7,50

Unto a Good Land

Unto a

Good Land

A HISTORY OF THE AMERICAN PEOPLE

David Edwin Harrell, Jr.
Auburn University

Sally Foreman Griffith
Independent Scholar

Edwin S. Gaustad
University of California, Riverside

Randall M. Miller
St. Joseph's University

John B. Boles
Rice University

Randall B. Woods
University of Arkansas

WILLIAM B. EERDMANS PUBLISHING COMPANY
Grand Rapids, Michigan / Cambridge, U.K.

WM. B. EERDMANS PUBLISHING CO.
255 Jefferson Ave. S.E., Grand Rapids, Michigan 49503 /
P.O. Box 163, Cambridge CB3 9PU U.K.

Printed in the United States of America

ISBN 0-8028-3718-2

www.eerdmans.com

Contents in Brief

Contents

21

THE POLITICS OF THE GILDED AGE   693

22

INNOCENTS ABROAD: EXPANSION AND EMPIRE, AMERICA AND THE WORLD, 1865-1900   723

23

IN SEARCH OF EFFICIENCY: THE VALUES AND IDEOLOGY OF PROGRESSIVISM, 1900–1917   749

30

IN THE SHADOW OF THE BOMB: THE COLD WAR IN THE TRUMAN YEARS   989

31

CONTAINMENT, CONTENTMENT, DISCONTENT: EISENHOWER REPUBLICANISM AND THE FIFTIES   1019

34

A NATION BESET: POLITICS FROM NIXON TO REAGAN   1111

35

A TURN TO THE RIGHT: THE REAGAN AND FIRST BUSH PRESIDENCIES   1141

36

THE POLITICS OF EQUILIBRIUM: THE CLINTON AND BUSH PRESIDENCIES   1167

37

AMERICAN SOCIETY IN THE NEW MILLENNIUM: A "CULTURE WAR," A STABLE CENTER   1195

Table of Features

Preface

HISTORY NEED NOT be left to the "experts," for everyone is to some degree a historian. To keep a diary, for example, is to perform some of the same tasks as the historian. Neither a diarist nor a historian records "everything that happened." Rather, each selects those events that have special significance or meaning, often arranging the happenings discussed in such a way as to emphasize what was truly important and why.

The task of the historian, in addition to selecting those events that have special significance, and arranging them in some sort of coherent pattern, is to convince readers that the story is not only *for* them but also *about* them. For Americans, the study of American history should have a special appeal; the story really is about you, just as surely as exploration of your own family background is another, if somewhat narrower, way of learning more about yourself.

In another sense, though, the study of history can help you to get outside of yourself, to enlarge your experience and escape the limitations of a given moment of time and spot in space. Patrick Henry said that the only light that guided his steps was the "lamp of experience." To some degree, that is true for us all, so that it makes much sense to broaden that experience as widely as possible. We do this by absorbing into ourselves the activities and aspirations of countless women and men who have preceded us. Their experiences become our own — if we allow them to.

Like the diarist, historians choose and select according to what they regard as most significant, what catches their interest and holds their attention. No two stories of the American past will be exactly the same, just as no two diary-keepers, even though they may describe the very same day in the very same town or school, will record the identical events in identical terms. The interests and background of each writer ensure the difference, thereby saving future historians from the horror of reading a hundred diaries with identical tales.

It is true, of course, that American history textbooks will share many items in common. None will omit the story of colonization, an account of the American Revolution, the development of the Constitution, westward expansion, the tragedy of slavery, the waves of immigration, economic struggles, military alliances, political quarrels, and so on. But all of this will be discussed within a pattern, and we will give particular attention to certain themes.

The most distinctive theme in *Unto a Good Land* — an attention to the persistence of religious faith in America — calls for more than a casual explanation. Most modern Americans know that religious zeal, mingled to be sure with less lofty motives, spurred on many of the early Europeans who explored the New World, where they encountered but generally did not appreciate the religious understandings of Native Americans. Most moderns also recognize that faith gave coherence to the earliest English families that settled New England, and that it later animated the clashes of the Scopes Trial. But faith has been a strong force throughout U.S. history, and as numerous recent events have made clear, the United States remains a bastion of religious beliefs. Various surveys point to the overwhelming majority who believe in God, the large plurality that regularly attend church, synagogue, temple, or mosque, and the roughly 40 percent who declare their religious beliefs to be life's most important value. At the close of the twentieth century, the United States stood as perhaps the most overtly religious society in the industrialized world.

The United States has never been a "Christian nation," as some enthusiasts have from time to time proclaimed; the country never became the shining city upon a hill that the Puritans aspired to build; the Constitution never proclaimed a specific religious stance, to the disappointment of some. At times, evangelical Protestants have wielded broad political influence, sufficient to make their own ideas and customs virtually define American character. But in other eras, different religious influences have worked in various ways to shape the American story.

Americans' generalized religious beliefs have been distilled from an ever broadening multiplicity of faiths. The nation's earliest consensus was Protestant, then generally Christian, then Judeo-Christian, then incorporating Islam and Asian faiths, and more recently becoming more of a vague theism in general. But in every age public servants have been obliged to offer obeisance to a generalized religion winnowed from the most broadly held beliefs of the people. Many Americans, hoping to persuade their fellow citizens to support some strategy or program, have felt compelled to square their arguments with the perceived will of God. This is not to imply that American political debate has been conducted on a notably high and moral level; it says only that Americans have understood and explained their common values in language laced with religious assumptions and terminology.

None of this emphasis on religion here is intended either to commend or to condemn—or to include or to exclude. To be sure, religion has not always been a force for righteousness. It has been employed as spiritual and moral uplift, but also as cynical rhetorical device or smooth rationalization. It has empowered the downtrodden, but it has also been allied in costly or cruel ways with civil or private power blocs. It has expressed deepest sincerity, but it has also sunk to the level of hypocrisy and manipulation. It has opened hearts, but it has also drawn battle lines. Religion can reveal its power in ways both inspiring and demeaning, but the power in either case is there and must not be ignored. Faith has moved mountains — as well as ships and nations, banners and borders, and hearts and minds.

This interpretive framework does not mean that this is a book about American religion. Nor is religion offered as a simplistic explanation for all that has happened in the nation's history. All of the authors have written in some way about American religion, and we believe that this vital subject has been grievously ignored in textbooks, but this textbook is about U.S. history. It is full of nonbelievers as well as believers; social, political, and economic forces as well as religious ones. We offer no simple hypotheses about ideological division or divine causation, nor do we embrace theories of divine national mission. Ours is only to tell the story. Regardless of your religious persuasion — and indeed, even if you remain unpersuaded by religion — this is your story, and we hope you enjoy it.

SPECIAL FEATURES

In addition to its unprecedented coverage of the religious dimension of American history, *Unto a Good Land* gives balanced attention to the social, political, and economic forces that have shaped the American people and nation. We have developed the book's features with both students and teachers in mind:

- **A clear and compelling narrative.** As authors of biographies and popular histories, as well as scholars of American history, we have shaped the book into a seamless narrative structure that restores the "story" to history and encourages students to read the story, not just memorize the facts.

- **A flexible two-volume format designed for varying classroom use.** In addition to the single hardcover edition, *Unto a Good Land* is available as two paperback volumes. While most other history texts divide the volumes at Reconstruction, we recognize that as our nation's history grows, each term of a two-semester course in that history will need to cover more ground. Thus, Volume 1 includes coverage up to 1900 for instructors who want to teach beyond Reconstruction, while Volume 2 still begins with Reconstruction for traditionally structured courses.

- **Informative and engaging special text features.** In every chapter, we have included "In Their Own Words" sidebars that feature excerpts from primary source documents to engage students' interest and illuminate key topics. Also, more than four hundred historical illustrations and forty informative maps placed throughout the book help students see, as well as read, our nation's history.

- **Reading aids to enhance student learning.** "At a Glance" chapter outlines help students plan their study of chapter material, and "Suggested Reading" bibliographies at the end of each chapter help students go beyond the text to learn even more.

- **Essential teaching aids.** To help you with class preparation, an Instructor's Manual and Test Bank prepared by Margaret E. Armbrester, University of Alabama at Birmingham, provides lecture notes, discussion questions, and multiple-choice and essay test items for each chapter. You can download it from the book's website, http://www.UntoaGood-Land.com, or contact your Eerdmans representative for a copy.

- **Primary documents.** Also available on the book's website are links to web-based texts of documents that have played key roles in our nation's history.

ACKNOWLEDGMENTS

For a project as large and complicated as this one, many people deserve thanks. James Miller deserves special recognition, as he shepherded the book from its early days at another publisher through its time in development at Eerdmans. His steady and informed guidance held the whole enterprise together at many key points, his careful reading and editing improved much of the original manuscript, and his advice was crucial

for Eerdmans to steer its way through new territory. Charles Van Hof had the vision to see that Eerdmans could join the ranks of U.S. history textbook publishers and was a passionate advocate for the book. At Eerdmans, Linda Bieze, David Bratt, Milton Essenburg, Jennifer Hoffman, Andrew Hoogheem, Kevin van der Leek, and Klaas Wolterstorff all helped to turn manuscript pages into the finished product you see here.

We also wish to thank the following for their generous assistance and support, in alphabetical order: David Allmendinger, Raymond Arsenault, Ronald Bayor, Paula Benkart, Kathleen Berkeley, Henry Bischoff, Nancy G. Boles, Patricia Dunn Burgess, David H. Burton, Maureen Carothers, Paul A. Cimbala, Dennis Clark, William Cohen, David Contosta, Merton Dillon, George Dowdall, Robert Engs, Drew Gilpin Faust, Melvin Garrison, Frank X. Gerrity, Howard Gillette, Jolyon Girard, Janet Golden, Rayna Goldfarb, Randal L. Hall, Maureen Ann Harp, John Higham, Sharon Ann Holt, Edward Johanningsmeier, Bethany Johnson, Charles Joyner, Kenneth Kusmer, Daniel Kilbride, Alan Kraut, Emma Jones Lapsansky-Werner, Francis Graham Lee, Sylvia Mallory, Scott Marler, Margaret Marsh, John McKivigan, Linda Patterson Miller, Gary Mills, Raymond Mohl, John M. Mulder, Evelyn Thomas Nolen, James Pringle, Mitchel Roth, Marion Roydhouse, Eric Schneider, Katherine A. S. Sibley, John David Smith, Sharon Strom, M. Mark Stolarik, Victor Taylor, James Turk, Jon Wakelyn, and Russell Weigley.

David Edwin Harrell, Jr.
Edwin S. Gaustad
John B. Boles
Sally Foreman Griffith
Randall M. Miller
Randall B. Woods

Reviewer Acknowledgments

We would like to thank the following reviewers, whose critical comments have helped to shape Unto a Good Land:

Margaret Armbrester
University of Alabama at Birmingham

Jean Harvey Baker
Goucher College

W. Roger Biles
East Carolina University

Terry D. Bilhartz
Sam Houston State University

S. Charles Bolton
University of Arkansas at Little Rock

Robert Brandfon
College of the Holy Cross

James D. Bratt
Calvin College

Richard D. Brown
University of Connecticut

Jon Butler
Yale University

Randolph B. Campbell
University of North Texas

Kathleen S. Carter
High Point University

John Milton Cooper
University of Wisconsin—Madison

J. Douglas Deal
State University of New York at Oswego

Jay Dolan
University of Notre Dame

Robert B. Ekelund
Auburn University

Merl Estep
Trinity Valley Community College

Eugene Genovese

Christopher D. Grasso
College of William and Mary

Allen C. Guelzo
Gettysburg College

Kermit Hall
Utah State University

David E. Hamilton
University of Kentucky

Richard L. Hume
Washington State University

Judith Ishkanian

Peter Iverson
Arizona State University

Harvey H. Jackson
Jacksonville State University

Kevin Klein
Harding University

Lawrence F. Kohl
University of Alabama

James B. LaGrand
Messiah College

Maxine Lurie
Seton Hall University

Clim Madlock
Southwest Tennessee Community College

Edward H. McKinley
Asbury College

Elizabeth Kimball McLean
Otterbein College

Clyde Milner
Arkansas State University

John A. Neuenschwander
Carthage College

Mark A. Noll
Wheaton College

Carol O'Connor
Arkansas State University

David P. Peltier
Ohio Northern University

Jonathan Prude
Emory University

Michaela Reaves
California Lutheran University

Leo P. Ribuffo
George Washington University

Marlene Rikard
Samford University

David W. Robson
John Carroll University

Carol Sheriff
College of William and Mary

Robert E. Shalhope
University of Oklahoma

John Staudenmaier, S.J.
University of Detroit Mercy

Samuel Stayer
Birmingham-Southern College

David C. Thomas
Union University

William Trollinger
University of Dayton

Arthur Worrall
Colorado State University

Neil L. York
Brigham Young University

About the Authors

David Edwin Harrell Jr. is Daniel F. Breeden Eminent Scholar in the Humanities at Auburn University. He has published seven books on American religious history, including the two-volume *Social History of the Disciples of Christ* and such pioneering studies of the Pentecostal and charismatic movements as *All Things Are Possible: The Healing and Charismatic Revivals in Modern America* and *Oral Roberts: An American Life*. He is also co-editor of a series entitled "Religion and American Culture" by the University of Alabama Press. He received his undergraduate degree from David Lipscomb College (now Lipscomb University) and his Ph.D. from Vanderbilt University, and has taught at, among others, East Tennessee State University, the University of Oklahoma, the University of Georgia, the University of Arkansas, and the University of Alabama at Birmingham.

Edwin S. Gaustad is Professor Emeritus of History and Religious Studies at the University of California, Riverside. He has also taught at Shorter College, the University of Redlands, Baylor University, and Auburn University. He received a B.A. from Baylor University and an M.A. and a Ph.D. from Brown University. He is the author of, among other works, *Sworn on the Altar of God: A Religious Biography of Thomas Jefferson, Liberty of Conscience: Roger Williams in America, Historical Atlas of Religion in America, The Religious History of America: The Heart of the American Story from Colonial Times to Today* (with Leigh Schmidt), and *Proclaim Liberty Throughout the Land: A History of Church and State in America.*

John B. Boles is William Pettus Hobby Professor of History at Rice University and Managing Editor of the *Journal of Southern History*. He has also taught at Towson State University and Tulane University. He did his undergraduate work at Rice University, and went on to earn a Ph.D. at the University of Virginia. He is the author of various books on the American South, including *The South Through Time: A History of an American Region; Black Southerners, 1619-1869;* and *The Great Revival, 1789-1805: Origins of the Southern Evangelical Mind,* reprinted as *The Great Revival: Beginnings of the Bible Belt.*

Sally Foreman Griffith graduated from Radcliffe College and received an M.A. and a Ph.D. in American history from Johns Hopkins University. Her first book, *Home Town News: William Allen White and the Emporia Gazette,* was awarded the Allan Nevins Prize by the Society of American Historians. She has taught at Grinnell College, Vassar College, and Villanova University, and since becoming an independent scholar she has authored studies of the Historical Society of Pennsylvania and Franklin and Marshall College.

Randall M. Miller is William Dirk Warren '50 Sesquicentennial Chair and Professor of History at Saint Joseph's University, having previously taught at Wesley College in Delaware. He is probably best known for his award-winning book *"Dear Master": Letters of a Slave Family.* He has co-edited the *Dictionary of Afro-American History, Religion and the American Civil War,* and *The Birth of the Grand Old Party: The Republicans' First Generation.* He serves as series editor for *Guides to Historic Events of the Twentieth Century* and *Major Issues in American History,* both published by Greenwood Press. He did his undergraduate work at Hope College and earned an M.A. and a Ph.D. from Ohio State University.

Randall B. Woods is a Distinguished Professor of History at the University of Arkansas and the author of *Fulbright: A Biography,* winner of the 1996 Robert H. Ferrel Prize for Best Book on American Foreign Relations and the 1996 Virginia Ledbetter Prize for Best Book on Southern Studies, and which was nominated for the Pulitzer Prize and the National Book Award. He has also written *A Changing of the Guard: Anglo-American Relations, 1941-1946* and *A Black Odyssey: John Lewis Waller and the Promise of American Life, 1878-1900,* and co-authored (with Howard Jones) *The Dawning of the Cold War: America's Quest for Order, 1945-1950.* He earned his B.A., M.A., and Ph.D. from the University of Texas at Austin.

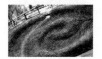

Prologue

The North American Continent and Its Native Peoples

ROUGHLY TWO HUNDRED million years ago, so geologists tell us, the earth's continents began to assume something like their present familiar shapes. Since they all did so at about the same time, the "New World" is no newer than the "Old World," only slightly more recent to acquire national boundaries, giant navies, and imperial pretensions thousands of miles distant.

The Western Hemisphere is also newer in acquiring human habitation. Anthropologists and biologists believe that the earliest hominids appeared in Africa at least 5 million years ago. A mere 30,000 years ago human wanderers from northern Asia migrated across a no-longer-existing land bridge[1] linking Siberia and Alaska and gradually moved down and across the Americas, North and South. Adapting to the widely different natural environments offered in this huge expanse, these ancient peoples created cultures as varied as the environments themselves.

The North American landmass of over nine million square miles makes it somewhat smaller than Africa, somewhat larger than South America, and vastly larger than all of Europe. Climate zones vary from the deserts of the Southwest to the tundra of Alaska, from the tropical humidity of southern Florida to the semi-arid northern plains of the Dakotas. Natural vegetation ranges from the mesquite and sage of West Texas to the giant sequoia of California and the dense subarctic

---

1. The land bridge disappeared as the immense icecaps covering much of the globe melted at the end of the last Ice Age 10,000 years ago. The water thus added to the world's oceans flooded many coastal plains, including the Siberia-Alaska land bridge.

180 million years ago

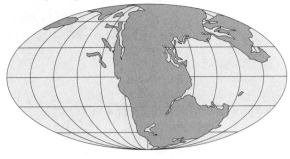

125 million years ago

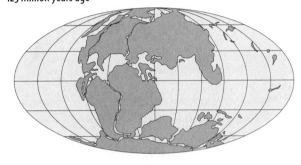

55 million years ago

Today

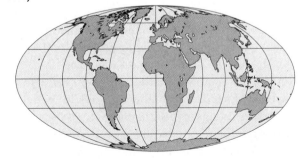

CONTINENTAL DRIFT

forests of Canada. Early explorers of the Atlantic Coast testified to the abundance of fish and game, of fruits and nuts, of berries and grain. Traders and trappers thought the continent's furs and hides inexhaustible: beaver, fox, deer, bear, otter, martens, rabbits, seals, buffalo, and more. Builders and shipwrights harvested tall trees for masts, pines for tar and turpentine, and hardwoods for bridges and homes.

But the earliest explorers also saw mountains and deserts that somehow had to be crossed, rivers that sometimes halted migration and at others eased it. For Europeans arriving by ship, eastern North America proved remarkably hospitable: broad, navigable rivers leading far enough inland to escape pirates or foreign enemies, but also penetrating far enough to allow for profitable importing and exporting of goods. Some rivers, such as the St. Lawrence, were navigable far enough inland as to permit — with a little portage — entry into the Great Lakes and eventually access, via the Mississippi River, all the way south to the Gulf of Mexico. Others, like the Delaware and the Hudson, offered shelter from the sea for untold miles northward, then further navigation into other great rivers upstream. Explorers recorded the great features of the landscape; settlers realized that these features would shape their way of life and determine the course that empire might take.

❧ Native Peoples

Few matters in early American history are as perplexing or highly controverted as those pertaining to the number of native Americans before European contact. The heaviest concentrations were in central Mexico, where agriculture developed about seven thousand years ago and where civilization reached its most sophisticated development. By modern standards, the vast area north of Mexico was sparsely settled, but by no means empty. Across it some five to ten million native North Americans are now estimated to have dwelled in log houses or wigwams, in pueblos or villages. Earliest migrants no doubt continued the pattern of migration for centuries, hunting, fishing, and gathering the natural vegetation. But by the beginning of the Christian era, if not several centuries before, a major agricultural civilization developed in the Ohio Valley, where the dramatic "Great Serpent Mound" survives as testimony to what is today known as the Hopewell culture. The later Mississippian culture, flourishing from perhaps the sixth century A.D. to the fifteenth, extended from the Mississippi and Missouri Rivers to Florida. Mississippian

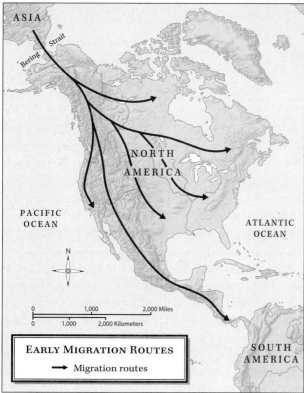

EARLY MIGRATION ROUTES
→ Migration routes

The Serpent Mound, Ohio People of the Adena Culture created this imposing mound — whose extent can only be appreciated from an aerial photograph — sometime around the beginning of the Common Era. Building it required enormous, sustained effort, but its purpose is still debated by experts.

mound-builders also created North America's first cities. The largest known urban center was Cahokia, near modern St. Louis, whose population about A.D. 1200 may have numbered 20,000 — larger than London at the same time.

In the arid Southwest, Indians also gathered in large numbers around a single site. The Anasazi reached a peak of community and cultural development in the thirteenth and fourteenth centuries A.D., leaving evidence of a large city in Chaco Canyon in northwestern New Mexico. Giant round kivas testify to elaborate religious rituals, even as the ruins reveal sophistication in both astronomical calculation and agricultural irrigation. Many of the surviving Pueblo Indians descend from this powerful and proud civilization.

Why these high cultures rose and fell is not totally clear, although major climatic changes are the most likely cause. Temperatures altered, rainfall declined,

An Anasazi Woman Dancing This wall painting from the Anasazi culture in the American Southwest, dating from roughly 1500 A.D., shows a woman performing a ceremonial dance and brandishing twigs.

Indians proved wondrously adaptable, creating political and social communities in places ranging from the hot, dry deserts of Arizona to the cold, wet forests of the Great Lakes. And the Hurons in that area would have had little in common with the southwestern Zuni, apart from the remarkable ability to draw from their surroundings not only a livelihood but also a whole system of ideas and values. Throughout the Western Hemisphere, pre-Columbian art and artifacts demonstrate a diverse people who were united in achievement and ability.

Historians are dependent upon archaeologists, anthropologists, and geologists for knowledge about these peoples and their movements before the Europeans' arrival. Chemists have also contributed to dating the age of organic material through application of the carbon-14 test. Newer methods of dating, including genetics, are also being developed to shed light on the mysteries of the continent's prehistory.

❧ Language Groups and the Land

Scholars no longer generalize about "*the* Indian culture" or "*the* Indian way of life." Indian ways were many, Indian myths strikingly different, the adaptations of each people ingenious in its own manner. Modern anthropologists have defined as many as thirty major linguistic groups of North American Indians. In the eastern half of what is now the United States, four language groups are known: Iroquoian (Great Lakes and upper South), Algonkian (New England, New York, Chesapeake Bay, and large segments of the Midwest), Siouan (Pennsylvania, Ohio, and portions of North Carolina), and Muskogean (most of the Southeast). Within these groups, each language was quite distinct, the Indians of one having no more ability to understand the spoken language of another than could newly arriving European settlers understand any. Indeed, North America

trade routes shifted — these and many more fundamental fluctuations forced a people to abandon long-occupied sites and even shift basic lifestyles.

That impressive Native American cultures flourished and skills multiplied, there can be no doubt. Bows and arrows, spears and stone axes, weaving and clothing, pottery shards, and cooking utensils offer abundant evidence of peoples grown wise and purposeful in the ways of their highly diverse worlds. North American

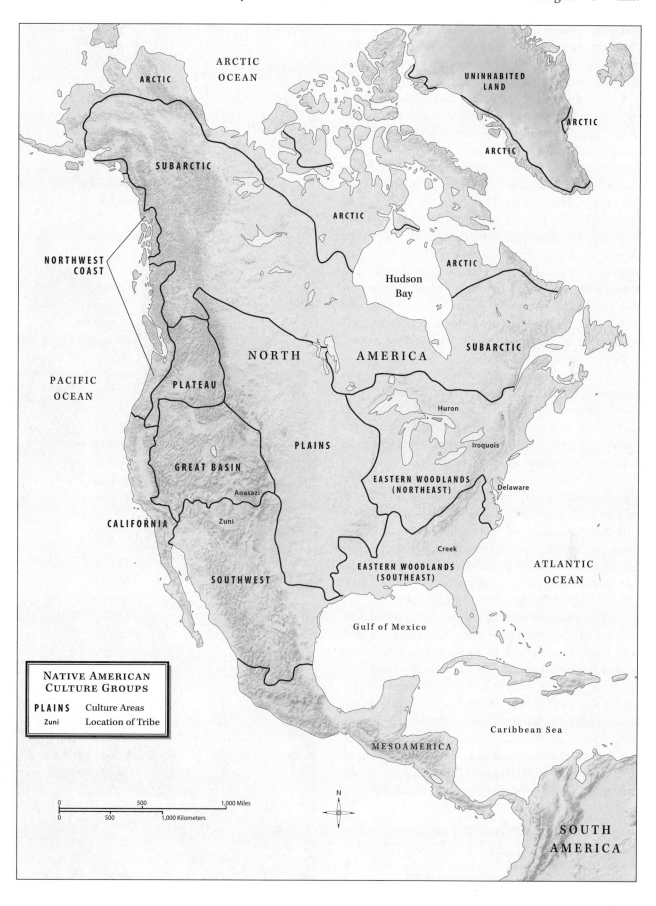

ARCTIC OCEAN

ARCTIC

SUBARCTIC

UNINHABITED LAND

ARCTIC

ARCTIC

ARCTIC

NORTHWEST COAST

Hudson Bay

ARCTIC

PACIFIC OCEAN

NORTH   AMERICA

SUBARCTIC

PLATEAU

Huron

PLAINS

Iroquois

GREAT BASIN

Anasazi

EASTERN WOODLANDS (NORTHEAST)

Delaware

Zuni

CALIFORNIA

Creek

SOUTHWEST

EASTERN WOODLANDS (SOUTHEAST)

ATLANTIC OCEAN

Gulf of Mexico

Caribbean Sea

MESOAMERICA

SOUTH AMERICA

NATIVE AMERICAN CULTURE GROUPS

PLAINS Culture Areas
Zuni   Location of Tribe

0   500   1,000 Miles
0   500   1,000 Kilometers

N

had even more linguistic diversity than Europe. One Christian missionary, despairing of this formidable multiplicity, wrote that if he could ask one blessing of the Holy Spirit, it would be the "gift of tongues."

Geography played the major role in defining the cultures of the almost innumerable Indian peoples in North America. When modern scholarship divides the Indian populations culturally, it names the major features of the land: arctic, plateau, plains, Caribbean, Eastern woodlands, and so on. The land first shaped the culture but eventually the culture reshaped or modified the land. That reciprocal relationship seldom badly abused nature, on which the very survival of the people depended. In most cases, moreover, nature was abundant, so that by careful husbanding of foodstuffs, native peoples insured an ample supply for the next year. Apart from natural calamities and severe climatic shifts, the land provided plenty for all. Following seasonal patterns, Indians generally migrated from place to place, traveling lightly.

Of course, Indians could quarrel about the land or by violence be driven from it. Such disputes tended to be tribal, not personal. Indian peoples went to war against each other, and likewise organized confederacies for mutual protection or collective aggression. The most famous of the confederacies, the Iroquois League of the Five Nations, which arose several centuries before the Europeans arrived in the Northeast, has similar, if weaker, imitations among the Virginia Indians and the Creeks in the Southeast. Before the pressures of European contact required some adjustments, many tribes placed political power in the clans, or kinship groups, as well as in the individual settlement or town. In this way enormous local autonomy was preserved.

Within Native American tribes, clans, and villages, women wielded far more power than the Europeans who made contact with them were willing to accept within their own societies. For example, when male Iroquois gathered in a council to make decisions, the senior women of the clan or tribe stood directly behind them, forcefully bringing their influence to bear. In most Indian societies, descent was through the mother's line, not the father's, and in many tribes female elders named the chiefs. Much of this powerful female influence probably derived from the women's control

Ruins of a Cliff Palace   This splendid dwelling, in what today is Mesa Verde National Park in Colorado, was constructed around 1200 A.D. It was probably only inhabited for a century or so, however; when drought struck the region in 1276, residents of the cliffs moved on to places where water was more plentiful.

over agriculture — a sphere that in European societies was always male-dominated (even though women did their share of field work at harvest time). Europeans were shocked and amused to see Native American men apparently lolling about the village while the women planted, tended, and gathered in the crops — forgetting, of course, that the men may have been "lolling" because they had just returned from an exhausting hunting or trading expedition. But Native Americans returned the scorn when they observed white men struggling to up-root rocks, plow fields, and plant crops (in ways that struck the Indians as highly inefficient), while their womenfolk stayed indoors, busy with housework and child care that Indians rarely witnessed. In these, as in so many other ways, profoundly different cultures and forms of social organization bred misunderstandings whose consequences were often tragic for both sides.

Among Native Americans, disputes did not concern "property rights," as Europeans would understand that term, but rather hunting and fishing rights, the division of a harvest, the capture of brides, or a convincing show of strength. Indian wars were not devastating sieges, but swift attacks and swift retreats, usually inflicting minimal damage to human life. Some tribes, it is true, had a reputation for greater ferocity, and the less aggressive groups attempted mainly to stay out of their way. The bounty and breadth of the land made staying out of the way a reasonable and not particularly difficult alternative. Most Indian groups moved freely and frequently, carrying with them what little they possessed in the way of tools, weapons, and modest food supplies.

For Europeans, these casual attitudes toward permanent residence upon or "ownership" of a particular bit of land created confusion and ever-increasing ill will. In some sense, Indians had a prior claim to all of North America — or did they? Certainly, every explorer who arrived on the shores of the New World regarded it as his first and most solemn duty to plant the flag and claim all that his eyes could see or his mind imagine in the name of his country and king. But what about those earlier inhabitants, those peoples who had roamed the land for thousands of years?

One of the problems was — from the European point of view — the very fact that the Indians "roamed." Did anyone acquire title to the land simply by walking across it? And what about land that at any moment was empty? Could Native Americans claim land that had never been cultivated or improved, fenced or cleared? To the European colonizers and their White

American successors, such claims made little sense. As with the ancient Israelites among the Philistines, a colonial Massachusetts clergyman explained, "there is room enough" for all. Europeans need not purchase such property, because land not being "used" was open to everyone. Or as the first governor of Massachusetts noted, "That which is common to all is proper to none." If Indians bought or sold property, what they sold was only the use of that property for a limited period of time. But when Europeans bought or sold property, they understood ownership to be permanent, boundaries to be fixed, and trespassers to be punished.

In such contrary perceptions lay the root of many misunderstandings — and much bloodshed. For the Indian, land was to be used, not owned. If Indians did sell land, they sold the use of it — all being welcome to share in the harvest of that good and fertile soil. If Indians did actually cultivate land, fertilize it, plant it, maintain it, then Europeans were generally willing to concede that in some sense that land was really theirs. As the Massachusetts General Court observed early in the seventeenth century, "what lands any of the Indians, within this jurisdiction, have by possession or improvement, by subduing of the same, they have just right thereunto, according to Genesis 1:28; 9:1; Psalms 115, 116." But of all those lands that were merely hunted and "roamed," of all those rivers and streams just fished or trapped, Europeans were not prepared to yield any prior claim to the Indians. Neither side understood the other's perspective, with the inevitable result that the views of the stronger side would prevail. In the sixteenth, seventeenth, and later centuries, possession remained at least nine-tenths of the law.

ஃ *Economy and Trade*

Indians did not need Europeans to teach them how to trade. Seacoast Indians traded shellfish for berries and nuts with inland tribes. Deer hunters exchanged venison for corn. Plains Indians bartered buffalo hides for baskets and bowls fashioned by the Anasazi. Whatever was abundant in one area (or season) could be traded for the surplus found somewhere else. The law of supply and demand operated equally everywhere. Barter was the chief mode of exchange, although gradually wampum — white or purple beads fashioned from particular seashells — came to be used more often as a kind of money as Europeans began to arrive. Of course, each village or tribe maintained a high degree of self-sufficiency, so that in pre-colonial days survival rarely depended on barter and trade. Still, the great Indian civilizations of the Ohio and Mississippi Valleys carried on extensive trade, extending as far south as the Gulf of Mexico and as far north as the Great Lakes.

In colder climates, men did most of the fishing and hunting, often far from home, while women and children worked close to the village gathering berries, birds' eggs, and shellfish scattered along the banks of lakes and rivers. In more temperate zones, women provided most of the food by planting and harvesting corn, then grinding it to flour and baking it. Men still hunted, but survival was not totally dependent on their success. Diet varied with the season, with the migration of bird and animal life, with the fertility of the soil and the rainfall. In winter, tribes lived on grain that had been stored, on meat that had been dried and smoked, and on what meager provisions might still be gathered. Life could be hard, to be sure, but not so hard as to preclude times of feasting and celebrations, especially in the fall and early winter when the crops were in and the animals were fat.

When the Europeans arrived, trading posts began to take on a life of their own and the newcomers' markets reshaped Indian (and colonial) economies. The native peoples' subsistence economy became a trading economy, as Indians began seizing more from the land than just what was necessary to satisfy their own needs. The wants of all Europe suddenly had to be met, and the abundance of animal life declined in order to meet this insatiable demand. This was most notably true in the fur trade. Whether carried on by the French, the Dutch, or the English, the result was the same: beavers, otters, martens, and fox were overhunted until they began to disappear from the land. With increased pressures for trade, traditional tribal patterns of clan and village autonomy began to break down, abetted by the Europeans' wish to negotiate with a single "chief," one often chosen not by the native people but by those with whom they bartered.

❧ Cultures and Religions

All Indians in their social organization took cognizance of the realities of birth, love, and death, and also of the unknown world beyond all the observable phenomena of nature. Certain tribal approaches to both the known and the unknown illustrate Native Americans' serious efforts to cope with the world around them, even as they suggest something of the notable cultural diversity in the Eastern woodlands alone.

In all cultures, ancient or modern, giving birth is a major event, accompanied by many anxieties and risks. Although birth is often also a public event, among the Iroquois the mother-to-be might go off into the woods, build a simple shelter by a stream, and there all alone deliver herself of her child. After a few days, she returned to the village to be welcomed by family and friends. European observers among the Narragansetts noted the ease of delivery, which they attributed in part to the women's excellent physical condition and sustained physical labor. "I have often known," one reported, "in one quarter of an hour a woman merry in the house, and delivered, and merry again." Others added, however, that drugs were sometimes administered to alleviate suffering and hasten delivery.

During nursing of the infant, conjugal relations between the mother and father were strictly avoided, which resulted in a natural birth control, but also in wandering husbands. Among the Delawares, many husbands during this time "have concubines, but not in the house." Ceremonial naming of the child, more elaborate in some tribes than in others, in every case paid careful attention to the clan (in some tribes determined by the mother's lineage, in others by the father's) and to all the relatives immediately gained through this kinship. Names frequently reappeared throughout the clan, or if a clan member had recently died, that person's name might be assigned to the newborn.

Marriage, always outside of one's own clan, united the two young people as well as their respective clans. Thus it had both its private and public aspect, the first usually marked by the exchange of gifts and the second by a public celebration. Premarital sex was tolerated, sometimes encouraged; adultery was not. Among the Narragansetts severe punishment was meted out not to an adulterous wife but to her lover; death occasionally resulted from the blows inflicted. Divorce came easily among the Hurons, since the economic investment (no bridal dowry as in Europe) was equal from both sides. Either husband or wife could take the step of announcing that the marriage was over — although this occurred much more readily before the arrival of children than after. The Ottawas, on the other hand, took monogamy seriously, accepting divorce only for some major and publicly recognized reason. Among some Great Lakes Algonkian-speaking Indians, a man might have more than one wife, while among the Senecas a wife could have more than one husband. The nearest thing to a uniform pattern among Native Americans was the prohibition of incestuous unions, which often included cousins. A man might, however, marry his wife's widowed sisters, thus placing them under his protection.

In death, native peoples sought to reintegrate the community as well as strengthen those who mourned. The tribal group took charge of the burial (usually in the fetal position), making offerings to assist the spirit's safe passage out of the body. A period of mourning ended with celebration, at which point the survivor's spouse was free to remarry and the deceased's name could be assigned to another member of the clan. Among the Ottawas, a dying man was decked out in all his ornamental finery, with his weapons placed at his feet. "They dress his hair with red paint mixed with grease, and paint his body and his face red with vermilion . . . and he is clad with a jacket and blanket as richly as possible." After death, the corpse was placed in a sitting position, and in that pose the departed warrior received family and friends. The women wept and sang mournful songs, and other ceremonies — depending on the rank of the deceased — took place. Then the deceased was either buried in a shallow grave or laid to rest in a tree or upon a scaffold seven or eight feet high in a ceremony known as "tree burial." Interment was attended by the entire village, with a kind of ritual reassertion of the power of good over evil, of life over death.

Most of these reports of native ceremonies have come to us from European missionaries, Catholic and Protestant alike, who sometimes indicated their approval or disapproval but at others simply recorded their own observations as accurately as possible. Next to trade and war, the missionary contact was the most sustained of the European associations with the Eastern woodland tribes, both in what became Canada and what became the United States. The missionaries also reported on the religions that they encountered, although most found it difficult to refrain from comparing native beliefs and practices with the ritual and theology of Christianity. A French Jesuit laboring in the Great Lakes region noted that the gods of the Indians, like those of the ancient Greeks, "live much in the same manner with us, but without any of those inconveniences to which we are subject." The native Americans' gods, in other words, were men and women writ large, agents of creation, instruments of blessings or curses, guides to immortality. The tribal members believed, this missionary added, that wherever they invoke their gods, they will be heard and the gods will respond accordingly. Often Indians offered sacrifices to make their prayers more effective, for example, by throwing

Native American Artifacts   Here are a variety of characteristic Indian objects from everyday life of the Pre-Contact Era, although not all of them actually date from that period. They include an Anasazi water jug and an Acoma bowl (both from the Southwest); a Haida owl mask, Columella beads, and a Sikyati bowl (Pacific Northwest); a Mississippian stone axe (Southeast); an Inuit water jar (Far North); a Key Largo carving of a cat (southern Florida); a Mimbres bowl (Great Plains); and Iroquois wampum (Eastern Woodlands).

tobacco or slain birds into a river. "When they happen to be without provisions, as often fall out in their voyages and hunting," one missionary recorded that Indians promised to the gods or their chief "a portion of the first beast they shall afterwards kill." All the festivals, songs, and dances among the Hurons and Algonkians, this same observer noted, "appeared to me to have their origin in religion."

One English historian who settled in the colony of Virginia wrote that the belief in immortality was widespread. The shamans[2] and priests, who "are looked upon as oracles," taught that "the Souls of Men survive their Bodies, and that those who have done well here enjoy most transporting Pleasures" in their version of heaven — one that had special appeal to the males. For hunting and fishing in that heaven will be amply rewarded, as will the desire for "the most charming Women, which enjoy an eternal bloom, and have an Universal desire to please." Hell, a subject on which many Indian tribes were silent, was among the Virginia natives conceived as a "filthy stinking Lake after Death, that continually burns with Flames, that never extinguish." In this as in other myths reported by explorer and missionary alike, some Christianizing influence on the beliefs in an afterlife can be detected.

Indian creation myths, too, came to reflect the influence of biblical accounts promulgated by European missionaries. The Cherokees told of a cosmos that once was all water; then a waterbeetle darted all over the water looking for some firm place to rest. Finding none, "it dived to the bottom and came up with some soft mud, which began to grow and spread on every side until it became the island which we call earth." Most of the earth remained soft and wet, so that birds (as from the story of Noah's ark) were sent forth to determine where it had become dry. "The Great Buzzard, the father of all buzzards we see now . . . flew all over the earth, low down near the ground, and it was still soft. When he reached the Cherokee country, he was very tired, and his wings began to flap and strike the

[margin handwritten note: Lake of Fire to describe hell]

2. Shamans, among Native Americans and many other peoples, were individuals credited by the community with special powers to communicate with natural forces and the spirit world.

ground." This action, the story-tellers concluded, led to the creation of mountains and valleys still to be seen throughout Cherokee country.

And so the Native Americans hunted and farmed, traded and fought, loved and acquired families, believed and celebrated in such a way as to give themselves a place in the universe and a meaning to their lives. They also adjusted, as necessary, to the rigorous demands of nature. Soon, even more radical adjustments would be required of them.

SUGGESTED READING

James Axtell, *The Invasion Within: The Contest of Cultures in Colonial North America* (1985). Axtell describes the "contest" among French, English, and Indian with conspicuous sympathy for the latter.

Harold E. Driver, *Indians of North America* (rev. ed., 1970). An anthropologist's fine introduction to a large subject.

Alvin M. Josephy, Jr., ed., *The American Heritage Book of Indians* (1961). A lavishly illustrated popular treatment.

Russell Thornton, *American Indian Holocaust and Survival: A Population History Since 1492* (1987). In the difficult area of population estimates for Native Americans, Thornton offers valuable guidance.

B. G. Trigger and W. E. Washburn, *The Cambridge History of the Native Peoples of America*, vol. 1: *North America* (1996). This work emphasizes the great diversity among the North American Indians: in their culture, their languages, and their historic experiences.

Wilcomb E. Washburn, *The Indian in America* (1975). A readable survey that is strengthened by an informed bibliographical essay and three helpful maps.

Wilcomb E. Washburn, ed., *The Indian and the White Man* (1964). A useful collection of documents that begins with the earliest instances of European contact.

Daniel J. Weber, *The Spanish Frontier in North America* (1992). Readable, balanced, and engaging, this excellent study is further enriched by 75 illustrations.

SUGGESTIONS FOR FURTHER READING

James Axtell, ed., *The Indian Peoples of Eastern America: A Documentary History of the Sexes* (1981).

Robert F. Berkhofer, Jr., *The White Man's Indian: Images of the American Indian from Columbus to the Present* (1977).

William Brandon, *The Last Americans: The Indian in American Culture* (1974).

Francis Jennings, *The Invasion of America: Indians, Colonialism, and the Cant of Conquest* (1975).

D'Arcy McNickle, *They Came Here First: The Epic of the American Indian* (1949).

David B. Quinn, *North American from the Earliest Discovery to First Settlements: The Norse Voyages to 1612* (1977).

Francis P. Prucha, *A Bibliographical Guide to the History of Indian-White Relations in the United States* (1977).

Nancy Shoemaker, ed., *Theorizing the Past in Native American Studies* (2002).

Ruth M. Underhill, *Red Man's America: A History of Indians in the United States* (rev. ed., 1971).

1

Discovery, Encounter, and Conquest, 1492–1607

ONE OF WORLD history's true turning points occurred in the course of the fifteenth and sixteenth centuries as the sharply differing cultures of Africa, Europe, and America encountered each other, clashed, mingled, and were forever transformed. The story of those years is filled with adventure and misadventure, with heroism and villainy, with promise and catastrophe. In these events human nature is revealed in all its wondrous and often perplexing variety. The curtain rises on the drama in the latter years of the fifteenth century. The two nations of Europe's Iberian Peninsula, Portugal and Spain, demonstrated the greatest interest and initiative in exploration into the Atlantic, while Portuguese adventurers also moved down Africa's west coast and on to South and East Asia. African and European cultures met — fatefully for the former, profitably for the latter — in these fifteenth-century Portuguese forays. Then, beginning in 1492, Native American and European ways of life confronted each other, with the technological superiority of the Europeans overpowering the limited defenses of the Indians.

While these world-changing encounters of previously separated peoples were getting underway, European culture itself was being transformed, first by the Renaissance's challenge to many prevailing assumptions and cultural patterns, then by the Reformation's demand for greater allegiance to Scripture than had been accorded by the preceding thousand years of medieval tradition. Explorers and conquerors carried with them the spirit or burden of both cultural upheavals — sometimes as advocates, sometimes as opponents. The

Tabula nouarum infularum, quas diuerfis refpectibus Occidentales & Indianas uocant.

The New World in 1540   The virtual separation of North and South America (joined only by the Isthmus of Panama) was for the first time recognized by a European mapmaker in this chart. Although much distorted, the two Western Hemisphere continents are clearly recognizable. They are labeled "the New World" in both Latin and German. Japan and East Asia, however, are still shown as lying just off the west coast of Mexico—testimony that the vast expanse of the Pacific Ocean was not yet understood, even after Magellan's voyage.

age of geographical discovery was one of self-discovery as well, both for Europeans and for Native Americans.

North America, as grasped by the European mind of the early sixteenth century, was both ill-shaped and incomplete. No Great Lakes, no Mississippi River, no Rocky Mountains, and certainly no Pacific Coast appeared on sketchy European maps of the "New World." What did appear was anything but clear: a roughly drawn Atlantic coastline with Florida shown as an island on some maps; and northern waterways on others promising passage all the way to the Orient. One map, drawn early in the sixteenth century, took the only hon-

orable course by tagging most of the continent as *terra ultra incognita,* acknowledging that of North America next to nothing was known.

If that was true of the land, it was likewise true of the peoples who had occupied that land for tens of thousands of years before the Europeans came. Who and from where were they? How numerous were they? What languages did they speak? What cities had they built? What customs did they follow? What skills, tools, and weapons did they possess? Perhaps most importantly, were they friends or were they enemies to outsiders from across the sea? And what was God's plan for them, now that Christendom had "found" them? Many years would pass before these questions began to get answers, and some answers are not settled yet.

Even before the fifteenth century, some Europeans left modest marks on North America. Scandinavian adventurers made their way across the Atlantic first to Iceland late in the ninth century, and in the tenth a

Viking named Eric the Red reached what he badly misnamed Greenland. By the year 1000 Leif Ericsson — son of Eric the Red — set foot on "Vinland," probably Newfoundland, where he found wild wheat (or rice), unusually large trees, and rich grazing lands. About ten years later an Icelandic merchant began trading with Vinland's inhabitants, first carrying on a useful commerce but quickly falling into conflict with them. To quote the saga of Eric the Red, the merchant and his men "realized by now that although the land was excellent, they could never live there in safety or freedom from fear, because of the native inhabitants. So they made ready to leave the place and return home." Return home they did, bringing an early end to Viking exploitation and exploration of North America.

Far more lasting consequences resulted from the much later penetrations of Portuguese and Spanish, French and English into the Western Hemisphere. For these nations, exploration led to the establishment of forts, the conquest or eviction of native peoples, the creation of trade routes as well as settlements, and unceasing contest between one another for the choicest treasures and largest territories. North America was a prize

to be plundered, with more promise of glory than even the mightiest Crusade. The "New World" was really not new at all, but by the sixteenth century it was about to enter upon what was manifestly a new age in its history.

THE EUROPEAN REDISCOVERY OF NORTH AMERICA

Centuries after the Vikings' first forays, Spain and Portugal took the lead in explorations out into the Atlantic Ocean. Portuguese mariners navigated down the west coast of Africa, then across the waters to Brazil. The Spanish monarchy, meanwhile, gambled on the dream of an Italian sailor — not that the earth was round (for all educated persons by this time knew that it was) but rather that the earth's circumference was not so great

The Vinland Map   Scientists and historians argued for decades about the authenticity of this map, which depicts America as a curious island called Vinland; today most consider it a modern forgery. Regardless, it serves as a reminder that Vinland was the name given to the New World by Leif Ericsson, who, along with other Scandinavian adventurers, reached it long before any other Europeans did.

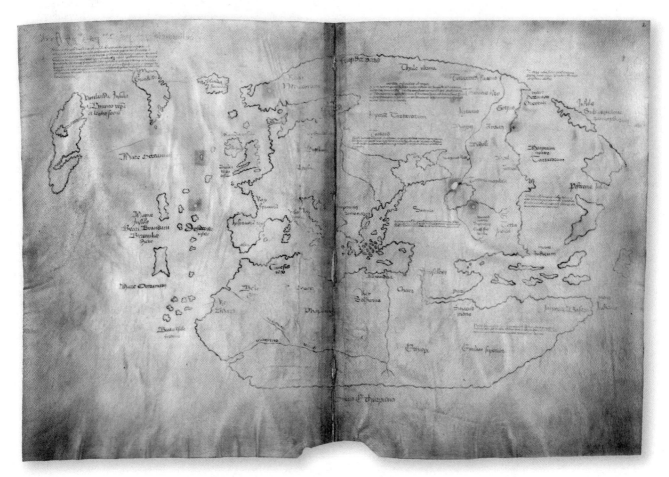

as to prevent an adventurer from reaching the East by sailing west. The gamble paid off handsomely: Spain planted her flag so widely in the Western Hemisphere that for a hundred years after Columbus her empire utterly dominated the new world.

ᴥ Early Iberian Adventures

Sailors from Spain and Portugal, strategically positioned as continental Europe's westernmost countries, ventured down the African coast and out into the Atlantic almost a century before Columbus's pivotal voyages. They could not have succeeded without the fifteenth century's new navigational instruments, techniques, and triangular sails that made it possible to tack against the prevailing winds. At the beginning of the fifteenth century, expeditions from Castile[1] began occupying the Canary Islands, and the Castilians kept control of these islands despite later Portuguese challenges. By 1432 the Portuguese Prince Henry (known as "the Navigator") was encouraging expeditions to the Azores Islands, about nine hundred miles out into the Atlantic, and a quarter-century later to the Cape Verde Islands. Both ventures resulted in acquisition and settlement of these islands by Portugal. A dynamic and imaginative adventurer, Henry collected maps (Arabic as well as European), searched records of all earlier European voyages, welcomed the invention of the compass and the astrolabe as aids to oceanic navigation, and stirred his own countrymen to dreams of world conquest and colonization. Before he died in 1460, he also pushed for further exploration southward along the coast of Africa, for that represented the most realistic route to India.

By 1488, long after Prince Henry's death, Africa's southernmost tip had been reached, and King John II — seeing India within

reach — promptly named it the Cape of Good Hope. A decade later Vasco da Gama planted a Portuguese trading post on India's soil. In Africa, the Portuguese found a world scarcely recognizable to Europeans. They found exotic animals such as the elephant and hippopotamus; they also found gold, as well as a more sinister source of wealth: slaves. Lisbon and other Portuguese cities became trade centers for ivory, gold, pepper, and slaves.

When African rulers discovered that the Portuguese were happy to exchange European goods for African men, women, and children, the Portuguese slave trade got off to a fast start. Europeans justified their traffic in human beings by claiming to be Christianizing those who had never heard the Christian message. Indeed, while the Portuguese would sell "heathen" slaves to other Europeans, they refused to sell to Muslims because, as one early chroni-

An Astrolabe This handsome instrument for observing the elevation of stars above the horizon was made in France about 1300. The astrolabe was invented in the Muslim world and copied by westerners. It was essential to the work of navigators, astronomers, and astrologers.

---

1. Castile was one of the two kingdoms — the other was Aragon — on the Iberian peninsula that in 1469 united to form Spain.

A New World Crusade

Christopher Columbus made no secret of his belief that his voyages of discovery were divinely ordained.

With a hand that could be felt, the Lord opened my mind to the fact that it would be possible to sail from here to the Indies, and he opened my will to desire to accomplish the project. This was the fire that burned within me when I came to visit Your Highnesses [Ferdinand and Isabella]. . . . Who can doubt that this fire was not merely mine, but also of the Holy Spirit who encouraged me with a radiance of marvelous illumination from his sacred Holy Scriptures, by a most clear and powerful testimony from the forty-four books of the Old Testament, from the four Gospels, from the twenty-three Epistles of the blessed Apostles—urging me to press forward? Continually, without a moment's hesitation, the Scriptures urge me to press forward with great haste.

---

cler reported, King John III, "a very Christian prince, ever more mindful of the salvation of souls than of the profits of the treasury . . . ordered the cessation of this trade, although he suffered great loss by this act." God quickly rewarded his faithful steward, the Portuguese historian added, by guiding him to the discovery of yet another gold mine farther down the African coast. So lucrative did the African trade become that Portugal demonstrated no great eagerness to hazard the risks of pushing westward farther out into the Atlantic.

CHRISTOPHER COLUMBUS

Portugal's reluctance became Spain's opportunity. Unified in 1469 through the teenage marriage of Isabella of Castile and Ferdinand of Aragon, Spain was now prepared to look beyond its internal struggles to destroy the remnants of Muslim rule at the peninsula's southern tip. Then, like Portugal, Spain could consider overseas conquests and settlements. In 1479 Portugal reluctantly recognized Spain's dominion over the Canary Islands off the west coast of Africa. By 1486 Queen Isabella was ready to listen to the schemes and dreams of the thirty-five-year-old Christopher Columbus. But she was not yet ready to act, for the undertaking was expensive, the Genoese sailor's demands audacious, and the results far from certain. So she did what any prudent administrator would do: she appointed a committee. It was a committee of churchmen, for the ranks of the clergy contained most of the well-educated Spaniards of the day: astronomers, geographers, cartographers, mathematicians, and other bookish scholars.

After several years of leisurely deliberation, the committee reported negatively. The voyage would take too long, a return voyage was virtually impossible, the probability of unknown islands being discovered so late in human history was quite remote. Deeply discouraged, Columbus, who had already been turned down by Por-

tugal, now prepared to leave for France to see if his luck would be any better.

At this critical juncture a Franciscan friar interceded on Columbus's behalf, urging Isabella to give him one more hearing and (alas) to appoint one more committee. This committee reported more promptly, but still negatively — with one important difference. The new group decided that such a voyage was conceivable and a return even possible; the crucial problem was cost. At this point Spain's general treasurer, Gabriel Sanchez, stepped into the breach to argue that the opportunity was too great to be missed, whatever the cost. This projected voyage "could prove of so great service to God and the exaltation of his Church," Sanchez informed the queen, that her failure to support such a cause would be "a grave reproach to her."

The Death of Columbus Still in chains, the emaciated and imprisoned Christopher Columbus takes his leave of his few remaining family and friends, including a faithful Indian, in this romanticized and fanciful illustration dating from the nineteenth century. Colonialism and mission work were never far apart in the European mindset, and idealization of Columbus as a visionary Christian hero was reaching its apogee by the time this image was created.

❊   **I N   T H E I R   O W N   W O R D S**

A Golden Age in a Golden New World, 1490s

Columbus in his journal marveled at the peacefulness of the people he found in the West Indies; ironically, he was in many ways a catalyst for the end of that peaceful way of life.

The people of this island [in the West Indies] and of all other islands which I have found and of which I have information, all go naked, men and women, as their mothers bore them, although some women cover a single place with the leaf of a plant or with a net of cotton which they make for the purpose. They have no iron or steel or weapons, nor are they fitted to use them, not because they are not well built men and of handsome stature, but because they are very marvelously timorous. They have no other arms than weapons made of canes, cut in seeding time, to the ends of which they fix a small sharpened stick...they are so guileless and so generous with all they possess, that no one would believe it who has not seen it. They never refuse anything which they possess, if it be asked of them; on the contrary, they invite anyone to share it, and display so much love as if they would give their hearts.

Convinced that the risks were worth it, Isabella in April 1492 commissioned Columbus as "Admiral of the Ocean Sea." Directing Columbus "to discover certain islands and mainlands in the ocean sea," Isabella sounded as uncertain as anyone else about just what lay beyond the western horizon. But whatever there was, Columbus would claim in the name of Spain for both the glory of God and the wealth of the nation. He would also, it was assumed, find his way through the islands to the Asian mainland, and so he was given a letter of introduction to the Great Khan.[2] By August, Columbus prepared to set sail from Palos in southern Spain with three ships under his command — the *Pinta, Niña,* and *Santa Maria.* Setting his course first for the Canary Islands, he thereafter sailed due west, the prevailing winds at his back.

In October 1492, thirty-three days out from the Canary Islands, a lookout on the flagship, *Pinta,* shouted the welcome word that land had been sighted. Soon after, Columbus and his men knelt on an island in the Bahamas that he promptly and gratefully named Holy Savior: San Salvador. From the European perspective, Columbus "discovered" these lands and their inhabitants. The latter, in turn, "discovered" ships and clothing such as they had never seen before. To demonstrate friendship, Columbus presented these islanders "some red caps and some glass beads, which they hung around their necks." Good will proceeded to the point that the natives even swam out to the ships, bringing "parrots and cotton thread in balls, and [reed] spears

and many other things." Indeed, they seemed ready to give all, though Columbus noted that really "they were a people very deficient in everything." But he resolved to take some "samples" of this world's population back to Spain, "that they may learn to talk." (Of course, they already knew how to talk, but not in any language that Columbus had ever heard.) Believing himself to be somewhere near the subcontinent of India, Columbus named these naked people Indians. After several more weeks of exploration in the Caribbean, Columbus headed back for Spain, forced by a storm into Lisbon on March 3, 1493.

Reports of the voyage aroused some envy in Portugal, great elation in Spain, and keen interest everywhere. None was more excited than Columbus himself, who wrote to Gabriel Sanchez (with what was surely false modesty) that the "great and marvelous results" should be credited not to him "but to the holy Christian faith, and to the piety and religion of our Sovereigns." With somewhat less modesty, he suggested that the successful venture be celebrated with processions, feasts, and decorations in all the churches. But no suggestion from him was necessary to stir other European capitals to seek their share in the probable spoils.

Hoping to forestall unseemly competition, Portugal and Spain appealed to the pope to determine the lawful rights to lands already found and not yet discovered. On the basis of these two countries' priorities in venturing westward, Pope Alexander VI in 1493 drew a line of demarcation 263 miles west of the Azores. Beyond that line, all would be Spain's; east of it, all would be Portugal's. That left Portugal with a lot of Atlantic Ocean, but little else. Therefore the two countries drew up the Treaty of Tordesillas and signed it on June 7, 1494, setting the line many miles farther to the west, thereby

---

2. In addition to being written in Latin, which no one in China could have read, the letter would have been useless from another perspective: there was no Great Khan, Mongol rule over China having ended in 1368. All this suggests how little Europeans knew of East Asia.

intercepting the hump of Brazil, and so determining the future of that country.[3]

ANCIENT CIVILIZATIONS ON NEW MAPS

With further voyages, by Columbus and by many others, mapmaking turned into a major industry, and the new craft of printing quickly circulated the letters, journals, and reports announcing the discovery of extraordinary lands. Some letters were genuine, others not: Who could separate incredible truths from incredible lies? One false letter gave credit to Amerigo Vespucci of Florence for having been the principal discoverer of the great continents, leaving to Columbus the honor of having been first to explore the Caribbean. Since Columbus still insisted all this great world was part of Asia (though he never found a Great Khan to accept his letter), and since Vespucci and others knew it was not, mapmakers in 1507 gave to that land the name it has ever since retained: America. Cartographers, desperate for information where none existed, put dragons or mermaids or extra islands where there was too much blank space; they also added names of voyagers and explorers, because it helped to sell maps. Amerigo Vespucci, as if by accident, won historical immortality. But behind this accident lay a sound judgment: These western continents were not a part of Asia, but belonged to another world altogether. By the time Columbus died in 1509, he alone among those knowledgeable of the "New World" clung to the idea that he had reached the gateway to China.

A near-obsession with Asia consumed Columbus

and many of his contemporaries. For fifteenth-century Europeans, the Orient cast an almost hypnotic spell: the promise of enormous wealth, the lure of a vast unknown, the quest for fame and power to be matched only by Europe's kings and queens. Ever since the move of the old imperial capital from Rome to Constantinople in the fourth century A.D., Europe had in some sense looked eastward. Until 1453, imperial Rome's successor, the Byzantine Empire, struggled to keep trade routes open and offered the West glimpses of distant wealthy civilizations. In the late thirteenth century, Marco Polo brought back to Venice stories of the riches of China that set the blood to racing. Muslim conquests in the Near East heightened emotions in another way, as Europe's Christians vowed in a series of extravagant crusades in the twelfth and thirteenth centuries to recapture Jerusalem and other holy sites from the "infidels." A failure in this as in so many other regards, the Crusades nonetheless kept Western attention focused on the East. When at last Constantinople fell in 1453, ending the Byzantine Empire, the immediate answer seemed to be yet another crusade to rescue the holy city and reestablish its rightful place as a major center of Christendom.

While dreams of recovering Constantinople soon faded, the notion that Europe's cause was that of Christianity, east and west, did not die. Columbus shared with many others the firm conviction that if the "islands and mainlands in the ocean sea" were populated, then Christianity must be brought to those too long deprived of it. Or perhaps lost enclaves of Christians existed in the West, as they were rumored to in Asia and Africa. Perhaps sailing across that trackless sea would turn out to be the greatest crusade of them all, doing more for the Christian cause than all the other crusades put

---

3. The fact that Portugal successfully pressed for a westward revision of the dividing line has led some historians to argue that the Portuguese already knew of Brazil's existence, but kept the information secret.

❋ **IN THEIR OWN WORDS**

Spanish Exploration of North America, 1541

In this cranky letter to His Majesty Charles I, October 20, 1541, Francisco Vasquez de Coronado expresses his disappointment with the New World.

And with only the 30 horsemen whom I took for my escort, I traveled forty-two days after I left the force, living all this while solely on

the flesh of the bulls and cows which we killed, at the cost of several of our horses which they killed, because (as I wrote your Majesty) they are very brave and fierce animals; and going many days without water, and cooking the food with cow dung, because there is not any kind of wood in all these places, away from the gullies and rivers, which are very few.

It was the Lord's pleasure that, after hav-

ing journeyed across these deserts seventy-seven days, I arrived at the province they call Quivira, to which the guides were conducting me, and where they had described to me houses of stone, with many stories. Not only are they not of stone, but of straw, but the people in them are as barbarous as all those whom I have seen and passed before this.

A Native American view of European "Discovery"

Handsome Lake was a Seneca Indian who in 1799 had a vision in which he was told that his people must retain their tribal ways and reject European ones. He taught that America was discovered in the following way.

A handsome man welcomed [a young man] into a room and bade him be of ease.... "Listen to me, young man, and you will be rich. Across the ocean there is a great country of which you have never heard. The people there are virtuous, they have no evil habits or appetites but are honest and single-minded. A great reward is yours if you enter into my plans and carry them out. Here are five things. Carry them over to the people across the ocean and never shall you want for wealth, position, or power. Take these cards, this money, this fiddle, this whiskey, and this blood corruption and give them all to the people across the water...."

The young man thought this a good bargain and promised to do as the man commanded him.... Now the handsome man who had appeared in the gold palace was the devil and when afterward he saw what his words had done he said that he had made a great mistake and even he lamented that his evil had been so enormous.

together. Lost colonies of Christians could be reunited with the larger Christian world or at the very least lost souls could be united in a worldwide Christian fellowship. Columbus's language grew religiously extravagant as he wrote that "God made me the messenger of the new heaven and new earth of which he spoke . . . and he showed me the spot where to find it." That Spanish missionaries joined with Spanish soldiers in the conquest of the newly discovered lands was no accident of history. On the contrary, in the fifteenth century the separation of religion from exploration and settlement would have been both inexplicable and intolerable.

❧ *France's First Probes*

From at least the fifteenth century through the twentieth, the fishing banks off Newfoundland have proved to be more profitable than a goldmine. The wealth of those waters fed Europe during much of that time. Fishing expeditions from France became an annual, state-regulated undertaking from at least the middle of the sixteenth century. Sailing from Normandy and other North Atlantic harbors, French mariners went ashore in what are now the Canadian Maritime Provinces to dry their cod before returning to Europe. In the process they learned something about both the Indians and the geography of the region. Such knowledge would prove useful when more serious exploratory efforts began.

Although French fishermen had plied their trade off the banks of Newfoundland for no one knows how long, the first official French expedition to the New World sailed in 1524. Not until the seventeenth century did anything resembling a French North American em-

pire begin to take shape, amid many difficulties and some serious reverses. Even then it came into existence slowly; for example, the population of New France fell far behind that of New England as early as the 1650s. But through the building up of a significant trade in furs and through the steady labors of French missionaries, France left its mark on the American North and Midwest as surely as did the Spanish in the Southwest.

Intrigued by the reports of great New World treasure pouring into Spain, King Francis I of France in 1524 commissioned an Italian sailor, Giovanni da Verrazzano, to explore the trans-Atlantic mainland north of the area of major Spanish activity, keeping a sharp eye out for that elusive route to Asia. Verrazzano sailed by a lot of territory, from around Carolina's Cape Fear River well past the mouth of the Hudson River (where now a handsome bridge across New York harbor bears his name). A learned and cultured man, this Italian captain faithfully reported all that he saw, or hoped that he saw. When he entered the Outer Banks of North Carolina, he thought he had found an eastern arm of the Pacific Ocean. He explored further, seeking to find some strait "in order to penetrate to those happy shores of Cathay [China]." Finding none, however, he continued northward, bestowing a French name on every major inlet or feature of the land. It was a civilized voyage: no slaughter of Indians, no trampling through the woods looting or burning or getting hopelessly lost. After a coastal cruise of several months, Verrazzano wrote: "Having now spent all our provision and victuals, and having discovered about 700 leagues [roughly 2500 miles] and more of new countries, and being furnished with water and wood, we concluded to return to France."

What Verrazzano "discovered" suggested to the

French authorities that more serious investigation was in order. In 1534 Jacques Cartier sailed west, exploring the Strait of Belle Isle between Newfoundland and Labrador. He totally missed the St. Lawrence River, but took two Indians back with him to France so they, too, could "learn how to talk." Returning in 1535 with three ships, over one hundred men, and his two interpreters, Cartier this time not only found the great northern waterway but also explored the St. Lawrence River some thousand miles inland, well past present-day Quebec and Montreal. If this river were not the fabled passage to the Orient, it certainly brought the Pacific Ocean much closer, Cartier reasoned. It also brought the Gulf of Mexico much closer. But many more years would pass before that became clear.

RENAISSANCE AND REFORMATION

While the Portuguese, Spanish, and French explorers were redrawing the maps of the world, European artists, writers, and theologians were reshaping the minds and hearts of many citizens within that world. The colonization of America took place in the midst of an intellectual and cultural upheaval that had far-reaching implications for the Western world. In the wake of that upheaval, kings and queens lost their heads, countries plunged into bloody civil strife, and the unity of Christendom shattered.

✣ *The Renaissance*

The fifteenth century was an Age of Discovery in more ways than one. Scholars recovered ancient texts from Greece and Rome, while artists took new pride in personal cultural explorations and achievements. The Renaissance (which literally means "rebirth") called attention and gave great impetus to the civilizing contributions of humankind, to the rich heritage of the past, both classical and Christian. Scholars insisted on reading Plato and Aristotle anew, preferably in the original Greek. And they turned to the Bible anew, reading it in the original Hebrew and Greek. Going back to the sources brought new inspiration to the time, but all this was joined with a vitality and fresh imagination that facilitated countless new discoveries of the mind and spirit.

Because Americans so often see the Renaissance as an aspect of European history and the Age of Discovery as the opening chapter of American history, it is easy to overlook their common features. Leonardo da Vinci was born in 1452, one year after Christopher Columbus; Niccolò Machiavelli the same year as Vasco da Gama in 1469; and Michelangelo in 1475, just a few years before Ferdinand Magellan, who led the first expedition to circumnavigate the earth. Europe's explorers, therefore, shared not only a temporal bond with Europe's artists and thinkers, but also their energy and freshness of vision. The Renaissance represented, among other things, a willingness to set out on unmarked paths, to do something for the first time, to throw off a tired tradition and overly familiar routine. Hugging the coastline of Africa was one way to see the world, but only a small portion of it. Clinging to the traditions of medieval scholasticism was one way to exercise the mind, but only a limited segment of it. In the fifteenth century, the uncharted waters, both geographical and intellectual, lured the adventuresome as never before.

✣ *The Reformation*

Throughout the fifteenth century, the Catholic Church was the sole ecclesiastical institution for all of Europe west of Russia and north of the Balkans. Just as the Holy Roman Empire symbolized a political unity, so the Roman Catholic Church symbolized (and, in fact, constituted) a churchly unity. "One church, one faith, one baptism" was not just an ideal but a reality in this region.

MARTIN LUTHER

All of that changed radically in the sixteenth century. In 1517, an Augustinian friar named Martin Luther (1483-1546) nailed ninety-five theses, or propositions for scholarly debate, on the door of the church in Wittenberg, a university town in northern Germany. So innocuous an action led to a cataclysmic result: a Holy Roman Empire divided and war-torn, and a Church Universal shaken and rent beyond all healing even a half-millennium later. Luther began with a relatively mild protest against the way in which the sacrament of penance was understood. Catholic practice and theology expected of sinners sincere sorrow and confession to a priest, followed by some form of satisfaction (offering alms or prayers, participating in a pilgrimage or crusade) in return and receiving forgiveness or absolution. In Luther's Saxony, however, sellers of "indulgences" offered forgiveness of sin for a price, and even offered a reduction in time spent in purgatory — the place where, after death, souls atoned for any residual guilt for their sins.

Martin Luther In an idealized nineteenth-century image, Luther appears as the steadfast man of God, fearlessly pointing to the New Testament.

Indulgence-selling struck Luther as a violation of fundamental Christian doctrine and a subversion of the true spirit of penance. Hoping to stop such irregular and degrading practices, he sought to bring the matter to the attention of the pope and of other church authorities. But when the corrective action that Luther sought was not taken, he steadily moved to more uncompromising positions. By 1520 he was rejecting the authority of the pope and even that of a church council. He took refuge, rather, in Scripture, defying centuries of medieval tradition. In his "Address to the German Nobility"(1520), Luther also appealed to the rising nationalism of his fellow Germans, arguing that they should reject the papacy as a foreign tyranny. The pope and his inner circle have, said Luther, "always abused our simplicity to serve their own arrogance and tyranny, and they call us mad Germans, who let ourselves be made apes and fools at their bidding."

In his study of Paul's letter to the Galatians in the New Testament, Luther found what he regarded as the theological key to his understanding of the relationship between God and his creatures: Men and women were no longer under the law — neither the ancient law of Moses nor the more recent law of the medieval church. For Jesus Christ had made human beings free, liberated from the impossible task of earning their salvation through good works or purchasing it through indulgences. Salvation was a gift of God, a free act of divine love. To try to win one's salvation by merit was to deny God's great gift and to mock Christ's selfless sacrifice. Justification by faith, not by works, became the touchstone of Luther's theological reform.

Taking equal advantage of German nationalism and of the newly invented printing press, Luther wrote not in the scholar's Latin but in the people's German, drawing many of his countrymen onto his side. He even translated the Bible into German so that the people might be able to read the Scriptures in their own language. By the time of Luther's death in 1546, the unity of the Roman Catholic Church had been shattered, as the numerous German principalities and city-states took sides either for Catholicism or for Lutheranism.

JOHN CALVIN

In France, a humanist scholar and theologian, John Calvin (1509-1564), soon introduced yet another mode of being Christian. Through his highly influential writings and by means of his direct leadership in the city of Geneva (on the border between France and Switzerland), Calvin made his presence felt in much of Western Europe and well beyond. Though Protestantism ultimately did not prevail in his native France, his version of the gospel came to dominate in the Netherlands, in Scotland, in several locales in Germany, Switzerland, and for a time in England and eastern Europe. Calvin's *Institutes of the Christian Religion,* first published in 1536 but repeatedly revised and enlarged until his death in 1564, was the first truly systematic presentation of Protestant theology. It was also by far the most important, as its influence extended powerfully to the North American continent.

In a long letter of dedication to King Francis I of France, Calvin argued strongly that Protestantism was not some new heresy. It was, rather, a return to the New Testament and would therefore be perceived as "new" only by those to whom the gospel of Jesus Christ was new. Artfully organized to develop the major themes of the ancient Apostles' Creed, Calvin's potent *Institutes* sought to defend his followers from unfair attacks — from cries for their "imprisonment, banishment, proscription, and flames, and [for them] to be exterminated from the face of the earth." By setting forth the fundamentals of New Testament Christianity as he understood it, Calvin dared to hope that Francis I would not be seduced "by those groundless accusations with which our adversaries endeavor to terrify you." Francis vacillated between harsh repression of the Calvinists and a somewhat more relaxed policy, but ultimately he came down on the side of the Catholic Church.

While Calvin clearly built on much that Luther had written and done, he just as clearly moved beyond Luther in several respects. Although both men rejected the Catholic view of the sacraments as the means by which God's grace is bestowed, Calvin moved farther away from the material and toward the spiritual. In the sacrament of the Lord's Supper, for example, Luther still saw the body and blood of Christ as physically present in the bread and the wine, though no priestly miracle created that presence on the altar. Calvin, on the other hand, saw the bread and the wine as spiritual symbols of Christ's presence, a presence to be received only through faith. Whereas the exuberant Luther saw justification by faith as a great liberation, the more austere Calvin saw the overarching sovereignty of God as the determining factor in all life, both here and hereafter. God's providence, not human freedom, shaped all destinies.

Neither Luther nor Calvin contributed directly to the American ideal of a separation between the church and the state. Luther put his trust in the German princes to enforce his reforms and restrain the rabble. Calvin, following the biblical injunction that "the powers that be are ordained of God," taught obedience to civil authority as a Christian duty. In his own Geneva, where he held positions of both civil and ecclesiastical power, clear lines between church and state were practically impossible to draw.

THE ANABAPTIST MOVEMENT

Such ideas of church-state separation as could be found in sixteenth-century Europe flowed from the radicals of the Reformation, most notably the Anabaptists. These sectarians, persecuted by Catholics, Lutherans, and Calvinists alike, taught that baptism should be administered to adult believers only, not to infants. Faith must be voluntary. And the church, likewise, must be a voluntary association, not governed by or under obligation to the state. Many of these radicals refused to vote or hold office; most also refused to bear arms, their pacifism bringing even more condemnation on their heads. Today's Mennonites and Amish are the direct descendants of this

The Pope Selling Indulgences This 1521 woodcut, printed in Wittenberg (the center of Luther's reform movement), makes the Lutheran case against Roman Catholicism. Here a wizened, demonic-looking pope and his cardinals authorize monks, identified by their tonsures, to take money from simple laypeople in return for assurances that their sins are not only forgiven but also will not be punished in Purgatory.

strain of the sixteenth-century Reformation; present-day Baptists are only indirectly related.

THE CHURCH OF ENGLAND

While much of continental Europe was being splintered by the Protestant Reformation and the Catholic forces that opposed the swift Protestant advances, England's King Henry VIII (1491-1547) was taking legislative steps to throw off all papal authority. In the 1530s the church *in* England became the Church *of* England, with the king taking unto himself full authority to "repress, redress, reform, order, correct, restrain, and amend" all errors in either theology or worship within his realm. Henry, motivated in part by his desire to marry Anne Boleyn and have his previous marriage to Catherine of Aragon annulled, wanted to prevent any legal appeals from his kingdom to any earthly authority beyond his domain. For Henry, as for Luther, the pope began to represent, if not a foreign tyranny, at least a foreign irritation and intrusion. He did depend on his nobles, but he ensured their support when he confiscated the extensive monastic lands belonging to the Catholic Church and distributed them to his favorites, keeping a fair amount for himself. When Henry died in 1547, the English Reformation had hardly begun. The next century or more, however, would see his nation strained and torn by competing forms and forces of religion.

CHANGING IDEAS

The Reformation was in part a political movement, in part a theological controversy, and in part a social transformation. From country to country, it moved in an uneven pace, sometimes affecting the individual parish or the individual worshipper hardly at all. Instead, it often seemed more like a treaty concluded at the upper echelons of the state. At other times, however, entire populaces got caught up in questions of access to the Bible, in debates about the presence of Christ in the Lord's Supper, in quarrels over conformity to this or that ritual requirement, and in battles for the rights of individual conscience. At a minimum, to embrace Protestantism meant to reject the authority of the pope, but it could and usually did mean far more: faith above works, Scripture over tradition, obedience to God above subservience to church leaders. In seeking to know exactly where it all led, men and women died as martyrs to their faith, Catholic and Protestant alike. Just as many lived in eloquent testimony to the vitality and reality of their faith.

Luther labored to break down the wall between the priesthood and the laity, arguing for "the priesthood of all believers." No special sacred class, he insisted, should be elevated above other Christians; no priestly caste enjoyed unique access to God, nor could members of this group bar others from the throne of grace. Other Protestant leaders followed Luther in giving greater prominence and authority to the laity, some groups later suggesting even that any clerical leadership was quite unnecessary.

In the Middle Ages, a "calling" meant that someone felt impelled to be a monk or a nun — to separate himself or herself from the world. In Protestantism, by contrast, the notion of "calling" was broadened to embrace any labor or service within the world. Christians, Protestantism asserted, served God by working in the world, not by escaping from it. Nor did those saved by grace take their ease, leaving all to God. On the contrary, Protestants were exhorted to work all the harder to convince the world (and themselves) that salvation had been granted. Diligent and dedicated labor, as a kind of divine calling, helped to create a capitalist society, thereby separating the medieval from the modern world.

✣ *European Powers and Perceptions*

By the end of the sixteenth century, the religious lines in Europe were fairly fixed. Northern Germany along with Finland, Denmark, Sweden, and Norway had opted for Lutheranism. Scotland, the Dutch Republic, portions of Switzerland, and various towns in France had chosen Calvinism. England had its independent Church of England, whose precise theological path was yet to be determined. If at one point it might have seemed that all of Europe was turning Protestant, the combined efforts of Catholic counter-measures and Catholic reforms saw that this did not happen. Ireland remained Catholic, as did most of southern Germany and most of France. Church and secular authorities in Italy and Spain repelled any tentative Protestant forays.

Indeed, Spain proved to be the most powerful force, both militarily and spiritually, for the Catholic resurgence. Spain's navy threatened England's in the late sixteenth century, and Spain's land forces fought hard to reclaim the Netherlands for Catholicism. A revival of Catholic piety, typified by such great Spanish mystics as St. Teresa of Ávila (1515-1582) and St. John of the Cross (1542-1591), gave new strength to a revitalized

PARIS

St. Bartholemew's Day   This contemporary illustration shows Catholic fanatics, loyal to the French king Charles IX and his mother Catherine de Medici, systematically massacring every Huguenot on whom they could lay hands in Paris on August 23, 1572.

Catholicism. Even more significantly, St. Ignatius of Loyola (1491-1556) founded the Society of Jesus in 1540. A military soldier wounded in battle, Ignatius vowed during his convalescence to create a company of spiritual soldiers for Christ: men who would serve the pope obediently and faithfully, anywhere in the world. And the Jesuits would prove their mettle, time and again, not just in Spain, but also in France, Belgium, in the East, and in the Americas.

France suffered serious distractions from religious controversies that resulted in religious wars. French Protestants (known as Huguenots), taking their message and convictions from their compatriot John Calvin, multiplied markedly by the middle of the sixteenth century. In 1572 a brutal massacre organized by the king on St. Bartholemew's Day resulted in the death of hundreds; over much of France, this ghastly event led to a virtual state of war between Protestants and Catholics. Ultimately, King Henry IV issued his Edict of Nantes in 1598 giving restricted rights to the Huguenots in quite limited areas, while the rest of France remained Roman Catholic. For a time, the edict brought a measure of peace to a religiously troubled land.

Many of Europe's deep and bitter divisions moved across the Atlantic to the New World. There, not only did nation become pitted against nation, but faith also fought faith. But despite these and other distractions, Spain, the Dutch Republic, England, France, and Sweden presented the strongest examples of nationalism in the era of discovery and exploration.

Only slowly did the enormity of the North American continent impress itself upon the European mind. At first the Great Western Sea seemed chiefly a route to the spices and riches of the East. None at first would have guessed that a huge land mass would block the fabled "Northwest Passage" to Asia. But ultimately the obstruction became an obsession to be possessed.

Nombra a Motzuma al Rey de España por succesor de su Imperio: le da la obediencia, y tributo.

Montezuma's Submission   This sixteenth-century painting shows a decidedly European view of the proud Mexican emperor Montezuma (Moctezuma) II as he kneels before the Spanish conqueror Cortés, submitting himself and his people to the rule of the Spanish king Charles I (Emperor Charles V).

SPAIN IN THE AMERICAS

Once a coastline had been identified, rivers probed, and landings made, the European powers thought of more than just sending explorers and missionaries to America. They began to see their presence in these lands as a more permanent venture. To trading posts, they needed to add settlements; to military forts, colonies. Spain set the pattern for others to follow, thinking of more than mere plunder or booty or purely symbolic planting of a national flag. Now Europeans dreamt of and planned for an overseas empire that would forever lend glory and wealth to their country.

❧ Spain's New World Possessions

Columbus followed his first venture of 1492 with three more voyages in 1493, 1498, and 1502–1504. Even more significant, however, from Spain's point of view were the beginnings of territorial control and the gathering of great wealth. In 1519 the Castilian nobleman and adventurer Hernán Cortés led a major expedition from Cuba to Mexico, landing at present-day Veracruz ("True Cross"). Striking inland, he proceeded to conquer the entire Aztec empire, including its capital at Tenochtitlán (now Mexico City). Mounted on his horse, a beast unknown to the Native Americans, Cortés made a dramatic figure in his full battle armor. The Aztecs regarded him as a sort of god, and Cortés did not disabuse them. In his more reflective moments, he settled for comparing himself with Alexander the Great of Macedon.

Making allies of Indian tribes chafing under Aztec domination, Cortés dramatically enlarged Spain's overseas dominion in a relatively short span of time. He also enlarged the domain of Christianity; he repeatedly explained to the Indians that they must give up human sacrifices, destroy their "idols," and embrace the religion of their conquerors. To his captains he gave captured Indian women as wives, piously cautioning his men that each maiden must first be baptized before marriages could be performed or cohabitation begun.

Cortés bargained with the Aztec ruler, Montezuma, for his kingdom and his life. Though Montezuma ultimately lost both, he tried to buy off the conqueror with heaps of gold and silver, precious stones, exquisite featherwork, and impressively carved solar calendars. So dazzled and hypnotized were Cortés and his men by the freely flowing gold that they could think of little else besides the capture and exploitation of the Aztec mines. When Cortés entered Tenochtitlán in late 1519, his men discovered treasures that staggered their imaginations. One soldier reported that he "had never seen such riches as those in my life before, [and] I took it for certain that there could not be another such store of wealth in the whole world." For his part, Montezuma soon realized that his vast wealth would find its way across the ocean to enrich Spain.[4]

Even before Cortés's conquest of Mexico, another Castilian, Ponce de León, had left Puerto Rico to explore Florida. Ponce de León had several possible motives: perhaps to search for gold, perhaps to gather Indian slaves (the supply having already been exhausted on several Caribbean islands), certainly to claim more land — both for Spain and for himself. Landing during Easter week (*pascua florida* in Spanish) near what later became St. Augustine, Ponce de León gave the region its lasting name. But neither this expedition nor a later one in 1521, when he was fatally wounded, yielded any significant return. Ponce de León found no gold, took no slaves — the natives there proving much less complaisant than in the Caribbean — and gained only the vaguest idea of the geography of the unfriendly land. But others would follow where he had failed.

In April 1527 Pánfilo de Narváez, sailing with five ships, plentiful horses and provisions, and six hundred men, landed at Tampa Bay with little clear sense of what to do next. Having been granted the lofty title of governor and captain general of the entire northern rim of the Gulf of Mexico, he decided to start at the eastern end of that rim and gradually to work his way back to Texas and northern Mexico.

But from the moment the men arrived in Tampa Bay, everything went wrong. First, they found no gold — only Indians assuring them that they must keep looking farther north. Second, they decided to split into two groups, one to explore overland along the northern rim, the other to sail in the general direction of the Texas coast. Third, they failed to make clear where the ships should pick up the land party. Fourth, the men on land soon ran out of food, gave up on gold (despite searching as far north as present-day Tallahassee), and soon decided that travel by water was much less arduous and dangerous. (It had taken more than two months to cover the two hundred miles from Tampa to Tallahassee.) So they turned westward to meet the Gulf waters near Panama City — a journey of another month, living off the land or Indian crops. Looking for their ships and seeing none (it would have been a miracle if they had), they decided to build new boats. But as one disgusted member of the party, Cabeza de Vaca, noted, "We did not know how to build them, nor did we have tools or iron or forge or oakum [hemp or jute fiber] or pitch or tackle." After eight years of hardship and near-endless wanderings, Cabeza de Vaca and three companions struggled back to Mexico City in 1536. Nothing they had seen even remotely resembled the glories Cortés had found in Mexico. North America had proved to be a major disappointment.

Spaniards, however, did not give up on the mainland. Three years after Cabeza de Vaca made his painful way back into Mexico, Hernando de Soto set out from Cuba to explore not only Florida but much of southeastern North America. Two goals obsessed de Soto: first, to find that great capital city of North America that would be comparable, somehow, to the capital city of the Aztecs and would, therefore, be laden with gold; and second, to find some great east-west river or waterway, opening up the long-wished-for passage to

Old Spanish Mission Church Soon after the Spanish began to colonize New Mexico, in the first years of the seventeenth century, friars built the mission of San Geronimo near Taos Pueblo. For generations the native people of that region resisted Spanish rule and attempts to Christianize them.

---

4. Actually the loot that the Spanish plundered from the Americas mostly found its way into the coffers of European bankers who financed Spain's endless wars in the sixteenth-century. This influx of American treasure helped spark and sustain a dramatic inflation known as the Price Revolution.

Asia. Cutting a wide swath through Georgia, Alabama, Mississippi, Arkansas, and Louisiana, de Soto found neither his capital city nor his watery way west. He did find the Mississippi River, on whose bank he was buried in 1542 after succumbing to a fever. His followers made their way to the Gulf of Mexico, then by barges to Mexico, returning after more than four years of pointless plunder empty-handed and utterly disillusioned. A sixteenth-century Spanish historian summed up the dismal results: de Soto, he wrote, "went about five years hunting mines, thinking it would be like Peru. He made no settlement, and thus he died and destroyed those who went with him."

The Spanish left little mark on the area through which de Soto roamed, though later the small settlement of St. Augustine, founded in 1565 in northwest Florida, gave them claim to the first "city" in North America. French Protestants who had settled along the St. John's River, just north of St. Augustine, were wiped out by the Spanish, who had no intention of sharing North America with anyone. But despite such pretensions, Spain's cultural impact on the southeastern corner of the present-day United States was minimal.

More significant by far were the Spanish settlements in the Southwest. The beginnings of Spain's explorations in this region — the expedition of Francisco Vásquez de Coronado in 1540-42 — were discouraging. Starting overland from his base in Mexico, Coronado and his troops traveled through Arizona and New Mexico, as ever in search of gold and great cities. He found, instead, poor pueblos and meagerly supplied Hopi and Zuni tribes. Exploring as far as Kansas, Coronado brought back reports no more hopeful than those coming from the earlier disastrous ventures to the east. For fifty years, Spain did little more with the parched southwestern lands. Only at the century's end did the Spanish decide that land should be subdued and held in the name of the crown.

In 1595 Don Juan de Oñate led the advance, a thousand miles north of Mexico City, into present-day New Mexico. By 1610 the town of Sante Fe arose to become the Southwest's chief political and spiritual center, which with one brief interruption it would remain. It embodied in North America the Spanish culture and power that more noticeably prevailed to the south. The missionary thrust of this conquest was the work of the Franciscans.[5] The brown-robed evangels had trouble

getting their message across to the Indians, provoking a revolt, for example, on St. Catherine's Island, Georgia, in 1597. But they also had trouble with *los conquistadores* — the Spanish military men who treated Indians with such brutality that any thought of missionary effectiveness vanished. One Franciscan friar complained bitterly to the Viceroy of Spain in 1601 about the behavior of Oñate, who with his soldiers looted, burned, enslaved, and oftentimes cut off the hands or feet of Indians who counterattacked or simply tried to defend their homes. "Because of these matters (and others that I am not telling)," the friar concluded, "we cannot preach the gospel now."

In 1680, in a secret and well-coordinated attack, the Indians of northern New Mexico revolted against both cross and crown, driving the Spanish all the way back into Mexico. But before the century ended, the Spanish returned in a celebrated reconquest that endured as long as Spain's political presence lasted in North America. With Spanish control reasserted and Santa Fe again Spain's northernmost outpost, the colonial economy rested on farming and raising sheep. But northern New Mexico also looked eastward, to trade with the Plains Indians and even with the French who in the late seventeenth century settled in Louisiana and Missouri (see below). Franciscan missionaries gave New Mexico its steadiest Christian presence and its most enduring ties with the distant culture of Spain. Ironically, gold would eventually be found in the West — but not until centuries later, and not by the Spanish.

❧ Imperial Government, Christian Missions, and Slavery

After Columbus explored the Caribbean, Spain quickly established commercial and administrative centers on the principal islands: Cuba, Jamaica, Puerto Rico, and Santo Domingo (also called Hispaniola). The first generation of Spanish officials established the *encomienda* system, which placed Indian villages under direct Spanish control and reduced the Indian people to virtual slavery. If Indians resisted, war resulted, with the outcome almost invariably favoring the invaders. A formal legal document called "The Requisition" was read in Spanish to the Indians (who could not understand it, of course), informing them that they must now obey the pope as well as the rulers of Spain, and must receive missionaries to instruct them in the rituals and doctrines of Christianity. The combination of land along with Indian serfs or slaves attached to it

---

5. Founded by St. Francis of Assisi in the thirteenth century, the Franciscans left their greatest mark in North America in the Southwest and Pacific West.

granted to the Spanish captains (or *encomienderos*) great political and economic power, though they always lusted for more.

Quite early in the Spanish occupation of the Caribbean islands, popes had tried to stop the inhumane treatment of the Indians. As early as 1510 Bartholomé de las Casas, a Dominican missionary in the Caribbean and South America, complained about the cruel injustices practiced against the indigenous people. It would be better, he cried, for the Indians to fall into the hands "of the devils of hell than of the Christians of the Indies." In 1516 las Casas received the title of "Defender of the Indians" for his bold stand. Some twenty years later he gained papal support and vindication in an edict of Paul III declaring that Indians were human beings, not animals, and were to be neither enslaved nor deprived of their property, but should enjoy their liberty "freely and legitimately."

Europe in general, and not just Spain, found a good measure of justification for New World conquest in the opportunity that it presented to bring the Christian gospel to those who had never heard it. But the tension between conversion and subjugation could not be easily resolved. Much of the theological rationale came across more as rationalization: a thin veneer of soul-saving covering a deep reservoir of private greed and national aggrandizement. And even where Franciscan missions dominated the landscape — as they did in Texas, New Mexico, and California — many questioned the techniques employed and the results that emerged.

The coming of missions required migrating tribes in the area to give up familiar patterns of hunting and gathering. Traditional rituals were now eclipsed by strange practices and even stranger ideas. Were the "mission Indians" victims of just another form of slavery or serfdom? And did all the rhetoric about carrying the gospel to a new world collapse before the hard realities of national rule, economic return, and simple survival? These questions would arise, again and again, among all the European explorers and propagandists.

Spain kept a tight rein on all her new colonies and territories, exercising authority through royally appointed viceroys and the Council of the Indies, established in 1524. Viceroys, as the king's deputies, exercised great power — in theory on behalf of the empire, in fact often on behalf of themselves. Their terms were short, however, so that their power and accumulated wealth would not rival that of the king himself. Initially, Spain appointed only two viceroys: one who from Mexico City administered Central America, North America,

and the Caribbean; the other who from Lima (in Peru) ruled all South America. The Council of the Indies, particularly in the sixteenth century, provided vigorous direction: passing laws, maintaining fiscal accounts, controlling shipping, and receiving appeals from local administrators of justice. Beneath these higher layers of governance swarmed many lesser administrators, but all were Spanish and most were born in Spain. *Creolos* — people of Spanish descent but born in the New World — were generally accorded lower social status.

Despite the subjugation of Indians as a whole, the Spanish population, predominantly male, intermarried freely with Indian women and produced children by native mistresses. The *mestizo* population of mixed Spanish and Indian ancestry was small in the sixteenth century but eventually would grow enormously. In the Caribbean in particular, the native population declined precipitously; European disease created a problem there as everywhere else in the Western Hemisphere. As the Indian population dwindled (and, in the Caribbean, disappeared), the demand for other sources of slave labor intensified. To fill the void, Spain soon began bringing black Africans to the major islands. Both Portugal and Spain exported slaves to the New World, the former mainly to Brazil and the latter initially to the Caribbean islands. Although accurate numbers are hard to come by, well before the first permanent English settlement arose in North America close to a million Africans had been enslaved in the Western Hemisphere. By the seventeenth century, well-established precedents were in place in the Portuguese and Spanish colonies that greatly influenced the English, Dutch, and French in developing slavery within the new domains that they established.

FRENCH COLONIZATION

As early as 1500, and perhaps even before, French fishermen pointed the way to the New World for their countrymen, but few chose to follow them. In the sixteenth century Verrazzano and Cartier carried the French flag to North America, but religious wars at home prevented their nation from taking advantage of what they had found. In the following century, France took up colonization with more seriousness, aided by domestic peace, supported by the Jesuits, and drawn by a lucrative trade in furs. By the end of the seventeenth century, North America harbored three great European powers: Spain, France, and England.

&ch; The French Empire

Attempts at French colonization were made in the 1540s and the 1560s, but none proved profitable or viable. The land was inhospitable and agriculture unproductive. Fur had not yet been recognized as the road to riches, and when discovered it would be the result of efforts by private entrepreneurs rather than those of the state. Above all, France, torn apart by the Wars of Religion (see above, p. 13), was in no position to sustain a policy of foreign colonization.

But in 1603, with the return of peace, the French crown gave Samuel de Champlain authority to survey the St. Lawrence Valley more thoroughly, with an eye to imperial gain and French colonization. Nowhere at this time did the continent sustain any European settlement north of Florida. For the next several years, Champlain laid the foundations for France's future empire in North America's interior. He established Quebec as part fortress, part trading post, and part winter residence. He also formed alliances with the Hurons against the Iroquois, securing his position along both banks of the St. Lawrence and learning from the Hurons of "great seas" — the Great Lakes — just beyond the rapids of Niagara Falls that prevented his ships from going farther upriver. In 1609, with the help of the Hurons, he explored the Richelieu River southward as far as Lake Iroquois in upstate New York, which, following a brief battle with the Iroquois, he renamed in his own honor Lake Champlain. By 1611 Champlain had planted French roots in Montreal, a settlement destined to become the principal base for exploration not only of the Great Lakes, but also of the upper Mississippi Valley.

Settlement in New France, although now permanent, remained far from spectacular despite Champlain's strenuous efforts both back in France and in Canada. In 1627 he persuaded Louis XIII's chief minister, Cardinal Richelieu, to support the creation of a Company of One Hundred Associates to encourage the development of New France. But just two years later Champlain's colony fell before English military power. England's occupation lasted only three years, but when France regained authority over the territory, colonization fell largely into the hands of private sponsors.

&ch; Jesuit Missions

France's religious struggles afflicted the New World as well. The home government sought to root out all Huguenots from the Newfoundland fisheries and the Canadian fur trade. The Edict of Nantes (see above, p. 13) did not guarantee toleration in the colonies, although enforcement for a time was lax. Then, in 1627, Richelieu determined that settlement in New France should be restricted to "natural-born French Catholics." When the French restored their authority in Quebec in 1632, Huguenot rights were pointedly not recognized. Instead, the Protestants became the object of powerful campaigns of repression and conversion, so that within two or three decades French Protestantism presented no challenge to Catholic ascendancy.

The earliest French missionaries were members of the Récollets, a branch of the Franciscan order. In 1639 Ursuline nuns also arrived in Quebec, along with nursing sisters; both hospitals and schools arose soon after. But beyond question the major spiritual force in New

---

✳ IN THEIR OWN WORDS

French Failure in Florida, 1565
Near the mouth of the St. Johns River, Frenchman Rene de Laudonniere writes of his country's defeat in Florida.

Thus briefly you see the discourse of all that happened in New France since the time it pleased the King's Majesty to send his subjects thither to discover these parts. The indifferent & unpassionate readers may easily weigh the truth of my doings, & be upright judges of the endeavour which I there used. For my own

part, I will not accuse nor excuse any. It suffices me to have followed the truth of history, whereof many are able to bear witness, who were there present. I will plainly say one thing: That the long delay that Captain John Ribault used in his embarking, & the fifteen days that he spent in roving along the coast of Florida before he came to our Fort Caroline, were the cause of loss that we sustained. For he discovered the coast the fourteenth of August, & spent the time going from river to river. . . . In my opinion, he should have had more regard

unto his charge, than to the devices of his own brain, which sometime be printed in his head so deeply that it was very hard to put them out. This also turned to his utter undoing, for he was no sooner departed from us, but a tempest took him, which in fine wrecked him upon the coast, where all his ships were cast away, & he with much ado escaped drowning, to fall into their [the Spaniards'] hands, who cruelly massacred him and all his company.

Rene de Laudonniere (near the mouth of the St. Johns River)

France after 1632 was the Society of Jesus. Jesuits even assumed control of the monastery formerly the property of the Récollets, taking over from them the education of Indian children and the missionary activities in selected Indian villages. But Indian boys, subjected to Jesuit discipline in Quebec schools, bolted like "wild asses' colts" whenever possible. Jesuits soon found that they could be most effective not by bringing the native people to them (as Spanish Franciscan missions did), but by themselves moving into the Indians' woods.

So, at great risk, Jesuits lived with the Indians. Some lost their lives; others returned dismayed and discouraged. Still others made painfully slow progress in winning converts, often struggling against their own countrymen with different priorities as well as against the native people's natural resistance. Even though the interest of Cross and Crown traversed the ocean together, generally even on the same ship, those interests were not evenly matched once trading began, conquest enlarged, and settlements grew. Commercial and national interests, stronger and ever more strident, eventually shaped the course of colonial life. Over time, the native population came to seem more an obstruction and irritation than an object of charity and evangelization.

Nonetheless, the Jesuits labored on, notably among the Hurons, who were not constantly on the move but were a settled agricultural group. By 1639 Jesuit fathers established a major mission center among those Indians living around Lake Huron. As many as 30,000 natives dwelled in "Huronia," the large settlement, and up to eighteen Jesuit missionaries labored in that one territory alone. One leader in this effort, Jean de Brébeuf, spent many months learning the Huron language, advising other Jesuits who might follow to let the study of the native tongue "be your Saint Thomas and your Aristotle." While learning the language, the new missionary's best tactic among the Indians, said Brébeuf, was simply to remain silent. At the end of much study and hard work, the neophyte would with luck "be able to stammer a little." Brébeuf showed similar sensitivity with respect to Huron customs and traditions, urging that great care be taken not to offend those whom the Jesuits sought to serve.

Was it worth it? Brébeuf had no doubt that it was, but wished to warn those contemplating the mission field in New France to come only if their souls burned with such fire that they counted it a great blessing to suffer for the gospel's sake. In 1649 war broke out between the Hurons and the Iroquois, resulting in the capture, torture, and death of Jean de Brébeuf. From

the perspective of the Iroquois, he deserved to die as an enemy of their god Areskoui and a friend to their enemies, the Hurons. But from the perspective of France and its church, he deserved the elevation to sainthood that came to him at last in 1930.

In the absence of a strong political figure such as Champlain, the Society of Jesus dominated New France's affairs from 1632 to 1659. The Society acquired valuable property that it proceeded to cultivate and harvest. Jesuits built mills to assist newly arriving settlers in constructing their own homes; they introduced a feudal system of rights and privileges; and they attracted wealth to New France in the form of donations from rich French patrons, from their own order, and from the king himself. Most enduring of all, they provided detailed reports of all activity — commercial, political, religious — that in the form of the famous *Jesuit Relations* still constitute the best record of Indian and French life that exists for New France.

❧ *The Fur Trade*

France was greatly aided in its bid for empire when a fur trader named Louis Joliet joined with the Jesuit Jacques Marquette to explore the upper reaches of the Mississippi River in 1673. They paddled down as far as the Arkansas River, where the Spanish presence blocked them from going all the way to the Gulf of Mexico. Marquette's maps and journals, however, later made possible France's ultimate reach all the way to the Gulf. Control of the entire Mississippi Valley gave France a territorial presence in North America that not only rivaled that of Spain and England, but for a time overshadowed both.

The success of New France hinged on the development and expansion of the fur trade, which proved to be lucrative. As with missions, so with trade: the most successful technique was to move into the forests and along the streams, trading with the Indians in their own locales, living with them and marrying their young women. (An Indian wife became a virtual necessity for survival.) These French *coureurs de bois* ("runners of the woods") collected furs far inland, transporting them to major collecting points for shipment to France. The fur traders also became explorers and mapmakers, interpreters, and on-the-spot diplomats. With birchbark canoes and snowshoes, some penetrated far north of the St. Lawrence, bringing back the pelts of beavers, otters, martens, elk, and bear. The traders operated without direction or control from either church or state, guided only by fluctuating market conditions. But so successful were they that by the end of the seventeenth century the strong alliance between the French and the Indians rested squarely on the trade in furs.

The French sent no great military expeditions to plunder or subdue the interior. Instead they depended on traders to bargain and buy, creating lasting and beneficial alliances. Many different tribes joined in the trade, the more migratory ones often being the most successful, or at least the most aggressive. Fierce Eskimos covered the area north of the Gulf of St. Lawrence, while Montagnais worked the wilderness between Quebec and the mouth of the river. Farther south and west, the Algonkians of the Ottawa River contributed heavily. While the Hurons did not migrate, they sat at the intersection of many trade routes, guaranteeing to the French an abundant and unceasing supply of furs.

The Indians did not need to be instructed in the nature of trade, but the arrival of the Europeans sharply altered the nature of their commerce. A Stone Age people suddenly entered the Iron Age; a people skilled in bows and arrows quickly learned the advantage of guns even as they prepared to exchange skins for woven cloth. At first the trade was neither organized nor sought out. It was more a matter of accidental meeting, and exchanging goods as a way of civil greeting, as a way of assuring each other that no harm was intended. No record survives of most of these incidental contacts, but some sixteenth-century reports do convey the flavor of the first casual meetings between curious Europeans and bewildered Indians. An early French explorer who arrived off the mainland of Canada in 1534, for example, led his crew in a friendly exchange of goods after each side demonstrated its peaceful intent. "Two of our men ventured to go on land to them, and carry them knives with other iron wares, and a red hat to give unto their captain. Which when they saw, they also came on land, and brought some of their skins, and so began to deal with us." Much of this kind of contact was more ceremonial than commercial.

But trading posts took on a life of their own as European markets began to shape the Indian and colonial economies. A subsistence economy for the Indian became a trading economy, as now Indians seized more from the land than just what was necessary for their own needs. The wants of all Europe proved insatiable, wiping out the abundance of North American animal life. This was most notably true in the fur trade, which whether carried on by French, Dutch, or English yielded the same result: beavers, otters, martens, and fox began to disappear. Indians began to disappear too, as guns and alcohol took their toll and as tribal patterns and traditional customs suffered disruption.

Disease, however, devastated Indian life most severely. Isolated from microbes of the Old World, Indians lacked immunity to Europeans' common ailments. Smallpox, chicken pox, measles, syphilis, malaria, yellow fever, and more besides decimated Indian populations wherever trade brought the two disparate populations into contact. The testimonies of the devastation wrought are as horrifying as the estimates of the death tolls: in some villages, 80 to 90 percent of the population succumbed to one or another of the diseases against which the Indians had no defense. Earliest European observers commented on the good health of the natives, their well-proportioned bodies, their physical vigor and remarkable endurance. Later observers would have occasion to speak (in the words of the Governor of Plymouth Colony) of the "lamentable condition" of the afflicted Indians "who lie on their hard mats, the pox breaking and mattering and running one into another." The story was endlessly and forlornly repeated, as the natives tried every traditional remedy, including that of burning and abandoning a plague-stricken village. European remedies were not much better; the only advantage that Europeans possessed was greater immunity built up over countless generations.

Trade brought contact, and contact brought disease. Distant tribes fared best if they maintained themselves in hunting and gathering, ignoring the temptations of trade, wampum, or a less strenuous life. But as trade networks broadened, few native peoples could remain aloof.

Whatever the Indians were paid for the pelts they brought in, the price multiplied ten times when the furs reached France — incentive enough to keep the trade going and to discourage all competition, whether from the Dutch or the English. For a time the Abenakis from Maine attempted to gather furs from other tribes for trading in New England. French authorities quickly put a stop to that by confiscating their boats and sending them home empty-handed. Sometimes the Algonkians got greedy and tried to shut the Hurons off from their trading, but in general the Iroquois gave the French the greatest trouble by sending frequent raiding parties along the St. Lawrence to rob canoes and other small craft.

Even changes of political fortunes or governmental administrations did little to interrupt the flourishing fur trade. The *coureurs de bois* were sufficiently remote to be undisturbed by events back in Quebec, to say

nothing of Paris. Throughout the seventeenth century, trade continued without serious hiatus. As it grew, France began to enjoy a degree of profitability from her colonies, especially after King Louis XIV took over direct control from the private companies in 1663. Even so, colonization seldom proved as remunerative as the merchants, princes, adventurers, and entrepreneurs fervently hoped.

HOLLAND AND SWEDEN JOIN THE RACE

Though small, Holland had a powerful merchant fleet and dominated many of the trade routes across the Atlantic. Freed from Spanish domination by the beginning of the seventeenth century, the Dutch Republic prepared to challenge Spain's powerful presence in the New World. While in general the Dutch were more interested in trade than in colonization, the North American opportunities seemed too good to pass up. Plenty of lands beckoned where neither Spanish nor French nor English had yet settled. Under an aggressive king, seventeenth-century Sweden also resolved to try its hand at New World settlements and profits.

ॐ *New Netherland*

Represented by English mariner Henry Hudson, the Dutch East India Company staked its first claim to some portion of North America's natural wealth. In 1609 Hudson sailed for Greenland, and soon thereafter explored the American coast as far south as the Chesapeake Bay. Briefly scouting out the Delaware River, he then sailed far up the river that now bears his name. From Manhattan Island to what would later become Albany, Hudson and his small crew traded with the natives, exchanging "knives and trifles" for green tobacco, maize, and furs. After a month's exploration of the land on both sides of the river, Hudson and his eighteen-man crew returned home. Amsterdam, delighted with the reports of his adventure, in 1621 created a Dutch

New Amsterdam, 1656   By 1656 New Amsterdam was already thriving as a place of trade, and its settlers brought their faith with them from the Netherlands. The first house of worship in New Netherland was, for fear of Indian attacks, built safely within the confines of Fort Amsterdam (above, center left). Completed in 1642, it remained until 1741, when it was destroyed by fire.

West India Company to seize the opportunities that Hudson had opened up.

In 1614, meanwhile, the Dutch established two North American fur-trading posts. One was at the Hudson River's mouth on Manhattan Island, providing excellent harbors for overseas commerce, while upriver Fort Orange (now Albany), still accessible by ocean-going vessels, was strategically located for access to the interior and its furs. A decade later the West India Company pushed the Dutch project beyond mere trade to actual settlement. With the purchase of Manhattan Island from the Indians in 1626, a small Dutch village at the southern end of the island became New Amsterdam, and the entire colony New Netherland. By the end of the 1620s enticements in the form of large land grants were being offered to patrons (in Dutch, *patroons*) who would lead a contingent of fifty or more people to settle on either side of a navigable river such as the Hudson. Granting a charter of "Freedoms and Exemptions for the Patroons, Masters, or Private Persons Who Will Plant Any Colonies in, and Send Cattle to New Netherland," the West India Company hoped to encourage widespread colonization. But by keeping a tight rein on the fur trade for itself, the company discouraged the most adventuresome. Finally, however, it followed the advice of its most successful patroon, Kiliaen van Rensselaer, that only a free trade in fur would encourage Dutch merchants and farmers to settle New Netherland. After 1638, when the company lifted its monopoly, the settlers grew from less than a thousand to about 10,000 within a generation.

Such population growth, especially on Manhattan Island itself, inevitably bred conflict with local Indians. In 1643, Governor Willem Kieft ordered a surprise attack upon the Algonkian Indians, killing as many as could be found in a single night. The Algonkians, understandably, responded with raid after raid on the Manhattan settlement. When Peter Stuyvesant arrived as governor in New Amsterdam in 1647, he found the village in deplorable condition and the two thousand Dutch residents thoroughly demoralized. Confronted with Stuyvesant's grim reports, the company decided to promote colonization even more vigorously, bringing in not just the Dutch settlers but persons of many nations and cultures. And in following that policy, the company gave Stuyvesant more than he bargained for.

This imperious governor wanted order, not diversity. He wished to create a model Dutch village, with model citizens who did not drink or fight on the Sabbath and who would remain loyal to the Dutch Reformed (Calvinist) Church. Before long, however, persons of other national and religious backgrounds began arriving, making a difficult colony even harder to govern. Germans, Swedes, and Finns brought with them their Lutheran theology and worship; Puritans on Long Island threatened to invade; followers of the radical Quaker sect from Rhode Island or England itself added to the explosive mixture.

In 1656, Stuyvesant published an ordinance that prohibited all unauthorized meetings of "sectaries," as well as condemning all "unqualified persons [who] presume in such meetings to act as teachers, in interpreting and expounding God's Holy Word, without ecclesiastical or secular authority." Two years before, when a dozen impoverished Jews arrived from Brazil, Stuyvesant invited them "in a friendly way to depart." But the company overruled him, decreeing that the Jews had every right to remain, "provided that the poor among them shall not become a burden to the company or to the community." Similarly, Stuyvesant sought to stamp out the Quakers who seemed to sprout up everywhere, but again the company patiently explained that only a policy of toleration and moderation would enlarge the population of New Netherland.

ஃ *New Sweden*

Four years before Stuyvesant arrived in New Amsterdam, a small party of Swedes sailed up the Delaware River to plant Sweden's flag near the present site of Wilmington, Delaware. Like the Dutch, the Swedes hoped to reap some profit from all this largely unoccupied land. Agriculture seemed the best place to begin. The first governor had instructions to plant grapes and make wine, to raise cattle of the best breed, to search

for metals and minerals, and to consider how Sweden might best profit from the country's abundant oak and walnut trees. Governor Johan Printz was also told to see that worship according to the practice of Sweden's own Lutheran church, "a true and due worship," be faithfully followed along the shores of the Delaware River.

By 1654 the colony of Fort Christina (named in honor of Sweden's young queen) had grown to the point that the settlers seized a nearby Dutch outpost. This so enraged Stuyvesant that he led seven armed vessels up the Delaware River and forced the surrender of Fort Christina. Stuyvesant, like other Dutch governors, thought the entire Atlantic coastline from Newfoundland to Florida to be his for the taking. And, so far as New Sweden was concerned, that proved to be the case. As we shall see in a later chapter, however, England had her own designs upon the lands between French settlements to the north and the Spanish holdings to the south. In 1664 England brought down New Netherland's Dutch flag as swiftly and bloodlessly as the Dutch had done with New Sweden's a decade before.

ENGLAND CATCHES UP

Except for the voyages of John and Sebastian Cabot just before 1500, England seemed to be leaving claims and state-sponsored colonization efforts in the Western Hemisphere largely to Spain and France. In the middle of the sixteenth century, England, like the Netherlands and France, was distracted by religious controversy and persecution. However, by the time of Elizabeth I (reigned 1558-1603) England was prepared to take more definitive action, particularly after the defeat of the Spanish Armada in 1588. By then, also, England had emerged as a proudly Protestant nation, opposed by nationality and religion alike to Catholic Portugal, Spain, and France. Yet the earliest English colonization efforts did little to suggest that North America was going to be any less disappointing to England than it had been to her rivals.

ஃ *The Cabots*

England's King Henry VII (reigned 1485-1509) had declined to support Columbus's venture, but listened with keenest interest to reports of the Genoese discoverer's voyages of 1492 and after. By 1496, Henry was ready to ensure that England was not excluded from the race for Oriental riches. He officially authorized another

Genoese, John Cabot, along with his sons, to sail and search under England's flag, claiming any lands not already ruled by a Christian prince. Cabot, according to Henry, could go anywhere north, east, or west (the king omitted the south as a courtesy to Portugal and Spain) with authority to "conquer, occupy, and possess" any "towns, castles, cities, islands, and mainlands" that he happened to come across.

In May 1497 Cabot sailed from Bristol in a single small ship, with a crew of only eighteen. (He had been authorized to take as many as five ships, but could not collect enough cash or credit to make that possible.) A month later he made landfall somewhere north of Newfoundland, sailed south and east, perhaps as far as Cape Breton Island at the southern rim of the Gulf of St. Lawrence. Although he failed to seize castles or locate the Great Khan, he did plant a cross and an English flag on the land — and that was enough to make King Henry very happy. Henry rewarded him with glory, money, and the promise to provide him the next year with ten armed vessels — at royal expense — along with as many prisoners as he might want for his crews and possible colonies. An Italian diplomat in London wrote that Cabot was now called "the Great Admiral, and vast honor is paid to him and he goes dressed in silk, and these English run after him like mad."

Cabot's second voyage in 1498 (with five vessels rather than the promised ten), backed with such eager anticipation and excitement, ended in tragedy. Following a severe storm, one vessel put in at Ireland; the other four, proceeding westward, were never heard from again. One of Cabot's sons, Sebastian, pursued the family interests by sailing for Labrador in 1508 or 1509, now aware that North America was not Asia but still looking for that waterway to the Orient. By around 1530, England along with the rest of Europe had a fair sense of the broad outlines of the North American coast, from Labrador all the way to the southern tip of Florida. But English sovereigns, caught up in their own religious turmoil, did not quickly take advantage of that knowledge.

❦ England on the Sidelines

English merchants, however, did not stand by idly. Developing overseas markets in the 1530s and 1540s, they broke into Spanish and Portuguese preserves in Africa as well as in the Western Hemisphere, building up a significant trade. This was illegal, not only from the perspective of Spain and Portugal, but from that of England as well. For England at this period had no wish to offend Spain, the land from which Henry VIII (reigned 1509-1547) had taken his first queen. Nonetheless smuggling operations continued, with profit offering great encouragement even where policy did not. Eventually government officials themselves began quietly to invest in the illicit trade.

England's religious allegiance meanwhile wavered. Henry VIII was succeeded by a sickly young son, Edward VI (reigned 1547-1553), who under his advisers' guidance intended to turn England sharply into a forthrightly Protestant land. During his brief reign, dissent (especially Roman Catholic dissent) was vigorously persecuted and all parishes were required to follow the newly adopted Book of Common Prayer. But when Edward died, the new queen, Mary I, daughter of Catherine of Aragon and Henry, insisted on reestablishing close ties with Spain and on returning England to Roman Catholicism. In the words of the 1554 Second Act of Repeal, it was her royal intent "to call us home again into the right way from whence we have all this long while wandered and strayed abroad." During her brief reign, from 1553 to 1558, dissent (especially Protestant dissent) was vigorously persecuted. Many Protestant leaders — the so-called "Marian exiles" — fled to John Calvin's Geneva or to other refuges in Switzerland. For a little over ten years, therefore, first under Edward and then under Mary, England was tossed first this way and that, with fines, imprisonments, and executions liberally inflicted on those holding the wrong religious views.

In the long and judicious reign of Elizabeth (1558-1603), some calm began to settle upon the troubled kingdom. No less the head of the church than Henry had been, Elizabeth (daughter of Anne Boleyn and Henry) chose to move cautiously — but toward Protestantism, away from Spain, away from the papacy, and to a degree away from Catholic thought and practice. The phrase *to a degree* offers the merest hint of the strongly differing opinions within England of just how Protestant the Elizabethan Church of England should be. During all of Elizabeth's reign as well as in the reigns that followed, those differences would do much to write England's subsequent history and that of America as well.

Although a great deal remained to be settled after Elizabeth, some changes were already fixed. England was a Protestant nation, prepared to carry Protestantism to any "towns, castles, cities, islands, or mainlands" to be discovered abroad. Moreover, in Scotland (still an inde-

New Amsterdam Becomes New York In 1664, when the English took over from the Dutch, the town once known as New Amsterdam and now renamed New York looked like this: only a few blocks at the tip of Manhattan. On the opposite shores lie what are now Brooklyn and Jersey City, New Jersey.

pendent kingdom) one of the Marian exiles, John Knox, returned from Geneva bent on transforming his small, impoverished country into a stronghold of Calvinism. In the following centuries, the history of those two Protestant nations would intertwine, and in their intertwining exert a powerful influence upon North America.

❧ Protestant Crusaders, Pirates, and Explorers

Early in Queen Elizabeth's reign, John Foxe published a large book destined to rank along with the Bible in the affections and interests of English-speaking people. Widely known simply as Foxe's *Book of Martyrs,* its full title speaks more eloquently to the temper of the time: *Acts and Monuments of These Latter and Perilous Days Touching Matters of the Church. Wherein Are Comprehended and Described the Great Persecutions and Horrible Troubles That Have Been Wrought and Practiced by the Romish Prelates, Specially in This Realm of England and Scotland, from the Year of Our Lord a Thousand unto the Time Now Present.* Besides confirming Elizabethan England's militant Protestantism (and its dominant counterpart, its stern anti-Catholicism), Foxe's bloody book inspired his fellow citizens to look upon their land as an "elect nation," set apart by God

for a divine mission on this earth. That mission, briefly, was to spread Protestantism around the globe as widely and as effectively as possible. After 1563, when the book first appeared, its popularity demanded eight more editions before the century was over. Drake carried the book aboard his ship, and the East India Company (founded in 1600) required that every shipmaster have his own copy. If a typical English home contained only two books, one would be the Bible and the other would be Foxe's.

Thus by the end of the 1560s, England no longer courted the favor of Catholic Spain. Repeated raids on Spanish shipping and infringement upon Spanish trade routes had soured the relationship. That relationship grew noticeably even sourer in 1570 when the pope issued a bull of excommunication against England's Protestant Queen Elizabeth. The next year, news of a Spanish plot to overthrow Elizabeth and return England to Catholicism made the widened breach irreparable. Although open war between the two nations had not yet erupted, the smugglers and pirates could be unleashed to do their worst.

The most famous of the "sea dogs," Francis Drake, had been nipping at Spain's heels since 1567. Every Spanish port in the Americas was subject to being looted and burned; every Spanish ship on the high seas invited capture. Learning that the Spanish sent treasures from Peru to the Isthmus of Panama, then crossed that narrow strip of land and reloaded the loot on ships bound for Spain, Drake awaited his opportunity. In 1573 he captured a pack train moving from Panama City to the port of Nombre de Dios, making off with some £20,000 of silver. Drake encouraged others to imitate him, even composing in 1577 for Elizabeth's edification a small tract entitled *How Her Majesty May Annoy the King of Spain.* It was easy to annoy: attack every ship, then run for the nearest Dutch port so that officially England would not be involved. If captured, make it clear that the ship operated under no flag at all; and if all goods and the ship itself were confiscated, remember that very quietly Her Majesty would reimburse.

After reaping great profits from ships sailing the

Spanish Main (the Caribbean coast of modern Colombia and Venezuela), Drake turned his attention to the western coasts of the Americas. Sailing around South America's southern tip and through the Straits of Magellan, in 1578 he descended upon the Peruvian coast, where his plundering could be even more direct. He first looted and burned Lima's port town, then headed off in search of a ship heavily laden with silver on its way to Panama. In a short time, he found one, which yielded him a fortune sufficient to pay for his entire expedition and still have some left over for Her Majesty's treasury. Fired with excitement, a contemporary reported: "We found in her great riches, as jewels and precious stones, thirteen chests full of royals of plate, four score pound weight of gold, and six and twenty ton of silver."

Continuing north in search of western approaches to the Northwest Passage, Drake put into a bay above San Francisco, repairing his ship and entertaining the Indians with his crew's singing of Psalms and reciting prayers. By 1581, this pious semi-official pirate had clearly earned the knighthood that the queen bestowed upon him. Now Sir Francis Drake, he had reduced the coffers of Spain, enlarged those of England, and irritated the Spaniards with such consistency and effect that annoyance virtually became the national policy. Beyond all that, however, Drake, with Foxe's *Book of Martyrs* always at his fingertips, took seriously his role as Protestantism's champion in the competition for New World position and profit.

Other Englishmen followed in his wake. Martin Frobisher made three voyages to the mainland; on the first in 1576 he skirted the southern tip of Greenland, sighting the land of northern Labrador. Sailing north to Baffin Island, he entered the bay that now bears his name, convinced that he had found the ever-so-elusive passage to the East. His captain, George Best, sounding more like a missionary than a mariner, exulted about the unknown lands being discovered where Christ's name might be spread, the gospel preached, "and infidels like to be converted to Christianity." Frobisher created much excitement in England by bringing back what he thought was a shipload of gold, but it turned out to be "fool's gold" (iron pyrites), as illusory as the route to the Orient.

The story of English colonization, as distinct from exploration, begins with Humphrey Gilbert and his half-brother, Walter Raleigh. A confidant of the queen, Gilbert was as obsessed with the potential of North America as with the Spanish threat in South and Central America. The Spanish Empire, Gilbert feared, would become so rich and so powerful that soon Catholicism and all the forces of the Inquisition would be turned against England. North America must be England's counterweight. In June 1578 Elizabeth granted her friend a patent (an official document conferring some right or privilege) of enormous sweep, Gilbert interpreting it as the right to possess any and all lands between northern Florida and the Arctic Circle. Raising funds privately, Gilbert by November of that year set sail from Plymouth with some five hundred men and ten ships. The expedition soon divided, however, some preferring to plunder Spanish shipping in the Caribbean rather than shove through icy waters near Labrador. A storm forced several other ships to turn back, so this venture achieved very little.

In 1583 Gilbert sailed once more, this time with three ships and with a specific view to arrange for settlements in New England. Subscribers had bought some twenty million acres from him — land in which neither they nor he had ever set foot. Arriving off Newfoundland, Gilbert made a great show of claiming the area around St. John's in the name of the queen, creating some amazement (if not amusement) among the Spanish, Portuguese, Basque, and French fishermen who had worked the waters for years and dried their catch on the banks where Gilbert now so proudly stood. He turned south toward Nova Scotia and New England when both the weather and the crews turned against him. After one of the three vessels was lost, a disheartened Gilbert set his sails homeward, going down with his own ship just off the Azores.

❧ Roanoke

The mantle now fell upon Walter Raleigh to continue and perchance execute the plans for North American colonization. In this he was encouraged and abetted by Oxford graduate and clergyman Richard Hakluyt, an enthusiast for English expansion, and cheerleader for bold adventuring. In 1584 he and Raleigh presented their carefully crafted arguments to the queen in a *Discourse of Western Planting*, stressing the need for actual settlements instead of mere forts, trading posts, or tentative probes along the Atlantic coast. Colonies gave permanence, constituting a genuine possession of the land. Colonies also gave settlers an opportunity to know their Indian neighbors, to share skills, tools, and information with them, to teach them and learn from them. Those seeking to spread the gospel to the Indians would also have a chance to move gradually, to study

The broyling of their fish ouer the flame of fier. 11 ᴮ

The Indian Method of Broiling Fish Europeans during the Era of Discovery were fascinated about virtually every detail of Native American life. This English image, one of John White's illustrations from Roanoke, shows how fish was broiled in the New World.

the languages and customs, to gain their confidence and trust. This would be far better, Hakluyt declared, than "to come unto them rashly without some such preparation"; the English had only to look at Florida and Canada, he added, to see the cruel consequences of preachers plunging too soon into an utterly foreign culture.

Giving precise point to this general message, Hakluyt noted that English sovereigns bore the title "Defender of the Faith." This must mean something more

than just protecting the status quo, he argued; to defend the faith of Christ must mean "to enlarge and advance the same." Just as the apostle Paul heeded the call from Macedonia, so England and its good queen must heed the call from North America. And should anyone worry about that papal line of demarcation drawn nearly a hundred years before? Certainly not in Protestant England, for, said Hakluyt, the pope had absolutely no authority to dispose of the New World's lands. Appealing to the Cabots' voyages, to the Bible, to history, and to common sense, Hakluyt waved aside all excuses and procrastinations. English prisons were filled with men and women, convicted of petty offenses, who wished only for some opportunity to show their diligence and worth. It was time for England to plant colonies and possess the land, thereby preventing "the Spanish King from flowing all over the face of that vast" wilderness, but such prevention could be effective only "if we seat and plant there in time, in time I say."

The queen agreed to transfer Gilbert's patent to Raleigh, who was already persuaded and had already been soliciting support for another colonization effort. In that same year of 1584 Raleigh sent out two ships to explore lands somewhere south of Newfoundland and north of Spanish Florida. The ships, one commanded by Arthur Barlowe, arrived at the Outer Banks off the North Carolina coast in June. Going ashore a few hundred yards from the sea, the men formally took possession of all they could see and even beyond in the name of both the queen and Walter Raleigh "according to her Majesty's grant and letter patent, under her Highness' Great Seal."

Prospects for English colonization appeared especially bright when Arthur Barlowe returned with reports of unrestrained, perhaps indiscriminate, enthusiasm. The land was so full of grapes that "the very beating and surge of the sea overflowed them." He saw fertile green soil on the hills, high cedars and botanical richness everywhere, and deer, rabbits, and birds "in incredible abundance." "I think," Barlowe exclaimed, "in all the world the like abundance is not to be found." After striking up some trading acquaintance with nearby natives, Barlowe and others later visited their main village where they were handsomely received. Barlowe's enthusiasm did not wane. "We were entertained with all love and kindness, and with as much bounty, after their manner, as they could possible devise. We found the people most gentle, loving, and faithful," Barlowe added, "void of all guile and treason, and such as lived after the manner of the Golden Age."

On the basis of such glowing observations, serious planning for a permanent colony could get underway. And serious Raleigh was. He consulted military experts on how the colony should be defended, builders on the techniques for erecting the fort and surrounding dwellings, physicians on the use of local herbs and plants, geographers on the art of cartography. He selected Thomas Hariot not only to direct the next voyage but to train other sailors in navigation and seamanship, and Hariot prepared himself by learning the Algonkian language from two Indians brought back to England in 1584. Along with Hariot, Raleigh chose a painter, John White, charging the two of them to record and draw everything that Englishmen back home would want to know: the flora and fauna, the natives and the landscape, the cultivation of and improvements upon the land. As a result of his choosing Hariot and White, Raleigh can be credited with the best visual and verbal record of sixteenth-century North America that has survived to this day. Raleigh also had the queen firmly on his side, as she bestowed knighthood upon him in January of 1585. In honor of the Virgin Queen of England, Raleigh gave the name Virginia to all that England now claimed in the New World.

In 1585, all plans carefully made, five well-provisioned ships set out from Plymouth in April under the leadership of Sir Robert Grenville. Severe storms, the dread of every Atlantic sailor, scattered the fleet off Portugal. One sank, but the others made their way separately to the North Carolina coast. In June and July, four of the five ships anchored in the somewhat protected waters around Roanoke Island, where the English erected a fort, planted a colony, spied on Spanish ships, and drew up full reports of the New World. As planned, Grenville

---

❋ IN THEIR OWN WORDS

English Excitement over Colonization, 1588

In his Briefe and true report, *Thomas Hariot reflected a zeal for colonization that was not uncommon among the English.*

I thought also good to note this to you, that you who shall inhabit and plant there [Roanoke Island] may know how especially that country's corn is there to be preferred before ours... For this I can assure you that, according to the rate we have made proof of, one may prepare and husband so much ground... with less than four and twenty hours' labour, as shall yield him [food] in a large proportion for a twelvemonth, if he have nothing else, but that which the same ground will yield... the said ground being also but of five and twenty yards square. And if need require, but that there is ground enough, there might be raised out of one and the selfsame ground two harvests or outcomes. For they [the Indians] sowe or set and may at any time when they think good from the middle of March until the end of June, so that they also set when they have eaten of their first crop. In some places of the country, notwithstanding, they have two harvests, as we have heard, out of one and the same ground.

returned to England to arrange for the colony's support and to harass Spanish ships. Hopes still ran high. But hard realities over the next several months dashed all hopes and mocked Raleigh's careful planning. Once again the Garden of Eden threatened to become the darkest pit of hell.

In the meanwhile, however, Hariot and White did their work as superb reporters. They were especially helpful in presenting a picture of Native American life as yet unmarred by protracted European contact. From Hariot we learn that the villages consisted of some ten to twenty houses, raised in a clearing in the forest, with a few long houses being sixty or seventy feet in length and half that in breadth. From John White's drawing of the village of Secotan we learn how such a community actually looked. There we also see the corn in various stages of growth and read how Hariot wondered at both the abundance of maize and the apparent ease with which it was grown. In that same sketch White portrayed a ceremony of prayerful thanksgiving, celebrated "when they have escaped any great danger by sea or land or have returned from the war." Here, as in impressive individual portraits and representations of skilled techniques in hollowing out boats and catching fish, White and Harriot with sensitivity, respect, and remarkable talent provide more information on the men, women, and children of coastal Carolina — indeed of North America — than is available from any other source.

The Indians and the English, having started out on such a high plane of mutual respect, learned to dislike and distrust each other. When the Indians provided food, then seed, and later fishing traps and techniques, the English came to accept it calmly as their due. When the English discovered the Indians guilty of some theft or discourtesy, they responded with fury, burning Indian dwellings and food supplies — and, indirectly their own. By the following June, the English had murdered the Roanoke chief, Wingina, on the rumor that he was plotting to destroy them. The truth is that they, through inattention to growing their own food, catching their own game, and trapping their own fish, were destroying themselves.

When Francis Drake, fresh from predatory activity against the Spanish in the Caribbean, sailed north in the summer of 1586 to see how the young colony was doing, he discovered they were not doing well at all. At first he thought that if he gave them new provisions and new small ships, they could be persuaded to stay. But again storms worked havoc, wrecking much of what

Drake had set aside for their use. The colonists had had enough. Accepting Drake's offer of transportation, they packed up and went home. Ironically, Grenville was at that very moment on his way back to resupply the colony. When he arrived a few weeks after Drake had left, he found the island deserted. Leaving a dozen or so soldiers behind to protect England's fragile claim, he departed for the more profitable business of challenging and boarding vessels to the south.

❧ A Lost Colony, A Saved Nation

Understandably, Walter Raleigh was deeply discouraged. Though a man of some wealth, he could not calmly contemplate the losses that these colonizing ventures entailed. Very likely he would have given up had it not been for John White. White, unlike most of the other colonists who returned, was ready to go back — indeed, he was ready to lead the next group, which this time would include women and children. Less of a military operation and more explicitly a colonizing venture, the group would be prepared to hunt, fish, and farm. White also decided that Roanoke Island was not the best place for a permanent settlement. First, as the colony grew, it would dispossess the local native population at the certain cost of ill will; and second, the surrounding waters were too shallow to accommodate England's large ships, while anchorage farther out left them exposed to the frequent and furious storms. A bit to the north, on the other hand, the Chesapeake Bay offered deep waters and less populous lands. This made more sense, and there White intended to plant a permanent settlement.

When nearing the coast in July with over one hundred settlers, however, the ship's captain had other thoughts. He was prepared to deposit them on Roanoke Island, but not to wait for days or weeks while they made themselves ready to go to Chesapeake Bay. Spanish treasures were calling, a lure stronger than the colonists' wishes could match. White, apparently accepting the inevitable, tried to make the best of the situation on Roanoke Island — where, ominously he found no sign of the dozen or so soldiers that Grenville had left behind the previous summer. As best he could, he offered encouragement and comfort to his charges, among whom was his own pregnant daughter, soon to give birth to England's first New World baby. "Because this child was the first Christian born in Virginia," White wrote, "she was named Virginia." If that happy event in August distracted White momentarily, he was quickly

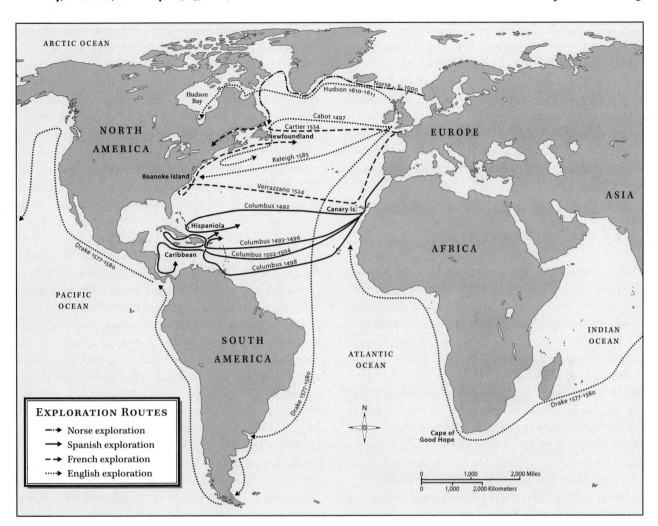

sobered by the anxieties of the settlers who knew that they needed more provisions and were worried that they might be delivered by mistake to the Chesapeake rather than to Roanoke. Someone, the council of assistants decided, must return to England to guarantee the sure supply of the group, and bring more colonists — especially wives and fiancées left behind — back to Roanoke. Reluctantly, White consented and sailed for England, arriving in November 1587.

He found an England busily engaged in preparing to fend off Spain's Philip II and the Armada he was constructing to crush the English navy and invade the island. No large ship could be spared for North America — no thought even could be given to the forlorn colonists entering upon their first North American winter. In one of the decisive battles of the century, the Armada was defeated in July 1588, contrary Channel winds this time working to England's advantage. The nation was saved, but the pitiful colony in "Virginia" was on its way to being lost.

Despite the signal defeat at sea, the war between England and Spain sputtered on, maintaining enough fury and consuming enough energy to frustrate White over and over in his attempt to return to his colony. After maddening delays, in August 1590 White arrived back in the shallow waters of the North Carolina coast in search for the colony he had last seen three years before. He found many signs of their former habitation, even some of his own now-buried trunks, but no daughter, no grandchild, no English colonists at all. What happened to them remains a mystery: most likely they were absorbed into neighboring native tribes or else died at the hands of nature or their neighbors. A colony was lost, and with it much of England's enthusiasm for the New World.

If there were to be any new English ventures, they would have to depend more on merchant initiative and investment than on royal direction or control. To help restore enthusiasm, in 1589 Richard Hakluyt published the first edition of his *Principall Navigations,* a collection of England's courageous adventures around the globe. This national epic was destined to inspire that Protestant nation to build on, not rest on, the past glories of Cabot and Frobisher, Drake and Grenville. When Elizabeth died in 1603, marking the end of the Tudor dynasty, a new royal house — the Stuarts — acceded to the throne. Perhaps the new Scottish-born king, James I, would somehow succeed where others had failed — in colonizing that promising but treacherous new land.

The Columbian Exchange

The encounter between the Old World and the New had profoundest consequences for subsequent human history. If North America was initially a great disappointment to Spanish, French, Dutch, Swedish, and English explorers, the European invasion brought tragedy of incalculable proportion to the native population. If much of the European "discovery" cloaked itself in the mantle of a religious crusade — Catholic or Protestant — that crusade seemed to take as many detours or to pursue other distractions as had those launched against Islam in the twelfth century. Neither Europeans nor Indians knew what to expect in the sixteenth century. Hopes alternated with fear, and much ended in calamity.

Those tribes who repeatedly traded with Europeans paid the highest price in terms of loss of life. When an epidemic struck, those who did not die directly from the disease might starve as a consequence of so many tribal members being stricken and prevented from planting or harvesting, hunting, or catching fish. Tribal organization suffered as leaders collapsed and died and as traditional healers — themselves fallen ill — lost all authority. Some villages were so reduced in population that a remnant of survivors threw themselves on the mercies of some other native community.

The biological contact, however, also had a more positive side. New arrivals from the Old World learned of plant and animal life not known in Europe, while Indians acquired skill in the use of the horse and dietary improvement through the tending of cattle. Having depleted their own forests for centuries, Europeans gloried in the abundance of trees along North America's eastern coast. Some would serve for fuel, some for building materials, some for food. Oaks, hickories, and pitch pines could keep the poorest Native Americans warmer than the wealthiest nobles at home. White and red cedar made excellent building material, while the very tall white pines were perfect for ships' masts. Walnut and cherry trees provided nuts and fruit to native and explorer alike. Domesticated cows, sheep, and hogs meant that Indian hunters could now enjoy a year-round food supply, and no longer be wholly dependent upon the luck of the chase or the breaks in the weather. At the same time, Indians could point out to Europeans the abundance of game as potential items in trade, even as they could instruct them in methods for tapping the seemingly inexhaustible supply of fish and oysters in the rivers, bays, and ocean. Crops unknown in Europe before Columbus greatly enriched the diet of Europeans, and indeed of the world. These included potatoes and sweet potatoes, peanuts and tomatoes, as well as a wide variety of peppers, beans, and squashes. In botany and zoology, the meeting of the two hemispheres could often bring benefit to both sides.

The horse was Europe's most conspicuous contribution to the Americas. Brought over in Spanish ships, the stallions and mares first had to withstand the hazard of voyages of six weeks or more from Spain to the Caribbean. Many animals did not survive, but those that did reproduced themselves in gratifying quantity. By the time that Cortés set out for Mexico in 1518, he could equip his expedition entirely from horses already in Cuba. The Spanish recognized how great a part the horse played in their conquests, affirming that they owed victory, "after God," mainly to their trusted mounts, even frequently listing them by name in their accounts of battle. Within half a century after Montezuma's surrender, a great many Indians of both Central and South America had become "horse Indians," adapting their cultural patterns to the use of the animals that often ran wild. In the next century, Indians on the Great Plains of North America — once dependent on dogs and their own feet for mobility — became skilled riders and even more skilled hunters.

Once contact had been made between widely differing cultures, events took on a momentum of their own. After Columbus, the human no less than the natural environment changed rapidly, both for good and ill.

Conclusion: A Time of Testing

The fifteenth and sixteenth centuries proved a severe testing time: for people and nations, and perhaps most of all for speculative theories. Those centuries revealed in sharpest outline a remarkable assortment of misunderstandings: about Asia, about the Americas, about geography, anthropology, and the role of religion in human affairs. That the Native American population came to be called "Indians" gave a persisting permanence to one of those misunderstandings. Other misunderstandings resulted in tragedy. Some misconceptions actually promoted discovery and exploration: for example, the indelible conviction that North America must possess great treasures and imposing cities comparable to those found farther to the south. Over the course of several generations, gradually a clearer picture of what the New World was all about slowly, often painfully, emerged.

To Portugal and Spain belong the undisputed honors of leading the way westward, charting paths where none existed before. Europe responded with wonder and with greed to new lands and undreamed-of riches. Native populations also responded with wonder to sights never seen before; the resulting culture shock led, more often than not, to the detriment if not the destruction of indigenous patterns of life and belief. Tentative offers of friendship from each side generally ended in the exploitation of the weaker by the stronger, with the institutional servitude employed in the Caribbean setting a grim pattern to be followed elsewhere.

If Spain prevailed in the southern latitudes, France found success in a more northerly direction, especially along the St. Lawrence River, and then later down the Mississippi. In between France and Spain, Holland and Sweden attempted to gain a modest foothold, but stronger national powers would soon prevail. The early efforts of the English in North America looked even less promising than those of the Dutch and the Swedes. By the middle of the seventeenth century, however, it was evident that England's stamp upon the North American continent would endure.

SUGGESTED READING

Colin G. Calloway, *New Worlds for All: Indians, Europeans, and the Remaking of Early America* (1997). Manages to treat the history of Europeans and Indians together, rather than in separate compartments; emphasizes the borrowings in both directions with the resulting "new worlds" for all involved.

Franco Cardini, *Europe 1492: Portrait of a Continent Five Hundred Years Ago* (1990). A lavishly illustrated volume that opens up the European world during the period of exploration and discovery.

William Cronon, *Changes in the Land: Indians, Colonists, and the Ecology of New England* (1983). A path-breaking book that takes seriously the intimate relationship between geography and culture.

D. W. Meining, *The Shaping of America*, vol. 1: *Atlantic America, 1492-1800* (1986). A remarkable contribution to cultural geography, with careful and instructive maps and lucid text.

D. B. Quinn, *Set Fair for Roanoke: Voyages and Colonies, 1584-1606* (1985). The life-long expert on English colonization offers extraordinary detail on the initial efforts in America.

Carl O. Sauer, *Sixteenth Century North America: The Land and the People as Seen by the Europeans* (1971). The story of discovery blended with the story of the land, its contours, cultivation, and natural endowments.

Kirkpatrick Sale, *Christopher Columbus and the Columbus Legacy* (1990). A highly critical view of the devastation wrought upon humanity and ecology by Columbus and his successors.

Russell Shorto, *The Island at the Center of the World: The Epic Story of Dutch Manhattan and the Forgotten Colony that Shaped America* (2004). A dramatic narrative accompanied by early portraits, landscapes, maps, and documents.

John Sugden, *Sir Francis Drake* (1990). An exciting recounting of Drake's remarkable adventures, with some attention to the religious ferment of his time.

Marcel Trudel, *The Beginnings of New France, 1524-1663* (1973). A careful history of the vision as well as the reversals of fortune characterizing the early history of eastern Canada.

Herman J. Viola and Carolyn Margolis, eds., *Seeds of Change* (1991). An excellent and elaborate portrayal of the agricultural changes in the North American continent as a result of the Columbus encounter; richly illustrated.

Delno C. West and August Kling, eds., *The Libro de las profecias of Christopher Columbus* (1991). The major vehicle for understanding the religious and apocalyptic assumptions that Columbus brought to his undertaking.

Louis B. Wright, *Gold, Glory, and the Gospel: The Adventurous Lives and Times of the Renaissance Explorers* (1970). An eminent historian recreates the excitement of the Age of Discovery, with considerable attention to the religious motivations of the time.

SUGGESTIONS FOR FURTHER READING

Felipe Fernándo-Armesto, *Columbus* (1991).

Alfred W. Crosby, *The Columbian Exchange: Biological and Cultural Consequences of 1492* (1972).

Miles H. Davidson, *Columbus Then and Now* (1997).

William W. Fitzhugh, ed., *Cultures in Contact: The Impact of European Contacts on Native American Institutions, A.D. 1000-1800* (1985).

Charles Gibson, ed., *The Black Legend: Anti-Spanish Attitudes in the Old World and the New* (1971).

Christopher Haigh, *English Reformations: Religion, Politics, and Society Under the Tudors* (1993).

David Heinege, *In Search of Columbus: The Sources for the First Voyage* (1991).

Alvin M. Josephy, *America in 1492* (1991).

Jay A. Levenson, ed., *Circa 1492: Art in the Age of Exploration* (1991).

Lyle N. McAlister, *Spain and Portugal in the New World, 1492-1700* (1984).

Alister E. McGrath, *Reformation Thought: An Introduction* (2nd ed., 1993).

William Manchester, *A World Lit Only by Fire: The Medieval Mind and the Renaissance* (1997).

Richard Lee Marks, *Cortés and the Fate of Aztec Mexico* (1993).

Ted Morgan, *Wilderness at Dawn: The Settling of the North American Continent* (1993).

Kenneth Nebenzahl, *Atlas of Columbus and the Great Discoveries* (1991).

Anthony Pagden, *Lords of All the World: Ideologies of Empire in Spain, Britain, and France, c. 1500–c. 1800* (1995).

Helen R. Parish, *Bartolomé de las Casas: The Only Way* (1992).

William D. Phillips, Jr., and Carla Rahn Phillips, *The Worlds of Christopher Columbus* (1992).

David B. Quinn, *North America from Earliest Discovery to First Settlements: The Norse Voyages to 1612* (1977).

George Sanderlin, ed., *Witness: Writings of Bartolome de las Casas* (1992).

Hugh Thomas, *Conquest: Montezuma, Cortés, and the Fall of Old Mexico* (1994).

Herman J. Viola, *After Columbus: The Smithsonian Chronicle of the North American Indians* (1993).

2 England's First "Foreign Plantations"
The Chesapeake and New England, 1607–1676

Tʜᴇ Nᴇᴡ Wᴏʀʟᴅ — both the unfolding reality and the rumors that made it seem a paradise — drew the English like a magnet. Its hypnotic sway entranced not just kings, queens, and ships' captains, but many segments of the populace. But whatever the New World's "pull," by itself it would probably not have been enough to draw men and women from their familiar homelands. A "push" was also needed — in the form of the difficulties and discomforts of seventeenth-century English life. So, first in droplets but soon in steady streams, English men and women began betting their lives and future fortunes upon the land called Virginia. At first Virginia covered the same vast swath of land as had Gilbert's patent — everything between Canada and Florida. Soon, however, some the borders of England's first permanent colony narrowed, chiefly as grants were made to other companies or proprietors.

Along its broad rivers, Virginia's first colonists settled and eventually prospered. Jamestown was the first permanent habitation — but just barely, for it came perilously close to repeating the tragic end of Roanoke. Soon Virginia had a neighbor, Maryland, initially more an opponent than ally. But once the two colonies survived their infancy, by the middle of the seventeenth century, the Chesapeake Bay region achieved a degree of economic success, though it also exhibited some serious and enduring social problems. One of those problems, the shortage of labor, brought significant numbers of white servants to the region, but eventually black slaves came in even greater numbers.

In what were earliest Virginia's northernmost

reaches, other English people created a New England, a region that by 1650 demonstrated reassuring stability and growth. Settlers there displayed a special religious commitment that stamped their culture unmistakably, and their efforts to enforce orthodoxy produced considerable dissent — and more variety in "the New England way" than is often supposed.

For all the early English settlers, the fundamental problem was survival. Meeting the most rudimentary needs of food, clothing, and shelter occupied virtually all of their waking hours. Nature in America, overadvertised by promoters as abundant and generous, often proved meager and miserly. Beyond that fundamental struggle, other themes gradually emerged. First, to the pluralism of Indian religion was added the pluralism of European religion, for even in these early decades of settlement Anglicans, Congregationalists, Roman Catholics, Baptists, and Quakers all made appearances. Second, no central London office guided, much less controlled, the several experiments in "foreign plantations." Whatever might work — merchant investments, proprietary grants, royal bailouts, religious refuges — became the pragmatic pattern. Finally, the steady deterioration of European relationships with the Native Americans transformed the high hopes of the sixteenth century into the grim realities of the seventeenth. At first, the Indians helped the English to survive; soon, however, they were seen as impediments if not enemies by every English settlement from Boston Bay to Chesapeake Bay. Efforts to convert the Native Americans yielded to wars designed to defeat them.

THE PUSH FOR EMIGRATION

Beginning in the sixteenth century and continuing long after, England suffered many difficulties and dislocations. Both population and unemployment grew, with the English economy seemingly unable to cope with either. Lands formerly held in common by villagers and their lords were now enclosed to facilitate landlords' raising of sheep, as the enclosure acts passed by Parliament shifted the balance between public and private lands and created an underclass of the disfranchised and chronically dissatisfied. Religious controversies aggravated a rapidly deteriorating situation. Men and women began to weigh their options, choosing between remaining in an old land "grown weary of its inhabitants" and going to a new land of alluring promise.

❧ *Upper Classes*

When James I arrived in England from Scotland in 1603, he found a country clearly divided. Royalty and nobility occupied the top rungs of the social ladder; the local earl, for example, drew loyalty and deference from the countryside surrounding his impressive estate. Beyond that, however, the nobility (there were only about fifty nobles at the beginning of the seventeenth century) sought wider areas of service — in the House of Lords, to be sure, but perhaps also in the inner circle of the king's trusted advisors, where service was rendered in hopes of handsome royal reward. Below the titled aristocracy, the country gentlemen,[1] about 5 percent of the male population, likewise were supposed to set an example of service and civility. The crown depended on them to staff local offices and courts, though many contented themselves with hunting, fishing, and entertaining their equals. The yeoman farmers who rented their land from noblemen or gentlemen (the word *farmer* meant a renter) were the most affluent of their class. At the lower levels, the yeomen were separated from poor tenants only by the accident of a good harvest and the extension of credit.

Merchants saw their fortunes rising in the course of the century, especially as royalty found overseas adventures abroad costing far more than they returned. If the aspirations of merchants for reward abroad increased, so did their social ambitions at home. Most successful merchants coveted land, which could be more safely passed on to posterity than a trade in risky commerce. But the merchant who hoped to acquire land, with all its social position and political influence, had first to make his fortune. This required shrewdness and daring, as he sought markets all over Europe and well beyond. Sometimes merchants even took up residence in foreign lands to direct and enlarge their commercial traffic.

As far back as the time of John Cabot, merchants led in encouraging expeditions and adventures far beyond England. The expense of some of these ventures was such as to require merchants to form regulated companies with a royal monopoly to trade in a given area. In 1553 the Muscovy Company was organized to carry on trade with the czar of Russia, a complex and costly enterprise beyond the means of any single merchant.

---

1. In the seventeenth century, "gentleman" indicated a certain social, economic, and educational status and was usually, though not invariably, associated with the ownership of land. Among the citizenry at large, only "gentlemen" had the right to bear arms.

Later the Levant Company pursued a similar purpose in Turkey.

More significant for the North American venture was the joint stock company, a form of business organization in which investors pooled their capital and shared in the profits — and losses. Many of Drake's expeditions sailed under the direction and with the support of some joint stock company, perhaps organized for that purpose alone. Unlike modern corporations, joint stock companies were designed to back specific undertakings. The most significant of all joint stock enterprises emerged at the dawn of the seventeenth century, and was called the East India Company. With heavy capitalization, this company assumed a central role in the expansion and control of English trade. It soon evolved into a center of power and influence, sometimes making loans to the state, other times serving as a prime mover in colonizing efforts abroad. By 1612, the East India Company resembled a modern corporation in that profits and losses from several business ventures were grouped together.

In 1606 the Virginia Company of London received a royal patent enabling it to sell stock to its members, all of whom hoped for a quick return on their investment. Within a few years, shares in the company were sold to the English public at large. Furthermore, if anyone did not have sufficient cash to invest in the venture, then that person literally could invest himself by going to Virginia at his own expense and trading his labor for a share in the profits. Later on, at its own expense, the company planned to send male and female servants who would carry much of the burden of labor, but would not share in the profits. All this was expected to happen just as soon as those shiploads of marketable goods — metals and minerals, furs and glass, dyes and tar — began flowing back to London.

❧ Land and Labor

In England, land meant economic standing and political power. Monarchs protected their positions by acquiring great blocks of land, while titled nobles could receive from those sovereigns no greater gift than land. Families with impressive land holdings preserved their position and privileges through the law of primogeniture, under which all family land passed to the eldest son. This practice saved magnificent estates from breaking into smaller pieces over the course of generations. However, for second and third sons it meant that owning land was a distant dream. Daughters might

marry well — provided their father gave them a handsome dowry — and younger sons might through their labors (or marriage) accumulate enough capital to buy land and eventually join the landed gentry. Nonetheless, the social and economic advantage clearly rested upon eldest sons.

The majority of English people did not own land outright. Many peasants, however, had secure hereditary rights to their holdings, called "freehold tenure." Other peasants' tenure, known as "copyhold tenure," was less secure and was subject to rent increases. As a vestige of the lingering feudal system, many villagers had access to land held in common: hunting and fishing rights, farming rights, and rights to the woodlands for timber and to the pastures for the grazing of cattle. In the sixteenth century, these common lands began to give way to privately held estates, as nobles hungrily added acres to make room for their deer parks and, as gentlemen, "enclosed" (surrounded with hedges) common land for grazing their sheep. This transition from common land to private land was made more gradual by the use of tenant farming, in which peasants held land from the lord of the manor, often for a long-term lease (either freehold or copyhold) that could be passed on from father to son. For this privilege the farmer paid a fixed rent; if land under this arrangement passed on from father to son, then the son had to pay a special fee, usually as much as a year's rent. The increased demand for land drove up prices, and for peasants without tenure the rents and fees levied also increased. Many were driven from the land, unable to pay the higher rents or secure holdings of their own. These displaced laborers wandered from place to place, seeking temporary rural employment. Often, they became chronically unemployed vagrants who begged for their food, or thieves who took it.

Unfortunately, the labor market was already oversupplied. A decline in the demand for English cloth, together with stiffer competition for foreign markets, caused unemployment to rise sharply, beginning around 1590 and extending well into the seventeenth century. Those lucky enough to find work discovered that wages had fallen so low that they could support neither themselves nor their families. Many textile workers, artisans, day laborers, and domestics found themselves at the edge of starvation, no better off than tenant farmers expelled from their homes. As clergyman Richard Hakluyt noted in the 1590s, England was "swarming at this day with valiant youths rusting and hurtful by lack of employment."

As a consequence, England's prisons swelled with men, women, and children whose only fault was that they could pay their debts or appease their stomachs only through petty crimes. Even minor crimes were punishable by death. "Look seriously into the land," one preacher advised, "and see whether there be not just cause, if not a necessity, to seek abroad." When in 1609 the Virginia Company wrote to the City of London to tell them that even "the meanest family" could receive "meat, drink, and clothing, with a house, orchard, and garden . . . and a possession of lands to them and their posterity," it sounded too good to be true. And in most respects it was. Nonetheless, if only half true, or a fraction of that, many could hardly pass up the chance. If persons were willing to pay their way, so much the better, but if not, they would sell themselves in servitude for however many years it took to escape what they could tolerate no more.

❧ *Population Growth and the Conquest of Ireland*

As if displacement and unemployment were not enough, the general population of England increased sharply in the sixteenth century, worsening the social and economic crisis. The country as a whole grew from under three million in 1500 to over five million by 1650. London's population alone rose from around sixty thousand in 1500 to more than three times that by 1600. Around the turn of the century, authorities began looking for ways to relieve the mounting pressures and solve their severe social crisis.

England's long war with Spain finally ended in 1604, and this moment of calm permitted King James I to resurrect hopes for expansion abroad. He looked first to Ireland. For centuries the English had tried to subdue, Anglicize, and colonize the large island to their west, establishing in the Middle Ages the Pale in eastern Ireland, a region where the English exercised some control. Outside the Pale there existed — to English eyes — no ordered society at all. The "wild Irish" organized themselves by clans, but to the English they seemed akin to the American Indians — if not to beasts — living "without any knowledge of God or good manners, in common of their goods, cattle, women, children, and every other thing." If instructed in the rules of Christian behavior, "I see no grace in them to follow it," one adviser wrote Queen Elizabeth in 1567. Yet the queen had made strenuous efforts to attach that land to her kingdom, sending such favorites as Sir Humphrey Gilbert and Sir Walter Raleigh to introduce the alleged benefits of Christianity and English civilization.

In 1607 the armies of King James crushed an Irish rebellion against English rule, then proceeded to tighten their control and establish colonies throughout that first foreign plantation. James, a Scotsman, gave Ulster (Northern Ireland) to fellow Scots to settle, distributing other land widely to wealthy merchant guilds of London. These new settlers would then assume the duty of subduing or driving out the native Irish. Many Englishmen, especially those active in Irish affairs, naturally thought of American colonization efforts in terms comparable to those applied to Ireland. In both places, native inhabitants had to be suppressed, English wealth rewarded and enhanced, and royal authority obeyed. In England, racism had deep roots long before its manifestations in the New World.

Apart from anxieties about Irish barbarism, the English faced division with the Welsh, whose land was supposedly totally integrated in the kingdom, and with the Scots, whose kingdom was linked to England only through a common monarch. Themselves a mixture of Britons, Normans, and Scandinavian-descended Jutes, the English by the time of James I thought of themselves as a race apart, just as geographically they were a land apart. Although they obviously shared a common culture with continental Europeans, they nonetheless saw England as unique — "This happy breed of men, this little world,/This precious stone set in the silver sea," as Shakespeare put it. But that happy breed itself was divided by a rigid class structure in place for centuries and by religious tensions now coming to a boil.

❧ *Religion and Rhetoric*

Not all reports of the New World were positive; indeed, the colony of Virginia suffered from much disrepute, especially given the costly failures prior to 1607. Gilbert lost his life, Raleigh his fortune, and countless merchants their ships. To many potential investors, the Native Americans were as wild as the untamed Irish — and who wanted another Ireland on their hands, with surly rebellions and a conspicuous lack of "good manners"? That faraway country, it seemed to many, had the capacity only to swallow up and destroy those who tried to tame it. So if the literature of promotion for America seems extravagant in its praise and fanciful in its promises, it must be remembered that the many negative reports required strong refutation.

To motivate James I, the merchants, and the potential settlers demanded stirring language. The words found in Thomas Hariot's *A Briefe and true report of the new found land of Virginia* (1588) were subject to constant repetition. Writers such as Hakluyt sought to inspire others by recalling what Elizabethan Englishmen had achieved: "which of the kings of this land before her Majesty," Hakluyt asked, "had their banner ever seen in the Caspian Sea? Which of them hath ever dealt with the emperor of Persia, as her Majesty hath done?" Hakluyt continued with a kind of doxology in praise of Elizabeth and her seamen: they reached Constantinople, traded with Babylonia, stretched the arm of England as far as India, sailed through the Straits of Magellan, ranged "along the coast of Chile, Peru, and all the backside of Nova Hispania, further than any Christian ever passed." In passing from Tudor to Stuart, should England pass from courage to cowardice? Hakluyt and others were prepared to lead a chorus shouting "No!"

An early arrival on the Virginia scene, Robert Johnson, wrote back to his fellow English to dismiss the "scandalous reports" that had been given of this hospitable land. The land offered new and abundant opportunity to be well housed and well fed, to own and cultivate land for the benefit of one's family and the steady progress of the community. What of hardships and difficulties? We should think, Johnson added, of not only the glories in Elizabeth's day, but of current challenges worthy of Alexander or Hercules and "those heathen Monarchs" who achieved so much that they were thought to be gods. In books and letters, in sermons and official charters, the message was the same: those who are bold and strong will reap the rewards of this once-in-a-lifetime opportunity.

Hariot's *Briefe and True Report*   Thomas Hariot's 1588 report was among the very first of many to encourage English colonization of the New World. The idealized Adam and Eve figures depicted on this front page reflect the belief that America would be a land of peace and prosperity.

Religion constituted a significant part of this rhetoric. Colonists were reminded that they took more than hoes and shovels with them: they took a gospel, a Protestant gospel, a "true and sincere religion" (in Hakluyt's words). "Advancing the glory of God" could be voiced in the very same breath with "enlarging the glory and wealth of England": no contradiction was perceived, only mutual reinforcement. Captain John Smith chided those who thought only of personal gain: if an Englishman "have any grain of faith or zeal in religion, what can he do less hurtful to any, or more agreeable to God, than to seek to convert these poor savages to know Christ and humanity?" And in 1610 early supporters of the Virginia effort declared roundly and clearly that their first purpose was "to preach and baptize" the Native Americans, rescuing them from the "arms of the Devil" as well as from an "almost invincible ignorance."

If the purposes of religion were to be served, so were those of morality. For London, the promoters argued, had become a sink of degradation and sin. Simply to survive, homeless young women became prostitutes and homeless young men took to assault and burglary. In Virginia, on the other hand, a whole and healthy family could work in the field, planting and reaping together, far from the temptations and cruelties of the city, far from the taverns and alehouses. People who in England had been "lewd and idle," enthused one pamphleteer, in the new country "not only grow ashamed of their former courses, but abhor to hear of them." Virtue, if lost, could be regained; innocence, if stained, could be made clean once again. People could begin life anew, with all the depressing memories of a former life wiped away.

Beyond these general motivations that pulled people toward America on behalf of religion and morality, England gave a "push" by requiring strict conformity to the Book of Common Prayer and its prescribed modes of worship and stipulated prayers. Little room for maneuver or dissent existed for Protestants, none whatsoever for Catholics. Those who wished to be even modestly innovative in religion — for example, offering spontaneous prayers or declining to kneel when receiving communion — quickly discovered that England in the early seventeenth century was not the place to try it. Many thought that perhaps in Holland, just across the English Channel, people might not be obliged to follow every procedure in the Book of Common Prayer to the letter. Even farther, across an Atlantic Ocean, Christians might dare to take another book, the Bible, as their only guide in constructing a true faith and a pure worship.

SUCCESS IN THE CHESAPEAKE

In planning overseas adventures, seventeenth-century English kings preferred to charter, bless, and promote more than to invest, support, and defend. The Virginia Company of London, a joint stock company, thus became the means to colonization. Jamestown resulted from their efforts, though within two decades King James found it necessary to assume direct control. The tobacco cultivation did rescue early Virginia's economy from disaster, but at the price of putting the colony's fortunes at the mercy of a wildly fluctuating market. Tobacco plantations also created a demand for labor ultimately met by slavery, casting a dark shadow across all subsequent American history. A generation after the launching of Virginia, England chartered another Chesapeake Bay colony. Maryland began with sharply different premises and under surprisingly different auspices.

✥ *The Virginia Company of London*

In April 1606, the king approved the creation of the Virginia Company of London, usually called simply the Virginia Company. By November 1606, the company had gathered its first complement of settlers. After outfitting three ships, the company drew up instructions for the group. Remembering the ill fate of Roanoke, the company urged special care in selecting a site for the colony, directing the group to take its time so that it would not be necessary to move in a few weeks or months. "Do your best endeavor," the merchants ad-

vised, "to find out a safe port in the entrance of some navigable river," choosing one that seems to go farthest inland. Sail up that stream until "you may make election of the strongest, most fertile, and wholesome place," keeping in mind not only possible Indian hostility but also Spanish ships marauding north from Florida. Above all else, the company firmly declared, do not allow anyone to write discouraging letters back to England. For this time, efforts must succeed.

By the end of December the small fleet was ready to sail, and after some time in the Caribbean, the ships sailed into Chesapeake Bay in April 1607. Looking around carefully, as they had been advised, the captain and his passengers chose a wide and navigable river, named it the James after their king, and sailed upstream about fifty miles where ocean-going vessels would still have no difficulty anchoring. One member of that first voyage, George Percy, reported with delight of the "goodliest Woods" of beech, oak, cedar, cypress, and walnut, as well as abundant strawberries, raspberries, and mulberries. In a few weeks, however, his mood changed. Disease and death struck again and again; foodstuffs brought from England quickly ran out; costly conflict with Native Americans threatened; no route to the Orient opened. Within the first six months, almost two-thirds of the 120 settlers had died. "There were never Englishmen left in a foreign country in such misery," Percy sadly concluded, "as we were in this new discovered Virginia."

✥ *Jamestown*

What went wrong? Nearly everything. The settlement called Jamestown proved not "wholesome," but a malarial swamp. Shallow wells yielded water that was brackish at best, contaminated at worst. Innumerable insects carried countless diseases: "swellings, fluxes, and burning fevers"; when food supplies dwindled, sickness ran wild. Questions of authority kept the community divided and fractious, as the company tried to assert its rights, the king his, and the local leaders theirs. All told, the colony's leaders rounded up very little obedience or discipline; more often they tended to cancel each other out, with the hundred or so settlers doing much as they pleased. About the only "achievement" of the first years was to alienate the Indians. To prove English superiority, the settlers burned villages, destroyed food supplies, and murdered men, women, and children.

This bloodshed need not have happened, for the

Smith's Map of Virginia John Smith's map, first published in 1612, remained the most influential map of Virginia throughout the seventeenth century and is an excellent example of the then-popular practice of using pictures rather than cartographic symbols to convey information. Many of the place-names he records are still in use today.

Indians did not initially insist on driving out the newcomers. Indeed, almost from the start, it was clear to the leader of the local Indian confederacy, Powhatan, that the situation of the English was so desperate that they would starve without access to his people's corn. "What can you get by war," he asked, "when we can hide our provisions and flee to the woods?" Trade and peaceful contact seemed far more sensible, both for Indian and English. "Think you I am so simple," Powhatan observed, "not to know it is better to eat good meat, lie well, and sleep quietly with my women and children, laugh, and be merry with you . . . than to be forced to flee from all, to lie cold in the woods, feed upon acorns and such trash, and be so hunted by you that I can neither rest nor sleep?" He proposed the kind of reciprocal gift-giving that Indians normally practiced among themselves to keep the peace. And indeed, while Jamestown was still small and struggling, it did make sense for both sides to exchange goods and "lie well,"

rather than destroy the ability of either to survive. Unfortunately, this promising pattern did not prevail. So desperate did the English consider their situation that military conquest seemed the only route to survival.

But all-out war did not begin at once, for a shrewd leader gradually emerged at Jamestown who, for a while, kept the settlers under control. This was Captain John Smith, one of the original six council members who assumed authority as the others died or departed. Smith, never a popular figure in Jamestown, was nonetheless a strong one. Twenty-seven when he joined the Virginia Company's great venture, Smith had already proved himself as a mercenary soldier fighting the Turks in Hungary. He had not hesitated in battle there, and he did not hesitate to take charge in Jamestown to prevent total disintegration. He improved relations with the Indians, notably with Powhatan, who had brought all neighboring tribes into a strong confederation. Without some food from the native inhabitants, he knew, the sickly colonists would die. Smith negotiated, haggled, and browbeat until some corn arrived in time. In addition, he explored, drew maps, wrote extensively, and demanded of his fellow colonists that they work at least as hard as he did. If they did not work, they would not eat — and he meant it. Those who failed to follow his example "the next day shall be set beyond the river, and forever be banished from the fort, and live there or starve."

Smith committed no serious atrocities against the Indians, although he envisioned a society in which the native people would do most of the work for the English. Impressed by the example of "stout Cortés" in Mexico, Smith concluded that Virginia Indians could also be led into a compulsory servitude that would permit some kind of coexistence. The Indians seemed to know how to make the land produce its fruit and the woods its game without extraordinary effort; they made cornbread and hominy, planted corn, peas, and pumpkins, boiled or broiled their fish and fowl, and generally lived well. With their help, Smith reasoned, the English could do the same. And, with their cooperation as well, trade patterns could develop, as in fact happened around the southern end of the Appalachian mountain chain.

By the fall of 1609, however, Smith returned to England to complain about the tangled lines of authority that threatened to sink the young colony. The Virginia Company, agreeing that a more direct control was required, persuaded the king to delegate all his authority to the company so that it, in turn, could delegate all its authority to a resident governor who would rule more like a military commander. First under Lord De La Warr (who gave his name to Delaware) in 1610, then under his deputy Sir Thomas Dale in 1611, martial law was imposed as the only hope for a colony beyond control. The settlers fell under a code of laws that made harsh demands and provided even harsher penalties. "That the Almighty God be duly and daily served," the code stipulated that "every man and woman" should attend services twice every day, be deprived of a food allowance for the first absence, be whipped for the second, and be sent to the galleys for six months for the third. All trading with the Indians or with ships sailing up the river would be carried on by the governor, not by private persons, for ship captains as well as ordinary sailors had been known to sell foodstuffs to an individual "at unreasonable rate, and prices unconscionable." All householders were ordered to keep their houses "sweet and clean" and also keep the street in front of their homes neatly swept. Stealing food from any garden, public or private, was a most serious offense, with capital punishment suitable to the crime.

Martial law could restore order, but it could not make Virginia attractive to new settlers. Something had to be done to provide incentive, so that the colony could grow and the company prosper. The company hoped to entice more settlers through grants of land, but also hoped to reap some profits from exporting lumber, wine, fish, and salt; from creating "silk farms;" from mining iron or coal; and from manufacturing glass. No longer starving themselves, the colonists should now provide some return on that hopeful investment made years before. One crop, above all others, suggested that real return was possible.

✑ *The Weed and the Economy*

While exploring Cuba on his first voyage, Columbus

✳ **IN THEIR OWN WORDS**

King James I on "this filthie noveltie," 1604
Smoking tobacco became very popular among the English—but not their king, who in A Counter Blaste to Tobacco *roundly condemned the habit.*

Have you not reason then to bee ashamed, and to forebeare this filthie noveltie, so basely grounded, so foolishly received and so grossly mistaken in the right use thereof? In your abuse thereof sinning against God, harming your selves both in persons and goods…by the custom thereof making your selves to be wondered at by all forraine civil Nations, and by all strangers that come among you, to be scorned and contemned. A custom loathsome to the eye, hatefull to the nose, harmefull to the braine, dangerous to the Lungs, and in the black stinking fume thereof, neerest resembling the horrible Stigian smoke of the pit that is bottomlesse.

and his sailors saw a curious sight: natives smoking some sort of weed unknown to Europeans, rolled up into a kind of cigar. Then, in the 1560s, an English pirate-explorer, Sir John Hawkins, after disposing of slaves in the Caribbean, visited the Florida coast where he observed that the natives, when they traveled, carried with them "a kind of herb dried." When they set fire to this mixture in an earthen cup, one of Hawkins's crew reported, they then placed a cane over it and "suck through the cane the smoke thereof, which smoke satisfieth their hunger, and therewith they live four or five days without meat or drink." Hawkins brought back to England some of the leaves of this novel plant; the custom spread, and soon Englishmen began to enjoy puffing a pipe of tobacco.

The Indians in Virginia also grew tobacco, using it for medicinal purposes as well as for recreational and ceremonial smoking. But Virginia's tobacco, having "a biting taste," was markedly inferior to that grown farther south. In 1611, colonist John Rolfe concluded that the problem in raising high-quality tobacco in Virginia lay not with the soil, but with the seed. He also recognized that the struggling colony needed something that could redeem its ever-declining reputation at home. To improve the odds for Virginia, Rolfe imported seeds from the Caribbean and present-day Venezuela, where the finest tobacco grew. From his small plot, he harvested his first tiny crop in 1612, then a slightly larger one the next year. By 1615 Virginia began to export tobacco to England, where its popularity continued to grow. That year, the export amounted to a pathetic 2,000 pounds; five years later, the export was a sizeable 40,000 pounds and, a decade after that, an astounding 1.5 million pounds. At last, Virginia had a product that would sell; at last, investors had a profit they could relish.

Everywhere Virginians planted tobacco, often ne-

Tobacco   This fine French illustration from the late sixteenth century claims that the American herb "petun," or tobacco, possesses wonderful medicinal properties as well as a delightful fragrance when smoked, and attests to its frequent use for these purposes by the Indians who cultivate it.

glecting to keep an acre or two for corn or some other foodstuff on which they could live. The governor had to order each grower to plant at least two acres of corn for himself (and two acres for each male servant) on pain of forfeiting his entire tobacco crop to the authorities. Rolfe worried too about what sort of Pandora's box he had opened, complaining that because Virginians know tobacco to be "very vendible in England" they risked their health and welfare by refusing to grow anything else.

❧ Demography and Representative Government

In its second decade, the small colony made some modest gains, both in population and in governance. By 1616 four new plantations had appeared: Henrico, fifteen miles below the falls of the James River (later the site of Richmond); Bermuda Hundred, about five miles below Henrico; West and Shirley Hundred, on the north side of the James River, just across from Bermuda Hundred; and Dale's Gift, on the eastern shore of Chesapeake Bay near Cape Charles. Yet their presence suggested more prosperity than in fact could be found. As ships brought new loads of immigrants, they often took back nearly as many as they brought. The building of crude homes in Jamestown hinted that many English came not to settle but to win a fortune and go home. And even without the fortune, large numbers left.

Natural increase in early Virginia came quite slowly because few families lived there. The proportion of males to females was approximately four to one in 1616 and no better a decade later. The Virginia Company advertised for "willing maids" to volunteer to sail for Virginia where men would pay the cost of their transportation in return for marriage. Yet growth was slow, for settlers confronted the additional difficulty of short life expectancy. Men died in their forties; women tended to live somewhat longer — if they survived the hazards of childbirth. Diseases such as malaria — "fever and ague" in the terms of the day — and typhus continued to destroy at a rate comparable to the great plagues of Europe. In the first twenty years of the colony's existence, the company sent more and more immigrants, and Virginia quietly absorbed them, as a great quagmire, without any sharp increase in population until after 1625.

The Virginia Company tried to make its feeble colony more attractive in two ways: first, by improving the terms for obtaining land; and, second, by introducing some measure of representative government. Thus the company gave residents who owned shares one hundred acres for each share. Those who had paid their own way to Virginia before 1616 also received one hundred acres, whether shareholders or not. Under a system introduced by Sir Edwin Sandys, who by 1619 directed the company's affairs, laborers who could not pay their own way became tenant farmers for seven years. During those years, they shared the crops with the landowner; then, at the end of the seven years, each laborer would get his own fifty acres, an estate beyond imagining for four-fifths of England's population.

To alleviate some of the problems inherent in governing a colony three thousand miles away, the company in 1619 provided for a General Assembly that, as John Smith observed, would be the beginnings of a kind of Parliament in Virginia. Twenty-two free male inhabitants, or "burgesses," were elected to serve under a governor appointed by the company. Even before this arrangement had been made, Virginia planters had already achieved a degree of independence by evading the company's orders or by claiming not to understand them; clarifi-

RELIGIOUS SERVICES AT JAMESTOWN.

Worship at Jamestown In this 1877 illustration, a book illustrator imagines how the earliest English settlers at Jamestown would have conducted an Anglican worship service. Note that the building is obviously meant to be temporary and that all the worshipers are men.

A "Gentleman" in Jamestown, 1619

John Pory, Speaker of the House of Burgesses, wrote to Sir Dudley Carleton in England to complain about the lack of culture he perceived in Jamestown.

At my first coming hither, the solitary uncouthness of this place, compared with those parts of Christendom or Turkey where I had been, and likewise my being seques-tered from all occurrences and passages which are so rife there, did not a little vex me. And yet, in these five months of my continuance here, there have come at one time or another eleven sail of ships into this river; but freighted more with ignorance than any other merchandise. At length, being hardened to this custom of abstinence from curiosity, I am resolved wholly to mind my business here; and, next after my pen, to have some good book always in store, [that] being in solitude the best and choic-est company. Besides, among these crystal rivers and odoriferous woods, I do escape much expense, envy, contempt, vanity, and vexation of mind. Yet, my good lord, have a little compassion upon me, and be pleased to send me what pamphlets and relations of the interim since I was with you, as your lordship shall think good. . . .

cation took months, by which time conditions often al-tered the case completely. Now the principle of "consent of the governed" won some formal recognition, even though the company affirmed that all legislation passed by the assembly had to be ratified in London before it became effective. In creating such a body, however, the company recognized that its effort at long-distance rule had failed, even as it recognized that colonists had some rights of their own.

❧ *Virginia and the Indians*

As English plantations expanded and as English pres-ence proved more than just a temporary nuisance, the Native Americans' resentment correspondingly in-creased. As early as 1609, Powhatan had expressed seri-ous misgivings to John Smith about what the English were up to. "Your coming is not for trade," Powhatan rightly observed, "but to invade my people and possess my country." Five years later, Powhatan still worried, but his daughter, Pocahontas, offered some promise as mediator between the two opposed cultures. Held hos-tage for many months in Jamestown in 1613 as a means of forcing Powhatan to return some captured Englishmen, Pocahontas learned more of the English language and English manners, and was even baptized into the Church of England.

General goodwill became particular when John Rolfe proposed to marry the nineteen-year-old Poca-hontas. Official English policy discouraged intermar-riage or other close contact with the Indians; indeed, Englishmen who on their own chose to live with the Indians were, if apprehended, often put to death. So Rolfe was careful to petition the governor, Sir Thomas Dale, for his permission, as well as that of Powhatan.

To Dale, Rolfe explained that he sought this marriage not "with the unbridled desire of carnal affection" but for the good of the colony and the glory of God. Such a marriage, he noted, might bring peace between the warring English and Indians, just as it would satisfy Pocahontas's desire "to be taught and instructed in the knowledge of God." Dale approved, and soon thereafter so did Powhatan, so that in April 1614 the wedding took place. It did, in fact, help keep the peace — for a time. But Pocahontas died in 1617, and Powhatan the follow-ing year. With those deaths, the old Indian anxiety re-turned: the English were, indeed, trying to possess their country. In addition, the English persisted in trying to transform "a rude, barbarous, and naked people" into models of English civility and Christianity.

Early on March 22, 1622, Indians came, as they so often did, to barter their goods with the English. But this time they had more than trade on their minds. As John Smith relates in his *History of Virginia,* the Indians "came unarmed into our houses with deer, turkeys, fish, fruits, and other provisions to sell us." In some cases, they even sat down to share breakfast with the settlers. But then they seized any tools or weapons lying about and "slew most barbarously, not sparing either age or sex, man, woman or child." They killed those that had already gone out into the fields to work, and would have razed Jamestown to the ground if a Christian In-dian had not warned inhabitants there of the carefully coordinated and wholly unexpected assault. When it was all over, about 350 settlers, about one-fourth of the colony's population, had fallen before the Indians' fury. Of those not killed, one survivor wrote, the Indians "burst the heart of all the rest." Now all talk of civility or Christianity with respect to the Indian ceased; gov-ernors and company officials spoke only of "extirpating the Savages" and rooting them out from being any longer "a people upon the face of the Earth."

The much-beleaguered Virginia Company attempted to put the best face possible on events in the colony where disease continued to account for more deaths than the massacre of 1622. But, company spokesmen pointed out, the Indian attack at least had the advantage of making any anxieties about English rights to the land purely academic. All natural rights claimed by the Indians were forever surrendered: the only right they retained was to be spared in combat in order to become slaves. To the company's enemies in England, however, the burden of Virginia's failure rested with the Virginia Company alone, which kept pouring in good money after bad, live immigrants after dead colonists. If the colony would be saved, the king must do it. So in 1624, after much legal wrangling, the charter granted the company in 1606 was formally withdrawn and Virginia became a royal colony.

King James had serious personal reservations about smoking. Nonetheless, by 1624 he was prepared to concede that tobacco was the only economic hope for his colony. The more land that could be planted and the more tobacco that could be exported, then the more profit for Virginia and for England, as well as for all middlemen along the way. With more land (no problem) and more servants (potentially a problem), profits could be wondrously and speedily multiplied. Large tobacco plantations required a large labor supply: where would it come from?

ஃ *Virginia Society*

Tobacco was both land- and labor-intensive. Because repeated crops of tobacco exhausted the soil within three or four years, early growers simply moved on to another section of cheap and readily available land. This discouraged the building of permanent residences, the planting of orchards, and the creation of towns. An alternative to moving on was to acquire so much land that portions of it could be farmed at different times, leaving some land to lie fallow and regain its fertility. As the price of tobacco declined in the second half of the seventeenth century, moreover, only the largest and most efficient tobacco growers could count on a steady profit. The large plantations that resulted shaped Virginia society and culture in the later colonial period.

In the absence of urban centers, each major plantation became a self-sufficient village. All life revolved around the plantation: children were born and edu-

cated there, young people were married there, and the dead were buried there. Most of the food was raised in the immediate neighborhood, and some of the clothing was woven on the local loom. Certainly the plantation provided the entertainment: gambling, horse racing, and hunting took place in or near the homes, some of which became commodious by the end of the seventeenth century. By then, at least among the well-off, brick homes were replacing the frame dwellings which had themselves supplanted the first settlers' simple cottages with thatch roofs and walls of poles held together with plaster or mud.

Virginia's four great rivers — the Potomac, Rappahannock, York, and James — dictated the patterns of settlements as well as trade. Plantations fanned out along the banks of these rivers in long narrow bands, keeping close to the water, but extending far enough back for extensive farming and safe building. Ocean-going vessels could anchor close to the plantation's "front door," which always faced the river. The plantation owner, with the help of his cooper, could pack the dried tobacco into great hogshead barrels, then load them from his dock onto a ship bound directly for European markets. Of course, the absence of major ports or shipping centers hampered the efficiency of the tobacco trade. Nonetheless, profits from those tobacco sales could be used to purchase luxury items from England, unloaded at that same front door. The rivers also served for travel within the colony as well as for easy access to the Chesapeake Bay and its riches of fish, oysters, crabs, and clams.

All of this eased the life of those who lived on the land below the fall line of the great rivers — the area called the Tidewater. Above those fall lines, in the Piedmont, a different and harder style of life developed. No roads carried travelers from the foothills to Jamestown (or, after 1699, Williamsburg), where settlers needed to go to have their legal cases heard and to make their views known. Small subsistence farms dotted the frontier, with Indians still a threat. Gradually, the strains developing between the older settlers in the Tidewater and the newer ones in the foothills reached a breaking point. With freed indentured servants looking for land, with Indians being driven farther west from their traditional homeland, and with the government in Jamestown seemingly indifferent to the concerns of the frontier, revolt erupted in 1676.[2]

Some attempts were made to compensate for the

---

2. On Bacon's Rebellion, see below, pp. 60-61.

A Tidewater Plantation   Tidewater Virginia offered many useful locations for plantations because of its many waterways with access to the sea. This illustration of a prosperous seventeenth-century plantation shows all paths leading to the water.

absence of major cities by decentralizing governance. Much government operated at the county level, even when this meant that a county courthouse had to stand all by itself in the countryside. The county court handled such vital matters as the building of roads and bridges, the operation of ferries, the supervision of local elections, the collection of taxes, and some administration of justice. At the parish level, the laymen who conducted the temporal affairs of the church, the vestry, looked after the widows and orphans, administered charity to the poor and disabled, and collected the tithe from all free male inhabitants, whether church members or not. To most Virginians, cities hardly seemed necessary.

Clergymen and schoolmasters, however, felt differently. Both groups required a significant accumulation of population to support them. In the early years, Virginia took little interest in building schools; one colonial governor rejoiced that no schools or printing presses could be found, "for learning has brought disobedience, and heresy, and sects into the world, and printing has divulged them, and libels against the best government. God keep us from both!" God, poverty, or inertia did keep most formal schooling out of Virginia through

the seventeenth century. Wealthier plantations might hire tutors for their own family, while poorer parents would send children out for an apprenticeship. The apprentice's status was similar to that of an indentured servant, but in addition to learning a trade, such children were also often taught how to read and write.

Clergymen fared somewhat better because the law was clearly on their side. The Church of England was by law the established church of the mother country and of colonial Virginia alike. This meant that church and state were intimately allied, that public taxes bought the land and built the churches and paid the ministers, and that official prohibitions discouraged competition from other religious groups. Anglican clergy had all the force and favor of English precedent behind them. The clergy of England's national church had little to complain about — or so it might seem. But in fact, they complained all the time.

Since they were often paid in pounds of tobacco — and since the price of that commodity went up and down — salaries were not stable. Accustomed to finer living in England than they found in Virginia, the clergy complained about their housing, about their hardships in travel, and (like everyone else) about the weather. Most of all, however, they complained about the absence of cities and towns. Try as they did to recreate in Virginia the kind of religious nurture that the English village enjoyed back home, they were frustrated at every turn. They were obliged to travel great distances to where the people lived; having done so (in some irritation), they found only a handful of parishioners prepared to attend divine service. Distances were so great and clergy so few that reaching every major plantation every Sunday was impossible. The whole religious enterprise struck the resident clergy as scandalously inefficient.

The laity also complained. As early as 1632 the Virginia Assembly found it necessary to order that "Ministers shall not give themselves to excess in drinking, or riot, spending their time idly by day or night playing at dice, cards, or any other unlawful game." Two decades later, a visitor found little improvement. The clergy, John Hammond wrote, dress themselves in black gowns so that they can "babble in a pulpit, roar in a tavern," and collect their salaries as though they were actually worthy of them. As Virginia's general economy and welfare improved, however, so did the vigilance and vigor of its Anglican ministry.

With legislative backing, parishes were laid out, glebes (farming lands whose harvest went to support the parish) were bought, and attractive country churches were built. By 1650 about thirty Anglican parishes had been created, though this did not always mean that a church had actually been erected or a minister installed. The parishes near the rivers measured some twenty to forty miles long, five to ten miles wide. Parishes away from the river could be as much as a hundred miles in length, and a single clergyman often had the responsibility of several parishes. Anglicanism was, therefore, thinly spread across the land; in some areas it existed in name only. The Church of England nevertheless expanded its network as throughout the seventeenth century more parishes came into being. Slowly, the parish church began to compete with the plantation home and the county courthouse as a center of rural life.

Yet Anglicanism never managed to rid the colony of all competition. Small pockets of Puritan or Quaker, Baptist or Presbyterian sentiment occasionally appeared. Moreover, some clergy who had not met all formal Anglican requirements for ordination nonetheless found themselves in Church of England pulpits. Clearly these churches concerned themselves more with their social function than with their denominational purity. Moreover, magic and witchcraft[3] served to deal with — or ward off — the powers of darkness. As late as the last decade of the seventeenth century, Governor Francis Nicholson required justices to examine carefully all cases of felonious crime, trespass, and witchcraft.

Catholicism and the Calverts

In its first sixty years Maryland, the second colony to be created in the South, did nothing to advance the Anglican cause. On the contrary, it was conceived as a refuge for England's Roman Catholics, an action so surprising as to shock not only Virginians but many

back in England as well. Two factors account for the surprise: first, the vehement sentiment against Catholicism throughout England and most of her colonies; and, second, the active persecution of Catholics in England, suggesting that no royal favor to that dreaded religion would likely be shown.

Charles I (who succeeded James I in 1625) maintained close connections with the Calvert family, even after George Calvert — the first Lord Baltimore — announced his conversion to Roman Catholicism the year that Charles came to the throne. And Charles had himself married a Roman Catholic. Earlier involved in efforts to colonize a portion of Newfoundland as a religious refuge, George Calvert in 1629 petitioned the king for some land in more temperate climes. In 1632, Charles granted Calvert a tract north of the Potomac River, stretching northward toward what would later become Philadelphia and inland for about one hundred miles to the sources of the Potomac. Before all formalities were concluded, George Calvert died, his title of nobility and his grant of land both passing to his twenty-six-year-old son, Cecilius Calvert.

The second Lord Baltimore was a sole proprietor, who had the power to establish what government he wished, grant land on his own terms, and rule his fiefdom without consultation or fear of contradiction. The proprietor functioned virtually as an independent monarch, though he could not pass laws contrary to those of England. In religion as well as in governance, America's first proprietary colony seemed set on a course that would distinguish it sharply from its very close neighbor. Before the century was over, however, Maryland and Virginia made up a Chesapeake society and a Chesapeake economy whose constituent parts could not be readily distinguished.

Yet in the early years Maryland seemed all too different. Several serious objections were raised against the very notion of a proprietary colony for Catholics. Baltimore and his advisers took up the objections, one by one, and their answers gave much insight into the temper of England in the 1630s. To the first objection that England was surrendering her battle to expel all "popery" from her soil, Baltimore responded that the nation had its own best interests in mind when it tried to increase colonization along the Atlantic, holding off the Spanish to the south and the Dutch to the north. To the second, Baltimore reminded his opponents that neither Virginia nor Maryland was all that wonderful a place to live. (Indeed, when criminals in England were given the choice between being hanged or be-

---

3. Between 1626 and 1705 nineteen Virginians were either charged with witchcraft or were referred to as witches. Charles City County had a "Conjurer's Field," while a pond in Princess Anne County was called "Witchduck."

ing sent to Virginia, many chose the gallows.) Finally, the challengers declared, Catholics situated between a Protestant Virginia and a Protestant New England would be tempted to make league with the Spanish and overthrow the Crown. Not so, said Baltimore, for the Protestants will outnumber the Catholics by more than three to one, and English Catholics, let it be remembered, were still English, still loyal to their flag and king. Besides which, the first settlers of Maryland, like the first settlers of Virginia, would be so busy just trying to survive that no time could possibly be found for foreign intrigue. Food, clothing, and shelter would be their preeminent concerns.

In 1634 two ships sailed up the Chesapeake Bay, landing at a cleared Indian village, renamed St. Mary's, the first capital of Maryland. While the colony certainly offered refuge to Catholics, Lord Baltimore recognized that it neither could nor should be limited to Catholics. So Protestants also boarded those first two ships, with Baltimore cautioning his fellow Catholics to avoid religious controversy and do nothing that would offend. Protestants were encouraged to settle in Maryland and, in fact, soon formed the majority, though the largest land holdings and major offices went to the Catholic relatives and close friends of the Calverts. A Protestant coup in the early 1640s temporarily wrested authority from the proprietor, but soon his authority was restored. To dampen religious tensions and please those in power after Charles I was beheaded, the Maryland Assembly passed an Act for Religious Toleration in 1649. This guaranteed to all Christians who professed belief in the Trinity the right to freely worship and freedom from coercion in religion. It was a limited toleration, to be sure, but nonetheless a step forward in an era of widespread persecution and intolerance.

Maryland faced the same economic challenges as Virginia: labor shortages, land distribution, and encouraging more colonists to cross the ocean. Maryland adopted the same headright system employed in Virginia, granting fifty acres to new settlers who paid their own way. Although Maryland's authorities did not have such sharp clashes with Indians, among whom Jesuit missionaries labored, that was counterbalanced by its severe clashes with Protestants who challenged or attempted to nullify Calvert's rule. On the whole, however, Maryland's early years were not as painful as Virginia's. Its population reached eight thousand within a single generation and exceeded thirteen thousand by 1670.

By that time tobacco had become the crop of choice and profit, as it had in Virginia. As long as tobacco prices held steady, all landholders gave their full attention to raising and exporting that single crop. Servants in Maryland, moreover, received fifty acres of land when their term of servitude expired (if they lived that long; many did not). Although settlers grew much of their own food and enjoyed a plentiful supply of timber, profits from tobacco bought whatever other goods and services were required. As the tobacco market declined toward the end of the century, Maryland planters diversified to wheat, corn, rye, barley, and peas; they also expanded their domestic industries, including such cottage crafts as shoemaking and cloth making. Carpenters and coopers had, of course, been present from the first generation of settlement. By the end of the century Maryland, economically, looked more and more like Virginia.

Politically, on the other hand, Maryland continued to be distinctive until 1692, since the governor and his council (composed of relatives and close allies) made sure that wealth and power stayed in Catholic hands. In 1635, the settlers, with Baltimore's approval, met in a General Assembly. Within three years this body sought the right to initiate legislation rather than passively accept whatever was sent over from England. Lord Baltimore, less enthusiastic about this idea, retained the right to summon or dismiss the Assembly as he chose. The popular body, however, argued for a status similar to that of England's House of Commons. Eventually the proprietors grudgingly conceded that argument.

Maryland's legislative house took advantage of the chaos of England's Civil War to assert its prerogatives and claims most vigorously, at the same time temporarily nullifying the authority of the proprietor. This Protestant group rejected the Catholic elites in Maryland even as it turned away from the Quakers who were growing in number. But its major struggle continued to be with the proprietor and his large family. Not until the Glorious Revolution of 1688-89 did royal sentiment shift away from the proprietor as another wave of anti-Catholicism swept England. When Maryland became a royal colony in 1692, a once uniquely Catholic enterprise looked for the most part like the rest of England's foreign plantations in the New World.

❧ Slavery and Servitude in the Chesapeake

Virginia's labor problems appeared quite early. From the beginning, Jamestown needed farmers and laborers to complement the relative abundance of artisans and gentlemen in the earliest immigration. In keeping with their social status in England, gentlemen were more inclined to hunt as a pleasant pastime, not to survive. They could, of course, plant corn, but as long as the Indians took care of that, it hardly seemed necessary. Some of the gentlemen even brought over servants, but they were trained to wait on their masters, not to work the soil. Ordinary laborers, who enjoyed no great reputation in England for their industry and persistence, found even less favor in Virginia. What steady source of labor could be counted on to make Virginia and Maryland prosperous colonies rather than failing dependencies?

One natural source of labor — the family's children — failed to

A Slave Sale in South Carolina This eighteenth-century newspaper notice employs the stock illustrations frequently used to depict slaves newly arrived from Africa. Notice the precautions that are supposedly being taken to ensure that the slaves do not spread smallpox, rightly feared in colonial America as a deadly disease. An outbreak of smallpox could wipe out a slave-trader's or a planter's entire investment and threaten his own family. So it would be reassuring to know that many newly arrived slaves carried the immunity conferred by having already contracted and survived the disease in Africa.

their labor for a specified number of years in exchange for passage to the Chesapeake and "freedom dues" such as tools, livestock, and land, when their term ended. A document known as an indenture spelled out the details of the contractual obligation, particularly the number of years to be served, varying from four to seven. Young children, however, could be indentured for a longer period, generally until twenty-one years of age. Bound labor was not a wholly novel idea in England, since many young people had served as apprentices to learn a trade. Normally, they received no income — only room, board, and the valuable instruction. So the indentured servants arriving in the Chesa-

materialize since the early immigrants were almost exclusively male. A second possible source, the Indians, seemed an obvious choice, except that Indians preferred to move into the interior during the humid summers, just when tobacco fields required the greatest and steadiest attention. Captain John Smith hoped that Indians might become useful laborers, but the native people showed no great interest in tedious chores even when they were nearby. Moreover, the colonists, ever fearful of Indian attack, resisted employing large numbers either in their homes or the fields. In 1619 the General Assembly warned that no more than five or six Indians should be put to work in any one place, and that only in the largest settlements; even then the Assembly advised that a "good guard in the night be kept upon them."

INDENTURED SERVITUDE

A third source of labor offered more promise. Unemployed or impoverished workers in England might sell

peake in the seventeenth century followed a tradition that was familiar, even if the country in which they served was not.

In 1619 Virginia's General Assembly stipulated that all contracts between masters and indentured servants be recorded and their provisions carefully enforced. One such agreement between the servant Roger Jones and his master, William Churchill, specified that Jones "is freely willing to serve his master seven years from his arrival," and that Churchill would put this servant to work in the store "and not employ him in common working in the ground." Brokers found it profitable to recruit indentured servants, receiving in exchange their headright to fifty acres. Hungry for colonists as well as for workers, the Chesapeake colonies in the 1640s and 1650s grew mainly through the large-scale importation of indentured servants.

For a generation or more, the system of white indentured servitude worked reasonably well, at least from the point of view of the master. The master had his labor supply, even if its temporary character required constant recruiting and re-supply. On the other side of the contract, the indentured servant could look toward the opportunity, after a few years, to start off in a new land with more promise of economic gain, even perhaps a measure of economic independence. Often, however, the high mortality rates prevented the servants from ever "cashing in" on the terms of their contracts. Moreover, the colonial courts busied themselves in trying to protect servants from abuse and masters from malingering. Male servants were prone to run away from hard and unfamiliar agricultural labor; if caught, they were punished, most often by the addition of months or years to their term. Unmarried female servants who became pregnant might also have their service extended, even if the master had gotten them pregnant. A pressing social problem arose late in the seventeenth century when large numbers of indentured servants began surviving long enough to fulfill their obligation, gain freedom, and threaten the

more established planters. But the decline of white indenture owed most to the dwindling supply of able-bodied excess workers in England and the rising supply of able-bodied, unfree workers from Africa or the West Indies.

ENSLAVING AFRICANS

Slavery was not invented in the Chesapeake, nor was it a significant feature of early modern English society. Accidents of history made it the distinguishing element of Chesapeake economic life. Greek and Roman societies made slaves of prisoners of war, a form of slavery that had nothing to do with race or tobacco. In the medieval world, pirates who plundered coasts made away with whatever booty they could find and sell, often including human beings. Only in the fifteenth century, however, did slavery become a transatlantic business, and only then did Africa, particularly its west coast regions, become the major supplier for the rapidly developing and degrading human traffic. Both Europeans

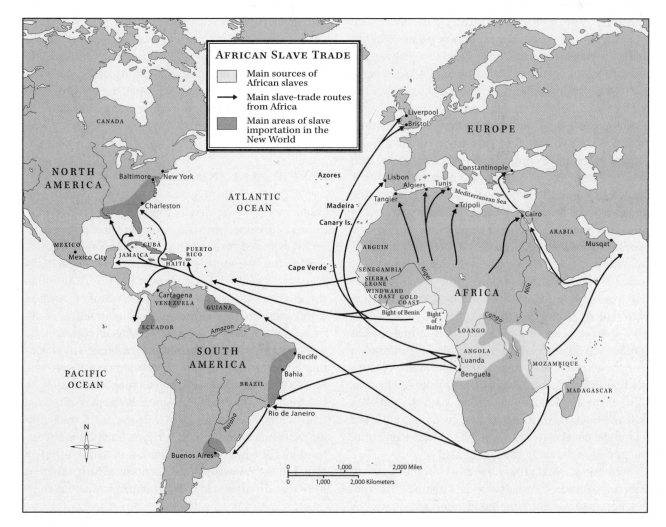

and Arabs participated in the slave trade, aided in each case by the cooperation or connivance of warring African rulers. Before Virginia was even founded, nearly one million African slaves had been dispatched to the New World, mostly to Brazil and the West Indies.

Africans arrived in Virginia quite early, even before 1619 when a Dutch ship arrived and sold twenty individuals who were aboard. Virginians, in turn, sold the "cargo" to various masters, in much the same way that indentures were bought and sold at dockside. This action established no precedent and attracted no comment from contemporaries in the colony: the use of unfree labor was a well-established practice. In the 1620s, as the need for labor grew, unfree white and black servants worked in the tobacco fields under similar conditions, suffered similar punishments, and — at first — were governed by similar laws. Some blacks gained their freedom when an agreed-upon term had expired, just as white servants did. Race relations in the earlier years were fluid, with fraternization and intermarriage routinely accepted. That situation, however, was quickly to change.

By the 1640s and 1650s, Africans were being seen as a category and class apart. Slavery became identified with blackness and slavery became a lifelong, hereditary status — features that created a racial caste in colonial Virginia that none could confuse with the fixed term of the white indentured servant. In so short a span of time, how had such clear and rigid distinctions been drawn? Because surviving records for those critical years are incomplete, no one can speak with absolute certainty of the evolutionary process that made blackness the functional equivalent of slavery and vice-versa. But step by step, "Negroes" (to use the term of Virginia's early laws) came to be treated as a race unto themselves: forbidden to bear arms, unable to petition the courts for redress of grievances, subject to extended terms of servitude, and legally prohibited from any sexual connection (including marriage) with whites. Racial prejudice on the one hand and a life sentence of servitude on the other mutually reinforced each other to create the "peculiar institution" of slavery, wherein black men and black women no longer had equal standing before the law nor in the eyes of Chesapeake white society. That society, moreover, rich and poor, servant and master, eventually achieved a political consensus from which the black segment of the population was routinely excluded.

Yet slavery at first grew quite slowly. By mid-century, only three hundred slaves toiled in Virginia. (The colony's population at the time stood at around 18,000.) By 1682, the total population had doubled, but the black population increased ten-fold. Early in the next century, the number of slaves rose to over 16,000, or approximately one-fourth of the total population, that ratio steadily rising in the eighteenth century. In Maryland, slave population, which also increased gradually in the seventeenth century, was unevenly distributed throughout the colony. Only the wealthiest landholders could afford the high initial investment required to purchase slaves. In the second half of the seventeenth century, one historian estimated that two-thirds of Maryland's slaves worked for only six percent of the planters. The wealth recorded on the wills of such plantation owners resided in two commodities above all others: land and slaves. Until 1715 or 1720, smaller landowners continued to rely upon indentured servants.

In the eighteenth-century Chesapeake, the problem of labor found its solution in slavery. As the price of white servants rose and the supply fell, the enslavement of black servants met the ever-increasing demand for agricultural labor. Slaves also reproduced themselves, sometimes in sufficient quantity to make further purchases unnecessary, and even on occasion provided the master with a surplus of labor that he could sell to others. Whereas indentured servants could look forward to freedom and economic opportunity, the slaves could anticipate only servitude without end, both for themselves and for their children.

A NEW ENGLAND WAY

What was first regarded as simply "northern Virginia" quickly developed an identity of its own. Captain John Smith explored the region in 1614 and soon began promoting it in the mother country as "New England." By 1620 the *Mayflower* made its way to Cape Cod. Although the Pilgrims' tiny colony grew quite slowly, it held on firmly, refusing to be dislodged by the cruelties of climate or the vagaries of humanity. A decade later, in the 1630s, the Puritans arrived in Massachusetts Bay with much greater force and even more impressive staying power. Not only did the Puritans refuse to be dislodged, but their imprint upon the American psyche exceeded that of any other colonists. While facing all the familiar problems of supply and survival, Puritans also confronted the challenge of religious dissent. Although New England developed an economy clearly different from that of Virginia and Maryland, in its relationships with the Native Americans it all too closely resembled its sister colonies to the south.

❧ *The Separating Pilgrims*

During Elizabeth's long reign, many persons within the Church of England tried valiantly to move that bureaucratic national institution toward a warmer embrace of the Protestant Reformation. Such persons wanted all remaining evidences of that church's long Catholic tradition utterly removed, such as bestowing special sacramental powers on bishops alone and diverging from the New Testament in matters of church order and worship. As petitioners to King James I put it in 1603, the true church ought not to be "governed by Popish Canons, Courts, Classes, Customs, or any human invention, but by the laws and rules which Christ hath appointed in his Testament." Some worked patiently to reform the entire church, moving it inch by inch and year by year closer to their goal. Others gave up hope that such a political-ecclesiastical entity would ever really change, and despairingly separated from the Church of England in order to fashion a fellowship of their own with the New Testament as their only guide. They likewise despaired of the state, seeing it as an obstruction to, not an instrument of, reform. Church and state, they thought, should have as little to do with each other as possible.

These "Separatists" did not take such a step lightly, for in becoming schismatics they fell afoul of English courts and jails. Conformity to the Church of England was not simply expected: it was demanded by law. Thus a convinced Separatist either had to leave the country or suffer the consequences of remaining. In Elizabeth's time, many left for Holland, where a good measure of religious toleration could be found. Even taking that course had its risks, however, for people could not receive permission to leave on the mere grounds of religious conscience.

One Separatist congregation meeting in secret in Nottingham, north of London, weighed its alternatives early in the seventeenth century. They had hoped that James I would be more lenient in religious matters than Elizabeth had been. But those hopes were dashed when James declared that all dissenters must conform

The Mayflower Compact   As envisioned by a nineteenth-century artist, the men aboard the *Mayflower* agreed to form "a civil body politic" — that is, a government — before disembarking in a place they knew they had no legal right to be. No women signed the document, but no male passengers on board were permitted to refuse.

in every way to England's worship and England's bishops — "else I will harry them out of the land, or else worse." "Worse" was clearly understood: it meant death. Yet to conform was impossible, for that meant a violation of conscience and a surrender of integrity. In 1607 the group fled to Leyden in Holland where they could worship in a manner that did no violence to their consciences. After some years in Holland, however, they found that solution unsatisfactory as they watched their children, heavily burdened with difficult labor, growing up to be Dutch, not English.

Aware of Virginia's colonization and of other English claims in the New World, the Pilgrims — as these Separatists became known — conceived of the ambitious and expensive plan to start a colony all their own across the sea. They received a land grant from the Virginia Company of London and some promise of merchant support, though neither came easily. The Pilgrims had to prove that they were not radical heretics; the merchants had to be assured that some return on their investments would be forthcoming. Being "knit together as a body in a most strict and sacred bond and covenant of the Lord," the group sailed at last from Plymouth, England, on September 6, 1620. Two months later, the *Mayflower* arrived off Cape Cod in Massachusetts, where these settlers would soon establish their own Plymouth.

The Virginia Company's patent extended no farther than around the southern tip of Manhattan Island. Thus the new arrivals realized that, being well north of that line, they needed some instrument of civil government, especially since some of their number, not sharing the same religious fervor, made "discontented & mutinous speeches." The resulting Mayflower Compact, dated November 11, 1620, pledged the group "solemnly & mutually in the presence of God and one another" to "covenant, and combine ourselves together into a civil body politic." The general good of the colony, not the private interests of any individual, stood as the guiding and sustaining principle.

Death took nearly half of the roughly one hundred *Mayflower* passengers during that first hard winter, when many continued to live aboard the ship. (It did not return to England until spring.) Only the intercession of the Wampanoag Indians, who taught the English how to plant and fish, kept the mortality rate from growing worse the following year. The Indians had seen their own mortality rate rise as disease, perhaps spread by European fishermen, weakened their ranks. The Pilgrims had superior firepower, to be sure, but their small numbers and isolation made them keenly conscious of their vulnerability. The only English allies along the Atlantic Coast were in faraway Jamestown, a fact that brought little comfort. And so these Pilgrims sought accommodation with the Wampanoags; they were assisted by intertribal rivalries that made such accommodation appealing to the native people as well. A modest trading in furs soon began.

The Pilgrim migration, unlike the settlement of Jamestown, included families from the beginning — families that needed to be housed and fed. So that first spring, crops were planted, houses built, and game hunted. No prolonged "starving time" haunted Plymouth as it had Jamestown, nor did the Indians conspire to attack as they did in Virginia in 1622. Rather, they assisted and advised, and even joined in the much-mythologized first Thanksgiving. In the following decades, tensions between the Indians and the English did develop in Plymouth, as they did elsewhere in New England. William Bradford, who was elected governor thirty times between 1622 and 1656, nonetheless proved to be a steady hand in directing the colony, as well as an able historian in telling of its courage and trials.

The colony was soon joined by those who were not "knit together" in a strict and sacred covenant. Persons who paid their own way over were not obliged to help pay off the indebtedness to the merchant company,

The New England Primer   The first textbook printed in America, the famous *New England Primer*'s crude woodcut illustrations and limping doggerel rhymes instilled into young minds in Puritan New England basic stories from the Bible and observations drawn from the often harsh realities of everyday life. The vocabulary it taught is, of course, far more complex than anything that modern children learn as they take their first steps toward literacy.

nor were they inclined to accept Bradford's authority. Especially in some of the outlying areas, challenges to the dominant religious vision frequently erupted. Bradford prevailed against all early uprisings, retaining his authority and giving Plymouth an executive continuity that Virginia sorely lacked. In 1627, the small colony of a few hundred felt secure enough to buy out its London backers, henceforth farming and trading for their own welfare and profit. Livestock and land held in common were now divided among all the settlers, whether they had been members of the company or not. This action both preserved the peace and gave great incentive to every landholder to produce as much as possible, for now it was all for his and for his family's use. The colony also prospered in a lucrative fur trade that reached from northern Maine to Long Island. By 1630, when streams of colonists began to settle in Massachusetts Bay, Plymouth had a market for its produce and livestock only forty miles away instead of three thousand.

❧ The Reforming Puritans

Charles I, who ruled from 1625 to 1649, asserted his authority over Parliament, church, and people with even more vigor than his father, James I. His archbishop, William Laud, joined in the effort to stamp out nonconformity and all religious dissent. Those Puritans who had not taken that dreaded step of separation from the Church of England continued to labor for the reform of the whole church from within. But they did so with increasing difficulty and an increasing sense that the odds against them were growing stronger. They, too, faced a hard alternative: They could conform, at great cost to their consciences; or they could defy, at great cost to their lives and fortunes. But motivated in part by a depressed textile industry in England, they chose a third alternative: migration to the New World.

Conscience required such a costly step. The whole effort to purify the national church rested on the assumption that a genuine reformation was required. A true church, these Puritans believed, did not result from political decisions made by the king and his advisers, from taking over the monasteries, or from preventing judicial appeals to the pope. A true church came only from a redeemed heart, from a faithful obedience to the New Testament standard of becoming a new creature in Christ. The church was not made up of all persons who happened to live in a certain locale or neighborhood. On the contrary, it was made up only of "visible saints," persons who had been saved by the grace of God and were prepared to testify before the entire congregation of their salvation. Social standing did not count, nor did wealth, nor good works. All that mattered was a new birth, a new life. "Therefore," the apostle Paul had told the church in first-century Corinth, "if any one is in Christ, he is a new creation; the old has passed away, behold, the new has come."

When in 1629 Charles dissolved Parliament after it tried to restrain his autocratic exercise of power, Puritans in the Church of England saw little hope for being heard in the higher echelons of either church or state. Just weeks before Charles's autocratic action, some Puritan members of the New England Company, chartered in 1628, applied directly to the king for a charter under the name of the Massachusetts Bay Company. With such a document in hand, the time seemed ripe for a migration of those who had for so long worked and prayed for a religious reformation that now was more remote than ever.

John Winthrop — lawyer, Puritan, and first governor of the Massachusetts Bay Colony — took great comfort in the fact that the sentiment to leave England for another world was so widely shared. If only a few were inclined to go, the colony would fail, but God "hath disposed the hearts of so many of his wise and faithful servants, both ministers and others, not only to approve of the enterprise but to interest themselves in it." The sheer number of people involved distinguished this colony from earlier English efforts. About seven hundred sailed with Winthrop in March 1630, another three hundred soon thereafter, and still another thousand before the year was out. The decade of the 1630s, producing what has been called the Great Migration, saw the population of Massachusetts Bay soar to nearly nine thousand. Since the colony did not lack immigrants, it therefore did not lack in labor, skills, productive farmers, and infusions of new blood and new strength.

The nature of the migration also set Massachusetts

❈ IN THEIR OWN WORDS

John Winthrop to his wife Margaret, 1630

From the beginning, Winthrop's Massachusetts Bay Colony was one in which it was expected that families would come and stay.

My dear wife,

Blessed by the Lord our good God and merciful father that hath preserved me in life and health to salute thee, and to comfort thy long longing heart, with the joyful news of my welfare, and the welfare of thy beloved children.

We had a long and troublesome passage, but the Lord made it safe and easy to us; and though we have met with many and great troubles (as this bearer can certify thee), yet he hath pleased to uphold us, and to give us hope of a happy issue. . . .

I shall expect thee next summer (if the Lord please) and by that time I hope to be provided for thy comfortable entertainment. My most sweet wife, be not disheartened, trust in the Lord, and ye shall see his faithfulness. Commend me heartily to all our kind friends at Castleins, Groton Hall: Mr. Leigh and his wife, my neighbour Cole and all the rest of my neighbours and their wives, both rich and poor.

from Charleston in New England, July 16, 1630

Bay Colony apart from Virginia and Maryland. The Puritan migration consisted of persons who planned to stay, not of those intent on making their fortune and returning to England as country gentlemen. Moreover, the Puritans came as families, not as single males nor as indentured servants, so that a natural increase of population accompanied the heavy influx of immigrants. Life expectancy in seventeenth-century New England, furthermore, far exceeded that of contemporary Virginia: roughly seventy-one years of age for males and seventy-six for those females who survived the dangers of childbirth. Though colder, the climate of coastal Massachusetts proved healthier than that of Chesapeake Bay, and death and disease never ravaged Massachusetts to the degree that it did early Virginia.

Literacy in New England was high, especially if we define literacy simply as the ability to read. (Many could read, but not write — writing and "doing sums" being a more advanced stage of education.) Because Puritans put so much stake in the Bible, reading was fundamental to the education of women as well as men; indeed, mothers were initially the chief teachers of reading and writing within the home. Soon every New England town had a grammar school for boys, while less formal "dame schools" saw to the education of girls. Then, in an astonishing act of courage, given the meagerness of their resources and the puniness of their number, the Puritans in the first decade of their colony founded a college that would soon take the name of Harvard. Patterned after Cambridge University, from which most of the Puritan ministers had graduated, Harvard College intended to bring as much liberal learning as possible into the New England wilderness.

The Puritan colony was also distinctive because the Massachusetts Bay Company was a "locally owned and operated" joint-stock company. London merchants neither directed nor owned it, nor did they drain profits from it. Those who migrated constituted the majority of stockholders, and they brought their charter with them. The charter gave stockholder-members (called "freemen") full authority to establish whatever form of government "which they shall find needful," and it stipulated that a General Court, consisting of all freemen, would meet four times a year.

The General Court functioned both as a court, trying cases and rendering verdicts, and also as a legislature, drawing up and passing laws for the governance of the colony. It elected the colony's governor who, together with his deputy and eighteen "assistants," met monthly as a kind of executive council with broad powers. Governor Winthrop extended the right to vote for assistants to all male landholders who were also church members, so that "freemen" quickly meant more than just stockholders in the company. This did not imply the creation of a democracy, for the officers so elected were accountable only to God, not to the people. But it did mean that a significant segment of the population had some voice in choosing those who ruled them. For over half a century, the Massachusetts Bay Company exercised its charter rights with minimal interference from abroad.

❧ Settlement Patterns

Unlike Virginians, the settlers of Massachusetts Bay built towns. One town, Salem, already existed as a port and fishing center before the Great Migration. Winthrop guided some of his group toward a peninsula just south of Salem that jutted out into Boston Bay. Here was more land than Salem could offer and more shelter from ocean gales and foreign ships. By the spring of 1631, crops had been planted and a modest fur trade begun

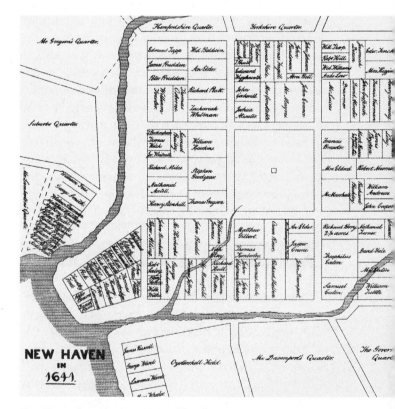

New Haven in 1641   New Haven, like all New England towns, was laid out according to an orderly plan, with the settlers' residential lots grouped around a central common. Beyond this core community stretched the villagers' fields. The whole settlement was modeled on what the settlers had known in their native England.

in Boston, which would quickly become the leading economic and cultural center for all New England.

In so swiftly creating their own towns, the Puritan migrants set the pattern for development of other towns, fanning out in a wide arc from Boston. Upon petition by a group of would-be settlers the General Court would grant a large (perhaps as much as 100 or 200 square miles) chunk of wilderness, at no cost, to be settled and subdued. Within this expanse, a village center would be planned, with its church, its school, and its "common" — land belonging to all. Each householder would receive a small house lot near the town center, in addition to farm and pasture lands that radiated out from it. No effort was made to carve up the entire wilderness, which would have meant granting each original settler several thousand acres. Rather, farms were kept small, chiefly for subsistence, and communities were supposed to remain closely knit. The precise amount of land bestowed on each household depended upon the size of the family and the type of service that each household could render to the community at large.

Thus the original settlers of Dedham, founded in 1636, did "mutually and severally promise amongst ourselves to profess and practice one truth according to that most perfect rule, the foundation whereof is everlasting love." That hardly sounds like a modern municipal charter — but the seventeenth century was not modern, and, moreover, the Puritan migration brought in its train a highly motivated, homogeneous, religiously dedicated group of people. To keep their town homogeneous and dedicated, Dedham's settlers further provided that any newcomers should not be "contrary minded," but "of one heart with us," prepared "to walk in a peaceable conversation with all meekness of spirit." Those not so prepared were advised to look elsewhere, preferably outside New England.

In a pattern repeated throughout the century, towns sprang up that imitated not only previous New England towns but also the small villages back in England. Each town exercised broad local control over the distribution of land, the education of its young, the calling of its minister, the training of its militia, and the oversight of both its economy and its morality. Of course, citizens paid taxes to the colony and provided militiamen as needed, though a new town often sought and received temporary exemption from both of these requirements as settlers made every effort to get houses and barns built, land cleared, and food supplied. Within a few years, the town and virtually all its inhabitants would normally be nearly self-sufficient.

With a hundred acres or so of land, a few cows, sheep, and hogs, a tightly built house, and unlimited firewood, each family could enjoy, if not prosperity, then a standard of living well above that of a majority of England's population.

Lacking the great rivers of Virginia to use as their highways, the Massachusetts settlers built roads, with each male resident expected to give a few days a year to the construction or repair of town roads and bridges. Long-used Indian trails furnished the initial pathway between towns. Through constant use, more than through expensive improvements, the pathways grew wider and somewhat smoother, though in the wintertime colonial roads everywhere became nearly impassable. But the rural farmers had little reason to get to faraway markets, since their agricultural surpluses were limited and their need for supplies from Boston minimal. Poor as these roads might be in the early years, they were good enough. In New England, only the north-south Connecticut River became a major commercial waterway.

❧ *The Puritan Ideology of New England*

Impressive immigration of both men and women, local governance, the creation of towns and small farms — these features set Massachusetts apart in the first decades of its existence from early Virginia. But what set the Bay Colony apart even more sharply was that complex web of ideas and ideology often called "the New England mind." In 1630, while still aboard the ship bringing them across the ocean, John Winthrop — though a layman — preached a sermon entitled "A Model of Christian Charity." "We are a Company," Winthrop observed, but one with the distinction of professing "ourselves fellow members of Christ." In undertaking to create a New World community, they were to establish "a due form of government both civil and ecclesiastical," keeping in mind that as they improved their lives, they did so in order to render better service to God. Just as one would avoid shipwreck at sea, so they must avoid similar calamity on land, and the only way to do that, said Winthrop, was to follow "the counsel of Micah, to do justly, to love mercy, to walk humbly with our God. For this end, we must be knit together in this work as one man," assisting each other, rejoicing together, mourning together, working together. If they so conducted themselves, "the Lord will be our God and delight to dwell among us." Let us all acknowledge,

Severall young men playing at foote-ball on the Jce upon the Lords-day are all Drownd

Puritanism and the Sabbath This 1671 woodcut, from a broadside entitled "Divine Examples of God's Severe Judgments upon Sabbath-Breakers, in Their Unlawful Sports," illustrates the importance Puritans placed on Sabbath observance. It depicts the sort of divine retribution many believed would be visited on those who violated the biblical command to rest on the Sabbath.

Winthrop advised, that "we are entered into covenant with him for this work."

Puritans believed that nations thrived only if they kept their covenant or agreement with God. With a strong sense of history, God's Providence, and divine destiny, Winthrop saw the Puritan venture as a way of demonstrating how not just colonies but nations could prosper and be blessed. God, Winthrop said, would "make us a praise and glory," so much so that "men will say of succeeding plantations: 'the Lord make it like that of New England.'" In short, "we must consider that we shall be as a city upon a hill, the eyes of all people are upon us." How much greater the burden, therefore, that rested upon Winthrop and his group. Because of that burden, government had the weighty task of seeing that the covenant was not broken, that in both behavior and belief one did nothing to offend a God of judgment no less than of mercy. The covenant bound the governed and the governors alike to know the will of God, as revealed in the Bible, and to follow that will as faithfully as human frailty would permit.

To help men and women in following God's will, ministers were chosen to interpret and, where necessary, to enforce that will. Meeting houses (Puritans did not call them churches) were built in every town for the purpose of collective praise and collective obedient ac-

tion. Church members, in making their own covenant, reinforced the more general public one. And church members, no less than pastors, had to study their Bibles, examine their souls, and make straight their paths. For the whole body of believers, the "fellowship of the saints," bore the responsibility for the obedience of and the integrity in the church. Each congregation directed its own affairs, hiring or firing its own ministers and setting the standards for church membership or dismissal. Neither bishop nor synod ruled over them. Thus the Puritans later assumed the denominational name *Congregationalism,* for each congregation governed itself.

This freedom from higher external authority, such as bishops or synods, gave church members the opportunity as well as the responsibility for running their own ecclesiastical affairs. Of course, that opportunity and responsibility could spread beyond the confines of the church — to the New England town meeting, for example. Yet the Puritans were not democrats. They recognized the social divisions routinely accepted in England, but more than that, they recognized that unredeemed, unregenerate individuals should not be put in charge of the affairs of state. The magistrate must be a *Christian* magistrate. And limiting the civil vote to church members, as the Puritans initially did, made eminent sense to people determined faithfully to keep a covenant with God.

The Puritan covenant was severe. Sunday was a day not for recreation and sport, but for worship and meditation. Puritans did not observe other holy days, saints' days, or even Christmas, all lingering elements of the papal calendar. They did not kneel at the sacrament of the Lord's Supper, for that too was "papist," suggesting the bodily presence of Christ in the elements of the wine and bread. Nor did they hear confession or treat marriage as a sacrament. Above all else, they did not consider salvation as something to be earned or worked for: it was a gift of God's grace, wholly unmerited and freely given to those whom God elected to save. In that as in all other dimensions of life and death, the Almighty Creator, not the pitiful creature, was in charge. Calvin's doctrine of predestination, often misconstrued as a kind of mindless fatalism, was on the contrary for the Puritans a comforting confidence in the sovereignty of a good and loving God.

Puritans left England to escape bishops, cleanse themselves of an impure worship, and strike out for a land where the "fountains of religion and learning" could gush forth anew. Harvard College, founded in

Massachusetts Law against Jesuits, 1647

The Puritans left England seeking purity of religion, and the laws they made in the New World reflect their desire to maintain that purity.

That no Jesuit, or spiritual or ecclesiastical person ordained by the authority of the Pope or See of Rome, shall henceforth at any time repair to, or come within, this Jurisdiction. And if any person shall give just cause or suspicion that he is one of such Society or Order, he shall be brought before some of the Magistrates, and if he cannot free himself of such suspicion, he shall be committed to prison, or bound over to the next Court of Assistants to be tried and proceeded with by banishment, or otherwise as the Court shall see cause; and if any person so banished shall be taken the second time within this Jurisdiction, upon lawful trial and conviction, he shall be put to death. Provided this Law shall not extend to any such Jesuit, spiritual or ecclesiastical person, as shall be cast upon our shores by shipwreck or other accident, so as he continue no longer than till he may have opportunity of passage for his departure. . . .

1636, faithfully reflected the Puritan community that created it; the "rules and precepts" of 1646 stipulated that every student "shall consider the main end of his life and studies to know God and Jesus Christ which is eternal life." The Bible was to be read twice a day, with all students expected to be "ready to give an account of their proficiency therein." But Harvard, though designed for the training of ministers, also offered education in the classics of antiquity, in the learned languages of the Renaissance, and in the study of Aristotelian physics, as well as natural and moral philosophy. When a site for the infant college was selected across the Charles River from Boston, the town was called Cambridge in memory of the Puritans' English past and with large hopes for their American future.

In transplanting themselves to Massachusetts Bay, the Puritans intended to re-create, as best they could, the New Testament church as they (and John Calvin before them) conceived it, to fashion what they still hoped the Church of England would turn out to be. They came not for freedom of religion in the abstract, but for *their* freedom of religion in particular. They never intended to found a colony where all religious dissidents of whatever persuasion, or none, would flock. Far from it: they would do their very best to keep "the New England way" as consistent, pure, undefiled, and undiluted as possible. To do this, they sometimes had to purge, sometimes persecute, sometimes even hang.

❧ Dissenters

Orthodoxy was never as complete as New England's clergy and magistrates would have wished. Side by side with it was a popular religion that believed in magic, followed astrological charts, and kept ancient superstitions alive — very much as many people continue to do today. Such popular religion did not noisily reject Puritan orthodoxy: it merely supplemented it, moving beyond the limited ritual of the meeting house to a more elaborate ritual of the field and the home whereby, for example, the fertility of the soil and of the marriage might be assured. The all-encompassing supernatural world could not be confined to the prayers of the clergy or the explicit promises of Scripture. Signs and portents, visions and wonders, fortunes told and illnesses strangely cured — these filled the seventeenth century world of all Europeans, Puritans included. As one author has recently written, orthodoxy and popular religion did not divide the culture between them, but together shared and shaped that culture.

More confrontational by far were those persons who did directly challenge the premises of Puritan orthodoxy, throwing down a gauntlet that could not be ignored. One such challenger, Roger Williams, took on the establishment by arguing (1) that the Puritan churches could not claim to be still a part of the Church of England, while trying all the while to transform it; (2) that the civil government had no business whatsoever meddling in matters of religion, enforcing the church's rules or punishing its detractors; and, (3) that all the Puritan settlers were trespassers because they had not purchased from the Indians the land on which they lived. In hurling these charges, Williams presented the authorities with a bill of indictment so threatening that the General Court of Massachusetts determined in 1635 that he could be tolerated no longer. He must be expelled: "It is therefore ordered," said the court in October, "that the said Mr. Williams shall depart out of this jurisdiction within six weeks."

But where to go, with winter approaching, with a pregnant wife and a two-year-old daughter? When it appeared that Williams would not go at all, the authorities prepared to ship him back to England. Williams, however, had traveled too far to turn back in that direction. So he struck out on foot, walking south through January's bitter cold, until he crossed the Bay Colony's sacred boundaries. For fourteen weeks, he wrote, "I knew not what neither bed nor bread did mean." He accepted meager fare from the Narragansett Indians, whose language he had learned and whose confidence he had won. At last, he came to the headwaters of the Narragansett Bay, where he bought some land from the natives and named his settlement Providence, "in a sense of God's merciful Providence unto me in my distress." And so the colony of Rhode Island was born, a colony that would be open to those of any religious persuasion or of none.

For Roger Williams believed that the finest liberty — the liberty on which all other freedoms rested — was the liberty of conscience. He despised the bloody religious wars afflicting continental Europe even as he abhorred the mindless persecutions in England: first of Protestants, then of Catholics, then of Protestants again, then of Separatists and Puritans. When will it ever end? Williams asked. And he answered: Only when the line between the world and the church is clearly drawn, only when Christ's command to Peter to "Put up thy sword" is fully understood, only when all recognize that conscience cannot be coerced or spiritual food shoved down the throat. Then, no longer will humanity practice "soul rape," no longer will we witness "the deflowering of chaste souls, and spilling the blood of the innocent," and no longer will we be obliged to hear the pathetic cries of thousands of "men, women, children, fathers, mothers, husbands, wives, brothers, sisters, old and young, high and low, plundered, ravished, slaughtered, murdered, famished."

Williams arrived at his passionate views on the separation of church and state not as a liberal secularist but as a devout follower of the New Testament. He read the parable of the wheat and the tares as the sifting and the winnowing of human souls. And he read the words of Jesus — "My kingdom is not of this world" — to mean that both believer and unbeliever should be untroubled by the sword of the state: leave it to God to do; human beings could never create such a thing as a Christian state, or a Christian kingdom, or a Christian civilization. *Christendom* was a word abhorrent to

him, for it pointed to that fatal mixture of politics and religion that had brought such ruin upon the world. Only if the conscience is free, he thought, can religion be pure and undefiled.

Williams was ahead of his time in this as in other respects: for example, his cultivation of good relations with the Indians, his respect for their culture, and his respect for the autonomy of their consciences. He would not participate in any forced conversion of the Indians. In a small tract called *Christenings Make Not Christians,* Williams complained about the "most inhumane conversions" thrust upon the Indians of both North and South America: "yea, tens of thousands of poor Natives, sometimes by wiles and subtle devices, sometimes by force compelling them to submit to that which they understood not." To have a dominant culture determining the religion of a powerless minority was to have learned nothing from Europe's bloody history.

Another dissenter, Anne Hutchinson, posed an even greater threat to the theological position of Puritanism. A midwife and member of Boston's congregation, Hutchinson simply wanted to take orthodoxy a little farther than it was willing to go. Salvation was by faith, not works, all agreed. But orthodoxy declared that, after salvation, a Christian's good works gave evidence of that salvation. In challenging that assumption, Hutchinson broke the essential bond between morality and religion, threatening to undermine the foundation of Puritan society. She was branded an "antinomian," literally one who is against the law. From the Puritans' point of view, she destroyed the very basis for law and therefore could not be tolerated. She set herself up as a source of religious truth equal or superior to that of the ministers of Massachusetts Bay, and felt herself to be in direct communication with God.

In 1637 the same General Court that exiled Roger Williams also brought Anne Hutchinson to trial and arrived at the same result: "she shall be banished out of our liberties and imprisoned till she be sent away." John Winthrop, speaking for the court, noted that she had "spoken diverse things . . . very prejudicial to the honor of the churches and the ministers thereof." Moreover, she had "maintained a meeting and an assembly in [her] house that has been condemned by the General Assembly." Perhaps above all else, however, she had said things and done things not "comely in the sight of God, nor fitting for [her] sex." With her family and a significant number of supporters, Anne Hutchinson fled to Rhode Island, where the Hutchinsonian party exercised considerable influence and where it contin-

John Winthrop   Winthrop, as this portrait makes clear, was a well-born seventeenth-century English man of the gentry. His austere bearing and dignified black velvet attire were what every gentleman of his day would have thought proper for a formal portrait, and are not in themselves characteristic of his Puritan faith.

ued to worry the authorities in Massachusetts. Later she moved to Long Island, where in 1643 a marauding band of Indians abruptly ended her life and that of some of her children.

Neither Williams nor Hutchinson saw the authority of the Massachusetts clergy and court as supreme. Both were as familiar with Scripture as their accusers, and both viewed biblical authority as higher than the opinions of mere mortals. Anne Hutchinson, moreover, suffered from the same liability that afflicted Joan of Arc: during her trial she admitted to having heard "voices," private revelations beyond the public revelation of the Bible. For Puritans, this was the ultimate presumption: to be so arrogant as to claim that God spoke directly to her. She was denounced as an enthusiast — that is, literally, as one filled with God — or at least proudly pretending to be.

Both Williams, who founded "Providence Plantations," and Anne Hutchinson, who settled in Portsmouth (on the island of Aquidneck), helped give Rhode Island an identity as a haven of dissent. In its earliest years, Baptists dominated the two major towns: Newport and Providence. Roger Williams helped create America's first Baptist church in Providence. Baptists had emerged in the first half of the seventeenth century from the Separatist tradition within Puritanism, abandoning the politically entangled Church of England to create the pure church of the New Testament as they understood it. After the middle of the seventeenth century, the much-despised, much-persecuted sect of Quakers (the Society of Friends, as they called themselves), originating in revolutionary England, also found refuge in Rhode Island. Williams, though he disagreed with the Quakers, determined that no arm of the state would be raised against them. Both Baptists and Quakers emphasized the voluntary and individual nature of religious belief. This assured that Rhode Island would attract devotees of many religious opinions, or of none. Roger Williams's colony would always be the defiant exception to "the New England way."

✤ *Expansion and Trade*

As Massachusetts Bay grew and prospered, other New England colonies came into being. As early as 1633 some restless citizens of the Bay Colony struck out in a southwesterly direction in search of larger parcels of land and easier access to the fur trade. The Dutch had earlier explored — and claimed as their own — the Connecticut River valley, at least as far upstream as present-day Hartford. But migrating Puritans paid little attention to that prior incursion as entire congregations moved into the valley. The river towns of Hartford, Windsor, and Wethersfield all sprang into existence in 1636. These formed the nucleus of what would become the colony of Connecticut three years later. Thomas Hooker, a major Puritan theologian and pastor of the church in Newtown (later Cambridge), led in the migration and in the formation of Connecticut's first government. To sustain them on their journey, Hooker and his party, said John Winthrop, "drove one hundred and sixty cattle, and fed of their milk by the way." Church membership, a condition of eligibility to vote in Massachusetts, was in Connecticut dropped as a franchise requirement. This gave Connecticut some claim as a more democratic society, but the bond between church and state was as intimate in this new colony as it continued to be in the Bay Colony.

A competing settlement along the coast had by 1638 assumed the name of the New Haven Colony. Including the towns of Guilford, Mitford, Stamford, and others, this colony had major commercial ambitions for trade in the West Indies and to Europe. Hemmed in by the Dutch in New York (still known then as New Amsterdam), leaders in New Haven pressed for England to dislodge the Dutch from their settlements and trading posts. By the time this finally took place in 1664, the New Haven Colony, forced to choose between the newly established New York and the closer colony of Connecticut, accepted absorption into the latter.

In that same decade of the 1630s, other Massachusetts Puritans migrated northward into what would become the colony of New Hampshire. Clergyman John Wheelwright, one of the early followers of Anne Hutchinson, was instrumental in founding Exeter, just north of the Bay Colony's border. For a time New Hampshire was under the jurisdiction of Massachusetts, but by 1679 it had won separate status as a royal colony. Although the coast of Maine was settled very early, it remained a part of the Bay Colony until 1820. In 1692 the Bay Colony also absorbed the much smaller Plymouth Colony. By the end of the seventeenth century, Massachusetts Bay had a population of over fifty thousand and Connecticut about half that many, with Rhode Island and New Hampshire boasting only about five thousand inhabitants each.

The "New England way" spread from Boston through all of the Bay Colony as well as into Connecticut and New Hampshire. Those three colonies cooperated closely with each other, sharing patterns of belief and behavior, and deepening the Puritan imprint on America. Rhode Island continued to be the exception. Indeed, during much of the seventeenth century it resisted repeated efforts of Connecticut and Massachusetts Bay to whittle away at its borders or, better, just to divide the small colony between them.

New England's trade quickly moved out of the Connecticut River valley and away from its own coastline to meet demands abroad. By 1644 New England sailing vessels showed great interest in the West Indies and in other English possessions in the New World, notably Bermuda, St. Christopher, and Barbados. Some New England merchants even took up residence in the Caribbean in order to facilitate trade between those islands and the mainland, or to use them as intermediary points of commerce and resupply in establishing commercial routes all across the Atlantic. Soon New England merchants transported timber and furs, cattle and horses, masts, and sometimes entire ships, to markets abroad. Some New England vessels also called at ports in Virginia and Maryland to pack their hulls with barrels of tobacco for England or the Continent. Similarly, others went north to Newfoundland in order to take on fish for the "wine islands" of Madeira, Azores, and the Canaries.

On Barbados the production of sugar became as much the all-consuming occupation as tobacco was in Virginia. On their way back from leaving their wares in England, New England captains from the 1640s on put in at the island to take on a load of sugar. Or they carried such exports as food and horses to Barbados and other islands, bringing back sugar or molasses that could be used as a sugar substitute. Molasses was used to manufacture rum, most of which was consumed in New England. Surplus amounts could be traded along the coast of Africa for slaves, ivory, and gold dust. Many of these slaves were then taken to Barbados where the sugar plantations required even more unfree labor than Virginia's tobacco ones. In fact, on eighteenth-century Caribbean plantations the importation of slaves rarely slackened, since mortality was high and natural increase low. Thus New Englanders' trading routes crisscrossed the Atlantic. Many merchants grew wealthy, but others plunged into bankruptcy when weather or pirates or a suddenly saturated market wiped out all profit. In Rhode Island, the deep-water port of Newport competed with Boston in the second half of the seventeenth century, though Boston soon returned to its former prominence.

New England's standard of living steadily rose, as traders brought back manufactured goods not otherwise available: fine cloth, iron tools and weapons, spices, quality glass, and luxury items of many sorts. In addition, of course, they imported slaves, mainly for export to colonies farther south, increasing their cash supply and thus making possible even more improvement in their lifestyles. Some merchants spent their fortunes on property, others on fashion and upper-class trappings. Some even grew so prosperous as to imagine that they could be accepted back in England as gentry. Most remained in New England, however, enjoying the privileges of wealth, the perquisites of political offices that frequently came their way, and the cultivation of contacts abroad upon which their success continued to depend. The evolution from town peddler to merchant prince had been slow (two or three generations), but it had been steady. For the most part it had also been peaceful — in marked contrast to New England's encounters with the Indians, which in the course of the seventeenth century deteriorated sharply and at great cost in life and property.

NATIVE AMERICANS AND THE ENGLISH

From the days of exploration to the early years of settlement, the native population offered Europeans a tempting target for conversion to Christianity. After some years of uneasy coexistence, however, those temptations gave way to quite another impulse: to take over land, to expand in power and numbers, and to reduce the Indians to total subservience. In Virginia, as noted above, Indian resentment resulted in a 1622 attack upon the settlers in or around Jamestown. But that clash of arms would not be unique, either in the history of Virginia or in English territories elsewhere.

❧ *Missionary Activity*

Like all other early colonists, those arriving in Massachusetts Bay in the 1620s and 1630s saw the evangelization of the Indians as both an obligation and an opportunity. Governor Bradford of the Plymouth Colony offered as the final reason for leaving Holland and England the Pilgrims' "great hope and inward zeal . . . for the propagating and advancing the gospel of the kingdom of Christ in those remote parts of the world." Puritans sent their missionaries to the Indians. The best known, John Eliot, managed to translate the entire Bible into the Algonkian tongue and, even more remarkably, got it printed on the primitive presses of Boston in 1663. He also assisted the Christianized "praying Indians" in forming fourteen small towns. From New England's point of view, it was a good, if modest, beginning.

While Massachusetts was more successful than the other New England colonies in evangelizing Native Americans, even there the establishment of Indian churches was severely limited. Puritans, with their emphasis on inculcating the ability and duty to read the Bible, held that Indians must first be taught to read and write, next be instructed in Christian doctrine, and finally be assisted in forming a church. All this took time, so that by 1674 only about a thousand Indians had associated themselves with the missionary effort. This

represented about one-sixth of the Indians then in the Massachusetts Bay Colony. An island off the Bay Colony coast, Martha's Vineyard, had one of the most vigorous missionary stations. Thomas Mayhew had created two Indian congregations there between 1647 and 1657, when he died at sea. In Plymouth Colony missionary Richard Bourne enjoyed a success similar to Mayhew's, making some five hundred converts by 1674. In Rhode Island, missionary activity was limited, largely because of Roger Williams's serious reservations about "forced conversions." And in Connecticut missionary activity was initially frustrated by the outbreak of war.

❧ *The Pequot War*

The Pequots, a tribe not native to New England, had in the sixteenth century moved from the upper Hudson River valley into the lower Connecticut River valley, roughly shoving aside other Indian tribes in their way and settling in Connecticut in the early 1630s. Stories of atrocities intensified the fears of English settlers in western Massachusetts and Connecticut, so much so that in 1636 those two colonies began preparations for war against the Pequots. These activities grew more hurried when rumors arrived that the Pequots were about to reach an alliance with the Narragansetts of Rhode Island, a potential confederacy of fearful power. Massachusetts Bay now turned to Roger Williams, whom they had exiled a short time before, urging him to act the role of diplomat and negotiator to prevent such a pact from being made. A trusted friend of the Narragansetts, Williams did as asked, and succeeded. He persuaded the Rhode Island tribe not only to abandon any thought of pledges to the Pequots, but to join in with the forces of Massachusetts Bay and Connecticut instead.

But the Pequots, even unaided, remained a threat to settlers eager to move into the Connecticut River valley, just as those land-hungry settlers posed a threat to the Pequots. In 1637, Massachusetts Bay, joined by Plymouth and Connecticut, declared war. In a series of devastating attacks, English forces emerged wholly victorious. The Pequots were destroyed as a tribal entity and their lands distributed to more friendly tribes or to English settlers. When the war formally ended in September 1638, the General Court congratulated itself on having taken such timely and definitive action in New England's first armed conflict with the native population. The Pequot War resulted, first, in the opening up of more land for settlement in Connecticut, evident in the founding of such towns as Fairfield, Farmington,

PHILIP. *KING* of Mount Hope.

P. Revere ff

Metacomet, or King Philip: An Eighteenth-Century Depiction This near-contemporary engraving accompanied a 1716 account of King Philip's War.

and Stratford; and second, in a great wariness among all Indians as to the ultimate intentions of the English and the ultimate fate of their own country.

☙ King Philip's War

For about thirty years, each side bided its time. Then in 1675 the great and calamitous Indian counterattack came. The chief of the Wampanoags, Metacomet (known to the colonists as King Philip), for several years had clashed with the Plymouth Colony over its continued encroachment upon his people's land. Repeatedly, each side prepared for battle; then, at the last minute, Metacomet would back down. By 1675 he vowed to retreat no longer, declaring "I am determined not to live till I have no country." Succeeding

where the Pequots had failed, Philip gathered a great many of New England's tribes into a massive but secret confederation. In June of that year, he launched a full-scale assault against English farms, villages, and towns throughout New England. For more than a year the war raged, destroying lives, houses, barns, crops, and cattle. Mary Rowlandson, captured in February 1676 along with her children from her Massachusetts home in Lancaster, wrote the first "captivity narrative." She explained how the difficult experience both tested and reinforced her faith: "I have seen the extreme vanity of this world," she wrote. "One hour I have been in health and wealth, wanting nothing, but the next hour in sickness, and wounds, and death, having nothing but sorrow and affliction." But, she concluded, "For whom the Lord loveth, he chasteneth."

New England had never suffered such a war, nor in percentage of lives and property lost has it suffered one of that magnitude since. Fifty-two of New England's ninety towns were attacked, and a dozen were burned or razed to the ground. While the attacking forces were outnumbered by about two to one, in the early phases of "King Philip's War" this made little difference. Only after the English recovered from their surprise and gathered all the militia together did their superior numbers begin to count. In August 1676, when Metacomet himself was killed, the war sputtered to an end. With that victory, English power was vindicated, just as Indian power in New England was forever broken. About six hundred English soldiers had been lost, with many times that many Indians — men, women, and children — slain or sold into slavery at the war's end. Beyond the cost in lives and property, one could not then or later calculate the cost in shattered relationships between those Americans who were here first and those who came later.

☙ Bacon's Rebellion

News of the devastation in New England reached Virginia within a few weeks, aggravating tensions between settlers and Native Americans there. The Indians had been pushed steadily westward, but every bit of ground they still held became an object of desire to settlers also pushing westward, especially newly freed indentured servants who found all the good land already taken. Indian population continued to decline; only around a thousand males remained in Virginia by the 1670s. English numbers, on the other hand, continued to grow, reaching around forty thousand in the same period. When in 1675 some Doeg Indians along the

Potomac River tried to steal cattle from a settler who refused to pay for goods he had traded from them, the frontier whites retaliated in force, killing ten Doegs and fourteen Susquehannocks who had not been directly involved in the dispute. For the nervous and grasping settlers, however, Indians were just Indians; tribal distinctions made no difference.

Two players dominated what ensued. Governor William Berkeley, who had directed Virginia's affairs on and off for over thirty years, had laboriously and conscientiously tried to fashion an Indian policy that would be fair to advancing settlers and retreating Indians alike. A 1646 treaty had granted the Powhatans land north of the York River in Virginia's western interior, and for a generation that treaty generally held. Fur trade developed and Indians settled in villages where they could raise both cattle and crops. But by 1676 Berkeley's policy had lost whatever popularity it had initially enjoyed among the frontier English. The opportunity arose for Nathaniel Bacon, a recent and reasonably well-to-do arrival from England, to take the part of the frontier folk against the Indians and, as it turned out, increasingly against Berkeley himself.

When the Susquehannocks, bent on revenge for the unprovoked murder of their people, took the offensive against the settlers in the winter of 1675-76 and killed some thirty-six of them, Bacon seized his opportunity. He gathered around him all the fighting men that he could to launch a series of attacks against the Indians, friendly or not, since (he claimed) those Indians taking aggressive action "have been so cunningly mixed among the several Nations [tribes]" that it was difficult to distinguish friend from foe. To be safe, Bacon concluded, simply slay them all. He applied to the governor for a commission to carry out this war of extermination, but Berkeley declined, repelled by the prospect of indiscriminate bloodshed. So Bacon declared that he would proceed anyway, which left Berkeley with little choice but to pronounce this frontier fighter a rebel.

As Berkeley struggled for a peaceful solution and sought to seal off the two cultures by a series of forts on the frontier, Bacon turned from intoxicating victories over the Indians to bring down the governor and his Indian policy along with him. In the summer of 1676, as forces supporting the two men squared off against each other, Bacon and his followers burned Jamestown to the ground. Berkeley ultimately prevailed, partly because British reinforcements were soon dispatched and partly because Bacon himself died of swamp fever in October. Meanwhile, the frontier rebels, having accomplished their main mission against the Indians, were eager to return home. With proper legal authority back in charge, many of Bacon's followers were tried and hanged as traitors. Yet Bacon's Rebellion left a lasting mark on Virginian and American history. First, the decimated, diseased, and dispossessed Indians now found their capacity to retain any degree of autonomy or tribal integrity further, perhaps fatally, reduced. Second, the struggle between the westerners of the Piedmont and the easterners of the Tidewater foreshadowed other sectional rivalries, as well as persisting tensions between the haves and the have-nots within colonial society.

CONCLUSION: DIFFERENTIATING CULTURES

In the earliest years of the seventeenth century, England thought of the entire Atlantic coastline as "Virginia." Gradually, however, Virginia became the name of only a single colony — like Maryland, or Massachusetts. But for two or three decades, Virginia stood alone as the example of English colonization in the New World. And a poor example it seemed to be: one of starvation, disease, massacre, political and financial failure. Only tobacco pulled these early colonists back from the edge of disaster. Learning from those hard lessons, Maryland moved quickly into tobacco cultivation and into a more stable form of political order. Both colonies searched hard for the laborers that would make their economies profitable; they found their source, ultimately, in slavery that soon was tied to a single race.

New England, in contrast, encouraged small farms, worked chiefly by the children of the farmer and his wife. Also, the development of towns (as opposed to the scattered river plantations farther south) enabled that region to re-create to a greater degree the small village life of the nation they had left behind. An identifiable "New England way" developed in Massachusetts, Connecticut, and New Hampshire that proved remarkably durable. Dissenters, however, notably in Rhode Island, provided a counterpoint to the dominant culture. In its relationships with the Native Americans, New England suffered even more severely than Virginia the scourge of war and the harvest of lasting enmity.

While the Chesapeake and New England colonies struggled toward maturity, England's society was being torn by its own fearful tensions. In 1640, royal authority faced a far greater threat than that posed by Bacon's Rebellion in Virginia. By 1649, when the king lost his crown and his life, Parliament had moved to the position of ultimate authority in England and over the colonies. Parliament, however, debated and divided as it desperately searched for the exact direction that the nation should take: in governmental structure, in religious affirmations, and in colonial administration. The turbulence of the 1640s and 1650s shook the kingdom to its core.

SUGGESTED READING

Richard Archer, *Fissures in the Rock: New England in the Seventeenth Century* (2001). With engaging narrative and sparkling prose, the author emphasizes the diversity even among New England's earliest settlers.

Francis J. Bremer, *John Winthrop: America's Forgotten Father* (2003). Though Winthrop was not really forgotten (see Edmund Morgan's earlier and excellent biography, *The Puritan Dilemma*) Bremer's book gives a fully rounded portrait of Winthrop, including his background in England.

Carl Bridenbaugh, *Vexed and Troubled Englishmen, 1590-1642* (1978). Offers a close look at English society as colonization gets underway.

John Demos, *A Little Commonwealth: Family Life in Plymouth Colony* (1970). Giving unusual attention to the material culture of a people, Demos looks at housing, clothing, furniture, and the human relationships within the home.

Stephen Foster, *The Long Argument: English Puritanism and the Shaping of New England Culture, 1570-1700* (1990). With steady attention to the England context, Foster shows how New England Puritanism did not so much decline as adapt to changing political and cultural patterns.

Edwin S. Gaustad, *Liberty of Conscience: Roger Williams in America* (1991). Shows the impact of Roger Williams both in old England and New, as well as the continuing thread of his impact and reputation in succeeding centuries.

David D. Hall, *Worlds of Wonder, Days of Judgment* (1989). A superb analysis of popular religion in seventeenth-century New England.

Ivor Noël Hume, *The Virginia Adventure: An Archaeological and Historical Odyssey* (1994). Archaeology made accessible to all by means of a lively style and engaging wit.

Kenneth A. Lockridge, *A New England Town: The First Hundred Years* (rev. ed., 1985). In following the fortunes of Dedham, Massachusetts, the author reveals the central characteristics of the New England town.

Edmund S. Morgan, *American Slavery, American Freedom: The Ordeal of Colonial Virginia* (1975). Not only tells more about the origins of slavery but also far more about the effect of slavery in creating a unified white political and social consensus.

Michael L. Oberg, *Dominion and Civility: English Imperialism and Native America, 1585-1689* (1999). The conflicting aims and methods of the English colonists with respect to the Indians here receive careful analysis and helpful explication.

Laurel Thatcher Ulrich, *Good Wives: Image and Reality in the Lives of Women in Northern New England* (1982). Provides a much-needed angle of vision with respect to colonial New England women.

Alden T. Vaughan, *American Genesis: Captain John Smith and the Founding of Virginia* (1975). A readable and informed synthesis of Virginia's earliest years.

Alden T. Vaughan, *New England Frontier: Puritans and Indians, 1620-1675* (rev. ed., 1979). Recounts the unhappy story of Indian conflicts in New England, from the Pequot War to King Philip's War.

SUGGESTIONS FOR FURTHER READING

Bernard Bailyn and Philip D. Morgan, eds., *Strangers Within the Realm: Cultural Margins of the First British Empire* (1991).

Ira Berlin and Philip D. Morgan, eds., *Civilization and Culture: Labor and the Shaping of Slave Life* (1993).

Warren M. Billings, *A Little Parliament: The Virginia General Assembly in the Seventeenth Century* (2004).

Francis J. Bremer, *Puritanism: Transatlantic Perpectives on a Seventeenth-Century Anglo-American Faith* (1993).

Theodore Dwight Bozeman, *To Live Ancient Lives: The Primitivist Dimension in Puritanism* (1988).

Alfred A. Cave, *The Pequot War* (1996).

Richard W. Cogley, *John Eliot's Mission to the Indians Before King Philip's War* (1999).

Cedric B. Cowing, *The Saving Remnant: Religion and the Settling of New England* (1995).

James Deetz, *In Small Things Forgotten: The Archaeology of Early American Life* (1977).

Andrew Delbanco, *The Puritan Ordeal* (1989).

Philip F. Gura, *A Glimpse of Sion's Glory: Puritan Radicalism in New England, 1620-1660* (1984).

Timothy L. Hall, *Separating Church and State: Roger Williams and Religious Liberty* (1998).

Ronald Hoffman, *Princes of Ireland, Planters of Maryland: A Carroll Saga, 1500–1782* (2000).

James Horn, *Adapting to a New World: English Society in the Seventeenth-Century Chesapeake* (1994).

Janice Knight, *Orthodoxies in Massachusetts: Rereading American Puritanism* (1994).

Allan Kulikoff, *Tobacco and Slaves: The Development of the Southern Cultures in the Chesapeake, 1600-1800* (1986).

J. A. Leo Lamay, *The American Dream of Captain John Smith* (1991).

Amy Schrager Lang, *Prophetic Women: Anne Hutchinson and the Problem of Dissent in the Literature of New England* (1987).

Philip D. Morgan, *Black Culture in the Eighteenth-Century Chesapeake and Low Country* (1998).

Francis Mossiker, *Pocahantas: The Life and the Legend* (1996).

Mary Beth Norton, *Founding Mothers & Fathers* (1996).

Anna Marie Plane, *Colonial Intimacies: Indian Marriage in Early New England* (2000).

3

The Empire
Torn, Restored, Enlarged, 1640-1732

ENGLAND PLUNGED INTO disorder and revolutionary turmoil during the 1640s and 1650s. King Charles I lost his head in 1649, and many within the kingdom and beyond thought that English citizens had lost their heads too. For religious chaos matched the political furies that saw armies arrayed against each other, Parliament and royalty fatally opposed, and all imperial ambitions critically delayed if not destroyed. The death of Charles threatened to end not only the monarchy but the secure position of the Church of England as well.

In the seething turbulence of these two decades, England's world was turned upside down. Insiders, including royalists, Anglicans, bishops, and nobles found themselves abruptly on the outside. Now all power was vested in the quarrelling committees of Parliament and in the military might of Oliver Cromwell and his army. Dissenters, accustomed to banging on the doors so regularly closed to them, suddenly found themselves at the centers of power, with a Civil War to conclude and a nation to run. But in 1660, the world was turned right side up once again, with a monarchy restored and a Church of England returned to its position of privilege. Those who had enjoyed unprecedented liberty in the time of the Long Parliament now felt the sting of repression and persecution. They had felt it all before, of course, but it hurt more after the years of heady freedoms briefly enjoyed.

For the majority of England's citizens, however, the Restoration came as a relief. The nation could again plan for something beyond whatever cataclysm or chaos each new day might bring. The nation could again find

Cromwell Dissolves Parliament   On January 22, 1655, Oliver Cromwell strode into the House of Commons, declared Parliament dissolved, and brusquely bid the members of that body (to which he had once belonged) begone. The king having been executed six years before, England now became an open military dictatorship, and Cromwell, as Lord Protector, exercised sovereign power.

refuge in the decency and order of its own Church of England. And the nation could take steps to reassert its position in world markets and replenish the depleted stores of wealth and goods at home. For a quarter of a century Charles II (1660-1685) would guide his restored kingdom on an ever-steadier course of empire.

With renewed attention to colonization prospects, Charles and his advisers encouraged the founding of Carolina, seized New Netherland from the Dutch, and repaid an old debt by offering an immense tract of land to William Penn. At the same time England strengthened the administration of its expanding dominions overseas by additional regulations of trade and by tightening the lines of political authority. By 1685, twelve

of the original thirteen American colonies (all except Georgia) had been launched on their way.

In that same year, Charles II died and was succeeded by his younger brother, James II, whose brief reign (1685-88) ended amid surging anxieties about the growth of his royal authority and the public display of his Roman Catholicism. The Glorious Revolution of 1688 — called glorious by the victors because it was bloodless — brought a new royal line to the English throne with the accession of William of Orange and his spouse Mary, daughter of James. As England's Parliament jockeyed for more political authority, England's colonies reacted against a kingly power too directly or too arbitrarily applied.

The Glorious Revolution had a widespread though uneven impact on the colonies. Rebellion against James II's royal authority broke out in Massachusetts and New York. In Maryland, the anti-Catholic dimension of England's Revolution had special force. In the midst of political maneuvers and anxieties, other religious uncertainties multiplied. Notably in New England, Puritan society suffered from theological and ecclesiastical controversy. One response to that tension was increased persecution of religious dissent; another response, even more grim, was the eruption of the witchcraft epidemic in Salem, Massachusetts.

The colonists on the fringe of the empire often benefited from the neglect while English attention was concentrated on crises at home or on the Continent. In such wars as those of William III and Queen Anne, however, colonists found themselves caught up in international affairs. William, moreover, resolved to make administration of the "foreign plantations" more efficient and more nearly uniform from colony to colony. With the arrival of the Hanoverian dynasty in 1714, the monarchy — and even more Parliament and its ministers — kept an eye out for ways in which the colonists could assist the empire. One of those ways turned out to be the founding of Georgia in 1732.

Thus in the late seventeenth and early eighteenth centuries England tottered and stumbled, only to emerge stronger on the world stage. On the other side of the Atlantic, colonization enterprises were both more assured and more assertive. And one of England's newer and most despised sects, the Society of Friends (Quakers), received an enormous grant of land in the New World that would bring to these dissenters both respectability and wealth.

TURMOIL IN ENGLAND

The English Civil War (1642-1646) brought to a head the struggle between royalist forces — broadly called by their enemies "Cavaliers" because of their reckless and haughty attitude — and the Parliamentary forces — called "Roundheads" because of the Puritan preference for short, unostentatious haircuts. For about a decade thereafter, Oliver Cromwell, commander of the successful Puritan troops, ruled as military dictator and Lord Protector. By 1660, however, Parliament, wearied of the years of strife and confusion, invited the son of the deposed and beheaded Charles I to bring the monarchy — never to be an absolute monarchy — back to England. One element of English life that especially troubled Parliament was the religious turbulence that spawned sects without number and theological disputes without end. Following the Restoration, the Church of England returned to its privileged position, as the nation began the long process of gaining world power.

❧ *The Civil War and After*

Since 1629, Charles I had ignored Parliament, displaying a stubborn determination to rule without legislative assistance or interference. Finally in 1639, when Archbishop William Laud, enemy of all religious nonconformity and dissent, tried to impose Anglicanism and its bishops upon Presbyterian Scotland, the furious Scots rose up in arms. Charles now needed Parliament's help. Accordingly, in 1640 he at last summoned Parliament to assist him in raising money and troops to crush Scotland. Parliament, for years denied any significant role in English rule, decided instead that the nation's difficulties stemmed not from Scotland but from the king himself. Continuing in session until 1653 — it refused to be called or dismissed at mere royal pleasure — this Long Parliament impeached Laud and sentenced the king's chief minister to death.

Parliament, in short, made clear that its voice would henceforth be heard. In 1642, when Charles ordered the arrest of five members of Parliament, the aggrieved legislature resolved that such royal arrogance would not be allowed. Since the king already had his own standing army, Parliament had to raise its own to resist Charles and his forces. So England was plunged into four years of civil war. Over those years, Parliament moved from protesting certain royal actions to absolving itself from loyalty to the king. Loyalty instead was pledged to Oliver Cromwell and his Puritan or New Model Army — a "new model" because of its stern and effective discipline, reinforced by firm religious commitment.

In 1645 Parliament ordered the beheading of Archbishop Laud, and once the Civil War went decisively in Cromwell's favor in 1646, the king's days were also numbered. In 1649 he followed Laud to the block. Now, as one dissenter noted, England would be ruled only by the "most High Eternal King of Kings." It seemed as though England was through with monarchy, now to be governed directly by its legislative body whose policies would be enforced by military might and religious zeal.

After Cromwell died in 1658, the effort of his less-capable son to carry on as Lord Protector failed. England again envisioned a more earthly sort of king. Royalists insisted that the time had come to restore civilian rule, stability, and order to a torn and melancholy land. In 1660, Parliament invited the exiled son of Charles I to return home from the Continent and to accept the crown.

When Charles II agreed to ascend the throne of England, he knew that it would be on Parliament's terms. Although he would possess considerable royal power, Charles shrewdly recognized that Parliament would henceforth be an active, vocal partner in the administration of the kingdom and its colonies. To follow any other course would risk the fate of his father, Charles I. But neither England nor Charles II could afford the repetition of those costly years. The nation had to make up quickly for all the dislocations suffered during the fitful years of turmoil and distraction. That was true with respect to internal affairs, to the foreign plantations — and to religion.

☙ Religion Unleashed and Religion Restrained

When in the 1640s the monarchy fell under attack, so did the Church of England. Anglicanism, with its Acts of Conformity, its Book of Common Prayer, and its battalions of persecuting bishops, had both reflected and enforced the royal will. A war against the king was a war against his church, as both sides recognized. Persecution, once aimed only at dissenters, now befell England's own national church. The imprisonment, then death, of William Laud symbolized the swift demise of Anglican privilege in both politics and society.

On the other side of the coin, dissent and non-conformity — so long suppressed, punished, and despised — suddenly found itself breathing a far freer atmosphere. Often quarreling among themselves, Puritans pursued differing forms of church government. Presbyterians reorganized their followers under synods and a general assembly, while Congregationalists (as in New England) saw each congregation as an independent entity. Presbyterians and Congregationalists (or Independents) dominated Parliament during the Cromwellian years. No longer fleeing before a royal army, non-conformists now *were* the army. No longer imposing a kind of Anglican imperialism upon the Presbyterians of Scotland, the new powers of England invited the Presbyterians to assist them in determining just what shape religious reform should take in a now kingless kingdom.

Already in the early years of the Civil War, Parliament summoned a large gathering of English clergy and laity to address the implications of the religious upheaval. The 150 Englishmen, joined by eight Scottish commissioners, constituted the important Westminster Assembly. Meeting steadily from 1643 to 1649, and then sporadically until 1652, the Assembly held more than 1,200 sessions, proposing a church structure that would substitute for bishops an ecclesiastical govern-

Fighting over True Religion   This scene from a 1641 Church of England pamphlet depicts the enemies of the church — an Anabaptist, a "Brownist" or Congregationalist, a familist, and a "Papist" or Catholic — endangering "true religion" (symbolized by the Bible in the middle) by pulling on the corners of its support.

ment of presbyteries and synods. Although this Presbyterian form never took hold over all of England (as it did in Scotland), the Assembly's work had wide influence on both the European and American scenes. This was especially true of the Westminster Confession of Faith, drafted in 1643 and adopted by England's Parliament in 1648. This significant creedal statement, accompanied by *A Larger* and *A Shorter Catechism,* would stand as Presbyterianism's standard doctrinal position for over three hundred years. Far more voluminous than the ancient creeds of the Christian church, the Westminster Confession consisted of over thirty detailed affirmations, ranging from the authority of Scripture to the nature of God and salvation and the authority of civil magistrates in religious matters.

The Westminster Assembly, however, could not begin to answer satisfactorily all the religious questions raised in the 1640s and 1650s, nor could it contain all the religious passions unleashed in that period. Presbyterianism was only one alternative to the Church of England; many other options arose too. Congregationalists, a small but influential minority in the Westminster Assembly, argued for greater freedom in church government, with each congregation having authority over its ministry and mode of worship. Baptists, not represented in the Assembly but prominent in Cromwell's army, called for far more religious freedom than anyone in authority was willing to grant — Anglicans, Presbyterians, or Congregationalists. In fact, Parliament in 1644, alarmed by the outbreak of new religious groups, sought to control or eliminate all "erroneous opinions, ruinating schisms, and damnable heresies." But the lid was off, and the religious pot boiled over.

Baptists arose even before the difficult days of England's Civil War. Branching out of Puritanism, especially the Separatists (as seen in the Plymouth Colony), Baptists argued not only for a free church government but for a free profession of faith. They insisted that only adults, never infants, should be baptized, for only mature persons could make a voluntary, personal Christian commitment. Although Baptists arose in England in the first decade of the seventeenth century, they found stimulation and hope in the freedom of the new Parliamentary rule. Indeed, they virtually made the Westminster Confession of Faith their own, altering the article on baptism to reflect their special convictions. Moreover, Roger Williams, back in London in these years in order to publish his major treatise on religious liberty, *The Bloudy Tenent of Persecution, for Cause of Conscience,* enjoyed the confidence and friendship of Oliver Cromwell. They even discussed theology together. This, along with the Baptist beliefs of many of Cromwell's most trusted army officers, assured that the sect would not be persecuted — at least not as long as Cromwell was in charge.

Many far more radical religious fellowships arose during the Civil War years. A group called the Levellers sought to abolish all distinctions of class and wealth. Another group, the Fifth Monarchists, prophesied an apocalyptic end to history and the establishment on earth of a kingdom of God. Seekers rejected all existing churches and looked for direct inspiration from God. Ranters turned away from all human law to find refuge in divine law alone. One group originating in the late sixteenth century, the Familists, emphasized the spiritual perfection to be achieved in this life and claimed that the biblical "resurrection of the dead" was an experience for the present, not the future. These and many other outbreaks of religious zeal lasted only briefly; most of them ended as mere historical curiosities.

One sect, however, the Society of Friends, survived the turmoil of the Revolution and the persecution of the Restoration. Led by George Fox, who began preaching in 1647, the Quakers gradually organized themselves in the early 1650s into a strongly evangelical body. These passionate proclaimers of a new vision seemed to some the ultimate expression of a radical Protestantism: no ordained ministry, no sacraments, no fixed mode of worship, no creed or confession of faith. Because they emphasized direct divine inspiration to every woman and man, Quakers seemed destructive of the social order as well as both civil and religious authority. Widely regarded as religious fanatics, the Quakers found themselves initially despised and later vigorously persecuted. Because they emphasized personal revelation (called the Inward Light) over biblical authority alone, these "fanatics" were fined, jailed, whipped, and executed in England, Scotland, Ireland — and America. Yet they held on, to become by the end of the eighteenth century significant and solid members of society both in Britain and abroad.

In general, restoration of the English monarchy meant the restoration of the Church of England to its former position of prestige and power. Enough of "ruin-

---

✴ **IN THEIR OWN WORDS**

England's Restoration and Renewed Religious Oppression

The Conventicle Act was one of many meant to restore the Church of England by repressing dissent.

For further and more speedy remedies against the growing and dangerous practices of seditious sectaries and other disloyal persons...be it enacted by the king's most excellent majesty, by and with the advice and consent of the Lords spiritual and temporal, and Commons . . . that if any person of the age of sixteen years or upwards, being a subject of this realm, at any time after the tenth of May next shall be present at any assembly, conventicle, or meeting, under color or pretense of any exercise of religion, in other manner than according to the liturgy and practice of the Church of England...then, where any five persons or more are so assembled as aforesaid, it shall and may be lawful for any one or more justices of the peace . . . by the best means they can, to dissolve, dissipate, or prevent all such unlawful meetings, and take into their custody such and so many of the said persons so unlawfully assembled as they shall think fit. . . .

The Conventicle Act, 1664, of the Clarendon Code

ating schisms" and "damnable heresies," most citizens concluded; the time had come for sobriety and order. Order, however, came at a price, and that price was once again a persecution of all those refusing to conform to the Church of England.

The Clarendon Code, a series of laws passed between 1661 and 1665, made rough indeed the path to dissent — or Non-Conformity, as it was now called. A Corporation Act limited election of local officers (and thereby to Parliament) to members of the Church of England. The Act of Uniformity required total obedience to all the rules in the Book of Common Prayer. The Conventicle Act prohibited any religious gathering whatsoever, except for those of the Church of England, with severe penalties for violation. Finally, the Five-Mile Act forbade all Non-Conformist clergymen from even teaching school or coming within five miles of any organized town unless they publicly pledged their support to the new religious order. Under the terms of the Clarendon Code, many dissenters were fined, jailed, or deprived of their living; the most famous of these prisoners was John Bunyan, who wrote his *Pilgrim's Progress* in the Bedford jail.

Memories of sixteenth-century Roman Catholic intrigues, with Spain as the villain, continued to haunt seventeenth-century England. Now, however, Louis XIV's France appeared as the power most likely to try to impose its policies and religion upon the Protestant island. Charles II returned to England with less anxiety about France and Roman Catholicism than most of his subjects harbored. That alone was enough to keep members of Parliament and others alert to any sign of favor to France or "softness" toward Roman Catholicism. When Charles II negotiated with France a secret Treaty of Dover in 1670, word gradually leaked that the monarch had not only pledged to join France in an attack upon Holland, but — far more frightening — agreed to embrace Catholicism himself and do all he could to bring his kingdom back under papal authority.

In 1673 Parliament responded with a Test Act that excluded from military or political office all persons who refused to receive the Lord's Supper according to the exact specifications of the Church of England. Although this act would obviously affect the Protestant dissenters no less than Catholics, its aim was to remove all Catholics from positions of influence or power. A "Popish Plot" in 1678 fanned public passions even more, as rumors spread of a conspiracy organized by the pope and the Jesuits to kill the king, set fire to London, and slay all stubborn Protestants. No such plot existed, but

twenty persons met their deaths before the hoax was exposed. Antipapal feelings did not subside, however, as concerns centered about the possible successor to Charles II. If it were to be his younger brother, James, Protestants found no comfort since James was soon to become a Catholic. Some members of Parliament promoted an Exclusion Bill to prevent just such a succession, but those efforts failed, and James II came to the throne in 1685 amid swelling anti-Catholicism.

❧ *Mercantilism*

No European political leader engaged in colonization entertained the slightest doubt about the basic purpose of colonies: they existed to benefit the mother country. Colonists should help to defend the parent nation against its enemies on land or sea; they should enlarge the territorial domain; and, most of all, they should establish a commercial network that would tip the scales heavily in favor of their sponsoring country. Such a favorable balance of trade would enable this sponsoring country to amass the gold and silver that everyone assumed was the key to prosperity. This policy of "mercantilism" was understood and, with varying degrees of effectiveness, implemented by all nations. As Sir Walter Raleigh had noted in the late sixteenth century, "Whosoever commands the sea commands the trade; whosoever commands the trade of the world commands the riches of the world, and consequently the world itself."

In England, Oliver Cromwell initiated the first of a series of Navigation Acts; Charles II and his successors merely built upon and expanded them. These acts provided the instruments and mechanisms that would make mercantilism work, strengthening England by increasing her wealth and protecting her trade. At the same time the trade of foreign competitors would be undermined or, preferably, eliminated. During England's turbulent revolutionary years, the Dutch gradually replaced Spain as the chief competitor in colonial trade. This threat Cromwell in 1651 wished to address.

Goods imported into England or her colonies had to be carried on English or colonial ships, with the majority of each crew also required to be English, and all foreign ships bound for the colonies had to stop first in England and pay a tariff. The colonists, in their turn, could not ship directly to foreign markets, but only by way of England where, once again, special taxes would be collected. These regulations applied to virtually all goods for which a market existed. The "enumerated commodities" started out by specifying such things as tobacco, wool, sugar, dyes, and various wood products. Each successive Navigation Act, however, added more commodities. The protection of England's trade monopoly and an enlargement of England's national treasury were the obvious and imperative points.

By the time of the Restoration, the colonies had reached a level of productivity that seemed to require even more control from London. In 1660 a new Navigation Act required that goods be shipped in English-built vessels whose crews were at least three-fourths English. Adding to the number of enumerated commodities, Parliament in 1660 and 1663 stiffened procedures that required all foreign goods to be taxed in England before passing on to the colonies. This, of course, added to England's wealth, while increasing the cost to colonists of all such foreign products. In 1673, tightening the economic noose once again, Parliament stipulated that any ship's captain taking on a cargo of tobacco, sugar, dyes or the like anywhere in the colonies must first post a bond to ensure that he sailed only to an English port.

Parliament and the king agreed that mercantilism required such laws. But to be really effective, mechanisms for supervision and enforcement were also needed. Like his predecessors, Charles II governed through the Privy Council, composed of royal favorites and heads of various departments of government. Large and unwieldy (it had some thirty to forty appointees), the Privy Council generally had so many pressing matters to attend to at home that it gave little systematic attention to colonial affairs. In 1675 Charles created out of his council a new committee, the Lords of Trade and Plantations, whose duties concerned the colonies alone. Now colonial governors, whether appointed by the Lords of Trade or not, would be responsible to them and would have to answer to them for any failure to enforce the Navigation Acts or other directives.

If the colonists could argue (as they regularly did) that governance from England made little sense since nobody there understood what was going on across the ocean, the Lords of Trade sought to amend that situation by repeated and relentless inquiries into all aspects of colonial enterprise. The king's committee conducted interviews, collected maps and books, issued orders, and intended to bring the rather freewheeling colonies into some uniform order, if not subservience. In 1679, for example, the Lords of Trade directed Massachusetts to withdraw all its officers from the four settlements in New Hampshire (Portsmouth, Dover, Exeter, and Hampton); the following year, upon the advice of his Lords, the king proclaimed New Hampshire a royal colony. In the pro-Anglican mood of the Restoration, moreover, the Lords saw no merit in indulging the Massachusetts Puritans. In fact, they wished to revoke that colony's charter altogether, requiring Massachusetts to amend all laws contrary to English law and to remove all legal impediments to Anglicanism.

Although prevented from doing all that they wished, the Lords of Trade did dispatch collectors of customs to all the colonies to see that England's sovereign will with respect to trade was neither flouted nor dodged — that England's revenues did not get lost in transmission. Smuggling and piracy would be squelched and trading with the French or Dutch would be halted forthwith. No longer would the Lords accept the promises or pledges or delaying tactics of colonial agents: They would send their own agents to enforce the Navigation Acts and bring to trial all who failed to abide by their detailed regulations.

In 1679 the Lords of Trade appointed Edward Randolph as customs collector in Massachusetts. This act aroused great resentment since for three years as a civil servant in Massachusetts, Randolph had regularly taken the side of England in every dispute and had even denounced the colony's leaders as "generally inclined to sedition, being proud, ignorant, and imperious." If the colonists regarded Randolph with suspicion and disdain, he returned the favor fully, seeing the colonists in general (and Puritans in particular) as defiant of all English laws and subversive of all English interests. As customs collector, he would set things aright. As the king's personal representative, he would assert authority where little or none had been exerted before.

Randolph proceeded to seize ships unauthorized to do business in Boston. He tried offenders, only to discover that local juries regularly acquitted those charged with violation of English laws. Getting broader authority, Randolph turned to courts administered by England's Admiralty (navy department). Such vice-admiralty courts, functioning without a jury, ensured that England's version of what justice required would be upheld. The Navigation Acts would be enforced with more vigor and effect than ever before.

These contests between the colonies and the king provoked a growing assertiveness among the colonial legislatures and colonial courts. Massachusetts manifested this perhaps more than most, but in other colonies just then coming into being, similar tensions soon appeared.

THE RESTORATION COLONIES AND THE DOMINION OF NEW ENGLAND

In 1660 England enjoyed a clear claim in North America only to Virginia and Maryland in the south and to New England in the north. In between, the Dutch had settled territory around the Hudson River, but had left much unexplored and unsettled. South of Virginia the Spanish flew their flag at St. Augustine, Florida, but great stretches of land awaited claim and conquest. Charles II and his advisers determined to fill those gaps, so that English rule would prevail all along the Atlantic coast from the French settlements in eastern Canada to the Spanish outposts in northern Florida. England wasted little time in executing this plan.

❧ The Carolinas

Although the restored monarchy was not an absolute monarchy, the king had wide discretion in administering overseas enterprises. Overseas, Charles II could make grants, set boundaries, and recognize claims. Moreover, old laws now had to be revised and repassed to restore royal authority to its status of earlier years. In setting up new colonies, Charles preferred to rely on proprietors (as in the case of Maryland) rather than on joint-stock companies (as in the cases of Virginia and Massachusetts). When a faithful royalist living in Barbados, Sir John Colleton, returned to England in 1660 to acclaim the restoration of the monarchy, he found his king fully receptive to further colonization. In March 1663 Charles granted Colleton and several other influential members of his court a charter for the expanse of land between Virginia and Florida that extended westward to the "South Seas." To honor their king, the proprietors named the colony Carolina (*Carolus* being the Latin form of "Charles").

These proprietors hoped to avoid the mistakes — and even more, the exorbitant costs — of England's earlier colonies. One important way to cut costs was to encourage settlement by those from nearby colonies. Tidewater Virginians in search of land had already cast their eyes as far south as Albemarle Sound, and a few New Englanders had ventured up the Cape Fear River to assess the possibilities of settlement. Carolina, it seemed, was ready to receive waves of settlers from the north.

Those waves, however, never reached Carolina's shores. Despite generous offers of land, of religious freedom, and a good deal of home rule, settlers de-

An Early Episcopal Church   St. James Church, in South Carolina's oldest Anglican parish outside Charleston, was built between 1711 and 1719. The rector at the time was a member of the Society for the Propagation of the Gospel in Foreign Parts, the English organization that promoted Anglicanism in the colonies.

clined to come in significant numbers or, if they came, to stay long enough to give the colony a solid start. Even efforts to attract non-British adventurers met with limited success. Within half a dozen years, most of the original eight proprietors had lost hope. One of their number, however, Anthony Ashley Cooper, vowed that Carolina must not be forsaken. Rallying the original backers to a personal level of investment that they had heretofore avoided, Lord Ashley — now the first Earl of Shaftesbury and the most significant member of the king's inner circle — sent three ships with settlers and supplies from England. After picking up additional colonists in Barbados, this contingent arrived in Port Royal, just north of the Savannah River, in the spring of 1670.

Lord Ashley labored with his physician, secretary, and friend, John Locke — later to win a great reputation as a philosopher — to draw up a detailed plan of government for Carolina. The Fundamental Constitutions of 1669 promised more than the proprietors were ever able to deliver. With elaborate structure and unique vocabulary, it envisioned three orders of society, all of whom would be supported with generous grants of land — up to 96,000 acres for the "baronies." Even small farmers received over one hundred acres apiece as further enticement to settlement. And dissenters would be as welcome in Carolina as in Rhode Island, for it was promised that "no person whatsoever shall disturb, molest, or persecute another for his speculative opinions in religion or his way of worship." Many Huguenots found refuge in Carolina, especially in its major settlement of Charleston (originally Charles

Town), founded in 1680. Scotch-Irish Presbyterians also settled in Charleston, Port Royal, and in the backcountry. Unlike the colonies founded in the first half of the seventeenth century, the Restoration colonies would embrace broader principles of toleration. Despite the generous terms offered, the Fundamental Constitutions within a generation lost the support of the settlers who preferred freedom to perceived structure.

By the 1690s Carolina was beginning to thrive. Charleston, at the juncture of the Ashley and Cooper rivers, grew to become not only a major port but also the colonial south's only city. By 1690 it had a population of over a thousand, and a generation later there were more than three times that number. Much of the early settlement came from Barbados where huge sugar plantations drove the price of land beyond the reach of the small farmer. White indentured labor quickly gave way to Barbados-style slavery, as the black population grew from less than one-fifth of the population in 1680 to over two-thirds by 1720. At first, Carolinians grew crops in the interior that they floated downstream to Charleston for transport to the Caribbean and England. In exchange for pork, peas, pitch, and tar, Carolinians imported sugar, molasses, wine, manufactured goods, and slaves.

By the end of the seventeenth century, however, rice became the crop of choice in Carolina. Slaves imported from West Africa brought with them the techniques of rice production, and became the labor force that made such production possible.

Coming directly from West Africa to the American mainland, these Carolina slaves brought much of their traditional culture with them. Especially on the large plantations where blacks lived in relative isolation from whites, West African languages, rituals, and mental outlooks lived on. In addition to a benevolent creator God, these Africans also believed in many lesser gods or spirits dwelling in rivers, trees, and ocean. Appeasing angry ancestors through sacrifice or improved behavior played a major part in regulating conduct. Dancing, drumming, and singing were persisting elements in this imported religion. Indeed, West African ritualism and ceremony has been called "danced religion."

Carolina's location near the southern end of the Appalachian Mountains offered another economic advantage: the trading of furs and hides. By going around the southern edge of the mountains, Carolinians reached far into the backcountry, ultimately all the way to the Mississippi River. In this expanse, traders established contact with many Indian tribes, setting up a commerce as profitable as that of the Dutch at the northern end of the mountain range. In their westernmost enterprises, Carolina traders discovered that they needed to worry about the French as well as the Spanish, for France's advance parties had established footholds in Biloxi as early as 1699, in Mobile in 1702, and even more firmly in New Orleans by 1718.

At the northern edges of the colony along Albemarle Sound, colonists had agitated since 1689 for a separate jurisdiction. By 1712, the area had its own governor and its own name: North Carolina. Lacking a major port or a principal urban center, North Carolina developed more slowly than either Virginia or South Carolina. Indeed, the slow-growing colony was often the butt of scorn from its near neighbors and from occasional visitors. One Anglican clergyman visiting the territory exclaimed that "the manners of the North Carolinians in General are Vile and Corrupt.... The whole Country is in a Stage of Debauchery, Dissoluteness and Corruption." This highly prejudiced observer explained North Carolina's difficulties by noting that it was settled by "outcasts" from the other colonies. But what chiefly

---

✳ **IN THEIR OWN WORDS**

Explorer John Lawson on North Carolina, 1709
By the beginning of the eighteenth century, the Carolinas were thriving colonies.

The Christian Natives of Carolina are a straight, clean-limb'd People; the Children being seldom or never troubled with Rickets, or those other Distempers that the Europeans are vis-ited withal.... The Vicinity of the Sun makes Impression on the Men, who labour out of doors, or use the Water. As for those Women that do not expose themselves to the Weather, they are often very fair, and generally as well feature'd as you shall see anywhere, and have very brisk charming Eyes, which sets them off to Advantage. They marry very young; some at Thirteen or Fourteen; and She that stays till Twenty is reckon'd a stale Maid.... The Women are very fruitful, most Houses being full of Little Ones. It has been observ'd that Women long marry'd and without Children in other Places, have remov'd to Carolina and become joyful Mothers.

from A New Voyage to Carolina

accounted for his venom was the simple fact that the Church of England was not effectively established there; for dissenters such as Baptists and Quakers had successfully invaded the land.

Despite population growth that by the end of the century reached about ten thousand in the northern and southern parts of Carolina, and despite a variety of profitable enterprises, the original proprietors did not fare well. Ignoring the Fundamental Constitutions, settlers seized more and more authority. Proprietors tried to control or eliminate the enslaving of backcountry Indians, but largely failed, at least until the Indians became less accessible and Africans more so. With some nudging from London, the proprietors also moved early in the eighteenth century to give the Church of England official status, even briefly barring all dissenters from the legislative assembly. As in Virginia, public funds went to the building of Anglican churches and the support of Anglican clergy. For a colony that started out with the offer of widest toleration, this favoritism implied a significant and disturbing retreat.

In addition to tensions over the official religion, Carolina suffered from deteriorating relationships with the Indians. In large part, this was due (according to Virginian William Byrd) to the traders who "don't only teach the honester Savages all sorts of Debauchery, but are unfair in all their dealings and use them in all kinds of Oppression." When Swiss immigrants settled New Bern in 1710, the Tuscaroras concluded that they were being pushed ever farther into the interior. As a consequence of that sentiment, these natives launched a fierce attack (the Tuscarora War) in 1711 that left over 130 settlers dead and all the rest thinking only of their safety. For the next three or four years, counterattacks conducted by both North and South Carolina militias together with their Indian allies killed about a thousand Tuscarora. Many of the remaining Tuscaroras moved as far north as New York, where they became the sixth nation of the Iroquois Confederacy.

South Carolinians, busy fending off Indians, also grew more anxious about the Spanish entrenched in Florida — especially when Spain encouraged Indian forays against them. This appeared to be the case dramatically in 1715 when the Yamassee, aggrieved over disappearing lands, launched an attack in which ninety Carolina traders and their families perished. The Yamassee War highlighted the vulnerability of this particular frontier. Since the proprietors seemed unwilling or unable to make Carolina more secure, the settlers in 1719 at last revolted against their patrons who, by "their

proceedings, unhing'd the Frame of government, and forfeited their Right to the same."

When South Carolinians petitioned England to be taken over directly by the monarch, the king obliged, making South Carolina a royal colony in 1720. (The decision became final when the proprietors sold their rights in 1729.) North Carolina, also under attack by the Yamassee, spent more for defense than the young and sparsely settled colony could afford and similarly it sought royal protection by encouraging England to buy out its investors. When these proprietors also consented to sell, North Carolina joined South Carolina as a royal colony in 1729.

New York and New Jersey

In 1664 Charles II granted to his brother, James, the Duke of York, sweeping charter rights to land that extended from parts of northern Maine to Long Island and south to the Delaware River. Much of this territory fell squarely across Holland's long established presence in New Netherland, most visibly on Manhattan Island and up the Hudson River to the present site of Albany (Fort Orange to the Dutch). England wanted not only the land that the Dutch occupied, but also the Hollanders' trade, particularly in furs. When the duke's expeditionary force of four frigates arrived off Manhattan Island in early September 1664 and demanded surrender, the Dutch complied peacefully. The generous terms of capitulation granted the Dutch West India Company the continued use of its property in the colony and, for a time, even permission to carry on trade through the port of New York — as the town of New Amsterdam was renamed. Dutch settlers could remain so long as they were willing to swear loyalty to the king of England, and the Dutch Reformed Church could continue to hold services. Thus while a Dutch cultural presence remained in New York and New Jersey, England accomplished its main objective of dominating the Atlantic shore from New England all the way down to Carolina. Only once, for fifteen months in 1673-74, did the Dutch reassert their authority on Manhattan Island. England had come to stay.

The Duke of York, as proprietor, had no patience for representative assemblies or democratic tendencies. His charter entitled him to rule as he wished, an authority that coincided neatly with his own predisposition. Yet local inhabitants believed that they should have some voice in matters that affected them directly. New England Puritans who had migrated onto Long Island pressed especially hard for something like their

The Surrender of New Amsterdam   This illustration, from a much later date, shows an illustrator's conception of the scene in which peg-legged Peter Stuyvesant, the last Dutch governor of New Netherland, in 1664 surrendered the colony to the English. They renamed it New York, and Stuyvesant retired to a farm on Manhattan Island.

familiar right of local governance. In response, the colony's governor, Richard Nicolls, drew up a body of laws in 1665 (the Duke's Laws) that offered assurances that English liberties would not be wantonly violated. Trial by jury was assured, with criminal penalties — less severe than those in England — carefully stipulated. Religious toleration was provided for, and likewise the right of local communities to determine which church should receive governmental support.

But even when his own governors urged him to relent, the duke continued to resist pressures for a popular legislative assembly. The people finally got their proprietor's attention when they began avoiding custom duties and other taxes by smuggling or by shipping and receiving goods through New England. In 1683 James informed his new governor, Thomas Dongan, that "I have thought fit that there shall be a General Assembly

of all freeholders, by the persons who they shall choose to represent them." The thought had not come without prompting. The Assembly would "have free liberty to consult and debate among themselves all matters as shall be apprehended proper to be established for laws for the good government of the said colony of New York." James would still have to consent to any laws passed by the assembly, but at the same time the Assembly could refuse all laws presented to them.

Although dominated by the continued Dutch presence, New York's populace revealed great diversity in language, in ethnicity, in religion. As tensions mounted between pro- and anti-British factions, both sides had to keep at least one eye out for French threats from Canada and Iroquois unrest along the Mohawk River. Economic rivalries aggravated ethnic divisions, and New York saw greater religious diversity within its boundaries than any other English colony. German Lutherans, English Quakers, Scots-Irish Presbyterians, and Dutch Calvinists were only the largest groups in a medley of faiths. A scandalized Anglican governor, Edmund Andros, complained in 1678 that the colony contained "religions of all sorts." A later Roman Catholic governor noted that though religious opinions of every variety could indeed be found, he suspected that most of the population had no religious opinions at all.

While New York was struggling for some measure of stability, even more complex developments took place just to the south. In 1664 the Duke of York granted what became New Jersey to two men who had been involved in the Carolina project: Sir John Berkeley and Sir George Carteret. The new colony, so named because Carteret had previously governed the Channel Island of Jersey,[1] seemed to get off to a promising start so far as local liberties and self-governance were concerned. In an effort to make New Jersey attractive to additional settlers, the two proprietors issued in 1665 certain "Concessions and Agreements" that provided for the election of a General Assembly, the privileges and responsibilities of which were spelled out in impressive detail. In addition, the proprietors promised generous grants of land "to every Master or Mistress" already residing in New Jersey, or arriving before January 1665, and likewise portions of land (ranging from 60 to 150 acres) to their servants or slaves, male or female, over fourteen years of age. Following the precedent set in the Rhode Island and Carolina charters of 1663, the proprietors also granted religious liberty beyond that currently enjoyed in England

---

1. An English possession just off the coast of Normandy.

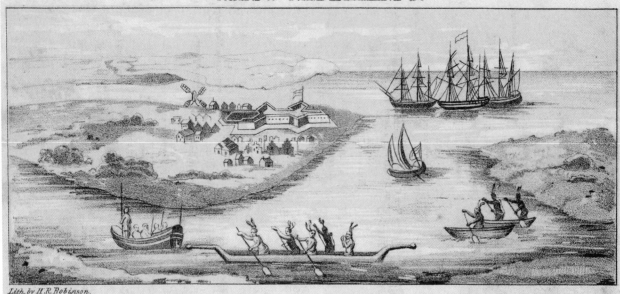

NIEUW NEDERLANDT.

Lith. by H. R. Robinson.

This view of Fort Amsterdam on the Manhattan is copied from an ancient Engraving executed in Holland. The Fort was erected in 1623 but finished upon the above model by Governor Van Twiller in 1635.

New Amsterdam Here is New Amsterdam before it became New York: a small island city where colonists from the Netherlands lived and traded.

or in most of the rest of America. So New Jersey's beginnings did seem most promising; nevertheless, here as elsewhere throughout the colonies the ability of a local legislative body to have a meaningful voice in government had to be fought for, inch by inch, year by year.

New Jersey's difficulties were compounded by the formal division of the colony into two halves in 1676. East Jersey, oriented toward New York, remained under Carteret's authority, while West Jersey, later oriented toward Philadelphia, came under the jurisdiction of two Quakers, John Fenwick and Edward Byllinge, to whom Lord Berkeley had sold his interest. When the two Quaker adventurers failed to make the sandy soil of West Jersey productive, their land fell into the hands of creditors, one of whom was William Penn. All of this shifting and transferring and dividing resulted in land titles of endless confusion and chaos. In East Jersey, moreover, the governor and his council in 1681 locked horns with the Assembly that clung stubbornly to the authority granted them in 1665, but which had been challenged or eroded ever since. Carteret "interpreted" the earlier concessions in such a way as to give most authority to the governor. To no one's surprise, the Assembly "interpreted" those concessions quite differently, thereby provoking the governor to bemoan the Assembly's "lack of understanding." The Assembly shot back that the gov-

ernor was either a liar or had not given the matter "due consideration." And so in New Jersey, as in New York, a restless populace vied with a defensive and increasingly authoritarian regime imposed from without.

When in 1685 the Duke of York became King James II, New York automatically became a royal colony. And when that same year James, joined by the Lords of Trade, created the Dominion of New England, over his colonial subjects' bitter opposition, he quickly added New York and New Jersey to this artificial union in the hope of bringing some order into both of those recent acquisitions. James and his advisers decided, moreover, that too much local control had not been good. New York's inhabitants, for example, had more voice in public affairs than had been agreed to in any other colony. In 1686, therefore, the citizens' "Charter of Liberty and Privileges" was withdrawn, to the consternation of the settlers and the growth of resentment directed toward the Crown. In 1702, a reunited New Jersey also became a royal colony, as England engaged in a major effort to reorganize its colonial household.

❧ *Pennsylvania and the "Lower Counties"*

Chartered by Charles II, the colony of Pennsylvania had many advantages over those that had preceded it. First, it enjoyed an enormous expanse of land; second, that land was wonderfully fertile; third, the inhabitants drawn to it were industrious and diligent;

fourth, it could benefit from more than fifty years of experience in the other colonies (much of it bad); and fifth, it was born of the vision of one remarkable man. William Penn, a wealthy English landowner, seemed destined for the comfortable life of a country squire; indeed, if his father could have controlled his destiny, Penn would have been precisely that. But in 1667, while in Ireland on a business trip for his father, something happened that radically altered the rest of Penn's life and refashioned a fair amount of early American history as well: William Penn became a Quaker.

The Religious Society of Friends, to use its proper title, had been in existence for only a dozen years or so when Penn cast his lot with them. Vigorously evangelistic, Quakers attracted much attention — and even more ridicule and scorn. In the Cromwellian years, "wild sectaries" abounded, so that Quakers could hardly be singled out. But after the 1660 Restoration, sectarian division was out of fashion, and conformity to the Church of England was in. Their limitless energies and unshakable convictions caused Quakers to suffer the heavy hand of persecution most visibly and most painfully, both in old England and new. Their doctrine of an Inward Light — the seed of God in all women and men, regardless of rank — threatened not only the authority of the Anglican clergy but the very order and stability of society itself.[2] Their refusal to take oaths, to bear arms, to show deference to their "superiors," their insistence on the equality of women[3] — all this and more infuriated just about everybody who was not a Quaker.

As one of those clearly visible and intolerable Non-Conformists, William Penn was himself imprisoned in 1668. Upon his release, he came to the defense of Quakerism with a 1670 publication entitled *The Great Case of Liberty of Conscience* where he argued strongly against any invasion by civil power into that tender and sacred reserve, conscience. A decade later he came to the Quakers' defense even more effectively when he petitioned Charles II for a colony in North America. Such a petition made sense only because the Crown owed a large debt (about £16,000) to Penn's father, first Lord of the Admiralty, who had backed the Restoration. What better way to discharge the debt than to give away land

William Penn   This 1666 portrait of William Penn at the age of twenty-two is indicative of the great wealth and privilege of his upbringing. Penn's membership in a new and embattled religious community called the Religious Society of Friends (which eventually became known as the Quakers) sensitized him to the need for a haven of religious liberty, a need that was fulfilled when the king granted him a large tract of land west of New Jersey to establish the colony of Pennsylvania.

that cost Charles nothing and might even bring him some return? So in 1681 the king granted Penn a huge tract south of New York, west of New Jersey, and north of Maryland. The western boundary, as with so many other colonies, would only be fixed when somebody learned what was out there.

ATTRACTING NEW SETTLERS

In addition to making some money from this venture (he liked to live well), Penn clearly intended that his colony would be a refuge for his fellow Quakers, but not for them only. Among the earliest laws he drew up while still in England was one that assured all settlers "who confess and acknowledge the one almighty and eternal God" that they would "in no ways be molested or prejudiced for their religious persuasion or practice in matters of faith and worship." Like Rhode Island, Pennsylvania would be a haven for religious dissent. Even more than Rhode Island, Pennsylvania attracted the most colorful variety of "religious persuasion or

2. For making similar claims Anne Hutchinson had been expelled from Massachusetts Bay Colony a half-century earlier. See Chapter 2.

3. Margaret Fell, an early organizer of the Quakers in England, in 1676 published a significant tract entitled, *Women's Speaking Justified, Proved and Allowed of by the Scriptures*. Women not only preached but took charge of the women's meetings, supervised the distribution of charity, and provided for the care of orphans, among many other duties.

William Penn and the Indians   This famous 1771 painting by American artist Benjamin West shows William Penn peacefully negotiating the purchase of land from the native people of his colony. For his time, Penn's relationship with the Native Americans was exemplary. Relations would deteriorate badly in the eighteenth-century colony.

practice" to be found in all of colonial America: Amish, Mennonites, Moravians,[4] Anglicans, Catholics, German Lutherans and Reformed, Scottish Presbyterians, Welsh Baptists, and Sephardic Jews, in addition to English and Irish Quakers who dominated the first waves of immigration in 1682.

Penn, however, was interested in attracting as many settlers as possible from wherever possible — so long

4. For these small Pietistic sects, see below, p. 81.

as they were willing to work. In his promotional pamphlets, he carefully avoided the excesses of those who, earlier in the seventeenth century, had promised woods full of deer, vines heavy with grapes, streams swarming with fish. Penn, on the contrary, urged prospective settlers to count on labor before harvest, winter before spring, two or three years before life would be as comfortable as what they left behind. He especially sought "industrious husbandmen and day laborers," artisans such as "carpenters, masons, smiths, weavers, tailors, tanners, shoemakers, shipwrights, etc., where they may be spared or are low in the world." Wages would be better in Pennsylvania, the proprietor promised, while the cost of food and housing would be less. And, of course, there was *land*. To those who could not afford to buy land, it would be rented to them at the price of one penny per acre — up to two hundred acres. Even servants would have fifty acres awaiting them "when their time is expired," for many hopeful settlers sold their services for five or seven years in exchange for passage across the ocean and labor for some master or mistress. To those who had better resources, Penn was prepared to sell five thousand acres for £100, assuring the prospective purchaser that the land would be "free from any Indian encumbrance."

A NEW APPROACH TO INDIAN RELATIONS
Having observed the great difficulties that Virginians and Puritans encountered with the Native Americans,

---

❋ IN THEIR OWN WORDS

William Penn as Landlord
His tenants did not repay William Penn's generosity as a landlord.

Loving Friend and Tenants,
I kindly salute you and wish you heartily well. I have sent the bearer, James Atkinson, to gather my quitrents [a rent paid in lieu of

services to the proprietor] among you, and you must not take it hard that I press you in this matter, for you know that I receive neither custom nor taxes, but maintain my table and government at my own cost and charges, which is what no other governor does besides myself. This makes me endeavor to get in my own dues for my winter supply. I expect you

will all strive to answer me herein, and so engage the kindness of

Your friend and landlord,

Wm Penn
Philadelphia, 9 November 1683

An Anglican Woman Encounters the Quakers

Elizabeth Ashbridge (1713-1755) immigrated to the colonies from England at age nineteen as an indentured servant after an elopement and a short-lived marriage. Though reared in the Anglican tradition, her search for spiritual truth led her to the Quakers.

Hence I came to Trenton Ferry, where I met with no small Mortification upon hearing that my Relations were Quakers, & what was the worst of all my Aunt a Preacher. I was Sorry to hear it, for I was Exceedingly prejudiced against these People & have often wondered with what face they Could Call them Selves Christians. I Repented my Coming and had a mind to have turned back. At Last I Concluded to go & see them since I was so far on my journey, but Expected little Comfort from my Visit. But see how God brings unforeseen things to Pass, for by my going there I was brought to my Knowledge of his Truth.—I went from Trenton to Philadelphia by Water, thence to my Uncle's on Horseback, where I met with very kind reception; for tho' my Uncle was dead and my Aunt married again, yet both her husband and She received me in a very kind manner. I had not been there three Hours before . . . my opinion began to alter with respect to these People.

Penn resolved upon a different course. In July 1681, Penn decreed that no one purchasing land in Pennsylvania "shall, by any ways or means in word or deed, affront or wrong any Indian." A few months later he urged his advance agents to make friendly overtures to the Indians in the area, "to be tender of offending" them and "to sit down lovingly among them." And to the Delawares themselves he wrote in October 1681 informing them "that I am sensible of the unkindness and injustice that has been too much exercised toward you by the people of these parts of the world." He would prefer to start off on a different foot, with fair purchase agreements, with fair adjudication procedures (appealing to a group composed "of an equal number of honest men on both sides"),

A Quaker Meeting   This undated North American image depicts the aspects of Quaker religion that critics found so unacceptable: The absence of a learned and socially respectable clergy, the Quakers' insistence that they could receive direct inspiration from the Holy Spirit, and the freedom that they accorded to women to speak in worship — all seemed to open the way to spiritual and social anarchy.

and with the explicit desire to "live together as neighbors and friends." All this Penn attempted before he himself left England for Pennsylvania. He even took the trouble to learn the Delaware language. And the Quaker conviction that pacifism, not war, was God's plan for humanity applied equally to the Indians. Every difficulty was not resolved, of course, but Pennsylvania in its early years was spared the equivalent of Virginia's 1622 Indian attack or New England's 1637 Pequot War. When later Penn did arrive in America, he concluded a treaty with the Indians in 1701 in hopes of ensuring that the new neighbors would not take advantage of the old inhabitants.

MAPPING AND REGULATING THE COLONY

If Penn tried to work out the conditions of settlement and relations with the Indians before setting sail, he also planned his "greene country towne" of Philadelphia with equal care. The exact site should be fixed, Penn noted, "where it is most navigable, high, dry, and healthy." Penn wanted oceangoing ships to be able to unload directly onto the docks, not requiring any unloading into small boats or barges. Located between the Delaware and the Schuylkill rivers, the city was laid out on a grid plan, with streets at right angles and with houses to be built in a line, "or upon a line as much as may be." This was so startling an innovation that, a century and a half later, London's Charles Dickens, strolling around Philadelphia, exclaimed, "I would have given the world for a crooked street."

Although Penn offered a wide toleration to religious beliefs, he was less tolerant of scandalous or immoral behavior — rather strictly defined. The Frame of the Government, adopted in 1682, declared that "a careless and corrupt administration of justice" would bring

God's wrath down upon the people; similarly, "the wildness and looseness of the people" would provoke the indignation of God against this new country. "Therefore," directed Penn, all "swearing, cursing, lying, profane talking, drunkenness, drinking of health, obscene words" would be "discouraged and severely punished." In addition to such major crimes as murder, duels, treason, and rape, the government banned stage plays, card playing, gambling with dice, "bull-baitings, cock-fightings, bear-baitings, and the like." These latter activities "excite the people to rudeness, cruelty, looseness, and irreligion." Sunday, "the Lord's Day," would be reserved for all persons "to worship God according to their understandings." Morality was to be as straight as the streets.

The Delaware River was fully navigable as far upriver as Philadelphia, but Penn saw a problem in the exclusion from his charter of the land below Philadelphia and Chester. This territory had already been granted to the Duke of York. But Penn and the duke had been friends from their youth, so it took no great power of persuasion to convince the future James II to convey the land across from New Jersey to William Penn. Claims by Maryland's Calverts were momentarily set aside, so that in 1682 the counties of Newcastle, Sussex, and Kent (the "lower counties" which much later constituted the state of Delaware) were added to Pennsylvania, assuring the colony unobstructed access to the sea.

PROSPERITY IN PENN'S COLONY

All the careful planning paid off. From its earliest years, Philadelphia enjoyed swift growth. When Penn himself arrived in October 1682, about four thousand persons lived in the area of his grant, some of them having arrived before the land was his. Three years later, Penn estimated that ninety ships had sailed for Pennsylvania since early 1682, with about eighty settlers per ship. This total of over seven thousand consisted, said Penn, of "French, Dutch, Germans, Swedes, Danes, Finns, Scotch, Irish, and English, and of the last equal to all the rest." Perhaps over half settled in the city itself, but many villages or townships of five thousand acres were created to accommodate a minimum of ten families each. When he visited such rural communities, Penn took comfort in seeing houses and barns go up, gardens planted, and corn harvested. Many a poor man, he noted, now knew the difference between being his own landlord and working only for others. Pennsylvania would prosper.

Penn, however, did not. Most settlers refused to pay their rents, modest though they were. Disagreements kept the wheels of governance from turning smoothly. Disputes with Maryland about the "lower counties" grew so intense that Penn in 1684 had to return to England in an effort to get that issue settled. During the fifteen long years he remained in England, local officials in the colony either mismanaged his affairs or sought more and more authority for themselves. Colonists enlarged their rights, while those of the proprietor steadily diminished.

The general prosperity that came to Pennsylvania resulted in part from the sober discipline and earnest efforts of the Quakers and like-minded, hard-working immigrants. Quakers were called to a simple life — but then Quakers grew wealthy. The "Quaker Grandees," as a modern historian has called them, moved away from the earlier rejection of the world and toward more conformity with it. One Quaker leader who had sorrowfully observed this transition reminded his fellow believers that once upon a time "Friends were a plain lowly minded people." Now, however, after twenty years or so in Philadelphia, the Society conformed "to the fashions of the world, true humility decreased, and their meetings in general were not so lively and edifying." Others, however, saw no contradiction in living well, while acknowledging that "every man ought soberly and discreetly to set bounds for himself, and avoid extremes, still bearing due regard to the society he is of."

Pennsylvania became a land of considerable social mobility. The average artisan in the 1680s could see himself as a gentleman by the first decade of the following century. As one merchant reported, even some who arrived as indentured servants had within two decades become "masters of great estates." Wealthy Quakers, it soon became evident, could not readily be distinguished in their clothing or housing from wealthy Anglicans or members of any other group. Yet, by the time of the American Revolution, many Quakers consciously turned from indulgence to austerity, from ornate living to plainness.

When Penn at last returned in 1699 to Pennsylvania, the Assembly was demanding an ever-larger role in the running of the colony. After long negotiation, Penn acceded in 1701 to the Charter of Privileges that created a unicameral (one-house) legislature and gave representatives the right to initiate bills. This charter continued to serve as the colony's chief instrument of government down to 1776. It reaffirmed liberty of conscience, provided for the annual election of legislators, specified that Pennsylvania's freemen would enjoy powers and privileges "according to the rights of freeborn subjects of England," assured that correct judicial procedures would be strictly observed, and stipulated that the Assembly would have the right of nomination for all local officers such as sheriffs and coroners.

In 1701 Penn returned to England for good. He grew ever more disillusioned as he heard that back in Pennsylvania even Quakers mistrusted each other, that even his own family embarrassed him, that even his appointed governors betrayed him. In 1718, he died a chastened, bankrupt, and broken man. His colony, however, had flourished: over ten thousand people arrived during its first decade of existence, and three times that number a generation later. As Pennsylvania quickly passed the colony of New York in population, Philadelphia was well on its way to becoming the cultural capital of the American colonies.

A HAVEN FOR PACIFISTS

In 1677 Penn had made a trip up the Rhine River in Germany to visit communities of Mennonites and other German pietists. He invited several of the persecuted groups — all pacifists — to settle in his colony when the time was ripe. One year after the founding of Pennsylvania in 1682, they began to come: Mennonites, then Amish, then Brethren and other offshoots of these Reformation-era sects. Germantown, begun in 1683, housed the first Mennonite congregation in America in that year and the first Brethren congregation in 1719. The Amish — an uncompromisingly strict group of Mennonites — sought refuge first in Berks County, though they quickly spread westward from that point. Like the Quakers, all these German bodies refused military service; they took their cue from Christ's clear command to "love your enemies, and pray for them that persecute you." From Saxony, the Moravians came later, settling in Nazareth and then Bethlehem. Also pacifists, the Moravians won wide admiration for their effective missionary labors among the Indians. Indeed, Pennsylvania became so great a haven for pacifists that the American Revolution posed special problems for the "Quaker colony."

❧ *James II and the Dominion of New England*

As Charles II lay on his deathbed in 1685, the Lords of Trade were busy creating a strong central colonial administration. In his brother, James II, they found a king just as interested in colonial control, but one who preferred to exercise that control more directly under his own authority. Eleven separate colonies, each with its own governor and each with, or trying to acquire, its own legislature, looked virtually ungovernable. A single administrative entity, or at most two or three such structures, seemed required to simplify and tighten the chain of command. New England — the most difficult to manage, and the most independent in its attitudes and actions — was surely the logical place to begin. Then, after a model of strong government had been firmly fixed there, the other colonies could be herded into comparable units. Of course, a strong proprietor such as William Penn might present an obstacle, but in time even that problem could be surmounted.

Soon after taking the throne, James II agreed to the plan that eventually created the Dominion of New England. James, who knew New York and New Jersey well, saw no reason not to add these colonies to the Dominion, especially since their governments were unstable and their political bickering endless. Even more important, these last two colonies could assist New England in fending off French attacks. An improvement in internal administration would enhance external security, a combination so fortuitous as to make the plan seem inspired. So James and his Privy Council imposed a single centralized government on New Hampshire, Massachusetts, Plymouth, Connecticut, Rhode Island, New York, and New Jersey. Over that expanse — larger than England itself — a single royal governor would rule along with his royally appointed council, and royally appointed judges benignly blessed it all. As for local legislative assemblies, James had the perfect solution: abolish them. Such assemblies, James had already decided from his earlier experience with New York, only delayed and blunted the efficient operations of government.

With the arrival of royally appointed Governor Edmund Andros in Boston in 1686, New Englanders quickly saw their worst fears realized. Taxes were levied with neither the colonists' advice nor their consent, trade suffered under the strict enforcement of the Navigation Acts, and justice turned sour when English common law and trial by jury gave way to the despised vice-admiralty courts. Beyond all that, royal quitrents[5] were suddenly demanded of every landholder. English liberty, at least as New Englanders had understood and enjoyed it, dissipated before their very eyes. When some aggrieved citizens (including the Reverend John Wise of Ipswich, Massachusetts) protested these unwelcome

---

5. Under old English law, a small annual fee owed by a freehold tenant; by the payment of this fee, he was considered "quit" or free of other feudal obligations for his land.

novelties, Andros fined them heavily and threw them in jail; and when Wise protested that English liberties recognized since the days of the Magna Carta were now being dishonored, one authority replied that colonists could hardly expect English liberties to be extended to the ends of the earth. But did colonists, simply because they were colonists, lose the birthrights guaranteed to English men and women at home?

Andros went out of his way to irritate Puritan Boston. First, he insisted on having his own church for Anglican worship, taking over a Congregational one temporarily for that purpose. Second, in a land where Sundays were spent in rest and worship, Andros celebrated major anniversaries with bonfires and fireworks. Third, he even allowed a maypole to be erected in Charlestown, a sacrilege signifying to all Massachusetts since the 1630s the triumph of unclean lives and impure thoughts. When Andros told New Englanders that they must pay for building a Church of England house of worship in Boston, the town's leading jurist, Samuel Sewall, replied that England's bishops "would have thought [it] strange to have been asked to contribute toward setting up the New England churches." Sewall may have had logic on his side, but Andros had the king on his. And so he prevailed, confiscating property and ordering the construction of New England's first Anglican church in 1688.

Andros was supported by the king, but the king was not supported by Parliament. In 1688 James II — who had promised to practice his Roman Catholicism privately — broke that promise in baptizing his newborn son as a Catholic. Faced with the prospect of a line of Catholic rulers and a return to the bloodshed of more than a hundred years before, Parliament abandoned James. The throne was offered to James's daughter, Mary, who had been raised a Protestant, and her husband, Prince William of Orange. In 1689 William and Mary as co-sovereigns ascended England's throne. The Glorious Revolution — as the events of 1688 came to be known — was quickly over. Much, however, had changed. James fled to France, from whence sporadic French-sponsored efforts would be made to return the Stuarts to England's throne. But English kings no longer enjoyed the prop of "divine right," as Parliament firmly asserted its prerogatives. Now sovereigns could not keep a standing army or levy taxes or suspend laws without Parliament's assent. The Toleration Act of 1689 softened the rigors of the Restoration years, granting toleration to all but Catholics and Unitarians. Finally, an Act of Settlement in 1701 explicitly ensured that all future kings or queens of England would be Protestant. For the island kingdom, the days of "popish plots" and Catholic coups were over. For the colonies, however, unsettled years loomed ahead.

COLONIAL UNREST AND PURITAN STRIFE

The effects of the Glorious Revolution rippled unevenly through the colonies. Even the Toleration Act had no immediate or general application across the ocean. In Massachusetts Bay, news of the Revolution resulted in the immediate overthrow of the much-despised Edmund Andros. In New York, ever-present factionalism erupted into rebellion that, though short-lived, shaped much of that colony's politics into the eighteenth century. The anti-Catholic aspect of England's Revolution had special meaning for the one colony governed by Catholic proprietors: Maryland. There, a non-Catholic majority supported a military coup that abruptly ejected all Catholics from local offices.

Meanwhile, American Puritanism faced internal discord and external challenge. In response to fears of its own weakness, New England's Puritan leadership sanctioned heavier penalties against such "outsiders" as Quakers and Baptists. Reproaching themselves and their people for moral failure or theological impurity, New England's Puritan divines turned inward, the infamous Salem witch hunt becoming the most enduring symbol of their tortured self-examination. Finally, Puritans debated vigorously the nature of church government itself, seeking to decide between a pure congregationalism and a more tightly controlled presbyterianism.

❧ *The Glorious Revolution in America*

The reign and religion of James II created anxieties in the colonies at least equal to those felt in England. The very year that a pro-French James came to the throne (1685), the French monarch, Louis XIV, revoked all toleration of Protestants in his country, driving thousands of Huguenots into exile. Catholic Spain continued to threaten Carolina on the southern frontier. If James were to succeed in returning England to the Roman Catholic fold, then what chance did the colonies have of maintaining their Protestant heritage? Hope lay only in the prospect of James's swift demise.

In 1688 and 1689 rumors of events transpiring or

Sir Edmund Andros on the Glorious Revolution in America, 1689

The Glorious Revolution was seen as less than glorious by Sir Edmund Andros, a loyal supporter of King James.

On the 18th of April, 1689, several of his majesty's council in New England having combined and conspired together with those who were magistrates and officers in the late charter government annually chosen by the people, and several other persons to subvert and overthrow the government and instead thereof to introduce their former common-wealth . . . [Andros is himself arrested, and] in the time of his confinement, being denied the liberty of discourse or conversation with any person, his own servants to attend him, or any communication or correspondence with any by letters, he hath no particular knowledge of their further proceedings, but hath heard and understands:

. . . [that] the confederates at Boston pos-sessed themselves of all his majesty's stores, arms, ammunition, and other implements of war, and disabled his majesty's man-of-war, the Rose frigate, by securing the commander and bringing her sails on shore. And at the same time, having imprisoned the secretary and some other officers, they broke open the secretary's office and seized and conveyed away all records, papers, and writings.

about to transpire kept the colonists edgy and suspicious. That it took weeks or months for reliable news to reach Boston or New York did not help matters at all. Ordinary citizens seemed to know what was going on before official channels informed royal governors or proprietors of exactly what was happening. This only aggravated suspicions and increased colonial unease. That overripe colonial rumor market, together with bureaucratic bungling and delay, led to open violence in Massachusetts, New York, and Maryland. Elsewhere, rebellion rumbled just below the surface.

In early April 1689, a newspaper arrived in Boston describing William of Orange's invasion of England. The person responsible for bringing in the paper from the West Indies was promptly arrested for spreading "Seditious and Treasonable" lies. Meanwhile, the taciturn and nervous Dominion governor, Edmund Andros, said nothing about the cataclysmic events abroad. Was Andros part of a plot to keep James on the throne or to bring him back from France? Were Massachusetts's liberties about to be scuttled by a royal governor resident in Boston?

Not if Bostonians could prevent it. On April 18 as many as a thousand armed men marched in the streets, arrested Andros, and threw him in prison along with several of his close advisers including the despised customs collector, Edward Randolph. It was time to call back the colony's aged governor, Simon Bradstreet, and return Massachusetts Bay to its traditional ways of governance. Randolph charged Cotton Mather and other local ministers with chief responsibility for the uprising, but it was in fact a widespread and popular rejection of royal authority, especially as manifest in the person of Andros. Acknowledging

that the local rebellion had broad support, Andros bemoaned the tendency of the colonists to assert their own will over England's. The Bay Colony, acting as though their old charter had never been revoked, proceeded (said Andros) to return to only those laws "made by themselves," to receive ships from "Scotland, Holland, Newfoundland, and other places prohibited," and to imprison all officials who tried to enforce the Navigation Acts.

When Massachusetts Bay received a second royal charter from William and Mary in 1691, it realized that its victory was not complete. The new charter gave the king the right to appoint the colony's governor, even as it severely restricted the broad powers of the General Court. Plymouth Colony and Maine were officially added to Massachusetts Bay, with royal control tightened over this enlarged territory. Also, property ownership rather than church membership became the essential qualification for voting; this change in the franchise weakened the influence of the churches in the affairs of state. The Bay Colony, though it had dislodged the Dominion of New England, had certainly not come close to overthrowing the authority of the empire itself.

In New York, unhappiness grew sharply when the colony was unceremoniously made an appendage to the Dominion of New England. Its own royal governor, Thomas Dongan, was recalled; Andros's subordinate, Francis Nicholson, became lieutenant governor. Most New Yorkers were no happier with James's Catholicism than Puritan New Englanders had been, and the Catholicism of former governor Dongan only further fanned the colony's restless anxiety. When Dongan was removed from office, moreover, he did not return to England, but stayed on in New York — with what schemes or plots in mind no one knew. That ignorance fed rumors rather than squelched them.

News of the April events in Boston reached New York in a few days, catapulting New Yorkers into action. Besieged by an angry and impatient citizenry who believed that they had not been told the truth about events in England, Nicholson decided in May to call a meeting of his councilors, city officials, and captains of the militia. Actions at this gathering indicated a government in total disarray, as well as one of questionable legal authority since Boston had thrown Andros into jail. Merchants on their own decided that customs duties should no longer be paid, partly because their government had no solid standing, partly because the customs collector was a Catholic, and partly because they did not want to pay duties in the first place. Still more rumors unnerved New York City, this time of a French and Indian attack upon Albany. That rumor proved false, but shaken colonists were ready for almost any sign of order and strength.

One of those militia captains, Jacob Leisler, arose as the man of the hour. The son of a German Calvinist minister, Leisler had emigrated to New Netherland in 1660, married the widow of a wealthy merchant, and during the years after Dutch rule collapsed moved in circles of influence and power. When Leisler led the militia in occupying New York City's fort, Nicholson and his advisers sailed for England. By early June Leisler ruled the city, and two months later he assumed the position of commander-in-chief of the entire colony. Leisler corrected Nicholson's "oversight" by publicly proclaiming William and Mary king and queen. This revolution in England, Leisler assumed, now gave legitimacy to his own in New York.

But legitimacy came begrudgingly from communities in New York — and not at all from the Privy Council back home. Leisler had to fight to get his authority recognized in Albany, which continued to be jealous of its own prerogatives, especially with regard to the fur trade. Drawing heavily upon Dutch support in New York City, Leisler alienated many of the English; some towns accused him of tyranny and some merchants sent petitions against him to England. When, finally, a new royal governor arrived in New York in March 1691, Leisler was ordered to surrender his forces and the fort that he controlled. Three times Leisler refused a direct order to surrender. When he finally did capitulate, he was arrested for treason and murder, tried, convicted, and hanged. Despite the apparent finality of this action,

an anti-Catholic, pro-Dutch Leislerian party remained a factor in New York politics for years.

Never a part of the Dominion of New England, Maryland had a different set of problems and grievances. Still a proprietary colony in 1688, Maryland had a Catholic proprietor (Lord Baltimore) and a Catholic governor. While many Marylanders were Catholic, the majority were not, giving to every grievance and suspicion a religious cast. In 1688 rumors flew that Catholics had allied themselves with Seneca Indians to destroy Protestants. When that same year James II's male heir was born, Marylanders were ordered to celebrate the birth of what was certain to be another Catholic monarch. Lord Baltimore demanded new oaths of fidelity as the ruling elite carefully explained that the divine right enjoyed by James had been conferred upon the proprietor and, through him, to his colonial Catholic officialdom. In January 1689 the proprietor's men called in all public arms for repair; given the circumstances, who could know whether the weapons would ever be returned?

By March 1689 all Maryland was in an uproar. Rumors flew that James II had been beheaded; other rumors had it that Lord Baltimore was supporting him in exile and fighting for his restoration. When Virginia in April declared William and Mary their lawful new sovereigns, Maryland made no similar declaration. When by July still no pledge of loyalty to the Protestant sovereigns had been voiced, another militia captain and member of the lower house, John Coode, seized the capital of Maryland, St. Mary's. Three months before, Coode had organized an "association in arms for the defense of the Protestant Religion." Having succeeded in his coup, Coode assured all that he fought only to save Maryland from Catholics and Indians, as well as to proudly proclaim William III and Mary II as king and queen of England and all its dominions.

Military actions swiftly over, the terms of surrender on August 1 dictated that no Catholic would hold military or civil office in Maryland. All those who had rebelled would be guaranteed safe passage to their homes, and all persons of the proprietary party who ceased struggling would be granted protection under the laws of England. In a long "Declaration of the Protestant Association," Coode and others reviewed their many grievances over Maryland's governance, pledged to call a "full and free Assembly" to build a new government, and promised that their colony would forever after be free of the "yoke of arbitrary government of tyranny and popery." By June 1691, Maryland had become

"A Witch Flies to the Sabbath on a Goat"   This woodcut from the late sixteenth or early seventeenth century depicted much of what was supposedly common knowledge about witchcraft. Here a naked woman who has surrendered her soul to demonic forces departs for a supernatural orgy, away on the back of a winged goat that symbolizes the Evil One. Her companions, male and female, prepare to follow her.

a royal colony, as both the Crown and the Protestant Association had hoped. No hangings or beheadings of the Maryland rebels took place; rather, the royal sovereigns not only commended them for their loyalty but also appointed several of their number to positions of authority in the new government. Lord Baltimore retained his land and his rents, but his power to rule had passed into other hands.

Behind all this upheaval lay the voice and authority of John Locke. In two treatises on civil government (in 1689 and 1690), Locke justified the Glorious Revolution in England. Civil government, he argued, was a compact — an agreement — by which the natural rights of humankind could best be preserved. Any government that failed to protect the fundamental rights of life, liberty, and property lost its legitimacy. Such a government not only *could* be overthrown, but *deserved* to be. Instinctively agreeing with Locke, Americans saw the Glorious Revolution as more than a change in England's royal rule. It led, colony by colony, to a greater assertion of rights against arbitrary or selfish authority; it promised a religious toleration for Protestant dissenters, though at the same time it strengthened anti-Catholic senti-

ments; and it convinced many that they were participants in the making of English history, rather than mere passive victims of directives from abroad. And in the eighteenth century, Americans would be quoting Locke again.

❧ Puritanism Under Pressure

The question of church membership received great attention in seventeenth-century New England and became, ultimately, the cause of serious division. Church membership should definitely not be, as in the Church of England, a mere formality, an indiscriminate inclusiveness that extended to all who lived in a particular parish. In Puritan society, the privileges of church membership should instead be extended only to those transformed by a profound and enduring spiritual experience.

THE HALF-WAY COVENANT

The logical demand that only "visible saints" be church members grew more difficult to defend when these members' infants were baptized, as they regularly were. For babies obviously could not undergo a conversion experience or profess a Christian creed. Yet they were in some sense part of the church covenant that bound together adult believers *and* their children. The normal expectation was that such children would later experience a conversion, at which point they could participate in the other sacrament of the Puritan church, the Lord's Supper. But what if these saints' children had no such experience and therefore never entered into the full communion of the church? That question became most acute when these young people themselves married and had children of their own. Should these *grandchildren* of the saints have the privileges of the covenant extended to them? Or was the purity of the church then sacrificed to some novel notion of grace "by heredity" rather than by personal and direct experience?

Such questions elicited neither easy nor unanimous answers. In 1657 and again in 1662 Puritans adopted a proposal that its opponents called the Half-Way Covenant. Under this agreement, children of the saints, if they accepted the discipline of the church and led morally respectable lives, could — even though unable to tell of their conversion — have their own children baptized. They could not, however, vote in church matters or participate in the Lord's Supper. Thus, these grandchildren of the first generation were within the church, but only "half-way." This compromise kept church membership from declining to a pathetic few, but it also raised questions about the loyalty of the second and third generations to the vision and conviction of the first. Adoption of this covenant remained controversial in New England, and most towns rejected it for years. Decades later, the standards for membership grew more relaxed and the necessity for these distinctions less pressing.

KEEPING PURITANISM PURE

If any should suggest, however, that Puritanism was growing soft, persecutorial vigilance would prove otherwise. When male and female Quaker missionaries penetrated the Bay Colony in the 1650s, alarmed authorities saw their preaching about an Inward Light as no better than the enthusiasm of Anne Hutchinson. Indeed, it was far worse, for of Anne Hutchinsons there had been only one; the Quakers, on the other hand, multiplied daily. Puritan authorities, therefore, exiled Quakers as soon as they identified them, warning such "fanatics" that, if they returned, they would suffer more than just exile. They did return: to be fined, flogged, mutilated, jailed, and exiled again — with more warnings that next time they would be put to death. Four Quakers nonetheless returned between 1659 and 1661, only to be hanged on Boston Common. One of the four, Mary Dyer from Rhode Island, urged those who sentenced her to die to "search with the light of Christ in ye" in order to determine who, in the end, had been "disobedient and deceived."

Baptists, pushing across the border from Rhode Island, also made Puritans uneasy, especially since they objected to all civil interference in religious affairs. The Half-Way Covenant dispute, moreover, played into the hands of Baptist evangelists who rejected infant baptism altogether, pointing out that church membership should consist only of baptized adult believers. No halfway compromise, therefore, was required. But Puritans were in no mood to be instructed by Baptists. When three Rhode Island Baptists ventured into Massachusetts territory in 1651, they were arrested, fined, and jailed — with one of their number flogged with thirty lashes in Boston's Market Square. This and other persecutions brought rebuke from Cromwellian England, which urged the Bay Colony to reconsider its rigid intolerance.

Two decades later, Puritans engaged in even more self-examination and self-criticism. The cost in lives and property during King Philip's War in 1675 caused many Puritans to wonder if that calamity came as a divine judgment upon a New England grown lax and indifferent. Added to that had been a series of major fires in Boston, the horror of a smallpox epidemic, and political pressures to impose Anglicanism on the colony. The hand of the Lord, many argued, seemed set against his people. In 1679 Increase Mather wrote of *The Necessity of Reformation, With the Expedients thereunto asserted,* which resulted in a "Reforming Synod" gathered to consider how New England and its people might best respond to the harsh turn of events. The Synod, meeting in the fall of 1679 and again in the spring of 1680, addressed itself to two questions: "What are the Evils that have provoked the Lord to bring his Judgments on New England?" and "What is to be done so that these Evils may be Reformed?"

In responding to that second question, the Synod called for a reaffirmation of faith in all its doctrinal purity, for a pledge to admit no one to the Lord's Supper "without making a personal and publick profession of their Faith and Repentance," and for a strict obedience to the discipline of the churches. The failure in moral discipline was, noted the Synod, the principal cause for the "degeneracy of the Rising Generation (so much complained of)." The clergy also took this occasion to point out that part of the problem lay in the failure to compensate ministers adequately, pay them promptly, and see that all churches were supplied fully. Indeed, some historians have argued that Puritanism was not so much in decline as was ministerial prestige and authority. The Reforming Synod, therefore, was designed to strengthen the clergy, especially the party associated with Increase Mather and his son Cotton.

THE SALEM WITCH TRIALS

Clerical prestige suffered even more a few years later when the witchcraft hysteria erupted in and around Salem, Massachusetts, in 1692. Even before this famous outbreak, New England courts had dealt with isolated cases of witchcraft — as indeed had courts all over Europe and in England. For in that mysterious realm beyond the world of the senses, great power resided: power for evil as well as for good, agents of Satan as well as of God. In the seventeenth-century Western world, the supernatural was neither distant nor dim, but immediately and forcefully at hand. Especially so in Salem in 1692.

The novelty in Salem was not the assumed reality of witches and wizards (women tended to outnumber men in this occupational specialty), nor was it that witchcraft was a crime, legally punishable by death — as the Bible prescribed. The novelty for America (not for Europe) was its singular persistence in Salem and its contagion. Anxiety over witchcraft took on epidemic proportions as charge followed charge, as seizure followed seizure, as court cases tumbled over one another, and as deaths by hanging inexorably increased. Before it was over, twenty persons died, most professing their innocence. Thus did Mary Bradbury assert that "I am the servant of Jesus Christ and have given myself up to him as my only lord and savior." But she was judged, nonetheless, to be the servant of Satan. Innocence was difficult to prove, since dreams of someone doing satanic deeds were initially accepted as evidence. Accusations, on the other hand, were easy to make, especially since they required little empirical evidence, only the dramatic recounting of visions.

Many explanations have been offered for Salem's witchcraft, from the psychological (mass hysteria) to the physiological (a bread mold that produced hallucinations). And many detailed studies have painstakingly traced the careers of the accusers and of the accused. It all began in the household of the Reverend Samuel Parris whose nine-year-old daughter, together with her eleven-year-old cousin, began behaving strangely. The concerned father did what any father would do: He called in a physician. Only after the doctor failed to find any physical explanation for the abnormal behavior did he — and the father — look elsewhere. "Elsewhere" today would probably mean psychiatric evaluation. But in the seventeenth century, "elsewhere" led to the world of evil spirits, of black magic, of persons knowingly or unknowingly functioning as agents of Satan. And so the girls, now including seven or eight more, were repeatedly asked, who or what was tormenting or bewitching them. By the end of February 1692, three names had been given, and three arrests were quickly made.

More and more accusations came, some probably provoked by the tensions between relatively impoverished Salem Village (where most of the accusers lived) and prosperous Salem Town, the home of most of the accused. What better way to even a score with an old enemy than by leveling a fearful charge so difficult to

disprove? Soon the jails were overcrowded and the docket of the local court jammed. As hanging followed hanging, some searched desperately not so much for the cause as for the cure. Two prestigious Boston clergymen, Increase and Cotton Mather — father and son — by the fall of 1692 threw their weight against proceedings that too readily accepted evidence that could at worst be faked, and at best was beyond proving or refuting. The Mathers, like most other learned people in Europe or America at the time, did not deny the reality of witchcraft. They only wished to limit if not suppress the raging epidemic that had broken out in Salem. They succeeded, no doubt helped by the royal governor, William Phips, who when his own wife was accused of witchcraft decided the time had come to bring the whole affair to an end. But for twenty victims and their families, the end had not come soon enough.

CONGREGATIONALISM AND LIBERTY

Late seventeenth-century Puritans disagreed, finally, over the precise form of their church government. Should their Congregational churches be truly independent, as the name implied, unhampered by any superchurch or even interchurch structure? Or should these separate institutions work together in a more coherent fashion "in supporting, preserving and well ordering the Interest of the Churches in the Country"? Those who answered affirmatively to the second question were accused of being presbyterianizers — that is, advocates of a more controlled church government. This position, embodied in the "Proposals of 1705," urged that all Massachusetts Bay clergy be gathered into regional associations that would in turn provide for a council that would meet, at least once a year, to "Inquire into the Condition of the Churches, and Advise such things as may be for the advantage of our holy Religion." But other Puritans believed that congregational liberty was endangered, as they asked what indeed was happening to "our holy Religion."

In Ipswich, Massachusetts, pastor John Wise took alarm at the effort — as he saw it — to turn Congregationalists into Presbyterians, to turn away from a precious freedom to an imposed order. As if royal authoritarianism from abroad were not enough of a problem, Wise argued, here were proposals that threatened an even more offensive homegrown authority. In so doing, this "law and order" party had "Out-King'd," "Out-Bishop't," and "Out-Pop't" all the kings, bishops, and popes that the Puritans and their ancestors had endured for the last hundred years. Could they no longer trust their own clergy to guide their own congregations? And if not, Wise thought, then perhaps the Puritans also needed to "advise" and "counsel" each other in their choice of marriage partners. "Why may not particular Beds be overruled, as well as particular Churches?" So strong were Wise's words on behalf of liberty that when revolutionary passions mounted in the 1770s, some Massachusetts patriots decided that his earlier tract required reprinting. Though the enemy had changed, the cause of liberty remained.

Imperial Wars, Imperial Interests

Colonists, often mired in the details of local politics, economic competitiveness, and religious faithfulness, did not necessarily see their activities or interests in a worldwide context. From the imperial point of view, however, such petty concerns deserved little if any attention. What mattered were the interests of Britain on the international scene: the empire's security and strength, its wealth and its national prospects for generations to come. Only to the extent that foreign plantations could help the mother country maintain its global position did they command the notice of statesmen and lords, of bishops and kings, of admirals and generals.

For most of the eighteenth century, Great Britain's chief preoccupation was with France. A series of Anglo-French wars pitted Europe's two most powerful nations against each other; and the two nations' North American colonists were inevitably drawn into the conflicts. Spain, though it could not match either England or France in military might in the eighteenth century, nonetheless continued to rule an enormous empire in the Western Hemisphere, cornering lucrative markets, threatening foreign ships, and resisting British territorial expansion. Spain's persisting presence in Florida constituted at best an irritant to English colonists in Carolina, at worst an active threat to life and property. To counter it, Great Britain established one more colony, this one named after George II.

❧ *King William's and Queen Anne's Wars*

When in 1689 William of Orange was named England's sovereign along with his wife Mary, he had already endured (as leader of the Netherlands) enough of Louis XIV's Catholic alliances and territorial ambition to ready him for an Anglo-Dutch front against the French.

England's first military encounter against his old enemy, King William's War (called in Europe the War of the League of Augsburg, 1689-1697), involved those colonies closest to and most wary of the French in Canada and the Mississippi Valley. For half a century, England and her colonies had anxiously watched France's efforts to establish a stronger presence in North America. The Jesuits had wielded enormous authority in New France throughout the first half of the seventeenth century, but in 1659 a papal representative brought greater centralization from the ecclesiastical quarter. On the civil side, France in 1663 moved to take direct control of its colony rather than administer it through the Company of One Hundred Associates. France took bold steps to create an orderly and rational plan of government, to encourage further emigration to North America, and to discourage bachelorhood among its settlers. In short, by 1670 France showed its determination to compete on even terms with other European states that had moved far ahead in the Western Hemisphere.

In this competition, France was greatly aided when a fur trader, Louis Joliet, joined a Jesuit, Jacques Marquette, in 1673 to explore the upper reaches of the Mississippi River. They paddled down as far as the Arkansas River, where the Spanish presence prevented them from going on to the Gulf of Mexico. Marquette's maps and journals, however, later made possible France's ultimate reach all the way to the Gulf. By the end of the century, probing the entire Mississippi Valley gave France a territorial claim in North America that threatened to rival Spain's and England's while the fur-trapping *coureurs de bois* had already given the French an important economic presence in interior America.

Led by such visionaries as Count Frontenac and La Salle, New France continued to assert itself, jeopardizing British interests in North America. The threat was real even though French colonial population — about ten thousand in the 1680s — lagged far behind that of New England, or even Massachusetts Bay. New England and New York, which had the most to lose, were readier than the other colonies to do their part in defending English claims against French in North America. They were even readier to encourage the Indians, notably the Iroquois, in attacks on French outposts and villages. The French, with their Algonkian-speaking western Indian allies, fought back — responding with a slaughter in Schenectady comparable to the one inflicted by the Iroquois on a French settlement near Montreal.

Massachusetts conceived a grand strategy to take Quebec, but the force under Sir William Phips, afflicted by storm, smallpox, and inadequate military might, retreated before Quebec's stubborn refusal to surrender. "Thus, by the evident Hand of Heaven," Cotton Mather wrote, "as well-formed an enterprise as perhaps was ever made by the New Englanders most unhappily carried." A treaty ending the European war (the Peace of Ryswick) settled nothing in North America: all conquests by either side were to be returned within six months.

The uneasy peace lasted only five years, and in 1702 an even longer war erupted. The War of Spanish Succession, known in the colonies as Queen Anne's War, raged until 1713. The earlier war had ended in a stalemate because the forces were so evenly balanced. In 1701, however, Philip V, grandson of France's Louis XIV, succeeded to the Spanish crown. This created the dismaying possibility that Spain and France might join against England, the Netherlands, or others in the endless contest to see who would dominate Europe and North America. When France and Spain concluded long-term trade agreements and cooperated in trying to subdue the rebellious Spanish Netherlands, England determined that it had no choice but to declare war, which it did in May 1702.

In North America, the French had already swept with greater assurance down the Mississippi, founding Biloxi in 1699 and Mobile in 1701. Carolina fur traders, accustomed to roam freely toward the Mississippi River, now suffered from an ever-stronger French presence. If western Indians hesitated over whether to throw their weight on the side of the French or the English, the French each passing year looked increasingly powerful — and the better ally. The Iroquois, having borne the brunt of French attacks and disappointed with the inconclusive outcome of King William's War, signed treaties of neutrality with both the French and the English. Since the Iroquois had traditionally been strong allies of the English, this neutrality only heartened the French. Eastern Indians, the Abenaki among others, cast their lot with the French, joining them in bloody raids upon Wells, Maine, in 1703 and Deerfield, Massachusetts, in the winter of 1704. In Deerfield, a village of fewer than three hundred, forty were killed, while more than one hundred colonists were taken prisoner and forced to march to Canada in a bitterly cold February.

Finding itself under attack, New England had to fight back, even as it called upon the other colonies for help. None came from that source, though the British by 1709 sent troops and ships to assist the beleaguered New Englanders. The French town of Port Royal

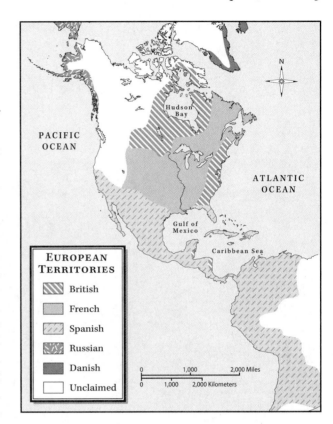

in Acadia (present-day Nova Scotia) fell before an English attack, leading English strategists to believe by 1711 that a massive strike against Quebec would bring New France to abject surrender and all of Canada into Queen Anne's domain. But the naval expedition against Quebec failed, undone by a timid admiral and contrary currents in the St. Lawrence River. Again, the battles in North America yielded indecisive results. By the terms of the Peace of Utrecht (1713), however, England did gain Newfoundland and most of Acadia south of the Bay of Fundy, except for Cape Breton. England also gained Hudson Bay. In Europe, France and Spain would remain separate and independent kingdoms, but they agreed to recognize — at long last — the legitimacy of the Protestant succession in England. For the most part, however, France's vast claims in the Canadian interior and in the Mississippi Valley went unchallenged.

Spain fought in Queen Anne's War as France's ally. Even before the fighting began, however, Spain found it necessary to defend its Florida foothold, especially around St. Augustine. When the English settled Carolina in the 1660s, Spain rightly suspected that their new neighbors would intrude upon their claims in Florida. The Treaty of Madrid in 1670 tried to forestall inevitable conflicts by promising that English claims would extend no farther south than Port Royal, South Carolina

Marquette and Joliet Discover the Mississippi River   Descending from the Great Lakes, the French fur trader Louis Joliet and the Jesuit priest Father Marquette in 1674 became the first Europeans to see the Mississippi River. Accompanied by Indians, they got as far south as the juncture with the Arkansas before retracing their route back north. This illustration dates from the late nineteenth century.

— just north of the Savannah River. But the Carolinians' Indian trade recognized no boundaries, and settlers began migrating beyond the Treaty of Madrid line. In 1680, without authorization from England, Carolinians led an Indian raiding party against a Spanish outpost on St. Catherine's Island, about one hundred miles south of Charleston and well beyond the treaty line. Three years later English privateers burned another Spanish outpost, this time near St. Augustine itself. The Spanish responded in 1686 by attacking a Scottish settlement near Port Royal, and only a violent storm prevented them from moving against Charleston by ship. The next year Spain responded further by building the solid stone fortress at St. Augustine (still standing) to thwart future forays from either Carolina or the sea. In fact, the Spanish presence in Florida then consisted of little besides missions and fortifications.

When England declared war upon both Spain and France in 1702, some Carolina settlers eagerly seized the opportunity to drive the Spanish out of Florida. In the fall of 1702 Governor James Moore of South Carolina led several hundred colonists and Indians to St. Augustine to obtain its surrender and cover himself with glory. With a force perhaps only half that size, the Spanish quickly sent a ship to Havana with an urgent plea for reinforcements. The Spanish retreated to the fortress, leaving the small town of St. Augustine undefended and deserted. A seven weeks' siege of the fortress brought Moore no closer to victory. When Spanish reinforcements did arrive, Moore had to content himself with burning the town and returning to Charleston. The next year, Moore, no longer governor, led an expedition into western Florida where he destroyed helpless Spanish missions, razed Indian villages, and brought about a thousand captive Indians back to Charleston, most of whom were sold into slavery.

In the Peace of Utrecht, Spain was obliged to cede Gibraltar and the Mediterranean island of Minorca to England. Britain also won the right to import nearly five thousand slaves annually into the Spanish colonies and once a year to send a single trading vessel, loaded with British goods, to South or Central America. But as with France, the treaty settled little of the North American contest for empire. Spain used her Indian allies to harass and harm the Carolinians, and especially to discourage any settlement south of Port Royal. (Spain was widely assumed to have been the off-stage instigator of the 1715 Yamassee War.) Clearly Spain stubbornly refused to be dislodged from North America, but equally clearly Spain would never accept Carolina agents and traders in the interior. England needed to take some bold step to secure the much-disputed lands between Florida and Carolina.

❧ *Colonial Reorganization*

While fighting colonial wars and pursuing diplomacy, England also took steps to tighten control over the colonies. Not only must the interests of mercantilism be served, but the interests of national defense as well. Colonial governors were held personally responsible for the strict enforcement of all navigation laws, with a heavy fine for any who failed. And whether appointed by the king or not, all governors were now required to answer directly to him and his Privy Council. If all abuses could not be eliminated, they could at least be "regulated."

Hoping to eradicate abuses entirely, England in 1696 created the Board of Trade. The new agency had a paid staff — unlike the Lords of Trade — for whom colonial matters were the primary, full-time responsibility. In the first decade or so of its existence, the Board played a central role in the approval of all colonial governors, in the review of all colonial laws, and in the hearing of all grievances concerning imperial policies or their local enforcement. With the Bishop of London as an *ex officio* member, the Board regarded colonial religious matters as well within its purview. Down to the American Revolution, all the colonies had to reckon with this powerful Board and its presidents.

Three years later king and Parliament cooperated against another irritant: piracy. In passing the Act for the More Effectual Suppression of Piracy in 1699, Parliament considered it wise not to depend upon local juries to bring pirates to justice. The act created special courts, without juries, to hear all pirate cases and to administer more justice than mercy to those who insisted on twisting the tail of the British lion. The famous Captain (William) Kidd, who was supposed to suppress piracy in King William's War, turned pirate himself and he

eventually was arrested, tried, and executed in London in 1701. But Kidd was only the most notorious offender, for many colonists were accused of aligning themselves with the pirates and sharing their booty.

Two religious agencies arose at the same time, both intended to bring an Anglican unity to the colonies' scandalous religious diversity. An organizer of great vision, clergyman Thomas Bray, in 1699 formed the Society for Promoting Christian Knowledge and, two years later, the even more important Society for the Propagation of the Gospel in Foreign Parts. Operating with state encouragement, as well as that of the Bishop of London, but with privately collected funds, both organizations hoped to make Anglicanism dominant everywhere from New Hampshire to South Carolina. The Society for the Propagation of the Gospel proved especially effective in hiring missionaries to establish stations in America and eventually build Anglican churches where none had existed. Bray's efforts complemented those of the Board of Trade; together they would bring to all the colonies a greater uniformity in political, economic, and religious life. Lords, Commons, king, and church alike agreed that the time had come not just to launch colonies, but to rule them as well.

❧ *Outpost of Empire: Georgia*

Near the beginning of the eighteenth century, the English government strengthened its home base by consummating a union with Scotland in 1707. At this point, Scotland lost its own legislature and acquired representation in Parliament. The resulting United Kingdom — Great Britain — was now spared distracting trade wars with its northern neighbor. In the same period the seesawing royal-parliamentary struggle for power finally came to an end in Parliament's favor. With the advent of Sir Robert Walpole in the new office of prime minister in 1721, the first minister and his cabinet overshadowed the king and his Privy Council in making policy. Walpole sought to keep Great Britain at peace — but not at any price. Disputes over the lands between South Carolina and Florida needed to be resolved before they led to open war between Britain and Spain, and in Walpole's view the resolution needed to be in Britain's favor.

The last British colony established in North America was founded with two goals in mind. First, the land between the Savannah and Altamaha rivers would be a buffer, keeping Spain and her Indian allies from terrorizing Carolinians, from interfering with their fur

Captain Kidd Howard Pyle, a famous American illustrator of children's books who strove for historical accuracy, painted this dashing image of the infamous pirate Captain Kidd at the turn of the twentieth century, capturing the spirit of the pirates who ravaged shipping in the Caribbean around 1700.

In 1732, King George II granted Oglethorpe and a board of trustees a charter for the colony. Having served his country honorably in war against Spain, Oglethorpe hoped to defeat or at least contain Spain by political means. His vision, however, was more than just political. Like many of the philanthropists and clergy of eighteenth-century England, the general wished to improve the status of Africans and Indians in America and strike a blow on behalf of religion and learning that would reverberate throughout the continent. Georgia would be different: no hard liquor would be allowed; no slavery of either Indians or Africans would be permitted; idleness and luxury would be scorned. The poor would have their way paid across the ocean, and land given them freely, along with cattle "and subsistence till such time as they can build their houses and clear some of their land." In this fashion, Oglethorpe proposed, "many families who would otherwise starve will be provided for and made masters of houses and lands."

In February 1733 Oglethorpe and forty families arrived to lay out the town of Savannah. Within five years, four other villages appeared. But all this sounds more prosperous and booming than Oglethorpe's efforts in fact turned out to be. Georgia did attract religious dissenters: persecuted Lutherans from Austria, Moravians from Saxony, Scottish Presbyterians who settled the town of Darien, and Jews sponsored by the London Sephardic community. But all this was not enough to save the utopian dreams of its founders or to promote prosperity. Restrictions on landholding were

trade, and from quietly advancing Spain's territorial ambitions northward. Second, the new colony would also alleviate a severe problem at home: jails filled with the "worthy poor" whose only crime was their poverty. Simply to obtain these wretches' release from prison was, in the words of the philanthropic General James Oglethorpe, to grant them "the privilege of starving at large." Something more needed to be done for them and Georgia could become that "something."

relaxed to encourage more settlers; slavery was permitted in 1750; liquor was imported to see if it might help the colony economically, but it did not. Settlers — about half of them debtors — complained that the colony had become "an object of pity to friends, and of insult, contempt, and ridicule to enemies." By 1752, Georgia could claim a population of just over 2,000 Europeans, at a time when Massachusetts had a population of over 180,000, Pennsylvania over 110,000, and South Carolina nearly as many. In that same year, the trustees of Georgia, disillusioned with their philanthropic venture, agreed that the colony, like so many private efforts before it, should be turned over to the king. Georgia's further evolution would be along lines far different from the vision of Oglethorpe.

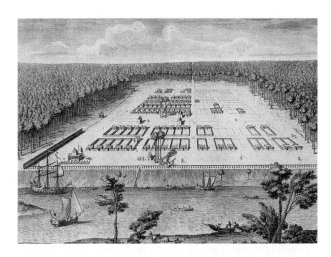

Savannah In 1733 the port of Savannah was hacked out of the surrounding forest and became the capital of the new British colony of Georgia. Savannah was laid out on an orderly grid plan, as this contemporary engraving shows.

CONCLUSION: ESTABLISHING STABILITY AND ORDER

In the century between the 1640s and the 1730s, England went through major transitions: from Civil War to Restoration, from a Glorious Revolution to union with Scotland, from alliances with the Dutch to wars with France and Spain. In that same period, colonial North America filled in the geographical gaps between New England and Virginia, so that English settlements dotted the Atlantic seaboard from Maine to Georgia. But French settlements had also enlarged, from Montreal to Mobile. The fate of the North American continent was not yet settled, nor was England's governance of its colonies uniform in operation or achievements.

By the middle of the eighteenth century, with Britain's last foreign plantation on the American mainland now just another royal colony, colonial life had in most places taken on a stability and order that would have been difficult to imagine a century before. Towns and plantations, schools and churches, marked and shaped the land. Families had seen parents, grandparents, and great-grandparents buried in American soil. Children for several generations had known only the local woods, meadows, and rivers, with memories of any other land as distant and irrelevant as were their seventeenth-century ancestors' memories of William the Conqueror or Charles the Bald. Colonial institutions had by 1750 developed a life of their own, molding in turn the lives of those that had fashioned them.

❈ IN THEIR OWN WORDS

Trustees of Georgia Encourage Settlers, 1735

The "worthy poor" with whom Oglethorpe intended to populate Georgia were promised the following to get them started in their new lives:

The Trustees intend this year to lay out a county and build a new town in Georgia. They will give to such persons as they send

upon the charity, to every man: a watch-coat; a musket and bayonet; a hatchet; a hammer; a handsaw; a shod [metal] shovel or spade; a broad hoe; a narrow hoe; a gimlet [drill]; a drawing knife; an iron pot, and a pair of pot-hooks; a frying pan; and a public grindstone to each ward or village. Each working man will have for his maintenance in the colony for one year . . . 312 lbs. of beef or pork; 104 lbs. of rice; 104 lbs. of Indian corn or peas; 104

lbs. of flour; 1 pint of strong beer a day to a man when he works and not otherwise; 52 quarts of molasses for brewing beer; 16 lbs. of cheese; 12 lbs. of butter; 8 oz. of spice; 12 lbs. of sugar; 4 gallons of vinegar; 24 lbs. of salt; 12 quarts of lamp oil; 1 lb. spun cotton; 12 lbs. of soap. . . . The trustees pay their passage from England to Georgia; and in the voyage they will have in every week four beef days, two pork days, and one fish day.

SUGGESTED READING

Francis J. Bremer, *Shaping New England: Puritan Clergymen in Seventeenth-Century England and New England* (1994). A major student of Puritanism successfully bridges the geographical gap between the northern colonies and the mother country; he demonstrates, among other things, how many of the Puritan ministers in the early years had studied together at Cambridge and maintained their friendship and mutual support, though separated by the Atlantic Ocean.

Paul Boyer and Stephen Nissenbaum, *Salem Possessed: The Social Origins of Witchcraft* (1974). Thoroughly researched, this book offers a novel and persuasive interpretation for the persistence of the Salem accusations and executions.

Harold E. Davis, *The Fledgling Province: Social and Cultural Life in Colonial Georgia* (1976). Discusses carefully the contrary purposes that coincided to bring Georgia into being.

David Eltis, *The Rise of African Slavery in the Americas* (2000). With an impressive use of quantitative data, Eltis has provided a superb history of his subject in North and South America, as well as the Caribbean.

Jack P. Greene, *Pursuits of Happiness: The Social Development of Early Modern British Colonies and the Formation of American Culture* (1988). With an emphasis on colonial evolution, the author contrasts the regional features of New England, the Middle Colonies, the Chesapeake, and the Lower South.

Douglas Edward Leach, *Arms for Empire* (1973). With meticulous care, the author covers the British colonies' military involvement prior to the Revolution.

Hugh T. Lefler and William S. Powell, *Colonial North Carolina: A History* (1973). Authoritative and engaging account of a colony that in the colonial period received more than its share of bad press.

James T. Lemon, *The Best Poor Man's Country* (1972). Giving an unusual amount of attention to the role of the land, the author throws an important light upon the early years of Pennsylvania's development, nicely joining the disciplines of history and geography.

Jill Lepore, *The Name of War: King Philip's War and the Origins of American Identity* (1998). The author sees this costly conflict as a defining moment in the relationships between the English and the Indians.

David S. Lovejoy, *The Glorious Revolution in America* (1972). A first-rate examination of the far-reaching reverberations of the 1688 events in England.

Mary Beth Norton, *In the Devil's Snare: The Salem Witchcraft Crisis of 1692* (2002). With careful attention to the context of conflicts on the frontier, Norton places the Salem episode — or better, Essex County — in a broader frame.

Robert C. Ritchie, *The Duke's Province: A Study of New York Politics and Society, 1664-1691* (1977). Examines the critical period after England seized from the Dutch their major possession on the American mainland.

Jean R. Soderlund, ed., *William Penn and the Founding of Pennsylvania, 1680-1684* (1983). With magnificent detail and carefully edited documents, this volume offers indispensable guidance to both the clear vision and the often confounding reality of Penn's colony.

John Thornton, *Africa and Africans in the Making of the Atlantic Slave World, 1400-1680* (1992). In a controversial study, the author argues that the slave trade could never have reached the scale that it did without the active cooperation and control of some African leaders.

John C. Van Horne, ed., *Religious Philanthropy and Colonial Slavery* (1985). Utilizing the correspondence of "Dr. Bray's Associates," Van Horne provides a novel perspective on both eighteenth-century England and the early years of Georgia.

SUGGESTIONS FOR FURTHER READING

Carol Berkin, *First Generations: Women in Colonial America* (1996).

Robert M. Bliss, *Revolution and Empire: English Politics and the American Colonies in the Seventeenth Century* (1990).

Francis J. Bremer, *Puritanism: Transatlantic Perspectives on a Seventeenth-Century Anglo-American Faith* (1993).

Elaine G. Breslaw, *Tituba, Reluctant Witch of Salem: Devilish Indians and Puritan Fantasies* (1997).

Kathleen M. Brown, *Good Wives, Nasty Wenches, and Anxious Patriarchs: Gender, Race, and Power in Colonial Virginia* (1996).

Lois Green Carr, Philip D. Morgan, and Jean B. Russo, eds., *Colonial Chesapeake Society* (1989).

John Demos, *Entertaining Satan: Witchcraft and the Culture of Early New England* (rev. ed., 2004).

Richard S. Dunn, *Sugar and Slaves: The Rise of the Planter Class in the English West Indies, 1624-1713* (1972).

J. William Frost, *A Perfect Freedom: Religious Liberty in Pennsylvania* (1990).

Judith S. Graham, *Puritan Family Life: The Diary of Samuel Sewall* (2000).

Francis Jennings et al., eds., *The History and Culture of the Iroquois Diplomacy* (1985).

Carol F. Karlsen, *The Devil in the Shape of a Woman* (1987).

Yasuhide Kawashima, *Puritan Justice and the Indian: White Man's Law in Massachusetts, 1630-1763* (1986).

Ned C. Landsman, *Scotland and Its First American Colony, 1683-1765* (1985).

Rebecca Larson, *Daughters of Light: Quaker Women Preaching and Prophesying in the Colonies and Abroad, 1700-1775* (1999).

Gloria L. Main, *Tobacco Colony: Life in Early Maryland, 1650-1720* (1982).

Robert Middlekauf, *The Mathers: Three Generations of Puritan Intellectuals, 1596-1728* (1971).

Daniel K. Richter and James H. Merrell, eds., *Beyond the Covenant Chain: The Iroquois and Their Neighbors in Indian North America, 1600-1800* (1987).

Robert C. Ritchie, *Captain Kidd and the War Against Pirates* (1986).

Jean R. Soderlund, *Quakers and Slavery: A Divided Spirit* (1985).

Laurel Thatcher Ulrich, *Good Wives: Image and Reality in the Lives of Northern New England, 1650-1750* (1982).

Richard Waterhouse, *A New World Gentry: The Making of a Merchant and Planter Class in South Carolina, 1670-1770* (1989).

Stephanie G. Wolf, *Urban Village: Population, Community, and Family Structure in Germantown, Pennsylvania, 1683-1800* (1976).

Peter H. Wood, *Black Majority: Negroes in Colonial South Carolina from 1670 Through the Stono Rebellion* (1974).

4

From Plantations to Provinces
The Evolution of American Society and Culture, 1660-1763

B Y 1760 COLONIAL population on the American mainland had reached well over one and one-half million, roughly one quarter of them African Americans. The major cities of Boston, New York, and Philadelphia boasted populations in 1760 of around 15,000, 18,000, and 23,000, respectively. Setting aside gigantic London, these urban populations compared favorably with most English or Scottish towns.

The population surge in the first half of the eighteenth century resulted to a great degree from the presence of *families*. The early days when the number of males greatly outnumbered females in the colonies had now passed; natural increase could begin to compete with the steady arrival of immigrants. Since the eighteenth century only slowly developed a passion for counting things, all the numbers are approximations; statistics on America become more reliable only after the first federal census in 1790. The informed guesses of a generation before, however, demonstrated that the American colonies had arrived at a position of some stature, no longer mere stragglers desperately clinging to a few feet of rocky or marshy coastline.

Nor were Americans by 1760 any longer of a single ethnic stock, even among whites. Germans had moved heavily into the Middle Colonies in the first half of the eighteenth century, with Scots and Scots-Irish in that same time period also becoming a conspicuous presence in New Jersey and Pennsylvania. In significantly smaller numbers, French Protestant exiles settled in Charleston, South Carolina, and New Rochelle, New York. The most conspicuous racial or ethnic diversity

New York City, 1742-1744　By the middle of the eighteenth century New York City was already fast becoming a cosmopolitan town with a busy harbor. The mapmaker has illustrated points of interest at the top of the map, among them City Hall, prominent individuals' homes, and several churches.

was, of course, created by the presence of Africans, who formed a majority of the population in South Carolina and a very sizable force elsewhere in the South. In Virginia, the slave population had grown from a modest 3,000 in 1680 to an imposing 120,000 by 1760. In all of New England, by contrast, out of a total population of nearly one-half million, slaves numbered only around five or six thousand.

Virginia, though it had no major cities, was nonetheless the most populous colony, with around 346,000 inhabitants, followed by Massachusetts and Pennsylvania (then including Delaware), each with more than 200,000 persons. The smallest colonies were Rhode Island, New Hampshire, and Georgia. All other colonies had populations of around 100,000 or more, with their inhabitants widely scattered in small villages and on family farms. All colonial cities were coastal cities; major urban centers would not develop inland until the nineteenth century. The colonial institutions that mattered most, therefore, were not those limited to the cities, but those that sprang up in small villages and the open countryside as well.

The colonial economy was essentially a rural economy. And the fundamental institution of the family made its living, reared its children, and established its values in far greater numbers on the farms than in the

cities. Some families met the demand for labor wholly within their own circle; others turned to servant and slave labor to maintain the household, clear the fields and plant the crops, and help with the harvest that might go to a market only a few miles away — or might reach commercial centers across the Atlantic. With all this gathering and spending, mothers and fathers also concerned themselves with the education of their children. Somehow, formally or informally, the values and knowledge of the present generation needed to be passed on to the next.

In the decades just prior to the American Revolution, colonial culture expressed itself in a variety of forms. Frequently viewed from abroad as a cultural desert, eighteenth-century America made significant contributions in literature and the arts, in religion and education, in science and in law. But quite apart from any recognition in the Western world at large, the colonists themselves enjoyed a cultural life of surprising vitality and depth. In the life of the mind and the spirit, citizens of the New World were not content to be mere borrowers and imitators. On their own, they would create a culture that would be something more than Europe once removed.

COLONIAL SOCIETY

In economic as in family life, the dominant white population developed more intricate patterns that revealed wide diversity from colony to colony. At the same time African slaves struggled with harsh codes, unfavorable environments, and numerous efforts to ignore or destroy their culture. In the midst of these tensions, attempts to provide appropriate education for children

Eighteenth-Century American Folk Art　This hand-painted pie plate, decorated in 1793, is a typical adornment of everyday household objects. The fanciful design conveys no higher symbolic purpose than a desire to bring simple enjoyment into family life.

took forms as varied as America's landscapes: from the southern plantations to the towns of New England.

❧ Pre-Industrial Colonial Economies

In treating colonial economic history, scholars tend to concentrate on foreign trade, for this was so often the friction point between England and its plantations. By the end of the seventeenth century, however, the colonial economy rested heavily upon the agricultural staples produced and consumed at home.

WORKING THE LAND

As in most of the Western world in this pre-industrial age, in the colonies the cultivation of land was the chief occupation and the chief source of wealth. The ready availability of land and generous early grants to settlers ensured that the American farmer tended to do well — much better than his European counterpart. About half the white population owned and worked their own farms with little or no slave labor. The large plantations that did employ great numbers of slaves engaged in the export business: tobacco and timber, rice and indigo, and later wheat and cattle. But the abundance of land made all the difference in the seventeenth century and well into the eighteenth — especially to farmers who were willing to move farther inland, beyond the initial areas of settlement. In addition, farmers could rise steadily on the social scale: more land, more political participation, more social and economic stability. Some indentured servants, if they survived their terms, might obtain land and thereafter acquire most or all of the privileges that England associated with the "freeholder."

Farmers managed to produce enough food to feed their families, their servants or slaves, with often enough left over to sell or barter locally. Planting corn, wheat, barley, oats, and rye as staple crops, the farmer (or more often his wife) also kept a vegetable garden and an orchard. Cattle, sheep, and hogs provided additional food, as well as hides and wool for clothing and other uses. Horses, which could feed on the grass or the agricultural surplus, were put to many tasks in transportation, hauling, and plowing. Chickens and other fowl added to the storehouse of food supplies on most farms. Crops flourished generally without extensive fertilizing; when the fertility of the soil began to decline, farmers simply moved to another plot of ten or twenty acres while the land lay fallow to regain fertility. Once initial supplies of farm animals were obtained, careful husbandry insured an ever-increasing number of cows, hogs, horses, sheep, and chickens to match the fertility of the soil. The rural population — the vast majority of all Americans — by 1760 could count on having the basic necessities of food, clothing, and shelter. Compared to most European peasants, they lived well.

Corn was an especially popular crop since it could be grown in all the colonies and since it could be harvested over a long season. Adopting the Indians' technique of "hilling" the land into small mounds, colonists planted corn in fields not yet completely cleared. After the corn stalk reached a satisfactory height, beans could be planted between the mounds; sometimes the cornstalks served as ready-made beanpoles. Wheat developed as a major export crop in the Chesapeake region as well as farther to the north in Pennsylvania, New York, and even into New England. Much of the wheat, however, was consumed locally since most colonists preferred wheat flour to either corn or rye flour. Rice was produced in the South, but more for export than for local consumption, while tobacco and indigo remained major exports for the foreign markets.

FAMILY FARMS

Farm families were economic units. At harvest time, the farmer called on all hands to bring in the crop — servants, children, and wives. Female labor, whether of wives or servants, was not limited to the home, even apart from the season of harvesting. In the absence of a major labor force, such as on the southern plantation, women helped till the soil, planted and cared for the garden, tended the orchard, milked the cows, gathered the eggs, cured the meat, dressed the hides — and so on. In the house, women cooked, washed, cleaned, sewed, and spun; all this, of course, was simply added to their unique tasks of bearing, nursing, and training the young children. As South

Dockside at a Virginia Tobacco Warehouse   Dating from 1777, this English illustration shows a typical scene as tobacco is loaded for shipment across the Atlantic. Because colonial Virginia lacked important seaports, tobacco was shipped from docks all along the navigable rivers and the Chesapeake Bay. Planters from the interior had their slaves roll cured tobacco to these docks in large barrels, called hogsheads, similar to those shown here.

Carolina's Eliza Lucas Pinckney wrote in the 1740s, "I am resolved to be a good Mother to my children, to pray for them, to set them good examples, to be careful both of their souls and bodys, to watch over their tender mind, to carefully root out the first appearing and buddings of vice, and to install piety, virtue, and true religion among them."

If all this was understandably a large order for the rural housewife and mother, urban women also sometimes had to assume additional specialized responsibilities. They ran inns, operated grocery stores, and sold millenary goods. When their husbands went to war or left their wives widows, then the wives became managers of the shop, small farm, or plantation. Unaccustomed as most were to economic independence, some grew to appreciate their new status and to advise other young women to pursue "as much independence as circumstances will allow."

AGRICULTURE AND TRADE

Since cash was in short supply in the eighteenth century, trade frequently took the form of barter. In addition, a single staple crop — tobacco, for example — might serve as money. Taxes, court fees, and even salaries were payable in tobacco. In Virginia, farmers who deposited their tobacco crop in warehouses received receipts that could circulate as readily as cash. Merchants, on the other hand, utilized a form of "book credit" that would be paid off with the arrival of the next shipment of goods, once again avoiding the necessity of hard currency or coin. In fact, since England forbade the export of her own coinage, the colonists used the silver and gold coins from Spain's New World when only a cash transaction would do.

Agriculture, of course, provided not only the livelihood for most Americans, but in addition a favorable balance of trade a good deal of the time. In 1700 the leading exports from the mainland colonies were tobacco, dyestuffs, skins, and hides. By 1725 rice had become an important export, its importance increasing steadily to 1760. Other less significant exports in the first half of the eighteenth century included timber, whale oil, and rum. But tobacco dominated the mainland exports, just as sugar did in the Caribbean.

Principally from the Chesapeake Bay, tobacco flowed to England and Scotland, and from there (after appropriate tariffs had been paid) to continental markets. Although Virginia tobacco was at first of poor quality, it improved so rapidly that by around 1700 Chesapeake tobacco was preferred above all others. Tobacco demanded careful cultivation, and small farmers and plantation owners grew more efficient in drying the leaf in a tobacco barn for three to six weeks, then grading, packing, and shipping the crop to a warehouse prior to transporting it abroad. Even a small farmer could, with the help of his wife and children, cultivate enough tobacco to bring in a cash income of around $1,000 per year, in addition to the foodstuffs grown and cattle raised. On

a large Virginia plantation such as that of Robert Carter, the amount of tobacco sold in a single year (1736) reached the equivalent of about $50,000 — an immense sum for the eighteenth century.

Tobacco made so much money for the farmer, the king, and all the middlemen in between that it became the measure by which the economy of the Chesapeake colonies rose or fell. Merchants extended credit to farmers who suffered a hard year, so that nothing would interfere with the next year's steady production. Or farmers could receive an "advance" on next year's crop, with which they could buy more land or slaves and keep production booming. London controlled the tobacco markets for the first century or so, but by 1740 Glasgow merchants were paying cash in Virginia as soon as the crop was loaded on the ship, rather than requiring the farmer to wait until the crop was sold in London weeks or months later. Since the centers for distribution remained abroad, and since Virginia and Maryland had such inviting waterways, no

cities developed in the Chesapeake region until the late eighteenth century.

From Pennsylvania northward, the farmers' surpluses often traveled no farther than the consumer markets developing in such urban centers as Philadelphia, New York, Newport, and Boston. Where large-scale foreign trade did grow, the products were more often processed commodities, such as rum and flour, rather than agricultural produce. Furs continued to be shipped from New York; lumber and wool from Philadelphia; horses and dairy products from Newport; whale oil, ship goods, and even ships from Boston or nearby ports. The Navigation Acts enriched England, but they did not prevent the colonists also from reaping a profit, sometimes, of course, through an avoidance of tariffs that the law imposed. The overarching reality of colonial economic life was that wealth accumulated gradually, that living standards improved steadily, and that colonists experienced an economic maturing to match their growing political assertiveness.

NEW WEALTH

Throughout the colonies, signs of affluence proliferated: more imported goods and finer clothing, dancing classes and French lessons, musical recitals, and, in Philadelphia, a theater that opened by the middle of

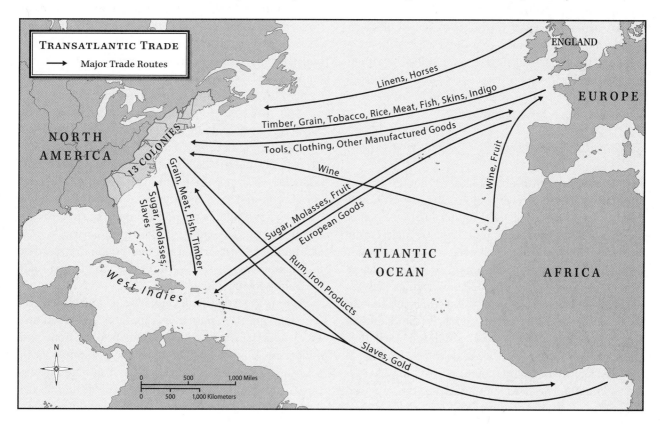

the eighteenth century. Even the muddy streets in that city were paved, and open sewers at last got covered. Income disparities persisted, of course, but in each region rising elites exerted their political power and set cultural standards that others strained to reach.

In the pre-Revolutionary generation, merchants in New England increased in wealth and eminence, outranked only by landed gentlemen and colonial officials. In the South, large plantation holders held the most wealth and, without question, the greatest political power. In the Middle Colonies, merchants also steadily strengthened their social position, followed by farmers and such professionals as doctors, lawyers, and clergymen. The wealthiest 20 percent of the population held nearly 70 percent of the total assets, a circumstance that did not vary widely throughout the eighteenth century.

But movement from the lower levels of society to a higher status did vary sharply. In Maryland, for example, about 90 percent of indentured servants became landowners at the end of their terms, and some of them ended with substantial estates. In Pennsylvania, on the other hand, only about one-third of contracted servants acquired land, and most of them only the prescribed minimum of fifty acres. Such limited holding did not allow them to enter even the middle class, much less the ranks of the wealthy. Yet in Newport, Rhode Island, a ship's cabin boy, Peter Harrison, managed in seven years' time — partly through a quite successful marriage — to join the local elite. Many may have dreamed of following Harrison's career curve, particularly since it was said that Newport "is as remarkable for pritty women as Albany is for ugly ones."

❧ Colonial Family Life

The most basic institution of all, the family, did not get off to an even start in every colony. The earliest immigrants, such as the English in Virginia and the Dutch in New Netherland, had been predominantly male: family formation had to await a more even sex ratio, achieved through the immigration of women. Elsewhere, in such regions as New England and Pennsylvania, families settled from the beginning, giving distinctive shape to the early social history of both areas. By the middle of the eighteenth century, however, family life — whether on plantation or farm, in village or town — provided the essential social foundation in every colony. In laying and building upon that foundation, women played the critical and determinative role.

GETTING MARRIED

In those societies where males greatly outnumbered females, marriageable women were spoken for at an early age, the average age in some Chesapeake communities being sixteen and a half. Moreover, when a husband died, the widow did not normally have a long widowhood, since proposals of marriage came quickly, especially if she now held considerable property. If after the second marriage the woman was still of childbearing age, then almost always a second family was added to the first. If she were beyond the age of childbearing, then her chances of survival greatly increased, as well as her chances of accumulating more wealth with the death of her second or even third husband. In choosing a mate in the Chesapeake, sons and daughters enjoyed considerable latitude since often one or both parents would have already died. Of course, the Anglican Church exercised careful supervision in the South: a 1662 Virginia law provided that "no marriage be solemnized nor reputed valid in law but such as is made by the ministers according to the law of England." These and similar regulations remained in effect down to the Revolution.

A more favorable gender balance obtained in New England, and consequently women did not marry quite so early; the age of nineteen or twenty tended to be the rule. And since New England males lived much, much longer (into their seventies, as opposed to the forties in Virginia), men as well as women remarried upon the death of a spouse. (Divorces were quite rare in the colonial period.) A wife's death in childbirth was all too common an experience; when it happened, the distraught husband searched quickly for a new wife to look after an orphaned infant together, perhaps, with other small children. New England parents regularly supervised their children's marital choices, and the increased life expectancy made it likely that they would be alive long enough to exercise their authority. Although the parish church and its Congregational minister provided their own oversight of proposed unions, the magistrate conducted the ceremony itself. Marriage was a civil ceremony in Puritan society even though the married life was blessed by God — indeed more blessed than bachelorhood or spinsterhood.

Among the Quakers of Pennsylvania and elsewhere, marriage and the choice of a mate was, if anything, even more saturated with religious prescriptions and concerns. A good Quaker marriage presumed both bride and groom to be of like faith and sufficiently mature to enter upon the responsibilities of faithfulness to each other and religious nurture for their children. "The

The Four Stages of Life   An eighteenth-century American woman created this homely, melancholy reflection on the crucial stages of her life: birth and infancy, betrothal and marriage, maturity, and death. Such thoughts about the essentials of the human experience formed a psychological foundation for most colonial Americans, surrounded as they were by ever-present reminders of both birth and death.

honorable marriage," said the Pennsylvania Quakers, "is when the bed is undefiled, transgression finished, freedom from sin witnessed, victory over the world known." These hard requirements did not prevent the vast majority of Quaker young men and young women from entering into matrimony, the women at around twenty-two years of age, the men at around twenty-six. Parental consent was required, of course, though it was not given in the face of either a son's or a daughter's opposition to the match. The Quaker meeting[1] also had to give its blessing and could, on occasion, intercede with a particularly obstinate parent. The Quaker meeting withheld its blessing from "mixed marriages," in which one of the partners was outside the faith. Not only would that marriage not be blessed, but also the Quaker partner stood in danger of being "disowned" or expelled from membership in the community. Quakers did not forbid remarriage, but encouraged the surviving spouse to wait at least one year, demonstrating "chastity, and virtue, and temperance."

For Quakers, blind romantic love was to be guarded against by a rational and deliberate consideration

1. The weekly session in which Quakers assembled without clerical guidance and remained silent until individuals were prompted by the Inner Light to speak.

of divine will. Marriage, William Penn warned, should be a "union of souls," not a "union of sense." Love, to be sure, was an appropriate emotion, but only as the object of that love was also appropriate. "Never marry but for love," Penn declared, "but see that thou lov'st what is lovely." And while one should never marry for money, it was folly to marry someone profligate and wasteful. In marriages between well-to-do Quaker families, much attention was given to the size of dowries. Nothing should be done in unseemly haste, but only as, step by step, the meeting gave its approval, the parents theirs, and the couple managed to find a happy conjunction of spiritual and more worldly interests.

PARENTS AND CHILDREN

For colonial Americans, the laws of nature directed that parents should provide food, clothing, and shelter for their children, just as the laws of the Bible commanded that children should "honor thy father and thy mother, that thy days may be long upon the land which the Lord thy God giveth thee." But in each colony or region, variations in these broad understandings manifested themselves, as religious backgrounds, economic necessities, and ethnic heritages modified fundamental patterns.

In New England, authorities worried so much about idleness that laws required children to be trained "in some honest calling, labor, or employment," beginning as early as seven years of age. At that age, daughters could readily assume household tasks, including those (such as sewing) that required some training and discipline. Sons might follow in their father's steps around the same time, but if they were to learn a trade outside the home they would be apprenticed to a journeyman or master when ten to fourteen years of age. After seven years of apprenticeship (or until the age of twenty-one), the young man would then be ready to assume his vocation, with little likelihood that he would ever forsake the one skill that he knew well. Girls might also be placed in another home, to work as servants, learn domestic skills, and escape being overindulged by their parents.

Vocation literally means "calling," and Puritans assumed that every honest employment should be a calling by God to work faithfully in the world. Puritans denied that God called persons out of the world or out of the family. On the contrary, the divine call was to work in the world — to marry, to be fruitful, to perform services useful to both God and humankind. From the Puritan perspective, monasticism was not a "higher" form of Christian dedication, but irrelevant and unprofitable. Just as God called men and women to salvation, so he called them to "worldly employments" that would honor the Creator more than "if you should have spent all that time in meditation, prayer, or other spiritual employment, to which you had no call." Given these presuppositions, parents took seriously their responsibility to guide their children into the proper life-work, urging them to listen for and heed their particular "call." And when God called, Puritans believed, he provided the necessary gifts for success in the chosen field. One way in which a person could decide if he or she had been called, therefore, was to examine carefully the talents and abilities that God had bestowed — a process curiously like modern vocational counseling.

If parents neglected their children, they were summoned before the magistrates for formal rebuke or, if necessary, punishment. If, on the other hand, children cursed or neglected their parents, the courts could again become involved. In some cases, children might even be removed from their own homes and placed in another family that "will more strictly look unto, and force them to submit unto government." When children resisted parental discipline or guidance, mothers and fathers might call upon the assistance of both the minister and the schoolmaster. All aspects of the child's life — work, play, education, religious training — revolved around the Puritan determination to uproot all sin and corruption and replace them with grace and salvation.

In the Chesapeake, the official Anglican Church hovered over all of life's major transitions: birth, marriage, and death. But given the scattered settlement in Virginia and Maryland, the ministrations of religion took place far more often in the home than in the parish church. By the middle of the eighteenth century, when the plantation system was in its full flower, great families dominated the political and social life of these colonies. In the seventeenth century, wives might give birth to five or six children — and be overjoyed if at least three reached adulthood and if they themselves survived the omnipresent dangers of childbirth. When these earlier bleak statistics of life expectancy turned more promising, families in the 1750s and beyond might have seven or eight children, most of them living to maturity.

Since all activity centered in the plantation manor, the celebration of a new birth also took place there. A few weeks after birth, parents arranged for a home baptism and christening. The ceremonies themselves, including the choice of godparents, were followed by the main event: sumptuous dining and joyous dancing. The tutor at Robert Carter's Nomini Hall in Virginia reported that a christening was "one of the chief times for Diversion here." Indeed, he put that ritual in the same category — as entertainment — with cockfights, fish-feasts, horse races, and fancy dress balls. Even in quite large families (seventeen children were born at Nomini Hall to Anne Tasker Carter) the arrival of each healthy child brought more festivities.

The pleasure continued as the family grew, with parents taking pride in their children's development and accomplishments. That same tutor for the large Carter family, Philip Fithian, reported that both parents had "a manner of instructing and dealing with children far superior, I may say with confidence, to any I have ever seen, in any place, or in any family." Fithian, a native of New Jersey and graduate of Princeton, wrote not as a proud Virginian but as a young outsider impressed with the warm, even indulgent, relationships between parents and children. Though the family patriarch, Robert Carter III, had some seventy thousand acres to oversee, along with artisans, tenant farmers, a dancing master, a music master, a tutor, and some five hundred slaves, he nonetheless found time for his children. The mother, Anne Carter, nursed her own children except when, overwhelmed by sheer numbers, she found it necessary to use a wet nurse, often a slave.

SONS AND DAUGHTERS

Planters' daughters shared in the family's affection and training more often than in its wealth. The rule of primogeniture — under which the eldest son inherited the land and the home — prevailed in the Chesapeake until Thomas Jefferson urged its abolition in Virginia in the 1780s. Even if land was divided among the children, that division was generally limited to the sons. The division of labor was more nearly even, with boys working outside the "great house," girls within. Imitating and directed by their mothers, girls worked at cooking, cleaning, knitting, spinning, and perhaps gardening. In larger and wealthier homes, both mother and daughters might confine themselves to supervising servants or slaves who performed the actual tasks. With girls' occupational roles thus clearly defined, Virginia's William Byrd II could in the early eighteenth century boast of his own daughters that "they are every Day up to their Elbows in Housewifery, which will qualify them effectually for useful Wives and if they live long enough, for Notable Women." Fithian noted that young girls also recognized their future role as mothers; they stuffed cloths and rags "under their Gowns just below their Apron-Strings, [and] were prodigiously Charmed at their resemblance to Pregnant Women."

By the age of five or six, boys no longer wore the long gowns of babyhood and put on "breeches" as a kind of initiation into the male world. More deliberate initiation came through the father's increased companionship with his son, as he took him not only outside into the fields, but on trips to neighboring plantations and into nearby villages. When a boy was old enough to ride a horse, he might be dispatched as a messenger, carrying instructions or invitations across the countryside. Visitors from other areas were impressed with the independence of young plantation sons, one commenting that "a Virginia youth of 15 years is already such a man as he will be at twice that age. At 15, his father gives him a horse and a negro, with which he riots about the country, attends every fox-hunt, horserace, and cock-fight, and does nothing else whatever." Most fathers, however, took satisfaction in a son's growing independence, just as most sons sought parental approval above all else. Beyond the bonds of affection, the bonds of economic reality held the family together, the sons in particular dependent upon their father's generosity in bestowing on them land. For although primogeniture remained the custom through most of the eighteenth century, more and more fathers found that the abundance of land allowed them to provide all their sons with some property, although the eldest received by far the greatest share, as well as the plantation house itself.

SLAVE FAMILY LIFE

The wealthy Chesapeake family stood in sharp contrast to the small farmer on the frontier, where large fortunes simply did not exist, and the contrast was even starker, of course, with respect to the slave family, in terms not simply of material welfare but also of parental authority and family integrity. Laws gave virtually no protection to the slave family — indeed, did not even recognize slave marriages. The separation of husbands from wives, and children from parents, occurred with tragic regularity. Yet somehow many slave families survived more or less intact, especially if the

white master saw some merit in allowing a father to help feed his children, a mother to cook for and clothe her own. But that this did not everywhere prevail is evident in a 1774 petition of Boston slaves to the Massachusetts legislature: "Our children are taken from us by force," they noted, "and sent many miles from us where we seldom or ever see them again, there to be made slaves of for life which sometimes is very short by reason of being dragged from their mother's breast." Boston's small slave population at least had a voice; even that was denied to the enslaved almost everywhere else.

Some masters took care to see that pregnant slaves were not overworked and that mothers giving birth had sufficient "lying in" time. The rate of deaths in childbirth was about the same for white and black women, but infant mortality was far higher in the slave family. Above all else, slaves who could not control their own destinies confronted the awful reality that neither could they control the destinies of their own children. When the New Jersey Quaker John Woolman traveled through the colonies in the 1750s, he was distressed to see the wretched condition of the slaves — and even more distressed to see many Quakers justifying their ownership of slaves. One justification he often heard was that slaves were being rescued from horrible circumstances in Africa. If so, Woolman wrote in 1757, that "would incite us to use them kindly, that, as strangers brought out of affliction, their lives might be happy among us." But that is not what he saw all around him. Rather, he saw a deplorable failure to recognize that "they are human creatures, whose souls are as precious as ours, and who may receive the same help and comfort from Holy Scriptures as we do."

ॐ Servants and Slaves

America in the seventeenth and eighteenth centuries attracted few immigrants from Europe's elite or privileged ranks. What it attracted, and what it so urgently required, was labor. Many immigrants, of course, worked for themselves, clearing the land, erecting a crude shelter, tilling the soil, and hungrily awaiting the first harvest. But an enormous number worked for others, either as servants or as slaves. Within the white population alone, one recent estimate suggests that about half of all immigrants arrived as servants. Within the involuntary black immigrant population, the percentage of slaves by the eighteenth century was virtually total.

Slaves Dancing This eighteenth-century watercolor shows slaves enjoying a moment of recreation — and preserving some of the culture of their homelands. The instruments the men play are African in origin and the patterns on the scarves the women wear on their heads are reminiscent of African tribal ones.

Both servants and slaves might be regarded as part of the master's extended family, but that is not to sentimentalize their roles. If children were under stern parental discipline, required to share in the field labor or sent away to outsiders to learn a trade, then other household laborers could certainly expect an authority that was at best firm and at worst inhumanly cruel. Parents who knew what was "best" for their children did not hesitate to enforce what was "best" on their servants and slaves.

THE EARLY SLAVE TRADE

During the entire colonial period, about 1.5 million slaves were imported into the British colonies, the majority sent to the Caribbean and the Southern Colonies. Between 1741 and 1760, some 267,000 slaves arrived in the West Indies, 63,000 in the Chesapeake, Carolinas, and Georgia, but only 1,000 in the Middle Colonies and about the same number in New England. New England and the Middle Colonies were certainly not hotbeds of abolitionist sentiment, nor was opposition to slavery widespread. The question was not morality, but economy. Other forms of labor sufficed on the small farm, or in the production of wheat, or in the raising of horses and cattle. Outside of the South, New York had the largest number of slaves, but most of these were employed as household servants, particularly among those wishing to flaunt their wealth by having slaves to serve their guests.

Patterns of bound labor varied widely from period to period and from area to area. In the British colonies, in massive numbers slave laborers came to be identified primarily with the Caribbean islands and the mainland South. Sugar in the former and tobacco and rice in the latter on the large plantations required enormous quantities of workers, a need that for a time was met with white indentured servants. By around 1680, however, three developments led to a sharp shift in the South away from white servants and toward black slaves. First, employment opportunities and wages both increased in England, drying up the ready supply of potential indentured immigrants. Second, the number of blacks captured in Africa and sold to the slavers increased to the point where the purchase of slaves (and their progeny) for lifetime servitude became more economically attractive than buying a white servant for a period of only four to seven years. Third, black slaves came to be seen as more tractable, less threatening to the social order, and less likely than whites to succeed in escaping.

In Virginia, for example, Bacon's Rebellion in 1676 demonstrated to the Tidewater elite what happened when armed frontier whites, newly released from bondage and deeply aggrieved over their inferior status, took matters into their own hands. "How miserable that man is," Governor William Berkeley noted, who had to govern a colony where six out of every seven inhabitants were "poor, indebted, discontented, and armed." Importing black slaves would alleviate this situation because they would not be armed, nor ever be released from their "contract." People of a distinctly different race and culture would become the workers, the laboring caste, allowing whites to achieve a greater degree of unity with each other. Whites might also come to a consensus on certain principles in which all — all of the non-slave caste, that is — could equally share. In colonial Virginia, as historian Edmund S. Morgan has pointed out, the paradox and cruel irony is that American freedom was born out of American slavery.

By the turn of the eighteenth century, slavery was flourishing in Maryland as in Virginia, and in 1750 blacks — overwhelmingly enslaved — accounted for more than one third of the population. In the tobacco-dominated Chesapeake region, the largest plantations developed labor forces of hundreds of slaves. By the second half of the eighteenth century, about 10 percent of plantations had more than one hundred slaves, another 10 percent more than fifty. Because tobacco used up land quickly, planters constantly needed more workers for clearing new land, planting corn in old land and restoring fertility by penning cattle in a given plot, meanwhile doing the time-consuming work of tending steadily to the newly planted tobacco seedlings. Tobacco planting could start as early as February, with all harvesting not complete until the first autumn frost. In the depths of winter, slaves kept busy pulling up stumps, making hogsheads for the tobacco, and mending fences that required constant repair.

REVOLTS AND RUNAWAYS

In South Carolina, where rice was the dominant crop, the black population exceeded that of whites by 1720 and for the remainder of the colonial period that black numerical dominance persisted. This demographic imbalance made South Carolinians especially fearful of slave revolts, though this anxiety was endemic to the South generally. In 1739 about twenty slaves broke into a warehouse near the Stono River in South Carolina, confiscated arms and ammunition, and the next day killed ten whites and burned several houses. The Stono rebels, now numbering about sixty blacks, then set out for St. Augustine, where the Spanish had promised them refuge. The South Carolina militia soon overtook them, however; the rebellion was brutally suppressed, and about forty blacks were killed. So extravagant was the punishment of blacks who had participated in the insurrection that the colonial Assembly in 1740 prescribed limits

for bodily mutilation or torture, scolding slave owners for conduct "highly unbecoming those who profess themselves Christians."

More often, rebellion took the form of fleeing. The best evidence for the frequency of runaways was the number of advertisements in colonial newspapers for the return of fugitives who might be identified by distinguishing marks or scars. Such an advertisement in South Carolina in 1770 called for help in locating a seven-months pregnant runaway "named Kate, about 32 years old, of a yellowish complexion, hollow jaw'd, a pouting look, all her upper fore-teeth gone, and speaks good English." Sometimes the newspaper notice indicated that the slave had recovered from smallpox, which left obvious scars. Distinctive clothing might also be noted, though often the description was of little help: he "has nothing on but an old rag about his middle."

When a black was caught away from his or her proper abode (and without a pass), the advertisement could take the form of a "found" rather than of a "lost." Thus the sheriff of Williamsburg, Virginia, in 1767 reported having several unclaimed blacks in his jail. Two had nothing with them "but an old Negro cloth jacket, and an old blue sailor's jacket without sleeves." Another, "named Sampson, about 5 feet, 10 inches high, about 25 years of age, well made, very black, ... is much marked on his body and arms with his country marks" — that is, the tribal scars he had brought from Africa. The sheriff urged the owners of these men "to come and pay the fees and take them away."

SLAVE "JUSTICE"

When runaways were caught, as they generally were, punishment was severe. Though it generally took the form of whipping, punishment could be more extreme, including imprisonment, exportation, or execution. Legal codes gave every protection to the master and his testimony, and little to the slaves, either individually

Advertising a Runaway Slave Public notices such as this were so routine in South Carolina and other major slave colonies that newspapers kept an image of a fleeing slave as part of their font of type. Notice how this advertisement warns other whites against harboring the runaway twelve-year-old slave girl, who speaks "pretty good English" despite being "newly arrived."

or collectively. Masters (whose records survive) explained at length their difficulties with slaves whom they described as lazy, drunken, disobedient, thieving, or malingering. Slaves (who left no records) were dependent upon neutral observers passing through the area to report the excessive mistreatment and pervasive distrust. One New Englander, traveling in South Carolina in 1778-79, wrote that "a man will shoot a Negro with as little emotion as he shoots a hare, several instances of which have come within my own knowledge." South Carolinians "have a brief way of trying Negroes for capital crimes," he continued. "The court consists of one Justice and two freeholders, who order the Negro placed before them at any place, try him, and hang him up immediately." The advantage of having a slave formally hanged rather than casually shot, the visitor explained, was that the government reimbursed the owner for his loss when the execution was legally carried out.

There were some legal efforts to mitigate the plight of the slave, such as declaring Sunday a day of rest for all, slave or free, and limiting the number of hours per day (twelve or fourteen) that a slave could be required to work. Often slaves were also permitted to live with their spouses and children, though any could be transferred to another part of the plantation or to another owner entirely. Males first greatly outnumbered females, though by 1770 the sex ratio was reasonably balanced. After that, with sufficient corn, meat, and possibly a small garden plot of their own, mainland slaves fared much better than their Caribbean counterparts. The natural increase that slave families provided their masters made the importation of new slaves less necessary in such places as Virginia and South Carolina.

WHITE SERVANTS

White indentured servitude generally met the unfree labor needs for the Middle Colonies and New England. And in the seventeenth century, England, Ireland, and Scotland provided most such servants, with nearly two hundred thousand arriving in America during that period. In the eighteenth century, Ireland, Scotland, and Germany took over as the major suppliers of this labor force as employment conditions improved in England. Some of the servants sent from eighteenth-century England (for example, to Georgia and Maryland) were imprisoned debtors or convicts. Ships from northern Ireland landed their human cargo mainly in the Middle Colonies, while those sailing from Catholic southern Ireland added Maryland to their other ports of call. German emigration, especially heavy to Pennsylvania in the period from 1749-1754, included many "redemptioners," or contract workers — persons who sold their own labor or that of their children to help pay for the Atlantic crossing. Boys in a German family might be bound over for their labor until they reached twenty-one years of age, girls until they were eighteen.

In the Middle Colonies white indentured labor resembled that of servants back in England. Men in the country tended to crops and farm animals, while those in the city engaged in some craft or trained themselves to become artisans. Women were more often engaged in domestic service, either on the farm or in the town. Up to the 1740s, the lot of such servants was fairly good, since labor was scarce and the contracts consequently generous. After that time, and up to the Revolution, labor was bountiful, resulting in lower wages and a smaller bonus of money or land at the end of the servant's term. Even in the better days,

✲ IN THEIR OWN WORDS

Virginia Code on Runaways, 1662
Servitude was so central to the Virginia economy that severe penalties were imposed for runaways.

Whereas there are divers loitering runaways in this country who very often absent themselves from their masters' service and sometimes in a long time cannot be found, [and whereas] that loss of the time and the charge in seeking them often exceeding the value of their labor, be it therefore enacted that all runaways that shall absent themselves from their said masters' service shall be liable to make satisfaction by service after the times by custom or indenture is expired: namely, double their times of service so neglected. And if the time of their running away was in the crop or the charge of recovering them extraordinary, the court shall limit a longer time of service proportionable to the damage the master shall make it appear he hath sustained.... And in case any English servant shall run away in company of any Negroes who are incapable of making satisfaction by an addition of a time, it is enacted that the English so running away in the company with them [shall serve additional time for the loss of the Negroes' labor as well as their own].

however, servants complained of masters who failed to meet their obligations, as masters complained of lazy, drunken, or dishonest servants. And servants, like slaves, also ran away; unlike slaves, they found it easier to blend into the wider population and remain at liberty. If caught, the servant might, like the slave, be whipped; even more likely, he or she might have the number of years under contract extended beyond the original agreement.

Labor needs in New England were met largely by native-born whites, so that there were neither great importations of slaves nor major influxes of white servants. In large farm families, all who were old enough worked either in the house or in the field as soon as age permitted. Fathers might delay allowing grown children to marry in order to keep them working longer. If servants were hired, they generally lived with the family as long as both parties found it advantageous. The worker, male or female, might be an unemployed artisan, an unmarried or widowed woman, an older son or daughter of fellow townsfolk, but in any case almost always another New Englander. In this manner, New England kept its ethnic homogeneity more successfully than the other mainland colonies. Serious labor dislocations tended to be a feature only of the coastal towns where shipping, privateering, and trading rose and fell in uneven waves.

By mid-eighteenth century, indentured servitude declined throughout the colonies as free labor became more accessible and even preferable. After all, masters had to provide indentured servants with food, clothing, shelter, and some freedom bonus. All this reduced the profit margin considerably, if not eliminating the profit altogether. Free labor, on the other hand, could be picked up as needed, and quickly dropped when no longer required. In contrast to white servitude, slavery did not decline before the Revolution, but continued to grow in both absolute numbers and geographic spread.

✧ Schools and Scholars

Reflecting their quite separate histories and distinctive cultures, the colonies offered a wide variety of educational options to their youth. New England — where building a town school had almost as high a priority as building a meetinghouse — achieved the greatest success. As early as 1647 the General Court of Massachusetts ordered that when any town grew to the number of fifty families, its citizens "shall then forthwith appoint one within their town to teach all such children as shall resort to him to write and read." When the number of families reached one hundred, a building to house a grammar school must be provided. Puritans not only valued literacy; they required it, so that all men and women could read the Bible, thereby (it was assumed) shielding themselves from superstition, heresy, and that "old deluder, Satan." In the grammar school, open to both boys and girls, subjects were divided into the "academical" (including Latin, Greek, logic, literature, and history) and the "useful" (including arithmetic, accounting, surveying, navigation, and bookkeeping).

After about seven years in a grammar school, attending from six to eleven in the morning and one to five in the afternoon year-round, young men could go on to the academy for education designed specifically to prepare them for admission to college. The student's own abilities and interests, the parents' circumstances and desires, and economic conditions or opportunities within the colony all helped determine whether a young man would attend an academy. Since young women were not admitted to college, no academy was created for them, though occasionally a private academy would allow girls to attend the school in the very early morning or late afternoon, when the "real scholars" were not present. Other private academies offered a full day of learning opportunities, though one Scotsman was disillusioned by his daughter's experience in such a school in Boston. In the first place, the young ladies — about twelve years of age — "do not get up even in this fine Season till 8 or 9 o'clock. Breakfast is over at ten, a little reading or work until 12, dress for dinner till 2, after noon in making or receiving Visits or going about the shops." He concluded: "Tea, Supper, and that closes the Day and their Eyes about 11." This particular father, at least, believed his money could be better spent in other ways.

Academies took the form chiefly of young men attaching themselves to the household of a minister, which offered a library as well as at least one person certain to have had a college education. Ministers likewise found it advantageous to supplement their meager salary by charging for room, board, and tuition, or perhaps working some of that out in the home or garden. As in any society, some ministers soon gained a reputation for being better tutors or having larger libraries, or perhaps for having a wife who prepared finer meals. In such cases, students might travel to some distant town for their academy training.

❋   I N   T H E I R   O W N   W O R D S

Promises for New England's "Dutiful Child"

Puritans required literacy so that all men and women could read the Bible — and, as this extract from the 1727 New-England Primer indicates, religion was the first subject about which children learned to read.

I will fear God, and honour the King.

I will honour my Father & Mother.

I will obey my Superiours.

I will submit to my Elders.

I will love my Friends.

I will hate no Man.

I will forgive my Enemies, and pray to God for them.

I will as much as in me lies keep all God's Holy Commandments.

I will learn my catechism.

I will keep the Lord's Day Holy.

I will reverence God's Sanctuary, for our God is a consuming Fire.

EDUCATION AND ASSIMILATION IN THE MIDDLE COLONIES

In the less homogeneous Middle Colonies, the orderly and regular New England pattern failed to develop. In New Netherland, the Dutch West India Company required the creation of a school in each Dutch village, although near the end of Dutch rule settlers in New Amsterdam complained that not enough was being done "in so wild a country" to see that youth were properly instructed not only in reading and writing "but also in the knowledge and fear of the Lord." Quakers, strongest in the Middle Colonies, overcame their suspicion of formal learning long enough to establish local schools for both sexes — sometimes taught together, but more often separately. Quakers recognized that creating their own schools was essential to maintaining their religious discipline and distinctiveness. Rules for Philadelphia boys adopted in 1748, for example, specified "That none shall at any time play or keep Company with the rude boys of the Town, but shall Converse, as much as they can, with their own Schoolfellows." Since Quakers had no professional ministry, the teaching of Latin and Greek seemed less important than inculcating practical skills. For the same reason, Quakers saw no reason to establish a college anytime during the colonial period.

Scotch-Irish made up a major element of Pennsylvania's population by the middle of the eighteenth century. Presbyterian Scots who had settled in northern Ireland (Ulster) and who suffered from economic deprivation and Parliament's discriminations cast about for other lands. Pennsylvania offered low taxes and beckoning lands. Beginning in the 1720s, these Scotch-Irish migrated in large numbers to America, most of them debarking in Philadelphia. Finding coastal land already occupied and very expensive, the newer arrivals moved on to the backcountry where they occupied empty lands without much concern for the niceties of legal title. Despite the primitive character of their frontier life, they steadily inculcated their children with the rudiments of education. Presbyterian ministers, like their Congregational counterparts in New England, also tutored college-bound young men or launched modest academies. As a result, literacy rates among the Scotch-Irish Presbyterians hovered around 90 percent, an astounding achievement considering the conditions of their life.

Germans constituted the other major non-English element in colonial Pennsylvania. Referred to as the "Pennsylvania Dutch" (a misunderstanding of the German word *Deutsch,* which means German), these immigrants also arrived in great numbers during the first half of the eighteenth century. Many of them preferred to maintain their own educational or vocational programs in isolation from the wider community, although in 1759 Mennonites in Germantown (near Philadelphia) opened a school "free to all denominations whatsoever without any regard to Name or Sect of People." This school, like most private schools, charged tuition, but every effort was made to reduce fees for children of the poor. In general, Germans operated their own schools with textbooks and instruction both in German. This so alarmed earlier settlers, especially after a sharp rise in German immigration in the 1730s, that some non-Germans lobbied Parliament to make it illegal to import German books or print anything in German in the colonies. Parliament refused, but many Pennsylvanians continued to worry.

Even the cosmopolitan Benjamin Franklin in the 1750s complained because the Germans failed to learn English or to assimilate to the surrounding culture. "Instead of their learning our language," Franklin wrote, "we must learn theirs, or live as in a foreign country." He supported a charity school movement, one of whose explicit purposes was to Anglicize the German population and make the learning of English mandatory. An early manifestation of the "melting pot" theory of Americanization, these charity schools, wrote one backer, would provide the same education to German and English boys and girls with the confident expectation that "acquaintances and connections will be formed, and deeply impressed upon them in their cheerful and open moments." Intermarriage would inevitably follow, thereby gradually erasing the "German problem." Though this particular movement was a failure, most Germans (except for the staunchest sectarians such as the Amish) did eventually adopt the English language and blend into the English-speaking Pennsylvania culture.

Ever mindful of education's importance in building a culturally and social stable society, Franklin continued to wrestle with plans for schooling the young, including blacks. He devised a "Plan for Improving the Condition of the Free Blacks," and commended George Whitefield's purchase of five thousand acres on the Delaware River "in order to erect a Negro School there." Likewise, he joined in Quaker efforts to see that young blacks received instruction in reading, writing, and the principles of religion. And in 1758 he contacted Dr. Bray's Associates to solicit their assistance in creating a school for blacks in Philadelphia. In all education, white or black, Franklin's interests tended toward the useful and away from the classical. The learning of Latin and Greek he regarded as little more than a showy ornament except for those going into the ministry.

In his *Proposals Relating to the Education of Youth in Pennsylvania,* Franklin in 1749 observed that "the good Education of Youth has been esteemed by Wise Men in all Ages, as the surest Foundation of Happiness both of private Families and of Commonwealths." He therefore urged that public-spirited citizens seek a charter for an academy and then supervise its founding and development. If some persons could take so much pleasure in gardening and horticulture that they forsook all other amusements, "why may we not expect they should acquire a Relish for that more useful Culture of young Minds?"

With his usual thoroughness, Franklin laid down the preferred curriculum that included good penmanship (learning to draw might help), good number skills ("Arithmetic, Accounts, and some of the first Principles of Geometry and Astronomy"), and certainly the English language. Quoting John Locke, he deplored forcing pupils "to learn the Grammars of foreign and dead Languages, and are never told of the Grammar of their own Tongues." Franklin also urged studying history as an excellent way to examine "Questions of Right and Wrong, Justice and Injustice," as well as to see the "wonderful Effects of Oratory." Above all, Franklin thought, history "will also give Occasion to expatiate on the Advantage of Civil Orders and Constitutions . . . the Advantages of Liberty, Mischiefs of Licentiousness, Benefits arising from good Laws and a due Execution of Justice, etc. Thus," he concluded, "may the first Principles of sound Politics be fixed in the Minds of Youth."

EDUCATIONAL CHALLENGES IN THE SOUTH
In the Southern Colonies, the absence of major towns (except for Charleston) precluded the establishment of urban schools or major academies. No taxes were levied for the support of education; private schools had to be financed by philanthropy, either from England or from local donors. As late as 1671 Governor William Berkeley rejoiced that Virginia had no free public schools, since he saw learning as the source of disobedience and heresy. Literacy rates, quite low in the South in the seventeenth century, remained low in the eighteenth. Perhaps half of the women in 1750 were literate, and about two-thirds of the men. For what little education the South provided went more generously to the male children; fathers in their wills set aside larger amounts of money to educate their sons than their daughters. On great plantations a tutor would be provided; neighboring children, especially if ties of kinship existed, might be included in the instructional program. Wealthy landowners could also send promising sons to an academy abroad.

Throughout the South, the serious lag in public education continued up to the Revolution and even beyond, a defect that caused Thomas Jefferson great anxiety in Virginia. In the midst of the Revolution, Jefferson took time to draft a legislative "Bill for the More General Diffusion of Knowledge," calling for all free youth to receive a grammar or general school education. Then academies should be created for those "whom nature hath endowed with genius and virtue" to prepare pupils for higher education. Jefferson lobbied hard for the passage of this bill ("the most important bill in our whole code," he wrote), but he failed to win its approval.

In all colonies, much education took place not in classrooms but in shops and on farms. Children serving their apprenticeships learned more than just a craft. They often also learned to read and write, either through the generosity of the master craftsman or because the contract required it. And if masters did not wish to assume that task themselves, they could send the youthful learner — as a typical contract stipulated — to "a good Evening School in Order to be well instructed in reading, writing, Accounting, and the like." From the middle of the eighteenth century on, vocational schools developed to help those who all day learned their crafts, but could spend some evenings in schools designed specifically for them. If the family failed to teach reading and writing, if the church in its catechetical instruction did not succeed in that instruction, and if academies remained restricted and elitist, then evening vocational schools, especially in urban centers, could still reach many of the working young.

THE AMERICAN ENLIGHTENMENT

By the middle of the eighteenth century, Americans demonstrated that they no longer merely survived on the fringes of civilization. At one level, the intellectual elites participated in the European Enlightenment, joining in its rebellion against tired tradition and reveling in its embrace of reason. At a more popular level, the colonists contributed to a sweeping wave of religious revivalism that united many fervent pietists[2] but at the same time divided some major denominations. The Enlightenment established one of the cultural boundaries of eighteenth-century America. The other boundary was defined by the intense religious excitement known as the Great Awakening.

Leading western European thinkers framed the discourse for Enlightenment thought. Those who considered themselves friends of the Enlightenment regarded all authority, both political and religious, with grave suspicion. For many intellectuals, experience and the scientific method became the only reliable avenues to truth. Many of those who embraced reason rejected

not only biblical revelation but also all abstract speculation and metaphysical system building. Plato was scorned and theology dismissed. The focus on reason tended to be of a special sort, favoring the axiomatic, the self-evident, the commonsensical — in short, the truths known to and demonstrable by experience. Intellectually, the world was being created anew.

The English thinkers who led the way to this new world were Francis Bacon, John Locke, and Isaac Newton. Bacon discarded the hoary authority of Aristotle and his deductive method of reasoning; in its place, he substituted experimentation and induction, or what we have come to call the scientific method. Locke likewise saw truth as something to be earned and learned — not inherited and not given. Truths did not descend upon us from heaven, nor were our tender minds filled with innate ideas. Truths awaited our pursuit, our discovery. Finally, Newton taught his contemporaries that God's world was orderly, regular, and predictable. By patient observation and careful mathematical calculation, one could uncover the secrets of the universe. Not in antiquity, but in modernity did one face — and create — the future.

In America, the Enlightenment expressed itself politically in such familiar figures as Thomas Jefferson (1743-1826) and John Adams (1735-1826). It expressed itself religiously in the non-institutional movement called deism, which accepted the central truths of "God, freedom, and immortality" because they supposedly could be found in nature and in reason. But no special revelation was required to perceive these great truths. This new excitement for learning and new willingness to consult nature directly infused literature, art, science, medicine, and law. By 1760, Enlightenment culture had come to the colonies.

❧ Literature: New Secular and Enduring Spiritual Concerns

Benjamin Franklin (1706-1790), a native of Massachusetts, moved to Philadelphia in 1723 as a young man. There he found the stage upon which he so successfully played his many roles. His enterprise as colonial printer gave him not only high visibility but sufficient fortune to follow many other pursuits: politics, science, social organization, diplomacy, and literary production. He was both product and promoter of the Enlightenment's penchant for new ideas, new observations, new approaches to every avenue of human endeavor. Of all his writings, none gained greater fame than his *Autobiog-*

---

2. Pietism places its emphasis upon the personal and experiential in religion; for fuller discussion, see below, pp. 121-23.

The Enlightenment and Slavery, 1773
Benjamin Rush saw slavery as anathema to Enlightenment ideals; tragically, almost another century would pass before the institution was abolished in the United States.

And now, my countrymen, what shall I add more to rouse up your indignation against slave-keeping? Consider the many complicated crimes it involves in it. Think of the bloody wars which are fomented by it, among the African nations. Or if these are too common to affect you, think of the pangs which attend the dissolution of the ties of nature in those who are stolen from their relations. Think of the many thousands who perish by sickness, melancholy, and suicide in their voyages to America. Pursue the poor devoted victims to one of the West India islands, and see them exposed there to public sale. Hear their cries, and see their looks of tenderness at each other being separated. Mothers are torn from their daughters, and brothers from brothers, without the liberty of a parting embrace. Their master's name is now marked upon their breast with a red-hot iron.

raphy, which he began writing in 1771 at sixty-five years of age. For so many in his own time and later, Franklin typified what it was to be an average American: no formal education, no "first family" nobility, no inherited fortune, but nevertheless succeeding at any chosen task by his own wits and energies and ultimately becoming the confidant of philosophers and kings. "Poor Richard," the pseudonym under which Franklin for years published almanacs filled with witty sayings and wise proverbs, ended up as "Rich Benjamin" — rich in honors, dignity, and enduring reputation.

In his *Autobiography* Franklin recounts how he helped bring learning and culture to his adopted city. In 1727 he formed "a club for mutual improvement which we called the Junto." Meeting on Friday evenings, members took turns reading original essays on "any point of morals, politics, or natural philosophy" that they might choose. The club, which lasted nearly forty years, Franklin pronounced to be "the best school of philosophy, morality, and politics that then existed in the province." Four years later, Franklin encouraged Junto members to pool their books to make a common library, which eventually became the Library Company of Philadelphia, still flourishing today. Of this achievement, Franklin later wrote that it "was the mother of all the North American subscription libraries, now so numerous." These libraries, he added, "have improved the general conversation of the Americans, made the common tradesmen and farmers as intelligent as most gentlemen from other countries, and perhaps have contributed in some degree to the stand so generally made throughout the colonies in defense of their privileges."

The move from discussing "morals, politics, or natural philosophy" to creating a library for "the common tradesmen and farmers" is typical Franklin. Theory must have its practical application; else it remains too far removed from everyday life and the ordinary concerns of women and men. Whether studying the gulf currents, observing the first hot air balloon crossing of the English Channel, considering the relationship between color and heat, or inventing bifocal glasses, Franklin was forever concerned with demonstrating that knowledge had consequences — not just for the scholar, but for all humankind. Moreover, scholarly pursuit could never justify the failure to be "a good Husband or Wife, a good Neighbour or Friend, a good Subject or Citizen." In 1760, Franklin wrote to a friend of his impatience with one Nicholas Gimcrack "who neglected the Care of his Family to pursue Butterflies." Such a man becomes a legitimate "Object of Ridicule" and fair game for satire.

In 1744 Franklin took the lead in creating the American Philosophical Society, the first learned society in the young country. While the Junto was limited to Philadelphia alone, the Philosophical Society was intended to be far wider in scope, even extending to interested parties abroad. Since "the first drudgery of settling new colonies . . . is now pretty well over," Franklin noted, men of curiosity and genius could begin "to cultivate the finer arts and improve the common stock of knowledge." Franklin, far more than a mere organization man, proceeded himself to take the lead in improving humankind's "common stock of knowledge."

KEEPING A RECORD

If autobiography as a literary form was unusual in Franklin's time (the very word belongs to the nineteenth century), the keeping of a diary was commonplace throughout the colonial period. Puritans were the most dedicated diarists, but southern gentlemen followed the practice as well. Of these, William Byrd II

A Virginia Gentleman, Early Eighteenth Century

Many colonists kept diaries, and William Byrd's offers a glimpse into the life of a learned, cultured Virginia planter.

July 7, 1709. I rose at 5 o'clock and read a chapter in Hebrew and some Greek in Josephus. I said my prayers and ate milk for breakfast. I danced my dance [did exercises], and settled my accounts. I read some Latin. It was extremely hot. I ate stewed mutton for dinner. In the afternoon it began to rain and blow

very violently so that it blew down my fence. It likewise thundered. In all the time I have been in Virginia I never heard it blow harder. I read Latin again and Greek in Homer. In the evening we took a walk in the garden. I said my prayers and had good health, good humor, and good thoughts, thanks be to God Almighty.

of Westover, Virginia, is best known for his wit as well as for his freewheeling observations of and experiments in plantation manners and morals. Born on the family estate, Byrd was sent to London for his education in the classics (he read Hebrew, Latin, and Greek, in addition to modern languages) but also in the ways of high society that he so clearly relished.

Although he could not spend all his years in the company of London's finest, he did his best to bring that flavor into Virginia generally and onto the Westover plantation specifically. His diary records this effort, along with the routine running of his huge estate and his not-so-routine dalliances with the opposite sex.

In his diary, William Byrd described such matters as choosing a gardener, disciplining his children, playing billiards, finding a good French wine, doing his accounts, reading Italian or Dutch literature, traveling to the colonial capital in Williamsburg, attending church, and saying (or forgetting) his prayers. For example, after a riotous night in London in 1718, he got home about five o'clock in the morning "and neglected to say my prayers." But after several hours of sleep, he rose about ten and sought to make amends as he "read a chapter [in the Bible] in Hebrew and some Greek in Homer. I said my prayers, and had boiled milk for breakfast."

For Byrd, the ritual of religion alternated regularly with the ritual of indulgence, as he felt compelled to catalogue every conquest of women, from servants and slaves to ladies and other gentlemen's wives. A male chauvinist without doubt, Byrd nonetheless seriously objected to his North Carolina neighbors because, said Byrd, they made their women do all the work. The women were sent out into the fields at sunup, while the men "lie and snore till the sun has risen one-third of his course and dispersed all the unwholesome damps." Even then, most men were content to smoke their pipes and stay close to "the chimney corner." In his extensive

diaries as well as in his carefully revised *History of the Dividing Line* (between Virginia and North Carolina), William Byrd produced lively prose, often laced with rich sarcasm and sharp observation.

THE POWER OF THE SERMON

The most prevalent form of literature in colonial America and the most widely printed, especially in the seventeenth century, remained the sermon. Sermons were heard not only in the meetinghouses and churches on Sundays, but at funerals, at midweek meetings, at the ordination of new ministers, and on occasions of public fasts or thanksgivings. Sermons, based on a biblical text, began by expounding the scriptural context, then asserting the doctrine that the text suggested. After considering all the possible objections against the doctrine being set forth, the minister concluded with a reassertion of its truth along with its immediate application to the lives of his parishioners. Sermons in New England labored to be "plain," that is, clear and convincing, free of fancy rhetoric or irrelevant musing. In the South, on the other hand, Anglican sermons featured rhetorical flourishes and "entertaining" conceits. Also in the South, the itinerant preaching of Baptists and Presbyterians elevated the extemporaneous sermon to a new art form; Patrick Henry was among those greatly influenced by this oratorical style. North and south, however, the effective preacher was one who drove doctrinal truths "into the hearts and consciences of men like an arrow." Sermons served to advertise the promises of the New World, to warn of impending doom when men and women failed to obey God's clear commands, to interpret the meaning of wars or earthquakes or plagues, but above all else to hold out the promise of God's ever powerful grace and saving love. If colonial Americans missed all other forms of literature, they rarely escaped the sermon.

❧ The Waning of Artistic Provincialism

Artistic representation, whether the Navajo sandpainting, the Hopi woven basket, the Seneca headdress, or the decorative jewelry of many tribes, is as universal as it is irrepressible. So it should occasion no surprise that American colonists, even without great artistic centers or teachers, nonetheless produced paintings that would ultimately win much admiration abroad. So also in architecture, after the period of earliest settlement — Franklin's "first drudgery" — had passed, colonists began consciously to improve the style of their homes, their churches, and their public buildings, resorting to copybooks from abroad and master craftsmen at home.

By the middle of the eighteenth century, the colonies had produced an abundance of folk art: portraiture, tombstone carving, elaborate calligraphy, painted tavern signs and wrought-iron weathervanes, knitting, needlework, and quilting. But also by that time, such prominent artists as Benjamin West, John Singleton Copley, and Charles Willson Peale had been born in (respectively) Pennsylvania, Massachusetts, and Maryland. Soon each of these men would come into his artistic maturity at about the same time that the colonies embarked upon an exercise of political maturity.

Born in 1738, Benjamin West by 1760 determined to study the great painters of the Renaissance. Journeying to Italy, he concentrated on Raphael and Titian, then by 1763 settled in London where he remained for the rest of his life. But his interest in things American and especially in budding American artists who chose to study with him never waned. In 1771 he decided to depict a battle he remembered from his youth: the successful assault of the British against Quebec in September, 1759, and the consequent fall of Canada to England. Though a major victory, it resulted in a bitter loss with the death of General James Wolfe. West would portray that poignant moment on the field of battle; however, he would clothe the men not in the classical togas of antiquity (for that was the fashion), but in the military uniforms of their own time and place, and the Indians

Benjamin West, *The Death of General Wolfe*   In a groundbreaking artistic move, West elected to render the soldiers in this painting in the uniforms of the day rather than in Greek and Roman battle dress. "The same truth that guides the pen of the historian," West observed, "should govern the pencil of the painter."

in their native dress. Strongly advised against so radical a departure from artistic convention, West replied that the Greeks and Romans knew nothing of the time or place that he chose to mark. The resulting masterpiece, *The Death of General Wolfe*, won widest acclaim not only in England, but throughout the Western world.

Born in the same year as West, John Singleton Copley grew up near the docks in Boston, helping his widowed mother to make a living in her tobacco shop. In his teens, he began painting extensively, teaching himself or learning from the occasional painter passing through the city. In his late twenties he submitted a painting to London's Society of Artists for possible exhibit there. The painting, *Boy with a Squirrel*, was unsigned, and neither Benjamin West nor Sir Joshua Reynolds had the faintest idea who could have submitted such a fine, natural, unstylized portrait. West recognized the flying squirrel as an American animal such as he had seen in Pennsylvania, then noted that the wood on which the canvas was stretched was American pine. So an American had done it, but who? Finally, the captain who had brought the canvas across the ocean came forward to say that the painter's name was Copley. The name meant nothing in London, but that would soon change. For after *Boy with a Squirrel* (painted in 1766) was exhibited, correspondence between West and Copley sprang up. Meanwhile, Copley married well in 1769 (into a Loyalist family), and became a wealthy and much admired portrait painter in Boston. His *Paul Revere* is perhaps his best-known work, but he painted other patriotic heroes such as Sam Adams, John Hancock, and Mercy Otis Warren. Ironically, his reputation as a painter of revolutionary leaders obscures the fact that in 1774 he left for London, never to return to his native land.

Charles Willson Peale, on the other hand, went to London in 1767 to study with West but by 1769 was back in his native Maryland. There, and in the cultural capital of Philadelphia, Peale painted before, during, and after the Revolution, as conspicuous in his patriotism as in his art. In 1772, he painted the first of some sixty portraits of George Washington, and soon after began the portrait of his still growing family. Deeply impressed by the great masters of Europe, Peale gave to his four sons the names Titian, Rubens, Raphael, and Rembrandt. (The first two became naturalists, the last two painters.) Like Franklin, Peale was an organizer, for he managed to form the new nation's first natural history museum (depicted in his famous self-portrait, *The Artist in the Museum*) as well as the Pennsylvania Academy of Fine Arts. Friend of Franklin, Washington, Jefferson, and other leaders, Peale never retreated from the political world, but plunged into it with vigor.

Colonial architecture, of necessity, had rude beginnings. Colonists used the materials at hand: chiefly wood, but also brick and stone. With an axe (sawmills were relatively rare in the earlier years), timbers could be split to erect the basic clapboard house with a large central fireplace on the first floor, a kitchen to one side, and a living room to the other. A ladder might lead to a second floor where two sleeping rooms accommodated the colonial family. By the eighteenth century, building plans grew more ambitious, as more people could afford homes that provided additional comforts and commodious space. Craftsmen faithfully copied or modified drawings found in such English books as James Gibbs's *Book of Architecture* or William Kent's *Designs of Inigo Jones.*

Peter Harrison, a native of England, settled in Newport, Rhode Island, in 1740, making his living as a merchant — not as an architect. In 1748 he designed the Redwood Library in Newport, introducing the neoclassical style associated with the sixteenth-century Italian, Andrea Palladio. Fourteen years later, he ex-

John Singleton Copley, *Boy with a Squirrel* The boy in Copley's famous painting is Henry Pelham, the painter's younger half-brother.

ecuted plans for what is now the nation's oldest Jewish house of worship, Touro Synagogue, also in Newport. Later in the eighteenth century, another American, more often thought of in a political context, took up architecture as a serious study. Thomas Jefferson, likewise influenced by Palladio, began work on his own home in Virginia in 1769, spending the next thirty or forty years — when other duties permitted — in modeling and remodeling his cherished Monticello. Architecture, whether in Richmond, Charlottesville, Washington, or France, continued to occupy and fascinate Jefferson who reported, simply but truthfully, that architecture "is my delight."

❧ *"And All Was Light": Science and the American Enlightenment*

The "scientific revolution" was predominantly a European event. Such names as Copernicus (1473-1543, Polish), Galileo (1564-1642, Italian), Kepler (1571-1630, German), and Newton (1642-1727, English) suggest the multinational character of a movement that so radically altered the way that people thought about the earth and the heavens of which it is a part. By the time of the Enlightenment, the results of fresh scientific investigations had been so widely absorbed into Western culture that even a few Americans readied themselves to join in that scientific revolution.

The early eighteenth-century English poet Alexander Pope wrote that "Nature and Nature's law lay hid in night;/God said, 'Let Newton be,' and all was light." This poetic compression honored Newton's noted achievement in bringing natural laws out of their dark obscurity. For example, Newton had helped to "tame" the comets by proving that they, like the planets, followed the regular order of nature. If the universe was truly orderly, human beings needed to know more about its origin, its size, and its "rules." A modest place to begin with those large — and still haunting questions — was with the earth's own sun: how far away, how far from the other planets orbiting it? In 1761 and 1769 European astronomers had two rare opportunities to observe the passage of Venus across the face of the sun. By a careful measurement of the time it took for this "transit of Venus," they could use Kepler's law to calculate the distance of Venus from the earth, the distance of Venus from the sun, and the distance of the earth from the sun.

David Rittenhouse of Philadelphia, a clockmaker by trade, trained himself to be an astronomer, even constructing a mechanical model of the solar system (an orrery) that showed the earth's motion in relation to that of the other planets. For the 1769 observation of the transit of Venus, Rittenhouse designed a special clock as well as a telescope that mechanically followed the planet's path across the sun. Aided by Franklin's American Philosophical Society, Rittenhouse — when all the mathematics were finally worked out — offered results that put the earth's distance from the sun at a remarkably accurate 92,800,000 miles. A few years later, Rittenhouse gave the same careful attention to the study of a total solar eclipse, with the consequence that eclipses would soon be seen more as objects of scientific investigation than as alarming signs of divine intervention.

Exploring the nature of electricity, however, gave colonial America the greatest opportunity for making a contribution to science and winning enormous respect abroad. Hearing a lecture on electricity in 1746, Benjamin Franklin decided that the subject needed more systematic study. Up to this point, such a familiar phenomenon as static electricity could be a subject for popular lectures, idle speculation, or mild amusement, but no one really understood what was going on. Franklin would change all that. He discovered that an electrical charge could be created by rubbing a glass sphere and then send the charge along a wire, storing it in a jar. For a new field, a new vocabulary was required: the glass sphere was the generator, the wire the conductor, and the Leyden jar the condenser. The amount of electricity that the jar could hold depended on the thickness of the glass, with the kind of charge (negative or positive) being different on the outside from the inside of the jar. Holding the jar and touching the wire gave a shock. "The knocking down of six men was performed with two of my large jars," Franklin reported, "not being fully charged."

Franklin's most famous (and dangerous) experiment was to fly a kite into a lightning storm in order to demonstrate that lightning and laboratory-made electricity were of the same stuff. In Franklin's words, the "experiment of drawing down the lightning" was conducted "in order to demonstrate its sameness with the electric fluid." He suspected a sameness because both in the laboratory and in the sky electricity produced light, swift motion, crooked direction, a tearing of whatever it passed through. There was also a "crack or noise in

---

❋   **I N   T H E I R   O W N   W O R D S**

Benjamin Franklin as Enlightenment Optimist

In this letter, written from France in 1780, Franklin views scientific progress with an almost religious awe.

Dear Sir [Joseph Priestly],

. . . I always rejoice to hear of your being still employ'd in experimental researches into nature, and of the success you meet with. The rapid progress *true* science now makes occasions my regretting sometimes that I was born too soon. It is impossible to imagine the heights to which may be carried, in a thousand years, the power of man over matter. We may perhaps learn to deprive large masses of their gravity, and give them absolute levity, for the sake of easy transport. Agriculture may diminish its labour and double its produce; all diseases may by sure means be prevented or cured, not excepting that even of old age, and our lives lengthened at pleasure beyond the antediluvian standard. O that more science were in as fair a way of improvement, that men would cease to be wolves to one another, and that human beings would at length learn what they now improperly call humanity! . . .

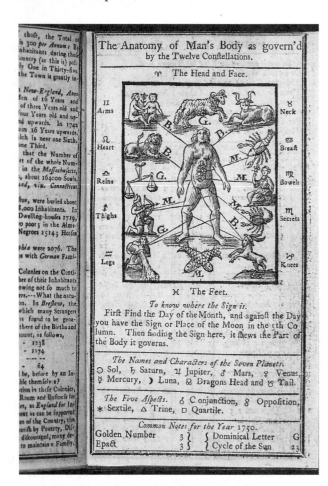

A Page from *Poor Richard's Almanack*, 1750 *Poor Richard's Almanack* is most widely remembered as a repository for Benjamin Franklin's countless aphorisms. But it also contained all the other information featured in almanacs of its day: calendar, weather, astronomical, and — as shown here — astrological data.

exploding" and a "sulphureous smell." Once he had shown that lightning was indeed a form of electricity, Franklin proceeded to invent the lightning rod to conduct lightning safely from a building's highest point into the ground, protecting both life and property. But some thought this impious, seizing from God's hands one of his weapons for chastising a disobedient people. After an earthquake struck the Boston area in 1755, one minister announced that this was divine retribution for those "iron points invented by the sagacious Mr. Franklin."

When a friend and fellow investigator in London, Peter Collinson, published Franklin's letters to him under the title of *Experiments and Observations on Electricity* (1751), the sagacious Franklin found himself the idol of Europe, admitted to England's Royal Society, to France's Academy of the Sciences, awarded medals, honors, and degrees. His own countrymen responded with honorary degrees to the man who had never attended college: Harvard, Yale, William and Mary, and Europe's universities all helped transform Ben Franklin into Dr. Franklin. Just as the world had been ready to understand the orderly motion of planets and the regular appearances of comets, so now the world was eager to learn more about this strange "fluid" and someday to harness its potential power. Though his work with electricity was enough by itself to make him a great celebrity, Franklin rested hardly at all, as he went on to introduce daylight saving time, to invent the "Franklin stove," and to anticipate the military use of aerial balloons. Beyond all that, of course, Franklin still had decades ahead to devote to his country's cause.

✌ *Practical Sciences: Medicine and Law*

If the motion of the heavens and the electrical fluid were becoming better understood in the eighteenth century, the fluids and fevers of the human body continued to mystify and confound. Contagions such as smallpox ravaged victims who turned in desperation to their physicians, who were — with equal desperation — seeking somewhere a cause and a cure. Along with greater understanding of the Newtonian sort, doctors sought greater professionalism and better medical education. Lawyers, gradually edging aside the clergy as the principal colonial profession, grew in significance and number during the eighteenth century as questions of English constitutionalism and American rights steadily gathered momentum. Just as Bacon had thrown off the mantle of Aristotle, so now a new class of lawyers might find it necessary to explore fresh understandings of the working of the body politic.

In the colonial period, many Americans treated their ills and defects just as they treated those of their farm animals or crops: that is, by reading some general handbook of practical remedies, or consulting their neighbors on the most expedient procedure. Learned doctors were rare, and even where they could be found, their advice was not at all clearly superior to folk wisdom. For most diseases, doctors prescribed harsh laxatives and extensive "letting" of blood — a treatment that more often dangerously weakened than benefited the patient. On the plantation, along the frontier, in much of rural America, the sick looked only to themselves or their families (or sometimes their ministers) for whatever medical assistance might be given.

In the treatment of disease, many theorists held that all diseases were related: that is, smallpox could become malaria, dysentery could become yellow fever.

And if diseases were of similar origin, then cures should be similar, if not identical. Such ignorance of specific causes and cures meant that the line between folk medicine and "professional" medicine in the eighteenth century was thin indeed. This helps to account for the low reputation that physicians ("Doctors of Physick") endured. Surgeons stood even lower in esteem, pursuing a craft that had traditionally belonged to barbers. Most colonials preferred to learn from the non-professional: their own slaves, or neighboring Indians, or trial and error at home. Jefferson bemoaned the "adventurous physician who goes beyond the 'scanty field of what is known'" into "the boundless region of what is unknown." Medical fashions come and go, Jefferson noted, "like the dresses of the annual doll-babies from Paris, becoming, from their novelty, the vogue of the day." It was a matter of sheerest luck when a patient was treated according to a vogue that actually worked; more often, Jefferson concluded, the patient "gets well in spite of the medicine."

In the cities, where most doctors could be found, most epidemics also erupted. Smallpox struck Boston with deadly force in 1721, as it had so often hit the crowded community before. While such a disaster might be seen by some as a just punishment from a wrathful God, such a view did not mitigate the suffering of the afflicted or the sorrow of bereaved parents. Was there no escape? Previously there had been none, but now a novel technique was being advocated in Europe that might mitigate the severity of the attack. The newly discovered and largely untried method, inoculation, seemed on its face irrational, if not mad: deliberately to transplant infected material from an ill person to the skin of a healthy person.

"SECURITY FROM A DISTEMPER BY RUSHING INTO THE EMBRACES OF IT"

"Madness" was precisely what a great many in Boston concluded when they heard about inoculation, among them the only physician with a real medical degree (from Edinburgh), Dr. William Douglass. Arrayed against him and the populace at large was the Congregationalist minister Cotton Mather, who as a member of the Royal Society of London had read in its *Transactions* of a Turkish doctor who had tried inoculation and discovered that, while the patient did get sick, the fever was much less severe than among those who caught the pox naturally. Mather, who read all this in 1714, immediately wrote to a doctor in London seeking more information about what England had done and what he, Mather, might do should an epidemic afflict Boston again. En-

gland, it turned out, had done nothing: the experiment remained unproven. On the other hand, the mortality rates with smallpox continued unacceptably high.

When the epidemic arrived aboard a ship from the West Indies in April 1721, Mather was determined to push hard for inoculation. He persuaded another doctor (who had been educated only as an apprentice), Zabdiel Boylston, to employ the paradoxical and highly controversial method. Boylston inoculated his six-year-old son and two black slaves. As evidence mounted that the resulting infections were mild and immunity from further infection long lasting, many other Bostonians got Boylston to inoculate them. Public outrage was enormous: the town's governing body even passed a law against further inoculations. Dr. Douglass thought

Benjamin Franklin   In this dramatic painting by Benjamin West, Benjamin Franklin captures the lightning from the storm and proves it to be electricity. Franklin gained fame all over the Western world for his scientific achievement. As the emissary of Revolutionary America in France, he would be called "the Electrical Ambassador."

Cotton Mather   One of the most formidable intellectuals of early eighteenth-century New England, Mather was a transitional figure between the stern Calvinist orthodoxy of the seventeenth century and the emerging rationalism of the Enlightenment. He took a deep interest in the natural sciences of his day, experienced a crisis of conscience in the Salem witchcraft controversy, and struggled with the Puritan faith of which he was one of the foremost guardians.

Damn you: I'll inoculate you with this, with a Pox to you." When, however, both the fever of public opinion and that of the pox subsided, statistics demonstrated the validity of what Mather and Boylston had done. Of the approximately three hundred persons inoculated, only five or six had died; of the five thousand who caught the disease naturally (almost half the population of Boston), nearly nine hundred perished. In other words, the chances for survival with inoculation were roughly ten times greater than for those stricken without it. Before the eighteenth century was over, the battle for inoculation had been won. The world of disease had its "rules" just as the heavenly bodies had theirs. Francis Bacon would have applauded another application of the scientific method.

A GROWING NEED FOR LAWYERS

Lawyers also came in for their share of sharp rebuke, often being grouped with doctors and clergymen as among the chief "scourges of mankind." One New Englander compared law to the lottery: "great charge, little benefit." Making a living off the misery of others struck colonists as inappropriate, if not vile. It was widely believed that law as a profession should only be followed by those who also pursued the "honest" labor of a farmer or merchant — for, said the Fundamental Constitutions of Carolina, it was "a base and vile thing to plead for money or reward." Such sentiments reflected a society suspicious of any elite and jealous of its own abilities to rectify wrongs and administer rough justice.

By the middle of the eighteenth century, however, estates had grown large, land titles had become contentious, and commercial transactions and maritime disputes had acquired considerable complexity. As the need for lawyers grew, so attention to their education and training increased. Most aspiring lawyers (Thomas Jefferson, for example) simply "read law" with a practicing lawyer or with someone well acquainted with the history of English Common Law as well as English local

the experiment scientifically absurd and theologically intolerable since it came from people faithful to "the prophet Mahomet." And people unquestionably did get sick from inoculation. How wild and absurd, to quote a South Carolina physician, to seek "Security from a Distemper by rushing into the Embraces of it."

Despite laws and outcries, Boylston continued to inoculate. By November public resentment reached a peak sufficient for a bomb (which did not explode) to be thrown through the window of Cotton Mather's home carrying the message: "Cotton Mather, You Dog,

law. In Jefferson's case, William and Mary College professor George Wythe served as his tutor and guide. John Adams studied with a practicing lawyer, Jeremiah Gridley, who (before the advent of more formal legal education at Harvard) trained many of Massachusetts's best legal minds. Other parents, if sufficiently affluent, sent their sons to London to be trained in law at the Inns of Court; William Byrd II was one such. By the 1760s, both Philadelphia and Charleston had around thirty young men studying law in London.

By that time — as we shall see in Chapter 5 — other tensions in the air suggested the need for sharp students of law. Local assemblies quarreled with their royal governors; colonists questioned their status as citizens in the British Empire; Parliament pushed its legal powers to the limit, or perhaps beyond, so far as the restless foreign plantations were concerned. Reason should be called upon here, as in other realms, to determine what new circumstances and new understandings should dictate. Just in time, the growing power, prestige, and number of lawyers spoke in behalf of not only a colonial culture but a colonial cause as well.

THE GREAT AWAKENING AND ITS CONSEQUENCES

Seventeenth-century colonists took religion seriously; so did their eighteenth-century heirs, as popular preaching and traveling ministers brought evangelical piety to a broad swath of the American people, white and black, rich and poor, urban and rural, educated and simple. Revivalism and concern for the soul's condition swept from Georgia to Maine, meeting only a few pockets of resistance or indifference. Before the high waters of zeal

and fervor subsided, churches had been enlivened or divided and the religious shape of British North America changed radically. African Americans joined in the Awakening, though they hardly needed that movement to convince them of the reality of personal and passionate experience of the divine. In higher education, the Awakening also had its impact, both on colleges already founded and in the creation of new ones. The Enlightenment largely moved among a limited elite; the Awakening, in contrast, found its audience in marketplaces and fields, in crowded churches and open assemblies. The first great popular movement spanning all the thirteen colonies, the Awakening helped create a sense of community that could begin to be called "American."

⅋ George Whitefield and Jonathan Edwards

When the Awakening erupted, the colonies already showed considerable religious diversity. Congregationalism (or Puritanism) dominated most of New England, while Anglicanism (or the Episcopal Church) held sway throughout much of the South. Both these official, "established" churches did their utmost to keep other religions far removed from their soil, but by the middle of the eighteenth century both had failed to maintain a religious monopoly. Baptists, Dutch and German Reformed, Jews, Lutherans, Presbyterians, Quakers, and Roman Catholics added their color to the religious painting. The diversity that prevailed when the revivals broke out would soon sharply increase both in number and direction.

NEW METHODS OF PREACHING
The catalyst in this all-colonial excitement was a young English minister named George Whitefield. An early

---

George Whitefield and the Great Awakening, 1739
Here is a typical day in the career of George Whitefield.

Friday, November 9 [in Philadelphia]. Read prayers and preached as usual in the morning, and perceived the congregation still increased. Visited a sick person, for whom I was sent for, and felt the power of the Lord

was present, both with him and those who attended him. Most wept at the preaching of faith. I was visited in a kind manner by the minister of the parish, and preached again in the evening from the Court House steps. I believe there were nearly two thousand more present tonight than last night. Even in London, I never observed so profound a silence. Before I came, all was hushed exceeding quiet. The night was clear, but not

cold. Lights were in most of the windows all around us for a considerable distance. The people did not seem weary of standing, nor was I weary of preaching. The Lord endowed me with power from on high. My heart was enlarged and warmed with Divine love. My soul was so carried out in prayer, that I thought I could have continued my discourse all night. . . . Surely, God is favourable unto this people.

associate of John and Charles Wesley — soon to lead a Methodist movement out of the Church of England — Whitefield while still in England turned to open-air evangelism. He would take the gospel message to the people rather than wait for the people to find their way into the churches. When he arrived in Philadelphia in November 1739, he moved quickly to "the Court-house Gallery in this City, about six at Night." There he preached "to near 6000 people before him in the Street, who stood in awful silence to hear him." So the local newspaper reported eagerly as virtually half the town's total population crowded around the much-heralded twenty-six-year-old evangelist.

And it was the same everywhere that Whitefield went, as he moved south from Philadelphia to Virginia, the Carolinas, and Georgia. The following fall, he strode into New England, preaching on Boston Common to five thousand people straining to hear every word. The next day, Sunday — September 21, 1740 — no Congregational church in Boston was large enough to accommodate the crowds that pressed to hear him, so "he went and preached in the Field to at least 8000 Persons." The next day repeated the dizzying excitement, and so did the day after that, as Whitefield, breathless with enthusiasm and inexhaustible in zeal, proclaimed his message (he reported) with "much Flame, Clearness, and Power." Even Benjamin Franklin, mildly skeptical of all that enthusiasm, testified to the power of Whitefield's oratory: "He had a loud and clear voice, and articulated his words so perfectly that he might be heard and understood at a great distance, especially as his auditories observed the most perfect silence." Even if one were not interested in the subject, Franklin added, "one could not help being pleased with the discourse."

Colonial America had neither seen nor heard anything quite like this before: extemporaneous preaching (not learned sermons read from a manuscript), powerful emotion (not dull doctrinal explication), and a concern about spiritual matters so intense as to fill the churches every week and require more services during the week. In New England the Awakening was as intense as it was brief: all over in a couple of years, the days of religious zeal were followed by months of recrimination and separation. But in the Middle and Southern Colonies, the movement continued well into the 1750s and even beyond. Penetrating every colony, the Great Awakening left few unmoved by its mighty surge.

To be sure, Whitefield did not do it all alone, though it is worth noting that the first individual to bring some degree of unity to the colonies was not a politician but a preacher. Whitefield had many admirers — and many critics. Several pastors took his cue by becoming "itinerants" who moved beyond their own parishes to travel widely through other parishes, preaching wherever invited to do so, and sometimes where not. Thus a New Jersey Presbyterian, Gilbert Tennent, attracted large crowds not just in the Middle Colonies but in New England as well. Like Whitefield, he often questioned the spiritual integrity of some of his fellow clergy, a questioning that — understandably — aroused great resentment. Carrying that crusade to even greater extremes, James Davenport, a Connecticut Congregationalist, called for books to be tossed into a bonfire and for parishioners to abandon their cold, formal, and "unconverted" pastors. Brought before the colony General Assembly for trial in 1742, Davenport was found guilty of disturbing the peace and order of the government, and expelled from Connecticut.

DEFENDING THE REVIVAL

Of Whitefield's many allies and of the Awakening's many defenders, none was more brilliant or influential than Jonathan Edwards. A graduate of Yale College and pastor of the Congregational church in Northampton, Massachusetts, Edwards had witnessed brief spurts of revivalism in his own parish years before George Whitefield arrived in America. Already inclined to support the movement, Edwards found himself having to defend it against its critics at the same time that he decried the excesses of fanatics like Davenport. One of the ablest critics of the Awakening, Charles Chauncy of Boston's First Congregational Church, thought that the unrestrained zeal threatened to upset all society, if not actually destroy it. For Chauncy, what Whitefield had begun in misguided sincerity, Davenport finished in inevitable anarchy. What persons in their right minds would tolerate the "Shriekings and Screamings, convulsion-like Tremblings and Agitations, Strugglings and Tumblings, which in Some Instances have been attended with Indecencies I shan't mention"? From Chauncy's point of view, it was time for the colonists to sober up after an unfortunate emotional binge.

From Jonathan Edwards's point of view, the fact that excesses had happened should not — must not — discredit the Awakening as manifestly a work of God. Clearly influenced by both Locke and Newton, Edwards strove to find order and "rules" even in the midst of all this excitement and emotion. We must learn to discriminate, Edwards argued, to separate the wheat from the chaff, the counterfeit from the genuine. In 1746, long after the furor had subsided in New England, Jonathan Edwards wrote the most sophisticated and profound defense of the movement that the eighteenth century produced. In his *Treatise Concerning Religious Affections,* Edwards dismissed all the "Shriekings and Screamings" as no sign, one way or another, of whether the Awakening was genuine. Some people, Edwards noted, are so afraid of emotion that they treat religion as though it were a matter of intellectual propositions only — a matter for the head alone and not for the heart. On the contrary, Edwards wrote, nothing ever changed a person's life without powerful emotions being clearly involved. "He who has doctrinal knowledge and speculation only, without affection [emotion], never is engaged in the business of religion."

So how to determine whether the revivalism was genuine or fake? Edwards expended hundreds of pages in his treatise in an earnest effort to answer that question, concluding that while many signs of true religious emotion could be noted, the most convincing and impressive sign was the quality of life that one lived after the temporary excitement had passed. Scripture, Edwards noted, teaches that a tree is known by its fruits. Common sense teaches the same thing. "Hypocrites may much more easily be brought to talk like saints, than to act like saints." So the genuineness of the Awakening, like the genuineness of a profession of love, was to be found not in tears or words but in the conduct of life.

Edwards did not convince everyone — not Chauncy, not all the members of his own congregation, which dismissed him in 1750. He spent the last eight years of his life in the frontier community of Stockbridge, Massachusetts, preaching to the Housatonic Indians and composing the major philosophical treatises upon which his enduring reputation rests. In 1758 he was invited to become president of the College of New Jersey (later Princeton University), but died within a few months of his taking up residence there. Colonial America could boast of no more learned theologian or philosopher than Jonathan Edwards.

✥ *Religious Realignments*

The Awakening revived religion, but also divided it. Two active denominations in the movements, the Congregationalists and the Presbyterians, fell apart over the issues of an itinerant ministry and intense emotionalism. The Congregational "New Lights" and the Presbyterian "New Side" supported the revival, while the "Old Lights" and "Old Side" opposed its sometimes disruptive zeal. In New England, the people had not been accustomed to seeing their own Congregational clergy so bitterly arrayed against each other. We are, Edwards regretfully noted, like "two armies, separated, and drawn up in battle array, ready to fight with one another; which greatly hinders the work of God." Division among the ministers led to schisms in the churches, as in many New England towns the single parish church became two. The second church, often called the Separates because they withdrew from the official tax-supported and now Old Light parish church, rejected what these pro-revivalists regarded as cold, compromised, second-hand religion.

In the Middle Colonies, the division between Old Side and New Side Presbyterians greatly troubled a relatively young denomination just beginning to be a major force in that region. Especially in New York and New Jersey, revivalist excitement resembled that found in New England, only with Presbyterian ministers such as Gilbert Tennent and Samuel Blair taking the lead. From the New Side point of view, none could properly object to the aroused interest in religion, the greater concern for personal salvation. From the Old Side point of view, however, several quite legitimate objections could be raised. First, many of the itinerant revivalists — "the strolling preachers" — had not been properly ordained; worse, they had not even been properly educated. Second, the authority of the church's own governing bodies, the synods, was not recognized, as parishes were invaded without permission and doctrine dismissed without warrant. Third, and most threatening of all, some Old Side ministers found their own spirituality and piety being questioned, to the discredit of all organized religion and sowing utter disorder in place of careful ecclesiastical control. The Old Side faction so completely dominated the Synod of Philadelphia that the New Side clergy withdrew to form in 1745 the competing Synod of New York. When these two "sides" came back together in 1758, the pro-revivalists prevailed.

Revivalism prevailed even more obviously and significantly in denominations that took their inspiration directly from the Great Awakening. Prior to the Awakening, the Baptists in America had experienced very little growth. A generation after the Awakening, however, the Baptists had multiplied four times over. This sharp increase rode the waves of a Calvinist theology that emphasized the sovereignty of God in contrast to the frailties of humankind. In New England, many of the New Light or Separate churches ended up becoming Baptist. In the Middle Colonies,

An Anti-Whitefield Cartoon George Whitefield was not universally admired during his lifetime. This savage English caricature accuses him and his followers of arrogance, hypocrisy, greed, and even (in the lower left corner) of consorting with prostitutes. The epithet "Dr. Squintum" refers to his eye disease.

Philadelphia continued to be a major Baptist center throughout the eighteenth century. But it was in the South, after the Awakening was over, that Baptist growth was phenomenal, notably in Virginia and the Carolinas. From around the 1770s on, the Baptists would be the dominant religious force in the South, emphasizing personal religious experience above creedal uniformity or institutional integrity. One Congregational Old Light explained the spectacular Baptist growth in altogether unflattering terms. "Many people," he noted, "are so ignorant as to be charmed with sound than sense." A preacher's lack of formal education, he added, "may easily be made up, and overbalanced by great zeal, an affecting tone of voice, and a perpetual motion of the tongue." There

was, of course, more to it than that, as growth both in the urban East and the frontier West would demonstrate in the nineteenth century.

The Methodists, not even a separate denomination at the time of the Awakening, also grew explosively in the late eighteenth century and beyond. Although not formally organized in America until 1784, well before that time Methodists operated within the Church of England as a pietist society bent on reviving religion and emphasizing personal spiritual development. Methodist "societies" and Methodist itinerant lay preachers gathered followers both in England and America, built chapels, and challenged established, formal ("cold and sapless") religion everywhere. From England, John Wesley dispatched lay evangelists in the late 1760s and early 1770s. The most famous of these was Francis Asbury, who arrived in America in 1771. Establishing his headquarters in Baltimore, Maryland, Asbury relied exclusively on traveling preachers or "circuit riders" to guide the impressive growth of this newest religious group. Unlike the predominately Calvinist Baptists, the Arminian[3] Methodists emphasized the free will of men and women who must accept a great deal of responsibility for seeking their own salvation. In less than a century, Methodists would outstrip all other Protestant denominations in gaining the allegiance of religious-minded Americans.

Among smaller religious bodies that joined in the Awakening were the Dutch Reformed, especially strong in New York and New Jersey. Under the leadership of Theodore Frelinghuysen, the Dutch heartily participated in the revivalism of the Middle Colonies and Frelinghuysen's son helped found Rutgers University. During the peak years of the Awakening in the 1740s, Count Nicholas Ludwig von Zinzendorf of Bohemia visited the colonies on behalf of the Moravians, or Society of Brethren. Zinzendorf hoped to bring German Reformed members closer to the Moravians, and bring both closer to the kind of spiritual renewal that he saw in the revivalism all around. But the German Reformed Church ultimately retained its own ecclesiastical identity. The common denominator in all these pro-revivalist groups was pietism: that is, an emphasis upon a personal, immediate, heart-felt religion. This stood in opposition to religion that was official and political, formal or merely intellectual, largely traditional and liturgical. For the pietist, neither denominational labels nor theological opinions counted as much as the spiritual health within. Thus the Awakening had the effect of creating a kind of unity of spirit that had important ramifications during the American Revolution.

This unity of spirit was, to be sure, far from complete. Not only did denominations divide, but many groups stood aloof from the Awakening. Anglicans generally resisted it, even though the most famous itinerant of all, George Whitefield, was himself an Anglican. Quakers, Lutherans, and Catholics could also be numbered among those not caught up in the revivalistic excitement. In the long view, however, those groups that did take their inspiration from the revivals dominated America's religious scene for generations after the original fires had cooled. Pietism even created alliances across the ocean, especially with fellow believers in Scotland and Germany. For a time, some dared even to hope that pietism could forge bonds strong enough to break through the toughest barriers of all: those of race.

3. The theological "school" of Arminianism represents a pulling away from Calvin's emphasis on God's sovereignty toward a greater stress on the freedom of the human will.

❧ *Slave Religion*

The black population in colonial America proved surprisingly susceptible to the message of Christianity — surprising because Christianity was, after all, the religion of their oppressive masters. These masters, moreover, made little systematic effort to convert the slaves and, in fact, often placed obstacles in the way of conversion. Missionaries in America generally found other tasks more pressing or other audiences more congenial. Masters worried about whether baptism somehow altered a slave's legal status, giving him or her some claim to freedom as a "brother or sister in Christ." In 1730 the secretary of the Society for the Propagation of the Gospel bemoaned how little the society's missionaries had done on behalf of those Africans forcibly removed to America. Masters, he explained, refused to give their slaves time off for religious instruction, except on Sunday when they had to plant and tend their own gardens. Some masters even argued that slaves became less obedient after baptism, and others opined that perhaps the slaves had no souls anyway. Apologetically, Secretary David Humphreys noted that he would not even mention such things "if they were not popular now," these arguments having absolutely "no foundation in reason or truth."

TRANSFORMING WORSHIP

The Great Awakening increased Christianity's attractiveness and accessibility to slaves. As preaching became more passionate, slaves — men, women, and children — found themselves readier to respond. And as itinerants gathered audiences whenever and wherever they could, blacks had many more opportunities to hear the gospel proclaimed. To those New Lights and New Side and new-born preachers, disdainful of formality and order, the slaves had as much right to join the church and participate in its ceremonies as anyone else. If uneducated, no matter; if conscious of their sinful and outcast state, so much the better; if desperate for a heaven offering release from earth's sorrow and suffering, then the preacher's words had an immediate relevance and healing power.

New Side Presbyterian Samuel Davies in Virginia took special satisfaction in the slaves' response to his preaching. In 1750 he personally baptized about forty slaves and, a few years later, administered the Lord's Supper to about sixty. In Maryland, the center of Methodism's early growth in America, circuit riders appealed equally to black and white; one itinerant joyfully reported his experience of "many hundreds of Negroes . . . convinced of sin, and many of them happy in the love of God." Baptists in the South found slaves as eager as whites to hear of a gospel open to all on equal terms. Some itinerants, so impressed with the slaves' keen interest in becoming Christians, questioned slavery itself, seeing it (according to Baptist John Leland) as "pregnant with enormous evils." This itinerant confessed that he could never be reconciled to slavery, and declared to the African American converts his hope "to meet many of you in heaven, where your melodious voices that have often enchanted my ears and warmed my heart, will be incessantly employed in the praise of our common Lord."

The Christianity to which the slaves were converted was, by that process, itself transformed. Though much of the African heritage was lost in the disruption of families and tribes in Africa and in the further separations and catastrophes of slavery itself, enough of the original culture survived to give black Christianity a distinctive character. Worship was an occasion not so much of solemnity as of joy. As one contemporary reported late in the eighteenth century, "the slaves praise Jesus with the lungs, hands, and feet." Both music and movement became prominent elements in the religious services. The Baptist emphasis on baptism by immersion — in a river, stream, or pond — also had much appeal to those of West African background, where water cults were commonplace.

As long as blacks worshiped under white leaders, some of the exuberance was discouraged or even suppressed. But soon both slaves and free blacks chose their own clergy, gathered in their own crude structures or brush arbors, and improvised their own services of worship. For generations, the ministry remained the only profession open to African Americans, and the black church the only institution where an oppressed people had a considerable degree of self-determination. Baptists attracted the greatest number of blacks as their form of church government permitted maximum congregational autonomy. Methodists were next in order of popularity, with separate black denominations formed even before the end of the eighteenth century. Presbyterians came in a distant third in attracting slaves and ex-slaves. Once enrolled in the ranks of the Christian religion, African Americans were never mere passive spectators or imitators. They contributed directly and powerfully to their adopted religion, nowhere more movingly than in such spirituals as "Nobody Knows the Trouble I've Seen" and "Steal Away to Jesus." If the Christianity of the masters supported and sanctioned slavery, the Christianity of the slaves enabled them to endure it and ultimately to survive it.

❧ Colleges: "Nurseries of Piety"

In the seventeenth-century colonies, only two colleges were founded, appropriately in the two most populous colonies: Massachusetts and Virginia. Harvard, the first of the two, began in 1636, as has been noted in Chapter 2. The College of William and Mary, the other seventeenth-century institution, was chartered in 1693, although instruction did not begin until nearly twenty years later. William and Mary's creation resulted from the steady labors of one man, Commissary James Blair, who had been appointed in 1689 as the Bishop of London's representative in Virginia. The leading Anglican cleric in the South, Blair spent much of his time trying to get the Church of England better organized and more strongly supported. But his other great goal was the creation of

---

✵ **I N T H E I R O W N W O R D S**

Raising Funds for the College of New Jersey (Princeton), 1754

Enlightenment and Great Awakening ideals are evident in this letter soliciting funds for the College of New Jersey.

Nothing has a more direct tendency to advance the happiness and glory of a community that the founding of public schools and seminaries of learning for the education of youth, and adorning their minds with useful knowledge and virtue. Hereby the rude and ignorant are civiliz'd and render'd humane; persons who otherwise would be useless members of society are qualified to sustain and honour the offices they may be invested with for the public service. Reverence of the Deity, Filial Piety, and Obedience to the laws are inculcated and promoted. . . . At length, several gentlemen residing in and near the Province of New-Jersey, who were well-wishers to the felicity of their country, and real friends of religion and learning, having observ'd the vast increase of those colonies, with the rudeness and ignorance of their inhabitants for want of the necessary means of improvement, first projected the scheme of a collegiate education in that Province.

an Anglican college. With the support of Virginia's governor and Assembly, and with some money collected locally to prove an earnest intent, Blair sailed for England to obtain royal permission, a charter, and more money. His best friend in court was King William's co-sovereign, Queen Mary, who backed his proposal and helped him secure funds, especially from the estate of Robert Boyle, the renowned British physicist and chemist.

When Blair died in 1743, the college had begun to attract many of the colony's best young men. In the 1750s and 1760s such future luminaries as Thomas Jefferson, George Washington, and Peyton Randolph received some of their education there, as it was the South's only colonial college. But the American Revolution created great hardships for a school so closely identified with an England and its sovereigns with whom the colonies were now at war. When the capital moved to Richmond in 1780, Williamsburg was left to the fringes of cultural and political life; its secondary status was further aggravated by the creation of the University of Virginia in the early nineteenth century. It was not until the twentieth century that William and Mary reemerged as a major institution.

At the very beginning of the eighteenth century, New England gained its second institution of higher learning with the founding of Yale in 1701. Connecticut citizens sought a school nearer than Cambridge as well as one less suspect of certain liberal leanings. Clergy took the lead in the creation of the school; the first eleven-man Board of Trustees were all ministers and all Harvard graduates. By 1716 the trustees finally settled on New Haven as the permanent location, and soon would agree to give their "Collegiate School" the name of Yale after Elihu Yale, a wealthy and childless official of the East India Company. Though Yale was himself an Anglican, others convinced him that if the Church of England really were the true church, what "better way to make men sensible of it than by giving them good learning"? Thus a second Puritan or Congregational school, receiving great help from a faithful Anglican, proceeded steadily on its path toward conspicuous success.

These three colleges preceded the Great Awakening, though two of them, Harvard and Yale, were tossed and turned in the spiritual turbulence. Of the remaining colonial colleges to be founded, five of the six schools had some connection with the revivalistic wave. Presbyterians created the College of New Jersey (later Princeton) in 1746, while Anglicans founded their second school in New York City in 1754: King's College (in Revolutionary days, patriotically renamed Columbia). Under the orig-

inal stimulus of George Whitefield and the later prodding of Benjamin Franklin, the College of Philadelphia (ultimately the University of Pennsylvania) received its charter in 1755. In 1764, with Baptists taking the lead, the College of Rhode Island (Brown University) became New England's third institution of higher learning. The Dutch Reformed in New Jersey in 1766 laid the foundation for a school of their own in New Brunswick: Queen's College, later Rutgers University. Finally, Eleazar Wheelock in 1769 created in New Hampshire Dartmouth College — a school intended originally for Indians.

With the exception of King's College in New York, the other five schools all revealed their sympathetic ties with the Great Awakening. By the time of the Revolution, New England and the Middle Colonies had four colleges each, while the South possessed only the College of William and Mary.

CONCLUSION: GROWTH, REVIVAL, AND CULTURAL MATURITY

In the last half of the seventeenth and the first half of the eighteenth centuries, the colonies grew steadily in population and in cultural maturity. That population remained predominantly rural, with agriculture being the principal occupation, the source of trade, and the avenue to modest wealth. The typical colonial family was a farm family, though exactly what this meant varied sharply from region to region. The slave family fought hardest for survival as a unit, but lost that battle repeatedly. Slavery itself, however tentatively adopted in the years of earliest settlement, had by the 1750s become deeply rooted, especially in the South. As slavery expanded, white indentured servitude slowly withered away.

The educational opportunities for children were most numerous in New England and least promising in the South; in the Middle Colonies, denominational and ethnic loyalties most often shaped the educational landscape. For the culture as a whole, sharp improvement could be seen in young America's contributions to literature, art, science, medicine, and law. These would be most evident in the urban centers of Boston, Newport, New York, Philadelphia, and Charleston. The mid-eighteenth century proved to be a lively time in religion, with revivalism — and strong reactions to it — disrupting and refashioning much denominational life in America. Many of the colonial colleges bore marks placed there by the Great Awakening.

In the crises to come later in the eighteenth century, the colonists would need all the learning that these colleges could offer, all the conviction and passion that the Awakening might provide, and all the power of reason ushered in during the Age of Enlightenment. In the world of politics, the challenges rose to unprecedented heights; the responses needed to match or scale those peaks.

SUGGESTED READING

Patricia U. Bonomi, *Under the Cope of Heaven* (1986). The best broad survey of religion in colonial America, with keen attention to its interaction with politics and society.

James T. Flexner, *America's Old Masters* (rev. ed., 1980). The authoritative discussion of artists Benjamin West, John Singleton Copley, Charles Willson Peale, and Gilbert Stuart.

J. William Frost, *The Quaker Family in Colonial America* (1973). An engaging and solid treatment of topics ranging from childhood discipline to marital "bargaining."

Brooke Hindle, *The Pursuit of Science in Revolutionary America, 1735-1789* (1965). A fascinating account of the colonial contributions to and gleanings from the scientific revolution.

Peter Kolchin, *American Slavery, 1619-1877* (1993). A broad survey that discusses the degree to which slaves managed to be culture creators on the one hand and cultural adaptors on the other.

Frank Lambert, *Inventing the "Great Awakening"* (1999). Lambert provides a clear picture of the role of the print media in helping to promote revivalism in America, England, Scotland, and Wales. Revivalists, as a conscious act of will, helped to create what in fact became a transatlantic Great Awakening.

J. A. Leo Lemay and P. M. Zall, *Benjamin Franklin's Autobiography* (1986). The most helpful edition of this classic, with maps, extensive notes, critical analyses, and a compendium of other Frankliniana.

George Marsden, *Jonathan Edwards: A Life* (2003). Yale University Press has provided (and is providing) excellent critical editions of Edwards's impressive corpus; utilizing these new works, Marsden gives us the best biography of Edwards now available.

Henry F. May, *The Enlightenment in America* (1976). The most sophisticated account of the several phases in the appropriation and extension of the European Enlightenment on this side of the Atlantic Ocean.

Jane T. Merritt, *At the Crossroads: Indians and Empires on a Mid-Atlantic Frontier, 1700-1763* (2003). A thorough treatment of interactions between colonists and Indians, with attention to war, trade, intermarriage, and the missionary enterprise — especially of the Moravians.

Philip D. Morgan, *Slave Counterpoint: Black Culture in the Eighteenth-Century Chesapeake & Low Country* (1998). This prize-winning study offers the most detailed and suggestive interpretation of African-American culture in Virginia and in South Carolina.

Harry S. Stout, *The Divine Dramatist: George Whitefield and the Rise of Modern Evangelicalism* (1991). A superb biography of the most conspicuous figure in the Great Awakening, treated in terms of the "theatre" of his performance and appeal.

Patricia J. Tracy, *Jonathan Edwards, Pastor: Religion and Society in Eighteenth-Century Northampton* (1980). The emphasis here is more on Edwards as pastor and revivalist than as philosopher or theologian; engaging narrative.

SUGGESTIONS FOR FURTHER READING

James Axtell, *The School Upon a Hill: Education and Society in Colonial New England* (1974).

Silvio A. Bedini, *Thinkers and Tinkers: Early American Men of Science* (1975).

Jon Butler, *The Huguenots in America: A Refugee People in New World Society* (1983).

Jane Carson, *Colonial Virginians at Play* (1965).

I. Bernard Cohen, *Benjamin Franklin's Science* (1990).

Lawrence A. Cremin, *American Education: The Colonial Experience, 1607-1783* (1970).

John Demos, *A Little Commonwealth: Family Life in Plymouth Colony* (1970).

Stephen Foster, *English Puritanism and the Shaping of New England Culture, 1570-1700* (1990).

Edwin S. Gaustad, *The Great Awakening in New England* (1957, 1968).

Philip J. Greven, *The Protestant Temperament: Patterns of Child Rearing, Religious Experience, and the Self in Early America* (1977).

Timothy D. Hall, *Contested Boundaries: Itinerancy and the Reshaping of the Colonial American Religious World* (1994).

Nathan O. Hatch and Harry S. Stout, eds., *Jonathan Edwards and the American Experience* (1988).

David Freeman Hawke, *Everyday Life in Early America* (1989).

Winthrop D. Jordan and Sheila L. Skemp, eds., *Race and Family in the Colonial South* (1987).

Ned C. Landsman, *From Colonials to Provincials: American Thought and Culture, 1680-1760* (2000).

Kenneth A. Lockridge, *The Diary and Life of William Byrd II of Virginia, 1674-1744* (1987).

Edmund S. Morgan, *The Puritan Family: Religion and Domestic Relations in Seventeenth Century New England* (1966).

Sharon V. Salinger, *"To Serve Well and Faithfully": Labor and Indentured Servants in Pennsylvania, 1682-1800* (1987).

Leigh E. Schmidt, *Holy Fairs: Scottish Communions and American Revivals in the Early Modern Period* (1989).

Daniel Blake Smith, *Inside the Great House: Planter Family Life in Eighteenth Century Chesapeake Society* (1980).

Mechal Sobel, *The World They Made Together: Black and White Values in Eighteenth Century Virginia* (1987).

Harry S. Stout, *The New England Soul: Preaching and Religious Culture in Colonial New England* (1986).

Helena M. Wall, *Fierce Communion: Family and Community in Early America* (1990).

Richard Warch, *School of the Prophets: Yale College, 1701-1740* (1973).

John F. Woolverton, *Colonial Anglicanism in North America* (1984).

5

Self-Governing Colonies in a Changing Empire, 1700-1775

A S BRITISH NORTH Americans were coming into social and cultural maturity in the mid-eighteenth century, they were simultaneously struggling to achieve political maturity. Sometimes those struggles went on within the individual colony; at other times colonial politicians contested the policies of the British Empire. Most often those policies took the form of periodic attempts to make the colonies more profitable to the mother country and to protect economic interests in Britain. But political authorities were rarely united. Parliament, more interested in asserting its authority over the king, passed more and more legislation — more than eighty acts in the first half of the eighteenth century — aimed at tightening control over colonial trade and such other aspects of colonial life as the sale of lands and the naturalization of foreigners. But if Parliament was more active, it was only rarely more effective. On the other hand, the royally appointed Board of Trade had to take a second place in colonial matters, even though its knowledge of the actual circumstances in the "foreign plantations" generally exceeded that of members of Parliament. And Parliament, ever vigilant in passing its laws, proved less vigorous in ensuring their enforcement.

In 1711, Parliament passed the first of three White Pine acts designed to preserve the forests of North America to meet the navy's incessant demand for masts, spars, and other ship timbers. Having denuded its own forests over the centuries, Great Britain now needed other sources of supply. North America surely constituted such a source — but it had to be preserved for imperial use. The provisions of these acts were so sweeping that they invited, if not demanded, evasion by the colonists. The Hat and Felt Act, approved in 1732, tried to limit competing colonial industry by restricting the sale of any hats made by colonists to the colony that produced them. The next year, 1733, saw the appearance of the Sugar Act (or Molasses Act) designed specifically to curb the growing colonial trade with the French Caribbean islands. Not only did Britain suffer from this trade, but France prospered — a doubly intolerable situation. By imposing a heavy tax on every gallon of foreign molasses, Parliament could theoretically stop this trade with the French. Again, however, enforcement was lax. Similarly, the Iron Act of 1750 and the Currency Act of 1751 were drawn up to serve British, not colonial, interests. In the end, they did more to irritate the colonists than to profit the mother country.

The empire, of course, had its own battles: internally, to be sure, but also externally against such formidable competitors in North America as France and Spain. In the first half of the eighteenth century, the fate of the North American continent still hung upon the fortunes of Europe's great powers. Ruling over all of Latin America (except Brazil), Spain's presence remained immense. In the area that would become the United States, Spain controlled Florida and by far the largest portion of the American Southwest. From the Atlantic to the Pacific oceans, Spanish soldiers and Spanish missionaries labored with the vision and sometimes with the reality of enormous empire.

In that same period, from 1700 to 1750, France consolidated its gains in Canada: starting from the Bay of St. Lawrence, French claims ran up that great river past the significant settlements of Quebec and Montreal, reaching as far as the Great Lakes. Later, as the French pushed south down the Mississippi Valley to New Orleans and Mobile, French territory stretched in a vast inland arc all the way from the North Atlantic to the Gulf of Mexico. The British colonies, by contrast, clung to the Atlantic shore, worrying about both French and Spanish imperial ambitions. The vulnerability of twelve mainland colonies in 1700 was shielded only by Britain's military might, both in Europe and in America.

The European competition for the North American continent reached its climax in the French and Indian War, known in Europe as the Seven Years' War (1756-1763). The American name for the conflict, the French and Indian War, identified Britain's principal European foe even as it also emphasized the crucial role of Native Americans in their shifting alliances or pledges of neutrality. No sooner had this "Great War for Empire"[1] ended in Britain's favor, however, than Britain discovered in its own settlements a spirit of restlessness and resistance that might prove even more troublesome than either Spain or France.

THE PRACTICE OF COLONIAL POLITICS

In each colony, voters and elected representatives strove to enlarge their voice in and control over their internal affairs — all within a broad frame of imperial policy. This search for more self-rule need not be seen as anti-British. Colonial politicians were just doing for their constituencies what members of Parliament were doing. Moreover, it simply made more sense for those who knew the local scene best to determine what worked best — both for the colony and for the empire. Parliament in faraway London resembled an absentee landlord: uninformed, inefficient, and sometimes uninterested. Parliament had its own differences of opinion, making unanimity there as elusive as in New York or Virginia. The radical Whigs in Britain saw liberty as their cause too, a cause aimed at an empire grown corrupt, autocratic, and self-indulgent.

❧ Politics at Home

By the 1730s, all thirteen original North American colonies except Georgia had been founded and set on their course of political development. Just as the terms and conditions of each colony in its first years had differed, so the local political development of each varied both in its nature and its rate of evolution. The days of joint-stock companies had passed; those of proprietorship were rapidly passing. Only in Pennsylvania, Delaware, and Maryland did the proprietor choose the governor. In other colonies, the king made his choice, and in the process met varying degrees of cooperation or resistance in the local legislatures.

EMERGING COLONIAL LEGISLATIVE POWER
The lower houses or assemblies in each colony saw themselves as roughly analogous to the House of Commons in Parliament. Just as the House of Commons struggled with the king over the boundaries of power, so the colonial assemblies jockeyed with a succession of governors for a clearer delineation of their authority. Within these assemblies, an increasingly assertive,

---

1. Modern historians' name for the conflict.

confident elite spoke with an ever stronger and more authoritative voice.

Connecticut and Rhode Island continued in the eighteenth century to operate under generous charters granted in the 1660s. These instruments of government granted virtually unlimited power to the assemblies — always provided, of course, that their local laws were not "repugnant" to the laws of England. But since their legislation did not require regular review in London, "repugnance" only came to anyone's attention if the sacrosanct Navigation Acts were violated. On occasion, however, persons aggrieved with the justice they received in either of these colonies might appeal directly to the Crown.

In Connecticut, for example, a property holder who died without a will had his property divided, not according to English Common Law, but according to the biblical Deuteronomic Law. Under the Common Law, all property would pass to the eldest son; but the Deuteronomic Law required that provision first be made for the widow and then that the property be divided equally among all the children, with perhaps a double portion to the eldest son.

In 1717 an eldest son, John Winthrop IV, took his case to George I's Privy Council, pointing out that Connecticut failed to follow the Common Law in this regard and had, in fact, often failed to obey parliamentary wishes in many other matters. After several years of litigation, the decision went against Connecticut. The colony, however, was accustomed to a great deal of latitude under its charter and so responded not by changing its laws but by appealing to Parliament to change its procedures — at least with respect to Connecticut. Although Parliament declined, Connecticut continued to do as it always had. The colony's authorities now took the precaution of securing agreement from all heirs that they would not appeal a judicial decision outside the colony — and if the heirs refused, the General Assembly simply delayed indefinitely making any property settlement whatsoever.

In Massachusetts, the lower house (operating under the new charter of 1691) participated in choosing the governor's council. This cooperative arrangement minimized conflict at the same time that it enabled the popularly elected body gradually to strengthen its own hand. Massachusetts, with its long tradition of independent operation under its original charter, worked hard to regain as much autonomy as possible. The best tactic was rarely to confront British authority directly. Like other colonies, Massachusetts strongly objected

Lord Cornbury? Political opponents of Lord Cornbury, royal governor of New York, circulated insinuations that the governor was fond of dressing in women's clothing, and this portrait was for many years thought to be of him in a dress. The painting is untitled and undated, however, so the identity of its subject will likely remain a mystery.

to the so-called "suspension clause," which stipulated that no legislative act went into effect until royal wishes concerning that act were known. Since such a suspension appeared to deny the very function of a legislature, elected representatives in the Bay Colony and elsewhere passed laws as needed without holding their collective breath to see whether the king approved. Royal governors admitted that the system was inherently defective, if not altogether obnoxious to the colonists. Consequently, the governors found themselves caught between their instructions from the king and the pressures from the legislatures.

The New York House of Assembly grew visibly restless when its royal governor proved arbitrary and autocratic. Under the imperious Lord Cornbury, governor from 1702 to 1708, conflict was inevitable. Cornbury took his royal prerogatives and himself so seriously as to object to any infringement — real or imagined — upon his authority. At the very time that Parliament was limiting royal power, Cornbury argued that in New York his power was absolute. When he arrested two Presbyterian itinerants for preaching without a license, one of the ministers, Francis Makemie, complained that England's Declaration of Religious Toleration (1689) made such arrest both illegal and improper. Cornbury pompously retorted that the act "does not extend to the Plantations [colonies] by its own intrinsic virtue, or any Intention of the Legislators, but only by her Majesty's Royal Instructions signified unto me." Since those instructions provided no specific exemptions for Presbyterian itinerants or other "strolling preachers," then you, Mr. Makemie, "shall not preach in my Government." But the tide ran against Cornbury, who was soon recalled, as the New York House continued to challenge and check its royal governors.

Pennsylvania's legislature built upon its Charter of Privileges that William Penn agreed to in 1701. Here the struggle was not against a royal governor but against a succession of appointed governors representing the Penn family. Pennsylvania's single legislative house moved to gain broad powers of appointment and taxation. By the 1730s and 1740s, the authority of the governor and his council sharply declined as that of the Assembly correspondingly grew. Quaker dominance in the Assembly also diminished as a diverse population burgeoned and as the Quakers' pacifism increased their unpopularity — especially on the frontier, where Indian warfare was commonplace. By 1756 the Quakers lost control of the legislature, so that it could now more confidently speak for the entire colony.

In Virginia the House of Burgesses throughout the eighteenth century steadily enlarged its governmental responsibilities. The House consisted of two burgesses elected in each county by the white male property owners, and it ruled in conjunction with — or in opposition to — the governor and his council. Although the council was sometimes compared to an upper house or senate, its twelve members were appointed by the royal governor, never elected by the people. So the voice of the voters had to be expressed in and through the House of Burgesses. The burgesses were specifically directed to hear the claims and grievances of the people. A 1727 history of the colony noted that the best way to "know the pressures, humors, common talk, and designs of the people" was to read the journal of the House and its committees.

As the century wore on, royal gubernatorial vetoes grew ever rarer and ever more difficult to enforce. Even if ultimately vetoed by the king, a Virginia law would have been in force in the colony for perhaps two years by the time the king learned of the law, imposed his veto, and sent official word of that action back across the ocean. Then the legislature could simply pass a slightly different law that would take effect immediately, even though it, too, might be negated a year or two later.

In South Carolina, the lower house took the name of Commons to make explicit the pervading sense that within the colony its power should be no less than that of the House of Commons within England. And indeed the South Carolina body proceeded to exercise its control over virtually every aspect of local administration and legislation. The royal governors were not so much opposed to this as frustrated by their own inability to govern as they had been instructed. For example, when the Board of Trade called upon all colonial governors to make certain that the Navigation Acts were strictly enforced, South Carolina governor James Glen responded in 1752 that this was virtually impossible. Such laws could be enforced in England, but not in South Carolina. In Charleston alone, Glen reported, fifty-nine ships could at the moment be found, "some loading, some unloading, at a dozen different wharves all along the bay, a street of half a mile in length." Only four officers of the realm had been commissioned to keep all this activity under close inspection. And that was just in Charleston alone. These four officers also had two other harbors to watch over, plus 150 miles of coastline "entirely open and full of rivers, creeks, and inlets where vessels may unload at pleasure without great risk of being disturbed." Colonial reality sometimes made a mockery of imperial policy, just as colonial legislatures labored to reduce colonial governors to a nullity.

INTRA-COLONIAL TENSIONS

Yet legislatures could nullify themselves when they turned into little more than subsidized debating societies. Colonial factionalism found its clearest expression in the lower houses, but also well beyond the walls of public buildings. Geography and ethnicity introduced disharmonies into many colonies. In Virginia, Bacon's Rebellion (1676) highlighted sectional tensions between the Tidewater and Piedmont regions, just as in New York Leisler's Rebellion (1689) underlined Anglo-Dutch ethnic strains.[2] Much later, in the 1760s, sec-

---

2. See Chapter 3.

tional tensions erupted in violent outbreaks in both South and North Carolina. There the so-called "Regulator" movement pitted backcountry people (chiefly Scots) against those living nearer the coast (chiefly English), who hoarded most of the power and suffered the fewest hardships.

In the South Carolina backcountry, settlers complained about the lack of support for roads and bridges as well as about inadequate representation in the Commons. When the Charleston authorities refused to come to their aid, in 1767 they created their own militia to drive out criminals and corrupt officials. These aggrieved citizens would virtually ignore the "eastern" authorities — as those authorities had ignored them. One approving observer noted that "the country was purged of all villains. The whores were whipped and drove off. The magistrates and constables associated with the rogues silenc'd and inhibited. Tranquility reigned." Although the picture was never that idyllic, within two or three years the Regulators' vigilante tactics had largely pacified the backcountry.

The violence and vigilantism were even worse in North Carolina. Backcountry grievances resembled South Carolina's: bad roads and bridges, and inadequate representation. Beyond that, however, the backcountry complained repeatedly about officials more interested in lining their own pockets than in ensuring justice and executing laws fairly. When these western settlers sought peaceful redress, they were either ignored or rebuffed. By 1771, protest turned violent as two armies of about one thousand men each clashed near Hillsborough, leaving nine men on each side mortally wounded. Americans killing other Americans bespeaks both the extremes of factionalism present in the colonies as well as a determination to protect popular sovereignty at the local level.

Quite apart from these most flagrant examples of intra-colonial divisions, specific legislation through much of the eighteenth century called attention to many other distinctions of economic status, ethnic loyalty, religious sentiment, and geographical interest. Merchants quarreled with farmers, creditors with debtors, property owners with the dispossessed, slaves with masters, Baptists with Anglicans, new immigrants with old settlers, frontier folk with Indians, and pirates with everyone who tried to punish or restrain them. Colonists had no shortage of issues to fight about, apart from any royal or parliamentary attempt to impose their respective wills.

THE THREAT OF AUTHORITY

But however divided and disputatious they were, colonists could find common ground when they faced particularly oppressive measures or obnoxious officials. As subjects of the British Empire, they thought of themselves as its beneficiaries, not its victims. They watched with interest the expansion of English liberty after the Glorious Revolution, and they wished to be included in that extension. They recognized the protection afforded by Britain's military power and from time to time they even demonstrated their willingness to become part of that armed force. They shared assumptions, values, traditions, and an intellectual framework that often did enable the colonial machinery to work, regardless of whether anyone was paying attention. But those same shared assumptions could threaten the imperial machinery when colonists felt themselves as separated from the broad mantle of English rights and liberties.

The churches, too, revealed some testiness about their own authority. Like the assemblies, they sought the maximum autonomy and freedom of action. Baptists and Congregationalists, of course, had long since elevated the authority of the local congregation into an honored principle. But even Anglicans, notably in the South, showed little inclination to accept the authority of a local bishop (had there been one), to say nothing of the Bishop of London. The laity who were in charge of Virginia Anglicanism very much preferred to keep it that way. Ministers served at the pleasure of the congregation. Just as the colonies had much to say about "home rule," so did the churches. In much of the eighteenth century, at any rate, it looked as though every church thought of itself as congregationalist.

❧ *Politics Abroad*

Ever since the mid-seventeenth-century English Civil War, radical Whigs had argued for greater individual freedom and tighter controls on the power of the state. Inspired by such remarkable figures in the 1640s as the Puritan poet John Milton and Roger Williams,[3] the "commonwealthmen" or radical Whigs worried about all entrenched power, be it of legislators, kings, or bishops. They also worried about England losing its moral standards, its self-discipline, and its public spirit.

In the Glorious Revolution of 1688-89 (see Chapter 3),

3. Williams, who returned from America to England in 1643 and 1651, played an important part in the intellectual and constitutional issues of revolutionary England.

Parliament restricted monarchical power — a restriction that Protestants felt the avowed Catholicism of King James II had made even more necessary. In justifying that revolution, the philosopher and political theorist John Locke dealt the final blow to the hoary "divine right of kings" doctrine. Kings, Locke argued, ruled not by power magnanimously bestowed from above but by power cautiously granted from below. The people held the ultimate power, and kings ruled only by their consent — a consent that could be withdrawn when tyranny threatened or fundamental rights were denied. Government did not create natural rights; government, therefore, could not deny natural rights. All authority rested on a voluntary agreement, and all authority bore watching. The colonists quoted Locke most frequently, but many other theorists also pressed for a quite different relationship between the rulers and the ruled.

In the early eighteenth century the more radical Whigs defended the right of dissenters from the Church of England. These dissenters most conspicuously included Congregationalists (or Independents), Presbyterians, Baptists, and Quakers. Radical Whigs also advocated freedom of the press and thought, praised the separation of powers, recognized the necessity of universal education, and worried — as had the Puritans — about basic weaknesses in human nature. Two great evils haunted the radical Whigs because they saw them as a threat to the survival of any nation, be it ancient Rome or modern England. The first evil was unchecked and arbitrary power. Evil was a part of human nature, but when one human being had enormous power, then the capacity for evil was magnified many times. Thus whenever people gave power to any ruler or body, they must take every precaution to see that the natural tendency to evil was blocked on all sides.

The second great evil was vice — the absence of virtue. All freedom-loving peoples must guard against the insidious growth of vice, just as they would against the rise of arbitrary power. One of the clearest signs that vice was defeating virtue was a decline in public spirit, defined as dedication to the welfare of all rather than the interest of a few. Another clear sign of vice was indulgence in luxury and self-regard. The signposts, the Whigs warned, should be read carefully in order to prevent Britain's ruin before it was too late for corrective measures. As Anglo-Irish philosopher and churchman George Berkeley noted in 1724: other nations had been wicked, but the English "are the first who have been wicked upon principle."

Two Whig writers living in London, John Trenchard and Thomas Gordon, gained great popularity in England and well beyond as they jointly satirized and attacked every abuse of power, every manifestation of political and public vice. Contemplating the nature of power, the authors in 1721 asserted that all government existed for the good of society. If that good were not served, the government could only be called a "Usurpation." The only difference between despotism and a proper government, they argued, was that "in free governments there are checks and restraints appointed and expressed in the Constitution itself." It made no sense — indeed it was nonsense — to talk of "absolute government." For, Trenchard and Gordon declared, absolutism no longer deserved the name of "government," but tyranny. No one should ever give power to another unless it was clear that the power would be used wisely and well; any who did otherwise "ought to be treated as idiots and lunatics."

If people were to be neither idiots nor lunatics, then they must — these Whigs tell us — so limit the exercise of power that it would never threaten to become absolute. People needed to remember that all men are wicked; in the words of Trenchard and Gordon: "Considering what sort of a creature man is, it is scarce possible to put him under too many restraints when he is possessed of great power. He may possibly use it well; but they act most prudently who, supposing that he would use it ill, inclose him within certain bounds, and make it terrible for him to exceed them." Power itself was not evil, but the abuse of power was the most terrifying evil that a free people had to confront and control.

These and other eighteenth-century Whigs looked to the republic of ancient Rome for lessons on how government might be constituted and for lessons on what went wrong. The answer to why Rome fell was simple: vice. Romans abandoned the pursuit of virtue to indulge themselves, to seek private good instead of the public good — that of the republic, or commonwealth. Instead of living simply, the Romans craved luxury. They built magnificent palaces, possessed a "prodigious number of slaves," wore magnificent jewels, and indulged themselves in food and drink served in the most opulent manner. And what, ask Trenchard and Gordon, did all the magnificence produce? Pleasure replaced temperance, idleness supplanted business, "and private regards extinguished that love of liberty, that zeal and warmth," which their ancestors had shown for the interest of the public. So given over were these later Romans to luxury and pride that,

Mission of San Xavier del Bac This imposing mission in the Sonoran Desert of present-day southern Arizona was built by Spanish Franciscan friars in the early eighteenth century, as the sphere of effective Spanish authority crept north of the Mexican heartland. It remains one of the finest examples of colonial baroque architecture in the United States.

"having before sold every thing else, [they] at last sold their country." No wonder that Rome fell. "Thus ended the greatest, the noblest state . . . that ever the Sun saw." And the authors would make the moral unmistakably clear: that "every other nation must run the same fortune, expect the same fatal catastrophe, who suffer themselves to be debauched with the same vices."

When these Britons, and later their American disciples, spoke of virtue, what they primarily meant was a public virtue that puts the welfare of others before the satisfaction of self. "Public spirit," the repeated refrain, as Trenchard and Gordon defined it, is "the highest virtue, and contains in it almost all others . . . it is a passion to promote universal good, with personal pain, loss, and peril; it is one man's care for many, and the concern of every man for all." Of course, citizens should give attention to family and friends and property, but not at the expense of the greater good for the nation. In continental Europe, the authors noted, the poor paid heavy taxes and tariffs "all to make a wanton and luxurious Court, filled with the worst and vilest of men." Half a province was starved to death in order "to make a gay garden!" That was not public spirit, but the conspicuous pursuit of vice and debauchery.

Colonists heard such rhetoric with eagerness and ready assent. Especially among Congregationalists and Presbyterians who took matters of public morality most seriously, and were more likely than others to have the capacity to enforce their standards, the radical Whig stance neatly coincided with their own. The depravity of humankind needed above all to be checked, not indulged. Kings, advisers, legislators, governors — all must be held to strict account for their allegiance to virtue. Moreover, if England were on a path to ruin, then perhaps it had surrendered its right to rule over a people more clearly dedicated to virtue than to vice. The Whigs, of course, fixed their eye mainly on reform within England, but their sharp criticism of an indulgent royalty and an arbitrary bureaucracy could have application well beyond their own island.

Meanwhile, the king and his advisers and many members of Parliament worried not so much about questions of vice and virtue as about matters of empire and national prestige. The most pressing question pertained not to ancient Rome but to modern European nations and their colonial possessions abroad. And the most immediate challenge was whether the British or the French would "own" the North American continent.

THE CONTEST FOR A CONTINENT

With the end of Queen Anne's War[4] in 1713, North Americans (except for a brief flare-up in 1739) enjoyed about a generation of release from Europe's exported conflicts. When fighting resumed in 1743 (King George's War), Spain had moved deep into the American West, and France had dispersed its traders, trappers, and missionaries through the Great Lakes and Mississippi Valley. Indeed, a map of North America for the middle of the eighteenth century would show Spain and France far ahead of Britain in territorial influence and domi-

4. In Europe this conflict was called the War of the Spanish Succession.

nance. The rivalry was real, and Britain seemed to be losing the race.

❧ *Spain: Safeguarding an Empire*

Since the beginning of Spanish presence in North America, notably in Florida and New Mexico, representatives of Cross and Crown marched or waded or rode horseback together. When in 1680 an Indian rebellion overran Santa Fe, New Mexico, killing settlers and Franciscan friars alike, the missionaries depended upon the state to bring about a reconquest in 1692. On other occasions, however, the state relied more on the church to explore, pacify, and hold territory for Spain. In Arizona, for example, the Jesuit Eusebio Kino staked out important territory as he turned cartographer and linguist, taught natives the techniques of farming, built chapels, and founded a major mission, Xavier del Bac, near Tucson.

Better known are the labors of a Franciscan missionary, Junípero Serra, who beginning in 1769 founded a chain of missions in California that extended all the way from San Diego to San Francisco. The missions became centers of training and catechizing, with the consequence that many Indians lost their tribal identity and patterns of culture. With the outbreak of European diseases in the confinement of the mission, many also lost their lives. Although only a fraction of California's Indian population lived under the control of the missions, that segment helped promote cattle and sheep grazing on a large scale, raised crops of wheat, corn, and beans, and contributed to the mission storehouses ample supplies of wine, leather, and wool.

In a futile effort to reclaim their traditional patterns of life, "mission Indians" frequently ran away or even attempted short-lived armed revolts. As a consequence, discipline was harsh, not greatly different from that imposed upon runaway or rebellious slaves in English colonies at the same time. The California mission friars readily employed shackles, hobbles, whippings, and imprisonment to keep the Indians in place and at work. And work they did, at great expense to their spirit and humanity. From all this, Father Serra has emerged a hero for some, a villain for others.

Beyond missionary activity, trading brought the Spanish and the Indians into frequent contact. Major centers in New Mexico such as Taos and Pecos enticed even the Plains Indians to the bartering grounds where they could obtain agricultural produce in exchange for their carefully crafted baskets and jewelry. Horses were also major items of trade, as earlier they had been prizes of war and raiding. At first, the Spanish had been reluctant to surrender the military value that horses offered, but in the vastness of the Southwest and Far West, maintaining a monopoly of the horse market proved impossible.

Often Spain would form an alliance with one tribe — the Comanches, for example — to help subdue more antagonistic tribes such as the Apaches. On other occasions, the Apaches would join the Spanish against the French in Louisiana. All these alliances were temporary, as Spanish officials concerned themselves above all with securing their empire's enormous land claims in the Western Hemisphere. If Spain could from time to time cast its lot with France to frustrate the imperial designs of Britain, so much the better. But the Spanish government could never relax its guard against European competitors that would happily gobble up portions of Spain's enormous empire.

While keeping one eye upon Europe, Spain needed another to watch its own colonies. There, the impulses toward self-governance grew in the eighteenth century until, in the early nineteenth, they broke the bonds of allegiance. After 1800, Spain's fall in the New World would be as dramatic as its rise after 1500.

❧ *France: Winning an Empire*

Economically, France's settlements in Canada and Louisiana proved about as disappointing in the first half of the eighteenth century as had the English colonies a century before. France's Canadian fur trade brought some profit at first, but soon warehouses in France were bulging with so many furs that prices plummeted. While fur trapping and trading continued, French Canadians also turned to farming, especially of wheat, both for sustenance and export. In Louisiana the French government expected private capital to develop natural resources, but initial high hopes of finding rich mines or encouraging large numbers of settlers soon collapsed. Like England, France resorted to clearing out its prisons for potential settlers, but this only gave Louisiana an even worse reputation. When Louisiana came under royal control in 1731, it had made money neither for its private investors nor for the Crown.

Nonetheless, if New France was expensive economically, politically it was even more difficult to abandon such impressive territorial claims. After all, France controlled the two greatest rivers of the continent, the St. Lawrence and the Mississippi, and as long as it held

Ursuline Convent The Old Ursuline Convent in the French Quarter of New Orleans was constructed in 1745 and is the oldest building of record in the Mississippi Valley.

those waterways it could cramp if not stifle further English expansion. For thirty years following the 1713 Treaty of Utrecht, France and England avoided war. Yet France did not seize the opportunities of this interlude to strengthen its imperial administration or improve its empire's economic prospects. Instead, bickering and intrigue continued to plague all the affairs of both church and state.

Peace ended in 1743 with the outbreak of King George's War, a war fought more in Europe than in America.[5] France did attack Nova Scotia, however, and New Englanders responded with a major expedition against the well-defended Fort Louisbourg on Cape Breton Island, just to the north of Nova Scotia. New Englander William Pepperell led a force of some ninety ships and about four thousand men against what had been described as the Gibraltar of North America. After a siege of seven weeks, Pepperell on June 17, 1745, seized

the now-crumbling fortress, captured more than a thousand prisoners, and gave the American fighting forces much to cheer about. But the cheering soon ended. In the Peace of Aix-la-Chapelle in 1748 all conquests were returned at the end of inconclusive fighting in Europe. But this only meant that Britain and France were fated soon to fight again for the right to rule the North American continent.

New France had been particularly successful in converting native peoples to Christianity. The Jesuits had left an indelible mark on Indian communities from the Great Lakes to New Orleans, and their impressive energies, along with those of Capuchins, Ursulines, and others, seemed to give French Catholicism a head start in the ecclesiastical conquest of interior America. That promising start was severely damaged in the early 1760s, when European politics resulted in the withdrawal of all Jesuits from their mission fields

5. In European history, this conflict is known as the War of the Austrian Succession.

and the abolition of the Society of Jesus in 1773. (It was restored by the pope in 1814.) In the Mississippi Valley, the order of expulsion asserted that the Jesuits could no longer wear distinctive clothing, that "all their property, real or personal, was to be seized and sold at auction." All sacred vessels or ornaments in New Orleans should be turned over to others and, in the country of the Illinois Indians, all chapels, once divested of valuable items, should be destroyed. The missionaries themselves were ordered back to France by the very first available ships. This religious reversal, independent of the military one, contributed to France's weakness in the New World; by 1765 French claims to Native American hearts and souls, no less than to lands, had dramatically declined.

A Plea for Union   Benjamin Franklin designed this image at the outset of the French and Indian War, urging the British colonies to support a united war effort by forming the so-called Albany Union. But each North American province had its own idea of its vital interests, and colonial cooperation remained an unfulfilled dream at that time.

POLITICAL THOUGHT AND POLITICAL PASSION IN BRITISH NORTH AMERICA

The last of the great Anglo-French conflicts of the eighteenth century, the French and Indian War (1756-1763), brought Great Britain enormous territories in North America, but also enormous debts. British efforts to secure colonial compliance in reducing those debts led to a series of confrontations and increasingly bitter disputes. Many of these clashes revolved around the Stamp Act of 1765 and the new departure in British policy that this law appeared to represent. The Stamp Act Congress and subsequent protests stimulated expressions of political philosophy that soon moved from quiet scholarly discourse to the noisy shouts of town hall and marketplace. All these economic and political arguments were aggravated by apparent religious aggression from London, as well as by potential religious oppression from Quebec. As colony after colony put forward repeated resolves, as mobs marched in the streets, and as sporadic violence broke out all along the Atlantic coast, some concluded that the time had arrived for united, intercolonial action. In 1774 the First Continental Congress gathered in Philadelphia — and the American Revolution gathered momentum.

The Great War for Empire

America's last colonial war was the most decisive for both Britain and France, to say nothing of the colonies themselves. And though that war began as a series of skirmishes in southeastern Pennsylvania, before it was over much of Europe as well as all of North America felt the full force of military struggle. This "Great War for Empire" tilted the delicate European balance of power sharply in Britain's direction. By the time the Peace of Paris was at last signed on February 10, 1763, the map of North America had taken on a surprisingly different look.

In the early 1750s, while French missionaries and soldiers moved steadily down from Canada into the Ohio Valley and the Illinois country, British traders and colonists were pressing steadily westward into those same areas. The fight for empire would first manifest itself in suspicious neighbors crowding each other in contests for the land, the trading privileges, and the critical loyalty of the Indian tribes. Pennsylvania and Virginia, which extended to the west without limit, felt the sharp edge of this international competition, as the French took steps to mark the West as indisputably theirs. To stake their claim, they buried in the soil leaden plates with inscriptions claiming ownership of the land for France. Meanwhile the Canadian governor, the Marquis Duquesne, ordered that a string of forts be built, not only in the Ohio Valley but also in what is today western Pennsylvania. Here was a challenge that could not be ignored.

Virginia felt as injured as Pennsylvania, since many Virginians had invested in the Ohio Company, a speculative venture designed to develop (and sell at a profit) vast western lands. Governor Robert Dinwiddie of Virginia in 1753 dispatched twenty-one-year-old George Washington to tell the French that they were encroaching upon long-standing British claims. After skeptically hearing out the young Virginian, the French authorities told him that they would not retreat from forts already erected and would, indeed, build more. The following year Dinwiddie sent Washington back with a small complement of troops to protect workers building an English fort. But the French routed first the builders and then, by the summer of 1754, Washington himself, forcing him to retreat. On the very spot where the British had hoped to establish a fort on the Ohio River in western Pennsylvania, the French built their own, Fort Duquesne. For Britain, the French and Indian War was off to a bad start.

England's Board of Trade determined that the colonial response to French adventurism must be a coordinated rather than a piecemeal action. To that end, the board summoned an all-colony congress to gather in Albany in June 1754. When this congress (in fact representing only seven colonies) met, a committee led by Benjamin Franklin presented a Plan of Union. Its clear purpose was to warn the French against trying to pick off Britain's colonies one by one: first, Pennsylvania or Virginia from the west, then New York or New England from the north. The colonies would stand together, not waiting for each local assembly to debate, to weigh its advantages, and at last to vote. "One principal encouragement to the French," Franklin wrote, "in invading and insulting the British American dominions was their knowledge of our disunited state." The Plan of Union would correct that disunity by providing for a president-general of the United Colonies, as well as a Grand Council to represent all the colonies. Although the congress and the colonial legislatures approved the plan, London did not. Political victories proved as elusive as military ones.

Britain's military fortunes continued to sink. In 1755 British authorities dispatched General Edward Braddock to stop the French advance in the west, particularly by forcing Fort Duquesne into a humiliating surrender. Moving men and supplies over mountainous

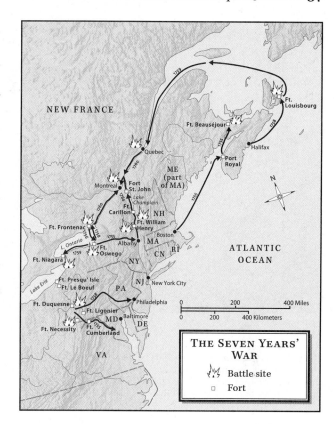

terrain and through heavy forests, Braddock (accompanied by Major George Washington) got within ten miles of the fort when a surprise ambush of Indians and French (themselves disguised as Indians) put the British forces to rout. The panic of retreat, said Washington, was like that of "sheep pursued by dogs." Braddock himself was killed along with some nine hundred other British casualties, killed or wounded. That July day of 1755 had indeed seen humiliation, but not of the French.

A second front, designed to take Fort Niagara on the southern shore of Lake Ontario and to thwart the arrival of further French enforcements at the mouth of the St. Lawrence River, fared no better. The British hung onto their fort on the northern tip of Nova Scotia and deported from that province some five thousand Acadians, many of whom made their painful way south all the way to French Louisiana. The exile of these Acadians (hence the name "Cajuns") marked their own heroism more than that of the British forces. The British won an ambiguous victory near the southern edge of Lake Champlain, encouraging them to bestow a new name — Lake George — on what the French had called Lac du St. Sacrement. But French victories outnumbered British ones, giving great encouragement to the few inhabitants of New France but more importantly

View of the Taking of Quebeck by the English Forces Commanded by Gen.l Wolfe Sep: 13.th 1759.

The British Attack on Quebec This 1760 engraving shows General James Wolfe's expedition against Quebec. Wolfe's army made a daring assault up steep cliffs to attack the seemingly impregnable French fortress in what became the decisive battle in the long Anglo-French struggle for empire in North America.

swinging Native American loyalties increasingly to France's side.

British fortunes began to change when William Pitt, appointed secretary of state by King George II in 1756, assumed the office of prime minister and took upon himself the overall direction of foreign and military policy. Pitt saw the colonial battlegrounds not as the fringes of imperial interests but as the very center. In Europe, Britain might be content to settle for a balance of power: supporting King Frederick the Great of Prussia here, resisting Austria and Russia there. But in North America, conquest must be the goal. Pitt, there-

fore, shifted British priorities and might to the North American theater, seeing the whole continent as the key to Britain's success as a world trader and global power. With his oratory, his geopolitical vision, and his adroit cultivation of the colonists, Pitt succeeded where others had failed. When Fort Duquesne fell to the British in 1758, it was promptly and appropriately renamed Fort Pitt. Today the place is called Pittsburgh.

The St. Lawrence River was New France's lifeline and the heavily fortified city of Quebec its heart. Take Quebec, and New France would fall. That simple strategy, however, had been frustrated repeatedly as Quebec, on a cliff high above the St. Lawrence and walled on the other three sides, proved virtually impregnable. When General James Wolfe arrived with a fleet and some nine thousand troops in June 1759, the opposing general, the Marquis de Montcalm, wisely decided to stay behind his city's stout walls. For two months Wolfe waited for the French to venture out, but to no avail. In early September he took the offensive, under cover of darkness moving about half his force up a steep cliff to the Plains of Abraham, just west of the city. Recognizing that in this position the British could cut off all supplies to Quebec, Montcalm had no choice but to attack. Both Montcalm and Wolfe perished in the bloody conflict that followed, but on September 17, 1759, the city of Quebec surrendered. A year later Montreal fell and then all of Canada.

In the Peace of Paris (1763), France ceded Canada

❋ IN THEIR OWN WORDS

The Fall of Quebec, 1759

Here Admiral Charles Saunders relates the fall of Quebec to Secretary of State William Pitt.

[British troops] embarked on board the ships and vessels above the town the night of the 6th instant [September], and at four in the morning of the 13th began to land on the north shore, about a mile and a half

above the town. General Montcalm with his whole army left their camps at Beauport and marched to meet [the other army]. A little before ten both armies were formed, and the enemy began the attack. Our troops received their fire and reserved their own, advancing till they were so near as to run in upon them and push them with their bayonets, by which, in very little time, the

French gave way and fled to the town in the utmost disorder, and with great loss, for our troops pursued them quite to their walls, and killed many of them upon the glacis [slope] and in the ditch. . . . If the town had been further off, the whole French army must have been destroyed. . . . I am sorry to acquaint you that General Wolfe was killed in the action. . . .

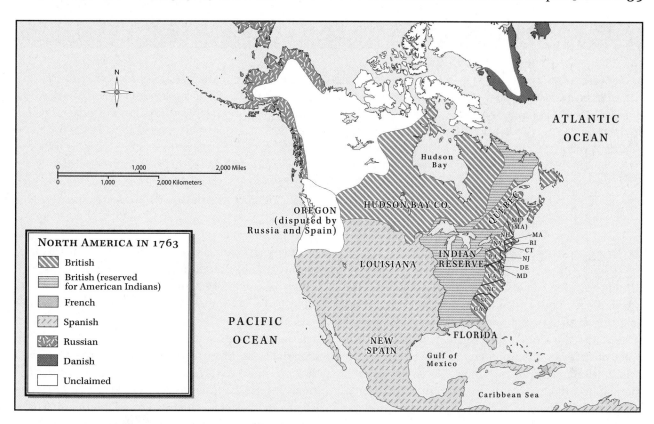

NORTH AMERICA IN 1763

- British
- British (reserved for American Indians)
- French
- Spanish
- Russian
- Danish
- Unclaimed

to Britain, along with all of the French claims east of the Mississippi River. Spain, which had allied with France in 1761, paid the price of being on the wrong side by losing Florida, although the French in a secret agreement gave New Orleans and Louisiana to Spain. But the British won full navigation rights to the Mississippi, which was to become the United States' own lifeline. France retained fishing rights off Newfoundland, along with two tiny islands in the Gulf of St. Lawrence, a pathetic remnant of what had once been both a proud and ambitious colonization effort in North America.

The Peace of Paris had important implications for India, for Africa, for Europe, and for scattered islands throughout the Caribbean, but its greatest impact, directly and indirectly, was on North America. The British found themselves in possession of a huge half-continent that must somehow be turned into a profit, not a loss; the humiliated French licked their wounds and awaited some opportunity for revenge; and the colonists, now convinced of their own strength, prepared to take advantage of the peace and of the newly accessible and inviting lands east of the Mississippi.

Those lands, however, were dramatically closed from the colonists by George III's proclamation of 1763. With a line drawn along the peaks of the Appalachian mountain chain, Britain decreed that the colonists would be confined to the territory east of that line, while the Native Americans would be reassured that all lands west of it would remain in their hands. Fur traders thought the line could work to their advantage, since it would keep settlers out. Land companies believed that they could make a profit from legitimate purchasers, as opposed to unauthorized migrants and squatters. Indians applauded the decision because it seemed to secure their rights to farm, fish, hunt, and rule from the Appalachians to the Mississippi. Since many tribes had recently defected from the French to the British, the proclamation rewarded them. Settlers east of the mountains, however, were far less happy with this royal edict. Not only did the line challenge or deny the boundaries accorded by the colonial charters, but the colonists living under those charters had for some time hungrily eyed the vast acreage on the western slopes and in the Ohio Valley. Here was land to be cleared, farmed, divided, and traded — in short, land that could lead to wealth. Expressing the hopes of many, George Washington regarded the 1763 line as only "a temporary expedient to quiet the minds of the Indians"; he urged Virginians and others not to delay unduly in staking out their claims across the Appalachians.

❈ IN THEIR OWN WORDS

The Board of Trade on New Western Colonies, 1768

England's Board of Trade saw the expansion of the American colonies westward as a profitable venture.

These arguments appear to us reducible to the following general propositions: namely, First, that such colonies will promote population and increase the demands for, and consumption of, British manufactures. Secondly, that they will secure the fur trade and prevent all illicit trade or interfering of French or Spaniards with the Indians. Thirdly, that they will be a defense and protection to the old colonies against the Indians. Fourthly, that they will contribute to lessen the present heavy expense of supplying provisions to the distant forts and garrisons. Lastly, that they are necessary in respect to the inhabitants already residing in those places . . . who require some form of civil government. . . .

❧ An Aggressive Kingdom

Britain, however, had other plans for the colonists. The war had been both long and expensive — seven years counting from 1756, but far longer than that if earlier sorties into the Ohio Valley were included. And the point of the war, Pitt would agree, was to enrich the British Isles, not impoverish them. No one objected if the colonies themselves prospered, but nearly everyone in Britain objected if colonial prosperity came at the expense of the empire itself. When George II died in 1760 (succeeded by his young grandson, George III), when Pitt retired in 1761, and when the Peace of Paris was signed in 1763, the stage was set for a new era in imperial relationships. The emphasis would now move from conciliation, compromise, and even what has been called "benign neglect," to ministerial directives and parliamentary coercion.

TAXING THE COLONIES

When George Grenville became chancellor of the exchequer in 1763, he determined to bring the colonists into compliance with the many Navigation Acts that had been passed during the preceding century. Smuggling would be stopped, taxes would be paid, delinquents would be tried (in vice-admiralty courts), and revenues would be collected and faithfully transmitted to England. In 1764 the Sugar Act levied a tax that, for the first time, had the express purpose of raising revenue — as its alternative name, the Revenue Act, clearly demonstrated. In addition to the tax on sugar or molasses, the 1764 legislation also imposed duties on wine, indigo, and coffee. Several colonies protested that such a tax represented a usurpation of the authority that each assembly jealously guarded for itself, just as Parliament jealously guarded its right — as opposed to the king's right — to tax citizens of the United Kingdom.

American colonists were not represented in the British Parliament. Therefore a growing number of colonial critics contended that they could not legitimately be subject to a tax imposed from abroad. As Massachusetts lawyer James Otis declared in 1764, the colonists had the same natural rights as all other persons, and if such rights be "taken from them without their consent, they are so far enslaved." The colonies, already suffering from a postwar depression, could not be expected "all of a sudden" (said Otis) "to bear all this terrible burden" of paying for the last war. If Parliament could tax America's trade, then, asked Otis, what was to prevent that body from taxing all its lands, its homes, and everything else? Furthermore, it was wrong to assume that the colonists had been freely living off the generosity and military might of Britain. On the contrary, Otis noted, "the colonies are and have been at great expense in raising men, building forts, and supporting the King's civil government here." Should even more money be required of the Americans, "it seems but equal they should be allowed to assess the charges of it themselves." In other words, said Otis, if the colonists were to be taxed further, then let their own legislatures — not a remote and uninformed Parliament — do it. Such would be fair, just, and "equal."

THE STAMP ACT

Neither impressed nor deterred, Grenville pressed on with an even more objectionable tax the next year. The Stamp Act of 1765 required the purchase of officially stamped paper for use in virtually anything printed in the colonies: deeds, legal judgments, almanacs, newspapers, advertisements, and, of course, certificates of compliance with the many customs regulations. At almost any point in the conduct of public business, Americans would confront the unwelcome novelty of a tax passed by Parliament aimed directly at the colonies. But more than mere novelty was involved: colonists argued that Parliament was attempting to do what it had absolutely no right to do. A principle was at stake. Colonists, they argued, could be taxed only by their own action. The colonists elected no members of Parliament. Any tax, however small or however rationalized, thrust upon them by Parliament without their consent deprived them of their natural rights as Englishmen and tended, as James Otis had said, to reduce them to slavery.

Protests multiplied. The act had passed in March of 1765; by May colonial newspapers were full of that news and equally full of the almost instantaneous negative reaction. In Boston, New York, and Philadelphia, popular "Sons of Liberty" movements threatened to take the law into their own hands. Mob violence frequently erupted. Composed chiefly of artisans or members of the lower classes, the Sons of Liberty represented a swelling populist resentment. But to many, they also represented ugly anarchy. As Thomas Hutchinson, lieutenant governor of Massachusetts, declared, widespread and spontaneous protests have "given the lower sort of people such a sense of their importance that a gentleman does not meet with what used to be called common civility, and we are sinking into perfect barbarism."

Protests came from others besides mobs. At the end of May 1765 the Virginia House of Burgesses resolved that the Stamp Act violated all charter rights granted to Virginia as well as those natural rights belonging to Virginians every bit as much as they belonged to those "abiding and born within the realm of England." If people no longer had the right to tax themselves or choose the representatives who will levy a tax upon them, then they had lost "the only security against a burdensome taxation."

Protesting against the Stamp Act, the young Virginian burgess Patrick Henry began to acquire his reputation for powerful, even inflammatory rhetoric. According to some reports, Henry declaimed to his fellow members of the Virginia House that "Caesar had his Brutus, Charles I his Cromwell, and King George III . . ." Immediately Henry's speech was interrupted by cries of "Treason! Treason!" — whereupon he finished more calmly: ". . . and King George may profit by their example." Whether apocryphal or not, the reporting does point to the distinction between attacking Parliament, which in 1765 was regarded as a safe target, and attacking the king, which in that year most Americans were unprepared to do.

Parliament, too, had its defenders, including to be sure members of that body itself. One such member,

The British Response Tarring and feathering was a humiliating, painful, and often dangerous, disfiguring, or even fatal punishment, depending on how hot the tar was. This British caricature attacks what was widely viewed in the mother country as the rabid fanaticism of the American patriots, shown here forcing tea down the throat of a tarred-and-feathered loyalist revenue agent — with a hangman's rope dangling ominously from a Liberty Tree.

Soame Jenyns, also an official of the Board of Trade, abruptly dismissed the notion that Parliament had no right to tax any Englishman anywhere. Parliament's right was so "indisputably clear" that it would seem utterly unnecessary to assert it except for the many arguments recently "flung out," their absurdity matched only by their insolence. All this talk about "liberty," Jenyns noted, was simply hiding behind a rhetorical smokescreen. "The liberty of an Englishman is a phrase of so various a signification, having within these few years been used as a synonymous term for blasphemy, bawdy, treason, libels, strong beer, and cyder, that I shall not here presume to define its meaning." One thing, however, that it surely did not mean was a repudiation of Parliament's right to legislate taxes for the entire empire.

George Grenville likewise saw Parliament's right to tax the colonies as beyond dispute. More than that, Grenville believed that the Americans were acting like ungrateful wretches. So did Charles Townshend, later to

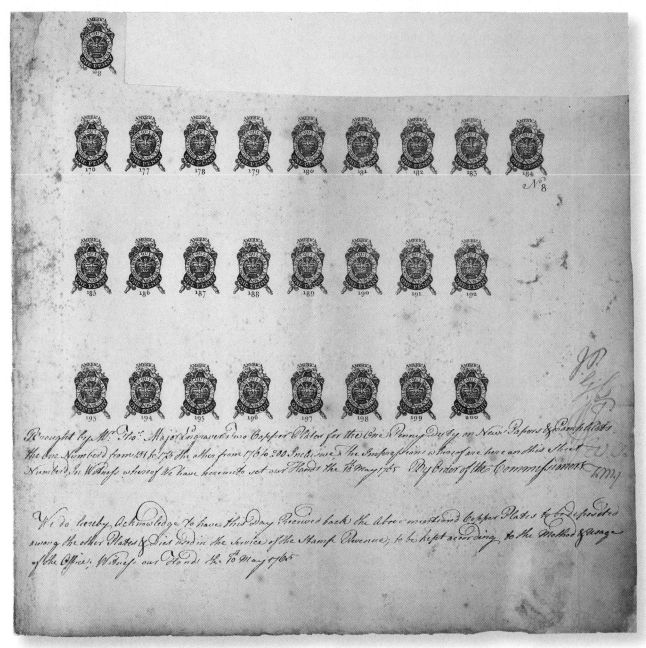

Stamp Act Stamps   This proof sheet of 1-penny stamps was submitted for approval to the Commissioners of Stamps by an engraver, May 10, 1765. According to the Stamp Act, the stamps were to be used on newspapers, pamphlets, and all other papers in the American colonies "being larger than half a sheet and not exceeding one whole sheet."

become Chancellor of the Exchequer. In defending the Stamp Act in 1765, Townshend allowed himself a concluding rhetorical flourish: "And now will these Americans, children planted by our care, nourished by our indulgence until they are grown to a degree of strength and opulence, and protected by our arms, will they grudge to contribute their mite to relieve us from the heavy weight of that burden which we lie under?" This performance stirred Isaac Barré, a former British army officer who had spent much time in America, to come passionately to the defense of the American view. "They planted by your care? No!" thundered Barré. "They fled from your tyranny to a then uncultivated and unhospitable country.... They nourished by your indulgence? They grew by your neglect of 'em.... They protected by *your* arms? They have nobly taken up arms in your defense...." Barré's speech did not dissuade Parliament from its path, but it did give much aid and comfort on the other side of the Atlantic Ocean.

Not all Englishmen voted for members of Parliament, but all Englishmen, so the British argument

Jonathan Mayhew on "The Powers That Be," 1750

In a "Discourse concerning Unlimited Submission and Non-Resistance to Higher Powers," the Reverend Jonathan Mayhew referenced the biblical Epistle to the Romans to draw a distinction between rulers who governed tyrannically and those who did not.

Let us now trace the apostle's reasoning in favor of submission to the higher powers, a little more particularly and exactly. For by this it will appear, on one hand, how good and conclusive it is for submission to those rulers who exercise their power in a proper manner. And, on the other, how weak and trifling and unconnected it is, if it be sup-

posed to be meant by the apostle to show the obligation and duty of obedience to tyrannical, oppressive rulers in common with others of a different character.

---

went, were nonetheless represented in Parliament. If the citizens of the new industrial city of Birmingham did not complain because their representation was not direct, why should Americans object? They, too, had a *virtual,* if not an actual, representation. A Maryland lawyer, Daniel Dulany, dismissed out of hand this British argument that Parliament did indeed represent the people of Boston, Massachusetts, as much as the people of Birmingham, England. Nonsense, Dulany replied: "The notion of a *virtual representation* of the colonies . . . is a mere cob-web, spread to catch the unwary, and intangle the weak." Dulany was willing to concede that Great Britain had the right to regulate trade, but it had no right to impose a direct tax — such as the Stamp Act — for the sole purpose of raising revenue. True, Dulany admitted, British interests and colonial interests were allied, but this did not mean a perfect congruence. "The connection between a freeholder of Great Britain and a British American [is] deducible only through a train of reasoning which few will take the trouble . . . to investigate." And the tie between the British American and a member of Parliament was even more remote: it was "a knot too infirm to be relied on."

The colonial clergy joined in the call for repeal of the Stamp Act. Stephen Johnson, pastor of the First Congregational Church in Lyme, Connecticut, preached a fast day sermon in December 1765 and published a series of newspaper articles all condemning what he saw as the growing arrogance of Parliament. If Parliament could impose a Stamp Act, then what other evils might follow? It could also afflict us with "a poll tax, a land tax, a malt tax, a cider tax, a window tax, a smoke tax, and why not tax us for the light of the sun, the air we breathe, and the ground we are buried in?" In Boston, the better-known Jonathan Mayhew, pastor of the city's West Congregational Church, condemned the Stamp Act on August 25 in such uncompromising terms that

many blamed him for the riots that erupted the following day. Taking his text from Galatians 5:12-13 ("For you were called to freedom . . ."), Mayhew spoke of the many dimensions of liberty and how a people must ever be on guard lest liberty degenerate into slavery.

Debate moved from the relative quiet of the spoken and printed word to the clamor of the milling mobs. On August 26, 1765, a Boston crowd stoned and tore apart the home of the official appointed to distribute the stamped paper. They also viciously attacked the house of Lieutenant Governor Thomas Hutchinson, smashing furniture, destroying books and private papers, and carrying off a great deal of loot. All of this was done on the basis of a rumor that Hutchinson, a fourth-generation American (and descendant of Anne Hutchinson), had supported and promoted the Stamp Act. He had, in fact, vigorously oppposed it, but as the symbol of royal power in Massachusetts he was a convenient if unlucky scapegoat. Riots also broke out in Newport and New York City. By October of that year it was clear that public passions needed restraining, that a resort to dignified discussion and debate was desperately required. In that month, representatives from nine colonies met in New York to raise a united and remarkably moderate voice in protest.

The Stamp Act Congress, repeating some of the same points that had been made colony by colony, gave greater force to those arguments by speaking in unison. The Congress, however, added new contentions of its own. Declaring themselves loyal sons of the empire, the twenty-seven men present vowed that their allegiance and their liberties were the same as all other English citizens: not more, not less. If Parliament levied a tax upon citizens living in Plymouth, England, that was well and good; if, however, Parliament levied a tax upon the people in Plymouth, Massachusetts, that was another matter altogether. "The People of these Colo-

IN THEIR OWN WORDS

Governor Thomas Hutchinson on Troubled Times in Boston, 1769

In this letter to a friend in London, Thomas Hutchinson confides his opinion that, for the sake of security, colonists in America should not share all the freedoms of those living in England.

I never think of measures necessary for the peace and good order to the colonies without pain. There must be an abridgement of what are called English liberties. I relieve myself by considering that in a remove from the state of nature to the most perfect state of government there must be a great restraint of natural liberty. I doubt whether it is possible to project a system of government in which a colony of three thousand miles distant from the parent state shall enjoy all the liberty of the parent state. I am certain I have never yet seen the projection. I wish the good of the colony when I wish to see some further restraint of liberty — rather than the connection with the parent state should be broken, for I am sure a breach must prove the ruin of the colony. Pardon me this excursion; it really proceeds from the state of mind into which our perplexed affairs often throws me.

nies," said the Congress, "are not, and from their local Circumstances cannot be, Represented in the House of Commons in Great Britain." Only their own respective legislatures, colony by colony, could tax them. The increased use of the vice-admiralty courts, moreover, had "a manifest Tendency to subvert the Rights and Liberties of the Colonists" since those courts denied that fundamental guarantee of a trial by jury. Arguing that the relationship between the colonies and the mother country must be "mutually Affectionate and Advantageous," this Congress concluded with "humble Applications" that the Stamp Act be repealed.

The following March it was. In May, Jonathan Mayhew delivered a sermon published under the title *The Snare Broken.* Here, he sought to absolve both king and Parliament of responsibility for the despised Stamp Act, explaining that it had been the work of "some evil-minded individuals in Britain who . . . spared no wicked arts, no deceitful, no dishonorable means to push on and obtain, as it were by *surprise,* an act so prejudicial." But not all colonists were so readily mollified. The repeal would have alleviated more resentments had not Parliament at the very same time passed the Declaratory Act that retreated not one inch from positions taken in 1764 and 1765, although Parliament artfully avoided using the word *tax.* Parliamentary rights had always been, and would always remain, uncompromised.

Nonetheless, the despised Stamp Act had been repealed. When that news reached the colonies several weeks later, celebrations erupted from Georgia to Maine. The Americans understood the repeal to be a parliamentary surrender to colonial principled argumentation. Britons' understanding, however, was far different. From the British perspective, a tactical concession had been made, but the principle held fast: Crown and Parliament remained wholly in charge of and responsible for the entire empire.

REASSERTING BRITISH AUTHORITY

In 1767 Parliament, under the guidance of now Chancellor of the Exchequer Charles Townshend, passed a series of revenue-raising laws known collectively as the Townshend Acts. The message of the Declaratory Act was translated into action, without giving British Americans much time to cool down from the passions of the previous two years. Special duties were imposed upon such items as lead, glass, paint, and tea, with a new Board of Customs Commissioners, headquartered in Boston, designated as the vigilant collecting agents. These actions were meant not to insult the colonists but to produce much-needed revenue for an empire still burdened with debt; and money would stay in America to cover the costs of administering justice and maintaining the appropriate agencies of government.

The colonists nonetheless felt insulted. They saw these new commissioners in the darkest light: persons who accepted bribes, seized ships, and utilized the vice-admiralty courts so as to arouse even more protests than before. Massachusetts's leading propagandist, Sam Adams, dismissed the commissioners as "a set of infamous wretches who swarm like the locusts of Egypt," growing fat while Americans grew lean. Pennsylvania lawyer John Dickinson, in his deceptively titled *Letters from a Farmer,* argued that duties for the purpose of regulating trade were quite acceptable, being necessary to "preserve or promote a mutually beneficial intercourse between the several constituent parts of the Empire." But what they had, as in the Stamp Act, Dickinson declared, was an entirely novel development, "a dangerous innovation": namely, an attempt to pass a tax for the sole purpose of raising revenue. If the colonists granted Britain this right, warned Dickinson, "the tragedy of American liberty is finished."

The commissioners, however, decided to make an example of John Hancock, probably Boston's richest merchant and large-scale importer. They charged him (whether the charge was trumped up or not never became clear) with failing to pay his taxes on a shipment of Madeira wine. Hancock's ship, the *Liberty,* was seized and Hancock himself brought to trial in 1768. The trial was not before a jury of his peers, that cherished British liberty, but before an English judge in the hated vice-admiralty court. Before the charges against Hancock were finally dropped, colonial defiance rose rapidly. And so did British determination to see that its rule was not flouted.

❧ A Roused People

In the next year, passions grew even hotter when Britain sent four regiments of soldiers to Boston to maintain law and order. This action flexed the muscles of the world's major military power in a way meant to communicate that they were in charge. Bostonians, like other colonists, deeply resented the presence of troops, who had not been sent in previous years when France threatened from the north, or Spain from the south, or Indians from the west. The Quartering Act, passed earlier, demanded that at colonial expanse His Majesty's troops be housed in barracks and supplied with bedding, cooking vessels, candles, salt, vinegar, and beer. New York was the headquarters for British troops in America, and the New York Assembly in 1766 agreed to everything but the salt, vinegar, and beer. This rebellious action led Parliament to declare all acts of that Assembly null and void until New York fully complied. In 1769, the New York Assembly grudgingly capitulated.

As official bodies knuckled under to British pressure, citizens at large showed little disposition to do so. One nonviolent way to demonstrate a growing disaffection with the empire was to join non-importation agreements calling for a boycott of British goods and British manufactures. American homespun became the clothing of choice and the symbol of protest. Beginning in 1768 newspapers reported proudly the activity of patriotic women, all wearing homespun themselves, gathered at their looms and in spinning bees to produce cloth in impressive quantities. If a British public had grown soft with self-indulgence and pampered luxury, a disciplined and determined force of women would prove that Americans were made of sterner stuff. "The industry and frugality of American ladies," the *Boston Evening-Post* reported in 1769, "must exalt their character in the Eyes of the World and serve to show how greatly they are contributing to bring about the political salvation of a whole Continent."

Although women did not hold political office in eighteenth-century America, or for some time after, letters and diaries reveal how keen was their interest in politics. In 1768, two planters' wives in Georgia campaigned widely for the election of one of their neighbors to the Assembly. In Edenton, North Carolina, in 1774 a Society of Patriotic Ladies did "Solemnly Engage not to Conform to that Pernicious Custom of Drinking Tea, or that we the aforesaid Ladys will not promote [the] wearing of any Manufacture from England untill such time that all Acts which tend to Enslave this our Native Country shall be repealed." No political innocents, women in large weaving and spinning groups vigorously denied that they wasted their conversation in idle gossip. Politics was their concern, American liberty their preoccupation. At one gathering of more than seventy women in Ipswich, Massachusetts, the local clergyman told the industrious laborers that the women by their example "might recover to this country the full and free enjoyment of all our rights, properties and privileges (which is more than the men have been able to do)."

Meanwhile, Boston citizens reflected on how best to respond to Britain's continued tightening of the screw. Other towns pledged their support, even offering to help block the landing of British troops. Although they considered staging a major protest when the four regiments arrived in September 1768, Bostonians held off. Yet the town was clearly unhappy that "troops are quartered upon us in a time of peace, on pretense of preserving order in a town that was . . . orderly before their arrival." Irritations steadily increased between the citizens and members of their "occupying army," as every insult — real or imagined — was eagerly reported in the local press. The suspicion steadily grew that the troops stayed in Boston not to enforce British law, but to subvert American liberty. Irritations reached a bloody climax in March 1770, when an aroused crowd began pelting regimental guards with snowballs and rubbish. The soldiers reacted, or overreacted, by firing into the crowd. When all confusion cleared, five Boston citizens lay dead and eight others

The Boston Massacre This nineteenth-century lithograph depicts the Boston Massacre, especially Crispus Attucks, an escaped slave who was the first of five men to be killed in the skirmish — and therefore the first to die for the cause of American independence.

had been wounded, two of them dying in subsequent days. The Boston "Massacre" lost none of its grimness in the telling and retelling, as other colonists wondered just when their turn would come.[6]

Subjected to withering attack, the Townshend duties (except for that on tea) were repealed in that same year, 1770. The colonists still maintained, however, that if today they could be deprived of property without their consent, then tomorrow they could be deprived of life

6. It should be noted that John Adams defended the British soldiers against the charge of murder; he pointed out that they had been provoked by a "motley rabble of saucy boys, negroes and mulattoes, Irish teagues and Jack tars." All but two were acquitted.

and liberty alike. Britain made other efforts at conciliation, removing the troops in Boston, for example, to an island in the harbor. But customs commissioners continued to exercise their authority, regularly perceived as arbitrary, while naval vessels never ceased their patrol of colonial waters to ensure compliance with British law. One British schooner, the *Gaspee*, while keeping a close watch for smugglers in Narragansett Bay, ran aground just south of Providence, Rhode Island. Angry and frustrated citizens seized the chance to board the vessel, capture its crew, and burn the ship to the water line. Britain's effort to identify and prosecute the offenders through the appointment of a special commission alarmed those who saw all commissions and vice-admiralty courts as agencies of enslavement, never of justice. A further aggravation was the announcement that the offenders, when caught, would be sent back to England for trial after indictment by a Rhode Island court or jury. The offenders, however, never were caught. Rhode Islanders professed no knowledge whatsoever of the incident.

Alarms raised in Rhode Island or Massachusetts spread to other colonies, Sam Adams ensuring that every British offense or indignity would be known up and down the Atlantic coast. Having served as tax collector in Boston from 1756 to 1765, Adams had resigned in protest against the Stamp Act. With a gift for keeping the public informed and alarmed, Adams gave to every plausible event a pro-American, anti-British spin. He had made the most of the Boston Massacre and of the *Gaspee* affair, seeing that each became a symbol of greater dangers that lay ahead. In 1772, he launched the committees of correspondence to keep all Massachusetts informed, if not inflamed, about every new development or threat. Adams candidly acknowledged

❋ IN THEIR OWN WORDS

Sam Adams Sounds the Alarm, 1771
In the October 14, 1771, issue of the Boston Gazette, *Sam Adams warned that the consequences of the dispute between England and the colonies would be far-reaching, whatever their outcome.*

The liberties of our country, the freedom of our civil constitutions are worth defending at all hazards; and it is our duty to defend

them against all attacks. We have received them as a fair inheritance from our worthy ancestors. They purchased them for us with toil and danger and expense of treasure and blood, and transmitted them to us with care and diligence. It will bring an everlasting mark of infamy on the present generation, enlightened as it is, if we should suffer them to be wrested from us by violence without a struggle or cheated out of them

by the artifices of false and designing men. Of the latter, we are in most danger at present. Let us therefore be aware of it. . . . Let us remember that "if we suffer tamely a lawless attack upon our liberty, we encourage it and involve others in our doom!" It is a very serious consideration, which should deeply impress our minds, that millions yet unborn may be the miserable sharers in the event!

his own purpose: "Where there is a spark of patriotic fire, we will enkindle it."

Britain gave Adams his chance to enkindle in 1773 when Parliament granted the all-but-bankrupt East India Company a monopoly on the importation of the still-taxed tea. When ships sailed into Boston harbor late that year loaded with tea, aroused citizens refused to let the merchandise be unloaded and sold. Some five thousand of them crowded into Old South Church on December 16 to decide what should be done next. What was done next is reported in the words of another Adams, John, who wrote in his diary under the date of December 17: "Last night three cargoes of Bohea Tea were emptied into the sea." But then, ceasing to be merely the reporter and becoming something of the prophet, Adams added: "This destruction of the tea is so bold, so daring, so firm, intrepid and inflexible, and it must have so important consequences . . . that I cannot but consider it an epoch [that is, a turning point] in history." If the Boston Tea Party were not an epoch in history, the British reaction to it early in 1774 does deserve that name.

The Boston Tea Party   With some inaccuracies, this engraving shows what happened when the Sons of Liberty dumped the East India Company's tea into Boston harbor. The actual Tea Party took place at night, and the crowd that assembled at dockside watched in silent awe as disguised "Indians" broke open tea chests and poured the contents into the water.

❧ Religious Imperialism

All the time that colonists suspected British motives and mechanisms with regard to taxation, they were beginning to suspect the mother country of a sinister plot to impose the Church of England upon every colony, regardless of its history or religious persuasion. Quakers in Pennsylvania would be forced to conform to England's national church; so would Baptists in Rhode Island, Catholics in Maryland, Congregationalists in Massachusetts and Connecticut. Such a plot sounded wildly improbable, but colonial paranoia made it credible. It grew more believable during the mounting campaign to send at least one Anglican bishop from England to America. For some Americans, importing taxed tea or molasses paled into insignificance when compared with the frightening possibility that Church of England bishops were about to be thrust upon dissenting colonists.

Why frightening? Because the spiritual lords of England's church were never simply church officials. Sitting in the House of Lords and on the Board of Trade, advisers to both king and Parliament, they also wielded enormous political power. Puritans, Quakers, and many others told their children and their grandchildren of bloody persecutions incited by — led by — imperious and powerful bishops. Had bishops changed all that much by the 1760s? Had the Anglican Church given up all efforts to establish and maintain a religious monopoly wherever England ruled? For most non-Anglicans in the colonies, the answer to both questions was strongly No. The Church of England was just as imperial, many concluded, just as aggressive, just as power-hungry and arbitrary, as the nation of England and its Parliament.

This inflammatory issue might have been submerged by Boston blood and sodden tea had not a New Jersey Anglican clergyman decided in 1767 to go public with a strong plea for bishops to be sent to America. Thomas Bradbury Chandler, in *An Appeal to the Public, in Behalf of the Church of England in America,* thought the time was ripe for bringing high-ranking churchmen from England to the colonies. It would strengthen the ties, Chandler argued, between the mother country and her sometimes wayward children; it would bolster the monarchy, for "Episcopacy and Monarchy are, in their Frame and Constitution, best suited to each other"; and, it would greatly enhance the ability of the American church to bring all the colonists into her welcoming fold. The time could not have been more unripe for sentiments such as this. Chandler misjudged the age as well as his countrymen.

One of those countrymen, a Presbyterian lawyer from New York, took up the gauntlet. William Livingston proceeded to organize in New York a Society of Dissenters dedicated to the defense equally of "civil and religious liberty," for the eighteenth century saw those two causes as inseparable. He published letters in the New York papers in order "to adminster an antidote to the poison" that Chandler's *Appeal* introduced. An "evil more terrible" awaited every American, Livingston wrote, "who sets a proper value on either his liberty, property, or conscience than the so greatly and deservedly obnoxious Stamp Act itself." When a bishop in England dared to enter the fray, Livingston was even more unsparing in his *Letter to the Right Reverend Father in God, John, Bishop of Landaff* (1768). Bishop John

Revolution and Religion　Probably made soon after the Boston Massacre, this needlework shows how many colonists understood political events in terms of familiar Bible stories. The biblical King David symbolizes King George III, playing his harp with no concern for the suffering of his subjects. David's rebellious son Absalom is seen as an American patriot. The figure executing Absalom — David's commander Joab in the Bible story — is dressed as a British officer.

— said Livingston — has affirmed that, lacking a complete establishment of the Church of England throughout America, the poor colonies languished in spiritual darkness. With little patience, Livingston exploded that "there is not a more virtuous, not a more religious people upon the face of the earth" than the Americans. Indeed, he would be glad to submit to any impartial judge a comparison between the spiritual health of those living in America and those living in England who "enjoy" a legal establishment "and are perpetually basking in the full sunshine of episcopal preeminence." Livingston concluded his letter with a sarcastic wish that the good bishop might never feel called upon to exchange his duties in England for similar episcopal responsibilities in America.

Livingston stood tall, but by no means alone, in the anti-episcopacy battle. Congregationalists gathered at Yale for commencement in 1769 confessed that they had "Reason to dread the Establishment of Bishops' Courts among us." Taxes would go up, of course, to support such bishops and their "palaces," but the real issue was liberty, civil and ecclesiastical: "Our civil Liberties appear to us to be in eminent Danger from such an Establishment," they wrote. If religious freedom was ever lost, then civil freedom would soon be gone as well. That had been the history of England, of the Continent, of most of the Western world. America's history, on the other hand, had up to this point been different, the Congregationalists concluded. "We have so long tasted the Sweets of civil and religious Liberty that we cannot be easily prevailed upon to submit to a Yoke of Bondage, which neither we nor our Fathers were able to bear." When a bill to broaden toleration for England's dissenters was tossed out by the House of Lords in 1772, Americans knew that their suspicions had been well founded. "I have so thoroughly studied the views and ultimate Designs of American Episcopalians," declared Yale President Ezra Stiles, "that I know I am not deceived."

With suspicions at such a height and religious sensibilities already rubbed raw, the colonists reacted with horror when Parliament in 1774 passed the Quebec Act. In calmer days, that too might have been viewed as a generous gesture, extending to French Canadians — now under British rule — the freedom to practice their Roman Catholic religion without hindrance or persecution. But in days that knew no calm, the Quebec Act was widely interpreted as a further British effort to cramp, confine, and coerce the stubborn colonies. For by the terms of that act, Quebec's boundaries were extended into the Ohio Valley, all the way to the point at which the Ohio River joined the Mississippi. Colonists speculating in western lands saw this as a cruel deprivation of their profit and property, while colonists bred for generations on fears of "popery" saw the Inquisition and Counter-Reformation lurking around the corner. If England could establish Catholicism in Quebec, could not that domineering nation do the same for Anglicanism in the thirteen colonies?

Not that most colonists needed to be reminded, but Samuel Adams in 1768 was willing to remind them anyway that "as you value your precious civil Liberty and everything that you can call dear to you, . . . be on your guard against Popery." Like William Livingston, Sam Adams abhorred the Stamp Act, but like him he also regarded any threat to religious liberty as even more terrifying. "Much more is to be dreaded from the growth of Popery in America," Adams noted, "than from the Stamp Act or any other acts destructive of civil rights."

Passage of the Quebec Act drove many Americans to believe that this was only part of England's larger plot to cancel out all colonial pretenses to liberty. Rumors flew: that Lord North (Britain's prime minister at the time the act passed) was busy recruiting an army of "Papists in Canada" who would "cut the throats of those heretics in Boston"; or, that Lord North was summoned to the Vatican to be honored by and perhaps received into the Roman Catholic Church. And the *Pennsylvania Gazette* declared that, despite this treacherous act, neither "the Gates of Hell, the Gates of Rome, nor the Gates of France" would ever prevail against the American colonies. That the rumors were all false and the fears all wildly exaggerated is largely beside the point. The passions were real, as real in the realm of religion as they were in the realm of politics. In 1774 Americans feared for their liberty — all liberty, civil and religious.

Colonists Convene a Congress

The Boston Tea Party confirmed the suspicions of many members of Parliament that Boston itself was the principal problem. To govern the colonies, Britain must first teach Boston a lesson, the argument went; and the others would quickly fall into line. Isolate Boston so that it does not infect the whole country: that was the British strategy. And so Parliament in 1774 passed a series of acts known collectively as the Coercive Acts (or, in American history, the Intolerable Acts). The first of these closed the port of Boston to all shipping; at the same time it required Bostonians to reimburse for the tea dumped in the harbor and the tax that would have otherwise been collected on it. This Boston Port Bill was soon followed by others that (1) permitted Americans to be taken to Canada or Nova Scotia for trial when local juries were likely to be "prejudiced"; (2) provided, once again, for troops to be quartered in Boston itself; and (3) allowed the governor to appoint his own council and rule with greatly expanded powers. One way or another, Boston would be brought to heel.

What had been intended to isolate, however, managed only to unite. The other colonies, which saw Boston's fate as potentially their own, pledged support, sent food, and roundly condemned the arbitrary actions of a Parliament that, increasingly, they disliked and distrusted. In Virginia, the House of Burgesses proclaimed June 1, 1774, as a day of fasting and prayer, when God's help might be sought "for averting the heavy calamity which threatens our civil rights, and the evils of civil war." Pennsylvania resolved "That their act of Parliament for shutting up the port of Boston is unconstitutional, oppressive to the inhabitants of the town, dangerous to the liberties of the British colonies." Women in North Carolina, already involved in sending

Sam Adams The son of a brewer, Sam Adams turned to politics for his own career. In addition to his role in calling the First Continental Congress he drafted many major protest documents, earning him the reputation of a radical.

relief supplies to Boston, vowed that they could not "be indifferent to whatever affected the peace and happiness of the country." And in Charleston, South Carolina (another port city like Boston), a leading citizen saw the Coercive Acts as a precedent for Parliament to cram down their throats "every Mandate which Ministers Shall think proper for keeping us in Subjection to the Task Master who Shall be put over us."

In July 1774 the youthful Thomas Jefferson made his literary debut, publishing anonymously the *Summary View of the Rights of British Americans*. Issued in Williamsburg, this patriotic piece was soon reprinted in Philadelphia and even abroad, giving Jefferson's sentiments wider currency than he expected. Virginia, which had passed strong resolutions against the Stamp Act and the Townshend Acts, saw its revolutionary reputation grow as well. Step by dreaded step, Jefferson warned, George III had placed all Americans under a kind of military rule: Boston first, but others surely

to follow. "His majesty," Jefferson wrote, "has expressly made the civil subordinate to the military." But how could a free people be placed under a military occupation? How could an English king, however powerful, "thus put down all law under his feet? Can he erect a power," Jefferson asked, "superior to that which erected himself?" Even a king must remember that "force cannot give right." And even a king must surely realize that a free people will not long submit to such oppression. "The god who gave us life," Jefferson concluded powerfully, "gave us liberty at the same time: the hand of force may destroy, but cannot disjoin them."

In that same summer of 1774 Samuel Adams presented to the Provincial Assembly in Massachusetts a resolution declaring "That a General Congress of Deputies meet at Philadelphia to consult together upon the present state of the colonies, and to deliberate and determine upon wise and proper measures for the recovery and establishment of their just rights and liberties, civil and religious." Since Boston already had its army of occupation, this legislative meeting had to be held in secret (in Salem) and the business accomplished before those loyal to Britain could spread the word of the treasonable activity under consideration. When the word did get out, General Thomas Gage, functioning as the military governor, dissolved the legislature, which was never again to meet under royal authority. But that action came too late: by a vote of 120 to 12, Sam Adams's motion had carried.

John Adams, Sam's cousin, was one of the five delegates elected to that First Continental Congress, scheduled to convene in September. John Adams's hopes were high for what he called "an assembly of the wisest Men upon the Continent, who are Americans in Principle, i.e., against the Taxation of Americans by Authority of Parliament." In early September, John in Philadelphia wrote to his wife Abigail reassuring her about his safety. "Be not under any Concern for me. There is little Danger from any Thing We shall do at the Congress. There is such a Spirit thro the Colonies," he added, "and the Members of the Congress are such Characters that no Danger can happen to Us which will not involve the whole Continent in Universal Desolation — and in that Case who would wish to live?" John feared not so much the British as his fellow delegates who seemed determined to debate every subject endlessly, tediously. To Abigail in October, he reported sarcastically that "This Assembly is like no other that ever existed. Every Man in it is a great Man — an orator, a Critic, a statesman, and therefore every Man upon every Question must show his oratory, his Criticism, and his Political Abilities."

Despite Adams's severe criticism and growing despair, the First Continental Congress did manage to hang together and take action. Most of all it demonstrated that Britain would not be allowed to play the colonies off against each other. Fifty-two delegates from twelve colonies[7] affirmed that the forcible denial of rights in one place threatened rights everywhere else. The Congress spelled out those rights belonging to all colonial Americans, first among them being "That they are entitled to life, liberty, and property, and they have never ceded to any sovereign power whatever, a right to dispose of either without their consent." Of the Coercive Acts and the Quebec Act, the Congress declared simply but firmly that "to these grievous acts and measures, Americans cannot submit."

The First Continental Congress also agreed that no longer would goods be imported from Britain or the West Indies, a measure that it hoped (though in vain) would do great damage to the British economy. More directly and more ominously, the delegates recommended that every colony arm itself and prepare its militia for whatever the future held in store. The Congress, which met for only seven weeks (September 5–October 27, 1774), cast its shadow over the next several months. During that time, events tumbled over each other with greater speed and fury than those anxious, word-weary men sitting in Philadelphia could possibly have imagined.

CONCLUSION: BATTLES FOR CONTROL

In the first half of the eighteenth century, Spain, France, and Britain continued to wage their contest for the control of the North American continent. And to all appearances, Britain — clinging to a narrow strip of land along the Atlantic coast — was losing that contest. This all changed most dramatically in the Seven Years' War, which reduced France to a secondary status in North America and would soon eliminate Spain as a military threat. Britain by 1763 had triumphed: its position in North America was secure.

Except that Britain's colonies resisted and resented the new efforts to make them pay for the costs of that long war and to play their assigned role as supporters of imperial policy and the imperial treasury. During de-

cades of benign neglect, each of the thirteen colonies had flexed its own political muscle and governed its own citizens, always of course within the broad parameters of an aloof British rule. Now, as England and its Parliament took renewed interest in colonial affairs, the efforts, especially to tax the colonists directly for the purpose of raising revenue, aroused immediate and growing resentment. Even in England itself, some sympathized with the colonial complaints, especially when British rule appeared arbitrary or corrupt.

In the 1760s, everything that Britain did lent itself to misunderstanding and misinterpretation. So also with the colonists, who were regarded as disobedient children at best, scheming traitors at worst. To the growing threats on civil liberties were added real or imagined threats to the religious liberties of all the colonists. Skillful propagandists kept the anti-British feeling brewing and boiling — not just in a single colony but also up and down the coast. By 1774 when the First Continental Congress gathered in Philadelphia, compromise and conciliation rapidly faded as realistic possibilities. With the assembling of the Second Continental Congress the following year, events took on an irreversible momentum of their own.

---

7. Georgia, distracted by a Creek Indian uprising, had sent no delegates.

SUGGESTED READING

Thomas C. Barrow, *Trade and Empire: The British Customs Service in Colonial America, 1660-1775* (1967). The central importance of economic anxieties and interests is clarified in this treatment of mismanagement and misunderstanding.

Jon Butler, *Becoming American: The Revolution Before 1776* (2001). Covering the period from 1680 to 1770, and giving full attention to the pluralism in early America, Butler skillfully shows how "modern" the colonists were before the Revolution plunged them into an even more challenging modernity.

J. C. D. Clark, *The Language of Liberty, 1660-1832: Political Discourse and Social Dynamics in the Anglo-American World* (1994). The author demonstrates, with respect to the subject matter of this chapter, how the ideas of religion could lead to the activity of open rebellion.

Peter M. Doll, *Revolution, Religion, and National Identity: Imperial Anglicanism in British North America, 1745-1795* (2000). The colonial anxiety over the possible appointment of Anglican bishops to the colonies was arrayed against the British determination to keep church and state allied in North America just as they were in Britain.

W. J. Eccles, *France in America* (1972). The major role played by France in eighteenth-century North America here receives full and reliable explication.

Jack P. Greene, *The Quest for Power: The Lower Houses of Assembly in the Southern Royal Colonies, 1689-1776* (1963). A persuasive account of the gradual development of local control during long periods of neglect from abroad.

Michael Kammen, *Empire and Interest: The American Colonies and the Politics of Mercantilism* (1970). Well written and well researched, this book crosses the Atlantic easily and frequently in analyzing the force of the separate "interests."

Pauline Maier, *From Resistance to Revolution* (1972). A skillful account of the steady growth in popular resentment against British encroachments upon colonial interests.

Amy R. W. Meyers and Margaret Beck Pritchard, *Empire's Nature: Mark Catesby's New World Vision* (1998). In 1747 Catesby published his remarkable *Natural History of Carolina, Florida, and the Bahama Islands.* The new book cited above, which introduces him to a much wider audience, is lavishly illustrated.

Edmund S. and Helen M. Morgan, *The Stamp Act Crisis: Prologue to Revolution* (1953). The authoritative account of the defining crisis in the decade before the Revolution.

Mary Beth Norton, *Liberty's Daughters: The Revolutionary Experience of American Women, 1750-1800* (1980). An important corrective to the prevailing accounts of events before and during the Revolution.

Howard Peckham, *The Colonial Wars, 1689-1762* (1964). In relatively brief compass, the author manages to clarify the muddled military picture prior to the Revolution.

Ellis Sandoz, ed., *Political Sermons of the American Founding Era, 1730-1805* (1991). A valuable collection of public rhetoric that reveals the close connection between religion and politics.

Barry Alan Shain, *The Myth of American Individualism: The Protestant Origins of American Political Thought* (1994). In a sharply revisionist study, the author gives far greater credit to communal Protestant thought for the unfolding events of the Revolutionary generation.

SUGGESTIONS FOR FURTHER READING

John K. Alexander, *Samuel Adams: America's Revolutionary Politician* (2002).

David Ammerman, *In the Common Cause: American Response to the Coercive Acts of 1774* (1974).

Fred Anderson, *Crucible of War: The Seven Years' War and the Fate of Empire in British North America, 1754-1766* (2000).

Patricia U. Bonomi, *A Factious People: Politics and Society in Colonial New York* (1971).

James E. Bradley, *Religion, Revolution, and English Radicalism: Nonconformity in Eighteenth-Century Politics and Society* (1990).

Stephen Brumwell, *Redcoats: The British Soldier and War in the Americas, 1755-1763* (2002).

A. Roger Ekirch, *"Poor Carolina": Politics and Society in Colonial North Carolina, 1729-1776* (1981).

Sylvia R. Frey and Betty Wood, *Come Shouting to Zion: African American Protestantism in the American South and British Caribbean to 1830* (1998).

Jack P. Greene, *Peripheries and Centers: Constitutional Development in the Extended Politics of the British Empire and the United States, 1607-1788* (1986).

Francis Jennings, *Empire of Fortune: Crowns, Colonies, and Tribes in the Seven Years' War in America* (1988).

Michael Kammen, *Deputyes and Libertyes: The Origins of Representative Government in Colonial America* (1969).

Douglas E. Leach, *Roots of Conflict: British Armed Forces and Colonial Americans, 1677-1763* (1986).

Lawrence W. Leder, *Liberty and Authority: Early American Political Ideology, 1689-1763* (1963).

Kenneth A. Lockridge, *Settlement and Unsettlement in Early America: Political Legitimacy Before the Revolution* (1981).

Peter N. Moogk, *La Nouvelle France: The Making of French Canada — A Cultural History* (2000).

Edmund S. Morgan, *Inventing the People: The Rise of Popular Sovereignty in England and America* (1988).

Gary B. Nash, *The Urban Crucible: Social Change, Political Consciousness, and the Origins of the American Revolution* (1979).

Alison G. Olson, *Anglo-American Politics, 1660-1775: The Relationship Between Parties in England and Colonial America* (1973).

Alan Rogers, *Empire and Liberty: American Resistance to British Authority, 1755-1763* (1974).

John H. Wigger, *Taking Heaven by Storm: Methodism and the Rise of Popular Christianity* (1998).

6 The Struggle for American Independence, 1775-1783

ALTHOUGH IT MET for only seven weeks, the First Continental Congress accomplished much. And what it could not achieve, it tried to anticipate by urging all the colonies to prepare as best they could for a future that appeared gloomy and threatening. After returning to their homes in the fall of 1774, the delegates soon saw their worst forebodings come true.

In the spring of 1775, war began. At first it seemed only a skirmish, a misunderstanding, a confusion about orders or intentions. By the end of June, however, each side had taken the measure of the other, and each had inflicted and suffered severe losses. The bloodshed and the rebellion had up to this point been exclusively a Massachusetts affair. Was it to be only that? Clearly, Britain would have preferred it that way.

The Second Continental Congress, which sat not for weeks but for years, was determined that this not be so. Some show of unity must be made, but this did not come easily as thirteen sovereign states for a time seemed intent only upon proving their independence from each other. The year of 1775 was a time for choosing: for taking sides in an impending war, or for taking sides, on religious grounds, against all war. Patriots, loyalists, and pacifists railed against each other, threatening to preclude any meaningful unity in sentiment or in action. England then could pick off the colonies, one by one, through concession or negotiation — or, if need be, by force selectively applied.

By the middle of 1776, however, the thirteen colonies had managed to agree on the Declaration of Independence, thereby thwarting British hopes of American

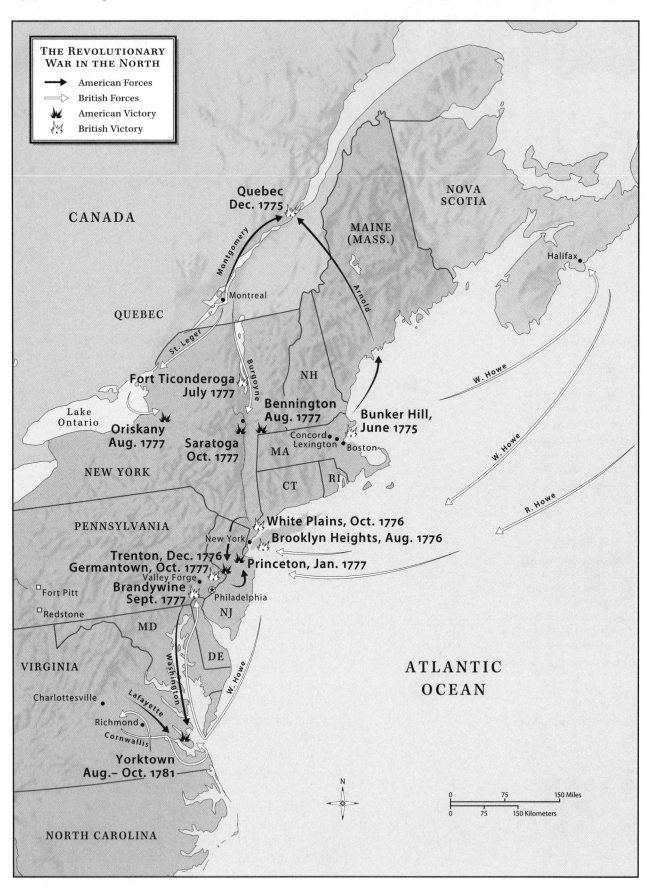

THE REVOLUTIONARY
WAR IN THE NORTH

→ American Forces
⇨ British Forces
💥 American Victory
💥 British Victory

CANADA

Quebec
Dec. 1775

NOVA
SCOTIA

MAINE
(MASS.)

Halifax

Montgomery

Montreal

QUEBEC

Arnold

St. Leger

Burgoyne

NH

Fort Ticonderoga
July 1777

Bennington
Aug. 1777

Bunker Hill,
June 1775

Lake
Ontario

Oriskany
Aug. 1777

Saratoga
Oct. 1777

Concord
Lexington

Boston

MA

NEW YORK

CT

RI

PENNSYLVANIA

White Plains, Oct. 1776
Brooklyn Heights, Aug. 1776

New York

Trenton, Dec. 1776
Germantown, Oct. 1777

Princeton, Jan. 1777

Valley Forge

Fort Pitt

Brandywine
Sept. 1777

Philadelphia

Redstone

NJ

MD

DE

W. Howe

W. Howe

W. Howe

R. Howe

VIRGINIA

Washington

Lafayette

ATLANTIC
OCEAN

Charlottesville

Richmond

Cornwallis

Yorktown
Aug.– Oct. 1781

N

NORTH CAROLINA

0　　　75　　　150 Miles
0　　75　　150 Kilometers

disunity or even anarchy. Thomas Paine helped to unify public opinion, even as Thomas Jefferson took the lead in expressing a political consensus for those supporting the American cause. Jefferson's rhetorical effort on behalf of consensus served both as a vital platform of domestic agreement and as an eloquent defense beyond the colonial borders of America's grievances and intentions.

If the British found early engagements more costly than they had expected, Americans found swift victory more elusive. The war stretched from months to years, with resolve faltering on both sides. Many soldiers suffered, grumbled, deserted, died; some managed to hang on to a measure of good cheer and brave hope. Civilians also suffered, although many found ways to serve "the glorious cause." Enslaved blacks were lured by both American and British promises of freedom; dislodged or threatened Indians sought alliance with the stronger or the nearer power. The absence of so many men from households and farms thrust special burdens and responsibilities upon the women left behind. And war, always a challenge to traditional structures and values, in this instance too presented new dangers and suggested new directions for society.

For many Americans, war against Britain was dictated by the necessities of history as well as by the Providence of God. England, once singled out for God's special favor, had forfeited its special place in the divine plan by becoming increasingly corrupt, vain, and autocratic. Earlier the battle between good and evil had been seen in strictly religious terms: a purified church (Protestant) against an unfaithful church (Roman Catholic), with the pope the convenient symbol of the Antichrist. In the days of revolution, however, oppressive civil government appeared as Satan's chief instrument on earth, drawing people from liberty into tyranny, from virtue into corruption, and from visions of eternity to indulgence in luxury and greed. To defeat the world's greatest military power, their preachers told them, Americans must rely on that even greater power that held all nations as dust in the hollow of his hand. Thus political resistance and religious assurance merged in a powerful partnership.

At last, the prospect of peace loomed ahead. Late in 1781, after their defeat at Yorktown, the British found their will to continue the struggle crumbling. The American determination to match a military victory with a diplomatic one correspondingly rose. After lengthy and difficult negotiations, the former colonists by 1783 had won not only their independence but much else besides.

GOING TO WAR

Resolves, protests, and congressional debates could carry the colonists only so far in their dispute with Parliament and George III. External events, outside the walls of legislative assemblies and even taverns, created a momentum of their own. These, in turn, led to more pressing and focused deliberations. Decision-making would soon pass from leaders down to citizens, who in ever-larger numbers joined in tense political debates.

❧ On Lexington Green

It was April 18, 1775. "Sir," read the military orders from British General Thomas Gage in Boston to his field commander, Lieutenant Colonel Francis Smith, "Having received intelligence that a quantity of ammunition, provision, artillery, tents and small arms have been collected at Concord, for the avowed purpose of raising and supporting a rebellion against his Majesty, you will march with utmost expedition and secrecy to Concord." Once they arrived at that small Massachusetts town, the British infantrymen were instructed to destroy any guns or artillery they discovered, to dump all gunpowder out of its barrels into the Concord River, to put captured lead musket balls into their pockets, "throwing them by degrees into ponds, ditches, etc.," and to burn tents and destroy foodstuffs. In this manner, the general back in occupied Boston had every reason to suppose that he could nip in the bud a brewing Yankee rebellion.

From a military point of view, the plan made perfect sense: destroy the means of war, and you avoid the war. The execution of the plan, however, left much to be desired. In the first place, the march toward Concord was anything but a model of "utmost expedition." The whole idea was to get the British troops out of Boston quietly and quickly under cover of darkness during the night of April 18. Then they would march with disciplined haste in the still-dark morning from Cambridge through Lexington (8 or 9 miles) and on quickly to Concord (another 6 or 7 miles), while the colonists still lay abed or only sleepily stirred. But it did not work out that way.

Nor did General Gage's call for secrecy have much effect. For the people of Boston and its surrounding countryside knew their territory intimately, watched all unusual developments carefully, and schemed intelligently to undermine all British attempts at secrecy. If all else failed, they could hang lanterns from the tower of the town's North Church (Congregational), signaling to those across the water what Smith's line of march would be. Would he go "by land" — that is, march across Boston neck, then around toward Cambridge; or would he go "by sea" — that is, take boats across the Charles River, arriving more quickly in the Cambridge area? The answer was "by sea," so two lanterns shone from the church tower. Determined to remove any possible confusion, silversmith Paul Revere rowed across the wide river that night to tell all whom he saw that the British indeed were coming.

At one o'clock in the morning, local farmer and militia captain John Parker received the news that British troops were or soon would be on the road through Lexington to Concord. Parker ordered the militia to gather on the common "to consult what to do." The initial conclusion was not to "meddle" with the troops "unless they should insult us." Meanwhile, since no lookouts had reported the British anywhere near, the militiamen could go home or rest inside the local tavern. When some three or four hours later, riders brought intelligence of the marchers' imminent arrival, drums summoned the sixty or seventy militiamen from their sleep to form two long thin lines, load their muskets, and wait uneasily for what the dawn would bring.

As the morning light broke, the first of Britain's infantry companies came into view, some 150 men or more. Parker's men did not run for cover, scurrying into barns or behind barricades or fences or trees. Rather, they stood as a show of force, as a silent statement of defiance, as men prepared to give some measure of reality to revolutionary rhetoric. The British, on their way to Concord, were equally unsure of just what to do. Although they could not ignore the armed men, they had no instructions to engage or capture them; perhaps the best tactic would be simply to surround and disarm

them, but not to fire.

But in all the maneuvering and surrounding, a shot was fired. Then more shots, and more, with both sides taking aim — or just shooting. Some of Parker's men broke to seek cover in the woods or behind any convenient house. Some of the advancing army heard and heeded orders to cease fire; others did not. When after fifteen or twenty minutes the smoke cleared and some semblance of order had been restored, four Americans lay dead on Lexington Green; four others had been killed nearby.

✺ The Road to Concord — and Back

When the rest of the British troops, some seven or eight hundred in all, arrived in Lexington, the pitiful little skirmish was over. The regulars drew themselves up in formation, fired a volley for effect, gave a shout of victory, and proceeded in military manner toward Concord where they could carry out orders to dump, burn, and destroy. The local militia initially withdrew, allowing the British troops to enter the town without opposition. But then a body of three or four hundred militia attacked the British defending Concord's Old North Bridge. Here the British clearly fired first — Emerson's "shot heard round the world" — and killed two Americans. The militiamen, in turn, killed three British soldiers and wounded nine.

Meanwhile the citizens of Lexington, much sobered and shaken, treated their wounded and buried their dead. In the midst of this somber activity, the citizens gradually realized that those same British troops, after doing their deeds in Concord, would come marching back along that very same road through Lexington. This time the militia and the other farmers and their

---

✺   **IN THEIR OWN WORDS**

The "Midnight Ride" of Paul Revere, 1775
Here is Paul Revere's own account of his famous ride.

Two friends rowed me across Charles River, a little to the eastward where the Somerset, man-of-war, lay. It was then a young flood, the ship was winding, and the moon was rising. They landed me on the Charlestown side. When I got into town, I met Colonel

Conant and several others; they said they had seen our signals. I told them what was acting and went to get me a horse. I got a horse of Deacon Larkin. . . . I set off upon a very good horse. It was then about eleven o'clock and very pleasant. After I had passed Charlestown Neck . . . I saw two men on horseback under a tree. When I got near them, I discovered they were British officers. One tried to get ahead of me and the other to take me. I turned

my horse very quick and galloped toward Charlestown Neck. . . . The one who chased me, endeavoring to cut me off, got into a clay pond where Mr. Russell's Tavern is now built. I got clear of him and went through Medford over the bridge. . . . In Medford I awaked the captain of the minute men, and after that I alarmed every house till I got to Lexington. I found Messrs. Hancock and Adams at the Reverend Mr. Clark's. I told them my errand. . . .

sons too young to serve would be ready for them. This time, the story would have a different end.

When Smith's army finally began its seventeen-mile march back toward safety in the early afternoon, his troops had been on the road or kept standing around waiting to get started since one o'clock that morning. Weary and anxious now only for the relative security of Boston, they began what was supposed to be an orderly retreat. Earlier word had sped throughout the countryside that more colonials were needed immediately to rally along the road back to Boston. Militia poured in from all over Massachusetts, and some even from Connecticut. Smith's retreat thereby soon became a rout, and a bitterly bloody one at that. On both sides along that suddenly long — endlessly long — road, militiamen and young boys gathered, hunching down behind stone fences, hiding behind large trees or in farmhouses and barns.

From cover, they fired, reloaded, aimed, fired again. Taking comparatively few casualties, the Yankees found their moment of revenge at hand and seized it without hesitation and without mercy. British soldiers, crowded together on the narrow road or even narrower bridges, presented tempting targets. As they fell, wounded or slain, discipline dissolved. Officers struggled to maintain order, to keep the march somehow still headed toward Boston, and to cope with a style of warfare for which they were ill prepared. Would the colonists never stop? Would the reinforcements from Boston never arrive? Would that seventeen-mile-long battlefield never end?

Finally reinforcements (under the command of Lord Percy) did arrive, as eventually did darkness, these twin allies helping Smith's much reduced ranks to reach Charlestown and the protection of England's warships nearby. The British had suffered nearly three hundred casualties, the colonial militia fewer than one hundred. Whoever looked upon that militia "as an irregular mob," Lord Percy pointed out, would "find himself much mistaken." They had learned to fight in their particular (and deadly) style against the Indians and Canadians, he added, and they knew how to use their own countryside to terrible advantage. The British now faced an aroused population that had had time to prepare, said Percy, and he concluded that "they are determined to go through with it, nor will the insurrection here turn out to be so despicable as it is perhaps imagined at home."

The road to Concord — and back — was a road that led to no quiet sanctuary or peaceful grove, either for the British or the Americans. On the contrary, it led to more battles, more bloodshed, more widowed and orphaned, more suffering and pain. It also led to more political resolve and a more united colonial response. New Yorkers by the thousands joined the Continental Association, originally created to support a trade boycott against Britain and to encourage Americans to develop domestic manufacturing and avoid importing any luxury items whatsoever. Americans could live simply, if that was what it took to be free. And in Virginia Patrick Henry responded to the news of Lexington and Concord by declaring in St. John's Church in Richmond that the time to choose had most certainly come: a choice between liberty or death.

❧ Toward Independence

When the First Continental Congress dissolved in October 1774, the delegates had agreed that a second Congress should meet the following May. This assembly would be able to determine what response Britain had made, what accommodations or compromises had been reached, what degree of quiet or calm prevailed in the land. When that Second Congress convened in Philadelphia on May 10, the events of Lexington and Concord were on every mind and on every tongue. Quietness and calm seemed a distant dream. And if those bloody events were not enough to transform a polite debating society into a resolute coalition, other bloody events quickly followed.

The British government also prepared for a showdown. Two weeks after the Second Continental Congress convened, Great Britain sent its most experienced military leaders to Boston: Major Generals William Howe, Henry Clinton, and John ("Gentleman Johnny") Burgoyne joined General Thomas Gage, already on the scene. Here were men trained in years of combat, mainly against France; here were men on whom Britain could presumably rely to bring a ragtag rebellion to a swift end. By mid-June martial law had been imposed in Boston and noisy "patriots" had been declared traitors to the king. British troops and British warships were now prepared to make a show of strength so dramatic as to penetrate far beyond the borders of Massachusetts, to all the contentious colonies up and down the Atlantic seaboard.

Militias, earlier created in every colony to train citizens and maintain order, now became the first line of defense. In the Seven Years' War, many militiamen gained valuable military experience as they created a semi-professional army. In 1774 some of the Mas-

The Battle of Bunker Hill, **by John Trumbull**   The son of the Revolutionary governor of Connecticut, John Trumbull saw active military service during the war and only later turned to professional painting. His dramatic depiction of the climax of the fight for Bunker (or Breed's) Hill, where he was present, shows the patriot commander Joseph Warren lying mortally wounded, while the British finally close in as the defenders' ammunition gives out. Notice the patriot officer's slave in the lower right corner.

sachusetts militia were reorganized as minutemen — ready for war "at a minute's warning." Colonel William Prescott, a minuteman officer, on June 16, 1775, led a force of about a thousand men from Cambridge Common after dark to the Charlestown Peninsula that stretched out toward Boston. With about two hundred troops from Connecticut along with a company from New Hampshire, Prescott's force embodied a growing colonial unity.

Prescott planned to dig in on Bunker Hill, where his forces could watch whatever the newly arrived generals were up to and, if necessary, challenge any movement of British troops. Prescott passed beyond Bunker Hill to Breed's Hill, which had the advantage of edging him even closer to Boston and the disadvantage of bringing him well within the range of the British warships' guns. Through the night the Yankees dug with pick and shovel, erecting a fortified rampart of earth and wood. Through the night, the British generals wondered and worried about just what the Yankees were up to.

By the dawn of June 17, it was all too clear what they had been up to: Prescott and his men had defiantly constructed a military stronghold only about a mile from Boston. Such a challenge could not be ignored. Of course, neither would it be met immediately. The British decided to wait until a high tide enabled them to land their troops farther up the soggy shore. Meanwhile, the Yankees kept digging, fortifying, and dodging the shells fired from the nearest warship. In the early afternoon General Howe at last put his troops on barges for the mile journey across the Back Bay, a force sufficient to outnumber the provincial army two or three to one, and to redeem the sullied reputation that His Majesty's army suffered on that road back from Concord. By three o'clock, Howe's redcoats began the march up Breed's Hill, impressive waves of well-armed infantrymen.

As the British began their close march up the hill, Prescott, well aware of the limited range of the muskets and of his limited ammunition, ordered his men to hold their fire. When at last he gave that long-awaited command to "Fire!" the effect was devastating. Having suffered a withering blow, the redcoats regrouped and marched closer so that the effect of the next volley was even deadlier. A third assault brought similar results, but with a crucial difference: the Americans had exhausted their supply of ammunition. Prescott's forces had no choice but to fight hand-to-hand to the death, which some did, or retreat to Bunker Hill and beyond, which more did. With the Americans in retreat, the British had won, but no one could find much joy in the misnamed "Battle of Bunker Hill." Prescott lost about one-third of his force of a thousand men, while the British suffered more casualties than Prescott had in his entire command. William Howe correctly observed that the British could afford no more such "victories." And Americans, both in Massachusetts and beyond, concluded correctly that this bloody beginning would have no swift or certain end.

Congress now took steps to create an army not just for New England but for all the colonies, one that somehow might compete with the ever-swelling British land and sea forces. In May 1775, after the encounters at Lexington and Concord, Congress offered the command of this yet-to-be-created army to Virginia's George Washington. Why Washington? For one thing, he had been a visible figure, in uniform, at the Congress itself, his very presence reminding the delegates of his availability and his stature. More importantly, the confrontations and battles had up to now been altogether a New England affair. It was important that a continental army be truly "continental," not regional, and the appointment of a Virginian would effectively make that point. Virginia's prestige and size (the most populous of all the colonies) likewise made the congressional move a prudent one. Finally, Washington seemed to many of the delegates that sort of moderate, rational, level-headed man whose selection would signal to the British that this rebellion was not simply the work of some

fanatical fringe, the hoarse cries of a few roughneck radicals. Washington would give leadership that would be respectable, intercolonial, professional, and — did any dare hope? — ultimately successful.

This continental army differed from the colonial militia in several respects, the most important being that the militia was local, informal, and only temporarily a collective force. Militiamen (consisting of most able-bodied free males) armed themselves, clothed themselves, and generally organized themselves into voluntary units. No central authority directed or controlled them. Like volunteer firemen today, they responded to an emergency, then quickly melted back into their ordinary civilian routine. Colonial Americans, confronted with the challenges of the frontier and the necessity of gathering game, found the musket as necessary as the hoe or axe. Already armed and already concerned about their own defense and their locality's, such citizens responded readily to their leader's call for some united action. They even trained periodically in order to be better prepared for whatever sudden necessity might arise. Since the militia was merely the community itself, armed and ready, colonists had no reason to mistrust or fear it.

It was otherwise with a standing army. Such a professional force, not subject to local control nor called out for a specific and limited purpose, hovered over a free citizenry as a potential weapon of oppression. That had been true in Cromwell's England in the seventeenth century; now it was true in King George's eighteenth century. Americans, having learned to fear the very idea of a standing army, feared even their own. Such an American army, moreover, implied that free citizens were not virtuous enough, not selfless enough, to perform whatever military service might be required voluntarily, without pay and without expectation of any reward beyond the safety and security of their community. A standing army meant taxes, then patronage, then pensions, then unchecked and therefore corrupt power. Such an "armed monster" became the instrument of tyranny, not its enemy. In addition to fighting the British, therefore, George Washington had to fight the deep-seated suspicions that throughout most of the war kept his army poorly paid, tentatively supplied, and never wholeheartedly embraced.

In early July 1775 Washington nevertheless took command of the only American army that existed, the one deployed at several staging areas around Boston. He had, perhaps, some fifteen thousand militiamen under his command, a respectable force for engagements on land, but for engagements on water Washington had little but a desperate hope that he could avoid such encounters altogether. Meanwhile, so much needed to be done to ensure supplies, to enlist troops on a regular (or "standing") basis, to appoint and unify a senior staff, to finance a major military undertaking of uncertain duration, somehow to draw from thirteen jealous colonies a trim, fit, fighting army.

That same July Congress, having boldly appointed Washington to lead a rebel army, attempted one more peaceful gesture. Parliament had been obnoxious, but perhaps the king would take the colonists' side. The "Olive Branch Petition," addressed directly to George III, represented the American moderates' last effort to find some alternative to all-out war. The king, however, declined even to give the petition a proper hearing, preferring to teach the Americans a lesson. He denounced the Continental Congress as an "illegal" assembly; negotiations, if ever there were to be such, would be conducted only colony by colony, never with the so-called United Colonies. Finally, Americans in general were declared traitors engaged in "an open and avowed rebellion." Even those who had long advocated reconciliation and forgiveness recognized that time had virtually run out.

❧ Loyalists, Patriots, and Pacifists

In Philadelphia John Dickinson had long advocated moderation. An English-trained lawyer who preferred the label "Pennsylvania Farmer," Dickinson had searched for ways to appease Britain on the one hand and preserve American liberty on the other. He wrote with careful and calm logic, pointing out where Britain had erred, where America had been injured, and awaited with confidence the rational resolution of an awkward situation. By 1775, no resolution had been achieved; nonetheless, Dickinson continued to believe that the colonies would never find happiness "for several ages to come but in a state of Dependence upon & subordination to our Parent State." Britain had defended the colonies in their infancy; Britain could and would continue to defend them in their budding maturity. Yet even Dickinson admitted that in late 1775 Americans must begin to arm themselves, prepare for war, and negotiate only from strength.[1] Sue for peace, but make ready for war. This

was a difficult position to maintain, and the difficulty only increased with time.

It was more forthright, more logical, and soon more popular to simply declare for one side or the other: patriot or loyalist. Lukewarmness or indifference no longer made sense. Everyone in those troubled days of 1775, declared one loyalist, "seemed to be on fire, either with rum, or patriotism, or both." And for those who had no sympathy for those patriotic fires, the safest path was flight: back "home" to Britain, or north to Canada — perhaps some sixty thousand or more "voting with their feet" in this fashion. Other loyalists, however, remained to argue still that Britain was not evil, only temporarily misguided; that independence was perhaps inevitable, but certainly not now; that, as a purely practical matter, the military defeat of the colonies was as certain as the setting of the sun.

One loyalist who stayed for a time, Samuel Seabury, made his most vigorous arguments in 1774 and 1775. A graduate of Yale and a missionary for the Church of England in New York, New Jersey, and his native Connecticut, Seabury found the actions of the Continental Congress not only illegal but also ridiculous. Americans were complaining about the rule of Parliament and the king, he wrote, all the while submitting themselves to the "slavish regulations" of Congress as well as to a wild assortment of "Committees, Riots, Mobs, Insurrections, [and] Associations." "A plague on them all," Seabury declared. They were all too ready to obey anybody in this country, no matter how foolish or weak or ill-chosen, the Connecticut clergyman argued. But, Seabury continued, "if I must be enslaved, let it be by a King at least, and not by a parcel of upstart, lawless Committee-men. If I must be devoured, let me be devoured by the jaws of a lion, and not gnawed to death by rats and vermin."

Understandably, the "rats and vermin" placed Seabury under house arrest. (Although his writings were issued anonymously, his authorship quickly became known.) Seabury managed to escape to New York City during the long British occupation of that port, then to England; the war years proved an unhappy period for him as they were for his church generally. Many other Anglican missionaries, employed by the London-based Society for the Propagation of the Gospel, also gave their fundamental loyalty to Britain, not to the colonies. Some, unlike Seabury, had no deep roots in America, having merely been sent out to the plantations for a few years to organize or strengthen the Church of England in the provinces. Like Seabury, however, these missionaries, especially when they insisted on continu-

---

1. At the time of the vote for independence, Dickinson declined to take his seat in the Congress so that Pennsylvania could vote unanimously in favor of the Declaration.

ing — even in 1776 — to read the prayers for the king, found themselves verbally abused, arrested, or tarred and feathered; often, they also saw their churches forcibly shut down. One such cleric in Pennsylvania reported to his London employer in 1776 that "every Clergyman of the Church of England who dared to act upon proper principles was marked out for infamy and insult." Some, he added, "have been dragged from their horses, assaulted with stones & dirt, ducked in water, obliged to flee for their lives." Clearly, it was a time for taking sides.

Some took sides early, some late, and some changed sides as circumstances altered. This makes any accurate estimate of the number of loyalists (or of patriots, for that matter) difficult. As historian John Shy has argued, moreover, the sentiment for loyalism or patriotism often shifted in response to the proximity of troops. When British troops were in the ascendancy and likewise nearby, loyalism tended to increase — and to shrivel as patriot troops marched victoriously into the neighborhood. To count loyalists and patriots, not only a calculator but also dated maps would be needed, revealing the movements of troops and the shifting fortunes of war.

On the patriot side, it was not enough to attack the loyalists or confiscate their property. Something had to be done to stir large numbers to support the American cause. The "silent majority" must be moved to abandon their silence; young men must be moved to leave their farms for service in Washington's meager army; merchants and artisans and wives and servants must be moved to lend voice and force to a cause not yet named, to an independence not yet declared. Unity must, somehow, be achieved, and without further delay.

COMMON SENSE

"'Tis not in numbers but in unity that our great strength lies," wrote Thomas Paine in January of 1776. Paine's in-

credibly popular tract, *Common Sense*, sold 150,000 copies, in a land with only about 500,000 households. And in that work, Paine offered "nothing more than simple facts, plain arguments, and common sense." The simplicity was real, the appeal enormous, the effect momentous. Paine, only recently arrived in America from England, managed to find not only the right words, but also the right rhythms that would strike responsive chords up and down the coast. He also managed to achieve far greater fame and worldly success than he had ever known in his previous thirty-seven years (or would ever enjoy again). The humble son of Quaker parents, Paine had endured only poverty and despair as he wandered from one menial job after another, as he drifted through two childless and unhappy marriages. Armed with a letter of introduction from Benjamin Franklin, he sailed for Philadelphia in the summer of 1774, arriving in October to try his hand at yet another trade: namely, journalism. With exquisite timing, he found his career, audience, and cause all at once.

The very idea of monarchy, Paine asserted, was absurd and contrary to the will of God, "for monarchy in every instance is the Popery of government." Employing such great words of his day as "reason" and "nature," Paine proved to his own satisfaction and his readers' that a continued dependence of the American continent upon the British island was both irrational and unnatural. "There is something palpably absurd," Paine declared, "in supposing a continent to be perpetually governed by an island. In no instance hath nature made the satellite larger than the primary planet." Britain should revolve around America, not the other way around. Men "of passive tempers" may still long for reconciliation, Paine wrote in this winter of decision, but "reconciliation is now a fallacious dream." The time had come for action, not debate; for resolution, not timidity. For at this moment, Paine promised, "we have it in our power to begin the world over again." Americans

❋ **IN THEIR OWN WORDS**

Anglican Loyalist in New York City, 1776
The Reverend Charles Inglis, rector of Trinity Church in New York City, maintained his loyalty to England and the Anglican Church throughout the war; after it, he was appointed bishop of Nova Scotia.

The present rebellion is certainly one of the most causeless, unprovoked and unnatural that ever disgraced any country — a rebellion marked with peculiarly aggravated circumstances of guilt & ingratitude. Yet amidst this general defection, there are very many who have exhibited instances of fortitude & adher-

ence to their duty, which do honour to human nature & Christianity — many who for sake of a good conscience have incurred insults, persecution & loss of property; when a compliance with the spirit of the times had insured them applause, profit & that eminence of which the human heart is naturally so fond.

could even create a New Order of the Ages, a *Novus Ordo Seclorum,* an independent republic and an end to monarchy. Such a moment must be neither delayed nor denied.

STAYING OUT OF THE FIGHT

Loyalty to Britain, or loyalty to America? That was the question, but not the only question. A significant number of Americans, notably in Pennsylvania, saw a higher loyalty. That was a loyalty to Christian principles as they understood them, to the New Testament command to "love your enemies, and pray for them that persecute you." These pacifists — Quakers, Moravians, Brethren, Mennonites, and others — had in many cases fled to America to escape persecution and oppression in their homelands, the oppression often taking the form of demands to bear arms in the service of the state. Pacifism at this period in America's history was not so much an individual decision as a corporate witness of the "peace churches." By becoming a member of one of these religious bodies, a person adopted its pacifist stance.

Mennonites, survivors of the radical wing of the Protestant Reformation, began to arrive in America as early as 1683, though significant growth did not come until the eighteenth century. By the time of the American Revolution, Mennonites were not a large group, though they were a highly visible one in Pennsylvania, Maryland, and Virginia. Sometimes in cooperation with other pacifist groups (such as the German Baptists, or Brethren) and sometimes alone, they petitioned legislative bodies for exemption from serving in a military capacity. In 1775, for example, Mennonites formally declared to the Pennsylvania Assembly that "We have dedicated ourselves to serve all Men in every Thing that can be helpful to the Preservation of Men's Lives but we find no Freedom in giving or doing, or assisting, in anything by which Men's Lives are destroyed or hurt." Recognizing that this was not a universal view and, in 1775, not a popular one, the petitioners added: "We beg the Patience of all those who believe we err on this point."

Like most other pacifists, Mennonites indicated a willingness to assist in those ways that did not require the taking of human life. They would continue to pay their taxes and would be ever ready to assist "those who are in Need and distressed Circumstances . . . it being our principle to feed the Hungry and give the Thirsty Drink." In this way, some of the resentment of neighbors was reduced, but not all. In northern Virginia, for example, a county committee protested that Quakers and Mennonites received special treatment, whereas (so the committee argued) they should be treated like everyone else. If drafted, they should serve, "and if they refuse to serve or provide able bodied Men to serve in their places respectively, that they be liable to the same Fine as other Militia Men in the like cases."

Benjamin Franklin, particularly sensitive to the potential unrest in Pennsylvania where pacifists were most numerous, urged a Moravian friend in 1775 to give the sect's young men some military training and not to hinder those who wished to serve. Such moderate action would, said Franklin, "operate in the Mind of the People very greatly in your Favour." Later that same year he urged that the Assembly adopt some general guidelines for conscientious objectors. They should help put out fires, assist in the evacuation of women and children from places where battles occurred, dig trenches for defense, and carry "off wounded Men to places where they may receive Assistance." The Assembly agreed to all these rules, but passed more of their own in the form of financial payments to be made to the colony.

Quakers constituted by far the largest pacifist group in eighteenth-century America, in 1776 numbering about forty thousand. They lived chiefly in Pennsylvania, but had a significant presence also in New Jersey. Moravians, Mennonites, and Brethren, on the other hand, each had memberships of only a few thousand. Even though numbers were limited, in the testing time of war every individual counted. It is all the more remarkable, then, that during the course of the Revolution the rights of the tender conscience, as they were often called, were recognized as something for which the states and ultimately the nation should stand. Several states, in fact, in writing new constitutions or formal bills of rights, offered specific guarantees to pacifists. Pennsylvania in 1776 declared: "Nor can any man who is conscientiously scrupulous of bearing arms, be justly compelled thereto, if he will pay such equivalent. . . ." In time of war, of course, the distinction in the public mind between pacifism and loyalism could readily be blurred, that between pacifism and treason almost as readily confused.

THE DECLARATION OF INDEPENDENCE

In January 1776 Paine argued that "we ought not now to be debating whether we shall be independent or not," but proceeding to establish independence "on a firm, secure, and honorable basis." Indeed, at this critical juncture, said Paine, only independence would unite Americans; it was the one tie that could bind the colonists and "keep us together." *Common Sense* did not immediately end all debate, but it did give an urgency and a focus to that debate throughout the colonies — especially within Congress, still meeting in Philadelphia. As a result, Thomas Jefferson, as chair of a drafting committee, put forward a proposed declaration that, after some amendment, was in July adopted and signed.

❧ *Getting Congress to Move*

An impatient John Adams goaded Congress toward some definitive action; an all-too-patient John Dickinson ("a piddling genius," Adams undiplomatically observed in a letter to Abigail) searched the horizons for signs that Britain was backing down; and a desperate George Washington pleaded for total, unified support — more money, more men, more munitions. Would Congress debate forever, or would it begin to act as though it had a nation to govern, a nation to save? Some demanded action now; others argued for action later — or perhaps none at all. The problem, said Adams, was how to get thirteen clocks to strike at exactly the same time.

In April 1776 Congress responded to Britain's closing of the port of Boston by opening all America's ports to trade with any nation, abruptly tossing out the theories and practices of mercantilism. If Britain insisted upon total capitulation and even humiliation, Congress would insist on total separation. The colonies, Congress advised, should set about scrapping their old royal charters and proceed to establish new state governments with new constitutions. Most of them did so. In May, Thomas Jefferson returned to Philadelphia after many months' absence in his own "country," Virginia. By the middle of the month, delegates in Philadelphia learned that Virginia's constitutional convention had in fact already passed a resolution of independence. Clearly New England no longer stood alone in its resistance to tyranny, but had been joined by the largest colony of all in calling for an end to interminable debate.

Virginia instructed her delegates in Philadelphia to propose that the Continental Congress "declare the United Colonies free and independent states, absolved from all allegiance to, or dependence upon, the Crown or Parliament of Great Britain." Virginia also urged that alliances be made as soon as possible with any nation willing to assist the Americans in their struggle for freedom. Even John Adams was surprised — but not so surprised that he could not swiftly prepare for the official resolution when it finally made its way north over the muddy roads from Williamsburg.

On June 7, Richard Henry Lee rose on behalf of the Virginia delegation to offer as a motion for debate: "that these United Colonies are, and of right ought to be, free and independent states." For those who had not taken sides up until now, no longer was there any place to hide. Some delegates pleaded for time so that they might receive instructions from their constituencies; some suggested that a vote of the people might be required in each colony. Questions tumbled one after another: What would Parliament do? What would the king think? What stance would Spain or France most likely adopt? What chance for total unity existed? The colonies could not move, some argued, until all were ready to move. They would never move, others argued, if they waited for everyone to move. How *does* one get thirteen clocks to strike at precisely the same time?

On June 9 a non-binding "straw vote" was taken. Seven colonies voted for independence: New Hampshire, Massachusetts, Connecticut, Rhode Island, Virginia, North Carolina, and Georgia. Five voted against: Pennsylvania, New York, New Jersey, Delaware, and South Carolina. Maryland abstained. Those voting against independence did not oppose the principle, only the timing. Those voting for independence believed that time had become a scarce commodity. Delay meant disaster. Yet seven colonies, the barest majority, were not enough to prosecute a war with any chance of success. What to do? Congress agreed to delay the final vote for three weeks. Meanwhile, in order that no precious time be lost, a committee was appointed to draw up some suitable statement or resolution for independence, should the final vote go that way.

Congress appointed five men to the committee: John Adams (Massachusetts), Benjamin Franklin (Pennsylvania), Thomas Jefferson (Virginia), Robert Livingston (New York), and Roger Sherman (Connecticut). As with all matters, the Congress had paid careful attention to regional balance. Three members represented colonies voting for independence on June 9, but two came from colonies voting against it. Now, how should the committee proceed with its work? Someone needed to prepare an initial draft, and Jefferson may have deferred to Adams, eight years his senior. But Adams preferred that Jefferson undertake the task for three reasons, as he recalled them. First, Jefferson was a Virginian and someone from the South "ought to appear at the head of this business." Second, "I," said Adams, "am obnoxious, suspected, and unpopular," while Jefferson was "very much otherwise." Third, Adams concluded that Jefferson could write "ten times better" and therefore deserved the honor — or the burden.

In a small second-floor apartment, Jefferson sat down to compose a draft that would reflect not his views but those of his fellow Americans at large. Turning "to neither book nor pamphlet while writing," Jefferson nonetheless drew upon the political rhetoric of the day as articulated in *Common Sense*, in Virginia's Declaration of Rights (composed just a short time earlier by George Mason), in the writings of England's radical Whigs, in the American pamphlets issued from the days of the Stamp Act onward, in his own *Summary View of the Rights of British America*, and in the impassioned oratory of Congress itself. On July 1, another straw vote was taken. This time nine colonies favored immediate independence, Maryland and New Jersey joining the original seven. It brought some consolation to the patriots, for though the movement was small, it was unmistakably a movement in the right direction.

The next day, July 2, a vote on independence was taken for the record. This time John Hancock sat in the president's chair, indicating that this was no mere straw poll but an official commitment, and the roll call of states began. New Hampshire led off with an "aye," to be joined in swift succession by the rest of New England. New York, alone among the Middle Colonies, abstained, not out of opposition but awaiting final instructions from its own Provincial Convention — and when it came, New York's vote was also affirmative. All of the southern states voted yes as well, so that when the day was done, endless debate had at last yielded to a gratifying if novel unity. Richard Henry Lee's motion put forward three weeks before had carried: the United Colonies were "absolved from all allegiance to the British Crown," and "all political connection between them and the state of Great Britain is, and ought to be, totally dissolved."

Having declared their own opinion in the matter, the delegates now turned to the document addressing "the Opinions of Mankind." Jefferson's draft was debated and amended on July 2, again on July 3, and once more on July 4. At last Congress voted, and at last America's first charter of liberty was dispatched to every colony, to be read from balconies, in crowded public squares, in legislative halls, wherever eager crowds could hear. Fireworks exploded, royal symbols fell, bells rang, prayers for the Congress replaced those for the king.

In New York on July 9 citizens demonstrated their support for the "unanimous Declaration" by tearing down the statue of King George III that had been erected only a few years earlier, while elsewhere effigies of the king were raised for all to see, then buried or burned.

✑ *Thomas Jefferson and the Declaration*

The thirty-three-year-old Virginian who drafted the Declaration of Independence was fairly new to the national scene. A graduate of the College of William and Mary, he had studied law there before in 1769 becoming a member of Virginia's House of Burgesses. Concerned with Virginia's response to Britain's imperial policies and with the growing tension between the royal governor and the burgesses, Jefferson kept his eye on the local political scene. But he, along with many fellow legislators, recognized that they could not ignore Britain's behavior elsewhere in the colonies. Boston's Tea Party, for example, and Parliament's swift closure of the port in retaliation, had aroused sympathy and keen interest farther south. In May 1774, Virginia's House of Burgesses declared a fast day in support of Boston's long suffering. An angry royal governor, Lord Dunmore, responded by dissolving the legislative assembly — which promptly adjourned to a nearby tavern to continue deliberations and call for an annual meeting of colonial delegates in a "general congress."

Jefferson had responded with his *Summary View*, as noted in Chapter 5. Now he assumed an even greater responsibility in being asked to speak in the name of the Continental Congress and on behalf of all the American people. Jefferson began by explaining that if Americans were about to leave the British Empire and assume their own "equal & independent station to which the laws of nature & nature's god entitle them" (as the first draft read), then "a decent respect to the opinions of mankind" required some formal declaration. In synthesizing the views heard all around him, Jefferson provided the nearest equivalent to a national creed that Americans have ever had. He penned, in words endlessly quoted and discussed, that there were certain self-evident truths (he first called them "sacred & undeniable"): that all men were created equal; that all had a fundamental right to life, liberty, and the pursuit of happiness; and that the essential business of government was to preserve or enlarge these rights, never to diminish them. When governments failed to discharge their sacred duty, then revolution was not simply a right, but a necessity. "When in the course of human

The Declaration of Independence, **by John Trumbull**   Trumbull spent many years completing this painting, executing a portrait from life for every one of the signers whom he could meet. In fact, many of those who eventually signed the Declaration did so much later in 1776, as they straggled into Philadelphia during the summer and fall. In this imagined scene, the drafting committee—Jefferson, Adams, Franklin, Robert Livingston, and Roger Sherman—present their work to John Hancock, president of the Continental Congress.

events it becomes necessary . . . ," Jefferson had written as the first words of the Declaration: necessary — not optional or preferable or defensible, but necessary. Just as the "laws of nature and of nature's God" were fixed and immutable, so the necessity to separate from the empire was set in the very nature of universal laws.

The rights that Americans claimed for themselves, moreover, had a similar necessity or inevitability about them. Life, liberty, and the pursuit of happiness were not privileges to be bestowed by some government out of its gracious indulgence, nor to be withdrawn by some government out of its pique or as a punishment. No, these rights were sacred, inalienable, axiomatic, self-evident, God-given. The idea of equality stemmed not from some political creed or philosophical treatise. It was essentially a theological position: that all human beings are equal in the eyes of God and the products of a single creation. Government granted none of this to its citizens; its only purpose was to protect and preserve that which had been originally given. Therefore, "when any Form of Government becomes destructive of these ends, it is the Right of the People to alter or to abolish it."

Drawing upon Locke and later Whig thinkers, Jefferson assumed the compact theory of government: that is, government was created not by "divine right" but by voluntary agreement of the people. Persons living in the state of nature could agree, if they so wished (for reasons of convenience or efficiency or mutual

interest), to surrender a portion of their individual liberty so that a government might guarantee an even larger liberty — against foreign invasion, for example. To dissolve a government was no fearful or immoral or heretical action. On the other hand, to endure a government that had forgotten whence its power was derived, that had substituted tyranny for liberty — this was the basest immorality and the grossest violation of the laws of nature and nature's God.

In earlier arguments with Britain, the colonists had generally made Parliament the object of their scorn. Parliament, after all, consisted of politicians, and politicians could be swayed, could be defeated in elections, could be divided against themselves, could be dismissed as the parochial, small-minded men that they so often were. But the king? The king did rise, or at least was supposed to, above petty politics and narrow interests. The king symbolized the empire in a way that Parliament failed to do. That, at least, was the distinction that the colonists made and even clung to in the late 1760s and early 1770s. By 1776, however, it had become clear that the distinction no longer made sense. America had only one king, Paine announced at the beginning of that year, and where was that king? "I'll tell you, friend," Paine wrote, "he reigns above, and doth not make havoc of mankind like the Royal Brute of Great Britain." Along with many others, Paine had earlier longed for reconciliation with the empire, but the events of April 1775 changed all that, he declared. From that moment, "I rejected the hardened, sullen-tempered Pharaoh of England for ever; and disdain the wretch that with the pretended title of FATHER OF HIS PEOPLE can unfeelingly hear of their slaughter, and composedly sleep with their blood upon his soul."

In the months that followed, many Americans abandoned the notion that only Parliament was to blame: the king had become their enemy too. So in the Declaration, Jefferson recited a damning litany of grievances and crimes against, not Parliament, but the king: "He has refused his Assent to Laws . . ."; "He has forbidden his Governors to pass Laws . . ."; "He has dissolved Representative Houses repeatedly . . ."; "He has obstructed the Administration of Justice . . ."; and, "He has plundered our seas, ravaged our Coasts, burnt our towns, and destroyed the lives of our people." No more hiding behind a Privy Council or a Parliament.

One more heinous crime Thomas Jefferson charged the king with, but on the nature and magnitude of this crime Americans found themselves deeply divided. The king, Jefferson wrote in his draft for Congress, "has waged a cruel war against human nature itself, violating its most sacred rights of life & liberty in the persons of a distant people who never offended him, captivating & carrying them into slavery in another hemisphere, or to incur miserable death in their transportation thither." All this horror was perpetrated, let all remember (Jefferson wrote), by the "CHRISTIAN king of Great Britain." What he had done was unworthy of the infidels, as he had vetoed or suppressed "every legislative attempt to prohibit or to restrain this execrable commerce." The king's only concern for blacks in America, Jefferson added, was to try now to incite them to rise against the rebels, thereby assisting the monarch who deprived them of *their* liberty to rob still others of theirs.

On this last point, Jefferson's rhetoric was strong — so strong, in fact, that Congress allowed none of it to survive in the final version of the document. The question of slavery and the slave trade divided the Second Continental Congress; it distracted and threatened to scuttle the Constitutional Convention eleven years later; and seventy-five years after that it rent the nation apart in civil war. Jefferson, himself a slaveowner, was in 1776 more vigorous in his condemnation of slavery than he would be later in his life. Paradoxically and tragically, the Declaration as Jefferson wrote it was a stronger statement than was the Declaration as Congress adopted it. And the final version only papered over America's deepest flaw.

THE CONTINENTAL ARMY: FRIENDS AND FOES

Outside the halls of the Philadelphia Congress, the battle was not one of words and resolutions, but of muskets and swords. The Americans, off to an encouraging start in the New England battles, quickly ran into difficulty and discouragement. The British, shaken by Lexington and Bunker Hill, geared up their powerful military engine to keep their empire intact. Yet the rebellious colonies that dared to take on mighty Britain were not without friends abroad: at first only potentially, but later in actuality.

❧ *American Strategy — Hit and Run*

When the Declaration of Independence was adopted, George Washington had been in command of the Continental Army for exactly one year. That year had not gone as badly as many expected, though neither had it gone well. Washington's best stroke was his occupation in early 1776 of Dorchester Heights, overlooking Boston. With a few pieces of heavy artillery, Washington took up a commanding position that kept British troops under the sights of his guns. General William Howe had enough troops to storm those heights, but not without cost, and the memory of Bunker Hill was still too fresh. Howe decided neither to attack nor to wait Washington out, but to leave. In March, a surprised but delighted Washington looked down upon the redcoated infantrymen packing up and boarding ships of the Royal Navy for a departure to New York. (About a thousand loyalists took this opportunity also to leave under the protection of the British flag.)

Quickly General Washington wrote to John Hancock in Philadelphia that on March 17, about nine o'clock in the morning, "the Ministerial Army evacuated the town of Boston, and . . . the forces of the United Colonies are now in actual possession thereof." With much modesty and good manners, Washington then proceeded to congratulate the Congress "on this happy event, and particularly as it was effected without endangering the lives and property of the remaining unhappy inhabitants." Perhaps this war, not yet declared, would be over even before it had properly begun.

But the Americans' luck swiftly ran out. They had already met disaster in Canada, when three months before the combined forces of Richard Montgomery (marching northward along Lake Champlain to Montreal) and Benedict Arnold (marching northward along the Kennebec River) attacked Quebec. Congress had ordered such an ambitious military maneuver in the hope that Canada, heavily settled by the French, would join the Americans in the struggle against Britain. French Catholics, however, feared the American Protestants who had so noisily protested the Quebec Act just the year before. The British who "owned" Quebec following the Seven Years' War were, of course, even less enthusiastic about this Yankee invasion. Even with limited forces, the practically impregnable city of Quebec could mount a strong defense, as James Wolfe had learned in 1759 (see Chapter 5). Against the invading forces, weakened by the long march, by winter, by disease, and by the lack of supplies, the British got the upper hand on De-

Washington at Trenton   General Washington leads the early morning attack on Trenton on December 26, 1776, in this lithograph commemorating the 100th anniversary of that battle.

cember 27 in a mere matter of hours. Montgomery was killed, Arnold severely wounded, and American hopes of winning over the "fourteenth colony" evaporated.

The heralded departure of the British from Boston represented, moreover, no large-scale retreat. Indeed, the build-up of His Majesty's forces in and around New York was enormous. Great Britain recognized New York to be the strategic center to be captured and held, perhaps to be the setting for a showdown battle with George Washington and his militia-dominated army. British strategy called for isolating New England, home to the most rebellious colonies. New York as the base of imperial strength was essential. Reinforcements under William Howe's command arrived in early July from Halifax, then still more under General Henry Clinton's command sailed up from their humiliating drubbing at the militia's hands in Charleston, South Carolina. By mid-July Howe's brother Richard, a Royal Navy admiral, sailed to Staten Island with a flotilla carrying yet more troops, including the well-trained, well-disciplined

mercenaries from the German principality of Hesse. A month after the Declaration of Independence, the British had over thirty thousand troops massed and ready for a climactic battle with Washington and his twenty thousand poorly equipped and scattered men.

A showdown was precisely what General Washington had to avoid. Greatly outnumbered on land, he could hardly conceive of an engagement at sea, although American ships on Lake Champlain would effectively delay a British invasion out of Canada. Once the British navy pulled back from New York, Washington dared to take up a position on Brooklyn Heights in August 1776. Badly outnumbered, Washington sought to embolden his troops by urging that they demonstrate a courage and spirit like that evident at Bunker Hill. Every soldier, he declared, should resolve "to conquer, or die, and trusting to the smiles of heaven upon so just a cause, . . . behave with Bravery and Resolution." But inspiring words did not suffice.

Dangerously outflanked by the more numerous British forces, Washington suffered a stinging defeat that could have been a disaster. Had General Howe pressed his advantage, he might have captured much of the Continental Army. But Washington executed a skillful retreat, under cover of night ferrying across the river to New York City over nine thousand troops, together with horses, cannons, and provisions. For the next two months, Washington found it necessary to order other retreats, first across the Hudson into New Jersey, then across the Delaware into Pennsylvania.

Washington was like a featherweight boxer in a ring with a giant. All he could do was stay out of reach, be light on his feet, move rapidly, surprise occasionally, insult his opponent's dignity now and then — but most of all, dodge those blows that could level him for good. In the second half of 1776, Washington became a master of retreat — and of little else. His other activity, not a strategy but a necessity, was to try to hold his army together, to persuade young men in the field to reenlist (perhaps for as little as an additional six weeks), to persuade older men in Congress that they simply must ensure that his troops were fed, paid, housed, and healed. Whatever spare moments that presented themselves could be used to promote a semblance of military discipline, to give those who needed it some instruction in shooting, and to train his men for swift and even surprising maneuvers.

In a brilliant attack on the Hessians in late December, the Battle of Trenton, Washington regained something of his reputation as a commander and restored bits and pieces of flagging morale, both in the army and out. Taking advantage of darkness, rain, and snow, Washington crossed the Delaware River on Christmas night 1776, with between two and three thousand troops. Washington stood poised by four o'clock in the morning for his surprise attack. Attack? This was the Washington who, so the British had concluded, knew only how to retreat. But early on the morning of December 26 in less than an hour of fierce battle, Washington did attack, and well-trained, well-disciplined Hessians fell before him. Taking nearly a thousand prisoners, Washington had in one swift stroke turned the mood from "darkness to light, from grief to joy!" as an army chaplain reported. Returning briefly to the Pennsylvania side of the Delaware River, Washington managed to acquire some militia reinforcements; with his enlarged army, he quickly assaulted the British garrison at Princeton and forced it into surrender. His weary troops had earned a rest, and went into winter quarters near Morristown, New Jersey.

❧ British Strategy — Occupy, Divide, and Conquer

The British continued to occupy New York City. They had left Boston, but took Newport in its place, so that New England would not be forgotten. Howe hoped to inflict enough damage on the colonists to force them to the bargaining table. He occupied Philadelphia, hoping loyalists would flock to him. They did not, and Congress only moved into the interior. Ultimately, His Majesty's forces seized Charleston as well — and indeed occupied every major colonial city at one time or another — and yet the Americans stubbornly fought on. Did they not know when they were defeated? What center of power could the British take that would signal to all Americans that the war was lost? Fortunately for the rebellious patriots, no such center of power existed. Disunity and localism had been a weakness; now it became a strength.

The other British strategy, in addition to occupying the major population centers, was the time honored one of "divide and conquer." If General Burgoyne's army could be sent down from Canada to the upper Hudson River, then General Howe's army marching up the Hudson from New York City could meet it and cut off all of New England and part of New York from the rest of the colonies. If New England fell, the rest would quickly collapse — or so the strategy went. Meanwhile, an unchallenged British navy could roam up and down the Atlantic coast, from New Hampshire to Georgia, threatening commerce and any military movement near the seaboard. But in executing this latter plan, British forces won a series of small victories, yet nothing seemed to make any great difference. And the British realized that as soon as they left Philadelphia, the patriot forces would slowly return and business as usual would resume.

❧ Saratoga and France

In September and October 1777 Britain's grand strategy fell apart. Burgoyne led his army down from Canada, as planned. Civilians — and some Continental soldiers as well — scattered from his path, alarmed at the heavy march of powerful troops. He crossed the Hudson River about thirty miles north of Albany, near Saratoga. On the American side, General Horatio Gates, assisted by the now-recovered but often-criticized Benedict Arnold, fortified Bemis Heights, just south of Saratoga and just west of the Hudson. With impressive numbers under his command (six to seven thousand Continentals, plus local militiamen), Gates faced a British army low in supplies and ammunition as well as weary from a long, difficult march. On September 19, the first large-scale battle in the campaign ended in an American victory, with Burgoyne suffering heavy casualties that could not be replaced. Gates, on the other hand, continued to receive fresh complements of men drawn by the long overdue news of an American victory. Burgoyne's only hope had rested in that grand strategy conceived months earlier: if General Clinton came north from New York City, Gates would have to divide his growing army to meet this new threat.

Clinton did march, but not far enough. So when the second battle erupted on and around Bemis Heights on October 7, Burgoyne found himself surrounded and outnumbered. He retreated to Saratoga, where he hoped to recross the Hudson and move back to safety in Canada. But the American forces were too strong, too persistent, too intoxicated by their promise of complete success. On October 17 Burgoyne surrendered, turning over to the Continental Army all remaining arms, artillery, and ammunition. Nearly six thousand British troops laid down their weapons — the worst humiliation they had yet seen. Shortly thereafter Burgoyne resigned from the army, devoting much effort in the months that followed to explaining "the disaster at Saratoga."

But the Battle of Saratoga's most significant effect

was neither on the careers of General Burgoyne nor General Gates, but on France. As Britain's implacable enemy, France was potentially the Americans' strongest ally. As early as December 1776, Benjamin Franklin arrived in Paris to represent American interests and specifically to seek French favor in the war against what now was their common enemy. Joined by other commissioners already on the scene, Franklin worked with his compatriots to persuade France by February 1778 to sign treaties of commercial and military assistance. Unofficially, of course, France was already much involved in the war, but now the alliance might become open. The three men in Paris were greatly assisted by the news that arrived from America of the Saratoga disaster, about two months after the event. This military defeat suggested to France that Britain was vulnerable and an American victory conceivable. Franklin skillfully played on French fears that Britain might quickly make peace with the colonies and on French hopes for a lucrative trade with America.

By June 1778 relations between France and Britain had deteriorated so far that both sides saw war as inevitable. While the British government hurriedly made peace overtures to the Continental Congress, France hastened to forestall that possibility by publicizing its alliance with America, officially recognizing the United States, and deliberately provoking hostilities with its rival superpower. Having no other choice, Britain declared war on France, and within a year Spain entered the war as France's ally. The American Revolution had become a world war. Even more to the point, Britain could no longer sail American waters with impunity. George Washington, at last, might have a significant (French) navy.

℅ *Defeat, Treason, Despair*

The recently concluded Franco-American alliance did not lead to immediate coordinated military activity, nor did defeat at Saratoga result in immediate curtailment of Great Britain's military forays. General William Howe occupied Philadelphia in September 1777, and

Valley Forge   This nineteenth-century engraving depicts soldiers in George Washington's ragtag army at Valley Forge during the winter of 1777-78. Washington's army persevered and survived at Valley Forge in spite of being short of basic necessities such as food and blankets.

the following October Washington engaged the British in nearby Germantown. A bruising battle, with Washington early pressing his advantage of surprise, ultimately turned in Britain's favor. Both sides absorbed heavy casualties, but the American side more so. Defeated and discouraged, Washington's soldiers limped a few miles farther to the northwest to a place called Valley Forge. There, in the manner of European armies, the Continentals spent the winter regrouping, retraining, and reassessing the military situation. There also, Washington could keep an eye on the British who had moved into Philadelphia for what appeared to be an indefinite stay.

Valley Forge had the advantage of offering defensible terrain — but virtually nothing else, being without food or clothing or shelter or warmth. No great battle was fought at Valley Forge — save one: the battle to survive. That Washington and his men somehow managed to win that struggle has given to Valley Forge all of the honorable associations generally reserved for dashing heroism and splendid victory. Washington saw his situation that winter of 1777-78 in rather different terms. Writing to Congress on December 23, 1777, the commander-in-chief looked for a miracle. Other-

George Washington at Valley Forge, December 29, 1777

When Congress failed him, Washington sent a circular letter to the states, requesting that they provide his army with the resources necessary to continue fighting.

. . . There is one thing more, to which I would take the liberty of soliciting your most serious and constant attention: to wit, the clothing of your troops and the procuring of every possible supply in your power for that end. If the several States exert themselves in the future in this instance, and I trust they will, I hope that the supplies they will be able to furnish in aid of those which Congress may immediately import themselves will be equal and competent to every demand. If they do not, I fear I am satisfied the troops will never be in a situation to answer the public expectation and perform the duties required of them. No pains, no efforts on the part of the States can be too great for this purpose. It is not easy to give you a just and accurate idea of the sufferings of the Army at large, and of the loss of men on this account. Were they to be minutely detailed, your feelings would be wounded, and the relation would probably not be received without a degree of doubt and discredit.

wise, he said, "this Army must inevitably be reduced to one of these three things: starve, dissolve, or disperse." The army needed help, and that desperately, Washington noted: food, supplies, reinforcements, "soap, vinegar, and other articles allowed by Congress," and medical assistance to deal with the typhus, typhoid, dysentery, and pneumonia that ravaged the ill-fed, ill-housed men.

From Congress, however, Washington got only complaints that more was not being done to defeat the British. America's top general was reduced to begging a Congress that in turn could only beg the states. Allowing a tone of bitterness to creep into his letters, Washington wrote: "I can assure those Gentlemen that it is a much easier and less distressing thing to draw remonstrances in a comfortable room by a good fire side than to occupy a cold bleak hill and sleep under frost and snow without clothes or blankets." But through that cruel winter, unrelieved by the knowledge that France was even then coming to his aid, Washington and his army somehow endured. The months had surely become, as Tom Paine had written the previous December, "the times that try men's souls." In the years just ahead, the times would prove even more trying.

In February of that bleak season, the deplorable lack of military discipline and order received an unexpected corrective. A Prussian soldier of fortune, Baron von Steuben, arrived in Valley Forge to assist Washington in whatever way seemed most useful. What was eminently most useful was somehow transforming Washington's men into a professional army. Despite barriers of language (von Steuben initially spoke only German), a few weeks of intensive training, close-order drills, and written manuals of arms made an amazing difference. Steuben formed a model company that, after a time,

could begin to instruct other companies. By spring the Valley Forge troops had not only survived but had remade themselves into an army that could recognize a command and execute it.

The next years continued to demand endurance and patience, faith and hope — with little success to sustain or warrant any of these. In June 1778 the British abandoned Philadelphia to reinforce their position in New York. Washington left Valley Forge to dog their footsteps, to pick a fight (for example, near New Jersey's Monmouth Court House in late June), to retreat and regroup as necessary. Meanwhile, Washington's other battles continued: to keep the army intact, supplies coming, his authority clear, and his commanders loyal.

Little did he know that even his own life was in danger from a plot fomented by Benedict Arnold. Soon after marrying a pro-British Philadelphia socialite in the spring of 1778, Arnold began a secret correspondence with British General Clinton, offering him vital military information and planning even more spectacular betrayals. Often passed over for promotion and commendation, the extremely ambitious Arnold had lost faith in the American cause even as he sought refuge in the British one. When he became commander of the strategic fort at West Point that dominated a stretch of the Hudson River, Arnold schemed to turn that post over to the British without a shot being fired. A British spy, carrying word of this plan as well as of a plot to seize George Washington, was captured and later hanged. Arnold escaped to British-occupied New York City, but West Point — and Washington — were spared.

Benedict Arnold's spectacular treason conceals the wider British efforts to lure many segments of the civilian population from the patriot side. If people could not be turned into loyalists, at least they might be transformed into neutrals. By 1780 the war had already proved long, difficult, and inconclusive. When British ships continued their plunder of all American shipping in rivers and along the coast, hardship mounted and resolve weakened. When the British offered bribes to many and pardons to more, the temptations to bring so unhappy a time to a merciful end grew almost irresistible. And if, in addition, the British managed to win dramatic military victories, then what folly it must be to continue to fight, run, starve, and die!

British luck in 1780, furthermore, ran high. In May the Americans suffered their worst defeat when Charleston, South Carolina, fell to the British, along with about five thousand troops. For some, Charleston represented as great a victory for the redcoats as Saratoga had for the Continentals. Many within the city, moreover, seemed to vindicate British expectations that most Americans, given a truly free choice, would reaffirm their loyalty to if not their love for the king. Three months later, General Gates confronted General Charles Lord Cornwallis at Camden, sustaining a bloodier American defeat than the Charleston debacle had been. Not from surrender but from musket, bayonet, and mortar, Gates lost a force of about two thousand men. Like Burgoyne, he was finished — but many concluded that so was the American cause. The War of Independence grew longer, drearier, and far less promising.

The War and American Society

Social dislocation and moral reevaluation are the inevitable companions to war, especially when that war is fought in the midst of a civilian population. In Revolutionary America, traditional patterns of behavior and thought no longer maintained their accustomed position, nor did deep-seated habits operate with their usual force. Some of the changes were deliberate and were applauded by most; others, however, were unforeseen, giving rise to anxieties and complaints. Before it was over, the American Revolution affected issues of race, gender, cultural leadership, morality, and religion.

❧ Race and the Revolution

Although the "divide and conquer" policy had not worked along the Hudson River, some British officers saw possibilities in another kind of division: black against white. A large African American population, mostly enslaved and with the rest vividly remembering oppression, seemed

ripe for plucking to the imperial side. This prospect looked especially bright in the South.

Most of the South's potential patriot leaders were off in military service, while many of those who remained worried about slave revolts or Indian attacks. Sectional rivalries between backcountry farmers and coastal plantation owners could perhaps also be exploited to Britain's advantage. Beyond all that, the South possessed a particular people, black slaves, whose discontent invited British manipulation. After the capture of Savannah, Georgia, late in 1778, the British army made systematic efforts to recruit escaped or captured slaves. Following the surrender of Charleston, so many blacks came under Cornwallis's charge that he was unsure how best to use them all. Clinton decreed that slaves belonging to rebellious masters were now to be housed, fed, and paid by the British; after faithful wartime service to the British, they would upon its successful conclusion be freed. Slaves belonging to pro-British masters would be returned to them, but only upon a promise that no punishment for their escape would be inflicted.

As long as the fortunes of war favored the Brit-

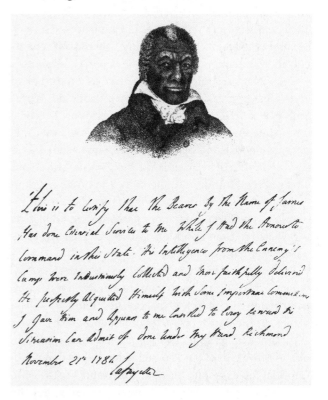

James Armistead Lafayette   A slave of General Lafayette, James Armistead Lafayette performed heroic acts of espionage on behalf of the Continental Army. He risked his life by pretending to supply Cornwallis with information damaging to the Americans, and was rewarded with a commendation from Lafayette (shown above) and manumission paid for by the General Assembly of Virginia.

ish, the number of blacks in their ranks increased. When fortunes reversed, the British endeavored to keep many blacks with them, even transporting some to the West Indies, Canada, or England. Other blacks made their way to British-controlled East Florida, while still others found themselves abandoned by the British "to face the reward of their cruel masters." By the end of the war, some fourteen thousand blacks left with the departing British.

Elsewhere blacks enlisted on the patriot side, especially when bearing arms could mean freedom. In Rhode Island, for example, a black regiment was formed, partly because that state had difficulty reaching its recruitment quotas. And there, as elsewhere, the legislature promised that slaves volunteering for military service would be "absolutely free" and entitled to all the benefits of the white soldier. This small regiment, one of the few units to see service throughout the entire war, distinguished itself repeatedly in military action from Rhode Island to Virginia.

Free blacks could, of course, enlist on terms of equivalent pay — if and when the army got paid. Washington, who had in 1775 banned the service of "Negroes" and "Vagabonds," soon recognized his error (and his military needs), and by the middle of 1778 blacks were serving in fourteen brigades of the Continental Army. These several hundred soldiers saw their own freedom and that of their country as mutual struggles. Their understanding of the cause, both personal and collective, is revealed in their adoption of such surnames as Freedom, Freeman, and Liberty.

In New England, more blacks were enlisted than elsewhere, with Virginia providing the next largest number, though more often of freed rather than of enslaved blacks. In the South promises of freedom to the slaves sometimes failed to be kept, or if kept, then a pension or a distribution of land could be delayed or denied. In Georgia, for example, black artilleryman Austin Dabney fought bravely, was wounded in 1779, and after the war gained his freedom. To some whites, however, this did not mean he should participate equally in the land lottery opened to Revolutionary veterans in 1819. The legislature, deciding otherwise, awarded Dabney 112 acres — much to the scorn of some whites in Madi-

British and Indian Allies   This engraving shows British General John Burgoyne commanding his Indian allies to make war in "civilized" fashion before their successful attack on Fort Ticonderoga in July 1777.

son County who protested that "it was an indignity to white men, for a mulatto to be put upon an equality with them in the distribution of the public land." Blacks also served in what passed for a Continental Navy, as well as on ships under the command of the several states. And blacks, like whites, discharged many other wartime duties, for example serving as guides, foragers, couriers, or spies.

Native Americans and the West

Another nonwhite group, the Indians, earlier pawns in the Anglo-French rivalry, again became pawns in the Anglo-American contest. Indians who had been pushed westward by the ever-enlarging colonial settlements concluded that their best hope of regaining lost territory lay in an alliance with the distant British rather than with the pushy Americans. Just as colonists living close to the Atlantic suffered most from the incessant prowl of British warships, so those on the western frontiers understood the Revolution chiefly in terms of fending off Indian attacks. Indeed, life on the western frontier was a daily hazard, Revolution or no. Southerners already reeled from the shock of the Cherokee War in 1760-61; Kentucky frontier settlers tried to hold off the Shawnee; New Yorkers edging westward encountered the Mohawks, despite British efforts after 1763 to restrict the colonists to land east of the Alleghenies.

In 1777-78 a young surveyor and soldier, George Rogers Clark, finally persuaded Virginia authorities to finance and equip an expedition into Illinois territory. There Clark attacked British strongholds and thwarted efforts to incite the Indians against advancing American settlers. On July 4, 1778, Clark with only 175 men surprised the English commander at Kaskaskia, just east of the Mississippi River. The commander had no choice but to surrender, given the ready willingness of French inhabitants to come to Clark's aid. For the next two years, Clark solidified his position, nullified English influence among the Indians, and even gained access to the upper reaches of that interior "highway," the strategic Mississippi. Although his fortunes and military budgets declined after 1781, Clark's conquest — it is not too strong a word — of the land north of the Ohio River had major consequences in the final treaty that marked the Revolutionary War's end.

British and Indian presence in the West nonetheless kept the American armies from focusing energy and firepower exclusively upon the British forces concentrated in the East. With insufficient forces for one front, George Washington was obliged to fight on two or more. Often, for example, he had to divert scarce supplies and even scarcer troops to western New York or the western Carolinas. In the fall of 1780 woodsmen and frontier fighters, a combination of militia and provincial forces, crossed the Blue Ridge Mountains to engage American loyalists (led by a British commander) encamped on Kings Mountain in South Carolina. These loyalists had long been busy stirring up the Indians and wooing the western settlers. The enemy drew up in formation atop an imposing and apparently impregnable ridge. Angered by the British commander's threat to hang all American officers and to "lay their country waste with fire and sword," and further enraged by the betrayal of some of their countrymen, the frontiersmen sought revenge and vindication. They attacked, not in formation, but in tested Indian-war fashion, moving from tree to tree, rock to rock, driving the British down from Kings Mountain, killing the commander and over two hundred more. The annihilation included the execution of a number of Tories captured in the company of the British soldiers. On this bitter and brutal occasion, the Americans lost fewer than thirty men.

The next year New Yorkers in or near Mohawk Valley, settlers who had often been disrupted by combined British and Indian raids, likewise sought revenge. When at last they received help from a seasoned regiment, they inflicted heavy casualties upon the rapidly retreating British and their Iroquois allies. This story, or some variation of it, repeated itself everywhere from New England to Georgia as Britain sought to press its advantage upon American forces whose attention was generally fixed elsewhere. Civilian suffering often exceeded that endured by the military, with the brunt frequently falling heaviest on both Indian and American women and children.

Women and the Revolution

Colonial women were far from passive spectators, whether in times of peace or of war. Experiencing the dangers of childbearing and the burdens of childrearing, they moved well beyond these roles to join actively in home-centered production. War redirected but did not create their energetic contribution to the demands of daily life. As early as 1774 an observer on a road near Boston reported that he saw "at every house women & children making cartridges, running bullets, making wallets, baking biscuit, crying & bemoaning & at the same time animating husbands & sons to fight for their liberties, tho' not knowing whether they should ever see them again."

During the war, women — the well-known Abigail Adams, for instance — often managed farms or businesses while also keeping their households together. In springtime, wives without husbands planted the fields, and in the fall they often bore the entire burden of reaping the harvest. Shopkeepers' wives now ordered and sold merchandise. Some women, like South Carolina's Eliza Wilkinson, organized discussion groups to raise political consciousness and exchange information. "None were greater politicians," she wrote, "than the several knots of ladies who met together." They also gathered for mutual support and encouragement, since so often "nothing but women and children" remained at home.

In Ipswich, Massachusetts, Sarah Hodgkins watched her husband leave for army service shortly after the bloodshed at Lexington. With two small children to care for and a farm to manage, the twenty-five-year-old wife tried to conceal from her husband her loneliness and near-despair, as she wrote to him throughout his years of service. "I look for you almost every day," she wrote, "but I don't allow myself to depend on any thing, for I find there is nothing to be depended upon but trouble and disappointments." In her anxiety that her husband would be killed, she confessed that "all I can do for you is to commit you to God . . . for God is as

**Abigail and John Adams
on the "ladies," 1776**
*While she may have made her husband
"laugh," Abigail Adams was prophetic in her
belief that women in America would eventually
insist on rights equal to men's.*

Abigail to John
Braintree, Mass., March 31, 1776
I long to hear that you have declared an independency — and by the way, in the new Code of Laws which I suppose it will be necessary for you to make, I desire you would remember the Ladies, and be more generous and favourable to them than your ancestors. Do not put such unlimited power into the hands of the Husbands. Remember, all Men would be tyrants if they could. If particular attention is not paid to the Ladies, we are determined to foment a Rebellion, and will not hold ourselves bound by any laws in which we have no voice or representation.

John to Abigail
Philadelphia, Penn., April 14, 1776
As to your extraordinary Code of Laws, I cannot but laugh. We have been told that our struggle has loosened the bands of government everywhere. That children and apprentices were disobedient — that schools and colleges were grown turbulent — that Indians slighted their guardians, and Negroes grew insolent to their masters. But your letter was the first intimation that another Tribe more numerous and more powerful than all the rest were grown discontented.

able to preserve us as ever, and he will do it, if we trust in him aright." Unlike other wives who watched and waited in vain, Sarah Hodgkins welcomed home her Joseph in 1779, unharmed in over three years of battle.

Other women took charge of the domestic economy in a manner that would directly assist the ordinary soldier. They would not only forsake fine garments for themselves and "wear as much of our own manufactory as pocible" (as eleven-year-old Anna Winslow of Boston observed with her uncertain spelling), but beyond that would spin and knit and weave for the use of the troops. This labor, self-consciously encouraged as part of the war effort, amounted to its own army of resistance. As a young woman from New York stated, women would help the whole country to "retire beyond the reach of arbitrary power, cloathed with the work of our own hands, & feeding on what the country affords." And where personal labor could not do enough, then money-raising efforts would do more. In Philadelphia, Esther DeBerdt Reed, author of *The Sentiments of an American Woman,* encouraged all women to provide additional funds for Washington's ill-clothed, ill-fed soldiers. Look to the examples of women in ancient Rome or in ancient Israel, Reed urged, and let us be useful warriors like "those heroines of antiquity."

Above all else, women as defenders of the home and its values stood for and honored that virtue upon which the Revolutionary cause rested. If patriots hoped to maintain virtue in the face of a decadent Britain, that hope rested heavily upon the role of women — as

instructors to their children, as models for their husbands and servants. The "Daughters of Liberty" served also as the mothers of virtue, rejecting extravagance and self-indulgence, embracing frugality and plainness. Patriots also lauded women as the great reservoirs of religious fervor, maintaining the centrality of the church even when excluded from offices of leadership within it. "The female breast is the natural soil of Christianity," Philadelphia patriot Benjamin Rush observed, and if religion was safely implanted there, he added, it could not be dislodged by all the radicals or infidels of the Western world. The "republican mother," loyal to her nation and her God, would raise sons and daughters to be citizens of impeccable virtue and deep devotion. Thus would the new nation be kept strong.

❧ *Soldiers at the Front, Citizens on the Line*

While officers fretted about their status and pensions, ordinary soldiers worried about exhaustion and exposure, disease and death. They also suffered from severe homesickness, for which the only cure at times seemed to be an unauthorized absence. For the most part lacking military experience, the soldier had to be trained in the rudiments of discipline, how to load, fire, or carry his weapon, and even how to march. Many also required some indoctrination in the basics of hygiene and sanitation. Many men did not bathe, except as an occasional recreation in a nearby river; many did not wash their clothes except under direct military com-

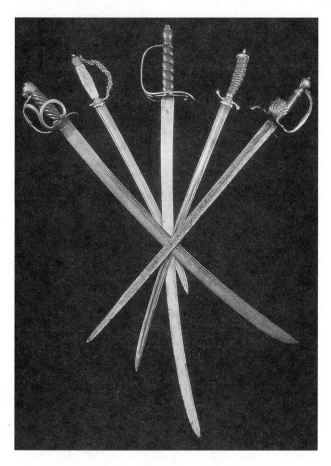

Swords and Sabers　　American swords and sabers used in the Revolutionary War.

mand. No wonder, then, that dysentery, disease, and "the Itch" spread uncontrollably. Also, no wonder that desertion proved virtually irresistible for so many. Most soldiers had never been far from home, nor forced to endure such deprivation. Officers tried everything from bribes to public whippings, even executions, to reduce the number of deserters, estimated in the early years of the war to be as high as 20 to 25 percent.

Yet to other soldiers the Revolutionary cause was just and their participation in it a source of immense personal satisfaction. Hardly oblivious to the suffering, they nonetheless took comfort in the part that they played in creating their new nation. Jonathan Rathbun of Connecticut joined the local militia at the age of sixteen, seeing action almost immediately in New London in 1781. There, Rathbun reported, "we witnessed a scene of suffering and horror which surpasses description": the city burned, the people devastated, and "more than forty widows made on that fatal day" in early September. "It was my melancholy duty," Rathbun wrote, "to assist in the burial of the dead, which brought me di-

rectly in the midst of these heart-rending scenes where the wife first recognized her husband, the mother her son, the sister her brother, in the body of a mangled soldier." The young soldier felt immediate sympathy for his fellow citizens, but also sensed an awakened love for his country.

The British, led by "the traitor Benedict Arnold," sacked Groton, Connecticut, at the same time, slaughtering those who surrendered their arms. Stephen Hempstead, severely wounded in the Groton struggle, noted that "the cruelty of our enemy cannot be conceived," with Arnold and other American loyalists ("our renegade countrymen") exceeding even the British in this respect. Yet, Hempstead wrote, "Never for a moment have I regretted the share I had in it," so much so that if for the sake of the country it were necessary to do it all over again, he would not hesitate. In Fairfield, Connecticut, redcoats "entered the houses, attacked the persons Whig and Tory indiscriminately, breaking open desks, runks [rundles, dish holders], chests, closets, and taking away everything of value; they robbed women of buckles, rings, bonnets, aprons, and handkerchiefs."

In Virginia, the hardships were no less, as English forces targeted soldier and civilian alike in an effort to destroy the tobacco crops in the field, the warehouses in which the harvest was stored, and the wharfs where the hogsheads were shipped. Foodstuffs, no matter whether guarded by women or children, were recklessly destroyed. Meanwhile, frontline soldiers suffered from bad water, typhus and smallpox, and wood ticks that "go thro one's clothes, creep into the pores of the skin, and cause it to swell to the degree of a bee sting, & are exceeding itching smarting." But Josiah Atkins in that summer of 1781 regarded the Revolution as a holy cause, with God guiding the deliverance of the Continental Army. Months before the final showdown at Yorktown, Atkins often experienced "Cornwallisean cruelty." One knew, however, Atkins concluded, that "there is a King superior to the British King, & a Lord far above their lords." In the end, Atkins — like so many others — found support in the conviction that God would grant ultimate victory to his special people chosen for such a time as this.

❧ Science, Art, and Literature amid the Carnage

Pre-Revolutionary Americans had imported technology more than they had developed it, but wartime conditions made continued importation problematic at best. "Yankee ingenuity" had to be called upon even before that phrase had become a tired cliché. A graduate of Yale in 1775, David Bushnell invented a kind of submarine ("Bushnell's Turtle") with which he hoped to "pulverize the British navy." Although unsuccessful in his attacks on enemy ships, Bushnell did identify a major military concern. So did Peter Townsend of New York, who designed a great iron chain to be stretched across the Hudson River to prevent the British from sailing north of West Point. Made of some 750 links, each weighing over one hundred pounds, the chain represented a manufacturing triumph, if not a military one.

More significant militarily, the long-barreled and carefully grooved "Pennsylvania rifle" won great respect during the Revolution, as did the western hunters who prized them and introduced them into battle. Permitting faster reloading and more accurate shooting than the smooth-bore musket, these rifles intimidated the enemy who never knew where the shots were coming from. The perennial shortage of gunpowder stirred the Continental Congress which, in turn, prodded the states to manufacture that essential product. But for this powder, as for heavy artillery pieces, the United States continued to draw upon French and other provisioners in Europe.

The Revolutionary War demonstrated the primitive character of medicine in general, of American military medicine in particular. Philadelphia physician Benjamin Rush, who held a bachelor's degree from Princeton and a Doctor of Medicine degree from Edinburgh, shared the limitations of his colleagues in diagnosing and treating disease. In 1777, as newly appointed physician general for the Continental Army, Rush "entered upon my duty with a heart devoted to the interests of my country." What he encountered, however, dismayed and depressed him: unclear lines of authority for running the hospitals, unsanitary conditions in those hospitals, inadequate medical supplies, and scanty clothing, bedding, and food. As Rush glumly reported to General Washington in the winter of 1777-78, "There cannot be a greater calamity for a sick man than to come into a hospital at this Season of the year." Indeed, Rush continued, "I am safe when I assert that 9 out of 10 who die under our hands perish with fevers *caught* in our hospitals." Rush's complaints went unheeded, at least unheeded to the degree that he thought essential. He therefore resigned his commission in 1778 to return to private life. His observations, however, of the wounded, of the melancholy and the malingering

in the army, led to his later contributions to the treatment of the physically and mentally ill.

Two American artists made the Revolution uniquely their own: Charles Willson Peale of Maryland (see Chapter 4) and John Trumbull of Connecticut. Trumbull served in the Continental Army early in the Revolution, then decided to study with the loyalist emigré Benjamin West in England in 1780. Since this was still during the Revolution, Trumbull fell under suspicion of being a double agent, was arrested, and briefly imprisoned. Upon his release, he sailed to Amsterdam where he completed a full-length portrait of Washington, the first authentic likeness that Europeans had seen. After a sojourn in America, he returned to London after the Revolution to produce the paintings by which that war is chiefly known: *The Battle of Bunker Hill, The Death of General Montgomery in the Attack on Quebec, The Battle at Princeton, The Surrender of Lord Cornwallis at Yorktown,* and others. His most famous painting portrays the signing of the Declaration of Independence; taking several years to complete and consisting of forty-eight individual portraits (thirty-six of them from life), this canvas that from photographs would seem to cover an enormous wall measures a mere twenty by thirty inches. Like Peale, Trumbull continued to combine his art with many other political and commercial activities.

Mercy Otis Warren of Massachusetts contributed much as both poet and dramatist, although she is even better known for her political activism (she was James Otis's sister) and for her subsequently acerbic reflections on the Revolution. Deeply involved in the public contentions and division during the long and uncertain years of war, she revealed little sympathy for those hesitant to support the patriotic cause. The year 1780 was especially dark, she noted, as the enemy pressed hard in open battle but equally hard in secret schemes to turn Washington's officers against him or lure soldiers away from their regiments. As paper money lost its worth and property values plummeted, public confidence sank to its lowest ebb. "The complicated forces of anxiety" at this time, she wrote, afflicted even General Washington himself. But most Americans, she noted, took courage in the confidence that the nation's affairs were under "the direction of an unerring hand" and that ultimately "the beneficent design of Providence" would be fulfilled.

South Carolina physician and patriot David Ramsay wrote of the Revolution first in his own state, but later broadened his account to encompass the country as a whole. Like Warren, Ramsay noted the extraordinary strain of the early days, but he remained impressed with the willingness of Americans to sacrifice, counting "everything cheap in comparison with liberty." The adversity of war drew Americans closer together, Ramsay explained; indeed, the Continental Army itself gave them a chance to know each other so that diverse citizens gradually "were assimilated into one mass." Thus, Ramsay argued, the very waging of war laid the foundation "for the establishment of a nation, out of discordant materials." Like Warren, too, Ramsay saw the hand of Providence assisting the American cause, drying the rain-soaked land around Trenton with a northwest wind so that when Washington's troops "took up their line of march, they were no more retarded, than if they had been on solid pavement."

But Revolutionary fervor was best caught in poetry and song. These literary vehicles served as a means of celebration, but even more as a means of keeping spirits high when there was so little to celebrate. A Boston singing master and composer, William Billings, in 1778 offered this hymn of encouragement:

> *Let tyrants shake their iron rod,*
> *And slavery clank her galling chains;*
> *We fear them not; we trust in God —*
> *New England's God for ever reigns.*

❧ Moral and Religious Values

In the eighteenth century especially, virtue commanded the attention of politicians, statesmen, clergy, and citizens at large. Public virtue, without which it was supposed neither a war could be won nor a republican government be maintained, required a regular accounting of the people's measuring up to the expected standards of civic responsibility, of commitment to the public good. This is what being a "republic" — and the Revolution — was all about. In wartime civilian and soldier alike would be tested even more severely regarding their dedication to the common good. Soldier Josiah Atkins, quoted above, agonized about the moral dimension of the Revolution. When as a New Englander he encountered widespread slavery in the South, he found the ideals of the war "strikingly inconsistent" with the realities of an institution that deprived persons "of that which nature affords even to the beasts." Civilian Benjamin Franklin saw public virtue as resting upon such virtuous private qualities as justice, temperance, fru-

Mercy Otis Warren   A close friend of John and Abigail Adams, Warren was one of the earliest — and best — of the contemporary historians of the American Revolution. She had astute judgment, a sharp tongue, and strongly nationalist sympathies.

gality, industry, and fortitude. On that firm foundation, a society could itself become virtuous, encouraging its citizens in devotion to the "science of virtue."

The war tested such sense of dedication to public virtue, especially as it required some sacrifice of personal freedom. Freedom was the Revolution's primary focus; yet paradoxically it called for a surrender of personal freedom on behalf of the larger good. To serve in the army involuntarily was to be coerced, not free; if so coerced, it should be only for the briefest amount of time, clearly an emergency of the moment. This sentiment made long-term enlistments difficult to obtain and made the notion of a permanent army intolerable. Surely a citizen must do his duty, but the individual and not the state had to determine just what that duty was. Despite the obvious tensions and despite Washington's difficulties in recruit-

Richard Allen The first independent institution for African Americans in the United States was the black church. Richard Allen was one of the leaders of a group of black Methodists who left an established Methodist church in Philadelphia when white church leaders attempted to restrict them to a segregated area of a new sanctuary to which black members had contributed. The church Allen established eventually became known as the African Methodist Episcopal Church.

the abrupt disestablishment of the Church of England in several colonies. In Virginia, where the Anglican establishment had its deepest roots, the sudden severance of all state support left the Church of England bereft and bewildered. It also left many old families of the Tidewater indignant that tradition counted for so little, that religion (in their view) would be so despised. But other Virginians, including the Baptists and Presbyterians, felt differently, judging that the cozy mixing of politics and religion had been good for neither, that religious harassment or persecution belonged to another age or another land. On different grounds, Thomas Jefferson and James Madison agreed that (in Madison's words) "Torrents of blood have been spilt in the old world, by vain attempts of the secular arm, to extinguish Religious discord, by proscribing all difference of Religious opinion." The mistakes of the Old World should not be duplicated in the New; rather, said Madison, Virginia and all America should offer "an Asylum to the persecuted and oppressed of every Nation and Religion." Dissenters joined with deists in Virginia to mount a combined attack against the state church as early as 1776, winning a total victory soon after the Revolution was over. Similar tactics, though neither as spectacular nor as influential, led to disestablishment in other southern colonies, as well as in certain counties in New York.

Congregationalism in New England — seen more as a "homegrown" religion than as an England-imposed one — maintained its official status for another generation.[2] The Congregational clergy (unlike the northern Anglican clergy) had moreover been conspicuous in their endorsement and support of the patriotic cause. Even in New England, however, the Revolution

ment, the dedication to freedom remained the fundamental goal. Resistance to tyranny was the clearest way to long-lasting freedom, and resistance to tyranny was also the prescribed path to public virtue.

The war tested traditional religious loyalties. The most obvious shock to tradition came in the form of

2. Congregationalism continued as the established church in Connecticut until 1818 and in Massachusetts until 1833.

produced calls for greater toleration of, if not complete freedom for, dissenting religions. The Baptist Isaac Backus, for example, as early as 1774 argued that a tax on conscience (requiring all citizens to support the Congregational church) was even more obnoxious than a tax on tea. Massachusetts, he said, had been as heroic in resisting the tea tax as it had been ignoble in imposing the conscience tax. Dissenters agree, he continued, with the principle of no taxation without representation; beyond that, they also assert that they cannot surrender to civil authority their consciences which belong only to God. "Here, therefore," Backus concluded, "we claim charter rights, liberty of conscience."

Some institutional religion did suffer during the Revolution, but on the whole the era saw great religious innovation and excitement. Methodists, a reforming movement born in the Church of England, took up much of the slack that followed the sudden disfavoring of Anglicanism. The Wesley brothers exercised general authority from abroad, but by the time of the Revolution Methodism had become an American enterprise. Methodist proselytizers, both male and female, traveled widely, preached boldly, and organized effectively in cities and on the frontiers. In the 1780s and 1790s Methodism grew at such a furious pace as to astonish observers. The growth included blacks as well as whites; in Philadelphia, to cite an important instance, Richard Allen directed a movement that ultimately became the African Methodist Episcopal Church. Evangelical religion generally — that is, religion that emphasized conversion above tradition and experience above reason — flourished north and south both during and after the Revolution. Indeed, this form of religion outdistanced all others in the decades immediately following the war.

The war itself floated on the waves of religious rhetoric, for religious discourse was the most commonly employed and the most widely understood form of public communication. Patriotic duty and religious duty frequently became one; fighting sin and fighting the British could be identified not only in pulpit oratory but also in personal resolve. Defeat on the battlefield called for more repentance, more humiliation, and days of fasting; victory required gratitude to God who had granted it. As Chaplain Ebenezer David wrote during the siege at Boston in 1776, "What God is about to bring to pass in the Kingdom of his Providence is known by him alone." The duty of Americans, said the chaplain, was to "wait upon him in the way of his judgments," keeping themselves faithful and doing all within their power to drive all "wickedness" out of the land. Chaplains preached and soldiers listened. Josiah Atkins noted on the occasion of a nationwide fast in 1781 that the chaplain's sermon "was the most excellent" he ever heard on this text: "Fear not, and be not dismayed at this great multitude, for the battle is not yours but God's."

Quite apart from the specific institutions of religion or the ministrations of army chaplains, the country as a whole thought of itself bound in a covenant with God. New England had long talked of the covenant between the creator and his creatures, but now others outside that region adopted the language and the concept. If citizens were obedient to God's law and submissive to his will, then God in turn would sustain and watch over them — and not this church or that, but the nation as a whole. America was on its way to becoming a "nation with the soul of a church," to quote a later British writer. If European tyranny became satanic, so the American republic became sacred, a holy community called apart for special tasks and conspicuous honor. In these terms, the future looked bright, so bright, in fact, that some were even willing to predict a new Golden Age, a renewed kingdom of God on earth.

VICTORY AND PEACE

After years of indecisive maneuver and inconclusive military encounters, in 1781 the War of Independence entered a sharply different phase. By the end of that year, George Washington was no longer the hunted, but the hunter; the British, from being the aggressors, became the conciliators. Soon the focus shifted from the battlefield to the bargaining table.

Diplomacy had long been a European art, not an American skill. To wage what eventually became a world war, Americans had quickly to hone that skill and find their way through the maze and treachery of international intrigue. If results can be taken as the principal standard for judgment, clearly by the end of the Revolution Americans had learned their lessons surprisingly well.

The treaty that in 1783 ended the Revolutionary War did far more than stipulate the cessation of hostilities. The United States gained new borders, new ambitions, and — once more in that complex world of foreign affairs — new dangers. The nation had come through one testing time with a creditable performance; other tests, such as maintaining a union and forging a central government, loomed ahead.

The *Bonhomme Richard* and the *Serapis* The fight between John Paul Jones's leaky old warship the *Bonhomme Richard* (donated by the French and named in honor of Franklin's "Poor Richard") and the British frigate *Serapis*, off the British coast in 1779, gave an exhilarating boost to patriot morale. Jones answered the British captain's demand for surrender with his famous retort, "I have not yet begun to fight," and went on to blast away at the *Serapis* until it was in flames. The battle was close enough to shore to be seen by many eyewitnesses.

❧ *The War at Sea*

George Washington's great difficulties maintaining his army were more than matched by his troubles keeping afloat anything that might properly be called a navy. Washington recognized the importance of sea power in fighting a successful war, but naval strategy without ships could not help. The Continental Congress also saw the need, but it was only one among many needs, most of which seemed more urgent. At first Congress, pressed by a shortage of funds, decided that any naval operation should be the business of the states. Quite soon, however, Congress authorized the fitting out of some merchant ships as armed cruisers. By 1777 a Navy Board, located in Boston, undertook a more systematic effort to establish an American fleet. Congressional interest and support, however, wavered. With the French entry on the American side in 1781, Congress gave up all thought of creating a true navy.

Washington, therefore, was left to his own devices. He commissioned many privateers to raid British shipping, particularly those ships carrying men and munitions to the British forces in North America. American seamen had long proved themselves skilled in working out of the many rivers, inlets, and ports of the eastern seaboard — sometimes legally and sometimes not. These skills now proved valuable, as vessels of many

types and varying degrees of seaworthiness, were pressed into service. British ships were raided in the West Indies, in the Bay of St. Lawrence, and even off the British Isles. Between March and December 1776, more than three hundred British ships were captured, and over four hundred the following year. By 1778, the British responded with armed convoys for their ships and tighter blockades of colonial ports, especially in the Middle Atlantic states.

Hungry for good news on any front, patriots took some comfort in the exploits of John Paul Jones in the early years of the war. A native of Scotland, Jones came to America at the outbreak of the Revolution, and in 1775 Congress commissioned him a naval lieutenant. In 1776 and 1777 he executed a series of raids on British shipping, capturing dozens of prizes and winning the confidence of supporters in Congress. In 1779 the French rewarded him with an older ship that Jones promptly renamed *Bonhomme Richard* in honor of Benjamin Franklin's "Poor Richard." In September he encountered a large British convoy off England's east coast, escorted by the heavily armed *Serapis*. Outgunned and often outmaneuvered, Jones succeeded after hours of bloody battle in forcing the surrender of the *Serapis*. So great a victory won him multitudes of admirers in France and in America. Still essentially without a navy, the Americans by 1779 at least had a naval hero.

❧ *The Road to Yorktown*

Although they occupied first Boston and later New York, Philadelphia, and Newport, as well as sought to isolate New England, the British for years neglected the South. That situation changed dramatically in May of 1780 with the disastrous American surrender of Charleston, South Carolina. The South would henceforth seem to be the soft underbelly of American resistance, the British clinging to the hope that rebellion there remained the active interest of only a small, readily outflanked minority. If Britain took advantage of intercolonial bickering, of restless slave populations, of Indian strongholds to the west, and of loyalist potential among the elite, then the South would fall. So the British reasoning went. And having seized control of the South, the British could move northward to bring the rest of North America to heel. Yorktown required major revision of that strategy.

Pacification of the southern countryside and education of the civilian population concerning their "true" (that is, British) interests seemed for a time to work.

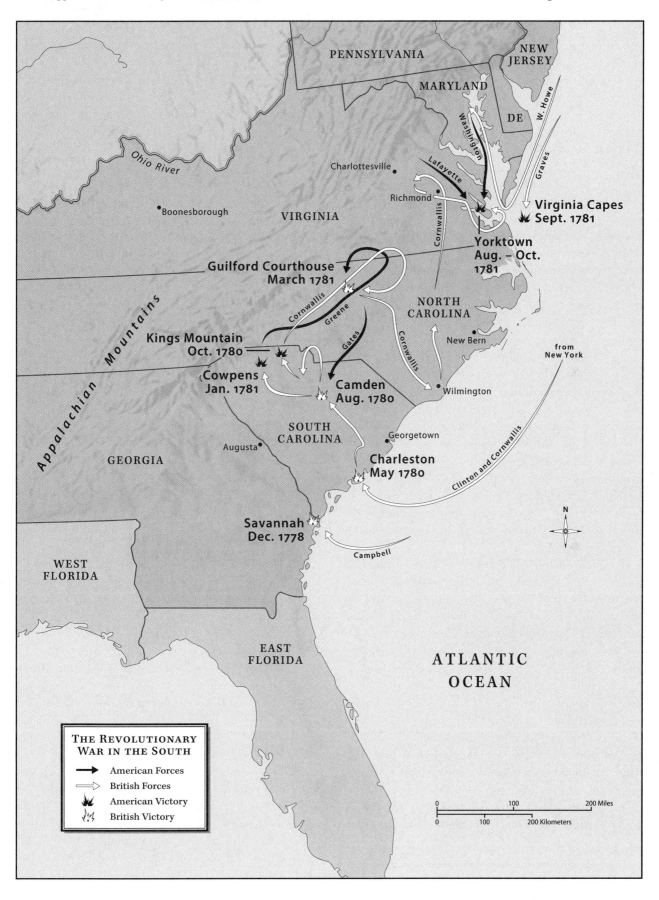

PENNSYLVANIA

NEW JERSEY

MARYLAND

DE

W. Howe

Washington

Ohio River

Charlottesville

Lafayette

Graves

Richmond

•Boonesborough

VIRGINIA

Cornwallis

Virginia Capes
Sept. 1781

Yorktown
Aug. – Oct.
1781

Guilford Courthouse
March 1781

NORTH
CAROLINA

Cornwallis   Greene

Gates

Cornwallis

New Bern

from
New York

Kings Mountain
Oct. 1780

Appalachian Mountains

Cowpens
Jan. 1781

Camden
Aug. 1780

Wilmington

SOUTH
CAROLINA

Augusta•

Georgetown•

Clinton and Cornwallis

GEORGIA

Charleston
May 1780

N

Savannah
Dec. 1778

Campbell

WEST
FLORIDA

EAST
FLORIDA

ATLANTIC
OCEAN

THE REVOLUTIONARY
WAR IN THE SOUTH

→ American Forces

⇨ British Forces

American Victory

British Victory

0   100   200 Miles

0   100   200 Kilometers

After Charleston surrendered in May, American militia and regulars suffered a costly defeat at Camden, losing some two thousand troops and devastating the patriots' morale. British strategy in the South never looked so good. To turn that tide, Washington late in 1780 appointed a new general for the southern campaign: Nathanael Greene[3] of Rhode Island. Working closely with state authorities and pressuring them for greater support of the army, Greene reorganized and revived a dispirited force. In January 1781, Americans won a reassuring victory at Cowpens, but two months later failed to win so convincingly at Guilford Court House in North Carolina. Greene's forces emerged from that contest, however, in better shape than Lord Cornwallis's. Apart from these battles, however, Cornwallis sensed a failure in the grand strategy. Loyalists did not join him; the civilian population neither willingly fed his army nor even offered intelligence about the movement of American troops.

So Cornwallis withdrew from North Carolina toward Virginia, and Greene slowly regained control of the Carolinas (except for Charleston) and Georgia (except for Savannah). Now the British strategy shifted once more: from tedious, piecemeal forays to a final showdown on the Chesapeake, where Cornwallis's forces would be reinforced by those of General Clinton from New York. Such would also allow the British navy — notably unhelpful in the Carolina countryside — to become a major factor, with its firepower placing the American military forces at a serious, perhaps disastrous, disadvantage.

But the French also had a navy and since early in 1780 Count de Rochambeau had some six thousand French troops with him in Newport, Rhode Island, waiting for the arrival of a French fleet. (The British had abandoned Newport the previous October.) Washington, with his army in and around White Plains, New York, waited for all the pieces somehow to come together, recognizing that he could not wait forever. As he wrote to a military aide in France in April 1781, "If France delays a timely, and powerful aid in the critical posture of our affairs, it will avail us nothing should she attempt it hereafter." Washington, more than anyone else, knew that little time remained: no more ignominious retreats, no more pleas to Congress, no more endurance begged of his men. "Our troops are approaching fast to nakedness," he wrote that April; "our hospitals are without medi-

cine, and our sick without nutriment." In a word, Washington concluded, "we are at the end of our tether . . . now or never our deliverance must come."

Meanwhile, Cornwallis from the South informed Clinton in New York that he proposed to move toward Williamsburg "where some subsistence may be procured," then look around for a suitable position on a river wide enough to accommodate British warships. "At present, I am inclined to think well of York." Both sides readied themselves for some sort of action that would bring the war to an end — and, indeed, shape the future of Europe and North America.

The French navy, long-promised and long-awaited, at last returned to North American waters in August 1781. Under the command of the Comte de Grasse, twenty-nine ships and more than three thousand troops stood ready to render assistance to Washington and Rochambeau, wherever they decided they most needed it, and provided they decided soon. The French naval force had been busy about France's business in the West Indies, and would need to be busy there again. But the Americans could have a few weeks, if they moved quickly.

Anticipating the necessity for speedy and definitive action, Washington and his advisers had met Rochambeau and his advisers in Wethersfield, Connecticut, in late May. Clinton and his forces, along with major elements of the British navy, still held New York; Cornwallis's men, promised strong reinforcements, were digging in along the York River in Virginia. Both positions presented formidable challenges and unique opportunities. New York at first appeared the better option. Although held by the British ever since 1776, it remained a vital commercial and mercantile center; moreover, through five years of war it stood as a symbol of British dominance and arrogance. Washington's forces, moreover, were heavily concentrated nearby. When in June Rochambeau marched his men down from Rhode Island to join Washington in New York, the combined army amounted to about eleven thousand. If Admiral de Grasse would sail into New York harbor with his ships and additional troops, New York might fall finally into American hands.

But if General Clinton withdrew all the forces in Virginia to New York, would Washington then prevail? And if the British navy outgunned the French navy, would any hope remain? What if de Grasse had other ideas about where the great offensive should occur and did not even arrive in New York harbor? The major component of the French navy did, in fact, sail from the West

---

3. Greene, a Quaker, abandoned the prevailing pacifism of his sect.

Indies to the Chesapeake, where in more open waters there was less chance of falling victim to British naval power, and where the French navy could help bring Cornwallis down. In August Washington learned that de Grasse was not coming to New York. Recognizing the need for sudden reevaluation, Washington wrote the admiral that "it has been judged expedient to give up for the present the enterprise against New York and to turn our attention towards the South." Therefore — and a consequential "therefore" it had become — "we have determined to remove the whole of the French Army and as large a detachment of the American as can be spared, to the Chesapeake, to meet Your Excellency there."

One strong argument against Virginia was the staggering challenge of moving all those troops in New York all those miles to Virginia. But no other choice remained. So the French and American armies marched from New York down to the headwaters of Chesapeake Bay. Washington left about four thousand men behind in New York to contain Clinton or at least to confuse him. The commander-in-chief also thoughtfully wrote several letters, at least one of which was sure to be captured, carefully explaining that New York remained the principal target and that de Grasse in fact was sailing for that harbor. By the time the troops reached Delaware, Clinton knew better, but Washington and Rochambeau had gained valuable time.

In early September most of the troops climbed aboard whatever boats could be pressed into service to continue the migration down the Chesapeake. They were soon joined by a small French naval force that Washington had for months tried to coax out of hiding in Newport. This force had boats with shallow enough draft to assist in the movement of troops down the bay and up the James River. Meanwhile, de Grasse had in fact arrived with his troops to discover the British navy, dispatched from New York, awaiting him. After four days' engagement, the badly hurt British ships limped back toward New York. Now de Grasse could block the entrance to the Chesapeake, preventing any assistance from reaching Cornwallis.

The stage at last was set for the battle that Washington had dreamed of since 1775: a battle in which forces under his command greatly outnumbered those of the enemy, with the navy now his ally rather than his nemesis, and, with a land war on terrain so familiar that he needed no map to interpret it. On September 27, he gave the order for "the whole Army" to march in one column "at 5 o'clock tomorrow morning precisely." And

if in marching toward Yorktown, "the enemy should be tempted to meet the army on its march," then General Washington commanded the troops to place their principal reliance upon the bayonet, proving to the British that they have no monopoly or "particular prowess in deciding battles with that weapon."

Bayonets were not needed, however, for Cornwallis was busy making his fortifications at Yorktown even stronger, busy writing to Clinton in New York for reinforcements in great numbers and in great haste. On September 30, Clinton assured a desperate Cornwallis "that I am doing every thing in my power to relieve you by a direct move," promising that ships would enter the bay no later than October 12 "if the winds permit, and no unforeseen accident happens." But the French navy turned out to be that "unforeseen accident" — a most happy one that prevented relief reaching Cornwallis by sea. "If things get worse, let me know," wrote Clinton, "and I will attack Philadelphia at once, forcing Washington to divide his army." Things did get worse, but with such swiftness and severity that no military diversion was either possible or useful.

With French engineers (Washington had none of his own), a classic military siege was conducted against Cornwallis. Americans and French together dug trenches in the daytime, just out of range of British guns. Then, at night, they extended each trench ever closer to the fortified British positions near the York River. Heavy guns could in that way be brought to bear upon British cannon. Swift attacks (one led by the young Alexander Hamilton) delivered brutal blows before the British learned just where the breakthrough had occurred. The Virginia militia joined in heartily; the small but hardened contingent of Virginians led by the twenty-four-year-old Marquis de Lafayette was ready; General Benjamin Lincoln, still smarting from his surrender at Charleston, awaited his revenge; General Henry Knox, an experienced artillery officer and Washington's trusted friend, brought all his valuable experience into play. From the left, the French advanced; from the right, the American army moved, pinning Cornwallis down between them. And to Cornwallis's rear lay the York River, with no navy that the British could call their own. In one last desperate move, Cornwallis attempted to get his troops across the river by raft or barge, but severe storms brought even nature into the fight against him.

"My situation now becomes very critical," Cornwallis wrote Clinton on October 15; "we shall soon be exposed to an assault in ruined works, in a bad position, and with weakened numbers." It was all true. And five days later, Cornwallis reported to his superior: "Sir, I have the mortification to inform your Excellency that I have been forced to give up the posts of York and Gloucester, and to surrender the troops under my command, by capitulation on the 19th inst. as prisoners of war to the combined forces of America and France." For the British, mortification; for the Americans, jubilation: the surrender of over eight thousand men, the capture of over two hundred artillery pieces, the acquisition of small arms and ammunition too bountiful to count. Even more important, however, was the boost Yorktown gave to American national pride and long-flagging morale. Victory in the war, in fact so precarious, seemed now inevitable, not only at Yorktown but everywhere that the hostile forces faced each other.

Yorktown was, of course, not the end, but it clearly signaled the beginning of the end. Although the war was to drag on for nearly two more years, the wind had gone out of Britain's sails just as it now filled those of America. The king still hoped for a complete American surrender, but Parliament and all the king's ministers hoped only for an end. Americans, too, if the terms were right (and above all other terms was independence), were agreeable to ending a very long war so that they might bring a very long-suffering people into a new era of peace and, someday, even prosperity.

❧ Diplomacy and Peace

Britain's earlier victory over France in the Seven Years' War (1756-1763) left the victor exhilarated, the loser humiliated and eager for revenge. Indeed, according to Benjamin Franklin, in 1777, "every nation in Europe wishes to see Britain humbled, having all in their turn been offended by her insolence." During the years of the American Revolution, the thirteen states benefited from these resentments, drawing much of Europe to their side, or at least gaining the assurance of a neutrality that would not work against them.

As early as 1775 the Continental Congress took steps to develop favorable foreign contacts, although its initial ventures into European diplomacy were rather amateurish. Diplomats abroad were old hands at the subtle games of bluff and bluster, compromise and maneuver, deceit and chicanery. It took most Americans some time to learn the rules (if indeed there were any). They had a great teacher in Pierre Augustin Caron de Beaumarchais — inventor, playwright,[4] master of intrigue. Beaumarchais travelled from Paris to London where he visited a Virginian, Arthur Lee, whom Congress had commissioned as its courier and its "ear" to determine, if possible, how European powers regarded the North American colonial "uprising." Beaumarchais, at least, was captivated by the romantic possibility of aiding a liberty-loving people, especially if by so doing he could twist the tail of the British lion, and twist it hard.

He hurried home to convince the French foreign minister, Comte de Vergennes, that France — for the sake of its own international interests, of course — should be ready to assist the Americans in any discreet way possible. All this occurred before even the Declaration of Independence had been proclaimed, so that France could hardly take any open or deliberately provocative action. But France could, under Beaumarchais's skillful guidance, set up a fictitious company that would send military supplies to America. This would be done "privately," of course, by a "company" — certainly not

4. He wrote *The Barber of Seville* and *The Marriage of Figaro*, famous satires on aristocratic pretensions.

❈ IN THEIR OWN WORDS

After Yorktown, a Congressional Proclamation, 1781

Whereas it hath pleased Almighty God, the Father of Mercies, remarkably to assist and support the United States of America, in their important struggle for Liberty against the long continued Efforts of a powerful Nation, it is the Duty of all Ranks to observe and thankfully acknowledge the Interpositions of his Providence in their behalf. Through the whole of the Contest, from its first Rise to this Time, the Influence of Divine Providence may be clearly perceived. . . .

It is therefore recommended to the several States to set apart the thirteenth Day of December next, to be religiously observed as a Day of Thanksgiving and Prayer, that all the People may assemble on that Day with grateful hearts to celebrate the Praises of our gracious Benefactor. . . .

Done in Congress this Twenty-sixth Day of October in the Year of our Lord, One Thousand Seven Hundred and Eighty-one, and in the sixth Year of the Independence of the United States of America.

the government of France. At the same time, American ships could be transformed into armed vessels in French harbors, enabling Americans to carry on a modest campaign against English commerce on the high seas. England, rightly guessing who was behind all this clandestine activity, complained often and vociferously. When the complaints grew particularly shrill, Vergennes would ostentatiously capture a few American ships and fine or jail the captains — then when things quieted a bit secretly pay off the ships' owner for losses and allow the vessels to "escape."

After the Declaration of Independence, the French grew even bolder, as did the Continental Congress. In September 1776 Congress dispatched an official diplomatic commission consisting, in addition to Arthur Lee, of Silas Deane of Connecticut and Benjamin Franklin. Seventy years old and a world-famous figure, Franklin was a wily sophisticate who, alone among the Americans abroad, needed no instruction in the diplomatic art. A smashing social success in Paris, Franklin exchanged the courtly powdered wig for the country beaver cap in order to make the American cause popular. Lee, Deane, and Franklin, having heard the good news of victory at Saratoga, managed early in 1778 to conclude with France those two important treaties noted above (p. 169). Henceforth, France's assistance would be more open, even flagrant, and more likely to lead to war with Britain. By June, that war had become a reality.

France pressured Spain to join in support of the American cause, or at least to oppose the British one. But Spain, which ruled so many colonies in the New World, was naturally reluctant to assist "rebellious colonials." Besides, if Americans won their independence, they might even cast an eye toward Spanish territory west of the Mississippi River. Finally, in April 1779, after France agreed to help drive the British out of Gibraltar, Spain reluctantly joined France as an ally. Unlike France, Spain did not officially recognize the United States and, unlike France, it rendered no assistance to the American rebels. Late in 1779 Congress sent the New Yorker John Jay to Spain to persuade that country to be more supportive. But in two and one-half frustrating, demeaning years, Jay gained only some hard lessons in the ways of European diplomacy.

Great Britain's preoccupations with her rebels opened the way for smaller nations to carry on a vigorous trade with the new states. The Netherlands was so successful in breaking the imperial monopoly that by the end of 1780 Britain felt obliged to declare war against it. Encouraged by the growing antagonisms between these two countries, Congress in the summer of 1780 dispatched John Adams to Holland to seek that country's official recognition and financial support. Unlike Jay, Adams actually won both objectives — but only after long and arduous negotiations. In fact, the American Revolution was nearly over before Adams managed to close the deal, but the tardiness did not diminish his enthusiasm as he in 1782 rejoiced that "the American Cause obtained a triumph more signal than it ever obtained before in Europe."

This was after Yorktown, of course, a stinging defeat that stimulated voices in Parliament calling for a settlement of what had become a protracted, increasingly unpopular war. Lord North was replaced as prime minister in March 1782 by the more conciliatory Marquess of Rockingham, who had long favored American independence. Hampered by factions within his own cabinet, Rockingham could accomplish little before his death that same July. He was succeeded by Francis Shelburne, who took personal control of the negotiations to end the war. Britain had long been willing to make every concession except one: independence. America had long been willing to compromise on almost every point except one: independence. Within a month of coming to office, Shelburne conceded that the time had come to discuss independence.

All the players now began to come together: Franklin, still in France, was joined by Jay, journeying north from inhospitable Spain, and by Adams, who took a coach south from the more helpful Netherlands. America had agreed not to make a separate peace with Britain apart from France. But as the British government prepared to make more and more concessions to the Americans, France drew back, alarmed that America might become too powerful in North America, too threatening to significant French interests there. As early as 1778 Vergennes had declared that "we ask independence only for the thirteen states of America. . . . We do not desire that a new republic shall arise which shall become the exclusive mistress of this immense continent." As John Adams wryly observed, Vergennes would hold "his hand under our chin to keep us from drowning, but not lift our heads out of the water."

The American negotiators thus found themselves facing a dilemma. Bound by treaty obligations and by instructions from Congress, technically they could not make a separate treaty with a favorably disposed Great Britain. But their own common sense and the necessity — given the excruciating slowness of communication across the ocean — of using their own judgments, they did what had to be done. Jay quietly left for England to discuss the terms of peace with that nation alone, technically observing protocol by declining to conclude an "official" treaty. During October and November, discussions between British negotiators on the one hand and Jay, Franklin, and Adams on the other moved ever closer to agreement. Finally, on November 30, 1782, the preliminary terms were set. "Unofficial" though the treaty might be, an enormous step toward peace had been taken.

When France learned of this backdoor diplomacy, Vergennes's response was restrained. He had grown increasingly unhappy about his commitment to help Spain drive the British from Gibraltar. Spain and France had tried to drive the British off the rock and had failed; France had no taste for prolonging that struggle. Besides, if those sly Americans had covertly concluded a separate peace, then (France could argue) taking Gibraltar would be even more costly, if not impossible. Vergennes protested to Franklin about the disgraceful behavior of the Americans and their utter disregard of their obligation to proceed only in league with France, but his heart was not in it. Nothing now stood in the way of signing the "official" Treaty of Paris on September 3, 1783. The war was truly over, and America's first venture into turbulent diplomatic waters had turned out remarkably well.

By the terms of the treaty, England acknowledged the rights of each of the states (named one by one) "to be free sovereign & independent states." Moreover, the territory of the United States now stretched west from the Atlantic coast not to the proclamation line of 1763 atop the Appalachian chain (as had been proposed in 1780), nor to a line drawn south from Lake Erie (as had been proposed early in 1782), nor to the Wabash River (as Vergennes had suggested later that year), but all the way to the Mississippi. That was more than France had wanted, and more than most Americans had dared to hope (though Franklin, that "old conjurer" as Adams called him, calmly asked for all Canada as well). Full navigation rights of the Mississippi "from its source to the Ocean" were also granted. To the south, the border would extend to Spanish Florida, a prize France had guaranteed to Spain as the price of its alliance; and to the north to roughly the present U.S.-Canadian border. With John Adams fighting vigorously for the right of New Englanders to fish off Newfoundland ("the gold mines of New England," he named them), the treaty conceded that the "People of the United States shall continue to enjoy unmolested

the right to take fish of every kind on the Grand Bank and on all other Banks of Newfoundland." Prisoners of war on both sides would be released, with Britain agreeing to withdraw all "armies, garrison & fleets from the said United States."

What, in turn, did the said United States grant and concede? Not much. British creditors should meet "with no lawful impediment" in collecting the £5 million sterling they claimed Americans still owed them. Congress agreed only not to pass any law that would prohibit collecting these debts, hardly a fiery pledge of cooperation. As for the loyalists who had fled America and lost all their property, the treaty's language was even more evasive. Congress would "earnestly recommend" to the separate states that they do something about making restitution to those who could show that they were "real British subjects." Congress itself would take no other action. The Americans had conceded virtually nothing — and had gained virtually everything.

It was, in short, a remarkably generous peace, and a remarkable diplomatic coup. England, at war with France, Holland, Spain, and her own colonies, was ready to call it quits. Besides, a nation of former British subjects might help contain both Spain and France in a land that Britain could not easily patrol or defend. Generous terms might, in addition, encourage the new nation to reestablish important commercial ties with a country with which it had traded for so many generations. Perhaps the economic war against France and Holland could be won, even if the military adventure could not.

Surprisingly, the Treaty of Paris was not universally acclaimed at home as a spectacular success. Congress, after all, had been ignored, France had been deceived, and England had been promised too much. Some factions in the Congress, acting under the recently adopted Articles of Confederation (see Chapter 7), even questioned whether the treaty should be ratified. To all this Franklin impatiently retorted that "there never was a good war or a bad peace." And when he returned home in 1785, he found himself celebrated, decorated, and immensely cheered. Jay, who had come back to New York the previous year, was appointed secretary of foreign affairs, replacing one of his sharpest critics, Robert Livingston. And when John Adams at last returned in 1788 (after the war he served as minister to Great Britain), he, too, received a hero's welcome. But the treaty itself was neither honored nor praised, then or later, as it so manifestly deserved to be.

CONCLUSION:
WAR AND NATION-BUILDING

The Revolutionary War began even before independence was declared. That abrupt, almost accidental beginning found Americans unprepared militarily and far from united in sentiment. George Washington, the Virginian, did much to shore up military defenses, while the Declaration of Independence and Paine's *Common Sense* helped create another kind of united front. Divided among patriots, loyalists, and pacifists, the budding nation needed all the unity it could get. And demoralized by a succession of humiliating defeats and retreats, American forces needed encouragement of any kind from any quarter.

That encouragement came, first, in the Battle of Saratoga, then in an alliance with France. Yet the war stretched on and on, with sacrifices at home often matching those of the battlefield. Britain held every major city or town, and when Charleston surrendered in 1780 it seemed as though British patience and strategy would at last be rewarded. But the surrender at Yorktown the following year did turn Britain's world upside down. Now Americans had breathing space and legitimate grounds for hope. The Treaty of Paris that concluded the war placed America on the crest of a wave that could propel it forward or crash it onto the shoals.

The critical era of nation-building had now begun, as Americans would continue to wrestle with the meaning and implication of the Revolution. The time had come to pay off the heavy war debts, to build a strong economy on the ruins of war, to meld states together into a genuine union, to correct factionalism and cure jealousies. Surely, the challenges were formidable and the wishes fervent. The hard-won peace of 1783, John Adams wrote Abigail, was the product of American labor and industry, purchased by the "firmness of her sons, and watered by the blood of many of them." "May its duration," he added, "be in proportion to its value, and like the mantle of the prophet descend with blessings to generations yet to come." Both Abigail and John Adams, along with countless others, recognized that much work remained to be done.

SUGGESTED READING

Catherine Albanese, *Sons of the Fathers: The Civil Religion of the American Revolution* (1976). With subtlety and a clear sense of the ambiguities of motives, the author traces the religious dimensions of Revolutionary fervor and rhetoric.

Joseph J. Ellis, *Founding Brothers: The Revolutionary Generation* (2000). It would be difficult to imagine a more engaging survey of the critical figures in the forming of the new nation. (Abigail Adams is included among the "brothers.")

David Hackett Fischer, *Washington's Crossing* (2004). A superb account of the attack on the Hessian mercenaries late in 1776. Extraordinarily helpful maps.

Don Higginbotham, *The War of American Independence: Military Attitudes, Policies, and Practice, 1763-1789* (1971). No narrow military history, the author's broad focus makes this book a stimulating exercise in social history.

Sidney Kaplan and Emma N. Kaplan, *The Black Presence in the Era of the American Revolution* (rev. ed., 1989). Providing many primary sources along with ample illustrations, the Kaplans shed much light upon an aspect of the Revolutionary period too often dimly lit.

John Keane, *Tom Paine: A Political Life* (1995). A brilliant biography of the best-selling author of the late eighteenth century: his dramatic rise, and his equally dramatic fall.

Linda K. Kerber, *Women of the Republic in Revolutionary America* (1980). This volume offers a provocative discussion of republican motherhood, along with attention to the changing legal status of women.

Pauline Maier, *American Scripture: Making the Declaration of Independence* (1997). A superb analysis of the "life and times" of the Declaration, with unique attention to scores of other "declarations" issued by provincial congresses, grand juries, militia associations, and a wide variety of counties and towns.

Robert Middlekauff, *The Glorious Cause: The American Revolution, 1763-1789* (2nd ed., 2005). A remarkably detailed and elegantly written account of the Revolution, buttressed by unusually helpful maps.

Richard B. Morris, *The Peacemakers: The Great Powers and American Independence* (1965). The classic treatment of the intricacies leading up to the Treaty of Paris in 1783.

Mary Beth Norton, *The British-Americans: The Loyalist Exiles in England, 1774-1789* (1972). A valuable study of the "other side" in the Revolution, with useful attention to such figures as Samuel Seabury and Thomas Bradbury Chandler.

Charles Royster, *A Revolutionary People at War* (1996). No stone is left unturned or unexamined in this excellent analysis of the Revolutionary drama and the players in it.

Gordon S. Wood, *The Radicalism of the American Revolution* (1991). This Pulitzer Prize winner rescues the American Revolution from those who would understand that event in essentially conservative — nothing really changed — terms.

Esmond Wright, Jr., *The Fire of Liberty* (1983). This handsomely produced volume presents eyewitness accounts of participants in and victims of the Revolution.

SUGGESTIONS FOR FURTHER READING

Bernard Bailyn, *The Ideological Origins of the American Revolution* (1967).

Benson Bobrick, *Angel in the Whirlwind: The Triumph of the American Revolution* (1997).

Wayne Bodle, *The Valley Forge Winter: Civilians and Soldiers in War* (2002).

W. Jeffrey Bolster, *Black Jacks: African American Seamen in the Age of Sail* (1997).

Colin G. Calloway, *The American Revolution in Indian Country* (1998).

Theodore Draper, *A Struggle for Power: The American Revolution* (1996).

Marc Egnal, *A Mighty Empire: The Origins of the American Revolution* (1988).

David Hackett Fisher, *Paul Revere's Ride* (1994).

Thomas Fleming, *Liberty! The American Revolution* (1997).

Eric Foner, *Tom Paine and Revolutionary America* (rev. ed., 2004).

William M. Fowler, Jr., *Rebels Under Sail: The American Navy During the Revolution* (1976).

Don Higgenbotham, *George Washington and the American Military Tradition* (1985).

Ronald Hoffman and Peter J. Albert, eds., *Religion in a Revolutionary Age* (1994).

Ronald Hoffman and Peter J. Albert, eds., *Women in the Age of the American Revolution* (1989).

Woody Holton, *Forced Founders: Indians, Debtors, Slaves and the Making of the American Revolution* (1999).

John Keegan, *Fields of Battle: The Wars for North America* (1995).

Richard M. Ketchum, *Saratoga: Turning Point of America's Revolutionary War* (1997).

Pauline Maier, *The Old Revolutionaries: Political Life in the Age of Samuel Adams* (1980).

Henry Mayer, *A Son of Thunder: Patrick Henry and the American Republic* (1991).

Holly A. Mayer, *Belonging to the Army: Camp Followers and Community during the American Revolution* (1996).

Richard B. Morris, *Seven Who Shaped Our Destiny: The Founding Fathers as Revolutionaries* (1973).

Gary B. Nash, *The Unknown American Revolution: The Unruly Birth of Democracy and the Struggle to Create America* (2005).

Mark A. Noll, *Christians in the American Revolution* (1977).

Mary Beth Norton, *Liberty's Daughters: The Revolutionary Experience of American Women* (1980).

Kenneth Silverman, *A Cultural History of the American Revolution* (1976).

Page Smith, ed., *Religious Origins of the American Revolution* (1976).

7

From Confederation to Federal Union, 1781-1788

URING THE AMERICAN Revolution, liberty had been the paramount issue. With independence assured, attention gradually shifted to the question of sovereignty. Just where did the center of authority lie? If in "the people," then how did the people make their will known? Did they voice their concerns directly, as in the New England town meeting? Or, did they, as in the various colonial assemblies, speak only through elected representatives? At every level of government — courts, councils, legislatures, executive officers — how should sovereignty be divided up?

A further desire haunted Americans searching for stability and order — for some center of gravity to replace king, Parliament, and established church. Liberty had been painfully won, but now steps must be taken to ensure that liberty did not turn into either anarchy or tyranny. What form of government could be adapted or invented that would preserve liberty, not eradicate it, but at the same time create a kind of order that would protect and promote the people's happiness?

In searching for that ideal form — that must somehow also become a reality — a pervasive uneasiness could be detected. That uneasiness pertained to the character or the quality of those persons chosen to represent or rule. We have already encountered the loaded word *virtue*, and in this chapter we will encounter it again and again. Public spirit and public good must prevail. For years, the revolutionaries had demanded sacrifice of private good for the welfare of the whole, for the "commonweal." That same dedication, that same selflessness, must now bring an uncertain people

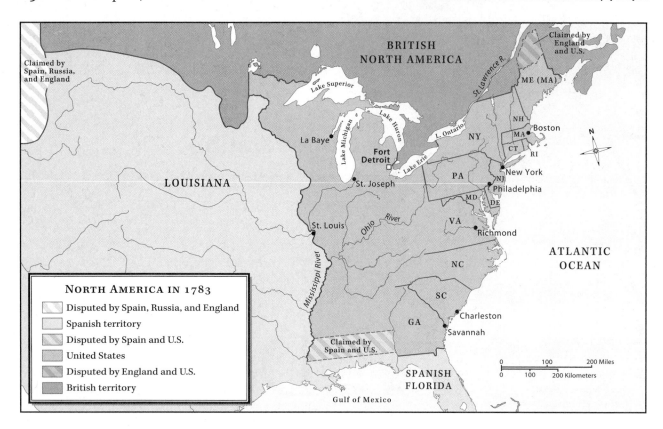

through troubled and difficult waters. After the clouds of war had vanished and the sunshine of peace warmed hearts everywhere, the danger was that Americans might grow soft. "Elated with success and blinded by prosperity," one orator proclaimed in 1785, "we too soon began to relax our manners, and to adopt the luxury, the follies, the fashions of that nation which so lately we had every reason to detest."

The thirteen states that had fought and won a war considered themselves sovereign countries, and they had surrendered little of their sovereignty to Congress. The issue now was whether the thirteen could in some sense, in any sense, become one. John Adams in 1776 had fretted about getting thirteen clocks to strike at the same time. A decade later he and many others urged that the separate machines be geared together so that they ran as a single mechanical model. Hopes for such an outcome rested to a great degree on the religious assurance that (in the words of Yale's president, Ezra Stiles) "God will not forsake this people, for whom he has done such marvelous things." In this 1783 sermon celebrating the peace that ended the Revolution, President Stiles took his text from Deuteronomy 26:19. "And to make thee high above all nations which he hath made, in praise, and in name, and in honor; and that thou mayest be a holy people unto the Lord thy God."

Struggling to sustain the war effort, Congress at the end of 1777 sent to the states a plan to create a somewhat stronger central government: the Articles of Confederation. But, bowing to the principle of state sovereignty, the Articles could not take effect until every state had ratified them. This did not occur until 1781 because small states like Maryland (the last to ratify) insisted that states with huge western land claims first surrender these territories to the central government. After the Articles were finally ratified, that thorny issue required immediate attention, along with other urgent domestic and foreign problems. In trying to solve these many issues, the weakness of the central government grew increasingly evident. As a blueprint for creating a nation "high above all nations," the Articles of Confederation clearly would not work. Congress, under that "management," could not even maintain law and order at home.

In the opinion of many, some more "energetic" form of government needed to be devised. Cultural and political leaders, living for the most part in East Coast cities, generally favored a stronger central government. Inland and rural dwellers, on the other hand, jealously guarded those liberties so recently won; just as surrendering rights to a British Parliament had been wrong, so surrender to some national American legislature would be equally wrong. Indeed, the very word *nation* stuck in the throat of many who saw in it too much centralization of power. A federated union might be acceptable; a national power was not.

Nonetheless, the cultural elites prevailed long enough to secure a call for a Constitutional Convention to gather in Philadelphia in May 1787. All were not of one mind on why they had been called together, nor on just what was expected of them. Delegates debated for months exactly what form any new government should take. When they finally finished debating, the people seized their turn to praise or denounce and ultimately to vote on what had been submitted to them. For more than a year and a half, that contest hung in the balance, with key states almost evenly divided between those favoring ratification and those opposed. When ratification at last came in 1788, Americans took a giant step in the direction of national government. That step led to another critical advance with the passage of a Bill of Rights.

THE SOVEREIGN STATES

Even though a war was raging, few Americans in the late 1770s and early 1780s worried much about that vague entity known as the United States of America — or as many preferred to say, these united States of America. Rather, states busied themselves with rewriting their own constitutions. Separation from Britain had made the language if not the substance of colonial frames of government obsolete. Few doubted that the former colonies, now independent states, had full responsibility for establishing new structures. Independent states should be no less responsible — indeed, more so — for the safety and welfare of their citizens than they had been as dependent colonies. Besides, prevailing political theory argued that a true republic must be small, close to the people, always subject to popular scrutiny and censure. If people were to be safe from tyranny, it would be through reliance upon and trust in their familiar, local governments. Only in the states, many believed, was sovereignty properly placed; only there were individual liberties most likely to be preserved. And only there could the virtue of citizen-neighbors ensure the success of republican government.

❧ *Revising the State Constitutions*

During the long decades of colonial rule, elected legislators had often tried to limit their governors' power while enlarging their own. So when it came to writing

new constitutions, the prevailing tendency was to maximize the power of the legislature (and that of the lower house if it existed) and to assign far less power to the executive. Under royal rule, moreover, colonists had long resented being placed under the authority of men who had been appointed (not elected) to tax or judge or govern them. Henceforth, Americans would agree to be governed only by those who they themselves had elected; and to keep the elective process meaningful, many states provided that elections be annual, at least for the lower house.

In May 1776 the Continental Congress recommended that the states set about forming new governments to protect the interests and promote the happiness of their citizens. Connecticut and Rhode Island continued to operate under charters that provided for elected governors and annual elections. But all the other states, sooner or later, wrote new constitutions; legislatures sometimes took the lead. At other times, special conventions were called for this purpose. In most cases, efforts were made to keep the people close to the process. "The people," to be sure, did not mean the masses, but those eligible to vote: in every case free males over twenty-one, and in most cases males who owned property. These voters either elected the members of their constitutional conventions or directly gave or withheld their approval in a ratification process. Popular sovereignty needed to be honored, not just in rhetoric but in practice.

Little New Hampshire led the way, adopting a new constitution a full six months before the Declaration of Independence. (Hedging their bets, the cautious New Hampshire legislators provided that the new constitution was "to be in Force during the present dispute with Great Britain, unless otherwise advised by the Continental Congress.") Replacing the ritualized "God save the King" with "God save the People," New Hampshire citizens allowed no ambiguity concerning where sovereignty lay: power descended not from above, but rose from the people. With no charter to fall back on, New Hampshire had to place its trust in a constitution that, ultimately, was submitted to the voters for their ratification. Gradually, property holding was eliminated as a qualification for voting as well as for holding office, even as direct representation was granted to towns long denied their rightful voice in government. Throughout the Revolution and long after, New Hampshire towns functioned as "little republics," enjoying a remarkable degree of autonomy.

In Pennsylvania, power shifted from the aristocratic

elites who continued to control the Assembly to western radicals and urban artisans who demanded a constitutional convention. This convention in 1776 adopted a declaration of rights and provided for a unicameral legislature without an aristocratic upper house. Roll call votes would let the people know how every legislator voted, and all major legislative proposals were to be printed and circulated so that the public will could be made known.

Other states, less torn by internal factions or tensions, opted more for stability than change. But, since the Revolution's central issue was Britain's denial of colonial rights and liberties, most states included a bill or declaration defining those rights as insulated from any governmental encroachment. Beyond these broad similarities, states expressed individuality (if not idiosyncrasy) as they constructed new fundamental frames of government.

Virginia, early to draw up a new constitution and bill of rights, in June 1776 set an example that many other states followed. Here, too, a special convention, not the legislature, assumed the task of creating a new government. Revolutionary stalwarts led the effort: George Mason, Edmund Randolph, Patrick Henry, James Madison, and Thomas Jefferson. (Jefferson soon left for Philadelphia to represent his state in Congress, although he would greatly have preferred to stay in Virginia for its vital task of drafting a fundamental frame of government.) The Virginia constitution-makers saw their role as creating a new government that would endure for generations and symbolize what the Revolution was all about. In drawing up their constitution, Virginia's leaders relied heavily on the advice of John Adams, currently in Philadelphia with the Continental Congress. Adams responded to the Virginians' and others' appeals for guidance, first in letters and later by publishing his *Thoughts on Government,* a small book that reveals much of the thinking behind the intense activity of the states in drafting their constitutions.

Adams believed that no activity could have greater consequences for the future than this composing, state by state, of new frames of government. "There can be no employment more agreeable to a benevolent mind," he wrote, "than a research after the best." And Adams, a voracious reader, had done his research well. He had pondered the political theory of such leading Englishmen as John Locke, Algernon Sidney, John Milton, and James Harrington; he familiarized himself with experiments in republicanism on the Continent (notably Holland); and, like many educated colonials, he knew intimately the successes and failures of the ancient republics of Greece and Rome. These days in America, Adams exclaimed, offered once-in-a-lifetime opportunities, days "when the greatest lawmakers of antiquity would have wished to live." Rarely have members of the human race been presented with the chance to choose a government "for themselves and their children." That chance is now given, Adams wrote, to some "three millions of people . . . to form and establish the wisest and happiest government that human wisdom can contrive."

Laying down some of the basic principles by which the new states might be guided, Adams understood that all wanted to create republics, not monarchies; all wanted to entrust power to the people, the surest protection against tyranny. But republics came in varying shapes and sizes, though all were (or should be) designed to ensure that reason, not passion, prevailed,

---

✳ IN THEIR OWN WORDS

John Locke on the True End of Government, 1690

The constitutions of the newly independent states owed much to the thought of Enlightenment political philosopher John Locke.

And hence it is evident that absolute monarchy, which by some men is counted for the only government in the world, is indeed inconsistent with civil society, and so can be no form of civil government at all. For the end of civil society being to avoid and remedy those inconveniences of the state of Nature which necessarily follow from every man's being judge in his own case, by setting up a known authority to which every one of that society may appeal upon any injury received, or controversy that may arise, and which every one of the society ought to obey. Wherever any persons are who have not such an authority to appeal to, and decide any difference between them there, those persons are still in a state of Nature. And so is every absolute prince in respect to those who are under his dominion.

For he being supposed to have all, both legislative and executive power in himself alone, there is no judge to be found, no appeal lies open to any one, who may fairly and indifferently, and with authority decide, and from whence relief and redress may be expected. . . .

and that power was carefully controlled, checked, and hedged to prevent corruption and abuse. Pomp, privilege, and royal patronage had no place in a republic; the time had come, Adams declared, for Americans to rid themselves forever of "the dons, the bashaws, the grandees, the patricians, the sachems, the nabobs — call them by what name you please." Citizens should be ruled by persons of integrity, property, virtue, and independence, to be elected annually, for "where annual elections end, there slavery begins." Standing for election every year had the further merit, Adams added, of teaching politicians humility and moderation, "without which every man in power becomes a ravenous beast of prey." Although it was desirable that legislators hold property, it was equally desirable that property be widely distributed, even in small amounts, so that power resided in the multitude, not in the few.

All colonists recognized that the central issue in creating a government pointed directly to questions of power. No government could exist without power, of course, but no government that abused its power deserved to exist. In constitution-making, therefore, the prime task was to exercise the greatest care in granting and controlling and — if need be — recalling power. For Adams and most others, the best security lay in a two-house legislature entrusted with such fundamental powers as levying taxes and declaring war. A single house was too much like a single individual, Adams reasoned, "subject to fits of humor, starts of passion, flights of enthusiasm, partialities, or prejudice, and consequently productive of hasty results and absurd judgments." A single house, moreover, even though initially elected, was prone to perpetuate itself year after year, even for life, as the histories of Rome, England (during the Long Parliament), and Holland demonstrated. The governor and the judges should be held accountable by the legislature, which in turn should be held accountable by the people.

In Virginia, the draft of a new constitution that George Mason submitted to the delegates followed much of Adams's thinking. The convention itself, more leery of executive power than either Adams or Mason, created a governorship notable for its weakness. (Jefferson even wished to call the executive merely an "administrator" to emphasize his subservience to the legislature.) As a consequence, Virginia's governor had no right either to veto bills or to suspend or adjourn a legislative session. Voting, as it had been for a generation or more, was restricted to free white males over twenty-one who owned at least one hundred acres

of undeveloped property or twenty-five acres with a dwelling. In Virginia, as elsewhere, universal suffrage still lay many decades away.

Other states found room for many variations on Adams's recommendations. Some redistributed representation more evenly, so that seaboard towns did not dominate legislatures. Pennsylvania, as we have seen, even ignored Adams's stern warning against the evils of a single legislative house. By the end of 1776 all states but three — New York, Georgia, and Massachusetts — had drawn up new constitutions or amended old charters. New York, distracted by the intensity of war within its borders or nearby, nonetheless proclaimed its first constitution in April 1777 and elected a governor and legislature in the summer and early fall. Georgia also established a new constitution in 1777, although the occupation of Savannah in 1778 and the reimposition of royal government in 1779 caused its suspension until the end of the Revolution.

Despite John Adams's vigorous promotion of new governments, Massachusetts did not adopt its constitution until 1780. (An earlier version, submitted to the voters in 1778, had been rejected.) Serving as the chief architect of the 1780 document, Adams provided for those divisions of power that would keep power tightly reined in. Like many Whigs (let alone traditional Calvinists), Adams entertained no romanticized notion of a pure and unsullied humanity. All people sinned; all people with power sinned gravely; all people with unlimited power sinned tragically. The best that a lawmaker could do was build strong safeguards around all users of power, making it terrible for any officeholder who violated the trust placed in him.

After a few stumbles, Massachusetts took significant strides toward popular sovereignty. On the question of holding a constitutional convention, all adult males, not just property holders, were declared eligible to vote. Also, the convention agreed to submit a draft of their deliberations to all the towns for an article-by-article review and response. And finally, to keep the voice of the people engaged, the convention provided for a further review of the final document in 1795, if two-thirds of the towns voted for it. Not only did Massachusetts honor popular sovereignty, but it also went beyond the other states in expanding the franchise where constitutional matters were concerned.

Obviously, not all the states understood the implications of the Revolution in the same way. Some, like New York, retained high property qualifications for voting, kept a strong governor, and put no confidence in frequent elections. Others, like Pennsylvania, saw the Revolution as requiring a purge of any lingering aristocratic tendencies. But virtually all interpreted the Revolution to demand a broadening of citizens' rights.

One mighty bulwark against absolute power was found in those declarations of rights that state after state proclaimed: rights that were inalienable and inviolable. The right to trial by jury (compromised before the Revolution by England's admiralty courts) was repeatedly asserted, with Virginia even calling for this right in civil as well as criminal cases. The right of all persons to life, liberty, and property — the essence of so many Revolutionary protests and resolves — was not granted by government and could not, therefore, be removed by any legitimate government. And if a government usurped these and other rights, then another fundamental liberty was claimed: that of a majority to change their constitutional structure, peaceably if possible, forcibly if necessary.

Because the states had sharply separate religious traditions and histories, no uniform assertion of religious views could be expected. But again, with fresh memories of England's ecclesiastical imperialism or insensitivity, the states pledged themselves to a wide toleration if not a full liberty in religion. Typically in 1776 New Jersey declared that "No person shall ever . . . be deprived of the inestimable privilege of worshipping Almighty God in a manner agreeable to the dictates of his own conscience"; at the same time, however, none should be compelled to attend or support any worship through "tithes, taxes, or any other rates."

So suspicious were several states of mixing religious and political power that they barred ministers from serving in the legislature or (in the words of New York's constitution) declared them ineligible for "holding any civil or military office or place within the State." On the other hand, many states granted specific constitutional exemption to those who, for reasons of conscience, could not bear arms or swear an oath in court; Maryland in this matter took specific note of the concerns of Quakers, Mennonites, and Brethren. Yet religious liberty was far from complete. Connecticut and Massachusetts continued to give official support to the Congregational church. Some states limited office holding to Protestants (Georgia), to Christians (Maryland), to believers in God (Pennsylvania), or to those who accepted "the divine authority" of the Bible (North Carolina). Tentative steps were being taken toward a full religious freedom in 1776, but years would pass before most states wholeheartedly embraced such liberty.

⚜ *Revising State Expectations*

In the enthusiasm of creating new constitutions, the states saw clearly what they were rejecting: royal governors and their cronies, Privy Council patronage, hobbled and often impotent legislatures, imperial interests at the expense of local needs. In that same enthusiasm, they also saw clearly — or at least thought they did — the only solid substitute for Britain's tyranny: the people. "God save the People," citizens of New Hampshire intoned, and though other colonies may not have adopted the slogan, they surely adopted the sentiment. If God saved the people, the people would save the states.

And that was the way it was supposed to work, until — especially after the War of Independence was over — you took a closer look at "the people." In the turbulence and upheaval of war, the cream did not always rise to the top. Indeed, as James Otis of Massachusetts noted, "When the pot boils, the scum will rise." In one state legislature after another, it appeared that "men of no genius or abilities" (to quote John Dickinson of Pennsylvania) had assumed control of government — with disastrous results. Regardless of how carefully constitutions had been drawn up, it could not be expected, Dickinson observed, "that things will go well when persons of vicious principles and loose morals are in authority." Governments can never be better than the people elected to run them. Or, as a South Carolinian observed, Americans after the War began "to fear that they had built a visionary fabric of government on the fallacious idea of public virtue."

In drawing up Virginia's Declaration of Rights, George Mason included one "right" that may strike the modern reader as somewhat odd: namely, the necessity for citizens to pursue "Justice, Moderation, Temperance, Frugality, and Virtue" in order to keep society free. But in making such a declaration in 1776, Mason was neither eccentric nor unique. In that same year, John Adams wrote to his cousin, Zabdiel Adams, that while statesmen "may plan and speculate for liberty . . . it is religion and morality alone which can establish the principles upon which freedom can securely stand." Constitutions were important, John Adams perhaps above all others would affirm; nevertheless, "The only foundation of a free constitution is pure virtue." Given such widely prevailing assumptions, therefore, it might readily be expected that frugal and virtuous citizens would elect legislators who, like themselves, would prove to be frugal and virtuous.

By the mid-1780s, such rosy assumptions withered.

Keeping the legislature close to the people by requiring annual elections seemed, at first, an excellent idea. The result, however, was a constant turnover, bringing new and untried persons into office, or often, in Madison's alarmist words, "men without reading, experience, or principle." Instead of persons of demonstrated "industry, economy, and good conduct," legislative halls swarmed with those wholly unskilled in running the machinery of state; many, moreover, seemed equally unskilled in the proper management of their own lives. A kind of "natural aristocracy" — persons of character, talent, and influence — was being ignored in a fanciful chase after an artificial equality of merit. Dumping all notions of British titles and nobility was good, but rejecting all sense of a natural nobleness of character was bad — and horribly costly to the cause of good government.

Society naturally divided itself into the "lower sort" and the "better sort," many acknowledged, though some in derision and some with approval. One champion of democracy, New York's Melancton Smith, disapprovingly recognized that American society had its differences as surely as Britain did. Here, said Smith, "birth, education, talents, and wealth create distinctions as visible . . . as [aristocratic] titles, stars, and garters." For a new nation dedicated to the idea of equality, these differences, Smith thought, were not healthy. For others, however, ignoring such natural, inevitable differences was even more unhealthy: it would allow the least qualified to become the most powerful. If state governments fell into the hands of "a set of unprincipled men who sacrifice everything to their popularity and private views," then the public good was forsaken and all that had been fought for was lost.

Competing theories concerning how "democratic" or how "aristocratic" the political and the social order should be began to divide each state, though this question rarely appeared in purest form. Every legislative debate was complicated by regional differences, occupational interests, personal loyalties (or antipathies), tax policies, intercolonial jealousies, and a host of other issues. But the central fact remained that state governments did not work as well as most had hoped. "Little republics" turned out to present large opportunities for graft and self-seeking, as the common good took second place to private gain. At the top of the social ladder, rich "nabobs" still exerted great influence for their own benefit, while at the bottom of that ladder the unworthy and the licentious looked after their own interests too. If government at the local level proved less than moderate, just, frugal, and virtuous, how was government doing at the national level?

THE UNION AND ITS LIMITS

Getting thirteen clocks to strike at precisely the same moment had indeed proved difficult in 1776, but seeing that those clocks kept time together in the years following presented even more obstacles. The Articles of Confederation represented the first tentative step toward an authoritative Timekeeper, but the voice of central authority was often muffled if not wholly silent. Yet between 1781 and 1789 some significant achievements for the union could be noted, especially with respect to the West. Such achievements, however, could not obscure the unsettling fact of the central government's virtual powerlessness in the face of any serious domestic rebellion or foreign intrusion. To some, such weakness was welcome. And to even more, the notion of a united nation came with difficulty, if at all.

❧ Articles of Confederation

The colonies, accustomed to defending themselves or promoting themselves alone, did on occasion recognize the need for unity. Although Benjamin Franklin's 1754 Plan of Union had gone nowhere, its favorable hearing in Albany indicated that momentous events might produce unified action. The Stamp Act Congress in 1765 and the Declaration of Independence in 1776 gave further support to the notion that Americans ought to unite. But *e pluribus unum* — "out of many, one" — remained a tantalizing and elusive goal. Americans had no interest in throwing off a foreign tyranny only to see it replaced by a domestic one. The states held all the power, and the "united States" (as the phrase appeared in the Declaration of Independence) held only as much power as the states chose collectively — and always reluctantly — to relinquish. An observer in 1776 could reasonably conclude that the phrase "united States" was just a phrase, not a viable political organism.

In that year, however, the Second Continental Congress appointed not only a committee to draft a declaration of independence, but also a committee to draft a constitution for these "united States." John Dickinson chaired the latter (as Jefferson had chaired the former), but the product of Dickinson's labors ran into even more difficulty than had Jefferson's Declaration. Congress argued for over a year before approving the

Articles of Confederation, a much-amended version of Dickinson's plan. And then the states argued for four more years.

The weak union created by the Articles would not go into effect until every state had ratified it. By July 1778, nine states accepted the Articles, and three more did so in 1779. Maryland, however, continued to hold out, concerned that the large states would become even larger unless they relinquished their claims to western lands that extended across at least half the continent. A gargantuan Virginia or New York would wholly smother states like New Jersey, Delaware, and Maryland, all of which lacked such claims. When in January 1781 Virginia agreed in principle to cede its western lands to the new union, Maryland finally joined the other twelve states in approving the Articles. Only in March 1781 could Congress ratify the Articles and declare itself formally to be "The United States in Congress Assembled."

That jealous regard for the sovereign independence of each state characterized — and shackled — the Articles of Confederation. Each state, regardless of population or wealth, would have the same single vote as every other state. Major decisions such as declaring war, coining money, or entering into treaties or alliances could be taken only if at least nine states agreed. States that had so scrupulously kept the power to tax in their own legislatures insisted that it stay right there. Congress could assess the states for a given amount based on property values, but if the states chose not to comply, Congress had no power to enforce its requests. So also with troops: after the war ended and the Continental Army disbanded, Congress had to turn to the states for its supply of soldiers — should the states in their wisdom, or at least in their sovereignty, see fit to provide any. "Each state," as Article 2 made perfectly clear, "retains its sovereignty, freedom, and independence."

Under the Articles, Congress was the central government's sole institution. The United States had no separate executive or judicial bodies. Congress did set up various departments to administer major areas of concern such as war, finance, and foreign affairs. First Benjamin Lincoln and then Henry Knox served as Secretary of War, Robert Morris as superintendent of finance, and Robert Livingston (later succeeded by John Jay) as secretary for foreign affairs. Congressional delegates themselves (at least two from every state) were elected annually, and no delegate could serve more than three years out of six. This guaranteed that power would not become entrenched, but it also guaranteed that valuable experience and expertise would regularly

be cast aside. Delegates were slow to be elected and even slower to arrive at wherever Congress happened that year to meet (New York, Philadelphia, Princeton, Annapolis), so that the nation's business was rarely executed with dispatch. Sometimes indeed, the nation's business could not be done at all because a quorum of seven states was absent. No center of government existed geographically, and no center of power manifested itself politically. American diplomats abroad discovered that the country they represented commanded little respect and provoked even less fear. Under such circumstances, the wonder is that the Articles of Confederation achieved anything at all.

In fact, however, major achievements can be credited to the central government between 1781 and 1789. One such accomplishment was, of course, the successful prosecution of the war and the achievement of independence. The Confederation Congress also helped guide the country through a severe postwar depression, even watching over a rise in population and national income. But perhaps its most impressive success pertained to that vexing problem of western lands: who owned them, who derived income from them, and under what terms should they be governed and eventually admitted to the Union.

❧ Western Lands and the Northwest Ordinance

The earliest colonial charters could not specify western boundaries in a "west" still unexplored and unknown. Virginia's original boundaries stretched westward all the way to the Pacific Ocean and north to the Great Lakes. All this meant little in the seventeenth century, of course, when settlers crept only a few miles inland. It still meant relatively little during much of the eighteenth century, when England, France, and Spain threw their ponderous weight around all of North America or when powerful Indian tribes dominated the unmapped West. This dramatically changed when the nation won independence and a western boundary on the Mississippi River. Here was enough land to arouse the interest of many a speculator (land companies had been busy even before the Revolution), to say nothing of the states themselves and of Congress.

From the speculators' point of view, lands purchased or seized from the Indians could be used to encourage settlement from the east and pay a handsome profit to the original investors. From the point of view of the large states, these lands were their charter rights; any settlement should be by their own citizens, and any profit should go into their own treasuries. From the point of view of a Congress charged with many responsibilities and possessing no income of its own, the acquisition of all those western lands seemed the solution to the Union's poverty and perhaps to its impotence. Amazingly, the point of view of Congress ultimately prevailed.

It prevailed in part because the small states kept up a steady barrage of argument against large states becoming ever larger. If that happened, the Union could no longer pose as a confederation of equals: there would only be burly giants and bullied midgets, the former growing ever richer, the latter steadily poorer. Moreover, the common effort of all the states had wrested these lands from Great Britain; land won by the blood of all belonged to all. Bounties in the form of land had been promised to many war veterans: should only veterans from states with large western claims benefit? Even many in those states having western claims argued that too great a size limited the effectiveness and the truly representational character of local government. So, one by one, the states turned over their vast claims to the central government: Virginia in 1781 (though not fully effected until 1784), New York in 1782, Massachusetts in 1785, Connecticut in 1786. In subsequent years additional grants came from North Carolina, South Carolina, and Georgia. Congress now owned land and — potentially — income as well.

If both the states and Congress were reasonably satisfied with the deal, neither the Indians nor the speculators were pleased. The Indians knew that the land had been theirs long before states or congresses had appeared on the scene; the speculators could see their hopes of profits dwindling away. The Shawnees raided settlements in the Ohio Valley in an effort to discourage westward migrations; the Miamis besieged Vincennes, Indiana; the Iroquois renounced an earlier treaty and threatened to go to war. Many years would pass and much blood would flow before whites settled in the West. Speculators had more success in regrouping their scattered forces, taking care to add many con-

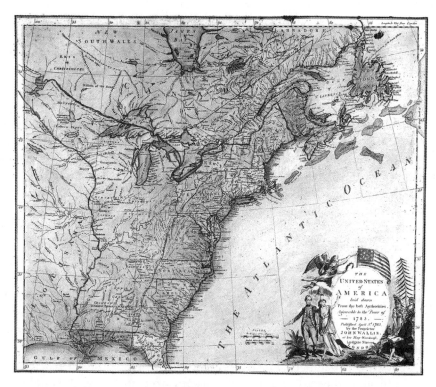

United States Map, 1783   This was the first specially engraved map of the United States, created after the declaration of peace with Great Britain.

gressmen to their ranks. In 1787 the Ohio Company, led by two Revolutionary War generals from New England, bought from Congress 1.5 million acres at the give-away price of less than ten cents an acre. But Congress did not have many buyers, nor did individual settlers necessarily feel obliged to pay anything at all. Although the Ohio Company was no model of fiscal or political integrity, it did recognize that sales of its land rested upon the creation of some regular and stable government north of the Ohio River and east of the Mississippi. Thus the company added its pressure upon Congress in 1787 to exercise a clear jurisdiction over western territories.

Well before then, in 1784 Thomas Jefferson had proposed an ordinance for the Northwest Territory, a vital principle of which asserted that new states formed out of this region should be admitted on the basis of full equality with the original thirteen. (The Union should have neither second-class citizens nor second-class states.) Jefferson also provided for self-government in the region and for the exclusion of slavery. This ordinance, though much amended, never passed; nevertheless, it formed the basis three years later for the more famous Northwest Ordinance. In this critical document Congress set policies and confirmed Jeffersonian principles that would shape not only the "Old Northwest" but most of the rest of the country as well. Indeed, in terms of far-reaching consequences, the ordinance of 1787 deserves to be ranked behind only the Declaration of Independence and the Constitution.

The Northwest Ordinance specified that no more than five nor fewer than three states could be formed out of this region, the point being to keep the new states roughly equivalent in size to the original ones. (Ultimately five were created: Ohio, Indiana, Illinois, Wisconsin, and Michigan.) Prior to statehood, the region would be governed by a General Assembly consisting of a governor, a Legislative Council, and a House of Representatives. Experience in republican forms of governance would begin as soon as five thousand free male adults had settled in the area. When the population of a future state reached sixty thousand, they could begin drawing up a state constitution and apply for admission to the United States.

The ordinance included a guarantee of fundamental liberties to all citizens — this before a Constitution or a Bill of Rights had been adopted for easterners. Religious freedom was guaranteed to all: this provoked no argument. Congress did argue at some length about whether the federal government should provide for the support of religion. Beginning in 1785, votes on this issue revealed deep divisions in the Congress. And in the final version of Article 3, something of that difference of opinion still survived. That article begins, "Religion, Morality and knowledge being necessary to good government and the happiness of mankind, Schools and . . ." Here, traditionally, the next words would have been ". . . and Churches shall forever be encouraged." But it does not read that way.

Some thought that government should not be in the business of promoting religion, even if religion was necessary to good government and human happiness. Others thought that, particularly in the uncivilized and disorderly Northwest, government simply *had* to be in the business of supporting churches no less than schools. The argument was real, and the vote was close. But what finally emerged was: "Religion, Morality and knowledge being necessary to good government and the happiness of mankind, schools and the means of education shall forever be encouraged."

The ordinance also guaranteed the right of trial by jury, stinging memories of Britain's violation of this fundamental liberty still lingering. Citizens in the Old Northwest, moreover, would have full access to the waters of the St. Lawrence and the Mississippi rivers, which "shall be common highways and forever free."

Finally, Article 6 declared that "There shall be neither slavery nor involuntary servitude in the said territory, otherwise than in the punishment of crimes whereof the party shall have been duly convicted." But this forthright declaration contained a fatal proviso that slaves escaping from any of the original states to this region "may be lawfully reclaimed and conveyed" to the original owner — an addendum that would cloud much of the country's history down to the 1860s.

A Land Ordinance of 1785 promoted law and order by ensuring that settlers knew exactly where the land they had purchased actually lay. Thus, it was hoped, true community and true nationhood might be preserved. This 1785 law also made effective the support for schools (but not churches) by setting aside a portion of land in each township for education. A township, six miles square, was divided into thirty-six lots of one square mile (640 acres) each, a "section" of land. The income from one of those sections was reserved for the support of schools. The aim of many of those in the East, especially in New England, was to see that the West did not become altogether another world or establish a sharply different way of life. Meanwhile, however, the East itself had its own difficulties with the notion of nationhood.

State Government, Shays's Rebellion, and the Crisis of Confederation

While the Articles of Confederation proved deficient in many areas, they were most glaringly defective in the field of commerce and trade. States had their own rules on imports and duties, their own currencies, and their own regulations for navigation and the collection of debts. Through all this Congress sat idly, or at least helplessly, by. Aggravating these difficulties was the inability of Congress to provide troops when emergencies arose in any one of the states. If the states had to defend themselves and to bear all the responsibility for trade and commerce, then of what purpose was the Union? The year 1786 only made that question more insistent, even as it made positive answers less plausible.

As states presented hard questions related to the central government, they were facing even harder questions within their borders. In most states, rival factions differed on virtually every issue before the legislatures: the salaries for judges, governors, or legislators; the confiscation of loyalist property and readmission of loyalists to citizenship; the printing of paper money; the interests of urban dwellers versus those of rural farmers; and, above all, the complex matter of taxation. Under the Articles of Confederation, most of the routine business of government rested upon the states. But as factionalism often brought the states to a kind of paralysis, the search for other remedies grew ever more urgent.

Having resigned his commission in a dramatic ceremony at the end of 1783, George Washington returned to private life at Mount Vernon, giving attention to his farm from which he had been absent so many years. He also did some land speculation and made daring plans to open up the Potomac River by a series of locks for navigation all the way to the Ohio Valley — any such venture would be in the national interest as well as in the even more direct interest of both Virginia and Maryland. Since it was unlikely that Congress could find the authority to undertake any such venture, Washington and others proposed that Maryland and Virginia send representatives to Alexandria to discuss the matter, as well as larger questions of boundary lines in the Chesapeake and the Potomac, the placement of buoys, the erection of lighthouses, and other practical matters. Meeting in March 1786, delegates from the two states soon accepted Washington's invitation to enjoy the hospitality of Mount Vernon, where in three days of deliberations they reached mutually acceptable conclusions. They also decided to invite Delaware and Pennsylvania to become involved, for navigation into the West crossed their territory. Indeed, they reasoned, were not these questions really *national* ones?

The growing conviction that such urgent matters required the broadest attention led Virginians James Madison and John Tyler (father of the future president) to urge all the states to meet in Annapolis, Maryland, the following September to deal with issues such as those raised at Mount Vernon. Eleven states responded to the invitation, indicating a widespread recognition of the critical problems. But only five states' commissioners actually showed up. Truly unified action remained extremely difficult.

For lack of a quorum, no official business could be conducted. Some thought the best course of action was simply to adjourn. But others saw too much at stake. Besides, the five states — New York, New Jersey, Pennsylvania, Delaware, and Virginia — had sent able men who were not prepared weakly to abdicate responsibility. Alexander Hamilton from New York, Madison from Virginia, Tench Coxe from Pennsylvania, and John Dickinson now from Delaware were among those who thought that questions of commerce demanded an-

swers, but beyond that, the question of union itself had to be addressed. "The power of regulating commerce is of such comprehensive extent," the commissioners declared, "and will enter so far into the general System of the federal government, that to give it efficacy . . . may require a correspondent adjustment of other parts of the Federal System."

In other words, far more was amiss than just who had the right to navigate what river. "Important defects" in the Articles of Confederation were acknowledged by all, the commissioners observed. As a result, in both domestic and foreign affairs, the only appropriate word to describe the United States of America in 1786 was *embarrassment:* embarrassment from British treatment of American ships in the West Indies, embarrassment from Spanish control of the lower Mississippi and the port of New Orleans, embarrassment from North African pirates capturing American ships and enslaving their crews. Ezra Stiles in 1783 had spoken of a nation "high above all nations." What had happened? Any sense that America could serve as a model to other nations seemed doomed. Spain tempted the westerners living in what would become Kentucky and Tennessee to cast their lot with a real empire and use the Mississippi freely; Britain tempted those living in what would become Vermont to join Canada and enjoy, once more, the protection of England's flag; discord and continental weakness tempted all thirteen states to consider regional confederacies and forget national union.

But even the states offered no sanctuary. In the midst of rampant inflation and deteriorating currencies, creditors turned in fury upon improvident debtors. Subject to intense lobbying and heckling, state legislatures did not resemble deliberative bodies so much as shouting contests. If democracy could ever work, it should do so at the local levels. Even there, however, "the people" did not appear the saving repository of sovereignty; they resembled more a mob swayed by interest and greed, by passion and demagoguery. This did not match the sacrifice of Revolutionary soldiers, nor the visions of Jefferson or Paine.

Under such unrelentingly dreary circumstances, the leading spirits among those gathered in Annapolis in September 1786 could not simply pack their saddlebags and wearily ride home. Everyone recognized the problems, the men in Annapolis wrote — problems "so serious" as "in the view of your Commissioners to render the situation of the United States delicate and critical." They therefore unanimously proposed that

Shays's Rebellion   Here is a contemporary woodcut of Daniel Shays and his lieutenant, Job Shattuck, taken from the cover of a pamphlet supporting the rebellion in western Massachusetts that they led. Both are shown wearing their Revolutionary War officers' uniforms.

another convention be called "to meet at Philadelphia on the second Monday in May next." That gathering should consider not only commerce but any further provisions "necessary to render the constitution of the Federal Government adequate to the exigencies of the Union." Recognizing that they could — at most — speak only for their five states, the commissioners nonetheless voted to transmit their conclusions to all thirteen states, as well as "to the United States in Congress Assembled."

Meanwhile, in western Massachusetts, restless farmers and dissatisfied Revolutionary War veterans began to mobilize against what they regarded as the greedy and manipulative easterners of their state. Legislative action reflecting the interests of conservative merchants and worried creditors increased taxes upon western farmers at the same time that it reduced their ability to pay. The result was that soon the jails in such towns as Worcester and Springfield began to fill with debtors — honest and able men who simply could not cope with the severe economic difficulties of the day. Some even volunteered to do roadwork for the state to pay off debts that they could not otherwise meet. Hard cash was virtually nonexistent and paper money virtually worthless. County courts charged high fees for their services, as did the "mercenary lawyers." Perhaps people would have willingly paid if only they perceived more justice in the system. But injustices

only multiplied. Farms were foreclosed, wages fell, debts mounted, and still the authorities demanded their pound of flesh.

Out of this seething cauldron of discontent, Daniel Shays emerged to rally debtors and harassed taxpayers ready to follow his lead — or that of almost any other likely candidate. A wounded veteran of Bunker Hill and Saratoga, and later a captain in the Revolutionary War, Shays had barely escaped a debtor's jail. By October 1786, he had moved into a position of authority. He drilled his troops carefully, paid them three shillings a day in cash, and quickly amassed as many as two thousand men. Where he got the money to pay his men no one has ever found out. But suspicions spread that the British in the interior, or perhaps Massachusetts Tories, funded the operation in the hope that the experiment in self-government would fail, beginning in Massachusetts. The peace treaty was, after all, only three years old: it was much too soon for Britain to give up on her "colonies" forever. With a little financial assistance, with a little internal dissension, with a little well-timed nudge — who knows?

In November a group of two hundred rebels stopped the proceedings of the court in Worcester, and in December another regiment interrupted the proceedings of the Hampshire County court. At the end of January 1787, Shays led an attack (not as coordinated as he had hoped) against the armory in Springfield, where he was swiftly routed by a special force of state troops. Within a few days, Shays's Rebellion was over; its leaders were tried for treason in the spring.

But Shays's Rebellion frightened respectable people everywhere. Signs of similar unrest or actual outbreaks of violence cropped up in New Jersey, Pennsylvania, Virginia, and South Carolina. A great many of the economic elite were prepared to agree with the Annapolis commissioners that the condition of the United States was both "delicate and critical."

The Confederation Congress demonstrated, once again, its inability to act decisively and swiftly. Massachusetts had appealed to Congress and to Secretary of War Henry Knox for troops to save the state's government from collapse and to put down a threatening insurrection. Congress, looking around for troops, discovered that it had none. Knox, desperate for help from any source, greatly exaggerated the size of the rebel army, adding for good measure (but with no evidence) that the Indians were flocking to the aid of the rebels. Moreover, Knox argued to any who would listen that, once the rebels conquered Boston, the rest of New England would soon fall to their radical, socially leveling demands. Despite such scary rhetoric, Congress still dallied, so that Massachusetts merchants and eastern landholders were required to raise money, pay troops, and hire General Benjamin Lincoln to defend the state against the threat of civil war.

Those favoring a stronger central government could not have asked for better timing. Those fearing a revolution that did not know when to stop could not have hoped for a more persuasive example. Abigail Adams, writing to Jefferson in Paris in response to his inquiry about the unrest, exploded that "Ignorant, restless desperadoes, without conscience or principles, have led a deluded multitude to follow their standard under pretence of grievances which have no existence but in their imaginations." Similarly, many other easterners viewed Shays's rebellion with darkest foreboding, as they did every other challenge to constituted authority. In his reply, the faraway Jefferson thought to calm anxieties, though he only inflamed them. Expressing his hope that the malcontents might be pardoned because "the spirit of resistance to government is so valuable . . . that I wish it to be always kept alive," Jefferson added: "I like a little rebellion now and then. It is like a storm in the atmosphere." Abigail Adams was not calmed.

Another Virginian stood closer to Abigail Adams than to Jefferson in his reflection on Shays's Rebellion. George Washington concluded that "we are fast verging to anarchy and confusion." Had anyone predicted in 1783 that such would have been the result of the War of Independence, "I should have thought him a fit subject for a madhouse." In the winter of 1786-87 the infant Union, trapped in the arms of death, was still fighting to stay alive.

RELIGION AFTER THE REVOLUTION

The Revolution left some elements of American religion devastated and desolate. Anglicanism felt the heaviest blows, but some other denominations similarly saw all religious order or control slipping away from them. On the other hand, new and rapidly growing religious bodies viewed the situation of the 1780s and beyond as challenging opportunities to expand their labors, to blend their mission in with the mission of America.

❧ Disestablishment and "Decline"

Hardly had the ink dried on the Declaration of Independence parchment before political leaders in Virginia began to abolish all special privileges enjoyed by the Church of England there. Although it took several years to accomplish the complete disestablishment, by the Revolution's end Anglicanism in Virginia and elsewhere was struggling just to survive. One minister glumly reported that the Revolution "has been fatal to the Clergy of Virginia. From a fixed salary they are reduced to depend upon a precarious subscription for bread." In 1785 a friend of Jefferson's complained to him that clergymen were starving as the state was caught between utter immorality on the one hand and "Enthusiastic Bigotry" on the other.

In 1784 Virginia's Anglicans reorganized themselves

✳ IN THEIR OWN WORDS

Power to the People, 1787

Shays's Rebellion induced fear in many of the new nation's leaders; Thomas Jefferson was not among them, as this letter attests.

The tumults in America [Shays' Rebellion] I expected would have produced in Europe an unfavorable opinion of our political state. But it has not. On the contrary, the small effect of those tumults seems to have given more con-fidence in the firmness of our governments. The interposition of the people themselves on the side of government has had a great effect on the opinion here. I am persuaded myself that the good sense of the people will always be found to be the best army. They may be led astray for a moment, but will correct themselves. . . . The way to prevent these irregular interpositions of the people is to give them full information of their affairs through the channel of the public papers, and to contrive that those papers should penetrate the whole mass of the people. The basis of our governments being the opinion of the people, the very first objects should be to keep that right; and were it left to me to decide whether we should have a government without newspapers, or newspapers without a government, I should not hesitate a moment to prefer the latter.

into the Protestant Episcopal Church in an attempt to end embarrassing ties to England's national church. The newly named Episcopalians, gathered in a state convention the following year, reported that their "churches stand in need of repair, and there is no fund equal to the smallest want." And, said the delegates, "for more than eight years our church hath languished under neglect. We will not, however, believe that her friends have revolted, and therefore trust that a knowledge of her present condition will rekindle their former affections." Affections were no doubt rekindled, but Virginia's old "Mother Church" never fully recovered from the shock of sudden disestablishment. From being the largest church in the South in the 1770s, the institution fell precipitously to fourth place in the early decades of the nineteenth century.

Once Anglicanism had aspired to be the established church of British North America. After the Revolution, this option no longer made sense. But could there be some other national church? Congregationalists in New England and Presbyterians in the middle and southern colonies might fill the vacuum. Working together (for little separated them theologically), they could possibly rise to the challenge of being "the American church." Yet Congregationalism had made too many enemies to appeal widely outside New England, and Presbyterianism alarmed others with its history of bloody battles in Scotland and of less bloody skirmishes in Pennsylvania. Above all, most citizens in the 1780s were at the very least quite unsure about the need for or wisdom of an "American church."

Feeling strongly a sense of responsibility for the good order and moral fiber of American society, these two denominations found the disorder and near-anarchy of the 1780s especially troubling. Congregationalists had for generations heard "jeremiads" — sermons bewailing the decline of piety and the rise of immorality. Nothing that the clergy saw in the 1780s impelled them to revise their opinions. Newport's Congregational minister, Samuel Hopkins, in his important *Dialogue Concerning the Slavery of Africans* (1776) strongly condemned the "public sin" of slavery, but also noted many other "public, crying sins found among us, such as impiety and profaneness . . . intemperance and prodigality and other instances of unrighteousness." And the Presbyterian General Assembly as late as 1798 warned that God had a controversy "with our nation," as the country faced "a bursting storm which threatens to sweep before it the religious principles, institutions, and morals of our people." Given those perspectives,

these two large denominations viewed religion after the Revolution as being in serious and steady decline. Yet the religious picture had a brighter side.

&ce; New and Vital Religious Forces

In 1784 Methodists meeting in Baltimore, Maryland, organized themselves into a distinct denomination, completely separate from the Church of England into which they had been born. Dedicating themselves "to reform the Continent, and to spread scriptural Holiness over these lands," these Methodists, under the leadership of Francis Asbury, moved with speed and in force up and down the East Coast, then, most significantly, out to the western frontier. Employing horseback preachers called "circuit riders," Methodists had no regular or settled clergy, but only itinerant spreaders of the Word who did not wait for a church to call them. They created the church. Or, even before the organization of a church, they preached, baptized, married the betrothed, buried the dead, and performed whatever other churchly services might be required — without the benefit of a church. "O America! O America!" exclaimed Asbury; "it will certainly be the glory of the world for religion." No "decline" here; no discouragement, but only opportunity.

As a continent opened up after the Revolution, Methodism was ready with its circuit riders to reach every settlement before tent stakes could be driven into the ground. Methodism and America were equally young, equally lively, equally ambitious. And the denomination's growth was phenomenal, to some even frightening. Congregationalist Jedidiah Morse, America's first geographer, tried to keep up with that growth, but despaired of doing so. In 1792 he wrote that "their numbers are so various in different places, at different times, that it would be a matter of no small difficulty to find out their exact amount." By the middle of the nineteenth century, Methodists had more churches by far than any other denomination.

A significant portion of that growth took place among African Americans. Richard Allen, later to play a major role in the organization of the African Methodist Episcopal Church, expressed his strong preference for Methodism as early as 1787. "I was confident," Allen wrote, "that there was no religious sect or denomination that would suit the capacity of the colored people as well as the Methodist." He explained that "the plain and simple gospel suits best for any people; for the unlearned can understand, and the learned are sure to understand." Allen happily concluded: "The Methodists were the first people that brought glad tidings to the colored people. I feel thankful that ever I heard a Methodist preach." Such a personal testimony could be multiplied many times over in the remaining years of the eighteenth century.

Baptists also represented a new vitality in American Christianity. Not a new denomination in the 1780s, they had, however, been invigorated by the Great Awakenings, north and south. Also preaching a "plain and simple gospel," Baptists found a ready audience among what Jedidiah Morse referred to as "the poorer sort of people." On the frontier, Baptists did not employ the traveling preachers that Methodists favored, but rather inspired earnest and pious farmers in sparse communities to help their neighbors create a church. What the farmer-preacher lacked in formal education, he made up for in enthusiasm and dedication. But Baptists also grew up and down the East Coast, forming associations for mutual encouragement and support. Like the Methodists, they grew: a tenfold increase in the three decades after the Revolution. No "decline" there, either.

Also like the Methodists, Baptists demonstrated a strong appeal within the black population. Baptist John Leland, preaching in Virginia, related in 1790 how he frequently saw slaves "walk twenty miles on Sunday morning to meeting, and back again at night." Attracted to Baptist calls for a full religious liberty and happy to affiliate with a denomination that did not place white bishops or superintendents above them, African Americans cast their lot with the Baptists in astounding numbers. And blacks did much more than simply join a white denomination: they made the denomination and the churches their own, bringing dance, music, and joy into their fellowships in a most impressive fashion. Unlettered white Baptist preachers sounded much like unlettered black Baptist preachers. Both spoke of a gospel open to all, of grace freely and fully given, of redemption that recognized no lines of race or gender. And both embodied a religion of the heart: religion tested not by bookish doctrine but by personal

Julianne Jane Tillman   Richard Allen, first bishop of the African Methodist Episcopal Church, recognized that some women possessed the gifts of preaching and teaching. One such woman was Julianne Jane Tillman, pictured here. Little is known about her except that she was a preacher in the first half of the nineteenth century.

experience and clear moral commitment. Together, Methodists and Baptists would do much to refresh and revive religion in post-Revolutionary America.

A CONSTITUTIONAL CONVENTION

Stung by Shays's Rebellion and the general weakness of the central government in 1786, people in Annapolis and elsewhere keenly anticipated the convention called for Philadelphia in May 1787. When the representatives selected by their state legislatures arrived in May, they brought with them a heritage of much political theory and considerable political practice. They also brought economic and local interests that, somehow, had to serve more effectively the interests of all. Because they were not all of one mind, concessions had to be granted and compromises somehow arranged. The guiding hand behind much of the deliberation and maneuvering was that of a thirty-six-year-old Virginian, James Madison.

❧ *Delegates and Principles*

Soon after the Annapolis convention ended in September 1786, Virginia and New Jersey (two of the five present at that gathering) had voted to send representatives to Philadelphia the following May. Pennsylvania, North Carolina, Delaware, Georgia, and New York took similar action when, on February 21, Congress added its timid voice to the call for another convention. Well aware that such a body might usurp its own limited powers, and more cautious than the commissioners in Annapolis, the congressmen stipulated that the Philadelphia group should confine itself to "the sole and express purpose of revising the Articles of Confederation." But only four states, in charging their own delegates, followed those narrow congressional instructions. By April, twelve of the thirteen states had made their choices. Only Rhode Island, torn by disputes over debts and paper currency, failed to send anyone to Philadelphia.

Baptism in the Hudson River This image, from the early nineteenth century, shows a Baptist community administering baptism by total immersion in New York. The public baptism of adult believers who could attest to a conversion experience was a distinctive, controversial practice of the Baptist movement. Other Christian denominations baptized infants soon after their birth.

As Annapolis had proved, selecting delegates did not automatically ensure that delegates would show up. Of the seventy-four chosen by the twelve states, only fifty-five ever made it to Philadelphia, and some of those chose not to stay throughout the five months of deliberations. In the end, fewer than forty men were prepared to put their signatures to the final draft, slightly more than half the total number selected. The quality of the men attending and the quality of their thought, nonetheless, kept them busy with their heavy task.

Virginia sent a particularly strong delegation of seven, with a reluctant Washington agreeing to head the group and then to preside over the convention itself. The highly visible presence of George Washington gave the gathering a legitimacy that it otherwise would have lacked. Washington was at first reluctant to attend because he had many projects under way at Mount Vernon that required his attention. On the other hand, he was so widely respected, even revered, that his presence alone would increase the odds for success immeasurably — as all his friends and neighbors insisted. Political theory was not Washington's strongest point, however, so that task fell to another Virginian, James Madison, an experienced legislator both in Congress and in his own state's House of Delegates. Other important Virginians included George Mason, architect of Virginia's constitu-

tion and Declaration of Rights; Edmund Randolph, sometime member of the Continental Congress and in 1787 governor of the state; and George Wythe, professor at the College of William and Mary and Jefferson's tutor in the law.

Pennsylvania sent an even larger delegation of eight, including the venerable Benjamin Franklin, now over eighty years old. Gouverneur Morris, formerly of New York where he had helped draft that state's new frame of government, had been influential during the Revolution, transferring his residence from New York City to Philadelphia. Robert Morris (no relation to Gouverneur) had been the financier extraordinaire of the Revolution, in which capacity he (like Washington) learned firsthand of the costly weakness of the Confederation Congress. James Wilson, an expert lawyer who had studied with John Dickinson, was James Madison's closest competitor as a political theorist and as a strong supporter of a national government with enough authority to do its proper job.

Although the delegations from the other states were not as large, they too included such able men as John Dickinson (Delaware), Roger Sherman (Connecticut), Rufus King (Massachusetts), Alexander Hamilton (New York), William Paterson (New Jersey), and John Rutledge and Charles Cotesworth Pinckney (South Carolina). Some of the more vocal members of the convention who ended up opposing its final product included two Virginians, Edmund Randolph and George Mason, Luther Martin of Maryland, and Elbridge Gerry of Massachusetts.

Two great figures of the Revolution were absent. John Adams, representing the interests of the United States as minister to England, would have gladly given his voice to the cause of stronger central government had he been present. And Thomas Jefferson, whose thoughts on the legitimacy of strong central government were more ambiguous, remained in Paris as the official envoy to the French court. Others were absent by choice. Patrick Henry, though named as a delegate, declined to attend because he "smelt a rat." Sam Adams had not been chosen, which was just as well since he acknowledged suspicions "of a general revision of the Confederation." And John Hancock, heavily involved in the local politics of Massachusetts and suffering from gout, likewise did not attend. "For God's sake," Rufus King wrote to Elbridge Gerry, "be careful who are the men" chosen to go to Philadelphia; "let the men have a good knowledge of the several states, and of the good and bad qualities of the confederation." On the whole, King's advice stood.

All the delegates brought to Philadelphia years of experience in either writing their own state constitutions or wrestling with the issues they raised. Many were lawyers and even more had studied law, and had grown learned in the tradition of English Common Law and familiar with Sir William Blackstone's bulky commentary on it. Eight had signed the Declaration of Independence, seven had served in the First Continental Congress, and far more than that in successive Congresses. At least thirty were veterans of the Revolutionary War, and nearly all had served their states in some civil capacity. Some were educated abroad (Edinburgh and Oxford); others had gone to colonial colleges. The delegates, in short, were not novices, not innocents, and certainly not dreamers. Certain that they knew what would *not* work, they hoped they knew what *would* work.

They knew they wished to preserve both liberty and property. Liberty in Revolutionary America was universally acclaimed even though not precisely defined; property was understood to mean at least (in the classic phrase) that a man's home was his castle. The delegates also wanted nothing to do with a hereditary monarchy or a hereditary nobility: "republicanism" (though variously defined) was their common goal. And for many, this meant that sovereignty rested ultimately not upon the states but upon the people. As a tactic to circumvent the intransigence or conservatism of the states, an appeal to the people was a useful strategem, although the "sovereignty of the people," taken too far, could itself lead to tyranny or anarchy. The delegates did not propose a democracy, for that was taking the people's sovereignty too literally and too directly. Furthermore, to the extent that some of the states had promoted democracy, the results had not been encouraging. Better a republic, like Holland or ancient Rome, that filtered the voices and wishes of the people through men carefully chosen — as Rufus King advised.

James Madison moved quickly, first to goad the Virginia delegation into action, then to arrange for Virginia to set the agenda for discussion. Deeply engaged in every aspect of the convention, Madison managed to keep the fullest notes on its secret proceedings. (By his own instructions, those notes were not published dur-

Benjamin Franklin   Though he was over eighty years old at the time, Benjamin Franklin agreed to serve as one of Pennsylvania's delegates to the Constitutional Convention. He is the only one of America's Founders who is a signatory of all three of the major documents of the founding of the United States: The Declaration of Independence, the Treaty of Paris, and the United States Constitution.

ing his lifetime.) In his *Notes,* Madison explained that he seated himself so as to hear every speech, that he was absent not a single day "nor more than a casual fraction of an hour in any day." He concluded his preface in these words: "I feel it a duty to express my profound & solemn conviction . . . that there never was an assembly of men, charged with a great & arduous trust, who were more pure in their motives, or more exclusively or anxiously devoted to the object committed to them, than were the members of the Federal Convention of 1787." Nevertheless subsequent historians have long debated the purity of motives: were the delegates more concerned with protecting their own property and privilege, or with disinterestedly advancing the cause of popular sovereignty?

No English political thinker was more widely admired in Philadelphia than John Locke. The late-seventeenth-century philosopher was revered not just for his justification of the Glorious Revolution, but also for his

Independence Hall   In Philadelphia's Pennsylvania State House (now known as Independence Hall, depicted here in a 1796 engraving), delegates representing twelve states — all except Rhode Island — negotiated the Constitution of the United States. To ensure secrecy, the windows were nailed shut despite the stifling summer heat and humidity.

reflection on the nature and purposes of government itself. By divine design, Locke wrote, men and women have been created as social creatures, God having put man "under strong Obligations of Necessity, Convenience, and Inclination to drive him into *Society,* as well as fitted him with Understanding and Language to continue and enjoy it." In this social state of nature, persons enjoyed equality in that no one individual had authority over another. One also enjoyed a natural right to property, but only as much as "a Man Tills, Plants, Improves, Cultivates, and can use the Product of." From this natural state, individuals can by mutual agreement or compact enter into a form of government whose only purpose is to guard and protect the "Lives, Liberties, and Estates" of those participating in the creation of a political order.

Another major source of ideas about government for those gathered in Philadelphia was the opposition or "country party" in eighteenth-century England, radical Whigs who denounced the excesses they found in British government and advocated various restraints on power (see Chapter 5). Such critics, ever fearful of conspiracies against liberty, had tried to develop structures that would make it difficult if not impossible to subvert the public good. They found especially attractive the notion of "mixed government," blending elements from all three classic forms: monarchy, aristocracy, and democracy. Separating the power to make laws from the power to execute the laws or to adjudicate them, also had great appeal to these Whigs. As a further check upon power,

they urged frequent rotation in office and demanded a ban on holding more than one office.

Some of the men in Philadelphia worried more about what a strong government *might* do; others feared what a weak government *could never* do. Power remained the central issue in the minds of the delegates: How was it to be divided between the central authority and the states, and how it was to be executed — or checked — at every level of government? A very few wanted to abolish the states altogether, entrusting all power to a new national government. Others — also a very few — would leave the status quo virtually untouched, with Congress obliged to beg from the states for every dollar, every soldier, every compliance with any federal law. Between those two poles ranged a great number of earnest orators and sometimes perplexed thinkers who may well have agreed with Madison that their plan, whatever it turned out to be, "in its operation would decide forever the fate of Republican Government."

The Critical Compromises

Almost from the beginning the convention found itself pulled by competing interests: those of large states and of small, those of merchants and of farmers, those whose economies were tied to slavery and those who were not, those who lived along the coast and those residing in the interior, those concerned chiefly with the interests of the nation and those preoccupied by local concerns. From the end of May until mid-September, the delegates listened or spoke, protested or agreed, departed in anger or remained with rising or falling hopes. No one could predict the outcome, but many wondered whether a document built on concession and compromise could possibly have enough integrity to be worthy of all their labor and sweat. And sweat they did. Philadelphia that summer was extraordinarily hot, black flies kept swarming, and the windows of the State House were nailed shut. The last step was taken to preserve secrecy, for the deliberations could not be placed at the mercy of a Philadelphia mob or bullying lobbyists. Although some disliked the secrecy rule, the Continental Congresses had established a clear precedent, and necessity dictated its adoption here.

By the scheduled opening day of the convention, May 14, 1787, delegations from only two states — Virginia and Pennsylvania — had arrived. It was not a promising beginning. While waiting in the fervent hope that others would soon arrive, the Virginia delegation got to work, preparing a proposal and an agenda for the rest of the delegates when (and if) they arrived. In fact, they did arrive, but slowly over rain-soaked, muddy roads. By May 25, men from seven states (a bare quorum) had shown up, permitting those gathered in Pennsylvania's State House to begin organizing the deliberative body. George Washington was quickly chosen as presiding officer. Each state had a single vote, but a simple majority of states would decide all questions. The secrecy rule could be enforced in the State House, but what about the dinners in the taverns and the informal conversations at the lodging houses? Most of the delegates honored the rule, but a few soon gained a reputation for speaking too freely. Others quickly learned who could be trusted with their confidences.

THE VIRGINIA PLAN

On the first day of business, the Virginia delegation rose to present its plan for a new frame of government. It chiefly represented the thought of young Madison. The Virginians envisioned a national legislature of two houses, with representation in both reflecting the population of each state or the amount of taxes each paid. The lower house would be elected by the people; the upper house would be chosen by the lower one, upon nomination by the state legislatures. The chief executive officer (or officers) would be elected by the legislature for a fixed number of years and would be ineligible for reelection. The legislature would also appoint the federal judges, serving during "good behavior" — in other words for life, barring serious charges proved against them.

Clearly the Virginia Plan represented a new beginning for governing the United States. Now all state officers would be bound by oath to support the central government, and the national legislature would even have the power to void any state laws that went against federal ones. The new Congress could make laws in all cases where "the separate States are incompetent" or where "the harmony of the United States" required unified action.

The nearly two weeks of ensuing debate on the Virginia Plan questioned many details and offered many modifications, but the essential features remained: a truly national government with real executive, legislative, and judicial authority. Since the legislature held the balance of power, and since the legislature was the branch of government closest to the people, much of the debate centered on how close to the people that branch should be. Should the people directly elect their representatives, or should the state legislatures, filtering public passions or fickleness, choose representatives to serve nationally? Connecticut's Roger Sherman, for example, argued that the people directly "should have as little to do as may be possible about the Government." James Wilson of Pennsylvania, on the other hand, believed that the federal government should rest on the broadest possible base: not on thirteen state legislatures, but on three million people. Such a broad base, said Wilson, would permit raising "the federal pyramid to a Considerable altitude."

As a large state, Virginia had naturally thought in terms of proportional representation. The small states, however, accustomed to the Articles' one-state-one-vote equality, strongly resisted any erosion of that sovereign equality. On June 15, New Jersey's William Paterson rose to present a plan that would preserve what the small states regarded as an essential principle. Under Paterson's New Jersey Plan, there would be only a single house of Congress where representation would be by states, not by population. Paterson did move beyond the Articles by providing for executive and judicial branches, but on the critical issue of representation he defended the status quo.

THE NEW JERSEY PLAN AND ALEXANDER HAMILTON'S ALTERNATIVE

Debate now grew heated. Paterson made it clear that New Jersey would never accept the Virginia Plan, for "she would be swallowed up." Paterson "would rather submit to a monarch, to a despot, than to such a fate." Wilson made it clear that the large states, including his own Pennsylvania, would never accept the New Jersey Plan. When former Pennsylvanian John Dickinson, now representing Delaware, suggested that the delegates really should limit themselves to revising the Articles, not jettisoning them, an impatient Alexander Hamilton rose on June 18 to present still another sweeping plan. Hamilton was prepared to reject state sovereignty altogether, even allowing the national government to appoint the governor of every state. Moreover, members of the Senate should be elected for life, as should be the "supreme Executive authority of the United States." When Hamilton finished his six-hour address, he probably left the delegates as breathless as himself. And though the Hamilton Plan found little support, it *did* make the Virginia Plan seem downright conservative by comparison. In any case, the Paterson Plan was the next day decisively defeated. The Philadelphia convention would do more than merely tinker with the Articles.

One vital aspect of the New Jersey Plan dealt with the knotty problem of competing loyalties to state governments and to the central government. In the event of conflict, who prevailed? Debate about that hard question raised other hard questions: the use of coercion against the states, the right of the federal government to review and if necessary void state laws, the role of the judiciary (federal or state) in examining legislation. The New Jersey Plan had declared that all acts of Congress and national treaties "shall be the supreme law of the respective States . . . and that the Judiciary of the several States shall be bound thereby in their decisions." But Madison and Wilson thought reliance on state courts too risky. On that most sensitive of all subjects, the sovereignty of the states, delicate balancing was required. What finally emerged in Article VI was more than many proponents of a stronger central government had dared hope for: a clear statement that the Constitution, together with treaties and national laws made under its authority, "shall be the supreme Law of the Land."

THE "GREAT COMPROMISE"

While the New Jersey Plan was defeated, the delegates did not wish to drive the smaller states away from the convention. On June 30, therefore, a committee was named to see whether some way could be worked out to honor, at least in part, the principle of state equality. When the convention re-convened on July 5, the committee (led by Roger Sherman) reported its famous compromise. In the lower house representation would be based on population; in the upper house, it would be equal for all states. All tax bills, however, would have to originate in the lower house, ensuring the people more power over the purse.

More than two hundred years after the "great compromise" was proposed, its acceptance seems a foregone conclusion. Such, however, was far from the case as the convention vigorously debated both details and substance. Large states thought too much had been given away; small states feared that not enough had been gained. Rancor erupted as some delegates suggested that the small states throw in their lot with some foreign country or be swallowed up by larger neighbors. For ten days, the convention vigorously wrestled with

the merits of the proposal until on July 16 the compromise narrowly carried. Connecticut, New Jersey, Delaware, Maryland, and North Carolina (predominantly small states) all voted for it; Pennsylvania, Virginia, South Carolina, and Georgia all opposed. Massachusetts was divided, New York did not vote since its delegates had left Philadelphia, and New Hampshire's delegates had not yet arrived. So the most critical hurdle had been cleared by the slimmest margin, a five-to-four vote.

Representation in the upper house would honor the principle of property, as well as of states' rights. In the lower house, people counted for more than property since representation was based on population. The districts were kept large in order to increase the probability that men of merit and virtue, not just local demagogues, would be elected. And by counting slaves both as property and as persons, the slave-holding states increased their political strength. Despite the rather benign language about slavery in the Northwest Ordinance, the Constitutional Convention in 1787 found slavery an explosive issue, requiring more compromises.

Clearly, the convention as a whole could not debate every power of Congress, every aspect of the Judiciary, and so on; thus, the delegates on July 23 appointed a five-man Committee of Detail that would draft a document that could then be either quickly approved, clause by clause, or revised as necessary. On July 26, the convention adjourned for ten days while the committee did its work, to report back on August 6. The "detail" now fell largely in the hands of practical men, as visionaries such as Madison played a less direct role.

COMMERCE AND SLAVERY

A sore point continued to be the issue that had prompted calling the Annapolis convention: trade. The Philadelphia body recognized that issues here demanded their close attention. But the states jealously guarded their right to export what they chose. The central government, on the other hand, needed some control over trade in order to make treaties, and the elimination of interstate trade barriers was essential to solidify the union.

Madison saw the difficulties in commerce as second only to the issue of western lands, with which the Confederation Congress had recently dealt. Those states without ports were especially aggrieved since they had to pay tariffs on goods imported through a neighboring state. Thus New Jersey, lying between the major ports of Philadelphia and New York, "was likened," Madison noted, "to a cask tapped at both ends;

and North Carolina, between Virginia and South Carolina, to a patient bleeding at both arms." If the states felt mistreated, the federal government felt ignored, dependent upon the voluntary compliance of thirteen separate states, each looking after its own interests. In the end, both sides made concessions, though many more came from the defenders of states' rights. States were now specifically prohibited from coining money or entering into agreements with foreign powers or even with other states. No state could levy import duties except with the approval of Congress. The federal government, however, would refrain from taxing exports and from prohibiting the migration or immigration of such persons "as the several states shall think proper to admit."

That last innocent-sounding phrase was a euphemism for the infamous slave trade. It pointed to another deep division in the convention, between North and South or, more accurately, between some parts of the North and some parts of the South. Only South Carolina and Georgia were determined that slavery — vital to their plantation economies — should be left alone. Indeed, Virginia's George Mason made the most passionate speech of the convention against slavery, seeing it as an unnatural cruelty certain to call forth divine retribution. Providence, said Mason, punishes "national sins by national calamities"; that being the case, "I hold it essential to every point of view that the General Government have power to prevent the increase of slavery." But South Carolina's John Rutledge countered that his state and Georgia would never agree to any plan of union that interfered with their right to import slaves. The compromise ultimately adopted was to abolish the slave trade, but not immediately, conceding to the two most interested states a twenty-year period during which slaves could still be imported. Allowing such trade ("this cruel war against human nature itself," as Jefferson had called it) until the year 1808 was "dishonorable to the American character," Madison protested — but in vain.

Neither Madison nor Mason contested another anomalous compromise: that of counting the slave population on a different basis from that of free whites. The so-called "federal ratio" meant that in any census count for purposes of representation, blacks would count for only three-fifths as much as whites. One hundred blacks, in other words, would be tallied as sixty when determining how many representatives a state was entitled to in Congress. All this caused little discussion in 1787 since the Confederation Congress four years earlier had arrived at this compromise in recognizing that the slave was both property and person. By such compromises, however ignoble, the Philadelphia convention was saved from complete disintegration.

THE BRANCHES OF THE FEDERAL GOVERNMENT

Some compromises were simple — almost automatic. Several state constitutions provided for the annual election of their legislators, while some delegates in Philadelphia thought the term should be of three years. The obvious solution was to provide two-year terms for the House of Representatives. In the Senate the term was set for six years, though suggestions varied from four years to service for life. One-third of the body was to be elected every two years — but elected by whom? By the people directly? By the lower house of Congress? Or by the state legislatures themselves, these bodies especially interested in that equal representation? The convention opted for the last method of election, and it remained in force until the adoption of the Seventeenth Amendment in 1913.

Many questions remained about the presidency. Should executive power be entrusted to a single individual or to a small council? Should the executive be elected by the people or by the national legislature? Should the office be severely limited in term, or for life, or for a specific number of terms? What veto powers should be granted to the executive branch? What war-making powers? These complex questions resulted in some complex (and ultimately unworkable) solutions. Thus the cumbersome provisions for separately electing the president and vice president lasted only until an amendment could be ratified in 1804 that made the whole process more viable (see Chapter 8). The small states feared that the Electoral College gave too much power to the lower house and, therefore, to the larger states. Ultimately, the decision to have votes for president and vice president counted by states represented another of those compromises between those who placed their confidence in the people and those who preferred to keep power in the states.

The judiciary occupied the convention's attention for less time in debate, and the final document offered relatively sparse definitions. It was quickly agreed that the legislature should not be its own court of last resort. Instead, this power should be granted (in Hamilton's words) "to distinct and independent bodies of men." Most states had set up their own supreme courts in this fashion, so the precedent was widely accepted. The U.S.

Supreme Court, moreover, would not displace the state courts but would have jurisdiction where the states themselves were litigating parties or where the interests of the nation were directly involved. Finally, the highest court had by implication the right to determine the constitutionality of all laws passed by Congress, thus giving it the final voice regarding "the supreme Law of the Land." But at least fifteen years would pass before that right was clearly enunciated, and not until then did the "third branch" of government acquire major importance.

By the end of August the delegates agreed to the procedures for the admission of new states, with the nation guaranteeing to every newly admitted state "a Republican Form of Government" and security against invasion. On September 10, the convention — proud as it was of its work — agreed to the procedures for amendments to a ratified Constitution, and two days later the delegates received the report from its Committee of Style. The time for one last vote was swiftly approaching.

❧ The Final Result

By the time the convention approved the basic draft of the Constitution on September 10 and handed it over to its Committee of Style for final phrasing, whispers and rumors were filling the streets of Philadelphia. But no one outside the State House knew the precise directions specified or the exact structure laid out. Even the delegates themselves did not know until the very last day, for changes continued to be made down to the end.

In naming the Committee of Style, the convention paid attention — as always — to geographical representativeness but it gave even more attention to the quality of its members. Here were men sensitive to the nuances of language and conscious of the power of proper, if restrained, rhetoric. Gouverneur Morris apparently took the lead in putting the Constitution into its final form, in condensing some twenty-three articles into seven. An awkward preamble became simply "We the people. . . ." And the long-range purpose of the convention's arduous labors included a securing of the "Blessings of Liberty," still so recently won, "to ourselves and our Posterity."

When the report came back on September 12, the delegates were not yet through with matters of either substance or style. They debated whether the override of a presidential veto should be by a two-thirds or three-fourths vote of both houses of Congress; whether the right to trial by jury in civil cases should be explicitly declared; and whether a Bill of Rights should be included. On September 13, the delegates focused on verbal niceties or ambiguities, and the next day worried about impeachment proceedings and standing armies. On Saturday, September 15, the convention struggled again with the question of representation, and how many congressmen should be allowed to each state in the first Congress. And now that the deliberations were coming to a close, some delegates said that — with regret — they could not put their signatures to that smoothly polished prose.

George Mason of Virginia believed that the national government was being made so strong that the country would "end either in monarchy, or a tyrannical aristocracy." That the convention's discussions had all been carried on in secret also bothered Mason. The people, he believed, needed to be consulted regularly, and since this convention had failed to do so, a second convention should be called. Governor Randolph thought that the draft should not be sent out to the people on a "take it or leave it" basis, but that state conventions might offer amendments for due consideration. Elbridge Gerry raised many objections, some peculiar to Massachusetts alone, but others concerned with arrogation of great powers to a national Congress, powers seemingly without limit or check. But these voices were minority ones, and by the day's end it was clear that most delegates intended to sign the final draft.

On Monday, September 17, the delegates for the last time gathered in the East Room of the Pennsylvania State House. Benjamin Franklin said that he, like most others present, could find this or that detail to object to, but no one should expect perfection. "Thus I consent, Sir, to this Constitution," Franklin declared, "because I expect no better, and because I am not sure that it is not the best." Franklin also urged each member to "doubt a little of his own infallibility, and to make manifest our unanimity."

Unanimity proved elusive, but thirty-nine delegates did sign their names. Of those present, all but three (Mason, Randolph, and Gerry) signed, although New York's delegation — except for Alexander Hamilton — had left in sharp disagreement. All states except absent Rhode Island had signatures on the document. Franklin, who during long days of debate and disagreement had looked at a carving of the sun in the back of Washington's chair, observed that artists did not find it easy to portray the difference between a rising and a setting sun. And so he had never been sure just which it was. "But now at length," on September 17, 1787, "I have the happiness to know that it is a rising and not a setting sun."

Yet many months would pass before the evidence trickled in, at an agonizingly slow pace, that would justify Franklin's confidence. The delegates had approved this new instrument of government, but what about the people? Having learned their lesson from the Articles of Confederation, which required unanimous approval before becoming effective, the delegates provided that the Constitution would automatically come into force when nine states had ratified it. But knowing the independence and stubbornness of the states, even approval by that number might be a long time coming.

THE ROCKY ROAD TOWARD RATIFICATION

One day after the Philadelphia convention adjourned, George Washington wrote to the Marquis de Lafayette that the Constitution was "now a Child of fortune, to be fostered by some and buffeted by others." A month later, after returning to Mount Vernon, Washington informed Henry Knox that the Philadelphia draft "is now before the Judgment Seat. It has, as was expected, its adversaries and supporters" — adding, less confidently than Franklin: "Which will preponderate is yet to be decided." And in a long letter to Thomas Jefferson on October 24 (which included a copy of the Constitution), James Madison noted that "The final reception which will be given by the people at large to the proposed System cannot yet be decided." All these expressions of anxious uncertainty were wholly appropriate. The question of whether the Constitution would win approval hung in the balance.

❧ *The Federalists*

In the battle for public opinion, labels can be as important as logic — perhaps more so. And those who favored ratification of the Constitution got the jump on their opponents by seizing the name "Federalist" to represent their position. "Nationalist" would have been a more accurate label, but a less winning one, for it suggested a degree of unity so high that it might fatally weaken the power of the states and threaten the indi-

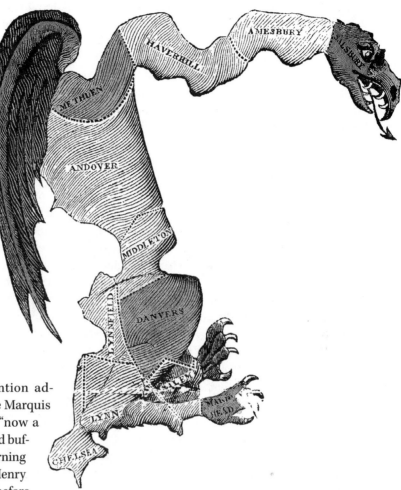

Elbridge Gerry and Gerrymandering Massachusetts delegate to the Constitutional Convention Elbridge Gerry opposed ratifying the constitution as it emerged from the convention, but he went on to serve in the first two Congresses and was eventually elected James Madison's second vice-president. His name is most associated today with the practice of drawing legislative districts so as to favor one party, known as "gerrymandering" after he drew up a district that resembled a salamander, as shown in the cartoon above.

vidual liberties. "Federalist" sounded like something not radically different from what the states had known under the Articles of Confederation, although — as Madison wrote Jefferson — everyone in the Philadelphia convention agreed that "the principle of confederation" was unworkable. Perhaps better terminology would have been that of the "ratifiers" versus those opposed to ratification — or, as Elbridge Gerry preferred to say, the "rats" against the "anti-rats."

The divisions into these two "parties," well before national parties truly emerged, did not follow predictable lines in every state. Often local issues (Shays's Rebellion in Massachusetts, paper money in Rhode Island, the Bank of North America in Pennsylvania) proved more persuasive. In Virginia, aristocratic Richard Henry Lee denounced the proposed Constitution as the work of "a coalition of monarchy men, military men, aristocrats and drones, whose noise, impudence and zeal exceed all belief." Federalists, on the other hand, tended to identify their opponents as demagogues, local politicians with narrow career concerns, and rural farmers who could not see beyond their immediate economic interest. But factions did not fall neatly into rigid categories; many variables, such as age, occupation, economic status, family background, political or military experience, and religion, made for shifting rather than stable alliances.

A little over a month after the convention adjourned, Madison, Hamilton, and John Jay adopted the Federalist tag as they wrote a series of letters between October 27, 1787, and May 28, 1788, to the New York newspapers. These eighty-five essays, collectively known as *The Federalist Papers,* were composed to persuade New York, a very doubtful state, to support the Constitution. But in making the case to New Yorkers, the three authors were making the Federalist case to the country at large. They made that case so well that, two centuries later, scholars and Supreme Court justices still turn to these *Papers* to determine the thinking of the supporters of the Constitution in that critical year of decision.

The best argument of the "rats" was the evident political debacles all around the country. The national government had no power, the state governments no honor. Madison exclaimed that "republican liberty" itself was endangered "under the abuses of it practiced in some of the states." The first experiments in self-government, at both the federal and the local levels, were just that: experiments, which now should be pronounced failures. After years of trial and error, the country could now benefit by its mistakes and swiftly repair its collapsing house. The second general argument favoring the Federalists was the quality of the men who had gathered in Philadelphia. The wide popularity of figures such as George Washington and Benjamin Franklin created an initially favorable disposition toward the Constitution. But neither of these arguments could stand up under heavy testing. True, the current situation was bad, but what proof was there that the Constitution would amend all the follies? True, good men favored the document, but other good men opposed it. Besides, the time had come to speak not in generalities but in specifics.

So in the *Federalist Papers* Hamilton, Madison, and Jay spoke of trade and taxes, of military weakness and diplomatic disarray, of the limits carefully placed upon power, of the need for "energetic" government, and of the ultimate responsiveness of the Constitution to the people. But they also wrote of the necessity for virtue, of the essence of a republic, of the appropriateness of a conciliatory and moderate spirit. Though Jay called for a "sedate and candid consideration," the debate often grew vitriolic and the tactics devious. Letter writers tried to enlist sympathizers or to change minds. Newspapers quickly filled with diatribes on both sides. Cried a pamphleteer in Pennsylvania: "Citizens! You have the peculiar felicity of living under the most perfect system of local government in the world. Suffer it not to be wrested from you — the inevitable consequence of the new Constitution." On the other side, George Washington urged the citizens of Georgia to consider their true interest. "If a weak State, with the Indians on its back and the Spaniards on its flank does not see the necessity of a General Government, there must I think be wickedness or insanity in the way."

The received wisdom of the day held that republics, to be safe and effective, had to be small, but here were thirteen states intending to join in one single republic. If such a notion were not preposterous, it was at the very least dangerous. This was the argument that the Federalists had to address and, with luck, overcome. In the most famous of the *Federalist Papers* (Number 10), Madison turned the argument about by declaring that the larger the republic the greater the possibility of its being represented by persons of wisdom, virtue, and ability. It was true that a pure democracy could not exist over a large territory, but a republic — that is, a representative government — could exist and even indeed flourish over a great expanse. Such a system, moreover, could better control the factions that arise in every society. Apart from a republic, the only way to eliminate factions or "interests" was to suppress liberty or rigidly control its expressions. But in a large republic, possessed of many factions, no one faction or clique could control the government or impose its will upon the majority. The many factions would contest against — and check — each other. In the proposed Constitution, therefore, "we behold," Madison concluded, "a Republican remedy for the diseases most incident to Republican Government."

Government needed to be so constructed that it checked not only its citizens but even its own exercises of power. "In framing a government," Madison pointed out in another famous *Paper* (Number 51), "the great difficulty lies in this: you must first enable the government to control the governed; and in the next place oblige it to control itself." This was the reason for separating the executive, legislative, and judicial powers, even though the separation was not total. Moreover, since in a republican form of government "the legislative authority necessarily predominates," it was vital to separate that authority into different houses, "and to render them, by different modes of election and different principles of action, as little connected with each other as the nature of their common functions . . . will admit." A bicameral legislature, joined with the protection of three branches of government, therefore provided a "double security" for the rights of the people.

Men were not angels, Madison acknowledged in Number 51, for if they were, "no government would be necessary." On the other hand, neither were they so benighted or vicious as to make it impossible for them to filter out those persons who could best represent them. Pure democracy allowed for no such filtering, and that was its fatal weakness. As Madison explained, "In all very numerous assemblies, of whatever characters composed, passion never fails to wrest the sceptre from reason." This had been true throughout history, Madison added, even in ancient Greece itself. "Had every Athenian citizen been a Socrates, every Athenian assembly would still have been a mob." A system of representation, on the other hand, built a shield against the tyranny of the majority or against "mobocracy."

Under the proposed Constitution (Jay argued), men would be called to their best, not their worst, just as were the delegates to the Philadelphia convention. These men, said Jay, pursued their arduous task "without having been awed by power, or influenced by any passions except love for their Country." Was it too much to believe that in all America one could not find similar men, similarly motivated, to fill the Senate and the House of Representatives? Madison refused to concede that the "present genius of the people of America" would choose and "every second year repeat the choice of sixty-five or an hundred men, who would be disposed to form and pursue a scheme of tyranny or treachery." Those who opposed the Constitution often did so, said Madison, on the assumption "that there is not sufficient virtue among men for self-government." If that be true, then the only option that remained was to accept "the chains of despotism," for they alone could prevent the people "from destroying and devouring one another." The argument about the nature of government became, in the end, an argument about the nature of humanity.

❧ The Anti-Federalists

Those who opposed ratification did so on many grounds, not least of which was their conviction that in the new government virtue would not prevail. The opportunities for indulgence of self-interest would be neither "checked" nor "balanced" but expanded to the detriment of the people. Every objection to a more energetic government was answered with the mere assertion that people would be "good," but there "is no security that they will be so, or continue to be so," said a North Carolina Anti-Federalist. And Robert Lansing of New York, who had stalked out of the Philadelphia convention, asserted that all the checks and balances were not needed if individuals were virtuous, but since they were not, the checks and balances were woefully insufficient. All free constitutions, he asserted, "are formed with two views — to deter the governed from crime, and the governors from tyranny." The proposed Constitution, he believed, did neither.

The executive power, moreover (the Anti-Federal-

❋ **IN THEIR OWN WORDS**

A Federalist Argument, 1787

Yes, my countrymen, I own to you that having given it attentive consideration, I am clearly of opinion it is your interest to adopt it [the Constitution]. I am convinced that this is the safest course for your liberty, your dignity, your happiness. I affect not reserves which I do not feel. I will not amuse you with an appearance of deliberation when I have decided. I frankly acknowledge to you my convictions, and I will freely lay before you the reasons on which they are founded. . . . It may perhaps be thought superfluous to offer arguments to prove the utility of the UNION, a point, no doubt, deeply engraved on the hearts of the great body of the people in every State, and one which, it may be imagined, has no adversaries. But the fact is that we already hear it whispered in the private circles of those who oppose the new Constitution, that the thirteen States are of too great extent for any general system, and we must of necessity resort to separate confederacies of distinct portions of the whole. This doctrine will, in all probability, be gradually propagated, till it has votaries enough to countenance an open avowal of it.

The Federalist Papers, Number 1 [Alexander Hamilton]

ists argued), was invested in a single ruler who could be elected and reelected without limit. And considering the power this ruler had — appointive, pardoning, veto, commander-in-chief, and so forth — how did he differ from King George III? Even Thomas Jefferson, receiving a copy of the Constitution sent by James Madison, wrote back in late December 1787, objecting to the abandonment of "the necessity of rotation in office, and most particularly in the case of the President." The president would in effect be elected for life, said Jefferson, and soon the office would become hereditary. When that happened, the republic would be no more. Jefferson was no Anti-Federalist, although he admitted he also was "not a friend to a very energetic government." His anxiety suggested, however, that here the Anti-Federalists had an argument that they could successfully exploit.

Other weaknesses, real or perceived, troubled those who wished to see the Constitution rejected. Since the days of Magna Carta, English liberty rested on the solid base of trial by one's peers. Yet, under the Constitution, the highest court in the land heard and decided cases without a jury present, which might well arbitrarily deny liberties to citizens and states alike. The Constitution contained no guarantees to a trial by jury, no protection against excessive fines or against cruel and unusual punishments, no certain security against the taking of life, liberty, or property without due process of law. What free people would vote for a "supreme Law of the Land" like that?

More highly praised was the representative character of the new government, but this — said the Anti-Federalists — deserved a closer look. In the first Senate, there would be 26 men; in the first House of Representatives, a mere 64. In the Senate, 14 men would constitute a quorum, and of that number 8 would be a majority. In the House, 33 would make a quorum, and only 17 a majority. Thus, if the 8 from the Senate were added to the 17 from the House, Richard Henry Lee of Virginia said, "the liberties, happiness, interests, and great concerns of the whole United States" would be "dependent upon the integrity, virtue, wisdom, and knowledge of 25 or 26 men." Further, considering the class from which these wealthy and powerful men would probably come, the country would have not a democratic republic but an aristocratic tyranny.

The Constitution said practically nothing about religion nor did it invoke God, and that bothered some people (especially in New England). But what little it did say bothered even more: namely, that "no religious test shall ever be required as a qualification to any office or public trust under the United States." No religious test, even for the president of the country! This meant, as one trembling New Hampshire Anti-Federalist pointed out, that "we may have a Papist, a Mohomatan, a Deist, yea an Atheist at the helm of government." Public servants who had no regard for the laws of God, he pointed out, "will have less regard to the laws of men, or to the most solemn oaths or affirmations." A Pennsylvania critic noted that no government survived unless built upon the foundation of religion: all the world knew that. But "what the world could not accomplish from the commencement of time till now," the framers of the Constitution, this critic sarcastically observed, "easily performed in a few moments." And Maryland's Luther Martin thought that "in a Christian country, it would be at least decent to hold out some distinction between the professors of Christianity and downright infidelity or paganism." If one were looking for reasons to vote against the Constitution, the "no religious test" provision joined with the silence on religious liberty generally would be quite enough.

Finally, though the Constitution was being submitted to "the people" for a vote, who were these people? And how were they to exercise their sovereignty in so vast a republic? Was all the talk about the "people" just a device for getting around the states? That tireless talker, Luther Martin, regarded the whole maneuver as suspect. In a federal government, he said, "the parties to the compact are not the *people,* as individuals, but the states, as states." It was the states that sent delegates to Philadelphia; once there, it was the states that voted, up or down, on every article or section of the Constitution. Now, with all that accomplished, the Federalists would dismiss the states altogether, replacing them with some fiction called "the people." Martin's argument had some merit, for the process of ratification did in fact pass over the heads of state legislatures to special conventions of the people called for the sole purpose of saying "yes" or "no" to this new instrument of government.

❧ The State Conventions and the People

When the Constitutional Convention adjourned on September 17, 1787, the text was transmitted to the Confederation Congress then meeting in New York. Congress was asked formally to submit the document to the states where the process of arranging for ratification conventions had to begin. Even that transmission was not accomplished readily, however, for some in Congress argued that the Philadelphia body had vastly exceeded its limited instructions to revise the Articles of Confederation. After several days of debate, Congress ultimately agreed on September 28 that the Constitution "be transmitted to the several legislatures in Order to be submitted to a convention of Delegates in each state by the people thereof." Since state legislators would more likely to protect their own powers and interests, the convention had proposed that approval or rejection be placed directly in the hands of popularly elected delegates, chosen to special conventions called for the sole purpose of ratifying or rejecting the Constitution. Federalists hoped for a swift approval, so that the "energetic" government could begin its effective operation with minimum delay.

It would take time, of course, for the states to set a date for an election of delegates, for that election to take place, and then for the winners to assemble, deliberate, and vote. It took time even for the congressional resolution of September 28 to reach all thirteen states. And when at last the voting did take place, the outcome often rested more on local interests than lofty principles. Political maneuvering became colorful and convoluted.

Before the year was over, three state conventions managed to meet and vote. Delaware and New Jersey voted unanimously for ratification on December 7 and 18, respectively. These small states felt that the Constitution protected them against incursions by the large states, and they took particular reassurance from their equal representation in the Senate. But in the third state to ratify that December, Pennsylvania, the vote was by no means unanimous — and the Federalist winners were by no means unsullied.

Although the Pennsylvania delegation had been consistently one of the strongest in the Philadelphia convention, the people of that state were not nearly so unified in their embrace of the Constitution. A powerful Anti-Federalist coalition, especially active in the western regions, regarded the Constitution as seriously defective. It should be defeated outright or, failing that, extensively amended. One Anti-Federalist arrived at the convention with a list of fifteen such amendments. But the Federalists who were in the majority managed to control the agenda and the procedures. When the final vote was taken on December 12, the tally showed 46 in favor of ratification and 23 opposed, exactly two to one. So while the vote was decisive, it was far from unanimous, hinting at still rougher waters ahead.

Two more small states ratified the Constitution at the beginning of 1788: Georgia and Connecticut. Georgia's vote on January 2, 1788, was unanimous in favor of ratification (the last such vote that the Constitution was to receive). Georgians favored a stronger central government (as Washington had urged) to protect them against the nearby Spanish and their Indian allies, and this vulnerability as well as a small population made it a "small" state. Next, on January 9, Connecticut ratified by a comfortable margin of 128 to 40.

In Massachusetts, however, the outcome was far more problematic. The men who had supported Daniel Shays in the western counties saw the Constitution as the creation of an eastern elite and mercantile interests. "These lawyers and men of learning and money men," complained one western delegate, "that talk so finely, and gloss over matters more smoothly, to make us poor illiterate people swallow down the pill, expect to get into Congress themselves." The vain John Hancock was won over to the Federalist side by vague talk that he might be considered for the presidency, especially if Washington's Virginia did not ratify. In addition to restless westerners, the counties in Maine (still a

---

❈ IN THEIR OWN WORDS

An Anti-Federalist Argument, 1788

All writers on government agree . . . that the origin of all power is in the people, and that they have an incontestible right to check the creatures of their own creation, vested with certain powers to guard the life, liberty and property of the community. And if certain selected bodies of men, deputed on these principles, determine contrary to the wishes and expectations of their constituents, the people have an undoubted right to reject their decisions. . . .

Some gentlemen, with laboured zeal, have spent much time in urging the necessity of government: from the embarrassments of trade, the want of respectability abroad, and confidence of the public engagements at home. These are obvious truths which no one denies. . . . But the most sagacious advocates for the [Federalist] party have not by fair discussion and rational argumentation evinced the necessity of adopting this many-headed monster, of such motley mixture, that its enemies cannot trace a feature of Democratic or Republican extract. . . .

Observations by a Columbian Patriot [Mercy Otis Warren]

part of Massachusetts) saw the Constitution as reducing or at least postponing their chances of statehood. So when the vote was taken on February 6, it was unnervingly close: 187 aye, 168 no.

A lull of more than two months followed before other state conventions could convene, but Federalists continued to organize. Then on April 28 Maryland ratified by 63 to 11, the carping voice of Luther Martin not counting for as much as he had hoped. Less than a month later (May 23), South Carolina ratified — but with a significant minority unhappy over the restriction on slave trade; the vote was 149 in favor, and 73 opposed. Eight states had now joined the Union.

The new plan of government would, according to the Constitution, become the law of the land when nine states had ratified it. The ninth state to do so, on June 21, was small New Hampshire — though reluctantly and narrowly, with a vote of 57 for and 47 against. Anti-Federalists were strong in this state of fiercely independent-minded local communities; Federalists, with their ties to Portsmouth's overseas trade, had to work hard and sometimes unfairly to prevail.

Technically the Constitution had now come into force, but Federalist joy at winning New Hampshire had to be muted. Who could imagine a successful union without Virginia and New York? The debate in Virginia had been especially intense, with such respected leaders as George Mason, Richard Henry Lee, and Patrick Henry notably effective in their opposition. Though Madison could not match Henry's oratory, he did outmatch Henry's mind, as he spoke with a knowledge so impressive and a logic so compelling that friend and foe alike acknowledged his sheer mental prowess. On June 22 James Madison revealed his concern in a letter to Alexander Hamilton. It would probably be necessary, he wrote, to agree to some future amendments to be passed just as soon as the new government got organized. Even with that concession, however, Madison calculated that the margin of victory would be as small as 3 or 4 votes. Almost in despair, Madison admitted that "the smallness of the majority suggests the danger from ordinary casualties which may vary the result." On June 26, the vote was taken: Virginia joined the Union with a slightly more generous vote than Madison had predicted — 89 for, 79 against. A crucial factor in the vote was western Virginians' hope that a stronger national government would subdue the Indians beyond the Ohio River. This, combined with solid support for union among tobacco-exporting tidewater planters, carried the day.

One month later it was New York's turn, where Ham-ilton had even less ground than Madison for optimism. Despite the fact that the *Federalist Papers* were directed explicitly to New York and that two of the three authors were New Yorkers, many suspicious citizens remained unconvinced. Some wanted to amend before ratifying; others wanted to join the United States tentatively, with a right to withdraw if certain conditions were not met or amendments not passed; still others took to the streets of Albany in bloody protest against ratification. When upstate Anti-Federalists, who dominated the convention, seemed about to prevail, Federalist New York City threatened to secede from the rest of the state. This threat persuaded some Anti-Federalists to switch their votes. Hamilton informed Madison on July 8 that "We have good reason to believe that our opponents are not agreed, and this affords some grounds for hope." But not much hope for either Hamilton or Madison, the latter replying on July 20 that "The Constitution requires an adoption *in toto,* and *for ever.*" Any condition attached to New York's vote, warned Madison, "must vitiate the ratification." One week later (July 27), New York voted by the closest margin of any of the states: 30 in favor, and 27 against.

Federalists could breathe much easier, with eleven states — more than a bare majority — now in the Union. Congress could be safely organized and a new government could begin, without waiting for the last two states to make up their minds. North Carolina initially voted against ratification, chiefly on the grounds of the absence of any Bill of Rights, a complaint voiced by the Anti-Federalists again and again. Much later, on November 21, 1789, when North Carolinians had been reassured on that score, they voted (194 to 77) in favor of the Constitution. Rhode Island, the first state to vote for a Declaration of Independence, was the last one to ratify the Constitution (by a vote of 34 to 22). By the time of that vote, May 29, 1790, President George Washington had already been in office for more than a year.

ஃ *The Bill of Rights*

Nothing about the Constitution raised more anxiety or caused more critical comment than its failure to provide clear guarantees of basic liberties. The matter had not been entirely overlooked in Philadelphia, but for a variety of reasons it had seemed best to set that assignment aside. The barrage of criticism during the ratification struggle, however, made it clear that the Constitution had to include a Bill of Rights. In adding these amendments to the Constitution, as in so much else, James Madison played a critical role.

Many arguments could be offered against including a Bill of Rights in the original Constitution. For instance, eight states already had their own declarations or bills, and if that many had arrived at such guarantees on their own, nothing should prevent the remaining five from following suit. Besides, fundamental civil liberties, like religion, were best dealt with at the state rather than the federal level. Hamilton argued that the preamble took care of the matter nicely: "We the people of the United States, to secure the Blessings of Liberty to ourselves and our Posterity. . . ." The whole point of the Constitution was liberty; it itself, said Hamilton, is a Bill of Rights, and did not require "a volume of those aphorisms" that many of the states had already enacted. In any case, such lists were more appropriate "in a treatise on ethics than in a constitution of government." Besides, he noted, the Constitution had no right to deny basic freedoms, so "why declare that things should not be done which there is no power to do?"

Many delegates at the Philadelphia convention, moreover, saw the Constitution as deliberately "incomplete." Blanks or deficiencies, they thought, should be remedied by the state legislatures or by special state conventions. By choice, most of the action in American government remained in the hands of the states. Those who complained about what the federal Constitution failed to do might be the very ones who would complain about its usurpations from local government and local control.

Others claimed that it would be difficult to get all the states to agree on just what rights ought to be specified — or to know when to stop a list of all the rights that should be protected. Noah Webster (of dictionary fame) ridiculed the whole idea of trying to enumerate all human rights. Should Americans go so far as to demand "that Congress shall never restrain any inhabitant of America from eating and drinking, at seasonable times, or prevent his lying on his left side, on a long winter's night, or even on his back?" But neither laughter nor logic quelled the demand for a Bill of Rights. It also became evident during those anxious months of ratification that unless private assurances were given that such a bill would be swiftly forthcoming, the new nation would never get off the ground.

In fulfilling these promises, Madison once again took the lead, urged on by the voters in Virginia as well as by his close friend in Paris. Jefferson's very first objection to the Constitution was "the omission of a bill of rights

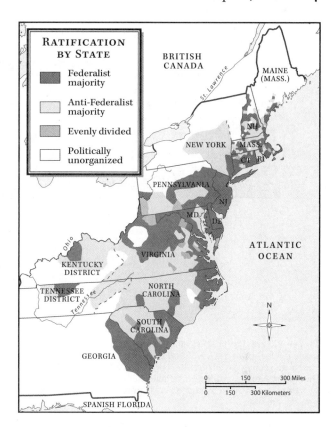

providing clearly . . . for freedom of religion, freedom of the press, protection against standing armies, restriction against monopolies, the eternal and unremitting force of the habeas corpus laws, and trials by jury." A Bill of Rights, Jefferson added, "is what the people are entitled to against every government on earth." For Jefferson, as for many other Americans, the preeminent purpose of a basic frame of government was not to make the government work, but to make it *safe*. Fundamental laws and constitutions were written, first of all, to protect the people from arbitrary exercises of power. All else was irrelevant, if not perilous.

When Madison was elected to the first House of Representatives early in 1789 (his election to the Senate was blocked by Patrick Henry and other Virginia Anti-Federalists), he saw as his first obligation the passage of a Bill of Rights. He had to work diligently, since the first Congress had many other important matters on its agenda. Soon after the House organized itself, Madison rose on June 8 to speak at length on behalf of such a bill. Noting the significant opposition to the Constitution encountered in several states, he urged the House to take action that would make that document acceptable "to the whole people of the United States" and not just to the (sometimes slim) majority. "It will also be a desirable thing," he added, "to extinguish from the

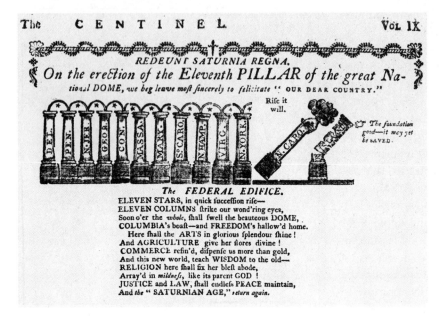

The CENTINEL.   Vol IX

REDEUNT SATURNIA REGNA.

On the erection of the Eleventh PILLAR of the great Na-

tional DOME, we beg leave most sincerely to felicitate " OUR DEAR COUNTRY."

Rife it will.

The foundation good—it may yet be SAVED.

The FEDERAL EDIFICE.

ELEVEN STARS, in quick succeffion rife—
ELEVEN COLUMNS ftrike our wond'ring eyes,
Soon o'er the *whole*, fhall fwell the beauteous DOME,
COLUMBIA's boaft—and FREEDOM's hallow'd home.
Here fhall the ARTS in glorious fplendour fhine !
And AGRICULTURE give her ftores divine !
COMMERCE refin'd, difpenfe us more than gold,
And this new world, teach WISDOM to the old—
RELIGION here fhall fix her bleft abode,
Array'd in *mildnefs*, like its parent GOD !
JUSTICE and LAW, fhall endlefs PEACE maintain,
And the " SATURNIAN AGE," *return again*.

Eleven Pillars Ratification of the Constitution by nine states made it "the law of the land," and the addition of Virginia and New York seemed to ensure that the Union would succeed. At that point, North Carolina and Rhode Island were still holding out. But — as the accompanying verse proclaims — Federalists' hopes were high.

bosom of every member of the community, any apprehensions that there are those among his countrymen who wish to deprive them of the liberty for which they valiantly fought and honorably bled." He concluded his appeal with a motion that a committee be appointed to draw up appropriate amendments that would then be submitted to the states for ratification.

For over three months, committees of both House and Senate labored and argued, sometimes over major substance and at other times over precise wordings. Many states sent in suggested amendments, and Madison offered his own thoughts, drawing heavily on Virginia's Declaration of Rights of 1776. While Madison can be credited as a prime motivator in the House, the amendments that finally emerged reflected the efforts of many Senators and Representatives. On September 25, 1789, the Senate approved the twelve amendments that the House had agreed to the day before. By December 15, 1791, three-fourths of the states (now including Vermont) had ratified the ten amendments that, collectively, are known as the American Bill of Rights.[1]

This same Congress passed the Judiciary Act of 1789. By

1. The two that failed dealt with re-enumeration of the House of Representatives and changing compensation for all congressmen, neither of these vital enough to make Jefferson's list of liberties to be preserved. The compensation amendment, which had no time limit for ratification, was finally adopted by three-fourths of the states in 1992, becoming the Twenty-Seventh Amendment.

its terms the courts had the responsibility of testing legislation against the Constitution, a power that Madison thought wisely invested in the third branch of the federal government. For the freedoms and guarantees spelled out in the Bill of Rights should not be vulnerable to legislative whim. Such freedoms as the First Amendment specified — freedom of speech, of the press, of assembly, and the right of petition — merely recognized rights that were natural and inalienable. So also freedom of religion, given a kind of double guarantee in that amendment: "Congress shall make no law respecting an establishment of religion, or prohibiting the free exercise thereof." This launched the uniquely American experiment: no national church, no interference with religious practices so long as public health and safety were not endangered. Government should do nothing to help religion, nothing to hinder.

The Second Amendment addressed the necessity of "a well regulated militia," assuring the states that their control and support of such militia would not be threatened. The Third Amendment, pertaining to the quartering of troops in private homes, has seldom required any litigation in subsequent centuries. On the other hand, the proscription "against unreasonable searches and seizures" (Fourth Amendment) has been repeatedly invoked, as has the Fifth Amendment's broad rules against double jeopardy, self-incrimination, and any denial of "life, liberty, or property, without due process of law." The "right to a speedy and public trial" is assured in the Sixth Amendment, and that trial shall be before "an impartial jury"; moreover, the accused has the right to confront his or her accusers, and the right of legal counsel. The right of trial by jury is also spelled out in civil cases, and all factual determinations in such a trial must be accepted by any other court (Seventh Amendment). The Eighth Amendment prohibits "excessive bail" as well as "cruel and unusual punishments." Finally, the Ninth and Tenth Amendments provided the most assurance to nervous states by limiting the rights of the central government, and reserving all other rights "to the States respectively, or to the people."

Madison did not win everything that he pressed for, but he — and the country — won much. Some of the guarantees went back to Magna Carta days of the early

Arguments for a Bill of Rights, 1789

Beginning with this speech to the House of Representatives on June 8, 1789, James Madison took the lead in adding a Bill of Rights to the new Constitution.

[I am] compelled to beg a patient hearing to what I have to lay before you. And I do most sincerely believe, that if Congress will devote but one day to this subject, so far as to satisfy the public that we do not disregard their wishes, it will have a salutary influence on the public councils, and prepare the way for a favorable reception of our future measures. It appears to me that this House is bound by every motive of prudence not to let the first session pass over without proposing to the State Legislatures some things to be incorporated into the Constitution, that will render it acceptable to the whole people of the United States, as it has been found acceptable to a majority of them. I wish, among other reasons why something should be done, that those who had been friendly to the adoption of this Constitution may have the opportunity of proving to those who were opposed to it that they were as sincerely devoted to liberty and a Republican Government as those who charged them with wishing the adoption of this Constitution in order to lay the foundation of an aristocracy or despotism.

thirteenth century, others back to England's own Bill of Rights of the late seventeenth century, while many more rested upon declarations drawn up in the several states. Together, these ten amendments (especially as they have been applied to the states through the Fourteenth Amendment)[2] are widely regarded as the bulwark of American liberty, the surest guarantee that government shall be an instrument for the preservation rather than the destruction of freedom.

CONCLUSION: A NEW REPUBLIC

In assessing the Constitution as a whole, Madison took the long view of its contribution to human history. Of course, this fundamental document addressed itself to current needs, dangers, and opportunities with respect to the thirteen states in 1787. But it also reflected a vision of the nature of man, of society, of human happiness. Best of all, perhaps, it reflected an optimism that refused to be beaten down by the naysayers and gloom-peddlers. The people should not hearken, Madison advised in *Federalist* Number 14, "to the unnatural voice which tells you that the people of America . . . can no longer live together as members of the same family; can no longer continue the mutual guardians of their mutual happiness; can no longer be fellow citizens of one great, respectable, and flourishing empire." As Lincoln would later urge, Americans should heed the "better angels" of their nature.

The Constitution did not create a democracy; *republic* was very much the preferred word. But the Constitu-

tion was flexible enough, "incomplete" enough, to allow for democratic developments in the decades that followed. Those developments harked back to the phrase with which the Constitution began: "We the people." If final sovereignty was vested not in any layer or level of government but only in the people, then this grand repository of power comprised the ultimate check and balance. In the inevitable jockeying that would occur among the executive, legislative, and judicial branches, all three were constrained by an awareness that behind and above them stood the people. As citizenship and voting rights expanded in the two centuries that followed, the people acquired ever larger opportunities, ever more awesome responsibilities.

For a dozen years, the American people had celebrated the adoption of the Declaration of Independence. Now in 1788, they had occasion for additional celebration: the birth or rebirth of a nation. Early in 1788 Boston set a pattern by organizing a major parade, with banners, floats, and marchers drawn from many occupational groups and levels of society. In city after city, once ratification in the particular state had been achieved, "Grand Federal Processions" commemorated the event, even as they sought to cement public sentiment. As one observer noted in 1788, the strength of any government depended on "the good opinion people in general have of it." Therefore, it was good "policy, and a sure mark of patriotism and public virtue, to endeavor that all ranks and orders of people should be pleased with, and should support it." To this end, he added, "nothing has a greater tendency to this than for the people of all conditions to assemble together, at certain times, to join in the celebration of the government under which they live." Under the new Constitution, the people had sober respon-

---

2. This "incorporation" or "nationalization" of the Bill of Rights has been one of the most notable developments in twentieth-century Supreme Court jurisprudence.

sibilities, but they could also have joyful festivities.

So in the final year of the 1780s, a nation had been reborn, a new form of government established, and a host of complex problems confronted, though not necessarily solved. Like Charles Willson Peale, raising the drape on his new museum in Philadelphia, Americans could look toward the remaining years of the eighteenth century with a sense that the curtain was going up on an altogether different drama in the history of the United States.

SUGGESTED READING

Ron Chernow, *Alexander Hamilton* (2004). A massive biography and major reinterpretation of Hamilton's contribution to the new nation.

Nathan O. Hatch, *The Democratization of American Christianity* (1989). A major reinterpretation of religion in the early years of the republic; provocative and indispensable.

Michael Kammen, ed., *The Origins of the American Constitution: A Documentary History* (1986). A convenient collection of private letters and public propaganda, along with excellent editorial guidance.

Forrest McDonald, *Novus Ordo Seclorum: The Intellectual Origins of the Constitution* (1985). With this book, one enters into the minds of the eighteenth-century framers, becoming for a moment a citizen of their world of ideas.

James Madison, *Notes of Debates in the Federal Convention of 1787* (1840, 1987). The most authoritative voice on what went on behind the closed doors of the Pennsylvania State House.

William Lee Miller, *The Business of May Next: James Madison & the Founding* (1992). Written in an engaging style, this book not only gives Madison his due, but also successfully re-creates the critical drama of the Constitutional Convention.

Edmund S. Morgan, *Benjamin Franklin* (2002). The most readable and reliable brief biography of America's ambassador of good will and good sense.

Richard B. Morris, *The Forging of the Union, 1781-1789* (1987). This careful study is as authoritative as it is readable.

Marvin Myers, ed., *The Mind of the Founder* (1981). A first-rate guide to the political ideas of James Madison.

Jack N. Rakove, *Original Meanings: Politics and Ideas in the Making of the Constitution* (1996). With pentrating insights, the author lays bare the several levels of meaning in the language of the Constitution-makers.

R. A. Rutland, *The Birth of the Bill of Rights* (1955). An illuminating discussion, in the context of other bills of rights, of the emergence of the first ten amendments to the Constitution.

Herbert J. Storing, *What the Anti-Federalists Were For* (1981). An introduction to the even more useful seven-volume collection edited by Storing, *The Complete Anti-Federalist*.

Garry Wills, ed., *The Federalist Papers* (1982). An inexpensive edition of the indispensable source, with introduction, outline, glossary, and bibliography.

Gordon S. Wood, *The Creation of the American Republic, 1776-1787* (1969). A profoundly impressive analysis of the process by which citizens created "a distinctly American system of politics."

SUGGESTIONS FOR FURTHER READING

Bernard Bailyn, ed., *The Debate on the Constitution*, 2 vols. (1993).

M. E. Bradford, *Original Intentions: On the Making and Ratification of the United States Constitution* (1993).

Roger H. Brown, *Redeeming the Republic: Federalists, Taxation, and the Origins of the Constitution* (1993).

John Butler, *Awash in a Sea of Faith: Christianizing the American People, 1550-1865* (1992).

Conrad Cherry, ed., *God's New Israel: Religious Interpretations of American Destiny* (1971).

Saul Cornell, *The Other Founders: Anti-Federalism and the Dissenting Tradition in America, 1788-1828* (1999).

Stanley Elkins and Eric McKitrick, *The Age of Federalism: The Early American Republic, 1789-1800* (1993).

Robert A. Ferguson, *The American Enlightenment, 1750-1820* (1997).

Edwin S. Gaustad, *Benjamin Franklin: Inventing America* (2004).

Ronald Hoffman and Peter J. Albert, eds., *The Bill of Rights: Government Proscribed* (1997).

James H. Hutson, *Religion and the Founding of the American Republic* (1998).

Ralph Ketcham, *James Madison: A Biography* (1990).

Frank Lambert, *The Founding Fathers and the Place of Religion in America* (2003).

Stuart Leibiger, *Founding Friendship: George Washington, James Madison, and the Creation of the American Republic* (1999).

Drew R. McCoy, *The Last of the Fathers: James Madison and the Republican Legacy* (1989).

Edmund S. Morgan, *Inventing the People: The Rise of Popular Sovereignty in England and America* (1988).

Merrill D. Peterson and Robert C. Vaughan, eds., *The Virginia Statute for Religious Freedom* (1988).

James H. Read, *Power Versus Liberty: Madison, Hamilton, Wilson, and Jefferson* (2000).

Jeffrey H. Richards, *Mercy Otis Warren* (1995).

Leonard L. Richards, *Shays's Rebellion: The American Revolution's Final Battle* (2002).

Richard A. Ryerson, ed., *John Adams and the Founding of the Republic* (2001).

Jonathan D. Sassi, *A Republic of Righteousness: The Public Christianity of the Post-Revolutionary New England Clergy* (2001).

Helen E. Veit et al., eds., *Creating the Bill of Rights: The Documentary Record from the First Federal Congress* (1991).

David Waldstreicher, *In the Midst of Perpetual Fetes: The Making of American Nationalism, 1776-1820* (1997).

Michael P. Zuckert, *Natural Rights and the New Republicanism* (1994).

8

First Presidents and Crucial Precedents, 1789-1809

WHEN GEORGE WASHINGTON accepted the presidency of the United States in 1789, he gave the untried new nation a symbol of unity that turned out to be more than just a symbol. The first federal census of 1790 revealed that the nation had nearly four million citizens, but no census was required to reveal much division and deep-seated differences among these millions. How could "these united States" become *the* United States? Some sought that unity in religious ideology, some in political structures. Alexander Hamilton saw banking, commerce, and manufacturing as the foundation on which a national government could unite sections and factions. John Adams tried to enforce a kind of political and (some feared) religious orthodoxy to make the many into one. But many others thought unity more a danger than a promise. Their concerns centered on state and local matters; a wobbly central government could fend for itself.

In the first wide-open presidential election in 1800, the supporters of Adams arrayed themselves against partisans of Thomas Jefferson in a contest so bitter that any optimism concerning national unity looked as if it would surely sink. Political parties, not envisioned by the Constitution, now moved onto the national stage. The Federalists, especially strong in New England and especially supportive of Washington and Adams, regarded themselves as destined to rule as (in their eyes) the men of virtue, the elite, the chosen of God. They believed in a government *for* the people, but not necessary *of* or *by* the people.

The Jeffersonian Republicans, on the other hand,

Copyright, 1876, by Currier & Ives, N.Y.

GEORGE WASHINGTON.   GEN'L HENRY KNOX, Sec'y of War.   ALEXANDER HAMILTON, Sec'y of the Treasury.   THOMAS JEFFERSON, Sec'y of State.   EDMUND RANDOLPH, Attorney General.

WASHINGTON AND HIS CABINET.

Washington's First Cabinet   Only four men sat in Washington's cabinet: Henry Knox (secretary of war), Alexander Hamilton (secretary of the treasury), Thomas Jefferson (secretary of state), and Edmund Randolph (attorney general), here depicted in an 1876 illustration. Together with a handful of clerks, a tiny army, the federal judges and Supreme Court justices, the members of Congress, and a modest cohort of postmasters and customs agents stationed throughout the nation, these men *were* the government of the United States.

male and female, black and white, young and old — anxious to see how the story might turn out.

GEORGE WASHINGTON AND NATIONAL UNITY

When General Washington resigned his commission on December 19, 1783, in Annapolis, Maryland, the country could not have felt more indebted to any other individual. He had prevailed in battle with dignity, honor, perseverance, and above all with a clear sense of the right relationship between military and civilian authority. Already "first in war," soon he would also be (in the memorable phrase of Henry Lee) "first in peace, and first in the hearts of his countrymen." Although he did much alone, he did appoint able, if sometimes quarreling, assistants, and he did benefit from a strong public sense of America as a nation of destiny and promise. In his relationships with Congress and with the ill-defined judiciary, Washington would set patterns that would be followed — or at least appealed to — by generations to come. Finally, in foreign affairs the first president would keep his young and vulnerable country out of war and the greedy grasp of Europe's expansionist powers.

❧ *The Executive: Washington and His Cabinet*

Just as the choice of Washington as presiding officer at the Constitutional Convention helped that body reach a successful conclusion, so the choice of Washington as president could set the country, under its new charter, on a hopeful path. There was no contest. On February 4, 1789, the Electoral College unanimously elected the one man around whom the country could unite. Then another two months passed before Congress could get itself together so that the votes could be officially counted in its presence. Washington waited at Mount Vernon until he could be formally notified of his election in April, and then set out for the temporary capital in New York City.

Washington's progression from Virginia to New York was a triumphal march, despite eight days spent on muddy, rutted roads. Crowds clamored to see and cheer him, banners welcomed the unblemished hero, pageants

sought votes from all levels of society, even from newly arrived immigrants not yet schooled in the ways of the new nation. Their "rule," if such should happen, would (Federalists said) be only a temporary and unfortunate interruption before voters returned to their senses and gave the reins of power back to those who deserved them. For the next three decades, however, the Federalists dissolved while the Jeffersonians held on to executive and legislative power. Over those years, the Jeffersonian party had its chance to give some substance and some definition to the American dream. How was the national character to be defined?

And what was recognizably "American" about politics, literature, religion, education, social structures, and moral purposes in the era of the Washington, Adams, and Jefferson presidencies? A wandering traveler in the 1790s, after traversing much of the new nation, observed that America was "a vast outline, with much to fill up." So it was when George Washington took his oath of office in New York City. How wisely and how well that outline was filled up involved not just the first three presidents but those four million Americans —

were given in his honor, and dinner parties planned at every stop. Flowers were strewn in his path and Handel's "See the Conquering Hero Come" was lustily sung. At the inauguration itself on April 30, church bells rang out, ships' cannons in New York harbor noisily burst forth, fire-crackers exploded, and loud cheers reverberated against the balustrades of Federal Hall on Wall Street. If pomp, pageantry, and good will could ensure success, then the new president faced only clear weather ahead.

The uncertain times, however, demanded more than pomp. Federal union was hardly more than a potentially powerful idea. But at the moment, power rested on the fortunes of one man and the durability of one document: the Constitution. Fortunately for Washington, those chosen or elected to serve with him were committed to making that one document work. The Anti-Federalists for the moment at least took to the sidelines, waiting for an opportunity to point out that they were right all along: a national government would never succeed.

In his inaugural address, Washington embraced the pervading view that a wise and merciful Providence watched over America. "No people," he declared, "can be bound to acknowledge and adore the invisible hand, which conducts the Affairs of men, more than the people of the United States. Every step by which they have advanced to the character of an independent nation seems to have been distinguished by some token of providential agency." He also called for a public virtue that, he and many others believed, was the only safe foundation for a free society. There is, he noted, "an indissoluble union between virtue and happiness, between duty and advantage, between the genuine maxims of an honest and magnanimous policy and the solid rewards of public prosperity and felicity." Like every subsequent inaugural address, Washington's was filled with hope. But also like all his successors, George Washington found political reality a sobering experience.

Everything was new, untested. As Washington pointed out even before taking the oath of office, "I should consider myself as entering upon an unexplored field, enveloped on every side with clouds and darkness." After taking that oath, the darkness did not disappear nor the apprehension diminish. Washington knew that he "walked on untrodden ground. There is scarcely any part of my conduct which may not hereafter be drawn into precedent." He must cautiously but wisely chart a path where none existed.

Not all choices were his to make. The vice presidency, for example, was determined not by the president (nor would it be until after the Twelfth Amendment to the Constitution in 1804) but by members of the Electoral College. On that ground, John Adams of Massachusetts was named to the position. Politically, it made sense to soften sectional rivalry by balancing a president from the South with a vice president from the North (just as the admission of Vermont to the Union in 1791 had to be "balanced" by bringing in Kentucky the following year). But Washington and Adams never developed a warm relationship. The vice president was given little authority or dignity, another precedent that endured well into the twentieth century.

In choosing persons to head the several departments of government — the president's "cabinet," though that word was not yet used — Washington named Jefferson as secretary of state and Alexander Hamilton as secretary of treasury. Exceptionally able as these two men were, they did not get along, and Jefferson resigned after Washington's first term. Hamilton, on the other hand, retained Washington's favor throughout the entire eight years, and exercised ever-increasing influence even when not in office. Washington was no king, but Hamilton nonetheless saw himself as a prime minister. A Revolutionary War hero, Henry Knox, who had served as secretary of war under the Confederation Congress, continued in that capacity in Washington's cabinet. As the nation's first attorney general, Washington appointed his old friend Edmund Randolph, who tried to keep the peace between Jefferson and Hamilton — and after Jefferson resigned, Randolph became secretary of state. (Soon, however, he was driven from office amid accusations of taking bribes.) Washington knew all his cabinet members personally, consulted them regularly, and regularly acted on their advice; this constituted another vital precedent.

In 1789 Washington entertained high hopes for the young republic, writing to Lafayette that "Nothing but harmony, honesty, industry and frugality are necessary to make us a great and happy people." That list of virtues, however, represented a severe demand not only on the population at large but also on the executive officers themselves. Washington would soon despair about the growth of a "party spirit," even as his anxiety mounted over the festering feud of his two trusted allies, Jefferson and Hamilton. In 1792 he wrote to both men, urging them to find some common ground. "I have a great, a sincere esteem and regard for you both, and ardently wish that some line could be marked out by which both of you could walk." Otherwise, Washington noted sadly, the nation might lose "the fairest prospect of happiness and prosperity that ever was presented to man." But even patriarchal pleas did not produce harmony. Was the nation, even in its tender youth, in danger of coming apart?

❧ Millennialism and the Republic

If the nation was to hold together, perhaps ideas more than personalities would make that possible. A biblically informed if not a biblically obedient people spoke and wrote of that much-prophesied kingdom of God on earth, of that thousand-year reign of peace and happiness ushered in by the omnipotent Creator in cooperation with his fallible creatures. Many during the Revolution and in the decades following clung to the conviction that America was uniquely part of God's plan. Yale's president, Ezra Stiles, in an election sermon preached in 1783, declared that all of America had now become that Puritan "city set on a hill." Tyranny was dethroned; liberty reigned. Stiles called on his audience to reflect on "how wonderful, how gracious, how glorious has been the good hand of our God upon us." A later Yale president, Timothy Dwight, in 1794 gave the sentiment poetic expression:

> O happy state! the state, by Heaven design'd,
> To reign, protect, employ, and bless mankind.

Just as God had guided ancient Israel, so God would direct the fortunes of America, "God's New Israel." The divine hand, evident in the American Revolution, was now revealed in the person of George Washington. "O WASHINGTON!" Stiles exclaimed, "how have I often adored and blessed thy God for creating and forming thee the great ornament of human kind!" For the future, many believed, the same divine hand will be demonstrated in the mission of the nation to all the world.

Just as Christians had received a "Great Commission" to go forth and make disciples of all peoples, so America now had its charge to promulgate the "Gospel of Liberty" that would forever bury all tyranny in ruins. In the seventeenth century, such language and religious optimism was most closely associated with New England and the Puritans. Now, in the late eighteenth century, republican ideology had joined with covenant theology to light a brighter beacon for the whole world to see. Northerners and southerners, Federalists and Anti-Federalists, could all join in a chorus of praise to that "Great Temple of Liberty" called America.

The earliest days of governance under the new Constitution were obviously experimental, and experiments could fail. But if Divine Providence smiled, the experimenters would not fail. Enormous psychological satisfaction could be found in the assurance that God would protect his New World Israelites just as he had those of the Old World. Politicians might quarrel, natural catastrophes might erupt, banks and crops might fail, but the gates of hell would never prevail against a divinely led people.

In the latter decades of the eighteenth century, the nation did not grow more secular-minded or profane, as has been widely assumed. Rather, the cloak of religious rhetoric and religious vision enveloped not just the churches, but the nation as a whole. A kind of political millennium gave promise and hope and perhaps some arrogance to the people at large: to their survival first of all, but well beyond that to their destiny across the continent and around the globe.

Even in the realm of language, Noah Webster of Connecticut tried to point the path to the unity of a nation. In his *Dissertations on the English Language* (1789), Webster not only standardized American spellings, but also pointedly drew distinctions between British English

---

✳ IN THEIR OWN WORDS

"God's American Israel"
In this sermon, preached at Hartford, Connecticut, on May 8, 1783, and entitled "The United States Elevated to Glory and Honor," Ezra Stiles encapsulates the widespread belief that God had a special plan for the new nation.

Already does the new constellation of the United States begin to realize this glory. It has

already risen to an acknowledged sovereignty among the republicks and kingdoms of the world. And we have reason to hope, and I believe to expect, that God has still greater blessings in store for this vine which his own right hand hath planted, to make us "high among the nations in praise, and in name, and in honour." The reasons are very numerous and conclusive....

Liberty, civil and religious, has sweet and attractive charms. The enjoyment of this, with property, has filled the English settlers in America with a most amazing spirit, which has operated, and still will operate, with great energy. Never before has the experiment been so effectually tried, of every man's reaping the fruits of his labour and feeling his share in the aggregate system of power.

(honour, colour) and American English (honor, color); the American version was simpler, clearer, more direct. That same year, Jedidiah Morse of Massachusetts published *The American Geography,* an immensely popular work suggesting that the nation had a geographical as well as a political destiny. Both Webster and Morse, firm Congregationalists, ardently supported a strong central government as the key to the fulfillment of the American millennial dream.

❧ *The Legislature: Washington and Congress*

The Constitution had much more to say about the powers of Congress than it did about the authority of either of the other two branches of government. The Constitution's First Article, by far its longest, detailed the wide scope of congressional authority. And Congress thought that only proper. Congress was closest to the people who were, of course, the ultimate base of all power in a republic. Only Congress could levy taxes, declare war, impeach and convict presidents, confirm the appointment of justices, and consent to treaties. Since Congress could do so much, the president obviously had to work closely with it.

Congress, jealously guarding its own powers, was immediately suspicious of any effort by the executive branch to assert its prerogatives. And since a president could be re-elected indefinitely, was there not danger that the newly elected American George could someday resemble the recently defeated British George? Congress would make certain that this did not happen. Although they may have trusted the George Washington who happened to be president, they harbored deep suspicions of what his successors might do.

Washington had no disposition to become a king. He thanked God for having led him "to detest the folly and madness of unbounded ambition." He knew how to exercise power responsibly, as well as how to limit it carefully. When in 1783 his long unpaid army officers contemplated marching on the government, Washington appeared, uninvited, to quell their threatened insurrection. In a carefully worded speech, he called upon those present "to express your utmost horror and detestation of the man who wishes, under any specious pretenses, to overturn the liberties of our country, and who wickedly attempts to open the floodgates of civil discord and deluge our rising empire in blood." No military coup took place. And as president Washington would see to it that no coup on behalf of royalty would ever occur. Besides, as he pointed out, he would make a

pathetic king since, being childless, he had no heirs.

Yet Congress worried. How should the president be addressed? How should he be received? Should they bow as he passed? William Maclay, a republican-minded Senator from Pennsylvania in the first Congress, kept a diary that reveals just how much attention was given to what now seems so trivial. That question of precedent, however, loomed large once more. On May 1, 1789, the minutes of the Congress referred to Washington's inaugural address of the day before as "His most gracious Speech." Appalled, Maclay rose to address the Senate: "We have lately had a hard struggle against Kingly Authority; the Minds of Men are still heated; everything related to that Species of Government is odious to the People. The words prefixed to the President's Speech are the same that are usually placed before the Speech of his Britannic Majesty. I know they will give offense; I consider them as improper." So convoluted did these and similar questions become that Congress found it necessary to appoint a Joint Committee on the Subject of Titles.

Richard Henry Lee of Virginia contended that all the civilized and, for that matter, the savage world found titles to be worthwhile. "There must be something in Human Nature," he suggested, "that occasioned this general Consent." Maclay responded that as knowledge increased, the need for titles correspondingly declined. The Constitution, moreover, specifically provided that "No Title of Nobility shall be granted by the United States." When the Joint Committee reported that the proper title of the president should be "His Highness the President of the United States of America and Protector of the Rights of the Same," Maclay was beside himself. If the title "His Highness" was going to be used because of the "high station" of the president, then such a title "belongs with more propriety to the Man in the Moon than Anybody Else, as his Station . . . is certainly the most exalted of any that we know of." Despite the sarcasm, Maclay was deadly serious: aristocratic tyranny lurked just around the corner. He blamed Lee along with Vice President John Adams for "all the fooleries, fopperies, fineries, and pomp of Royal etiquette." And he won. The most exalted title by which the chief executive officer of the United States would henceforth be known was, simply, "Mr. President."

More critical issues than mere titles shaped the relationship between the president and Congress. The Senate had the right to give its consent to presidential appointments, but could it dismiss appointees once in office? Many Senators thought such a right was implied; if granted, it would greatly weaken the executive

---

❋ **I N   T H E I R   O W N   W O R D S**

"That Species of Republick"

I also am as much a Republican as I was in 1775. I do not "consider hereditary Monarchy or Aristocracy as Rebellion against Nature." On the contrary, I esteem them both Institutions of admirable wisdom and exemplary Virtue in a certain stage of Society in a great Nation. The only Institutions that can possibly preserve the Laws and Liberties of the People, and I am clear that America must resort to them as an Asylum against Discord, Seditions and Civil War, and that at no very distant Period of time. I shall not live to see it — but you may. I think it therefore impolitick to cherish prejudices against Institutions which must be kept in view as the hope of our Posterity. I am by no means for attempting any such thing at present. Our Country is not ripe for it in many respects, and it is not yet necessary, but our ship must ultimately land on that shore or be cast away.

John Adams to Benjamin Rush, 1789

---

office. James Madison, as close adviser to Washington (as well as a member of the House of Representatives), urged the House to vote against such a senatorial privilege, which it promptly did. In the Senate, where the matter was much more hotly debated, a tie vote was broken by the presiding officer, Vice President Adams, in favor of the stronger executive. This precedent, too, was of critical significance.

Washington, on the other hand, was reluctant to use the veto power to thwart the will of Congress. In his view, the veto should be used not over policy differences, but only when an action of Congress seemed to violate the Constitution. As a "president above party," Washington saw himself as the neutral, impartial judge of the constitutionality of a legislative act. Later, when presidents became party leaders, then it fell to the Supreme Court to determine the constitutionality of the acts of Congress.[1]

The president made some attempt to gain the Senate's consent by meeting with them face to face early in his presidency to discuss a treaty with the southern Indians. But the process was so tedious and the results so unsatisfactory that Washington determined to let the Senate operate on its own leisurely timetable while he — at some remove — would operate on his. When, despite his presence, the Senate decided to refer the whole matter to a committee, Washington rather angrily responded that "This defeats every purpose of my coming here." In deciding never again to visit the Senate for such a reason, Washington fixed yet another precedent.

❧ The Judiciary and the Supreme Court

The Constitution had less to say about the judicial branch than about either the legislative or executive branches. That so little was explicitly set forth aroused more suspicions than it allayed. For after all, here was the highest court in the land in which that most precious of judicial liberties, trial by jury, was absent. Here also was a court that potentially could rob the state courts of any genuine power.

Debates in the Constitutional Convention gave considerable attention to judicial appointments. Should they be by the Senate, by the president, or — as ultimately agreed — by the president with the consent of the Senate? Gouverneur Morris conceived of the chief justice of the Supreme Court as serving on a Council of Advisers to the president and chairing it in his absence. He had also urged that the chief justice propose such laws as "may promote useful learning and inculcate sound morality throughout the Union." But none of these notions found their way into the Constitution, which spoke only of the Court's judicial power extending to all cases "arising under this Constitution, the Laws of the United States, and Treaties made."

Alexander Hamilton, in *Federalist* Number 78, had tried to reassure an anxious public that the Supreme Court, having neither the power of the sword nor of the purse, was the least dangerous branch of government. "It may truly be said to have neither Force nor Will but merely judgment; and must ultimately depend upon the aid of the executive arm even for the efficacy of its judgments." Hamilton did suggest, however, that the Court would necessarily get involved when any legislative act contravened the Constitution; in such an instance, "the Constitution ought to be preferred to the statute, the intention of the people to the intention of their agents."

Washington appointed John Jay as the first Supreme Court chief justice. A lawyer and former chief justice of New York, Jay was also an ardent nationalist who had argued forcefully for approval of the Declaration of In-

---

1. See below, pp. 244-45.

dependence and for ratification of the Constitution. He joined with Hamilton and Madison in writing *The Federalist,* though he contributed the least of the three. Because he had served as secretary of foreign affairs during the Articles of Confederation period, Washington thought him the logical choice for secretary of state in his new "cabinet." Jay, however, preferred becoming chief justice, and Washington quickly accommodated him.

But what kind of institution had Jay agreed to direct? Later in 1789 the Judiciary Act spelled out the detail absent from Article III of the Constitution. In addition to the chief justice, the Supreme Court would have five associate justices. Thirteen federal district courts were established, as well as three circuit courts. States could appeal to the Supreme Court if any of their own laws were challenged as being unconstitutional. Most significantly, the Judiciary Act of 1789 made it clear that federal laws and federal treaties would be "the supreme Law of the Land" and that state sovereignty would in every case yield to national sovereignty.

In 1793, however, in *Chisholm v. Georgia,* Jay's Court ruled that the Constitution explicitly allowed a citizen of one state to sue another state. This seemed too harsh a blow against the rights of the states, with the result that in 1794 the Eleventh Amendment was proposed, and was ratified in 1795. Here the federal judicial arm was shortened to block it from reaching down to hear suits against a state by citizens of any other state or foreign power.

In 1793 Jay also declined an invitation to advise the executive branch on the interpretation of foreign treaties. Jay pointed out that the Constitution had drawn clear lines between the three branches and that these lines would inevitably be blurred if the Court became a party either to executive decisions or to congressional deliberations. Within a year, Jay had even more reason to be sensitive about treaties and their interpretation: while still chief justice, he was asked to negotiate a treaty with Britain. "Jay's Treaty" proved exceedingly unpopular. After five years as chief justice, Jay resigned to become governor of New York. Washington appointed in his place Oliver Ellsworth of Connecticut, principal author of the Judiciary Act of 1789 and a jurist of broad experience.

During Washington's administration, the Supreme Court did not manage to define itself as a major branch of government. Hamilton's words were fully vindicated: namely, that "the judiciary is beyond comparison the weakest of the three departments of power." That situation, however, would change soon after 1800.

❧ Alexander Hamilton and Economic Structures

As Washington's secretary of the treasury, Hamilton had clear responsibility for economic matters. But his concern in this area went well beyond mere official duty. Alexander Hamilton, more than anyone else in Washington's entourage, had a single-minded vision of where the United States should be headed as an economic power and of the steps necessary to take the country there. Only thirty-five years old when named secretary, Hamilton, the illegitimate son of a Scottish merchant, was fired by extraordinary ambition and thirst for glory. Not guilty of trying to line his own pockets with federal money, he allied himself with merchants and manufacturing interests who managed to fill theirs. But, from Hamilton's point of view, it was all in the interest of national unity. Without capital, without credit, without economic strength at home or fiscal respect abroad, the new nation could quickly collapse.

In 1790-91, Hamilton presented to Congress four significant reports: on credit (including duties and taxes), on a national bank, on a mint, and on manufactures. Here his vision took on reality. And here, too, Hamilton's design to weaken the power of the states by strengthening the power of the nation grew clear. Hamilton had the immense advantage of a fixed sense of direction and of remarkable boldness in putting the new nation on a solid economic foundation.

The first economic problem confronting the country was its enormous debt — about $54 million — accumulated during the course of the Revolution. Congress had sold certificates to fund the war effort or had given certificates (in effect, IOUs) to its soldiers in lieu of salary. Over the years, much of this paper had been resold at far below face value, and most of them had passed into the hands of speculators, some of whom were also members of the first Congress. Many assumed that the certificates would be redeemed at some discount — say, fifty cents on the dollar — but Hamilton felt strongly that the integrity of the nation required that the "funding" (as the paying off was called) be at full value, even if it did enrich the speculators. Madison and Jefferson vigorously opposed Hamilton's program, but Congress seemed disposed in its favor. An additional advantage, Hamilton believed, was that the sudden accumulation of wealth in the hands of speculators could make money available for lending to the government or to those prepared to begin industrial development.

Continental Currency This 1777 five-dollar note is typical of the paper money issued by the Continental Congress to pay for the costs of the American Revolution. Because the new government issued more paper currency than it could back up with gold or silver reserves, the currency eventually became nearly worthless.

Continued European demand for American foodstuffs delayed this investment of capital that Hamilton envisioned.

Tied to the "funding" issue was the related question of "assumption": that is, the federal government taking over or assuming the debts accumulated by the individual states during the course of the war. Even more unpopular than funding, this proposal of Hamilton's ran into stiff opposition not only from Jefferson and Madison but also from many others as well. Staunch Federalist Gouverneur Morris, for example, thought it made no more sense to take over the debts of the states than to take over the debts of businesses or individuals. Several states, moreover, principally in the South, had already repaid much if not all of their debts. It was

grossly unfair for citizens of these states to have paid taxes once to retire their own debts, only to be federally taxed a second time to pay off the debts owed by other states. Hamilton, on the other hand, argued that the New England states, if their debts were not assumed, might withdraw from the Union. John Adams commented, "It is a rapture to see a returning disposition to respect treaties, to pay debts, and to do justice by holding property sacred and obeying the commandment, 'Thou shalt not steal.'"

For weeks Congress wrestled and worried and searched for an acceptable accommodation. A complex tangle grew more complex as the question of the permanent location of the nation's capital turned into a toy tossed around to win a vote here, a vote there. The compromise ultimately arrived at between Hamilton and Jefferson gained the votes of two Virginia congressmen for Hamilton's assumption plan, but only if the national capital was fixed along Virginia's northern border. According to the agreement reached at a dinner attended by Hamilton, Jefferson, and Madison, the capital would move from New York City to Philadelphia for ten years, then after that to a new ten-mile-square Federal District on the Potomac River, carved out of land granted by Maryland and Virginia.

In all this jockeying between Hamilton and his opponents, battle lines had been drawn: northern and mercantile interests versus southern and agricultural interests. Not yet having broken with Hamilton, Jefferson conceded in conciliatory tones that "in general I think it is necessary to give as well as take in a government like ours." Yet even Washington felt the rare sting of criticism: he had sold out his troops by not supporting Madison's proposal to reward only the original holders of the certificates; then, he had sold out again by bargaining to get the permanent capital, almost within view of his Mount Vernon acres. But Washington was only glad to have the contentious issues resolved.

Buoyed by his legislative victories, Hamilton pushed on to questions of currency and a national bank. While the narrow issue was the creation of a bank, the broader issue — that reverberates down through all subsequent American history — was one of constitutional interpretation. How "loosely" or how "strictly" should that fundamental document be interpreted? True, the Constitution said nothing about a national bank or charters of incorporation. On the other hand, the Constitution did say that Congress had the power to "make all Laws which shall be necessary and proper for carrying" out the specified powers (Art. I, Sec. 8). As "strict" constructionists (as least on this issue), Madison and Jefferson held that it was unconstitutional to take any action that the Constitution did not expressly allow. As a "loose" constructionist, Hamilton found in the "necessary and proper" clause plenty of room for a national bank and no doubt many other innovations as changed circumstances might warrant.

Both sides advised Washington: the two strongest members of his cabinet, Jefferson and Hamilton, as well as his trusted adviser, James Madison. Washington even asked Madison to prepare a veto message should he decide that the proposal for a national bank really was unconstitutional. Jefferson, at Washington's request, prepared a memo in opposition to the national bank, explaining that granting a monopoly to such an entity would set a dangerous precedent — that moving beyond the clear constitutional language was "to take possession of a boundless field of power, no longer susceptible of any definition." Privately, his language was even less restrained: "There are certainly persons in

all the departments who are driving too fast," with the "monied interests" greatly favored over the agricultural interests. Or as Senator William Maclay stated bluntly: "Congress may go home; Mr. Hamilton is all-powerful, and fails in nothing he attempts."

The president invited Hamilton to respond to Jefferson and Madison, which he did — at great length and with superb reasoning. Any government that ties itself to a literal text, said Hamilton, is frozen in place; it has no flexibility, no adaptability, no life. Scoring an effective debating point, Hamilton noted that even Madison recognized this fact in *The Federalist* when he wrote that "No axiom is more clearly established in law, or in reason, than that wherever the end is required, the means are authorized; wherever a general power to do a thing is given, every particular power for doing it is included" (Number 44). What had changed Madison from a loose constructionist in 1788 to a strict constructionist in 1791? The answer, of course, is that Madison and Jefferson saw the Hamilton juggernaut as driving toward an America that neither wished to see realized.

George Washington received the bank bill on February 14, 1791, and had ten days to sign or veto it. During those ten days, Madison prepared the possible veto message and Hamilton composed his lengthy response. At the last possible moment, Washington, having been pulled in opposite directions, signed the bill into law. The nation now had a bank that, though largely private, could issue notes, provide credit, service the national debt, handle government finances, and make loans — even to the nation itself. At this point, Jefferson concluded that only an organized party could resist or thwart a Hamilton program that seemed invincible.

Now the secretary of treasury turned his agile attention to making the United States a major industrial and manufacturing power. In his famous "Report on Manufactures," written in 1791, Hamilton argued that the nation should not be dependent on imports from abroad, but should be a producer not just of agricultural goods but of manufactured items as well. Such a move would "afford a more ample and various field for enterprise," just as it would create "a more certain and steady demand for the surplus produce of the soil." Protective tariffs could give infant industries a chance to succeed. Hamilton took refuge in the broadest constitutional language of all: the "promote the general Welfare" clause of the preamble. The national bank was, at least, a single institution, but claiming a right to do anything that, however vaguely, promoted the general welfare, threw the doors very wide open indeed. Madison wrote in some despair to Virginia's Governor Henry Lee, "The federal government has been hitherto limited to the specified powers, by the greatest champions for latitude in expounding those powers. If not only the *means,* but the *objects* are unlimited, the parchment had better be thrown into the fire at once." But Congress felt that it had moved far and fast enough in Hamilton's direction: the report was shelved, and the Jefferson-Madison alliance could retain some hope still for an agrarian and small-town America.

❧ Foreign Affairs and Bitter Final Days

President Washington seriously considered retirement at the end of his first term in 1793, and asked Madison to draft an address suitable for the occasion. Though only sixty years of age, Washington had suffered severe illnesses. As the duties of the office grew more tiresome, he wrote to Jefferson, "retirement and tranquillity became an irresistible passion." He also feared dying in office, for that would set the precedent of the president serving for life. But all his friends and advisers declared that his departure at this critical time would be a disaster, and the Electoral College on February 13, 1793, unanimously named Washington to a second term.

RELATIONS WITH FRANCE AND BRITAIN

Two weeks before, France had declared war on Great Britain. The French Revolution of 1789 had run its course, becoming ever more radical, reaching a climax of sorts in the beheading of Louis XVI early in 1793 and of Queen Marie Antoinette many months later. Britain, along with Austria and Prussia, wanted to restore monarchy to France; the French republicans wanted to steer their own course. And President Washington hoped that the United States could steer its own course so as to avoid being drawn into a war for which it was surely not ready. Neither France nor Britain made it easy for America to stay aloof, as both treated the United States with contempt on the high seas and in the interior of the North American continent alike.

Nor was Washington's burden lightened by his secretary of state's vigorous partisanship for agriculture and France, while his secretary of treasury with equal passion supported commerce and England. Both Jefferson and Hamilton agreed that the United States should stay out of the war, but each saw the nation's sympathies as resting in different places. In April 1793 Washington issued a Proclamation of Neutrality that, in effect, canceled the Franco-American Treaty of 1778 that theoreti-

cally made the two countries allies "forever." Jefferson thought that treaty should still be honored; Hamilton thought otherwise since it had been made with a king now overthrown. In any case, the proclamation should keep the young nation out of war.

Or so it seemed, until the British grew increasingly callous in their treatment of America. To the Americans' continued irritation Britain retained control of military posts in the interior that, by the terms of the treaty ending the Revolutionary War, should long before have been abandoned. With consummate gall, they even built a new fort in Ohio, near what is today Toledo. British fur traders competed — much too successfully — with American fur traders, even as they armed and formed alliances with the Indians to frustrate further advancement of the western frontier. By impressing — that is, seizing sailors off American ships at sea, men who they claimed were Royal Navy deserters — the British deeply offended American feelings. Then in 1793 Britain confiscated dozens of American ships trading with the French West Indies, an act that so enraged the American public that war appeared inevitable.

Relations with France fared no better, mainly because the new republic, recognized by the United States at Jefferson's urging, sent as its first ambassador Edmond Charles Genêt — the worst possible choice. Genêt acted not so much like an ambassador as a petty ruler who could make or break laws as he wished, who could use American waters as staging areas for forays against British shipping. Jefferson and other Francophiles first tried to defend Genêt, but he ultimately became such an embarrassment that none came to his rescue. In August 1793, Washington demanded his recall. He resigned, but did not return to France where he likely would have been executed. He stayed in the United States, deflated and ignored. Yet France could not be ignored. And a position of neutrality, even of civility, grew ever harder to maintain.

JAY'S TREATY

Meanwhile, relations with Britain deteriorated to the point that Washington determined to send John Jay as special emissary to see if some calming agreement could be reached. But Jay's Treaty (with Hamilton as the real force in the background) calmed practically no one. England gave up little. Jay had been instructed to seek an opening of British West Indian trade to American ships, to settle disputed terms of the 1783 treaty that ended the Revolutionary War, and to arrive at a commercial agreement with England. All he got were promises (1) to abandon the forts in the Old Northwest — promises that had been made before; (2) to compensate the U.S. for the vessels seized in December 1793, but only if the British creditors collected debts owed before the Revolution; and (3) to allow some trade from American ports to the British West Indies, but only in vessels less than seventy tons and only if they carried no sugar, molasses, coffee, cocoa, or cotton. Britain did reaffirm to Americans their right to navigate the Mississippi River, but this concession came more at the expense of Spain than of Britain.

The treaty found no welcome in America. When at last the details of the agreement leaked out, Jay was condemned in every market place and hanged in effigy in nearly every town. Sentiments painted on a fence in Taunton, Massachusetts, revealed the public mood: "Damn John Jay! damn every one that won't damn John Jay!! damn every one that won't put lights in his windows and sit up all night damning John Jay!!!" Appropriately, Hamilton came in for his share of damning, too, since he had taken Britain's part so improperly, even giving the British ambassador private information that gravely weakened Jay's hand as a negotiator.

But the Senate still had to consent to the treaty and the president still had to sign it. Amazingly, despite all the inflammatory rhetoric and ill will, in 1795 the Senate mustered the two-thirds vote of concurrence (with no votes to spare), though it did delete the clause regarding trade with the West Indies. The president signed, chiefly on the grounds that war with England had been avoided. (As it turned out, it had only been postponed until 1812, but that was long enough to permit the nation to grow stronger.) He also signed because the one member of his cabinet most opposed to his doing so, Edmund Randolph (Jefferson's successor at the State Department), had been implicated in taking French bribes, and was forced to resign. Even after presidential and senatorial approval, the treaty was threatened by an effort in the House to deny the necessary funding. Washington, ever concerned about precedent, argued that the House had no constitutional basis for frustrating or nullifying a treaty agreement: that was a matter for the Senate and the executive. After prolonged debate, the House on April 30, 1796, approved the required funds, but by the slim vote of 51 to 48.

The bitter controversy surrounding Jay's Treaty put Washington's administration under such a cloud that it was difficult to find men who would step into vacant cabinet posts or even accept nomination to the Supreme Court. A federal job was made even more unattractive

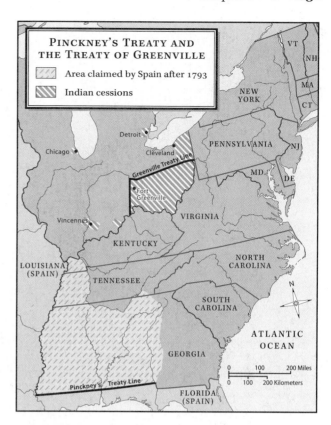

by the severe yellow fever epidemic that infected much of Philadelphia in 1793; thousands fell before the devastating disease, and the federal government was even forced to flee inland. For Washington, the second term could not end soon enough. If he thought that patriots could rise above party, he was virtually alone in that lofty position. Jeffersonian Republicans gathered strength in the rural areas, emphasized equality of classes, and saw the rise of cities as akin to sores afflicting the human body. Hamiltonian Federalists, on the other hand, vested their confidence in the elite and well-born, the "natural aristocracy," in the wealth of the rising mercantile class, and in the political strength of the cities. Republicans favored local control, Federalists centralized control. And while both groups initially resisted adopting party labels or platforms, both ultimately turned from Washington's complete disdain of "party."

THE WHISKEY REBELLION

Washington enjoyed somewhat greater success in asserting federal power within the United States. In western Pennsylvania, frontiersmen vigorously protested the new federal excise tax on liquor. This tax aggravated many other grievances of those living in the West: burdensome and ill-paid militia duty, continued conflicts with the Indians, elite members of eastern officialdom

Negotiating the Treaty of Greenville   Native American chiefs ceded their ancestral lands to General Anthony Wayne of the United States for 1/6-cent per acre. This picture of the transaction was painted from a sketch by one of Wayne's officers. Wayne is the figure in the center; to his left is William Henry Harrison, who would later be president.

drawing good salaries in their towns, and the especially onerous requirement of journeying all the way to York or Philadelphia to stand trial for non-compliance with the federal tax. Since exporting whiskey was one of the few means that westerners had to turn into a small amount of cash (hauling wagonloads of corn over the mountains to eastern markets was prohibitively expensive), this tax struck western farmers as just another example of federalism gone mad. The central government was treating its subjects as Parliament and the king had a few decades earlier treated theirs. Rural

protest escalated into the violent episode called the Whiskey Rebellion: armed men defying government authority and shedding blood. It was Shays's Rebellion all over again, and Washington would have none of it. If a minority could defy and dictate to the majority, then, said Washington, "there is an end put at one stroke to republican government, and nothing but anarchy and confusion is to be expected thereafter."

Washington, who had fought over the terrain around the small village of Pittsburgh before, determined to lead the troops himself. Calling out militiamen from Virginia, Maryland, Pennsylvania, and New Jersey, Washington commanded an immense force of nearly fifteen thousand troops in the fall of 1794. The rebellious frontiersmen, when confronted with such a show of governmental muscle, faded into the forest and no pitched battle was ever fought. Leaders were tried, found guilty, but — having received a presidential pardon — never put to death. Hamilton, serving as Washington's chief of staff on this occasion, exulted over so clean and clear a victory. Even some Jeffersonian Republicans agreed that "all attempts to oppose the execution of constitutional laws by force are improper, dangerous to freedom, and highly unbecoming good citizens." Such activity unchecked would, said these Republicans, inevitably "produce anarchy and civil war." Yet, in the election of 1800, the Republicans denounced this heavy-handed display of federal power. The whole episode demonstrated to Hamilton the need for a standing army; to Hamilton's opponents, it kept just that fearful spectacle in clear view.

SUCCESS IN THE WEST

Another show of force in the Old Northwest likewise yielded results in which President Washington took satisfaction. On August 20, 1794, General Anthony Wayne crushed the Miamis in in the Battle of Fallen Timbers in Ohio. As a consequence, most of what was to become the state of Ohio came under federal control, as was spelled out a year later in the Treaty of Greenville. Eager settlers and land speculators could now move freely into lands north of the Ohio River. By the end of the year Washington believed that the infant nation had demonstrated to the skeptics abroad that "republicanism is not the phantom of a deluded imagination; on the contrary, that under no form of government will the laws be better supported, liberty and property better secured, or happiness more effectually dispensed to mankind."

In dealing with Spain, Thomas Pinckney had far greater success than Jay had with the British. By Pinckney's Treaty of 1795, Spain (1) granted free U.S. navigation of the Mississippi; (2) undertook mutually with the United States to restrain Indians from attacking each other's settlers; and (3) conceded that the U.S. border extended all the way to the thirty-first parallel (roughly the northern border of Florida) and all the way to the Mississippi River. This agreement had the further virtue of winning the restless citizens of Kentucky (admitted to the Union in 1792) and Tennessee (admitted in 1796) back into the good graces of the United States.

As long as the Spanish authorities at New Orleans had manipulated American access to the Gulf of Mexico, both Kentucky and Tennessee had flirted with transferring allegiance to Spain. Some residents had even talked of creating a separate Allegheny Nation in the transmountain west. At least until Pinckney's Treaty was signed, westerners continued to feel neglected by the urban East and thought that it made sense to look more to Spain than to Philadelphia for economic support and commercial outlet. Pinckney's Treaty was much more warmly received in the United States than Jay's. On March 3, 1796, the Senate voted its unanimous approval.

WASHINGTON'S FAREWELL ADDRESS

By that time, George Washington was already at work on drafts for a final address to his fellow citizens. He had asked Madison to draft remarks when he was thinking of retiring at the end of the first term, and that draft he still possessed. But much had happened in the second term that needed to be taken into account, and for help at this stage he turned to Alexander Hamilton. By now, he was unequivocal that the second term would be his last. He would, he wrote in response to a query from Hamilton, "close my public life on March 4 [1797], after which no consideration under heaven that I can foresee shall again draw me from the walks of private life." Once more, a powerful precedent was set: a maximum of eight years as president, even though the Constitution had placed no limit on the number of terms. (This precedent stood until Franklin D. Roosevelt's election to a third term in 1940.)

What is known as Washington's "Farewell Address" was never delivered as a speech — for Washington was no orator. Rather, it was published in a Philadelphia newspaper in September 1796, and rapidly reprinted thereafter, both at home and abroad. Washington wished it to be his final legacy, and Hamilton also labored to make it "*importantly* and *lastingly* useful." Washington, distressed by growing political partisanship, emphasized over and over the necessity of union, of common purposes, of oneness as Americans. "You have in a common cause fought and triumphed together," he told the American people. "The independence and liberty you possess are the work of joint councils and joint efforts, of common dangers, sufferings, and successes.... every portion of our country finds the most commanding motives for carefully guarding and preserving the union of the whole." "Union," "common," "joint," "together" — these were the words that Washington would return to repeatedly. If rhetoric could make the Union one, the president in his last months of office would do all within his power to provide that cement.

The United States must look to its own interests, Washington continued, not confusing those with the interests of any other nation. "Against the insidious wiles of foreign influence . . . , the jealousy of a free people ought constantly to be awake." Temporary foreign alliances might be necessary, but not permanent alliances. And in looking to itself for unity and wholeness, America must not forsake virtue. "'Tis substantially true that virtue or morality is a necessary spring of popular government." Moreover, "reason and experience both forbid us to expect that national morality can prevail in exclusion of religious principle." Here was no voice of party or faction, of region or of class, but of a patriarchal Moses trying to lead his children out of the wilderness of foreign domination and moral confusion into the promised land of a true and lasting liberty.

Washington left office in March 1797, and a little over two years later he was dead. Despite the bitter partisan attacks he had endured in the last years of his presidency, his funeral and the unrestrained bounty of praises poured out upon him constituted his country's own Farewell Address. And it too lacked all spirit of party or faction. Almost deified, certainly sanctified, Washington ascended into heaven, according to one famous artistic rendition, accompanied by a host of angels. When Timothy Dwight delivered his eulogy, he chose his biblical text with care: "And there arose not a prophet since in Israel like unto Moses, whom the Lord knew face to face" (Deuteronomy 34:10).

JOHN ADAMS AND THE RISE OF POLITICAL PARTIES

George Washington's last official words had warned against the rising "party spirit"; John Adams's first presidential words bemoaned the persisting "party spirit." Despite these high-level cautions, parties would ultimately become the most familiar feature of American political life. Since John Adams had served George Washington faithfully if quietly as his vice president for eight years, his election to the presidency in 1796 might be regarded as inevitable. That this was far from the case, however, testified not only to party differences but even more to serious divisions among the Federalists. For a variety of reasons, the presidency of John Adams was not a happy time for him, although the country fared somewhat better than he did personally. The Washington precedent of two terms did

not work its magic for Adams; in 1800, in a bitter election battle, Adams would lose to his own vice president and political rival, Thomas Jefferson.

The Party Spirit

The notion of political parties, not envisioned by the Constitution and welcomed neither by Washington nor by Adams, found little favor generally in the final decades of the eighteenth century. In the first place, in England and on the Continent, dedication to a party interest meant loyalty to a private, selfish faction. A party's good stood in contrast to the public good. In the second place, what Americans needed in the 1780s and 1790s was, above all else, *unity*. For the new nation to survive, it seemed, all Americans had to rise above parochial interests of region, class, or occupation. The nation was a land of differences: in creed, in race, in language, in blood. If it could not achieve unity on the *political* level, then (almost everyone agreed) oneness was only a phantom or a fantasy. Rejecting the whole idea of political parties not only made sense: the alternative made no sense.

Nevertheless, and it is a critical *nevertheless*, the seeds of party division began to sprout almost from the beginning. The seedlings were most evident in the "party platform" of Alexander Hamilton and his program for national economic development. If Washington held the real reins of power in his hand, Hamilton was the party boss — a role to which he diligently and disastrously clung during Adams's term as president. The party that he led came to call itself the Federalists, with Hamilton's own loyal following often designated the High Federalists. It aligned itself with the rich and powerful, the merchant and urban class, and aristocratic tendencies that distrusted anything smacking of democracy. "The mass of the people," said Hamilton, "are turbulent and changing — they seldom judge or determine right."

As Hamilton grew more insistent in the pursuit of his program, he galvanized opponents to organize, too. Madison and Jefferson, differing sharply with Hamilton, argued that the mass of the people must be brought into the political process, not shut out from it. Government should not grant favors to the chosen few, but rather must guarantee equal rights for all. Above all, it should protect the farmers. "Cultivators of the earth are the most valued citizens," Jefferson informed Jay in 1785. "They are the most vigorous, the most independent, the most virtuous, and they are tied to their country, and wedded to its interests, by the most lasting bonds." Jeffersonian Republicans favored equality, individualism, freedom, farmers, and France; Hamiltonian Federalists admired hierarchy, order, authority, merchants, and England. And each faction had its own newspaper to disseminate the "party line": the *Gazette of the United States* for Federalists, and the *National Gazette* for Republicans.

The fierce arguments over Jay's Treaty revealed, among other things, the two movements in the process of becoming two parties, with the geographical divisions now evident. New England in general favored ratification of the treaty; the South and West generally opposed it; the states in between were divided. This roughly corresponded to the sectional divisions of the two parties; Federalists were the treaty's main supporters and Republicans, its principal opponents. Later, the French Revolution similarly divided Federalists and Republicans. The former abhorred that radical revolt, seemingly so different from the American Revolution; the Republicans, on the other hand, supported it as another great — if bloody — blow on behalf of liberty around the world.

Democratic-Republican societies sprang up to support France in its struggles, even as they saw themselves as a necessary counterweight to the growing assertiveness of the urban and capitalistic East. Their voices, often strident and sometimes radical, aggravated the anxieties of those concerned above all with the unity of the new nation. Even Washington turned more and more to the safety and order of the Federalists, though never admitting, even to himself, that he might be a party member.

The Apotheosis of Washington   American painter Rembrandt Peale created this image of George Washington, after his death in 1799, rising triumphantly to heaven, and cheap lithographs (like this one) were widely distributed throughout the nineteenth century. Federalist-era politics had made even Washington a polarizing figure, but death transformed him into an icon of patriotism, piety, and republican rectitude.

By 1795, Jefferson concluded that political parties were not deplorable — only inevitable. "Were parties here divided merely by a greediness for office, as in England," he observed, "to take a part with either would be unworthy of a reasonable or moral man." But that was not the case in the United States, he insisted. Here where the difference was one of principle, a difference "as substantial and as strongly pronounced as between the republicans & the Monocrats of our country, I hold it as honorable to take a firm & decided part, and as immoral to pursue a middle line." He would be a party man with pride, not with apology, Jefferson concluded, and many fellow citizens agreed.

Newspapers also became increasingly partisan, and as their numbers multiplied, so did their political passions. As a Baltimore editor unapologetically explained near the end of the eighteenth century, "The American people have long enough been imposed upon by the pretended impartiality of printers; it is all delusion." He added that "every party will have its printer, as well as every sect its preacher; and it is as incongruous for a publication to be alternately breathing the spirit of Republicanism and Aristocracy as for a clergyman to preach to his audience Christianity in the morning, and Paganism in the evening." Battle lines, evident in 1796, grew vehemently more so in 1800.

❧ The Contest of 1796

Adams won the election, but by the slimmest of margins. The Federalists fielded two candidates: John Adams and Thomas Pinckney; the Republicans, also two: Thomas Jefferson and Aaron Burr. Both "tickets" had geographical balance, with Adams from Massachusetts and Pinckney from South Carolina on one side, with Jefferson from Virginia and Burr from New York on the other. But at that time "tickets" did not run as such; instead, the electors in each state voted separately for two candidates for president. Voters did not voice their choices directly for president, but voted for electors pledged to support a particular man or (by 1796) even a "Federal" or "Jefferson" ticket. After counting the Electoral College votes, Congress would declare the person with the largest number of votes to be president, and the runner-up to be vice president. By this awkward mechanism, soon to be corrected,[2] Adams, with 71 electoral votes, was named president; Jefferson, with 68 votes, became vice president.

2. By the Twelfth Amendment in 1804.

It was not auspicious for the Adams presidency to win by so narrow a margin, and to have as his second in command the leader of the opposition party. Like Washington, Adams had serious reservations about the rise of parties. In 1780 he declared that "There is nothing I dread so much as a division of the republic into two great parties, each arranged under its leader, and concerting measures in opposition to each other." He saw this as a danger in Massachusetts under its newly adopted constitution, and a danger in the new nation under its fundamental frame of government. Parties were bad.

But for Adams in 1796 the news got worse. A political manipulator of endless energies, Hamilton had decided that Thomas Pinckney would be more pliable than stubborn John Adams. Hoping to make Pinckney president, Hamilton persuaded the South Carolina Federalists to cast all their votes for Pinckney. But New England electors, getting wind of this legerdemain, withheld enough votes from Pinckney to ensure that the larger number went to Adams. (In the final tally, Pinckney received 59 electoral votes.)

Still the humiliations grew. In his cabinet Adams retained many who had served Washington, for to have a wholesale housecleaning would suggest a party spirit. Few of them manifested leadership or brilliance; worse, few of them demonstrated a primary loyalty to Adams. They either took their cues directly from Hamilton or looked back with defeatist nostalgia to the days when the country had a *real* president: George Washington. A vice president of another party, a cabinet of dubious loyalty, and a populace that compared the second president disadvantageously to the first. All of Adams's resources of character and training would be called upon just to survive.

Adams brought a wealth of experience to his new position, and he had thought and written much about the nature of government in general and the Constitution in particular. A man of voracious intellectual appetite, he read more widely and more thoughtfully than almost any other statesman of his generation. Then he had served for eight years as vice president, and though he described it as "the most insignificant office that ever the invention of man contrived or his imagination conceived," it kept him fully immersed in public affairs. Few men have ever come to the presidency more thoroughly prepared for the office. But the presidency required its occupant to be both a consummate politician and a statesman. Adams was more the latter than the former.

❧ War with France?

The overriding concern and external pressure confronting the Adams administration was the nation's relationship with France. When Adams became president on March 4, 1797, the most urgent question was whether war with France could be avoided. France had reacted negatively to the ratification of Jay's Treaty, for it seemed both a repudiation of the Franco-American alliance dating back to 1778 and a submission to British interests at the expense of French interests. In a single year, from June of 1796 to the summer of 1797, France had seized more than 300 American ships and imprisoned many of the crewmembers. When the very pro-French minister, James Monroe, was replaced by a more neutral envoy, C. C. Pinckney of South Carolina, the French arrogantly refused to recognize him and threatened even to arrest him.

By the fall of 1797 Adams convinced Congress to send a three-man commission to France, consisting of Pinckney, Elbridge Gerry of Massachusetts (a Republican), and John Marshall of Virginia (a Federalist). The French condescended, ultimately, to deal with this commission, though so far as mutual relations were concerned it would have been far better had they not. For the three anonymous French agents (dubbed X, Y, and Z by John Adams) demanded huge bribes for France before substantial negotiations could proceed. This insolence infuriated the commissioners, the president, and the American public. Adams said that the United States must choose "between actual hostilities on our part or national ruin." But the administration chose a "qualified hostility" over an outright declaration of war. In the summer of 1798, Congress authorized the capture of armed French ships and cut off all commercial activity with that difficult nation. On June 13 the president vowed that "I will never send another minister to France without assurances that he will be received, respected, and honored as the representative of a great, free, powerful, and independent nation." Four weeks later Congress formally announced that all former treaties with France were now null and void. It was not war, but it was so close as to be virtually indistinguishable.

Seeing these dangerous developments, Adams argued for an American navy — more than for a much-feared standing army — to guard American shores. Such a force would be a first line of defense against any European powers, but it could also, where necessary, see to it that a hostile power felt America's sting. Within two years, more than eighty armed French vessels were captured, mostly in the West Indies. Congress also created the new Department of the Navy in 1798. Adams appointed Maryland merchant Benjamin Stoddert as the first secretary of the navy, giving him at least one cabinet officer not caught up in either Washington's or Hamilton's orbit. Under Stoddert's leadership, the building of naval vessels and the establishment of naval yards proceeded rapidly.

If a full-scale war actually did break out, however, something would have to be done about an army, no matter the reluctance of Adams himself and much of the public to pay for "idle men." When Congress authorized a force of 10,000 men to serve for three years, Adams turned to the nation's favorite retired general to take command. Washington agreed, but only if Hamilton served as second-in-command. Adams had no choice but to take yet another bitter dose of Hamiltonianism, although he understandably thought that as commander-in-chief he, not Washington, should have made the choice. The army never went to war, however, no doubt to the real regret of Hamilton who had visions of leading an impressive force into the Floridas and Louisiana to expel the French.

Public resentment against France was so strong and Hamiltonian hatred of France so intense that only Adams's rigid determination kept the United States out of war. He was stubborn, in this instance fortunately so. Hearing that France might be more amenable to some calming compromises, Adams — without consulting anybody — appointed a special envoy to Paris. Caught off guard, the High Federalists predictably reacted with fury. But Adams stuck to his position. When the commissioners finally arrived late in 1799, they found themselves dealing with the newly ascendant Napoleon Bonaparte. After months of tiresome maneuvers, in the Convention of 1800 (ratified by the Senate the next year), both sides agreed simply to settle for a cancellation of all treaties between them.

That agreement seemed minimal indeed — with two exceptions. First, it did avoid a costly war for which the United States was ill-prepared. Second, it helped make it possible in the next administration for the United States to negotiate the extraordinary purchase of the entire Louisiana Territory. But the immediate effect was a further decline in the popularity of John Adams. By refusing to go to war, he put country ahead of personal ambition and severely damaged his chances for re-election. Yet he never regretted his action. Years later, he wrote that he found such satisfaction in the outcome of the negotiations that "I desire no other inscription over my gravestone than 'Here lies John Adams, who took upon himself the responsibility of the peace with France in the year 1800.'"

❧ Adams and the Ordeal of Liberty

Despite his great familiarity with government and human nature, Adams did not come into office with any domestic agenda clearly in mind. He responded to circumstances more than he attempted to shape or anticipate them. And whenever opportunity presented, he escaped to his homestead in Quincy, Massachusetts. He saw himself more as an umpire between quarreling factions than as initiator of legislation. He also saw himself as much put upon by a critical press, badly mistreated by his enemies in government, and — like every president — repeatedly let down by his friends. During his presidential years, both he and Abigail suffered from serious bouts of ill health. And when the capital was moved from Philadelphia to Washington, D.C., in 1800, the cold, empty, unfinished White House only added to the unhappiness of its first occupants. "This House," Abigail Adams wrote to her sister, "is built for ages to come." Meanwhile she hung her wash to dry in the empty reception room.

Adams, when first elected, asked his vice president to attend the cabinet meetings. But after consulting Madison and others, Thomas Jefferson declined on the grounds that it might compromise his role as leader of the loyal opposition. Declining also spared him the agony of meetings that, more often than not, took positions that Jefferson abhorred. But respectfully excusing himself from regular cabinet meetings also brewed suspicions in Adams's mind that this man was not loyal — certainly not in the way that Vice President Adams had been loyal to Washington. When some private opinions of Jefferson's critical of Adams became public knowledge, Adams saw his one-time friend as his enemy. "You can witness for me how loath I have been to give him up," Adams wrote to his son, John Quincy, in 1797. "It is with much reluctance that I am obliged to look upon him as a man whose mind is warped by prejudice and so blinded by ignorance as to be unfit for the office he holds."

Many thought that Adams was unfit for the office *he* held, and these critics were by no means all Jeffersonian Republicans. Hamilton had done his best to keep Adams from becoming president. He had failed, but would succeed in seeing that Adams never had a sec-

ond term. In 1800, Hamilton (who in general preferred to operate craftily behind the scenes) published a most impolitic "Letter from Alexander Hamilton concerning the Public Conduct and Character of John Adams, Esq., President of the United States." While praising his patriotism and his integrity, Hamilton concluded baldly that Adams "does not possess the talents adapted to the Administration of Government, and that there are great and intrinsic defects in his character, which unfit him for the office of Chief Magistrate." Adams, accused of having a violent temper, held it in check at this time, though years later he denounced Hamilton as "a bastard brat of a Scotch pedlar" who was so consumed by ambition that he "hated every man young or old who Stood in his Way."

No question about it, John Adams had real enemies. Well he might from time to time believe himself surrounded by them. From that conviction he could easily move to the corollary belief that the country, too, was surrounded by enemies. Many Federalists thought of themselves as the only legitimate interpreters of the Constitution; therefore criticizing them meant criticizing and perhaps condemning the republic itself. Although he did not author the bills that came to be known collectively as the Alien and Sedition Acts of 1798, Adams sympathized with their purpose and promptly signed them into law. Under them, the residency requirement for citizenship was extended from five to fourteen years. In time of war or threat of war, the president could expel all aliens who were citizens of the enemy nation.

The Sedition Act, far broader in its sweep, made it a crime to threaten "any officer of the United States Government with any damage to his character, person, or property." Penalties were provided for all found guilty "of printing, writing, or speaking in a scandalous or malicious way against the government of the United States, either house of Congress, or the President." Since both Federalist and Republican newspapers had for years been printing the vilest diatribes against each other's rival candidates, this action obviously represented a major change from what had been widely understood as fundamental constitutional rights.

And while these changes drove Jeffersonian Republicans right up the wall, they also drove many of them into jail, as editors of Republican presses found themselves repeatedly charged with violation of the Sedition Act. Jefferson and others came to the rescue of editors deprived of their livelihood, making contributions for their needs and complaining loudly of the injustices they suffered. In June 1798 Benjamin Franklin Bache, grandson of his namesake, was arrested for slandering Adams. Long an object of Federalist contempt for his anti-government diatribes, Bache charged Adams with being "blind, bald, toothless, and querulous." He was arrested since one charge was obviously false: Adams was not blind.

James Madison condemned these congressional actions as not only unauthorized by the Constitution but also specifically prohibited by it. Giving such sweeping powers to the federal government, said Madison, ought "to produce universal alarm, because it is levelled against that right of freely examining public characters and measures, and of free communication thereof, which has ever been justly deemed the only effectual guardian of every other right." Jefferson saw a Federalist coup at work, ushering in America's own "Reign of Terror." If the public tolerated this extreme legislation, then next, said Jefferson, "we shall immediately see attempted another act of Congress, declaring that the President shall continue in office during life . . . and the establishment of the Senate for life." A deadly poison had been inserted into the body politic; Madison and Jefferson felt obliged to find an antidote — and quickly.

The two Republican leaders, protecting the ideals of the republic as they envisioned them, proceeded at the state level to thwart or "nullify" these unacceptable federal actions. Madison prepared resolutions for Virginia, while Jefferson secretly did the same for Kentucky. The point of these "resolves" in both cases was to give states the right to determine the constitutionality of federal actions and, if they so chose, to void the application of the odious law in their own territories. As parties to the compact that had created the Union, states could withdraw from that compact when they found it necessary. In Jefferson's proposed language for Kentucky, ". . . every state has a natural right in cases not within the compact . . . to nullify of their own authority all assumptions of power by others within their limits." This was strong language — so strong that it did not survive in the final wording of the Kentucky Resolutions. But the principle did survive, not only in 1798 but decades later when threats to the unity of the nation proved more serious and even disastrous (see Chapters 12 and 14).

Jefferson and Madison believed that other states should be consulted, but none chose to follow the lead of Virginia and Kentucky. If the possibility of secession was implied in the language of either man, neither intended to go that far. As Jefferson wrote to John Taylor in November 1798, "For the present, I should be for resolving the alien & sedition laws to be against the constitution & merely void, and for addressing other States to obtain similar declarations." Then he added, "I would not do anything at this moment which should commit us further." But in the minds of many, too much had been done already, and party divisions never seemed deeper or more dangerous.

The Republicans, or "Jacobins"[3] as Adams called them, not only clung to their love of France but, said Adams, were convinced that the Federalists were their enemy and the country's. Rumors spread that state militias in the South were arming for any eventuality. Adams deemed it "prudent and necessary to order chests of arms from the War Office" to be brought quietly through the back doors of the executive mansion. On the other hand, the High Federalists, who clung to their love for England, pushed for war against France; such a war, said Adams, would give them an opportunity to attack the Republican opposition at home. (The High Federalists, said Jefferson, "have had their heads shorn by the harlot England.") By April of 1799, Adams thought it expedient to declare a national day of fasting, urging the Almighty to "withhold from us unreasonable discontent, from disunion, faction, sedition, and insurrection." The days were dark with gloom, and for Adams they would grow gloomier still.

❧ Defeat and Disillusionment

When John and Abigail Adams moved into the presidential home in Washington, D.C., in the fall of 1800, it was clear that the family would not be spending another four years in what would later be called the White House.[4] Formal political campaigning was not the Federalist style, but what hurt Adams more than anything else was the irreparable split in his own party. Hamilton campaigned, but not for Adams. His presidential choice this time was General Charles Cotesworth Pinckney, brother of Thomas Pinckney, whom he had supported in 1796. As inspector general of the army, Hamilton lost no opportunity to tell any troops that he saw that Adams was too weak to be president and that a mili-

3. An emotionally laden term of abuse, *Jacobin* referred to the radicals of the French Revolution. In America, the tag when hurled at anyone during these years aroused great fear.

4. As we shall see in Chapter 9, the mansion acquired this name after the War of 1812.

THE PROVIDENTIAL DETECTION

Anti-Jefferson Propaganda   The elections of 1796 and 1800 set the tone for most subsequent presidential contests with their vicious mudslinging. In this broadside from the 1800 campaign, Thomas Jefferson is about to sacrifice the United States Constitution on the "Altar of Gallic [French Revolutionary] Despotism," already blazing with deistic writings and encircled by the devil's tail. In his other hand he brandishes a letter he had written to his Italian radical friend Philip Mazzei, supposedly defaming George Washington. Under the ever-vigilant eye of God, however, the American eagle thwarts the infidel Jefferson's wickedness. Jefferson's supporters replied in kind, accusing the Federalists of being crypto-monarchists.

tary man was needed for the office. "This intriguer," Abigail Adams wrote, has been "endeavoring to divide the Federal party — to create divisions and heart burnings against the President, merely because he cannot sway him or carry such measures as he wishes."

Adams, who had put up with Hamilton's "intriguing" and with a disloyal cabinet far longer than anyone believed that he could or should, finally reached the breaking point. In May 1800 he dismissed Secretary of War James McHenry and Secretary of State Timothy Pickering for having given total allegiance to Hamilton and incessantly scheming against Adams. Hamilton responded with his damning letter, and friends of Adams bounded to his defense. Dictionary-maker Noah Webster rebuked Hamilton sharply, asking whether all men would not "believe that your ambition, pride, and overbearing temper have destined you to be the evil genius of this country." Other friends came to Adams's rescue

as well, but the damage was done as a bitterly divided Federalist party presented to the voters its ticket of Adams and Pinckney.

Still hoping for victory, the Federalists made religion a central campaign issue and Jefferson presented a most tempting target. Condemning the vice president as a skeptic, deist, and "enemy to pure morals and religion, and consequently an enemy to his country and his God," the Federalist press unleashed its barrage. "Anyone who has so little shame as to vote for Thomas Jefferson," editorialized the *Gazette of the United States,* "insults his maker and his redeemer." The election boiled down to a simple issue, Federalist partisans exclaimed in screaming headlines: "GOD — AND A RELIGIOUS PRESIDENT; or . . . JEFFERSON AND NO GOD!!!" The Republicans responded by noting that Jefferson had publicly declared that America's "liberties are a gift of God." Also, the man who in his Statute on Religious Freedom had referred to the "Holy Author of our Religion" as "Lord both of body and mind" was no enemy to God, though he was no friend to Calvinist orthodoxy. (Neither, indeed, was John Adams, although his New England admirers chose to overlook this.)

In December 1800, as the electoral votes trickled in, the early returns gave encouragement to the Jeffersonians. New England solidly supported its native son, but New York went Republican, and Pennsylvania split. Virginia weighed heavily on behalf of its native son, as did the rest of the South. When the tally was completed, the Adams-Pinckney ticket had 65 votes, while the Jefferson-Burr ticket claimed 73. Not only had Adams lost, but the Federalist party as well received a body blow from which it never recovered. John and Abigail Adams heard that grim news at the same time that they learned of the death of their son Charles in New York City. "My little bark has been oversett in a squall of thunder & lightning & hail," the president wrote to another son. "I feel my shoulders relieved from a burden" and "the short remainder of my days will be the happiest of my life." The "short remainder" (which lasted for another quarter-century) did see a considerable degree of equanimity return to the much-besieged second president of the United States.

THE REVOLUTION OF 1800 AND A JEFFERSONIAN REPUBLIC

John Adams had been defeated — but had Thomas Jefferson been elected? That question was not so readily answered because Jefferson and Aaron Burr ended up with exactly the same number of Electoral College votes. When that matter was finally worked out, Jefferson had another problem: namely, putting his own stamp on the judicial branch of government. On the domestic front, Jefferson gave more than lip service to his dictum, "That government is best which governs least." The one exception to his reining in of the federal establishment was the pivotal Louisiana Purchase, an eventuality not explicitly authorized by the Constitution. In foreign affairs, Jefferson, having now lost some of his ardor for the French Republic, tried to bring both France and Great Britain into a more acceptable posture toward to the United States. And, unlike Adams, Jefferson did win a second term, giving him the opportunity to put a Jeffersonian stamp on the still malleable nation.

❧ The Election and Jefferson's First Inaugural

As distinct from the Federalists, who never wanted to get too close to the masses, the Republicans — although not Jefferson himself — campaigned with an almost modern vigor. They also depended on the "Democratic-Republican Societies," which had arisen in the mid-1790s among friends of the French Revolution and admirers of Thomas Jefferson. In 1800, these grassroots organizations could function as local headquarters of the Jefferson-for-President movement. Federalists dismissed the membership of these clubs as "butchers, tinkers, broken hucksters, and trans-Atlantic traitors." The last phrase indicated the Federalist conviction that these groups imitated the radical Jacobin clubs of Paris, but, in fact, they also had roots in such homegrown popular precedents as the Regulators in North Carolina and the Sons of Liberty in Massachusetts. Far broader than these societies, however, Republican campaigning spread to the marketplace and the fields,

to city centers and village crossroads. Another Federalist reported with disgust that "Every threshing floor, every husking, every party work on a house-frame or raising a building, the very funerals are infected with bawlers or whisperers against government." But the bawlers and whisperers proved the practical political wisdom of getting and staying close to the people.

DEADLOCK

The victory of the Jefferson-Burr "ticket" clearly showed the geographical division of the two parties. New England went solidly for the Federalists, and the South — except for North Carolina and Maryland — went just as solidly for the Republicans. The middle states followed no simple pattern: New York fell into the Republican column, New Jersey and Delaware into the Federalist column, while Pennsylvania split almost evenly (8 votes for the Republicans, 7 for the Federalists). The relatively narrow margin of the Republican victory (73 to 65) was wider in the House races of 1800 where Republicans won 66 seats to only 40 for the Federalists. But the margin of victory did not grip the public's attention so much as the perplexing tie in Electoral College votes between Thomas Jefferson and Aaron Burr. Each man received 73 votes. Which one should be president?

That was a question for the House of Representatives to settle, if it could. And if it could not, then some officer in the federal government might be designated a temporary president until another election was held. Such a course of action would paralyze the country for many months; as it turned out, government virtually ground to a halt anyway in December and January. The whole awkward situation was not anticipated because one elector from South Carolina was supposed to cast a vote for George Clinton of New York instead of Burr. That would have brought Burr in at 72 votes to Jefferson's 73, thus avoiding the entire crisis and making runner-up

---

❋   **IN THEIR OWN WORDS**

Jefferson's First Inaugural Address, 1801

Let us then, fellow citizens, unite with one heart and mind; let us restore to social intercourse that harmony and affection without which liberty and even life itself are but dreary things. And let us reflect that, having banished from our land that religious intolerance under which mankind so long bled and suffered, we have yet gained little, if we countenance a political intolerance, as despotic, as wicked, and as capable of as bitter and bloody persecutions. During the throes and convulsions of the ancient world, during the agonizing spasms of infuriated man, seeking through blood and slaughter his long-lost liberty, it was not wonderful [surprising] that the agitation of the billows should reach even this distant and peaceful shore; that this should be more felt and feared by some, and less by others, and should divide opinions as to measures of safety; but every difference of opinion is not a difference of principle.

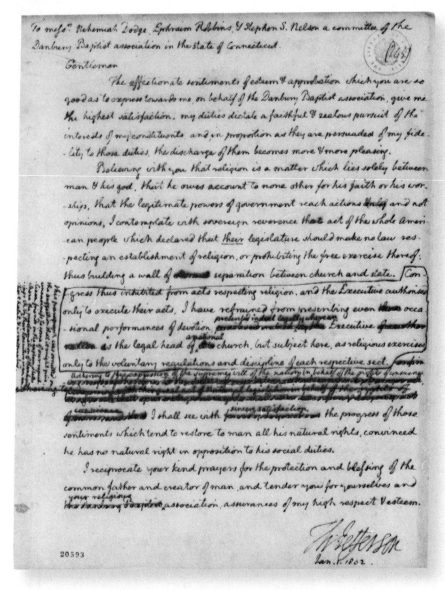

Jefferson's "Wall of Separation" In 1802 Thomas Jefferson wrote this letter to the Danbury Baptist Association, supporting their assertion of religious freedom in a state — Connecticut — that still officially established the Congregational Church. "Believing with you that religion is a matter which lies solely between man & his god," Jefferson wrote, "that he owes account to none other for his faith or his worship, that the legitimate powers of government should reach actions only and not opinions, I contemplate with sovereign reverence that act of the whole American people which declared that *their* legislature should make no law respecting an establishment of religion or prohibiting the free exercise thereof, thus building a wall of separation between church and state."

dent. Most Federalists preferred Burr, if only to spite Jefferson. But one influential Federalist — who else but Hamilton? — argued for Jefferson. Although he despised Jefferson, he despised Burr even more. Damning with faint praise, Hamilton opined: "Jefferson is to be preferred. He is by far not so dangerous a man, and he has pretensions to character." Adams too, though he largely stayed out of the fray, despaired over the prospect that Burr, this "dexterous gentleman," might rise "like a balloon filled with inflammable air."

The electoral votes were officially counted on February 11, 1801. At this point, the House of Representatives, still controlled by the Federalists, could begin its task of deciding between the two men. The vote would be by states, of which there were now sixteen. The Republican states would vote for Jefferson, the Federalist states — despite Hamilton — for Burr. And the count was eight states for Jefferson, six for Burr, and two delegations divided and therefore not voting. Jefferson had only half the states — not the required majority. For six days, and through thirty-five ballots, the House tallied the same monotonous results. Finally, on the thirty-sixth ballot, the Federalists in the divided delegations of Vermont and Maryland abstained, thus giving the Republican Representatives in those states the opportunity to cast their votes for Jefferson. South Carolina and Delaware turned in blank ballots, leaving Burr with only four New England states. This brought Jefferson's number of states to ten and the requisite majority was at hand. Finally, on February 17, only two weeks before the inauguration, Jefferson was named president-elect. Like Adams in 1796, it did not seem the best of beginnings.

DIFFERENCES BETWEEN ADAMS AND JEFFERSON

In those many weeks of uncertainty, Jefferson had the confidence (or optimism) to consider what he would say

Burr the vice president. But for reasons unknown, the elector failed to do what was expected of him.

As soon as the tie between Jefferson and Burr became public knowledge, political maneuvering began. Most Republicans assumed that the "ticket" meant that Jefferson would become president and Burr vice presi-

to the nation when, and if, he were chosen as its third president. The sentiments that divided Republicans from Federalists were already well known. While Jefferson would be loyal to his supporters, he would not exile or disparage his opponents. The differences between Adams and Jefferson had, however, become personal as well as philosophical. Adams preferred to talk of the glories of the past, as in the republic of ancient Rome or the vision of early Puritanism; Jefferson preferred to talk about the promise of the future, as in the optimism of the Enlightenment and the emancipation of reason. Jefferson later noted that the two parties viewed progress very differently, the party of reform seeing no limit to the horizons of the human mind. "The enemies of reform, on the other hand," Jefferson wrote, "denied improvement, and advocated steady adherence to the principles, practices and institutions of our fathers, which they represented as the consummation of wisdom and acme of excellence, beyond which the human mind could never advance."

In the realm of religion, the two men also differed sharply. Adams preferred to cultivate ties between the government and churches; Jefferson wanted to sever them. Adams as president declared national days of fasting and of prayer; Jefferson as president left such matters to the clergy, not the politicians. Adams cultivated the clergy and curried their favor. Jefferson, on the other hand, was depicted by Federalists as atheist, infidel, and arch-demon determined to destroy all religion.

Jefferson was, to be sure, the enemy of all efforts to enforce religious conformity. State-protected religion, he had written in 1787, had only one effect: to make "one half the world fools, and the other half hypocrites." Jefferson was no atheist and Adams no Calvinist, but their approaches to and attitudes toward religious structures did set them apart in 1800. Adams's political strength lay in New England, and it was just there that Jefferson found the most powerful alliance between church and state. Congregationalism remained the official religion of Connecticut and Massachusetts, and Congregational clergy — Jefferson was convinced — still harbored ambitions to create a national church. For all their tactical differences, however, in the realm of religious ideas, both Jefferson and Adams were deists. They emphasized the role of reason in religion, questioned the divinity of Jesus and the Christian doctrine of the Trinity, and devalued the authority of revelation and miracles.

A PEACEFUL TRANSFER OF POWER

On March 4, 1801, the new capital city of Washington heard its first inaugural address. Intending to make a statement both in his dress and his demeanor, Jefferson walked to the inauguration wearing a plain black suit. He presented himself as the simple Virginia farmer, acceding to the wishes of the people — not a king to be crowned with pomp and parade. And after his speech, he walked to the boarding house where meals were served, sat at the foot of the table, and took no notice of status or rank, neither his nor that of others around the table. America should set itself on a deliberately different course from the monarchies of Europe.

Those attending the inaugural probably appreciated the speech more in the reading than in the hearing of it, for Jefferson, like his two predecessors, was no spellbinding orator. He was, however, a spellbinding and gifted writer. Calling for wholeness in the troubled body politic, as had Adams and Washington before him, Jefferson urged his fellow citizens to "unite with one heart and one mind." "We have called by different names brethren of the same principle. We are all Republicans; we are all Federalists." Then, with one eye cast on the hated Sedition Act, he added: "If there be any among us who wish to dissolve this Union, or to change its republican form, let them stand undisturbed as monuments of the safety with which error of opinion may be tolerated, where reason is left free to combat it."

Jefferson noted with gratitude that the nation, thus far, had been spared direct involvement in Europe's nearly incessant wars. America, he said, was "kindly separated by nature and a wide ocean from the exterminating havoc of one quarter of the globe." He clearly hoped that this removal from European strife would continue, as the nation maintained "honest friendship with all nations" but rejected "entangling alliances." Indeed, nature had so richly blessed the United States that it had all the ingredients for great happiness ahead. The nation now needed only "a wise and frugal government, which shall restrain men from injuring one another, shall leave them otherwise free to regulate their own pursuits of industry and improvement, and shall not take from the mouth of labor the bread it has earned."

In crisp and compact language, Jefferson laid out what he believed to be the "essential principles of our government." He emphasized the role of the states as "the surest bulwarks against antirepublican tendencies," but he also honored and staunchly defended "the preservation of the general government in its constitutional vigor, as the sheet anchor of our peace at home and safety abroad." Rights and liberties fought for in the American Revolution, and freedoms guaranteed in the Bill of Rights, were no less precious in 1801.

John Adams heard none of these words, having left town early that morning, bound for his quiet home in Massachusetts. But this first real transfer of power was peaceful: no heads rolled, no troops were mustered, no blood was shed. In marked contrast to what was happening in France at the end of the century, the United States allowed the machinery of government to operate as the framers had foreseen or, at least, had hoped.

The "revolution" of 1800, as Jefferson himself had called it, did not reach everyone. In his own state of Virginia, Gabriel, a slave and legally the property of a plantation owner, in 1800 planned a general slave uprising in and around Richmond. Perhaps as many as five thousand slaves knew of the plot, but only a fraction of that number armed themselves and prepared to revolt. Before their elaborate plans could be carried out authorities learned of the plot and arrested its leaders. Twenty were executed, with the sentences of the Henrico court monotonously repeated: "[The Court] sentences Will, a negro man slave, the property of John Mosby, Senior, of Henrico, to death on charge of conspiracy and insurrection, and orders that he be hung on the 12th [September] at the usual place of execution." Slaves in particular, African Americans in general, watched the Jeffersonian revolution from afar, not participants in its vibrant optimism and only tardily heirs to its promise.

✥ John Marshall Leads the Supreme Court

The night before leaving town, John Adams made several appointments to the federal and other courts in the District of Columbia, the so-called "midnight appointments." The Federalists had lost the presidency and lost their majorities in Congress; but, reasoned Adams, they should not lose the judiciary too. Two weeks earlier, the Federalist Congress had passed the Judiciary Act of 1801, among other provisions creating twenty-three new federal judgeships. With alacrity Adams proceeded to offer nominees for these positions so that the outgoing Senate could confirm them before it expired on March 4. These appointments, together with the last-minute recommendations for the District, stacked the courts with Jefferson's enemies. And Jefferson did not look kindly upon his former friend's action. The nominees, he noted, "were from my most ardent political enemies, from whom no faithful cooperation could ever be expected. . . . It seemed but common justice to leave a successor free to act by instruments of his own choice." Much of Adams's hurried appointment of "midnight judges" was undone the very next year

when a Republican Congress repealed the act of 1801. With their offices abolished, those who had briefly held them were abruptly turned out.

One appointment of Adams, however, endured throughout Jefferson's two terms and far beyond: John Marshall, the new chief justice of the Supreme Court. A distant kinsman of Jefferson's and a fellow Virginian, John Marshall was a Federalist. He and Jefferson, therefore, were political opponents, and while that made life more difficult for the president, it did help to establish the judiciary as an independent branch of government. Marshall's tenure on the Court was so long (from 1801 to 1835), and his leadership so firm that he left it a far different institution than he found it.

A former soldier in the Revolutionary War, Marshall returned to Virginia to practice law. Financially, he married well and politically he was soon identified as the leading Federalist in Virginia. In 1800 he accepted appointment as Adams's secretary of state. A year later, when Chief Justice Oliver Ellsworth resigned from the Court, Adams offered the position first to John Jay, who declined, and then to John Marshall, who accepted. Adams had apparently considered some older men, but he decided that the Federalists needed someone who could look after their cause for years to come. At the age of forty-five, Marshall fit the bill nicely.

A personable and persuasive figure, with a reputation for conviviality and ready humor, Marshall brought the other justices wholly within his orbit. He spoke for the Court, literally, handing down a long succession of mostly unanimous opinions. Justices lived outside Washington except during the Court's relatively brief sessions. Then they lived in rooming houses, often the same one, giving them a kind of off-bench unity as well as while they were sitting. Under Marshall's guidance, the Court maintained a Federalist line: curb the power of the states and magnify the authority of the national government; protect private property and money interests; and make the Court permanently strong. Marshall accomplished this feat not in a single stroke, but virtually so in the celebrated case of *Marbury v. Madison*, decided in 1803.

William Marbury, a justice of the peace in Washington, was one of Adams's "midnight judges." James Madison served as Jefferson's secretary of state. Marbury, along with three other justices, sued Madison when he refused to give them their duly signed (by Adams) commissions of appointment — normally a formality falling within the secretary of state's purview. It was a minor case, but the Supreme Court agreed to hear it — much to Jefferson's irritation. Marshall faced a tough dilemma: if he ruled against Madison, his decision might be defied; if he ruled against Marbury, he weakened the orderly operations of the national government. Marshall found an excellent way out that did not defy Jefferson, without diminishing the Court.

To the question, Did Marbury deserve to receive his commission? the answer was "yes." To the further question, Can the laws of the Congress come to his rescue? the answer was also "yes." But to the question, Can the Court offer him remedy? the answer was "no." The reason for the negative was that the Judiciary Act of 1789 had extended the jurisdiction of the Supreme Court beyond that stated in the Constitution. Therefore, (1) the law in question was in part unconstitutional, (2) the case could not properly be heard by the Court, and (3) the Court could render no final verdict on the matter. Marshall denied one power to the Court but asserted a far greater one: the right of *judicial review*. Henceforth, the Constitution would stand as the supreme law of the land, and the Supreme Court would be the final authority on what that document said and, even more importantly, what it meant.

❧ *Economics and Politics at Home*

In his First Inaugural, Jefferson spoke of a "wise and frugal" government. Frugality he emphasized by cutting costs and eliminating offices; wisdom he sought through careful appointments and prudent policies. His two most important cabinet choices were his fast friend, James Madison, as secretary of state, and Swiss immigrant Albert Gallatin as secretary of treasury. Both men gave Jefferson solid and significant service throughout his two terms. Levi Lincoln held the office of attorney general only during Jefferson's first term, but proved both able as a lawyer and supportive as a politician.

Jefferson began his governmental frugality with his own personal lifestyle. Instead of moving about Washington in a coach with six or eight horses, he rode horseback, generally alone. He disdained fancy clothes, dinners, and lofty titles. His predecessors wore wigs and worried about protocol; he did not. By 1801, even such modest titles as "master" and "servant" no longer seemed suitable to a republic in which all citizens could advance themselves through hard work and honest effort. Contemporaries noted that Americans now spoke of the "help." Clothing no longer would designate rank, and if ordinary people wanted and could afford to wear silk, gold, and lace (forbidden by colonial sumptuary

laws), then let them do so. Officers of government now abandoned knickers in the style of the English aristocracy, instead wearing long pants in the style of French workingmen. (Federalist John Marshall was a conspicuous exception.) Women, except for a few dedicated Federalists, forsook corsets and cut their hair. The British minister was offended to be received by President Jefferson attired "in slippers down at the heels, and both pantaloons, coat and underclothes indicative of an indifference to appearance."

Economy was, of course, more than manners. Cost-cutting, the president believed, was essential not just to balance the budget but to rid the nation of the debt that corrupted its politics and reduced the power of its government. Jefferson restricted the number of positions in the executive department and urged Congress to abolish public offices under their jurisdiction. He trimmed foreign missions back to a mere three: Britain, France, and Spain. In eliminating the hated excise taxes, such as had provoked the Whiskey Rebellion, he also eliminated the even more despised tax collectors. He could not immediately cut the standing army, but he notified Congress that he intended to rely on the state militias as the first line of defense, which in an emergency could hold until "regulars" were recruited and armed. Moreover, the Republican president argued that a standing army in peacetime was neither "needful [n]or safe." Jefferson reduced the number of sailors, sold some of the ships, and stopped construction of others. The United States needed only enough of a navy, he said, to defend the American shores or perhaps make a preemptive strike against insolent pirates. America, in Jefferson's view, must not aspire to be a great sea power like England or France.

Jefferson had serious reservations about keeping Hamilton's national bank, but Secretary Gallatin persuaded him that it would be convenient and useful to do so. Gallatin played an even more determinative role in retiring the national debt. When Jefferson took office, the public debt stood at around $83 million, and Gallatin conceived of a plan to retire that debt within sixteen years, chiefly through the sale of western lands and the collection of import duties. By the end of Jefferson's first term, the federal treasury had a surplus of $1 million. A cherished Jeffersonian principle held that one generation had no right to bind posterity. If one generation carelessly accumulated a large public debt, those that followed were subjected to fiscal servitude. "By the law of nature," Jefferson asserted, "one generation is to another as one independent nation is to another."

The issue of political patronage rendered Jefferson perplexed and indecisive. Presumably a change of parties would mean a change of personnel — everywhere. Legally, however, not all offices were open to presidential plucking. Politically, Jefferson still wanted to "rise above party" where possible, though his moderation angered many of the Republican faithful. Moreover, Jefferson still bristled at all the appointments that Adams made after he knew of his defeat. He would, so he explained to James Monroe, remove all Federalist leaders from office, but those serving quietly in the ranks could stay until they vacated their office, either by death or by resignation — though he was disappointed that resignations were few and deaths none. Loyal Republicans Charles Pinckney of South Carolina and Robert Livingston of New York won appointments as minister to Spain and France, respectively; but beyond that Jefferson came under intense pressure to increase his pace of removal of Federalists. Demands from New Jersey and Delaware were, he said, "moder-

ately importunate," and in Pennsylvania he was told of serious discontent. He looked forward to the day when he could ask regarding potential candidates for office only three questions: "Is he honest? Is he capable? Is he faithful to the Constitution?"

The despised Alien and Sedition Acts of the previous administration had been written to expire in 1801 — cleverly, so that a hostile new administration would not have the opportunity to use them against its Federalist political opponents. When the expiration date arrived, the Jeffersonians allowed them simply to lapse. Jefferson even saw to it that the Republican editors who had been convicted under the Sedition Act were discharged from prison, and he supported the refunding of their fines. Jefferson worked with Congress carefully on this and many other matters, proving himself to be a master of persuasion. He held regular informal dinners for the Republican legislators, many of whom were or became good friends. Under such winsome leadership, Congress gave his domestic agenda its benign blessing.

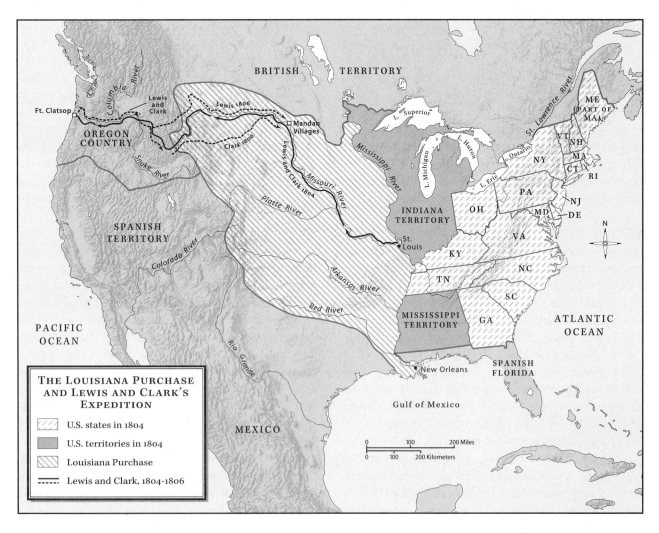

THE LOUISIANA PURCHASE AND LEWIS AND CLARK'S EXPEDITION

- U.S. states in 1804
- U.S. territories in 1804
- Louisiana Purchase
- Lewis and Clark, 1804-1806

That leadership outwitted the Federalists at every turn. They grew steadily weaker, ever more regional, ever more remote from the people. To the extent that they had any power, it was in New England where, in their utter frustration, they periodically threatened to secede. New Englanders even involved Jefferson's vice president (and presidential rival), Aaron Burr, in a plot to include New York in the secession. Hamilton learned of Burr's collusion, exposed the scheme, and dashed Burr's hopes of becoming governor of New York. An enraged Burr challenged Hamilton to a duel that took place on July 11, 1804, in which Hamilton received a fatal wound.

The Republicans, finding themselves scarcely opposed, began to quarrel, dividing into factions associated with a dominant individual or a forgotten principle. Some, deciding that "party" was not such a great idea after all, vowed to listen to the still small voice of conscience (or idiosyncrasy) and to no one else. Still others waited for an opportunity to make league with disgruntled Federalists on some issue or other. Still, Jefferson's leadership went unchallenged and his popularity undiminished. He had stopped listening to Burr as early as 1802, so he was in no danger of being betrayed by a man whom he no longer trusted. "I never thought him an honest, frank-dealing man," Jefferson later wrote, but considered him as "a crooked gun . . . whose aim or shot you could never be sure of."

Domestically, Jefferson's administration reached the pinnacle of success in the Louisiana Purchase in 1803. No accomplishment enhanced his presidency more, and nothing else so radically changed the history of his country.

✥ *The Louisiana Purchase and the West*

The admission of Ohio to the Union in 1803 gave ample testimony that America's interest in the West was both steady and strong. The Old Northwest, east of the Mississippi and north of the Ohio River, was now beginning to acquire a white population as relations with the Indians and the British permitted. But the Mississippi River, as a political boundary, was a great barrier to westward migration, just as the waterway served as a great "highway" for the region west of the Allegheny Mountains. Americans living there viewed with special concern the matter of who controlled the port of New Orleans.

The vast Louisiana Territory, including New Orleans, had been France's pride in the interior of North America. But in 1762 France ceded it to Spain as com-

A Sketch from the West Meriwether Lewis covered pages and pages of his expedition journal with sketches and descriptions of the wildlife he observed in the West. This bird is just one fine example.

pensation for that ally's losses in the Seven Years' War. Napoleon Bonaparte's rise to power correspondingly revived visions of a great French overseas empire. Louisiana, named in honor of France's Louis XIV, seemed a logical place to begin imperial rebuilding. So Bonaparte persuaded Spain to cede the vast and hard-to-defend American wilderness territory to France. Preliminary terms were agreed to in 1800, although the transfer did not become official until the fall of 1802.

Jefferson feared the change, for it put a power much more ominous than Spain in control of New Orleans. Although France, said Jefferson, had hitherto been our "natural friend," its occupation of New Orleans and threat to Mississippi shipping made that friend now a natural enemy. "The produce of three-eighths of our territory must pass to market" through New Orleans,

Jefferson observed, and nothing must be allowed to obstruct it. If Jefferson could not prevent the transfer, perhaps he could neutralize some of its impact by buying West Florida and New Orleans from the French. After Congress appropriated $2 million for this purpose, Jefferson dispatched James Monroe of Virginia to join the American minister to Paris, Robert R. Livingston, to discuss such a deal with the French. Jefferson authorized his negotiators to go as high as $10 million, if necessary. But, he added, if the talks broke down, the United States would have no choice but to turn to Britain to help keep the French in check.

The talks did not break down, but they took a wildly unpredictable turn when Charles Maurice de Talleyrand-Perigord, the French diplomat, asked the Americans if the United States would be interested in buying *all* of Louisiana. Livingston and Monroe could hardly believe what they were hearing. When they recovered sufficiently from the shock, they began discussing terms, ultimately arriving at a figure of about $15 million for land that would double the size of the United States. The purchase price worked out to about three cents an acre, at a time when the federal government was charging settlers in the Old Northwest two dollars an acre.

Why did France sell? Bonaparte's troops had failed to put down a slave uprising in Haiti; the attempt was costing him dearly, and Louisiana might cost him more. Besides, he now needed more money to rebuild his army and prepare for the new war with Britain he was planning. Bonaparte wished neither to drive America into the arms of the British nor to go to war with the United States (or even the aroused and belligerent westerners) to defend his distant wilderness. Thus a combination of motives — for the United States, a happy combination — led Bonaparte to move quickly. On April 30, 1803, Livingston and Monroe, exceeding their instructions, signed on behalf of the United States an agreement to buy some 800,000 square miles of land. Livingston commented that this, "the noblest work of our whole lives," would enable the United States to move into the first rank of world powers.

News of the purchase set the western settlers to rejoicing in the summer of 1803. Kentuckians, worried that the United States might be too weak to defend "their" river and "their" port, had even considered raising a vigilante army to "free" New Orleans, although the realists among them admitted that, without a genuine army or navy, their cause was doomed. Not now, however. Suddenly the president had become in their eyes

"The Immortal Jefferson."

Jefferson, the strict constructionist of earlier days, now found himself obliged to do something not specifically authorized by the Constitution. It would be possible, of course, to amend the Constitution to make explicit the president's authority to purchase new territory, but such a process would take months if not years. He could find refuge in the "general welfare" clause or in the power to make treaties, or he could think of pushing through an amendment after the fact. But now was the time to act, before the French ruler changed his mind. Now was not the time, said Jefferson, to get hung up on "metaphysical subtleties."

But Federalists, formerly advocates of a loose construction of the Constitution, now became the strict constructionists. One New England Federalist grumbled that "we are to give money of which we have too little for land of which we already have too much." Another complained about paying any amount for a "great waste, a wilderness unpeopled with any beings except wolves and wandering Indians." What troubled the New Englanders most was that this sudden expansion of "the West" would necessarily come at the political expense of "the East." New England would witness the gradual erosion of its influence in national affairs.

But a bargain was a bargain, and this one was simply too good to pass up. The treaty officially reached American shores in July 1803, and the following October the Senate ratified it by a lopsided vote of 26 to 6. What, exactly, had the United States bought?

EXPLORING THE WEST

Even while Louisiana was still in foreign hands, Jefferson, a man of enormous intellectual curiosity and scientific interest, had persuaded Congress to appropriate funds to explore all the way to the Pacific Ocean. This expedition, Jefferson assured Spain, France, and Britain, was not motivated by territorial ambitions: its purposes were strictly geographical and scientific. In 1803 Jefferson appointed his private secretary, Meriwether Lewis, to head the trek, to be assisted by another Virginia neighbor, William Clark. The secretary of war supplied Lewis and Clark with equipment and provisions, as well as volunteers from the army to help explore and, if need be, defend the expeditionary corps, which eventually grew to about fifty. The leaders carried French and English passports that "will entitle you to the friendly aid of any traders of that allegiance with whom you may happen to meet."

Jefferson's detailed instructions to Lewis and Clark

revealed the president's questing mind. The men were to observe all flora and fauna and to take notes (with illustrations, if possible) of what they saw. Jefferson added that "Your observations are to be taken with great pains & accuracy, to be entered distinctly & intelligibly for others as well as yourself." Many copies should be made, so that if one set were lost or captured, another might survive. All encounters with Native Americans should be as friendly as possible: "allay all jealousies as to the object of your journey, satisfy them of its innocence." In urging Lewis and Clark to take extensive notes on the various tribes they met, Jefferson made the expedition one of ethnology, as well as of geography, botany, zoology, soil science, and even astronomy.

Of course, the expedition had serious political and military purposes as well. First, territorial claims needed to be established for as much of the West as possible. Second, that old lure of a northwest passage to the Pacific, with all its commercial possibilities, continued to attract. Third, a U.S. presence in the Pacific Northwest would keep Britain and the Hudson Bay Company in check — or at least under closer observation. Above all, mapping the West would make that vast region accessible for future settlement and territorial expansion.

From Pittsburgh, the explorers first made their way to St. Louis late in 1803, then ascended the Missouri River north to the Dakotas. Turning westward, Lewis and Clark crossed the Rockies, ultimately joining the Columbia River and descending its course until they at last sighted the Pacific. "Ocian in view! O! the joy," rhapsodized Clark in uncertain spelling. In their twenty-six-month march, they had been immeasurably aided by a French trader's Indian wife, Sacagawea, who served as interpreter and, when necessary, negotiator. Returning along a similar route, the expedition reached St. Louis in September 1806, three years after setting out.

Politically and scientifically, the Lewis and Clark expedition had been an unqualified success. Although it would take years for all of the *Journals* to be published and for their information to be absorbed, the American public could begin to think of that unknown wilderness as now their own. And Thomas Jefferson could plant seeds at his beloved home, Monticello, that Meriwether Lewis had carefully gathered along the way.

Jefferson sent another explorer, Zebulon Pike, into the West in 1805 and 1806 — first up the Mississippi in search of its source, then up the Arkansas River to present-day Colorado. (The name Pike's Peak there testifies to the unsuccessful effort to reach the top.) Pike also pushed into New Mexico where uneasy Spanish authorities brought Pike and his followers into Santa Fe under arrest. Pike persuaded his interrogators that his interests, like those of Lewis and Clark, were geographical, not political.

BURR'S TRIAL FOR TREASON

Aaron Burr's interests in the West, however, were decidedly political. Exactly what direction (or directions) they took was less clear. The vice president, having fled New York to escape justice following his killing of Hamilton, went south and then west. The newly acquired West, not yet fully bound into the Union, seemed ripe for plucking — by somebody. Maybe in collusion with Spain, Burr could promote a separate government with himself at its head. Or with France. Or with England. Or with the unscrupulous commander of the U.S. Army, James Wilkinson. Himself a master of deceit and intrigue, Wilkinson for years had plotted with Spain for his own advancement and enrichment in the West. He and Burr were natural allies. But when Burr was about to be exposed, Wilkinson decided to turn against him and support a charge of treason. When Jefferson learned of all this, he commented that "Burr's enterprise is the most extraordinary since the days of Don Quixote. It is so extravagant that those who know his understanding would not believe it if the proofs admitted doubt."

Having been tried and acquitted in territorial courts, Burr was brought to Richmond in 1807 to be tried for treason before Chief Justice John Marshall, sitting as a circuit judge. Since Jefferson so desperately wanted Burr to be found guilty, his nemesis Marshall hewed to the narrowest possible definition of treason, and found the evidence insufficient for conviction. He so instructed the jury, which not surprisingly concluded that Aaron Burr "is not proved to be guilty." For some years, Burr lived abroad, returning to New York in 1812 to spend the rest of his days, more or less quietly, in legal practice. Burr, having failed in domestic politics, failed in foreign intrigue as well. He even failed in his marriage; when in his eighties, his wife divorced him on the charge of adultery.

THE TRIUMPH OF JEFFERSONIAN POLITICS

Jefferson's victory for his second term was more impressive than in 1800. In fact, it demonstrated the perilous state of the Federalist Party as Jefferson tallied 162 electoral votes to Charles Pinckney's 14. Jefferson's choice as vice president, George Clinton of New York,

A View of the Rockies   Lewis and Clark's expedition fueled American interest in the West, which only grew as more expeditions generated romantic images of rugged vistas like this one.

represented the anti-Burr faction in that state. This time, no question arose as to who should be president and who should have the second office. For the Twelfth Amendment (adopted in September 1804) clarified a previously murky situation by requiring electors to vote for a president and a vice president. From that year on, presidents had this much power at least: they could name their own vice president.

For the next twenty years, the Jeffersonian party would control the presidency. This long-term party control reinforced the Jeffersonian impact on America. The Federalist Party, on the other hand, virtually retreated from the national scene, surviving only in New England. Their opposition to the Jefferson embargo of 1807 (see below) gave the Federalists some new life, but their resuscitation was temporary. Not until Andrew Jackson in the 1830s, did a vigorous two-party system reappear in American politics.

✥ To the Shores of Tripoli — and Beyond

Beyond fretting about Aaron Burr, Jefferson also was burdened by troubles with foreign powers. The Barbary pirates, who controlled the mainland of northwest Af-

rica and menaced shipping in the Mediterranean, made an excellent living raiding the commerce of any country — including the United States — that did not pay them tribute. Jefferson found this bribery offensive, degrading, and costly, and he was even more outraged when the Pasha of Tripoli cut down the American flag in front of the nation's consulate. Insisting that national honor be satisfied, Jefferson dispatched a naval fleet to Tripoli in 1801 and, after years of negotiation, in 1805 wrung from the reluctant ruler the concession that tribute would no longer be demanded from American commercial vessels sailing in what he claimed as his territorial waters. It was a minor international incident, but it — along with much later settlements with the other Barbary States of Algiers, Tunis, and Morocco — increased visibility and respect for the United States abroad. It also honored Jefferson's careful monetary calculation: sending the navy cost money, but in the long run that cost less than paying off the Pasha, year after year.

France's declaration of war against Britain in 1805 presented more serious problems. Once again the task was not to decide between the two warring parties but to stay aloof from both. American traffic on the high seas increased sharply as England and France locked in combat. Much of the increase in American shipping came at the expense of the British, who determined to stop it by forbidding goods from being shipped from

Meriwether Lewis to Thomas Jefferson

Dear Sir.
 Fort Mandan [North Dakota],
April 7th 1805
 Herewith inclosed you will receive an invoice of certain articles which I have forwarded to you from this place. Among other articles, you will observe by reference to the invoice, 67 specimens of earth, salts and minerals; and 60 specimens of plants;

these are accompanyed by their respective labels expressing the days on which obtained, places where found, and also their virtues and properties when known. . . . These have been forwarded with a view of their being presented to the Philosophical Society of Philadelphia, in order that they may under their direction be examined or analyzed. After examining these specimens yourself, I would thank you to have a copy of their labels made out, and retained until my return. The other

articles are intended particularly for yourself, to be retained, or disposed off as you may think proper.
 You will also receive herewith inclosed a part of Capt. Clark's private journal, the other part you will find inclosed in a separate tin box. This journal is in it's original state. . . . Captain Clark dose not wish this journal exposed in it's present state, but has no objection that one or more copies of it be made . . . correcting it's grammatical errors &c.

the West Indies directly to France. The British rule did permit ships that unloaded West Indian goods at an American port and at least theoretically paid duty to sail on to France. However, in the notable case of the *Essex* in 1805, the British Court of Appeals ruled that so-called "broken voyages" like this were actually continuous voyages violating an old international rule that trade that was not open in time of peace could not be permitted in time of war.

To this financial blow, the British added a psychological blow by boarding American ships on the high seas and forcibly taking any Englishman, or anyone who they thought might be English, to serve on their own undermanned ships. This practice of "impressment" was seen as insolence to the highest degree, an insolence hardly softened by the fact that many British sailors preferred service on American commercial vessels to the harsher service in the Royal Navy. If thousands of Americans were impressed into British service, it was — Britain responded — only because tens of thousands of English sailors had deserted, often with the encouragement of American captains.

Jefferson tried diplomacy, sending a special commission of James Monroe and William Pinkney to make concessions that would induce Britain to give up the hated business of impressment. Britain would not budge. Jefferson's emissaries came home with a treaty the president found so unsatisfactory that he would not even submit it to the Senate.

Then on June 22, 1807, the British illegally, and without permission, boarded the American frigate, the *Chesapeake*, to retrieve four sailors who had deserted in Norfolk, Virginia. In the ensuing struggle, three Americans were killed and eighteen wounded. Ameri-

can pride was more than wounded. "Never since the battle of Lexington," Jefferson declared, "have I seen this country in such a state of exasperation." The British, he added, "have often enough, God knows, given us cause of war before; but it has been on points which would not have united the nation. But now they have touched a chord which vibrates in every heart."

What would the choice be: national humiliation or war? The first was unthinkable, the second almost inevitable. But the nation needed more time, Jefferson strongly believed — time to grow stronger in population, in produce, in financial resources. Jefferson took what seemed like the only way off the horns of a harsh dilemma. In December of 1807 he persuaded Congress to pass the Embargo Act, which prohibited the export of almost all goods from the United States; this, Jefferson argued, would injure both belligerents, but especially Britain, which was more dependent on goods from abroad.

The embargo backfired terribly. It hurt American shipping cruelly, especially in New England, where it was called the "dambargo." So devastating were its results that it threatened to bring the moribund Federalist party back to life. "The Immortal Jefferson" in four short years became "You Infernal Villain." Federalists complained that the Embargo Act was like "cutting one's throat to cure the nosebleed." On the Fourth of July New Englanders sang a song that included this stanza:

> *Our ships, all in motion,*
> *Once whitened the ocean,*
> *They sail'd and returned with a cargo;*
> *Now doomed to decay*
> *They have fallen a prey*
> *To Jefferson, worms, and Embargo.*

Unemployed American sailors now joined the British crews, mitigating the impressment problem but not in the way Jefferson envisioned. Smugglers evaded the force of the act, especially by sending goods through Canada. France showed no gratitude for the hardships imposed on England, but instead seized American ships in French ports on the hollow pretext that they must be British ships in disguise. Nothing worked. Fifteen months after the embargo was passed, Jefferson signed its repeal. "Peaceable coercion" had avoided war, although that would have been a more popular course of action. Unhappily, it only postponed war with England from Jefferson's administration to that of his successor, James Madison.

THE JEFFERSONIAN LEGACY

Though never quite becoming the American icon that George Washington did, likenesses of Thomas Jefferson appeared on medals, in waxworks, innumerable etchings, and paintings; in statuary, and even on Liverpool potter ware. Europeans joined Americans in giving artistic honor to America's third president. His home in Monticello eventually became a national shrine, and the Jefferson Memorial in Washington, D.C. (dedicated by Franklin D. Roosevelt in 1943), today draws visitors by the tens of thousands. Yet what he left to the nation has much more to do with his ideas, compromises, and political philosophy than with monuments and images.

✣ Art and Architecture

Jefferson was both a patron of the arts and a contributor to artistic development. His years in France honed an already keen aesthetic sense as he collected, observed, sketched, and stimulated his fellow citizens to move toward cultural sophistication. His first library contained many books on painting, sculpture, architecture, and theories of aesthetics, and when he went to Paris in 1785 his mind was well stocked and his eye well trained.

Meeting France's noted sculptor, Jean-Antoine Houdon, Jefferson quickly concluded that this must be the artist to create the statue of George Washington authorized by the state of Virginia. He brought home from Paris in 1789 seven of Houdon's plaster portrait busts, including one of himself. Most of these ended up at Monticello, which began to resemble an art museum with original paintings (both European and American),

silver, marble, and porcelain objects gathered in Paris, and highest quality examples of French craftmanship. With some enthusiasm, Jefferson wrote during his first year in Paris: "Were I to proceed to tell you how much I enjoy their architecture, sculpture, painting, music, I should want words. It is in these arts they shine."

Jefferson's contributions in architecture laid the foundation for a greater appreciation for quality and style among his fellow citizens. When still in his twenties, Jefferson began constructing Monticello. Greatly influenced by the sixteenth-century Italian architect Andrea Palladio, Jefferson worked on his classical design for years, modifying or enlarging the building over most of his lifetime. He was so captivated by a small Roman temple in southern France (the Maison Carrée) that he quickly determined this should be the model for Virginia's state capitol in Richmond.

When it was agreed to build the new "Federal City" of Washington, D.C., Jefferson immediately suggested a French engineer and surveyor, Pierre Charles L'Enfant, to plan it — after models of great European capital cities. When L'Enfant withdrew from the project, Jefferson took over, designing the Mall and deciding on the locations of the Capitol and the executive mansion. When the time came to build the presidential residence, Jefferson anonymously entered the competition for its design. Though his plan was not selected, when he later moved into the structure he added the two porticoes and other elements to the structure. While president he also pushed architect Benjamin Latrobe to complete the imposing Capitol, which in its unfinished condition suggested some tentativeness to the life of the young republic itself.[5]

Jefferson's most stunning architectural achievement came in the last years of his life: the design of the University of Virginia in Charlottesville. He laid out the grounds of his "academical village," with close attention to classical motifs and obvious deference once more to the ideas of Palladio. The rotunda, initially the library and modeled after the Roman Pantheon, has been called "the greatest example of French visionary architecture in North America." State capitols across the country as well as other public buildings imitated Jefferson's striking rotunda design. Jefferson would have been remembered as one of America's great architects even if he had done nothing in any other field.

---

5. The Capitol was not finished, however, until Lincoln's administration. The completion of the dome despite the raging Civil War had symbolic implications that Lincoln understood as fully as Jefferson.

Jefferson's Wheel Cipher   Cryptography was one of Thomas Jefferson's many interests, and he designed this wheel cipher while serving as George Washington's secretary of state. Made up of twenty-six cylindrical wooden pieces on an iron spindle, it worked essentially like a combination lock, allowing words to be scrambled and unscrambled. Jefferson abandoned use of this cipher after 1802, but in the 1920s the United States Army developed one that was remarkably similar and used it until the beginning of World War II.

❧ Education and Science

"If a nation expects to be ignorant and free," Jefferson wrote in 1816, "it expects what never was and never will be." His commitment to education was virtually an obsession. Like other figures of the American Enlightenment, Jefferson fought strenuously to remove all shackles from the human mind. But if the mind were simply left free, and all paths to inquiry left open, with no disciplined pursuit of knowledge as a consequence, then the battle — though seemingly won — had been lost. The goal of education, said Jefferson's close friend, Benjamin Rush, was "to convert men into republican machines."

At every level of education, the South lagged behind New England in the eighteenth century. Conscious of Virginia's deficiencies, Jefferson introduced into the state legislature in 1779 a Bill for the More General Diffusion of Knowledge. He labored and lobbied hard for its passage, but his fellow Virginians found it too costly, or too egalitarian, or too ambitious. Jefferson envisioned a system of public education open to all free citizens, rich or poor, and set into a competitive frame that would allow the best students to be sent to a "grammar school" that, despite the name, was akin to a preparatory academy for higher education. The state must not neglect its finest resource, Jefferson argued, but avail itself of "those talents which Nature has sown as liberally among the poor as the rich, but which perish without use if not sought for and cultivated."

Jefferson's educational reform plan from the first half of his life failed, but the grand design of the second half of his life, the University of Virginia, succeeded magnificently. Back home in Monticello after retiring from the presidency, Jefferson decided to establish a public university that would be faithful to Enlightenment ideals and serve the needs of the new republic. At first he sought to make his own alma mater, the College of William and Mary, *the* state university, but only if his old college abandoned all ties to the Episcopal Church. When it refused, Jefferson started afresh with an entirely new institution that was very much a Jeffersonian creation.

Not theology and metaphysics, but science and the practical arts, were the foundation of the University of Virginia's curriculum. He determined the site, laid out the grounds,[6] designed the buildings, devised the courses, chose the faculty, raised the money, selected the books for the library, and even kept track of the construction by telescope from his hilltop home a few miles away. "Mr. Jefferson's University," it is still called.

Jefferson set the example for his university by being, if not a scientist in the strict sense, a man consumed with scientific curiosity and an abiding interest in the world around him. To a friend in 1791 he had described politics as his "duty," but science as his "passion." And to Pierre-Samuel du Pont de Nemours (the French entrepreneur who founded what is today the DuPont Corporation), he wrote in 1809: "Nature intended me for the tranquil pursuits of science by rendering them my supreme delight." "But," he added, "the enormities of the times in which I have lived, have forced me to . . . commit myself on the boisterous ocean of political passions." At Monticello he installed busts of the "three greatest thinkers" in the world: Francis Bacon, Isaac Newton, and John Locke.

Jefferson's one book, *Notes on the State of Virginia* (1787), gave more attention to scientific observations and the collection of data than to any other subject. Besides the state's flora and fauna, Jefferson described its geography, its rivers and streams, its climate (he kept temperature records at Monticello for over fifty years), its mountain ranges, and its natural resources. In his own scientific reflections, he borrowed from Europe where possible and applied his own creative genius where not. His inventions included a dumbwaiter (a small elevator for bringing wine from the cellar to the dining room), a great clock that indicated not only the time but also the days of the week, a revolving chair, a portable writing desk, and a machine that made du-

6. What is called the campus at every other American university is still known as "the grounds" at the University of Virginia.

Monticello Jefferson spent much of his lifetime and fortune designing, building, tearing down and rebuilding, and embellishing his home, Monticello, which crowns a low mountain overlooking Charlottesville, Virginia. It is the complete embodiment of Jefferson's exquisite artistic taste and innovative personality. Lacking any water source except rain collected from the roof and buckets and barrels that slaves lugged up from a spring at the foot of the mountain, it was also a wildly impractical place to build a home.

plicate copies as he wrote. To encourage gathering information about scientific developments abroad, Jefferson opposed placing tariffs on books and periodicals brought into the United States. And to encourage the dissemination of scientific information at home, he joined Franklin's American Philosophical Society in Philadelphia and served as its president from 1797 to 1815.

He collected scientific objects as he collected art: avidly. At Monticello he displayed fossil bones, wild animal heads, remarkable geological specimens, and a variety of cultural artifacts of Native American tribes. He launched the science of paleontology and promoted a uniform standard of weights and measures. Like his father before him, he acted as his own surveyor in projects that interested him; he made regular astronomical observations, and at one time even planned to build an observatory atop his "little mountain." With an ever-restless, ever-grasping mind, Thomas Jefferson, as scientist, would no doubt have preferred to go on the Lewis and Clark expedition himself; as president, however, he had to settle for making of that expedition a boon and stimulus to the development of science throughout America. When critics pointed out that American contributions to science were rather minimal, Jefferson

responded that when the United States had been in existence as long as the Greeks before they produced a Homer, or as long as the English before they produced a Shakespeare, then it could legitimately be asked what this new nation had managed to accomplish.

❧ Gender and Race

Brilliant as Jefferson's legacy to America might be in the realms of science and culture, in the troubled spheres of gender and race relations his imprint was mixed at best, tragically flawed at worst. In so many avenues of thought, Jefferson moved well ahead of his times. In others, however, he never wholly escaped the age and place of his upbringing.

In his thinking about women, Jefferson took some steps forward, but some backward as well. He did believe that they deserved an education, certainly in the domestic arts, but also in art, music, and dance. They should learn French, the language not only of diplomacy but the "depository of all science." Mothers should be educated in sufficient depth to enable them to educate their own daughters, and sons too, if need be, in the absence of formal schooling. Jefferson, moreover, favored abolishing the traditional law of primogeniture (by which all property passed to the eldest son) in favor of younger sons and all the daughters as well. This would provide some measure of economic independence, from which other kinds of independence could more readily flow.

On the other hand, Jefferson thought of women largely in terms of their ability to assist and comfort men. They should not engage directly in politics other than "to soothe and calm the minds of their husbands, returning ruffled from political debate." Women should not mix in public assemblies or dance after marriage, for to do so would lead to moral decline and "ambiguity of issue." To his secretary of the treasury, Albert Gallatin, Jefferson wrote in 1807 that appointing a woman to public office was "an innovation for which the public is not prepared" — and added, "nor am I." It is impossible to make a feminist out of Jefferson.

Notwithstanding Jefferson, women did make major strides in the new nation, both in contributions rendered and recognition won. In the early years of the republic, many women emphasized the sacrifices that they, no less than the soldiers in battle, had been called upon to render and had willingly made. Gender roles, while admittedly different, did not elevate one above the other in value. Moreover, women played the major role in preserving moral values, in seeing within the family that the rhetoric regarding virtue had some visible reality. Husbands, fathers, sons, daughters — all would be held to a strict moral account that would preserve virtue in the republic for generations to come. Evangelical women, after the Revolution, pointed out that the real war confronting the nation was against sin and the devil. In an anonymous pamphlet published in Boston in 1787, a "Daughter of America" explained that Satan "has done more harm already, than all the armies of Britain will ever be able to do." She concluded that "we shall all be destroyed or brought into captivity, if the women as well as the men, do not oppose, resist, and fight against this destructive enemy." In the battle against vice and for virtue, women served in the trenches and on the front lines.

In writing about the Indians, Jefferson took a more egalitarian line, though his politics and his science frequently pulled him in opposing directions. Artists and authors of his day often portrayed the Indian as the quintessential American. To demote or degrade the Indian was somehow to degrade America. Jefferson spent much time refuting French armchair anthropologists who argued that all species in North America were inferior to those of Europe. Nonsense, Jefferson replied, disproving the charge by weighing, measuring, counting, and recording in great detail. Not in South America, where Indians had been held in slavery for centuries, but in North America Europeans should look "to seek their original character." On the basis of his own close scientific observation, Jefferson judged the Indian "to be in body and mind equal to the whiteman." Even more surprising for the time, he saw white-Indian intermarriage as altogether appropriate. In an address to several tribes in 1808, he stated that "we shall all be Americans; you will mix with us by marriage, your blood will run in our veins, and will spread with us over this great land." Yet this vision remained only that: a vision.

For political realities kept intruding — upon the nation in general, but on Jefferson in particular. When he served as Washington's secretary of state, he joined in the move to drive the Indians farther westward. "I hope we shall drub the Indians well this summer," he wrote to Madison in 1791; then, we can "change our plan from war to bribery." Europeans had not treated Indians fairly, Jefferson readily acknowledged, but Americans would do no better. Jefferson the politician agreed that the Indians must first be conquered, then pacified, then civilized. They would enjoy liberty as soon as they allowed knowledge to displace ignorance and "reformed" behavior to supplant native tradition. Jefferson the anthropologist saw no reason why Indians and whites could not live together as equals. Unhappily, the science and the politics never merged into a single, consistent approach.

Jefferson's attitudes toward blacks and slavery had the grimmest consequences. Here theory and experience seemed totally at odds. As author of the Declaration of Independence, Jefferson exalted the idea of equality: all men (meaning human beings) are of an equal creation. More than that, he condemned the slave trade (that "cruel war against human nature itself") in language so strong that it had to be stricken from the Declaration before the Continental Congress would accept it. In 1783 Jefferson urged his fellow Virginians to provide freedom for all children born of slaves after 1800. And the next year he fashioned the language of the Northwest Ordinance that "neither slavery nor involuntary servitude" would be allowed anywhere in that large western expanse. But the year 1784 would mark the high point of Jefferson's efforts toward abolition.

✹ I N   T H E I R   O W N   W O R D S

An American Language

In a copious list of names of places, rivers, lakes, mountains, &c. which are introduced into this work, no labor has been spared to exhibit their just orthography and pronunciation, according to the analogies of our language, and the common usages of the country. The occurrence of Indian names has not, in every instance, been well adjusted by American authors. Many of these names still retain the French orthography, found in the writings of the first discoverers or early travellers; but the practice of writing such words in the French orthography ought to be discountenanced. How does an unlettered American know the pronunciation of the names Ouisconsin or Ouabasche in this French dress? Would he suspect the pronunciation to be Wisconsin and Waubash? Our citizens ought not to be perplexed with an orthography to which they are strangers.

Noah Webster, *The American Spelling Book*, 1803

In his *Notes on the State of Virginia,* published in 1787 but composed as early as 1785, Jefferson revealed his gloomy doubts about the prospect of blacks in America. He saw them, unlike the Indians, as improbable prospects for intermarriage or complete integration. His political enemies seized the opportunity to expose what they saw as utter hypocrisy. For they charged him with keeping a mulatto mistress, Sally Hemings, by whom he had several children. Many generations later, scholarly investigators — not political enemies — have examined these charges with great care, and with mixed results.

But the most damning evidence of Jefferson's racism comes from his own pen. Admitting that his observations of African Americans had been severely limited, he nonetheless suggested, "as a suspicion only," "that the blacks, whether originally a distinct race, or made distinct by time and circumstances, are inferior to the whites in the endowments of both body and mind."

Here Jefferson sank ever deeper into his native southern social milieu. Slaveholders throughout the South had a mean opinion of the mental capacities of their labor force. Blackness itself was widely interpreted, both in Europe and America, as a sign of inferiority. The eminent Scottish philosopher David Hume declared as simple fact that "there never was a civilized nation of any other complexion than white." Thomas Carlyle, the Scottish historian of the nineteenth century, carefully explained that in the divine plan blacks had been created to serve whites, and this fact was firmly fixed in the laws of nature. So much was blackness identified in popular thought with inferiority that James Madison once told a friend that "if he could work a miracle, he knew what it would be. He would make all blacks white; and then he could do away with slavery in twenty-four hours."

In the *Notes,* Jefferson did forthrightly condemn slavery. Whatever the talents of the blacks, he wrote, it was "no measure of their rights." Slavery diminished both master and slave, he noted, creating "the most unremitting despotism on the one part, and degrading submissions on the other." If Jefferson could not embrace equality, he could at least extol liberty — but it was a liberty *postponed.* For the eradication of slavery, "we must await with patience the workings of an overruling Providence," Jefferson wrote, "and hope that that is preparing the deliverance of these, our suffering brethren." Never has Jeffersonian rhetoric sounded so hollow, or rung so false a note. Slavery was an abomination, yes, but leave it to heaven. Blacks are of an equal creation, yes, but somehow still inferior. My scientific observations are quite limited, yes, but nonetheless my mind is made up. Concerning both slavery and the blacks, Jefferson, the great libertarian and egalitarian, failed to measure up to his own high ideals and moral claims.

✾ Reason and Religion

So strongly is Jefferson identified with the cause of political liberty that it is difficult to believe that his devotion to religious liberty ran even deeper. For Jefferson, the Enlightenment represented above all else freedom for the human mind. And, in his view, religion had historically been the leading enemy of freedom of thought. The bigoted clergy, Jefferson wrote, had had the advantage for centuries of "stated and privileged days to collect and catechize us, opportunities of delivering their oracles to the people in mass, and of molding their minds as wax in the hollow of their hands." In the Jefferson Memorial in Washington, D.C., Jefferson's famous words are carved in stone: "For I have sworn upon the altar of God, eternal hostility against every form of tyranny over the mind of man." That sentence comes from a letter to Benjamin Rush, written in 1800, in which the context makes clear that the tyranny he most feared was a religious one. "Almighty God hath made the mind free," Jefferson declared in his Statute for Establishing Religious Freedom (1786), and he would do all in his power to keep minds free. With Madison's help, he persuaded the Virginia legislature to pass the statute, with its promise that no one would be "compelled to frequent or support any religious worship, place, or ministry whatsoever." Nor would any person be restrained or molested or burdened simply because of his or her religious opinions. The union between church and state, as had prevailed in Virginia for nearly two hundred years, must be broken and never put back together again.

When Jefferson published his *Notes* the next year, he included the statute in an appendix — one measure of his pride in having struck a blow for religious liberty. Another measure may be found in his letter to Madison in 1787 where he revealed his delight in "seeing the standard of reason at length erected, after so many ages during which the human mind has been held in vassalage by kings, priests & nobles."

Virginia had taken the first giant step in 1786; Jefferson encouraged Madison to see that the nation took a similar step in the First Amendment to the Constitution, proposed in 1789 and ratified two years later. The amendment began: "Congress shall make no law respecting an establishment of religion, or prohibiting the free exercise thereof." Government should neither favor religion nor oppress it, but leave it alone. On his tombstone, Jefferson asked to be remembered for only three accomplishments: the Declaration of Independence, the Statute for Establishing Religious Freedom, and the University of Virginia.

His contribution to religious liberty was enormous, but he did not stop there. He wanted to bring about a theological reformation as well, to create a climate in which religion would be as rational as it was free. To forward this enterprise, he spent many evenings in Monticello, after retiring from the presidency, creating what has been called "the Jefferson Bible." Working with the four Gospels in the New Testament, and comparing the Greek, Latin, French, and English versions, Jefferson restricted his "bible" to the sayings of Jesus, especially those that offered moral counsel. There should be no conflict between faith and reason, for reason must be in charge. But religion, he thought, is the foundation and enforcer of morality, and there should be no conflict between them.

Over the centuries, Christianity, Jefferson argued, had departed widely from the simple teachings of Jesus. It had been weighted down by philosophical abstraction and metaphysical speculation. "Our savior did not come into the world to save metaphysicians only," Jefferson noted. What was once so simple and clear had been made so complex and mysterious. The essence of Christianity was "Fear God and love thy neighbor," but that essence had been encrusted by layers of priestly absurdities and "scholastic subtleties." Jefferson was neither infidel nor atheist, but a radical reformer who would have all persons return "to the plain and unsophisticated precepts of Christ." So confident was Jefferson about the Age of Enlightenment and the promise of rational religion that in 1822 he asserted "that the present generation will see Unitarianism become the general religion of the United States." He went even further: "I trust that there is not a young man now living in the U.S. who will not die an Unitarian." One reason why that never happened was the popular wave of evangelicalism that was sweeping over the nation even as Jefferson was making his confident — and utterly mistaken — prediction.

CONCLUSION: BUILDING AND NURTURING THE NEW NATION

When Washington was unanimously chosen as president of the United States, it was unclear how much unity among the thirteen sovereign states was possible. For many, it was equally unclear how much unity was desirable. But Washington did manage to put a *national* face on many of the actions that he and the Congress undertook. The new nation addressed the problems of war debts and war obligations, created a national bank, stimulated manufacturing, and determined the permanent location of the capital. The first president, pulled in opposite directions, also kept the nation out of war, and firmly put down internal rebellion. He did much in his two terms to mark the path toward nationhood.

The single term of his successor, John Adams, also managed to keep a young and vulnerable people from being caught in the furies of European wars. On the domestic front, his troubles were many, as his own vice president, Thomas Jefferson, led the opposing political faction, and his own cabinet, dominated by Alexander Hamilton, gave very little loyalty to the president. The Constitution did not anticipate the rise of political parties, and Washington personally deplored the "party spirit." Nonetheless, within a remarkably brief period of time, political parties became a permanent feature of the nation's life.

Nothing demonstrated this more clearly than the hard-fought campaign of 1800, pitting President Adams against Vice President Jefferson. The victory of Jefferson heralded the growing influence of his Republican Party, with the gradual decline of Adams's Federalist Party. The most dramatic single event of Jefferson's presidency, the Louisiana Purchase, doubled the size of the United States and thrust it closer to its role as a major player on the world stage. During his two terms, the U.S. Supreme Court also shed its minor role to become a major player on the American stage.

The twenty years covered by the nation's first three presidents did much to determine the future political destiny of the American people. As President Washington observed, he walked upon "an unexplored field, enveloped on every side with clouds and darkness." After his labors, as well as those of his two successors, the clouds had parted enough to allow a good deal more light to shine through.

SUGGESTED READING

Stephen E. Ambrose, *Undaunted Courage: Meriwether Lewis, Thomas Jefferson, and the Opening of the American West* (1996). A highly readable, delightfully detailed account of the nation's most significant overland exploration; excellent maps.

Ruth Bloch, *Visionary Republic: Millennial Themes in American Thought, 1756-1800* (1985). A sophisticated analysis of both the sweep and the power of millennial ideas in the new republic.

Richard Brookhiser, *Founding Father: Rediscovering George Washington* (1996). A "moral biography," this book seeks not to denigrate or dismiss Washington, but to retrieve him for our own time.

Lester J. Cappon, ed., *The Adams-Jefferson Letters,* 2 vols. (1959). An endlessly engaging correspondence between the two political allies, then political enemies, then friends again; the range of subjects covered by these two omnivorous readers staggers the imagination.

Joseph J. Ellis, *Passionate Sage: The Character and Legacy of Adams* (1993). An appreciative, insightful examination into the inner Adams that would rescue him from partial obscurity.

Joseph J. Ellis, *American Sphinx: The Character of Thomas Jefferson* (1997). Rejecting myth-making and sentimentality, the author offers instead a solid, sensitive portrayal of the complexities of our third president.

James T. Flexner, *Washington: The Indispensable Man* (1969). A one-volume condensation of Flexner's four-volume and authoritative biography of the first president; readable and wise.

Edwin S. Gaustad, *Faith of the Founders: Religion and the New Nation, 1776-1826* (1993). Gives special attention to the role of Adams, Franklin, Jefferson, Madison, and Washington in setting the republic on its daring and experimental religious path.

Donald Jackson, *Thomas Jefferson & the Stony Mountains: Exploring the West from Monticello* (1981). Provides excellent context, with over a dozen maps, of the expedition of Lewis and Clark, along with others moving westward at Jefferson's behest.

Linda K. Kerber, *Women of the Republic: Intellect and Ideology in Revolutionary America* (2nd ed., 1986). A persuasive case for the real, if limited, emancipation of women in the latter decades of the eighteenth century; also, a fresh assessment of their major contributions.

Ralph Ketcham, *Presidents Above Party: The First American Presidency, 1789-1829* (1984). Probes the earnest efforts, ultimately unavailing, of the first presidents to put "party spirit" far behind them.

John Chester Miller, *The Wolf by the Ears: Thomas Jefferson and Slavery* (1977). A thorough and balanced analysis of the most haunting and troubled issue of Jefferson's career.

Merrill D. Peterson, ed., *Thomas Jefferson: A Reference Biography* (1986). Pursuing a topical approach to the many-sided Jefferson, this volume gives attention to such interests as art, architecture, education, religion, science, slavery, the West, agriculture, political thought, and the American Indians.

James Morton Smith, *The Republic of Letters: The Correspondence between Jefferson and Madison,* 3 vols. (1995). Absolutely essential reading for the vital public roles of these two Virginians, as well as the light it sheds on their long-lasting friendship.

Francis N. Stites, *John Marshall: Defender of the Constitution* (1981). In brief compass, this volume provides a readable introduction to the life and thought of not the first chief justice but the first one that anyone remembers.

SUGGESTIONS FOR FURTHER READING

Joyce O. Appleby, *Capitalism and a New Social Order: The Republican Vision of the 1790s* (1984).

Joyce O. Appleby, *Liberalism and Republicanism in the Historical Imagination* (1992).

Joyce O. Appleby, *Inheriting the Revolution: The First Generation of Americans* (2000).

Lance Banning, *The Jeffersonian Persuasion: Evolution of a Party Ideology* (1978).

Kenneth R. Bowling and Helen E. Veit, eds., *The Diary of William Maclay* (1988).

R. B. Burnstein, *Thomas Jefferson* (2003).

Andrew Burstein, *The Inner Jefferson: Portrait of a Grieving Optimist* (1995).

Edward H. Davidson and William J. Scheick, *Paine, Scripture, and Authority: The Age of Reason as Political and Religious Idea* (1994).

Joseph J. Ellis, *His Excellency: George Washington* (2004).

John Ferling, *Adams vs. Jefferson: The Tumultuous Election of 1800* (2004).

John R. Fitzmier, *New England's Moral Legislator: Timothy Dwight, 1752-1817* (1998).

Jack Fruchtman, Jr., *Thomas Paine and the Religion of Nature* (1993).

Edwin S. Gaustad, *Sworn on the Altar of God: A Religious Biography of Thomas Jefferson* (1996).

Felix Gilbert, *The Beginnings of American Foreign Policy* (1961).

Annette Gordon-Reed, *Thomas Jefferson and Sally Hemings: An American Controversy* (1997).

Christine Leigh Heyrman, *Southern Cross: The Beginnings of the Bible Belt* (1997).

Charles F. Hobson, *The Great Chief Justice: John Marshall and the Rule of Law* (1996).

James Horn et al., eds., *The Revolution of 1800: Democracy, Race, and the New Republic* (2002).

John R. Howe, Jr., *The Changing Political Thought of John Adams* (1966).

Leonard W. Levy, ed., *Freedom of the Press: From Zenger to Jefferson* (1966).

Paul K. Longmore, *The Invention of George Washington* (1988).

Charles A. Miller, *Jefferson and Nature: An Interpretation* (1988).

Peter F. Onuf, *Jefferson's Empire: The Language of American Nationhood* (2000).

John Rhodehamel, *The Great Experiment: George Washington and the American Republic* (1998).

James P. Ronda, *Finding the West: Explorations with Lewis and Clark* (2001).

Laurel Thatcher Ulrich, *A Midwife's Tale: The Life of Martha Ballard, Based on Her Diary, 1785-1812* (1990).

Kerry S. Walters, *The American Deists: Voices of Reason and Dissent in the Early Republic* (1992).

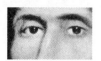

Nationalism, Capitalism, Sectionalism, and Religion in the Early Republic

THOMAS JEFFERSON LEFT the executive mansion in March 1809, but as a political era the Age of Jefferson continued for at least sixteen years. Jefferson was succeeded by two of his close Virginia friends and political lieutenants, James Madison (1809-1817) and James Monroe (1817-1825). His party, the Democratic-Republicans, became the nation's only viable party as the Federalists rapidly lost influence. By 1819 the Jeffersonians could look with some pride upon their achievements. For the first time in history there had been a peaceful transfer of political power in 1801, and in 1803 the nation had doubled its size with the Louisiana Purchase. Jefferson consciously tried to soothe political differences and to attract opponents by his powerful ideas and luminous personality. To a substantial extent, he succeeded.

But trouble brewed after Jefferson laid down the presidency. Relations with Great Britain continued to deteriorate until a second war with the old mother country broke out. This conflict, the War of 1812, at first went badly for the young nation, but it concluded in January 1815 with a spectacular victory over the British at New Orleans. A wave of exuberant nationalism swept the country. Along with this burst of national pride came far-reaching economic changes. But these changes soon began to create in different sections a renewed sense that they did indeed have separate and competing interests. The result was the emergence of a divisive sectionalism, culminating in bitter political struggle in 1819 over the question of admitting Missouri as a state — a controversy so intense that even the normally optimistic Jefferson felt premonitions of coming disunion and civil war.

At the beginning of the nineteenth century, the North and South resembled each other far more than they differed, and political alliances stretched across the nation. Federalists dominated most of the North and had a stronghold in South Carolina; Jeffersonians dominated the rest of the South and were also strong in New York. The South at this time represented the liberal, progressive mainstream of American politics; New Englanders had the more narrow perspective, threatening secession if they did not get their way. But different patterns of economic development and urbanization occurred in the North and the South. Capitalism and the market economy expanded in the North, along with a far-reaching transformation called the transportation revolution; the South experienced the rise of a distinct form of evangelical religion and the rapid spread of cotton cultivation and of slavery into the new territories west of Georgia. These factors, working beyond the pale of politics, were creating two distinct regions, the North and the South, with the West being subsumed into these two. The fate of the nation came to rest on how the people of these various regions interacted with each other, perceived their own interests, and turned to politics to defend their position.

ASSERTING INDEPENDENCE: FROM THE WAR OF 1812 TO THE MONROE DOCTRINE

Thomas Jefferson was succeeded as president by his closest friend, James Madison, diminutive in stature but a giant in intellect. Like Jefferson, Madison had a record of long and distinguished public service before becoming president. More than anyone else at the 1787 Constitutional Convention and in the first Congress, he was responsible for the form of the new government and for the Bill of Rights. Later he had been President Jefferson's most trusted political operative as Jefferson was pioneering a new role for the president as party leader.

Yet as president Madison proved weak and inept. Attempting to continue Jefferson's policies, he lost control of events and by 1812 found himself waging "Mr. Madison's War" with Great Britain, a conflict that badly exacerbated sectional strains. From the War of 1812 the United States was lucky to emerge intact and with its borders undiminished.

⮞ *"Peaceful Coercion" Fails*

As Jefferson's secretary of state, Madison had struggled along with his president to find some resolution to the problem of French and British commercial interference with American neutral rights. These two superpowers of the era were locked in a life-and-death struggle over the fate of Europe. Relative to them, the United States was a minor power for which neither showed respect, and which neither feared. Anything the United States did to protect its rights as a neutral — short of completely shutting down its foreign trade with both — irritated one side or the other. Both were in a position to show their displeasure by threatening American ships with capture. And Jefferson had already discovered how damaging to national prosperity and ominous for national harmony it could be to attempt a total embargo of trade with both sides. Unless the United States simply decided to avoid permanently all trade with France and Great Britain, war was probably inevitable with one or another — if not with both.

Madison, like Jefferson, hoped, however, that economic coercion — withholding trade — could replace warfare as the way of settling differences between nations. But their idealism seemed ineffectual in the face of the naval and military might of Great Britain and France. Weeks before Madison took office, Congress repealed the Embargo Act and the Non-Intercourse Act, which permitted American trade with all countries *except* France and Britain and promised that the United States would resume trading with whichever of those nations ceased to violate American commercial rights as a neutral. But when both belligerents ignored the United States's weak policy of a tiny carrot and no stick, Madison had almost no recourse left. Casting about for *something* that worked, Congress too drifted for months. Finally in May 1810 it replaced the Non-Intercourse Act with Macon's Bill No. 2, which reopened American trade with both Britain and France — but threatened that if one of these warring enemies dropped its restrictions on American trade, the United States would halt all trade with the other. France's Emperor Napoleon clearly fooled the Americans by pretending to repeal French prohibitions against their trade, and the desperate Madison fell into the trap by quickly banning trade with Britain.

By early 1811 Madison faced an economically ominous situation. All commerce had been suspended with the nation that had been by far America's largest trading partner — while the duplicitous Napoleon continued to capture American ships found in ports that France controlled. The embargo against British trade actually hurt Americans more, although in 1811 and especially in 1812, the embargo began to damage the British economy as well. Within Great Britain, domestic merchants began appealing for a relaxation of the anti-American policies. But at first the government would not bend, fearing to benefit France and compromise Britain's accustomed domination of the seas; it did not think the Americans would resort to war and little feared the prospect if they did. Ironically, American economic coercion finally achieved results in June 1812. A new British cabinet came to power that took steps to cool down the quarrel with the United States. Napoleon, it feared, was ending France's most offensive trade policies against the Americans, behooving Britain to conciliate Madison. But — as we shall see — it was too late.

In some ways an American declaration of war against France would have been as justified as the one against Britain. Both powers had interfered with American commerce and treated the United States contemptuously. But the American grievances against Great Britain did not end with the Revolutionary War. In many ways the British had not yet accepted the legitimacy of American independence. To many Americans, British disrespect rankled at least as deeply as trade disputes. How could the United States survive in a hostile world if it could not defend its honor? National pride demanded an end to British impressment of American sailors — seizing them for the Royal Navy — and interference with its commerce; the matter was not narrowly economic. In this sense, war with Britain would be a kind of Second War for Independence, perhaps necessary for the nation to achieve its self-respect.

❧ *American Expansionists*

Indian wars and land hunger also contributed to many Americans' increasing determination to stand up to perceived British slights. The 1810 elections brought to Washington a group of young congressmen who had not fought in the American Revolution and were thus all the more eager to reassert American independence. Among these "war hawks" were John C. Calhoun of South Carolina, Felix Grundy of Tennessee, Henry Clay and Richard M. Johnson of Kentucky, and Peter B. Porter of western New York. The confident, highly nationalistic Clay, only thirty-four years old, was elected Speaker of the House. Clay and his cohorts in-

tended to cease trying such half-measures as Macon's Bill No. 2 and instead resolutely defend their country's honor and interests. They wanted to push Spain out of Florida and England out of Canada, and these western and southern demands ultimately proved as strong a motivation for war as the festering problems of international commerce.

Spanish-held Florida in 1810 included not only the peninsula but also a panhandle section extending along the Gulf Coast all the way to the Mississippi River. The section east of the Perdido River, including the peninsula, was known as the colony of East Florida; West Florida extended from the Perdido to the Mississippi. In 1803 Jefferson had failed to ensure that the Louisiana Purchase included West Florida. Weakened after 1808 because it was occupied by Napoleon, Spain could not effectively defend its Florida territories. The exiled king of Spain was allied with Britain against Napoleon, but the British government had little interest in Florida. So when American settlers living near Baton Rouge — part of Spanish West Florida — revolted in 1810 and requested annexation by the United States, President Madison quickly proclaimed all of West Florida to be American territory. Spain was helpless to prevent West Florida's loss, but it clung desperately to its fort on Mobile Bay. Emboldened by Congress, Madison sent General George Mathews to seize East Florida in 1811, although the president later expressed some regrets about this high-handed action. Southerners wanted the region in order to prevent runaway slaves from joining the Seminole Indians in East Florida, but the United States had no legal claims to it; and Spain made feeble noises about war. This was enough for the New England states to threaten secession if the United States persisted in its aggression. Madison thereupon withdrew General Mathews. So Spain kept its tenuous hold on East Florida and Mobile Bay, while southerners cast covetous eyes on the whole territory.

❧ *Indian Resistance to White Expansion*

Settlers in the Midwest, the former Northwest Territories, were no less expansionist. In 1811 and 1812 they insisted that the British were instigating and supporting spirited Indian resistance against American farmers in the Indiana Territory. "The British scalping knife," charged a Kentucky newspaper, "has filled many habitations both in this state as well as in the Indiana Territory with widows and orphans." There was some truth in such accusations, although the Indian resurgence

Tecumseh An unknown painter captured this image of the great Native American leader. Notice how he has dressed his hair and adopted white dress—signs of the assimilation that otherwise he strongly opposed.

ance continued after the war. The Treaty of Paris of 1783 required that the British withdraw their troops from the region. However, the British authorities, protecting their fur-trading interests and contemptuous of the United States, not only continued to occupy forts at Detroit and Michilimackinac but also built a new fort in northwestern Ohio. Moreover, they kept alive their alliance with the Shawnee by supplying these people with weapons with which to fight American settlers.

To the Shawnee, white Americans were invading their homeland, justifying armed resistance; to the Americans, the Shawnee warriors were simply agents of the nefarious British. Actually, the Shawnee felt little loyalty to the British and were defending their traditional way of life. As white settlement pushed deeper into the Northwest Territory in the 1780s, skirmishes with the Shawnee intensified. The frontier blazed with Indian-white conflict, with white casualties running as high as 1,500 a year. Finally, after 1790, a strengthened American military force turned the tide in a series of battles, climaxing in a crushing defeat of the Shawnee by General Anthony Wayne in 1794 at the Battle of Fallen Timbers in northern Ohio. The resulting Treaty of Greenville in 1795 apparently opened the Northwest to peaceful white settlement.

Whether to accept the whites' victory split the Shawnee. One large group was led by Chief Black Hoof, who urged his people to acknowledge defeat and begin to assimilate. But numerous other Shawnee resisted accommodation, retreated into the backcountry, and tried to live in their traditional manner. Slowly disease contracted from the whites, alcoholism, and shrinking of their hunting lands threatened to destroy even the Shawnee who had fled westward into Indiana Territory. From 1801 to 1809 the territorial governor of Indiana, William Henry Harrison, by devious means persuaded bands of Indians to give up larger and larger stretches

would have happened even without British support. Nevertheless, the prospect of an Anglo-Indian alliance frightened white Americans.

In the Northwest, as in the Southwest, most Native Americans in the late eighteenth century began a slow process of accommodation to white ways of life. The Cherokee in the Southwest led the way. However, two native peoples — the Southwestern Creeks and the Shawnee of the Ohio Valley — in the last half of the eighteenth century tenaciously opposed the advance of white civilization. During the American Revolution the Shawnee had sided with the British, and this alli-

of their ancestral lands. Indians of various nations found themselves being crowded in upon one another. This process culminated in 1809 with the Treaty of Fort Wayne, by which the native peoples surrendered another 3 million acres.

Two brothers, leaders in different ways of the traditional Shawnee, now began a momentous struggle against the destruction of their people's way of life. One was a religious mystic, the other an organizational genius. Tenskwatawa had failed as a warrior and medicine man, and he was overweight, blind in one eye, and a helpless alcoholic. In 1805 he collapsed into a trance so deep that he seemed to be dead. When he awoke, he related that he had been taken to heaven and hell and had received a vision of salvation for all Indians. They must stop drinking, fighting among themselves, using white man's clothes, tools, and artifacts of all kinds, and return to completely traditional ways. In particular, the Shawnee should repudiate the white custom of individual land ownership and accept the Great Spirit's wish that the land belong to them in common. Their break with the past must include the traditional religious ritual of extinguishing and relighting all their fires. Once the Indians had totally renounced all accommodations to white ways, Tenskwatawa taught, God would restore them to their traditional greatness. The attractiveness of this revitalization movement was so strong among the Shawnee that hundreds flocked to "the Prophet," as Tenskwatawa was now called. He traveled among the Shawnee, converting many to his vision of recaptured glories, and in 1809 he established a town named Tippecanoe ("Prophet's Town") in northwestern Indiana.

The Prophet's brother, Tecumseh, was a gifted warrior who built on this religious message to create a military alliance linking the Shawnee with the remnants of other Indian tribes in the Northwest. Tecumseh even traveled into the South, carrying his militant message of armed resistance and his brother's message of spiritual regeneration to the Choctaw, Chickasaw, Cherokee, and Creek. A north-south Indian coalition, Tecumseh urged, could halt the westward advance of the white population. With his powerful oratory, Tecumseh's indictment of the whites amounted to a call to arms: "The white race is a wicked race. . . . The mere presence of the white man is a source of evil to the red men. . . . The only hope for the red man is a war of extermination against the paleface."

By 1811, Anglo-American tensions had heightened. Anticipating a clash with the United States, the British had begun to supply some weapons to the Indi-

ans in the Northwest. Tecumseh was less interested in British policies than in arming his forces against U.S. encroachment, and in early 1811 he had gathered more than a thousand warriors at Tippecanoe to defend traditional Indian civilization. Americans in the Northwest, primed by years of conflict to fear and hate Indians, saw in Tecumseh's movement not only Indian savagery but also — exaggerating British involvement — the old mother country's treachery. With another war with Britain looming over the gnawing issues of maritime commerce and impressment, western Americans in particular felt they had to crush Tecumseh's Indian confederacy quickly to secure the frontier against a possible British invasion from Canada.

Indiana Territory governor William Henry Harrison made the first move. Commanding more than a thousand soldiers, he surrounded Tippecanoe in November 1811. Tecumseh was still away recruiting Creek Indians allies, and in his absence the Prophet foolishly called for a surprise attack against Harrison's troops, promising that his magical powers would bring certain victory. The battle raged all day, but Harrison won a resounding victory, killing over a third of the attacking Indians and burning Tippecanoe; the fame he won would, many years later, carry him to the presidency. The Prophet's reputation was effectively destroyed; he tried to blame the defeat on his wife, who (he said) had been ritually impure while she helped him perform ceremonies. This excuse convinced no one; the Prophet narrowly escaped death at the hands of angry Indian warriors and fled into Canada, his influence ended. Tecumseh, however, returned from the South to lead his Shawnee warriors — armed by the British and even stiffened with British soldiers — in a series of devastating raids against American settlements in Indiana and Michigan.

The rapidly escalating war on the Northwest frontier in 1811 and early 1812 led many western politicians to conclude that the Indians would not be "pacified" until the perfidious British were driven from North America.

❧ *"Mr. Madison's War"*

Despite the British and French depredations against American maritime commerce that mostly harmed the Northeast, New England was not keen to fight. Many merchants there believed they had more to lose by taking on Great Britain — the world's mightiest naval power — than by suffering her interference with Amer-

Tenskwatawa, "the Prophet"   This lithograph, produced in 1836, two years after Tenskwatawa's death, is perhaps rather fanciful and is meant to portray his image at the time of his greatest influence, on the eve of the War of 1812. Together with his brother Tecumseh, "the Prophet" exercised an enormous influence over the Native American peoples of the Old Northwest and Old Southwest.

ican trade. One reason northern merchants tolerated British depredations is that their profits from one successful voyage often repaid the losses of several unsuccessful ones. Moreover, the region was home to many Federalists and Congregational clergy for whom Napoleon and the "godless French" presented, in the long run, a far greater danger to European and American freedom than England. New England ministers and politicians opposed a war "against the nation from which we are descended, and which for many generations has been the bulwark of the religion we profess." The Federalist Party, almost dead by 1804, made a comeback.

Thus it was the southern and western War Hawks, elected in the congressional elections of 1810, who vociferously led the call for war to protect American prestige and honor, to defend America's international trade, to prevent further British encouragement of Tecumseh, and to scotch the Federalists. "The honor of the nation and that of the party are bound up together," wrote a Democratic-Republican editor, "and both will be sacrificed if war not be declared." The War Hawks were also clearly expansionist: they coveted both Spanish territory and British Canada and saw war as a means to satisfy their hunger for additional land. Moreover, many southern and western Baptists, having bad memories of the Church of England that had once persecuted them, were quick to believe that the British government was "corrupt, arbitrary, and despotic" and hence considered war "just, necessary, and indispensable." Madison, a profound political theorist, was not a shrewd politician. Outmaneuvered by the French and the British governments into going to the brink of war, he ultimately caved in to War Hawk demands that he fight.

Madison's State of the Union address reflected the pressure of the War Hawks especially and of most members of the Democratic-Republican Party in the states south of Pennsylvania when he accused Britain of "trampling on rights which no independent nation can relinquish." But he revealed his restricted vision of presidential authority by inviting Congress to put the United States "into an armor and an attitude demanded by the crisis." In effect, he gave the initiative to the legislature. Congress responded in April 1812 by increasing the army from 6,000 men to 35,000 and authorizing the president to call up 50,000 state militia troops if needed. Congress did not, however, increase the pitifully tiny United States navy; doing so would, it was thought, be futile given the overwhelming strength of the Royal Navy. Congress also enacted a ninety-day embargo of American shipping, intended primarily to get American ships safely back into port before hostilities broke out. Then on June 1 Madison sent to Congress a message in which he outlined what he thought were sufficient reasons to declare war against Great Britain. The final decision, however, he carefully left up to Congress.

Madison thus failed to exercise any restraining influence. Had he done so, events might have moved more slowly, until the news crossed the Atlantic that the British government had at last backed down on the infuriating infringement of American neutral rights. As it was, sentiment in the Northeast overwhelmingly opposed a declaration of war. Congressman Josiah Quincy of Massachusetts was typical of his region in considering the War Hawks barbaric "backwoodsmen" eager to wage a "cruel, wanton, senseless and wicked war" simply to grab Canada's land. Not a single Federalist would vote for war, and many Republicans in the North opposed the declaration because they believed negotiations should be tried somewhat longer. The passion for war flamed hottest in the South and the West, where the issues were national honor, fear of Indian attacks, and expansionism. Led by the War Hawks, on June 18, 1812, the House voted for war by 79 to 49, and the Senate by 19 to 13. The next day President Madison declared war.

Never before or since has America gone into a foreign war so politically divided and so militarily unprepared. The maritime regions of the country vehemently opposed a struggle that was supposedly being waged to defend their interests. The American people, moreover, had been simply unwilling to pay sufficient taxes to create an effective military. And because the charter of the Bank of the United States had expired in 1811 without being renewed, the government was scarcely able even to secure loans and pay its wartime bills.

❧ The Failed Invasions of Canada

Nevertheless, for those Americans who favored war, seizing Canada appeared easy. The United States had a population six times that of Canada, three-fifths of whom were recent American emigrants with no strong loyalty to Britain. Many of the remainder of Canadians were of French ancestry and presumably anti-British. Fewer than 2,300 British regulars guarded the thousand-mile-long U.S.-Canadian border. Niagara Falls prevented the powerful British ocean fleet from sailing into the Great Lakes, and supplying Upper Canada (Ontario) presented apparently insuperable logistic problems for Britain. Thomas Jefferson said that conquering Canada was "a mere matter of marching."

What seemed so easy in theory foundered in practice. The Canadian people did not rally to the American invaders; indeed, both Catholic French Canadians and Anglican English-speakers were repelled by brash American Protestant enthusiasm. At least some of the emigrants from the United States living in Canada were loyalists or their descendants, who had no reason at all to favor a United States takeover and every reason to fear it. Moreover, the commanders of the invading American armies were mostly elderly Revolutionary officers who had lost the zest for battle, and the American militia had no stomach for tough fighting against Britain's fierce Indian allies. To make matters worse, the state militiamen were unwilling to fight far from home.

The first indication that the invasion of Canada was not going to be a cakewalk came in July 1812, when General William Hull attacked Upper Canada only to find his communications and progress stymied by Tecumseh's Indian forces, who seemed to roam the countryside at will. Fort Michilimackinac in northern Michigan had already fallen to Tecumseh, whose reputation for viciousness frightened Hull. The American general paused, then quickly retreated to Detroit with Canadian general Isaac Brock in hot pursuit.

Brock skillfully exploited Hull's inordinate fear of the Indians. He warned Hull that "the numerous body of Indians who have attached themselves to my troops will be beyond my control the moment the contest commences." Foreseeing an Indian massacre, Hull surrendered 2,200 troops on August 16, 1812, without firing a shot! (Later he was court-martialed for cowardice.) Meanwhile Indian forces captured Fort Dearborn (now Chicago) and massacred its garrison. Far from sparking an uprising among Canadians or routing their small forces, the Americans had suffered a string of embarrassing defeats. Anglo-Canadian-Indian troops now controlled much of the northern portion of the Old Northwest (Illinois, Indiana, and Michigan Territories and the state of Ohio).

Things went no better when the second U.S. inva-

"Old Ironsides"   Here the U.S.S. *Constitution* is towing the *Cyane*, which it captured in battle February 28, 1815. Though it was made of wood, the *Constitution* came to be known as "Old Ironsides" because it appeared to be invulnerable even to cannon shots. It captured twenty-four enemy ships and never lost a battle.

sion of Canada began in early October. Captain John Wool led a detachment of regular army troops across the Niagara River, planning to push deep into Canada with the aid of New York militia who were supposed to follow him. Wool's invasion caught the British off guard, and he won an early battle in which General Brock was killed. The British quickly reorganized, however, and counterattacked. Unwilling to cross their state line, New York militia stood by and watched as a larger British force crushed Wool's U.S. regulars on October 13. A twenty-six-year-old officer, Winfield Scott, negotiated the American surrender as Mohawk Indians were pressing their advantage.[1]

The third American invasion attempt on Canada began on November 19. General Henry Dearborn, another Revolutionary War veteran (grown so fat that he had to be transported in a cart), led an army of militiamen north from Plattsburg, New York, intending to take Montreal. But after marching nineteen miles to the Canadian border, the militiamen refused to go farther. On November 14 a despondent Dearborn returned with his soldiers to Plattsburg. Canada stood safe, and much of the northern U.S. frontier was at risk to Anglo-Indian marauders.

∞ *The Naval War*

Ironically, while the invasion of weak-looking Canada was proving a fiasco, in the early months of the war the United States won several signal engagements against

---

1. Scott would later prove his mettle in the Mexican War and develop Union strategy at the beginning of the Civil War.

The Battle of New Orleans　Andrew Jackson made his reputation as the hero of the new American nationalism in his stunning victory over the British at New Orleans. This scene shows the death of British commander Sir Edward Pakenham in the foreground. Had the outcome of the battle been different and the British kept New Orleans—as they intended to do—the history of nineteenth-century America might well have been greatly altered.

the mighty Royal Navy. The British had far more frigates than the Americans, who only had seven, but three of the U.S. frigates were among the world's largest, fastest, and most maneuverable. British attention was concentrated on Napoleon, and the Royal Navy was primarily engaged in patrolling European waters. Nevertheless, American morale rose on August 19 when the U.S.S. *Constitution* defeated H.M.S. *Guerrière* off the coast of Nova Scotia. The news eased some of the humiliation of the ignominious American surrender of Detroit. Then in mid-October a U.S. sloop-of-war, the *Wasp,* took the British brig *Frolic* some 600 miles out from Virginia, and the frigate U.S.S. *United States* captured H.M.S. *Macedonian* near the Madeira Islands on October 25, sailing her into New London, Connecticut, as a prize. And at the very end of the year, on December 29, the U.S.S. *Constitution* notched another triumph when she

destroyed H.M.S. *Java* near the coast of Brazil, gaining for the *Constitution* the name of "Old Ironsides."

But these startling victories barely affected the overall dominance of the Royal Navy. The British quickly concentrated their naval forces and clamped a total blockade on the American coasts — except for New England. The Chesapeake Bay was closed up by Christmas of 1812; New York and the South, by the spring of 1813. By at first exempting New England from the blockade, the British apparently hoped to push that disaffected and strongly anti-war section into seceding from the United

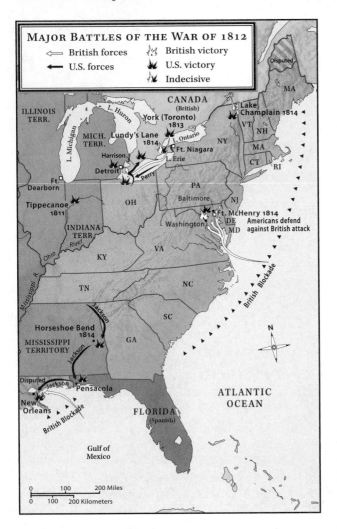

MAJOR BATTLES OF THE WAR OF 1812

⟸ British forces   British victory
⟵ U.S. forces   U.S. victory
                    Indecisive

poleon in Europe, and to British strategists Canada seemed far away and relatively incidental. Dearborn launched another invasion attempt in April 1813, this time with initial successes. American troops took York (present-day Toronto), the capital of Upper Canada, capturing 600 British troops and burning the Parliament houses and the residence of the governor. Several months later — and after the ailing Dearborn had been replaced by Winfield Scott, recently promoted to general — American forces began their march from York toward Montreal. But on November 11, 1813, they suffered a stinging defeat in the Battle of Chrysler's Farm. The American invasion of eastern Canada thereupon collapsed, leaving as its only real result a significantly heightened Canadian nationalism in the wake of the needless burning of the government buildings at York.

Simply recovering Detroit, which they had lost in the first year of the war, now became American strategists' main objective. President Madison made William Henry Harrison, the hero of Tippecanoe, a major general and put him in command of U.S. forces in the Northwest. Unlike Hull, Harrison was not paralyzed by fear of the Indians. But he had to postpone his planned invasion of Canada until he could strengthen his position, and meanwhile an Anglo-Indian force defeated American troops in January 1813 and pressed into Ohio. Harrison quickly realized that he could not retake Detroit as long as a British naval squadron controlled Lake Erie, and to contest it President Madison authorized Captain Oliver Hazard Perry to construct an American fleet as rapidly as possible. Perry soon commanded nine vessels, and after a ferocious battle in September 1813 against better-armed British ships at Put-in-Bay (at the western end of Lake Erie), he destroyed the enemy fleet. Although Perry's forces suffered heavy casualties, the victory was complete. In a famous communication Perry wrote General Harrison, "we have met the enemy and they are ours."

When British general Henry Proctor heard of Perry's victory, he promptly abandoned Detroit and began a quick retreat up the Ontario peninsula before Harrison's troops could be ferried by ship across the lake to cut off his retreat route. Proctor's retreat was opposed by the aggressive Tecumseh, who wanted the British-Indian army to stand its ground. Tecumseh gave in after Proctor promised eventually to get into a better position and fight. Harrison followed, Perry's ships having transported his 4,500 men across Lake Erie. At Moraviantown on the north bank of the Thames River, Harrison attacked the outnumbered Canadians on

States and perhaps even joining up with Canada. Not until the spring of 1814 did the Royal Navy blockade New England. By that time the entire U.S. navy — including the *Constitution* and the *United States* — was bottled up in American harbors. After early 1813 only small, quick American privateers (privately owned ships licensed by Congress to attack enemy vessels) slipped through the blockade to harass British shipping. (There were no privateers in New England, where the blockade was slow to be enforced.) These privateers, more or less legalized pirates, were especially effective operating out of Baltimore and the countless small harbors of the Chesapeake. Altogether they did significant damage to enemy shipping, capturing more than 1,300 British vessels.

❧ The Shifting Fortunes of War

In 1813 American military prospects brightened somewhat. Britain was still preoccupied with crushing Na-

❋ **IN THEIR OWN WORDS**

Evacuating the President's House, 1814

In a letter to her sister, dated August 23, 1814, First Lady Dolley Madison described what happened after President Madison, on horseback, left the President's House (as it was then called) in a futile effort to rally the defenders of Washington, D.C. Soon after Mrs. Madison dispatched this letter and fled, the British occupied the city and burned the presidential mansion.

Wednesday Morning, twelve o'clock. — Since sunrise I have been turning my spy-glass in every direction, and watching with unwearied anxiety, hoping to discover the approach of my dear husband and his friends; but, alas! I can descry only groups of military, wandering in all directions, as if there was a lack of arms, or of spirit to fight for their own fireside.

Three o'clock. — Will you believe it, my sister? we have had a battle, or skirmish, near Bladensburg, and here I am still, within sound of the cannon! Mr. Madison comes not. May God protect us! Two messengers, covered with dust, come to bid me fly; but here I mean to wait for him. . . . At this late hour a wagon has been procured, and I have had it filled with plate and the most valuable portable articles, belonging to the house. Whether it will reach its destination, the "Bank of Maryland," or fall into the hands of British soldiery, events must determine. Our kind friend, Mr. Carroll, has come to hasten my departure, and in a very bad humor with me, because I insist on waiting until the large picture of General Washington [by Gilbert Stuart] is secured, and it requires to be unscrewed from the wall. This process was found too tedious for these perilous moments; I have ordered the frame to be broken, and the canvas taken out. It is done! and the precious portrait placed in the hands of two gentlemen of New York, for safe keeping. And now, dear sister, I must leave this house, or the retreating army will make me a prisoner in it by filling up the road I am directed to take. When I shall again write to you, or where I shall be to-morrow, I cannot tell!

October 5, 1813. Tecumseh's Indian warriors bore the brunt of the American attack. The Canadians were defeated, with a mounted regiment of Kentuckians under Colonel Richard M. Johnson crushing the Indians and killing Tecumseh. This battle had far-reaching consequences, for it destroyed Tecumseh's Indian confederacy and ended the Indian threat to white settlement of the Northwest. Johnson would ride the fame of having killed the hated Tecumseh (with his own hands, he bragged) to repeated political victories. In 1836 he became vice president.

The year 1814 was a momentous one in the war that had torn Europe for so long. Napoleon's rash 1812 invasion of Russia had failed, and the following year one previously conquered European state after another rose against him. In March 1814 the victorious allies occupied Paris, and Napoleon abdicated. The British army was now free for action in North America. Fourteen thousand British troops sailed to Canada, prepared to launch a wiping-up operation against the United States. New England now came under the British blockade, and in the summer of 1814 a three-prong British offensive unfolded, designed to vanquish the Americans.

The first British strike was to send a sea-land force into the Chesapeake to sack Washington, D.C., largely in retaliation for the American destruction of York. After that, the British planned to capture the rich port of Baltimore and punish that "pirate's nest." Madison appointed Baltimore lawyer William H. Winder to command a hastily assembled troop of militia in defense of the national capital. But when the crack British forces slammed into the ill-trained American militia at Bladensburg, Maryland, on August 24, the militia ran so fast that the battle came derisively to be known as "the Bladensburg races." The same day the British marched unopposed into Washington, and President Madison fled leaving his dinner uneaten. Exacting revenge for York, British soldiers systematically torched most of the official government buildings, including the President's House.[2] Then, expecting the same easy pickings, the invaders moved on to Baltimore in the first week of September. But the city on the Chesapeake proved to be another story. American general Samuel Smith had 13,000 troops under his command, and a barrier of sunken ships blocked direct access to Baltimore harbor, in the heart of the city. Another 1,000 Americans held strongly built Fort McHenry at the harbor's mouth. The redcoats landed some fourteen miles from Baltimore, but General John Stricker halted their advance, the British general himself receiving a fatal wound. Then, on September 13-14, an all-night rocket and artillery bombardment from the British ships

---

2. When the presidential mansion was rebuilt after the war, it was painted white. Ever since, it has been known as the White House.

failed to crack Fort McHenry's defenses. (A Maryland lawyer, Francis Scott Key, whom the British were holding hostage on one of their ships, watched the fearsome bombardment. At the break of dawn, seeing the giant U.S. flag still flying, he was moved to write a poem, "The Star-Spangled Banner," which was soon set to the tune of a popular British drinking song, "To Anacreon in Heaven." Congress made it the national anthem in 1931.) Stopped at Baltimore, the British withdrew their land forces and sailed for Jamaica. The first major British invasion had failed.

The second phase of the British attack was launched from Canada. British troops under General Sir George Prevost began making preparations for a full-scale invasion of New York and New England, but in July 1814 American commanders Jacob Brown and Winfield Scott struck first. Invading across the Niagara River, they defeated the British at the battles of Chippewa and Lundy's Lane. For the British, this was a foretaste of the difficulties that lay ahead. Prevost's main operation was to be a coordinated land-and-water attack of 11,000 veteran soldiers across Lake Champlain, taking Plattsburg, New York, and marching into the heart of New England, cutting that section off from the rest of the United States. But heroic action by Captain Thomas Macdonough, skillfully employing a small flotilla of boats on Lake Champlain, inflicted a stunning defeat on Prevost's forces near Plattsburg on September 11. They retreated to Montreal.

Thus the second major British invasion had been stopped, and the war seemed stalemated. But the third enemy blow was still to fall.

Making Peace and Winning a Victory

Even before Britain's 1814 offensive had got underway, both sides had agreed to discuss peace terms at Ghent, in present-day Belgium. Hoping that Prevost's offensive would tilt the advantage, Britain was in no hurry to conclude negotiations, which were entrusted to relatively minor diplomats. (The top British negotiators were at the Congress of Vienna, wrangling with the other great powers' representatives over the shape of post-Napoleonic Europe.) To Ghent, however, the United States sent five distinguished and shrewd men, including Speaker of the House Henry Clay, Secretary of the Treasury Albert Gallatin, and the American minister to Russia, John Quincy Adams.

Both sides opened with tough demands. The British side called for the Americans to hand the North-

west over to the Indians; the Americans stuck to their insistence that Great Britain acknowledge U.S. neutral rights and end impressment. Then came news of the British defeat at Plattsburg. Weary after the long war with Napoleon, the British government received discouraging military advice about defeating the Americans in the Great Lakes region: impossibly long supply lines would be required. And with Napoleon defeated, the British had little reason to intercept American trade or impress American sailors. Thus, even though a peace treaty might ignore the Americans' chief grievances, ending the war itself might be possible. By December both negotiating teams were moving toward agreement, and on December 24, 1814, they agreed to cease fighting, saying nothing about neutral rights and impressment, returning to boundaries that had existed before the conflict started, and leaving a number of minor issues undecided. The agreement, however, would not take effect until it was formally ratified by both governments.

The greatest battle of the war occurred after the peace treaty was signed — but before its formal ratification. On November 26, 1814, some 7,500 British regulars, fresh from defeating Napoleon, sailed from Jamaica headed for New Orleans. The British commanders, of course, knew nothing about the negotiations at Ghent, and they had orders to conquer New Orleans and Louisiana as a permanent British beachhead. On board the British ships were the staff for a complete civil government, a document declaring the Louisiana Purchase fraudulent, and a plan to proclaim as governor of the new British province General Sir Edward Pakenham, the invasion's commander. Had the invasion succeeded, the whole subsequent history of the United States might have been very different.

The American general defending the region was Andrew Jackson, already known as a formidable fighter against both the Indians and the British. In 1811 Tecumseh had managed to gain as southern Indian allies for his offensive against white settlement a group of young Creek warriors who called themselves "Red Sticks" because of their painted war clubs. In 1813 the Red Sticks had massacred whites at Burnt Corn and Fort Mims in what would later become Alabama, in retaliation for which American militia under Jackson had swept through Alabama with a vengeance. In March 1814 Jackson annihilated the concentrated Red Stick forces at the Battle of Horseshoe Bend, and five months later he forced the Creeks to accept a harsh treaty transferring some 23 million acres in Alabama

The Star-Spangled Banner   Francis Scott Key's words, fitted to a well-known English tune, made this "pariotic song" an instant hit in the emotional days of the War of 1812. This sheet music was first printed in Baltimore, soon after the failed British attack on Fort McHenry. Almost immediately, it became the United States's unofficial national anthem, although Congress did not officially designate it as such until the twentieth century.

and Georgia to the United States. By then Jackson was in control of virtually the entire Southeast, and hearing that a tiny advance force of British had occupied the formerly Spanish town of Pensacola in the Florida panhandle, Jackson led 3,000 troops to capture it easily. Then Jackson moved westward to Louisiana, first establishing himself near Baton Rouge.

General Pakenham and the commanding British admiral had decided not to wend their way slowly up from the mouth of the Mississippi to New Orleans. Instead they tried to seize the city by marching overland from the east, by way of Lake Borgne and a network of shallow bayous. But the British were painfully slow in assembling their forces, giving Jackson time to mobilize 5,000 additional troops — militia from Kentucky and Tennessee, free blacks from Louisiana, friendly Indians, and even a smattering of local French pirates. Jackson's men quickly constructed a sturdy breastwork just south of New Orleans, directly in the path of the British. Early on the fog-shrouded morning of January 8, 1815, as the redcoats were making their move, a sudden breeze swept away the covering fog. The British troops paused, in full view of Jackson's riflemen and cannoneers. With the enemy suddenly revealed on the open ground, the American forces directed devastating fire that cut them to shreds as Jackson's military band tauntingly played "Yankee Doodle." In five minutes, even before it could call a retreat, the British army was destroyed and Pakenham lay dead. In less than an hour the battle was over, with the British suffering more than 2,000 casualties to a mere 71 for the Americans.

Jackson's spectacular victory at New Orleans convinced the British government that the United States could not be subdued without paying unacceptable costs. After news arrived that the British government had formally accepted the Treaty of Ghent, the Senate ratified it unanimously on February 11, 1815. Two days later, President Madison proclaimed peace. The last war between Great Britain and the United States was over, and Andrew Jackson was an American hero.

❧ A Burst of Nationalism

Historians today see the war as having ended more in stalemate than in actual American victory, and the British defeat at New Orleans appears at least as much the result of British mistakes as of American prowess. But that is not how Americans interpreted events in the immediate aftermath of the war. News-

paper headlines across the nation screamed: "Almost Incredible Victory!! Glorious News," and "Splendid Victory: Rising Glory of the American Republic." Having defeated the British twice, Americans believed they had clinched their right to be recognized as an independent nation. It was easy for them to assume that the American republic had a special destiny. Thus they had an obligation to nurture the new nation's sense of cultural identity complete with heroes and to promote its growth in security, prosperity, and international stature. American writers and painters began to turn to American themes for their artistic endeavors. The *North American Review,* a literary journal to rival those of Great Britain, began publication in 1815. Jackson was transformed into a military genius, hailed as somehow both a man of God and a force of Nature, an embodiment of the American people. Legends arose about his Kentucky sharpshooters who supposedly cut the British forces to shreds. (Actually, regular riflemen and the artillery did most of the damage to the British troops.) Songs like "The Hunters of Kentucky," portraying a common-man army of militiamen triumphing over the professional British army — a victory of democracy over aristocracy — became a national hit, sung or hummed everywhere. Henry Clay, still in Paris after negotiating the Treaty of Ghent, reportedly said, "*Now,* I can go to England without mortification." In the warm afterglow of victory, sectional feelings dissipated and political leaders recognized that national interests should prevail over narrow concerns. As Swiss-born Albert Gallatin, also an American negotiator at Ghent and soon to be named minister to France, summed up recent events and the rise of national pride, "The War has renewed and reinstated the national feelings which the Revolution had given and which were daily lessened. The people . . . are more American; they feel and act more like a nation; and I hope that the permanency of the Union is thereby better secured."

❧ The End of the Federalists

The Battle of New Orleans had at least as great a significance for American domestic politics as it had for securing the peace. New England's opposition to the war had breathed new life into the dying Federalist Party. In sermon after sermon, New England Congregational clergy condemned the war against Britain. To these alarmed preachers, only Great Britain's armed might blocked the French Antichrist from taking over the world; Americans, they said, should accept the small price of British interference in neutral waters.

Other New England Yankees had economic reasons for being pro-British. Some local merchants carried on an illegal but thriving trade with Canada, putting personal profit before American national interest. Various rich New Englanders lent money to the Canadians rather than buying United States war bonds. The New England states refused to send their requested quota of militia, and several New England leaders urged outright resistance to the war effort. In 1814, after the British extended their blockade to include the region, some New Englanders even spoke of secession. They had suffered from Mr. Jefferson's embargo, they had warned against fighting, and now "Mr. Madison's War" caught them in the vise of the Royal Navy.

Hotheads among the New England Federalists called for an assembly in Hartford, Connecticut, to vent their frustrations and plan a separate New England Confederacy. Delegates from Massachusetts, Rhode Island, and Connecticut convened in Hartford on December 15, and the convention continued until January 15. Moderates outnumbered the secessionists, so talk of leaving the Union gave way to strong states'-rights arguments. Even so, the convention passed a series of resolutions that put in bold relief New England's disaffection with the rest of the nation in general and with Madison's Democratic-Republicans in particular. The convention announced that each state had the right "to interpose its authority" against national legislation with which it disagreed. The convention wanted to cancel the Three-Fifths Compromise, which gave the slave-holding South over-representation in Congress; it wanted to bar naturalized citizens (usually Democratic-Republicans) from holding office; and it wanted to require a two-thirds majority of both houses of Congress before war could be declared, new states admitted, or foreign commerce banned. All these measures indicated how defensive the New Englanders were and how concerned they were to protect their interests from the growing South and West.

Three New England commissioners brought the Hartford Convention's demands to Washington, D.C., just as the bracing news of Jackson's victory in New Orleans arrived from the other direction. Amid the waves of patriotism washing over the capital, the sour-grapes New England Federalists looked self-serving, negative, and unpatriotic. And the war's end had cleared away most of their grievances. The fizzling out of the Hartford Convention effectively killed the

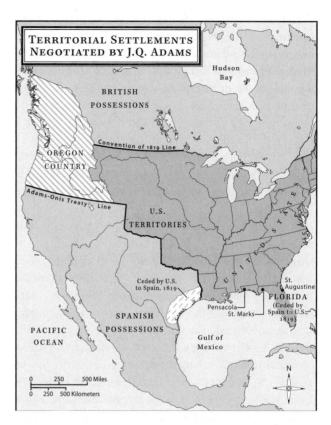

Federalists as a national party. They fought their last presidential campaign in 1816, and even though they managed to find a candidate who had supported the War of 1812 — Senator Rufus King of New York — they carried only Massachusetts, Connecticut, and Delaware. James Monroe, the Democratic-Republican heir to Madison, won the electoral vote 183 to 34. Monroe consolidated Democratic-Republican dominance as the Federalists shrank; in 1820 he would win with all but one electoral vote — one elector, believing that only George Washington should have the glory of a unanimous Electoral College victory, cast a vote for John Quincy Adams, who was not even in the running for the presidency. For all intents and purposes, there was only one national political party during the Monroe administration.

❧ *John Quincy Adams's Continental Diplomacy*

In the flush of confidence and patriotism after the Treaty of Ghent and Jackson's convincing victory, Monroe and the Democratic-Republicans in Congress turned to unfinished business in both international diplomacy and internal economic policy. Monroe was fortunate to be served by the man who was probably the greatest secretary of state in the nation's history,

John Quincy Adams. This eldest son of John Adams had uncommon intellect and foresight, and he was a tenacious negotiator and a dedicated nationalist. At Ghent in 1814 Adams had sought unsuccessfully to win British agreement to disarmament along the U.S.-Canadian border. In March 1816, now secretary of state, he tried again, and Britain, keen to avoid a naval race on the Great Lakes, agreed. The resulting Rush-Bagot Treaty of 1817 limited both nations to four warships on the Great Lakes. This agreement, the first mutual disarmament in modern history, removed a source of Anglo-American friction.

The next year Adams — worried by rumors Russia might push south from its territory of Alaska all the way to San Francisco Bay, forever blocking the United States from having a port on the Pacific with lucrative trade routes to China — arranged a Boundary Commission that fixed the Canadian-American boundary in the Northwest. The line ran from the Lake of the Woods westward along the 49th parallel to the Rocky Mountains. Both countries agreed to a joint occupation of the territory west of the mountains, called Oregon, for ten years. Not forgetting his native New England's fishing interests, in 1818 Adams also persuaded Great Britain to extend fishing rights to Americans off the coasts of Labrador and Newfoundland, and even to permit Americans to dry their catch along stretches of the coast.

Adams next turned his attention southward, to the United States's perennially difficult relations with Spain. That formerly great imperial power faced a stubborn, increasingly successful revolt by most of its Latin American colonies, beginning in 1808. Just before the War of 1812, the U.S. had simply seized West Florida. Spain's tenuous occupation of East Florida still rankled with Americans, although Spain could neither prevent local Indians from raiding southern Georgia nor return runaway slaves who took refuge in Florida. Spain still ruled Mexico, however, and the royal government that regained power in Spain after Napoleon's defeat refused to accept the legitimacy of the 1803 Louisiana Purchase. It wanted to save Mexico's northern province, Texas, and to push the Louisiana boundary as far east as possible. Adams wanted to define a secure western boundary for Louisiana and to acquire all of Florida. Alert to Spain's precarious situation both in Europe and Latin America, Adams adroitly kept up heavy pressure on the Spanish minister to the United States, Luis de Onís, who desperately wanted to hold Texas.

In the midst of the negotiations, Andrew Jackson charged into Florida like a rampaging bull, demonstrating the flimsiness of Spanish control. Constantly irritated by Indian raids against both cattle and slaves, Georgia in 1817 requested federal help. Monroe authorized Jackson to punish the Seminoles for their incursions into Georgia, and Jackson followed his orders overzealously. He chased the Seminoles back into Florida, burning Indian villages and hanging chiefs as he went. Along the way he encountered two British citizens who Jackson thought traded too freely with the Indians, so he hung them too. Then Jackson moved to-

❈ IN THEIR OWN WORDS

The Monroe Doctrine, 1823

Transmitting this message, written by Secretary of State John Quincy Adams, to Congress was the most important action by President James Monroe, and it ensured his name immortality. It became the cornerstone of American foreign policy until World War II.

... [T]he occasion has been judged proper for asserting, as a principle in which the rights and interests of the United States are involved, that the American continents, by the free and independent condition they have assumed and maintain, are henceforth not to be considered as subjects for the future colonization by any European powers....

With the existing colonies or dependencies of any European power, we have not interfered and shall not interfere. But with the governments [of Latin America] who have declared their independence and maintained it, and whose independence we have, on great consideration and on just principles, acknowledged, we could not view any interposition for the purpose of oppressing them, or controlling in any other manner their destiny, by any European power in any other light than as the manifestation of an unfriendly disposition toward the United States....

Our policy in regard to Europe, which was adopted at any early stage of the wars which have so long agitated that quarter of the globe, nevertheless remains the same, which is, not to interfere with the internal concerns of any of its powers; to consider the government *de facto* as the legitimate government for us; to cultivate friendly relations with it, and to preserve those relations by a frank, firm, and manly policy, meeting in all instances the just claims of every power, submitting to injuries from none....

ward Pensacola, where the Spanish royal governor of Florida resided. Jackson removed the governor, took control of the town, and claimed East Florida for the United States. Spain and Great Britain were furious, and Jackson's foes in Monroe's cabinet denounced Jackson's brutal highhandedness.

But wily John Quincy Adams approved of Jackson's actions, reminding both his cabinet colleagues and Onís that if Spain could not control its Indians, then it forfeited control of Florida. The Spanish and British governments acknowledged that Spain was helpless in the face of a determined United States. Willing to give up Florida in order to keep Texas, the Madrid government authorized Onís in February 1819 to sign a treaty with Adams renouncing all claim to Florida. In return, the United States assumed $5 million in claims by its citizens against Spain. The boundary of the Louisiana Purchase was defined as following the Sabine River to the 32nd parallel, then zig-zagging north to the Red River, the 100th meridian, and the Arkansas River to the Rocky Mountains, north again to the 42nd parallel, and finally due west to the Pacific. By accepting the treaty's boundary, the United States gave up all claims to Texas, and Spain still controlled the vast territory from Texas to California. This Adams-Onís (or Transcontinental) Treaty confirmed the United States as a transcontinental nation stretching from the Atlantic Ocean and the warm water of the Gulf of Mexico to the pounding breakers of the Pacific on the Oregon coast (although Oregon was held in joint occupation with Great Britain). Secretary of State Adams confided to his diary his hopes for the treaty: "May its future influence on the destinies of my country be as extensive and as favorable as our warmest anticipations.... The acquisition ... of a definite line of boundary ... forms a great epoch in our history."

❧ The Monroe Doctrine

Adams had one more diplomatic triumph. Many Americans (Henry Clay among them) had been clamoring since 1818 for the United States to recognize the independence of Spain's now-rebellious American colonies, but Monroe and Adams had gone slowly until the Florida matter was worked out. With the ratification of the Transcontinental Treaty in February 1821, Monroe and Adams were ready to accede to popular pressure. In March 1822 Monroe asked Congress to recognize the independence of Argentina, Peru, Colombia, Mexico, and Chile. But trouble

loomed in Europe. In November 1822 representatives of the monarchies that had defeated Napoleon began discussing how to help Spain restore her New World empire. There were even noises about France sending a large army to South America to aid the Spanish. Great Britain, which had begun to profit mightily from the opening of trade with the formerly closed Spanish colonies, objected to the other European powers intervening in Latin America. Great Britain was beginning to move away from mercantilist thinking and toward the principle of free trade, the American position. But the British, with their own colonial empire to safeguard, did not wish to recognize the independence of the former Spanish colonies. United States officials reacted with dismay to any talk of European intervention in Latin America.

To break the dilemma in which he found himself, British Foreign Secretary George Canning devised a clever plan. In August 1823 he proposed that the United States and Great Britain issue a joint statement opposing any European intervention in the New World and pledging that neither would annex any of Spain's former colonies. There was significant American sentiment to go along; Jefferson, Madison, and many other senior statesmen approved. But John Quincy Adams disagreed. He was unwilling to forgo any future United States acquisitions in the region (especially Cuba), and he was concerned about Russian intentions along the coast of California and French ambitions in Latin America. Rather than "to come in as a cock-boat in the wake of the British man-of-war," Adams insisted, it would be more honest — and in the United States's interest — to declare unilaterally that the New World was off limits to European intervention. (Actually, Adams knew that British interests dictated that they keep an Atlantic fleet positioned to prevent the French and Spanish from invading South America, in effect enforcing the proposed American position.) Adams's nationalistic arguments convinced Monroe, who in December 1823 used his annual message to Congress to spell out the bold policy that later came to be known as the Monroe Doctrine.

Following Adams's logic, Monroe announced four major points. First, the American continents "are henceforth not to be considered as subjects for future colonization by any European powers." Second, Monroe followed this hands-off warning with a claim that the political system developing in the New World was "essentially different" from that in monarchical Europe; the two should remain separate. Third, he warned, any attempt by European powers to extend their control or system to any place in the Western Hemisphere that had won its independence would be considered a direct threat to the United States. And fourth, Monroe promised that the United States would not interfere with the European powers' remaining New World colonies, nor would it in any way interfere with strictly European matters. That is, the United States would keep hands off European events.

At the time, Monroe's words seemed more bluster than policy, the ultimate announcement of United States independence from Great Britain and the Old World. Although the Marquis de Lafayette called the statement "the best little bit of paper that God had ever permitted any man to give to the World," the United States had no practical way of enforcing its warning about European involvement in the Americas. These policies were to Great Britain's advantage too, and it was the Royal Navy that made Monroe's doctrine a reality. But decades later, after the U.S. had grown into its role as a world power, asserting and enforcing the Monroe Doctrine became the centerpiece of American foreign policy.

An American Farm Homestead, about 1810   This engraving, showing rural life in central New Jersey, offers a much-idealized depiction of the self-contained mode of production in the United States before the Industrial Revolution and the market economy made self-sufficiency obsolete.

BUILDING A UNITED NATION: THE MARKET ECONOMY AND THE MARSHALL COURT

A tide of optimistic nationalism swept over the United States in the years immediately following the triumphant conclusion of the War of 1812, and with the dangers of war with Britain in the North and with Spain along the Gulf soon removed, Americans began to address the problems attendant to being masters of a transcontinental empire. Before the war, Presidents Madison and Monroe had fully supported the Jeffersonian idea of strictly limited government, but the difficulties encountered in executing any kind of military strategy had shown the utility of, for example, a national bank and an improved system of transportation to link together the far-flung nation. The Bank of the United States had been established a year after Alexander Hamilton's 1790 "Report on a National Bank," but when its twenty-year charter expired in 1811 the Jeffersonians — who had opposed Hamilton's original proposal — happily let it die. But by 1816 events had proved Hamilton right. Likewise, first the embargo and then the effectiveness of the British blockade had forced Americans to become more self-sufficient in manufactured goods and shown the dangers of remaining dependent on European sources for such goods. The result was that the Jeffersonians came to adopt the essentials of Alexander

Hamilton's 1791 "Report on Manufactures," supporting a tariff to protect American factories from cheap British competition and a plan of "internal improvements" in transportation to expedite commerce.

❧ The Emergence of a Capitalist National Economy

Although Americans living in the years 1815-1820 did not fully comprehend the magnitude of the change, the U.S. economy was in the midst of a profound transformation. Modern historians for several generations have analyzed various aspects of these changes, whose combined result has recently been given the grand title of *the Market Revolution*. Different regions and classes felt the transformation in different ways. But almost everywhere an older America of farmers producing only to feed their families was giving way to a world in which farmers specialized in producing certain products for sale to markets — local, regional, national, or international. The Market Revolution meant that American farmers were tending to surrender their self-sufficiency and economic independence, instead tying themselves to the marketplace where they sold their crops and bought the kinds of goods they had once either made for themselves or bartered for with a local hand worker.

The Market Revolution had far-reaching consequences for American society. The ultimate consumers of farmers' products often lived far away, as did the manufacturers of the goods these farmers bought in stores. To work smoothly, these long-range economic exchanges needed a stable currency and system of credit. Quicker and cheaper means of transportation became necessary to speed goods to market. Inviolate corporate charters and easy incorporation procedures had to replace earlier, haphazard, and often corrupt arrangements if larger-scale manufacturing and transportation systems were to be put on a firm foundation. All this was happening in the years after 1815. Both private behavior and government policy changed to accommodate the growing economy. Inventors and entrepreneurs saw their roles magnified. Americans' mental horizons widened both in space and time, for market-oriented production required longer-range planning and consideration of supply and demand far beyond one's neighborhood.

Thus the Market Revolution lifted the veil ever so gingerly upon what we have come to know as the modern capitalist economy. The way to wealth for the nation was trade between its regions, transporting the food and raw products that each could best produce to another, in exchange for the other's produce or manufactured goods. By concentrating on those products for which its climate, geography, or workforce gave it an advantage, each section would prosper, just as the nation's aggregate wealth increased. An ever-growing volume of commerce lowered prices to consumers, created new economic opportunity, and absorbed a rapid population growth, further accelerated by European immigration.

The Market Revolution concept has proven very useful to understanding the processes that created a significantly new American nation in the decades following 1815. Premonitions of one result of the Market Revolution exploded in 1819, when the nation found itself embroiled in controversy over a severe economic depression and Missouri's admission to the Union. Once the War of 1812 was over and the Napoleonic wars ended, renewed British shipping curtailed what had developed into an American commercial boom. This economic downturn was exacerbated when the Second Bank of the United States, attempting to control a frenzy of western land speculation based on easy credit, called in its loans to many state banks, forcing them to foreclose on overextended buyers. The growing interconnectedness of the economy meant that hardships in one region easily affected other regions: policies that made sense for one region could harm another. Coming on top of these economic fears, the Missouri Crisis revealed a sudden and shocking division of the United States along starkly sectional lines — slave states versus free states.

In complicated ways, the Market Revolution helped build the modern America we all recognize: an urban, industrial, capitalist powerhouse that is today the world's superpower. But ironically, the Market Revolution — by maximizing the efficiency of economic specialization — may also have been a precondition for the American Civil War. The South's comparative advantage (its soils, climate, and slave workforce) in growing cotton for tremendous worldwide markets meant that the South became far more dependent on the international market for its basic export than the remainder of the nation. Most of New York City's exports were southern-grown cotton, bound for British textile mills. As southerners shipped out their cotton, either directly to Britain or by way of New York, in exchange they imported a higher proportion of their manufactured needs. Because millions of black southerners, being enslaved, earned no wages, consumer demand in the

South was comparatively weak, further depressing the need for the region to manufacture goods or develop cities. Thus even though the South specialized in one crop and produced for the world market, its market economy came to differ significantly from the North's.

◈ An Economic Policy for Capitalist Development: The American System

By embracing the basic policies of Alexander Hamilton in the aftermath of the War of 1812, the Democratic-Republican presidents Madison and Monroe were responding to needs made evident by wartime problems (transportation bottlenecks, credit shortages, and the federal government's lack of ready access to capital) while at the same time spurring economic changes already underway. The prospects for the new nation seemed unlimited, and the grand expanse of western and southern lands now taken from Indian and foreign control promised a long harvest of new states. Louisiana had become a state in 1812; then quickly after the war came Indiana (1816), Mississippi (1817), Illinois (1818), and Alabama (1819). In anticipation of such growth, President Madison developed a program of federal support for economic growth. Two slave-owning congressmen who had been War Hawk leaders in 1812, John C. Calhoun of South Carolina and Henry Clay of Kentucky, still heady with nationalism, pushed Madison's program. Clay gave it a name: the American System.

Stable credit and a trustworthy currency were central to economic growth and national development. But as yet the federal government did not print paper money, and the only currency was gold and silver coins (except for state bank notes that fluctuated wildly in value). To ensure a reliable credit and monetary system, in 1816 Calhoun sponsored an act to charter, for twenty years, the Second Bank of the United States, or B.U.S. It would be headquartered in Philadelphia but could establish branch banks as needed. The federal government would provide $7 million of its initial capital of $35 million, would appoint one-fifth of the B.U.S.'s directors, and would deposit its normal resources in the bank, also using the bank to pay its bills. The bank could make the kinds of private commercial loans that the growing nation needed to build factories, turnpikes, mills, and other infrastructure. The bank's loans were in the form of notes — pieces of paper that legally circulated as currency. Unlike the notes of unregulated state banks that often plummeted in value on the rumor that the banks might fail, B.U.S. notes were stable currency,

acceptable at face value in payment of debts. Hence they provided the much-needed expansion of currency that the market economy so desperately needed.

The second leg of the American System was "internal improvements." This phrase — much used at the time — meant federally sponsored improvements in the transportation system of toll roads (turnpikes) and canals. Calhoun, remembering how transportation difficulties had hampered troop movements in the War of 1812, strongly supported transportation improvements for nationalistic reasons. "Let us, then," he told Congress in 1815, "bind the nation together with a perfect system of roads and canals. Let us conquer space." Presidents Madison and Monroe were constrained by their strict-constructionist constitutional principles from supporting with federal funds transportation projects that were not clearly national in scope. Calhoun and Clay were much more willing to discern a national interest in creating a network of local transportation links. On grounds of military necessity, in 1816 Madison signed a bill to construct the National Road, built of crushed stone and stretching from Cumberland, Maryland, on the Potomac, to Wheeling, Virginia,[3] on the Ohio River. But in 1817 Madison vetoed an internal improvements bill that did not meet his exacting standards. In the future, most internal improvement projects would be funded either by states or by private corporations, made possible in part by refinements in the legal definitions of both charters and corporations. Clay remained a strong proponent of federally funded internal improvements.

The American System had a third leg — a tariff on imported goods to create the federal revenue needed to fund both internal improvements and military defense. And that was not all. By raising the price of British goods that were being dumped on the American market at below cost to bankrupt new American factories, tariffs would protect these "infant industries" until they could compete equally with the better established British manufacturers. In other words, in addition to producing federal revenue, the tariffs would protect and promote private manufacturing interests. Support for the tariff came from the West, the Middle Atlantic States, and most of New England. Calhoun, still in his nationalistic mood, strongly supported the tariff.[4] He and other nationalists, even if they were not from manufacturing regions like New England, understood that it was not in the nation's interest to depend upon for-

---

3. Now West Virginia.
4. As we shall later see, Calhoun eventually became a southern sectionalist and opposed tariffs.

eign powers for manufactured goods. The British blockade had demonstrated that such dependence meant military disadvantage as well as private inconvenience. Calhoun and a few other southerners embraced the tariff for explicitly nationalistic reasons, not because it potentially benefited the southern economy (although some southerners thought it conceivable that the South might someday manufacture cotton textiles). But Calhoun assumed that the tariff would not be so high as to enrich artificially the manufacturing interests, nor did he expect it to last long after American manufacturers had become fully competitive with the British. In both respects he would later have reasons to regret his pro-tariff stance in 1816.

ॐ *John Marshall and National Supremacy*

While Presidents Madison and Monroe, supported in Congress by many former War Hawks, were pushing through strongly nationalistic legislation, one influential Federalist still held office. This was Chief Justice John Marshall — a tall, extremely thin man with a head that seemed too small for his long body and so loose-jointed that when he walked he had the jerky movements of a puppet — who led the Supreme Court from 1801 to 1835. Marshall too was a Virginian, but he was an ardent personal foe of Jefferson and the later Virginia Republicans. Yet in his firmly Hamiltonian advocacy of a powerful central government and the protection of property rights, Marshall as much as anyone furthered the Market Revolution. He dominated the Supreme Court as no chief justice since has done, and himself wrote most of his Court's major opinions. Marshall understood the need to achieve consensus on a case before issuing a decision so that the Court spoke with one voice, authoritatively. He thus discouraged political attempts to manipulate the Court and gave it greater stature by the weight and unanimity of the decisions rendered. More than any other person, Marshall established the role and sanctity of the Supreme Court in American political life. The Court, he wrote in one decision, had a duty "to say what the law is." He also believed that the business community was the engine driving national progress and interpreted the Constitution to further business interests. The legislation enacting the American System and the sweeping decisions of the Marshall Court worked together to reshape the American economy.

From the first years of his tenure, Marshall had expanded the role of the Supreme Court and the federal government. In *Marbury v. Madison* (1803) he had led the Supreme Court in ruling that it — as the ultimate arbiter of constitutionality — could strike down acts of Congress.[5] Similarly, in *Fletcher v. Peck* (1810), he and the other justices declared that the Supreme Court could overrule a state law that violated the sanctity of contracts.

Beginning in 1819 came another series of the Marshall Court's fundamental decisions, all upholding the sanctity of contracts and defending the "loose" interpretation of the Constitution. In the case known as *Dartmouth College v. Woodward,* New Hampshire attempted to change Dartmouth's original charter granted by King George III. Representing the college (of which he was an alumnus), the prominent Massachusetts politician Daniel Webster argued before Marshall's Court that Dartmouth must keep its original charter. Webster's famous concluding plea — "It is, sir, as I have said, a small college. And yet there are those who love it" — supposedly brought even the stern Marshall to tears. In February 1819 Marshall's decision for the Court's majority ruled that a state could not amend a charter. Once entered into, a charter or acts of incorporation were sacred and could not later be changed or interfered with at the whim of one party. Any charter granted by a state or by the federal government to a private corporation — a turnpike or canal company or a textile factory, for example — enjoyed the full protection of the Constitution's contract clause (Article VI, clause 1).

Almost simultaneously, the Marshall Court's decision in *Sturges v. Crowninshield* overruled a New York bankruptcy law by which one Richard Crowninshield attempted to get out of repaying debts incurred before the law was passed. Marshall voided the New York law because it had been written to apply to such previously contracted debts. Marshall ruled that debts were a form of contract and therefore could not be later canceled: the law remained valid for debts incurred after its enactment.

In an even more far-reaching decision in 1819, handed down less than five weeks after *Dartmouth,* Marshall squarely faced an issue bringing a state government into collision with the federal government. The Maryland legislature, pressured by local banking officials who resented competition and regulation by the Baltimore branch of the Bank of the United States, levied a $15,000 annual tax on all "foreign" banks. The cashier of the Maryland branch of the B.U.S., John W.

5. See Chapter 8.

McCulloch, refused to pay the tax. Thereupon Maryland sued McCulloch for payment. The case eventually reached the Supreme Court, starkly posing the question of the constitutionality of the Bank of the United States versus the constitutionality of a state taxing a federal agency. Marshall dealt with both issues emphatically and convincingly. First, he argued that the Constitution gave Congress the power "to make all laws which shall be necessary and proper for carrying into execution" the legitimate purposes of the government. These "implied powers," Marshall ruled, included the right to establish a national bank — the Constitution, that is, had *implied* or *discretionary* powers in addition to those specified in writing. In essence, Marshall argued that the Constitution was a living, flexible instrument, intended to be adjusted to the changing needs of the people of the United States. "Let the end be legitimate," he wrote, "let it be within the scope of the Constitution, and all means which are appropriate, which are plainly adapted to that end, which are not prohibited, but consistent with the letter and spirit of the Constitution, are constitutional." Moreover, he declared, "the power to tax involves the power to destroy." Thus no state could be allowed to tax an operation of the national government — and the Maryland legislature's action in taxing the branch bank was unconstitutional and void.

The Marshall Court had put federal supremacy on an unassailable foundation, and the powerful defense of the legality of the bank in *McCulloch v. Maryland* gave the young national economy a strong thrust forward.

Five years later, in 1824, another milestone Supreme Court decision spurred internal improvements and the entrepreneurial boom again. A disputed New York law gave a monopoly to steamboat owner Aaron Ogden to operate a ferry service between New York and New Jersey. When a competitor, Thomas Gibbons, who had a federal license to operate a coastal line, sought to provide service to New York, Ogden sued him. Ogden claimed an exclusive right to operate a ferrying service on the New York side of the Hudson River, barring Gibbons from docking in New York. When the case of *Gibbons v. Ogden* reached the Supreme Court, Marshall ruled in favor of Gibbons on the grounds that only the federal government could regulate interstate commerce. A state could still regulate commerce solely within its borders, but if a trip began or ended outside the state, then federal laws governed it. When commerce of any kind — and here Marshall had in mind more than just steamboats — crossed a state line, it ceased being a state matter and fell under federal jurisdiction. This decision prevented states from interfering with interstate commerce and freed entrepreneurs to develop competitive enterprises of all kinds.

State Law and Corporations

On the state level, sweeping legal changes were also under way. States were becoming far more willing to issue charters, usually for public purposes: bridges, ferries, turnpikes, banks. Often these charters gave exclusive rights to the holders, protecting the interests, say, of the builder of a toll bridge. As the scale and scope of business enterprise increased after 1815, state legislatures issued an ever-growing torrent of charters. But investors soon began pressuring legislatures for incorporation procedures intended more to protect their own liability than to limit competition. (Before, when a business or investment failed, individual investors were liable to the full extent of their assets regardless of the size of their original investment. A business collapse often bankrupted even minor investors and could land them in jail.) In the years following the War of 1812, state after state routinized incorporation laws (previously, incorporation was available only by special negotiation with the legislature) and passed legislation specifying that in case of the corporation's financial failure, an investor was liable only up to the amount of his initial investment. This safeguard was intended to attract investors — although some critics saw corporation law as a scam that allowed debtors to escape their creditors should their enterprise fail.

The great advantage of the newly emerging corporation was its ability to pool resources and finance larger enterprises like the Boston Manufacturing Company, which in 1823 built the nation's largest textile factory. John Marshall had guaranteed the security of charters and acts of incorporation, and in turn the state legislatures were transforming the corporation. Whereas once they had been special privilege buffering a monopoly from competition, corporate charters became the engines of competitive enterprises. The huge expansion in the number and variety of corporations in the decades after 1815 both contributed to and emblemized the successes of the Market Revolution.

New Technologies and the Transportation Revolution

Even before incorporation smoothed the path of would-be entrepreneurs and inventors, a variety of

factors had freed Americans to adopt innovation and improve manufacturing technology. In 1790 Samuel Slater imported and improved secret British textile technology, which enabled him to build in Rhode Island the nation's first modern textile factory. Oliver Evans developed the first fully mechanized flour mill in Delaware in the 1790s. Eli Whitney not only invented the cotton gin in 1793, with enormous consequences for the South;[6] in the later 1790s he also secured a large government contract to build muskets assembled by relatively unskilled artisans using a system of interchangeable parts. This idea had originated in Europe, but Whitney and other Americans so perfected the concept that it came to be known as the American sys-

6. See Chapter 11.

American Stage Wagon   Bouncing over rutted, rocky, axlebreaking roads such as are shown in this 1792 engraving, "stage wagons" like this were the main way—apart from riding on horseback—that Americans traveled overland in the early republic.

tem of manufacturing. In Europe and Britain associations of craftsmen and artisans called guilds slowed innovation because they saw change as a threat to existing interests, but there were no restrictive guilds in America. The United States's institutional openness to innovation, its growing national markets, the improvements in its means of transportation, its guarantees of sanctity for contracts, its easy procedures for incorporation, and the ready access to credit and loans that its financial system provided, worked together to produce a transformation of America in the decades following the War of 1812.

Water Power at Slater's Mill   Mill chases such as this were the main source of power at the dawn of the American Industrial Revolution. This engraving shows the first true American factory, Slater's Mill, at Pawtucket, Rhode Island, dating from 1791.

NEW ROADS

In colonial times and the first years of the new republic, transporting passengers or freight overland had been excruciatingly slow and expensive. A federal government analysis in 1816 determined that a ton of goods could be shipped across the Atlantic for $9, but that overland that same ton of goods could only be moved thirty miles for the same amount of money. It took three to four weeks for a wagonload of wheat to rumble from Buffalo to New York City — and it would cost three times more to haul it this distance than it could sell for at its destination. Transportation costs meant that only nearby farmers could produce for the New York City markets. Similarly high transportation costs westward often made manufactured goods prohibitively expensive, forcing farmers either to rely on home manufacturers or those produced by local artisans. Given these transportation difficulties, no regional market economy could develop.

The first efforts to conquer distance — and mud — were turnpikes. In 1794 an all-weather toll road was built from Philadelphia to Lancaster, Pennsylvania. This type of road, invented by John L. McAdam in England, was extremely expensive to build and maintain, requiring expensive tolls. The construction of these roads involved putting down layer after layer of crushed stone, each layer packed together by a heavy roller and the crown finished off with a fine coating of rock dust mixed with water. When hardened, the sur-

face of "macadamized" roads formed a kind of waterproof cement. Since heavy wagons still had to be pulled by teams of horses or oxen, freight costs remained high. But herds of cattle and hogs could be efficiently driven along the turnpikes to eastern urban markets. Despite the continuing disadvantages, by 1825 most of the Northeast, including Pennsylvania, New York, New Jersey, and southern New England, was linked by a network of turnpikes, usually financed at least in part by the states. The federally funded National Road (begun in 1811) eventually extended all the way to Vandalia, Illinois, near the Mississippi River, in 1838.[7]

THE ERIE CANAL

Clearly, however, animal-powered land transportation remained an inefficient and expensive way of distributing goods over large distances. Waterborne transportation was far less expensive. But except for coastal trade along the eastern seaboard and for floating flatboats and barges down the Ohio and Mississippi Rivers, natural water routes did not link the eastern population centers with the farming regions of the Old Northwest. Canals seemed the answer. In 1817 the farsighted governor of New York, DeWitt Clinton, conceived what seemed to many the crazy idea of a 363-mile canal linking the Hudson River at Albany with Buffalo on Lake Erie. Such a project, Clinton realized, would connect the Old Northwest (the Midwest) by water to New York City. The result, he argued, would be "the greatest inland trade ever witnessed." And as a consequence, New York City would become "the granary of the world, the emporium of commerce, the seat of manufactures, the focus of great money operations ... [and] the whole island of Manhattan, covered with habitations and replenished with a dense population, will constitute one vast city." Critics ridiculed Clinton's idea — at the time the longest canal in America was but twenty-eight miles in length — and called it "Clinton's Big Ditch" and "the Governor's Gutter," but he persuaded the state legislature to issue some $7 million of bonds, mostly subscribed to by British and New York City merchants.

Construction on the Erie Canal got underway in 1819. Thousands of workers (local farmers and 3,000 Irish immigrants) dug a canal forty feet wide and four feet deep. A system of eighty-three locks lifted the canal over ridges, and great stone aqueducts carried it across rivers. Along the way the engineers and workmen had to solve a variety of construction problems, and they

7. I-70 and U.S. 40 mostly follow this route today.

invented solutions as they worked, including a device for pulling up stumps and using blasting power manufactured at the Du Pont works in Delaware to break through rocks. They also came up with a form of waterproof cement. The canal was the most stupendous engineering feat in the nation, and when completed all the way to Buffalo in 1825 it proved an enormous success. Within seven years its tolls had paid for its construction. Cutting transportation time by two-thirds and freight rates by as much as 90 percent, the canal enabled commerce to boom. Instant cities like Rochester and Syracuse sprang up, and an astonishing volume of goods and passengers flowed along the route. By 1830 as many as fifty thousand people annually were traveling along the canal to farmland in the Midwest. Colorful songs and folklore arose about the builders of the canal and the powerful keelboat men — like the legendary Mike Fink — who poled their craft along its route. The commerce flowing into New York City made it the nation's leading port and largest city.

The Erie Canal's spectacular success touched off a canal-building boom throughout Pennsylvania and much of the Midwest. Maryland, Massachusetts, and Rhode Island also entered the sweepstakes. Soon much of the Midwest was linked either to the Lake Erie or the Ohio-Mississippi River system, though no other canal was remotely as successful as the Erie. The most grandiose of all was the Chesapeake and Ohio Canal, intended to link Washington, D.C., by way of the Potomac valley with Ohio by crossing the Appalachian Mountains. President John Quincy Adams turned the first spade on the Fourth of July, 1828. Altogether, between 1815 and 1840 more than three thousand miles of canals were built at a cost of $125 million, a prodigious sum at the time.

STEAM ENGINES AND STEAMBOATS

But long before the C&O Canal reached the Ohio River, it (and most other canals) became largely obsolete. In Baltimore — ironically on the same day, July 4, 1828 — aged Charles Carroll of Carrollton, the sole surviving signer of the Declaration of Independence, helped lay the first foundation stone of the Baltimore and Ohio Railroad. Eventually, the railroad, rather than the canal or turnpike, would serve as the highway for the maturing market economy.[8]

8. See Chapters 10 and 14.

✳ IN THEIR OWN WORDS

The Mississippi Steamboat

Mark Twain grew up in a Mississippi River town (which he later immortalized in Tom Sawyer *and* Huckleberry Finn), *and in his* Life on the Mississippi *he recalled the way in which a gaudy steamboat's arrival brought the excitement of the greater world outside into these otherwise somnolent communities.*

Presently a film of dark smoke appears . . . ; instantly a Negro drayman, famous for his quick eye and prodigious voice, lifts up the cry, "S-t-e-a-m-boat a-comin'!" and the scene changes! The town drunkard stirs, the clerks wake up, a furious clatter of drays follows, every house and store pours out a human contribution, and all in a twinkling the dead town is alive and moving. Drays, carts, men, boys, all go hurrying from many quarters to a common center, the wharf. Assembled there, the people fasten their eyes upon the coming boat as upon a wonder they are seeing for the first time. And the boat *is* rather a handsome sight, too. She is long and sharp and trim and pretty; she has two tall, fancy-topped chimneys, with a gilded device of some kind swung between them; a fanciful pilot-house, all glass and "gingerbread," perched on top of the "texas" deck behind them; the paddle-boxes are gorgeous with a picture or with gilded rays above the boat's name; the boiler deck, the hurricane-deck, and the texas deck are fenced and ornamented with clean white railings; there is a flag gallantly flying from the jack-staff; the furnace doors are wide open and the fires glaring bravely; the upper decks are black with passengers; the captain stands by the big bell, calm, imposing, the envy of all; great volumes of the blackest smoke are rolling and tumbling out of the chimneys — a husbanded grandeur with a bit of pitch-pine just before arriving at a town; the crew are grouped on the forecastle; the broad stage is run far out over the port bow, and an envied deck-hand stands picturesquely on the end of it with a coil of rope in his hand; the pent steam is screaming through the gauge-cocks; the captain lifts a hand, a bell rings, the wheels stop; then they churn back, turning the water to foam, and the steamer is at rest. Then such a scramble as there is to get aboard, and to get ashore, and to take in freight and to discharge freight, all at one and the same time; and such a yelling and cursing as the mates facilitate it all with! Ten minutes later the steamer is under way again, with no flag on the jack-staff and no black smoke issuing from the chimneys. After ten more minutes the town is dead again, and the town drunkard asleep by the skids once more.

Even as new transportation networks were being planned and constructed, technology was turning the nation's great natural transportation system, its network of western rivers, into another corridor for commerce. Invented and perfected in early nineteenth-century America, the steamboat seemed as miraculous as the airplane would a century later. Flatboats and keelboats, hitherto the only way of transporting goods on the western rivers, could easily float downstream. But rowing, towing, or poling them upstream was extremely laborious and slow. Barges and flatboats were usually dismantled in New Orleans and sold for lumber, and the crew walked or rode horseback home to Cincinnati or Pittsburgh. River-borne commerce upstream was essentially impossible. Steamboats changed all this.

The Erie Canal, 1830   This painting by John William Hill shows the canal in operation, a little over a decade after its completion. Notice the thriving town and farm that the canal has brought to life.

Beginning in the 1780s, various American inventors had experimented with the steam engine to propel a boat. But it was New Yorker Robert Fulton in 1807 who first successfully demonstrated the practicality of a steam-powered boat when his *Clermont,* 142 feet long and driven by two side paddlewheels, puffed clouds of smoke as it churned up the Hudson River at an impressive five miles an hour.

Fulton went into business with his fellow New Yorker Robert R. Livingston, who had arranged an exclusive state charter to operate steamboats in the waters of New York City. Fulton and Livingston made such spectacular profits that soon competitors elsewhere were tinkering with their design and improving it. Henry Miller Shreve in Louisiana developed a flat-bottomed, shallow draft steamboat perfectly adapted to western rivers, and in 1815 his vessel the *Enterprise* made the first steam-driven voyage from New Orleans to Pittsburgh. Then the 1824 Supreme Court decision

in *Gibbons v. Ogden* prevented such monopolies as Livingston's and Fulton's from stifling competition. Thereupon investors and entrepreneurs promoted steamboats throughout the nation and opened up a huge new transportation network in the heart of the country. Two-way commerce along the Ohio-Mississippi-Missouri River system became feasible. Where in 1820 sixty-nine steamboats worked on the western rivers, there were hundreds by the 1830s.

Even the smaller rivers soon supported steam-driven traffic, and millions of tons of river-borne commerce enriched the port cities from New Orleans to Saint Louis to Louisville and Pittsburgh. Flatboats and barges, along with huge rafts of logs tied together, still floated down the rivers, and in fact such downriver commerce actually increased in volume as the steamboat age blossomed. (In 1828 the young Abraham Lincoln contracted a partnership to deliver a flatboat of farm products from Rockport, Illinois, to New Orleans, and it was on this trip that he first witnessed slavery — an experience that affected him the rest of his life.) Except for New York City and Baltimore — seaports with good transportation links to the interior — all of the most impressive urban growth in the United States between 1800 and 1850 occurred in river cities. Steamboats were indispensable to the Market Revolution by providing quick, inexpensive transportation to the whole mid-section of the nation. Before the steamboat, most water commerce had been along the Atlantic and Gulf coasts; the shift to interior commerce bound the Midwest to the Northeast as never before, with political implications that would not be fully realized until the Civil War.

The smoky behemoths also caught the public's imagination. Soon the Ohio-Mississippi-Missouri boasted steamboats that resembled floating palaces, three or more decks high and with giant lounges and saloons as long as a football field. Most passengers slept on the deck, perhaps atop a cotton bale, but the affluent could travel in opulent comfort. Fancy food and drink, gambling, and music helped pass the time. (Passengers lazily watching the scenery, however, were always in danger: steamboats were notorious for running aground, hitting underwater snags and sinking, or blowing up with great loss of life.) When a steamboat docked, sleepy river towns suddenly came to life, as Mark Twain memorably described in *Life on the Mississippi*. Steamboat races upstream drew huge interest, and the size and magnificence of the later vessels, matching the majestic power of the Mississippi as it rolled toward the sea, gave the whole industry of steamboating a ro-

mance that endures in American folklore. Riverboat musicians, at first primarily white brass players, introduced their instruments to black musicians, at first mainly banjoists; years later, black musicians in river cities, playing instruments like the trumpet, invented that quintessential American musical form, jazz.

The Seeds of Sectionalism

Turnpikes, canals, and steamboats combined to make the transportation revolution that was essential to the emergence of a national market economy. Urbanization and factory production followed, above all in the North and Midwest. There, the Market Revolution quickly meant a proliferation of commerce, busy shops and artisans, and the first factories, all tied together by improved transportation and ever-widening lines of credit. Spurred by easy credit and new transportation networks, the Market Revolution also gripped the South — but with far different consequences. There the economy became increasingly dominated by the production of staple crops for export — especially cotton — and the use of slave labor. John C. Calhoun, the War Hawk and fervent nationalist who in 1815 had written optimistically of binding the nation together by a system of transportation, by 1828 defensively declared that "On the great and vital point, the industry of the country, which comprehends nearly all the other interests, the two great sections of the Union are opposed." That fundamental shift in viewpoints reflected profound changes that had occurred in the nation in little more than a decade.

❧ *"A Fire Bell in the Night"*

An unusual combination of events — political, economic, and legal — came together in 1819 with far-reaching consequences. As a result, for the first time significant numbers of white southerners started to believe that their essential interests differed from those of other Americans. From this date can be traced the origins of southern self-consciousness, and former nationalists like John C. Calhoun began their inexorable intellectual and political shift toward regionalism and eventually sectionalism. No one saw it coming, and except for the dramatic convergence of events in 1819 the ebullient young United States might have continued to vaunt the optimistic nationalism released by the victory at New Orleans. Even so, no one who lived through

The Case Against Admitting Missouri, 1819

Rufus King, a Federalist Senator from New York (and a veteran of the 1787 Constitutional Convention), offered these reasons against admitting Missouri as a slave state in 1819. His argument against opening the West to slavery would continue to resound in the North until the Civil War.

The motives for the admission of new states into the union, are the extension of the prin-ciples of our free government, the equalizing of the public burdens, and the consolidation of the power of the confederated nation. Unless these objects can be promoted by the admission of new states, no such administration can be expedient or justified.

. . . If Missouri, and the other states that may be formed to the west of the river Mississippi, are permitted to introduce and establish slavery, the repose, if not the security of the union may be endangered; all the states south of the river Ohio and west of Pennsylvania and Delaware, will be peopled with slaves, and the establishment of new states west of the river Mississippi, will serve to extend slavery instead of freedom over that boundless region.

Such increase of the states, whatever other interests it may promote, will be sure to add nothing to the security of the public liberties; and can hardly fail hereafter to require and produce change in our government . . . .

---

the crisis could foresee the actual chain of events that, in retrospect, now seems to lead from the confrontation of 1819 to the outbreak of civil war in 1861.

The westward march of statehood seemed an orderly and predictable process in the second decade of the nineteenth century, steadily adding to that "star-spangled banner" of which nationalists sang. Louisiana had become a state in 1812, and within two years after the War of 1812 two more states — Indiana and Mississippi — had joined the nation. The admission of new states generally followed the precedent established by the Northwest Ordinance. As their population grew, frontier regions passed through two grades of territorial organization and thence to statehood. Upon entering the Union, they were equal in every way to the original thirteen. Used to this procedure, no one anticipated anything unusual when the citizens of Missouri Territory began petitioning Congress in 1817 for elevation to statehood. On April 3, 1818, a House committee reported an enabling act for Missouri's admission.

Then trouble erupted. The very next day a congressman from New Hampshire, Arthur Livermore, proposed a constitutional amendment barring slavery in any future state. Livermore and other New Englanders feared the future population growth of additional slaveholding states in the West and South would further weaken New England's already diminishing position in Congress. Livermore's resolution to prohibit the spread of slavery failed, but the enabling act for Missouri never got passed before Congress adjourned.

When Congress reconvened in November 1818, it received a new resolution requesting statehood for Illinois, carved out of the original Northwest Territory. New York Representative James Tallmadge, Jr., a Jeffersonian Republican, bitterly opposed the resolution because the proposed state's constitution did not expressly prohibit slavery — to Tallmadge, a clear violation of the Northwest Ordinance. Nevertheless, the House approved the resolution to admit Illinois without the new state banning slavery. But before Speaker of the House Henry Clay could introduce a resolution from Missouri citizens seeking permission to adopt a constitution and become a state, antislavery advocates convened an emergency meeting in Philadelphia. Calling itself "The American Convention for Promoting the Abolition of Slavery, and Improving the Condition of the African Race," this special meeting petitioned Congress opposing the introduction of slavery into *all* new states and territories.

Premonitions of trouble gathered as 1819 dawned. In January, Pennsylvania congressman John Sergeant introduced a vaguely written resolution instructing the House Judiciary Committee to study an ordinance guaranteeing certain basic civil and religious rights to all inhabitants of territories. South Carolinian William Lowndes, however, quickly saw in the innocent-sounding resolution an antislavery intention. Clearly, the admission of Missouri had become entangled in a gravely important issue that had seldom before been publicly acknowledged: Was slavery to expand, or was it to be contained and eventually allowed to expire? For those who favored limiting slavery and encouraging its demise, Missouri seemed the logical extension of the Northwest Territory, where bondage was already prohibited. For those who favored extending slavery,

Missouri's location made it an essential symbol of slaveholders' right to move westward with the growing nation. The whole destiny of the West, and the nation, seemed at stake. The Missouri question, wrote the editor of the New York *Daily Advertiser,* "involves not only the future character of our nation, but the future weight and influence of the free states. If now lost — it is lost forever." Pressure built over the winter of 1818-1819 as legislators, considering principles and politics, jockeyed for position: both North and South were coming to understand themselves as possessing interests distinct from one another. Yet still no one was quite prepared for what was to happen.

In early 1819, the House took up bills introduced to create two new states: Missouri and Alabama. There was no controversy involving Alabama; given its location, it would obviously be a slave state. Moreover, admitting Alabama would produce an equal balance between slave states and free: eleven of each. (The population of the northern free states, however, was larger by more than 600,000, and growing more rapidly.) But Missouri was a different matter. How it came in — slave or free — would shift the balance of power in the Senate, where each state had two votes. During consideration of the Missouri Enabling Bill on February 13, 1819, Congressman Tallmadge arose once again to move an amendment of the bill. Tallmadge sought to block the further introduction of slaves into Missouri and to provide for the eventual emancipation of the slave children already there when they reached the age of twenty-five. Like a bolt of lightning, this issue, discussed for the first time in two decades openly on the floor of Congress, cleaved the body sectionally. Southern congressmen indignantly rejected the Tallmadge amendment but were outvoted. By a strictly sectional vote the House on February 17 passed the controversial amendment. But the fiercely contested issue failed in the Senate ten days later. When Congress adjourned on March 3, 1819, the festering issue of Missouri's status lingered.

Thomas Jefferson, quietly retired at his beloved Monticello, fully grasped the seriousness of the issue — even his own party was split by the crisis — and began a campaign by correspondence to promote compromise. Almost unconsciously, Jefferson was moving toward a southerner's view of the slavery issue. Writing to a friend, Jefferson admitted that "this momentous question like a fire bell in the night, awakened and filled me with terror. I considered it at once the [death] knell of the Union."

❧ *The Panic of 1819*

The new Congress would not convene until December 1819, but between the introduction of Tallmadge's amendment and the resumption of debate, a major economic crisis exacerbated sectional tensions. With the end of the Napoleonic wars in 1815, European agriculture had at first recovered, reducing the Continent's dependence on grain imported from the United States; and Great Britain now resumed its dominance of worldwide shipping, hurting New England's maritime interests. A recession in Britain, however, depressed the market for cotton just as hard-pressed British manufacturers dumped their goods on the American market. To protect themselves, American manufacturers demanded higher tariffs. All these shocks hit different sectors of the American economy hard, hammering home the lesson of the United States's new dependence on international trade.

Homegrown troubles added to the Americans' growing economic woes. The years immediately following the War of 1812 had seen a speculative mania as buyers scrambled for western lands. Land sales in the West tripled between 1815 and 1818. As prices skyrocketed, get-rich-quick speculators borrowed ever-larger sums from ill-regulated state banks. Public land officially valued at $2 per acre zoomed to $80 and even $100 per acre. The Cincinnati and Lexington (Kentucky) branches of the Bank of the United States succumbed to the speculative mania, and the president of the B.U.S., William Jones, proved a lax administrator. As the amount of state bank loans — issued as negotiable notes — increased at a dizzying rate, Jones resigned in early 1819. His successor, Langdon Cheves of South Carolina, was far more cautious. The B.U.S. began demanding that the notes it received from state banks be paid for in specie — actual gold or silver coin. (The money in circulation — much of it improvised: warehouse receipts, promissory notes, private scrip, state treasury notes — had become so "puzzling to traders," wrote a Scotch traveler in 1820, that a merchant, "when asked the price of an article, instead of making a direct answer, usually puts the question, 'What sort of money have you got?'") State banks could meet this requirement only by forcing their creditors to pay off their notes in specie. The result was a collapse of the national money and credit system. The speculative boom in western lands crashed. Thousands of shady speculators and honest farmers alike were wiped out by the monetary contraction. The result of all these factors, national and international, was a bruising six-year depression known as the Panic of 1819. As one contemporary observed critically, "the Bank was saved and the people were ruined."

The Panic hit western and southwestern farmers particularly hard, and they soon found their villain: the B.U.S. A tradition of western hatred of the B.U.S. — "the Monster Bank" — and of banking in general was kindled, destined to survive long into the twentieth century. And because manufacturers from the same northeastern region that harbored the Philadelphia-based B.U.S. began pushing for tariff increases, westerners and southerners quickly concluded that their interests were antithetical to the northeastern capitalists'. Cotton growers especially, utterly dependent upon exporting their product and fearing British retaliation to American trade barriers, ceased to see tariffs as a nationalistic necessity. Instead, they believed, protectionism unfairly enriched one section of the nation while jeopardizing the exports of another.

ॐ The Missouri Compromise

Southern nerves had already been touched by Tallmadge's antislavery amendment and the costs of the Panic of 1819 when Marshall in March 1819 announced the Supreme Court's decision in *McCulloch v. Maryland*. Capping a series of earlier Marshall decisions that established the Supreme Court's superiority over state governments, *McCulloch* boldly defended the constitutionality of the B.U.S. by stretching the definition of federal powers. Many southerners now saw a frightening specter: might not the federal government, with its ever-expanding powers, someday decide to interfere with slavery, the South's "peculiar institution"? Exactly such an alarm filled a series of highly critical essays published in the Richmond *Enquirer* within a month of the *McCulloch* decision. Marshall himself answered these criticisms in a biting reply in the Philadelphia *Union* in April, and in turn an eminent Virginia judge, Spencer Roane, replied to Marshall in the *Enquirer*. Marshall responded with nine essays in the Alexandria *Gazette*. Neither side convinced the other, but the whole exchange aggravated the fears of increasing numbers of Virginians and other southerners about the dangers to slavery inherent in the federal government's growing power. States'-rights rumblings began to be heard in the South.

Such was the atmosphere of economic misery and constitutional uncertainty in which Congress gathered in December 1819. Political passions had not cooled. Passionate debates rehearsed all the arguments over slavery that would echo for decades to come, and the intense feeling about the issue frightened moderates. Northerners openly argued that slavery was a contradiction of the Declaration of Independence and had no legitimate place in America. White southerners just as defiantly argued that their freedom meant the freedom to own slaves; indeed, they *defined* their liberty in terms of their right to enslave others and hold them as property. Such southerners believed that their region's economy — their very way of life — depended upon black slavery. Never before had the raw tensions dividing the nation stood so starkly revealed.

Enter a determined Henry Clay in early 1820. Using his office as Speaker of the House and his warm personality, Clay devised a series of compromise measures that, each by different majority coalitions, passed both the House and the Senate in February 1820. The result, known as the Missouri Compromise, admitted two new states. One was the free state of Maine, hitherto part of Massachusetts. Balancing Maine was the state of Missouri, in which slavery was permitted. Slavery was prohibited from the rest of the Louisiana Territory lying north of Missouri's southern boundary, formed by the latitude of 36° 30′. South of that line, in the Arkansas Territory and the eventual Oklahoma Territory, slavery would be legally permissible if the actual settlers so desired. This compromise arrangement — the idea of Senator Jesse B. Thomas of Illinois — of course left the greater part of the Louisiana Territory, north of 36° 30′, free of slavery, but this seemed acceptable at the time because most of the Great Plains was considered a desert, unfit for settlement or agriculture. For the moment, the balance of power in the Senate remained, and with a kind of theoretical balance of future slave and free states west of the Mississippi, the explosive issue seemed uneasily settled. Many Americans heaved a huge sigh of relief. But as Jefferson recognized, the issue had not been really resolved. In ways not completely understood, perceptive Americans sensed that the nation now contained several differing regional economies — and perhaps even rival cultures.

THE EVANGELICAL RESURGENCE

The rapid development of the market economy in the northern states created a real division between the

North and the South, and the dominance of a slave-based staple crop economy in the South further drove a wedge between the regions. It is also now evident that the development of a different religious tradition in the South also contributed to both cultural and political divergence between the sections, although, like so many of the other changes that were occurring, the full implications were not immediately clear to contemporaries. In both regions there was a democratization of religion in the first quarter of the nineteenth century, with theology, church leadership, and lay involvement evolving.

The changes were first more dramatic in the South, the region that previously had had the weakest religious infrastructure; a Great Revival that began in 1800 transformed the region's religious landscape and ensured the dominance there of the Baptist and Methodist churches. In New England, theological adjustments began in the 1790s that came to fruition more than two decades later in the religious movement known as the Second Great Awakening, but before this series of revivals occurred new denominations arose to rival the Congregational-Presbyterian dominance that had prevailed before. There was far more religious diversity in the northern states, both because of immigration and because the transformative economic and social change led many people to reconsider older ways of thinking and doing. Even so, the persistent Puritan tradition in New England (which followed settlers into upstate New York and across the upper Midwest) in subtle ways influenced the tone of even the more democratic new denominations in the North. The much weaker Episcopal Church in the South had less influence on the revivalistic ethos of the Baptists and Methodists who came overwhelmingly to dominate the southern society.

In the two decades before the Civil War the South came to see itself set apart from the North as truly in religion as in economic and political matters. The seeds of that distinctive religious culture were planted in the first decades of the nineteenth century.

❧ Northern Protestantism Responds to Challenges

The mainstream northern religious tradition at the beginning of the nineteenth century — before large-scale European immigration brought significant numbers of Catholics and later Jews to the northern states — was a Congregational-Presbyterian common front. The Con-gregational church had evolved from the colonial Puritan church, and the Presbyterian stronghold was in Pennsylvania and New Jersey, with Princeton its intellectual citadel. Both churches were part of the political, economic, and intellectual establishment. Both shared traditions of a learned clergy and proclaimed a sophisticated Calvinist theology that emphasized God's role in human salvation. Both saw conversion more as an individual's assent to key doctrines than as an emotional confrontation wherein one felt swept away by the Holy Spirit.

Yet the First Great Awakening in the 1730s and 1740s had led to religious controversy and the strengthening in New England of the Baptist denomination. Baptists pushed for churches supported voluntarily, not by state taxes, and they put more emphasis on the individual's role in discovering his or her own salvation. The Methodist movement, an evangelical offshoot from the Church of England, also began to make inroads in New England and such colonies as Maryland and New York just before the American Revolution. The Methodists were even more insistent that salvation began with the individual's desire to put away the old person and discover a new being in Christ — being born again, as the Gospel of John (3:3) expressed it. Both Baptists and Methodists employed lay ministers who had no formal education, only a deep commitment to their faith, and their religious services were long, loud, disorderly (in comparison to the more formal churches), and apt to be conducted anywhere, even within the parish boundaries of the older established churches. What is more, their services attracted ordinary people, especially as the American Revolution unleashed powerful democratic urges in the nation.

Congregational and Presbyterian leaders in New England took worried notice of these developments that threatened their domination of the religious life of the region. Yale University president and Congregational minister Timothy Dwight began to suggest revisions in the orthodox Puritan theology: humans had a greater degree of agency with regard to their salvation than hitherto recognized and were not automatically and hopelessly mired in sin. Dwight also suggested that humans could define a life of duties that were broader than simple devotion to God. The full implications of these deviations from orthodoxy not even Dwight understood, but he had begun a democratizing tradition that later, under evangelist and reformer Charles G. Finney, made conversions a routine result of organized revivalism and social reform the expectation of Christian endeavor. Other Congregationalists, dissatisfied with the rigidities of the older orthodoxy and upset by the emotional excesses of revivalism, argued that morality should be achieved by "character building"; they portrayed Jesus more as a model of behavior than as the divine mediator for sinners. These liberal religious thinkers emerged in the early nineteenth century as Unitarians.

Long before the Congregationalists and Presbyterians could see the consequences of Dwight's theological accommodations, they decided to act as one in response to the missionary needs of the rapidly developing West. The first three presidents of Princeton had been New England Congregationalists, and in 1801 the two denominations, faced with significant migration into western New York and the Northwest Territory, had strengthened their ties by signing a Plan of Union. This cooperative agreement, whereby the two denominations shared pulpits, ministers, and delegates between their ecclesiastical associations, essentially merged the two denominations. In 1808 this unity was furthered by the "Accommodation Plan" that made their forms of church government uniform. For the next generation the Presbyterians and Congregationalists acted as a single group in New York, Ohio, Indiana, Illinois, Michigan, and Wisconsin. Combined with their strength in the Middle Atlantic and New England states, the "Presbygationalists" virtually defined mainstream Protestantism in the North.

Growing out of their roles in colonial New England, the Congregationalists and Presbyterians understood the responsibility of the church to be far broader than just seeing to the state of the souls of their members. They believed churches had a responsibility for the condition of the larger society. As such, they simply took it for granted that civil government and the churches should work together to achieve a moral, just society. The churches believed that they as an institution should address the evils of society as well as individual sins, and they believed one of their goals was to stiffen the backbone of government officials; similarly, they expected the government to enforce morality. Hence there was a long tradition of election day sermons, an expectation that church and state had a mutual obligation to maintain a godly order.

In important ways, the dominant northern religious tradition focused as much on the churches' societal roles as on their roles as agents for individual conversion. For that reason, northern religious bodies often found themselves supporting reform movements aimed at "saving" a society or class of people rather than only emphasizing personal evangelism. Even northern Methodists, for whom active evangelism remained the primary mission, came to emphasize personal holiness that evolved in the direction of social perfectionism. This comprehension of the social dimension of religion, rather than exclusive concentration on individual conversion, led to a battery of religiously inspired reform movements in the North, and much later to the origins of the Whig, Know-Nothing, and Republican parties. Many New England Congregationalists, strident opponents of the War of 1812 only to see the U.S. emerge unscathed, came to believe that God had preserved the nation in order to give the Congregationalists/Presbyterians one more chance to reform society. They interpreted the need for godly reform to be especially severe given the population movement to the newer states in the Northwest and Southwest. The result was the organization of the American Bible Society and the American Education Society in 1816, the first of a phalanx of reform or benevolent societies that over the next generation would attempt to shape and discipline American society (see Chapters 10 and 12). This willingness to employ the joint forces of church and state to effect moral reform of the nation was, however, a characteristic of the northern, Calvinistic, Protestant tradition. In contrast, the southern evangelical or pietistic tradition was primarily focused on the necessity of converting individuals, with the societal dimension of their mission drastically reduced.

❧ The Great Revival in the South

Institutional Protestantism had been far weaker in the colonial South than in the northern colonies. The southern colonies from Maryland to Georgia had an established church, that is, a church supported by tax revenues and the civil arm of the law, but the Anglican (or Church of England) churches had large parishes, were not heavily attended, and their largely English-trained ministers had little appeal to the mass of southerners. Local church governance was controlled by the planter elite, and neither the ministers nor the boards of vestry made energetic attempts to reach out to the unchurched or the underchurched. At best, the Anglican Church in the South was a nominal religious establishment. For that reason, the so-called Great Awakening that swept the New England and Middle Atlantic colonies in the 1730s and 1740s only lightly touched the southern colonies.

A Camp Meeting   A British artist exhibited this watercolor at the Royal Society in London in 1839. He claimed to have sketched the scene "on the spot," though exactly where or when is not clear. American revivalism was of considerable interest — usually not very sympathetic — to the British public.

Partly as a secondary effect of the Great Awakening, however, beginning in the 1740s and 1750s, active, energetic outposts of Presbyterians and Baptists took root in South Carolina and Virginia, and within a decade the Methodists — then a radically evangelistic arm of the Anglican Church — began to carve out a foothold in Virginia, Maryland, and North Carolina. The Baptists and Methodists criticized the planter aristocrats' opulent lifestyle and ownership of slaves, for the evangelical denominations were very much a religion of the common folk.

A proliferation of religious revivals so widespread as to have the effect of a Great Awakening never occurs in a vacuum. Instead, there must be in place a network of ministers and churches, a shared idea about how God works in history, and a perceived social crisis so severe that devout people believe the only solution is a kind of divine intervention. Neither of these prerequisites was sufficiently in place in the South in 1740 — in contrast to New England — to allow the sprinkling of small revivals to grow into a region-wide religious awakening. But by the 1790s a network of ministers and churches was in place, and the fifteen years after the American

---

An Indiana Camp Meeting, 1832

Frances Trollope, an intrepid Englishwoman, was one of many Europeans who traveled widely in the United States in the 1820s and 1830s to observe democracy in action. She provided this astonished but essentially condescending glimpse of a revival in her book Domestic Manners of the Americans, *published in London in 1832.*

The prospect of passing a night in the backwoods of Indiana was by no means agreeable, but I screwed my courage to the proper pitch, and set forth determined to see with my own eyes, and to hear with my own ears, what a camp-meeting really was. I had heard it said that being at a camp-meeting was like standing at the gate of heaven . . . [or] finding yourself within the gates of hell; in either case there must be something to gratify curiosity, and compensate one for the fatigue of a long rumbling ride and a sleepless night.

We reached the ground about an hour before midnight. . . . [She peeked into a tent and saw men and women kneeling on the straw-covered ground.]

Out of about thirty persons thus placed, perhaps half a dozen were men. One of these, a handsome-looking youth of eighteen or twenty, kneeled just below the opening through which I looked. His arm was encircling the neck of a young girl who knelt beside him, with her hair hanging disheveled upon her shoulders, and her features working with the most violent agitation; soon after they both fell forward on the straw, as if unable to endure in any other attitude the burning eloquence of a tall grim figure in black, who, standing erect in the center, was uttering with incredible vehemence an oration that seemed to hover between praying and preaching; his arms hung stuff and immoveable by his side, and he looked like an ill-constructed machine, set in action by a movement so violent as to threaten its own destruction, so jerkingly, painfully, yet rapidly, did his words tumble out; the kneeling circle ceased not to call, in every variety of tone, on the name of Jesus; accompanied with sobs, groans, and a sort of low howling inexpressibly painful to listen to. . . .

Revolution had ushered in an onslaught of change that persuaded many people that the society was in crisis.

First the ratification of the federal Constitution and then the writing and ratification of new state constitutions had inaugurated an era of intense political controversy. Economic change was remaking the South, as rice and indigo planters, no longer having privileged access to British markets, began a long decline. The cotton gin, on the other hand, had introduced a new boom crop, with farmers clamoring for fresh land and more slaves. The opening up of new settlements in Kentucky and Tennessee, spurred by Revolutionary land bounties, created a massive human migration westward, threatening to depopulate sections of the seaboard states, whose soil was exhausted from generations of planting tobacco. Population growth in sections of the new states outpaced the ability of churches, schools, and civil government to keep up, just as dreams of new land, more slaves, and fortunes in cotton crowded religion from the minds of many frontiersmen. Moreover, news from Revolutionary France brought frightening images of infidelity and destruction of clerical institutions, and these rumors, highly exaggerated, led many in America to fear for the future of religion. From today's perspective, these economic and political changes appear to be quite normal responses to the conclusion of the Revolution and the beginning of a new nation. But to many churchgoers in the 1790s the changes were frightening and disrupting because no one knew where the change would lead or when it would end. It was the widespread interpretation by southern ministers and devout laypersons that the late 1790s were a period of religious decline and societal crisis. Among such people, convictions grew that God would soon intervene to set things aright.

Out of this matrix of events, perceptions, and fears, southern evangelical clergy constructed in the final years of the 1790s an expectation that at any moment God would effect an all-transforming religious revival. It was with that interpretative schema in place that ministers and laypersons responded to a series of emotionally intense revival meetings that began in Kentucky in 1800. Within a year or two the revivals had spread into all the southern states. "Hell is trembling, and satan's kingdom falling," wrote a South Carolina Methodist in 1802, "the sacred flame . . . is extending far and wide." Out of these interdenominational revivals came the camp meeting, where hundreds of people would come and camp out for religious services that would last for days, with dozens of preachers speaking throughout the campgrounds from makeshift pulpits and preaching stands. The singing and sermons attracted great attention, as did the size and scale of the meeting. Even more notoriety came from what were called the physical exercises: people fainting, having spasms of shaking and grunting, and laughing hysterically.

Partly a result of crowd hysteria, partly in response to intense religious feeling and a hunger to experience a life-transforming conversion, partly legitimated by the instant interpretation of the camp meeting revivals as the long hoped for, long expected divine intervention into society, the size, novelty, and emotional power of the revivals that began in Kentucky initiated what is usually called the South's Great Revival. As a result of this series of revivals and camp meetings — in truth the South's First Great Awakening — church membership doubled, tripled, even quadrupled in many parts of the South. New churches were organized, and many young men felt called to the ministry. The Presbyterians soon pulled back from the emotional intensity of the outdoor revival meetings, and the Baptists began to focus on annual revivals in individual churches, leaving the camp meeting as the preferred instrument of evangelism of the Methodists in both the South and the North.

But the power and efficacy of the camp meeting style of preaching had a profound impact on all three dominant southern churches, especially on the Baptists and Methodists. Theological precision and doctrinal matters were minimized as preachers sought to speak directly to the heart and emotions of listeners in order to gain a conversion. As dramatic, story-telling sermons became the center of the religious service, ritual and theology were minimized. Reacting to their perception that when religion was in consort with the state, religion could be perverted — a reaction to the evangelicals having suffered persecution at the hands of the established churches before the Revolution — the Baptists and Methodists tended to privatize religion. After 1800, as the cotton-fueled slave economy closed its vise on the South, both Baptists and Methodists quickly realized that if they continued to attack slavery their ability to prosper and spread the gospel in the South would be sharply curtailed. More evangelical than reformist in nature, both churches decided to minimize their antislavery message in order to maximize their evangelical opportunities. They rationalized that religion was more a matter of the soul, of the spirit, than of earthly issues.

The primary purpose of the churches was to gain conversions, to focus more on the sins and failings of individuals than on the problems of society. To involve the churches in political or economic issues, evangelicals believed, was to risk the central mission of the church. Out of this combination of theological perspective and rationalization came the central southern religious tradition, the belief that the churches' chief roles were individualist, private, and confined to nurturing inner piety. Southern churches had a far more limited conception of their societal responsibilities than did northern churches, and as a result the dominant southern evangelical churches were slow to address the institutional evils of society. The variety of benevolent societies that were sponsored by the northern churches found relatively few members in the rural South. (Only in southern cities would northern-style religious reform emerge.) This southern religious tradition helped to set apart the slaveholding South from the free labor society of the North, and although no one fully understood the significance of these regional religious differences in 1819, over the next four decades the churches would also help widen the sectional breach.

CONCLUSION: OPTIMISM AND CHALLENGES

Varying degrees of support for the War of 1812 had revealed different sectional interests in the nation, but the final victory at New Orleans allowed a flowering of nationalism that had more than symbolic effects. Politicians, including southerners, supported rechartering a national bank, levying tariffs to protect infant American industries, and funding some internal improvements. Meanwhile, the American economy was being transformed; and what historians now call the Market Revolution would lead to the growth of transportation networks, manufacturing, and cities, especially in the North. In the South, the agricultural revolution made possible by the invention of the cotton gin and the opening up of new territories in the Southwest was creating the Cotton Kingdom.

Yet this period of nascent nationalism also set into motion myriad factors that would later divide the nation into antagonistic sections and the controversy over the admission of Missouri in 1819-1820 marked the opening round of the debate over slavery. Economic, constitutional, and religious differences soon emerged, and the nation that had seemed relatively unified in 1816 would enter the second quarter of the nineteenth century with sectional and political tensions ready to erupt.

No one in the early 1820s was farsighted enough to glimpse accurately the future, and for many Americans the next decades were optimistic ones of economic and population growth, political democratization, cultural and intellectual maturation, religious conversion, and a flowering of reform movements. The South would grow and thrive as a related but essentially different society, one dominated by slavery. The northern free society, resting on an increasingly modern market economy, would find itself in constant and often congenial collaboration with the southern slave society — also capitalistic, but dependent on agricultural exports. These two maturing societies, dependent on but increasingly wary of one another, must be understood in depth before we can fathom the political, territorial, and moral differences that eventually led to the Civil War.

Suggested Reading

John B. Boles, *The Great Revival, 1787-1805: The Origins of the Southern Evangelical Mind* (1972). The standard account of the series of revivals that transformed the religious life of the South.

Christopher Clark, *The Roots of Rural Capitalism: Western Massachusetts, 1780-1860* (1990). A thorough, multi-faceted examination of how the economy was changed by the so-called Market Revolution.

R. David Edmunds, *Tecumseh and the Quest for Indian Leadership* (1984). A detailed, sympathetic portrait that emphasizes the role of Indian culture.

Donald R. Hickey, *The War of 1812: A Forgotten Conflict* (1989). The most satisfactory overall narrative of the war — causes, battles, and conclusion.

Glover Moore, *The Missouri Controversy, 1819-1821* (1953). An older but still extremely useful analysis of this critical episode.

R. Kent Newmyer, *John Marshall and the Heroic Age of the Supreme Court* (2001). The best study of Justice Marshall and his shaping influence on both the Court and American life.

J. C. A. Stagg, *Mr. Madison's War: Politics, Diplomacy, and Warfare in the Early Republic, 1783-1830* (1983). Especially good on the origins of the war.

Gordon S. Wood, *The Radicalism of the American Revolution* (1992). A brilliant analysis of the long-range consequences of the Revolution, a period that Wood sees stretching to the Jacksonian era.

Suggestions for Further Reading

Doron S. Ben-Atar, *The Origins of Jeffersonian Commercial Policy and Diplomacy* (1993).

Jeanne Boydston, *Home and Work: Household, Wages, and the Ideology of Labor in the Early Republic* (1990).

Robert F. Dalzell, *Enterprising Elite: The Boston Associates and the World They Made* (1987).

George Dangerfield, *The Awakening of American Nationalism, 1815-1828* (1965)

John Mack Faragher, *Sugar Creek: Life on the Illinois Prairies* (1986).

William Gribbin, *The Churches Militant: The War of 1812 and American Religion* (1973).

Joseph Haroutunian, *Piety versus Moralism: The Passing of the New England Theology* (1932).

Nathan O. Hatch, *The Democratization of American Christianity* (1989).

Christine Leigh Heyrman, *Southern Cross: The Beginnings of the Bible Belt* (1997).

Brooke Hindle and Steven Lubar, *Engines of Change: The American Industrial Revolution, 1790-1860* (1990).

Morton J. Horowitz, *The Transformation of American Law, 1780-1860* (1977).

Paul Johnson, *A Shopkeeper's Millennium: Society and Revivals in Rochester, New York, 1815-1837* (1978).

Walter LaFeber, ed., *John Quincy Adams and the American Continental Empire* (1965).

Walter Lord, *The Dawn's Early Light* (1974).

Ernest R. May, *The Making of the Monroe Doctrine* (1992).

Robert V. Remini, *The Battle of New Orleans* (1999).

Charles Sellers, *The Market Revolution: Jacksonian America, 1815-1846* (1991).

Ronald E. Shaw, *Canals for a Nation: The Canal Era in the United States, 1790-1860* (1990).

Steven Watts, *The Republic Reborn: War and the Making of Liberal America, 1790-1820* (1987).

William Earl Weeks, *John Quincy Adams and American Global Empire* (1992).

G. Edward White, *The Marshall Court and Cultural Change, 1815-1835* (1991).

10 The Modernizing North

A MIDDLE-AGED PERSON who had lived his or her entire life in Massachusetts or Pennsylvania would, by 1800, have seen remarkable political changes. But in terms of how most people actually lived — how they earned their living, did their work, obtained their clothes, traveled, thought of their future — change would have been imperceptible to such a person. Most Americans in the North as well as the South still lived in rural areas, most of them were engaged in agriculture, and most made their own clothes or purchased items like shoes from artisans who made the entire product by hand. Everyone traveled on foot, by animal, or by boats propelled either by wind, by the current, or by human or animal labor. In most of their day-to-day activities, ordinary people in 1800 lived very similarly to the way people had lived a century or more before. Most children were expected to make their livings in ways quite similar to those of their parents even if they had to move away to find sufficient land to cultivate. Work roles, gender roles, and class roles would, it was assumed, remain relatively constant. No one could foresee in 1800 or even 1810 that they were on the cusp of a series of interrelated developments that would fundamentally reshape the lives of countless people, especially in the northern states.

Nowhere in the nation was change over the course of the next five decades more rapid, or more transforming, than in the northern states, especially those stretching from Massachusetts southward to Pennsylvania and westward to Ohio. A new North was the result, and the cumulative effect of these changes was to very significantly widen the gap between the moderniz-

New England Cloth Makers This eighteenth-century depiction of making cloth in an American household shows a way of production that would become largely obsolete when the Industrial Revolution spurred the creation of textile mills in New England.

ing northern states and the more traditional southern states that continued, largely unchanged, to depend on staple crops and slave labor.

The rate of change is a relative matter, and change even in the Northeastern and Middle Atlantic states was rapid only from the perspective of what had gone before, when decades had little affected how most people lived. The half century following 1810 would see more far-reaching changes in technology, industry, and transportation than the previous two centuries, although the pace seems slow from the perspective of today. Change, moreover, was very uneven, varying from one region to another, between urban and rural areas, and from one industry to another. Even those persons

whose lives were most enmeshed in the related series of developments that produced change were seldom completely aware of exactly what was happening and of its implications for the future.

THE INDUSTRIAL REVOLUTION

Work is more than simply how people make a living or how goods are produced. Work shapes people's lives; it determines the pace of their activities, affects the timing of social and religious events (in agricultural societies, for example, major revivals and camp meetings are scheduled after crops are laid by, that is, no longer in need of cultivating), influences the acculturation and training of children, helps create social identity and political and economic interests, and much more. Working conditions and expectations of success (or failure) contribute to social stability (or unrest), create expectations of hopefulness (or hopelessness), influence family size, and inspire people to strive for upward mobility or depart for greener pastures — or to rebel, or to sink into passivity. In the opening decades of nineteenth-century America, every aspect of work — from production techniques to laboring conditions to the composition of the workforce to marketing mechanisms — was transformed. No one foresaw the changes; no one directed the overall transition. But the result was a nation that by 1850 barely resembled what it had been only a half-century before.

ஃ *Traditional Production*

At the opening of the nineteenth century, 97 percent of the nation's population lived on farms. Most people made the things they needed or purchased them from local artisans — often by bartering goods or work effort rather than by paying cash. For example, a farmer might barter eggs or butter or pigs or even firewood with a blacksmith for an ax or hoe; similar goods might be exchanged for shoes with the local cobbler. Often imported goods were available in crossroads stores or in small trading communities, but just as often barter was the means of commerce here too. Local artisans such as saddlers, blacksmiths, hat makers, and gunsmiths operated small shops with an apprentice or two and perhaps several hired hands, and the artisan supervised every aspect of the craft. Larger shops might employ a journeyman — in a sense, a graduated apprentice who received a wage. The artisan gathered his raw materials, did the most skilled labor himself and supervised the rest, and sold his product from his shop with no middleman between the workshop and the consumer. The farmer bargained directly with the artisan for the goods, and whether money or farm products or labor was exchanged, the transaction was face to face.

The market for an artisan's products was local, and the artisan only supplied those goods impractical for a typical farm family to make for itself. For example, most farmwomen made their family's clothing but purchased their shoes; a farmer would build utilitarian tables and benches but purchase metal tools and nails. Only in cities were there specialty artisans making luxury goods, but silversmiths and cabinetmakers who produced for the economic elites tended to deal more commonly in money, and their skill level was higher. In 1800 most manufactured goods were still imported from England and made available through merchants rather than artisan-manufacturers.

Another kind of industry were mills of various sorts, ranging from grist mills to saw mills, all of which had to be located near running water. Here too local farmers often bartered — for example, paying to have their corn or wheat ground by giving the miller a percentage of the meal or flour. The exchange was direct and personal, and the market local.

The first inklings of an emerging industrial system were so carefully adapted to the local, household nature of earlier production that it did not seem a significant break with the way things had been done before. Technological developments in the production of thread and cloth, brought to America from Britain by what we would now call industrial espionage, initiated the factory system. Samuel Slater, an apprentice in a British cotton spinning mill, slipped out of the country in disguise, came to Providence, Rhode Island, and there — funded by two wealthy Providence investors — reconstructed from memory the secret British machinery. Yet this mill that Slater helped build did not produce finished cloth; rather, it transformed broad folds of cotton into yarn. This yarn was "put out," as the phrase went, to hundreds of households in Providence and the surrounding farming neighborhood, where housewives and daughters, working at their own pace on home looms, wove it into cloth. Agents of Slater's mill contracted with the women, delivered the yarn, and later picked up the finished cloth and sold it. The women worked by the piece and the rate was low, but it was assumed by their employers that they had the financial support of husbands and fathers and that their wages only supplemented the family income. Because most of the actual workers in the cloth industry still toiled in private homes, Slater's mill represented only the entering wedge of modern industry. It preserved many of the features of traditional home production.

As Slater's operations expanded, he began to locate mills in rural areas and bought extensive tracts of land surrounding the mill sites. Then he would recruit entire farm families, renting out land to the fathers and employing the children and wives in his mill; children, whose nimble fingers changed the spindles, made up half his work force, women about a quarter, and men (at higher pay and with the most skilled jobs) a final quarter. By bringing farms and families into the industrial process, Slater and other mill owners who followed his example consciously sought to avoid the perceived evils of English industrial cities (and what the English poet and mystic William Blake called their "dark, Satanic mills"); they tried to preserve as much as possible of traditional New England home production even in an industrial context. The output of the home looms, of course, belonged to the mill owners, and they were responsible for its marketing, which reached far beyond the local community. The larger scale of total production (hundreds of home looms) overseen by the mill owners and the improvements in transportation that allowed expanded markets had subtly transformed the former domestic work of wives and daughters into a commodity whose ultimate consumers were as far away as the South and the West.

The putting-out system that Slater had originally adapted was closely related to developments in the making of shoes. Traditionally master artisans called cobblers had purchased leather, made the entire shoe in their shops with the assistance of apprentices and

helpers, and then sold the finished shoes at the front of their shop. By 1800, shoemakers in eastern Massachusetts, eyeing larger markets for simple shoes in the slave South, began to expand their operations even as they deskilled the process. At first master artisans organized networks of small workshops, in towns such as Lynn and in the countryside, run by journeymen and apprentices with their entire families providing labor. The master artisans at their centralized shop would cut out shoe leathers and distribute the parts to the home workshops, where wives and daughters would sew the upper part of the shoe together; journeymen sewed the uppers to the soles, and apprentices helped as necessary. Then the master artisans would collect the finished shoes, paying by the pair, and market them either in their central shop or through merchants in such cities as Boston, which had trade links with southern cities.

As markets grew, artisans constructed larger production centers. There skilled craftsmen still cut out the shoe leathers, then shipped them out for sewing

Cotton Mills This illustration from the front page of the May 29th, 1852, issue of *Gleason's Pictorial* shows the Boott Cotton Mills of Lowell, Massachusetts. The mill is now a National Historic Park that chronicles the history of Lowell and its role in the Industrial Revolution.

to dozens or hundreds of homes, gathered up the sewn uppers, and put them out again — often to farms where during the long winter evenings hundreds of farm men and their older sons sewed the uppers to the soles. This process, employing a large number of relatively unskilled men and women in scattered rural homes, enormously increased output. One British traveler noted that "A stranger who has not been enlightened upon the ways of the place would be astonished at the number of small square erections, like miniature schoolhouses, standing each as a appendage to a dwelling house. These are the shoe shops, where the father of the family and his boys work. . . ." The Massachusetts cobbler who finished the entire shoe was no more; shoes were now mass-produced by unskilled laborers, each of whom worked on only one stage of production. The shoe manufacturer who employed skilled craftsmen to cut the leather and hundreds of household workers who participated only to supplement farm income was no longer a master artisan. Rather, he was a merchant/businessman whose skill lay in procuring materials, adjusting the scale of production to economic fluctuations, and finding new markets. The master cobbler hung on, making luxury shoes or working in isolated rural markets untouched by the advances in transportation, but by the mid-nineteenth century shoe manufacturing was more an industry than a craft. Despite the continuities with the past in the putting-out system for both textiles and shoemaking, and the modest use of mechanization, quite consequential innovations in work rhythms and discipline resulted that foreshadowed later industrialization.

❧ Emergence of a New Industrial System

The initial evolution in cloth and shoe production — away from home production for family consumption and toward home production for mass consumption — represented a local adaptation to American traditional values. But international events soon played a role in enlarging the scale and changing the workforce of New England mills. Transatlantic commerce had brought great wealth to the leading New England merchant families during the two decades before 1807, but the disputes with both Britain and France that culminated in embargoes and the War of 1812 sent New England merchants' incomes plummeting even as the demand for American-made goods expanded. With profits to invest and alert to new opportunities, some New England

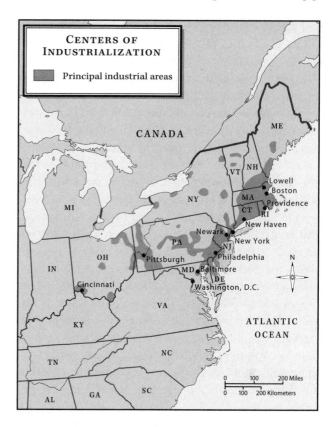

merchants reallocated their funds from shipping to factories. Francis Cabot Lowell, scion of a wealthy Boston family, made an ostensibly casual tour of British textile mills in 1811, where the newest technological advances in production were guarded as national secrets. Lowell asked intelligent questions, observed closely, and each night in his room wrote down from memory what he had seen and heard. Returning to Boston with sketches and knowledge, Lowell teamed up with a skilled Boston artisan, Paul Moody, and they proceeded to reproduce and improve the British machinery. In fact, Moody's mechanical genius and Lowell's vision enabled them to create the power loom, a water-powered series of machines that allowed all aspects of cotton textile production, from spinning to weaving and finishing the cloth, to be completed under one roof. No longer, as with Slater's mills, would the yarn have to be sent out to hundreds of homes for the weaving of cloth. Lowell's system required a much higher start-up cost, but his family connections to wealthy Boston merchants allowed his group, the Boston Associates, to create the Boston Manufacturing Company in 1813 with stock valued at $400,000. The next year in nearby Waltham, the Boston Associates opened the first modern factory, integrating every stage of the operation within one large building. The factory was a success from the beginning, and with the tariffs placed on British goods in 1816 following the War of 1812, the protected American market guaranteed the future prosperity of the enterprise. The Boston Associates acted to take advantage of their niche in textile production.

Although the family mills, as the Slater system was called, seemed an ideal compromise between factories and the traditional rural communities, problems soon developed. Local people often did not like the new families attracted to the leased farms on mill property, and disputes arose about roads, dam sites to enhance the water power, and even the financing and control of schools for mill children. The Boston Associates devised an entirely new method of supplying their labor needs. In 1823 they built a complete town at the confluence of the Concord and Merrimack Rivers and named it Lowell. The site had six mills and housing for all workers. The most skilled workers and all the managers were men, who lived in individual homes. But the innovation at Lowell was the employment of young single women from farming communities of northern New England. The infertile, rocky soil of the region made agriculture hard and unprofitable, and many young men were migrating westward to better soils and opportunities. The fathers and brothers left behind were switching from crops to livestock and had less need for family labor. As a result, there appeared a seeming excess of young, unmarried farmwomen, whom the Boston Associates targeted for their labor needs. The mill owners built boarding houses at Lowell. The young women were attracted to the jobs; they earned wages that initially seemed generous; and they were held to strict moral standards, complete with housemothers in the boarding houses, curfews, prohibitions against alcohol, and requirements to attend church. In fact the young women policed themselves, organized literary societies, dressed attractively, attended lectures, and were perceived as a wholesome alternative to child labor or to the reports from England of vile industrial conditions. Visitors from across New England and even Europe journeyed to Lowell to see what seemed the future of industrial arrangements. Harriet Martineau, an eminent British traveler in the early 1830s, marveled that "the girls have, in many instances, private libraries of some merit and value."

The wages were attractive at first, and neither the physical labor nor the workday seemed excessive to farm daughters accustomed to hard work and long hours. But the factories were noisy, the workplace was kept artificially humid to prevent threads from breaking, and, as competition increased and the overall economy faltered in the mid 1830s, owners cut wages and speeded up the pace of work. In both 1834 and 1836 substantial numbers of the Lowell girls, as they were called, stopped work to protest deteriorating conditions. (In 1824 women millworkers in Pawtucket, Rhode Island, in one of the very first work stoppages, had led their co-workers, male and female, on strike in response to wage cuts and lengthened hours.) Eventually immigrants replaced the New England farm girls at Lowell and in many other textile mills. By the 1850s, over half the New England textile workers were immigrants, and mainly Irish. The Lowell mill girls did not, as was originally expected, work for a few years and then return to their farming communities to marry, their wages having been sent home perhaps to educate their brothers. Instead, they tended to spend the money on themselves, established dowries that their families could not provide, and in many cases began lives of involvement with labor and other reform movements. About a third of the mill girls married men in Lowell and remained town dwellers, and those who ended up returning to their home communities tended to marry older men who pursued non-farm occupations.

❧ The Factory System Evolves

For all the attention Lowell garnered, New England mills were not the only mode of manufacturing or labor organization in the industrializing North in the decades after 1820. Although cities like New York and Philadelphia lacked access to waterpower and had to await the development of the stationary steam engine before many kinds of manufacturing were possible within their limits, these cities had other advantages that were soon turned to industry. Their ports, and the construction first of canals and later of rail networks, gave these cities access to a rapidly expanding market, and the merchants and artisans who were turning into entrepreneurs and businessmen were quick to recognize the size of the retail market to be served. The growing population of New York and Philadelphia, fed by migration from rural areas and by substantial European immigration, meant that plentiful workers were available at low wages, and the urban density meant that potential workers lived close by and did not have to be artificially concentrated in mill villages or large factories. Expanding markets and convenient workers allowed merchant/artisans to reconceive the shop format. Finished cloth, leather, or other materials processed elsewhere could be brought to an urban location, cut into shape by a relatively small number of skilled workers in one large building, and the parts then easily distributed to hundreds of individual workers — widows, immigrants, impoverished families — scattered across the city. Anywhere there was space to work and a window to provide light, this elastic workforce, easily hired or fired and paid by the piece, could assemble parts into finished products, or at least could perform one aspect of the finishing process. The result was a kind of dispersed factory, with managers seeing to it that the constituent parts of goods were sent to the workforce, then reaggregated at a central location either for special finishing touches or for retail distribution.

In this manner New York City emerged as the nation's major producer of ready-made clothing. Everywhere in the United States before about 1810, wives and mothers usually made all the family's clothing, although the more affluent had their clothing specially made to fit them by tailors, and some cheap ("slop") ready-made clothing could be bought. But the opportunities for expanding their business led tailors — master artisans — to focus their skills on cutting out the patterns of cloth, then contracting out to hundreds and later thousands of women in New York homes, rooms, and basement hovels to sew together the parts into inexpensive, standard-sized clothing, much of it destined for western farmers or southern slaves. Conditions in these home workshops were crowded, squalid, and dimly lit, with children often underfoot as the mother or father sat bent over the workbench. Master tailors soon employed lower-skilled journeymen tailors to cut the pieces, and the women doing the basic needlework came to have their occupations simplified to performing only one aspect of the actual assembling of clothing. This deskilling meant that the women involved in the needle trade required less training and could be paid lower wages. Many tailors and journeymen found themselves becoming something akin to shop foremen, with certain master tailors emerging more as managers, salesmen, and retailers. By 1850, about 18,000 women in New York worked in the needle trade, and New York was the leading manufacturer of clothing. Along the way a new class of white-collar workers — legions of clerks, accountants, and lower-level managers — developed to service this form of dispersed manufacturing that reached far beyond clothing. A wide variety of products were made in variations of this process in New York and other large cities.

In Philadelphia, for example, manufacturing output increased 88 percent in the three decades after 1810.

The next step toward enlarged production and greater efficiency was to build large centralized factories that consisted of a number of separate rooms where low-skilled, low-paid employees, often women and immigrants, performed one simple task. The net result of all the tasks performed in the right order was the finished product. By separating the manufacturing into a number of discrete, easily learned tasks, the necessary skill level (and hence wages) dropped. Population density provided sufficient workers within walking distance, but the growth and concentration of such worker-intense factories (with little machinery) increased urban population density even more.

❧ The American System

Another innovation at the beginning of the nineteenth century eventually would revolutionize industrialization. This was the so-called American System of manufacturing, although actually the concept had arisen first in England. The idea was to break up the manufacture of what were then high-tech items (rifles, later watches, steam engines, and even Cyrus McCormick's reapers) into a number of discrete parts so that unskilled workers could make absolutely identical individual parts. These interchangeable parts could then be assembled into a finished product. This required accurate standardization of all the parts and hence improvement in what are called machine tools, which manufacture metal parts. Eli Whitney in 1798 had contracted with the government to make 10,000 rifles in a little over a year; he planned to utilize this new system of interchangeable parts, devising molds to make precise pieces of the guns. His idea was better than his execution, and it took ten years to fulfill his contracted order, but the point was made. Later mechanics moved beyond Whitney's use of molds to creating technologically superior machine tools — for example, steam-powered lathes that followed a pre-arranged pattern — and thereafter a series of American mechanic-inventors and creative industrialists pioneered the development of the modern manufacturing of metal goods. Europeans were amazed at how open Americans were to new ways of doing things, how eagerly they accepted new machines and techniques. A German visitor quipped in the 1820s that "the moment an American hears the word 'invention' he pricks up his ears."

These gains in efficiency, accompanied by improve-

Irish Immigrants, 1836

A British traveler in the United States, Charles Latrobe, looks beyond the rowdy reputation of the ragged-looking Irish immigrants of his day and discerns an enduring pattern of the immigrant experience in America.

From New York they go in swarms to the canals, railroads, and public works, where they perform that labor which the Americans are not inclined to do. Now and then they get in a fight among themselves in the style of old Ireland, and perhaps kill one another, expressing great indignation and surprise when they find that they must answer for it though they are in a free country. By degrees, the more thrifty get and keep money, and diving deeper into the continent, purchase lands; while the intemperate and irreclaimable vanish from the surface.

The Americans complain, and justly, of the disorderly population which Ireland throws into the bosom of the Union, but there are many reasons why they should be borne with. They, with the poor Germans, do the work which without them could hardly be done. Though the fathers may be irreclaimable, the children become good citizens — and there is no finer race in the world, both for powers of mind and body, than the Irish, when favored by education and under proper control.

ments in transportation, allowed huge increases in production and decreases in prices. Soon the ordinary family had machine-made clocks,[1] and men carried inexpensive pocket watches (which, however, were notoriously inaccurate). This greater attention to precise time was itself an outgrowth of the factory system, which required that all laborers be at their workstation at starting time.

In 1851, when the British held a great international fair at the famous Crystal Palace in London to showcase the newest marvels of technology and industry, the crowds were astonished at the sophistication of American machinery and manufacturing techniques. The American System had proven itself on the world stage. Two years later, in 1853, the British sent a special parliamentary commission to study the American System on location. By the eve of the Civil War, a band of six northern states sweeping from Massachusetts to Ohio, including New York and Pennsylvania, had significantly industrialized, even though they were still primarily rural in terms of population numbers.

The causes and effects of this industrialization were multiple. Americans had taken technological breakthroughs in England — the spinning jenny, the steam engine, the concept of interchangeable parts — and perfected them. Improvements in transportation broadened the markets of manufactured goods. The availability first of farm families, then of the New England mill girls, and still later of immigrants desperate for jobs, provided a plentiful labor source. The re-

chartering of the Bank of the United States in 1816 and the maturation of banking in most states provided a source of credit necessary for investment. Merchants with an eye for trading markets helped transform manufacturing from an artisan activity to a marketing activity that distributed mass-produced and hence cheaper products. The older craft-oriented production declined, and the number of artisan/craftsmen shrank proportionally as workingmen and women became more numerous. Growing cities provided local markets and sources of workers, and as adjacent rural areas boomed and sent raw products back to the port cities by rail and canal either for additional processing or for the international trade, cities expanded still further.

Like a magnet, the great abundance of cheap western land drew European immigrants and eastern farmers' sons alike, and settlers on the moving frontier both produced cereal grains for export and for feeding the exploding American cities and formed a practically limitless market for the goods manufactured in the eastern and northern factories. Improving job opportunities produced by the expanding industrial economy also attracted immigrants. The whole process was synergistic, with industrialization both depending on and feeding the rise of immigration and the growth of cities and the prosperity of the West. The adoption and proliferation of the coal-burning, stationary steam engine after 1810 soon allowed more cities to have manufacturing (rather than assembly) factories that utilized power-driven machinery — no longer did such processing have to take place at the falls of rivers. The combined result was a transformation of the northern states in the half-century following 1810.

1. Handmade clocks, which today are prized antiques, before the early nineteenth century were found only in the wealthiest households.

IMMIGRATION

Every person of European or African ancestry in the United States in 1820 either had immigrated (the blacks involuntarily) or was the descendant of immigrants, but in that year the overwhelming majority of people living in the nation had been born there. During the thirty years before 1820, only a quarter of million Europeans had entered the nation, and the international slave trade, which had dwindled to a trickle by 1790, was outlawed in 1808. But with the end of the Napoleonic era in Europe in 1815, the pace of immigration accelerated. Many Europeans wanted to escape religious or political persecution; others sought better economic conditions when they found themselves displaced either from farms as a result of agriculture shifting from crop cultivation to livestock or from craft occupations as a result of industrial mechanization. Word already had spread that in America good farmland was plentiful and cheap and that jobs were to be had everywhere. Often the prospects for advancement in America were exaggerated, but desperate people felt the whip of persecution and poverty and imagined the carrot of American prosperity. The result was a sig-

A German Beer Hall in New York City   This image dates from 1864, but German immigrants had been creating establishments like this ever since they began arriving in force in the United States in the 1840s. Beer halls were an ordinary part of urban life in Germany. However, their boisterous conviviality (into which whole families, including children, were welcomed), and the large quantities of beer that patrons consumed, scandalized American moralists.

nificant upswing in immigration, at first mainly from Ireland and England but followed by huge numbers of Germans.

During the 1820s, some 150,000 Europeans came to the United States, and the flow soon increased to a torrent. In the next decade Irish immigration increased fourfold and German more than twentyfold, helping bring total immigration to 600,000. In the final two decades before the Civil War, immigration reached numbers that to many old-stock Americans threatened to inundate the nation. People were coming from Scandinavian countries, from England and Scotland, from the Netherlands, and especially from two more longstanding sources: Ireland and Germany. A long-building transformation of the Irish rural economy at the hands of the British caused severe poverty. To make matters worse, a devastating potato

blight in Ireland produced a famine that killed a million people from starvation, and even more fled Ireland for the United States, pouring into cities like New
York and Boston — 781,000 in the 1840s alone, and a
total during the 1840s and 1850s of 1,795,000. During
the same two decades almost 1.5 million Germans entered. The proportions that these numbers represent
are today difficult to comprehend: between 1840 and
1860, some 4.3 million European immigrants settled
in the nation, most in the North. This was more people than had lived in the United States in 1790, and
foreign-born persons represented 11.2 percent of the
total American population in 1860.[2] Even more strikingly, one out of three white males in the North in
1860 was an immigrant, and over half the population
of Boston and New York had been born abroad. Most
large northern cities had majority or near-majority
immigrant populations, and more than half the total foreign-born population lived in three northern
states: New York, Pennsylvania, and Ohio. Overall,
however, far fewer immigrants came to the South, for
few wanted to stay in the region and compete with
slaves for work. The much-smaller southern cities
also had substantial foreign-born populations. But
most immigrants who came to New Orleans — a major port of entry — proceeded up the Mississippi River
to settle in Missouri or the Midwest.

∾ *The Immigrants*

Although the lives of immigrants were greatly changed
when they came to the United States, their lives also
helped change the nation. For example, most of the
Irish hoped to find land and become farmers; but purchasing land, supplies, and supporting themselves
before the first crop came in was simply beyond the
means of most Irish, who seldom could move beyond
their port of arrival. There, necessity forced them to live
in squalid, cheap housing, often no more than a damp,
dark cellar room, and to take low-skilled, low-paying,
jobs. Upon arrival, the Irish had to avoid being swin-
dled by con men of all sorts who swarmed the docks
waiting to take advantage of frightened, bewildered
immigrants. Irish men accepted the hardest, dirtiest
jobs, like building roads, drainage ditches, and canals,
while Irish women either replaced New England mill
girls in towns like Lowell and Waltham, found jobs in

the needle trades in cities like New York, or became
cooks and maids. Industrial growth, population and
agricultural growth to the west, and the need to build
not only thousands of homes and factories in the cities
but also the transportation infrastructure of canals and
railroads gave jobs to hundreds of thousands of Irish
men, and they slowly overcame prejudice and poverty
to begin moving up the income ladder. Bad as conditions were in urban slums, they were better than back
in Ireland, and Irish settlers sent optimistic letters urging loved ones at home to come to the New World, too.
But because they often competed with black laborers
in northern cities, many Irish wanted to keep slaves in
the South and opposed abolitionism. In the Civil War,
many Irish would also strongly resent being drafted to
fight to free the slaves, for in large part they saw freed
slaves (who might come north) as rivals for the kinds
of jobs on which many of them still depended.

Because of their poverty, and hence their willingness to take the worst jobs and live in the worst housing conditions, the Irish in the eyes of many old-line
Americans seemed inferior people, and they attracted
myriad stereotypes about filthiness, violence, criminal-
ity, and drunkenness. Often they faced discrimination
when attempting to find jobs outside the stereotypical
"Irish trades." Their Catholicism only magnified prejudice against them. The Irish responded quite naturally
by living close together, strongly identifying with their
Catholic parish, establishing parochial schools for their
children, and organizing mutual aid societies (whose
members contributed small amounts of money weekly
or monthly to provide support for one another when
in need) and social clubs for both men and women.
This networking intensified old-line Americans' fear
that the Irish were and would remain a foreign presence in their midst. It was the perceived threat of the
Irish to supposed American civilization that gave rise
to the nativist Know Nothing, or American, Party in
1852 (see Chapter 14). But in fact, Irish immigrants'
survival strategies provided them with avenues for advancement both within the church and, through local
politics, within American secular society. Most became
Democrats because that party welcomed or tolerated
them far more than did the Whig Party.

If poverty drove the Irish to America but trapped
them for the first generation or two in the port cities, other European immigrants, less strapped financially, were able to move beyond the cities to carve
out farms in the interior. The relatively few Dutch
who came concentrated in Michigan and to a lesser

---

2. In 2000, amid another great surge in immigration, 10.4 percent of the U.S. population (not counting illegal immigrants) was
foreign-born, following a low of 4.7 percent in 1970.

extent in Wisconsin. The Scandinavians, mostly Lutheran, tended to settle in the upper Midwest, where their Lutheran descendants are still numerous. Immigrants from England, Wales, and Scotland continued to come throughout the period, their number rising to over 400,000 arriving in the 1850s. Many mechanics and artisans were among the early English immigrants, and they fit in well with the dominant population. Welsh miners and English ironworkers often pursued the same occupations in America. But after the Irish, the next largest and most important source of immigrants was the various states that make up what is now Germany.

German immigrants had been coming to the United States since the early eighteenth century, and they were considered by their old-line American neighbors to be ideal farmers. Members of the German-speaking Moravian sect settled in North Carolina, and Pennsylvania had a particularly heavy German settlement. But in the early nineteenth century German immigration dwindled, becoming insignificant compared to British or Irish. The numbers began to pick up in the 1830s, then more than 400,000 came in the 1840s, and in the 1850s German immigrants actually outnumbered Irish, 952,000 to 914,000. Unlike the Irish, few left Germany in dire straits because of famine, but the commercialization of agriculture did displace many farmers, and thousands of craftsmen and artisans lost their jobs because of early industrialization. The great majority of Germans were either Lutheran or Catholic, and there were a fair number of German Jews, but a significant minority of German immigrants were atheists — socialist revolutionists driven into emigration by the collapse of the Revolution of 1848. Because they were not as impoverished as the Irish, most German immigrants, even though they entered through the same port cities as the Irish, generally did not remain there. (Baltimore was an exception.) They could afford to move farther west. Many settled in the riverport cities of the Midwest — Cincinnati and St. Louis, for example — but most developed farming communities throughout the Midwest. State immigration offices and railroad and steamship companies often advertised in German for settlers to come to their states (and buy their tickets), and these words of enticement, combined with enthusiastic letters from earlier settlers, helped turn the stream of German immigration into a flood.

The Germans tended to cluster together, settling in small communities with their farmlands beyond. In this fashion they could maintain their language, their churches, and their clubs and social organizations. They had beer gardens, singing and music clubs, gymnastic clubs, and societies for debate and political discussion. Even old-line Americans considered them industrious, and their cultural, literary, and educational impact on a number of towns and cities was substantial. Initially old-stock Americans were put off by the Germans' propensity to frequent beer gardens on Sundays — this was seen as a profanation of the Sabbath — and the German example gave credence to the temperance movement to forbid or limit alcohol consumption. But because Germans scattered across the vast territory of the Midwest rather than remain concentrated in several port cities, they never seemed as threatening to American values as did the Irish. Except for an enclave in central Texas (where they were antislavery and would oppose secession), practically no Germans settled in the South. As producers of agricultural products both to feed the teeming cities of the North and for export, and as markets for American manufacturing jobs, the 1.5 million German immigrants between 1830 and 1860 contributed significantly to the demographic and economic transformation of the North in the generation before the Civil War.

URBANIZATION

Still another great change in the North before the Civil War was the development of towns and cities, and this urbanization was both a cause and a result of industrialization and immigration. Together, urbanization, industrialization, and immigration, as well as the availability of the West for settlement by millions of farmers who produced grain for the emerging cities and for export — and were themselves ample markets for goods manufactured by urban factories — were the reason why the North changed from a mostly rural, agricultural region in 1800 to one with significant cities and a growing manufacturing base in 1860, even though the majority of the population still were farmers.

While the cutting edge of change was in the cities, it is important to remember that for many rural Americans the crops grown, the homes lived in, and the work routines performed remained the way they had been for generations. In many parts of the North, industrialization, profits, and "modernity" in general met social, cultural, and religious opposition. Older ways of ordering society did not mesh easily with the emerging society represented by factories, immigrants,

Five Points, New York City   New York, like most other large cities of early nineteenth-century America and Europe, had its dangerous neighborhoods. "Five Points," an ethnically and racially mixed district on the Lower East Side, was notorious for its crime, prostitution, poverty, and squalor. This picture dates from 1859.

and crowded cities, and the clamor for "progress" and profits was interpreted at first as sinful greed. Quickly, however, religious leaders came to terms with the new era and learned to accept prosperity as a blessing that supposedly accompanied hard work, thrift, and proper behavior. This religious accommodation to the newly emergent capitalist society weakened the ability of religious leaders to be moral critics of societal institutions. Poverty and other social maladies caused by the rapid growth of cities and factories attracted relatively little attention from ministers, who were quicker to chastise

the poor than the conditions that produced poverty. Not until the Social Gospel movement after the Civil War[3] did religious leaders apply their critical insights to the urban-industrial system that had transformed rural America. However, what most struck contemporaries about the era was the astounding pace of urban growth.

❧ Urban Growth

Numbers illustrate the rate of urban growth. In 1820, only 6 percent of Americans lived in urban regions (defined at the time by the Census Bureau as places with 2,500 people or more); by 1860, 20 percent did. Never be-

3. See Chapter 19.

fore — and never again — did the nation undergo such a proportionately large move from the countryside to the town and the city. The change is even more impressive if one examines individual cities. New York swelled from 124,000 inhabitants in 1820 to just over a million in 1860 (counting Brooklyn, which was then a separate city). Philadelphia grew from just under 100,000 people in 1820 to more half a million in 1860. Even more remarkable was the growth of brand new cities like Rochester, which literally mushroomed from a small village before the Erie Canal opened in 1825 to a city of 22,000 by 1850. Chicago, likewise an instant city, catapulted from nothing to a population of 100,000 in 1860, eighth largest in the nation. Only five cities in the Northeast had as many as 25,000 people in 1820; by 1850, twenty-six cities were that large. There was even more rapid growth in cities whose population had been between 10,000 and 25,000, and the number of census-defined urban places of between 2,500 and 10,000 inhabitants increased almost fivefold. By 1860, one-third of the people living in the Northeast were urban residents, compared to 7 percent of southerners. And unlike the South, many northern cities were inland.

The four largest cities in 1860 had been the four largest a half century before. All of them — New York, Philadelphia, Boston, and Baltimore — were major Atlantic seaports. All had long been commercially important, exporting American products and importing manufactured goods from Europe. Only Baltimore, with a series of flour mills lining Jones Falls as it coursed through the city, had from the beginning been a major manufacturing center. Maritime commerce had been the secret to all these cities' early growth.

New York City leaped ahead forever by 1810, and developments in the next decade would ensure its commercial dominance. In 1817 merchants there founded the Black Ball Line, the first regularly scheduled packet ships to cross the Atlantic. At first they had trouble keeping to schedule, but even the relative dependability of the Black Ball ships induced merchants to direct their trade through New York. The New York state legislature's action in 1817 funding the construction of a canal connecting the Hudson River to Lake Erie also proved decisive. Although the Erie Canal was not finished until 1825, it opened up to New York City the vast markets of the Midwest, with the Great Lakes serving as a natural extension of the canal. Finally, in 1817 the New York Stock Exchange was reestablished on a sound basis, making New York from that moment on the nation's financial and banking center. This ability to

extend credit allowed New York merchants to capture the cotton carrying trade of the South. New York ships sailed to New Orleans or Mobile to load up with cotton and carry it to Britain, there exchanging it for other goods that were brought back to New York for distribution either in the city or, via the Erie Canal, to the West. The South produced three-fourths of the world's cotton, and most of it was handled by New York merchants, driving the city's growth.

Other northeastern cities also thrived. Philadelphia prospered from its location in an agriculturally rich region. It retained its Atlantic commerce, and its manufacturers found many markets to the west and south. Boston discovered ready markets for cloth and shoes in the South, still had strong trade with Europe, and so thoroughly dominated the China trade that Americans there were at first called "Bostons." Baltimore initially suffered in competition with New York after the Erie Canal opened, but Baltimore entrepreneurs and investors responded first by the Baltimore and Ohio Canal (which never paid off), next by improved roads, and finally by developing the Baltimore and Ohio Railroad, which successfully linked the markets of the Midwest to Baltimore and hence the sea.[4]

But as fast as the growth of these traditional large American port cities was, even more impressive was the record of cities in the interior. Initially the largest inland cities were river towns, where like the ocean ports they facilitated trade in raw products and manufactured goods. Pittsburgh, Louisville, St. Louis, and New Orleans all lay on the banks of the Ohio-Mississippi River system that, served by flatboats and later steamboats, formed a vast water transportation network in the heart of the nation. Each of these cities had special reasons for prosperity. Pittsburgh's proximity to coal and iron deposits early made it a leading industrial center, famous for its smog; French traveler Michel Chevalier in 1831 referred to the "dense, black smoke" that poured from the foundries and forges of "the dirtiest town in the United States." St. Louis was the commercial center of the West, the starting point for caravans westward and the eastern terminus of the Sante Fe Trail. New Orleans, near the mouth of the Mississippi, profited from immense shipments of corn and other produce from the American heartland that were transferred to ocean-going vessels on the wharves lining the Mississippi River. Cincinnati — popularly known as "Porkopolis" — became the nation's leading

4. See Chapter 9.

meatpacking center (before Chicago), and along with pork processing a manufacturing base undergirded the city's diverse economy. Of the original major river cities, Louisville alone failed to keep pace with the nation's urbanization.

A new kind of interior port city arose after completion of the Erie Canal. Now that the Great Lakes through the Erie Canal offered a water route to New York City and hence the Atlantic world, lake ports grew rapidly as transshipment centers both for the produce of the Midwest and the manufactured goods of Europe and the East. Buffalo, where the canal connected to Lake Erie, was the prototype lake port, soon afterwards followed by Cleveland and Detroit and eventually by Chicago. Incorporated in 1837, Chicago became the era's greatest boomtown, the juncture of a huge rail network linking it to the South and West with the water route of the Great Lakes. By the early 1850s, ninety-six trains a day were entering the city. With its rail connections to the wheat farms to the west, Chicago became the nation's leading grain-shipping center by 1858, and soon thereafter it surpassed Cincinnati in the meat trade. As Midwestern farmers began to reorient their trade (grain exports and manufactured imports) away from the south-flowing Ohio-Mississippi River system and toward the east-west rail and water routes, the West became firmly linked not with the South but with the urbanizing and industrializing Northeast. This economic and trade nexus would prove crucially important during the Civil War.

❧ Urban Life

Cities swelled so rapidly in early nineteenth-century America that their population surge overwhelmed their ability to handle the problems of growth. Urban dwellers especially in the eastern seaboard cities consisted of both former rural dwellers who had come in search of jobs and thousands of immigrants from overseas. The cities were compact in area, and historians call them *walking cities* because workers lived close enough to walk to their jobs. Hence they were densely packed. The onrush of impoverished immigrants pushed wages down, and entire families often lived in tiny rooms or unfinished basements — as many as a quarter of the poorest families shared such rooms with another family! A Boston doctor described "one cellar . . . occupied nightly as a sleeping-apartment for thirty-nine persons. In another, the tide had risen so high that it was necessary to approach the bedside of a patient by means of a plank which was laid from one stool to another; while the dead body of an infant was actually sailing about the room in its coffin."

City streets were mostly unpaved, and in the absence of modern water or sewage systems, sanitary conditions were horrible. Even in those cities that developed water works, piped water (untreated, of course) was available only for the houses of those who could afford to pay for the plumbing connections. The vast majority of people had to depend upon public hydrants along the streets or upon shallow water wells. Behind teeming tenement houses and crowded shacks stood stinking outhouses, which often overflowed and polluted nearby wells. With no sewage system, people emptied their garbage and chamber pots into the streets. Herds of hogs swarmed through the streets, scavenging human waste materials but leaving behind their own manure, which, combined with that of the horses that pulled the carts, wagons, and street railroads, produced a stench that on warm days could be overwhelming. Overcrowded, fetid neighborhoods became breeding grounds for disease of all sorts, and practically every city suffered periodic cholera and typhus epidemics and constant problems with more mundane public health issues. There were no effective, organized fire departments, and the mostly wooden houses and shacks, crowded together, often burned in conflagrations that destroyed scores of city blocks.

Destitution and disease led to crime, as despairing people turned to robbery, prostitution, and vandalism. The notorious Five Points slum in New York City had conditions more desperate than any in London, shocking even visitors like Charles Dickens, who had wide experience with urban squalor. So-called street rats — children and young men without families — roamed the larger cities, living off petty thievery, begging, and scavenging and sleeping in doorways, on bales of hay, in attic crawlways, and in coal bins. None of the cities had adequate police forces. Until the end of the era most of them tried to rely on traditional night watchmen, although New York finally organized a uniformed police force in 1845. Terrible working conditions stimulated mob attacks against Irish and blacks, for artisans who had lost their jobs and their status and saw their wages fall lashed out at them as scapegoats. The cities displayed stark contrasts in wealth, with a tiny minority at the top enjoying luxurious housing, paved streets, and running water, and the vast majority living in poverty. For example, in New York City in 1845 the wealthiest 4 percent of the population owned fully 80 percent of the city's wealth. Yet despite horrid living conditions, the economic might of the cities still attracted newcomers, and the cities continued to grow.

LABOR MOVEMENTS

Rapid social and economic changes always produce winners and losers in society, especially initially. Certainly western farmers benefited from the transportation revolution, for they now had better markets for their grain and other products, and they profited from the lower prices of manufactured goods. Urban merchants who adapted to the changes in production and merchandising saw their total wealth and status rise, and some master craftsmen, particularly those with access to credit and with entrepreneurial skills, became industrialists/merchants who oversaw the work of others and marketed their goods to great profit. But many urban workers found that the conditions of their labor, even their relationship to their craft, fundamentally changed for the worse, and their wages fell, their housing conditions worsened, and their pride in their trade diminished. In many ways, urban laborers bore the brunt of the wrenching changes that were beginning to transform the North into a modern industrial society.

❧ From Artisans to Workers

In preindustrial society, a boy usually learned his trade by being apprenticed to a skilled artisan by his parents. As he gained in skills to the point that he could make a living at the trade, he set out (journeyed) to find a shop in which to work. At that point he was known as a journeyman. If he was lucky, worked hard, and had business acumen, he might within a few years be able to set up his own shop and work as an artisan, with journeymen and apprentices under his direction. But in the emerging industrialized society, a handful of artisans emerged as manufacturers/businessmen, and division of labor and the factory system reduced the skill requirements of workers. No longer did the path to success carry one from apprenticeship to artisan; child labor replaced apprentices, low-paid laborers (both men and women) replaced journeymen, and upward mobility largely ceased. Former journeymen might become the equivalent of shop foremen, but they seldom could expect one day to own their own shop. No longer did journeymen/workers sell the finished prod-

ucts of their labor; instead, they simply sold their labor for wages. Pride in their work product disappeared as workers became anonymous, interchangeable laborers who never saw customers (and probably not even their employer) face-to-face. With mobility nipped and pride of accomplishment diminished, many laborers found work unfulfilling.

The new factory system of production changed the workplace in more subtle ways as well, continuing the erosion of workers' pride initiated by the earlier putting-out system; and laborers felt an increasing loss of control over their lives. In both farm labor and in early artisan shops, workers more or less followed their own schedules. They could pause during the workday for a break (usually a "refresher" with alcohol), do another chore, tend to their children, interact with a customer. But the factory system put them under the tyranny of time: everyone had to be at his or her place when the work began, and no one could pause, run an errand, get a drink, or attend to a child once the factory day got under way. Often a whistle blew first to awaken the workers in a mill village; again when everyone had to be at the workplace or machine, and yet again for lunch and for the resumption of work. Laborers who had once felt in charge of their lives and took pride in their work now felt that the whistle, bell, or clock had made them inconsequential cogs in the industrial process. Drinking on the job was forbidden, not only because it was dangerous amid the machinery but also because it slowed down work. As owners responded to increased competition by speeding up the factory and shortening the lunch breaks, workers' anger rose at their sense of being manipulated and mistreated. Women at some of the first textile mills pioneered the work protest, simply refusing to go to work in 1824 at a mill in Pawtucket, Rhode Island, and a decade later (as we have seen) walking out of the Lowell mills to protest a wage cut. Few of these efforts succeeded because mill owners simply replaced protesters with immigrant laborers. Unskilled workers in several cities formed loosely organized workingmen's associations in the late 1820s and early 1830s, protesting not only work conditions but their larger situation — they called for free public schools, access to land in the West, and the end of government-sponsored monopolies like banks. They were fiercely opposed by the factory owners, many artisans-become-businessmen, and even craft specialists who no longer sensed a connection to the masses of unskilled workers beneath them.

⅋ *Labor Unions*

The first tentative labor unions began as trade unions of former artisans in specialty crafts like shoemaking, printing, and the building trades, and they organized more to protest their declining status and shrinking mobility than to defend the wages and working conditions of unskilled laborers. Craftsmen from a variety of trades organized the National Trades Union in 1834, but it had only limited, local success before it collapsed in the depression that began in 1837. Worker organizations across a variety of trades in a single city, so-called General Trade Unions, developed in most of the largest northeastern cities in the mid-1830s, but they too fell victim to the depression. Frequent protests, however, did gradually lead in the late 1830s and early 1840s to a reduction in the normal workday from twelve or more hours to ten. More important, in 1842 the right to form a union organization and to strike were guaranteed by the Massachusetts Supreme Court in the decision *Commonwealth v. Hunt,* striking down laws that declared union activities criminal conspiracies. Yet this decision only applied to Massachusetts, and employers elsewhere continued to fire workers suspected of union activities. Several states also passed mechanic's lien laws, giving workers first claim on the assets of bankrupt employers. Yet despite the shortening of the workday and enhanced legal rights in some states, the majority of urban workers saw little improvement in labor conditions. In 1860 less than 0.1 percent of American workers belonged to unions of any sort.

In the traditional artisanal environment, shop and home were usually the same structure, and leisure and work intertwined. Similarly, in agricultural settings, leisure and work were often interrelated in such activities as log rollings and barn raisings. But this blending of sociability and labor disappeared in urban workplaces. Community recreational and social gatherings common in traditional society also lagged, and increasingly spectator sports like boxing and baseball, along with such commercial entertainments as operas, minstrel shows, and circuses, arose to provide amusement for the urban working class. Irish workers, almost all Catholics, also frequented taverns, and later German workers enjoyed Sundays strolling through beer gardens. Old-line Protestant Americans — and Whig politicians — saw such behavior as unruly, practically un-American, and conducive to absenteeism at work. Democratic politicians, somewhat less concerned to discipline and reform society, were more open to diverse ethnic habits. As a result, the immigrant laborers and workingmen in general flocked to the Democratic cause, and Democratic Party activities became a kind of school of Americanism for immigrants and urban workers. The Democrats' opposition to the Bank of the United States and to privilege in general, and their support of opening the West to settlement, meshed with the priorities of the working class. In the Democratic Party workers found a voice, and gradually they — the Irish in particular — learned how to use local politics to better themselves. Many laborers, too, and especially their children, gained some social mobility through hard work. The Irish especially strained their resources to buy homes for themselves. Such limited upward mobility, undergirded by continual waves of new immigrants willing to take the lowest-paying jobs, prevented powerful class conflict from arising. Most workingmen also held out the hope of eventually moving up in life and thus did not feel themselves to be part of a permanent underclass. The expectation of individual improvement served to ameliorate potential class tensions. But the age was, nevertheless, also one of religious and social reform, especially among the middle class. Few accepted the status quo.

RELIGIOUS REVIVALISM AND SOCIAL REFORM

The eminent French political theorist Alexis de Tocqueville traveled throughout the United States in 1831 and 1832, closely observing political and cultural institutions and behavior in preparation for writing his great book, *Democracy in America.* One of the characteristics of the nation most striking to him was the role of religion. He wrote that he knew of "no country in the world in which the Christian religion retains a greater influence over the souls of men than in America." Analyzing the way that religion seemed to reinforce American attitudes toward democracy and liberty, he concluded that religion was "the foremost of the political institutions" of the nation. Tocqueville had arrived in the United States in the midst of a new kind of religious revivalism that was sweeping through portions of the North, and this revivalism was both result and cause of a series of theological reconsiderations that were rapidly remaking the theory and practice of religion. Protestant Christianity was being democratized, responding to the changes in American society and preparing to address the dynamic social conditions of the nation that ranged from the teeming industrial cities in the Northeast to the raw farming communities of the upper Midwest, the Mississippi Valley, and the new states and territories west of the Mississippi River.

᭪ *The Democratization of Christianity*

This quickening of religious interest in the northern states is often called the Second Great Awakening, but the movement is really too long, too diffuse, and too diverse to accurately be subsumed under such a label. In some ways the movement began in the 1790s when religious leaders like Timothy Dwight, president of Yale University, began to preach a spirited series of sermons in defense of traditional Christianity, as opposed to the deism widely associated with the Enlightenment and the French Revolution. Using that supposed foreign threat as a foil, Dwight and other ministers energetically promoted what they initially took to be Christian orthodoxy. But as so often happens, these defenders of the faith found it necessary to make slight adjustments in theology and application to fit changing times. In the context of a nation that had declared and won its independence from Britain and in which voters democratically chose their leaders, older conceptions of hierarchy, authority, and divine control needed reconsideration.

Dwight himself was primarily interested in smiting deism and infidelity, and in doing so he developed a four-year cycle of lectures on Christian religion that were eventually published in 1818. Dwight subtly began to emphasize, more than orthodox theologians had before, that humans had both moral and intellectual agency. They were not necessarily and automatically bound to sin, and Dwight wrote of their having a "system of duties" that implied a human-defined notion of happiness rather than narrow religious virtue defined as love of God. Dwight had unconsciously begun a school of thought that came to be known as the New Haven Theology. This new way of thinking was continued by Nathaniel Taylor, Dwight's one-time assistant who became an eminent preacher in New Haven and later professor of theology in Yale's Divinity School, founded in 1822. Taylor, too, either did not recognize how innovative his ideas were or could not admit it, but he moved beyond the orthodox Calvinist idea that humans were depraved by their essential nature. In other words, humans might do wicked things, but doing so was a result of their own actions, not of an inner nature over which they had no control. Sinning was common

and perhaps to a degree universal, but rational, moral humans had "power to the contrary" — that is, people could choose to live differently. Men and women were not, in a passive or deterministic sense, part of nature; rather, they controlled their own destiny. The lives they chose to live resulted from their decision, not from some arbitrary act of God even before the foundations of the world had been laid. Here, clearly, was an intellectual rationale for revival preaching intended to persuade people to choose Christ and the Christian life.

Asahel Nettleton, who left his graduate studies in religion at Yale to take a preaching assignment, proved so effective at winning converts that he was ordained by a Congregational consociation as a traveling evangelist in 1811. Again, he did not frontally assault older theological precepts but was so persuasive a preacher that he inadvertently helped undermine the idea that revivals were mysterious works of God. Nettleton only moved a short step toward the role of revivalist: he preached in regular churches, stayed in the regular minister's home during his visit, and discouraged unseemly emotionalism either in his sermons or in the listeners' responses. Nettleton demonstrated almost accidentally that conversions were the result of certain kinds of preaching and could practically be expected if ministers skillfully called people to repentance. Lyman Beecher, another student of Dwight and a more exuberant evangelist than Nettleton, took the New Haven Theology to the West. After preaching revivalism and reform for years, arguing that God worked not by arbitrary power but through his mercy and love, Beecher popularized the idea of "disinterested benevolence." Humans were attracted to Christ and were converted by the example of God's love toward them, and they in turn exemplified their converted state by living lives devoted "disinterestedly" to others. Beecher later moved to Cincinnati to become president of Lane Theological Seminary, where he trained a whole generation of ministers to associate evangelism and revivalism with moral and social reform. Beecher was especially committed to "saving the West from the Pope," and he had spelled out in *A Plea for the West* (1835) how important he deemed it for like-minded Protestants to convert the great heartland of the nation to his version of activist Christianity.

Note how far religion had moved from the orthodoxy of the seventeenth century: now it was argued that humans were attracted to God because of his demonstrated love toward them, they could choose or will to overcome their habits of sinfulness, and in their new lives as Christians they could — and should

**Charles Grandison Finney
on Revivals, 1835**

A lawyer by training, Charles Grandison Finney here presents a lawyer-like brief in defense of the revival. Success, Finney argues, is the result of the preacher's skillful human effort, not a divine miracle.

Religion is the work of man. It is something for man to do. It consists in obeying God. It is man's duty. It is true, God induces him to do it. He influences him by his Spirit, because of his great wickedness and reluctance to obey. If it were not necessary for God to influence men — if men were disposed to obey God, there would be no occasion to pray, "O Lord, revive thy work." The ground of necessity for such a prayer is, that men are wholly indisposed to obey; and unless God interpose the influence of his Spirit, not a man on earth will ever obey the commands of God.

A "Revival of Religion" presupposes a declension. Almost all the religion in the world has been produced by revivals. God has found it necessary to take advantage of the excitability there is in mankind, to produce powerful excitements among them, before he can lead them to obey. Men are so sluggish, there are so many things to lead their minds off from religion, and to oppose the influence of the gospel that it is necessary to raise an excitement among them, till the tide rises so high as to sweep away the opposing obstacles. They must be so excited that they will break over these counteracting influences, before they will obey God.

— reform society. Salvation was available to whoever really wanted it, and human agency was central both to individual conversion and to the betterment of society. Christianity was already being democratized by the time Tocqueville came to America.

❧ Charles G. Finney and Modern Revivalism

The person who exemplified both the new theology and the expanded role of the revivalist was Charles G. Finney, whose impact on American religion was immense. Finney had been born in 1792 in Connecticut, but his parents moved to New York State while he was still an infant. Finney returned to Connecticut for his education and then moved back to New York, beginning to practice law there in 1818.

Finney, a remarkably skilled lawyer, had become a religious skeptic. But he was also friendly with a young Presbyterian minister in Adams County, New York, named George W. Gale, with whom he had theological discussions. Strongly disagreeing with Gale's theology, Finney began a systematic reading of the Bible to back up his own points. In the course of these ongoing debates, Finney one day while walking to his law office was struck with an idea that changed his life: salvation was not a complex matter that involved God's providential plans or mastery of a body of theology. All it required, Finney wrote that he instantly saw, was "my own consent to give up my sins and accept Christ." Finney decided then and there to do so if he possibly could, and that night he felt a powerful wave of what he called the Holy Spirit roll over him in response to his prayerful decision to change his life forever. The next

morning, when someone reminded him that he had a court case to argue, Finney replied that as of last night he had "a retainer from the Lord Jesus Christ to plead his cause." And that Finney undertook to do with the rhetorical skills of a hardheaded lawyer. As a lawyer he was accustomed to doing whatever it took to win a case; as an advocate for God's cause, he would likewise make use of any means at his disposal to move people toward deciding to become Christians. He consented to some informal training by Gale, but began preaching almost immediately. The St. Lawrence Presbytery officially ordained him as a Presbyterian minister on July 1, 1824.

Finney changed evangelism's rhetorical style. He spoke the forceful, colorful, blunt language of the street and preached without notes. Looking directly at his listeners, when he spoke of sin and sinners he bluntly said "you," not the less offensive "they." He spoke as though he was trying to convince a jury: he pointed, used body language, and both shouted and whispered. He was by turns witty, logical, informal, pleading. He used a pithy, vernacular style to make formerly complicated ideas crystal-clear, and his language was so vivid that when he spoke of unrepentant sinners descending into hell, pointing downward with his finger, listeners in the back aisles supposedly stood up to catch a glimpse of hellfire. Enthusiastic hymn singing got everyone in the audience involved in the service. Unlike Nettleton, Finney understood the role of emotion and used it effectively to persuade people to make a decision. The decision was theirs, not God's, and so important did Finney consider their choice that he invented new techniques of pressuring the indecisive toward commitment. He called them down to the front of the audience, right before the pulpit, and while they cowered on what he called the "anxious bench" Finney directed all attention to them and used their example to dramatize what he portrayed as the great conflict between heaven and hell. Shocking contemporaries, Finney asked women to pray and testify in public. Finney was consciously applying psychic pressure to the unconverted in an attempt to force them to choose Christ.

Finney's revival career attracted regional, then national attention after 1826 when he initiated the first of a series of preaching campaigns in the small cities that were emerging along the Erie Canal. At Utica, Rome, Auburn, Troy, Vernon, and other commercial centers growing by leaps and bounds along with the traffic on the canal — and filled with newcomers who missed the comfort of home churches and the support of kin networks but were nonetheless determined to make their own future in the economic boom — Finney preached no-nonsense sermons that appealed to the age's can-do spirit. He adapted the revival to urban life: he publicized his appearances, he organized groups of mostly middle-class women (who had the leisure to pursue the cause) to spread the news of the meetings (his wife Lydia was active in such visitations), he arranged for teams to visit workers in their homes, and he mobilized churches both to bring people to his preaching and to welcome them after their conversion. Finney preached not just on Sundays or perhaps Wednesdays, but every night of the week, and his services went on for hours with special "inquiry sessions" that were intended to bring home to any curious person the importance and possibility of his or her conversion then and there. These nightly services, several hours long, lasting for weeks, came to be called "protracted meetings," and in a real sense they were the urban equivalent of rural camp meetings.

When Finney came to a town with his organization of local co-workers, his employment of publicity, and his series of nightly meetings featuring his own persuasive preaching and the anxious bench, he learned that plentiful conversions were automatic. In fact, Finney argued that precisely because people's salvation was in their own hands and that old-fashioned Calvinism was a "theological fiction," conversions were exactly what one should expect. The revival was not — as had been thought during the First Great Awakening — a miraculous event sent by God and something for which ministers could only hope and pray. To the contrary, as Finney later wrote in a practical handbook entitled

Lectures on Revivals of Religion (1835), a revival "is not a miracle, or dependent on a miracle, in any sense. It is a purely philosophical [scientific] result of the right use of the constituted means — as much so as any other effect produced by the application of means." In other words, the revival was a human mechanism that, properly used, would produce conversions as surely as a coffee pot produced coffee.

❧ Religion and Reform

With his fame soaring and a trail of revival successes behind him in 1830, Finney was invited to Rochester, New York. Here he brought together techniques he had been perfecting in the smaller towns. His appeal was mostly to the merchants, shopkeepers, master artisans, factory owners, and professional people who were prospering most from the commercial/industrial revolution that was remaking American life. These individuals saw that the new evangelicalism's stress on self-discipline and individual achievement fit the new business conditions, and they could demand — or at least urge — the same behavior from their workers. If the workers chose the new discipline, they would prosper too, but if they persisted in less ideal behavior, they would fail and deserve their poverty. Success, the businessmen argued, was each person's responsibility, and they celebrated the new theology. In six months church membership in Rochester doubled, and other ministers elsewhere, adapting the mechanisms Finney had pioneered, were stoking the fires of revivalism throughout New York and into neighboring states. The region along the Erie Canal became known as the "Burnt Over District" because of the succession of "scorching" revivals in the years after 1826. But his revival techniques were not the most radical of Finney's ideas. Believing that sin was voluntary and that people could will to reject it, he reasoned that if they were properly motivated they could become perfectly holy — untainted by the shadow of sin that the orthodox clergy felt still affected converts and produced backsliding.

Moving far beyond Lyman Beecher's idea of disinterested benevolence, Finney argued that because Jesus had told his disciples to "be perfect, even as your Heavenly Father is perfect," he obviously meant that they *could* be so, and hence gave the converted the special power — grace — that would enable them to achieve moral perfection. Finney argued that the purpose of the church was to reform the world. Mobilized individuals,

Mission to Sailors. Missionary societies in nineteenth-century America left no stone unturned or no place unattended to convert their fellow Americans. This church was built by the Young Men's Church Missionary Society of New York in 1844 to minister to visiting seamen. A floating church, built to a similar design, was moored on the Philadelphia waterfront.

using the right means, could avoid evil themselves and work to eradicate it from the world. This optimistic, democratic idea that hardworking Christians could so improve and reform the world that they could bring on the millennium — a thousand-year reign of godliness on earth, after which Christ would return — contributed to an enormous wave of revivalistic and reform activity in the North and Midwest. Finney himself moved to the Midwest in 1835 to become professor of theology at Oberlin College and eventually its president. He, his followers, and the college turned out a phalanx of (unconsciously elitist) devoted moral reformers in the three decades before the Civil War. Finney had overreached in his prediction that "if the church will do her duty, the millennium may come in this country in three years," but such fervor characterized much of the Christian impulse in the northern states in the second quarter of the nineteenth century, producing an outpouring of reform activity.

❧ Catholic Revivalism

Protestantism was not alone in adapting new techniques to reach the unchurched. The Catholic Church too recognized that many immigrants were slipping from their Old World connection to Roman Catholicism either because they found themselves in regions — on the frontier or in newer cities — where there were few opportunities for traditional worship or because they were so pressed for economic survival that religion was ignored. Other immigrants no doubt chose, once in the United States and removed from parents or traditional ties to the church, and given the popular American prejudice against Catholicism, to move toward either secularism or even some form of Protestantism. Such drifting away from moorings in European Catholic culture was labeled "Americanization" and recognized as a genuine threat to Catholic faith. Catholic leaders sought ways to defend the church's cause, and one result was the rise of the Catholic press. The Catholic hierarchy, centered in Baltimore, and regional bishops also energetically sought to recruit more priests from Europe and raise up home-grown clericals to staff more local parish churches.

More akin to Protestant revivalism was the proliferation of parish missions, which first appeared at the end of the eighteenth century, spread slowly during the second quarter of the nineteenth century, and then blossomed after 1850. The concept of the parish mission had arisen in Europe, but it seemed perfectly adapted to the American situation. The idea was to utilize special mission priests — often from the Redemptorist, Jesuit, or Paulist orders — who would travel about, spend one or two weeks at one location, and attempt both to revive immigrants' dormant attachments to the Catholic faith and to call them together to promote the formation of permanent parish churches. Unlike regular Catholic worship service, which was heavily ritualistic and sacramental in nature and placed relatively little emphasis on the sermon, the parish mission priests emphasized the sermon and used it — replete with emotion, vivid word imagery, and memorable depictions of hellfire and brimstone — to wake Catholics up to their perilous fate if they neglected religion and to attract them back to their traditional church. The focus was on awakening listeners to their spiritual plight, leading them to conversion, and persuading them to enter a life of regular devotion and worship — intentions identical to that of Protestant revivalists. During the 1850s hundreds of parish missions, similar to frontier and urban revival meetings, were held, revivifying Catholic religion and culture in the growing northern cities especially and — as an unintended consequence — intensifying Protestant fears about the encroachments of what was seen as a foreign religion. A virulent anti-immigrant (and specifically anti-Catholic) political movement flourished briefly in the 1850s (see Chapter 14).

❧ *An Age of Reform*

Many factors helped kindle the spirit of reform that spread through the nation after 1825. From its Puritan origins, New England had inherited a strong sense of mission to reform this continent and the world — a vision of being the redeemer nation that the Revolution secularized. The Declaration of Independence and the mythology that grew up following the achievement of independence and the writing of the Constitution suggested that America's political idealism would eventually transform the world. In less grandiose terms, a strong tradition of down-to-earth reformism had inhered in such examples as Benjamin Franklin's do-good essays. Images of political millennialism permeated Jefferson's writings, and the rhetoricians who touted both Jacksonian and Whiggish politics found it easy to slip into rhapsodic portrayals of the kind of society and nation that would result if only their leaders were voted into office. Workingmen's unions and other secular groups identified social maladies or needs and organized movements with specific purposes. Certainly middle-class, old-line Americans of the sort who made up the leadership of the Whig Party had in mind disciplining, correcting, and reforming their society. The rapid change associated with industrialization, urbanization, and immigration frightened many conservatives into thinking that the nation had to be shaped and reformed lest it fall into corruption and chaos. Parents in an age of mobility and change who were concerned about the different world their children would grow up in were often ready participants in reform activity.

While the Finneyite movement provided much of the moral fervor of the reformers, empowered women to join and promote good causes, and led most of those involved to feel sure they were on God's side, and vice versa, the organizational techniques widely associated with reform originated before Finney with the initial wave of disinterested benevolence. In one of his most famous comments about America, Tocqueville remarked on the propensity of its citizens to organize associations for every cause. By "the principle of asso-

ciation," Tocqueville meant the interlocking network of voluntary societies that had begun growing up earlier in the century to address a huge range of issues. The glory of the voluntary societies was their single-issue nature, permitting people to work together on the issue to which the society was dedicated even though they disagreed on many other topics. Since the societies were supported by voluntary contributions, they did not have to wait for government support or approval. Like-minded men and women could cooperate raising funds, dispensing information, and addressing perceived evils ranging from an absence of Bibles on the frontier to the existence of slavery in the South. A variety of voluntary associations were formed after 1816 — the American Bible Society and the American Education Society that year, then the American Colonization Society (founded in Virginia in 1817), the American Sunday School Union (1824), the American Tract Society (1825), the American Temperance Society (1826), the American Peace Society (1828), and the American Antislavery Society (1833). Most had a clear Protestant agenda: the Protestant version of the Bible was distributed, the tracts were evangelical pamphlets, the Sunday schools were intended to teach literacy and progressive Protestant values. The goal was to transform America into a vast community of self-regulating Protestant Christians.

The leaders of the societies (and their primary financial backers) tended to be mainly northeastern Presbyterians and Congregationalists, and many board members served on the directories of several voluntary societies. This so-called Benevolent Empire channeled the interests and energies of thousands of well-meaning Christians — a majority of the rank-and-file were women — who, motivated both by charity and by fear of America's future unless they acted to shape it, created a climate in the North in which reform activity reached into almost every corner. "A restless, prying, conscientious criticism," wrote Ralph Waldo Emerson, "broke out in unexpected quarters." Real social ills were identified and ameliorated, and imaginary evils attacked. It was assumed that the problems of society were significantly large, that earlier and individualistic reforms efforts had been insufficient, and new methods were needed, combining the efforts of many like-minded persons. The reformers assumed that they knew what was wrong and what was necessary to improve society. And most of them believed that social evils were the result of individual moral failure, but that even the most dissolute of people could have their consciences pricked and their souls touched, so that they

Temperance Propaganda   George Cruikshank, a well-known anti-liquor crusader, produced a series of sensational engravings entitled simply "The Bottle." "The Husband, in a State of Furious Drunkenness, Kills His Wife with the Instrument of All their Misery," reads the original caption of this 1847 image.

could turn around their lives. The result of this constellation of attitudes was the Age of Reform.

❧ Temperance

One of the most popular reform movements attacked what was called Demon Rum, a generic epithet for all forms of spirituous drinks. Americans had always drunk a lot by today's standards, and traditionally many farmers west of the Appalachians had turned their corn into liquor because in that form it was more profitable to transport it to eastern markets. By the late 1820s the average per capita consumption of hard liquor was over five gallons annually — more than twice today's rate. This heavy drinking had social consequences: men drank up their wages and, coming home inebriated, beat their wives and children. Often they could not keep their jobs in the newly routinized factories. Moralists had always deplored excessive drinking, but in the mid-1820s Protestant reformers broadened their

attack. In 1826 Lyman Beecher preached a series of six hard-hitting sermons calling not just for temperance but for complete abstinence. That same year the American Society for the Promotion of Temperance (read: abstinence) was founded. This new cause caught on, with other revival leaders like Charles G. Finney and Theodore Dwight Weld calling abstinence a necessary precondition to conversion.

Particularly for middle-class reformers, upset by urban saloons, drunken workingmen, and the growing presence of Irish and German immigrants who held different cultural attitudes toward social drinking — and convinced that much urban poverty, prostitution, and juvenile delinquency were the result of excessive drinking — the temperance campaigns were bold strokes for social improvement. By the mid-1830s more than a million Americans had joined national, state, and local temperance societies and had taken a pledge not to imbibe. Irish and Catholic immigrants often and understandably saw the temperance movement as a stalking horse for nativist persecution, and indeed many reformers saw immigrants as besotted foreigners sinking the nation under a wave of Catholicism and liquor. Because temperance advocates tended to be Whigs in the 1840s, Catholic immigrants flocked to the Democrats.

More than with most reforms, the temperance movement had a dimension of social control. The reformers sought to change the behavior of the masses who supposedly had difficulty controlling their appetites, but their methods were primarily persuasion. Pamphlets, sermons, rallies, and testimony meetings all tried to witness to the evils of drink and motivate drunkards to will a change of their behavior. During the severe economic downturn following the Panic of 1837, many workingmen — convinced that they would have to be more punctual, thrifty, and motivated to survive in the new workplace — came to see temperance as a kind of secular salvation. Moved not by religion but by economic concern, workingmen founded the Washingtonian Society in 1840 to promote abstinence. They organized parades, rallies at which reformed drunkards gave impassioned testimonies about how their lives had changed for the better since becoming teetotalers, and plays and minstrel shows with a temperance theme. Their wives, organized into Martha Washington Societies, worked to spread the antidrinking message. (Other workingmen, however, such as the so-called Bowery Boys, resisted reformers' efforts and stuck deliberately to working-class ways, including comradeship accompanied by heavy drinking.) By the mid-1840s the national consumption of alcohol had been cut by more than half, to less than two gallons per capita annually. Still the method was largely one of moral suasion, based on appealing to the common sense and natural morality of the public to give up the evil of drink. Timothy Shay Arthur's lurid exposé, *Ten Nights in a Bar-room, and What I Saw There* (1845) would, in the next decade, be second only to *Uncle Tom's Cabin* in sales. Then in 1851 the movement took the next step, calling on the state and local governments to prohibit the manufacture and sale of alcohol (except for medical use). Maine, led by Neal Dow, pioneered legal prohibition, and by the eve of the Civil War all the New England states had similar "Maine laws," as did New York, Pennsylvania, Ohio, Indiana, Michigan, and Iowa. Irish and Catholic immigrants rightly detected an undercurrent of nativist prejudice in some of the temperance fervor.

❧ Horace Mann and the Educational Crusade

All the intensity of the temperance crusade was also evident in the national movement to provide public schooling for the mass of the nation's children. The earliest organized efforts on behalf of tax-supported schools for all children were by artisans and journeymen in Philadelphia. The Philadelphia Working Men's Party in 1829 advocated free public schools for their children, and within several years similar calls came

---

❋ IN THEIR OWN WORDS

Abraham Lincoln,
Temperance Advocate, 1842

Young Abraham Lincoln — lawyer, aspiring politician, and abstainer from alcohol — made this speech to a group of Washingtonians in 1842, two years before he was elected to one term in Congress. Already his characteristic moderation was evident, as well as his ability to use humor, common sense, and folk-wisdom to make a profound point.

When the dram-seller and drinker were incessantly told — not in accents of entreaty and persuasion, diffidently addressed by erring man to an erring brother, but in the thundering tones of anathema and denunciation with which the lordly judge often groups together all the crimes of the felon's life, and thrusts them in his face just ere he passes sentence of death upon him — that they were the authors of all the vice and misery and crime in the land; that they were the manufacturers and material of all the thieves and robbers and murderers that infest the earth; that their houses were the workshops of the devil; and that their persons should be shunned by all the good and virtuous, as moral pestilences — I say, when they were told all this, and in this way, is it not wonderful that they were slow, very slow, to

acknowledge the truth of such denunciations, and to join the ranks of their denouncers in a hue and cry against themselves.

To have expected them to do otherwise than they did — to have expected them not to meet denunciation with denunciation, crimination with crimination, and anathema with anathema — was to expect a reversal of human nature, which is God's decree and can never be reversed.

When the conduct of men is designed to be influenced, persuasion, kind, unassuming persuasion, should ever be adopted. It is an old and true maxim "that a drop of honey catches more flies than a gallon of gall." So with men. If you would win a man to your cause, first convince him that you are his sincere friend. . . .

from workingmen's parties in New York, Boston, and scores of smaller industrializing cities. But soon economic grievances replaced schools as their main cause, and the increasing identification of urban workers with Catholic immigrants also limited support for the issue.

The foremost educational reformer of the age was Horace Mann, the secretary of the state board of education in Massachusetts from 1837 to 1848. Like other reformers, Mann insisted that democracy could work only if Americans took education seriously. He gave what could be called educational sermons, portraying in vivid terms not sin or hellfire or the results of too much time spent in the barroom. Rather, for Mann the evil was an ignorant, uneducated public in this, a nation where voters controlled the government. "Ignorance is a crime in a republic," Mann exhorted, and he spelled out the social disasters that would result: "If we do not prepare children to become good citizens — if we do not develop their capacities, if we do not enrich their minds with knowledge, imbue their hearts with the love of truth and duty . . . then our republic must go down in destruction. . . ." It is clear that educational reformers like Mann, Catharine Beecher, and Harry Barnard had in mind not just the "three Rs" but teaching proper Protestant, Whig cultural ideas and character as well. Despite the leadership of such reformers, class issues complicated the drive for public education, and many employers had no enthusiasm for keeping young potential workers in school. Child labor was simply too attractive to many employers, who doubted in any case the working class's potential for full citizenship. Educational reformers fought these prejudices.

Part of the educationalists' agenda was developing a standardized curriculum so that all students would learn a uniform body of information. The reformers never developed a formal system of national stan-

Punishment at Sing-Sing   Hopes that model antebellum prisons would reform inmates quickly faded. This image shows a prisoner at Sing-Sing Prison (Ossining, New York) being subjected to water torture for an infraction of prison rules. Harsh discipline became the rule in these institutions; many prisoners died or went insane as a result of their treatment.

dards, but nearly identical sets of textbooks came to be assigned across much of the nation, especially in the North where the public school movement was strongest. For two generations the majority of school children grew up with the McGuffey readers, and these collections of English, European, and American classics, wholesomely Protestant, became in effect a common curriculum that advocated sobriety, patriotism, hard work, honesty, and steadfastness to duty.

Instead of the often common practice of holding school for only two to three months annually, Mann and other reformers wanted to lengthen the school year to eight or ten months. They also wanted to compel attendance by law and to do away with the old ungraded schools in which all children, from six to eighteen or older, sat in the same room with one teacher. The reformers called for graded schools, the children separated by age, and taught more gently. Women had previously been considered inappropriate to control classrooms that included practically full-grown boys, in which strict physical discipline seemed necessary. But reformers like Mann and Beecher argued that young children in particular, whose minds were more plastic and could be molded with love, patience, and understanding, should be taught by women — considered natural nurturers. This meant that the new graded schools had a special need for women teachers, and this in turn created an acceptable career, almost a mission field, for young, educated, unmarried women. By the 1850s women came to dominate the teaching in the lower grades, and a number of northern states — beginning with Massachusetts in 1852 — passed compulsory school attendance laws.

Like the temperance crusade, the public school movement sowed tensions between Catholic immigrants and old-line Americans. The public schools tended to open with Protestant prayers and to assign readings from the King James Bible, not the Douay translation that Catholics used. Catholics who sent their children to voluntarily supported parochial schools resented paying taxes to support public — in their eyes, Protestant — schools. Many Catholic parents simply disobeyed the school laws, refused to enroll their children in the public schools, and had them attend Catholic schools for as many months a year as they could afford. Protestants saw immigrants as backward and un-American; Catholics viewed the public school officialdom as dictatorial. These conflicts would roil urban politics into the twentieth century, and their reverberations are still felt.

❧ A Smorgasbord of Reforms

While the temperance and public school crusades affected most citizens in the northern states and generated the most organizational support, the Age of Reform exhibited a wide range of efforts to identify and ameliorate social evils. Most of them sought to assist "worthy" unfortunates. Thus Thomas Gallaudet devoted his life to educating the deaf. He devised methods of instruction, opened his first school in Connecticut in 1817, and advocated similar institutions throughout the region. By the early 1850s there were schools for the deaf in fourteen states. In like fashion Dr. Samuel Gridley Howe dedicated himself to developing methods of teaching the blind. Louis Braille's system of raised dots had not yet been invented, so Dr. Howe worked with books that had raised letters. He was able to open his first school in Boston in 1832, though most of his efforts were in Worcester, and the fruits of his work attracted widespread attention both in the United States and abroad. Similar schools were soon established in the northern states. Other movements tried to reform prostitutes, to provide food and housing for the urban poor, to minister to lonely sailors in seaports, to advocate all kinds of health and eating fads. Sylvester Graham, among other things a dietary reformer, invented and marketed graham crackers in hopes that they would help maintain sexual purity and control excess sexual desire, which he believed caused disease, insanity, and death; he found many buyers.

For centuries the insane had usually been confined at home, locked away in a closet or kept in chains, presumably for their own and others' safety and to prevent them from embarrassing their family. Some were considered so incorrigible that they were jailed along with vicious criminals. Cure was not expected, and the feebleminded hardly seemed human. Evangelical reformers, eager to see the possibility for redemption of every sort in every person, had their consciousnesses raised about this state of affairs and came to be appalled by the conditions around them that everyone had silently accepted. Dorothea Dix, teaching Sunday school in a Massachusetts jail in 1841, was horrified to discover the plight of several insane people warehoused in the building. She then investigated conditions elsewhere in the state and was shocked to learn of how the insane were treated. In a heart-felt memorial to the state legislature in 1843 she graphically portrayed what she had seen: "*insane people confined within this* Commonwealth, *in cages, closets, cellars, stalls, pens! Chained, naked, beaten with rods, and lashed* into obedience." That very year the legislature voted funds to enlarge the state hospital, and Dix spent the next decade traveling throughout the nation advocating humane treatment for the insane. At least moderate rehabilitation was expected as a result of kind treatment and adequate food. Dix was joined in her cause by other reformers, and largely as a result of her crusade by the time of the Civil War twenty-eight states, including several in the South, had public institutions for the insane, and many cities had local hospitals as well.

Criminals too had been treated much as the insane, with the more vicious locked away in jails and the worst put to death; lesser crimes were normally punished by whipping and branding. Jails were simply places to quarantine criminals so they could do no harm to society. But in the early nineteenth century reformers came to believe that human behavior was at least partly determined by social environment. People, it was felt, could be shaped and disciplined by the right influences. This was particularly true in the United States, insisted Philadelphia lawyer and former congressman Charles Jared Ingersoll in his 1823 publication, *Discourse Concerning the Influence of America on the Mind,* and such environmental arguments undergirded a variety of reform endeavors. It stood to reason — so he claimed — that if criminals were removed from society and brutal jails, placed under close supervision, disciplined, and forced by doing solitary time to think about their evil ways and repent, they could reform and redeem their lives. Acting on such assumptions, the state of New York built model prisons at Auburn in 1819 and Ossining (Sing Sing) in 1825. Here prisoners worked in groups during the day under military discipline but were not allowed to speak to each other; at night they were confined to tiny, windowless cells where they were expected to contemplate their evil ways. They also received "moral and religious instruction." Some reformers believed that this so-called Auburn system allowed for too much contact between prisoners during the day. An alternative prison model developed in Pennsylvania, where all prisoners were held in absolutely solitary confinement and allowed no human contact. Both systems seem unbelievably harsh by today's standards, but the defenders of each assumed that the system would bring convicts to reform themselves. These American experiments to reform criminals attracted attention from European observers (Tocqueville was sent from France for this purpose), but they failed. Many criminals went mad, committed suicide, or otherwise never left their cells to return to society. Rising expenses, understaffing, and recidivism all made prisons increasingly overcrowded. By the eve of the Civil War the hope of criminal reform was largely forgotten, and prisons became the hopeless institutions they have remained, although the rehabilitation ideal still lives on.

Antislavery

Antislavery began as simply one among many do-good movements in an Age of Reform, but as it grew and evolved it became an issue that absorbed many other issues and affected politics as did no other cause. It touched a raw nerve in the body politic, and the debate it unleashed ultimately led to the Civil War.

The Quakers, a small perfectionist and pietistic religious group, in the mid- to late eighteenth century first identified slavery as a grave moral sin afflicting the land. They organized efforts to eradicate it in states like Pennsylvania, and the relatively few Quakers living in such states as North Carolina, Virginia, and Maryland began freeing their slaves in the aftermath of the American Revolution. The radical revivalism of the early Baptists and Methodists in the South at this time also produced a principled stand against slavery. Many early evangelicals freed their slaves and a few, unwilling to live in a slaveholding society, fled the South. Political ideology, too, caused many in the North, where slavery was less central to the economy, to question the rightfulness of the institution, and the "contagion of liberty" that spun out of Revolutionary-era protest led the northern states, beginning in 1780, either to end slavery immediately in their jurisdictions or to begin a process of gradual emancipation. The Northwest Ordinance, representing this viewpoint, banned slavery from the territory and the states that eventually would be created out of it. Many southerners like Thomas Jefferson advocated these moves against slavery. The Constitution did not outlaw slavery, but it did allow Congress to prohibit the importation of slaves after 1808, and Congress, following the explicit urging of Jefferson, did pass legislation (which Jefferson signed into law on March 2, 1807) — effective January 1, 1808 — making it illegal to import additional slaves from abroad. Thereafter only a relatively few slaves were illegally smuggled in from Africa and Cuba.

❧ The Colonization Movement

By 1804 every state north of Maryland and Delaware had put slavery on the road to extinction, but in the Deep South slavery was getting a new lease on life because of the cotton gin and geographical expansion. In the Upper South states, however, slavery did seem anachronistic as farmers shifted from tobacco to wheat and corn. Neither Quakers in Pennsylvania nor white farmers in the Upper South felt much concern for the slaves them-

Illustrations of the American Anti-Slavery Almanac for 1840.

"Our Peculiar Domestic Institutions."

Northern Hospitality—New-York nine months law. [The
Slave steps out of the Slave State, and his chains fall.
A Free State, with another chain, stands ready to re-
enslave him.]

Burning of McIntosh at St. Louis, in April, 1836.

Showing how slavery improves the condition of the female sex.

The Negro Pew, or "Free"   Mayor of New-York re-
Seats for black Christians.   fusing a Carman's license
                                 to a colored Man.

Servility of the Northern States in arresting and returning
fugitive Slaves.

Selling a Mother from her Child.

Hunting Slaves with dogs and guns.   A Slave drowned
by the dogs.

" Poor things, ' they can't take care of themselves.' "

Mothers with young Children at work in the field.

A Woman chained to a Girl, and a Man in irons at work in
the field.

Branding Slaves.

Cutting up a Slave in Kentucky.

Paid.   Unpaid.

Antislavery Propaganda, 1840   The American Anti-Slavery
Society directed a constant barrage of propaganda at northern
audiences in the decades leading up to the Civil War. Among
themes constantly stressed were those illustrated by this "Alma-
nac": the separations by sale of children from their mothers, the
beatings, the use of bloodhounds to track down fleeing slaves, the
complicity of northerners in returning runaways to their masters,
the persecutions of abolitionists, and the lynching (sometimes by
burning alive) of free blacks. The intended result was to keep before the northern public the realization that slavery was a terrible
moral blot on the nation. Until the 1850s, however, most northerners tended to "tune out" abolitionist propaganda.

Trouble Brewing   This cartoon caricatures William Lloyd Garrison along with David Wilmot, Horace Greeley, and John Calhoun as gathered around a bubbling cauldron like the witches in Shakespeare's *Macbeth*. The cauldron is filled with sacks labeled with the names of issues that were divisive in the antebellum period. Garrison adds to the pot a bag labeled "abolition" and urges slaves "strong as goats" to "cut your masters' throats."

selves; rather, they worried about how the institution harmed white society, and they wanted to send both free blacks and newly emancipated slaves back to Africa. In 1816 Quakers and many slave owners in the Upper South founded the American Colonization Society and began making preparations to ship free blacks to West Africa; in 1820 they established Liberia as a colony to receive them. This movement was impractical and racist from the beginning, and also prohibitively expensive. One of the colonizationists' reports described the nation's free black population as "notoriously ignorant, degraded and miserable, mentally diseased, [and] broken spirited." The intent was to purge the land of free blacks, not to end slavery. And most free blacks, recognizing the racist motivation, refused to go. As one black pastor put it, "we are *natives* of this county. We only ask that we be treated as well as *foreigners*." On the whole, blacks repudiated the colonization movement and began instead organizing antislavery societies. Over fifty were founded by the late 1820s, and the decade ended with a Boston free black, David Walker, publishing a bold *Appeal to the Colored Citizens of the World* (1829) that called on blacks to resort to violence if necessary to free themselves. The colonization movement was wholly ineffective. In 1830, when the population of slaves totaled more than 2 million, only 259 free blacks were sent to Liberia. In no conceivable way could colonization have even made a dent in the growing slave population.

Simultaneously with the rise of the colonization movement, a number of antislavery societies were organized in the South during the 1820s. Most of the antislavery societies in the nation in 1827 were in the South (106) rather than in the North (only 24), and southern members outnumbered northern ones by almost four to one. But these were gradualist organizations, and the mostly religious members pinned their hopes on moral suasion to get slaveholders to surrender their slaves.

Yet the window of opportunity during which southern abolitionists might have been effective was rapidly closing. The Nat Turner slave revolt of 1831 really ended the period during which thoughtful southerners would discuss the issue.[5] Already southern states were passing laws to prohibit antislavery agitation, and the cotton curtain began to descend around the South, keeping out critical discussion of the issue. At the same time northern antislavery spokesmen were becoming bolder. After 1830 antislavery was almost completely a northern sentiment, and nothing proved to be more divisive between the regions.

❧ *The New Antislavery Movement*

Northern antislavery changed for a number of reasons. Many critics of slavery had finally lost patience with the colonization movement. In late 1830 a young, idealistic, morally intense abolitionist from Boston, William Lloyd Garrison, left his position with a moderate antislavery newspaper in Baltimore, returned to his home city, and on January 1, 1831, began publication of a forthright abolitionist newspaper, *The Liberator*. In bold type Garrison shouted his intentions to stop at nothing until he had driven slavery from the land: "I will be as harsh as truth, and as uncompromising as justice," his initial editorial screamed. "I am in earnest — I will not equivocate — I will not excuse — I will not retreat a single inch — AND I WILL BE HEARD." With those brave words a new abolitionist movement in America began. That August came the Nat Turner insurrection in Virginia, and a massive slave revolt in Jamaica followed in December — ammunition for white southerners who

5. See Chapter 11.

argued that even discussion of the issue was dangerous for the southern way of life. In 1833 Parliament enacted a gradual-emancipation plan to free the slaves in the West Indies colonies. There seemed to be international movement for the great cause of abolition. That year Garrison, with a group of sixty-two other whites and blacks, organized the American Anti-Slavery Society in a Boston church basement. As black abolitionists had always urged, Garrison now rejected moderate plans of gradual emancipation and calls for colonization. He demanded immediate emancipation, to begin right then with no compromising, and he called for complete equality for freed persons.

The sources of the new abolitionism varied from concerns about the economic backwardness of the institution of slavery to the example of Great Britain, but in the early 1830s in the northeastern United States the primary motivation was religious. Here all the zeal and moral fervor of Finneyite revivalism and the organizational apparatus of the benevolent empire came to a point. Slavery was seen as a sin, a moral cancer that had to be obliterated instantly. Abolitionists employed all the techniques of the skilled revivalists with their tried and true methods: Mass meetings were held; the horrors of slavery were expounded; former slaves like Frederick Douglass, Henry Bibb, and William Wells Brown gave personal testimonies; millions of tracts were printed and distributed; women formed local societies, raised funds, and provided moral staying power. As with other evangelical reformers, the abolitionist leaders assumed that if people really understood the horrors of slavery, they would voluntarily take a stand against it and free themselves from its evil. Just as evangelicals thought that drunkards would give up drink, that criminals after contemplation of their ways would reform their be-

havior, and that "sinners" would turn away from sin at a revival meeting, so too they hoped that converted slaveholders and those who benefited from slaveholding would instantly reject their involvement in the practice. Abolitionists spread their message in many creative ways, including children's games and candy wrappers with antislavery warnings. This idealistic expectation minimized the hard economic and social rationale behind slavery in the South. Optimistic reformers could not understand why those profiting from the evil institution would not seize the opportunity to liberate themselves from bondage to this particular form of sin.

The absence of quick success did not stymie the movement, and abolitionism spread far beyond Boston. No one did more to make it a religious crusade than Theodore Dwight Weld, who in 1834 organized a band of students at Lane Seminary in Cincinnati into an antislavery society and sent them across the Midwest seeking converts to abolitionism. This upset the more moderate antislavery president of Lane, Lyman Beecher, who tried to suppress the student movement. Weld thereupon led the students en masse to Oberlin College in northern Ohio, which became an idealistic, racially integrated college prominent in the antislavery cause for decades. Many northern reformers joined the movement — ministers and laypeople, men and women, poor and rich, like the philanthropic brothers, Arthur and Lewis Tappan, who underwrote many reform causes, especially abolition. In 1838 Weld co-edited with his wife, Angelina Grimké — a southern-born abolitionist and feminist — an eye-opening book entitled *American Slavery As It Is*, a stirring indictment of slavery based on documentation from southern sources.

Antislavery had become a moral crusade, and opposition to it developed everywhere. Southern states

---

❋ IN THEIR OWN WORDS

William Lloyd Garrison
Defends Himself, 1831

Here the abolitionist William Lloyd Garrison staunchly rejects the notion that he should temper his antislavery rhetoric. Contrast this with Abraham Lincoln's tone, quoted earlier in this chapter.

I am aware that many object to the severity of my language; but is there not cause for

severity? I *will be* as harsh as truth, and as uncompromising as justice. On this subject, I do not wish to think, or speak, or write, with moderation. No! no! Tell a man whose house is on fire to give a moderate alarm; tell him to moderately rescue his wife from the hands of the ravisher; tell the mother to gradually extricate her babe from the fire into which it has fallen;—but urge me not to use moderation in a cause like the present. I am

in earnest — I will not equivocate — I will not excuse — I will not retreat a single inch — AND I WILL BE HEARD. The apathy of the people is enough to make every statue leap from its pedestal, and to hasten the resurrection of the dead.

It is pretended, that I am retarding the cause of emancipation by the coarseness of my invective and the precipitancy of my measures. *The charge is not true.*

moved to prevent the post office from distributing abolitionist tracts, white southerners verbally and sometimes physically attacked antislavery spokesmen, and a bounty was placed on Garrison and other abolitionists. In the North anti-abolitionist mobs disrupted antislavery rallies, a mob dragged Garrison through the streets of Boston, Weld and his whole band were attacked and threatened almost constantly, and in Illinois abolitionist editor Elijah P. Lovejoy was murdered and his printing press destroyed. These attacks, if anything, seemed to ennoble the cause and increase the zeal of the antislavery reformers. By 1840 more than 200,000 northerners belonged to more than 2,000 abolition societies. But a movement this large and addressing such a complex issue could not avoid fissure.

The group of abolitionists associated with Weld and the Tappan brothers believed that real progress on achieving antislavery was possible without bloodshed or completely reshaping society. Moral suasion, spread by well organized, energetic reformers using all the publicity at their disposal, could effect a social conversion on the matter of slavery. When proslavery forces attempted to squelch the antislavery message by automatically tabling all petitions to Congress so that the issue would not be discussed by that body (the so-called gag rule) and by trying to pass a law to ban antislavery pamphlets from the mails, they inadvertently made abolition into a free-speech issue in the North. Former president John Quincy Adams, after 1831 a Representative from Massachusetts, led a fight for almost ten years in Congress to kill the gag rule. The proslavery forces' heavy-handedness, ranging from violations of free speech to mob action and violence in the North, turned northerners lacking personal experience with slavery into antislavery activists. Slowly the Weld forces came to see that political pressure could aid their cause, and they moved to transform at least partially the voluntary reform movement against slavery into a political organization. In 1840 they established the Liberty Party with James G. Birney as its presidential candidate.

❧ *The Radical Abolitionists*

Garrison had by now given up on the existing society addressing the issue of slavery. Becoming ever more radical, he began to attack the entire hierarchical arrangement of society, government, and the family. Garrison believed that all relationships based on power were evil, from the patriarchal father dominating his family and the police power of government to human

bondage. He supported complete racial and gender equality, further widening the gap between himself and his few followers and the larger antislavery movement. In 1838 he helped found the New England Non-Resistant Society, which called for a complete moral remaking of society, and in 1840 he supported the election of a woman, Abby Kelley, to a previously all-male committee of the American Anti-Slavery Society (AASS). This was the final straw for the moderate Weld-Tappan-Birney wing of the antislavery movement, and they broke away from the AASS and formed the American and Foreign Anti-Slavery Society.

Garrison grew, if anything, still more radical. He could brook no compromise with social or economic forces, and in a famous scene in 1854 he publicly burned a copy of the Constitution — "a covenant with death and an agreement with Hell" that "should be immediately annulled." Garrison also broke with prominent black abolitionist Frederick Douglass. Garrison wanted Douglass simply to recite his autobiographical depiction of slavery, but Douglass had a mind of his own and wanted to do more: he was more practical than Garrison and supported the translation of antislavery into a political cause.

In 1845 Douglass published the first edition of his famous autobiography, *Narrative of the Life of Frederick Douglass,* and in 1847 he started his own newspaper, the *North Star.* Thereafter he spoke widely and eloquently on behalf of abolition. Douglass addressed the problems of discrimination against blacks in the North almost as much as he did slavery in the South. Unlike Garrison and more like Weld and the Liberty Party, Douglass decided to fight slavery and racism from within the system. He wrote that the Constitution was created "to establish Justice, insure domestic Tranquility . . . and secure the Blessings of Liberty," as its preamble stated, so it could not have been intended to support something as evil as slavery. He then used the principles of the Constitution to attack bondage.

The splits in the abolitionist movement ultimately did not harm the crusade. The black abolitionists, with their public lectures and published memoirs, brought home vividly to many northerners the inhumanity of slavery. The political abolitionists kept the cause in front of the American people and maintained pressure on Congress, and the Liberty Party convinced many northerners, even those not really concerned about slavery and the plight of blacks, that there really was a Slave Power conspiracy in the South that would trample on the rights of northern whites to defend their

The "Declaration of Sentiments," 1848
In the "Declaration of Sentiments," Elizabeth Cady Stanton uses the language of the Declaration of Independence to call for equality between the sexes.

When, in the course of human events, it becomes necessary for one portion of the family of man to assume among the people of the earth a position different from that which they have hitherto occupied, but one to which the laws of nature and of nature's God entitle them, a decent respect to the opinions of mankind requires that they should declare the causes that impel them to such a course.

We hold these truths to be self-evident: that all men and women are created equal; that they are endowed by their Creator with certain inalienable rights; that among these are life, liberty, and the pursuit of happiness. . . .

The history of mankind is a history of repeated injuries and usurpations on the part of man toward woman, having in direct object the establishment of an absolute tyranny over her. To prove this, let facts be submitted to a candid world.

He has never permitted her to exercise her inalienable right to the elective franchise.

He has compelled her to submit to laws, in the formation of which she had no voice.

He has withheld from her rights which are given to the most ignorant and degraded men — both natives and foreigners.

Having deprived her of this first right of a citizen, the elective franchise, thereby leaving her without representation in the halls of legislation, he has oppressed her on all sides. . . .

---

peculiar institution. Many northerners also feared and disliked African Americans even as they opposed slavery. Northern negrophobia led many to see blacks as inferior, and racist stereotypes abounded in popular jokes and minstrel shows. Most abolitionists did not support full equality between the races, and at least some northerners advocated abolition because they worried that otherwise runaway slaves would come north, where they would compete for jobs and "pollute" society. A wide range of motivations lay behind the antislavery movement. The abolitionist movement in all its permutations succeeded in placing slavery so centrally in the public imagination that it simply could not be ignored. And the radical perfectionism of Garrison, because it did seem so wildly extremist, made other positions look moderate by contrast. The abolitionists eventually reshaped the cultural and political landscape of antebellum America.

WOMEN'S RIGHTS

One unanticipated result of the reform movement in general and of abolitionism in particular was the emergence of a movement to expand the rights of women. Antebellum women were called upon to organize and raise funds for a variety of causes, gave oral reports and testimonies, helped distribute tracts, and pondered how legal and social restraints inhibited the free activity of bondspeople. It was an easy step from portraying how slaves were dependent on the will of their owners to understanding how wives were dependent on the will of their husbands. As Abby Kelley wrote in 1838, "In striving to strike . . . [the slave's] irons off, we found most surely that *we* were manacled *ourselves.*" That vivid realization occurred to many women active in the reform currents of the 1830s and 1840s. Married women had no control over their own property (even inherited property) or their own income, were barred from higher education and all professions, and enjoyed almost no legal rights. The general consciousness-raising that occurred as women considered the plight of slaves caused some women to question the dependent status of women in American society.

❧ The Women's Movement

Angelina and Sarah Grimké became lighting rods in the movement. Moving north from their native South Carolina and speaking out against slavery, these sisters found themselves bitterly attacked for addressing mixed (male and female) audiences. This opposition only strengthened their protofeminism, and they began to defend the right of women to organize, speak out, or do anything men could do. As Sarah Grimké wrote in 1837, "men and women were CREATED EQUAL. . . . whatever is right for a man to do, is right for woman." Other courageous women, willing to risk opprobrium, also advocated improvements in the rights of women. The final straw for two women abolitionists, Lucretia Mott and Elizabeth Cady Stanton, came in 1840 when they journeyed to London to attend the World Antislavery Convention, only to be told they could not be seated in the assembly. After intense complaint the women were allowed to sit in the balcony behind a curtain so they could neither see nor be seen. This indignity drove Mott and Stanton to create an organization that would "speak out for *oppressed* women," as antislavery organizations did for black slaves. Opposition was stronger than they expected, some even coming from women, and the pressures on them to soft-pedal their complaints so as not to jeopardize other reform movements (like antislavery) delayed their cause. But in 1848 Mott and Stanton finally held their national convention on the rights of women at Seneca Falls, New York.

The hundred assembled delegates issued a Declaration of Sentiments closely modeled on the Declaration of Independence: "We hold these truths to be self-evident: that all men and women are created equal." They called for economic rights and the right to vote (controversial even among the delegates), and while by 1860 women in a number of states did acquire increased control over their property and income, not for seventy-two years, in 1920, would women win the right to vote nationally. Mississippi passed the first Married Women's Property Act in 1837, and other states followed soon thereafter, but the motivation was to prevent unworthy sons-in-law from seizing control of and squandering family assets, not to enhance the economic role of women. This issue had become more acute as more young couples were marrying for love and not as a result of careful (and supposedly more sensible) parental arrangement. In general, the women's movement, unlike the reforms promoting temperance, public schools, and antislavery, had little effect in the antebellum period and did not really bear fruit until the twentieth century. But the early women's movement raised many of the right questions about the nature of their status.

***Rubens Peale with a Geranium,* by Rembrandt Peale**　This portrait, executed in 1801 in the neo-classical style then very popular in Europe, shows one of the sons of the famous American painter Charles Willson Peale (1741-1827). All of the elder Peale's sons were named for famous European painters, and all were themselves painters. The son who did this painting, Rembrandt (1778-1860), achieved the greatest reputation.

❧ *The Cult of True Womanhood*

The women's movement faltered not just because many women were more involved in other movements like temperance or because many males felt their gender roles threatened by strong, active women. An alternative model of women's role also emerged during this period, in part reflecting how the male workplace became physically separated from the home as a result of industrialization. Less often now did a husband and wife jointly operate a small shop; the woman tended now to stay at home with the children as the man went to a workplace in another building. This spatial separation created the concept of different spheres: the male sphere, which was competitive, market-oriented, and secular; and the female sphere, which was nurturing, domestic, and religious. The woman's prescribed role was to make the home a moral oasis — safe from the strife and temptations of the world. The woman should seek to be a moral emissary to her husband, nurture the children so that they would grow up moral citizens, and maintain Christian standards in the midst of a changing, chaotic world.

This domestic prescription of the proper woman's role might today seem a weak substitute for greater economic and political rights, but for many women in the second quarter of the nineteenth century the result was a role of heightened importance. It was up to women to protect the morality of their husbands and to raise children who would be moral, responsible adults. Women were the agents of civilization, unofficial ministers working to promote a democratic Christian society — in effect, a Protestant society whose standards of behavior were decidedly middle class and critical of immigrant, Catholic, and working-class lifestyles. What has been called the "cult of true womanhood" — strongly supported by most men and by ministers and publicists galore and also by most women reformers — was a more attractive model for many women than that of activist for enhanced secular rights. Ironically, while the two-spheres ideology crimped the women's movement, it helped propel many middle-class urban women into a variety of moralistic reform movements to "improve" the society outside the home. In the welter of so many competing causes, the more secular women's movement never achieved the momentum required to challenge legal restrictions against women. And increasingly in the years after the mid-1840s, abolitionism became the reform crusade that consumed most of the North's moral intensity. Even many sympathetic radical abolitionists in the Garrison camp who strongly supported the cause of women put that issue on the back burner in the critical years after 1850. In that decade, antislavery was the Cause of causes.

ARTS, LETTERS, AND UTOPIAS

Considering the urban-industrial-immigration interrelationship during the four decades following 1820 and the simultaneous proliferation of reform movements, it would be easy to imagine that in the midst of so much invention, movement, struggle, and action, the life of contemplation and culture was neglected. In Great Britain, the haughty *Edinburgh Review* snidely asked in 1820, "In the four quarters of the globe, who reads an American book?" But that would soon change. As emblematic of this age as reform or social flux was an intellectual discovery of American landscape, of the American character, and of both a popular and high culture. It was as if, having finally established political independence at the conclusion of the War of 1812 and with an expansive West beckoning, the nation set about self-consciously to establish its personality and declare its cultural independence.

Although the first generation of writers following the American Revolution sought to commemorate the new nation and its potential, they were so wedded to the fashionable European styles that their writings seemed false. Poets like Joel Barlow and novelists like

---

✳ **IN THEIR OWN WORDS**

Walt Whitman, "One's-Self I Sing," 1867
While not in the original edition, this poem eventually came to open later editions of Leaves of Grass.

One's-Self I sing, a simple separate person,
Yet utter the word Democratic, the word En-Masse.
Of physiology from top to toe I sing,
Not physiognomy alone nor brain alone is worth for the muse, I

        Say the Form

complete is worthier far,
The Female equally with the Male I sing.

Of Life immense in passion, pulse, and power,
Cheerful, for freest action form'd under the laws divine,
The Modern Man I sing.

Walden Pond   Henry David Thoreau built his famous cabin (long since vanished) near this spot; the shore of Walden Pond is in the background. Admirers have piled up stones to form a cairn as a spontaneous memorial. Woods have encroached much more on the spot than during Thoreau's lifetime. The railroad of which Thoreau complained in *Walden* still runs close by, now carrying commuters between their suburban homes and their jobs in downtown Boston.

Charles Brockden Brown chose American settings, but their results were too dependent on English styles. Nor could the first American painters and sculptors escape Old World fashions, as exemplified by the paintings and sculptures of George Washington portrayed draped in the flowing robes of antiquity.

James Fenimore Cooper was the first novelist of substantial merit to take advantage of an American setting, and his books *The Spy* (1820), *The Pioneers* (1823), and *The Last of the Mohicans* (1826) were vivid, colorful, and memorable adventures of frontier life. His character Natty Bumppo exemplified the contrast between nature and civilization, a motif that would

intrigue American readers for a century to come. Another successful interpreter of the American past was Washington Irving, who found comic themes in the depictions of the Dutch settlers along the Hudson River. In *The Sketch Book* (1819) he gave to American literature the character of Rip Van Winkle and "The Legend of Sleepy Hollow." Artists John Singleton Copley, Gilbert Stuart, and Charles Willson Peale (and especially Peale's son Rembrandt) found in portraiture a way to capture something authentically American about their subjects. Another group of artists discovered in the lush landscape of the Hudson River Valley a rich metaphor for the beauty and possibility and freshness of the American people and nation, and artists such as Thomas Cole, Asher Durand, and Frederic Church in the half century after 1820 created a movement known as the Hudson River School that depicted melodramatic scenes from the region with all the sense and sensibility of the romantic movement that was sweeping Europe. And innumerable folk artists depicted American scenes and personalities, but their work was so different from high art as to constitute a separate genre.

❧ *The New England Renaissance*

The intellectual who as advocate and writer/lecturer most shaped the achievement of American literary independence was Ralph Waldo Emerson. A former Unitarian minister trained at Harvard but living in the Massachusetts town of Concord, Emerson came to think that Unitarianism — the penultimate product of the tradition of religious liberalism that had begun with Timothy Dwight and Asahel Nettleton revising Calvinist orthodoxy — was too cold and formalistic. He became part of a movement known as transcendentalism, an emotionally warm, open, almost pantheistic philosophy that held that all people could experience divinity in nature and, if they obeyed the impulses of their hearts, discover truth. As the Northeast in particular grew more urban and industrial, Emerson exulted in the beauty and re-creative properties of nature. He also glorified the individual, free of all artificial constraints from tradition or government. Emerson urged Americans to have the courage to strike out on their own, to follow their own intuitions, and to create art forms that were consistent with their inmost being and with their American setting. In a famous lecture entitled "The American Scholar," which Emerson delivered dozens of times after he became the first star of the lyceum[6] lecture circuit in the North, the epigrammatic speaker preached a message of independence, individualism, and self-reliance. In modern vernacular, Emerson told his fellow writers and artists and citizens to "do your own thing" and to not worry about convention and consequences. Emerson's fame, his gentle nature, and his literary grace emboldened dozens of literary and artistic Americans to do just that, and the result has come to be known as the "American Renaissance."

Closely associated with Emerson was his Concord neighbor Henry David Thoreau — a loner and a gentle, introverted man who so valued his independence that he essentially rejected involvement in the world. Families, jobs, pursuit of wealth — all seemed to him to produce the "lives of quiet desperation" that he saw people all around him leading. Rather than simply think about issues, he acted on them. In order to pare

life down to the basics and contemplate what he considered truly important, Thoreau constructed and for almost two years lived in a simple cabin on the shores of Walden Pond, about a mile from Concord center. There he looked inward to contemplate cosmic issues, and the result was a work widely recognized today as an American classic, *Walden* (1854). Thoreau excluded all non-essentials from his life and thought hard and honestly about the bedrock issues of existence. "I went to the woods," he wrote, "because I wished to . . . front only the essential facts of life, and see if I could not learn what it had to teach, and not, when I came to die, discover that I had not lived." Earlier he had composed an account of a trip he and his brother had taken (*A Week on the Concord and Merrimack Rivers* [1849]), and this memoir too was an occasion for Thoreau to muse about the problems of life and his theories of literature. He was such an individualist that he went Jefferson one better: "That government is best," Thoreau wrote, "which governs not at all." True to this philosophy, he spent a night in jail in 1846 rather than pay poll taxes that he believed would support the U.S. war against Mexico. Drawing on this experience he wrote *Civil Disobedience* (1849), a defense of disobeying laws one considers unjust. Many Americans came to know this philosophical stance better in the 1960s when Martin Luther King, Jr., employed it in opposition to southern laws mandating racial segregation. No society could exist if every person were a Thoreau, but no society would be worth much without the leavening influence of such rare people.

Emerson's call for American individualism received in the person of the poet Walt Whitman a more earthy and democratic exemplification. Born on Long Island, Whitman left school early, worked in print shops, wrote for a number of newspapers, did carpentry for a while, and came to know and love the vast variety of people and occupations that made up the American public. Following Emerson's call to be himself, freed from all artificial constraints, Whitman broke loose from the normal standards of poetic meter and rhyme. He wrote free verse and about mundane, even vulgar, matters, experimenting with language and topic. He wanted to capture the soul, the ethos, of the typical American, and he imagined that he in some fashion represented the average man. Using slang, speaking bluntly, and breaking all conventions, Whitman's expanding and evolving collection of poems entitled *Leaves of Grass* (first published in 1855) constituted an optimistic hymn to the American people.

---

6. An association providing public lectures, concerts, and discussions.

❧ *Probing Human Nature*

But in contrast to the optimism and can-do philosophy of both Emerson and Whitman, three literary geniuses probed the darker side of human nature. Nathaniel Hawthorne of Salem, Massachusetts — site of the famous witch trials of 1691-1693 — had a sad, lonely childhood, and as an adult he disliked the easy optimism of the transcendentalists. He was intrigued by the consequences of mistakes, pride, and sin, and the guilt in which they culminated. Hawthorne first revealed his preoccupation with guilt in *Twice-Told Tales* (1837), with their New England setting, but it was in two powerful novels, *The Scarlet Letter* (1850) and *The House of Seven Gables* (1851), that his mordant thoughts about the lingering effects of sin and greed received full expression. His *Scarlet Letter* condemned less the Puritan woman guilty of adultery, Hester Prynne, than the judgmental society in which she found herself.

Even less enamored of the bright and sunny side of life was New Yorker Herman Melville; his father, like Hawthorne's, died while the future author was still a child. Melville, like Hawthorne, dropped out of school as a young teenager, held a variety of jobs, and eventually found himself first aboard a whaling ship and then among a tribe of South Sea cannibals. Two of his early books, *Typee* (1846) and *Omoo* (1847), adventurous portrayals of this exotic locale, were popular successes. But Melville's masterpiece, *Moby-Dick* (1851), achieved little appreciation until the twentieth century. It is a dense, brooding account of the all-consuming obsession of Ahab, a whaling captain, with hunting down and killing a giant white whale, Moby Dick. The white whale symbolized the mystery, beauty, and evil in nature, and Ahab's passion for defeating the whale led to his own death. Life had to be endured; one could not shape destiny in one's favor, and nature was ultimately both omnipotent and unknowable. Melville held out no easy promise of becoming one with nature and learning its truths as if by osmosis.

Boston-born and Virginia-raised Edgar Allan Poe exemplified the troubled, even crazed, literary genius. Addicted to gambling, alcohol, and drugs, and deeply pessimistic about life in urbanizing America, Poe skirted both insanity and poverty as he pursued a brilliant career as editor, reviewer, and author of hauntingly original short stories and poems. He gave romanticism and sentimentalism a dark tone by setting his stories amid a background of urban life marked by terror, the bizarre, and tragedy, made the more be-lievable because he often based them loosely on stories he read in the urban press. His writing, unlike his life, was notable for its careful discipline — he was a consummate craftsman. Poe was no easy optimist, no singer of democracy. Rather he focused on murderers, on the insane, on people desperately disturbed by manias or guilt. The macabre was his forte, and in a series of stories Poe succeeded in painting dark, horrifying, portraits of tormented characters unlike those found anywhere else at the time in American literature: "The Premature Burial," "The Fall of the House of Usher," "The Pit and the Pendulum," to name a few. In addition to being the master of the horror story, Poe also essentially invented the detective story with such tales as "The Gold Bug" and "The Purloined Letter." Poe was actually widely read in his own time, and poems like "The Raven" were instantly popular. Had he been personally stable, Poe might have made a good living with his creative writing and skillful editing. But how much of his genius was wrapped up in his own tormented soul? In 1849 he was found unconscious on a Baltimore street and died shortly thereafter in a delirium — only forty years old.

❧ *Popular Culture*

These are the writers whose names and works are known by all students today, but the most widely read mid-nineteenth-century American authors were that "damned mob of scribbling women," as an envious Hawthorne once complained — popular women writers who took advantage both of the religious and sentimental currents of the time, and reaped a fortune from the cheap paperback book market made possible by the steam press. They produced a stream of phenomenal best sellers. No one (except historians) today reads such authors as Catharine Maria Sedgwick, Susan Warner, Maria Cummins, and Elizabeth Phelps, but these were the authors who best understood and catered to the public taste of antebellum America. Warner's *Wide, Wide World* (1851) went through fourteen editions in only two years.

The heroines of these novels were usually women who seldom left the domestic hearth, but who through courage, piety, and self-reliance reached out to others among their kin and community and helped them overcome hardships of every kind. They lived quiet, unassuming lives of great drama and tragedy, but love and faith brought them through their tribulations to peace and resolution. It was this tradition of sentimental domestic literature that Harriet Beecher Stowe utilized so powerfully in her great abolitionist novel, *Uncle Tom's Cabin* (1851).[7]

The steam press also made newspapers and magazines less expensive, and the result was a tremendous expansion of publications that catered to the rapidly growing urban masses. At the same time, new city dwellers avidly sought excitement in sports such as baseball and bloody, bare-knuckle prize fights. Theaters sprang up across the land, but these were arenas for rowdy, boisterous, even bawdy presentations as well as Shakespeare and dramatic versions of best-selling novels like *Uncle Tom's Cabin*. Diarist Philip Hone described a disturbance in a New York playhouse in 1849 that erupted when a certain actor came on stage: "he was saluted with a shower of missiles, rotten eggs, and other unsavory objects, with shouts and yells of the most abusive epithets. In the midst of this disgraceful riot the performance was suspended." Unlike today, when Shakespeare is regarded as a sacrosanct icon of high culture and dreaded by high-school readers, the bard found a ready and receptive audience among the urban populace. People who had never read a line of "literature" loved Shakespeare's great plays, and in deference to their audiences managers "dumbed down" some of the language, highlighted the sword fights and romance, cut minor (and occasionally even major) characters, shortened scenes, and sometimes gave tragedies happy endings. But workers and artisans in the 1830s knew the basic plotline and characters of Shakespeare the way their counterparts today know television series.

Even more democratic in taste were the minstrel shows, which proliferated after the 1850s in northern cities. Here black-faced white entertainers danced, sang, and performed humorous sketches while masquerading as southern blacks. To a degree they introduced northern audiences to the music and dance of slaves, but this was black culture once removed: white men supposedly interpreting black art to northern crowds. The depictions of blacks in the sketches was stereotypical and demeaning, filled with stock characters like Uncle Ned, the humble, devoted slave in disheveled dress, and Zip Coon, the debonair urban black and confidence man. (Stowe's *Uncle Tom's Cabin* was notable for presenting, for the first time in American history, a black hero — Uncle Tom himself — endowed with the virtues that whites of the time found

7. See Chapter 14.

noble.) Something of the rich black music tradition did get relayed through the white-dominated popular culture, and white songwriters like Stephen Foster borrowed from minstrel tunes to create their music. But one of the cultural tragedies of the era is that black art in its multiform richness was not allowed to find its own public expression.

❧ *Utopianism*

This was an age when reformers sought to engage society and correct observed evils like slavery and drink, when writers like Emerson emboldened individuals to be self-reliant and live out their dreams, when even more radical literary individualists like Thoreau sought to escape society — at least briefly — in search of the true meanings of life. This was an age when many people, seeing the progress of settlement westward across the landscape and the harnessing of steam to power machines and electricity to send messages, came to believe that people could shape and mold society at will. There was, remarked Emerson, "not a reading man but has a draft of a new community in his waistcoat pocket." There was an optimism to some of the radical reform schemes that hid the intractability of many human failings. A distinction must be drawn between the reform societies in which idealistic people organized to achieve practical, obtainable improvements in the larger society and the utopian and communitarian movements in which wildly optimistic individuals — many with a strong religious motivation — sought to separate themselves and their followers from society and set up cooperative communities of like-minded perfectionists, isolated and insulated from the presumed evils of the rest of the world.

SOCIAL ENGINEERING

One of the most ambitious of such utopian communities was New Harmony, established in Indiana in 1825 by Robert Owen, a wealthy Scottish industrialist. In Scotland, Owen had become a radical opponent of competitive industrialism and an advocate of what would today be called social engineering. He planned — and in the wilds of southern Indiana actually built — a small, carefully organized cooperative community where the workers bartered their labor for goods at the community store. But mismanagement, conflicting goals, lazy workers, and Owen's frequent absences led to quick economic failure. There was simply too much turnover in population and too much diffusion

Catharine Maria Sedgwick,
Hope Leslie, **1827**
Novels like Sedgwick's Hope Leslie, *set among the Puritans, took advantage of the religious and sentimental currents of their day — and sold millions of copies. In this excerpt, Magawisca, a young Indian woman, saves the life of Everell Fletcher, a young colonist taken hostage by her father.*

"Stand back!" cried Magawisca. "I have bought his life with my own. Fly, Everell — nay, speak not, but fly — thither — to the east!" she cried, more vehemently.

Everell's faculties were paralyzed by a rapid succession of violent emotions. He was conscious only of a feeling of mingled gratitude and admiration for his preserver. He stood motionless, gazing on her. "I die in vain, then," she cried, in an accent of such despair that he was roused. He threw his arms around her, and pressed her to his heart

as he would a sister that had redeemed his life with her own, and then, tearing himself from her, he disappeared. No one offered to follow him. The voice of nature rose from every heart, and, responding to the justice of Magawisca's claim, bade him "God speed!" To all it seemed that his deliverance had been achieved by miraculous aid. All — the dullest and coldest — paid involuntary homage to the heroic girl, as if she were a superior being, guided and upheld by supernatural power. . . .

of organizing motivations to fuse the participants into a unified community. Moreover, Owen became too radical for the community's good, attacking marriage, private property, and mainstream Christianity as "absurd and irrational systems of religion." With no available leader to hold them together and no coherent philosophy, New Harmony soon disintegrated in the face of public attack.

Even more harshly criticized was Nashoba, the biracial Owenite community in Shelby County, Tennessee, established in 1826 by Englishwoman Frances Wright as a refuge where slaves could work to purchase their freedom. When Wright began to attack marriage and religion, and a popular magazine published a story about interracial free love at Nashoba, it was simply more than the public could accept. After the experiment broke down, Wright sailed with the few slaves to Haiti and they were emancipated. Yet despite the collapse of the two Owenite communities, Owen's basic idea that social environment, not original sin, shaped human character survived to influence many later reformers and government planners.

When during the hard times of the depression of the late 1830s and early 1840s people again sought to change their social circumstances, the ideas of another secular engineer of society became popular. Charles Fourier was a French socialist utopian thinker opposed to the principles of competitive capitalism, but he did not attack popular conceptions of marriage and religion. Instead, he advocated rearranging society into small, cooperative communities of laborers called phalanxes where all work was valued and the most distasteful chores were the best paid. Fourier

combined a practical idealism with an emphasis on the dignity of work.

In the 1840s more than forty phalanxes were organized in the nation, although none lasted for long. The best known was Brook Farm, near Boston, formed in 1841 by a group of literary idealists — most of them friends and admirers of Emerson — who sought to show that manual labor could be fruitfully combined with the cultivation of the mind. Brook Farm quickly evolved into a Fourierist phalanx, but although it attracted many visitors and became a cultural sensation, its blend of mental and manual labor proved less financially productive than the intellectuals hoped; Brook Farm's population never exceeded one hundred. The community finally failed in 1847 after a destructive fire, but not before Nathaniel Hawthorne had lived there for a while and turned the experience into a satiric novel, *The Blithedale Romance.* The secular communities influenced by Owen and Fourier demanded a degree of submersion of the individual into the group that was difficult for a nation of individualists to accept.

NEW RELIGIOUS MOVEMENTS

The most successful utopian communities proved to be those based on shared religious convictions, and several of them attempted to reorder not only attitudes toward property but also those toward sexual relationships and the concept of family. Strong religious commitments did, at least for a while, prove able to mold many followers into disciplined communities where individualism was harnessed to the command of religious leaders or community-chosen authorities.

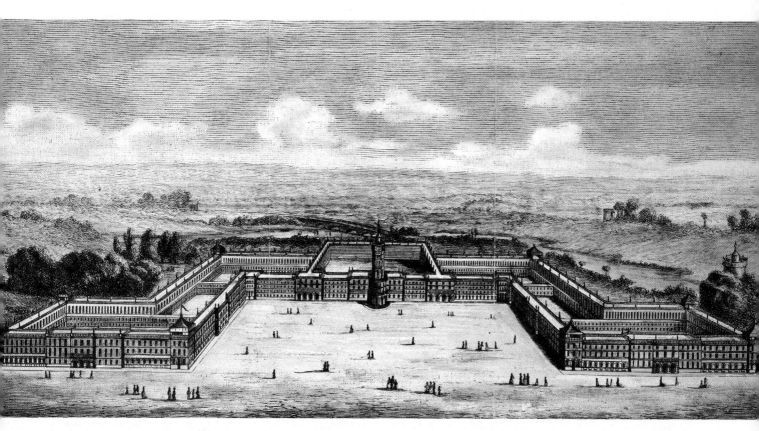

Several smaller movements originated abroad and either brought most of their adherents to the United States or appealed to ethnic American communities isolated by language from the larger society. Thus the Rappites at Harmony in western Pennsylvania and later at Harmony in Indiana (Robert Owen purchased the defunct Harmony for his New Harmony), the followers of George Rapp who wanted to rule their community by the absolute, literal commands of the Bible; the Separatists of Zoar in Ohio; the Swedish immigrant community founded by Eric Janson at Bishop Hill in Illinois; and the Amana Society first in New York and later in Iowa — all these were representative of the utopian experimental communities that sprang up across the North and Midwest. Two other religious movements, the Shakers and the followers of John Humphrey Noyes, had longer histories, and the most successful of all, the Mormons,[8] today constitute a major American religious body.

The Shakers, or the United Society of Believers in Christ's Second Appearing, had their origins in England. Ann Lee, the illiterate and abused wife of a blacksmith in Manchester, suffered greatly as one after another of her four children died in infancy. In 1770 she

8. See Chapter 13.

Design for a Fourierist Phalanx Charles Fourier, a French theorist whose combination of brilliant and strange ideas forms one of the foundations of the nineteenth-century science of sociology, advocated gathering humanity into communities of exactly 1,620 men and women. This number corresponded to the precise number of different human "types," of whose existence he convinced himself and many of his readers. Each such community should be housed in a "phalanx." One of his German followers prepared this drawing of such a utopian community. Of course, none of these communities were ever built, but the idea attracted much attention throughout the Western world, including the United States, as an alternative to the abuses of early industrial capitalism.

had a revelation that the sex act was the root of all human evil and that celibacy was the path to happiness. Her vision also revealed to her that Jesus' second coming was near, and it would be in the womanly form of "Mother Ann" Lee herself, thus completing the male-female incarnation of the Christ. Mother Ann quickly attracted followers, and her visions led her also to attack private property. In 1774 she and a small group of adherents emigrated to Watervliet, New York, where they established a community. A Christian revival in nearby New Lebanon created a number of eager seekers after spiritual renewal, and many followed their minister Joseph Meacham into Mother Ann's community. By now they were being called Shakers because their characteristic worship service featured stylized dancing, with hands extended up and out and shaken, symbolically both shedding sinful thoughts and ac-

❈ **IN THEIR OWN WORDS**

John Humphrey Noyes Advocates "Complex Marriage," 1853

John Humphrey Noyes here presents "complex marriage" as it was practiced in the Oneida community as superior to both monogamy and polygamy.

The similarity and the difference between monogamy and polygamy, may be illustrated thus: Suppose slavery to be intro-duced into Pennsylvania, but limited by law, so that no man can own more than *one* slave. That might be taken to represent monogamy, or the single wife system. In another State suppose men are allowed to own any number they please. That corresponds to polygamy. Now what would be the difference between these two States, in respect to slavery? There would be a difference in the details, and external limitations of the system, but identity in principle. The State that allowed a man to have but one slave, would be on the same general basis of principle with the State that allowed him to have a hundred. Such, we conceive, is the relation between monogamy and polygamy; and as we understand the New Testament, the state which Jesus Christ and Paul were in favor of was neither, but a state of entire freedom from both.

cepting spiritual blessings from above. After Mother Ann died in 1787, Meacham became the head of the Shaker movement. He systematized their doctrines, drew up a constitution for communal governance, and organized the growing believers into several "families" or communities. In addition to complete celibacy, the Shakers gave their private property to the community as a whole, lived according to strict rules, and sought earthly perfection in the belief that the millennium was nigh. The movement spread into Kentucky and the Midwest after the Great Revival of 1800 — many revival converts were swept into the Shaker fold — and by the 1820s about twenty Shaker communities stretched from New England to Ohio, with approximately 6,000 members. They became noted for their simple but beautiful furniture and for their cultivation and marketing of seeds. Their practice of celibacy meant that they could grow only by attracting converts or raising orphaned children, and by the 1850s a steady decline in their numbers had begun. A few Shakers still survive.

John Humphrey Noyes, a charismatic young Finney convert and divinity student at Yale, took the evangelical conception of perfection to its logical conclusion. He believed that complete perfection and freedom from sin was possible given correct discipline. Noyes concluded that the millennium had really been instigated in A.D. 70 but had been obscured by false teachings; it could, however, be rediscovered and put into action. He also believed that primitive Christian communism was the ideal for true believers, a complete sharing of goods and marriage partners. Noyes argued that marriage represented the "exclusive possession of one woman to one man," and such selfishness was a main barrier to human perfection. Hence he advocated

"complex marriage," whereby all the saved mutually loved each other as husband and wife. Still he called for sexual restraint, calling on all but the most perfect men to withdraw from their wives before ejaculation. He called for cooperative childcare, communal ownership of property, and, through his leadership, the achievement of complete perfection.

Noyes attracted a small following in Putney, Vermont, in the early 1840s, but public outrage forced him in 1848 to move his community of fifty-one followers to Oneida, New York. By good luck one of the early converts, Samuel Newhouse, had invented a highly efficient small-animal trap, and the community's manufacture of this trap made it economically solvent. Prosperity, childcare, careful discipline, and the promise of perfection gained more members, and later the production of silverplate continued the community's prosperity. But Noyes's advocacy of complex marriage brought criticism, especially as word got out that he and several elders decided who could actually father children — as it mainly turned out, "Father" Noyes himself. Charges of "free love" and adultery caused Noyes to flee to Canada in 1879. Within two years the Oneida community shed its religious identity, reorganized as a joint-stock company, and distributed the shares among the former community participants. It continues today as a completely secular company producing silverplated tableware.

It is notable that most of the utopian movements, whether religious or secular, proposed to reject the private ownership of property and revised conceptions of marriage, ranging from the complete celibacy of the Shakers to the complex marriage of the Oneida community to the polygamy of the Mormons. While the utopian experiments founded on religious ideals and

Shaker religious greeting, watercolor, January 1853. An example of a spirit or inspirational drawing shared between Shakers as gifts. Spirit drawings expressed the emotional feelings within the artist and were inspired by symbolic expressions of religious experiences. It is believed that the drawings were created by women for a very limited audience, such as the artist's family or immediate circle. They were not circulated throughout the larger Shaker community, as Shaker rules prohibited hanging the drawings or other decorative items.

CONCLUSION: DRAMATIC SHIFTS AND UNPRECEDENTED CHANGES

The four decades after 1820 saw unprecedented change in the North. The physical landscape was changed as cities grew, canals were dug, roads were built, and railroads spread out to tie the nation together. Demographically the region underwent dramatic shifts, as rural people moved to cities, Americans of all sorts moved west, and immigration from Europe modified the ethnic homogeneity of northern society. How people earned a living, how they purchased goods, where they chose to live — all were transformed during these years. The resulting tensions led to religious revivals, reform movements, and a whole range of attempts to control and reshape a society that seemed to be in flux. All the old assumptions, from expected occupations to gender roles to the use of slave labor, were up for reconsideration. In the midst of being pulled by tradition and pressured by the forces of change, people sought new ways of expressing their hopes and fears in a fresh American literature that broke from European models and discovered creative new topics and ways of expression. In ways no one at the time fully realized, the North was undergoing modernization, and though the process was still underway in 1860, all at that time who looked back a few decades could understand that they were living in a far different country than that over which Thomas Jefferson had presided. The North and South were both changing but at vastly different rates, and the mutual awareness that the regions were in effect moving apart from each other was the context for much of the political disputation of the era. These were creative, chaotic, contentious years, and in the northern states of this era we see the birth of modern America.

promoted by religious leaders lasted longer than the secular experiments, ultimately their radical attacks on marriage and private property caused them all to fail unless, like the Mormons, they fled to a distant frontier, established a community that really worked, and were so geographically isolated that there was practically no opportunity for members to backslide into the "gentile" world. Eventually the Mormons internalized their "way" so successfully that they could survive the outside world forcing them to move to Utah and eventually to give up polygamy.

SUGGESTED READING

Mary Kupiec Cayton, *Emerson's Emergence: Self and Society in the Transformation of New England, 1800-1845* (1989). An insightful analysis of one writer placed in the context of his wider world.

Alan Dawley, *Class and Community: The Industrial Revolution in Lynn* (1976). A model local study of the transformation of artisinal to wage labor.

Ann Douglas, *The Feminization of American Culture* (1977). An influential analysis of the role of reform-oriented middle-class urban women and liberal Protestant ministers.

Oscar Handlin, *Boston's Immigrants: A Study in Acculturation* (rev. ed., 1959). A pathbreaking account of the impact of immigration on a northern city and the impact of America on the immigrants.

Curtis D. Johnson, *Redeeming America: Evangelicals and the Road to Civil War* (1993). A brief, clearly argued interpretation of the role of evangelical religion in northern life, culture, and politics.

Bruce Laurie, *Artisans into Workers: Labor in Nineteenth-Century America* (1989). A general examination — with many illustrative examples — of the fundamental change in the nature of paid work that occurred in this era.

Charles G. Sellers, *The Market Revolution: Jacksonian America, 1815-1848* (1991). An essential synthesis of economic, political, and cultural change that popularized the concept of "market revolution."

Kathryn Sklar, *Catharine Beecher: A Study in American Domesticity* (1973). An influential biography that illustrates both the scope and limitation of women's reform possibilities in the mid-nineteenth century.

Ronald G. Walters, *American Reformers, 1815-1860* (1978). A wide-ranging, judicious survey of the variety of reforms and the motivations of the reformers.

Sean Wilentz, *Chants Democratic: New York City and the Rise of the American Working Class, 1788-1850* (1983). An important social history of how an emerging working force changed the texture and tone of urban life.

SUGGESTIONS FOR FURTHER READING

Paul F. Boller, *American Transcendentalism, 1830-1860* (1974).

Nancy F. Cott, *The Bonds of Womanhood: "Women's Sphere" in New England, 1780-1835* (1977).

Whitney R. Cross, *The Burned-Over District: The Social and Intellectual History of Enthusiastic Religion in Western New York, 1800-1850* (1950).

Jay P. Dolan, *Catholic Revivalism: The American Experience, 1830-1900* (1978).

Ellen C. DuBois, *Feminism and Suffrage: The Emergence of an Independent Women's Movement in America, 1848-1869* (1978).

Barbara Leslie Epstein, *The Politics of Domesticity: Women, Evangelicalism, and Temperance in Nineteenth-Century America* (1981).

Michael Fellman, *The Unbounded Frame: Freedom and Community in Nineteenth-Century American Utopianism* (1973).

Karen Halttunen, *Confidence Men and Painted Women: A Study of Middle-Class Culture in America* (1982).

Mark Y. Hanley, *Beyond a Christian Commonwealth: The Protestant Quarrel with the American Republic, 1830-1860* (1994).

Julie Roy Jeffrey, *The Great Silent Army of Abolitionism: Ordinary Women in the Antislavery Movement* (1998).

Paul E. Johnson and Sean Wilentz, *The Kingdom of Matthias: A Story of Sex and Salvation in Nineteenth Century America* (1994).

John R. McKivigan, *The War Against Proslavery Religion: Abolitionism and the Northern Churches, 1830-1865* (1984).

Steven Mintz, *Moralists and Modernizers: America's Pre–Civil War Reformers* (1995).

Barbara Novak, *Nature and Culture: American Landscape Painting, 1825-1875* (1982).

Nell Irvin Painter, *Sojourner Truth: A Life, A Symbol* (1996).

Edward Pessen, *Riches, Class, and Power: America Before the Civil War* (rev. ed., 1990).

Benjamin Quarles, *Black Abolitionists* (1969).

Leonard L. Richards, *The Slave Power: The Free North and Southern Domination, 1780-1860* (2000).

Steven J. Ross, *Workers on the Edge: Work, Leisure, and Politics in Industrializing Cincinnati, 1788-1890* (1985).

Mary Ryan, *Cradle of the Middle Class: The Family in Oneida County, New York, 1790-1865* (1981).

Christine Stansel, *City of Women: Sex and Class in New York, 1789-1860* (1986).

William R. Sutton, *Journeymen for Jesus: Evangelical Artisans Confront Capitalism in Jacksonian Baltimore* (1998).

Robert C. Toll, *Blacking Up: The Minstrel Show in Nineteenth-Century America* (1974).

Barbara Tucker, *Samuel Slater and the Origins of the American Textile Industry, 1790-1860* (1984).

Anthony F. C. Wallace, *Rockdale: The Growth of an American Village in the Early Industrial Revolution* (1978).

11

The Old South

MOVIES AND POPULAR fiction have created in the American mind a powerful image of the Old South that combines romantic elements with deep tragedy, good manners with racial violence, elegant plantation mistresses with unkempt poor white "crackers." All these ingredients were present in the antebellum South, but not in equal measure. The region and the time have been so fixed in American memory that it has proven difficult for historians to unscramble the stereotypes and present a more historically accurate portrayal of the South as it changed over time in response to events. By the end of the era it was widely perceived, both by itself and by outsiders, to be the most distinct region of the nation, but that had not always been so.

In truth, the South may have remained more unchanged than did an industrializing and urbanizing North, which after the Revolution abolished slavery within its bounds and was becoming increasingly peopled by immigrants from Europe. Yet one result of dissimilar rates of change between the northern and southern regions was a South that appeared to be departing from the emerging American mainstream. Spokespeople from both regions believed that the other was taking an errant path away from the founding ideals of the nation. The political and cultural responses to this splitting of the national vision have long preoccupied historians almost as intensely as they did the actual participants in the original controversies. In order to understand the nature and scope of these debates that eventually led to a tragic division in the nation and four long, bloody years of civil war, we must address the economies and societies of the two great regions of the nation in the two generations before the Civil War.

PLANTATION ECONOMIES

There is no consensus on exactly when one should date the beginning of the Old South. If one means by that term a region self-consciously aware that its society and economy were so different from the rest of the nation that its regional interests were incompatible with the national interests, then perhaps the Old South began about 1820. If one means that the Old South was that unique part of the nation where slave labor existed, then it began shortly after the conclusion of the American Revolution, when the states to the north of Maryland began, through a variety of processes, to end slavery within their borders. (Although slavery had existed in all the colonies before 1780, nowhere north of Maryland did it dominate agricultural production or determine the social status of whites.) If one means by the term a region whose economy and society were grounded in the production of staple crops, often grown on such a scale that the farming units were styled plantations, with the labor force on these plantations being largely black slaves, then the Old South began in the early seventeenth-century Chesapeake colonies of Virginia and Maryland, and somewhat later in South Carolina and Georgia. Usually the term *Old South* implies roughly the first half of the nineteenth century for the states to the south of Pennsylvania, where the legendary Mason-Dixon line was surveyed in 1767 to end a boundary dispute between Maryland and Pennsylvania and became the unofficial boundary between northern and southern states. We will define the Old South as referring to the period that began in 1793 with the invention of the cotton gin and ended in 1861 with the outbreak of the Civil War, but this era and region can only be understood in the context of the previous century and a half.

It is one of the supreme ironies of American history that the region we see as atypical — the slaveholding, staple-producing South — was in the viewpoint of England the typical colony, whereas New England was the exception. According to mercantilist theory, overseas colonies were to produce goods that could not be produced in the mother country and would otherwise have to be purchased from England's rival nations, which meant that in the exchange English money would flow into the treasuries of the competing European nations.

The southern colonies, because of their longer growing seasons and fertile soils, produced exotic goods — tobacco, rice, indigo, and naval stores (timber, tar to apply to ropes to prevent their decay, and pitch to paint the keels and sides of wooden ships to stop leakage) — that could not be grown in the British Isles. The New England colonies, to the contrary, had rocky soils and a short growing season, so the New England economy came to be based on fishing and commerce — direct competition with the home country. The southern colonies, not the northern ones, served the intended purposes of overseas empires. Moreover, the southern colonies, with their landed gentry emulating the lifestyles of English country gentlemen and worshiping in the established Anglican church, seemed much more the reflection of English ideals after the late seventeenth century than New England with its dissenting Puritan tradition. So, from the British perspective, at the time of the American Revolution the South was the normative section, the North the eccentric section. In the decades that followed, the northern states emerged as a modern, urban-industrial market economy open to new peoples and new ideas; to a much greater extent, the South developed along the lines already in place, and a new crop and new territory primarily strengthened its traditional economy, labor system, and social arrangements.

This basic system of large, efficient agricultural units that specialized in the production of a single so-called staple crop for the international market (although the crop differed by region: tobacco in the Chesapeake, rice or indigo in South Carolina and Georgia, and sugar in Louisiana) and whose labor source was primarily black slaves had been developed in the southern colonies by the early eighteenth century. Most tobacco farmers cultivated few acres and owned no slaves, but most tobacco was grown on large, slave-operated plantations. Rice, indigo, and sugar were mostly grown on large, capital-intensive plantations. But the one crop whose cultivation most characterized the Old South did not become important until the very end of the eighteenth century, and its rise was related to technological achievements in the textile industry in England and a simple invention in Georgia. Together, these made cotton production economically feasible in the South.

♪ Rise of King Cotton

Cotton is an old crop. It was grown in ancient Egypt, where it was used to make soft garments for the priestly class. It was known in Europe for centuries as a botani-

cal curiosity and was sometimes grown as an ornamental plant, but its fibers were not used to make clothing. Europeans associated cotton cloth with exotic places in South Asia like Calicut and Madras, and the names of cotton goods — calico and madras — revealed their Indian sources. English woolgrowers fought the importation of competitive fibers, and the tradition-bound guilds that dominated woolen manufacture opposed the import of new materials. But entrepreneurs in the early eighteenth century began importing raw cotton fiber to create a new kind of industry to meet the need for cheap clothing. Because the emerging cotton industry was less subject to the pressure of guilds, which opposed gains in production efficiency that might threaten jobs in their craft, technological innovation led to the development of labor-saving machinery. The cheaper cloth that resulted found such a growing mar-

The Cotton Gin   Whitney's invention was ingeniously simple, easy to operate, and uncomplicated to repair. It enabled the cultivation of short-staple cotton to spread far across the interior of the South. In this contemporary illustration, slaves put the gin to work while two white men in the background talk about it.

ket that the new cotton industry could not satisfy its need for fiber by imports from faraway India.

Minute amounts of cotton had been grown in the American South since the first settlement at Jamestown, but it was never a commercial crop. The fiber was so difficult to separate from the seeds that labor costs made anything other than home consumption impossible; small patches were often cultivated for domestic use, and women and children would painstakingly separate the lint from the seed by hand. Two kinds of cotton were known in the southernmost states: the black-seed variety had smooth seeds and relatively

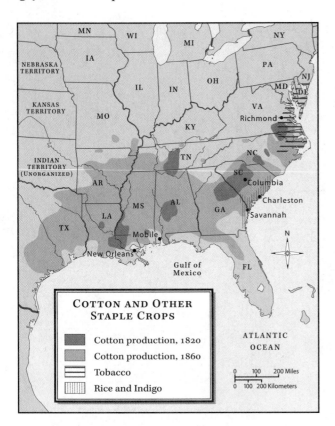

COTTON AND OTHER STAPLE CROPS

- Cotton production, 1820
- Cotton production, 1860
- Tobacco
- Rice and Indigo

ATLANTIC OCEAN

0   100   200 Miles
0   100   200 Kilometers

giously in the sandy islands along coastal South Carolina and Georgia. This so-called sea-island cotton could be profitably processed either by hand or by the clumsy roller gins, and such cotton from South Carolina and Georgia found a ravenous market in Great Britain. Between 1784 and 1791 British imports of southern cotton increased 216 percent, and they doubled again before 1800. But sea-island cotton could only be grown in the narrow geographical range of the coastal islands and hence could never become the dominant crop even in the southern seaboard colonies. The problem remained of how to separate the lint from the green-seed cotton, with its adaptability to a wide range of soil types — this species of cotton had the potential to be cultivated across the entire southern region. The surging imports of sea-island cotton vividly illustrated the market that existed for cotton lint. If only the processing bottleneck with green-seed cotton could be solved, then cotton held promise to be a bonanza crop that would bring great wealth to the region. A young Connecticut-born tutor in Georgia set about to solve the problem.

Eli Whitney in 1793 was visiting Mulberry Grove in Georgia, the plantation of the late Nathanael Greene of Revolutionary War fame, where he heard (as he wrote his father) much talk about the "extreme difficulty of ginning cotton." Several men told him that "if a machine could be invented that would clean cotton with expedition, it would be a great thing both to the Country and to the inventor." Whitney set his mind to the task and, as he told his father, "struck out a plan of a Machine in my mind." His solution was a brilliantly simple refinement of the traditional roller gin. On one of the cylinders he added wire teeth, and he fixed this cylinder against a slatted box so that the teeth grabbed cotton that was stuffed in the box and pulled the lint through the slits in the side of the box that were too narrow to allow the seeds to pass. Then to the second cylinder, rotating in the opposite direction, he added small brushes that whisked the cotton from the teeth into a container below. Both cylinders were rotated by a single hand-turned crank connected to the cylinders by a simple gear mechanism. One person turning the crank could gin far more cotton in a day than fifty could by pulling the lint from the seeds by hand. This machine was so elegantly simple in principle that others quickly improved it further.

long lint easily pulled from the seeds, but this variety of cotton was extremely susceptible to a fungus disease known as the rot; consequently it had little commercial value. Green-seed cotton was hardy enough to grow in various types of soils and climatic conditions, but its much shorter lint adhered with stubborn tenacity to its fuzzy seeds, making the processing of the lint disappointingly time consuming and costly. Everyone realized that green-seed cotton had commercial possibilities if a way could be found to separate the lint from the seed efficiently, but the device commonly used — related to a centuries-old machine called the "charka" in India — worked like an old-fashioned wringer washing machine. An operator fed cotton bolls between two cylinders turned toward each other by a gear mechanism; the idea was to mash the cotton through the narrow slit between the two cylinders, with the pressure of the cylinders squeezing the seeds apart from the lint. Unfortunately much cotton was left sticking to the seeds, and fragments of crushed seeds contaminated the lint.

Then, in the half decade following the conclusion of the American Revolution, returning loyalists who had fled to the West Indies brought back with them to South Carolina and Georgia a West Indian variant of the black-seed cotton that was far more resistant to the rot. This cotton, with its long and luxuriant lint, grew prodi-

Soon farmers across the piedmont of South Carolina and Georgia, knowledgeable about commercial agriculture from earlier experience with tobacco in their native Virginia and North Carolina, quickly adopted

A Louisiana Sugar Mill, 1853 Sugar growing required a large capital investment, not only for land and slaves but also for the mills and boiling vats in which the cane was crushed and the sugar refined into molasses. Slaves who worked on sugar plantations were kept busy by difficult routines throughout the year.

green-seed cotton as their cash crop. Almost instantly cotton cultivation began its inexorable sweep westward. Within two years of Whitney's invention, a skilled slave mechanic near Natchez on the banks of the Mississippi River replicated the gin, and planters there, an outpost of British settlement in what had been Spanish territory, began their cotton empire too.

Cotton proved to be an ideal crop for the South. It required no expensive infrastructure before or after cultivation — unlike rice, which required extensive levees and dikes for flooding and draining fields, and sugar, which needed elaborate mills for boiling and refining the cane. It could be stored inexpensively without spoiling or being consumed by vermin. Its value in relation to its weight was high, thereby decreasing transportation costs. And it could be cultivated at almost equal efficiency at any scale of production, from the family farm to the large plantation. (Small farmers paid a portion of their production to have their cotton ginned either by independent gin operators or large plantation owners who also had gins.) Cotton throughout most of its cultivation was not as labor-intensive as tobacco, although at harvest time came a labor crunch. At any

scale of production, farmers could plant and cultivate more cotton than they could pick: picking was the labor constraint that determined the size of a cotton farm or plantation. Small farmers restricted their cotton acreage to the picking ability of their family.

The Old South had no surplus population of free laborers ready to jump in at harvest time. Farming units could be expanded beyond the size of family farms only by acquiring slaves. Slave laborers, whose availability was guaranteed by their owner, were considered necessary for the expansion and the anticipated prosperity of cotton plantations. Most southern whites — certainly those whose scale of operation, real or intended, was larger than the family farm — simply assumed that slave labor was essential to carve fields out of the forests, to plant, hoe, and plow the cotton, and especially to supply the high labor needs at picking time. Cotton and slavery marched in lockstep across the South, from the piedmont of Georgia and South Carolina to the fertile black soils of Alabama and Mississippi, across the broad Mississippi River all the way to central Texas by the 1850s. Cotton and slavery came to define the Old South the way no other crop ever had characterized a broad region of the nation. "Cotton and negroes are the constant theme," wrote one observer of the region, "the ever harped upon, never worn out subject of conversation of all classes."

In the nineteenth century tobacco continued to be the major crop in Maryland, Virginia, and North Carolina, although wheat had displaced tobacco from primacy in many regions of Virginia and Maryland. Baltimore and Richmond became great flour-milling centers. Rice and to a far lesser extent indigo continued to be cultivated in the coastal regions of South Carolina and Georgia, though neither crop ever completely replaced the British markets lost during the Revolution. Kentucky as well emerged as a major tobacco-growing region, and hemp was also grown there commercially, its fibers being used to make the rope and baling cloth for cotton transportation. In semitropical south Louisiana, sugarcane had long been cultivated, but the nine-month-long growing season did not allow the cane to mature sufficiently for sugar production; only syrup could be made from the cane. Then in 1795, almost simultaneous with Whitney's invention of the cotton gin, a French émigré planter named Étienne de Boré, who had a sugarcane plantation near New Orleans on the site of present-day Tulane University, perfected a process of crystallizing sugar from the juice of the immature cane. Thus was born the sugar industry in Louisiana, and within a decade large-scale sugarcane plantations employing thousands of slaves brought great prosperity to this special region of the South.

So before 1800, at both the eastern and western edges of the South, technological breakthroughs allowed the rise of a staple-crop slave society to sweep the region. Sugar was confined to one region in Louisiana (and for a short time also along the southern reaches of the Brazos River in Texas), but cotton was almost the universal crop in the states from South Carolina to Texas. There it soon became king — and later a tyrant.

WHITE SOUTHERNERS

Unlike small farms on which were cultivated a variety of mostly food crops primarily for home consumption, plantations and large farms from Maryland to Texas specialized in one commercial crop, which varied by region. All the commercial agricultural operations also grew foodstuffs, especially corn, and often were self-sufficient. The smaller farmers — called plain folk or yeomen — were self-sufficient. After all, these farmers had no financial resources to fall back on in case the price for the commercial crop fell, and for these small farmers the first priority was growing enough foodstuffs to feed their families, their livestock, and if they owned one or several slaves, their workforce. These farmers grew a variety of crops, raised cattle, hogs, and chickens for food, and, if they had the surplus labor and saw a ready market, would put in a few acres of cotton or a small tobacco patch, and would sell their excess cattle, pigs, eggs, milk, butter, and honey either to local planters or, if possible, to nearby town residents. So-called subsistence farmers were as alert to dollar-and-cents opportunities as were planters (or northern businessmen), and both paid attention to the respective markets for their goods. All were eager to "get ahead." It is important to realize that the South as a whole, despite its economic dependence on staple-crop production, was self-sufficient in foodstuffs and even exported grain and livestock for northern consumption. Cotton itself contributed in a backhanded way to the adequacy of the food supply because corn could be planted, cultivated, and harvested around the peak labor demands of cotton. (Cotton farmers limited their planting of the crop to the amount they could pick, leaving them with excess labor most of the year.) With fixed land and labor costs and flexible cultivation schedules, corn could be grown at practically no cost on cotton farms and plantations. Little wonder that corn was the basic food crop in the South for humans and livestock alike.

❧ Plain Folk and Planters

It was not always possible to delineate precisely who was a planter, a large farmer, and a so-called "plainfolk farmer." Even historians have not always agreed upon definitions. However, the rule of thumb is that one had to have a minimum of twenty slaves (and sufficient acreage of land to cultivate) in order to qualify as a planter; obviously, this is a very rough estimate, because the age and sex distribution of those slaves had more to do with labor output and crop production than numbers alone. An owner of four adult male slaves, four adult female slaves, and twelve slave children may very well have had a smaller agricultural production unit than another owner who had only seven or eight males. Also by common agreement, owners of less than twenty but more than five slaves are generally referred to as large farmers, while yeoman or plainfolk farmers had fewer than five slaves. Almost half of all slaveholders possessed fewer than five slaves, and the most commonly owned number of slaves was one. Farmers with only one or two slaves usually employed them in the household, helping with cooking, washing, and gardening.

It is seldom realized today that the majority of whites in the Old South did not own any slaves, and the percentage of whites who owned bondspeople was steadily declining over the last three antebellum decades. In 1830, only 31 percent of white heads of households owned slaves, and by 1860 this percentage had declined to 25 percent. Many who did not own slaves were young men who had not yet received their inheritance. But the minority ownership of slaves should not

A Plantation Manor of the Mid-Nineteenth Century   Most slave owners lived in more modest homes than this. Notice the broad verandahs. The owner's family and visitors would have spent much time on them, trying to catch breezes that could lessen the stifling summer heat and humidity.

deceive one into thinking that the commitment to slavery was weak: practically every white aspired to slave ownership, and almost no whites could imagine any other labor system that could control the existing slave population. Even so, the majority of southern farmers were nonslaveholding family farmers, most of whom owned their own land, and these small farmers grew mainly food crops and supplemented their diet with hunting and fishing; they were also quick to sell any surplus goods they produced or gathered, and they picked up seasonal employment on larger plantations if available.

Many contemporary observers left jaundiced descriptions of poor whites. Typical was Bishop Henry Benjamin Whipple's comment that "there is not a more ignorant & debased white population in the United States than the lower classes of whites in Georgia." But to think of nonslaveholders as "poor white trash" or "crackers" — shiftless, propertyless ne'er-do-wells — is as false as to think of all whites as plantation aristocrats. Considering the Old South, modern readers must look beyond the mansions that are tourist attractions today and the trashy whites of popular fiction and comic pages. Nonslaveholding whites who did not till the soil found other ways of making a living, from fishing along the coasts of North Carolina to splitting shingles, from working in turpentine forests to gathering moss for furniture stuffing. Some small farmers became quite well off by raising herds of cattle that grazed the unfenced lands of the South, while others raised large herds of hogs that, like the cattle, were driven overland to markets. The cattle herder and the hog drover were common types in the Old South, even though they hardly ever appear in the novels and movies that have so fixed the region and time in the American imagination.

Difficult as it has been for historians to define planters and farmers, one must also realize than many people changed categories over time, either moving up or sliding down the economic ladder. Often young men started out as propertyless farmers, even overseers, before they inherited slaves from their parents. Many small farmers moved to regions of fertile, virgin soil, worked hard, prospered, bought a slave or two, expanded the size of their operation even as they worked alongside their slaves, then bought more land and slaves and planted more cotton, in an upward spiral of success. Such determined, hardworking, healthy, lucky whites made the transition from being essentially pioneers on new soil to successful farmers and eventually made it to the level of planter. One Mississippian characterized this process: "To sell cotton in order to buy negroes — to make more cotton to buy more negroes, 'ad infinitum,' is the aim and direct tendency of all the operations of the thorough-going cotton planter; his whole soul is wrapped up in the pursuit." The size of homes often marked this transition, but the two-story, planked home with a verandah might well have started out as a two-room dog-run log cabin, later expanded to two stories, with plank siding added later to cover the original log construction. In much of the Old South — except along the eastern seaboard — the frontier was only a short remove from plantation society. The dispersed pattern of settlement caused by plantation agriculture, and the consequent discouragement of towns and manufacturing, actually prolonged frontier-type conditions in the region.

Some planters with bad luck, poor skill, or ill health slid into a downward spiral, selling their slaves and lands in a desperate attempt to pay their debts. Other small, landless farmers moved around geographically but never improved their economic status. The whole time and region were ones of flux, with a significant population shift westward ultimately all the way to Texas, but the movement up and down the ladder of success complemented the geographical movement. Often younger sons of wealthy eastern seaboard slave families would move, caravan-like, to new opportunities in the western states of the South or Florida, bringing with them their families, some slaves, livestock, and supplies. It was common for groups of people related by kin to move together to a new region, or sometimes for several members of a church to make the trek in company. Moving along with people one knew made the leap west or south less lonely, provided assistance in times of need, and in the earliest days offered protection against Indians.

In the older states from Maryland to Georgia, and in Kentucky, there were established families for whom gentility was more than pretension. The tradition of the English country gentleman was replicated, sometimes to a surprising degree, and there were plantations with private tutors, impressive libraries, and learned planters and cultivated mistresses who could serve a meal according to the latest fashion, sustain witty conversation, and dance the latest step. A few planters did have handsome, architecturally pleasing mansion houses, their sons received good educations in England or at Princeton, the University of Virginia, or the University of North Carolina, and their daughters had their manners and their artistic skills polished in local academies. (Girls were not educated for the professions or for plantation management, though they did often, along with their social graces, have enough native intelligence to run the plantation with skill when necessity demanded. And many girls of well-to-do families studied literature, art, and languages with private tutors or at female academies; certainly some of them, as evidenced by their letters and diaries, became quite well read and sophisticated.) Scattered across the fabulously rich soil of the black belt were prosperous cotton plantations that were home to cultured even if often self-educated planters; and certainly in the Louisiana sugar region there were impressive, gracious planters living in opulent mansions. But these great plantations — these white-columned mansion houses, these rich, Tara-like plantations of wealth and parties and fine clothes — were extraordinarily atypical. There are more multimillionaires in the southern states today than there were plantation aristocrats in the Old South. These are the homes that have survived and tourists today visit, but these important artifacts of the past can mislead the unwary about the nature of the southern society and economy.

❦ Daily Life in the Old South

Most southern farmers, whether they operated small family farms or large plantations manned by dozens of slaves, considered themselves first and foremost farmers. Their diaries and daybooks were filled with meteorological notations, details about how various crops were doing, records of chores completed or planned — the nitty-gritty details that related primarily to crop production. Worries about prolonged bouts of rain, an unusually late freeze, devastating droughts — such were the concerns of southern farmers at almost any scale of production. The small farmer and the wealthy slave owner alike realized that the price cotton fetched affected their prospects for the coming year, and they often went about the same tasks at the same time: planting, hoeing, laying by, picking. This commonality of interests, this self-identity with certain similar tasks, tended to create a sense of community that blurred class lines. No one was unaware of class — that in every neighborhood there were families with better reputations, more land, greater wealth — and these worthies were duly acknowledged and respected. But nearly universal involvement with agriculture helped to create ties that stretched across economic bound-

aries. Whites high and low met at the market or country store; at the polling place and on court days; they often worshiped at the same churches. Most wealthier families had relatives who were poor; many poorer families could point with pride to better-off kin. Kinship did count for much, and kin helped out their blood relations when sickness or hard luck or poverty made assistance necessary.

What is more, by common consent from the late seventeenth century on, even the poorest white man knew that southern racial mores counted him superior to the black slaves. White skin always conferred a presumption of cultural privilege and explicit legal superiority over blacks. In the Old South race trumped class nearly every time, and a kind of "white-folks democracy" shaped political attitudes. Kinship, common agricultural schedules, religion, and race molded a society that submerged potential class tensions. Elite whites and skilled politicians realized that it was essential to at least outwardly demonstrate respect for all manner of white people. A rich planter who "put on airs" earned the contempt of the plain folk, and a politician who did so courted sure repudiation at the polls. In the South as in the North, democracy was the ideal among whites. Only in the stress of the Civil War did this potential for class conflict — a tiny minority of wealthy slaveholders dominating the region politically and economically — break into open animosity.

Yeoman farmers (who often owned several slaves) and nonslaveholding whites had living conditions that were very similar. Geographical mobility was a hallmark of the time, with a steady stream of migrants from the older seaboard states moving west. It was not uncommon for parents, having been born in South Carolina or Georgia, as a young married couple to be living in Alabama, where the first children would be born; a decade later the family would be in Mississippi, where other children were born, and in old age the parents would be living in Louisiana, Texas, or Arkansas, often with grown children nearby. All the Deep South states west of Georgia had been in the Union for less than half a century when the Civil War came, and small farmers still typically lived in log cabins. Wealthier farmers and planters, along with town dwellers, often lived in homes made of lumber and even brick, but such construction was a sure sign of affluence. Most of the early homes in the region were more similar than different: dimly lit because of the expense of glass and the inefficiency of candles and lamps; ill-heated by fireplaces or wood stoves; very small compared to today's ideas of

A Planter's Week, 1838

Bennet Barrow was a wealthy, successful cotton planter in northern Louisiana who ran his plantation with an iron hand. He offered incentives to slaves who worked well while severely punishing slackers and rule-breakers. These diary entries, employing his idiosyncratic spelling and punctuation, recount typical activities in January 1838.

21   Cloudy verry cold, pressed 9 Bales

22   Making plough lines — threatened with Rheumatism

23   White Frost

pleasant day — during my stay at Mr Joors last week my House servants Jane Lavenia & E. jim broke into my store room — and helped themselves verry liberally to every thing — Center — Anica — & Peter had some of the good drink "as they say" — I Whiped the first three worse that I ever Whiped any one before

24   Showery day. Finished Ginning yesterday started 15 ploughs for oats [space] near 450 Bales — putting up stalles for work horses — my House boy E. Jim the meanest, dirtiest boy I ever had about

me — women and trash gang cleaning up

26   ploughing for corn since yesterday warm — too wet to plough

27   Mistey morning. Cleared beautifull Put up the Tombstone over my Father — removed from Washington City Fall of 1836

28   Cloudy cool morning left Home for Woodvill — took with me Eleven Fox hounds shall com'ce [commence] hauling my last lot Cotten to morrow . . .

---

how much space a family needs and affording little privacy; and sparsely furnished with simple, homemade pieces. Cooking was done in the fireplace or on a wood stove, although the better homes had a free-standing kitchen for protection against all-too-common fires. Water came from a well or spring and was brought to the house in buckets, and bathing was usually a weekly event. The better homes had outhouses, though at night most people used chamber pots discreetly kept under beds. Many of the people living in cabins simply went to the woods to relieve themselves. No one had screened windows, so mosquitoes, flies, and similar pests were part of everyday life, and microorganisms and disease flourished.

Even when food was plentiful, it no doubt became monotonous. Families grew all their own food or bargained for items with neighbors. Refrigeration did not exist, so meat had either to be eaten quickly or preserved, usually through salting or curing in a smoke house. Hog meat was much preferred, and few southerners either white or black developed much taste for salted beef. Everyone ate fish and occasionally wild game like rabbit or squirrel. Fresh vegetables were available only in season, so in winter people ate dried peas and fruit preserves, while potatoes were carefully spread out and stored so as not to rot, and people looked forward to springtime and a new supply of vegetables. Corn was consumed fresh on the cob, in pudding, ground as meal and baked into cornbread and cornpone, soaked in a lye mixture to change it into hominy and eaten that way or ground into grits. Food

was often fried, salads were almost unheard of, and some version of corn appeared at most meals. As one English traveler wrote condescendingly of dining in the South, "No one seems to think that there is any thing better in the world than little square bits of pork fried in lard, bad coffee, and indifferent bread." Actually, coffee and tea were luxuries not always available to plain folk. Affluent planters had somewhat more variety, and slaves and the poorest whites less, but everyone's diet was constrained by simple availability.

❧ Towns and Industry

The Old South's economy was overwhelmingly agricultural, but there were villages, towns, and several cities, most of which served the processing and marketing needs of the agriculturists, and there was industry, mostly of an extractive nature — mining and logging, for example. Hence there were southern storekeepers, artisans, and transport workers such as stevedores and wagoneers. There were publishers, doctors, lawyers, ministers. Most of these professionals supported and profited from slavery, and most owned slaves for domestic service. Indeed, almost every affluent white owned slaves and operated a plantation as much for the status as for the income. Prosperous artisans often owned or leased slave laborers and as a result tended to identify with the landed planter class. Nothing conferred respectability in the Old South better than owning slaves and running a plantation. As J. H. Ingraham, who had recently moved from Maine to Mississippi, wrote in 1835, "A plantation well stocked with hands, is the *ne plus ultra* [the ultimate] of every man's ambition who resides at the south. Young men who come to this country, 'to make money,' soon catch the mania, and nothing less than a broad plantation . . . can fill their mental vision. . . ."

Yet one should not let the dominance of the plantation economy hide the existence of a wider range of occupations and skills. For example, a crop like cotton depended on agents to buy and transport it from the fields to southern port cities or, later, to gin sites. Large plantations and sometimes store owners in crossroads villages often operated gins, where the lint was shaped into bulky bales for transport farther on. At port cities, cotton presses compacted the bales before they were loaded on ships bound for the bustling mills of either the Northeast or England. The bales were wrapped and tied in cloth and ropes made primarily from hemp, itself grown and processed in Kentucky. Ironworkers and blacksmiths made and repaired the plows, hoes, and other tools, while saddle makers provided harnesses and yokes. There was also local demand for wagons and carriages. Local carpenters and brick masons — many of them slaves or free blacks — also served both plantation owners and town dwellers.

There was a brisk internal economy within the South, with hogs driven to market and crops like hay, oats, and apples shipped from higher, mountainous regions to the larger market towns of the lower South. Farmers in states like Kentucky and Tennessee raised and trained hundreds of thousands of mules, which were sold into the Deep South states as the draft animal of choice. Lumber was cut and sold locally, as were shingles and barrel staves, and in states like Maryland and Virginia there were coal mines and ironworks making pig iron for local fabrication into tools and nails. In the port cities there were rope makers, ship carpenters and caulkers, and stores that provisioned the ships. And of course there were merchants, doctors, lawyers, and bankers, many of whom invested their profits in slaves and land. But prosperity everywhere was heavily dependent on the staple crops, and even mule drovers in Kentucky and farmers gathering apples in the alpine region of North Carolina understood that their markets improved when the price of cotton was high and

New Orleans in 1850   New Orleans at mid-century was a bustling and cosmopolitan commercial center, and the most important city in the South. A strong residue of French culture still lent the city a unique character. This view shows Lafayette Square in the heart of the French Quarter, with the spires of the city's Roman Catholic cathedral rising in the background.

knew that their prospects were tied to the institution of slavery. The market-oriented slave-labor agricultural system in the antebellum South was unmistakably capitalistic in nature.

But the clear dominance of the plantation society should not keep one from noting the commercial and cultural significance of cities in the Old South. Baltimore, Richmond, Charleston, Savannah, Memphis, Lexington, and New Orleans had impressive cultural institutions, numbers of educated citizens, diverse economies (manufacturing for local needs, artisans' shops, a wide range of services for the agricultural hinterland), and substantial numbers of European immigrants that, though small by northern standards, contrasted sharply with the southern countryside. Urban lawyers, merchants, and ministers read books, subscribed to literary and philosophical reviews, and were often as up-to-date in their ideas as were the best-educated classes in the North. Opera houses, musical societies, theaters, and lending libraries gave a cosmopolitan sheen to these cities, and except for their defense of slavery, southern urbanites felt at one with their northern counterparts. Women like Mary Chesnut and Louisa McCord were abreast of the newest intellectual and literary fashions of Europe. New Orleans-born composer Louis Gottschalk blended music from the European romantic movement with black rhythms and Creole tunes from Louisiana, and his exotic melodies became a sensation in both France and the United States. The South seemed different, not backward, and southern novelists, poets, and essayists — far less known today than the luminaries of New England — nevertheless published and found a limited regional audience. William Gilmore Simms of Charleston and John Pendleton Kennedy of Virginia and Maryland, for example, wrote important novels of southern life, and the *Southern Quarterly Review* published essays and reviews on a wide range of current topics and books. Yet despite the undeniable importance of southern urban life, the society's center of gravity rested squarely in its plantation economy.

⁊ *White Women in the Old South*

Perhaps no stereotype of the Old South is more vivid than that of the southern lady, either the flighty plantation belle concerned with little besides balls and beaus or the plantation mistress who added grace to the household and ministered to the sick slaves. The mistress of legend is long-suffering, devout, kind, and competent, yet she hovers in the background and quietly supports her husband. These images of southern white women found their most memorable form in the best-selling novel and most popular movie of all time, *Gone With the Wind* (1939). As though with a laser beam these fictional characterizations of the southern white lady have been burned into the consciousness of most Americans. Yet they distort and conceal more than they reveal historical reality. In fact, this almost mythical depiction of the southern lady was not just a creation of a novelist; this was the way southern rhetoric described the lady, especially in the romanticizing days of the post–Civil War South when many whites looked back to a lost era and infused it with an idealism sadly lacking in their own time. Perhaps, too, southern males, who expected women to be subservient dependents, subject to the authority of their husbands, constructed this mythical version of ladyhood as a form of compensation to women for their constricted social, political, legal, and economic roles. Perhaps also creating the image of the saintly plantation mistress was an attempt by white men to compensate their wives for male sexual relationships with slave women — or maybe even a form of male rationalization for such behavior by deliberately de-sexing white women. Of course, the great majority of white women did not reside on plantations and led lives vastly different from the ideal type.

Real plantation mistresses seldom had idle, leisurely lives. A small number of white women lived on plantations large enough to supply them with a substantial retinue of servants, but most had only a slave woman to do much of the cooking and one or two slaves for the most unpleasant household tasks of washing and cleaning. Again, on the largest plantations a slave woman or teenager would often help with child care. But even on these atypically affluent plantations, the mistress had to administer the home, setting slaves to their tasks and supervising canning vegetables and fruits for the winter. The great majority of white women did not have the services of any slaves, and these women had lives filled with labor. They gardened and gathered the produce, prepared it for cooking, and cooked all the meals; they washed and mended clothes; they supervised often a household full of children — all without the conveniences we today take for granted. White farm women had to help in the fields, chopping and picking cotton, or helping transplant the tobacco slips from the seed bed to the fields, or assisting in any variety of agricultural emergencies that could strike isolated farms.

Women had many gender-specific roles. When neighbors gathered for a barn raising or hog killing — as in all agricultural societies, major tasks involving several families working together had recreational and social overtones — women did certain chores, men others. While the men and older boys constructed the barn or cleared the fields, the women and older girls cooked the meal that would end the day in a festival of food and frolic, often with someone breaking out a fiddle to accompany tired but happy feet. Women working together talked about womanly concerns, shared recipes and folk remedies, and discussed their (and others') children. Gossip not only spread information but also shaped community standards of behavior by defining actions held up for shame. This mechanism was one means of teaching community moral standards to the younger girls who helped the older women busily preparing food for the social dinner following the day of labor.

❧ Religion as an Institution

Prevailing social conventions held women to be more openly religious than men, and this expectation mirrored the reality of southern churches, where active female members outnumbered males two to one. In part because they were less involved in the pressures and temptations of public life outside the home, women were thought to be more pious than men and better situated to be good Christians; and they were held to higher moral standards, especially with regard to lesser sins such as swearing and drinking. The churches disciplined both men and women for obvious sexual infractions, but the larger society tended to judge women more harshly for such transgressions as out-of-wedlock pregnancy. A woman's virtue was considered her most precious possession.

The evangelical churches particularly took very seriously the churches' role as moral exemplars, and members were held to account for behavior deemed unchristian as well as injurious to the larger society and the general reputation of the church itself. Churches took disciplinary actions against members who profaned the Sabbath by doing unnecessary work, who fought among themselves, who lied to another church member, who refused to pay their just bills, and so on. Such discipline was not so much a censorious moralizing as a community effort to establish the bounds of proper behavior necessary for harmonious living. Certain behavior was by definition sinful, but usually a church committee met with accused members and tried to work out ways of ending harmful actions and mending relationships. Common sense and a spirit of forgiveness generally marked church disciplinary proceedings, and the proceedings were conducted with a degree of democratic participation — men and women, white and black — unique to church government and absent from civil government.

Not everyone in the Old South was a church member or even tried to live by the churches' moral standards. Actual church membership as a percentage of the total population was about half what it is today, but that may say more about the relative ease — and few demands — of membership today than about the relative influence of religion in the Old South. Far more people attended church services in the nineteenth century than actually belonged to churches, and summertime revivals and camp meetings attracted throngs of people and for many were the highlights of the season. Even those with no active church life seemed to understand the social and political importance of outwardly supporting the churches and conforming to the basic Christian worldview. Still, many whites subscribed to an ethic of honor in which one's worth was determined by others' opinion or how one was treated. In this secular calculus of self-valuation, constant vigilance was necessary to protect one's reputation; any unrequited slight detracted from one's honor. Any act of disrespect had to be answered, either by a duel for the upper class or by a fist- or knife-fight for the underclass. This culture of honor, which had ancient roots in Europe, produced a culture of violence. According to this culture, only men possessed honor; women possessed virtue. Many male churchgoers opposed this secular valuation of worth, arguing instead that one's essential worth was recognized by God and maintained by one's relationship to Jesus. Women and ministers frequently criticized the cult of honor and often campaigned against dueling. Many Christian men also valued their good name and the resulting respect they had in the congregation and community above a worldly esteem based on instant violent defense of their so-called honor. Overall, the religious culture was far more influential and universal in the Old South than the cult of honor.

In terms of religion, the South was not monolithic. Pockets of Catholic strength endured in Maryland and Kentucky, and Catholicism dominated much of south Louisiana and the Spanish-influenced regions of Texas. There was also a Catholic presence in most larger cities, such as Charleston and Savannah. The Jewish presence was much smaller, although influential synagogues existed in Baltimore, Richmond, Charleston, Savannah, and New Orleans. But the South as a whole was overwhelmingly Protestant. After the Great Revival at the beginning of the nineteenth century had revitalized the evangelical denominations and especially the Baptists and Methodists, those two denominations rose to dominance in the South. Both churches had to make accommodations to the region, primarily by first downplaying and then almost completely reversing their early opposition to slavery. Because the most insistently antislavery ministers found it difficult to get and keep positions in the South, they were gradually replaced by evangelical preachers who were willing to accept slavery in order to be allowed to preach more widely in the region. The ministers changed in other ways as well. Their strictures against fine dress, fiddle-playing and dancing, prosperity, architecturally elaborate churches, and a whole variety of creature comforts and social amenities moderated as their membership increased and became more affluent.

These adjustments to the rising social status and prestige of the evangelical churches were both a cause and a result of the churches' widening their appeal to encompass a broader cross-section of society. The Episcopal Church along the eastern seaboard of the South retained its leadership position among the wealthiest white southerners even as its percentage of membership declined, and in other regions the Presbyterian Church had the highest social prestige and the most affluent members. But the greatest rise in social position occurred among the Baptists and Methodists, who since their founding days in the mid-eighteenth century had come to dominate the region both in numbers and in cultural influence. By the 1830s they counted many prominent persons among their members. Southern Protestantism adjusted its method and its message to what had brought it success during and shortly after the Great Revival. In the persons of James Henley Thornwell and Benjamin M. Palmer the Presbyterians produced learned theologians, but most southerners did not have such divines as their ministers. Baptist and Methodist preachers usually de-emphasized formal theological argumentation and focused instead on retelling in an infinite variety of ways the story of God's love and Jesus' redemptive death. The major point of sermons in the popular evangelical churches was to effect a conversion experience. Religious services were oriented more toward evangelism than toward worship, and the social message was more moralistically directed toward individual behavior than prophetically focused on failings of social institutions.

❧ Religion and Slavery

This individualistic ethos perhaps made it easier for southern churches to move from attacking slavery during their founding days to defending it by the 1830s. At the beginning almost no Baptists or Methodists owned slaves, and many impoverished evangelicals identified more with the slaves than with the planter aristocrats. But slaveholders, fearful of the impact of antislavery evangelical religion on their slaves, quickly restricted ministers' access to the blacks. Because evangelical ministers honestly believed that blacks were far more at risk for living outside the gospel than for living in bondage, they strategically limited their antislavery views in order to be able to preach more freely to slaves. (For these preachers such compromise was not an act of hypocrisy but rather of principle — nothing was more important, they believed, than saving knowledge of the gospel, not even earthly freedom. Ministers who could not accept this compromise simply gave up on the South and took their ministry elsewhere.)

And as the evangelical churches grew, soon including both more affluent members who owned slaves and more slaves themselves, the institution of slavery came to look less evil to the ministers. As the churches gained devout slave members, the ministers gradually came to accept slavery as the mechanism by which Africans were introduced to Christianity. When abolitionists began attacking the southern churches for tolerating slavery, the southern clergy, feeling besieged, defended themselves (and slavery) by pointing to the number of slaves in their churches. This soon led them into defending southern society in general and to a systematic religious defense of slavery as an institution often mentioned in the Bible and never specifically condemned either by God or by Jesus. Before slavery was attacked, few white southerners had felt it necessary to think much about defending human bondage: it was simply a given of their time and place. But when the issue was raised, most slaveholders were pleased to discover the institution grounded in history and religion.

In the Old South most whites — men and women, rich and poor, urban and rural — found it easy to accept the legitimacy and morality of slavery. For those few who might have harbored some concerns about the institution's rightness, reasons of practicality and concern for social order dampened almost all public criticism

A "Christian" Apologetic for Slavery, 1850

James Henley Thornwell (1812-1862) was one of the South's leading theologians prior to the Civil War. This extract is from a sermon probably more convincing to Thornwell's original hearers than it is to readers today.

The fundamental mistake of those who affirm slavery to be essentially sinful, is that the duties of all men are specifically the same. . . . The argument, fully and legitimately carried out, would condemn every arrangement of society, which did not secure to all its members an absolute equality of position; it is the very spirit of socialism and communism.

The doctrine of the Bible, on the other hand, is that the specifick duties — the things actually required to be done, are as various as the circumstances in which men are placed. . . . Some are tried in one way, some in another — some are required to do one set of things, some another — but the spirit of true obedience is universally the same — and the result of an effectual probation is, in every case, a moral sympathy with the moral perfections of God. The lesson is the same, however different the textbooks from which it has been taught.

of human bondage. Ever since the initial shift to large-scale slavery at the very beginning of the eighteenth century, few whites had questioned it. For those who had worries, there was the example of English slaveholding on the West Indian island of Barbados, where within several decades during the seventeenth century the workforce had become composed almost entirely of African slaves. As blacks became increasingly available, it seemed easier to subject them to harsh discipline and brutal work routines because they were so obviously different from the English, and it was simple to translate difference into inferiority. For whites, blacks came to be seen as natural slaves — and for those whites who sought further assurance about their labor system, ministers and ideologues pointed out that the Bible made many uncritical references to slavery, that slavery had apparently existed in all known societies, and that by creating income and freeing some whites from most physical labor, slavery contributed to the flowering of white culture. Moreover, slavery provided discipline and order presumed so necessary to a society containing a workforce that had little reason to defend the society and many reasons to run away or rebel.

Whites quickly sprang to slavery's defense on grounds of practicality, necessity, and morality. Religion eventually became the surest defense strategy, with planters and ministers alike arguing that slavery was divinely sanctioned. This was not special pleading — the Bible read literally can be seen to provide a solid justification of slavery, and proslavery ministers could rebut the abolitionists verse for verse. When they were most honest, Christian slaveholders understood that the divine — as they saw it — sanction of slavery included a responsibility to treat their slaves humanely

(as befitted persons in that status) and provide them Christian instruction. Hence slavery was only provisionally acceptable in the eyes of God. But this principle was often neglected in practice. Although economic rationalization, religion, and racism made strange bedfellows, together they eased most southern whites' consciences. White males even defined their own freedom as the liberty to own slaves, thereby further wedding democracy to slavery. Moreover, many whites assumed that hierarchy was the natural order, with white male husbands and fathers having natural authority over all dependents in the plantation household — women, children, and slaves (whom they saw, in effect, as permanent children). When slaveholders included their slaves under the rubric of family, they had in mind this conception of dependent relationships, of course, not actual biological kinship (although, as we have seen, such kinship was not always lacking).

BLACK SOUTHERNERS

A cousin to the stereotype that all whites were planters and slaveholders (except for a few shiftless and sickly poor whites) is the belief that all blacks in the Old South were slaves performing only menial labor on broad-acred plantations. Not all blacks were slaves, not all slaves worked on farms, and not all slaves were unskilled.

❧ *Diversity within Slavery*

All slaves were unfree, but diversity was as much a characteristic of the slave population as of the white.

Since only 12 percent of white slaveholders in 1860 held twenty slaves or more and hence qualified as planters, and almost half of all slaveholders owned five or fewer slaves, obviously many slaves lived in groupings that were not plantations. Yet despite this distribution of slave ownership among whites, a majority of slaves actually lived on plantations. This apparent paradox is easily explained: one plantation of fifty or one hundred slaves accounted for more enslaved people than twenty small farms with one or two bondspeople apiece.

Most agricultural units with one or more slaves were farms, not plantations (that is, large establishments with over twenty slaves), and the owner of such farms often worked in the fields alongside and supervised the slaves — the fewer slaves he owned, the more likely the white master worked with them, and his supervision increased in proportion to the number of bondspeople

Slaves and Overseers Harvesting Cotton   The pace of work picked up frantically during the cotton-picking season as slaves raced to bring in the crop before rain or hail could damage it. Every available hand—often including those of house servants—was pressed into the job. This contemporary scene shows the harvesting of cotton on a relatively large plantation. Overseers were usually hired from among the poorer white population. Their job was to make sure that the slaves put out maximum effort, and they carried (and used) whips to ensure results.

he owned. Again, if a small farmer owned one or two slaves, usually these would be women, perhaps with a child, who was used primarily for domestic work to ease the life of the owner's wife. Besides helping with cooking, washing, and child care, the slaves on very small farms often worked in the garden and with food gathering and preparation. When there were one or two slaves, they usually lived in a lean-to attached to the white people's cabin or slept in the attic. In such close quarters, relations between owner and enslaved could vary from relatively harmonious to embittered. It was not unknown for something like real affection to grow between the white woman and her slave, or between the slave woman and the white children, but close proximity could also produce tension, anger, and hatred. The cabins of small farmers were small, cramped, and uncomfortable, and even more so for the slave crowded into the attic. The slave usually had the same diet as the owners, but obviously the choice cuts and whatever was in least supply went first to the whites, with the slave taking what was left. If a slave woman did the cooking, perhaps she secretly augmented what would be left over.

When one or two slaves lived literally under the roof

Slavery Days

Delia Garlic said she was more than a hundred years old when in the 1930s her story was taken down in African American dialect by an interviewer at her home in Montgomery, Alabama. Here she recalls growing up a slave in Virginia; she lost her brother William in a sale and never saw him again.

"Dem days was hell. . . . I was growed up when de war come," she said, "an' I was a mother befo' it closed. Babies was snatched from dere mother's breas' an' sold to speculators. Chilluns was separated from sisters an' brothers an' sisters never saw each other ag'in.

"Course dey cry: you think dey not cry when dey was sold lak cattle? I could tell you 'bout it all day, but even den you couldn't guess the awfulness of it.

"It's bad to belong to folks dat own you soul an' body; dat can tie you up to a tree, wid yo' face to de tree and yo' arms fastened tight aroun' it; who take a long curlin' whip an' cut de blood ever' lick.

"Folks a mile away could hear dem awful whippings. Dey was a terrible part of livin'. . . ."

---

of the white owner, the slaves were under almost constant supervision. Slaves on small farms had little opportunity to meet other black people, to develop anything like a separate slave community and culture, or even to find a spouse. Slave marriages were not recognized by law in the South, and on rare occasions masters selected mates for slaves for breeding purposes. But such interference in conjugal relations was certainly atypical. Most slaves found their own partners, and both masters and ministers often recognized slave marriages and even blessed them with approval and festive ceremony. However, such marriages were not legal no matter how binding and meaningful they proved to be to the couple involved. And most whites, if they felt economic convenience required it, were willing to sunder slave marriages by selling away one of the members.

White owners generally understood well enough normal human needs to allow their slaves limited time to visit other slaves, although slaves off the farm had to carry a note from their owner giving them permission to travel. It became very common for husband and wife to live on adjoining farms, with the husband needing his owner's permission to visit his wife and children on weekends or even (if proximity allowed) at the end of a long workday. There is much evidence that slaves preferred having a spouse on an adjoining farm or plantation because it was difficult for slave husbands to deal with having their owner control the slaves' wives. As slave Henry Bibb wrote in his memoirs, "If my wife must be exposed to the insults and licentious passions of wicked slavedrivers and overseers; if she must bear the stripes of the lash laid on by an unmerciful tyrant; if this is to be done with impunity, which is frequently done by slaveholders and their abettors, Heaven forbid

that I should be compelled to witness the sight." Even on plantations when it would have been possible to find a local spouse, slave men and women often chose partners "abroad." This practice may have had some connection also to cultural traditions in Africa, where sometimes the men of a village lived in separate quarters from the women, with the children living with their mothers.

Life and Labor

Historians once believed that living conditions were better for slaves on small farms, but this interpretation may have been based on a threat that antebellum slaveholders often used to frighten their slaves into better behavior — the threat of being sold to a big plantation in the Deep South, or Louisiana, where supposedly conditions were much worse. For a slave on a small farm, the threat of being sold was no doubt frightening because it would destroy his family, but contemporary whites and early historians alike seem to overlook the matter of family splintering and focused instead on the supposed harshness of larger plantations.

Today, historians are in general agreement that for most enslaved persons, life was more bearable on a plantation, or at least on a larger farm with a dozen or more slaves. Such farms or plantations had separate housing for the slaves, usually family-sized cabins a hundred yards or so from the owner's house. This distance gave at least some leeway for slaves (with the exception of the few house slaves) to have time to themselves, out of constant sight or hearing of their owners. Slaves could reveal their feelings, sing their songs, tell their tales, have social maneuvering room to be them-

Nanny and Child The children of large plantation owners probably spent at least as much time with their black nannies as with their own parents. This photograph of a slave woman and the white child for whom she cares dates from about 1850. It underscores the complexities of race, gender, and power relationships in the antebellum South.

selves rather than be what their masters demanded. It must have been some comfort to retreat to a black environment after a daytime of work under white supervision. In larger groupings slaves were better able to find friends, mates, protectors, and nurturers among their own people. In this supportive community of fellow blacks, slaves were able to reconstruct or create synthetic versions of older African cultural traditions, dimly recalled personally or from their elders' memo-

ries. And because the larger planters tended to have more financial resources, they were better able to survive bad crop years without having to cut rations or clothing allowances or, worst of all, sell slaves and disrupt black families. To be a slave in any circumstance was horrible, but if one had to be a slave, then it was generally better to be enslaved on a plantation than on a small farm. Yet all such generalizations are liable to many exceptions, with slave treatment running the gamut on both farms and plantations.

Work was central to the experience of all adult slaves. Work routines, the actual kinds of labor, and seasonal variations in hours worked varied according to a number of factors, including the staple crop grown on the plantation, the number of slaves and both the male/female ratio and the age distribution, the personality of the planter and his overseers, and the geographical location of the plantation itself. It is easier to discuss a range of situations than to try to determine average conditions. With working conditions, as with several other aspects of slave treatment, often the extreme conditions — either atypically bad or good situations — caught the attention of contemporaries and were recorded in letters or diaries. Thus "normal" conditions are often more difficult to uncover. Generally the task of the historian is to concentrate on the broad middle of the spectrum rather than the extreme ends. On small plantations and on farms with several slaves, bondspeople often had to perform a variety of tasks according to the crop season and the gender of the slave.

Female slaves typically worked in the fields, the dairy, in food preparation, and in the laundry, as well as taking care of the white children. In the winter, when their labor was not needed in the fields, slave women often wove cloth, helped with the butchering and salting of hogs, and perhaps assisted male slaves in clearing new fields. During the crop season slave women transplanted tobacco plants, chopped cotton (cutting away the grass with a hoe), and planted rice. At harvest time especially, every slave woman picked cotton except the specialized house slaves on the very largest plantations. Cotton harvesting was extremely labor-intensive over a period of several months, and every available slave worked long hours, their hands at first bleeding from being scratched by the hardened cotton bolls and their backs aching every day from bending and pulling the heavy cotton sacks along the rows. Women worked alongside men, too, for the several-days-long frenzy of sugarcane harvest, with the laborers toiling practically around the clock to cut the cane and cook it into sugar before the crop spoiled. Occasionally on cotton plantations, women plowed — some even appeared to prefer to plow — but usually plowing and driving wagons were reserved for male slaves.

During the winter months enslaved men cut and hauled firewood, built wooden fences, cleared woodlands for new fields, ditched low areas to improve drainage, or perhaps dug and hauled marl, a naturally occurring mineral deposit in several regions of the South that was spread on the soil to improve fertility. Men usually did most of the plowing, so the early spring saw male plowers breaking the land and other men, most of the women slaves, and black teenagers planting the crops, then hoeing them to keep the grass under control, cutting away the so-called sucker plants from tobacco, removing tobacco worms, and then again at harvest season turning all available labor to getting in the crops. Male slaves built and repaired barns, fences, slave cabins; cared for the livestock (older children often helped tend the livestock); and assisted with any chores that were specific to an individual farm or owner's needs. Male slaves worked at sawmills in the off season, cut hay, gathered apples, hauled crops or other goods to market, and on larger plantations often operated the cotton gins and supervised the cooking of the cane juice. In other words, slaves worked at every task that needed to be done, not just the most menial chores. On some of the atypically large plantations, male slaves specialized as highly skilled blacksmiths or carpenters, but much more commonly slave men were jacks-of-all-trades, their tasks varying according to seasonal labor demands. There is abundant evidence that white owners and overseers recognized the competence of various slaves, assigned them work appropriate to their abilities, and often took pride — as did the slaves themselves — in their skills. When slaves were sold they were priced according to their abilities, along with their age, gender, strength, and health. A small percentage of slaves were literate — some taught by owners or owners' children, some essentially self-taught — and occasionally planters recognized that the ability to read enhanced the usefulness of certain slaves and even corresponded with them about crop matters. But most slaves, by state laws, were kept illiterate.

❧ *Urban and Industrial Slavery*

The South was an agricultural society, and cities and towns were fewer, smaller, and less important than in the North. Southern cities were more commercial entrepôts than centers of manufacturing, and they were the focus of southern cultural life. Planters and their families journeyed to towns and cities to shop, to socialize, and to attend concerts and the theater, and often planters sent their children to academies in towns for their education. There, too, slaves (and free blacks) lived, worked, and shaped separate communities for themselves.

The size of slave holdings in towns was smaller than in agricultural units, although the percentage of whites who actually held slaves ran slightly higher. Most urban slaves were women (except in the industrial city of Petersburg, Virginia, with its tobacco factories employing male slaves), and they typically engaged in domestic work of various kinds. Owners of restaurants, hotels, inns, and other service institutions also owned or leased slave women. Warehouses, factories, liveries, and prosperous artisans often owned or hired (from white owners) male slave laborers, and town and city streets were filled with slaves driving wagons, delivering goods, and performing an astonishing variety of jobs. Slaves built and repaired roads, homes, and shops; they fabricated wrought iron; they staffed vegetable stalls and butcher shops. Most white slaveholders had accommodations at the rear of their homes, perhaps within walled spaces containing a patio, for their slaves, and many slaves who hired themselves out as carpenters, masons, tanners, or artisans of any number of sorts (returning a portion of their wages to their owner) found separate lodging on the outskirts of towns. There existed an entire subculture of shops, businesses, and cultural-social institutions for slaves and free blacks in southern cities.

The agricultural South was not heavily industrialized, and much of what industry did exist complemented agriculture: cotton gins and presses, for example. But wherever industry was found, there too were skilled slave laborers. The coalmines and ironworks of Maryland and Virginia, for example, had used slave laborers since the seventeenth century. In the salt works of the Kanawha River Valley in western Virginia (now West Virginia), where brine water was pumped to the surface and boiled away in huge vats to leave the residue of salt — a hot and dangerous job — slaves worked as laborers and foremen. Skilled slave workmen toiled in the lumber industry throughout the South — cutting logs, sawing them into lumber, floating rafts of logs down river to cities like New Orleans for sawing into planks, splitting cedar shingles, manning the turpen-

Tredegar Ironworks, Richmond, Virginia Slaves in urban areas often worked long hours in industrial settings like this one, performing all manner of dangerous and unpleasant jobs. Ironically, it occasionally also happened that skilled slaves would be foremen overseeing unskilled poor white workers.

tine forests of North Carolina, and producing tar and pitch. At brickworks, in smelly tanyards, in shipyards, in the contaminated atmosphere of the Maryland Chemical Works in Baltimore, in the massive Tredegar Ironworks factory in Richmond — slaves worked at every imaginable industrial task in the South, often in positions requiring skill and managerial ability and sometimes — as strange as it might seem — even with supervisory authority over less-skilled whites. Owner/employees were more concerned with production and profits than logical consistency. Skilled slave artisans as well as laborers at ironworks and many other trades worked for a customary amount, measured in terms of

a measurable output and agreed upon by master and slave alike. For labor over and beyond that accepted norm, slaves were paid for overtime. From such funds slaves were able to purchase extra food or clothing, household luxuries for themselves or loved ones, items to increase their income (like tools, boats, livestock), and even on some occasions put money into bank accounts. Although slaves were at times used for dangerous and difficult jobs, often the most hazardous labor was reserved for free Irish workers.

There were persistent shortages of slave labor at some industrial sites, which were often far from the largest concentration of slaves in the coastal regions along the eastern seaboard or in the cotton-rich black belt across the Deep South. These tightened labor markets allowed slaves to negotiate better working conditions or other advantages. In both urban and industrial settings, slaves were often responsible for hiring themselves out, returning an agreed-upon portion of their annual wages to their owner. Urban slaveholders in particular often leased their slaves on annual contracts, and slaves essentially made their own deals, bargaining for the situation that seemed most advantageous in terms of location, work assignments, extent of tasks, and so on. Often competition among industrial or other employers gave slaves some choice. Slaveholders too, who obviously wanted the slaves they hired out to receive adequate food and be treated in such a way that they would not be prone to run away or apt to be injured, also helped their slaves shop for the best situation. All this is to say that in limited ways slaves on the market for hiring out their labor had some control over their working conditions, and they made the most of their opportunities. In a variety of ways slaves used their creativity, their ingenuity, and their wiles to carve out more social and cultural breathing space than their legal situation seemed to allow. But this was more the result of black agency than of white leniency. White employers offered limited advantages and monetary bounties to employed slaves to guarantee an adequate number of workers, not because they were philanthropic.

❧ Free Blacks

About a quarter million blacks were legally free in the South in 1860. Ever since the mid-seventeenth century some blacks had not been slaves. This number grew both from normal population increase and from manumissions — the act whereby a slave was formally freed from bondage. The status of a small number of blacks in the seventeenth century had been unclear before slavery became a rigid and legally prescribed institution. At least some blacks in early Maryland and Virginia appear to have been free from the beginning; others served for several years as indentured servants and then became free, just as did white indentured servants. A small number of blacks who initially were held as slaves were able to prove that they had converted to Christianity (either in the colonies or perhaps in England while serving their masters on a visit), and since it was originally presumed that only heathens could be enslaved, courts manumitted some Christian slaves. The law was quickly changed to close this escape clause, and after 1667 a slave's religion did not affect his legal status. Still, throughout the late seventeenth and the eighteenth centuries it was relatively easy for a white slaveholder to free his slaves, either for reasons of con-

science or for meritorious service, so that the number of free blacks increased slowly. As their numbers increased, it became more common for free black families to emerge, enlarging still more this population of people who were an anomaly in a society that normally considered slavery to be the natural state of blacks.

During the American Revolution the contagion of liberty led a few slaveholders to free their slaves for reasons of political ideology, and the growth of evangelical religion in the decades following caused still other owners to free their slaves for religious reasons. The result was a surge in the population of free blacks, whose numbers in the South increased from 32,357 according to the census of 1790 to 61,241 in 1800. Owners in the Upper South occasionally freed all their slaves in the aftermath of the American Revolution, while those in the Deep South normally freed only special slaves, including mulattos born of interracial sexual relationships.

The laws allowing manumission were tightened after the 1820s. Most states now required that owners freeing their slaves post bonds, and often insisted that freedpeople leave the state. These laws were not always enforced — occasionally slaves were virtually freed even though the owner still technically owned them — but they did greatly slow the increase in the free black population. Conditions of virtual but not legal freedom, allowing whites to escape posting bond and blacks to remain near loved ones, were of course fragile and could be ended by the death of the white or a change of mind; to pay off their creditors, debtors could still claim those who had become virtually free. On occasion other white patrons who knew the intention of a deceased slaveholder would intervene to protect the favored situation of a black who had been allowed to live as virtually free, but such slaves constantly worried that antagonistic whites could end their favorable but tenuous special status.

Despite the increase in restrictions against manumission, by the 1830s there was a demographically significant number of free blacks living as individuals, as free black families, and in mixed marriages (with one partner enslaved) throughout most areas of the South. A small majority of the free blacks were farmers, and a handful were even planters who owned slaves and cultivated the normal staple crops. But free blacks were most noticeable in southern cities. In such places as Charleston, Richmond, Savannah, and New Orleans they were quite numerous, occasionally even dominating certain skilled professions like brickmasonry or ship caulking. Free blacks served as barbers, restaura-

Patrollers Slaves taking unauthorized leave — either to flee or to visit a spouse or other family members at another plantation — had to evade the slave patrols on the roads, day and night. In the South, all white men were expected to do patrol duty. Slaves were by law forbidden to travel without carrying papers from their owner giving them permission to be away. If they lacked such permission, they were assumed to be runaways or otherwise up to no good.

teurs, draymen, mechanics, blacksmiths, and ironworkers — in fact practically every occupation. Most were poor, but in every city some became prosperous, even wealthy, and lived in substantial homes in the better parts of the cities. William Johnson of Natchez, to cite an extreme example, was a wealthy barber, had a handsome home in the white section of the city, belonged to the elite jockey club and attended horse races, entered into business transactions with whites, owned a farm and several slaves, attended concerts and circuses, and was a well-respected citizen. Free blacks never enjoyed the full range of freedoms available to whites, but they could own property, make contracts, travel, and generally lead lives far different from those of slaves. But free blacks could not testify against whites in court: William Johnson, the barber of Natchez, was murdered by

a white man who went free because all the witnesses to the crime were black.

The wealthy free black who owned black laborers was highly atypical. Most free blacks owned only one "slave," often a spouse who had been a slave of a white owner and had been purchased to cement the marriage. If the wife of a free black craftsman, for example, was a slave, she could be sold at the whim of her white owner regardless of her affection for her husband, for slave marriages were neither recognized nor protected by law. Yet there were wealthy free blacks who had large slaveholdings and employed their bondspeople on plantations or in artisanal labor. These black slaveholders generally treated their slaves no differently than whites did.

The largest southern cities had substantial numbers — up to 20 percent of their population — of free blacks. Their presence as workers, skilled laborers, and residents was quite visible and economically indispensable. Whites often fretted about the number and influence of free blacks, for they understood that skilled and prosperous free blacks were living refutations of white arguments about blacks being natural slaves. Whites feared that the presence of free blacks could under-mine slavery by reinforcing slaves' desire for freedom. Free blacks, who were more often literate than slaves, could — whites worried — be conduits of rebellious in-formation, if not actual fomenters of rebellion, as in the reputed case of Denmark Vesey in Charleston in 1822. In fact, free blacks were usually so well aware of the fragility of their situation and of white dominance that they were often conservative forces rather than leaders of rebellion. That did not prevent cities and towns from passing legislation and proclamations to keep free blacks theoretically under control — laws circumscrib-ing free blacks' behavior that, after the Civil War and emancipation, became the prototypes of official rules maintaining racial segregation.

Still, free blacks, like slaves, learned how to create and maintain surprising degrees of autonomy within a discriminatory society. Free blacks often owned their homes and created a series of mutual support institu-tions such as churches, savings and burial societies, musical societies, recreational and social organiza-tions. They also practiced behavior patterns designed to cultivate protective relationships with white pa-trons who could intervene to ameliorate or finesse le-gal impediments. In today's vernacular, free blacks, like slaves, were "survivors." Slavery and racial discrimina-tion were only too real, but both slaves and free blacks were always more than victims. They found islands of autonomy, individual agency, and creative protection of their own family prerogatives in the midst of a sea of oppression.

❧ Slaves as Human Property

So varied were the conditions of slave life that it is difficult to generalize about it, other than to say that slavery always meant ultimately not being free — and being the property of someone else. In every mea-surable way, slaves were worse off than any others in the Old South, but the real determinant of slavery is not daily caloric intake, square feet of living space, or length of work hours. The lack of control over one's own destiny is the most devastating aspect of being enslaved. Yet it is important, even while emphasiz-ing the lack of freedom, not to minimize the physical hardships of slavery. Slave treatment is a complicated issue, and the matter of food supply and its diversity, or the delivery of health care, for example, sometimes was beyond the control of white slaveholders and even society at that time. But even when the situation lay

beyond slaveholders' conscious control, the institu-tion of slavery in various ways always worsened condi-tions for the enslaved.

By southern law, enslaved persons were property, not people. They could be sold, gambled away, given away, or used as collateral; they were listed in wills and on tax rolls just like livestock and farm implements. This denial of the humanity of slaves was recognized by whites as a legal fiction used for commercial or inheri-tance purposes only, because they also knew that slaves had human emotion, initiative, and personality. In the seventeenth and eighteenth centuries some whites had speculated about slaves being something less than hu-man; but by the nineteenth century enslaved persons were typically referred to by whites as family depen-dents — a kind of permanent children who supposedly needed white authority, discipline, and nurturing. The patriarchal family model, based on biblical precepts and deeply entrenched in English society, assumed that white males as heads of household had a proper su-pervisory role over natural dependents, that is, wives, children, servants, and slaves. But race, not class, con-trolled the categorization of slaves as a permanent de-pendent class, and slavery was seen by almost all white southerners as a natural condition, supported by the Bible. Thus whites convinced themselves that slavery did not contradict the precept of all (white) men being created equal in the eyes of the law. Individual slaves were often appreciated, sometimes loved, understood to have special skills, and on occasion trusted implic-itly. But as a group slaves (that is to say, blacks) were judged irresponsible, immature, and childlike, hence needing white discipline for their own good. This did not rule out the administration of cruel punishments such as whippings and even more brutal "discipline," but the purpose of slavery was not intended to be the physical destruction of enslaved persons — quite the contrary, considering their high replacement cost.

❧ Slave Family Life

Slavery was filled with contradictions and inconsis-tencies, such as people defined as property but often treated as humans. Marriage and the slave family were usually not recognized by law, but Christian and Vic-torian-era models of behavior as well as practical ex-perience led most slaveholders to recognize the family relationship of slaves, even when spouses lived on dif-ferent plantations and husbands needed special visit-ing rights. Most slaveholders came to appreciate their

A Slave Family   Despite the threat of breakup by sale or a division of property among heirs, slaves tried to maintain the integrity of their nuclear family units. This photograph, from South Carolina, shows three generations of a single slave family.

slaves' own desires to live in family groups. Certainly slaves living as families were more outwardly content and less likely to run away. Moreover, allowing slaves to form families seemed morally right to whites — another way in which whites' practice reflected their unconscious understanding that blacks were humans and not livestock.

By the early eighteenth century the normative living arrangement of slaves was by family grouping, although "the family" was defined more broadly than the twentieth-century American nuclear family. Most white slaveholders tried to keep family groups together, seldom sold small children away from their mothers, and allowed family visitation; in effect, owners usually accepted the legitimacy if not the permanency of slave marriages. The evangelical churches also promoted the legitimacy of slave marriages and disciplined slave members for committing adultery, even though the concept relevant to slaves had no reality in the civil law of the region. However, when economic adversity forced the breakup of slave families by sale, most whites put their own comfort or profit first. No doubt some slaveholders felt bad in such situations, but their

feelings did not prevent the sale or assuage the impact on the broken families. Every slave lived with the fear of separation, because even a slaveholder who for religious or other reasons supported the slave family could die or go into debt or bankruptcy, allowing slave families to be splintered by white laws. With the fragility of their families always in mind, slave parents maintained extended kinship networks to try to cushion such ruptures. Broad definitions of "aunt" and "uncle" beyond actual biological connection, as well as similarly generous conceptions of cousinry, represented an attempt to spread a quasi-family support system expansive enough to include individuals separated from their biological kin.

This recognition and inadvertent support of the slave family is revealed in how slaves were often listed in plantation records (that is, by family groupings) and by the size of slave cabins. Slaves usually lived not in gender-specific barracks but in family-sized cabins, often with unattached adults who might be either young single adults or elderly ones. Only rarely were slaves fed at the equivalent of soup kitchens; normally, slave wives and mothers cooked for their own families, treasuring this means of strengthening family bonds even at the end of a long and tiring day. Parents socialized their children into the harsh realities of slave life by teaching them survival and coping skills, often expressed through folk tales and songs. The so-called Uncle Remus tales, for example, were lessons for dealing with life under bondage, not just entertaining yarns. Slave parents sacrificed to protect their children as much as possible from the hardships of bondage, and they sought ways to augment the food and clothing of their children. Slave children often ran around almost naked in the summer months until they were five or six years old, then for another couple of years they often wore unisex shifts. Slave children often played with the white children in relative equality until about the time the white children started school. That was a harsh moment of truth for many slave children, and sometimes it even troubled the white children. But just as often, young whites about that age began to mimic the behavior of the adult whites around them, "playing" at ordering slave children around and threatening to beat them in cruel imitation of the adults they knew. Yet it was not unknown for something akin to real affection to exist between former playmates of different color even as social conditions allowed the master-slave relationship to dictate interpersonal relations after the childhood years.

❧ *Housing, Food, and Health Care*

Slave cabins of course varied among plantations and in different geographical regions. On some of the oldest, largest, and wealthiest plantations in Virginia and Maryland, for example, they were often brick. More commonly, they were built of either sawn lumber, logs, or (along the South Carolina and Georgia coasts) an indigenous building aggregate called tabby. The houses were tiny by today's standards, sometimes not much larger than a modern bedroom, and furnishings were sparse and utilitarian, many objects serving several purposes. Floors were often dirt, and windows lacked glass panes and screens. Cooking was usually done over a fireplace, whose chimney was sometimes constructed of mud and sticks. The size, dimensions, even shape of the slave cabin may have come from African sources. Life was lived mainly outdoors; slave cabins (like those of small white farmers) were primarily places to sleep. Firewood needed be cut and hauled, and water had to be drawn from wells or collected at springs, then carried to the cabin in buckets. Both were hard work; indeed, every aspect of everyday life was labor intensive. The crowded cabins afforded no privacy, and they were hot in summer and cold and drafty in winter. The cabins were usually grouped together, with garden plots nearby and perhaps fenced areas for pigs owned by the slaves. Chickens roamed freely. On the better managed plantations a communal outdoor toilet was located nearby also, but just as often slaves had to relieve themselves in the woods.

There has been much confusion about slave food supply because earlier historians assumed that slaves ate only what their owners gave them. Most planters reasoned that it was only sensible to provide their bondspeople an adequate — if monotonous — diet. As one Alabama planter wrote, revealing an unintentional callousness, "I make it a rule to feed them well, as I think it poor economy to starve laborers or stock." Certain staple goods like corn meal and pork were distributed to slaves by their owners, averaging about a peck (a quarter bushel) of corn meal per week, along with three to four pounds of pork. Corn meal and pork — with slaves given the fattier portions because it was incorrectly assumed that they preferred it and were better off eating it — was usually kept under lock and key and distributed by the owner or his agent. But certainly other food — fresh vegetables, molasses, rice, yams — was given out by the owner when available or when in season.

Enslaved people did not merely sit back and subsist only on the food officially distributed. As creative, ingenious providers for themselves and their families, slaves found a number of ways of supplementing their diets. Most cultivated their own garden plots and often had pigs, chickens, and guinea fowl of their own. They fished; caught oysters, crabs, and crayfish; hunted squirrel, raccoon, opossum, and birds (slaves sometimes had access to guns for hunting, and they often used dogs, clubs, or small traps); and gathered nuts, polk weed for greens, sassafras roots for tea. Solomon Northup, a free black captured and sold into slavery in Louisiana, described how he devised a fish trap and reported that "the flesh of the coon is palatable, but verily there is nothing in all butcherdom so delicious as a roasted 'possum." Such augmentation of their diet is more a testament to slave efforts than to planter design, and it was yet another way slaves learned to make the most of a bad situation. Even so, during the long winter months when fresh vegetables were unavailable, slaves sometimes suffered from protein-deficiency diseases like pellagra. This was partly a result of the dietary deficiencies of corn and partly caused by the genetic inability of many African-descended people to metabolize the lactose in milk.[1] In periods of drought or depression, when white owners had to cut back, slaves were the first to feel the pinch.

Disease is no respecter of persons, and microorganisms spread from master to slave and vice versa, but certain conditions accentuated the disease susceptibility of blacks. African Americans have a heightened susceptibility to respiratory diseases (bacterial pneumonia was unknown in Africa before the arrival of Europeans, and Africans had developed no immunities to it), and being confined in small cabins where human sputum could spread tubercular bacteria may have posed a greater health hazard for blacks than for whites similarly housed. We know that many enslaved persons suffered from pneumonia and tuberculosis (then called consumption). Slaves often suffered from a variety of arthritic or rheumatoid conditions, and the rigors of their work routines no doubt accentuated infirmity. Many blacks, on the other hand, do not suffer from malaria or yellow fever at the same rate as do whites, and particularly in coastal regions where rice was cultivated in stagnant pools of fresh water — ideal breeding grounds for the mosquitoes that spread the microorganism causing malaria — slaves' relative immunity was quickly noted by whites and indeed used

---

1. This inability is also found among many Jews and people of East Asian ancestry.

as a supposed divine justification for slave labor in the rice fields. (The resistance to malaria resulted from a hemoglobin abnormality known as the sickle cell trait that had apparently developed in Africa, where malaria had been endemic for thousands of years. However, in the South in those regions beyond the malarial swamps, and later after malaria was eliminated as a major health threat, blacks who inherited the sickle trait from both parents often suffered from sickle cell anemia, a chronic and ultimately fatal condition.)

Blacks and whites alike fell victim to dysentery, cholera, hepatitis, typhoid fever, diarrhea, salmonella, and intestinal worms, but because slaves tended to have worse diets, did harder physical labor, and got (for what it was then worth) less care from physicians, their morbidity rates were higher. Whites and blacks both resorted to home remedies and self-cure first and only called upon doctors when the condition failed to respond. Whites learned that disease easily spread from slaves to whites (although they did not know precisely by what mechanism this happened), so they usually brought in medical experts to attend persistently infirm slaves — being aware also, of course, of the economic costs of sick or deceased slaves. But medical care in the Old South (as elsewhere in the nation) often was of little help, and in some case the prescribed treatment — purging or bleeding — actually worsened a patient's condition. No one knew about microorganisms, understood how impure water or food could cause illness, took care to locate wells a safe distance from toilets or animal pens, or had access to refrigeration to prevent food spoilage. As a result, disease constantly tormented the Old South, and anyone who reads letters, diaries, or account books from the time will be astonished at the pain and suffering that seemed to afflict practically everyone. Still, there is no doubt that in this democratic disease environment, slaves for a number of reasons were burdened with more than their share of sickness. Heavy labor and frequent childbirth often caused enslaved women to age quickly. Broken bones incorrectly set, hernias resulting from heavy labor, and toothache caused by poor dental hygiene were all common — and avoidable — afflictions among enslaved persons.

❧ Work Routines

The actual labor organization of plantations differed according to size, crop, personality of the master, and many other factors. On small farms, with only one or two slaves available to work in the fields, the owner typically worked alongside the slaves, although he determined the tasks and the work hours, and probably at times did more supervising than actual hand labor. There are examples of master and several slaves working together at such tasks as cutting poles to build a barn, fencing, butchering hogs, plowing, and picking cotton. Labor was so necessary at peak times on small farms that no owner could be just a supervisor. As farms increased in acres and number of slaves, the distance between the owner and the physical labor also widened. On large farms and small plantations, the owner was more a labor supervisor. He probably had one or two trusted male "slave drivers": slaves who roused the others in the morning, took them to the fields, supervised their labor, and saw to it that tasks were done and that no one slackened. Such drivers often incurred the animosity of their fellow slaves but received some benefits from their owners: additional wages, special favors like enhanced visiting rights to their spouses on adjoining plantations, and a degree of prestige. The owners of the largest plantations might employ a white overseer, with several black drivers under him. Both drivers and overseers deflected slave anger away from the owner and toward themselves, and slaves learned how to manipulate the system by complaining to owners about a cruel or overly demanding driver or overseer. White owners who wanted to see themselves as kind, paternalistic patriarchs often intervened on behalf of their slaves: They could dismiss overseers and demote drivers, but their slaves were usually permanent.

The system seemingly allowed slave laborers no rights and little power, but artful slaves devised means partially to control the work pace. By complaining, by malingering, or by feigning illness, slaves might pressure planters into some form of accommodation. The whole workforce in the field could silently slow down the routine so that the weaker women — not the strongest workers — set the pace. The result came to be commonly accepted work paces and hours. On rice plantations in particular, a slave's expected daily output was unofficially codified as a "task," which an efficient male slave could often complete by early afternoon and have the remainder of the day free. Most owners did not want to gain the reputation among other whites of being hard or cruel masters and so accepted community norms for workdays. Certainly slaves worked long hours and often at physically tiring jobs, but agricultural tasks were seasonal and not as methodical and time-urgent as modern assembly-line labor might suggest. On days when it was too wet or cold to work outdoors, slaves did minimal chores around the cabins, such as feeding livestock. There were times of peak labor, such as planting and especially harvest, but at other times labor demands were less pressing. As in all agricultural societies, certain tasks combined work and play. Repeatedly, aged former slaves in early twentieth-century interviews recalled that corn shucking could be nearly as festive an occasion as a dance. During the regular season, slaves learned to pace themselves when hoeing, plowing, or picking cotton. Shorter winter days also diminished the time spent in the fields. Still, at the end of the workday slaves had to gather and prepare their food, cut firewood, wash and mend their clothes, and care for their children. One does not have to assume fieldwork from sunup to sundown all year long to understand the exhaustion many slaves must have often experienced.

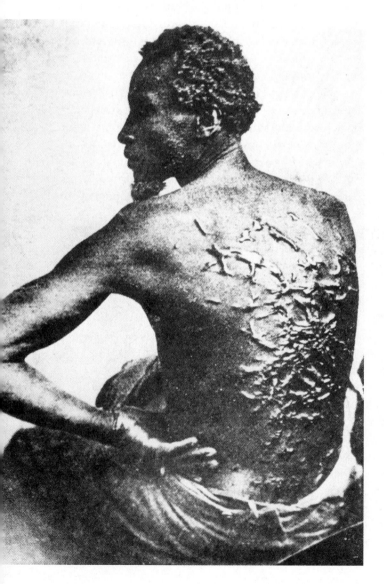

The Scars of Slavery After the Civil War an older slave named Gordon posed in North Carolina for this photograph, showing on his back the evidence of many floggings.

❧ *Discipline*

No topic is more difficult to discuss than slave discipline because the topic is both repugnant and complicated. It is helpful to imagine discipline as a spectrum: At one end was brutal, violent whipping, with salt poured into wounds, maybe even branding and the cutting off of ears, fingers, toes, and sexual organs. At the other end of the spectrum was behavior so mild as almost to blur the distinction between slavery and freedom. Both ends of the spectrum existed, and both were atypical. For the great majority of slaves and masters, discipline lay somewhere in between, nearer the brutal end than the center, but few slaves were habitually brutalized by evil owners. The institution of slavery is evil enough in its denial of basic freedoms and its everyday humiliations and unrewarded labor to condemn itself; there is no need to construct demonized stereotypes of vicious owners.

Every slave understood that force — punishment — was never far away. Even kind owners could withhold privileges, or administer mild whippings, or sell "recalcitrant" slaves; and kind owners could die, leaving slaves subject to far harsher behavior. Even owners who wanted to think of themselves as benevolent masters on occasion whipped slaves violently. Practically every slave either had been whipped, knew another who had been whipped, had witnessed whippings, or had seen the scars of earlier whippings. The threat, the fear, of whippings made them an ever-present psychological reality even for those plantations or slaves that never directly experienced a whipping.

Slavery rested on the *potential* of brutality without practical legal recourse, and that more than the undeniable existence of some relatively benevolent owners defined the institution. Although not all slaves were frequently or ever beaten, and few were worked to death, and their living conditions and food supply were not markedly worse than that of the poorest whites, the institution was evil because it denied black people their identity as people. It deprived them almost completely of the most basic freedoms.

Nevertheless, many owners honestly believed that slavery as an institution was ordained by the Bible. They saw slavery as the mechanism by which God intended to bring Africans to America and teach them Christianity and civilization. This attitude assumed that slavery was a divinely ordained institution and that slaveholders had a Christian responsibility toward their slaves. But few owners lived up to these professed ideals. Owners could whip slaves and rationalize their behavior as that of a father justly chastising his disobedient children; owners could separate families and justify such action as economic necessity. Slaves caught between, on the one hand, a harsh economic reality that defined them as property and valued them primarily for their productivity and, on the other hand, a Christian ideology that justified their bondage as providential, might be expected to have lived violent, nihilistic lives of desperation and self-consuming anger. That they on the whole did not is one of the great human victories of history. How did slaves survive slavery without becoming psychologically enslaved? How did they hold on to their humanity in the midst of an inhumane institution?

SLAVE CULTURE

By law, slavery was a system that deprived slaves of their essential identity as human beings and denied them the sanctity of marriage and family. As a cultural and social institution, it also attempted to obliterate the African culture of the first imported slaves. African slavers along the coast of Africa stole and purchased Africans from interior regions for sale to waiting Arab or European slave traders; to those stolen were added war captives. This network of capturing and selling Africans by Africans for slave markets in Arabia predated European penetration of the market, but then the destination of African slaves began to shift to the New World. Given the diverse sources of this human cargo, slaves corralled in pens called barracoons awaiting shipment often had no common language, and those gathered from common sources found themselves sold in small lots along the southern seaboard, where they were mingled with earlier captives with whom they could not converse. The disorienting tragedy compounded being ripped out of a homeland and away from kin and subsequently being brought to a strange country, among utterly alien people. Surely many enslaved persons in this predicament must have thought their life was worse than death. Early eighteenth-century whites found them strange, frightening laborers and treated them with a harshness that would have shocked planters in the mid-nineteenth century. The slave population in the late seventeenth century through the early eighteenth century was overwhelmingly composed of young males. Because few female slaves were sent across the Atlantic, marriages were uncommon and children scarce. Life for many male slaves was nasty, brutish, and short. Yet out of this was to evolve slave families, a more equal sex ratio, and a distinctive slave culture — partly African, partly American — that allowed enslaved persons to

---

❋ IN THEIR OWN WORDS

Sarah Grimké Learns About Slavery, Early Nineteenth Century

Sarah Grimké (1792-1873) was born to a wealthy family in Charleston, South Carolina. In the 1820s she and her younger sister Angelina became Quakers and moved to Philadelphia, where both became outspoken abolitionists and feminists. Here, in a famous book of eyewitness accounts of slavery that circulated widely in the pre–Civil War North, she testifies to some of what she saw as a young woman, which turned her against slavery forever.

A punishment dreaded more by the slaves than whipping, unless it is unusually severe, is one invented by a female acquaintance of mine in Charleston — I heard her say so with much satisfaction. It is standing on one foot and holding the other in the hand. Afterwards it was improved upon, and a strap was contrived to fasten around the ankle and pass around the neck; so that the least weight of the foot resting on the strap would choke the person. The pain occasioned by this unnatural position was great; and when it continued, as it sometimes was, for an hour or more, produced intense agony. I heard this same woman say, that she had the ears of her waiting maid *slit* for some petty theft. This she told me in the presence of the girl, who was standing in the room. She often had the help-

less victims of her cruelty severely whipped, not scrupling herself to wield the instrument of torture, and with her own hands inflict severe chastisement. Her husband was less inhuman than his wife, but he was often goaded on by her to acts of great severity. In his last illness I was sent for, and watched beside his death couch. The girl on whom he had so often inflicted punishment haunted his dying hours; and when at last the king of terrors approached, he shrieked in utter agony of spirit, "Oh, the blackness of darkness, the black imps, I can see them all around me — take them away!" and amid such exclamations he expired. These persons were of one of the first families of Charleston.

develop a sense of self-worth and humanity, countering the depersonalization of bondage. This signal accomplishment was of immense importance for African Americans. It would prove to be a kind of cultural rebellion that allowed black Americans to survive the travail of slavery and minimized psychological damage. The creation of African American culture was a triumph of the human spirit.

Africa Forgotten and Reclaimed

Although they were relatively uncommon, some females were among the earliest slave arrivals in the North American mainland, and from the beginning some male slaves found mates and formed families. The resulting children, more equal in sex ratio, better adapted to the climate, and hence healthier, grew to maturity, and as the first generation of American-born, or "creole," slaves, they more easily created their own families. With the second generation of creole slaves, an indigenous slave population arose in the colonies, and by about 1715 the number of slaves born in the southern colonies outnumbered those being imported from Africa. The normative grouping of slaves in the South was then by family, and as young males and their wives now typically had children, the adults began to seek ways of recovering dimly remembered African cultural traditions.

All over the world, human societies seek ceremonial ways to ritualize the natural transitions in life — birth, puberty, marriage, death. With marriage and the common presence of children, eighteenth-century African Americans from many different cultural traditions found themselves in a strange land, lacking the ritual specialists, and even among themselves faced with a complex variety of competing memories of proper ritual. How was tradition to be recovered when there was no uniform African practice and no exact replication of Old World ingredients in the American landscape? Cultural synthesis, including the development of a so-called pidgin language, became the foundation for creating the African American way of life in the South.

When slaves found themselves stranded on plantations surrounded by other blacks who spoke mutually unintelligible African languages, their loneliness and sense of abandonment must have been almost overwhelming. The communication logjam was broken by the development of an artificial second language for all the speakers, what linguists call a *pidgin* — a language created out of words and phrases gathered from many

other languages, in this case, the multiplicity of African tongues, as well as many Spanish, English, and Portuguese words sprinkled in by slaves who had been captured, sold, or enslaved in other New World colonies. (Other pidgins emerged elsewhere in the hemisphere — Haitian Creole, for example.) The African American pidgin language had its own simplified grammar, and it was the process by which the earliest blacks began to share their thoughts and create a black community. Pidgin language was not true to any of its source languages, but it became the first language of the second generation of slaves born in the colonies. Because of the increasing presence of English and the diminishing and diluted presence of various African tongues, the pidginization process migrated toward English, eventually becoming what is known today as Black English. In isolated regions of the South, such as the sea islands of South Carolina and Georgia, where enslaved persons had less frequent contact with whites, pidginization did not go as far. The resulting dialect, known as Gullah in South Carolina and Geechee in Georgia, became the common language of the local blacks and never evolved into Black English.

The pidginization model, taking words and phrases from many sources and blending them into a new language, suggests what happened across the cultural spectrum. Imagine slaves from culturally distinct areas in Africa thrown together for the first time in the southern colonies. A man and woman form a family and have a child, and each parent knows that the birth must be ceremonially recognized. But with whose rituals? They remember different practices. And where is the ritual specialist — in the Old World, usually a wise older person — who can perform the correct rites? (Slavers would have rejected wizened ritualists and brought only young workers to the New World.) Even if the parents knew the correct ritual ingredients and their symbolic values — perhaps the feather from a bird that flew at great heights, the bark from a tree renowned for its hardness, the fur from an animal known for its cunning or speed — the flora and fauna in Virginia or South Carolina did not match that of the remembered homeland. The solution, we can hypothesize, was a blending of practices and ingredients that scrambled the parents' two cultures (and maybe snatches of English or Native American culture) and substituted American ingredients for those of the Old World. The resulting ritual would therefore not truly replicate any African one, yet would correspond to the same cultural values and purposes. It would be a New World adaptation

— partly old, partly new, partly borrowed, and partly improvised. It was a new creation, an African American cultural artifact that gave meaning and a sense of wholeness to the young slave family.

The process of creating African American cultural moorings seems to have been ongoing, so that slaves created their own communities and their own culture and did not become merely the creature of their owners. Each time enslaved people devised their own values system, developed their own cultural practices, or employed their own naming system for their children, they were making a statement about their humanity — defining themselves as individuals and not chattel property.

Historians now see a rich array of African cultural traditions reflected in subtle ways in slave basketry, music, dance, quilts, hair styles, food, naming practices, aesthetic preferences, folk tales (Uncle Remus stories, for example) and folk medicine, and religion. On the rice plantations, for example, the slaves were directed to make baskets for the harvesting and winnowing of rice. The slaves apparently learned from nearby Indians how to use the tall marsh grasses, long-leaf pine straw, and palmetto fronds, all of which were similar to materials available in portions of Africa, to make broad, flat baskets for harvest use. The patterns woven into the baskets were African. Owners saw the baskets but not the cultural transmission, and until recently neither did scholars. The quilts that slave women made had patterns that consisted of irregular rectangles, not the symmetrical pattern of the quilts made by English women. White observers commented that slaves did not know how to create lovely patterns, not understanding that the use of brightly colored rectangular patterns was a cherished African aesthetic practice.

✧ *Black Christianity*

The rise of Christianity among enslaved Americans was of great importance, and religion became and continued to be one of blacks' major refuges from the dehumanizing tendencies of slavery and later of segregation. In the earliest days of slavery, whites saw Africans' presumed "paganism" as a justification for enslaving them. But when some slaves either converted to Christianity in the seventeenth-century South or could show that, before being sold into the colonies, they had spent some time in England and had been baptized, colonial courts freed them upon the assumption that only heathens

could properly be held in bondage. Because this prospect threatened some whites' slave property, the law in Virginia was conveniently changed in 1667 so that "the conferring of baptism doth not alter the condition of the person as to his bondage or freedom." This did not result in massive missionary campaigns to the black laborers, although on occasion devout masters did attempt to convert their bondspeople. In the opening decades of the eighteenth century Anglican reformers in England, roused by the Reverend Thomas Bray, helped fund the Society for the Propagation of the Gospel in Foreign Parts, which emphasized missionary efforts toward the slaves in the colonial South. But these attempts were doomed to slight success because of the Anglican ministers' general contempt for the blacks, and because the emotionally austere Anglican religious services had little to attract the mostly young male slaves.

There had been many different religious beliefs among the West African cultures from which most slaves in the American South came, but several common features appeared in all traditional African religions. Apart from those who were Muslim, most animistic West Africans had a three-part conception of the supernatural, worshiping ancestral gods, nature gods, and an all-powerful but more distant omniscient divinity. Ancestral and nature gods seemed friendlier and easier to approach, while the omniscient god seemed the supernatural force to which humans should turn only in situations of absolute extremity. The nature gods often were thought to live in special places associated with water, in part no doubt because water was obviously so essential to life. Hence religious rites and practices frequently involved water. The confirmation of a religious experience was generally thought to be some kind of spiritual possession, marked by emotional ecstasy. These common attitudes toward religious life were shared by many enslaved persons in the South. (Some slaves came from Islamic backgrounds, but they were always too small and scattered a minority to reestablish the communities essential to maintaining Islamic life. Other Africans came with memories of a Catholic faith that had been introduced into their homeland by Portuguese missionaries, and aspects of this Catholic tradition — as with the Islamic — lingered for several generations in the eighteenth-century South.)

By the mid-eighteenth century the increasing prominence of slave families and the resultant willingness to discover a ceremonial and religious dimension to their lives meant that the growing slave population in the South was receptive to a hybrid of Christian and Afri-

A Secret Slave Prayer Meeting Beyond their suspicious owners' eyes, slaves gathered on plantations for their own religious services, presided over by charismatic preachers—themselves drawn from the slave community. Here they could worship as they thought fit, praying for strength to bear the burdens of slavery and for deliverance from bondage.

can religious appeals. At the same time, religious developments in the white society were paving the way for a remarkable growth of evangelical Christianity among southerners that would also prove highly attractive to enslaved persons.

For more than two decades following the mid-1740s, three successive waves of evangelical church growth occurred in the southern colonies: the Presbyterians came first, then followed by the Baptists and finally by the Methodists. The latter two groups in particular appealed to the poorer whites: Their lay ministers believed they were called to spread the gospel to all persons, especially the poor and forlorn, and their sermons and services were noticeable for their emotional abandon as people shouted, cried, and sank to

the floor "stricken" by conviction of sin. Baptism, either by sprinkling with water or full immersion in a pond or stream, figured prominently in the services, and the devout spoke and shouted of Jesus, the Holy Spirit, and the powerful role of God the Father who answered all prayers and was sufficient for all emergencies. This three-part conception of the holy, this emotional spiritual possession, this respect for an all-powerful Jehovah, this prominent use of water in the ritual of baptism — all this resonated with traditional

Slave Spirituality: "Lay Dis Body Down"
This slave "spiritual" speaks for itself.

I know moon-rise, I know star-rise
   I lay dis body down.
I walk in de moonlight, I walk in de starlight
   To lay dis body down.
I walk in de graveyard,
I walk troo de graveyard,
   To lay dis body down.

I lie in de grave and stretch out my arms,
   I lay dis body down.
I go to de jedgement in de evenin' of de day
   When I lay dis body down,
An' my soul an' your soul will meet in de day
   When I lay dis body down.

African religion. Slaves hungering for a religious structure and evangelical ministers reaching out to convert those around them represented a fortuitous meeting of need and intention, as well as shared generalized conceptions of the supernatural.

African American slaves found this new kind of white Christianity attractive, and they flocked to the churches. Over and over again, white ministers wrote of the religious affections of the blacks, of their evident emotional response to sermons that often put whites to shame. Between about 1750 and 1810, the slave population in the American South made a large-scale transition to evangelical Christianity, and that religious orientation was full of import to the slave community and to the white community alike. As with whites, membership numbers are difficult to analyze for an era in which (unlike today) far more people attended church than actually belonged. But evidence suggests that most slaves were either active or passive Christians, and that the Christian worldview became dominant in the slave community — even though for many blacks (and whites) Christianity remained in uneasy tension with a range of superstitions: good-luck charms, ghosts, magic, and astrology.

By the 1830s slave Christianity found institutional expression in a variety of ways. Perhaps the majority of enslaved persons at least occasionally worshiped in what might be called biracial churches. There, slaves usually sat in the balcony or at the rear of the church, and on days with especially high attendance might crowd around outside the windows and doors; but they heard the same sermon as did the whites, took communion from the same minister (but following the whites), and were buried in the same cemeteries. Second, almost as many slave narratives reported attendance at secret, or at least black-only, services in the cabins or in so-called brush arbors in the woods near the plantation. Slave narratives indicate that the same blacks attended both kinds of services, and the theology seems

to have varied little although enslaved Christians surely spoke out more freely and exhibited more emotion at the brush arbors. As one slave recalled of such clandestine services, "they used to sing songs what came a-gushing up from the heart." Third were what might be called adjunct churches, black-run churches adjacent to white churches and nominally under the authority of the white minister. The adjunct church might have its own pastor, Sunday school classes, and disciplinary proceedings. Fourth were, in the cities, the completely autonomous black churches, like the African Baptist Church in Richmond, which had a seating capacity larger than any white church in the town. Free blacks sometimes controlled these independent churches, but they had many slave members.

Most rural slaves belonged to biracial churches and in them slaves may have found more nearly equal treatment than anywhere else in southern life. This semblance of equality was all the more valued for its rarity. In the disciplinary meetings in Baptist churches, for example, blacks could testify against whites, and whites were occasionally disciplined or exonerated on the basis of black testimony — this in an era when blacks could not testify against whites in the civil and criminal courts (in the seventeenth century, before the institution of slavery hardened, some slaves may have testified in court against their masters, but this was not possible in the eighteenth and nineteenth centuries). The procedures for admission to the churches by transfer of letter also were the same for whites and blacks, with the same terminology employed. Whites and blacks were often referred to with the identical use of "brother" or "sister" before their names — an equality of address unique in the South. Blacks did sit segregated in the balconies and at the rear of the church, but they probably preferred to sit together rather than amid the whites. Attendance at church was almost the only safe opportunity that slaves from a variety of plantations and farms had to visit and socialize, and these black back benches were one of the places the larger slave community was created and nurtured. Whites were evidently unaware of the community-building in progress under their noses on Sunday, but this was only one way in which black Christians used the opportunity of worship to create their own brand of Christianity.

White ministers appear regularly to have addressed a specific portion of their sermons to the slaves in the congregation, much like special children's sermons today. Perhaps the minister paused, either at the beginning or near the end of the service, to say something like "And now a word for our black brothers and sisters." One can almost see the black worshipers roll their eyes back and sigh — here it comes — as the minister uttered some words about how slaves should obey their masters. But enslaved worshipers seem to have expected these condescending words, to have discounted them with disdain, and endured them because also in the church service they heard the full sermon and gospel. Slaves ignored the heavy-handed message of social control and absorbed the news of salvation from sin and spiritual empowerment. Certain themes took on added importance for the enslaved worshipers: the concept of Jesus as friend, the story of Moses leading the enslaved Israelites out of bondage, the concept of just rewards in the afterlife, when devout slaves would be in heaven and cruel white masters in hell. Religion provided an arena far larger than the plantation in which slaves were ultimately judged by a just and forgiving God rather than a self-serving owner.

Over and over again slaves heard the message that in God's eyes all are equal, and while white preachers may have meant this abstractly, slave listeners took it to heart. Such messages gave slaves a sense of self-worth, offered a means for moral improvement and the feelings of approval and contentment such self-mastery promoted, gave meaning to life, and suggested that in the end devout slaves would prevail over their earthly masters. Religion also helped create a sense of special community. It provided avenues for leadership: There were black ministers, blacks known for their ability to pray, and black singers who in their spirituals inspired all their hearers and brought a proud sense of accomplishment. Religion also taught how to lessen the tensions and very human disagreements that erupted between individual slaves on a plantation or in a neighborhood. The positive functions of Christianity were manifest in the slave community, and enslaved Christians found a purpose for their lives and even a joy in

their everyday living of it that offered solace against the inhumanity inherent in their bondage.

✣ Slave Rebellion

Rebellion is another very complex aspect of slavery in the Old South, and it too needs to be understood as a spectrum of behaviors: at one end, armed insurrection; at the other end, passive resignation. No slave was always at the same point on the spectrum. A supposedly resigned slave could be driven to various forms of active rebellion by outrageous behavior, and many tended to move in either direction along the spectrum in response to specific treatment. Slaves developed consummate skills at hiding their true emotions from whites. Charles C. Jones, a white minister, was acute enough to admit that "Persons live and die in the midst of Negroes and know comparatively little of their character. . . . [they] are one thing before the whites, and another before their own color."

Most black resistance took the form not of physical insurrection, but of a more subtle, nuanced kind of cultural or psychological resistance that prevented the complete internalization of white expectations. When slaves held on to portions of their own culture or created new forms of African American culture, they were resisting simply becoming what the white owner wanted them to be or become. When they persisted in their own aesthetic preferences about quilts or music or naming their children, they were making a statement about their own value and self-determination. When their Christianity allowed them to value themselves and see that they were valued in the sight of God, they escaped the most dehumanizing tendencies of bondage. The rise of the black family and the efflorescence of black culture represented a profound resistance to the institution of slavery.

Frequently white owners had no idea about the ways that slaves found to escape depersonalization. For example, owners often gave their worn-out, out-of-fashion, or outgrown clothing to their slaves, and then ridiculed them for the way they utilized these hand-me-downs: a brightly colored vest worn without "matching" coat or shirt, a colored pocket sewn on a jacket, silky sleeves attached to an otherwise drab shirt, a patch of sheen here and there. Whites read the result as comical. What slaves were doing was disassembling — deconstructing — the masters' clothes and reassembling them in their own fashion to add a bit of color or style or individuality to their own wardrobe.

$150 REWARD

RANAWAY from the subscriber, on the night of the 2d instant, a negro man, who calls himself *Henry May*, about 22 years old, 5 feet 6 or 8 inches high, ordinary color, rather chunky built, bushy head, and has it divided mostly on one side, and keeps it very nicely combed; has been raised in the house, and is a first rate dining-room servant, and was in a tavern in Louisville for 18 months. I expect he is now in Louisville trying to make his escape to a free state, (in all probability to Cincinnati, Ohio.) Perhaps he may try to get employment on a steamboat. He is a good cook, and is handy in any capacity as a house servant. Had on when he left, a dark cassinett coatee, and dark striped cassinett pantaloons, new---he had other clothing. I will give $50 reward if taken in Louisvill; 100 dollars if taken one hundred miles from Louisville in this State, and 150 dollars if taken out of this State, and delivered to me, or secured in any jail so that I can get him again.   **WILLIAM BURKE.**

Bardstown, Ky., September 3d, 1838.

A Runaway Slave, 1838   This advertisement gives full particulars about a slave, trained as a house servant and tavern worker, who is suspected of fleeing to Louisville, Kentucky. His owner thinks that he is looking for work on a steamship or for a chance to escape across the Ohio River to freedom in Cincinnati.

They were using pieces of the hand-me-down clothing not to copy their owners but to create a sense of their distinct personality. In the sense of the aphorism that "clothes make the man," slaves were taking what the whites gave them and rearranging it, reconceiving it, and refashioning it to make a statement about their individuality. Here again was a kind of resistance to the inhumanity of slavery right under the owners' noses, but the whites never understood it.

Yet such cultural resistance was not all that occurred. Slaves did find physical ways to fight back. They could organize a work slowdown; they could break tools or let mules escape so that plowing was impossible the next morning; they could "accidentally" chop down a cotton plant. Barns or sheds mysteriously burned; provisions unaccountably disappeared from storehouses or smokehouses. Slaves occasionally ran away, usually not to escape to freedom in the North (which would mean never seeing family and loved ones again) but to protest behavior the slave deemed inappropriate, and such flight was common enough that owners did not even advertise for the runaway unless he or she had been absent for several weeks. Such temporary runaways usually stayed nearby, perhaps hiding out in the woods or in a barn, and the other slaves would slip the runaway food. Sometimes such runaways were going to visit loved ones who had been previously sold several miles distant. Owners came to see this form of running away as just expected slippage in the system, but for those slaves seeking this momentary escape, it provided a way to get back at an owner, to make a statement, to visit relatives sold away.

Then there were some occasions where slaves were driven to the extreme of lashing out at cruel owners, striking them with their fists, a tool, or a weapon. In the seventeenth and eighteenth centuries such slaves may have poisoned their owners, but this method seems to have lapsed. Desperate or angered slaves sometimes fled to escape slavery, but the likelihood of success was small. The total number, mostly from the border states, who successfully escaped north via the Underground Railway is in the low thousands, contrary to legend and myth that exaggerate the impact. On a handful of

Confessions of Nat Turner   After his attempt to lead a slave uprising was defeated and he was arrested, Nat Turner was interviewed by Thomas R. Gray, a southern physician, and out of this interview came this book. It described how Turner had taken an eclipse of the sun as a sign that "I should arise and prepare myself, and slay my enemies with their own weapons."

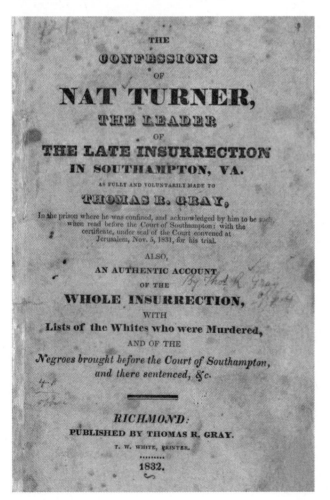

occasions — in 1739 with the Stono Rebellion in South Carolina, in 1795 and again in 1811 in the Pointe Coupée region of Louisiana, and in 1831 in Southampton County, Virginia, with the Nat Turner revolt — there were armed insurrections involving several dozens of slaves, but these protests were brutally suppressed by whites, with many non-participating slaves killed in the aftermath. And the rebellions may have been in response to particular incidents that angered the slaves instead of a planned attack against the entire system of slavery. As a result, in the American South, unlike the Caribbean and Brazil, there was no tradition of successful slave rebellions. Moreover, the American South, unlike other areas where slavery prevailed, lacked an isolated interior to which successful slave rebels could flee to establish independent "maroon" communities that stood as a symbol to other slaves of alternatives to bondage. In the southern states, the interior was filled with whites or Indians who were only too glad to capture runaways, either for their own use or to be returned for a reward. There were small maroon communities of escaped slaves in some of the remote, swampy regions of the Deep South, and larger numbers of slaves escaped to freedom in Florida when it was under Spanish and then British control, eventually intermarrying there with Creeks and forming the Seminole tribe. Still, armed insurrection was more a vague fear in white minds than an active possibility for most southern slaves. Cultural resistance usually brought better results, and explosive pressure occasionally could be released by temporary running away or in acts like sabotage that did not threaten the entire slave community with harsh reprisals. The relative absence of armed slave insurrections in the Old South is not an indicator that the system was benign.

CONCLUSION: THE STARK ANOMALY OF SLAVERY

For a nation that prided itself on equality and freedom, slavery, with its denial of all basic freedoms, was a stark anomaly. White southerners struggled to defend the institution and found in the Bible and in their insistence that blacks were a kind of permanent children beliefs and rationalizations that eased their consciences. Blacks saw the contradictions between ideal and practice. "No one who has not been in slavery," wrote one former slave, "knows the real curse of it." They worked to salvage their sense of humanity from an institution that legally defined them as property, and they devised a whole set of actions, behaviors, patterns of dissimilitude, and alternate value-systems that allowed them largely to survive psychologically intact. Their creation and preservation of their own culture, their skillful coping with life in extreme conditions, their understanding of their moral and religious worth, even superiority, represents a victory of humanity over inhumanity.

SUGGESTED READING

Ira Berlin, *Many Thousands Gone: The First Two Centuries of Slavery in North America* (1998). The best modern synthesis, and a very interpretative one, of the evolution of the institution of slavery, alert to regional variations.

Ira Berlin, *Slaves Without Masters: The Free Negro in the Antebellum South* (1974). A pioneering synthesis of the free black experience, with careful attention to both chronology and region.

Clement Eaton, *The Growth of Southern Civilization, 1790-1860* (1961). An older classic of southern history that in its social and cultural sweep has not been superseded.

Drew Gilpin Faust, *James Henry Hammond and the Old South: A Design for Mastery* (1982). A masterful biography that illuminates the culture, society, and politics of antebellum South Carolina.

Elizabeth Fox-Genovese, *Within the Plantation Household: Black and White Women of the Old South* (1988). An influential interpretation of southern women, with an emphasis on class and race.

Eugene D. Genovese, *Roll, Jordan, Roll: The World the Slaves Made* (1974). The most influential history of slaves and their culture: stunningly researched, broad in scope, and vigorously interpretative.

Suzanne Lebsock, *The Free Women of Petersburg: Status and Culture in a Southern Town, 1784-1860* (1984). A well-written, impressively researched, and analytically sophisticated interpretation of urban women in the South.

Ann Patton Malone, *Sweet Chariot: Slave Family and Household Structure in Nineteenth-Century Louisiana* (1992). The best study of the varieties of slave family life.

Gavin Wright, *The Political Economy of the Cotton South: Households, Markets, and Wealth in the Nineteenth Century* (1978). An indispensable study of the South that extends beyond the minority of whites who owned slaves; it explains how the society worked on many levels.

Bertram Wyatt-Brown, *Southern Honor: Ethics and Behavior in the Old South* (1982). A wide-ranging analysis of an influential cultural ideal in the region, at least with regard to white men.

SUGGESTIONS FOR FURTHER READING

John W. Blassingame, *The Slave Community: Plantation Life in the Antebellum South* (1972).

John B. Boles, *Black Southerners, 1619-1869* (1982).

John B. Boles, ed., *Masters and Slaves in the House of the Lord: Race and Religion in the American South, 1740-1870* (1988).

Charles C. Bolton, *Poor Whites of the Antebellum South: Tenants and Laborers in Central North Carolina and Northeast Mississippi* (1994).

Orville Vernon Burton, *In My Father's House Are Many Mansions: Family and Community in Edgefield, South Carolina* (1985).

Jane Turner Censer, *North Carolina Planters and Their Children, 1800-1860* (1984).

John Patrick Daly, *When Slavery Was Called Freedom: Evangelicalism, Proslavery, and the Causes of the Civil War* (2002).

Drew Gilpin Faust, *A Sacred Circle: The Dilemma of the Intellectual in the Old South, 1840-1869* (1977).

Lacy K. Ford, Jr., *Origins of Southern Radicalism: The South Carolina Upcountry, 1800-1860* (1988).

Eugene D. Genovese, *The Political Economy of Slavery: Studies in the Economy and Society of the Slave South* (1965).

Michele K. Gillespie, *Free Labor in an Unfree World: White Artisans in Slaveholding Georgia, 1789-1860* (2000).

Sally E. Hadden, *Slave Patrols: Law and Violence in Virginia and the Carolinas* (2001).

Steven Hahn, *The Roots of Southern Populism: Yeoman Farmers and the Transformation of the Georgia Upcountry, 1850-1890* (1983).

Walter Johnson, *Soul by Soul: Life Inside the Antebellum Slave Market* (1999).

Charles W. Joyner, *Down by the Riverside: A South Carolina Slave Community* (1984).

Jan Lewis, *The Pursuit of Happiness: Family and Values in Jefferson's Virginia* (1983).

Donald G. Matthews, *Religion in the Old South* (1977).

Stephanie McCurry, *Masters of Small Worlds: Yeoman Households, Gender Relations, and the Political Culture of the Antebellum South Carolina Low Country* (1995).

Sally G. McMillen, *Southern Women: Black and White in the Old South* (1992).

Christopher Morris, *Becoming Southern: The Evolution of a Way of Life, Warren County and Vicksburg, Mississippi, 1770-1860* (1995).

Albert J. Raboteau, *Slave Religion: The "Invisible Institution" in the Antebellum South* (1978).

Marie Jenkins Schwartz, *Born in Bondage: Growing Up Enslaved in the Antebellum South* (2000).

Mark M. Smith, *Mastered by the Clock: Time, Slavery, and Freedom in the American South* (1998).

Mitchell Snay, *The Gospel of Disunion: Religion and Separatism in the Antebellum South* (1993).

Randy J. Sparks, *On Jordan's Stormy Banks: Evangelicalism in Mississippi, 1773-1876* (1994).

Brenda E. Stevenson, *Life in Black and White: Family and Community in the Slave South* (1996).

Steven M. Stowe, *Intimacy and Power in the Old South: Ritual in the Lives of the Planters* (1987).

Elizabeth R. Varon, *We Mean to Be Counted: White Women and Politics in Antebellum Virginia* (1998).

12 The Coming of Democratic Politics
Andrew Jackson and the Second Party System, 1824-1844

FROM GRADE SCHOOL, American students have learned to think of folksy Andy Jackson as a man of the people, the president who somehow ushered in the so-called Age of the Common Man. Just over six feet tall, extremely thin, with a pointed nose and broad brow topped by a mane of reddish hair (gray by the time he became president), Jackson had a violent temper that only with difficulty did he keep in harness while in the White House. Occasionally political events and politicians triggered his passion, and Jackson would vigorously squelch whatever offended him. And he was extraordinarily sensitive about any hint of scandal associated with his wife. Jackson had married Rachel Robards in 1791, actually before her divorce from another man had become final. Because under the law Jackson could not legally be married to Rachel before the divorce had become final, legal sticklers and political enemies sometimes charged them with living in an adulterous relationship — but if Jackson ever got wind of such talk, the result could be explosive.

In his early roisterous days he earned the reputation of a brawler, and he never backed down from what he considered a slight to his honor. As Jackson said of himself, "I was born for a storm and a calm does not suit me." In 1806 Jackson got into an argument with Charles Dickinson over a horse race, and Dickinson insulted Rachel. Jackson challenged Dickinson to a duel. Knowing how good a shot his opponent was, Jackson wore an extremely loose coat to mislead Dickinson's aim. Dickinson fired and hit Jackson in the chest, but Jackson stayed on his feet, took his bead, pulled the

Andrew Jackson This portrait, made for wide distribution, admiringly depicts Jackson as a wise and powerful statesman — with his sword close at hand. Jackson was both the most admired and the most hated American in public life in his day.

trigger — and the pistol did not fire! By the rules of the duel, this did not count as a shot, so Dickinson was required to stand until Jackson got off a real shot. Coolly, Jackson recocked and shot Dickinson dead.

Again in 1813, Jackson, while serving as the second to a man dueling with Thomas Hart Benton's brother Jesse, took offense at Benton's comments toward him. Jackson physically attacked Thomas Benton over this perceived insult, only to have Jesse shoot Jackson in the arm and shoulder (the bullet in the arm was removed during Jackson's presidency). Yet this same tough old soldier and Indian fighter, known popularly as "Old Hickory," "the General," and "the Hero," could break down in tears when enemies insulted the memory of his mother or beloved wife.

Obviously Jackson was no learned gentleman in the mold of Thomas Jefferson or James Madison, but instead a son of the rough-and-ready frontier. The era named after him, it is now widely believed, was a time of increasingly democratic politics, in part inspired by his efforts and personality. Yet Jackson the man and the Age of Jackson are both paradoxical: Jackson was a

wealthy slaveholding planter and an autocratic leader who bristled at opposition. Certainly no one called him Andy to his face. His election was more the result of democratizing tendencies in American politics than a cause of it. Still, by sheer force of personality and by being a lightning rod for political controversy, he so dominated the two decades after 1824 that the label "Age of Jackson" accurately stamps the period. Even Henry Clay, no friend of Jackson, wrote at the end of his administration that the president had "swept over the Government, during the last eight years, like a tropical tornado." The mythic Jackson seemed to overwhelm the real man, and that partly explains his influence on the times. Powerful cultural and economic forces helped reshape national politics, intensifying partisan identification, increasing voter turnout, and infusing politics with a new moral urgency. During these years we can in retrospect see bubbling beneath the surface of events the issues, tensions, and fears that would erupt to cause intense sectional controversy and — three decades later — a long and bitter Civil War.

THE DEMOCRATIZATION OF AMERICAN POLITICS

The federal Constitution and the first state constitutions had acknowledged that in some profound way the people were sovereign. The people's voice, expressed through the vote, was, however, rather muffled. Nowhere, of course, could women or slaves vote in 1789; in most states the few free blacks were also barred, and nearly every state imposed property or tax-paying requirements even on free white male voters. In every state wealthy merchants and (in the South) slaveholders dominated both politics and office holding. Kinship ties, personal relationships, and financial influence weighed heavily on how men voted, especially given the practice in nearly every state of what was called *viva voce* voting, or voting by voice. By this method the voters assembled before the electoral judges and walked up one by one, standing before an official who checked the voting list, and announced their vote aloud, with all onlookers — including the local men of power and prestige and perhaps the candidates themselves — looking on and taking note. It was easy for powerful men to exert influence, and understandable that poorer men sometimes felt either awed or pressured into voting as the local bigwigs wanted. Low rates of participation suggest that they often tried to evade the whole business by staying away.

All in all, politics in the United States was more democratic than anywhere else in the world at the time, but it failed to meet modern standards or even long satisfy the voters of the young nation. Between the 1790s and 1821, several original states (Connecticut, Maryland, Massachusetts, New York, and South Carolina) modified their suffrage requirements, scaling back property requirements and often only assessing a minimal poll tax. The new states of the West led the way in providing for universal white male suffrage, beginning with Kentucky (which entered the Union in 1792), Tennessee (1796), and Ohio (1803). In fact, none of the eight new states that were formed between 1796 and 1821 had property requirements for voting. As the population of these newer states surged, many older states liberalized their rules for voting in a futile effort to stem the westward migration of voters. Westward migration also disrupted traditional hierarchies in established eastern communities and raised the problem of whether hierarchies should be acknowledged at all in the new communities. Leadership came to be seen as a right to be earned, not inherited. Those who were carving out new communities in the West learned to trust their own abilities more and became less willing to defer to others. The use of the paper ballot rather than the voice vote also became widespread as a means of minimizing the influence of the powerful and wealthy, although even ballots did not render voting altogether secret.

Politics was being democratized in other ways besides increasing the number of voters. Even contemporary shifts in religious thought and practice away from the idea that sinners could do nothing about changing the state of their souls and toward the newer assumption that they had an active role in choosing to be saved — the whole point of revivalistic preaching — had a political consequence. If most people were wicked sinners predestined to hell, as traditional Protestant theology assumed, how could they be entrusted with governing the community? But if people were able to make a decision about their eternal life, and could choose to reform their earthly lives, were they not also able to make valid decisions about mere political matters? Political democratization influenced the direction of religious change, but the influence worked in both directions. The unfolding Market Revolution also suggested that if ordinary people could on their own make reasonable decisions about selling their crops and purchasing necessary goods, then they had no need to defer to political leadership by a ruling elite.

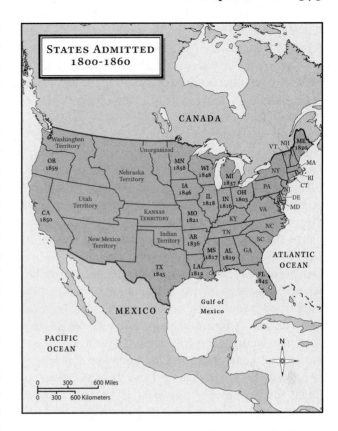

Another result of the increasing democratization was that many more political offices became elective rather than appointive. As the electoral college initially was intended to work, state legislatures chose the presidential electors who would name their choice for president in a private meeting. Ordinary citizens therefore did not vote for presidential candidates or even for electors pledged to a candidate. Yet the party struggles after 1800 gave impetus to allowing voters to choose pledged presidential electors. By 1824, all but a half-dozen states had democratized the electoral college to this extent, and only South Carolina resisted after 1832 by having its legislature alone choose its presidential electors. This meant that, far more directly than previously, the popular vote determined the outcome of presidential contests.

❧ The End of the Virginia Dynasty

James Monroe was the last of the Founding Fathers to hold the presidency. Like his predecessors Jefferson and Madison, he had served as secretary of state before ascending to the presidency. He was the last president to wear knee britches, and on special occasions he donned his Revolutionary War uniform. He embodied the politics of the past, and everyone knew that, following Washington's precedent, he would not seek a third term in 1824. But who would be his successor? Now that the Federalist Party was dead, the Republicans had a variety of potential leaders but no automatic choice, no clear mandate — and certainly no one who had been a Revolutionary leader.

The Virginia Dynasty of presidents, which had begun with Washington himself, was ending. Although only Jefferson's Democratic-Republicans triumphed, the party's unity had become unglued. As the nation's population moved westward and economic interests diversified, politicians grew impatient with the established custom of having a handful of party leaders in Congress — the "caucus" — pick a practically obvious person as the Democratic-Republican candidate for the presidency. Such an undemocratic selection might have seemed reasonable in an earlier political age, but now with a number of potential candidates available, and with the role of the people in the political process being magnified by the newer conception of party, some method other than a backroom caucus ought to be employed to choose the people's leader. Later, in 1831, an ephemeral protest group, the Anti-Masonic Party, would come up with the idea of a party presidential convention, whose delegates were elected precisely for the purpose of democratically choosing a party nominee,[1] and this would become the accepted technique for choosing presidential candidates. But no clear means were at hand in 1824.

It used to be fashionable to call Monroe's administration the "Era of Good Feelings" because in it the Federalist Party practically died, leaving the Republicans (who had dropped *Jeffersonian* from their label) seemingly the only political party on the scene. In fact, Monroe's second term was dominated by political maneuvering as several able would-be Republican presidential contenders angled for election, and feelings got to be quite bad. When the usual congressional caucus met and chose William H. Crawford of Georgia, only a quarter of the congressmen participated. Crawford had a distinguished career in government; he had been a cabinet officer, American minister to France, and, as a supporter of limited government and states' rights, was supported by Thomas Jefferson and much of the Virginia establishment. But in the midst of the election campaign he suffered a debilitating stroke that essentially eliminated him as the front-runner.

Crawford, the caucus candidate, faced several rivals,

1. For anti-Masonry, see below, pp. 399-400.

each of whom could depend upon strong support from his own section of the country. First out of the chute came "Gallant Harry of the West" — Kentucky's Henry Clay, vivacious, a master of legislative leadership and compromise, and the proponent of the vigorously nationalistic "American System" of canals, turnpikes, and protective tariffs. Clay expected that his advocacy of "internal improvements" would cement his support in the West, while his proposal for funding them by tariff revenues would garner the votes of eastern manufacturing interests. Clay envisioned southern cotton and western grain flowing to the urban manufacturing centers of the Northeast, while goods manufactured there flowed back to growing markets in the South and West, as a result diminishing sectional rivalries. The second regional candidate, John Quincy Adams — brilliant, reserved, an experienced diplomat and politician from Massachusetts, and son of the second president — was New England's favorite son. Third, in the early stages of the contest, John C. Calhoun put himself forward. A rigorously intellectual former congressman from South Carolina and currently Monroe's secretary of war, Calhoun rivaled Crawford for southern support. But soon the ever-logical and ambitious Calhoun realized that he had a lock on the vice presidency and calculated that from it he could later gain the presidency, so he dropped out of the presidential contest and made sure he won the second office.

These jockeying Washington "insider" politicians suddenly got a rude shock. Out of the West came charging Andrew Jackson, the hero of the Battle of New Orleans yet widely considered a legislative lightweight, hardly taken seriously at first by his more accomplished competitors. Jackson was known in the western states as an inveterate Indian fighter, the man who had pacified much of the Old Southwest for white settlement. Critics saw him as a hothead, a man who had killed an opponent in a duel, and a tavern brawler who had married his wife under questionable circumstances. (Thomas Jefferson, remembering Jackson in the Senate in 1797, said of him in 1824: "His passions are no doubt cooler now . . . but he is a dangerous man.") Even his early supporters had considered him a mere stalking horse for their own political interests. But Jackson proved to be an astute politician, a man who sensed how to position himself as a national military hero, an opponent of internal improvements, a champion of "the common man," and a spokesman for the democratic West. He boasted of being untainted by the wheeling and dealing of the established politicians.

Yet much of Jackson's image was the result of sleight of hand, for this so-called representative of the common man had prospered mightily as a lawyer, land speculator, and cotton planter, and at "the Hermitage" — his plantation near Nashville, Tennessee — he owned more than a hundred slaves.

Promoted by close advisers as the true spokesman of the Age of Democracy, in the state-by-state voting for presidential electors Jackson outscored Adams, Clay, and Crawford. (Calhoun ran as the sole candidate for the vice presidency.) Jackson's popular votes (153,544) and electoral votes (99) topped those of the next leading candidate, Adams, with 108,740 popular votes and 84 electoral votes. But in this four-way race, Jackson lacked the electoral-college majority necessary for outright victory. The Twelfth Amendment to the Constitution provided that in such a case the House of Representatives would choose the president from among the top three winners of electoral votes. Despite being incapacitated, Crawford had come in third with 41 electoral votes, eliminating Clay with his 37 electoral votes. But as Speaker of the House, Clay would play a major role in the House's choice of the next president. Crawford's condition put him out of contention, bringing the choice down to Adams or Jackson. Clay approved of Adams's forthright nationalism and saw in his presidency an opportunity to weld together the Northeast and the West; he probably also foresaw that such an alliance would keep alive his own unextinguished presidential aspirations. In addition, Clay felt a genuine contempt for Jackson's political inexperience and his military background, remarking that he could not conceive how "killing 2500 Englishmen at New Orleans" qualified the general for the "difficult and complicated duties of the Chief Magistracy." After a brief conference with Adams, Clay put his legislative prowess to work for him, and the House subsequently chose Adams as president.

Ꝫ President John Quincy Adams

One of Adams's first acts in office was to appoint Clay his secretary of state. It seemed a logical choice. Clay had received valuable foreign experience by serving with Adams as one of the American commissioners at the Ghent peace negotiations in 1814. The high-principled Adams almost certainly did not dangle this position before Clay earlier in exchange for the Speaker's support in the House's presidential decision. Yet Jackson had garnered the most popular and electoral votes,

only to lose the presidency, and he and his supporters immediately saw a payoff for a stolen presidency — a "corrupt bargain," as Jackson labeled it, that had snatched the election from him and the plurality of American voters. So Adams entered the White House under a cloud of suspicion. Jackson, easy to anger and slow (if ever) to forget, began almost immediately to maneuver for what he considered his rightful office in the next election, 1828.

John Quincy Adams was probably the most learned, cosmopolitan man ever elected president after Thomas Jefferson. But he was decidedly the wrong man for the times in this the dawning age of mass politics. The idea of aggressively seeking election was anathema to Adams: "If the country wants my services," he once said loftily, "she must ask for them." Yet under his very nose Jackson's supporters began organizing campaigns in every state to win popular support for Old Hickory, and in the 1826 midterm elections Representatives friendly to Jackson captured control of Congress, further complicating Adams's presidency. Moreover, in an age of growing sectional interests, Adams was a confirmed and visionary nationalist. He proposed congressional funding for a great national university, a national astronomical observatory, scientific expeditions of all sorts, a far-sighted system of internal improvements, all to promote what the Constitution called "the common welfare." Given his lack of a popular mandate and his midterm repudiation, all his proposals to Congress were politically dead on arrival.

Adams saw internal improvements as a logical way to bind the West to the East, facilitating the interchange of agricultural and manufactured goods. To Andrew Jackson, such schemes came too close to Henry Clay's "American System." The general branded federally funded internal improvements as waste and an unconstitutional expansion of national government, and his attack on Adams's proposals found favor elsewhere. The state of New York, for example, also opposed Adams's program because it had spent its own funds to dig the Erie Canal, which opened just as the president introduced his proposals. Naturally, New York saw no need to spend federal money so that other states could compete with it for western commerce. Martin Van Buren, one of the state's chief politicians, led the New York opposition and promoted Jackson's candidacy.

Then Adams unintentionally upset southerners, already edgy about the future of slavery following the recent controversy over Missouri's entry into the nation and a presumed 1822 slave revolt in Charleston supposedly led by Denmark Vesey and that never happened (and probably had been only a figment of the imagination of worried whites). Adams, supported by Clay, urged that the United States send delegates to a conference of newly independent Western Hemisphere nations in Panama. Southerners argued that the presence of United States delegates would imply recognition of the black republic of Haiti, as the former French colony of St. Domingue was now known after a successful slave rebellion. In all these issues Adams might have gained support had he been willing to compromise and build new coalitions. Yet intellectually able though he was, Adams was clumsy in politics, and he rejected on grounds of principle the give-and-take of bargaining. He thought the mere rationality of his policies would sell them to the nation. But times had changed. The simultaneous death on July 4, 1826 — the fiftieth anniversary of the signing of the Declaration of Independence — of Thomas Jefferson and John Adams, the two principal authors of the document, seemed to many Americans an awesome and providential sign that one era had ended and another begun. A new political world was being born. The broadening of the franchise had dropped the level of policy debate and made image more important than substance. John Quincy Adams, like his father a reserved, formal man, lacked the common touch, and he found himself thrust unprepared into the Age of the Common Man.

***Politics in an Oyster House* by Robert Caton Woodville**   This humorous American painting from 1848 comments on (many) Americans' love for political debate, which was in high gear during the Jacksonian era. The older gentleman seems less than happy to be receiving his tablemate's harangue, but he endures it patiently.

❧ *Martin Van Buren and the Rise of the Political Party*

The primary architect of a new conception of political parties was a young New York politician named Martin Van Buren, the son of a tavern-keeper in the Dutch-dominated hamlet of Kinderhook. Despite his lack of family connections or wealth, Van Buren rose in state political circles thanks to his remarkable amiability and political shrewdness. ("The Little Magician," many would call him.) When the ambitious Van Buren entered state politics, powerful cliques of great families controlled the scene, and aristocrats like De Witt Clinton ruled the state like a personal fiefdom, doling out patronage on the basis of personal loyalty rather than loyalty to ideas or policies. Van Buren conceived of the political party as the voice and agency of the people, a method of identifying, representing, and expressing the popular will.

Thus understood, parties derived their power from the people, and it followed that party leaders were bound to obey the dictates of the party. In theory, such parties stood for the interests of a broad cross-section of the populace. Unlike European parties that were responsible to aristocratic cliques, and unlike older conceptions of Anglo-American parties that represented narrow interests, the new idea of the party was a means of embodying democratic intent — expressing the voice of the people. And, particularly after the Missouri Crisis of 1819 had threatened a North-South rending of the Union, the idea of broad parties binding people together across a wide range of issues seemed an antidote to what Van Buren called "geographical differences founded on local instincts or what is worse, prejudices between free and slaveholding states." Well-disciplined parties could safely channel political differences, and party organizations, newspapers, and spokespeople could use such differences to weld together the kind of group identification that mobilized voters and influenced government policies. As a state legislator and then New York State attorney general before he went to Washington in 1821 as a Senator, Van Buren revolutionized his state's politics. In Monroe's last years as president, the Little Magician prepared to bring what became known as mass political participation to the national arena, a process that would eventually yield what historians now call the Second Party System. Van Buren recognized that political parties were essential to a democracy, and that insight — more than the rather dismal results of his own presidential administration (1837-1841) — makes him a great figure in American political history.

❧ *The Election of Andrew Jackson*

The "Old Hero," Andrew Jackson, had already proven himself a master of the new politics of symbolism. As Indian fighter, British basher, enemy of big government, and straight-talking representative of the plainfolk pioneers of the West, he took the nation by storm. Martin Van Buren, who understood the new style of politics better than anyone else at the time, served as Jackson's campaign manager. Van Buren saw to it that in countless towns and village crossroads, Jackson supporters — who shortened their party name from Democratic-Republican to Democratic — came to identify their

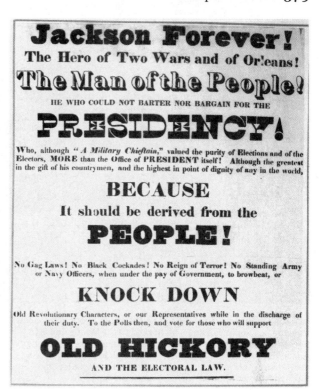

Jackson for President   This poster from the 1828 election sums up the case for Jackson as the incorruptible people's candidate for president. Notice the scornful allusions to the "corrupt bargain" by which Jackson's 1824 rival, John Quincy Adams, is said to have unworthily gained the presidency.

candidate (a veritable force of nature, they called him), with freedom and equality of opportunity (for whites only) and hundred-proof democracy. In Pennsylvania, where an embryonic party machinery had already been created and the caucus method of choosing a presidential candidate had been rejected, the popularly elected convention delegates unanimously picked Old Hickory as their presidential candidate. Jackson's party managers like Van Buren were masters of the emerging political system, and with blockbuster states like New York and Pennsylvania in their camp, Jackson's election looked certain.

Jackson supporters also used popular songs, broadsides, pamphlets, and symbols to forward their cause, and Jackson men marched in torchlight parades brandishing hickory sticks and brooms, suggesting the need to sweep Washington clean of corruption and privilege. The ditty that practically became the theme song of the campaign had been written several years before 1828 to commemorate the victory over the British at New Orleans. Jackson so appreciated the song that he had thousands of copies printed and distributed. No campaign event was complete without a rousing rendition

Jackson's Inauguration   The crowd of muddy-booted, tobacco-chewing Jackson partisans who flocked to the White House to celebrate the Hero of New Orleans's accession to the presidency shocked respectable citizens of the day and, indeed, portended the transformation of the presidency into the one office that claimed a direct mandate from the American people.

of the ballad, and when the final couplet stanza was belted out, the audience always responded with loud and enthusiastic huzzahs:

> *But Jackson, he was wide awake,*
> *And was not scared at trifles,*
> *For well he knew Kentucky's boys,*
> *With their death-dealing rifles,*
> *He led them down to cypress swamp*
> *The ground was low and mucky,*
> *There stood John Bull in martial pomp*
> *And here stood old Kentucky.*
>
> *Oh! Kentucky, the hunters of Kentucky!*
> *Oh! Kentucky, the hunters of Kentucky!*

The new style of politics was not just gimmicks and entertainment, however, for the stakes were high. Supporters of both Adams and Jackson resorted to vicious innuendo and hyperbolic charges. Jackson men sought to associate Adams (and his National Republican Party) with aristocracy and privilege at war with the interests of the average person. Consequently Adams was portrayed sipping expensive wine from golden goblets, and he was accused of wearing fancy silk underwear — imagine the contrast with manly Jackson, war hero and tamer of the West! Adams was lampooned as a rich, ef-

fete, intellectual dilettante more at home in the salon than in the halls of power; Jackson, retorted the other side, was a brute, a brawler, a cockfighter, a drunken gambler more at home in the saloon than in the legislative chamber, a deadly duelist, and a man of loose morals who had lived in adultery. The Adams forces simply believed that neither on the basis of character, nor experience, nor ability was Jackson worthy of the presidency, and hence his election should be thwarted.

Symbols became all-important in mobilizing voters. One of Jackson's supporters summed up the contest as "the *democracy* of the *country*" against the "*lordly purse-proud aristocracy.*" But the more the Adams forces portrayed Jackson as common, unsophisticated, and unlearned, the more the mass of voters identified with him. Particularly in the South and West did Jackson find appeal. Winning in those regions upwards of 80 percent of the popular vote, and 56 percent nationwide, he was swept into office in the first presidential landslide. Jackson outpolled Adams more than two to one in the electoral college (178 to 83). The people had spoken, and in Andrew Jackson democracy had found its voice. On his inaugural day, while Adams slipped unnoticed out of town, a raucous crowd of well-wishers mobbed the White House, standing on the chairs to see the Old Hero, tracking mud across the rugs and floor, pushing and shoving to get to the refreshments until the food and drink were put out on the lawn. "Ladies fainted, men were seen with bloody noses, and," reported an appalled society matron, "such a scene of confusion took place as is impossible to describe." The spectacle of unruly celebrants jumping through the White House windows to get to the cake and punch told doleful Adams supporters that a new political order had arrived. As one unhappy observed noted, "the reign of King Mob" had begun.

THE JACKSON ADMINISTRATION

Andrew Jackson's election symbolized the changes that were reworking the American political process, and as president he significantly changed the role of that office. Jackson broke the tradition of scholar-statesmen in the White House, for he was self-consciously a representative of the common man. Because he was the only official of the nation elected by a vote of all the people (that is, of all who *could* vote), Jackson saw himself as the embodiment of the nation's political will. In that capacity he believed he had both the right and the duty to be the nation's leader. He promptly reversed a tendency toward executive weakness and political passivity, thereby significantly reshaping the presidency. He used the veto more frequently than any predecessor, and in doing so he showed his independence of both Congress and the Supreme Court. He clearly dominated his cabinet and did not hesitate to change its membership to advance his policies. Jackson took strong stands on major issues that faced him, like nullification and internal improvements, and he proved to be a polarizing president. But his strongly partisan stands helped reorient politics away from local issues and toward national ones. As a powerful political figure, Jackson also followed in Jefferson's footsteps by strengthening the role of the president as party leader who set the political agenda for the party and nation. His authoritative style made it possible for political opponents to attack him as dictatorial, but his personal style allowed him to garner popular support as the people's spokesman. As one of Jackson's backers said of his ability to maintain public affection in the face of mounting criticism, "Old Hickory shines brighter the more they rub him."

The "Spoils System" and the New Presidency

During the campaign Jackson's managers and supporters had railed against government officeholders as often lazy and corrupt parasites, men who used their privileged position for private gain rather than the public good. Moreover, Jackson saw his personal foes as enemies of the people who deserved to be driven from the public coffers. Martin Van Buren, who resigned as governor of New York to become Jackson's secretary of state and chief political and policy adviser, channeled this desire to get undesirables out of office into the broader purpose of rewarding personal and political friends. This had long been the rule in state politics, and ever since Jefferson's victory over John Adams in 1801 had brought a major political shift at the federal level, removing foes and rewarding supporters had been normal procedure. In truth, the politically inept and stiffly principled John Quincy Adams had exercised so little patronage that he injured his own backers, mak-

ing Jackson's shake-up seem more radical than it really was. But in the past such partisan restaffing had been done quietly. Jackson made it high-profile policy.

Jackson gave his purge a new name — "rotation in office" — and claimed that it represented democratic government at work. No entrenched bureaucracy had a permanent hold on government, he argued, and the theoretical losses in efficiency and competency that resulted from removing experienced officeholders was negligible. In Jackson's words, "the duties of public offices" were so "plain and simple" that average men could easily perform them. As one Jackson supporter put it, "The barnacles shall be scraped clean from the ship of state; every 'traitor' must go." In fact, Jackson only removed about 10 percent of the slightly more than 10,000 civilian government employees — postmasters, collectors of customs, Navy Yard workers, and holders of similar jobs. The turnover represented only a little more than the normal that took place after the previous changes in administrations — and most of Jackson's appointees were, in affluence, education, and background, little different from those they replaced. But there was one exception: they were all friends of Jackson. Old Hickory was putting his stamp on the government. Moreover, Jackson's rhetoric about the appropriateness of average men for government positions fit a broad contemporary hostility to so-called experts. In 1830 the Jackson forces brought Francis Preston Blair from Kentucky to Washington to edit a pro-administration newspaper called the *Washington Globe,* and government workers who earned more than $1,000 annually were required to subscribe or be fired.

Of course, not all the men removed from office were incompetent or corrupt, and not all the new appointees were honest. One, Samuel Swartout, named Collector of the Port of New York, eventually sailed for Europe with more than a million stolen dollars. But claims by the pro-Adams press that Jackson had mounted a new reign of terror and indiscriminately purged good and decent officeholders were overblown. The change was primarily that Jackson now publicly acknowledged and labeled the process as democratic rotation in office; his enemies, picking up on a phrase actually used by one of Jackson's jubilant supporters ("to the victor belong the spoils"), gave the practice a name that stuck: the spoils system.

Jackson claimed to be the only nationally elected leader of all the people. As such, he believed he represented the national will. Neither Congress nor the Supreme Court nor the cabinet officers had his almost mystical connection to the body politic. His was a new conception of the presidency, enormously enhancing its leadership role and executive authority. It seemed appropriate to him, therefore, that federal workers should owe their job and allegiance to him. While he was not a man of many ideas, he knew what he believed in and pushed his positions forcefully. Except for Van Buren, his official cabinet appointees were a weak group. One critic dismissed them as "the Millennium of the Minnows." His real advisers were the insiders, called the Kitchen Cabinet, whom he assembled informally. They held approximately the same relationship to congressionally approved cabinet officers as do present-day White House advisers and staffers. Jackson felt no compunction to have their role authorized by locally elected congressmen. Both the justification of rotation in office and the use of the Kitchen Cabinet were authentic expressions of Jackson's strong personality and harbingers of a radically new conception of the American presidency — in large measure, the one to which Americans still hold. It truly is accurate to call the era ca. 1828-1844 the "Age of Jackson."

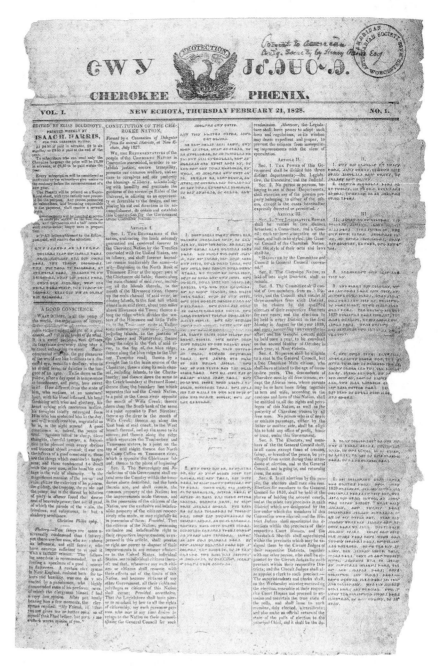

❧ Jackson's Indian Policy

The president's policy toward Native Americans reflected his innermost beliefs. Like most white settlers of the Old Southwest, Jackson felt that the Indians' desire to use their land for hunting and subsistence should yield to Anglos' hunger to spread agriculture and commerce westward. His dramatic victory over Creek warriors at Horseshoe Bend in central Alabama in 1814 — which earned him the ephithet of "Mad Dog Jackson" from the Creeks — had opened up much of the Alabama and Mississippi territories to white farmers and their slaves, while also convincing him the Indian nations were weaker than previously thought.

The *Cherokee Phoenix* On February 21, 1828, the first issue of the newspaper the *Cherokee Phoenix* was printed. It used both English and the Cherokee language, the latter in the new alphabet invented by Sequoyah. The rapid development of the Cherokee as a "modern" people, practicing white-style agriculture, handicrafts, and commerce, unnerved southern whites, who feared them as economic competitors.

The federal government's official arrangements with the native peoples took the form of treaties, not agreements. From earliest colonial times, most whites had conceded that the Indians were peoples with original claims to their land. Recognizing that, first the British authorities and later the American government believed that Indian land had to be purchased from tribal leaders before it could be opened to white settlement. Regarding the Indian tribes as sovereign nations, American officials assumed that negotiation with them must be handled by the national government, not by individual states. After all, the federal Constitution (Article I, Section 10) explicitly forbade a state from entering into "any treaty, alliance, or confederation." Jackson was never deterred by the Constitution when it did not suit him, and he had little patience with negotiating with Indians. The Creek collapse at Horseshoe Bend brought Jackson increasingly to consider Indian nationhood a farce. To him, Indians were simply individual members of tribal groups who could be dealt with by states, whose land could be purchased or claimed by state governments, and who could be persuaded or forced either to give up their cultural identity as Indians and totally accept white ways, or else to sell their lands and with government help relocate in the so-called Indian Territory west of the Mississippi River.

The issues were enormously complex. Well-meaning whites found it difficult to accept the Indians' understanding of tribal lands, which did not include the concept of private ownership. The Indians' dependence on vast hunting grounds seemed to whites an unacceptably inefficient use of the land. Whites believed that God intended fertile soils to support stable homesteads, with the fields tilled for maximum production. Indian or "savage" ways must be replaced, and in order that rapacious frontiersmen not corrupt Indians with liquor and steal their lands, the native peoples should be removed farther west into designated regions. There, white well-wishers hoped, Indians would be free from white greed long enough to adopt white attitudes toward property ownership, settled agriculture, and other essentials of Anglo civilization. In other words, the Indians could be saved only if they ceased being Indians, because the westward migration of whites was inevitable. "Who can arrest the march of our population to the West?" asked the Democratic newspaper the *Washington Globe*. "HE only, who can thrust out his arm and arrest the sun in its course. It will roll on, until stopped by the western ocean." Such were the benign if ironic assumptions behind the government policy of Indian removal, a policy originally developed by Thomas Jefferson, who sincerely believed himself a friend of the Indians. Later, whites advocated removing Indians to the West less to protect them as a people than to get to their lands.

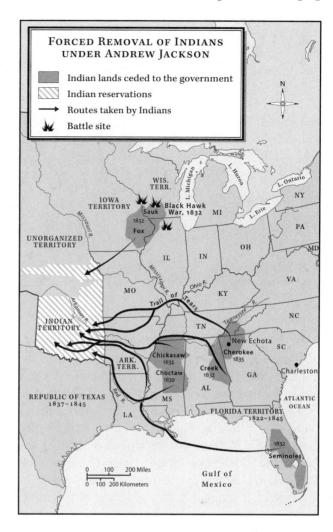

Among Indians, too, various assumptions competed about how best to respond to the pressure of white settlement and cultural imperialism. Many whites and Indians had intermarried, and all the Indian nations contained "mixed-bloods," many of them quite willing to abandon most Indian traditions and accept white ways, even if this meant selling tribal lands and moving west. But the majority of full-blooded Indians resisted complete assimilation. Most of the Indians in the South were members of five large groups, by whites commonly called the Five Civilized Tribes: the Choctaws, Cherokees, Creeks, Chickasaw, and Seminoles. Responding reluctantly to governmental incentives and public pressure, these tribes had ceded most of their lands to the federal government by 1830 and had already moved a substantial portion of their populations to the West.

Consolidating ideas and policies inherited from Jefferson and Monroe, Jackson sought to speed up the process. His first message to Congress in December

The Trail of Tears This 1850 wood engraving from an American textbook illustrates the removal of the Cherokee people to the West some twelve years earlier in 1838.

1829 laid out a disingenuous rationale for moving the Indians. Jackson declared that "the condition of the Indians within the limits of the U.S. is of a character to awaken our sympathies, and induce the inquiry if something cannot be done to better their situation." But pressured by land-hungry whites, believing (like most other whites) that Indians were not yet ready for "civilization," and having little respect for Indian people themselves, Jackson's primary goal was getting their land for the advance of white farmers. In 1830 he pushed through Congress the Indian Removal Act, which provided agents to negotiate removal plans, appropriated money to pay nominal sums for the land vacated, and gave the military authority to force recalcitrant Indians to surrender their claims to tribal lands.

Jackson moved quickly to use the power Congress had given him. Between 1831 and 1833, approximately 15,000 Choctaws were forced out of their homes in Mississippi and made a sad trek to the Indian Territory.[2] The United States Army forced the Creeks, many in chains and handcuffs, to leave their lands in Alabama and Georgia in 1836, and the following year the Chickasaws were driven from their ancestral lands in north Alabama. The Seminoles resisted, fighting a long guerrilla campaign in the Florida Everglades until 1842. But the most poignant and tragic story of all is that of the Cherokees, whose homeland lay in northeastern Georgia, westernmost North Carolina, and the southeastern corner of Tennessee.

2. Present-day Oklahoma.

The Cherokees, in part counseled by northern Protestant missionaries who had converted many of them to Christianity, took at their word the philanthropic promises of Presidents Jefferson and Monroe. They aggressively accepted white civilization by adopting white dress, establishing Christian churches, developing farms, raising cattle, growing cotton (sometimes with black slaves), and building saw and grist mills. They created an alphabet and began publishing a newspaper in their own language, the *Cherokee Phoenix*. In 1827 they wrote their own constitution and sought to form themselves into a separate independent nation (within the borders of the existing state of Georgia), with their capital at New Echota in northwest Georgia and their own government and court system.

Georgia and its governor, George M. Troup, ignored the Cherokee claims and declared the Indians' constitution and laws null and void. Having dismissed their land titles, the Georgia government began to survey the Cherokees' lands for sale to whites by a state lottery. Since colonial days the federal government had mediated between Indian and state conflicts. But with a thinly veiled reference to slavery, Governor Troup declared that federal claims to jurisdiction over Indians that superseded state authority raised the danger that "jurisdiction claimed over one portion of our population may very soon be asserted over another." Troup had shrewdly united land greed and proslavery sentiment behind state claims for control of the Indian lands and rejected federal jurisdiction.

The discovery of gold in the Cherokee lands in 1829 exacerbated white hunger for the Indian lands. Soon some 3,000 whites trespassed upon Cherokee lands with scant regard for Indian crops or homes. Vainly the Cherokees sought redress in Georgia courts, only to have the state pass a law prohibiting them from seeking gold on their own lands. Earlier presidents, faced with disputes over Indian lands, had insisted that the federal government had sole authority to enter into treaty and land-purchase agreements with Indian nations, but Andrew Jackson disparaged Indian claims of nationhood and sided with Georgia's declaration of authority over Indian affairs within its borders.

The Cherokees tried to fight Georgia with white legal procedures. Relying upon earlier conceptions of the federal government's sole authority to enter into agreements with Indian nations, in 1830 they sought a Supreme Court injunction to stop Georgia's extension of its legal system into Cherokee territory and its seizure of tribal lands. Writing for the majority in *Cherokee Nation v. Georgia* (1831), Chief Justice Marshall rejected the traditional practice and ruled that Indian tribes were not truly like foreign nations with whom treaties were negotiated. Rather, he wrote, Indians were something unique, "domestic dependent nations," and as such could not sue in federal courts. So he rejected the Cherokee request for an injunction to stay Georgia's actions. But the Marshall Court went on to assert that only the federal government had sovereignty over the lands of these "domestic dependent nations." Hence Georgia had no legal jurisdiction over Cherokee lands and could not enforce its laws against Indians who lived on them.

The following year Marshall strengthened the Court's assertion of federal authority over the Indians. In *Worcester v. Georgia,* a case involving two missionaries who had refused to obtain licenses from Georgia before pursuing their call to the Cherokees, Marshall's Court held that the Indian nation was a legitimate entity that the state could not summarily overrule. Indeed, the Indian nation was subordinate only to the national government. For many states'-rights Georgians, such a ruling again raised the fear that, using similar logic, the Supreme Court might interfere with or even outlaw slavery. Georgia officials did not intend to let

the Supreme Court limit what they believed to be the sovereignty of the state, especially when white Georgians coveted the land both for its fertility and for its gold. Jackson, tilting toward maximizing the rights of the states, reportedly said, "John Marshall has made his decision. Now let him enforce it." Whether or not he actually used such words (there is some doubt), Jackson certainly did not intend to enforce Marshall's ruling — clearly violating the Constitution's definition of the executive as the federal government's enforcement arm.

Jackson got his way. Although the Indians had advocates in Congress, although Protestant missionaries called for patience and humanity, and although the distinguished lawyer and former United States attorney general William Wirt argued their cause, Jackson and the supporters of quick and forced removal carried the day. In 1838, the Van Buren administration sent a contingent of 7,000 soldiers to "escort" some 16,000 Cherokees to the Indian Territory west of the Mississippi, watching as perhaps 4,000 men, women, and children died of hunger and exposure along what was called "The Trail of Tears." Although several hundred Cherokees surreptitiously fled into the Great Smoky Mountains of western North Carolina (where their descendants still live), and although the Seminoles fought on for several years in Florida, by the early 1840s the Indian presence was essentially eliminated from the Southeast.

Indian removal followed the same course in the Northwest Territory. A Winnebago uprising, led by Red Bird, was crushed by the army in 1827, and the Sac

---

❈ IN THEIR OWN WORDS

An Indian Voice on Removal, 1854
John Mannuaucon Quinney (1797-1855) was a Mahican Indian. This eloquent plea is part of an address delivered on July 4, 1854, to a white audience.

Let it not surprise you, my friends, when I say, that the spot on which we stand, has never been purchased or rightly obtained; and that by justice, human and divine, it is the property now of the remnant of that great people from whom I am descended. They left it in the tortures of starvation, and to improve their miserable existence; but a cession was never made, and their title has never been extinguished. . . .

What are the treaties of the general Government? How often, and when, has its plighted faith been kept? Indian occupation forever, is, next year, or by the next Commissioner, more wise than his predecessor, re-purchased. One removal follows another, and thus your sympathies and justice are evinced in speedily fulfilling the terrible destinies of our race.

My friends, your holy book, the Bible, teaches us, that individual offences are punished in an existence, when time shall be no more. And the annals of the earth are equally instructive, that national wrongs are avenged, and national crimes atoned for in this world, to which alone the conformations of existence adapt them.

These events are above our comprehension, and for wise purposes. For myself and for my tribe, I ask for justice — I believe it will sooner or later occur — and may the Great and Good Spirit enable me to die in hope.

John C. Calhoun The most familiar portraits of Calhoun are photographs from his old age that show him as a grim-faced, grizzled sectionalist fanatic — "the cast-iron man," one English-woman called him. But this painting from about 1825, when he was J. Q. Adams's vice president, shows him as a strikingly hand-some, but no less strong-willed, American nationalist.

and Fox Indians in Illinois, Iowa, and Wisconsin, led by Black Hawk, resisted for several years before being almost destroyed in a battle with regular army and militia forces in 1832. (Lieutenant Jefferson Davis of Mississippi commanded regular troops in this so-called Black Hawk War, and Captain Abraham Lincoln participated as a volunteer in the Illinois militia.) Subsequently the Winnebago, the Sac, and the Fox ceded their lands and moved west of the Mississippi into what is now Nebraska.

By the 1850s a federal policy had evolved that envisioned creating reservations for most of the surviving native peoples in the trans-Mississippi West. This policy was designed to clear the vast territory for permanent white settlement. The tragic result was the Indian nations' demoralization, impoverishment, and depopulation.

Nullification

By defending the principle of rotation in office and by supporting Georgia's sovereignty over all the land within its boundaries, Jackson seemed to minimize federal authority and to support grassroots democracy and states' rights. In several highly publicized decisions regarding federally funded internal improvements, he again seemed to show himself a critic of government centralization. For example, he vetoed the Maysville Road Bill in 1830 because it would have required the federal government to buy stock in a private company that would build a road entirely in one state, Kentucky.

Jackson knew his veto would be popular in northern states that had funded their own internal improvements, and he phrased his veto message in such a way that it seemed to defend what the Constitution called "the reserved powers" of the states. This pleased the southern states, which also opposed the tariffs that generated the revenue for internal improvements. (Not incidentally, the denial of funds to Kentucky gave a backhanded slap to that state's Senator, Henry Clay, and his vaunted American System.) On other occasions, Jackson did approve large federal appropriations for river and harbor improvements that could be rationalized as helping national commercial interests rather than the economy of one state, and, not incidentally, many of these projects were in key states that strongly supported Jackson.

But these instances of Jackson siding with the states misled some southerners into supposing that Jackson was at heart more a states'-righter than a unionist. In fact, in the most critical conflict between those two positions — a conflict that threatened to divide the nation — Jackson came down emphatically on the side of the Union. The conflict itself, arising from a dispute over tariffs but grounded in South Carolina's declining economic fortunes and exacerbated by escalating personal antagonism between Jackson and John C. Calhoun, gave a preview of the future Civil War. This conflict, the nullification controversy, laid bare regional rivalries and demonstrated how central the issue of slavery had become to South Carolina's conception of its destiny. It left severely discontented southern states with secession as apparently their only option.

HELPING ONE SECTION, HURTING ANOTHER
John C. Calhoun had first come to Congress from South Carolina in 1811 as a "War Hawk," aggressively defending American interests in what soon became the War of 1812. As we saw in Chapter 9, the (then) strongly nationalistic Calhoun had supported the tariff of 1816, designed to protect American manufacturing interests from a postwar British commercial policy aimed at destroying American competitors by dumping low-priced goods on the United States market. But he had seen this tariff as conducive to the national good: it would allow American manufacturers to mature to the point that the nation no longer depended on British products, and revenue raised by the tariff would be used for military preparations.

Yet although by 1826 American manufacturers had grown strong enough to survive on their own, they were by no means willing to forgo the extra competitive advantage that tariffs provided. South Carolina, on the other hand, was in slow economic decline. Charleston had seen its primacy among southern ports give way to

Webster's Reply to Hayne   With the gallery packed and hawk-eyed Vice President Calhoun presiding, Daniel Webster rises in the Senate on January 26, 1830, to deliver his impassioned answer to South Carolinian Robert Hayne's defense of nullification. Webster's speech is one of the masterpieces of American political oratory and a powerful statement of the emerging nationalism of the Jacksonian Era.

New Orleans and Mobile, and the tens of thousands of acres of fertile new lands in Alabama and Mississippi not only attracted many of the most ambitious young South Carolinians but also had a higher cotton yield per acre. Economically hard-pressed South Carolinians came increasingly to see the tariff as simply raising the price of their imports and imperiling their exports. How disastrous to their state would it be if, for example, Great Britain retaliated against American tariff policies by restricting its imports of southern cotton and rice?

The tariff clearly helped one part of the nation and hurt another. If the national government could thus unfairly discriminate against a minority region, what would prevent the majority section from passing other kinds of legislation that could cripple the minority

Webster's Reply to Hayne, 1830

Rejecting South Carolina Senator Robert Hayne's defense of nullification, Daniel Webster's ringing oration appealed to the North's growing sense of nationalism, as embodied in the federal union. Here is Webster's climactic closing. Flowery, dramatic language such as this thrilled audiences everywhere in the nineteenth-century United States, even when — as was emphatically not true of Webster's speech — it was devoid of sense or real content. To get the full effect, imagine a sonorous, booming voice, a slow, stately pace, a flashing eye, and dramatic pauses and gestures.

While the Union lasts we have high, exciting, gratifying prospects spread out before us — for us and our children. Beyond that, I seek not to penetrate the veil. God grant that in my day, at least, that curtain may not rise! God grant that, on my vision, never may be opened what lies behind!

When my eyes shall be turned to behold, for the last time, the sun in heaven, may I not see him shining on the broken and dishonored fragments of this once glorious Union; on states dissevered, discordant, belligerent; on a land rent with civil feuds, or drenched, it may be, in fraternal blood! Let their last feeble and lingering glance rather behold the glorious ensign of the Republic, now known and honored throughout the earth, still full high advanced, its arms and trophies streaming in their original luster, not a stripe erased or polluted, not a single star obscured, bearing for its motto no such miserable interrogatory as "What is all this worth?" nor those other words of delusion and folly, "Liberty first and Union afterward"; but everywhere, spread all over in characters of living light, blazing on its ample folds, as they float over the sea and over the land, and in every wind under the whole heavens, that other sentiment, dear to every true American heart — Liberty *and* Union, now and forever, one and inseparable!

— for example, federal limitations on slavery? The 1819 controversy over the admission of Missouri had already put nervous South Carolinians on edge; next came the panic in 1822 when white Charlestonians believed they had discovered and thwarted free black Denmark Vesey's plans for slave rebellion in Charleston. (The "conspiracy" was mostly in the minds of the white authorities, for they were alert to every conceivable threat to slavery, real or imagined.) In the late 1820s Calhoun had come to see his earlier support of tariffs as ill conceived, in part because he had not foreseen his own changed political situation or the economic decline of his home state.

At this moment the politics of the 1828 election disrupted national tariff policies. Taking for granted that Jackson would win the southern vote against President Adams, the Democratic Congress began to seek ways to win for him the Middle Atlantic States with their manufacturing interests, as well as the farm states of the Old Northwest (today's Midwest). The Democrats' solution was to concoct a tariff that, by placing stiff levies on imported textile goods, iron, raw wool, flax, molasses, hemp, and distilled spirits, clearly helped the Mid-Atlantic States and the Northeast. In other words, they abandoned the theory that tariffs should simply protect the national interest and gave an economic bonus to two regions in exchange for their political support. One critic accurately described the tariff bill's blatant political purpose as promoting "manufactures of no sort, but the manufacture of a President of the United States." Jackson's managers assumed that southern anger at what one politician called the "Tariff of Abominations" would be directed toward Adams. They were too smart by half: Calhoun and other southerners blamed Jackson.

Calhoun, however, did not want to break openly with Jackson. He was running for the vice presidency and reasoned that, once in office, he would be able to influence Jackson to lower tariffs. Moreover, Calhoun assumed that Jackson would serve only one term, after which Calhoun himself would don the party's presidential mantle. For that reason, Calhoun kept secret his authorship of an anonymous pamphlet, the *South Carolina Exposition and Protest,* which appeared later in 1828. In the pamphlet, Calhoun argued that the Union was a voluntary compact of states, that the states could decide the constitutionality of federal laws, and that specially elected conventions (like those that had originally ratified the Constitution) were the proper venue for voiding or nullifying particular federal legislation that a state might decide to be fatal to its interests. In a way, Calhoun echoed arguments first advanced in 1798-1799 by the Virginia and Kentucky Resolves and in 1814 by the Hartford Convention.[3] Neither of these protests had seriously threatened the Union, but Calhoun's ideas might. Yet Calhoun largely kept his thoughts to himself during the early years of Jackson's administration because he needed Jackson's political support in 1832 and

3. See Chapters 8, 9.

hoped that Jackson would, of his own initiative, work to reduce tariffs. Then a personal rift opened between the two that shattered the façade of good will and disrupted the political landscape.

THE JACKSON-CALHOUN RIFT

The first precipitating event was one of the silliest controversies ever to divide a presidential administration. Jackson's secretary of war, John H. Eaton, in 1829 had married a perky young widow, Peggy O'Neal Timberlake, daughter of a Washington tavern keeper, shortly after her naval officer husband's suicide. The Washington rumor mill spread the word that Peggy had flirted (and more than that) with Eaton while her husband was away at sea. She herself admitted that she was "frivolous, wayward, [and] passionate." John C. Calhoun's scandalized wife Floride did not believe Peggy Eaton had a place in polite society. The stiffly proper Mrs. Calhoun and her friends among the other cabinet wives thereupon snubbed Mrs. Eaton socially. Instantly there resurrected in Jackson's memory ugly rumors about his dear-departed Rachel and how they had supposedly lived together immorally. So Jackson quickly sprang to the defense of Peggy Eaton and her marriage with the secretary of war. Angrily Jackson struck out at the venomous "conspiracy" and "dark and sly insinuations" that he felt really were aimed past Peggy — at himself and his administration. It was easy, given Floride Calhoun's leadership in the spat, somehow to see John C. Calhoun's hand in the affair. Van Buren, a widower, was quick to glimpse the wedge developing between Jackson and Calhoun over what he called "the Eaton malaria," and he widened the breach. Van Buren showed sympathy for the Eatons by including them in social functions and thereby cemented his own position with the president.

The second event that precipitated a Jackson-Calhoun rift was an exchange of orations between Senator Robert Y. Hayne of South Carolina and Daniel Webster of Massachusetts in January 1830. Hayne, speaking more passionately than wisely, hoped to attract the political support of the West to the southern cause. What he said tended to isolate the South. Spokesmen from the West, led by Senator Thomas Hart Benton of Missouri, had long advocated the sale of public lands to settlers at the cheapest possible rate, eventually hoping to reduce the cost to 50 cents an acre and thereafter graduated downward until it would be free to pioneers. Northeastern industrial interests feared that cheap land would lure the working class to the West, raising

factory owners' labor costs. On the other hand, if land prices remained high, income from its sale would still swell the federal treasury, thus negating the argument that high tariffs were required to produce needed government revenues. Steep land prices could lead to reductions in tariffs.

Recognizing this conundrum, a Connecticut Senator introduced a resolution in December 1829 calling for a moratorium in the surveying of federal lands and limiting future sales. Westerners were outraged. Seeing a chance to widen the chasm between the West and the East, Senator Hayne sought, by defending the principle of cheap land, to unite the political interests of the West with the South. But in his Senate address Hayne got carried away with his rhetoric and launched into an attack on the principle of the tariff. Borrowing freely from Calhoun's anonymously authored *Exposition and Protest,* Hayne lambasted the tariff as unconstitutional, dangerous to the economic future of the South, a threat to the Union, and an example of the tyranny of the majority that must be countered by individual states' declaring it unconstitutional. Hayne transformed a controversy over the price of western lands into a divisive debate over the constitutionality of the federal tariff.

The staunch defender of eastern business and industrial interests was Daniel Webster, and the galleries of the Senate chamber were crowded with listeners on January 20 and 26, 1830, as Webster, the greatest American orator of the age, demolished Hayne's position that individual states should be the arbiters of the law of the land. That was the role of the Supreme Court, and to argue otherwise would result in the dissolving of the nation. In a powerful conclusion Webster evoked the frightful vision of a nation "drenched . . . in fratricidal blood" if Hayne's counsel was taken, as contrasted with a nation gleaming in peace and prosperity if he was heeded. Then came the famous ending, memorized and declaimed by schoolchildren for the rest of the century: "Liberty *and* Union, now and forever, one and inseparable."

The third event that heralded a growing break between the president and his vice president was a much-talked-about set of toasts at a banquet in Washington on April 13, 1830, honoring Thomas Jefferson's birthday. Jackson, always an aggressive, even combative man, came to the dinner in the wake of the Webster-Hayne debate. With Webster's eloquent words ringing in his head, the president rose to toast the assembly. Looking directly at Calhoun, Jackson defiantly held up his glass and spoke: "Our Federal Union — It must be preserved!" Momentarily stunned, Calhoun rose immediately afterward, every eye turned to him and every breath held. His hand quivering ever so slightly as he held up his glass, the South Carolinian's voice in reply was strong: "The Union, next to our liberty, most dear!" Then he continued: "May we all remember that it can only be preserved by respecting the rights of the States and distributing equally the benefit and the burthen of the Union!"

The dramatic exchange of toasts openly revealed the fissure that had split the administration. Soon Jackson even knew of Calhoun's authorship of the *Exposition and Protest*. When, shortly afterwards, Van Buren supporters showed Jackson solid evidence that in 1818 Calhoun as secretary of war had criticized Jackson's unauthorized military incursion against Spanish Florida,[4] the break became total. At that moment Van Buren offered Jackson a way to purge his cabinet of Calhoun supporters by tendering his own resignation and maneuvering most of the others into resigning, too. Jackson replaced them all with men who unwaveringly supported him, and subsequently he rewarded Van Buren by nominating him to be minister to Great Britain. Vice President Calhoun, presiding over the Senate, simply for spite handled the Senate vote in such a way that he cast the tie-breaking vote that denied Van Buren confirmation. When, shortly afterwards, Jackson advocated a new tariff in 1832 that would reduce most rates, Calhoun denounced Jackson's revised tariff because it still affirmed the legitimacy of tariffs. Resigning the vice presidency, Calhoun — growing less supportive of Democratic government by the year — returned to South Carolina. Jackson named Van Buren as his vice presidential candidate for the 1832 election and let it be known that Van Buren would succeed him as the Democratic presidential candidate in 1836.

"NULL, VOID, AND NO LAW"

Calhoun was back in South Carolina when the tariff of 1832 passed. For white South Carolinians the issue was less the exact levies of the tariff than what enactment of the tariff said about the fragility of the state's long-term best interests, as defined by its slaveholders. That the federal government could pass legislation — without the state's or the South's support — that was binding on the state and regulated (or interfered with) the state's economy raised the specter of the federal government regulating or hindering other aspects of the

4. Chapter 9, pp. 272, 274-75.

state's economy, or even imposing restrictions against slavery within the state.

South Carolinians kept in touch with the slaveholders of the British Caribbean islands (some of them relatives), who had seen slavery successfully attacked by Parliament without their having any effective political recourse. Parliament was by then moving toward abolishing slavery in the British colonies, an action that it was to take in 1833. Equally, feared South Carolinians, federal legislation could do the same thing in their state. And they had other worries, closer to home. In Boston in January 1831 William Lloyd Garrison had launched his abolitionist newspaper, *The Liberator*, stridently affirming the goal of immediate emancipation. In August of that same year, Nat Turner's slave revolt erupted in Virginia. Outnumbered by their slaves, their numbers eroding as their younger sons migrated westward to more fertile soils, their economy in a slow descent, worried about slave insurrections, and now fearing a federal assault on what they defined as their basic institution, white South Carolinians were in no mood to show restraint in their opposition to the tariff. For them the tariff had become a stalking horse for abolitionism. The South Carolina legislature decided to put into practice the concept of nullification that Calhoun had spelled out in the *Exposition and Protest*.

Had some kind of convention gathered representing all the southern states, South Carolina might have been forced to moderate its position. As it was, the state forged ahead, expecting or at least hoping that other southern states would follow. Delegates were elected to a special convention that, on November 24, 1832, approved an Ordinance of Nullification declaring the tariffs of 1828 and 1832 "null, void, and no law, nor binding upon this state." The South Carolina legislature then met and forbade the collection of tariff duties after February 1, 1833 — and, it threatened, if the federal troops attempted to enforce the payment of duties, the state would secede from the Union. As if that were not enough, the legislature chose the intemperate Senator Hayne as the new governor and appointed Calhoun as his replacement in the Senate.

REACTION AND COMPROMISE

Andrew Jackson may in the past have sent signals suggesting that he was a states'-righter, but in this crisis he understood instinctively that the Union was at stake. Nullification, he proclaimed, "strikes at the root of Government and the social compact." From his boyhood days during the Revolution, and again in the War of 1812, Jackson had fought for the nation, and he was certainly not about to brook anti-unionist activities engineered by his enemy, Calhoun. Jackson took nullification talk personally, and he responded personally. He sent word through a congressman that he would come to South Carolina, hunt down the nullifiers' leaders, and hang them from the nearest tree. Calhoun actually feared for his life. Jackson began making military preparations to dispatch a force of 50,000 men to South Carolina to enforce federal laws, then spoke elsewhere of 200,000 men. He denounced nullification as an "abominable doctrine" and called treasonous the idea of South Carolina using force to resist national laws. Then, behind the harsh talk, Jackson used a carrot-and-stick approach to defuse the crisis.

Jackson pushed through the Senate a so-called Force Bill authorizing the federal government to use the army and navy to collect the customs if necessary. The bill dissuaded the other southern states from giving South Carolina any support at all. "Fear not," Jackson told fellow unionists. "The Union will be preserved." Then Jackson gave his support to Henry Clay, who once more, as during the Missouri Crisis, lived up to his reputation as the Great Compromiser by introducing a new tariff bill that gradually reduced tariffs over a ten-year period. In late January, some ten days before nullification was to go into effect, the South Carolina legislature postponed the effective date of nullification. No other southern states had come to its defense, and Jackson clearly meant what he said about crushing with overwhelming armed force the principle of nullification and its leaders. Fearing for his personal safety in the event of either secession or war, Calhoun shifted his support to Clay's compromise tariff. After passing the tariff, the House added its support to the Force Bill, making it law. Then, responding to the tariff compromise, the South Carolina legislature repealed the Ordinance of Nullification. The crisis passed. To save face, South Carolina also nullified the Force Bill, but with the tariff issue settled, Jackson was wise enough to ignore this meaningless last gesture of defiance. The Union had been saved — for the moment.

THE BANK WAR

The Old Hero's last great political battle raged over the complicated issue of banking. Jackson knew little about the intricacies of finance (and was mistaken in what he thought he knew), but he had a masterful understanding of the national mood and how to appeal to it. Through adroit actions he won his short-term politi-

cal battle that he picked over the future of the Bank of the United States. But the consequences of his victory would be very damaging to the nation's economy and to the political fortunes of his successor. It is necessary to examine the nature of the banking industry in the first third of the nineteenth century in order to understand how the seemingly arcane matter of the congressional rechartering of the Bank of the United States could precipitate a political controversy so severe that it reshaped national politics.

The Second B.U.S. and the Nation's Banking System

The original Bank of the United States had been chartered for twenty years in 1791 as an essential element of Alexander Hamilton's economic plan to put the new nation on solid financial and political footing. Yet while Hamilton had argued that the bank was necessary for national prosperity, Jefferson and his supporters (including James Madison) had argued against the constitutionality of the bank and raised fears about its centralizing tendencies. So when the charter expired in 1811, President Madison made no effort to continue the bank or its functions. Then came the War of 1812, revealing how important the bank was in stabilizing the economy and maintaining the value of the variety of privately issued paper money that circulated in lieu of government-backed paper money (such as we have today). In the surge of nationalism at the war's end, the Democratic-Republicans had moved, along with levying a protective tariff, to reestablish the national bank. The Second Bank of the United States (B.U.S.), headquartered like the first in Philadelphia, won a twenty-year charter in 1816. Although it got off to a rocky start and helped precipitate the Panic of 1819,[5] the bank's constitutionality seemed secure following the Marshall Court's great 1819 decision, *McCulloch v. Maryland*.

By the early 1820s the Second B.U.S. was performing its functions confidently and competently. In 1823 a brilliant and aristocratic young Philadelphian, Nicholas Biddle, accomplished in literature and law as well as finance, became its president. Biddle fully understood the bank's role in stabilizing the national economy, and he was not at all hesitant to use his institution's power and wealth to regulate the sometimes questionable practices of the dozens of small state banks. Since paper money backed by the federal government did not

5. See Chapter 9.

then exist, the most secure form of money was gold and silver coins, called specie. But specie was in short supply. To provide the circulating currency that the growing economy needed, state banks augmented the specie in the money supply by issuing loans in the form of bank notes to borrowers. Holders of these notes paid interest on them, but they could also spend bank notes as paper money.

People normally bought goods and paid their debts with these bank-issued notes, and as long as the various state-chartered banks that issued the notes were sound, they circulated roughly at face value from person to person, just as paper money does today. But if an issuing bank failed or was rumored to be on the verge of failing, then the value of its notes plummeted, leaving those who held them completely at risk. Because banks collected interest upon the initial issuance of notes, they were usually tempted to issue more notes than they had gold or silver deposits in reserve should the owners of notes come to the bank and demand — as they legally could — specie coins in exchange for the full stated value of the note. Essentially, banks gambled that never at any one time would many holders of notes demand such reimbursement in coin, so the banks tended to issue paper notes with abandon, inflating the money supply and fueling the 1820s economic boom with cheap money. In the background, however, lurked two great risks to the national economy. If too much paper money circulated, hyperinflation could be unleashed; and if an epidemic of bank failures occurred, a disastrous collapse in the money supply would follow, causing a deep depression. It was precisely to head off such a panic that Biddle ran the B.U.S. as a central bank with the aim of controlling the loose lending practices at the many state-chartered banks throughout the nation.

In the normal course of business, most of the state banks' paper notes came across the counters of the twenty-two branches of the B.U.S. By accumulating notes from a state bank and then presenting them to that bank for conversion into specie, Biddle or his agents could force banks either to keep sufficient gold and silver reserves on hand or face severe curtailment of their lending practices. Holding this whip over potentially irresponsible banks, Biddle could make state banks exercise discipline. When necessary to slow down the expansion of the economy because it threatened to become wildly excessive, the B.U.S. could demand repayment of its loans, that is, "call them in." This would reduce the money in circulation and sharply limit expansion. Using such tactics, the B.U.S. under Biddle's direction played a positive and responsible role in stabilizing the economy.

Yet the very success of the B.U.S. automatically made enemies among some directors and owners of state banks. The bank's restraining discipline also irritated many farmers and would-be entrepreneurs, particularly in the West and Midwest, who benefited from cheap money because it made it easier both to get loans and to pay debts. Urban workers blamed the bank's calling in of loans in 1819 for causing the Panic, and in truth the bank's policy on that occasion, although probably justified, had exacerbated the immediate economic problem. Senator Thomas Hart Benton of Missouri soon arose as an early and forthright critic of the policies of the B.U.S. Andrew Jackson especially identified with these western interests who favored easy access to money. Moreover, having gone through a near-disaster in financial speculation as a young man, Jackson had long been suspicious of institutions that seemingly made a profit just by bookkeeping and by issuing paper money. Somehow they did not seem to him to do any real work.

❧ Jackson Takes on the B.U.S.

Early in his administration Jackson had been frank with Biddle. "I do not dislike your Bank any more than all banks," said the president — meaning banks in general. But the more Jackson learned about the B.U.S., the more he disliked it in particular. The B.U.S. was a private bank, headquartered in Philadelphia, not Washington; its stockholders were private citizens, and only a minority of its directors were appointed by the federal government. And yet this privately owned and controlled bank was the official depository for federal funds, which gave it a commanding position and allowed it, by making loans to businesses and individuals, to reap handsome profits. Jackson came increasingly to see it as an aristocratic institution, representing an evil concentration of power. And because foreigners owned just less than a quarter of the bank's stock, he (unreasonably) feared foreign domination of the American economy. In his view, the B.U.S. neither represented nor benefited the ordinary American citizen.

For all these reasons Jackson let it be known that he opposed the B.U.S., and in his first message to Congress in 1829 he attacked the "constitutionality and expediency" of the bank. The B.U.S. and its powerful political supporters, in turn, branded Jackson as the enemy of

sound finance and of rational economic policy — and, for that matter, of constitutional government. The Supreme Court had already decided that the B.U.S. *was* constitutional; Jackson had no mandate or authority to question that decision. The bank's supporters determined to shore up the long-term prospects of the B.U.S., whose current charter would expire in 1836. Henry Clay and Daniel Webster, strong proponents of the B.U.S., devised an election strategy that they believed would not only embarrass Jackson and preserve the B.U.S. but also promote Clay's ardent presidential aspirations.

Mistakenly assuming that the B.U.S. was so strongly supported by knowledgeable business leaders and bankers nationwide that Jackson would not dare torpedo it in an election year, in 1832 Clay and Webster persuaded a reluctant Biddle to make an early application for rechartering the bank. Since the 1816 charter would not expire until 1836, there was some risk in antagonizing Jackson four years earlier than necessary. But Clay really believed that his strong advocacy of the B.U.S. would be his ticket to the White House, and he pushed the rechartering bill through Congress in June and early July of 1832. Jackson, however, saw the scheme as more a threat to his incumbency than a defense of the bank. "The Bank," he told Van Buren, "is trying to

"'Let Every One Take Care of Himself' — As the jack ass said when he was dancing among the chickens." This political cartoon satirizes Andrew Jackson's campaign to remove federal funds from the corrupt Second Bank of the United States and redistribute them in the state banks. Jackson is shown as a jackass dancing among the chicks (the state banks) in a barnyard. Vice President Martin Van Buren is shown as a fox, sneaking up on a chicken that is labeled the U.S. Bank. The baying dogs in the corner represent the newspapers sympathetic to Jackson's plan.

kill me, but I will kill it!"

Assisted by three of his closest advisers, Amos Kendall, Francis Preston Blair, and Roger B. Taney, on July 10 Jackson vetoed the B.U.S. rechartering bill with a powerfully written veto message. Instantly his message became an effective campaign tool for his reelection. Jackson, who always believed himself the embodiment of the people, cast the B.U.S. as a public enemy, "unauthorized by the Constitution, subversive of the rights of the States, and dangerous to the liberties of the people." Dismissing the *McCulloch v. Maryland* decision, he said that the president had as much right as the Supreme Court to determine what was constitutional or not. He then raised the specter of foreign control, which could "impoverish our people in time of peace, . . . disseminate a foreign influence through every section of the Republic, and in war . . . endanger our independence." As if that were not enough, this monstrous bank would

Jackson Takes on the B.U.S., 1832

Jackson's veto of the bill to recharter the Bank of the United States rested on a gross misunderstanding of economics, but it flowed directly from his political philosophy and was couched in language that resonated with ordinary Americans' sense of justice.

It is to be regretted that the rich and powerful too often bend the acts of government to their selfish purposes. Distinctions of society will always exist under every just government. Equality of talents, of education, or of wealth cannot be produced by human institutions. In the full enjoyment of the gifts of heaven and the fruits of superior industry, economy, and virtue, every man is equally entitled to protection by law.

But when the laws undertake to add to these natural and just advantages artificial distinctions, to grant titles, gratuities, and exclusive privileges, to make the rich richer and the potent more powerful, the humble members of society — the farmers, mechanics, and laborers — who have neither the time nor the means of securing like favors to themselves, have a right to complain of the injustice of their government.

There are no necessary evils in government. Its evils exist only in its abuses. If it would confine itself to equal protection, and, as heaven does its rains, shower its favors alike on the high and the low, the rich and the poor, it would be an unqualified blessing. In the act before me [for rechartering the B.U.S.] there seems to be a wide and unnecessary departure from these just principles. . . .

enrich a select few who, not "content with equal protection and benefits," sought to make themselves "richer by act of Congress." Standing forth as the champion of the ordinary citizen — of the men on the make as opposed to the entrenched establishment — Jackson concluded by taking "a stand against all new grants of monopolies and exclusive privileges, against any prostitution of our Government to the advance of the few at the expense of the many. . . ."

Jackson's use of the presidential veto for policy reasons was a shocking innovation in 1832, and many of his opponents regarded it a grave abuse of power. Moreover, Jackson's charges against the bank were inaccurate and unfair. They made little financial sense. But they made great political sense. While Webster might attack the veto message for attempting to "inflame the poor against the rich" and threatening the very Constitution, Jackson knew his constituency. Spokesman for the striving majority against the elites, he swept the election of 1832, beating Clay resoundingly by an electoral vote of 219 to 49 and taking 55 percent of the popular vote.

Safely reelected and reading the vote as a mandate to finish off the B.U.S. even before its scheduled expiration in 1836, Jackson moved to drive a stake through the heart of the "Monster Bank." He decided to remove all federal funds from the B.U.S. and deposit them in seven specially chosen state banks. He gave the necessary orders to his secretary of the treasury, Louis McLane. But McLane, like most cabinet members,

thought Jackson's plan was certainly unwise and possibly illegal, and he refused. Jackson believed cabinet officials should be his personal lieutenants and promptly transferred McLane to the recently vacant position of secretary of state, naming William J. Duane secretary of the treasury. And when the president learned that Duane agreed with McLane, he too was summarily fired. Finally, Jackson turned to Roger B. Taney, who had helped write the bank veto message. Taney was as suspicious of banks as Jackson, so once in office he quickly transferred the current government deposits and made sure that new federal funds would also go to the seven named state banks — in one of which Taney owned stock and whose president was his close friend. Hence critics soon called the favored institutions "pet banks." By 1833 there were twenty-three of them. And in 1835 Taney got his reward when Jackson appointed him chief justice of the Supreme Court after John Marshall's death.

Nicholas Biddle, correctly understanding that as matters stood the B.U.S. had no future, incorrectly reasoned that he could still manage his bank so as to bring maximum pressure on Jackson to relent in his war. Biddle therefore began to call in all the outstanding loans, insisting that they be paid off in specie, and he sharply curtailed making new loans. Predictably, great economic distress ensued as businessmen, land speculators, farmers, and westerners in general found themselves caught in a dramatic deflation. The winter of 1833-1834 was a season of panic and depression. But

The Bank War This mock bank note was created to parody the often worthless currencies issued by banks, businesses, and the government in lieu of coins during the Panic of 1837. It features caricatures of Van Buren, Jackson, Benton, and Calhoun.

when the victims screamed to Jackson, the stubborn president told them to talk to Mr. Biddle. Ultimately they did, so that the pressure intended to be exerted against Jackson ended up being turned against Biddle. Capitulating, Biddle began to make loans again, with the result that the economy that had been jerked almost to a standstill now spurted ahead. Biddle had hoped the result of such manipulation would prove to Jackson the importance to the economy of a national bank, but Jackson read the results as further proof of the B.U.S.'s disproportionate capacity for economic mischief.

❧ *The Consequences: The Panic of 1837*

As the economy lurched from a brief but disastrous slowdown into a rapid acceleration, a speculative mania swept the nation in the years 1835-1836. Land speculators laid out tens of thousands of house lots around such cities as New York and Chicago, and investors spent wildly on land in the Midwest and in the South. The "Flush Times," people called these years in Alabama and Mississippi. The causes for this investment extravaganza were many, but with no strong central bank to restrain the excess, the ups and downs of the economy turned into an exaggerated boom-and-bust cycle. This was just what Jackson had feared and opposed, but ironically it was what his policies had encouraged. By

1836, ninety state banks had federal deposits, and most of them used their windfalls of government money to expand the number and amount of loans they offered. Few exhibited much caution or ensured an adequate backing in specie. Federal profits from land sales and tariff collections produced a revenue surplus, and in 1836 some $37 million in unspent federal money was distributed to the states. By spending the money on a variety of internal improvements, the states simply put more money into circulation, increasing inflationary pressures. British banks, attracted by high American interest rates, invested heavily in the nation, particularly in firms handling the cotton trade.

To Jackson and the hard-money supporters closest to him, this wild boom, with its rampant speculation fueled by paper money (bank notes), was absolutely horrifying. Jackson tried to throttle the expansion on July 11, 1836, by issuing the Specie Circular. After August 15, he ordered, all large parcels of land purchased by speculators or investors had to be paid for in either gold or silver specie. Actual farmers who were buying parcels of less than 320 acres had an additional four months to pay with bank notes for the land they were farming.

This presidential order caused the land market to crash. Speculators did not have the specie to continue buying land, and investors feared that the new policy would slash the market price of their existing land-holdings. Simultaneously, a worldwide recession had begun, causing British banks to start calling in their American loans. The resulting credit crisis, combined with the collapse of the land boom, produced the Panic of 1837. There ensued six years of economic misery, with a temporary respite in 1839 — the deepest depression the American economy had yet experienced. Jackson by then was out of office, but his successor, Martin Van Buren, was left to face the disaster and take the blame.

Hundreds of banks nationally suspended operations, precipitating thousands of business failures especially in commercial and port cities. In cities like New York the unemployment rate soared as high as one-third of the workers, leaving many breadwinners and their families in abject poverty. For those who retained their jobs, wages fell as much as 50 percent. There were food riots in several cities, and some desperate people turned to the millennial teachings of William Miller, who prophesied the end of the world on October 22, 1843; believers even sold their possessions, donned white robes, climbed atop their houses and barns, and got ready to ascend into heaven. (By the predicted millennial date the economy had begun to improve.)

"Martin Van Ruin's" administration became a hopeless failure. He saw no federal responsibility to act to ease the human hardships: there were no public soup kitchens, no unemployment insurance, no efforts to save banks, no increase in public works to provide jobs. Neither did the states offer any relief. Private charity helped as possible, but the role of government had not yet expanded to include responsibility for the people's well-being. Van Buren, who had substantial political skills but not Jackson's popular appeal, and who was equally ignorant of economics, did not know what to do. True to the hard-money, anti-bank philosophy of Jackson, however, Van Buren believed that putting government funds in the "pet banks" (which had been Jackson's idea) had led to the overheated economy and then the collapse. His solution was to divorce all federal moneys from the banking system. He proposed to Congress an Independent Treasury consisting of a series of branch treasury offices located in the largest cities. Federal funds would be deposited in these so-called sub-treasuries and disbursed as necessary from them. The plan also required that both tariffs and land purchases be paid for in gold and silver coins or in notes from banks that paid in specie. Van Buren fought throughout his entire presidency to get his Independent Treasury scheme approved by Congress, succeeding in 1840, the final year of his administration. The result was to lock up federal funds, the spending of which might have marginally eased the economic distress of the times. The Whigs, who won the presidency in 1840, repealed the act as soon as Congress met in 1841. Van Buren had not found a way to address the economic woes of the nation, but he had succeeded in polarizing the voters so completely that political lines were hardened. Ironically, while Van Buren had earlier proved himself to be a consummate politician, he failed at presidential governance.

THE ORIGINS OF THE SECOND PARTY SYSTEM

The intense partisan struggles of the Jackson years solidified the two-party political system that still remains intact. The political party was maturing as a concept and gaining acceptance as a positive good. The older view was fading that parties were mere organized factionalism that promoted narrow self-interest above the general interest. Although the Whigs — as the anti-Jacksonian opposition party came to be called — tended to be more prosperous and urban and the Democrats more humble and rural, both parties appealed to a range of voters across all economic classes and in all sections of the nation. These were national, not sectional parties, and the very diversity within the parties produced healthy internal conflict that required compromise and served as a moderating influence. Both parties developed effective methods of finding candidates, mobilizing voters, and generating electoral enthusiasm. Voter turnout reached unprecedented levels. Although the parties offered clear choices to the voters, they were nationalizing forces. When in the 1850s this Second Party System began to come apart, the nation's unity was sundered, and civil war loomed.

❧ *Traditional Political Opposition to Jackson*

Jackson's intemperate, personal, and largely uninformed war against the B.U.S. not only had catastrophic consequences for the nation's economy; it also led to a fundamental political realignment. The B.U.S. was the flashpoint of ferocious political combat for almost ten years, and two of the most powerful Senators of all time,

Daniel Webster and Henry Clay, spearheaded opposition to Jackson. Apart from their own frustrated ambitions, their resistance largely reflected economic considerations, broadly defined. Webster was the greatest orator of his day, a man of humble origins who had learned to love the finer things of life and found that unwavering support of the mercantile and industrial interests of his home state of Massachusetts brought personal rewards. Though he and the president were allies in the nullification crisis, he opposed Jackson's anti-bank and anti-tariff policies — primarily because they hurt his state and his backers.

Henry Clay, also an accomplished orator but even more skilled at backroom negotiation and legislative bargaining, and a man who enjoyed gambling, horse racing, and extravagant living, had for years promoted a far-reaching set of policies agreeable to business interests. His American System, which promised to use government powers to create a unified national economy tied together by internal improvements and stimulated and stabilized by a central bank and protective tariffs, was for its time essentially a sound idea. Jackson opposed every aspect of Clay's system, and the president's 1830 veto of the Maysville Road plan in Kentucky had seemed to Clay an act specifically to humiliate him. So Clay opposed Jackson because he believed the Old Hero's whole notion of government was flawed, backward-looking, and injurious to the glorious future that the Kentucky Senator foresaw for the nation.

But opposition to Jackson had roots deeper and broader than the personal piques of Webster and Clay, or the interests of the nation's leading businessmen. Jackson's election in 1828 brought to the White House a kind of frontier Jefferson for the common man, more a "symbol for an age" (as one historian has called him) than the usual political leader with specific views and policies. Jackson's actions as president quickly showed

BORN TO COMMAND.

OF VETO MEMORY.

HAD I BEEN CONSULTED.

KING ANDREW THE FIRST.

King Andrew the First This cartoon, from the time of the presidential election of 1832, gives the emerging Whig view of Jackson as an arrogant king, wielding his veto to thwart the will of Congress. Jackson vetoed more bills in his first term than had all the presidents before him combined. He was the first president to use the veto to advance his own political agenda. That — although expected of presidents today — was considered a high-handed abuse by his political opponents in Congress like Clay, Webster, and Calhoun.

that his beliefs and combative personality had real and negative consequences — which, many people discovered, outweighed whatever gratification they saw in Jackson's triumph as a vague democratic symbol. Jackson's attacks on federally funded internal improvements — canals and roads — economically hurt specific regions and damaged actual farmers and merchants. Industrialists and merchants in New England understood the importance of transportation links to the West, and both consumers and producers in the Midwest knew that they benefited from transportation improvements. The largest cotton planters in the South and the South's urban merchants also supported federally funded internal improvements, both to keep up with the growth of the North and to give them the money they needed to invest in slaves.

Similarly, Jackson's war against the B.U.S. and the economic instability that it unleashed disturbed not simply northeastern industrialists and great mercantile houses but also would-be entrepreneurs throughout much of the North and Midwest. These men needed a source of stable loans for business expansion. Young Abraham Lincoln, for example, was an enterprising anti-Jacksonian who admired Clay's American System. In the South too, bankers, merchants, and large planters supported the B.U.S., feared the consequences of unregulated pet banks, and opposed Jackson's knee-jerk anti-bank prejudice.

The third great Senator who led resistance to Jackson was John C. Calhoun. After Jackson's threat of military power had forced South Carolina's nullifiers to back down, Calhoun's personal hatred of Jackson and his abstract fear of federal power grew furiously. From then on, Calhoun opposed Jackson personally and politically with every ounce of his being. Many South Carolinians and not a few other southerners actually agreed with most of Jackson's basic policies yet opposed him simply because of his strong stand against nullification.

Many Americans worried about Jackson's concept of presidential power. He made much of the fact that he alone was elected by all the people, which he claimed gave him authority far greater than that of Congress and even the Supreme Court. In the aftermath of the Peggy Eaton affair he had called for the resignation of cabinet members (who after all had won congressional confirmation) in such a manner as to suggest that pleasing him was their primary function. Editor Hezekiah Niles protested Jackson's treatment of his cabinet secretaries "only as ... *clerks*" and his imperial references to them as "my cabinet." No earlier president, from Washington to John Quincy Adams, had treated his cabinet in such a way. His rather high-handed assumption that cabinet members worked only to effect his purpose became even clearer when Jackson ejected two successive secretaries of the treasury who balked at transferring federal deposits from the B.U.S.

And when John Marshall issued a Supreme Court decision defending the Cherokees in Georgia that Jackson disagreed with, the Old Hero simply refused to use his office to enforce the law. To his critics, in short, Jackson seemed a raging, self-willed tyrant, subject to no restraints except his own interpretation of the people's will. Hostile cartoons began to appear showing King Andrew I trampling on the Constitution. In that atmosphere Jackson's opponents gradually coalesced into an opposition party that chose the name Whigs, consciously reviving the British opposition party of the Glorious Revolution and the colonial American critics of King George III. The Jacksonians continued to identify their party with the interests of the struggling common man as opposed to the comfortable elite, and upon occasion General Jackson was compared to General Washington, but the Whigs had identified a potent political theme.

Forces were at work, older and broader even than King Andrew or the Monster Bank, that caused many Americans to fear for the future of the republic. In the decade and a half following the War of 1812 the nation had experienced immense changes. The Market Revolution had begun to alter the scale and the manner of how countless Americans made their living. Improvements in transportation — first better roads, then a spreading network of canals, and eventually railroads — expanded farmers' opportunities for selling their produce and brought them manufactured goods far beyond the offerings of local artisans or traders. Soon economic decisions in faraway places determined not only the price that farm produce fetched but also the style and cost of goods purchased locally.

Prices and credit no longer depended directly on a man's good name. Distant, impersonal forces, over which no single person had any influence, were now crucial. Artisanal jobs were changing; factory work was increasing; cities were growing; immigrants with strange languages, cultures, and religions were flocking into northern and Middle Atlantic cities. Looking back, historians give these changes such abstract labels as progress, or urbanization, or the Market Revolution; to contemporaries, however, the changes were often wrenching and bewildering.

One significant group of Americans largely accepted the inevitability of change but worried about the consequences of undirected, willy-nilly development. Such Americans came to believe that the nation needed ordering, disciplining, and reshaping by government or organized forces of religion and morality if it were to fulfill its providential destiny. Two seemingly unrelated episodes — the sudden rise of the anti-Masonic movement and a boiling controversy over Sunday mail — pointed to the cultural tensions and concerns permeating Jacksonian-era politics. These cultural issues, along with a variety of reform impulses, soon got swallowed up in the larger political matrix and helped draw the line between the emerging Democratic and Whig parties.

∞ Anti-Masonry

Masonic lodges had a long history in the United States. Prominent politicians of every persuasion (including George Washington) had been members, along with reputable men of most local communities, all of whom joined together in the fraternal organization replete with secret symbols, handshakes, and rituals. Such was the benign setting of a bizarre, still-unsolved murder. In 1826 an upstate New York stonemason, one William Morgan, disappeared and was apparently killed, probably because he had threatened to reveal certain Masonic secrets. Local officials who were Masons did little to find the perpetrators — who, in fact, have never been identified — and suddenly Morgan's case became a *cause célèbre.*

Humbler Americans had always felt some resentment against the Masons, who tended to be wealthier and more influential than the average citizen. Suspicions had arisen that through their secret fraternity Masons pledged mutual aid and shared information that gave them unfair advantages over non-Masons. Masonry in fact did profess a mixture of Enlightenment rationalism, religious toleration (except toward Roman Catholicism), and mysticism that made it a quasi-religious movement. False rumors spread that the Masons were opposed to Christianity. Masons drank, it was darkly hinted, and they plotted and practiced strange, unbiblical rituals at their lodge meetings; indeed, it was whispered they represented a nefarious, European-based conspiracy against the basic liberties of average Americans. The Morgan murder turned all these rumors into a flood of real fears. Masonry, to many Americans, had now been revealed as an enemy to the American way of life. Intervention was necessary to preserve republican government.

Presumably the anti-Masonic hysteria would have benefited the people's hero, Andrew Jackson, but Jackson's enemies turned the movement to their behalf. For one thing, Jackson himself was a Mason. In New York,

newspaper editor Thurlow Weed, a virulent enemy of Martin Van Buren, seized upon the worries about a Masonic conspiracy and stirred up a fear campaign that connected Van Buren's political power in the state and the economic clout of his supporters with the frightening image of powerful men meeting in secret to control the state. There was no substance to the charge that Van Buren was antidemocratic. But Weed, a master propagandist, succeeded in combining opposition to Van Buren with fear of a Masonic conspiracy. Because rumors against the Order included charges that lodges were dens of drunken iniquity, temperance supporters tended to gravitate to anti-Masonry.

Soon reformers who wrung their hands over a variety of (mostly urban) vices and social problems began to see the anti-Masonic movement as a vehicle for purging society of its many evils. Practically out of nowhere, the anti-Masons became a factor to be reckoned with in such northern states as Massachusetts, New York, and Pennsylvania. The anti-Masonic movement evolved into a diffuse party of moral reform, identifying sin in many urban behaviors and looking to governmental power to correct the evils, promote republicanism, and shape an evolving society into a more orderly America. The Anti-Masonic Party pioneered techniques of organization — including a political convention rather than a caucus to choose a presidential candidate[6] — and it mastered the creation and manipulation of publicity in ways that would be widely used by later political parties and reform movements, particularly abolitionism. The anti-Masons were among the first fully to appreciate the influence of public opinion and to learn how to exploit it for their purposes. Although there had been fears of evil conspiracies before in American politics (for example, during the American Revolution, the fear of a parliamentary plot to extinguish American liberties), anti-Masonry became the first of the great "X-power" bugaboos in American history. Not long after would come the so-called Catholic Power, the Abolitionist Power, the Slave Power, and the Money Power, down to and including various Red Scares and conspiracy theories of the twentieth century. The image of secret conspirators plotting villainies behind the scenes has proven a convenient way for both right-wingers and left-wingers to explain behaviors and political actions they both disliked and found otherwise difficult to understand.

6. See above, p. 376.

RELIGION IN JACKSONIAN POLITICS

Almost immediately, the real aims of the Anti-Masonic Party came into focus as a range of social issues rather than an exclusive phobia about Masons. In fact, William Wirt, the party's rather reluctant presidential candidate in 1832, had himself been a Mason. Soon anti-Jacksonian politicians followed Thurlow Weed's lead in downplaying the issue of Masonry, instead beginning to shape the grab-bag of anti-Masonic grievances into the emerging anti-Jackson Whig Party. Social and religious reformers — men and women who were willing to employ governmental power, or church bodies, or great national multidenominational organizations to shape and discipline society — slowly began to see that the Whig Party shared their willingness to use government. And so rival camps of reformers coalesced in Jacksonian America. Like Henry Clay with his American System, anti-Jackson moral reformers aimed to remold the nation. The Whig Party proved especially congenial to the mind-set of the primarily northern religious reformers who wanted, through persuasion and the law, to make the nation conform to their Protestant image of a Christian republic. The Whigs wanted to promote change through an interventionist government. Their rivals, the Jacksonian Democrats, in important respects envisioned a very different American future: the expansion across geographical space of an empire of small farmers and entrepreneurial men on the make; and they also stressed the individual white person's right to be let alone in matters of conscience. Jackson supporters prized their local independence, disliked special privilege of all kinds, and opposed pressure or influence on them by agencies or forces outside their control. Whigs and moral reformers, on the other hand, envisioned the future in terms of, over time, improving — socially, morally, economically — the population within the nation's existing borders. Whigs were the party of peace, governmental activism, and collective reform. Jacksonian Democrats favored territorial expansion, individualism, a hands-off attitude toward the economy, and white supremacy.

❧ *Sabbatarianism*

In the first decades of nineteenth-century America a running controversy over the Sunday delivery of the U.S. mail came to epitomize broader debates about the future of the republic and the proper roles within it of church and state. This debate foreshadowed the development of the Second Party System, in which the Democrats and Whigs replaced the earlier Federalists and Republicans as broad coalitions dominating the political scene for two decades. The religious dimension of the Sunday mail controversy not only added a moral element to politics, thereby significantly raising the stakes of party disputes, but it also helped perfect techniques of mass appeal that revolutionized electioneering. In the course of the Democratic-Whig rivalry, American politics switched from being a gentry-based leisure pursuit to a mass-based enterprise with professional leaders and the aura of a participatory sport. Political participation swelled enormously, and partisanship became fully accepted — rather than condemned as anti-republican "factional intrigue." No longer appealing to narrow regional or class "interests," the two great national parties now sought out adherents in all sections of the nation, and they essentially subsumed all the divisive issues of the day into struggles between two competing party conceptions of right policy.

The Sabbatarian controversy had its origins in a law that Congress passed in 1810, requiring post offices to be open on any day that mail was delivered, including Sundays. Earlier, Congress had not mandated such a policy, leaving hours of post office operation up to the postmaster general. Many stagecoach lines had not run on Sunday, and most small post offices therefore stayed closed on that day. But for post offices at key distribution points along the major routes, where the stagecoaches ran seven days a week and delivered mail daily, the postmaster general required that postmasters (or their clerks) sort the mail to expedite its transportation. This did not necessarily require post offices to be open to the public. In 1809, however, a Presbyterian elder who happened to be the postmaster in a Pennsylvania town ordered his clerks actually to keep the office open on Sunday so that townspeople could pick up their mail. His church asked him to stop, claiming that he was profaning the Sabbath. The postmaster, a certain Hugh Wylie, appealed his case all the way to the national assembly of the Presbyterian church, which in 1810 ruled against him. Wylie was, in effect, given the choice of either working in the post office or remaining a Presbyterian.

In 1809 Wylie had not been required to open his post office to the public, but the 1810 federal legislation gave postmasters no such choice. By federal law, patrons could now expect to pick up their mail even on the Sabbath. The U.S. postmaster general, sensing political trouble, interpreted the law as narrowly as possible: he ruled that only those post offices that actually received mail deliveries had to be open, and only for an hour. The opening, moreover, must be delayed until after the close of morning worship services. Even so, many devout Christians were shocked by this federal law, which flew in the face of what they believed God required: to keep holy the Sunday Sabbath. These persons interpreted the federal law as not only an infraction of the Ten Commandments but also as an infringement of their religious liberty. If they worked for the post office, they would have to break either the Second Commandment or Congress's law.

Hundreds of petitions signed by thousands of persons poured into Congress protesting the Sunday mail law. These petitions often went beyond merely attacking compulsory opening of post offices on Sundays; the petitioners also wanted to stop the Sunday stagecoaches, the sorting of mail on Sunday, and every other vestige of postal labor on the Christian Sabbath. Yet this flurry of protests had hardly begun before the nation found itself at war with Great Britain, and it was impossible to deny, in the midst of the War of 1812, that the nation's self-interest often required the quickest possible delivery of the mail. So the controversy over the Sunday mails (or, as some would style it, over whether the government could profane the Sabbath and force believers to participate in that profanation) petered out by 1817 without really being resolved.

The Sunday mail controversy erupted again in 1826, the year after Congress reenacted the law requiring post offices to open on Sunday if they received mail. In the fifteen years since 1810, the number of post offices and the miles of postal roads had more than tripled. The volume of commerce and mail had kept apace with the Market Revolution, enormously swelling the amount of postal business. Because all other government and non-essential offices closed on Sundays, and because on Sundays traditional Protestant worshipers refrained from work, travel, and most forms of recreation, towns and villages were almost eerily quiet on Sundays. Few people ventured out.

The very peacefulness of small-town American Sundays was rudely shattered by the bustle and noise of the arrival of the mail coach and the scramble of more secular (or at least less rigidly Sabbatarian) persons to hurry to the post office. For the traditionally devout, gathering up mail and all the accompanying neighborly visiting and talking corrupted the sanctity of the Lord's Day. But it was the series of revivals in the North and Northeast, collectively called the Second Great Awakening, that emboldened many church leaders to want to strengthen the nation's observance of the Sabbath. Urban growth, by providing anonymity and removing the disciplining influence of family elders, also tended to encourage, from the perspective of more traditional village life, profanation of the Sabbath. The burgeoning growth of new immigrant (and mostly Catholic) populations that saw Sunday as a day of recreation, visiting, and good-natured camaraderie, as well as a time for worship, also profoundly upset traditional Protestant leaders.

A Christian counterattack was spearheaded by Presbyterian and Congregational churches of the urban Northeast, beginning in 1826 with a second campaign against the Sunday deliveries of mail and promoting strict Sabbath observance. Many religious leaders feared that God would somehow punish the nation for violating the Sabbath. The campaign began by attempting to convince laypersons to avoid unnecessary Sunday activities. In this, as in most other reform movements, the effort was more to inspire self-discipline than to enforce social control on unwilling people. Nevertheless, the intention in either case was a remade society. In 1826 the Presbyterian General Assembly urged its members to boycott any business that stayed open seven days a week. A prominent Presbyterian in the great Erie Canal city of Rochester, Josiah Bissel, even organized a stagecoach and canal packet company called the Pioneer Line. It promised to be so efficient that it could beat competitors even though it did not operate on Sundays.

Soon the Sabbatarian movement became a big-time operation. In 1828, aiming to persuade the public to use his line and boycott companies that violated the Sabbath, Bissel and other moral reformers founded the General Union for the Promotion of the Christian Sabbath (GUPCS). The year before, Presbyterian minister Ezra Styles Ely in Philadelphia, concerned about a number of supposed moral failings on the part of society, had called for *a Christian party in politics.* Ely argued that if the old-line Protestant denominations united at the ballot box, they "could govern every public election in our country." The GUPCS did not answer Ely's call for a political party, but it was one of the first pressure groups organized to affect public opinion and thereby politics. It distributed tens of thousands of brochures and, expanding its appeal to factory workers and artisans, argued that closing businesses on Sunday would give workers a needed day of rest.

By December 1828 the GUPCS had embarked on still another way to protect the Sabbath. Moving beyond efforts at moral suasion through publicity, it now embarked on a campaign to petition Congress to repeal the law that kept post offices open on Sundays. Hundreds of petitions signed by tens of thousands of laypersons from all sections of the country flooded into Congress. Most came from New England, the Midwest, and the Middle Atlantic States, but the South also contributed a good number. The campaign against the Sunday mails was national, as was the general effort to promote old-time Protestant observance of the Sabbath. Apart from occasional overtones of coercion, the basic thrust of the campaign was to appeal to citizens' consciences to police themselves by inner discipline.

❧ The Anti-Sabbatarianism Backlash

Coming on the heels of Rev. Ely's proposal for a Christian party, the crusade against the Sunday mails frightened the country's few unbelievers, its slowly growing numbers of Roman Catholic immigrants, and large numbers of its many pietistic evangelicals such as southern Baptists, Methodists, and Disciples and Church of Christ members (all of whom tended to be individualistic and skeptical of ruling hierarchies). In addition, the Sabbatarian movement antagonized most of the political and economic supporters of Andrew Jackson, whose orientation was decidedly localistic and laissez-faire (that is, opposed to government intervention in economic affairs). Atheists and agnostics were an insignificant political force in the 1820s, but such advocates of these persuasions as the English-born radicals Frances Wright and Robert Owen joined Christian dissenters in attacking the Sabbatarian movement as an attempt to squelch all dissent and subvert the First Amendment's prohibition of a religious establishment.

Many pietistic evangelicals who fully supported the strictest individual observance of the Sabbath nevertheless were deeply suspicious of Presbyterian-Congregationalist efforts to mandate any kind of religious observance. For such Christians, legal compulsion in religious matters conjured up memories of an unholy alliance between church and state that had persecuted Baptists and Methodists in colonial times, and smacked of a theocracy (government by clergy or by officials who are considered divinely guided). Any effort by either the churches or the government to control behavior and direct society seemed to pietistic evangelicals a limitation on individual religious freedom. (A tiny group of so-called Primitive Baptists in the West and South even opposed efforts to establish Sunday schools, seminaries, mission societies, and all other human agencies to spread the gospel, believing that doing so would "dethrone God; sap the foundation of the Christian religion; raise anti-Christ to his full power . . . and . . . bring on an awful persecution . . . against the true Church of Christ.") Catholic immigrants — already wary of reformers who advocated temperance and demanded public schools that would inculcate Protestantism along with reading — rightly saw the legal proscription of Sabbath observation as a Protestant attack on what they considered acceptable Sunday behavior, which included convivial relaxation in beer gardens after Mass. And all these groups, in common with most Jacksonians, opposed any attempt to impose standardized behavior or national systems of transportation or banking. Indeed, they resisted any sort of national uniformity. As Irish Catholics flocked to the Democratic Party, old-line Protestants turned away from the party precisely because it was becoming "foreign." Ethnic and cultural concerns shaped party affiliations at least as much as economic concerns.

All the petitions against the Sunday mail flooded into the offices of the Senate Committee on the Post Office, chaired by a Jackson partisan from Kentucky, Colonel Richard M. Johnson. A famous Indian fighter who promoted himself for having personally killed in battle Tecumseh, the great Shawnee chief, Johnson was also a friend of evangelicals who feared the overweening influence of national church organizations. Moreover, Johnson represented the economic interest of many in the South and West who feared that stopping the mails on Sunday would increase their competitive disadvantage with eastern merchants, who always got first word of European markets. Johnson embodied the basic Jacksonian belief in localism, which implied opposition to standardizing national systems. Johnson had a strong preference for limited government, in contrast to moral reformers or to economic nationalists like Henry Clay with his American System. Such reformers and planners found more congenial the idea of harnessing the power of government or of organized "benevolence" to change society.

Laissez-faire in outlook, Johnson and most other Jacksonians believed that maximizing freedom of choice was the best way to ensure a good and just society. If the Whigs were the party of reform, the Democrats were the party of westward expansion. They saw the future in terms of an ever-expanding empire of

MATTY'S PERILOUS SITUATION UP SALT RIVER

family farms and small-scale enterprise. Reformers, repelled by the nation's growing cities and by the rawness of its frontier life, often feared the consequences of such unbridled, undisciplined freedom, from which they expected only social chaos. Expressing his fundamental disagreement with the Sabbatarians, Johnson in two powerful committee reports (probably written for him by a Baptist named Obadiah Brown), one in 1829 and one in 1830, attacked the Sabbatarian movement as an enemy of freedom.

Johnson's attacks on those who sought to prohibit Sunday mail deliveries were withering. Pointing out that different religious groups disagreed as to which day was the Sabbath (Saturday or Sunday), Johnson argued that the Sabbatarians in effect wanted to draw the government into a religious debate and decide a theological issue. But he saw a still more menacing threat behind the Sunday mail crusade — an effort to establish a theocracy by combination, organization, and petition. In other words, Johnson portrayed the effort to promote the Sabbath and restrain the Sunday mails as a Trojan horse that would deprive most Americans of their reli-

"Matty's Perilous Situation Up Salt River"   In this cartoon from the 1840 presidential election, Martin Van Buren is drowning in the Salt River under the weight of various controversial political issues (Salt River was a slang term for political failure). His opponent, William Henry Harrison, is paddling over on a barrel of hard cider to save him. Harrison is commenting that he'll try to save him—but he's only good enough to be appointed inspector of cabbages in his hometown of Kinderhook, New York.

gious freedom. "Extensive religious combinations to effect a political object are, in the opinion of the committee, always dangerous." Warming to his subject, Johnson cautioned that "All religious despotism commences by combination and influence; and when that influence begins to operate upon the political institutions of a country, the civil power soon bends under it; and the catastrophe of other nations furnishes an awful warning."

Johnson's first report produced a rash of petitions to Congress defending the Sunday mails; but his second report, issued on March 4, 1830, seemed so persuasive even to the foes of the Sunday mails as almost to render further controversy counterproductive. Perhaps, most Sabbatarians concluded, those who wished to promote strict Sunday observance should simply rely on moral suasion and local resolutions, not the federal government. The last gasp on behalf of the GUPCS came in an address to the Senate on May 8, 1830, by Senator Theodore Frelinghuysen of New Jersey. In his apparent support of coercive state laws, however, Frelinghuysen weakened his case. The reelection of Andrew Jackson in 1832 and the strengthened position of the Jacksonians in Congress doomed the crusade against Sunday mails, and the GUPCS disbanded in late 1832. Once again the Sunday mail controversy quickly disappeared from the public scene. Ironically, decades later the cause was resurrected by the defenders of working people, who secularized the argument: at last the effort succeeded in the late nineteenth century, and the post offices were closed on Sundays as part of broader efforts to shorten the work week and provide people with more time for recreation.

❧ Ethnic and Cultural Origins of the Whig Party

Even though the Sunday mail controversy and the anti-Masonic movement both failed in their immediate purpose and indeed proved ephemeral, both became cultural agents that helped weld together a broad anti-Jackson coalition. Fearing the tumultuous changes that their society was experiencing, many Americans came to accept the anti-Masons' claims about elite or secret control of American life, or responded enthusiastically to the religious reformers' crusades for temperance, Sabbath observance, antislavery, and public schools. Behind all these impulses lay the conviction that American society needed controlling and shaping, and those who thought in such terms generally opposed the live-and-let-live attitudes of the Jacksonians. Such powerful cultural worries, as well as objection to specific Jacksonian policies — Old Hickory's war against the B.U.S., his denunciation of certain federally funded internal improvements, his genocidal actions towards the Indians, his tariff policies, and his crushing of nullification — all flowed together to create a patchwork opposition party. The glue that held all the disparate Whigs together was fear and hatred of that purported tyrant, King Andrew I.

DIVERSE GROUPS, COMMON ISSUES
As a result, American political attitudes largely polarized into two great parties, both of which drew supporters from all regions, from all classes, and from a broad spectrum of social, religious, and cultural groups. One party saw government as a necessary,

positive force for reform; the other party wanted to limit the power and role of the national government and privilege unrestrained individual initiative. Even the issues that at first glance seem essentially economic or fiscal were perceived at the time to have moral consequences. Extravagant investment and speculation, defaulting on debts, and supporting or opposing tariffs on self-interested grounds all have ethical dimensions. It was easy for religious and social reformers to infuse moral weight even into debates over economic policy.

Despite the diversity within the two parties, each displayed a surprising degree of cohesion around opposing sets of policy issues. By the middle of Jackson's second term the new Whig Party was crystallizing out of the many strands of opposition to Jackson. By 1836, it had become a national party and had begun planning how to oppose the election of Jackson's hand-picked successor, Martin Van Buren. Essentially a party of reformers, the Whig Party found its supporters mostly among those most affected by the market economy: urban merchants, bankers, and factory owners; farmers who grew crops for the national or international markets; and clergy (as well as many cultural conservatives among the general population) dismayed by the social, moral, and cultural flaws they perceived in America's emerging capitalist, multicultural society. Even in the South, many Whigs appeared in the urban banking and commercial circles and among the largest planters (especially Louisiana sugar planters who wanted tariff protection). The Democrats, on the other hand, found great strength among urban workingmen, Catholic immigrants, small farmers, and upwardly mobile entrepreneurs in the South and West who chafed under presumed domination by older northeastern elites.

In 1836 the new Whig Party was less a unified opposition than a collection of angry interest groups. Whigs came together largely on account of their mutual dislike of Jackson and what he represented — democracy run amok. Whig opposition had not quite jelled behind a manageable number of issues or a single candidate. Instead, the party ran four sectional candidates against Van Buren, hoping that such a strategy would deny the Little Magician a majority of electoral votes and throw the election into the House of Representatives. So William Henry Harrison of Ohio, Hugh Lawson White of Tennessee, W. P. Mangum of North Carolina, and Daniel Webster of Massachusetts all ran as Whigs; but only Harrison proved an effective vote-getter. Against

Tocqueville Fears the Tyranny of the Majority, 1835

Alexis de Tocqueville did not, like many European observers of the American scene during the Jacksonian era, contemptuously reject democracy. He understood that democracy was probably the wave of the future both in America and in Europe. He sought to understand it, and in so doing wrote one of the most profound and enduring books on public affairs in the nineteenth century, Democracy in America. *Here, he puts his finger on one of the recurrent issues in American politics—one which confronted the Framers of the Constitution, and which still poses an important dilemma: how do we reconcile the majority's wish to govern with a minority's wish to safeguard its rights?*

My greatest complaint against democratic government as organized in the United States is not, as many Europeans make out, its weakness, but rather its irresistible strength. What I find most repulsive in America is not the extreme freedom reigning there but the shortage of guarantees against tyranny.

When a man or a party suffers an injustice in the United States, to whom can he turn? To public opinion? That is what forms the majority. To the legislative body? It represents the majority and obeys it blindly. To the executive power? It is appointed by the majority and serves as its passive instrument. To the police? They are nothing but the majority under arms. A jury? The jury is the majority vested with the right to pronounce judgment; even the judges in certain states are elected by the majority. So, however iniquitous or unreasonable the measure which hurts you, you must submit. . . .

I am not asserting that at the present time in America there are frequent acts of tyranny. I do say that one can find no guarantee against it and that the reasons for the government's gentleness must be sought in circumstances and in mores rather that in the laws.

---

all four, Van Buren retained enough of the aura of Old Hickory to win 170 electoral votes to 124 for the combined Whig candidates. Richard M. Johnson, who had led the attack against the Sunday mail protesters, became Van Buren's vice president.

THE LOG CABIN AND CIDER CAMPAIGN

Van Buren's popular majority had been thin — less than 51 percent of the total vote. He lost two southern states. Even had his administration not been soon beset by the economic catastrophe caused by Jackson's bank war and Specie Circular, Van Buren's electoral prospects were not rosy for 1840. For by that date the Whigs had moved beyond a loose coalition of grumblers who believed the hurly-burly nation somehow needed discipline and direction; they had become as modern a political party as the Democrats. They had perfected the electioneering skills first introduced by the Democrats in 1828, and they had found a candidate — in their own version of General Jackson — perfect for the new style of campaigning. Many Whigs, veterans of a number of religiously inspired benevolent associations, had learned in those earlier moral crusades how to mobilize volunteers, produce persuasive literature, raise money, and organize a campaign.

Smelling victory in early 1840, the Whigs decided to nominate one candidate unencumbered by well-known and firmly held views (such as those that burdened Clay and Webster, their best-known leaders). Their choice fell upon Ohioan William Henry Harrison, who had proved himself popular in 1836. Harrison superficially resembled Jackson: the now sixty-seven-year-old general was an old Indian-war hero whose fame rested on his victory over Tecumseh at the Battle of Tippecanoe in 1811. For sectional balance, the Whigs chose Senator John Tyler of Virginia, about whom they knew little except that he was a vigorous foe of Andrew Jackson. Coining the slogan "Tippecanoe and Tyler Too," party managers ran the campaign with no platform and a presidential candidate who professed no firm opinions about anything. When a Democratic journalist, meaning to ridicule the Whig candidate for having no positions and being unfit for the highest office in the land, sneered that Harrison would be content to spend the rest of his days sitting on the front porch of his cabin sipping hard cider, the Whig symbol machine saw its opening.[7] The Democrats had given them the image of a folksy, humble candidate whose heroism and simple tastes commended him to the public more effectively than any bundle of policies or sterling credentials.

Perfecting the campaigning techniques the Jacksonians had pioneered in 1828, the Whigs launched their Log Cabin and Cider campaign. Campaign songs and torchlight parades featured miniature log cabins and huge cider barrels rolled along the streets. A campaign newspaper called the *Log Cabin* kept supporters up to date, and Harrison actually campaigned vigorously, even traveling about by rail for the first time for a

---

7. In truth, Harrison had practically retired and was living in near-poverty, so the jibe was not far from the mark.

presidential candidate. In contrast to "Old Tip's" simple tastes, the Whig press hooted at Van Buren as an eastern aristocrat, lolling on Turkish divans and drinking expensive foreign wines. Charges were flung that he "put cologne on his whiskers," and he was mockingly called "Sweet Sandy Whiskers." While Harrison contentedly dined on hog meat and hominy grits, Van Buren (it was said) employed a fancy French chef to prepare his gourmet meals at public expense. Both images were as inaccurate and unfair as those of Jackson and Adams in 1828, but the Whigs were paying the Democrats back for the Jackson forces' treatment of Adams in 1828. A Whig campaign song summarized the spirit of their campaign:

> *Old Tip he wears a homespun suit*
> *He has no ruffled shir-wir-wirt!*
> *But Van he has the golden plate,*
> *And he's a little squir-wir-wirt!*

As one Democratic newspaper lamented in June 1840, "We have taught them to conquer us."

The result was a huge expansion of the electorate. Twice as many voted in 1840 as in 1828, and almost 80 percent of eligible white men actually cast ballots — probably the highest rate of registered voter participation in American history. Harrison carried nineteen out of twenty-six states, winning victories in every region from Maine to Louisiana and from Michigan to Georgia. Harrison was swept into the White House with an electoral college landslide of 234 votes to 60.

TYLER'S SURPRISE

The Log Cabin campaign was a cynical means to an end, which was the very intentional use of government to effect political, fiscal, and cultural change. Clay and Webster, the most powerful Whig leaders, expected to dominate the administration and govern energetically with Harrison as a figurehead. In the first several weeks of his administration Clay and Webster's plan seemed to be working to perfection. But then, on April 4, 1841, exactly a month after taking the oath of office (and delivering history's longest inaugural address, bareheaded in a cold rain), President Harrison died of pneumonia.[8] Vice President Tyler ascended

to the presidency, making it clear that he intended to be a real president, not an "acting" one.[9] And now the Whig leaders learned that they should have paid more attention to Tyler's principles before they put him on the ticket. Tyler objected to the entire Whig program and had only opposed Jackson because of Old Hickory's autocratic style. Within a week of taking office, Tyler issued an address that made clear that he was not really a Whig. In June, Senator Clay introduced a set of resolutions to Congress outlining an aggressive Whig economic policy, including repealing the Independent Treasury Act that Van Buren had passed in continuation of Jackson's bank war and reincorporating a bank of the United States, along with authorizing higher tariffs to create federal revenue for internal improvements.

Tyler and Clay had thus staked out diametrically opposing policy positions. With differences between the Whig leaders in Congress and President Tyler out in the open, the Whigs essentially read Tyler out of their party. In reality a conservative Democrat rather than a reformist Whig, Tyler vetoed every aspect of Clay's program, including two versions of the bank incorporation bill. In part because the general economy was improving, the national bank faded out of American politics for a generation. In any case, the Whig program was politically dead. By September 1841, Tyler's entire Whig cabinet had resigned except Secretary of State Webster, who stayed in office long enough to conclude the Webster-Ashburton Treaty with Great Britain.[10] Tyler replaced the departing Whigs mostly with southern Democrats. Eventually John C. Calhoun became his secretary of state (after Abel P. Upshur of Virginia, who had followed Webster, was killed in 1844 in an accidental explosion aboard the warship *Princeton*). Calhoun's appointment marked his return to the Democratic fold and the rise to dominance of the South in the Democratic Party. As the election of 1844 neared, the Whigs who had looked so invincible in 1840 were divided and confused; the Democrats were determined to regain the presidency. But the political landscape was about to be changed by the explosive issues of slavery and expansion.

---

8. Learning of the Whig president's death, unforgiving Andrew Jackson considered it an "act of an overruling providence . . . to preserve and perpetuate our happy system of republicanism and stay the corruption of this combined cliqe [sic]."

9. Since this was the first time that a president had died in office, there was some uncertainty as to whether the vice president should succeed to the office or merely be a passive caretaker. Tyler set the precedent that he should fully assume the office.

10. See Chapter 13, pp. 411-12.

Conclusion:
Emerging Sectionalism

For the two decades between 1824 and 1844, the major issues dividing the nation were controversies over banking, the tariff, and internal improvements. Temporarily at least, the danger to the Union of nullification and even secession was crushed by a president willing to threaten drastic retaliation. Meanwhile, competing visions for safeguarding the future of the Union had arisen. On one side were those who wanted to shape, control, and reorder the population through social and religious reform that would produce a self-disciplined citizenry. On the other side stood advocates of localism, of limited government, and of entrepreneurial spirit as the surest guarantees of democracy and opportunity. Two major political parties took shape to represent coalitions of voters who agreed in broad philosophical outline, and these parties developed techniques to identify party leaders, motivate voters, and gain intense partisan loyalty. The nation's basic divisions were mostly ethnic, cultural, and religious, *not* sectional. Both Whigs and Democrats had significant supporters in both North and South, and on the state level Whigs and Democrats battled almost to a draw in the South in the decade after 1840. Both were national parties in 1844. Issues that were narrowly sectional, such as territorial expansion and the continuation or abolition of slavery, had not yet become central to national politics. In some instinctive way, both Clay with his American System and Van Buren with his advocacy of national political parties understood that political conflicts needed to be channeled away from sectional divisions.

Yet this was about to change. Andrew Jackson died in the summer of 1845, symbolizing also the passing of his political era. After 1844, banking, tariffs, and internal improvements would recede as the key markers of political identification, replaced by a new range of issues that would bedevil the American political system until the Union broke apart in civil war. Matters of reform, specifically antislavery, would play a major role in defining the new issues, but the immediate cause of trouble would be territorial expansion and the future — not simply the present existence — of slavery. And, for many northerners, soon a new "Power" would threaten the republic's future: the "Slave Power," the code word for southern extremists allegedly determined to control the Union for the benefit of a few slaveholding aristocrats. In the Jacksonian era territorial expansion had seemed an uncontroversial process by which farmers seeking to better themselves moved westward to carve new homes out of the wilderness. The Jacksonians saw such expansion as the elixir of democratic progress. But by the 1840s expansion escalated into conflict with other nations, disputes between the Whigs and Democrats, a war with Mexico, and a political upheaval that exacerbated every real and perceived difference between the North and South. The Second Party System eventually would prove unable to defuse the multiple controversies that arose over territorial expansion. Its collapse would ultimately bring on the Civil War.

SUGGESTED READING

Donald B. Cole, *Martin Van Buren and the American Political System* (1984). Details how Van Buren helped shaped the emergence of the modern party system.

Donald B. Cole, *The Presidency of Andrew Jackson* (1993). A revisionist account of Jackson's presidency that is more critical of his policies and accomplishments than earlier works.

Richard E. Ellis, *The Union at Risk: Jacksonian Democracy, States' Rights, and the Nullification Crisis* (1887). The most complete and judicious treatment of this complex event.

Bray Hammond, *Banks and Politics in America from the Revolution to the Civil War* (1957). An older but still unsurpassed history of the bank war in Jacksonian politics.

Michael F. Holt, *The Rise and Fall of the American Whig Party: Jacksonian Politics and the Onset of the Civil War* (1999). A magisterial, exhaustive, and very lengthy analysis of practically every imaginable aspect of the Whig Party.

Richard Johns, "Taking Sabbatarianism Seriously: The Postal System, the Sabbath, and the Transformation of the American Political Culture," *Journal of the Early Republic* 10 (Winter 1990): 517-67. The most complete, insightful, and wide-ranging analysis of a little-known controversy that helped reshape antebellum politics.

Richard P. McCormick, *The Second American Party System: Party Formation in the Jacksonian Era* (1966). The classic depiction of the breakup of the party system associated with the Age of Jefferson and the emergence of another party system in the 1820s and 1830s.

John Niven, *John C. Calhoun and the Price of Union* (1988). An accessible biographical treatment that places Calhoun squarely in the matrix of national politics.

Arthur M. Schlesinger, Jr., *The Age of Jackson* (1945). One of the great landmarks in American historical scholarship that lauds the democratizing forces at work during the era.

SUGGESTIONS FOR FURTHER READING

Glenn C. Altschuler and Stuart M. Blumin, *Rude Republic: Americans and Their Politics in the Nineteenth Century* (2000).

John Ashworth, *"Agrarians" and "Aristocrats": Party Political Ideology in the United States, 1837-1846* (1983).

Jean H. Baker, *Affairs of Party: The Political Culture of Northern Democrats in the Mid-Nineteenth Century* (1983).

William J. Cooper, Jr., *The South and the Politics of Slavery, 1828-1856* (1978).

George Dangerfield, *The Era of Good Feelings* (1949).

Ronald P. Formisano, *The Birth of Mass Political Parties, 1827-1861* (1971).

William W. Freehling, *Prelude to the Civil War: The Nullification Controversy in South Carolina, 1816-1836* (1966).

Paul Goodman, *Toward a Christian Republic: Antimasonry and the Great Tradition in New England, 1826-1836* (1988).

Richard Hofstadter, *The Idea of a Party System: The Rise of Legitimate Opposition in the United States, 1780-1840* (1969).

Daniel Walker Howe, *The Political Culture of the American Whigs* (1979).

Lawrence F. Kohl, *The Politics of Individualism: Politics and the American Character in the Jacksonian Era* (1989).

Shaw Livermore, *The Twilight of Federalism: The Disintegration of the Federalist Party, 1815-1830* (1962).

Marvin Meyers, *The Jacksonian Persuasion* (1960).

Merrill D. Peterson, *Olive Branch and Sword: The Compromise of 1833* (1982).

Norma Lewis Peterson, *The Presidencies of William Henry Harrison and John Tyler* (1990).

Donald J. Ratcliffe, *The Politics of Long Division: The Birth of the Second Party System in Ohio, 1818-1828* (2000).

Robert V. Remini, *The Life of Andrew Jackson* (1988).

Ronald N. Satz, *American Indian Policy in the Jacksonian Era* (1975).

Joel H. Sibley, *The Partisan Imperative: The Dynamics of American Politics before the Civil War* (1985).

Ian Tyrrell, *Sobering Up: From Temperance to Prohibition in Antebellum America, 1800-1860* (1979).

Harry Watson, *Liberty and Power: The Politics of Jacksonian America* (1990).

John G. West, Jr., *The Politics of Revelation and Reason: Religion and Civic Life in the New Nation* (1996).

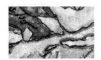

13

Territorial Expansion, Manifest Destiny, and the Mexican War

TO MOST CITIZENS of the modern United States, their nation's march from the shores of the Atlantic Ocean across the continent to the Pacific seems a foreordained, absolutely natural progression. Though it came to be so argued in the 1840s, in earlier decades the dimensions of the nation had not been conceived of in such expansive terms. President Jefferson's acquisition of the Louisiana Territory had seemed extraordinarily bold, and the millions of acres thus purchased from France seemed to most Americans adequate for the nation's population growth for centuries yet to come. After the western boundary of the Louisiana Purchase had been fixed in 1819 by the Adams-Onís Treaty and the issue of free versus slave states in the region had been settled the next year by the Missouri Compromise, the major issues dividing the nation had been not territorial but internal: tariffs, banks, moral reform. The only threats of war were thought to come from Europe, and military expenditures were concentrated in building coastal fortifications sufficient to withstand naval attacks. When a territorial issue arose in the late 1830s, the risk was not internal division but rather war with Great Britain. Yet within less than a decade, territorial expansion had ballooned into an issue of explosive internal controversy, setting into motion a train of events that would have tragic consequences for the nation.

CONTROVERSIES WITH CANADA

Despite — or perhaps because of — two successful wars against Great Britain, American citizens felt a kind of love-hate relationship with England. They were still in many ways intellectually dependent upon English books but independent enough to ignore British copyright law and publish dozens of pirated editions of English books — infuriating British authors, who saw Americans as irresponsible and lawless. When in the midst of the economic difficulties following the Panic of 1837 many states defaulted on their debts to British firms, Americans came in for severe denunciations in the British press. Writers like Charles Dickens mocked American pretensions to greatness. After Britain had emancipated the slaves in its colonies in 1833, it portrayed the United States, with its millions of slaves in the South, as a backward land of hypocrisy. American opinion-makers seethed at English condescension, looked for any opportunity to poke John Bull in the eye, and meanwhile were quick to take offense at any supposed lack of respect for this country's independence. Against this antagonistic backdrop, Canadian-American relations took an ominous turn in the late 1830s.

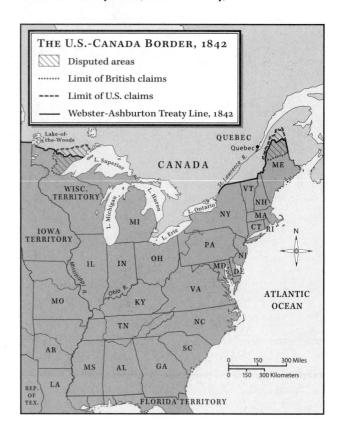

❧ *The* Caroline *Incident*

The British had never paid much attention to, nor expected much from, their Canadian colony. In large part, what remained of British North America was seen, from London, as a bulwark against the United States and a possible staging ground for British armies in the event of war. Then, in 1837, some Canadians, resenting their low priority in the British scheme of things and seeing the fruits of colonial rebellion in the prosperous states to their south, began a rebellion against British rule. Loyal Crown forces quickly put an end to the insurrection, but before the fires were extinguished, American citizens from New York and Vermont came to the aid of the revolutionaries by providing supplies; by offering the use of a small steamer called the *Caroline* to ferry material aid to the insurgents; and by serving as a haven for refugees fleeing British troops. All this was completely illegal. In response, a band of loyal Canadian militia on the night of December 29, 1837, crossed the Niagara River to the American side, where the *Caroline* was docked, boarded her, threw off the crew, set the steamer afire, and then put the vessel adrift. In the course of the struggle an American citizen, Amos Durfee, was killed.

This so-called *Caroline* affair ignited a storm of protests against Britain's alleged violations of American neutrality, but the British Foreign Office ignored American concerns, arguing that in aiding Canadian

insurrectionaries the Americans had gotten what they deserved. Charges and countercharges flew between the two nations, with Americans incensed by what they took to be British hauteur. A group of Americans several months later even boarded a British steamer, the *Sir Robert Peel,* on the American side of the St. Lawrence River and burned it, while secret groups organized for the purpose of overthrowing British rule in Canada. President Van Buren acted to suppress the American depredations against Canada and sent General Winfield Scott to patrol the region. By 1839-1840 the tension had lessened, but then it was inflamed again in November 1840 by the arrest in New York of Alexander McLeod, a Canadian deputy sheriff who was charged with being involved in the 1837 attack on the *Caroline* and for having murdered Amos Durfee.

Lord Palmerston, the British foreign secretary, said that the raid against the *Caroline* had been officially planned to prevent continued American involvement in the Canadian insurrection, and that therefore McLeod, who was following official orders, must be released. If he were executed for murder, declared Palmerston, war would result. Secretary of State John Forsyth retorted in December 1840 that the courts of New York had jurisdiction (though New York governor William H. Seward promised to pardon McLeod should he be convicted). A possible international incident was avoided when the New York jury on October 12, 1841, acquitted McLeod.

✣ *The Aroostook War*

Meanwhile another dispute had erupted between American and Canadian citizens, and it too threatened to eventuate in war. The Treaty of Paris of 1783, which had ended the American Revolution, had not definitively settled all the boundary problems between the United States and Canada. A subsequent series of commissions in 1818 had set the 49th parallel as the boundary from the Lake of the Woods in present-day Minnesota to the ridge of the Rocky Mountains. No agreement could be reached on the territory west of the Rockies, the so-called Oregon Territory, so both sides agreed to a ten-year period of joint occupation. Two other problem areas remained, the territory between Lake Superior and the Lake of the Woods, and the northern border of Maine, where both Maine and the Canadian province of New Brunswick claimed the rich timberlands of the Aroostook River Valley.

British troops' efforts to suppress the Canadian insurrectionary movement in 1837 had been hampered by the thick winter ice obstructing the St. Lawrence River. Accordingly, British military planners decided to build a road from St. John, New Brunswick, on the Bay of Fundy, to Quebec and Montreal — the best route for which lay through territory claimed by Maine. When Canadian lumberjacks arrived in the winter of 1838-1839 to start cutting a path for the military road and harvesting the timber, Maine citizens took it as an invasion and tried to expel the foreigners. The Canadian lumbermen fought back, capturing a Maine posse and the official Maine land agent. Soon both Maine and New Brunswick were mobilizing their militia, and the result was the so-called Aroostook War.

There were no casualties, but the dispute threatened to get out of hand when Congress appropriated $10 million and authorized President Van Buren to call up 50,000 volunteers. Luckily, Van Buren sent to the scene General Winfield Scott who, experienced in such matters in the aftermath of the *Caroline* affair, persuaded the governor of Maine and the lieutenant governor of New Brunswick to accept a truce in March 1839. But before Britain and the United States could permanently settle the issue by means of a boundary commission, another unrelated controversy further poisoned Anglo-American relations.

In late 1841 an American brig, the *Creole*, left Virginia headed for New Orleans with a cargo of approximately 130 slaves. En route the slaves mutinied, killing a white crew member, and took the vessel to the port of Nassau in the British Bahama Islands, knowing full well that slavery had been abolished there and in all other British colonies. The slaves went ashore certain that they had escaped their bondage, and the British did accept as free all those who had not actually participated in the takeover of the ship. American officials and the owners of the *Creole* protested, claiming that the slaves were "mutiners and murderers" and still the property of American citizens. The British ignored the protests of the Americans, and the property claims were not settled until 1855.

Britain had for years been engaged in suppressing the Atlantic slave trade, and though the *Creole* case involved the internal movement of slaves from one state to another, rather than slaves being imported from Africa, the British were not interested in strict definitions of immorality. Southerners were outraged, but sectional political feelings were inflamed when an Ohio congressman, Joshua R. Giddings, used the occasion to attack slavery and the coastal trade in humans. With strong southern backing the House of Representatives censured Giddings in March 1842, but a southern nerve had been touched. While slavery had receded as a political issue since the debate in 1819 over the admission of Missouri, the sensitivity remained. The *Creole* affair simply complicated British-American relations.

✣ *The Webster-Ashburton Treaty*

In September 1841 Sir Robert Peel became prime minister, ending Palmerston's tenure (not for the last time) as foreign secretary. Peel — more conciliatory toward the United States than Palmerston — sent a special envoy to Washington, D.C., Alexander Baring, the First Lord Ashburton. Ashburton had headed a major bank with large American investments, and he realized that for commercial reasons alone the disputes between the two nations ought to be settled.

By this time John Tyler was president, and his secretary of state, Daniel Webster, agreed with Ashburton on the overriding importance of good Anglo-American commercial relations. Even though the political war between Tyler and the congressional Whig leaders had caused the rest of the new president's cabinet to resign, Webster stayed in office to complete negotiations with Ashburton. Personally simpatico, they sought to defuse the controversy over the Aroostook River Valley, and the compromise that resulted, although giving most of the disputed land to Maine, allowed sufficient acreage for the British to build their military road from New Brunswick to Quebec. Webster used a fraudulent map to gain the approval of the Maine commissioners. Meanwhile the secretary of state and the British envoy skillfully devised language to assuage the lingering tensions over the *Caroline* and *Creole* affairs and to clarify the border controversy in northern Minnesota. The resulting Webster-Ashburton Treaty was ratified by Congress on August 20, 1842, one of the few genuine accomplishments of the Tyler administration. The treaty did much to ease the hard feelings between the two nations.

THE NEAR WEST: TEXAS

In the 1830s a territorial issue arose concerning the acquisition of territory controlled by Mexico, a province called Texas and forming part of the huge Mexican state of Coahuila. The controversy became both a political problem within the United States and ultimately a foreign policy dispute that culminated in war with Mexico. The whole cluster of events related to Texas became one of the turning points of American history, and it shifted the basic orientation of the nation's politics to sectional issues. None of these complications were foreseen in the 1820s, when the first American settlers began to trickle into the former Spanish — and now Mexican province — of Texas.

❧ *Spanish Texas*

Spanish explorers de Soto and Cabeza de Vaca had traversed what is now known as Texas in the sixteenth century, but Spanish officials were extremely slow to develop the vast region. Fearing European competition for the land after French explorer La Salle landed there (by mistake) in 1685, in the next decade Spanish authorities established two short-lived missions in eastern Texas. Two decades later, threatened by French colonists in Louisiana, Spanish authorities founded six more mission settlements in eastern Texas, including one near the Indian town named Nacogdoches. In 1718 they established a supply depot in central Texas at San Antonio. Within three more years a number of Spanish towns and missions were founded. Even so, the Span-

ish population of Texas grew very slowly, and the colony never prospered.

Officials in Mexico City paid scant attention to the distant colony, even when, in the early nineteenth century, a few Anglo pioneers began to dribble across the Sabine River and plant crops on the fertile river and creek bottomlands. During the Monroe administration, Secretary of State John Quincy Adams had been involved in difficult negotiations with Spain both to settle the ownership of Florida and the western boundary of the 1803 Louisiana Purchase; the resulting Adams-Onís Treaty of 1819 unambiguously defined the Mexican-American boundary as following first the Sabine River, next a line drawn north to the Red River and then along the eastern edge of the Rocky Mountains to the 42nd parallel, and finally west to the Pacific. Under this treaty, Texas clearly lay beyond the limits of American authority, and no one in Washington had any inclination to change that. Nevertheless, settlers from the southern states continued to cross the Sabine, some of them fleeing debts (particularly after the Panic of 1819), the law, or unhappy marriages. By 1823, perhaps as many as three thousand American citizens were living on the Mexican soil of Texas. Spanish authorities winked at the illegality of this settlement and hoped, by treating the pioneers leniently, to attract their allegiance to Mexico and thereby form a buffer against future American expansion.

❧ *Stephen F. Austin and Anglo Settlement in Texas*

Once Mexico gained its independence from Spain in 1821, it pursued more aggressively the old Spanish policy of attracting U.S. settlers, in part because American economic interest in the commerce along the Santa Fe Trail to New Mexico had raised the specter of Yankee ambitions to take over all of Mexico's lightly governed northern provinces. Connecticut-born Moses Austin, whose lead mining operations in Missouri had gone bankrupt in the Panic of 1819, was quick to see the potential of migration to Texas, and after traveling to San Antonio to talk with Mexican officials he was awarded a charter in January 1821 granting him 200,000 acres of land if he would bring in 300 families. Moses Austin died before he could fulfill his contract, but his son, Stephen F. Austin, arrived, took up his mantle as the founder of Anglo Texas, and won additional concessions following a series of trips to Mexico City. The terms of the settlement contracts changed several

Texas in 1822   Stephen F. Austin drew this map of the Mexican province of Texas in 1822, labeling it in Spanish. Austin, a recent immigrant from the United States, at that time intended to keep Texas loyal to Mexico. The Nueces River, not the Rio Grande, forms the southern boundary of Texas.

times, and additional contracts were granted to a number of other land promoters. The government of Mexico was extremely unstable, and there were a series of mini-revolutions — sometimes several changes of rulers in a single year. But in 1824 a new liberal Mexican constitution was approved, Texas was organized as a province of the state of Coahuila, and in March 1825 the territory was opened up to colonization. Settlers were expected to profess the Catholic faith, have no slaves, obey the laws of Mexico, and essentially become Mexican citizens, but few balked at these conditions because the land grants were so generous — more than 4,600 acres per family. Migration from the United States soared, and by 1830 Texas contained as many as twenty thousand Anglo settlers.

Problems soon arose because most of these Yankees really had no intention of becoming culturally Mexican. They nominally became Catholic but continued Protestant worship surreptitiously, they "freed" their slaves and then "hired" them as lifetime servants, and few bothered to learn Spanish. In the mid-1820s there were no more than three or four thousand Mexican settlers — called Tejanos — in Texas, concentrated in San Antonio, Goliad, and Nacogdoches and on large ranches in the central and southern portion of the state. These Mexican settlements were controlled by an elite of traditional ranching families, and the relatively few Anglos who came to San Antonio or the ranching centers often intermarried, adapted Mexican ways, and became in effect Tejanos. James Bowie, who later died in the Alamo, was one of these adapted Tejanos, and he married the daughter of the vice governor of Texas.

It was from the Mexican ranching families that the later Texas ranching empire developed. Thus the cattle-raising techniques and terminology of Texas and the West were of Spanish-Mexican origin. The first Texas cattle drives began in the region south of San Antonio, and later herds were driven to Nacogdoches and from there to the United States. As a result of this interaction with Tejanos, Anglos in Texas adopted certain aspects of the Spanish-Mexican legal codes (particularly with respect to water rights, a critical matter in the region's arid climate) and retained the use of mounted militia to police the far-flung province. The fabled Texas Rangers were an adaptation of Tejano practices. But most of the Anglo settlers were to the east of San Antonio. They were more interested in cotton farming than in ranching, and for cotton cultivation they assumed that slaves were necessary. They saw themselves as transplanted southerners, not as would-be Mexicans or Tejanos.

Perhaps the first hint of trouble came in Nacogdoches in 1826, when land promoter Hayden Edwards led a revolt against Mexican authorities in a dispute over land laws and established the short-lived "Republic of Fredonia." Stephen F. Austin, who honestly wanted the settlers to live up to their obligations under Mexican law, helped squelch the Fredonia rebellion. But the episode showed the potential for conflict between the expectations of the Mexican authorities and the Anglo settlers. Austin was a skilled diplomat, and throughout most of the 1820s he was able to keep the rumblings of trouble under control, even though a Mexican study commission in 1829 warned that Anglos vastly outnumbered Tejanos and flagrantly ignored Mexican laws.

In 1830 the unstable government in Mexico City again changed, and strong centralizers gained control. It was their policy to tighten the rules over the far-flung provinces and emphatically to enforce existing laws. Texas was closed to further immigration from the United States. Immigrants were solicited instead from Switzerland, France, England, and Poland to counter American influence, adding to Texas's rich multicultural heritage. When Mexico emancipated its own slaves in 1829, the importation of more slaves into Texas was outlawed and steps were taken to enforce the emancipation of slaves already there. Mexican officials also tried to collect the customs duties on trade to and from Texas that the Anglo settlers had simply ignored. However, Mexico lacked the military power to enforce these laws except very sporadically, and so the effect

was to anger the Anglo settlers without changing their behavior. Americans continued to flow into the region. Austin got the restriction against immigration lifted in late 1834, and by the following year Anglos were coming to Texas at the rate of a thousand a month. At the end of 1835 there were approximately 30,000 Anglos in Texas, 5,000 black slaves, and only 4,000 Tejanos. This disproportion in Anglo population, and the inability to enforce Mexican laws, worried authorities in Mexico City. The Texas situation was growing out of control.

The Texas Revolution

In 1834 General Antonio Lopez de Santa Anna became dictator of Mexico, abolished the federal system of government created by the constitution of 1824, and accelerated the centralization of authority. Rumors spread to Texas of draconian measures about to be applied, including disfranchisement, the complete abolition of slavery, the collection of taxes and customs, and even the expulsion of the Anglo settlers. Both Tejanos and Anglos resisted the intended changes and began to talk of rebellion against Santa Anna's rule. Santa Anna prepared to send troops to Texas to enforce the collection of customs, but the settlers in Texas acted first, seizing a small Mexican garrison at Anahuac. At first Stephen F. Austin counseled patience; he hoped to work with liberals in Mexico City who opposed Santa Anna and wanted to restore the constitution of 1824. But events outpaced Austin's efforts at compromise, and when Santa Anna began to invade Texas, Austin sided with the Texas rebels. Under Austin's leadership a small force of Texans captured San Antonio in December 1835. Thinking they had won the skirmish, the Texans let down their guard. Austin, whose skills were diplomatic rather than military anyway, departed for the United States, where he hoped to arrange support for the cause of Texan independence.

But Santa Anna, commanding more than 4,000 Mexican troops, laid siege to the city on February 23, 1836. Most of the population had a chance to flee, but 187 men, commanded by Colonel William B. Travis and including Davy Crockett and Jim Bowie, undertook a courageous defense of their position by occupying a stoutly walled mission called the Alamo in the heart of the city. For ten days the outnumbered Texans kept Santa Anna's army at bay and inflicted heavy casualties. But finally, on March 6, the Mexican artillery breached the walls, and the Mexican army, with its band playing "El Deguello" (the centuries-old song that was a signal for the total destruction of the enemy), made its final assault. In a fury of desperate hand-to-hand combat the Texan defenders were vanquished. Every single defender was eventually killed and their bodies burned in a giant pyre.

Unbeknownst to the men in the Alamo, who believed they were fighting to restore the constitution of 1824, Anglo and Tejano delegates met at the tiny village of Washington-on-the-Brazos and on March 2 declared independence of Mexico and wrote a new constitution. The new government named Sam Houston commander in chief of the army, but Houston realized it was too late to attempt a rescue of the men defending the Alamo. Shortly thereafter Santa Anna captured a small force of about 350 Texan defenders near San Antonio and, after marching them southeastward to the town of Goliad, massacred them all.

Sam Houston and the ragtag Texas army retreated eastward from the vicinity of San Antonio, headed in the direction of the San Jacinto River. Houston, despite the criticism he received for not turning and fighting, was slowly increasing his army as he retreated by picking up volunteers, and, knowing Santa Anna was in pursuit, bided his time for an opportunity to counterattack. Then, on the afternoon of April 21, near the western bank of the San Jacinto near Galveston Bay, just at siesta time when Santa Anna and his men were taking a confident nap, Sam Houston's small army surprised the far larger Mexican army. Yelling "Remember the Alamo" as they scattered Santa Anna's troops, the Texas army won the battle in just seventeen minutes. Half Santa Anna's men were killed, the remainder were taken prisoners, and Santa Anna himself, rudely awakened from his siesta, was captured wearing only a silk shirt and his underwear. Subsequently on May 14 he signed a treaty recognizing the independence of Texas and the Rio Grande as the border with Mexico. In fact, the Mexican government refused to accept either the treaty or the border. Texas's independence was fragile, its ultimate status unclear.

∞ *The Texas Nation*

Sam Houston was elected president of the Republic of Texas and instantly sent out feelers to his old friend, President Andrew Jackson, about annexation by the United States. Jackson favored annexation, and before the Texas Revolution had even offered Mexico $5 million for the territory, but Jackson was a good enough politician to realize how controversial the annexation

The Siege of the Alamo   This nineteenth-century illustration shows the attack on the Alamo by a much larger force of Mexican troops.

of another slave state would be. At the moment there were thirteen free states and thirteen slave states. Southerners of course approved of annexation, but many northerners, the growing antislavery forces, and the emerging Whig Party all opposed admitting Texas to the Union. Jackson knew that if he pushed for annexation, he would likely jeopardize the election of his successor, Martin Van Buren.

So Jackson did not attempt to annex Texas, and he even waited until after the election to recognize it diplomatically, on his final day in office. Van Buren, lacking the mandate Jackson had enjoyed and soon buffeted by the political repercussions of the Panic of 1837, completely ignored the controversial issue.

✳ IN THEIR OWN WORDS

The Anglo-American Settlers in Texas Revolt, 1836

This call to arms is typical of the hopes and fears of the Texas rebels as they declared independence of Mexico in 1836.

Fellow Freemen,

The despot dictator [Santa Anna], and his vassal myrmidonns [sic], are fast displaying their hostile colums [sic] on the frontier of our heretofore happy and blessed Texas. Their war cry is, "death and destruction to every Anglo-American, west of the Sabine"; their watch word, actually, "beauty and booty." Many of you met the veteran soldiers of Europe, when [in the War of 1812] they dared to invade the land of our fathers, under the same sacrilegious watch word — you chartered and gloriously drove them back to the ocean; you made tyrants tremble at the name of American freemen, and taught them that the soil of an independent people is not to be polluted by the footsteps of a mercenary soldier. And will you *now*, as Texian freemen, as fathers, as husbands, as sons, and as brothers, suffer the *colored* hirelings of a cruel and faithless despot, to feast and revel, in your dearly purchased and cherished homes? Figure to yourselves, my countrymen, the horror and misery that will be entailed on you should the ruffians once obtain foothold on our soil? Your beloved wives, your mothers, your daughters, sisters, and helpless innocent children given up to dire pollution, and massacre at the hand of barbarians!! Your farms redeemed by you from the wilderness, with so much pain and labor, laid waste! and where now flourish the rich products of the husbandman, will be seen the briar and bramble, and our *garden of Texas* again become a dreary wild, occupied only by the savage of the desert, and the cruel animals of the forest; and the *name of Texas* will only be remembered by its fearful sufferings, and as having been once inhabited by a civilized, but unfortunate people. . . .

Thereafter southern congressmen made sporadic attempts to bring up annexation. But the southerners in Congress gave up after Congressman John Quincy Adams (who as president had once tried to purchase Texas for $1 million but now saw Texas as simply an extension of the empire of slavery) in a heroic three-week-long speech brought about the defeat of an annexation resolution.

Rebuffed in their attempt to gain annexation to the United States, Texan officials prepared to create a permanent independent nation. Texas established its own army and navy and successfully sought diplomatic recognition from both Britain and France. Mexico had not recognized Texan independence but took no action against the new nation, so Texas looked forward to peace and prosperity as an independent republic. Britain was happy to see Texas succeed, seeing in the new republic an impediment to future U.S. expansion, a plentiful new source of cotton, and a market for manufactured goods free of the tariffs of the U.S. Some Texans began to dream of expanding westward, perhaps all the way to California and the Pacific harbor of San Francisco. Given Britain's claims to the Oregon Territory, the idea of a pro-British Texas to the south of Oregon made the new republic seem even more attractive to Britain. However, some British antislavery spokesmen wanted to stem the spread of slavery and stop the trans-Atlantic slave trade. These British antislavery proponents saw Texas, like Canada, as a possible refuge for free blacks. Even some U.S. abolitionists dreamed momentarily of developing the nation of Texas as a brake on the expansion of southern slaveholding. These contrasting conceptions of Texas, as a giant transcontinental empire blocking U.S. expansion and reaching to the Pacific, or as a barrier to the expansion of southern slavery, were soon to inject the Texas issue once again into American politics.

❧ The Failed Attempt to Annex Texas

President John Tyler, repudiated by the Whig leaders and opposing the entire Whig program, sought to redefine his administration by attracting southern support. He had already replaced most of the cabinet he had inherited from the ephemeral Harrison administration with southern Democrats, and he seized upon the annexation of Texas as the issue that would attract almost unanimous southern backing. Tyler and his new southern secretary of state, Abel P. Upshur (who replaced Daniel Webster after Congress ratified the Webster-Ashburton Treaty), promoted Texas annexation as a patriotic enlargement of the nation. Indeed, there was significant interest among northeastern merchants in the idea of a transcontinental empire with the great harbor of San Francisco beckoning the trade of the Orient. Upshur believed he had the votes in Congress to get a treaty of annexation approved, but before he completed the treaty, he was killed in an accidental explosion aboard the U.S.S. *Princeton*. Tyler promptly appointed John C. Calhoun to replace Upshur as secretary of state.

Calhoun moved with typical aggressiveness to complete the negotiations with Texas. He offered Texas equality with other states, and in return for handing over its public lands to the federal government the latter would assume Texas's national debts up to a maximum of $10 million. The treaty was concluded on April 12, 1844, and ten days later President Tyler submitted the annexation treaty to the Senate with an attached message defending the action in terms of its general good for the nation. But then Calhoun made a fateful mistake. He released to the press a letter he had written several days before to the British foreign minister in Washington, Richard Packenham, defending the annexation of Texas as necessary to protect the institution of slavery — which he called "essential to the peace, safety, and prosperity" of the nation.

Calhoun's indiscretion suddenly made the annexation of Texas seem less a national good than a proslavery move. Both northern Whigs and northern Democrats quickly stepped back from support of expansion because Calhoun had sectionalized the issue. Some Whigs also wanted to deprive Tyler of any sort of a political victory. Abolitionists convinced many northerners who had paid little attention to annexation that Texas was part of a slaveholders' conspiracy. In short, the issue blew up in Calhoun's and Tyler's faces, and the Senate rejected the treaty on June 8 by a more than two-to-one vote. Tyler tried then to annex Texas by a joint resolution of both houses of Congress, but Congress adjourned before Tyler could get the measure to a vote.

So in the summer of 1844 Texas, and the general issue of national expansion, had became a political hot potato. Tyler had failed in his effort to use Texas annexation to recoup his political fortunes, but it was yet to be seen how the issue would play itself out. Clearly, however, Texas was not the only territorial issue hanging fire. The entire region west of the Rocky Mountains had, in the last decade, come to occupy a powerful place in the American imagination. National expansion was a cause far broader than the visions of cotton fields and slaves that southerners entertained. Daniel Webster once said that the San Francisco harbor alone was worth twenty Texases. Expansion and politics became conjoined in the summer of 1844, with results no one could have predicted.

THE FAR WEST: OREGON AND CALIFORNIA

❧ *Spanish California*

In the early seventeenth century Spanish officials developed permanent colonies in what is now New Mexico, and a thriving Hispanic community developed there. As we have seen, in the early eighteenth century Spanish colonization and mission activities reached into Texas, but population growth was slow among the Tejanos until they were augmented by Anglos coming from the United States after the 1820s. Spanish interest in California was even slower to awaken: There were no mission activities until about 1770, when some twenty-one missions were established reaching from San Francisco Bay to San Diego. The Hispanic population, called Californios, centered at first near the missions and protective forts called presidios.

Early in the nineteenth century the Mexican government essentially gave up on the missionary enterprise in California and began a slow process of secularizing the Hispanic presence. Californio settlers developed huge cattle ranches called rancheros and, using forced Indian labor, made great fortunes and enjoyed an aristocratic, seemingly carefree lifestyle in the comfortable climate of southern California. But the Californio population was negligible in comparison to the size and obvious wealth of the province — which, lying more than a thousand miles from Mexico City, received little support from and owed little allegiance to Mexican officialdom.

Along the entire western coast of North America are three great natural harbors: the Strait of Juan de Fuca that opened into Puget Sound, San Francisco, and San Diego. At the beginning of the nineteenth century the harbors were so attractive and Spanish occupation so light that a number of European nations — France, Great Britain, and Russia — along with the United States coveted the region and made claims for the territory. The collapse of the Napoleonic Empire in 1814-1815 removed France from the scene. By the terms of the Adams-Onís Treaty of 1819 Spain gave up its claims to the Oregon Territory north of the 42nd parallel, the northern boundary of California. Russia in 1824-1825 relinquished its claims to the land south of 54° 40′ latitude, the southern boundary of Alaska. That left England and the United States in disputed joint occupation of the Oregon Territory and Mexico with legal control over California.

New England merchants had already explored the harbors of the West Coast and begun to develop a trade empire in the Pacific. Ships exchanged American goods for the pelt of the sea otter in the Oregon Territory, then traded the pelts to China in exchange for tea and silks. Vessels even earlier had begun the habit of stopping along the California coast for provisions, and soon there was a brisk trade in exchanging American manufactures for cowhides and tallow (rendered cattle fat used to make candles and soap) produced on the rancheros of the wealthy Californios who hungered for American goods. In the normal course of trade, some American sailors and merchants remained in California, attracted by the money to be made, the climate, and the unhurried lifestyle. Some intermarried with the Californios and began to create a small multicultural society. Richard Henry Dana's classic autobiographical account, published as *Two Years Before the*

Mast (1840), captured the fascination California had for adventurous Americans. This small, prosperous, laid-back Anglo-Californio society numbered perhaps 3,200 persons in the mid-1830s. Given the obvious promise of the land and the merely nominal Mexican rule, California came to seem like a plum ripe for the picking in the mid-1840s. Many northeastern merchants, determined to avoid the consequences of another economic downturn like that begun in 1837, saw vastly expanded trade to the Orient as a guarantee of American prosperity, and such commerce across the broad Pacific required ports on the California and Oregon coast.

&cp; The Fur Trade and Mountain Men

Despite the climatic and lifestyle attractions of California, Anglo settlement grew more quickly in the Oregon territory. One of the motivations that brought Anglo pioneers was the desire of Christian missionaries to convert the Indians. Like the earlier Catholic missions in California, this conversion effort in Oregon met little religious success, but the missionaries ended up attracting permanent settlers to establish farms.

The Presidio at San Francisco, 1816 In the early nineteenth century, San Francisco consisted of little more than this fortified Spanish presidio (military post), a Catholic mission, and a tiny settlement called Yerba Buena on an island in San Francisco Bay. The spot shown in this sketch is now in the heart of the city of San Francisco, looking north, with the bay in the background.

However, the very first European visitors to the Oregon Territory in the late eighteenth century had been shipboard merchants buying sea otter skins from the indigenous Indians. Disease microorganisms from these initial European contacts killed the majority of the Indians in the Northwest and weakened their ability to resist the infusion of land-based beaver trappers from Canada, primarily British agents of the Hudson Bay Company.

At first, French fur trappers — often married to Indian women and culturally almost Indian — dominated the fur trade. But by the opening decades of the nineteenth century the fur trappers had become a polyglot population, with French, French-Indian, British, and American white and black men all roaming the West seeking to satisfy the demand for beaver pelts driven by European fashion. In 1821 the Hudson Bay Company bought out its largest rival and dominated the entire fur business of North America, operating primarily out of a series of trading posts scattered across Canada and the Northwest. John Jacob Astor's competing U.S. firm, the Pacific Fur Company, was forced from the Oregon Territory in 1812. Because of British dominance in the beaver trade, there were more British agents and trappers in the Oregon Territory than there were Americans, and although the United States and Great Britain agreed to joint occupation of Oregon in 1818, in sheer numbers the British had the better claim to the region. Throughout the 1820s and 1830s, Oregon was occupied and controlled primarily by the British, and the American presence was slight indeed.

The great expanse of the Rocky Mountains, reaching from Santa Fe to the Canadian border, remained virgin territory for the trapping of beavers. The American William Henry Ashley of the Rocky Mountain Fur Company out of St. Louis developed the practice of employing American men who worked as fully independent agents. For most of the year these men worked alone (or with their Indian wives and families) in the mountain valleys and along the stream beds that attracted the beavers, but once a year they met at a well-publicized rendezvous site to exchange their pelts for cash, guns, ammunition, tobacco, trinkets for Indian gifts, and whiskey. These annual rendezvous events, held at

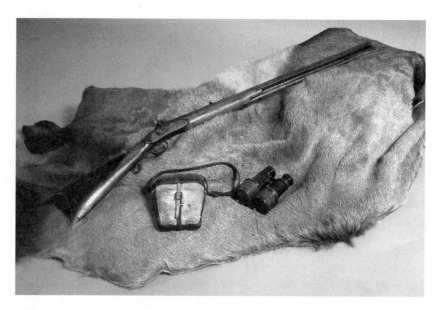

Rifle and Binoculars   This Hawken rifle and pair of binoculars belonged to Jim Bridger, one of the famed Mountain Men of the early nineteenth century.

such places as Jackson Hole, Wyoming, were boisterous, ethnically diverse occasions.

The fur trappers, known as mountain men, wearing leather clothes and speaking a variety of Indian tongues, were a colorful and exotic tribe of individualists. Such trappers as Jedediah Smith, Jim Bridger, Tom Fitzpatrick, James Ohio Pattie, and Kit Carson have come to occupy a permanent place in American folklore. These men were the unofficial explorers and trailblazers of the Rocky Mountains, and the trails they discovered, learned no doubt from Indians, often became the routes later permanent settlers followed to Oregon and California. They found the mountain passes, the shortcuts, the waterholes, the obstacles to avoid. The number of mountain men was never large, and as European fashions turned from beaver skins to silk, their role changed after the 1830s. They turned their geographical knowledge and survival skills from tracking beaver to guiding army exploratory expeditions and later wagon trains of settlers. Tales of the exploits of the mountain men and their expertise helped place the West before the American imagination and helped beckon the adventurous to come conquer and occupy the vast territory.

The Santa Fe Trail

Long antedating and far outnumbering the storied mountain men of the Rockies were the southwestern ranching families of Spanish descent. But by the early nineteenth century the forty thousand Hispanic settlers of New Mexico, more than a thousand miles from Mexico City, found themselves in need of markets for their products and eager to buy manufactured goods. American merchants out of St. Louis, seeking to recover from the Panic of 1819, were eager to find new markets. And St. Louis was four hundred miles closer to Santa Fe than was Mexico City. In 1821 a trade route was established linking Santa Fe with St. Louis, and mule-driven wagons commenced an immensely profitable trade. Soon goods shipped to Santa Fe were being distributed further south into the northernmost provinces of present-day Mexico, and the operators of silver mines in Chihuahua and Sonora began sending Mexican silver to the United States via the Santa Fe Trail in exchange for much-needed goods. By 1825 the trade was so prosperous that Congress voted to provide military protection for the trains of cargo wagons on the Santa Fe Trail, even though the passage was not through American territory. By about 1830, several hundred American merchants had taken up permanent residence in Santa Fe and at a trading post called Bent's Fort in what is now southeastern Colorado, often marrying Hispanic wives and becoming acculturated to the Hispanic way of life. These trading opportunities opened the eyes of other American merchants to possible broader markets in the American West, and the wagon trains of goods to and from Santa Fe certainly proved that people and supplies could be successfully transported great distances over land.

❧ Army Exploration of the West

The American government and public also learned about the American West through government-sponsored scientific and surveying expeditions. Thomas Jefferson had begun the process when scientific curiosity had largely motivated him to send Meriwether Lewis and William Clark on a three-year expedition from the Ohio River down to the Mississippi River and thence up the Missouri River, eventually crossing the northern Rockies and finally reaching the Pacific Ocean in November 1805; then they returned by a somewhat different route to St. Louis. The congressional appropriation stated that Lewis and Clark would cultivate friendly relations with the Indians (and, presumably, wean them from alliances with the British) and promote American commerce. Their detailed published reports were a significant contribution to science and naturalism and

popularized the American West as a land of almost infinite size and promise.

A number of such army exploratory expeditions were undertaken in the early decades of the nineteenth century. Among the leaders were Lieutenant Zebulon Pike (who was the first Anglo to discover the Colorado mountain named after him and who traveled through the Rockies into northern Mexico and thence across Texas), Major Stephen Long (who explored the Great Plains that are now portions of Nebraska, Colorado, Kansas), and John C. Frémont (who became known as the Pathfinder for his three significant expeditions in the northern Rockies, the Great Basin, and the Sierra Nevadas in the early 1840s). These military explorers published reports filled with maps, engravings, and fascinating descriptions of the terrain and wildlife of the West. (Frémont's gifted wife, Jessie Benton Frémont — daughter of the expansionist Missouri Senator, Thomas Hart Benton — wrote much of Frémont's widely read reports.) Accounts of such wonders as the geysers of the Yellowstone, the Grand Canyon, the giant redwood trees, and the great herds of buffalo entranced readers throughout the nation and stirred up some Americans to think of the West as a land of mystery and opportunity. But the reports also emphasized that, except for dwindling numbers of Indians (dying from the whites' diseases) and a sprinkling of Hispanic settlers and occasional Anglo merchants and mountain men, most of the West was empty of human beings.

❧ Early Settlement of the Oregon Territory

From the earliest decades of permanent European settlement on the North American mainland, farmers had pushed west to fertile new lands, usually staying in approximately the same latitudes (with similar climates) and choosing familiar soil types and terrain. The farmers expected to break the soil with light plows, to plant corn, wheat, and peas in the Midwest and cotton across the South, and to use felled trees to build houses and barns, fence crops, and burn for fuel. But beyond the 98th meridian of longitude lay the Great Plains, where the soil was difficult to plow, rain was scarce, and trees rare except along watercourses.

Army explorers and other pioneers beyond the 98th meridian were perplexed by the huge expanse of treeless plains that they found there. Since the earliest colonial days, folk assumption had it that treeless land was no good — would not grow crops. Settlers in seventeenth-century Maryland, for example, had skipped over a section of treeless land in the north-central portion of the state, assuming it was unfit for agriculture. So when would-be settlers contemplated the Great Plains, a region they tellingly called the Great American Desert, they likewise assumed the region was a wasteland and made little or no effort to settle there. Familiar forest and terrain extended further west in Texas, so cotton-growing farmers eagerly pushed westward there in the 1820s and 1830s. But the tide of migration westward halted geographically near the western border of Missouri. From there, would-be western farmers leapfrogged across the Great Plains to the fertile valleys of the Pacific Coast. The plains region would be settled only decades later, as the last frontier of the mainland United States.

The Oregon country, despite its great distance, seemed far more inviting to American immigrants than the High Plains region. From the moment of the initial settlement in the mid-1830s until the early 1840s, Oregon's reputation spread as a paradise for family farmers. Britain's population dominance of the region was about to end.

Missionaries were the first to spread the word of Oregon's promise. In 1820 the American Board of Foreign Missions established Protestant churches in Hawaii, and one of the more famous of the missionaries there began writing back to friends in Massachusetts that the Protestants should do something about planting mission churches in the barely developed Oregon Territory. These calls to awaken the Congregational church were heard by a Boston schoolmaster, Hall J. Kelley, who had been fascinated by the West since first reading the reports of Lewis and Clark. In 1831, Kelley organized the American Society for Encouraging the Settlement of the Oregon Territory. Kelley used the society to distribute promotional literature that glowingly described the climate, the soil, the opportunities for trade to the Orient. This advertising campaign caught the attention of Nathaniel J. Wyeth, a young Boston entrepreneur who had already made a fortune by inventing a device to cut ice

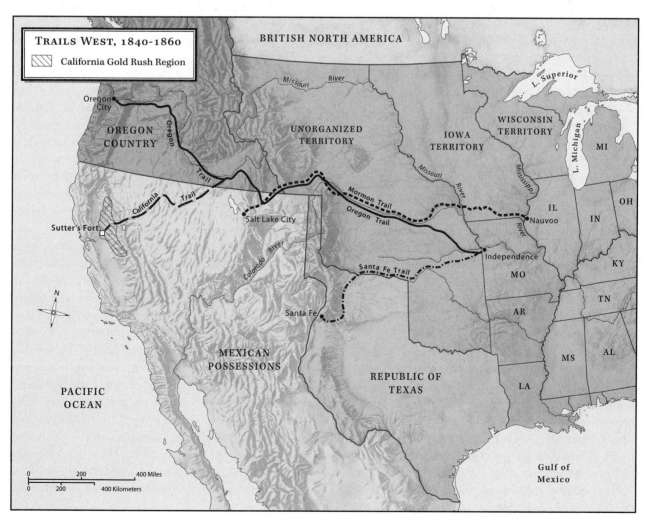

The Great American Desert and the Rocky Mountain Barrier, 1821

In 1820, Major Stephen Long led an army expedition westward from what is now Council Bluffs, Iowa (across the Missouri from Omaha) to the Pikes Peak region of Colorado. This is his discouraging report on what he found.

In regard to this extensive section of country, I do not hesitate in giving the opinion, that it is almost wholly unfit for cultivation, and of course uninhabitable by a people depending on agriculture for their subsistence. Although tracts of fertile land considerably extensive are occasionally to be met with, yet the scarcity of wood and water, almost uniformly prevalent, will prove an insuperable obstacle in the way of settling the country. This objection rests not only against the section immediately under consideration, but applies with equal propriety to a much larger portion of the country. Agreeably to the best intelligence that can be had, concerning the country both northward and southward of the section, and especially to the inferences deducible from the account given by Lewis and Clarke [sic] of the country situated between the Missouri and the Rocky Mountains above the river Platte, the vast region commencing near the sources of the Sabine, Trinity, Brases, and Colorado, and extending northwardly to the forty-ninth degree of north latitude, by which the United States' territory is limited in that direction [i.e., the present-day U.S.-Canadian border], is throughout of a similar character. The whole of this region seems peculiarly adapted as a range for buffaloes, wild goats, and other wild game; incalculable multitudes of which find ample pasturage and subsistence upon it.

This region, however, viewed as a frontier, may prove of infinite importance to the United States, inasmuch as it is calculated to serve as a barrier to prevent too great an extension of our population westward, and secure us against the machinations or incursions of an enemy that might otherwise be disposed to annoy us in that part of our frontier.

---

from the ponds near Cambridge, Massachusetts, which was then sold to thirsty customers in the West Indies and South America. Ships heavily insulated with sawdust from Maine lumber mills transported the blocks of ice to equally heavily insulated icehouses in the tropics. Before refrigeration, this was the only way to have cool drinks in hot climes, and wealthy planters would pay a pretty penny for such a soothing treat. Fresh from this triumph, Wyeth decided to try his hand at adding to his wealth by developing a colony in Oregon.

In 1832 Wyeth set out overland to Oregon with twenty-four men, guided by mountain man William Sublette, following paths partly explored by Lewis and Clark and traversing the South Pass through the Rockies, which the mountain man Jedidiah Smith had discovered. Wyeth also sent a cargo vessel around Cape Horn at the southern tip of South America, intending to rendezvous in Oregon, but the ship was lost at sea. Disappointed, Wyeth returned to Boston and organized another two-prong expedition. On this trip the Reverend Jason Lee and four other Methodist missionaries accompanied Wyeth overland. This time the ship also arrived safely, though only after the lucrative salmon season had ended. So, with no immediate way to turn a profit, Wyeth gave up on Oregon and returned to what he knew best, the ice business.

The missionaries stayed, however, and founded a small but permanent farming community in the Willa-mette River Valley. The Indians had little interest in the missionaries' message, and before long the missionaries began to devote more effort to developing the farming community and attracting Anglo settlers. In 1838 Lee returned to the East Coast to gather more settlers. He launched a promotional magazine that sang the praises of the Oregon country, and even sent a memorial to Congress requesting U.S. protection for the American citizens along the Willamette. Wyeth and Lee had definitely proven that it was feasible to transport both people and goods long distance by ox-drawn wagons and reproduce a typical farming community in the Northwest.

In 1834 the American Board of Foreign Missions, recognizing the economic and religious opportunities offered by the West and responding to a call from four Flathead Indians, sent Congregationalist missionary Dr. Marcus Whitman and his young wife, Narcissa, to the eastern part of the Oregon Territory, in what is now Washington State. Accompanied by another missionary family, the Spauldings, the two Whitmans came overland, with Narcissa becoming the first Anglo woman to cross the Rockies, and arrived at Fort Walla Walla in September 1836. Together, the Whitmans and the Spauldings established a mission for the Nez Percés near what is now Lewiston, Idaho. For about ten years the Congregational missions enjoyed modest success, and the Whitmans wrote back east enticing additional Anglo farmers.

Protestants were not the only Christian missionaries active in the Pacific Northwest, for American Catholics also recognized the Oregon Territory as a mission field. Two Franciscan priests, Frances Blanchet and Modeste Demers, arrived in 1838, and in 1840 Jesuit priest Father Pierre-Jean de Smet established Sacre Coeur Mission among the Flathead Indians in the Coeur d'Alene country of what is now western Montana. By 1847 there were some fourteen Jesuit missionaries active in the far Northwest.

In the mid-1840s, however, the tide of westward migration began to bring less scrupulous and greedier white settlers to the Northwest. Meanwhile the Protestant missionary leaders quarreled among themselves, as well as with the Catholics. The Indians felt threatened and confused, especially when a measles epidemic struck that primarily killed them but largely spared the whites. The Cayuse accused Dr. Whitman of administering poison in the guise of medicine. In the fall of 1847 the frustrated and disillusioned Cayuse massacred Marcus and Narcissa Whitman, along with most of the other mission workers. The resulting white retaliation almost exterminated the Cayuse.

The Oregon Trail   In this extraordinary 1860 photograph, settlers, horses, and covered wagons head west along the Oregon Trail.

❧ *Oregon Fever and the Oregon Trail*

The letters of the various missionaries back to co-believers in the East, along with the promotional activities of Hall J. Kelley and others, suddenly struck a responsive chord among Americans suffering from the economic and social devastation of the Panic of 1837. Tales of lush fields, bountiful rainfall, beautiful mountains of timber and game, rivers thick with salmon, and the mighty Pacific reaching toward the mystery and markets of the Orient, all combined to create a veritable Oregon Fever in 1842. The next year a thousand emigrants, largely from the farm states of the Upper Mississippi and Ohio River valleys, made the two-thousand mile overland trek from embarkation points along the western edge of Missouri — towns such as Independence, St. Joseph, and Kansas City in Missouri and Council Bluffs in Iowa. In 1844 another thousand came to Oregon, traveling in giant, canvas-covered Conestoga wagons called "Prairie schooners" because, like ships at sea, they traversed the endless ocean of grass that stretched to the horizon and beyond.

The wagon trains that brought settlers westward on the Oregon Trail have acquired an indelible place in the American memory. By 1845, some five thousand people, traveling mainly in family groups, often three gen-

Emigrants to Oregon, 1846

In 1846, young Francis Parkman, a Boston blue-blood, set out to improve his health by traveling the Oregon Trail on horseback and then published a famous account of his encounters with emigrants, Indians, and the vastness of the American West. Later he would become one of nineteenth-century America's greatest historians. Here, from his The Oregon Trail, is his description of a wagon train in western Nebraska.

Far off, on the other side [of the Platte River], was a green meadow, where we could see the white tents and wagons of an emigrant camp; and just opposite to us we could discern a group of men and animals at the water's edge. Four or five horsemen soon entered the river, and in ten minutes had waded across and clambered up the loose sand-bank. They were ill-looking fellows, thin and swarthy, with care-worn anxious faces, and lips rigidly compressed. They had good cause for anxiety; it was three days since they first encamped here, and on the night of their arrival they had lost one hundred and twenty-three of their best cattle, driven off by wolves, through the neglect of the man on guard. This discouraging and alarming calamity was not the first that had overtaken them. Since leaving the settlements, they had met with nothing but misfortune. Some of their party had died; one man had been killed by the Pawnees; and about a week before, they had been plundered by the Dahcotahs [sic] of all their best horses. . . .

The emigrants re-crossed the river, and we prepared to follow. First the heavy ox-wagons plunged down the bank, and dragged slowly over the sand-beds; sometimes the hoofs of the oxen were scarcely wetted by the thin sheet of water; and the next moment the river would be boiling against their sides, and eddying fiercely around the wheels. . . .

It is worth noticing, that on the Platte one may sometimes see the shattered wrecks of ancient claw-footed tables, well waxed and rubbed, or massive bureaus of carved oak. These, many of them no doubt the relics of ancestral prosperity in colonial time, must have encountered strange vicissitudes. Imported, perhaps, originally from England; then, with the declining fortunes of their owners, borne across the Alleghanies [sic] to the remote wilderness of Ohio or Kentucky; then to Illinois or Missouri; and now at last fondly stowed away in the family wagon for the interminable journey to Oregon. But the stern privations of the way are little anticipated. The cherished relic is soon flung out to scorch and crack upon the hot prairie.

---

erations together, had come to Oregon, and by 1848 another three thousand had forked south from the main trail to reach California. Overall, between 1840 and 1860 some 300,000 persons crossed the Great Plains in wagon train caravans, producing ruts that can still be seen in places. These were overwhelmingly middle-class farm families from the Midwest, for it cost from $600 to $1,000 to outfit the wagon, buy supplies, and hire guides (usually veteran former fur trappers who knew well the mountain passes and trails). Urban poor and working-class families could not afford to make such a journey.

The journey was exceedingly arduous. Women and small children usually traveled in the crowded, bumpy wagons, while the men and older children walked or rode horseback. Each family usually had several cattle on hoof accompanying them. Typically, it took six months to reach Oregon. The trail first crossed luxuriant prairies of grass, but then came the higher, drier plains, the dangerous mountain slopes and narrow passes, and the harsh, arid, desert-like stretch beyond South Pass. The last phase often included rafting down the Columbia River to their welcome destination. No matter how many emigrant guidebooks they had read in preparation, families usually started out with too much furniture and too many heirlooms, treasures that had to be abandoned along the trail as the road got harder and the oxen became famished and exhausted.

The trip seemed absolutely interminable as day after day the jolting wagon, the eye-stinging and throat-clogging dust, the wearisome preparation of food and doing the family wash in inhospitable, makeshift circumstances took their toll on everyone — and especially on the women, who had to maintain their usual domestic routines. Cooking meals at the end of a tiring day, and having to gather and use dried buffalo dung for fuel because the plains were devoid of firewood, removed much of the romance from the evening camp. Men were usually more enthusiastic about the trip and the prospects for creating new farms in Oregon. Women sometimes shared the sense of excitement for a new life and the hope for financial improvement; but more often they mourned the loss of ties with kin back home. Children mostly experienced the whole trip as a great adventure. There were dangers, although far more died from accidents than from Indian attacks. The wagon trains, consisting of upwards of a hundred wagons, formed little self-contained communities for the duration of the overland voyage. They often drafted a constitution of sorts, elected officers, enforced discipline, hired an experienced guide, and set forth making about fifteen miles on a good day. On rare occasions trains met delays, encountered terrible hardships, and the whole enterprise turned into a disaster. Thus members of the Donner party, which foolishly tried to cross the Sierra Nevada Mountains after the snows had begun to fall, got stuck in a blizzard. The few survivors resorted to cannibalism before they were rescued.

But the majority of pioneers on the wagon trains made it to their destinations. Even though they arrived too late that first year to put a crop into the ground, the settlers who had arrived in previous years supported the newcomers the first winter, and then the new Oregonians or Californians the next spring were able to plant and soon prospered. As early as 1843 the farmers in the Willamette Valley began to organize themselves into some kind of provisional government, and that same year the Senate passed a resolution organizing Oregon as a territory. The House, however, did not pass it. Meanwhile, the British threatened that they would consider such a unilateral annexation of Oregon a declaration of war. Little aware of these larger events, the American settlers in Oregon continued to make tentative steps toward self-government, and, borrowing heavily from the constitution of Iowa, they held a special election in July 1845 to approve a provisional government and elected a governor.

Many Americans by the 1830s did profit from the prospects of the Far West. The earliest trading vessels to visit the ports of Juan de Fuca, San Francisco, and San Diego both to pick up sea otter skins for the China trade, or hides and tallow in California, or provisions for long whaling voyages in the Pacific, had alerted promoters and publicists in New England to the importance to American commerce of gaining a foothold on the Pacific Coast. Oregon Fever had convinced many midwesterners that the course of empire demanded that the United States acquire the Pacific Northwest. Tales of fur trappers and reports of army expeditions further informed politicians and policy makers of the promise of the West. John L. O'Sullivan, a Jacksonian newspaper editor, in 1839 wrote that "We are the nation of human progress, and who will, or what can, set limits to our onward march?" A midwestern expansionist argued that "the nation that possesses Oregon will not only control the navigation of the Pacific, . . . but the trade of China itself." President Jackson tried to purchase San Francisco and the surrounding region

from Mexico, Calhoun predicted San Francisco would one day be "the New York of the Pacific Coast," and commercially minded Whigs in New York and Boston dreamed of a trade empire reaching from New England via the West Coast to the practically infinite markets of China. Politically, expansionism found adherents far beyond the South. For example, many prominent northern Democrats, including Stephen A. Douglas in Illinois, Lewis Cass in Michigan, and James Buchanan in Pennsylvania (all future candidates for the presidency), became vocal expansionists. For many ordinary citizens in the North, the Far West was a mission field, a farmers' paradise, the commercial entrepot of tomorrow. In short, as the election of 1844 neared, expansionism was an idea whose time seemed to have come.

THE ELECTION OF JAMES K. POLK

❧ *Victory of a Dark Horse Candidate*

John Tyler had hoped to cement his chances for reelection with a triumphant annexation of Texas, and there were northern Democrats and Whigs who supported expansion for a number of important reasons. But, as we have seen, in early 1844 Secretary of State Calhoun's mishandling of the treaty negotiations by his ill-advised letter to the British minister emphatically sectionalized expansion. Suddenly Calhoun had made expansion look like a plot merely to expand slavery. Tyler had long been at odds with the Whig Party, and now his advocacy of Texas removed even the remotest chance that he could get the party's nomination for the presidency in 1844. Tyler momentarily toyed with the idea of running as an independent, but that hope quickly evaporated. The Whigs gleefully discarded their accidental president, Tyler, and turned to their old war-horse, Henry Clay, who seemed so deserving at last of his party's nomination. But Clay, adroit politician though he was, misjudged the strength of the national sentiment for expansion, as distinct from support for Texas annexation. Moreover, by naming as their vice-presidential candidate Theodore Frelinghuysen — who had in the early 1830s been so outspoken on behalf of the Sabbatarian movement and all manner of Protestant reforms — the Whigs unintentionally motivated Catholic voters to turn out en masse in states like Pennsylvania, New York, and Massachusetts to vote for the Democratic ticket. The Whigs had hoped to balance

Clay's worldly reputation with Frelinghuysen's obvious piety, but the effort backfired on them.

Martin Van Buren confidently expected to win the Democratic nomination, but he too was cautious about the Texas question. Van Buren feared that annexation might cause war with Mexico, and he was concerned that the proslavery turn the issue had taken might seriously aggravate the sectional issue. New Yorker Van Buren was no ardent defender of slavery, and his lukewarm attitude on the Texas issue convinced Calhoun and the southern Democrats to derail his nomination. The southern Democrats pushed through a resolution at the Democratic convention requiring that a candidate must receive two-thirds, not a simple majority, of the delegate votes in order to win the nomination — a rule to which the Democrats would cling until 1936, effectively giving the South a veto over the party's presidential nominations. Van Buren, the first northern Democrat to feel the brunt of this veto, failed to get the necessary two-thirds; but he could block expansionists like Cass and Buchanan from winning. On the eighth ballot a new name appeared on the ballot, James K. Polk of Tennessee. Polk, former Speaker of the House and governor of his state, was a staunch Jacksonian and a strong expansionist (as opposed to being just a southern defender of the annexation of Texas). Southern delegates and northern expansionists alike could support him, and so could the Jackson traditionalists. So on the ninth ballot the delegates began to stampede to Polk's cause, and he won the unanimous vote of the convention. Pointing up national support for expansion, the Democrats named George M. Dallas of Pennsylvania as their vice-presidential candidate.

Clay, the Whig candidate, began to waffle on the Texas question, sensing that there was significant support for annexation among southern Whigs. But by hedging his previously announced opposition to Texas Clay gained few southern Whig votes while outraging most northern Whigs. A sizable number of northern Whigs most opposed to annexation and slavery broke away from their party and joined the antislavery Liberty Party, which had first appeared in 1840. The national popular vote was close, even with Frelinghuysen driving many urban Catholic and immigrant voters to the Democrats. The Liberty Party only polled 62,300 votes, but they were concentrated in a handful of pivotal states. The 15,812 votes the Liberty Party won in New York State cost Clay the state and its thirty-six electoral votes. Without New York in his column, Clay lost the election to Polk by less than 40,000 popular votes, but by an electoral margin of 105 to 170. New York's electoral votes made the winning difference for Polk.

❧ The Annexation of Texas

Polk, the Democrats, and lame-duck President Tyler all interpreted the election of 1844 as a mandate for both expansion generally and for the annexation of Texas in particular. Tyler sought to recoup his fading administration by trying once again to bring Texas into the Union. In December 1844 Tyler sent Congress a bill asking that Texas be annexed not by formal treaty but rather by a joint resolution of both houses of Congress. After some debate, both northern and southern Democrats united behind Tyler's proposal, and on February 27-28 the House and the Senate respectively approved the resolution, giving the Republic of Texas until January 1, 1846, to respond. France and Britain immediately began to woo Texas, vastly preferring a friendly independent Texas to an expanded United States, but Texan sentiment for joining the United States was too strong. Texas president Anson Jones convened his country's congress and proposed a resolution accepting annexation, while also calling for a convention to draft a new state constitution. The annexation resolution passed unanimously, a constitution was quickly drafted and was accepted by Congress, and on December 29, 1845, just two days before the deadline expired, President Polk signed the act making Texas the twenty-eighth state of the Union.

Mexico had broken diplomatic relations with the United States shortly after the annexation resolution had passed in February 1845 and took steps to increase the size of its army. An immediate irritant was the exact southern boundary of Texas: Mexico claimed that the Nueces River was the border, whereas Texas and the United States both claimed the Rio Grande. Polk understood that war with Mexico over the border dispute and the larger issue of Texas annexation itself was very possible, but he did not shrink from the prospect. First, however, he had to settle another possible international crisis with Great Britain over the Oregon Territory.

MANIFEST DESTINY

❧ The "All of Oregon" Movement

Polk had taken office with an aggressively expansionist inaugural address. "Our title to the country of the Oregon is 'clear and unquestionable,'" exclaimed Polk defiantly but inaccurately. "Already our people are preparing to perfect that title by occupying it with their wives and children." Referring briefly to the onrush of American settlers to Oregon, Polk continued: "The world beholds the peaceful triumphs of the industry of our emigrants. To us belongs the duty of protecting them adequately where they may be upon our soil. The jurisdiction of our laws and the benefits of our republican institutions should be extended over them in the distant regions which they have selected for their homes." But Oregon was not uncontested terrain, and Polk was unwilling to risk two wars simultaneously. He sought to finesse the Oregon question with a masterful combination of bravado and conciliation. He cared about Oregon, but his heart was set on California and the harbor at San Francisco. First, though, Oregon had to be peacefully acquired. Then Polk could risk war with Mexico, not only to save Texas but also to acquire California.

In 1843 and 1844, as Oregon Fever swept over the Midwest, Democratic leaders began to talk expansively of "all of Oregon." By this they meant American annexation of the whole territory, all the way to the southern border of Russian Alaska. At first the Whigs had mocked this definition of American territory as "fifty-four forty or fight," referring sarcastically to the latitude of Alaska. The U.S. had no legal basis for this claim. The treaty of 1818 with Great Britain settled the 49th degree of latitude as the Canadian-U.S. border as far west as the ridge of the Rocky Mountains, and early Anglo-American discussions about the future of Oregon had implicitly assumed that this 1818 line might be extended, thus partitioning the territory. Drawing the border at the 49th parallel gave the U.S. control of the deep-water harbor of Puget Sound and access to the Pacific by the Strait of Juan de Fuca. Despite the Whigs' ridicule of the "All Oregon" claims of 54° 40′, the grandiose vision of Oregon was politically popular, especially for Democrats who could use the issue to attract northern Democrats and defuse the claim that Democratic expansionism was simply a ruse to gain Texas as a slave state. Claiming all of Oregon — the ports for northeastern commercial interests and the land for the midwesterners aflame with Oregon Fever — was a way for James K. Polk to nationalize expansionism. Knowing a winning campaign issue when he saw one, Polk had championed the call for reasserting the claim of the United States to all of Oregon, from the northern border of California to the southern tip of Alaska.

The election of 1844 saw expansionism emerge as a national cause. Even many Whigs who had mocked staking of land claims far into northwestern Canada understood the commercial importance of gaining Pacific ports for American shipping. A group of Democrats inspired a Young America movement that argued that God himself ordained the spreading of American values across the continent. John L. O'Sullivan, editor of the *United States Magazine and Democratic Review*, gave legendary expression to this viewpoint in an article in the summer of 1845. It is, Sullivan wrote, the nation's "manifest destiny to overspread and to possess the whole of the Continent which Providence has given us for the development of the great experiment of liberty." John Quincy Adams, no reckless follower of fashion and no friend of reckless expansion or of the annexation of Texas, nevertheless believed that the settlement of American farmers and missionaries in Oregon gave the U.S. a stronger right to the region than Britain with only an occasional fur trapper to back its flimsy claim. Perhaps reflecting the language of American mission that had first been used by his Puritan forebears, Adams said the United States was the appropriate nation, "at the first behest of God Almighty . . . to make the wilderness blossom as the rose, to establish laws, to increase, multiply, and subdue the earth." *Manifest Destiny* was an accurate term for Americans' belief in the inevitability and rightness of their nation's expansionist ambitions.

✣ Polk's Campaign for Oregon

Polk, like his hero Andrew Jackson, believed he embodied the sentiment of the people, and the surging approval for expansion in 1844 and 1845 only strengthened his resolve. He was certain that Great Britain could be bluffed, in part because of Oregon's distance from Great Britain and in part because so many American citizens had by now settled in the territory. Polk was convinced that by talking tough he could prevail. Britain still held out for the joint occupation of the Oregon Territory and generally claimed that American rights only extended to the Columbia River, almost two hundred miles south of the 49th parallel. Polk understood that to insist upon the "fifty-four forty" demand of the election campaign would surely lead to war with Great Britain, and in truth he did not think that what is now British Columbia was very promising farm land. (Most American settlers in fact lived south of the 46th parallel.) So in July 1845 Polk instructed Secretary of State James Buchanan to offer Britain a compromise, the 49th parallel all the way

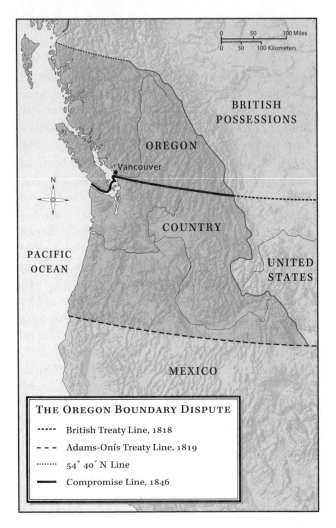

The Oregon Boundary Dispute

- - - - -   British Treaty Line, 1818
- - -   Adams-Onís Treaty Line, 1819
········   54° 40′ N Line
————   Compromise Line, 1846

formation of a government agency to handle Indian affairs in the region west of the Rocky Mountains. Speaking more generally than just of Oregon, Polk expanded the Monroe Doctrine by adding what became known as the Polk Doctrine. First, he stated that "the people of this continent alone have the right to decide their own destiny." Then he said that the United States would not allow a European nation to prevent an independent state from entering into union with the United States.

British minister Pakenham well understood the point of Polk's message to Congress. In a spirit of reconciliation Pakenham asked Polk to again tender his compromise offer and submit the issue to international arbitration, but Polk huffily refused. Polk intended to increase the pressure on Britain in order to win flat-out concessions, not uncertain arbitration. After months of debate, Polk's resolution for terminating joint occupancy passed Congress in April 1846, and on May 21 Polk submitted the notice to Pakenham.

Great Britain realized the time had come to either fight or compromise. Britain decided to take the diplomatic initiative, but just in case negotiations failed, it sent a squadron of warships toward North America. Britain understood that the great preponderance of American settlers over British fur trappers in the disputed region significantly favored the American position. In addition, years of overtrapping had diminished the productivity of the fur trappers and lessened the need for trading posts. The commercial prospects for trade to China and the Canadian interior made it more important to gain transient rights through the Strait of Juan de Fuca and access to ports along Puget Sound than to annex land already occupied by American farmers. So Britain offered a new version of Polk's July 1845 agreement. The boundary would be the 49th parallel all the way to Puget Sound, then loop down and go through the middle of the Strait of Juan de Fuca to the Pacific. This would give all of Vancouver Island to Britain, allow both nations access to Puget Sound, and award to the United States the disputed region between the Columbia River and the 49th parallel. Britain also claimed navigation rights on the Columbia River.

The president doubtless realized that this British offer gave the United States everything it really wanted, and because war with Mexico had just been declared, he wanted to settle the Oregon controversy. The commercial realists of the Northeast understood that the British were handing over to the United States the valuable ports. As one spokesman from Massachusetts argued in support of accepting the British offer, "We

to the Pacific. This would surrender American claims above the 49th parallel (as much a compromise as the "all Oregon" expansionists would accept), and would still give the United States the coveted port at Puget Sound. But Richard Packenham, the British minister in Washington, summarily turned down the offer because it did not give Britain all of Vancouver Island and said nothing about navigation rights on the Columbia River, a long-time British demand.

Infuriated, Polk withdrew his offer. He believed he had offered Britain a good-faith compromise by backing away from his election demands. Bluffing war, Polk in his first message to Congress on December 2, 1845, again claimed all of Oregon. He recommended that the United States give Britain the required one-year notification that the joint-occupation agreement of the Oregon Territory, in place since 1818, was now ending. Polk called for formally extending United States jurisdiction to the American settlers already living in the region, offered army protection of the Oregon Trail, and asked for the

need ports on the Pacific. As to land, we have millions of acres of better land still unoccupied on this side of the mountains." Some of the "all Oregon" extremists in the Midwest were opposed, but most northern and southern Democrats favored the agreement, as did the Whigs. John C. Calhoun took the lead in advocating acceptance. Calhoun always believed he was a nationalist, and this he saw as a way of cementing legitimate northeastern commercial desires with the necessity, as he saw it, of southern expansion into Texas.

The combination of American pioneers spreading Christianity, family farms, and American laws into the Northwest, along with the acquisition of ports beckoning the China trade, made acceptance of the British compromise seem the obvious realization of the nation's Manifest Destiny. The Senate on June 15, 1846, ratified the agreement with Britain, with the stipulation that Britain's navigation rights to the Columbia River were only temporary. But Polk's diplomacy had worked: Britain had backed down, Polk had got all he really wanted out of Oregon, both the region where the American settlers lived and the major port, and every-

thing had been achieved without war. Polk could turn his full attention to the expanding crisis with Mexico.

✣ Polk Maneuvers for California

More even than Oregon, Polk coveted California and its wonderful ports of San Francisco and San Diego. But unlike with Oregon, the United States had absolutely no legal claims to the territory. The huge expanse, lightly governed by Mexico, had perhaps ten thousand Hispanic settlers (the Californios), twice that many Indians, and approximately five hundred "Americanos" who inhabited California as traders, merchants, and adventurers. Polk conceived of a plan to obtain California by the same process by which Texas was acquired. If the Americanos and Californios successfully revolted

"Present Presidential Position"   This lithographic cartoon criticizes President James K. Polk as stubborn. His head is shown on the body of a donkey studying the proposed 54°40′ boundary of the Oregon Territory. Two boys in the foreground coax Polk with cabbage labeled "re-election," but he will not budge. In the background, three groups of prominent Democratic politicians debate the merits — or lack thereof — of Polk's steadfastness.

against Mexican rule and subsequently approached the United States, then (Polk thought) the nation could follow the Texas precedent and simply annex the territory — Mexico's claims to the contrary notwithstanding.

Polk took a series of steps designed to carry out this scenario. First, in July 1845 he ordered Commodore J. D. Sloat, the commander of the United States naval fleet in the Pacific, to seize San Francisco should Mexico declare war on the United States in the ongoing Texas imbroglio. Second, hearing rumors from his agent in California (Thomas O. Larkin, a merchant in Monterey and proponent of American expansion) that both Britain and France had secret plans for acquiring California and maintained consulates there for purposes certainly unfavorable to the United States, Polk secretly authorized Larkin to connive to maneuver a rebellion — should one break out among the Californios — toward declaring independence and asking for American protection. Finally, Polk ordered John C. Frémont, who commanded a heavily armed contingent of cartographic engineers, to move into California to protect American interests in case of trouble.

Frémont met some resentment, withdrew temporarily northward to Oregon, then reentered California. By early summer he was moving toward San Francisco. Interpreting his orders liberally, Frémont in June backed a small group of insurgent Americanos in the town of Sonoma who resisted Mexican rule and proclaimed the Bear Flag Republic, so-called because their makeshift flag depicted a grizzly bear and a star on a white background. On July 5, 1846, the small band of rebels chose Frémont to direct the affairs of what they called the Republic of California. By this date the U.S. had declared war on Mexico, Commodore Sloat had taken San Francisco and Monterey, and Mexican opposition in California was proving to be ephemeral. Before the end of summer, the Stars and Stripes had replaced the Bear Flag in most of California. By early 1847 Stephen Kearny and his troops arrived fresh from taking Santa Fe, and the American occupation and control of California was completed.

THE MEXICAN WAR

❧ Mr. Polk's War

Polk had not deliberately sought war with Mexico in order to protect the annexation of Texas and acquire California, but he was willing to resort to war if negotiation failed to win these objectives. One problem was that the Mexicans were furious with the United States for having, in their opinion, stolen Texas. As early as 1818, while drawing its internal borders, Mexico had defined the Nueces River as the boundary of the province of Texas. To Mexico, the American claim that the border lay on the Rio Grande was simply an attempt at international extortion. Hostility was so severe that Mexico had made several vindictive raids into Texas in the early 1840s, inflaming the Anglo Texans' anti-Mexican sentiments to such a point that they turned against even the Hispanic Tejanos who had helped them win independence. At the same time, Mexican animosity toward the United States ran so high that no Mexican government could afford to be seen negotiating with the hated Yankees. It was in this context that in mid-1845 Polk was informed that the Mexican government would secretly meet an American agent.

Already, in May 1845, Polk had ordered General Zachary Taylor, commander of American forces in the Southwest, to move his "Army of Observation" into Texas, and on July 31 Taylor set up camp at Corpus Christi, just south of the Nueces River, and thus beyond the line that Mexico considered the legal border of Texas. From the Mexican viewpoint, Taylor had invaded Mexican territory. Within three months Taylor had stationed almost half the entire U.S. Army, some 3,500 troops, in the disputed territory.

Learning of the possibility of negotiations despite the growing threat of war, in November Polk sent Louisianan John Slidell on a secret mission to Mexico. With full approval of his cabinet, Polk authorized Slidell to offer Mexico, in return for recognizing the Rio Grande as the Texas border, full American assumption of all Mexican debts owed U.S. citizens. Moreover, Slidell offered to purchase California and New Mexico for $25 million or, if that were not possible, New Mexico alone for $5 million.

But word of Slidell's mission leaked out in Mexico, and the weak government in Mexico City, clinging to power by the skin of its teeth, turned away Slidell lest popular anger at the prospect of negotiations topple it. Hoping to strengthen his diplomatic hand, Polk ordered General Taylor to advance deeper into the disputed territory — all the way to the northern bank of the Rio Grande. Of course this only further infuriated the Mexicans, who understandably saw Taylor's advance as a flagrant invasion. In early 1846 Slidell tried to negotiate again, with a new government that had taken office in Mexico City, but it too dared not even receive him. So in late March Slidell returned empty-handed to Washington. No Mexican government was stable enough to negotiate with the United States.

Perhaps Polk should have exercised some patience, but he was not patient where expansion was concerned. He had determined to go to war if necessary to defend Texas and gain California, and on May 9, 1846, he told his cabinet that he intended to ask Congress to declare war against Mexico on the trivial matter of debts owed to American citizens. Several of his advisers cautioned delay, at least until there was some evidence of open Mexican hostility. At that moment word arrived that a contingent of Mexican troops had crossed the Rio Grande and on April 25, 1846, run into a small patrol of sixty-three American troops. Shots had been fired, and eleven Americans were killed, five wounded, and the remainder captured. General Taylor sent word to Polk that "hostilities may now be considered as commenced."

This was exactly what Polk wanted to hear. On May 11 Polk sent a message to Congress charging that Mexico had "invaded our territory and shed American blood upon the American soil." Polk of course neglected to mention that the bloodshed had occurred on disputed soil — soil that Mexico had long claimed and had never relinquished. Two days later, on May 13, Congress declared war on Mexico and authorized the president to call up 50,000 volunteers.

Partisan feelings about the war ran high. At the outset, even many Whigs felt that, with Taylor under attack on the Rio Grande, they had no choice but to support Polk's policies. But as time passed, the war became extraordinarily unpopular in the North, and disputes involving the ultimate disposition — slave or free — of the territory gained from the war later ignited a sectional split that threatened as never before to divide the na-

tion. Polk's single-minded attention, however, was focused on prosecuting the war so as to defeat Mexico and achieve his territorial ambitions for the nation.

❧ Military Success in Mexico

General Zachary Taylor did not wait for a congressional declaration of war to retaliate for the Mexican attack on his troops. After quick victories in Texas, he commenced a major invasion of Mexico, heading for Monterrey. (Monterrey was a small, isolated town until a railroad was built there — from Laredo — in the late nineteenth century.) The terrain was incredibly rugged and Taylor's troops were outnumbered, but the Americans, led by a number of young, aggressive, West Point-trained officers eager to put their education to work, were far better trained and disciplined than the Mexican forces. After several sharp skirmishes, a skilled artillery attack, and a frontal assault, Taylor captured Monterrey on September 25, 1846. Taylor chose to treat the defeated Mexican army with leniency, assuming that would promote the chances for diplomacy.

Reinforcements reached Taylor from San Antonio, and by the end of the year he had conquered most of northeastern Mexico. Taylor's success alarmed Polk, who feared that the general, a Whig, would be able to translate his battlefield victories into political success in the next presidential election. Santa Anna, of Alamo fame, had meanwhile regained power in Mexico — in part because Polk had believed a rumor that Santa Anna might be willing to negotiate an end to the war and had helped him return to Mexico City. But Santa Anna, back in power, ignored all American peace overtures. In February 1847 Santa Anna thought he saw an

---

❋ **IN THEIR OWN WORDS**

**Henry David Thoreau,
"Resistance to Civil Government," 1849**
Like the Vietnam War in the twentieth century, there was much citizen resistance to the Mexican War, as Thoreau noted a few years later in his famous essay.

I heartily accept the motto, — "That government is best which governs least"; and I should like to see it acted up to more rapidly and systematically. Carried out, it finally

amounts to this, which also I believe, — "That government is best which governs not at all"; and when men are prepared for it, that will be the kind of government which they will have. Government is at best but an expedient; but most governments are usually, and all governments are sometimes, inexpedient. The objections which have been brought against a standing army, and they are many and weighty, and deserve to prevail, may also at last be brought against a standing govern-

ment. The standing army is only an arm of the standing government. The government itself, which is only the mode which the people have chosen to execute their will, is equally liable to be abused and perverted before the people can act through it. Witness the present Mexican war, the work of comparatively a few individuals using the standing government as their tool; for, in the outset, the people would not have consented to this measure.

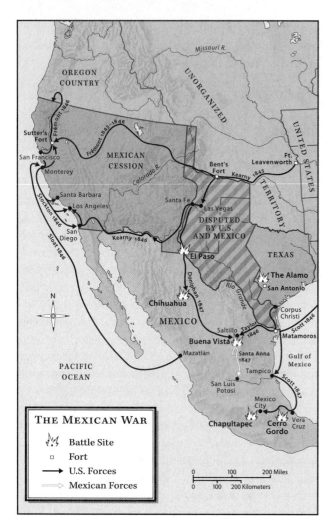

bulk of his army in two different directions, one group headed south into Mexico proper and the other west toward California. The eight hundred men dispatched south marched to El Paso and then into the Mexican province of Chihuahua where, against extremes of desert heat, impossible mountainous terrain, and superior Mexican forces, they won a series of one-sided victories and joined up with General Taylor at Monterrey.

Kearny himself took three hundred of his troops and headed due west, across the deserts of what is now Arizona along the Gila River. En route Kearny ran into former mountain man Kit Carson, who had been John C. Frémont's guide in California. Carson was headed east to Washington with the announcement that California had been occupied and was practically in the control of American troops. Realizing that California was almost in the bag, Kearny sent two hundred of his troops back to Santa Fe and hurried on with the remainder. He arrived in southern California on November 25, 1846, just in time to finish off the last remnants of Mexican opposition. By early January the Mexican forces surrendered and signed a treaty of capitulation with General Frémont. California was completely in the hands of U.S. forces.

Militarily the war was going better than Polk could have dreamed, but diplomatically and politically it was proving a disaster. There seemed little prospect that any conceivable Mexican government would be stable enough to negotiate — let alone get the populace to accept — a peace treaty with the hated United States. Even Polk's efforts to get Congress in August 1846 to approve $2 million to underwrite negotiations turned into a political disaster: A young Pennsylvania congressman, David Wilmot, attached a rider to the administration bill providing that "neither slavery nor involuntary servitude shall ever exist in any part of . . . [the] territory" acquired as a result of the war. This Wilmot Proviso (as it is known in history) caused an explosion of outrage and opposition among southern politicians, and, as we shall see in the next chapter, transformed American politics. If this were not enough trouble for Polk, Taylor's continuing successes threatened to overshadow the president. Polk desperately wished he had a victorious Democratic general, and he even toyed with the silly idea of appointing Missouri's expansionist Democratic Senator, Thomas Hart Benton, to lead the American troops. But good sense finally won out. Polk, angry with Taylor, took some of his troops and reinforced General Winfield Scott, a tall, handsome, skilled leader — but also a Whig in his political sympathies.

opportunity to destroy Taylor's forces near Saltillo, but after vicious fighting near Buena Vista, Taylor held his position. Santa Anna withdrew, leaving Taylor in command of northeastern Mexico for the duration of the war. Taylor's brilliant victory at Buena Vista (where Jefferson Davis, the later Confederate president, also distinguished himself) only gained him more fame and popularity, to Polk's dismay.

From the beginning, Polk had more on his mind than just the border dispute about the Nueces River. Two days after Congress had declared war, Polk ordered Colonel Stephen W. Kearny to march down the old Santa Fe Trail from Fort Leavenworth (in what is now Kansas) to take Santa Fe. By mid-August, without firing a shot, Kearny had captured Santa Fe. The local residents — far from Mexico City and long accustomed to profitable trade with the Yankees — apparently had no objections to Kearny's claiming New Mexico for the United States. Kearny then divided his troops, leaving a small contingent to occupy New Mexico and sending the

Scott's mission was to land at the coastal city of Vera Cruz with an invading force of 12,000 and march overland to take Mexico City. The poorly led Mexican armies had taken a severe beating, but they refused to surrender and continued to fight bravely. The invading Americans were outnumbered but had the advantage of being superbly led. In addition to the capable senior commanders, Taylor and Scott, the American junior officers — the pride of West Point — were eager to prove their worth. The roster of officers who honed their skills on the battlefields of Mexico included such future Civil War leaders as Robert E. Lee, Ulysses S. Grant, P. G. T. Beauregard, George B. McClellan, Braxton Bragg, George G. Meade, Jefferson Davis, William T. Sherman, and Thomas J. Jackson.

In March 1847 Scott landed near Vera Cruz, which after an eighteen-day siege fell to his bombardment. He then prepared to move directly toward Mexico City. Santa Anna had recovered from his defeat at Buena Vista and rushed to set up what looked to be an absolutely impregnable position commanding the highway through Cero Gordo pass. By all odds, Scott's advance was stymied. Then an able young engineer in Scott's army, Robert E. Lee, found a way around Santa Anna's left by a route that led to a small peak. From this position, Scott was able to get howitzers in position to bombard Santa Anna's defending forces. After a sharp bombardment, Scott's forces rushed the Mexican defenders, defeated them in bloody combat, and moved through the pass to Mexico City, where the defenders outnumbered Scott's forces three to one. Again, it seemed that Scott might be stopped. But in a series of brilliant attacks Scott secured victories in battles at Contreras, Churubusco, Molino del Rey, and Chapultapec. On September 14, 1847, Mexico City fell to the American troops, and a battalion of U.S. marines stood guard over the National Palace — "the halls of Montezuma," as the Marines' Hymn still celebrates. Even European observers (who before the war had expected the Mexicans to win) were much impressed by Scott's achievement.

❧ Treaty of Guadalupe Hidalgo

By early 1847 Polk was desperate to bring the war to a conclusion. Not only was it promoting the fame and political prospects of two Whig generals, Zachary Taylor and Winfield Scott, but it also become extremely unpopular in the North. Whigs — who at the outset found themselves politically obliged to support Ameri-

can troops under fire — had always believed that Polk had trumped up the cause of the war simply to fulfill his own expansionist ambitions. Early on, northeastern Whigs viewed the war as little more than a plot to gain new territory for the expansion of slavery. For example, the obscure Illinois Whig congressman Abraham Lincoln had ridiculed Polk's justification of the war effort, and in Massachusetts Henry David Thoreau had gone to jail in an act of civil disobedience rather than pay a tiny tax to support the war.

As one military success followed another, even Polk was momentarily tempted by the heady talk of vast territorial expansion. Some proslavery fanatics began to talk of annexing much of Mexico — even "all of Mexico." John C. Calhoun, who had opposed going to war, was very much opposed to such extreme expansionism, in part because he knew it would exacerbate sectional tensions and in part because he did not believe that "inferior" Mexican nationals could ever be assimilated into the American white population. The controversy over Wilmot's Proviso was a prelude to the sectional animosities that erupted, and Polk feared the political division might even disrupt the Democratic Party. Polk resisted the "all Mexico" calls, but how could one negotiate a peace treaty with a nation whose governments kept collapsing?

Obviously no official ambassador would be received, so Polk had sent (along with General Scott's invading army) a special agent: South Carolinian Nicholas P. Trist, who had once been Andrew Jackson's private secretary. The president authorized Trist to offer Mexico $15 million for all of California and New Mexico, and assume (up to $3.25 million) the debts Mexico owed American citizens; in return, Mexico would recognize the Rio Grande border and surrender all claims to California and New Mexico. After being rebuffed several times, and even ignoring Polk's letter recalling him in the early fall of 1847 (the president thought his envoy might settle for less than he was authorized to accept), Trist continued to work with the Mexican government that had succeeded Santa Anna's. Staying on despite Polk's recall, Trist signed the Treaty of Guadalupe Hidalgo with the Mexican government February 2, 1848. By this treaty, Mexico accepted virtually all of Polk's original terms: the Rio Grande border, the cession of all California and New Mexico, and $15 million compensation and the United States's assumption of all Mexican debts to American citizens.

Polk was furious at Trist for ignoring his instructions to break off negotiations, but the president also feared the political storm that would erupt at home if he did not accept the treaty. Reluctantly Polk submitted the treaty to the Senate, which voted 38-14 to accept it on March 10, 1848. Seven of those in opposition were Democrats who rejected the treaty because they wanted to hold out for all of Mexico. The other seven objectors were Whigs who opposed the treaty because they did not want to add to the Union even California or New Mexico. The war had limped to an end, and no one — Democrat or Whig, northerner or southerner — was fully satisfied. Few could yet foretell what additional problems would result from the acquisition of millions of acres of new land for the nation. In fact, Pandora's box had been opened.

GROWTH OF UTAH AND CALIFORNIA

The sectional controversy that arose over whether slavery should be allowed to expand into the new territory acquired from Mexico became a major cause of the Civil War, but independent of the parade of events that led to Fort Sumter two other of the most amazing stories in American history occurred in the course of populating the West during the 1840s and 1850s. Americans striving to please God and to find gold led to two significant migrations to the West, one to Utah and the other to California, and to a fourfold increase in the combined populations of Utah and California in the years 1850-1860. In writing the history of the United States there is a tendency to subordinate everything after the Wilmot Proviso to the coming of the Civil War, but the migration of the Mormons to Utah and the Gold Rush "forty-niners" to California lie beyond the political mainstream, even though in interesting ways they also contribute to the story.

⇝ *Joseph Smith and the Origins of Mormonism*

Born in 1805, a poor Vermont farm boy named Joseph Smith grew up to found what became the largest religious denomination started in the United States, a movement that today has more than 4.5 million members in this nation and millions more worldwide. When Smith was a teenager his parents, classic ne'er-do-wells, moved to Palmyra, New York, but the boom times associated with the building of the Erie Canal bypassed them. This part of upstate New York was a region — the so-called Burnt Over District — so caught up in a series of evangelical revivals and people proclaiming ec-

static conversions that a young, impressionable, highly imaginative boy with a mind like Velcro could easily be confused by the welter of religious impressions. In fact Joseph Smith had a vision in which both God and Jesus came to him and warned him to reject as apostasy the swirl of religious sentiments. He must wait, they said, until in good time truth would be revealed to him.

Sure enough, as Joseph Smith later recounted his story, in 1823 the angel Moroni appeared to him and led him to a hidden cache of manuscripts, buried in the Hill Cumorah near Palmyra. The manuscripts were written on thin gold plates in strange hieroglyphics. But Smith was not allowed to handle the gold plates until he had undergone a four-year period of moral testing. Buried along with the golden tablets were two magical seer stones, and by placing them in a contraption somewhat like spectacles Smith was able to translate the "reformed Egyptian" symbols.

Beginning in 1827 and continuing for the next two years, Smith spent hundreds of hours hidden behind a curtain or blanket translating these divine writings, dictating what he was reading first to his wife and eventually to three other copyists. No one who was not a convert in almost a religious trance ever saw the actual golden plates, and as soon as Smith had finished his task of translation and transcription, the angel Moroni returned and took them away. Smith, along with several close associates who had come to believe Smith had indeed received a new revelation from God, raised money and in 1830 paid a printer to publish 5,000 copies of the *Book of Mormon.*

In 500 pages of dense, convoluted prose, heavily reminiscent of the King James Version of the Bible, the *Book of Mormon* told a number of incredible stories. A part of the *Book of Mormon* was entitled the Book of Ether, which recounted the story of an ancient, pre-Hebraic people called the Jaredites who, following the confusion attendant to the attempt to build the Tower of Babel, had journeyed to America aboard submarine-like crafts. Here they established a flourishing civilization, but eventually fratricidal wars led to their almost total destruction, and Ether was the last surviving prophet of the Jaredites who recounted their story and predicted that a promised city of Zion would eventually arise on this continent.

Most of the *Book of Mormon,* though, relates the history of a later group of Hebraic peoples who came to America about 600 B.C., shortly before the Babylonian captivity of the Jews. Two sons of a Jewish prophet named Lehi were the most influential of these newcomers, but the descendants of the two sons, named Nephi and Laman, quarreled, and though the descendants waxed and waned in their righteousness, eventually the Lamanites essentially exterminated the Nephites. Long before their final conflict, Jesus — after his crucifixion and resurrection — visited America and worked miracles. But even his example was not enough to extinguish the animosity between the Lamanites and the Nephites. To punish their evil ways, God darkened the skins of the Lamanites, and they became the progenitors of American Indians.

In one great final battle in A.D. 384, the Lamanites decimated the Nephites. The surviving Nephite prophet and leader, Mormon, wrote on the golden plates the history of his people. Some years later, in 421, Moroni, the son of Mormon, supplemented Mormon's history with some details of his own and hid the total accumulation of sacred writings in a hillside in New York, where they were to remain until the times were providentially propitious. Enter Joseph Smith in 1823.

Despite the astounding outline of this story, the *Book of Mormon* quoted liberally from the Bible and made a number of unexceptional references to orthodox theology. In fact Mormon theology was closer to mainstream Christianity in 1830 than it would ever again be, for Joseph Smith would continue to receive revelations that drew his movement further away from Christian orthodoxy. In 1830, however, the *Book of Mormon* seemed to harmonize a number of competing denominational issues, its cadence seemed completely biblical, and the aura Joseph Smith effected as one who had received new revelations fresh from God and the angel Moroni recommended the new religion as the answer to the prayers of many devout searchers for truth and certainty. Here, with the authority of a person who had a direct conduit to God standing before them, was the pathway to holiness.

❧ *Opposition to the Mormons*

Joseph Smith's movement grew rapidly. In 1834 he formally organized the Church of Christ, soon renamed the Church of Christ of Latter-Day Saints. But along with devotees, Smith attracted opposition both because of his authoritarian leadership (for example, he tended to ignore local, state, and federal laws with which he disagreed) and because he suggested that the *Book of Mormon* had supplanted the Bible as the final word of God. Aware of the seriousness of the opposition, in 1831 Smith began the first in a long and fateful series of

The Angel Moroni Reveals the Golden Plates to Joseph Smith   This lithograph illustrates the moment when, in Mormon belief, an angel led young Joseph Smith to the upstate New York hiding place of the golden plates, which Smith then translated and published as the *Book of Mormon* — the hitherto unknown history of ancient America.

westward moves. Initially he settled in Kirtland, Ohio, where he gained a number of new converts, including a former Baptist and Church of Christ minister, Sidney Rignon, who later contributed to Smith's evolving theology. Smith founded a savings bank in Kirtland but refused to get a state charter; when the bank failed in the Panic of 1837, hundreds of families — not just Mormon families but non-Mormons whom Smith called "gentiles" — lost their savings. The community outrage forced Smith and his followers to flee Ohio.

Already Mormons had begun to move to Missouri, and in 1838 Smith joined them. But the "gentile" neighbors there were already furious at the Mormons, in part because they erroneously feared the New Yorkers and Ohioans might be closet abolitionists. Shortly before Smith arrived, the bulk of the Missouri Mormons had abandoned their first settlement and moved to a more northern portion of the state. But Smith's stated intention to wreak vengeance on the Mormon enemies, complete with the statement that he would be "a Second Mohammed," only flamed the anger of the Mormon opponents. A Missouri state militia practically declared war on the Mormons, fearing their theology, the autocratic rule of Smith, and their growing prosperity. The Mormons fled again, this time eastward to Illinois, where on the banks of the Mississippi they were allowed in 1839 to establish the city of Nauvoo. Here the Mormon leaders laid out a model city, complete with plans for an impressive temple. The Whigs and Democrats, evenly matched in the state, vied to court the Mormon vote. Thus allowed to proceed, the Mormon city enjoyed remarkable growth. By 1844 Nauvoo was the largest city in Illinois, with a population of 15,000.

Again Smith allowed his community's prosperity to fuel his ego. He ruled the community with an iron fist, commanded its militia (the Nauvoo Legion), experienced new visions (which for a while he kept secret from most of his followers) that promoted polygamy or plural marriage, and even announced plans to run for the presidency of the United States. Rumors mounted that Smith planned to take over the Northwest and establish a Mormon empire. Opposition again began to arise in Illinois against Smith's leadership style and his community. When Smith crushed a flicker of internal opposition within the Mormon community and destroyed the printing press of a dissident group, a troop of Illinois militia began to move against him. The militia dissolved into a mob, Smith and his brother were jailed, and the mob stormed the jail, lynching the two Smith brothers on June 27, 1844.

❧ The Mormons' Deseret Empire

The Mormon movement, or, as they called themselves, the Latter-Day Saints, might have ended had its charismatic leader died a natural death, but lynching turned him into a martyr. Another charismatic leader, Brigham Young, emerged, a man with superb organizational skills. Even before his death Smith had realized that his movement would have to leave Illinois and find a refuge far beyond the disapproving eye of non-Mormons. He investigated the possibility of establishing a settlement in a remote section of Texas on the Rio Grande, and he sent secret feelers to France and Russia about some refuge in the far Northwest or elsewhere. As the Mormons' new leader, Young considered these plans and decided to move more than a thousand miles from the United States, into the valley of the Great Salt Lake in what was then Mexican territory, protected from interference by U.S. authorities by rugged mountain ranges and the great expanse of barren prairie.

Before the end of 1845, Young had sent an advance party to the Great Salt Lake region, mapped out a trail from Illinois to Utah that included way stations with planted crops and dug wells, and made preparations to sell all the Mormon property at huge discount and begin the great trek westward. In one of the most dramatic folk migrations in American history, by the summer of 1846 more than twelve thousand Mormons were on the move, driving cattle along with them and accompanied by almost four thousand wagons. The bulk of the migration moved very slowly, camping at the way stations to harvest the crops and collect food and forage for the next stage of the journey. When Young himself, with another advance party, finally came to the top of a mountain ridge and surveyed the great valley before him, he announced, "This is the place." Over the next few years thousands of Mormons arrived, and not just from Illinois but also from England, where Mormon missionaries had found many converts in the teeming industrial towns.

Brigham Young was a true visionary, and by the power of his personality — supported by devout lieutenants and obedient believers — he organized the Mormon settlement in the West with genius-like efficiency. He directed the people to dam up mountain streams, diverting water through canals to the dry but fertile desert floor, and the desert literally bloomed. The church owned the land, which it parceled out in small lots for intense cultivation, made the laws, and organized community life so that all worked together for the common good. In 1849 a constitution was written for the completely autonomous state of Deseret. Soon the Mormons began to prosper, in part by selling provisions to Americans attracted to California by the discovery of gold in 1849.

Within a decade more than ninety Mormon communities dotted the West. Salt Lake City's broad streets and preparations for the construction there of a mighty temple suggested the Mormons' confidence and ambition. Mormon settlements stretched north from Salt Lake City, as well as southwestward along what was called the Mormon corridor — past Provo, Cedar City, and Las Vegas, all the way to San Bernardino, California. Young envisioned future settlers from England coming by sea to San Diego or Los Angeles, then overland along the corridor of Mormon settlements. Others came from England to New York and then by train to Missouri; from there they pushed wheelbarrow-like carts holding their worldly belongings all the way to the Great Salt

Lake. Clearly, by the early 1850s the Mormon community in the West, a virtual theocracy, was the most successful religious communitarian experiment in American history. The rapid development of the Mormon empire in the climatically inhospitable West was one of the most remarkable accomplishments in American history.

✸ *The Mormon War*

The rationale for the Mormon migration to the isolated desert valley of the Great Salt Lake was to escape involvement with the United States. But history caught up with the Latter-Day Saints in 1850 when, according to the terms of the Compromise of 1850, the entire region was organized as the Territory of Utah. (Congress ignored the Mormon name of Deseret.) Most Americans considered the Mormons to be so far away that they cared little about them or their empire, and President Millard Fillmore's appointment of Brigham Young as territorial governor reassured the Mormons themselves that having become once more citizens of the United States would effect little change. But trouble soon erupted. The Mormon Church expected to continue nominating candidates for office and judges and directing devout church members how to decide in jury cases. On the other hand, the federal government expected to appoint the government officials, most of whom were non-Mormon.

Non-Mormons tended to be contemptuous of Mormon practices, especially polygamy, and they usually showed their feelings; Mormons in turn resorted to (or averted their eyes from) violence against so-called gentiles and harassed federal judges and other officials so badly that most of them gave up and fled the territory. More than anything else — more than the Mormons' theocratic government, more than their ignoring federal officials — the practice of plural marriage shocked and outraged Americans in general. Brigham Young, for example, at one time had twenty-seven wives. The 1856 Republican Party platform even contained a plank attacking polygamy and slavery as the "twin relics of barbarism" in the nation. As much as southern slavery, many Republicans considered Mormon polygamy a "peculiar institution" basically at odds with American values. But Democrats too, like Stephen A. Douglas of

Salt Lake City　Already by 1868, as this early photograph indicates, Salt Lake City had begun to look like a substantial urban oasis in the great Western desert.

Illinois, referred to Mormonism as a "loathsome ulcer" that should be excised from the nation. In 1857 Democratic president James Buchanan, determining that the Mormons were substantially in rebellion against the laws of the nation, sent an armed force of U.S. troops under the command of Albert Sidney Johnston (later a Confederate hero) to suppress the Mormon leaders and bring them into conformity with U.S. legal practice.

Colonel Johnston led a force of 2,500 men across the plains, wintered near Fort Bridger in the northeast corner of the Utah Territory, and by the summer of 1858 marched into the valley of the Great Salt Lake. The Mormon population retreated from the soldiers' path, but Mormon guerrillas impeded the army by setting the prairie and army wagons on fire. The so-called Mormon War saw almost no bloodshed, but Johnston set up an occupation base between Salt Lake City and Provo at a place he named Camp Floyd (after Secretary of War John B. Floyd). A war of nerves resulted, and Brigham Young resisted giving in to U.S. authority, but Johnston was firm. He determined to uphold the laws of the federal government, writing to another officer that the Mormons "have with premeditation placed themselves in rebellion against the Union and entertain the insane design of establishing a form of government thoroughly despotic and utterly repugnant to our institutions." To a friend he wrote — again unaware of the irony of his words — that "The people of the Union must now . . . act with . . . vigor and force . . . against those who raise a parricidal hand against their country." After about a year of army occupation and uneasy truce, President

Buchanan offered to pardon the Mormon leaders and Brigham Young agreed to obey U.S. officials. The Mormon War was over, and Colonel Johnston prepared to return to his home in Texas. He left Utah on March 1, 1860, riding on horseback to California, where he planned to board a ship and return to his family.

❧ California and the Gold Rush

Johnston had hardly returned to Texas before he was called to Washington. There he learned that the military commander of the Department of California had just died, and Secretary of War Floyd appointed Johnston to report to San Francisco and take command of the Department of the Pacific. Johnston returned to Texas, picked up his family, and sailed for California (via Central America) in late December 1860. Three weeks later the Johnston family arrived in San Francisco, a thriving, cosmopolitan city of almost 57,000 persons, and on January 15, 1861, assumed his command. The California that he encountered in the winter of 1861 was a far cry from the unstable Bear Flag Republic in 1846. In the interim the region had been annexed under the Treaty of Guadalupe Hidalgo in 1848, gold had been discovered near Sacramento, and California had become the destination of tens of thousands of would-be millionaires.

John Sutter, a Swiss-born Mexican citizen who had come to California in 1839, had a huge ranch, a fort, and a variety of support operations in the Sacramento Valley. In January 1848 a carpenter working near the millrace of Sutter's sawmill accidentally noticed small, gold-colored flecks. The news spread rapidly back to San Francisco, then a tiny port village, and from there back to the East Coast and eventually to the world. Thousands of people from all over the world began to converge on California, many coming overland by what had been called the Oregon Trail but turning southwest in what is now Idaho and heading toward the Mother Lode, which ran for more than 150 miles along the western slopes of the Sierra Nevada mountains. Thousands more came by sea.

Almost 100,000 "Forty-Niners" arrived in California in 1849 alone, most from the United States but thousands also from Mexico, Latin America, Europe, and China. The first American gold rush had been in North Carolina and Georgia more than a decade earlier, so many southern whites, experienced with panning

---

❋ IN THEIR OWN WORDS

Mormon Polygamy, 1860

Sir Richard Burton, a British world traveler (also famous for his translation of The Arabian Nights)*, visited the Mormons in 1860 and was fascinated to see how polygamy supported the Latter Day Saints' religious and social life. Burton's attempt to understand and describe sexual practices regarded as "deviant" shocked his Victorian contemporaries but is considered pioneering anthropological research today.*

The "chaste and plural marriage" being once legalized, finds a multitude of supporters. The anti-Mormons declare that it is at once fornication and adultery — a sin which absorbs all others. The Mormons point triumphantly to the austere morals of their community, their superior freedom from maladive influences, and the absence of that uncleanness and licentiousness which distinguishes the cities of the civilized world. . . .

All sensuality in the married state is strictly forbidden beyond the requisite for ensuring progeny — the practice, in fact, of Adam and Abraham. During the gestation and nursing of children, the strictest continence on the part of the mother is required. . . .

Besides religious and physiological, there are social motives for the plurality. . . . To the unprejudiced traveler it appears that polygamy is the rule where population is required. . . .

The other motive for polygamy in Utah is economy. Servants are rare and costly; it is cheaper and more comfortable to marry them. Many converts are attracted by the prospect of becoming wives, especially from places where, like Clifton, there are sixty-four females to thirty-six males. . . .

For the attachment of the women of the Saints to the doctrine of plurality there are many reasons. The Mormon prophets have expended all their arts upon this end, well knowing that without the hearty co-operation of mothers and wives, sisters and daughters, no institution can live long. They have bribed them with promises of Paradise — they have subjugated them with threats of annihilation. With them once a Mormon always a Mormon; . . . the apostate Mormon is looked upon by other people as a scamp or a knave, and the woman worse than a prostitute. . . .

Another curious effect of fervent belief may be noticed in the married state. When a man has four or five wives with reasonable families by each, he is fixed for life: his interests, if not his affections, bind him irrevocably to his New Faith. But the bachelor, as well as the monogamic youth, is prone to back-sliding. Apostacy [sic] is apparently so common that many of the new Saints form a mere floating population. He is proved by a mission before being permitted to marry, and even then women, dreading a possible renegade with the terrible consequence of a heavenless future to themselves, are shy of saying yes.

and operating sluices, came to apply their skills in the western mountains. Often they brought slaves with them. The non-southern gold miners greatly resented the slaves for giving what the miners felt was an unfair advantage to southern gold seekers. This resulted, in 1849, in a California constitution that outlawed slavery less for reasons of humanity than for greed, although southern politicians saw it erroneously as an act of hostility against southern institutions. Californians soon turned their racial prejudice against the Chinese who came in following the gold rush, and they too were attacked for their willingness to work for cheap "coolie wages."

Within a decade a half-billion dollars' worth of gold was shipped from California, bringing great wealth and a number of social problems to the region. Instant towns and mining camps sprang up along the Mother Lode. The workers, overwhelmingly young men, worked hard, fought, got drunk, made and lost small fortunes, gambled, and rarely remained rich. Soon the heyday of the individual miner who panned for gold in mountain streams was past, and expensively equipped corporate mining took over. The real fortunes were made by the merchants, for the tens of thousands of miners needed to be fed, clothed, housed, financed, transported, and entertained, and the men and women engaged in these mundane trades were the ones who prospered and built the state of California. One, for example, was Levi Strauss, a German Jewish immigrant who came to San Francisco to manufacture cheap but durable work pants that still remain a characteristic American product.

In 1850 probably one-fifth of all the Anglo women in rip-roaring California were prostitutes, and more of them died young than became wealthy matrons. But many hardworking wives of miners took in boarders, opened simple restaurants, did laundry, and supplemented the family budget by their steady income. San Francisco became the great entrepot of the entire gold region, and by the early 1850s California was no longer a leisurely ranching state but a frantically bustling mining and mercantile empire. Its growth, as well as the constitutional prohibition against slavery, made California statehood a political issue that could not be avoided in 1850.

The western mining frontier shifted eastward to Colorado with the discovery in 1858 of gold near Denver and shortly thereafter at Central City, and to Utah Territory in 1859 with the discovery of the famous Comstock Lode, a rich vein of silver at Virginia City in what is now Nevada. Still other states in their turn became

Advertising the Gold Rush   Almost as soon as the discovery of gold in California was announced, posters like this began going up on the East Coast, advertising the speediest possible passage to the gold fields — in this case, via a Nicaraguan crossing. Notice how "jack asses" are also promised as part of the cargo, so that would-be miners can be assured of a pack animal on their arrival at San Francisco. The advertised price of passage — $90 — was a very considerable sum for the day, much more than the average eastern worker's monthly wages.

the scene of other gold and silver rushes. Each time, wild boom times always characterized the mad search for instant wealth in gold and silver — and each time, corporate mining eventually took over.

As early as the 1850s San Francisco, with its magnificent harbor — "a marvel of nature," a Spanish diarist had called it in 1776 — became the leading city on the Pacific Coast. The diverse national background of those rushing to California made San Francisco a stunningly international city, and its wealth, its distance from other major urban areas, and the booster-like pride in the beauty of its setting and the seeming miracle of its growth made citizens enormously pleased both with themselves and their instant city.

It was to this enterprising and accomplished city that Colonel Johnston brought his family in January 1861. San Francisco supported more than a dozen newspapers (including French and German papers), two libraries, two historical societies, a variety of theaters, and the California Academy of Science.

CONCLUSION: NEWS FROM THE SOUTH

Johnston and his wife were enthusiastic about their new home, and Elize Johnston even said she hoped her children would make California their permanent home. But already, far away in the American South, states were beginning to secede from the Union. A rumor arose that southerners in California were plotting a Confederate coup to take over the state. Johnston quickly and emphatically spoke against such secessionist conspiracies and wrote to the governor of the state that "I have spent the greater part of my life in the service of my country . . . and not a cartridge or a percussion cap belonging to her shall pass to any enemy while I am here as her representative."

Again Johnston did not appreciate the irony of his words. On April 9, 1861, he received the news that his home state of Texas had seceded from the Union. Immediately deciding that he could not bear arms against his people, later that day he resigned from the U.S. Army. Less than a year later, on April 7, 1862, Confederate General Albert Sidney Johnston would die at the Battle of Shiloh leading a southern army against the forces of the United States. The coming of that great conflict in which he perished dominated American politics in the slightly more than a decade following the nation's territorial realization of its Manifest Destiny. The optimism and adventure that had marked the opening of the West soon turned to the fatalism and tragedy of the American Civil War.

SUGGESTED READING

Leonard J. Arrington and Davis Britton, *The Mormon Experience: A History of the Latter-Day Saints* (1979). A modern, detailed, fair-minded account of a unique American religious-social experiment that succeeded.

H. W. Brands, *The Age of Gold: The California Gold Rush and the New American Dream* (2002). Colorfully tells the impact on California and the rest of the nation of the discovery of gold at Sutter's Mill.

Bernard De Voto, *Across the Wide Missouri* (1947). A broadly conceived, beautifully written book deservedly regarded as a classic of American letters.

Thomas R. Hietala, *Manifest Design: Anxious Aggrandizement in Late Jacksonian America* (1985). A reassessment of Manifest Destiny stressing party politics and economic impulse driving expansion.

Robert W. Johannsen, *To the Halls of the Montezumas: The Mexican War in the American Imagination* (1985). A lively, accessible history of the war with much attention to the domestic impact of the conflict.

Merrill D. Peterson, *The Great Triumvirate: Webster, Clay, and Calhoun* (1987). A masterful political biography of the three great Senate leaders and the world they lived in.

John I. Unruh, Jr., *The Plains Across: Overland Emigrants and the Trans-Mississippi West, 1840-1860* (1979). A richly detailed social history of the westward movement.

David J. Weber, *The Mexican Frontier, 1821-1846: The American Southwest under Mexico* (1982). Places the acquisition of Texas in a broad political-social context.

SUGGESTIONS FOR FURTHER READING

Barton H. Barbour, *Fort Union and the Upper Missouri Fur Trade* (2001).

William Benemann, ed., *A Year of Mud and Gold: San Francisco in Letters and Diaries, 1849-1850* (1999).

Gregg Cantrell, *Stephen F. Austin, Emprasario of Texas* (1999).

Malcolm Clark, Jr., *Eden Seekers: The Settlement of Oregon, 1810-1862* (1981).

Tom Dunlay, *Kit Carson & the Indians* (2000).

John S. D. Eisenhower, *So Far from God: The U.S. War with Mexico, 1846-1848* (1989).

William H. Goetzmann, *Exploration and Empire: The Explorer and Scientist in the Winning of the West* (1966).

R. Douglas Hurt, *The Indian Frontier, 1763-1846* (2002).

Julie Roy Jeffrey, *Converting the West: A Biography of Narcissa Whitman* (1991).

Theodore J. Karaminski, *Fur Trade and Exploration: Opening of the Far Northwest, 1821-1852* (1983).

Paul D. Lack, *The Texas Revolutionary Experience: A Political and Social History, 1835-1836* (1992).

Frederick Merk, *Manifest Destiny and Mission in American History* (1963).

Leonard Pitt, *The Decline of the Californios: A Social History of the Spanish-Speaking Californians, 1846-1890* (1999).

Brian Roberts, *American Alchemy: The California Gold Rush and Middle-Class Culture* (2000).

David Roberts, *A Newer World: Kit Carson, John C. Frémont, and the Claiming of the American West* (2000).

John H. Schroeder, *Mr. Polk's War: American Opposition and Dissent, 1846-1848* (1973).

Charles G. Sellers, *James K. Polk: Continentalist, 1843-1846* (1966).

Wallace Stegner, *The Gathering of Zion: The Story of the Mormon Trail* (1964).

Robert M. Utley, *Frontiersmen in Blue: The United States Army and the Indians, 1848-1865* (1967).

Elliott West, *Growing Up with the Country: Childhood on the Far-Western Frontier* (1989).

14

Sectionalism and Slavery's Dark Cloud: The Coming of the Civil War, 1846-1861

SELDOM DO HISTORICAL actors fully understand the long-range consequences of events in which they participate. But in 1846 two thoughtful observers of the national scene, one southern, the other northern, had a fateful premonition of the repercussions that would result from the war in Mexico. In South Carolina, John C. Calhoun had opposed action against Mexico in part because he anticipated that war would increase the size, authority, and expense of the national government, all of which he interpreted as working against the interests of the South. More important, Calhoun feared that northern opposition to the war would escalate to the point of threatening the Union. Meanwhile, a thousand miles away in Massachusetts, Ralph Waldo Emerson confided to his diary at the beginning of the war that "the United States will conquer Mexico, but it will be as the man who swallows the arsenic, which brings him down in return. Mexico will poison us."

These eerily accurate predictions grew out of understandings of how deeply entrenched were the fundamental divisions that existed in the nation, divisions that the political parties had tried to paper over or ignore. But in the aftermath of the Mexican War these divisions became no longer vague abstractions but practical problems that demanded policy decisions. Politicians and political parties had to come up with answers, and the attempt to solve the problem led to the famous Compromise of 1850, which a generation of hopeful Americans wanted to believe had settled the disruptive issues for good. Yet events soon proved the compromisers wrong and the pessimists like Calhoun and Emerson right. Slavery — the question of whether it was right or wrong, the question of whether it should be confined to the South or allowed to spread, the question of whether it should be abolished everywhere — raised questions so momentous that it ultimately became impossible to sustain a compromise. The result was the poison Emerson had feared: Disunion.

CONFRONTING "THE SLAVE POWER"

Modern, aggressive abolitionism had begun in the early 1830s, and abolitionist spokesmen (including former slaves, such as Frederick Douglass), ministers, newspapers, public rallies, and formal organizations had all worked to spread the conviction that slavery was a sin, a cancerous disease in the body politic. During the first wave of abolitionism that had begun in the northern states at the end of the American Revolution, those who urged ending slavery were willing to accept gradual emancipation, sometimes stretching out over years. But abolitionists in the 1830s and 1840s were less willing to be patient and compromise with what they considered a flagrant sin against humanity and God; they pushed for immediate and total emancipation. The most radical white abolitionist, William Lloyd Garrison, condemned the U.S. Constitution itself as an "agreement with hell" because it implicitly accepted the institution of slavery, but most abolitionists focused on preventing the spread of slavery into new territories that would become states, reasoning that if slavery were confined it would somehow wither and die. Actually, southern proslavery spokesmen also believed that the health and vitality of their peculiar institution depended on its ability to spread westward. Proslavery advocates were convinced that slavery was a moral institution, even a providentially inspired institution planned by God as the mechanism to civilize and Christianize the so-called heathen of Africa. Such southern publicists of course also defended slavery as a practical, economic institution and believed that slave labor, by relieving certain whites from much manual labor, allowed a flowering of white civilization. But slavery's defenders were also more than willing to dispute the abolitionists' claims that slavery was immoral by parading biblical passages in its defense. Yet these intellectual and religious arguments regarding slavery occasioned few real political disputes as long as the issues were theoretical.

✣ *Slavery in the Territories*

The slavery issue became concrete when it involved the potential expansion of human bondage into new territories and future states. The abolitionists, despite their reservations about the Constitution's acquiescence in slavery where it already existed, saw the legal means to prevent slavery's expansion in the second paragraph of Article III, Section 2, of the Constitution: "The Congress shall have power to dispose of and make all needful rules and regulations respecting the territory or other property belonging to the United States...." Even southerners and slaveholders had accepted this reading of the Constitution for more than fifty years. The precedent for Congress's right to limit slavery's expansion had been the Northwest Ordinance of 1787, which banned the introduction of slaves into the territories north of the Ohio River (although the status of the few slaves already in the region remained unchanged). The validity of the Missouri Compromise line of 1820, prohibiting slavery in the Louisiana Purchase territories north of the southern boundary of Missouri, had rested on this right of congressional authority over territories.

But in the decades after the Missouri Compromise (1820), the rise of aggressive abolitionism and of combative southern proslavery doctrines intensified mutual antagonisms and kindled sectional fears. Then, in 1846, the outbreak of war with Mexico raised the possibility that the United States would acquire millions of acres of new territory. Would the new states to be created there be slave or free? In the 1840s, northern migration to the fertile soils of Oregon, and later the onrush of settlers to California following the discovery there of gold, accelerated the movement toward statehood in the Far West and exacerbated the slave state–free state conflict. Territorial expansion was the catalyst provoking the conflict over slavery that erupted in national politics in the midst of the Mexican War. The conflict threatened as nothing ever had before to divide the nation into warring factions. By 1850, the very survival of the nation seemed at stake.

CONCERNS OVER THE "SLAVE POWER"
The northern appeal of abolitionism broadened as the movement began to focus less on the evils of slavery for the blacks and more on the potential harm the institution might do to northern whites. The idea arose in the North that slaveholders and their political supporters constituted a nefarious cabal dedicated to taking over

The Free Soil Ticket, 1848   Under the slogan "Free Soil — Free Labor — Free Speech," Martin Van Buren and Charles Francis Adams ran for president and vice president. Adams was the son of John Quincy Adams; during the Civil War he would ably serve as Abraham Lincoln's minister to Great Britain. Notice that the Free Soil appeal is directed entirely toward the interests of northern white farmers and laborers; it deliberately avoids abolitionist themes and imagery.

lic expression of abolitionist ideas, and through the Gag Rule, passed by Congress in 1836 with solid southern support, which required that all petitions regarding slavery be automatically tabled. Some proslavery defenders even called for the reopening of the international slave trade, overturning the Constitution's ban against importing new slaves into the nation after 1808.

The idea of a Slave Power conspiracy also came to include a fear among many northern whites — who had no strong opinions about the morality of slavery in the South per se — that southern desires to extend slavery into new territories or even existing northern states would mean unfair competition for free white laborers and farmers. Large slave plantations in the Northwest would harm the interests of small free farmers, and slave laborers would certainly force down white wages. Therefore many northern whites, even those who disliked blacks, became opponents of slavery because the Slave Power conspiracy seemed to threaten their well-being. Antislavery in the form of a fear of Slave Power had expanded beyond a religious or moral concern and become a matter of self-protection to countless whites in the North. War with Mexico and the corresponding potential that the nation would acquire a vast new western territory — most of it south of the Missouri Compromise line and hence open to the expansion of slavery — opened a political Pandora's box. And once opened, the troubles proved very difficult to confine.

and controlling the Union. This conspiracy of the "Slave Power" (the phrase was coined in 1844 by James Birney of the Liberty Party) would supposedly stop at nothing to expand its sway. It was said to advocate the expansion of slavery into the western territories, the Caribbean, and Central America. Proslavery advocates certainly did deprive opponents of the freedom to express their views through southern state laws against distributing antislavery tracts, through mob action against the pub-

THE WILMOT PROVISO

During a sultry nighttime session of Congress on August 6, 1846, a young Pennsylvania congressman named David Wilmot finally raised the lid of the box. The House was debating an innocuous appropriation request by President Polk for funds to underwrite negotiations with Mexico. In the midst of the discussion, Wilmot stood and, after briefly saying that he was no opponent of territorial expansion itself, attacked slavery in moralistic terms. Then, borrowing language directly from the Northwest Ordinance of 1787, he moved to attach a rider to the appropriations bill: in any land that might be acquired from Mexico, Wilmot proposed, "neither slavery nor involuntary servitude shall ever exist in any part of said territory, except for crime, whereof the party shall first be duly convicted."

Wilmot's bombshell stunned the political establishment. Although the measure passed in the northern-dominated House, the Senate adjourned (August 10) before it could vote on the rider. But the issue would not die. Time after time the formula, called the Wilmot Proviso, was added to bills in the House, and each time debate reverberated throughout the nation. For many northerners, the Proviso was necessary to prevent the Slave Power plot from taking over the nation. To defensive southerners, who saw northern efforts to put parameters around slavery as a flagrant attempt to restrict the rights of southern property holders, Wilmot's Proviso threatened the essential southern institution and the whole southern way of life. Southerners well knew that admission of Iowa and Wisconsin to the Union as free states was just then pending, with Minnesota and even Oregon waiting in the wings. Four possible new free states would tip irreparably the balance of power to the North. Clearly flouting the Missouri Compromise, Wilmot and his northern compatriots sought to prevent the South from extending slavery to the potential new states that might be formed out of territory conquered in the war with Mexico. Opposing Wilmot's Proviso head-on, Senator John C. Calhoun on February 19, 1847, offered a resolution that Congress could not restrict slavery from any territory, arguing that to do so would deprive southern citizens of their constitutionally guaranteed property rights in one part of the Union. The South and the North were clearly heading toward a collision over slavery's expansion.

Democratic Senators Lewis Cass of Michigan and Stephen A. Douglas of Illinois sought to defuse the explosive issue. Instead of arguing about whether Congress had the right to decide if a territory would be slave or free in advance of the territory's actual settlement, they suggested another method of determining the issue. In part these two prominent leaders simply wanted to finesse the politically controversial issue, but they also sincerely believed that their proposed solution, called "popular" or "squatter sovereignty," was the more truly democratic method of handling the controversy. Their idea was to let Congress simply approve the organization of states without reference to slavery; afterwards, the people who actually lived in the prospective state should decide for themselves whether or not they would allow slavery. On the surface this seemed straightforward and fair. But actually popular sovereignty raised as many problems as it settled. When exactly would the people decide? Would slaveholders be willing to move into a region if they knew their human property might be disallowed sometime in the future? Would it be simply a matter of which side got there first with the most supporters? Or would the outcome hinge on which side was the best organized, the most determined, or the most fanatic? Would not this lead to chaos and violence?

THE FREE SOIL PARTY

The two major political parties tried to evade the explosive slavery issue as the presidential election year of 1848 approached. Both national parties realized how risky it would be to take a firm position either way on slavery. Both parties blinked as they faced the central issue of the time, hoping against hope that it would somehow go away. And neither party nominated a presidential candidate with strong views about slavery. The Whigs chose an absolutely unpolitical Mexican War hero, General Zachary Taylor, who had never before even voted in a presidential election[1] and flatly refused to express a position on any substantive matter; his party did not even produce a platform. The Democrats were no more forthright. President Polk was not available because he had long before plainly stated that he would only serve one term, so the Democrats turned to Lewis Cass of popular sovereignty fame — but the party itself refused to endorse even that namby-pamby position.

In the face of such political equivocation a new party emerged out of the remnants of the Liberty Party, which had been avowedly committed to ending slavery wherever it existed. The new group called itself the Free Soil Party. It was a coalition of principled antislavery Democrats angered at Cass both for his earlier support of Polk's expansionism and for being willing to accept slavery under the guise of popular sovereignty, and of so-called Conscience Whigs who opposed slavery and abhorred their old party's abandonment of principle in

---

1. In the nineteenth century, professional American military officers typically refused to vote in national elections in order to maintain a nonpartisan image and to honor the principle of civilian control of the military. Such abstention from political activity, including voting, continued until World War II, and was practiced by such notable American officers as George C. Marshall and Dwight D. Eisenhower.

nominating the slaveholder Taylor. Free Soilers were in fact more opposed to the expansion of slavery into new territories where it would compete with free laborers than they were against slavery for the sake of its black victims. In this sense the Free Soil Party was less abolitionist than had been the Liberty Party of 1844, but in so positioning their party the Free Soilers appealed to a wider spectrum of northern voters. Martin Van Buren, despite his earlier reputation for political opportunism, gained the support of the Free Soilers because as president he had opposed the annexation of Texas. Now, angry at the Democrats for refusing to nominate him in 1844, the ex-president was more than willing to carry the Free Soil banner against both his former party and the principle of expanding slavery. The Free Soil Party garnered fewer than 300,000 votes (about 10 percent of the total) and really did not affect the outcome of the election, which Taylor won narrowly. But the advent of the Free Soil Party suggested the resiliency of the slavery issue and the possibility that a purely sectional party might arise on the strength of that issue should one of the two national parties, Democrats or Whigs, falter.

❧ From the California Gold Rush to the Uneasy Compromise of 1850

In January 1848 a carpenter helping to build a sawmill along the western foothills of central California's Sierra Nevada range turned up a handful of gold nuggets. Word got out, and suddenly no one in the Far West could think of anything else than striking it rich. Plows stood abandoned in the fields in Oregon and shops emptied in San Francisco as men rushed to the gold fields. Soon the electrifying news swept back to the East, unleashing a gigantic rush of men to the West. Within a year California's unruly, fortune-seeking population numbered more than 100,000. Among the newcomers were southerners from earlier gold fields of North Carolina and Georgia, some of them having brought their slaves with them to pan for gold and construct the sluice gates that would mechanize their search for the precious metal. White settlers from other regions objected to competing with slave panners and sluice operators, and they complained about the "degradation" of having to work side by side with any blacks, free or slave.

Virulent antiblack sentiment resulted in the 1849 California constitutional convention following the example of Iowa's just-written constitution by prohibiting slavery. California's opposition to human bondage rested on racist antipathy toward black laborers in the gold fields, not for any concern about the fate of enslaved people; but all the same, southern proslavery forces read the results to mean that one more state had joined the antislavery ranks. Oregon had earlier experienced somewhat similar racist opposition to black settlers, with the result that its provisional government in 1844 had prohibited blacks in the region; again, southerners lumped Oregon's racist opposition to the presence of black settlers with principled antislavery.

In 1849, southern resistance to any form of antislavery, whether racist or principled, exploded. The politically naive President Taylor sought to have Congress avoid the controversial issue of slavery by suggesting that California be promptly admitted as a free state without going through a formal territorial phase — and that the rest of the former Mexican territory be organized as the states of New Mexico and Utah without Congress making any determination as to whether slavery would exist in them or not. Himself a Louisiana slave owner, Taylor could not imagine cotton or sugar plantations in the arid Southwest and considered the issue of slavery expansion there an empty abstraction. But most southern politicians disagreed. The real result, they saw, would be the same as though the Wilmot Proviso had been passed: There would be a parade of new antislavery states, swelling the northern majority in both houses of Congress and sharply confining the slave portion of the nation to its present size. Increasingly the South would find itself a minority region, rapidly losing its political ability to protect its special interests against the tyrannical aims of an antislavery majority.

John C. Calhoun, who unlike Taylor thrived on abstractions, saw the issue as a life-and-death matter for the South. Calhoun rejoiced that the California controversy had so awakened and united southern opposition across both the Whig and Democratic parties, and in the Senate he demanded absolute purity on the ideology of proslavery. He even promoted a meeting of southern delegates in Nashville in 1850 who would threaten secession as the only viable southern alternative should the Senate fail to pass an ironclad guarantee of slaveholders' rights to take their slaves anywhere in the nation. Raising the specter of disunion, Calhoun wanted to shock the nation into giving the South total assurance that slavery would be safe from national interference. He personally considered himself a nationalist, but he believed the only way to ensure the nation's future was for the North to acquiesce to slavery forever in the South. Far less devoted to the Union than Calhoun, a younger group of southern politicians, the so-called fire eaters, were eager to secede to save slavery. Meanwhile in the North there was powerful and growing opposition to making any more compromises with the moral sin of slavery and an increasing willingness to oppose the Slave Power. As never before the Union was on the verge of rupture during the winter of 1849-1850.

The great national debate for several dramatic months seemed to be personified by the words of three aging Senators, the last hurrah by the great triumvirate who had often dominated Senate debate over the past three decades. Henry Clay, known as the Great Compromiser for his role in settling the Missouri conflict in 1820 and the nullification controversy in 1831, now at age seventy-three once again felt destiny's call to save the Union. Clay saw himself, not President Taylor, as the nation's rightful leader who must play his proper role at this moment of crisis. Accordingly Clay crafted a series of congressional measures, combined into one large "omnibus" bill, that he planned to have the Senate vote up or down.

Clay's bill tried to resolve all the outstanding issues that so threatened the Union. First, he proposed to admit California as a free state. Second, he would organize the remainder of the Mexican cession into two territories, New Mexico and Utah, with "no restriction or condition on the subject of slavery." Third, to settle a dispute that had arisen because Texas claimed a large chunk of New Mexico, he established the present western border of Texas. Fourth, to mollify the Texans for this loss of land (stretching from present-day New Mexico into Colorado), Clay proposed that the federal government assume $10 million in debts that had been incurred by the Republic of Texas. Fifth, attempting to settle a constant irritant to antislavery northerners incensed by the spectacle of slavery and slave traders in the national capital, Clay proposed the abolition of professional slave trading there — but would allow slavery to continue so long as the people of the District of Columbia and Maryland approved of it. (Compensation was promised to owners should these jurisdictions ever vote to end slavery in the capital.) Finally, in a last effort to sweeten the entire deal for southerners, Clay proposed a much stronger Fugitive Slave Act, beefing up the provisions of the original 1793 act by requiring more cooperation from northern state and federal officials in helping southerners recover slaves who had escaped to the North. Clay assumed that by siding with the North on some issues and with the South on others, he could attract sufficient political support to steer the entire package through Congress.

Gaunt and so near death that he had to have someone else read his speech, Calhoun replied to Clay that the South could not make any more compromises that limited the spread of slavery. Secession, even if the South had to fight for it, would be his region's only option. Then the third senatorial giant, Daniel Webster, weighed in. Delivering his famous "seventh of March" reply to Calhoun's thinly veiled threat, Webster thundered there could be no such thing as peaceful secession. In a great and eloquent closing passage in praise of the Union, Webster drew back from the horror of division and warfare. The North, he pleaded, should accept the compromise, especially those provisions that did not legally exclude slavery from the New Mexico and Utah territories. Believing that climate would effectively prevent slavery's expansion there, he saw no reason for needless government action that would rub salt in the wounds of southern sensibilities.

Audiences thronged the Senate balconies to hear Clay, Calhoun, and Webster in what everyone assumed was their last battle. But newer Senators were about to crowd them off center stage. New York Whig Senator William H. Seward answered Webster (and also broke with President Taylor) by giving full political voice to a bold abolitionist stance toward slavery in the territories. Dismissing what the Constitution said, Seward scandalized southerners particularly by declaring that "There is a higher law than the Constitution ... the common heritage of mankind." This seemed to open up floodgates of possible threats to the southern position, as well as to undermine the authority of the Constitution itself. Meanwhile, President Taylor opposed Clay's omnibus bill and continued, hardheadedly, to push his own approach. Clay's vaunted compromise bill seemed to be going nowhere; political opposition to the whole was simply too strong.

Then the logjam broke. Unbending Senator Calhoun died on March 31. On July 9 President Taylor followed him to the grave, a victim of gastroenteritis after having gorged on fresh fruit and cold milk at a hot July Fourth celebration. He was succeeded in the White House by Vice President Millard Fillmore, a veteran New York Whig politician who strongly favored Clay's system of compromises and quickly appointed Webster secretary of state. And Clay, himself ill and completely exhausted by his strenuous efforts on behalf of the compromise package, handed over floor leadership of the bill to Stephen A. Douglas, Democratic Senator from Illinois. An adept politician in his own right, Douglas saw that the bill as a whole was too much for forces in either section to swallow. So he broke apart the package into its separate components. Then, adroitly maneuvering and cobbling together temporary alliances, he got each part of the compromise passed by shifting coalitions. By the end of September the deal was done; no genuine consensus across the sections had been achieved, and there was division within the major parties themselves. Still, Americans desperately wanted to believe that the great issues had been solved (or at least evaded) and the Union saved. But the Compromise of 1850 soon began to unravel, and the ultimate consequences proved as dire as Webster had feared in his seventh of March speech.

❧ Uncle Tom's Cabin

While the national political parties had tried to avoid focusing on the slavery issue because they knew it touched political nerves both North and South, and even the Clay/Douglas compromise had been unwilling to countenance a congressional decision on slavery in the New Mexico and Utah territories, slavery was a festering issue that could not be wished away. As Ohio Senator and antislavery Democrat Salmon P. Chase rightly warned, "The question of slavery in the territories has been avoided. It has not been settled." And the Fugitive Slave Act, under which northern authorities had to aid southern slaveholders in recovering runaway human property, forced northerners to see people they knew being rounded up and forcibly returned to bondage. Slavery was to them no longer a faraway abstraction but instead a horrifying act of injustice against a flesh-and-blood individual. The prospect of slaveholders' surrogate hands reaching into northern neighborhoods and re-enslaving blacks had been raised by the Fugitive Slave Act of the Compromise of 1850. Among the many it outraged were two New England women. Soon after the compromise had passed Congress, Mrs. Edward Beecher, incensed over Congress's capitulation to the interests of the Slave Power and in particular feeling betrayed by what she saw as Daniel Webster's caving in to southern pressure, penned an impassioned letter to her sister-in-law, Harriet Beecher Stowe, an experienced professional writer. "Hattie," she scribbled, "if I could use a pen as you can, I would write something that will make this whole nation feel what an accursed thing slavery is." Supposedly Mrs. Stowe, upon reading this heartfelt message, rose from her chair, clutched the letter in her fist, and resolved "I *will* write something . . . I will if I live."

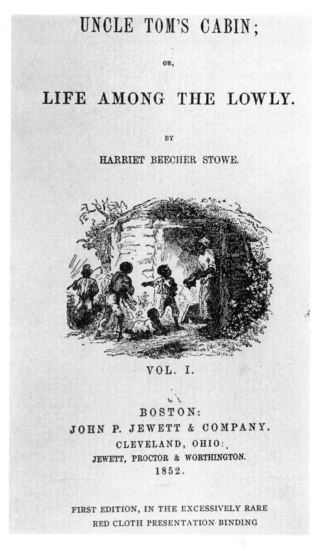

Title Page of the First Edition of *Uncle Tom's Cabin*   To northern readers, the great appeal of Harriet Beecher Stowe's 1852 novel was its portrayal of black people as Christian heroes with whom whites, accustomed to the moralizing and sentimental fiction of the day, could readily identify. The book's searing indictment of slavery—and of what the institution did even to well-intentioned slave owners—came straight from testimony that abolitionists had been collecting for a generation.

In June 1851 the Washington *National Era* began serializing the results of her defiant resolution to the acclaim of a growing northern audience of readers. By the following spring, *Uncle Tom's Cabin* was published in book form and became a runaway bestseller. Soon a dramatized version was enthralling audiences across the nation. Both the book and the play became sensations in London. In moving prose, touching the heartstrings of evangelical Protestantism and paying homage to popular beliefs in the sanctity of the home and the special virtue of women, the book devastatingly and memorably indicted the intrinsic evils of slavery

Harriet Beecher Stowe,
***Uncle Tom's Cabin*, on the Guilt of the "Good" Slave Owner, 1854**

Much of the power of Uncle Tom's Cabin *came from Harriet Beecher Stowe's ability to appeal to the moral values of northern women and from her demonstration of how slavery forced even well-intentioned men and women into complicity with its evils. In this scene, early in the novel, a debt-ridden slave owner, Mr. Shelby, finds himself obliged to sell to a shady slave-trader named Haley the pious, elderly Uncle Tom and the young son of Mrs. Shelby's favorite servant, Eliza. Mrs. Shelby is horrified, but cannot resist her husband's logic.*

Mrs. Shelby stood like one stricken. Finally, turning to her toilet, she rested her face in her hands, and gave a sort of groan.

"This is God's curse on slavery! — a bitter, bitter, most accursed thing! — a curse to the master and a curse to the slave! — I was a fool to think I could make anything good come out of such a deadly evil. It was a sin to hold a slave under laws like ours, — I always thought so when I was a girl, — I thought so still more after I joined the church; but I thought I could gild it over, — I thought by kindness, and care, and instruction, I could make the condition of mine better than freedom — fool that I was!"

"Why, wife, you are getting to be an abolitionist, quite."

"Abolitionist! If they knew all I know about slavery, they *might* talk! We don't need them to tell us; you know I never thought that slavery was right — never felt willing to own slaves."

"Well, therein you differ from many wise and pious men," said Mr. Shelby. "You remember Mr. B.'s sermon, the other Sunday? . . . But now, my dear, I trust that you see the necessity of the thing, and you see that I have done the very best that circumstances would allow."

"O yes, yes!" said Mrs. Shelby, hurriedly and abstractedly fingering her gold watch, — "I haven't any jewelry of any amount," she added, thoughtfully; "but would not this watch do something? — it was an expensive one, when it was bought. If I at least save Eliza's child, I would sacrifice anything I have."

"I'm sorry, very sorry, Emily," said Mr. Shelby, "I'm sorry this takes hold of you so; but it will do no good. The fact is, Emily, the thing's done; the bills of sale are already signed, and in Haley's hands; and you must be thankful it's no worse. That man has had it in his power to ruin us all, — and now he is fairly off. If you knew the man as I do, you'd think that we had had a narrow escape."

even in the hands of "good" slave owners. Filled with memorable characters, narrow escapes, incredible coincidences, terrible villains, and moralistic asides to sympathetic northern readers, the book vastly multiplied the pervasiveness and strength of antislavery sentiment in the North.

Beecher attempted to appeal to a southern audience, too. She made her worst villain, Simon Legree, a transplanted Yankee living in the South, and she sympathetically portrayed several of the slaveholders. But southerners read the novel with undiscriminating anger, seeing it as abolitionist poison threatening every nook and cranny of southern civilization. Millions of northerners who had never seen a slave, never heard an abolitionist lecture, or never thought twice about popular sovereignty suddenly through Mrs. Stowe's fictional characters understood powerfully and vividly that slavery was wrong and had no place in the nation. Abolitionism had spread from beyond the assembly of zealots to the hearths of millions of average northerners. It was quickly becoming a tenet of morality that would admit of no worldly compromise. Such was the morally supercharged atmosphere in which the presidential election of 1852 took place.

⚭ *The Collapse of the Whig Party*

The year 1852 witnessed the last contest between the Whig and the Democratic parties, which had dominated national politics for two decades. The Whig Party was falling apart. Henry Clay died in June 1852; and Daniel Webster followed him to the grave in October. William H. Seward of New York became the titular head of the party, to the consternation of southern Whigs who remembered Seward's dictum that a higher law than the Constitution condemned the expansion of slavery. Southern Whigs had survived in their region by arguing that they were more effective defenders of the peculiar institution in the halls of Congress than the Democrats were, but Seward's ascendancy compromised their viability in the South. Seward and similarly minded northern Whigs disliked the softness of President Fillmore on slavery. At the Whig convention, a fifty-two-ballot battle over the presidential nomination ended with the dominant Seward faction finally getting General Winfield Scott chosen as the party's standard-bearer. Scott, like Zachary Taylor and before him William Henry Harrison, was an apolitical military hero, first in the War of 1812 and later in the Mexican War. Although from Virginia, he just went through the motions of endorsing slavery and, heavily influenced by Seward, offered only token support to the Compromise of 1850. Southern Whigs found themselves in a real quandary, and most either did not vote or cast a despondent protest vote for the Democratic candidate. The Whig Party, in effect, had ceased to be a national political institution.

The Democrats had a trio of possible candidates — Lewis Cass with his morally ambiguous position of popular sovereignty on the slavery issue; Stephen Douglas, fresh from his successful management of the Compromise of 1850 through Congress, and Pennsylvanian James Buchanan, a slippery fellow whose supporters touted him as a "Northern man with Southern principles." Each had significant strength, but not enough to win, and so the three canceled each other out — Douglas perhaps mostly for pursuing the ring somewhat too aggressively. Finally, on the fiftieth ballot, the exhausted Democrats turned to a dark-horse candidate: handsome, likable, and mediocre Franklin Pierce of New Hampshire, a man so little known that he had no powerful enemies. Though a New Englander, Pierce opportunistically announced that he solidly supported every part of the Compromise of 1850 — even the Fugitive Slave Act, the provision that most upset northerners and loomed largest in symbolic importance for slaveholders.

The Democratic Party already had strong machines for getting out the vote in northern cities, and these machines were particularly effective in winning immigrant support. The strongly Protestant Whig Party made some efforts to appeal to immigrant and Catholic voters, but in doing so it offended old-line Protestant Whigs, who tended to see urban Catholics as a mortal threat to the nation. Many Democrats who in 1848 had gone for the Free Soil Party returned to the Democratic fold. The result was a resounding Pierce victory: he won the electoral vote 254 to 42 and was the last candidate to win both the popular and electoral vote in North and South until another Democratic Franklin (Roosevelt) repeated the feat in 1932.

Never again would the Whig Party compete in a presidential election. Whig voters would in the next few years splinter — some pursuing Free Soil ideals, others turning to the nativist American, or "Know-Nothing," Party. On the eve of the 1856 presidential election, most northern Whigs (and a growing number of antislavery northern Democrats) would find a political home in a new sectional political organization, the Republican Party. In the tumultuous 1850s, events drove politics — and politicians reacted rather than led.

❧ The Storm Over Fugitive Slaves

Southern efforts to enforce the newly strengthened Fugitive Slave Act, and northern outrage at the consequences, would alone have been enough to keep the pot of animosity and distrust between the sections boiling.

✳ IN THEIR OWN WORDS

A Southern Woman Reflects on *Uncle Tom's Cabin*, 1862

The wife of a U.S. Senator who resigned when tensions between North and South grew insurmountable, Mary Boykin Chesnut in her diary, prepared for publication after the Civil War, expresses a popular southern view of Harriet Beecher Stowe and her novel. (Topsy and Eva, mentioned by Boykin, are idealized characters — an enslaved girl and a rich plantation owner's daughter — in the novel.)

Read *Uncle Tom's Cabin* again. These negro women have a chance here that women have nowhere else. They can redeem themselves — the "impropers" can. They can marry decently, and nothing is remembered against these colored ladies. It is not a nice topic, but Mrs. Stowe revels in it. How delightfully Pharisaic a feeling it must be to rise superior and fancy we are so degraded as to defend and like to live with such degraded creatures around us — such men as Legree and his women.

The best way to take negroes to your heart is to get as far away from them as possible. As far as I can see, Southern women do all that missionaries could do to prevent and alleviate evils. The social evil [that is, prostitution] has not been suppressed in old England or in New England, in London or in Boston. People in those places expect more virtue from a plantation African than they can insure in practise among themselves with all their own high moral surroundings — light, education, training, and support. . . . There are cruel, graceful, beautiful mothers of angelic Evas North as well as South, I dare say. The Northern men and women who came here were always hardest, for they expected an African to work and behave as a white man. We do not. . . .

Topsys I have known, but none that were beaten or ill-used. Evas are mostly in the heaven of Mrs. Stowe's imagination. People can't love things dirty, ugly, and repulsive, simply because they ought to do so, but they can be good to them at a distance; that's easy. You see, I can not rise very high; I can only judge by what I see.

CAUTION!!

COLORED PEOPLE

OF BOSTON, ONE & ALL,

You are hereby respectfully CAUTIONED and
advised, to avoid conversing with the

Watchmen and Police Officers
of Boston,

For since the recent ORDER OF THE MAYOR &
ALDERMEN, they are empowered to act as

KIDNAPPERS
AND
Slave Catchers,

And they have already been actually employed in
KIDNAPPING, CATCHING, AND KEEPING
SLAVES. Therefore, if you value your LIBERTY,
and the *Welfare of the Fugitives* among you, *Shun*
them in every possible manner, as so many *HOUNDS*
on the track of the most unfortunate of your race.

Keep a Sharp Look Out for
KIDNAPPERS, and have
TOP EYE open.

APRIL 24, 1851.

The Fugitive Slave Act   In April 1851 Theodore Parker, a well-known Unitarian minister and abolitionist, wrote and posted this handbill warning the black population of Boston to be on the lookout for "slave catchers and kidnappers," who now included the Boston police. Parker was stirred to action after a fugitive slave from Georgia was caught in Boston and forcibly returned to his master under the terms of the Fugitive Slave Act of 1850. Attempts to enforce this law in their midst turned many New England whites into ardent abolitionists.

Many northern communities were determined to resist the letter of the law because they felt a higher principle — human dignity and freedom — gave them a moral duty to defend liberty. When in February 1851 a runaway slave named Shadrach was captured in Boston, an organized group of free blacks rushed the courtroom, overwhelmed the federal marshals, and whisked Shadrach away to Canada and safety. Having learned a lesson, two months later federal officials employed 300 soldiers to prevent a similar rescue of another fugitive slave, Thomas Sims, who was then returned unshackled to the South and slavery. Across the North in town after town, citizens were shocked to find professional slave catchers hunting down runaways. Occasionally, completely unscrupulous slave catchers kidnapped long-time free black residents of the North and illegally sent them back South as runaways. Under the Fugitive Slave Act, so-called runaways were denied due process and had no legal defense. Solomon Northup was one of those free black citizens of the North who was spirited away to the South and sold as a slave, but after ten years of bondage he was rescued and subsequently wrote a powerful indictment of the institution of slavery. In towns such as Oberlin, Ohio, public outrage at the evils of the Fugitive Slave Act intensified opposition to the Slave Power interests in every form. Many northerners, their moral concerns stirred up by *Uncle Tom's Cabin,* saw that the effect of the Fugitive Slave Act was to attempt to force them into complicity with slavery.

No case better exemplified the deleterious effect of the act on national politics than that of Anthony Burns, a former Virginia slave who had escaped his bondage and fled to Boston, where he found a job in a clothing store. He indiscreetly wrote a letter to his brother, still a slave, which fell into white hands. Burns's old owner learned of his whereabouts and came to Boston to reclaim his human property, as was his legal right under the Fugitive Slave Act — which, moreover, required local government officials to aid Burns's owner. Burns was arrested in May 1854 and thrown in jail on bogus charges; preparations were begun to ship him back to Virginia. When a committee of Boston abolitionists protested and even attempted to batter down the jail door, President Pierce sent federal troops to Boston to enforce the highly unpopular law. Friends of liberty in the city raised funds and tried every legal maneuver they knew to win Burns's case, but Pierce and the local U.S. attorney were determined to carry out the law. Burns's owner even agreed to sell Burns to the committee (who of course would legally set him free), but the U.S. attorney would not allow the issue to be so circumvented. At the conclusion of the trial in June federal troops marched Burns — to the sound of tolling bells — through Boston streets lined with protesters, upside-down American flags, and black-draped buildings, as though the entire city was mourning the death of liberty. A federal revenue cutter waited in the harbor to carry Burns back to slavery.

Wealthy textile manufacturer Amos A. Lawrence spoke for many when he wrote of this occasion that "we went to bed one night old fashioned, conservative, Compromise Union Whigs & we waked up stark mad Abolitionists." In Massachusetts, Ohio, Michigan, and Wisconsin, strong "personal liberty" laws were soon passed to counter the Fugitive Slave Act by giving blacks increased legal protection and rights. The North increasingly saw southerners as man stealers and rabid slavery expansionists, and the South saw the northerners more than ever as incorrigible opponents to slave owners' legal rights.

It was in the vortex of this swirling passion that another political thunderstorm broke, the result of the Kansas-Nebraska Act. Southerners and northerners alike saw the Kansas crisis as emblematic of slavery's future. Either slavery or freedom would be victorious in Kansas — the issue admitted no compromise. "Bleeding Kansas" was the result, an ominous omen for the nation.

✧ Douglas's Kansas-Nebraska Bill

It was a dangerous moment. The Whig Party was disintegrating, leaving many of its supporters in search of a new political home, fearful of the future, and receptive to talk about threats to the nation. Meanwhile sectional concerns about slavery were inflamed by the constant uproar provoked by the fugitive slave controversy. Fatefully, Illinois Senator Stephen A. Douglas introduced what initially seemed an absolutely routine bill in Congress — thereby making one of the greatest political miscalculations in American history.

Douglas was ambitious for himself and for his state. He was eager to build a transcontinental railroad linking his hometown of Chicago to the Pacific, but to do this the land west of Iowa and Missouri must first become organized territory, with a regular form of civil government in place and white citizens in residence.

Originally a portion of the Louisiana Purchase that under the terms of the Missouri Compromise of 1820 would be forever free of slavery, the region for twenty years or more had been legally "unorganized" Indian territory. Tribe after tribe had been moved there, and treaties had guaranteed the land to them permanently. But the commitment to Indian occupation was of little concern to Douglas — as, for that matter, was the fact that in 1853 the U.S. government had bought from Mexico some 29,000 square miles of land (the Gadsden Purchase) along the southern boundary of the New Mexico territory, precisely to accommodate the best rail route from Louisiana to the Pacific. Douglas, who also had personal financial interests in land through which his favored northern transcontinental railroad route would pass, was willing to violate promises to the Indians and build a rival to the southern Pacific route to benefit Chicago. But because the territory Douglas wanted to organize lay north of the Missouri Compromise line and would presumably be free, Douglas knew that he had to find some way of attracting southern congressional support for his schemes.

Why would southerners support such a move that would both compete with the southern rail route and pave the way for another free state? Anticipating their objections, Douglas proposed in January 1854 a bill to organize all the land north of the Missouri Compromise line as the Nebraska Territory (the land south of the line, today Oklahoma, remained as "unorganized" Indian territory). To attract the necessary southern support, Douglas proposed to modify the Missouri Compromise itself. Under his bill, the region's inhabitants, as they prepared for statehood, would vote on whether the new states would be slave or free on the basis of popular sovereignty. In effect, Douglas was seeking to extend the 1850 compromise solution of the Utah and New Mexico territories retroactively to land whose permanent free status had been established in 1820. To be sure, Douglas believed that climate and terrain would keep slavery out of the region, so in fact the states ultimately carved out of the Nebraska Territory would not be slave. But Douglas soon learned that southerners would not support him unless he explicitly removed the slavery prohibition section of the Missouri Compromise. Under fierce southern pressure, Douglas then proposed to organize two territories, Nebraska to the west of Iowa and Kansas to the west of Missouri. Because Missouri was a slave state, presumably slaveholders would move into the Kansas Territory — balancing slavery there alongside free-soil Nebraska.

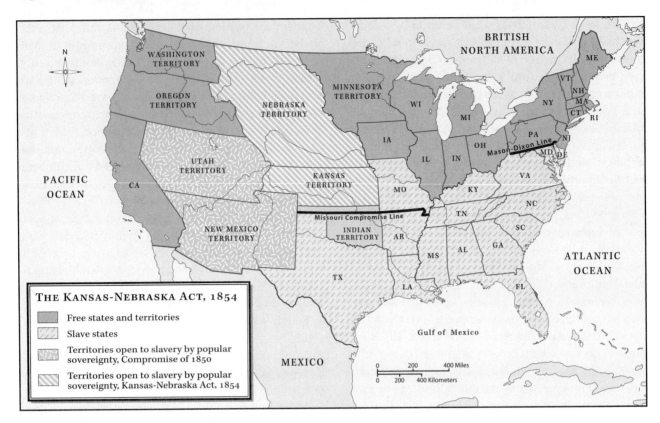

THE KANSAS-NEBRASKA ACT, 1854

- Free states and territories
- Slave states
- Territories open to slavery by popular sovereignty, Compromise of 1850
- Territories open to slavery by popular sovereignty, Kansas-Nebraska Act, 1854

Douglas's Kansas-Nebraska bill ignited a firestorm of protest in the North. It seemed a blatant attempt to buy southern support by voiding a thirty-four-year-old compromise and throwing to the Slave Power land that had been vouchsafed to freedom. Within a day of Douglas's second version of the bill, on January 24, the *National Era,* which had serialized Harriet Beecher Stowe's eye-opening novel, published an "Appeal of the Independent Democrats in Congress to the People of the United States," written by six antislavery congressmen, including Senator Charles Sumner of Massachusetts. In purple prose the appeal attacked the bill as a part of a southern Slave Power plot, and editorials and addresses across the North took up the charge. A one-term former Whig congressman from Illinois, now practicing law and semi-retired from politics, Abraham Lincoln, was roused as never before, and Senator William Pitt Fessenden of Maine confided that "it needs but little to make me an out & out abolitionist."

The antislavery Conscience Whigs opposed the bill unanimously, and nearly all other northern Whigs also refused to support it. These other Whigs, often called Cotton Whigs because they had economic interests in the South and were normally upset by abolitionist activities, opposed the bill because they feared its pas-

sage would only worsen relations between the sections. Even a group of northern Democrats opposed the bill, which they too saw as threatening to disrupt an uneasy sectional peace over the slavery issue. Old Liberty Party members, Free Soilers, Conscience Whigs, dissident Democrats — all mounted a furious assault against the bill. Many southerners, Whigs and Democrats, who before had been lukewarm to Douglas's proposal, in the face of this antislavery and anti–Slave Power agitation, rushed to defend the proposal and counter every threat, real and imagined, to the southern position on slavery. With solid southern support and the support of the Pierce administration, Douglas was able to guide the Kansas-Nebraska bill through both the Senate and House (where the vote was extremely close). But the spirited opposition the bill had aroused drove one more nail into the Whig Party's coffin and caused the Democrats to lose two-thirds of their northern congressional seats in the fall 1854 elections. The Whigs were so split that they collapsed as a national party, and the Democratic Party had taken a terrible beating in the North. The demise of the Whigs and the sectionalization of the Democrats opened a wedge for a new political party in the North. The Second Party System — pitting Whigs against Democrats — was dead, but the future political system was not yet born.

THE PARTY SYSTEM IN FLUX

Before the party breakup, both the Whigs and Democrats had national organizations, and the necessity of attracting votes and candidates in both sections effectively moderated both parties on the slavery issue. Even in the South the Whigs and Democrats had been almost equally in balance, with no clearly dominant party throughout the 1830s and 1840s. But with the eruption after 1854 of harsh divisions over race, many erstwhile Whigs in the North began to oppose the expansion of slavery and thus broke with their party's traditional attempts to straddle the issue. With large elements of the northern Whigs moving toward antislavery, many southern Whigs felt abandoned and drifted toward the Democrats. In practice, this meant that as the Democrats became the only party in the South, there were no moderating political tendencies in the section. Moreover, because the Democrats suffered grievous losses in the North in 1854, losing sixty-six of ninety-one seats outside the South, the Democratic Party in effect was quickly becoming a sectional — a southern — party, feeling little pressure to develop a more moderate, "national" position on the explosive issue of slavery.

With the serious fraying of the Democratic Party in much of the North, and with the southern Democrats becoming identified with the Slave Power, former northern Whigs and others opposed to the direction of national politics had no obvious political home. In this political vacuum two new parties began to coalesce, one born in the Northeast and one in the Northwest. The northeastern party grew with amazing speed, and collapsed just as quickly; the northwestern one was destined to survive.

❧ Anti-Catholicism and the Know-Nothings

The mid-1840s had seen a dramatic rise in European immigration, with almost 3 million immigrants arriving in the decade after 1845. Many of these were Irish or German Catholics, and as their numbers grew, Catholics in many northeastern cities often chose to live close together, both to be near their churches and schools and to avoid Protestant discrimination.

Until now the nation had been overwhelmingly Protestant, and this was nowhere more true than in Puritan New England. But as the old cities of the North and East — Boston, New York, Philadelphia, Baltimore — began to gain large and rapidly growing populations of ethnic Catholics from Europe, and especially as ag-

gressive Catholic leaders like Bishop John Hughes of New York City mounted campaigns to defend Catholic positions on matters such as parochial schooling, the Protestant majorities in the northern states began to fear the emerging Catholic minority. The religious revivals of the Second Great Awakening had persuaded many Protestant evangelicals that the survival of American republicanism depended on converting the whole nation to Protestantism, and they suspected any groups that supposedly put allegiance to an institution or organization above individual moral choice. For that reason some Protestants had previously opposed the Masons and the Mormons, and now the Catholics looked equally menacing. A fictitious and salacious "confession" entitled *Awful Disclosure of Maria Monk* purported to expose the outrageous behavior inside convents, where priests turned the gospel upside down and did all manner of unspeakable things to and with nuns.

Moreover, former Whigs who had learned to fear a Slave Power conspiracy now began to worry about a Catholic conspiracy as well. Protestants tended to see the Catholics as a foreign population who had no experience with democratic principles and were subject to authoritarian control by the pope. Catholics had different religious customs that Protestants often equated with pagan superstitions. Instead of respecting the Constitution, thought many Protestants, Catholics had sworn a secret allegiance to the pope. Samuel F. B. Morse, better known as an artist and for his invention of the telegraph, was also a virulent nativist, and his 1835 book, *Imminent Dangers to the Free Institutions of the United States Through Foreign Immigration*, helped popularize the fear of Catholicism. American observers were aware that in Europe the Catholic Church very much supported the undemocratic Old Order, and the papacy at that time seemed unshakably reactionary and uncompromisingly anti-Protestant. In truth the Catholic Church in America quickly became Americanized, but many concerned Protestants were slow to recognize that acculturation process. And whatever their political allegiance, Irish and German Catholics tended to pay a social allegiance to a saloon culture that to abstemious Protestant Whigs meant only disorder and drunkenness. No wonder, sniffed respectable old-stock Americans, these heathen foreigners voted in unthinking blocs for whatever Democratic-Party demagogue bought their support. The new arrivals, so the saying went, "landed on Monday and voted on Tuesday."

In short, many traditional-minded northern voters,

A Know-Nothing Cartoon This cartoon illustrates the Know-Nothing charge that Irish and German immigrants were stealing American elections and running the big-city political machines. It also plays up contemporary stereotypes among nativists of excessive drinking in German and Irish immigrant cultures.

ner arose in the Northeast in 1849 to combat the perceived Catholic threat to the republic, and when members were asked what their organization stood for or promoted, they were supposed to answer: "I know nothing." Hence the name — the Know-Nothings — by which the organization became popularly known.

Opposition to Catholics and other immigrants was broader and more fervent than either Democratic or Whig leaders imagined, and it tended to rise up from the general populace, not be directed by recognized leaders. Members of secret organizations like the Order of the Star-Spangled Banner mounted what can only be characterized as a stealth political campaign in many parts of the Northeast in the election of 1854, conducting write-in campaigns to get previously unknown candidates elected to a wide variety of offices before the regular parties even knew they were going to be opposed in the elections. As the anti-immigrant or nativist groups got into office, they coalesced into the American or Know-Nothing Party. Coming almost out of nowhere, they attracted 63 percent of the popular vote in Massachusetts in 1854 and won the governorship, most of the legislative seats, and the entire congressional delegation. Within a year the Know-Nothings controlled most of New England and had gained substantial influence in Kentucky, Maryland, and Missouri. The primary motivation behind Know-Nothing support was fear of a Catholic conspiracy against democracy, which easily combined with that other, long-standing northern hobgoblin, a Slave Power conspiracy.

But just as the Know-Nothing Party blazed up suddenly and spectacularly in 1854 and 1855, it fizzled just as completely after 1856. The causes for this collapse are difficult to explain. For all their fulminations, the Know-Nothings actually could do little to stop immigrants from flocking in and had little effect on the existing Catholic populations. Know-Nothings, it turned out, were Do-Nothings when it came to urban realities. The movement's leaders tended to be political amateurs who did not understand how to organize and discipline a party, to mobilize workers, or to govern once in office. The tendencies toward secretiveness in the party also served to make it seem not wholly unlike other

along with reform-minded Whigs who favored temperance and progressive politics and reform-minded Protestants who associated the spread of their faith with the perfecting of society, came to see the rapidly growing Catholic population as a distinct threat to the future of the nation and to democracy itself. Violent armed rioters attacked Catholics and Catholic institutions in a number of northern cities. One of the first riots in August 1834 ended with the burning of the Ursuline convent and school in Charlestown, Massachusetts. In the mid-1840s bloody anti-Catholic riots broke out in a number of northern and midwestern cities. A May 1844 riot that erupted in Philadelphia resulted in the torching of two Catholic churches and a number of private homes and a final casualty toll of thirteen dead and more than fifty wounded. In response, Bishop John Hughes of New York City urged Catholic men to arm themselves and stand guard around every Catholic church.

Many groups were organized among Protestants to oppose the influx of immigrants, and vague proposals were floated to control their influence, such as extending to twenty-one years (rather than the existing three years) the period of residency required before they could obtain the right to vote. One such secret anti-Catholic organization called the Order of the Star-Spangled Ban-

Archbishop John Hughes Cautions Against Organizing Catholic Settlement in the West, 1856

Born in Ireland, John Hughes (1797-1864) was the first archbishop of New York. Here, responding to Catholic clergy and laypeople who wanted to promote the resettlement of poor Irish Catholic immigrants in the Buffalo area and farther west, Hughes voiced his objections to uprooting his flock from the urban environment in which they had settled. By moving west, they would risk falling victim to their inexperience with frontier life, to financial trouble, and to illness — and would also lose the familiar support of their church and community life.

It must not be inferred that the writer [Hughes] is opposed to the diffusion of emigrants into those portions of the country in which land may be obtained and in which living is cheap and labor has its fair recompense. But there is a natural process by which this result is perpetually going on. Poor emigrants not finding employment in one place seek it in another. And then when they go westward especially, acquire a certain practical knowledge of the production of the soil or the mines in the neighborhoods in which they find themselves. With their limited knowledge as far more important capital than the limited amount which they have economized from their labors, they sometimes acquire a title to lands, or in interests by which their temporal prosperity is increased. But the idea of disturbing the minds of those, who may be already established, whether in the East or in the West, by a gilded and exaggerated report of theoretical blessings, which are in reserve for them, provided they can acquire the nominal ownership of 60 or 100 acres of uncultivated land, not infrequently teeming with fever and ague — remote from the church — remote from the school — remote [from] the Post Office — remote from the physician — remote from the neighbors — this idea is dangerous, just so far as any Catholic emigrants thereby them besides, our convention have [sic] understood that capital, more or less will be necessary, for those who shall be found simple enough to follow their advice. This being the case, that advice is tendered to those who, wherever they are located whether in the East or the West, have been already to some extent successful in their industrial efforts. One might suppose that if they are doing well, it would be unwise for them to give up the certainty which they have for the uncertainty which is proposed for them. . . .

potential conspiratorial forces, even the Catholics and the Slave Power, whose allegiances to constitutional democracy seemed uncertain. And the potential threat to democracy of a mysterious and distant pope came to many northerners to seem much less menacing than the threat at home of the Slave Power. Antislavery had disintegrated the Whig Party, and it proved just as corrosive to the American Party. The central divisive issue of the day was slavery, not popery, and on that issue nativism crashed and the Republican Party was born.

❧ *The Rise of the Republican Party*

It seems that many northerners, profoundly unhappy with the Whig Party and indeed disillusioned with politicians in both major parties because of their avoidance of a strong moral stand against slavery, flirted briefly with Know-Nothingism. But most quickly became disgusted with the American Party because it was more prejudiced against Catholics than supportive of core democratic principles. Illinois ex-congressman Abraham Lincoln, still a relative unknown, asked of former antislavery Whigs who now supported the Know-Nothings, "How can anyone who abhors the oppression of Negroes be in favor of degrading classes of white people?"

Lincoln, referring to the Declaration of Independence's phrase about all men being created equal, went on to say in characteristically pithy language that "We now practically read it 'all men are created equal except Negroes.' When the Know-Nothings get control, it will read 'All men are created equal, except Negroes and foreigners and Catholics.'" The basic anti-Americanism of the American Party's central issue caused it quickly to fade when another new political party, genuinely antislavery and infused with much of the progressive economic and moral reform sentiment of the Whig Party but cleansed of its ties to the South, emerged in the Northwest. That new coalition was the Republican Party.

In a variety of midwestern states such as Wisconsin and Michigan, opponents of the Kansas-Nebraska Act began coming together in 1854. Conscience Whigs opposed to the expansion of slavery and northern Democrats upset with the knee-jerk proslavery of the southern Democrats began to create a new party with a symbolic name, the Republican Party, a name that harkened back to the values of the American Revolution. Because the northern Democrats included Catholics and recent immigrants, the Republican Party deemphasized nativism even though many of its former Whig supporters were Protestant temperance advocates and Sabbatarians who still harbored suspicions of immigrants. Old Liberty Party abolitionists joined the new party despite its being more opposed to the expansion of slavery into free territories than to the existence of slavery in the South itself. The northern Democrats generally disagreed with former Whigs' inclination to support internal improvements, so the Republican leaders, at least in the beginning, also soft-pedaled their pro-business, pro-tariff tendencies. What really held together this uneasy coalition of persons unhappy with their former parties was the prospect, unleashed by the Kansas-Nebraska Act, that slavery might manage to expand into territory long thought guaranteed as free soil. Many if not most of these Free Soilers were prejudiced against blacks and wanted to preserve the territories exclusively for whites. They feared competition with the slave-labor plantations and the cheap-labor slave artisans that southerners might bring into the region. The Republican Party was created by political pros from the Whig and Democratic parties who knew how to create effective party organizations, manage campaigns, get out literature, and mobilize voters. Hence the Republican Party had a range of issues and a skilled leadership that allowed it, unlike the amateurish and bumbling American Party, to grow into a permanent and influential political machine. The American Party had found moderate support in the South so in a sense had been a national party, but the Republican Party was entirely a sectional party — all its support came from the northern states.

There were some true abolitionists in the Republican Party, but their voices were drowned out by the noisy clamor of those white racists who simply wanted to keep blacks, slave or free, out of new territories. The glue that really stuck together all the various elements of the Republican Party was this commitment to maintaining the territories as a land of opportunity for whites only — *all* whites, including European immigrants, but whites only. Southerners tended to see all Republicans as rabid abolitionists, but they misperceived their opponents. Likewise, Republicans tended to see all Democrats as rabid agents of the Slave Power conspiracy. The events in Kansas following 1854 gave credence to both misperceptions and fed the flames of distrust. All positions hardened in the aftermath of the Kansas-Nebraska Act, and the normal political process of compromise became increasingly impossible. Two sectional parties, the Republicans in the North and the Democrats, present in the North but totally dominant in the South and dominated by their southern adher-

ents, controlled national politics as the nation lurched into unprecedented conflict over the possible expansion of slavery in the Kansas Territory. Storm clouds hovered on the horizon.

✖ *The Road to Civil War*

Even before Kansas turned bloody, events in late 1853 and 1854 lent credence to northern fears of a Slave Power conspiracy to expand slavery. Several times between 1849 and 1851 a colorful expatriate Cuban adventurer named Narciso Lopez had gathered southern support for attacks on Cuba, hoping to conquer this Spanish colony with its half-million slaves for southern annexation. After officials there captured and executed Lopez in 1851, southern expansions waited until a friendlier president sat in the White House. Pierce was more to their liking, and for a time he supported southern calls for taking over Cuba. His minister to Spain, Louisianan Pierre Soulé, incautiously trumpeted American claims to acquire Cuba. In late 1853 and early 1854 Pierce encouraged firebrand John Quitman's quixotic plot to invade Cuba and precipitate a revolutionary movement there that would presumably result in calls for annexation by the United States. After the political turmoil of the Kansas-Nebraska Act, Pierce tried to rein in such activities, but he did authorize Soulé in Madrid to offer Spain as much as $130 million for the sugar-and-slave-rich island. When the Spanish government declined, the enterprising Soulé met with the American ministers to Britain and France at Ostend, Belgium, in October 1854 and persuaded them to sign the so-called Ostend Manifesto, a semi-secret document calling Cuba vital to the United States and claiming a divine right to buy or otherwise obtain the island. When word of the memorandum leaked to the press, northern newspapers and public opinion were livid. Pierce had to back down, recall Soulé, and abandon all Cuban schemes. But the damage had been done, for southern proslavery expansionists seemed to show no limits in their ambitions.

✖ *Bleeding Kansas*

Congress opened Kansas up for non-Indian settlement in May 1854, even before the treaties voiding Indian title to the lands had been ratified and the public land had been surveyed. The first settlers came from Missouri, the slave state that lay adjacent to the entire eastern border of Kansas. Senator David Atchison of Missouri, a southern extremist, took a leave from Congress to promote slaveholder immigration to the Kansas Territory. "If we win," wrote Atchison, "we carry slavery to the Pacific Ocean; if we fail we lose Missouri, Arkansas, and Texas and all the territories; the game must be played boldly." With his aid, hundreds of slaveholding Missourians stormed across the state line, less to settle Kansas than to seize it. Antislavery forces, seeing the "bold" game being played, raced to get their own sympathetic settlers in before the slavery advocates could set up a government and write a constitution. As could have been predicted, popular sovereignty meant a contest to see which side could get there first with the most. Boston-based abolitionists raised funds, recruited settlers, and founded the New England Emigrant Aid Society to facilitate migration; expecting violence, they shipped west Sharps repeat-

ing rifles packed in wooden crates labeled "Bibles." But although abolitionist forces managed to move perhaps a thousand New Englanders to Kansas, more Missourians got there earlier, and their numbers swelled once people like Senator Atchison heard about the New England Emigrant Aid Society. An election was scheduled for November 1854 to elect a territorial delegate to Congress, and Atchison herded hundreds of Missourians across the border expressly to vote. As a result, a proslavery delegate was elected.

The Sack of Lawrence   This lurid print shows the attack on Lawrence, the leading Free Soil settlement in Kansas, by a band of proslavery men on May 21, 1856. Widely publicized in the North, the sacking of Lawrence convinced many northerners that a civil war had already begun between forces dedicated to keeping the West open to freedom and those who wanted to impose slavery on the frontier.

When the time came in March 1855 to elect a territorial legislature, proslavery forces mounted an invasion of some 5,000 "border ruffians" who promptly made a mockery of the principle of popular sovereignty. The 2,905 legal voters cast 6,307 votes! Not surprisingly, a proslavery legislature was elected, it promptly passed a slave code and made even *criticism* of slavery illegal. Actually, by this time the normal westward migration of settlers from the midwestern states had produced an antislavery majority of permanent inhabitants in the state, and they felt disfranchised and unrepresented by the proslavery legislature sitting in the town of Lecompton. The antislavery forces held their own elections and created a rival government at Topeka. By 1856 the Kansas Territory had a fraudulently chosen proslavery

The Caning of Charles Sumner Sumner had a sneering, supercilious personality, and he was an insufferable snob and a self-righteous moralist, but the brutal attack on him on May 22, 1856, by hotheaded South Carolina congressman Preston Brooks made the Massachusetts Senator a martyr to freedom and civilized values in most northern eyes. Notice the beatific expression on Sumner's face as Brooks beats him, the pen in the hand he raises to shield himself, and the jeering faces of other proslavery politicians who watch and allow the assault to proceed. The fact that this attack occurred on almost the same day as the Sack of Lawrence was not lost on northerners, convinced that the Slave Power was at last revealing its true colors.

government and an extralegal antislavery (or more accurately, Free Soil) government.

President Pierce should have intervened to enforce a new and fair election, but he was too beholden to southern voters to risk their displeasure. Even many proslavery people who genuinely believed in the principle of popular sovereignty were offended by the high-handed election fraud in Kansas. But Pierce nevertheless condemned the antislavery government in Topeka and, in effect, encouraged the proslavery forces to solidify their shaky control of the territory. In May, some 800 of them raided the antislavery town of Lawrence, burning homes (including the home of the Free Soil governor) and businesses and destroying two antislavery presses. But no one was killed. This raid, soon known as "the sacking of Lawrence," particularly enraged a recent antislavery settler, John Brown, who — almost insane in his principled opposition to slavery — believed himself appointed by God to wreak vengeance upon the sinister forces of slavery. Shortly after the Lawrence raid, Brown gathered together his four sons along with two other accomplices and, under cover of darkness, raided a series of farmhouses belonging to proslavery settlers along Pottawatomie Creek. Brown and his followers

SOUTHERN CHIVALRY — ARGUMENT versus CLUB'S.

dragged five men and boys from their beds and hacked them to pieces with broadswords. The consequence of this retaliatory raid was a small-scale war in the Kansas Territory, with hundreds of men on both sides taking up guns. Within several months, as many as 200 settlers lay dead. As one-sided pro- and anti-slavery press accounts of the violence in Kansas spread, opinion was inflamed in both the North and the South. Each side increasingly saw the other as fanatics who condoned murder and bloodshed to achieve their purpose. Civility vanished in the fray — along with prospects for peaceful compromise.

Extremism was the order of the day in the halls of Congress, congressmen on both sides hurling charges at one another and abandoning the normal trappings of courtesy. One of those most given to verbal excesses was Senator Charles Sumner of Massachusetts, a brilliant, arrogant, and exceedingly complex man who was devoted in principle to the rights of others but seldom respected any individual with whom he disagreed. Events in Kansas boiled his blood, and he reached new heights of verbal pyrotechnics as he assailed the proslavery forces abroad in the nation and seated in Congress. Sumner was particularly intemperate in his attacks on elderly Senator Andrew P. Butler of South Carolina, slandering him for having taken "the harlot, slavery" as his mistress and ridiculing the elderly man who had lost some muscular control of his lips and drooled; Sumner sneered at "the loose expectoration" of Butler's speeches. Even antislavery stalwarts were stunned by Sumner's rhetorical excess, and Congressman Preston S. Brooks, Butler's nephew, decided to take action. Brooks did not consider Sumner a gentleman, so a formal duel was inappropriate under the southern code of honor. Brooks decided that Sumner, as a common cur, deserved a beating. Two days following the insult to his uncle, Brooks entered the Senate chamber after it was adjourned and crept up behind Sumner, seated and writing at his desk. With his gold-headed cane Brooks beat Sumner about the head and shoulders until the blood-splattered Sumner ripped his desk from its moorings and collapsed on the floor. Sumner was not seriously injured physically, though it took him almost three years to overcome the psychological trauma. Returning to South Carolina, Brooks was lionized: brass bands met his train, and dozens of admirers presented him with replacement canes. Such incidents inflamed sectional hatred. Northern public opinion learned of the sacking of Lawrence and the Brooks assault on Sumner and decided that the Slave Power brutes were contemptuous of freedom; southern public opinion learned of John Brown's massacre at Pottawatomie Creek and Sumner's intemperate attack on Butler and decided that the northern antislavery forces were contemptuous of southerners' property rights in slavery. In this poisonous political context the nation faced the 1856 presidential election.

❧ The Ominous Election of 1856

The Democratic Party had two obvious candidates, but both were unelectable because of their association with the Kansas-Nebraska Act. President Franklin Pierce had angered too many northern Democrats with his precipitate support of the proslavery side in the settlement process in the Kansas Territory. He had been too politically indebted to southern Democrats to do otherwise, but his cavalier disregard of the honest application of popular sovereignty had infuriated even some proslavery advocates who saw popular sovereignty as a genuine way to reflect the wishes of the actual settlers of a territory. The other Democrat with high name recognition was Senator Douglas; but although he still had support in both the North and South, he had simply miscalculated too extravagantly in pushing his plans to organize the Nebraska Territory, offending too many voters. So the Democrats turned to a colorless political professional, James Buchanan, a longtime congressman from Pennsylvania, former minister to Russia, and secretary of state under Polk, who had the good luck of having served in the immediately previous years as minister to Great Britain (and had signed the Ostend Manifesto). Hence he had been out of the country during the complicated brouhaha over Kansas and was untouched by the controversy. His promoters boasted that this "northern man with southern principles" could be elected as a truly "national" candidate.

This was the new Republican Party's first presidential campaign, and the sectional nature of its appeal was reinforced when only a sprinkling of delegates showed up from just four Upper South states. The Republicans chose as their candidate the dashing but none-too-intelligent John C. Frémont, "the Pathfinder," an adventurer who had explored much of the westernmost territories and been a hero in the conquest of California during the Mexican War. Frémont was a forthright opponent of the expansion of slavery into new territories, and he fit perfectly the Republican Party's antislavery platform plank. The campaign slogan became a catchy "Free Soil, Free Speech, and Frémont." The northern wing of the expiring American Party somehow was convinced to endorse Frémont (though his wife was Catholic), and the southern wing, finding itself the halfway house of former southern Whigs who were not yet ready to become Democrats, nominated former president Millard Fillmore (who apparently had never even attended a Know-Nothing meeting prior to getting the nomination).

The presidential election was no three-way contest: in effect there were two sectionalized elections, Buchanan versus Frémont in the North and Buchanan versus Fillmore in the South. Buchanan, the only "national" candidate, won with a minority of the total popular vote but a majority of the electoral college votes because he carried four northern states (Pennsylvania, New Jersey, Indiana, and Illinois) and all the southern states except Maryland. (Fillmore won there.) Fillmore had attracted about 40 percent of the total southern vote, but because Frémont was not even on the ballot in the South, Buchanan won the region handily.

Frémont, although he did not gain the presidency, did remarkably well for the candidate of a party waging its first presidential campaign. He won substantial majorities in eleven of the sixteen northern states, swept New England completely — and had he eked out a victory in Pennsylvania and either Illinois or Indiana, he would have won the presidency without a single vote from the South. That possibility of a sectional president, made possible by the North's population advantage (and hence advantage in the electoral college), frightened thoughtful proslavery politicians even as they welcomed the victory of James Buchanan.

As president, Buchanan hoped to calm the political storms and restore peaceful compromise as a means of settling political differences. Instead, he was rendered almost helpless to control a series of events that swirled to hurricane force, blowing away all chance of compromise and convincing both sections that the

Dred Scott and his Family Like the fictional characters in *Uncle Tom's Cabin*, the flesh-and-blood protagonists of the Dred Scott case humanized the horrors of slavery for countless northern whites, who hitherto had thought of slaves only as distant and alien abstractions. Publicized in the national media of the day, such as *Frank Leslie's Illustrated Newspaper*, the story of Scott's efforts to break the chains of slavery became a powerful personal drama—especially when Scott's claims to justice were thwarted by a pro-southern Supreme Court that, critics charged, meant to impose slavery throughout the United States.

other was incorrigibly determined to have its way. The South came to see the North as the land of abolitionism run wild, and the North grew to see the South as under the control of a Slave Power that would stop at nothing until slavery ruled nationwide.

Buchanan had some forewarning of the first problem that confronted him, but he mishandled it, as he would mishandle many others in the future. Although this was no time for a bumbling president, in truth events were in the cockpit and no presidential pilot could have brought the ship of state through safely.

❧ The Dred Scott Decision

More than two decades earlier, in the mid-1830s, army surgeon Dr. John Emerson of St. Louis was transferred first to Illinois and then to a post in the Wisconsin Territory. Accompanying him was his slave, Dred Scott, who while serving as Dr. Emerson's manservant in the Wisconsin Territory married a young slave woman, Harriet Robinson, originally owned by the local Indian agent. Eventually Dr. Emerson died, and Dred and Harriet found themselves back in St. Louis. There, in 1846, several abolitionist friends urged them to sue Emerson's widow, Irene, for their freedom on the grounds that their long-time residence in the free state of Illinois and the free territory of Wisconsin had voided their bondage. At first Dred and Harriet brought separate but related suits, but for financial reasons in 1850 they decided to pursue the case only in Dred's name with the explicit understanding that if he were successful, Harriet would win freedom too. Irene Emerson, and of course slaveholders in general, held that simply taking a slave to a free region for a period did not bestow freedom on the slave, and that the slave's permanent status was determined by the state to which he or she returned — and Missouri was a slave state.

This case, filled with political significance, went from court to court, from decision to appeal, until it reached the Supreme Court in 1854. There it languished until finally arguments were heard in 1856, but the justices — possibly hoping to prevent any decision from becoming a political football in the election year — held it over in order to hear the arguments again in the 1856-57 session. The case received widespread newspaper coverage, and politicians in both sections closely followed the process and awaited the decision of the southern-dominated Court, presided over by Chief Justice Roger B. Taney of Maryland. The justices themselves were deeply divided over the case, and in fact wrote nine separate opinions. But Taney persisted until he was able to claim to have crafted a final "Opinion of the Court." There is evidence that President-elect Buchanan — who desperately wanted the Court to decide the issue of slavery in the territories in order to take the pressure off him — had some sense of the Court's wrangling within its chambers and pressured it to shape the final decision to his liking. In particular, Buchanan seems to have persuaded Pennsylvania justice Robert C. Grier to join the five southern-born justices in concurring with Taney's decision. Several days before Buchanan was to take the oath of office on March 4, 1857, Taney apparently leaked the imminent decision to Buchanan — totally unacceptable behavior for a justice. Anticipating northern opposition to the decision, Buchanan in his inaugural address took the somewhat disingenuous step of announcing that he would "cheerfully submit . . . in common with all good citizens" to the Supreme Court's ultimate decision, with the clear implication that all other good citizens should do likewise. Then, two days later on March 6, the Supreme Court announced its verdict.

First, the Court ruled that as a black — free or slave, it made no difference, Taney argued, because of how the authors of the Constitution had conceived of blacks — Dred Scott was not a citizen and therefore was ineligible to bring suit in a federal court. Second, the Court accepted the southern principle that a slave's status was determined by the laws of the state to which he returned. Third, the Court ruled that the congressional prohibition of slavery in the territories that was the key provision of the Missouri Compromise was unconstitutional because it deprived a citizen (that is, a white slaveholder) of his Fifth Amendment guarantee of property rights. In other words, the Missouri Compromise, by declaring certain territories free of slavery, in effect had deprived a slaveholder of the use of his property should he move to that territory. Therefore the Missouri Compromise itself had been unconstitutional. And fourth and most controversially of all, the Supreme Court moved beyond the substance of the case at hand: In a misguided effort to settle the issue of slavery expansion once and for all — and in a way favorable to the southern position — the Taney Court ruled that neither Congress, nor certainly a territory, inferior to Congress, could deprive slave owners of their property rights in humans in a territory. In other words, the Missouri Compromise prohibition of slavery in the territories of the Louisiana Purchase was invalid, and so would be a popular-sovereignty decision against slavery. The Supreme Court had come perilously close to accepting the John C. Calhoun position that the federal government should give the South an ironclad guarantee of slavery's right to exist everywhere, for all time.

National Divisions Widen

But rather than settle the political issue, the Dred Scott decision produced a firestorm of protest in the North. To many opponents of slavery it seemed irrefutable evidence that the Taney Court was but a tool of the Slave Power conspiracy, determined ultimately to force slavery into every region and state. Many political and religious leaders, newspaper editorials, and even state legislatures in the North denounced the decision as invalid. Abraham Lincoln (who was becoming a prominent Republican spokesman) reminded his listeners that the Supreme Court had reversed itself before, suggesting that once new, fairer-minded justices were appointed in the future (presumably by a Republican administration) this pernicious decision would be overruled. Even northern Democrats like Stephen Douglas, who wanted southern support but really believed in the principle of popular sovereignty as a way of letting the people of a territory have a voice in the laws of their region, objected to the Court's decision. Desperate to find a way to dissent from the unpopular ruling but not wanting actually to deny the Court's authority, Douglas in May 1857 came up with an awkward straddle. He admitted that the Court determined the law — but he also suggested that the people of any territory, by simply refusing to pass the necessary police and regulatory legislation, could in practice prohibit slavery there. Dashing Buchanan's hopes, the Supreme Court had inflamed the issue of slavery.

MORE TROUBLE IN KANSAS

In the midst of the Dred Scott uproar, Kansas once again entered the public spotlight. A proslavery legislature sat in Lecompton, and an antislavery one sat in Topeka, each vehemently antagonistic toward the other. By this time the Free Soil forces were a large majority of the population of the territory, and Buchanan, just installed in the White House, faced the problem of what to do about Kansas. Buchanan wanted a convention of duly elected delegates to meet, draw up a constitution (slavery could be voted up or down, the president did not care), and he would submit this constitution to Congress, which would admit Kansas to statehood. But the Free Soil forces had been so burned in the past by election fraud by the Lecompton government that antislavery men simply boycotted the election for delegates to a constitutional convention: proslavery forces, they said, would steal the election anyway. Of course, with antislavery voters sitting out

the election, the proslavery men (representing perhaps 10 percent of the eligible voters) totally dominated the constitutional convention, which proceeded to write a constitution that established a state government, protected slaveholders' rights to the slaves already living in the territory, and submitted to the voters of the state not the entire constitution but merely the right to have a referendum on whether future slave imports would be prohibited or accepted. Voters would have no say about the continuation of the slavery already existing in Kansas.

Of course by restricting the voters to deciding only upon the issue of future slave imports and no other aspect of the constitution, the Lecompton convention had made a mockery of popular sovereignty. So the Free Soil majority in the state again boycotted the ratification election, and a small proslavery minority voted to accept the flawed constitution and allowed continued slave imports. But by now the Free Soilers had gained political control of the territorial legislature — the honest territorial governor, a Mississippian appointed by Buchanan, threw out so many fraudulent proslavery votes that the Free Soil majority actually won the election — and they authorized a second ratification vote, this time on the entire constitution. With antislavery forces now voting, the Lecompton constitution went down to a resounding defeat. But President Buchanan had already come out in support of the Lecompton constitution, despite its evident unpopularity in the territory, because he was dependent on southern Democratic support; more than two-thirds of his electoral votes had come from slave states. He simply ignored the second ratification election that rejected the constitution and submitted the Lecompton constitution to Congress, asking that it accept Kansas as a slave state.

Northern public opinion was incensed by Buchanan's succumbing to proslavery forces. Even many members of his own party, northern Democrats, felt he had betrayed all principle on the altar of political expediency. Stephen Douglas, who to realize his White House ambitions would need southern Democratic support, courageously broke with the president of his own party. True, Douglas was in a no-win situation: If he supported Buchanan's position on Kansas, he would lose all hope of winning northern Democratic support in 1860; if he opposed Buchanan, southern Democrats would label him a traitor to the South. But in the meantime, Douglas was up for reelection to the Senate from Illinois in 1858, and Illinois was overwhelmingly opposed to the Lecompton constitution. In addition, Douglas also saw

Buchanan's support of the Lecompton constitution as an insult to the principle and practice of popular sovereignty. Hence for reasons both of principle and of political necessity (he had to stay in the Senate to keep alive his presidential hopes), Douglas fiercely fought Buchanan's equally tenacious effort to have Congress accept the Lecompton constitution.

Bleeding Kansas bled once again, with armed violence and death in the territory. (Kindling memories of Bully Brooks's assault on Sumner, a brawl also broke out in the House of Representatives involving thirty members.) Under intense pressure from the president, the Senate narrowly accepted Buchanan's Kansas proposals, but in the House a coalition of Republicans and Douglas Democrats defeated the bill on April 1, 1858. As a sort of compromise, Congress sent the Lecompton constitution back to Kansas for another popular referendum, and even though by the terms of the election set by Congress, Kansans knew that, if the constitution failed, Congress would not reconsider admitting Kansas to statehood until it had a population of 90,000, the voters of the territory rejected the proslavery Lecompton constitution by a ratio of more than six to one. Kansas now faded from the national scene, though it did become a free state in 1861. But the results of the ugly conflict were striking. Buchanan's political future was bleak; the Democratic Party had effectively split into southern and northern parties; and Douglas, perhaps the last potential "national" Democratic nominee, had by his opposition to the Lecompton constitution and his objections to Taney's Dred Scott decision fatally wounded his chances in the South.

The bitter political fighting over Kansas showed just how divided the nation had become less than ten years after the Compromise of 1850 had seemed to promise that the slavery-expansion issue was resolved. But there were pressures, tensions, and cultural attitudes abroad in the land that boded ill for a peaceful solution; slavery had become an issue that precluded compromise in the best of times.

ECONOMIC STRAIN

And these were not the best, nor the easiest, of times. Late 1857 and 1858 saw a severe economic depression cripple the North particularly. The end of the Crimean War in 1856 (France, Great Britain, and Sardinia aiding Turkey in a war against Russia) had depressed international demand for northern agricultural exports, and this in turn ultimately led to the failure of a major Ohio investment bank in August 1857. As the telegraph sped word of this failure to Wall Street and beyond, other financial markets panicked. After a wave of selling off stocks, business failures and cutbacks swept across the North, forcing thousands to lose their jobs. When Republicans and northern Democrats proposed raising tariffs to prop up northern industries, southern Democrats — harmed by tariffs — scuttled the attempt. Angry northern spokesmen attacked the South and its congressional representatives for failing to raise tariffs: this was but one more example of the Slave Power forces dominating the government to their advantage. Because the international market's demand for cotton was not as affected as it was for northern grain, the South escaped the worst ravages of this depression, the so-called Panic of 1857. Many southerners took this as evidence of the superiority of the southern cotton-slave economy to that of the North, and it led to exaggerated interpretations of the power of what was called King Cotton. Southern firebrands vaunted King Cotton and the society that produced it as invincible.

THE CULTURAL DIVIDE

More than politics and economics were pushing the sections apart. Southern novelists like William Gilmore Simms authored proslavery polemics, and other novelists like John Pendleton Kennedy created a new literary genre, plantation novels, that were highly romanticized accounts of life and labor on southern plantations, with plantation masters and mistresses portrayed as cultured and aristocratic, uncontaminated with the race for profits, and slaves portrayed as happy, childlike dependents. (Ironically some northerners, opposed to the emergent industrialization and urbanization of the Northeast, also wrote romanticized plantation novels to critique what they felt their region was becoming.) Many of the leading northern men of letters — Ralph Waldo Emerson, Henry David Thoreau, James Russell Lowell, Herman Melville — published essays, poems, and speeches highly critical of slavery, and of course continuing sales of *Uncle Tom's Cabin* brought home to millions of northerners the evils of the institution of slavery. Another new genre of writing, the memoirs of former slaves like Frederick Douglass and Solomon Northup, in vivid, firsthand accounts transformed slavery from an abstraction to what increasingly was seen in the North as an evil cancer afflicting the body politic. Southerners, of course, saw the popularity of such works as further evidence of an abolitionist conspiracy gripping the North. Romantic plantation novels and the contrasting depictions of the institution by such writer-orators as Frederick Douglass widened the chasm in public opinion between the North and South.

The demise of the Whig Party and the split of the Democrats into southern and northern factions, along with the rise of the completely sectional Republican Party, meant that no other major institutions reached across sectional lines to hold the nation together. The great national churches that had substantial adherents in the South — the Baptists, Methodists, and Presbyterians — had in fact or in effect been rent sectionally by the 1850s, severing one more tie that had traditionally united Americans. Prominent northern religious leaders — ministers like Henry Ward Beecher and Theodore Parker — attacked not only slavery but also the southern churches for defending slavery, and southern society in general. But if northern ministers pointed to slavery as an evil, a sin, and a violation of the Golden Rule of doing unto others as you would have them do to you, southern ministers preached an entirely different message. Slavery in their sermons had become a divine institution, God's method of bringing Christianity to pagan Africans, and they searched the Scriptures diligently (and successfully) to find biblical defenses that seemed to legitimate the institution in ancient Israel and the Roman Empire. Southern religious leaders accused their northern brethren of blasphemy for condemning slavery because southern ministers believed the Bible supported the institution. Religion became one of the factors driving the sections apart.

The Presbyterian Church never split formally into sectional parties, but an intense schism tore apart the church nevertheless. Two factions arose in the national church, an Old School group, dominant in the South, that was conservative and in effect proslavery, and a New School group, dominant in the North, that was liberal in theology, oriented toward social reform, and antislavery. Southern churchmen feared that the "Presbyterian Church [was] becoming an Abolition Society." By 1838 the schism had essentially created two Presbyterian churches. Just before the final division into Old School and New School factions, a prominent Kentucky Presbyterian minister moaned that "Our people are no longer one body of Christians" — and, he soon could have added with much accuracy, no longer one nation.

In 1845 the Methodist churches and the Baptist churches formally split into separate sectional churches, and for them the split was very literally caused by controversies over slavery. The Southern Methodists broke away on May 1 after the national church had demanded that a Methodist bishop from Georgia,

The Lincoln-Douglas Debate   Despite a great deal of conventional political hoopla — bands playing, food and drinks distributed to supporters, and occasionally demagogic language used by both candidates — the series of public debates between Lincoln and Douglas as they contended for the Senate offered voters a serious exchange of views on a national and a moral issue of the utmost seriousness. Appropriately, it attracted national attention and made Lincoln a celebrity throughout the North. This is a contemporary illustration.

James O. Andrew, either give up his slaves (whom he had inherited, not bought) or resign his church position. For the Baptists the breaking point occurred when the denominational governing body had ruled in 1844 that a southern slaveholding minister, James E. Reeves, also of Georgia, could not be appointed a missionary by the Home Mission Society. Upset southern Baptists began to make provisions for withdrawing from the national body, and on May 7, 1845, one week following the Methodist breakup, the Southern Baptist Convention was established. Now that the dominant Protestant churches in both sections no longer had members from the other section in their organization, neither had moderating influences. The result was that churches became strongly identified with their respective regions and in effect became agents of sectionalism — and eventually secession.

✥ Lincoln and Douglas Debate

Against this backdrop of ever-widening sectionalism, with the division over slavery becoming more heated, a spectacular contest between Abraham Lincoln and Stephen A. Douglas for the Illinois Senate seat captured the nation's attention, with widespread press coverage in both sections. At the time state legislatures actually elected the state's two Senators (this would be the case until 1913), so the campaign between Lincoln and Douglas was not for popular votes but for the election of candidates for the state legislature who were pledged to vote for them for the Senate seat. Douglas, next to Buchanan, was the country's best-known Democrat, and despite his opposition to the Lecompton constitution that had infuriated southerners, he still had some semblance of national sup-

port. Nevertheless, Buchanan was so angry at Douglas that he actively worked against his senatorial election in Illinois. Lincoln was unknown nationally but widely recognized in his own state; he had served for eight years in the Illinois legislature and for one term in the U.S. House of Representatives. An underdog, Lincoln challenged the famed Douglas to a series of political debates, seven in all, and Douglas accepted. The central topic turned out to be slavery, and thousands of Illinois citizens traveled to the debates, held between August 21 and October 15, 1858, which featured parades, brass bands, floats, and much hoopla in addition to the three-hour debates wherein Lincoln and Douglas argued mightily over the great issue of the day. Here was democracy at its best, in effect a statewide political science seminar offered by two political masters.

Physically, the two candidates were very much unalike. Douglas was as short and stocky as a tree stump; Lincoln, a foot taller, was as thin as a stick. Douglas was an immaculate dresser, neat and always wearing the newest styles; Lincoln wore loose-fitting, wrinkled black suits with a tall stovepipe hat that exaggerated his height. Douglas campaigned in a private railroad car and always made an impressive entrance to the debate site; Lincoln rode in a simple passenger car and walked from the station to the speaking stand. Douglas wanted to portray himself as the accomplished and experienced master of the Senate and imply that Lincoln was just a local politician who would be out of his depth in Washington; Lincoln wanted to suggest that Douglas was devoted to the fashion and political fads of the day with no firm moral mooring, and that he himself was a true man of the people.

In fact, Lincoln and Douglas agreed on most basic issues. Both were opposed to the expansion of slavery into the territories and believed it an outmoded, inefficient labor system; both were conventionally racist; both were more interested in reserving the territories for free white inhabitants than in attacking slavery where it existed. But as debaters they had to magnify their differences and try to suggest that the other was more extreme than in fact he was. Douglas painted Lincoln as a radical abolitionist and called him a Black Republican to suggest that he advocated social equality between the races. Lincoln replied that "I am not in favor of negro citizenship" and made clear that he did not accept the principle of social equality, that he did not want to repeal the Fugitive Slave Act, and that he took no stand on the admission of additional slave states. Lincoln's strategy was to argue that Douglas was

The Lincoln-Douglas Debates, 1858

Before a crowd of voters at Ottawa, Illinois, who were white racists but uneasy about the prospect of slave labor competing with free labor or preempting new land in the West, Abraham Lincoln responded in these words to Stephen Douglas's attempts to "define" him as a race-mixer and abolitionist.

. . . Anything that argues me into his [Douglas's] idea of perfect social and political equality with the Negro is but a specious and fantastic arrangement of words, by which a man can prove a horse chestnut to be a chestnut horse. (Laughter.)

I will say here . . . that I have no purpose directly or indirectly to interfere with the institution of slavery in the states where it exists. I believe I have no lawful right to do so. I have no purpose to introduce political and social equality between the white and the black races. There is a physical difference between the two, which in my judgment will probably forever forbid their living together upon the footing of perfect equality, and inasmuch as it becomes a necessity that there must be a difference, I, as well as Judge Douglas, am in favor of the race to which I belong having the superior position.

I have never said anything to the con-trary, but I hold that, notwithstanding all this, there is no reason in the world why the Negro is not entitled to all the natural rights enumerated in the Declaration of Independence, the right to life, liberty, and the pursuit of happiness. (Loud cheers.) I hold that he is as much entitled to those as the white man. I agree with Judge Douglas he is not my equal in many respects — certainly not in color, perhaps not in moral or intellectual endowment. But in the right to eat the bread, without leave of anybody else, which his own hand earns, *he is my equal and the equal of Judge Douglas, and the equal of every living man.* (Great applause.)

---

a fanatical proslavery man, the implications of whose policies would be to spread slavery to all the states. Even before the debates, in the "House Divided" speech announcing his campaign, Lincoln had stated that "I do not expect the Union to be dissolved — I do not expect the House to fall — but I do expect it to cease to be divided. It will become all one thing or all the other. Either the opponents of slavery will arrest the further spread of it, . . . or its advocates will push it forward, till it shall become alike lawful in all the States, old as well as new, North as well as South. Have we no tendency to the latter condition?" Lincoln's message was, by implication, that a vote for Douglas was a vote to allow the Slave Power conspiracy to dominate the nation on behalf of the South's interests.

At the debate in Freeport, Illinois, just north of Chicago, held on August 27, Lincoln asked Douglas a calculated question. Mr. Lincoln put the hypothetical to Mr. Douglas: Could the people of a territory legally exclude slavery before their territory became a state? If Douglas said no, then he in effect agreed with the Dred Scott decision and lost Free Soil support in Illinois and northern support generally; if he said yes, he lost all prospect of southern support for his presidential ambitions. An able and quick-thinking debater, Douglas attempted to split the difference with a variation of something he had suggested first in May 1857. Without condemning the Dred Scott decision, Douglas said that slavery in practice could exist in a territory only if there were certain regulatory laws in force; if the territorial legisla-ture simply refused to pass the necessary police legislation, slavery could not exist. Hence popular sovereignty still lived, Dred Scott decision or no. This artful dodge, which became known as the Freeport Doctrine, infuriated the South, and proslavery stalwarts never forgot or forgave Douglas for implying that slavery's expansion could be halted. But this compromise went over well in Illinois, where Free Soil but racist sentiment was strong, and by this calculated waffling Douglas sealed his victory in the state. When the votes were counted for the legislative seats, Douglas supporters were in the majority (although their cumulative vote was less than the vote for Lincoln supporters). So Stephen Douglas won reelection to the Illinois Senate seat. But the Freeport Doctrine would come back to haunt him in 1860, and Lincoln's eloquence, his ability to raise the slavery debate to the plane of morality and express those moral issues in the powerful cadence of the King James Bible, presaged his mastery of words in the White House.

❧ John Brown's Raid

As if the political waters were not turbid enough, one high-strung individual who saw himself as God's avenging angel invaded Maryland to exact revenge from the sinful South. John Brown, who had brutally murdered southerners in Kansas in 1856, had since then concocted a plot to arm southern slaves with pikes, start a small insurrection that he assumed would spread like wildfire down the Appalachian backbone of the South, and

John Brown Although it dates from the twentieth century, this mural painting by John Steuart Curry (1897-1946) seems to capture the larger-than-life fury of John Brown (with a Bible in one hand and a gun in the other) as he roused western farmers to drive slavery from the land.

develop a free-black refuge in the mountain valleys. On October 16 he along with twenty-two black and white followers, including two of his sons, raided the federal arsenal in Harpers Ferry, Virginia (now West Virginia), capturing the arsenal and a huge stockpile of arms. But there his plot fizzled. He had neglected to alert the slaves in the vicinity in advance, he had brought no food for the next day, and when no support swelled among the slave population, he was left surrounded by a hastily gathered white militia. His invasion was over by the second day, and Brown and his men were trapped in the Baltimore and Ohio Railroad engine station just at the foot of the rail bridge crossing the Potomac River. Word of his raid had quickly reached Washington, D.C., and President Buchanan sent a military detachment —

headed by Colonel Robert E. Lee and Lieutenant J. E. B. Stuart — to recapture the arsenal. After a skirmish, Brown himself and five of his men were captured; all the rest were killed.

The Virginia government withstood efforts to lynch Brown and instead indicted him for treason, murder, and instigating slave insurrection — the worst nightmare of the white South. Brown in his life had been mostly a failure, and clearly his deep-felt opposition to slavery in his own mind legitimated almost indiscriminate slaughter of whites. But this probably deranged man at his trial found within himself great courage, profound dignity, and a surprising eloquence. As the judge prepared to pronounce his sentence of death after Brown's conviction, Brown — seizing the role of martyr — said: "Now, if it is deemed necessary that I should forfeit my life for the furtherance of the end of justice, and mingle my blood further with the blood of my children and with the blood of millions in this slave country whose rights are disregarded by wicked, cruel, and unjust enactments, I say, let it be done." He then died bravely on the gallows. Correspondence was discovered linking Brown to a who's who of northern intellectuals, ministers, and abolitionists, who evidently had supported him with funds and encouragement even though they seemed to take care not to know exactly what he intended.

Most northerners, especially northern politicians, condemned Brown's raid at Harpers Ferry and his insurrectionary schemes. They took pains to separate their opposition to the expansion of slavery from his violent plans. But a smattering of very eminent northern intellectuals praised Brown as a martyr for black freedom. Ralph Waldo Emerson wrote that Brown would "make the gallows as glorious as the cross," while Henry David Thoreau irresponsibly referred to him as "an angel of light." Southerners were outraged by the minority of support for Brown in the North, and they failed to grasp how limited and unrepresentative of northern public opinion such commendation was. But most southerners were past rational discrimination; they saw Brown's murderous plot as typical of what abolitionists had in mind for the South, the isolated but very visible praise of his actions as representative of northern sentiment, and the Republican Party as the logical extension of radical abolitionism. Nothing had yet so inflamed the South and tended to make southerners distrustful of all their northern brothers and sisters. As one North Carolinian wrote, a man who had always conceived of himself as a strong unionist, "I confess the endorsement of the Harpers Ferry outrage . . . has shaken my fidelity. . . ." Newspaper editorials blasted the North and called for southerners to prepare to defend themselves. Local southern militias began to stockpile arms and to train. Voices hitherto calm now called for considering secession. The election year of 1860 began on an ominous note.

❧ *The Fateful Election of 1860*

As if the slaveholders of the South needed anything else to sour their attitudes toward the North as a new election year approached, a faction of some sixty-eight Republican members of the House of Representatives poured oil on the flames. In 1859 they caused to be reprinted and distributed as election material 100,000 copies of an abridged version of southerner Hinton Rowan Helper's 1857 book *The Impending Crisis of the South: How to Meet It*. Utilizing data from the census of 1850, Helper had argued that slavery impoverished the

South and especially degraded and impoverished the majority of southern whites, the nonslaveholders of the South. He called upon this silent majority to overthrow planter dominance and, in their own interest, to abolish slavery. Planters, aware that the percentage of heads of southern white households who owned slaves was decreasing, saw this book as a call for internal revolution, for class warfare — as more dangerous, in fact, than *Uncle Tom's Cabin*. "Helperism" was feared by slaveholders as much as calls for slave insurrection, and it made southern whites condemn the entire North as the enemy of the South. When the Republican majority in the House in December 1859 sought to elect John Sherman from Ohio as Speaker, the southern members were outraged because he had endorsed the campaign compendium of Helper's work. Their fervent opposition cost Sherman the speakership and further indicated that national politics had reached unprecedented levels of misunderstanding and intersectional suspicion. John Sherman's defeat and John Brown's hanging in December 1859 brought to a close a dismal year. But matters were to go from bad to worse.

The clear front-runner for the Republican presidential nomination was Senator William H. Seward of New York. But along with Seward's high name recognition came much ideological baggage and a hint of corruption raised by his association with New York State's Whig (and later Republican) Party boss, Thurlow Weed. Seward had been very visible for a long time, and his forthright condemnation of nativism had won him the enmity of the remnants of the Know-Nothing movement that otherwise leaned toward the Republican Party. But more than anything, Seward was known as an outspoken critic of slavery. He had used such phrases as "an irrepressible conflict" in describing the political differences between the sections and had spoken of "a higher law" than the Constitution that justified opposition to the South's peculiar institution. Consequently, Seward was absolutely anathema to the South and to southern sympathizers in the North, and even northern moderates were queasy about him. Republican Party leaders gathering in mid-May for their presidential nomination convention in Chicago wanted to win the election, and they were determined to moderate their antislavery stance and widen their appeal to northern voters. They were fully aware that if in the last presidential election they had carried Pennsylvania and either Illinois or Indiana, they would have won the White House.

The Republican platform was clearly intended to

THE POLITICAL GYMNASIUM.

Published by Currier & Ives, 152 Nassau St. N.Y.

pick up the additional northern support necessary to capture the presidency. Planks called for raising tariffs (popular in Pennsylvania with its manufacturing interests), for internal improvements like an intercontinental railroad (popular in midwestern states like Illinois), for a homestead law offering 160 acres of free land to settlers in the West, including immigrants (intended to diminish any residual animosities that might have attached to the Republican Party), and for unrestricted immigration (to woo immigrant voters who normally went Democratic). And to nail down its core support from Free Soil advocates who wanted to keep slavery from expanding, the Republican platform declared categorically that "the normal condition of all the territory

Politics as Usual, 1860   This cartoon, published by Currier & Ives, treats the campaigns of Lincoln, Douglas, John Breckinridge, and John Bell (the Constitutional Union candidate) for the White House in 1860 as a stunt-filled exhibition of "political gymnastics." During the campaign, a great deal was made of Lincoln's image as "the rail-splitter"; hence the light-hearted treatment here of chinning bars and the like. Most voters in 1860 did not appreciate how deadly serious was the drift toward civil war that the presidential contest portended, and they were shocked when slave states began to secede after the outcome was announced.

of the United States is that of freedom, . . . and we deny the authority of Congress, of a territorial legislature, or of any individuals, to give legal existence to slavery in any territory of the United States."

The Republican platform, in short, revealed the party's determination to win. That determination prevented front-runner Seward from securing the nomination on the first ballot. By the second ballot, a combination of unease about Seward's electability and the skillful machinations of Lincoln's campaign strategists brought Lincoln and Seward even in the delegate count. By the end of the third ballot, Lincoln was within a couple of votes of capturing the nomination; then, amid a backdrop of furious deal-making by his agents, delegates began to switch their votes to Honest Abe. The movement instantly snowballed, and shortly Lincoln was named the unanimous choice of the Republican convention for the presidential race.

Then (as today), image-making counted heavily in politics, and for all his moral depth Lincoln was also one of the shrewdest politicians in American history. He and his managers presented him as Honest Abe, the simple "rail splitter," an Everyman who had risen from poverty to political distinction, an exemplar of what free white men could accomplish in a land of opportunity — just the same image-making that in earlier decades had propelled Andrew Jackson and William Henry Harrison into the White House.

As the Democratic Party made preparations to journey to Charleston, South Carolina, for its convention in April, Stephen Douglas anticipated defeat. Earlier in the year Senator Jefferson Davis of Mississippi had offered a series of resolutions in the Senate essentially demanding that the nation unequivocally guarantee to southern whites a permanent right to take slavery into all territories. Of course, there was no way that the Senate would pass such resolutions, but they indicate the mood of the southern Democrats. They would support the Union only so long as the Union supported their right to own slaves everywhere in the nation. Douglas came to Charleston as the only candidate who had a chance to win substantial votes in both regions, but he could not compromise on the principle of popular sovereignty without losing his northern support. When a large bloc of southern extremist Democrats insisted on a party plank demanding that neither Congress nor territorial legislatures could legally limit slavery, the die was cast. Douglas controlled a majority of the delegates but not the two-thirds necessary to win the nomination, and he would not capitulate to the extremists' demands. Even when the delegates from eight southern states walked out of the convention, Douglas would not budge. The convention decided to have a cooling off period of six weeks, after which they would reconvene in the Border State city of Baltimore.

Before the Democrats reassembled, another party, newly formed, held a brief, somber convention in Baltimore. Groups of older, conservative Democrats and former Whigs, unhappy with the tendencies in both major parties and fearful for the Union's survival, coalesced as the Constitutional Union party. They promised nothing but support of the Constitution and the Union as it existed, and enforcement of the laws. They really hoped against hope that by ignoring or denying the divisive issues of the day they could somehow finesse the crisis and save the nation from division and bloodshed. The colorless convention nominated two bland candidates, John Bell of Tennessee for the presidency and Edward Everett of Massachusetts as his running mate.

By the time the Democrats reconvened, they thus faced two opposition parties. It was even more obvious that with Republican Party strength concentrated exclusively in the North, and with the Constitutional Union Party expected to do best in the Border States, the Democratic Party had an opportunity by appealing to supporters in both sections to solidify its role as the only national party. But that depended on the Democratic candidate and the party platform. The party bolters had decided to meet in Richmond a week before the Baltimore meeting, but they could decide on nothing and so came to Baltimore. In their absence the Douglas Democrats had quickly put together several new state parties and elected new delegates; since the Douglas forces controlled the Baltimore convention, they ruled in favor of most of the new, pro-Douglas delegates. The anti-Douglas delegates, who had bolted in Charleston, were still in a rule-or-ruin mood, and once more they walked out when they saw that they still could not dictate an ironclad guarantee of slavery as a platform plank. The remaining delegates nominated Douglas on a popular-sovereignty platform, while the southern Democrats convened in another Baltimore hall and nominated for the White House Vice President John C. Breckinridge of Kentucky on a platform demanding congressional protection of slavery in the territories. With the Democrats thus split into sectional parties, the election of Lincoln seemed a foregone conclusion.

Following the normal pattern for nineteenth-century presidential elections, Lincoln did not campaign for the White House. Instead, tens of thousands of Republican volunteers spread the good word about how Honest Abe would maximize opportunities for whites in the North and the western territories. Constitutional Union candidate John Bell drew his support mostly from the Border States. Lincoln's name was not even on the ballot in ten southern states, and Breckinridge did not campaign in the North. Only Douglas broke with tradition by barnstorming in both sections — not that he expected to win, but putting the national interest above personal ambition, he spoke on behalf of the Union in both sections, trying to persuade voters to support the nation however the election turned out. Courageously campaigning through the South with no chance of winning, he risked ridicule at best and assassination at worst, and in fact fatally undermined his health.

With northerners convinced of the radical perfidy of the Slave Power forces, and with southerners likewise convinced that the entire North seethed with radical abolitionism, voters were in no mood to be magnanimous. They did turn out in huge numbers; 81.2 percent of eligible voters cast ballots. But they voted their sectional interests. Lincoln, capturing only 40 percent of the nationwide vote but 54 percent in the northern states, won 180 electoral votes, a comfortable margin of victory in the electoral college. Douglas got the second largest total of popular votes and attracted support from all over the nation, but he carried in just Missouri and part of New Jersey, garnering a mere 12 electoral votes. Breckinridge gained the 72 electoral votes of eleven southern states, and Bell won the Upper South and Border States of Tennessee, Kentucky, and Virginia, for a total of 39 electoral votes. For the first time, the nation had a completely sectional president, elected without a single vote from the Deep South states. Nothing could have filled the slave states with a greater foreboding.

President-Elect Lincoln   Lincoln sat for this photograph by Mathew Brady, probably immediately after he arrived in Washington, D.C., on February 24, 1861, shortly before his inauguration. At the time, the secession crisis had already begun, yet Lincoln was saying nothing in public about the issue. He had begun to grow a beard, hoping to add a touch of *gravitas* to his public image — hitherto that of the lanky prairie rail-splitter.

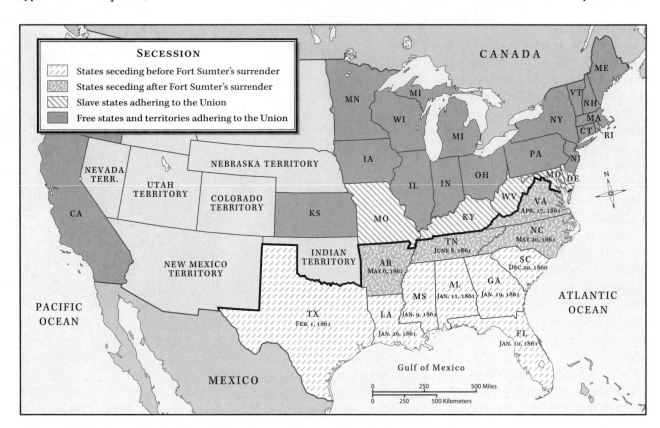

⤚ Lincoln and the Secession Crisis

Lincoln considered himself a moderate on the slavery issue, and both as a candidate and as president-elect he took pains to emphasize that he would do nothing to attack slavery where it existed. But in part because Douglas had painted him as an abolitionist Black Republican in the 1858 debates, and in larger part because southern whites could no longer tell the difference between moderate Free Soilers and radical abolitionists, the white South saw Lincoln as an aggressive threat to their whole way of life. Most southern whites — and certainly the political leaders and shapers of opinion — implicitly understood that their way of life rested on the institution of slavery. Surely the policy differences between the two sections found a variety of expressions: conflicts over taxation, tariffs, internal improvements, the status of territories, an industrial-urban vision of the future as opposed to an agrarian one. But in every case at the bottom of the disagreement lay slavery. The consensus among historians over the past three or four decades has unequivocally come around to the position that the root cause of secession and the Civil War was slavery.

Lincoln, moderate that he was, and cautious if not passive by nature, played his cards extremely close to his vest in the months between his election in November 1860 and his inauguration in March 1861. For one thing, he was convinced that the South was bluffing in its bold talk of secession. Even after the first seven Deep South states seceded, he thought they were attempting to pressure him into accepting ironclad guarantees of the right to take slaves into present and future territories. If he could simply hold out long enough, he believed, the noisy hotheads would lose their support in the South and the presumed silent majority of Unionists, many of them like himself former Whigs, would emerge to seize the political initiative. So a mostly quiet Lincoln seemed for fateful months to do nothing — irritating many northerners — while events swirled around him.

One group of moderate Senators, led by Kentucky Senator John J. Crittenden, who aspired to be a latter-day Henry Clay and devise a nation-saving compromise, tried to defuse the ticking political time bomb. On December 18, 1860, Crittenden introduced a peace resolution in the Senate, but the "compromise" it offered was in effect a complete surrender to the South. It called for a constitutional amendment that would restore the Missouri Compromise line protecting slavery below that boundary; for another constitutional amendment that would prohibit the federal government from ever

The Case for Secession, 1860

Immediately after the votes were counted in November 1860, southern newspapers began calling for secession. Here is one such appeal, from the Richmond Examiner.

It would seem that the sectional game has been fairly played out in the North. New York has gone for Lincoln by a majority larger than she cast for Fremont in 1856. Of the free States we see no reason to hope that the Black Republicans have lost more than two, and they amongst the smallest and weakest in political power — those on the Pacific.

The solid, compact mass of free States has solemnly given its sanction and its political power to the anti-slavery policy of the Black Republicans. — The idle canvass prattle about Northern conservatism may now be dismissed. A party founded on the single sentiment, the exclusive feeling of hatred to African slavery, is now the controlling power in this Confederacy. Constitutional limitations on its powers are only such, in its creed, as its agents and itself shall recognize. It claims power for the Government which it will control, to construe the measure of its own authority, and to use the entire governmental

power of this Confederacy to enforce its construction upon the people and States of this Union. No man can fail to see and know this who reads and understands what he reads. The fact is a great and perilous truth. No clap trap about the Union, no details of private conversations of Northern men can alter it or weaken its force. It is here a present, living, mischievous fact. The Government of the Union is in the hands of the avowed enemies of one entire section. It is to be directed in hostility to property of that section.

What is to be done, is the question that presses on every man.

---

interfering with slavery in the South; for the repeal of various northern states' personal-liberty laws that tried to void the Fugitive Slave Act of 1850; and for federal compensation to owners of runaway slaves. The so-called Crittenden compromise was no compromise at all; all the "give" would come from the North.

And give way Lincoln refused to do, in part because he still expected a Unionist resurgence in the South. When he responded negatively to a Senate feeler on the issue of the extension of the Missouri Compromise line, the other northern Senators balked. Then the southern Senators, who had announced at the beginning of the process that they would support the compromise measure only if it won strong Republican approval, refused to endorse the resolution. Hence on December 31 the compromise proposal failed to clear the committee established to consider it. In a last-gasp effort, Virginians called for a special convention to meet in the national capital to search for some way to find a compromise, and several states sent representatives. But this effort failed too because the central issue — the theoretical right of slavery to expand into new territories — was no longer amenable to compromise.

South Carolinians knew their state had a reputation for extremism. Several times earlier they had called for the other southern states to follow them only to find themselves embarrassingly standing alone. This time South Carolinians were determined not to risk having egg on their faces; they would wait for several other states to secede before they acted precipitately. But in the excitement of the moment South Carolina got

ahead of itself and rushed into calling a secession convention, convinced that this time the other southern states were right behind them. On December 17 — one day before Crittenden introduced his ill-fated peace resolution to the U.S. Senate — the South Carolina secession convention convened, and three days later, December 20, it voted unanimously for a secession ordinance voiding "the union now subsisting between South Carolina and the other States."

Word of South Carolina's action was telegraphed across the South, and within days the other Deep South states chose delegates to their respective secession conventions. Secession sentiment was by no means unanimous even in the Deep South — many thought the North would eventually back down — but prosecessionist delegates dominated the conventions and voted overwhelmingly for separation from the Union. Between January 9 and February 1 the six Deep South states followed their fiery leader, South Carolina, in voting to leave the Union. In a number of states prominent ministers added their prestige to the secession bandwagon, none more influentially than Presbyterian Benjamin M. Palmer of New Orleans, whose thunderous sermon on behalf of the southern cause (God's cause, he called it) was widely reprinted throughout the region. But the Upper South and Border States — Delaware, Maryland, Virginia, North Carolina, Kentucky, Tennessee, Arkansas, and Missouri — held back at the fateful brink. They represented the preponderance of the South's population, food production, and industrial might. The future of the incipient Confederacy, and the sundered nation, hung precariously in the balance.

Even before the other southern states had acted, South Carolina had sent commissioners all across the South, instructing them to propose that each state, as it seceded, prepare to send delegates to a special convention for the purpose of creating a provisional Confederate government. This constitutional convention was scheduled to open in Montgomery, Alabama, on February 4. By that date seven states had voted to secede, and the convention began even before the delegates from Texas could arrive. In only three days the convention produced a provisional Confederate constitution, closely modeled on the U.S. Constitution with the exception that it expressly guaranteed slavery and expressly invoked God, a reference to the supposed providential nature of the Confederate cause. Two days later, on February 9, Senator Jefferson Davis of Mississippi was chosen the provisional Confederate president and Alexander H. Stephens vice president; both had been moderates in the secession crisis. A real election was scheduled for the fall of 1861 in which Davis and Stephens were duly elected, and the constitution ratified, by the voters of the Confederacy.

This was the problem looming before president-elect Lincoln as he contemplated putting together his cabinet and tried to decide exactly how he should react to the emergency of seven Deep South states having formally left the Union and proclaimed themselves a new nation. Whatever he did with regard to those states that had already left, the critical issue was how to reach out to the Upper South and Border States whose future status was yet uncertain. Could he somehow entice, cajole, or force the seven departed states to return to the Union without irritating one or more of the fence-sitting states to choose secession? Or even if there was no way to reclaim those already seceded, could any additional secessions be prevented? Was it better to be patient, or to demand and threaten? Lincoln opted for patience even as many of his fellow northerners called for action. Others in the North, particularly those with commercial ties to the South, at first recommended that the South be permitted to leave peacefully for the sake of good business. Still others, glad to be free of the Slave Power politicians in Congress, basically said "good riddance." General Winfield Scott of Mexican War fame wrote "Wayward sisters, depart in peace!" Just-appointed Secretary of State William Seward even advocated provoking a war against France or Spain hoping that a surge of patrio-

tism would restore the Union. Lincoln had to take his own counsel in the midst of such divided opinion.

Rumors of an assassination plot forced Lincoln to slip by darkness into Washington, D.C., just before he had to take his oath and deliver his inaugural address on March 4, 1861. The North and the South were eager to hear what he had to say, eager to discover what course of action he intended. Lincoln knew the burden his address had to carry and crafted it with great care. First he spoke of the perpetuity of the Union and said that secession was illegal: "No State upon its mere motion can lawfully get out of the Union." The South had participated fairly in the 1860 election; it could not simply leave because it did not like the democratic outcome, and to permit it to do so was to condone anarchy, to accept the end of the whole American experiment in democratic government. He was as conciliatory as he could be, pledging not to interfere with slavery where it already existed; he would even support a constitutional amendment to that effect. But he went on to say that he had a constitutional obligation to "hold, occupy, and possess the property and places belonging to the Government," a potent claim since four federal forts in the Confederacy as yet remained in Union control. Nevertheless, Lincoln clearly did not want war; he still hoped, somehow, for a peaceful resolution of the crisis. Speaking to the South near the conclusion of his address, Lincoln added, "In your hands, my dissatisfied fellow-countrymen, and not in mine is the momentous issue of civil war." Then, reaching out once more in a moving and conciliatory gesture, he said:

> I am loath to close. We are not enemies, but friends. We must not be enemies. Though passion may have strained, it must not break, our bonds of affection. The mystic chords of memory, stretching from every battlefield and patriot grave to every living heart and hearthstone all over this broad land, will yet swell the chorus of the Union, when again touched, as surely they will be, by the better angels of our nature.

CONCLUSION: OUTBREAK OF WAR AT FORT SUMTER

Yet only one day after his inauguration, Lincoln learned that Fort Sumter, in the middle of Charleston's harbor, had at the most only ten days of supplies left. Lincoln's pledge to hold and occupy federal property quickly came to a head.

Fort Sumter's importance was purely symbolic, not military. If Lincoln acquiesced to its surrender, the Union would look impotent and the Confederacy would be both emboldened and legitimated and better able to attract the other southern states to its banner. For the Confederates, eager to establish themselves as a real nation both in the eyes of the other southern states and potential allies in Europe, it was essential to drive Union occupiers out of the harbor of their flagship city, Charleston. Not to be able to do so would suggest the so-called Confederate States of America was ephemeral, a bluster that would soon fade as passions cooled. Lincoln believed that if he could somehow hold on to the fort without thereby seeming to initiate hostilities against the South, then perhaps he could buy enough time to let Unionist support grow in the Border States and Upper South, ultimately defusing the secession crisis — perhaps as the nullification crisis had defused in the days of Andrew Jackson.

Lincoln developed a plan. He would send food and medical supplies to Major Robert Anderson, in command at Fort Sumter, but not military reinforcements, and he would notify the Confederate officials unambiguously that this was a peaceful resupply, intended only to maintain the status quo. To that effect he sent a telegram and had a letter hand-delivered to the governor of South Carolina. In truth Lincoln doubted that South Carolina would accept such an offer and would probably initiate hostile action against Fort Sumter — thus becoming the aggressor. But he thought there was a chance South Carolina would accept his proposal, that hostilities could be avoided over Fort Sumter, and perhaps that the secession crisis could be blunted.

Confederate president Jefferson Davis and his advisers, however, determined that their new nation could not accept the maintenance of the status quo. Hence southern officials decided to reject Lincoln's offer. At President Davis's command, the southern general in charge, General P. G. T. Beauregard, on April 11 sent Major Anderson an ultimatum to surrender. Anderson refused to do so by a set time, saying only that he was soon to run out of supplies. The southern leaders decided they could not afford to wait for Lincoln to resupply Fort Sumter and ordered an attack to commence against the island fortress. Sharply at 4:30 A.M. on April 12 a fierce bombardment of Fort Sumter began; thirty-four hours later Major Anderson surrendered. The first shots of the Civil War had been fired.

Two days later, on April 15, President Lincoln issued a proclamation declaring that "combinations too powerful to be suppressed" by normal means existed in the seven Deep South states, an unlawful rebellion against the federal government, and he called for seventy-five thousand volunteers to join the militias of the loyal states to put down the rebellion. Much of the North approved of his action against forces that had fired on the American flag, and thousands thronged to quell the rebellion and restore the Union. Ralph Waldo Emerson, touring a naval base in Massachusetts, exulted that "Sometimes gunpowder smells good." But Lincoln's proclamation horrified the South. Even those Upper South states like Virginia that had doubted the wisdom of secession now faced the prospect of Union militiamen marching through their state to crush their Deep South brethren. More than John Brown's raid, more than Lincoln's election, more than the firing of Fort Sumter, this was the straw that broke the camel's back.

Reluctant secessionists now had to make a decision, and in nearly every case — whether as states like Virginia that could not side against their slaveholding neighbors or as individuals like Robert E. Lee who opposed both secession and slavery but could not side against their state — southerners sided with the secession. Four crucial Upper South states now joined the Confederacy: Virginia on April 17 (two days after Lincoln's proclamation), Arkansas on May 6, North Carolina on May 20, and Tennessee on June 8. After much internal conflict, Missouri and Kentucky stayed in the Union even though many of their sons joined the Confederate army. Delaware easily remained loyal to the Union. The westernmost portion of Virginia broke away from the state and proclaimed its loyalty, being admitted to the Union as West Virginia in 1863. Lincoln, aware of how essential a loyal Maryland was to the security of the District of Columbia, used military force to arrest secessionist leaders in the state and hold them in jail without trial, simply refusing to risk the state's deciding to support the Confederacy.

The Union was now sundered, divided into two nations. No one knew if or what kind of war would result, or how long it would last, but war seemed certain. And so it was.

SUGGESTED READING

Charles B. Dew, *Apostles of Disunion: Southern Secession Commissioners and the Causes of the Civil War* (2001). Argues convincingly that the root causes of the Civil War were the issues of slavery and racism.

William L. Barney, *The Secessionist Impulse: Alabama and Mississippi in 1860* (1974). A detailed political history of how two southern states reacted to Lincoln's election, and why.

Don E. Fehrenbacher, *Slavery, Law, and Politics: The Dred Scott Case in Historical Perspective* (1981). Essential reading on one of the most fateful Supreme Court decisions in the nation's history.

Eric Foner, *Free Soil, Free Labor, Free Men: The Ideology of the Republican Party Before the Civil War* (1970). A pioneering study of the role of free labor ideology in the rise of the Republican Party.

William W. Freehling, *The Road to Disunion: Secessionists at Bay, 1776-1854* (1990). A lively, vigorously interpretive account of the personalities, issues, and events leading to the Kansas-Nebraska Act.

John Mayfield, *Rehearsal for Republicanism: Free Soil and the Politics of Antislavery* (1980). A political-cultural analysis of an emerging northern sentiment against the spread and continuation of slavery.

Stephen B. Oates, *To Purge This Land with Blood: A Biography of John Brown* (1970). A well-written, rigorously analytical account of the forces — personal and national — that drove John Brown to do violence in the desire to achieve good.

David M. Potter, *The Impending Crisis, 1848-1861* (1976). A balanced, comprehensive, and wise account of the coming of the Civil War — an enduring classic of American historical scholarship.

Gunja SenGupta, *For God and Mammon: Evangelicals and Entrepreneurs, Masters and Slaves in Territorial Kansas, 1854-1860* (1996). The fullest account of the troubles in "Bleeding Kansas."

SUGGESTIONS FOR FURTHER READING

Tyler Anbinder, *Nativism and Slavery: The Northern Know-Nothings and the Politics of the 1850s* (1992).

Stanley W. Campbell, *The Slave Catchers: Enforcement of the Fugitive Slave Law, 1850-1860* (1970).

Richard J. Cawardine, *Evangelicals and Politics in Antebellum America* (1993).

William J. Cooper, Jr., *The South and the Politics of Slavery, 1828-1856* (1978).

Daniel W. Crofts, *Reluctant Confederates: Upper South Unionists in the Secession Crisis* (1989).

Richard N. Current, *Lincoln and the First Shot* (1963).

David B. Davis, *The Slave Power Conspiracy and the Paranoid Style* (1969).

David H. Donald, *Charles Sumner and the Coming of the Civil War* (1960).

Ronald I. Formisano, *The Birth of Mass Political Parties: Michigan, 1827-1861* (1971).

William E. Gienapp, *Origins of the Republican Party, 1852-1856* (1987).

C. C. Goen, *Broken Churches, Broken Nation* (1985).

Thomas F. Gossett, *Uncle Tom's Cabin and American Culture* (1985).

Maury Klein, *Days of Defiance: Sumter, Secession, and the Coming of the Civil War* (1997).

Bruce Levine, *Half Slave and Half Free: The Roots of the Civil War* (1992).

John McCardell, *The Idea of a Southern Nation: Southern Nationalists and Southern Nationalism, 1830-1860* (1979).

Anne C. Rose, *Voices of the Marketplace: American Thought and Culture, 1830-1860* (1995).

Mitchell Snay, *Gospel of Disunion: Religion and Separatism in the Antebellum South* (1993).

Kenneth M. Stampp, *America in 1857: A Nation on the Brink* (1990).

J. Mills Thornton, *Politics and Power in a Slave Society: Alabama, 1800-1860* (1978).

Eric H. Walther, *The Fire-Eaters* (1992).

15

"This Mighty Scourge"
The Civil War Years

THE FIRING ON Fort Sumter opened four long, bloody years of warfare — with destruction and death on a proportional scale unprecedented in the American historical experience before or after. But in April 1861 few Americans expected such a turn of events. It was not clear to them that April morning, with the sound of cannonading still ringing in the ears of Charlestonians and with smoke rising from the shelled ruins of the fort in the city's harbor, that no last-minute compromise would prove possible — that additional conflict could not be avoided. And though the reactions, North and South, to the surrender of Fort Sumter quickly multiplied the dangers and soon made it at least probable that war would result, few believed prolonged hostilities lay in the future. Most southerners were confident that a firm show of resolve would dissuade the North from interfering with the Confederacy's desire for independence, and most northerners either said good riddance to the South or believed the Confederacy would soon collapse.

In assessing their chances, southern leaders did not take a good, hard look at the population, industrial, and transportation advantages possessed by the North. Confederate leaders expected a quick, decisive war — not a war of attrition. The world had not yet seen the kind of war that was soon to reveal itself in the four dozen months following the shelling of the little fortress in Charleston's harbor. Men on both sides were filled with confidence and bravado early in 1861, believing that right — and thereby God — was on their side. But death and destruction eventually brought

Lincoln and His Cabinet Ponder the Emancipation Proclamation. The decision to issue the Emancipation Proclamation was one of the gravest that Lincoln and his advisers ever faced. Here he is shown considering that fateful decision. Secretary of State William Seward sits facing him.

despair, especially in the South, and even theological reconsiderations. After the end of armed conflict, both regions interpreted a new divine purpose for themselves. One of the universal functions of religion is to provide a larger sense of meaning for everyday happenings, and many people during the era of the Civil War turned to religion in an attempt to understand the wrenching events they were witnesses to and participants in.

MOBILIZING AND NATION-BUILDING

❧ *The North-South Balance Sheet*

The word *war* immediately brings to mind images of soldiers and battles. But the ability to put troops in the field and supply them requires a governmental structure, and while the United States of America had to stretch its understanding of government functions and mobilize its resources, the Confederate States of America (CSA) faced an even heavier task: not only to create itself and all the sinews of government action, but also to generate from scratch the manufacturing and support infrastructure necessary to provision its armies. The North and the South had to devise means to raise sufficient manpower to keep their armies at strength, had to discover ways to finance the war effort, and had

to deal with unprecedented social strains. Ultimately, Abraham Lincoln proved a far greater political leader than Jefferson Davis, though given the disparity in resources it is unfair to suggest that Davis's leadership failures had much to do with the war's outcome.

Lincoln took office possessing little charisma or even respect among Union politicians. Yet he proved wise beyond expectation. He put together a cabinet consisting of several of his strongest critics, but his personality and openness slowly brought them to his side. In time William H. Seward as secretary of state, Salmon P. Chase as secretary of the treasury, and Edward M. Stanton as secretary of war — three extremely able men — came to be instrumental in helping to mobilize the financial, industrial, and moral resources of the North for victory. Lincoln's sense of humor, his marvelous political skills, his ability to put into words the nation's evolving purpose allowed him to oversee a major expansion of government power and authority, necessary not only for military victory in 1865 but for the imminent emergence of modern America.

Given the size and diversity of the North's industrial resources, the government contracted with private businesses to supply the military's needs. At first it faced corruption, delays, and shoddy goods, but in the end government diligence generally overcame these problems. By the final year and a half of the war, the northern manufacturing machine was going full blast, bountifully supplying the army. Many northern industries that had originally suffered because they had lost southern markets ended up enjoying a wartime boom. Paying for the supplies was another problem that the historically undertaxed nation had to face. With the southern Democrats out of Congress, protectionist-minded northern Republicans raised the tariff rates, but this only cut back on tariff revenues. Direct taxes assessed on the individual states brought in little. In August 1861 the nation's first federal income tax was begun; the rate of 3 percent was assessed only against the affluent — those with annual incomes of over $800. Secretary of the Treasury Chase was also averse to borrowing money, so the North resorted to printing more money.

Until then paper money had been privately issued by banks, and the value of these bank notes was determined by the solvency of the banks. But early in 1862, following Chase's recommendation, Lincoln signed the Legal Tender Act, making government-issued greenbacks legal currency, backed by the U.S. treasury. Some $150 million in greenbacks were initially printed, and, because they largely retained their value, they proved their value in paying for the massive war effort.

To raise the necessary number of troops, after the first surge of volunteers had served their term and the patriotic bloom of military service had wilted, Lincoln's government moved toward a draft. First, on July 17, 1862, Congress enacted a law that allowed the president to assign troop quotas to the individual states; then, in March 1863, it passed the Enrollment Act that made eligible to draft all able-bodied white males, aged twenty to forty-five — eleven months after the harder-pressed Confederate Congress had passed the nation's first conscription act. Without planning to do so, the

Confederate Recruits These Confederate soldiers from Louisiana relax as they pose for this photograph, taken in 1861. One man plays a violin.

United States in developing the managerial procedures for raising and equipping a huge military force, in creating a modern paper currency system, and in extending the supervising hand of government beyond where it had ever reached before, was creating the foundation of modern nationhood.

But if the North had problems to meet in 1861, they were minor compared to those facing the Confederacy. Jefferson Davis and his associates literally had to create a new nation; they had to summon willing publicists and preachers to help generate feelings of true nationalism; they had to put together a governing structure, complete with such mundane necessities as a postal system. The Confederacy in part did so simply by taking over the post offices previously built and maintained by the U.S. and Confederizing them, often with the same employees. Diplomatic relations had to be established — an endeavor the CSA put great hopes in — and agencies and procedures had to be cobbled together to do the nation's normal business as well as conduct a war for national survival. Jefferson Davis was not as skilled as Lincoln was in putting together and managing an effective cabinet, and he was hampered because, in the

absence of political parties in the CSA, he could not use party discipline to keep potential dissenters in line. As a result his administration, and the Confederate war effort, was crippled by dissent, obstructionism, and states-rightsism. Relations between Davis and his vice president, Alexander H. Stephens, were poisonous; Davis constantly battled with state governors like Joseph E. Brown of Georgia and Zebulon Pike of North Carolina; and he could be haughty and petty when he met opposition, lacking Lincoln's gifts of self-deprecating humor and common sense. At least in his ordinance chief, General Josiah Gorgas, Jefferson Davis found an organizational genius who helped the South arm itself. Gorgas supervised the development of government arms manufactories, and while Confederate soldiers occasionally were hungry and went barefoot, Gorgas saw to it, almost miraculously, that they had sufficient weapons and ammunition.

❧ Raising Armies

In the first blush of wartime enthusiasm, both North and South had more volunteers than the military authorities could train and equip. But the South too soon found itself facing manpower shortages after the boredom, loneliness, and death of war erased romantic images of adventure and quick victory. Southerners who had always argued in defense of limited government intrusion and direction in life now faced a situation in which the primacy of state over national government hampered efforts to recruit and supply a large

army. Inevitably, therefore, the South's new national government had to make unprecedented efforts to marshal the Confederacy's economic, manufacturing, and transportation resources. Factories and cities mushroomed, and even the ideal of the volunteer army withered: in April 1862 the CSA passed its first (and the nation's first) conscription act. Initially all able-bodied white males, aged eighteen to thirty-five, were eligible to be drafted, but as the Confederacy's fortunes plummeted and casualties mounted, the ages were eventually broadened to include all males between seventeen and fifty. Political and economic considerations led to exempting certain occupations as well as the owner or overseer of twenty or more slaves, which led to much grumbling among poorer southern whites. Actually the draft served mostly to inspire enlistment before men were actually drafted.

Even more hated than this extension of government power was the Impressment Act of 1863, giving often desperate southern military commanders the legal right to take food and other necessities from civilians at prices that were prescribed by law but seldom considered fair by the civilians directly affected. And to raise the requisite revenues for the war effort, the Confederate government — even more disinclined

Confederate Currency   Confederate political leaders and romanticized scenes of southern life are featured on these ten- and twenty-dollar bills.

IN THEIR OWN WORDS

Strains in the South, 1862

In this entry in her diary, Mary Boykin Chesnut comments on the suffering Confederate economy and plummeting morale after the defeat of the Merrimack *by the* Monitor.

Cotton is five cents a pound and labor of no value at all; it commands no price whatever. People gladly hire out their negroes to have them fed and clothed, which latter can not be done. Cotton osnaburg at 37 ½ cents a yard, leaves no chance to clothe them. Langdon was for martial law and making the bloodsuckers disgorge their ill-gotten gains. We, poor fools, who are patriotically ruining ourselves will see our children in the gutter while treacherous dogs of millionaires go rolling by in their coaches — coaches that were acquired by taking advantage of our necessities.

This terrible battle of the ships — Monitor, Merrimack, etc. All hands on board the Cumberland went down. She fought gallantly and fired a round as she sank. The Congress [a Union warship] ran up a white flag. She fired on our boats as they went up to take off her wounded. She was burned. The worst of it is that all this will arouse them to more furious exertions to destroy us. They [the North] hated us so before, but how now?

In Columbia [South Carolina] I do not know a half-dozen men who would not gaily step into Jeff Davis's shoes with a firm conviction that they would do better in every respect than he does. The monstrous conceit, the fatuous ignorance of these critics! It is pleasant to hear Mrs. McCord on this subject, when they begin to shake their heads and tell us what Jeff Davis ought to do.

than the North to utilize income taxes — resorted to the printing press to provide money. This currency too was backed up, in theory, by the government's presumed ability to pay, and as the CSA's prospects looked increasingly bleak, the value of the Confederate dollar plummeted to less than two cents in gold, wreaking great hardship upon southern society. The North's blockade prevented southern cotton from reaching either northern or English markets, destroying the South's economy, and prevented most imports of needed goods. Jefferson Davis urged southerners to cultivate food crops, but the rail network had been devised to expedite the transportation of cotton to seaports, not move bulk grains from west to east. The South would eventually lose the war on the battlefield, but its ability and willingness to continue fighting were sapped by internal divisions, financial and economic problems, and transportation difficulties.

The First Battles

Patriotism soared in both the North and the South in the weeks following Fort Sumter, with volunteers overrunning the capacity of the military organizations to make use of them. Hotheads in both sections wanted action, northerners expecting the Confederacy quickly to collapse and southerners expecting northerners, once they met spirited resistance, to capitulate to the South's desire for independence.

In a series of minor skirmishes in May and June 1861, Union troops under General George McClellan defeated small Confederate forces in western Virginia, which helped guarantee the subsequent separation of that part of the state and its organization in 1863 as a Unionist state, West Virginia. Yet distant action in western Virginia failed to satisfy Republican politicians in

The *Monitor* and the *Merrimack*. The engagement of the Federal *Monitor* and the Confederate *Virginia* (as the northern-built *Merrimack* had been renamed) on March 9, 1862, at Hampton Roads, Virginia, was the first encounter in naval history between ironclad warships.

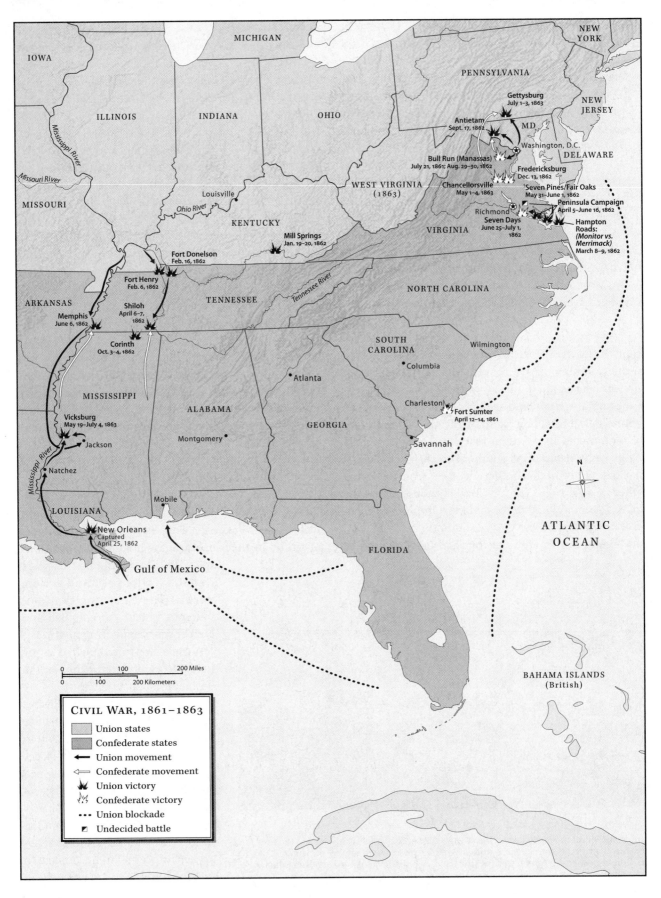

CIVIL WAR, 1861–1863

- Union states
- Confederate states
- → Union movement
- ⇐ Confederate movement
- Union victory
- Confederate victory
- ··· Union blockade
- Undecided battle

Washington, who noisily pressured Lincoln for prompt movement against Richmond.

President Lincoln had few pretensions to knowledge about military matters and at first left strategic planning to the aged General Winfield Scott, a hero of the Mexican War. Scott was devising a general plan to close off Confederate maritime commerce by means of a naval blockade, control the border states, then move down the Mississippi River, cutting the South in two, followed by a relentless squeezing of the Confederacy into near submission. The time gained by this process would allow the mobilization of the North's massive resources and the training of soldiers for later forays into the heartland of the South, bringing the Rebel nation to its knees. But the clamor in Washington for a quick victory overwhelmed Scott's patient timetable, and he sent green Union troops under the command of General Irvin McDowell against equally green Confederate troops commanded by General P. G. T. Beauregard.

On July 21, just twenty miles from Washington near the little town of Manassas Junction, Virginia, McDowell's troops engaged the Rebels at Bull Run Creek. Victory at first seemed sure to the Union army, but southern forces held firm after a stirring defense led by General Thomas J. Jackson — "Look, there is Jackson with his Virginians, standing like a stone wall against the enemy," exclaimed another southern general, inadvertently giving Jackson his nickname — and then, late in the day, southern forces were reinforced when General Joseph E. Johnston's troops rushed in by railroad from the Shenandoah Valley. The tide turned, and the exhausted northern army turned back. Suddenly Union near-victory collapsed into chaotic defeat as soldiers abandoned their positions and equipment and began a headlong retreat back toward Washington, getting tangled up with the carriages of civilian battle spectators who had ridden out for an afternoon of picnicking and excitement. Beauregard's army was too tired, and too inexperienced, to follow up the rout with a decisive and annihilating attack, even though Stonewall Jackson supposedly wanted to capture Washington itself. President Davis, who also had journeyed to the battle site, had his own strategy. He believed the South should simply defend its territory, not be the aggressor, and that the North would soon tire of the conflict and let the South go its own way. So both armies simply moved

Antietam In the Civil War era, photographers could not take "action" shots due to long exposures required to record an image. But they could eloquently photograph the aftermath of battles. This photograph of the battlefield at Antietam speaks for itself.

apart, licked their wounds, and made preparations for better supplying and training their armies according to their respective plans for the future.

STRATEGY AND BLOODSHED IN THE WEST

For months afterward, the battle theater shifted westward, all the way to Kentucky and Tennessee. In January 1862 General George H. Thomas turned back a Confederate incursion into Kentucky at Mill Springs, helping insure that Kentucky remain in the Union. Meanwhile another Union general, Ulysses S. Grant, whose rumpled appearance seemed to belie his West Point training, made preparations to cut the South in two by thrusting southward through the breadbasket region of middle Tennessee. Utilizing Commodore Andrew H. Foote's fleet of gunboats to ascend the Tennessee River from the Unionist staging point of Cairo, Illinois, Grant won a signal victory on February 6 by taking Fort Henry, just below the Kentucky line, then followed up that success by forcing the surrender ten days later of Fort Donelson with its fourteen thousand Confederate troops, the biggest victory of the still young war and a serious blow to Rebel hopes, whose army for the time was pushed out of Tennessee.

The cigar-chewing Grant knew his objectives and knew how to strike boldly when his opponent was reeling. He now pushed southward toward Corinth, Mississippi, just below the Tennessee line and a major junction on the rail line that linked Memphis to the East. Intent on severing the Confederate nation, Grant's army moved relentlessly toward Corinth as another Union general, Don Carlos Buell, moved to join him in a concentrated force. Southern general Albert Sidney Johnston, with forty thousand men, had moved from Tennessee to Corinth; and knowing Grant was headed that way but had not yet been augmented with Buell's army, Johnston decided to make a preemptive strike against the northern forces early on the morning of April 6.

Surprising Grant's men near Shiloh Church, just north of Corinth outside the little Tennessee town of Pittsburg Landing, the southern forces seemed almost to win a decisive victory as evening approached, having pushed Grant's forces back to the river despite heroic efforts by Grant's lieutenant, William T. Sherman. But with success seemingly in hand as night fell, Johnston fell, fatally injured. His army, momentarily stunned, delayed a potentially crushing assault, and during the night Buell's reinforcements arrived. The next morning the reinvigorated northern soldiers pushed back the de-moralized southern army, whose apparent victory had turned into defeat. The Rebel force retreated to Corinth, which they soon evacuated. Grant did not pursue and crush the wounded southern army, a hesitation that cost him personal command of the northern armies in the West as General Henry W. Halleck took active control of the western theater. But neither army had seen such carnage as they experienced at Shiloh. This had been the bloodiest battle yet in American history, with the two competing forces suffering a staggering total of twenty thousand casualties in two days of fighting. No one had ever seen or imagined a war this terrible, and this battle by the small country church foreshadowed many deadly months ahead.

Within weeks another northern force, a fleet under the command of Captain David G. Farragut, blazed its way past Confederate fortifications at the mouth of the Mississippi River and, in tandem with land troops commanded by General Benjamin F. Butler, captured New Orleans on April 25, 1862. Soon only a stretch of the Mississippi between Port Hudson, Louisiana, and Vicksburg, Mississippi, remained in Confederate hands. The Union had almost succeeded in slicing through the middle of the South.

MCCLELLAN'S COMMAND

Back in the East, Lincoln was beside himself with insistence that the Union forces move effectively against southern armies and the Confederate capital at Richmond, Virginia. In the aftermath of the humiliating Union defeat at Bull Run, Lincoln had replaced General McDowell with General George B. McClellan. McClellan seemed the ideal leader to whip the inexperienced Union soldiers into an effective fighting force. A West Point graduate and veteran of the Mexican War, McClellan had even been a member of a study group that had gone to Europe to learn the newest military training and strategic ideas. Arrogant, handsome, and an organizational wizard, McClellan set about creating an army out of his raw recruits. But McClellan proved to have a serious flaw — an organizational and preparedness perfectionist, he never felt sufficiently ready to use his forces aggressively. Lincoln nevertheless insisted that the Union forces move to take Richmond, demanding that McClellan move his huge army overland directly toward the Confederate capital. McClellan, worried about the terrain and southern defenders and hesitant to approach Richmond in such uncompromising fashion, decided to transport his army of 112,000 men by ship down the Potomac River and thence by water to Fortress Monroe at the tip of the peninsula formed by the James and York rivers. This plan became feasible in early March 1862, after the Union ironclad gunship, the *Monitor,* successfully rebuffed the Rebel ironclad, the *Merrimack,* thence opening up the harbor near Fortress Monroe.

At last, in early April 1862, McClellan's giant force began cautiously inching up the peninsula toward Richmond, with McClellan always imagining that the Confederate forces were larger than they in fact were and hoping for reinforcements from Washington. But Stonewall Jackson was ravaging Union forces in the northern Shenandoah Valley, and Lincoln, fearful that Jackson might raid Washington, kept forty thousand Union troops nearby to defend the capital. Still McClellan kept up his snail's pace, reaching within five miles of Richmond. Suddenly southern general Joseph E. Johnston caught a portion of McClellan's forces separated from the main body by the flood-swollen Chickahominy River. At a place called Seven Pines on May 31 – June 1, the Confederates came within a hair of destroying a goodly portion of McClellan's army. Despite this success, General Johnston was wounded, and Jefferson Davis replaced him with the incomparable Robert E. Lee. Lee soon moved aggressively against McClellan's larger army, and in a bloody week of assaults (called the battle of Seven Days, June 25 – July 1, 1862), Lee, though he suffered grievous losses, succeeded in convincing McClellan that he would not be able to take Richmond without absolutely unacceptable casualties. McClellan, who had come so close, then retreated twenty miles back down the James to a fortified defensive position. Richmond was safe, Lincoln was disgusted, and Lee readied his army to strike again.

Lincoln called off McClellan's aborted campaign and removed him from overall command of Union troops in the East. The new Union general in chief, Henry W. Halleck, following his president's wishes, soon sent McClellan and his now smaller force to join with General John Pope for an overland campaign against Richmond. Lee, though, quickly moved his army toward Pope and got to him before McClellan did. In the second battle of Bull Run, fought on August 29-30, 1862, the Confederates won a significant victory. Lee, who just months before faced a threatening Union army only five miles from Richmond, now appeared to be on the verge of taking Washington. Halleck seemed no better than McClellan, so a doubly frustrated Lincoln reappointed McClellan — who at least knew how to train his troops — to head the Army of the Potomac.

Perhaps he could learn from both his mistakes and Lee's successes.

Lee understood by mid-1862 the scale of the war, and he knew that unless the South won quickly, it would probably lose a lengthy war of attrition. As bold and aggressive as McClellan was cautious, Lee began to hatch an ambitious plan. A powerful thrust through western Maryland into Pennsylvania could, if successful, have important payoffs for the South. Much-needed supplies of food and weapons could be captured; volunteers for the Confederate cause might be garnered from the Border States; the fall elections in the U.S. might turn more favorably for peace candidates; and a signal military victory on northern soil could very well so stun the North — and convince northerners that persisting at war with the South would bring unacceptable human costs — that the disheartened Yankees would acquiesce in southern independence. The risks were high, for Lee was proposing abandoning the South's policy of defensive warfare, and by becoming the obvious aggressor, the Confederacy would lose some of its possible cachet with potential supporters in England. But Lee believed, and he convinced Jefferson Davis of this, that the South's best hope for ultimate success lay in turning the tables on the North by invading it.

In early September Lee divided his army into several units and sent them toward Maryland. A Union officer found a copy of Lee's battle orders wrapped around a cigar that had fallen from a Rebel's pocket, so that McClellan became aware of Lee's plans and began to move toward Lee before all his troops could be rejoined. Still McClellan was slower than he should have been, and by the time he met Lee's troops near the small town of Sharpsburg, Maryland, on September 17 (Stonewall Jackson had already taken Harpers Ferry and its supplies), most of the southern armies had come together again. There, in the beautifully rolling farmland surrounding Antietam Creek, Lee's forty thousand troops crashed into McClellan's seventy thousand. The result, associated to this day with battle sites named after the cornfield, the Dunker church, Bloody Lane, and Burnside's bridge, proved to be the bloodiest single day of the Civil War. When night finally fell on the exhausted armies, more than twenty-three thousand casualties littered the fields. Had McClellan in the cover of dark or on the next morning attacked Lee's crippled army, the war might well have ended there. But McClellan, strangely, again proved too cautious. The following night Lee's army crossed over the Potomac and limped back to Virginia and safety. Lee did live to fight another day, but his

"Contrabands" Runaway slaves like these kept fleeing to Union lines, and before the Emancipation Proclamation northern commanders had no official guidance about how they should be treated. This photograph shows "contrabands" in the camp of a Rhode Island regiment in the District of Columbia.

high-stakes invasion had failed. Lincoln, bolder than his generals, dismissed McClellan and took advantage of the victory to change the moral course of the war.

STALEMATE

ᢏ Slavery and the War

Most southerners in 1861 had understood that, at its most fundamental level, the war was over slavery. Confederate vice president Alexander H. Stephens had frankly stated that slavery was the "cornerstone" upon which the Confederate States had been founded. Yet while some abolitionists would have disagreed, most

northerners were hesitant to claim that the war was about slavery; rather, like Lincoln himself, they argued that the purpose of the war was the reunification of the Union. With little opposition, Congress in the summer of 1861 passed a resolution to that effect, disavowing any intention of interfering in what were euphemistically called the domestic institutions in any region. Lincoln was morally opposed to slavery, but his political instincts told him that he had to move slowly. Four Border States, where slavery was still legal, had sided with the Union cause, and precipitous action against slavery would likely drive them out of the Union. Many if not most northerners were insufficiently concerned about slavery to fight a war to end the institution, and most of them were sufficiently racist to fear the consequences for the North if slavery were ended and millions of blacks moved northward to compete for white jobs. Lincoln understood that if he got too far in front of northern public opinion, he and his party would suffer in the 1862 congressional elections — he was, after all, a minority president. In addition, Lincoln knew that, strictly speaking, he had no unambiguous constitutional authority to strike against slavery. So Lincoln was careful to assure the public that he would not try to effect a social or racial revolution and instead was engaged in war for conservative purposes, to put the nation back together again.

Yet political and military pressures soon complicated Lincoln's cautious strategy. Abolitionists, emancipationist Republicans in his own party, and outspoken black activists in the North criticized the president for what they interpreted as his moral cowardice in the face of a clear evil and argued that, in return for having instigated a war and taken Union lives, at the very least the South should have to give up slavery. Lincoln, the northern public, and certainly the northern armies also came to realize that slavery was proving a military advantage to the Confederacy. Because the South could count on slave labor in the fields, in the factories, and in building military fortifications, a higher proportion of white males in the South than in the North were available for combat. In a very direct way, southern slavery therefore cost northern lives. Moreover, as long as northern war aims were less moral than political, that is, intended to reunite the nation rather than free the slaves, then the Confederacy had some hope of attracting English or French aid. Finally, as northern armies moved into such slave-rich regions as the South Carolina Sea Islands (which fell into Union hands in late 1861), Union commanders faced the problem of how to handle slaves who suddenly were behind Union lines. Should they be freed or returned to their previous owners? This practical dilemma was multiplied as thousands of slaves — men, women, and children — began fleeing their owners and coming to Union forces. The slavery problem was no longer an abstraction but an emergency that demanded a solution.

When northern commanders first found themselves with the dilemma of inadvertently capturing

Lincoln Drafts the Emancipation Proclamation These two illustrations convey northern and southern views of the Proclamation. In the northern view, Lincoln is inspired by the Constitution and the law; the South viewed the Proclamation as inspired by the devil, drink, and the ghosts of John Brown and the Haitian slave rebels.

slaves, they essentially improvised by calling the slaves "contraband" — just like the rest of the slaveholders' property now in their possession. Slave contraband was often put to work aiding the Union military, but they were not freed. Congress attempted to regularize matters in August 1861 by passing a Confiscation Act that authorized Union armies to seize all Confederate property actually employed militarily against the U.S., including slaves put to quasi-military use. But neither did this official act explicitly free those slaves captured, and it apparently applied only to slaves who had been engaged in materially assisting Confederate troops. Clearly a problem remained: What about the general slave population whose owners fled and who now found themselves in Union hands? Again in late 1861 and in the spring of 1862, field commanders, facing a human emergency for which they had no exact instructions, freed slaves who came into their possession. But this angered northern conservatives, and Lincoln, fearing the political consequences, overrode the commanders' decisions.

✢ The Emancipation Proclamation

Still, the slavery issue demanded resolution, and slowly the North moved toward a decision that it may not have been fully conscious it was making because of its piecemeal nature. On April 16, 1862, emancipationist Republicans, already called Radical Republicans, passed a bill outlawing slavery (but compensating owners) in Washington, D.C. Two months later another bill ended slavery in the U.S. territories but did not compensate owners. Then on July 17, 1862, Congress passed a Second Confiscation Act liberating all slaves coming into Union hands who had been owned by persons in rebellion against the Union (that

Marching Song of the First Arkansas (Negro) Regiment

The black soldiers of the First Arkansas, a Union regiment, proudly sang this rousing song to the tune of "The Battle Hymn of the Republic," with its familiar chorus "Glory, glory hallelujah." In addition to kindling martial valor, it also echoed black hopes as word of the Emancipation Proclamation spread.

Oh, we're the bully soldiers of the "First of Arkansas,"
We are fighting for the Union, we are fighting for the law,
We can hit a Rebel further than a white man ever saw,
As we go marching on. (Chorus)

See, there above the center, where the flag is waving bright,
We are going out of slavery; we're bound for freedom's light;
We mean to show Jeff Davis how the Africans can fight,
As we go marching on. (Chorus)

We have done with hoeing cotton, we have done with hoeing corn,
We are colored Yankee soldiers, now, as sure as you are born;
When the masters hear us yelling, they'll think it's Gabriel's horn,
As we go marching on. (Chorus)

They will have to pay us wages, the wages of their sin,
They will have to bow their foreheads to their colored kith and kin,
They will have to give us house-room, or the roof shall tumble in!
As we go marching on. (Chorus)

We heard the Proclamation, master hush it as he will,
The bird he sing it to us, hoppin' on the cotton hill,
And the possum up the gum tree, he couldn't keep it still,
As he went climbing on. (Chorus)

They said, "Now colored brethren, you shall be forever free,
From the first of January, Eighteen hundred sixty-three."
We heard it in the river going rushing to the sea,
As it went sounding on. (Chorus)

Father Abraham has spoken and the message has been sent,
The prison doors he opened, and out the pris'ners went,
To join the sable army of the "African descent,"
As we go marching on. (Chorus)

Then fall in, colored brethren, you'd better do it soon,
Don't you hear the drum a-beating the Yankee Doodle tune?
We are with you now this morning, we'll be far away at noon,
As we go marching on. (Chorus)

Source: *Soldier Songs and Home-Front Ballads of the Civil War,* compiled and edited by Irwin Silber (NY: Oak Publications, 165 W. 46th St., NY, 1964), p. 38.

is, it did not liberate the slaves held by Union supporters in the Border States). This act also authorized the use of freed slaves by the Union army. In the midst of these events, Lincoln drafted an emancipation proclamation and submitted it to his cabinet in July. Lincoln argued that if he termed the proclamation a military necessity, he could find constitutional justification for his action. However, Secretary of State Seward did not think that the right moment had arrived to announce the decision. In the aftermath of the defeat of McClellan's Peninsula Campaign, to do so might seem an act of desperation. Seward's caution seemed even more pertinent a month later, when Union troops were again humiliated at the Second Battle of Bull Run. Lincoln accepted the political wisdom of Seward's counsel and awaited an opportune time to announce his momentous proclamation.

Finally, on September 17-18, 1862, Lincoln learned that General Lee's invasion of the North had been thwarted at Antietam. Lincoln's chance to act from a position of Unionist strength had come. On September 22, Lincoln released what was called the Preliminary Emancipation Proclamation, announcing that on January 1, 1863, a hundred days later, all slaves in states and areas under Rebel control would be free. By now Lincoln had northern public opinion behind him — in fact, Radical Republican sentiment was pushing him — and by his proclamation he could preempt calls for possibly more revolutionary action and give conservatives some time to come to terms with the rising demand for action against slavery. Lincoln tempered his moral outrage against bondage with his desires for democratic acceptance of necessary change. In December 1862 he even proposed to Congress a bill that would provide compensation to those states that would rejoin the Union and voluntarily end slavery, immediately or gradually, and, to relieve racist fears in the North, he again promised to seek funds to underwrite the colonization of ex-slaves outside the continental United States. But none of the Confederate states accepted the offer. Consequently, on January 1 the official Emancipation Proclamation declared that, "as a fit and necessary war measure, . . . all persons held as slaves within . . . states and parts of states wherein the people . . . are . . . in rebellion . . . are and henceforth shall be free. . . . And . . . such persons . . . will be received into the armed service of the United States."

The document did not possess the simple eloquence that Lincoln's prose often exhibited, but behind the politically calculated language — couched in terms of military necessity and thereby constitutional law — burned a moral and transforming purpose. Henceforth the war was clearly about the discontinuation of slavery, and this was but the initial first step. Abolitionists might think Lincoln should have moved earlier, but he *had* moved; English and French public opinion shifted away from support of Confederate independence and to support of the cause of emancipation; blacks now had powerful reason to join the actual fight for freeing their brothers. Ultimately almost 180,000 blacks fought as Union soldiers, and although they fought in separate black units, had white officers, and at first were underpaid and disrespected, their courage and heroism soon gained for them the admiration of many northern white soldiers.

Critics, both in 1863 and today, have argued that Lincoln's Emancipation Proclamation in a technical sense freed no slaves — it applied only to regions in rebellion where he was powerless to effect any change. But such criticism misreads how the announcement subtly and profoundly changed northern war aims, southern diplomatic fortunes, and black military resolve.

❧ *Turning the Tide*

Even though blocking Lee's invasion attempt at Antietam had given President Lincoln the opening he needed to issue the Preliminary Emancipation Proclamation, northern military fortunes seemed to revert to their normal dismal course in the months following the carnage upon the Maryland countryside. Lincoln, disgusted with McClellan again for not having crushed Lee's crippled Army of Northern Virginia after Antietam, sacked the overly cautious general and replaced him with General Ambrose E. Burnside, who suffered from the opposite failing: a too-reckless willingness to attack Lee's forces. In mid-December, Burnside threw his massive army of 120,000 men against Lee's strong defensive positions at Fredericksburg, Virginia. Lee had 75,000 men, but they devastated the superior Union numbers, particularly at Mayre's Heights, a defeat so overwhelming that it moved the victorious Lee to mutter: "It is well that war is so terrible — we should grow too fond of it." Following his failed assault, a tearful Burnside retreated. Lincoln replaced him with General Joseph Hooker, a boastful drunkard who promised to have no mercy on Lee. Hooker readied his forces, even larger than Burnside's had been, and made preparations to attack Lee at Chancellorsville, ten miles west of Fredericksburg. But Lee, with less than half as many troops, pounced first. While sending Stonewall Jackson to attack Hooker's flank, Lee ordered his own men to engage Hooker's front. The battle was fierce, but Lee won the day. On May 5 Hooker accepted defeat and his army, its morale broken, retreated to beyond the Rappahannock River. Yet the southern armies had not escaped unscathed; along with a fearful 12,000 casualties, Stonewall Jackson was mortally wounded by

---

✴ IN THEIR OWN WORDS

Thoughts on the Eve of Battle (undated)
An Irish-born Confederate infantryman named John Dooley had these thoughts as he marched toward the battle of Gettysburg.

We know how straight into the very jaws of destruction and death leads this road of Gettysburg; and none of us are as yet aware that a battle is before us; still there pervades our ranks a solemn feeling, as if some unforeseen

danger was ever dropping darksome shadows over the road we unshrinkingly tread.

For myself, I must confess that the terrors of the battlefield grew no less as we advanced in the war, for I felt far less fear in the second battle of Manassas than at South Mountain or even at Fredericksburg; and I believe that soldiers generally do not fear death less because of their repeated escape from its jaws. For, in every battle they see

so many new forms of death, see so many frightful and novel kinds of mutilation, see such varying fortunes in the tide of strife, and appreciate so highly their deliverance from destruction, that their dread of incurring the like fearful peril unnerves them for each succeeding conflict, quite as much as their confidence in their oft tried courage sustains them and stimulates them to gain new laurels at the cannon's mouth.

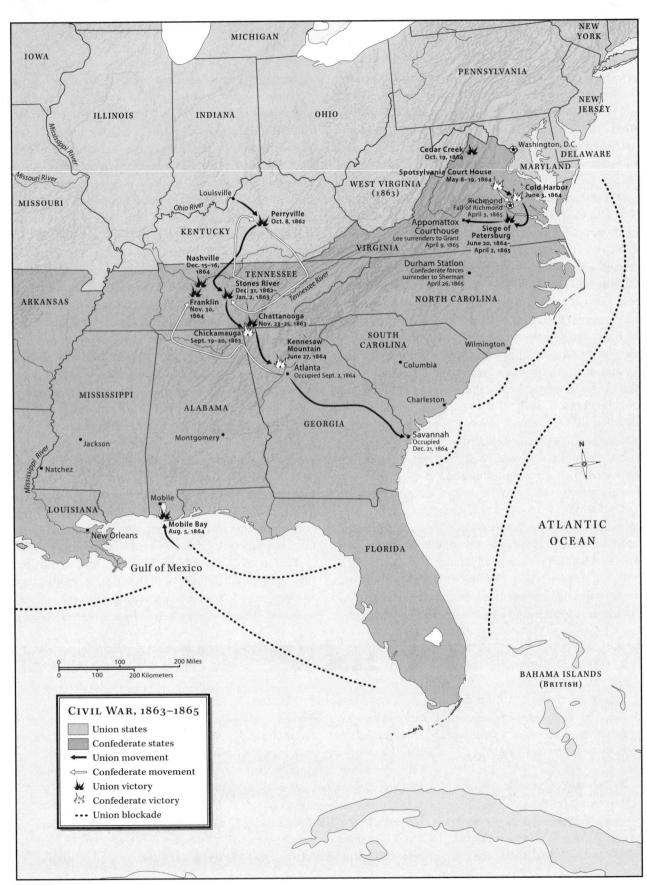

CIVIL WAR, 1863–1865

- Union states
- Confederate states
- → Union movement
- ⇦ Confederate movement
- Union victory
- Confederate victory
- ••• Union blockade

accidental friendly fire. And Confederate news from the West was not good.

For many months, General U. S. Grant had been preparing to take Vicksburg, seemingly invincible atop the bluffs overlooking the Mississippi River. Grant's strategy was so audacious that even Lincoln argued against it, but Grant pushed ahead. Moving south down the Mississippi, in late March he crossed to the west bank, opposite Vicksburg and some distance north of the city. Then his troops made a long loop west and south, coming back to the river twenty-five miles south of Vicksburg. Now his gunboats and supply ships shot downriver, past Vicksburg and a terrible shelling from Confederate guns, to rendezvous with Grant's troops and ferry them across the Mississippi. On the east side of the river again, Grant's army this time looped east and north, capturing the Mississippi capital, Jackson, along the way. Then turning west, on the relatively narrow dry access to Vicksburg, Grant bore down upon the city, putting it under siege on May 22. As Lee and Davis savored the Confederate victory at Chancellorsville and contemplated future strategy, the Rebel forces and civilians at Vicksburg were beginning to undergo a pounding siege that reduced the starving southerners to eating their mules and even rats.

GETTYSBURG

Lee and Davis feared that Vicksburg might fall, and they knew that before they could get reinforcements there it would probably be too late. Lee once more dared a boldly aggressive strike against the North. While his army still had the capacity to fight — and Lee and his fellow generals now considered the Army of Northern Virginia practically invincible — Lee persuaded Davis that an all-out attack on the North might score such a stunning victory that it would outweigh the probable loss of Vicksburg. Such a victory would fatally undermine northern morale and at last might earn European recognition for the Confederacy. In short, it might quickly win the war. Davis accepted the gamble. In early June, while Vicksburg stoically endured its savage bombardment, Lee's forces crossed the Potomac once more, marching northward. General Hooker thought he now saw his chance to take Richmond, but an exasperated (and utterly correct) Lincoln scolded him that his proper target was Lee's army, not the Rebel capital. Soon Lincoln replaced Hooker with General George G. Meade and sent him into Pennsylvania in pursuit of

Lee, careful to keep his army between Lee and Washington, D.C. By June 29 Lee was within ten miles of Harrisburg, Pennsylvania, and began to scout out the best location for the anticipated climactic battle with the Union army.

The next day a portion of Lee's cavalry, looking for shoes and other leather goods at the rail crossroads town of Gettysburg, accidentally stumbled upon two brigades of Union cavalry. Neither army had really wanted trouble here, and Lee was woefully ignorant both of the size and location of Meade's troops because his chief reconnaissance officer, the dashing cavalry commander Jeb Stuart, was off creating havoc near Baltimore. Nevertheless, the unintended exchange of gunfire attracted reinforcements, and as though pulled by an invisible attraction toward the pleasant little village known chiefly for its Lutheran seminary, Lee's main forces and Meade's moved toward collision. On July 1 Lee took control of the town, and Meade arranged his troops along high ground just south of the town, with either end of his line occupying small hills. Meade had the better position, and several of Lee's lieutenants pleaded with him to back away, to get between Meade's Union army and Washington, and wait for the proper moment to engage. But Lee had simply marched too far, risked too much, and come to believe too completely in his intrepid soldiers to retreat. There followed two days of the most awesome artillery bombardment and the fiercest fighting ever seen in North America. There was death and bravery in abundance on both sides. Finally, toward mid-afternoon on July 3, after another long artillery bombardment, Lee sent General George E. Pickett with some fifteen thousand men from the Confederate line, which held Seminary Ridge, across broad open fields and up the slope toward Cemetery Ridge, where the Union army was entrenched. The gunfire was withering, and although a handful of Rebels momentarily broke through the Union lines, the whole Confederate charge was soon broken and driven back down Cemetery Ridge. In an hour the South had lost ten thousand of its bravest men, and Lee's second invasion was crushed. Lee lost a total of seventeen generals, over a third of his army, and as he retreated on July 4 toward Virginia his ambulance train stretched nineteen miles long. Casualties for both armies reached over fifty thousand. Gettysburg had been the nation's deadliest battle ever.

When the retreating Lee reached the Potomac, he found it flooded and temporarily unfordable. Had Meade moved quickly, he could have annihilated the

Army of Northern Virginia and probably ended the war. Yet once more, as with McClellan at Antietam, the Union lost a golden opportunity. Lincoln said later of the occasion, "Our army held the war in the hollow of its hand and would not close it."

But as word was telegraphed back to Washington on July 4 telling of the great victory at Gettysburg, that same day the news flashed along the telegraph lines from the West. On July 4, Vicksburg also had fallen to Grant, and Confederate general John C. Pemberton had surrendered his army of thirty thousand to Grant. The Confederate capital was as stunned by the bad news as Washington was exulted by the good. Yet even though its fate in hindsight was sealed by those two victories, the South was still unwilling to concede, and the North knew that ultimately victory had to be won on the battlefield against a tenacious adversary.

❧ *The Diplomatic and Naval War*

The Union victory at Gettysburg also tipped the balance finally against the South in both the diplomatic and naval aspects of the war. In early 1861, Confederate leaders had some reason to expect assistance from both England and France — England, primarily because they assumed its textile industry was dependent on southern cotton; and France, because Emperor Napoleon III had imperial ambitions in Mexico and hoped to curry favor with the South in case its independence gambit succeeded. A Confederate nation friendly to France would perhaps support French plans for a Mexican puppet empire, or so the French emperor supposed. The initial indications were that the South would win concessions from England and France, both of which recognized the Confederacy as a belligerent, though not as a full-fledged nation. This half-victory for the South meant that the European powers would not accept the North's boycott as a legitimate exercise of a nation's powers over its own ports; rather, Europe officially saw the blockade as a wartime measure that the Union government had to physically enforce.

Yet ultimately the threat of a cotton embargo had little effect. Textile manufacturers in England had stockpiled supplies and were finding alternative sources of cotton in India and Egypt. Poor grain harvests in Europe gave Yankee wheat more diplomatic clout than Dixie's cotton. France was unwilling to go it alone in extending diplomatic recognition to the Confederacy, and when England hesitated, France held back.

The Union almost blew its diplomatic advantage in the fall of 1861 when an overly aggressive U.S. naval captain stopped the British steamer *Trent* on the high seas and seized two southern envoys (James M. Mason and John Slidell) en route to England and France. British leaders were outraged by this belligerent act, but cooler heads prevailed, and Lincoln, judging that one war at a time was enough, released the emissaries and permitted them to travel to Europe.

Some English aristocrats, disdainful of democratic America, were pleased by the Civil War — indeed, had long expected democracy would come to such a pass — and in effect said to the American belligerents, "A plague on both your houses." British workers, who had little political influence anyway, favored the North and emancipation. The Emancipation Proclamation won the wider public relations battle in England for the North. And Gettysburg, serving as a premonition of ultimate Union victory, determined the future outcome of the naval war, too.

The North had moved quickly to enforce the naval blockade, taking Port Royal Sound among the South Carolina Sea Islands in November 1861 as a staging point for the blockade. Within the next few months, it captured additional Confederate ports along the Virginia and Carolina coasts. By April 1862, Admiral David G. Farragut also had control of New Orleans. Blockade runners continued to get through, but the traffic was drastically reduced and became so risky that the light, fast-moving ships soon preferred to carry high-profit luxury goods rather than the medicines, foods, and military supplies the Confederate government and home front desperately needed. The South's belligerent status allowed it to purchase warships from English shipyards. The most famous of these vessels was the C. S. S. *Alabama,* which across three oceans ran down, outmaneuvered, and destroyed dozens of Union merchant ships before it was sunk in the final year of the war. The *Alabama* and several sister ships in total destroyed over 250 Union vessels.

The Confederate secretary of the navy, Stephen R. Mallory, was meanwhile negotiating with Britain's famous Laird shipyards — builders of the *Alabama* — in early 1863 for two ironclad vessels that had deadly underwater pointed rams intended to devastate enemy ships in close-order naval combat. Union officials knew how destructive these ships could be to their commerce, and the American minister to Great Britain, the courtly Charles Francis Adams, soberly threatened England with a U.S. declaration of war if these vessels were delivered to the Confederacy. With the news of Gettysburg in their minds, English authorities backed down and bought the Laird rams for the British navy, dooming what remained of the South's hopes for overcoming northern naval supremacy. When in August 1864 Admiral Farragut succeeded in taking the well-protected and fiercely defended harbor of Mobile, Alabama, the last major Confederate port on the Gulf of Mexico, total Union naval supremacy was guaranteed.

❧ Wartime Social Strains

By 1863 the scale and duration of the war had brought to both northern and southern societies stresses and changes on a scale undreamed of during the heady days of April 1861. The changes were most wrenching in the South. The prewar southern economy had been dominated by cotton exports, and southern leaders had assumed that the English textile industry was so dependent on southern cotton that England would be a ready source of loans, diplomatic support, and perhaps even military assistance by supplying war materiel. This assumption took for granted that the South could ship its cotton overseas. But the northern military blockade was sufficiently effective to shut off this possibility both for cotton diplomacy and for maintaining the lucrative markets cotton planters had long depended on for their personal prosperity. Moreover, before the blockade became practically unbreachable, Jefferson Davis had wanted to control cotton exports abroad precisely to put economic and diplomatic pressure on potentially supportive foreign governments. In fact, as already mentioned, English stockpiles of cotton and even greater dependence on northern wheat than on southern cotton rendered southern diplomatic hopes void, regardless of Union or Confederate actions. Confederate policy, Union blockade, and English needs thereby devastated the cotton-based southern economy, and Davis's actions, while necessary national policy for the Confederacy, angered planters who cared more about individual profits than common purpose. Likewise, when Davis tried to pressure southern planters to forsake cotton and grow badly needed foodstuffs, he met opposition to what was termed government intervention. Many planters, it turned out, had supported secession to avoid the threat of federal interference with their presumed right to own slaves, and they did not like the Confederate authorities' interference with their presumed right to grow cotton with those slaves.

FOOD SHORTAGES AND CLASS DIVISIONS IN THE SOUTH

Self-serving southern planters also maneuvered to trade cotton illegally for goods with Union officials in those sections of the South where proximity of Union agents allowed such commerce, and Texas cotton planters rushed to profit by sending cotton abroad through the Mexican port of Matamoros. Private interests quickly undermined Confederate policy, and small farmers, lacking the means of profiteering and suffering grievously from food shortages and the absence of many males who were away at war, soon chafed at what they termed "a rich man's war and a poor man's fight." As the northern blockade tightened its grip on the southern seacoasts, imports such as coffee, salt, and medicines were cut off — in part because southern blockade runners preferred to import high-price luxury items rather than risk their ships for the common good. Poor southerners experimented with a variety of ersatz coffee products like burned peanuts and shifted their diet away from salted beef to chicken. Such minor inconveniences escalated the hardship of war, and food shortages and high prices disproportionately affected the poorer folk of the South, inflating their frustration and animosity toward both Confederate political leadership and the war itself. Emergent class conflict hindered the South's ability to maximize its manpower resources, and by the final year of the war as many as half the southern soldiers were deserters at any one time.

Transportation failures worsened the South's food distribution problems. Even at the beginning of the war, the South's rail lines had not been effective because the tracks were of many different widths and had been built to link cotton-growing regions to seaports, not to provide a network connecting far-flung sections of the South. As the war wore on, the rail system wore out, exacerbating the problems with the actual rail routes. Draft animals necessary for farming were also increasingly impressed for service in the Confederate armies, crippling small farms particularly, the very ones that before the war had emphasized food production. The conscription of white men as soldiers and slaves as military laborers also cut farm production. As Union armies captured ever-larger parts of the South — the coastal areas of South Carolina and Georgia, much of the Mississippi Valley, the fertile central portion of Tennessee — the Confederacy lost valuable agricultural regions and suffered the dislocation of slaves and their owners, further disrupting crop production. Women were not as experienced or effective at maintaining slave discipline in the absence of their husbands, and women, children, and older men were often unable to maintain farm output at prewar levels. And when armies of either side marched through a region, tearing down fences and trampling crops, they often took (sometimes with pay, sometimes not) exactly what they needed: livestock, meat and grain, and wagons.

The combined result was massive hardship, hunger, and growing frustration with war in the southern countryside; and absolute desperation in southern cities. In April 1863 women almost maddened by food shortages rioted in Richmond, the Confederate capital. When an onlooker, mistaking a mob for a crowd, asked a young girl if some sort of celebration was in process, he was told: "There is. We celebrate our right to live. We are starving. As soon as enough of us get together we are going to the bakeries and each of us will take a loaf of bread." Ultimately Jefferson Davis had to come out and personally intervene to quell the bread riot. Such urban women, along with farm women trying to raise a crop, feed their families, and keep body and soul together in the face of absent husbands and ever-lengthening war, found that privation and anger gnawed away at their Confederate patriotism, and as the women became disillusioned, their sentiment quickly and profoundly affected the southern troops. By the final year and a half of the war, southern morale slumped severely, and not even Lee's military leadership skills could completely overcome plaintive appeals from wives to their husbands in the ranks. As northern forces grew larger and better supplied, southern forces thinned, grew hungrier, and began to desert in increasing numbers. It had become, at last, a war of attrition.

CHALLENGES TO SLAVERY

The institution of slavery began to disintegrate in the midst of war. In those expanding regions where Union armies were in control, white owners generally fled. Slaves very seldom sought vengeance against their former masters, and little wanton destruction of plantation mansions occurred. Rather, blacks often wanted to in effect withdraw from the whole system of staple crop production for world markets and sought the independence of a peasant-like subsistence economy. Northern military commanders and soon agents of various northern philanthropic endeavors, come south to provide assistance and direction to the ex-slaves, or freedmen (whether they desired such help or not), ex-

perimented with redistributing land, found northern white managers to employ the former slaves in cotton production, and hoped to imbue blacks with the supposed habits of Yankee industry and thrift. Blacks, just out from under southern white owners, were seldom eager to submit to northern white supervision. But in Union-held areas of the South, southern slavery as it had existed prior to 1861 was no more.

In Rebel-controlled areas, the absence of so many white men who had previously managed farms and plantations and disciplined the slave workforce led to a sharp decline in agricultural output. Slaves, eager for self-control, quickly took advantage of the slackening supervision and moved, often cautiously and subtly, to carve out new arenas for independent action and limited freedom. The Confederate government also impressed the labor services of thousands of slaves, putting them to service on behalf of the government or the military. In so doing the Rebel government abolished the old idea that the white owner's control over his slaves was complete. Many slaveholders, anticipating the advance of Union forces, moved their households — including slaves — to the interior of their states or even westward toward Texas to avoid capture and emancipation, and such dislocation and the resulting confusion weakened discipline and provided many creative slaves with opportunities to seize increased initiative and avoid older forms of subservience. The institution of slavery depended on stability and the unquestioned authority of experienced white owners, and in the chaos of total war both prerequisites withered away. Slavery was dying from changes occurring within the Confederacy even as the Confederacy fought desperately to hold on to the institution.

JOBS AND RACIAL TENSIONS IN THE NORTH

Northern society was also affected by the war in ways little foreseen at the outset. Initially many northern businesses suffered, some because they lost southern markets (for example, for the kind of rugged shoes slaveholders purchased for their slaves) and others because financial and investment markets were disrupted by the uncertainty of the future. The textile industry suffered from the interruption of cotton supplies, although eventually Union army purchases of woolen goods allowed textile manufacturers to return to prosperity. During the first winter of the war, 1861-1862, the substantial loss of more than $300 million in uncollectible southern debts caused a brief depression in the North. There were some temporary shortages of laborers, but continued European immigration helped replace men then in uniform, and the expanding use of labor-saving technology allowed smaller numbers of rural workers to increase farm production. For example, the mechanical mowers and reapers perfected by Cyrus and William McCormick replaced four, five, even six farmhands, and during the war years the McCormicks doubled their sales to seventy thousand machines annually. Crop failures in Europe so increased demand for American grains that even with enhanced production, prices continued to rise — undermining, by and by, southern hopes for so-called cotton diplomacy.

Of course, the North was not free of racism. Many Peace Democrats objected to the continuation of the war and worked to end the conflict by accepting southern secession. Opposition to the war sometimes originated in something like pacifist sentiment, but more often there was hostility to the Republican Party, abolitionism, and the disruption of normal business channels. Troops generally did not fight their southern brothers for an abstraction like the Union, and many were not opposed to the South's acceptance of slavery. As the war dragged on and deaths mounted, this northern weariness with war threatened Lincoln's presidency and his reelection in 1864. After the war aim became emancipation, northern opposition to the war became more militant. So-called Copperheads in sections of the Midwest actively tried to impede the war effort, in large part because they feared that the abolition of slavery would lead to the migration northward of blacks. Copperheads and their supporters opposed the anticipated competition with blacks for jobs and feared their social presence.

The word *miscegenation* was coined in reference to a fear and repulsion toward expected racial intermarriage. Irish immigrants often shared these racial fears because they knew they would suffer most from job competition with blacks, and, because they were generally too poor to purchase exemptions from the draft, they felt they had to bear too heavy a brunt of the burden of conscription. This anger boiled over in four days of brutal rioting in New York City beginning on July 13, 1863. A mob of mostly Irish Catholics rampaged through the city, striking out against blacks, wealthy Republicans, draft offices, and even an orphanage for black children. Federal troops fresh from the Union victory at Gettysburg had to be rushed to the nation's largest city to quell the violence. By the time the riot was squelched, over a hundred people were dead. Many northern citizens were horrified by the violence and racism exhibited in New York and raised funds to assist victims, but the riots vividly indicated the depth of racial tensions and the frustration with the war.

As northern industry adjusted and adapted to wartime needs, the economy began to boom. Wages did not keep up with inflation, so some workers suffered, but the number of jobs, overall production, and profits all grew. The expansion was not just in the total number of small mom-and-pop operations but rather in the scale of production. Wartime contracts proved a boon to many manufacturers, and along with the increased scale came improved managerial and accounting techniques, the application of rudimentary statistics to such things as clothing manufacturing — determining the optimum range of sizes among a specified lot of uniforms, for example — and more sophisticated methods of planning, organization, communication, and application of labor-saving technology within large-scale enterprises. Distraught workers, suffering from wages that did not keep up with prices or fearing displacement by technology, showed a new militancy by striking and organizing labor unions. Some thirteen national unions organized by occupation resulted, and manufacturers responded by blacklisting union members, hiring strikebreakers, and sharing information about labor activities. Union members won some of their demands, but manufacturers held the upper hand and even on occasion could call on federal troops to help. Company profits soared as wartime demand increased their markets.

NATIONAL LEGISLATION FOR THE NATIONAL ECONOMY

The pro-business Republicans, completely in control of Congress since the departure of the southern members, pushed through a series of acts that served to modernize and centralize the national economy, with long-range implications only imperfectly understood at the time. In 1861 the Morrill Tariff Act of March 2, 1861, raised duties generally from 5 to 10 percent, and subsequent revisions of the tariff in 1862 and 1864 increased duties substantially, benefiting company owners more than the consumers, but the result strengthened the nation's industrial base. On May 20, 1862, Congress passed the Homestead Act, offering 160 acres of public land free to any person who would reside on (and presumably farm) the land for five continuous years. That same year Congress created the Department of Agri-

The Gettysburg Address

Abraham Lincoln's unheralded "remarks" following Edward Everett's lengthy oration at the dedication of the cemetery for the Union war dead at Gettysburg in November 1863 are generally considered the greatest speech ever delivered in the United States, and one of this nation's defining statements of purpose. This is the complete text.

Fourscore and seven years ago our fathers brought forth on this continent, a new nation, conceived in liberty, and dedicated to the proposition that all men are created equal.

Now we are engaged in a great civil war, testing whether that nation, or any nation so conceived and so dedicated, can long endure. We are met on a great battlefield of that war. We have come to dedicate a portion of that field, as a final resting-place for those who here gave their lives that that nation might live. It is altogether fitting and proper that we should do this.

But, in a larger sense, we cannot dedicate—we cannot consecrate—we cannot hallow—this ground. The brave men, living and dead, who struggled here, have consecrated it, far above our poor power to add or detract. The world will little note, nor long remember what we say here, but it can never forget what they did here. It is for us the living, rather, to be dedicated here to the unfinished work which they who fought here have thus far so nobly advanced. It is rather for us to be here dedicated to the great task remaining before us—that from these honored dead we take increased devotion to that cause for which they gave the last full measure of devotion—that we here highly resolve that these dead shall not have died in vain—that this nation, under God, shall have a new birth of freedom—and that government of the people, by the people, for the people, shall not perish from the earth.

---

culture and by the terms of the Morrill Land Grant Act of that year gave each state thirty thousand acres of public land per congressman; this land could be used or sold, the proceeds of which had to be employed to promote agricultural, engineering, and military education in the various states. From this legislation came the series of land-grant universities that still serve hundreds of thousands of students.

The business-dominated Congress passed on July 1, 1862, the Pacific Railroad Act, authorizing the first transcontinental railroad, running from Omaha, Nebraska, to Sacramento, California, and connecting at Ogden, Utah. This act was complemented in 1864 with the Northern Pacific Railroad Act. Both acts chartered corporations to construct the rail lines and gave them loans valued at millions of dollars and generous grants of millions of acres of land. The complete line linked the West Coast to the East, and the Homestead Act seemingly had primed the land in between to prosper.

The proposed transcontinental railroad enjoyed other advantages, too. For example, it used the rail gauge (the distance between the tracks) of many northern rail lines that had already been standardized, making it possible for rail cars to move from line to line as need arose.

As previously noted, early in the war Congress had, by passing the Legal Tender Act (1862), authorized the

Confederate Dead   Rebel troops killed in the bloody battle of Fredericksburg here are interred in December 1862 as a chaplain says prayers.

issuance of paper currency that was guaranteed by the federal treasury as legal tender — that is, acceptable in payment of debt. The National Banking Acts of 1863, 1864, and 1865, which allowed a series of national banks to issue uniform currency and by a tax on state bank notes essentially drove out of circulation competing paper currencies of fluctuating value, both standardized the banking system and created a more dependable and straightforward money supply.

If measured simply in terms of output, the early dislocations that the war caused in the northern economy were, in the last year and a half of the war, cancelled out by the growing boom in war-related productivity. The war did not spur northern industrialism if one simply compares the rate of growth in the economy during the war years (1861-1865) with the immediately preceding years. But if one considers the institutional, infrastructural changes in the northern economy during the war years — the development of a standardized banking and currency system, the creation of a nationwide rail network, the better environment for industrial success provided by more than ample tariff protection, the growth in agricultural production that resulted from the Homestead Act and the application to agriculture of new technology, and the development of entrepreneurial, managerial, and accounting expertise — then clearly these years laid the foundation for the phenomenal economic and industrial growth that characterized late nineteenth-century America. Here occurred the birth of modern America.

ᦿ A New Kind of War

The scale and destructiveness of the battles at Antietam, Gettysburg, and Vicksburg brought home to civilian and military leaders that this was a new kind of war. The telegraph permitted instantaneous communication. The railroad allowed the rapid movement of troops and supplies over long distances. Introduction of the rifled musket made obsolete older military tactics, though officers were slower to recognize this change than were foot soldiers. The military tactics that commanders had learned at West Point assumed the use of muskets firing the so-called minié ball. Such muzzle-loading weapons had an effective range of less than a hundred yards, and so poor was their accuracy that defenders fired in volleys, hoping that a random minié ball might hit an onrushing enemy. Given the short effective range and the time it took to reload, onrushing troops, if they were numerous enough to withstand the initial volley, could by rushing forward with fixed bayonets overrun defenders before the latter could reload. Hence traditional military wisdom taught that massed attackers could overwhelm even well-positioned defenders. So Civil War leaders often ordered infantry offensive moves in the expectation that the defenders would break.

But over and over again, as with the Union infantry attacks against Confederate defenders at Mayre's Heights or Pickett's charge on the Union line at Gettysburg, the defenders more than held their ground and inflicted horrendous casualties on the charging enemy. A new kind of weapon had fatally changed the calculus of combat. The rifled musket, utilizing grooves inside the barrel that cause the bullet to spin, offered — like a spinning as opposed to a tumbling football — far better accuracy and extended the effective killing range out to four hundred or more yards. The improved accuracy and range now meant that soldiers in a defensive posture could get off two, three, or even four deadly volleys before attackers came within bayonet range. Suddenly the advantage had shifted drastically to the defenders, and officers continued to use the old tactic of infantry charges only at the cost of staggering losses. Thousands of soldiers on both sides needlessly lost their lives in futile charges before commanders finally comprehended the changes new weapon technology demanded in military strategy. And, in the brutal months following Gettysburg and Vicksburg, the Union forces learned how to wage a new kind of combat — total war, a method of combat whose object was not simply to defeat opposing armies but so to damage the opposing societies that they would lose the will and the means to continue fighting. The Civil War entered a new and even more terrible final phase.

The concept of total war, put into practice in the final year of the war, was not the only lesson learned from the wholesale death rates of the Civil War. Soldiers north and south discovered that something they had previously believed was wrong. At the beginning, soldiers had a romantic attitude toward war: it would be filled with adventure, high camaraderie, courage, and a certain etiquette wherein one held back from brutal murder. Courage was initially understood as almost a magical concept, practically a shield that protected its bearer from death. Courage allowed officers to stand and direct the action of their men seemingly oblivious to the hail of gunfire; courage meant that men could advance toward opposing ranks confident that their lives would be spared if they remained steadfast. The new rifles, however, riddled the romantic, magical mantle of courage. Men who saw thousands of their comrades mowed down in a single day, who came face to face with the harsh impersonality of death, suddenly realized that courage was obsolete, even useless. The good and true died along with the cowards; the brutality of war was blind to individual merit.

ᦿ The Grapes of Wrath: Faith in Battle

The experience of war also transformed many soldiers' religious beliefs. Most mainstream clergy in both regions had forthrightly supported the war in religious terms. A significant component of northern abolitionism had been Christian opposition to slavery as sinful, and most abolitionists saw the war as a religious crusade to free the nation from a terrible evil. Others in the North felt just as strongly that the nation was the expression of divine will, that secession was practically a form of blasphemy, and that God would ensure Union victory. This northern view of the Civil War as a moral and religious endeavor was captured in Julia Ward Howe's great hymn, "The Battle Hymn of the Republic," written in the fall of 1861:

Mine eyes have seen the glory of the coming of the Lord;
He is trampling out the vintage where the grapes
of wrath are stored;
He has loosed the fateful lightning
of his terrible swift sword:
His truth is marching on.

Many Union soldiers went off to war with the full blessings of their families and churches, confident they were doing God's will and sure of success. Individual Union soldiers often expected to be protected by Providence from danger and death.

Early defeats strained this confidence in Union victory and personal safety, but in the final year of war northern ministers returned to the theme of providential purpose as they sought to reconcile the terrible costs in deaths with the concept of a just God. In his second inaugural address, President Lincoln pondered the cause and continuation of the war. "The Almighty has His own purposes," he suggested. If the nation supposed, he said, that slavery was the cause of the war and an offense against God that must be punished, then God might will that "this mighty scourge of war . . . continue, until all the wealth piled by the bondman's two hundred and fifty years of unrequited toil shall be sunk, and until every drop of blood drawn with the lash, shall be paid with another drawn with the sword, as was said three thousand years ago, so

still it must be said 'the judgments of the Lord are true and righteous altogether.' "

Southern clergy also had supported slavery, secession, the Confederacy, and the felt necessity of war, certain they too were doing God's will. Both forming the new nation (God was explicitly invoked in the Confederate constitution) and fighting for its independence were interpreted as legitimate acts of Christian duty. Clergy in each region often condemned the enemy in harsh language, and both were quick to find biblical justification for their position and confident that God would ultimately grant them victory. On an individual level, southern soldiers also believed that, if they were Christians, God would protect them from danger even in the midst of combat. Presbyterian minister R. L. Dabney told Stonewall Jackson's troops that "you need not be trying to dodge shot or shell or minié. Every one strikes just where the Lord permits it to strike, and nowhere else, and you are perfectly safe when the missiles of death fly thickest until Jehovah permits you to be stricken." The implication was that Jehovah would not choose to have a devout disciple stricken.

❈ IN THEIR OWN WORDS

Lincoln's Second Inaugural Address

A month before his assassination, Lincoln delivered his second inaugural address, reaching back to ancient Hebrew prophecy in an attempt to fathom the enormity of the struggle through which the nation had passed and the meaning of slavery for its people. Here are the concluding paragraphs of his brief speech.

. . . One-eighth of the whole population were colored slaves, not distributed generally over the Union, but localized in the southern part of it. These slaves constituted a peculiar and powerful interest. All knew that this interest was, somehow, the cause of the war. To strengthen, perpetuate, and extend this interest was the object for which the insurgents would rend the Union, even by war; while the government claimed no right to do more than restrict the territorial enlargement of it. Neither party expected for the war, the magnitude, or the duration, which it has already attained. Neither anticipated that the cause of the conflict might

cease with, or even before, the conflict itself should cease. Each looked for an easier triumph, and a result less fundamental and astonishing.

Both read the same Bible, and pray to the same God; and each invokes His aid against the other. It may seem strange that any men should dare to ask a just God's assistance in wringing their bread from the sweat of other men's faces; but let us judge not that we be not judged. The prayers of both could not be answered; that of neither has been answered fully.

The Almighty has His own purposes. "Woe unto the world because of offenses! For it must needs be that offenses come; but woe to that man by whom the offense cometh!" If we shall suppose that American slavery is one of those offenses which, in the providence of God, must needs come, but which, having continued through His appointed time, He now wills to remove, and that He gives to both North and South, this terrible war, as the woe due to those by whom the

offense came, shall we discern therein any departure from those divine attributes which the believers in a living God always ascribe to Him? Fondly do we hope—fervently do we pray—that this mighty scourge of war may speedily pass away. Yet, if God wills that it continue, until all the wealth piled by the bondman's two hundred and fifty years of unrequited toil shall be sunk, and every drop of blood drawn with the lash, shall be paid by another drawn with the sword, as was said three thousand years ago, so still it must be said "the judgments of the Lord are true and righteous altogether."

With malice toward none; with charity for all; with firmness in the right, as God gives us to see the right, let us strive on to finish the work we are in; to bind up the nation's wounds; to care for him who shall have borne the battle, and for his widow, and his orphan—to do all which may achieve and cherish a just, and a lasting peace, among ourselves, and with all nations.

But as with the concept of courage, through wartime experience of the confusion and chaos of battle, with men left and right falling victim to rifled bullets and artillery shellings, soldiers learned that devout Christian soldiers often fell in combat, too. Whatever God's ultimate plan was for the cause of North or South, individual soldiers — courageous, Christian men — clearly met instant death on the battlefield and died more slowly but just as horribly from wounds, disease, and injury. Recognition of this reality affected army morale and increased soldiers' fear and dread of battle, but it also contributed to waves of religious revivals in both armies, especially in those of the South. Most of a soldier's life was spent waiting, with short episodes of battle usually separated by weeks or months of camp life. Here men — lonely and bored and with time on their hands — had time to think about the fearful possibility of death, and the scale of combat and the escalating casualties evaporated earlier confidence that their courage or faith would insulate them from danger. Such troops represented a fertile field for ministers, who could approach the men at the point of their immediate concern and offer them, through conversion and the Christian promise of eternal life in heaven, both ultimate victory over death and the assurance that they would see loved ones again. Officers quickly noted and approved of revivals and conversions among their troops because it made for more contented soldiers, more willing to risk their lives in combat. After 1863 massive revivals swept through both armies, producing thousands of converts and helping define the character of the participants' final comprehension of an event that otherwise was so huge and overwhelming that it passed understanding. In the final months of the war, clergy on both sides helped civilians and troops come to terms with how the great conflict seemed to be concluding, a resolution that was understood in the context of competing versions of God's plan for the nation.

TOWARD UNION VICTORY

The year 1863 had begun with the issuance of Lincoln's Emancipation Proclamation, made politically feasible by the Union victory three and a half months earlier at Antietam, which profoundly altered the northern war aim and destroyed the Confederacy's hopes for European intervention on its behalf. The great Union victory at Gettysburg in July of that year provided the occasion, on November 19, 1863, for ceremonies dedicating a national cemetery for the Union dead at Gettysburg. A huge crowd gathered at the site, a gently rolling hillside just to the south and east of the small town, to hear the major address by Edward Everett, a renowned orator (and the Constitutional Union Party's vice-presidential candidate in 1860), who for two hours delivered a flowery speech from memory. President Lincoln, invited almost as an afterthought, had also been asked to give remarks, but clearly Everett was intended to be the main attraction.

In fewer than three hundred words, however, Lincoln captured the meaning of the occasion and the purpose of the American experiment in liberty with stunning eloquence, and his address is one of the great orations in history and a gem of American literature. As the Emancipation Proclamation had changed the purpose of the Civil War, so the Gettysburg Address revised the ultimate meaning of the American nation. Subtly amending the Constitution by the moral power of his language, Lincoln made equality as well as freedom the ultimate goal of the nation.

⬥ Grant's New Strategy

Yet the Civil War was still to be decided in late 1863, and the decision would be made on the battlefield. In ret-

rospect it is evident that the combination of southern losses at Gettysburg and Vicksburg, and the ascendancy of General Grant, presaged final Union victory. But the beginning of the end became even clearer after a Union defeat of Confederate forces at Chattanooga on November 25, 1863, opened the entire heartland of the South to Union control.

Following Grant's capture of Vicksburg, Lincoln had named him commander of all Union troops west of the Appalachians. Quickly Grant moved to shore up Union troops near Chattanooga, where Confederate success under General Braxton Bragg, reinforced by troops sent via rail by General Lee, threatened a major southern victory that might recoup some of the morale lost at Gettysburg and Vicksburg. But Grant also rushed in additional troops by rail, and the Union forces broke the siege that the Confederates had placed on Chattanooga and daringly attacked southern positions on Lookout Mountain, sometimes with the battles taking place amid and above low-lying clouds. The Union victory gave the North control of Tennessee, and Atlanta lay little over a hundred miles to the southeast. On March 9, 1864, Lincoln elevated Grant to lieutenant general and commander in chief of all Union armies. As the year began Grant and Lincoln laid plans to take both Atlanta and Richmond, tightening the vise on the remaining Confederate forces. Lincoln had finally found a general who knew how to fight, and jointly they resolved to bring the war to a conclusion by coordinating Union armies in the West and the East and bearing down on Rebel forces in Virginia with such unrelenting determination that Lee would not be able to spare troops to send to the West. The war was about to enter an even more brutal, horrible stage.

In early May Grant sent the 100,000-man Army of the Potomac, under the immediate command of General Meade, across the Rapidan River and directly into the Wilderness, a thickly forested wasteland just west of Chancellorsville. On May 5-7, 1864, Lee, with sixty thousand men, attacked Grant's right flank. The fighting was fierce. Lee outmaneuvered Grant and inflicted more than eighteen thousand Union casualties (while suffering ten thousand casualties in his own army). Unlike previous Union generals, Grant did not panic and retreat; instead, he moved his army to the left, attempting to outflank Lee. But Lee moved rapidly, just in time to get his forces in defensive trenches near Spotsylvania Court House. Again Grant attacked frontally, and after five more bloody days (May 8-12) and another twelve thousand Union casualties, Lee's outnumbered army still held its positions. Grant, though, with bulldog tenacity, was not about to call off his advance. "I propose to fight it out along this line if it takes all summer," he wrote to General Halleck in Washington.

Grant intended to wear down Lee's forces no matter how many casualties he took, grimly realizing that the North could afford the losses and that Lee could not. Backing away from the field of battle at Spotsylvania Court House, Grant once more looped south and east before turning again to attack Lee's new, and solid, defensive positions at Cold Harbor, a scant nine miles east of Richmond. A breathtakingly bold but foolish Union assault against Lee's defenders cost Grant seven thousand men in one cruel hour — his troops had pinned the addresses of their next of kin onto their uniforms before they marched toward the enemy. Grant again backed away but made preparations to sweep to the south and then west once more. This time he crossed the James River and aimed at Petersburg, Virginia's rail center south of Richmond. He began to coordinate a long siege operation against Petersburg and Richmond,

Sherman's Army in Georgia   Marching across Georgia, Sherman's troops destroyed everything in their path that was militarily useful or whose destruction might damage civilian morale. Here, "Blue Bellies" rip up railroad tracks. This image was reproduced as a "stereopticon" so that a viewer, with the help of a cheap hand-held device, could see it in three dimensions.

both now defended by Lee's intrepid troops, so reduced in number that they could no longer risk offensive action against Grant's forces. In one savage month Grant had suffered sixty thousand casualties — more men than Lee commanded — but fresh reinforcements swelled the Army of the Potomac to a larger size than it had had at the beginning of the campaign.

Although superior northern resources were now showing their effect, to the war-weary northern public Grant appeared to be outmatched by Lee time and time again. Grant, called by northern critics "the butcher," was widely thought to be sending his soldiers to death with almost reckless abandon. Opposition to Lincoln mounted along with Grant's rising casualty figures. Lincoln believed in Grant and the eventual success of his dogged method of fighting, but would the disconsolate public vote him out of office and settle for peace at any price, even at the price of maintaining slavery in the South? Could Lincoln politically outlast Lee militarily? Lincoln feared not, as Grant's siege of Petersburg and Richmond settled into the misery, death, and seeming intractability of trench warfare. As the 1864 presidential elections loomed, Lincoln seriously expected to lose.

Developments on another military front ultimately saved Lincoln's presidency. Within days of the Army of the Potomac's crossing of the Rapidan to begin its slow, crunching movement toward Richmond, General Sherman on May 7, 1864, launched his fateful operation to move from southeastern Tennessee toward Atlanta. The Confederate defense of northwest Georgia was led by the shrewd Joseph E. Johnston, who, although distrusted by President Davis, effectively used his army — about two-thirds the size of Sherman's hundred-thousand-man force — to slow down Sherman's progress even if he was unable to defeat the Union invasion. But Jefferson Davis needed more than delaying tactics. He knew the South was running out of manpower, military materiel, and even the civilian will to continue the war, and Lee was pinned down in Richmond. Davis reasoned that the Confederacy's last best hope was to win a dramatic victory during the election summer; perhaps then the northern public, war-weary too, frustrated with Lincoln, and angry with Grant for his expenditure of men, would reject Lincoln in the fall 1864 elections and choose a Peace Democrat for president.

Davis kept waiting for news of victory from Johnston, but Johnston, uncommunicative in the best of circumstances, could send his president no news of success and instead slowly kept falling back, retarding Sherman but unable to defeat him. Finally a success-starved Da-

vis removed Johnston in mid-July and replaced him with General John B. Hood, whose aggressive nature was suggested by the fact that, although he had lost an arm at Gettysburg and a leg at Chickamauga, he still had himself strapped into his saddle so he could lead his men into battle. Hood, following Davis's wishes, changed from Johnston's wily defensive strategy to a daring offensive one, attacking Sherman's superior numbers in several futile engagements. Hood's losses were more than double Sherman's. Sherman crushed Hood and took Atlanta on September 2, 1864, telegraphing Lincoln that "Atlanta is ours, and fairly won." The news buoyed both Lincoln and the northern public and carried Lincoln to a solid victory in the November elections.

∞ Bringing the War Home to the South

The South was now to learn what total war meant. Early in the summer, Jefferson Davis had sent Jubal A. Early out of the northern Shenandoah Valley to make a desperation raid through Maryland — Early got to within five miles of Washington — hoping to take pressure off Lee in Richmond. But Grant did not relax his siege; instead, he sent battle-hardened Philip H. Sheridan to the Shenandoah with orders not only to defeat Early's army when it returned but also to so destroy the valley that it could no longer participate in the war. Sheridan's orders were to leave the area so barren that a crow flying over it would have to carry its own rations, and Sheridan carried out those orders with grim determination.

With Sheridan having proven the possibility and effectiveness of that kind of total warfare against an entire society, not just an army, Grant and Sherman now proposed to turn loose total war on Georgia. General Hood had pulled his army back together and moved into Tennessee, hoping both to cut Sherman's supply lines and perhaps even to lure Sherman into chasing after him. But Sherman ignored the loss of supplies and the temptation to track and defeat Hood's reduced forces; he had bigger fish to fry. Sherman meant to live off the land as he sent two giant columns of troops on a 285-mile trek across the state toward Savannah, destroying everything his own armies did not need along a 60-mile-wide swath. The destruction that Sherman wrought stunned Georgians and even many of his own soldiers. Livestock were killed not only to feed the Union troops but also simply to deprive southerners of their use; barns, bridges, fences, public buildings, and crops were burned; railroads were torn up and their rails heated and wrapped around trees — "Sherman neckties" — so they could never be reused. Even private homes were ransacked, clothes scattered, and pictures cut out of their frames. Sherman wanted to make war so unspeakably brutal, so hellish, that he would totally demoralize Georgians and by extension all southerners. Pioneering a new kind of warfare, Sherman broke the back of southern resistance. Seeing what was about to befall them, the leaders of Savannah had the good sense to surrender on December 21, in advance of Sherman's actual arrival, hence protecting the beautiful city from total destruction. Sherman again telegraphed Lincoln with good news: "I beg to present you, as a Christmas gift, the city of Savannah." Within weeks Sherman turned north, bringing his trademark devastation through South Carolina — a state he really wanted to punish — and into North Carolina, planning to join forces with Meade and Grant in Virginia for the final crushing of Lee and the Confederacy.

The northern public may have despaired of the war ever ending in the spring of 1864, but their woes were as nothing compared to those of the southern home front. Widespread destruction of homes, farms, and cities; severe shortages of everything from coffee and salt to necessary medicines; near famine in many areas; displaced people white and black who voluntarily (or involuntarily, in the case of most blacks) had fled the advance of invading armies; a general wearing out of the social infrastructure and the individual commitment to the war — all were taking their toll on southern morale. Thousands of Confederate soldiers had left their posts and returned home, at least for a while, to give desperately needed help to loved ones. Lee's armies at the end were at less than half strength. Southern women, who early in the war had supported the cause and been willing to bear the sacrifice, by 1864 wondered if the sacrifices being asked of them were not too great. When the womenfolk began to give up hope and expressed their despair in pitiful letters to their husbands, their congressmen, even to Jefferson Davis himself, it is not surprising that soldiers' motivation to continue fighting wilted. In the midst of the despondency and defeatism many southerners began to reconsider two cornerstones of their original optimism, their certainty that God favored their cause and that slavery must be defended at all costs.

❧ The Last Days of Southern Slavery

In 1861 most southern clergy had been certain that God supported both the institution of slavery and the cause of secession, and clergy had helped create and sustain southern nationalism. Southern patriots assumed that they would win because God was on their side. But the succession of defeats and the lengthening casualty lists began to sap southern confidence. As morale sagged and then collapsed, southerners tried to understand their change in fortune, and as one would expect in a nineteenth-century society in which Christianity was the overwhelmingly dominant religion and shaper of worldviews, many southerners turned to their religion and religious leaders for insight and explanation. If God controlled everything ultimately to his purpose, then he must have a hand in Confederate losses. Because of earlier expectations that as a Christian slaveholding society the South could expect military success, perhaps military defeats were the consequence of the South not being sufficiently Christian — or of slaveholders slipping in their responsibilities as Christian masters. Perhaps God was causing the South to be defeated as chastisement for its moral failings. Hence, as the war moved into its final stages, southern ministers began calling laypeople to renewed piety and warning slaveholders that they must be kind masters and promote the spread of the gospel among their bondspeople. Religious leaders' calls for reforming the master-slave relationship included protection for slave families and marriage and teaching slaves to read so that they might study the Bible. Southern greed, violence, and profanity were also attacked as possible reasons why God might be withholding his protective hand from the Confederacy. Religion did not cause a collapse in southern morale; defeats did. Instead, religion sought to offer southerners some possible explanation for their wartime plight. The search for religious meaning also carried the suggestion that God's purposes were larger than the success or failure of the Confederacy itself, and following final defeat many southerners returned to this theme, the search for God's ultimate plan for the South.

After the Emancipation Proclamation, and as thousands of northern blacks joined the Union armies and hundreds of thousands of southern slaves fled to Union lines where many either became soldiers or performed valuable noncombatant work, thoughtful southerners also came to understand that blacks offered yet another advantage to the North. For by now southern manpower and resources were running thin. In the aftermath of Gettysburg, southern newspapers occasionally began to suggest what months before had been unthinkable — that the South should free a portion of its slaves who would then fight in the southern army on behalf of Confederate independence. In other words, the South's war aim was shifting from support of slavery at whatever the cost to support of independence, even at the price of giving up slavery. Initially this seemed a preposterous argument to most southerners, but in late 1863 practical individuals, looking both at the battlefield and the homefront, began to examine all alternatives that might produce military success.

In January 1864, Confederate general Patrick R. Cleburne formally proposed using black soldiers to his commanding officer, General Johnston. Without making any decision, Johnston simply forwarded Cleburne's proposal to President Jefferson Davis. Other Confederate generals protested Cleburne's idea, arguing that if slaves (whom they considered a race of permanent children) could become real "men" and effective soldiers, then the whole southern conception of slavery and the character of blacks was flawed — a possibility they could not entertain. Davis was enough of a politician to be cautious of public discussion at first of such an explosive concept, but he was also enough of a soldier to understand that only such a bold casting aside of old ideas and traditions might be able to secure the South's independence. In the final desperate months of 1864, other southern leaders began to reach a similar conclusion.

On November 7, 1864, Davis sent the Confederate Congress a message calling for increased utilization of blacks by the army. The government, he suggested, should buy the slaves so impressed, presumably prior to freeing them. This measure met violent opposition in Congress, and not until General Lee himself in a letter on February 18, 1865, supported the arming and freeing of slaves was passage of the bill ensured. On March 13, 1865, five days before it adjourned for the last time, the Confederate Congress passed and President Davis signed "An Act to increase the military force of the Confederate States." The act did not actually provide for freeing the black soldiers, but the orders eventually issued by the War Department made emancipation clear. Several weeks later, recruiting and training of black troops began in Richmond and other Virginia towns. But now it was too late. Military resistance ended before any black Confederates could see military action.

❧ The War Ends

Throughout the bitter winter of 1864-1865, with Union and Rebel forces locked in deadly combat around Richmond, conditions in the trenches brought indescribable hardship and horror to the soldiers. As the southern troops were slowly running out of supplies, the news of the loss of Atlanta, then of Savannah, and finally that Sherman was marching northward to unite his forces with Grant's caused southern troop morale to plummet. By the late winter months, hundreds of Confederate soldiers were deserting every night, and Lee's army at the end had shrunk to only thirty thousand men. By contrast, Grant's armies stood at 115,000, larger than when the campaign to take Richmond had begun.

Lee understood that he could not hold Richmond much longer, and in the last days of March 1865, he was planning to pull his men from their defensive position in the trenches, move quickly west to the rail connection at Lynchburg, and from there try to move his troops by train south into North Carolina where he could reinforce General Johnston's army. But Union armies moved before Lee could effect his final move. On April 2, Sheridan took the last railroad into Richmond, and his forward units began to cut their way through the thin Confederate defenses on the outskirts of the city. All that Lee could do was wait for the cover of darkness and then evacuate his remaining troops from Richmond, abandoning the city.

As Jefferson Davis sat worshiping in church that cold Sunday morning, a messenger slipped in and whispered to the president of the Confederacy that Lee could hold the city only a few more hours. Davis quietly got up and left the service. All over town versions of this scene reoccurred, as government officials scurried to gather essential papers. That evening the Confederate government, together with such of its archives as could be hurriedly packed up, was on a train to Danville, escaping just hours before the capital fell to Grant. Lee's army fled west, too. Famished and with their clothes in tatters and their cause hopeless, they marched only out of respect for General Lee. Grant was fast on their trail. The day after Lee and Davis left, with the city still smoldering from fires the departing Rebel soldiers had set, Union forces entered the city and hoisted the American flag. The following day President Abraham Lincoln himself came to the Confederate capital and walked through the streets, thronged by jubilant slaves. The long war was at last winding down, and Lincoln could begin to taste the fruit of his determination and leadership.

Lee's intention was to hurry to Lynchburg, some sixty miles west. But Grant's troops pushed west too; there were several minor skirmishes, and by April 7 it became clear to Lee that Grant had scotched his desperate attempt to get to Lynchburg and had cut off escape routes to the south. Further fighting would be senseless and futile. That day Lee indicated to Grant that he was willing to discuss terms for surrender. Some of Lee's staff suggested dispersing the army into the mountains and

launching guerrilla warfare, but Lee knew full well that the South was already devastated and that such "bushwhacking" would "take the country years to recover from." No, the time had come to end hostilities.

By an exchange of letters Lee and Grant arranged to meet in the parlor of a private home near the little village called Appomattox Courthouse. Lee, a strikingly handsome man, arrived looking splendid in his finest uniform, a sword at his side. Grant, mud-splattered, a cigar in his mouth, and characteristically disheveled, came to Appomattox to discuss the final terms magnanimous in temperament. Lincoln had ordered Grant to be generous: "Give them the most liberal terms," Lin-

A Western Sod House   Prairie sod was frequently used as building material to construct a warm home on the treeless western prairie during initial settlement in the Civil War era and after. This photograph was taken in Dakota Territory.

coln had written. "Let them have their horses to plow with, and, if you like, their guns to shoot crows with. I want no one punished." Grant, sensitive beneath his gruff exterior, agreed with such generosity. When Union troops began to fire their guns in celebration and shout hurrahs, Grant put a stop to such demonstrations out of regard for the feelings of the defeated southern troops. Later that day Grant sent rations to the hungry Confederate soldiers. Men in blue and gray mingled with a surprising lack of animosity, their hate spent in combat. Three days later, on April 12 — four years to the day since the firing on Fort Sumter that had begun the war — Lee's troops marched across the field to stack arms, the symbol of surrender. The Union troops at the ceremony began a bugle call and shifted their arms to an honor salute out of respect for their defeated enemy. The southern commander, in reply, saluted and ordered his men to march forward in honor formation. The war, which had in its fighting turned brutal and savage, ended with dignity and mutual respect between the armies.

Within a month the final hostilities had ceased. Less than a week later, General Johnston surrendered his remaining troops to General Sherman at Durham Station, North Carolina. On May 4 the last of the Confederate troops east of the Mississippi River surrendered at Citronelle, Alabama, and on May 26, General Edmund Kirby Smith, who had often roamed the trans-Mississippi South as though it were his own fiefdom, surrendered in New Orleans.

Jefferson Davis did not give up so easily, urging southern soldiers to become guerrilla fighters in the hills and woods. But the southern people could not stand any more fighting, as Lee accurately recognized. On May 10 the fleeing Davis was captured in Irwinsville, Georgia, and subsequently imprisoned for two years. And on April 14, just five days after Lee and Grant had exchanged terms at Appomattox Courthouse, Major Anderson once again raised the American flag over Fort Sumter.

Civil War Nurses Both women and men, many of them volunteers, served as nurses for men wounded or sick during the Civil War. Though primitive by today's standards, care of the sick and wounded made great advances over the standards that were possible during the Revolutionary War and other earlier conflicts.

That same evening in Washington, President and Mrs. Lincoln, celebrating at last the happy conclusion of the killing, went to Ford's Theatre for a bit of well-deserved relaxation. General Grant and his wife turned down an invitation to accompany them because Julia Grant did not enjoy Mary Lincoln's company. In the middle of the performance a deranged, unemployed, pro-Confederate actor, John Wilkes Booth, entered the presidential box and shot Lincoln point-blank in the head. Booth jumped from the box to the stage (breaking his leg in the fall) and with characteristic theatricality shouted to the audience before he escaped into the night, *"Sic semper tyrannis,"* the Virginia state motto that means "Such is always the fate of tyrants." That same evening a second conspirator wounded Secretary of State Seward with a knife. A third accomplice lost his nerve and failed to attack Vice President Andrew Johnson, as had been planned. The next day Lincoln died. Two weeks later Union troops found Booth, and either they shot him or he killed himself. Eight other accused accomplices were subsequently found and tried; four were hanged, the others imprisoned.

Despite northern suspicions at the time, Lincoln's assassination had been no official Confederate plot, no conspiracy inspired by the southern government or military leaders. Rather, a small band of crazed pro-Confederate fanatics had acted out their frustrations, totally unaware that the consequences of their action would not be favorable for the South. Lincoln was a man of great generosity of spirit, a superb politician with a perfect sense of timing, a master of using the English language to inspire and to heal. Never had the nation more needed his special gifts than in the aftermath of this great war. And now he was gone. Andrew Johnson took the oath of office on April 15, becoming president, and on April 21 the train left Washington carrying Lincoln's body back to Springfield, Illinois. Along the way thousands of citizens thronged the tracks, many in tears, to mourn his loss. No one could predict, at that sad moment, exactly what the depth of his loss would mean to the nation as it attempted in the coming months to heal the wounds and bitterness of secession and war.

Conclusion: The Meaning of the Civil War

What were the effects of the war? In some ways this is an easy question to answer, in other ways immensely complex. For many families the most immediate effect was the loss of loved ones. The total deaths resulting from the conflict add up to more than 620,000 (364,222 Union soldiers, 258,000 Confederates), almost equal to the total death toll of all other American wars combined, and when measured against the population by far the highest casualty rate in the nation's history. Approximately another 400,000 combatants were wounded but survived. Total casualties thus amounted to about one million — in a nation whose population, north and south, was thirty-one million. Hardly a fam-

ily was spared from this toll of death and injury, and for decades after the presence of men missing an arm or a leg bore silent testimony to the scale of the great conflict that had rent the nation.

Other losses were far more evident in the South than in the North. Many former Confederate soldiers seem to have lost confidence in themselves and in their abilities. As a result they responded to the need for economic and political change after the war with less creativity and less entrepreneurial skill than might otherwise have been the case. Some of them had learned in the midst of combat a callousness toward brutality and death that boded ill for political enemies and blacks in the period of Reconstruction; the terrorist activity of the Ku Klux Klan was one of the sad results. The wartime physical destruction in the South had been severe: homes, farms, churches, colleges, and public buildings had been destroyed or damaged on a massive scale. The total number of livestock in the South fell dramatically, with consequences not only for farming in an age of draft animals but also for food. Confederate financial losses were $2 billion in loans, and far more was lost in other assets. Southern slaveholders suffered an economic blow from the end of slavery, whatever the tremendous moral gain emancipation represented. Hardly a church, college, or family escaped the war unscathed financially.

But the changes wrought by the war were more significant than such tabulation of losses can suggest. Many of the changes turned out, in the long run, to be positive.

First and foremost was the end of slavery. It is hard to imagine slavery ending for decades without the war, and despite the difficulties that still remained for blacks, emancipation was the necessary first step. Most white southerners were not yet ready to accord blacks equal civil and social rights, and racism in the North as well meant than in many states there blacks could not vote and in a wide variety of other ways were not equal under the law. Yet limited freedom was better than chattel slavery, and Lincoln in the Gettysburg Address held out the promise of full equality. That promise had yet to be completely fulfilled, and the central agenda of the Era of Reconstruction that followed the Civil War was working out the place of blacks in American society. Although the most important consequence of the Civil War was emancipation, the slow and incomplete achievement of full equality has been a tragic theme throughout much of the nation's history ever since 1865.

Union victory in the Civil War made it practically

unthinkable forever after to talk of secession, and the balance of power between state sovereignty and national authority was permanently altered. No longer was the United States a union of States — rather, it had become a Union of states, a powerful nation whose central authority was clearly dominant. Individual states still had responsibilities for many local functions, but it was understood after 1865 that federal authority — as defined and limited by the Constitution — was supreme. No state could decide which national laws to follow.

The centralizing effect of the war was most evident in the realm of economics. As a result of wartime needs, the national government had devised a centralized banking system, a national currency, a system of high tariffs, and an income tax. Economic policy was advanced through promoting a transcontinental railroad network, the settlement of public lands by means of the Homestead Act, and the establishment of a system of colleges that emphasized a practical curriculum — primarily agriculture and engineering. Wartime necessity had also taught the nation methods of organization, habits of bureaucratization, and skills of administration that had not existed in prewar America.

Along with this increase in the scale of doing business came a subtle intellectual transformation, exemplified by the rise of large-scale voluntary agencies like the Sanitary Commission and the Christian Commission. The appearance of such volunteer agencies demonstrated a shift in national priorities from an almost uncritical emphasis on the individual to an acceptance of organized, cooperative action on the part of voluntary or government agencies. Government could be seen as a positive agent of economic or moral progress, whether promoting railroad construction across the western plains or supporting higher education or protecting the rights of former slaves in the South. In the North the Civil War exerted a permanent modernizing influence that shaped the nation's development over the next century. But the Confederacy, too, had modernized over the course of the war: It had strengthened its central authority in such matters as the draft and impressment of supplies, had promoted industrialization and urbanization, and had directed economic development to aid the war effort. How permanent these changes might have proved had the South won its independence can never be known, for southerners saw them simply as wartime measures. But in the decades after 1865, economic, organizational, and governmental changes originating in the North came to

influence the South also. In the largest sense, the Civil War created the modern American nation in the place of the prewar federation of states.

In subtle ways too, the lives of women were changed by the Civil War. In thousands of households throughout the land — and especially in the South — women had to become the primary providers for their families in lieu of men who were away at war. This proved a severe hardship to many women, but these women serving as temporary heads of household often found a sense of self-confidence and competency they had not known before. Many of these women were so exhausted by their wartime hardships that they were willing to give up their expanded roles when their husbands returned home after the war. (Often southern war veterans seem to have found it psychologically important to reassert their dominant male roles as some sort of compensation for having lost militarily.) North and South, women found employment in factories, in government offices, and in the offices of the bureaucracies that grew up to handle the enlarged scale of private business and industry. But even though women learned new skills and their efforts were understood to be essential to both military and private enterprise, they were not paid equal wages and seldom were allowed administrative authority commensurate with their skills or contributions. Their proper sphere of activity was not expanded permanently, even if wartime emergency sometimes gave them expanded opportunities for employment. Women performed particularly important service as nurses in military hospitals and pioneered nursing (hitherto a male domain) as a profession for women, but the medical profession — like law and the ministry — was still entirely for males only, and nurses were categorized as a species of domestic help for decades yet.

No one in mid-1865 fully comprehended the changes they had experienced already or knew how these changes would affect the national future or their personal lives for good or ill. Most people did not even possess methods of analysis, categories of explanation, or vocabulary sufficient for interpretation. Instead, in both regions people often turned to their ministers and to their religions in an attempt to find larger meaning for what they had experienced and suffered. If we respect the men and women who lived through that era, then we should try to understand their experience in their own terms. That means taking seriously what leading and representative ministers said in an age when mainstream Protestantism was overwhelmingly the dominant form of American religious expression.

As white southerners had tried to cope with a lengthening string of defeats after mid-1863 and the collapsing morale that resulted, they had turned to their assumptions about how God dealt with people in history. They could only interpret their losses, and God's evident approval of such losses, in terms of divine punishment for transgressions. Southern society was insufficiently moral, or slaveholders had not been properly Christian masters, or southerners had been too consumed with greed — that is, the cause of their emerging defeat could be found only in God's will, and because (they reasoned) he never acted arbitrarily, God must be chastising the South for a purpose. Ministers often used the imagery of purification by fire, of metal being pounded into shape on an anvil, to explain what they interpreted God to be doing, or having done, to the South. He was using the experience of war, the shedding of blood and the resultant purification, to reshape the South and redefine its mission to the world. That mission, the ministers discovered in the midst of defeat, was to be a spiritual example to the rest of the nation. The South was to model a form of evangelical religious expression that eschewed the things of this world and emphasized the purely spiritual role of the church. This church would have no involvement with secular or social issues, would repudiate the materialism and corruption of the war years, and would instead focus on the necessity of individual conversion. In effect, the southern ministers provided a way for many devout southerners to discover moral victory in the face of military defeat. The South's true destiny was not to establish an independent nation but to be an exemplar of conservative Protestantism and revivalism.

In the final year of the war and in its aftermath, northern ministers sought not to explain defeat but rather to interpret the providential purposes of victory. It was an easy assumption that victory signaled that God favored the Union and the end of slavery, but ministers wanted to explain to what end God saw to it that the nation was reunited. Boston minister and theologian Horace Bushnell spelled out most clearly a theological interpretation of northern victory. Bushnell saw the nation almost as a living organism, called into being by God before the Declaration of Independence. Yet this organism had not yet really understood itself as a corporate unity, had not really — in the years since 1776 — actualized the true identity that God had in mind for it. Hence the war had happened for purposes grander than the elimination of slavery or the simple reunification of the nation as a group of federated states. Emphasizing the

Judeo-Christian themes of sacrifice and the shedding of blood being necessary for atonement, Bushnell saw the Civil War as God's calling the American nation to self-actualization as a new being, a corporate nation with unity of purpose and identity. Therefore the death and bloodshed were a necessary experience for the American people, for only thus could a true nation — "God's own nation," in Bushnell's language — be created. The Civil War was thus the occasion during which God was molding the final destiny of the American nation; in a real sense for Bushnell, the war had created a modern nation. For Bushnell and those who agreed with him, that divine purpose both helped justify the scale of the sacrifice to contemporaries and empowered the victorious nation to face the future with confidence.

Hence in both regions of the nation ministers provided laypeople with a language and a divine purpose with which they could make moral sense of the otherwise incomprehensible and individually overwhelming experience of the Civil War. We today are not required to accept either explanation as valid, but we should understand that most people of that era sought or accepted generally religious explanations for the events of the time. In letter after letter of Civil War soldiers, we read comments to the effect that human language could not describe the horrors of the battle scenes. Soldiers, laypeople, and even President Lincoln himself ultimately fell back upon religious concepts and religious language in their attempt to understand the causes of the war and accept its outcome. Today, after more than a century, though most commentators no longer use a religious vocabulary, the Civil War is still seen as a major turning point in American history.

SUGGESTED READING

Paul D. Escott, *After Secession: Jefferson Davis and the Failure of Confederate Nationalism* (1978). Critical of Davis, this work reveals the unraveling of the Confederacy during the maelstrom of war.

Drew G. Faust, *Mothers of Invention: Women of the Slaveholding South in the American Civil War* (1996). An influential account of how women managed to hold body and soul together, adapted to new situations, and contributed to the Confederate war effort, and how their eventual exhaustion if not impatience with the sacrifice required helped undermine Confederate morale.

J. Matthew Gallman, *The North Fights the Civil War: The Home Front* (1994). A survey of how the North was changed by wartime events: the need for troops and materiel, the response to political pressures, and the confrontation with mounting casualties.

Joseph T. Glatthaar, *Forged in Battle: The Civil War Alliance of Black Soldiers and White Officers* (2000). A pioneering study of the role of black troops in the Union cause.

Gerald F. Linderman, *Embattled Courage: The Experience of Combat in the American Civil War* (1987). An original, provocative analysis of the changing role of courage in the Civil War.

Leon Litwack, *Been in the Storm So Long: The Aftermath of Slavery* (1979). A vigorously interpretative, impressively documented history of emancipation, beginning with wartime developments and continuing into Reconstruction.

James M. McPherson, *Battle Cry of Freedom: The Civil War Era* (1988). The best modern account of the war — comprehensive, balanced, analytical, and eminently readable. Covers political, military, and social history equally well.

Randall M. Miller, Harry S. Stout, and Charles Reagan Wilson, eds., *Religion and the American Civil War* (1998). A collection of insightful essays on many aspects of religion during the Civil War era, with attention to both North and South and the battlefront as well as the home front.

Clarence L. Mohr, *On the Threshold of Freedom: Masters and Slaves in Civil War Georgia* (2001). A gripping account of how wartime exigencies affected both the white and black populations, with one result being proposed reforms to the institution of slavery.

Charles Royster, *The Destructive War: William Tecumseh Sherman, Stonewall Jackson, and the Americans* (1991). A thought-provoking interpretation of why the war turned so brutal, and its effect on the combatants.

Suggestions for Further Reading

Michael C. C. Adams, *Our Masters the Rebels: A Speculation on Union Military Defeat in the East, 1861-1865* (1978).

Herman Belz, *A New Birth of Freedom: The Republican Party and Freedmen's Rights, 1861-1866* (1976).

Richard G. Beringer et al., *Why the South Lost the Civil War* (1986).

Ira Berlin et al., *Slaves No More: Three Essays on Emancipation and the Civil War* (1992).

William Blair, *Virginia's Private War: Feeding Body and Soul in the Confederacy, 1861-1865* (1998).

Catherine Clinton and Nina Silber, eds., *Divided Houses: Gender and the Civil War* (1992).

William J. Cooper, Jr., *Jefferson Davis, American* (2000).

LaWanda Cox, *Lincoln and Black Freedom: A Study in Presidential Leadership* (1981).

Drew Gilpin Faust, *The Creation of Confederate Nationalism: Ideology and Identity in the Civil War* (1988).

Michael Fellman, *Inside War: The Guerrilla Conflict in Missouri During the Civil War* (1989).

John Hope Franklin, *The Emancipation Proclamation* (1963).

George M. Fredrickson, *The Inner Civil War: Northern Intellectuals and the Crisis of the Union* (1965).

Gary W. Gallagher, *The Confederate War: How Popular Will, Nationalism, and Military Strategy Could Not Stave Off Defeat* (1997).

Louis S. Gerteis, *From Contraband to Freedom: Federal Policy Toward Southern Blacks, 1861-1865* (1973).

Joseph T. Glatthaar, *The March to the Sea and Beyond: Sherman's Troops in the Savannah and Carolinas Campaign* (1985).

Allen C. Guelzo, *Abraham Lincoln: Redeemer President* (1999).

Herman Hattaway and Archer Jones, *How the North Won: A Military History of the Civil War* (1984).

William S. McFeely, *Grant: A Biography* (1981).

James M. McPherson, *What They Fought For, 1861-1865* (1994).

Reid Mitchell, *Civil War Soldiers* (1988).

Reid Mitchell, *The Vacant Chair: The Northern Soldier Leaves Home* (1993).

James H. Moorhead, *American Apocalypse: Yankee Protestants and the Civil War* (1978).

Robert M. Myers, ed., *The Children of Pride: A True Story of Georgia and the Civil War* (1972).

Stephen B. Oates, *With Malice Toward None: The Life of Abraham Lincoln* (1977).

Phillip Shaw Paludan, *"A People's Contest": The Union and the Civil War, 1861-1865* (1988).

George C. Rable, *The Confederate Republic: A Revolution Against Politics* (1994).

James L. Roark, *Masters Without Slaves: Southern Planters in the Civil War and Reconstruction* (1978).

James I. Robertson, *Stonewall Jackson: The Man, the Soldier, the Legend* (1997).

Willie Lee Rose, *Rehearsal for Reconstruction: The Port Royal Experiment* (1964).

Gardiner H. Shattuck, Jr., *A Shield and Hiding Place: The Religious Life of the Civil War Armies* (1985).

Emory M. Thomas, *The Confederate Nation, 1861-1865* (1979).

Emory M. Thomas, *Robert E. Lee: A Biography* (1995).

V. Jacque Voegeli, *Free but Not Equal: The Midwest and the Negro during the Civil War* (1967).

Bell I. Wiley, *The Life of Billy Yank* (1952).

Bell I. Wiley, *The Life of Johnny Reb* (1943).

Bell I. Wiley, *The Plain People of the Confederacy* (1943).

Gary Wills, *Lincoln at Gettysburg: The Words that Remade America* (1992).

16 Reconstruction and the New South

THE WAR WAS over, but no one yet knew what kind of Union had been saved by blood and arms. Clearly the United States of 1865 differed in fundamental ways from that of 1861. Slavery had died so that the Union might live. Many northerners also had gained new confidence in the latent power of the *nation,* and like Abraham Lincoln at Gettysburg and in other public addresses, now spoke of the United States in the singular rather than the plural. So, too, the way the Union had won reconfirmed the vitality of democratic processes and institutions, not only in defeating secession, which Lincoln had properly called the antithesis of democracy, but also in the fact that in the North elections and party politics had continued uninterrupted during the war. To those northerners who had made "The Battle Hymn of the Republic" their anthem, victory also reaffirmed their belief in America as a land chosen by God — how else explain, they asked, the trial by fire that led to the promise of "a new birth of freedom"? Such experiences also fostered hope that, as Lincoln had prayed in his second inaugural address, in March 1865, the nation might finish its task "With malice toward none; with charity for all; with firmness in the right, as God gives us to see the right." But no one in 1865 quite knew how such confidence and conviction would bring seceded states back into the fold while securing the newly won freedom of the emancipated slaves, the Republican wartime legislation promoting westward expansion, education, and economic growth, and the sense of common purpose among different people the war had encouraged (political, ethnic, and racial partisanship notwithstanding).

On such questions hung the meaning of the war — and the fate of the republic.

WARTIME RECONSTRUCTION

Questions about reconstructing the South began before the war was over. The emancipation of the slaves meant that Union victory would bring fundamental social and political changes to a defeated South. The days of plantation slavery were past, "gone with the wind." But the scope of those changes remained unclear during the war. The need to win the war overrode considerations about building a postwar society. Until Union victory was assured, Reconstruction remained largely an instrument of military policy, a way to gain support for the Union and emancipation and undermine the Confederacy. As long as military exigency drove Reconstruction policy, the president held the initiative in his capacity as commander in chief, but in 1864, with Confederates in retreat across a broad front, Congress sought a larger role.

For two years, President Lincoln had tried to nurture Unionism in those areas of the South that came under federal control. In the Border States, western Virginia (which became the separate state of West Virginia in 1863), and occupied parts of Tennessee, Louisiana, Arkansas, and elsewhere, Lincoln used political patronage and advice in an effort to move southerners toward accepting the end of slavery and making friendly governments. These were, in Lincoln's words, "experiments" adapted to the circumstances of each state rather than mandates or a uniform policy. As Republican James G. Blaine observed, "Mr. Lincoln had no fixed plan for the reconstruction of the States."

On December 8, 1863, President Lincoln laid out his first comprehensive proposal for Reconstruction when he issued his Proclamation of Amnesty and Reconstruction. Lincoln's proclamation established a process whereby a seceded state might return to the Union. It proposed that when, in any such state, the number of qualified voters taking an oath of allegiance to the Union and pledging to accept the abolition of slavery equaled 10 percent of the number of people in that state who had voted in the 1860 presidential election, that minority might create a new state government. The constitution of that government had to be republican in form (as required in the Constitution), abolish slavery, and provide for African American education. Upon completion of these terms, the president would recognize the new civil government.

Lincoln hoped a conciliatory approach would win over former Whigs and southern Unionists as a way to shorten the war and lay the groundwork for a Republican Party in the South. Thinking that "we would sooner have the chicken by hatching than smashing the egg," Lincoln foreswore a punitive policy. To be sure, his "Ten Percent Plan," as it became known, prohibited high-ranking Confederate civil and military officers, persons who had resigned from Congress or federal commissions, and persons who had mistreated Union prisoners of war from taking the loyalty oath, but it did not exclude them from public life once "loyal" governments had been established and did allow them to regain their full citizenship with a presidential pardon. To those who took loyalty oaths and received presidential pardons, Lincoln also promised a restoration of all property, except slaves or confiscated property already transferred to third parties, and even hinted that some compensation for slave property might be possible. On the other side, he ruled out any blanket enfranchisement of former slaves, although in one instance he later suggested to the Unionist governor of Louisiana, where a large class of educated free blacks lived, that it would be good politics generally to enfranchise "the very intelligent [black men] and especially those who have fought gallantly in our ranks." But Lincoln did not push the idea lest he alienate the whites he was courting.

Lincoln's plan proved too radical for conservatives and too conservative for radicals. The first signs of opposition came from states unaffected by Lincoln's proclamation — West Virginia and the four slave states that stayed in the Union. There, slaveholders clung to their human property even after its liberation was evident, and Unionists, many of them nonslaveholders resentful of slaveholders' antebellum political and economic dominance, demanded more power and a proscription of former Confederates. One of the first political lessons of the war was that Reconstruction would require a difficult balancing act that had to include the competing interests of former slaves, former slaveholders, and white small farmers in each state.

Meanwhile, abolitionists bristled at the easy terms Lincoln promised for readmission and especially for failing to make explicit provisions for black enfranchisement and civil rights. Lincoln's plan, said abolitionist Wendell Phillips, "frees the slave and ignores the negro." But, with the war in doubt, most Radical Republicans in Congress held their criticism until they saw the plan in operation. Lincoln's "experiments,"

Freed Slaves This group of newly freed slaves was photographed in Richmond immediately after the war. Some of the ruins of the city after the disastrous fire, which broke out at the time of its fall to the Union army, are visible in the background. Freed slaves often tested their liberty by seeking jobs for wages, marrying, looking for relatives and spouses who had been separated by sale, or simply moving about and socializing as they pleased — all forbidden actions while they had been in bondage.

meanwhile, failed to rally much white Unionist support or to protect blacks. By summer 1864 such Radicals as Congressman George W. Julian and Senator Charles Sumner had seen enough of southerners' intransigence and Lincoln's Reconstruction in practice. They demanded more rigorous terms for readmission. Also, as Union armies advanced, so, too, did Congress's interest in establishing Reconstruction policy. The Congress was no longer willing to concede that function to the president's prerogative alone. Whereas Lincoln had exercised his authority in emancipating the slaves and issuing his Proclamation of Amnesty and Reconstruction largely under his war-making power, the Congress now insisted on a preeminent role because of its con-

stitutional responsibility to ensure republican government in the states.

In July 1864, Congress passed the Wade-Davis Bill, which summed up the minimum terms most Republicans, and likely the majority of northerners, demanded of former Confederate states for readmission to the Union. Whatever differences Republicans had among themselves over matters of the tariff, banking, and other policies, they were united in their belief that Reconstruction must give southern Unionists the upper hand in establishing new governments in the former Confederate states, that the Republican Party should get a fair chance to organize in the South, and that the abolition of slavery and the repudiation of secession should be accepted as facts. On those matters, Lincoln and his party agreed. Radical Republicans wanted more. They also pressed for assurances that the former planter class would not return to power and that the newly freed slaves (called "freedmen") would be secure in their basic civil rights. Arguing variously that the seceded states had committed "state suicide" or should be treated as "conquered provinces," the Radicals insisted that the former Confederate states would be readmitted on such terms as Congress established. Radicals determined to slow the readmission process until they had secured their objectives.

The Wade-Davis Bill spoke to such concerns by providing that each former Confederate state would be ruled by a military governor until it could be organized under a two-stage process of oath-taking and constitution-making. Under the congressional plan, no state could begin the Reconstruction process until all resistance to the Union had ceased there and a majority of eligible voters in that state took an oath of allegiance to the Union. At that point, only those southern whites who swore an "iron-clad oath" that they had never voluntarily aided or supported the Confederacy could vote for delegates to a state constitutional convention. Once convened, such a convention had to repeal secession, repudiate all debts incurred by the Confederate government, and abolish slavery. The Wade-Davis Bill guaranteed blacks equality before the law but was silent on African American suffrage and made no provision for either education or land for the freedmen.

Lincoln pocket-vetoed the Wade-Davis Bill,[1] claiming he did not want to be bound to one policy, though he added that any "loyal" state might still choose to accept it. None did. The Republican-controlled Congress, in turn, refused to accept the governments formed under Lincoln's "Ten Percent Plan," and several Radicals blasted him for overstepping his authority. The president and Congress stood at loggerheads. But, with the war all but over, Lincoln suggested in cabinet meetings that he might accept more demanding terms for readmission. On

April 11, 1865, in what became known as his "last speech," he gave a qualified endorsement of limited black suffrage. He also acknowledged that Reconstruction would be "fraught with great difficulty," because southerners remained "disorganized and discordant" while northerners disagreed "as to the mode, manner, and means of reconstruction." Four days later he was dead.

❧ *The Thirteenth Amendment*

While Lincoln and the Radicals differed over the pace and punitiveness of Reconstruction, they did agree that the abolition of slavery had to rest on more secure constitutional footing than the Emancipation Proclamation and wartime confiscation acts. Lincoln strongly supported an amendment that would definitively end slavery everywhere. In January 1865, amid shouting and jubilation during which some congressmen "wept like children," Congress finally approved such an amendment and sent it to the states for ratification, which was achieved in December 1865. In one sentence, the Thirteenth Amendment did away with an institution that had existed since the dawn of the republic and had cost untold misery to millions. In its second sentence the amendment did more by authorizing Congress to "have power to enforce this article by appropriate legislation." Therein lay the concept of "positive liberty" that some abolitionists, Radical Republicans, and even Lincoln had claimed was government's responsibility. Where the Founding Fathers and most nineteenth-century Americans had viewed the relationship of liberty and government in negative terms — that is, government had to be kept from encroaching on liberty — wartime emancipation had shown that government might expand freedom. How government might do so — and for many detractors, whether government ought to do so — became the burning political question of Reconstruction, and one that has survived to this day.

For some, the Thirteenth Amendment settled "the question of the age." In 1865 abolitionist William Lloyd Garrison called on the American Anti-Slavery Society to disband because its work was done; "thank God," he exulted, the vocation of abolitionist "is ended." Others disagreed. Most abolitionists and Radical Republicans pointed to much work left undone, especially the need to guarantee the freedmen equal rights before the law and the franchise. As Frederick Douglass warned, "Slavery is not abolished until the black man has the ballot." The politics of Reconstruction now superseded the moral issue of slavery.

---

1. That is, he refused to sign it within the ten days required by the Constitution, while Congress in the meantime adjourned.

The assumed power of the Thirteenth Amendment itself remained more a promise than a recognized constitutional and political principle. Did the amendment confer citizenship on African Americans and effect a constitutional revolution by bringing a reunited nation under "one law impartial over all," as some Radicals claimed? Did it demand special efforts to lift the ex-slaves to equality? Or did it merely end the institution of slavery and leave the freedmen to their fate? And what was government's proper role in securing rights during peacetime? Although Radicals believed that the nation, as the "custodian of freedom," required more strength, most northerners, including many reformers, who had accepted an expansion of federal governmental authority in order to save the Union expected that authority to shrink when the troops came home. Laissez-faire principles, after all, still governed American thought. So, too, from some blacks' perspective, a dependency on government and white benefactors would limit blacks' freedom and likely incite a white backlash if blacks were seen as wards of the state. Frederick Douglass thus answered the question of what government should do for the ex-slave by saying, "Do nothing. . . . Give him a chance to stand on his own legs! Let him alone!" He believed that with the ballot and basic civil rights, African Americans could make their own way.

❧ Andrew Johnson and "Restoration"

The need to define citizenship, defend freedom, and determine the Reconstruction of seceded states soon forced the government to do something. Through the spring, summer, and fall of 1865, that task fell to a southerner, the new president, Andrew Johnson of Tennessee. Because he refused to call Congress into special session, Johnson claimed for himself the principal role of communicating the terms of readmission expected by northerners. Unfortunately for all concerned, Johnson proved unsuited to the complex issues before him.

Despite a surface similarity to Lincoln, Johnson lacked Lincoln's political skills and moral vision. Both had grown up in poverty without formal education, but Lincoln's humble origins had taught him humility, while Johnson's bred resentments and insecurity. Born in North Carolina and early orphaned, Johnson moved to Tennessee at age seventeen and worked as a tailor before acquiring land and slaves. He entered politics as a Jacksonian and rose rapidly to become governor and then United States Senator. He reveled

in the rough-and-tumble politics and stump-speaking style of eastern Tennessee, promising to raise up the "honest yeomen" by knocking down the "purse proud" aristocrats. When Tennessee seceded, Johnson refused to resign his Senate seat. He stood with the Union, and alone. His action was based on principle, but it also spoke to his own political history. Throughout his life, Johnson was a political maverick even within his own party. Stubborn and overbearing, he was unable to make compromises. Where Lincoln had acquired the ability to study human nature and put ego behind interest in his years riding the Illinois circuit as a lawyer, Johnson remained unbending in his conviction that he alone knew the right way. As one biographer observed, Johnson seemed happy only in opposition.

Johnson's actions during the war belied his rigid personality and later troubles with Republicans. While serving as military governor of Tennessee, he called for harsh treatment of secessionists. In 1864 he thundered that treason was a crime that "must be made odious and traitors must be punished and impoverished." Although Johnson had no interest in antislavery except to strip slaveholders of their wealth and power, he accepted the abolition of slavery and during the war assured blacks in Tennessee that he would be their "Moses." Lincoln, the former Whig, liked what he saw in Johnson and added the lifelong Democrat to the presidential slate to create a "National Union" ticket for the 1864 presidential election.

Within a month of being sworn in as president, Johnson announced his own plan for Reconstruction, and in principle stuck to that course over the next three years. Johnson believed that the war had been fought to save the Union and end slavery, not to ensure blacks' equality before the law. Slavery was dead, so that, to Johnson's mind, the main goal of Reconstruction was restoring loyalty to the Union. He also thought that revenge served no purpose once the war was over. Rebuilding the nation should take precedence over all considerations, he argued, and a speedy "restoration" of government in the former Confederate states would achieve that end. Significantly, in describing the readmission process, Johnson preferred the term "restoration" rather than the implicitly more sweeping term "Reconstruction." He also viewed the restoration process as primarily an executive responsibility — thus his decision not to call Congress into special session. Most important, Johnson was a strict constructionist. The former tailor gave the Constitution "a snug fit" in arguing for limited government and rejecting the Radical Republicans' broad claims of

Thaddeus Stevens A veteran abolitionist, Stevens became the leader of the Radical Republicans in the House of Representatives and the advocate of remaking the conquered South into a yeoman society. He was also one of the relatively few Northern politicians to have a genuine sense of social justice toward African Americans.

federal authority to extend protection to the freedmen and remake the South.

Insisting that he was continuing Lincoln's plan, Johnson issued two proclamations in May. The first required that white southerners would have to take loyalty oaths to regain their civil and political rights and their property, except slaves. His plan followed Lincoln's in excluding various categories of ex-Confederate civil and military officials from the general pardon; to those, Johnson added all ex-Confederates with taxable property worth $20,000 or more, hoping thereby to give the "humble men" of the South control of the new governments. Those excluded from the general pardon would have to apply individually to the president for special

pardons. The second proclamation outlined the terms of readmission. A provisional governor in each state, appointed by the president, was charged with calling a convention to amend the state's antebellum constitution to ensure republican government and provide for regular elections. Privately, Johnson later urged state conventions to repudiate secession and any Confederate debts and to ratify the Thirteenth Amendment, but initially he did not insist on those terms as a condition of readmission. Once states had complied with his terms, Johnson would recognize their governments and "restoration" would be complete. He also accepted the governments organized under Lincoln's "Ten Percent Plan" as already having completed the process of readmission.

Johnson's mild terms sent the wrong message to white southerners. At war's end, the South lay prostrate and pliable, though still hostile. Hatred of northerners did not abate, but few southerners were so extreme as the old Virginia fire-eater Edmund Ruffin who committed suicide rather than be ruled by "damn Yankees" or those former Confederates who fled to Brazil to set up a new plantation society in that slaveholding country. In 1865 most southerners simply wanted to get the Reconstruction process over and gritted their teeth expecting the worst. "Tell us what we must do," General Wade Hampton of South Carolina wrote Radical Thaddeus Stevens in an acknowledgment that a defeated South would have to submit to the victor's terms. In the critical year of 1865, Johnson's plan answered the question.

❧ *A Defiant South*

Offered generous terms for readmission, white southerners seized the moment to try to recover as much power as possible. Johnson helped them along by being overly solicitous of their requests and blind to the needs of Unionists and freedmen. Prominent ex-Confederates and planters flattered Johnson by praising his policy as in the best interests of a true re-union and by begging his favor, to which he responded by issuing pardons liberally (on average 100 a day in September 1865 and almost 13,500 over two years). They appealed to Johnson for a restoration of property seized during the war. Johnson obliged them by instructing army officers to return abandoned lands to former Confederates, which led to the ouster of many African American farmers from fields they had been working. When blacks resisted, as they did along the Georgia coast, Johnson ordered them forcibly removed. He backed the provisional governor of Mississippi, over the protests of the Union general there, when the governor used Confederate veterans to organize the state militia, thereby humiliating the general and endorsing the rearmament of white southerners.

Johnson ignored warnings that, far from easing tensions and fostering loyalty, his lenient approach was inspiring southern truculence. In summer 1865 Governor W. W. Holden of North Carolina wrote Johnson that "much of a rebellion spirit" persisted there, and a North Carolina innkeeper echoed the sentiments of many southerners when he told a northern journalist that although the Yankees had killed his sons and destroyed his property, they had left him "one inestimable privilege — to hate 'em. I git up at half-past four in the morning, and sit up till twelve at night, to hate 'em." Later in 1865 Republican leader Carl Schurz, whom Johnson had sent south on a fact-finding mission, reported that he found the region teeming with "incorrigibles" who opposed any "progressive ideas," glorified their southern past, and, most worrisome, insisted that, emancipation notwithstanding, "the blacks at large belong to the whites at large." Still, Johnson refused to adjust his policy.

The evidence of an "unreconstructed" South cropped up everywhere in 1865. In launching new governments under Johnson's plan, southerners thumbed their noses at Republican conditions for readmission. Led by South Carolina, several states merely "repealed" their ordinances of secession rather than disavow the principle; South Carolina and Mississippi refused to repudiate the Confederate debt; Mississippi and Texas failed to ratify the Thirteenth Amendment; and Georgia reserved the right to claim compensation for emancipated slaves. Northern public anger, even from some Democrats, at such "rebellion feeling" forced Johnson to wire several southern governors instructing them to insist that the conventions formally repudiate secession and Confederate debts and ratify the Thirteenth Amendment.

When he did so, the southerners complied, suggesting that a more forceful policy would have been "accepted" in 1865 if Johnson had made it an unequivocal condition of readmission.

Also troubling was the new southern governments' treatment of the freedmen. Southern whites feared emancipation threatened complete social upheaval and economic chaos. Beginning with Mississippi in November 1865, each southern state passed a series of laws known as "black codes" to regulate the labor and civil arrangements of the freedmen. The codes varied from state to state, but they followed a similar pattern everywhere of wanting to ensure a ready supply of dependent black labor and blacks' subservience to whites. The codes did permit blacks to sue and be sued in state courts and to testify in court cases involving other blacks, to legalize marriages, and to hold certain kinds of property. But the codes excluded blacks from juries, generally prescribed more severe punishment for blacks than whites for similar crimes, prohibited blacks from suing or testifying in interracial legal actions, and in some places segregated public facilities. The codes also prevented blacks from owning weapons and horses and limited their rights of assembly. Criminal offenses included using "insulting" language and preaching the gospel without a license. Many similar restrictions also existed in northern states, so that southerners could rightly claim they were simply following accepted practice in limiting blacks' civil rights. But the zeal with which the southerners rushed such codes into law worried Republicans.

Rather than moving African Americans toward responsible citizenship, the southern states seemed "hell-bent," as one Alabaman confessed, on keeping them "in their place" as the "bottom rail" of society. Revealingly, the southern states made no provision for black education. More ominous were the harsh laws on vagrancy, labor, and land that all reeked of slavery. Most whites believed that only physical force and close supervision could move blacks to productive labor. The attitude was summed up by a planter in Georgia who scoffed at Republican intentions to aid the freedmen by saying that "moral elevation, social equality and political superiority do not increase the African's capacity to weed a row." White southerners wrote the black codes accordingly. South Carolina and Mississippi led the way with laws limiting blacks to agricultural and domestic service and requiring blacks to sign year-long labor contracts or be subject to arrest as vagrants; any "vagrant" unable to pay his or her fine could be bound over to work on a chain gang or hired out to a planter to pay off the debt. Apprenticeship laws bound out black minors to work for planters without pay. Mississippi forbade blacks from buying or renting farmland, and several states made it a crime for employers to offer wages that might entice black workers away from other jobs. Fence laws requiring livestock owners to fence their animals rather than let them graze freely, as was the practice before the war, made it virtually impossible for landless blacks to raise pigs or cattle. Many of the racially discriminatory parts of the black codes did not go into force because the Union army and the Freedmen's Bureau suspended them wherever possible, but the labor provisions revealed how little "freedom" white southerners would tolerate for supposed "freedmen."

Finally, from the northern point of view, southern voters under Johnson's plan spat defiance by electing governors, state legislators, and members of Congress who were prominent ex-Confederates, some of whom had not even taken loyalty oaths to the Union and one of whom, Alexander Stephens, former vice president of the Confederacy, was still in prison. When a small army of ex-Confederate military officers and political leaders marched to Washington in December 1865 to claim their seats in Congress, northern public opinion rebelled. Seeing the black codes as a brazen attempt to undo the crowning achievement of the war, the *Chicago Tribune* warned "that the men of the North will convert the State of Mississippi into a frog pond before they will allow such laws to disgrace one foot of the soil in which the bones of our soldiers sleep and over

which the flag of freedom waves." In surveying southern responses to Johnson's plan, a Boston newspaper warned, "What can be hatched from such an egg but another rebellion?"

The First Congressional Reconstruction Plan

When the thirty-ninth Congress gathered in December 1865, Republicans decided to take Reconstruction into their own hands. The Republican-controlled Congress refused to seat the delegates from the "restored" states and created a Joint (House and Senate) Committee on Reconstruction to formulate a Reconstruction policy. Republicans could at least agree on a holding action until they sorted out their own priorities regarding Reconstruction and worked out an accommodation with the president. Beyond that, Republicans did not yet know what to do.

A small group of conservative Republicans, who feared a break with Johnson and wanted a speedy reunion to facilitate commerce, joined with Democrats in arguing for Johnson's plan. Radical Republicans, meanwhile, had given up on Johnson, whom some decried as "a traitor." They called for the thorough overhaul of southern institutions and equal rights and the franchise for the freedmen, lest, in the words of Thaddeus Stevens, "all our blood and treasure have been spent in vain." But the Radicals were a minority within the party. Moderate Republicans such as Senators William Pitt Fessenden of Maine, John Sherman of Ohio (General William Tecumseh Sherman's brother), and Lyman

---

✳ IN THEIR OWN WORDS

Letter to Freedmen's Bureau, 1865

Ex-slaves protested the "black codes" that threatened to return them to bondage. Union veterans, such as this author, Private Calvin Holly, often took the lead in demanding the federal government win the war by securing the peace.

Suffer me to address you a few lines in reguard to the colered people in this State. From all I can learn and see, I think the colered people are in a great many ways being outraged beyond humanity. Houses have been tourn down from over the heades of women and Children — and the old Negroes after they have worked there till they are 70 or 80 yers of age drive them off in the cold to frieze and starve to death. . . .

Some are being knocked down for saying they are free, while a great many are being worked just as they ust to be when Slaves, without any compensation. Report came in

town this morning that two colered women was found dead [be]side the Jackson road with their throats cot lying side by side. . . . The Rebbles are going a bout in many places through the State and robbing the colered peple of arms, money and all they have and in many places killing.

So, General, to make a short of a long story I think the safety of this country depenes upon giving the Colered man all the rights of a white man, and especialy the Rebs. and let him know that their is power enough in the arm of the Govenment to give Justice, to all her loyal citizens.

Trumbull of Illinois made up the largest bloc in the Congress and controlled the key committees. Nothing could be done without their support, as was made clear when Fessenden rather than the Radical Charles Sumner was named chairman of the Joint Committee on Reconstruction. Moderates found Johnson's plan defective, but they wanted to find ways to cooperate with him on a policy that would ensure basic civil rights for the freedmen, favor Unionists in the South, and build a national Republican Party. On the latter point, they were especially concerned because, with the abolition of slavery, the readmitted ex-Confederate states would gain fifteen extra seats in Congress from reapportionment (former slaves now counting as whole persons for purposes of representation). Moderate Republicans feared that without a Republican foothold in the South, southerners would join hands with northern Democrats to overturn all the Republican wartime legislation on land, education, banking, and transportation.

The question of African American rights forced everyone's hand. Witnesses trooped before the Joint Committee on Reconstruction telling of growing lawlessness and violence against blacks and Union officials in the South. Clara Barton, for example, reported in painful detail seeing a pregnant black woman lashed mercilessly. The testimony convinced Republicans that additional federal legislation was necessary to protect blacks, restore order, and foster loyalty. Moderate Republicans, led by Lyman Trumbull, drafted two bills in early 1866 "to destroy" the "discriminations" of the black codes and establish respect for law.

The first bill extended for three years the life of the Freedmen's Bureau, a War Department agency largely staffed by army officers, which had been created in March 1865 to aid refugees (black and white) and put ex-slaves to work on abandoned or confiscated lands. The bill also authorized the Bureau to build and support schools in the former Confederate states and to establish special courts to settle labor disputes involving freedmen. Despite almost unanimous Republican support for the Freedmen's Bureau bill, Johnson vetoed it on the grounds that it illegally established military courts for civilians in peacetime. Johnson also dismissed the bill as an "immense patronage" that would bankrupt the government and breed indolence among the freedmen. Four days after his veto, Johnson harangued a crowd outside the White House with a speech accusing Radical Republicans of treason and conspiring to kill him.

The second bill, known as the Civil Rights Act of 1866, was Congress's first attempt to define freedom under the Thirteenth Amendment. Intended to nullify the Dred Scott decision and the black codes, the bill defined as national citizens all persons (except Indians) born in the United States and guaranteed them "full and equal benefit of all laws and proceedings for the security of person and property as is enjoyed by white citizens." The bill also gave the federal government the right to intervene in state courts if they discriminated against black citizens. In constitutional terms, the Civil Rights Act signaled a dramatic potential change in federal-state relations. It retained the traditional conception of states having the primary responsibility for law enforcement but introduced a federal claim to monitor state actions on behalf of national citizens. Johnson vetoed the bill charging that it gave black citizens greater protection than white citizens and that it violated the exclusive jurisdiction of state courts.

Johnson's vetoes dismayed Republicans, especially because they believed the laws expressed the majority thinking among northerners regarding fairness and because they thought the laws enforced the basic provisions of presidential Reconstruction. Johnson had complained that no such legislation should be passed while southerners were excluded from Congress, but his argument won over no Republicans now distrustful of Johnson's intentions and suspicious of his allies. Johnson's vetoes made him the darling of southerners and Democrats. If his purpose was to build a broad coalition of conservatives and moderates that would isolate Radicals, the strategy failed. The vetoes dashed the moderate Republicans' hopes of working with the president.

The extent to which Johnson had miscalculated Republican unity was made clear when Congress easily overrode his veto of the Civil Rights Act, the first time in American history that a major bill became law over a presidential veto. Congress then passed an amended Freedmen's Bureau Bill, which Johnson vetoed and Congress then repassed with a two-thirds majority vote. Johnson, soon dubbed "Andy Veto," thereafter assumed an obstructionist role, vetoing congressional measures on Reconstruction, only to have his vetoes overturned. More important, Johnson's actions pushed moderate Republicans toward more radical positions. The moderate Republicans' dominant presence meant congressional Reconstruction never became truly radical — there was no confiscation of land, trials of ex-Confederates for treason, or wholesale, permanent political excommunication of southerners — but Reconstruction did become more radical than it otherwise would have been had Johnson and white southerners not been so obstinate.

◈ *The Fourteenth Amendment*

In an effort to put basic civil rights beyond nullification by the Supreme Court or simple repeal should Republicans lose control of Congress, and to settle outstanding issues with the president, in April 1866 Republicans proposed a sweeping constitutional amendment. The Fourteenth Amendment, which Congress passed in June and sent to the states for ratification, consisted of five parts, each addressing a particular concern of Reconstruction. The most important, and the one that has occasioned the most litigation over time as to its meaning and application, was Section One. The first section defined American citizenship in such a way as to include blacks: "All persons born or naturalized in the United States, and subject to the jurisdiction thereof, are citizens of the United States and of the state wherein they reside." It then prohibited any state from making or enforcing "any law which shall abridge the privileges or immunities of citizens of the United States," from depriving "any person of life, liberty, or property, without due process of law," and from denying "to any person within its jurisdiction the equal protection of the laws." The ambiguity of some of the language over time led to an expansion of the amendment's application — for example, the "due process" clause was invoked by corporations (legal "persons") in the late nineteenth century to limit state regulation and the "equal protection" clause was used by civil rights advocates during the twentieth century to attack racial and other discrimination. In 1866, however, the first section was directed at the black codes and discriminatory treatment in the courts, not against segregation in schools, public places, or public transportation. At the same time, there was no ambiguity about the framers' intent to prevent the states from abridging the basic rights of citizens.

The remaining sections of the amendment addressed a host of Reconstruction issues. Section Two provided for proportional reduction in a state's congressional representation if it denied suffrage to any adult male citizens. Section Three disqualified from state and national office all ex-Confederates who had violated their prewar oaths to uphold the U.S. Constitution, though Congress might remove any such disability by a two-thirds vote. Section Four guaranteed the national debt,

repudiated the Confederate debt, and disallowed all claims for loss of property, including slaves. Section Five empowered Congress to enforce the amendment "by appropriate legislation."

Sections Two and Three provoked immediate controversy. The handiwork of moderates who wanted to avoid alienating northern voters, the two sections were intended to build loyalty, and the prospects for a Republican Party, in the South by changing the southern electorate. Their effect was to anger Radicals who complained that they did not go far enough to remake the South and Democrats and southerners who thought they went too far in asserting a federal role in defining suffrage at all. Radicals had sought a blanket enfranchisement of blacks, but moderates preferred the formula that would allow northern states, with their small black populations, to continue to restrict black suffrage at little cost while forcing southern states, with their large black populations, to enfranchise blacks or risk significant loss of representation. Radicals denounced the second section as "a swindle" and a "wanton betrayal of justice and humanity," but moderates had their way. Meanwhile, women reformers felt betrayed because the clause explicitly limited suffrage to males. Elizabeth Cady Stanton warned that the introduction of the word "male" into the Constitution threatened "an antagonism between black men and all women" and showed that woman "must not put her trust in man." Rather than conceding that Reconstruction was, as Frederick Douglass insisted, "the negro's hour" and that women's rights had to yield to black rights lest black suffrage be lost altogether, many women reformers began to think of separating their cause from Reconstruction. The Fifteenth Amendment in 1870 would finally push them in that direction (see below). Democrats and white southerners, in turn, decried the second and third sections of the Fourteenth Amendment as vengeful and called any effort at black suffrage "an insulting outrage." Southern legislatures refused to ratify the amendment.

President Johnson denounced the Fourteenth Amendment and urged southern legislatures to reject it. With the amendment the central issue, he made the congressional elections in the fall of 1866 a referendum on his versus Congress's Reconstruction policies. In August, Johnson embarked on a whistle-stop train tour to rally opposition to the amendment and to persuade northern voters to throw the Radicals out of office. Johnson's "swing around the circle" brought out the worst in the president's character and revealed the

THIS LITTLE BOY WOULD PERSIST IN HANDLING BOOKS ABOVE
HIS CAPACITY.

AND THIS WAS THE DISASTROUS RESULT.

extent to which he had completely misread northern public opinion. During the summer of 1866, northern feelings regarding southern attitudes and lawlessness had hardened after news of murderous white mob attacks on African Americans in Memphis and New Orleans. Clearly, under Johnson's plan southern whites could not be trusted to respect blacks' basic freedom. Union veterans especially felt betrayed by events and organized the Grand Army of the Republic, in part to deliver the soldiers' vote to Republicans and also to lobby for their pension claims. Johnson responded by saying Radicals had instigated the riots to embarrass him and by calling Radicals "traitors." Intemperate in language, humorless, and self-pitying, Johnson traded insults with hecklers who taunted him with chants of "Don't get mad, Andy." In reverting to his Tennessee stump-speaking style of personal invective, he lost both his dignity and his following. Johnson's hope of forging an alliance of Democrats and conservative Republicans into a new National Union Party was stillborn, and even his supporters shied away from him in public. As one southerner lamented, Johnson's speeches and actions had cost him "the moral power

President Johnson Squashed This cartoon in *Harper's Weekly*, a staunchly Republican journal, taunts Johnson as a foolish boy who was "handling books above his capacity" — such as the United States Constitution. Most Republicans quickly realized that it had been a mistake to make Johnson, a Unionist Democrat, Lincoln's running mate in 1864.

of his position, and done great damage to the cause of Constitutional reorganization."

Northern voters overwhelmingly rejected Johnson and embraced the Republican appeal to "Stand by Congress." Republicans rolled up more than a two-thirds majority in both houses of Congress, gaining thereby a "veto-proof" Congress to forge their own Reconstruction policy. Republicans also won every northern governor's race, majority control of every northern legislature, and significant power in West Virginia, Missouri, and Tennessee. As one Republican in Tennessee gloated, Johnson was now a "dead dog in the White House." Johnson's ineptness and intransigence and southern rebelliousness did more than win the day for Republicans. They ensured that congressional Reconstruction policy would be more "radical" than what had been proposed, and rejected, earlier. The minimum terms for readmission now included the Fourteenth Amendment.

❧ The Second Congressional Reconstruction Plan

Fortified by the election returns, Republicans determined to have their own Reconstruction plan in 1867, two years after Appomattox. They did so in a flurry of legislative activity on March 2, 1867. The Republicans first pushed through the Reconstruction Act, which invalidated the state governments formed under the Lincoln and Johnson plans and divided the ten remaining unreconstructed states (Tennessee had been readmitted to the Union after ratifying the Fourteenth Amendment) into five military districts, each under the command of a major general with authority over civil and judicial matters. The army officers, though backed by only 20,000 soldiers, were charged with maintaining order, supervising the administration of justice, and protecting the civil rights of "all persons." The act also established the procedure whereby a state might be readmitted to the Union. The officers were to enroll all eligible voters (adult black men and white men who had not been disqualified under the Fourteenth Amendment), who could elect delegates to a state convention to write a new state constitution that must guarantee universal manhood suffrage and might disqualify prominent ex-Confederates from office. Once a state presented an acceptable constitution to Congress and ratified the Fourteenth Amendment, Congress would admit the state's elected representatives and military rule would end in that state. Congress also passed the Habeas Corpus Act, which expanded the rights of citizens to remove cases from state to federal courts.

Congress then moved to limit Johnson's ability to obstruct the enforcement of the laws. As president, he still had the power to appoint and remove military and civil officers. To ensure congressional control over the army, Congress added a rider to the Army Appropriations Act, directing the president to issue all orders to the five military commanders in the South only through the general of the army, Ulysses S. Grant, who could not be dismissed without the Senate's consent. In an effort to stop Johnson from removing Republican officeholders who supported congressional Reconstruction and to protect Edwin M. Stanton, the secretary of war who endorsed the congressional plan and was responsible for administering much of it, Congress enacted the Tenure of Office Act, which required the Senate's consent for the dismissal of cabinet officers and anyone else who originally had been appointed with the Senate's approval.

Congressional Reconstruction did not take immediate effect because most white southerners preferred to remain under military rule rather than participate in a constitution-making process that guaranteed black suffrage. They refused to trade their "honor" and "manhood" for readmission on Republican terms. President Johnson also slowed enforcement of the new law by replacing army officers sympathetic to the congressional plan with more conservative men. Congress remedied the defects in its Reconstruction Act by passing three subsequent Reconstruction acts that required the military commanders in the South to register eligible voters and made it easier for a simple pro-Unionist majority in any state to set in motion the constitution-making machinery. The passage of those acts cleared the way for a combination of southern blacks, Unionist southern whites, and northerners in the South to organize state governments and begin forming local Republican Party structures. Congress dealt with Johnson by impeaching him.

❧ The Impeachment of Johnson

Radicals had been trying to impeach Johnson for some time, but moderates had balked at so extreme a measure. By early 1868, however, many moderates also came to believe that congressional Reconstruction would never succeed as long as Johnson stood ready to block it. During the summer 1867 congressional recess, Johnson tried to test the constitutionality of the Tenure of Office Act by removing Secretary of War Stanton, but in early 1868 Congress did not concur with Stanton's removal. Johnson dismissed Stanton anyway and named the more conservative General Lorenzo Thomas in his place. Stanton, in turn, refused to leave his post; he barricaded himself in his office and for two months lived off the encouragement of Republicans and food sent up in a bucket. Johnson's defiance of Congress opened the door to his impeachment. An exasperated Austin Blair spoke for moderate Republicans when he charged that Johnson "has thrown down the gauntlet to Congress, and says to us plainly as words can speak it: 'Try this issue now betwixt me and you; either you go to the wall or I do.'"

On February 24, 1868, the angry Republican majority in the House voted unanimously to impeach Johnson for "high crimes and misdemeanors in office." Nine of the eleven articles of impeachment against Johnson dealt with the removal of Stanton and violations of the chain of command in issuing military orders. The crux

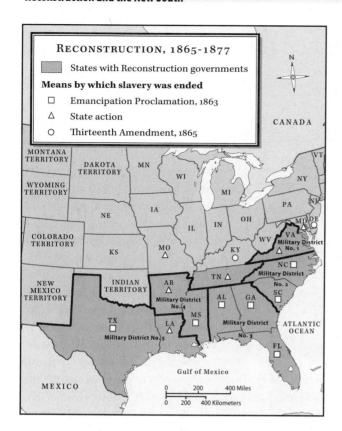

RECONSTRUCTION, 1865-1877

States with Reconstruction governments

Means by which slavery was ended

☐ Emancipation Proclamation, 1863

△ State action

○ Thirteenth Amendment, 1865

dignity during the trial. Chastened by impeachment, he promised to enforce the laws, which he thereafter did. Although the Radicals lost in their effort to drive Johnson from office and use impeachment as a political club, they gained in finally subduing their nemesis. At last, congressional Reconstruction could go forward unharried by the president.

❧ The Fifteenth Amendment

But by 1868 many northerners had grown tired of the wrangling over Reconstruction and worried about too much power passing into black and Radical hands. In elections for state offices in 1867, Democrats made impressive gains in several northern states by using race as an issue. Republican editor Horace Greeley of the *New York Tribune* conceded that "we have lost votes in the Free States by daring to be just to the Negro." The election of 1868 pointed to further erosion of general support for the Republicans. Northerners who wanted to get on with other issues resented the Radical Republicans' constant harping on "moral obligations" to the freedmen. During the presidential contest, the Democrats and their candidate Horatio Seymour of New York found a responsive chord among many northerners by interlacing the themes of race, Republican constitutional "excesses" in Reconstruction, and the "corruption of politics" by black enfranchisement in the South, which they mixed with promises to issue cheap money, called "greenbacks," to help debt-ridden western farmers. The Republican candidate, Ulysses S. Grant, rode his popularity as a military hero into office, handily winning the electoral vote. But the general's popular vote margin was surprisingly thin, only 300,000 out of roughly 6 million votes cast. Newly enfranchised southern African Americans had delivered 450,000 votes to the Republicans, which meant that a majority of white voters had preferred Seymour. Shocked Republican leaders scurried to save the day by retreating from Radical positions (see below) and by locking in black enfranchisement.

of the Republicans' indictment was the tenth article charging Johnson with obstructing congressional Reconstruction and attempting to bring Congress into "contempt and reproach." The eleventh article summed up the previous ten charges. In his trial before the Senate, Johnson's lawyers argued that Johnson could only be tried for an indictable crime and added that he technically had not broken the Tenure of Office Act in any case because Lincoln, not Johnson, had appointed Stanton so that Johnson was free to replace him. Radical Charles Sumner replied that impeachment was, as the Founding Fathers intended, "political in character" and thus not limited to criminal offenses.

For eleven weeks, the trial packed the Senate galleries with onlookers. Finally, in mid-May, the Senate voted 35-19 to convict, one vote short of the two-thirds majority necessary to remove the president. Seven Republicans had broken party ranks to vote for acquittal. They did so because they feared Johnson's removal would weaken the constitutional balance of powers in the federal government. They also recoiled from the prospect of the rabidly Radical women's rights and labor supporter "Bluff" Benjamin Wade of Ohio, the president pro tempore of the Senate, succeeding to the presidency upon Johnson's removal. Johnson helped his own cause by conducting himself with uncommon

For two years, Radical Republicans had argued for universal African American suffrage as a basic right, but moderates had rejected such pleas as too radical. Northern voters might accept black enfranchisement in the South as necessary for freedmen to protect themselves, but they wanted none of it at home. In a democratic society, enfranchisement implied social as much as political equality. For that reason, white southerners considered black suffrage to be complete degradation and never forgave Republicans for forcing it on them.

Johnson's Impeachment Trial   The galleries were always packed with ticket-holding spectators during Andrew Johnson's trial, and the nation followed events closely through newspaper accounts. The trial itself was conducted with dignity, and Johnson refrained from his characteristic public outbursts of bad temper.

Likewise, between 1867 and 1869, white northerners defeated nine referenda on enfranchising blacks in their own states. But the 1868 election returns also awoke moderate Republicans to the possibility of losing control of Congress and the presidency if they did not have black votes. Close elections in such key states as Indiana suggested that black votes might assure Republican majorities. And, as one Republican noted, by making the voting right national, "party expediency and exact justice coincide for once." Moderates thus backed a constitutional amendment to enfranchise blacks generally.

In 1869 Congress passed the Fifteenth Amendment and sent it to the states for ratification. Bitter battles over ratification ensued. Democrats howled that the amendment was the ultimate federal usurpation of states' rights, and opponents of ratification in mid-Atlantic, midwestern, and border states with large African American populations warned of "black over white" if the amendment became law. Whether out of justice, a desire to settle the Reconstruction question once and for all, partisan self-interest, or (as in the four ex-Confederate states that voted for it) a condition of readmission, the Fifteenth Amendment was ratified in 1870. Church bells rang across New England where support for the amendment was strongest, and Repub-

licans cheered the victory as proof that God had "willed" the outcome as the way to end prejudice. Most Republicans thought they had now fulfilled their duty to the freedmen, and themselves, and had freed national politics from the vexing "Negro question." As the *New York Tribune* concluded in April 1870, in assaying a quarter century of sectional strife ending with the enfranchisement of blacks, "Let us have done with Reconstruction. The country is tired and sick of it.... LET US HAVE PEACE."

In fact, the amendment proved flawed and peace did not come. Instead of barring discrimination in suffrage based on "race, color, nativity, property, education, or religious beliefs," as Radicals had proposed, the amendment the moderates crafted simply forbade the states from denying or abridging the right to vote "on account of race, color, or previous condition of servitude." Moderates believed a more sweeping guarantee of the franchise would infringe on northern states' suffrage qualifications, which kept the Chinese from voting in California and forced immigrants and the poor to meet literacy and property tests in other states. The amendment also left women out — the final indignity to women's rights advocates, who then went their own way. A disgusted Elizabeth Cady Stanton argued against the amendment because it allowed unlettered foreign-born and black men access to the ballot box while denying the same right to educated women: "Think of Patrick and Sambo and Hans and Ung Tung, who do not know the difference between a Monarchy and a Republic, who never read the Declaration of Independence ... making laws for Lydia Maria Child, Lucretia Mott, or Fanny Kemble." The irony of the amendment was that by allowing for inequalities affecting whites, it did not even protect blacks. Before the century closed, southern whites would use literacy tests, property qualifications, and poll taxes to deny blacks the vote.

❧ *The Supreme Court and Reconstruction*

Congressional Reconstruction went into place without any sustained challenge from the Supreme Court. In 1866, to be sure, the Supreme Court had seemingly nullified the Freedmen's Bureau courts when it unanimously ruled in *Ex parte Milligan* that civilians could not be tried in military courts when the civil courts were open. Republicans derided the decision as a "piece of judicial impertinence which we are not bound to respect," and, in fact, the Freedmen's Bureau courts continued to operate for several years. The Court also invalidated the use of loyalty oaths in two 1867 cases. Congress, in turn, attempted to reduce the Court's size, limited its jurisdiction in certain civil rights cases, and even talked of abolishing the Court altogether. But the Court avoided a collision with Congress by dismissing suits intended to prevent enforcement of the Reconstruction Acts and by ruling in *Texas v. White* (1869) that secession was illegal and that Reconstruction was a political rather than a constitutional problem. The Court left it to Congress to guarantee republican governments in the states.

❧ Forming Reconstruction Governments in the South

Republican Reconstruction in the South began in 1867. In 1868 all but Virginia, Mississippi, and Texas had been readmitted to the Union, and by 1870 all the former Confederate states had completed the process of constitution-writing under Republican eyes and rejoined the Union. (Georgia was readmitted in 1868, then disqualified for unseating elected African American legislators, and readmitted in 1870.) Republican rule, however, lasted less than a decade. In some states, Democrats regained power within a few years, and in all states, conservative white resistance to Republican ideas and programs limited their application. However brief and incomplete, Republican Reconstruction did lead to constitutional reform and a new biracial southern electorate.

The conventions that met in 1867 and 1868 to draft new constitutions signaled a potential revolution in politics because blacks participated in them. Nowhere else in the world where slaves had gained their freedom did ex-slaves acquire democratic political rights so soon or fully. At the same time, the fact that blacks had any political say caused conservative southern whites to reject the new constitutions and the Republican governments formed under them as illegitimate. Indeed, from the outset, conservative whites hurled racial slurs at what they called the "Bones and Banjoes Conventions." They disparaged the delegates as "baboons, monkeys, and mules" and their handiwork as a

"base conspiracy . . . of ignorant Negroes co-operating with a gang of white adventurers." Anyone associating with blacks became suspect. Conservative whites sneered at southern whites who joined the process as "scalawags" (a term for scrawny, worthless livestock) and northern whites as "carpetbaggers" (a term for interloping hustlers who carried all their possessions in a cheap bag made of carpet), or used other terms such as "white Negroes" and "black Republicans" to mark all white Republicans as racial turncoats, or worse. They were, in the words of one Democrat, "the mean, lousy, and filthy kind that are not fit for butchers or dogs." The caricatures of the delegates and southern Republicans stuck in the public mind — and thereafter much historical writing about the period — and suggested how difficult it would be to build a broad base of public support for the new constitutions and governments.

In fact, the delegates and supporters of the Republican Party were anything but the "vultures," "ragamuffins and jailbirds" the conservative white southerners would have contemporaries believe. The "scalawags" largely consisted of wartime Unionists from small farm upcountry regions who wanted to improve their economic prospects and who, despite their own misgivings about allying with African Americans, risked social ostracism for supporting Republicans. As one Georgian remarked, "It costs nothing for a Northern man to be a Union man, but the rebuff and persecution received here [by scalawags] . . . tells a horrible tale." Scalawags also included former Whigs who opposed secession and a few prominent planters and politicians eager to promote railroad and industrial improvements in a "new South." "Carpetbaggers" were mostly Union veterans, businessmen, teachers, and missionaries who came south willing to invest capital in land, factories, and railroads and reputation in encouraging reform, or to improve their health in a warmer climate. Most African American delegates were literate, many having been free before the war. They were drawn largely from the clergy and the artisan class and included several college graduates. Despite differences in background and interest that eventually would undermine the Republican alliance, black and white came together in their initial forays into constitution-writing and government-making to demand a new politics and a "new South." The modern, democratic constitutions they wrote were hardly products of disorder and demagoguery, as the conservatives claimed. Indeed, some of their constitutional provisions stood long after the Republicans fell from power.

The new constitutions, in historian James McPherson's estimation, ranked "among the most progressive in the nation." All the constitutions provided for statewide public education for both races. Many states assumed responsibility for such previously local or private concerns as hospitals, asylums, and charity. Several states reformed their criminal codes and penal systems. The rights of women also gained in several states. South Carolina, for example, instituted its first divorce law, and most other states guaranteed property rights to women. The constitutions redistributed political power. Legislative districts were redrawn to give more representation to small farmers, many previously appointed offices were made elective, and property qualifications for voting or holding office were abolished or reduced. Voting reforms led to universal adult manhood suffrage in much of the South. The constitutions were generally non-punitive toward former rebels. Black delegates especially insisted that no further penalties be imposed on ex-Confederates. Five states refused to disqualify ex-Confederates outright for their participation in the rebellion, and two others repealed their disfranchisement clauses in 1868. Also dramatic were the changes in taxation. States shifted the tax burden to real property while providing homestead exemptions and other protection to small property holders. For the first time, large landholders would have to carry a significant portion of taxation. Yet no state authorized any confiscation or redistribution of land, fearing that any attack on property rights would scare off needed investment.

The new constitutions were not so progressive as to attack racial discrimination fully. White delegates, and later elected officials, showed little interest in using government to encourage "social equality." Only South Carolina and Louisiana, where blacks were well organized politically, prohibited segregation in public schools, though in practice the ban largely went unenforced. Up-country whites everywhere opposed any proposals explicitly forbidding segregation. The prevailing thinking was stated by one North Carolinian, who observed, "There is not the slightest reason

A Carpetbagger Thomas Nast, the gifted and acerbic caricaturist for *Harper's Weekly,* was a staunch Republican and foe of President Johnson, but in this cartoon he lampooned the Yankees who supposedly went into the postwar South in search of loot, carrying all their belongings in a cheap suitcase called a carpetbag. One of Nast's favorite targets was corruption in public life. But northerners who went south in search of opportunities were not always corrupt.

why blacks and whites should sit in the same benches, in Churches, school houses, or Hotels. Each can have the equal protection and benefits of the law without these." The vast majority of black leaders agreed that social integration was not on their agenda. Their concerns remained more practical — gaining equality before the law, access to land and schools, and protection of basic civil and political rights. Blacks did, however, object to constitutional language explicitly requiring segregation because, as North Carolina's James Hood prophesied regarding education, "Make this distinction in your organic law and in many places the white children will have good schools . . . while the colored people will have none." Some blacks also viewed Reconstruction as a time ripe for spiritual and social conversion of whites from their racial prejudices. For that reason, they tried to keep segregation laws off the books lest such laws lock in attitudes before a change of heart could occur.

❧ *The New Southern Electorate*

Even more far-reaching than the new constitutions was the new southern electorate. Unwilling to disfranchise all former Confederates and unable to win over a majority of whites, Republicans turned to African Americans to build their party in the South. Republicans recruited black support through Union Leagues, Grant Clubs, and patriotic organizations. The Union Leagues were most active in reaching out to prospective voters with hell-fire speeches, torch-light rallies, and evocative posters, while also schooling them on issues such as taxation and education. Political meetings went on late into the night, after the farmers had tended their stock, eaten supper, and walked several miles to the schoolhouse or church where the meeting was held. Black men came in droves because they wanted to hear debates first-hand and decide for themselves the future of their communities. Black women, too, participated in parades and rallies. Even though they could not vote, they showed their support by waving flags and wearing campaign buttons supporting Republicans and urging their men to march to the polls.

A sense of divine purpose and urgency fired blacks' early political efforts. Indeed, many black preachers and orators spoke in apocalyptic terms when discussing politics. For example, in a July 4, 1865, sermon delivered to 10,000 freedmen in Augusta, Georgia, A.M.E. minister James D. Lynch warned that if whites refused justice to the freedmen, "there will be an army marshaled in the Heavens for our protection, and events will transpire by which the hand of Divine Providence will wring from you in wrath, that which should have been given in love." With evangelical fervor, black leaders preached the importance of voting as the way to bring on a "new age" of racial harmony and progress. By 1867 events had moved many blacks to realize that only through political power might they do their duty by God to save the republic and help themselves.

The main source of African American political mobilization came from black-run institutions, none more so than the churches. African Methodist Episcopal (A.M.E.) churches, with their large following and organizational structure of classes, societies, and bands, proved especially well suited for spreading political ideas and gaining voters. Ministers across the South opened their pulpits to Republican appeals, and church picnics, classes, and club meetings often were converted into voter drives. In the initial flush of Republican Reconstruction, some black ministers worried that building the Republican Party threatened to crowd out building the church. The Reverend Houston Holloway, for one, recalled that "Politics got in our midst and our revival or religious work for a while began to wane." Still, ministers led the way into politics. As the Reverend Charles H. Pearce of Florida observed, "A man in this State cannot do his whole duty as a minister except he looks out for the political interests of his people." Minister-politicians such as Georgia's Henry M. Turner and Tunis G. Campbell, South Carolina's Richard H. Cain, and Mississippi's James D. Lynch emerged as the most significant element of black political leadership, parlaying their prestige within the black community and their organizational and oratorical skills into successful runs for office.

Turner, for example, won election to the Georgia legislature, and the northern-born Campbell, who had come south during the war "to instruct and elevate the colored race," established a virtual political fiefdom in McIntosh County, Georgia, that lasted to the end of Reconstruction. Over the course of Reconstruction, more than 100 black ministers won election to legislative seats, and many more served in other political capacities.

The Republican Party benefited enormously from such ministers' "missionary" work. African Americans seized the ballot as the Holy Grail. In the 1867 elections, the first time southern blacks could vote, almost 90 percent of eligible black voters laid down their hoes, trowels, and other tools to step up to the ballot box. As one Alabaman put it, "The negroes voted their entire walking strength." They would continue to do so throughout Reconstruction, providing the mainstay of the Republican Party in the South. Indeed, along with the church and the school, blacks regarded the Republican Party as vital to defining and defending what freedom would mean. As Alabaman George Houston, an ex-slave and state legislator, averred, "I say the Republican Party freed me, and I will die on top of it."

The emerging Republican Party proved to be a rickety structure, built on three unequal legs. Up-country whites distrusted the economic motives of former Whigs and often disliked the carpetbaggers' preaching on racial justice. Although scalawags held the most political offices during Reconstruction, the carpetbaggers' political skill, connections with the federal government, and capital gave them a disproportionate influence within the party, especially in statewide races — to the eventual resentment of native-born southerners. Blacks provided roughly 80 percent of the votes across the South that made Republican rule possible, but they never held offices commensurate to their voting strength. Over the course of Reconstruction, most of the roughly 2,000 black officeholders served at the local level as sheriffs, members of town councils and school boards, justices of the peace, and county tax collectors. These were important positions at the point of contact for most blacks (and whites) with government, but they were not policy-making offices. Black officeholders largely implemented laws made by others. As long as blacks accepted such minor offices while deferring to white leadership, the scalawags stayed in the Republican fold. But blacks chafed at the paternalism of the carpetbaggers and the overt racism of the scalawags. They grew impatient "holding the hind legs" and demanded fairness. When blacks challenged whites for leadership positions, winning legislative seats and even congressional races in such states as South Carolina and Mississippi, the three-legged Republican coalition collapsed. Many scalawags went over to the Democrats, who had been simultaneously wooing them with promises of "redemption" and chastising them for apostasy in bedding down politically with blacks.

By contrast, as the southern Republicans came apart, the southern Democrats grew increasingly united. Race overcame all other considerations among Democrats, and the single purpose of driving the hated "black and tan" Republicans from office gave Democrats a mission equal in their minds to the conversion of souls. Indeed, from church pulpits and campaign stumps came the same admonition to "beat back the Devil" by ending the "unholy" Republican alliance of black and white. As a group of South Carolinians explained to Congress in 1868, whites would "never quietly submit to negro rule." They would resist until they "regained the heritage of political control handed down to us by honored ancestry. That is a duty we owe to the land that is ours, to the graves that it contains, and to the race of which you and we alike are members — the proud Caucasian

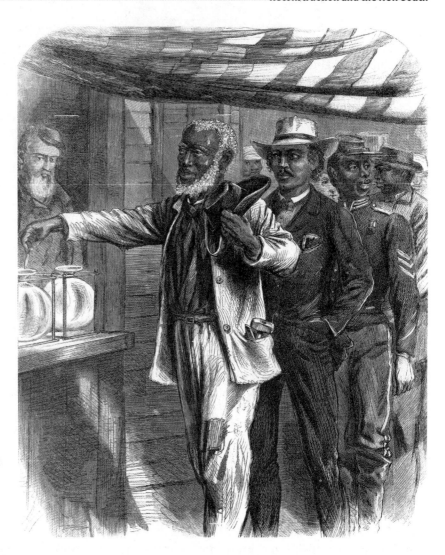

Southern Black Men Voting   In 1867 *Harper's Weekly* published this memorable drawing of blacks casting their first votes under the watchful eye of a Union soldier who guards the polling place. Notice the variety of voters lined up to cast their ballots, including a laborer, a well-to-do man, and a war veteran.

race, whose sovereignty on earth God has ordained." So intent were Democrats on "redeeming" the South from Republican rule that they justified any means, even violence, to do so.

❧ *Republican Governments in Action*

The new governments tackled enormous problems of relief, recovery, and rebuilding. All the states committed to establishing statewide systems of public education, often from scratch. The Freedmen's Bureau and such northern aid societies as the American Missionary Association provided teachers, books, and supplies, sometimes for several years, but the states assumed the lion's share of the cost and responsibility for public education and did not altogether forsake such responsibility even after Democrats regained control (though many Democratic regimes cut education outlays significantly). The governments also undertook large public improvements programs. The charred and gutted ruins of public buildings had to be cleared away and new ones put up in their places. Levees, bridges, roads, and other public works needed to be repaired. Established banks were allowed to scale down their war-inflated debts, and new banks were chartered in an effort to foster new investment. The governments also launched ambitious transportation and industrial development programs. To attract investment, states floated railroad bonds, established industrial commissions, and offered loans, subsidies, and other benefits to prospective manufacturers. The physical results were impressive when considering how much had to be rebuilt. Over 6,000 miles of railroad track was laid during this period, and the number of manufacturing establishments doubled between 1860 and 1880. But such gains were also deceptive, for much of the investment went into restoring what had been destroyed by war and neglect. Inexperience led to waste and other problems. And governments added to their own costs simply by creating the bureaucracies necessary to oversee the new responsibilities.

Taxes at all levels soared to meet the mounting obligations and debts of government. By 1870 the tax rates of southern governments had risen to three to four times their prewar level. States increased poll taxes and passed new taxes on luxuries, sales, and occupations, but they relied mainly on property taxes. Amid falling land and crop prices and rising fears of foreclosures, southern landowners faced what seemed to them a crippling tax burden and a loss of their "independency." Despite attempts to protect small property holders from excessive taxation, the net effect of the tax laws was regressive. That is, people with less money had to pay proportionately more of their limited incomes in taxes. Although southern tax rates, on average, were no more than those in most midwestern states, southerners cried foul when forced to pay the taxes. Before the war, most southerners had paid almost no taxes. Now they were asked to fund a host of new government projects, pay the salaries of what seemed to many a bleating "no property herd" of politicians and bureaucrats, and cover the debt obligations from bond sales to northern capitalists. In their taxing policies, the Republican governments seemed to be at cross-purposes with the new

democratic order promised in the state constitutions. That some states mismanaged their funds, defaulted on obligations, and suffered from corruption added to a growing sense of betrayal and discredited Republican governments, even among their erstwhile supporters. Democrats made hay on the taxation issue, which they mixed with charges of corruption and race to convince whites that the "black and tan" Republican legislatures were bent on the complete ruin of southern society.

Corruption plagued the new governments and further weakened their political credibility. Corruption abounded during the Gilded Age (see Chapter 18), and southern politicians shared in it. Expanding public responsibilities and a postwar "get-rich-quick" mentality fueled opportunities for graft. Part of the corruption was due to inexperience and ignorance in guarding against it, part to outright greed. Republicans in the South admitted that the rush to rebuild often led to "bargains with the devil." Bankers, railroad men, and others seeking charters, franchises, and government business greased many legislators' palms to smooth the passage of bills favorable to their special interests. With little personal wealth, too many legislators made deals to get something for themselves while in office. Carpetbagger governor Henry Clay Warmth of Louisiana, accused of having pocketed thousands in kickbacks, explained the corruption that teemed in his state by observing that "everybody is demoralizing down here. Corruption is the fashion." Democrats joined in the feast. One Louisiana Democrat informed a northern party leader that "You are mistaken if you suppose that all the evils [in government] result from carpetbaggers and negroes — democrats are leagued with them when anything is proposed which promises to pay."

The corruption proved disastrous for Republicans. In perspective, the corruption of "black Republican" legislatures paled by comparison to the thieving of such scoundrels as "Boss" William Marcy Tweed of New York City, whose Democratic "ring" probably stole more money in a few years than all the southern Republican governments did in a decade. But the Democrats did not care about degrees of corruption. And thoughtful southern Republicans understood that even a whiff of scandal and corruption on their part would hand the Democrats an issue that would as surely end northern support for southern Republicans as it would outrage southerners. Democrats made "scandal" and "corruption" bywords in describing Republican rule and laid the blame in the "pact with the Devil" that let blacks vote and hold office. They embellished tales of black legislators hiring retinues of clerks and hangers-on, and laying out exorbitant amounts for spittoons and other accessories, and they pointed with derision to the hams, perfumes, whiskey, wine, suspenders, and even corsets one assembly purchased as "legislative supplies." They repeatedly cited the instance of the South Carolina legislature voting its Speaker of the House a bonus of $1,000 to pay off a bet lost on a horse race, and they snickered at how one drunken governor supposedly was persuaded by "a fancy lady in a burlesque show" to sign a bond issue. And they mocked the seriousness of black and white Republican legislative deliberations as buffoonery and posturing. After visiting the South Carolina assembly in 1873, influential journalist James S. Pike called it "the installation of a huge system of brigandage." Such governments, the Democrats insisted, deserved neither respect nor obedience. It was white southerners' "democratic duty" to overthrow them.

❧ White Violence

The Democrats waited until southern states had been readmitted to the Union to mount concerted efforts to overthrow Republicans. Unused to being outside the inner circles of power, Democrats were at first frustrated by their own impotence. By 1868, however, they determined to reclaim what they believed was rightfully theirs. They challenged the legality of elections, sowed discord among Republicans, and beat the drums of white supremacy. Democrats profited from factionalism within the Republican Party and from the failures of Republican rule. Democrats blamed high taxes and low levels of public morality on the Republicans — a campaign that not only mobilized southern whites but also convinced many northerners that southern Republicans were unfit to govern. More than anything else, Democrats pounded away at black empowerment, which, to them, meant white debasement. Whites must stand together, they declared, or surely the South would be "Africanized" and sink into "barbarism." Often calling themselves conservatives, the Democrats promised to restore "a Christian order" to politics and return prosperity to the region. More to the point, conservative white southern men and women ostracized whites who helped freedmen or Republicans, and welcomed back into the racial fold those who left them.

Conservative white southerners also turned to violence to drive Republicans from the South and African Americans back into submission. Violence had been widespread across the South since 1865, but by 1868 it assumed a more focused, political form. Numerous vigilante groups such as the Regulators, the Pale Faces, and the Knights of the White Camelia rose up to keep blacks from the polls and reassert "respect" for white supremacy. As nightriders, they threatened black families in their isolated cabins, disrupted meetings, and intimidated Republicans en route to do public business or vote. Vigilantism spread because it had the support of all classes. Planters, merchants, even ministers, locked arms with poorer whites to restore Democrats to office and put blacks "in their place."

The most notorious paramilitary group was the Ku Klux Klan. It began in Pulaski, Tennessee, in 1866 as a social club but soon degenerated into terrorism. Its elaborate rituals, outlandish garb, and mumbo-jumbo of passwords appealed to men's club spirit, and its loose organization of dens, each headed by a Grand Cyclops, gave it an adaptability to local circumstances that helped the Klan spread rapidly into every southern state. The Klan's presence was most keenly felt in those areas where black and white populations were roughly equal and violence might defeat Republicans. Terror was the Klansmen's trade. Sheet-clad Klansmen posing as ghosts of Confederates appeared before cabins late at night to menace the occupants. They singled out Republican leaders, black and white, for physical attack, even murder, and left a string of corpses across the South to warn anyone who might sell a farm to a black person or stand up as a Republican that there was a price to pay for such "sins."

Outgunned and respectful of legal processes, African Americans alone could not fend off the vigilantes. When they did resist, they often suffered worse violence. On Easter Sunday 1873, more than fifty blacks were massacred in Colfax, Louisiana, after a three-week siege by whites. Republican governments outlawed vigilantism but lacked the military or police power to suppress it. The few federal troops in the South were mostly stationed in or near the larger towns, away from the countryside where most southerners lived and where attacks on isolated cabins, churches, and meetinghouses could go unpunished. When several state governments armed black militias to restore order, the actions only served to infuriate whites more. Republican weakness emboldened the vigilantes to commit more brazen crimes, sometimes even in daylight. Desperate Republicans appealed to the federal government for help.

In 1870 and 1871 Congress passed three Enforcement Acts to protect black voters by providing federal supervision of southern elections and giving the president the power to suspend the writ of habeas corpus and use federal troops to enforce the law in areas he declared to be in rebellion. Congress also held hearings in which black and white victims of the Klan's outrages testified to the campaigns of terror across the South. In 1871 President Grant invoked the Ku Klux Klan Act, as the third enforcement bill was known, in nine counties of South Carolina, and by 1872 federal marshals there and elsewhere made enough arrests, and got almost six hundred convictions, to suppress the Klan and encourage blacks to vote in the 1872 elections.

The Ku Klux Klan　Horsemen in Ku Klux Klan garb are shown riding along a road with their horses at a gallop in this 1875 photograph.

But the Klan and similar vigilante groups had achieved their main goals. Violence had thrown many local Republican organizations into disarray. Blacks suffered disproportionately from the violence because the murder or exile of a prominent local black leader, particularly a minister-politician, affected the entire community infrastructure of church, school, mutual aid societies, and political party. The loss of a respected black voice in the freedmen's still largely oral culture might effectively silence them politically. At the same time, the violence also drove whites away from political involvement, making some feel that trying to build a Republican Party in the South was a "fool's errand." Finally, the violence discredited the Republican governments. Their inability to protect themselves made southerners more contemptuous of Republican claims to legitimacy and disgusted northerners anxious to be rid of the Reconstruction question.

And the violence did not end. Intimidation became a regular feature of the "redemption" process, bequeathing a legacy of violence that would corrupt southern politics for almost a century thereafter. Draped in the mantle of southern honor, conservative white men determined to show their manhood by standing up to "insolent" blacks and "rapacious" white Republicans. In Louisiana, the White League formed to beat and bully Republicans away from the polls, and in Mississippi "white liners" entered politics with a vengeance, openly proclaiming in 1875 that they would "Carry the election peaceably if we can, forcibly if we must." The "Mississippi Plan" emerged as a combination of disciplined Democratic political mobilization, making it "too damned hot" for any white to stay out of the Democratic Party, and constant intimidation of black voters. White landowners told black laborers and sharecroppers that anyone supporting Republicans would be thrown out of work and off the land. Whites instigated riots, disrupting political rallies, as in Vicksburg in December 1874, when thirty-five blacks were killed. Whites armed with knives would stalk blacks heading to the polls, threatening them with death or mutilation if they did not turn away or vote for a Democratic candidate. Most violence preceded election days as warnings to anyone who ran against the Democrat "redeemers." In Macon, Mississippi, for example, the Republican candidate for country treasurer was "shot down walking on the pavements, shot by the Democrats because he made a speech and said he never did expect to vote a Democratic ticket, and also advised the colored citizens to do the same." In South Carolina, Red Shirts and "rifle clubs" followed Mississippi's lead with armed threats against Republicans, with the rifle clubs, for example, practicing marksmanship by shooting at targets in or near Republican rallies.

What distinguished such violence and intimidation from the Klan variety was that it operated openly. It also succeeded in overthrowing Republican governments. When the governor of Mississippi appealed to President Grant for aid, the U.S. attorney general replied, "The whole public are tired out with these annual autumnal outbreaks in the South," and advised the governor to "Preserve the peace by the forces in your own state" to show that Republicans in Mississippi "have the courage to fight for their rights." The governor had courage but few resources, and the Democrats carried the state. By 1876 only Louisiana, Florida, and South Carolina remained under Republican control.

❧ *The Disputed Election of 1876*

By 1876 most northern Republicans had lost the political will to reform the South and had washed their hands of Reconstruction. The party itself had been transformed from its early reform days. The generation that had fought slavery's expansion, freed the slaves, and written congressional Reconstruction had passed from the scene by way of retirement, defeat at the polls, or death. Radicals like Thaddeus Stevens, now buried in a black cemetery in Pennsylvania, survived only in memory. Even the Civil Rights Act of 1875, prohibiting racial discrimination in all public accommodations, transportation, and juries, was more gesture than conviction. Republicans did not press for its enforcement. The new generation of Republicans was more attuned to organization than ideology, to building up business and brokering the competing claims of economic and ethnic groups in the North rather than breaking down prejudices and bringing justice to the South. And in the interests of promoting investment, it was willing to buy stability by placating white southerners. At the same time, the party had lost much of its moral stature because of a series of scandals in the Grant administration and in Congress. Indeed, *Grantism* had come to mean wholesale corruption and gorging at the "great barbecue" of public money. The party almost split apart in 1872 as reform-minded "Liberal Republicans," wanting to clean up politics and promote the free trade principles of liberal capitalism, backed the quixotic Horace Greeley for president, who was subsequently endorsed by the Democrats. The Liberal Republican faction died with Greeley after Grant's re-election in 1872, but it had frightened many Republicans into thinking they had to refocus their party's interest and identity. So, too, did the Panic of 1873, which sent the economy plummeting and the Republicans reeling. In 1874 Democrats won control of the House for the first time since before the Civil War. Money matters now counted more than protecting black voters in the South. As one Republican observed, "Hard times and heavy taxes" made white voters wish blacks "were in hell or Africa." The northern public clamored for attention to issues closer to home — of industrialization, labor unrest, immigration. The northern Republicans took stock of the situation and acted to save themselves.

To white southern conservatives, the centennial

❋ IN THEIR OWN WORDS

"Brute Force," 1874

Democratic-controlled newspapers railed against Republican Reconstruction, arguing that the governments were illegitimate because they were imposed by northerners and sustained by black votes. This Atlanta News *editorial was representative of such thinking. It endorses any means, even violence, to overthrow the governments and resist further federal civil rights legislation.*

Let there be White Leagues formed in every town, village and hamlet of the South, and let us organize for the great struggle which seems inevitable.... The radicalism of the republican party must be met by the radicalism of white men. We have no war to make against the United States Government, but against the republican party our hate must be unquenchable, our war interminable and merciless.... By brute force they are endeavoring to force us into acquiescence to their hideous programme. We have submitted long enough to indignities, and it is time to meet brute force with brute force. Every Southern State should swarm with White Leagues, and we should stand ready to act the moment Grant signs the civil-rights bill. It will not do to wait till radicalism has fettered us to the car of social equality before we make an effort to resist it. The signing of the bill will be a declaration of war against the southern whites.... We have been temporizing long enough. Let northern radicals understand that military supervision of southern elections and the civil-rights bill mean war, that war means bloodshed, and that we are terribly in earnest, and even they, fanatical as they are, may retrace their steps before it is too late.

year of American independence promised the final liberation from "foreign rule." Already in southern states "redeemed" from the Republicans, the Democrats had begun the process of repealing Republican policies and reasserting control over African Americans. The Democrats lowered taxes, pared governmental expenses, cut back or eliminated social programs, and reduced aid to education. They reinstituted vagrancy laws and passed new provisions binding debtors to landholders and merchants. And they restricted black mobility and property holding, down to limits on hunting and fishing rights and owning dogs. With three states still in Republican hands, though, much "redemption" was yet to be achieved. The Democrats looked to the presidential and congressional elections of 1876 as the best chance since the war to regain control over their "country."

When Grant declined a third term and Republican factions could not get their own favorites nominated for a presidential run, the party settled on the relatively unknown and unexciting but also untarnished Rutherford B. Hayes. As a bewhiskered Union veteran, a fiscal conservative, and, most important, a three-time governor of the important swing state of Ohio, Hayes brought a proper Republican pedigree to the ticket. Hayes promised "home rule" in the South and protection of civil and political rights "for all" without bothering to explain how both contradictory goals might be achieved. The Democrats put forward Samuel J. Tilden, a millionaire governor of New York who already had won civic reformers' hearts by smashing the Tweed Ring and attacking graft in the state. Tilden also campaigned on pledges of a "sound money" fiscal policy, an end to political corruption and governmental waste, and peace.

The election proved anything but peaceful. Conservative white southerners left nothing to chance. The Mississippi Plan operated wherever Republicans still competed for office. In South Carolina, for example, armed Red Shirts broke up Republican rallies, flogged and murdered prominent blacks and Republicans, and so disrupted the democratic process that one Democrat described the election as "one of the grandest farces ever seen." Post-election investigations suggest that violence kept as many as 250,000 Republicans from the polls in the South.

At the national level, Tilden had won the popular vote by roughly 250,000 votes, but his electoral vote count was only 184, one short of the 185 needed for election. The Republicans contested the returns from South Carolina, Florida, and Louisiana, and Republi-can-controlled returning boards in those states disqualified enough Democratic votes to give the states to Hayes. Along with one contested vote he received from Oregon, Hayes now claimed the presidency by one electoral vote. The Democrats erupted with charges of fraud and threats of civil war if the Republicans did not give back the "stolen election."

Congress attempted to resolve the dispute by forming a special electoral commission to determine which votes were valid. The fifteen-member commission was equally divided between Republicans and Democrats from Congress and the Supreme Court, with the fifteenth seat reserved for Justice David Davis, an independent. But Davis resigned after being elected to the Senate by the Illinois legislature, whereupon the Congress replaced him with a Republican Supreme Court justice. The commission then voted along strictly party lines, giving the election to Hayes by an 8 to 7 vote. Democrats in Congress refused to certify the result and threatened a filibuster to block any election. Meanwhile, Democratic "Minute Men" armed themselves and pledged to have "Tilden or blood" on inauguration day.

In truth, few Americans had any stomach for a new civil war. Behind the scenes, in the proverbial "smoke-filled rooms" of such places as the luxurious Wormley House, a Washington hotel owned by the black restaurateur James Wormley, important Republicans and southern Democrats worked out a series of understandings, later known collectively as the Compromise of 1877. Hayes's supporters agreed that in exchange for the Democrats conceding the disputed southern states, Hayes as president would remove federal troops and not stand in the way of Democratic takeovers of those states. The Democrats, in turn, pledged to respect the rights of the freedmen and accept Hayes as president. In sidebar negotiations, southern politicians lobbied for federal support for railroads and other internal improvements and for federal patronage, including a cabinet post. The deal was struck, and the Congress ratified Hayes's election.

Hayes honored some of the promises his supporters had made. Eager to conciliate the South, promote business investment there, and build a political alliance of southern Democrats and conservative Republicans, he named a southern Democrat as postmaster general and appointed many former southern Whigs, now Democrats, to federal offices. The administration also supported many internal improvements appropriations for the South, which received more federal money during Hayes's administration than ever before. Most

Rutherford B. Hayes   A former governor of Ohio who had gained a reputation as a scrupulously honest man, Hayes was a welcome relief after the corruption that President Grant had tolerated. But a taint of illegitimacy overhung Hayes's victory in the disputed election of 1876, and he was never able to rally the country behind him.

important, Hayes ordered federal troops in the capitals of Louisiana and South Carolina back to their barracks, whereupon the Republican governments in those states collapsed. A small number of federal troops remained in the South but no longer as a protector of civil rights. Republicans and Democrats agreed that the army was needed to fight Indians in the West and railroad strikers in the East. Home rule meant leaving southerners alone to settle their own affairs. By 1877 the entire South had fallen into Democratic hands.

Hayes made three trips to the South during his presidency to underscore the theme of sectional reconciliation. In a speech in Atlanta in 1877, he asserted that blacks would be "safer" if whites were "let alone by the general government." White southerners greeted Hayes

with Rebel yells and cheers. "Let alone" fit the age of "laissez-faire," and soon became the prevailing creed in the government's approach to race relations and economic policy. Political Reconstruction was over.

❧ Democratic Governments in a "Redeemed" South

African Americans had less to cheer about. In the states already under Democratic control, the conservatives had shown what they intended to do about protecting blacks' civil rights. The newly redeemed states followed suit in reintroducing many of the restrictive provisions of the old black codes of 1865-1866 and adding new discriminatory laws, especially in the criminal codes. During the 1870s and after, ever more onerous laws weighed on blacks and the poor across the South. In several states stealing livestock and crops became felony offenses; Mississippi's infamous "pig law" made the theft of any livestock a grand larceny crime punishable by up to five years in prison. Trespass laws in many states also had severe penalties. Most states adopted convict-lease systems whereby black prisoners were leased out to private contractors, such as coal-mining operators, road construction concerns, and planters, who often exploited the workers to the point of exhaustion and even death. Segregation became more common, though no state as yet introduced a comprehensive system of state-regulated racial segregation. Such institutions as schools, asylums, hospitals, orphanages, and prisons were segregated. Blacks and whites did continue to share public parks and public transportation, such as railroad and streetcars, but there, too, segregation was becoming the rule by the 1880s.

That conservative-ruled governments did not go farther in restricting blacks' civil rights owed to the fact that African Americans continued to vote well into the 1890s. Some also continued to serve in elective and appointive offices, especially at the local level but also in a few legislative and congressional districts. Conservatives who had "redeemed" their states by driving blacks from the ballot box now looked to black votes to keep themselves in power. Conservatives used bribery, coercion, and fraud to "win" black votes. When such tactics failed to deliver the votes, blacks were summarily disfranchised by force or legal means (see below). The net effect of "let alone" was to leave blacks at the mercy of conservative whites who would use them to advance their own interests, at best, and abandon them when counting black votes no longer paid. For a time, though, blacks escaped systematic state-endorsed public humiliation by way of segregation laws and disfranchisement. Southern politicians eager to attract northern capital pointed to such facts as proof that the "let alone" policy of "home rule" was working.

Conservatives needed black votes because they were losing white ones. Once restored to power, the Democrats lost the unifying force of race that had muted otherwise internal class differences over economic development and taxation, among several issues. The depression of the 1870s and the dependence on one crop pitted small farmers hungry for relief from taxes against large black-belt planters and supporters of banking, manufacturing, railroad construction, and other capital projects. Democratic factions jockeyed for black votes, but the general pattern was for the black-belt interests and their business and industrial allies to use black votes to maintain control over state governments.

The volatility of southern politics burst forth repeatedly during the 1870s and 1880s. Politicians in states heavily burdened with debt tried to buy off small farmers' unrest by revoking land grants to railroads, ending tax exemptions to corporations, and cutting back on other support for business. Government expenses were also trimmed in many states, to the point that some states, such as Alabama, limited the legislature to biennial sessions and slashed both the size of the payroll and the pay for all officials.

Retrenchment proved a two-edged sword. The tax system became more regressive, with few exemptions for small farmers and many for large ones. The cutbacks in public spending for schools, hospitals, and asylums hurt poor whites as well as blacks; indeed, the drop in educational support in Louisiana was so severe that white literacy actually declined between 1880 and 1890. Unless local communities resorted to self-help programs, as occurred through black and white churches, education suffered from under-funding. As one observer noted in 1888, "The typical Southern free school is kept in a log house, with dirt or puncheon floor, without desks or blackboards." Such was the cost of retrenchment to the poorer classes regardless of color.

The most significant split among Democrats occurred in Virginia, with the rise of the Readjuster Movement. Led by William Mahone, a former Confederate general, railroad promoter, and deft politician, the Readjusters sought to scale back — to "readjust" — the state's large debt by lowering interest rates on it and repudiating part of it. Such a readjustment, Mahone argued, would lift Virginia's heavy tax burden while also freeing up state money for public schools and development projects. Black and white small farmers rallied to the Readjuster Movement, which gained control of the state in 1879 and over the next two years rewrote its laws to increase aid to education, but also repealed the poll tax, reformed the penal code, and revised the tax system. The Readjusters appealed directly to the broad mass of Virginians, and even joined with Republicans. Most of all, they embraced the idea of an activist government capable of promoting both economic development and social improvement. Conservatives countered by summoning up the ghost of "black Republican" rule and resorting to violence to disrupt Readjuster meetings. The appeal to race shattered the Readjuster alliance and returned the state to conservative Democratic control in 1883, but not before the Readjusters had shown how vulnerable the economic elites were to rumblings from below and how precarious was their grip on the black vote.

Elsewhere, dissatisfaction also spurred independent reform movements, though none so successful as the short-lived Readjusters. The usual targets were the corrupt Democratic courthouse gangs who ruled local politics, inequitable tax systems, and the need for agricultural relief and reform. Such movements as the Patrons of Husbandry (known as the Grangers) cropped up to provide advice on scientific farming, purchasing and marketing, and finally politics. Even the churches were rent by class strains. The holiness movement among Methodists, for example, was as much a protest by farmers and mill workers against the allegiance of the red-bricked Methodist establishment with the business elites as it was a revival of spirituality and a return to "the simple life" (see Chapter 21). The politics of the "redeemed" Democratic South shook under the social and economic discontents.

✧ The Populist Challenge and the End of Black Voting

Against the background of farmer unrest and rapid economic and social change, a new wave of agrarian reform, known as populism, swept across the South. The causes of populism were many and varied according to region (see Chapter 21). In the South decades of falling cotton prices, growing indebtedness, and rising rates of tenancy, when combined during the 1890s with a new economic depression and the arrival of the cotton-destroying boll weevil, led southern farmers to question their social and political leaders, and in some cases even their way of life. Many small farmers had become especially vulnerable to the vicissitudes of markets over which they had no control because they had moved from self-sufficiency to commercialized agriculture. As cash earnings from cotton became more important, and the production of food for domestic consumption less so in their yearly plantings, southern farmers became ever more enslaved to those who controlled credit and markets. They felt abandoned by a politics that catered to the interests of big planters, bankers, and industrialists and by organized churches and cultural institutions that increasingly spoke the language of modernism and business order. As the editor of *Southern Farmer* noted in 1891, "the farmer has about reached the end of his row."

Harking back to the Granger movement of self-help and political protest, and drawing on such "renegade" political movements as the Readjusters and the "Greenback" Party, farmers looked to themselves for economic and cultural redemption and political power. Unlike such previous movements, which remained localized, the farmer protests of the late 1880s and 1890s became region-wide and eventually national. The principal agency for such expression and mobilization became the Southern Alliance movement, which sprang up during the 1880s in various local forms and during the 1880s coalesced into a broad regional "alliance" (see Chapter 18). By the 1890s more than a million southern farmers had joined the Alliance movement, which preached a message of respect for farmers' values and of governmental intervention to regulate prices, interest rates, and railroads and to increase the money supply. In Alliance rallies much akin to religious camp meetings, farming men and women discovered a common ground of conviction and purpose. Using the pulpit-pounding language of religious revival, Alliance speakers celebrated the moral and social worth of the small farmer and chastised the greed of unchecked free market capitalists. And they organized — not only to share information about farming, marketing, and other concerns, but also to challenge both local Democratic politicians who ignored their interests and the concept of limited government itself. Alliance people then went forth with evangelical ardor to spread the word.

Eventually, Southern Alliance people hooked up with westerners in a third-party movement, the People's (or Populist) Party, that would shake the complacency of traditional national politics and the idea of laissez-faire and prod the nation into making significant electoral reforms. In the South, the Populists first tried to take over local Democratic organizations, but having failed they moved to rewrite southern politics altogether. They did so by banding together on the basis of class, even patching over racial divisions in an effort to mobilize the "one-mule farmer" vote to unseat the "man in the big house." Indeed, in many states, the black vote held the key to victory. As one black delegate to the Texas state Populist convention observed, "If you are going to win, you will have to take the negro with you."

A string of local Populist successes, and the realignment of the major political parties (see Chapter 21), unsettled the southern political order. Across the South, conservatives fought back by stuffing ballot boxes, threatening economic reprisals, and driving wedges between factions among their opponents. Out of habit, if not interest, many white farmers were reluctant to forsake the Democratic Party they had supported for years. Moreover, the conservatives broke up the Populist alliances by using violence and fomenting racial discord. In Wilmington, North Carolina, in 1898, for example, the conservatives routed a Populist-Republican black majority coalition from office, in the process killing eleven blacks and injuring many more. Conservatives made blacks the scapegoats for all the political and social problems afflicting the South and pointed the way to electoral "reform" and renewed respect for the white farmer.

The failure of the Populists and their friends in the 1896 elections dealt the Populist Party a mortal blow. The party limped through another election, and populist rhetoric echoed for years in southern politics, but the separatist political movement was dead. Amid recriminations about the cause of the failure, white southerners moved to "clean up" southern politics by keeping blacks from any role in it, and thereby letting whites fight it out "fairly" among themselves without the distraction, and "disruption," of black votes. To end fraud, the argument went, it was necessary to take the franchise from blacks so that no one could use their votes to stuff ballot boxes.

From the 1890s through the early twentieth century, all the southern states disfranchised African Americans under the guise of "good government." To deny the ballot without running afoul of the Fifteenth Amendment, they used such devices as literacy and property qualifications, poll taxes, and registration laws. Although most states provided loopholes whereby illiterate and poor whites might qualify — for example, by being able to demonstrate to a voting registrar that one "understood" the state constitution when read to him, or by having a grandfather who had voted in 1860 or 1866, before blacks were enfranchised — the net effect of the disfranchisement laws was to reduce drastically the voting strength of all poor people. Blacks were stripped of the vote in all but a few localities, eliminating them as a factor in southern politics for half a century. Blacks also disappeared from public offices and jury boxes. White voter participation also dropped dramatically, by over 25 percent in many states. Opposition parties also collapsed. The South emerged as a one-party, Democratic (but un-democratic) "solid South." It would remain so until the modern civil rights movement led to the re-enfranchisement of blacks and a fundamental reorganization of southern politics during the late 1960s and the 1970s.

THE RISE OF JIM CROW

What poor whites lost at the ballot box was supposedly made up with state-mandated racial segregation. Segregation was widespread in the South before the 1890s, but it was not systematically applied, nor did it carry the full weight of state law. In a rural society, where blacks and whites already had separated in their churches and social activities and where they generally lived and worked apart (see below), custom and function kept black and white segregated much of the time, but as more blacks and whites moved to towns and cities and competed for jobs and public space, the lines of status became blurred. More galling to whites was that a new generation of blacks, not born in bondage, had grown up demanding respect. The increasing independence of blacks in building their own churches, mutual aid societies, and other institutions and in their persistent efforts to participate in public life convinced a new generation of whites that only the power of the state could maintain racial boundaries.

Beginning in the 1890s, southern states moved to fix blacks' status by enacting a universal system of segregation by law. State laws and local ordinances, known as Jim Crow[2] laws, detailed rules on racial etiquette that governed virtually every public activity. Blacks were by law confined to segregated areas in public parks, theaters, music halls, hotels, or kept from such places altogether; forced to sit in the rear

2. "Jim Crow" was originally a generic name for African Americans, particularly those whom whites considered "uppity." It referred to a stock comic character in blackface minstrel shows.

of streetcars and ride in special "colored only" railroad cars, even when they purchased a first-class ticket; and more. So complete did segregation in law become that it included separate entrances to public places, separate water fountains, and even separate Bibles in courtrooms. White lawmakers went to absurd lengths to keep the races apart. Atlanta's new city zoo, for example, built separate aisles on each side of the animal cages so that there would be "no communication" between black and white. (The animals were free to confront both.) Curfews kept blacks off the streets in several cities, and residential codes confined blacks to certain districts. The purpose of such laws was to do more than rely on custom to dictate social relations and standing. The laws were intended to elevate whites by debasing blacks.

Where the law left off, mob rule took over. Beatings, mutilations (even castration), and murders occurred with frightening regularity, but lynching increasingly became the weapon of racial control in the rural South. The number of lynchings rose along with white anxieties about political, social, and economic changes. During the hardscrabble 1890s, the number of lynchings peaked, averaging 187 annually in the nation, with three quarters of those occurring in the South and the vast majority of victims being black (on average, two blacks a week were lynched during this time). Lynchings were often public spectacles witnessed by large crowds, including women and children. In some cases, refreshments were served, and souvenirs, including body parts from the victim, sold or seized. The public lynching served as a demonstration and a ritual of the white community's power and a closing of racial ranks. Although some white southerners protested the barbarity, and black journalist Ida Wells-Barnett launched a crusade against it, most whites accepted lynching as a way to preserve the racial order. In the words of Georgia women's rights advocate and prohibitionist Rebecca Latimer Felton, "if it takes lynching to protect women's dearest possession from drunken, ravening human beasts, then I say lynch a thousand a week if it becomes necessary."

The victims were accused of any of a host of "crimes," from theft to being "uppity," which is to say anyone judged to have crossed the line by acting independently. In many instances, black men were charged with sexual advances against white women, thereby threatening "the purity" of the white race. The racial stereotypes of the day depicted blacks as a jumble of contradictions, at once placid watermelon-eating "Sambos" and bestial predators, but to many white southerners, blacks seemed more the beast than the buffoon. Their consorting with Republicans had proved their essential "depravity," and thus, argued whites, justified any means to hold their base instincts in check. Such thinking was enshrined in such immensely popular potboilers as the Reverend Thomas Dixon's *The Leopard's Spots* (1902) and *The Clansmen* (1905), which painted Reconstruction as a dark plot to destroy Christianity and "mongrelize" the South and ballyhooed the rescue of white women and southern honor by the Klan. Such thinking also lay behind disfranchisement, segregation, and lynching.

❧ *The Supreme Court and Jim Crow*

Over the last quarter of the nineteenth century, the Supreme Court helped open the door to segregation by cutting away at the promise of civil rights and the broadened definition of freedom that had underscored Republican Reconstruction. In a series of decisions, the Court narrowed the application of the Fourteenth Amendment. In the slaughter-house cases (1873), which dealt with state regulations of butchers, the Court decided that states, in establishing rules to regulate matters of public interest, did not necessarily infringe on the privileges of citizenship, as protected under the Fourteenth Amendment. In practice, this ruling limited the ability of private citizens to appeal to the federal government for relief from state and local governments' claims to jurisdiction over a host of public activities. The Court also struck down the ability of governments to forbid segregation. In *Hall v. De Cuir* (1878), the Court invalidated a state law barring segregation on riverboats because such a law interfered with interstate commerce. In the civil rights cases (1883), the Court declared unconstitutional the Civil Rights Act of 1875, which had guaranteed citizens the right to use public facilities, ruling that hotels, theaters, and railroads were not "public" institutions. The Court argued that the Fourteenth Amendment protected citizens from violation of their civil rights by governments, not by private citizens. And in *Plessy v. Ferguson* (1896), the Court upheld a Louisiana statute that required separate racial accommodations on railroad passenger cars. In *Plessy*, the Court argued that as long as accommodations for both races were equal, segregation did not violate the equal protection clause of the Fourteenth Amendment. The "separate but equal" doctrine stood until 1954 and provided the constitutional cover for racial segregation by law, which in practice meant separate but very unequal facilities.

The Court had affirmed Jim Crow, with but the lone dissenting voice of Justice John Harlan, a former slaveholder, insisting that "The Constitution is colorblind." In 1898, in Williams v. Mississippi, the Court approved of Mississippi's disfranchisement restrictions, arguing that such devices as poll taxes and literacy tests with the "understanding clause" did not "on their face discriminate between the races."

The Court's decisions reflected the changing attitudes of northerners as much as continuing a limited conception of government. In their own discriminatory practices toward blacks, immigrants, and labor unions, many northerners echoed the racial arguments of white southerners. As the eminent Yale economist William Graham Sumner remarked, "The Negro's day is over. He is out of fashion." Whether in the Indian wars to "open" the West; the "white man's burden" to justify imperial ventures in Asia; or the Chinese Exclusion Act and efforts to keep southern, central, and eastern Europeans out of the country, the attitude of whites had hardened decidedly against "people of color" everywhere.

BLACK EXERTIONS FOR FREEDOM

The boundaries of freedom so painfully fought over in politics and in the courts were also being defined in less formal, though often more indelible, ways by blacks and whites as they reordered southern society after emancipation. "Freedom," averred one black Georgia minister, "burned in the black heart long before freedom was born." Being free, as one ex-slave shouted in 1865, meant that "Now I am for myself." It carried the connotation of being reborn, which is why many ex-slaves took new names. Even as slavery unraveled during the war, blacks began to test what freedom meant by doing what had been denied them in bondage. For some, it was attending a religious meeting without whites present; for others, buying a gun or swilling liquor — all forbidden under slavery. Freedom, said the Reverend Henry M. Turner, meant no less than enjoying "our rights in common with other men. . . . If I cannot do like a white man I am not free."

Among the first actions of newly freed slaves was simply to walk about on their own account, to "stretch my legs" for liberty, as one African American said, without the permission of a master. Newspapers reported that in 1865 and 1866 especially, the freedmen were a people in motion. Many blacks left their home plantations to try their luck in nearby towns (the urban black population tripled after emancipation) or on land not owned by their former masters. They also did so, as one astute Freedmen's Bureau agent in South Carolina observed, "not so much for wandering, as for getting together . . . every mother's son among them seemed to be in search of his mother; every mother in search of her children."

Reuniting families riven by slavery and war became a major social force in the immediate postwar years. African Americans went to great lengths to locate spouses, children, and other relatives sold away. One man, for example, walked over 600 miles to North Carolina following a rumor that his wife and children were there. For years after 1865, black newspapers were filled with advertisements for lost family members, some who had been separated for twenty years or more. Blacks also sought to secure their hold on families by legalizing slave unions and by contesting efforts of former masters to claim their children under apprenticeship laws.

Ida Wells-Barnett   African American journalist Ida Wells-Barnett was a fearless leader in the resistance of Jim Crow laws in the post-Civil War South. In 1884 she refused to give up her seat on a train to a white man, and beginning in the 1890s — after three of her friends were lynched — she crusaded against that horrific practice.

Family needs even decided who would work for whom. Black men asserted their claim to manhood by refusing to let their wives and children work in the fields for whites or in any way be subject to white authority. Although such refusal cut family income, black men and women valued it as an essential definition of freedom. As one white planter reluctantly recognized, "The [black] women say they never mean to do any more outdoor work, that white men support their wives and they mean their husbands shall support them." Black preachers, editors, and other male leaders emphasized the importance of maintaining the father-headed family and reminded women of their special duty to make the home a "place of peace and comfort" and to obey their fathers and husbands. Only when blacks set up for themselves as sharecroppers or farmers did black women and children return to the fields. Still, by 1870 the pattern of the black family was set, especially in the cotton-producing regions, with most blacks living in a two-parent household in which men and women had separate spheres of responsibility. That pattern would remain intact until the great migration of African Americans out of the South to the industrial urban North in the twentieth century.

❧ *The Church*

The church emerged as the matrix of black community life in the postwar South. In a remarkable exodus, black Baptists and Methodists left biracial churches to form their own congregations so that by 1867 virtually all "churched" blacks worshiped in all-black churches. One indication of the scope of the change was that in 1860 42,000 blacks had belonged to biracial Methodist churches in South Carolina alone, but by 1870 only 600 did so. The "self-separation" of blacks from biracial churches was a reaction to the unwillingness of white-run churches to admit blacks on an equal basis as members, though many such churches reached out to blacks in other ways and lamented their leaving. More important was the freedmen's quest for autonomy. As one white northern missionary astutely observed, "the Ebony preacher who promises perfect independence from White control and direction carries the colored heart at once." The recruiting efforts of northern white missionaries, who otherwise helped set up schools and provided aid to freedmen, fell on deaf ears, no doubt in part because many such ministers ridiculed black religious practices of "shouting" (dancing), clapping, and calling back to preachers as "heathenish habits." Many blacks joined the African Methodist Episcopal Church, which vigorously organized across the South, but the majority found independent black Baptist congregations most congenial. In them, blacks could worship as they wished and run their own affairs free of any ecclesiastical or white oversight.

The black churches provided practical services as well as fellowship. They were principal venues for political meetings and mobilization (see above) and self-improvement. Churches dispensed relief, ran schools, sponsored social events, and established a wealth of self-help and mutual-aid associations, including burial societies, temperance clubs, and debating and literary societies. Some churches even housed savings banks. By the early twentieth century, especially in towns and cities, many such activities went on outside church doors, but the ties to the churches survived in the prominence of ministers and church leaders in running social, cultural, and economic organizations and in the reiteration of the self-improvement theme resounding from black pulpits. The churches set and maintained moral standards, disciplining wayward members and "backsliders" and thereby minimizing white intrusion into blacks' private lives. Self-reliance fed the blacks' messianic sense of their own history. By managing their own affairs through so many church-related activities, blacks gained confidence in their own abilities — and their destiny. Black ministers and lay people alike often cast themselves as the "children of Zion" or God's "chosen." The "promised land" was at hand, if they would but take it. At the same time, the blacks' separation from biracial Christianity and their push for autonomy also cut them off from shared religious experiences and direct communications with white Christians that might have formed the basis for common social and political interests.

White southerners were also turning inward after the war. In most white evangelical Protestant churches, the emphasis was on repairing both faith and physical structures. The need to rebuild churches burnt and ravaged from war consumed much energy in the postwar era. So, too, did revivals intended to revitalize a people's faith shattered by defeat. White ministers feared, in the words of one South Carolina Baptist, that defeat had caused "almost general demoralization, and a general apathy" that was "preying upon the vitals of religion itself." Veterans wracked by wounds and self-doubt, especially as they faced unemployment and the inability to resume their "manly" station as providers after the war, were reported "brooding over blighted hopes" and taking "to their cups or to gambling shops, and are now to be seen on the plain highway to destruction." And women who during the war had faced alone marauding soldiers, recalcitrant slaves, and an unyielding land no longer could so readily believe in the old "truths" about God as a protecting Father and their southern men as patriarchs. After the war, white churches had much work to do to restore even the faith in themselves.

To meet the spiritual, psychological, and social needs of their congregants, white churches wove as full a web of social institutions as did black ones. Churchgoing whites became increasingly absorbed in an evangelical Protestant culture of clubs, benefit associations, and church picnics and outings. Camp-meeting revivals, some lasting days, increased the spiritual tenor of white society, and hard preaching and love feasts harvested many souls for Christ. Churches imposed discipline on their members and assumed leadership roles in defining morality for white society at large. In the rebuilding process, men reasserted their "patriarchal" authority as ministers and church elders and deacons, but women acquired increasing authority by their numbers — more women joined churches than men — and by running Sunday schools, charities, and numerous other church-based social functions. As more southerners moved to

---

✳ IN THEIR OWN WORDS

"When Woman Gets her Rights Man Will Be Right," 1867

Sojourner Truth, born a slave in New York in 1797, was a powerful voice for black and women's rights before and after the Civil War. In this speech, she argued that equality for black women should follow naturally from emancipation of slaves.

I come from another field — the country of the slave. They have got their rights — so much good luck. Now what is to be done about it? I feel that I have got as much responsibility as anybody else.... There is a great stir about colored men getting their rights, but not a word about the colored women; and if colored men get their rights, and not colored women get theirs, there will be a bad time about it. So I am for keeping the thing going while things are stirring; because if we wait till it is still, it will take a great while to get it going again....

You have been having our right so long, that you think, like a slaveholder, that you own us. I know that it is hard for one who has held the reins for so long to give up; it cuts like a knife. It will feel all better when it closes up again. I have been in Washington about three years, seeing about those colored people. Now colored men have a right to vote; and what I want is to have colored women have the right to vote. There ought to be equal rights more than ever, since colored people have got their freedom.

towns by the late nineteenth century, it also became possible for women church members to enlarge their "sacred circle" and engage in a host of reform activities, such as temperance, child welfare, and poor relief.

Some southern white churches dealt with defeat and despair by denying them. Beginning in 1866, with the publication of Edward Pollard's book *The Lost Cause,* many white southerners defended secession as constitutional and the Confederacy as a noble enterprise. By the 1870s, the Lost Cause had evolved into a civil religion, with its own institutions and rituals. Many southern clergymen embraced the idea, arguing that the Confederacy was a Christian society, "baptized in blood," and that the money-grubbing North and its "Yankeefied" followers in the South were sunk in "Mammonism." In memorials and monuments, the Lost Cause advocates worshiped the memory of the Confederate soldier, especially Robert E. Lee and Stonewall Jackson, who were depicted as Christian knights; "redeemed" southern state governments declared Lee's birthday a holiday. Organizations such as the United Daughters of the Confederacy, founded in 1895, kept the sanctified version of the past alive in history textbooks and public pageants well into the twentieth century. The prominence of white ministers and church clubwomen in celebrations of the Lost Cause, such as Confederate Memorial Day, lent religious authority to its claims and emboldened the "redeemers," who invoked the Lost Cause mythology to justify the violent overthrow of Republican governments. The involvement of white clergy in the Lost Cause movement also contributed to southern whites' conviction that they were God's chosen to provide moral and political leadership, just as it condemned white churches in blacks' eyes as unreconstructed.

❧ *The School*

The freedmen equated education with freedom. Denied access to education while slaves, African Americans rushed to makeshift and missionary schools during and after the war to acquire "the talisman of power" that would make self-improvement — and, thus, liberty — possible. Teachers reported adults as old as eighty years sitting next to small children, avidly learning to spell and do arithmetic. Typical was the observation of one Freedmen's Bureau officer who noted that "A negro riding on a loaded wagon, or sitting on a hack waiting for a train, or by the cabin door, is often seen, book in hand delving after the rudiments of knowledge." The initial impetus for founding schools came from

"The Good Shepherd"   On April 3, 1875, *Harper's Weekly* published this drawing and the following caption: "It was known here [in Richmond] Sunday morning that the Civil Rights Bill had passed both Houses of Congress and needed only the signature of the President to become a law. On this very morning in Manchester, just across the river from Richmond, a negro woman marched into the Meade Memorial Episcopal Church just before the service began and took a front seat beside a lady. The lady at once rose, went into the vestry-room, and informed the rector, Rev. Mr. SAMMS. Mr. SAMMS considered the situation for a few moments, and then determined that, as the easiest way out of the difficulty was perhaps the best way, he would dismiss the congregation without any service, which he did promptly."

northern church-based philanthropic organizations, especially the American Missionary Association, and the Freedmen's Bureau, which provided supplies and sometimes paid the salaries of teachers. The northern-born teachers who came South to staff schools imbued their work with a powerful sense of mission, "as if we were in India or China," said one. That reform impulse underscored education thereafter, though with a vital difference from foreign missions in that blacks in the South soon took over control of their own schools. Blacks raised money to buy land, build schoolhouses, purchase books and supplies, and hire and pay their own teachers. To provide their own teachers and ministers, blacks and their friends opened advanced schools, including such colleges as Howard, Fisk, and Hampton. The schools, like the churches, became hubs of black enterprise and political activity. Black teachers, for example, negotiated and mediated labor con-

Freedmen's Bureau Teachers Under the auspices of the Freedmen's Bureau, high-minded northern women came south to teach not only literacy and other basic school subjects (to adults as well as to children), but also vocational skills. Here, in the Freedman's Union Industrial School in Richmond, black women learn to be seamstresses, widening their opportunities for finding paid employment.

tracts and prepared political tracts. Despite strenuous effort, black schools lagged behind white ones, especially after conservative Democratic governments cut public support for education. Few public or even church-based schools reached far into the countryside where most blacks, and whites, lived, and the demands of planting and harvest interrupted the short school year in any case. Still, the desire for learning remained intense and spurred repeated efforts to found schools as the means of promoting self-improvement.

❧ Booker T. Washington and Self-Help

The theme of self-improvement through education was especially popular among the small class of black

businessmen and professionals that had grown up serving a black clientele. Among them, no one embodied the self-help theme more visibly and vocally than did Booker T. Washington. Born a slave in Virginia in 1856, Washington had attended a freedmen's school in Hampton, Virginia, and in 1881 established his own industrial school for blacks at Tuskegee, Alabama. There he gathered promising young black scientists, such as George Washington Carver, and other teachers to provide blacks with vocational skills in agriculture, industry, and the trades. At Tuskegee, in countless speeches, and in his autobiography *Up From Slavery* (1901), Washington preached the gospel of self-help through hard work, integrity, and practical education. Washington gained national prominence in 1895 with a speech, later known as the "Atlanta Compromise," which he delivered to a racially mixed audience at the Atlanta Exposition. In it, he urged blacks to "throw down your buckets where you are" rather than flee the South, and to turn from the siren song of political equality to the real power that would come from economic success.

Conceding the racial prejudice of his day, he argued that economic betterment was the route to acceptance, that only wealth, "a little green ballot," would earn respect and power. Then, raising his hand, he reassured his listeners that "in all things that are purely social, we can be separate as the fingers, yet one as the hand in all things essential to mutual progress."

White southerners enthusiastically applauded Washington's speech as an endorsement of the conservatives' policies, while northern white philanthropists sought out Washington for advice on how best to help uplift southern blacks. Washington translated his acceptance among southern whites and his access to northern philanthropists into support for his brand of practical education, even as he secretly was funneling money and advice to lawyers and civil rights organizations to challenge Jim Crow and black disfranchisement in the courts. Many southern blacks admired Washington for his personal success and national attention, even if they did not accept his seeming capitulation to white racism, and Washington thus became the "spokesman for his race" in white eyes.

As violence against blacks continued and poverty spread, black support for Washington eroded and criticism arose. Led by the northern-born, Harvard-educated scholar W. E. B. Du Bois, black intellectuals and journalists pointed to the impracticality of the Tuskegee approach in the face of mechanizing agriculture and modernizing industry and to the implacable racism of whites. In *The Souls of Black Folk* (1903), Du Bois rejected Washington's emphasis on patience and manual skills and argued that only through the leadership of a liberally educated elite, a "talented tenth," and the ballot could blacks gain equal rights and justice. But in the South where over 90 percent of blacks continued to live until World War I, most blacks followed Washington's public accommodationism and efforts at self-improvement rather than Du Bois's political activism into the next century. Their ties to the land and dependence on whites for capital dictated such a course.

Booker T. Washington   One of the greatest educators of his day, Washington founded and served as president of the Tuskegee Institute, an academic and vocational school for African Americans.

❧ Land and Labor

Essential to securing black freedom was control over their own land and labor. As one black minister informed General William Tecumseh Sherman during the war, land-ownership held the key to liberty: "We want to be placed on land until we are able to buy it and make it our own." How, indeed whether, blacks would acquire land became a burning question after the war. During the war, the War and Treasury departments and benevolent organizations had tried various experiments using black labor on abandoned plantations, in an effort to restore production, to introduce blacks to concepts of wage labor, and to demonstrate that black free labor could be as profitable as had been black slave labor. In practice, the government generally leased the plantations to former masters and white overseers who were bent on making a crop more than remaking the South. From such experiences, blacks became wary of relying on government or benefactors to gain their economic "independency." They wanted "forty acres and a mule" and then to be left alone to set themselves up on their own small farms.

W. E. B. Du Bois The greatest black intellectual of the post–Civil War era, Du Bois studied at the University of Berlin and earned the first Ph.D. granted to a black by Harvard University.

Few freedmen got land. Proposals by such Radical Republicans as Thaddeus Stevens to confiscate the lands of the wealthiest and most notorious Confederates went nowhere in a Congress that prized the sanctity of property as the cornerstone of liberty. Congress did pass a Southern Homestead Act in 1866, which set aside roughly 44 million acres of land for the freedmen and white Union men, but the land was poor and often inaccessible. In any case, the freedmen lacked the capital or credit to buy and improve any acreage and the seed and tools to plant it. And white landholders were loath to sell land to any blacks who might have had capital. Planters wanted the freedmen to return to the fields as gang laborers under white supervision — thus, the black codes of 1865-1866.

Although African Americans largely remained a propertyless class, they resisted all attempts to return them to the conditions of bondage. Planters tried to sign the former slaves to yearlong contracts at almost subsistence wages, often payable in shares of the crop at year's end — the planter to provide housing, clothing, and other essentials and the laborer to submit to the almost complete authority of the landowner. The Freedmen's Bureau often endorsed such contracts as the first step toward recovery and an apprenticeship in free labor responsibility. But many blacks refused to sign on, and those who did shirked their duties and worked at their own pace, left the plantations before harvest, and in other ways asserted their own social and psychological independence in the midst of their economic dependence. "I mean to own my own manhood," declared one South Carolina freedman, who rejected a labor contract of 25 cents a day. Blacks used their mobility as leverage to negotiate better terms, and some left the South altogether during the 1860s to settle in all-black towns in Kansas or, as "Exodusters," headed west to try farming on the Plains. The Freedmen's Bureau tried to mediate disputes between planters and workers, and agents drew up contracts that gave workers a lien on the crop to ensure they would be paid. But planter pressure and government policy weakened the Bureau's enforcement capacity, as did the planters' distrust of the agents' intentions and the freedmen's resentment of the Bureau's attention to planters. By 1867, earlier in some places, freedmen were making their own arrangements with landholders.

Across the cotton and tobacco South individual landholders and freedmen hammered out new work arrangements. Some freedmen rented land on an annual basis for a cash payment and worked the land as tenants, retaining complete control over the crops planted and the money earned. The most widespread practice, though, was sharecropping. Under this system, the landowners subdivided their plantations into thirty- to fifty-acre farms that could be worked by a single family, and rented the unit on an annual basis for a share of the crop. The terms of the contract varied widely, depending on whether the "cropper," as the tenant was known, or the landowner provided tools, livestock, seed, and other necessities, but the normal division was for half a crop to the cropper and half to the landowner. Short of cash and reluctant to assume any obligations to care for the freedmen's dependents, the planters welcomed the sharecropping system as a way to get workers on the land to guarantee a crop. Because the sharecropper's return depended on the harvest, the planter was assured his "workers" would not leave before the crops were brought in and also gained the extra labor of the cropper's family, who now returned to the fields. Planters also retained a measure of control over the freedmen because they could refuse to renew the lease of an unsuccessful or "uppity" tenant, including any whose politics displeased the planters. By controlling the cotton ginning and marketing of the crops grown on his land, the planter also exercised considerable control over the net return the cropper would get, and those planters who also supplied credit to their tenants reaped other returns from them as well. Most important, systems of farm tenancy meant that the planters kept their land. The sharecroppers, in turn, were freed of the daily oversight by whites, gained a larger return for their labor than under the wage system, and retained the hope of acquiring their own land some day, if cotton prices held and they could hold on to some of their earnings.

Sharecropping and tenancy altered the sociology of the South. In areas where plantations had dominated before the war and blacks clustered in slave quarters on each plantation, the social landscape changed from blacks living together to blacks living apart on separate farms. The physical dispersal of the freedmen made the family the center of social organization and the churches central to black community life in the rural South. Churches and church functions were often the only places where blacks regularly came together. At the same time, the social relations between former masters and ex-slaves changed perceptibly. Planter paternalism had no place in a world governed by written contracts and the market. Former masters expressed hurt and bitterness that their former slaves, especially their most "trusted servants," had gone over to the Republicans and insisted on their own land. Planters were slow to give up their assumptions of the right to command blacks in all ways, but they did renounce the "obligations" of paternalism. As one southern editor observed, "the Law which freed the negro at the same time freed the master" of any due to his former slaves except kindness. Too often, kindness also was a casualty of business decisions, as dollar-starved planters evicted elderly and disabled blacks who could not pay their own way. The hard-edged racial politics of Reconstruction and after was in part an outgrowth of hard-nosed social relations, as well as hard times.

The credit system that underwrote farm tenancy undercut the possibilities for African American self-sufficiency and took a toll on the land. The farmer had to borrow against the fall harvest to get seed, tools, and essentials for spring planting. Rural merchants running "crossroads country stores" stepped in to fill the need by advancing supplies, feed, and other items to farmers and tenants on credit. To secure the loans, the merchant attached a lien on the tenant's crop and insisted that the tenant grow only a marketable cash crop, especially cotton. The merchants, who had to borrow capital from northern concerns at exorbitant rates in a highly competitive postwar economy, in turn charged crushing interest rates of 50 percent or more for goods sold on credit at inflated prices to farmers who had nowhere else to go. When cotton prices collapsed in 1869 and stayed low through the 1870s, it became impossible to repay the debts, which were then carried over to the next year. As one writer observed, once the farmer entered the cycle, "he had usually passed into a state of helpless peonage." Planting decisions shifted from farmer to merchant, many of who were planters, and new laws protected the landlord's and the merchant's claims to the crop over the tenant's. The crop-lien system cheated almost everyone. Farm tenancy and reliance on cash crops prevented crop diversification and use of fertilizers and depleted the soil, further driving down prices and individual yields. More southerners grew cotton after the war than during the heyday of "King Cotton" but profited less from it. The depressed economy mired black and white farmers in debt and tenancy, perpetuated outdated agricultural practices, and left the region backward and frustrated. Such was the breeding ground for angry politics and populism.

THE "NEW SOUTH" PROMISE

In the face of wartime destruction and declining agriculture, some southerners looked to the North for capital and ideas about how to build a "New South." Led by such newspaper editors as Henry Grady of the *Atlanta Constitution* and Henry Watterson of the *Louisville Courier-Journal*, New South advocates pledged to "out-Yankee the Yankee" by investing in manufacturing and adapting northern values of thrift and industry to southern conditions. Even as editors such as Grady paid their respects to the nobility of the Lost Cause, they sought to replace the "tired" old planter class with a new business class, the plantation house with the factory as the standard of wealth and status. In the spirit of laissez-faire capitalism, they called on southern governments to promote industry by keeping business free of regulations and high taxes and by capitalizing on the region's natural advantages of cheap labor and abundant natural resources. The Redeemer governments obliged, and northern capital followed with significant investment in railroads, mining, lumbering, and textile manufactures.

New South advocates pointed to the "progress" of a fourfold increase in railroad mileage from 1865 to 1890 that promised to open the southern interior to development and by 1900 even stretched into the South Florida wetlands. Coal and iron ore dug from northern Alabama, Tennessee, and Virginia filled train cars, as did sulfur, bauxite, and phosphate dug from the southeastern states. Even more impressive were the riverboats and railroad cars piled high with lumber; by 1910 the South accounted for 45 percent of the nation's lumber supply. Huge blast furnaces belched progress in Birmingham, the "Pittsburgh of the South," which by 1898 was the largest producer of pig iron in the country, and hundreds of thousands of cotton spindles whirred and looms clattered in the many textile mills dotting the Piedmont region. By 1900 the South was the nation's leading producer of cloth, and southern textile mills employed more than 100,000 workers. New industries promised new wealth. The oil that gushed from Spindletop, in Beaumont, Texas, in 1901 bathed the Gulf region in hopes of cashing in on a new kind of "black gold." Meanwhile, James "Buck" Duke of North Carolina made a fortune promising, as one admirer said, "clean, quick, and potent" pleasure with his machine-rolled cigarettes, which he marketed to a growing urban America through deft advertising that included alluring "cigarette girls" wooing customers with smoke. The

rise of cities such as Atlanta and Charlotte heralded the potential new wealth of the interior, and the population movement from farm to factory and town bespoke a promised shift from an agrarian to an industrial, urban society that might in time rival the North.

But the New South Creed proved a false promise for regional renewal. Much of the southern "boom" came at a fearful cost to the land and the people. Most of the industrial activity was in extracting raw materials, with the final, more profitable, processing of products done elsewhere. Mining, lumber, cloth production, and agriculture tended to be low-wage industries. Low-paid miners risked their lives gouging out coal and iron ore that made northern investors rich and left the Appalachian hills with played-out mines, leached soil, and fouled water. Northern lumber and logging syndicates hired mobile lumber-cutting teams, made up of young, poorly paid black and white men, to hew down virgin hardwood and yellow pine forests in giant swaths. In the words of historian Edward Ayers, the lumber companies "quickly took what they wanted and moved on," leaving in their wake deserted sawmill towns and entire counties denuded of wood. Soil erosion usually followed.

In the cotton-mill towns, the companies employed whole families but often relied on women and children to tend the machines, which kept wages down. Indeed, it was the prospect of cheap labor, even more than low taxes and proximity to raw materials, that led New England textile manufacturers to relocate their mills down south in the late nineteenth century. Largely drawn from

---

❋ IN THEIR OWN WORDS

"The New South," 1889

Henry Grady, more than anyone else, was the advocate of a "New South," arguing that the South must free itself from economic bondage by adopting "Yankee" ways of industry and commerce. In doing so, New South advocates appealed to northerners for investment and a reconciliation of sectional differences.

I attended a funeral once in Pickens county in my State. . . . This funeral was peculiarly sad. It was a poor "one gallus" fellow, whose breeches struck him under the armpits and hit him at the other end about the knee

— he didn't believe in *décolleté* clothes. They buried him in the midst of a marble quarry: they cut through solid marble to make his grave; and yet a little tombstone they put above him was from Vermont. They buried him in the heart of a pine forest, and yet the pine coffin was imported from Cincinnati. They buried him within touch of an iron mine, and yet the nails in his coffin and the iron in the shovel that dug his grave were imported from Pittsburgh. They buried him by the side of the best sheep-grazing country on the earth, and yet the wool in the coffin bands and the coffin bands

themselves were brought from the North. The South didn't furnish a thing on earth for that funeral but the corpse and the hole in the ground. . . .

Now we have improved on that. We have got the biggest marble-cutting establishment on earth within a hundred yards of that grave. We have got a half-dozen woolen mills right around it, and iron mines, and iron furnaces, and iron factories. We are coming to meet you. We are going to take a noble revenge . . . by invading every inch of your territory with iron, as you invaded ours twenty-nine years ago.

white tenant farmers and agricultural workers fleeing poverty, southern cotton mill workers had to learn the discipline of the clock and survive the boredom, choking heat and cotton dust, and cramped, noisy conditions of indoor work before they became competitive with factory hands elsewhere in the United States and western Europe — and employers paid them accordingly. In 1890 the typical southern textile worker averaged 85 cents-a-day pay for a sixty-hour work week, far below northern pay scales. Workers lived in company towns in which the mill owner provided the housing, the store, the school, and sometimes even the church, in addition to the work. As bad as the pay was the social ostracism of becoming a "linthead," a mark of having failed in a culture that still much admired agrarian over industrial values.

Workers fought to retain their dignity by building their lives around family and church and to claim a bigger wage and better working conditions by organizing. Strikes and labor violence became a regular feature of coal-mining areas, and in the early twentieth century cotton mill workers struck several times in bloody confrontations. Mine- and mill-owners crushed such uprisings ruthlessly and pocketed the profits (see Chapter 23).

Southern industries lagged behind industry in the rest of the country and did not provide sufficient foundation for dramatic regional economic development. Most textile mills, for example, produced yarn and coarse fabrics, which were shipped northward for weaving and final processing. As a result, late nineteenth-century southern mills did not develop high skill levels in their workers or retain enough capital earnings to serve as a "multiplier industry" as textile mills had done earlier in New England. Southern mills spun out no machine-tool makers, as had occurred in the North, and the South generally lacked technological innovators and home-grown modern managers. At the same time, the growing concentration of industries nationally in a few hands (see Chapter 18) conspired to retard southern industrialization. Northern companies jealously guarded their patents, and discriminatory freight rates hampered southern manufacturing. The system of freight differentials established by railroad companies in the 1870s and 1880s especially discriminated against southern-produced steel, thus keeping it out of the national market, while offering favorable rates for raw materials, thus encouraging investment in the South. The lack of local capital made southern industries dependent on northern credit. Only cotton textiles, furniture-making, and tobacco manufactur-

ing drew on significant local capital outlays. Most debilitating was the overall poverty of the region, saddled with one-crop agriculture and debt-crippled farmers. The net result was a region that boasted of its industrial progress but in 1900 remained an economic colony of the more vigorous, more capital-rich industrial North.

CONCLUSION:
THE SOUTH AT CENTURY'S END

As the half-century after the Civil War closed, the South had been "remade," though not in the ways Radical Republicans wanted. Plantation days were over, except in the wistful memories of the Lost Cause and Joel Chandler Harris's "Uncle Remus" tales, and southern politicians no longer bullied the nation with threats of disunion. Sectional reconciliation had come, at least publicly. White northerners had returned the South to "home rule" and, in the midst of a massive "new immigration" of eastern European Jews, Catholics, and others, had come to accept white southerners' arguments about the need to keep all "colored people" and aliens "in their place." Southerners returned to national service, rallying to the flag during the 1898 Spanish-American War. Reconciliation was symbolized and affirmed as Confederate veterans clasped hands with their Union counterparts at reencampments at Gettysburg and other Civil War battlefield sites in 1888 and regularly thereafter. A host of mass-produced products entered the South, along with northern advertising and capital, to bind the South increasingly to the national market economy and consumer culture. The rising interior cities and villages and towns cropping up across the region also pointed southern growth in the same direction as the urbanizing North. Most important, slavery was dead. If freedom for blacks was not so free as it was for whites, at least blacks had gained recognition as citizens of the republic and had found in their own families, churches, and self-improvement associations the matrix for a self-sustaining, independent black community life. Also, the Reconstruction amendments had laid the constitutional basis for a second "new birth of freedom" in the modern civil rights movement after World War II.

Yet, the South in 1900 was in many ways a blighted land. Neither real progress nor racial progress had gone very far beyond words. Differences among people had widened, and distrust between the races and among classes soured human relations and degenerated into violent politics. Poverty gripped much of the region and crushed the psychological and physical health of southerners as much as it strangled the region's economy. For all the "New South" boosterism, the South remained largely agricultural and rural, with overworked soils and underpaid labor. In education (human capital), wealth, and living standards the South had not kept pace with northern development. Indeed, in that regard, as historian C. Vann Woodward has observed, the Union was more of a "house divided" in 1900 than in 1860. A real "new South" would not emerge until a "second Reconstruction" some sixty years later.

SUGGESTED READING

Edward L. Ayers, *The Promise of the New South, 1877-1906* (1992). A major recasting of the social, economic, and cultural reconstructions of southern life, with special emphasis on the role of modernization on folkways, law, and social relations.

David W. Blight, *Race and Reunion: The Civil War in American Memory* (2001). A close consideration of the competing images, ideas, and interests in "remembering" the war, slavery, and Reconstruction.

Eric Foner, *Reconstruction: America's Unfinished Revolution, 1863-1877* (1988). The now standard history of Reconstruction that centers the story on blacks' aspirations for and movement toward freedom and the social, economic, and political forces retarding a true "revolution" in Reconstruction.

Steven Hahn, *A Nation Under Our Feet: Black Political Struggles in the Rural South from Slavery to the Great Migration* (2003). A revolutionary rethinking of the ways African Americans drew on a political sensitivity and culture from slavery to create community foundations for political activism in freedom.

Leon F. Litwack, *Been in the Storm So Long: The Aftermath of Slavery* (1979). A sensitive survey of African Americans' efforts to define freedom and their interactions with whites in the crucial first years of emancipation.

Heather Cox Richardson, *The Death of Reconstruction: Race, Labor, and Politics in the Post-Civil War North, 1865-1901* (2001). A valuable charting of the decline of northern support for Republican Reconstruction amid rising race consciousness, labor unrest, and concerns about a changing economic order that remade party politics.

Daniel W. Stowell, *Rebuilding Zion: The Religious Reconstruction of the South, 1863-1877* (1998). An original reading of the visions northern and southern churches and the freedpeople had of Reconstruction and how such views and interests shaped society, politics, and religion.

Joel Williamson, *A Rage for Order: Black-White Relations in the American South since Emancipation* (1986). An abridgment of *Crucible of Race* (1984) that points to the persistence and pervasiveness of racism that ruled law and society in the postwar South.

Charles Reagan Wilson, *Baptized in Blood: The Religion of the Lost Cause, 1865-1920* (1980). A discovery and examination of the civic religion of the "Lost Cause" and its effects on the "New South" ideology and white southern identity.

C. Vann Woodward, *The Origins of the New South, 1877-1913* (1951). The classic study of southern race relations, business development, labor arrangements, political power, and society after "Redemption" and the failure of the populist revolt to remake the South.

SUGGESTIONS FOR FURTHER READING

James A. Baggett, *The Scalawags: Southern Dissenters in the Civil War and Reconstruction* (2003).

Michael Les Benedict, *The Impeachment and Trial of Andrew Johnson* (1973).

Edward J. Blum, *Reforging the White Republic: Race, Religion, and American Nationalism, 1865-1898* (2005).

Dan T. Carter, *When the War Was Over: The Failure of Self-Reconstruction in the South, 1865-1867* (1985).

Jane Turner Censer, *The Reconstruction of White Southern Womanhood 1865-1895* (2003).

Paul A. Cimbala, *Under the Guardianship of the Nation: The Freedmen's Bureau and the Reconstruction of Georgia, 1865-1870* (1997).

Richard N. Current, *Those Terrible Carpetbaggers: A Reinterpretation* (1988).

Don H. Doyle, *New Men, New Cities, New South: Atlanta, Nashville, Charleston, Mobile, 1860-1910* (1990).

Katharine L. Dvorak, *An African-American Exodus: The Segregation of Southern Churches* (1991).

Laura F. Edwards, *Gendered Strife and Confusion: The Political Culture of Reconstruction* (1997).

Robert F. Engs, *Educating the Disfranchised and Disinherited: Samuel Chapman Armstrong and Hampton Institute, 1839-1893* (1999).

Carol Faulkner, *Women's Radical Reconstruction: The Freedmen's Aid Movement* (2004).

Gaines M. Foster, *Ghosts of the Confederacy: Defeat, the Lost Cause, and the Emergence of the New South* (1987).

Jacquelyn Dowd Hall et al., *Like a Family: The Making of a Southern Cotton Mill World* (1987).

Louis R. Harlan, *Booker T. Washington: The Making of a Black Leader, 1865-1901* (1972).

Gerald D. Jaynes, *Branches without Roots: Genesis of the Black Working Class in the American South, 1862-1882* (1986).

Michael Perman, *Struggle for Mastery: Disfranchisement in the South, 1888-1908* (2001).

Nina Silber, *The Romance of Reunion: Northerners and the South, 1865-1900* (1993).

Brooks D. Simpson, *The Reconstruction Presidents* (1998).

Allen W. Trelease, *White Terror: The Ku Klux Klan Conspiracy and Southern Reconstruction* (1971).

Michael Vorenberg, *Final Freedom: The Civil War, the Abolition of Slavery, and the Thirteenth Amendment* (2001).

Harold D. Woodman, *New South, New Law: The Legal Foundations of Credit and Labor in the Postbellum Agricultural South* (1995).

17

Remaking the Trans-Mississippi Wests

EVEN BEFORE THE American republic was founded, Europeans and then "Americans" had imagined and espied the "great West" beyond the Mississippi River to the Pacific Coast. The Spanish laid early claim to the whole of the region, and for over two centuries attempted to assert their authority through Catholic missions and military presidios posted widely among native peoples. The French *coureurs de bois* and black-robed Jesuit missionaries in the upper plains and soldiers and traders along the lower Mississippi River and Gulf of Mexico fed imperial notions of a "new France" extending into the prairies. The British pushed the French out of Canada in 1763 and later made good their own claim to the area, spreading out from the mouth of the Columbia River by establishing trade with various native peoples and building trading posts and forts. The Russians, too, had ambitions along the Pacific coastline, though such interest remained more word than deed.

Sustained exploration, exploitation, and occupation of the vast and varied trans-Mississippi region did not come until the United States acquired the Louisiana Purchase in 1803 and sent out scientific and military expeditions to map the area, inventory its resources, make contacts with native peoples, and ready itself for expansion through public policies promoting westward settlement. By the mid-nineteenth century, the annexation of Texas, the war with Mexico, the northern boundary treaty with the British, and the Gadsden Purchase had redrawn the map generously for American claims. Many Americans justified westward expansion by arguing it was the republic's "Manifest Destiny" to occupy and reap riches from a continental empire. That dream, the thinking went, required only that nature and the native peoples be "tamed," Mexicans and other "interlopers" removed, and transportation improved. Such was the public agenda for the next half-century as Americans marched across and remade the trans-Mississippi West.

Although the mountain man and cowboy came to symbolize a West where the individual roamed free, in fact the federal government and high-finance capital played a huge role in developing the trans-Mississippi West. The government sponsored scientific expeditions and geological surveys that mapped the region, identified its resources, and channeled migration and development, and later even determined which lands might be national parks because they were unfit for mining or farming. The federal government organized the region into territories under the authority of the secretary of the interior, who charged the federally appointed territorial governors to promote order and settlement. States emerged from the territories in two clusters of admission into the Union — Oregon (1859), Kansas (1861), Nevada (1864), Nebraska (1867), Colorado (1876), North Dakota (1889), South Dakota (1889), Montana (1889), Washington (1889), Idaho (1890), Wyoming (1890), and Utah (1896). Oklahoma (1907), New Mexico (1912), and Arizona (1912) soon followed. Still, the federal government continued to own most of the land in the region, controlled water rights on key rivers and tributaries, maintained forts, subsidized transportation, carried the mail, and plowed significant resources into local economies. The federal government also sometimes intervened in private matters to shape the culture of the region. It did so most aggressively in the 1880s when Congress passed legislation, supported by Supreme Court decisions in the so-called Mormon cases, effectively disfranchising and excluding from office Mormons practicing polygamy and seizing the church's assets to force compliance with anti-polygamy laws; only after the Church of Jesus Christ of Latter Day Saints leadership capitulated on polygamy in 1890 did Congress consider Utah's statehood, which it granted in 1896 with the requirement that Utah's constitution expressly guarantee religious tolerance in the state and "forever" prohibit "polygamous or plural marriages."

Investment bankers and businessmen developed the West by providing much of the capital, while corporations provided the managerial and technical expertise that built the railroads, operated the mines, harvested the forests, organized the markets for hides, grains, and cattle, and even moved many people onto the land. In the half-century from the admission of California to the Union in 1850 to the Alaska gold rush of 1897 and the annexation of Hawaii in 1898, much of the West was transformed into commercial farms and ranches, large-scale mining operations, and towns and cities that established the new industrial order, and was settled by diverse peoples from the Americas, Europe, and Asia. Yet at the same time, other Wests persisted in the American imagination and in early efforts at preservation and environmental conservation.

Native Peoples

When Americans began moving across into the trans-Mississippi West in large numbers at mid-century, they did not enter an empty continent waiting for "civilization." An estimated 360,000 Indians then lived in the region between the Mississippi River and the Pacific Coast. Contrary to popular stereotypes about "the Indian" as "wild" and "savage" and all cut from same cloth, the native peoples varied considerably in culture and society across the vast area as each group adapted to local resources and shaped its own environments in the process. Lewis and Clark had noted such diversity in their search for the headwaters of the Missouri and a Northwest passage to the sea, and numerous other explorers, traders, and trappers provided similar descriptions of a diverse landscape and many peoples — for anyone who would heed their advice about going west.

❧ Diverse Ways of Life in the Southwest and Northwest

In the Southwest, the Hopis and Zunis practiced an intensive agriculture, herded sheep, and traded with the Mexican *rancheros* (ranchers), with whom they had worked out an accommodating coexistence. By the nineteenth century, the Navajos were shifting from a nomadic and raiding culture to a more sedentary one, bartering produce for tools, cloth, and other items. Like the Pimas and others, they used irrigation systems to farm the arid region. The Pueblos continued to live in their tiered towns, fending off Apaches and others and working the ground to grow maize, beans, and squash. The Comanches, Kiowas, Arapahos, and Apaches in present-day Colorado, eastern New Mexico, and western Texas, as well as Shoshone, Utes, and others in the deserts of the Great Basin, hunted game and raided Spanish and Indian settlements but mostly scratched out a spartan subsistence on dogs, rabbits, insects, snakes, and wild plants, which they sometimes sustained by diverting water from streams.

Farther north in the forests along the Cascade Mountains and in the foothills of the Rockies, natives such as the Chinook and Yurok burned the woods to create grasslands and spaces for the deer, elk, moose, and bear they hunted. In the river valleys, the Yakima and other native peoples caught fish, including great quantities of salmon during the salmon runs on the Columbia River. Indians such as the Tlingits on the Pacific Coast hunted bear, beaver, and porcupine, gathered clams, fished the ocean, and speared whales and seals to provide food, clothing, shelter, and all manner of materials.

❧ Hunting Buffalo on the Great Plains

On the Great Plains lived various tribes, many of them Sioux-speakers but also Cheyenne, Blackfeet, and Crow. Plains peoples organized their physical, social, and spiritual lives around the buffalo hunt. The men hunted, and the women followed to butcher the slain animals and then hang the meat on racks to dry. The buffalo (or American bison), which numbered over 12 million at mid-century, provided the natives with food, clothing, shelter, bedding, boats, tools, weapons and armament, ornaments, rattles, drums, glue, fuel, and more. The conical *tipi* (tepee), made from buffalo hides, was an effective shelter, easily put up and taken down and transported, just as the shield, made from hides, was an effective armor capable of stopping a bullet. Buffalo dung ("chips") burned well, if not very aromatically. Bones might be made into knives, awls, fishhooks, amulets, toys, and myriad other items for fashion and fashioning. A stretched buf-

Tanning Hides   Women followed men on the buffalo hunts, skinning and cutting up the slain animals. Here a Blackfoot woman tans a buffalo hide.

falo hide served as a canvas to record events. The skull became a religious totem.

The introduction of the horse by the Spanish late in the sixteenth century, and later the acquisition of firearms and metal products from the French and British, made the Plains Indians more migratory, warlike, and efficient hunters. The horse prospered on the grasses of the plains and gave the Plains Indians a new ability to track and chase down buffalo, carry more goods, and extend their range across a wide area. The use of metal-tipped arrows and guns increased the natives' killing power and efficiency in hunting and war. No more would they have to stampede whole herds of buffalo over cliffs into ravines, as was the practice before the natives adopted the horse and adapted European goods. The horse further transformed Plains Indian cultures by emphasizing the heroic way of life of the mounted hunter-warrior, who became almost a mythical centaur. Young men joined warrior societies, sought visions to ensure success in the hunt and battle, and counted personal bravery as the true mark of a man. No people were more successful in taking to the horse than the Lakota (or Teton) Sioux, who by the mid-nineteenth century dominated the northern plains, having seized the Black Hills, forged alliances with the northern Cheyennes and Arapahos, driven the Pawnees and others southward, and gained control over the fur trade along the Missouri River.

✣ *Tribal Beliefs, Relations, and Practices*

Despite their diversity, Indian peoples shared a common respect for nature. They endowed the land, animals, and plants with sacred meaning, all part of an interconnected world. Humans, as part of that unity, must live in accord with nature and honor it with ceremonial rituals. Indeed, some plants and animals had special or superior powers that particularly demanded human recognition and respect. Man would not be nature's master; thus, the Judeo-Christian account of God giving man dominion over nature made no sense to Indian thinking about the creation of all life. Indian belief "systems" did not prohibit farming or hunting, but they did discourage the accumulation of wealth for its own sake. To be sure, some natives abjured farming as a violation of the earth, while others hunted and trapped animals for trading purposes. Overall, though, trans-Mississippi Indians believed that land, plants, and animals were not commodities to be exploited for profit. Sustained contact with European/American traders and settlers threatened such a worldview and native life.

Most Indians also shared a similar emphasis on kinship and tribal relations. They held common ideas about the centrality of community and the importance of cooperation. Across the West, with only a few exceptions among the wholly sedentary peoples, tribes tended to be small, roughly 300 to 500 people, which came together for summer encampments and broke into clans or bands for winter. Until the disruptions of over-hunting, war, displacement, forced migration, and disease that came with European/American intrusion, most natives lived their entire lives within the group of their birth. Within each tribe people were bound together by extended kinship ties. Children learned to respect their elders, who exercised a collective influence over the tribe. Most Indians thus grew up in cultures emphasizing loyalty, obligation, and duty to the group over any individual aspirations. Decision was by consensus rather than command, a practice that later caused much confusion in Indian-white relations.

Indian life was hardly static or stuck in a Stone Age trance before European and American traders brought new goods to the region. Inter-Indian exchanges were common and sometimes spanned long distances. As they moved about following game or searching for better conditions, native peoples discovered new ways of hunting, growing crops, building shelter, and crafting clothes and objects for wear and display. Natives absorbed new goods and ways into their own cultures because they wanted them, just as they would later seek European goods, even to use in ways the makers had not intended. Indians, for example, cut up metal pots to make spear and arrow points and other tools, thereby saving much taxing labor in chipping, scraping, or grinding out stone and bone implements. Like the Europeans and Americans, many native peoples were explorers, discoverers, and traders, and their ability to incorporate new materials and ideas into their cultures made them more adaptable and resilient than common stereotypes would have them.

Over time the new ways became the old ways. In the folklore and creation stories of various Plains peoples, for example, the horse was present from the beginning. Similarly, the Navajo reworked their origin stories as hunters to fit the southwestern environment on which they settled and farmed. They thus "forgot" their northern roots in claiming they had always lived in *Dine Bikeyah,* or Navajo country, that stretched across a wide area marked in its corners by four sacred mountains. Such recastings of myths and traditions bespoke changeability and adaptation in native cultures.

Too few Europeans or Americans understood or appreciated the Indians' ways of organizing their societies and sharing decisions. Instead, they applied their own ideas about political structure and authority to the natives, mistaking the influence of an elder, or chief, for absolute power and insisting that agreements made with such chiefs had the force of law. Europeans and later Americans also misread territorial disputes among Indians as being traditional or fired by distinct, exclusive claims to land and resources akin to European rivalries. In fact, most disputes among natives were transient, and concepts of territory were based on use rather than any proprietary ownership.

THE INDIAN WARS

Until the mid-nineteenth century, American and native contacts in the trans-Mississippi West were limited and largely peaceful. Americans regarded the Great Plains as the "Great American Desert" after explorer Zebulon Pike dismissed the region as an arid wasteland. Instead, Americans eyed the Oregon Territory and California as the best places to settle. The wagon trains rumbling over the Oregon Trail during the 1840s and after cut across Indian lands, but the emigrants initially had little trouble with the natives, except for petty thievery and a few brushes with bands of braves wearing warpaint. The pioneers traded with the natives for food and supplies and hired them as guides, and some few among them even came to respect the natives for their mastery of the horse and ability to survive in a seemingly inhospitable environment.

Indian-white conflict came soon enough. The swelling stream of settlers moving to Oregon in the 1840s and 1850s and the mad rush of gold-hunters to California, starting in 1849, disrupted native life. Along the wagon trails west, the emigrants depleted scant timber resources for fuel, over-hunted or drove away game, interrupted animal migration patterns, and inadvertently infected Indians with cholera, measles, and other diseases; meanwhile, their livestock ate up the plains grasses the buffalo needed. Clashes between natives and westering emigrants became more common by the 1860s as the Indians worried about the increased pace and size of the Americans' movement westward and the federal government determined to push Indians aside to make way for "progress."

❧ *Challenges of White Settlement*

As tensions increased, the United States government resolved to ensure safe passage across the plains, reduce intertribal warfare, and secure the region for future settlement by persuading the Plains Indians to accept designated tribal boundaries that the government pledged to protect and respect. As early as 1851, at Horse Creek near Fort Laramie in present-day Wyo-

ming, roughly 10,000 Indians from all the major northern Plains tribes gathered in a great "council" to make a treaty with Thomas Fitzpatrick, a mountain man and highly regarded U.S. Indian agent known as "Broken Hand" to the Indians because he had lost three fingers in a gun accident. In the Treaty of Fort Laramie, each tribe represented there accepted the American proposals for specific limits on hunting grounds in return for annual payments, gifts, and the American pledge never to violate the arrangements. Two years later, at Fort Atkinson on the Arkansas River, Fitzpatrick held another "big talk" (council), this time reaching a similar accord with Kiowas, Comanches, and Plains Apaches. These two treaties were intended to create northern and southern concentrations of Indians separated from one another by an American passageway across the plains.

This policy, known as "concentration," was built on a false premise that the government could, and would, direct the propulsive American westward surge away from the protected lands and that the Indian chiefs signing the treaties at Fort Laramie and Fort Atkinson spoke for their people. In fact, even those who signed the "treaties" had doubts about them. In the words of one Sioux chief at Fort Laramie, "You have split my land and I don't like it." Agent "Broken Hand" Fitzpatrick, whose skill and reputation made the treaties possible, also did not believe in their premise; rather, he thought diplomacy a poor substitute for military power in dealing with Indians. Within three years of the Horse Creek council, fighting broke out when Brule Sioux killed several soldiers who impetuously had sought to punish them following a misunderstanding over the butchering of a Mormon emigrant's stray cow. In 1855 the U.S. Cavalry in turn attacked an Indian village at Ash Hollow. At the same time, passage of the Kansas-Nebraska Act signaled new efforts to open the plains to settlement, and in 1858 and 1859 the Pikes Peak gold rush spurred a new wave of gold-seekers clamoring into Colorado, onto land guaranteed by treaty to the Arapaho and Cheyenne in 1851. The government, meanwhile, reneged on its promises of payments and protection by tolerating gross corruption and mismanagement in the Indian Bureau of the Department of the Interior, the governmental agency in charge of Indian affairs. Bureau agents cheated natives in trade, shortchanged them in payments and support, and allowed trappers, miners, and hunters on Indian lands. Thus began a generation of warfare on the plains.

Local Militia

During the Civil War, most of the U.S. Army went east to fight the Confederacy, leaving local militia and volunteers to police the frontier. Misunderstandings and frustrations rapidly escalated into violence, with no significant federal government authority to maintain order and honor its own commitments. Knowing of the weakened military presence and angry at the federal government's continued failure to provide annual payments or honor other treaty provisions, the Santee Sioux in the Minnesota Territory, in 1862, moved onto their former hunting grounds, once "ceded" to the United States. War broke out in August 1862, when the Santee Sioux attacked and killed roughly 500 settlers there, and the surviving settlers, aided by reinforcements from the U.S. Army, lashed out at the Sioux in two weeks of violent retaliation. General John Pope, commander of U.S. forces in the territory, instructed his officers to treat the Indians "as maniacs or wild beasts, and by no means as people with whom treaties or compromises can be made." Soldiers and settlers acted accordingly. The government tried and convicted more than 300 captured Indians for murder, but President Abraham Lincoln commuted the death penalty for all but 38 of them after an appeal for mercy by the Episcopal bishop in the territory, who pointed to the "rascality of the Indian business" as the cause of the troubles. In December 1862, the government hanged the Indians still sentenced to death and exiled the rest to reservations in the Dakota and Nebraska territories. The settlers and army hounded the remaining Santee Sioux out of Minnesota, so that the population had been reduced from its prewar number of 7,000 to fewer than 400 in 1866.

Meanwhile, in Colorado Territory, the Arapahos and Cheyennes had been harassing gold miners and others who had encroached on the natives' supposedly treaty-protected lands. The governor of Colorado wanted to end all land treaties with the Indians and open the territory to settlement, and white settlers feared a general Indian war. At dawn on November 29, 1864, militia colonel John Chivington and his force of almost 1,000 militiamen attacked a sleeping band of Cheyenne at Sand Creek, slaughtering men, women, and children and disemboweling and mutilating their bodies in an orgy of hatred. The Cheyennes under Chief Black Kettle thought they had army protection, and Black Kettle even raised a white flag to signal peace when the assault began. Chivington ignored the flag, ordering his men to "Kill and scalp all, big and little. Nits make lice."

Breaking Resistance *Execution of the Thirty-Eight Indians,* an 1883 painting depicting the hanging of the Minnesota Sioux after the "uprising of 1862," was widely circulated as a lithograph and quickened interest in Indian affairs among easterners. During the American Civil War, the government intended the public spectacle of the mass execution to discourage further Indian resistance at a time when U.S. military forces were spread thin in the West.

News of the Sand Creek massacre outraged public opinion in the East, and a joint congressional investigation later condemned Chivington for the excess.

Total War

After the Civil War, the federal government beefed up military forces in the West. The cavalry regiments were composed mostly of men hardened to difficult duty and battle during the Civil War, many of them Irish, some of them former Confederates, and two regiments of them black Civil War veterans, whom the Indians called

"buffalo soldiers." The army never developed an innovative strategy of Indian warfare or much understood the difference between conventional and unconventional war when fighting on the plains. Rather, the military practiced "total war" akin to what Grant, Sherman, and Sheridan had used to defeat the Confederacy.

The army strategy was simple. As explained by one officer, victory came by "permitting the Indians no rest and rendering any and every hiding place insecure." The military relentlessly dogged the enemy, broke up his camps, and disrupted or destroyed his food supply. The mounted Plains Indians, armed with short bows capable of driving an arrow through a horse, were superb guerrilla fighters and gave as good as they got. Indeed, in all the Indian wars of the trans-Mississippi West, Indians killed more men in battle than did the U.S. Cavalry. But the army had more men in reserve to fight than did the Indians, so that Indian losses were more damaging in the long run. The army wore down the Indians. For more than twenty years the cavalry chased down bandits, cattle thieves, and "hostiles" (as Indians off reservations were called). Within two years of the Sand Creek massacre, exhausted Cheyennes, Arapahos, Kiowas, and Comanches had surrendered their claims to the area.

The events in Minnesota and Colorado and the opening of the Bozeman Trail to the gold fields in Montana, in the Powder River country, led combinations of Teton, Oglala, and Lakota Sioux under Red Cloud to launch attacks against miners, emigrants, and soldiers intruding on Sioux lands. Red Cloud warned that he and the other warriors would not give up their "last hunting ground" and would "prefer to die fighting rather than by starvation." For two years (1865-1867) the Powder River region was aflame with war. In December 1866, outside Fort Phil Kearney, the Indians ambushed Captain William Fetterman and his command, killing all 80 men and mutilating their bodies in reprisal for atrocities against the Sioux.

❦ Negotiations and Reservations

The annihilation of Fetterman's force, and ineffective military efforts elsewhere, sobered the federal government to a reassessment of policy in 1867. So, too, the investigation of the Sand Creek massacre stirred public debate about the conduct of Indian affairs in the West. Clearly, "concentration" — the idea of a permanent Indian country separating whites and Indians along an east-west axis — had failed. What followed was a patchwork reservation system, intended to keep Indians and whites apart, prevent expensive wars, and open lands to white settlement and use. The policy, said General William Tecumseh Sherman, was to effect a "double process of peace *within* the reservation and war *without.*" A deeper purpose was to isolate Indians on small reservations. There, through moral and religious education and practical example, the Indians might be converted into "Christian farmers." Doing so meant breaking the natives' individual tribal identities, yet the government undermined the principle by negotiating separate treaties. In attempting to get land concessions from the various Indians, the government recognized each tribe as an independent nation.

Congress little comprehended its own contradictory purpose. It urged peace negotiations with the Sioux, which resulted in a temporary halt to construction of the Bozeman Trail and a treaty at Fort Laramie in 1868 in which the government promised to abandon its forts in the Lakotas' territory and Red Cloud later agreed to keep his Oglala warriors in check. Red Cloud had toured the eastern United States in 1870 and came away convinced that he could save his people only by reconciliation; the power of the United States was too much to resist with mounted warriors alone.

In the Southwest, American military effort and intertribal warfare left a trail of death and devastation and forced treaties on some native peoples. For almost ten years, beginning in 1861, soldiers and the Chiricahua Apache, led by Cochise, traded atrocities, and Apache raids kept the region in a state of terror. The U.S. military defeated the Mescalero Apaches, but the Chiricahua warriors fled into the mountains to harass ranchers, miners, and travelers for another twenty years. The army had more success against the Navajos. Led by former mountain man Kit Carson, New Mexican volunteers destroyed Navajo crops, orchards, and livestock and allowed Pueblos, Utes, Hopis, and Zunis to attack the Navajos wherever they found them. In 1864 defeated and demoralized Navajos surrendered to Car-

Negotiations The Peace Commission backed its arguments with the threat of the U.S. Army, then led by General William Tecumseh Sherman in the West. In this Alexander Gardner photograph, Sherman (center, second white person to the right of the pole in the tent) and several peace commissioners negotiate with northern Plains Indian "chiefs" at the Fort Laramie, Wyoming, spring 1868 "big talk."

lations among different northwestern peoples. Out of the way and living in stable communities, the northwestern tribes posed no immediate threat to American ambitions and were of little interest to whites, except for Christian missionaries.

Elsewhere, Indian-white relations remained troubled. In a series of treaties with the Apaches, Arapahos, Bannocks, Cheyennes, Kiowas, Navajos, Shoshones, and Sioux, the federal government persuaded the Indians to remove to reservations in return for provisions and money payments. The northern Plains Indians were to go to the "Great Sioux Reserve" in the Dakota Territory and the southern Plains Indians to the Indian Territory in present-day Oklahoma. The treaties collectively replaced the old Indian policy of "concentration" with a new one of "small reservations."

son. He then sent them on what the Navajo thereafter remembered as the "Long Walk," a forced march away from their homes south to a reservation at Bosque Redondo, where they were supposed to take up farming and learn the "truths of Christianity." Four years later, the survivors returned to the now much-reduced Navajo lands. Hemmed in, they raised sheep and made woolen blankets and rugs for the market, which allowed them a precarious existence into the twentieth century.

Only in the Pacific Northwest did the local tribes largely escape the crush of settlers and the rush of U.S. Cavalry. Most of the northwestern peoples lived where whites did not yet go, until the early twentieth century. Their ability to fish the rivers, bays, and ocean for food, and their skills in bartering, gave them advantages the plains and desert Indians lacked. The elaborate practice of gift-giving known as *potlach* also smoothed re-

Many Indians refused to accept the terms. The Oglala chief Crazy Horse returned to the plains to hunt buffalo and vowed to fight the "piecemeal penning" of his people that the government's reservation policy demanded. Sitting Bull, a Lakota Sioux war chief and holy man, mocked those Sioux who accepted government handouts as "fools to make yourselves slaves to a piece of fat bacon, hard-tack, and a little sugar and coffee." Rather than renounce their way of life, Sitting Bull and like-minded Indians stayed off the reservations. Known as "Dog Soldiers," they fought ferociously, fired by a powerful sense of religious purpose in refusing to give up their land and culture. The tie between respect for the old ways and staving off whites was exemplified by a warrior at the battle of Summit Springs in 1869, who faced the enemy with one ankle tethered to a sacred stake. Many westerners also refused to accept the terms of the new "small reservation" policy. They wanted no limitations on their "rights" to go where they pleased, even on reservations, and sneered at the easterners' concern for the Indians as misguided meddling. As one westerner remarked in a letter to the *Chicago Tribune,* "Give us [General] Phil Sheridan, and send Phil-anthropy to the devil." War continued in the West.

miners, suppliers, saloonkeepers, prostitutes, and others eager to gouge wealth from the ground or from each other. They all demanded protection from Indians.

When the federal government failed to intimidate the Sioux into accepting a new treaty that would cede the Black Hills, President Ulysses S. Grant in 1875 ordered the cavalry to force all "hostiles" back to the reservations and open the area to prospectors and settlers. In response, the Sioux allied with the Cheyenne, who had their own grievances with aggressive settlers and unfulfilled treaty obligations.

ॐ *The Great Sioux War*

The most blatant violation of the treaty promises occurred in the Dakota Badlands. The Fort Laramie treaty of 1868 supposedly had forever closed the area to white intrusion, but rumors of gold and silver in the Badlands trampled such promises. Indeed, mining strikes in the West invariably led to invasions of native lands and governmental efforts to remove Indians from the area. And so it was in 1874, when miners stormed into the Black Hills of the Sioux to scratch for gold supposedly as close as "the grass roots." Colonel George Armstrong Custer had planted the notion of easy wealth there after leading a military expedition into the area. A rich lode of ore at the Homestake Mine fed the frenzy, and soon the town of Deadwood boomed with over 10,000 gold-mad

They pledged, in Sitting Bull's words, never to sell or give away so much as "a pinch of soil." Sitting Bull also had a dream, following a Sun Dance ceremony, in which he saw dead American soldiers falling into Indian hands. The Great Sioux War of 1876-1877 had begun.

The most famous incident of the war was "Custer's Last Stand," as the Battle of the Little Big Horn became known in popular culture thereafter. The vainglorious Custer wanted to gain public adulation by bold actions, much as he had done in a famous cavalry charge during the Civil War and in a murderous attack on a village of Cheyennes on the Washita River in Kansas in 1868. Custer's 600-man Seventh Cavalry moved ahead of the two main army columns sent to subdue the "hostile" Indians. Roughly 12,000 Sioux and Cheyenne had encamped along the Little Big Horn River, in Montana

"A Talk with Sitting Bull," 1881

Sitting Bull (Tatanka Iyotake), the famous holy man and chief of the Teton Sioux who won the Battle of the Little Big Horn in 1876 and then retreated with his band to Canada until the lack of supplies forced his "surrender" to the U.S. Army in 1881, gave an interview to a Minnesota newspaper reporter in August soon after his return. Speaking through an interpreter, he explained he was not surrendering his identity or right to live in the traditional ways.

Reporter — The white man admires your conduct in a battle. You showed yourself to be a great chief in the Custer fight.

Sitting Bull — There was a Great Spirit who guided and controlled that battle. I could do nothing. I was sustained by the great mysterious One. [Here Sitting Bull pointed upward with his forefinger.]

Reporter — You conducted the battle well; so well that many thought that you were not an Indian, but that you were a white man and knew the white man's ways.

Sitting Bull [pointing to his wrist] — I was not a white man, for the Great Spirit did not make me a white skin. I did not fight the white man's back. I came out and met him on the grass. . . .

I do not want aid or assistance from the whites or anyone else. I want them to stay from my country and allow me to hunt on my own land. I want no blood spilled in my land except the blood of the buffalo. I want to hunt and trace for many moons. You have asked me to come in. I wanted the white man to provide for me for several years if I came in. You have never offered me any inducements to come in. I did not want to come. My friends that come got soap and axe-handles, but not enough to eat. I have come in, and want the white man to allow me to hunt in my own country. That is the way I live. I want to keep my ponies. I can't hunt without ponies. . . . The white man wanted me to give up everything.

Territory, during the summer buffalo hunt. On June 25, 1876, after the major army force had charged the camp and retreated, Custer, in a flanking movement, met a large body of warriors riding out from the camp. Not knowing there were thousands, rather than hundreds, of Indians coming toward him, he had divided his forces and with roughly 200 men under his immediate command met the Indians shouting "Hurrah, boys, we've got them." All Custer and his men got was a hailstorm of bullets and arrows and death. As the Cheyenne chief Two Moons recalled the fight, "The shooting was quick, quick. Pop-pop-pop, very fast. Some of the soldiers were down on their knees, some standing. Officers all in front. . . . We shoot, we ride fast, we shoot again. Soldiers drop, and horses fall on them."

News of Custer's defeat reached the nation readying to celebrate its centennial. Desperate for heroes amid the miseries of a depression, labor violence, the failure of Reconstruction, and the corruptions of the Grant administration, the public embraced Custer as a martyr to a noble cause. Custer already had prepared the ground by publishing his autobiography, *My Life on the Plains* (1874), in which he styled himself as a western hero akin to Davy Crockett and Kit Carson, and he even invited newspaper reporters along on his campaign

against the Sioux to record the supposed opening of the West. With his long flowing reddish-blond hair, buckskin coat, and haughty air, he embodied the cockiness of the Americans' insistence that the West was theirs by right. Custer's reputation grew as the battle was recast by celebrants of American Manifest Destiny as the necessary sacrifice of good men on a divine mission. Custer's widow, Elizabeth Bacon Custer, burnished the image with her own account of life with a man she described as God-fearing and generous, first in public appearances and then in her widely read book *"Boots and Saddles"; or Life in Dakota with General Custer* (1885). For over a half-century thereafter in popular culture "Custer's Last Stand" was synonymous with American bravery and Indian "savagery." Open criticism of Custer did not begin until the 1930s after the death of his widow. Not until the 1990s did archaeological evidence and new respect for Indian accounts right the record of the battle and rewrite its history.

Little Big Horn was almost the last stand of the Sioux. By 1876 it was no longer possible for Indians to hold back the ceaseless swarm of settlers and constant hounding of the federal forces. The soldiers kept the Indian men from hunting the buffalo and the women from drying meat, preparing hides, and gathering wild foods. Within a year of Custer's defeat, most of the Sioux had returned to the reservation, the reservation chiefs had ceded the Black Hills, and Crazy Horse had been killed while a prisoner at an army post, the victim of a soldier's bayonet stab in his back. Sitting Bull escaped to Canada for a time, but after the government there refused to supply him with food or land he returned to the United States and fell into the army's hands in 1881. After his release, Sitting Bull personified the defeat of the once mighty Sioux by appearing in 1885 as an attraction in Buffalo Bill Cody's Wild West Show. In their annual chronicle of events, painted on buffalo hides, the Lakota Sioux summed up their plight by depicting 1876-1877 as the year the soldiers took their horses.

ᘛ Devastation of the Buffalo Herds

Hunting buffalo proved as effective as hunting Indians and taking their horses in "winning the West" for Americans. Already reduced in numbers by drought, the disruptions of emigrants' overland traffic, and increased and more efficient hunting by Plains Indians, the vast buffalo herds were declining by the 1860s. The coming of the railroads and market hunting sealed their fate. The transcontinental railroads used their "rights-of-way" across the plains to build lines that employed thousands of workers, all needing to be fed, and to haul goods and move people that settled the West, but the railroads also interrupted buffalo migrating patterns. In 1872 Secretary of the Interior Columbus Delano applauded the slaughter of the buffalo herds by professional hunters hired by railroad companies to supply hungry road gangs with meat and by "sportsmen" who rode the trains across the plains, shooting at buffalo from railroad cars for the "sport" of it. To his mind, the "rapid disappearance of the game" would force the Indians to "return to the more reliable source of subsistence furnished at their agencies." When Congress passed a bill in 1874 to limit buffalo hunting, President Grant refused to sign it, thinking any curb on hunting would undercut the military's effort to control the Indians.

The demand for buffalo hides in eastern markets — the skins for robes or as a source of leather for shoes and industrial belts — added to the systematic "harvesting" of the animals. Commercial hunters could kill more than 100 buffalo in an hour, and the railroads could

Shooting Buffalo from the Train   The systematic slaughter of the buffalo hastened the demise of the Plains Indians. Railroad companies hired hunters to kill buffalo for meat, hides, and other products, and they also sponsored "sporting cars" that "sportsmen" might rent to shoot buffalo.

haul hides in carloads. By the late 1870s, eastern tanneries were buying up buffalo hides in lots of 50,000 at a time. Over 10 million buffalo hides came to market during the 1870s and 1880s. Such slaughters, General Philip Sheridan rightly observed, effectively destroyed "the Indians' commissary" and were the army's most effective weapon in forcing "hostiles" on the plains to surrender or face starvation. The Plains Indians understood this. In the words of Two Leggings, a Crow warrior, after the disappearance of the buffalo, "Nothing happened. . . . We just lived. There were no more war parties, no capturing horses . . . , no buffalo to hunt. There is nothing more to tell."

✎ *Surrender and Flight*

Elsewhere, too, the military starved and pursued "hostile" Indians into submission. In 1875, on the southern plains, the Americans won the Red River War against the Cheyennes, Comanches, and Kiowas by preventing the Indians from hunting, gathering, or trading for food. Against the Apaches in the Southwest, the army employed Apache scouts to hunt down every Indian who had left the reservation. For years, the brilliant and ill-tempered Geronimo and his Chiricahua Apache warriors eluded the military. He was captured in 1881, escaped the reservation in 1885, was recaptured the following year, and then exiled from his native land. With the defeat of the Sioux, Comanches, and Apaches, the federal government seemingly had "won the West."

Symbolic of that victory was the treatment of the Nez Perce in the Oregon region. The Nez Perce had grown rich raising livestock along the Snake River, and in 1877 resisted government efforts to force them onto a small reservation. Rather than give up their way of life, young warriors attacked settlers pushing onto Nez Perce land. Following a U.S. Army reprisal, several hundred Nez Perce men, women, and children fled toward Canada with the cavalry hot on their heels. The desperate Nez Perce defeated the soldiers in a series of encounters, but they could find no succor from their old allies the Crows, now serving as American scouts, and did not reach Sitting Bull's Sioux in Canada. After trekking more than 1,300 miles through mountains and rough terrain, the Nez Perce under Chief Joseph were trapped by the army and surrendered. In his surrender speech, as related (and perhaps exaggerated) by an interpreter and reported in the press of the day, Chief Joseph provided an epitaph for all Indians who had tried to survive in the face of the American advance and the

military's pursuit: "I am tired of fighting. Our chiefs are killed. . . . Our old men are dead. It is our young men who say yes or no. . . . It is cold and we have no blankets. The little children are freezing to death. . . . Hear me, my chiefs! I am tired. My heart is sick and sad. From where the sun now stands, I will fight no more forever." General William Tecumseh Sherman, then in charge of the military in the West, ordered the defeated Nez Perce sent to Fort Leavenworth, Kansas. In a series of forced relocations, the Nez Perce survivors were marched to Indian Territory in Oklahoma. In 1885 the government allowed the remnants of Chief Joseph's band to return to Idaho territory.

Warfare with western Indians ended as it had with Indians east of the Mississippi River a half-century earlier. Most Indians were removed by force to a bleak "Indian country" or confined to reservations, where starvation, disease, and disruption of the old ways took a fearful toll. Like their eastern counterparts, the western Indians had their own "trails of tears."

ATTEMPTS AT ASSIMILATION

During the Indian wars, humanitarian reformers waged a different kind of war on the natives — a "conquest by kindness," as one reformer put it. They sought to "save" the Indians by remaking them into Christian "Americans." Most Americans believed that the Indians' days were numbered. The question for the trans-Mississippi Indians echoed the issue for those east of the Mississippi in the early nineteenth century — namely, whether to assimilate or annihilate the natives. Few Americans outside the West argued for annihilation, preferring instead proposals to remove Indians to places where they might adopt farming and give up their "savagery" for American ways. Reformers, most of whom were well-educated, Protestant easterners, pressed the government to end what they regarded as a legal fiction of recognizing, and thus perpetuating, Indian tribes as "domestic dependent nations." Instead, the reformers urged the government to stop negotiating any more treaties, to abrogate those already in existence, and to treat all Indians as individual wards.

✎ *Partnership of Church and State*

By the 1870s, the government's broad policy increasingly favored the reformers' insistence that the way to end the "Indian problem" was to eliminate the Indian as a distinct cultural identity. A partnership between government and Protestant churches promised to do so. Already in 1869 President Grant had established the Board of Indian Commissioners to help resolve conflicts among Indians and spread Christian values. Protestant churches chose the board members, and the government gave over the administration of some Indian agencies to churches. In 1871 Congress ended the treaty system, though the government continued to negotiate "agreements" with Indians to get land concessions from them. Contradiction and confusion abounded as questions of the status of old treaties and new agreements seemingly clashed with the policy of ending Indian autonomy, and civil and military authorities quarreled over who should control Indian relations in the West. No confusion existed over the government's policy of banning "pagan" religions, breaking up Indian religious ceremonies, and seizing religious objects on the reservations — all in an effort to destroy the Indians' communal identity and weaken their traditional leaders.

During the 1870s the churches lost their direct control in administering Indian agencies, but the Protestant reformers' influence over Indian policy actually increased. The Women's National Indian Association, established in 1874, lobbied for a policy of assimilation, and its offshoot, the Indian Rights Association, sponsored missions on the reservations. Catholic missions in the northern plains and the Southwest stayed in places where they were already established before the federal government and Protestant churches became interested in running the reservations and schools, and they continued on their own accounts to convert and protect Indians. But the Catholic Church and its missionary societies remained outside the circle of policymakers in Washington and left out of Indian Bureau allocations of food and supplies. The new movement to remake the Indian was largely a Protestant enterprise.

❧ Arousing Public Concern

In the East, public concern for saving the Indians was aroused after lecture tours by such Indians as Standing Bear of the Ponca tribe and Susette La Fleche,

Geronimo's Surrender   Geronimo and his Chiricahuas escaped capture for many years, raiding American and Mexican settlements and striking fear across the Southwest. In this illustration an aging Geronimo (far right) still shows his defiance before the Canyon de los Embudos meeting with General George Crook, March 1886, during which he agreed to surrender to the innovative general who had tracked him relentlessly using pack mules and Indian scouts.

daughter of an Omaha chief, who complained of mistreatment and pointed to bloody atrocities in the Indian wars. Adding to public concern was novelist and poet Helen Hunt Jackson's best-selling *A Century of Dishonor* (1881), an exposé of government fraud and corruption in Indian affairs, a litany of broken treaties, and a call to end the reservation system. Photographers chronicling the demise of "the Vanishing American" further pricked the consciences of easterners. Images of dour Indians dressed in combinations of native and Western garb made Indians appear as sad relics of a bygone era but also as prospective converts to American ways. But, reformers warned, time was running against the Indians, unless the government would change its policies and turn over Indian affairs to the true "friends of the Indian." That sense of urgency also hastened reformers' efforts to expand their missions and to create new institutions to convert the Indians.

❧ A Three-Pronged Approach: Education, Suppression, and Allotment

The reformers had a three-pronged approach to saving the Indians. Simultaneously, reformers wanted to suppress Indian culture, community, and religion; inculcate middle-class, Protestant values of individual responsibility; and break up tribal landholdings in favor of individual allotments. The emphasis was on replacing tribal/communal identities with individual ones. American Protestantism placed a heavier emphasis on individual identity than traditional Indian beliefs did. After all, Protestant evangelicalism demanded individual salvation, just as American citizenship demanded individual accountability.

Fundamental to their plans was the establishment of Indian schools where Indian children especially might be trained in the skills and cultural attitudes necessary to function in the modern world. The most famous such school, and the prototype for others, was Carlisle Indian School, in Pennsylvania, founded in 1879 by Richard H. Pratt, a former cavalry officer who had commanded a unit of "buffalo soldiers" in Oklahoma and worked with "reforming" Indian prisoners in Florida. At Carlisle, Pratt proposed to "kill the Indian and save the man" through a rigorous program of industrial education akin to that practiced at black self-help institutions such as Tuskegee in the rural South, and through a policy of "Americanization," akin to the Progressives' later approach to immigrants in the urban North. The key was removing the children from the supposedly contaminating influences of their families and stripping them of any vestiges of Indian identity and loyalty. That meant cutting the Indians' long hair, dressing them in stiff uniforms, giving them new names, speaking to them only in English, and converting them to Christianity.

The results were mixed. There were not enough schools and not enough government interest to apply the reforms widely, and there was little evidence that such education improved the natives' prospects for success. More important, most Indians resented and resisted the forced acculturation. At the same time, Indian youths subjected to such education, on and off the reser-

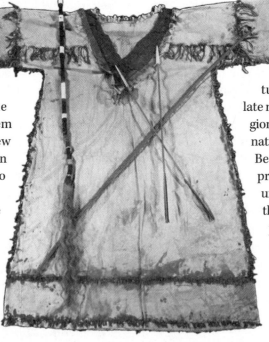

Ghost Dance Shirt   The religion of the Ghost Dance brought the promise of Indian resurgence if only its adherents would purify themselves of white influences, especially alcohol, and engage in the Ghost Dance ritual. Ghost Dance shirts like this one were believed to protect wearers from the white man's bullets.

vations, were caught in between two cultures, unwelcome in the white world but changed enough so as to be no longer comfortable in the Indian one. Zitkala-Sa (Red Bird), a Sioux woman who was taken at age eight from the Pine Ridge reservation to a school in Indiana, recalled the pain of that process in her autobiography. Upon returning home to her mother she discovered that "Even nature had no place for me. I was neither a wee girl nor a tall one; neither a wild Indian nor a tame one." Zitkala-Sa, using her married name of Gertrude Bonnin, later solved her dilemma by becoming a civil rights advocate for Indians. Others like Charles Eastman, a Dakota Sioux, determined "to know all that the white man knows" and gave up his "bow and arrows for the spade and pen." Eastman went to college and later medical school. Likewise, among the Dakota Sioux and Nez Perce, converts to Presbyterianism found Christianity liberating, and their camp meetings and preaching appealed to natives for their emotional content much like the ecstatic Dream Dance and other native revivals. Other natives slipped back to tribal life or into alcohol and despair.

Still other Indians, caught in a cultural crisis and in a state of shock over their diminished state following the Indian wars, found release in revivals of traditional religions or in new pan-Indian religions that promised a return to Indian autonomy. In the late nineteenth century visionary religions grabbed many natives' imagination. Medicine men such as Sword Bearer of the Crow had visions and preached apocalyptic prophecies, until the army stepped in to quash them. In the 1870s and 1880s, the peyote religion, which blended elements of Christian mysticism and found many takers among Indians returning from the boarding schools, emphasized mystical powers gained through abstinence from alcohol and use of the peyote, a small, spineless cactus with hallucinogenic qualities, to purify oneself. The peyote religion spread rapidly from the southwestern plains northward and eastward, as far as the Great Lakes, and continued as a potent force well into the twentieth century.

In the Southwest a Paiute shaman named Wovoka reported revelations from the Great Spirit, which came to him as a vision during a total eclipse of the sun in 1889. He foretold that all Indians who followed the mystical rituals of "the Ghost Dance," prayed fervently, gave up alcohol, and practiced the old ways would see the return of the buffalo, the resurrection of the Indian dead on judgment day, and the flight of the whites. As Wovoka's message moved across the plains, alarmed settlers reported Indians dancing and chanting trancelike in circles for days. To the U.S. Army and Indian agents committed to ending all traces of "pagan ritual" among the Indians, the Sioux embrace of the Ghost Dance especially bode ill. Indeed, Sioux chiefs such as Sitting Bull and Big Foot had transformed the Ghost Dance into a militant religion, with ghost dancers wearing white "ghost shirts" that supposedly could stop a bullet and ghost dancers awaking from their trances claiming special powers to kill whites. Fearing another uprising, in December 1890 the army sent the Seventh Cavalry, Custer's old regiment, to the Sioux reservation to stop the rituals and arrest Sitting Bull. Reservation police

murdered Sitting Bull, and the Seventh Cavalry tried to disarm Big Foot's band at Wounded Knee Creek in South Dakota. The cavalry used machine guns to rake the Sioux camp, killing 146 Indians. A deep snow then covered the bodies until they were dug up and dumped in a mass grave in January 1891. With the Wounded Knee massacre, the army had silenced the Ghost Dance. Thereafter, Indian resistance was more covert.

The reformers recognized that schools alone would not redeem the Indians; nor would suppression of Indian religions. The third part of the reformers' program was the elimination of tribal identity by ending the reservation system. That came in 1887 with the passage of the Dawes Severalty Act (more properly, the General Allotment Act). The act centered on Senator Henry Dawes's premise that "Selfishness is at the bottom of civilization." Until Indians were landowners, they would never know progress. The act intended to transform Indians into independent farmers by breaking up the reservations into individual allotments of private property — 320 acres for grazing or 160 acres for farming to each head of a household, and lesser amounts to unmarried adults and orphans. Surplus reservation land could be sold to anyone. To prevent swindling, the government would hold title to the land for 25 years.

✳ IN THEIR OWN WORDS

"The School Days of an Indian Girl," 1900
Zitkala-Sa (Gertrude Simmons Bonnin), a Lakota Sioux from the Yankton reservation in South Dakota, was sent to a Quaker school in Wabash, Indiana, as a young girl, and returning to her people discovered she had lost her identity, being "neither a wild Indian nor a tame one." She later attended a Quaker college, returned again to live among the Sioux, married, and then left the reservation to become an advocate for Indian civil rights. Her autobiography, excerpted here, captures the isolation many such Indians felt caught between two worlds.

As I hid myself in my little room in the college dormitory, away from the scornful and yet curious eyes of the students, I pined for sympathy. Often I wept in secret, wishing I had gone West, to be nourished by my mother's love, instead of remaining among a cold race whose hearts were frozen hard with prejudice.

During the fall and winter seasons, I scarcely had a real friend, though by that time several of my classmates were courteous to me at a safe distance. . . .

At this stage of my own evolution, I was ready to curse men of small capacity for being the dwarfs their God had made them. In the process of my education I had lost all consciousness of the nature world about me. Thus, when a hidden rage took me to the small white-walled prison which I then called my room, I unknowingly turned away from my one salvation.

Alone in my room, I sat like the petrified Indian woman of whom my mother used to tell me. I wished my heart's burdens would turn me to unfeeling stone. But alive, in my tomb, I was destitute!

For the white man's papers I had given up my faith in the Great Spirit. For these same papers I had forgotten the healing in trees and brooks. On account of my mother's simple view of life, and my lack of any, I gave her up, also. I made no friends among the race of people I loathed. Like a slender tree, I had been uprooted from my mother, nature, and God. I was shorn of my branches, which had waved in sympathy and love for home and friends. The natural coat of bark which had protected my oversensitive nature was scraped off to the very quick.

natives, and reservation lands not allotted were opened to non-Indian homesteaders. The principal result of the Dawes Act was the transfer of Indian lands into white hands. In 1881 Indians held over 155 million acres of land in the trans-Mississippi West; in 1900 they had less than 78 million acres. Most Indian tribes opposed allotment, but the government rebuffed their efforts to forestall it. When Lone Wolf, a Kiowa chief, sued to halt the division of lands as a violation of treaty guarantees, the U.S. Supreme Court in 1903 declared that Congress had absolute power to regulate Indian affairs, even to violate its own treaties, because Indians had no legal status as tribal entities. Not until 1934 did Congress end the allotment system and return to a policy of tribal ownership of land.

With much of their land gone, their religion and culture under assault, their tribal systems in disarray, their population reduced by disease, dislocation, starvation, and war, and their West invaded and remade by miners, ranchers, and farmers who used up the land and killed the buffalo, the Plains Indians in white eyes seemed a "vanishing race" more to be pitied than feared. Many Indians also worried they were passing away. As the visionary Black Elk observed, "The nation's hoop is broken and scattered. There is no center any longer, and the sacred tree is dead." In fact, Indians survived, and some few outside the plains and the allotment system even prospered, into the next century. Indian sovereignty also weathered the legislative, military, and reform efforts to kill it, assuming new vigor in the twentieth century in the Indian rights movement.

The act further provided that all Indians who accepted allotments, gave up their tribal ways, and became "civilized" were to be granted citizenship. The act was not implemented in the Pacific Northwest or the Southwest to any degree. Its main impact was on the plains.

Theodore Roosevelt once described the allotment system as "a vast pulverizing engine" to crush "the tribal mass." The act succeeded all too well in demoralizing native cultures, but it did not lift Indians from dependency. The allotments were too small for effective farming or herding on the plains, and few Indians had any collateral to get started or enough experience with farming, marketing, and managing money in any case. ~culators got around the title restrictions by "leasing" ~ost arable land from unsuspecting or desperate

NEW SETTLERS IN THE WEST

The process of unsettling the Indians made possible the settling of the trans-Mississippi West by several million foreign-born immigrants and native-born migrants during the second half of the nineteenth century. Much of the flow was westward and then fanning across the region, although peopling the West also meant Mexicans moving northward, Asians eastward, and Canadians southward. Those venturing to the trans-Mississippi West did so to try their luck at mining, ranching, and, mostly, farming. Some came as single men in a mad rush for gold and silver to California, Nevada, Colorado, Dakota Territory, and wherever rumors of a new strike led, with jobbers, suppliers, saloonkeepers, and prostitutes hanging on. More came as families or even members of congregations and communities intending to make the West shimmer with amber waves of grain. Some few, especially the Mormons, sought escape from religious persecution, and others from a troubled past, but most went to the trans-Mississippi West to find new wealth in a new land. That much was promised in reams of advertisements, pamphlets, newspaper stories, and personal accounts extolling the riches to be had by crossing the mighty Mississippi to follow the sun.

❧ Long Overland Journeys

Getting there was an arduous process. The quarter million pioneers who trekked overland to Oregon and California in ox-drawn covered wagons, laden with household goods, farm implements, and supplies, suffered under weather extremes of broiling sun and cramping cold, insect infestation, dysentery and other diseases, breakdowns of wagons and exhaustion of animals, and sometimes near starvation on a trip that took six to eight months at mid-century. Cast-off goods from too heavily loaded wagons, bones of dead draft animals, and crudely made crosses of gravesites marked the routes westward. Poor planning, broken axles, bad maps, and other problems might lead to disaster, as befell the Donner party that got caught in the snows in the High Sierras en route to California in 1846 and in desperation resorted to cannibalism to survive. Trying to control costs, the Mormon church in 1856 ordered its members to walk and use handcarts, rather than oxen-driven wagons, to push their goods across the plains and mountains. The experiment failed miserably when 225 people died en route to Salt Lake City and the survivors had to be rescued. In other instances, single men packed what they could on their backs and hiked to the gold fields or farms.

❊ IN THEIR OWN WORDS

A Visit to Salt Lake City, 1893

The Mormon "kingdom" of Deseret was both a mystery and a marvel to non-Mormons. In 1893 journalist Julian Ralph visited Utah on a fact-finding tour and reported that the Mormons, after giving up polygamy, seemed indistinguishable from other "Americans" in habits, except for their remarkable ability, like the Israelites of old, to make a garden bloom in the desert. In this excerpt Ralph relates both the Mormons' character and the way they gathered water in their famous irrigation system.

Afterwards, when I employed a photographer and asked him if he was a Mormon, the man of the camera said that he was, indeed, and why did I ask? Was it because I did not see his horns? Well, as to his horns, he was sorry to say he had none. He supposed they would begin to grow out when he got older.

"I told a man once," he added, "that I was a Mormon, and he said 'You don't say so! I thought Mormons were queer-looking people and had horns.'"

Since my reader may wonder what sort of persons they really are, suffice it if it is noted here that they are precisely like the people of the West generally—the Americans being very American indeed, the Germans being more or less German, the Scandinavians being light-haired and industrious as they are at home, and so on to the end. . . .

After being introduced to many Mormons it came to be luncheon-time, and I was invited to join the family circle of one of my new-made acquaintances. . . . The husband, as he approached his garden gate, called my attention to the sparkling water coursing down the street gutter, and then to a bit of board beside it. He took up the board, dropped it into a pair of slots in the side of the gutter, and turned it instantly and full head into his garden. The performance was a familiar one to me, but perhaps the reader does not understand it. The street gutter was an irrigation ditch. The water was that of a mountain stream, tapped high up in the hills. There was the secret of the rich greenery of Salt Lake City, and, for that matter, of the marvelous transformation of Utah from desert to garden.

✤ *The Rise of the Railroads*

Promise of the West John Gast's 1872 painting, *American Progress*, which was reproduced as a print and widely distributed, summed up the promise of the West. Miss Liberty leads the way for prospectors and farmers, who drive the Indians into retreat in the march westward, using all manner of transportation. Telegraph lines, the pony express, and the railroads link the new land with the old and assure that civilization will follow the plow.

The railroad changed the pace and scale of overland travel and the reach of settlement, effectively remaking the West. On May 10, 1869, at Promontory, Utah, when a golden spike was driven wedding the Union Pacific tracks with the Central Pacific tracks, church bells across the country rang out the news that America had entered a new age. The transcontinental lines shortened the journey from coast to coast from several months to a week's time, linked the region to the market economy, and made possible hauling more and heavier goods, and more people. Farmers especially benefited as railroad companies opened new land for settlement, but miners, engineers, cattlemen, itinerant salesmen of wares, and preachers of the gospel also took to the rails. In 1869 Secretary of the Interior Jacob D. Cox predicted the fundamental ways the railroads would propel western settlement: "Instead of a slowly advancing tide of migration, making its gradual inroads upon the circumference of the great interior wilderness, the very center of the desert has been pierced. Every station upon the railway has become the nucleus for a civilized settlement, and a base from which lines of exploration for both mineral and agricultural wealth are pushed in every direction."

During the long overland journey, men were principally responsible for transportation and protection, while women assumed new tasks in tending livestock, setting up and maintaining the camps, and driving the teams when men got hurt, died, or left. The wagon trains operated as covenanted communities, usually drawing up and agreeing among themselves on the general regulations for good order. As overland emigrant Catherine Haun remarked in her diary, in the wagon train, "Each family was to be independent yet a part of the grand unit and every man was expected to do his individual share of general work and picket duty." As more people ventured west, their diaries and letters sent back to family and friends charted the path and made preparations more responsive to true conditions on the overland trails. Forts and trading posts provided some protection and the possibility of resupply, though often at fearfully high prices. But trudging along the rutted routes remained a difficult, long journey through the 1860s.

The railroads not only moved goods and people, but they also became the largest private holders of real estate in the region. As such, they did much to determine the direction and shape of settlement in the West. Under the terms of the Pacific Railroad Act, passed in 1862 to promote the construction of transcontinental railroads, Congress granted land, 10 to 20 square miles, and other subsidies to railroads for each mile of track they laid. The government parceled the land out in a checkerboard pattern of alternate squares so as to reap its own benefit from the increased value of public lands with transportation nearby, but Congress also gave away huge tracts of land outright as rights of way to favored railroads. By 1872 Congress had doled out 170 million acres in land grants to encourage railroad construction. States and territories also deeded over as much as a fifth to a quarter of their public land to get rails laid across prairie and plains. Always with an eye to profit, the railroads sought the most arable land, close to water, as the "best" route for their lines, and the governments obliged. Without transportation such land was worthless. With it, the land rose in value. And the railroads cashed in.

❧ Settlers from Overseas and Eastern States

The railroads peopled the West by accident and design. The railroads hired thousands of Irish, Chinese, Mexican, and other workers to dig roadbeds, blast rock, burrow tunnels, and lay rail, and many such workers stayed on in western depot towns that rose up along the rails or destination cities such as San Francisco. More purposeful were the railroad companies' recruitment efforts to lure people to their lands. They sent agents eastward and across the Atlantic to recruit settlers, and established land bureaus to facilitate the transfer of land. To prospective settlers, the railroad companies offered easy credit, low land prices, free transportation west, and agricultural advice and assistance. States and territories

Lure of Western Lands   Railroads and other businesses promoted western settlement vigorously, sometimes with unabashed hyperbole, as this 1888 poster, which starkly contrasts the "New World" and the "Old World," indicates. Europe is depicted as a land of famine and oppression; the Dakota Territory is described as the "Land of Golden Grain."

furthered the promotion by publishing guidebooks for prospective settlers, sending their own agents to Europe to pitch the bounty to be had on their land, and hitching up with railroads to promise transportation and access to markets. In advertisements and promotional literature written in many languages, the railroad companies and state and territorial immigration agencies painted the West as the Promised Land of milk and honey. In the words of the governor of Wyoming Territory, in 1887, the rich soils there promised a new Garden of Eden to all "practical every-day farmers, who will put their hands to the plow and not look back."

The combined efforts of railroad and government promotions worked especially well in drawing over

2 million foreign-born settlers to the trans-Mississippi West between 1870 and 1900. Europeans usually came as groups to work soils similar to those in their native countries. Whole villages were transported from Europe to settle on the plains. Some groups were preferred to others for their steady habits and farming knowledge. Among promoters, Russian German Mennonites and Catholics (German-speakers who had settled in czarist Russia in the eighteenth century but

Exodusters Homesteading peopled the plains and promised a new life for migrants and immigrants. Black homesteaders went west to take up land under provisions of the Homestead Act or as part of the Exoduster movement, organized by clergymen, to escape racism and poor prospects in the post–Civil War South and build self-sustaining black communities in the West.

east of the advancing frontier. Some came from as far away as the Deep South. Black Exodusters, first led by the "Black Moses" Henry Adams of Louisiana in 1879, left sharecropping, debt peonage, and racism in the postwar South in search of land and freedom in Kansas and westward, and even set up all-black towns. The people came in bursts, known as "booms," first into the river valleys and along the railroad lines and then farther out onto the grasslands. By 1889, after several boom years in crop prices and with the "frontier" approaching the semi-arid lands from Kansas to Texas, farmers and railroad companies persuaded Congress to open the Indian Territory to settlement. In spring 1889, nearly 100,000 "Boomers" came by train, wagon, buggy, muleback, horseback, and on foot to what had been the heart of the territory, waiting to claim their share of the 2 million acres Congress was about to throw open. Some "Sooners" jumped the gun, sneaking into the area to beat the swarm of "Boomers" to the new promised land, but finally on April 22 the gun sounded and the "Boomers" stormed in. Over the next few years, Congress created the Oklahoma Territory to provide government and opened millions more acres of land there, which soon was almost wholly claimed by non-Indian farmers and ranchers. Other areas of the plains also began to "fill up," so that the superintendent of the federal census, after reviewing the 1890 census map, reported that for the first time in American history, there was "no frontier line."

suffered persecution in the nineteenth) were the most sought after, and in 1905 the Sante Fe Railroad won a bidding war with the Burlington and Missouri Railroad to bring over 60,000 Russian German Mennonites from the Ukraine to Kansas. Other groups hitched their own desire to escape poverty and persecution in Europe to railroad companies' interests in building stable communities. Thus, groups such as the Jewish Colonization Association and the Hebrew Emigrant Aid Society sponsored Jewish agricultural communities on the plains. The plains was a crazyquilt of immigrant/ethnic communities of Swedes, Norwegians, Danes, Germans, Russian Germans, Poles, Czechs, Russians, Eastern European Jews, and others. By 1900 the northern plains region had the highest proportion of foreign-born in its population of any region in the nation and a religious diversity equal to any city in the land. The patterns of settlement allowed for the maintenance of many Old World customs, and the languages of the old country were the lingua franca in towns, schools, and churches for many years.

The bulk of the newcomers to the Great Plains, though, came mostly from the states immediately

MINING THE WEST

Underscoring Manifest Destiny was the assumption that the great wealth of the West waited only for American genius and energy. The gold and silver strikes that immediately followed the American seizure of California from Mexico seemed only to confirm that conceit, and the mining booms set the pattern for the other western bonanzas in lumbering, ranching, and commercial farming. From the 1840s through the 1880s the opening of gold and silver mines from California into

Canada fed the "gold fever" that drew legions of fortune hunters from as far away as China and Europe in search of quick riches. The scale and rapidity of wealth taken from western mines dwarfed all previous gold mined in America, indeed in the world. In 1852, for example, miners panned and dug out $81 million worth of gold from the Sierra Nevadas in California, and in the single decade from 1849 to 1859 they took $555 million from the "golden state" alone. By the end of the century, California had yielded $1 billion in gold. Here was wealth to rival the Midas-sized fortunes the robber barons were amassing in manufacturing and merchandising back east. And like the robber barons, miners brought an anything-goes mentality to stake their claims and claw their way to wealth.

In fact, few miners got rich, and the mining bonanzas were often short-lived and soon monopolized by corporations with the capital and resources necessary to extract and process the richest deposits from deep-lying veins of quartz. Hydraulic drilling replaced surface mining as corporations pulverized the Sierra Nevada Mountains to squeeze out gold. In mining first, and then in other extractive industries, the resources of the West were incorporated into the machinery of industrial capitalism. But the popular press and rumor kept thousands of prospectors scouring gullies and hillsides for the next big strike.

❧ Dreams of Gold

The first of the great western bonanzas was the California gold strike of 1849 (see Chapter 13). In 1858 a strike on the Fraser River in British Columbia sent thousands scampering northward, and also in 1858, prospectors working the Clear Creek, near present-day Denver, discovered gold and silver, which set off a scramble of 50,000 men to Colorado shouting "Pikes Peak or Bust." Most of those hopefuls busted, but there were major strikes elsewhere to compensate. In 1858 and 1859, prospectors such as Henry "Old Pancake" Comstock made a series of independent finds along the Carson River in

Oklahoma Land Rush The federal government's decision to open millions of acres to white settlement in what became Oklahoma Territory brought a flood of settlers to stake claims to the land. The government subsequently opened more lands in the territory; this is a depiction of settlers racing into the newly opened "Cherokee Strip" in 1893.

4357. "We have it Rich." Washing and panning gold, Rockerville, Dak. Old-timers, Spriggs, Lamb and Dillon at work. Photo and copyright by Grabill, 1889.

Panning for Gold   In the first stages of gold strikes intensive labor and luck were the key requirements. Miners used relatively simple techniques, like pans, as shown here in the Dakota Territory, to separate gold from gravel.

Nevada that resulted in the fabulous Comstock Lode, the richest single vein of gold and silver in history. Gold strikes followed in western Nevada, Idaho, Montana, Wyoming, and South Dakota. Almost as a rite of passage, men raced from strike to strike, pocketing disappointment as they took off for the next "big one." The last great strikes occurred in Alaska, with the first important discovery in 1880, thanks to the Tlingit Indians, and later strikes in 1886 near the Yukon River, and the biggest in the Klondike region in 1896. Soon "Seward's Folly" was filling up with the same kinds of polyglot gold bugs as swarmed over the rest of the West.

Each new strike added to the gold mania that gripped the American imagination and boosted the national economy. It was impossible to resist the lure of a strike. Newspapers teemed with accounts of great finds each surpassing its predecessor in easy riches, and the glitter of new wealth in mining towns drew hordes in search of their own pots of gold. During the long economic depression set off by the financial Panic of 1893, the cry of "Gold in the Klondike" sent thousands of men to frozen tundra. In the Pacific Northwest, which was especially hard hit by the depression, many of the area's men hopped boats and trains heading northward, and the nation cheered the prospect of gold in the midst

of the bitter "free silver" populism of the day (see chapter 21). In addition to the psychological boost each strike gave, the strikes added to the nation's money supply without causing any significant inflation, fueled booms in each area where gold and silver were found, and hitched the mining West to the growing international market economy.

❧ Booming Towns and States

The California gold rush, for example, spurred the state's economic and demographic take-off that began in the mid-nineteenth century and lasted until the Panic of 1873, after which agriculture sustained growth. Into California poured thousands of people from across the globe. As journalist Louisa Amelia Knapp Clappe wrote in a series of articles on the gold rush, walking through a mining camp was a lesson in "national variety," for she heard people speak in English, Spanish, German, French, Irish, Italian, Chinese, Hawaiian, and various American Indian languages. Diversity did not mean harmony. When the surface gold played out and competition for good sites intensified, tensions rose and racism raged. The new government in California expelled Mexicans, and American miners also forced Chinese and Indian miners off their claims. Still, people came. And suppliers came to serve the needs of burgeoning and hungry populations.

San Francisco rapidly expanded as the key portal through which flowed wheat (increasingly grown in California as farmers settled in the valleys), fish from the Pacific coasts, coffee and cocoa from Mexico, rice from China, lumber from inland, and countless other products to satisfy the appetites and egos of people chasing money. The populations exploded almost overnight, and jerrybuilt structures cropped up to serve every need or appetite. One observer described the hurly-burly boom town as having been "hatched like chickens by artificial heat."

San Francisco soon had much to crow about. Within a few years of the gold rush it became the dominant city in the trans-Mississippi West and a colonizer of its own. Its local capitalists used mining wealth to underwrite a host of real estate, agricultural, manufacturing and other projects in the West, Hawaii, Alaska, and abroad, giving San Francisco an independence from eastern investment bankers rare among western cities. San Francisco developers bought up thousands of arid acres in southern California, linked the village of Los Angeles to the Southern Pacific and the Santa Fe railroads in 1887, and thus to the transcontinental railroad network, and promoted the town and area as an earthly paradise with what one guidebook boasted as "hedges of geraniums, fifteen feet high … heliotrope grown in trees, forty feet high, . . . [and] roses of a thousand varieties, by the million." Tourists and speculators rushed in, much like gold-seekers, to gawk and buy. Even after the real estate bubble burst in 1889, Los Angeles and other southern California towns grew, and San Francisco capitalists continued to lead the way.

Likewise, the Comstock Lode led to the rapid rise of Virginia City, Nevada, which became the most famous of all mining towns. San Francisco silver kings from Nob Hill invested heavily in the mines there and developed Virginia City from a shantytown in 1859 to a city of some 20,000 in 1873. At its height, the town boasted four banks, an opera house, hotels, well over 100 saloons, a dozen breweries, numerous dance halls and bordellos, a half-dozen jails, and, wrote Mark Twain, "some talk of a church." Everyone was after a fast buck. In his book *Roughing It* (1872), Twain caught the temperament of Virginia City and every boom town like it when he observed that "there was a glad, almost fierce intensity in every eye, that told of the money-getting schemes that were seething in every brain and the high hope that held sway in every heart."

❧ *Boom and Bust Economies*

Hopes were often dashed, and miners reduced to becoming wage laborers for large-scale mining companies or moving on. Comstock, for example, sold his claims for a few thousand dollars and two mules before heading off to new strikes in Oregon and Idaho. Boom towns, known

Impact of Mining   The Comstock Lode at Virginia City, Nevada, shown here in a cutaway view, yielded more than $500 million in silver and gold ore between 1859 and 1877. The environmental toll was heavy, however; mining and logging operations denuded the land and hastened erosion and pollution.

as "Helldorados," went bust, becoming ghost towns with names such as Deadwood Gulch that spoke volumes on their rough-hewn history. Some few became important trading or manufacturing centers and prospered even after the mines played out. A railroad link often decided a town's future, too, for railroads not only tied a town to the markets but also brought in "civilization" in the form of traveling entertainers, preachers, and purveyors of luxury goods, books, and finery. Denver made its fortune in smelting and machine-making for mining. Helena started as a mining camp at Last Chance Gulch, and survived as a commercial center because of its location on the trade route between Forts Benton and Bannock and Virginia City. Where ore veins lasted, as in the copper mining center of Butte, Montana, a permanent city took root. Virginia City, though, no longer shined by 1900. The big lode was mostly gone, and the hangers-on numbered roughly 4,000.

Much of the money made in Virginia City and the other mining towns went to those who sold food, supplies, liquor, and fantasy. Miners complained that the cost of food and supplies ate up all their earnings. As one prospector in California remarked, "I would have made money if I could have lived without eating." Eggs sold for $5, a loaf of bread for $10, and men would pay anything in the camps for nails and tools. In the Yukon, "Klondike King" Charles Anderson once paid $800 for "a small keg of bent and blackened nails salvaged from a fire" so he could build a sluicebox. In mining camps and towns across the West, shippers, many of them Mexicans, hauled out the ore and carried in the supplies in ox-driven wagons or on mulebacks. Merchants, many of whom were German Jewish immigrants, provided all manner of goods and services and often moved into banking, transportation, and real estate. Saloonkeepers, barbers, cooks, laundresses, blacksmiths, assayers, lawyers, gamblers, and others plied their trades.

Prostitution abounded in the mining towns, like the cattle towns (see below), where men often outnumbered women by three or more to one. In Helena, Montana, for twenty years after the Civil War, for example, prostitution was the principal source of paid employment for women, until a combination of a shift from a mining base to commerce and reform government curtailed the demand and the ubiquity of the service there. From the 1860s into the 1890s, probably as many as 50,000 so-called fancy girls worked in western brothels,

"cribs," saloons, and dance halls for roughly $30 a week for white women and less for Mexicans, blacks, Chinese, and Indians. Whoring was a profitable business for the madams who owned brothels and other property, but few prostitutes got much for giving up their bodies. Countless numbers sank into lives of violence and abuse, disease, alcoholism, and drug addiction, and many committed suicide. Other women did better running boarding houses, restaurants, and laundries.

❧ Establishing Law and Order

Drifters, deserters, desperadoes, down-and-outers, and other dangerous people flocked to the mining camps and towns, along with gamblers, con men, and thieves, for the lure of fast money and fast times there. Stealing another's strike, known as claim-jumping, was common at strikes. So, too, was violence. In the early days of mining towns, lawlessness ruled. As one observer described Last Chance Gulch in 1864, "braggart oaths filled the air," the "crack of the revolver was often heard above the merry notes of the violin," and "fights, quarrels, wounds, or murders" happened daily.

The mining towns' highly transitory population of young men engaged in hard labor and hard living brought missionaries who tried to save them but

---

✳ IN THEIR OWN WORDS

"Formation of the Vigilance Committee," 1865

Thomas J. Dimsdale, an Englishman, came to Virginia City in 1863 and in 1864 was named the first superintendent of public instruction in Bannack, the temporary capital of Montana Territory. He also became the editor of the Montana Post, *the first newspaper in the territory. In a series of articles first published in 1865 and reprinted in book form a year later, Dimsdale relates the purpose and usefulness of vigilante committees on the mining frontier.*

The reasons why the organization was so generally approved, and so numerously and powerfully supported, were such as appealed to the sympathies of all men who had anything to lose, or who thought their lives safer under the dominion of a body which, upon the whole, it must be admitted, has from the first acted with a wisdom, a justice, and a vigor never surpassed on this continent, and rarely, if ever, equalled. Merchants, miners, mechanics, and professional men, alike, joined in the movement, until, within an incredibly short space of time, the road agents and their friends were in a state of constant and well-grounded fear, lest any remarks they might make confidentially to an acquaintance might be addressed to one who was a member of the much-dreaded Committee....

Reviewing the long and bloody lists of crimes against person and property, which last included several wholesale attempts at plunder of the stores in Virginia and Bannack, it was felt that the question was narrowed down to "kill or be killed." "Self-preservation is the first law of nature," and the mountaineers took the right side. We have to thank them for the peace and order which exist today in what are, by the concurrent testimony of all travellers, the best-regulated new mining camps in the West.

The record of every villain who comes to Montana arrives with him, or before him; but no notice is taken of his previous conduct. If, however, he tries his hand at his trade in this region, he is sure of the reward of his crimes, and that on short notice; at least such is the popular belief.

proved poor soil for planting church establishments. The missionaries' call for support to tame a lawless land and newspaper and literary accounts of the mining camps and towns as the Devil's dens did much to create the popular image of the West as "unchurched" and even ungodly.

Absent organized government, police forces, and religious establishments, miners and townspeople dealt with the problems of law and order by creating their own crude justice in vigilante law. They set up codes of conduct for themselves, and self-appointed vigilante committees chased, beat, and hanged interlopers, criminals, and brigands who disturbed the camps and towns. The vigilante "justice" sometimes masked racial discrimination, as whites drove Chinese, blacks, and Mexicans from the strikes, but it also established "order." As the ramshackle towns grew into more prosperous communities, women came as wives, teachers, and boardinghouse keepers, and merchants, suppliers, and others with property also tried to cool tempers and build more stable communities. Police departments and courts replaced vigilantes, banks secured wealth, and schools and churches opened. Towns confined saloons, gambling dens, and brothels to distinct districts. They also segregated the races thinking such was the way to good order. Pendleton, Oregon, went so far as to require the Chinese to live in an underground city, where the laundries, groceries, opium dens, and other Chinese businesses were located and Chinese had to go after dark. Over time local codes and informal practices yielded to state laws. Indeed, the need for law and order was a primary stimulant to establish territorial and then state governments in the West.

The transformation from frontier fort or trading post to city was further proof of America's destiny in the West. Typical of the wonderment were the remarks of a traveler to Cheyenne, Wyoming, who in 1876 celebrated the city as "another American miracle." Cheyenne had got its start in mining and then a second life as a cattle town, before it settled into a civil prosperity as a regional commercial center. In ten years Cheyenne had grown from a motley collection of portable shacks and rough-and-tumble characters that earned the town the nickname "Hell on Wheels" into "a substantial, thriving city with friendly wide streets, splendid hotels, banks, jails, insurance companies, opera house and churches!" Each faith had "its own church in a city that, five years ago, consisted of dugouts and moveable shacks." By century's end, the boom-and-bust mining towns existed only in Alaska, a few pockets in the West,

and in popular dime-novel literature and magazine images relating tales of big strikes, bad men, fancy girls, and fast guns. But all was not glitter and gold in the West made by mining. Less noticed in public depictions of the mining frontier but more significant for the future of the land were the gouged-out hills, mercury-laced water and soil, mining debris, excessive run-off, and other forms of environmental degradation that came faster, cost more, and lasted longer than any wealth dug out of the ground.

CATTLE AND COWBOYS ON THE PLAINS

The glitter of gold lured many across the Rockies, but the Great Plains also offered its own promise. The removal of Indians, the destruction of the buffalo herds, and the arrival of railroads opened the plains to cattlemen and later to farmers. The harsh, arid climate, unfamiliar soil, few trees, and thin vegetation on the Great Plains at first had discouraged farmers from settling there. Cattlemen from Texas, however, found the vast plains grasslands a stock-raisers' paradise for grazing their herds during the long cattle drives to market, and soon claimed the area for themselves. From the 1840s on cattle and oxen from overland migrants, teamsters, and army suppliers mingled with cattle that had drifted from Texas onto the plains, but the massive march of cattle onto the plains and as far as Canada was the product of the railroad and growing urban markets for meat and hides after the Civil War. During its heyday through the 1880s the cattle industry brought fat profits to western cattlemen, middlemen shippers, and midwestern and eastern slaughterhouse owners. Grass dethroned cotton as America's "king," and the cowboy replaced the farmer as America's beau ideal.

❧ Driving Cattle to Market

The cattle industry traced its origins to Mexican ranchers and the ecology of south Texas. There Mexicans perfected open-range ranching. During the year they let their cattle move freely from feeding ground to feeding ground on the treeless, unfenced green grasslands. In the spring *vaqueros* (cowboys), with their lariats for roping, herded the cattle on horseback and "rounded up" the cattle into corrals. There they marked the calves with brands and selected the steers to send to market. At the same time, the Texas longhorn evolved. These lean, ill-tempered animals with long legs and horn spreads as much as five feet across grew slowly and rarely gained more than 1,000 pounds, and their meat was tough — "80 pounds of hamburger on 800 pounds of bone and horn" was the common description. But they proved perfectly adapted for long drives to market. The hardy beasts were able to survive without much water, needed little winter feeding, and were inured to the tick carrying splenic fever (popularly known as Texas or Spanish fever) that devastated domestic dairy herds, oxen, and breeding stock elsewhere. Midwestern and eastern markets bellowed for meat after the Civil War, and enterprising Texan rangers recognized that cattle purchased for $3 to $4 per head in Texas, or even rounded up from tens of thousands of unbranded mavericks roaming as far north as the Texas panhandle, could fetch $40 per head — if you could bring them to market. The railroads provided the way and the plains grasses provided the fuel for the long drives. Cattlemen moving north stocked the range with longhorns and managed the herds with cowboys.

The annual cattle drives northward from Texas to railheads connecting to eastern markets began in earnest after the Civil War. Nature and commerce dictated the routes. The overland expeditions followed trails that had grass for cattle grazing along the way and stayed behind a quarantine line established by states such as Missouri and Kansas to protect domestic livestock from splenic fever. Abilene, Kansas, was the first cattle town to profit from its location, beyond the tick line, at the end of the Chisholm Trail from Texas, and on the Kansas Pacific Railroad, which connected to Kansas City and eastern markets. Thanks largely to the foresight of Joseph McCoy, a young cattle dealer from Illinois who invested heavily in the site, Abilene was transformed almost overnight in 1867 from a dusty village to a bustling bovine entrepot with stockyards, cattle pens, loading ramps and chutes, stables, and barns for the animals and saloons and hotels for the cowhands. Soon, Wichita, Dodge City, Cheyenne, and Caldwell rose as competing cattle towns as the long drives grew in size, herds spread into the Texas panhandle, the Indian Territory (Oklahoma), eastern New Mexico, and as far as Colorado, Montana, and Wyoming, and railroads pushed deeper onto the plains.

❧ Cowboy Culture

The famous long drives from Texas lasted from early spring to late fall. The team consisted of a trail boss, a cook and his chuck wagon, wranglers with spare horses, and fifteen to twenty cowboys (roughly one for every 300 to 500 head on the trail) and a herd of two to three thousand steers trailing. The cowboys kept the cattle moving across as much as a thousand miles of territory, protected them from predators and thieves, rounded up strays, prevented stampedes, and sang at night to soothe the cattle and keep from falling asleep while on watch. Cowboys lived in the saddle from sunup to sundown, all for a lump sum payment of roughly $30 to $40 at the end of the drive. They faced heat, pests, thieves, and even gun-slinging outlaws and murderers who stole and killed almost gleefully. They then faced unemployment until the next roundup.

The hard life attracted few older men. The cowboys of the long drive and the open range were usually in their teens and twenties, and they rarely stayed on for more than two or three drives. They were also a mixed lot of Mexican vaqueros, Indian horsemen, African American freedmen from the South, and whites, many of them former Confederates. Despite the differences, the cowboys developed a crude camaraderie on the drives. When wages fell and the cattle industry shifted to ranching closer to railheads during the 1880s, Anglo cowboys sought to exclude blacks, Mexicans, and Indians from the ranches and drives at the same time employers tried to hire them because they worked hard for less. The cowboys also formed unions to get higher wages. By then, though, the cattle industry had become reorganized as a rationalized industry and the day of the long drive and cowboy was past, except in popular literature.

At the end of the drive, the boss sold his herd to a cattle dealer or rancher, paid his workers, and headed back to Texas with whatever profit was left. With cash to spend and time to spend it, the cowboys and wranglers wasted no time buying food, liquor, and outfits (new denim jeans shipped from the Levi Strauss company of San Francisco, Stetson hats from Philadelphia, and Justin boots from Texas), and whooping it up in the cattle towns. Any number of rogues and criminals came to the cattle towns to fleece or rob the cowboys and their patrons, and for a time the cattle towns earned reputations as violent, unruly, and ungodly places. As one proverb had it for Kansas, "There's no Sunday west of Junction City and no god west of Salina." Another popular western saying spoke to the violence of the early cattle towns: "God did not make all men equal. Colonel Colt [inventor of the Colt revolver] did." Owners of stables, dry goods stores, banks, barber shops, hotels, saloons, gambling houses, and other businesses depended on the infusion of money the cowboys brought and tolerated rowdy and randy behavior as long as it meant profits and did not tear the town apart.

Soon enough businessmen with large investments to protect in buildings, stockyards, and depots tamed their West by incorporating their towns and bringing in churches, schools, and police. Families came, often with Victorian-era religious and social values of order, and women reformers pressed to clean up the morals and the dirt. Cattle towns passed laws banning the carrying of guns, restricted in number and location brothels, dance halls, and other places where trouble might occur, and hired lawmen. The raucousness that still occurred was seasonal and limited, and the number of gunfights declined. During his days as a lawman in Dodge City and Wichita, Wyatt Earp killed only one man, and "Wild Bill" Hickok, who served as town marshal in Abilene in the early 1870s, killed only two men while there (one his own deputy by mistake), before moving on to Deadwood, a mining town where violence was more common and where Hickok would be gunned down while playing poker, holding aces and eights (thereafter the "deadman's hand"). Only in dime novels did the cow towns continue to be wide open and wild.

❧ Fences and Water Rights

Cattle shipments slowed during the depression years of the 1870s but revived by 1876. The cattle industry moved westward and northward as the railroads stretched across the plains. Cattle grazed freely on public lands, wintered on the range, and needed only crude corrals for the spring and fall roundups, and they obligingly dropped calves to keep the herds stocked. Low costs, rising cattle prices, and hungry consumers as far away as Europe clamoring for more and better beef made cattle raising seem like a sure bet. Books and newspapers promised a "beef bonanza" to investors, and in the 1880s eastern and European capital underwrote large ranches in Colorado, Wyoming, Montana, and the Dakotas. Future president Theodore "Teddy" Roosevelt, for one, pumped $50,000 into the Elkhorn Ranch in the Dakota Territory and, almost unique among such investors, went out to ride the range as a cowboy, clad in

Cowboys Though a significant element of the western economy for only a short time, cowboys who drove cattle to market became one of the dominant symbols of the rugged individualism thought to thrive in the West.

buckskin and armed with a six-shooter and a hankering for run-ins with rustlers and desperadoes. Ranchers on the northern plains responded to market demand by improving their breeds, for example, crossing white-faced Herefords with longhorns to get cattle that carried more, and more tender, meat and fattened quickly on grasses. The beef rush was on.

The improved breeds needed water, abundant grass, and proximity to railroads. As elsewhere in the West, water was the key. Whoever controlled water "owned" the open range. Large ranchers seized on homestead provisions to amass critical parcels of range by using their cowhands as "dummy" homesteaders to file fraudulent claims along water and then transfer the land to the cattlemen, thereby keeping rivals from the grass and the water. As one rancher explained, "I have 2 miles of running water, . . . [and] the next water from me in one direction is 23 miles; now no man can have a ranch between these two places. I have control of the grass, the same as though I owned it." Large ranchers and cattle corporations soon monopolized huge tracts of public land they considered their own preserves. The Matador cattle company of Texas, for example, used its ownership of 100,000 acres of waterfront to claim a range of over a million and half acres.

To keep rivals out, prevent overcrowding and overgrazing, and impose "order," the cattle kings formed livestock, or cattlemen's, associations. The associations regulated "water rights," tried to limit the number of cattle, provided for the quarantine of infected animals, supervised and coordinated spring and fall roundups, protected the brands of members, fought prairie fires, set up courts to settle disputes among members, and chased down and dispensed "vigilante justice" of summary judgment and lynch law to cattle rustlers and horse thieves. The associations became powerful political forces in their own states and territories as well, ensuring favorable policies in legislation and the courts. The large ranchers also strung thousands of miles of barbed wire across the range to keep their improved breeds in and predators, thieves, and interlopers out. In one act of grasping that spoke volumes on big ranchers' claims to the range, Charles Goodnight ran a fence from the Texas panhandle into New Mexico. Signs posted on the fences warned of a quick and violent penalty to any interloper. The cattle barons hired cowboys to "ride the line" daily, checking and repairing fences, gathering in stray cattle, and punishing any fence cutters or "trespassers" they caught.

Small ranchers, sheepherders, cowboys, and others were unwilling to cede the range to the cattle barons. They tore down the signs, cut the fences, and took what water, grass, and cattle they thought were theirs by right. Like prairie fires, range wars broke out across the northern plains and then into New Mexico and Arizona that pitted rancher against rancher, rancher against sheepherder, rancher against farmer, rancher against cowboy, and various other combinations of animosity. With more resources and often more ruthlessness, the big ranchers usually outlasted the small ranchers, cowboys, and others who opposed them. Representative of the pattern was the series of long-running and bloody conflicts that raged across New Mexico and Arizona from 1880 to 1910 — the most famous of which was the Lincoln County War that gave rise to the legend of Billy the Kid — in which the big Anglo and Hispanic (*ricos* in local parlance) ranchers and companies employed militia, hired gunmen such as the Earp brothers, and exploited contacts in territorial capitals and Washington, D.C., to put down the challenges.

❧ Natural Changes and Challenges

In the end, Nature and the railroads decided who ruled the range. Cattlemen had increased their herds to cash in on the beef bonanza, but in doing so ruined themselves. Too much beef began to glut the market at the same time that cattle producers in Canada and Argen-

tina reached American markets because of improved rail and ship transportation. Prices fell. Meanwhile, the swelling herds of cattle literally consumed the plains, with some sections so overgrazed that they had no ground cover. The cattle ate up the buffalo and grama grasses that had replenished the plains for generations, and in their stead grew less nutritious, unpalatable cheat grass, thistle, and weeds. Soil erosion followed. Undernourished cattle weighed less and took longer to prepare for market, were more susceptible to disease, and were less able to withstand wintering. By the mid-1880s in many areas of the plains, it required ten times the area to feed a steer as what was needed in the early 1870s. Costs rose.

Nature dealt the hammer blow. During most of the 1880s, winters on the plains had been mild, which contributed to the growth and spread of the herds and the overgrazing that followed. Disaster struck the southern plains in 1884-1885, when blizzards killed off tens of thousands of cattle already weakened by inferior feeding. The barbed-wire fences now trapped the animals; unable to move away from the storms, the cattle ran into and piled up against the barbed wire, and then froze or starved to death. In the northern plains, the drought and scorching heat of the 1886 summer claimed tens of thousands of cattle. Then, as one cattleman observed, "An overstocked range must bleed when the blizzards sit in judgment." Judgment came in the winter of 1886-1887, the worst on record, that gripped the plains from Canada to Texas and sent temperatures plunging to 68 degrees below zero in some areas. Cattle froze standing. When spring came, the rot and gagging stench from tens of thousands of carcasses stacked against barbed wire and in gullies bore grim witness to the greed of the cattlemen. The surviving animals were so emaciated that they were unmarketable. The same cycle of a very dry summer and a very cold winter causing large-scale cattle losses occurred in the Great Basin in 1889-1890, where Californians had sent their cattle after switching to cereal production in the 1870s and where too many cattle grazed on denuded land by the 1880s. In Colorado, Wyoming, Montana, and the Dakotas, the losses ran to 90 percent of the herds, and elsewhere to 30 percent or more. In the Great Basin area, ranchers reported losses of 50 to 75 percent of their herds. The scenes of slaughter and suffering disgusted even hardened ranchers such as Montana's once mighty cattle king Granville Stuart, who now found "distasteful" a business that had fascinated and profited him before the winter disaster and who now pledged never again to "own an animal that I could not feed and shelter."

The market more than conscience decided the result. Banks frightened by the losses called in loans, and ranchers had to sell at whatever their depleted livestock would get on an already falling market. In Chicago, cattle brought only $1 a hundred-weight in 1887, down over $8 from prices in the early 1880s. Bankruptcies rolled across the plains like tumbleweeds and forced a reorganization of the industry. The surviving cattlemen gave up the idea of the open range and the cattle drive. The corporations with capital and planning, like the King Ranch of Texas, bought and leased land for water and grazing, upgraded their stock, raised hay for winter fodder, and learned to market animals more quickly by selling steers younger to feeding lots. Selective breeding of small herds of 200 head or so became the industry norm. Cowboys became wage-earners who spent more time fixing fences, digging irrigation ditches, and cutting hay than riding herd. Like mining, cattle raising was strictly business.

❧ Sheep versus Cattle

Further indicative of a transformed West was the steady expansion of sheep raising from its original foothold in the Mexican borderlands of California, New Mexico, and Texas into and across the Great Plains. Sheep proved hardier than cattle. They needed little water and thrived on weeds cattle would not eat. Sheep also required less attention than cattle — a single herder and several dogs could control up to 3,000 sheep — and less initial capital investment. Their wool did not spoil and might be stored for long periods, allowing for some control over prices, and wool was protected by tariff from foreign competition.

Cattlemen despised sheep. They complained that the sheep ruined the grasses by close cropping and smelled so bad that cattle would not go where sheep had been. The cattlemen hated the sheep raisers as much as the sheep. Indeed, human prejudices figured much in the Anglo cattlemen's and cowboys' denigration of sheep as inferior animals, because the owners and shepherds of the sheep were usually Mexicans, Basques, Scots, or Mormons, all of whom Anglos considered "un-American." Cattlemen tried to keep the sheep off the range by driving them over cliffs and killing them in droves and by attacking the shepherds in a series of range wars that raged for years. As the territorial governor of New Mexico observed in 1886, "I understand very well . . . what a cow-boy or cattle herder with a brace of pistols at his belt and a Winchester in his hands means when he 'asks' a sheepherder to leave a given range." Violence succeeded in some places, such as in the long-running Lincoln County War in New Mexico that drove out Mexican herders and earned the county the reputation as "Little Texas." Elsewhere, the cattlemen retreated in the face of encroaching sheepherders, and also farmers, and an ever less accommodating Nature.

The sheep kept coming. The changing ecology of the plains and mountain grasslands and the high prices for wool and mutton favored sheep over cattle. Some cattlemen bowed to market forces by diversifying their own stock to include sheep raising. By 1900 sheep raising had succeeded cattle raising as the leading agricultural industry in Wyoming and Montana, and in northern Arizona and New Mexico sheep outnumbered cattle by ratios of four and eight to one. The sheep and the shepherd never earned public adoration as symbols of western toughness and individualism as did steers and cowboys. But they did represent a changing West, as well as the continued importance of environmental and market forces in shaping that West.

FARMING THE WEST

Simultaneous with mining, lumbering, cattle raising, and sheep raising, farming remade the West. The farmers came along with, in the wake of, and often in contest with the other "pioneers" seeking wealth from the land. Farmers going to the well-watered, well-treed areas of the Pacific Northwest and California found the soil and climate there sufficiently compatible with what they had known in the midwestern and mid-Atlantic areas to adapt readily to their new homes. Farming on the Great Plains, however, required new techniques and tools to succeed. An invisible line separated the tall grass prairie from the bunch grass plains, and crossing it meant adapting to a new world of semi-aridity and isolation. The "sodbusters" who ventured onto the Great Plains after the Civil War entered an environment with little wood for barns, fences, houses; no stands of trees to provide shelter from blizzards or storms; and little rainfall for crops (the annual precipitation west of the 98th meridian was below the 20 inches needed to grow corn or wheat by methods practiced by eastern farmers). New machines and science made profit possible on the "last frontier," and the railroads connected the farmers with markets and products of the world they left behind, but in the end it would be well-capitalized agribusiness concerns more than single-family farms that reaped the richest harvest of grains and survived.

❧ Free Land, Harsh Conditions

The siren song of "free land" lured many farmers to the Great Plains during the 1860s and after. As in so much of western development, the federal government smoothed the path. The Homestead Act of 1862 provided the essential lure for farmers to go to an area previously regarded as inhospitable and unarable. Under the terms of the act, which the wartime Republican Congress passed to promote the rapid settlement of the West as a bastion of small farms and free labor, 160 acres of surveyed public land was available "free" to any person who paid a $10 registration fee, cultivated and improved the land, and built a habitation and lived on the land for five years, or a person could buy the 160-acre parcels outright for $1.25 an acre. Between 1865 and 1900 almost 400,000 heads of household (mostly families, but several thousand unmarried men and

unmarried women as well) claimed land under the provisions of the Homestead Act. Five times as many farmers bought land directly from railroad companies, speculators, and states that promoted settlement (see above). On the dry plains a 160-acre farm was too small to make a living, but homesteading provided an essential push for settlement and opened areas where the railroads initially were reluctant to go.

Farming on the plains and in the Great Basin proved difficult. Harsh weather, crop pests, drought, prairie fires, competition from abroad, overproduction, and other problems plagued the farmers. Blizzards piled snow so high it covered houses, and melting winter snows created river torrents that washed away crops and improvements. Dust storms lashed the plains, stripping all vegetation and covering everything with blankets of dirt. Locust swarms so blackened the sky that one could not tell night from day. During the 1870s plains farmers reported seeing grasshopper clouds a mile long; grasshopper invasions ate everything in their path, including clothes and the bark off trees.

Farmers prayed for relief, which sometimes came and was remembered as a miracle — none more so than the "miracle of the gulls," when gulls ate up the grasshoppers that threatened crops in Mormon settlements

---

❋ IN THEIR OWN WORDS

Swedish Immigrant Diary, 1870-74

In the 1870s Swedish immigrant Ida Lindgren moved with her husband to Nebraska and then Kansas following the lure of the land, only to find, like many immigrant women on the plains, that the climate, conditions, loneliness, and crop pests led to a hard life.

May 1870

What shall I say? Why has the Lord brought us here? Oh, I feel so oppressed, so unhappy! Two whole days it took to get here and they were not the least trying part of our travels. We sat on boards in the work-wagon packed in so tightly that we could not move a foot, and we drove across endless, endless prairies, on narrow roads; no, no, not roads, tracks like those in the fields at home when they harvested grain. No forest but only a few trees which grow along the rivers and creeks. And

then here and there you see a homestead and pass a little settlement. The Indians are not so far away from here, I can understand, and all the men you see coming by, riding or driving wagons, are armed with revolvers and long carbines, and look like highway robbers.

July 1870

Claus and his wife lost their youngest child at Lake Sibley and it was very sad in many ways. There was no real cemetery but out on the prairie stood a large, solitary tree, and around it they bury their dead, without tolling of bells, without a pastor, and sometimes without any coffin. A coffin was made here for their child, it was not painted black, but we lined it with flowers and one of the men read the funeral service, and then there was a hymn, and that was all.

August 25, 1874

We have not had rain since the beginning of June, and then with this heat and often strong winds as well, you can imagine how everything has dried out. There has also been a general lamentation and fear for the coming year. We are glad we have the oats (for many don't have any and must feed wheat to the stock) and had hoped to have the corn leaves to add to the fodder. But then one fine day there came millions, trillions of grasshoppers in great clouds, hiding the sun, and coming down into the fields, eating up *everything* that was still there, the leaves on the trees, peaches, grapes, cucumbers, onions, cabbage, everything, everything. Only the peach stones still hung on the trees, showing what had once been there.

in Utah. They also got false hopes during the early 1880s when the plains received above normal rainfall and farm prices rose, spurring movement onto the land by convincing many farmers that rain followed the plow. Supposedly, the thinking went, farming would alter the climate. Amid such hopes and torments, people moved to the plains but also off it in cycles of boom and bust. And despite drought, depressions, and despair some farmers stayed on even during the darkest days of the 1890s, waiting for the next boom. As the old joke said: "Living in Nebraska is a lot like being hanged; the initial shock is a bit abrupt, but once you hang there for a while you sort of get used to it."

New Technologies and Tactics

Important technological innovations made possible farming on the new lands. Sod-busting on the prairies and plains benefited from a period of rapid modernization of agriculture. Cyrus McCormick's horse-drawn reaper, developed in the 1830s and mass-produced in the McCormick works in Chicago by the 1850s, led the way. It cut the grain stalks in large swaths. The harvester, invented in the 1870s, followed. It drew the cut stalks to a platform for binding into sheaves. At the same time, new milling techniques using steel rollers to separate cleanly the husk from the bran produced a smooth white flour that became highly prized among urban consumers, increasing demand for wheat and making Minneapolis the flour-milling capital of America. From mid-century on, the U.S. Patent Office reported numerous agricultural inventions and improvements, including steel-tipped plows for "busting" through the sod, mechanized corn planters, mechanized rakes, improved reapers and harvesters, combines, and wire binders. The inventions and improvements allowed farmers to farm more acres with fewer hands — by 1880, for example, a single combine could do the work of twenty men — and by the last quarter of the nineteenth century, a farmer using the new implements to grow wheat and corn could produce almost ten times more than a farmer before the Civil War. By enclosing their acres with barbed wire, perfected by Joseph Glidden in the 1870s, farmers could keep cattle from trampling crops.

On the plains, the lack of surface water and adequate rainfall led to efforts at irrigation, the use of windmills, and "dry farming." Irrigation worked on the eastern fringe of the plains and in the Great Basin, and was eventually aided by federal legislation, especially the Newlands Reclamation Act of 1902, underwriting

irrigation projects to "reclaim" water resources supposedly only waiting to be discovered and released by man's genius. After much experimentation trying to adapt eastern methods of drawing water from wells, plains farmers turned to windmills with thin blades to capture the ever-blowing "free" wind power needed for deep-drill wells. A big boost to plains farming came when farmers learned to plow furrows deep enough to cause capillary action in the loosened soil and then to harrow the field to create a dust mulch to hold the moisture. This "dry farming" technique opened much of the plains to agriculture. Over time, it also sowed seeds of a whirlwind, for the repeated turning of the soil contributed mightily to dust storms and eventually the Dust Bowl of the 1930s.

Science played a vital role in "opening the West" to farming. Much of the science was funded by government. Knowledge about soils, plant development, and weather increased dramatically during the last half of the nineteenth century. The land grant colleges established by the Morrill Act of 1862 trained a host of agronomists, botanists, soil experts, and other scientists who adopted an applied scientific philosophy. The U.S. Department of Agriculture, established during the Civil War, promoted "scientific farming" in its experimental agricultural stations, publications, and agents. The Weather Bureau provided fuller and more accurate information on weather patterns.

Knowledge brought by immigrant farmers also seeded the plains with people, plants, and procedures suited for the soil and climate there. Russian Germans from the steppes, for example, already knew how to use manure and grass for fuel, how to build a house from sod, how to plow to hold moisture in the soil, how to drive grasshoppers from fields by using flails, and what to plant. They brought over the hardy, drought-resistant Turkey Red variety of wheat that grew well in heat and cold. Scandinavian immigrants carried similar knowledge and experience to the northern plains. Farmers from all lands learned to prosper on the plains by planting more sorghum and other drought-resistant grains and less corn per acre.

The Rise of Agribusiness

Growing wheat or other grains on the plains required land enough to justify the expense and labor of dry farming and machines enough to harvest crops intended for market. Agricultural journals pounded home the theme that farming was now a business that must leave nothing to chance. As one journal editor wrote, "Farming for business, not for a living — this is the motif of the New Farmer." Plains farmers needed to succeed as specialists growing cash crops for sale on world markets. As such, they became cogs in the wheels of the industrial revolution that dictated the means and the market for their farming. What happened in New York counting houses, Chicago railroad yards and grain exchanges, Rockford agricultural machine factories, and other points in the intricately intertwined industrial economy affected life on the farm — and even whether there would be a farm. The 160-acre homestead was too small to return a profit on the plains. Farmers bet on high prices to borrow for more land and for the machines. The ocean of wheat soon hid a mountain of debt.

From the 1870s on, large agricultural combinations assumed an increasing share, and much of the profit, of cereal production on the plains. Bankers and railroad investors sought new outlets for investment after bond failures in the early 1870s, and the cheap land of the plains beckoned as grain prices rose. Investors set up "bonanza farms" of 10,000 to 15,000 acres or more and operated them with all the efficiency the managerial revolution had at hand. Some bonanza farms were so large that managers strung telephone lines to keep in touch with suppliers, workers, and staff. In the Red River valley of North Dakota, for example, the Cass-Cheney-Dalrymple farm extended for six miles, had over 100 employees, and, in factory-like rhythms, ran 66 plows, 125 seeders, 200 harrows, 30 self-binding harvesters, five steam-powered threshers, and other equipment over 25,000 acres of land. Wheat production soared through the 1880s and spread from Minnesota, across the Dakotas, into Montana and Colorado, and as far as California. In California, by 1890, thanks to government aid in diverting water to irrigate the Central Valley, bonanza farms were producing more wheat for export than any state but Minnesota.

America became the world's breadbasket. Farmers rushed to and across the plains to grow their own pots of gold from grain. But economies of scale favored the bonanza farms in the highly competitive world of wheat. Large-scale operations could wring concessions from railroads and processors and buy supplies in wholesale while small farmers had to pay whatever the market dictated for transportation, handling, processing, and supply. When wheat and corn prices fell, such inequities reaped a crop of bitter anger toward the railroads, processors, and owners of capital that fueled the radical farm politics of the 1890s (see Chapter 21).

Specialization extended to other products in the West. Fruit and vegetable production especially profited from modern business organization and method. Growers combined in cooperative marketing associations to send their apples, grapes, cherries, and oranges to market. California orange growers set the standard. They used the new refrigerator railroad cars to ship their produce safely to eastern markets, which they cultivated by selling their product as a healthy and exotic food and branding it as a quality product. California growers stamped the "Sunkist" trademark on oranges to identify the brand in the public mind. Likewise, large California grape growers were trademarking "Sun Maid" raisins, which they sold in boxes for a nickel.

Such specialization included importing and controlling labor, which proved more difficult to manage than machines. In California, half the state's agricultural workforce was Chinese by the 1870s. Fruit growers and packers especially depended on the industry and artistry of Chinese workers in wrapping individual fruit in a way that appealed to grocers and consumers. When white farm workers and vigilantes attacked the Chinese as interlopers, the large growers tried to hold onto their workers, whom they regarded as industrious but docile, but the growers bucked against an inexorable nativism. By the end of the century a combination of the Chinese Exclusion Act of 1882 and violence had driven most Chinese from the fields to urban Chinatowns (see Chapter 19). Growers countered by bringing in Japanese and Mexican workers. In turn, the Japanese used their own special skills to start up vegetable and fruit farms on leased land and sold their produce to growing California urban markets.

The vagaries of the market and Nature took their toll on even the most efficient farmer. Bonanza farms and family farms alike suffered from drought, severe winters, and swarming insects. More damaging were falling prices, due especially to overproduction but also to deflation and foreign competition from Russia and Argentina. The costs of land, maintenance of draft animals, and equipment continued as wheat prices declined during the late 1880s and collapsed in the Panic of 1893. Many families could not outlast the debts and left the Great Plains, with population losses in some counties reaching 50 percent. Large-scale grain producers weathered the natural and economic disasters better than most small farmers and recovered in the early twentieth century, but the boom days never returned and the family farms that relied on wheat as a cash crop were doomed.

Farm Life and Community on the Plains

The treeless plains demanded a new way of living. Short on wood, farm families burrowed into dugouts or cut sod into blocks that they laid edgewise to create walls for sod-houses, which replaced the log cabin as the symbol of the "new farmer." They adapted stoves to burn dung, sunflower stalks, and scrub brush to heat their houses, which they shared with the livestock during winter, and learned to make wool from the hair of wild animals, soap from combinations of pork rinds and grease, and bandages from cobwebs. And they lived apart from other families on their individual rectangular homesteads that bobbed on the undulating plains as if adrift on the sea.

❧ Challenges of Settling Down

Under such harsh conditions, turnover was high on the plains. Native-born American settlers were the most unsettled among plains farmers. Unlike many immigrant farmers who had moved as members of communities (see below), many of the native-born farmers emigrating from the Mississippi River valley region or from points farther east usually came as individual families or even as unmarried men and women. Although such migrants sometimes had moved in chain migrations with connections to either an extended family or a relocated rural neighborhood from their home place, their stay in any one place was conditional. They were capitalists ready to sell their improved land to the next settlers. Lacking common roots with an established community, they also more readily moved on when fortunes changed. But even immigrants were not immune from feelings of isolation and failure, which, as later described by Norwegian novelist O. E. Rolvaag in his best-selling *Giants of the Earth* (1927), could lead to madness, and which in reality led to movement to new farms or to towns.

Women especially felt the burdens of the hard plains living that offered none of the "romance" of the independent farm so celebrated in American culture. Often they had not wanted to leave families and communi-

Faith on the Plains   Churches were often the first community structures put up in plains settlements. Church-building depended much on lay initiative in raising the money and providing the materials, skills, and labor in putting up a church. In 1869 the congregation of the first Episcopal church in Wichita, Kansas, posed proudly before the crude sod-and-timber church as testimony to the community they had gathered there.

ties behind when the men had determined to try their luck on the plains, and as one forlorn farm wife wrote in a letter home, now they faced a hard life of mosquitoes as fat as birds, hailstones "as big as hen's eggs," choking dust, and searing heat and numbing cold that the houses could not keep out. Throughout the West, women deserted their husbands or initiated divorce proceedings in numbers that far exceeded per capita rates elsewhere.

Movement, however, was not confined to either sex. Many counties in western Iowa, Kansas, Nebraska, and the Dakotas lost half their residents between 1880 and 1890, for example. Some left to try their luck farther west, but many others simply departed because they could no longer carry the debt and disappointment. The frustration was summed up in a sign posted on one Texas plains dwelling: "Two hundred miles to nearest post office, one hundred miles to wood, twenty miles to water, one mile to hell. God bless our home. Gone to live with the wife's folks."

Still, many people stayed. Some even came to appreciate the subtle beauty of the plains, as later did Willa Cather in her novels set in Nebraska. As transportation improved, farmers brought in wood for housing and filled their homes with the bric-a-brac of Victorian domesticity and carpets, lamps, upholstered chairs, and sundry utensils to make life "civilized." They thus would prove they had not become "savage" by living on the plains. And, as one Swedish woman in Dakota Territory wrote home to her parents, in America she worked hard but "was considered a human being" so that that she had "no wish ever to return to Sweden."

❧ *Coming Together as Communities*

To fight isolation, families clustered their houses on the adjoining corners of their homestead plots. They cooperated in fighting prairie fires, putting up fences, repairing outbuildings, nursing the sick, and more. They gathered for husking bees, group threshings, holiday celebrations, and camp meetings, the latter of which might last several days if a particularly effective itinerant preacher came.

They went to the towns that cropped up along the railroads to serve the rural population with dry goods stores, banks, legal and medical services, insurance agencies, libraries, churches, and even graveyards. Some, such as the Jews who first came to the plains as members of agricultural communities, removed from the farms to the towns altogether, where they might support rabbis and meet their religious needs. In the towns, churches and Sunday schools meant regular religious worship and instruction that promised a stable moral compass and opportunities for socialization. Along with town dwellers, the men joined clubs or fraternal orders, such as the Masons and the Benevolent and Protective Order of Elks, and the women joined in auxiliaries to such organizations or in their own sewing, musical, and literary societies. They also formed reform associations to fight "demon rum" and other social evils that threatened family and community. Plains women also joined in efforts to secure the suffrage and gain a larger voice in public affairs, often with more success at the local and state level than women back east. To be sure, in such places social hierarchies emerged based on education, wealth, religion, and race, and townspeople and farmers never fully commingled. But community was possible on the plains.

❧ *Immigrant Settlements and Americanization*

Immigrants were often more successful in adapting to plains living than native-born Americans. Some, such

as the German Hutterites who moved to South Dakota in the 1870s and the Poles who settled central Nebraska in the 1880s, sought seclusion, and so dug in. Many immigrants who adapted well to plains living did so because they came as members of covenanted communities wherein a church served as the institutional cement holding the people together. In their physical isolation on the prairies and plains, the settlers found community through faith. They set up churches and schools, with preaching and teaching in their homeland languages. As one Norwegian farmer explained in surveying Lutheran churches that blossomed across the northern plains: "Nobody made us build them [the churches], and they weren't put up with tax money [as in Norway]. We scraped the money together for them, not from our surplus, but out of our poverty, because we needed them." The plains landscape was soon dotted with churches of many faiths — Eastern Orthodox, Roman Catholic, Lutheran, Mennonite, Reformed — and church rituals and worship served to perpetuate the old ways in a new land. Amid the denominational diversity, Lutheran churches emerged as the plurality and gave the Great Plains a Lutheran character that still survives in many places. The churches also acclimated many settlers to a new life of individual family farms, separated from the village context they had known in Europe. Within the churches the settlers struggled with assimilation, as the American-born second and third generations inched toward "Americanization." Swedish congregations in rural Minnesota for a time debated whether God would hear prayers in English, and eventually conceded the possibility by having bilingual services.

Whatever God's linguistic preferences, the children of the immigrants increasingly became "Americanized." This was due in large part to their increasing involvement in the market economy. They could hardly escape it, for the railroads had lent money to the immigrant settlers and moved them to the plains to grow cash crops, not to worship God. The railroads' god was commerce, and the railroads encouraged the farmers to specialize in cash crops — wheat on the northern plains, corn in the central plains, and cotton in the southern plains — that the railroads might haul to market. The vicissitudes of staple crop prices, and the torments of droughts and locusts, would test the farmers' faith and by the end of the century drive many to populism or off the farm altogether.

THE WESTS OF IMAGINATION

No single West emerged from the last half-century of exploitation. Nor did any single image encompass the vast promise of the West and the hard realities of it. The various "frontiers" in mining, trapping, logging, ranching, and farming had their own heroes of enterprise, individualism, and derring-do, but in fact all succeeded through coordinated effort, governmental support, and, in the end, organized capital.

During the nineteenth century art and literature figured mightily in imprinting ideas about the West on the public mind. Some authors still viewed "the West" as an antidote to corrupting civilization. From the *Leatherstocking Tales* of James Fenimore Cooper through Mark Twain's *Huckleberry Finn,* the West of imagination was a place free of society's entanglements where men might find adventure and solitude. The trans-Mississippi West became a grander stage to realize such freedom. The awe-inspiring power of western rivers, the majesty of the mountains, the sheer scale and emptiness of the land were captured in the reports and drawings of American explorers and scientists from Lewis and Clark on their "voyage of discovery" to John Wesley Powell in his geo-logical surveys. Photographers such as William Henry Jackson added to the sense of the Great West as counterpoint to the East with awe-inspiring images of unsullied landscapes and grand canyons that surely were the handiwork of God. In his crusades for preservation for purposes of recreation, naturalist John Muir, founder of the Sierra Club in 1892, rhapsodized on Nature's redemptive powers with the promise that "the clearest way into the Universe is through the forest wilderness." In paintings, sculpture, photography, and fiction that West still beckoned in 1900, though it also demanded stewardship of its beauty and resources. Such a West inspired efforts at conservation and the creation of the first national parks, where people might contemplate Nature and refresh themselves from hurried modern lives.

At the same time, the West served as a metaphor for redemption, a place to build a new society. This was the place where faith would be tested. In this mythi-

The Mythical West Buffalo Bill Cody's wildly successful "Wild West" show popularized the cowboy as the rugged individual and featured staged battles with Indians, shooting exhibitions with Annie Oakley and other dead-eyes, and riding and rodeo tricks that delighted eastern and European audiences and imprinted a dashing West on the popular imagination that lasted for generations.

John Wesley Powell Reports on the Grand Canyon, 1875

John Wesley Powell, a one-armed Civil War veteran, gained fame for his daring geological surveys of a previously uncharted West of grand rivers and canyons. His calls for conserving land not otherwise useful for farming, ranching, mining, or timber made him an early champion of a national conservation policy for the West, and along with the images of a pristine West by such photographers as William Henry Jackson, Powell's rhapsodies of a sublime and majestic Nature made the as yet unspoiled West a place of spiritual renewal in the popular mind.

All the scenic features of this cañon land are on a giant scale, strange and weird. The streams run at depths almost inaccessible; lashing the rocks which beset their channels; rolling in rapids, and plunging in falls, and making a wild music which but adds to the gloom of the solitude. . . .

The varying depths of this cañon, due to the varying altitudes of the plateaus through which it runs, can only be seen from above. As we wind about in the gloomy depths below, the difference between 4,000 and 6,000 feet is not discerned, but the characteristics of the cañon — the scenic features — change abruptly with the change in the altitude of the walls, as the faults are passed. . . .

In the very depths of the cañon we have black granite, with a narrow cleft, through which a great river plunges. This granite portion of the walls is carved with deep gulches and embossed with pinnacles and towers. Above are broken, ragged, nonconformable rocks, in many places sloping back at a low angle. Clambering over these, we reach rocks lying in horizontal beds. Some are soft; many very hard; the softer strata are washed out; the harder remain as shelves. Everywhere there are side gulches and cañons, so that these gulches are set about ten thousand dark, gloomy alcoves. One might imagine that this was intended for the library of the gods; and it was. The shelves are not for books, but form the stony leaves of one great book. He who would read the language of the universe may dig out letters here and there, and with them spell the words, and read, in a slow and imperfect way, but still so as to understand a little, the story of creation.

cal West a kind of Darwinian calculus operated in the struggle between good and evil where only the strongest survived. Good conquered evil, provided individual men acted to claim the land, impose law, and build responsible, respectable communities. There was no room for slackers and cowards. This was the West popularized in the dime novels from the 1870s on. In such novels, directed to urban readers hungry for adventure and eager to believe individual character still counted, the western heroes stared down gunslingers, lassoed horse thieves and cattle rustlers, drove off Indians, and protected women and children from all manner of two-legged and four-legged beasts. The cowboy hero cast in many of Frederic Remington's bronze sculptures and in Owen Wister's hugely successful novel *The Virginian* (1902) epitomized the virtues of steady habits, moral clarity, and courage that promised a West made safe for God-ordained communities.

Other images crowded the mind. Most powerful among them was that of a vanishing West. William F. "Buffalo Bill" Cody traded on his life as an army scout and pony express rider, made famous in a Ned Buntline dime novel, *Buffalo Bill: King of the Border Men* (1869), to mount his wildly successful Wild West Show in 1883. The show ran for many years. It featured Cody capturing Indians in mock battles and included various rodeo and circus-like acts of steer roping, gun shooting, and horsemanship. The Wild West Show played to tens of thousands of people in exhibitions across eastern America and Europe and reinforced the idea of seeing "the West" before it was gone. Indeed, one year, Cody hired Sitting Bull, the Sioux chief who had defeated Custer, to stand mute and glaring, almost like a cigar-store Indian, as testimony to the fact that the wild West was over, with the "good guys" winning.

CONCLUSION: PROFITS AND "PROGRESS"

More perceptive was the recognition that such mythical Wests as morality plays were gone, if they ever existed. In their place, boosters, speculators, railroad men, government agents seeking settlers, and a host of others reminded Americans why the West always mattered. It was a place for progress through profit, the latest and greatest resource for American capital and might. They still saw gold in the hills and cash in crops and hardly blinked over the removal of Indians, the blasting of mountains, and the wholesale harvesting of animal hides, timber, mineral resources, and anything else Nature had bestowed on the land. Their heroes were engineers, railroad builders, finance capitalists — men of grand vision and ambition. Such men might even make the desert bloom. Such a view of conquest was summed up in a 1906 issue of the *North American Review* that was an epitaph for the old West and an invitation for a new one:

> The old cabins and dugouts are replaced by modern dwellings. The great ranges are fast passing into orderly farms, where cultivated crops take the place of wild grasses. Steadily is man's rational selection directing the selection of nature. Even the cowboy, the essential creation of Western conditions, is rapidly passing away. Like the buffalo, he has had his place in the drama of civilization. The Indian of the plain must yield to civilization or pass away. Custer, Cody, Bridger, and Carson did their work and passed on. Pioneers of the old school are giving place to a young and vigorous group of men of intellect, will and ceaseless activity, who are turning the light of scientific discovery on plain and mountain. . . . [A] nation of two hundred millions of freemen, living under American Common and Statute law, stretching from the Atlantic to the Pacific, fifty millions of whom occupy the arid region of the continent, where the word "desert" is unknown, will soon be a mighty reality.

That was America's true Manifest Destiny.

And so it was to be in the twentieth century. But at what cost to Nature and the verities of the older America that survived more in myth than fact? That question haunted Americans as they scanned the far horizons and contemplated a future after the frontier was "closed" and industrial capitalism seemingly had triumphed.

SUGGESTED READING

Richard A. Bartlett, *The New Country: A Social History of the American Frontier 1776-1890* (1974). A vivid account of the peoples seeking and settling on American frontiers, filled with useful information on topics as varied as the technology of migration and farming, immigrant recruitment, land policy and use, railroads, church-building, and community life.

Sarah Deutsch, *No Separate Refuge: Culture, Class and Gender on an Anglo-Hispanic Frontier in the American Southwest, 1880-1940* (1987). A pioneering study that views the frontier as a place of symbiotic cultural and social interactions, in this case of Anglo-Mexican relations in New Mexico and Colorado, and places women, including missionaries, at the center of community formation.

William H. Goetzmann and William N. Goetzmann, *The West of the Imagination* (1986). A stunning display and discussion of the artistic imaginings and re-visionings of the West that fed interest, migration, settlement, conservation, and popular culture in contradictory ways over several centuries.

Robert V. Hine and John Mack Faragher, *The American West: A New Interpretive History* (2000). The "new Western history" at its best, with ample illustrations and a wide sweep of interest in cultural, environmental, ethnic, social, and women's issues.

Frederick E. Hoxie, *A Final Promise: The Campaign to Assimilate the Indians, 1880-1920* (1984). An ethnohistory measuring the social and cultural costs of assimilation policy and the clashing ideals of reformers and Indians regarding their own best interests.

Andrew C. Isenberg, *The Destruction of the Bison: An Environmental History, 1750-1920* (2000). A telling cultural, economic, and ecological examination of the ways men and nature interacted to cause the drastic decline of the bison (buffalo).

David Alan Johnson, *Founding the Far West: California, Oregon, and Nevada, 1840-1890* (1992). An innovative, detailed account of the charter groups that established government, community, and interests in three states that suggests ways to observe similar developments elsewhere.

Rodman W. Paul, *The Far West and the Great Plains in Transition, 1859-1900* (1988). An important overview of the mining, agricultural, and settlement histories of the region, with much attention to land use patterns, race relations, and conflicting economic interests.

Francis Paul Prucha, *American Indian Policy in Crisis: Christian Reformers and the Indian, 1865-1900* (1976). A close examination of the federal government's changing policy regarding Indian assimilation and the Protestant churches' role in shaping interest and policy.

Glenda Riley, *The Female Frontier: A Comparative View of Women on the Prairie and the Plains* (1988). A provocative argument that traditional values and practices of women's domesticity created a common women's experience in settling the West, irrespective of the physical environment.

Robert M. Utley, *The Indian Frontier of the American West 1846-1890* (1984). Still the best survey of the changing "frontiers" of the West due to the entanglement of Indians and non-Indians, assayed from a dual perspective, with much on Indian-American conflicts, government policies, and military actions.

Donald Worster, *Under Western Skies: Nature and History in the American West* (1992). A groundbreaking series of essays on the complex relationships between man and nature, with particular attention to migration patterns and habits of animals and people, the ways cultures informed uses of the land, the centrality of water to western development, and the changing human and natural worlds.

Suggestions for Further Reading

David Wallace Adams, *Education for Extinction: American Indians and the Boarding School Experience, 1875-1928* (1995).

Patricia Albers and Beatrice Medicine Albers, *The Hidden Half: Studies of Plains Indian Women* (1983).

Lewis Atherton, *The Cattle Kings* (1961).

Donald J. Berthrong, *The Cheyenne and Arapaho Ordeal: Reservation and Agency Life in the Indian Territory, 1875-1907* (1976).

Everett Dick, *The Lure of the Land: A Social History of the Public Lands from the Articles of Confederation to the New Deal* (1970).

Robert A. Dykstra, *The Cattle Towns* (1968).

David M. Emmons, *The Butte Irish: Class and Ethnicity in an American Mining Town, 1875-1925* (1989).

Mark Fiege, *The Making of an Agricultural Landscape in the American West* (1999).

Gilbert C. Fite, *The Farmer's Frontier, 1865-1900* (1966).

Morris W. Foster, *Being Comanche: A Social History of an American Indian Community* (1991).

Stan Hoig, *The Oklahoma Land Rush of 1889* (1984).

Paul Andrew Hutton, *Phil Sheridan and His Army* (1985).

Julie Roy Jeffrey, *Frontier Women: The Trans-Mississippi West 1840-1880* (1979).

Alvin M. Josephy, Jr., *The Civil War in the American West* (1991).

Joy S. Kasson, *Buffalo Bill's Wild West: Celebrity, Memory, and Popular History* (2000).

Lawrence H. Larsen, *The Urban West at the End of the Frontier* (1978).

Frederick C. Luebke, ed., *Ethnicity on the Great Plains* (1980).

Chris J. Magoc, *Yellowstone: The Creation and Selling of an American Landscape, 1870-1903* (1999).

Paul Mitchell Marks, *Precious Dust: The True Saga of the Western Gold Rushes* (1995).

Janet A. McDonnell, *The Dispossession of the American Indian, 1887-1934* (1991).

Douglas Monroy, *Thrown among Strangers: The Making of Mexican Culture in Frontier California* (1993).

James C. Olsen, *Red Cloud and the Sioux Problem* (1965).

Catherine Price, *The Oglala People, 1841-1879* (1996).

Peter J. Rahill, *The Catholic Indian Missions and Grant's Peace Policy, 1870-1884* (1953).

Paul Reddin, *Wild West Shows* (1999).

Richard W. Slatta, *Cowboys of the Americas* (1990).

Elliott West, *The Contested Plains: Indians, Goldseekers, and the Rush to Colorado* (1998).

Donald Worster, *Rivers of Empire: Water, Aridity, and the Growth of the American West* (1985).

Mark Wyman, *Hard-rock Epic: Western Miners and the Industrial Revolution, 1860-1910* (1979).

Liping Zhu, *A Chinaman's Chance: The Chinese on the Rocky Mountain Frontier* (1997).

18

The New Industrial Order

I N 1876 THE world came to Philadelphia to celebrate America's 100th birthday. Philadelphia hosted the spectacular Centennial Exhibition that drew over 10 million people to the exposition grounds in Fairmount Park to see art, agricultural produce, and whatever else the various states of the United States and foreign countries chose to display. Most of all, they came to see the machines. At the fair, the Americans made the usual bows to farming in Agricultural Hall and to democracy in speeches, but it was the burgeoning American industrial might that the American sponsors sought to project and the crowds paid to see. In Machinery Hall, a building covering 14 acres and filled with devices of all types from many nations, the Americans stole the show with Alexander Graham Bell's telephone, Thomas Alva Edison's Quadruplex Telegraph (capable of transmitting several messages simultaneously), and other mechanical marvels.

At the center of the American exhibit stood the massive two-cylinder, 1,400 horsepower Corliss Engine that supplied the power for the other 800 machines at the exposition. From its first hiss of steam on opening day, the great gleaming engine also drove the American exhibit's underlying assumption that technology was the author of progress. Machines secured freedom by liberating humanity from dulling labor and by increasing material bounty. The crackling voices on Bell's "speaking telegraph" and the long-and-short dashes of the Morse Code broadcast the message that machines could conquer space and time. American power seemingly knew no bounds.

The centennial gave the nation a chance to look

backward and forward. In celebrating the machine, Americans chose the future over the past. Technology — the steamboat, the telegraph, the railroad — made America strong. It saved the Union during the Civil War, and it was winning the West. The Centennial Exhibition traded on history in its advertising, concessions, and souvenirs (pictures of George Washington were everywhere) but by featuring technology, it symbolically placed the republic's happiness in the hands of captains of industry rather than Jefferson's simple farmers and artisans. Industrial America was coming of age.

The Centennial Exhibition itself provided a practical demonstration of the technological and organizational genius rapidly transforming post–Civil War America from an agricultural republic into the industrial rival of Great Britain and Germany. Planning for the exposition took five years. Mindful that the previous American world's fair, the 1853-1854 Exhibition of the Industry of All Nations, had been a commercial failure, the centennial fair's organizing committee, comprised largely of businessmen, relied on modern promotional devices and underwriting to ensure the exposition's success. In America, even a birthday party should be made to pay.

The fair's businessman organizers financed the extravaganza by selling stock, at ten dollars a share, to over 20,000 Americans and by lobbying city and state governments for subsidies. They enlisted women veterans of the Civil War Sanitary Fairs to raise money and send petitions to legislative bodies. They oversaw the design and construction of 200 buildings — including a Woman's Hall that the women fundraisers demanded as a consequence of their services. They advertised the fair in magazines and through the sale of patriotic souvenirs.

In managing so large an enterprise, the organizers borrowed managerial practices of centralized command from the railroads and military, and they used the latest technology in communications to orchestrate their solicitations and arrangements with foreign and state governments and countless contractors. Already, through their use of the telegraph and typewriter, the fair's organizers were applying the technology of information collection and control that was revolutionizing the office. To move the millions of people who attended the fair, the organizers arranged for expanded service from Philadelphia's streetcars, and an elevated train was built on the grounds to handle the extra load. The Pennsylvania Railroad ran special excursion trains from New York, Baltimore, and Pittsburgh to its Market Street station in city center, and then carried passengers to the fair on newly arranged commuter trains. The organizers knew how to tap a national audience and to bring it to a central place.

The success in promotion and transportation made the Centennial Exhibition the nation's first mass tourist enterprise. Americans were fascinated by scientific and technological advances and eager to learn about them. From the 1830s on they attended lectures, read magazines and books, and went to exhibitions on science and technology. The Centennial Exhibition capitalized on that enthusiasm by providing the means to travel to the fair in comfort and then making the event itself informative and fun. Although the fair did not reward its sponsors with large financial returns, it did show that centralized management, telecommunications, and integrated transportation could reach a vast national market. Here were the elements of a new industrial order.

POST–CIVIL WAR NATIONAL ECONOMIC EXPECTATIONS

The "heroic age" of American industrial growth represented at the Centennial Exhibition reflected the positive attitude most Americans held toward business following the Civil War. Businessmen emerged from the Civil War as heroes. Their roles in financing the war, producing both "guns and butter," and distributing goods had contributed mightily to Union victory. Businessmen reminded the nation of that fact by draping themselves and their products in patriotic symbols at public events, such as Fourth of July parades and centennial celebrations, and in advertising their wares. Southerners, too, dressed their own thinking with newfound pro-business attitudes. Even in the muddled logic of the "New South creed" (see Chapter 16), businessmen were lifted to pedestals just below those for Confederate generals. Supposedly, businessmen practicing "Yankee" thrift and enterprise would redeem the South from northern rule and preserve southern values.

The war had taught Americans to think big and nationally in terms of economic development. They learned that decisions about credit made in New York or Philadelphia banking houses affected the output of midwestern farms and factories. Soon enough, western resentment toward eastern bankers would explode in the farm revolts of the 1870s and 1890s, and labor too would resist the growing consolidation of financial and industrial power into a few hands, but the immediate thrust after the Civil War was toward national development at all costs. Indicative of such attitudes was the popularity of such board games as Milton Bradley's "Checkered Game of Life" that rewarded the player who landed on the square marked "Industry" with a move to the square marked "Wealth," which was worth twice the value of the one marked "Honor."

The scale of expectations rose, and with it, the definition of wealth. The war inured Americans to spending millions and accustomed them to measuring wealth and status by the new standard. Great generals moved armies in the tens of thousands; big businessmen counted fortunes in the millions. Americans once impressed by 100-mile-long railroads now laid out transcontinental lines of a thousand miles or more. The size of the country, which at one time had seemed a disadvantage to building a nation, became an advantage as Americans discovered ways to exploit the abundant natural resources of coal, iron, timber, and the land itself in their continental empire. Senator John Sherman of Ohio summed up the new attitude and vision in a letter to his brother, General William T. Sherman: "The truth is, the close of the war with our resources unimpaired gives an elevation, a scope to the ideas of leading capitalists, far higher than anything ever undertaken in this country before. They talk of millions as confidently as formerly of thousands."

The war also drilled millions of Americans in the virtues of regimented work. Nationalism and regimentation marched together in mass armies outfitted with standard-issue rifled muskets, blue uniforms, and boots. Young men who fought, worked, and ate and slept together understood that discipline and coordinated movement through hierarchical command determined victory. Organized relief, such as the legions of women nurses and Sanitary Commission workers, further attested to the benefits of concerted effort. Success demanded system. The large-scale, integrated supply and management of Union forces defeated the less well-organized, more "democratic" southern foe in the end — a victory that affirmed the superiority of "modern" bureaucracy and national order over paternalism and localism (embodied in the planter-dominated, states' rights Old South). Although few industrial workers accepted the logic of an "industrialized" work ethic that would reduce them to machines, the ethic gained much from the war. By working together, patriotic Americans not only saved the world's "last, best hope" for republican government but also made it strong.

The old values of hard work and individual responsibility still echoed in public discourse and in the Horatio Alger stories and other popular fare where fate rewarded diligence, sobriety, and honesty with riches. But such tales belied the truth about the new industrial order. More accurate was the observation of novelist William Dean Howells's hero Silas Lapham, who upon returning from the war to take up the family business realized: "I found that I had got back to another world. The day of small things was past, and I don't suppose it will ever come again in this country." The world of the small producer was yielding to the huge factory, the small-town merchant to the big-city retailer. The merchant-dominated economy of the early nineteenth century, with merchants functioning as middlemen (wholesalers, commission salesmen, importers, retailers) in the many exchanges that brought the goods of producers to consumers, was being replaced by a national distribution network. Although most Americans continued to work on farms or in shops and mills organized along craft lines, it was the likes of big steel, big oil, and big sugar that dominated the national market and seized the public imagination after the Civil War. Andrew Carnegie rather than Andrew Jackson came to embody the ideal of the self-made American.

THE RAILROADS

More than any other single industry, railroads set the rate and scale of American industrial growth and defined the new industrial order. Indeed, from the 1850s to the 1890s railroads symbolized the new industrial culture, evoking a mixture of awe and anger from the American public. No industry received more attention in pictures and print. As early as 1848 Ralph Waldo Emerson observed that the railroads were "the only sure topic of conversation, . . . the only one which interests farmers, merchants, boys, women, saints, philosophers, and fools." For the rest of the century, public interest grew apace with the increase in the railroads' track mileage and economic power. Reflecting on the post–Civil War age of which he was a part, historian Henry Adams mused that, from 1865 to 1895, in order "to make the continent habitable for civilized people," Americans "dropped every thought of dealing with anything more" than building "a railway system." That task alone consumed "the energies of a generation, for it required all the new machinery to be created — capital, banks, mines, furnaces, shops, powerhouses, technical

Chinese Laborers　In this 1867 photograph, Chinese men with picks and hammers are shown at work on the Central Pacific Railroad. The transcontinental lines employed large numbers of Chinese and Irish immigrants in the arduous and dangerous work of laying track through mountains, over canyons, and across deserts.

knowledge, mechanical population, together with a steady remodeling of social and political habits, ideas, and institutions to fit the new scale and the new conditions." Adams's generation mortgaged itself to the railways, he said, "and no one knew it better than the generation itself."

America needed the railroad. In time, need also caused Americans to fear it. Steam locomotives, with their whirring wheels and billowing smokestacks, were the standard metaphor for America's thrust toward industrial might, while railroad magnates, by their greed and corrupt business practices, became the personification of unchecked economic power. Frank Norris's widely read novel *The Octopus* (1901) about the struggle between wheat farmers and the Southern Pacific Railroad for control of California caught the paradox of need begetting fear. On the one hand, Norris hitched progress to western farmers loading produce on railcars headed east; on the other, he condemned the heartless railroad monster for strangling the wheatgrowers trapped in its monopolistic grip. As Norris understood, the profound ambivalence Americans felt toward the railroad mirrored their own hopes and

fears about the post–Civil War industrial order. Americans did not know where the industrial revolution was taking the nation, but they did know that the railroads were pointing the way.

The railroads were America's first big business. The size of their operations dwarfed all other industries. The principal railroads in the 1850s were capitalized from $17 to $35 million each, at a time when the largest textile mills rarely exceeded $1 million in capital and the largest plantations even less. Railroads became America's single largest employer, with almost three-quarters of a million workers by 1890. The first great fortunes of the era were made in laying track and selling shares in railroad companies, and the first rounds of brass-knuckled capitalism were fought by railroad "robber barons" beating up on competition and unloading watered stock and badly built roads on the public. The thousands of miles of train tracks crisscrossing the United States (166,000 miles of track by 1890, nearly 200,000 by 1900) created an integrated national market and opened the South and West for development. By their huge purchases of iron and steel, coal, wood, rubber, leather, and glass, the railroads functioned as the great multiplier industry from the 1850s to the days of Henry Ford and his automobile.

Railroads further stimulated national economic growth by lowering transportation costs. If nothing else, railroads shortened travel time between cities. A steamboat leaving New Orleans wended its way 1,484 miles on the Mississippi and Ohio rivers to reach Cincinnati, while a train took a more direct route of 922 miles and traveled at more than three times the speed of water transport. Railroads offered the added benefit of year-round service — a competitive advantage over canals, which were often closed three to five months a year by low water, winter freezes, and repairs.

Railroads also standardized time. In order to coordinate train schedules through a thicket of local reckonings of time, the American Railway Association, on November 18, 1883, divided the continent into four standard time zones. Despite howls from Americans wanting to live by "God's time," which they measured by sunrise and sunset, millions of Americans adjusted their watches and clocks to "railroad time." Congress ratified the railroads' action in 1916. Similarly, uniform specifications for basic railroad equipment and signal systems, cooperative billing among competing railroads, and a national standard track gauge of 4 feet 8½ inches (which on the last night of May 1886 was established when southern roads shifted one rail three inches closer to the other to comply) further facilitated the movement of goods and people across the country. If the Civil War had made a nation, the railroads were forging its essential links.

❧ Building an Integrated Railway System

From mid-century on, railroad executives wanted to develop integrated systems and system in management. Fixed costs (e.g., track maintenance, salaries of office and supervisory staffs, taxes, and interest on bonds) were much higher than variable costs (e.g., labor) and had to be paid whether the trains rolled or not. High fixed costs dictated close attention to detail to keep expenses down and aggressive recruitment of capital and customers to keep revenues up. Because it cost almost as much in fuel and labor to pull a short train as a long one, railroad executives sought ways to haul more cars over their tracks. That meant tapping into the major east-west flow of commerce.

Before the Civil War no single railroad connected an eastern port directly with a midwestern city. The need to load and unload goods several times on different companies' lines, each with a separate gauge track, en route from New York to Chicago or St. Louis, for example, caused bottlenecks that added to shipping costs and made scheduling and control of transportation unpredictable. To draw traffic to their main lines, railroads bought or built feeder lines, but organizing trunklines between major markets seemed to railroad men the best way to fill train cars and control expenses.

East of the Mississippi, the emphasis was on buying and merging existing lines to create integrated systems. In 1851 the New York & Erie ran a line from Albany to Dunkirk, on Lake Erie, but the first true trunkline directly tying Atlantic coastal cities to midwestern commercial centers was the New York Central, organized

A Western Timber Trestle   The rapid construction of the transcontinental lines included such herculean feats as putting up large wood frame trestles, such as the one in this 1860 photograph. Unfortunately, much of the work was shoddy and later had to be redone—sometimes after causing disastrous accidents.

by New York iron magnate and political boss Erastus Corning. Corning used his influence in the state legislature to combine several New York lines into a new corporation known as the New York Central, which he supplied with rails, spikes, and other hardware produced by his own iron firm. Commodore Cornelius Vanderbilt, who had amassed a fortune in shipping and steamboats before turning to railroads in 1862, wrested control of the Central from Corning in 1867. Through a combination of bribery, stock-watering, and ruthless acquisition, Vanderbilt made another fortune gobbling up smaller lines in five states and extending the Central to New York City, thus completing the New York Central system. In 1875 it had over 4,700 miles of track connecting New York City with several midwestern sites. Other big railroad companies such as the Baltimore & Ohio (B&O) and the Pennsylvania established similar control over parallel through-routes to the Midwest. By the 1880s several competing trunklines ran along the east-west corridors of commerce. Likewise, in the South some 400 small companies, averaging not more than forty miles each, were welded into five major systems that linked southern traffic to the national railway network.

Eastern railroad companies poured more traffic into their systems by acquiring steamship lines. Improvements in steamship design and power enlarged cargo capacity and reduced the time of transatlantic travel to ten days or so by the 1880s, contributing to the threefold increase in American exports between 1870 and 1900. With access to markets from the American plains to the Russian steppes, the trunkline railroads pulled America deeper into the international commercial nexus.

West of the Mississippi, transcontinental lines had to be built from scratch across 1,800 miles of sparsely populated, treeless plains and rugged mountains. Railroad builders there faced staggering start-up costs of buying engines and cars, acquiring land, putting up depots, and laying track where only the buffalo roamed. They had to beg and borrow huge sums in a highly competitive capital market.

Railroads everywhere were voracious consumers of capital. The big railroads borrowed heavily by selling bonds, largely to British and eastern banks. The Pennsylvania Railroad, for example, issued $78 million worth of securities to finance its expansion during the 1870s. In 1897 the combined value of all American railroad stocks and bonds was over 8½ times the *national* debt. Such capital needs could not be met from private sources alone. Western transcontinental lines especially looked to the government for aid, because, without local traffic to sustain them, they had to lay track in advance of settlement and to compete with established eastern companies for risk capital.

✧ Government Aid to Railroad Construction

Railroads had a long history of government support. Since the 1840s railroad companies, like turnpike and canal companies before them, had lobbied state and local governments for rights-of-way and capital. Local lawmakers eager to link their communities to a burgeoning transportation network obliged by donating land for terminals and stations, buying railroad stock, and abating taxes. At the same time, companies running interstate tracks petitioned the federal government to help defray construction costs. Beginning in 1850 with land grants to Illinois, Mississippi, and Alabama, which those states in turn gave to the Illinois Central to build a line from Illinois to Mobile, railroads were the first industry to receive large-scale federal government subsidies. In the 1880s, they also became the first big business to come under federal regulation (see below).

To encourage building transcontinental lines, Congress, in 1862, passed a federal land-grant bill. During the thirty years of the program, 79 railroads received over 131 million acres, which, when added to the 49 million acres of state land grants, roughly equaled the combined acreages of California and Nevada. Railroad companies gained control over large swathes of the West's most arable and well-watered acres and grew fat selling the land (estimated total earnings from sales were $500 million) or using prospective land grants to secure loans. By ceding rights-of-way along favorable routes, allocating to railroad companies alternate sections of surveyed public land along those routes, and providing military protection for and encouragement of western settlement, the federal government effectively subsidized railroad construction across the plains and the Southwest (see Chapter 17). In turn, by requiring railroads to carry the mail and military shipments at low rates as a condition of getting land grants, and having its own alternate sections rise in value due to their location near transportation, the government recouped its investment and spurred settlement and economic growth in the West.

With so much money to be made from government largesse, scoundrels joined the more honest railroad

Palace Car   As the interior of the 1875 "Palace Car" of the Ohio Railway reveals, railroad companies tried to bring the comforts of middle-class homes to train travel in order to induce more people to take to the rails.

men in the rush to the federal trough during the 1870s. Scandals followed. None was more famous than the bribery of congressmen by the Crédit Mobilier, the construction company set up by the major stockholders for the Union Pacific. Crédit Mobilier exhausted all the Union Pacific's capital and drove it into bankruptcy while paying its own stockholders handsome dividends from money made laying track. When exposed, the scandal dogged the careers of a vice president, a Speaker of the House, and two Republican Senators with presidential ambitions. The revelations raised public concerns about conflicts of interest for the first time and, coming during the major business recession of the 1870s, temporarily dampened public support for railroad construction. Crédit Mobilier entered the nation's political lexicon as the catchword for corruption and made railroads synonymous with scandal.

The collapse of Jay Cooke's Philadelphia banking house, triggering the Panic of 1873, further rocked public confidence. Cooke's failure resulted from the rampant speculation and pyramiding of paper credits common to railroad financing based on government grants. Cooke and other investors in the Northern Pacific Railroad had over-extended themselves to

the amount of $100 million on a project that laid less than 500 miles of track from Minneapolis to Bismarck, North Dakota. The Panic dried up railroad investments for almost five years.

Popular support revived with the end of the business recession. In the 1880s, the great decade of railway expansion, public and private sources underwrote 73,000 miles of new track. A nation on the move regarded transportation as a divine right and demanded railroad construction whatever the cost. For all the corruption, shady transactions, and shoddy construction that went with it, land grant and other government assistance programs did get trains rolling across the trans-Mississippi West.

❧ Travel by Train

From the driving of the golden spike at Promontory, Utah, in 1869, that joined the nation together by rail, to the automobile age, Americans took to the trains to see

river, stared upward at geysers in Yellowstone, and attended world's fairs in Philadelphia, Chicago, and St. Louis. The integrated railway system made tourism possible for millions of Americans and profitable for railroad companies and concessioneers. Although passenger revenue declined in importance relative to freight revenue, because freight shipments increased dramatically after the Civil War, passenger miles per year went from almost 5 billion in 1870 to 12 billion twenty years later.

Railroad companies lured riders by offering cheap fares, convenience, and comfort. By the 1880s an individual could travel from New York to San Francisco and back in a few weeks, for less than $50, on a ticket booked by a single agent. Persons riding first-class on one of the transcontinental lines feasted on seafood, fruits, chocolates, and other delicacies served in the dining cars during the day and climbed into cozy berths, with their tucked sheets, in Pullman sleeping cars at night. Coal stoves and then steam heating in the 1880s kept passenger cars snug from winter chills or mountain frosts. Steel rails, standardized car couplings, and the Westinghouse air brake, introduced in the 1870s, made rides smoother and safer. The introduction of the flexible covered passageway, or vestibule, in 1887, freed passengers to move safely from car to car.

The Brooklyn Bridge Bridges made movement across town and across the country faster and safer. The Brooklyn Bridge stood as an American engineering achievement equal to the skyscraper (see Chapter 19). This view of the bridge on a midday in 1898 also reveals how dependent various modes of transportation were on the bridge and how incomplete was the transition from horse to steam and electric power in moving goods, especially over short hauls.

their country. Railroads going from sea to shining sea made America comprehensible and fostered national identity and pride by allowing people to experience the immensity and variety of the land. By train excursions, sightseeing Americans traveled from the slag heaps of the Pennsylvania coal region to the purple-mountained majesty of the Rockies, gazed down at Niagara Falls from Roebling's suspension bridge spanning the

Bowing before the locomotive god, cities replaced dingy train sheds with cathedral-like stations, where red-capped porters welcomed travelers to concourses of restaurants, service shops, and money and ticket exchanges. Part of the romance of the rails was the bustle and the din in the great train depots filled with panting iron horses, barking vendors, and buzzing crowds. Standing in a place such as the massive and magnificent St. Louis Union Station, with its 42 stub tracks and 18 different railroads, gave the American traveler a sense of almost infinite power and possibility. Americans, the railways were saying, could go anywhere.

THE MANAGERIAL REVOLUTION

To get Americans and their goods somewhere safely and on time required good management. Railroad executives confronted unprecedented problems of coordinating far-flung operations extending over hundreds, even thousands of miles. They had to maintain huge inventories of rolling stock, buildings, and supplies; to make countless daily decisions regarding freight shipments and passenger schedules; and to monitor untold daily financial transactions (from paying salaries and rents to purchasing fuel and supplies to selling tickets and renting space). In the absence of any indigenous examples of large-scale business bureaucracies, the railroads devised new and ever more intricate systems of control. The scale and complexity of running a railroad led to the managerial revolution that would fundamentally alter the way Americans did business.

In the traditional family-owned firms of antebellum America, the owner(s) ran the business, from buying raw materials to selling the finished product. With a limited product line, a few employees, and a narrow market, it was possible for one person to know virtually every aspect of the business and to pass that knowledge along to an heir. Running a railroad involved many and more complex decisions than any one owner or manager could attend. Indeed, it was a full-time occupation, demanding specialized skills, just to watch the payroll of a company like the Pennsylvania Railroad, which in the late 1880s employed almost 50,000 workers, roughly 25 times more than any single manufacturer before the Civil War. Railroads recruited salaried professionals and organized them into hierarchical bureaucracies responsible for day-to-day operations.

At first, railroad executives looked to the military for hierarchical management models, and many military officers parlayed their engineering and administrative experience into railroad careers — a relationship strengthened by the Civil War. Early railroad executives borrowed from the army the concept of dividing operations into geographical departments that reported regularly to a central command. In the 1830s the Baltimore & Ohio Railroad, for example, used army engineers to survey its routes; from them, the B&O executives learned military accounting and reporting techniques.

Daniel McCallum of the New York & Erie refined the practices during the 1850s by insisting that agents, conductors, and engineers file daily reports, from which

Rural Depot   The railroad depot became the communications hub of small towns and rural counties and, as exemplified in this interior shot of the Solway, Minnesota, station at the turn of the century, the working example of the new industrial order, with its regimentation of time and compulsion for order. The union of railroad and telegraph brought goods and information to otherwise isolated places.

managers could prepare accurate and timely financial statements and rate adjustments each month. To that end, he drew the first table of organization for an American business to show the route information and decisions must take in the chain of command. When the *American Railroad Journal* offered lithographed copies of McCallum's chart, for the price of one dollar apiece, readers snapped up the supply. Railroad men hungered for ways to impose system in management. Meanwhile, the Pennsylvania Railroad under Herman Haupt and J. Edgar Thomson created separate accounting, treasury, legal, and secretarial departments and regional divisional offices responsible to a central office. The basic principles of modern business management were in place by the Civil War.

✜ *Managerial Control*

Managers also asserted control over their companies by contriving new accounting methods. Railroad executives developed capital accounting, which allowed them to recover depreciation expenses, and cost accounting, which identified specific expenses and problems so that rates could be adjusted monthly, even weekly, to particular markets. In so doing, railroad exec-

"Design for a Union Station" The robber barons were popularly caricatured as ruthless industrial magnates whose efforts to destroy competition and raise prices put liberty itself in danger. Edward R. Harriman, attacked here, was a Wall Street tycoon who battled to control many of the nation's railroads. In 1907, when this cartoon was produced, Theodore Roosevelt was bitterly denouncing him as a monopolist.

utives took the first steps toward administering prices rather than letting invisible market forces determine them. The "visible hand" of railroad management tried to brush aside Adam Smith's proverbial invisible hand of the market, once perfected principles of standardized decision-making and accounting gained currency in the industry. By way of comparison, few merchants and manufacturers as late as the 1850s even knew the extent and sources of their own profits or losses until they closed their books at year's end.

The capital needs of the trunkline railroads further propelled the managerial revolution underway. By issuing large amounts of stock, they spread ownership among many investors. Ownership of large companies became increasingly passive as shareholders yielded authority to boards of directors who appointed skilled managers to run the organizations. The rolled-up-

sleeves and face-to-face business world of the small town merchant or mill owner was passing in favor of the impersonal, tightly structured order of green-visored modern management. Throughout industrializing America a class of managers arose whose principal concern was organizational rather than entrepreneurial. By the early twentieth century, climbing the bureaucratic ladder, rather than starting one's own business, was the route to success. In big business skill and experience counted more than family, organization more than personal character.

✃ Information and Management

System in management depended on reliable, up-to-date information. In this, too, railroads led the way. At a time when a single track carried traffic in both directions, safety alone required more efficient means of signaling trains than relying on flagmen to prevent rail disasters (or, as in the case of one Erie train headed toward collision in 1854, a woman waving her red woolen underdrawers to warn of imminent danger). Recognizing the need for effective communications to move freight and passengers over long distances, railroad executives seized on the telegraph.

The railroad and the electromagnetic telegraph, patented by artist and college professor Samuel F. B. Morse in 1841 and put into commercial service in 1844, grew up together. In exchange for free telegraphic service, railroads let telegraph companies string their wires along railroad rights-of-way, transported telegraphers and their equipment without charge, and shared space in train stations. By 1870 telegraph wires reached across the nation, making possible almost instantaneous communications between a booking agent in San Francisco and one in New York. The transatlantic cable (1857) and, by the 1870s, cables to Japan and China facilitated international trade and travel.

Equally important were communications in and between offices. By the 1870s, business communications had swollen from the trickle of a few letters a week, written by hand, of antebellum days to a deluge of memoranda, reports, and letters, dictated to stenographers who, in turn, transcribed them on typewriters. Companies such as mail-order houses that corresponded directly with customers at first resisted the use of the typewriter, patented in 1868, as too impersonal, but railroad and other executives who dealt frequently with agents and managers made "machine writing" standard business practice by the late 1870s. Such innovations, along with carbon paper (1872) and an improved mimeograph (1890), allowed businesses (or any organization from church bodies to political parties) quickly and cheaply to generate the multiple copies that bureaucracy demanded. Information flowed relentlessly. Gregg "speed-writing," or shorthand, introduced in the 1880s, helped secretaries keep pace with the torrent of words. The ticker tape machine (1867) gave managers immediate access to price fluctuations, and the adding machine (1898) gave then fast tallies of accounts payable and due. Pneumatic tubing sped the paperwork between desks, up and down in tall office buildings.

Just as the paper trail of information and decision lengthened in the modernizing office, the telephone closed social distance in many daily business transactions. Alexander Graham Bell, a Scottish-born immigrant teacher of deaf persons, perfected the device in 1876. Western Union, the telegraph giant, initially dismissed his invention as an "electrical toy," so Bell and his backers organized their own company and hired Theodore N. Vail, a former railway mail superintendent, to run the business. Bell's toy soon transformed communications. New Haven, Connecticut, opened the first telephone exchange in 1878, and New York and Boston completed the first intercity hook-up the same year. Telephone poles sprouted across urban America. Western Union installed 56,000 telephones in 56 cities in 1879 alone, before losing a patent war with the Bell Telephone Company.

Banking on the promise that a people who believed time was money would pay for fast communications, Bell Telephone's Vail set out to improve service and create a national phone system. He chartered the American Telegraph and Telephone Company (AT&T) in 1885 as a subsidiary of the Bell Company to build and run a long-distance network, and switched from iron to copper wire, which carried sound over a much greater distance. Where independent phone companies and stubborn provincialism of local business interests hindered such efforts, as in the South, Vail and his lieutenants denied them access to Bell lines and equipment. Meanwhile, Vail imposed long-distance system requirements on local Bell affiliates, forcing them into the AT&T national network. The Bell organization secured its monopoly by purchasing patents and competing companies and by renewing patents on basic equipment. Although rural areas were left without phone service until the twentieth century, the industrializing, urbanizing parts of the nation had 1.5 million phones in 1900, and in 1915 AT&T completed a transcontinental line between New York and San Francisco.

❧ Business Education

The first generation of managers learned by doing. No schools or books about management existed to provide workable models for business organization on a national scale. Expert knowledge and experience in the great corporations put together in the nineteenth century — from railroads to food processing to steelmaking — generally remained with those who had built the businesses. Their continued growth and prosperity, however, depended on training a new generation of managers to handle the problems of large-scale bureaucracy and nationwide, even international, competition. As businesses and organizations grew in size and complexity, they required specialists in accounting, advertising, engineering, law, marketing, production, sales, and scientific technology. Whether shipping stoves to Sheboygan or Bibles to China, businessmen saw sound management principles as crucial for success. Extensive enterprises could not be left in the hands of amateurs.

The need for specialists led businessmen to establish and endow schools geared to training young men in engineering, mechanics, machinery, and management. Before the Civil War engineers principally acquired their skills as apprentices and on the job; only West Point offered regular instruction in surveying and civil engineering. Business methods were taught haphazardly in some public high schools and private commercial schools in larger cities. By the end of the century a young man could attend such schools as the Massachusetts Institute of Technology (1861), the Columbia School of Mines (1864), and the Leland Stanford, Jr., University (1891), which had curricula devoted to applied science, mining, and engineering rather than the classical studies of traditional colleges. As graduates from such programs moved into prominent industrial positions, especially in the fields of telecommunications, chemicals, and electricity, the ties between industry and technical education tightened.

The first collegiate school of business and the prototype for American business schools was the Wharton School of Finance and Economy, established at the University of Pennsylvania in 1881. Its founder, Joseph Wharton, ruled an empire that included steelmaking and nickel mining in Pennsylvania, gold mines in Nevada, dredging operations in Idaho, and railroad interests stretching from the mid-Atlantic to the Pacific Northwest. The Quaker Wharton subscribed to the Protestant work ethic as the way to wealth, but he realized that he needed engineers, lawyers, and managers more than an ethic to run his many and varied investments. To get them, Wharton helped found what later became Lehigh University to train engineers, and by making a $100,000 contribution in 1881, persuaded the University of Pennsylvania to start a school that combined the liberal arts, and so an awareness of society, with courses in accounting, finance, and management. By the mid-1890s, the Wharton School had a full range of business courses. The impetus for business higher education never slackened.

Training professional managers itself rapidly became a big business. In 1898 the University of Chicago and the University of California launched schools of business, followed in 1900 by the Tuck School of Administration and Finance at Dartmouth College, which offered the first postgraduate management education, and in 1908 by the Harvard Graduate School of Business Administration. John D. Rockefeller, the major supporter of the University of Chicago business school, organized the General Education Board in 1902 to convert colleges and universities to "practical education." The Board channeled millions of dollars to schools that developed courses in banking, engineering, insurance, law, mechanics, medicine, and sciences.

The entrepreneurs who endowed the schools named or sat on their boards of directors and informed the curricula. Business schools rarely bucked parental authority, even in maturity. Joseph Wharton continued to provide substantial gifts to the school that bore his name, gifts that he used to hold it to its principal mission. When Wharton later became dissatisfied with his creation, he revoked a $500,000 bequest he had assigned to it, but by then the school had attracted other wealthy benefactors and served them loyally. In the classroom as in the boardroom, business held sway.

The swelling demand for white-collar workers at every level of business also affected general education. White-collar clerical work was the fastest growing sector of the urban labor force in the late nineteenth century. Corporate offices, banks, utilities, and retail stores needed thousands of men and women for office work — with men generally assigned to bookkeeping, sales, and management and women to stenography and filing. As conditions in factories worsened for blue-collar workers and as skilled workers and unions lost control over the workplace (see below), many working-class parents encouraged their children to take commercial courses in public schools and find jobs in offices, where clerks generally earned higher wages, had better working conditions, and faced fewer layoffs than factory workers. Business was the "god" of America, a young Russian Jewish immigrant astutely observed in 1914, so that "in all the schools business and not labor is pointed out as the ideal occupation." High schools introduced business courses, from bookkeeping to typing, and increasingly stressed the vocational side of formal schooling. By 1910 the United States had 30 university-level business schools, and scores of colleges and even some seminaries boasted business-related courses that promised the "science" of management applied to almost any endeavor.

⁊ Taylorism and Scientific Management

"Scientific" management was what factory owners wanted in the highly competitive economic world of the late nineteenth century. As the scope of the market expanded nationally, so, too, did the scale of industrial production. Big factories muscled aside small ones in the manufacture of mass-market goods. Size had its advantages. Large factories could produce more efficiently and cheaply than small ones because, with more capital resources, they could purchase new technology that sped up assembly lines and reduced the number of high-paid skilled laborers (see below). Also, they could use their size to get discounts in buying raw materials in quantity and shipping in bulk. Such "economies of scale," however, put a premium on management. Large factories had to operate close to full capacity simply to recover the huge capital outlays for machines and materials. High-volume manufacturing depended on low per-unit production costs to turn a profit. Wasted motion idled machines.

Industrial managers came to realize that just as standardization of parts made mass production possible so standardization of work tasks could make it profitable. Organizing the factory became as important as outfitting it. In factories, as in railroads, everyone from managers on down had to think and work in concert and with precision.

Given the high fixed costs of the machines, factory engineers and managers looked for ways to control, and reduce, such variable costs as labor. Steelmaker Andrew Carnegie, for example, repeatedly admonished his managers to watch costs, not profits. "Show me your cost sheet," he commanded, for it was "more interesting to know how well and how cheaply you have done this thing than how much money you have made, because the one is a temporary result . . . but the other means a permanency that will go on with the works as long as they last." More than anything else, businessmen believed labor costs had to be controlled. Indeed, by the twentieth century, making workers more "cost-efficient" became the single most important management goal in large-scale industries. Everywhere in industrial America managers were drafting work rules and designing tasks with an eye to increasing worker output.

The high priest of productivity was Frederick Winslow Taylor, whose time-and-motion studies revolutionized the industrial workplace and whose writings, especially *Principles of Scientific Management* (1911) became holy writ among industrial engineers and factory managers. Taylor was obsessed with order and efficiency. Pundits quipped that he had been born with a stopwatch in his hand, and, in truth, as a boy, he measured his stride to improve his hiking, experimented with various overhand pitching deliveries to throw a baseball accurately, and even devised a new croquet stroke to cut down excess swing. Taylor also grew up at a time when the processes of motion fascinated many Americans. Artists such as Thomas Eakins were painting the human form in ways that showed its dexterity. In the 1870s, in California, the English-born photographer Eadweard Muybridge was developing a multiple-camera technique to record an animal in motion. Muybridge's experiments, which laid the groundwork for motion pictures, started out to settle a bet whether all four of a racehorse's hooves simultaneously left the ground at some point during its stride (he showed that they did), but they attracted national attention for demonstrating that machines could measure movement. Frame-by-frame Muybridge revealed what the naked eye could not see, and by breaking down complex movement his cameras made it comprehensible and subject to control. Amid such interest, Taylor became an engineer.

In the iron and steel works he entered during the 1870s and 1880s, Taylor's calibrating vision saw only anarchy on shopfloors where skilled workers controlled the rhythms and division of labor. Taylor believed that scientific study could break down the industrial process into its simplest components, which, once understood, would allow managers to increase production and lower costs by eliminating unnecessary motion and workers. Stopwatch in hand, he recorded the time workers spent on each particular task and then proposed changes in the jobs to improve efficiency. In his most famous demonstration, at the Bethlehem Steel Company in 1898, Taylor designed 15 kinds of ore shovels, each for a specific task and each to be used in a specific way. He was able to show that 140 men could do the work of 600. The company thereupon fired the "excess" shovelers, cutting its ore-shoveling costs by half. It also gave the remaining shovelers a raise.

The other side of Taylor's plan was to provide incentives for workers to exceed production goals by rewarding them with extra pay when they did so. Under Taylor's scheme, however, workers lost. Jobs became more tedious and monotonous, and the character and pace of work were defined by management rather than the workers themselves. Skill and tradition yielded to "scientifically" ordained rules from which workers could not deviate. Managers, the "white shirts" in workers' parlance, were not able to be on the floor all the time observing work, so, instead, they measured output. They weighed the tonnage of coal, for example, in determining the "efficiency" of miners, rather than going into the mines themselves. By approaching worker input principally by looking at output, managers lost effective contact with the work culture and failed to appreciate and respect the difficulties or skills involved in producing. Managers also adopted Taylor's ideas piecemeal, preferring the emphasis on worker productivity while ignoring his calls for pay incentives. Indeed, most managers looked for ways to cut wages for slack work rather than raising them for better work.

"Taylorism," as Taylor's ideas came to be known, did not take hold everywhere. His program called for redesigning the physical layout and work patterns of the whole factory and for precise record keeping and cost accounting to monitor every aspect of the flow of goods and work there. Few manufacturers could bear the costs of complete retooling and reorganization of heavy industries, and workers resisted management's efforts to reduce them to cogs in a wheel (see below). Also, the mechanization of industry itself was an uneven process. Such basic industries as logging, for example, continued to rely on manual labor and horse-

The Great Inventor   In 1877, Thomas A. Edison had himself photographed in this pose after five days and nights of continuous work perfecting the phonograph. It sums up his famous dictum that invention was "one percent inspiration and ninety-nine percent perspiration." This was precisely the image that Edison wished to project to the world.

drawn transportation into the early twentieth century. The wholesale adoption of Taylorism waited until the twentieth century, especially the 1920s, when a "cult of productivity" and the widespread replacement of steam power by electricity encouraged fuller mechanization of both capital and finished goods industries.

THOMAS EDISON AND INDUSTRIAL TECHNOLOGY

From the end of the Civil War to the turn of the century Americans thought they were living through a new scientific revolution. It was a time of unprecedented technological innovation and invention. Indeed, the U.S. Patent Office issued over 500,000 patents between 1860 and 1890, as compared to only 36,000 in the previous seventy years. In 1892 the commissioner of patents justly boasted that America was "known the world around as the home of invention." The outpouring of inventions and innovative processes testified to Americans' inveterate search for practical new ways of doing and making things, going back to the days of Benjamin Franklin and Thomas Jefferson. But most of the new patents now came from organized research laboratories rather than individual tinkerers working in small machine shops and backrooms. Many of the new in-

ventions involved expensive equipment and sophisticated scientific knowledge beyond the means of any one person. In science, as in business, the individual was being shunted aside in favor of system. Enjoying a wealth of new consumer goods and mechanical wonders, most Americans applauded the change and called it progress.

More than anyone else, Thomas Alva Edison showed how organized research could be productive and profitable and yet, by his gift for self-promotion, also kept alive the comforting idea that individual effort mattered. Born in 1847, in Milan, Ohio, Edison left school early to become a telegraph operator. Edison was a prodigy, experimenting with telegraphs and electricity as a youth and by age twenty-two patenting his first invention, an electrographic vote recorder. A year later, while working in a New York brokerage house, he developed an improved stock-ticker, for which he received a $40,000 bonus from his employer. With two like-minded colleagues he established an electrical engineering company, but he sold his interest in that concern to organize a research laboratory in Newark, New Jersey, that promised to unlock the "mysteries of electrical force." Edison focused on the electrical transmission of messages, for in fast-paced, fast-growing urban, industrial America, one could get rich improving communications. By 1876 Edison was turning out two inventions a year. Among his patents were an "electric pen," an early model of the mimeograph, and the multiplex telegraph.

Edison always sought practical applications for his work, but he was no Franklin willing to share his inventions for the public good. Edison believed science should pay. "Anything that won't sell," he once said, "I don't want to invent." In 1876, in a long wooden shed in Menlo Park, New Jersey, he set up his "invention factory," initially staffed by fifteen young, ambitious experimental scientists and engineers committed to industrial technology as a business. There, Edison predicted, the research team would produce "a minor invention every ten days, and a big thing every six months or so." This was no idle boast. Edison's industrial-research laboratory cranked out hundreds of inventions or improvements, ranging from the storage battery to an electric dynamo, and made the "wizard of Menlo Park" a rich man and a folk hero.

Edison cultivated the image of the lone genius hatching wonders by a combination of "one percent inspiration and ninety-nine percent perspiration," but in fact he was a shrewd businessman and systemizer who spent much of his time promoting his products and himself and running a modern company. Edison played to the myth by putting his name on his products and having himself photographed alone by each new invention that came from the laboratory. At the same time, he divided his research team into departments to maximize production and planned his projects systematically, always with an eye to changing market forces.

Edison, like Theodore Vail in telephones and the Du-Ponts in chemicals, wanted complete control over the process of scientific production in order to monopolize the products of industrial technology in the market. He aggressively bought out competitors or hounded them with lawsuits charging patent infringements, even when his own claims were rather dubious. He traded on his fame to stake claims to ideas he had not perfected, as in the case of the motion-picture camera, which was being developed by others. Such was the power of Edison's name that the inventor of a motion-picture projector could find no buyers for his machine because they were expecting Edison to come out with his own, which he did in 1893 (the kinetoscope). Edison was not always so farseeing as the myth would have him. He originally marketed his phonograph (patented in 1877) as an improved dictaphone for business rather than a form of home entertainment. By the 1890s, when he finally recognized the phonograph's real appeal, others had encroached on his idea, denying Edison the monopoly over idea and product that he sought in all his inventions.

And then there was light. In 1877 Edison turned his attention to a "big thing" by seeking a way to light the American home with electricity. Finding a cheap, reliable, and safe means of indoor illumination promised handsome rewards. As late as the 1840s Americans relied on daylight to conduct their affairs. Most private dwellings were lit dimly, if at all, after dark, unless the owners were willing to burn expensive candles or whale oil lamps. Beginning in the 1850s, gas lighting systems were installed in several cities, but high installation and maintenance costs for pipes and meters limited gas lighting to large urban areas and to middle- and upper-class customers. During the 1860s kerosene became abundantly available once the western Pennsylvania oil fields were tapped for a dependable source of oil, from which kerosene was refined. Kerosene was cheap but also dirty and dangerous, posing a major fire hazard in crowded cities built of wood. If electricity could be harnessed and delivered to individual outlets in homes and businesses, the problems of pollution and fire would be controlled.

The available electrical lighting — arc lamps used for street lighting — was unsuited for indoor use. What was needed was a means to take electricity from a central power source and convert it into small usable amounts for individual customers, switches to control the flow of electricity within circuits, insulated wiring to prevent fire, a meter to record usage, and, most basically, an incandescent glass lamp to give off bright light. To make home electric lighting viable, and to draw customers from natural gas, it was necessary to establish a system (of generators, circuits, meters) that encompassed a wide area of users. Edison's genius was recognizing that the technical problems of indoor electric lighting were inextricably bound up with organizational and commercial considerations. To ignore the latter while concentrating on the former would short-circuit the scientific effort.

Other researchers before Edison had experimented with passing electricity through a filament in a vacuum tube to produce light, but no one had found a fiber that did not crumble quickly from the heat. With a brashness that trumpeted the spirit of the times, Edison boldly declared he would solve the problem. He formed the Edison Electric Light Company in 1878 and assigned the various tasks of developing an economical light bulb to his teams of engineers and scientists. Edison thus positioned himself to market an "incandescent lamp" even before he invented it. After trying hundreds of different fibers, the Edison company developed a carbonized filament capable of burning brightly for up to 170 hours.

Ever the showman and promoter, Edison "announced" his discovery in 1880 by stringing his lights in front of his house and turning them on when news of James A. Garfield's election as president was flashed across telegraph wires, and at Christmastime he decorated the Menlo Park laboratory grounds with forty of his incandescent bulbs. Thousands of people made the pilgrimage to see the light created by the wizard of Menlo Park and came away dazzled. Science, worshipers of technology were saying, rivaled God in separating light from darkness.

Edison moved rapidly to capitalize on his discovery, but he never realized its full potential. In 1882 he opened a power station, designed for maximum public

"The Scientific Splendors of This Age," 1871

In a June 1871 journal entry, Ralph Waldo Emerson caught the Americans' worship of technology as the agent of progress. Such a belief underscored public support for industrial advance and encouraged investment in new technology throughout the century.

The splendors of this age outshine all other recorded ages. In my lifetime have been wrought five miracles, namely, 1, the Steamboat; 2, the Railroad; 3, the Electric Telegraph; 4, the application of the Spectroscope to astronomy; 5, the Photograph; — five miracles which have altered the relations of nations to each other. Add cheap postage; and the mowing-machine and the horse-rake. A corresponding power has been given to manufactures by the machine for pegging shoes, and the power-loom, and the power-press of the printers, and in dentistry and in surgery, Dr. Jackson's discovery of Anaesthesia. It only needs to add the power which, up to this hour, eludes all human ingenuity, namely, a rudder to the balloon, to give us the dominion of the air, as well as of the sea and the land. But the account is not complete until we add the discovery of Oersted, of the identity of Electricity and Magnetism, and the generalization of that conversion by its application to light, heat, and gravitation. The geologist has found the correspondence of the age of stratified remains to the ascending scale of structure in animal life. Add now, the daily predictions of the weather for the next twenty-four hours for North America, by the Observatory at Washington.

---

exposure, on Pearl Street near New York City's financial district and began to supply direct current for lighting to several banking houses and to both the *New York Herald* and the *New York Times,* which in turn supplied Edison with investment capital and publicity. Edison's system, however, had a fatal limitation; it ran on direct current, at low voltages capable of traveling only a mile or two. This necessitated building some 60 generating stations in New York alone to meet demand.

Meanwhile, inventor George Westinghouse had developed a system of high-voltage alternating current, which could be carried over long distances and then through transformers reduced to safe voltages for business and household use. Edison was slow to correct his error, warning that the Westinghouse system would "kill a customer every 6 months." Edison and direct-current advocates fought Westinghouse by staging public demonstrations at which they electrocuted horses with high-voltage charges (for a time, "to Westinghouse" meant to electrocute) and by suing Westinghouse for patent infringements. Undaunted, Westinghouse, through his Westinghouse Electric Company (1886), persisted in efforts to make alternating current safe, efficient, and cheap. The Westinghouse system lit the Chicago World's Columbian Exposition in 1893 and became standard in the industry.

By the turn of the century almost 3,000 power stations were feeding alternating current to American homes and businesses, and American life was never the same. Night was transformed into day, lengthening the hours for work and play and making possible night shifts in factories, nightlife in cities, and night-time entertainment at home. The development of the alternating-current electric motor by Westinghouse and Croatian immigrant Nikola Tesla in 1888 increased the demand for electricity by creating new uses for it. Businesses adapted to electrical power, and electrically driven gadgets and machines relieved some of the drudgery of housework and added new kinds of recreation.

Edison got out of the electric lighting business in the late 1880s. He capitulated to Westinghouse and to finance capitalists J. Pierpont Morgan and Henry Villard, eager to impose more system on the development and distribution of electricity. The bankers bought up patents in electric lighting and, in 1892, Morgan arranged for the merger of the Edison Illuminating Company, which he had helped to organize for Edison ten years earlier, with several electrical equipment companies to form the General Electric Company (GE).

General Electric and Westinghouse Electric ran research laboratories to improve equipment and discover new uses for electricity. By the early twentieth century they began to produce electric appliances (e.g., stoves, refrigerators), in effect, creating a new consumer goods industry. In 1896 GE and Westinghouse assured their control over the national market by agreeing to pool patents. Invention in the electrical industry became the virtual monopoly of the two giants. Independent inventors, such as Granville T. Woods, a mechanical engineer from Columbus, Ohio, who invented the automatic circuit breaker, among a host of useful innovations he patented in electronics, found that the only viable outlet for their ideas was sale to the big electric companies.

Similarly, George Eastman in photography, the Du-Ponts in chemicals, and John D. Rockefeller in petroleum used systematic industrial research to dominate their industries by creating new products and controlling patents. The American industrial research laboratory, modeled after Menlo Park, made invention the servant of business and contributed to the dominance of a few companies in each industry. One effect was to discount innovation in favor of consolidation. By World War I, the independent "dream plants," where innovator-entrepreneurs like Edison chose their own problems to solve and risked time and resources to discover a "big thing," were themselves being absorbed by expensive industrial "research and development" laboratories run by corporate giants such as GE and AT&T, more interested in improving existing systems than investing in potential scientific breakthroughs.

BIG BUSINESS AMERICA

From the late nineteenth century through the early twentieth century American big business emerged. Giant industrial organizations brought together in national organizations all the processes of production and marketing. Large companies spread downward and upward (owning and running every stage of the business from the acquisition of raw materials to the sale of the finished product) and outward (buying up rival companies) in their efforts to increase profits and impose order in their industries. New legal instruments such as the "trust" and the "holding company" allowed big businesses to combine several enterprises and consolidate separate companies in ways that achieved significant control over the market. The prevailing attitude of "laissez faire" (or "let alone") encouraged a hands-off policy from government so that combination and consolidation went almost unchecked. By the end of the century, the concentrations of power that developed in big business left smaller rivals gasping, if they survived at all, and crying for relief.

❧ *Andrew Carnegie and Big Steel*

More than anyone else, Andrew Carnegie embodied the new industrial order of the Gilded Age. Only his rags-to-riches story and his diminutive frame (he stood 5′4″ and weighed but 130 pounds) distinguished him from the other industrial titans of the day. Carnegie's devotion to integrated systems of production and sales

bespoke the logic of the new industrial order. So, too, did his ruthless management style and attention to detail. And the great personal fortune of this steel-plated Midas, valued in the hundreds of millions of dollars by 1900, made Carnegie, along with the other big-business magnates, seem larger and more powerful than the republic itself.

Carnegie was born the son of a Scottish handloom weaver who had been thrown out of work by the rise of mechanized mills and had emigrated with his family to western Pennsylvania in 1848. At age twelve Andrew worked as a bobbin boy in a Pittsburgh factory, and later as a messenger boy and telegrapher. In 1852 Thomas A. Scott, local superintendent of the Pennsylvania Railroad, hired Carnegie as his personal telegrapher and secretary. After Carnegie hitched his fortune to Scott and the railroad, he rose rapidly. When Scott became vice president of the line in 1859, Carnegie became local superintendent. The railroad business taught Carnegie the importance of system in management, while Scott taught him the advantages of inside information in investment. Carnegie invested shrewdly in railroad-related enterprises — bridge construction, sleeping cars, a locomotive factory, oil, and, especially, iron foundries. Carnegie was already a wealthy man when he left the railroad business for finance in 1865. But he considered himself a builder more than a broker and thought that amassing wealth for its own sake was "one of the worst species of idolatry." He entered the steel business.

During a trip to England in 1872 he had observed the Bessemer process, which converted iron ore cheaply and easily into steel by forcing a blast of cold air through the molten iron to burn off excess carbon. The huge blast furnaces fired his imagination, and Carnegie returned to America with big plans to build the world's largest, most advanced steel mill. Carnegie recognized that once the stronger, more durable and elastic steel could be produced in high volume at low cost, it would replace iron in industry, construction, and transportation.

Before the Civil War, producing steel was an expensive, tedious process requiring highly paid skilled craftsmen. In 1847 William Kelly, a Kentucky ironmaster, had devised a method for burning out impurities during the blast to make steel quickly, but he was unable to exploit his insight. A patent dispute with Englishmen Henry Bessemer slowed the application of the similar Kelly and Bessemer processes in the United States. By the early 1870s, however, the consolidation

The Bessemer Process These engravings from 1876 show steel being made by the Bessemer process. At the top, steel is refined in the blast furnace. At the bottom, molten steel is poured out to form ingots. The work was fraught with danger for the workers, who lacked protective equipment and clothing.

the runners on sleds scooting down hills in New Hampshire.

Carnegie played the pivotal role in moving America into the age of steel. He emerged as the principal steel-maker in America as early as the 1880s. Between 1890 and 1900 he increased his annual production over nine-fold, from 322,000 to 3 million tons. By 1900 his mills accounted for a third of the total American output and turned out more steel than all British mills combined.

He succeeded, in part, by exploiting the ups-and-downs of the economy to his advantage. While others cut back on inventories and postponed plant expansion during recessions, Carnegie bought equipment and materials at bargain-basement prices from suppliers desperate to sell. Carnegie also located his steel mills close to raw materials and at junctures of competing transportation systems. His huge steel-making complex near Pittsburgh, on the Monongahela River, gave him immediate and excellent river and rail connections to local coking coal deposits and to the vast, newly developed iron ore ranges in Minnesota, reached by way of the Great Lakes and railroads. The competition between the Pennsylvania and B&O railroads for his shipments allowed Carnegie to negotiate special low freight rates. Superb salesman that he was, he constantly scouted out new uses for steel and ways to advertise the superiority of his product. Thus, for example, Carnegie gained heightened symbolic, as well as monetary, returns by supplying the skeletal frame for the Washington Monument and the plate for the all-steel navy the government launched in the 1890s. Steel was the spine of a rising American power.

Carnegie also sought internal ways to reduce production costs and religiously reinvested earnings in plant expansion and new technology. By management techniques borrowed from the railroads (and managers hired away from the railroads), he almost single-handedly drove down the cost of producing steel in America. He ran the most efficient steel mills anywhere. An astute judge of talent, he surrounded himself with able,

of the Kelly and Bessemer patents made large-scale steel production possible. As a former railroad man, Carnegie understood how the railroads' insatiable demand for track, bridges, and rolling stock promised to make such steel production both practical and immensely profitable.

Carnegie's prescience paid off, for railroads became the principal consumers of steel through the 1890s. Steel rails alone made up three quarters of the American steel output. As the cost of steel went down from $100 a ton in the 1870s to $12 a ton by 1890, and the quality of steel went up with the development of the open-hearth furnace method (slowly cooking molten pig and scrap iron by exterior heat, which allowed for more sampling), Americans found ever more uses for it. By the turn of the century steel was being used in everything from girders holding up skyscrapers on Wall Street to

ambitious managers such as Henry C. Frick, Charles M. Schwab, and Alexander Holley. By using the most advanced systems of cost-accounting and record-keeping, he pinpointed inefficiencies and held managers accountable for the performance of their departments. By pitting managers against one another — the winners earning fat bonuses and partnerships and the losers harsh rebukes — he stepped up production.

Carnegie spoke much about the welfare of his workers, but he practiced a hard line. He used scabs and strikebreakers to hold labor unions at bay, and when that failed, as during the Homestead strike of 1892 (see below), he crushed the union. During business slowdowns he reduced wages and furloughed workers and introduced new work rules, and he dismissed workers whenever production efficiency made them redundant. Withal, he listened to his workers to get fresh ideas. From immigrant workers, for example, Carnegie learned of the latest European advances in metallurgy. Also, following up on suggestions workers made, he instituted the eight-hour day, established cooperative stores in his plants, and paid his workers every two weeks instead of once a mouth, as was standard in the industry. Such accommodations were good business. Carnegie's workers stayed on the job more than those at rival mills.

❧ Vertical and Horizontal Integration

Carnegie's operations expanded, too, because he kept expanding. He pioneered vertical integration, acquiring control over the raw materials, transportation, and sales of his products. To ensure a reliable supply of iron ore, Carnegie's company bought up almost two-thirds of the fabulous Mesabi Range in Minnesota and ran its own fleet of Great Lakes steamers, a railroad connecting Pittsburgh and the Great Lakes, and a docking company. It also owned 40,000 acres of coal land and had its own limestone quarries. Carnegie steel was sold through company-owned sales offices rather than wholesalers. Thus, Carnegie established the backward and forward linkages that provided control over every phase of making steel, from mining to marketing.

Carnegie plowed the profits from vertical integration back into plant expansion. He subscribed to the simple maxim that "in human society" the "one truth clearer and more indisputable than another ... is that the cheapness of articles ... insures their general distribution" and cheapness "is in proportion to the scale of production." Unlike other big businessmen, he did

American Heavy Industry   This view of the steel works at Homestead, Pennsylvania, in the early twentieth century suggests the scale of operations, the reliance on water and rail transportation, and the pollution that all characterized American heavy industry.

not convert his company into a corporation or turn to bankers for the enormous sums necessary to purchase new equipment and buy out competitors. He retained a majority of shares in his company, which he ran as a limited partnership until he sold out in 1901, and he used the company's profits — $5.4 million in 1890, $40 million in 1900 — to integrate horizontally, buying more and building bigger mills.

In their efforts to control the market and keep profits within their own firms, large companies in other industries also practiced vertical integration. Producers of such items as cigarettes, canned goods, and especially perishable goods seized on vertical integration as a way to take advantage of new national markets created by modern communications and transportation.

In food-processing during the 1880s, for example, Henry Heinz arranged with farmers to grow improved seeds for his cucumber plants at a set price, and had the cucumbers shipped on Heinz-owned freight cars to Heinz pickling and canning operations and then on to grocery stores, where Heinz fixed the prices of his products. Van Camp's and Franco-American followed suit. Meanwhile, meatpacking rivals Philip Armour and Gustavus Swift were buying up livestock, slaughterhouses, and refrigerator cars to get their beef to market without interruption. Swift's and Armour's

UCAS GUSHER
t Spindle Top
w in about 10:00 a.m.
January 10th 1901

Gusher   When this wildcat test drilling "blew," on January 10, 1901, near Beaumont, Texas, the fabulous Spindletop Oil Field was born. Pictures like this confirmed public confidence in America's as-yet-untapped riches and spurred development of the industry and the Southwest.

when he wrote that "a cow goes lowin' softly into Armours and comes out glue, gelatins, fertylizer, celoolid, joolry, sofy cushions, hair restorer, washin sody, soap, lithrachoor, and bed springs, so quick that while aft she's still cow, for'ard she may be anything fr'm buttons to pannyma hats." Small butchers and packers simply could not match the economies of scale practiced by the big packers.

By the early twentieth century a few large processors and packers dominated the food industry — for example, Armour and Swift as well as Morris & Cudahy in meatpacking, General Mills and Pillsbury in flour milling, United Fruit Company in tropical fruit, and Campbell's in soup. Further, by their efficiency they made plants and animals just another commodity to be purchased in attractive, tightly wrapped packages and cans. Distanced from the acts of growing and killing, the consumer was encouraged to eat more, with no physical or moral costs paid out in the process.

Vertical integration required huge investments small companies could not afford, and the lower prices the big companies charged for their products at the market drove small competitors from the field. John D. Rockefeller, whose Standard Oil Company epitomized the power of vertical integration, explained the advantages: "We had taken steps of progress that our rivals could not take. They had not the means to build pipelines, bulk ships, tank wagons; they couldn't have their agents all over the country; couldn't manufacture their own acid, bungs, wicks, lamps, do their own cooperage — so many other things; it ramified indefinitely. They couldn't have their own purchasing agents as we did, taking advantage of large buying." And Rockefeller might have added that his smaller competitors could not establish their own grocery stores, as he did, to sell their kerosene (the principal product refined from oil in the late nineteenth century). Rockefeller induced customers to buy kerosene at his stores by marking down the prices on all groceries, in the process ruining competing grocers and oil-refining rivals alike.

Hand-in-hand with vertical integration went horizontal integration as producers tried to lessen competition and impose order in their industries. Horizontal integration involved companies within an industry combining to control the market by setting production and/or pricing levels. A crude device used by many firms during the 1870s and 1880s was the "pool," whereby several competing companies privately agreed to divide the market and to limit production

large slaughterhouses, situated at railheads close to the Great Plains ranches that supplied their cattle or by the vast Union Stock Yards in Chicago ("the great bovine city of the world"), kept down production costs, and their refrigerator cars ensured quality and reduced spoilage. In addition, in their war on waste, the big packers profited from the sale of animal by-products used in making leather, fertilizer, soap, glue, and other products. The humorist Finley Peter Dunne, speaking as his fictional Irish saloonkeeper "Mr. Dooley," caught the many sides of modern meatpackers' efficiency

and fix prices, but lacking any legal standing such gentlemen's agreements could not be enforced. Amid bruising competition and falling prices generally in the late nineteenth century, businessmen reneged on promises in order to save themselves at the first sign of hard times.

More durable were the "trust" and the "holding company," legal instruments perfected by John D. Rockefeller. In the volatile oil-refining industry slugging matches among competitors repeatedly disrupted operations and unsettled prices. When he was not crushing them, Rockefeller tried to convince his rivals to share business peaceably. To that end, a Rockefeller lawyer converted the trust, which originally meant a fiduciary arrangement, into a device for centralizing management. In 1882 Rockefeller's Standard Oil Company of Ohio and forty other refining companies exchanged the common stock in their companies for stock issued by nine trustees who in turn supervised the collective operations and distributed the earnings of the trust among the shareholders.

Securing combinations was made easier by compliant state governments, which relaxed incorporation restrictions. Commenting on the bribery that went with favorable legislation, one wag quipped that Rockefeller had done everything to the Pennsylvania legislature except refine it. In 1889 New Jersey became the first state to amend its incorporation laws to allow one company to own stock in another. It was now legally possible to merge management and ownership in the form of a holding company. Rockefeller incorporated the Standard Oil Company of New Jersey as a holding company that then bought up the stock of the Standard Oil trust of 1882. By 1900 Standard Oil of New Jersey controlled over 90 percent of the nation's oil-refining facilities.

Such combinations occurred in other industries as well. Indeed, from the 1880s on, something of a merger mania swept America. Gigantic combinations became especially prominent in the metal, rubber, leather, chemical, farm machinery, electrical machinery, transportation, cottonseed oil, sugar-refining, and tobacco-processing industries, creating "oligopolies" in which a few companies dominated the market. The business depression of 1893 forced widespread sellouts, with big companies gulping down smaller ones at a frightening rate, but even large concerns were devoured by rivals. Between 1894 and 1904, one-third of all existing companies "disappeared" in mergers.

The most dramatic merger came amid economic recovery. In 1901 Wall Street financier J. Pierpont Morgan put together the first $1 billion company, when he bought out Carnegie Steel for nearly $500 million to form the United States Steel Corporation. U.S. Steel, which combined more than 200 different manufacturing establishments, vast iron ore and coal holdings, fleets of ships and other freight carriers, and more, controlled three-fifths of the nation's steel-making capacity. Although not a monopoly (other large steel producers competed in the field), U.S. Steel symbolized the concentrated power of a few large companies within American industry that had shifted control of the economy from the small-town merchant or village smithy under the chestnut tree to the boardrooms of corporate management and banking houses.

To be sure, in fields that did not require large capital investments in equipment or benefit from economies of scale, small businesses continued to proliferate and prosper. Businesses relying on simple production and marketing processes (such as furniture-making and publishing), producing specialty items (such as toys), or delivering services (such as retailing) resisted the trend toward combination and remained vital parts of the American economy. But in the public mind, as in the national market, big business ruled.

❧ Competition and Combination

The movement toward combination grew out of wasteful competition and almost anarchic conditions in key industries. A continuing deflationary trend in prices, which lasted from the depression of 1873 through the depression of 1893, aggravated the situation. Prices went down because the nation's ability to produce outpaced its ability to consume.

Businessmen tried to stimulate consumption by advertising their products in new ways. Improvements in photoengraving and the reach of mass circulation newspapers and catalogs allowed businesses to display their goods attractively to a national audience. Some manufacturers succeeded in creating demand for new products through advertising. Advertising worked especially well in introducing consumer goods. James B. Duke, for example, used gimmickry, attractive packaging, and aggressive advertising to build an empire on smoke. In the 1880s Richmond cigarette-making companies had refused to replace conventional hand-rolling with the newly invented Bonsack cigarette-rolling machine because they could not imagine how to sell so many cigarettes, whereupon Duke bought the machine and then created a market for its output with a vigorous nationwide advertising campaign that promoted smoking as both democratic (available to all) and fashionable. In most industries, however, increased production soon glutted markets and drove down prices, thereby further exacerbating the basic problem.

Nowhere was the problem more acute and visible than in the railroads. The railroads had built hastily during the 1860s and 1870s and overbuilt during the 1880s. In making grants to transcontinental lines, the federal government had put a premium on speed by awarding competing rights of way to different companies and rewarding the ones that laid the most track with extra grants and loans. In the race between the Central Pacific and the Union Pacific for example, each line threw down track almost without regard for terrain. The Central Pacific imported 7,000 Chinese laborers to gouge out a route through the Sierra Nevadas, and even kept them at work in winter under twenty-foot snow drifts so as not to lose ground to the rival Union Pacific, which was surveying, grading, and laying track in hundred-mile strides across the Plains. A chorus of hammers and anvils sang out their progress. Soon a chorus of complaints rang out from ship-

pers. The poorly engineered roads slowed traffic because of the need for frequent repairs, especially along steep grades. All the transcontinental lines, except for James Hill's privately funded Great Northern, had to be re-laid within a few years, bankrupting the companies and disrupting traffic.

Competition among railroads led to desperate attempts to increase volume and to destroy rivals. To get the traffic of the "big shippers" along trunk lines where several railroads competed for business, railroad managers gave preferred customers free passes, built sidings and connectors directly to the big shippers' factories without charge, offered free land to draw businesses to their territory, and, most of all, manipulated freight rates. Big shippers received low rates for bulk shipments on long hauls and rebates (reductions off the posted rates). Such practices ran railroads into the ground, especially during business recessions when railroads engaged in rate wars that reduced many to bankruptcy. Railroad failures were the principal catalysts for the depressions of the 1870s and 1890s. Sixty-five lines went under and two-fifths of all railroad bonds were in default in the Panic of 1873, and almost

❋ IN THEIR OWN WORDS

John D. Rockefeller Testifies before Congress, 1898

The new industrial order concentrating wealth and power in corporate hands much worried Americans by the end of the century. Following passage of the Sherman Anti-Trust Act in 1890, Congress began investigating corporate practices. In his testimony before Congress, John D. Rockefeller justified the methods he used to gain control over oil refining, including the advantages of rebates wrung from the railroads, and pointed to the necessity of industrial combinations.

Q. To what advantages, or favors, or methods of management do you ascribe chiefly the success of the Standard Oil Company?

A. I ascribe the success of the Standard to its consistent policy to make the volume of its business large through the merits and cheapness of its products. It has spared no expense in finding, securing, and utilizing the best and cheapest methods of manufacture. It has sought for the best superintendents and workmen and paid the best wages. It has not hesitated to sacrifice old machinery and old plants for new and better ones. It has placed its manufactories as the points where they could supply markets at the least expense. It has not only sought markets for its principal products, but for all possible by-products, sparing no expense in introducing them to the public. It has not hesitated to invest millions of dollars in methods for cheapening the gathering

and distribution of oils by pipe lines, special cars, tank steamers, and tank wagons. It has erected tank stations at every important railroad station to cheapen the storage and delivery of its products. It has spared no expense in forcing its products into the markets of the world among people civilized and uncivilized. It has had faith in American oil, and has brought together millions of money for the purpose of making it what it is, and holding its market against the competition of Russia and all the many countries which are producers of oil and competitors against American oil. . . .

It is too late to argue about advantages of industrial combinations. They are a necessity. And if Americans are to have the privilege of extending their business in all the States of the Union, and into foreign countries as well, they are a necessity on a large scale, and require the agency of more than one corporation.

200 railroads failed and one-third of all the nation's track mileage was lost to foreclosure in the Panic of 1893. At the same time, railroads experienced much labor unrest and industrial violence, further discrediting them in the public mind (see below).

Savage competition and discriminatory practices benefited few people and angered many. Small shippers paid the price in higher rates for short hauls. Producers in areas where there was no railroad competition found themselves overcharged to the point of ruin. During the 1870s, for example, commercial wheat farming in upstate New York, which was served only by the New York Central, collapsed because farmers there paid 10 cents more to ship a barrel of flour to New York City than did midwestern farmers who had access to several lines. Likewise, in oil-refining, Rockefeller's strategically located operations along the main east-west railroad corridor and near the Great Lakes gave him a competitive advantage in transportation that his less favorably situated rivals could not match. But the big shippers, too, disliked the instability of rates and distrusted the railroads.

The selfish activities of railroad buccaneers who tried to eliminate rivals by violent or illegal means disgusted even the jaded public of the Gilded Age and hurt the railroads themselves. The "Erie Wars" during the 1860s were only the most outrageous of several such affairs. Jay Gould (whose presence, wrote one newspaper, made "millionaires tremble like innocent sparrows . . . when a hungry hawk swoops down on them"), Daniel Drew, and Jim Fisk (a former circus vendor) — all directors of the Erie — conspired to seize the New York Central from Cornelius Vanderbilt, who was trying to win control of the Erie. Each side built roundabout roads solely to force the other to buy them, issued watered stock, and bribed officials, hired toughs, and even fought pitched battles in the streets. The expensive wars disrupted traffic and finally sank the Erie line in 1877 under the weight of mismanagement and an ocean of watered stock.

Railroad managers tried to bring order to their industry by pooling arrangements and treaties among themselves. The strongest lines also bought up weaker ones to establish interregional systems. In the West the Atchison, Topeka and Santa Fe acquired control over 9,000 miles of track between Chicago and the Pacific. Such efforts succeeded only during the prosperous 1880s. Saddled with large debts, even the largest and best-managed railroad combinations went under during the Panic of 1893.

❧ Competition and Government Regulation

The disorder in the railroad industry led to efforts by government and finance capitalists to restore order. Several New England states had established railroad commissions before the Civil War to investigate grievances and monitor rates, but such agencies had only limited advisory powers. Their purpose was more to publicize the affairs of the railroads than to fix rates. After the war, regulation by public commission became stricter and more widespread. In several midwestern and southern states during the 1870s, small merchants and businessmen resentful of rebating and farmers angry over discriminatory freight rates and overcharging at grain elevators (often owned and run by the railroads) combined politically in the "Granger" movement (see Chapter 21) and won control of state legislatures. Where before the Civil War local farmers, merchants, and real-estate interests had once supported railroads to spur local economic development, by the 1870s the railroads were increasingly viewed as menacing forces invading local markets and bleeding small producers with unfair rates. The Granger-controlled legislatures sought to reassert local authority over the impersonal railroad corporations by classifying railroads as a "public interest" subject to state regulation. They established commissions with the authority to set maximum rates and to punish wrongdoers.

Railroads bitterly contested such laws in the courts. Their lawyers invoked the Fourteenth Amendment, arguing that the Granger laws deprived the railroads of their private property without due process of law. In *Munn v. Illinois* (1877), the United States Supreme Court upheld the constitutionality of such legislation, declaring that when private property served a public interest "it must submit to be controlled by the public for the common good." In *Wabash Railway v. Illinois* (1886) the Court weakened *Munn* by ruling that Congress alone had the power to regulate interstate commerce. The *Wabash* case pointed up the basic defect of the Granger laws. Individual state action was powerless to regulate nationwide rail systems, and efforts to do so added to transportation costs and confusion by creating crazy-quilt regulatory patterns from one state to the next. Effective and constitutional regulation of the railroads demanded federal involvement.

Railroad executives and shippers alike turned to the federal government to stabilize prices. The result was the Interstate Commerce Act (1887), which required railroads to publish rate schedules, prohibited

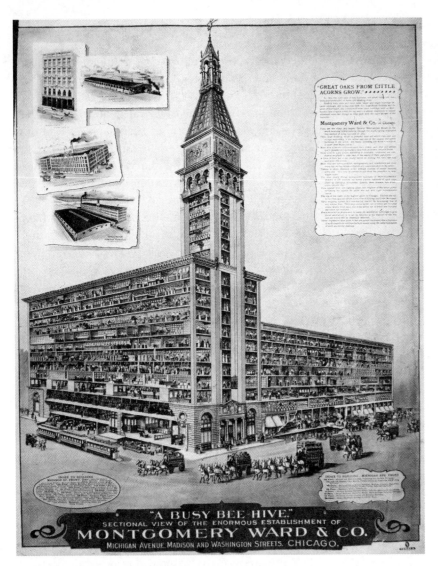

"A BUSY BEE-HIVE."
SECTIONAL VIEW OF THE ENORMOUS ESTABLISHMENT OF
MONTGOMERY WARD & CO.
MICHIGAN AVENUE, MADISON AND WASHINGTON STREETS, CHICAGO.

Montgomery Ward   Together with rival Sears, Roebuck and Co., Montgomery Ward dominated the nation's catalogue sales business at the turn of the century. This 1898 lithograph advertises the company's Chicago department store and mail-order headquarters, from which it reached deep into rural and small-town America. Unwise business decisions after World War II eventually led to the demise of the company colloquially called "Monkey Wards."

sonable and just" rates. The Interstate Commerce Act had signaled a legislative breach in the philosophy of laissez-faire in its assertion of federal regulatory authority, but it was essentially a conservative and palliative measure intended to restore competition rather than rethink the premises of unchecked big business growth.

The concern for competition led Congress to pass the Sherman Anti-Trust Act in 1890, which outlawed "every contract, combination in the form of trust or otherwise, or conspiracy, in restraint of trade or commerce." The act reflected a growing fear among Americans that big business combinations threatened America's republican character. Many Americans still subscribed to laissez-faire notions that harked back to the days of Thomas Jefferson, when it was believed that the small producer was the foundation of a free society. To the late nineteenth-century public mind, the trusts embodied the corruption of American politics and economy; indeed, the popular press often caricatured trusts as bullying, barrel-bellied plutocrats gorging themselves on small producers and exercising monopoly. The Sherman Anti-Trust Act, in the words of its sponsor, Senator John Sherman of Ohio, would protect the individual consumer and small business proprietor from such "associated and corporate wealth and power."

During the 1890s, the Sherman Act failed of its purpose. Its sponsors had framed the act as a statement of general principles rather than a blueprint for regulation. Congress left it to the courts and the president to enforce the act. The pro-big-business Supreme Court soon eviscerated even the spirit of the act by ruling in favor of the "sugar trust" (*U.S. v. E. C. Knight*, 1895), when it declared that although the sugar trust controlled over 95 percent of the sugar-refining capacity in the United States such a production monopoly did not violate the Anti-Trust Act because manufacturing was not commerce. Attorneys general did not bring suits

discriminatory rates and pooling arrangements, declared rates must be "reasonable and just," and most important, established the Interstate Commerce Commission (ICC), the first federal independent regulatory agency, to investigate complaints. The act satisfied no one. The ICC lacked enforcement powers and so proceeded cautiously and functioned largely as an information agency. In the laissez-faire world of late nineteenth-century jurisprudence, the Supreme Court handed down a series of decisions during the 1890s that emasculated the commission by giving the courts exclusive authority to decide what constituted "rea-

against business under the Sherman Act, and corporation lawyers found loopholes to escape its provisions. Indeed, attorneys general hostile to labor unions actually used the act to end strikes and break up unions by charging them with restraint of trade. Senator George Hoar of Massachusetts, one of the principal authors of the act, lamented in 1902 that "the grave evil" of large fortunes being concentrated in few hands had in fact "increased rapidly during the last twelve years." Not until the Progressive movement did the Sherman Act serve as an effective instrument of regulation. Meanwhile, combination continued unabated.

❧ The Bankers Step In

Big business required enormous amounts of capital. The unprecedented scale of production and the many competing industrial systems starting up at the same time drove up demand for investment capital far beyond the ability of individual companies to supply it. For most of the nineteenth century, merchant capital and savings of the firms themselves had met investment capital needs, but by the 1870s large-scale industry turned to external sources for the money necessary to purchase land, buildings, and machinery. Sales of stocks and bonds became the principal source of new investment capital by the 1890s.

Increasingly, big business turned to finance capitalists to serve as the broker for individuals and institutions with money to invest, and the banks themselves bought up corporate bonds and securities. The price for such aid, however, was acceptance of banker control. During flush times bankers supplied capital for expansion and improvement, but during hard times they often assumed new responsibilities of rescuing failing enterprises by negotiating mergers or reorganizing companies with terms that assured bankers the dominant interest in ailing companies.

In railroads, especially, bankers reorganized the industry. Led by Drexel, Morgan & Company at 23 Wall Street, New York (a partnership joining the resources and acumen of J. Pierpont Morgan with Anthony Drexel of Philadelphia which gave the partners access to the major financial markets of New York, Philadelphia, and also England), large banking houses from New York, Philadelphia, and Boston stepped in to save the railroad system during the 1890s. The banking houses wanted to protect their bondholder interests and restore predictability and profitability to the railroads, so essential for the economic health of the nation. To do so, they ex-

Advertising, 1894 Advertisers began to emphasize brand name identification and loyalty in the late nineteenth century. In this advertisement promoting the comforts of an Ohio railroad's dining car, the advertiser crams in testimonials for a carriagemaker, a brand of cigars, a beer label and a whiskey brand, a safe manufacturer, and an "Oriental Powder Mill."

tended credit to railroads in receivership on condition that the bankers got a majority of seats on the railroads' boards of directors. Once installed in power, the bankers tried to revitalize the bankrupt lines by refinancing their debt, by opposing rate wars, rebating, and the other favors to shippers, by eliminating or consolidating competing trunk lines, and by forcing mergers whenever feasible. Most of the nation's railroad system was "Morganized" by the early twentieth century. Indeed, by 1905 New York banking houses had consolidated more than a thousand railroad lines into six combinations worth over $10 billion. Morgan alone controlled the boards of principal railroads in the East, the South, and the West. Likewise, in such industries as public utilities, agricultural machinery, electrical machinery, rubber, and steel (and also insurance), bankers provided essential financial services. The more dependent industrialists got on finance capitalists, the more control banks demanded. Combined with the eagerness of banks to invest in industrial stocks and bonds and the appeal of "bigness" for its own sake, the major banking houses exercised ever stronger influence over the investment of industry's earnings and the direction of big business. Banker control was supposed to put railroads, indeed American industry generally, on a sound footing and to end the wild swings in the economy that caused major business depressions during the 1870s and 1890s. In fact, the finance capitalists could not deliver on their promise of order and stability.

Banking policies provoked panics in 1873, 1884, 1893, and 1907. In each case, banks called in loans to meet depositers' withdrawals during periods of tight money. The country's dramatic economic growth repeatedly led to capital shortages, which strained the banking system and forced companies to put off spending on capital improvements. At the same time, workers' purchasing power did not keep pace with increasing productivity because employers did not distribute their profits sufficiently among workers. The American business cycle of boom and bust continued well into the twentieth century.

≌ The Character of Wealth

Many Americans worried that the money power threatened to end all competition by concentrating American industrial production in the hands of bankers alone. Further, the bankers' preference for investments in industry and their ability to manipulate credit nationwide, when combined with the big banking houses' reluctance to support agricultural investment (where loans were secured by land), bred resentment among southern and western farmers hungry for credit. Earlier admired for their energy and foresight, bankers became, to the public mind by 1900, grasping monsters. With his piercing eyes and intensity, the massively built Morgan more than anyone else personified the image of the "money trust" drawing all economic power unto itself.

Yet at the same time Americans remained ambivalent about wealth-getting ways of banks and big businessmen. Many Americans equated wealth with respect. While decrying the corrupting power of banks in one voice, in another Americans acknowledged

them as symbols of national success and prosperity. Significantly, toy banks were among the most popular toys sold in America after the Civil War. Even on the plains, where farmers likened bankers to locusts, get-ahead children played bankers. Newspaperman William Allen White recalled his boyhood days in Kansas during the 1870s when the "banker" acquired most of the marbles: the enterprising lad who set up "a fancy marble for boys to shoot at from a hazardous distance" and charged two or three common marbles a shot, with the promise of "giving the prized marble to the man who hit it, . . . accumulate[d] marbles faster by running this thing he called a bank than he could by playing for keeps, although he was fairly deft at it." The other boys admired "the banker" for his risk-taking. Likewise, "money" games found wide appeal in middle-class homes. The board game "Moneta, or Money Makes Money" (advertised in the 1889 Montgomery Ward catalog) traded on Americans' desire to pile up riches, as did popular dime magazines such as the *Young Hal Morton of Wall Street* series that told tales of an alert, eager teenager amassing a fortune by following stock tips and listening to bankers. Young Hal never dirtied his hands breaking sod on the prairie or splitting rails; there was no money in that.

Lest anyone doubt that money was necessarily corrupting, some Christian moralists intoned that great wealth could do great good and that rich men were themselves the products of good character. The Reverend William Lawrence, Episcopal bishop of Massachusetts, reassured doubters that "in the long run, it is only to the man of morality that wealth comes." Occasionally, the wicked might prosper, but, he concluded, "Godliness is in league with riches," and material prosperity made "the national character sweeter, more joyous, more unselfish, more Christlike."

ORGANIZED LABOR

The enormous changes in the scale, pace, and nature of work affected workers in countless ways. Workers' responses to industrialism varied according to their skills, geography, values toward work, ethnic, racial, and religious identities, and the culture and kind of work. Many workers continued to work in small factories and family-run businesses to century's end. There, workers' skill, knowledge of the product, and personal relations with the owners gave workers significant control over the workplace and pride in their work. But increasingly across America large factories were pushing aside smaller manufacturers in capital and finished goods production, and machines were replacing skilled workers with semi-skilled and unskilled workers. The American worker was becoming a wage earner rather than working for himself. In 1860 one-half of all workers were self-employed, but by 1900 two-thirds worked for wages. Between 1860 and 1890 the industrial work force grew from 885,000 to over 3.2 million, and the lion's share of that growth came in large industries. Many new industrial workers were immigrants (see Chapter 19), and such industries as textiles, garment-making, food-processing and canning, hat-making, and toy manufacturing relied heavily on women and children. The 1890 federal census counted roughly 600,000 children between the ages of ten and fourteen employed in mining and manufacturing. In cotton textile mills and coal mines children commonly began work as young as eight or nine years of age.

Taking the long view, industrial workers improved their standard of living because of increases in productivity over the half-century from the 1860s to World War I; indeed, for those who had jobs, real wages increased steadily after the 1870s. Such long-term data disguise the complexity and precariousness of industrial work during the late nineteenth century. During good times work was plentiful, though unevenly shared, with unskilled workers facing at least one or more months without work even in the most prosperous years. Depressions in the 1870s and 1890s, the wild swings of the economy, and the frequent disruptions in work due to breakdowns in machinery, failed shipments of needed materials, and mismanagement threw legions out of work at a time and reduced workers to desperation. In their daily lives many workers struggled to survive. Wages were low for unskilled work, working conditions often dangerous, and protections such as workmen's compensation and disability pensions almost unknown. The buying power of one's wages was further limited in those "company towns" where workers were paid in scrip or chits redeemable solely at the company store. Only by sending everyone to work, taking in boarders, or making do with far too little might the average industrial working family earn and save enough to buy a house and provide for old age in a factory town; prospects were even less bright in industrial cities. Even relatively well-paid skilled workers in large-scale industries felt keenly their loss of bargaining power, status, and control over the workplace.

As machines became more important, workers became more expendable for factory managers looking for ways to cut costs and speed production to recover the huge investments in technology. Hours were long—ten to eleven for the normal six-day week in most northern industries, more in southern ones by the 1880s—and the workplace was too often unsafe and unhealthful. Pollutants, dust, and chemicals filled the factory air and mineshafts and left countless workers with respiratory diseases and other afflictions and killed thousands during the heyday of the new industrial order. Accidents added to the toll of injury, dismemberment, and death. Between 1880 and 1900 industrial accidents cost an average of 35,000 workers' lives each year. The common law protected employers from most liability, and employers argued that workers contracted for work on their own account, thereby loading the cost and burden of recovery from any work-related injury or malady onto the workers. Workers who did not contribute to the many ethnic, religious, or occupational mutual aid and burial societies working-class people founded to protect themselves were left to beg from charity when trouble came, which it did with frightening regularity in mining and heavy industry.

The size of the factory operations, the monotony and regimentation of work, and the impersonal relations with management further alienated workers. Especially galling was the tendency of capital to view labor as a commodity subject to the laws of supply and demand in a laissez-faire world where the "devil took the hindmost." As one Connecticut labor official observed in the 1880s, a "feeling of bitterness" and a "distrust of employers" now ruled among workers.

Workers' discontents burst forth in a series of bitter battles between labor and capital that rocked America after the Civil War. Workers also sought to assert their own interests by organizing unions. To be sure, by 1900 less than 2 percent of all workers and no more than 10 percent of industrial workers were members of unions; still, by 1900, with the advent of the American Federation of Labor, craftsmen at least had laid the foundations for modern trade unionism. And even in the face of bloody defeats in several major strikes in the 1890s, labor recognized that the strike constituted its best, if imperfect, weapon to wring concessions from capital and gain respect from workers. At the same time, labor realized it needed to shape public opinion and win political power to create a favorable social and legal framework for effective organizing in the next century.

❧ *Working-Class Protests and Strikes*

During the last half of the nineteenth century, tens of thousands of workers' protests, shutdowns, mobbings, and strikes occurred, many ending in violence. The 1870s were an especially volatile decade, but labor-capital conflicts continued unabated throughout the period. In 1891 the Bureau of Labor Statistics estimated that almost 10,000 strikes and lockouts took place between 1881 and 1890 alone. Most such actions were spontaneous and local, growing out of a particular grievance in a mine or factory, but as labor became more organized, strikes became more planned and more nationwide in their implications. Protest and violence were hardly new to America, but the intensity, frequency, and destructiveness of the strikes in railroads, mining, and steel especially shook the nation and caused sober reassessments of the new industrial order (see Chapter 20).

Factory, mine, and railroad owners used spies, Pinkerton detectives, strikebreakers (known as "scabs"), and thugs to break up strikes, and played on ethnic, racial, and religious differences among workers to keep them from organizing. They organized themselves in the General Managers Association and similar associations to coordinate efforts to put down strikes and pressure governments to act on their behalf. They also stepped up efforts to strengthen governmental police powers to maintain order. The use of the injunction against strikers, the organization and improvement of the National Guard in northern industrial states, the construction of fortress-like armories in cities to stockpile arms (often located on the borders of working-class areas), and the dispatching of federal troops to quash strikes all signaled an increased national concern with curbing labor protest.

LABOR STRIFE IN MINING AND RAILROADS

The depression of the 1870s was a time of bitter labor strife. Strikes in Massachusetts textile mills and the Pennsylvania anthracite coal region set the tone. None was more famous than the anthracite miners' strike that broke out in 1875 and ended in 1877 with the execution of twenty Irish miners, members of the Ancient

---

❊ IN THEIR OWN WORDS

"Labor's Catechism," 1887
Writing under pseudonyms, two Rhode Island power-loom weavers and labor activists with ties to Christian Socialism and the Knights of Labor, Bobba Chuttle and Betty Reedhook, drafted this popular catechism to recruit and instruct workers on the moral foundations of union organizing and mocked the new morality of the marketplace espoused by factory owners. By using the form and cadences of a religious catechism, the labor organizers appealed to the religious sensibilities of many workers and set up the common good of workers as a moral principle.

Q. What did thy masters promise thee?
A. They did promise and vow many things in my name: First: — That I should renounce the comforts of life through working for less wages than the weavers in other towns, and starve my wife and hunger my children for the same cause. Second: — That I must not in any way try to better my condition, but be content to work at any price which they think proper to give; neither must I join the Knights of Labor as that is contrary to their by-laws. Third: — That I must bear patiently the insults of all that are put in authority over me, and a host of other things too numerous to mention.

Q. Dost thou not believe that thou art bound to do as they have promised for thee?
A. No, verily; for I have come to the determination to free myself, and to strive to get as much for my work as the weavers in other places for the same kind and quality, and that is the Knights of Labor's duty.

Q. Rehearse the articles of thy belief.
A. I believe in the Golden Rule — do unto others as you would have them do unto you — and in Honesty, his only son, who was conceived by our Common Rights, born of the Virgin Truth, suffered under Cotton Treason, was crucified, dead, and buried in Rhode Island, for many years, but is now risen again, and sitteth on the right hand of Justice and Liberty.

Q. What dost thou chiefly learn from these articles of they belief?
A. I learn to believe that the time has now arrived when I must make a firm stand for a fair share of the profits of my industry, which is nothing less than the Union List, have nine hours' work, seven hours' play, eight hours' sleep, and fair wages every day.

Order of Hibernians (known as the Molly Maguires), convicted of murdering their coal mine managers. The strike grew out of longstanding distrust and disputes that pitted Irish Catholic miners against Welsh and Scottish Protestant mine owners, who were determined to break the union. The sensational trial and hangings in 1877 made the Molly Maguires martyrs to labor and to many Irish Catholics thereafter, who recalled them in song, verse, and folklore. But organized labor strikes did not begin significantly to affect the American economy until the Great Railroad Strike of 1877.

In July 1877, after eastern and midwestern railroads cut wages between 10 and 20 percent, firemen and brakemen from the Baltimore & Ohio Railroad took over the depot in Martinsburg, West Virginia, and blocked all traffic through this vital link. Local militia, many of whom were railroad workers, refused to clear the tracks because they sympathized with the strikers, whereupon the governor persuaded President Rutherford B. Hayes to send in federal troops with a court order to break the strike. That tactic failed when railroad workers elsewhere shut down other trunk lines, thus paralyzing the nation's rail system. As described by James A. Dacus, a newspaper reporter who followed the strikes closely, railroad workers and their sympathizers, including many women, thought "they had been wronged and oppressed beyond all endurance," and stood ready to bring on Armageddon rather than submit to humiliation and starvation. Workers lashed out at the railroads. In Pittsburgh strikers and their friends destroyed $5 million worth of Pennsylvania Railroad engines, rail cars, tracks, machine shops, grain elevators, roundhouses, and stores, carrying off food, clothes, and even Bibles, before troops dispersed them, with heavy casualties. The strikes spread rapidly across the country, inducing sympathy strikes by coal miners. In St. Louis strikers seized control of the city government for two days, and it took twelve days of fighting for federal troops to defeat the strikers there and retake the rail yards. In Chicago over 20,000 people assembled at a rally sponsored by the Workingmen's Party in support of the strikes. Black and white workers locked arms in several cities to keep freight from moving. Armed with Gatling guns, troops assailed strikers and eventually restored "order," but at a fearful cost in lives and property. When the Great Railroad Strike was over, one hundred people were dead, more than $10 million of property was destroyed, and many Americans shuddered at the thought, as one newspaper editor observed, that another "great civil war"

was about to divide the country—this time between classes rather than sections.

Railroad owners and conservative critics called for beefing up the U.S. Army to deal with the grave internal threat. In their minds, the labor solidarity of the strikers across racial, ethnic, and geographic lines seemed to bode class war. Much of the national press ignored the causes of the workers' discontent and focused on the violence, thereby casting strikers as enemies of order and democratic government. Typical of the angry disparagement was the *New York Times*'s characterization of the strikers as "hoodlums, rabble, bummers, looters, blacklegs, thieves, ruffians, incendiaries, enemies of society, brigands, rapscallions, riffraff, felons & idiots." Although not of one chorus, the religious press chimed in with worries about lawlessness, which several editors attributed to workers' selfishness and to workers' having fallen under the spell of anarchism, socialism, and communism. In the words of one Congregational magazine, the violence demanded a strong hand to discipline workers, concluding that "Napoleon was right when he said that the way to deal with a mob was to exterminate it." Still, unionism grew, and a raised labor consciousness following the 1877 strikes increased labor militancy.

HAYMARKET AND HOMESTEAD

In 1886 a riot at Haymarket Square in Chicago raised fears of labor radicalism to a white heat. The trouble began when the McCormick Harvester Company locked out 1,400 members of the Knights of Labor for demanding a wage hike and an eight-hour day, as part of a five-year campaign for reduced hours in Chicago's factories. Workers attacked the strikebreakers the company tried to bring in, and, in turn, police fired on the workers, killing four. Following the police attack, August Spies, a German-born anarchist, called for a mass meeting at Haymarket Square to protest the violence and "destroy the hideous monster" of capitalism before it destroyed labor. On May 4, roughly 3,000 men and women gathered in the rain at Haymarket, listening to fiery speeches but otherwise orderly. As the meeting broke up, the police advanced on the crowd. Someone then threw a bomb at the police, wounding sixty-seven, seven of whom eventually died. Four civilians were killed in the ensuing melee, and seven more later died from injuries. The police arrested hundreds, and the government indicted ten anarchists for conspiracy to commit murder. Two of the indicted were members of the Knights of Labor. With its large Ger-

The Haymarket Affair The labor movement suffered a black eye in American public opinion with the 1866 riot in Haymarket Square in Chicago. Following a relatively peaceful meeting of men and women gathered to protest police violence surrounding a strike, the police advanced on the crowd, and someone threw a bomb. Several were wounded and eighteen people eventually died from the blast and the violence that ensued.

city newspapers across the country looked upon organized labor with suspicion, worrying that anarchists and their atheism lurked behind every labor protest and effort at organizing. "Haymarket" soon became the "bogeyman" in popular parlance that the captains of industry invoked thereafter to justify ruthless suppression of strikes.

In the 1890s, violent clashes between strikers and police, company-hired Pinkerton detectives or private guards, and federal troops intensified public fears of anarchism and social upheaval. In 1892 at the silver mines of Coeur d'Alene, Idaho, striking miners and company guards waged war using dynamite and rifles before federal troops drove the strikers from the mines. More in the public eye, in 1892, members of the newly formed Amalgamated Association of Iron and Steel Workers walked out of the Carnegie steel works in Homestead, Pennsylvania, protesting Carnegie's introduction of new labor-saving technology and reduced piece-rates. Unskilled workers joined the strikers and sealed off the plant. Henry C. Frick, the manager, determined to end the strike and break the union, brought in 300 Pinkerton detectives armed with Winchester rifles. The detectives arrived on two barges, but the waiting strikers sent them fleeing with blasts from a brass cannon and a barrage of gunfire. The detectives surrendered. Frick appealed to the governor of Pennsylvania for help, who obliged by sending 8,000 state militia to march on the strikers and putting Homestead under martial law. Frick hired scabs to replace the strikers, and the troops beat back the workers and guarded the mills. The union offered to give up its economic demands in return for recognition, but Frick refused any negotiations, which caused public opinion to shift to the union's side. Then in July an anarchist broke into Frick's office and shot and stabbed him repeatedly. Miraculously, Frick survived, and an outraged public turned on the strikers, now irrevocably tied to anarchism and violence in the public mind. In November, the union gave up. The union's defeat at Homestead ended effective labor organizing in the steel industry until the 1930s.

man population, Chicago had become the nation's center for anarchist and socialist activities, a fact that worked against the accused and fed the public hysteria calling for crackdowns on "foreign wretches" and anarchists and socialists of all kinds. The Illinois attorney general insisted Chicago needed to make examples of the anarchists: "Hang them, and you save our institutions." Also, during 1886, over 600,000 workers in the country went on strike, a number three times the average of the preceding five years and, to many Americans, a harbinger of increased labor unrest that needed to be checked. Although no evidence linked those charged with the bomb-throwing, eight of them were convicted because they had made "incendiary" speeches. The court handed down death sentences to five of the anarchists and stiff prison sentences to the others.

The "Haymarket Riot" (labor remembered it as the "Haymarket Massacre") did much damage to the Knights of Labor and the eight-hour-day movement. In the public mind, the union became linked to the anarchists, and it never recovered its reputation from the "ungodly" association. Recruitment dried up, and the union limped through the next decade a shadow of its former strength, which had commanded 730,000 members in 1885. The eight-hour-day movement also suffered from its now bloody image of anarchist violence. Cities beefed up their police forces, and the religious press and most

THE PULLMAN STRIKE OF 1894

The Panic of 1893 and the ensuing years of depression

led to deep wage cuts, massive layoffs, and lengthy work stoppages across America. In 1894 workers lost jobs in unprecedented numbers, and labor and management were spoiling for a fight on many fronts. That fight came especially in the Pullman Strike of 1894, one of the most important strikes in history for its defeat of the railroad brotherhoods, use of the federal injunction, and emergence of Eugene V. Debs as a national leader.

The strike began when factory workers at George Pullman's model factory town, near Chicago, struck the company in protest over wage cuts, layoffs, and Pullman's refusal to negotiate. Especially galling to the Pullman workers, who had to live in the town as a condition of work, was Pullman's insistence on keeping rents and utility rates high on company housing despite the wage cuts and layoffs. With its tree-lined streets, neat brick houses, and public gardens and park, the town of Pullman bespoke owner George Pullman's Christian belief that a healthful environment begat good morals and good work. Workers appreciated the physical setting but resented Pullman's stern moralism and prying into their private lives (he forbade alcohol and smoking), high-handed dismissals of any workers who objected to town policies, and almost feudal lordship over them. Pullman workers had joined the new American Railway Union, headed by Debs, and sought redress from Pullman. When Pullman refused to discuss workers' concerns, the union voted to refuse to handle Pullman cars. Because Pullman cars ran on many railroads, the strike effectively shut down rail traffic coming out of Chicago, the nation's railroad hub. The strike spread to twenty-seven states and territories and threatened to stop the nation in its tracks. The railroad systems that had created the integrated national economy now faced the undoing of that economy unless the strike could be settled.

Railroad owners sought to smash the union rather than bargain with it. Acting in concert through the General Managers Association, they persuaded President Grover Cleveland that the strike obstructed mail delivery (even though strikers had promised to handle any freight trains that did not have Pullman cars), and Cleveland's attorney general, Richard Olney, a former railroad lawyer, secured a court injunction, citing the Sherman Anti-Trust Act of 1890, to break up the "conspiracy in restraint of trade." Cleveland then ordered 2,000 federal troops to Chicago to enforce the injunction. Their arrival led to clashes with strikers, and angry mobs burned and stole property and destroyed Pullman cars. The soldiers "gave the butt" of their rifles in beating back strikers—images of which artist Frederic Remington made famous in a series of widely reprinted illustrations, much akin to his renditions of U.S. soldiers winning the West against Indians and fighting the Spanish to free Cuba. Twelve people died, several scores were arrested, and the union was defeated.

Debs and other union leaders were tried and convicted for contempt of court for disobeying the injunction, a conviction that made the injunction a powerful weapon against strikes. The strike and the trial thrust Debs's name into the national limelight; his experience turned him against capitalism and toward socialism. He complained of the "debauching power of money" and founded the Socialist Party of America in 1897. But the industrial capitalists still ruled the roost.

❧ National Unions

The Civil War gave a boost to the idea of organizing national unions. Before the war, hundreds of workingmen's parties, craft unions, and local brotherhoods operated in an economy where much work was localized, but the rise of an integrated national economy with capital increasingly concentrated forced workers to consider national alliances and new national organizations. As one Pennsylvania newspaper put it in 1877, labor needed to combine against the combinations of capital to have any power in the new industrial order. But welding the interests of craft and unskilled workers into a common union movement or organizing workers by industry would be difficult.

NATIONAL LABOR UNION

The idea of bringing skilled and unskilled workers together in a nationwide organization got its first test with the National Labor Union (NLU), founded in 1866 by William Sylvis, a big-chested iron molder who traveled across America stumping for the eight-hour day and workers' cooperatives so that workers would manage their own factories, and railing against the wage system. The union grew to over 600,000 in a few years, but it came apart just as quickly because of Sylvis's death in 1869, hard times during the depression of 1873, and its sometimes-conflicting goals. Like many antebellum workingmen's parties, the NLU was at once practical and visionary, wanting currency and banking reform, restrictions on immigration (particularly Chinese immigration), national political reform rather than strikes, and a return to the simpler life.

KNIGHTS OF LABOR

Likewise, the Knights of Labor, founded in the 1860s by Philadelphia garment workers as a Protestant secret society with elaborate rituals to bind members together, looked backward and forward in its proposals to secure labor's place. After the union ended its secrecy in 1881, it opened its membership to Catholics, men and women, whites and blacks—indeed, to every working person except lawyers, doctors, bankers, liquor sellers, stockbrokers, and professional gamblers, who, in the Knights' calculus were all thieves. The union grew rapidly under the banner that "An injury to one is the concern of all." Membership swelled to over 700,000 after the Knights won a strike against the hated Jay Gould and his Wabash Railroad in 1885. The Knights espoused a moral vision that emphasized the need to give up greed and dishonesty, practice temperance, and engage in worthwhile work in order to end class divisions and foster democracy (see Chapter 20). But the Knights were never able to reconcile their insistence on cooperatives and the reservation of the public lands with their radical proposals for the eight-hour day, equal pay for the sexes, government ownership of railroads and telegraph lines, a graduated income tax, and the prohibition of child labor, among several interests. More problematic, the Knights' national leaders eschewed boycotts and strikes as their principal weapon, preferring arbitration, running cooperative workshops, and endorsing political candidates as the way to gain power. Local chapters did not share the leaders' preferences. Without endorsements from the national leadership, local chapters engaged in work stoppages, attacked strikebreakers, and destroyed property when companies refused to negotiate and set guards or soldiers on them. The spectacular failure of several key strikes, especially against Jay Gould's Texas and Pacific Railroad, and the reputation that stuck to the Knights as a haven for anarchism following the Haymarket riot hastened their demise. In the end, the union collapsed because it was too ambitious and too unwieldy.

AMERICAN FEDERATION OF LABOR

The American Federation of Labor (AFL), founded in 1886 by several former socialists, succeeded the Knights of Labor as America's most significant union. It did so by operating under a different philosophy than the Knights regarding the strike and by organizing as a federation of individual trade unions, each representing a specific trade (e.g., bricklayers, carpenters, cigarmakers, tailors, typesetters), rather than trying to bring all industrial workers under one canopy. Led by Samuel Gompers, a London-born Jew from New York's Lower East Side and member of the tough Cigar Makers Union there, the AFL abandoned ideas of a workingmen's party and utopian social reforms to focus on bread-and-butter issues of wages, hours, safety, and benefits. This was, in Gompers's words, "pure and simple" trade unionism. Gompers insisted that workers needed to accept that they would remain wage earners all their lives and had to give up notions of some day becoming capitalists. To that end, the AFL promoted unionism as a way of life, insisting that the members of the craft unions pay high dues to commit them to the cause and that they support one another in strikes. The AFL sought accommodation with capital by getting owners to recognize the union as the collective bargaining agent and pledge to maintain a "closed shop" (one in which workers must be union members as a condition of being hired). Decisions on strikes and boycotts rested with the individual member unions, but the AFL national office provided money and legal aid and encouraged affiliated unions to support any strike by another AFL member union. The AFL also lobbied Congress for a bill to protect strikers from antitrust actions, and presented itself as moderate by limiting membership to native-born white men (only two member unions enrolled women). The AFL grew steadily, so that by 1904 it counted 1.2 million members, more than half of all union members of any kind in America.

The success of the AFL pointed up the limits of organizing labor. In 1900 most immigrants and virtually all unskilled workers were unorganized. The ethnic, racial, and religious divisions among them and the impermanence of so much work kept workers on the move and apart. By the late 1890s, too, the failures of unions also made them bad bets for workers fearful of risking jobs, and even lives, on organizations under siege by management and too often short-lived. Partly, too, the limited number of workers in unions was due to the persistent hope and faith many workers retained in progress. Prosperity had returned by 1900, and some states had begun to pass laws to protect workers from the worst abuses, to limit child labor, and to improve working conditions. Labor was gaining new respect too, as the public accepted its value. In 1894 Congress made Labor Day a legal holiday. Enlightened employers exhausted from labor strife also moved to provide minimum benefits, clean up their plants, and recognize workers' right to speak on their own behalf in disputes. The costs of labor troubles suggested such thinking was good business. But overall, big business held the upper hand and resisted all efforts of workers to organize. The day of the big union was yet to come.

CONCLUSION: NEW DIVIDES

The increased industrial production of the United States, the national networks of distribution, and the efficiencies of centralized management did raise living standards generally and create new wealth. But the very nature of the new industrial order divided Americans, even as the mass consumer culture and transcontinental transportation system bound the nation together. Doubts about the benefits of unregulated capitalism accumulated as rapidly as the chits on J. P. Morgan's desk. Concentrated wealth and ownership violated sacred American commonplaces about a republican order based on dispersed wealth and individual enterprise. Further, the abuses of big business in exploiting labor and corrupting politics and the growing gap separating rich and poor in the nation raised a host of corporate critics during the late nineteenth century who warned that the trend toward giantism was unnatural, immoral, and fatal to American democracy and Christian values.

The responses to industrialism would include efforts by workers to combine in unions against the business combinations and by farmers to organize in political parties — in the words of populist Mary Ellen Lease, "to raise less corn and more hell." The principal response would be Americans' efforts to rethink the premises of the economic order. In pulpits, pulp novels, and public debate Americans would challenge the assumptions of a laissez-faire capitalism that begat Rockefellers and Morgans while devouring the proverbial yeoman farmer and artisan, and they would call for a return to the simple life. Many Americans, as varied as native-born evangelical Protestants in rural places and Catholic and Jewish "new immigrants" in urban ones, would take on modernism itself.

SUGGESTED READINGS

Alfred D. Chandler, Jr., *The Visible Hand: The Managerial Revolution in American Business* (1977). A seminal discussion of the rise of modern management, first in railroads, and of attempts to organize and control the integrated national market.

David A. Hounshell, *From the American System to Mass Production, 1800-1932: The Development of Manufacturing Technology in the United States* (1984). A revealing survey of the invention, adaptation, and application of technology in the modern factory system.

Alice Kessler-Harris, *Out to Work: A History of Wage-Earning Women in the United States* (1982). A sweeping survey of women's increased engagement in work outside the home, their participation in labor organizations, and the changing perceptions of women's place and work in society.

William Leach, *Land of Desire: Merchants, Power, and the Rise of a New American Culture* (1993). A broad-gauged, suggestive treatment of the ways business managers, retailers, preachers, and others purveyed the cult of mass consumption.

Albro Martin, *Railroads Triumphant: The Growth, Rejection, and Rebirth of a Vital American Force* (1992). A paean to the "Romance of the Rails" and the significance of railroad systems to American economic growth.

David Montgomery, *The Fall of the House of Labor: The Workplace, the State, and American Labor Activism, 1865-1925* (1987). A probing examination of labor-management conflict, with special attention to the militancy and diverse interests of workers.

R. Laurence Moore, *Selling God: American Religion in the Marketplace of Culture* (1994). A revealing study of the ways religious leaders adapted commercial practices to religion and the ways businessmen employed religion to sell goods and a consumer culture.

David F. Noble, *America by Design: Science, Technology, and the Rise of Corporate Capitalism* (1977). A penetrating examination of modern technology and the links between management and engineering that made possible large-scale industry.

Daniel T. Rodgers, *The Work Ethic in Industrial America, 1850-1920* (1978). A pioneering study of the adaptations of older concepts of work to the regimentation and anonymity of modern industrial labor and efforts to restore faith in work as a moral good.

Susan Strasser, *Satisfaction Guaranteed: The Making of the American Mass Market* (1989). A sprightly discussion of the ways advertising, marketing, and product development encouraged mass consumption.

Alan Trachtenberg, *The Incorporation of America: Culture and Society in the Gilded Age* (1982). An interdisciplinary reading of the economic, social, and literary expressions of mechanization and the emergence of a corporate-based middle-class culture.

Olivier Zunz, *Making America Corporate, 1879-1920* (1990). A probing examination of the rise of corporate capitalism and the ways it shaped a national consumer culture.

SUGGESTIONS FOR FURTHER READING

Paul Avrich, *The Haymarket Tragedy* (1984).

David Bain, *Empire Express: Building the First Transcontinental Railroad* (1999).

Richard F. Bensel, *The Political Economy of American Industrialization, 1877-1900* (2000).

David Brody, *Steelworkers in America: The Nonunion Era* (1960).

Robert V. Bruce, *1877: Year of Violence* (1959).

Ron Chernow, *The House of Morgan: An American Banking Dynasty and the Rise of Modern Finance* (1990).

Ron Chernow, *Titan: The Life of John D. Rockefeller, Sr.* (1998).

Marjorie W. Davies, *Woman's Place Is at the Typewriter: Office Work and Office Workers, 1870-1930* (1982).

Thomas C. Cochran and William Miller, *The Age of Enterprise: A Social History of Industrial America* (rev. ed., 1968).

William Forbath, *Law and the Shaping of the American Labor Movement* (1991).

David M. Katzman, *Seven Days a Week: Women and Domestic Service in Industrializing America* (1982).

Paul Krause, *The Battle for Homestead, 1880-1892: Politics, Culture, and Steel* (1992).

Pamela Walker Laird, *Advertising Progress: American Business and the Rise of Consumer Marketing* (1998).

Naomi R. Lamoreaux, *The Great Merger Movement in American Business, 1895-1904* (1985).

A. T. Lane, *Solidarity or Survival? American Labor and European Immigrants, 1830-1924* (1987).

John Laslett, *Labor and the Left: A Study of Socialist and Radical Influences in the American Labor Movement, 1881-1924* (1970).

Walter Licht, *Industrializing America: The Nineteenth Century* (1995).

Martin V. Melosi, *Thomas A. Edison and the Modernization of America* (1990).

Daniel Nelson, *Frederick W. Taylor and the Rise of Scientific Management* (1980).

Philip Scranton, *Endless Novelty: Specialty Production and American Industrialization, 1865-1925* (1997).

Shelton Stromquist, *A Generation of Boomers: The Patterns of Labor Conflict in Nineteenth-Century America* (1987).

Cecelia Tichi, *Shifting Gears: Technology, Literature, Culture in Modernist America* (1987).

Sarah Lyons Watts, *Order against Chaos: Business Culture and Labor Ideology in America, 1800-1915* (1991).

Robert E. Weir, *Beyond Labor's Veil: The Culture of the Knights of Labor* (1996).

Irwin Yellowitz, *Industrialization and the American Labor Movement, 1850-1900* (1977).

19 The Modern Industrial City, 1850-1900

THE MODERN CITY rose as the site and symbol of the new industrial order after the Civil War. Before the war commerce largely had fueled urban growth. Whether as hinges in the Atlantic export trade or entrepots for the rich American hinterlands, cities had depended on the exchange of goods produced, and often processed, elsewhere. Cities had served the countryside in an agricultural republic. In the postwar era, the advent of steam power, railroads, and large-scale steel production made possible the industrial city, while centralized management, communications, and finance capitalism shifted authority from the farms and mill villages to city centers. By the 1890s, when historian Frederick Jackson Turner was musing on the closing of the American frontier, smokestacks, railroad yards, department stores, investment houses, and skyscrapers already heralded the triumph of the modern city and a new American identity. Although less densely populated than the nations of Europe and Asia, the United States had become one of the most urbanized countries on the globe and, as such, had begun to seem less different from the Old World. Historian Henry Adams, who lived through the change, observed in 1905: "The American boy of 1854 stood nearer the year 1 than to the year 1900."

PEOPLING THE MODERN CITY

Between 1850 and 1900 American cities exploded in population. The Civil War had slowed city growth, but the irresistible pull of the city that had been drawing

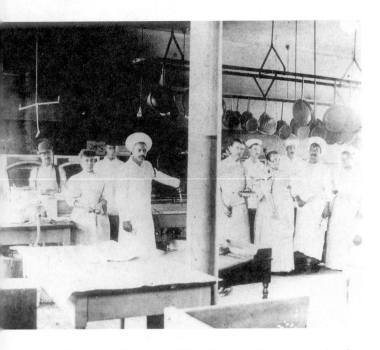

A Catering Company Although excluded from most craft and factory jobs, some urban African Americans were able to carve out niches in the service trades. The Baptiste family of Philadelphia, pictured here, was one of several black catering families who ran independent businesses over several generations.

rural migrants and immigrants since before the war magnified many times over after Appomattox. Upheavals of war drove black and white southerners to towns where boosters such as Henry Grady of the *Atlanta Constitution* promised a "New South" that would banish poverty and defeat. Midwestern city fathers trumpeted their own advantages of access to farm producers and eastern markets because of improved railroad and water connections. And industrial cities everywhere clanged with the sounds of progress. The expectation of work brought people to town, and, in turn, the huge influx of job-seekers stimulated the economic growth that made cities so attractive. The process fed itself, as newcomers brought brains and brawn to industries and small businesses and, by sheer numbers, dramatically expanded the urban market for goods and services.

What distinguished postwar urban growth was the scale and variety of population. Industrial cities had populations in the tens and hundreds of thousands and people from many backgrounds and countries. In the industrial city the face-to-face, small-town world of the village smithy yielded to the impersonal, clock-time regimen of the factory manager, and the hum of familiar sounds to the din of jostling traffic and confusion of foreign tongues. The migrants and immigrants

streaming into industrial cities in search of work found the urban environment both beguiling in its many diversions and bewildering in its diversity. Yet many urban newcomers did not abandon the rural or village worlds they left behind. By concentrating together in particular neighborhoods near their places of work — anchored by churches, clubhouses, saloons, and small businesses — they struggled to transplant their native values and associations on the mean streets of the industrializing city. That migrants and immigrants were able to resist being melted down altogether in the industrial urban crucible, even as they were being changed by it, added to the dynamism that made postwar cities so compelling to so many different people.

Urban Growth

As early as the 1830s the rate of urban population growth had begun to exceed that of the rural population, but not until the industrial era did it take off. Between 1850 and 1900 the population of the United States quadrupled, while the urban population multiplied sevenfold. In 1790, the year of the first census, only 1 American in 30 lived in a town with a population of 8,000 or more people (from 1870 on, the census definition of a city). By 1840 the ratio was 1 in 12; by 1870, 1 in 4; and by 1900, 1 in 3. Nearly half the nation lived in a city at the time of the 1910 census. The once rural America had come to town.

Much of that population resided in small cities with populations of 25,000 or less, but from mid-century on the big city dominated the urban landscape. Between 1860 and 1890 the number of cities with 100,000 or more people had increased from 9 to 26; by 1910 there were 50 such places. On the eve of the Civil War only 2 American cities had populations of 500,000 or more; forty years later there were 6, including New York, Chicago, and Philadelphia with more than a million each. Neither Europe nor Asia could then match the pace of American urbanization.

The rapid growth of American industrial cities distinguished them from their commercial forebears. Whole new cities arose in response to industrial demand. Birmingham, Alabama, illustrated the interplay of technology, transportation, and finance capital that built the industrial city. Founded in 1871 at a confluence of coal, limestone, and iron ore deposits, Birmingham was the product of the Louisville & Nashville Railroad, which sought to develop the north-central Alabama economy to feed its trunkline, and of northern capitalists eager to underwrite steel production in the South. The city boomed. Property speculation was so rampant in the 1880s that the same piece of land might change hands several times in one day. By 1900 the city had almost 40,000 people; twenty years later it counted more than 178,000.

Most remarkable was Chicago, the world's fastest growing city in the late nineteenth century. For its unabashed self-promotion Chicago would earn the nickname "Windy City," but the city's progress more than realized its boosters' bluster. Because of its position on the Great Lakes and at the terminus of several railroads, Chicago commanded much of the midwestern trade. When Cyrus McCormick moved his manufacturing operations there in 1847, he signaled the industrial stage of Chicago's development. In addition to the manufacture of agricultural machinery, Chicago's location made it the nation's slaughter- and packing-house capital and granary. By the 1880s steel-making and other industries further diversified Chicago's economy. In the next decade, with the Marshall Field store and the Montgomery Ward and Sears, Roebuck mail-order houses, Chicago established itself as a major retailing center. Even the great Chicago fire of 1871, which left 100,000 people homeless and razed most of the commercial district, did not slow the city's expansion or dampen its "I will" spirit. Architects flocked to the lakeside city to build it anew. Chicago's population doubled in the 1870s and tripled between 1880 and 1900. What had been a swampy trading post with a handful of families in 1831 had swollen to a city of over 109,000 people by 1860 and to a metropolis of over 1.5 million by 1900, dominating the Midwest and ranking second only to New York in size and wealth among American cities. Little wonder that Theodore Dreiser, in his novel *Sister Carrie* (1900), sent his young heroine to Chicago to seek her fortune.

Urban growth occurred unevenly across America. The most industrialized regions were also the most urbanized ones. The Northeast and Midwest were home to more than 80 percent of the nation's city dwellers in 1890, while the South Atlantic states accounted for less than 8 percent. Where local economies were stagnant, cities did not grow. Sharecropper agriculture, poverty, and disease especially burdened southern river and port cities. In 1876 a yellow fever epidemic in Memphis killed over 5,000 people, drove away almost 18,000 more, and ended foreign immigration. At the same time, railroad development, the shift from self-sufficiency to market agriculture in the Piedmont, and industrialization fed the growth of interior southern cities and effected a significant change in postwar southern leadership from the Low Country to the Up-country (see Chapter 16). Besides Birmingham, Atlanta, Augusta, Macon, Chattanooga, Charlotte, Nashville, Houston, Dallas, and Fort Worth all recorded striking population gains in the South. In every region medium-size cities registered impressive growth rates during the period of industrialization, and no section lacked a big city by 1900.

In the West, railroad connections spurred dramatic urban growth. The great transcontinental railroad men were city builders. Seattle, for example, thrived once it became the terminus for James J. Hill's Great Northern Railway. Likewise, Albuquerque, Cheyenne, Phoenix, and Reno owed their fortunes to railroads. Both Los Angeles and San Francisco capitalized on the combination of good transportation, climate, and nearby agricultural development. Los Angeles grew from 5,700 in 1870 to over 100,000 by 1900, and San Francisco from almost 57,000 in 1860 to over 298,000 in 1890.

Some cities prospered because of a peculiar geographical advantage that gave them a competitive edge in exploiting natural resources. Minneapolis built on its location in the grain trade to dominate flour milling in its region. So, too, Kansas City became a great livestock, packing, and grain center because railroads connected it to the cattle kingdom and sod-house frontier. Denver cashed in on Colorado gold and silver strikes; Tulsa rose along with the oil rigs in Oklahoma; and in Richmond and Durham cigarettes were rolled from local tobacco. Other cities were identified with a specific product: Akron, Ohio, for rubber; Bridgeport, Connecticut, for corsets; Corning, New York, for glass; Grand Rapids, Michigan, for furniture; Hershey, Pennsylvania, for chocolate; Pittsburgh for steel; Tampa, Florida, for cigars — all ringing up profits on cash registers made in Dayton, Ohio. Culture also affected a city's character and economy. The German immigrant concentration in the Midwest made Milwaukee and St. Louis famous for beer and Cincinnati for sausage. Generally, though, larger cities had more diversified economic bases. Philadelphia, for example, produced 211 of the 264 manufactured articles listed in the federal census of 1910. It led the nation in the production of cigars, hats, hosiery, leather, locomotives, rugs, saws, streetcars, steel ships, and textiles, and ranked second in the production of chemicals, drugs, fertilizer, foundry castings, petroleum products, and sugar.

❧ The Lure of the City

The city's abundance and variety of work drew migrants and immigrants to town. In Europe and America alike, millions of people left farms and villages for cities during the nineteenth century. Between 1880 and 1910 some 11 million Americans did so. The commercialization of agriculture pushed surplus farm workers off the land, as reapers, harvesters, and other machines increased yields per acre and replaced human hands. In the United States agricultural depressions in the 1870s and 1890s quickened the migration.

An oppressive farm tenancy and racial discrimination drove rural southern blacks to nearby towns and cities during the late nineteenth century, the first step in what would become the "great migration" of blacks to northern industrial cities during and after World War I (see Chapter 22). Before 1910, however, blacks' movement to town remained a southern and border state phenomenon. The railroad development in the southern Piedmont led the migration toward inland cities (see Chapter 16). Between 1880 and 1910 the black population of Atlanta increased an average of 48.7 percent each decade, Chattanooga an average of 63 percent, and Birmingham (between 1890 and 1910) an average of 131 percent. So, too, the physical expansion of Washington, D.C., and attempts by Washington capitalists to develop local industry created construction and factory jobs that black southerners rushed to fill in the late nineteenth century. But even as southern and border city populations became more black, northern ones became less so between 1880 and 1910. Blacks numbered fewer than 4 percent of the northern urban population during that period. Foreign immigrants swelled northern industrial cities and left little room for black job aspirants until World War I.

Young men and women especially wanted to trade the monotony and poor prospects of rural life for the wonders and wages in the city. Farming lost its allure in the late nineteenth century as an urban culture spread over the land. Popular magazines, pulp novels, and mail-order catalogs advertised the glitter, gadgets, and goods of city life, and the city's bright lights, amusements, department stores, theaters, and newspapers all beckoned. At the same time, writers decried the loneliness and despair of farming life, where, in the words of novelist Hamlin Garland, "beautiful youth" became "bowed and bent."

Most important, though, was the promise of urban employment that offered higher pay and shorter hours than farm work. Cities needed armies of industrial, white-collar, trade, and service workers. The physical expansion of cities demanded tens of thousands of workers, from hod carriers to steam fitters. So, too, did private maintenance. The Widener Estate in Elkins Park, Pennsylvania, kept six men busy full time just to mow and tend the lawn. In real estate alone, the paperwork required legions of agents and clerks. Young women, who had even fewer opportunities in rural America than did young men, could find employment as sales clerks in department stores, domestics in hotels and private homes, laundresses, waitresses, office clerks, factory operatives, and, if fortune failed them, as prostitutes.

THE NEW IMMIGRATION

The promise of American cities reached across the oceans to attract roughly 25 million immigrants to the United States between 1866 and 1915. The vast majority of the newcomers congregated in the industrial Northeast. Since mid-century, immigrants had constituted a significant percentage of eastern and midwestern urban populations. The trend accelerated over the next fifty years. In 1890 the number of immigrants in Chicago was almost equal to the total population of the city just ten years earlier, and in 1900 one-third of Chicago was foreign-born. In 1890, 80 percent of New York City's population consisted of immigrants or their children, and by 1900 New York City boasted the largest foreign-born population in the world. As immigration increased dramatically over the next twenty years, urban concentrations became even denser. In 1910 more than 70 percent of the inhabitants of New York, Chicago, Boston, Cleveland, Detroit, Buffalo, and Milwaukee, and over 50 percent of the residents of St. Louis, Cincinnati, Pittsburgh, Newark, Philadelphia, and San Francisco were immigrants or their children.

After 1880 most immigrants came from southern, central, and eastern Europe, where industrialization, the mechanization of agriculture, and the recent abolition of serfdom were transforming rural and village-based economies. Peasants and village artisans could no longer make a living from their meager landholdings and sought work as wage earners on large landlords' estates or in growing urban areas. The prospect of steady work and much higher wages ultimately lured many of them to America. The telegraph and improved mail service spread information about opportunities in the New World, and the railroad opened the once landlocked interior to port cities. Transatlantic steamship lines offered reduced rates in the competition for passengers to fill the steerage section below decks on the ships crossing the ocean. For many, the destination was not the United States but Argentina, Brazil, or Canada, where immigrants from southeastern Europe and Asia were being actively recruited. A huge migrant labor force moved across the European and American continents in the late nineteenth and early twentieth centuries.

Most emigrants from Europe were young men between the ages of fifteen and thirty-five, either unmarried or traveling without their families. Many of them viewed their migration as temporary, a sojourn in the industrial United States, or elsewhere, to earn sufficient money to set up favorably in the place of their birth. Among immigrants to the United States, as many as one-third or more from such places as Hungary and southern Italy returned to their homelands. Many such "birds of passage" entered, left, and re-entered the United States in search of work (making an accurate count of the number of permanent immigrants impossible). With the ocean crossing taking only from one to two weeks in modern steamships and admission to the United States virtually a certainty, migration back and forth became common. After several years in America, most immigrants chose to stay, starting families here or bringing over their spouses and children.

Others came to America to escape political or religious persecution. Eastern European Jews particularly fled onerous restrictions on work and government-tolerated attacks, or pogroms. Prohibited from owning land in the Russian empire, Jews living in small villages known as *shtetlach* or in crowded urban ghettos found too few opportunities to use their skills as artisans and merchants. Unlike the "birds of passage," they left eastern Europe with their families, never to return.

❧ The Golden Door

Two-thirds of all immigrants entered the United States by way of New York City, "the golden door," where the Statue of Liberty greeted them. By the early twentieth century the statue had become a symbol of America's welcome for, in the words of poet Emma Lazarus, Europe's tired, poor, "huddled masses yearning to breathe free." To many immigrants' thinking, however, the greeting was not so friendly. They realized that federal control over immigration reflected a change in Ameri-

Inspecting an Immigrant   The Ellis Island experience could be embarrassing to people from peasant backgrounds. Authorities required immigrants to pass a medical examination. The eye chart in the background is in the Cyrillic (Russian) alphabet.

can attitudes toward them. To handle the staggering numbers of immigrants, in 1891, the United States government took control of admission procedures away from the states and set up its own processing stations at the principal ports. State officials and private agencies largely had sought to protect immigrants against abuses, but the federal role was judgmental, intended to protect America from the "wrong" kinds of immigrants.

Ellis Island embodied the new approach. From July 1892 on, most immigrants coming to America in steerage were processed there. A three-acre mud flat and formerly the site of a naval arsenal, by 1902 Ellis Island was a complex of red-brick buildings capable of handling at least 5,000 arrivals per day. Between 1892 and 1924, the peak years of immigration, roughly 12 million immigrants passed through Ellis Island's portals. (In 1990 census officials estimated that 100 million people, or 40 percent of the U.S. population, could trace their ancestry to at least one of those 12 million immigrants.) At Ellis Island the casual paternalism of the states in admitting immigrants yielded to the impersonal bureaucracy of the federal government. Immigration authorities there prided themselves on their efficiency in moving people along in an assembly-line fashion.

Although the inspection process lasted only a few hours on average, immigrants often found the experience humiliating and frightening. Strangers pinned tags on them, separated them from their baggage, and then marched them through narrow aisles, set off by iron-pipe railings (which reminded the immigrants of a prison), toward the inspection stations. There they suffered through interviews that poked into personal histories and physical examinations that pried open mouths and peeled back eyelids and sometimes required immigrants to bare their torsos to inspectors. Unhappy immigrants covered the walls with graffiti lamenting their decision to emigrate or offering advice to those who would follow them. One Italian summed up the disillusionment: "Damned is the day I left my homeland."

In fact, few immigrants failed to gain entry. Over 80 percent of those passing through Ellis Island were admitted without difficulty, and most of the rest were detained only a short while, waiting for funds or a relative to arrive or for a minor health problem to heal. Also, immigrants successfully resisted the depersonalizing inspection process by clinging to their Old World memories, their faith, and the knowledge that they soon would be reunited with family and friends at the "kissing booth" on the first floor of the Ellis Island inspection station. Typical was the experience of Myron Surmach, a seventeen-year-old immigrant from the Ukraine who, in 1910, came to work in the Pennsylvania coal mines: "At Ellis nobody changed my name, nobody bothered me. Right away I liked America. I made money and felt good."

Criminals and sharpers preyed on the new arrivals, selling them bogus documents and unnecessary services, overcharging them at concession stands, or hustling them off to work at low wages. Unscrupulous fellow-countrymen used their language and cultural affinities to entice ignorant peasants into unfair labor contracts. The *padrone* system, though helpful to many southern Italians eager for work, was open to abuse as labor bosses packed immigrants off to boarding houses and then "sold" their labor in lots to railroad companies, public works contractors, or strikebound factories. The *padrone* took a commission out of each worker's pay or pocketed the difference between what employers bid for the gangs of workers he assembled and the low salaries actually given to the immigrants. Most immigrants, however, did not need such middlemen to find their way in America. Before emigrating, they had made employment and housing arrangements through relatives and friends. Thus, for example, Poles from Gdansk knew to go to the Polish Hill section of Pittsburgh because relatives there had sent them money for passage and instructions on travel connections.

The immigration authorities tried to banish the middlemen from Ellis Island and to replace them with social reformers and religious missionaries. In 1907, for example, the Young Men's Christian Association began a comprehensive program of health inspection and relief. Soon the religious and reform groups were in stiff competition both among themselves and with other organizations that considered the immigrants their own. Denominational societies provided aid and the American Bible Society and the American Tract Society distributed literature, printed in various European lan-

---

❋ IN THEIR OWN WORDS

"The New Colossus," 1883

Emma Lazarus's poem became synonymous with the promise of America held out by the Statue of Liberty. It received scant attention when it was published, at a time when the restrictions of Ellis Island more than the beacon of the Statue of Liberty reflected American attitudes about immigrants, but by the 1930s it was fixed on the statue and in American popular thinking as the true meaning of America.

Not like the brazen giant of Greek fame,
With conquering limbs astride from land
    to land,
Here at our sea-washed, sunset gates
    shall stand
A mighty woman with a torch, whose flame
Is the imprisoned lightning, and her name
Mother of Exiles. From her beacon-hand
Glows world-wide welcome; her mild eyes
    command
The air-bridged harbor that twin cities frame.

"Keep, ancient lands, your storied pomp!"
    cries she
With silent lips. "Give me your tired, your poor,
Your huddled masses yearning to breathe
    free,
The wretched refuse of your teeming shore.
Send these, the homeless, tempest-tost
    to me,
I lift my lamp beside the golden door!"

guages and Hebrew, in support of efforts to convert Catholic, Eastern Orthodox, and Jewish immigrants to Protestantism. At the same time, German Catholics could find succor from their own St. Raphael's Society, and blue-capped members of the Hebrew Immigrant Aid Society gave verbal advice and printed information about inspection procedures to fellow Jews as they disembarked from the ferryboats at Ellis Island.

✑ Restrictions on Immigration

Entry into the United States had been almost unrestricted before a federal law in 1882 excluded convicts, "lunatics, idiots, paupers or persons likely to become public charges." Later, the Foran Act of 1885 barred contract laborers brought over by private companies. Congress expanded the criteria for exclusion again in 1891 to keep out polygamists and "persons suffering from a loathsome or dangerous contagious disease," in 1903 to prevent beggars, prostitutes, and anarchists from entering, and in 1907 to ban the "feebleminded," children under sixteen when unaccompanied by their parents, and people with tuberculosis, among others. Significantly, Congress never applied any religious test for admission, and it retained the principle of providing a haven for persons escaping political persecution.

Rising nativism put pressure on Congress to impose literacy tests and other barriers to stanch the immigrant flow, but before World War I the United States maintained its open admission policies for Europeans. People from the Western Hemisphere had no restrictions placed on them until 1965; indeed, in the late nineteenth through the early twentieth century, a sizable Mexican migration was deemed necessary for the agricultural development of the Southwest.

Only Asians were shut out. To appease western nativists, Congress passed the Chinese Exclusion Act of 1882,

The Last Yankee   This cartoon from 1888 shows the forlorn "last Yankee" standing amid a crowd of gaping, jeering, and rather sub-human foreigners who have overwhelmed the United States thanks to unrestricted immigration. Late nineteenth-century American nativists envisioned the coming twentieth century in such — to them — frightening terms unless the tide of immigration was stopped.

which virtually ended Chinese immigration until World War II (see Chapter 17). Many easterners applauded the policy. Even Jacob Riis, the Danish-born champion of the urban immigrant poor, denigrated the Chinese of New York City's Mott Street as given over to opium dens, white slavery, and an unyielding "paganism." Such stereotypes were applied universally to Asians, including

Letter of Protest, 1885

The national campaign to raise funds to build the pedestal for the Statue of Liberty, a gift from France, came not long after the Chinese Exclusion Act (1882), at a time of growing repression of racial minorities. Saum Song Bo, a Chinese-American writer, noted the irony and appealed to Christians to right the wrongs by ending immigrant exclusion.

A paper was presented to me yesterday for inspection, and I found it to be specially drawn up for subscription among my countrymen toward the Pedestal Fund of the Bartholdi Statue of Liberty. Seeing that the heading is an appeal to American citizens, to their love of country and liberty, I feel that my countrymen and myself are honored in being thus appealed to as citizens in the cause of liberty. But the word liberty makes me think of the fact that this country is the land of liberty for men of all nations except the Chinese. I consider it as an insult to us Chinese to call on us to contribute toward building in this land a pedestal for a statue of Liberty. That statue represents Liberty holding a torch which lights the passage of those of all nations who come into this country. But are the Chinese allowed to come? As for the Chinese who are here, are they allowed to enjoy liberty as men of all other nationalities enjoy it? Are they allowed to go about everywhere free from the insults, abuses, assaults, wrongs, and injuries from which men of other nationalities are free? . . .

Whether [the Chinese Exclusion Act] or the statue to Liberty will be the more lasting monument to tell future ages of the liberty and greatness of this country, will be known only to future generations.

Liberty, we Chinese do love and adore thee; but let not those who deny thee to us, make of thee a graven image and invite us to bow down to it.

---

those who had come to America under the auspices of Christian missionaries. In the early twentieth century, as a result, congressional laws and presidential policies closed off legal entry to nearly all Asians.

The "new immigrants" from southern, central, and eastern Europe struck native-born Americans as different from the "old immigrants" from northern and western Europe, who once had been the principal source of immigration to the United States and who still continued to arrive in great numbers until the mid-1890s. Native-born Americans remarked on the "new immigrants'" poverty, swarthy complexions, and peasant cultures and worried that the largely Catholic, Eastern Orthodox, and Jewish newcomers would overwhelm Protestant America.

❧ *Immigrant Employment and Destinations*

More than any other factor, the American industrial city, with its prosperity and variety of jobs, was the distant magnet drawing the immigrants. Immigrant destinations in America were not random: the employment patterns of particular cities directed the immigrant flow. Thus Poles and Slovaks, who often lacked specialized craft skills, largely bypassed Philadelphia, whose local economy was based on workshops, handicrafts, and household industries requiring workers with specific skills and where the Irish and blacks already had secured a foothold in the unskilled labor market. Instead, the Poles and Slovaks went to the coal-mining towns of northeastern and southwestern Pennsylvania or to the steel cities of Bethlehem, Pittsburgh, and the Great Lakes region, where strong backs and willing hands were the main requirements for work. Because they did not like to work underground, unskilled southern Italians avoided coal-mining jobs in favor of work as longshoremen and construction laborers. Italians laid and maintained streets, railroad tracks, subways, and streetcar lines in numerous northeastern and midwestern cities, and rebuilt San Francisco after the 1906 earthquake. Eastern European Jews drew on previous experience in the needle trades to set up as garment workers, tailors, and clothiers in such textile and clothing centers as New York and Philadelphia, and readily parlayed other skills as jewelers, butchers, bakers, and shopkeepers into jobs in many cities. Some Scandinavians and Germans continued to settle on midwestern farms, but many groups (especially Slavs, southern Italians, and Greeks) rejected farming — which they had come to associate with "donkey and goat" labor in the Old World — for the ready wages of urban employment.

Religious, cultural, and racial prejudices also ruled employment patterns. Protestant Scandinavian girls were preferred over Catholic Irish girls as domestic help in many Protestant homes. Employers widely viewed western and northern Europeans such as Germans to be more honest, industrious, and reliable than the "new immigrants" and paid them accordingly. In the West railroad recruiters from the Southern Pacific and other lines replaced Asians on the section gangs

A New York City Sweatshop   An immigrant family sews garments in their tenement apartment in 1913. Working at home in sweatshop conditions allowed mothers and children to contribute to family incomes, but at the cost of keeping children out of school and at exploitative piecework wages.

with Chicanos from El Paso and northern Mexico, whom the recruiters thought more docile, orderly, intelligent, and cheap. Virtually everywhere blacks were excluded from factory jobs, except when employers used them as strikebreakers, and were left to compete in the precarious world of day labor or in small-scale service enterprises. In southern cities race often determined job categories. Blacks monopolized such jobs as railroad porters and domestic servants, which whites considered beneath them. Throughout the country black married women worked outside the home to compensate for the low earnings of their husbands.

Working-class immigrants tended to cluster in neighborhoods close to their work and to people from their native villages or provinces. By means of letters home, notices published in foreign papers, or the accounts of returned sojourners, prospective emigrants

in the Old World learned where to find jobs and companionship in the New. In a typical example of "chain migration" an individual "pioneer" from a village would venture to a city, followed by relatives and friends until the village itself appeared to have been transplanted to one particular street or block. Mexicans traveled in the steps of fellow villagers along railroad lines leading to Los Angeles and other southwestern cities. Black rural migrants to northern cities likewise followed the railroads, reconstituting southern ways and church communities in the alleys of Washington, D.C., Philadelphia, and New York.

Migration chains formed along occupational as well as kinship lines. Thus between 1880 and 1914, immigrants from the wheat-raising town of Sambuca in western Sicily parted company in America, as peasants headed for the sugar parishes of Louisiana and artisans went to Brooklyn, Tampa, Chicago, or Rockford, Illinois. Old World prejudices also governed emigrants' decisions about where to locate. In New York, for example, northern Italians lived on 69th Street west of Broadway, and Genoese clustered on Baxter Street, both avoiding the Neapolitans and Calabrese, whom they despised, in the Mulberry Bend section.

❧ The Immigrant Enclave

In the urban immigrant enclaves, it was possible to retain much of the Old World culture. Grocers, peddlers, and specialty shops catered to traditional tastes of the immigrants (and helped to introduce new foods into the American diet over time). Merchants let customers haggle over prices and buy on credit, further binding immigrant consumers to sellers who spoke their language and respected their ways. Even after moving out of the immigrant neighborhood, the immigrants and their children returned to its stores to buy foods and goods, such as religious objects, they could get nowhere else. Wherever they lived, Chinese who wanted soy sauce, bean curd, dried mushrooms, snow peas, bamboo shoots, giblets, and other basic ingredients for Chinese cooking continued to patronize groceries in Chinatown.

Foreign-language newspapers and entertainments also kept Old World languages and customs alive. So, too, did a host of mutual-aid societies, religious institutions, social clubs, workers' organizations, and saloons — many organized on the basis of provincial identities from the Old World. In Providence, Rhode Island, between 1874 and 1914, eastern European Jews established twenty-four different Orthodox congregations along Old World regional lines. Immigrants might mix with members of other groups at work, but the ethnic neighborhood and its separate institutions often formed the boundaries of their social universe.

❧ Immigrant Religion

At the center of the immigrant enclave stood the church or synagogue. Religion was an important, usually a central, component of one's identity in the Old World, and it remained so in the New. In addition to articles of clothing and tools for a trade, immigrants invariably packed religious objects to sustain them in America — liturgical sheet music from Poland, a sacramental wine cup from Lithuania, a baptismal bonnet from Sicily. In a typical remembrance now inscribed at Ellis Island, Czech-born Sam Auspitz recalled that in 1920 his mother "brought her candles, . . . her Bibles . . . the things that were near and dear to us."

Amid the swirl of the industrial city, religion promised continuity with the world the immigrants had left behind. They gathered in their houses of worship to observe the traditional holy and feast days, to gain recognition through ritual, and to hear the familiar chants of the Latin or Eastern rite liturgy, readings in Hebrew from the Torah, or sermons in their own language. At picnics and club meetings they enjoyed the camaraderie and gossip of others of like tongue and faith and sought suitable mates for their children. Women often found sustenance and special meaning in congregational life, with religious organizations and social functions calling upon them for charitable work and offering them support outside the home. In the immigrant world, not only marriage but also such rituals as baptism and first communion or circumcision and bar mitzvah had both social and religious significance, for the vows and ceremonies bound the individual and the family to a larger community.

The church or synagogue was the meeting place, and often the spawning ground, for a variety of nonreligious organizations such as mutual-aid societies, insurance companies, athletic teams, secret lodges, and musical and dramatic groups. In an age of few public services, religious organizations built and staffed urban hospitals, orphanages, and welfare organizations. Parish banks underwrote church and school construction and lent mortgage money to would-be homeowners and businessmen.

But the church also became the battleground where different immigrant groups competed for space and recognition, and the very associations that drew believers to the church in time spun them outward away from it. Indeed, differences among the immigrants showed up most markedly in their churches. A common Catholicism, for example, did not prepare the southern and eastern European immigrants for the austere, formalistic practices of the Irish-American church. The southern Italians brought centuries of folk religious customs to the church — charms to assure fertility and prevent illness, amulets to ward off "the evil eye," and festivals to celebrate particular saints. To honor the Virgin Mary or the patron of their home village, the Italians would carry a statue of the Madonna or saint through the neighborhood, followed by brass bands, weeping women, excited children, and believers rushing to pin money on the holy effigy. The American bishops, who usually were of Irish descent, recoiled from what they regarded as heathenism and sought to convert the "new immigrants" to Irish-American ways. In San Francisco the Irish hierarchy drafted Italian priests to convince the immigrants to abandon the processions and "superstitions" of saint days, but the Italians continued to prefer their Madonnas and local festivals to Sunday Mass.

The issue of Americanization reverberated throughout the immigrant church (see Chapter 20). While the church hierarchy insisted on uniformity, each immigrant group demanded preaching and pastoral care in its own language. Disaffected groups, including a contingent of the Rusins (Ukrainians) who practiced one of Catholicism's Eastern rites that allowed priests to marry, left the unsympathetic American Catholic church to affiliate with the Russian Orthodox church in this country. Italians in Buffalo lapsed into non-observance and avoided the parochial schools until they got their own priests. The Italians and many other groups fought for and won the principle of the "nationality parish," a major concession to ethnic pluralism within

the Roman Catholic church. In Boston, New York, and St. Paul, for example, Italians resentful of being shooed into basement chapels in Irish-run churches forced bishops to establish Italian parishes.

The very size and diversity of the industrial city and mobility of the population militated against religious and cultural unanimity and cohesion. In most cities, no single immigrant group stayed long enough or was numerous enough wholly to control any neighborhood. The proverbial "Jewish" Lower East Side of New York in fact teemed with Italians, Germans, Slavs, and other immigrants. Likewise, at no time did Swedes make up a majority of Chicago's "Swede Town." The heterogeneity of the industrial city, more than anything else, made the New World unlike the Old. The steeples and domes of Russian, Greek, German, Italian, Irish, Polish, and other churches overlooking the immigrant wards throughout urban, industrial America bore witness to the ethnic variety, and the religious choices, in the immigrant city.

❧ Community and Identity

Immigrant neighborhoods were in flux, immigrants a people in motion. Migration to American cities was

---

✳ IN THEIR OWN WORDS

Letters Home, 1902

Immigrant letters home sent advice and information, and often remittances. Letters were a way of keeping contact with family and community and providing the means for relatives and others to follow to America. They also reveal the ways America was changing the immigrants as to social relations and identity, as these two letters from Polish immigrants to Chicago, Konstanty and Antoni Butkowski, suggest.

November 11 [1902]

Dearest Parents:

... Family remains family only in the first time after coming from home, and later they forget and don't wish any more to acknowledge the familial relations; the American meat inflates them....

I beg you, describe to me about our country, how things are going on there. And please don't be angry with me for this which I shall write. I write you that it is hard to live alone, so please find some girl for me, but an orderly [honest] one, for in America there is not even one single orderly girl....

Konstanty Butkowski

Chicago, December 31, 1902

Dear Parents:

If Konstanty wrote you to send him a girl, answer him that he may send a ship-ticket either to the one from Popów or to the one from Grajewo. Let the one come which is smarter, for he does not know either of them, so send the one which pleases you better. For

in America it is so: Let her only know how to prepare for the table, and be beautiful. For in America there is no need of a girl who knows how to spin and to weave. If she knows how to sew, it is well. For if he does not marry he will never make a fortune and will never have anything; he wastes his work and has nothing. And if he marries he will sooner put something aside. For he won't come back any more. In America it is so: Whoever does not intend to return to his country, it is best for him to marry young; then he will sooner have something, for a bachelor in America will never have anything, unless he is particularly self-controlled....

Antoni Butkowski

matched by movement between and within cities. Between 1880 and 1890 almost 800,000 people moved into and out of Boston. Within Chicago, according to a 1915 survey, almost half the residents of the Polish and Italian districts moved each year. In Omaha at the turn of the century, nearly 60 percent of all ethnic groups who stayed in the city had changed addresses three or more times in a fifteen-year span. Everywhere in the United States high turnover rates were especially common in working-class neighborhoods, principally because of unstable and seasonal employment and high rents.

Some city dwellers, however, remained trapped in sections of the city where movement was restricted. Social and economic discrimination confined Mexicans to barrios, Chinese to Chinatowns, and blacks to ghettos. White violence and restrictive covenants (clauses in deeds that prohibited resale of a property to members of certain groups) kept them there. In southern cities segregation denied blacks access to many public places, while inferior education and limited job opportunities built further barriers between the races. In northern ghettos storefront churches, small businesses, social clubs, and taverns formed the marrow of a new black urban culture. In ghettos everywhere, the growth of religious and cultural institutions and businesses dependent on racial consciousness and group patronage bred group unity while increasing social isolation.

Even within a particular nationality group, fundamental differences kept immigrants apart, and rivalries among religious and ethnic leaders tore at congregational and community unity. Germans, for example, were divided by religion (Protestants of several denominations, Catholics, Jews, and free-thinkers), occupation, class, and culture (e.g., patrons of beer gardens and Sunday concerts versus teetotalers and sabbatarians). Inside those divisions, German Protestant and Catholic churches, like the churches of even the most homogeneous groups, could be split by schisms rooted in doctrine or clashes of personality. After a typical battle over lay versus clerical authority, Polish nationalists left Chicago's St. Stanislaus Kostka parish for Holy Trinity, one of the member congregations that made up the new and independent Polish National Catholic Church in the United States.

Poverty and the economic necessity of the family economy reinforced the immigrants' hold on family and church, while the desire to escape those constraints weakened the family's and organized religion's grips on the second or third generation. Sweatshop conditions

combined with the preferences of some immigrant groups to keep women and children at home — the women to take care of the children and the women and children both to contribute to family income. Cigars, clothing, buttons, and other sewing notions were all made or prepared for sale by families working long hours in their own homes. To fulfill social obligations to relatives and friends from the "old country" and to bolster meager family incomes when children were too young to work, immigrant families took in boarders, further crowding already cramped living quarters and adding to women's responsibilities at home.

The communal basis of immigrant life encouraged children working outside the home to turn over all their wages to their parents and to forgo individual advancement in favor of group allegiance. Slovak Catholics, for example, preferred to send their children to Slovak parochial schools, where the children would learn catechism, obedience, and "family values," rather than to public schools, where they would be introduced to American ways to wealth. The value of formal education varied among immigrant groups. Eastern European Jews, Armenians, Germans, and Romanians tended to keep their children in school whenever possible to encourage their economic success in America. Slavs and southern Italians often traded formal education for steady income, pulling children out of school early to draft them into the workforce. Among all groups, fathers used their connections at work or among fellow immigrants to secure jobs for their progeny and so to direct their career paths. Thus as late as World War II, Germans tended to be over-represented as toolmakers, Poles as steelworkers, Serbs as miners, and Jews and Italians in the apparel industry.

Becoming American in the Immigrant City

At the same time, the fluidity of industrial and urban employment with its rapid job turnover and expanding opportunities for work outside the local neighborhood pulled many immigrant children away from the family. Amid the secular amusements of vaudeville, moving-picture shows, spectator sports, and more, children resented their parents' claims to all their hard-earned wages. Public schools taught children to value the dollar and to get ahead. So did many churches. By portraying themselves and their immigrant congregants as a "pilgrim people," church leaders encouraged upward mobility and progressive attitudes. German churches in Chicago taught "American business skills" along with catechism. Ethnic newspapers that touted the successes of local immigrant businessmen added another voice to that litany. The *Jewish Daily Forward* was among several ethnic newspapers that responded to readers' requests for help in negotiating the "American way of life."

American interests and identities eventually prevailed over Old World ones. Other Americans — both the native-born and those from different immigrant groups — principally saw the immigrants in terms of a single nationality and ignored regional differences: thus, Germans were German, whether from Bavaria, Prussia, or Württemberg; Irish were Irish, whether from Limerick, Cork, or Donegal. The children of immigrants came to view themselves in similar ways. Over time, Old World distinctions waned, especially after restrictions in the 1920s effectively ended European immigration. Foreign-language newspapers, for example, survived at first by downplaying Old World regional differences in favor of a common cultural identity, and later by increasing their use of English and coverage of local events.

The children of immigrants became members of *American* ethnic groups. Children learned English in school and on the street; families mixed American foods into ethnic dishes; musicians blended American and Old World folk music (polka bands, for example, replaced violins with accordians and trumpets to play louder in the American style); and all lived in American settings. In America, different Italians discovered they were Italian, then Italian-American, rather than Calabrese or Genoese. Finding common bond in their mother tongue and a similar brand of Catholicism, they accepted the notion of marrying someone from a different regional background long before they could contemplate marrying outside the Italian-American group.

Likewise German Jews in America — who had over two generations established themselves comfortably in commerce and civic life and built up a Reform Judaism adapted to American circumstance — put aside their initial unease that the poor eastern European Jewish immigrants would embarrass American Jews and invite anti-Semitism with their strange ways and religious Orthodoxy. The German-American Jews reached out to the newcomers through such relief agencies as the Hebrew Immigrant Aid Society. They also provided jobs for the immigrants. Although the eastern Europeans' religious Orthodoxy, lower employment status, and vibrant Yiddish culture slowed the convergence, in the 1920s and 1930s common concerns about the fate of Jews in Europe and the perceived need for a Jew-

ish homeland drew American Jews of all backgrounds together.

Among all immigrant groups, children began to speak, dress, dream, and even pray differently than their parents did. As Polish immigrant Helena Brylska-Dabrowska lamented in 1908, her children no longer listened to her, preferring to "run everywhere about the world," and so had lost their innocence. "They were good in the beginning but now they know how to speak English, and their goodness is lost," she concluded. Urban life dangled so many distractions that for many rural migrants and immigrants religious life became increasingly compartmentalized — something for the Sabbath and holy days only. Fathers spent time at work and then in saloons or social clubs. The culture of progress that brought people to town competed with the culture of faith, over time confusing the two. One Slovene immigrant in Milwaukee appreciated the paradox when he compared the masses of shoppers clogging the streets with Old World pilgrims crowding their way to a shrine. They passed department-store window displays showing what clothes and accessories to buy for Sunday services.

THE NEW FACE OF THE CITY

The sheer size and growing population density of the industrial city forced dramatic changes in its physical shape and social character. The influx of hundreds of thousands of new urban dwellers drove up real estate prices and strained already overburdened city services. The mixed-use patterns of the antebellum cities gave way to economic and social segregation. Real-estate developers, builders, and urban architects reordered city space, building commuter rail and trolley lines that radiated outward in a wheel-spoke pattern from the downtown hub, dividing and subdividing old housing stock to cram in new arrivals close to the city core, building upwards via skyscrapers, and expanding housing at the city's edge and beyond. The pace of life quickened in the industrial city, as workers punched time clocks and met train schedules, and the efficiency and impersonality of modern urban life often elbowed aside the sense of common values and kinship that had once marked small-town life.

Before the development of cheap, reliable urban transportation, city size had been limited by the distance people could comfortably walk to work. In such "walking cities," the radius rarely extended beyond a few miles, and people of all classes lived and worked close to one another. Handsome townhouses faced the streets, but beside or behind them stood modest structures where artisans resided and plied their trades. The lower classes found housing in the nearby shacks and flimsy buildings that filled alleys. Countinghouses and warehouses clustered along the docks, and noxious industries such as tanning, brewing, and meatpacking located on the city outskirts. Otherwise, small industry, business, and residence were jumbled together. No overarching city design guided development. In the markets, on the streets, and in the public squares of the walking city, class and ethnic lines blurred enough so that city dwellers might feel part of the larger community. Poverty abounded in the walking city, but it had a familiar human face. In 1856 Philadelphia patrician Sidney George Fisher remarked in his diary that he knew personally more than five thousand people of all classes in the city.

By the turn of the century the walking city had metamorphosed into the sprawling, segmented city. Economic function and income divided the city roughly into a concentric pattern. A central business district, or downtown core, where few lived, was ringed by a manufacturing and wholesaling district, where immigrants and the working poor jammed into tenements and subdivided old houses. Beyond them was a stretch of lower-middle-class to middle-class rowhouses or apartment buildings, where skilled, clerical, and some factory workers resided. Then came the fringes of the city, where professionals, managers, and businessmen retreated to their spacious Victorian homes, leading "upholstered lives" and tending their manicured lawns and shrubs away from the stench, noise, dirt, and push-and-shove of the city.

❧ The Development of Mass Transportation

New means of transportation made possible the new urban geography of economic integration and social segregation. As early as the 1820s and 1830s such eastern cities as Boston, New York, and Philadelphia had operated horse-drawn public carriers called omnibuses. Omnibus systems spread rapidly through the 1850s, but the slow, heavy, vehicles accommodated few passengers and their high fares limited ridership. By mid-century, steam-powered commuter railroads were pushing city boundaries outward for the affluent. The New York & Harlem Railroad connected the suburban village of Harlem with New York, and the Chicago & Mil-

waukee Railroad linked such North Shore communities as Evanston, Wilmette, and Lake Forest with Chicago.

At the same time, many cities had switched to horse-drawn streetcars. Rails smoothed the ride, compared to the jostling of omnibus wheels over cobblestones, and they made possible larger conveyances and more rapid movement. By establishing fixed routes, the horse railways promised riders predictability. They also broadened the compass of the city to five miles or more. With lower fares, the horsecar systems attracted a middle-class clientele, who commuted to work downtown from newly developed residential areas, or suburbs, on city borderlands. By the 1880s, horse-drawn streetcars were carrying almost 190 million passengers annually in the United States. Transit schedules and rail lines increasingly ordered urban lives as city dwellers acquired the "riding habit."

Horsecars did not meet the demand for cleaner, cheaper, and more reliable urban transportation. Horse manure (ten pounds per day per horse) fouled the air, and exhausted animals dropped dead pulling heavy cars over hills. Technology soon replaced the horsecars with cable cars, pulled by steam-driven, underground wire rope clamped to the car. Introduced in San Francisco in 1873, cable cars proved especially effective there and in such other hilly cities as Pittsburgh and Washington, D.C.

The most important advance in urban transit was the electric trolley. In 1888, on a twelve-mile track in hilly Richmond, Virginia, Frank J. Sprague, a naval engineer and former associate of Thomas Edison, demonstrated the practicality of powering streetcars with electrical currents transferred from overhead wires to the vehicle by a four-wheeled spring device, or *troller*. A frenzy of construction and conversion to electricity followed Richmond's success, as city governments awarded generous trolley franchises to transit entrepreneurs. Trolleys rolled along at twice the speed of horsecars, and the American system of flat-fee fares with free transfers encouraged mass ridership. For a nickel, one could escape the soot and smells of the city on a daily commute or, for the poor, on a Sunday outing.

Mass ridership encouraged construction. In 1890 the nation had 5,700 miles of horse-drawn track and only 1,260 miles of electrified track; twelve years later, just 250 miles of horse-drawn track remained in service, while the total length of electrified track had grown to 22,000 miles.

Transit companies tried to increase ridership by developing the urban periphery. By the 1890s, the

Peoples Railroad trolley in St. Louis ran out to Grand Boulevard, a dirt road amid cornfields that the transit company was transforming into an avenue worthy of its name. The company laid out private streets with fountains, and it planted shade trees and shrubs to lure prospective homebuilders and buyers. Everywhere in urban America, transit companies invested heavily in such suburban real estate speculation, encouraging the very population dispersal that in the coming Automobile Age would be their downfall. Henry Huntington, who built a vast street railway network in Los Angeles, likened his work to that of his uncle, the railroad baron Collis P. Huntington, whose Central Pacific Railroad had helped to settle the West. In the late nineteenth and early twentieth centuries streetcar companies made more money selling real estate in outlying areas than running their lines. Many, in fact, went bankrupt once they no longer had suburban land to sell.

To lessen traffic congestion, in the 1870s New York City experimented with steam-powered elevated trains running on trestles high above the streets, and several midwestern cities followed. Because the "els" were expensive to build and maintain, and city dwellers resented their noise, soot, and ugliness, most cities resisted constructing the steam-powered version. But the advent of electricity encouraged several cities to introduce electric-powered elevated railways or subway systems, or a combination of both. Beginning in Boston in 1897 and then in New York in 1904 and Philadelphia in 1908, elaborate subways snaked underground, sometimes for hundreds of miles within a city.

Aboveground loomed complexes of river bridges, often built by railroad companies. Such spans as St. Louis's Eads Bridge, with its steel arches and massive stone piers, exalted the power of the nationally integrated rail systems and ended the reliance on inefficient river ferries. Most remarkable of all was the Brooklyn Bridge, a steel-cable suspension bridge designed and built by John and Washington Roebling to span the East River. When completed in 1883, after thirteen years of construction and at a cost of twenty lives, the mile-long structure could accommodate two railroad lines and other traffic. More than three hundred suspension bridges were built during the next twenty-five years.

✣ *The Skyscraper*

The trolley lines, els, subways, bridges, and commuter railroad systems operated as centrifugal forces pulling middle- and upper-class residences ever farther from city centers while simultaneously making the downtown more accessible to all. Although small business strips emerged at outlying transfer points, urban transit systems converged downtown with spectacular economic impact. The central business district rapidly developed as the principal location for banks, insurance companies, corporate headquarters, government agencies, professional offices, and retail stores, as well as for hotels, theaters, and other places of entertainment. The divided city thus had a vital center held together by a web of rail and streetcar lines.

Soaring values at the city center forced up the height of buildings. The pressure to build upward began around mid-century, but construction technology did not catch up to demand for several decades. The thick walls necessary to bear the weight of masonry structures limited floor space and capped the height of buildings at about twelve stories. The development of cast-iron and, later, the more elastic steel frame-and-girder skeletal construction freed internal space by removing the need for thick walls and made it possible to erect "skyscrapers" of thirty or more stories. Then the substitution of glass for masonry brought in light and gave the skyscraper the basic look it would have thereafter. The safety elevator, electrified in the 1880s, made the taller buildings practical. In fact, renters were willing to pay extra for the prestige and privacy of top floors in a crowded city.

Chicago became the architects' mecca for the new construction. William Le Baron Jenney's ten-story Home Insurance Building (1885), Louis H. Sullivan's Schlesinger and Mayer (now Carson, Pirie, Scott) department store (1889-1904), and Daniel Burnham's Reliance Building (1894) marked the epoch. Out of the ashes of the Great Fire of 1871 arose opportunity and a new urban vision. The "Chicago School" of architects not only rebuilt the midwestern metropolis but also created an American urban style. Admiring engineers for their practicality and influenced by pragmatism, these architects urged builders, in the words of Sullivan, to discard "books, rules, precedents, or any such educational impedimenta" borrowed from Europe. The American tall office building, Sullivan wrote, "must be every inch a proud and soaring thing, rising in sheer exultation that from bottom to top it is a unit without a single dissenting line." Sullivan's Wainwright Building (1890) in St. Louis and Prudential Building (1895) in Buffalo pointed the way. By the early twentieth century skyscrapers studded urban skylines across America.

⁊ *The Palace of Consumption*

The emergence of a "ready-made" clothes industry by mid-century and a cornucopia of other mass-produced goods, from prefabricated household furnishings to children's toys, encouraged an urban lifestyle of consumption and display that found its fullest expression in the department store. Although modeled after French shopping arcades, the department store was an American institution. In its democratic appeal to shoppers of all classes, in its variety and wealth of consumer goods, and in its scale, the department store stood as a testimony to American industrial genius.

It also transformed city space. The large glass display windows, clean sidewalks outside, and easy accessibility by means of streetcars and trains (John Wanamaker built his Philadelphia "Grand Depot" above a train shed) — all combined to invite women downtown to shop and work, to see and be seen. In a culture of consumption, shopping became a social art and the smart and smartly dressed shopper the embodiment of the *modern* city dweller.

To attract and hold customers, the department store relied on marked, fixed prices and newspaper advertising. Department stores advertised aggressively; indeed, department stores bought so much space in newspapers that, by the early twentieth century, advertising had surpassed circulation as the revenue basis for metropolitan dailies. By means of advice columns about fashion and etiquette, storeowners further used the press to educate consumers on what and how to buy.

In department stores everywhere, service was the storeowners' credo. "Honest" John Wanamaker, who chose retailing over the Presbyterian ministry, thought of his business as a public service. He pledged his clerks to respect all customers by honoring the "Golden Rule" and Wanamaker's "trinity of square-dealing": "All goods

The Flatiron Building, New York City The steel frame is still visible as the skyscraper goes up. Built between 1901 and 1903, the Flatiron was when completed the world's tallest building — over 300 feet high. It still stands at the intersection of Broadway, Fifth Avenue, and Eighteenth Street.

to be sold openly, / All traders to be treated alike, / All fraud and deception to be eliminated." Likewise, Marshall Field, who personally greeted customers and listened to their complaints, employed numerous floorwalkers to welcome and assist anyone who entered his Chicago store. Marshall Field's motto summed up department store merchandising: "Give the lady what she wants."

Shoppers were encouraged to roam freely in stores, to inquire about goods from the many floorwalkers and sales clerks, and to exchange or return purchases that did not satisfy them. Lay-away plans made it possible to buy now, pay later. The cavernous, multistoried emporiums, often occupying an entire city block, were divided into departments (hence the name) arranged by product. Bargain basements served the poor and economy-minded, and exclusive dress shops and salons catered to the affluent. By staffing the counters with "salesgirls" — usually young working-class women taught and dressed to be models of fashion and elegance — the stores put women shoppers of all classes at ease. Restrooms, reading and smoking rooms for men, nurseries for children, beauty parlors, and restaurants lured middle-class customers downtown to spend the day away from their isolated domesticity. Instead of drudgery, shopping was convenient and fun.

The stores promised luxury and welcomed all comers, except blacks who were relegated to basements or barred altogether in cities as far north as Baltimore. The grand marble stairways, vaulted foyers, and wide, well-lighted interiors allowed working-class shoppers to escape their own drab surroundings. The displays instructed immigrants and new arrivals to the city on proper dress and behavior, showing them the way to middle-class respectability. To trade a peasant's babushka for a hat, which in the old country only a lady wore, was democracy made real. Democratic customer service reinforced the illusion. Miss Leslie's *Behaviour Book* (1857) reminded ladies not to show any impatience "if a servant-girl, making a six penny purchase" was served before them, because in American stores "the rule of 'first come, first served,' is rigidly observed."

The mass consumer culture sold in the department stores spread outward along the rail lines that carried the goods and customers to city centers. Rural free delivery of mail (1898) and parcel post (1913) opened distant markets to urban advertising and promotions. By means of mail-order catalogs and branch stores, Marshall Field and

other urban merchants attempted to capture small-town markets.

More important were the mail-order houses of Montgomery Ward and Sears, Roebuck, both strategically based in the nation's railroad nexus of Chicago. Montgomery Ward started in the 1870s as an outgrowth of the Granger movement (see Chapter 21), selling agricultural supplies and household wares. By the 1890s the company offered over 10,000 items. "You think of it, Ward's has it" was its motto. In the early twentieth century Sears, Roebuck commanded the mail-order field. Known as "The Cheapest Supply House on Earth" and run by Richard W. Sears, "the Barnum of merchandising," who could "sell a breath of air," Sears, Roebuck blanketed the country with its robust, handsomely illustrated catalogs, filled with detailed descriptions of thousands of products and advice on how to use them. It distributed upwards of 6 million catalogs annually. Only the Bible had a wider reach.

Along with such chain stores as F. W. Woolworth's "five-and-dimes," mail-order houses pulled small-town,

Electric Streetcar, Washington, D.C.   About 1895, this streetcar was the latest innovation in mass transit, conquering urban space and leading to the dramatic geographic expansion of late nineteenth-century cities. It drew its power from a "skate" at the front of the vehicle, which touched an underground "third rail."

rural America into the urban, consumer nexus. Mail-order catalogs brought the city to the country, and rural consumers consulted them to shake off rusticity. Yet the catalogs also could be a reminder of the constraints and limits on rural consumerism. Hard-pressed schoolteachers, who wanted to use outdated catalogs as arithmetic and spelling texts, competed for back issues with farm families, who still had outhouses and recycled the paper there.

❧ Urban Lifestyles

The urban culture of consumption affected not only public space but private lives. Lives that intersected downtown at work or in stores diverged at home. Class divisions showed in housing styles and personal lifestyles. The upper and middle classes increasingly retreated to the privacy of mansions, apartments, or suburban homes, emphasizing lives of consumption and domesticity over public involvement. The poor were left to themselves.

Before the Civil War prosperous merchants and financiers had lived handsomely, but modestly, on annual incomes of $10,000 to $20,000. The industrial age created new personal fortunes in the millions and fostered attitudes of "conspicuous consumption" that isolated the rich from the general society. The new rich rented front pews in fashionable churches and mouthed homilies about good works' being pathways to heaven, but few of them joined Andrew Carnegie in practicing a "gospel of wealth" (see Chapter 18). The parvenus preferred to spend money on themselves.

The very rich occupied exclusive sections within the city, such as Fifth Avenue in New York, the "Gold Coast" north along Lake Michigan in Chicago, and Nob Hill in San Francisco. In stately mansions or in Renaissance-style apartment buildings, the millionaires overindulged in lavish entertainment and gaudy display. Amid the depression of the 1890s, one New York hostess spent $369,000 on a ball, and Harry Lehr staged a sumptuous dinner for his friends' dogs. Even in death, the elite proclaimed their wealth. Between 1897 and 1899, New York's monied aristocracy spent more than $1.5 million on mausoleums. The rich measured status by the artwork, silverware, and numbers of servants they collected.

However much those with material splendor disdained the common folk below, they could not escape public scrutiny. Society pages in newspapers tallied the personal and financial assets of debutantes, and reporters noted, in lurid detail, the extravagance and

Domestic Music-Making   Families like these middle-class New Yorkers were still dependent on a piano or other instruments, as well as their own voices, for musical entertainment around 1900. The advent of the phonograph, to be followed after 1920 by radio and after 1945 by television, revolutionized family life.

debauchery in the world of white gloves and cummerbunds. The excesses of the rich, when compared with the misery of the poor, would become a staple of muckraking journalism and a call to reform (see Chapter 23).

Middle-class city-dwellers — managers, shopkeepers, professionals, public employees, clerks, and salespeople — also developed a distinctive urban lifestyle. In the cities they lived in apartments or two- and three-story row houses. Luxury apartment houses, modeled after the European flats, had become popular among the rich by the 1870s, and by the 1880s cheaper models caught on among middle-class residents who lacked the money or incentive to buy their own homes. Clusters of apartment houses formed the cores of residential districts.

Apartment-house living afforded middle-class families privacy and room and promised them some of the same luxuries the rich enjoyed. The perfection of the radiator in the 1870s and improved water circulation through pipes allowed for central heating and indoor plumbing. So, too, innovations such as the trap in sinks (which ended the danger of sewer gas being vented upward into homes) and the flush toilet brought the duties of kitchen and bathroom indoors. Hot-and-cold running water made getting up for work less painful than in the days of cold splashes from a washbowl. Gas and electric lighting extended the day into the evening, so that after the family supper and then prayers or Bible reading, parents could retire to the living or sitting room to read — father, the newspaper, and mother, one of the popular mass-circulation magazines, a "pulp" romance novel, or a quasi-religious advice book — or to sing or listen to music, play cards, or view natural scenes through stereoptical slide lanterns, while perhaps munching on Cracker Jacks and sipping Canada Dry ginger ale.

Apartment living encouraged what novelist William Dean Howells called "the moral effect of housekeeping." The apartment, like the row house, became the home, where middle-class women practiced domesticity, piety, and order. At home, Protestant and Catholic middle-class women arranged sacred space — alcoves or walls with religious objects and Bibles prominently displayed and even stained-glass windows and Gothic arches added. Mothers taught children catechism and led daily devotions. The home as private chapel endowed women's duties with moral authority and purpose. By the end of the century, however, secular concerns and furnishings were crowding out time and space once reserved for sacred matters.

In the middle-class apartment or row house mothers became "managers." With the aid of live-in servants and modern conveniences, women brought discipline and order to the home. They got everyone up to the clang of a mechanical alarm clock and after break-

Two Crazes of 1902 The man on the left is taking a photograph — actually a three-dimensional "stereograph" — of the group of fashionably dressed women cyclists, probably out for a spin on a Sunday afternoon. Cycling and photography were two of the most popular leisure activities of prosperous turn-of-the-century urbanites.

fast, which usually included some packaged cereal, sent children to school and father to work, each with a sandwich or cold meal prepared from meats kept in the icebox and such treats as Fig Newtons, Hershey chocolate bars, Tootsie Rolls, or Wrigley's Juicy Fruit chewing gum purchased from the local grocery store.

Apartment living, combined with smaller family sizes, allowed middle-class women to spend more time outside the home. Reading clubs, charities, and sports (lawn tennis, ice skating, and especially bicycling) kept minds and bodies busy in a middle-class culture that put increasing emphasis on personal growth and learning how to play. At the same time, the urban milieu encouraged middle-class women to organize. Women's clubs, the American Association of University Women, the Young Women's Christian Association, church groups, aid societies, and suffrage lobbies grew apace with the expansion of middle-class women's time away from domestic duties.

The middle-class lifestyle extended out to the suburbs. Streetcars made outlying areas accessible, and cheaper suburban land values and mass-production building techniques made housing affordable. In the late nineteenth century the vast majority of suburban dwellers rented their homes, but clerks and skilled workers, earning on average $1,000 a year during the 1890s, could afford to buy in the less fashionable areas where houses ranged in price from $1,000 to $5,000. In their homes, the middle-class suburban dwellers lived much like their city-dwelling counterparts, though the distance from downtown and the detached houses kept women at home more than in the city and added to household chores the burden

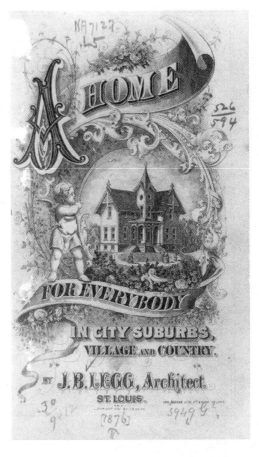

"A Home for Everybody" The idealization of suburbs was a common theme of architecture books promoting new home construction, as the title page of this 1876 publication suggests.

of keeping up the grounds. Still, the city remained within reach for work, shopping, and recreation, and so middle-class families continued to clutter their houses with Victorian bric-a-brac and their lives with commercial entertainment after they joined the residential exodus.

The appeal of the suburbs was as much spiritual as functional. The suburbs promised to redeem the nation from the drabness, crime, and social dislocation of the city. Trimming hedges and mowing lawns would regenerate effete office workers by getting them back to nature, or so claimed the garden and home magazines advertising lawn and garden supplies. The fresh air and tree-lined streets offered not only health and recreational benefits to children but also relief and renewal to tired and harried adults. Developers and landscape architects laid out curved street patterns to free suburb dwellers from the stultifying rigidity and monotony of the urban gridiron. Real-estate promoters argued that detached houses would strengthen family unity and that owning a home would ensure social stability. Village as-

sociations preached the virtues of a return to small-town community and the simple life.

The reformers, however, expressed a profound ambivalence about the city. Even as they extolled the benefits of escaping urban problems, they traded on the suburbs' proximity to urban advantages. Suburbs, after all, were extensions rather than rejections of urban life. Suburban dwellers wanted city services, and because it was cheaper to connect new developments to existing municipal water and sewer systems, outlying areas did not resist annexation by cities. One of the principal ways in which nineteenth-century cities grew was by absorbing unincorporated surrounding lands, thereby capturing population movement and also unifying such crucial services as police, fire, and water into metropolitan systems. In 1898, for example, Greater New York City was created by consolidating Brooklyn and the boroughs of Manhattan, Queens, Staten Island, and the Bronx. Annexation kept the country tied to the city.

The supposed redemptive effects of the natural landscape also inspired efforts to bring the country to the city. From mid-century on, landscape architects such as H. W. S. Cleveland, George E. Kessler, and Frederick Law Olmsted planned urban parks as places of healthful recreation. Olmsted's Central Park in Manhattan became the model for a park-building mania that spread westward to Cincinnati, Indianapolis, Chicago, Minneapolis, Kansas City, Omaha, and San Francisco. With its trees and sunken roadways, hiking and riding trails, a lake for boating and skating, a variety of vistas, and a mall for concerts, Central Park exercised, in Olmsted's words, "a distinctly harmonizing and refining influence . . . favorable to courtesy, self-control and temperance."

The urban park promised to civilize nature and humanity and to restore community in the divided city. In planning parks and suburbs, Olmsted emphasized the need to create physical environments that would afford a Christian people the means "of coming together, of being together, and especially of recreating together on common ground." This vision translated into broad vistas and no fences. In reality, however, different classes competed for space in the parks. Because they thought that the middle classes sought repose, while the lower classes wanted "boisterous fun and rough sports," planners often located parks away from working-class areas. Natural settings remained the preserve of "the better sort," and commercial amusement parks, such as Coney Island, served the masses.

❧ *Slums*

While urban America's middle and upper classes reached for open space, the lower classes suffered from ever more crowded, unsanitary conditions. Landlords capitalized on the crush for space near city centers by subdividing existing buildings or putting up cheaply built four- and six-story tenements and charging high rents. In 1890 more than 1.4 million people lived on Manhattan Island, and the Tenth Ward on the Lower East Side had a population density of 900 people per acre, the highest concentration in the world.

Although many poor people lived in shacks, shanties, or subdivided older houses, the slum tenement

became the common urban form in large industrial cities and the literary symbol for working-class areas everywhere. In *Maggie: A Girl of the Streets* (1893), novelist Stephen Crane aptly described it as a barracks that "quivered and creaked from the weight of humanity stamping about in its bowels." Slum housing dulled the senses with its unimaginative and repetitive designs and high density. Tenements stood like gloomy prisons for the millions of urban newcomers. Jammed side-by-side on 25-by-100-foot lots, they choked out light and air. Most tenements lacked indoor plumbing and adequate heating. Families shared outdoor privies and drew water from private wells and hydrants. Sewage systems, if they existed at all, were so overloaded that tenement areas reeked of human waste and decomposing garbage.

Such filthy, cramped conditions bred disease and social suffering, and urban death rates soared. Respiratory ills especially afflicted slum districts. One corner

A Suburban Family, 1880s   The three generations of this prosperous family sat for a photograph in their garden-like back yard, whose shrubbery added to middle-class privacy and created a sense of country living. They would have been among the pioneers in relocating out of the crowded central city. Obviously, mowing the grass was a low priority. And the youngest member of the family could not keep his head still long enough for the slow-exposure camera that was used.

THE POLO GROUNDS
NEW YORK

SEASON OF 1887.

HOME GAMES OF THE NEW YORK BALL CLUB FOR THE LEAGUE CHAMPIONSHIP.

April 28, 29,	with Philadelphia,	June 9, 10, 11,	with Washington,	Aug. 22, 23,	with Pittsburg,
May 5, 6, 7,	" Boston,	" 13, 14, 15,	" Philadelphia,	" 25, 26, 27,	" Chicago,
" 9, 10, 11,	" Washington,	July 7, 8, 9,	" Detroit,	" 29, 30, 31,	" Indianapolis,
" 14,	" Philadelphia,	" 11, 12, 13,	" Pittsburg,	Sept. 1, 2, 3,	" Detroit,
" 16, 17, 18,	" Indianapolis,	" 15, 16, 18,	" Chicago.	" 5, 6, 7,	" Washington,
" 20, 21, 23, 24,	" Pittsburg,	" 19, 20, 21,	" Indianapolis,	" 26, 27, 28,	" Boston,
Decoration Day " 30 A.M. & P.M., 31.	" Detroit, Chicago.	" 23, 25, 26,	" Boston,	Oct. 5, 6. 8.	" Philadelphia

Professional Baseball　In 1887, the Polo Grounds were the home of the New York professional team shown here. The club went on to become the New York Giants of the National League, which played in this Bronx stadium until 1957. The team then became the San Francisco Giants. Notice the very deep left field and shallow right field — consequences of the park having been originally designed for polo. To judge from this picture, the male and female fans are decidedly middle- and upper class.

of New York was known as "lung block" because of the high incidence of tuberculosis. Typhoid, diphtheria, and cholera also plagued the lower classes. Infant mortality rates were high. In 1900 as many as 60 percent of the babies born in one Chicago district did not survive

their first year. Everywhere, poor diets debilitated slum dwellers. In 1906 social reformer Upton Sinclair found that for the poor living near Chicago's stockyards, a typical grocery list included "pale-blue milk . . . watered and doctored with formaldehyde," canned peas "colored with copper salts, and their fruit jams with aniline dyes." Heavy alcohol consumption among the lower classes further weakened their resistance to fatigue and disease. Alcohol, one of the few "cheap" means of escape from the stresses and despair of poverty, also contributed to the violence that exacted a heavy toll in slum districts. Inexperience with urban living, crime, social dislocation, and ignorance about public health all added to the misery and death tolls.

Housing and health problems demanded public response. New York City led the way, establishing a municipal health authority (1866) and passing the first significant building code for tenements (1879), which specified minimum requirements for light and air for every room. The code inspired the so-called dumbbell tenement, designed as a reform measure by architect James E. Ware. The tenement, consisting of 24 to 32 four-room apartments, was shaped like a weightlifter's dumbbell with an indentation at each side of the building to create an airshaft of five feet between abutted buildings. Such airshafts in fact let in little air or light and often became fire hazards and trash silos.

Tenement codes never addressed the need for a thorough overhaul of inner-city urban housing. The codes covered only new construction. Reformers and public officials alike refused to challenge the private property rights of landlords, either by imposing safety and building codes on existing structures or by underwriting public housing of any kind. Further impeding housing reform were the distance and dissociation of the middle and upper classes from the working-class areas. In popular parlance, *tenement* had become a pejorative term, its residents likened to the vermin and diseases that flourished in the buildings. Real housing

reform awaited an awakened social conscience and the Progressive movement (see Chapter 23).

More immediately successful in alleviating urban ills were practical improvements that benefited business and middle-class residents. Wherever a genuine public interest was recognized, support for improvement was possible. By the end of the nineteenth century, cities were paving thoroughfares (first with cobblestones and then with the quieter asphalt), lighting streets (first with gas, then with electric arc lighting, and eventually with Edison's incandescent lamps), and planting trees along public boulevards. Such improvements made cities safer and more attractive places to do business, but they rarely extended to poor sections.

In the area of public health, the middle class did come to recognize a common interest with the immigrant and working-class inhabitants of the slums. City dwellers of all classes sickened on the filth and foul odors of the city. In Baltimore no one could escape the suffocating stench of the Back Basin, into which flowed the city's sewers. Baltimore journalist H. L. Mencken remembered that his native city smelled "like a billion polecats" during the summer. In Cleveland the combined noxious fumes from outdoor privies, street offal, and the Cuyahoga River, which ran as "an open sewer through the center of the city," so offended the mayor that he called for public action in the 1880s. Microbes

---

✳ IN THEIR OWN WORDS

***Our Country,* 1885**

In his immensely influential book, Our Country, *Congregationalist minister Josiah Strong warned that the concentrated power of bosses, the "saloon," the Catholic church, and the rich threatened democracy and Christian order. His mix of nativism, anti-Catholicism, and progressivism underscored much early middle-class social consciousness and social conscience in addressing the problems of the city.*

The city is the nerve center of our civilization. It is also the storm center. The fact, therefore, that it is growing much more rapidly than the whole population is full of significance. . . .

The city has become a serious menace to our civilization. . . . Because our cities are so

largely foreign, Romanism finds in them its chief strength.

For the same reason the saloon, together with the intemperance and the liquor power which it represents, is multiplied in the city. . . .

The rich are richer, and the poor are poorer, in the city than elsewhere; and as a rule, the greater the city, the greater are the riches of the rich and the poverty of the poor. Not only does the proportion of the poor increase with the growth of the city, but their condition becomes more wretched. . . .

Socialism centers in the city, and the materials of its growth are multiplied with the growth of the city. Here is heaped the social dynamite; her roughs, gamblers, thieves, robbers, lawless and desperate

men of all sorts, congregate; men who are ready on any pretext to raise riots for the purpose of destruction and plunder; here gather foreigners and wage-workers who are especially susceptible to social arguments; here skepticism and irreligion abound; here inequality is the greatest and most obvious, and the contrast between opulence and penury the most striking; here suffering is the sorest. As the greatest wickedness in the world is to be found not among the cannibals of some far-off coast, but in Christian lands where the light of truth is diffused and rejected, so the utmost depth of wretchedness exists not among savages who have very few wants, but in great cities, where, in the presence of plenty and of every luxury, men starve.

did not respect class lines. Unsanitary water systems carried disease into middle- and upper-class homes alike. By the 1890s doctors had widely accepted the germ theory of disease, and the general public was ready to support water-filtration systems, sewage treatment plants, and public-health inspection and quarantine. City health boards and newspapers advocated proper personal hygiene and diet, milk and meat inspection, and improved health care.

THE STRUGGLE FOR CONTROL OF THE CITY

Cities were unable to respond to many urban problems because decentralized, fragmented political power compounded the ethnic and class divisions. During the nineteenth century city government was in disarray. Still fearful of strong executives, a democratically inclined people instead enlarged city councils and parceled out government responsibilities on an ad hoc basis to special independent boards. State legislatures further cramped city governments by refusing them home-rule charters, which would have given municipalities more autonomy, and by limiting their taxing and borrowing powers. Yet the burgeoning urban populations needed schools, police and fire protection, water, and paved streets. The city had become, as *Harper's Weekly* complained about New York as early as 1857, "a huge semi-barbarous metropolis . . . not governed at all." The power vacuum at the center of city government almost invited strong men to seize power through organization, and out of the confusion emerged urban boss politics, or the city "machine."

Arrayed against the machine would be shifting alliances of middle-class reformers, civil engineers, and city planners eager to improve city government and attack social ills. Much like the Mugwumps campaigning for political reform at the national level (see Chapter 20), the reformers lacked staying power during the 1870s and 1880s. At the local level they failed to appreciate the sources of the machine's support among the immigrants and poor, instead spouting pious sermons about the need for temperance, fiscal economy, and civil-service reform. Still, by the end of the century new power blocs were emerging that challenged the hegemony of machine politics by promising order and efficiency in city services and compassion and relief to the urban poor. Businessmen who depended on municipal services pressed for centralized management and professional-

ism at city hall. Thus, for example, insurance underwriters demanded professionally run fire departments free of the ethnic tribalism and patronage that had characterized so many of them during the nineteenth century.

To meet citywide demands for water, sewage treatment, trash collection, and public health inspection, city governments increasingly depended on technical experts, whose expertise insulated them somewhat from the vicissitudes of local politics and whose loyalties anyway were to their professions rather than to particular ethnic or political interests. Civil engineers viewed the city in panoramic terms, understanding that the issues involved in paving roads, building bridges, and providing water required metropolitan cooperation. They allied with city planners, a profession then in its infancy, in calling for comprehensive plans for metropolitan development. Engineers and planners profited from the late nineteenth-century American emphasis on efficiency (see Chapter 18), and in their insistence on bringing expert bureaucrats into city administration, they won support from moral reformers. Such reformers also sought structural changes in city governance that would allow for an invigorated central administration to oversee the social and physical renovation of the whole city. The creation of metropolitan water and sewer districts in several cities and the construction of massive city halls in numerous cities during the late nineteenth century seemed to herald the triumph of those wanting municipal responsibility and power to emanate from the center. But the "service city" run by professional bureaucrats was more hope than reality before the Progressive movement of the early twentieth century (see Chapter 23). Most citizens continued to trust their local ward leader or alderman and remained reluctant to impart too much authority to distant managers and executives. Small vendors worried more about the disposition of sidewalk space and peddlers' licenses than about sweeping plans for broad boulevards and city plazas. Even as the administration of city services was coming into the hands of engineers and bureaucrats, the politics and power of the city remained balkanized. While the new urban planners saw the new city halls as signals of their own rising fortunes, savvy "machine" politicians were using them as sources of jobs, payoffs, and patronage to maintain their grip on city government as a whole.

❧ City Machine Politics

Most city machines were loosely knit coalitions organized on the ward level, though by the twentieth cen-

"Ingratitude in Politics," 1905

Tammany Hall district leader George Washington Plunkitt was unusual in revealing the art of politics in a candid, public way in a series of interviews with journalist William Riordan. In this excerpt he sums up the principal rule of the kind of personal politics of reciprocity that ruled boss-run cities everywhere.

"The politicians who make a lastin' success in politics are the men who are always loyal to their friends — even up to the gate of State prison, if necessary; men who keep their promises and never lie. . . .

"The question has been asked: is a politician ever justified in goin' back on his district leader? I answer: 'No; as long as the leader hustles around and gets all the jobs possible for his constituents.' When the voters elect a man leader, they make a sort of contract with him. They say, although it ain't written out: 'We've put you here to look out for our interests. You want to see that this district gets all the jobs that's comin' to it. Be faithful to us, and we'll be faithful to you.'

"The district leader promises and that makes a solemn contract. If he lives up to it — spends most of his time chasin' after places in the departments, picks up jobs from railroads and contractors for his followers, and shows himself in all ways a true statesman — then his followers are bound in honor to uphold him, just as they're bound to uphold the Constitution of the United States. But if he only looks after his own interests or shows no talent for scenting out jobs or ain't got the nerve to demand and get his share of the good things that are goin', his followers may be absolved from their allegiance and they may up and swat him without bein' put down as political ingrates."

tury several machines had evolved into well-integrated political structures. The machines nominated candidates and got out the vote. Their power rested on a style of personal politics and social services that delivered jobs and assistance to inner-city neighborhoods in exchange for ballots. The bosses converted the ballots into cash by selling licenses and franchises, by taking kickbacks from contractors on public works projects, and by getting payoffs to ignore gambling, prostitution, and illegal drinking. City machines arose and prospered because immigration was creating a vast new electorate, unfamiliar with democratic processes and ripe for exploitation, while the physical growth of the cities was generating abundant opportunities for graft.

The bosses thought of politics in terms of service rather than issues. They understood that the immigrant and poor masses had little interest in national issues like imperialism, free silver, or civil-service reform. The people's needs were more basic. The machine's philosophy was simply stated by Martin Lomasney, boss of Boston's South End: "I think that there's got to be in every ward a guy that any bloke can come to — no matter what he's done — and get help . . . none of your law and justice, but help."

The successful ward boss was visible and available. Observed George Washington Plunkitt of New York's Tammany Hall (the city's dominant Democratic political organization), politics was the boss's occupation "every day and night in the year." His headquarters bore the inscription "Never closed." Plunkitt's "office" was a bootblack stand in the county courthouse off Foley Square; Tammany's Charles Francis Murphy's, a lamppost on Second Avenue; Chicago's John Coughlin's, a bathhouse in the city's levee district.

The boss was ready at hand to dispense aid to victims of a fire (fires were "great vote-getters," said one boss), distribute food baskets and coal to the needy, plead with authorities for an immigrant who broke some minor law, and, above all, find work for men on the docks, on the streets, or with one of the many public and private projects in the expanding city. The bosses attended baptisms, weddings, and funerals and presented gifts on special occasions (one New York boss gave a pair of shoes to each newborn child in his district). In clubhouses and especially saloons, they socialized and kept abreast of local gossip. The bosses thus cultivated support by remaining close to their constituents. "Study human nature and act accordingly," counseled Plunkitt. They knew the everyday needs of poor people and worked to fill those needs at a time when government performed few public services, workers had no workmen's compensation despite high on-the-job injury rates, and an indifferent, even hostile, middle class showed little inclination to tax itself to increase relief.

In addition to providing charity and employment, bosses courted voters by playing to their vanities and aspirations. Machines sponsored glee clubs for those of a musical bent, boxing and baseball for athletic boys, and a host of amusements for everyone. "Big Tim" Sullivan of New York's Lower East Side arranged summer ferry cruises, picnics in the park, clambakes, and fireworks displays to lift the spirits of people otherwise burdened with long hours of toil and a dreary tenement environment. The bosses also made politics itself entertaining. They put on rousing Fourth of July celebrations, parades, and torchlight processions and dressed up party workers and supporters with campaign buttons, sashes, feathers, handkerchiefs, and hats.

Boss politics thrived in a male working-class culture of hard drink and personal honor. The corner saloon served as headquarters for many ward bosses. Large brewers owned most saloons and by offering free lunches and occasional free drinks encouraged the heavy drinking that went on there, but it was the bosses who capitalized on the relationship between drink and camaraderie to make the saloon synonymous with the machine. Boss-run saloons were places where workingmen could get checks cashed, deposit and borrow money, and leave and pick up messages. More so, they were places where men could gamble and strut. Prodigious feats of drinking, betting on prizefights, and verbal sparring showed one's toughness and prowess. Bosses encouraged such behavior by selling liquor licenses generously, lobbying against liquor-control bills in state legislatures, and tolerating, indeed profiting from, the vices such as gambling and prostitution that drew men to saloons. To the working classes, bosses were akin to John L. Sullivan, the bare-knuckled heavyweight champ, whom they admired for his strength and willingness to take on all comers. In the masculine world of barrooms, brothels, and ballot boxes, deed counted more than character, action more than thought, and victory more than anything else. Bosses understood all that and acted accordingly.

Urban politics offered a social ladder for ambitious youth. The rags-to-riches stories of the bosses themselves made politics an inviting profession. Richard Croker was an Irish immigrant who rose from the slums of Lower Manhattan, through the Fourth Avenue Tunnel Gang, to head Tammany Hall, and George B. Cox was a child of British immigrants who worked his way from newsboy to runner for gamblers to saloonkeeper before heading the Republican machine in Cincinnati. Second-generation immigrants raised on an American schoolbook diet of upward mobility were especially attracted to machine politics. The machine offered prestige and the opportunity to serve, with the prospect of making money besides.

The most colorful, best-known bosses were Irish. The Irish claimed that political leadership came naturally to them. The success of the Irish, in fact, largely derived from their familiarity with the English language and political system, their tendency to move less than other immigrants, and their early mastery of the ecclesiastical labyrinths of the Catholic church, the first primer in bureaucracy in the American city. Irish bosses tended to favor other Irish in the organization, and virtually all machines excluded blacks, but otherwise the machine was open to anyone who could deliver votes. In fact, bosses came from varied backgrounds — for example, the Episcopalian Ferdinand Latrobe of Baltimore, the Jewish Abe Reuff of San Francisco, and the Jewish-born Catholic convert Martin Behrman of New Orleans — and both political parties.

City bosses styled themselves as city builders. In deflecting criticism about the graft, bribery, and thievery of their machines, bosses pointed to the new streets, transit lines, utilities, docks, bridges, parks, zoos, city halls, and other public works built by machine patronage. Machines, the bosses said, were good for business. By imposing some order on structurally decentralized municipal governments, the machines did aid those businesses dependent on government decisionmaking, but they received kickbacks and other payoffs in return and drove up the cost of the improvements to customers and taxpayers. Real-estate developers, builders, and transit companies merged their interests with those of city machines just as the saloonkeepers, gamblers, and prostitutes did. Only the saloons served a "free" lunch, however.

Modern urban sports were part of the machine's legacy. Organized sports of all kinds benefited from boss-run police departments that winked at violations of Sunday blue laws, and horse racing and boxing prospered wherever bosses allowed the illegal gambling and liquor sales that made those sports profitable. Baseball had an especially intimate relationship with the machine. In addition to sponsoring amateur and professional baseball teams (the Giants started in New York as a Tammany club), machines controlled the streetcar lines to the new urban ballparks. As investors in streetcar companies and owners of baseball teams, the bosses cashed in on the game's enormous popularity. Grateful fans did not forget them on election day.

The bosses' protestations of good will and public improvements notwithstanding, the machine was not good for the city. Most bosses were thieves. The most notorious was Tammany's William Marcy Tweed, who with his henchmen in the Tweed Ring stole millions of dollars between 1869 and 1871. Tweed had a yacht, a mistress, a Fifth Avenue mansion, and a huge appetite for boodle. The excesses of bribery and display made the bald, big-bellied Tweed an easy caricature for cartoonist Thomas Nast, who satirized him relentlessly in *Harper's Weekly.* After Tweed went to jail, bosses were less ostentatious, though no less greedy. The popularity of the bosses disguised their selfishness. Machine politics lowered the tone of civic life and saddled cities with large debts and habits of unpunished crime and vice. Machine politics did not lift the masses from poverty. Only rarely did nineteenth-century bosses sponsor reform legislation to improve the lives of their constituents or to safeguard them at work. They saw no profit in ending dependence.

Boss rule fit the age. In the laissez-faire world of individualism, bosses were little different from businessmen who pursued self-interest over public welfare. Many businessmen cooperated with the bosses to gain favors, franchises, and freedom from regulation. Reformers, such as anti-saloon and civil-service advocates, who attacked the boss system for its immorality failed to understand that boss rule was deeply rooted in the conditions and attitudes of the day. Instead, patricians shunned city politics because, as Theodore Roosevelt's socialite friends scornfully observed when he proposed cleaning up New York City, "the organizations were not controlled by 'gentlemen.'" The middle and upper classes barricaded themselves behind shrubs and iron fences, ignoring the suffering of the urban masses. With everyone out for themselves, the city cried out for reform.

AWAKENING SOCIAL CONSCIENCE

The miseries and corruption of city life eventually stirred the middle-class social conscience to action. Since mid-century, middle-class church leaders, reformers, and concerned citizens had decried the urban ills around them and tried to rally support for good government and doing good. However much the middle class was becoming secularized by urban culture and enamored of individualism, many Protestants still retained a sense of civic responsibility and charity. In the post–Civil War era, Protestants expanded their earlier relief efforts and launched new ones. Enthusiasm and organization were the keywords of their voluntarism, and personal salvation and moral uplift the goals.

❧ *Early Efforts at Reform*

Much of the early postwar reform effort blamed the victims for their suffering. In medical books and sermons,

disease was viewed as a divine judgment and poverty as a sin. According to the moral calculus of the Reverend Henry Ward Beecher, as explained to his suburban Brooklyn congregation during the labor strikes of 1877, a man who did not smoke or drink beer could support a wife and five children on a dollar a day, and a man who could not live on bread and water alone "is not fit to live." Frugal people, he added, "can scarcely help accumulating" no matter how miserable their condition.

Nativism colored the middle-class response. Protestant ministers, among others, fulminated against the culture and social habits of the immigrants, who danced, drank, and did not keep the Sabbath. In his best-selling book, *Our Country; Its Possible Future and Its Present Crisis* (1885), the popular Congregationalist minister Josiah Strong argued that the city was "a menace to society," in large part because it was being overrun by immigrants and Catholicism. Strong urged Protestant churches to stand together against "the elements of anarchy and destruction." Unwilling to concede his Protestant "civilization" to the "barbarism" of religious pluralism, he prescribed a hardy regimen of moral improvement, temperance, and immigration restriction. Most of all, he urged evangelism: "Christianize the immigrant, and he will be easily Americanized."

The humanitarians' hostility toward, and ignorance of, immigrant and working-class culture led to missionary work and an emphasis on "Americanization," personal redemption, individual effort, and self-control rather than social change. The thrust was ameliorative and conservative rather than radical. Many nineteenth-century urban reformers shared a faith in laissez-faire economics that further made them unwilling to attack poverty and social ills on a broad front. The suburbanization of Protestantism compounded the difficulties by cutting off many church members from personal contact with the suffering in the city and by absorbing them in church building and Bible study in their own areas. More than one suburban pastor worried that such isolation led to "spiritual destitution" and urged his flock to look to the city as a field "for the exercise of Christian energy." Still, by focusing on their public responsibility, the middle-class churchmen and reformers moved toward an ethic of community cohesion and helped lay the groundwork for the Progressive era (see Chapter 23).

TEMPERANCE

The Protestant reform impulse poured new energy into the temperance movement. Middle-class Protestants and some Catholics believed that America's urban ills would be solved by closing down the saloons. Good-government reformers (sometimes derisively tagged by their enemies as the "goo-goos") attacked the saloon because it was the city machine's base of operations. Moral reformers hated it because it fostered alcoholism, gambling, prostitution, and, added the Anti-Saloon League, because it dulled religious consciousness and prevented personal salvation. Native-born Protestant women took the lead in post–Civil War temperance reform, which was especially relevant to women's domestic sphere. Strong drink often led not only to poverty, but also to domestic violence and broken homes. Church women founded the Woman's Christian Temperance Union (WCTU) in 1873 to "preserve the individuality, the privacy, and sanctity of the home." Led by Frances Willard, a devout Methodist who served as its president from 1879 until her death in 1898, the WCTU grew to be the largest women's organization in the nation and expanded its concerns from temperance to women's education, support of labor unions, social-welfare reform, and women's suffrage. (Willard rallied women to support suffrage by calling for "the ballot for Home Protection.") Drying up the city demanded that women get involved in politics to press for passage and enforcement of licensing and closing laws for saloons. Appeals to conscience and self-discipline were not enough to break demon rum's grip on the immigrant and working classes. Temperance required coercion, and coercion required getting control of government.

PUBLIC SCHOOLS

The Protestant establishment continued to run the public schools as an agency to instill social order and middle-class values. In addition to teaching such basic English-language skills as reading and writing, the public school encouraged cultural assimilation. By the late nineteenth century, schools regularly included patriotic programs and opened the day with the Protestant version of the Lord's Prayer, salutes to Old Glory, and pledges of allegiance to the United States. Urban school systems reached downward through the age ranks, adding kindergartens, in the words of one writer, "to catch the little Russian, the little Italian, the little German, Pole, Syrian, and the rest and begin to make good American citizens of them." The schools reached upward with vocational and shop training to make older students good American workers. Supervised play in playgrounds and on athletic teams was intended to teach children to respect rules and order. In

the classroom middle-class Protestant values reigned in the continued use of scriptural and denominational texts and in the curriculum's emphasis on punctuality, cleanliness, industry, thrift, temperance, and respect for authority. The public school preached conformity and self-discipline as the means of overcoming urban poverty. Wanting to impose such discipline on immigrant and working-class youths, who ordinarily attended school haphazardly and left formal education by age thirteen for full-time work, urban school systems in the early twentieth century increasingly turned to truancy laws to corral as many children as possible.

SUNDAY SCHOOLS AND CHILDREN'S AID

Outside the public school, most Protestants looked to the Sunday school as their principal mission to the "unchurched" and the way to promote moral improvement in society. The Sunday school underwent profound change after the Civil War, moving from an emphasis on religious conversion to one of Christian nurture and spiritual growth, but evangelism always was central to its mission. By the 1880s instruction was regularized so that a uniform lesson could be taught to people of various backgrounds. Sunday school leaders introduced "decision days" and "rally days" to galvanize the faithful and win new souls to Christ. Both adults and children went to Sunday schools, forging a more united Protestant front and an agency of widespread but organized evangelical outreach.

Much of the middle-class urban reform effort was directed toward the young. It was widely believed that families could be reached through their children and that young people were more receptive to evangelism and moral improvement. In several cities, Protestant reformers established charitable societies to find useful work for street orphans and transient youths, and also to visit their parents to press on them the need for temperance and discipline. Charles Loring Brace's New York Children's Aid Society, founded in 1853, provided a model copied in other cities. Brace sought to remove waifs and "street arabs" from the "dangerous classes" and from the "snow and mud of the street." To foster self-help among the poor children, the society ran workshops and reading rooms and also arranged employment and foster care in the Midwest, away from the city's corrupting environment.

THE YMCA AND YWCA

Other evangelical organizations established urban missions. A major effort at moral suasion was undertaken

The Origins of Basketball   In this photograph from 1891, James Naismith, who invented the game, sits wearing a suit (as many basketball coaches still do) at the center of his team at Springfield College in Massachusetts. The basket into which shots were made was originally just that — a peach basket.

by the Young Men's Christian Association (YMCA) and Young Women's Christian Association (YWCA). Imported from England at mid-century, the Ys sought to save urban youth by building the whole person — "physical, mental, social, and spiritual." The YMCA particularly espoused a "muscular Christianity" that respected the body as a temple of God. To abuse the body with alcohol or bad social habits was to blaspheme God. Strong bodies could go forth to spread the gospel. The YMCAs built gymnasiums, dormitories, reading rooms, and night schools across the urban United States to fend off the debilitating effects of urban life with wholesome recreational and educational opportunities. By 1900 the nation had more than 1,500 YMCAs with a quarter-million members. Although less

widespread, Young Men's Hebrew Associations built similar facilities to serve Jewish youth.

PROTESTANT AND CATHOLIC URBAN MINISTRY

Saving the poor from physical and moral destitution required organization and a willingness to go directly into the slum districts. Various holiness and pentecostal groups established rescue missions in the cities, but such efforts were uncoordinated. In the East London slums, Methodist "General" William Booth began a mission that became the Salvation Army in 1878; it dispatched forces to America in 1880. Its "slum brigades" of uniformed volunteers, women prominent among them as "soldiers" and "officers," marched into skid rows and tenement neighborhoods to evangelize, using brass bands and fervent preaching to command attention. By the 1890s the Army's leadership mounted a more systematic assault on poverty and sin. Under its "social scheme," the Army opened soup kitchens, shelters for prostitutes and the homeless, second-hand stores, dispensaries, and job-training schools and camps. In addition, it provided temporary employment for the jobless. The Army's principal purpose remained evangelism, however, and its message was the old refrain of temperance, personal salvation, and moral uplift.

Urban revivalists likewise hammered away at intemperance, immorality, and lapses from Christianity. From mid-century on, Catholic "revivalists," who visited urban parishes to conduct "missions," urged Catholics to trade indifference for devotion, alcohol for the altar, and sin for sacraments. Many more Protestant evangelists trod the sawdust trail of revivalism. The most famous and successful was Dwight Moody, a Massachusetts-born former shoe salesman of immense size (he weighed 300 pounds) and heart. Teamed with chorister Ira David Sankey, Moody launched a revival in Great Britain (1873-1875) that reached an estimated 3 to 4 million souls. He then brought the campaign to America, preaching his simple optimism that individual conversion would solve social problems. Moody used a homey storytelling style that effected thousands of conversions as he and Sankey carried their crusades across the continent. Because the world was "a wrecked vessel" in Moody's eyes, he had only one charge from God: "save all you can." Urban America shook with revivals in the 1870s and 1880s. So energized, Moody and other evangelists established schools, such as Moody Bible Institute (1889) in Chicago, to train lay people to expand the urban ministry.

CHALLENGES AND FAILURE

Although Protestant church membership doubled between 1880 and 1900, the revivalists failed to convert or reform urban America. Protestants counted few conversions among the immigrants or their children. This was not for lack of effort. Tract societies, Sunday schools, and urban revivalists adapted their message to try to appeal to immigrants, and Christian businessmen funded urban ministries and outreach among the foreign-born. Fearing immigrant radicalism and wanting to do good among the poor, Chicago meatpacker Joseph F. Armour established the Armour Mission in 1886. Similarly, John Wanamaker set up Presbyterian churches in working-class areas of Philadelphia. But such individual acts did not meet the needs of either relief or reformation. Even Moody once despaired, after a discouraging response in New York, that the immigrant city was no place for his ministry. The Protestant revivalists and reformers failed to see the world from

the perspective of the immigrants and the poor, many of whom resented the middle-class intrusions into their lives and most of whom were too preoccupied with trying to survive to listen to preachments on temperance, keeping the Sabbath, and getting right with the Protestant God. Old-time religion alone could not save the cities.

The depth and tenacity of urban poverty troubled even the most hardened old-school moralist. By the 1890s urban problems were obvious to anyone who would but see. In 1890 the Danish-born journalist Jacob Riis, an active churchman, awakened the public conscience with his book *How the Other Half Lives*, a powerful indictment of tenement conditions. Riis pioneered the use of photography to promote reform. Having taught himself how to use the camera, he prowled the alleys and cellars of New York's Lower East Side tenement district to record on film, and in angry prose, the horrors and suffering he saw. He made his photographs into lantern slides and gave a series of illustrated lectures, not unlike revival meetings, where he exposed wrongs and called upon his middle-class audiences to make things right. The combination of photographs and words became a powerful weapon in the reform arsenal during the Progressive era. By bringing the viewer into the tenements, the pictures and words of Riis and other moralists moved the middle-class conscience to action. So, too, did reminders of Christian duty and brotherhood. In his enormously popular novel *In His Steps* (1896), Charles M. Sheldon, a Congregationalist minister in Topeka, Kansas, asked readers to consider only one question when they faced the social problems of slum life: "What would Jesus do?"

❧ The Social Gospel

Instead of seeing sin and poverty as the result of personal guilt, some Protestant pastors and thinkers blamed societal causes for the urban problems of their day. They began to assail middle-class Protestants for their complacency and the rich for their abuses of the working classes. They rejected the moral-purity approach of such organizations as the Anti-Saloon League that said excessive drinking was the cause of poverty, and instead viewed drinking as endemic to desperate, hopeless slum conditions. The problem was not the drinker, who needed help, but the sweatshop operators and "slumlords" who profited from keeping the poor down.

As early as the 1870s a few Protestant clergymen had begun to call for an "applied Christianity." The Christian, in other words, must change society, not just seek personal salvation. A reformed environment was necessary to create a moral society. To attend to the needy, Christians should stay in the city and make the church the community center in which a new sense of fellowship through service might grow.

An early example of such thinking was the work of William S. Rainsford, who transformed his St. George's Episcopal Church on New York's Lower East Side into a

Bandits' Roost   Jacob Riis first photographed Bandits' Roost on New York's Lower East Side in 1888 and later asked, "What sort of an answer, think you, would come from these tenements to the question, 'Is life worth living?'"

school for industrial training, a boys' club, and a relief station. Rainsford helped organize the interdenominational Institutional Church League, which spread nationwide the gospel of social activism, popularly known as the "social gospel." The league ran dispensaries for food and clothing, youth clubs, employment services, home economics classes, savings banks, and colleges.

"Hull-House," 1898

Florence Kelley, daughter of pro-labor Pennsylvania congressman William "Pig Iron" Kelley, moved to Hull House in 1891, where she learned to appreciate "charity work" as an instrument for social action. Here she describes the importance of advocates of social action living with and among the people to understand their needs and speak for them.

The question is often asked whether all that the House undertakes could not be accomplished without the wear and tear of living on the spot. The answer that it could not, grows more assured as time goes on. You must suffer from the dirty streets, the universal ugliness, the lack of oxygen in the air you daily breathe, the endless struggle with soot and dust and insufficient water supply, the hanging from a strap of the overcrowded street car at the end of your day's work: you must send your children to the nearest wretchedly crowded school, and see them suffer the consequences, if you are to speak as one having authority and not as the scribes in these matters of the common, daily life and experience....

Nowhere is the individual so left to himself as in the cosmopolite medley of a great working class district in an American city; and nowhere does the devil clutch more voraciously after the hindmost....

The isolation, the apathy, the lack of initiative, the social downdraft, as it has been well called, that unsocialize a great industrial neighborhood, cannot be replaced with light and life by any spasmodic effort. Only when the whole community persistently does its part can the slum be outgrown and transformed, as the ugly stages of the hobbledehoy are outgrown and left behind in growing manhood; while for arousing the whole community to do its part, surely the resident group contributes a stimulus limited in value only by the interpretative skill and wisdom of the residents.

More widely influential was Washington Gladden. First in Springfield, Massachusetts, and then, from 1882 to 1914, as pastor of the First Congregational Church in Columbus, Ohio, Gladden moved from providing social services to criticizing the laissez-faire economic system that tolerated injustice and fostered greed. Churches, Gladden insisted, must do more than try to close saloons and attack corruption; they must embrace the poor and challenge unfettered capitalism itself.

Walter Rauschenbusch, a German-American Baptist whose social conscience was awakened during his pastorate near New York's Hell's Kitchen slum, gave theological substance to the social gospel movement. Although influenced by Henry George and Edward Bellamy and theological liberalism (see Chapter 20), Rauschenbusch grounded the social gospel in the tradition of the Old Testament prophets, Jesus' ethical teachings, and millennial expectations of a revived "kingdom of God." Rauschenbusch called for nothing less than "the Christian transfiguration of the social order."

Such thought led the social gospel in two directions. One was toward an interdenominational and international outreach, which took form in 1908 in the Social Creed of the Federal Council of Churches. The other was toward a growing reliance on politics as an instrument of social change. The social gospel ministers believed there were Christian solutions for social problems, but they discovered that eliminating crowded and unsafe tenements, poverty, crime, and disease all required the effective mobilization of public resources. They sought to purge government of machine politics, believing that only then could it protect the masses with "social legislation" abolishing child labor, establishing minimum safety conditions at work, writing and enforcing tenement codes, and recognizing labor unions.

The social gospel movement represented a minority position in Protestantism, and it had little influence on Catholicism or Judaism. Most Protestants still believed that the church should concern itself with individual salvation, and many middle- and upper-class Protestants grew uncomfortable with the social gospel's seeming drift toward Christian socialism. But its reform impulse gave Christian purpose to later reform and was a means whereby Protestants tried to reclaim moral leadership in an increasingly worldly and religiously plural urban America.

Theological conservatism discouraged Catholics from social activism until late in the century. Individual Catholic priests lobbied for labor reforms and passage of social legislation, and Cardinal James Gibbons of Baltimore defended the Knights of Labor as a legitimate organization. (The Vatican, however, condemned the Knights as a "secret society.") At the same time, the church's parish structure and religious orders of nurses and teachers helped make traditional forms of charity and neighborhood action responsive to local needs. But many bishops clamped down on activist clergymen. In New York a popular priest, Father Edward McGlynn, was excommunicated in 1887 for supporting "socialist"

Henry George's bid for mayor against a Tammany Hall candidate friendly with the archbishop.

After Pope Leo XIII issued his liberating encyclical *Rerum Novarum* ("Concerning the New Conscience") in 1891, the Catholic church assumed a more tolerant stance toward social causes. While strongly condemning socialism, the pope nonetheless criticized the "greed of unchecked capitalism." He called for justice toward organized labor and for both church and government to care for the poor. In 1893 Rome lifted the excommunication of Father McGlynn, and by 1900 Catholic periodicals were publishing denunciations of great wealth and urging "a new kind of conscience." Into the twentieth century, however, the church's reform effort remained hobbled by limited resources (Protestants "had the wealth, we had the poor," observed one Catholic reformer), internal struggles over Americanization, and the inbred conservatism of the American church hierarchy.

❧ The Settlement House

The settlement house marked a bold experiment in urban reform. The idea was borrowed from London's Toynbee Hall, a residence in the London slums where young intellectuals lived and worked to bring education and the arts to the poor. After visiting Toynbee Hall, several young Americans organized similar projects in the United States. Important settlement houses were started by Stanton Coit, Vida Scudder, and Lillian Wald in New York, Robert A. Woods in Boston, and Graham Taylor in Chicago. By the turn of the century more than 100 settlement houses were operating in America; ten years later the number had grown to more than 400. The settlement idea appealed strongly to Protestants influenced by the social gospel, but by 1900 Catholics and Jews had established their own settlement houses in New York, Los Angeles, and elsewhere.

The most famous and influential settlement house was Chicago's Hull House (1889), an old mansion on South Halsted Street, amid sweatshops and crowded run-down housing. Hull House was the work of Jane Addams and Ellen Gates Starr, who embodied the settlement-house movement. They were among the first generation of college-educated women who left school imbued with a missionary spirit and eager to apply to real problems the new social sciences they had learned in college. Initially, they assumed a patronizing attitude toward their subjects. They wanted to promote social harmony and cooperation by bringing small-town middle-class values to the city's immigrant working class; the goal was to bridge the gap between the classes by making the poor into self-reliant individuals. Hull House and the other settlements set up home economics classes to teach budgeting, nutrition, and preparation of American foods; sponsored civics classes to teach about American democracy; ran kindergartens, nurseries, and recreational programs to inculcate orderliness in young charges; and preached self-discipline to all. The very look of the settlement house was intended to encourage middle-class propriety. Flower boxes outside and reading chairs and books and magazines casually spread on tables inside all suggested the comforts of middle-class domesticity.

The settlement-house movement had a largely Protestant social gospel impulse, despite the many Jewish settlement-house workers in New York. Most settlement-house workers belonged to a church. But Addams and others came to realize that the Protestant cast of the settlement house jeopardized its mission in the predominantly Catholic and Jewish immigrant neighborhoods. Without abandoning their personal Christian beliefs, settlement-house leaders cut the houses' formal ties to Protestant denominations and moved toward a broader program of social reform. In response. the home mission boards of the denominations set up their own neighborhood houses, which combined the educational and recreational programs of the settlements with religious services, Sunday schools, and other forms of evangelization.

Soon, the young, well-educated settlement-house workers discovered that they themselves had much to learn from the immigrants. Recognizing the value of ethnic culture in preserving family unity, Hull House opened a labor museum where immigrants could practice and show their Old World craft skills and thereby gain a sense of self-worth and respect from their children. Addams wanted "our foreigners" to "project a little of the historic and romantic into the prosaic quarters of our American cities." The settlement house, wrote Addams, was rooted in the principle of community. Its purpose was to establish a sense of neighborhood among different classes. Indeed, Addams maintained an open-door policy at Hull House. Neighborhood residents could come and go as they pleased. Addams made getting to know the Italians, the Germans, and the Russian and Polish Jews of her district a top priority. She also encouraged the resident settlement-house workers to get out to know the neighborhood.

The settlement, Addams insisted, should be an organism spreading its influence outward. Hull House grew from one building to several, including a dormitory for single women, a medical dispensary, and a theater. More important, it became a command center for reshaping the city. After viewing the problems of poverty firsthand, settlement-house workers became agents for reform. The problems of slum life so crushed the poor that many workers found the art shows, classes in English, and amateur concerts at Hull House irrelevant. Addams and other settlement-house leaders therefore became involved in politics and began to work for a complete overhaul of the American city. At Hull House Addams sponsored debates on public education, machine politics, and workers' rights. She demanded enforcement of sanitation regulations, better police protection, and improved schooling. On one occasion, she got herself appointed garbage inspector to ensure that the trash in her ward would be picked up.

The settlement house became a laboratory and school for social action. At Hull House, for example, Julia Lathrop learned the techniques of lobbying for juvenile courts and health care for children that later made her so effective as a member of the Illinois State Board of Health, and Florence Kelley's investigations of Chicago's sweatshops and child labor abuses led to the passage of the model Illinois Factory Act in 1893. The profession of social work was spawned in the settlement house. In campaigning for tenement laws, public health care, playground construction, and good government, settlement-house workers emerged as a powerful phalanx of Progressive reform (see Chapter 23). But the principal function of the settlement house remained educational. As *The Commons*, a magazine for reformers, editorialized in 1900, the settlement house would realize its mission by "teaching its neighborhood to demand better housing, better public facilities, better conditions of industry, more educational privileges, good books, lectures, music, art, recreation, indoors and out, means of cleanliness, public and private, leisure for these things, etc., etc., and by educating its outside constituency to see the righteousness and reasonableness of these demands."

One of the most far-reaching effects of the settlement-house movement was the application of social sciences to urban problems. Initially, Addams once noted, settlement-house workers came to "do something about the social disorder," but soon enough they determined the need "to investigate something." The settlement houses obliged by conducting extensive surveys of the immigrant wards and working conditions, which in turn attracted muckraking journalists in search of more precise information on the lives of Riis's "other half." In the industrial and financial world, after all, only numbers mattered. Statistical inquiry became a means of identifying problems so that they might be resolved systematically. In 1894 Hull House, at the behest of the U.S. Department of Labor, conducted an intensive flat-by-flat survey of every tenement in one district that resulted in the nation's most comprehensive canvass of urban housing. Researchers completed community surveys in other cities, the most notable being sociologist and historian W. E. B. Du Bois's classic *The Philadelphia Negro* (1898), which he compiled while a resident of the Philadelphia College Settlement, and *The City Wilderness* (1898) by Robert Woods and his colleagues at Andover House in Boston. The utility of such surveys encouraged foundations to sponsor others. The Russell Sage Foundation funded the six-volume Pittsburgh Survey (1907-1908), the most complete profile of city life and work.

The use of sociology, economics, and history to document social problems brought scholarly rigor and the power of numbers to the reform effort. During the Progressive era the statistical investigative survey would be the spine of social and economic reform legislation, showing the middle class how the different parts of the city related to one another so that it was possible to see the city as a whole.

THE CITY ENTERS THE NEW CENTURY

At the close of the century Americans held two contrasting views of the city and its future. One view posited the city as the engine of American power, a dynamo like the Corliss Engine at the Philadelphia Exposition of 1876, which had celebrated progress and promised a better life of consumption and convenience. The second view saw the city as disorderly, the breeding ground for the forces of demagoguery, disparity, and moral decay.

The two opposing views were most clearly evident in 1892-1893 when Chicago hosted the World's Columbian Exposition. Twenty-one million people paid to visit the shining "White City" of wooded lanes, parkways, lagoons, and plaster-of-paris and whitewashed pseudoclassical buildings built especially for the occasion in Jackson Park, on Chicago's southern lakefront. Louis Sullivan was appalled by the confusion of styles and sprawling grounds, which contrasted with his own urban vision of clean lines shooting upward, but the public loved the fair. Hamlin Garland wrote to his parents on their Dakota farm: "Sell the cook stove if necessary and come. You must see this fair."

The White City laid out by Frederick Law Olmsted and Daniel Burnham was an urban landscape designed to show that it was possible to bring order to the city. With its electric railway and ferry boats, its own sewer and water systems, and its uniformed teams of sanitation workers cleaning up the grounds each day, the White City was a statement of what planning and good management could do. Order could banish poverty and urban ills. As one visitor remarked, in the White City there was no room for poverty. In stark contrast to its triumph, however, stood the crowded, corrupt gray city being surveyed by Jane Addams not far away.

The view from the White City prevailed. City planning was then in its infancy and largely concerned with fashioning new communities rather than reshaping old ones, but by the turn of the century Burnham and others were drafting comprehensive plans for park systems and urban design that guided development in Washington, Chicago, Kansas City, Denver, and Seattle for decades thereafter. Engineers were creating unified sanitary administrations, such as the 185-square-mile district for metropolitan Chicago (1889) and the centralized Metropolitan Sewage Commission in Boston (1889). Even the urban religious revivals — Moody launched a major crusade in Chicago in 1893 — and the settlement houses bespoke a belief that the city could be "tamed" and made to do good if people would but come together. All demanded that people consider the city as a whole, and all believed that the city was worth saving.

CONCLUSION: POINTS OF CONVERGENCE IN THE AMERICAN CITY

Despite growing class divisions, ethnic and racial diversity, and the functional segregation of space, the American city had many points of convergence. At parks, department stores, ballparks, museums, concerts, and vaudeville shows people of different backgrounds shared similar experiences and developed a public etiquette that made for civility. Ethnic, racial, and class lines did not disappear, and, indeed, in some ways they were widening, but they blurred whenever different people found common purpose at civic events. Thus, for example, cheering for the home team at the ballpark bonded all fans together, whether seated in box seats or bleachers. Public schools and metropolitan newspapers gave students and readers a common language, and by reporting on citywide matters, mass-circulation dailies broadened their readers' compass of interest and identity. During the nineteenth century uniquely urban institutions and experiences fostered a modern city culture, distinct from rural worlds lost and demanding a new appreciation of common humanity.

Historian Henry Adams, in his autobiography, remarked on the effect of the World's Columbian Exposition and what it symbolized about American urban promise. "Chicago was the first full expression of American thought as a unity; one must start here." The key word was "unity." The question for Americans entering the new century was whether they would follow the lead of revivalists, planners, and social reformers in search of a unified public order or continue in the ways of individual self-interest and unplanned growth. The answer came with the Progressive movement.

SUGGESTED READING

Tyler Anbinder, *Five Points: The 19th-Century New York City Neighborhood That Invented the Tap Dance, Stole Elections, and Became the World's Most Notorious Slum* (2001). An ambitious, intensive neighborhood study that examines the private worlds and public conflicts of the black, immigrant, and native-born white populations in Lower Manhattan and the ways their experiences defined urban culture.

Gunther Barth, *City People: The Rise of Modern City Culture in Nineteenth-Century America* (1980). A brisk but informed survey of urbanizing institutions such as the department store, apartment house, ballparks, and newspapers.

John Bodnar, *The Transplanted: A History of Immigrants in Urban America* (1985). A sensitive and rich treatment of immigrants' lives and work in industrial cities.

Paul S. Boyer, *Urban Masses and Moral Order in America, 1820-1920* (1978). A probing account of reformers' values and efforts in shaping urban life.

William Cronon, *Nature's Metropolis: Chicago and the Great West* (1991). A brilliant reorientation of urban and American development that shows the economic interdependence of urban and rural America, the connections between urban, industrial growth and politics and power, and the centrality of Chicago to the nation's progress.

Raymond A. Mohl, *The New City: Urban America in the Industrial Age, 1860-1920* (1985). A detailed, informed survey of the rise of the industrial city, with an excellent bibliography.

Robert Orsi, *The Madonna of 115th Street: Faith and Community in East Harlem, 1880-1950* (1986). A telling exploration of the faith, folkways, and community among Catholic immigrants and migrants and the ways "local people" interacted with the church and urban institutions.

Roy Rozenzweig, *Eight Hours for What We Will: Workers and Leisure in the Industrial City, 1870-1920* (1983). A study of the development and uses of the city park as the site for cultural and class contestation over the meaning and use of public space and community resources.

Carl Smith, *Urban Disorder and the Shape of Belief: The Great Chicago Fire, the Haymarket Bomb, and the Model Town of Pullman* (1995). An examination of the ways in which public perceptions of cities and the urban masses were shaped by perceptions of urban disasters, labor troubles, and disorders.

Jon Teaford, *The Unheralded Triumph: City Government in America, 1870-1900* (1984). A penetrating view of urban government and services and the fragmentation of city and suburbs.

SUGGESTIONS FOR FURTHER READING

Aaron Abell, *American Catholicism and Social Action: A Search for Social Justice, 1865-1900* (1960).

Charles Cheape, *Moving the Masses: Urban Public Transit in New York, Boston, and Philadelphia, 1880-1912* (1980).

Susan Curtis, *A Consuming Faith: The Social Gospel and Modern American Culture* (1991).

Richard Griswold del Castillo, *The Los Angeles Barrio, 1850-1890: A Social History* (1980).

Allen Davis, *Spearheads for Reform: The Social Settlements and the Progressive Movement 1890-1914* (1967).

Sarah Deutsch, *Women and the City: Gender, Space, and Power in Boston, 1870-1940* (2000).

Perry Duis, *The Saloon: Public Drinking in Chicago and Boston, 1880-1920* (1983).

Steven Erie, *Rainbow's End: Irish-Americans and the Dilemma of Urban Machine Politics, 1840-1985* (1988).

Donna R. Gabaccia, *From the Other Side: Women, Gender, and Immigrant Life in the United States, 1820-1990* (1994).

James Gilbert, *Perfect Cities: Chicago's Utopias of 1893* (1991).

Caroline Golab, *Immigrant Destinations* (1977).

John F. Kasson, *Amusing the Millions: Coney Island at the Turn of the Century* (1978).

Thomas Kessner, *The Golden Door: Italian and Jewish Immigrant Mobility in New York City, 1880-1915* (1977).

Alan M. Kraut, *The Huddled Masses: The Immigrant in American Society, 1880-1921* (1982).

Margaret Marsh, *Suburban Lives* (1990).

Donald L. Miller, *City of the Century: The Epic of Chicago and the Making of America* (1996).

Randall M. Miller and Thomas D. Marzik, eds., *Immigrants and Religion in Urban America* (1977).

Ross Miller, *American Apocalypse: The Great Fire and the Myth of Chicago* (1990).

Steven A. Riess, *City Games: The Evolution of American Urban Society and the Rise of Sports* (1989).

Mark H. Rose, *Cities of Light and Heat: Domesticating Gas and Electricity in Urban America* (1995).

Roy Rozenzweig and Elizabeth Blackmar, *The Park and the People: A History of Central Park* (1993).

Thomas Schlereth, *Victorian America: Transformation in Everyday Life* (1991).

David Schuyler, *The New Urban Landscape: The Redefinition of City Form in Nineteenth-Century America* (1986).

John R. Stilgoe, *Borderland: Origins of the American Suburb, 1820-1939* (1988).

Virginia Yans-McLaughlin and Marjorie Lightman, *Ellis Island and the Peopling of America* (1997).

Olivier Zunz, *The Changing Face of Inequality: Urbanization, Industrialization, and Immigrants in Detroit, 1880-1920* (1982).

20 Post–Civil War Thought and Culture

AMERICANS TRANSFORMED THEIR world in the generation that followed the end of the Civil War. No corner of the nation, no aspect of daily life was left untouched by changes in transportation, in finance, in technology, in the organization of work, and in the production of food. For many, these changes were summed up in the powerful symbol of the railroad. As a young boy in the 1870s, William Allen White witnessed the arrival of the railroad in his pioneer Kansas town. He recalled that it brought to an end "a rather competent civilization." From his child's point of view, "it meant that homemade sleds and little homemade wagons would pass; that the bows and arrows which boys made by seasoning hickory behind the stove and scraping and polishing them with glass, would as an art disappear forever out of the life of American boys." Yet it is not clear how Americans *perceived* and *responded to* such changes. Were they welcomed as progress, or feared as destructive of accustomed ways of living?

New forms of transportation, communication and trade created technological bonds that brought the United States ever more closely together in a material sense. Despite the expectations of many, this union did not translate directly into uniformity in ways of thinking or living. In fact, the post–Civil War period saw increased cultural diversity among the inhabitants of the immense nation. Immigration, of course, brought to America people from new regions of Europe, who practiced different religions and followed different customs. The nation's economic development also brought greater occupational diversity, which often encouraged differences in points of view. Furthermore, the transformation of America's cities into giant metropolitan areas magnified already-existing cultural differences between city, town and rural people. It was, in short, a time of widening divergence in the thinking and the ways of life among the peoples of the United States.

This diversity was sometimes hard to see, however, because the postwar period marked the increasing prominence of *metropolitan,* or the national- and urban-oriented, culture that had taken shape in the North during the Civil War. Representing the interests and values of mainly urban people and organizations whose outlook was primarily national rather than local or regional, this metropolitan culture celebrated the virtue and the inevitability of increasing centralization and homogenization in American life. Its spokesmen extolled corporate giants like Carnegie and Rockefeller as agents of progress and proclaimed the coming dominance of values of rationality, efficiency, productivity, and national power. Although the national media gave greatest play to these metropolitan ideas, many Americans continued to adhere to other values, emphasizing the continuing importance of local distinctiveness, decentralization, and democratic decision-making.

NATIONAL CULTURE AND FAITH IN PROGRESS

The tension between centralization and localism had a long tradition in American life and thought, but the growing power of national corporations brought it into greater prominence in the later nineteenth century. The conflict was also highlighted by advances in the technology of printing. Beyond immediate face-to-face conversation, print was the medium for the exchange of ideas in nineteenth-century America, where nearly all adults were able to read. Publishing books, magazines and newspapers was a business like any other, subject to economic and technological forces. It was, at the same time, the source of income for a large number

THE PROGRESS OF THE CENTURY.
THE LIGHTNING STEAM PRESS. THE ELECTRIC TELEGRAPH. THE LOCOMOTIVE. THE STEAMBOAT.

Progress   The popular lithographic firm Currier & Ives in 1876 printed this icon extolling some of the inventions that had transformed nineteenth-century life: the steam press, the electric telegraph, the steamboat, and the railroad. Notice also the thick black smoke belching from the factory. In the nineteenth century that was always a symbol of jobs, prosperity, and progress. It would take a century for such a smokestack to evoke automatic thoughts of pollution and disease.

of writing men and women, and the principal means through which Americans as a nation expressed and debated their ideas.

Just as they were becoming centers of the nation's financial institutions, the cities of the Northeast grew in their influence over national publishing after the Civil War. Tensions between North and South before the war had hindered the emergence of a truly national reading audience — *Uncle Tom's Cabin,* after all, had been a runaway bestseller in the North, but was banned in the South. After the war, large publishing firms in New York, Boston, and Philadelphia took advantage of the national market made possible by the expanding network of railroads by adopting ever-larger and faster steam driven printing presses. These, along with new methods of manufacturing paper, continually lowered costs and made printed materials available to more people. Prominent book publishers such as Scribners and Harper Brothers launched national magazines in which they featured serial versions of their books. The continued growth throughout the late nineteenth century of the circulations of national magazines makes

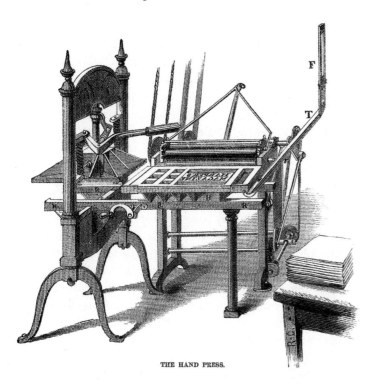

THE HAND PRESS.

The Old Ways   While the steam press was considered one of the nineteenth century's symbols of progress, local newspapers were printed on hand presses like the one in this 1865 engraving from *Harper's New Monthly Magazine*. Type had to be set by hand, and every sheet was individually printed by laboriously turning the crank.

it possible to think for the first time in terms of a truly national medium.

❧ *Publishing: National and Local*

Yet there were limits to the penetration of this national press. Unlike the nations of Europe, the United States was too large and decentralized in the nineteenth century to have national newspapers. In the emerging metropolitan areas, however, the great concentration of population made possible the emergence of cheap daily newspapers that appealed to a broad cross section of the population. To get the latest stories to newsboys on the streets before their competitors, they employed ever more powerful presses and experimented with new typesetting machines to turn out more papers in the shortest possible time. Buttressed by advertising revenues from the burgeoning urban department stores (see Chapter 19), these daily newspapers attracted a diverse readership by means of illustrations, sports stories, special sections for women and children, and (by the end of the century) comic strips.

Meanwhile, other newspapers and magazines proliferated throughout the country, using less advanced and cheaper printing machinery to communicate with smaller, more specialized audiences. Every hamlet boasting a population of a hundred or more had at least one, and often two or three, weekly and biweekly newspapers that published local news. Lacking economies of scale, smaller newspapers were printed in short runs on small, hand- or water-powered presses. The cost of setting up such a print shop was relatively low, and it was possible for individuals and groups to establish journals to represent their particular perspective. The telegraph, which quickly came to be controlled by the Western Union monopoly, distributed fast-breaking national and international stories, but it was expensive. Most of the news and commentary in smaller papers was copied from paper to paper, while state and local stories were covered by local reporters. These smaller publications co-existed with the new national mass-market publications, meeting the special needs of foreign-language immigrants, African Americans, and religious organizations as well as rural readers. They made it possible for sub-cultures to thrive despite the prominence of the metropolitan-based national media.

Thus a pattern of increasing centralization at the national level and diversification at the local was in part a reflection of the contrasting implications of developments in communication technologies. It is important to keep both patterns in mind when considering how post–Civil War Americans responded to the changes around them. Moreover, though the postwar period was an age of print, it was also the last great age of public speaking in American history. As they had in the decades before the Civil War, men and women still turned out regularly to be educated and entertained at public lectures by well-known writers and ambitious local leaders alike. Like Emerson with his famous essay "Self Reliance," many men and women of letters made handsome livings traveling about the country delivering their famous lectures repeatedly, just as musicians today are expected to perform hits from their latest albums. Orators may have expressed popular attitudes, but they also aimed to touch their audience's emotions through their performances.

The historian's difficulty in describing precisely what ordinary people thought is complicated by the growing recognition that, even when Americans *read* the same nationally distributed books and magazines, they often *interpreted* them in different ways, according to personal contexts and concerns. Hence, we cannot assume that even a best-selling book was a simple, straightforward reflection of the convictions of a broad segment of the American people. Instead, it might have been successful because it was able to appeal in different ways to different audiences. In exploring American thought and culture, then, we must look to see ideas expressed not only in what people read but also in their actions.

❧ Modern Metropolitan Culture: The Growing Authority of Science and Progress

Despite these reservations, it is possible to say that the defining feature of the emerging national culture of post–Civil War America was an exuberant faith in progress. In responding to the myriad changes they saw around them, Americans could draw on several traditions of thought about the nature of change over time. In many cultures, any alteration in accustomed ways of doing things is perceived as threatening, representing a decline from time-honored standards. Since the Renaissance, some social observers had argued that civilizations followed a cyclical pattern of rise and decline analogous to the human life-cycle. A third possibility, the idea that change was part of a continuous process of improvement, or *progress,* was relatively new, taking root among Enlightenment thinkers in the eighteenth century and becoming more general in Europe and the United States only in the nineteenth.

FAITH IN PROGRESS

Christian beliefs had played a part in the general acceptance of the idea of progress, as periodic religious awakenings in the eighteenth and early nineteenth centuries were seen by many Protestant evangelicals as signs of the approaching millennium. On the other hand, other mid-nineteenth-century revivalists like Dwight Moody (see Chapter 18) gave greater emphasis to the Book of Revelation's predictions of great turmoil and destruction before the final triumph of Christ. Such revivalists took a much more pessimistic view of the direction of change in America.

Many Americans blended religious thought with more worldly perceptions of the changes taking place around them. They viewed the impressive expansion of white settlements across the continent, the founding and growth of towns and cities, the conversion of once-open lands into fruitful farms and mines, and the increasing productive power of manufacturing enterprises as obvious evidence that history followed a progressive, or upward path. For many in the antebellum

North, slavery had represented a tragic mistake that stood in the way of the nation's progress. The war eliminated it, and many viewed the suffering war brought as atonement for slavery's sin. Afterward, the idea of progress became firmly entrenched in the national culture as the expansion of productive forces seemed destined to continue indefinitely.

Science actually had relatively little to do with the impressive material changes taking place, but it gained in popular respect because many assumed that it was responsible for progress. Although few understood scientific method, many believed that as the world became more "modern," people would abandon irrational superstitions and let themselves be guided by the findings of science. It is commonly thought that the new Darwinian interpretation of evolution was instantly perceived as a challenge to traditional Christian ideas of Creation, but most of those who were aware of Darwin's new theory in the immediate postwar period did not see it as incompatible with religious belief.

Since the eighteenth century, leading Protestant ministers such as Cotton Mather and Jonathan Edwards had pursued scientific research as a supplement to the study of scripture in understanding God's purposes for creation. Scientists and ministers alike asserted that evidence of His design could be found everywhere in nature. A generation before the publication of Charles Darwin's *Origin of Species* in 1859, however, the new science of geology called into question the accuracy of Biblical accounts of the creation and the age of the Earth. Religiously-inclined scientists responded in many different ways, but some evangelical researchers had no difficulty harmonizing their religious beliefs with the mounting evidence that change in biological forms had taken place over time. Darwin's principal argument, that changes in biological species occurred by means of the "natural selection" of new variations, offered an explanation for these changes. Some believed that the idea of natural selection challenged divine design, but a number of evangelical Christians, such as botanist Asa Gray, promoted Darwin's theory. He argued that the Bible should not be thought of as a scientific textbook, and pointed out that Darwin's theory did not explain *how* variations occurred in the first place. Divine design could be seen not only as compatible with natural selection but as necessary to give Darwin's theory coherence. "Natural selection," he wrote, "is not the wind that propels the vessel, but the rudder which, by friction, now on this side and now on that, shapes the course." The wind, for Gray, was God. In the early debates over Darwin's theory, many of his most active proponents were religious men, including ministers; among those who attacked him were scientists who thought that there was not enough evidence for some of his conclusions.

During the rest of the nineteenth century, terms of the debate gradually shifted, not so much because of Darwin's ideas themselves but as a reflection of the nation's widening cultural differences. Many educated, predominately urban Americans accepted the theory of natural selection as part of a package of ideas about evolution. They did so because these ideas had received the stamp of scientific authority, and because they were consistent with a general perception that progress was part of God's design. On the other hand, for religious leaders who increasingly attacked Darwinism, the theories were in some ways symbolic of the growing power of science and of the general direction of change in postwar society. By upholding the authority of scripture, Darwin's religious critics declared their opposition to all that they saw as wrong with the Gilded Age.

It is important to note that Darwin did not argue that changes occurring through the process of natural selection were necessarily good or moral. Rather, it was the English writer Herbert Spencer who shaped the popular understanding of *evolution* as a word and a concept. He, not Darwin, coined the popular catch phrase "survival of the fittest." Largely self-educated, Spencer had worked as civil engineer on a railroad and as a magazine editor before taking up philosophical writing. His voluminous works attempted to apply what he thought of as the techniques of science to developing an all-inclusive philosophy based on evolution. (His methods actually owed more to the deductive reasoning of the idealistic tradition in philosophy.) After the appearance of the *Origin of Species,* Spencer set out to apply to all the sciences what he termed the "law" of evolution. For him, this meant that all forms of life gradually "progressed" from simple forms through a series of stages characterized by greater complexity, specialization and integration. He even compared human society to an organism, and argued that it was subject to the same forces of evolution. Although he believed that all societies must eventually decline and die, his assertion that Western civilization was just reaching a mature stage of development reinforced an optimistic attitude toward the direction of change.

Some Americans read Spencer's books, but many more were exposed to his ideas through populariza-tions by disciples such as John Fiske and Edward Livingston Youmans. Fiske noted similarities between the idea of natural selection and traditional Calvinism: "it elects the one and damns the ninety and nine." But he insisted that in human society the progressive forces of love and idealism channeled the random operation of natural processes. Youmans founded the magazine *Popular Science Monthly* in 1872 to promote the latest scientific findings. He proclaimed Spencer's ideas of cosmic evolution as "a great and established fact" that accounted for everything we see around us. Moreover, Youmans asserted that science was vastly superior to religion in affording self-understanding: "Human beings should be studied exactly as minerals and plants are studied, with the simple purpose of tracing out the laws and relations of the phenomena they present."

Ultimately, Spencer's ideas were so far-reaching and indeed so vague that they could be and were used to justify a wide range of social agendas in Europe, Asia, and the United States. In America, his belief in the inevitability of progress helped to mute the pessimism inherent in Darwin's own interpretation of natural selection, and as we shall see, his opposition to government interference in the economy was trumpeted by critics of specific regulations. But it must be said that overall Spencer's ideas and slogans such as the "survival of the fittest" did not so much influence postwar Americans as provide useful ammunition for debates over the direction of change. Invoking Spencer did, however, enable a wide range of social commentators to lay claim to the prestige of "science."

In discussions in the major national media, science superseded religion or morality as the most authoritative basis for argument. In the early part of the century, proponents of change, whether westward expansion or moral reform, had been most likely to invoke divine sanction, as in the case of "Manifest Destiny." By the end of the century, it would be more common for the spokesmen for the new corporations and the educated urban middle classes to proclaim that "immutable natural laws" supported their positions. Such appeals were considered vastly more hard-headed and realistic, powerful attributes in postwar culture. Writing in magazines of opinion like the *North American Review,* published in Boston, and the *Independent,* from New York, such commentators as Yale economist William Graham Sumner asserted that the new power of giant national corporations only reflected the process of natural selection in economic life. Interference with the operation of these natural "laws" by means of dem-

ocratic legislation, he insisted, would only slow progress. Yet, even as he relied upon the scientific prestige
of Darwin's ideas, Sumner applied them inconsistently.
His view of "fitness" in human beings, for example, was
not a matter of inherited traits but of the conscious
willingness to work hard and delay gratification.

WRITING FOR "THE BEST MEN"

Such journals of opinion did not have a wide readership, but they both reflected and guided the thinking
of their educated urban, upper middle-class audiences,
what they described as "the best men." The weekly
newspaper *The Nation,* for example, was influential despite the fact that its circulation never exceeded 12,000.
This did not trouble its opinionated editor E. L. Godkin, who professed no intention of mixing with common folk on the "democratic plan," but envisioned his
readership as "thoughtful, educated, high-minded men
— gentlemen in short." Bostonian Charles Eliot Norton
declared that *The Nation* stood, with "Harvard and Yale
Colleges," as "almost the only solid barriers against the
invasion of modern barbarism and vulgarity."

The Nation was established in 1865 to stand "independent of mere party politics, and upholding sound
principles of loyalty and nationality." It promoted the
cause of a unified national economy and culture, even
as it paid greatest attention to events and institutions
in New York City. Initially, its Radical Republican backers hoped to use it to promote the cause of civil rights
for the freedmen in the South. But as it became clear
after the war that New York's working men were intent
on using democratic means to promote laws in their
interests, the journal quickly converted to laissez-faire
principles. This was an easy transition for Irish-born
Godkin, who had been schooled in classical political
economy in Belfast. He denounced the rising influence of working-class and ethnic voters in New York
politics and advocated measures such as immigration
restriction and civil service reform (see Chapter 21) to
protect the influence of the cultured classes. A fear of
radicalism aroused by riots in New York and the short-
lived Commune in Paris in 1870-71 soon colored his
perception of all politics in America. George William
Curtis, editor of *Harper's Weekly,* also shifted abruptly
from government intervention to laissez-faire. Largely
in response to local developments, these metropolitan
editors attempted to redefine the domain of legitimate
political debate, reducing its territory by invoking the
higher authority of "natural economic laws."

In fact, many men of wealth in the Northeast followed the same pattern. One of *The Nation's* wealthy
backers, John Murray Forbes, was a Boston financier
who controlled the vast Burlington Railroad system
in the Midwest. He watched with alarm in the early
1870s as Midwesterners began to complain about his
railroad's discriminatory rates. One of his chief executives was his cousin Charles Perkins, who similarly denounced all local efforts to regulate railroad rates as
"communistic" interference with "the Natural laws of
trade." Their friend Bostonian Charles Francis Adams
was a frequent contributor to *The Nation* and president
of the Union Pacific Railroad — and son and grandson,
respectively, of former Presidents John Quincy Adams
and John Adams. He argued that protective tariffs
contradicted divinely ordained economic laws, and
warned, "When you meddle with eternal laws, you are
more likely to mar than help, and if you mar, you must
undergo the punishment." He noted darkly in 1884 that
the tendency for government interference that had begun with protectionism had even now inspired a Massachusetts law providing free school textbooks!

SOCIAL DARWINISM AND THE
ROOTS OF LIBERAL PROTESTANTISM

Despite such grim pronouncements, many if not most
Americans continued to support government involvement in many aspects of their lives, particularly
at the state and local levels. Nor was there anything
approaching consensus on the question of whether,
in economic matters, progress was more helped by
greater concentration or open competition. In fact, it
is hard to say precisely how widespread or influential
was what critics later termed "Social Darwinism." The
idea of evolution itself gave rise to contradictory policies. One of the few business leaders who made a careful study of Darwin and Spencer, steel magnate Andrew
Carnegie (see Chapter 18) argued in "Wealth," a famous
essay in the *North American Review,* that growing economic inequality was inevitable and "essential for the
progress of the race." He concluded that "the Law of
Accumulation of Wealth, and the Law of Competition,"
however unjust, were "the best and most valuable of
all that humanity has yet accomplished." Yet, in direct
contradiction to the pronouncements of Sumner and
Adams, Carnegie urged that the wealthy had a moral
duty to use their resources "for the public good," by
establishing institutions such as public libraries to enable the poor to help themselves. Through wise philanthropy, he concluded, wealth could become a "potent
force for the elevation of our race."

The career of Henry Ward Beecher (1818-1887), the most famous minister in the United States in the decades following the Civil War, reflects the somewhat muddled response of urban, middle-class Americans to ideas of evolution. Son of Lyman Beecher, one of the leading figures in the Second Great Awakening (see Chapter 8), and brother of novelist Harriet Beecher Stowe, he had inherited the mantle of leadership of New England Protestantism. Beginning his career in the Midwest, he moved in 1847 to Plymouth Church in the growing middle-class suburb of Brooklyn, New York, where he gained national attention as an abolitionist. A dynamic and eloquent preacher who exerted a strong emotional appeal over his audiences, he was in demand throughout the nation as a lecturer, but also spread his ideas through a best-selling novel *Norwood* (1867) and numerous published collections of sermons.

Beecher was much attracted to the idea of evolution. He played a major role both in popularizing Darwin and Spencer and in integrating evolutionary concepts into liberal Protestant theology. Insisting that both science and religion were evolutionary, he proclaimed to clergy troubled by Darwin, "you must be sure to meet the Lord when He comes in the air, when He moves in the providences of the world, when He is at work in natural laws . . . when He is shining in great scientific disclosures." In *Evolution and Religion,* a collection of sermons published in 1885, Beecher provided a moving and accessible explanation of natural selection, adapted to his American audience, that concluded, "Design by wholesale is grander than design by retail."

In part, Beecher was convinced that Protestantism must embrace science in order to keep pace with change in the modern world. In an 1872 speech to Yale theological students he argued that ministers must be educated in the new social sciences in order to retain the allegiance of "the intelligent part of society." He continued:

> I think that our profession is in danger, and in great danger, of going under, and of working effectively only among the relatively less informed and intelligent of the community. . . . The study of human nature is not going to be left in the hands of the church or the ministry. It is going to be part of every liberal education, and will be pursued on a scientific basis.

Less defensively, he also stated that study of a "science of management" provided ministers with knowledge of human nature that could serve as a practical

Henry Ward Beecher   The most esteemed Protestant preacher in post–Civil War America foreshadowed, both in his theology and in his personal life, many of the crises that twentieth-century Christianity would face.

professional tool. "You must know what men are in order to reach them, and that is part of the science of preaching."

Beecher also embraced the idea of evolutionary progress because it enabled him to promote doctrinal change while still honoring the stern Calvinism of his ancestors. His famous 1873 sermon "Through Fear to Love" applied evolution to the field of morality. He asserted that some people, particularly in the cultured

"Wealth," 1889

Steel magnate Andrew Carnegie wrote this essay as he grappled with what to do with the financial returns from his industrial enterprises. He concluded that "the surplus wealth of the few" was best put to use in creating public institutions like libraries and schools, "the ladders upon which the aspiring can rise."

The problem of our age is the proper administration of wealth, so that the ties of brotherhood may still bind together the rich and poor in harmonious relationship. The conditions of human life have not only been changed, but revolutionized, within the past few hundred years. In former days there was little difference between the dwelling, dress, food, and environment of the chief and those of his retainers. . . . The contrast between the palace of the millionaire and the cottage of the laborer with us to-day measures the change which has come with civilization. . . .

The price which society pays for the law of competition, like the price it pays for cheap comforts and luxuries, is also great; but the advantages of this law are also greater still, for it is to this law that we owe our wonderful material development, which brings improved conditions in its train. But, whether the law be benign or not, we must say of it, as we say of the change in the conditions of men to which we have referred: It is here; we cannot evade it; no substitutes for it have been found; and while the law may be sometimes hard for the individual, it is best for the race, because it insures the survival of the fittest in every department.

classes, had reached a "higher plane" where a primitive morality based on fear was being replaced by a morality of love. By smoothing over the "harsh," "rigid," and "gloomy" doctrines of original sin and future punishment, Beecher sought to make religion more acceptable to his middle-class urban congregation of more than 3,000. Similarly, the principal theme of *Norwood* was that because God was present in Nature, religious truths were more approachable through intuition and feeling than through reason. Ironically, by shifting the foundation of religious experience from doctrine to sensibility, he ceded the realm of reason to science, leaving his authority as a minister dependent on his ability to stir his listeners' emotions. At this he was highly successful, for the members of Plymouth Church remained devoted to him despite a widely publicized trial in 1875 for adultery with one of his parishioners that ended in a hung jury. Notwithstanding the national notoriety of the scandal, he remained a popular spokesman for liberal Protestantism until his death in 1887.

❧ *Expertise*

Even for the urban middle classes, however, all change was not progress. The increasing availability of consumer goods could be unsettling as well as liberating, as upwardly mobile men and women sought to refashion their identities in a society of constantly changing values. Men struggled to build careers in the midst of economic fluctuations and evolving definitions of middle class work. Women, on the other hand, were charged with making homes out of the dizzying array of manu-factured goods offered by the new department stores (see Chapter 19). As consumer goods became ever more widely available, status hierarchies were maintained by constantly shifting distinctions in taste, which the aspiring middle class woman must struggle to keep up with. Meanwhile, advertisers learned to subtly transform "luxuries" into "necessities" and to persuade readers that progress simply meant more of everything. For middle-class urban women, the shift from domestic production to shopping was greeted with concern in a Protestant culture that had long associated excessive consumption with moral danger. Reflecting the media's ambivalence toward this new world of consumption, the *New York Times* reported a conversation between an English visitor and a Philadelphia matron. According to the *Times,* the Englishwoman noted that whenever she was "dull or cross," she found solace in a half hour's meditation at Westminster Abbey. The American woman smilingly reassured her, "Why can't you do that in Philadelphia? — there's Wanamaker's!"

To address this unease with the pace of material change, the publishing world offered hosts of self-styled "experts." Etiquette books promised to tell aspiring matrons how to act, dress and furnish their houses; advice books for men promised secrets to scrambling up the new corporate ladders. On a more elite level, writers for the genteel magazines proclaimed that the antidote for social disorder was "Culture" with a capital C. Through the careful study of great art and literature and the cultivation of good taste and high ideals, the rough edges of American materialism could be smoothed. To carry out this program, the postwar period saw the founding of the great metropolitan art museums, opera houses and symphony orchestras. Similarly, men in the forefront of expanding higher education argued that their institutions would prepare a new elite of educated men and women to reclaim America's culture from vulgar materialism. Harvard's Charles Eliot claimed that the university represented "plain living against luxury."

THE RISE OF UNIVERSITIES AND PROFESSIONS

In fact, the development of a new form of higher educational institution, the research university, played a crucial role in the rising authority of scientific language and methods in post–Civil War America. Previously, hundreds of colleges had been established in towns and cities throughout the nation. Most were founded by religious denominations and heavily oriented toward a classical curriculum of Latin and Greek, moral philosophy, and rhetoric, and were intended principally to train young men for the ministry and for public life. Typically headed by formidable clergymen, who personally taught the capstone senior course on moral philosophy, antebellum colleges sought to pass on traditional values as defined by Christian doctrine and classical philosophy. Science received little attention. In fact, the pioneering scientific research of the antebellum period was most often done by independently wealthy gentlemen and other amateurs.

After mid-century, a number of related changes came to higher education. Within undergraduate education, the emphasis began to shift from the classics to the natural and social sciences. When the chemist Charles W. Eliot became the first non-minister to head Harvard in 1869, he expanded the elective courses that students could take and hired Spencer's popularizer John Fiske despite the misgivings of his trustees. Meanwhile, the Land Grant Act of 1862 enabled the states to establish publicly-supported universities designed not only to make higher education more widely available, but to promote research in practical areas like engineering and agriculture. In New York, Andrew Dickson White persuaded the wealthy philanthropist Ezra

GENTLEMAN MEETING A LADY.

Etiquette, 1880s Middle-class manners were exquisitely fine-tuned in the late nineteenth century. This illustration, from a popular manual of etiquette, shows how a proper lady and gentleman should gracefully acknowledge each other when they chanced to meet on the street: "either by bowing or words of greeting, a gentleman lifting his hat."

Cornell to support his vision of a university combining vocational education with the best features of the modern German research university. Although he met with fierce political resistance from denominational colleges, White succeeded in opening Cornell University in 1868. (White wrote a popular lecture, "The Battle-fields of Science," about the perennial conflict between "religious dogma" and free inquiry; translated into articles in *Popular Science Monthly* and later books, it helped foster the mistaken impression among historians that religious leaders had opposed Darwinism from the beginning.)

Beginning with Johns Hopkins University in 1876, new private universities were also established with graduate programs directly modeled on those in Germany. These were made possible by the benefactions of wealthy industrialists like Carnegie, Vanderbilt, John D. Rockefeller, who supported the University of Chicago, and railroad tycoon Leland Stanford, who founded a university in memory of his son.

Such new and renovated institutions became cen-

College Students   Two students relax in their room at Harvard in 1870. The detailed wallpaper, the ornate furniture, the framed pictures covering the walls — not to mention the suits and serious demeanors on the students themselves — all attest to a college experience quite unlike what most students today have.

ters for research in America, both drawing strength from and reinforcing popular faith in science. They were the seedbed for a new kind of middle class, one based upon possessing expert knowledge rather than owning a business. Implicitly and sometimes explicitly antagonistic to traditional forms of knowledge, the universities were dedicated to the discovery of new truths rather than the transmission of eternal verities. Complementing the natural sciences were new disciplines — sociology, economics, political science, psychology, anthropology — dedicated to the scientific study of human behavior. Although new scholarly

journals were founded to publish scientific research, leading academics like Sumner also reached a broad general audience through the metropolitan media. Their research had not yet moved beyond the comprehension of educated men and women, and they felt it a duty to offer their insights on current issues. Consequently, academics participated actively in media debates about politics and reform as well as education and religion.

The concrete result of this expansion was a striking increase in the numbers of young men and women with college education: in 1870 there were 52,000 undergraduates in the United States; by 1890 there would be 157,000. Although the proportion of college and university students never rose above 5 percent of their age group in the nineteenth century, this increase produced a generation with experiences and expectations that differed from their prewar parents. For some, the university experience uprooted them from local ties and set them on careers that demanded geographical mobility, giving them a national perspective. Many academic researchers went a step further and were drawn into a widening international intellectual community among scholars throughout Europe, the Americas, Australia and New Zealand.

Meanwhile, the older denominational colleges continued to enroll thousands of students, drawn from a smaller geographical area and from within the ranks of the religious group. Often facing strong pressure to emulate the universities and abandon their traditional classical curriculums, many gradually adopted alternative B.S. degree programs and allowed some choices of electives. But even as they allowed students to emulate the larger institutions in organizing fraternities and football teams, they retained a religious framework that had been abandoned elsewhere. In the later part of the century, such schools became centers for the emergence of the Y.M.C.A. movement that embraced a more strenuous kind of religiosity, "muscular Christianity."

Yet career paths for new college graduates were not clearly defined. The expansion of higher education itself created thousands of salaried positions for graduates interested in a career that combined intellectual activity with a sense of public service. Other college graduates, such as Lincoln Steffens, Ida Tarbell and Ray Stannard Baker, drifted awhile after undergraduate and post-graduate training until they found important careers in journalism. They defined their work as applying the skills they had first learned in science laboratories to the investigation of social issues.

The increase in the college-educated population combined with the rising authority of science to transform professional work. During the Jacksonian period, egalitarian challenges weakened or eliminated laws regulating entry to the traditional professions — the ministry, medicine and the law — to the point where anyone could practice who gained a certain amount of knowledge through apprenticeship and who attracted sufficient clientele. In the postwar period, the prestige of scientific knowledge became a counterweight to democratic principles, by emphasizing the importance of specialized training and expertise. The movement toward the modern professional system began with the founding of the American Social Science Association in 1865. With the goal of establishing what one historian has described as "communities of the competent," the ASSA brought together college graduates with more traditional elites in a number of northeastern cities. It promoted "scientific" reforms in civil service, charity and prisons. Then in the 1880s, more specialized groups like the American Historical Association and the American Economic Association were launched, marking a shift away from public policy issues and toward the kinds of technical investigations being done in the research universities.

The American Medical Association was one of the most successful of the new associations founded to strengthen professional boundaries. Although it had existed as an ineffectual trade group since 1846, the AMA seized upon the revolution launched in Europe in 1876, when Louis Pasteur and Robert Koch connected specific diseases with particular microorganisms, to argue that only scientifically trained physicians should be

---

❄ **IN THEIR OWN WORDS**

"The Status of Athletics in American Colleges," 1890
This 1890 Atlantic Monthly *essay by Harvard professor Albert Bushnell Hart explained recent changes in college life. The popularity of athletics fostered more physically assertive norms of masculinity in the urban middle class.*

The chief seat of amateur sport is in the colleges. Here are assemblages of young men having unusual control over their own time; here is a strong feeling of *esprit de corps;* here,

out of the many players offering themselves, a first-rate team may easily be formed. . . . College authorities acknowledge, willingly or unwillingly, that athletic sports must be allowed and even encouraged. There is a growing sentiment that exercise is essential for the most efficient use of the mind. . . .

The first distinct result of athletics, as seen in the colleges, is a considerable increase in the average of bodily strength. The popular caricature of the college student is no longer the stoop-shouldered,

long-haired grind, but a person of abnormal biceps and rudimentary brains. As a fact, the most popular man in any college class to-day is usually a good student who can do something in athletics better than anybody else. The effect of this accepted standard of complete manliness is seen on men who never take part in athletic contests. The bodily vigor and health of students in the colleges have visibly risen in twenty years. . . . Experienced directors and trainers apply scientific methods of developing the body.

allowed to practice. Beginning in the 1890s, local AMA chapters gained in power and persuaded local governments to allow doctors themselves to restrict entry into the profession to those with scientific credentials. Similarly, the American Bar Association was founded in 1878 "to advance the science of jurisprudence." In 1894 New York became the first city to set up a central examining board of lawyers to control admission to legal practice. Increasingly, lawyers were trained in universities instead of through clerkships. In 1870, only one quarter of new lawyers had attended law school; by 1910, two-thirds did so.

New professions also arose under the protective banner of science that came to epitomize, in the words of historian Thomas Haskell, "the very essence of the professional idea — expert authority, institutionally cultivated and certified." Overall, 234 national professional associations were established between 1870 and 1900. Although rarely as successful in achieving control over entry into their occupations, these associations helped to establish standards of excellence and to defend their members' jurisdiction against encroachment by workers in overlapping fields.

WOMEN AND PROFESSIONALISM

The rising authority of science and professionalism was to have mixed implications for the status of women in American society. The prewar women's rights movement had drawn on equal rights ideology and Christian doctrines of the equality of all believers, but "science" as it was used in the late nineteenth century more often than not justified *inequality* between the sexes as well as between social classes and races. Darwinian theories were often cited as "proof" for assertions that would be deemed highly unscientific today. For example, prominent Boston physician Edward Clarke announced in 1873 that women's unique reproductive organs, the result of an evolutionary process of sexual specialization, were so delicate that they could be severely damaged by the mental exertion of higher education. Allowing young women access to college education, he warned, ran the risk of rendering them sterile and imperiling the very future of the nation. Although a number of women's colleges, including Vassar and Bryn Mawr, were founded in the postwar period, and women were admitted to many of the new universities, the "scientific" theories of Dr. Clarke were reflected in physical education requirements and, in some cases, separate curricula for women.

On the one hand, some women were able to find jobs as well as training in the expanding universities, and a number of female researchers played significant roles in the development of such fields as psychology and anthropology. On the other, as social science disciplines evolved in the later nineteenth century, women would often be deemed less capable of theoretical work and relegated to more "practical" subfields. Women found positions more readily, for example, in the new professions of social work, education, and home economics, than in the more purely academic fields of sociology, psychology, and economics.

Nonetheless, participating in these emerging professions allowed college-educated women to play a larger role in public life. More than any other person, Jane Addams was responsible for the creation of the profession of social work (see Chapter 19). But her en-

---

✳ IN THEIR OWN WORDS

Twenty Years at Hull House, 1910

Having had the opportunity to gain a college education, many women like Jane Addams found little opportunity to use it. In her memoir, she described how, after years of seeking, she and friends founded a settlement house in Chicago modeled after Toynbee Hall in London.

I gradually reached a conviction that the first generation of college women had taken their learning too quickly, had departed too suddenly from the active, emotional life led by their grandmothers and great-grandmothers; that the contemporary education of young women had developed too exclusively the power of acquiring knowledge and of merely receiving impressions; that somewhere in the process of "being educated" they had lost that simple and almost automatic response to the human appeal, that old healthful reaction resulting in activity from the mere presence of suffering or of helplessness. . . .

It is hard to tell just when the very simple plan which afterward developed into the Settlement began to form itself in my mind. . . . but I gradually became convinced that it would be a good thing to rent a house in a part of the city where many primitive and actual needs are found, in which young women who had been given over too exclusively to study might restore a balance of activity along traditional lines and learn of life from life itself; where they might try out some of the things they had been taught and put truth to "the ultimate test of the conduct it dictates or inspires."

try into the field of public service came only after an extended period of inactivity and depression following her graduation from a women's college in 1881, as she attempted to fulfill the expected role of the well-to-do Victorian woman. Later, in *Twenty Years at Hull-House* (1910), she strongly criticized what she described as "the snare of preparation," believing that pursuing personal "cultivation" kept young people from active participation in life. Through Hull House's work on behalf of its poor neighbors, Addams and a community of reform-minded women found a constructive role in society. They also provided social scientists such as John Dewey at the University of Chicago with a laboratory to investigate contemporary problems, which laid the groundwork for Progressive-Era reform programs.

William James   The founder of modern American psychology, James was also one of the principle architects of the philosophical school known as Pragmatism. Altogether, he is one of the most formidable figures in American intellectual history.

❧ *Pragmatism and Religion*

For most of the postwar advocates of one variety or another of the new authority of science, they emphasized science as a superior form of knowledge, a source of "fact" far in advance of traditional "superstitions." Only a few of the most perceptive thinkers of the late nineteenth century — particularly philosophers Charles Sanders Peirce, William James, and John Dewey — perceived that science offered more properly a "culture of inquiry" rather than a source of absolute knowledge. They understood that the achievement of modern science was a *method* of investigation within a community of researchers, where findings were always subject to further research and revision. But they did not, as popularizers claimed, offer the certainty of absolute *laws*. In addition, recognizing better than most the philosophical implications of the Darwinian account of random variation and natural selection, they envisioned a universe of chance and accident, offering neither solace of traditional religious doctrines nor new theories of evolutionary progress. They understood that the real meaning of Darwin's theory was that change was merely *change,* not progress.

William James, the best known of the three in the late nineteenth century, first applied the name *pragmatism* to this perspective in 1907. But he had already exemplified the experimental approach in his previous psychological studies, including *The Varieties of Religious Experience,* in which he asserted that the reigning scientific rationalism was incapable of dealing with human spiritual life. Acknowledging that a personal conception of God was "incredible to our modern imagination," James asserted that though spirituality should not be reduced to its physical manifestations, its truth could be judged from its effects, especially its ability to bring forth a "difference of emotional atmosphere." As a young man, James suffered greatly from depression. At first he hesitated to undertake scientific study, fearing it would rob him of "blind trust" in the universe, but he came to believe that the scientific worldview itself, seemingly so "rugged and manly" in its adherence to facts, masked a childish longing for certainty. As a scientist who thought through the implications of his own practices, he was too aware of the limitations of his calling to adopt the agnosticism that was fashionable among social scientists. He explained:

> When I look at the religious question as it really puts itself to concrete men, ... then this command that we shall put a stopper on our heart, instinct, and courage, and *wait* — acting of course meanwhile more or less as if religion were *not* true — till doomsday, or until such time as our intellect and senses working together may have taken in evidence enough, — this command, I say, seems to me the queerest idol ever manufactured in the philosophic cave.

James attacked "the airy and shallow optimism of current religious philosophy" for glossing over the harsh realities of industrial society. But he insisted that theories of any sort, whether religious or scientific, should be seen as "instruments" and truth as "the practical consequences of acting on a belief." Given those definitions, he embraced a heroic religious sensibility in which "all is well, in *spite* of certain forms of death, indeed *because* of certain forms of death — death of hope, death of strength, death of responsibility, of fear and worry, competency and desert, death of everything that paganism, naturalism, and legalism pin their faith on and tie their trust to." Not, in short, the kind of optimistic faith in progress preached by the national media.

DISSENTING VIEWS OF PROGRESS

Despite the impression of increasing homogeneity and centralization conveyed in the national media, Americans' lives became if anything more diverse during the postwar era. Even in this period of rapid urbanization, nearly three-quarters of the population of the United States in 1890 lived in rural areas or towns under eight thousand people. Although few Americans were untouched in some way by the economic and social changes of this period, responses of rural and small-town residents and of workers and immigrants in the cities differed in important ways from those of the dominant national culture. There was less agreement that all changes were signs of progress. Some vociferously resisted most changes as threats to their way of life, while others approached it warily, incorporating innovations in a piecemeal fashion and rejecting others. Above all, they sought to retain as much local control as possible over their everyday lives and refused to grant primary authority to the spokesmen of the urban, national culture.

᪪ Rural and Small-Town North

Though defined by the Census Bureau as "urban" places, towns and smaller cities in the later nineteenth century were in many ways distinct from both the emerging metropolitan centers and the embattled farms. As the economic and social bridge between these worlds, small-town residents often saw themselves as occupying a happy cultural medium, without the backwardness of the country or the corruption of the city. Small-town leaders included merchants, small manufacturers and professionals who depended upon the surrounding countryside for their business. For them, progress meant an increase in population and trade, but increasing centralization of power in large corporations and faraway urban centers threatened their autonomy as much as that of neighboring farmers.

Small-town businessmen suffered from the dominance of big city merchants, largely because of the advantage their location — the result of consolidation in the great regional railroad systems — gave them over markets and transportation costs. The businessmen's position was complicated by the fact that they had long been staunch advocates of progress, particularly when it came to improvements in transportation. For decades, local boosters in the Midwest tried to persuade farmers in their regions to approve bond issues to pay for new railroads by arguing that everyone gained from increased trade and property values. After the Civil War, however, these railroads came under the control of Northeastern financial groups like that led by John Murray Forbes, and began to discriminate in their rates against the very communities that had founded them. The railroad regulations first passed in the Midwest in the 1870s were described by their critics as "Granger Laws," in an attempt to discredit them, but they were actually the brainchildren of local businessmen who had been feeling the withering effects of railroad rate structures since the Civil War.

Late in 1865, the Burlington, Iowa, *Hawk-Eye* predicted that "the West" could soon become the center of power in the United States:

> Every careful observer must see that this great valley of the West is to be the seat of empire for the continent.... In the West lies the undeveloped wealth, material, mental, moral, and physical that is to control the future destinies of the Republic. The monopolies of Eastern corporations, manufacturing and transportation companies must give way before the irresistible march of improvement and progress in the West.

The answer, the editors thought, was not only to gain state aid for more railroads to compete with the monopolies, but to encourage economic diversification through the introduction of local manufacturing enterprises. "Sending our grain, wool, cattle, hogs, etc., East," they noted, "and then bringing them back in the shape of woolen goods, boots, shoes, hats and caps, agricultural implements, steam engines, etc., etc., is a very expensive way of getting on in life." Over the next half-century, this dream of economic diversification was blocked by the market power of industries in the Northeast and the Great Lakes region, but after the turn of the century manufacturing in agriculture-related industries such as meat-packing began to move back into the countryside.

By the 1870s, local business leaders in many Midwestern towns energetically lobbied their state legislatures to outlaw the rate discrimination they believed stood in the way of "the irresistible march of improvement and progress." In states like Illinois and Iowa, these efforts coincided with the mushroom growth of Granger organizations (see Chapter 21), whose members were also alarmed by the railroads' power over their lives. But the interests of farmers and merchants sometimes diverged — farmers benefited from lower prices brought by mail-order purchasing and from lower rates offered for long-haul shipping that bypassed local merchants. Debates in the state legislatures centered less on *whether* to regulate railroads and more on *how,* from the standpoint of different economic and regional interests, to do it most effectively. In Iowa in 1874, for example, businessmen in cities along the Mississippi River wanted to set mandatory schedules of maximum rates in order to lower charges between themselves and interior points; the state Grange organization, on the other hand, supported a limited commission system that was also backed by railroad lobbyists. In public, railroad leaders denounced any form of regulation and attempted to stigmatize the movement by connecting it with agrarian radicalism. It was they, in fact, who dubbed the legislation "Granger Laws." John Murray Forbes of the Burlington discounted criticism of rate discrimination as the product of the "slow agricultural mind." E. L. Godkin wrote in *The Nation* that advocates of state regulation were guilty of "spoliation as flagrant as any ever proposed by Karl Marx." Pro-regulation businessmen rejected charges of radicalism; they simply argued that the railroads were common carriers built with public funds and pointed to the long tradition of government support for the economic well-being of its people.

PRODUCERISM AND LOCAL RELIGION

In fact, small businessmen, farmers and workers alike challenged the economic theories that dominated the national media. Although regional, class, racial and religious differences often prevented effective political alliances among them (see Chapter 21), most members of these groups believed that there was indeed a "natural economy," but one governed by the moral claims of the producer, not the workings of abstract "laws." Though in favor of economic growth, they denied that the present path of increased economic centralization and inequality represented true progress. Instead they proposed the growth of a decentralized and balanced economy along the lines of the philosophy laid out by Philadelphia economist Henry Carey, which is often termed producerism. Carey, who had been influential in the antebellum Whig party, refused to accept postwar academic economists' distinctions between science and morality. His advocacy of the Greenback cause and rejection of the gold standard made him unfashionable in the metropolitan media, but he continued to publish works promoting the idea that society must be considered as a whole in the interest of maximizing true "happiness," not simply aggregate "wealth." He believed that a nation of small and medium-sized producers, though perhaps less efficient, would support a truly just, democratic, and stable society. It was the responsibility of a democratic government to enact policies, such as tariff protection and an abundant currency, to ensure the survival of such an economic system.

Meanwhile, religious culture was being reshaped in the small towns as well as the cities, but local religion followed a number of different, diverging paths. Although economic differences were less pronounced in the small towns than in metropolitan areas, every place had its local "gentry" of well-to-do merchants and farmers, doctors and lawyers and ministers of the larger churches. Its members were the people most likely to be affected by the cities' changing intellectual climate, but diffusion of the new media was uneven. The son of one of the leading citizens in the village of El Dorado, Kansas, young William Allen White did not encounter national magazines like *Harper's* and *The Atlantic* until the mid-1880s, when he was a college student in the larger town of Emporia. Even though he had not yet been exposed to the new evolutionary ideas, as a youth he was uncomfortable with public displays of emotion associated with evangelical religion. While a student at the Presbyterian College of Emporia, White and a friend formed a pact to resist the appeals of a Moody revival that swept through town. They "were scared stiff that it would get us and pledged ourselves to stand against it." On summer evenings, he watched curiously at camp meetings attended by "the workers, the failing farmers, and their fading wives." He was both excited and repelled by the "emotional upset, the hallelujahs and the imprecations to the Lord for forgiveness — all the outbursts of overwrought minds and burning hearts that made the spectacle so weird, so terrible, so fascinating."

Jane Addams grew up in the village of Cedarville, Illinois, daughter of a prominent businessman who was not a church member even though he taught Bible class in the nondenominational community church.

Nearby Rockford Seminary, which she attended in the late 1870s, was known as "The Mount Holyoke of the West" because of its religious intensity. One of the few "unconverted" girls in the school, Addams was the recipient of "every sort of evangelical appeal." She remained unresponsive to them, however, having adopted "a sort of rationalism" from her father and from an "early reading of Emerson." Nonetheless, she was attracted to "an ideal of mingled learning, piety, and physical labor" formed from her reading of medieval history, an ideal that would find secular expression in her settlement house work. In fact, many other men and women like White and Addams who would play prominent roles in the turn-of-the-century Progressive movement were products of small-town or rural childhoods. Though they rejected what they saw as the narrow doctrines and unseemly emotionalism of evangelical Protestantism, their participation in Progressive reform programs was driven by a semi-secularized "religion of humanity" that had its roots in evangelical Protestantism.

CHAUTAUQUA

For others in the rural and small-town middle classes the issue was not secularization but how to respond to proliferating opportunities for amusement afforded by an expanding economy. The Chautauqua movement, which demonstrated the potential of blending piety and entertainment, illustrated the contained experimentation with change undertaken by many Americans. Over the nineteenth century, Methodism had grown to become one of the major Protestant denominations despite its bans on drinking, dancing, gambling and nearly all types of commercial entertainment. One reason was its inventiveness in creating alternatives to these forbidden activities. Methodists originated Vacation Bible School, for example, and held their camp meetings in attractive spots like Martha's Vineyard and the Jersey Shore. They founded the Chautauqua Association in 1873 as a vacation camp to train Sunday school teachers. Located on the shores of spectacular Chautauqua Lake in western New York State, its two-week "institutes" offered lessons, sermons, devotional meetings *and* concerts, humorous lectures, bonfires and fireworks, plus access to a full range of recreational activities. One of its founders, Methodist minister John Vincent, explained that the institute's organization of activities refused to distinguish between sacred and secular activity. His goal was "to turn all secular nature into an altar for the glory of God." The enthusiastic response soon broadened the Association's audience far beyond Sunday school teachers, and for the next five decades hundreds of thousands of rural and small-town Americans made the pilgrimage to western New York to see many of the nation's most prominent thinkers and doers, including six presidents.

The Institute's ability to reconcile relaxation, religion and self-improvement was an example of the roundabout process by which many mainstream Protestants adopted a more positive attitude toward leisure in the late nineteenth century. Social Gospel leaders Washington Gladden (see Chapter 19) recalled his joy at realizing as a twelve-year-old that salvation did not require "the sacrifice of baseball." He remained convinced, however, that diversions must be "wholesome," and "educational"; he distrusted purely commercial amusements and of course forbade any such activities on Sundays.

The movement quickly generated spin-offs, including smaller week-long institutes at attractive rustic sites throughout the Northeast and Midwest. The Chautauqua Literary and Scientific Circle was set up in 1878 to provide materials for home-study groups that met in private homes. A monthly magazine, *The Chautauquan,* offered help in running these groups. Dedicated to "the Promotion of True Culture," it described itself as a "high-class literary magazine adapted to the needs of practical people." Those completing the study programs were invited to come to Chautauqua for a special "Recognition Day," which for many men and women who were not able to attend high school or college represented a special moment of achievement. Although the standardized reading provided by the Circle might be seen as evidence of cultural centralization, *Chautauquan* editors were careful not to offend the norms of its rural and small-town readers. The Circle lists included safe "information reading" in nonfiction subjects like history, geography and art. Novels, still scandalous to some, were omitted, though *The Chautauquan* judged that individuals might read one or two "good novels" a year without damage to "a well-organized mind." The egalitarian method of learning in the Circles, where members took turns presenting the assigned readings to the rest of the group, also ensured that the readings would be translated into terms that made sense within local perspectives. The overarching framework remained religious: members of the Vincent Chautauqua Literary and Scientific Club in Indianapolis, for example, heard Bishop Vincent himself deliver a lecture, "How to Grow Intellectually," which "emphatically pronounced that secret to be found in prayer."

LATE NINETEENTH-CENTURY REVIVALISM

The Moody revival that Kansan William Allen White resisted was part of the series of crusades conducted throughout the United States in the decades after the Civil War (see Chapter 19). Although revivalist Dwight Moody continued to believe in Biblical infallibility and premillennialism, he generally avoided controversial doctrinal issues in his sermons because his primary goal was to achieve conversions. He emphasized the love of God and kept his message simple: "Ruin by sin, Redemption by Christ, and Regeneration by the Holy Ghost." He did not mention hellfire or God's wrath, not because he rejected the doctrine of eternal punishment but because he thought it was not effective. He explained pragmatically, "Terror never brought a man in yet." Instead, he offered sentimental music and "living truths for head and heart," dramatized with "thrilling anecdotes and incidents, personal experiences, touching home scenes, and stories of tender pathos." Moody was most interested in individual salvation, but he was ambivalent about the direction of change in America. At the least, the supposed progress of postwar culture offered new opportunities for sin. In a sermon on temptation, he identified the "four great temptations that threaten us to-day": the theater, disregard of the Sabbath, Sunday newspapers, and atheistic teachings like evolution.

Others in rural and small-town America were more appalled by the falling away from true religion that they observed in the cities, and more willing to openly attack it. Before the Civil War, Jonathan Blanchard was an abolitionist ally of Henry Ward Beecher. Afterward, he continued the struggle to make America a "Christian nation," but found a widening gulf between how he and urban ministers defined this idea. As president

A Holiness Revival Service   A woman prays for the family of a convert at a late nineteenth-century holiness camp meeting. The Holiness Movement taught that, after conversion, believers could become, through the power of the Holy Spirit, entirely free from sin. Allowing women to preach was still unusual at the time this image was made.

of Wheaton College in Illinois and editor of a religious magazine, *Christian Cynosure*, he publicly attacked what he viewed as growing doctrinal laxity among Congregationalists. He was particularly vehement in his criticism of Beecher, noting, "If Mr. Beecher's teachings are the gospel of Christ, what need had Christ to be crucified." He ridiculed Beecher's efforts to modify his Puritan heritage: "When he is about to assail some fundamental truth, held and suffered for by the Puritans, he always begins by proclaiming himself their descendant." By the end of the 1870s, Blanchard's estrangement from the direction of the New England Congregationalism brought him into alliance with Moody and his Bible Training Institute in Chicago. Blanchard's son Charles succeeded him as president of Wheaton in 1882 and cemented the transition to a new outlook that formed the foundation of modern fundamentalism after the turn of the century. Such critics of "progress" no longer hoped to redeem the entire nation but to preserve a saving remnant until the final coming of Christ. Among Charles Blanchard's favorite texts was "Come out from among them and be separate." Increasingly, he looked for true disciples of Christ among those whom progress had left behind, the very people whom the adolescent White had ridiculed.

The third "R" in Moody's formula, "Redemption by the Holy Spirit," reflected an increasing emphasis among some evangelical Protestants upon a direct personal experience of God's grace. A number of parallel movements, including a separatist Holiness Revival among the Methodists, emerged in the postwar period to establish a tradition that after the turn of the century became known as Pentecostalism. Holiness teachings were spread through books, including Asa Mahan's *The Baptism of the Holy Spirit* (1870), which illustrated a shift in focus from Christ to the Holy Spirit, and through camp meeting revivals such as those White observed. They were also fostered and spread by a series of conferences in both Britain and the United States, in which like-minded clergy and laymen from a number of different Protestant denominations developed new interpretations of sin and grace. These included the belief that the experience of holiness translated into "power for service," which gave rise to a wide variety of philanthropic organizations in the cities that emphasized aid to the poor as well as evangelism. Such organizations were at least as numerous as those inspired by the more liberal Social Gospel spokesmen.

Negotiating Change in the Rural North

In long-settled areas of the rural Northeast and Midwest, farmers had been integrated into a market economy well before the Civil War. The continued importance of the family farm and the local community, however, sustained long-held Jeffersonian beliefs in individualism, independence, and local autonomy. Farmers valued the relative freedom that agriculture allowed them, and continued to think of theirs as the most virtuous way of life, not simply a way of earning a living. Moreover, they continued to believe that agriculture was fundamental to the virtue and well-being of the nation as a whole. In order to preserve it, they resisted changes that meant enlarging government, fearing both higher taxes — often hard for cash-poor farmers to pay — and interference from outside experts.

For example, throughout the nineteenth century rural roads were local institutions. They were maintained by the farmers themselves, through a system in which they paid off road and poll taxes with their own labor and use of their teams and equipment. Designed to meet local needs, the often-meandering and sometimes impassable system of country roads was the bane of the long-distance traveler. Rural voters rejected all efforts to centralize the system or shift it to a cash basis. They were nonetheless quick to adopt new technologies in the form of inexpensive patent road scrapers, introduced in 1879, which made possible improved roads without administrative changes. In the 1880s and 1890s, however, increased pressure for improved rural roads came from a new quarter: urban enthusiasts for the new sport of bicycling who wanted to escape into nature on smooth, permanent road surfaces. Represented by the nationwide League of American Wheelmen (generously funded by bicycle manufacturers), bicyclists agitated for the construction of macadamized (hard-surface) roads and a shift in authority to professional engineers at the state and federal levels. Farmers, who would bear the bulk of the costs of these vastly more expensive crushed-stone surfaces, adamantly opposed roads that they did not need. An 1893 Iowa farmers' convention made their feelings clear: "We don't want any eastern bicycle fellers or one-hoss lawyers with patent leather boots, to tell us how to fix the roads that we use." The resulting impasse was not broken until after the turn of the century, at the dawn of the automobile age, when the states began to pay directly for paved roads.

Of even greater concern was the issue of country schools. Like the roads, these were governed locally in the nineteenth century by tiny subdistricts within each township, each run by an elected school board with the power to set taxes, establish curricula, and hire teachers. Here too rural residents wanted to keep costs low, but school issues were even more contentious because they aroused people's anxieties about their children's future. Many farmers feared that inappropriate schooling — anything going beyond the "three R's" — would draw their children away from an agricultural way of

One-room Schoolhouse Rural schools faced many challenges in the late nineteenth century. One-room schoolhouses, like this one in Montana, made it difficult to separate students by grade. Large blackboards and new books were too expensive for many rural schools, which struggled to keep costs down. And parents often insisted that school calendars conform to agricultural cycles so that children could be available for farm work.

life; others wanted schools to prepare their children to succeed in a fast-changing world that might be vastly different from their own.

Beginning in Massachusetts before the Civil War, school reformers sought to eliminate the multitude of tiny districts in favor of township-wide systems. They hoped that larger districts would make it possible to hire better-trained and professionally certified teachers and superintendents and to purchase more modern materials. They also wanted to eliminate one-room schools in favor of larger buildings where students could be separated according to grades, and to establish high schools. Massachusetts farmers, however, resisted these changes as a threat to their ability to shape their

children's education. They wanted, for example, school terms to complement agricultural cycles, so that children could participate in farm work. To save money, they preferred the custom of having students furnish their own school books, which were often handed down within extended families, instead of adopting the newer standardized texts advocated by reformers. And they wanted to retain the one-room schools, not only to keep their children closer to home, but because the buildings also served as community centers for their rural neighborhoods, hosting singing schools, debating societies, public lectures and religious meetings when school was out. In the patronizing characterization of a reform advocate, farmers viewed the large districts as "an entering wedge to centralization and despotism." Opposing them, he reported, "backwoods orators in town meetings eloquently appealed to the memory of Patrick Henry and the heroes of Lexington and Bunker Hill"; they succeeded in fending them off for several decades.

Rural depopulation, however, accomplished what the reformers could not. As declining numbers of children made the tiny districts financially burdensome, they were gradually phased out. This happened first in Massachusetts in the 1880s, soon followed by the rest of rural New England. In the 1890s a subsequent push for school consolidation, or the merging of rural and town schools, was fought even more strongly through the Northern states generally. In many places in the late nineteenth century, the population of villages and towns grew faster than that of the farms even in agricultural areas, bringing to a head tensions between the competing perspectives of farmers and townspeople. Reform advocates were fortified by the increasing emphasis among postwar professional educators upon education as a means of socializing children into the broader world, defined in urban terms. Farmers opposed consolidation not only because the graded schools and high schools generally brought higher taxes, but because it meant transporting their children into town in hired hacks. A correspondent to the *Ohio Farmer* protested that this was "monumental stupidity. Instead of education we get jobbery and the minds of the children are fed upon false ideals and error." Although they were able to block consolidation until after the turn of the century, the reorganization of rural schools was accomplished during the Progressive period by means of an all-out campaign by professional educators and state and federal agencies to solve what was officially defined as "the rural school problem."

For many rural Americans in the second half of the nineteenth century, the schoolbooks handed down through generations of school children were most likely *McGuffey's Readers*. This was a series of six volumes of short stories, essays and poetry compiled by William Holmes McGuffey, a Cincinnati teacher, arranged in rising levels of difficulty. They were sold throughout the nation, but were ubiquitous in the Mid-

west; well into the twentieth century, autobiographers from that region assumed that their readers knew precisely what they meant when they wrote, as did William Allen White, that at the age of ten he was "in the second reader, but had read all the readers through to the fourth."

Although the wide use of McGuffey's readers might seem another sign of standardization, in many ways it reflected a decentralized rural life that was knit together not by modern bureaucracies but by a set of shared general beliefs. The *Readers* were popular because they embodied a simple moralism and avoided offending the sensibilities of a diverse readership. (The *Readers* are, for example, still used today in Amish schools.) Their contents did not attempt to impart current information, but exemplified what were considered unchanging producerist values — assumed to be particularly prevalent among rural people — of hard work, practicality, and simple living. They extolled the greatness of all things American, but stayed away from partisan or regional issues. Family life was celebrated and the importance of obedience upheld, as in the popular poem "Casabianca," where a young boy dies on a burning ship rather than defy his father's order to stay there until he returned.

Though farmers had adopted some mechanical aids to production, agriculture remained dependent upon nature in all its vagaries. They were less touched than urban Americans by the general atmosphere of material progress that encouraged secularization in religious thought. The *McGuffey's Readers* preached a generalized Christianity as the basis of a prosperous, orderly society. The *Sixth Reader* asserted:

> If you can induce a community to doubt the genuineness and authenticity of the Scriptures; to question the reality and obligations of religion; to hesitate, undeciding, whether there be any such thing as virtue or vice; whether there be an eternal state of retribution beyond the grave; or whether there exists any such being as God, you have broken down the barriers of moral virtue, and hoisted the floodgates of immorality and crime.

Published in 1857, these words were more a statement of the central place of religion than a comment upon developments in doctrine. They reflected the thinking of ordinary Protestant Americans through much of the century. Indeed, as late as 1905 a leading Baptist writer estimated that "the vast majority" of lay Baptists throughout the country were simply unaware that there had been any change or challenges to orthodox theology.

The world presented in McGuffey's readers seemed to be entirely innocent of change. It was agrarian and small-scale, and the individual prospered or failed according to his own efforts. The city, on the other hand, was portrayed as the source of moral danger, where young men were routinely ruined by being tempted into such dissipated activities as dancing, card playing, and attending the theater, which led inexorably to drinking, gambling, crime, prison and early death. Although the reality of rural life in the nineteenth century suggests that people were not necessarily more moral or sober than urban residents, the ideals embodied in *McGuffey's Readers* fostered the perception that at basis the world was simple, sure and fundamentally unchanging. This was far different from the world manifested in the urban media.

❧ *The Distinctive South*

The wartime destruction of the Southern economy and its failure to recover fully afterward meant that most Southerners did not face the same kinds of cultural changes encountered by Americans in other regions. Despite the efforts of New South promoters (see Chapter 16) there were fewer and smaller towns and cities. Those that did develop, moreover, adopted fewer of the cultural manifestations of northern urbanism. The dominant tone of public life after the end of Reconstruction was set by rural creeds and customs of localism, self-sufficiency, and suspicion toward change.

Nonetheless, significant cultural changes did occur in the postwar South, although obscured by its isolation from the national media. For example, the giant camp meetings that had been an innovation of the region earlier in the century gave way to local revivals conducted outside the limelight of the national tours of prominent figures. Where antebellum evangelism had focused on individual conversion and avoided the kinds of social reform movements that were common in the North, it broadened after the war to include precisely these kinds of issues. Antebellum revivalists in the South, faced with the reality of slavery and a male code of honor that demanded aggressiveness and self-display, had been less successful in spreading the disciplined behaviors that were becoming the hallmark of the northern middle class. Men of all classes followed the lead of the planters in prizing hunting, horserac-

ing and cock-fighting, drinking, and fighting. After the war, southern churches provided a bulwark in a time of chaos. Membership in evangelical denominations grew dramatically. Moral legislation, once spurned because of its ties to abolition, now flourished. Most southern states passed laws allowing local bans on alcohol, swearing, cock-fighting, gambling, and sporting events on Sunday. Many of these recreations continued outside the law, and crimes of violence were more prevalent than in the North, but Protestant morality nonetheless had achieved a dominant position in the public culture of the South.

Organized in their own denominations, African American churches played an even more prominent role in the postwar period. (See Chapter 16.) In the face of violent suppression of nearly all efforts at self-determination, ministers of black churches were de facto leaders of their community, charged with caring for the material and spiritual well-being of their flocks. Despite the racial separation of the churches, the centrality of musical expression in African American spirituality presented an important doorway of influence into national white culture. Jubilee songs, first sung by the Fisk Jubilee Singers as they traveled throughout the United States and Europe to raise funds for all-black Fisk University in Nashville, introduced northern white audiences for the first time to African American spirituals, albeit somewhat altered and "smoothed" to suit white tastes. Fisk students were

The Fisk Jubilee Singers   The nine original members of the Jubilee Singers from Fisk University pose in this 1871 photograph. Notice the singers' proper middle-class dress. They were the first internationally acclaimed African American singers, introducing "slave songs" to the world and preserving this fine music from extinction. They also gained legitimacy in white eyes by singing classical European music.

trained to sing classical and popular music of the day, but tour organizers quickly learned white audiences were fascinated by spirituals. Billed as a "healthful pleasure," Jubilee concerts drew men and women who were generally wary of commercial theater. Other African American colleges soon followed suit, and white revivalists introduced spirituals into their meetings. By 1903, W. E. B. Du Bois would complain in *The Souls of Black Folk* that "the mass of 'gospel' hymns which has swept through American churches and well-nigh ruined our sense of song consists largely of debased imitations of Negro melodies made by ears that caught the jingle but not the music, the body but not the soul, of the Jubilee songs."

Despite their differences, neither white nor African American churches in the South experienced the kinds of economic and social conditions that fostered change in the urban North. Fewer southern ministers felt the need to reconcile science and received beliefs, and those who did were quickly silenced. For example, James Woodrow, the uncle of future president Woodrow Wilson, was dismissed from Columbia Theological Seminary in Columbia, S.C., for claiming that evolution was compatible with Scripture. Nor did Protestant churches encounter the growing religious diversity brought to both urban and rural North by immigration (see below). In fact, the strongest influence from the North in this period may have been the migration into the region, particularly the Appalachians, of new Protestant groups like the Seventh-Day Adventists and Holiness movements.

DIVERGENT SUBCULTURES

Increasing differentiation within American culture in the second half of the nineteenth century was not only the result of differences between regions or between cities and countryside. Within the cities and towns themselves, immigration and the emergence of distinct working-class communities made for even greater diversity in ways of living and thinking. All of these groups were excluded from the dominant metropolitan culture, and sought to work out their own interpretations of the idea of progress.

Native-born, Protestant Americans greeted the swelling numbers of immigrants in the late nineteenth century with profound ambivalence (see Chapter 19). On the one hand, immigrants helped provide the workers and consumers required for the nation's material progress.

Andrew Carnegie estimated the economic contribution of each immigrant at $1,500, and outside the Northeast nearly every state established agents or boards of immigration to attract foreign settlers. Moreover, Americans had long pointed proudly to their nation's attractiveness to migrants as ultimate proof of the success of their experiment in republican government. Unlike nineteenth-century European nations that defined themselves in terms of a common ethnicity, Americans had espoused — at least officially — an ideological form of nationalism that required only an acceptance of democratic institutions. (Even today, the absence of an ethnic basis for citizenship distinguishes the United States from nations such as Germany and Japan.) Americans even derived a sense of national identity from their ability to assimilate many types into one: Oliver Wendell Holmes, Sr., boasted, "We are the Romans of the modern world, the great assimilating people."

But increased postwar immigration brought a further proliferation of languages, religions, and customs that prompted many to ask whether the nation could absorb, even survive such diversity. Even before the Civil War, the anti-Catholicism that had greeted Irish immigrants (see Chapter 14) had exposed a widespread assumption that the United States was a *Protestant* nation. The predominance of Catholic migrants from southern and central Europe threatened the widespread assumption that the United States was a *Protestant* nation, and the arrival of large numbers of eastern European Jews aroused fears for the future of the nation's *Christian* character. The anxieties that accompanied these realizations demonstrated the extent to which many assumed that a shared Protestant culture was essential for the success of democratic society.

The rising authority, among members of the urban upper classes, of Darwinism and supposedly "scientific" ideas about racial differences added a new racial strand to the older religious strand of nativism in the United States. Particularly in New England and the Northeast, writers proclaimed that America's greatness lay in the dominance of its "Anglo-Saxon stock." Families that had been prominent for generations attempted to distinguish themselves from social-climbing parvenus by emphasizing their descent from English nobility. John Fiske, the popularizer of evolution, for example, claimed to be a direct descendant of ninth-century England's King Alfred. For most of the postwar period, however, Anglo-Saxonists remained confident in the ability of their "race" to assimilate newcomers. Not until the crises of the 1890s would anxieties about the future of their multi-ethnic population supersede this optimism. Then, increasing demands were heard, particularly in the Northeast, for immigration restrictions.

❧ Immigrants Encounter the New World

The thinking of native-born Americans about the fate of immigrants seemed to resolve into opposing poles of complete assimilation and some sort of persistence as an "undigestible" foreign mass within the national body. As with rural Americans, however, immigrants followed a path of selective change. The very act of migration, of course, entailed fundamental changes. But once in America, newcomers had to decide how much change to accept, and how to interpret the changes that occurred. In the interest of preserving key aspects of their way of life, they accepted, even embraced, some changes while resisting others. There is irony here as well. In the process of transforming an "immigrant" into an "ethnic" culture, each group created an identity based in varying degrees on a sense of distinctiveness, of being "outsiders" in America. Yet over time the combined influence of the new diversity of cultures transformed the very definition of what it meant to be "an American."

For Catholic newcomers, whether from "old" immigration sources such as Ireland and Germany or the newer regions of southern and eastern Europe, the church was the most important institution mediating between immigrants and America. By 1850, Catholics were already the nation's largest single denomination, and despite recurrent anti-Catholicism they were a political force in key cities and states. Yet because a majority of Catholics in the postwar period were foreign-born, the church itself faced the task of defining its own identity in the midst of the proliferation of national cultures. Its leadership, moreover, was divided over how best to accommodate to American culture, or indeed how to envision the kind of America they wanted to accommodate to.

One source of anti-Catholicism throughout the nineteenth century was the church's close ties in Europe with reactionary or autocratic governments and its expressed opposition to democratic ideas. (See Chapter 14.) This supposed mistrust of the Catholic's ability to be a "real" American received fresh impetus in 1870 when the First Vatican Council proclaimed the dogma of papal infallibility. (There was considerable opposition to this step among liberal Catholics in Europe, who also dissented from the church's reactionary

politics and often advocated the separation of church and state.) In America, some Catholic leaders, styling themselves "Americanizers," argued that the church must distance itself from its ties to reactionary foreign powers and embrace "Anglo-Saxon" manners and institutions. Orestes Brownson, a former Transcendentalist who converted to Catholicism before the Civil War, warned, "If Catholics choose to separate themselves from the great current of American nationality, and to assume the position in political and social life of an inferior, a distinct, or an alien people, or of a foreign colony planted in the midst of a people with whom they have no sympathies," the church would miss its potential to transform American society. He was succeeded as spokesman of the Americanizers by the archbishop of St. Paul, Minnesota, John Ireland, who proclaimed, "Progress is the law of God's creation," which the church must follow.

Catholics who opposed this approach were more critical of the dominant American culture, with its lack of order and discipline and its excessive individualism and materialism. Nonetheless, they were careful not to challenge the nation's fundamental institutions. They avoided the thorny issue of the separation of church and state, to which Rome was unalterably opposed, but embraced the principle of freedom of conscience. Since Catholics were still a minority, it was a strategically useful position, but ironically it served to promote the further secularization of public life in America. Catholic writers pointed out that in the United States it was Protestant evangelicals who posed the most significant threat to free religious practice by seeking to legislate their norms of Sabbath observance and to inject their forms of worship into public ceremonies. They noted that the Protestants in Massachusetts and Connecticut had been the first in America to establish state-supported churches and had clung to them longest, until the 1830s. Catholic leaders opposed the public schools, not because they were secular but precisely because of the prevalence of Protestant religion there.

These Catholics professed themselves to be as patriotic as the Catholic Americanizers and Protestants who attacked them for disloyalty. They simply did not accept the right of the dominant majority to equate Americanism and Protestantism. In so doing, they articulated a more pluralistic way of understanding American culture. They emphasized the important role that Catholics had played in the New World, a role minimized by Protestant historians. The Columbian Catholic Congress held in conjunction with the Chicago ex-

Immigrants Shopping, 1895   Immigrants to the United States all wrestled with questions of assimilation. But they also lived their lives from day to day, as this 1895 photograph of crowds of people shopping for food at a Hester Street market in Manhattan's Lower East Side attests. Such a scene could just as well have been photographed in eastern Europe, although there more women would have covered their heads with scarves.

position in September 1893 reminded Americans that "it was a Catholic monk who inspired Columbus with hope; it was Columbus and a Catholic crew that first crossed the trackless main; that it was a Catholic queen who rendered the expedition possible; and that it was a

Catholic whose name has been given to the entire continent." Catholic historian John Gilmary Shea argued that it had been the Catholics of Maryland who had introduced religious liberty to colonial America. The standard claim that the Puritans of New England had pioneered religious liberty he deemed "a farce too contemptible for consideration." Rather, he characterized them as "narrow-minded, tyrannical, and intolerant in religious thought," and "grasping and avaricious" in their treatment of the Indians.

Despite their criticisms of American society, Cath-

olic critics did not seek a permanent isolation of immigrant cultures within their own communities. They
sought instead the right to define the terms of their
assimilation. Anton Walburg, a German-born pastor
in Cincinnati, published a controversial pamphlet *The
Question of Nationality in Its Relation to the Catholic
Church in America* in 1889. Like so many travel books
by European writers, it attacked Americans' worship
of money, their ridiculous obsession with size instead
of quality, and their unsophisticated culture. Yet Walburg's purpose was not simply to criticize but to improve. Pointing to the nation's destiny for greatness, he
attempted to distinguish a "false Americanism" from a
"true," pluralistic one that would admit of "no distinction of color, rank, condition, or nationality." He hoped
that by maintaining a sense of pride in their heritage,
instead of embracing the lowest forms of popular
American culture, immigrants could enrich their adopted homeland.

If the idea of cultural pluralism challenged the
claims of Protestants to represent the core tradition
in American history, it was also suspect to the more
conservative church hierarchy in Rome. Francesco
Cardinal Satolli, the first apostolic delegate to the
United States, blessed the Catholic Congress in Chicago in 1893: "Christian truth and American liberty will
make you free, happy and prosperous." But he attacked
America's ranking Catholic prelate, James Cardinal Gibbons of Baltimore (see Chapter 19), for attending the
World's Parliament of Religions at the same exposition,
because he feared that such ecumenism fostered "in-
differentism," or the blurring of religious distinctions,
which would weaken Catholic identity. Debates within
the church culminated in 1899 in *Testem Benevolentiae*,
the letter of Pope Leo XIII denouncing "Americanism,"
or an overemphasis on personal liberty as "hostile to
Catholic doctrine and discipline." Like the same pope's
1891 encyclical, *Rerum novarum*, the letter emphasized
that American Catholics must obey traditional principles of mutual obligation, not American notions of
individual freedom.

Like Catholic immigrants, the Jews who came to
the United States in the postwar period also debated
how best to respond to the new world they encountered. Unlike Catholics, they had a long history of being "outsiders," a persecuted minority within Europe's
Christian societies. In the relatively more tolerant environment of America, Jews faced a new problem: how
to preserve a sense of cultural identity that had been
shaped by centuries of exclusion. Within the ghettos of

Europe, cultural uniformity had been enforced, but it
could not be taken for granted in the New World. Although, as for many other migrants, piety was often not
a primary characteristic among those Jews who chose
to emigrate, in their new homeland religion became
central to their identities. Yet the precise character of
that religion remained to be determined.

In 1877, about quarter of a million Jews lived scattered thinly throughout the country. Because Judaism
had no centralized hierarchy, the individual synagogue
became the most important unit, although Hebrew
Union College in Cincinnati represented an important
center of Jewish culture. Before large numbers of eastern European immigrants began arriving in the later
part of the century, most American Jewish immigrants
had come from Germany. Many had prospered, and
the worship practices in their congregations began to
look more like liberal Protestantism, with the introduction of family seating in place of the separation of the
sexes and the embellishment of stained glass windows
and organ music. In 1885 a rabbinical conference met
in Pittsburgh to establish a national organization and
agreed on a set of defining beliefs for what was called
Reform Judaism. It ratified the congregational structure that had emerged and stated that the laws of the
Torah and Talmudic commentary should be adopted
"only as far as they can be adapted to the institutions of
the Society in which they live and enjoy the blessings of
liberty." This in effect permitted Jews to abandon many
aspects of worship and daily life, such as special dietary
practices, that had for centuries defined Jewish identity. Noting this, a number of rabbis at the conference
refused to join, laying the foundation for what emerged
in the twentieth century as Conservative Judaism.

By 1885, the new patterns of immigration made
Reformed Jews a minority. The number of Jews quadrupled by the end of the century, reaching 3 million
by World War I, with the majority clustered in the
Northeast. These new immigrants were much poorer
and shared, in Yiddish, a common language. (Yiddish
is the German dialect spoken by central and especially
east European Jews.) With greater numbers to support
the preservation of their distinctive way of life, they rejected the Reformed path of adaptation to American
culture. The result was a growing diversity in definitions
of what it meant to be a Jew in America. While some in
areas like New York City, with the greatest concentration of Jewish immigrants, chose to adhere strictly to
all laws of the Torah, others adapted more selectively
to the dominant culture. For many, Yiddish provided a

common urban sub-culture, with its own books, newspapers and theater. Others, while retaining a sense of Jewish identity, were attracted to secular labor radicalism (see below).

Many Jewish immigrants transferred intellectual skills, honed by a culture that emphasized Talmudic study, to the pursuit of education through the public schools. In New York they were so successful that by the turn of the century Jewish students dominated the publicly funded City College. They gained admittance to upper class Columbia University in such numbers that the institution, fearing for its elite reputation, adopted a "selective admission" policy — in effect a quota system — to reduce the proportion of Jewish undergraduates. Columbia's deans revealed their view of the undergraduate liberal arts program as a socializing experience for "gentlemen" of the upper classes when they explained that the children of eastern European Jews lacked the "social advantages" to make "pleasant companions" for the college's "natural constituency." Moreover, the deans said, Jewish students were a bit too "enthusiastic" about "accomplishment." The problem seemed to be that these children of immigrants had adapted too well to the new culture of intellectual inquiry being shaped in the emerging universities.

To varying degrees, each group of immigrants arriving in postwar America conducted a similar internal and external debate over change. Like native-born farmers, they negotiated contentiously with the agents of centralization and homogenization over how far and on whose terms they would become "assimilated" to the national American culture. Although no group of immigrants in the process of becoming an "ethnic" group was able to preserve unchanged the way of life they had known in their homelands, they were able to resist pressure to submerge their cultures into some "Anglo-Saxon" mainstream.

For other groups of immigrants, as well as longtime Americans such as blacks and Indians, issues of race made assimilation far more complicated. After the Civil War, for example, no group sought assimilation more eagerly than the former slaves, only to meet the intractability of white racism. The differences between Du Bois and Booker T. Washington (see Chapter 16), for example, involved different formulas for racial progress and assimilation. Du Bois resisted Washington's program of working within segregated communities, for he wanted to see talented African Americans participating as equals within the dominant metropolitan culture. He envisioned black leaders becoming "co-worker[s] in the kingdom of culture," by "fostering the traits and talents of the Negro, not in opposition to, but in conformity with, the greater ideals of the American Republic." Yet the foreboding that racism would continue to make his people outsiders within their own nation gave rise to Du Bois's famous statement about their divided consciousness: "One ever feels his twoness — an American, a Negro; two souls, two thoughts; two unreconciled strivings; two warring ideals in one dark body, whose dogged strength alone keeps it from being torn asunder."

❧ Workers Respond to Industrial Progress

If many immigrants were skeptical about Americanizers' claims that "Progress" was "the law of God's creation," so were the working men and women whose lives were transformed by the industrialization of manufacturing in the postwar period. Change was not uniform, however, differing in type and intensity according to the industry and the region. In areas of the South and West to which railroads came late in the century, if at all, artisanal forms of production that had disappeared from the Northeast in the Market Revolution (see Chapter 9) survived until late in the century. Compounding this regional diversity in rates of development, each manufacturing area had its own unique mix of industries, attracting differing patterns of ethnic and religious settlement. As in other aspects of American culture, the proliferation of local differences belied a surface impression of homogenization.

Nonetheless, workers everywhere responded skeptically to the visions of progress proffered by spokesmen for the new industrial order. The ideal of many continued to be a world of small-scale, independent producers, comparable to the agrarian world celebrated by *McGuffey's Readers*. They looked back to the artisanal system of production as it had operated before the Market Revolution and the emergence of the factory system. There, young boys had learned their trade by apprenticing to master craftsmen, working for little pay but in exchange being taught the complicated skills of production. After completing his apprenticeship, the young man continued to work for somewhat higher wages until he saved enough to establish a workshop of his own. In this world the possession of a certain amount of property, within the context of a rough general equality, ensured a balance of independence and equality that was the foundation of a democratic society. Robert MacFarlane, a mid-century labor leader, argued that a "small but universal ownership" was the "true foundation of a stable and firm republic." This artisanal ideal sought to balance individual rights with communal responsibilities, and work was done for the public good as well as personal gain.

This was the ideal, at least. In the crowded cities of the Northeast, reality had already begun to diverge from the ideal in the decades before the Civil War. The hope that westward expansion brought increased opportunities for young journeymen had attracted many artisans to the Free Soil ideology before the war. For some, it worked: Jane Addams' father had begun life as a miller's apprentice in Illinois, and novelist William Dean Howells started as a printer's devil (assistant) in rural Ohio.

But in industry after industry after the war, industrialization destroyed the traditional crafts. By breaking up manufacturing into smaller, simpler steps and by introducing new technologies, factory owners eliminated the need for artisanal skills. This allowed the employment of less-skilled workers, including immigrants and — anathema to many artisans — even women, who received lower wages. Mass-production lowered the quality of goods but also the price; those who had not been able to afford handmade goods might see this as progress, but not the craftsman whose skills were no longer demanded. In those industries where mass-production overwhelmed or eliminated traditional craft skills, workers could no longer hope to climb the artisanal ladder to achieve an independent livelihood as a small-scale producer. Instead, they faced the likelihood of a lifetime of working for wages. In a culture that had traditionally equated permanent wage-labor with slavery, this was a bitter pill.

Even if their trades were not immediately threatened, artisans in postwar American observed industrial changes with alarm. Their analysis of the problem and their proposed solutions were consistent with their producerist tradition, however. Rejecting the new Marxist socialist argument that class was determined by ownership of private property, they attributed the growing economic ills to a small group of wealthy capitalists who did no productive work but manipulated the system to control the labor of the vast "middle classes" of artisans, farmers and small businessmen. They feared that industrialized manufacturing would destroy this virtuous middle group through "the encroachments of both . . . the extremely rich and the extremely poor."

The Knights of Labor was established by a small group of Philadelphia garment cutters in 1869. It was a time

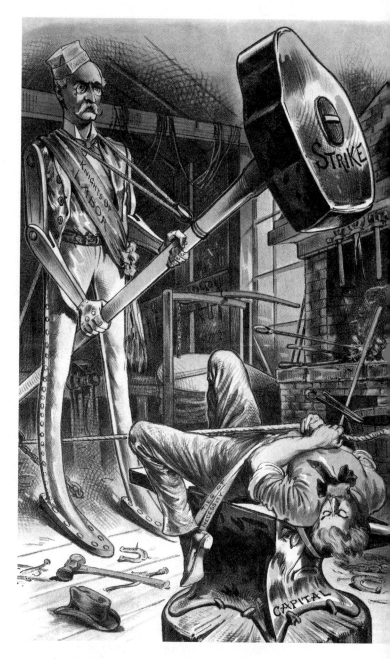

Anti-Labor Cartoon, 1890   Here, a monstrous, mechanical figure representing the Knights of Labor threatens to crush employers on an anvil labeled "Capital." By this time, however, the Knights were already fading as a force in the labor movement.

when organized labor movements were in disarray but fraternal societies flourished. Its first leader, Uriah Stephens, had been studying to become a Baptist minister when the Panic of 1837 forced him out to work as a tailor to support his family. Strongly attracted to fraternal rituals, he was a Freemason, an Odd Fellow, and a Knight of Pythias. The other founding members were also active in a variety of fraternal orders, and together they fashioned a secret, ritualistic brotherhood dedicated to "education"

The Haymarket Poster In English and German, this poster summons workers to the fateful Haymarket Square "mass meeting" on May 4, 1886. Notice that those coming to the meeting are urged to "arm yourselves."

industrial areas of western and northeastern Pennsylvania and into New York. The failure of the 1877 railway strikes and the brutal suppression of unions brought additional workers into the Knights, finally prompting the creation of a national organization in 1878. The preamble of the constitution written at its first General Assembly proclaimed its goal as making "industrial and moral worth — not wealth — the true standard of individual and national greatness." In place of strikes and partisan politics, the Knights advocated nothing less than the end of the wage system through its own version of evolution: They looked toward "the organization of all laborers into one great solidarity, and the direction of their united efforts toward measures that shall, by peaceful processes, evolve the working classes out of their present condition in the wage-system into a cooperative system." The preamble also called for equal pay for women, abolition of child labor, an eight-hour day, a graduated income tax, and government ownership of natural monopolies such as telegraphs, telephones, and railroads. For the present, it focused on transforming workers themselves through mystical ritual and doctrines. At the beginning of each meeting the assembly's head, the "Master Workman," solemnly intoned:

> In the beginning the great Architect founded the
>   Universe;
> The governing principle of which is Immutable Justice.
> In its Beautiful proportions is displayed Omniscient
>   Wisdom;
> And sealed His work with the signet of Everlasting
>   Truth;
> Teaching that everything of value, or merit, is the result
>   of creative Industry;
> And the cooperation of its harmonious parts evermore
>   inculcates perfect Economy.

The Knights' ceremonies created a semi-religious experience for many workers who had been alienated from mainstream Protestant churches because of the latter's support of the new economic system. The order emphasized the dignity of labor by pointing out that Christ had been a carpenter, and vowed that its primary enemy was the "idolatry of wealth."

As the assemblies proliferated, the movement began to diversify. The Knights welcomed members of all "productive" groups, including women and African Americans, barring only bankers, lawyers, speculators, gamblers, and liquor dealers. Despite its inclusiveness,

in the values of universal brotherhood, cooperation, and honor. Like the other popular fraternal orders, the Knights created in their meeting places, literally called "sanctuaries," places untouched by the ruthless competition of the day. The postwar popularity of fraternal organizations, each claiming in some way to defend such "chivalric" qualities as courage, loyalty, truthfulness, deference to legitimate authority, justice and care for the vulnerable, offered an eloquent challenge to the reigning doctrines of progress. The Knights of Labor offered an additional element in its vision of one day establishing an alternative culture based on its principles.

For its members' protection, the Knights' founders insisted on absolute secrecy, and the new order grew slowly by establishing additional chapters, called assemblies. Its principles and rituals were passed on only by word of mouth. Gradually, the organization began to spread beyond the Philadelphia region, into the heavy

particular assemblies tended to be dominated by a particular trade or ethnic group, giving rise to conflicting interests. Although the original Knights had been native-born, Protestant craft workers, newer members were more likely to be unskilled industrial workers, many of them foreign-born Catholics. Under the umbrella of the organization were assemblies of Marxists in New York City, anarchists in Chicago and Denver, Germans in Cincinnati, French Canadians in New England mill towns, and black coal miners in Ottumwa, Iowa. Tensions grew between radical and trade-unionist factions. Many newcomers, like railroad machinist Terence V. Powderly, began to agitate to abandon the order's "veil" of secrecy, streamline the ritual, and take on a more public role.

In 1879 Powderly became national head and moved the Knights away from secrecy. An Irish-born Catholic, he hoped to keep the church from including the Knights in its blanket condemnation of all ritualistic secret societies. (In this he failed, as both the American bishops and the Vatican denounced the Knights in the mid-80s. Only in 1891 did Pope Leo XIII reverse the condemnation, at the urging of Cardinal Gibbons.) But Powderly maintained the order's vision of transforming economic relationships by educating workers and developing methods of workplace democracy to restore their "personal dignity." After going public in 1882, the order grew within three years from fewer than 43,000 to 111,000. But increasingly its locals defied the ban on strikes. In the early 1880s a few, such as Philadelphia shoemakers and Union Pacific shopmen, were victorious, but many, including miners in Pennsylvania, Ohio, and Indiana, textile spinners in Fall River, Massachusetts, and iron molders in Troy, New York, were defeated. Then, in 1885, Knights led and won a highly publicized strike against Southwest Railway Conglomerate, owned by the widely detested financier and "robber baron" Jay Gould. Practically overnight, membership swelled to over three-quarters of a million. Many of these new members came with raised expectations and little interest in the order's cooperative vision. Despite Powderly's continuing emphasis on education, new members demanded strike leadership and support. But industrial employers vowed to fight back, and a second strike against Gould failed disastrously in 1886, followed by other defeats.

The most damaging blow to the Knights' vision of a brotherhood of all producers came in May 1886, when a dynamite bomb exploded as policemen attempted to break up a protest meeting of workers in Chicago's Haymarket Square. The toll eventually rose to eighteen killed and many more wounded, most of them policemen. Unable to discover the bomb-thrower's identity, the authorities nevertheless convicted eight anarchists, two of whom were members of the Knights, of conspiracy in the bombing. (Seven of the eight were German immigrants, adding fuel to nativists' fears as well.) Despite Powderly's refusal to defend the accused men, the national press took advantage of the situation to vilify the order, while internal divisions between radical and conservative wings ripped the organization apart. Although the Knights played an important role in the emergence of the rural Farmers' Alliance movement in the late 1880s (see Chapter 21), national membership quickly melted away.

The order's attempt to offer an alternative vision

✳ IN THEIR OWN WORDS

"The Secret Work of the Knights of Labor," 1870s

Like the many other fraternal organizations that proliferated in the nineteenth century, the Knights of Labor drew heavily upon religious language and beliefs in its secret rituals. It also hoped to channel the sense of brotherhood into economic transformation.

In the beginning, God ordained that man should labor, not as a curse, but as a blessing; not as a punishment, but as means of development, physically, mentally, morally, and has set thereunto his seal of approval in the rich increase and reward. By labor is brought forward the kindly fruits of the earth in rich abundance for our sustenance and comfort; by labor (not exhaustive) is promoted health of the body and strength of mind, labor garners the priceless stores of wisdom and knowledge. It is the "Philosopher's Stone," everything it touches turns to wealth. "Labor is noble and holy." To glorify God in its exercise, to defend it from degradation, to divest it of the evils to body, mind, and estate, which ignorance and greed have imposed; to rescue the toiler from the grasp of the selfish is a work worthy of the noblest and best of our race.

You have been selected from among your associates for that exalted purpose. Are you willing to accept the responsibility, and, trusting in the support of pledged true Knights, labor, with what ability you possess, for the triumph of these principles among men?

of progress may have foundered because of its effort to balance universalism with local autonomy. Its emphasis upon the "honor" and "nobility" of work and its inclusiveness brought together thousands of workers, who often had very different goals. But for a time its rituals, publications and public activities formed an alternative culture that challenged the authority of the dominant view that workers deserved to be poor. In the twentieth century, union organizers for the IWW and the CIO returned to the ideal of an inclusive brotherhood of skilled and unskilled workers. For the moment, however, emphasis shifted to the pragmatic "bread and butter" unionism championed by Samuel L. Gompers. Gompers had joined the Knights of Labor in 1873 while a cigar-maker in New York City. He soon parted ways with the order and in 1886 helped found the American Federation of Labor, an organization exclusively for craft unions. Recognizing that employers were more vulnerable to strikes by skilled workers, who were harder to replace, Gompers and the AF of L focused on improving wages, hours, and conditions for them, while ignoring unskilled industrial operatives. In 1888 Gompers publicly attacked the Knights' cooperative vision as utopian. In effect, he urged workers to accept that "progress" had made the wage system inevitable and seek a secure place within the new order. "The way out of the wage system," he stated, "is through higher wages."

ঔ *Radical Visions of Progress*

Though agreeing with Gompers that the self-sufficient artisan was a thing of the past, other Americans developed visions of progress far different from those purveyed by the metropolitan press. The postwar period witnessed a proliferation of radical voices in the United States, some influenced by European thinkers and many others home-grown, who argued that the capitalist system of industry was merely a transitional stage in social evolution.

Although the image of the bomb-throwing anarchist, the legacy of Haymarket, became a stereotype for all radicals in the national media, critics of American society held a wide variety of positions. Anarchists themselves drew upon the writings of a number of different European philosophers and ranged between extremes of libertarianism and collectivism, and between advocates of violence and pacifism. All, however, rejected the authority of government and advocated a society based on voluntary institutions. They differed over whether this society would be achieved

through revolution or the gradual spread of cooperatives as envisioned by the Knights of Labor. As we have seen, many American anarchists lived in metropolitan immigrant communities and published newspapers in English and German. By the end of the century a growing number of workers in western mining and industrial areas had embraced anarchism. Native-born Americans were also drawn to anarchism through the writings of nonconformists such as Thoreau, Emerson, and Whitman. They spread their ideas by publishing newspapers with titles like *Truth* and *Free Comrade* and utopian romances such as *The Dwellers in Vale Sunrise* and *The Natural Man.* They also founded a number of communes in the West, including Home (Washington State) and Kaweah (California).

Socialists occupied an even more varied spectrum of philosophical positions, although all agreed that the path of social evolution lay in collective ownership of industrial wealth. Many were followers of the "scientific" socialism developed by the nineteenth-century German philosopher Karl Marx, who argued that "laws" of economic development dictated the eventual overthrow of the capitalist system by a revolution of the impoverished masses it had created. Just as Sumner dismissed economic reformers as sentimental moralists, Marx ridiculed other forms of socialism as "utopian." Nonetheless, thousands of Americans, from impoverished immigrants to prosperous intellectuals, adhered to a belief that some form of state control of economic institutions would bring about a just society. Many rejected Marx's belief in revolution, however, in favor of a more evolutionary vision. After the defeat of his American Railway Union in 1894 (see Chapter 21), Eugene V. Debs turned his energies to founding a non-Marxist Social Democracy party, dedicated to the achievement of socialist goals through acquisition of political power. Groups of socialists established colonies, such as Equality, in Washington State, seen as a "vanguard of the army that was to cover the thinly-populated State of Washington with a network of cooperative settlements and quietly and peaceably — and quite legally — transform it into a cooperative commonwealth."

In fact, creating alternative visions of progress — through fiction, in utopian novels, and through the founding of new communities in the West — was a major method of social criticism in late nineteenth-century America. The inspiration behind most of these was *Looking Backward,* the hugely popular novel published in 1888 by Edward Bellamy. Bellamy found it difficult to fit into postwar society, rejecting careers in the ministry, law and journalism. Suffering from tuberculosis and prone to bouts of nervous exhaustion, he found escape in imagining fantasy lands, which he captured in romantic short stories that he published in newspapers and magazines. *Looking Backward* began as one such story, but as he wrote amid the unrest of 1886, there came into his mind the image of a great "industrial army" organizing the nation's production in the same way that the Union Army had conducted the war. Bellamy seized upon the military model as the answer to all the ills of the day. *Looking Backward* told the story of the Boston patrician Julian West, who in the year 2000 awakens from a hypnotically induced sleep. He finds that society has been transformed, not merely through the introduction of marvelous new technologies but through a complete reorganization according to principles of cooperation, public service, and economic justice. With the protagonist West standing in for the skeptical reader, the novel demonstrates in precise detail how such a society would operate, down to a system of credit cards to regulate purchases in a magnificent department store of the future.

Like the Knights of Labor, Bellamy hoped that cooperation would replace the injustice and disorder of the 1880s, but he lacked their faith in the virtue of working people. Like many members of the middle class, he distrusted strikes and saw socialist political parties as misguided. Instead, he was attracted to the image of a vast army of industrial workers as a more efficient and orderly way of organizing society. Like the Knights' vision, it would be based on principles of mutual obligation and equality, but would be directed from the top down by an enlightened corps of officers. (Bellamy had sought to enroll at West Point in 1867 but was turned down because of poor health.) He labeled his ideal "nationalism," to convey the sense both of national ownership and transcendence of narrow special interest. Like a well-calibrated machine, the national industrial army would be carefully organized to provide just the right combination of incentives and punishments to produce compliance. All production would be controlled by a single organization, elimi-

Edward Bellamy *Looking Backward* combined utopian idealism with many of the techniques of sentimental popular novel-writing to achieve an unprecedented success with the American public in the troubled 1880s and 1890s.

nating "the wastes which resulted from leaving the conduct of industry to irresponsible individuals." In a world without class, industrial work would be performed by young people as a form of universal service, with greater rewards accruing to the most difficult. Decisions would be made by officers who had risen through the ranks; older adults were free to choose occupations that suited their interests. Women were organized in a sort of auxiliary army, with tasks deemed suitable to their different needs and abilities, but all received equal "credits"; neither they nor their children depended upon men for support. All received ample resources to ensure access to the array of consumer goods that the industrial system produced.

The novel was immediately successful, becoming one of the most widely read books of the century. Its sales were surpassed only by *Uncle Tom's Cabin* and the religious historical novel *Ben-Hur*. Readers were clearly attracted to Bellamy's detailed description of a far happier, juster society. The novel, unfortunately, was much vaguer about exactly *how* the transformation had taken place. Bellamy leaves the explanation to a sermon preached by one of his characters. Noting that by the late nineteenth century "the vast majority of men had agreed as to the crying abuses of the existing social arrangement," it was still tolerated because they failed to perceive a viable alternative to competitive individualism. Then, when at an unspecified time it was generally recognized that a reorganization of society "on a higher ethical basis" was in the interests of all, "the dawn" finally came. "From the moment men allowed themselves to believe that humanity after all had not been meant for a dwarf, . . . but that it stood upon the verge of an avatar of limitless development, the reaction must needs have been overwhelming. It is evident that nothing was able to stand against the enthusiasm which the new faith inspired." The sermon alludes to a "stormy epoch of transition, when heroes burst the barred gate of the future and revealed to the kindling gaze of a hopeless race, . . . a vista of progress whose end, for very excess of light, still dazzles us." But the implication is that the revolution was swift and nearly bloodless. True to his New England Protestant roots, Bellamy presents the revolution in terms of a mass intellectual conversion, a secular millennium.

Many of his readers did indeed respond enthusiastically to the vision. John Dewey and Charles Beard both placed *Looking Backward* second only to Marx's *Capital* on their lists of the most influential books of the late nineteenth century. The WCTU, the National Council of Women, the National Farmer's Alliance, and the Knights of Labor all distributed copies to their members. It was translated into more than fifteen languages and inspired an international debate. Readers founded hundreds of Nationalist Clubs to promote the vision; characteristically, their goal was the voluntary conversion of capitalists through persuasion rather than political engagement. They published a magazine, *The Nationalist,* to promote the cause. Bellamy himself, however, began to believe that the movement must take on practical issues, and founded his own journal, *The New Nation,* to advocate government ownership of coal mines, telegraph and telephone companies, and the railroads, and equal and compulsory education.

A popular writer and lecturer, Charlotte Perkins Gilman extended Bellamy's ideas to present a more radical feminist vision. She argued that it was, in fact, women's economic dependence upon men that was holding up the final evolution of society into socialism. Applying evolutionary ideas, she noted that women's dependent position resulted in an unhealthy exaggeration of gender differences that required men to be ruthlessly competitive, both to the detriment of society. Her ideas were developed in speaking to Nationalist Clubs and writing poetry and articles for *The Nationalist* and other "progressive" periodicals. They were summarized in a best-selling book *Women and Economics: A Study of the Economic Relation between Men and Women as a Factor in Evolution* (1898). Gilman's ideas influenced the women's rights movement, then regaining momentum, though she was little interested in winning the vote. More moderate women's suffragists believed that receiving the franchise was an essential step in the progress of both their gender and the nation as a whole.

Radical Critiques of Progress

Other social critics went farther, rejecting entirely the dominant faith in progress. Henry George, a middle class Philadelphian, had traveled widely throughout the United States and worked as a seaman, a printer, and a newspaperman. His observations of the tremendous changes of the 1860s and 1870s led him to write a book, *Progress and Poverty* (1879), challenging the very foundations of the idea of progress. George presented his own version of "scientific" history to refute the "hopeful fatalism" of laissez-faire economics. He believed that repeated cycles of "growth and decay of civilizations" throughout history belied the popular theory of continuous progress, the view that "improvement tends to go on unceasingly, to a higher and higher civilization." Instead, it showed that nations tended to rise and fall, as division of labor and the accumulation of wealth steadily widened the gap between classes. As an increasing proportion of the civilization's resources were devoted to the support of an idle ruling class, it invariably collapsed. In his idea of a "single tax," George claimed to have discovered the key to eliminating these cycles. This was a tax on what he defined as unearned wealth in land, which would prevent growth in inequality. His thinking reflected his roots in the agrarian and artisanal producerist ideal of a small-scale, egalitarian economy and widely diffused political power. The book was dismissed by the national media but inspired a small but dedicated band of Single Taxers, and his general analysis of the nation's problems had a much wider readership. In 1886, with support from the Knights of Labor and other workers' and radical groups, George ran for mayor of New York as the candidate of the United Labor party. He was narrowly defeated by Democrat Abram S. Hewitt but ran ahead of a wealthy young Republican named Theodore Roosevelt.

George's analysis also inspired the Farmers Alliance and Populist movements (see Chapter 21). His vision of a civilization in decline also underlay *Caesar's Column,* a disturbing futuristic novel published in 1891 by

Minnesota Populist writer Ignatius Donnelly. One of the most widely read books of the early 1890s, it was an apocalyptic, anti-utopian premonition of society as it would be in 1988 if trends continued. Evoking the worst fears of rural America, Donnelly portrayed the city as a den of hypocrisy, sexual debauchery, grinding poverty, and explosive violence. The world is ruled by a small group of plutocrats and policed by hired bands of "Demons," who drop poison-gas bombs from dirigibles to suppress opposition. Under this oppression, both urban workers and farmers have become brutalized. Ultimately, the civilization is consumed in a bloody revolution, leaving a small number, a saving remnant, to flee to Africa, where they form a new society based on Christian socialist principles.

Donnelly's vision, fusing radical politics with evangelical millennialism, was further manifested in his preamble for the 1892 Omaha platform of the People's Party:

> A vast conspiracy against mankind has been organized on two continents, and it is rapidly taking possession of the world. If not met and overthrown at once, it forebodes terrible social convulsions, the destruction of civilization, or the establishment of an absolute despotism.

Donnelly's apocalypse illustrates the role of evangelical culture in the emergence of the Alliance movement and Populism. A shared Protestant culture provided a fertile medium for nurturing the agrarian movements to challenge the economic and cultural power of Northeastern financial elites. The Alliance's traveling lecturers spoke a language and employed organizational forms shaped by generations of revivalists. The experience of working together within the Alliance movement helped farmers withstand the withering ridicule of the metropolitan press.

By the mid-1890s, however, it had become difficult for even the most optimistic middle-class American to dismiss the voices of critics of progress. Of the financial panic of 1893, Henry Adams wrote of his Boston friends, "Men died like flies under the strain and Boston grew suddenly old, haggard, and thin." His eccentric younger brother Brooks was in the midst of writing his own book, entitled *The Law of Civilization and Decay* (1895). It reasserted a cyclical theory of historical development, in which societies alternated between periods of civilized "concentration" and barbaric "dispersion." In the early stages of centralization, he believed, the characteristic "mental types" were religious, military, and artistic; as it continued, the capitalist, or moneylender, became dominant. At some point, concentration can go no farther, and disintegration sets in. Brooks Adams made no effort to conceal his contempt for the commercialism of his day, idealizing the art and chivalry of the Middle Ages. He perceived incipient disintegration even in the era's art.

> The ecstatic dream, which some twelfth-century monk cut into the stones of the sanctuary hallowed by the presence of his God, is reproduced to bedizen a

---

✱ IN THEIR OWN WORDS

Caesar's Column: A Story of the Twentieth Century, 1890

Populist writer Ignatius Donnelly created one of the first "dystopian" novels in 1890 to show the logical outcome of the nation's concentration of wealth. Set in 1988, the story climaxes in an apocalyptic riot by the urban poor, brutalized by oppression and deprivation.

Civilization is gone, and all the devils are loose! No more courts, nor judges, nor constables, nor prisons! That which it took the world ten thousand years to create has gone in an hour. . . .

But still the work of ruin and slaughter goes on. The mighty city, with its ten million inhabitants, lies prostrate, chained, helpless, at the mercy of the enraged *canaille*. The dogs have become lions.

The people cannot comprehend it. They look around for their defenders — the police, the soldiery. "Where are they? Will not this dreadful nightmare pass away?" No; no; never — never. This is the culmination — this is the climax. . . . These are "the grapes of wrath" which God has stored up for the day of his vengeance; and now he is trampling them out, and this is the red juice — look

you! — that flows so thick and fast in the very gutters.

You were blind, you were callous, you were indifferent to the sorrows of your kind. The cry of the poor did not touch you, and every pitiful appeal wrung from human souls, every groan and sob and shriek of men and women, and the little starving children — starving in body and starving in brain — rose up and gathered like a great cloud around the throne of God; and now, at last, in the fullness of time, it has burst and comes down upon your wretched heads, a storm of thunderbolts and blood. . . .

warehouse; or the plan of an abbey, which Saint Hugh may have consecrated, is adapted to a railway station.

Adams made no specific predictions about the United States, though he referred pointedly to the growing power of the banker, referred to as "the monied type," and "the usurious mind." Theodore Roosevelt, reviewing the book for *Forum* magazine, admitted that it contained a "very ugly element of truth." But he attempted to put Adams in his place by concluding that the idea that moneylenders were crushing American farmers was "really quite unworthy of Mr. Adams, or of anyone above the intellectual level of Mr. [William Jennings] Bryan, Mr. Henry George, or Mr. Bellamy."

From the new world of the research universities came other challenges to the reigning faith in progress, all the more troubling because they were couched in the dominant language of science itself. Thorstein Veblen, son of Norwegian immigrants, had grown up on farms in Wisconsin and Minnesota, isolated from native American culture. He did graduate work at Johns Hopkins, Yale, and Cornell and taught at a number of prominent universities, but never lost the sense of being an outsider in metropolitan culture. His most famous book, *The Theory of the Leisure Class* (1899), applied the tools of evolutionary science to modern American business. But unlike Spencer or Sumner, who equated dominance with superior "fitness," Veblen mustered evidence from philosophy and the new fields of psychology, sociology, anthropology, and economics to show that the "leisure class" controlling America was made up of those who excelled in "pecuniary" and "predatory" traits that were "survivals" from barbaric stages of development. It had been engineers, mechanics and workmen, not the financiers, he argued, who wrought the industrial advances of the nineteenth century. They possessed what Veblen called the "instinct of workmanship," motivated by "a taste for effective work, and a distaste for futile effort." But their achievements were now controlled by a leisure class that performed no productive work. Unlike the Alliance or the Knights of Labor, Veblen claimed to be purely objective and scientific in his treatment of this class, but he ruthlessly satirized the behavior of "captains of industry" as barbaric. The great institutions of late nineteenth-century culture, including the modern university, as well as the opulent displays of the wealthy (see Chapter 19), he ridiculed as forms of "conspicuous consumption," and even "conspicuous waste."

Son of a pioneer Wisconsin businessman, historian Frederick Jackson Turner too was something of an outsider to metropolitan culture. As a graduate student at Johns Hopkins he resisted his professor's theory that American democracy was merely the result of "Anglo-Saxon" traditions. As a professor at the University of Wisconsin, Turner developed his own evolutionary theory about American culture that reflected his Midwestern origins. Like an increasing number of late nineteenth-century evolutionists, he thought that environment played a greater role than heredity. He attributed all that was distinctive in American culture, especially its democratic and pluralistic character, to the influence of the frontier. "Up to our own day," he wrote, "American history has been in a large degree the history of the colonization of the Great West." For Turner, who largely ignored the existence of native Americans, the continuous "advance of American settlement westward," the taking up of "free land," had set up a repeated cycle of "progress" from frontier simplicity to civilized complexity that enabled Americans to develop a culture unlike that of Europe. "American social development has been continually beginning over again on the frontier. This perennial rebirth, this fluidity of American life, this expansion westward with its new opportunities, its continuous touch with the simplicity of primitive society, furnish the forces dominating American character."

Turner presented his ideas in a paper, "The Significance of the Frontier in American History," read before a meeting of the American Historical Association in conjunction with the 1893 Chicago Columbian Exposition. In some ways, Turner simply translated a popular vision of expansionary progress into the measured language of social science, and his tone was similarly upbeat. Yet the evolutionary pattern he traced was not linear, but cyclical. Throughout its history, Turner believed, American culture had been reinvigorated through a return to the primitive wilderness and through the exertion of transforming it.

Even as it celebrated the frontier's importance, Turner's paper began with the Superintendent of the Census' 1890 announcement that there was no longer a frontier — a line separating settled from unsettled regions in the United States. "This brief official statement marks the closing of a great historic movement," Turner acknowledged. As he intended, his paper defined a new frontier in research, which occupied professional historians for the next half century. But it left unanswered the crucial question: what would replace the frontier in American society? Did the disappearance of the "gifts of

The Chicago Exposition, 1893 The glittering white buildings and a vast array of industrial and technological wizardry on display dazzled the public, which flocked to tour the Exposition. Visitors carried away a vision of past and future progress that belied the grim realities of the depression that struck the U.S. just as the Exposition was closing.

free land" mean the end of American uniqueness? Had progress itself ended the special qualities that Turner identified? The only thing certain was that if progress was to continue, Americans would have to find an environmental equivalent to the frontier.

CONCLUSION: VOICING ALTERNATIVES

Even as America became more physically unified in the generation after the Civil War, its increasing diversity was reflected in a wide range of responses to change. A metropolitan culture, disseminated through national media and educated in the new university system, extolled the growing power of science and efficiency over all aspects of life. But those who shared less in the nation's growing industrial wealth, in urban working-class neighborhoods, small towns and rural areas, found ways to communicate alternative points of view that often rejected change or found ways of influencing

how it shaped their lives. Farmers, workers and immigrants all refused to accept dominant interpretations of progress and used their own publications and organizations to preserve a degree of choice over changes in local ways of life.

By the end of the century, the chorus of voices criticizing the idea of progress mounted to overwhelm the "fatalistic hopefulness" of the dominant postwar national culture. Some Americans continued to speak with the moral language of traditional values, but they were joined by a younger generation of university-trained men and women more comfortable with the arguments of evolutionary science. In the face of persistent industrial conflict and financial crises in the 1890s, even many middle-class Americans began to ask whether the limits of progress had been reached. Together, these voices clamored increasingly for reform of politics and the economy. The fact that many rejected the complacent materialism of the Gilded Age should not obscure, however, that they had little else in common. The diversity of values among Americans, even of definitions of what it meant to be an American, became increasingly apparent after the turn of the century, as many Americans of all types set out to reform their society.

Suggested Reading

Hal S. Barron, *Mixed Harvest: The Second Great Transformation in the Rural North, 1870-1930* (1997). Describes the mixture of encouragement and resistance in farm families' attitudes toward change.

Thomas Bender, *New York Intellect: A History of Intellectual Life in New York City, from 1750 to the Beginnings of Our Own Time* (1988). The middle chapters provide a detailed analysis of the postwar emergence of influential metropolitan cultural institutions in New York City.

Sally F. Griffith, *Home Town News: William Allen White and the* Emporia Gazette (1989). Illustrates the multifaceted role of a community newspaper in mediating between metropolitan and small town culture in late nineteenth-century Kansas.

David N. Livingstone, *Darwin's Forgotten Defenders: The Encounter between Evangelical Theology and Evolutionary Thought* (1987). Describes the varied and changing responses to Darwinian theories.

George M. Marsden, *Fundamentalism and American Culture: The Shaping of Twentieth-Century Evangelicalism, 1870-1925* (1980). An influential study of the development of a distinctive evangelical subculture in the United States.

Wilfred M. McClay, *The Masterless: Self and Society in Modern America* (1994). Early chapters highlight the powerful attraction of many American intellectuals to the idea of a centralized national government.

William G. McLoughlin, *The Meaning of Henry Ward Beecher: An Essay on the Shifting Values of Mid-Victorian America, 1840-1870* (1970). An examination of the influential role of a popular preacher and writer in the shaping of liberal Protestantism.

R. Laurence Moore, *Religious Outsiders and the Making of Americans* (1986). Demonstrates that groups outside the Protestant mainstream have repeatedly redefined what it means to be American.

Robert E. Weir, *Beyond Labor's Veil: The Culture of the Knights of Labor* (1996). Details the transitional role of the fraternal order that served as an important forum for the expression of producerist opposition to industrialization.

Suggestions for Further Reading

Andrew Abbott, *The System of Professions: An Essay on the Division of Expert Labor* (1988).

Elaine S. Abelson, *When Ladies Go a-Thieving: Middle-Class Shoplifters in the Victorian Department Store* (1989).

Lewis Atherton, *Main Street on the Middle Border* (1954).

Thomas Bender, *Intellect and Public Life: Essays on the Social History of Academic Intellectuals in the United States* (1993).

Robert S. Fogarty, *All Things New: American Communes and Utopian Movements, 1860-1914* (1990).

Lawrence Goodwyn, *Democratic Promise: The Populist Moment in America* (1976).

Thomas L. Haskell, *The Emergence of Professional Science* (1977).

John Higham, *Strangers in the Land: Patterns of American Nativism, 1860-1925* (1955, 1988).

John Lauritz Larson, *Bonds of Enterprise: John Murray Forbes and Western Development in America's Railway Age* (1984).

James R. Moore, *The Post-Darwinian Controversies* (1979).

R. Laurence Moore, *Selling God: American Religion in the Marketplace of Culture* (1994).

Clifford Putney, *Muscular Christianity: Manhood and Sports in Protestant America, 1880-1920* (2001).

Gretchen Ritter, *Goldbugs and Greenbacks: The Antimonopoly Tradition and the Politics of Finance in America, 1865-1896* (1997).

John H. Roberts, *Darwinism and the Divine in America: Protestant Intellectuals and Organic Evolution, 1859-1900* (1988).

Rosalind Rosenberg, *Beyond Separate Spheres: Intellectual Roots of Modern Feminism* (1982).

Thomas J. Schlereth, *Victorian America: Transformations in Everyday Life* (1991).

Alan Trachtenberg, *The Incorporation of America: Culture and Society in the Gilded Age* (1982).

Laurence R. Veysey, *The Emergence of the American University* (1965).

Altina L. Waller, *Reverend Beecher and Mrs. Tilton: Sex and Class in Victorian America* (1982).

William Allen White, *The Autobiography of William Allen White* (1946, reprinted 1990).

21   The Politics of the Gilded Age

I N HIS NOVEL *The Gilded Age* (1873), written with Charles Dudley Warner, Mark Twain gives a tour of the nation's capital. It teems with schemers, lobbyists, jobbers, and other rogues eager to fleece the public and an equal number of innocents abroad gullible and greedy enough to be easy prey. Men and women intrigue for congressional favors and patronage and push countless false hopes for the fast buck, from eyewash ("the Infallible Imperial Oriental Optic Liniment") to railroad land grants, all under the guise of the public good. Bribery, vote stealing, and gaseous oratory distinguish the successful politician. An honest person is a fool. So corrupting is the political and social world Twain describes that it transforms the once virtuous orphan girl heroine of his story into a hardboiled lobbyist who ends her life in scandal. An air of impermanence and swindle blows everywhere through the seat of the Republic. Washington, by Twain's count, also has "more boarding-houses to the square acre . . . than any other city in the land," but if you try to pass yourself off as a congressman in seeking a room in any one of them, the landlady will say "full" or demand payment in advance. The public cannot trust its elected servants.

Twain's burlesque of government and the national political culture, based on real scandals and thinly disguised portraits of real members of Congress, caught the mood of the times. It gave the period from the end of Reconstruction to 1900 its name — the "Gilded Age," glitter on the outside, base metal below. It colored the way many historians have viewed the politics of the era thereafter. But the emphasis on the venality and banality of national politics misses the other great current surging through national public life. Amid all the disarray and dissembling in government, there also was a search for order. By the end of the century, many Americans would look to Washington with hope rather than disgust. Reforms in voting, office holding, and management would transform the electorate and public life. The process was in many ways undemocratic, but it did position American politics, government, and society to enter the Progressive era.

POLITICAL PARTIES AND POLITICAL STALEMATE

The period from the election of Abraham Lincoln in 1860 to that of William Howard Taft in 1908 has often been characterized as the era of Republican ascendancy. The Democrats, after all, managed to elect only one president during that time — Grover Cleveland twice, in 1884 and again in 1892. Such a view distorts the political picture. Political instability rather than Republican monopoly ruled much of the day. The two major national parties were evenly matched. With power within the grasp of each party, they fought fierce battles for the White House and congressional seats. Third parties also arose to challenge the two-party hegemony and to push into the political arena such issues as monetary policy, civil service reform, labor relations, and farm support.

✵ *A Delicate Balance of Power*

Sometimes large electoral majorities in presidential contests disguised the thin popular support for the victors. No Republican presidential candidate ever won a majority of the popular vote in any election from 1876 to 1892, and in both 1876 and 1888 the defeated Democratic candidates outpolled the Republican winners in popular votes. Single-term presidencies broke the continuity of policy-making and fostered excessive politicking and brokering by ambitious political chieftains in Congress and in the states. After Ulysses S. Grant's retirement from office in 1877, no incumbent president was re-elected until William McKinley in 1900. In such a rickety political structure, politicians shied away from bold stands. And on issues such as currency reform and regulation of the industrial economy, where Republicans and Democrats feared to tread lest they alienate moneyed interests and the broad electorate each

courted assiduously, third parties entered. A seeming politics of stalemate resulted until farm radicalism and economic depression reshaped the political landscape in the election of 1896.

National politics seesawed because it rested on a delicate balance of power. The two major parties consisted of alliances of regional and interest groups that held together by avoiding clear-cut positions on potentially divisive issues that might tear the parties apart and by invoking common symbols and interests that might unite their disparate factions. The Republicans held sway in rural and small-town New England, Pennsylvania, the upper Midwest, and southern California, and they generally won over white-collar, middle-class workers and professionals in northern cities. As the party of emancipation, Republicans also had unwavering support from African Americans, as long as they could get to the polls. The Democrats counted on the "solid South," once they had overthrown Republican rule there, and they regularly tallied the votes of the southern counties in Ohio, Indiana, and Illinois and, with some exceptions, the boss-ruled machine votes in northern cities with large immigrant populations. Each party also tried to cut into the other's strongholds. After Reconstruction, for example, Republicans periodically made overtures to southern whites, promising to support regional economic development and to relax still further their ever-diminishing interest in the fate of blacks, while southern Bourbon Democrats appealed to blacks, promising to shield them from lower-class white violence (see Chapter 16). Such strategies rarely succeeded. Party loyalties generally held firm until the 1890s.

In six states, neither party had an advantage. Those "swing states" — Connecticut, New York, New Jersey, Ohio, Indiana, and Illinois — determined the outcome of national elections. They became the focus of both major parties' undue attention. In blatant attempts to woo their votes, both parties consistently nominated their presidential and vice-presidential candidates from the "favorite sons" of those states. Every president who served during the Gilded Age came from Ohio (three), New York (two), or Indiana (one).

✵ *Muted Differences*

The national political alignments and the potential internal divisions within the major parties muted the differences between the parties over such issues as the tariff, currency reform, public land policy, support for

A Political Treadmill This cartoon from an 1883 issue of *Harper's Weekly* captures the frustrations of the Democratic Party in the Gilded Age. A donkey walks on a treadmill, which is called the "Democratic Platform." Parts of the platform are labeled "Free Trade," "High or Low Tariff," "Hard or Soft Money," and "Anything for Success." Off in the distance, seemingly unattainable, is the White House — which, however, Democrat Grover Cleveland would narrowly win in 1884.

railroads and internal improvements, and the civil service. Both major parties also tended to be dominated by their eastern wings, which favored business interests and decried labor and farmer radicalism. And, periodic bows to civil service reformers notwithstanding, neither party wanted to kill the federal patronage cow that fed the party faithful with jobs and contracts. It would take an assassin's bullet to bring about change on that score.

The generally agreed upon assumptions of laissez-faire — or "let alone" — kept both parties from endorsing reformers' calls for federal regulation of the new industrial order. Laissez-faire did not mean do nothing. Far from it. To politicians of the Gilded Age, it was a call for government to unlock the riches of the continent by providing access to public lands and natural resources, subsidies for internal improvements, and protection from foreign competition, and by removing such "obstacles to progress" as Indians, Mexicans, or anyone else who stood in the way. In the words of one senator: "One of the highest duties of Government is the adoption of such economic policy as may encourage and develop every industry to which the soil and climate of the country are adapted." In national campaigns and in Congress, the parties disagreed over the

details, but Democrats and Republicans agreed on the basic assumptions of the age.

The tariff is a case in point. The historically divisive tariff issue should have pointed to clear, persistent party differences over economic policy during the Gilded Age. But that happened only erratically. To protect American manufactures and agriculture from foreign competition, lawmakers had steadily raised duties on imported goods and products since the Civil War. Republicans generally urged protective tariffs in order to promote economic growth. They equated "protection" with Victorian domestic virtues and patriotism, intoning how it kept the American home free of "corrupting alien" influences and favored American production over foreign imports. Democrats, on the other hand, generally sought reduced tariffs in order to encourage foreign trade and benefit American farmers. Huge Treasury surpluses that piled up during the 1880s, largely from customs house revenues, further angered Democrats who wanted smaller government. In rhetoric at least, Democrats made lowering the tariff sound like a holy crusade. In 1887, for example, President Grover Cleveland denounced the protective tariff as "the vicious, inequitable and illogical source of unnecessary taxation," and Democrats ran on a low-tariff platform in the election the following year. The Republicans won and promptly solved the "problem" of the surplus by dishing out generous pensions to Union veterans, subsidies to steamship lines, and "pork" in the form of river and harbor improvements and fat premiums for government bondholders. In wiping out the surplus, the Republican "Billion Dollar Congress" (1889-1891) kept the tariff question in the public eye.

Still, tariff interests cut across party lines, blocking tariff reform and confusing the tariff as a defining party issue. Regardless of their own party affiliation, industrialists pushed for ever-higher tariffs as a way to keep foreign goods out and prices up, and labor endorsed high tariffs as a way to keep their jobs. Republican and Democratic farmers alike wanted high rates for agricultural products they sought to sell and low ones for manufactured goods they needed to buy. Middle-class consumers everywhere complained about artificially high duties that jacked up prices.

Each party made its bows to history and then drafted rate schedules favorable to its diverse followers. Democrats, for example, spouted their traditional low-tariff principles amid the clinking of glasses at party gatherings such as the annual Jefferson and Jackson Day dinners, but those same Democrats got trowel in hand to

The Blue and the Gray   In this engraving from an 1887 newspaper, Union and Confederate veterans gather to commemorate the Battle of Gettysburg. One of the men has brought his wife. As veterans from either side aged and made peace with one another, politicians were less and less able to count on getting votes simply by either invoking the Confederate Lost Cause or waving the Union's Bloody Shirt.

add their own bricks to the tariff wall whenever they needed to protect anything grown or made in their own districts. Legislation brought neither clarity nor logic to tariff policy. In 1890 Congress enacted the McKinley Tariff that both lifted schedules to absurd heights, even posting rates on some goods and products that Americans neither produced nor consumed, and invited foreign trade by introducing a reciprocity clause authorizing the president to lower rates for any country that did likewise for American imports. When the Democratic-controlled House of Representatives passed the first significant postwar rate reduction in 1894, the Republican-controlled Senate tacked on almost 600 amendments restoring most cuts. In practice, the parties agreed to disagree on the tariff but kept the protective principle firmly in place.

⚖ Political Culture

Despite the seeming similarity of the major parties, party loyalty was intense during the Gilded Age. Voter turnout averaged almost 80 percent of eligible voters for presidential elections and even higher for some state ones during the Gilded Age, in part because people believed politics — and the victory of their party — mattered. One of the principal reasons for such loyalty was that real differences in philosophy, personality, and policy separated Republicans from Democrats. Republicans, for example, countenanced a fuller array of federal activism than did Democrats, who espoused states' rights and more limited government. More than anything else, though, religion, ethnicity, and culture defined party ties and stirred voter passions.

Republicans, sometimes called the "Party of Piety," drew heavily from native-born Anglo-Saxon Protestant groups who put their faith in strict codes of personal morality. Harking back to Puritan forebears and antebellum reformers, members of such moralistic groups did not make sharp distinctions between private and public virtue. They accepted public intervention into private life as a way to impose a uniform moral standard on society. They attacked the "saloon power" of immigrants and Democratic city machines, urging temperance laws and strict licensing to check the corrosive political effects of "demon Rum." They also preached sabbatarianism, demanding Sunday-closing laws and the end to Sunday postal service.

Democrats, sometimes called the "Party of Personal Liberty," opposed governmental intrusion into private morality and ethnic culture. Such a philosophy found favor among Roman Catholics, Jews, and Lutherans, who acknowledged the imperfect nature of humanity and society and vested responsibility for morality in the individual and the family rather than the state. Efforts to force them into English-only public schools, to give up Sunday entertainments, and to abstain from alcohol all smacked of nativism to such groups. The Democrats capitalized on such feelings by opposing any such restrictions.

Religion and ethnic issues generally played out in local and state politics. They often pitted immigrant city ward bosses against downstate rural legislators and added to the already fevered pitch of American politics. Aid to parochial schools and English-only public education were especially explosive issues that divided states along ethnic and religious lines. Wisconsin, for example, almost broke apart in the late 1880s and early 1890s when Catholics and Lutherans refused to obey a state law requiring attendance at English-only schools.

Although religious and ethnic issues did not directly involve the federal government, they did intrude in national politics. The devoutly Republican and Presbyterian Postmaster General John Wanamaker (1889-1893), for example, became a color cartoon centerfold in such Democratic illustrated weeklies as *Punch* that pilloried "Holy John" for phasing out Sunday postal work and preaching sabbatarianism in the federal government. Democrats never failed to accuse the Republicans of nativism and a "holier than thou" attitude, while Republicans responded in kind that Democrats reeked of "Rum, Romanism, and Rebellion." And since winning the presidency and Senate seats hinged on winning states and state legislatures, state party organizations and identities decided national elections. Aspirants for national office who flouted the religious and ethnic values of the party they represented did not get nominated.

❧ Lingering Effects of the Civil War

For a quarter century after Appomattox, memories of the Civil War also affected political loyalties and congressional politics. No Democrat in the South ever regretted wearing his tattered gray uniform and summoning up the ghosts of the Lost Cause while on the stump. Republicans, meanwhile, waved the "bloody shirt" shamelessly during campaigns, as much to find a common ground among otherwise competing factions and to distract voters from Republican failures as to remind northern veterans and their families that the party of Lincoln had saved the Union. Republican orators made it seem almost treasonous to vote for a Democrat. Typical of the histrionics is the following excerpt from a bloody shirt speech in 1876: "Every man that endeavored to tear the old flag from the heaven that it enriches was a Democrat. Every man that tried to destroy this nation was a Democrat.... The man that assassinated Abraham Lincoln was a Democrat.... Soldiers, every scar you have on your heroic bodies was given you by a Democrat." The Republicans reinforced their claim to wartime loyalties by regularly running former Union officers for the presidency and for governorships.

Invoking Civil War memories worked only so long as veterans made up a significant part of the electorate. By the 1890s, a new generation of voters had emerged with other interests. Also, the veterans themselves had begun burying wartime hatreds in a series of reencampments at battlefield sites. Legions of veterans from both sides returned to such fields of carnage as Gettysburg during the 1880s and 1890s to honor one another for their bravery. The presidential election of 1884 pitted two candidates who had not served during the war, and successful Democratic presidential candidate Grover Cleveland's majorities in both the popular and electoral vote count further signaled the fading of the bloody shirt in national politics.

The bloody shirt remained a political factor in Congress far longer because Union veterans expected returns on their votes. The Grand Army of the Republic

"The Bloody Shirt," 1876
Republicans traded on memories of the Civil War and the martyred Lincoln to divert attention from divisive issues such as the money question, tariffs, and regulating the new industrial economy. They waved "the bloody shirt" in speeches and images to remind voters of their obligations to the Union. Robert Green Ingersoll's stirring speech is an example of the practice.

I am opposed to the Democratic party, and I will tell you why. Every state that seceded from the United States was a Democratic State. Every ordinance of secession that was drawn was drawn by a Democrat. Every man that endeavored to tear the old flag from the heaven that it enriches was a Democrat. Every man that tried to destroy this nation was a Democrat. Every enemy this great republic has had for twenty years has been a Democrat. Every man that shot Union soldiers was a Democrat. Every man that starved Union soldiers and refused them in the extremity of death a crust was a Democrat. Every man that loved slavery better than liberty was a Democrat. The man that assassinated Abraham Lincoln was a Democrat. Every man that sympathized with the assassin — every man glad that the noblest president ever elected was assassinated, was a Democrat. Every man that wanted the privilege of whipping another man to make him work for nothing and pay him with lashes on his naked back, was a Democrat. Every man that raised blood-hounds to pursue human beings was a Democrat. Every man that clutched from shrieking, shuddering, crouching mothers, babes from their breasts, and sold them into slavery was a Democrat.... Soldiers, every scar you have got on your heroic bodies was given to you by a Democrat. Every scar, every arm that is lacking, every limb that is gone, every scar is a souvenir of a Democrat.

(GAR), a northern veterans' organization that numbered more than 400,000 men in 1890, lobbied tirelessly for pensions for all former Union soldiers to compensate them for disabilities and poor pay during the war and for support for the widows and orphans of those whose shirts truly had been stained with blood. Congress responded dutifully to GAR petitions by appropriating generous pensions, some of which were still being paid out in the middle of the twentieth century.

GETTING OUT THE VOTE

With so much at stake in terms of patronage and principle, and with elections so close, the major parties resorted to any means to enlist supporters and to get out the vote. Politics was war, and the major parties waged it that way, with chains of command, strategic planning, and military rhetoric. Parties, like armies, demanded obedience and unflagging loyalty from their men, which meant voting the straight party ticket. Rallying the troops was essential for success. Mass meetings, torchlight processions, parades, and ox-roasts drew thousands at a time for entertainment and instruction. The British diplomat Lord James Bryce, whose book *The American Commonwealth* (1888) had little good to say about the American "democratic" party system in action, marveled at the spectacles: "For three months processions, usually with brass bands, flags, badges, crowds of cheering spectators, are the order of the day and night from end to end of the country."

✍ The Spectacle of Campaigns

Bryce and like-minded American political reformers derided the seemingly mindless character of campaign pageantry, but they missed the point. At a time when few outdoor amusements were available, campaigning provided a form of mass martial entertainment that was combination spectator and participant sport. Politics also was serious business. Eager to please, party managers followed the lead of such entertainment impresarios as Phineas T. Barnum in using newspapers to promote their events and in giving the public what it wanted. Nothing was left to chance. Parties blanketed the country with lavishly illustrated campaign literature extolling the virtues of their party and its slate of candidates and lampooning their opponents. Wire services, improved printing techniques, multiple copying of documents, and office machines allowed state party bosses to coordinate nationwide campaigns. To satisfy the demand and package the goods, parties changed their political rhetoric from the windy orations of antebellum days to short speeches of five to ten minutes in length, delivered with energy and efficiency in several towns each day. Train schedules in hand, party managers booked speakers at stops across the country.

In getting out the vote, local political clubs played vital roles. They organized the hands-on politics of paraphernalia and parades that roused voters' interest. They raised grass-roots support for the party slate and produced an astonishing variety of political objects

Republican Convention Several contemporary scenes from the 1880 Republican Convention that suggest the bustle, fanfare, and politicking of the event. James Garfield and Chester A. Arthur emerged as the nominees for president and vice president.

to distinguish their candidates. Badges, buttons, and brooches pinned on lapels, and bandanas, kerchiefs, feathers, and shawls worn or waved, along with customized lanterns, banners, bunting, bottles, and all manner of clothing, ceramic objects, and even toys contributed to the festive air of campaigning, but equally important they physically and psychologically linked supporters to their party and its candidates. At barbecues and picnics spellbinders fed crowds with memories of glories past and visions future, all of which went down easily with generous helpings of pork and alcohol served up by party organizers.

Such rhetoric and rallying were not just show. Political gatherings competed with religion in bringing people together to reaffirm their values and shore up group solidarity. Partisanship paradoxically created at least the illusion of unity and real participation in political society. Speaking in the plain style made popular by evangelical preachers (direct, candid, and laced with folk wisdom and humor), candidates reached out to their audiences, simultaneously flattering and instructing in order to win them over. When men of property locked arms in parades, shared beer and beef at barbecues, and spoke frankly with those below them in wealth and station, they closed the distance between the classes during the political season.

For white men, political clubs and corner saloons offered camaraderie and a sense of belonging in an in-

The Ticket　　James A. Garfield and Chester A. Arthur, the Republican presidential and vice-presidential candidates in 1880, adorn a bright red cotton bandana. The political parties distributed everyday household items such as this to reach out to women — though they could not vote in national elections — and to middle-class voters.

creasingly fragmented world. Saloons served as hiring halls and recruiting stations for ward bosses eager to line up immigrant and working-class voters, a fact that made anti-saloon campaigns the principal focus of urban reformers (see Chapter 19). Party loyalty was a currency that could be traded anywhere, and like church membership, it could be "proof" of one's good reputation when moving to a new neighborhood or locality. On Election Day, men marched to the polls in unprecedented numbers, never yet equaled in American history. With printed ballots in hand, they showed their true colors as Americans and as men.[1]

ℂ Women's Influence

Women too enjoyed the hoopla and fanfare of street parades and picnics. Women were more than mere onlookers to political life. During the Gilded Age, much campaign literature and many campaign mementos were directed to women, even though few women could vote. The parties fashioned shelves of decorative

1. Before the introduction of the secret or "Australian" ballot at the end of the nineteenth century (see below), voters voted by dropping preprinted ballots — supplied by the party for whose ticket they intended to vote — into boxes. Voting a "split ticket" meant having to scratch names off the party ballot. These voting practices made it much easier for each voter's choices to be publicly known.

glass, textiles, and household objects keyed to Victorian women's tastes. More important, they celebrated "family values" in campaign portraits of candidates with their families and in tokens, handkerchiefs, plates, and posters featuring the wives of candidates. Minor parties added their own trinkets. The Equal Rights Party, with Belva Ann Lockwood as its presidential candidate in the 1880s, invented several unique items, including a card with a pop-up skirt showing a suffragist underneath.

Appeals to women obliged parties to put up candidates and espouse values that would not offend women's Victorian sensibilities. That campaigns often degenerated into mud-slinging matches pointed up the limited power of women's supposed tempering effects on American public behavior. Politics remained principally a man's game, as much a blood sport and rite of passage as a demonstration of democracy. Still, the cascade of objects and images aimed at women bespoke the party managers' belief that married women, at least, strongly influenced their husbands' voting behavior.

In the end, it mattered that women did not vote, except in several sparsely settled western states. Women's rights advocates understood that influence was not power. In a political environment where people felt keenly the difference between insiders and outsiders, women wanted access. Undeterred by their exclusion from the Fifteenth Amendment (see Chapter 16) and by a Supreme Court decision, *Minor v. Happersett* (1875), that allowed states to deny women the ballot, women's rights advocates lobbied for the suffrage.

The debate over the Fourteenth and Fifteenth Amendments had split women's rights advocates over means and ends in seeking enfranchisement. Two rival suffrage groups had emerged in 1869, but such women remained united in their belief that women needed and deserved the vote. The American Woman Suffrage Association, led by Lucy Stone and Julia Ward Howe, concentrated on adding enfranchisement amendments to state constitutions and emphasized women's supposedly superior moral nature in bidding for support. The more militant National Woman Suffrage Association (NWSA), led by longtime women's rights advocates Elizabeth Cady Stanton and Susan B. Anthony, sought universal suffrage by federal enactment and a broad program of reform. The NWSA and its supporters demanded the ballot as a basic human right. The NWSA especially kept the suffrage issue in the public eye. Anthony staged public demonstrations trying to vote, and she and the

NWSA persuaded friendly senators to introduce a woman's suffrage constitutional amendment several times in Congress between 1878 and 1896, though to no avail. The men were not ready to share political power or to expand further federal authority over voting rights.

In 1890 the two branches of the woman's suffrage movement united in the National American Woman Suffrage Association (NAWSA). Under the pragmatic Carrie Chapman Catt, elected president in 1900, the NAWSA shifted the suffragists' argument from demanding the franchise as a basic human right to one emphasizing its benefits to society. With the ballot, women could improve the character of public life and could protect and educate their families by selecting boards of health and public education. Women did not win the suffrage easily. Several states actually defeated referenda and constitutional amendments to enfranchise women.

Women did, however, score modest gains elsewhere. The increased attention to political issues by such temperance organizations as Frances Willard's powerful Woman's Christian Temperance Union and by such settlement houses as Jane Addams's influential Hull House in their struggles against the saloon and machine politics in the cities (see Chapter 19) inspired many middle-class women to join the suffrage ranks. Women's clubs debated such political issues as boss rule, prostitution,

WCTU Members Praying Members of the Woman's Christian Temperance Union kneel in prayer outside a saloon in a western town in this 1885 photograph.

gambling, alcohol sales, bad schools, and poor health and living conditions in their communities. During the 1880s women were winning the right to vote at the local level, especially in school-board elections. By 1890 women could vote on school issues in nineteen states

❊ IN THEIR OWN WORDS

Campaigning for Women's Rights, 1876

Excluded from the ballot box and public forums, women drew on their organizing experience in social reform, churches, and civic celebrations to get their interests noted in public discourse and the public record. They staged protests and rallies as part of their "outdoor politics." The scene from the Centennial Fourth of July celebration in Philadelphia, from which women's interests had been excluded, shows the tactics that won woman suffrage advocates notice and notoriety.

That historic Fourth of July dawned at last, one of the most oppressive days of that terribly heated season. Susan B. Anthony, Matilda Joslyn Gage, Sara Andrews Spencer, Lillie Devereux Blake and Phoebe W. Couzins made

their way through the crowds under the broiling sun to Independence Square, carrying the Woman's Declaration of Rights. . . . Their tickets of admission proved open sesame through the military and all other barriers, and a few moments before the opening of the ceremonies, these women found themselves within the precincts from which most of their sex were excluded.

The declaration of 1776 was read by Richard Henry Lee, of Virginia, about whose family clusters so much of historic fame. The close of his reading was deemed the appropriate moment for the presentation of the woman's declaration. Not quite sure how their approach might be met — not quite certain if at this final moment they would be permitted to reach the presiding officer

— those ladies arose and made their way down the aisle. The bustle of preparation for the Brazilian hymn covered their advance. The foreign guests, the military and civil officers who filled the space directly in front of the speaker's stand, courteously made way, while Miss Anthony in fitting words presented the declaration. Mr. Ferry's face paled, as bowing low, with no word, he received the declaration, which thus became part of the day's proceedings; the ladies turned, scattering printed copies, as they deliberately walked down the platform. On every side eager hands were stretched; men stood on seats and asked for them, while General Hawley, thus defied and beaten in his audacious denial to women the right to present their declaration, shouted, "Order, order!"

and on tax and bond issues in three. More important, the experience of lobbying for the ballot and for reform and the organization of women's clubs schooled a new generation of women in a politics of pragmatism that would lead the way to the Nineteenth Amendment during the Progressive era.

REINING IN THE SPOILSMEN

One of the most pressing concerns during the Gilded Age was reforming politics and cleaning up the federal government. As the size and complexity of the federal bureaucracy grew, the need to bring it into line with modern management techniques and to appoint capable professionals became more apparent, at least to businessmen who had to deal with federal agencies. The cronyism-bred corruption in bureaus running Indian affairs, military procurement, and railroad grants that had infected the Grant administration (see below) and the constant infighting among party chieftains over patronage vitiated public confidence in government while adding to its inefficiency and cost.

Since the beginning of mass political parties, however, government jobs had been handed out as rewards for party loyalty. The attitude toward government service was summed up in the political maxim, "To the victor belong the spoils." Often incompetent and unqualified applicants swooped down on Washington after elections hunting jobs "like vultures for a wounded bison." When President James A. Garfield took office

in 1881, he was overwhelmed by hungry office-seekers. "My God!" he lamented, "What is there in this place that a man should ever want to get into it?" The answer was power. Without patronage to dispense, politicians feared they would be unable to recruit workers or dun the grateful officeholders for the "contributions" that filled party coffers. Party bosses who headed the state machines that picked the candidates and got out the vote defended the spoils system as democratic and as a means of keeping government attuned to the people. They resisted all efforts to dilute or abolish what one forthright boss called "the mother's milk" of politics.

Powerful factions within each party vied for control of the national organizations in order to distribute the patronage. In part because they won the presidency more than the Democrats, the Republicans especially suffered from personal feuds and factional disputes over federal patronage during the 1870s and 1880s. The two most powerful rivals were the "Stalwarts," led by Senator Roscoe Conkling of New York, often caricatured in the press as a gobbling turkey because of his arrogant strut, and the "Half-Breeds," led by Senator James G. Blaine of Maine, the "Plumed Knight," famous for his charisma and ceaseless quest for the White House. About Blaine it was said that "men went insane over him in pairs, one for and one against." Although the Half-Breeds pushed a more vigorous economic nationalism than the Stalwarts, divvying up the spoils of office rather than philosophy was the real reason they hated one another.

The nastiness that often marred Gilded Age politics

❋ IN THEIR OWN WORDS

"Woman and Temperance," 1876

Cleaning up society by reforming the ballot was a common theme among "good government" advocates, and women seeking the franchise played to that tune. Frances Willard perfected the argument that responsible, Christian women needed the ballot to save the home from drink and dissipation by attacking the saloon power. In her first major temperance speech, she outlined the basic themes.

In our argument it has been claimed that by the changeless instincts of her nature and through the most sacred relationships of

which that nature has been rendered capable, God has indicated woman, who is the born conservator of home, to be the Nemesis of home's arch enemy, King Alcohol. And further, that in a republic, this power of hers may be most effectively exercised by giving her a voice in the decision by which the rum-shop door shall be opened or closed beside her home. . . .

Nothing worse can ever happen to women at the polls than has been endured by the hour on the part of conservative women of the churches in this land, as they, in scores of towns, have plead with rough,

half-drunken men to vote the temperance tickets they have handed them, and which, with vastly more of propriety and fitness they might have dropped into the box themselves. . . . I spent last May in Ohio, traveling constantly, and seeking on every side to learn the views of the noble women of the Crusade. They put their opinions in words like these: "We believe that as God led us into this work by way of the saloons, HE WILL LEAD US OUT BY WAY OF THE BALLOT. We have never prayed more earnestly over the one than we will over the other. One was the Wilderness, the other is the Promised Land."

was not reserved for contests between Republicans and Democrats. Candidates routinely smeared their opponents as thieves, traitors, and worse. Intraparty machinations included spying, blackmail, and bribery. In one of the most celebrated cases, New York's Thomas Platt, a Stalwart and a public churchgoer, withdrew from a Senate race after having been discovered in the arms of "an unspeakable female" while residing at the Delavan Hotel in Albany. Platt's dalliance had been reported by a dozen Half-Breed New York state assemblymen, who, in stocking feet, had climbed a stepladder to watch Platt's couplings through a transom window. With such tactics, rival factions lowered the tone of political discourse and helped make character assassination a regular feature of public life.

❧ The Appeal of Civil Service Reform

Against the Stalwarts and Half-Breeds stood the "Mugwumps," so named (they said) from an Algonquin term meaning "great men," though their opponents scoffed that the term really meant fence-straddlers, with their "mug" on one side and their "wump" on the other. Largely eastern and elitist, these earnest reformers sought to rid politics of corruption by introducing a civil service system that would return government control to men of good breeding and education — like themselves. They lobbied for a law that would place federal jobs on a civil service list immune from partisan politics by limiting jobs only to those applicants who had the specific technical qualifications necessary to perform their duties and by preventing promotion or dismissal of such federal employees except on the basis of merit. They especially wanted to lift the morality of public service.

The Mugwumps were, in part, heirs to the Liberal Republicans, a group of Republican dissidents who denounced corruption within the Grant administration and in Republican-ruled southern governments and the spoilsmen in general. The Liberal Republicans broke with the "regular" Republicans when they could not reform the party from within. In 1872 they fielded their own candidate, Horace Greeley, editor of the *New York Tribune* and political gadfly. He exhausted himself making ardent speeches (he died a few weeks after the election) but brought little consistency or credibility to his message. The Democrats also nominated Greeley (a life-long scourge of Democrats) as their candidate, thereby blunting the reform thrust of the Liberal Republicans' effort to remake party politics by stepping outside the spoilsmen-run major parties. The Liberal

Republicans also raised questions related to the Republican conduct of Reconstruction that further distracted voters from the civil service reform message. The Liberal Republicans' campaign slogan, "Anything to Beat Grant," summed up their scattershot approach. Grant won handily, with 56 percent of the popular vote and electoral victories in all the northern states. The Liberal Republican debacle left civil service reformers confused and disorganized. Soon enough, though, the continued abuses in government and a new group of reformers refocused attention on the civil service issue.

A growing federal bureaucracy, which doubled in size between 1871 and 1881 and reached over 160,000 workers by the early 1890s, and the need for special skills in management, gave civil service reform an urgency that it had lacked in the Liberal Republicans' moral calculus. Reformers reminded the public that the government had assumed significant engineering, technological, scientific, and information-gathering responsibilities since the Civil War. The demands of such newly established programs as the Department of Agriculture, the Bureaus of Statistics, of Weather, and of Education, and the Commissioner of Immigration, to name several, could not safely be let to amateurs. Mugwumps believed that the federal government should follow business in relying on trained professionals to manage its increasingly complex functions. They argued that "incompetent hacks" whose only qualification was party loyalty weakened both the administration and moral tenor of public service.

❧ Newspapers and Reform

The national magazines *The Nation* and *Harper's Weekly* provided regular outlets for reformers' ire. Cartoonist Thomas Nast filled the pages of the latter with poison-ink barbs ridiculing Democratic and Republican corruption. Equally important was the emergence of a more independent "watchdog" journalism, freed from dependence on local party patrons and critical of government. By stationing regular correspondents in the capital and using the new wire services such as the Associated Press (AP), newspapers got regular and quick access to national news. They thus helped focus attention on national politics and government. Editors also learned that lurid descriptions of corruption sold newspapers. The "lords of linotype" obliged by covering the daily doings in Congress and cultivating habits of investigative reporting that later developed into the "muckraking" style of the Progressive era. Stories on government regularly decried corruption and inefficiencies begging for reform. Typical was a report about the House of Representatives in 1882 that read: "As I make my notes I see a dozen men reading newspapers with their feet on their desks.... 'Pig Iron' Kelley of Pennsylvania has dropped his newspaper and is paring his fingernails.... The vile odor of ... tobacco ... rises from the two-for-five-cents cigars in the mouths of the so-called gentlemen below.... They chew, too! Every desk has a spittoon of pink and gold china beside it to catch the filth from the statesman's mouth." To escape censure, politicians learned soon enough that they needed to assume at least the appearance of disinterested public service.

Reformers and politicians both tried to manipulate the news during elections. In 1884, for example, Republican presidential hopeful James G. Blaine, the symbol of the spoils system in reformers' eyes, was burned by newspaper allegations that as Speaker of the House during the 1870s he had received railroad stock in exchange for political favors and by the publication of the "Mulligan letters" linking him to a corrupt bargain with a southern railroad. The Democratic *New York World* printed contradictory Blaine statements in parallel columns and, using new reproductive processing techniques for cartoons, ran front-page caricatures of Blaine as "the tattooed man" for his many peculations and as "the continental liar from the state of Maine" for his denial of such dealings. Blaine suffered further embarrassment when a stenographer, who the Democrats put on Blaine's trail hoping to catch him in a misstep, recorded that at a meeting of 400 Protestant ministers in New York, staged by Republicans to win their endorsement, an over-zealous preacher had condemned the Democrats as the party of "Rum, Romanism, and Rebellion." Later that day, Blaine had attended a banquet of millionaires at Delmonico's Restaurant, which Blaine's detractors quickly tagged "Belshazzar's feast." Democrats flashed the news of the two events across the wires, casting Blaine simultaneously as an enemy of immigrants, Catholics, and southerners and a friend of plutocrats. The newspaper depictions probably sealed Blaine's defeat in the election. They surely enhanced the power of newspapers to define the character of politics.

Reformers did not rely on journalism alone to educate the public and transform politics. They organized reform associations to focus sustained attention on a single issue, be it civil service, tariff, currency, or municipal reform. Through education, the reformers hoped to lift politics from partisanship and to introduce a new political style in America. Instead of emotions and

blind party loyalty, they urged a sober politics of independent judgment, individual conscience, and modern business methods. Reformers also compiled statistics to show the debilitating effects of political corruption on the economy and society. In the age of "numeracy," in which numbers mattered, the social sciences lent credibility to the reformers' calls. In the end, though, civil service reformers emphasized morality more than mathematics in their attacks on the party system.

Such efforts rarely won over the mass of voters, who preferred drum-thumping parades and saloon politics and looked to the promise of jobs and favors as a reward for turning out on Election Day. The often erudite and aloof Mugwumps, after all, preached a politics of exclusion that ran against the democratic appeal of mass political participation. They also threatened to undo the masculine world of privilege. Party regulars who railed against the elitism of "the snivel service" and the reformers' calls for non-partisanship often used sexual innuendo to remind men they would lose much with reform. Non-partisans, they charged, were "a third sex," and civil service would emasculate the electorate by introducing "political hermaphrodites" into the body politic. With party interests firmly against any change that would diminish their power, the prospects for passing significant civil service reform were dim.

ᢒ *Impetus for Reform*

Fate gave civil service new life. The assassination of President James A. Garfield by a deranged and disappointed office-seeker in 1881 forced the Congress to take up the civil service issue. While walking through a Washington train station, Garfield was shot twice in the back by Charles J. Guiteau, who thought that the Stalwarts would reward him with a job and thank him for removing the man who had denied the Stalwarts control over the lucrative patronage of New York port. When he was seized by authorities, Guiteau reportedly boasted, "I am a Stalwart, Arthur is President now." The handsome, athletic Garfield, who had gained a reputation for courage as a Civil War general and honesty as a governor in Ohio, became a martyr to the cause of reform as he lingered in pain for eleven weeks before dying of blood poisoning in September 1881. The trial of Guiteau in November added to the moral imperative of righting the great wrong. Guiteau's lawyers argued that Guiteau was not guilty by reason of insanity (one of the first instances of such a defense). The judge and jury refused to accept the plea, despite abundant evidence about Guiteau's delusionary history, because they viewed the assassin's actions in moral terms. Guiteau was judged responsible for his deed, convicted, and hanged. The nation now bore the obligation to cleanse itself of the corruptions that gave rise to spoils-seekers such as Guiteau — or so the civil service reformers argued.

The reformers capitalized on the popular indignation over Garfield's assassination to make civil service reform the test of responsible government. Angry with the feuding Republicans, voters in 1882 gave the Democrats a majority of nearly 100 seats in the House of Representatives. Political survival as well as principle now compelled Republicans to act. President Chester A. Arthur, a flashy dresser and big eater hardly known for restraint in his personal appetites or in his generous dispensing of patronage to fellow Stalwarts in New York, surprised many observers who expected him to follow Conkling's lead. But Arthur understood the moral obligation Garfield's death had thrust upon him. To office-seekers coming for favors he reportedly announced, "For the Vice-Presidency I was indebted to Mr. Conkling, but for the Presidency of the United States my debt is to the Almighty." Arthur steered an independent course, prosecuting post office frauds and supporting civil service legislation.

In 1883 Congress passed the Pendleton Civil Service Act, which had been drafted by the National Civil Service Reform League, organized in 1881 to lobby for such a reform. The Act created a bipartisan civil service commission to prepare and administer competitive examinations and to establish merit standards for appointment and promotion. It also prohibited politicians from making financial assessments on officeholders. Although the Pendleton Act initially covered only about 10 percent of federal offices, presidents steadily expanded the list of protected employment. By 1900, more than 40 percent of all federal government jobs enjoyed civil service protection. More important, civil service had become a fixed principle in government. States and municipalities also began to adopt civil service and other governmental reforms.

Civil service reform helped change the character of the governmental workforce and workplace. The growing executive departments of government, like the corporate offices of railroads and banks, employed large numbers of clerks, many of them women. In the office men and women negotiated new rules of workplace etiquette, challenging Victorian, middle-class conventions that kept "proper ladies" from vying with men for

Garfield's Assassination   Charles Guiteau, who was probably insane, shot Garfield in the back at Union Station in Washington, D.C., on July 2, 1881. Garfield died three months later, and Guiteau was later executed.

wages. In principle, though not always in practice, the civil service system opened jobs to women with stenographic and other office skills and protected them from flagrant abuse by offering procedures for complaint. In the interest of efficiency, managers insisted on gentlemanly deportment from the men, which meant no more drinking, cussing, tobacco chewing, or cigar smoking in the office. Even as middle-class women in federal clerkships became more "masculine" by competing with men for pay and promotion, the office became more "feminine" as men learned to be gentlemen while on the job. The office also became more modern. Both men and women subscribed to uniform codes of behavior, submitted to managerial authority, and made merit rather than cronyism the means of advancement. Such an ordered environment made possible the systematic collection and processing of more information and, as Progressives would realize in the twentieth century, the assumption of more regulatory responsibility. Civil service poised government to act.

Civil service reform also signaled a shift in governmental authority and decision-making away from decentralized congressional politicians and party bosses responsive to local interests and toward executive management and bureaucracy committed to establishing uniform national standards. The civil service law in practice increased the influence of corporate business and national professional groups. A new breed of party leaders turned to lobbyists and big business for the money to run campaigns and sustain party organizations. Rather than shifting political power from "the interests" to "the people," as so much reform rhetoric had promised, civil service reform favored those with access to information and skill. The growth of bureaucratic, managerial power in decision-making occurred in state governments as well, and even in national church bodies. The adoption of the corporate management model for government of the state and national organizations lessened grassroots influence and alienated many people from the leadership. The farmers' revolt against "the interests" during the 1890s — with the populist proposals for direct election of Senators, initiative and referendum, recall, and primaries — represented, in part, a movement to restore local, grassroots authority (see below).

Civil service reformers joined with other critics of the spoilsmen and the popular party system to reorder American political life by emphasizing responsibilities over rights. Their efforts included not only driving out the corrupt politician but also reforming the electorate. In doing so, they put much weight on the moral meaning of voting. They argued that only "responsible, deserving citizens" who shared their middle-class values and who were beholden to no one but God should be entrusted with the franchise. They wanted to take politics out of immigrant and working-class saloons and pool-halls and put it in middle-class parlors and pews. Instead of parades and partisanship, reformers urged an educated electorate, knowledgeable about issues and above self-interest. Dissatisfied with the pace of reform within their own party, some reformers joined third-party movements, such as the Prohibition Party, which insisted that citizenship should be defined by moral rules.

The connection between anti-saloon politics and woman's suffrage was especially strong. By 1900 nearly all women suffragists espoused prohibition as essential for political reform. Heavily Protestant in membership and morality, and tinged with nativism, the movement to get the ballot for literate, sober middle-class women went hand-in-hand with efforts to take it away from the supposedly untutored, unwashed immigrants and poor whose whiskey-soaked ballots kept the bosses in power. Ballot reform, with the move toward the Australian, or "secret," ballot in the 1890s and early 1900s, like civil service reform, was intended to limit political participation and government to "the best sort."

Civil service reform, ballot reform, and woman's suffrage, in varying degrees, encouraged a politics of privilege in America. Disfranchisement of blacks and poor whites in the South following the failure of the Populist revolt (see Chapter 16) and trimming voting lists in cities as part of the Progressive movement's civic reform recast American politics by the early twentieth century. The exuberant, masculine marching-arm-in-arm braggadocio of the Gilded Age yielded to the more scientific canvassing and impersonal polling of modern campaigns. Until such changes occurred, however, Gilded Age politics provided one of the most visible and vocal expressions of popular values and interests.

THE PRESIDENCY AND CONGRESS REMADE

In public estimation and historical memory, Gilded Age presidents seemed weak. The postwar presidents labored in the ever-lengthening shadow of Abraham Lincoln's memory. As the martyred president's stock rose, particularly among northerners commemorating the Union victory in public squares crowded with statues of wartime heroes and bookstores crammed with soldiers' memoirs, other leaders had to measure up to Lincoln. No one met that test. The impeachment of Andrew Johnson, the corruption in Ulysses S. Grant's administration, and the disputed election of Rutherford B. Hayes all sapped the moral authority of the office. Narrow victory margins and frequent turnover in office contributed to a decline in presidential prestige from the Lincoln standard. Presidents seemed less commanding, and due to their personalities and their own limited conceptions of the office, they sought to command less.

Such actions reflected public opinion. Wartime necessity had led to a temporary expansion of executive authority and federal governmental activity. With the threat of disunion settled by the Civil War, most Americans retreated to prewar notions of government. However much Americans sought leaders of Lincoln's stature and moral character, they did not want to endow them with new powers. By the 1870s many Americans had come to admire Lincoln especially for his restraint and respect for the Constitution — virtues seldom perceived in him during the war. Postwar presidents took all this to heart.

Public expectations of national government generally still ran in nineteenth-century constitutional channels toward laissez-faire policies and away from activist executives. Most Americans looked to state and local governments for regulation. According to the creed of laissez-faire, the federal government should spur economic growth and protect, and perhaps expand, America's shores. It should not help the downtrodden. President Grover Cleveland summed up such thinking when he vetoed a bill to aid drought-stricken Texas farmers in 1887. Said Cleveland, "Though the people support the government, the government should not support the people." Until economic depression, labor unrest, and agrarian radicalism forced a change in the 1890s, the opportunities for presidential initiative remained constrained.

Structural limitations further hemmed in presidential authority. Presidents lacked the resources to dictate national policy. After the Civil War, no president until William McKinley in 1897 had both houses of Congress under the control of his own party for his entire term. Congress kept the presidents out of the annual budget-making process. The White House did not have the staff necessary to lead in any case. Nor did presidents compensate by expanding significantly the "informal" powers of the office. No president since Lincoln used language to shape public discourse in ways that moved people to action. As a senator, William McKinley had gained a reputation for writing tariff schedules that read like poetry, but once in the White House, even he did not rise to Lincoln's rhetorical eloquence. It would take Theodore Roosevelt to show modern presidents the ways to use the "bully pulpit" of the office.

Political corruption also weakened presidential authority by eroding public confidence in the executive office. A string of scandals during Grant's administration (1869-1877) embarrassed the presidency and haunted the office thereafter. In 1869 two financiers and railroad "robber barons" — James ("Jubilee Jim") Fisk, Jr., known for his stable of fast horses and his reputation with fast women, and Jay Gould, a conniver so feared that Wall Street bankers shuddered at his approach — attempted to corner the gold market with the help of President Grant's brother-in-law, a New York trader. They bid up the price of gold to dizzying heights, confident from inside information that the Treasury Department would not sell gold. When Grant learned that his sister and his wife had entered the gold speculation, he ordered gold released from the Treasury. The gold bubble burst on "Black Friday," September 24, 1869, ruining many honest investors while Fisk and Gould salvaged their fortunes. A congressional investigation cleared Grant of any wrongdoing, but the association of his family with the gold scheme damaged the president's reputation.

Copyrighted 1893 by F. Miller.

Pⲅⲉsidⲉnt and Mⲅs Clⲉvⲉland

President Cleveland and His Bride   In history's first wedding of a sitting president, seemingly confirmed bachelor Grover Cleveland married an attractive young woman, Frances Folsom, midway through his first term.

In 1872 the press revealed blatant buying of favors in which members of Congress accepted railroad stock from a fraudulent construction company, the Crédit Mobilier, so they would look the other way as the company skimmed off money building a transcontinental line with government subsidies. Vice President Schuyler Colfax was among the many prominent political figures implicated in the scheme. Although Grant dumped Colfax as his running mate in 1872, the Crédit Mobilier scandal further tarnished the Grant administration. Then in 1875 the public learned that the president's private secretary, Orville Babcock, was among the government officials getting payoffs from the "Whiskey Ring," a group of distillers who used bribery to avoid paying excise taxes. Grant's reputation suffered anew when he appealed to the jury on Babcock's behalf, helping his friend escape punishment. In 1876 the press discovered that Grant's secretary of war, William E. Belknap,

Visiting Benjamin Harrison, 1892

Julia Foraker, married to a prominent Republican, was a close observer of White House politics and personalities. She noted that the most successful politicians combined the personal touch and popular image-making with modern campaigning. In this excerpt she explains why Benjamin Harrison was not re-elected.

The Harrison administration, beginning in 1889, was marked by one of the strangest personalities that ever found a place in the sun. Benjamin Harrison was a Presbyterian with a firm, doctrinal belief, which he was heard to express, that he had been predestined to occupy the presidential chair. Unfor-

tunately, predestination failed to provide for a second term; indeed, it hardly insured the predestinee temperament enough to get him through the first. If "anything in the shape of a human being" interested Abraham Lincoln, nothing much in the shape of one brought a gleam to the eye of our aristocratic twenty-third President. . . .

Harrison spoke extraordinarily well; probably no presidential candidate ever spoke better. He was always clear, forceful, vigorous, and always fresh. . . . Harrison was the first to make popular the front-porch campaign which later McKinley carried on at Canton. Each delegation was received with a speech that directly appealed to the district

it represented and which captivated by its sympathetic, intimate understanding of individual conditions and its mastery of facts. The fine Harrison homestead in Indianapolis was devastated by the crowds which flocked to hear the candidate speak; Republican fans even carried off the fence. Harrison in 1888 did as much by his front-porch eloquence to help his cause as McKinley did to help his in 1896. If people could have just heard those splendid speeches, just heard Harrison, and then gone straight home and remembered how fine it was and never, never tried to shake the speaker's hand that was so like a wilted petunia — well, history might have been different.

had accepted bribes from the "Indian Ring," suppliers who got exclusive trading rights to supply Indians under government control. Belknap resigned in disgrace. Grant, ever loyal to his subordinates, expressed regret over the loss of his cabinet member. Grant was personally honest, but the corruption within his administration, when combined with the many revelations about scandals in Congress and state governments, caused reformers and newspapers to blame the president for the low level of public morality.

The circumstances of Rutherford B. Hayes's election in the disputed election of 1876 and his policies in office added little to presidential stature. To Democrats, the Compromise of 1877 stank of cigar smoke and whiskey from what they saw as a backroom intrigue that stole the office for the Republicans (see Chapter 16). Critics flayed "Rutherfraud" Hayes and "His Fraudulency" unmercifully and refused to accept his rightful claim to the presidency. His public policies won him few supporters. He pursued a conservative monetary policy, refusing to increase the money supply by coining silver, and he retreated almost completely on any Republican commitment to southern African Americans. His inability to respond effectively to the economic depression of the 1870s, his use of federal troops to restore order during the violent railroad strikes in 1877, and his veto of a bill to restrict Chinese "coolie" immigration in 1879 all angered labor interests. Meanwhile, he clashed with congressional Republicans over patronage. Al-

though genial by nature, Hayes's political ineptness left him, as one congressman said, "almost without a friend" in Congress and no prospects for another presidency. Hayes did not choose to run again in any case.

The chastening effects of corruption, congressional opposition, and low public esteem for presidential leadership, in time, brought modest reform to the presidency. Presidents from Hayes to McKinley sought to restore the moral leadership of the White House as a way to reclaim its influence over American life. Since Lincoln's day, the press had focused attention on the presidential family and suggested that its behavior carried moral weight in the nation. Hayes, along with his wife and childhood sweetheart, Lucy Webb Hayes, led the way in remaking the image of the "first family" and banishing any hint of "Grantism" and whiskey politics from the White House. The Hayeses and their children prayed daily and sang hymns in the Red Room after dinner. They also made the White House the center of the American domestic circle by introducing such "family" rituals as the annual Easter egg roll on the White House lawn, which proved so popular that by 1904 Edith Kermit Roosevelt complained privately that the roll caused "a needless destruction to the . . . grass." More important politically, the president and "Lemonade Lucy" were temperance advocates. When Hayes threw a dinner party, "the water flowed like champagne." Subsequent presidents restored spirits to the White House beverage list, but they and their families publicly paraded their piety by attending church and avoiding scandal.

Even Grover Cleveland met the new standard, despite his admission during the verbally vicious 1884 presidential campaign that, as a young man, he had fathered an illegitimate child. Republicans had chanted, "Ma!, Ma! Where's my pa?" during the campaign, to which the Democrats retorted, "Gone to the White House, Ha! Ha! Ha!" Cleveland won the election over Republican James Blaine in part because he instructed his supporters "to tell the truth" when his past was uncovered, while Blaine danced around accusations of his own checkered history of spoils and bribery. The public dubbed the rotund, bewhiskered bachelor "Grover the Good." Cleveland's honesty continued in office. He also brought romance to the White House by marrying the beautiful young Frances Folsom during his first term. A gracious hostess, the new First Lady made the White House bright with social activity and domestic charm and became a political asset to her husband.

The personal morality of presidents in office did not end the rough-and-tumble campaigning that outraged reformers during the Gilded Age. In the 1888 election, for example, the Republicans resorted to "dirty tricks" and shameless electioneering to swing the election for "Young Tippecanoe" Benjamin Harrison, the grandson of William Henry Harrison. Known as "the human iceberg" for his frigid personal manner and limp handshake, Harrison seemed above the political fray. Indeed, in his innocence he had boasted to Matthew Quay, his campaign chairman and the Republican boss of Pennsylvania, that Providence had given the election to the deserving Republicans. Quay knew better. "Providence hadn't a damn thing to do with it," Quay remarked, adding privately that Harrison "would never know how close a number of men . . . were compelled to approach the gates of the penitentiary to make him President." Still, appearances mattered. In office the hard-working, psalm-singing former Presbyterian deacon, "Young Ben" Harrison ran his administration without scandal and conducted himself with dignity. At a time when newspapers were reporting scandals in private lives and public affairs, and after such a prominent churchman as Henry Ward Beecher was entangled in a highly publicized, drawn-out adultery trial (1874-1877; see Chapter 20), the White House was becoming a model of probity by comparison.

Slowly, presidents also began to wriggle free from congressional domination by using the veto power, drafting legislation, hosting dinners and having consultations with congressional leaders to win influence among them, supporting executive commissions, and intervening in labor strikes. In his two terms (1885-1889 and 1893-1897), Grover Cleveland proved the most energetic. The burly Cleveland wielded the veto club with vigor, knocking down more legislation than all previous presidents combined. He thus exercised a negative power by forcing Congress to consider his wishes in crafting legislation. In prosecuting a veterans' pensions racket scheme and ending patronage abuses, he showed that a principled president could stand against powerful lobbies. He dismayed his conservative business supporters by denouncing the absurdly high rates of the protective tariff, and he angered labor by using federal troops to crush the Pullman strike in 1894 and by pressing for federal arbitration of labor disputes. In 1887 Congress laid the basis for executive regulatory functions when it passed the Interstate Commerce Act, creating the Interstate Commerce Commission to monitor railroad rates and practices. Cleveland balked at exercising the new authority. He signed the bill "with reservations," and he and the courts narrowly construed the commission's power. But the regulatory die had been cast.

Many problems persisted. Especially vexing were the low pay, uncertain tenure, and long hours that dispirited and exhausted government workers. As one Post Office official complained in 1891, "I average at my desk — without a moment's absence from the building — more than ten hours a day, besides night work." The poorly ventilated, cramped offices and suffocating heat and humidity in the nation's capital further drained workers. Before the installation of electric fans and window screens, not much was done to make the offices more habitable, but civil service protection and modern management techniques brought some relief in wages and working conditions. So, too, did administrative reforms and the introduction of modern office technology that improved efficiency and made possible centralized management. The White House, for example, installed a telephone in 1878 and bought its first typewriter in 1880. Private power (e.g., corporations, business associations, lobbies) remained more effectively organized than public power and presidential activism remained limited, but the potential of the executive branch to mobilize the nation's vast energies became increasingly evident by the time of William McKinley's election in 1896. The government needed only the political will to do so.

Congress also became more orderly, though not necessarily more trusted. By the 1880s the Senate had so many wealthy members drawn from business and industry and responded so dutifully to big business interests that newspapers called it "the Millionaires Club." The House, though, was the prime subject of ridicule. Lacking effective leadership, the House seemed incapable of conducting the people's business and stumbled through a string of scandals during the 1860s and 1870s. In 1878, for example, the members of an important committee, and their clerks, held up the House's adjournment because they were too drunk to present the final appropriations bill for passage. The House functioned largely as an extension of state-run political machines. Congressmen spent their days running errands and pushing claims for constituents and supporters and had little time, or inclination, to address the pressing economic and social issues of a rapidly industrializing society. Surveying the field of party hacks and overworked clerks, reformers despaired for good government. Indeed, Mark Twain's quip that "Congressmen are less educable than fleas" echoed throughout the Gilded Age.

In an effort to tighten party discipline, as much as a response to criticism, House Speaker Thomas Reed of Maine brought order to the House. The hulking "Czar" Reed (he stood 6'3") pushed through a series of rules changes in 1890 that concentrated the power over committee appointments and House business in the Speaker's hands. So powerful was Reed that congressmen whispered that they dared not breathe without his permission. The Senate, too, instituted new rules to ensure party discipline and smooth the legislative process. Senate caucuses named committee members and established the calendar of business. Such changes in Congress did not make government more democratic. As the interests of government broadened, Congress relied increasingly on specialists (and lobbyists) to provide information about complex subjects. Both House and Senate committees turned to experts to help draft legislation. The Congress became simultaneously more beholden to lobbyists and special interests as it became more able to legislate.

THE MONEY QUESTION

More than any other issue, the money question forced government to act and led to a significant political realignment during the populist revolt of the 1890s. The money question involved matters of political economy and morality. American money policy was based on

bimetallism — that is, money was coined from both gold and silver — and on a distrust of paper money not backed by specie. The nation's expanding economy and population increased the need for currency just to keep pace with demand, but adjusting the money supply was fraught with political peril. Tight money appealed to creditors such as bankers and bondholders and to industrial workers who feared inflation would erode their real wages. Many farmers, however, argued that the government was morally obligated to increase the money supply enough to keep farm prices from falling and to make it easier to borrow. Some industrialists also favored increasing, or "inflating," the money supply as a way to help them pay off their debts and to spur consumers' purchasing.

The Panic of 1873 brought on the first money crisis. The failure of the New York banking firm of Jay Cooke & Company led to a financial panic. Thousands of businesses failed, and tens of thousands of workers lost their jobs. Desperate unemployed men roamed the streets of cities demanding work and clashing with police called out to protect private property and maintain "order." Farmers were hit especially hard. Many northern and western farmers had borrowed heavily during the wartime boom to expand production, and southern farmers generally carried a heavy debt load trying to rebuild their lives. All felt the pinch of declining prices for their crops. Adding to their frustrations were the inequities of freight rates and the farmers' relative loss of buying and cultural power in a rapidly industrializing, urbanizing America. Farmers fought the latter issues during the 1870s through such state governmental action as the Granger laws (see Chapter 19). They joined with workers to push the money issue into electoral politics.

During the 1870s the money question centered on whether to issue more paper money, known as "greenbacks" because it was printed on green paper, which was not redeemable in gold or silver. During the Civil War, Congress had issued $450 million of greenbacks out of necessity, but the public distrusted the unbacked currency and the Treasury steadily withdrew $100 million of the "folding money" after the war. The debt-weary farmers and out-of-work laborers found new value in the greenbacks during the 1870s. The major parties fudged the issue, and Congress refused to reissue greenbacks to satisfy inflationists' demands. Greenback movements sprouted across the South and West. A national Greenback Labor Party polled over a million votes and won fourteen seats in Congress in 1878. Congress's decision in 1879 to convert the remaining greenbacks to gold and, more important, the prosperity of the 1880s ended the greenback controversy.

It did not end the money question. Silver became the "sacred white metal" that debtors and silver miners insisted would save America from financial and moral ruin. Traditionally, the government had bought and minted both silver and gold into coins, but by the early 1870s so little silver was being offered to the Treasury that Congress, in the Coinage Act of 1873, ordered an end to coining silver dollars. The effect was deflationary: prices fell and the value of the dollar rose. New silver strikes in Nevada made more silver available just when Congress had put America on the gold standard. Debtors eager to increase the money supply so they could pay their debts with inflated dollars joined with silver miners in denouncing the "Crime of '73" and demanding the resumption of silver purchases. Thanks to the handiwork of Representative Richard P. ("Silver Dick") Bland of Missouri, Congress passed the Bland-Allison Act of 1878, authorizing the Treasury to buy and coin between $2 million and $4 million worth of silver each month.

Creditor interests cried foul and warned of dire consequences if inflation occurred. They, too, said God was on their side in the controversy. The pressure for "soft money" (greenbacks and silver coinage), they argued, threatened civil unrest and encouraged profligacy. At least one Protestant magazine chimed in that "Atheism is not worse in religion than an unstable or irredeemable currency in political economy." Monetary conservatives in the government saved the day for "sound money" — and, they thought, the nation's soul — by purchasing only the minimum amount of silver each month. Silverites continued their own crusade for inflation, and in 1890 Congress appeased them with the Sherman Silver Purchase Act, which obligated the government to buy 4.5 million ounces of silver every month regardless of price and to issue treasury notes, paper redeemable in gold or silver, equal to the value of silver purchased. In practice the government redeemed the notes only in gold, and new silver strikes continued to drive down silver prices. Silverites felt betrayed, while "gold bugs" thought that any concessions to silver undermined America's credit abroad and discouraged investment at home.

THE DEPRESSION OF 1893 AND THE GOLD STANDARD

In 1893 the nation fell into the worst economic depression of the century. The depression lasted four years and shook public confidence in the new urban and industrial order. Labor violence and farmers' protests seemed to augur a general outbreak of class warfare. Doubts about the social and economic cost of industrialization swirled everywhere. During the crisis the money question emerged as the defining element in politics. Neither party could avoid taking a stand on silver or gold, which had come to symbolize where one stood on industrialization and modernization generally. The two-party system almost cracked under the strain. Angry farmers and unemployed workers abandoned the major parties for the Populists or drove the "gold bugs" from the Democratic party leadership and made silver the new standard of political and moral rectitude.

The depression was caused by structural imbalances in the economy. The ability to produce was outpacing the ability to consume. The economy had been in decline since 1890, but the immediate crisis was triggered by the failure of the Philadelphia & Reading Railroad in 1893. Railroads had led the way in building the industrial and corporate order. To many Americans, the destiny of America rode on the rails (see Chapter 18). Over-speculation in railroad stocks, overbuilding of rail lines, and sometimes underhanded management practices had combined to slow railroad growth by the 1890s. The multiplier effect of railroads now roared backwards. Railroads slashed their demand for iron, steel, lumber, coal, and all the other products necessary to build and run the lines. As the economy contracted, overextended railroads went bankrupt, carrying public confidence and many other businesses down with them. A selling mania swept the New York Stock Exchange. Panic-stricken investors dumped stocks at any price, converting their holdings to gold. By the end of 1893, seventy-four railroads, 600 banks, and over 15,000 businesses had failed.

The causes of the Panic of 1893 were complex, but many businessmen and President Cleveland blamed the crisis on the silver issue. They charged that the silverites' demands had weakened investors' confidence in the American economy. In fact, the nation's gold reserves had become dangerously depleted by the generous outlays of the "Billion Dollar Congress" and the flow of gold overseas, after British investors had converted millions of dollars of their American investments into gold in the wake of the failure of an important British banking house that had invested heavily in American railroads. Also, as silver prices declined, many holders of silver certificates had exchanged them for gold from the Treasury.

HARPER'S WEEKLY

LOOKING UP THE PANHANDLE RAILROAD.—From a Photograph by J. W. Taylor.

IN THE PANHANDLE RAILROAD YARDS.—From a Photograph by J. W. Taylor.

The Burned Viaduct.

WRECKING-CREW AT WORK IN THE CINCINNATI, BURLINGTON, AND QUINCY RAILROAD YARDS, LOOKING EAST.—From a Photograph by R. D. Cleveland.

THE GREAT RAILWAY STRIKES—MILES OF BURNED FREIGHT-CARS IN THE RAILROAD YARDS ABOUT CHICAGO.

704

Burned Freight Cars These three photographs of burned freight cars during the Pullman strike were originally published in *Harper's Weekly* on July 28, 1894. The strike's violence and its threat to disrupt the nation's mail service thoroughly frightened middle-class Americans.

Cleveland had a simple solution to the crisis: repeal the Sherman Silver Purchase Act of 1890 and put America squarely on a single gold standard. Amid furious debate, a special session of Congress finally repealed the Act in October 1893, but the economic gain proved minimal. If anything, the repeal hurt the economy by contracting the money supply further. The drain on the gold reserve continued. Cleveland tried to shore up the gold reserves with bond sales, to little effect. In 1895 the gold reserve had sunk to only $41 million. In desperation, the president agreed to let a syndicate of bankers, headed by J. P. Morgan, lend the government gold in exchange for U.S. bonds at discount. The bankers resold the bonds to the public, earning a handsome profit for themselves and yielding $65 million to the Treasury, half of it in gold from Europe. Another bond sale for $100 million in 1896 sold quickly. Cleveland's policies saved the gold standard. They did not restore prosperity.

While Cleveland tried to build up the gold reserves, the depression deepened. Railroads continued to go bankrupt (by 1897 a third of the nation's railroad mileage was in receivership) and banks and businesses to fail. Farm prices plummeted, bringing ruin to an already depressed and over-mortgaged rural America. Corn prices, for example, fell from 50 cents to 21 cents a bushel between 1890 and 1896. At least farmers could eat what they could no longer sell. In the cities, the depression threatened starvation. Unemployment rose to 25 percent of the urban workforce in 1895. Desperation gripped the land. Armies of ragged unemployed men tramped about looking for any kind of work, pleading for aid, and, when hungry enough, stealing to provide something for their families. Where men could not find work, women and children left home to take jobs as domestics, in the needle trades, or in mills for subsistence wages. Families took in boarders and sewing, anything to survive. Still, the suffering mounted. By 1895 one out of five industrial workers had no job and no savings to meet his most basic needs. Soup kitchens, bread lines, handouts from ward bosses, church and Salvation Army food banks, and other forms of private relief could not answer the demand as the depression settled into its second and then its third winter.

Anger rose along with despair. Riots broke out in numerous cities. Labor militancy exploded across America. A generation that remembered the mass violence of the railway strikes of 1877 and the gun battles between strikers and strikebreakers at Homestead, outside Pittsburgh, in 1892 and the armed resistance of striking silver miners in Coeur d'Alene, Idaho, in 1892, now shuddered at the widespread breakdown of law and order in 1894. From the West came reports of men seizing trains, looting, and gathering in swarms to march eastward to take over the capital. In eastern and midwestern cities fiery radicals blazed against the ruling class and the state that served it. In New York City, anarchist Emma Goldman thundered for laborers to "demonstrate before the palaces of the rich; demand work. Demand bread. If they deny you both, take bread. It is your sacred right!"

Labor did act. One of the most widely circulated news stories was the coal miners' strike that shut down Pennsylvania and the Midwestern mines when 170,000 workers walked off the job to protest cutbacks. The workers battled state militia units called out to protect the mine-owners' property and crush the strike, and they blew up coal trains and dropped dynamite into mine shafts. In 1894 the nation's railway brotherhoods, under the lead of the American Railway Union (ARU), staged a sympathy boycott in support of factory workers who had struck the Pullman Sleeping-Car Company in a dispute over massive lay-offs, drastic wage cuts, and poor living conditions in Pullman's "model" factory town outside Chicago. By refusing to load or haul any trains with Pullman cars, the railway brotherhoods effectively stalled train traffic in much of the eastern United States. The government moved quickly to derail the strike. U.S. Attorney General Richard Olney used the Sherman Anti-Trust Act to obtain a court injunction against the boycott; federal marshals arrested Eugene V. Debs, the ARU's charismatic president, when he refused to order his men back to work; and President Cleveland dispatched federal troops to Chicago to smash the strike, over the protest of the pro-labor Illinois governor, John Peter Altgeld. The government's actions ignited a round of violence. Mobs burned railroad cars and even part of the Columbian Exposition in Chicago. To many laborers, the promise of a new America and the bounty of products displayed at the "White City" in the Chicago exposition mocked the workers' reality of low or no wages and frightful working conditions. Labor walkouts continued, crippling many industries. More than 1,400 strikes occurred in 1894. Labor would be heard.

Worried businessmen cried "anarchism" and demanded federal intervention to break up strikes and unions and restore order. But public sympathies increasingly ran with labor as employers cut wages, laid off workers, and used strong-arm tactics against striking workers and their supporters. The insensitivity of some among the upper class toward the suffering of those below them fueled growing resentments toward the rich as a class. Perhaps the most publicized act of upper-class arrogance was the lavish costume ball put on by one New York socialite in 1894, while poor men and women shivered and begged for food in one of the city's harshest winters. The rich socialite met with widespread public scorn.

Many Americans also began to rethink older assumptions about the causes of poverty. The idea that individuals brought poverty on themselves because of their bad habits and immorality began to yield to a broader criticism of the economic environment. Blaming poverty on individual sin no longer seemed a rational explanation for the desperation of decent people who wanted to work but could not find any employment. The Social Gospel movement gained wider appeal (see Chapter 19). Christian socialism also grew amid the suffering. Frances Willard, head of the Woman's Christian Temperance Union, flirted with socialism and urged working people to unite in political action. Some Christians saw Armageddon coming, as the century closed in violence. One popular Iowa evangelist evoked a chorus of "Amen's" whenever he likened the "moral conceit" blinding America to the need for social justice in the 1890s to the arrogance of wealth that brought down the Israel of old. The influential Presbyterian journal *The Churchman* warned: "There are a thousand evidences that the present state of things is drawing to a close, and that some new development of social organization is at hand." Calls for a larger governmental responsibility in tackling the depression and its attendant evils rang out from church

Coxey's Army on the March   Coxey's Army of unemployed workers marches past a lumberyard en route to Washington, D.C., early in their 1894 trek from Ohio. This was one of the first of the great public demonstrations that would frequently be held in Washington throughout the twentieth century.

pulpits, union halls, middle-class women's clubs, and elsewhere. Many people now looked to the national government to provide both leadership and compassion in the crisis.

The boldest proposal for governmental action came from "General" Jacob Coxey and his "Commonweal Army of Christ" in 1894. A self-taught monetary expert and businessman from Ohio, Coxey used apocalyptic language to argue that the federal government could end unemployment and save the country from the "usurers" by issuing $500 million in legal-tender greenbacks to state and local governments to hire men to build roads. When Congress ignored his "Good Roads Bill," he launched the "Tramps March on Washington" to "send a petition to Washington with boots on." Starting with a band of men, women, and children from Massillon, Ohio, Coxey's "Army" gathered thousands of sympathizers en route, as his force converged with others who had set out from the West. But only 500 people actually arrived in Washington with Coxey in April. Coxey and two other leaders were immediately arrested for trespassing on the Capitol grounds,

and club-wielding police sent his followers scurrying. Coxey's army disbanded, but other "armies" later descended on Washington during the depression (as many as seventeen "industrial armies" marched on the capital in 1894 alone). Even in defeat, Coxey's Army had shifted public attention to Washington to resolve the economic crisis.

The public did not like what it saw there. Cleveland's devotion to the gold standard and his response to the Pullman strike and Coxey's "invasion" heartened some businessmen, but they infuriated many citizens, who viewed the president and his philosophy of laissez-faire as heartless. A series of reactionary decisions by the Supreme Court defending monopoly and striking down a recently passed federal income tax sealed public distrust of the conservative forces ruling Washington. Cleveland bore the brunt of the criticism. Agrarian reformers and silverites castigated him as a traitor to the working people of America and a stooge of Wall Street — "Morgan's errand boy," as one put it. The image of the United States government being bailed out by Wall Street in the sale of bonds struck many Americans as a sellout. Silverites and farmers in the Democratic Party vowed to take over the party from Cleveland and the "gold bugs." Southern Democrats cheered the words of Governor "Pitchfork Ben" Tillman of South Carolina, who successfully campaigned for the Senate on a pledge to "stick my pitchfork into his [Cleveland's] ribs" to get "that old bag of beef" and Wall Street out of government.

Democrats paid dearly for Cleveland's policies. In the 1894 elections Republicans drowned the Democrats in a torrent of votes in one of the largest congressional swings in American history. The Republicans won a 140-seat majority in the House. A major political realignment was under way. In twenty-four states no Democrats won any national office, and even immigrant workers were cutting their traditional ties to the party. Meanwhile, populism was making inroads in both parties. The party system began to become unglued.

THE POPULIST CHALLENGE

Political discontent had been brewing for two decades among farmers and others who felt left out of the profits and social benefits of the new industrial order. Farmers were confused and angry about their declining fortunes and status and their mounting debts. Farm prices steadily fell and farm debt steadily rose during the late nineteenth century. The South wallowed in poverty, scarce money, and low cotton prices since the end of the war. The crop-lien system added to southern farmers' woes by tying them further to a one-crop economy and burdensome mortgage rates they could never hope to repay. Many southerners lost their land, becoming sharecroppers or tenants or abandoning agriculture altogether (see Chapter 16). Meanwhile, farmers on the Great Plains saw their amber waves of grain taken over by corporations and prices for wheat, corn, and other staples fall in another round of boom-or-bust Plains agriculture (see Chapter 17). Farmers had overextended themselves during the 1880s. The agricultural depression of the 1870s had ended in the early 1880s when failures in wheat crops overseas led to increased demand for American farm products. The boom lasted six years. Abundant rain and bumper crops brought feast and many hopeful migrants to the Plains. Land in Kansas that had sold at $15 an acre in 1881 went for $270 in 1887, and agents from eastern banks roamed the ranges almost begging farmers to borrow. The day of reckoning came, first with the blizzards and ice storms of 1886-87 that ruined the cattlemen and then with the hot and dry summer of 1887 that began almost a decade of drought on the Plains. Just as the choking winds and scorching sun withered the farmers' wheat and locusts and other pests ate up

what little survived, wheat prices collapsed worldwide. Many bankrupt farmers gave up. Over 30,000 farmers left South Dakota between 1888 and 1892, and many more departed from western Kansas, lamenting that "In God we trusted, in Kansas we busted." Farmers farther east who had a greater stake in their land and improvements dug in. They would join with southerners to form the backbone of farm radicalism.

Farmers Come Together

Farmers blamed the eastern banks, the railroads, and "middlemen" rather than overproduction for their troubles. During the 1870s midwestern farmers had fought back by organizing the Grange to eliminate the middleman's profits. Grangers ran cooperatives that bought goods in bulk and sold them to farmers at cost, milled and stored grain, provided insurance, and lent money. The Granger lodges soon became political as well, as members screened candidates and lobbied for legislation to control freight rates and charges at grain elevators. The Grangers scored some modest, short-term successes, but the movement collapsed under the mismanagement of the cooperatives and the futility of trying to regulate national industries with state legislation (see Chapter 18). With the return of prosperity, the Grange lost members. Still, the Granger movement laid a seedbed for other farmers' organizing efforts.

The most powerful and significant of the farmers' organizations that followed was the Farmers Alliance. The alliance movement grew from a variety of farmers clubs that had cropped up during the 1870s depression. The first "alliance" began in Texas in the 1870s, when ranchers banded together to catch stray cattle and "rustlers." Poor farmers joined as local alliances spread northward and turned their attention to a host of problems facing the debt-heavy Texas plains. The movement rapidly moved eastward across the cotton South in the late 1880s, once the persuasive Dr. Charles W. Macune, a self-taught physician and lawyer from Texas, took charge. Under Macune's energetic leadership, several regional alliances merged to form the National Farmers Alliance and Industrial Union in 1889. Also known as the Southern Alliance, Macune's organization experimented with farmers' cooperatives to buy equipment and supplies for members and to market their products, especially cotton. A more loosely organized Northwestern Alliance emerged on the Plains and also tried its hand at cooperatives. The experiments failed. Banks refused to lend money to the credit-starved farmers, and local merchants opposed the cooperatives. The experience in trying to run cooperatives and get loans hardened Alliance members in their distrust of the "money interest." It also led them to politics. Southern and Northern Alliance members rejected the idea of a political union at first. Sectional prejudices separated them, as did the southerners' emphasis on debt relief and lowering tariffs and the northerners' emphasis on railroad regulation and protection from foreign competition. Southerners wanted to work within the Democratic Party, while northerners talked of starting a third party. Still, the alliances shared common interests and styles. In 1890, at a meeting in Ocala, Florida, they agreed on the need to inflate the currency and coin silver at generous ratios to gold, to abolish the national banks, to reduce tariffs, to establish a graduated federal income tax, to regulate the railroads and telegraph companies closely (and, if necessary, to nationalize them), and to set up a subtreasury system. The subtreasury idea was Mac-

une's plan to manipulate the market by letting farmers hold their goods until prices rose. Farmers would deposit nonperishable crops in government-owned warehouses and receive low-interest loans, with the crops as collateral. The farmers would repay the loans when they sold their crops later at higher prices.

The alliances sold their "program," known as the "Ocala Demands," with all the fervor and organization of a revival. The National Alliance prepared the way for action by distributing literature to its many chapters and training a cadre of local men and women to teach members the ins and outs of the money issue and how to run an organization. The Alliance maintained its own press, which fed stories to the hundreds of local alliance weeklies, and carried news from the locals as a way to build common bonds. The papers used straight talk to make the complex issues plain and to stir their readers. As one editor described the situation in 1890: "There are three great crops raised in Nebraska. One is a crop of corn, one is a crop of freight rates, and one a crop of interest. One is produced by farmers who by sweat and toil farm the land. The other two are produced by men who sit in their offices and behind their bank counters and farm the farmers." At the same time itinerant Alliance speakers roused supporters at county

Caricature of the Populists, 1896 This anti-populist cartoon envisions the Supreme Court as a group of whittling, cider-swilling, tobacco-chewing farmers. The millionaires J.P. Morgan, Rockefeller, Sage, John Jacob Astor, Vanderbilt, and Jay Gould are not caricatured, but rather presented as individuals prevented from getting a fair hearing because of the agenda of the populists.

THE SUPREME COURT,—"AS IT MAY HEREAFTER BE CONSTITUTED"
IF THE SILVERITES EVER GET A CHANCE TO PUT THEIR POPULISTIC AND REVOLUTIONARY PLATFORM INTO FORCE.

fairs, picnics, and local alliance gatherings. Georgia's red-headed Tom Watson, a planter's son, pounded his fist and cracked his whip in furious speeches lashing the money interest and urging black and white farmers to put aside race and march together. From the Plains came firebrand Mary Elizabeth ("Mary Yellin'") Lease, a Wichita lawyer, prohibitionist, and suffragist, who stormed across Kansas telling farmers to "raise less corn and more hell." "Sockless Jerry" Simpson, a bankrupted Kansas rancher, also pitched his speeches directly to the class and cultural identities of the one-plow poor farmers who made up most of the Alliance's membership by boasting he wore no silk stockings.

Emboldened by the strong language and the sense of righteousness they felt in their cause, Alliance members entered the political arena in 1890. In the South, Alliance-backed candidates took over numerous local Democratic Party organizations and won control of eight state legislatures, four governorships, and forty-four House seats. In the Plains, Alliance men swept the Kansas races, where they ran under the banner of the newly formed People's party, seized control of both houses of the Nebraska legislature, and gained many seats in the Minnesota and South Dakota assemblies. The electoral successes of 1890 raised the political stakes everywhere and bred a third-party movement. The failure of the Alliance-sponsored candidates once in office to honor their pledges to the farmers or to make much difference in federal policies further convinced Alliance leaders that only a separate national party would give farmers the clout necessary to discipline their representatives and redirect America.

In February 1892 a convention of Alliance delegates, labor leaders, women's rights advocates, money and tax reformers, prohibitionists, and others met in St. Louis to map a common political course for the disaffected and "disenfranchised." They organized the People's Party, which soon became known as the Populists, and readied themselves for a national campaign. At the party's nominating convention in Omaha, in July, the delegates adopted the Alliance's "Ocala Demands" of 1890 and added proposals for the direct election of Senators, initiative and referendum, and other electoral reforms to return government "to the hands of 'the plain people.'" The Alliance-dominated convention also reached out to organized labor by calling for the eight-hour work-day and the restriction of "undesirable" immigration. The party nominated James B. Weaver of Iowa, a former Union general and Greenbacker, for president, and balanced the ticket with James Field of Virginia, a former

Confederate general who had lost a leg in the war. Ignatius Donnelly, the frothy Minnesota Populist savant and author of the popular utopian novel, *Caesar's Column* (1891), about a dark future of class oppression, set the tone for the party's national mission. He described the nation as on "the verge of moral, political, and material ruin," with corruption everywhere, the people demoralized, and justice impatient. The People's Party wanted nothing less than national redemption.

❧ *Populist Themes*

Conservative critics painted the Populists as a monstrous hybrid of hayseeds and socialists. Admittedly, populism presented a tangle of contradictions, at once radical in economic proposals and conservative in social ones, demanding an expansion of federal authority and a restoration of local power. Calls for inflation did not sit well with many workers, and the movement's anti-Semitism (speakers like Lease railed against what they called "the international Jewish banking conspiracy"), nativism, and extreme rhetoric alienated Catholic, Jewish, and other immigrants. But the real reason conservatives feared populism was the Populist Party's insistence on a collective, national responsibility for people's well-being and its assault on the principle of laissez-faire. The Populist Party posed a real threat to politics as usual. In the South, for example, the Populists openly courted African Americans. A parallel alliance movement, the Colored Farmers' National Alliance and Cooperative Union, had grown to a quarter million members, with branches in every southern state, by 1892. Populists wanted their votes. Several bold Populist speakers attacked lynch law and emphasized the common interests of poor farmers that transcended race.

The Populists' fervid campaigning and calls for a re-ordering of the economy and politics did not bring electoral victory. Weaver garnered a million popular votes nationwide, and Populists won local races in Kansas and other western states. The Populists failed in the South, however, as race-baiters drove a wedge into the movement by conjuring up fears of "Negro rule." Watson lost his congressional seat, and racial antagonisms intensified as a result of the election. The immediate legacy of the Populists' broken bid for African Americans' support would be disfranchisement and "Jim Crow" (see Chapter 16). In the former Granger states of the Midwest, the Populist party also fared poorly. Farmers there had shifted to dairy, truck, and other kinds of farming during the 1880s and rid themselves of the debt loads that had driven farm radicalism elsewhere. Those farmers rejected populism as the rantings of, in the words of one anti-Populist Kansas editor, "misfits," "neurotics" filled with hate, and ne'er-do-well farmers who did not paint their barns. Industrial workers also stayed away. As a third-party movement, populism had spent its force in 1892.

Within the two-party system, however, populism grew. Western Republicans threatened to bolt the party unless the dominant eastern bosses made some concessions to inflate the currency and meet other farmers' needs. The Democratic Party was especially ripe for takeover. The depression of the 1890s and the Cleveland administration's policies hurt the party badly. The split between the conservative, pro-business eastern wing of the party and the increasingly desperate westerners and southerners was almost irreparable after the 1894 elections. Not since 1860 had the party faced such deep internal divisions. Southerners and westerners plotted to make the party their own. They fastened on the silver issue to galvanize support for a populist Democratic party. To do so, they circulated pro-silver pamphlets, especially William H. "Coin" Harvey's immensely popular booklet, *Coin's Financial School* (1894), which reduced the money question to a "conspiracy of Goldbugs" and the promise that the free coinage of silver would end debt and rejuvenate the economy. The way to the Promised Land, said the silverites, was not down the "yellow brick road"; rather, a silver rod pointed the way.

"Coin's Financial School" The popular 1894 booklet mocked the "gold bugs" and equated the free coinage of silver with prosperity and moral redmption. In this illustration, readers are urged to "take [their] choice" between prosperity and poverty — the former a direct result of bimetallism, the latter of "monometalism."

While silver miners operated from narrow self-interest in pressing the claims of silver, many westerners and southerners viewed the money issue more broadly. Where one stood on gold or silver was tantamount to where one stood on the meaning and destiny of America. In the public mind, gold had become synonymous with big business and eastern capital, with the world of bureaucracy and modernism; silver, in turn, had come to represent the "work-worn" and "dust-begrimed" farmers and laboring people, a return to a simpler time when the proverbial Jeffersonian yeoman farmer and artisan ruled. The money issue now defined political categories. The major parties had to face the issue squarely. Within such an intellectual and political context, the election of 1896 loomed as a critical moment in American history.

THE CROSS OF GOLD AND THE ELECTION OF 1896

The Democrats met in Chicago in July. The western and southern delegations drove the Cleveland "gold bugs" from the floor, adopted a platform calling for "the free and unlimited coinage of silver and gold" at the ratio of 16 to 1, and picked a thirty-six-year-old former congressman from Nebraska as their candidate. The epiphany of the Chicago meeting came when William Jennings Bryan addressed a still deadlocked convention. Already a well-known orator and silverite, described by one admirer as "a young divine," the handsome Bryan repeatedly brought the cheering audience to its feet in a booming speech that filled the great hall with defiance to eastern capital, invoked the memory of Jefferson and Jackson by comparing "our farms" to "your cities," and called on "the plain people of this country" to join in "a cause as holy as the cause of liberty — the cause of humanity." Pressing his fingers to his brow, he closed his speech in the cadences of the King James Bible with the prophecy that the "producing masses of this nation and the world, supported by the commercial interests, the laboring interests, and the toilers everywhere" would answer eastern capital's "demand for a gold standard by saying to them: You shall not press down upon the brow of labor this

A Cross of Gold   William Jennings Bryan, catapulted into the spotlight because of his "Cross of Gold" speech, speaking more calmly just before the presidential election of 1896.

crown of thorns, you shall not crucify mankind upon a cross of gold." Bryan stood at the podium with his arms outstretched in mock crucifixion. The audience sat in stunned silence, and then erupted in wild applause and thronged Bryan as he returned to his seat. The convention nominated him for president the next day.

The victory of "silver" in Chicago left the Populists in a dilemma. The silver issue carried much symbolic weight among Populists, but it was one of several important issues. Alliance members and southerners, especially, thought silver a distraction from the more sweeping reforms they had proposed in 1890 and 1892. Western Populists favored Bryan and "fusion" with the

Democrats. Running a separate candidate, they warned, would take votes from Bryan and throw the election to the Republicans. The Populists bitterly yielded to the fusion plan, nominating Bryan as their presidential candidate and preserving the appearance of independence by selecting Tom Watson as their own vice-presidential candidate. For all practical purposes, fusion swallowed up the People's Party as a separate organization. As Watson explained it: "The Democratic idea of fusion is that we play Jonah while they play the whale."

Meanwhile, at their convention in St. Louis, the Republicans had chosen William McKinley to head their ticket. A former congressman and then governor of Ohio, McKinley brought pro-business principles, sympathy for labor, and personal integrity to the campaign. He also brought the political ambition and deep pockets of fellow Ohioan "Dollar Mark" Hanna, a businessman who spent a small fortune to engineer McKinley's nomination on the first ballot and who would raise millions for his election. Republicans endorsed the gold standard and a high tariff. Only "sound money" could end the depression, they said. The nation braced for "the battle of the standards."

The election of 1896 offered voters a real choice in substance and style. Bryan, "the Great Commoner," barnstormed the country in a new style of campaigning. He traveled 18,000 miles by train and delivered as many as thirty speeches a day in a direct bid for votes. He brought the campaign to the people, clasping hands eagerly and preaching the virtues of small-farm, small-town America. Although he harped on silver (he had "silver on the brain," said one observer), Bryan also spoke about the need to regulate railroads, ease credit, and raise crop prices. The enthusiastic crowds mobbing his train at the whistle stops seemed to promise victory.

The Republicans countered Bryan's popular personal appeal by waging a campaign based on a combination of fear and modern marketing. The Republican press used the Populists' nomination of Bryan to caricature him as a radical (which he was not) and to warn of dire economic and social consequences if Bryan and his ragtag followers gained the White House. Republicans went for the "belly vote" in their "Stop Bryan, Save America" campaign. They told farmers and laborers that a Bryan victory would mean mortgages would not be renewed and factories would close, and they reminded anyone who would listen that the Democrats had brought on the depression. McKinley, in turn, promised Americans "a full dinner pail."

More important, the Republican Party, led by Mark

McKinley on the Front Porch Though they could not vote, many women enthusiastically joined the crowd at one of William McKinley's speeches during his 1896 "Front Porch" presidential campaign. This was one of the great mobilizations of voters during the nineteenth century, and — like Bryan's barnstorming by train — it foreshadowed the kinds of campaigns that twentieth-century presidential candidates would wage.

Hanna, orchestrated a masterful, dignified "front porch" campaign. Borrowing from techniques used in the 1880s, Hanna sat McKinley on his porch in Canton, Ohio, and brought the voters to him. Hanna understood that by using the wire services and newspapers McKinley and his message could reach everywhere in the nation without the candidate leaving Canton. Working on a pre-arranged schedule in conjunction with the railroads, Republicans trooped delegations from various and different interest groups to Canton to deliver speeches and presents (including five eagles) and receive McKinley's blessings and handshake. Some 750,000 persons made the pilgrimage to McKinley's door — lumbermen one day, women's rights advocates the next, the Colored Republican League the next, and so on, even the "40,000 Pounds for McKinley Club" boasting "40,000 pounds for McKinley, not one ounce for Bryan." It all had the air of public spontaneity. In fact, each speech had been written by Republicans beforehand, each McKinley homily crafted to satisfy a particular interest group. McKinley exuded the image of the knowledgeable, concerned public servant, and with his wife and children flanking him in posed photographic "opportunities," he appeared as the consummate family man. Several days before the election, the Republicans added a final patriotic touch. By promoting Flag Day as a national celebration, they wrapped McKinley and the party in "Old Glory." An admiring

Theodore Roosevelt summed up Hanna's strategy: "He has advertised McKinley as if he were a patent medicine."

Hanna also assessed fearful businessmen millions of dollars to build a huge war chest. He understood that the old politics of patronage was past and that the new politics of organization had arrived. Money held the key to political power. With the money, the Republicans hired over 1,400 speakers to go into doubtful districts selling McKinley and Republicanism. Using social scientific methods to identify voters' interests down to the ward level, and drafting speeches in different languages tailored to particular groups, the Republicans made politics a science. In doing so, they did not forget the old politics of parades, posters, and paraphernalia. Only now the events were more carefully staged by central party management and the symbols more calculated in their appeal. Republicans and the new politics won resoundingly in 1896. Both presidential candidates won more votes than any other candidate in history, but McKinley won many more than Bryan. McKinley swept the populous industrial Northeast and Midwest, four border states, five upper Mississippi Valley "cornbelt" states, and California and Oregon, leaving only the Solid South, the Plains, and Rocky Mountain states to "the Boy Orator from the Platte" and the Democrats. Bryan had the acres, McKinley the votes, one observer noted. Settled farmers, the urban middle class, and industrial workers went for the Republicans. Bryan offered them little, except the prospect of devalued money, lower real wages, and higher food prices. Equally important were urban America's suspicions of rural America. Catholic and Jewish voters, for example, cringed at the pulpit-pounding politics of populism, and Bryan's moral condemnations of urban life served only to offend immigrants. The Democrats seemed out of step with the age, mired in a nostalgic past of a yeomanry that never was. Never again would agrarian votes alone pave the way to the White House. Indeed, for all but eight of the next thirty years, the Republicans would dominate national politics on the strength of the new voter alignments forged in the 1890s. Middle-class values, big business, and big cities now ruled. The Democrats languished in the one-party South and the sparsely settled western states.

The return of prosperity in 1897 and gold strikes in Alaska and elsewhere buried the silver issue until the Great Depression of the 1930s. In 1900 McKinley easily won reelection on the promise of another full dinner pail. In his second bid for the presidency, Bryan dredged up populist ideas in 1900, to little effect. Foreign policy more than domestic issues colored the next campaign, and the more forward-looking Republicans were in power to stay. Populism was not altogether dead. Its national democratic moment had passed, but it survived regionally in the South as a cultural force and a political style for generations. And many of the Populists' reform proposals were later enacted by the Progressives, who, in the words of William Allen White, "caught the Populists in swimming and stole everything except the frayed underdrawers of 'free silver.'" Even the sub-treasury plan found new life in the twentieth century, when it became the basis for New Deal farm support policy.

CONCLUSION: THE END OF THE OLD AND THE RISE OF THE NEW

McKinley in office embodied many of the new trends toward modern management and national purpose that had been unfolding during the late nineteenth century. He drew on the professions, journalism, and business to staff his administration. He used government mediation, rather than force, to resolve potentially violent labor strikes, and he proposed a government commission to study the possibility of regulating monopoly. He recognized the importance of good public relations. McKinley, in white vest and with flowered lapel, charmed the Washington-based press corps, lobbyists, and voters alike. The press treated McKinley's ideas and actions kindly in print, and Congress dared not ignore the popular president. With the Republicans in control of both houses of Congress and the presidency, they could act in concert to legislate policy. In a series of savvy machinations within the party, McKinley lessened the power of state bosses while enhancing the national party organization. Just as Mark Hanna had used modern communications and marketing to get McKinley elected, the president used his office in ways that established him as the first "modern" president. At the same time, the effects of the civil service and ballot reforms began to take hold. Voter participation declined, party organizations centralized, and interest groups gained ascendancy after McKinley's term. The future of politics, as in everything else, lay in organization.

The nineteenth century closed on a note of hope and anticipation. Although serious class and cultural divisions and gross social injustices cried ever louder for redress and sank many Americans into pessimism, prosperity and political stability held out the promise of a national response in the new century. The instruments for governmental action and public persuasion were in place. Soon enough, the Progressives would use them. Americans by 1900 also had a wider vision

The "Cross of Gold" Speech, 1896

William Jennings Bryan's brilliant and electrifying "Cross of Gold" speech secured Bryan the Democratic nomination in 1896, but more importantly, it summed up the worldview of the populist-oriented elements of the party and the nation, with their distrust of the eastern business interests and politics as usual.

Ah, my friends, we say not one word against those who live upon the Atlantic coast, but the hardy pioneers who have braved all the dangers of the wilderness, who have made the desert to blossom as the rose--the pioneers out there [pointing west], who rear their children near to Nature's heart, where they can mingle their voices with the voices of the birds--out there where they have erected schoolhouses for the education of their young, churches where they praise their Creator, and cemeteries where rest the ashes of their dead--these people, we say, are as deserving of the consideration of our party as any people in this country. It is for these that we speak. . . .

You come to us and tell us that the great cities are in favor of the gold standard; we reply that the great cities rest upon our broad and fertile prairies. Burn down your cities and leave our farms, and your cities will spring up again as if by magic; but destroy our farms and the grass will grow in the streets of every city in the country. . . .

If they dare to come out in the open field and defend the gold standard as a good thing, we will fight them to the uttermost. Having behind us the producing masses of this nation and the world, supported by the commercial interests, the laboring interests, and the toilers everywhere, we will answer their demand for a gold standard by saying to them: You shall not press down upon the brow of labor this crown of thorns, you shall not crucify mankind upon a cross of gold.

of their national responsibilities, not only for their own personal profit but also for society generally. And, as the new century dawned, so, too, did Americans begin to imagine an empire across the seas.

SUGGESTED READING

Glenn C. Altschuler and Stuart M. Blumin, *Rude Republic: Americans and Their Politics in the Nineteenth Century* (2000). A complete overturning of conventional historical writing on the extent of public interest and involvement in politics, arguing that small-town, middle-class America was largely indifferent to and ignorant of national politics and issues and voted largely out of a sense of civic duty and pressure from party activists.

Cindy Sondik Aron, *Ladies and Gentlemen of the Civil Service: Middle-Class Workers in Victorian America* (1987). A study of the ways government bureaucracies grew and adapted to middle-class values and employment and the managerial revolution, thereby making government more modern and capable of information gathering and regulation and informing private business culture and practice.

Robert Cherny, *American Politics in the Gilded Age* (1997). A description and analysis of the ethnic, religious, and institutional foundations and interests of politics and their effects on the political process.

Rebecca Edwards, *Angels in the Machinery: Gender in American Party Politics from the Civil War to the Progressive Era* (1997). A path-breaking exploration, using newspapers, political cartoons, and campaign material culture, to discover the ways parties and political activists appealed to and engaged women in politics by converting issues and candidates into concerns about family and morality and the ways women, in turn, steered politics and government toward their interests.

Gaines M. Foster, *Moral Reconstruction: Christian Lobbyists and the Federal Legislation of Morality, 1865-1920* (2002). A forceful argument on the means and ends of Christian lobbyists in their increasingly effective efforts to combat vice with law and the effects of such lobbying in expanding federal regulatory interest.

Lawrence Goodwyn, *Democratic Promise: The Populist Movement in America* (1976). Influential reading of populism as a radical movement rooted in economic experience of Alliance culture and cooperatives and democratic ideology.

Michael McGerr, *A Fierce Discontent: The Rise and Fall of the Progressive Movement in America, 1870-1920* (2003). A major reinterpretation of the origins and evolution of the Progressivism as a broad middle-class social movement trying to reshape the values and behavior of Americans of all classes.

H. Wayne Morgan, *William McKinley and His America* (rev. ed., 2003). A life-and-times study that casts McKinley as a modern president in political sensibility and style in cultivating the press and public and in managing government, the architect of a new national Republican majority, and the clarion for a renewed sense of national destiny and purpose.

Mary P. Ryan, *Women in Public: Between Banners and Ballots, 1825-1880* (1990). An important reorientation of women's places in public life, showing how women practiced "outdoor politics" by organizing and managing social reform, civic celebrations, and public events in ways that informed politics, civic engagement, and public discourse.

Michael Schudson, *Discovering the News: A Social History of American Newspapers* (1978). An engaging and perceptive look at the ways the democratization of public, political, and social life affected news coverage and reporting that made the press the Fourth Estate in public life.

Mark W. Summers, *Party Games: Getting, Keeping, and Using Power in Gilded Age Politics* (2004). A reexamination of the ways parties and public interest groups made politics a business by the sophisticated use of popular culture, the press, managerial techniques, patriotism and civic duty, money, patronage, and other means of persuasion.

Robert H. Wiebe, *The Search for Order, 1877-1920* (1967). A still invaluable interpretation of the age that emphasizes the pull and power of professionalization and bureaucratization in public and private life and the dominance of national institutions and interests over local communities.

SUGGESTIONS FOR FURTHER READING

Peter Argersinger, *The Limits of Agrarian Radicalism: Western Populism and American Politics* (1995).

Ruth Bordin, *Woman and Temperance: The Quest for Power and Liberty, 1873-1900* (1981).

Sean Dennis Cashman, *America in the Gilded Age: From the Death of Lincoln to the Rise of Theodore Roosevelt* (1984).

Robert F. Durden, *The Climax of Populism: The Election of 1896* (1965).

Elisabeth Griffith, *In Her Own Right: The Life of Elizabeth Cady Stanton* (1984).

Matthew F. Jacobson, *Barbarian Virtues: The United States Encounters Foreign Peoples at Home and Abroad, 1877-1900* (2000).

Ari Hoogenboom, *Outlawing the Spoils: A History of the Civil Service Reform Movement, 1865-1883* (rev. ed., 1982).

Ari Hoogenboom, *Rutherford B. Hays: Warrior and President* (1995).

Morton Keller, *Affairs of State: Public Life in Late Nineteenth-Century America* (1977).

Paul Kleppner, *The Third Electoral System, 1853-1892: Parties, Voters, and Political Cultures* (1979).

Gerald W. McFarland, *Mugwumps, Morals, and Politics, 1884-1920* (1975).

Michael McGerr, *The Decline of Popular Politics: The American North, 1865-1928* (1986).

Robert McMath, *American Populism: A Social History, 1877-1898* (1993).

H. Wayne Morgan, *From Hayes to McKinley: National Party Politics, 1877-1896* (1969).

Joanne Reitano, *The Tariff Question in the Gilded Age: The Great Debate of 1888* (1994).

Elizabeth Sanders, *Roots of Reform: Farmers, Workers, and the American State, 1877-1917* (1999).

Carlos A. Schwantes, *Coxey's Army: An American Odyssey* (1985).

Theda Skocpol, *Protecting Soldiers and Mothers: The Political Origins of Social Policy in the United States* (1992).

John G. Sproat, *"The Best Men": Liberal Reformers in the Gilded Age* (1968).

Mark W. Summers, *The Press Gang: Newspapers and Politics, 1865-1878* (1994).

Irwin Unger, *The Greenback Era: A Social and Political History of American Finance, 1865-1879* (1964).

Richard E. Welch, Jr., *The Presidencies of Grover Cleveland* (1988).

R. Hal Williams, *Years of Decision: American Politics in the 1890s* (1978).

22

Innocents Abroad: Expansion and Empire, 1865-1900

IN THE IMMEDIATE post–Civil War era, few Americans worried much about the world beyond the seas. There were enough troubles at home in settling the "southern question," conquering the West, building a new industrial order, and assimilating millions of new immigrants. Even in the age of steam, the oceans provided "free security" from a hostile world. So, too, the idea of American "exceptionalism" — of America being anointed by God and history to play a special role in the world as "a city upon a hill," creating a successful republic that might be a model for human redemption everywhere — fostered American "isolationism." America's destiny supposedly demanded avoiding foreign entanglements — ideas echoed from Thomas Paine's *Common Sense* in 1776, through George Washington's "Farewell Address," to the Monroe Doctrine — lest America lose its way in the moral corruption, rivalries, and confusions of European affairs. Better, the thinking went, that the United States chart its own course and secure its continental empire. America's future thus looked principally to keeping European powers from further intrusions in the Western Hemisphere while also developing the American economy and increasing exports.

By 1900, however, the United States had stretched out across North America and extended its interests in the Western Hemisphere and Asia. It had moved from the expectation and habit of continental expansion, within the framework of American isolationism, to the first strides to plant the flag overseas. The United States had acquired an "empire" and had asserted its claim to stand among the great nations. Those shifts set off a full-blown debate among Americans about the republic's place in the world and the moral, political, and social burdens and duties of expansion and empire — a debate that continued well into the next century.

The new direction occurred almost by accident. Until the 1890s, at least, the United States lacked the trained diplomatic personnel and military and naval power to direct, manage, and enforce a coherent foreign policy. Identifying American interests and involvement "overseas" was largely the handiwork of Protestant missionaries, businessmen, journalists, intellectuals, and naval officers. Incidents rather than policy too often dictated where and how the United States entered the world. Little wonder that Europeans dismissed American pretensions to greatness. Indeed, trying to explain the Americans' improbably easy victory in the Spanish-American War in 1898, German Chancellor Otto von Bismarck summed up the Europeans' disdain when he quipped, "There's a special providence that exists for drunkards, fools, and the United States of America."

But providence alone did not decide American affairs. By the 1890s, new men and new ideas about American responsibilities and opportunities in the world came to the fore, and a new professionalism in the foreign service and naval affairs informed American diplomacy and military policy. Also important was the sense of urgency to enter the race for empire and to ensure American access to overseas markets, in Asia especially, at a time when European powers were seizing control of land and trade in large parts of Asia and Africa. Changing intellectual currents, especially the spread of Social Darwinism among prominent educational and political leaders at home, and the growing influence of missionaries on American thinking about the world order and commerce, further extended American interests overseas. All such factors converged in the late nineteenth century to effect basic shifts in American policy and to provide the will, skill, and tools to make possible new American ambitions in the world.

LIMITS ON EXPANSIONISM AND EMPIRE

A general public ignorance of the world beyond American borders kept foreign policy issues out of mind until the end of the century. To be sure, politicians sometimes whipped up public anger by exaggerating some alleged insult to American territorial integrity and pride, a tactic especially productive of votes from Irish immigrants still resentful of British rule and arrogance. No one ever lost votes by "twisting the Lion's tail." Immigrants brought knowledge of and interest in their homelands with them to the United States, but the sheer diversity of immigrants muted any single immigrant/ethnic group's ability to make its native country a subject of American support and governmental favor. American politics continued to focus on domestic questions, reinforcing Americans' inward gaze. Even ostensibly foreign questions, such as Chinese exclusion, turned on domestic issues. Only the religious press regularly reported on events and needs overseas, largely in an effort to support missionary work or organize relief for victims of disease, famine, and religious persecution. American newspapers carried little sustained coverage of non-European affairs and generally reported only the wars, calamities, and problems of other peoples — all of which no doubt confirmed many Americans in their seeming splendid isolation from a troubled world.

Structural problems also limited the ability of the United States to develop a forceful foreign policy. Chief among them were the ignorance and incompetence of American diplomats and consular agents, the weakness of the American military, and the miserable state of the American navy until its rebuilding program began in the late 1880s.

American diplomacy suffered especially from overtaxed and ineffectual diplomatic officials. The State Department was understaffed; in 1885, for example, it had only sixty employees, including clerks. In an age when many diplomatic posts were still one or more days away in communication from Washington, consuls and envoys had significant influence in shaping "policy." Many ministers and consular agents were political appointees who viewed their offices as temporary rewards and hardly bothered to learn the history, culture, language, or interests of the countries to which they were posted. The State Department compounded the problem by providing little instruction and only general, uniform guidelines rather than specific concerns for their assignments, and by tolerating outrageous behavior and stupidity in the field. Examples of Americans' blundering and arrogance were legion. One consul in Tokyo, for example, disgusted his Japanese hosts with his habit of carrying a pistol in public and cracking a whip at pedestrians while he sped along in his carriage, and an American ambassador in Ecuador plotted to assassinate the British minister there and to have Ecuador annexed by the United States. In the words of Mark Twain, Americans got the foreign service

"GIVE IT ANOTHER TWIST, GROVER — WE'RE ALL WITH YOU!"

that befitted a people ignorant and contemptuous of the outside world: "Under our consular system we send creatures all over the world who speak no language but their own, and even when it comes to that, go wading all their days through the blood of murdered tenses, and flourishing the scalps of mutilated parts of speech. When forced to it we order home a foreign ambassador who is frescoed all over with . . . indiscreetness, but we immediately send one in his place whose moral ceiling has a perceptible shady tint to it, and then he brays when we supposed he was going to roar."

The army also was too weak to advance American interests abroad. After the Civil War, the rapidly demobilized army shrank to less than 30,000 men and remained small and dispersed until the Spanish-American War in 1898. The United States Army was deployed in fighting Indians and exploring the West. Although the army was becoming more professional in training its officers, the emphasis at West Point remained on engineering. The government simply did not prepare the army to serve as an instrument of American foreign policy. Even when war came in 1898, the army struggled to recruit, outfit, and organize 200,000 men for duty in Cuba and the Philippines. The concept of the volunteer army still ruled military policy and limited military influence.

"Twisting the Lion's Tail"   President Grover Cleveland is depicted challenging the British Empire, a move that never failed to stir up support or gain votes in the United States. Britain was a dominant power in the world at the time, such that provoking it was compared to provoking a lion.

For a two-ocean nation, a strong navy was more important than an army for defense and diplomacy, but until the rebuilding campaign of the late 1880s, the American navy was shockingly out-of-date in technology and had few seaworthy vessels. In 1881 the navy's five major ships were over a quarter century old. The once-proud American navy of Civil War days had become, in the words of one naval observer, "an alphabet of floating washtubs" by the 1880s. American ships limped along at less than 5 knots per hour because their boilers were obsolete and poorly maintained. The major European powers meanwhile had embarked on their great naval arms race and far outpaced and outclassed American naval building. The United States had to rely on fulmination rather than firepower to get its way in Latin America and Asia. That it succeeded at all was due to circumstance and the potential of American power, not, as many Americans opined, the "rightness" of the American cause and God's special providence.

FORCES FOR EXPANSION AND INTEREST OVERSEAS

Amid all the weaknesses of American diplomacy and power, several "givens" informed American interests in foreign affairs and several new forces stirred public opinion about America's need to become more actively engaged in the world. Among those givens was the constant American urge to expand outward. A people on the move needed new frontiers. With the continental frontier "closed," as announced by the Census Bureau in 1890 and echoed by historian Frederick Jackson Turner in his famous 1893 address on the significance of the American frontier, Americans might now chart new directions for progress.

Businessmen helped lead the way. The expanding American industrial economy strained to find new markets, especially during business downturns in the United States such as the devastating Panic of 1893. Improved communications with Europe after the laying of the transatlantic cable sped exchanges in information, facilitating sales and investments and improving management of distant interests, as it also improved coordination of missionary work among churches. One Protestant minister preached that the laying of the transatlantic cable was a call to evangelize the world, for it promised to end the confusion of languages from the days of Babel. Laying a Pacific cable to Asia had similar effects on exchanges in commerce and ideas. Railroad companies with shipping lines also propelled the movement of goods, people, and ideas across the oceans. Businessmen operating within the American national market soon learned to think globally, as the linkages improved and markets opened up. By the end of the century, for example, more Singer sewing machines were being sold outside the United States than within, literally stitching Americans to overseas production and exchanges.

At the same time, the sizable American missionary work in Asia, the Middle East, Africa, and South America increasingly bound the United States to the

Missionaries to China   Women missionaries were especially prominent in the foreign mission movement, making up over two-thirds of the foreign mission contingents in the 1890s. Many women missionaries found work in China and other Asian missions liberating, as they applied their schooling and religious training to remaking the world.

larger world. Expansion was central to American evangelical Protestantism. Committed to spreading the gospel, churches took up world evangelization with a renewed sense of urgency after the American Civil War. Missionary fervor swept colleges and seminaries, and organizations such as the intercollegiate Student Volunteers for Foreign Missions recruited missionaries and support for the "evangelization of the world in this generation." In the last thirty years of the nineteenth century, Protestant missions abroad increased fivefold. Over and over again, Protestant leaders chanted the familiar refrain, in the words of one missionary, that the "full hour of opportunity" was now at hand to save humankind. Americans took up the call. Between the 1880s and 1920, thousands of Protestant missionaries went forth to proclaim the Good News of salvation through Christ.

In doing so, they also pointed to the good news of capitalism and lighted the way for commerce. Many missionary efforts allied with businessmen in introducing American goods and setting up vocational schools and Western-style colleges as part of a "civilizing" process necessary to prepare the "heathen savage" for a meaningful spiritual conversion. Missionaries openly appealed to businessmen to support their work. As one missionary wrote, by underwriting schools, dispensaries, and other works of the mission stations, businesses would make "Everyone thus helped . . . a drummer for your goods, and the great church they represent at home would be your advertising agents."

But Protestant missionaries were not in far-off places to hawk American products. They went to save souls. Home churches, mission boards, the YMCA and YWCA, and women's clubs sponsored missions and outfitted them with books and supplies. In turn, missionaries in remote places made the "dark continents" known through church publications and public presentations on their visits home. Each missionary report on hospitals built and souls saved, and each missionary appeal for support from the home church or denomination, reminded countless Americans of "the mission" to share God's blessings. They also linked their work to the "mission" theme of America going back to the Puritans and recast during the American Revolution. By redeeming the world, American missionaries were, in

the words of one Congregationalist leader, "laying the foundations of empires, and we are shaping the future of great populations and mighty states." Even some Catholics shared that vision of American outreach. In the words of Archbishop John Ireland, "America is too great to be isolated from the world around her and beyond her" and must spread both its Christian witness and civic institutions.

Echoing such purpose were advocates of the "white man's burden," who drew on Social Darwinism to argue that the Anglo-Saxon "race," as the finest product of natural selection, had a "duty" to bring order and uplift to the benighted "darker" peoples everywhere. Social Darwinism was a contradictory, misapplied jumble of ideas claiming lineage to Charles Darwin's *On the Origin of Species* (1859), which included the concept that only the fittest of any species survived through a process of natural selection. As popularized and adapted to society by such writers as the Episcopal clergyman and professor William Graham Sumner of Yale University, Darwinian laws supposedly also ruled the social order. Such thinking justified the ruthless competition of the marketplace, they argued, but paradoxically it also demanded imperial conquest as a way to lift the savages from their own misery and

---

❋ IN THEIR OWN WORDS

Theodore Roosevelt's
American Ideals, 1897

An ardent nationalist and expansionist, Theodore Roosevelt used his office, friends, and pen to push for an aggressive "manly" policy of "robust Americanism" to remake the world and restore moral and physical vigor at home. Linking American foreign policy with moral strength was a common theme in American thinking about the republic's place in the world that continued through the Cold War in the twentieth century. Here Roosevelt especially denounced the timidity of educated men at a time that demanded moral courage—a telling argument during the later debates over annexing overseas lands.

There are many upright and honorable men who take the wrong side, that is, the anti-American side, of the Monroe Doctrine

because they are too short-sighted or too unimaginative to realize the hurt to the nation that would be caused by the adoption of their views. There are other men who take the wrong view simply because they have not thought much of the matter, or are in unfortunate surroundings, by which they have been influenced to their own moral hurt. There are yet other men in whom the mainspring of the opposition to that branch of American policy known as the Monroe Doctrine is sheer timidity. This is sometimes the ordinary timidity of wealth. Sometimes, however, it is peculiarly developed among educated men whose education has tended to make them over-cultivated and over-sensitive to foreign opinion. They are generally men who undervalue the great fighting qualities, without which no nation can ever rise to the first rank. . . .

It is an evil thing for any man of education to forget that education should intensify patriotism, and that patriotism must not only be shown by striving to do good to the country from within, but by readiness to uphold its interests and honor, at any cost, when menaced from without. Educated men owe to the community the serious performance of this duty. . . .

It is through strife, or the readiness for strife, that a nation must win greatness. We ask for a great navy, partly because we think that the possession of such a navy is the surest guaranty of peace, and partly because we feel that no national life is worth having if the nation is not willing, when the need shall arise, to stake everything on the supreme arbitrament of war, and to pour out its blood, its treasure, and its tears like water, rather than submit to the loss of honor and renown.

THE COSMOPOLITAN.

The first step towards lightening

The White Man's Burden

is through teaching the virtues of cleanliness.

Pears' Soap

is a potent factor in brightening the dark corners of the earth as civilization advances, while amongst the cultured of all nations it holds the highest place—it is the ideal toilet soap.

All rights secured.

"The White Man's Burden" Imperialism, racism, and commercialism came together in this 1899 Pears' Soap ad, which traded on Admiral Dewey's impeccable reputation to line "the white man's burden" of moral, cultural, and political uplift with American toilet soap. Such attitudes of American superiority suffused policymaking and the public's acceptance of the obligations of empire.

barbarism. In the hands of Congregationalist minister Josiah Strong, such ideas became a command for expansionism. In his hugely popular book *Our Country* (1885), Strong insisted that the Anglo-Saxon was "divinely commissioned to be, in a peculiar sense, his brother's keeper" and that God was thus "training the Anglo-Saxon race for its mission" of Christianizing and civilizing the "weaker races." If America acted, American civilization would "move down upon" Mexico and Latin America and across the seas to bring everywhere the happy result of the "survival of the fittest" in social efficiency. To such thinkers, time was running out for the Anglo-Saxons to save the world, and thus themselves.

Also important in giving currency to the commer-

cial, Christian, and Anglo-Saxon imperatives of expansion was an elite group of well-connected, well-educated men in public office. Drawn principally from the patrician class, bonded by school ties, especially Harvard, and almost all Republicans, the group included such politically prominent expansionists as Senator Henry Cabot Lodge, Senator Albert Beveridge, Assistant Secretary of Navy (and future president) Theodore Roosevelt, Captain Alfred Thayer Mahan, Secretary of War Elihu Root, and Secretary of State John Hay. In books, articles, speeches, lectures, and sermons, these advocates of a "large policy" of American expansion preached the importance and urgency of Americans standing with the great powers. They pressed for a muscular Christianity of missionizing as a way to reinvigorate the Anglo-Saxon people who had gone soft in their luxury, and they countenanced war as a way to reassert masculinity amid the "feminizing" trends of modern life and to test American will. Indeed, as war clouds gathered over the Cuban question in 1897, Theodore Roosevelt thundered, "I should welcome almost any war, for I think this country needs one." But theirs was no blind rush into imperialism. They studied history, geography, political science, and economics to map America's destiny. And they insisted the United States must prepare for greatness.

Central to the preparation was building a modern navy. The principal architect of a new navy policy, known as "navalism," was the strategist and historian Captain Alfred Thayer Mahan. In two important books on the influence of sea power in history, he argued that great nations had increased their wealth and enhanced their security through foreign trade. Great nations had great navies. Applying his logic to contemporary American problems of wild swings in the economy, he urged a naval building program to modernize the decrepit U.S. fleet and the acquisition of bases in the Caribbean and the Pacific to maintain the ships. He further called for an American-run inter-ocean canal connecting the Atlantic and Pacific Oceans. Mahan's ideas hit a responsive chord in Congress, which in the 1880s already had launched a naval building program to replace the wooden-hulled navy with a steam-powered, steel fleet of cruisers and battleships, and among businessmen eager to expand their markets. Henry Cabot Lodge, who had married into a naval family and was a strong supporter of the new Naval War College, especially championed Mahan's strategic concepts. In the Senate, he prefaced his own arguments for expansion by invoking navalism: "Sea power is essential to the greatness of every splendid people." Theodore Roosevelt also strongly endorsed Mahan's ideas and moved to implement them as Assistant Secretary of the Navy in the McKinley administration.

The missionaries, businessmen, Social Darwinists, and navalists did not constitute a foreign policy establishment. They disagreed among themselves on specific concerns, and some among them even balked at annexing places in the Caribbean and Pacific when the chances came in the 1890s. But together they did provide a strong push for expanding American interests abroad. Especially during the 1890s, expansionists, dubbed "jingoes" by their critics, found ample opportunity to exert American power overseas and led the U.S. into what one called "a splendid little war" with Spain in 1898 that ended with a victory showcasing the might of the new navy, the acquisition of the Philippines and Puerto Rico, and the swelling of American pride.

SECURING NORTH AMERICA

However far Americans might dream of extending U.S. interests, the government never lost sight of the need to ensure national security by promoting stability in North America. The Union victory in the American Civil War not only forged the nation-state of the United States and freed the slaves but also effectively cleared the continent from "foreign" intrigue and intervention. The British finally recognized American supremacy in North America. Rather than risk losing Canada to American territorial ambitions or nascent Canadian separatism, the British granted Canada dominion status and self-government in 1867. The demilitarization of the United States–British Canadian border that had begun with the boundary commission following the War of 1812 was now assured. Americans still eyed Canada covetously, but they expected it to fall into American hands "like a ripe apple" and gave up any ideas about a forceful takeover.

Complicating Anglo-American relations were the American claims against Great Britain for damages done by British-built raiders, such as the *C.S.S. Alabama,* sold to the Confederacy during the war. After much blustering on both sides about their respective rights under international law, the Americans and British agreed to submit their dispute to an international tribunal. In 1871 the tribunal awarded the U.S. $15.5 million in damages.

PATIENT WAITERS ARE NO LOSERS.

UNCLE SAM. —I ain't in a hurry; — it 'll drop into my basket when it gets ripe!

New Territories   American ambitions in the Western Hemisphere began to awaken in the years after the Civil War. This 1897 cartoon, entitled "Patient Waiters Are No Losers," shows Uncle Sam waiting for Cuba, Canada, Hawaii, and Central America to fall into his possession.

The settlement of the so-called *Alabama* claims, along with the establishment of a Canada that would not be subject to American encroachments, helped clear the decks of longtime Anglo-American discord in the region. But new troubles in the hemisphere soon threatened the budding Anglo-American accord. In the 1880s bitter arguments over Canadian and U.S. rights to kill seals in the Bering Strait and over fishing rights in the North Atlantic led to much sword-rattling that did not end until 1898, and U.S. intervention in a British boundary dispute with Venezuela in 1895 almost caused the U.S. and Great Britain to come to blows. Still, in North America at least, the beginnings of an Anglo-American rapprochement that would bloom in the twentieth century had been planted.

Immediately after the American Civil War, the United States also turned its attention southward to force the French from Mexico. During the American Civil War France had installed the Archduke Maximilian of Austria as "emperor" of Mexico in a French bid to regain power in the Western Hemisphere. The United States had opposed the move as a violation of the Mon-

"Seward's Folly" Reconsidered American public opinion largely scorned the purchase of Alaska by Secretary of State William Henry Seward in 1867 as "Seward's Folly," but the discovery of gold there sparked a gold rush in the Klondike region in 1896, making the purchase seem less foolish.

as "Seward's folly" and "Frigidia" because they saw no benefit in the icy reaches of a far-off Alaska, but the acquisition of the northern "ice box," as some called it, removed a potentially dangerous power from the continent, gave Americans control over important fishing and whaling areas, and by way of the newly laid telegraph line across Alaska and into Siberia, promised in Seward's words to "extend throughout the world American ideas and principles of public and private economy, politics, morals, philosophy, and religion." With North America "secure," and the continent filling up with settlers, Americans might turn their imagination to expansion overseas.

LATIN AMERICAN RELATIONS

Latin America always remained a primary concern of American policymakers. Proximity alone dictated the interest. The strategic importance of Central and South America was a self-evident truth to

roe Doctrine and Mexico's sovereignty. With the war over, Secretary of State William Henry Seward, who had broad ideas about expanding American influence in the region, demanded the French withdraw from Mexico. Lest the French doubt American resolve, the U.S. sent 50,000 soldiers to the Rio Grande in 1866. The French yielded and left Maximilian to his fate. Mexican nationalists led by Benito Juarez soon captured and executed Maximilian in 1867 and restored Mexico to republican rule.

Seward meanwhile went angling for Alaska. In 1867 the United States bought Alaska from the Russians for only $7.2 million, a move Seward made without even informing the president. Critics mocked the purchase

any thinking American. Also, Americans felt a special kinship with Latin America as part of the American conceit that the New World would redeem the Old. Although Americans foreswore intervention in European, Asian, and African affairs, they did claim special prerogatives in the Western Hemisphere to foster republics and drive out colonialism. The Monroe Doctrine was but one expression of that self-willed hemispheric responsibility. By the late nineteenth century, however, the United States briefly shifted its attitude and policy toward Latin America from strong-arm tactics to deep-pocketed ones, the war with Spain excepted. Americans would secure the hemisphere by way of investment dollars and trade rather than military force to build up Latin American economies as markets for American goods, strengthen republican interests in the region, and check European colonial ambitions. Influence was cheaper than empire, and it sold better. In the words of the New York *Commercial Advertiser* in

1898, the United States should promote "a new Monroe Doctrine, not of political principles, but of commercial policy. . . . Instead of laying down dogmas, it figures up profits." Regarding Cuba, though, the United States used war and intervention to drive out the Spanish, protect American investments, and bring "order" to its island neighbor so that significant investment and good government might follow. Likewise, the United States flexed its muscles to ensure an American-controlled inter-ocean canal in Panama.

Securing American interests in Latin America was neither easy nor inevitable. Latin American peoples distrusted the United States for its bullying past of filibustering expeditions, invasions, and territorial seizures and resented the still predominantly Protestant American press and public leadership for lecturing them on good government and deriding their Catholicism as ignorant and a drag on progress. Also, many competing interests within Latin America made a unified approach difficult. What counted in Spanish-held Cuba was different than what mattered in independent Venezuela. Americans did not always appreciate the distinctions, or even bother to learn the particulars of each country. European powers also controlled most of the Caribbean and exercised significant commercial influence almost everywhere. Except for the island of Hispaniola, shared by the independent Haiti and Santo Domingo (the Dominican Republic), all of the Caribbean basin was in European hands as late as the mid-1890s. The Spanish clung to the last remnants of their once great empire, and the French, Dutch, and Danish colonies were thinly planted, but the British were a dominating presence in the Caribbean and elsewhere in the region. Britannia ruled the waves — and the markets.

❧ Pan-Americanism

The United States tried to exert its influence in the hemisphere by a combination of cautious Pan-Americanism, aggressive challenges to European claims, and investments. In 1889, for example, Secretary of State James G. Blaine sponsored a Pan-American Conference in Washington to discuss common hemispheric problems and foster hemispheric unity. More particularly, Blaine hoped the meeting would open Latin American markets to American trade. At the time, the United States was importing almost three times as much from Latin America as it was selling there. No general trade treaty came, though the U.S. did negotiate bilateral agreements with several nations that provided for

reciprocal tariff reduction. Pan-Americanism was a tough sell among Latin American nations tied to European, especially British, investment and trade. Whatever goodwill had been created by Pan-Americanism was lost in 1891 when the United States demanded, on threat of war, a formal apology and damages from Chile for the murder of two American sailors and injury to seventeen others attacked by a mob while the sailors were on shore leave in Valparaiso. Chile yielded on all counts, much to its humiliation. But the American victory over Chile came at the price of Latin Americans' anger over the United States's high-handed actions. It would be fifty years before Blaine's brand of Pan-American agreements found widespread acceptance.

Also, American imperialism was too recent to be forgotten. Indeed, in 1869, the Ulysses S. Grant administration had tried to annex Santo Domingo, the Spanish-speaking territory on the island of Hispaniola, in an effort to promote trade, provide American business access to mining and commercial opportunities, and promise a refuge for American blacks. Grant's scheme foundered in 1870 due to his administration's clumsy handling of the proposal, intraparty squabbles among Republicans, and fears of adding more "dark-skinned" people to America's population. Although a political fiasco in the United States, the Dominican episode fed fears among Caribbean and Latin American peoples that the United States still had designs on taking lands in the region.

Other American actions undercut any incipient Pan-Americanism. At all costs, the United States was committed to building an inter-ocean canal, which Americans thought essential to national security and commerce. Whereas earlier in the century the U.S. sought cooperation in any such project, after the Civil War it was ready to go it alone. In 1880, two years after the Colombian government had authorized a company organized by the French engineer Ferdinand de Lesseps, builder of the Suez Canal, to dig a canal across the Isthmus of Panama, President Rutherford B. Hayes unilaterally declared that the United States would not allow any European power to control an inter-ocean waterway. Hayes's announcement directly contradicted the 1850 Clayton-Bulwer Treaty with Great Britain, by which each nation had agreed never to "obtain or maintain for itself any exclusive control" over such a canal. The British sniffed at the American announcement, but the U.S. persisted in having its way. A North American company got a contract to build a canal across Nicaragua and cut the British, French, or anyone else out of the project. The daunting engineering problems and costs of building any canal soon bankrupted both the French and American companies. Nevertheless, the U.S. had made clear its position on an inter-ocean canal. Early in the twentieth century, the U.S. virtually seized Panama from Colombia by sponsoring a revolution, and built the canal across the isthmus. Commerce soon flowed, but at the cost of inter-American distrust. In 1921 the United States paid Colombia $25 million by way of apology for its high-handed actions.

❧ Rattling Sabers at the British

The United States also assumed a new role as self-appointed arbiter of hemispheric conflicts. The telling example occurred in 1895 when the United States intervened in a border dispute between Venezuela and British Guiana. The British had refused to submit their grasping territorial claims to an international body for arbitration, whereupon the U.S. Secretary of State Richard Olney warned the British that any invasion of Venezuela or seizure of its territory would be a violation of the Monroe Doctrine. To the world's mightiest naval power, Olney further declared that "Today the United States is practically sovereign on this continent, and its fiat is law upon the subjects to which it confines its interposition." Unless the British agreed to arbitration, Olney continued, the Congress would take up the matter. The U.S. letter was a virtual ultimatum to the British. The British foreign minister, Lord Salisbury, after waiting four months to reply, scoffed at the Monroe Doctrine as having no standing in international law and being unenforceable. The British flatly refused to submit the dispute to arbitration. With his political fortunes flagging at home because of a failing economy, an otherwise irenic but always self-righteous President Grover Cleveland made the British response a point of national honor. He asked Congress to authorize and underwrite an American boundary commission to settle the British-Venezuelan dispute and bellowed that the U.S. would "resist by every means in its power" any British violation of Venezuelan territory, as decided by the United States. Congress unanimously voted for the commission, and the public clamored for a showdown with the British in

---

❊ IN THEIR OWN WORDS

Olney Corollary to the Monroe Doctrine, 1895

The American-British dispute over Venezuela borders led the United States to infuse the Monroe Doctrine with new moral and military meaning by warning that the United States was "practically sovereign" in the Western Hemisphere and would defend its interests forcefully, as Secretary of State Richard Olney communicated in this cable to the American ambassador to Great Britain. The British blustered in response, and both sides rattled swords before agreeing to an accommodation that helped pave the way for Anglo-American rapprochement generally.

That America is in no part open to colonization, though the proposition was not universally admitted at the time of its first enunciation, has long been universally conceded. We are now concerned, therefore, only with that other practical application of the Monroe doctrine the disregard of which by an European power is to be deemed an act of unfriendliness towards the United States. The precise scope and limitations of this rule cannot be too clearly apprehended. . . .

Is it true, then, that the safety and welfare of the United States are so concerned with the maintenance of the independence of every American state as against any European power as to justify and require the interposition of the United States whenever that independence is endangered? The question can be candidly answered in but one way. The states of America, South as well as North, by geographical proximity, by natural sympathy, by similarity of governmental constitutions, are friends and allies, commercially and politically, of the United States. To allow the subjugation of any of them by an European power is, of course, to completely reverse that situation and signifies the loss of all the advantages incident to their natural relations to us. But that is not all. The people of the United States have a vital interest in the cause of popular self-government. They have secured the right for themselves and their posterity at the cost of infinite blood and treasure. They have realized and exemplified its beneficent operation by a career unexampled in point of national greatness or individual felicity. They believe it to be for the healing of all nations, and that civilization must either advance or retrograde accordingly as its supremacy is extended or curtailed. Imbued with these sentiments, the people of the United States might not impossibly be wrought up to an active propaganda in favor of a cause so highly valued both for themselves and for mankind. But the age of the Crusades has passed, and they are content with such assertion and defense of the right of popular self-government as their own security and welfare demand. It is in that view more than in any other that they believe it not to be tolerated that the political control of an American state shall be forcibly assumed by an European power.

the hemisphere. Olney's warning to the British and Cleveland's threat to use force was the boldest claim that the United States had made up to that time regarding the authority of the Monroe Doctrine.

The British woke up to the danger of a direct confrontation with the United States, which they hardly wanted. They were feeling isolated in the complex new alliances forming in Europe and frustrated with many troubles in the Middle East and South Africa. Fighting over some remote tropical land now seemed foolish. The British wanted friends. Great Britain signed a treaty with Venezuela that provided for international arbitration, which largely settled the claims to the British liking. The war drums went silent. The consequence of the affair was that the United States had puffed up its national pride by getting its way with words, feeding a dangerous delusion that such practice would work anywhere. But the British concession to arbitration did pay large dividends in fostering Anglo-American friendship. By "patting the eagle's head" in tacitly accepting American hegemony in the hemisphere and America's responsibility for promoting stability within it, the British furthered a process of building an Anglo-American unity that would be the foundation of both nations' policies over much of the next century. The rapprochement paid early dividends in three to four years, when both countries supported each other's respective imperial wars in Cuba and Africa.

❧ *American Business Interests*

Less dramatic but more significant in tying American interests to the hemisphere was the increase in American investments. Much of the focus was on the Caribbean basin, with Mexico an especially attractive prospect. U.S. capital entered Mexico rapidly, especially after Porfirio Diaz seized power in 1876. American capitalists hardly blinked at the ruthless methods Diaz used to maintain "order" over the next thirty-plus years, for they thought the seeming political stability in Mexico an invitation for investment. Although many Mexicans resented the American capital "invasion," Americans bought up land and mines, built railroads, established businesses, and expanded trade. By 1900 U.S. trade with Mexico had in-

"No Trespass" This *Judge* cartoon spoke to public opinion supporting the strong American stance in the 1895 Venezuela dispute. In this decidedly American view, Uncle Sam defends the hemisphere from European bullies and interlopers.

creased more than nine-fold, from $7 million in 1870 to $64 million annually by 1900, and by 1910 U.S. companies and citizens owned 43 percent of Mexico's property. Likewise in Central America, Americans, led by the railroad entrepreneur Minor Keith, whose holdings later became the United Fruit Company, bought out British concessions and muscled aside local interests in building an empire of banana plantations, ranches, mines, and railways. The growing dollar investment in Mexico and Central America forced American policymakers to consider how to protect such interests from foreign rivals and domestic disturbances. Supporting political regimes friendly to American investments and building up American naval strength in the region became policy by the end of the century. From there it proved but a short step during the twentieth century to intervening in Latin American countries to secure or assert American economic investments, build and control an inter-ocean canal, and shore up regimes supportive of American interests.

ISLAND HOPPING IN THE PACIFIC

America's reach into the Pacific Ocean extended back to the China trade of the early republic. During the nineteenth century whalers, merchants, missionaries, and others brought back reports of bounties to be had across the vast ocean. China was foremost in Ameri-

Queen Liliuokalani A strong proponent of Hawaiian nationalism and independence, Queen Liliuokalani came to power in 1891, but she was overthrown in a revolution sponsored by American business interests two years later. After she was deposed, and even after the United States annexed Hawaii in 1898, she continued to live on as a symbol of Hawaiian culture.

cans' interest in Asia, but from mid-century on Americans cast a wider net in thinking about possibilities in the Pacific. Commodore Matthew Perry's opening to Japan in the 1850s had stirred the American imagination of new markets in Asia, and the subsequent visit of Japanese dignitaries to the United States had set off a brief infatuation with Japanese art and fashion. During the 1870s the U.S. helped Japan modernize by supporting industrialization and offering Japan tariff relief, much to the dismay of the British, who feared an Asian rival. The United States was betting on Japan as a friend in Asia. In 1882 the U.S. also signed a treaty with Korea, which Europeans once called the "Hermit Kingdom" for its self-imposed isolation, opening its ports to

Western trade, establishing favorable Korean-American tariff reciprocity, and promising protection of Korean territoriality. The new relationship with Korea also opened the door to Protestant missionaries there, which led to the growth of a substantial Christian community that had long-range implications for American interest in the peninsula country. Some of these missionaries later worked to keep Korea free from Chinese, Japanese, and Russian political intrusions. Hawaii and far-off islands in the South Pacific also danced in the American mind as places where the intrepid might find profits and even paradise.

The sun-glistened islands of Hawaii early caught the American eye. Since the 1790s Hawaii was a way station for whalers and shippers. Protestant missionaries followed in the 1820s, and by the 1840s Yankee missionaries and merchants had made Honolulu into a little New England port town. The original missionaries sought to convert the native people to Christianity, which also meant weaning them from their Polynesian culture and fitting them out in Yankee cloth. They had mixed success in their efforts. The children of the missionaries and the merchants thought more about acquiring huge tracts of land to grow sugar than winning souls for Christ. American investors, such as Samuel Dole, established large sugar and pineapple plantations worked by Chinese and Japanese laborers and prospered under favorable trade arrangements with the United States.

But fortune faded in 1890 when the McKinley Tariff ended the duty-free status of Hawaiian sugar, plunging Hawaiian sugar prices downward 40 percent in a year. At the same time, a resurgent Hawaiian "nationalism" grew as natives, resentful of foreign wealth and threats to their own culture and autonomy, cheered Queen Liliuokalani's ascension to the Hawaiian throne in 1891. The autocratic queen was an ardent Hawaiian nationalist hostile to the Americans. To protect their interests, the planters, assisted by American troops, staged a successful "revolt" in 1893, deposing the queen and proclaiming an independent Republic of Hawaii. They then appealed to the United States for annexation. The American representative to Hawaii, John L. Stevens, cabled Washington that "The Hawaiian pear is now fully ripe, and this is the golden hour for the United States to pluck it."

The hour passed. Democratic President Grover Cleveland believed in "national honesty," and he doubted the Americans in Hawaii spoke for all the people. Cleveland sent a special investigator to Hawaii, who reported back the collusion of Stevens and the American planters in unseating Queen Liliuokalani and

KING KAMEHAMEHA V. LAYING THE CORNER-STONE OF THE BISHOP'S CHURCH AT HONOLULU.—[SKETCHED BY G. H. BURGESS.]

the opposition of the Hawaiian natives to annexation. Annexation stalled, but restoration of Hawaiian rule did not follow. American public opinion would not allow Cleveland to "give back" Hawaii to the natives, and Cleveland would not use force to reinstall the deposed queen. Cleveland suffered much abuse for not taking the ripe Hawaiian pear, stings that no doubt influenced his thinking in other foreign policy incidents such as the British-Venezuela boundary dispute.

The United States would never relinquish its grip on Hawaii. Hawaii figured prominently in American designs for linking the United States and Asia. In 1867 the United States had occupied Midway Island as a naval stop in the Pacific, but the splendid Pearl Harbor near Honolulu offered a perfect place for refitting ships. In the 1840s the U.S. had warned other powers to keep out of Hawaii, and by granting Hawaiians trade and tariff advantages in the 1870s had tied them to the American market. The British and the Germans backed off in Hawaii. They did so in part because they had reached an understanding with the United States elsewhere in the Pacific. In 1889 the United States and Germany had almost clashed over control of the Samoan Islands, but a hurricane destroyed both the American and German warships there and forced the quarreling parties to the

Hawaiian Church American Protestant missionaries were present in Hawaii from the 1820s on. Early generations earnestly sought conversions to Christianity, though some of their descendents turned their interests more to financial investments in the islands rather than spiritual ones.

bargaining table. The British, Germans, and Americans agreed to a three-way protectorate of the islands, with the U.S. keeping the port of Pago Pago, which it wanted as a refueling station. Meanwhile, in 1887, the U.S. had negotiated a treaty with the Hawaiians by which it got the exclusive right to build and fortify Pearl Harbor. The United States was going to share Hawaii with no one, especially not Japan, which had sent a warship to protest Hawaii's exclusion of new Japanese immigrants in 1897. Expansionists insisted it was only a matter of time before the United States annexed the islands, for in the words of the New York *Post* in 1894, "The policy of annexation is the policy of destiny, and destiny always arrives."

Destiny arrived in 1898, riding the high tide of expansionism during the McKinley administration. The United States formally annexed the islands in 1898 when, by joint congressional resolution, the Congress made Hawaii an American territory and the U.S. sent a territorial governor to take charge there. The queen lived on for many years, a symbol of Hawaiian culture to the natives

Boxer Rebellion When Westerners, including American missionaries and business interests, appeared to be making inroads in China, Chinese nationalists, called "Boxers," struck back, as depicted in this Chinese woodcut.

and an irritant to the planters. The American Pacific fleet found a haven in Pearl Harbor, and America's reach to Asia was shortened by thousands of miles.

AN OPEN DOOR TO CHINA

For most Americans, Asia meant China. The acquisition of Hawaii and the Philippines (see below) in 1898 made sense in the larger context of American interest in gaining a foothold in China. Indeed, throughout the nineteenth century China was the prize and the preoccupation of American missionaries, traders, and policymakers who looked westward across the Pacific. The vast potential of the China market beckoned merchants and investors, and the huge mass of "heathen Chinee," as Westerners derisively called them, offered churches and foreign mission boards a prospect for conversion and uplift equal to their ambitions to save the world. But in China the United States entered a tangled terrain of European powers jostling for empire and trade and Chinese people suspicious of foreigners and resistant to change. After the 1850s China was sinking into the depths of its secular decline vis-à-vis the Western world and seemed to Europeans especially ripe for the picking. The United States was a latecomer to the mad rush by European powers, especially Great Britain, France, Germany, and Russia, to carve out spheres of influence and dominate China. And the United States lacked the naval power to force its way.

After its defeat by Japan in 1894-1895, China lay open to European powers and Japan eager to grab economic concessions and establish spheres of influence in which each power would be supreme commercially and militarily. European imperialism directly threatened American interests in China. American manufacturers and exporters, still reeling from the economic depression of 1893, opposed any partition of China because they feared losing access to valuable Chinese ports and markets. American Protestant churches also warned that the breakup of China would interrupt their Christianizing activities there, and they feared too that prior Catholic missions in China would gain a foothold if American Protestants were left out. Indeed, since the 1840s American Protestant churches had invested heavily in mission work in China, establishing schools, hospitals, and stores to carry the Christian message and refit the Chinese into Westerners in consumption as well as faith. American churches had cooperated with British ones in some overseas efforts, but in the 1890s American Protestant missionaries flocked to China as a special field of calling. Between 1890 and 1895 over 1100 Protestant missionaries, mostly Americans, answered the call for a new evangelization effort and service in China. American missionaries regularly reported on their progress in China and in doing so won much sympathy for China's "special place" in God's plan for worldwide salvation. The churches preferred persuasion to military or political force to gain China for the West, and the religious press lobbied hard in the United States to prevent European aggrandizement in China. In all this, the U.S. was joined by the British, who already controlled much of the Chinese export trade and sought to keep China open to "free trade." Complicating matters in China, though, was the new American interest in the Philippines, recently "acquired" in the victory over Spain (see below), and the furious debate within the United States about the extent to which America should plant the flag beyond North America, if at all.

Secretary of State John Hay, keen to American public feeling and a clever writer, caught the moment with a deft maneuver and a catchy phrase that cast American interests in the form of principled disinterest. He played on circumstances to offer the appearance of American resolve with no demand to demonstrate it. In 1899 Hay addressed the first of two "Open Door" notes to the imperial powers with economic interests in China, laying out the principle of the "Open Door." Hay asked only that the powers keep their spheres of influence in China open to all nations and not establish discriminatory trading, transportation, or tariff policies within them. This "Open Door" note reiterated what had been the United States position during the nineteenth century, but its bald statement now made it seem like new policy. Americans applauded the note for its clarity and fairness. The British accepted the note conditionally because it echoed their own free trade position, Russia politely declined, and Germany, France, and Japan responded coolly by saying they would sign on only if all powers agreed to do so. Italy agreed to the note because it had no sphere of influence in China. Rather than admit that the U.S. had little leverage in making China policy, Hay blithely announced that the imperial powers had accepted the "Open Door" as policy and Americans in China might proceed with business as usual.

The Chinese had their own say. In 1899 Chinese super-nationalists, whom Western journalists called the Boxers because their symbol was a fist, rose up to drive the "foreign devils" from their land. The Boxers murdered hundreds of Christian missionaries and Chinese Christians and countless Europeans and others. In June 1900 they occupied the capital Beijing (Peking) and laid siege to the district housing foreign diplomats and citizens. The imperial powers mounted a rescue force of 18,000, to which the United States sent 2500 Americans, to relieve the Westerners holed up in the compounds in the capital. The American contribution to the joint military operation, along with Hay's first note, seemed a bold advance beyond America's traditional isolationism outside the Western Hemisphere. Coming at a time of bitter debate within the United States about acquiring an overseas empire, and amid the horrible costs in lives lost fighting Filipinos (see below), the direct involvement in China caused concerns that the U.S. was rushing blindly into an Asian morass.

After the Westerners were freed from the Boxer siege in August 1900, though, the United States feared the conquering powers would demand territorial concessions from the feeble Manchu government of China. Hay dispatched a circular, which historians often refer to as the second Open Door note, to the imperial powers, this time calling on them to respect China's territorial integrity, withdraw troops after the defeat of the Boxers, limit punitive damages to be exacted from China, and foreswear further expansion of their spheres of influence there. This note was a significant extension of American policy in Asia, but Hay had no hope of enforcing it other than through diplomacy and prayer. Although no other power endorsed the proposal, Hay proclaimed it accepted principle anyway. Circumstance favored the American position. The imperial powers did not want to fight among themselves over Chinese territory and agreed to accept indemnities in money. Americans interpreted this as an acceptance of the Open Door notes and a vindication of the Americans' "unselfish" contribution to restoring order to China. The Open Door principle soon rose in the American mind to the status of the Monroe Doctrine as an unassailable truth and foundation of policy. Without fully appreciating the implications of its assertion of authority in Asia, or allocating the resources to make good its assertions, the United States was committed to maintaining stability in China. Such thinking later informed the American response to Japanese expansion on the Asian mainland in the 1930s.

Explosion of the *Maine* This lithograph depicts the explosion of the *Maine* in Havana harbor February 15, 1898. The still-unexplained explosion and subsequent sinking of the American vessel was the pretext for war against Spain.

The imperial powers assessed China a huge indemnity of over $300 million. America's share of $24.5 million exceeded the actual expenses and damages due Americans, whereupon the United States returned over $10 million to the Chinese government. A grateful Chinese government put the money into a special trust for educating Chinese students in the United States and China. Several such students would figure prominently in China's freedom struggles in the next century.

THE CUBAN CRISIS

Closer to home, Cuba loomed large in American concerns about maintaining order in the Caribbean and enforcing the Monroe Doctrine. Only ninety miles southwest from the tip of Florida, Cuba always had been in the sights of American expansionists. American adventurers had sponsored Cuban rebels during the nineteenth century, and American investors smelled sweet profits if they could gain entrance to the sugar-rich island. The Spanish stood in the way. The Spanish had brutally crushed rebellions there from 1868 to 1878 and had drained wealth from the island, leaving much of the population poor and angry. A new revolution in 1895 led by Jose Marti soon became a popular cause in the United States.

American newspapers wanting to get stories to grab readers reported in gory detail the atrocities the Spanish committed in trying to quell the rebellion. William Randolph Hearst's *New York Journal* and Joseph Pulitzer's *New York World,* especially, used the war to boost circulation by sending reporters and artists to Cuba to provide human-interest stories and images, and other papers followed suit. This "yellow journalism" sometimes exaggerated atrocities and ignored the rebels' own outrages. Hearst, for example, reportedly told Frederic Remington, then on hire as a newspaper artist: "You furnish the pictures, and I'll furnish the war." But Spanish brutality was real enough. Indeed, beginning in 1896, Spanish General Valeriano Weyler's "reconcentration" policy of herding Cubans into barbed-wire enclosures to keep them from aiding the rebels led to over 200,000 civilian deaths from disease and starvation by 1898. The newspapers won much support for the rebels among Americans and whipped up war sentiment. In the words of the *Omaha World-Herald,* the Americans, as God's chosen people, must act, for only they might free Cuba by "working out a pure intent." The "jingoistic" expansionists chimed in, calling on Americans to liberate a fellow hemispheric people from colonialism and open Cuba to American investment and democracy.

San Juan Hill Dismounted African American cavalry supporting the Rough Riders at the Battle of San Juan Hill, July 1, 1898, bore the brunt of the battle but got little of the glory in newspaper accounts. This illustration provided a rare recognition of black soldiers' contribution to victory.

The government was not going to be bullied or rushed into war by headlines. President Grover Cleveland resisted such pressure. He refused to give the rebels belligerent status, which would have been almost tantamount to recognizing the rebel government. Nor was the business community of one mind on Cuba, where American investment reached $30 million by 1896. Business especially feared an American war for Cuba would derail the recovery from the Panic of 1893. Even the Republican ascendancy in 1897, with the election of William McKinley as president and the greater administrative and congressional influence of expansionists such as Hay, Roosevelt, and Lodge, did not immediately move the United States to a collision with Spain over Cuba. Republicans were in fact divided over Cuba. The Spanish also sought conciliation, removing "Butcher" Weyler and offering the Cubans a degree of self-government. Unsure which direction the Cuban crisis would go, Washington sent the armored cruiser the *U.S.S. Maine* to Cuba in 1898 to stand ready to protect Americans there and appease jingoes at home.

Two events forced the Americans' hand. One was the publication, with much fanfare by Hearst's *Journal,* of a letter stolen from the Spanish ambassador in Wash-

ington, in which the minister urged further repression in Cuba and dismissed McKinley as a "would be politician" who catered only to the crowd. Six days later, on February 15, 1898, the *Maine* blew up in Havana harbor, with a loss of 260 men. The cause of the explosion was never discovered (and remains a mystery, although most scholars agree that it is highly unlikely the Spanish did it), but Americans concluded that the Spanish did the dastardly deed. The jingoes and the yellow journalistic press screamed for war, crying "Remember the *Maine!* To hell with Spain."

McKinley sought a peaceful resolution by calling on Spain to end its reconcentration policy, grant an armistice, and accept American mediation of the conflict, and later by adding that he expected Cuban independence to result from any negotiations. Spain agreed to comply with the former requests but could not promise independence, for to do so would cause the Spanish government to fall. The Cuban rebels, now confident of American intervention, refused any concessions short of complete independence. Critics of McKinley's policy complained

"Latest Greatest Shortest War" This 1898 magazine cover commemorated the swift victory of United States forces over the Spanish in the Spanish-American War, which swelled national pride and patriotism.

the U.S. needed to act; indeed, an overanxious Roosevelt claimed McKinley "had no more backbone than a chocolate eclaire" and urged Americans to show their manliness by standing up for Cuban independence and revenge on the Spanish for their perfidy. McKinley spent many sleepless nights praying what to do. It helped that by 1898 trade journals pointed to the potential of the war to invigorate American industry and transportation, and that much of the established Protestant press now looked on a war with Spain as a way to free Cuba and the Philippines from Catholicism and "barbarism." Meanwhile, the assistant secretary of the Navy Roosevelt had cabled Commodore George Dewey, chief of the U.S. squadron in Asia, to head for the Philippine Islands, then a Spanish colony and a gateway to China.

In April McKinley finally yielded to the war pressure because he understood American objectives would not be satisfied any other way. He presented a war message to Congress, and Congress, by joint resolution, recognized the independence of Cuba and authorized force to push the Spanish off the island. Without dissent, Congress also adopted an amendment, proposed by Senator Henry M. Teller, that renounced any "sovereignty, jurisdiction, or control" in Cuba once Cuban independence was achieved. But, even as the Teller Amendment foreswore annexation of Cuba, the senator reminded his colleagues that Spain had "some other islands" that were fair game in war. Significantly, too, the declaration of war did not include any specific recognition of the rebel government. Americans wanted a free hand after the war, and McKinley believed the Cubans needed American guidance. Four days later, on April 24, 1898, Spain declared war. The United States returned the favor the next day.

A "Splendid Little War"

European observers predicted the Americans would be overmatched in a war with Spain, but Americans thought otherwise. Americans went to war with bands playing popular tunes such as "Hail, Hail, the Gang's All Here" and "The Stars and Stripes Forever" (the battle song of the war), confident that the moral superiority of the republic would readily beat the "corrupt" Old World power. As one American general boasted while en route to Cuba, "This is God Almighty's war, and we are only His agents." The victory also seemed assured because the war seemed to patch up northern and southern sectional differences; white southerners endorsed the war effort and signed up for service, and Congress sang both "The Battle Hymn of the Republic" and "Dixie" in authorizing the war and announcing sectional reconciliation. Victory did come fast and sure in a war that lasted less than four months and wrested islands from Spain in the Pacific and the Caribbean. This "splendid little war," as John Hay described it, also got a romantic gloss from the reporting of American heroics in Cuba by Stephen Crane and Richard Harding Davis and in drawings by Frederic Remington, among others, and it made heroes of Teddy Roosevelt and George Dewey.

In fact, the actual war was anything but splendid for those who served in the American army. The army was ill-prepared for war. The regular army, which numbered only 28,000 men and 2100 officers when the war broke out, rapidly swelled to unmanageable size with the rush of 200,000 volunteers to arms. Corruption and incompetence combined to keep supplies, uniforms, food, and weapons from the soldiers. Volunteers arriving in Tampa, Florida, the main staging area for the invasion of Cuba, were issued Civil War vintage rifles, rotten and diseased rations, and woolen uniforms to fight a summer campaign in a tropical climate. The general disorganization and poor planning cost lives. Indeed, mismanagement and diseases such as dysentery, yellow fever, malaria, and typhoid largely accounted for the almost 5500 men who died during and immediately after the war. Only 379 Americans were killed in battle.

Adding to the confusion in organizing for war was the presence of several thousand black volunteers in Tampa and Lakeland, Florida. They were part of the almost 10,000 African Americans raised to help free Cuba from Spanish oppression. But they found oppression of their own in the segregated towns of Tampa and Lakeland and in their segregated status in the army. Tensions exploded in a race riot between white and black soldiers in June 1898 that threatened the expeditionary force readying to leave for Cuba. Once in battle, the "smoked Yankees," as the Spanish called the black soldiers, performed ably, and racial tensions subsided.

The invasion of Cuba was almost a fiasco. Eager to get glory, aggressive volunteer regiments such as Colonel Leonard Wood's and Lt. Colonel Teddy Roosevelt's "Rough Riders" muscled aside other soldiers to grab supplies and commandeer space on transports heading to Cuba. By June 30, over 17,000 Americans had landed to face a Spanish army superior in numbers and weapons. But the Americans had the good fortune of a strong naval unit under Rear Admiral William T. Sampson that, in May, had bottled up the Spanish battle fleet in the harbor of Santiago de Cuba, and by blockading Cuba had ended any threat to the expeditionary force from the water. The Spanish also obliged by having detailed only 13,000 of their 200,000 men to Santiago, which became the major theater of the land fight. Although poorly led and unable to resupply their forces, and operating amid a hostile local population, the Spanish fought bravely and almost defeated the green American volunteers anyway.

On July 1, the Americans broke through the Spanish lines to seize the Spanish garrisons on El Caney (Kettle) Hill and San Juan Hill above Santiago harbor. Leading the way up San Juan Hill was Roosevelt, who had resigned his post in the Navy department to raise a regiment for the war. The squeaky-voiced Roosevelt urged on his horseless regiment of cowboys, toughs, adventurers, and young men of privilege wanting to show their mettle, which with support from two black regiments seized San Juan Hill. The Americans suffered heavy casualties but won laurels in the public imagination for their daring. Roosevelt, never bashful, boasted how he shot a Spaniard during this "bully fight" and wrote his friend Senator Henry Cabot Lodge that he and his men deserved medals of honor. Adoring reporters and illustrators such as Davis and Remington celebrated such exploits and promoted Roosevelt and the "Rough Riders" as the embodiment of manly courage.

The American exploits did force the Spanish fleet from Santiago. The Spanish had ordered Admiral Pascual Cervera never to surrender, so on July 3 he steamed his seven aging black-hulled ships from the harbor hoping to reach open sea. Sampson caught Cervera fleeing westward along Cuba's southern coast and in four hours sank the entire Spanish fleet, with the loss of no American ships and only one American life. Americans at home crowed over their success in Fourth of July speeches that blared the triumph of American strength and virtue. With their Cuban forces completely exposed, the Spanish surrendered the island.

Meanwhile, an American expeditionary force numbering 17,000, led by the former Indian fighter General Nelson A. Miles, occupied Puerto Rico in a campaign one American humorist described as a "gran[d] picnic an' moonlight excursion." The local population collaborated with the Americans, who they viewed as liberators, and the Spanish put up little resistance. When the armistice ending the fighting in the war came on August 12, the Americans already had control of the island and little intention of giving it up.

Across the ocean, the Americans scored equally striking victories. Commodore Dewey had responded quickly to the threat of war with Spain by readying his squadron of cruisers and support vessels to move from Hong Kong to Manila, in the Philippines, all according to an American naval war plan developed in 1896. Upon learning that war had been declared, Dewey ordered the Asiatic Squadron to Manila to confront the Spanish fleet. At daybreak, May 1, 1898, in Manila Bay, the Americans put the Spanish ships anchored there in their gunsights, and Dewey gave his famous order, "You may fire when ready, Gridley," whereupon the Americans raked the Spanish fleet with five passes of deadly fire. By noon, the Americans destroyed the entire Spanish fleet without the loss of a single American in the battle (one sailor died of a heart attack). News of the triumph set off a Dewey mania in the United States, with Dewey hats, canes, spoons, paperweights, and

Anti-Imperialism Speech, 1898

Anti-imperialists countered arguments for annexation of the Philippines and other territories by invoking morality, constitutionalism, race, and efficacy among several arguments. Religious leaders played important roles on both sides of the debate, particularly in terms of moral obligations in the world and at home. A member of the Anti-Imperialist League, the Reverend Charles G. Ames in this address sounded a common warning that imposing military government abroad eventually would corrupt free government in the United States.

We are told that it is "our duty" to extend to the struggling people of the Philippines the same help and protection we have pledged to Cuba. Did we take a pledge to conquer and annex Cuba? We laid much stress on the fact that the suffering was "at our very doors"; then, almost before we have lifted a finger to deliver Cuba, we set up a claim to Spanish possessions on the other side of the globe! American interests were deeply involved in the Cuban disorders; can we give any similar reason for laying hand on the Asiatic Archipelago?...

Let us face the facts and the underlying problem. We speak with contempt of the Spanish title to the islands. What other title can we acquire by conquest? Next we must govern either with or without the consent of the people. If with their consent, it must be expressed through republican forms; that is, by suffrage. Is there a man in America who wishes those seven millions of Malays, Negritos and Chinamen for fellow-citizens and joint rulers of this Republic? But if we govern them without their consent, it must be by military occupation, — by force; that is, by the Spanish method, though we shall not copy the Spanish cruelty. There is no third possibility....

What will be the effect on our domestic policy? How can we undertake to rule subject provinces in distant parts of the globe without trampling on the principles of free government? Once accepting this way of dealing with other people, how long will it be before some occasion will arise for applying it at home? In committing ourselves to permanent military methods of government anywhere, we give up the republic, for we abandon its fundamental principle, even while boasting of the name.

---

other items selling briskly in souvenir shops. One poet summed up the exuberance when he wrote, "Dewey! Dewey! Dewey!/Is the hero of the Day/And the *Maine* has been remembered/In the good old-fashioned way" by smashing the Spanish "In Manila's crooked bay."

The swiftness and completeness of the naval victory actually confused the Americans as to what to do next. Dewey earlier had established secret contacts with the Filipino rebel leader, Emilio Aguinaldo, to coordinate any attack on the Spanish-held Philippine Islands, but Dewey had not brought any American troops to invade the islands. He now asked for troops to seize and occupy Manila. Without fully realizing the implications of authorizing an invasion force, President McKinley ordered 11,000 soldiers sent to the Philippines. The Americans, supported by Aguinaldo's insurgents, took Manila on August 13.

The day before, August 12, Spain already had ceded Puerto Rico and remote Guam, in the Mariana Islands, to the United States and conceded Cuban independence. The Philippines proved a more nettlesome problem. The Spanish did not want to give up the island archipelago, even though Americans and Filipino nationalists controlled Manila and the main islands and the last vestiges of Spanish authority in the Philippines had collapsed. In the end, in the treaty signed in Paris December 10, 1898, Spain was forced to give up the Phil-

ippines for $20 million and formally turn over Puerto Rico and Guam to the United States.

The war with Spain was over, but the question over the future of the Philippines and America's place in the world remained.

THE GREAT DEBATE OVER IMPERIALISM

The U.S. victory established it as a great power, but Americans were not sure what that "power" meant. The advocates of a "large policy" wanted the United States to keep what it had won by arms. The stunning naval victories in Cuba and the Philippines justified the "navalism" of Mahan and the expansionists and emboldened some among them to demand more in the race for empire. Others balked at outright imperialism, for Americans had gone to war with Spain to fight colonialism, not embrace it.

The annexation of Hawaii in 1898 pointed toward empire. Newspapers argued that Hawaii was essential to American interests in Asia as a halfway station to the Philippines and China. McKinley concurred and readily signed the joint congressional resolution annexing the islands in 1898. Moving westward from Hawaii, the United States now had a string of strategic islands —

Midway, Wake, and Guam — as stepping-stones to the Philippines and the Asian mainland.

Events in the Philippines almost undid American ambitions in Asia. The Filipino nationalists under Aguinaldo expected the Americans to leave the Philippines, and rebelled rather than submit to American authority. Americans controlled the capital, but the rebels held the countryside. A bloody guerrilla war broke out in 1899 just as Americans back home were debating the obligations of empire beyond the seas. The Philippine Insurrection, as Americans called it, lasted over three years and cost over 4,000 American and almost 20,000 rebel soldiers' lives, and between 100,000 and 200,000 civilians died because of the struggle. The combatants waged a war of savage ferocity, with atrocities on both sides. The Filipinos frustrated American forces with ambushes and raids, and the Americans responded with attacks on rebel bases and villages friendly to the insurgents and with penning supporters of the insurgency in concentration camps. In 1901 the Americans captured Aguinaldo, but the rebels fought hard for another year before surrendering. Scattered resistance persisted thereafter. The "insurrection" had a paradoxical effect on American thinking. At once it made it impossible for policymakers to withdraw, lest they seem

weak and open the islands to European imperialists by default, while it also made the case for Americans disengaging from the bloody business of empire. Similar difficulties would haunt America's entanglement in Vietnam sixty years later.

❧ *Annexation?*

The Philippines question especially vexed McKinley. Not a few months before, one wag quipped, Americans did not know if the Philippines were "islands or canned goods," and the president had only an old school geography textbook to locate them on a map, but now the fate of the Philippines dogged the president at every turn. He went about the country testing various ideas as to annexation and control, and as a devout Methodist, he sought God's guidance as to how to end the war and realize what he had termed America's "duty" to destiny. McKinley did not think the Filipinos were yet fit for self-rule, and he refused to return the islands to Spanish misrule. He also worried that American inaction in the Philippines would invite European and Japanese interference there. Annexation pressures mounted. Republican senators pressed for annexation as necessary to secure American trade in Asia and as the fulfillment of the divine command of

---

❋ IN THEIR OWN WORDS

"Speech on America's Destiny," 1900
In a widely circulated and much-quoted speech, the historian and first-term Republican senator from Indiana, Albert Beveridge, starkly stated the case for annexation in terms of Anglo-Saxon racial superiority, American commercial interests in Asia, and the nation's "divine mission" to organize and uplift the benighted peoples of the world. During the nineteenth century, and after, invoking the mission theme proved especially effective in American arguments first for Manifest Destiny in North America and then for expansion overseas.

Mr. President, the times call for candor. The Philippines are ours forever, "territory belonging to the United States," as the Constitution calls them. And just beyond the Philippines are China's illimitable markets. We will not

retreat from either. We will not repudiate our duty in the archipelago. We will not abandon our opportunity in the Orient. We will not renounce our part in the mission of our race, trustee, under God, of the civilization of the world. And we will move forward to our work, not howling out regrets like slaves whipped to their burdens, but with gratitude for a task worthy of our strength, and thanksgiving to Almighty God that He has marked us as His chosen people, hence forth to lead in the regeneration of the world. . . .

Mr. President, this question is deeper than any question of party politics; deeper than any question of the isolated policy of our country even; deeper even than any question of constitutional power. It is elemental. It is racial. God has not been preparing the English-speaking and Teutonic peoples for a thousand years for nothing but vain and

idle self-contemplation and self-admiration. No! He has made us the master organizers of the world to establish a system where chaos reigns. He has given us the spirit of progress to overwhelm the forces of reaction throughout the earth. He has made us adept in government that we may administer government among savage and senile peoples. Were it not for such a force as this the world would relapse into barbarism and night. And of all our race He has marked the American people as His chosen nation to finally lead in the regeneration of the world. This is the divine mission of America, and it holds for us all the profit, all the glory, all the happiness possible to man. We are the trustees of the world's programs, guardians of its righteous peace. The judgment of the Master is upon us: "Ye have been faithful over a few things; I will make you ruler over many things."

What to Do with the Philippines?   After freeing the Philippines from Spain, Americans faced native Filipinos who wanted independence from the United States. In the ugly guerrilla war that ensued, both sides committed atrocities, and Americans at home came to doubt the "benefits" of having the overseas territory, depicted here as a white elephant.

manifest destiny. The Protestant religious press echoed such sentiments in calling for an "imperialism of righteousness." The Catholic Philippines, the press insisted, was ripe for Protestant evangelism that would make the natives good Christians and, in time, good candidates for self-government. Even the First Lady, Ida McKinley, to whom the president was devoted, urged annexation for humanitarian reasons, believing the Filipinos could not take care of themselves. President McKinley finally decided he had no choice but to keep the islands to help "our little brown brothers" and protect American interests. As he later explained his decision: praying to God for light on the subject, "one night late it came to me this way . . . [that] there was nothing left for us to do but take them [the Philippine Islands] all, and to educate the Filipinos, and uplift and civilize and Christianize them and by God's grace do the very best we could by them, as our

fellow-men, for whom Christ also died. And then I went to bed, and went to sleep, and slept soundly." While McKinley's remarks offended Catholics (for many Filipinos were Catholic), anti-imperialists, and others, they galvanized support for annexation in Congress.

McKinley had made up his mind that the United States must "not shirk the moral obligation of our victory" over Spain. But McKinley's resolve and the proposed treaty with Spain did not decide the issue. The new American commitments in the Caribbean and Asia needed both the Senate to ratify the treaty, and thereby endorse the policy, and the American people to sign on to the idea. Senators and most Americans who commented on the question focused largely on the Philippines. Holding onto Puerto Rico and Guam was a given in the debates. Cuba also posed little concern, for the United States intended to honor the Teller Amendment there. The Philippines proved a more troublesome claim, as the Filipino insurrection demonstrated. This distant tropical area, with a population of "dark-skinned" Asians so different in customs, language, and religion from "Americans," raised fundamental questions about the character of the United States. All previous territories of consequence acquired by the United States, save Alaska, had been geographically contiguous, thinly populated, and presumably intended for settlement and eventual statehood. The acquisitions from the Spanish-American War did not fit that bill. Puerto Rico was made a protectorate with only a vague prospect of an improved status at some future date. Concerns about race, religion, and culture especially bedeviled the question of the Philippines. In the debates on empire, attention fixed on the Philippines because of an active independence movement there and an immediate need to settle the islands' status before other powers interfered.

Opposition to annexation formed quickly. Opponents of annexation, known as "anti-imperialists," included many prominent Americans, including such otherwise unlikely allies as steel magnate Andrew

Carnegie, trade unionist leader Samuel Gompers, former president Grover Cleveland, reformer Jane Addams, novelists Mark Twain and William Dean Howells, intellectuals William James and William Graham Sumner, Republicans George Boutwell, Carl Schurz, and Charles Francis Adams, and Democrat William Jennings Bryan. Some among them organized an Anti-Imperialist League to sell the American people on their ideas and to lobby against the treaty. The anti-imperialists warned that annexation of the Philippines would drag the United States into Asian intrigues and possibly war with Japan or China in the future. They invoked the Declaration of Independence, pointing out that annexation would violate the "consent of governed" principle Americans held dear. They saw in imperialism the corrosion of American moral purpose and republican virtue and feared imperialism abroad would erode freedoms and morality at home. Women reformers, who made up a sizable body of anti-imperialists, sided with the Filipinos as disfranchised people, like women in the United States. Important African American newspaper editors worried that tolerating brutality against the Filipinos encouraged brutality against blacks in the United States and warned that an imperialism premised on notions of racial superiority corrupted everyone. Many opponents of annexation also warned that the Filipinos were unable to be assimilated by reasons of race and religion. The anti-imperialists, though, never managed a sustained, coherent criticism of American imperialism. Many did not oppose American imperialism per se, only the Philippines annexation. Southerners in the United States emphasized racial arguments, westerners and labor leaders emphasized the threat cheap Filipino labor posed, and northerners emphasized the economic and geopolitical costs of annexation.

Most public opinion supported annexation. McKinley and the expansionists made the case that there was no practical alternative to annexation, and that Americans dare not fail in their obligations to manifest destiny and moral uplift. The "white man's burden" argued for annexation, as did prospects for trade. And rather than adding to American costs, the Philippines would open Asia further to American interests. The Supreme Court also helped allay concerns about any need to incorporate the peoples of new territories into the full body politic when it ruled, in the Insular Cases in 1900 and 1901, that the Constitution did not follow the flag. The United States thus might retain territories with no promise of statehood or guarantees of other basic rights to the peoples therein. Senator Henry Cabot Lodge dismissed the anti-imperialists' charges of any immorality in expansionism by reminding them that the United States already had gained much by conquest in taking the American West, and Teddy Roosevelt mockingly asked if anyone proposed returning New Mexico to the Apaches. Might sometimes made right. Other Senators repeated what was becoming a core belief of expansionists — namely, that independence and "consent of the governed" were principles reserved only for those few people "fit" to have them. Republican Senator Albert Beveridge caught the mood of American expansionism in 1900 when he argued in a speech that the United States must hold the Philippines because God "made us the master organizers of the world to establish a system where chaos reigns. He has given us the spirit of progress to overwhelm the forces of reaction throughout the earth. He has made us adept in government that we may administer government among savage and senile peoples. Were it not for such a force as this the world would relapse into barbarism and night. And of all our

"School Begins" Anti-imperialists variously appealed to patriotism, racism, and nativism to argue against trying to incorporate the Philippines, Puerto Rico, Hawaii, and the South Pacific islands into American life and government. In this 1899 *Puck* cartoon, the supposed limits of the new people are suggested in showing a black person cleaning the windows, an Indian with a book upside down, and a Chinese youth staring in, while the unkempt non-whites from the new acquisitions seem to promise only trouble for Uncle Sam. White students read quietly at their desks.

race He has marked the American people as His chosen nation to finally lead in the regeneration of the world." Annexation of the Philippines was nothing less than God's command, just as McKinley had concluded. It also reflected the ethos of an emerging Progressivism to "clean up" inefficiency and corruption.

In getting the treaty ratified, McKinley relied on politics and patronage rather than God's hand. He had appointed three senators, including a Democrat, to the peace commission, and he had lobbied hard for the treaty. The anti-imperialist William Jennings Bryan, the likely Democratic presidential candidate again in 1900, helped McKinley's cause when he refused to use his influence to defeat the treaty in the Senate. He argued that the Senate should approve the treaty to end the war with Spain and then have the question of empire decided in a national referendum, presumably the 1900 election. The Senate narrowly ratified the treaty in February 1899. The national referendum never came. Presented with the fact of Philippines annexation, Americans going to the polls in 1900 had no way to undo what was done. And the political parties had not divided along neat lines on expansionism, making it difficult to mobilize a clear referendum on foreign policy. Other issues, such as the old "free silver" cause, also distracted Americans from any new debate on the Philippines. McKinley's reelection in 1900 seemingly settled the question of annexation and distant empire in presidential politics.

❧ A Foundation for Nation-Building

The American administration of the new acquisitions confirmed the "rightness" of the imperial course, to many Americans, and laid the institutional and intellectual foundations for "nation-building" during the twentieth century. In the Philippines, under the civilian governorship of William Howard Taft, beginning in 1902, the United States improved public health, education, transportation, and civic institutions and negotiated the sale and transfer of lands from the Catholic church to Filipino farmers. The United States also prepared the Philippines for eventual self-government by providing for an elected Filipino assembly in 1902, though the United States also assured its presence in the region by building a naval base at Subic Bay, where it would remain for almost ninety years. In 1933 Congress set up a timetable for the Philippines' independence, which finally came on July 4, 1946.

In Cuba, the United States Army under Leonard Wood stayed on the island to build economic infrastructure, schools, and "good government" on an American model, necessary for American investments and Cuban independence. In the troubled waters of the Caribbean, with European rivals ready to seize advantages, the United States did not trust the Cubans to protect themselves or American interests. In 1901 the United States forced the Cubans to accept a permanent treaty with the United States, known as the Platt Amendment, that limited the power of Cuba to change currency, fiscal, and other economic policies established by the Americans, except with American consent, and granted the United States the right to intervene in Cuba, at American discretion, to preserve Cuban independence and protect "life, property, and individual liberty." In 1902 the United States turned over the government to the Cubans, but Americans stayed, with heavy investments in sugar plantations and commercial concessions, and on several occasions in the early twentieth century sent troops to occupy parts of the island to restore "order" when Cubans did not follow American policy or threatened American property. The U.S. also strengthened its place in the region, and over the island nation, by establishing and maintaining thereafter a naval base in Guantanamo Bay.

In the Philippines and Cuba, the American objectives to bring order, investments, and self-rule were achieved, but not without fostering resentments among Filipinos and Cubans impatient to go their own ways and dividing Americans about the moral and political costs of empire. And for all their congratulating themselves on good intentions in nation-building, Americans did not appreciate the enlarged and continued role as protector the United States now had assumed in the Pacific and the Caribbean. Those obligations became painfully evident in the next century.

CONCLUSION: AMERICA AND THE WORLD IN 1900

In surveying the results of American war and diplomacy as the new century dawned, one French diplomat observed that "The United States is seated at the table where the great game is played, and it cannot leave it." Surely, the half-century from the 1850s through 1900 had altered America's course from its traditional "isolationism" to one of wider interests and involvement in the Atlantic and Pacific worlds. Diplomacy was now in the hands of professionals, and the government developed broad policy objectives and tried to allocate the intellectual, political, and military/naval resources to implement them. Yet many of the old verities about American purpose and place remained. Despite all the push for expansionism, the United States's imperial acquisitions were few, and even short-lived. The anti-imperialists had lost the argument on annexing the Philippines, but the debate had made outright colonialism more difficult to defend. American churches and businesses wanted access to foreign places rather than outright ownership of them, and the costs of empire, such as killing Filipinos in order to free them, were more than most Americans wanted to bear. Also, as some progressives suggested, the United States did not have to get into the business of owning colonies in order to prosper from expansionism. Promoting free trade, encouraging Western values, and supporting good government abroad would reap dividends enough for the United States. Americans soon surprised the Europeans by largely getting out of governing Cuba and by moving the Philippines toward independence. American expansion thus did not follow the European style of imperialism. The United States came to the table of power politics, but it did so still believing America was to follow a different drummer in matters of war and policy. With the assassination of William McKinley in 1901, it also came to the table with the Rough Rider and expansionist Teddy Roosevelt as president. Roosevelt believed in American "greatness" (a word he invoked often in speaking of duty and destiny) and was not afraid to exert force, but he sought balance more than domination, and he demanded preparation as the predicate for policy. No longer would Americans be innocents abroad.

SUGGESTED READING

Robert L. Beisner, *From the Old Diplomacy to the New, 1865-1900* (2nd ed., 1986). The best overview of the period, stressing the structure, thought, and practice of foreign policy but downplaying the role of missionaries and business in shaping policy, with a superb bibliography.

Robert L. Beisner, *Twelve against Empire: The Anti-Imperialists, 1898-1900* (1985 ed.). A thorough and balanced survey of the anti-imperialist movement with recognition of its religious impetus but also its elitism.

Michael Hunt, *The Making of a Special Relationship: The United States and China to 1914* (1983). An excellent analysis of Sino-American relations with due attention to non-governmental and religious interests and the Chinese role in the relationship.

Jane Hunter, *The Gospel of Gentility: American Women Missionaries in Turn-of-the-Century China* (1984). An exploration of evangelical Protestants' engagement with empire, arguing that women missionaries sought to impose American middle-class culture on the Chinese.

Matthew Frye Jacobson, *Barbarian Virtues: The United States Encounters Foreign Peoples at Home and Abroad, 1876-1917* (2000). A provocative and sweeping argument on how the connections between Americans' search for markets and cultural influence and their experiences with immigrants and expansion shaped perceptions and policy.

Walter LaFeber, *The New Empire: An Interpretation of American Expansionism, 1860-1898* (1998 ed.). Although heavily weighted toward an economic interpretation of American interest and interests in foreign affairs and expansion, still an essential grounding in the issues of the age.

Walter LaFeber, *The Cambridge History of American Foreign Relations,* vol. 2: *The American Search for Opportunity, 1865-1913* (1993). A readable and original reading of American policy, noting the interplay of cultural, economic, and political interests informing American thinking about and movement into foreign affairs.

Ernest R. May, *Imperial Democracy: The Emergence of America as a Great Power* (1961). A still reliable overview of American thought, policy, and practice in the rise to great power ambition and status, based on a thorough mining of American and European archives.

David M. Pletcher, *The Diplomacy of Trade and Investment: American Economic Expansion in the Hemisphere, 1865-1900* (1998). An examination of governmental interest and role in and support for expanding trade and gaining markets and influence in the region.

Joseph Smith, *Illusions of Conflict: Anglo-America Diplomacy toward Latin America, 1865-1896* (1979). A careful study of American assertiveness and British concessions that led to American "supremacy" in the hemisphere.

Anders Stephanson, *Manifest Destiny: American Expansion and the Empire of Right* (1995). An excellent synthesis emphasizing the mission theme in American expansion.

David F. Trask, *The War with Spain in 1898* (1981). An informative diplomatic and military history that also casts McKinley as a reluctant war president.

SUGGESTIONS FOR FURTHER READING

David L. Anderson, *Imperialism and Idealism: American Diplomats in China, 1861-1898* (1985).

Jules R. Benjamin, *The United States and the Origins of the Cuban Revolution* (1990).

H. W. Brands, *Bound to Empire: The United States and the Philippines* (1992).

Charles Brown, *The Correspondents' War: Journalists in the Spanish-American War* (1967).

Kenton J. Clymer, *Protestant Missionaries in the Philippines, 1898-1916: An Inquiry into the American Colonial Mentality* (1986).

Graham A. Cosmas, *An Army for Empire: The United States Army in the Spanish-American War* (1971).

John M. Dobson, *America's Ascent: The United States Becomes a Great Power, 1880-1914* (1978).

Willard Gatewood, *Black Americans and the White Man's Burden, 1898-1903* (1975).

David Healy, *Drive to Hegemony: The United States in the Caribbean, 1898-1917* (1988).

Patricia R. Hill, *The World Their Household: The American Woman's Foreign Mission Movement and Cultural Transformation, 1870-1920* (1985).

William R. Hutchison, *Errand to the World: American Protestant Thought and Foreign Missions* (1987).

Stanley Karnow, *In Our Image: America's Empire in the Philippines* (1989).

Brian M. Linn, *The U.S. Army and Counterinsurgency in the Philippine War, 1899-1902* (1989).

Thomas McCormick, *China Market: America's Quest for Informal Empire, 1893-1901* (1967).

Stuart Creighton Miller, *"Benevolent Assimilation": The American Conquest of the Philippines, 1899-1903* (1982).

Ian Mugridge, *The View from Xanadu: William Randolph Hearst and United States Foreign Policy* (1995).

Thomas J. Osborne, *"Empire Can Wait": American Opposition to Hawaiian Annexation, 1893-1898* (1981).

David S. Patterson, *Toward a Warless World: The Travail of the American Peace Movement, 1887-1914* (1976).

Thomas Schoonover, *The United States in Central America, 1860-1911* (1991).

Robert Seager II, *Alfred Thayer Mahan: The Man and His Letters* (1977).

Mark Russell Shulman, *Navalism and the Emergence of American Sea Power, 1862-1893* (1995).

Merze Tate, *The United States and the Hawaiian Kingdom: A Political History* (1965).

E. Berkeley Tompkins, *Anti-Imperialism in the United States: The Great Debate, 1890-1920* (1970).

Paul Varg, *Missionaries, Chinese, and Diplomats: The American Protestant Missionary Movement to China, 1890-1952* (1958).

Richard E. Welch, Jr., *Response to Imperialism: The United States and the Philippine-American War, 1899-1902* (1979).

Marilyn B. Young, *The Rhetoric of Empire: American China Policy, 1895-1901* (1968).

23

In Search of Efficiency:
The Values and Ideology
of Progressivism, 1900-1917

IN 1900, THE editors of the *Christian Oracle*, a small Chicago magazine that was destined to become the most influential Protestant publication in the twentieth century, renamed the paper *The Christian Century*. That title reflected the expectations of the white Protestants who had led the United States in the nineteenth century. They believed that the U.S., with God's help, would become the twentieth century's preeminent Christian nation. Their forecast proved to be both right and wrong. They correctly anticipated the global preeminence of the United States in the twentieth century, but their dream of a culturally united, Christian nation became more illusory with each passing decade.

The decades before and after the turn of the twentieth century were a watershed in American history. Looking back, the nation was overwhelmingly rural, Protestant, and, save for the disfranchised and segregated African American community and Native Americans, composed mostly of people descended from northern Europeans. Before 1890 American politics had been concerned largely with domestic affairs; internationally, the United States had played a minor role. Just ahead lay a very different landscape. By 1920, the United States had become an industrial giant, producing more than England, France, and Germany combined; in that year, the census confirmed that the United States had become an urban nation, its cities filled with an extraordinary mixture of ethnic, racial, and religious types. And the country was destined to be the most powerful international presence in the twentieth century.

Cultural diversity and class tensions were not new in 1900, but the bewildering pluralism of American society in the early twentieth century troubled older-stock Americans who believed that ethnic, class, and religious discord threatened the nation's identity as never before. These perils were not imaginary. The widespread economic inequality caused by industrialization raised fundamental questions in the minds of fair-minded people about the American promise of equality of opportunity; political corruption at every level of government threatened the concept of popular democracy; the nation's increasing ethnic and cultural pluralism undermined the idea of an American character.

In the midst of these momentous social, economic, and political changes, Americans faced the most unsettling intellectual crisis of modern history. The scale and import of these intellectual changes was not so obvious at the time, partly because the most divisive issues were debated mostly by intellectual elites in the nation's developing university system. Thus, during the first two decades of the twentieth century much of the nation continued to look and act like a Protestant Empire. But the revision of traditional Christian ideology triggered by Darwinianism in the late nineteenth century broadened in the first two decades of the twentieth century. By the end of World War I, the nation's elite educational institutions were dominated by secularists for whom natural science was the supreme standard of truth.

The triumph of secular thought did not undermine national pride or confidence in the future. American intellectuals gave new life to the old ideas of Manifest Destiny and American exceptionalism, clothing in scientific garb the notion that the nation was especially blessed and chosen to lead. A generation of scientists, mostly social science experts, replaced theologians as the discoverers and interpreters of truth and became the caretakers of the optimistic belief that institutions could be changed for the better. The language describing the nation's destiny was a telltale sign of the shift in intellectual authority; America's mission became "progressive" rather than "providential."

Resulting from and contributing to the social and intellectual ferment of the early twentieth century was a proliferation of new organizations — voluntary associations that gave order to people's lives and raised to new levels the noise of interest-group debate. For a century Americans had liked to join voluntary associations that provided them with a sense of identity and gave cohesion to life's rituals, most often churches and ethnic associations, but the variety of the nation's organizational infrastructure became much more complex during the first two decades of the new century.

Many old-stock Americans, shocked by the squalor of urban poverty, the inhumanity of modern industrialism, and the power and arrogance of the rich, became leaders in a political crusade to reform the country in the name of God and progress. The rhetoric of a majority of the churchmen, politicians, and social reformers of the twenty years that came to be called the Progressive Era was laced with an intense moral seriousness. But the white, Protestant political leaders of the years 1900-1920 formed only one part of the progressive movement. Immigration, urbanization, and industrialization also created clusters of self-conscious minorities whose reform programs were quite narrow. Immigrants, organized labor, women's rights advocates, and African Americans each collected supporters. By 1900, a wide variety of Americans were demanding reform. Politicians, ministers, labor leaders, social workers, feminists, writers and others offered plans designed to impose moral order on an increasingly diverse and seemingly disorderly society.

These reformers, collectively called progressives, had different agendas and used different methods; most often their solutions depended on the authority of the new social sciences rather than on the religious verities of earlier years. Perhaps the one assumption that progressives shared was a belief in "progress"; in that sense, they all clashed with those who wanted to protect the economic and political position of people with property and wealth or who in other ways feared or resented change. These were heady times, not because everything was right but because so many people believed that it was possible to remedy what was wrong. Even the discontented still believed in America's destiny and in democracy, and all progressive reformers appealed to higher truths to support their causes.

THE PROMISE OF A NEW CENTURY

As Americans most recently discovered on January 1, 2000, there is something exhilarating about turning a new century. According to Senator Chauncey Depew, there was not a man in the Senate who did not "feel 400 per cent bigger in 1900 than he did in 1896, bigger intellectually, bigger hopefully, bigger patriotically, bigger in the breast from the fact that he is a citizen of a country that has become a world power for peace, for civilization and for the expansion of its industries and the products of its labors."

It was easy to sell Americans on the idea of progress in 1900. At the beginning of the new century, the nation was widely viewed as the world's greatest success story, and the pace of development quickened after 1900. The country's population was growing rapidly, from 76.1 million in 1900 to 106.5 million by 1920. The production of manufactured goods increased nearly 75 percent in the first decade of the century, and technological changes dramatically improved the quality of life for most Americans and allowed more leisure time for ordinary people — progress was everywhere apparent. Americans were confident that they were both a great people and a prosperous and powerful nation; that national pride and confidence offered a solid foundation for national unity.

❧ Foundations of the American Dream

The American spirit seemed indomitable during the first two decades of the century. When an earthquake and fire devastated San Francisco in 1906, destroying 25,000 buildings, citizens began clearing the wreckage and rebuilding the city while the flames still burned. If some critics of American society during the Progressive Era were angry and demanding, almost all believed in the American dream and tempered their protests with sunny visions of the future.

There was good reason for optimism. In the early twentieth century, the United States was the richest and most dynamic nation in the world. In spite of the problems targeted by reformers, the success of the American experiment was evident everywhere. The gross national product spiraled upward; estimated at $18.7 billion in 1900, in 1910 it was $35.3 billion, and by 1920 reached $91.5 billion. In 1908, the magazine *Literary Digest* published a rosy profile of the average American male, noting that the country's $227 per capita income was the highest in the world. Advances in medicine and public health had led to an increase in life expectancy from forty-nine years in 1901 to fifty-four in 1920. The rapid growth of savings accounts (from $3.4 million in 1900 to $17.4 million in 1920) attested to the continued expansion of the urban middle class. Millions of immigrants viewed the United States as the Promised Land; in spite of the difficulties they encountered when they arrived, most thought they had found it.

Turn-of-the-century American optimism was rooted also in the perception that the country was still ethni-

5342   San Francisco Earthquake, April 18, 1906. Houses on Howard Street after the earth quaked.   Copyright 1906 by C. H. Graves.

The San Francisco Earthquake   These handsome houses collapsed immediately in the earthquake on April 18, 1906.

cally and culturally homogeneous. Despite the large influx of immigrants in the late nineteenth century, that perception had a basis in fact. In 1900 nearly nine out of ten Americans were descended from one or more northern European nationalities, mostly those from the British Isles, Germany, and Scandinavia. About eight out of ten professed a Protestant faith, and more than six out of ten (45.8 million) resided either on farms or in small villages. In 1900, most Americans and most foreign observers correctly viewed the United States as a predominantly Anglo-Saxon, Protestant state.

❧ Prosperity and Industrial Concentration

The American economic success story in the first two decades of the twentieth century was based on a continuation of the industrial and financial growth of the late nineteenth century. By the middle of the 1890s the United States had a favorable balance of trade, exporting more goods and capital than it imported, and by the outbreak of World War I the United States was no

J. P. Morgan   J. P. Morgan angrily shakes his cane at someone (perhaps the photographer) on a New York City street. He never worried about his image as an imperious tycoon who always intended to get exactly what he wanted.

longer a debtor nation. The building of the railroads, particularly, had created the essential infrastructure for expansion. Efficiency continued to be the goal of good businesses, as experts streamlined production methods and increased output in many of the nation's factories. Frederick W. Taylor's book *Scientific Management* (1895) was so widely respected around the world that "Taylorism" became a synonym for "efficiency"; indeed, after the Bolshevik Revolution, Lenin, who admired Taylorism, tried to introduce the American efficiency expert's ideas in Soviet factories (see Chapter 18). Impressive new consumer industries appeared, led by the fledgling automobile manufacturers. In 1900 fewer than 10,000 people were employed in the manufacture of automobiles; in 1920 around 200,000 were working in the industry.

Greater productivity and increasing consumer spending produced a bonanza for the advertising business. Advertising had been used sparingly in nineteenth-century America, when it seemed more important to expand production than to boost distribution. But by

1900 American companies spent around $95 million promoting their wares, and by 1920 the figure reached nearly $500 million.

During the years around 1900 American businesses consolidated at a furious rate, and the basic structure of the twentieth-century American economy took shape. By 1910, 1 percent of the industrial firms in the nation produced 50 percent of the country's manufactured goods, and monopoly (the control of an entire industry by a single firm) and oligopoly (control by a few big companies) dominated most areas of American industry. International corporations also had begun to appear. After 1905, the tendency toward consolidation abated somewhat. Rapid technological advances and changing consumer tastes once again made the economy more competitive and unstable. At the time of its organization in 1901 the United States Steel Corporation accounted for 62 percent of the nation's output of steel, but by 1920 its share had declined to 40 percent and more than 400 different firms were manufacturing steel. Nonetheless, consolidation remained the aim of American business.

The huge outlays of money required for industrial combinations placed increasing power into the hands of financiers, none of them more widely respected and feared than J. Pierpont Morgan. A congressional investigation in 1912 revealed that the J. P. Morgan & Co. banking firm had a larger influence on the American economy than the federal government. Morgan and his associates were directors in forty-seven corporations, including the country's largest railroads, steel companies, shipping companies, General Electric, American Telephone and Telegraph, and International Harvester.

To some extent, the individualistic businessman remained an American hero in the early twentieth century. Millions of small businesses still provided important services in the American economy, and most small entrepreneurs aspired to break into the ranks of the rich and powerful. The names of the wealthy were as famous as those of the presidents. The greatest popular heroes were the geniuses of invention such as Thomas A. Edison (see Chapter 18), Alexander Graham Bell, and Henry Ford (see Chapter 26), but most Americans offered grudging admiration even to the likes of J. P. Morgan. As a rule, the wealthy continued to view themselves as the finest products of the American dream and, although many approved progressive appeals for efficiency and order and supported some progressive reforms, they feared that the rising tide of government regulation would undermine their privileged status. The beliefs of the wealthy, like those of other groups seeking to mold American ideals, were fraught with inconsistencies. Although still capable of ruthless, unjust, and occasionally illegal business practices, many wealthy industrialists and financiers won a measure of public favor by lavishly underwriting hospitals, universities, museums, libraries, and other civic projects.

The immense power of business concentrations concerned even some political conservatives, and the wealthy were intensely scrutinized by journalists, social scientists, and politicians. In periods when a majority of citizens believe that the nation has strayed from its central commitments, reformers often identify one group as the principal source of society's problems. The barons of industry and finance who controlled the huge corporate empires were billed as the quintessential villains in the progressive political melodrama, and many of them exhibited an arrogance and public irresponsibility that made them easy targets. On the other hand, by 1900 the still-powerful political influence of business was no longer as pervasive as it had been in the late nineteenth century; anti-business rhetoric sometimes served the purpose of other interest groups seeking to press their own agendas.

Beginning in 1907, the economic success story of the early twentieth century was broken by a serious recession caused by an over-expansion of the nation's industrial productive capacity. Bank failures rose sharply during the Panic of 1907, and a serious banking disaster was averted largely because Morgan organized a pool of funds that saved threatened New York banks. The economy never sank into a full-fledged depression like that of the 1890s, but conditions remained far from rosy for nearly a decade. Non-farm unemployment rose from 3.9 percent in 1906 to 16.4 percent in 1908 and remained in double digits for the next four years; by 1914 non-farm unemployment had again risen to double digits and remained there until war in Europe began to stimulate American industry in 1916. In fact, all through the Progressive period inequality in the distribution of the nation's wealth increased; in 1913, 15 percent of the national income went to the richest 1 percent of the population, and these owned about half of the nation's wealth.

❧ Advertising the Nation's Success

The American success story was widely publicized in the early twentieth century. Newspapers remained the most influential dispensers of news and molders of public opinion during the Progressive Era; average daily newspaper circulation reached an all-time high just before World War I at about 32 percent of the population. William Randolph Hearst was the most successful consolidator in the newspaper industry, buying the *New York Journal* in 1895 and building an empire of mass-circulation papers throughout the country, which he used to sway public opinion on many issues, including the Spanish-American War. The newspaper business remained competitive and publishers used sensational journalism to build circulation, highlighting crimes, disasters, and scandals. At the same time, newspapers began printing separate sections catering to special interests such as sports, women's fashions, and clubs.

Improvements in printing technology and a burgeoning market for mass reading materials greatly increased the number of magazines and books published in the early twentieth century. Most of the reading material in the first two decades of the twentieth century differed little in tone from that of earlier years. Except for a distinctive genre of reform writing closely identified with progressive politics and labeled "muckraking" by Theodore Roosevelt (see Chapter 24), American writing was conventional in style and optimistic

**Marcel Duchamp,
*Nude Descending
a Staircase, No. 2***
In 1912, this key
work in the rise of
the Cubist move-
ment caused a
sensation — and
attracted much
ridicule — when
it was displayed at
the Armory Show.

in spirit, celebrating traditional values and a national mission. Art and literary historians have generally regarded these years as a creative lull before the sweeping literary innovations of the 1920s. It was subject matter rather than style, however, that prompted William Dean Howells to chastise the writers of these years for exploring only "the smiling aspects of life."

The popular fiction of the day, both children's and adults' books, continued to depict traditional heroes in simple tales of virtue triumphing over adversity. The plot thickened a bit beyond Horatio Alger's Gilded Age simplistic luck-and-pluck motif. The heroes and heroines of the Progressive Era generally succeeded through skill and ingenuity, or at least personal charm and good looks. Edward Stratemeyer, creator of the Rover Boys series, employed a panel of formula writers who ground out a steady stream of popular books about pristine heroes and heroines, including the Bobbsey Twins and Tom Swift. The era's most notable addition to the family story tradition for young women was Kate Douglas Wiggins's *Rebecca of Sunnybrook Farm* (1903).

The best selling adult fiction of the early twentieth century featured romance, religion, adventure, and a fascination with the outdoors — pretty much a catalog of what was judged important and interesting by most Americans. Zane Grey, the foremost writer of western stories, was the Progressive Era's most popular author. Fifty Grey novels kept his name on the bestseller list for nearly two decades.

Most serious American writers also celebrated American life and the American dream, even when they portrayed the problems of the era. Some novels, such as Owen Wister's *The Virginian* (1902), extolled the nation's landed heritage, but the era's dominant strain of fiction exalted political, social, and moral reform. Wister's writing, which was greatly admired by most Americans, including President Theodore Roosevelt, helped to form the genre of the American western novel and also embodied the moralistic and optimistic tone of writing during the Progressive Era. While progressive fiction sometimes probed the evils in modern society and the darker side of human nature, it uniformly featured moral, triumphant heroes and heroines. American writers endorsed the spirit of civic and ethical responsibility that sparked progressive reform, and they imbibed deeply of the age's optimism.

One may fault American writing in the Progressive Era because its offerings were so optimistic as to be unfaithful to life. But in that respect the writers mirrored the times. The nation's best writers did grapple with the sins of American society in their novels; but, like most Americans, they saw a stark divide between good and evil. They portrayed America as a battleground between corporate brutality and popular virtue, but they seldom doubted the final triumph of right.

American writers were aware of the blooming modernist movement in Europe, and there were foreshadowings of the artistic revolt that would sweep the United States in the 1920s. Greenwich Village, the New York City neighborhood that constituted America's first Bohemia, was a caldron of jazz, free love, political radicalism and literary experimentation in the years before World War I. Perhaps the most influential book written in this iconoclastic artistic community was Van Wyck Brooks's *America's Coming of Age* (1915). Anticipating the favored targets of the intellectuals of the twenties, Brooks blamed the nation's Puritan heritage for Americans' worst character faults — repressive moralism and greedy materialism. Brooks contributed to an avant-garde magazine published in the Village, *Seven Arts,* as did other promising young writers.

The sharpest jolt to the progressive spirit in the arts came in February 1913 when the International Exhibition of Modern Painting opened at the Sixty-Ninth Regiment Armory in New York City. Most of the art in the exhibit was American and realistic, but among the 1,600 art objects were samples of post-impressionism, expressionism, and cubism created by the leaders of European modernism, including Picasso and Matisse. Most Americans, including most art critics, were repulsed by the new techniques, seeing in them a spirit of anarchy and irrationality that was disgusting and politically dangerous. The slogan of the Armory Show was "The New Spirit," but most progressive Americans agreed with Theodore Roosevelt that modern art was the work of a "lunatic fringe," the epitome of European decadence.

❧ The Mass Pursuit of the Good Life

Urbanization, the rise of mass production industries, and technological advances continued to work great changes in the way people lived, and, to some extent, made more and more people feel they were participants in the American dream. Labor saving inventions cut the workweek of manufacturing workers from about sixty hours in 1890 to forty-seven in 1920. White-collar workers typically worked long hours, but they often had weekends off. Leisure time and the availability of consumer goods brought within the reach of ordinary people many products considered luxuries for the wealthy a few years earlier, ranging from ready-made cigarettes and silk stockings to flush toilets.

The spread of a mass culture in which more and more people engaged in shared forms of recreation and entertainment, and mass consumerism, in which more and more people bought the same commodities, endowed efficient, modern industry with awesome, god-like qualities. The makers of material things were the source of present blessings and offered the promise of an ever-grander future. At the same time, mass entertainment offered escape from the harshness of laboring like a cog in the assembly line, relief from time clocks and efficiency. Past generations of Americans had been taught self-control, self-denial, and frugality; twentieth-century consumers were encouraged to self-indulge and spend. This mighty transformation in American values did not go unnoticed. Many middle-class professionals and religious leaders were deeply disturbed by the materialistic demon, consumerism.

OUTDOOR ACTIVITIES

Nothing better symbolized the marriage of technology, business resourcefulness, and the mass culture boom than the development of amusement parks. At the turn of the century, Luna Park and Dreamland Park on Coney Island, a beach resort in Brooklyn, became models for hundreds of family entertainment centers. Made accessible by streetcars and automobiles, parks were built in cities around the country. They showcased modern technology, particularly the marvels of electrification. Dreamland advertised that it was lit by a million light bulbs.

Organized sports flourished in the early twentieth century, a perfect expression for the temper of the times. Some team sports, particularly baseball, were played in small towns, but the growth of professional sports as a business was an urban phenomenon. Streetcars and automobiles made the ballparks accessible, and newspapers provided coverage of the games, replete with statistical analysis. The psychological underpinnings of organized sports reflected many of the values of the Progressive Era. Generally played in open fields, ball games reminded Americans of their rural roots and appealed to their competitive nature. Like modern life, the games were organized and regulated but also called for specialized skills. Endless statistical analysis gave sports a scientific aura.

Baseball continued to be the most popular team sport. In 1903 the Boston Red Sox defeated the Pitts-

Coney Island   The illumination of Luna Park at Coney Island permitted patrons to amuse themselves far into the evening. This photograph dates from 1910.

burgh Pirates in the first World Series played between the National and American Leagues. Football changed from an elitist game for college boys to a spectator sport in the early twentieth century, though college teams, rather than professionals, made the game popular. Football was plagued by scandals at the turn of the century because colleges often used illegal players, and unregulated violence resulted in the death of fifteen players in 1905. President Theodore Roosevelt, a staunch preacher of "the strenuous life" and a booster of football, convened a conference to reform the game and the Intercollegiate Athletic Association (renamed the National

College Athletic Association in 1910) was formed. The NCAA revised the rules of the game into something close to their modern form, legalizing the forward pass and outlawing the dangerous "flying wedge" formation.

Americans loved playing games in their leisure time, as well as watching them. Thousands of communities supported amateur and semipro baseball teams, and pickup games at picnics often found both men and women in the field. Other athletic activities also brought the sexes together. Some ten million Americans owned bicycles in 1900, and couples often rode together on bicycles built for two. Croquet, a genteel game that combined the outdoors, careful rules, and friendly competition, was probably the most popular game at family outings.

SHOW BUSINESS

Like sports, show business expanded and changed in cadence with technological advances, business strategies, and the growth of mass consumerism. Long a staple of popular entertainment, circuses flourished early in the century as railroads opened up more of the countryside to the big tops. During the first decade of the century circuses reached the peak of their popularity, but by the time the Ringling Brothers and the Barnum and Bailey shows merged in 1918 to form "The Greatest Show on Earth," circuses had fallen behind other forms of show business.

The most widely viewed stage performances of the early twentieth century were vaudeville, a type of variety show that featured acrobats, magic shows, animal acts, comedy skits, and song and dance performers. Vaudeville theaters and traveling companies of performers multiplied early in the century, bringing entertainment to thousands of towns and villages. The most spectacular of the vaudeville shows, the Ziegfeld Follies, included elaborate sets, headline performers, and an alluring parade of Ziegfeld Girls. Vaudeville was a boon for black and immigrant performers, although, particularly in the case of blacks, the most successful entertainers pandered to the prejudices of the day in stereotypical and demeaning "darkie" routines, and many vaudeville shows continued to feature white performers in blackface.

The theater rage of the early twentieth century was musical comedy. Featuring popular music, humor, and dancing, musicals were typically patriotic and moralistic. Like vaudeville, the theater was a door of opportunity for talented immigrant writers and performers. George M. Cohan, the son of Irish vaudeville entertainers, earned a reputation as a leading song writer and the quintessential American patriot with songs such as "Yankee Doodle Boy" and "You're a Grand Old Flag." Irving Berlin, whose Russian Jewish parents, named Balines, immigrated to America in 1893 when he was five years old, was a genius at synthesizing the varied musical traditions of the country. Untrained as a musician and never able to read music, during his long career Berlin wrote thousands of popular songs. In 1911 he contributed music and lyrics to the popular show, *Alexander's Ragtime Band;* by 1921 his songs were so popular that he built and operated his own theater to produce his plays.

THE MUSIC BUSINESS

The success of musical comedies was a reflection of the enormous popularity of music in the early twentieth

The Ziegfeld Follies   The dance company, a favorite on the vaudeville circuit in the early twentieth century, was considered risqué. Their female dancers' display of bare legs was barely within the bounds of respectability. Here they perform a "Russian" number.

organs and pianos, many equipped with automatic player rolls. By 1920, quite modest homes often boasted a piano or organ, and even working-class children suffered through piano lessons.

Technological improvements made phonographs and records increasingly popular. The recording industry was extremely competitive, but by 1920 consolidations made the Victor Talking Machine Company (which merged with RCA in the 1920s) and Columbia Phonograph, the successor of Alexander Graham Bell's Volta Graphophone Company, the largest distributors of phonographs and records. Symbolizing the growing ethnic diversity of the nation, the most popular records of the early twentieth century were operatic arias and popular songs recorded by the Italian tenor Enrico Caruso and the Irish singer John McCormick. The sale of records spiraled in the second decade of the century in conjunction with a dance boom.

DANCE HALLS AND MOVIE HOUSES

Dancing was the most popular social activity in the country. Dancing forms varied widely depending on region, ethnicity, and class. In high society the waltz remained stylish, while immigrant dance halls reverberated with the polka and other ethnic dances. But popular music, particularly ragtime, produced new dance forms that were peculiarly American, most of them rooted in black culture and introduced by black performers. The public embraced wave after wave of new steps; even refined young people danced the Turkey Trot, the Fox Trot, the Bunny Hug, and the Grizzly Bear.

In 1905 a new age in mass culture began with the opening of the first nickelodeon, a Pittsburgh establishment that allowed customers to drop a nickel into a machine that would show them a full program of short motion picture films. Public movie theaters appeared soon thereafter, the last block needed to build the modern motion picture industry.

Movie making developed quickly after 1900. Thomas Edison's studio pioneered many of the early innovations in film making; *The Great Train Robbery* (1903), a western filmed by Edison in New Jersey, used dissolves

century. More than anywhere else in American life and culture, music was a melting pot. The American musical imagination was energized by the nation's cultural pluralism; the country's music was probably its most original cultural contribution of the twentieth century. The most popular new music of the early twentieth century was ragtime, a precursor of jazz whose marriage of harmony and rhythm drew upon classical traditions but was rooted in African American music. Around the turn of the century, Scott Joplin, a classically trained African American musician, wrote the first popular ragtime tune, "Maple Leaf Rag." Ragtime was adapted and modified by white synthesizers like Berlin into the popular music of the day.

The mass consumption of popular music was promoted by an organized music business. By 1900 a number of publishers located on New York City's 28th Street (called Tin Pan Alley) had built a flourishing sheet music industry based on market research that tried to discover and mold public taste. As in other industries, one business success fostered related industries; the popularity of sheet music fueled a piano-playing rage. In 1910 piano manufacturers produced more than 350,000

to develop the story and cross cutting to show both bandits and posse at the same moment in time. D. W. Griffith, first employed by Edison as an actor, produced the first long feature in 1915, *The Birth of a Nation*. A film set in the Civil War and Reconstruction, the picture scandalously glorified the KKK and reeked with race prejudice, but it was a production triumph, using for the first time such techniques as closeups, fade-outs, and the filming of huge battle scenes.

Some of the best films during these early years were comedies. Mack Sennett's Keystone Company, formed in 1912, became famous for innovative techniques and slapstick comedy featuring the Keystone Cops. Sennett also introduced such future comedy greats as Ben Turpin and Charlie Chaplin. The British-born Chaplin, whose first major film success was *The Tramp* (1915), combined acrobatic skills, a fine comic sense, and a degree of social commentary to become the foremost persona of early motion pictures.

Sports, music, film, and other forms of mass recreation and entertainment had a homogenizing effect on American culture, breaking down ethnic, sectional, and class barriers. For several centuries the music, art, literature, and games of the rich and the poor had been quite different. Not since pre-industrial times had rich and poor come so close to sharing the same cultural world as in the twentieth century. To some extent, this shared culture allayed the growth of class consciousness in the country.

Despite mass culture's homogenizing effect and its general affirmation of things American, the nation's multiculturalism showed through. Sports teams often had regional and ethnic identities; outings at Coney Island and other entertainment parks rarely included ethnically or culturally mixed groups. Ethnic and race prejudice was a given in much of the vaudeville and movie entertainment of the period, and a few entertainers, most notably Charlie Chaplin, subtly expressed the frustrations of working people.

THE SEARCH FOR ORDER AND A PLACE IN THE REPUBLIC

If economic success and mass culture brought Americans together, other forces pushed them apart. The pluralism of American society expanded at a dizzying pace during the Progressive Era. Many middle-class Americans fretted over the growing concentration of wealth and the arrogance of big businessmen, but they were equally troubled by the country's new cultural diversity and the growth of class consciousness. The consolidation of business in the late nineteenth century encouraged other groups such as farmers, laborers, and professionals to organize. Defining one's place in society became a preoccupation in Progressive America. Confident and patriotic as they were, most Americans felt a deep need to identify with a more immediate community that shared their interests and advocated their rights in the forum of politics. Of course, local and regional voluntary associations had flourished in the United States for a century. These older organizations continued to be of great importance, but increasingly they had powerful competitors for people's loyalty.

❧ Diluting the WASP Consensus

The transformation of American cities from white, Anglo-Saxon, Protestant strongholds into islands of ethnic pluralism, which had begun in the years after the Civil War, gained momentum after 1900. The massive migration of Europeans to American in the late nineteenth century (see Chapter 19) continued unchecked. The first fifteen years of the twentieth century witnessed one of the largest movements of population in modern history as the swarming westward migration of Europeans, begun in the late nineteenth century, reached its peak. The number of immigrants seeking political freedom and economic opportunity in the United States topped a million for the first time in 1905, peaked in 1907 at 1,285,349, and surpassed a million in four other years (1906, 1910, 1913, and 1914). Only the outbreak of World War I stanched the flow. In 1910, more than 13 million Americans were foreign born, the largest proportion (nearly 15 percent) of the nation's population in the twentieth century.

Some regions were dramatically changed by the migrations of the late nineteenth and early twentieth centuries. Most northeastern states had heavy concentrations of foreign-born populations in 1910: 32.8 percent in Rhode Island, 31.2 percent in Massachusetts, and 29.8 percent in New York. Many of the agricultural states of the Northwest also had large foreign-born communities; in North Dakota the figure stood at 27.1 percent and in Minnesota at 26.2 percent. In many states, the number of "foreign-stock" residents (persons with at least one foreign-born parent) exceeded 50 percent.

More than 70 percent of these immigrants were coming from southern and eastern Europe. Between 1900 and 1920 the number of foreign-born in the United

States from England, Germany, and Ireland declined; on the other hand, the number of Polish immigrants increased from 383,000 (14,000 in 1870) to 1.13 million, from Italy 480,000 (17,000 in 1870) to 1.6 million, and from Russia 423,000 (4,600 in 1870) to 1.4 million. Smaller numbers but similar percentage increases were recorded from Austria-Hungary, Finland, Romania, and Greece. Large numbers of the immigrants from Russia and eastern Europe were Jews fleeing persecution. Like those who had preceded them in the late nineteenth century, many immigrants were skilled workers, but most were of peasant origin and had to accept low-paying unskilled jobs in factories or menial tasks in the growing cities.

IMMIGRANT COMMUNITIES

Large numbers of immigrants continued to cluster into self-contained communities in the cities — in "Little Italy" or "Polonia." Those ethnic ghettos were much more complex than most older Americans imagined; the new arrivals often had roots in provincial cultures that were marginally related to larger national groupings. Immigrant communities were far from static; in the early twentieth century around 50 percent of the people in any given Polish neighborhood had disappeared ten years later, having either returned to their homeland or moved elsewhere in the United States in search of economic opportunity. A government study concluded that of the approximately 10 million immigrants entering the country between 1908 and 1923, nearly 3.5 million returned home.

Ethnic businesses and parish churches continued to be the focus of life in immigrant communities, as businessmen competed with priests for community leadership. Mutual aid societies and fraternal bodies that provided minimal insurance to dues-paying members more or less defined national groupings and gave them a political voice. Such societies flourished in the late nineteenth century; by 1910 American Poles had founded around 7,000 ethnic organizations and about three-fourths of the Polish-American popula-

Temple Emanuel, New York City This ornate temple stood until 1927 at Fifth Avenue and 43rd Street. It was built in 1868 and described by a contemporary critic as "the finest example of Moorish architecture in the Western world." In the Progressive Era, nearly every northeastern city was home to impressive synagogues.

tion belonged to such voluntary association. The largest, The Polish National Alliance (1880), claimed more than 200,000 members by 1920. Eastern European Jews created at least 3,000 societies, known in Yiddish as *landsmanshaften.* The solidarity of ethnic neighborhoods formed the basis for the political machines that amassed increasing power in the cities in the late nineteenth century.

Religion remained near the heart of the immigrant experience. American Judaism was much less uniform than outsiders imagined. During the first two decades of the twentieth century over 1.5 million Jewish immigrants arrived in America, around 95 percent of them from eastern Europe. These new immigrants were separated from Jewish descendants of nineteenth-century German immigrants by barriers of class, language, education, politics, and religion. Most of the older Jewish community had embraced Reform Judaism; like liberal Protestants, they quickly adjusted themselves to modern thought. Orthodox Judaism was given a new vitality by the influx of Yiddish-speaking eastern Europeans, many of them refugees from the violent and officially tolerated anti-Semitism of czarist Russia and Romania. The reorganization of the Jewish Theological Seminary in 1902 marked the formal beginning of Conservative Judaism, a middle-of-the-road effort to preserve the observance of Jewish ritual while making it easier for succeeding generations to adapt to American society. Others in the new Yiddish-speaking immigration were defiantly anti-religious and socialist or anarchist.

As more and more synagogues appeared in American cities, their architecture defined Jewish communities. Reform synagogues adopted the architectural and worship styles of American Protestant churches. In their early years of poverty, Orthodox Jews worshiped in storefronts, but before World War I most cities in the Northeast boasted impressive orthodox synagogues built in the Byzantine-derived styles of Greece and Russia.

The strongest unifying force in American Judaism early in the twentieth century was the spread of Zionism, a movement that arose in late nineteenth-century Europe that aimed at reviving Hebrew culture and founding a modern Jewish national state, preferably in Palestine. Many prominent American Jews, including Supreme Court Justice Louis Brandeis, supported Zionism, seeing it as an extension of American idealism. Although Zionism united disparate groups (including some of the Jewish socialists), the movement was not uniformly embraced by American Jews in the early twentieth century. Some powerful Jewish-rights organizations, including the American Jewish Committee (1906) and the Anti-Defamation League of the B'nai B'rith (1913), opposed Zionism, believing that it threatened to destroy the hard-won goodwill enjoyed by successful American Jews.

NEW IMMIGRANTS, NEW CHALLENGES

The Roman Catholic Church was overwhelmed by the new immigration. The church grew so rapidly that in 1908 the Vatican declared that the United States was no longer a mission field. Nonetheless, the American church continued to suffer a chronic shortage of priests as the ratio of clerics to parishioners hovered at around one for every thousand. The burst of Catholic church construction that had begun in the late nineteenth century continued. Because Catholic parishes often had thousands of members, the new parish churches were frequently impressive in size and grandeur, and typically they included facilities for a parochial school. In most American cities, impressive new cathedrals, generally built in the city center, became proud symbols of legitimacy for the poor immigrants crowded in urban slums and made it impossible for other Americans to ignore the growing presence of the American Catholic church. The National Conference of Catholic Charities, founded in 1910, valiantly struggled to provide relief for the worst cases of deprivation among orphans and widows.

The huge numbers of immigrants posed perplexing problems for church leaders. While some Catholic immigrants became thoroughly Americanized, most continued to live in ethnic neighborhoods and retained strong loyalties to the distinctive practices and celebrations of the Catholic Church in their country of origin. The church found it impossible to supply suitable priests for the 2 million newly arrived Italians; some church leaders feared that these tensions would lead to wholesale defections, but unless they were political radicals most Italians remained loyal to the church. Polish Catholics proved an even more difficult minority for the Catholic Church to digest. The shortage of Polish priests was particularly acute; the ratio of priest to parishioners among Polish Catholics was about 1:4,000. The Irish predominance in the American priesthood constantly caused friction that in many Polish parishes erupted into open hostility against the "One, Holy, *Irish,* Apostolic church." The most visible focus of discontent was the lack of Polish-American bishops, and the first such appointment did not occur until Paul Rhode became an auxiliary bishop in Chicago in 1908. Rhode, who was both a loyal priest and an ardent Polish nationalist, skillfully united the Polish Catholic community and became a voice for Polish causes both in America and in Europe.

Before Rhode's appointment, several splits had occurred in the Polish Catholic community, some led by lower clergy and some by dissident lay leaders who objected to the church's authoritarian tactics. The Old Catholic group, which had left the church in 1897 under the leadership of Antoni Kozlowski, claimed 75,000 adherents by 1907. Under the leadership of Francis Hondur, other dissident congregations united in 1904 to form the Polish National Catholic Church in America, which by 1916 claimed nearly 30,000 communicants.

Immigration not only caused huge growth in the American Catholic church, it also contributed to a great multiplication of Orthodox and Protestant denominations. Immigrants organized American branches of the

Russian and Greek Orthodox churches early in the century. In 1917, after the democratic first phase of the Russian Revolution had toppled the czar, Tikhon Bellavin, the Russian Orthodox bishop of San Francisco and New York City, became the first patriarch of the Russian church in Moscow since the days of Peter the Great (who had abolished the patriarchate and brought the Russian church under the control of lay bureaucrats). Orthodox churches seemed to older-stock Americans to be islands of exotic mysticism, but they provided cultural continuity for millions of Balkan and other east European immigrants.

Lutheranism also grew rapidly. American Lutheranism claimed nearly 4 million members by 1926, but Lutherans were divided into more than thirty denominations by ethnic, linguistic, and theological differences. Like the Catholic Church, Lutheran congregations were dominated by newly arrived immigrants, and the churches' leaders seemed oblivious to the theological debates ravaging the other branches of American Protestantism. American Lutherans (who were mostly of German or Scandinavian ancestry) were divided by sharp ethnic and minor theological differences, but all remained tied to the theology of the Reformation. Estranged from other American Protestants by language, theological tradition, and culture (beer-drinking Lutherans were appalled by the prohibition crusade), the Lutheran churches of America were spiritual and cultural havens for millions of unassimilated north European settlers. The tight-knit familial culture of these immigrants could be seen in their churches. Charting the percentage of male members in American churches in 1926, the Census Bureau noted that seven out of ten of the denominations with the highest percentages of men were Lutheran.

Immigration and the burgeoning cities brought into sharp contrast the hopes and discontents of the early twentieth century. The flow of new people into the nation and the buzzing vitality of the cities advertised that America was the world's best hope. The millions of foreigners who arrived with great hopes contributed mightily with their lives and with their sons and daughters to the building of America. In the minds of many, particularly among the new arrivers, the vision of America as a melting pot remained as compelling as ever. Coining a durable phrase, the Russian-born author Israel Zangwill wrote enthusiastically in 1908: "America is God's Crucible, the great Melting-Pot where all the races of Europe are melting and re-forming!" Whatever the difficulties they encountered in urban ghettos or

on the remote and desolate farms of the Great Plains, most of the Great Migration of immigrants who came from Europe during these years made it clear that they loved America, their chosen Promised Land.

Although young progressives embraced the notion of cultural pluralism rather than the melting pot as a basis for national existence, the concept still seemed dangerously un-American in the early twentieth century. Most Americans, including progressives, believed that the polyglot of new peoples in the cities threatened the country's existence and its "racial purity" unless they could be efficiently Americanized. Public school educators staunchly opposed the spread of ethnic and religious private schools that taught children in languages other than English, and several states required that English be the medium of instruction in all schools. Older Americans were appalled by the ethnic-based urban political machines, by what they considered the cultural backwardness of the new immigrants, and by the unfamiliar faiths that the new arrivals brought with them. Furthermore, American labor leaders were alarmed by the continued flow of cheap labor into the United States, convinced that immigration was undermining the bargaining position of unions. In the minds of many Americans, the immigrant flood jeopardized the religious, racial, economic, and political assumptions of the American majority.

✌ Sectional Variations on the American Theme

The regions of the nation continued to vary widely in culture and thought. The region east of the Mississippi and north of the Mason-Dixon line contained 45 percent of the nation's population and far exceeded the South and the West in economic, educational, and social development. But while increasing numbers of Americans were urban laborers, millions of others were cowboys, farmers and farmers' wives, fishermen and village shopkeepers. Even the cities were filled with the sons and daughters of rural America. In 1910, nineteen southern and western states remained two-thirds rural; in a half-dozen southern states more than two-thirds of the people still worked in agriculture. The rhythm of life changed slowly in the sleepy villages of the Midwest and on the sultry, impoverished farms of the South. In the first two decades of the century, millions of Americans lived and died knowing little of the squalor of slums or of the political battles raging in the state capitals and in Washington, D.C. Their lives resonated more with the century past than with the one

09371. A SOUTHERN BAPTISM.

ahead, and they continued to revere the individualistic ideals they had inherited from their grandparents.

The South remained the most culturally isolated section of the country, and most white southerners felt a keen sense of regional identification. Affected only slightly by the industrial expansion of the late nineteenth century and preoccupied with racial issues, the South constituted a land apart, virtually untouched by the waves of immigration that were making the United States so strikingly diverse a society. Except for Texas, where the percentage of foreign-born population in 1910 was 6.2 percent, and Florida, where it was 4.5 percent, the proportion of foreign-born in the South was minuscule. In seven southern states less than 1 percent of the state's population had been born outside the United States.

During the late nineteenth century, southerners came closer than any Americans ever had to constructing an alternate set of ideals to those of the rest of the nation. Religion was at the heart of the southern self-understanding. By 1900, the South had become the "Bible Belt," the most churched and solidly Protestant section of the country. Largely untouched by the pluralizing effects of immigration, self-conscious over its history and mired in poverty, the white South constructed

A Baptismal Service in South Carolina   By 1900 the South had become the solidly religious "Bible Belt," and many southerners, white and black, felt more kinship with old ways than they did with progressivism.

its own evangelical civil religion that united regional identity with the God of the Confederate "Lost Cause." The religion of both whites and blacks in the South had a distinctive regional flavor, as did the lives of southerners of both races. Even the forward-looking leaders of the New South embraced the section's sense of Christian mission. "The hope of the world is America," wrote Edwin Mims in a 1926 book entitled *The Advancing South,* "the hope of America is evangelical religion of the most orthodox type, the hope of the American church is the southern Evangelical churches."

While southern Presbyterians and Methodists increasingly identified with their northern counterparts (and joined the Federal Council of Churches), the Southern Baptist Convention rejected cooperation outright. The secretary of the Arkansas Baptist Convention urged Baptists to "smite, smite, hip and thigh, the 'bastard' Union movement, dear preachers of God's Book, by calling every Baptist soul under the reach of your prophetic voice to toe the denominational line." Southern Baptists focused single-mindedly on converting the lost and

The NAACP's "Silent Protest" Parade, July 1917   Speaking out against the violence that African Americans routinely suffered in early twentieth-century America, the NAACP held this "silent protest" parade up Fifth Avenue in New York City. The United States had already entered World War I, and few whites were interested in "colored people's" grievances. Yet this march was a harbinger of the great civil rights demonstrations and other acts of non-violent protest that would shake the nation's conscience in later generations.

building churches, and they succeeded, in the first two decades of the century doubling their numbers from 1.65 million to 3.1 million. The staunch orthodoxy of Southern Baptists, and of other southern groups such as the Churches of Christ, helped make the South a bastion of religious and political conservatism.

∾ African Americans — the Invisible Americans

African Americans were the nation's most isolated and alienated minority in the early twentieth century. During the first two decades of the century, the social and political oppression of African Americans accelerated and patterns of segregation spread in North and South alike. In the South the disfranchisement of blacks was virtually total, and racist demagogues dominated the region's politics. On the Senate floor in 1900, Ben Tillman of South Carolina candidly described the disfranchisement of blacks in his state: "We have scratched our heads to find out how we could eliminate every last one of them. We stuffed ballot boxes. We shot them. We are not ashamed of it." Fanned by race prejudice, lynchings fluctuated from a low of sixty in 1905 to a high of seventy-nine in 1915. During the first two decades of the century about 500,000 African Americans migrated out of the South to the North. The remarkable migration was spontaneous and uncoordinated, and it left some rural regions of the South with serious labor shortages. The great migration was like a Biblical exodus in the minds of many African Americans, and they took their religion with them into the cities of the North. During these years around 500,000 more African Americans left southern farms to settle in the cities of the South. Although migration provided a limited degree of economic opportunity for African Americans, they generally were greeted in the North by prejudice and discrimination in housing, jobs, and education. The combination of white racism and black discontent sparked nearly a dozen race riots between 1900 and 1915 in cities in both sections of the country, and the violence took its heaviest toll in black neighborhoods.

Booker T. Washington remained the most influential spokesman for blacks at the turn of the century. Washington won the support of northern philanthropists and southern civic leaders for his program of black pride and self-help that seemed to call for very gradual changes in patterns of segregation and race relations. Actually Washington, a canny politician, quietly backed a variety of efforts to secure black constitutional rights, including contributing financial support to civil-rights cases in the courts.

Increasingly, however, Washington came under fire from black critics who regarded him as an authoritarian figure with a limited vision. In the early twentieth century Washington's leadership was challenged by two northern-born, Harvard-trained blacks, William Monroe Trotter, the publisher of the *Boston Guardian*, and W. E. B. Du Bois, a sociologist and historian who had studied in Germany and became the first black to earn a Ph.D. from Harvard. Both Trotter and Du Bois demanded immediate recognition of the constitutional rights of blacks and criticized Washington's emphasis on industrial education.

While teaching at all-black Atlanta University in 1905, Du Bois helped to organize the Niagara Move-

❋ IN THEIR OWN WORDS

Debate over African American education, 1896-1902

From 1896 to 1902, Booker T. Washington and W.E.B. Du Bois carried on a debate in the pages of The Atlantic *magazine over the educational goals that would best serve the black community. Washington believed blacks should cultivate self-reliance through the mastery of technical skills.*

We must admit the stern fact that at present the Negro, through no choice of his own, is living in the midst of another race, which is far ahead of him in education, property, and experience: and further, that the Negro's present condition makes him dependent upon the white people for most of the things necessary to sustain life, as well as, in a large measure, for his education. In all history, those who have possessed the property and intelligence have exercised the greatest control in government, regardless of color, race, or geographical location. This being the case, how can the black man in the South improve his estate? . . .

Let us help the Negro by every means possible to acquire such an education in farming, dairying, stock-raising, horticulture, etc., as will place him near the top in these industries, and the race problem will in a large part be settled or at least stripped of many of its most perplexing elements. This policy would also tend to keep the Negro in the country and smaller towns, where he succeeds best, and stop the influx into the large cities, where he does not succeed so well. The race, like the individual which produces something of superior worth that has a common human interest, wins a permanent place, and is bound to be recognized.

Du Bois, on the other hand, considered Washington's emphasis on technical training to be insufficient and ultimately dehumanizing.

[W]hen turning our eyes from the temporary and the contingent in the Negro problem to the broader question of the permanent uplifting and civilization of black men in America, we have a right to inquire, as this enthusiasm for material advancement mounts to its height, if after all the industrial school is the final and sufficient answer in the training of the Negro race; and to ask gently, but in all sincerity, the ever recurring query of the ages, Is not life more than meat, and the body more than raiment? And men ask this to-day all the more eagerly because of sinister signs in recent educational movements. The tendency is here born of slavery and quickened to renewed life by the crazy imperialism of the day, to regard human beings as among the material resources of a land to be trained with an eye single to future dividends. Race prejudices, which keep brown and black men in their "places," we are coming to regard as useful allies with such a theory, no matter how much they may dull the ambition and sicken the hearts of struggling human beings. And above all, we daily hear that an education that encourages aspiration, that sets the loftiest of ideals and seeks as an end culture and character than bread-winning, is the privilege of white men and the danger and delusion of black. . . .

[T]his is certain, no secure civilization can be built in the South with the Negro as an ignorant, turbulent proletariat. Suppose we seek to remedy this by making them laborers and nothing more: they are not fools, they have tasted of the Tree of Life, and they will not cease to think, will not cease attempting to read the riddle of the world. By taking away their best equipped teachers and leaders, by slamming the door of opportunity in the faces of their bolder and brighter minds, will you make them satisfied with their lot?

ment, a civil-rights group that demanded the "recognition of the principle of human brotherhood as a practical present creed" and won the support of such white progressives as Jane Addams. The Niagara Movement merged with other reform groups in 1909 to form the National Association for the Advancement of Colored People (NAACP). Du Bois became the Director for Publicity and Research in the new organization and for twenty-four years edited its magazine, *The Crisis*. A prolific writer, in 1903 he wrote a pioneering study of black religion, *The Souls of Black Folk*. He quickly established himself as the preeminent black intellectual of the first half of the century.

Churches were as central to the African American subculture as they were in immigrant communities. According to Du Bois, in the South nearly "every American Negro is a church member." The ministry was one of the few professions open to African Americans, and preachers were the most influential leaders in the black community. Black churches were predominately Baptist and Methodist; the 1906 census reported that those two denominations included 95 percent of all black Christians. Local Baptist and Methodist churches generally had fraternal relations with their white counterparts, but by 1900 religious racial segregation was as complete as that in southern society as a whole. In the late nineteenth century, a few leaders in the major black denominations sought to find, in the words of Benjamin Tucker Tanner, editor of the African Methodist Episcopal *Review,* "a theology for themselves." But, generally speaking, black churches remained theologically conservative; to the extent that their weak financial condition allowed, black denominations participated in the evangelical missions movement of the early twentieth century. African American worship combined elements of evangelical revivalism and African religion; differences in patterns of worship separated black and white churches as effectively as the law. The rhythms and rhetoric of the church influenced the style of African American religion and politics throughout the twentieth century.

❧ Women — Americans Who Would Be Heard

The group that made the clearest gains during the Progressive Era were advocates of women's rights, even though Victorian views of "woman's sphere" remained strong in the early twentieth century. In a 1904 article in *Ladies Home Journal,* former president Grover Cleveland expressed a view that was still common among men and

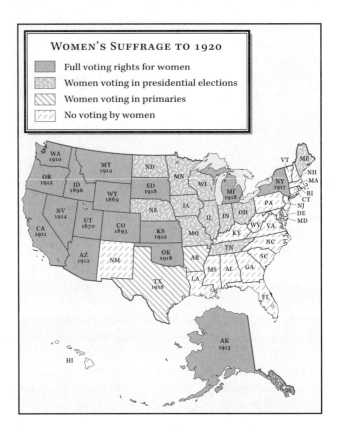

women alike: "Sensible and responsible women do not want to vote, their role having been assigned long ago by a higher intelligence than ours." Millions of Americans, including many women, continued to believe that women were best suited to be wives and mothers, and should stay out of the corrupt world of politics.

However, times were changing. Women had been entering the American labor force for years, and by 1900 women workers had established a foothold in many areas of the economy, but the biggest percentage increase — from 23.5 percent to 28.1 percent — occurred from 1900 to 1910. The "feminization" of secretarial jobs during these years increasingly placed poorly-paid young women, who were presumed to have superior talents in the use of typewriters, in positions that had long been reserved for young men. By 1920, women held 64 percent of all stenographic jobs in the nation and 92 percent of all secretarial positions. The new consumer society also opened to women positions as sales clerks in department stores; by 1920 around one-third of the nation's 1.5 million clerks were women. Increasing numbers of women were educated at state universities and in women's colleges, and many attained leadership positions in progressive reforms, particularly those that attacked liquor and prostitution and that advocated labor laws. Perhaps more notable, women reformers building on the pioneering work of Jane Addams gained attention as leaders in areas that challenged traditional views. Katherine Bement Davis, a widely respected expert in penal reform, served a term as New York City's commissioner of corrections. Margaret Sanger, a thirty-year-old nurse who had seen her mother's health destroyed by overwork and a seemingly endless series of pregnancies, founded the Birth Control League in 1914. Two years later she opened the nation's first birth control clinic in Brooklyn and was arrested for the first time in her controversial career for distributing birth control information.

The women's club movement had become nationally organized in the 1890s with the founding of three separate groups: the General Federation of Women's Clubs, the National Council of Jewish Women, and the National Association of Colored Women, and those organizations grew increasingly vocal. By 1917 the General Federation had more than 1 million members. Mostly hailing from the middle and upper classes, during the Progressive Era the club women moved from non-controversial discussions of literary and cultural topics to lobbying for woman's and child labor legislation, pure food and drug laws, and, beginning in 1914, woman's suffrage.

Despite support for suffrage from several presidents of the period, in 1914 women could vote in state and local elections in only twelve states, all of them west of the Mississippi. When Susan B. Anthony retired as the head of the National American Woman Suffrage Association (NAWSA) in 1900, she was succeeded by Carrie Chapman Catt of Iowa. Married to a civil engineer who strongly supported her efforts, Catt was an organizational genius whose political skills were crucial in the drive for suffrage. Dr. Anna Howard Shaw, a Methodist minister and the first woman in America to hold degrees in both medicine and divinity, replaced Catt as president of the organization in 1904. She remained in that position until 1915, bringing a sense of religious fervor to the crusade. The leaders of NAWSA lobbied, distributed literature, and organized rallies and parades all over the country. Nonetheless, support came slowly, even from the masses of women.

The woman's suffrage movement got its biggest boost from its historic alliance with the prohibition movement. While some feminist leaders were non-traditionalists who flaunted smoking and new sexual attitudes, the strongest supporters of suffrage were middle-class women and men with traditional Protestant values who viewed women as a potential base of support for moral legislation, particularly prohibition. In every region except the South, women were leaders in the prohibition movement.

"A Christian People"

"Our boast has been that we are a Christian people," read the opening line of a 1908 temperance lecture; similar assertions launched innumerable political orations during the Progressive Era. In some respects, the claim rang true. In hundreds of communities, businesses closed on Sunday as prescribed by law, thousands of public school systems required teachers to read the King James Bible in class, and in scores of other informal acts Americans publicly displayed religious faith. At the popular level, faith in God still stood beside faith in nation as the pillars of the American conscience. At the same time, the faith preached in the more liberal Protestant churches was less restrictive than the faith of the fathers had been, and it demanded less single-minded devotion to spiritual things.

Churches continued to thrive, but they also slowly, almost imperceptibly, moved toward the periphery of society. Among the professions, only ministers lost prestige during the early twentieth century. The multiplication of organizations during the Progressive Era sometimes complemented churches, as in the case of temperance societies, but they sometimes competed with churches for individuals' loyalty. Protestantism remained a powerful lobbying force, but a disproportionate amount of the church's influence went into the prohibition campaign. In countless ways Protestant leaders began to sense that they were becoming cultural outsiders, a station long occupied by Roman Catholics and Jews. Increasingly, Protestant churches served and defined particular communities of faith rather than the nation.

In spite of some decline in their influence, churches remained the broadest institutional framework within American society. In 1916 over 42 million Americans claimed affiliation with some religious body. Synagogues and Catholic churches continued to be the cultural focal points for enclaves of urban immigrants, guiding lights for everyday routines. Millions of other Americans, urban and rural, white and black, found in their religious bodies the most intimate institution in their lives, the only organization that many would ever join. Churches still touched the lives and consciences of most Americans. From a Lutheran confirmation in Minneapolis, to an Easter mass in Boston, a bar mitzvah in Brooklyn, a Baptist dinner-on-the-grounds in Flat Creek, Tennessee, and a Pentecostal revival in Los Angeles, the noise of solemn and joyous assemblies resounded from sea to sea.

❧ *Protestants*

In spite of the formidable cultural and intellectual challenges swirling about them, the nation's most powerful Protestant denominations, composed overwhelmingly of old-stock Americans who shared in the nation's prosperity, faced the twentieth century with unbridled optimism. Protestant churches grew steadily in size and wealth during the Progressive Era; in 1916, an estimated 26 million adult Americans belonged to Protestant denominations. Denominations built fewer new buildings during these years than in the remarkable construction boom of the late nineteenth century, but the value of Protestant church edifices more than doubled between 1916 and 1926. Virtually every downtown came to be graced by majestic Gothic and Romanesque Protestant sanctuaries, monuments to the success of their members, to the stature of the "Princes of the Pulpit" who preached in them, and to the continued prominence of religion on the American landscape. These sprawling church plants grew larger and larger in the early twentieth century, adding Sunday-school classrooms and, as the social gospel made its way into practice, recreational facilities.

In 1900, the two great popular churches of the nineteenth century, the Methodist and the Baptist, were swollen with the children and grandchildren of the religious pioneers who had strewn the frontier landscape with plain country church buildings. The Methodist family of churches (including both white and black denominations) counted 6 million members and Baptist churches 5 million, making them the largest Protestant groups. Growth slowed in other older denominations — the Presbyterians, Congregationalists, Disciples of Christ and Episcopalians — but those bodies continued to increase in wealth and prestige. In 1908, thirty-three historic Protestant denominations, later called the "mainstream churches," formed the Federal Council of Churches of Christ in America, an ecumenical organization with no powers over the member churches but with a strong claim to speak for American Protestantism. Although some large Protestant groups, most notably the Southern Baptists, did not join the FCC, it was a remarkable ecumenical achievement. At the World Missionary Conference in Edinburgh in 1910, American liberals played an important role in launching a worldwide ecumenical movement. The burgeoning ecumenical spirit gave a powerful public voice to the leaders of the major Protestant denominations.

❧ *Catholics*

The American Catholic church was a towering presence in American society in the early twentieth century, having grown to more than 14 million members by 1910 and nearly 18 million by 1920. Yet it was neither as visible nor as influential as its size would suggest. American Catholic leaders contributed little to the progressive consensus; indeed, the church veered to the right in the early twentieth century. Partly, Catholic conservatism was a reaction to the growing tide of anti-Catholic nativism and to its own need to digest the huge tide of immigrants, but partly the American church also reflected the theological conservatism of its own hierarchy and of Rome.

In the 1890s, the encyclicals of Pope Leo XIII (1878-1903) to the American church had given qualified support to labor and social reform but squelched a liberal Catholic ideology that the Vatican had labeled "religious Americanism." Having earlier condemned the notion of the separation of church and state and the growing acceptance of "naturalistic" ideas, in 1907 the Vatican issued a syllabus detailing the errors of Modernism. Leo's successor, Pius X (1903-1914), warned that modernists were "enemies of the Cross of Christ, who, by arts entirely new and full of deceit, are striving to destroy the vital energy of the Church." The Vatican's rejection of modern thought blocked the path for Catholic theologians to enter the modernist-fundamentalist debate that was dividing Protestantism. Catholic colleges and universities remained solidly conservative, as did the growing network of parochial schools. By 1900 the church was operating more than 3,800 parochial schools in the United States and more than 650 schools for girls. Almost all were staffed by sisters who influenced (both positively and negatively) a generation of Catholic youngsters. Generally speaking, the church's hierarchy was conservative on social as well as theological issues, opposing an array of things modern ranging from socialism to divorce, motion pictures, and woman's suffrage. Some Catholic leaders, such as the influential archbishop of Baltimore, Cardinal James Gibbons, worked hard to soothe nativist prejudices, going so far as to become a public advocate of prohibition.

❧ *The Growth of Class Consciousness*

To some extent the prosperity of the Progressive Era was felt throughout the society, muting class antagonisms. Nonetheless, class consciousness was a principal cause of the proliferation of voluntary associations that characterized the era. The organization of big business provided both a model and powerful motivation for others to form national organizations to represent class interests. The National Association of Manufacturers was founded in the 1890s to promote the interests of small businesses, and in 1903 that organization sponsored an ultraconservative Citizens Industrial Association to fight the spread of unions. Scores of smaller associations provided organizational umbrellas for other groups — lumbermen, druggists, dairymen, and so on.

Farmers, who had suffered through depression in the late nineteenth century, at last enjoyed a moderate prosperity during the first two decades of the new century. Capitalizing on that prosperity, farmers formed producer cooperatives to control prices and to help them drive better deals with the manufacturers of agricultural equipment. Farmers with large investments in land and equipment increasingly looked upon themselves as businessmen rather than laborers. The American Farm Bureau Federation, founded in 1920, gave the cooperative movement a strong national voice. As farming increasingly became a heavily capitalized business, farmers abandoned the anti-monopolistic rhetoric of the nineteenth century and began to fortify their own protectionist enclave.

Of course, business people and farmers had been organizing for decades, and to some extent both had worked their will with the American political system. Middle-class professionals and skilled laborers were the most successful new organizers during the Progressive Era, but even the poorest Americans created new organizations that gave them space to speak their minds.

❧ *Religion from the Bottom Up*

As in most times, few people in the early twentieth century spoke for the poor, and the poor controlled few institutions where they could speak for themselves. The avenue for self-expression most open to the poor was religion, and in the first two decades of the century American religion went through another period of democratization as the rural and urban poor founded their own churches.

One of the clearest symptoms of the nation's ethnic and class divisions was the sharp decline of mainstream Protestantism in the cities. Protestant churchpeople were deeply concerned by the specter of "Godless" (meaning non-mainstream Protestant) neighborhoods that seemed impervious to traditional methods of evangelization. In one way or another, every Protestant-led reform of the early twentieth century, from the social gospel to prohibition, addressed the sprawl of Catholicism and secularism in the cities.

Poor native-born Americans were as ill at ease in the comfortable downtown Protestant sanctuaries and the neat chapels in the suburbs as were immigrants. Increasingly, the poor sought God in urban storefront missions and in rural brush arbors and ramshackle buildings, and they established new denominations that they controlled, giving them access to professional clerical status not through education but by gifts and calling. One such religious rebellion, the holi-

✳ IN THEIR OWN WORDS

Pentecostal Revival at the Azusa Street Mission, 1906

The birth of the modern Pentecostal movement can be traced to a revival in a run-down building on Azusa Street in downtown Los Angeles in 1906. Among those who participated was Glen A. Cook, who described his experiences.

I could feel the power going through me like electric needles. The Spirit taught me that I must not resist the power but give way and become limp as a piece of cloth. When I did this, I fell under the power, and God began to mold me and teach me what it meant to be really surrendered to Him. I was laid out under the power five times before Pentecost really came. Each time I would come out from under the power, I would feel so sweet and clean, as though I had been run through a washing machine. . . . My arms began to tremble, and soon I was shaken violently by a great power, and it seemed as though a large pipe was fitted over my neck, my head apparently being off. . . . About thirty hours afterwards, while sitting in the meeting on Azusa Street, I felt my throat and tongue begin to move, without any effort on my part. Soon I began to stutter and then out came a distinct language which I could hardly restrain. I talked and laughed with joy far into the night.

ness movement, was already well under way at the turn of the century, calling Methodists back to the earlier Wesleyan emphasis on the doctrine of entire sanctification and personal Christian experience. Several new holiness denominations appeared around the turn of the century, including the Church of the Nazarene, the Christian and Missionary Alliance, and the Church of God (Anderson, Indiana). Other Protestant families also spawned new churches among the poor. The religious census of 1906 separated the Churches of Christ from the more liberal Disciples of Christ. While the doctrinal basis of the division was the former's rejection of the use of instrumental music in worship and the formation of missionary societies, the schism was also economic and sectional. The Churches of Christ were the poorest, the most rural, and the most southern segment of that movement. These new churches joined such nineteenth-century groups as the Church of Jesus Christ of Latter-Day Saints (Mormons), Seventh-Day Adventists, and Jehovah's Witnesses to provide alternate religious havens for the most alienated Americans.

More important in the long run as an expression of the religious aspirations of the rural and urban poor and working class was the birth of the Pentecostal movement. In 1901, in a prayer meeting at a Bible school operated by Charles G. Parham in Topeka, Kansas, a young woman spoke (and wrote) in what Parham and his students judged to be a miraculous language. The Pentecostal movement was based on the belief that speaking in tongues was the "initial evidence" of the baptism of the Holy Spirit, but it also emphasized divine healing and the imminent return of Christ. In 1906 William J. Seymour, a black preacher trained by Parham, led a revival at the Azusa Street mission in Los Angeles that lasted for nearly three years. Several thousand people from all over the world visited the revival and returned to preach the new Pentecostal message at home; the dilapidated building at 312 Azusa became the most revered landmark in the birth of Pentecostalism. Pentecostals were fiercely anti-modern, condemning pleasures that were either inaccessible or inadvisable for their working class converts, including wearing jewelry, moviegoing, drinking, and fashionable dressing. Their little churches provided professional opportunity for talented people whose economic and educational backgrounds made them ineligible for ordination in mainstream churches — men and women, whites and blacks. In 1920 around one of every ten Pentecostals was an ordained minister.

For nearly half a century Pentecostalism would languish in little churches in rural areas and in small urban congregations, but as early as 1914 several substantial denominations had been formed: the Assemblies of God, the Church of God, and the Pentecostal Holiness Church. The Church of God in Christ, led into Pentecostalism in 1907 by its influential founder, Charles H. Mason, quickly became one of the largest predominantly black denominations.

❧ The Growth of Professionalism

Middle-class professionals were the leaders of the progressive movement. The development of the professions was well under way at the turn of the century (see Chapter 20), but the number of white-collar workers in American cities, many of them highly trained specialists, increased from 5.1 million in 1900 to 10.5 million in 1920. Like populists, many middle-class progressives looked back nostalgically to the nation's agrarian past. Troubled by the rise in class-consciousness and by widening economic inequality, they longed for the supposedly more egalitarian conditions of the past. Although most lived in cities, they mourned the loss of such real and imagined agrarian virtues as neighborliness and honesty.

Middle-class progressive leaders were made uneasy by the visibility and power of wealthy businessmen, by labor organizations, and by the squalor of urban poverty. In general, middle-class professionals disdained great wealth, seeing materialism as the dominant sin of the day. At the same time, many feared the organized labor movement. "Captains of industry" and "labor bosses" were both undermining the American dream of a classless society. Increasingly, middle-class progressive intellectuals turned to politics to defend their vision of a moral and democratic nation.

The continued growth of professional organizations, well under way by 1900, provided the educated middle-class with platforms from which to speak. These associations controlled entry into the professions and gave an aura of authority to the pronouncements of such specialists as economists, historians, political scientists, and sociologists trained in Ph.D.-granting universities. Social scientists produced floods of studies offering supposedly detached and scientific critiques of American society, backed by the authority of the new professional associations. Historian Frederick Jackson Turner idealized the linkage between the professionals and political progressivism: "By training in science, law, politics, economics, and history, the universities may supply the ranks of democratic administrators, legislators, judges, and experts for commissioners who shall disinterestedly and intelligently mediate between contending interests."

Several older organizations, including the American Medical Association (1847), the National Education Association (1857), the American Bar Association (1878), and the American Historical Association (1884), grew rapidly during the Progressive Era. Scores of new professional associations also arose, such as the U.S. Chamber of Commerce (1912), the American Association of University Professors (1915), and the National Association of Accountants (1919). All of these middle-class groups claimed responsibility for the supervision of reform in their field of expertise. The American Medical Association, reorganized in 1901, brought standardization to medical education, reducing the number of medical schools (by eliminating inferior ones) from 166 in 1904 to 95 in 1915, and becoming a powerful voice for health reform.

The professional associations reacted jealously to any challenge to their authority. When grocery-store owner Daniel David Palmer developed an alternative medical theory based on "adjusting vertebrae, using the spinous and transverse processes as levers," which he called chiropractic, the medical profession successfully lobbied for legislation making it illegal in many states. According to one insider, in 1922, the AMA "met in secret conclave in Chicago and adopted the slogan, 'Chiropractic must die.'" In the years ahead, chiropractic survived, and eventually established better relations with the medical community, but at times it appeared that the power of the AMA would suffice to destroy such an "unscientific" rival. Even some physicians criticized the arrogance of the AMA's efforts to regulate the profession; one Chicago doctor dubbed the society's leaders "impertinent porcine trust-monopolists."

Professional groups spoke with such scientific authority, and exercised such stringent control over their areas of expertise, that they increasingly came to be more influential in the formation of public policy than older voluntary associations. Often professional associations provided a more dominant institutional focus in the lives of individual professionals than did churches or ethnic associations — one's status as a lawyer frequently was more consequential in his or her life than being a Baptist or a German-American.

Although professional associations enforced new standards of competence and training, they were also self-consciously elitist, protecting the status and privileges of particular groups. Some erected barriers that kept women, blacks, Jews, and other minorities out. On the other hand, the Progressive Era saw the creation of female professions such as nursing and social work, and the field of home economics was created by women excluded from the "scientific" professions.

✖ *Labor Gains and Labor Radicalism*

In current dollars, the wages of industrial laborers rose markedly during the early twentieth century, although real wages probably stayed about the same. A majority of the nearly 40 million men and women in the American labor force in 1910 still labored long hours for low wages (an average of over fifty hours a week in industrial jobs and more than sixty hours a week in many other areas). Even in the best circumstances factory labor was likely to be strenuous and boring, and often it was dangerous.

Child labor remained a visible sore; in 1900 an estimated 1.5 million children between the age of ten and fifteen were employed as non-farm laborers. In the cities, entire immigrant families often labored as a unit to earn sufficient money for survival. Safety was such a low priority for most employers that thousands of workers died every year in accidents. In 1911, a shocking fire at the Triangle Shirtwaist Company factory in New York City stunned the nation, intensifying demands for safer working conditions and for worker's compensation laws. The fire broke out in the factory just thirty minutes before closing time and management had locked the doors to assure that none of the workers left early. In the panic that erupted 147 workers died, mostly women and children, many of them jumping to their death to escape the flames. By 1916, partly in response to the Triangle fire, more than thirty states had enacted workmen's compensation laws.

Much about the climate of the Progressive Era encouraged unionization. Skilled laborers strengthened their unions and gained political clout during these years. Some large businesses began to see the advantages of having a unified and contented labor force, although anti-union sentiment remained very strong. In the relatively stable economic environment at the beginning of the century, union membership grew from less than 800,000 in 1900 to more than 2 million in 1910 and more than 5 million in 1920. The American Federation of Labor led the advance, reaching 1.5 million members by 1910. By that time, the A.F. of L. spoke

Child Labor Working in a dark, unventilated space, these "break-er boys" separate slate from coal in a Pennsylvania mining district. The work was terribly unhealthy — it ravaged lungs and distorted proper skeletal development — and of course paid only a pittance, most of which went to help support their families. Abuses such as this were targeted by Progressive-Era child-labor legislation.

for a substantial portion of the nation's skilled labor-ers and the union increasingly became a political force, supporting the Democratic presidential tickets in 1908, 1912, and 1916. The times were suited for the moderate agenda of AFL leader Samuel Gompers; the A.F. of L. continued to focus narrowly on bread-and-butter is-sues such as higher wages and shorter hours and lob-bied for legislation exempting unions from prosecution under the Sherman Antitrust Act. Moderate unionism won support from some, but by no means all, progres-sive politicians.

While a majority of skilled American laborers were contented with the moderate goals of the craft-ori-ented A.F. of L., around 90 percent of the nation's indus-trial labor force remained unorganized before World War I, either ignored or consciously excluded by the A.F. of L. During the first two decades of the century, a more radical labor movement attempted to unionize unskilled workers and received widespread publicity. William D. "Big Bill" Haywood gained prominence by organizing Western lumberjacks, miners, and other harshly exploited laborers who often were housed in isolated, primitive camps, and in 1905 he helped form the Industrial Workers of the World (IWW) — "Wob-blies" to friends; "I Won't Work" to enemies. In the next decade this radicalized union made some headway in recruiting textile workers in the East.

Openly advocating the overthrow of capitalism, the union proposed the establishment of a worker-led co-operative commonwealth. The IWW was riddled with internal dissension and linked to several violent incidents. In 1906, Haywood and two others were charged with assassinating former Idaho governor Frank Stennenberg, but defense attorney Clarence Darrow won their acquittal. In 1911, union members were charged with bombing the building of the *Los Angeles Times* during a strike by printers, killing twenty-one people. Once again, Darrow defended the union members, but this time they were convicted. During World War I almost the entire leadership of the union was jailed. Haywood jumped bail and fled to Russia, and the union collapsed in the 1920s.

The successes of the labor movement in general and the high visibility of the Wobblies in particular revealed an incipient class-consciousness that frightened middle-class Americans, even though the IWW failed to garner a substantial base of support among American laborers. Nonetheless, the growing visibility of unions made it increasingly difficult to ignore the fact that America had become a society with a small class of wealthy financiers and business people at the top and at the bottom a huge and growing body of impoverished laborers, including millions of blacks and new immigrants. Unions also highlighted the expanding organizational pluralism in the nation; they joined business and professional associations, churches, and ethnic associations in demanding a voice in the reshaping of the common American conscience.

FROM PROVIDENCE TO PROGRESS

By 1900 an intellectual revolution was under way that would change the country as dramatically as had industrialization and immigration. The first two decades of the twentieth century witnessed the beginnings of a profound transfer of intellectual leadership in America. Secular notions had long diluted the religious underpinnings of American culture and thought, but by 1920, theologians, long the chief interpreters of the nation's moral code, had been consigned to the fringe of American academic life. A secularist perspective, bolstered philosophically by scientific naturalism and a broad acceptance of the general explanatory powers of evolution, had gained ascendancy in most American universities. Sometimes the new secularism simply ignored religious ideas; sometimes social

The Rebel Girl   Elizabeth Gurley Flynn, whose autobiography *Rebel Girl is* a fascinating memoir of the American Left, speaks at the famous Lawrence (Massachusetts) Strike in 1912. A spellbinding orator as a young woman, after 1935 she became one of the most prominent figures of the American Communist Party and remained an unabashed Stalinist until her death, while visiting Moscow, in 1964.

scientists saw religion as a residue of superstition that soon would be vanquished by objective truth. Secularists used naturalistic science to reinvigorate the American public's confidence in the ideas of progress and national destiny.

The term *progressive* describes a variety of early twentieth-century reform movements anchored in the faith that the nation's problems could be rationally solved. The progressive movement's intellectual, religious, and political roots are visible in the decades before 1900, but a unique combination of circumstances and personalities shaped the spirit of the social and political reform movements after the turn of the century.

Progressive leadership came overwhelmingly from young, college-educated, middle-class men and women whose families had lived in the United States at least for several generations, and often since colonial times. Reform leaders had been reared on the morality of evangelical Protestantism and educated in secular universities. The progress they sought was theoretically based in the new social sciences — principally sociology, economics, and psychology. But progressivism was never a unified or consistent movement. Pressures for change emanated from a wide variety of organized groups seeking to further particular causes.

✂ The Populist Heritage

Progressivism, observed Kansas editor William Allen White, was populism with the whiskers shaved off. To be sure, much of progressivism's political agenda had been anticipated in the Populist party platform of 1892. The passage of the Interstate Commerce Act and the Sherman Anti-Trust Act owed much to the populist hatred of big business. Some prominent progressive politicians had cut their political teeth as populists, and many honored the crusading spirit of William Jennings Bryan. The continuity between populism and progressivism was most obvious in the South and West, where popular discontent focused on resentment of railroads and other monopolies. On the other hand, a majority of

progressive leaders had been conservative prior to 1900 and had little direct connection to populism. Indeed, they had generally opposed it.

Although progressivism and populism shared some common aims, important differences distinguished the two movements. Populism addressed the grievances of farmers; progressive concerns focused on urban problems. The demands of the populist movement were "belly reforms," designed primarily to rectify farmers' economic grievances. Progressivism, on the other hand, was a movement of the head and the heart, rooted in the intellectual and ethical climate of the day. Its interests ranged far beyond the economic well-being of a single class, and often set its goal as overcoming America's widening class divisions.

✂ Muckrakers

As in many periods of reform, a new form of popular communication flourished and played an important role in identifying society's demons and saviors; in the Progressive Era it was muckraking journalism. Literary realism was a well-established genre before the turn of the century. In the late nineteenth century Theodore Dreiser, Stephen Crane, and Hamlin Garland had sought to portray social and economic problems with brutal realism in their novels. Henry Demarest Lloyd wrote a famous exposé of Standard Oil Company in 1894, and in 1901 Frank Norris published *The Octopus*, a novel attacking the monopolistic railroad barons of California. Soon, the literary assault

---

❋ IN THEIR OWN WORDS

Conditions in Meatpacking Plants, 1906
"Muckrakers" set out to expose horrible working conditions in American industry at the turn of the twentieth century. The Jungle, Upton Sinclair's fictional account of life in a meatpacking plant, was intended to point out the exploitation of immigrant labor and the need for socialism, but it had its greatest impact on laws concerning food preparation. Sinclair later wrote, "I aimed at the public's heart and by accident hit it in the stomach."

There were the men in the pickle rooms, for instance, where old Antanas had gotten his

death; scarce a one of these that had not some spot of horror on his person. Let a man so much as scrape his finger pushing a truck in the pickle rooms, and he might have a sore that would put him out of the world; all the joints of his fingers might be eaten by the acid, one by one. Of the butchers and floorsmen, the beef boners and trimmers, and all those who used knives, you could scarcely find a person who had the use of his thumb; time and time again the base of it had been slashed, till it was a mere lump of flesh against which the man pressed the knife to hold it. The hands of these men would

be criss-crossed with cuts, until you could no longer pretend to count them or to trace them. They would have no nails, — they had worn them off pulling hides; their knuckles were swollen so that their fingers spread out like a fan. . . .

This is no fairy story and no joke; the meat would be shovelled into carts, and the man who did the shoveling would not trouble to lift out a rat even when he saw one — there were things that went into the sausage in comparison with which a poisoned rat was a tidbit.

on social injustice broadened into an unprecedented impetus to reform.

In the first decade of the twentieth century, a large body of social reform literature was published in mass-circulation magazines read by middle-class Americans, providing the kind of readership needed to sustain a major reform movement. *McClure's* magazine launched the era of muckraking journalism in 1902 with the first of a series of articles on political corruption written by Lincoln Steffens, "Tweed Days in St. Louis." The next month, *McClure's* began running a series on the high-handed tactics of Standard Oil Company written by Ida Tarbell. "Capitalists, workingmen, politicians, citizens — all breaking the law, or letting it be broken," wrote publisher S. S. McClure. "Who is left to uphold it? . . . There is no one left; none but all of us." Soon other magazines — *The Arena, Munceys, Hampton's, Cosmopolitan,* and *Everybody's* — joined *McClure's* in offering a steady diet of exposés of business and political corruption.

Frustrated by the "irresponsibility" of the popular writers, in 1906 Theodore Roosevelt pejoratively called them "muckrakers," a name that stuck. Roosevelt believed that the writers were sensationalists with little interest in solving the nation's problems. William Howard Taft's judgment was even harsher. He charged that the muckrakers created a "pathology of hysteria" that hindered those seeking "affirmative action and the enactment of beneficial legislation."

It is difficult to assess the lasting significance of the muckrakers. They fanned the fires of resentment against unfair business practices and probably helped to defeat some corrupt political machines. On the other hand, the muckrakers offered little in the way of solutions, and few of them were the unbiased and objective critics of society that they pretended to be. By 1910, muckraking had lost much of its popular appeal.

The Secularization of the American University

American philosophy came of age at the turn of the century. In the 1890s the young English philosopher Bertrand Russell — destined to be one of the preeminent intellects of the twentieth century — concluded that the Harvard philosophy department had become the most distinguished in the world. In 1907, a member of that department, William James, published *Pragmatism,* among the most influential philosophical books of the early twentieth century. Arguing that truth must be tested by practical consequence, pragmatism was an ideal foundation for the practical reform spirit of progressivism.

John Dewey was more important in the development of modern thought; his philosophical elaboration of Pragmatism, called Instrumentalism, emphasized the vital role that ideas played in forming a society and the need to constantly test the instrumental value of those ideas. After a distinguished career at several midwestern universities, Dewey moved to Columbia University in 1904. During his long subsequent academic career in New York City he became best known for his advocacy of "progressive education." In a book published in 1900, *The School and Society,* Dewey argued that "education is the fundamental method of social progress and reform." Dewey's educational theories preserved the cherished American belief that education had a moral as well as an intellectual aim, though the new progressive morality (which was often quite Christian in content) was legitimated by scientific thinking rather than theological assertions. The rapid expansion of public school systems in the late nineteenth and early twentieth centuries gave great practical significance to Dewey's educational ideas.

Dewey's influence extended far beyond his role as the father of "progressive education." He cast a long shadow across the entire intellectual life of the nation during the first half of the century. As popularized by social scientists, Dewey's ideas gave a new vocabulary and new secular meanings to assumptions that formerly had been laden with religious content. He secularized the idea of freedom of the will, arguing that human preferences determined the future, but in place of divine purpose Dewey substituted a world with harmonies and meanings discoverable by human endeavor. Moral purpose remained in Dewey's naturalistic world, but it was to be discovered not by revelation or theology but by a sublime scientific method that offered guidance in the moral as well as the physical world. Academicians were not of one philosophical mind in the early twentieth century, but virtually all social scientists acknowledged John Dewey as the nation's preeminent thinker.

The centerpiece of the intellectual revolution of the early twentieth century was the modern, autonomous, research-oriented university with its tight-knit disciplines, hierarchies of specialists, and claims of being the source of objective truth. These influential institutions left imprints on generation after generation of twentieth-century leaders of American politics and thought. The number of students in colleges and universities rose from around 150,000 in 1890 to 600,000 in 1920. Within the universities naturalistic philosophical views, emphasizing non-religious, scientific thinking, proved particularly congenial to the burgeoning natural and social sciences. On the other hand, after 1900 conservative Bible-believing views virtually vanished from university campuses; such ideas were considered anachronistic vestiges of a pre-modern past. Even religious liberals attempting to accommodate Christianity to modern thought generally found themselves isolated far from the center of the university's intellectual life.

Naturalistic theory identified the state as the laboratory where humanity's moral meaning was to be discovered. In naturalistic moral debates the state became the highest altar, the nation the sanctuary to be cleansed. In the first half of the twentieth century, according to British historian Arnold Toynbee, an "unavowed worship of parochial states was by far the most prevalent religion in the Western World." Of course, from the days of the Puritan journey "unto a good land" Americans had endowed the state with divine purpose, but in the nineteenth century few Americans felt any sense of competition between the adoration of American democracy and the religious faith of Protestantism. By the end of the twentieth century Americans would be more apt to speak of the nation's destiny in secular rather than in religious language.

Church and state did not become rivals until the second half of the twentieth century, but during the Progressive Era the state came to depend less and less on religion for moral authority. It would be easy to overstate the shift to secular authority in the first two decades of the century, for American political rhetoric and the American social conscience remained saturated by religious faith. But the pendulum was swinging. In 1900 the proportion of clergy to professors was 118,000 to 7,000; by 1930 the figures were 149,000 to 62,000. Preachers were still respected in local communities, but professors now trained the nation's experts.

❧ Progressive Education

The great majority of school-age children during the Progressive Era ended their formal education in the eighth grade, or even earlier. Still, beginning in the 1890s the growing concentration of the American population in urban areas, as well as parents' desire to see their children advance in a world that valued specialized skills, combined to spur a rapid growth of high school enrollments. By 1900, about 10 percent of all children aged fourteen to seventeen were attending high school, and by 1920 more than 30 percent were. Higher education remained restricted to middle- and upper-class white families.

Traditionally, training in ancient languages and mathematics had been the essential prerequisites for higher education, but in the 1890s American high schools were rapidly supplementing these subjects with science, modern languages and literature, and history. Because many turn-of-the-century high school graduates did not go on to college, "practical" subjects like bookkeeping and woodshop were being added to the curriculum, but academic subjects remained the core. (Latin, for example, was taken by a third of all high school students in 1890 and by half of them in 1900, and some 80 percent of high school students studied some foreign language.) Parents valued this curriculum for inculcating mental discipline and broadening life choices even for non-college-bound children.

Against this background of far-from-universal schooling, the Progressive Era was roiled by acrimonious public debate about education, revealing much about the progressives' attitudes and aims. Teaching methods, curriculum, and the fundamental purpose of education all became objects of important Progressive-Era educational controversies — debates that still continue, with enormous implications for American society and still little prospect for resolution.

The typical high school classroom at the turn of the twentieth century did not look much like its present-day counterpart. Students sat in rows of desks bolted to the floor, discipline was strict (although seldom involving corporal punishment), teachers interacted with pupils in a generally authoritarian manner, and instruction relied heavily on memorization and recitation. Dewey's celebrated "laboratory school" at the University of Chicago between 1896 and 1904 introduced much-needed reforms, symbolized by his unbolting of desks so children could gather around their teacher in a friendly circle. Dewey encouraged teaching in a relaxed, informal manner that made school more fun, although the subject matter remained solidly academic. He and his student teachers obtained impressive results with these methods, which he continued to advocate throughout his long career.

Dewey's innovations dovetailed with the theories of educationists like G. Stanley Hall, the president of Clark University and the first prominent American champion

Vocational Education   These young men and women in Baltimore, some of them probably recent immigrants, are being taught the practical skills that were a goal of Progressive education. On the left, the boys use tools; on the right, the girls learn cooking, with an eye to employment either in well-to-do households or in restaurants.

of Freudian psychology. Liberating children from unnecessary tension and paying attention to their physical and mental health were among the cornerstones of Hall's influential "child study" movement, whose rallying cry was for educators to learn the needs of children and avoid imposing adult values on them. Hall's concern about "overstressing" children included opposing homework and claiming that excessive pressure on girls endangered their biological destiny — motherhood. Indeed, Hall railed against trying to teach any academic subjects to most students, whom he lumped in "a great army of incapables, shading down to those who should be in schools for dullards or subnormal children, for whose mental development heredity decrees a slow pace and early arrest." Dewey, though he was never so blunt, thought that the typical child need

not become literate before the age of eight.

Dewey aimed to make schools the instrument of social reform, not simply the vehicle for inculcating knowledge. And while he was elaborating his complex ideas (in lectures so murky that few students could follow his thoughts), other progressive education experts were invoking his authority to mount a full-scale assault on "bookish" education, which they dismissed with progressivism's supreme condemnation: "inefficiency." Thus the superintendent of schools at Cleveland and his deputy in 1910 decided that although 1 percent of students were destined to be managers and 4 percent would become "lawyers, doctors, preachers, teachers, men of science, of art, and officeholders," the other 95 percent should be tracked into vocational education, as befitted their future as "industrial and commercial workers." But how to identify the 5 percent? Look at their neighborhoods, for "where the streets are well paved and clean, ... where the language of the child's playfellows is pure, ... — it is obvious that the educational needs of such a child are different from those of the child who lives in a foreign and tenement section."

Advocates of such elitism considered themselves progressives and democrats, and they attacked traditional education as "authoritarian," even "monarchical." Their purpose, they said, was to train ordinary students for the working lives they would lead, rather than stuffing their heads with useless information. Any subject without immediate social utility was suspect. Education, said the president of Columbia University, must adapt "the larger proportion of the population to their environment." In 1907, the superbly educated Theodore Roosevelt announced that "our school system is gravely defective in that it puts a premium upon mere literary training and tends therefore to train the boy [sic] away from the farm and the workshop. Nothing is more needed than the best type of industrial school, the school for mechanical industries in the city, the school for practically teaching agriculture in the country."

Half-consciously, Roosevelt was echoing the views of the nation's business leaders, for whom the best educational system would be a vocational one, turning most young people into "efficient" workers. That was one reason why Booker T. Washington's vocationally oriented educational program for black youths received such enthusiastic endorsement from the white power structure. Similarly, the junior high schools that began to proliferate around 1910 were intended primarily as vocational institutions, more suitable than academic high schools for the mass of children whose education would terminate upon entry into the labor force. The author of the standard textbook on school administration acknowledged in 1916 that demand for "efficient" vocational rather than academic education was coming from business and was being resisted primarily by "ultraconservative schoolmasters," incapable of understanding "democratic" needs. Articles in popular magazines like *The Saturday Evening Post* echoed such experts in denouncing "our medieval high schools" that prepared students for the twelfth, not the twentieth century. "Democracy's high schools," it was proclaimed, would teach girls "domestic science" and boys "industrial arts," preparing them to be useful and meanwhile saving the taxpayer money that would otherwise be squandered on Latin.

But teachers and students in many of these "medieval high schools" and their tax-paying parents stoutly resisted the progressive theorists, clinging to hopes that a traditional, content-rich education offered young people their best chance for upward mobility. "Anyone who suggests that by sneering at books and 'literary courses' that the great heritage of human thought ought to be displaced for the reason of teaching the technique of modern industry is pitifully wrong, and if the comparison must be made, more wrong than the man who would sacrifice modern technique to the heritage of ancient thought." So wrote the great black intellectual W. E. B. Du Bois in 1917, angrily reacting to a federal report recommending universal vocational education for black children. William C. Bagley, one of the few white educational experts who rejected progressivism, did so in the name of keeping opportunities from closing in the faces of ordinary children.

But Du Bois and Bagley were fighting for a losing cause. Increasingly, the cause of progressive education spread as the administrators of a school district, worried about not being "up to date," called in educational experts to conduct a survey of how well their children's needs were being met. Invariably, these experts — drawn from a small group of elite schools of education — would recommend some useful reforms (such as improving school safety and children's health, and increasing public funding). But they would also insist on sweeping curricular reform, attacking hidebound "absolutists" who advocated a single academic curriculum for all students and lauding reform-minded "experimentalists."

Progressive education did not sweep the boards all at once. Despite the experts, many teachers went on teaching the subjects they knew with the methods they had always used. In 1920, enrollments in academic subjects remained high. But by then the educational establishment was busy training a new generation of teachers and administrators whose interpretation of Dewey's "child-centered" pedagogy insisted that traditional content-oriented education served only to "accentuate class distinctions and fit an aristocracy for awing and ruling the masses." What many modern critics now call "dumbed-down" schooling, progressives told the nation, was "progressive," "efficient," and "democratic." It was one of the most dubious products of the progressive mind-set — and one of the most durable.

❧ A Theoretical Base for Progressivism

In education as well as many other areas of thought, progressive theories rested on the spirit of scientific naturalism that ruled in American universities. The writings of sociologist Lester Frank Ward and economist Richard T. Ely in the late nineteenth century had opened the way for assaults on the rigid "survival of the fittest" social Darwinism that had equated success with biological fitness. By the beginning of the twentieth century, "reform social Darwinism," the idea that society could be molded by rational efforts, reigned supreme among social scientists.

Perhaps the most influential social scientist of the early twentieth century was Charles A. Beard, who in the 1920s would be president of both the American Historical Association and the American Political Science Association. Beard contributed to the reform spirit in an influential book that examined the motives of the framers of the Constitution, *An Economic Interpretation of the Constitution* (1913). Proposing an interpretation generally rejected (or at least heavily modified) by later generations of historians, Beard argued that the Constitution had been "originated and carried through principally by four groups of personal interests: ... money, public securities, manufactures, and trade and shipping." Beard intended to strip politics of its pretensions and rationalizations and to reveal it as an arena of conflicting group interests. Group tensions were not bad in themselves, Beard believed; by objective study social scientists could reveal the best uses of governmental power in mediating conflicting interests. Progressive historians appealed to Beard's theory to champion revising the Constitution to protect broader interests in the twentieth century.

The idea of firmly set, absolute truth was nowhere more entrenched at the turn of the century than in the legal profession. Basing their judgments on common law, precedent, and conservative interpretations of the Constitution, judges rendered verdicts that weighed heavily in favor of those who controlled society. This conservative legal tradition was challenged in the early twentieth century by Oliver Wendell Holmes, Jr., whose ideas came to be called "Legal Realism." A distinguished Massachusetts supreme court justice and Harvard law professor who was descended from a patrician New England family, Holmes was appointed to the United States Supreme Court by Theodore Roosevelt in 1902. His ideas, often expressed in dissenting opinions, supported a pragmatic interpretation of law summarized in a much-quoted dictum: "The life of the law has not been logic; it has been experience." Legal history, Holmes believed, was "the history of the moral development of the race."

Herbert Croly was the most influential progressive political theorist; his book *The Promise of American Life*, published in 1909, became the charter for Theodore Roosevelt's presidential progressivism (see Chapter 24). Reviving the central political debate of the nation's earliest decades under the Constitution, Croly explored the historic friction between Jefferson's defense of individualism and fear of government and Hamilton's exaltation of the state over the individual. He believed that the future demanded a combination of the two philosophies. The realities of modern life demanded "an increasing amount of centralized action and responsibility," but Croly embraced these Hamiltonian principles as a means of protecting Jeffersonian ideals. Croly's writing epitomized the optimism of the progressive period: the promise of American life, he declared, was bright. He called for national unity, including governmental coordination of the nation's economic life, in order to achieve the greatness that was America's destiny.

A recent Harvard graduate, Walter Lippmann, emerged as another influential political writer who supported Croly's progressive views in two brilliant books, *A Preface to Politics* (1913) and *Drift and Mastery* (1914). Beginning as a socialist, and often a critic of progressive politicians, Lippmann chided the slow "drift" toward a better society that many progressives accepted, calling for "mastery" through a more aggressive "scientific" management of the nation's economy. In 1914, Croly collected an impressive editorial

corps (joined in 1917 by Lippmann) and began publishing a sophisticated magazine, *The New Republic*, which became — and remains — an influential voice for reform ideas.

The Heyday of American Socialism

Orthodox Marxism won few converts in the United States, but some thinkers during the Progressive Era, mostly writers and labor leaders, drew directly on socialist ideology and many others were influenced by the socialist critique of modern society. In 1901 the Socialist Party of America was formed by a coalition of labor leaders and intellectuals (including Lippmann). The party advocated a moderate "cooperative commonwealth" in which the government would control production and distribution for the welfare of all, but would also preserve many of the rights of private property. American socialists rejected violent revolution and advocated change through democratic political methods. In its 1904 platform the party pledged "to rescue the people from the fast increasing and successful assault of capitalism upon the liberty of the individual."

Its moderate aims made the Socialist Party seem little more than the left wing of progressivism. Before World War I several American cities, including Milwaukee, elected socialist mayors. Many of the reforms advocated by socialists were later embraced by moderate reformers, including woman's suffrage, a graduated income tax, and public works projects for the unemployed. At its peak the Socialist Party had about 1,200 officeholders in some 340 municipalities and dominated about one-third of the craft unions in the A.F. of L. While political socialism was most successful in cities, the Socialist Party also had strong organizations in Oklahoma and a number of Upper Midwestern states.

To a remarkable degree the socialist movement of the Progressive Era attracted both immigrants and old-stock American workers and farmers, and it supported an active press. Reform-minded, middle-class people disgusted by political corruption often voted for socialist candidates in the cities, but the party was never able to build a permanent coalition. The national spokesman for socialism was union leader Eugene V. Debs. Mild-mannered but a charismatic orator, Debs ran for president on the Socialist Party ticket in five elections beginning in 1900, receiving 6.5 percent of the total vote in the election of 1912.

The moderate, reform-minded socialism of the Progressive period influenced many social scientists, particularly economists, and progressive politicians borrowed from socialist proposals. The movement also left behind a legacy of publicly owned utilities; by 1915 two-thirds of American cities owned their own water works, and around one-third owned electrical power plants.

In spite of these significant triumphs, most Americans never embraced socialist ideas. The United States alone among the major western nations failed to develop an enduring socialist movement in the early twentieth century. The reason for the failure of leftist ideologies in America is complex. To some extent, economic opportunity and the availability of land hindered the development of class-consciousness. A republican and democratic political culture had taken deep roots in early nineteenth-century America, before European-style socialism and theories of social democracy emerged, making America less receptive to radical alternatives. To a remarkable degree, even as class divisions deepened and class consciousness rose in the country, most Americans, including the swarms of newly arriving immigrants, sought to better their own status and to assure the upward mobility of their children.

Other factors hindered socialist efforts to build on the growing class-consciousness in the early twentieth century. The American two-party political system seriously curtailed the ability of third parties to launch electoral challenges at the national level. Many American intellectuals during the Progressive period, optimistically predicting progress based on the application of scientific principles, dismissed socialist ideas as subjective theories or pseudo-science. The repression of socialist organizations during and after World War I seriously damaged the movement, as did internal intellectual squabbles following the 1917 Bolshevik Revolution in Russia.

Perhaps most important, socialism and more radical leftist ideologies seemed to challenge the core content of the American democratic creed. A large majority of Americans viewed socialism as an inherently un-American, foreign idea. Indeed, the leaders of the American socialist movement were generally either middle-class and well-to-do intellectuals or else working-class immigrants who had embraced socialist ideas in Europe. Americans during the Progressive Era wanted to refurbish the American dream, but not many wanted to abandon it.

❧ The Divided Mind of American Protestantism

The body of American thought most directly challenged by the enormous intellectual changes in the early twentieth century was Protestant theology. Church leaders reacted in two ways. Most liberal churchmen continued to revise Protestant theology in an effort to make the Christian faith acceptable to educated people and to contribute to the formulation of the progressive reform movement. On the other hand, conservative churchmen refused to compromise long-held convictions and rallied the faithful for a counterattack against modernity. In many ways, the deepening division in Protestant thought was symbolic of the growing gulf between the increasingly obscure knowledge of specialists and the "common sense" beliefs of the less educated masses.

American Protestant leaders were slow to grasp the degree to which their thought was being marginalized among intellectuals. There was some uneasiness in the American religious empire about the declining influence of God, but no sense of emergency. Neither did Protestant leaders recognize the depth of internal tensions within their community. Protestant theologians continued to believe that they spoke for America, and, at the popular level, they often did. But increasingly their voice was only one of many seeking to influence the national conscience, and their pronouncements would never again in the twentieth century seriously challenge science as the final arbiter of truth.

Whatever the nation's problems, the leaders of the country's large Protestant denominations were optimistic, progressive, and liberal, thoroughly in tune with the reform spirit of the age. By 1900, theological liberalism (so-called because it stressed freedom from the traditions of the past) was increasingly called modernism, indicating that it aimed at accommodating modern thought. Well entrenched in most of the older Protestant seminaries, this "New Theology" was a dogged

effort to rescue the core truths of Christianity from the erosion of secular thought and to reinterpret the individualistic faith of the nineteenth century into a usable theology in the urbanized, industrialized society of the twentieth century.

The social gospel was liberal Protestantism's contribution to the progressive mind. In many of the nation's most prestigious Protestant pulpits the polemical preaching of the early nineteenth century gave way to the social gospel (see Chapter 19). In the first two decades of the twentieth century, Walter Rauschenbusch fleshed out his social-gospel theology in a series of influential books, including *A Theology for the Social Gospel* (1917). He argued that the kingdom of God would arrive when "humanity organized according to the will of God." Increasingly, Rauschenbusch and other social gospel leaders were attracted to the writings of European Christian Socialists, inspiring them to denounce the growing concentration of wealth in America and the injustices of the modern class system. The number of social gospel theorists

Billy Sunday Evangelizing   Sunday was a mesmerizing speaker. Here — the figure standing next to the chair on the podium, back to the camera — he addresses a large audience in New York City in 1917.

within Protestantism was never large, but they were well placed and articulate. Their voices were influential within the Federal Council of Churches; its "Social Creed" demanded "equal rights and complete justice for all men in all stations of life." The Federal Council was strongly pro-labor and backed the peace movement that gained strength in the pre–World War I years.

If liberal Protestant theologians were slow to recognize that they were being outflanked by a rising tide of secularism, most were somewhat aware that deep fissures were developing within the Protestant community. The differences among Protestants were more than simple disagreements about the intellectual challenges of science; "two types of Christianity" had appeared that were sharply different "in spirit, aim, point of view, comprehensiveness." One was individualistic and emphasized the truths of the nineteenth century; the other was social and imbibed of the new learning. Nearly every major Protestant denomination included people of both types.

By and large, the Protestant Empire avoided open warfare in the first two decades of the twentieth century. Most of the largest denominations tried to accommodate both liberals and conservatives by emphasizing both traditional evangelism and social activism. After a fierce modernist-fundamentalist war broke out in the 1920s (see Chapter 26), a prominent clergyman looked back on the years before World War I as a sort of "Truce of God." While many liberal theologians embraced the social gospel, others were relatively conservative on social issues; Shailer Mathews, a respected University of Chicago modernist, urged social reform as a way to "allay discontent" and "forestall radicalism." On the other hand, conservatives were not without compassion for the urban poor; they founded hundreds of "rescue missions" during the Progressive Era that offered real aid to the destitute, both physical and spiritual. Symbolic of this balance, in 1912 the Federal Council of Churches of Christ added a commission on evangelism to its already active commission on social service.

Protestants were also united in the early twentieth century by their continued fear of the growing presence of the Roman Catholic Church and by strong anti-Semitic prejudices. Most Protestant leaders during the first two decades of the twentieth century joined in the campaigns to curb immigration and to enact prohibition. Many clergymen were active in such organizations as the American Protective Association, whose members pledged never to vote for a Catholic, hire one if a Protestant was available, or join with Catholic workers in a strike.

While the liberal leaders of the mainstream churches were the weightiest spokesmen for American Protantism, popular evangelists were far more visible. Touring revivalists flailed away at evolution, which they deemed the intellectual nucleus of modernism, and warned of the corrupting influence of modern mass culture. They pretty well identified the enemies; modern thought eroded religious influence among the educated and the rage for comfort and pleasure undermined the church's influence on working people. They also clearly spoke the mind of many ordinary people who felt alienated both from the ideas and the lifestyle of the educated and the well-to-do.

At the turn of the century Billy Sunday was the nation's most celebrated evangelist (see Chapter 19).

Originally a roistering, hard-drinking outfielder for the Chicago White Stockings (the early name of the White Sox), Sunday was converted and began his evangelistic career in 1893. Early in the twentieth century Sunday set records for conversions that would stand until the post–World War II ministry of Billy Graham. Sunday's success was based on theatrical preaching and the organizational skills of his wife, Helen Amelia Thompson, better known as "Ma" Sunday. During his heyday, Sunday's crusades were conducted in specially constructed "tabernacles" with sawdust floors. Millions of Americans heard and saw Sunday's performances and around 300,000 "hit the sawdust trail" in the tabernacles to accept Christ. Sunday published "box scores" of the results of his revivals; he calculated that the price of a soul won in his campaigns was around two dollars, making him the most efficient soul-winner in a society that had made efficiency a moral virtue.

While conservative Protestants resisted modern ideas and culture, including the social gospel, many were lower-middle class working people who recognized the growing inequities in American society. A few, most notably William Jennings Bryan, were important political reformers. Most religious bodies, Protestant, Catholic, and Jewish, had a benevolent side — supporting rescue missions, orphanages, and hospitals. Nonetheless, most conservative evangelical Protestants continued to believe that a better world demanded eradicating individual evil. Scorning social gospel concepts, they shared Billy Sunday's opinion that "we've had enough of this godless social service nonsense."

Some serious theologians fought a rearguard action against modern ideas at the turn of the century. Theological conservatism remained particularly strong in the Northern Presbyterian church; a majority of the faculty of Princeton Theological Seminary, led by the brilliant young New Testament scholar J. Gresham Machen, was staunchly orthodox. In 1908 conservative Protestant leaders formed the World's Christian Fundamentalist Association, which between 1910 and 1915 published a twelve-volume series of pamphlets entitled *The Fundamentals*. Later called fundamentalists, the conservatives defended historic evangelical theology and demanded conformity on five basic points: the inerrancy of the Scriptures, the virgin birth of Jesus, the physical resurrection of Jesus, the vicarious atonement, and the physical second coming of Jesus.

Millennialist speculations (theories based on Biblical predictions of an imminent return of Christ to establish an earthly kingdom) flourish during periods of rapid change; during the Progressive Era a premillennial the-ory called dispensationalism was embraced by millions of evangelical Protestants. Dispensationalism had its beginnings in England and was widely popularized in the Scofield Reference Bible published in 1909. Based on a literal reading of prophecy, dispensationalism divided history into seven periods, or "dispensations." The sixth period, "the dispensation of grace," began with Christ's resurrection and would end with his return to establish a millennial kingdom, which most dispensationalists believed was imminent. Dispensational premillennial-ism was pessimistic, predicting a cataclysmic end to society rather than a period of reform. In that respect, the spread of premillennialism was another signal that millions of ordinary Americans never bought into the idyllic Progressive vision of the future.

CONCLUSION: PROGRESS AND PROGRESSIVISM

The Progressive Era was one of those critical periods when a large majority of Americans agreed that the nation was in danger, that equality of opportunity and democracy were threatened by social instability and economic injustice. Yet the air was filled with confi-dence and optimism during these years, partly because economic prosperity and mass production introduced more and more luxuries into people's lives. Among the educated, modern science seemed to have divine pow-ers capable of bringing social improvement. Progress would not be easy to bring about, but it seemed inevi-table. Americans still believed that they lived in a great country that was destined to be greater.

On the other hand, many people were deeply trou-bled about the nation's perplexing pluralism — by the vast cultural and economic chasms that separated cul-tures, sections, faiths, races, sexes, and classes. Hundreds of voluntary associations were signposts of subgroups that organized people's lives amid society's disorder. Many of the debates of the period pitted newly-empow-ered groups, such as professional associations and la-bor unions, against older elites.

The intellectual transition of the Progressive Era was as profound as its economic and social changes. The modern, secular university took its place at the center of American thought, furnishing a scientific rationale for ideas of progress and national destiny. Progressive political rhetoric was laced with the language of Prot-estant morality, and traditional Christian ideas perme-ated the thought of ordinary people, but increasingly the judgment of science served as the ultimate author-ity for change

The variety and ambiguity of the period has led some recent historians to argue that the phrase *Pro-gressive movement* serves no useful purpose — there was no movement, only scores of shifting causes that fashioned distinctive coalitions. It is possible, however, to talk of the Progressive Era, a period when diverse interest groups emerged that permanently changed American society. For all its diversity, common themes weave through the period. It was a time when every personal and national act required public justification before God and corroborating evidence from experts. Sometimes this moralistic temper led to efforts that protected the weakest from the strong; at other times it justified efforts to impose the moral beliefs of the ma-jority on the entire nation.

Older special interests did not collapse easily before the assaults of reformers during the Progressive Era. Conservatives struggled to retain control of the federal, state, and local governments of the country. But, above all, progressives were skilled political reformers, and it was in the nation's political arenas that they wrought great changes in American society.

SUGGESTED READING

John Milton Cooper, Jr., *Pivotal Decades* (1990). A lucid survey of the first two decades of the twentieth century that offers a balanced interpretation of progressivism.

Richard Hofstadter, *The Age of Reform: From Bryan to FDR* (1958). A book that long dominated interpretations of the era, Hofstadter saw progressivism as a reform instigated by a middle-class elite concerned about its loss of status.

Gabriel Kolko, *The Triumph of Conservatism: A Re-Interpretation of American History, 1900-1916* (1963). An interpretation of the period that sees progressivism as a strategy to protect business interests.

Arthur S. Link and Richard L. McCormick, *Progressivism* (1983). A discussion of the varied interpretations of progressivism by historians.

Martin E. Marty, *The Irony of It All: 1893-1919* (1986). A sweeping survey of American religion at the beginning of the twentieth century.

Sidney M. Milkis and Jerome M. Mileur, eds., *Progressivism and the New Democracy* (1999). A collection of essays by leading scholars surveying current interpretations of progressivism.

Diane Ravitch, *Left Back: A Century of Failed School Reforms* (2000). A blistering attack on the progressive legacy in twentieth-century American education.

SUGGESTIONS FOR FURTHER READING

Aaron I. Abell, *American Catholicism and Social Action: A Search for Social Justice, 1865-1950* (1963).

Karen J. Blair, *The Clubwoman as Feminist: True Womanhood Redefined, 1880-1914* (1980).

Dorothy M. Brown and Elizabeth McKeown, *The Poor Belong to Us: Catholic Charities and American Welfare* (1997).

John W. Chambers II, *The Tyranny of Change: America in the Progressive Era, 1900-1917* (1980).

Elizabeth L. Clapp, *Mothers of All Children: Women Reformers and the Rise of Juvenile Courts in Progressive-Era America* (1998).

Willard B. Gatewood, *Aristocrats of Color: The Black Elite, 1880-1920* (1990).

James R. Goff, *Fields White unto Harvest: Charles G. Parham and the Missionary Origins of Pentecostalism* (1988).

Donald K. Goffell, *The Age of Social Responsibility: The Social Gospel in the Progressive Era, 1900-1920* (1988).

Lynn D. Gordon, *Gender and Higher Education in the Progressive Era* (1990).

Dewey W. Grantham, *Southern Progressivism: The Reconciliation of Progress and Tradition* (1983).

William R. Hutchison, *The Modernist Impulse in American Protestantism* (1976).

Morton Keller, *Regulating a New Society: Public Policy and Social Change in America, 1900-1933* (1994).

T. Jackson Lears, *No Place of Grace: Antimodernism and the Transformation of American Culture, 1880-1920* (1981).

David Levering Lewis, *W. E. B. Du Bois: A Biography of a Race* (1994).

Michael E. McGerr, *The Decline of Popular Politics: The American North, 1865-1928* (1986).

Nell L. Painter, *Standing at Armageddon* (1987).

Marc Lee Raphael, *Profiles in American Judaism: The Reform, Conservative, Orthodox, and Reconstructionist Traditions in Historical Perspective* (1984).

William Seraile, *Fire in His Heart: Bishop Benjamin Tucker Tanner and the A.M.E. Church* (1998).

Milton C. Sernett, *Bound for the Promised Land: African American Religions and the Great Migration* (1997).

Edward Stettner, *Shaping Modern Liberalism: Herbert Croly and Progressive Thought* (1993).

24 Progressivism in American Politics, 1901 to World War I

THE ANXIETIES CAUSED by rapid social and economic change at the turn of the century defined the Progressive Era as a time of causes and crusades. The reform sentiment of the period took on added significance because most progressives looked to government to restore the American dream, and they relished political combat. The governmental reforms of the Gilded Age, including civil service reform and the growing professionalization of the Washington bureaucracy, had set the stage for the progressive movement, and the election of 1896 had provided an agenda for the progressive presidents of the early twentieth century — Theodore Roosevelt, William Howard Taft, and Woodrow Wilson. Progressives backed a broad array of social, economic, and political reforms; no one person was likely to embrace all of them. The federal government enacted the era's most far-reaching legislation, but progressives won their first political successes at the local and state levels.

Nationally, the Progressive Era witnessed a renaissance of presidential leadership, conspicuously lacking in the Gilded Age. Roosevelt and Wilson are generally ranked among the nation's greatest chief executives, and Taft was a competent (if politically clumsy) and somewhat underrated president. Surrounding these presidents were a colorful and vigorous cast of political characters whose thought and actions helped shape modern America.

While all progressives agreed that reforms were needed, Roosevelt and Wilson, the Republican and Democratic leaders of presidential progressivism, appeared to have deep-seated philosophical disagreements about the proper path to progress. In practice, however, both Republican and Democratic administrations enlarged the role of the federal government in regulating the nation's economy as a means of restoring equality of opportunity. Loyalty to the American democratic tradition, coupled with a determination to restore equality of opportunity, outweighed fears of government regulation in the minds of almost all progressives. The expanding power of the federal government and the augmentation of the presidency were the chief legacies of political progressivism, and these became dominant themes in twentieth-century American domestic history.

National progressivism crested in the election of 1912, an exciting campaign that pitted all three of the era's presidents against each other and for good measure added a vigorous challenge from the Socialist party. World War I brought domestic reform to an end in 1917, but, if we can refrain from imposing postwar moods on earlier times, the Progressive Era was a time of lofty aspirations and notable accomplishments.

THE CORE OF THE PROGRESSIVE AGENDA

Although certain common threads ran through progressive thought — a confidence in progress and the ability of human beings to change society for the better, a belief in a moral social and economic order, and a nostalgia for the individualism and egalitarianism of America's agrarian past — the specific causes backed by progressive reformers varied, as did their solutions. Some reforms received nearly universal support and were widely debated political issues during the Progressive Era; others failed to attract the kind of coalition necessary to demand serious political consideration.

Two complexes of individuals and organizations were centers of lobbying influence — one primarily secular, the other religious. The urban social justice movement, led by social scientists, fostered crusades for political efficiency and honesty, the acceptance of cultural pluralism, and fairness in providing opportunity for the poor. Protestant churches, equally disturbed by the disarray of American society, urged government restrictions on immorality as a means of restoring order.

❧ The Urban Social Justice Movement

In 1900 crusading journalist Jacob Riis observed that the worst of New York City's slums were gone, replaced by parks, playgrounds, and improved housing. Late nineteenth-century urban reform had improved many neighborhoods. But despite this progress, in most cities in 1900 slums remained filthy, unhealthy, and dangerous places to live.

The growth of cities continued at a rapid pace in the first two decades of the century, highlighted by the census report in 1920 that, for the first time, more than 50 percent of the population lived in towns with populations of more than 2,500. That landmark of the transition to an urban society had probably been reached around 1914 and, excluding the still overwhelmingly rural South, had occurred early in the twentieth century. Some cities grew to enormous size; the population of New York City reached 5.6 million by 1920, Chicago 2.7 million, and Philadelphia 1.8 million. About half of the nation's urban dwellers lived in cities with a population of 100,000 or more.

The plight of the urban poor pricked the consciences of some Americans and stirred fears among others. The wealthy, regarded by many reformers as the chief instigators of the nation's social ills, were not completely unmoved by the suffering of the poor and many engaged in philanthropic giving on an unprecedented scale. Businessmen provided the funds for thousands of local charities. Symbolizing the progressive drive for efficiency, Andrew Carnegie and John D. Rockefeller established foundations to coordinate their philanthropy. Rockefeller's first foundation, established in 1902, funded mostly education projects, as did a foundation begun by Carnegie in 1905. The giant Rockefeller Foundation, begun in 1913, funded hundreds of millions of dollars in grants for medical research and education. Scores of other wealthy individuals and families established smaller foundations. While there is some truth to the critical judgment that this outpouring of philanthropy from the captains of American industry was sometimes a self-serving effort to improve businessmen's public image, forestall radical discontent, and exercise power in new spheres, it was also an expression of consciences whetted by the Protestant ethic.

The expansion of private giving in the early twentieth century funded a variety of religious and secular relief agencies. For instance, by 1900 the Salvation Army, an evangelical movement organized along quasi-military lines that only recently had come to the United States

Public Playground in New York City, ca. 1900 Providing playgrounds where working- and middle-class urban children could get healthy exercise and fresh air was the goal of one typical Progressive campaign at the turn of the twentieth century. Notice the way in which these children are dressed for school — all the boys in knickers, for example.

from England, was supporting more than 20,000 workers to dispense relief (as well as Christian teaching) to the urban poor. Perhaps the most important by-product of this proliferation of charitable agencies was the fact that they employed a new genre of specialists, social workers and statisticians, who collected data used to rally public support for many progressive causes.

Settlement houses continued to be important institutional centers of the Protestant social justice movement. The settlement house movement blossomed in the first two decades of the century, their numbers growing from around 100 in 1900 to more than 400 by 1920. Chicago's Hull House (1889) remained the most influential model, and its founder, Jane Addams, one of the most respected voices in the social justice movement. Settlement house workers found that they could not transform their own neighborhoods without becoming involved in state and local politics; the sweep of issues they addressed included child and women's labor, juvenile delinquency, penal procedures, poverty, the problems of the foreign born, the exploitation of women, public education, and

the plight of African Americans. A remarkable number of progressive politicians and social activists lived for a time in a settlement house.

Settlement houses were only one part of the network of institutions that contributed to the spirit of urban reform. Countless local civic federations, municipal leagues, women's organizations, and government research bureaus provided occasions for social scientists and business leaders to discuss ways to reform governance in the cities. They frequently drafted plans that made city administrations operate more honestly and efficiently.

The social justice movement gained many political victories during the Progressive Era. Much of the legislation passed by local and state governments was drafted by urban activists. But the movement also con-

Child Labor, 1910

One of the many causes Jane Addams championed as a result of her experiences at Hull House was the establishment of child labor laws.

Our very first Christmas at Hull-House, when we as yet knew nothing of child labor, a number of little girls refused the candy which was offered them as part of the Christmas good cheer, saying simply that they "worked in a candy factory and could not bear the sight of it." We discovered that for six weeks they had worked from seven in the morning until nine at night, and they were exhausted as well as satiated. The sharp consciousness of stern economic conditions was thus thrust upon us in the midst of the season of good will.

During the same winter three boys from a Hull-House club were injured at one machine in a neighboring factory for lack of a guard which would have cost but a few dollars. When the injury of one of these boys resulted in his death, we felt quite sure that the owners of the factory would share our horror and remorse, and that they would do everything possible to prevent the recurrence of such a tragedy. To our surprise they did nothing whatever, and I made my first acquaintance then with those pathetic documents signed by the parents of working children, that they will make no claim for damages resulting from "carelessness."

The visits we made in the neighborhood constantly discovered women sewing upon sweatshop work, and often they were assisted by incredibly small children. I remember a little girl of four who pulled out basting threads hour after hour, sitting on a stool at the feet of her Bohemian mother, a little bunch of human misery. But even for that there was no legal redress, for the only child-labor law in Illinois, with any provision for enforcement, had been secured by the coal miners' unions, and was confined to children employed in mines.

---

tributed several broader ideas to the twentieth-century American reform mentality. First, urban reformers viewed cities as interesting and exciting places to live, shunning the nostalgia for things rural and simple that pervaded some progressive thought. Some urban progressives also embraced cultural diversity, insisting that it posed no threat to American democracy, and they encouraged immigrants to preserve their ethnic heritage. Finally, in an age when most whites assumed the inferiority of blacks, a few urban reformers were among the first to challenge racist notions. Three white settlement workers, Mary White Ovington, William English Walling, and Henry Moskowitz, initiated the organizing of the National Association for the Advancement of Colored People (NAACP) in 1909.

❧ Saving the WASP Empire

While many progressive reformers attacked social evils such as poverty and child labor, others believed that the breakdown of order in American society was caused by individual immorality, a failure of basic values. They believed that the rise of secular ideas and mass consumerism had driven the Protestant faith and traditional values from the center of the American conscience; the result was rampant greed and self-indulgence. Thus, believing themselves to be reformers as surely as secular advocates of social justice, many middle-class Christians backed campaigns to coerce moral conduct.

American Protestant churches united almost as one behind a bevy of moral reform movements in the early twentieth century. The growing progressive confidence in efficiency fueled the continued growth of organizations such as missionary societies and the Sunday School Union. Churchmen backed a variety of moral reform crusades in cities, including efforts to censor the new movie industry and campaigns to eradicate the nation's "social evil," prostitution. John D. Rockefeller, Sr., an active Baptist, financed a series of studies of vice and venereal disease, and numerous localities passed laws against prostitution. In 1910 Congress enacted the Mann Act making it illegal to transport a woman across state lines for loosely defined "immoral purposes."

The cause that most unified Protestants at the turn of the century was prohibition, a reform backed by evangelicals since the 1830s. Some saw prohibition as a means of reforming individuals, and others as a broader reform that would transform society, but, whatever their motives, the cause of prohibition united Protestant America as it had rarely been in the past. The intensity of the crusade sapped much of the energy of the nation's Protestant churches; the unity it brought among the churches obscured the impending division within the Protestant Empire.

A variety of motives led progressives to support laws prohibiting the sale and consumption of alcohol, and thus bring to a successful conclusion a crusade that had gained strength throughout the last half of the nineteenth century. The Protestant doctrine of moral perfectionism, anti-Catholic prejudices, and a genuine desire to protect families and improve the health and safety of the nation all surfaced in prohibitionist rhetoric. Prohibition could easily be viewed as an effort to transform society and thus a means of progress. The Women's Christian Temperance Union (WCTU) and the Anti-Saloon League, working in combination with thousands of local Protestant churches, exerted enormous pressure at every level of American politics. Critics of the movement reacted to the narrowest and most repressive side of prohibition, seeing it as an attempt to impose the moral standards of evangelical Protestants on the rest of the nation. Despite the opposition of each of the presidents during the Progressive Era, by 1916, nineteen states and hundreds of local communities had enacted prohibition laws.

Efforts to restrict immigration drew on many of the beliefs that supported the prohibition movement. Many Protestants believed that immigration had undermined public and private morality in the cities. While some progressives argued that liberal immigration policies were symbolic of the American dream, all acknowledged that the migration of millions of non-English-speaking people created social problems. Further, the American Federation of Labor (A.F. of L.) lobbied strongly to stop the flow of cheap labor into the country.

The movement to restrict immigration was supported by some progressive social scientists, for varied reasons. A presidential commission in 1911 strongly urged restrictions, partly because of the assumed "moral degeneracy" of the new immigrants. The racist assumptions underlying immigration reform were blatantly expressed in the writings of Madison Grant, a sophisticated New Yorker who gained a reputation as a progressive because of his support for the conservation movement. In *The Passing of the Great Race* (1916), Grant wrote a spurious version of world history

The Salvation Army   During the Christmas season of 1906, a well-dressed woman drops a contribution into a Salvation Army kettle at West Thirteenth Street and Seventh Avenue in New York. "The Salvation Army. Free Christmas Dinner to 25,000 Poor of This City. 'Keep the Pot Boiling,'" reads the sign.

that attributed all cultural advances to "Nordics" and arranged other ethnic groups in a descending order of worth. Grant mourned the "mongrelization" of the early American racial stock (ostensibly Nordic) and claimed that "racial suicide" could be averted only by restricting immigration.

In the early twentieth century environmental or genetic explanations seriously challenged older religious

Eugenics Display   Popularizers of the pseudoscience of eugenics would exhibit flashing-light displays like this one at state fairs to reach a broad rural audience, sometimes even sponsoring contests to determine which families were the most genetically fit.

understandings of human motivations, giving support to various racist ideologies. The most ominous outgrowth of racist ideas in the early twentieth century was the spread of eugenics, a pseudo-science that contended that desirable human characteristics were spread unevenly through the races and that society could be improved through controlled reproduction. In 1904 the Center for the Study of Eugenics was founded with support from the Carnegie Foundation. Presided over by Charles B. Davenport, a well-known zoologist who was also a racist and proponent of immigration restriction, the center gave a degree of scientific legitimacy to eugenics. While eugenics never gained widespread support as a tool for improving society, it appealed to some progressives, including Theodore Roosevelt, and was the basis in some states for legislation permitting the sterilization of certain criminals and the insane

LOCAL AND STATE POLITICAL REFORM

The social justice movement gave powerful impetus to reform at the local and state levels. Led by the new professional classes of social workers and social scientists, social justice reformers addressed a wide range of urban issues, ranging from slum housing to the working conditions of women and children. These profes-

sionals furnished philosophical authority for government action and greatly enhanced their own stature and visibility in the process.

Progressives also embraced the cause of honesty and efficiency in government, a concern that led to a variety of reforms of state and local governments, as well as campaigns to eliminate electoral corruption. Some progressives championed the expansion of political democracy, leading to such changes in the electoral process as the direct election of U.S. senators in 1913. On the other hand, the progressive emphasis on efficiency and honesty in government had the undemocratic effect of reducing the electorate, a development that many middle-class reformers welcomed.

State and local governments also sought to bring order to the unregulated business environment. During the Progressive Era, state and local governments grew larger and more efficient in an effort both to facilitate business growth and to regulate it. State regulation was not new in 1900, but the myriad of experiments launched by local and state governments in the first two decades of the twentieth century gave a sense of permanence to the concept. At the same time, it became increasingly clear that the sprawling growth of large corporations made it impossible for state and local governments to regulate them.

❧ Reorganizing American Cities

American cities, widely seen in 1900 as hotbeds of political corruption and graft, attracted much attention from the muckrakers. When the mummy of Rameses II went on display in New York City in 1907, one reporter sardonically predicted that the pharaoh would vote in the next election. Fanning nativist prejudices, many old-stock Americans blamed urban political corruption on immigrants, but in reality urban political corruption had little to do with the percentage of foreign-born population; it spread rather evenly through American cities of various size and ethnic makeup.

Political corruption was only one urban problem that stirred progressives. Cities were also magnets of crime and vice, a fact that reinforced Protestant beliefs about the inherent immorality of urban life and added momentum to such moral campaigns as prohibition. The burgeoning cities also housed the generation of new rich whose gaudy materialism and ostentation alarmed progressives as much as did crime and political corruption.

Urban political reform was well under way at the turn of the century, but the progressive movement greatly accelerated feelings of civic responsibility and demands for efficient local government. A group of reform mayors elected around the turn of the century, including Thomas L. Johnson in Cleveland, Samuel E. "Golden Rule" Jones in Toledo, and James D. Phelan in San Francisco, had successfully attacked corrupt machines and were providing efficient municipal services. Johnson and other urban reformers favored public ownership of such services as mass transportation, water, and power. These urban ventures in what reformers approvingly called "gas and water socialism," some of them initiated by socialist politicians, encouraged many Americans to accept the principle of governmental regulation.

Some of the progressive urban reforms had an undemocratic effect, and, indeed, an undemocratic intent; they were designed to transfer power into the hands of experts who would presumably act rationally and honestly. In 1900 Galveston, Texas, adopted a city-commission form of government, the most widely embraced urban political reform of the Progressive Era. After a hurricane and tidal wave had devastated the city, the Texas state legislature appointed a five-member commission to govern the city. Each commissioner assumed responsibility for a single department of government, greatly reducing the possibility of corruption. The Galveston experiment combined the progressive goal of eliminating corruption with the business community's interest in promoting governmental efficiency. So successful did this innovation appear that by 1915 more than four hundred other cities had adopted it. In a further search for efficiency, in 1908 the commissioners of Staunton, Virginia, hired a city manager. By 1923 more than three hundred cities were employing trained professionals as city managers to administer the routine operations of urban government.

❧ Progressivism in the States

State governments at the turn of the century were often as corrupt and inefficient as those of cities. One newspaper regularly labeled the Pennsylvania legislature the "larcenylature"; another reported that while Con-

The Galveston Hurricane   Measured by deaths and property damage, the hurricane that leveled Galveston, Texas, in 1900 was one of the worst natural disasters in American history — probably a Level 5 storm (the highest measure on the scale) that struck without warning, for scientific weather forecasting was only in its infancy. In the wake of the storm, Galveston adopted a new city-manager form of government, widely seen as a more "efficient" and less corrupt way to administer cities.

gress might open with 100 bills, the Missouri legislature opened with the "introduction of $1,000 bills." Powerful senators, often aligned with and supported by local business interests, controlled state political machines. State legislators, who elected senators, were easily corrupted by wealthy office seekers. "Some people are born rich," wrote a reporter in Tacoma, Washington, in 1900, "while others have the good fortune to engage in a Montana senatorial contest."

The most important progressive victory at the state level came in 1900 when Robert M. La Follette defeated the Wisconsin political machine to win the governorship. By the time La Follette finished three terms in 1906, Wisconsin had enacted a system of business taxation and regulation and social services that led Theodore Roosevelt to call the state "the laboratory of democracy." Elected to the first of three terms in the Senate in 1906, La Follette was the nation's most relentless advocate of reform until his death in 1925.

La Follette's success in Wisconsin became a model for other progressive victories, particularly in the Midwest and the West. A number of governors, most notably Albert Cummins of Iowa and Hiram Johnson of California, later joined La Follette in the Senate to form

Battling Bob La Follette   With his mighty shock of pompadour hair, his stern and humorless rectitude, and his never-ending crusade against corrupt big-business interests, Governor (and later Senator) Robert La Follette was the archetypal Progressive of the early twentieth century. As this caricature shows, he was seen as the architect of Wisconsin as "the model state" and "the laboratory of democracy."

James K. Vardaman in Mississippi, Hoke Smith in Georgia, and Benjamin Tillman in South Carolina. These new-breed southern governors were classical demagogues, fanning racial intolerance and supporting the disfranchisement of blacks (similarly, West Coast progressives often catered to anti-Asian bigotry), but they also sponsored reforms. Most were middle-class supporters of the idea of the New South; they were generally backed by the region's educators, editors, and professional classes. Mississippi became the first state to establish a primary system, albeit for whites only, and several southern states passed laws regulating railroads and other powerful businesses.

❧ Electoral Reform — Democratic and Undemocratic

Calls for the democratization of politics led to the institution of statewide primaries in thirteen states and the legalization of women's suffrage in nine states by 1912. In addition, twenty western states enacted initiative laws, allowing voters to force legislatures to vote on specific legislation; a similar number provided for legislation by popular referendum; and eleven states adopted a recall provision that allowed voters to force a public official to stand for reelection before his term had ended. Progressives also targeted the Senate, known as the "millionaire's club," for reform. Senate elections were notoriously corrupt — a late nineteenth-century aphorism asserted that "it is harder for a poor man to enter the United States Senate than for a rich man to enter Heaven." By 1910 over half of the states required state legislators to cast their votes for Senate candidates who had won popular primary elections (known as the "Oregon system"). The Senate had successfully beaten back efforts to mandate direct elections on several occasions since the idea was first introduced in 1826, but in 1912 a Senate investigation into charges or bribery and corruption in the election of Illinois Senator William Lorimer pressured Congress into submitting to the states a constitutional amendment revising the method of selecting senators. Riding

a progressive core in that formidable bastion of conservatism. Western progressive politicians tapped into the popular prejudices that had fostered populism — clashing economic interests of farmers and industrial wealth, and a long-standing western distrust of the intelligentsia. Progressivism did less well in the states of the East, although New York elected reformer Charles Evans Hughes as governor in 1906 and Woodrow Wilson won in New Jersey in 1910. The relative failure of political progressivism in the eastern states highlighted the inability of the primarily Protestant, middle-class reform movement to act in common cause with the labor movement or with newly arrived Roman Catholic immigrants, who often supported urban political machines.

At the turn of the century the South witnessed a political revolt similar to that in the West. As in the West, southern conservative political regimes were challenged by popular reform governors — Jeff Davis in Arkansas,

a wave of state support for reform, the Seventeenth Amendment was ratified in 1913.

Although these political innovations were motivated by a kind of democratic zeal, the Progressive Era was not a time of unbridled confidence in the masses nor of expanding popular participation in politics. On the contrary, the rise of powerful interest groups with specific political agendas destroyed the broad party alliances of the nineteenth century that had politicized immigrants, the poor, and the uneducated and had raised voter turnouts to record heights. Whereas nineteenth-century urban political machines had been adept at rallying popular support, reformers' attacks on corruption often meant reductions in voting totals and the effective disfranchisement of powerless urban groups.

The first two decades of the twentieth century mark the beginning of a long period of declining voter participation that has been labeled by political scientists "an era of electoral demobilization." In the presidential elections of 1896 and 1900 the average voter participation was 83.8 percent; in the presidential elections from 1900 to 1916 the average declined to 75.4 percent. Partly, this decline reflected the completion of black disfranchisement in the South; in these same elections voter participation in the South declined from 49.9 percent to 32.4 percent and black voting in presidential elections fell to less than 2 percent. Percentage declines were smaller elsewhere, but in every section of the nation voter participation steadily dropped during the Progressive Era.

There is no simple explanation for the decline in voting during the Progressive Era, a trend that became even more exaggerated in the 1920s and has continued almost unbroken to today (in 2000, barely half the eligible voters participated). Partly, it revealed a slow breakdown in the cohesion of the ethnic-religious enclaves in urban slums: the first generation of Americans who were descendants of immigrant parents were both less willing to support political machines and less likely to vote. Voter turnout also declined because the Republican victories in 1896 and 1900 had so rearranged party alignments that many districts that had been very evenly divided in the late nineteenth century became safe Republican districts — and wherever one party had a safe majority, voter turnout declined.

Dwindling voter participation also owed something to the progressives' desire to purge the electorate of what they considered its most unfit elements. Even the disfranchisement of blacks in the South fit the progressive ideological pattern. In the cities, the undesir-

able voters were, in the words of Theodore Roosevelt, "the lower grades of the foreign population." In the late nineteenth and early twentieth centuries the Republican Party successfully labeled the Democrats the party of economic radicalism, the "saloon," and depression. Republican progressive reformers who set out to eradicate political corruption understood quite well that most of the "undesirable" voters were foreign-born and Democratic. Gradually, they diminished the ability of urban political bosses to deliver large blocs of Democratic votes.

❧ States Provide Models for Progressive Legislation

Although much progressive reform at the local and state levels focused on increasing efficiency or democracy in government, hundreds of social and economic reforms were also enacted. State governments, in particular, became (in La Follette's phrase) "laboratories for reform," establishing hundreds of regulatory commissions and planning agencies that became models for programs later introduced by the federal government. The multiplication of specialized agencies tied progressive politics firmly to university-trained intellectuals and advocates of "scientific" reform.

La Follette's Wisconsin was the model Progressive state. In a step imitated by other progressives elsewhere, La Follette called on experts at the state university to draft reform legislation, and John R. Commons, a noted Christian economist at the University of Wisconsin, took a particularly important role in constructing the Wisconsin model. By 1915 Wisconsin not only had passed a direct primary law but also raised taxes on railroads and other corporations, established a railroad regulatory commission, enacted a law controlling lobbying, inaugurated a state civil service system, and adopted a state income tax.

Progressive states established scores of regulatory commissions in an effort to control railroads and other monopolies. Southern progressives led the way in establishing powerful elected commissions: Georgia became the first state to install a rail commission in 1879. By 1914, state railroad regulations had become so complex and irregular that company executives backed federal regulation to escape the harassment of state commissions. Progressive states also established regulatory commissions in other public service industries and began supervision of insurance and investment companies.

The scope of progressive concerns was sufficiently

wide to give hope to diverse advocacy groups. Progressive state legislatures enacted a variety of women's and child labor laws. By 1914 every state had established a minimum age limit for child labor, ranging from fourteen to sixteen. In 1903 Oregon mandated a ten-hour workday for women, and by 1917 thirty-nine states had passed similar laws. Progressive states also passed more general labor legislation, setting maximum hour and minimum wage standards in certain industries, requiring safety standards, and forcing employers to furnish accident insurance. Maryland passed a workmen's compensation law in 1902; by 1920, all but six states had similar legislation.

By the outbreak of World War I, progressive state legislatures had transformed the United States into one of the most highly regulated nations in the world. Progressive legislation at the state level anticipated virtually every subsequent program initiated at the national level. Nonetheless, progressive regulations at the local and state level varied widely from place to place, and sometimes were contradictory. The problems spawned by industrialization and urbanization were not local or regional, they were national, and it became increasingly clear that only the federal government could address them successfully. Even American businessmen, threatened by the crazy quilt of state and local regulations, increasingly appealed to the federal government for arbitration.

THEODORE ROOSEVELT AND THE SELLING OF NATIONAL PROGRESSIVISM

To a large degree, the injection of progressivism into national politics coincided with the charismatic leadership of Theodore Roosevelt. Dynamic and engagingly eccentric, Roosevelt became one of the most popular public leaders in American history; he also was one of the country's shrewdest practical politicians. Roosevelt sometimes posed as an extremist, partly as a ploy to maneuver conservatives into action, but more often and more accurately he pictured himself as a conservative trying to save the American way of life. Nonetheless, the changes begun during Roosevelt's presidency transferred primary responsibility for the oversight of the nation to the federal government, continuing the transformation of the American political system into its twentieth-century form and creating the activist, media-savvy modern American presidency.

❧ *Theodore Roosevelt Takes Center Stage*

On September 6, 1901, while making a speech in Buffalo, President William McKinley was shot by an anarchist. His death eight days later brought to the presidency forty-two-year-old Vice President Theodore Roosevelt, the youngest man in American history to hold the office. Roosevelt would be an electric presence in American politics for more than a decade.

Theodore Roosevelt was a child of the American elite: of New York Dutch ancestry that ran back to colonial times, Roosevelt had been born to an "old money" family, was educated at Harvard, traveled widely, and developed deep intellectual interests. Sickly as a boy, Roosevelt's iron will enabled him to overcome his physical problems through exercise and adherence to "the strenuous life," a regimen reminiscent of Puritan morality. He loved hunting, hiking, and swimming, but his interest in nature, like everything in his life, had a strong intellectual side. Roosevelt was insatiably curious; as a child he spent countless hours collecting natural specimens and reading Darwin. When he entered Harvard, he was already a skilled naturalist, and throughout his life his reading of Darwin informed his social and political outlook as well as his thinking about science. The first of ten books written by Roosevelt, a history of naval engagements in the War of 1812, was published two years after he graduated from Harvard in 1880. An extremely rapid reader, Roosevelt could converse on nearly any subject, spoke three foreign languages, and could read four others. Probably no other presidents except Thomas Jefferson and James Madison have been so broadly and deeply learned.

Early in life Roosevelt decided to seek a political career. Because this would involve contending in the public arena with corrupt and uncouth urban bosses, his was an uncommon choice for young men of his social class during the Gilded Age, although not for a Roosevelt. In 1882, he was elected to the New York State Assembly. Two years later, Roosevelt's first wife died giving birth to their daughter, Alice. To recover psychologically from this blow, he spent the next two years on a ranch in Dakota Territory that he had purchased the year before. Reinvigorated by two years of ranching, hunting, and serving as a deputy sheriff in the Badlands, he returned to New York City and ran unsuccessfully for mayor. Then he toured Europe, married Edith Carow, and began rearing a large family at his Sagamore Hill home on Oyster Bay, Long Island. Appointed to the Civil Service Commission by Benjamin Harrison in 1889, he established himself as a member of the reforming group within the Republican Party.

Having built a reputation as a loyal party man, in 1895 Roosevelt was appointed police commissioner of New York City. In that role he gained a reputation as a champion of reform and also revealed a talent for winning the attention and favor of the press. Appointed assistant secretary of the Navy by McKinley in 1897, he became, in Mark Twain's words, the "chief promoter of a war with Spain." When war erupted, Roosevelt enlisted and recruited a cavalry battalion of former football players, cowboys, professional gamblers, and polo players, all of them devoted to him. These "Rough Riders'" diversity symbolized Roosevelt's personal, visceral understanding of America's growing pluralism. The highly publicized (and considerably overstated) participation of the Rough Riders in the charge up San Juan Hill (actually Kettle Hill) in Cuba vaulted Roosevelt into the national limelight.

Coming home triumphantly from Cuba in September 1898, Roosevelt was eager to test state politics. With some misgivings, New York political boss Senator Thomas C. Platt backed Roosevelt's nomination as the Republican candidate for governor. Elected as a war hero, Roosevelt showed considerable political skill in establishing a working alliance with the party machine in the state. Nonetheless, Platt remained uneasy about the energetic Roosevelt and pressed party leaders to select him as McKinley's vice-presidential running mate in 1900, which would remove him from state politics and relegate him to an office that at the time meant political oblivion. Roosevelt had reservations about giving up his governorship to accept such a dubious honor, but he proved to be a "bully" candidate, drawing more press attention than either McKinley or William Jennings Bryan, who again headed the Democratic ticket. While McKinley remained an aloof campaigner, Roosevelt delivered 673 speeches in 567 cities

TR Speaks The new President Roosevelt regales his audience from a tabletop in this photograph.

and towns in 24 states. "When the campaign is over," wrote a Philadelphia reporter, "Mr. Roosevelt will have to train down to the Vice-Presidency."

When President McKinley died in 1901, Senator Mark Hanna expressed the shock of many of the Republican leaders who had opposed Roosevelt's nomination: "Now look! That damned cowboy is President of the United States." Party bosses had good reason to worry about Theodore Roosevelt's accession to the presidency. Although he was deeply committed to an orderly world and often was conservative in action, the new president's rhetoric was heavy with moral pronouncements. Equally unsettling to the Republican power structure was Roosevelt's energy and impulsiveness. "TR" — as newspaper headlines and political cartoonists immediately began calling him (he hated "Teddy") — loved to give speeches bristling with superlatives, and his vocabulary provided colorful descriptions of his adversaries that lesser men could only envy. Historian Henry Adams, in perhaps the most quoted contemporary description, called Roosevelt "pure act"; a reporter suggested that a new verb should be added to the English language, "to Roosevelt." While president, Roosevelt championed an amazing variety of causes, including an ill-fated attempt to simplify spelling that had been endorsed by the National Education Association. He set off a national craze for jujitsu when he brought a Japanese instructor to the White House to give him lessons in that martial art. His energy and flair endeared him to the public and to the press. "Nothing strains the credulity of the American people more," reported the *Washington Post,* "than a news dispatch reading: 'the President spent a very quiet day.'" At the time of his death in 1919, one of Roosevelt's former associates on the New York Police force spoke for millions of people: "It was not only that he was a great man, but, oh, there was such fun in being led by him."

For Roosevelt, life had more to do with responsibility than with fun. His family's patrician and Dutch Reformed heritage imbued him with a deep sense of duty. Privileged people such as himself, he was convinced, had a special obligation to do their duty with a strong will and a cool head. "If a man has the right stuff in him," he once observed, "his will grows stronger and stronger with each exercise of it." Roosevelt displayed the will and vitality that most Americans believed epitomized the national character. The White House came alive as the home of the Roosevelt family. Alice, the oldest of the six children, was a high-spirited and sharp-tongued young woman immortalized in the song "My Alice Blue Gown." The Roosevelt boys kept ponies and played baseball on the White House lawn. Roosevelt himself was far more accessible and quotable than any of his presidential predecessors. In effect, Roosevelt turned the presidency into what it has remained — an office best filled by someone able to become a celebrity.

Roosevelt's actions in his early months in office — announcing that he would carry out McKinley's programs and retain McKinley's cabinet — calmed conservative worries. His cautious early approach was partly dictated by his desire to be elected president in his own right in 1904, but it also showed his skill in the art of political compromise. He was fascinated by the mechanism of government, by the give-and-take required for political success in America's pluralistic society. Throughout his career Roosevelt shrewdly balanced moral absolutes and a calculated quest for power.

❧ *The Extension of Regulation and Trustbusting*

In 1903 Congress, at Roosevelt's urging, passed the Progressive Era's first major extension of the federal government's regulatory powers — the Elkins Act, which strengthened the Interstate Commerce Commission and forbade railroads to grant rebates to favored customers. Although passage of the Elkins Act signaled a victory for reform and the president, business did not view it as a major blow. Railroad owners did not relish government regulation, but they were happy to be rid of the confusing rate systems that had resulted from discriminatory pricing. Roosevelt also got Congress to enact an important piece of conservation legislation, the National Reclamation (or Newlands) Act, which set aside revenue from the sale of public land in sixteen western states to finance reclamation projects in the West. But otherwise Roosevelt's first term showed relatively scanty legislative results.

On some reform issues, such as tariff revision, Roosevelt was never willing to do battle. He insisted that the tariff question was one of "expediency and not of morality" and that the political costs of pushing reductions through Congress would be so high that other progressive reforms would be jeopardized. As a result, under Roosevelt the United States continued to maintain the high protectionist barriers that had been raised by McKinley. The president was more intent on vigorously enforcing the public policy enacted at the end of the nineteenth century — especially the Sherman Anti-Trust Act of 1890. Although Roosevelt railed against trusts in his first State of the Union Address in 1901, he won his lasting identification as a "trustbuster" with the government's antitrust suit against the Northern Securities Company, which his attorney general, Philander C. Knox, shocked the financial world by announcing on February 19, 1902. Roosevelt's administration brought the suit in order to force the dissolution of the Northern Securities Company, a giant holding company bent on creating a monopoly of northwestern railroads, that had been put together by the most visible business magnates in the country — J. P. Morgan, William Rockefeller, James J. Hill, and E. H. Harriman. The government's suit outraged the arrogant Morgan, who confidentially told Roosevelt that "if we have done anything wrong, send your man to my man and they can fix it up." The Supreme Court's 5-4 verdict against the company in 1904 rejuvenated the Sherman Anti-Trust Act as a means of controlling financial concentration.

Roosevelt relished his fame as a trustbuster, though he probably got more credit than he deserved. The Northern Securities case had been planned and approved by McKinley before his assassination, and it was prosecuted by McKinley's appointees. Nor did Roosevelt ever intend to destroy the huge accumulations of wealth that seemed to him necessary for modern industrialization; rather, he wanted to make them serve "the public good." The only way to bring "arrogant capitalists to heel," he believed, was by using the Sherman Act. During Roosevelt's seven years as president, the attorney general filed antitrust suits against forty-four companies, including Standard Oil Company, the American Tobacco Company, and the DuPont Corporation.

Roosevelt again pitted the presidency against business interests during a strike by miners in the anthracite coalfields of Pennsylvania in May 1902. The strikers, demanding recognition of the United Mine Workers Union, higher wages, and other benefits, were confronted by a coalition of railroad owners who controlled about 70 percent of the mines. After workers refused to accept pay cuts, the owners closed the mines and refused to negotiate. As winter approached, the nation faced a severe shortage of heating fuel, and coal prices soared. The owner's spokesman, George Baer, issued a series of uncompromising and arrogant statements demanding that the government support the mining companies against union "outlaws." In one of his more notorious dictums, Baer revealed the self-righteous mind-set of many wealthy businessmen, an attitude that rested firmly on the individualistic Christian ethic of the nineteenth century: "The rights and interests of the laboring man will be protected and cared for, not by the labor agitators, but by the Christian men to whom God in his infinite wisdom has given the con-

" JIU-JITSUED "

"Jiu-Jitsued"   Among his many other colorful and well-publicized activities in the White House, TR took lessons from a Japanese master in jujitsu (initiating a nationwide craze for that martial art). In this 1906 cartoon, he applies his skill to the railroad trust.

trol of the property interests of this country." If Baer was correct, quipped a reporter, stealing coal was not larceny, "it was heresy."

On October 3 Roosevelt summoned the leaders of both sides to the White House. The president was infuriated when the "arrogant stupidity" and condescension of the owners wrecked the discussion. Roosevelt then persuaded the governor of Pennsylvania to request federal troops to preserve order in the mining districts, promptly dispatched them and announced that, if necessary, the troops would dig coal. The owners, faced with this veiled threat to nationalize the mines, agreed to the appointment of a presidential commission that arbitrated a compromise solution.

Roosevelt's swashbuckling handling of the coal strike did not end the labor movement's problems, for it continued to get mixed treatment from the Supreme Court. In the *Danbury Hatters* case in 1908 the Court ruled that a secondary boycott (that is, a strike action by one union in sympathy with the grievances over which another union was striking) violated the Sherman Anti-Trust Act. This was the first time that labor unions had been subjected to antitrust regulation. On the other hand, in another 1908 case, *Muller v. Oregon,* the Supreme Court upheld an Oregon law limiting the working hours of women. Attorney Louis Brandeis (who would later become a distinguished Supreme Court justice) defended the Oregon law with statistical, historical, economic, and sociological data rather than traditional legal precedents. This "Brandeis brief" opened a new era of legal argument for social legislation.

Roosevelt's actions in the *Northern Securities* case and the coal strike endeared him to much of the public as a trust-buster. In fact, the president was no doctrinaire radical, nor was he overly fond of organized labor. In later years, union supporters often accused Roosevelt of being anti-union. The only clear messages in the president's early actions were that he demanded fairness in class disputes, or a "square deal" as he called it, and that he would use the government against powerful interests when they threatened the nation's democratic ideals.

℘ *Political Victory and the Square Deal*

Roosevelt was preoccupied during his first term with ensuring that his party would nominate him for a second term. (At the time, such nomination was not a foregone conclusion. All previous vice presidents — Tyler, Fillmore, Andrew Johnson, and Arthur — who had been vaulted into the White House by their predecessor's death were denied their party's subsequent nomination for the presidency.)

His chief competitor within the Republican Party was Senator Mark Hanna of Ohio, who coveted the presidency. But Hanna's sudden death in 1904 removed all obstacles, and Roosevelt was unanimously nominated at the Republican convention.

A badly divided Democratic party nominated little-known New York Supreme Court justice Alton B. Parker to run against Roosevelt in 1904. A lackluster candidate with a conservative record, Parker was no match for the charismatic Roosevelt. TR won in a landslide, with a popular vote of 7.6 million to Parker's 5.1 million, and the Republicans gained majorities in the Senate and the House. On the evening of his victory, the elated

Progressive-Era Class War A fist, punching through from the lower depths, sends a shockwave through a crowd of carefree plutocrats in this dramatic turn-of-the-century image, warning of dire social conflicts ahead if calls for reform were not heeded.

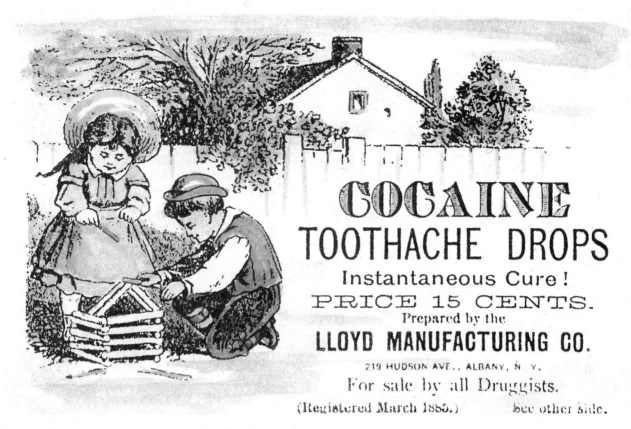

COCAINE TOOTHACHE DROPS

Instantaneous Cure!

PRICE 15 CENTS.

Prepared by the

LLOYD MANUFACTURING CO.

219 HUDSON AVE., ALBANY, N. Y.

For sale by all Druggists.

(Registered March 1885.)　　　　See other side.

Roosevelt announced to the press that "under no circumstances will I be a candidate for or accept another nomination." He would later regret it.

Roosevelt's astonishing margin of victory was an omen of the growing importance that personality would play in presidential elections in the twentieth century. It also signaled that many of the old political issues of the nineteenth century, such as currency and civil service reform, had lost their appeal. More important, the victory made clear the dominance that the Republican Party had gained at the end of the nineteenth century. Touting themselves as the party of prosperity, Republicans entered the new century as champions of the American dream, while they blasted the Democrats as the party of foreigners and radicalism. The election of 1904 showed strong Republican gains in the Northeast and Midwest, where increasing numbers of assimilated immigrants left the Democratic Party to vote for the party of prosperity and Americanism. In many districts where elections formerly had been hotly contested, the Republicans gained a safe majority.

After his election, Roosevelt pressed Congress, which was still dominated by conservative Republicans, to pass legislation securing his "square deal." His inaugural address in 1905, much more forceful than his earlier speeches, devoted over half its space to requests

Advertising Cocaine, about 1885　Cocaine was one of several dangerous drugs (heroin was another) that were widely advertised and freely sold over the counter in the late nineteenth century. In their legal heyday, these substances must have addicted hundreds of thousands of unsuspecting consumers. Establishment of the Food and Drug Administration finally began to bring them under scrutiny and control.

for economic and social legislation.

Roosevelt stressed the need for legislation giving the government more control over railroads. Railroads had been the target of reformers ever since the passage of the Interstate Commerce Act in 1887, but the Supreme Court had weakened the powers of the Interstate Commerce Commission so severely that it had often been ineffectual. In 1905 Congress debated a bill broadening the powers of the commission, but defeated it in spite of Roosevelt's support. The next year, however, after skillful negotiations and compromises by the president, the legislation passed. This Hepburn Act empowered the ICC to intervene in two of the areas long considered sacrosanct by private business: the right to set rates and the right to inspect company books. Although the law disappointed newly elected progressive Senator Robert La Follette, who wanted much more drastic regulation of the railroads, the Hepburn Act nonetheless was a landmark in the expansion of the federal government's regulatory powers.

Theodore Roosevelt's "Square Deal," 1903

Theodore Roosevelt embraced the progressive ideals of the early twentieth century. He sought to balance the needs of workers and business leaders, believing that Americans at all levels were entitled to fair treatment — what he called "a square deal."

In his turn, the capitalist who is really a conservative, the man who has forethought as well as patriotism, should heartily welcome every effort, legislative or otherwise, which has for its object to secure fair dealing by capital, corporate or individual, toward the public and toward the employee. . . . For in no way is the stability of property better assured than by making it patent to our people that property bears its proper share of the burdens of the State; that property is handled not only in the interest of the owner, but in the interest of the whole community.

We must act upon the motto of all for each and each for all. There must be ever present in our minds the fundamental truth that in a republic such as ours the only safety is to stand neither for nor against any man because he is rich or because he is poor, because he is engaged in one occupation or another, because he works with his brains or because he works with his hands. We must treat each man on his worth and merits as a man. We must see that each is given a square deal, because he is entitled to no more and should receive no less.

One day after the Hepburn Act became law, Roosevelt signed two bills authorizing governmental regulation of food and drugs — the Pure Food and Drug Act and the Meat Inspection Act. Congress had debated such legislation for years; under Roosevelt, Dr. Harvey Wiley, the chief chemist of the Department of Agriculture, with the support of the American Medical Association, had accumulated abundant evidence that the public needed protection. Popular support grew after the publication of Upton Sinclair's novel, *The Jungle* (1906), which included a lurid account of unsanitary conditions in the Chicago stockyards and meat-packing industry, and progressives used the public outrage to prod Congress into action. Roosevelt, who had read and was sickened by the book, appointed a commission to study the packing industry and threatened to release its damaging report if Congress failed to act. The unregulated sale of drugs posed an equally dangerous threat to public health. A *Ladies Home Journal* exposé of patent medicine revealed that Mrs. Winslow's Soothing Syrup for babies contained morphine and was labeled "poison" in Great Britain. The establishment of the Federal Food and Drug Administration to oversee the labeling of foods and drugs sold in interstate commerce and the provision for meat inspection by the Department of Agriculture joined the Hepburn Act as the major legislative achievements of Roosevelt's second term.

Roosevelt and his progressive Republican successor ignored some areas of potential reform. Although the Republican Party — the party of Lincoln — continued to win black votes in the North and in the few places where they could still vote in the South, African American pleas for equality of opportunity and justice received little attention. Roosevelt touched off a thunderous protest among white Southerners when he invited Booker T. Washington to the White House for a conference and dinner in 1901. But — perhaps in acknowledgement of that white protest — he initiated no serious civil-rights reform. Although the president resented the demagogic southern attacks on Washington's White House visit, it was not repeated. Moreover, in a highly-publicized incident in 1907, Roosevelt discharged "without honor" an entire African American regiment, including a number of Medal of Honor winners, after one black soldier had been accused of committing a murder in Brownsville, Texas. The incident occurred during a wild shooting spree, and all of the soldiers refused to testify against one another. The president's action humiliated African Americans and their supporters. While blacks continued to play a decisive role in Republican Party politics in the South, younger black leaders, disgusted by a lack of support from national Republicans, began to explore the possibility of an alliance with the Democratic Party.

Overall, the legislative accomplishments of Theodore Roosevelt's seven years in office were limited. But the progressive legislation that did pass was a tribute to his political skills in dealing with the conservatives who still dominated the Republican Party and to his ability to further public acceptance of government regulation.

❧ A Beginning for Conservation

Roosevelt's promotion of conservation was probably the most important and lasting contribution of his presidency, and it marked a major expansion of public interest in environmental issues. The Census Bureau's announcement in 1890 that the frontier had closed awakened many Americans to the finiteness of the nation's natural abundance, causing some reformers to recognize that nineteenth-century plundering of the nation's natural resources had imperiled its future. The Forest Reserve Act of 1891 gave the president the authority to close timber areas to settlers and to establish national parks. President Benjamin Harrison reserved 16 million acres, and each of his successors added new lands to the park system; by the time Roosevelt became president in 1901, approximately 45 million acres had been set aside. In his first presidential address, Roosevelt emphasized the urgency of measures to conserve the nation's water and forest resources. During the next seven years, the president set aside nearly 150 million acres of forestlands and protected against sale an additional 80 million acres of mineral lands.

The chief architect of the administration's conservation program, Gifford Pinchot, had become head of the small federal Forestry Bureau in 1898. A Yale graduate, Pinchot spent three years studying forestry in Ger-

Theodore Roosevelt and John Muir   Hiking up to the promontory that overlooks Yellowstone Falls, President Roosevelt poses with Muir, the bewhiskered founder of the Sierra Club and ardent champion of wilderness preservation at the beginning of the twentieth century. Roosevelt, a conservationist who favored the "efficient" exploitation of natural resources, often disagreed with Muir's more radical environmentalist agenda.

many and Switzerland. In 1905, Roosevelt enlarged the Forest Bureau, renaming it the United States Forest Service. As chief forester, Pinchot organized the Forest Ranger program (including personally designing the uniforms and badges) and built the service into a powerful, semi-autonomous agency in the Interior Department. In 1907, Roosevelt appointed as secretary of the interior James R. Garfield, Pinchot's friend and fellow naturalist. Roosevelt, Garfield, and Pinchot hiked and played tennis together, reinforcing one another's sense of urgency about conserving the nation's natural resources.

In a final contribution to the conservation cause, Roosevelt convened the National Conservation Congress in Washington in 1908. Attended by forty-four governors and about 500 experts and dignitaries, the congress drafted a report urging support for conservation at the state and national levels. Within eighteen months, forty-one states had established conservation agencies.

Conservation was a complex political and philosophical issue that would vex all of the presidents of the Progressive Era. Like most political issues during these years, it did not simply pit two opposing groups against one another. Pinchot, in typically progressive language, supported a "rational, planned exploitation of nature." But he had enemies on both his right and his left, whose opposition foreshadowed the political battles over environmental protection that would be fought during the twentieth century. In the conservative camp, representatives from western states increasingly objected to the government reserving huge tracts of land and resisted the conservation movement as a hindrance to their region's economic development. On the left, Pinchot's emphasis on a "reasonable" exploitation of public forest lands inspired passionate dissent from wilderness preservationists, chief among them John Muir, a well-known nature writer who in 1892 helped organize the Sierra Club — still an influential champion of sweeping environmental protection. In 1911, Muir submitted plans for a national park system to President William Howard Taft, and the establishment of the National Park Service in 1916 (two years after Muir's death) provided a conservation approach more satisfactory to preservationists. However, in 1913 a lasting split in the conservation movement developed when Muir unsuccessfully protested using part of Yosemite National Park as a water reservoir for San Francisco, a project that had been approved by Pinchot.

❧ *Roosevelt Drifts to the Left*

During his last years as president, Roosevelt and Congress reached a virtual stalemate. Each year the president asked for more and more legislation — and Congress passed less and less. A recalcitrant Congress, repeatedly offended by what it considered presidential usurpations of power, even refused to fund the printing costs for the reports of the presidential commissions that Roosevelt convened. In spite of the president's immense personal popularity, the Republican Party was deeply divided, and a conservative majority in the Senate blocked reform legislation.

Nonetheless, Roosevelt's proposals in his last two years as president, including such ideas as inheritance and income taxes, and his increasing attacks on the "malefactors of great wealth," set an agenda for progressives. Told that the closing years of most presidential terms were periods of "stagnation," Roosevelt retorted that during the last year of his administration "stagnation continued to rage with uninterrupted violence." Roosevelt bequeathed to his successor a full set of progressive objectives, a sharply divided Republican party, and a Congress bristling over the tactics of an active, energetic president.

COMPETING PROGRESSIVE VISIONS

Political progressivism was still difficult to define in 1908. Many politicians who sometimes described themselves as progressives embraced change with restraint, desiring only a smattering of reform sufficient to save the nation from what they perceived as radicalism. Some of Roosevelt's closest advisers, including William Howard Taft, his secretary of war, were just such cautious progressives. As the reform rhetoric of progressives like Senator Robert La Follette grew more strident, these deliberate progressives found themselves more comfortable in the company of conservatives.

Furthermore, by 1910 progressives had defined sharp philosophical differences among themselves. Most important, they disagreed about how to deal with big business. Roosevelt became the chief spokesman for the concept of using big government to regulate big business, distinguishing "good trusts" from "bad trusts." His ideas came to be called the New Nationalism. On the other hand, Democratic progressives built on the populist notion that bigness was intolerable because it destroyed the American belief in equality of opportu-

nity. By 1912 that theory had an eloquent new spokesman in Woodrow Wilson, who called his platform the New Freedom.

❧ *Roosevelt Picks His Successor*

Despite his battles with the conservative Republican Congress, Theodore Roosevelt could have had the Republican nomination in 1908 for the asking. He was only fifty and relished being president, but he was genuinely committed to the two-term tradition. By 1906 Roosevelt had chosen William Howard Taft as his successor, and he used him more or less as an assistant president during his last two years in office.

Taft was an able constitutional lawyer who held a number of important appointed offices, including a successful term as governor of the Philippines, before becoming secretary of war in 1904. Three times Roosevelt offered Taft Supreme Court appointments, but his presidential ambitions led him to decline each time. A loyal supporter of Roosevelt's progressivism, Taft never hinted at disagreement with the president.

Roosevelt's support assured Taft his party's nomination. Although the Republican platform paid lip service to Roosevelt's progressive agenda of ensuring justice for all classes, and at Taft's insistence called for the progressives' goal of tariff reduction, the conservative "Old Guard" still dominated the GOP convention. The Democrats nominated William Jennings Bryan for the third time, returning to the magnetic popular leader after the conservative Parker's poor showing four years earlier. The Democrats pictured themselves as the party of the people against "special privilege" and pledged to create a Department of Labor. Bryan campaigned vigorously on a platform calling for lower tariffs, stronger antitrust laws, and more government regulation of business. With Samuel Gompers complaining that labor had been "thrown down, repudiated and relegated to the discard by the Republican party" — and with the Republicans charging that the Democrats were drifting "toward socialism" — the election of 1908 marked the beginning of organized labor's move toward open support of the Democratic party.

Campaigning did not suit Taft's judicial temperament, although Roosevelt goaded him into making some speeches. Taft detested political posturing, conceding in all honesty that both parties were "trying to do the same thing." Despite his lackluster qualities as a politician, Taft won easily, with a 321-162 majority in the electoral college, but his margin of victory in the popular vote, 7.6 million to 6.4 million, was far less than Roosevelt's four years earlier. The closer vote reflected concerns over the recession that had begun in 1908, to some degree tarnishing the Republicans' image as the party of prosperity. Most Americans, including Taft, felt that the Republican victory had more to do with the popularity of Roosevelt than with the strengths or weaknesses of either party's candidate.

Everyone knew that the new president lacked the flair of his mentor. Taft's presidential ambition had been fed by his wife, and her debilitating stroke shortly after they settled in the White House deprived him of a valued political adviser. A man of unswerving honesty and integrity, Taft was temperamentally ill suited for the presidency. He disliked political maneuvering (repeatedly writing to his friends that "politics makes me sick") and was uncomfortable in the limelight. Taft was the first golfing president, but compared to the presidents before and after him, he seemed remote and lethargic — and terribly overweight.

On the other hand, Taft had many characteristics that would have commended him in the Gilded Age. An amiable and self-effacing conversationalist, jovial about his 300-pound figure, Taft boasted that he was the politest man in the country because he once had given up his seat to three women. Universally regarded as a man of sound judgment, Roosevelt had depended on his friend Will more than any other adviser. The legislative achievements of his administration attest to Taft's considerable political skill.

At heart, Taft was a conservative, and that proved to be a political liability in a time when sentiment for reform ran strong. He had a deep reverence for the law, and he respected orderly and slow change. Once Roosevelt's influence had faded, Taft turned for advice to those who shared his temperament. His cabinet appointees included five corporation lawyers.

President William Howard Taft   Politicians in the Progressive Era did not always worry as much about looking physically fit as would their counterparts a century later. Taft enjoyed both golf and a good meal, weighed almost 300 pounds, and lived happily to the age of seventy-three.

❧ Taft Alienates the Progressives

No one could have foreseen Taft's political problems in 1909, for most progressives believed that he would be an ally. Within a year, however, Taft had alienated most congressional progressives and had aligned himself with some of the most conservative "Old Guard" Republicans in Congress.

The rift opened during an attempt by progressives in 1909 to unseat Speaker Joseph Cannon in the House of Representatives. Cannon was a coarse and ruthless dictator who, like his predecessors, used his powers of appointment to control the House and block progressive legislation. Taft disliked Cannon and promised support for an uprising led by progressive Republican George Norris of Nebraska. But when pressured by conservative senators whose support he needed for tariff reduction, Taft reversed himself, and the progressive representatives suffered a humiliating defeat. The Republican progressives deeply resented Taft's desertion and his subsequent cordial relationship with Cannon. Without the president's backing, a bloc of progressive Republicans, called the Insurgents, resumed the battle against Cannon in 1910 — and this time, in alliance with the Democrats, they won. They passed a Norris-sponsored rules amendment that removed the speaker from the powerful House Rules Committee and deprived him of the power to appoint members of standing committees. Never again would speakers of the House have the sweeping powers that Cannon had wielded.

The deepest wedge between Taft and the progressive Republicans in Congress was driven by the passage of the Payne-Aldrich Tariff in 1909. Taft considered tariff reduction his first priority upon taking office, and he called a special session of Congress to address the issue. The bill that passed the House after months of haggling and political compromise ostensibly reduced the tariff, particularly the rates on some important products such as iron ore, coal, and oil. But in the Senate conservatives mutilated the original bill by attaching more than 800 amendments, and the resulting Payne-Aldrich Tariff actually raised rates on many items. Although the final compromise that Taft signed was so complex as to defy simple characterization, Taft threw his support behind the law, declaring it a "good bill" that revised the tariff "substantially downward." Taft did not like all of its provisions, but he felt that its conservative architects, Senator Nelson Aldrich of Rhode Island and Speaker Cannon, had fairly considered his views. He was particularly pleased that the law allowed the president to seek revisions of the tariff through international negotiations. Progressives in Congress and the press, however, were outraged both by the Payne-Aldrich bill and by Taft's cooperation with the likes of Aldrich and Cannon.

The third incident that alienated Taft from the progressives, a clash between Gifford Pinchot and Secretary of the Interior Richard A. Ballinger, tainted Taft's reputation as a conservationist and overshadowed his sponsorship of $20 million in western irrigation projects. During Roosevelt's administration Pinchot had been a personal friend of both Secretary of the Interior James R. Garfield and the president. ("Sir Galahad of the Woods," the newspapers took to caricaturing the energetic idealist Pinchot.) Pinchot enjoyed no such privileged position in the Taft administration, and his relationship with Ballinger was soon strained. On Ballinger's recommendation, Taft returned more than a million acres of reserved forestland to the public domain. Pinchot became ever more convinced that Ballinger was a foe of conservation, and when a former government official charged that Ballinger had been involved in an illegal attempt to seize coal lands in Alaska, Pinchot joined a crusade to oust him.

Like many other Republicans, Taft considered Pinchot "a radical and a crank," but he tried to mollify him, not wanting him to become a martyr. Nonetheless, in January 1910, when a letter from Pinchot criticizing Ballinger was read on the Senate floor, Taft's patience was exhausted, and he ordered Pinchot removed from office. A Senate investigating committee exonerated Ballinger of any wrongdoing, though it also raised serious questions about his commitment to conservation. Progressives in Congress and the muckraking press loudly backed Pinchot.

Despite the widening rift between progressives and the administration, the legislative accomplishments of Taft's first two years compared favorably with those of Roosevelt's administration. Disappointing as the Payne-Aldrich Act was to tariff reformers, it contained two historic riders. One provided for a corporation tax, for the first time empowering the government to regulate corporate behavior through taxation. The second rider provided for the submission to the states of a constitutional amendment authorizing Congress to levy an income tax. It was ratified in 1913 as the Sixteenth Amendment.

The president backed a number of new laws expanding government regulation of business. In 1910 Congress passed the Mann-Elkins Act, further expanding the powers of the Interstate Commerce Commission. The law shifted the burden of proof to corporations in rate disputes, and it brought telephone, telegraph, cable, and wireless companies under the jurisdiction of the ICC. The Mann-Elkins Act expanded the Hepburn Act so dramatically that it received the unanimous vote of the progressives in Congress.

Taft's commitment to Roosevelt's policies was clearest in his prosecution of antitrust suits. Attorney General George W. Wickersham initiated ninety antitrust suits, more than twice as many as had Roosevelt's two administrations, including cases against U.S. Steel Corporation and the American Tobacco Company. Once again, however, Taft's good intentions backfired. The government's case against U.S. Steel argued that Roosevelt had been misled when he approved the company's 1907 acquisition of the Tennessee Coal and Iron Company. The implication that he had been hoodwinked by the corporation infuriated Roosevelt.

Taft had tried to follow a "policy of harmony," and he was remarkably successful in securing the support of conservatives for important reform legislation. But by 1910 the Republican Party was hopelessly divided. The Insurgents, a vocal minority in Congress, claimed the Roosevelt legacy and lambasted conservative Republicans as tools of the trusts. Outspoken progressive senators, particularly Robert La Follette, exasperated the mild-mannered president. As midterm elections approached in 1910, Taft decided to purge the party of progressive zealots, and many Republican primaries turned into bitterly fought contests between conser-

Roosevelt on His African Safari   After he left the White House, TR advertised his long safari in Africa as a collecting and scientific expedition, and some of his trophies are still displayed in New York's American Museum of Natural History. But he also enjoyed himself immensely and was never far from the public eye.

vative candidates supported by the president and progressive opponents.

✥ The Rift between Roosevelt and Taft

Roosevelt made an honest effort not to overshadow his less glamorous successor. Immediately after leaving office, he sailed for Africa under the auspices of the Smithsonian Institution on a hunting and collecting expedition funded by Andrew Carnegie. But he did not leave the eye of the American public. The press reported TR's journey in luxurious detail, beginning with his departure with nine pairs of glasses, a gold-mounted rabbit's foot given to him by boxing champion John L. Sullivan, 200 rockets in case his safari got lost, and a veritable library of books. In Africa, Roosevelt bagged 296 animals, including nine lions, eight elephants, thirteen rhinoceroses, seven hippopotamuses, six buffalos, fifteen zebras and twenty-eight gazelles, and brought back the most complete collection of East African flora and fauna to be found outside Africa. "Somewhere in the wilds of Africa," reported the *Cleveland Leader* in 1909, "a perfectly good three-ton hippopotamus has become a historical character." Afterwards, Roosevelt toured Europe with his family, meeting most of Europe's royalty. When Roosevelt returned to the country in June 1910, he and Taft gave no public hint of any tension between them.

A split between Roosevelt and Taft was probably inevitable, even though both men sincerely wanted to avoid it. Shortly after he returned to the United States, Roosevelt found his faith in Taft shaken. When the details of the U.S. Steel case became public in 1910, Roosevelt felt that he had been personally attacked, left to appear as either "a fool or a knave."

Roosevelt and Taft avoided open hostility before the congressional elections of 1910, but in August Roosevelt delivered a series of speeches attacking conservative Republicans. In an important address at Osawatomie, Kansas, Roosevelt outlined a bold new program of reform that he began calling the New Nationalism. Far more progressive than anything he had advocated while president, the New Nationalism called for sweeping social legislation and unequivocally declared that the government's right to regulate for the public welfare outweighed individuals' rights to private property. Roosevelt had continued to move to the left in his thinking. On the other hand, Taft's conservative temperament was strained to its limits to support the programs he inherited from the Roos-

evelt of 1907 and 1908. The two Republican leaders had drifted in different directions. The same split divided the entire GOP.

The midterm election of 1910 was a bitter defeat for Taft and for the Republican Party in general, for his effort to purge progressive congressmen failed embarrassingly. Forty incumbent conservatives lost to progressives in the primaries. Then, in the general election, the GOP lost fifty-seven House seats and ten seats in the Senate. For the first time in sixteen years the Democrats gained control of the House. While Republicans continued to hold a slight majority in the Senate, control passed into the hands of a coalition of Democrats and progressive Republicans. Factionalism played havoc with the Republican Party's dominant political position over the next decade, affording the Democrats a window of opportunity for important gains.

During his final two years in the presidency, Taft's party was in disarray. In 1911, Insurgent Republicans formed the National Progressive Republican League, which drafted a platform, endorsed Robert La Follette as a presidential candidate in 1912, and began organizing to defeat Taft's renomination.

✥ The Election of 1912

The presidential campaign of 1912 marked an auspicious moment in American political history, more critical even than the election of 1896 in solidifying the transformation of ideas and institutions that shaped twentieth-century American political life. It marked the high water mark of progressivism. The election pitted against each other the three presidents of the Progressive Era and offered some of the most sophisticated political discussions in American political history.

Despite insurgent gains in 1910, conservatives controlled the Republican convention that met in the summer of 1912. With characteristic enthusiasm — "My hat's in the ring! The fight is on and I am stripped to the buff!" — Roosevelt made an all-out effort to win the party's nomination. He entered twelve primaries, won nine, attended the convention personally (unheard-of for a presidential candidate at the time), and had far more delegate votes committed to him than did Taft. However, the party's national committee refused to recognize many of Roosevelt's delegates, and Taft won renomination. Roosevelt's supporters condemned the nomination as a fraud and called on the former president to accept a third-party nomination.

Taft entered the 1912 campaign with no illusions

about his chances. He was embittered that Roosevelt had deserted him, and he believed that it would have been cowardly to refuse his party's nomination. Indeed, Taft and other conservatives were fighting primarily to save the Republican Party from what they saw as radicals. Once the campaign began, Taft made a few speeches to remind the public that he had favored lower tariffs and fair business practices, but he made no serious effort to win reelection.

Insurgent Republicans had already begun organizing a third party, called the Progressive Party, and La Follette had coveted and worked hard to secure its presidential nomination. But his physical collapse in February 1912 had given many of his supporters an excuse to throw their support to Roosevelt in his battle with Taft and the Republican Old Guard. The new party's leaders delayed holding their convention until August, after the GOP convention had given its nomination to Taft. Having failed to win the Republican nomination, Roosevelt reappeared at the Progressive convention in Chicago. It resembled a gigantic religious revival more than a political gathering, opening its sessions with stirring choruses of "Onward, Christian Soldiers" and "The Battle Hymn of the Republic" sung by a "Jane Addams chorus." Enthusiastically nominated by the Progressives, Roosevelt entitled his acceptance speech a "Confession of Faith."

The Progressive party adopted a sweeping reform platform that endorsed direct primaries, a National Health Service, a system of insurance for the unemployed, the ill, and the elderly, and woman's suffrage. Roosevelt had hitherto kept his distance from the women's movement, but now he embraced it. Jane Addams gave a speech seconding Roosevelt's nomination, and women reformers played an important role in the convention. Frances Kellor, head of the New York State Commission of Industries and Immigration and a former Hull House resident, helped manage Roosevelt's campaign. Despite the fanfare, however, Roosevelt had accepted the third-party nomination reluctantly, recognizing the political peril that he was running. As long as there remained a possibility that the Democrats would nominate a conservative southern candidate, TR had hopes of forging a victorious alliance of the reforming elements in both major parties, and when this hope faded with the Democrats' nomination of a progressive Roosevelt still believed that a new reform coalition would emerge in the wake of a failed Democratic presidency. Roosevelt's Bull Moose campaign was the best-funded third-party

race in American history; Progressive expenditures were equal to about 60 percent of the average of the two major parties.

Roosevelt's calculations were not entirely unrealistic, for a conservative did lead in the early balloting at the Democrats' convention. But the two-thirds rule prevented his nomination, and then William Jennings Bryan and his supporters threw their support to the leading progressive Democratic candidate, the governor of New Jersey, Woodrow Wilson. After forty-six ballots, Wilson finally won, and the fate of Roosevelt's third-party bid for the White House was sealed.

Wilson, the former president of Princeton University, had emerged as a leading Democratic contender in 1910 when he won the governorship of New Jersey as a full-fledged progressive. His impressive intellectual credentials made him an ideal opponent to conduct a national debate with Roosevelt over their contrasting progressive visions — TR's "New Nationalism," with its advocacy of a powerful, activist government, and what Wilson called the "New Freedom," which called for a somewhat more limited governmental role and for more competition in the economy.

The campaign of 1912 was in fact a race between Roosevelt and Wilson, both of whom launched energetic campaigns on the same day — August 7, 1912. In October, the nation reeled in shock when Roosevelt, while making a speech in Milwaukee, was shot by a deranged bartender. Nevertheless, the indomitable TR spoke for eighty minutes with a bullet in his chest. (It had been deflected by Roosevelt's steel eyeglass case and the folded pages of his speech.) However, he was forced to convalesce most of the remainder of the campaign, and Wilson canceled his speaking tour out of respect for his wounded opponent.

Wilson's chief adviser, the celebrated progressive attorney Louis Brandeis, urged him to challenge what both perceived to be a fatal flaw in Roosevelt's New Nationalism: TR's acceptance of "good trusts" as a fact of modern life. Brandeis believed that their excessive concentration of power made all giant corporations inherently oppressive and that economic efficiency could be preserved and promoted only by encouraging competition among smaller firms. Competition was wasteful and inefficient, Brandeis and Wilson agreed, but so was democracy; the protection of freedom was more important than monopolistic efficiency. Wilson's New Freedom denounced all trusts and proposed a return to an economy of small entrepreneurs. Roosevelt believed that Wilson's stand bordered on demagoguery, appealing to nostalgia for a vanished agrarian past.

In practice, both Wilson and Roosevelt supported an expanding federal state, and they differed little about how that power should be used. The profoundest difference between the two men was their contrasting views of human nature. Roosevelt, while optimistic that society could be changed, was a twentieth-century Hamiltonian who viewed human nature as essentially perverse, requiring governmental control. His New Nationalism called for hammering out a new national consensus, eliminating divisive sectional, ethnic, and class conflicts. Wilson, on the other hand, was a latter-day Jeffersonian, believing that "this great American people is at the bottom just, virtuous, and hopeful; the roots of its being are in the soil of what is lovely, pure, and of good report." Wilson's New Freedom accepted the nation's cultural diversity and even saw it as an asset (although both the candidate and a large segment of his party held racist views toward African Americans).

An overwhelming majority of voters in 1912 supported either reformers or radicals farther to the political left. Wilson received a popular vote of 6.3 million and 435 electoral votes. Roosevelt ran second, with a popular vote of 4.1 million and 88 electoral votes. Eugene V. Debs, the eloquent candidate of the Socialist party, running for the third time on a ticket that called for "collective ownership and democratic management of communication and transportation systems," received more than 900,000 votes — the high point of Socialist fortunes in American politics. The conservative candidate, Taft, won only 3.5 million votes and 8 electoral votes.

The electorate had overwhelmingly repudiated the perceived conservatism of the Taft years. Beyond that, the results were unclear. Wilson won by the largest electoral majority yet amassed in a contested presidential election, but he got only 41.8 percent of the popular vote, actually polling 109,411 fewer votes than Bryan four years earlier, and many of his votes were piled up in the Solid South, which would have supported virtually any Democratic presidential nominee. Wilson had defeated a Republican party crippled by internal strife and weakened by a continuing recession. On the other hand, if one views the combined votes of Wilson, Roosevelt, and Debs as an endorsement of reform, about three-fourths of the American electorate can be said to have supported change. In short, while it appeared that the vote gave Wilson a mandate for reform, the results clearly had been skewed by the unusual cast of candidates and the bitter split in the Republican Party.

WILSONIAN PROGRESSIVISM

President Woodrow Wilson assigned a high priority to the passage of new legislation that would solidify and broaden the progressive reform movement. In the first two years of Wilson's presidency (1913-1914), Congress enacted laws reducing the tariff, establishing a national banking system, and strengthening federal antitrust powers. In the next two years (1915-1916), Congress passed a number of less far-reaching laws that further expanded the government's regulatory powers. Given sweeping powers by this legislation, Wilson left behind a broadly expanded executive branch.

By 1917, American involvement in World War I inevitably drew the country's attention to foreign affairs and marked an end to the Progressive Era of domestic reform. By then, however, the movement had accomplished many of its goals and had forged a new consensus on American democratic values.

❧ *The Scholar President*

Woodrow Wilson, a product of the academic and intellectual milieu that gave birth to much of the ideology of the progressive movement, was eminently qualified to be the nation's leader during the hopeful and idealistic years from 1913 to 1919. After receiving a Ph.D. in history and political science from Johns Hopkins, Wilson taught at Bryn Mawr College and Princeton University. In 1902 Wilson assumed the presidency of Princeton at a time when he was still flirting with political conservatism. He entered politics only after losing a bruising battle in which the university's board refused to support his reform of the Graduate School and his efforts to curb the university's prestigious and snobbish student "eating" clubs (in effect, fraternities). Wilson, the only American president to have earned a Ph.D., not only was erudite, but was also an artist with words, capable of swaying the public (and, remarkably, even his fellow politicians) with lofty speeches. Wilson made more public speeches than any other president, and his soaring appeals to right and morality both shaped the age and expressed its spirit.

Born in a Presbyterian rectory in Staunton, Virginia, in 1856, Wilson was the first southerner to be elected president since Zachary Taylor in 1848. He spent most of his youth in Virginia and South Carolina, and while practicing law in Atlanta he married Ellen Louise Axson, the daughter of a Georgia Presbyterian minister. While some of Wilson's political acts (for instance, his refusal to support black civil rights) may have been related to his southern roots and political base, he rejected the region's harshest racial views. His southern upbringing had less effect on Wilson's intellect than did his adult experiences in the North, where he was educated and spent most of his life. Both of his parents were reared in Ohio and his mother was born in England.

Religion left a deeper imprint on Woodrow Wilson; he clearly mirrored the values of the liberal Protestant majority in the nation. The son and grandson of Presbyterian ministers, Wilson was unashamedly Christian; his father was one of the founders of the Southern Presbyterian Church and during his presidency Wilson regularly attended the Central Presbyterian Church in Washington, where he served as an elder. In 1913, speaking before an assembly celebrating the tercentenary of the translation of the Bible into English, Wilson observed that, as a "Christian nation," the United States had striven throughout its history to "exemplify that devotion to the elements of righteousness which are derived from the revelations of Holy Scripture."

Religious belief formed the core of Wilson's innermost character. Upon being informed that he had won the Democratic nomination in 1912, Wilson dismayed his weary campaign manager with the statement: "I am a Presbyterian and believe in predestination and election. It was Providence that did the work." Wilson was never a narrow Calvinist; his belief in predestination mingled with liberal Protestant assumptions and he fully agreed with prevailing notions of evolutionary progress. Wilson proved to be a wily politician and was skilled in the art of compromise, but more than most politicians he found compromise morally burdensome. His incorruptibility and rigid commitment to principle endowed him with great stature as a leader but also proved to be his most vulnerable political trait. Wilson's religious faith presupposed a moral order; like most moralists, he generally identified his own views with divine law. At best, Wilson's portrayals of public events as struggles between good and evil were inspirational; at worst, his moralizing was inconsistent and self-serving.

Woodrow Wilson's presidential style was actually a mix of Christian idealism and hardheaded realism. Some of his close associates felt that Wilson was too dogmatic, shunning critical advice. On the other hand, Wilson changed his thinking on important issues during his public life, leading some critics to view him as a temporizer with few real convictions. Roosevelt detested Wilson, charging that he spoke with "deliber-

ately involved weasel words" that allowed him to opt for the most expedient political course. "For heaven's sake never allude to Wilson as an idealist or altruist," Roosevelt wrote to a friend, "he is a doctrinaire when he can be so with safety to his personal ambition and he is always coldly selfish; he hasn't a touch of idealism in him." Even a Wilson admirer, economist Richard T. Ely, complained that the president "could speak beautifully and say nothing, if he wished." While Wilson's blend of idealism and realism infuriated his critics, it proved to be a remarkably successful political formula.

Wilson's management of the Democratic Party was the key to his political success. An admirer of British government, his most noted book, *Congressional Government* (1885), was a laudatory treatment of the parliamentary system. Wilson believed that the president should function as the head of the dominant legislative party, using party solidarity to pass his programs. Wilson did try to win the bipartisan support of progressives in Congress, but it was his success in uniting his own party that marked him as a consummate politician.

⅋ Congress Backs the President

Woodrow Wilson's extraordinary success during his first term took most Washington observers by surprise. His stirring inaugural address highlighted his oratorical skills, but Wilson entered the presidency keenly conscious that he, like Taft, lacked the personal charisma of Roosevelt. Wilson had a dry wit and was fond of limericks, but his political contemporaries and the public perceived him as cold and aloof. During his early months in office Wilson held weekly press conferences and established a good rapport with the press, but he did not like such exchanges and ended them in 1915.

Despite these personal limitations, Wilson was a stunning success on Capitol Hill. Partly, circumstances played into his hands. Democrats gained control of Congress for the first time in sixteen years in 1912, and party leaders were eager to appear decisive. A large number of first-term congressmen were elected in the Democratic sweep, and they were amenable to cooperating with party leaders and the president. Wilson astutely appointed William Jennings Bryan secretary of state, assuring the support of Bryan's substantial following in the Democratic Party, or, at least, forestalling open opposition.

Immediately after his inauguration, Wilson called Congress into special session to enact a revision of the tariff. For the first time since John Adams, the president appeared personally before the joint houses, delivering an impassioned call for Congress to face up to the task of reducing the protective tariff, the mother of special privilege and monopoly in America.

Tariff revision had been advocated in the Democratic platform and by progressives for years, but in the battle over the Payne-Aldrich tariff regional protectionist interests and a strong pro-business bloc in the Senate thwarted realistic reductions. When Congress convened in 1913, lobbyists once again descended on Washington; most political observers assumed that the president's proposals would fail. As the discussions headed toward deadlock, Wilson politically flanked Congress; in a bold public address he hinted that the Senate had fallen under the control of selfish lobbying interests. The embarrassed Senate launched an internal investigation that revealed no wrongdoing, but under the glare of public attention Congress passed the Underwood-Simmons Tariff in October 1913.

The new tariff reduced rates by about 25 percent and placed a number of important items, including iron, steel, and raw wool, on the free list, significantly lowering the tariff for the first time since 1857. Almost as stunning, a rider attached to the Underwood-Simmons Tariff enacted the first income tax based on the newly ratified Sixteenth Amendment. Proposed as a means of recovering revenue lost through tariff reduction, the income tax affected mostly the wealthy; the rates began at 1 percent on gross incomes of $3,000 per year and increased to 6 percent on incomes over $50,000, exempting about 96 percent of the population.

Equally as pressing and complicated as tariff revision was the need to reform the banking and currency system. The nation's disorganized banking system had proven incapable of responding in times of financial crisis. Banking facilities were particularly inadequate in the South and the West, and farmers in both sections suffered from a lack of credit. While banking problems were clear, solutions were not. Two major questions loomed: whether the nation would have a centralized or decentralized banking system and whether the system would be controlled by the federal government or by private banks. Differing combinations of answers left politicians supporting four different financial plans. Powerful Republican Senator Nelson Aldrich favored a centralized private banking system; Democratic Senator Robert L. Owen, chairman of the Senate Banking Committee, favored a centralized bank controlled by the government; Carter Glass, the chairman of the House Banking Committee, favored a decentralized system of banks under private control.

With Wilson's support, Congress passed a fourth option, establishing a decentralized system of reserve banks under the control of a federal board. The Federal Reserve Act authorized the establishment of between eight and twelve regional banks to serve as "banker's banks," depositories for the cash reserves of national banks. In addition, the reserve banks rediscounted the commercial and agricultural loans of member banks and issued a new currency based on that collateral, Federal Reserve notes. The federal reserve banks had the power to expand and contract the money supply in keeping with changing requirements. At the head of the system was a powerful Federal Reserve Board composed of seven members (later eight) appointed by the president. That board was empowered to raise and lower the interest rates at which commercial banks borrowed money to lend to the public. The board also controlled the money supply, and could shift reserves from one region to another, thus diminishing the domination of the powerful private Eastern banks. Generally regarded as the most important single achievement of the Wilson administration, the Federal Reserve System soon won the support of its most outspoken critics, including the private banking community.

In 1914 Wilson pressed Congress for legislation strengthening government control of trusts. In September Congress authorized the establishment of the Federal Trade Commission, a presidential board empowered to investigate corporations and to issue cease-and-desist orders when it suspected unfair business practices that suppressed competition. The Federal Trade Commission bill was drafted by Louis Brandeis, and progressives viewed it as the culmination of the crusade to control big business. With some exaggeration, Wilson boasted that the commission would "make men in a small way of business as free to succeed as men in a big way and kill monopoly in the seed." To the consternation of his progressive supporters, Wilson appointed conservatives friendly to banking and business to the Federal Trade Commission, and the board exercised little of its regulatory powers.

Three weeks after establishing the FTC, Congress passed the Clayton Antitrust Act. The new antitrust law significantly expanded the Sherman Act; it prohibited strategies for combining corporate power such as interlocking directories and exempted labor organization from prosecution under antitrust laws. Samuel Gompers, having long lobbied for such protection for labor, called the Clayton bill "labor's charter of freedom." In practice, the establishment of the FTC and the passage of the Clayton Act marked Wilson's acceptance of the concept of federal regulation of big business. Although Wilson and his Democratic supporters had not completely abandoned the individualistic rhetoric of the New Freedom by the end of 1914, they had begun the realistic task of building an enlarged federal bureaucracy to regulate society.

ᴣᴼ *Expanding the New Freedom*

The congressional elections of 1914 gave no clear signals about public reaction to the accomplishments of Wilson's first two years in office, but Democratic Party losses were significant in the House of Representatives — a total of fifty-nine congressmen. The Democrats actually gained five seats in the Senate and retained control in the House of Representatives by a reduced margin. Conservative Republicans gained most. In the new political environment of 1915, Congress passed no legislation that rivaled in importance the major bills of the preceding term.

Nonetheless, the volume of reform legislation passed by Congress actually increased in 1915 and 1916; many of the laws reflected congressional and presidential acceptance of a broader progressive philosophy. In 1916 Congress expanded government responsibility for the welfare of several specific groups. The burst of legislation included a law controlling merchant marine shipping rates, the Federal Farm Loan Act establishing a land bank system to provide loans for farmers, the Keating-Owen Act banning child labor in businesses engaged in interstate commerce, the Adamson Act mandating an eight-hour day for most interstate railroad workers, and the Workmen's Compensation Act that brought 500,000 federal workers under its umbrella. Congress also revised the tax laws, raising the income tax and imposing an inheritance tax, effectively shifting a larger share of the nation's tax burden to the wealthy and to the Northeast.

The legislative flurry of 1916 marked a clear shift in emphasis for Wilson. Some progressives had labeled Wilson a "sham reformer" after his first two years in office, particularly because of his opposition to child labor laws and to woman's suffrage. But whether his conversion was political or ideological, by 1916 the president embraced broader progressive aims. The progressive legislation of 1915 and 1916 brought into focus the dilemma that divided progressivism, and

Louis D. Brandeis   Nominated by President Wilson and confirmed after a bitter fight in the Senate that stirred up ugly anti-Semitic sentiments, Brandeis was confirmed as the first Jew to sit on the United States Supreme Court. He is regarded as one of the greatest and most influential justices of the twentieth century.

twentieth-century liberalism — deciding whether the government should favor one class above another in an effort to protect the weak and compensate for past injustices, or should simply open opportunities for all. By 1916 most progressives agreed that two groups in American society, labor and farmers, deserved special protection and support from the federal government. To a large degree, the Wilsonian reforms welcomed the organized labor movement as a partner in defining the American ideals of equality and morality.

Some oppressed groups fared no better during the Wilson administration than they had under Roosevelt and Taft. W. E. B. Du Bois, William Monroe Trotter, and other black leaders supported the Democratic Party in the election of 1912, but they were soon disenchanted with President Wilson. Wilson had no sympathy for racist demagogy, but he condoned segregation and acquiesced when his Texas-born postmaster general, Albert S. Burleson, expanded segregation among postal employees. Furthermore, while the number of blacks

The Fight for Women's Suffrage, 1917

More than any other individual, Carrie Chapman Catt was responsible for women gaining the right to vote in America in 1920. Her address to Congress in 1917 challenged the nation to live up to its ideals by granting women's suffrage.

The American Revolutionists boldly proclaimed the heresies: "Taxation without representation is tyranny." "Governments derive their just powers from the consent of the governed." The colonists won, and the nation which was established as a result of their victory has held unfailingly that these two fundamental principles of democratic government are not only the spiritual source of our national existence but have been our chief historic pride and at all times the sheet anchor of our liberties.

With such a history behind it, how can our nation escape the logic it has never failed to follow, when its last unenfranchised class calls for the vote? Behold our Uncle Sam floating the banner with one hand, "Taxation without representation is tyranny," and with the other seizing the billions of dollars paid in taxes by women to whom he refuses "representation." Behold him again, welcoming the boys of twenty-one and the newly made immigrant citizen to "a voice in their own government" while he denies that fundamental right of democracy to thousands of women public school teachers from whom many of these men learn all they know of citizenship and patriotism, to women college presidents, to women who preach in our pulpits, interpret law in our courts, preside over our hospitals, write books and magazines, and serve in every uplifting moral and social enterprise. Is there a single man who can justify such inequality of treatment, such outrageous discrimination? Not one....

---

employed by the federal government increased during the Wilson years because of growth in the bureaucracy, the percentage of African Americans holding federal jobs declined during Wilson's presidency. After a visit to the White House in 1914, Booker T. Washington reported: "I have never seen the colored people so discouraged and bitter."

African Americans had good reason to be discouraged on the eve of World War I. The death of Booker T. Washington in 1915 robbed the black community of its most respected leader. Although the Supreme Court in 1915 ruled unconstitutional Oklahoma's "grandfather clause" restricting black voting rights, marking a beginning of judicial defense of civil rights, southern states continued to resort to other means, such as poll taxes, to disfranchise black voters. In 1915, no group of Americans had been so thoroughly ignored by the progressives as blacks; throughout the nation race relations grew more and more tense.

The woman's suffrage movement fared better; in 1916 Wilson became a strong supporter of a constitutional amendment allowing women to vote. Nonetheless, the amendment did not pass until the patriotic spirit during World War I cast women in a favorable light. Wilson urged Congress to pass a suffrage amendment in 1918 as a "vitally necessary war measure." Despite the general recognition of women's contributions to the war effort, the amendment was defeated by the Senate in 1918; resubmitted the next year, the amendment passed by exactly the necessary two-thirds vote.

In August 1920 Tennessee became the thirty-sixth state to ratify the Nineteenth Amendment (Kentucky having been the only other southern state to ratify it), just in time for women to vote in the national election.

The entry of the United States into World War I also added a patriotic aura to the prohibition crusade because of the prominence of German-Americans in the brewing industry. Despite the vigorous opposition of Wilson, many progressives supported prohibition and in 1917 Congress passed a constitutional amendment prohibiting the manufacture, sale, or transportation of alcoholic beverages. By January 1919 the required twenty-nine states had ratified the Eighteenth Amendment. Wilson vetoed the enabling legislation, the Volstead Act, but Congress overrode his veto and prohibition went into effect in January 1920.

Congress also overrode presidential objections in passing new restrictions on immigration, once again with the support of many progressives. Nineteenth-century laws had excluded certain undesirable groups, such as the mentally ill, paupers, and criminals, from immigrating to the United States. In the early twentieth century pressure mounted for passage of a "literacy test" that would require aliens over age sixteen to be able to read at least thirty words in some language before admission. Such laws were passed in 1894, 1913 and 1915, only to be vetoed by Presidents Cleveland, Taft, and Wilson. Nonetheless, the growing strength of the immigration reform movement became apparent in 1917; Congress passed a literacy test over the veto of Wilson.

From Wilson's point of view, the legislative achievements of 1915 and 1916 were all the more remarkable because of his involvement in two serious political squabbles. First, in June 1915 Secretary of State William Jennings Bryan resigned because of a widening disagreement with Wilson over American neutrality policies, thus jeopardizing the unity of the Democratic Party. The next year, in perhaps the hardest political fight of his first term, Wilson secured the confirmation of his friend and adviser Louis D. Brandeis to the Supreme Court. Brandeis, the first Jewish justice to serve on the Supreme Court, was feared by business leaders because of his advocacy of public causes and many of the nation's leading lawyers also opposed his appointment. Anti-Semitism also played a significant role in galvanizing opposition. Confirmed in 1916 by a narrow vote, Brandeis served on the court until 1939, becoming a brilliant defender (often in dissenting opinions) of government social action.

During these critical months, Wilson performed brilliantly as a political leader, more and more identifying the Democrats as the party of progressive reform. Wilson increasingly referred to his party as Progressive Democrats; to a remarkable degree Democratic congressmen followed the president's lead. In the critical Brandeis vote only one Democrat voted against confirmation and only four Republicans voted for the progressive justice. In view of the increasing power of conservatives in the Republican Party and Wilson's progressive leadership of the Democrats, by 1916, a major party realignment had taken place.

CONCLUSION: THE LEGACY OF POLITICAL PROGRESSIVISM

"We stand at Armageddon," Theodore Roosevelt told progressives in 1912, "and we battle for the Lord." That battle, progressives increasingly acknowledged, would be won or lost in the arena of national politics. Armed with consciences inherited from their Protestant ancestors and sheaves of statistics and reports from professional social scientists, progressive leaders sought to rescue the American ideals of democracy, equality of opportunity, and moral destiny. Of course, for all the high-flown rhetoric, the motivations of political progressivism were not devoid of self-interest. While much of the legislation passed during these years can be traced to progressive fervor, nearly every reform was a product of pragmatic compromise negotiated among the increasingly vocal religious, ethnic, economic, and professional subgroups within American society. This morally-driven, practically-compromised politics reigned from Roosevelt to Wilson; uniformly the intent of progressive politicians was to save the American dream by eradicating the evils of modern life. The most fundamental result of their efforts was a permanently expanded federal government, launching, in the minds of some experts, the modern American welfare state.

In the political battles of the first two decades of the twentieth century progressivism wrought turmoil and change in both of the nation's major political parties and came closer than any other movement in the twentieth century to launching a successful third party. What was accomplished by political progressivism? Not much, if one answers from a radical perspective. The progressives were not revolutionaries; they were reformers who believed profoundly in the nation and its future. They never intended to change the American economic system or to destroy private industry and finance. Often their reform vision did not extend much beyond their own interests; it barely included women and generally ignored African Americans and other minorities. Generally speaking, progressives did not like class distinctions and made little effort to address the issue of class inequalities. The social and economic legislation passed during the progressive period lagged far behind that enacted in Europe, where old-age pensions and unemployment insurance had already appeared. If true reform demands visionary changes in the basic structures of society, the progressives were failures, or, perhaps more accurately, they were successful conservatives who helped to perpetuate older American political and economic beliefs.

From a less radical perspective, progressives wrought great changes in the American governmental system, modifying its structure into its twentieth-century form. Some of the agencies established during the Progressive Era continue in operation at the end of the twentieth century. The Federal Reserve System has been revised, but it remains the basis of the American banking and currency system, and federal antitrust policies are still based on the Clayton Antitrust Act. The progressive emphasis on government regulation in the public interest became a permanent addition to American political thought, accepted in later years by Democrats and Republicans alike. The progressives also played a role in transforming the American concept of charity into a public obligation, a notion that underlay the late twentieth-century concept of "entitlement" — the notion that the government, in certain circumstances, was the guarantor of economic security.

The progressive experiment in big government crested during World War I. In many ways World War I became the ultimate progressive crusade, the real Armageddon. However, the sobering ordeal of war and the unsatisfactory peace that followed left behind a nation far removed from the embattled kingdom of God summoned into action by Theodore Roosevelt.

Suggested Reading

Several of these works provide surveys of national politics during the Progressive Era:

Sidney M. Milkis and Jerome M. Mileur, eds., *Progressivism and the New Democracy* (1999).

John Milton Cooper, *Pivotal Decades* (1980).

Richard Hofstadter, *The Age of Reform: From Bryan to FDR* (1958).

Gabriel Kolko, *The Triumph of Conservatism: A Re-interpretation of American History, 1900-1916* (1963).

Four other works offer perceptive interpretations of the two major figures in national progressive politics, Theodore Roosevelt and Woodrow Wilson:

John M. Blum, *The Republican Roosevelt* (1954).

John M. Blum, *Woodrow Wilson and the Politics of Morality* (1956).

John M. Blum, *The Progressive Presidents* (1980).

John Milton Cooper, Jr., *The Warrior and the Priest: Woodrow Wilson and Theodore Roosevelt* (1983).

Suggestions for Further Reading

LeRoy Ashby, *William Jennings Bryan: Champion of Democracy* (1987).

Kendrick A. Clements, *Woodrow Wilson* (1987).

Margaret Finnegan, *Selling Suffrage: Consumer Culture and Votes for Women* (1999).

Willard B. Gatewood, *Theodore Roosevelt and the Art of Controversy* (1970).

Paul W. Glad, *The Trumpet Soundeth: William Jennings Bryan and His Democracy, 1896-1912* (1960).

Lorine Swainston Goodwin, *The Pure Food, Drink, and Drug Crusaders, 1879-1914* (1999).

Sara Hunter Graham, *Woman Suffrage and the New Democracy* (1996).

Elna C. Green, *Southern Strategies: Southern Women and the Woman Suffrage Question* (1997).

Samuel P. Hayes, *Conservation and the Gospel of Efficiency* (1959).

Kenneth W. Hechler, *Insurgency: Personalities and Politics of the Taft Era* (1940).

Steven J. Holmes, *The Young John Muir: An Environmental Biography* (1999).

Lawrence J. Holt, *Congressional Insurgents and the Party System, 1909-1916* (1967).

Suzanne M. Marilley, *Woman Suffrage and the Origins of Liberal Feminism in the United States, 1820-1920* (1996).

David G. McCullough, *Mornings on Horseback* (1981).

John M. Mulder, *Woodrow Wilson: Years of Preparation* (1976).

James Penick, Jr., *Progressive Politics and Conservation: The Ballinger-Pinchot Affair* (1968).

David Sarasohn, *The Party of Reform: The Democrats in the Progressive Era* (1989).

Theda Skocpol, *Protecting Soldiers and Mothers: The Political Origins of Social Policy in the United States* (1992).

Peter Temin, *Taking Your Medicine: Drug Regulation in the U.S.* (1980).

David P. Thelen, *Robert La Follette and the Insurgent Spirit* (1976).

Edwin Weinstein, *Woodrow Wilson: A Medical and Psychological Biography* (1981).

25

A Sense of Mission: The United States in World Affairs, 1900-1920

A T THE BEGINNING of the twentieth century a number of emerging industrial nations, including Germany, Japan, and the United States, challenged the commercial dominance of the older imperial powers, Great Britain and France. Since the 1880s, all the major developed nations had been competing intensely for markets and colonial possessions in Asia, Africa, and the Pacific. Amid this pattern of shifting international power, nations formed new coalitions — usually sealed by secret treaties, further heightening tensions. America's emergence as a world power coincided with this period of international instability, and to a minor extent contributed to it.

The Spanish-American War clearly marked the United States as an emerging world power, but most Progressive Era American politicians focused on domestic problems rather than international issues. In some respects, the rhetoric of American foreign policy from 1900 to 1920 echoed the moralism of domestic progressivism: Americans wanted order and justice for others as well as themselves. International affairs had also attracted Americans' interest since the 1890s because of a growing belief that American industry needed access to foreign markets to avoid the cycle of depressions that had racked the nation in the late nineteenth century — and especially during its final decade. This economic concern found formal expression in Secretary of State John Hay's Open Door notes of 1899.

The American debate over imperialism subsided early in the twentieth century. In 1901, the Supreme Court rendered a series of decisions in the *Insular*

Cases, ruling that the territories recently acquired by the United States did not automatically gain the protection of the Constitution, thus establishing an American empire. Nonetheless, few Americans supported seeking additional major territorial expansion.

But if colonial acquisition lost its luster for Americans in the early twentieth century, the desire to expand American influence around the world gained momentum. Sometimes this expansionism had the clear economic motive of winning new markets for American industry and agriculture, but its impetus was much more broadly based. None of the Progressive Era presidents were simple tools of American businessmen, and frequently business leaders lagged behind other proponents of internationalism. Andrew Carnegie, for instance, supported the international peace movement and other anti-imperialist causes. But most Americans entered the twentieth century confident that all of their ideas and institutions would benefit humankind everywhere, in every way — in the arts, industry, religion, and politics.

The idea of national mission was never stronger than in the early twentieth century, giving a high calling to international affairs. Two competing visions of America's international mission survived through World War I. The more aggressive version saw the United States as an active, civilizing force in the world. So conceived, America had both the right and the responsibility to exert its influence. On the other hand, for many Americans commitment to a strong peace movement replaced anti-imperialism. Believing that war, like other social evils, was the product of irrational drives that progress would ultimately supplant, peace advocates urged the settlement of national disputes by arbitration and began exploring the idea of an international organization of nations to preserve order.

Theodore Roosevelt and Woodrow Wilson became symbols of these two approaches. In broad strokes, Roosevelt stood forth as the bellicose and energetic spokesman for American expansion, with the idealistic Wilson championing international cooperation. But such neat characterizations distort the ideas and policies of both men. All of the Progressive Era presidents were knowledgeable internationalists who attempted to protect the strategic interests of the United States. On most critical questions arising during the first two decades of the century — first building and then protecting the Panama Canal, keeping markets open for American products around the globe, maintaining a stable world order, and entering World War I on the side of the British and French — the tactics and timing of the progressive presidents differed, but their strategic aims were identical.

In short, American foreign policy in the early twentieth century was based neither on New World innocence and idealism nor on a calculated and ruthless quest for economic and political power. Despite important policy differences between the three progressive presidents, each desired to reform the world in America's image and to export the ideals and institutions that each believed had made the United States a great and righteous nation. Remaking the world in America's image became — and would remain — a leitmotif of twentieth-century national policy. Such an egocentric intent may be selfish by definition, but progressive leaders found it a noble, missionary calling, and they often pursued it selflessly.

In the wake of World War I, events at home and abroad brought to the fore the serious disagreements among progressives about how best to further America's international mission. Wilson hoped to build a cooperative world order working through an international organization, and he believed that the foundation for that dream had been laid with the drafting of the Treaty of Versailles in 1919. However, his opponents — who included both conservatives and progressives — were convinced that neither morality or national interest would be served by American involvement in European affairs. In the months after World War I, economic and social dislocation at home and the specter of communist revolutions abroad so fractured American politics that the United States never ratified the international treaties that ended the war. Once again, American foreign policy was powerfully influenced by political developments at home.

ROOSEVELT, TAFT, AND THE WORLD

The seemingly high-handed foreign policy of the progressive Republican presidents, particularly Theodore Roosevelt, appeared to clash with the humanitarian domestic crusades of the period, but both policies were rooted in the moralistic and self-confident patriotism of the age. During the Progressive Era, most Americans believed that they were morally bound to build a haven for democracy and equal opportunity at home, while at the same time to help the rest of the world achieve the same blessings.

Theodore Roosevelt, like many other turn-of-the-century American leaders, divided the world into "civilized" and "uncivilized" nations. To America, he thought, had been given the responsibility of bringing order to the unruly and civilization to the benighted. In a Senate speech in 1900 that echoed Puritan appeals to God's providence, Indiana Senator Albert Beveridge expressed the prevailing blend of morality and nationalism undergirding American foreign policy: "It is ours to set the world its example of right and honor. . . . It is ours to execute the purpose of a fate that has driven us to be greater than our small intentions. We cannot retreat from any soil where Providence has unfurled our banner."

✥ Missions Lead the Way Abroad

The broad base of American interest in international affairs in the early twentieth century was illustrated by the rise of a powerful Protestant missionary enterprise. In 1900, the humorous British magazine *Puck* reported a fictitious dialogue: "'Your majesty,' said the right-hand man of the native king, 'there is a missionary working his way along the coast.' 'Well, we don't want to have any trouble,' said the king. 'Ask him if his people won't be satisfied with a coaling-station.'" In fact, the appearance of Western missionaries had often been the first step in the imposition of imperial control over non-Western peoples during the nineteenth century. By 1900, to many Americans the Christianization of the entire world seemed a realistic goal.

Although most denominational missionary societies had been founded in the early nineteenth century, in 1890 only about 900 American missionaries resided in foreign countries. By 1900 the number rose dramatically, to nearly 5,000, and by 1915 it reached nearly 10,000; the American missionary movement would crest at about 13,000 in 1925. By then, American churches were supporting about half of the Protestant missionaries in the world. Symbolically, in 1900 President McKinley addressed an Ecumenical Missionary Conference in New York City that included representatives from more than 200 agencies, probably the largest such assembly ever convened. The directors of these well-funded mission boards were as efficiency-minded as progressive reformers. A stream of "sociological reports on foreign missions," bolstered by charts and statistical profiles of remote populations, flooded local churches with information about the blessings that Westernization and Christianization had brought, or could bring, to the world.

The Ultimate Cause   On December 19, 1900, the American satirical magazine *Puck* ran this cover, commenting on American laws against Chinese immigration. The caption reads: "'But why is it,' asked the thoughtful Chinese, 'that I may go to your heaven, while I may not go to your country?' The American missionary shrugged his shoulders. 'There is no Labor vote in heaven,' said he." American mission work was often viewed in places like China as a form of Western cultural imperialism.

The Student Volunteer Movement (SVM), launched in 1886 to encourage college students to become foreign missionaries, provided a steady stream of volunteers for missionary societies. The SVM became the organizational base for the remarkable career of one of its founders, John R. Mott, a noted ecumenist and the most famous promoter of missions in the twentieth century. By 1920, 8,140 young American college students, SVM volunteers, had gone abroad. Increasingly, church colleges and seminaries offered professional training for missionaries, and some missions took on a social service cast, providing medical and educational aid as well as the gospel.

Missions leaders typically spoke of the expansion of western culture in millennial language: the reign of Christ would be introduced by the spread of western

The Student Volunteer Movement

Key to American missionary hopes at the turn of the twentieth century was the Student Volunteer Movement. Arthur T. Pierson, an American missionary leader, believed that the enthusiasm and vitality of young Christians would be a catalyst for the evangelization of the entire world.

Perhaps it is [God's] will to produce such an army of volunteers to knock at the gates of the Church and say, 'Here we are! Send us!' that the Church, long apathetic and lethargic, shall wake up to the fact that her present agencies and instrumentalities are inadequate; that her present gifts are disgracefully disproportionate to the needs of the work and the destitution of perishing millions; that the world never can be evangelized at the present rate of progress; that after long and patient waiting, God is taking the matter out of the hands of those who are older, more conservative, over-cautious, and who lack the daring of a courageous faith, and Himself leading on the younger men of our generation to take up the great work of evangelizing the world. To the young men who flamed with enthusiasm for the country, we owe the successful issue of the late war for the Union. To the young men, under God, the world may yet be indebted for the universal proclamation of the Gospel.

civilization. Usually missionaries not only sought to Christianize non-western peoples but also to modernize and westernize them. Many financial backers came to view the westernizing role of the missionaries as the primary justification for the mission enterprise, and the American belief in the superiority of Protestant Christianity was inextricably linked with broader notions of cultural and racial superiority. Perhaps partly for this reason, American missionaries won few converts in places such as China, where Christianity was popularly perceived as a tool of western imperialism.

It was logical that missions enthusiasts would view the political supporters of expansionism as allies; to a large degree, the potential of a mission field depended on imperialist successes. American missionaries most often followed the flag; in some cases, they were attracted to areas where the British colonial system had already spread the English language. American missionaries played particularly important roles in the nations where American diplomatic and commercial interests were strongest, including Hawaii, Japan, and China.

In fairness, it must be said that missionaries frequently opposed economic and political exploitation in the non-western world, and that many of them came to support and appreciate the cultures where they spent their lives. The thousands of American missionaries of the early twentieth century, most of whom were not trained academics, made important scholarly contributions as translators, linguists, lexicographers, and amateur anthropologists and ethnographers. Their children, deeply influenced by the foreign cultures in which they had been reared, became a highly visible presence in the professional foreign service and in American universities throughout the remainder of the twentieth century.

Churchwomen were particularly important in the mission movement; before the outbreak of World War I they had formed forty women's foreign mission societies with more than 3 million members. Women also became important workers in missions, often filling roles that were closed to them at home. Generally denied ordination, women served as doctors, teachers, nurses, and social workers in mission stations around the world. No doubt their examples revised the thinking of thousands of women and men in non-Western societies about the status of women.

In the 1890s, American Catholics began to organize counterparts to Protestant missionary societies. Pressed by European church leaders to give more active support to the international Catholic mission program, by 1920 American Catholics were contributing around $1 million a year to the church's worldwide work. The first American order specifically devoted to foreign missions, the Catholic Foreign Mission Society (the Maryknoll Fathers), was established in 1911 and sent its first missionaries abroad in 1918. It was not until after World War I, however, as the American Catholic church increased in wealth and prestige, that the church's support for foreign missions rose dramatically.

❧ Roosevelt and the Expansion of American Influence

No president before him was better versed in world history and foreign cultures than Theodore Roosevelt, whose assessments of the balances of power in the Pacific and Europe correctly anticipated much that would happen in the twentieth century. Roosevelt viewed international affairs as a competitive struggle between a few great and wealthy nations. He believed that negotiation and arbitration should be used to settle disputes between those nations, maintaining an orderly balance of power. Roosevelt did recognize differences among smaller countries, acknowledging, for instance, the stability of some of the Latin American democracies. But he expected that the weaker "civilized countries," including the smaller European states, would seek security in the great powers' shadow. Beyond the pale of civilization, he thought, lay the rest of the world — a mass of semi-barbarous countries that the big powers needed to police.

Roosevelt's foreign policy reflected the best and worst characteristics of late nineteenth-century middle-class Americans. Deeply committed to morality and justice, he also was unabashedly nationalistic, viewing the United States as a moral policeman in a disorderly world, and he imbibed the white racism of the age. Although his condescension toward the "weaker races," like his patronizing attitude toward individuals he considered his social inferiors, seemed good spirited, his rhetoric and his policies often reeked with patriotic and racist prejudice. He felt a grudging admiration (mixed with apprehension) toward the Japanese, but he considered other non-whites decidedly inferior. Roosevelt agreed that "peace is generally good in itself," and he correctly believed that he made real contributions to world peace during his presidency. On the other hand, he remained convinced that "only the warlike power of a civilized people" could maintain order in the world. Roosevelt's contemporary critics — today echoed by most historians — condemned what they saw as an arrogant abuse of American power during his presidency. But Roosevelt saw no moral inconsistency in using might to bring "progress" to the world and forcing uplift on those too backward to act in their own interest. Indeed, in Roosevelt's mind, not to do so would have been immoral.

❧ *Peacemaking in the Pacific*

American interest in a formal empire weakened in the first years of the twentieth century, partly because the Filipino Insurrection did not end until 1901 and ultimately required the deployment of thousands of American troops in the islands. For more than three years after the end of the Spanish-American War, a rebel army led by Emilio Aguinaldo, who claimed to be the legitimate head of the Filipino nation, waged a guerrilla campaign against the American army of occupation, resulting in the death of more than 4,000 American soldiers — far more than the number killed during the Spanish-American War. When they learned about it, Americans were sickened by the brutal suppression of the rebellion, which left more than 50,000 Filipinos dead and forced thousands into concentration camps. After he was captured in 1901, Aguinaldo issued an appeal for peace that effectively brought an end to the insurgency. In the summer of 1901 William Howard Taft became the first civilian governor of the Philippines. He announced that the United States would assist Filipinos to prepare for independence and initiated a program of building an infrastructure of roads, schools, and health facilities in the islands. Filipinos also received increasing autonomy in local government. This was the first time that an imperial power announced a long-range decolonialization plan aiming at total independence, and although the process was interrupted by World War II, it was ultimately achieved on schedule, on July 4, 1946.

American interest in protecting foreign markets and maintaining a balance of power in the Pacific was an established policy when Roosevelt became president. Confident of American abilities to compete in an open market, and realizing that American national interests required continuous economic growth, the nation's political leaders worked to curtail the other imperial powers' colonial expansion in Asia. When a major Chinese popular uprising against imperialist encroachments, the Boxer Rebellion, presented a grave threat to foreign lives in China in the spring of 1900, McKinley dispatched American troops as part of an international force to subdue the insurrection. At the same time, Secretary of State John Hay pressed diplomatically for assurances that the other great powers would not exploit the Boxer Rebellion as an excuse for partitioning China.

Roosevelt was aware that American influence in the Pacific was limited by distance and by the entrenched power of Japan and the European nations that had already staked claims there, but he hoped to serve as a broker in the region. During his first years in office, Roosevelt saw Russia as the most serious threat to American interests in Asia because of its control over the huge Chinese province of Manchuria. In 1904 this situation changed dramatically when Japanese torpedo boats attacked the Russian fleet at Port Arthur at Manchuria's southern tip, virtually destroying it. At the

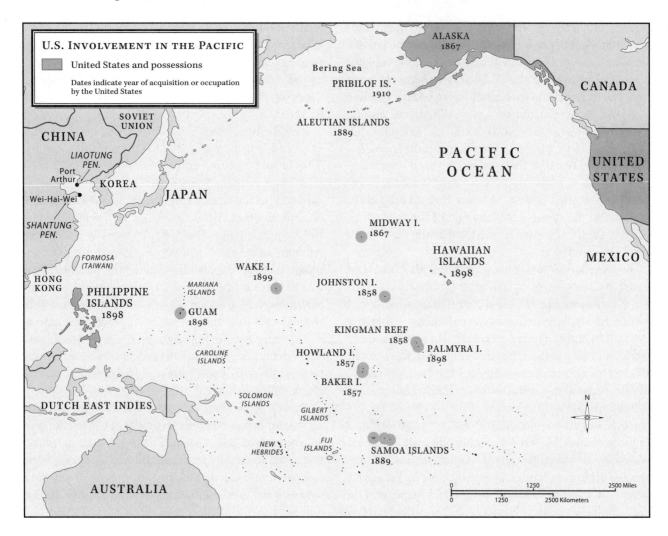

U.S. INVOLVEMENT IN THE PACIFIC

United States and possessions

Dates indicate year of acquisition or occupation by the United States

beginning of the ensuing Russo-Japanese War, American public opinion favored the "underdog" Japanese, at least until Japan's stunning success threatened to tilt the balance of power. Partly because of these concerns, Roosevelt persuaded the two countries to open peace negotiations in Portsmouth, New Hampshire. The president played an active and tactful role in the negotiations that ended the war, and for his efforts became the first American to be awarded the recently established Nobel Peace Prize in 1906. Although some Japanese felt cheated by the Portsmouth Treaty, at the moment most appeared to be satisfied by the measure of control in Korea and Manchuria that victory gave to Japan.

Immigration persisted as the most unsettling problem in America's relations with Asian nations. After the United States had closed the door to Chinese immigration in 1882, more than 20,000 Japanese immigrants settled in California in the 1890s. Racial discrimination ran rampant on the West Coast, partly because of economic and religious prejudices against Asians

and partly because some Americans were beginning to view Japan as a potential military threat — "the yellow peril." In 1906, the San Francisco School Board triggered an international crisis when it ordered the segregation of all Japanese, Chinese, and Korean children into a separate school. Although furious with the "idiots in the California legislature," Roosevelt used the crisis to secure an amendment to the Immigration Act of 1907, which allowed him to negotiate individually with nations to exclude immigrants who might detrimentally affect labor conditions. In a diplomatic exchange in February 1907, known as the Gentleman's Agreement, Japan agreed to cease issuing passports to Japanese laborers. Japanese enforcement of the agreement was so strict that in 1908 more Japanese left the United States than entered it.

American-Japanese tensions remained high in 1907-8, and Roosevelt used these tensions to generate congressional support for a naval building program. In December 1907 Roosevelt dispatched America's modern navy on a global tour. The "Great White Fleet's" cruise around the world began with a stop in Tokyo's harbor, Yokohama, sending an unsubtle message to the Japanese that the gains they had made in Korea and Manchuria by the Portsmouth Treaty did not imply an American withdrawal of interest from the region. Japanese-American tension eased somewhat in 1908 after the signing of the Root-Takahira executive agreement, with both countries pledging themselves to maintain the "existing status quo" in the Pacific, to respect the territorial possessions of one another, and to acknowledge the independence of China. In effect, the agreement gave the Japanese a free hand to develop their economic control of Manchuria, and it secured American interests in the Philippines, where Japan had long been considered a potential interloper.

❧ Tensions in Europe

While many Americans had some understanding of the country's longstanding diplomatic and economic interests in the Pacific, few except those with strong ethnic ties to Europe felt that the United States had a stake in the boiling national disputes that were constantly erupting across the Atlantic. Roosevelt, however, was keenly aware that the rising ambitions of Germany threatened world stability and that German financial expansion in Latin America directly challenged American interests.

American relations with Great Britain had been improving steadily since the war scare during Cleveland's second administration in the early 1890s, partly because of a common cultural heritage and partly because both English-speaking nations had begun to fear the rise of Germany. These improving relations got a boost when the British government signed the Hay-Pauncefote Treaty (1901), conceding to the United States the right to build, maintain, and control a Central American canal. Although the enormously significant Anglo-American political and military alliance of the twentieth century was only beginning to form, Roosevelt clearly envisioned the United States as an ally of the British in any European showdown.

European peace was threatened in 1904 when France, shortly after signing the Anglo-French Entente (a treaty that isolated Germany in the European power struggle), announced its intention to intervene in the affairs of Morocco. The Germans objected. At the behest of the German Kaiser, Roosevelt persuaded the British and French to meet with delegates from thir-

teen nations, including the United States, in Algeciras, Spain, to arbitrate the dispute. The settlement of April 1906 primarily satisfied the French, who gained control over the Moroccan police, but Roosevelt helped persuade Germany to accept the agreement. Trivial as the dispute seemed to most Americans, the Moroccan affair was the first of a series of crises crystallizing the major power rivalries that would trigger World War I nine years later.

Roosevelt's chief interests in the Algeciras settlement were the preservation of peace in Europe and curtailing German aggressiveness. Although the Moroccan agreement did establish an open door policy for the area, Americans had scant economic interest in North Africa. American reaction to the Algeciras Conference sent mixed signals; the agreement was ratified by the United States Senate, but only after a proviso was added stating that the United States accepted no responsibility for enforcing the agreement and did not intend to become involved in European disputes. A Chicago newspaper dismissed Roosevelt's role in the Algeciras Conference as an indication that TR "does not want any wars in which he cannot mix." Such public apathy disturbed Roosevelt, for he believed that in the twentieth century the United States would play a critical role in maintaining the balance of power around the world.

❧ Wielding a "Big Stick" in Latin America

While Roosevelt's intercessions in Asia and Europe made the United States a highly visible international power, his boldest foreign-policy decisions involved the Western Hemisphere. In 1902 Roosevelt quoted an old saw — "speak softly and carry a big stick; you will go far" — to describe his foreign policy. The slogan proved a boon for cartoonists; the press also labeled his policies "cowboy diplomacy." These caricatures encouraged an inaccurate stereotype (that still persists) of Roosevelt's foreign policy as impetuous and irresponsible; in fact, most of his actions represented thoughtful reactions to particular crises. Nonetheless, Roosevelt found his popular image useful on occasion. He believed that Congress was not "fitted for the shaping of foreign policy," and he used his executive powers with a dramatic flair. Willing to compromise with congressional opponents on domestic issues, Roosevelt made his most audacious foreign-policy decisions early in his presidency.

The acquisition of the Panama Canal Zone was

Taking the Panama Canal In 1906, inspecting work on the Panama Canal, President Roosevelt — sporting an immaculately white tropical suit and a Panama hat — posed at the controls of a huge steam engine. This was the first time a sitting American president had traveled outside the United States.

Roosevelt's most daring and successful venture in Latin America. American interest in a canal across Central America reached far back into the nineteenth century, and the Hay-Pauncefote Treaty in 1901 paved the way for action. Roosevelt immediately pressed Congress to authorize negotiations for the rights to begin constructing a canal. Engineers identified two feasible routes, one through Nicaragua and the other across the Isthmus of Panama, at the time a province of Colombia. Though longer, the Nicaraguan passage posed fewer serious engineering obstacles. Further complicating the Panama route were the rights and franchises owned by the New Panama Canal Company, a corrupt and now bankrupt French venture that had tried but failed to build a canal across the isthmus in the 1880s. Only when the French company lowered its price from over $100 million to $40 million did Congress back the Panama route. In 1902 the president was authorized to purchase the assets of the New Panama Canal Company and to proceed with negotiations with Colombia. The following year, Secretary of State Hay signed with the Colombian government the Hay-Herran Convention, giving the United States a ninety-nine-year lease on a canal across the isthmus in return for a payment of $10 million to Colombia and a yearly rental of $250,000. The convention was ratified by the U.S. Senate, but then, unexpectedly, the Colombian Senate rejected it. Chagrined that the U.S. had offered the French company four times as much, the Colombians demanded $20 million and a share in the payment to the New Panama Canal Company.

Roosevelt raged at the "contemptible creatures in Bogotá," calling them "foolish and homicidal corruptionists." Threats abounded. Congress authorized the president to investigate the possibilities of a Nicaraguan canal, and Roosevelt hinted that he might take the canal zone from Colombia by force. But on November 3 the deadlock was broken when a revolution established Panama's independence from Colombia. The insurrection was funded and coordinated from New York City by a junta headed by Philippe Bunau-Varilla, a French citizen and lobbyist for the French Panama Company. Although the inside workings of the plot will probably never be known, it is clear that the United States government was informed in advance of the impending revolution. An American warship, the *Nashville,* put into port at Panama City on November 2, 1903, the evening before the uprising, ostensibly to maintain "free and uninterrupted transit" across the isthmus, landed Marines, and prevented Colombian troops from moving into Panama. On November 6 the United States recognized Panamanian independence and the next week received Bunau-Varilla as minister from the new Republic of Panama. On November 18 the Hay–Bunau-Varilla Treaty was signed, granting the United States the right to build a canal on the same terms offered to Colombia but adding an American guarantee of Panama's independence. Although Roosevelt later contradicted himself about his role in the revolution, on one occasion he stated that "getting Panama as an independent Republic ... was done by me without the aid or advice of anyone," and in a 1911 speech in Berkeley, California, he boasted: "I took the Panama Canal." Work began almost immediately; in 1906 Roosevelt approved the final plans for a lock canal and visited the site himself. Completed in 1914 at a cost of $365 million, the canal was not only a remarkable engineering feat but also a major stimulant to commerce in the Western Hemisphere.

The American acquisition of the Panama Canal was not a senseless display of self-interest and power, in spite of Roosevelt's self-serving statements about his role. Canals had come to be a universal symbol of the civilizing possibilities of modern technology, and many Americans and Europeans agreed with Roosevelt that "ignorant and backward" people should not be allowed to block the march of civilization. Furthermore, the political situation in Colombia was chaotic, making negotiations very difficult, and Panama had a longstanding tradition of revolt and independence-seeking. In short, Roosevelt's actions in 1904 were not so impulsive as he himself pictured them; they were a predictable outcome of the tenor of the times and of the president's own intellectual assumptions.

The Panamanian episode symbolized a growing American interest in Latin America. Of particular concern to the United States was the economic and political instability that made many of the Latin American republics subject to coercion and intervention by their European creditors. Most Americans viewed the South American republics with condescension, speculating that a species of Latin American mosquito communicated "revolutionary bacillus." A financial crisis in Venezuela in 1901, which threatened foreign investments, resulted in a blockade by British, German, and Italian warships and the bombardment of Venezuelan ports and shipping. Upon appeal from the Venezuelan president, Roosevelt persuaded all parties to submit the dispute to international arbitration, but the region's instability remained.

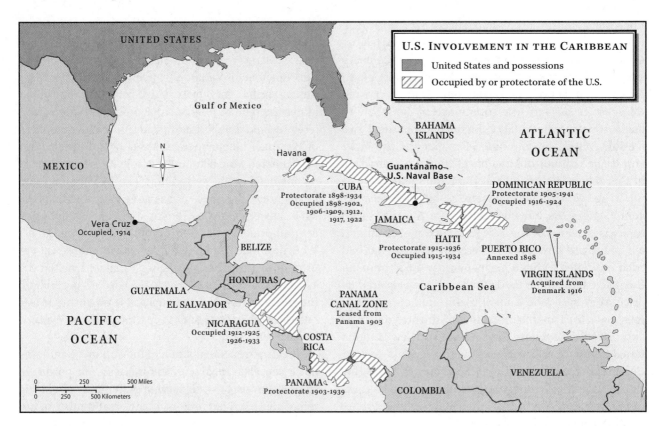

In 1901 Roosevelt did not interpret the European powers' intervention to protect their investments as a violation of the Monroe Doctrine. But when a similar situation arose in 1904 in Santo Domingo, he changed his mind. With characteristic bluster, the president stated his new view, quickly dubbed the Roosevelt Corollary to the Monroe Doctrine, in his annual message to Congress: "Chronic wrongdoing, or an impotence which results in a general loosening of the ties of civilized society, may in America, as elsewhere, ultimately require intervention by some civilized nation, and in the Western Hemisphere the adherence of the United States to the Monroe Doctrine may force the United States, however, reluctantly, in flagrant cases of such wrongdoing or impotence, to the exercise of an international police power."

In the early nineteenth century the Monroe Doctrine had been intended to protect the weak Latin American republics from the reactionary monarchies of Europe. The Roosevelt Corollary, on the other hand, announced that the United States would protect both its own interests and those of European creditor nations from the financial and political irresponsibility of the Latin American republics. A series of American interventions in Latin America in the years that followed had strong economic motives. In 1931, retired Marine

General Smedley D. "Old Gimlet Eye" Butler, told an interviewer: "I helped make Mexico safe for American oil interests in 1914. I helped make Haiti and Cuba a decent place for the National City Bank boys to collect revenue in. I helped purify Nicaragua for the international banking house of Brown Brothers. . . . I brought light to the Dominican Republic for American sugar interests in 1916." But, again, American actions were never purely economic; the desire to build stable, democratic, capitalistic nations in Latin America rested on broad notions of national mission.

❧ Taft's Dollar Diplomacy

William Howard Taft was well prepared to direct American foreign policy. Particularly knowledgeable about the Philippines and China, he was known and respected throughout East Asia, as well as in Panama and Cuba. Taft shared the general foreign-policy perspective of Roosevelt, though he acted more cautiously and patiently than his predecessor.

Taft's most noted diplomatic strategy took its name from his 1912 message to Congress, in which he called for "substituting dollars for bullets" abroad. Although the phrase "dollar diplomacy" did not gain currency until Taft's message, Roosevelt's actions in Latin

America, in spite of his fulminations about honor and righteousness, served quite well to further American economic interests. Although easy to caricature, dollar diplomacy was not simply a plan to protect American foreign investment with military might, as some of the president's critics claimed. Rather, Taft saw American economic expansion in China and Latin America as a means of cooling anti-American feelings and as a strategy for breaking the grip of traditional isolationism in the United States, using investments to stimulate American involvement in areas of the world where he believed the country had a strategic interest. Taft encouraged wealthy Americans to invest abroad and persuaded American bankers to furnish loans to a number of Latin American countries. In the end, the weakness of dollar diplomacy was not that it envisioned a raw use of American power to benefit the wealthy, but simply that it did not work. Businessmen were not willing to risk millions of dollars abroad without assurances that the government would protect their investments.

Compared to Roosevelt, Taft was restrained in using force. He dispatched American marines to Nicaragua in 1912 in the wake of a rebellion that roiled that strategically important country. On the other hand, in 1911, when a revolution in Mexico threatened American economic interests by bringing to power the democratic reformer Francisco I. Madero, Taft recognized the new regime and carefully avoided any hint of intervention. Thus Taft's presidency provided something of a transition from TR's bellicose policies to the more conciliatory philosophy of Wilson.

WILSON DEFINES AMERICA'S MORAL MISSION

A cosmopolitan and learned man, in 1913 Woodrow Wilson brought to the White House a sophisticated understanding of the world. On the other hand, in the decade prior to his election Wilson's attention had focused exclusively on domestic reform, and he had manifested little interest in foreign affairs. "It would be an irony of fate," he wrote to a friend shortly after his election, "if my administration had to deal chiefly with foreign affairs."

In August 1914 a hideous war erupted in Europe, destined to last more than four years and to shape most of twentieth-century global history. As the world's most powerful remaining neutral nation, the United States inevitably became embroiled in quarrels with both

sides. For more than two years, Wilson sought to defend American neutral rights and to persuade the warring nations to end the savage conflict; his efforts were sometimes clumsy and at other times were botched by subordinates who did not share his hopes for peace, but his dramatic and stirring speeches urging peace and justice captured the world's attention. Before the United States entered the war in 1917 Wilson had broadly outlined the terms of the peace.

The Flowering of the American Peace Movement

American foreign policy in the first two decades of the twentieth century was indirectly influenced by a growing peace movement. Before 1900 the peace movement drew supporters mostly from religious groups, but between 1900 and 1914 progressive lawyers, editors, and professional educators joined clergy in founding nearly fifty new peace organizations. In some ways, this new reform was an extension of the anti-imperialist sentiment of the first years of the century, but it was more clearly akin to progressivism's broader confidence in a rational and efficient world. In 1910 Andrew Carnegie — a veteran anti-imperialist — established the Carnegie Endowment for International Peace with a $10 million gift, and in 1914 he gave an additional $2 million to establish the Church Peace Union.

Like domestic progressives, leaders of the peace movement looked to government to correct international as well as national injustices. Optimistically, Frederick Lynch, secretary of the Church Peace Union, predicted that the twentieth century would be "the age of treaties rather than the age of wars, the century of reason rather than the century of force." The membership in peace societies spanned the political spectrum, furnishing a socially respectable outlet for those with mildly reforming inclinations. Peace groups supported a broad array of causes during the first two decades of the century, such as arbitration treaties with England and France signed during the Taft administration and an international peace conference that met in The Hague in 1907, and they opposed American military interventions in Latin America, whether by Roosevelt, Taft, or Wilson. Increasingly, the movement came to champion a world political organization, and in 1915 pacifist leaders founded the League to Enforce Peace to promote that idea.

None of the nation's Progressive Era political leaders was directly involved in the peace movement, but all of them, including Roosevelt, supported the rational settlement of international disputes by arbitration. The idealistic tenor of the peace movement and its call for a world organization increasingly alienated Roosevelt and attracted Wilson, who addressed the first national gathering of the League to Enforce Peace. The practicality of establishing a league of nations would not be fully debated until after World War I, but the prewar peace movement helped define a boundary between the balance-of-power assumptions of Roosevelt and Taft and the moralistic, almost missionary approach of Wilson.

❧ Wilson as Moralist and Realist

Woodrow Wilson was, in the words of his biographer Arthur Link, "primarily a Christian idealist." Wilson's idealist rhetoric soared highest when he set out to define America's moral mission in the world. Over and over, Wilson announced that the United States would never again selfishly expand its power and wealth by the use of force; on the contrary, he called on Americans to support right against wrong and to help the weak against the strong. Wilson deplored balance-of-power politics, holding it responsible for Europe's repeated entanglement in bloody wars. Although Wilson had supported imperialism in the 1890s, his enthusiasm receded in the early twentieth century, and by 1915 he had become an advocate of a cooperative world order based on moral principles. The first American president to seek the protection of human rights abroad, Wilson championed the principle of "self-determination" — "the right of peoples with a common language, culture, and history to govern themselves." In keeping with this presidential emphasis on self-determination, in 1916 Congress passed the Jones Act granting limited self-government to the Philippines and promising later independence.

Wilson labeled dollar diplomacy immoral. In a 1913 speech in Mobile, Alabama, he declared his intention to make friends in Latin America and promised that "the United States will never again seek one additional foot of territory by conquest." Lashing out at selfish nationalism, Wilson warned: "It is a very perilous thing to determine the foreign policy of a nation in terms of material interest. . . . Human rights, national integrity, and opportunity as against material interests . . . is the issue which we now have to face." In 1914 Wilson delighted peace advocates and enraged Roosevelt by appearing before Congress to ask, on grounds of national honor, for changes in the Panama Canal's discriminatory toll

structure. The Wilson administration subsequently negotiated a new treaty with Colombia that expressed "sincere regret" for any injustices perpetrated during the Panamanian revolution and agreed to pay Colombia $25 million. Roosevelt's friends blocked ratification of the treaty until after his death in 1919.

Wilson's appointment of William Jennings Bryan as his secretary of state was a political move designed to ensure Democratic unity in support of the president's progressive agenda, but as fellow moralists Bryan and Wilson also shared a Christian view of the world. Bryan secured Wilson's support for his plan to negotiate bilateral arbitration treaties that committed the signatories to six months of discussion before either side resorted to force. Before the European war came to dominate American concerns, Bryan negotiated thirty such "cooling off" treaties, much to the delight of peace advocates.

Yet despite his idealistic rhetoric, Wilson proved to be a realist when it came to using force in defense of American interests abroad. During his presidency, the U.S. Navy and Marines intervened in Latin America more often than during the terms of Roosevelt and Taft. Without treaty sanction and over the protest of the local governments, American troops occupied Haiti in 1915 (after eight revolutions in four years) and the Dominican Republic in 1916, and the Marines remained in Nicaragua throughout Wilson's presidency, turning that country into a virtual American protectorate.

Wilson's aggressive actions in Latin America, like those of his predecessors, were dictated by the need to safeguard the Panama Canal and by the general desire to protect American interests in the Western Hemisphere, forestalling European intervention. Despite his condemnation of dollar diplomacy, in a general way Wilson was as supportive of American economic expansion as his Republican predecessors had been. Nonetheless, Wilson's idealistic rhetoric was not a hypocritical facade; he wanted deeply to remake other nations in America's image. But like Roosevelt and Taft, he sometimes resorted to force to achieve this lofty goal.

❧ Wilson and the Mexican Revolution

The ongoing revolution in Mexico tested Wilson's resolve to support only those who "act in the interest of peace and honor, who protect private rights, and respect the restraints of constitutional provisions." The overthrow of Mexico's long-time dictator Porfirio Diaz in 1911, threw that nation into a decade or more of political turmoil. A little more than a year after his fall, Diaz was replaced by liberal reformer Francisco Madero, raising American hopes that a responsible democratic government would be established in Mexico. Then, in February 1913, Madero was deposed and murdered in a military coup led by General Victoriano Huerta. Despite pressure from business leaders to recognize Huerta, outgoing President Taft refused.

Wilson inherited the Mexican quandary. For many months American relations with Mexico posed questions that seemed more pressing than the war that erupted in Europe in the summer of 1914. Wilson was outraged by the murder of Madero and refused to recognize Huerta's "government of butchers." Although some Americans urged Wilson to depose Huerta by force, Wilson instead initiated a policy of "watchful waiting," placing an arms embargo on Mexico and urging Huerta to relinquish power and hold free elections. When a promising revolutionary movement emerged under the leadership of Venustiano Carranza, Wilson permitted arms shipments to reach the rebels and stationed American naval vessels off the Mexican coast to block arms shipments to the Huerta forces.

Two incidents in April 1914 provoked Congress to approve a presidential request for authority to use troops in Mexico to protect American rights. The first, in Tampico, involved no more than a brief arrest of several American sailors and an alleged insult to the American flag. A second incident in Veracruz proved more serious. Trying to intercept a shipment of munitions from Germany, the American navy bombarded Veracruz and landed a detachment of Marines who seized control of it. Mexican resistance was heated, resulting in the deaths of nineteen American servicemen and more than a hundred Mexicans. These incidents made it clear that most Mexicans resented the use of American force, regardless of its intent. In June the United States agreed to submit the dispute to mediation and to withdraw all troops in November. Huerta repudiated the negotiated settlement, which called for his resignation, but his government had become so weak that it fell before the end of the year. Wilson then recognized Carranza as the lawful leader of Mexico. But the situation remained volatile.

Pancho Villa, at times a revolutionary supporter of Carranza and at other times a bandit chieftain, coveted American support. In 1915-1916 he became a destabilizing force. Disappointed by Wilson's recognition of Carranza, Villa's band raided villages throughout northern Mexico, killing a number of American citizens. Then, early in 1916 Villa raided several border towns in Texas and New Mexico. His attack on Columbus, New Mexico, in March resulted in seventeen deaths. Pressure mounted on Wilson to abandon his policy of watchful waiting and take action against Villa. Reluctantly, President Carranza granted permission for American forces to pursue Villa into Mexico, but he was stunned when Wilson ordered 15,000 troops into northern Mexico under the command of General John J. Pershing and summoned another 150,000 militia to assemble along the border.

The American army pushed into Mexico but failed to capture Villa. Wilson's resort to force met increasing resistance, not only from Villa but also from other Mexicans. By the end of 1916, as events in Europe were bringing the United States ever closer to entry into World War I, the American army's presence in Mexico had become highly undesirable. Even though no settlement had been negotiated with the Mexican government, in January 1917 Wilson ordered the army out. Shortly thereafter, Carranza was elected president in a democratic election and Villa was captured by Mexican authorities. American-Mexican relations remained strained in the 1920s but slowly improved as Mexico regained political stability.

❋ IN THEIR OWN WORDS

**Report to Woodrow Wilson
on the War in Europe, 1914**
Colonel Edward M. House, President Wilson's chief adviser, was sent to Europe to assess and report back on the situation in Europe.

The situation is extraordinary. It is militarism run stark mad. Unless someone acting for you can bring about a different understanding, there is some day to be an awful cataclysm. No one in Europe can do it. There is too much hatred, too many jealousies. Whenever England consents, France and Russia will close in on Germany and Austria. England does not want Germany wholly crushed, for she would then have to reckon alone with her ancient enemy, Russia; but if Germany insists upon an ever increasing navy, then England will have no choice. The best chance for peace is an understanding between England and Germany in regard to naval armaments and yet there is some disadvantage to us by these two getting too close.

A Steamer Is Sunk   In these photographs taken around 1916, an Allied steamer is sunk by U-boat torpedoes. Though the Germans agreed to halt submarine warfare after this incident, they resumed the practice in early 1917. It was the terrifying, unbridled attacks of the German U-boat submarines that finally brought America into World War I.

The debacle in Mexico illustrated the perils inherent in U.S. relations with Latin American countries. Wilson intended well in Mexico; he supported reformers even when they were unresponsive to American overtures, but he ultimately resorted to armed intervention. Events in Mexico revealed the limits of America's ability to impose reform in Latin America and the internal contradictions in Wilson's moral diplomacy. Anti-American hostility united disparate Mexican elements against the United States. The withdrawal of American troops in 1916 was a tacit admission that, whatever Washington's intentions, Latin American countries meant to make their own mistakes and solve their own problems.

∽ Keeping Us Out of War

The assassination of Archduke Franz Ferdinand of Austria-Hungary in Sarajevo by a Serbian nationalist in June 1914 set off a chain of events that ultimately aligned the Central Powers — Germany, Austria-Hungary, Bulgaria, and Turkey — against the Allied Powers: France, Russia, Great Britain, Italy, and Japan. By early August Europe was engulfed in a conflict that the British called the "Great War." Ultimately thirty-five nations around the world mobilized 65 million men to engage in one of history's most deadly and ghastly struggles, in which defensive positions fortified by machine guns mowed down waves of attacking forces. By 1918 the flower of European youth lay buried along the German-French border, in Italy, and in Russia; 10 million young men had

died and another 20 million had been wounded and mutilated. Directly and indirectly, the war cost over $300 billion. For Europe, World War I was the prophetic Armageddon.

NEUTRALITY

In an address on August 19, 1914, President Wilson declared the United States a neutral and called on Americans to be "impartial in thought as well as in action." He designated October 4 "Peace Sunday" and asked all citizens to pray for peace. Such detachment was hardly possible, particularly for the millions of recently arrived immigrants who strongly supported one side or the other. Nonetheless, many Americans were disdainful of the ancient European hatreds that had once again erupted into war. In Congress, a vanguard of progressive Republican senators still seeking solutions to domestic problems — Robert M. La Follette, George W. Norris, Hiram Johnson, and William E. Borah — formed a phalanx of opposition to American involvement.

As the Central Powers and the Allies launched propaganda campaigns to win American sympathy, each could count on significant blocs of supporters in the United States. The Central Powers drew backing from millions of Americans of German descent, as well as from many Irish-Americans who wanted to see their ancestral homeland win independence from England.

Few Americans felt ties of kinship with France in 1914 — many, in fact, scorned France as a land of decadence and sin. On the other hand, a shared culture, language, and history tilted much American sympathy toward Great Britain in spite of Wilson's call for neutrality in thought. With the exception of Secretary of State Bryan, Wilson's cabinet was strongly pro-Allied. The American ambassador in London, Walter Hines Page, soothed tensions between the United States and Britain, and Wilson's close confidant and adviser, Colonel Edward M. House, favored intervention on the Allied side. When Bryan left the cabinet in 1915, he was replaced by a strong Anglophile, Robert Lansing.

In the early months of the war, the Allied Powers encroached on American neutral rights more frequently than did Germany. As it had done a century before in the Napoleonic wars, Great Britain blockaded its Continental enemies, the Central Powers, early in the war, and the Royal Navy's high-handed enforcement of the blockade angered American shippers. International law forbade shipping munitions and other "contraband of war" from neutrals to belligerent countries, but Britain barred the shipment of many items, including food, under the heading "conditional contraband." The British also enforced the blockade with unprecedented tactics, including intercepting American ships bound for such neutral nations as the Netherlands and the Scandinavian countries. The British foreign office defended its actions as courteously and inoffensively as

possible, and Ambassador Page helped to defuse each crisis by slowing the exchange of notes, allowing time for emotions to cool. Thus, although British violations of American neutral rights were annoying, they never threatened a serious confrontation.

By comparison, early in the war the United States and Germany clashed only infrequently. Americans were shocked when Germany invaded neutral Belgium, seeking to outflank French defenses — an immoral act of aggression that all but staunchly pro-German Americans condemned and that left in its wake a trail of (generally false) atrocity stories, well publicized by Allied propagandists. A young American engineer then living in London, Herbert Hoover, organized a volunteer relief effort, the Commission to Relieve Belgium (CRB), which at its peak distributed $25 million a month in food and medical supplies to the stricken Belgians.

PUBLIC OPINION BEGINS TO SHIFT

The first decided shift in American neutrality followed a German announcement in February 1915, declaring the waters around the British Isles a war zone in which all enemy ships would be attacked without warning.

❋ **IN THEIR OWN WORDS**

Woodrow Wilson's Declaration of Neutrality, 1914

When war broke out on the European continent in 1914, Woodrow Wilson declared the United States neutral. He was determined to keep the U.S. out of the struggle between European alliances. Two years later, he won reelection on the slogan, "He kept us out of war."

The effect of the war upon the United States will depend upon what American citizens say and do. Every man who really loves America will act and speak in the true spirit of neutrality, which is the spirit of impartiality and fairness and friendliness to all concerned. The spirit of the nation in this critical matter will be determined largely by what individuals and society and those gathered in public meetings do and say, upon what newspapers and magazines contain, upon what ministers

utter in their pulpits, and men proclaim as their opinions upon the street.

The people of the United States are drawn from many nations, and chiefly from the nations now at war. It is natural and inevitable that there should be the utmost variety of sympathy and desire among them with regard to the issues and circumstances of the conflict. Some will wish one nation, others another, to succeed in the momentous struggle. It will be easy to excite passion and difficult to allay it. Those responsible for exciting it will assume a heavy responsibility, responsibility for no less a thing than that the people of the United States, whose love of their country and whose loyalty to its government should unite them as Americans all, bound in honor and affection to think first of her and her interests, may be divided in camps of hostile opinion, hot against each other, involved in the war itself in impulse and opinion if not in action.

Such divisions amongst us would be fatal to our peace of mind and might seriously stand in the way of the proper performance of our duty as the one great nation at peace, the one people holding itself ready to play a part of impartial mediation and speak the counsels of peace and accommodation, not as a partisan, but as a friend.

I venture, therefore, my fellow countrymen, to speak a solemn word of warning to you against that deepest, most subtle, most essential breach of neutrality which may spring out of partisanship, out of passionately taking sides. The United States must be neutral in fact, as well as in name, during these days that are to try men's souls. We must be impartial in thought, as well as action, must put a curb upon our sentiments, as well as upon every transaction that might be construed as a preference of one party to the struggle before another.

International law (dating from the era of sailing vessels) required that unarmed merchant ships be sunk only after provisions had been made for the safety of noncombatant passengers. Germany claimed that the development of the submarine as a weapon had rendered obsolete the old rules of naval warfare. Wilson warned that Germany would be held to "strict accountability" for any loss of American life. Most Americans thought that the German threat was a bluff, and in fact Germany had only twenty-one submarines in 1915. Only a few minor incidents occurred in the first weeks of the German blockade, but in March an American was killed when a British liner, the *Falaba,* was sunk. Bryan urged Wilson to ban American travel on all belligerent ships, but the president refused, reluctant to abandon the traditional rights of a neutral.

Then, on May 7, 1915, a German submarine, firing one torpedo, sank another British liner, the *Lusitania,* off the coast of Ireland, igniting a wave of indignation in the United States. The ship had sailed from New York City with a crew of 667 and 1,257 passengers, 188 of them Americans, who ignored the German Embassy's public warning that the ship was subject to attack. The torpedo struck as the passengers were finishing lunch; viewing through his periscope the "throng of humanity attempting to save themselves," the German commander refrained from firing a second torpedo. The ship sank in twenty minutes, taking 1,198 people to their deaths, including 114 Americans, among them socialite Alfred Gwynne Vanderbilt and Charles Frohman, one of the nation's most respected theatrical producers.

The sinking of the *Lusitania* shocked Americans. An Iowa editor called the attack "deliberate murder," and Roosevelt branded it "piracy, pure and simple." On the other hand, the overall public reaction to the sinking was distinctly non-belligerent. Out of a thousand editors asked to telegraph their views to the New York papers, only six called for war. Secretary of State Bryan, fearing the possibility of American involvement, again urged Wilson to frame a conciliatory protest that included a warning to Americans not to travel on belligerent vessels, but Wilson rejected Bryan's appeal and demanded that Germany stop the submarine campaign, apologize, and pay reparations. The German reply was unsatisfactory, arguing that the *Lusitania* was armed (untrue) and carrying contraband (true). Wilson followed with a stronger note that provoked the resignation of Bryan, and a third that was a virtual ultimatum.

Even after the *Lusitania* incident, public opinion favored neutrality. Three days after the tragedy, in one of his most celebrated messages to Congress, Wilson sought the high ground: "There is such a thing as a nation being so right that it does not need to convince others by force that it is right. . . . There is such a thing as a man being *too proud to fight.*" Pro-Allied militants demanded more decisive action; Roosevelt compared Wilson's approach to writing a note of protest to a man who had slapped his wife. On the other hand, peace supporters, led by Bryan and La Follette, called for a more sympathetic hearing for the German position, noting that British violations of neutrality, particularly the food blockade, were as arbitrary and inhumane as submarine warfare.

The German submarine campaign continued into the spring of 1916, and in March Wilson threatened to break diplomatic relations. That ultimatum precipitated a crisis in the German high command, already divided about the effectiveness of the submarine campaign, and resulted in a decision to comply with the American demand. German military leaders believed they could win the war with a huge offensive in the summer of 1916 and that the blockade was no longer needed.

WILSON AS MEDIATOR

In the meantime, Wilson attempted to mediate the European conflict. In December 1915 he sent his friend and adviser Colonel Edward M. House to talk with both sides, but, partly because of House's pro-Allied duplicity, the initiative was ineffective. House led the British to believe that Wilson was prepared to use the American peace proposal as a means of entering the war on the Allied side. The House-Grey memorandum, which Wilson's envoy signed with British Foreign Secretary Sir Edward Grey in 1915, promised American entry into the war if the Germans refused peace talks. But Wilson gutted the memo by penciling in "probably" beside the promise of American entry into the war. In truth, the British had little interest in Wilson's proposals. Like the Germans, the British believed that they could win the war in 1916.

Wilson used consummately idealistic language in defining American neutrality during the first year of World War I. "My interest in the neutrality of the United States," he told a press gathering in April 1915, "is not the petty desire to keep out of trouble. I am interested in neutrality because . . . there is a distinction waiting for this Nation that no nation has ever got. That is the distinction of absolute self-control and self-mastery." Of course, Wilson's policies served more mundane national interests as well. American economic interest in an Allied victory, or at least a status quo peace, grew each month as Britain and France accumulated huge debts in America. In a more general way, Wilson's foremost war aim was a stable postwar world; he believed that the British fleet was indispensable for the maintenance of global order.

In the early months of the war Wilson believed that neutrality would give America a critical voice in framing a peace when the war stalemated. By 1915, however, the president had become a convert to the idea of "preparedness," originally the brainchild of Roosevelt and his militantly pro-British friends. Now Wilson, too, supported bills expanding the army and navy. When peace advocates in Congress, particularly the Bryan Democrats, blocked a military buildup, Wilson appealed to the public. In the process, Wilson discovered that international tensions had transformed him into a popular leader whose idealistic rhetoric swayed public opinion at home and around the world. After the *Lusitania* crisis, public opinion swung strongly behind preparedness, and in the summer of 1916 Congress passed bills expanding the army and the National Guard and authorizing a large naval building program. In October Wilson appointed a Council of National Defense to provide expertise on strengthening American forces.

As a by-product of growing American concern about the European war, the United States acquired the Danish West Indies, today known as the American Virgin Islands. The United States had tried to purchase the islands on a number of previous occasions, but World War I made the acquisition strategically compelling. In August 1916 Wilson agreed to pay the exorbitant price of $25 million, and the Virgin Islands became American territory in early 1917.

❧ The Election of 1916

From President Wilson's point of view, events in Europe had reached a favorable political balance as the election of 1916 approached. Germany had ceased its submarine campaign, and while British actions continued to annoy the United States (particularly the brutal crushing of the Irish independence movement in the Easter Rebellion in Dublin in 1916), America's neutrality seemed secure. Wilson had won a worldwide reputation as a spokesman for peace, and he had pushed the preparedness program through Congress.

Wilson's personal life also had taken a happy turn. In 1914, he was shattered by the death of his wife, Ellen. But in March 1915 he met a forty-three-year-old widow, Edith Galt, and, at age fifty-seven, Wilson fell madly in love. The two were married in December 1915 in the White House. Wilson was boyishly exuberant about the new relationship; Edith became his most trusted friend and, to some extent, adviser.

Even though the times were favorable for Wilson, he had to fight hard for reelection in 1916. The Democratic Party's campaign slogan arose unexpectedly when, in a passing remark, the convention's keynote speaker brought an uproar of approval with the observation that Wilson had kept the nation out of the European war. Wilson had no sympathy for peace radicals like Bryan, who had proposed a constitutional amendment requiring a national referendum to declare war except in case of invasion, and he chafed somewhat at being the peace candidate, knowing full well that America's continued neutrality depended more on the decisions of European leaders than on him. Nonetheless, the Democratic campaign slogan became "he kept us out of war."

Still bitter about the Bull Moose rebellion of 1912 and wary of TR's eagerness to jump into the war at the first opportunity, the Republicans ignored Roosevelt and nominated Supreme Court Justice Charles Evans Hughes, formerly the progressive governor of New York. Because the Democrats had appropriated the peace issue, Hughes was obliged to campaign in defense of national honor. Hughes had a good reform record as governor, supported women's suffrage (which Wilson still opposed), and on the Supreme Court had become the chief advocate of black civil rights. Nonetheless, domestically, the Republicans attacked the reforms passed by Congress in 1916, particularly the income tax and the Adamson Act, thus identifying themselves as the nation's conservative party.

The election was the closest in three decades. Wilson's electoral college victory of 277 to 254 was determined by his cliffhanger win in California, where he had expected to lose. His razor-thin victory was a remarkable political triumph for the president. Compared to 1912, Wilson's popular vote had increased from 41.9 percent to 49.4 percent of the total. (Hughes received 46.2 percent, with Eugene Debs and various minor-party candidates dividing the remainder.) In California the Democratic vote almost doubled. Still a minority president, Wilson nevertheless was the first Democratic incumbent to be reelected since Andrew Jackson's victory in 1832.

At the time, it appeared that the Democratic Party had reduced the huge edge gained by the Republicans at the turn of the century, but Wilson's win was more a reaction to world tensions in 1916 than a fundamental party realignment. Wilson did profit from persisting disaffections among Republicans who had voted for Roosevelt in 1912, and in a number of western states the Republicans continued to be torn by conservative-progressive feuding that played into Democratic hands. Ominously for Wilson, however, the GOP remained the nation's dominant political party.

MAKING THE WORLD SAFE FOR DEMOCRACY

Six months after the 1916 election, the United States declared war on Germany. In the minds of most Americans, including Woodrow Wilson, the United States entered World War I with noble intentions. Wilson asked Congress to declare war only after months of peacemaking proposals; it was not a rash act. In the 1930s isolationist critics of World War I would argue that America's entry into the war was self-serving, induced by profiteers seeking to protect their investments. More perceptive critics would later insist that the U.S. entered the war because Germany threatened the orderly, free-market world that Americans identified with the nation's mission. Some Americans had transparently selfish motives for wanting the United States to join the Allies, and most Americans believed that their own interests would be best served by an outcome that would extend democracy, equality of opportunity, and economic freedom. Nonetheless, American entry into World War I was strongly motivated by idealism, and many American soldiers answered a high call to aid what they perceived as a just cause. More than most nations in most wars, the United States entered World War I with no self-evident ambition for national gains.

Although American armed forces played a limited role in World War I, the nation's entry into the conflict was probably decisive, for the arrival of fresh American troops at the front in 1918 would deal a heavy psychological blow to the war-weary German army. Equally important, Wilson's speeches brought to the war a new sense of moral purpose that bolstered the Allies and undermined the German will to fight.

Overwhelmingly, the American people rallied behind the war. In fact, World War I hastened the acculturation of many ethnic and religious minorities intent on proving their loyalty to the nation in time of crisis. Support for the notions of democracy, equality, and national mission reached high tide during the Great War. The current of patriotism ran so strong that the government seriously encroached on the constitutional rights of unpopular groups — German-Americans, conscientious objectors, and socialists. Only after patriotic fervor began to cool did the severity of the abuses become clear.

World War I altered the lives of most Americans. The millions of men — and thousands of women — who served in the armed forces learned much about their country and the world; the millions who worked in the wartime factories and shipyards were exposed to only slightly less dramatic cultural changes. The social and economic transformation wrought by America's relatively brief participation in the Great War was undone with remarkable speed at its end, but millions of wartime experiences had weakened American provincialism and sectionalism.

❧ Germany's Fateful Decision and Wilson's Troubled Choice

After his electoral triumph in 1916, Wilson hoped to persuade the Europeans to cease fighting. The war remained stalled, and both sides had suffered devastating losses. The British and French were so deeply indebted to American businesses and financiers that they were having difficulty floating loans. In December, Wilson launched a "peace offensive," sending a note to the Central Powers and the Allies asking each side to state its war aims, observing (somewhat naively) that the objectives of the two seemed "virtually the same." Both sides regarded Wilson's note as presumptuous. The British government replied politely but without commitments, whereas the Germans, who once again anticipated a military victory in the spring, brusquely dismissed his inquiry.

In an unexpected appearance before Congress in January 1917 Wilson delivered an eloquent speech urging "peace without victory" and a "peace between equals." Wilson's old political foe, Senator La Follette, pressed through the crowd to grasp the president's hand and tell him gratefully: "We have just passed through a very important hour in the life of the world." Wilson's address also called for "a new international order" to replace the balance-of-power treaty system that had aligned the Allies against the Central Powers.

Fatefully, however, on February 1, 1917, Germany resumed unrestricted submarine warfare, an act that led directly to America's entry into World War I. The Germans were taking a calculated risk. The Kaiser's high command believed that a massive offensive in the spring of 1917 would end the war before American forces could be mobilized and used in Europe, and that in the meantime a well-prepared submarine campaign would cut the Allied supply line. It was a wrongheaded decision, for the Germans underestimated the Allies' desperate condition. Russian resistance would collapse in the course of 1917, and Britain and France were on the verge of financial ruin when the Germans provoked American intervention. In hindsight, Germany traded probable victory for almost certain defeat.

When the German decision was announced, Wilson broke diplomatic relations, but public opinion remained sharply divided about America's next step. The president announced a policy of "armed neutrality," asking Congress for permission to arm American merchant vessels. His request was passed overwhelmingly by the House but was killed in the Senate by a filibuster of twelve peace senators — a "little group of willful men," Wilson called them, and soon he concluded that he had authority to arm merchant ships without congressional approval. By March German submarines had begun sinking American ships, and the president

summoned a special session of Congress to meet on April 2.

Then a colossal German diplomatic blunder hastened America's march toward war. On January 19, the German foreign secretary, Arthur Zimmermann, had secretly cabled the German ambassador in Mexico City to seek an alliance with Mexico should the United States enter the war. In return, Germany promised to aid Mexico in recovering "the lost territory in New Mexico, Texas, and Arizona." Intercepted and decoded by British naval intelligence, the message was passed on to ambassador Walter Hines Page. The U.S. government confirmed the note's authenticity and released it to the press on March 1.

Words such as *solemn, tragic,* and *grave* filled Wilson's address on April 2 as he spoke to the hushed chamber for a prolonged period before revealing what his recommendation would be. Finally, he announced: "There is one choice we cannot make. . . . We will not choose the path of submission." A storm of applause erupted. "It is a fearful thing to lead this great peaceful people into war," Wilson continued, but the United States could not refuse to fight for "democracy and freedom," to bring "peace and happiness" to the whole human race. The president assured the world that the

---

❋ **IN THEIR OWN WORDS**

Woodrow Wilson Asks for a Declaration of War, 1917

Despite President Wilson's determination to remain neutral in the conflict in Europe, German attacks on American ships in the North Atlantic finally left him with little recourse but to ask Congress for a declaration of war.

The present German submarine warfare against commerce is a warfare against mankind. It is a war against all nations. American ships have been sunk, American lives taken in ways which it has stirred us very deeply to learn of; but the ships and people of other neutral and friendly nations have been sunk and overwhelmed in the waters in the same way. There has been no discrimination. The challenge is to all mankind. . . .

Armed neutrality is ineffectual enough at best; in such circumstances and in the face of

such pretensions it is worse than ineffectual: it is likely only to produce what it was meant to prevent; it is practically certain to draw us into the war without either the rights or the effectiveness of belligerents. There is one choice we cannot make, we are incapable of making: we will not choose the path of submission and suffer the most sacred rights of our nation and our people to be ignored or violated. The wrongs against which we now array ourselves are no common wrongs; they cut to the very roots of human life.

With a profound sense of the solemn and even tragical character of the step I am taking and of the grave responsibilities which it involves, but in unhesitating obedience to what I deem my constitutional duty, I advise that the Congress declare the recent course of the Imperial German government to be in fact nothing less than war against

the government and people of the United States; that it formally accept the status of belligerent which has thus been thrust upon it; and that it take immediate steps, not only to put the country in a more thorough state of defense but also to exert all its power and employ all its resources to bring the government of the German Empire to terms and end the war. . . .

The world must be made safe for democracy. Its peace must be planted upon the tested foundations of political liberty. We have no selfish ends to serve. We desire no conquest, no dominion. We seek no indemnities for ourselves, no material compensation for the sacrifices we shall freely make. We are but one of the champions of the rights of mankind. We shall be satisfied when those rights have been made as secure as the faith and the freedom of nations can make them.

United States entered the war without "rancor," that Americans felt no ill-will toward the German people. After asking Congress to declare war, Wilson solemnly counseled that the nation had no other choice: "God helping her [America], she can do no other." Perhaps a majority of Americans did not understand the historical resonance of the phrase, but most Germans would have recognized it as a paraphrase of Martin Luther's words that launched the Reformation.

On April 4 the Senate endorsed the war resolution. Six "irreconcilables," including La Follette, voted against it. Two days later, on Good Friday, the House passed the declaration of war, 373-50. Wilson had moved slowly and reluctantly toward war; even so, American entry into World War I aroused the strongest opposition in Congress since the War of 1812.

In April 1917 relatively few Americans perceived the European conflict as a direct threat to the security of the United States. Some American intellectuals, most notably *New Republic* editor Walter Lippmann, believed that American security was linked so directly to British sea power that the nation was seriously jeopardized by German submarines. Roosevelt also insisted that the United States was fighting for strategic, not altruistic, motives: "First and foremost we are to make the world safe for ourselves. This is our war, America's war." Still, America faced no direct military threat. Wilson and the American public might have vaguely sensed that a German victory would imperil American interests, but the president's call to make the world "safe for democracy" was profoundly idealistic. It is not surprising that such a moral appeal stirred a less uniform reaction than would a clarion call to defend hearth and home.

❧ *The Call to Arms*

America's entry into World War I brought a new exuberance to the depressing struggle. Jauntily, a famous song by Broadway's George M. Cohan promised that "the Yanks are coming, and we won't come back 'til it's over, over there." More than 2 million Americans volunteered for service. Roosevelt asked for command of a division, advertised for recruits to serve in it, and in May announced that he had nearly 250,000 names to select from. Wilson and Secretary of War Newton D. Baker declined Roosevelt's offer, both for political reasons and because they wisely decided to place military command in the hands of professional soldiers. Gifford Pinchot wrote to the disappointed Roosevelt: "At least, he kept *you* out of war."

It came as a genuine surprise to many Americans that Wilson intended to dispatch an American army to the Western Front. "Good God, you're not going to send troops over there, are you?" gasped one senator when his committee was informed of the administration's plans. He, like many of the public, had thought that American participation in the war would be limited to naval action. But Wilson insisted that American men go into the thick of the carnage.

It was soon apparent that volunteers would not satisfy the need for troops, and in May Congress agreed to create the Selective Service Administration, which would conduct America's first draft since the Civil War. The administration established 4,500 local draft boards, each staffed by community volunteers. Draft registration took place in June, and on July 20 the secretary of war drew the first draft number, 258. Throughout the country, registrants with that number received a letter designed to sound friendly and homey: "Greetings from the President of the United States: You have been selected by a committee of your neighbors for service in your country's armed forces."

By and large the World War I draft law worked well. About 24 million men registered, some 44 percent of the country's male population, and 2.8 million draftees served in the military. Draft evasion was a reasonably low 11 percent, although in some localities dodging ran much higher. Partly, the draft law succeeded because most of the economic discriminations that marred the Civil War statute had been eliminated and its enforcement in local communities was (with some glaring exceptions) generally fair and equitable. More important, the brevity of American participation in the war did not require drafting many of those who seriously objected to serving. However, willingness to perform military service was waning rapidly in the last months of the war, and draft resistance might have mounted had the conflict gone on much longer.

A small number claimed the conscientious objector status allowed by the draft law for ministers and members of historic "peace churches," such as Quakers and Mennonites. Local draft boards granted conscientious objector status to 57,000 young men; about 21,000 of that number accepted non-combat duty. Only around 4,000 men refused induction on religious grounds; they were forced to do menial labor in military camps. Most of these radical pacifists came from the ranks of the young Pentecostal churches and the International Bible Students (later called Jehovah's Witnesses). Ironically, Alvin York, the war's greatest American military

Decorated American Heroes   This group of African American doughboys from the 369th U.S. Infantry, more gallantly known as the "Harlem Hellfighters," were decorated for their exceptional bravery under fire — with the coveted French *Croix de Guerre*. They got no recognition from their own army, and returned to face virulent racism in 1919.

hero, who single-handedly killed 14 Germans and captured 132, was a devout Tennessee hill man who declared himself a conscientious objector before being persuaded that the Allied cause was just. Sometimes the "persuasion" that draft boards exerted on would-be COs was quite abusive. Men who claimed to be conscientious objectors on philosophical, political, or other non-religious grounds were almost invariably turned down, and if they persisted in resisting service were dealt with very harshly.

Blacks had a bittersweet military experience during the war. Black enlistments ran high, spurred both by patriotic fervor and the rare economic opportunity offered by a military career. More than 350,000 blacks served in the armed forces during the war, all of them segregated into all-black units that were often poorly trained and commanded by white officers who resented the assignment. Under pressure from civil rights leaders, the military established a training center for black officers, and by the end of the war about 1,200 black officers had been commissioned.

Although many blacks served in menial service jobs such as cooks and stewards, NAACP pressure led to the formation of two black combat divisions, one of which saw action in France. Although some black units fought

with valor, others — demoralized by poor training, inadequate equipment, and inferior leadership — left war records that did little to ease prejudice against black soldiers. Even those blacks who had positive experiences overseas resented returning to a segregated society. Overall, the military experiences of blacks worsened postwar American race relations.

African Americans were not alone in suffering negative stereotyping because of their wartime experiences. Progressive Era obsessions with gathering "facts" and seeking "efficiency" culminated in a policy of testing the intelligence of all draftees, and those whose scores were too low were rejected. The instrument that was used was the Stanford-Binet Intelligence Quotient (IQ) test, recently devised and full of cultural biases that favored American-born and -educated whites. Draftees were asked, for example, about the French painter Rosa Bonheur, whom middle-class high school students might have studied but who would have stumped a poor rural Southern youth (black or white) or a Polish immigrant. Not surprisingly, both blacks and white "ethnics" often scored abysmally low and later found themselves labeled as "morons." In the 1920s, "findings" such as these would be triumphantly cited by nativists and racists as "proof" that the nation must take drastic steps to save itself from "mongrelization" and idiocy, as well as by progressive educators convinced that most public school students were too stupid to take a rigorous curriculum.

Mobilization of the armed forces proceeded smoothly. In a little over a year the services swelled from 200,000 "regulars" to some 5 million men and women. The military built thirty-two camps across the nation to train the new recruits, exposing many for the first time to modern technology and such basic hygiene as regular bathing and shaving (with the newfangled safety razor, replacing the straight razors that most men of the day used). Those soldiers who actually served abroad (for many others, the war was over before they got there) experienced an even greater culture shock, summed up by the famous question: "How are you gonna keep 'em down on the farm after they've seen Paree?"

Military training emphasized moral uplift. Although

World War I camps did not witness religious revivals like those that had erupted among soldiers during the Civil War, chaplains conducted regular religious services, and most camps had clubs operated by such organizations as the Red Cross and the YMCA. A variety of organizations coordinated religious activities in military camps — the General Wartime Commission of the Federal Council of Churches, the Knights of Columbus, the National Catholic War Council (later the National Catholic Welfare Conference), the Jewish Welfare Board, and the Young Men's Hebrew Association. The prominence of these organizations in the war effort, coupled with the strong Protestant moralism that pervaded American progressivism and with legitimate public-health concerns about venereal disease, ensured that illicit sexuality got presented to the troops as an enemy almost as dangerous as the Kaiser. "How can you salute the flag when you're filthy with gonorrhea?" demanded a typical poster aimed at recruits. Every effort was made (not always successfully) to keep prostitutes away from the training camps. And when French premier Georges Clemenceau offered to provide the American troops in France with the officially inspected brothels that routinely serviced other Allied soldiers on leave from the front, his letter elicited alarm from Secretary of War Baker: "Don't show this to the president, or he'll call off the war."

✐ The American Expeditionary Force Contributes

American military efforts in World War I were more efficient and professional than they had been in most of the nation's earlier wars. Wilson and Baker left major military decisions in the hands of the commander of the American Expeditionary Force (AEF), General John J. Pershing. The Allies were never satisfied by the rate at which American troops reached France, and they were openly displeased when Pershing refused to send early arriving troops to the front and insisted that the AEF fight as a unit under American command. Despite these spats, the U.S. military made a weighty contribution to the Allied victory. At the war's end, more than 2 million American troops were in France and nearly 1.4 million were on the Western Front.

The American navy played a significant role in transporting American troops to France, although the British did much of that job because of the small size of the American merchant marine. The navy's most vital contribution to the war was the escort service by which it protected troop convoys from German submarines, which in the spring of 1917 took a frightful toll on Allied shipping. American naval commanders threw their weight behind the adoption of a convoy system proposed by a group of junior British naval officers. Grouping troop ships closely together and escorting them with British and American destroyers, the convoy system sharply reduced the submarine threat and brought losses to bearable levels.

American troops began arriving in France in June 1917. A few units went to the front in October, just before the fighting came to a standstill in the winter of 1917-1918. By May 1918 around 500,000 American troops were in France and the pace of shipment had quickened. In July, more than 300,000 Yanks arrived.

They got there just in time, for the moment was ripe for a great, final German offensive. After suffering some 9 million casualties, Russia had already collapsed during the previous twelve months. Weakened by military catastrophes and his own incompetence, the czar had been overthrown by a popular uprising in March 1917 (February, according to the Russian calendar). A provisional government then tried to keep Russia in the war on the Allied side — to its own ultimate undoing — but it was overthrown by the Bolshevik Revolution in November (October) 1917. In March 1918 the Bolshevik government withdrew from the war, signing the humiliating Treaty of Brest-Litovsk. The Italians had also suffered crushing defeats at Austro-Hungarian hands in late 1917 and now could offer little real resistance. Then, in March 1918, hoping to win the war before more American troops got across the Atlantic, Germany launched a massive offensive along a fifty-mile stretch of the Western Front, endeavoring to split the French and British armies and drive through the gap to Paris.

Reeling from the German attack, the Allies persuaded Pershing to begin sending American units to the front in small numbers in March and in division-strength units at the end of May. American Marines played a heroic role in stopping the Germans in a battle at Belleau Wood in June; of the 8,000 Marines engaged, more than 5,000 were killed or wounded. The German offensive was finally stopped in July in the bloody Second Battle of the Marne, in which 85,000 American troops fought.

In July and August 1918 the Allied armies went on the offensive, strengthened by a steady stream of fresh American troops. In September the American army was assigned a sector of the battle line. Pershing was an aggressive commander, eager to break the stale-

The Western Front In 1918, American fighting men proved their mettle by holding a crucial segment of the Western Front as the Germans attempted their last breakthrough, then spearheaded the Allied counterattack. This photograph suggests the desolation of the World War I battlefield, where every inch was bitterly contested. The American soldiers pictured here, incidentally, belonged to an all-black regiment.

mate on the Western Front with the kind of overwhelming assault that under World War I conditions was almost guaranteed to yield enormous casualties. However, the German troops that the American soldiers faced were themselves exhausted and often in overextended positions. So when Pershing thrust about 550,000 American troops into the first independent American offensive to recapture St. Mihiel, they made dramatic gains, though at a high price. Between September and November about 1.2 million American troops battled along a twenty-five-mile line in the Allies' huge Meuse-Argonne Offensive that pushed the Germans back all along the Western Front. By early November, Allied troops were poised to drive into Germany. At that point the imperial regime collapsed, the Kaiser fled to Holland, and representatives of the newly proclaimed German Republic signed an armistice on November 11.

At the end of the war Pershing commanded forty-two American divisions in France, twenty-six of them at the front. Around 50,000 Americans had been killed in action — almost as many as would die in the Vietnam War — and more than 200,000 others were listed as casualties. Another 60,000 Americans perished from non-combat causes, mostly in an influenza epidemic that decimated all World War I armies.

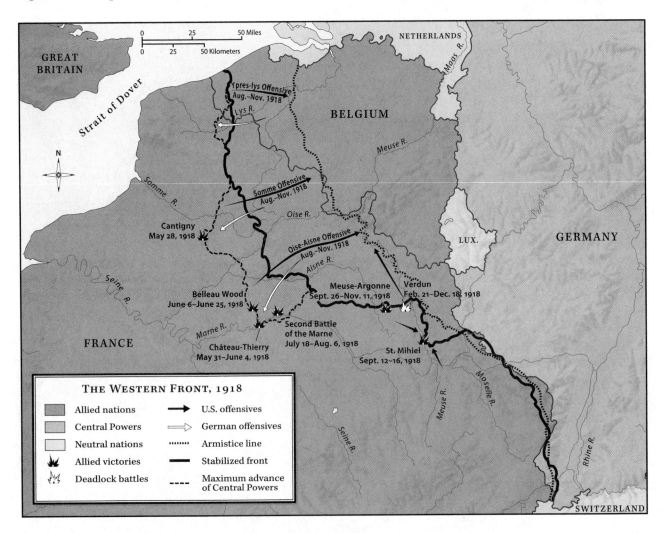

A generation of future American leaders played roles in the war. Herbert Hoover, already famous for leading the enormous American volunteer effort to feed starving civilians in Belgium (he would later perform the same service in civil war–wracked Russia) during the period of American involvement in the war, spearheaded an important federal program to ensure the nation's food supply. Franklin Delano Roosevelt occupied his distant cousin Theodore's old position of Assistant Secretary of the Navy. His future vice-president, Harry S Truman, rose from lieutenant to major while serving with his Kansas City buddies in the 129th Field Artillery. Captain Dwight D. Eisenhower, a young professional soldier, had requested an overseas assignment but was ordered to organize a number of training centers in the United States and ended the war with the temporary rank of lieutenant colonel. George C. Patton commanded an American unit of British-built tanks. Flamboyant Douglas MacArthur won many honors and much publicity for his heroics as the commander of the famous 42nd (Rainbow) Division in France and was promoted to general.

❧ Organizing the Nation for War

The task of shifting the American economy to wartime production was as challenging as military mobilization. The war accelerated economic changes that were already at work in American society — industrial growth, technological progress, and the expansion of agricultural production — and it provided a laboratory for testing progressive efficiency, which was one reason that certain progressives like Walter Lippmann enthusiastically endorsed the war effort. The need to coordinate the economy led to unprecedented government planning and regulation. The government dismantled wartime regulations hastily in 1919, but World War I gave the United States its first taste of a planned economy, which would be remembered during the Great Depression and World War II.

In many ways, America's most important contribution to World War I was financial. The American treasury made a series of emergency loans to the Allies that sustained their ability to wage war and left behind a legacy of over $10 billion in Allied debts. By 1919 Britain had borrowed more than $4 billion and France $3.4 billion. The United States's position as debtor nation ended (in 1914 it had owed foreigners a net sum of more than $3 billion), and World War I left it one of the globe's leading economic powers — almost the equal of Great Britain.

Despite his soaring rhetoric, Wilson took a hard-headed view of the leverage that he believed the Allies' indebtedness was handing to the United States, and he did his best to use wartime circumstances to expand American economic influence not only in western Europe but also in Latin America. His efforts were greatly resented by other Allied governments, which saw them as blatantly hypocritical. However, the war ended before Wilson was able to exploit America's newfound economic clout to the full.

World War I brought the United States its first experience in huge deficit spending. The direct cost of America's war effort was nearly $22 billion; between 1915 and 1920 the national debt soared from $1 billion to $20 billion. Early in the war the government depended on large financiers for funds, but that strategy placed too much power in the hands of a few wealthy institutions. Secretary of the Treasury William McAdoo proposed financing a major portion of the war cost through taxes, and in 1917 and 1918 Congress levied new taxes on corporations, individual income, and inheritances, putting a much heavier burden on the wealthy, who paid most of the taxes. Federal taxation raised about $9 billion and paid approximately one-third of the cost of the war.

Borrowing paid for the rest. The government conducted five campaigns of selling small-denomination bonds to the citizens. A stable of celebrities, including actor Charlie Chaplin, singer Enrico Caruso, and baseball stars Ty Cobb and Babe Ruth, hawked the bonds in huge rallies throughout the country. These drives were both financial and psychological successes, raising more than $21 billion and fanning wartime patriotism.

Gearing up the nation's industry for wartime production was an enormous challenge. The Allies, the American military, and the private sector jammed factories with orders. In some industrial areas the response was impressive, as American manufacturers sharply increased production of clothing, small arms,

and automobiles. American shipyards expanded their labor force from 50,000 to 350,000. On the other hand, American industry supplied almost no tanks, airplanes, or heavy guns to the Allied war effort.

The Wilson administration coordinated the nation's economic transformation through presidentially appointed boards. The most powerful of these, the War Industries Board (WIB), established in July 1917, was charged with increasing industrial production and eliminating waste. Congress granted broad domestic powers to the president. The Lever Food and Fuel Control Act, passed in August 1917, authorized him to control the production and distribution of food and fuel. Congress also established the Bureau of Investigation in 1917 (renamed the Federal Bureau of Investigation in 1923) as a national police force to enforce wartime laws. Its first head was a young lawyer named J. Edgar Hoover, who would hold the job until his death in 1972.

In most economic areas the president appointed academicians and businessmen to lead boards that encouraged voluntary cooperation. Known as dollar-a-year men because they accepted only token compensation, many of the executives did laudable work. Herbert Hoover, head of the Food Administration, was the most successful, tripling the amount of food available for export. Hoover resorted to some price fixing, but relied mostly on voluntary food conservation — asking citizens, for example, to observe wheatless Mondays and Wednesdays, meatless Tuesdays, and porkless Thursdays and Saturdays. Providing a patriotic example, Wilson grazed sheep on the White House lawn.

Voluntary cooperation proved less successful in controlling major industries. Competition among the nearly 3,000 American railroad companies badly snarled the nation's transportation system. In early 1918 the U.S. Railroad Administration, headed by treasury secretary McAdoo, began operating American railroads as a unified system. The Railroad Control Act, passed by Congress in March 1918, fixed the compensation to be received by each private railroad company and provided for the dissolution of government control no later than twenty-one months after the ratification of a peace treaty.

Appointed chairman of the WIB in March 1918, Bernard M. Baruch was the chief architect of the American industrial conversion. A southerner and an independently wealthy stock trader, Baruch was a warm friend of the president. Although the powers of the WIB were never well defined, Baruch coordinated the actions of other boards, assigned raw materials, awarded contracts, set prices, and demanded compliance with government guidelines. Combining an extraordinary mastery of detail, great personal charm and persuasiveness, and a close personal relationship with Wilson, Baruch faced down anti-Semitic prejudice and effectively coerced cooperation from American industrial leaders. In spite of business resentment of government intervention, big business profited from the war both directly and indirectly. The war opened the era of huge government contracts that wedded industry to federal spending, and saw the appearance of the cost-plus contract that guaranteed profits. The same approach would be used during World War II, and it foreshadowed what President Dwight D. Eisenhower in 1961 would call "the military-industrial complex."

Wilson asked Congress for bipartisan support during the war, declaring that "politics is adjourned." Most Republicans felt that Wilson continued to play politics, however, particularly during the congressional elections of 1918, when he called on the American public to endorse his leadership by electing a Democratic Congress. He failed, for the Democrats lost both houses of Congress. While Wilson's stature as an inspirational wartime leader was beyond challenge, as the war in Europe drew to a close, it became clear that the Republicans were neither a vanquished nor an intimidated opposition.

✑ Rallying around the Flag

Most Americans patriotically backed World War I. Progressives had feared cultural diversity before the war, and patriotism made national unity seem even more imperative after American entry into the war, especially because millions of Americans had ancestral ties to enemy — or at least anti-British — nations. The organized labor movement offered critically important support; American Federation of Labor head Samuel Gompers was an exemplary patriot. Most unions agreed to submit labor disputes to arbitration before the National War Labor Board, co-chaired

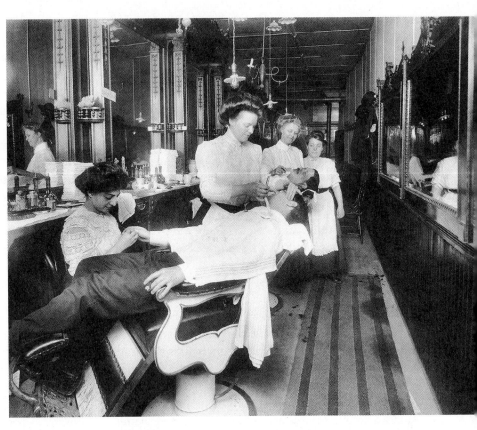

Women Barbers of World War I   Women helped with the war effort by taking over jobs that had previously been held by men, now gone to serve in the military. Here women barbers shave and manicure clients. By invading barbershops, a traditional space for male bonding and camaraderie almost as sacred as the saloon, women barbers shocked many men's sensibilities.

by Frank P. Walsh and ex-president Taft. Overall, the board was sympathetic to labor; during the war A.F. of L. membership soared from 3 million in 1917 to 5 million in 1920.

Women played a crucial role in the wartime transformation of the economy. Around 16,500 women served overseas during the war, mostly as ambulance drivers, canteen workers, clerical workers, telephone operators, and nurses. Many thousands of other women entered the work force for the first time during the war, often filling industrial jobs traditionally occupied by men. Although women laborers contributed to winning the war and served as an example for later generations, most industrial jobs were reclaimed by men at the end of the war.

African Americans also viewed the war as an opportunity to better their lot. In addition to those who volunteered or were drafted in the military, thousands more migrated out of the South to work in the factories of the North. While many found jobs, they also encountered race prejudice and discrimination. Race tensions triggered an ugly riot in East St. Louis, Illinois, in July 1917 that resulted in the deaths of nine whites and an uncounted number of blacks.

Most of the nation's churches strongly supported the war. Although the traditional peace churches dissented, backing for the war was almost universal among Catholic, mainline Protestant, and Jewish leaders. World War I was a milestone in the Americanization of the Catholic Church, for the church's leaders seized the crisis as an opportunity for Catholic immigrants to prove their loyalty to the nation. In April 1917 James Flaherty, head of the Knights of Columbus, promised Wilson the support of his organization, and American Catholic bishops rivaled their Protestant counterparts in blessing American entrance into the war. Eventually, more than a million Roman Catholic young men served in the American military, and only four claimed conscientious objector status (which their church's leaders did not encourage). Even those Irish and German Catholic communities that had opposed American entry into the war quickly rallied behind the flag. Another outsider religious group that won respect during World War I was the Church of Jesus Christ of Latter-Day Saints, probably the most despised and ridiculed religious group in the nation in the late nineteenth century. Utah regularly went over the top in buying war bonds and oversubscribed volunteer enlistments, and during the war Mormons began their transformation from outsiders to supremely patriotic Americans.

Vigilance, 1917 In addition to the officially sponsored Committee on Public Information, independent groups like this one sprung up in response to widespread fear of spies and disloyal aliens. "Will you not," the poster demands, "join with other patriotic Americans in organizing a Vigilance Corps in your community?" The hysteria that such "vigilance" unleashed produced endless snooping, some violence, a number of deaths, and countless violations of basic civil liberties.

Most liberal Protestants viewed World War I as a part of the quest for the kingdom of God. Frank Mason North, president of the Federal Council of Churches of Christ in America, urged Christians to back the war: "The war for righteousness will be won! Let the Church do her part." Sometimes religious rhetoric turned vengeful, as when a leading New York City preacher demanded a postwar settlement calling for "the sterilization of 10,000,000 German soldiers and the segregation of the women."

Many fundamentalists viewed World War I as the cataclysm prophesied to precede the return of Jesus. Despite this theological pessimism, however, most fundamentalists were as patriotic as other Protestants. No one more emphatically pronounced God's blessing on the war than Billy Sunday. "If you turn hell upside down," Sunday told an audience in 1917, "you will find 'Made in Germany' stamped on the bottom." In a prayer before the House of Representatives, the popular evangelist gave the Lord a strong reminder about Germany: "Thou knowest, O Lord, that no nation so infamous, vile, greedy, sensuous, bloodthirsty ever disgraced the pages of history."

Although organized religion played a role in building patriotic support, the job of selling the war at home and abroad fell primarily to the Committee on Public Information, established by Wilson in April 1917. The committee was headed by George Creel, a muckraking journalist who had won Wilson's confidence. Secretary of War Newton Baker described the work of the committee as "the whole business of *mobilizing the mind of the world*." The committee issued news releases, published pamphlets, and employed some of the nation's best-loved artists to design patriotic posters. Creel recruited around 75,000 leaders to deliver brief prepared speeches at public gatherings in their communities; these clergymen, lawyers, teachers, and other prominent citizens, nicknamed "Four Minute Men" because of the length of their prepared texts, supplied every community with the loftiest justifications for the war combined with blood-curdling portrayals of Germans as modern "Huns." At its worst, Creel's propaganda oversimplified the war's causes and linked all doubt with treason.

In the long run, the most important work done by the Committee on Public Information was the printing and widespread circulation of Wilson's speeches. Translated into scores of languages, pamphlets containing presidential statements were distributed around the world. Creel smuggled more than a million copies of Wilson's Fourteen Points speech (see below) into Germany and Austria-Hungary, where it greatly stimulated peace sentiment. American propaganda contributed to Wilson's emergence as a cult hero in Europe, so that by the end of the war the American president's picture was displayed on the walls of humble homes all over the continent, and workers were idolizing the president as the champion of democracy and a just peace. In all, the Committee on Public Information was the first coordinated effort by the American government to manipulate public opinion.

❧ Patriotism and Repression

The liberties guaranteed by the Constitution are often imperiled by war, and World War I proved to be an especially difficult time for these liberties as Congress and the president sanctioned numerous violations of citizens' rights. By "selling" the war as an idealistic crusade to cleanse the world of the evil allegedly encapsulated in "Prussian militarism" and "Hun barbarity," the American authorities were in fact unleashing an ideological struggle and whipping up a public hysteria that had no rational bounds. Wilson himself set the tone in his war message on April 2, 1917, threatening "disloyal" elements with resolute repression — and he meant it. With his encouragement, Congress passed four laws in 1917 and 1918 designed to restrict freedom of speech and action, and the administration enthusiastically enforced them. The Espionage Act, passed in June 1917, empowered the postmaster general to bar from the mail "treasonable" or "seditious" materials and provided fines and imprisonment for spying, sabotage, or activity detrimental to the military. The Trading with the Enemy Act, passed in October, forbade trading with Germany and gave the postmaster general the right to censor materials going to and from enemy nations.

The Alien Act and the Sedition Act followed in 1918. The first gave broad powers to the commissioner of immigration to deport non-citizen residents suspected of hostile actions. The Sedition Act was the most sweeping of the repressive laws. It imposed fines and prison terms on persons found guilty of interfering with the prosecution of the war or war production, including those using "disloyal, profane, scurrilous, or abusive language" about the American government, the Constitution, the flag, the military forces, or industry.

These wartime acts were vigorously enforced. The publications of socialists, political radicals, and pacifists became special targets for suppression. By the war's end, more than two thousand persons had been imprisoned under the Espionage Act and about a thousand were convicted under the Sedition Act. Socialist Eugene V. Debs, the most notable public figure convicted under the Sedition Act, in 1918 was sentenced to ten years in prison for saying in a speech: "They tell us that we live in a great free republic; that our institutions are democratic; that we are a free and self-governing people. This is too much even for a joke."

State and local governments often suppressed dissent even more vigorously than the federal authorities.

"Spies and Lies," 1917

One key factor in getting Americans behind the war effort was the work of the Committee on Public Information, which designed posters and pamphlets to spread its message of support for the American cause — sometimes feeding anti-German hysteria in the process.

German agents are everywhere, eager to gather scraps of news about our men, our ships, our munitions. It is still possible to get such information through to Germany, where thousands of these fragments — often individually harmless — are patiently pieced together into a whole which spells death to American soldiers and danger to American homes....

Do not discuss in public, or with strangers, any news of troop and transport movements, or bits of gossip as to our military preparation, which come into your possession....

Send the names of such [suspicious] persons, even if they are in uniform, to the Department of Justice, Washington. Give all the details you can, with names of witnesses if possible — show the Hun that we can beat him at his own game of collecting the scattered information and putting it to work. The fact that you made the report will not become public.

You are in contact with the enemy *today*, just as truly as if you faced him across No Man's Land. In your hands are two powerful weapons with which to meet him — discretion and vigilance. *Use them.*

Some states seriously curtailed the rights of German-American citizens; Nebraska, for example, passed a law forbidding the teaching of German in public schools. Informal and extra-legal repression by public opinion at large or by self-appointed super-patriot groups ranged from the silly to the awful. Sauerkraut had to be referred to as "liberty cabbage," symphony orchestras refused to perform the works of German composers like Beethoven, German books were banned from public libraries and sometimes burned, and German-Americans could find themselves publicly humiliated. In one particularly horrifying incident, a young man in St. Louis whose only offense was his German birth was brutally lynched, and the leaders of the mob were subsequently acquitted.

As a consequence of the World War I repression, the National Civil Liberties Union (now known as the American Civil Liberties Union) was founded in 1917 by Roger Baldwin, a young social worker and conscientious objector who was imprisoned for refusing to register for the draft. The organization became the foremost defender of civil liberties and of unpopular causes in twentieth-century America.

Cases involving the wartime laws began to reach the Supreme Court in 1919, and at first the Court gave its approval to much of the official repression campaign. In March the court upheld the Espionage Act in *Schenck v. United States.* Justice Oliver Wendell Holmes wrote the decision defending the government's right to restrict freedom of speech in times of crisis, especially war. Holmes argued that free speech was always subject to a certain amount of restriction and that in determining when speech was unacceptable the standard should be "a clear and present danger" that it would cause unlawful behavior. The Sedition Act was also upheld in *Abrams v. United States* (1919), although in that case Holmes was joined by Brandeis in a dissent that urged that the government carefully avoid suppressing "the free trade of ideas." "The best test of truth," wrote the eloquent Holmes, "is the power of the thought to get itself accepted in the competition of the market." To Holmes, though, that marketplace did not always function efficiently, and the government had the ultimate authority to decide when it needed to be temporarily shut down.

FROM VICTORY TO DISILLUSIONMENT

Rarely in history have war aims been stated with more grace and idealism than in Woodrow Wilson's wartime addresses. In 1919, Wilson went to the Peace Conference in France with concrete notions about building a cooperative world order, but the Treaty of Versailles turned out to be a compromise that satisfied few. By 1920 the Senate had rejected the treaty, and the grandiose hopes of the war years vanished with amazing rapidity.

While the Senate debated the treaty, the nation struggled with the problems of adjusting to a peacetime economy. Postwar dislocation in 1919 and 1920 was exacerbated by anxieties caused by the Marxist revolution in Russia. Preoccupied with the fight over the treaty and weakened by a severe stroke, President Wilson offered little leadership during the critical months of demobilization at home. In the eighteen

The Big Four   Formally dressed (as diplomats then customarily did) in morning coats and striped trousers, the leaders of the Allied and Associated Powers posed at the Paris Peace Conference. Left to right: David Lloyd George of Great Britain, Vittorio Orlando of Italy, Georges Clemenceau of France, and Woodrow Wilson of the United States.

months following the armistice, the unity of purpose of the wartime years was replaced by a divisive and angry mood.

❧ From the Fourteen Points to the Peace of Paris

During both the war and the peacemaking process, Woodrow Wilson tried to position himself above the convoluted politics of Europe. After it entered the war, Wilson insisted that the United States should be called an "associate power" rather than an ally, a distinction that did not sit well with the British and French. Exasperated by Wilson's moralistic detachment, King George V allegedly asked: "Do we have a co-belligerent or an umpire?"

Had he heard this, Wilson probably would have re-torted that indeed "an umpire" was needed and that the United States, under his leadership, must be it. The Allies' war aims did include extensive annexation — an intention made clear at the end of 1917 when the new Bolshevik regime in Russia published the czarist government's wartime treaties with the Western powers. Was it for these nationalistic and imperialistic goals that so many millions were dying? Wilson knew that the Allies must either regain the moral high ground or allow the Bolsheviks to exploit Europeans' profound war-weariness with their offers of "peace without annexation or indemnities" — and with their calls for turning this "imperialistic war" into an international class struggle. Implicitly answering the Bolshevik leader V. I. Lenin, and indeed opening the Soviet-American contest for global leadership that would continue for the next seventy years, in January 1918 Wilson dramatically went before Congress to outline peace terms that, he said, should bring the war to a just conclusion. The "Fourteen Points" setting forth these terms made Wilson and the nation he headed seem a beacon of hope for a peaceful world.

TERRITORIAL ADJUSTMENTS,
OPEN COVENANTS, AND "A GENERAL
ASSOCIATION OF NATIONS"

Some of the Fourteen Points dealt specifically with questions of territorial adjustments, including restoring Belgium's independence, returning to France the "lost provinces" of Alsace-Lorraine that Germany had annexed in 1871, and ensuring an independent Poland access to the sea. Although the breakup of the Austro-Hungarian and Ottoman Empires was not directly called for in the Fourteen Points, leaders of the national minorities of eastern Europe took heart from Wilson's call for the "autonomous development" of new nations in that region along "clearly recognized lines of nationality." Indeed, as the end of the war approached in October 1918, Wilson would support the flurry of nationalistic uprisings in the region that swept away Austria-Hungary and left in its place the new nations of Poland, Yugoslavia, and Czechoslovakia, as well as a swollen Romania. Wilson in fact deeply believed in the principle of "national self-determination," and he would fight hard for it in the process of negotiating a peace settlement. Yet, as subsequent history has demonstrated, establishing clear-cut and just national boundaries in eastern Europe was impossible. This was one more instance of American progressive ideals clashing with the harsh realities of history and international politics.

The more general of the Fourteen Points also reflected an American progressive's hopes of achieving a lasting peace, but each of them carried the seeds for future disagreement. "Open covenants of peace openly arrived at" meant forgoing supposedly cynical diplomatic bargaining behind closed doors and instead negotiating the peace treaties in the full glare of publicity, so that people could see what their representatives were doing — but what if some people wanted their representatives to do things that other people regarded as unjust? "Freedom of navigation of the seas" had been an American demand since the War of 1812, but it clashed with Great Britain's vital need to dominate the high seas in wartime. Arms reduction was another point that almost everyone agreed was desirable — but what about each nation's desire for military security? "The establishment of equality of trade" was an important plank in the Democratic party's platform, sure to stir the opposition of protectionists everywhere, including the United States.

Point Fourteen was for Wilson the capstone of all his demands. In it he called for "a general association of nations . . . for the purpose of affording mutual guarantees of political independence and territorial integrity to great and small states alike." This demand was directly inspired by the prewar American peace movement, and Wilson sincerely believed that such a "general association of nations" would ensure that international disputes were settled justly, preventing future wars. But would any nation, including his own, surrender any of its sovereign power to defend its vital interests to such an international umpire?

TREATY NEGOTIATIONS

Although the American military contribution to victory had been secondary, Wilson emerged from the war as the most commanding political figure in the world. He decided to go personally to France to participate in the treaty negotiations. Accompanied by an entourage of historians, geographers, political scientists, and economists, on December 4, 1918, Wilson sailed aboard the *George Washington* (an ocean liner confiscated from Germany and patriotically renamed), and upon his arrival in Europe he received a popular reception that bordered on hysteria.

But even as this euphoric scene was unfolding in the winter of 1918-1919, other events were undermining the American president's power to work his will at the peace talks. Wilson had hoped that Germany would remain strong enough to resist the most punitive demands of the British and French, but the collapse of the Kaiser's government in late October destroyed the possibility of a "peace among equals." Moreover, the Bolshevik Revolution in 1917-1918, as well as the subsequent intervention of Allied troops in Russia in 1918, clouded the future of that nation, now sinking into a bloody civil war. The possibility that communist revolution would spread westward from Russia into central Europe haunted the peace conference. Back in the United States, meanwhile, the congressional elections of 1918 left the Republicans in control of both houses of Congress. What was seen abroad as Wilson's political defeat played into the hands of European politicians seeking to undermine his influence.

While Wilson's personal presence at the peace conference no doubt added prestige to his peace proposals, the president's critics judged it a mistake. The tense and grueling negotiations continued for over six months, taking a heavy physical toll on the president and appearing to weaken his resolve. Even worse, Wilson's absence from the United States during these critical months permitted his political opponents to build support that would complicate ratification of the treaty. In hindsight, it appears clear that Wilson should have stayed home, sent a bipartisan delegation to France, and used his influence to lobby for a realistic League of Nations.

Wilson's extended absence from the country was a well-meaning mistake, but his choice of peace commissioners to accompany him to France was a calculated and unnecessary political gaffe. He appointed no senators to the commission, snubbing the body that would be called on to ratify a peace treaty. Equally imprudent, he appointed no notable Republican to the commission. These omissions were needless (several important Republicans, including ex-president Taft, supported Wilson's peace plans), and they appeared politically spiteful. Whatever his reasons, Wilson's peace commission was neither bipartisan nor a strong support for him during the negotiations.

The Peace Conference opened on January 18, 1919, in impressive ceremonies at the Palace of Versailles, but it soon settled into day after day of closed-door negotiations in Paris between the "Big Four": Wilson, Georges Clemenceau of France, David Lloyd George of Great Britain, and Vittorio Orlando of Italy. Wilson's stated war aims collided head-on with French and British vindictiveness toward Germany and with Italian territorial ambitions. Clemenceau proved to be a particularly wily adversary, stalling for time while portraying Wilson as a naïve American whose moral revision of the world, he sneered, demanded four more points than God had required in the Ten Commandments.

Five issues dominated the treaty discussions: (1) Germany's fate and its borders, (2) reparations, (3) Germany's colonial empire, (4) Japanese ambitions in China, and (5) territorial promises made to Italy by Great Britain, France, and Russia. Humiliated and devastated by German invasions in 1870 and again in 1914, France wanted to weaken Germany forever; Clemenceau advocated dividing Germany into several small states, each of them barred from having armed forces, as well as compelling the Germans to pay huge reparations to compensate for the ravages of the war. Lloyd George was less extreme, seeing an intact postwar Germany as a necessary piece in the European balance of power, but he had his own set of punitive demands — to destroy Germany as a naval power, to strip away German colonies in Africa and the Pacific, and to force the Germans to pay huge reparations. In the wake of the collapse of the Austro-Hungarian Empire, Italy viewed itself as the major power in southern Europe

and greedily claimed territory. On the other hand, the new nations born of nationalist uprisings after the war — Poland, Yugoslavia, and Czechoslovakia — sought assurances of protection. Finally, Japan, the Allied partner in Asia, coveted the German colonies in the Pacific and wanted to retain the Chinese province of Shandong (Shantung), a former German sphere of influence that Japanese troops had occupied during the war.

COMPROMISE

Confronted with this cornucopia of self-interest, Wilson compromised. The Treaty of Versailles dealt much more harshly with Germany than Wilson's wartime rhetoric had proposed. Germany was forced to accept sole guilt for causing the war (exactly what the American propaganda machine had argued) and to assume the burden of paying for wartime devastation — a figure set by an international commission in 1920 at a then astronomical $35 billion. The treaty stripped Germany of its colonies and lopped off border areas inhabited largely by non-Germans: Alsace-Lorraine to France, part of Schleswig to Denmark, and part of eastern Prussia to Poland. The Rhineland was demilitarized, and Germany had to surrender its navy and to restrict its army to a puny 100,000 men. At Wilson's insistence, the former German colonies were placed under the control of the League of Nations as "mandates" slated for eventual independence. But harsh as the Treaty of Versailles was, Germany remained a potentially powerful nation — wounded, weakened, and above all angry, but not so seriously damaged that it could not recover.

Wilson found the principle of self-determination even more difficult to protect and was repeatedly driven to compromise. He persuaded the Japanese to promise to withdraw from Shandong in 1922 in return for economic concessions there. In Europe the principle of self-determination was violated repeatedly by the treaties (named for various palaces around Paris) that were forced on the other former Central Powers. Millions of German-speaking people were incorporated into Poland, Czechoslovakia, France, and the newly constituted but small Austria (which was barred from uniting with Germany). Several million Hungarians were also handed over to Czechoslovakia, Yugoslavia, and Romania to give these new countries strategically advantageous borders. In a blatant violation of the principle of self-determination, Italy annexed strategic South Tyrol, populated by 200,000 German-speaking Austrians. Italy prompted the ugliest confrontation at the Versailles conference in an unsuccessful bid to take the Adriatic port of Rijeka (Fiume) from Yugoslavia.

In the midst of the hard bargaining at the conference table, Wilson clung to one irreducible demand — there must be a global organization to keep the peace, and so it was done. At his insistence, the last section of the Treaty of Versailles consisted of the Covenant — note the biblical terminology — of the League of Nations. The League's structure included an Assembly in which all nations had an equal voice, a nine-member Council that included as permanent members the United States, Great Britain, France, Italy, and Japan, and a permanent Secretariat located in Geneva. The most critical section of the Covenant, Article X, granted the Council power to impose military sanctions to deter aggression.

In later years, the Paris peace settlement was criticized as an impractical compromise — neither generous enough to reconcile Germany nor harsh enough to forestall later German aggression. Almost immediately, the treaties raised howls of protest on all sides. Most Germans felt that they had been duped into signing the armistice on generous terms and being punished even after they had replaced the Kaiser with a democratic republic. Among the victors, neither the Italians nor the Japanese were satisfied with their substantial gains. Equally ominous was the defection of many British and American intellectuals who had applauded Wilson's Fourteen Points and supported American entry into the war but now recoiled in disgust from what they decided were the peace treaties' "immoral" compromises. For example, the liberal American magazine *The Nation* wrote that Wilson, "the one-time idol of democracy, stands today discredited and condemned."

In retrospect, it is difficult to defend a settlement that preserved peace for only two decades. And yet, for all of their flaws, the Paris treaties can be judged too harshly. Years later Winston Churchill marveled that so much of Wilson's idealist rhetoric had been incorporated into the treaty. Most important, the League of Nations stood in 1920 as a cornerstone for building a new world order. Whatever the weaknesses of the 1919 settlement, the collapse of world peace in the 1930s reflected more the lack of resolve on the part of the world's major powers than the shortcomings of the postwar treaties.

❧ America Rejects the Treaty of Versailles

Woodrow Wilson knew that the Treaty of Versailles was in political trouble in the United States long before he returned home in June 1919. And yet the president had been so focused on conference negotiations that he had done little to keep the Senate or the American public informed, or to prepare Americans for the compromises he had to make. Returning from France, Wilson used stirring biblical rhetoric to urge the Senate to ratify the treaty: "The stage is set. The destiny disclosed. It has come about by no plan of our conceiving, but by the hand of God who led us into this way." Within weeks the president was involved in the bitterest and most disappointing fight of his political career.

The Senate divided into three factions in the fight over ratification. The Democratic minority supported the president's call to "accept what is offered us, the leadership of the world." But their number fell far short of the two-thirds necessary to ratify the treaty. Some distinguished Republicans, including Taft, also supported the treaty, but few Republicans in the Senate were willing to let Wilson have his way entirely. A second group of senators, mostly Republicans, agreed to vote for ratification if certain "reservations" were added. The most substantial of the reservations demanded Congressional approval before the United States would be bound by the collective security provisions of the Covenant's Article X. These opponents of the treaty were not isolationists: they believed that the United States should continue to exercise world power, but they saw the Covenant as a seriously misguided forfeiture of national prestige and power. Furthermore, like liberal critics of the treaty, these nationalists condemned the Paris peace settlement as an unrealistic effort to freeze the world political structure as it existed in 1918. This was not an unreasonable assessment: most historians today would agree.

The third Senatorial faction, a group led by progressives such as La Follette and Idaho's William Borah, opposed the treaty as a betrayal of tradition of American isolationism that had been enunciated by George Washington in his Farewell Address and by James Monroe and John Quincy Adams in the Monroe Doctrine. They also pointed out — correctly — that it violated the principle of self-determination for other nations. The isolationists' moral vision soared as high as Wilson's. America, they said, must set its own house in order to provide a model of morality and democracy, but the United States neither could nor should attempt to make the world safe for democracy. Known as the "irreconcilables," sixteen of these senators voted against the treaty both without and with reservations.

The chief antagonists in the debate that raged in the summer and fall of 1919 were President Wilson and the powerful head of the Senate Foreign Relations Committee, Henry Cabot Lodge of Massachusetts. The debate turned into an ugly confrontation marred by mutual hatred between Wilson and Lodge, a conservative and arrogant intellectual with a sophisticated knowledge of world affairs. In their own ways, each was loyal to his principles and his understanding of what was best for the country. But in the end, sheer stubbornness, moral principle, and personal rancor mingled to preclude compromise.

Instead of entering serious negotiations with the Senate, Wilson decided to appeal to the American people. In September, as the president scheduled a three-week speaking tour, his opponents in the Senate smugly reminded him that they, not the people, would vote on the treaty. Several irreconcilable senators followed Wilson from city to city, making rebuttal speeches.

The tour was one of Wilson's most distinguished oratorical efforts. He brilliantly defended his vision of a new world order, although reluctantly he also pointed to selfish national justifications for ratification. A rejection, he warned, would create commercial conflict and international rivalries that would draw the United States into another war; but American industry would gain new access to markets if the nation accepted its proper role of world leadership. Never the unrealistic dreamer that his critics painted him, Wilson was convinced that the United States would prosper in a free world market. His appeals for international morality were not hypocritical, but they had always combined with a canny eye to American strategic and economic interests.

On September 25, Wilson faltered during a speech in Pueblo, Colorado. Later that evening he experienced blinding headaches and at the insistence of his physician returned to Washington. On October 2 the president suffered a massive stroke. Wilson lingered near death for several days but then began a surprising improvement. Nonetheless, he received no visitors for four weeks. For the remainder of his life he was partially paralyzed on his left side and suffered from a loss of vision. He also showed diminished powers of concentration and less control of his emotions.

Wilson's illness doomed hopes for a treaty compromise. Public confidence in the president plummeted. Vicious rumors circulated that Mrs. Wilson was running the government (and she did in fact exercise considerable influence on her stricken husband), despite a report from a group of Republican senators who visited Wilson and found him in good spirits. More important,

his illness made the president less flexible than ever, more embittered, and deeply disillusioned.

On November 19 the Senate voted on the Treaty of Versailles twice. Submitted with reservations, it was defeated 39-54, the irreconcilables and the Democrats opposing it. Without reservations, the treaty lost again by a vote of 38-53, defeated by the irreconcilables and Republicans demanding reservations. The stunning rejection of the treaty was followed by months of maneuvering to find a compromise. Lodge once again submitted the treaty for a vote in March 1920, this time with a less stringent set of reservations. The Senate voted 59-35 to ratify, seven short of the needed two-thirds. Twenty-one Democratic senators defied the president's instructions to vote against the treaty as submitted, but it was not enough. In any case, Wilson had vowed that he would not sign any version of the treaty that included reservations.

The American failure to ratify the Treaty of Versailles deflated hopes for a stable world order in the 1920s and 1930s. Both Lodge and Wilson shared the blame. Lodge was determined to preserve America's right to act independently as a traditional world power; Wilson had a vision of a new order of international cooperation. But the two could easily have compromised on middle ground, for both wanted the United States to play a major role in world politics. Indeed, both sought to extend American principles and power around the world. In the end, Lodge savored victory over his despised foe more than a responsible world peace. Wilson, crippled physically and emotionally, clung to his sense of moral superiority. He had bargained and compromised for months in Europe but now he refused to cut a deal with his hated American political enemies.

The rejection of the treaty brought to an unfortunate end American participation in World War I, a far cry from the heady idealism of a few months earlier. In 1920, official Washington ground to a virtual standstill, national politics reached an impasse, and the national mood boded ill for reformers and moralizers.

❧ A Troubled Society

Bad news abounded in 1919. In what came to be known as the "Black Sox" scandal, eight members of the Chicago White Sox baseball team, including legendary hero "Shoeless" Joe Jackson, were banned from baseball for allegedly conspiring with gamblers to lose the World Series. Bloody race riots in more than twenty American cities killed hundreds of blacks and whites.

All year long, the nation counted the death toll from the devastating "Spanish influenza," an epidemic that spread around the world in the war's aftermath. About 20 million Americans contracted the "flu," and over 500,000 died. In Philadelphia, the death rate rose 700 percent in 1919, with as many as 650 dying in the city in a single day.

Against this somber backdrop, Americans began the difficult transformation back to a peacetime economy and society. Economically, the United States had profited from the war. The gross national product rose from $62.5 billion in 1916 to $73.6 billion in 1919, and the United States had become a major creditor nation. On the other hand, dismantling the wartime economy caused a severe shock. Despite recommendations from a variety of sources, including the National Catholic War Council, that the government retain some of the federal bureaucracy that had kept the economy operating efficiently, Congress quickly dismantled the wartime agencies in 1919 and 1920. Dramatic inflation followed. Consumer prices rose 77 percent between 1916 and 1919. Factories slowed production as wartime orders ended, just as the demobilization of the armed forces was pouring workers into the labor market, raising unemployment to about 7 percent. By the end of 1920, the nation lay in the grip of a severe recession. Returning veterans found that their hero's welcome included no economic guarantees.

Farmers found themselves in an even worse plight. During the war they had thrived as the United States shipped huge consignments of food to its hungry allies, and American farmers optimistically incurred large debts to buy land and equipment. But in 1919, most European nations abruptly cancelled their orders and began erecting high tariff barriers to protect their own food producers. This devastated the American farm economy, which would not recover until World War II.

Thus World War I left an ambiguous economic legacy. Because of labor scarcity, unskilled workers improved their lot slightly, but skilled labor's relative economic standing had deteriorated during the war years. Many workers were frustrated when postwar economic conditions further eroded their purchasing power. The result was a massive confrontation between organized labor and an intransigent management. During the war strikes had been rare, but in 1919 the dam burst and unions called more than 2,500 work stoppages, more than in any other year in American history. More than 4 million American workers went on strike. Some were successful, but most gained little.

Two major strikes in 1919 seriously damaged the public image of organized labor. In November 1919 the United Mine Workers, led by a militant, flamboyant, and charismatic young organizer named John L. Lewis, shut down the nation's coal mines. The workers won higher wages, but their triumph set off a wave of resentment against the union and the adversarial tactics of Lewis, a colorful leader of whom the nation would hear much during the next thirty years. In Pittsburgh 250,000 steel workers, poorly paid and often compelled to work in dangerous mills, struck under the leadership of William Z. Foster. The owners hired strikebreakers and crushed the strike in a little more than three months. Two other strikes, neither of major economic significance, fanned fears of union radicalism. In early 1919 the Central Labor Council of Seattle, dominated by remnants of the IWW, brought the city to a virtual standstill when 60,000 workers stayed home in a general strike. Seattle mayor Ole Hansen announced that the city was on the verge of anarchy, charged that the leaders of the strike were Bolsheviks, and asked for troops to protect Seattle. The strike failed to gain the support of more moderate union leaders and collapsed after nine days. The IWW, already weakened by wartime repression, never recovered from this disaster.

Equally portentous — and equally disappointing to its participants — was a strike for shorter hours by Boston policemen in September 1919. After two nights of looting and vandalism, Massachusetts Governor Calvin Coolidge called in the National Guard with the sonorous statement that turned him into a conservative hero: "There is no right to strike against the public safety by anybody, anywhere, any time." The strike was crushed, but the resulting discharge of the entire Boston police department caused a serious deterioration of law enforcement in the city.

The low level of tolerance for dissent in 1919 and 1920 also touched off race riots. Black aspiration rose in the months after World War I, particularly among returning veterans, but blacks soon discovered that the war had not changed their status. Sixteen lynchings were recorded in 1919, including those of ten veterans. Chicago was the scene of the bloodiest riot in 1919. Already seething from race tensions that followed the influx of blacks from the South during the war, the city was torn by sixteen days of violence after an African American youth was attacked by whites and subsequently drowned in Lake Michigan. Fifteen whites and twenty-three blacks died in the Chicago riot, and many blacks found themselves homeless.

Red Scare, 1919 In this cartoon, a bearded Bolshevik brandishing the torch of "anarchy" creeps under the American flag. For a year, the nation was convulsed with fears of radical conspiracies and of "Reds" almost literally hiding under beds, until the scaremongers overplayed their hand by predicting specific disasters that never happened. In fact, true anarchists hated the Bolsheviks as ruthlessly authoritarian, and fought them bitterly in the Russian Civil War.

❧ The Red Scare

The seizure of power by the Bolsheviks in Russia in October 1917 exacerbated American fears of radicalism. The success of Bolshevism challenged Americans' most cherished political and economic assumptions; Wilson refused to recognize the Soviet government, a policy that remained in place until 1933. In 1918 Wilson reluctantly sent American troops to participate in an abortive attempt by a fourteen-nation Allied military force to prop up anti-Bolshevik forces in Russia, but they were withdrawn in 1920. Meanwhile, left-wing socialists and other admirers of the "Soviet experiment" organized two pro-Bolshevik parties, which under pressure from Lenin united in the Communist Party of the United States in 1921. Its most notable early leader was John Reed, a left-wing journalist who had written

a romantic account glorifying the Russian Revolution, *Ten Days That Shook the World*. Reed returned to Soviet Russia, where he died in 1920 and was entombed among the Communist heroes in Red Square. Clearly, the United States faced no danger of a Communist takeover after World War I, but fears of revolution nonetheless spread widely, feeding a hysterical reaction against socialism and other leftist ideas and organizations — and also against foreigners, who dominated the radical ranks and were identified in the public mind with interminable and incomprehensible troubles abroad.

In April and May 1919 an unknown person or persons, probably Italian anarchists, mailed package bombs to thirty prominent Americans, including senators, cabinet members, Supreme Court Justice Oliver Wendell Holmes, Jr., and capitalists John D. Rockefeller and J. P. Morgan — all of them identified rightly or wrongly as enemies of political radicals. Not a single bomb harmed its intended victim, but one seriously injured the wife and the maid of Georgia Senator Thomas Hardwick. In June an Italian immigrant was killed attempting to deliver a bomb to the residence of Attorney General A. Mitchell Palmer. Palmer's house was severely damaged, though he and his wife escaped injury. These acts of terror incited public outrage and fanned fears of Bolshevism.

The right-wing backlash in 1919, labeled the Red Scare, found its champion in Attorney General Palmer. He took the lead among citizens and government officials in lumping together all radicals — the IWW, communists, socialists, and anarchists — as a single "red menace." In November 1919 the Justice Department raided the offices of socialist and communist political organizations in twenty cities, seizing files and arresting 250 people. All these "Palmer raids" were conducted with little regard for legality. In December, 249 aliens were deported to Russia, including veteran anarchists Alexander Berkman and Emma Goldman. (Goldman became deeply discouraged by witnessing the growing dictatorial control of the Communist Party and the Soviet bureaucracy, and she later wrote a perceptive account entitled *My Disillusionment in Russia.*) Palmer's actions brought public acclaim; he was popularly dubbed the "Fighting Quaker," and there was talk of running him for president in 1920. Evangelist Billy Sunday recommended harsher measures: "If I had my way with these ornery wild-eyed socialists and IWWs, I would stand them up before a firing squad and save space on our ships." A second series of raids in thirty-three cities in January 1920, orchestrated by Palmer's protégé, J. Edgar Hoover of the department's Bureau of Investigation, resulted in the arrest of some 2,700 people; by May the number of detainees had reached 4,000. Local and state governments also pushed the attack on radicals. In January 1920 the New York state legislature expelled five elected members who were democratic socialists.

Palmer, a former Pennsylvania congressman with a good record as a progressive, had mixed motives in pressing the Red Scare. The extreme measures he used, which were at least tolerated by Wilson, were prompted partly by his genuine fear of Bolshevism. Indeed, as early as 1915 Wilson had warned that political radicals were "creatures of passion" and that "disloyalty and anarchy . . . must be crushed out." But public support for Palmer's flamboyant methods proved short-lived. Groups ranging from law school faculties to liberal clergymen complained that the raids were illegal, and in January 1920 the Supreme Court barred the use in court of illegally seized evidence. Palmer's credibility plummeted when he predicted massive radical violence on May Day 1920 and nothing happened. Now ridiculed by the press as the "Quaking Fighter," Palmer saw his political boom collapse, and fears of radical revolution began to abate. By the end of 1920, however, the raids and deportations had virtually destroyed the Italian anarchist movement in America and had weakened leftist political parties and the union movement generally.

CONCLUSION: THE UNITED STATES BECOMES A WORLD POWER

American foreign policy from 1900 to 1920 foreshadowed the nation's global role in the twentieth century. All three progressive presidents were internationalists who believed that American power would play a crucial role in the new century. They identified Germany and Japan as the unstable nations in the European and Asian balances of power and fostered the Anglo-American friendship that is still a cornerstone of both nations' foreign policies. All of America's political leaders believed that it was this country's mission to export — whether by force, arbitration, or example — its version of political and economic democracy.

By the end of World War I, however, the nation's political leaders held three contradictory views of America's tactical role in the world, all of them having precedents in the thinking of past political leaders. In the early twentieth century William Jennings Bryan had pushed the Democratic Party toward isolationism, and progressive Republicans like Borah, Johnson, and La Follette joined them. By 1919, the "irreconcilables" best represented that tradition. On the other hand, the Republican Party under Roosevelt and Taft supported a more ambitious American global presence. TR died in early 1919 — prematurely old, sick, and grieving for the son who had been killed in the war — but his defense of a nationalistic foreign policy was adopted by the more conservative Republicans and became the basis for their opposition to the Treaty of Versailles.

Woodrow Wilson believed that World War I would remake the world, and he believed that the United States had been called by God to establish a new, moral world order. In domestic policy, Wilson had built on the reform tradition that Bryan had first fostered within the Democratic party, but his internationalist vision rejected Bryan's equally moralistic, almost pacifist, and thoroughly isolationist legacy. Thus, by 1916, a foreign policy realignment was under way. Republicans drifted toward the nationalism of Roosevelt, while Democrats abandoned Bryan's isolationism for the broad internationalism of Wilson.

World War I, like other American wars, had a powerful homogenizing effect on American society, but the months immediately after the war reversed that trend. Many groups that had felt strongly alienated from the mainstream of American society, such as Roman Catholic immigrants, Mormons, African Americans, and organized labor, rallied around the flag and proved their allegiance during the war. In the war's aftermath, these minorities felt that they had earned a larger voice in the American democratic process. In varying degrees, they were disappointed.

The transition from the lofty optimism of the Progressive Era and World War I to the sour disillusionment of the 1920s came with shocking suddenness. The social turmoil in America in 1920 was not an isolated aberration — the entire western world was in disarray in the wake of the Great War — but in America the anxiety caused by postwar economic dislocation was exacerbated by the bitter debates over the peace conference and the treaty. In 1920 Republican presidential candidate Warren G. Harding's soothing calls for social peace and "normalcy" signaled the end of an epoch of progressive reform and soaring hopes for world peace.

SUGGESTED READING

John Milton Cooper, Jr., *The Causes and Consequences of World War I* (1971). An excellent overview of the events surrounding American entry into World War I and the war's aftermath.

John M. Dobson, *America's Ascent: The United States Becomes a Great Power, 1880-1914* (1978). A study that shows how American expansionist foreign policy was based on a combination of economic interest, moralism, and missionary zeal.

Robert H. Ferrell, *Woodrow Wilson and World War I* (1985). An excellent overview of Wilson's diplomacy and the peace conference.

Frank Freidel, *Over There: The Story of America's First Great Overseas Crusade* (1964). A good account of American participation in World War I.

William E. Leuchtenburg, "Progressivism and Imperialism: The Progressive Movement and American Foreign Policy, 1898-1916," *Mississippi Valley Historical Review* 39 (1952): 483-504. An influential article that views moral idealism as the basis for both the domestic and foreign policies of progressives.

Arthur S. Link, *Woodrow Wilson: Revolution, War, and Peace* (1979). A sweeping analysis of Wilson's philosophy by the leading Wilson scholar.

David M. Kennedy, *Over Here: The First World War and American Society* (1980). An excellent study of the home front.

SUGGESTIONS FOR FURTHER READING

Ray H. Abrams, *Preachers Present Arms: The Role of American Churches and Clergy in World Wars I and II* (1969).

Arthur E. Barbeau and Florette Henri, *The Unknown Soldiers: Black American Troops in World War I* (1974).

William J. Breen, *Uncle Sam at Home: Civilian Mobilization, Wartime Federalism and the Committee for National Defense* (1984).

Charles Chatfield, *For Peace and Justice: Pacifism in America, 1914-1941* (1971).

Kenton J. Clymer, *Protestant Missionaries in the Philippines, 1898-1916: An Inquiry into the American Colonial Mentality* (1987).

Richard H. Collin, *Theodore Roosevelt's Caribbean: The Panama Canal, the Monroe Doctrine, and the Latin American Context* (1990).

Daniel M. Crane and Thomas A. Breslin, *An Ordinary Relationship: American Opposition to Republican Revolution in China* (1986).

Patricia R. Hill, *The World Their Household: The American Woman's Foreign Mission Movement and Cultural Transformation, 1870-1920* (1985).

William R. Hutchinson, *Errand to the World: American Protestant Thought and Foreign Missions* (1987).

John Keegan, *The First World War* (1998).

Kathleen Kennedy, *Disloyal Mothers and Scurrilous Citizens: Women and Subversion during World War I* (1999).

Thomas Knock, *To End All Wars: Woodrow Wilson and the Quest for a New World Order* (1992).

Mark Meigs, *Optimism at Armageddon: Voices of American Participants in the First World War* (1997).

Ivan Musicant, *The Banana Wars: A History of United States Military Intervention in Latin America from the Spanish-American War to the Invasion of Panama* (1990).

David J. O'Brien and Stephen S. Fugita, *The Japanese American Experience* (1991).

Gerald W. Patton, *War and Race: The Black Officer in the American Military* (1981).

Richard Polenberg, *Fighting Faiths: The Abrams Case, the Supreme Court and Free Speech* (1988).

Ronald Schaffer, *America in the Great War* (1992).

Stephen L. Vaughn, *Holding Fast to Inner Lines: Democracy, Nationalism, and the Committee on Public Information* (1980).

Susan Zeiger, *In Uncle Sam's Service: Women Workers with the American Expeditionary Force, 1917-1919* (1999).

26

An Exhilarating Decade
American Life in the 1920s

ONTHS BEFORE THE landslide victory of Republican Warren G. Harding in 1920, it was clear that the electorate's mood had changed and that the progressive political coalition had collapsed. Politically, the nation veered to the right in the 1920s, electing a sequence of Republican presidents. Progressivism did not vanish, and many of the political changes wrought in the preceding decades remained in place; the federal government, particularly the executive branch, continued to grow in size and prestige. Progressives remained a powerful force in Congress, and the last of the decade's Republican presidents, Herbert Hoover, was the leader of the reforming side of his party. Nonetheless, the prevailing political sense of the twenties was that the government should act as cheerleader, and perhaps coach, to the nation's successful business team, but should not attempt to be a referee. The Republican presidents claimed credit for sowing the decade's prosperity, but after 1929 Hoover had to reap the economic whirlwind.

A long boom began in 1922, producing a new surge of consumerism and euphoric optimism. Exhausted by years of crusades for reform culminating in the bitter treaty debate, most Americans opted for getting on with the business of living; satisfied consumers formed the majority that turned the reins of government back to conservative Republicans.

If large numbers of Americans were contented with their economic state during the twenties, the level of social anxiety was nonetheless high, sparking ferocious debates. Indeed, as wartime patriotism faded, the nation seemed more divided than ever. The strikes, the race riots, and the crackdown on leftists in 1919 laid bare deep-seated popular apprehensions about the nation's ethnic and cultural diversity. In addition, the surge of consumerism, long regarded by religious leaders as the most menacing modern challenge to morality, continued to alter traditional behavior and, many believed, the American character. Other social and intellectual trends, none of them really new, added to the decade's controversies. Urbanization continued. Most Americans were aware that in 1920 the Census Bureau reported that for the first time a majority of Americans lived in cities and small towns. With the end of World War I, moreover, immigration began to increase again, rekindling anxieties in the white, Anglo-Saxon, Protestant majority.

The divisive scientific idea most debated in the twenties, the Darwinian theory of evolution, had been pondered by intellectuals for decades, but in the 1920s open controversy about it erupted in the nation's churches and schools. Among other new scientific ideas, Freudian psychology and Einstein's theory of relativity posed serious challenges to traditional beliefs.

Chroniclers of the twenties have been fascinated by the decade's social clashes, seeing them as harbingers of America's escalating twentieth-century encounter with modernity. The decade has been labeled "The Age of the Flapper," "The Jazz Age," and "The Roaring Twenties." Its most engaging characters were the cynical, disillusioned young intellectuals who ridiculed their more conventional contemporaries, flailing away at Prohibition and preachers, "rubes" and Rotarians, democracy and do-gooders. They scorned America's Puritan past as repressive and explored personal freedom with a youthful zest and flamboyance, permanently influencing American fashion, music, literature, and public morality. But interesting and influential as they were, the talented literary rebels of the twenties numbered in the hundreds and did not speak for or to most Americans.

The majority of Americans were social and political conservatives, and many of them launched ferocious counterattacks. Indeed, the intensity and extremity of conservative causes in the twenties was a measure of

American Leaders, 1921　From left to right, Henry Ford, Thomas A. Edison, Warren G. Harding, and tire manufacturer Harvey Firestone enjoy a break. During the 1920s American businessmen once again became popular heroes.

the anxiety felt by many old-stock Americans. Their crusades in the twenties had the appearance of last-ditch battles. Prohibition came to symbolize the conservative desire to establish legally a purer and more Christian society. Protestant fundamentalists tried to ban the teaching of evolution in public schools, and the revived Ku Klux Klan, an extraordinary success in the early twenties, appealed to a variety of people who resented the pace of social change. Alarmed and angered, millions of Americans joined to defend the customs of an earlier and more orderly time. Throughout the United States, the sound of battles between defenders of the old order and champions of a new order resounded through the schools, the churches, and the governing boards of nearly every county and village.

A DECADE OF RELATIVE PROSPERITY

By 1922 the economic boom that gave coherence to the twenties was well under way. The industrial accomplishments of the decade provided a real basis for giddy optimism. The wealthy profited most from the boom, but prosperity altered the lives of most Americans and provided an environment for the decade's social conflicts.

Technological improvements continued to increase factory productivity; during the twenties industrial output in the country doubled. While some older industries, such as coal and textiles, declined slightly, dramatic increases occurred in automobile manufacturing, chemicals, and electrical equipment. The chemical industry, under the leadership of such giant corporations as DuPont and Union Carbide, capitalized on the growing market for synthetic fibers and plastics. The expansion of the electrical equipment industry was tied to new consumer products such as household appliances and radios, as well as to increases in the use of industrial electrical equipment.

The economic boom of the twenties had profound social consequences. Improvements in transportation and communication continued to break down provincial barriers and speeded the spread of news and new ideas. In addition, the wide array of technological advances provided increased leisure time for the public.

❧ *Welfare Capitalism and the Decline of Unionism*

The businessman resurfaced as an American hero in the twenties. Henry Ford, Harvey Firestone, and Thomas A. Edison were names as familiar as those of presidents. Popular magazines were filled with the success sagas of the captains of industry. Furthermore, the names of the wealthy were attached to countless civic and humanitarian projects. In the 1920s and 1930s the huge Rockefeller and Carnegie Foundations provided more than 85 percent of the external funding for scientific research in American universities.

Ironically, this idealization of the rugged individualist businessman came at a time when American corporations were becoming more managerial in style. In most corporations the sale of vast amounts of stock to the public had separated ownership from management; company executives were experts trained in efficiency and marketing. When Alfred P. Sloan became the head of General Motors in 1924, he challenged the leadership of the still privately held Ford Motor Company by creating a modern corporation featuring team management and an emphasis on research and marketing.

The managerial revolution that accompanied the emergence of large, publicly owned corporations did not dramatically change the tactics of American business leaders. A new wave of business concentration raised the share of total corporate income going to the largest 5 percent of the nation's companies from 79.6 percent in 1918 to 84.3 percent in 1929. Even more portentous was the imbalance in the distribution of national income. The share of national income going to capital rose during the decade from 19.6 percent to 25.5 percent, while the share going to labor slipped from 77.9 percent to 72.9 percent.

To some extent, other sectors of the economy, particularly skilled laborers, shared in the prosperity of the 1920s. Wages rose steadily throughout the decade, though never at the rate of increases in business profits, and only a few industrial areas suffered significant unemployment. Per capita income rose from $672 in 1922 to $857 in 1929, and for a majority of the labor force real wages — income measured against the prevailing price level — also rose.

For semiskilled and unskilled workers (who filled many factory jobs), the picture was bleaker. Over the decade, the families of most such workers barely clung to their existing standard of living and the income of every potential wage earner had to count, causing some hardship every time there was a short-term layoff — a frequent occurrence even in these good years, as companies tried to keep costs under tight control.

Between 1921 and 1929 total union membership dropped by 30 percent, to about 3.5 million. This decline had complex causes. The relative prosperity of some American workers partly explained it, as did public hostility to unions, born of the bitter and disruptive postwar strikes.

But much of the decline in proportion of workers belonging to unions was caused by the narrow focus of the unions themselves, which remained bastions of ethnic prejudice — Irish workers dominating transportation; Italians, construction; and Jews, the needle trades. Blacks were accepted in only a handful of AFL locals and accounted for less than 2 percent of the membership in 1930. Narrowly focused on bettering the lot of skilled workers, the AFL craft unions generally rejected political activity, favored immigration restriction, and opposed a minimum wage for unskilled laborers. Indeed, they had no interest in organizing the laborers in the nation's great heavy industries such as steelmaking. Unable to organize and bargain collectively, these workers were not only low-paid relative to their productivity, but often lost ground in their living standards over the course of the decade.

Employers, of course, had no reason to favor worker-led unions, and every reason to resist them. Many large corporations short-circuited labor organizers by launching "company unions," which by the end of the decade enrolled around 1.5 million workers. This paternalistic movement, labeled "welfare capitalism" or "industrial democracy," sometimes gave workers real improvements: a five-and-a-half-day workweek and paid vacations, employee recreation halls and cafeterias, more equitable grievance procedures and a curbing of the arbitrary power of foremen, stock-ownership plans, and in a few cases profit-sharing schemes. But these

Advertising the New Electrical Age　Ads like this frequently appeared in American magazines and newspapers in the 1920s, aimed at both middle- and working-class consumers. Notice the very "wordy" style of advertising copywriting, in contrast to the use of a few arresting slogans and images today.

improvements touched only a small percentage of the American labor force. And even for these workers, "welfare capitalism" looked better on paper than it functioned in practice. Its basic purposes were to outbid union organizers, to discourage job-hopping, and to persuade workers to give their loyalty to the company rather than to ethnic, religious, or community organizations, let alone independent unions. Employers rarely showed a corresponding loyalty to their workers when it came to layoffs in slack times. Nor did most workers put much faith in their companies' pension plans; in the absence of Social Security and unemployment insurance (which did not exist before the 1930s), workers had to depend on their savings, their families, and their church and community organizations to take care of them in old age or sickness.

Not all corporate opposition to unions was so benign. Companies employed thousands of spies and private agents to discourage union organization, and generally the government could be counted on to back management in labor disputes. In most company towns the authority of the government and of the employer became virtually indistinguishable. Companies circulated "blacklists" that excluded labor activists from jobs, and used many other repressive techniques to curtail union growth.

❧ The Consumer Boom Gathers Steam

Prosperity was sufficiently widespread among the middle class and skilled workers in the twenties to support a consumer boom, out of which grew a mass culture that

Fueling Up   On a rainy day in 1927 a man and two women fill their car's gas tank at a station in New Jersey. Gas stations proliferated across the nation's landscape during the 1920s, responding to a huge consumer need and inspiring cultural critic H. L. Mencken to rail about Americans' "libido for the ugly."

cash rather than make major purchases on installment. Thus there was a class and an ethnic dimension to the divisive cultural stresses posed by the twenties' consumer boom and its homogenizing influence.

The engine that drove the consumer boom was advertising, a profession that gained growing respect in the twenties. As the mass consumer culture expanded, the distribution of goods became as important as the production of goods. While selling Americans on the virtues of material comfort and consumption, advertisers softened the impact of change by stressing the traditional values of individualism and community, appealed to buyers to dare to smoke cigarettes or drive an automobile — and to use Listerine mouthwash to avoid social embarrassment. Bruce Barton, an advertising wizard of the twenties, boasted that his profession was responsible for the higher standard of living and more. "Advertising," he wrote, "sustains a system that has made us leaders of the free world: The American Way of Life." In 1925, Barton published a best-selling book, *The Man Nobody Knows,* an interpretation of the New Testament that portrayed Jesus as a master salesman. Barton's Jesus was not an ascetic prophet but "the most popular dinner guest in Jerusalem," who "picked up twelve men from the bottom ranks of business and forged them into an organization that conquered the world." Needless to say, all Americans did not see advertising as such a blessing. Veteran muckraker Upton Sinclair warned that advertising undermined the will of the press to critique big business advertisers, and many saw advertising as a not-too-subtle attack on all independent thinking.

❧ *Americans on the Road and in the Air*

The gaudiest business success story of the 1920s was the automobile. The rapid development of the industry was one of the greatest achievements of modern technology, for until Henry Ford designed the Model T in 1908, automobiles had been expensive toys of the rich, built by hand in small quantities. Ford and other

tended to homogenize American society in countless ways. Automobiles led the way, but scores of other consumer products dramatically changed millions of lives. Radios and telephones revolutionized communications; ready-made clothing standardized dress; refrigerators, washing machines, and vacuum cleaners reduced the drudgery of housework. Especially for the middle class, installment buying made possible such large purchases as a home or a car, which hitherto most Americans could buy only for cash. By the end of the decade, chain stores catering to mass tastes — the A & P, Safeway, Woolworth, J. C. Penney, and Walgreen — were displacing small merchants in middle-class neighborhoods. The new stores offered nationally advertised brands and were clean and "up-to-date," but they neither allowed haggling over prices nor extended credit — time-honored practices that kept many ethnic and working-class families loyal to "mom-and-pop" groceries in the urban neighborhoods that the chains generally ignored. Likewise workers, made cautious by the ever-present chance of layoffs, were still inclined to save up and pay

American inventors simplified automobile construction, and by World War I the United States was producing far more cars than any other nation. Not until the twenties, however, did the industry really burgeon. New car sales, still fewer than 500,000 per year in 1913, reached nearly 2 million in 1920 and 4.5 million in 1929. By that time the nation had more than 26.5 million registered vehicles. The value of the automobile industry, compared to that of other sectors of the economy, rose from 150th place in 1900 to first place in 1925. The industry's expansion spawned similar growth in related products; for instance, the manufacture of tires and inner tubes doubled, and gasoline refining quadrupled. Cars changed the American landscape, as service stations and garages became landmarks in both town and country. Different oil companies built identifiable structures adorned with symbols such as the Texaco star and Mobile's flying horse.

The acknowledged hero in putting the nation on wheels was Henry Ford. In 1907, Ford made a famous and dramatic announcement: "I will build a motor car for the great multitude. . . . It will be so low in price that no man making a good salary will be unable to own one — and enjoy with his family the blessing of hours of pleasure in God's great open spaces." After designing the Model T, Ford began exploring more efficient methods of production. In 1911, he opened an assembly-line plant in Highland Park, Michigan, and began turning out cars at an unprecedented rate. He continued to perfect the assembly-line technique; by 1920 half of the motorcars in the world were Model Ts. By the time the Model T was discontinued in 1927, Ford had sold about 15 million austere but dependable "Tin Lizzies."

As Ford's manufacturing methods became more efficient and the volume of his output rose, the price of his Model T steadily dropped — from $950 in 1909 to about $260 in 1925.

Ford's frontal assault on the conventional business wisdom that a product should be priced as high as the market would bear revealed his grasp of the potential of mass consumption. Even more stunning was Ford's action in 1914 doubling his workers' wages and reducing their workday from nine to eight hours. This bold decision contradicted the long-held assumption that wages must be rigidly tied to productivity. The most dramatic single event in the history of welfare capitalism, Ford's hike of wages was possible only because his company issued no publicly traded stock and remained his personal property. The canny Ford understood that his workers were also potential customers, but "Fordism" was heatedly debated before being accepted as good business practice.

Nor did Ford impress all of his workers as a benevolent boss. Work on his assembly lines was boringly repetitious, high-pressured, and exhausting. One Chicago employee summed up the feelings of many workers: "Ford, that son of a bitch, he's hard to work for. Soon as work slack, lay off, doesn't give a damn for men." And as events a decade later would vividly show (see Chapter 27), Ford was an implacable enemy of the union movement.

Ford's stranglehold on the automobile industry was successfully challenged in the 1920s. Among scores of short-lived companies, two formidable new competitors arose by the middle of the decade: General Motors, the producer of the Chevrolet, and the Chrysler Cor-

---

✳ IN THEIR OWN WORDS

"Don't Be a Dust Eater," 1925

By the mid-twenties so many Americans drove cars that highways and cities were becoming crowded with them. One editor had the following words of encouragement to share with drivers succumbing to an early version of "road rage."

Have you heard the call of the open country?

Does the thought of green fields and invigorating breezes stir something in you which starts you planning the next weekend away from the city?

Then in the midst of your plans does the nightmare of dust-driven highways clotted with slow-moving, complaining traffic take all the joy out of the picture and cause you to leave your car in the garage? . . .

Crowded roads are unpleasant, but, after all, the driver is to blame for not choosing his route more carefully. What American car owners should do is get off the main highways and onto the secondary roads.

The beauty of the back road awaits the driver who will dispense with his inclination to follow the leader over gas-laden, oil-smeared thoroughfares, which carry nearly ninety per cent of our traffic. No wonder the main roads are insufferable.

Get away from the wheel-to-wheel procession. Find the byways and lanes of the countryside, where you need not be afraid of overcrowding even on the sunniest of summer Sundays.

Don't be a dust eater.

poration, which built Dodges and Plymouths. Massive GM posed a particularly dangerous threat to Ford. Catering to new demands for comfort and style (it was the first to offer cars in colors other than black), GM's market share rose from 12.7 percent in 1921 to 43.9 percent in 1931. Faced with this challenge, in 1927 Ford stopped producing the Model T, closed the assembly line for a year, and returned to the market only in 1929 with the more luxurious Model A. Such was the Ford legend that 500,000 people made down payments on the new model before seeing the car or knowing the price. Nonetheless, Ford's market share fell from 55.7 percent in 1921 to 24.9 percent in 1931.

Automobiles became virtual necessities for the upper and middle classes in the 1920s, though most families only had one car. (Two-car families would not become common until the 1950s.) Probably a majority of the nation's skilled workers and better-off farmers also bought cars. By the end of the decade, even 24 percent of the lower-income families in the typical industrial city of Joliet, Illinois, were reported to own an automobile.

The popularity of automobiles created a pressing demand for better roads. At the beginning of World War I, the American highway system was still a patchwork of disconnected and muddy roads. The Progressive Era had spawned a "Good Roads Movement," and by 1917 every state had a Highway Department. In 1921, the Federal Highway Act expanded the availability of federal matching funds for highway construction, and as early as 1923 a system of national highways was planned. (One of the first federal officials to study the problem was a young army officer assigned by the War Department to assess transportation needs from the perspective of national defense: Dwight D. Eisenhower.) Still, in 1930 less than 25 percent of the nation's roads were "surfaced," and only about 5 percent were paved by modern standards. Not until the 1950s, during the Eisenhower presidency, would there be a massive federal program to construct a network of high-speed roads.

Automobiles changed American society in a variety of ways. Skilled workers could live farther from their jobs, and the middle class continued its migration to the suburbs that had been begun in the late nineteenth century with the building of streetcar lines. Early symptoms of urban flight included a sharp decline of interest in public transportation and declining incomes in central cities. No class was affected more by the transportation revolution than farmers. Rural isolation eroded as Model Ts chugged in from the farm to the city, and

Henry Ford's Great Innovation In 1923 Ford introduced the first moving assembly line, on a conveyor belt, at his automobile plant in Dearborn, Michigan. It greatly speeded up production, even as it also reduced work to a mind-numbing series of repetitive motions from which the worker could not take even a moment's break.

rural mail carriers regularly brought the outside world to farm families.

Although they had less immediate impact on the average American's daily life, airplanes symbolized the promise of technology. The successful flights of Orville and Wilbur Wright near Kitty Hawk, North Carolina, on December 17, 1903, put the United States in the vanguard of aviation. In 1909, the Wright brothers received a contract from the United States Army to manufacture airplanes. World War I greatly stimulated interest in the military potential of airplanes, and for a while Europeans became the leaders in aircraft development. (All the planes flown by Allied fighters, including famed American "aces" such as Eddie Rickenbacker, were British or French machines.) In the early twenties, however, the United States passed several aviation milestones. The first airmail flight was made in 1918 from New York to Washington, and only two years later transcontinental airmail service commenced, using short city-to-city hops. By 1926, when the Air Commerce Act began federal supervision of air traffic, such improvements as radio beacons at airports had begun to appear.

An enchanted moment in the history of global aviation came on May 21, 1927, when Charles A. Lindbergh, Jr., completed the first solo transatlantic flight from New York to Paris in the *Spirit of St. Louis.* "Lucky Lindy's" carefully planned flight of more than 2,000 miles took him thirty-three and a half hours. After receiving a hero's welcome and a prize of $25,000 in Paris, Lindbergh returned home to an outpouring of affection. He became the foremost celebrity of a hero-worshiping decade, embodying much that Americans valued in the twenties — mechanical precision and skill, a disciplined personality, and commercial success.

∞ A Leisure Society

While air travel was for the few, huge numbers of Americans were affected by developments in the field of radio. Although radio had been invented around the turn of the century, KDKA in Pittsburgh, the first commercial station, was not launched (by Westinghouse) until 1920. In November 1920, WWJ, another Westinghouse station in Detroit, broadcast national election returns, introducing Americans to live news coverage with its announcement of Warren G. Harding's elevation to the White House. Hundreds of stations were built in the next few years; by the end of the decade approximately 10 million American homes had radios.

Radio in the early 1920s was often a hobby, popular in working-class families. Cheap kits were sold widely, allowing any reasonably dexterous person to build a simple crystal set. Often not-for-profit, stations were

Valentino, "the Sheik" In 1926 Rudolph Valentino appeared in his last and most popular silent film, *The Sheik*, costarring the swooning Vilma Banky.

mostly low-powered and local, oriented toward audiences defined by social class, ethnicity, or religion. Fraternal lodges and union locals often maintained stations, and in large cities many national associations filled the airwaves with foreign-language broadcasts. Fundamentalist ministries such as Chicago's Moody Bible Institute became an important presence on the air, and so did Catholic organizations reaching out to Italian, Polish, Hispanic, and other non-WASP audiences.

This essentially local, amateurish approach to radio broadcasting began to succumb to homogenizing national and commercial interests by the mid-twenties. A new strategy of selling advertising time to pay for entertainment became well entrenched, greatly expanding the scope of commercialization, turning performers into employees of business sponsors, and encouraging a trend toward the development of independent religious radio ministries. In 1926, the National Broadcasting Company (NBC) became the first major network, followed the next year by the Columbia Broadcasting System (CBS). Both figuratively and literally, the big national networks overpowered local broadcasting, although some special-interest stations remained on the air until the Great Depression (and a few even later). With its relentless advertising of national brands and its attractive programming, network broadcasting became one of the most powerful instruments of cultural homogenization by the end of the twenties, and its influence would grow even mightier during the Depression (see Chapter 28).

The direction taken by the American radio industry owed much to Herbert Hoover, who, as secretary of commerce in the early twenties, claimed regulatory powers over the medium. In the mid-1920s Hoover coordinated a series of conferences that defined broadcasting as a business enterprise rather than a government service, as many European nations defined the medium. In 1927, the Federal Radio Commission was established to regulate the expanding industry. Its influence greatly strengthened national, as opposed to local and special-interest, broadcasting.

Paralleling the rise of commercial radio, the motion picture industry flourished in the twenties, and American filmmakers became the world's leaders. The growing demand for movies required larger and larger capital investment, and by 1920 a film industry, centered in Hollywood, California, was well established. The giant production companies that would dominate the industry in future years, including Paramount, Metro-Goldwyn-Mayer (MGM), Warner Brothers, and Columbia, were in existence by 1929. By the end of the

decade, 28,000 movie theaters were scattered throughout the nation; average weekly attendance at the movies had risen from 40 million in 1922 to 90 million in 1930. The Hollywood studios fostered a star system that catered to an insatiable public appetite for news of the romances, marriages, divorces, and extravagant lifestyles of such legends of the silent screen as Charlie Chaplin, Mary Pickford, Clara Bow, Douglas Fairbanks, Rudolph Valentino, and Greta Garbo. In theaters across the nation, these superstars competed for audiences with Tom Mix and other cowboy heroes of the Western movies. In 1927 Warner Brothers' *The Jazz Singer,* the first movie featuring synchronized speech and music, assured the success of the "talkies."

Both radio and the movies reflected the nation's love of music and did much to form public tastes. It was fitting that the first widely viewed talkie featured jazz; musically, the twenties belonged to jazz, and the decade was appropriately labeled "The Jazz Age." In many ways the most significant contribution of African Americans to culture in the twentieth century, jazz was neither African nor American; it was distinctly African American, a product of the melting pot. The precedents for jazz can be found in the blues, sad songs that featured

The Jazz Age   In this photograph, from about 1922, the great young jazz trumpeter Louis Armstrong poses with "King Oliver's Creole Jazz Band." Groups such as this regularly performed in Harlem's Cotton Club, but (apart from those who waited on tables and washed dishes) they were the only black people who could enter such clubs with their all-white audiences.

"blue" notes that were deviations from the tempered scale; and in ragtime, the heavily syncopated music of the early twentieth century that imposed African motifs on the American brass band tradition.

A musical form characterized by improvisation and a syncopated rhythm, the word "jazz" most likely began as a euphemism for sexual intercourse. It captured liberated youth's free spirit and lust for life, as did the decade's most popular dances such as the Charleston. Born before the turn of the century in New Orleans (where talented black musicians found work performing in brothels patronized by well-to-do white men), the closing of that city's famed red-light district known as Storyville as a wartime "purity" measure in 1917 hastened the spread of jazz up the Mississippi River to Memphis and St. Louis, and from there to the cities of the North — above all, to Chicago and to New York's Harlem. Enthusiasm for jazz throughout the American population was also spread by another of the great consumer-oriented machines of the era, the phonograph. Jazz recordings, which the white businessmen who ran the industry disparagingly called "race records" until they realized how much money they brought in, sold equally well among whites and blacks, giving a strong boost to African American racial pride. A generation of creative black musicians — including W. C. Handy, Joe "King" Oliver, Jelly Roll Morton, and Louis Armstrong — became musical legends in the twenties. Oliver's all-black Creole Jazz Band made its recording debut in 1923. The band's featured cornetist, Armstrong, was the quintessential jazz soloist, and during his long life became known as the jazz ambassador to the world. Harlem's Cotton Club became a magnet for affluent whites excited by jazz's exuberant, "primitive" vigor — although it was a bitter commentary on the era's racism that the only African Americans allowed in the Cotton Club were the great performers themselves and the menial service personnel. (It was, incidentally, run by the Mafia.)

Many of the most popular songs of the decade were introduced in Broadway musicals. Russian-born Irving Berlin collaborated with the Marx Brothers to produce his first great musical hit, *The Coconuts* (1925), but the most prolific and talented musical writer of the decade was George Gershwin. Gershwin's greatest hit was probably the song "Suwannee," sung by Al Jolson in *The Jazz Singer*. But he teamed with his brother, Ira, to write a steady stream of hit musicals, including *Lady Be Good* (1924), *American in Paris* (1925), *Funny Face* (1927), and *Strike Up the Band* (1927). Gershwin displayed his virtuosity by writing a highly acclaimed semiclassical symphony in jazz style, *Rhapsody in Blue* (1924). A number of white performers, including Benny Goodman and Bix Beiderbecke, became accomplished jazzmen by playing alongside black performers.

The popular dancing boom of the early twentieth century expanded into a full-blown craze in the twenties. Enterprising entrepreneurs built dance halls all over the country, ranging from the elegant Roseland and Savoy in New York City to rural juke joints in the South. Civic groups and social clubs sponsored dances; some public dance halls attracted stag men by selling tickets for dances with female partners. *Variety* magazine estimated that more than 60,000 dance bands performed throughout the nation during the twenties. Almost without exception, black performers introduced the decade's new dances — the Black Bottom, the Shinny, and the Varsity Drag, in addition to the Charleston.

Increased leisure time induced a voracious appetite for news. The New York *Daily News,* established in 1919,

quickly became the nation's leading tabloid, reporting sensational crime and sex stories. *True Story* magazine, begun by Bernarr McFadden in 1919, had 300,000 readers in 1923 and more than two million by 1926, titillating readers with articles such as "The Confessions of a Chorus Girl" and "What I Told My Daughter the Night Before Her Marriage." Americans embraced one fad after another — mah-jongg, crossword puzzles, contract bridge, the Charleston, beauty contests, roller skating, dance marathons, and flagpole sitting, in which intrepid publicity-seekers vied to see who could remain perched atop a flagpole the longest.

Most of all, the twenties was the golden age of American sports, peopled by a generation of legendary heroes. Robert Tyre ("Bobby") Jones, winner of golf's "grand slam" in 1930, and "Big Bill" Tilden, the first great American tennis champion, piqued popular interest in those formerly aristocratic sports. At the other end of the social spectrum, in 1921 draft-dodging American Jack Dempsey drew boxing's first million-dollar gate (and loud boos) in defending his heavyweight championship by knocking out the French war hero Georges Carpentier. Dempsey's second loss to Gene Tunney in 1927 was witnessed by over 100,000 spectators and grossed well over $2 million. Heroes abounded — not only Tunney but also Harold "Red" Grange, the "Galloping Ghost" of the University of Illinois and the Chicago Bears; Johnny Weissmuller, who set scores of world swimming records before retiring to portray Tarzan in the movies; and even Man-o'-War, the magnificent chestnut horse that was unbeatable in 1920. There were also sports heroines, reflecting the changing image of women in the twenties. Helen Wills sparked an interest in women's tennis, and in 1926 Gertrude Ederle shocked the world by breaking the male record for swimming the English Channel.

The undisputed king of sports in the twenties was baseball. Automobiles, radios, and leisure time helped secure its place as "the national pastime." The decade had begun horribly for baseball following the Black Sox scandal in 1919, but better times were just ahead. That same year the New York Yankees paid a record $100,000 to purchase the contract of young pitcher-outfielder George Herman Ruth, Jr., from the financially troubled Boston Red Sox (bringing down, so Sox fans believed, a curse on the team. It did not win another World Series until 2004).

The "Babe" became the supreme sports idol of the twenties, a man whose larger-than-life talent and personality made him instantly recognizable throughout the nation. He hit over forty home runs in eleven seasons between 1920 and 1932 and a record sixty home runs in 1927. His offensive skills — which were aided by the introduction of the "live ball" — changed the basic strategy of baseball, from a game of pitchers' duels and strategic singles to a contest of muscular sluggers, swinging for homers. A child of recent immigrants who had learned the game while being brought up in a Baltimore home for wayward boys, Ruth was a fun-loving, affable, bighearted man with awesome appetites for food, alcohol, and sex. When the Babe collapsed in 1925 from a reported attack of influenza and indigestion (apparently the real cause was syphilis), the nation waited expectantly for reports on the state of his health. Throughout the decade, between nine and ten million baseball fans each year flocked to see Ruth and a long list of heroes only slightly less formidable.

WINDS OF CHANGE

Political reform languished in the twenties, but there was no moratorium on debate about American society. A majority of the decade's social activists, like most of its politicians, worried about the changes that had been wrought during the Progressive Era and sought a return to an earlier, more orderly time. The dangers that frightened these embattled conservatives were not illusions. Protestant American culture had fallen under siege, beset by a science that undermined its most cherished beliefs, taunted by a young intelligentsia who flaunted a new morality (and successfully peddled it to the younger generation), and overwhelmed in the burgeoning cities by immigrants with cultural values far different from those of the nation's earlier settlers. In short, the cultural clash of the 1920s was not contrived — it was real. Some of the decade's debates would appear trivial in the years of depression and war that followed, but most of the cultural quarrels of the twenties would resurface throughout the twentieth century.

The New Science

Perhaps the most curious folk hero of the twenties was Albert Einstein. From the moment of his first visit to the United States in 1921, the mild-mannered and eccentric physicist captivated the American public. The disheveled, odd-looking Einstein became synonymous with the word *genius.* Few scientists, much less the general public, understood Einstein's theories of relativity, made public in 1905 and 1916 and formulated in the deceptively simple equation $E = mc^2$. When the scientist visited President Harding in 1921, the *New York Times* reported in a comically understated headline: "Einstein Idea Puzzles Harding."

Einstein's theory of relativity illustrated that time, space, and motion are not absolute, but rather are relative to the observer and the observer's motion. Relativity posited a radically different universe from the orderly machine described by Isaac Newton more than two hundred years earlier. The Einsteinian universe made possible predictions, however, that Newtonian theory failed to anticipate. In May 1919, British astronomers at the Palomar Observatory in California confirmed that the mass of the sun

Babe Ruth   Playing against the now-defunct Washington Senators, "the Babe" crosses home plate after slugging another home run. Ruth was the most beloved baseball player of the 1920s.

caused light rays to curve as they passed, thus slowing time and bending space as predicted by the general theory of relativity. Newton's clocklike and orderly universe was being replaced by a universe that seemed shockingly relativistic to nonscientists.

Even more unsettling, though at first little known, was the new theory of the quantum, first formulated in 1900 by Max Planck, a German physicist. Planck demonstrated that energy is emitted discontinuously in certain discrete amounts, or quanta. Based on Planck's finding, a mathematical theory called quantum mechanics was worked out beginning in the 1920s that permitted a widening inquiry into the nature of the atom and of subatomic matter. Quantum mechanics uncovered a world of particles whose movement is unpredictable and not bound by the rules that were assumed to govern all matter. Einstein was troubled by the randomness of the theory; convinced that God "does not play dice" with the universe, he would spend the last thirty years of his life (he died in 1955) unsuccessfully seeking a "unified field theory" to explain both the behavior of subatomic particles and the geometry of gravity.

If physicists were undermining older understandings in profound ways, other intellectual challenges came with stunning rapidity as the twentieth century began. Nowhere were they more disturbing than in the field of psychology. The guru of the intellectuals of the twenties was the Austrian psychologist Sigmund Freud, who explored the influence of hidden drives and sexual repression on behavior. Freud and his colleague Carl Jung (who later broke with Freud) both lectured in the United States in 1909, but psychoanalysis gained its first broad hearing — and acceptance among influential segments of the public — in the twenties. The idea that areas of human behavior lie outside of conscious control suggested that humans were not primarily rational beings — a sentiment shared by many in the wake of the horrors of World War I.

The rise of behavioral psychology was more important in the universities than psychoanalysis was, but it was no less unsettling to older understandings of human conduct. As explained by the American experimenter John B. Watson, the human personality responded predictably to clear stimuli, and Watson boasted that, given a free hand, he could bend any child's personality in whatever direction he chose. The irrational, conditioned response of the human personality, as asserted by behaviorists like Watson, opened new vistas for advertisers and propagandists, but it deeply troubled those who believed in a world of rea-

son and absolute truth. As the new findings in science and psychology became popularized, all time-honored values were increasingly subject to reexamination. Novelist Willa Cather wrote, "The world broke in two in 1922 or thereabouts."

❧ *The Literature of Revolt*

American literature in the twenties launched a withering attack on formalism, the idea that eternal verities and natural laws governed society. The decade's artistic modernism was sweeping, embracing new forms of writing such as free verse poetry and stream-of-consciousness novels. The intellectuals of the twenties viewed themselves as a generation liberated from the constraints of culture, and they were relentless critics of the foibles of the times — the dehumanizing effects of modern life, the evils of big business and factory working conditions, the reign of materialism and greed, the American fascination with success. Coining a memorable expression, writer Gertrude Stein termed the disenchanted artists of the postwar years a "lost generation," groping for meaning in a collapsing world.

Several avant-garde American cultural centers flourished during the decade, including the South Side in Chicago and Greenwich Village in New York City. But a number of important American writers felt more at home (and found that they could live more cheaply) in Europe than in America. Gertrude Stein, who moved to Paris in 1903, and Ezra Pound, who lived successively in London, Paris, and Italy, were the Lost Generation's mentors, championing experimentation in poetry and prose. The foremost expatriate poet was St. Louis–born T. S. Eliot, who eventually became a British citizen. Eliot's poem *The Waste Land* (1922) lamented the shattering of Western civilization by the ravages of World War I.

Increasingly recognized as the most talented of the expatriates was Ernest Hemingway, who was encouraged by Gertrude Stein while he was working in Paris as a reporter for the Kansas City *Star*. Hemingway wrote of American expatriates in Paris in his first novel, *The Sun Also Rises* (1926). His second novel, *A Farewell to Arms* (1929), portrayed the irrationality of wartime life. Hemingway's characters struggled to find meaning in a world filled with capriciousness and tragedy.

While many authors in the twenties wrestled with the intellectual unraveling of the world, others challenged the American character. Baltimore journalist H. L. Mencken raised the art of criticism to new heights of elegant, witty vitriol. From 1914 to 1923 Mencken edited *The Smart Set,* an avant-garde magazine with a small circulation, but in 1925 he and drama critic George Jean Nathan founded and began editing *The American Mercury,* a large-circulation magazine designed, in his words, for the "civilized minority." Walter Lippmann judged Mencken to be "the most powerful influence on this whole generation of educated people." Mencken's iconoclasm and criticism of middle-class America and its "booboisie" betrayed an undiscriminating elitism that reflected both his social-Darwinist view of life and his libertarian opposition to any restrictions on free thought and expression. An outspoken agnostic, he jeered at religious faith as "an illogical belief in the occurrence of the improbable," and he denounced democracy because it put power into the hands of "dunderheads, cowards, trimmers, frauds, and cads." Puritanism, long a revered part of the American past, became in Mencken's words "the haunting fear that someone, somewhere might be happy." Mencken and his fellow debunkers viewed "Puritanism" as a repugnant part of the nation's heritage, so distorting the word that decades passed before it regained any resemblance to historical reality. Asked why he continued to live in an America that he ridiculed so relentlessly, Mencken retorted: "Why do men visit zoos?" In the pages of *The American Mercury* and his Baltimore *Sun* newspaper columns, Mencken lustily championed iconoclastic writers such as Sinclair Lewis, Theodore Dreiser, and Eugene O'Neill, and hammered with caustic wit at Prohibition, the South, fundamentalism, and practically everything else except German music and Chesapeake Bay cuisine.

Sinclair Lewis's 1920 best-seller, *Main Street,* depicted the monotony and meanness in a small Minnesota town. This he followed with a series of novels laying bare other American duplicities. *Babbitt* (1922) mercilessly attacked boosterism and the hollowness of success, and *Arrowsmith* (1924) caricatured the medical profession. *Elmer Gantry* (1927), Lewis's most unforgiving exposé, skewered revivalistic religion. It was the story of a brazen ex-football player who became a successful evangelist by flaunting his physical attractiveness, preaching half-plagiarized sermons, and shamelessly promoting himself. Denounced by church leaders, the novel captured the religious hypocrisy and materialistic greed that the intellectuals of the twenties labeled philistinism. Lewis insisted that his books were not muckraking and that they underscored the strengths of American character, as well as the weak-

nesses. In 1930, he became the first American to receive a Nobel Prize for literature.

Probably the best-known American writer in the twenties was F. Scott Fitzgerald; his third novel, generally considered his best, *The Great Gatsby,* won critical acclaim in 1925. The story of Jay Gatsby's quest for wealth and social standing, the book described the hero's defilement by the hypocrisy and greed that characterized the decade's seemingly carefree high society. Fitzgerald's books earned him sufficient fame and money to make him a part of the hedonistic but hauntingly empty society he chronicled. He and his glamorous wife, Zelda, came to be symbols of the Jazz Age — extravagant, rebellious, and haunted by his alcoholism and financial failures and by her mental illness.

Playwright Eugene O'Neill explored psychological and sociological uncertainties. O'Neill won a Pulitzer Prize in 1920 for his play *Beyond the Horizon;* he wrote seventeen other plays during the decade. O'Neill's work was deeply influenced by Freud, and his critics agreed that he was at his best when his characters were tragic or at least unhappy. He introduced expressionism to the American stage in *The Emperor Jones* (1921), a tour de force of imaginative theater.

Other talented writers were ending and beginning careers during the twenties. Theodore Dreiser, already acknowledged as a master of literary realism, produced his most ambitious novel in 1925, *An American Tragedy.* Other authors wrote penetrating novels with regional settings: Edith Wharton studied New York society in *The Age of Innocence* (1920); Ellen Glasgow wrote of Virginia in *Barren Ground* (1925); and Willa Cather, whose earlier books had described the frontier experience, wrote movingly about the Catholic culture of the Southwest in *Death Comes for the Archbishop* (1927).

❧ *The New Morality and the New Woman*

Some of the titles given to the 1920s — "The Age of the Flapper," "The Era of Flaming Youth," "The Roaring Twenties" — reflected a perception that the basic values of American society were changing and that the rebellion was being led by the young and by women. Among the popular songs of the decade were "Hot Lips," "I Need Lovin'," and "Burning Kisses," and *Flaming Youth* was a popular film. While the actual "flaming youth" were never more than a small minority in American society, they were visible and, to some extent, emulated.

The 1920s' image of the assertive young woman, or flapper (Mencken coined the word), seriously challenged traditional moral values. She smoked cigarettes, danced the Charleston, listened to jazz, took joyrides in automobiles, and flaunted her sexuality. By the end of the twenties, flapper styles were featured in the Sears catalog as well as on the cover of *The Smart Set*. Conservatives saw symptoms of moral decay everywhere around them. One preacher warned that if skirts climbed at the same rate for two more decades, the hem line would be "fifteen feet above the head." Older Americans deplored the sensuous jazz music, the wild dancing, and the petting parties favored by the younger generation.

The moral revolution of the twenties was tied to the broad social transformation of the decade. As a majority of Americans became city dwellers, they discovered that the urban environment weakened the ties of the extended family. In addition, the ever-expanding public school system came to assume many of the child-training duties that had formerly been family responsibilities. High school enrollment doubled in the 1920s, as more working-class teenagers remained in school rather than entering the workforce early to help support their families, and increasingly young people were introduced to ideas and values at odds with their parents'. Of course, most public school teachers in the 1920s were themselves quite conservative, but many parents for the first time came to sense that school was displacing family authority in some realms, and religious conservatives made their first concerted effort to control the intellectual content of the classroom by passing laws banning the teaching of evolution.

Women led the dramatic change in lifestyle in the twenties. The availability of consumer goods helped emancipate women from the drudgery of housework. The automobile was an ideal laboratory for sexual experimentation, and in it one could escape the community-enforced moral code of the small town. Perhaps most important, the dissemination of information about birth control, promoted vigorously by Margaret Sanger, somewhat undermined the pillar of the double standard of morality, woman's fear of pregnancy. Birth control gave women new sexual freedom and also contributed to a declining national birth rate and the lengthening of women's life expectancy.

The intellectual oracle of the new morality was Sigmund Freud. To be sure, few Americans really understood Freud, but psychoanalysis encouraged uninhibited discussions of sex that would have been unthinkable a decade earlier. At the popular level, the lesson read into Freud was the urgency of escaping from sexual repressions.

To some extent, the changing role of women was tied to the perception that women had become financially less dependent on their husbands. Actually, women made few economic gains during the decade. They entered the workforce in unprecedented numbers during World War I, but most of them left again after the war. The image of the economically self-reliant working girl of the twenties is largely a myth. The total number of women in the labor force of the country rose from 8.3 million in 1920 to 10.6 million in 1930, but that represented a gain of less than one percentage point — to 23.6 percent of the total labor force. The number of married women working did increase significantly during the decade, from 23 percent of women workers to 28.9 percent. But most women continued to live in traditional families and to work in low-paying female occupations — nurses, teachers, secretaries, sales clerks, waitresses, and domestic servants. Women did make up a majority of those employed in the emerging field of social work, and many held leadership positions in the profession.

The triumph of woman suffrage defused the women's rights movement. Actually, the women's movement had suffered a bitter split before ratification of the Nineteenth Amendment. The moderate National American Woman Suffrage Association, headed by Carrie Chapman Catt, claimed most of the credit for pushing through the suffrage amendment by the narrowest of margins. After ratification the association transformed itself into the League of Women Voters, losing much of its feminist identification. Catt declared that the suffrage amendment had "nearly completed the emancipation of women in America."

A second, more radical feminist movement was led by Alice Paul, who insisted that the women's movement had "just begun." Paul's confrontational tactics antagonized moderate women's rights reformers. Her group, known after 1915 as the National Woman's Party, set a new agenda for feminism in 1923 with the demand that Congress pass an Equal Rights Amendment that would eliminate all legal distinctions between the sexes. Her efforts were largely ineffectual, at least partly because many feared that such an amendment would annul hard-won progressive legislation protecting the rights of working women.

❧ The "New Negro"

During the twenties the total African American population grew by more than 1.5 million, but the number of rural blacks fell by 300,000. This difference was reflected in the massive migration of blacks out of the South into the cities of the North, which had begun during World War I and accelerated in the twenties. Newly arrived blacks continued to find discrimination in northern cities almost as pervasive as in the South, but they had greater economic opportunity in the North and a new freedom to express rising expectations. The political implications of the black migration were illustrated in 1928 by the election of Republican Oscar DePriest, a black alderman from Chicago, to the House of Representatives. He was the first black elected to Congress since the collapse of Reconstruction and the first ever from outside the South.

New leaders and a revised self-image called the "New Negro" emerged in the black community after World War I. Booker T. Washington died in 1915, and political leadership among blacks passed to the National Association for the Advancement of Colored People and W. E. B. Du Bois, editor of *The Crisis* and the organization's unchallenged intellectual leader. The NAACP continued to battle in the courts for the enforcement of the Fourteenth and Fifteenth Amendments, but had few successes.

Harlem emerged in the twenties as a center of black thought and culture. For the first time, a group of black writers gained national recognition. In *Harlem Shadows,* poems published in 1922 by Jamaica-born Claude McKay, the themes of black pride and defiance set the tone for a movement labeled the Harlem Renaissance. An anthology published in 1925, entitled *The New Negro,* introduced a variety of talented writers, including poet Langston Hughes and author Jean Toomer. Toomer's collection of stories, *Cane* (1923), told of black life in rural Georgia in the 1880s and was considered by many to be the finest literary achievement of the Harlem Renaissance.

Marcus Garvey became a symbol of black aspirations in the twenties. A Jamaican, Garvey formed the United Negro Improvement Association two years before coming to the United States in 1916. By 1920, the association had over thirty chapters in the United States, and by 1923, Garvey claimed it had 6 million members. The membership was probably never so large, but Garvey's newspaper, *Negro World,* was widely read by blacks, particularly among the urban working classes. Garvey preached black pride and condemned American society as too racist for redemption. Urging blacks to leave America to establish "an African nation for Negroes" in Liberia, he organized the Black

The Harlem Renaissance   African American painter Malvin Gray Johnson, one of the notable talents of the Harlem Renaissance, painted this self-portrait in 1934. Largely dependent on wealthy white patrons, the Harlem Renaissance suffered a severe setback during the hard times of the 1930s, but it left a lasting imprint on American culture and life.

Star Steamship Line and sold stock to thousands of blacks.

Garvey was pictured as a charlatan and a buffoon by his detractors, including many black leaders who believed that integration and constitutional equality were the proper black agenda. Garvey's penchant for uniforms and parading made him an easy target for ridicule. More crippling to his reputation was the collapse of the Black Star Steamship Line. Convicted of mail fraud and confined in a federal penitentiary in 1925, Garvey was deported to Jamaica in 1927. While Garvey remains an enigmatic figure, he clearly tapped an emerging spirit of black pride. In many respects, Garvey and his organization were black counterparts to the fraternal and "booster" organizations in contemporary white society. Groups such as the Shriners, the Odd Fellows, and the UNIA all provided identity, importance, and mission amidst the impersonal bustle of the modern city.

CONSERVATIVE BACKLASH

As in other periods of rapid social change, defenders of older values fought back. Many of the restrictive measures of the twenties — Prohibition, immigration quotas, antievolution legislation — were tied to the nation's Protestant heritage, but they were also products of popular democracy. Most intellectuals in the twenties condemned these efforts to regulate society as unwarranted assaults on personal liberty, but to many ordinary Americans they were simply democracy in action. William Jennings Bryan, the old hero of populist democracy, cast his defense of the Tennessee law prohibiting the teaching of evolution in the public schools in just such terms: "The tax-payers must decide what shall be taught.... So

Modernism through Fundamentalist Eyes This caricature, published in a widely read fundamentalist magazine, expressed the alarm and disdain many conservative American Christians of the 1920s felt about the mainstream churches' embrace of theological and social modernity.

a man can believe anything he pleases but he has no right to teach it against the protest of his employers." In one sense, Prohibition was a quintessential example of the majority trying to rule. During his visit to the United States in 1921, Albert Einstein was asked if he found Prohibition an intolerable violation of personal liberty. As naïve an idealist in politics as he was a genius in physics, he replied incredulously, "How could that be in America? You have a republic.... Nothing that is done by a democratic Government could be done against freedom." In the minds of many Americans, moral legislation was the people's answer to the condescension of intellectuals and the immorality of foreign radicals.

The major conservative counterattacks were over by 1925. In some cases, including the efforts to restrict immigration, unions, and booze, conservatives attained their objectives, thus allaying anxieties. On the other hand, in 1925 the antievolution campaign permanently stalled.

❧ Religious Diversity and Confrontation

In 1920 the nation held vast reservoirs of people clinging to traditional beliefs and values. A national religious census in 1926 reported that the country had 232,154 congregations claiming nearly 55 million members. But the depth of religious faith in the nation was hardly captured by those statistics. In 1927, President Calvin Coolidge wrote to an Episcopal Sunday school teacher in Washington, D.C., "The foundations of our society and Government rest so much on the teachings of the Bible that it would be difficult to support them if faith in these teachings should cease to be practically universal in our country."

THE GROWING CATHOLIC CHURCH

Though a majority of Americans did not realize it, those values were nowhere more deeply rooted than in the immigrant-swollen American Catholic church. The church passed 20 million members in 1929, making it nearly three times as large as any single Protestant denomination. Still struggling to digest the millions of immigrants of varying nationalities who had arrived in the past twenty-five years, the Catholic Church developed a strong hierarchy. Having survived earlier fears that the church might splinter as a result of "Americanizing" influences, during the twenties American Catholicism was tightly controlled by the clergy. The laity seemed content, in the words of Pope Pius X (1903-1914), "like a docile flock, to follow the Pastors."

In some Slavic, Italian, and German areas the church remained a bastion of Old World culture, but increasingly the Irish-American hierarchy fostered an English-speaking communion through parochial education. In 1926 the American Catholic church operated nearly 5,500 parochial school systems enrolling 1.8 million students; generally English was the language of instruction. While the expansion of parochial education speeded acculturation, it also provided a buffer against the dominant Protestant culture and, more important as the decade wore on, against secular values. On many controversial social questions, Catholics were more conservative than their Protestant neighbors. For instance, Catholic leaders strongly opposed woman suffrage, fearing that it would alter the traditional role of women.

Despite their number, American Catholics remained, to some extent, an alienated minority. Partly, Catholics were separated from their Protestant neighbors by religious culture — by homes that were decorated with statues and pictures of saints, by frequent oral confession, by meatless Fridays, and by celebrations of holy days that had been "sanitized" from Protestantism by the Puritans. Partly they were separated by the vast network of institutions that the church had founded — not only schools but also hundreds of hospitals and orphanages. And partly Catholics were isolated by prejudice. Catholics and Protestants continued to rouse mutual suspicions, and the decade's legislation restricting immigration and prohibiting drinking was aimed at Catholic immigrants and their culture. From their side, many Catholics felt conscience-bound to keep their children out of the "Protestant-dominated" or "secular" public schools. The Catholic Church opposed both immigration restriction and Prohibition, although the slowing of immigration was probably a blessing to the church, allowing it time to digest a century's growth.

However conservative its overall role in American society might be, during the 1920s the Catholic Church was going through its own internal battles over the pace of modernization. "The people of the United States must be Americans or something else. They cannot serve two masters," declared Chicago's Archbishop Mundelein — himself a fifth-generation German-American — in throwing the church's influence against the ethnic isolation to which many "hyphenated-American" Catholics clung during the twenties. In Chicago and other "melting-pot" cities, church authorities tried to discourage ethnic fragmentation by redrawing parish lines and demanding that English be the language of preaching, teaching, and ordinary parish business. (Latin, of course, was still the liturgical language.) The largely Irish- and German-background episcopate was openly suspicious of the "superstition," even "paganism," that they detected in the street processions and saints'-day festivals that many Italian Catholics had brought to America from their native Naples or

---

❋ **IN THEIR OWN WORDS**

"The Secret of Success," 1925
The United American, *a popular magazine, had the following advice for immigrants joining the American workforce.*

The secret of success is not a secret. Nor is it something hard to secure.

To become more successful, become more efficient. Do the little things better. So work that you will require less supervision. The least supervision is needed by the person who makes the fewest mistakes.

Do what you can do and what you should do for the institution for which you are working, and do it in the right way, and the size of your income will take care of itself.

Let your aim ever be to better the work you are doing without bettering yourself.

The thoughts that you think, the words that you speak, and the deeds you perform are making you either better or worse. Realize with [Victorian poet William] Henley that you are the master of your fate and the captain of your soul. You can be what you will be.

Sicily, making the Little Italies of American cities noisy and colorful. Church authorities' attempts to discourage these celebrations caused great bitterness and even the threat of schism in the Italian and Polish communities, and were not entirely successful.

Despite these tensions within the church, increasing numbers of American Catholics entered the post–World War I years with a new confidence about their place in American society. When the church's International Eucharistic Congress was held in Chicago in 1926, for the first time coming to America, it attracted nine cardinals and was attended by an estimated 500,000 Catholics. For five days the display of pageantry received national attention. The church entered a new "brick-and-mortar" period in 1920. Scores of impressive new cathedrals were constructed, and between 1916 and 1926 the value of the average Catholic church building more than doubled.

SUCCESSES AND CHALLENGES FOR AMERICAN JUDAISM

The Jewish community grew from slightly more than 1 million in 1900 to nearly 3.5 million by 1920, with nearly half living in New York City. Between 1916 and 1926 the number of synagogues doubled, to more than 3,100. Jewish congregations were independent, and in the 1920s only about 20 percent of them were formally united with one of the unions representing the three branches of American Judaism — Reform, Conservative, and Orthodox. Nonetheless, the three theological wings of Judaism were defined by networks of synagogues and by social and benevolent organizations that served Jews of diverse ethnic and economic backgrounds. Like Catholics, many American Jews continued to live in insulated enclaves in the twenties. Jewish congregations in the United States operated more than 500 school systems enrolling 70,000 daily students and another 70,000 who received religious training one day a week.

Many Jews, regardless of whether they were Orthodox, Conservative, or Reform — and even regardless of how religiously observant they were — felt strong concerns about the homogenizing, assimilationist pressures of modern American society. Their response to these trends echoed the worries of countless Catholics and Protestants, that their young people were being sucked into a secularist, materialistic culture devoid of the anchor of traditional values. "What will become of our children?" asked a Chicago rabbi in 1925, sounding much like his conservative Christian peers. "Do we want them to grow up men and women who have an understanding of the problems of life, who know the history of their ancestors, who are proud Jews, and who will be a credit to us? Our children are running away from us. . . . Let us build houses of worship, social centers and Hebrew schools, and let us provide the means for the coming generation to learn and to know."

Zionism — the international movement to create a Jewish homeland in Palestine — continued to flourish in the United States. By 1926 the Zionist Organization of America claimed 71,000 members; between 1918 and 1926 American Jews contributed more than $15 million to support various projects in the Holy Land. In the years after World War I American Jews also contributed more than $67 million to aid European Jews dislocated by the war and by postwar persecution in Russia, Poland, and Romania. Jewish self-consciousness was heightened by the virulent resurgence of anti-Semitism, most visible in Henry Ford's newspaper, the *Dearborn Independent,* and in the rise of a frightening new version of the Ku Klux Klan. Anti-Semitism was deep-rooted in Western history, but it was bolstered in 1920s America by nativist prejudice and fears that linked Jews with political radicalism, as well as by the sheer number and visibility of Jews in American society.

PROTESTANT MODERNISM AND FUNDAMENTALISM

Liberal Protestantism was the segment of American religion most willing to embrace modernism but at the same time most buffeted by the rapid intellectual and social changes of the twenties. The optimistic hopes of the social gospel, like those of progressivism in general, seemed out of place in the postwar world. As theological liberals strove to square their beliefs with scientific thought — the magnificent Riverside Church built in New York City during the twenties included on its west portal the carved figures of Charles Darwin and Albert Einstein — they increasingly found themselves under attack from both the left and the right. By the mid-1920s a growing group of academic agnostics, calling themselves humanists, labeled modernism a "half way reform" that only "flirts with science." In *The Twilight of the Gods,* social scientist Harry Elmer Barnes advised that "nothing better could happen to American religion than for progressive young divines in Methodism to forget about Jesus." In turn, liberal churchmen warned that humanists would find it impossible to preserve hope and a belief in values in a world purged of a personal God.

At the other end of the spectrum, Protestant fundamentalists waged war on liberals for abandoning the doctrine of inerrancy, the belief that the Bible was absolutely precise and free from all factual error. Conservative Princeton scholar J. Gresham Machen argued in his book *Christianity and Liberalism* (1923) that the liberals' abandonment of "one Christian doctrine after another" had created a new religion "so entirely different from Christianity as to belong in a distinct category."

Liberal churchmen vigorously defended themselves against fundamentalism. In a famous sermon preached in 1922 that ultimately cost him his pastorate at the First Presbyterian Church of New York, "Shall the Fundamentalists Win?" Harry Emerson Fosdick, a professor at Union Theological Seminary, warned that fundamentalism was "immeasurable folly." Arguing that religious faith had nothing to fear from "scientific thought" and specifically embracing evolution, Fosdick called for a progressive Christianity that "saves us from the necessity of apologizing for immature states in the development of the biblical revelation."

The modernist-fundamentalist conflict divided two of the largest northern Protestant denominations, the Northern Baptist Convention and the Presbyterian Church in the United States of America. Until 1925, conservatives controlled the denominational boards and agencies in both churches, but there was a growing concern that liberals had undue influence on the missions supported by the churches. In the early twenties conservatives conducted minor purges of liberals.

In 1925, moderates disenchanted by the increasingly caustic tactics of the fundamentalists deserted the conservative alliance. Both denominations suffered defections, but by the end of the decade they had joined the Methodists and Episcopalians in tolerating, if not promoting, more modernistic views of Christian theology.

THE SCOPES TRIAL

Generally taken as symbolic of the routing of fundamentalism in mainstream Protestantism in the twenties was the trial of John T. Scopes in Dayton, Tennessee, in July 1925. The trial contested a newly passed Tennessee law prohibiting the teaching of evolution in the public schools. Five southern states passed antievolution laws in the twenties, and similar bills were introduced in states from Maine to California. Evolution became a public focus for the modernist-fundamentalist controversy after half a century of theological debate because conservative Protestants, many of them uneducated, saw quite correctly that Darwin's ideas had broad moral consequences. These Bible-believing masses insisted that they were proprietors of the public schools and demanded control of the curriculum.

When Scopes, a coach and science teacher at Central High School in Dayton, was charged with violating the Tennessee antievolution law, the American Civil Liberties Union retained several famous trial attorneys to defend him, including Clarence Darrow. Himself a fundamentalist Christian, and alarmed by the elitist and social-Darwinist implications of evolutionary the-

---

✳ IN THEIR OWN WORDS

An Obituary for William Jennings Bryan, 1925

H. L. Mencken attended the Scopes trial in Dayton, Tennessee, and wrote scathing reports for the Baltimore Sun. *None of those articles, however, better captured the venom of Mencken's pen, or the condescension he felt for rural America, than an article he wrote reflecting on the death of William Jennings Bryan.*

There was something peculiarly fitting in the fact that [Bryan's] last days were spent in a one-horse Tennessee village, beating off the flies and gnats, and that death found him

there. The man felt at home in such simple and Christian scenes. He liked people who sweated freely, and were not debauched by the refinements of the toilet. Making his progress up and down the Main street of little Dayton, surrounded by gaping primates from the upland valleys of the Cumberland Range, his coat laid aside, his bare arms and hairy chest shining damply, his bald head sprinkled with dust — so accoutred and on display, he was obviously happy. He liked getting up early in the morning, to the tune of cocks crowing on the dunghill. He liked the heavy, greasy victuals of the farmhouse kitchen. He liked country lawyers, country

pastors, all country people. He liked country sounds and country smells. . . .

. . . His career brought him into contact with the first men of his time; he preferred the company of rustic ignoramuses. It was hard to believe, watching him at Dayton, that he had traveled, that he had been received in civilized societies, that he had been a high officer of state. He seemed only a poor clod like those around him, deluded by a childish theology, full of an almost pathological hatred of all learning, all human dignity, all beauty, all fine and noble things. He was a peasant come home to the barnyard.

ory as it was often presented in the 1920s, the aging William Jennings Bryan offered his services to Tennessee as prosecuting attorney. The stage was set for high drama.

The nine-day trial was a national spectacle, perfectly calculated to caricature fundamentalism. For the first time, live radio broadcasts reported on the progress of a trial, and scores of reporters, including the acerbic Mencken, roamed the village's unpaved main street, mingling with rural evangelists like T. T. Martin from Blue Mountain, Mississippi, who had journeyed to Dayton to "drive hell out of the high school." The scene, Mencken wrote to a friend, was "far worse than anything you can imagine, even under the bowl. Every last scoundrel in sight is a Christian, including the town Jew."

Despite the sideshow surrounding the trial, the outcome was never in doubt. Convicted of violating the law, Scopes received a token sentence. On appeal, the Tennessee Supreme Court reversed the decision on a technicality, refusing to rule on the larger question of the constitutionality of the law. But the fundamentalist cause had been subjected to a withering barrage of ridicule from journalists — above all Mencken, whose syndicated daily reports called the residents of Dayton "gaping primates" and "yokels" and described their religious beliefs as "simian gabble." After Bryan collapsed and died in Dayton on the Sunday following the trial, Mencken wrote an unusually nasty (even for him) obituary: "It was hard to believe, watching him at Dayton, that he had traveled, that he had been received in civilized societies, that he had been a high officer of state. He seemed only a poor clod like those around him, deluded by a childish theology, full of an almost pathological hatred of all learning, all human dignity, all beauty, all fine and noble things. He was a peasant come home to the barnyard." The antievolution movement had lost its celebrity leader, and many felt that both Bryan and the fundamentalist movement had been crushed in Dayton, never to rise again.

ENDURING REVIVALISM

Despite its setbacks in the northern churches and the embarrassment of the Scopes trial, fundamentalism was far from dead. Conservative Protestantism remained the folk religion of the nation and continued to show its strength in the revivals of Billy Sunday and other evangelists. Sunday dismissed evolution as "jackass nonsense": "If a minister believes and teaches evolution, he is a stinking skunk, a hypocrite, and a liar." Fearful of the fate of the cities, fundamentalists believed that they still controlled the countryside. Wrote preacher John

Roach Straton in 1925: "The religious faith and the robust conservatism of the chivalric South and the sturdy West will have to save America from the sins and shams and shames that are now menacing her splendid life."

The most striking new evangelist to appear on the scene in the 1920s was Aimee Semple McPherson. A flamboyant and attractive Pentecostal who held large healing campaigns in the United States and Canada in the early twenties, in 1923 "Sister Aimee" settled in Los Angeles and built a large church, Angelus Temple, which by 1930 had 12,000 members. In 1926 McPherson was allegedly kidnapped, only to reappear mysteriously a month later. The press, and others, charged that she spent the time with her lover and business manager, and after an investigation she was charged with conspiracy to obstruct justice and subornation of perjury. The sensational case received more press attention than any other event during the decade, but in 1927 the charges against McPherson were dropped and she emerged more popular than ever. Shortly afterward, she founded a new denomination, the International Church of the Foursquare Gospel, and remained a model for later generations of faith-healing revivalists.

❧ Nativist Fears and Immigration Restrictions

World War I slowed to a trickle the flow of European (though not Mexican) immigrants, but the numbers of transatlantic migrants rose again after the war, reaching 805,228 in 1921 and 706,896 in 1924. As before the war, a majority of the Old World immigrants were laborers from the poverty-stricken southern and eastern European countries. Nearly a third were Italians, and Poles constituted the second-largest nationality.

Congressional restrictions on immigration prior to the twenties had excluded certain "undesirable" groups such as criminals and had reflected prevailing racist prejudices by targeting Asians. In 1921, a quota system was imposed for the first time, limiting the number of immigrants from any nation to 3 percent of the citizens of that nationality in the population in the census of 1910. The Immigration Act of 1924, culminating half a century of nativist pressure, reduced quotas to 2 percent of a nationality's numbers in the census of 1890, before millions of southern and eastern Europeans had begun flocking to America. Subsequent modifications changed the quotas slightly and based them on the census of 1920, but, taken together, the acts sharply reduced the tide of immigrants from Europe. The laws excluded

Aimee Semple McPherson   Pictured here in a dramatic portrait taken at an evangelistic meeting in London, Aimee Semple McPherson was a media star whose theatrical preaching and divine healing services inspired a later generation of American televangelists. She also won praise for her relief of the poor during the Depression, and she left behind a major Pentecostal denomination, the International Church of the Foursquare Gospel.

Japanese immigration but, apparently by oversight on the part of nativist radicals, did not establish quotas for the Western Hemisphere. Because of that omission over 1.5 million immigrants from Canada and Mexico made those countries the largest sources of new immigrants in the 1920s. These migrants did something to replace the cheap labor supply cut off by exclusion.

The 1924 law highlighted the pervasiveness of racism, anti-Catholic prejudice, anti-Semitism, and fear of political radicalism and signaled that most Americans had lost faith in the ideal of a "melting pot." Lothrop Stoddard's *The Rising Tide of Color* (1920) built on the pseudo-scientific racism of Madison Grant's earlier works (see Chapter 23) in warning against "mongrel-

ization." Although some scholars challenged popular theories advocating racial purity and white supremacy, most notably anthropologist Franz Boas of Columbia University, not until Nazi Germany took this racist thought to its horrifying conclusion of genocide in the 1930s and 1940s did such theories fall into general disrepute in America. In the 1920s, even many people who considered themselves progressives were also racists and scorned non-WASPs.

❧ *The Case against Foreigners*

On April 15, 1920, two people were killed during a robbery at a shoe factory in South Braintree, Massachusetts. Three weeks later, two Italian immigrants, Nicola Sacco and Bartolomeo Vanzetti, were arrested and charged with the murders. Before being executed on August 23, 1927, the two came to symbolize for conservative Americans the evils of foreign radicalism, and their case became a *cause célèbre* for liberals in America and indeed all around the world. A body of protest literature grew out of the trial, including novels by Upton Sinclair and John Dos Passos.

The facts of the case are still disputed. Both Sacco and Vanzetti had probably been involved in the anarchist bombings of 1919, and most modern experts think that Sacco was involved in the South Braintree incident, but the evidence against them in the murder trial was mostly circumstantial. Less problematic is the question of whether the defendants received a fair trial. The prosecution case was flimsy, but much more dubious was the conduct of Judge Webster Thayer. In private, the judge referred to the defendants as "those anarchist bastards," and his charge to the jury sounded like an order to convict. Thayer denied eight appeals before the two died in the electric chair.

The compelling question surrounding the Sacco and Vanzetti case is why the trial of two Italian immigrants for murder roused such an international furor. Clearly, at issue was more than the guilt or innocence of Sacco and Vanzetti. The defendants were Italian immigrants, atheists, avowed anarchists, and pacifists. The case stirred the deepest fears and fanned the most ardent prejudices of the twenties. The injustice of their execution (which drew a public apology from Massachusetts Governor Michael Dukakis in 1977 on the fiftieth anniversary of the pair's death) was that the defendants were tried on the basis of who they were rather than on the facts of the case.

ঌ The Ku Klux Klan Defines "Pure Americanism"

The most flagrant example of the rising tide of "100 percent Americanism" in the twenties was the Ku Klux Klan. Inspired by the Reconstruction organization, but with a wider range of targets, the new KKK was founded on Thanksgiving Night 1915 at Stone Mountain, Georgia. William Joseph Simmons, a salesman, part-time preacher, and promoter of fraternal organizations, was the first Imperial Wizard of the Invisible Empire. The Klan grew slowly at first and in 1920 still had only about 5,000 members. In 1920, Simmons employed as publicity experts Edward Clarke and Elizabeth Tyler, who introduced a pyramid recruiting system based on financial incentives. The KKK membership mushroomed in the early twenties, reaching a peak of around 4.5 million members in 1924. The Klan was strongest in the South, West Coast, and Midwest.

Like the Sacco and Vanzetti case, the rise of the KKK

defies simple explanation. To some extent, the KKK built on the American love for fraternal organizations. During its peak years the Klan had around 500,000 women members, for many of them providing "a way to get together and enjoy." The Klan's hierarchy of "wizards," "kleagles," and "goblins," and its robes, hoods, and torchlight parades paralleled the pageantry that attracted Americans to completely harmless and often benevolent secret associations, like the Odd Fellows and Elks. Furthermore, the KKK had been romanticized in the popular movie, *The Birth of a Nation,* and its overt aims — "to protect and maintain the distinctive institutions, rights ... and ideals of a pure Americanism" — unquestionably lured many responsible citizens into membership. In many localities the Klan's membership was dominated by respectable middle-class citizens (a majority nonfundamentalists) who sincerely wanted to improve their communities.

Lurking beneath the surface, however, were more sordid appeals to prejudices that were widely embraced by middle-class white Americans — anti-Catholicism, nativism, anti-Semitism, and racial bigotry. For the most part, the Klan used pressure tactics to gain its objectives, intimidating school boards and politicians and promoting lectures by alleged "escaped nuns" and other rabble-rousers. Such tactics had little real impact on the politics of the nation; almost no laws can be directly traced to the influence of the Klan. More troubling was the Klan's propensity for violence. In 1921, the *New York World* published an exposé of Klan violence that included charges of flogging, kidnapping, and murder. Ironically, the series probably helped Klan recruiting by giving the organization its first national publicity. The Klan began to decline in 1925, however, after revelations of a savage rape and murder committed by David Stephenson, a KKK leader in Indiana. Responsible citizens abandoned the organization, and in the last half of the twenties its membership virtually disappeared.

ঌ The Failure of Prohibition

Prohibition seemed to many — liberals, sophisticates, urban dwellers, newly arrived immigrants, and others outside the orbit of evangelical Protestantism — the quintessential expression of twenties repression. Mencken called the Prohibition period (from 1920 until 1933) "the thirteen awful years." Yet the "Noble Experiment" (Herbert Hoover's expression) was a social reform that harked back to the optimistic spirit of the nineteenth century. Taken in its most favorable light,

A Flapper and Her Flask   Long Russian boots became fashionable during Prohibition, for reasons this young woman demonstrates. (The swastika that forms part of the floor tile design is without significance; this image was sometimes used as a decorative motif long before the 1930s, when the German Nazis made it a hated and feared symbol of their movement.)

Prohibition represented an early effort to confront a major public health problem. Few of Prohibition's opponents (the "wets") denied the lamentable personal and social cost of drunkenness, particularly on the poor. Furthermore, Prohibition was a democratic reform. By the time the Volstead Act implemented Prohibition (1919), forty-six out of forty-eight states had ratified the Eighteenth Amendment. To the wets' charge that Prohibition restricted personal liberty, its supporters (the "drys") countered that for good reason many other laws regulated individual rights — from traffic ordinances to the prohibition of dueling and the use of narcotics. In spite of such rational defenses, by the end of the decade there was a clear national consensus that the experiment had failed.

By the 1920s, prohibitionist rhetoric sometimes appealed to the same prejudices that supported immigration restriction and the KKK. Prohibition, charged some critics, was the vengeance of Protestant farmers on the hordes of Catholic, Jewish, and atheist immigrants in the unruly and ungodly cities. It was, in effect, an exclusion act directed at the cultures of immigrants already in America.

It was not true, as wets taunted, that the consumption of alcohol went up during the twenties. Drinking probably fell sharply. But there were massive violations of the law. The Prohibition Bureau, charged with enforcement of the law, never employed more than 3,000 agents, while the nation had more than 18,000 miles of border to patrol. All through the twenties the ships of bootleggers were anchored just outside the twelve-mile international limit, and the proximity of many of the nation's big cities to Canada and Mexico made smuggling impossible to control effectively. In most major cities, hundreds of "speakeasies" (illegal bars and nightclubs) operated almost openly throughout the decade. Furthermore, the production of alcoholic beverages was relatively simple; for $500 anyone could purchase a still capable of producing a hundred gallons a day, and thousands of amateurs learned to make home brew and bathtub gin (sometimes poisoning themselves with the product).

In the final analysis, Prohibition failed because the law was openly violated by too many large groups within the American populace. Millions of urban immigrants and their descendants, brought up in cultures where alcohol was a staple of the diet and a symbol of conviviality, were perplexed by Prohibition. They, joined by millions of other Americans who never repudiated their taste for John Barleycorn (as liquor came to be personified), voided the law by disobeying it. Prohibition proved, for a very brief period, that the political center of gravity in the nation was not in New York City and San Francisco, but in Brown's Hollow, Smith's Crossing, and countless other small towns. In the long run, the experiment proved, as have other restrictive laws, that a society rarely can enforce a law that is flaunted by a substantial minority.

❧ The Spread of Organized Crime

The Eighteenth Amendment did not create organized crime in the United States, but it greatly expanded its reach and its profitability. Furnishing major cities with daily supplies of alcohol was a large business enterprise, and because of its bulk, beer running required a huge organization. Crime bosses became major employers, operating caravans of trucks escorted by gangs armed with Thompson submachine guns (nicknamed "Chicago pianos") to protect them from other mobsters trying to encroach on their territories.

The most famous criminal of the twenties was "Scarface" Al Capone. He controlled more than 160 speakeasies in the Chicago area and by the early twenties employed over 700 men. Capone rode in an armored car and quartered his men in a hotel in the suburb of Cicero; at the age of thirty-two he was reputedly worth more than $20 million. Throughout the twenties the Capone gang waged a war with the rival Dion O'Banion gang that featured scores of sensational shootouts. In 1929, the entire nation was shocked when seven O'Banion garage workers were machine-gunned to death by Capone gangsters disguised as policemen. The brutality of this St. Valentine's Day Massacre shocked a nation that had become accustomed to the violent escapades of gangsters.

Unfortunately, organized crime bred worse evils than the operation of speakeasies. The wealth of the mob bosses encouraged payoffs to law enforcement officers. Having hundreds of gunmen on their payrolls, mobsters used intimidation and violence to bully legitimate businessmen. Chicago's Republican mayor, the demagogic "Big Bill" Thompson (most famous for delighting Irish-American voters with his pledge to punch England's King George V in the nose if he ever set foot in the city), was allegedly Capone's stooge. In the cities, protection rackets forced businesses to pay commissions to organized crime under the threat of violence, and in a single year Chicago experienced over 150 bombings of business establishments. Many factors contributed to the growth of organized crime during the twenties, including the size of modern cities, technological developments such as the automobile and submachine guns, and the Mafia tradition among Italian immigrants, but Prohibition provided the economic base to support its flowering.

HIGH REPUBLICAN POLITICS

The Republican presidential tickets in the 1920s won overwhelming victories, returning the party to the dominance it had enjoyed before its split over progressivism had allowed Wilson to take the White House. The reasons for this ascendancy were curiously captured in Warren G. Harding's malapropism when in the 1920 campaign he called for a return to "normalcy." (He had meant to say "normality.") The rhetoric of the Republican presidents often sounded like pre-McKinley Republicanism. But in fact Harding, Calvin Coolidge, and most of all Herbert Hoover built on the foundation laid in the Progressive Era.

Political dissent did exist in the twenties. Progressives continued to champion old causes, and in some states they remained politically potent. But at the national level progressive successes were few. The Democratic Party seemed permanently divided into a northern wing that was urban, Catholic, and wet and a southern wing that was rural, Protestant, and dry. The conservatism of the electoral majority often led Democratic candidates to sound and act much like Republicans. It was a contented majority that elected the presidents, bought the automobiles, and gave the decade its generally conservative character.

❧ The Election of 1920

The presidential election of 1920 was the first since the enactment of woman suffrage, so it was hardly surprising that the popular vote was more than double that recorded four years earlier. But neither the issues nor the candidates inspired strong feelings in the electorate.

The Democratic convention met in San Francisco in June 1920 and nominated progressive Governor James M. Cox of Ohio on the forty-fourth ballot. The vice-presidential nomination went to Wilson's young assistant secretary of the navy, Franklin Delano Roosevelt. Tall, handsome, a distant cousin of TR, and something of a social lion in Washington, the Democratic Roosevelt had the respect of leaders throughout his party, but was not regarded as a political heavyweight.

At the Republicans' Chicago convention, several of the leading presidential contenders (including Herbert Hoover) were eliminated because they seemed to have excessively progressive pasts. With no strong front-runner, Ohio party boss Harry M. Daugherty predicted that the choice would be decided in a hotel by "some fifteen men, bleary-eyed with lack of sleep." Indeed, after a deadlock on the first day of the convention, Senator Henry Cabot Lodge summoned the party's most influential leaders to a meeting in the Blackstone Hotel room of editor George Harvey. The gathering in the "smoke-filled room," heavily weighted toward conservative senators, conferred with state leaders all through the evening before deciding to support Senator Warren G. Harding of Ohio. Harding was nominated the next day on the tenth ballot. The Ohio senator's chief strengths were his membership in the Senate (a group still smarting from Wilson's snubbing), his handsome countenance, and his transparent desire to work the will of his betters in the party. The vice-presidential nomination went to Calvin Coolidge, the governor of Massachusetts who had become something of a national hero by squelching the Boston police strike in 1919.

The clearest issue in the election of 1920 was the Democratic endorsement of the Treaty of Versailles, but even on that point, both parties spoke ambiguously. Change was the issue in the election; Republicans ran against Wilson rather than Cox. Harding set the tone of the campaign in an oft-quoted dictum: "America's present need is not heroics but healing; not nostrums but normalcy; not revolution but restoration . . . not surgery but serenity."

The only surprise was the size of the Republican victory. Harding received 16,152,200 popular votes to Cox's 9,147,353. In the electoral college the vote was 404 to 127. Republicans won large majorities in both houses of Congress as well. Eugene V. Debs, running for the fifth and final time on the Socialist Party ticket, polled more than 900,000 votes while still incarcerated in the federal penitentiary in Atlanta for violating the wartime Espionage Act, a clear signal that dissent had not vanished from the land. But overall the election was a resounding proclamation that a new conservative era had begun.

❧ *Harding and the Return to "Normalcy"*

Harry Daugherty first encountered Warren G. Harding when the future president was the editor of the Marion (Ohio) *Star*. Catching a glimpse of the handsome Harding waiting for a shoeshine at the local hotel, Daugherty allegedly mumbled: "Gee, what a President he'd make." Under the tutelage of Daugherty, Harding was elected to the Senate in 1914 and distinguished himself as a loyal party man. He was fond of making flowery speeches, described by former Secretary of the Treasury William McAdoo as "an army of pompous phrases moving over the landscape in search of an idea." An ordinary man, Harding was a member of the Elks, the Odd Fellows, the Hoo Hoos, the Moose, the Masons Lodge, the Red Men, and the Baptist Church. He entered the presidency enjoying widespread public favor.

Harding wanted to serve his country well. Several of his cabinet appointees proved to be capable public servants: Secretary of State Charles Evans Hughes, Secretary of Agriculture Henry C. Wallace, and Secretary of Commerce Herbert Hoover all served with distinction, and so did Harding's secretary of the treasury, the

---

❋ **IN THEIR OWN WORDS**

"A Few Don'ts," 1918

Ezra Pound was one of the Lost Generation's literary mentors. Many poets of the day would have followed the iconoclastic advice he offers here, originally published in the premiere issue of Poetry *magazine.*

An 'Image' is that which presents in intellectual and emotional complex in an instant of time. . . .

It is better to present one Image in a lifetime than to produce voluminous works.

All this, however, some may consider open to debate. The immediate necessity is to tabulate A LIST OF DON'TS for those beginning to write verses. I can not put all of them into Mosaic negative.

To begin with, consider the three propositions (demanding direct treatment, economy of words, and the sequence of the musical phrase), not as dogma—never

consider anything as dogma—but as the result of long contemplation, which, even if it is some one else's contemplation, may be worth consideration.

Pay no attention to the criticism of men who have never themselves written a notable work. Consider the discrepancies between the actual writing of the Greek poets and dramatists, and the theories of the Graeco-Roman grammarians, concocted to explain their metres.

wealthy banker and industrialist Andrew Mellon, who was as adept and competent as he was conservative.

Unfortunately, some other appointees betrayed Harding's compulsion to reward unqualified and unsavory friends. Harding's surgeon general was Dr. Charles ("Old Doc") Sawyer, a homeopathic physician from Marion, and as superintendent of prisons he appointed his brother-in-law, Heber H. Votaw, a former missionary. More disastrous were his choices of Harry Daugherty as attorney general and Senator Albert B. Fall as secretary of the interior. Dubbed the Poker Cabinet and the Ohio Gang, these cronies quickly became the president's closest advisers. Washington was soon adrift with rumors of all-night poker sessions at the White House and carousing presidential visits to Daugherty's apartment at 1625 K Street.

The landslide Republican victory in 1920 marked the return of business leadership to government. The complexities of balancing the rights and interests of business and labor that had held sway since Theodore Roosevelt's administration gave way to the notion that the health of the nation should be gauged by the prosperity of business. The architect of the decade's conservative economic agenda was Treasury Secretary Mellon. Mellon's strategy, most of it enacted after 1925 because of persistent progressive opposition in Congress, called for balancing the budget, reducing the national debt, cutting income taxes, and raising tariffs to protect agriculture and industry. The income tax cuts overwhelmingly benefited the wealthy, but this was because at the time no one but the affluent paid income taxes at all, and rates had been raised considerably to finance World War I. Mellon also urged government efficiency, and in June 1921 Congress passed the Budget and Accounting Act, establishing the Budget Bureau in the Treasury Department to prepare an annual budget and the General Accounting Office to audit government accounts. These agencies greatly simplified the task of Congress in allocating money and for the first time allowed the federal government to estimate its total expenditures.

Under the leadership of Herbert Hoover the Department of Commerce fostered scientific planning in industry as a means of eliminating waste. Hoover believed that the government's role in economic planning should be strictly advisory, but he encouraged voluntary cooperation, called associationalism, in the private sector. Hoover's innovative policies, Mellon's introduction of efficient budgeting practices, and the resourceful foreign policy of Secretary of State Charles Evans Hughes gave a positive cast to the early Harding years.

Harding died on August 2, 1923, seized by a sudden convulsion in a San Francisco hotel room while returning from a trip to Alaska. The official cause of death was listed as a cerebral hemorrhage. As Harding's body was transported across the nation by train, mourners lined the tracks to pay him final honor. He died a beloved man, the public outpouring of sympathy rivaling the mourning that followed the assassination of Lincoln. The New York *World* (a Democratic paper) praised Harding's "winning character growing toward greatness under the stern tutelage of experience in office."

Unfortunately, the major legacy of Harding's presidency was not legislation or lasting public esteem, but a series of scandals uncovered after his death by congressional investigations that began in 1924. Harding had premonitions of what was coming. "My God," he had confided to journalist William Allen White shortly before his death, "this is a hell of a job! I have no trouble with my enemies. . . . But my damned friends,

---

❈   IN THEIR OWN WORDS

Coolidge on the Role of Government, 1920

Coolidge delivered this famous "Law and Order" speech while campaigning for vice president; it sums up the view of government he brought to the presidency three years later.

. . . There are strident voices, urging resistance to law in the name of freedom. They are not seeking freedom for themselves, they have it.

They are seeking to enslave others. Their works are evil. They know it. They must be resisted. The evil they represent must be overcome by the good others represent. Their ideas, which are wrong, for the most part imported, must be supplanted by ideas which are right. This can be done. The meaning of America is a power which cannot be overcome. Massachusetts must lead in teaching it. . . .

Laws are not manufactured. They are

not imposed. They are rules of action existing from everlasting to everlasting. He who resists them, resists himself. He commits suicide. The nature of man requires sovereignty. Government must govern. To obey is life. To disobey is death. Organized government is the expression of the life of the commonwealth. Into your hands is entrusted the grave responsibility of its protection and perpetuation.

President Coolidge In August 1927, Calvin Coolidge donned this Sioux headdress during a celebration in Deadwood, South Dakota.

Daugherty was finally pressured into resigning as attorney general in March 1924 by Harding's successor, Calvin Coolidge. In 1927, he was formally charged with taking bribes and defrauding the government. Daugherty invoked his Fifth Amendment right to refuse to testify, and his conspiracy trial ended in a hung jury.

By far the most publicized of the Harding scandals resulted in the conviction of interior secretary Albert Fall in 1927 on charges of conspiracy and bribery. He was sentenced to a year in prison — the first cabinet member to be imprisoned. Fall was found to have accepted bribes from oil moguls Edward L. Doheny and Harry F. Sinclair in return for granting favorable leases to them on government oil reserves at Teapot Dome, Wyoming, and Elk Hills, California. A congressional investigation dragged on for months, uncovering evidence that Fall had received repeated loans and gifts from the two businessmen — about $100,000 from Doheny and more than $300,000 from Sinclair. Doheny and Sinclair were also tried on charges of bribery but were acquitted, although Sinclair was sentenced to nine months in prison for contempt of court.

In 1927, as both Harry Daugherty and Albert B. Fall faced trials for conspiracy, Harding's reputation reached its nadir with the publication of a sensational book, *The President's Daughter*. Written by a young woman named Nan Britton, it told of the birth of Harding's illegitimate daughter, conceived in the Senate cloakroom. The seamy private life of this ordinary man, lurking about Washington's seedy hotels and carousing with the Ohio Gang, seemed a sorry disgrace to the presidential office. Alice Roosevelt Longworth, Theodore Roosevelt's salty daughter, offered what became the most-quoted appraisal of the departed president: "Harding was not a bad man. He was just a slob."

... they're the ones that keep me walking the floor at night." Ultimately, charges were made against officials in the Departments of Justice, Navy, and the Interior, as well as the Veterans' Bureau and other smaller agencies. Before he died, Harding probably knew that he and the nation had been betrayed by Harry Daugherty.

❧ *Calvin Coolidge Rides the Boom*

On the day that Warren G. Harding unexpectedly died, Vice President Calvin Coolidge was visiting his parents in Plymouth, Vermont. When the news came, his father, a justice of the peace, administered the oath of office with memorable symbolism by the light of an oil lamp.

Taciturn and parsimonious, "Silent Cal" Coolidge was a stereotypical Yankee. He had graduated cum laude from Amherst College and practiced law in Northampton, Massachusetts, but his ascent from mayor to governor to president owed more to his uncanny luck than to any superior political instincts. Like everything else in his career, his elevation to the presidency was perfectly timed.

Coolidge's transparent honesty made him a refreshing alternative to the excesses of the Harding era, and he guided the Republican Party through the years of scandalous revelations with dignity, though with little enthusiasm for the investigations. Most historians have judged Coolidge harshly for his inactivity (he worked four hours a day and took long naps), his personal stinginess (he kept close check on the White House servants to see that they did not overstock the pantry), and the banality of some of his comments ("When more and more people are thrown out of work, unemployment results," he once solemnly intoned). Herbert Hoover summarized Coolidge's character: "He was a fundamentalist in religion, in the economic and social order, and in fishing." But it would be a mistake to dismiss Coolidge as a buffoon. Though conservative and conventional, he was no fool.

Calvin Coolidge's flaws as president had less to do with his New England character than with the economic and political assumptions that he shared with many Americans. To him, political radicals were those who believed "that in some way the government was to be blamed because everybody was not prosperous, because it was necessary to work for a living, and because our written constitutions, the legislatures, and the courts protected the rights of private owners." The business of the government was to support business and to protect society against radicals. He believed that "civilization and profits go hand in hand."

Coolidge was a popular president. To be sure, his popularity rested partly on an economic boom that was careening toward worldwide disaster. Nonetheless, to many Americans "Silent Cal" seemed the epitome of Yankee shrewdness, and he sometimes revealed a wry New England sense of humor. When Mrs. Coolidge was having her portrait painted by Howard Chandler Christy, the president said that he didn't like the bright red dress she was wearing. Christy insisted that it was needed to add color. With a deadpan expression, the president asked the artist: "Why not paint her in a white dress and paint the dog red?"

Riding a tide of public contentment, Coolidge won the Republican nomination in 1924. The Democrats, on the other hand, were hopelessly divided into northern and southern wings, and the requirement that a candidate needed two-thirds of the delegate votes for the nomination gave southerners, as intended, a veto. Catastrophically in this new era of live radio broadcasting, the convention went through two weeks of rambunctious wrangling before nominating John W. Davis, a moderate corporation lawyer from West Virginia whose most important government position had been the ambassadorship to Great Britain. Davis was a bland compromise after the South's candidate William G. McAdoo and New York's "wet" governor Al Smith cancelled each other out in a mind-deadening 103 ballots.

Disgruntled progressives formed a third party and nominated the old warhorse Robert La Follette. The pro-labor, pro-farmer Progressive platform called for government ownership of railroads and utilities. In what would be his last political campaign, "Fighting Bob" received the endorsement of both the Socialist Party and the AFL — not normally political bedfellows.

The electorate was content to "keep cool with Coolidge." Electoral participation continued to fall. Fewer than 50 percent of the eligible electorate had voted in 1920, and the rate declined further in 1924. But the Republican victory was overwhelming. Coolidge received 382 electoral votes, and Davis carried only the twelve states of the Democrats' "Solid South," for 136 electoral votes. La Follette won nothing but his native Wisconsin, with 13 electoral votes. Coolidge collected over two million more popular votes than his two competitors combined, and the Republicans retained control of both houses of Congress.

On succeeding to the presidency, Coolidge had asked Harding's cabinet to remain, but several members resigned in 1924, including the soon-to-be-disgraced Daugherty. Remarkably little important legislation was passed during Coolidge's presidency His most notable accomplishment was to cut the budget drastically, partly by reducing military spending. The administration's financial policies first balanced the budget and then began retiring the national debt at the rate of about $500 million per year.

The relatively slight legislative achievements of the Harding and Coolidge years were in part a reflection of the continued strength of progressivism in Congress and in state governments. Old-time progressives continued to press for the regulation of big business, usually unsuccessfully, but they did hinder the dismantling of the regulatory structure that had been created during the Progressive Era.

On August 2, 1927, while visiting a South Dakota Indian reservation, Coolidge, in typically terse prose,

informed the press that "I do not choose to run for President in 1928." Whether Coolidge expected to be drafted by his party or simply wanted to return to private life, most Republicans were delighted to accept the president's decision. Columnist Heywood Broun exulted: "At last eloquence has gushed from the Vermont granite."

The Coolidge Boom

America's prosperity in the twenties was deceptively fragile. A chronic farm depression, regarded by many as a nagging exception to the good times, was only one symptom of a troubled economy. The international creditor status of the United States and the profits of American business in the early 1920s provided vast sums of capital that were used to expand the nation's productive capacity, as well as to speculate in stocks.

Lindbergh and His *Spirit of St. Louis* Before he took off on his epoch-making transatlantic flight, Charles A. Lindbergh posed for this photograph beside his frail single-engine airplane, striking a note of calm confidence.

But because workers and farmers did not share equally in the decade's prosperity, the nation's capacity to consume lagged far behind its ability to produce.

The skewing of economic regulation in favor of business and the wealthy was obvious in Mellon's strategy, but the pro-business bias of the era was much more broadly based. Secretary of Commerce Herbert Hoover's trade associationalism encouraged businesses to pool their expertise for the sake of efficiency, while at the same time purportedly remaining competitive in the marketplace. The federal government contributed to economic development by aiding businesses through conferences and the collection of information. The Supreme Court supported associationalism in the 1920s, holding that it was constitutional for businesses to cooperate so long as some measure of competition survived. Presided over by former president William Howard Taft, who became chief justice in 1921, the court rendered a steady stream of pro-business decisions during the decade. In 1922, the court struck down a federal law curtailing child labor *(Bailey v. Drexel Furniture Company)*, and in 1923, the justices invalidated a law fixing a minimum wage for women in the District of Columbia *(Adkins v. Children's Hospital)*.

At the international level, the huge World War I debts owed to the United States by European nations, the accumulation of gold reserves in America, and the raising of American tariff barriers set the stage for a world economic crisis. The Fordney-McCumber Tariff in 1922 brought rates back to levels as high as those existing before the passage of the Underwood Tariff in 1913 (see Chapter 24). The return of protectionism was predictable in view of the influence of business interests in the conservative Republican administrations, but high tariffs also came to be a leading demand of the powerful congressional Farm Bloc.

The most troubling economic issue of the 1920s was declining farm profits, even though many farmers shared in the boom mentality of the twenties. In the first two decades of the century American farmers had prospered, and during World War I, when European agriculture suffered serious disruption, prices had soared — only to crash when these markets were suddenly closed by European tariff barriers beginning in 1919 (see Chapter 24). However, the technological advances of the early twentieth century encouraged ever-larger farms (the number of tractors increased ten times during the twenties), and farmers increasingly identified themselves as businessmen rather than laborers. Cooperative arrangements for buying and marketing expanded

during the decade, but European demand for American farm products declined, and prices plummeted.

Farm discontent led to the formation of a powerful Farm Bloc in Congress composed of southern and western congressmen. This congressional group lobbied throughout the decade for legislation to aid farmers, and every Republican president recognized the farm depression as the nation's foremost economic problem. In 1921, an Emergency Tariff raised duties on most agricultural products, and the following year the Fordney-McCumber Tariff granted to the president the power to raise existing tariffs by as much as 50 percent if he deemed foreign competition unfair. Although such tariff legislation generally brought reprisals from abroad, American farmers, facing increased competition from such new agricultural exporters as Canada and Argentina, continued to support tariff hikes. In 1922, the Farm Bloc secured the passage of a Cooperative Marketing Act that exempted agricultural cooperatives from prosecution under antitrust laws.

The most sweeping proposal for agricultural reform in the twenties was the McNary-Haugen Farm Relief Bill, first introduced in 1926. The bill proposed the establishment of a Farm Board empowered to buy excess crop production, either storing it for future sale or unloading it in foreign markets at prevailing prices. Essentially, the scheme envisioned dumping excess agricultural products abroad. The prices farmers would receive for these commodities would be determined by a complicated formula that compared farm income with other areas of the economy between 1910 and 1914. Any differential between the price support and the world market price would be covered by an "equalization fee" to be paid by farmers. The bill was defeated in 1926. The Farm Bloc passed it the following year, only to encounter a presidential veto. Coolidge insisted that the McNary-Haugen Act legalized price-fixing and unfairly benefited special groups. Farm conditions continued to deteriorate, and the bill was passed again in 1928, once again being vetoed by Coolidge.

☙ *The Election of 1928*

By 1928 the clear leader of the Republican Party was Herbert Hoover. From impoverished beginnings, Hoover had worked his way through Stanford University and pursued a brilliant career as an international mining engineer, making enough money to retire at forty in 1914 and become a public servant. His work during World War I as the chairman of the American Relief Committee in Belgium and as the United States Food Administrator had won widespread acclaim and talk of his presidential candidacy in 1920. During his eight years as secretary of commerce in the Harding and Coolidge cabinets he turned the department into a highly visible agency for the promotion of business efficiency and trade associations. Hoover began campaigning immediately after Coolidge's announcement and was nominated on the first ballot at the Republican convention in Chicago.

Although the Democratic Party was still divided into northern and southern wings in 1928, the delegates, meeting in Houston, nominated Governor Alfred E. Smith of New York on the first ballot. A Tammany Hall Democrat who supported the repeal of Prohibition, Smith was the first Roman Catholic ever nominated for the presidency. After the Democrats balanced the ticked by naming Senator Joseph T. Robinson of Lonoke, Arkansas, the emblematic Democratic donkey was said to have a "WET head and a DRY tail." Nonetheless, Smith's nomination clearly marked the growing ascendancy of the eastern, urban wing of the party. In the South, Republicans made the most of running against "Alcohol Al."

Once again, the party platforms in 1928 offered few real differences. Hoover insisted that Smith's support of farm legislation and a government-operated power plant in Muscle Shoals, Alabama, was dangerous radicalism, but Smith was, in fact, a conventional conservative, and the only real campaign issue was Republican prosperity. Noted the liberal *New Republic* ironically, "Prosperity is a prerogative which God has bestowed, subject to certain limitations, upon the American people if they remain Republican." Probably more important than the issues, the personalities of the two candidates provided stark contrasts. Smith's candidacy spawned a vicious anti-Catholic whispering campaign — one rumor reported that plans had already been drafted to construct a tunnel from the White House to the Vatican. Smith insisted that his Catholic faith would not interfere with his execution of the office of the president, and Hoover agreed that the issue was irrelevant. Nonetheless, the nomination of Smith brought Catholic-Protestant tensions into clear focus. Smith's candidacy affected the American Catholic community in contradictory ways: anti-Catholic attacks exacerbated the alienation felt by many Catholics, but at the same time church leaders celebrated Smith's nomination as a milestone in the journey of American Catholics into the national mainstream.

Besides religion, other personal differences also weighed in Hoover's favor. Smith's New York brogue was a decided liability. For the first time in American history, radio ("rad-dio," as Smith pronounced it in his nasal New York accent) was an important factor in the campaign. Smith, a witty and garrulous professional politician, sounded like a foreigner to Midwesterners and was virtually unintelligible to Southerners.

Once again, the only surprise in 1928 was the size of the Republican victory. The electoral vote was 444 to 87, with Hoover receiving 21 million votes to Smith's 15 million. Hoover carried Smith's home state of New York (although Democratic gubernatorial candidate Franklin Delano Roosevelt won). Even more surprising, the Republicans breached the Solid South, carrying Florida, Texas, North Carolina, Tennessee, and Virginia, and almost winning Alabama. But, though not of much comfort to the Democrats in 1928, there were other symptoms of change in the election that boded well for the future of the party. Smith polled 60 percent more votes than any previous Democratic candidate, won nearly every major city, carried such traditionally Republican states as Massachusetts and Rhode Island, and drew support from the progressives who had supported La Follette in 1924.

❧ *The Great Engineer at the Wheel*

Herbert Hoover, the ablest of the Republican presidents of the twenties, had a well-developed and coherent philosophy for a cooperative society. In 1922, while serving as secretary of commerce, Hoover wrote *American Individualism,* a book that the *New York Times* praised as "among the few great formulations of American political theory." The book is today forgotten, but the ideas it expressed have recurred perennially in the nation's history. Hoover believed that individualism had reached its most positive form in America. "The ideal of service," he wrote, was a "great spiritual force poured out by our people as never before in the history of the world."

Hoover's book called for a rationalized economy that offered equal opportunity to all. He urged voluntary cooperation between government and business as a modern alternative to laissez-faire capitalism and socialism. The government was to be the partner of the trade associations, stimulating the economy by educating and organizing businessmen to respond to expert advice. As secretary of commerce, Hoover sponsored government agencies to bring order to new industries, including the Bureau of Aviation and the Federal Radio

Advertising a Tractor   In 1921 a dealer in Washington, D.C., advertised his tractors with this catchy promotional idea. Tractors driven by internal-combustion engines were still relatively novel in 1921, but many farmers went into debt to acquire them.

Commission. Beginning his presidency in a climate of unbridled optimism, "the Great Engineer of the New Order" set out to collect information and funnel ideas to business leaders. Some progressives viewed Hoover's election as a ray of hope in the conservative decade. Yet in the end, Hoover's ideas depended on business prosperity as much as those of his predecessors.

During the campaign, Hoover promised to call a special session of Congress to deal with the farm depression. Out of that session came the Agricultural Marketing Act, a compromise measure that established a Federal Farm Board to promote the marketing of farm products through agricultural cooperatives and stabilization corporations. This plan, like others during the period, failed to stabilize farm prices because farmers did not reduce their acreage in production. In 1930, in a further effort to aid farmers, as well as protect American industry, Republicans pushed through the Hawley-Smoot Tariff. The law raised tariffs on agricultural products nearly 50 percent, and also raised tariffs on other commodities. But whether or not the protection of American agricultural products from foreign imports ever held any promise for helping farm prices, by the time the law passed it had a very unfortunate effect on the deepening depression.

∞ Boom and Bust in the Stock Market

American stocks, fueled particularly by the profitability of such new consumer industries as automobiles and communications, rose steadily in the twenties. By the middle of the decade, much corporate capital was being used to purchase stocks, and the American market also attracted large foreign investments. In 1927, just as the American economy was slowing perceptibly, a bull market began. As prices shot up, the market became increasingly speculative. Estimates of the number of Americans who bought stock range as high as 15 million, although only one-tenth of that number were active traders. More important, the boom mesmerized the nation, and its optimistic assumptions were widely accepted. In an article published in the *Ladies Home Journal* just two months before the crash, John J. Raskob, chairman of the Democratic party and a former General Motors executive, inscribed one of the prime artifacts of the boom: "Everybody ought to be rich." President Hoover worried that the boom might be getting out of hand, but he felt he could not intervene openly without destroying business confidence and involving the government too closely in the free market.

Encouraging buyers' get-rich-quick hopes, various political and institutional factors fueled the Great Bull Market. In 1927 the Federal Reserve System stimulated speculation by lowering interest rates, while political leaders and leading economists made euphoric predictions about the future. There was much talk that a "new economy" had arrived, supplanting the old "boom-and-bust" business cycle and ensuring that economic expansion was on a "high plateau" of unending growth. Margin buying contributed powerfully to the frenzy — the easy credit that allowed buyers to purchase stock with as little as 10 percent down. (The catch was that if the value of shares fell below a certain level, brokers could demand immediate payment in full — and if the buyer could not come up with the cash, the stock was automatically sold. Excessive marginal speculation therefore served as a built-in time bomb in the event of a crash.) Finally, the information on which speculators relied in buying stock was often incomplete, if not deceptive or downright false, and unscrupulous insiders often manipulated the trading in shares. Because of the almost total absence of government regulation in securities markets, ordinary investors had no idea how closely stock speculation now resembled gambling in a crooked casino.

The stock euphoria of the late twenties was also foolhardy in the light of economic conditions. In 1926 a highly speculative Florida land boom had burst, ruining many investors, but the disaster did little to restore sanity. Many areas of American industry, particularly housing and automobile production, had slowed markedly by 1927; in almost every industrial area more goods were being produced than could be consumed. As inventories built up, factories closed and workers were laid off, further shrinking the consumer market. Ironically, the market continued to climb, pushed partly by investments by businesses with no other outlet for their profits.

Against this ominous background, and with the underlying economy moving toward recession, a final market surge began in March 1928. Stocks often rose ten to fifteen points a day, and so many shares were traded that the Wall Street ticker ran minutes behind the bidding. The Standard and Poor's average of 414 industrial stocks rose from less than 100 in 1927 to above 250 in September 1929.

In September 1929 stock prices began to fluctuate wildly; then in October they moved steadily downward. Canny investors began to sell, but others saw the retreat as an opportunity to snap up bargains before the next market ascent. Then, on October 23, the market dropped 50 points, and on the next day — "Black Thursday" — Wall Street plunged into chaos. Brokers unloaded huge blocks of margin stocks with orders to sell at any price. Bankers formed a pool of $240 million in an effort to restore confidence (a pool of $25 million had stopped a panic in 1907), but Tuesday, October 29, was the worst day in the history of the stock exchange up to that time. By the middle of November 1929, about $30 billion had been erased from the market value of stocks listed on the New York exchange; before the decline stopped in 1932, the loss reached about $75 billion.

CONCLUSION: A DECADE OF PROSPERITY AND SELF-ANALYSIS

Was the twenties a particularly factious and belligerent decade? All of the decade's disputes had been brewing for years; even the intellectual revolt was well under way in Greenwich Village before World War I. Furthermore, some of the shrillest arguments of the twenties never stirred broad popular response. A majority of Americans were neither members of the KKK nor rebellious flappers nor carousing speakeasy customers nor irresponsible stock market speculators. Most ordinary citizens behaved much like their grandparents. All in all, relatively few people danced the Charleston or read *The Great Gatsby;* far more sang hymns and read the Bible. On the other hand, few mature adults in 1920 would have denied that the nation had changed dramatically in their lifetime. By the end of the decade, writes historian William E. Leuchtenburg, the years before World War I seemed a "lost Acadia."

This acute sense of change goes far in explaining why the decade was such fertile soil for extremist ideas. The changes wrought by urbanization, immigration, consumerism, and intellectual relativism were so well defined by 1920 that older Americans joined in last-ditch efforts to stem the tide of modernity. Millions drew lines in the sand around the religious, social, and patriotic fundamentals that they would not yield.

The "Lost Generation" was not the first group of American young people to challenge traditional values. Nativism predated the KKK by decades; the clash between fundamentalist religion and modern science was half a century old. To understand why these issues reached new levels in the twenties one must consider the sum total of intellectual, economic, and social forces at play during the decade. World War I fostered an illusory view of America's cultural unity, but then the Red Scare and the treaty debate shattered earlier optimism. Rural-urban tensions reached new heights, highlighted by the report of urban population surpassing rural in the census of 1920. Scientists, ranging from Einstein to Freud, posed new ideas as disconcerting as those of Darwin. Perhaps more than anything else, the stage for the decade's dramatic debates was set by prosperity. In good times, when most people possess basic economic necessities, social groups become bellicose about power. Freed from threats from abroad, and to a large degree free from extreme economic deprivation, Americans looked inward. On both the left and the right, those with an acute sense of social responsibility set about to remake the nation in their own image. The harsh realities of the thirties would bring the nation's attention back to the much more basic questions of survival.

Neither was the politics of the twenties a sharp disruption from the past. In some ways, the political conservatism of the period marked a reversal of progressivism and the economic planning of the war years, particularly the Republican emphasis on a strictly limited role for government. This bias against regulation encouraged the decade's uneven economic development. On the other hand, most politicians in the twenties saw a need for greater economic cooperation and standardization. Herbert Hoover's notion of a planned market economy, albeit a voluntary one, marked the 1920s as a transitional period between progressivism and the New Deal and a stepping-stone on the path to modern liberal capitalism.

Suggested Reading

Charles C. Alexander, *Here the Country Lies: Nationalism and the Arts in Twentieth Century America* (1980). A sweeping survey of American art during the early twentieth century that emphasizes the continued search for a national culture.

Frederick Lewis Allen, *Only Yesterday* (1931). This venerable book, iconoclastic but good-spirited, remains an entertaining excursion through the twenties.

Paul Carter, *The Twenties in America* (1968) and *Another Part of the Twenties* (1977). Carter is a judicious and careful scholar who is unwaveringly fair to the decade's extremists on the right and the left. His sympathetic vignettes of fundamentalists and prohibitionists help balance the caricatures such groups often receive.

Morton Keller, *Regulating a New Economy: Public Policy and Economic Change in America, 1900-1933* (1990) and *Regulating a New Society: Public Policy and Social Change in America, 1900-1933* (1994) provide broad overviews of public policy developments during the 1920s.

William E. Leuchtenburg, *The Perils of Prosperity, 1914-1932* (1970). A comprehensive, elegantly written, and sophisticated interpretation of the 1920s.

George M. Marsden, *Fundamentalism and American Culture* (1980). An excellent survey of the fundamentalist-modernist religious clash in the 1920s.

Michael Parrish, *Anxious Decades: America in Prosperity and Depression, 1920-1941* (1992). A good recent overview of the decade.

George Soule, *Prosperity Decade: From War to Depression* (1947). An excellent survey of economic developments from World War I to the Stock Market Crash.

Suggestions for Further Reading

Paul Avrich, *Sacco and Vanzetti* (1991).

Susan D. Becker, *The Origins of the Equal Rights Amendment: American Feminism Between the Wars* (1981).

Kathleen M. Blee, *Women of the Klan: Racism and Gender in the 1920s* (1991).

Norman H. Clark, *Deliver Us from Evil: An Interpretation of American Prohibition* (1976).

Elton C. Fax, *Garvey: The Story of a Pioneer Black Nationalist* (1972).

James J. Flink, *The Automobile Age* (1988).

Willard B. Gatewood, Jr., *Controversy in the Twenties: Fundamentalism, Modernism, and Evolution* (1969).

James R. Grossman, *Land of Hope: Chicago, Black Southerners, and the Great Migration* (1989).

John Higham, *Strangers in the Land: Patterns of American Nativism, 1860-1925* (1955).

K. Austin Kerr, *Organized for Prohibition: A New History of the Anti-Saloon League* (1985).

Edward J. Larson, *Summer for the Gods: The Scopes Trial and America's Continuing Debate over Science and Religion* (1997).

I. Jackson Lears, *Fables of Abundance: A Cultural History of Advertising in America* (1994).

David L. Lewis, *When Harlem Was in Vogue* (1981).

Bradley J. Longfield, *The Presbyterian Controversy: Fundamentalists, Modernists, and Moderates* (1991).

Carole Marks, *Farewell — We're Good and Gone: The Great Black Migration* (1989).

Lary May, *Screening Out the Past: The Birth of Mass Culture and the Motion Picture Industry* (1980).

Kathy J. Ogren, *The Jazz Revolution: Twenties America and the Meaning of Jazz* (1989).

John B. Rae, *The American Automobile Industry* (1985).

Steven A. Riess, *City Games: The Evolution of American Urban Society and the Rise of Sports* (1989).

David E. Ruth, *Inventing the Public Enemy: The Gangster in American Culture, 1918-1934* (1996).

Milton C. Sernett, *Bound for the Promised Land: African American Religions and the Great Migration* (1997).

Louise M. Young, *In the Public Interest: The League of Women Voters, 1920-1970* (1989).

27

The Great Depression and the New Deal

I**N THE SPRING** of 1933 the nation lay wounded amidst the deepest and most bewildering depression ever to grip the modern industrial world. On March 4, the day that Franklin Delano Roosevelt was inaugurated president, Illinois and New York suspended banking, joining thirty-eight other states that had earlier declared "banking holidays." On the same day, the New York Stock Exchange closed its doors for the first time in history, and an eerie silence spread through deserted canyons in the hubs of the nation's urban centers. "There was something awful — abnormal — in the very stillness of those streets," a resident of downtown Chicago remembered. "I recall being startled by the clatter of a horse's hooves on the pavement as a mounted policeman rode past."

During the 1930s and ever since, experts have debated which demons — individual, institutional, or structural — were responsible for this numbing decade. Many of those trapped by the economic collapse of the 1930s blamed financiers and industrialists. It could hardly have been otherwise. Wealthy businessmen and conservative politicians had predicted a never-ending cycle of progress. So, justly or unjustly, public opinion saddled them and "the Great Engineer," President Herbert Hoover, with responsibility for a disaster that devastated not just the United States but the entire industrial world.

However, the central question of the 1930s was not who had caused the Great Depression, but rather how to solve it. To answer that question, the people turned to the consummate politician of the twentieth century, Franklin Delano Roosevelt. Roosevelt's antidote was the New Deal, a torrent of laws that created a bewildering array of federal agencies. The New Deal greatly enlarged the size and power of the national government, particularly the executive branch. Perhaps as important as the New Deal in allaying the suffering of the Depression was the persona of FDR himself. The president's optimism, courage, vitality, and willingness to experiment sustained hope in the midst of desperation.

On the surface, the New Deal was an impenetrable maze of legislation and bureaucracy, most of it economic, some of it contradictory. The reforms of the Roosevelt era were not driven by a single underlying theory; they were rooted in political compromise and a spirit of experimentation. Although many contemporaries pictured the New Deal as dangerously radical, socialism never seriously tempted Roosevelt or his chief advisers. The New Deal's single-minded intent was to reform capitalism and the market economy in its moment of deepest crisis. It sought to protect the legitimate profits of business as well as the dignity of the poor. In the short run, the New Deal was a limited success, bringing relief but not curing the Depression. Only World War II would restore industrial production and wipe out unemployment.

But viewed in a century-long perspective, the Depression and the New Deal permanently changed the United States. While most post-Depression Americans still paid lip service to an earlier gospel of individualism and self-reliance, the nation had adopted the system of political economy that it still retains: a regulated "mixed economy" and a welfare state, in which almost everyone accepts the federal government as the arbiter in society's search for a more "moral" capitalism. That was the New Deal's most enduring legacy.

HOOVER STRUGGLES WITH A DEEPENING DEPRESSION

Herbert Hoover did not cause the Depression, as many of his fellow citizens believed, nor was he singularly inept in seeking solutions, as many of his political critics charged. Hoover was a bright, compassionate, thoughtful public servant who believed that enlightened capitalism would provide ongoing prosperity in the modern world. Of course he, like every other actor in this tragic drama, made some serious mistakes. More broadly, his theory did not work in the 1930s, partly because the business and financial leaders who controlled economic decisions were neither so informed nor humane

as Hoover. Few of Hoover's contemporaries — Democrats or Republicans, economists or politicians — were more knowledgeable about the workings of modern capitalism, nor did his critics have better remedies once the Depression began.

Except for a slight upturn in the late summer of 1932, the Depression deepened all through the Hoover presidency, reaching its depths in the months between his defeat in the election of 1932 and Roosevelt's inauguration in March 1933. The government did not come to a standstill during these months. Hoover encouraged voluntary relief and sponsored a program of government spending that the Democrats denounced as wildly irresponsible; these efforts formed a bridge to the broader federal programs of the New Deal. But Hoover's actions were too little too late. By 1932 a shroud of gloom had enveloped the president; Secretary of War Henry Stimson told colleagues that "it was like sitting in a bath of ink to sit in his room."

Hoover's Democratic opponent in the election of 1932 was the governor of New York, Franklin Delano Roosevelt. A patrician courageously battling back from a crippling attack of polio, the smiling Roosevelt cast a bright beam of light on the grim realities of the times. But what could he do? His campaign speeches were so void of substance that many of his supporters viewed him as an intellectual lightweight who would likely be a figurehead president; Justice Oliver Wendell Holmes hoped that Roosevelt's "first class temperament" might compensate for his "second-rate intellect." Hoover thought Roosevelt's rhetoric was so vague and contradictory that he was an amoral demagogue. In 1932 it would have been difficult to predict that the nation was about to enter a dramatic period of domestic reform under the leadership of one of its strongest and most revered presidents.

❧ The Great Depression and Its Causes

In spite of the stunning dimensions of the stock market crash in the fall of 1929, no one envisioned the severity of the economic collapse that ensued over the next forty months. By March 1933, the dimensions of the Great Depression were coldly suggested by a statistical litany: the nation's industrial production had been cut in half; one-third of the country's railroads were bankrupt; the steel industry was operating at 12 percent of capacity; more than 5,000 banks (about one-third of the nation's financial institutions) had closed their doors, wiping out the savings of millions; unemployment reached around 13 million (around one-fourth of the entire American industrial labor force) and millions more worked reduced hours in order to stretch payrolls as far as possible. U.S. Steel, the nation's largest corporation, employed 225,000 workers in 1929, 54,000 in 1931, and none on April 1, 1933. Thousands of farmers had been pushed from their land because of foreclosures (on a single day in 1932, according to one report, one-fourth of the land in the state of Mississippi was offered for sale at auction); 81 percent of the rural schools in Alabama were closed and 170,000 children in Georgia were without education; emigration out of the country exceeded immigration into it by 103,000 to 35,500 in 1932, and on a single weekend transatlantic liners boarded four thousand emigrants leaving the United States for Europe. Viewing the wreckage of the American economy, Calvin Coolidge remarked, "In other periods of depression it has always been possible to see some things . . . upon which you could base hope, but as I look about, I now see nothing to give ground for hope — nothing of man."

During the 1930s many judged that the Depression was the harvest of profligate wrongdoings in the twenties. Surmised a prominent business leader: "Business depressions are caused by dissipation, dishonesty, disobedience to God's will — a general collapse of moral character." He was greatly exaggerating, but his assessment was frequently implied in the aftermath of the 1929 crash. Inasmuch as immorality contributed at all to the Depression, the sins of financiers seemed the most scarlet. A special Senate committee investigating the Wall Street collapse exposed an array of crooked dealings among investment bankers that damaged the image of financiers for decades to come.

But other factors contributed more to the Depression than the villainy of financiers. Hoover believed that reckless speculation in the U.S. stock market and events abroad were the primary causes of the economic calamity, and he was partly right. Other factors contributing to economic instability and eventual collapse at the end of the 1920s and in the early 1930s included the basic unsoundness of the American banking system, the rigidity that the gold standard imposed upon international finance, the high tariff barriers that discouraged international trade, and the loose credit policies of the Federal Reserve throughout the twenties.

Few informed people believed that the Depression had been caused merely by the shenanigans of dishonest businessmen, or by a conspiracy of international bankers; after all, the worldwide economic decline be-

gan in the U.S. According to economist John Kenneth Galbraith, the American economy in 1929 was "fundamentally unsound." Many influential people in the 1930s, including Roosevelt, believed that the cause of the collapse was over-production: modern productivity had overrun itself, demanding retrenchment. "Our industrial plant is built," Roosevelt observed during the 1932 campaign, "the problem just now is whether under existing conditions it is not over built. Our last frontier has long since been reached." Seemingly ratifying this gloomy prognosis of the national future, gross investment in the United States declined from $16.2 billion in 1929 to an anemic $300,000 million in 1932. Few people in the 1930s could imagine the new period of economic growth that would soon revitalize the economy, and the concept of planned growth had few advocates. Such thinking failed to challenge the early Depression at its most fundamental level, promoting economic growth.

Stated another way, the most obvious problem of the 1930s was under-consumption. From this point of view, the chief culprit was the unequal distribution of income during the 1920s. During the twenties, corporate profits grew at three times the rate of wages, thus increasing industry's ability to produce while reducing the amount of money available to consumers. When credit began to tighten in 1929, buying fell, workers were laid off, and the downward spiral accelerated — decreasing consumption lowered investment opportunities, thus cutting employment, thus decreasing consumer buying further.

However one views the root causes of the Depression, ruinous flaws in the world economic system contributed to the depth and intensity of the collapse. Unsound and fraudulent corporate organizations had flourished in the late 1920s, international finance and trade were disorganized, and the Federal Reserve Board was totally inept in handling credit both before and after the crash. Few American politicians judged that capitalism itself had failed, but most acknowledged that the touted "New Era" system of the 1920s had failed.

ஃ Hoover's Considered Response to a Worsening Collapse

The Wall Street crash in 1929 shattered confidence, but it did not necessitate the Great Depression. President Hoover was much ridiculed for his October 25, 1929, statement: "the fundamental business of the country, that is, production and distribution of commodities, is on a sound and prosperous basis." In a speech to Congress in December, the president maintained that the economic crisis was merely a "problem of growth and progress" and that it would be resolved "in a spirit of conciliation" once "the facts" were digested by experts. In retrospect, such statements appear reasonable and responsible. Stock prices stabilized in early 1930, unemployment edged up only slowly, and that March Secretary of Commerce Robert P. Lamont predicted: "Business will be normal in two months."

Amid these optimistic signals, Hoover summoned to the White House the nation's business and labor leaders and asked them to voluntarily maintain production to ward off a depression. He urged state and local political leaders to increase public works to stimulate the economy. This strategy worked for a few weeks. As the downturn appeared to stabilize, Hoover remarked in May: "I am convinced we have passed the worst and with continued effort we shall rapidly recover." Greeting a delegation representing national charitable organizations that urged him to support a federal public works program, the president told them: "Gentlemen, you have come sixty days too late. The depression is over."

Part of Hoover's optimism may have come from the hopes he and congressional Republicans put in the Smoot-Hawley Tariff, which they touted as a stabilizing measure that would seal off the United States from foreign economic problems and protect American jobs against cheap foreign competition. But a thousand economists at the time signed a petition denouncing the new tariff as folly, and ever since the verdict of historians and economists has been that this was perhaps the Hoover administration's most disastrous mistake. Smoot-Hawley raised tariffs to an all-time high, but it almost immediately began provoking retaliation by the nation's trading partners, which raised their own protective barriers.

Perhaps in anticipation of the new tariff's consequences, U.S. business confidence collapsed in July 1930, sending stock prices plummeting. Within twelve months of the Wall Street crash, the sharp but overdue market correction and the economic slowdown were turning into a chronic depression. With protectionism strangling international trade, the chances of recovery dimmed rapidly.

Hoover never wavered from his faith in a protective tariff, and at first he rejected the idea of active government coordination of industry — dreading, he said, a regimented, subsidized economy. On the other hand,

he was far more energetic and creative in seeking other remedies than is generally pictured. Basically, Hoover hoped to rally voluntary support that would slow the economic decline and relieve suffering without government intervention. He appointed a President's Emergency Committee for Employment and urged business leaders to stop the vicious circle of layoffs. He also supported a tax cut, encouraged more liberal credit for businesses, asked Congress for a large increase in public works spending, and urged local and state governments to expand their relief efforts. In hindsight, Hoover's efforts appear woefully inadequate, especially when set against the great blunder of raising tariffs, but at the time the Boston *Globe* gave thanks that the White House was occupied by "a man who believes not in the philosophy of drift, but the dynamics of mastery."

The president was touched by the personal tragedy unfolding around him in 1930, but, fearing the creation of a permanent welfare class, he resisted calls for a massive federal funding for relief. To encourage private charity, in 1931 he appointed the President's Organization for Unemployment Relief. However, no private charity organization in existence could have met the growing needs of the unemployed. The Red Cross, while big and efficient, insisted that relieving the unemployed was not the type of emergency that it was founded to address. Churches relieved suffering in many localities, mostly by dispensing food and fuel. A Quaker himself, Hoover asked the Friends Service Committee to expand its charity activities, and the Philadelphia Meeting worked heroically to stem suffering in the mining communities of Pennsylvania. During the early months of the Depression, cities supplied the only public relief. Such help never reached a majority of the poor, and it was soon exhausted. No state had a Department of Welfare until Governor Franklin D. Roosevelt organized one in New York in 1929, before the onset of the Depression.

Probably no more than 25 percent of the needy received any public help during these months. Others were tided over by relatives and friends or scrounged for food and housing, and millions did without adequate clothing and medical care. A curious, black humor arose amidst the suffering — most of it aimed at Hoover. The shantytowns that had appeared in the cities were called "Hoovervilles"; unemployed drifters carried "Hoover bags"; if someone smiled, it was witty to ask, "Is Hoover dead?"

Many families had always depended on faith-based charities to help them through hard times, and in the cities ethnically-oriented benevolent and savings institutions — "immigrant" banks, insurance companies, burial associations, and the like — were not only community pillars but also the repositories of hard-won savings. Ordinarily these institutions had the resources to sustain their clients through economic downturns and personal misfortunes, although their finances were sometimes rather disorderly. But economic collapse on the scale of the Great Depression overwhelmed them. Charities simply could not accommodate the throngs of working families that suddenly found themselves without a livelihood. Mutual-aid societies and small community savings banks were often among the first such institutions to collapse, as depositors ceased to save, borrowers defaulted, investments failed, and creditors called in loans. The loss of such institutions struck one more heavy blow at the infrastructure of countless communities across the nation, leaving in its wake lost savings, broken hopes, and widespread bitterness.

In the mid-term elections in the fall of 1930, the continued decline in the economy caused the Republicans to suffer their first electoral defeat since 1916. Democrats won nineteen of the thirty-one gubernatorial races. The Republican majority in the House of Representatives fell from 103 to 2, but by the time the new Congress finally convened, in December 1931, deaths among GOP members gave the Democrats formal control of the House.[1] The Senate was evenly split, although the Republicans could organize it thanks to Vice President Charles Curtis's deciding vote. However, an informal coalition of Democrats and liberal Republicans actually dominated the Senate.

❧ Too Little Too Late: Democrats and Republicans Attempt Reform

By enacting the Smoot-Hawley Tariff, Hoover and the Republican Congress were not the only policymakers to make a grievous mistake in the name of restoring economic confidence and growth. Ignoring Hoover's pleas, the New York branch of the Federal Reserve tightened credit. It was trying to support the dollar's value relative to gold, but its tight-money policy had the predictable result of further stifling recovery.

Falling economic dominoes abroad deepened the Depression. In the spring of 1931 France blocked the democratic German Republic's attempt to form a customs

union with neighboring Austria — a shortsighted action that contributed to the collapse in May 1931 of central Europe's economic structure. As a result, Germany, which was now deprived of the flow of American credits that during the twenties had enabled it to meet its international obligations, defaulted on its reparations. Bowing to the inevitable, in June Hoover declared a moratorium on all reparations. These actions effectively killed the international monetary system of the 1920s, as well as hopes for a quick recovery — and Germany staggered toward the economic shipwreck that would help bring Adolf Hitler to power at the beginning of 1933.

These European disasters had a ripple effect within the United States. In the fall of 1931 the Depression became worldwide, and for the next eighteen months economic indicators plunged downward. In October 1931 alone, more than 500 American banks failed. Hoover feared that the nation's economic system was nearing collapse. He secured promises from business leaders to refrain voluntarily from foreclosures, but month after month the Depression deepened, and the foreclosures never ceased.

Before the crash, tariffs and taxes had brought in enough revenue for the federal budget to show a considerable surplus. But the economic collapse dried up tax revenues at all levels of government, and not even the Smoot-Hawley tariff could make up the difference for the federal treasury. Hoover's 1932 federal budget ran a deficit that soared to $2.7 billion — 60 percent of total federal expenditures, proportionately a far more unbalanced budget than any of his successors'.

To Hoover's economically orthodox mind, balancing the federal budget was an obligation as sacred as defending the gold standard, maintaining a protective tariff, and saving American workers from the dole. His solution, which he presented to the new Congress when it convened in December 1931, was a substantial federal sales tax. This the Democratic-dominated Congress refused to grant him, arguing correctly that the burden would fall heavily on those least able to pay. However, the Democrats were as wedded as Hoover to the sanctity of balanced budgets — they would make a big issue of the president's "extravagance" in the next election — and so they enacted a large hike in income taxes, tilting the burden toward the upper-income brackets. Considering the desperate need for economic stimulus, raising taxes in either form was the wrong thing to do. But the conventional economic theory of the day gave no guidance toward meeting the unprecedented emergency that the Depression had now become.

---

1. Before the ratification of the Twentieth Amendment in 1933, more than a year normally elapsed between the election of a new Congress and its first meeting.

Hoover also presented Congress with the most ambitious program of federal economic action ever proposed in peacetime. He called for an expansion of public works, for extending the lending power of Farm Loan Banks, for creating a home-loan program to slow foreclosures, and for establishing a huge, federally funded reconstruction corporation that would lend money to threatened businesses and banks. Considering the small size of the federal government, which in 1929 accounted for around 3 percent of GNP, the second phase of Hoover's program to relieve the Depression was dramatic and innovative.

The Reconstruction Finance Corporation (RFC), which at Hoover's urging Congress chartered in January 1932, did some good. It provided an initial capital of $500 million and authorized an additional $1.5 billion to be raised through the sale of tax-exempt bonds. Within a year the RFC had loaned about $1.5 billion, clearly helping to bolster the tottering economy. Although the RFC was criticized for lending mostly to large businesses, some of them controlled by members of the agency's board, the RFC remained a crucial stim-

The Bonus Army　Despite attempts by a few radicals to exploit the marchers' despair, the Bonus Army displayed remarkable restraint and dignity when they converged on Washington in the summer of 1932. Here a contingent ascends the Capitol steps to petition their representatives for relief.

ulus to economic recovery for a decade. During the subsequent Roosevelt presidency, under the leadership of Texas banker Jesse Jones the RFC would become the New Deal's biggest single investor, pouring about $15 billion into the economy.

But in 1932 the RFC alone was clearly inadequate to reverse the Depression. Democrats in Congress, as befuddled as the Republicans, criticized Hoover relentlessly but offered no alternate program. Most Democrats in Congress in 1932 probably stood to the right of Hoover, and generally they believed their best strategy was to avoid "committing our party to a definite program." They were content to criticize Hoover and wait for the elections of 1932. Speaker of the House John Nance Garner boasted, "I fought President Hoover with everything I had, under Marquis of Queensberry, London prize ring and catch-as-catch-can rules." Hoover had been as flexible and innovative as his economic philosophy and conscience allowed. In July he vetoed a bill for direct federal relief and a massive public works program, clinging grimly to his conviction that a new era of enlightened capitalism was on the horizon.

Hoover's growing frustration combined with his naturally stiff personality to make him appear inflexible and unfeeling. His tragic loss of rapport with the public was highlighted during the summer of 1932 by his overreaction to a rally of unemployed veterans in Washington, variously estimated at between 12,000 and 20,000, which petitioned Congress to pay bonuses that were not due until 1945. This "Bonus Army" built a shantytown on the mud flats of the Anacostia River, and some spilled over into vacant government buildings on Pennsylvania Avenue. Most of the veterans and their bedraggled families went home when Congress refused their petition, but a few hundred remained. During a demonstration two veterans and two policemen were killed. Losing all sense of proportion, Hoover ordered General Douglas MacArthur to lead a detachment of cavalry, infantry, and six tanks to clear the camp and burn the veterans' shanties. Although MacArthur called the marchers "a mob . . . animated by the essence of revolution," they offered no real resistance. Probably less than a hundred were political radicals; the rest were a pathetic band of despairing victims.

❧ *The Election of 1932*

Dispersing bedraggled World War I veterans cast a pall over Hoover's reelection campaign. The Republican

Franklin D. Roosevelt Campaigns for Change, 1932

While campaigning for the presidency in 1932, Franklin D. Roosevelt told the Oglethorpe University Class of 1932 that he believed the country was ready for the government to take bold steps to address the deepening economic crisis.

The year 1928 does not seem far in the past, but since that time, as all of us are aware, the world about us has experienced significant changes. Four years ago, if you heard and believed the tidings of the time, you could expect to take your place in a society well supplied with material things. . . .

How sadly different is the picture which we see around us today! If only the mirage had vanished, we should not complain, for we should all be better off. But with it have vanished, not only the easy gains of speculation, but much of the savings of thrifty and prudent men and women, put by for their old age and for the education of their children. With these savings has gone, among millions of our fellow citizens, that sense of security to which they have rightly felt they are entitled in a land abundantly endowed with natural resources and with productive facilities to convert them into the necessities of life for all of our population. More calamitous still, there has vanished with the expectation of future security the certainty of today's bread and clothing. . . .

The country needs and, unless I mistake its temper, the country demands bold, persistent experimentation. It is common sense to take a method and try it: If it fails, admit it frankly and try another. But above all, try something. The millions who are in want will not stand by silently forever while the things to satisfy their needs are within easy reach.

Convention met in Chicago in June and nominated the president with little enthusiasm. The keynote speaker, quipped humorist Will Rogers, could hardly boast of "accomplishments," and would not view the situation with "alarm," leaving the possibility that the delegates would "get two solid hours on the weather." The Republican platform called for reductions in federal spending, a balanced budget, and cooperation with efforts to stabilize international finance.

The Democratic convention that met in Chicago two weeks later adopted a platform blasting Hoover's "extravagance" but in many other respects mirroring the Republicans' promises. It called for drastic cuts in federal spending, a balanced budget, and participation in a conference to stabilize world currencies. However, the Democrats also pledged an expanded program of relief and — perhaps more significant politically — called for repealing Prohibition. In spite of the Depression, Prohibition was a hotly debated issue; philosopher John Dewey complained that "in the midst of the greatest crisis since the Civil War . . . the only thing the two national parties seem to want to debate is booze."

Most of the Democratic presidential contenders, including House Speaker John Nance Garner, were conservatives. One exception was Oklahoma's shaggy governor "Alfalfa Bill" Murray, a radical populist in the Bryan tradition who spoke for the stricken farmers of the Great Plains. New York's Franklin D. Roosevelt — a frontrunner primarily because of his landslide reelection in 1930 as governor of the nation's most populous state — was impossible to characterize ideologically.

Roosevelt campaigned for the nomination for months, calling for "bold, persistent experimentation." But no one knew what he might actually do in the White House. He seemed to the influential journalist Walter Lippmann "a pleasant man who, without any particular qualification, would very much like to be president."

Roosevelt owed his success at the convention mainly to the support of the party's leading political bosses, who sensed that he was "a winner." On the fourth ballot he reached the two-thirds necessary for the nomination, thanks to a deal by which Garner became his running mate.

Breaking with tradition, which dictated that presidential nominees stay discreetly at home and be ceremoniously informed by a delegation of party elders that they had been chosen, Roosevelt immediately flew from Albany to Chicago to make an acceptance speech that electrified the convention delegates. In it, he promised: "I pledge you — I pledge myself to a new deal for the American people." The term *New Deal*, devised by lawyer Samuel Rosenman, was a happy combination of Woodrow Wilson's "New Freedom" and Theodore Roosevelt's "Square Deal." Still, what his "new deal" might be no one could say — least of all Roosevelt himself.

Few candidates in American political history have savored campaigning as did Franklin Roosevelt — despite his physical disability, to which the media scarcely ever drew attention. As the Democrats' nominee in 1932, FDR traveled 17,000 miles and delivered more than a thousand speeches. But his campaign oratory was vague and contradictory, promising something to everyone. Echoing the most persistent Democratic theme — Hoover's allegedly profligate spending — Roosevelt promised to balance the budget and cut federal spending by 25 percent.

Roosevelt was vague for a variety of reasons. Although he was deeply committed to the progressive tradition of an activist and "caring" government, his vagueness in part simply reflected his lack of any settled plan for recovery. But he was also vague because his political instincts told him to conduct a campaign that would win the election without entering into controversial specifics. In the end, it was not Roosevelt's incoherent proposals that carried the day. He owed his success to his irrepressible optimism, to his captivating smile, to the glib slogans that offered a "new deal" for the "forgotten man at the bottom of the economic pyramid" — and to the fact that he was not Herbert Hoover.

Hoover realized that the American voters were in a mood to repudiate him. Tired and grimly focused on defending the gold standard and a balanced budget, he vainly tried to make Roosevelt debate basic economic principles. He was convinced that Roosevelt was a charlatan proposing "changes and so-called new deals which would destroy the very foundations of our American system." He believed that Roosevelt would end forever the system of voluntarism and individual rights that had made America a great nation. In his last important speech, Hoover warned that if the Democrats won "the grass will grow in the streets of a hundred cities, a thousand towns; the weeds will overrun the fields of millions of farms." But all this availed him nothing. It was the Depression, not party platforms nor campaign rhetoric, that decided the election of 1932.

Roosevelt was elected in a landslide, collecting 22.8 million votes to Hoover's 15.7 million, and winning the electoral college by 472 to 92. Save for 1912, when the GOP had been split, no Republican had ever been beaten so badly. The Democrats won huge majorities in Congress, outnumbering Republicans in the House by nearly three to one.

Many intellectuals who saw little difference between the two candidates on important issues voted for Socialist Norman Thomas (whose vote totaled 882,000) or for Communist William Z. Foster (103,000). Still, considering the severity of the Depression, the number of Americans who voted for radical political change was remarkably low. The Communist Party worked vigorously to recruit workers, the unemployed, and blacks, but with little success. In 1932 the party claimed only 13,000 members, a disproportionate share of whom belonged to "cells" that had been organized among students and intellectuals — and many of these, repelled by the Communists' dogmatism, quit soon after joining.

The charm and political style of Franklin D. Roosevelt proved to be a strong asset, but the discernable shift of new groups of voters to the Democrats, which would make it the nation's dominant party for several generations, followed rather than preceded the arrival of the New Deal. Voter turnout in the presidential race remained virtually unchanged from 1928. Many Americans still believed, with Hoover, that the Depression was a short-term adjustment and that recovery would begin soon. Even those most adversely affected did not perceive that the Democrats offered a significantly different choice from the Republicans. Given no clear alternatives, the most oppressed classes appear not to have voted in large numbers in 1932. Millions of Americans, however, held the Republicans liable for the Depression, and they simply voted against the party in power, whether its candidates were progressives or conservatives.

ॐ The Interregnum — the Depression's Darkest Hour

The four months between the election of Roosevelt and his inauguration on March 4, 1933, called "the interregnum," was the nation's winter of despair. Three years of depression had cut national income in half, and in December 1932 America's European debtor nations announced that they were in default. While prices, wages, and employment tumbled, mortgage payments and taxes remained fixed, and the crescendo of foreclosures on homes and farms reached staggering levels. As the number of failed banks passed five thousand, the nation's financial system tottered on the brink of collapse.

Hoover blamed worsening conditions on public uncertainty following Roosevelt's election. He urged Roosevelt to assure the world that he would support sound economic measures at home and cooperate with European efforts to stabilize international currencies at an upcoming conference in London. In two notorious meetings between the president and the president-elect, Hoover lectured Roosevelt on his elaborate and sophisticated views on international recovery, but Roosevelt refused to issue the assurances that Hoover wanted. Thus Hoover's presidency ended in a precipitous economic spiral downward that he was incapable of influencing.

In many ways, Roosevelt's actions during the interregnum are difficult to understand. He was so unresponsive to Hoover's requests for cooperation that he was later charged with purposely allowing the economy to collapse as one last symbol of Republican incompetence. Other explanations are more plausible. Roosevelt was no theorist; he probably never understood the intricacies of Hoover's ideas, nor did he like what he did understand. Above all, Roosevelt feared making commitments that might later limit his freedom to act.

During the interregnum Roosevelt assembled a team of advisers and drafted legislative proposals. Early in the campaign Roosevelt had commissioned his attorney, Samuel Rosenman, to seek fresh ideas. Rosenman recruited Barnard College professor Raymond Moley who, in turn, brought to Roosevelt's advisory team two friends from Columbia University, Rexford Guy Tugwell, an expert on agriculture, and economist Adolph A. Berle, Jr. These men formed the core of Roosevelt's inner circle of advisers, and the *New York Times* gave them a name that stuck: the "brains trust." This group was bolstered by a stream of talented and idealistic people who brought a potpourri of ideas and plans — sometimes mutually contradictory — to Hyde Park during the interregnum. Invigorated by his victory, Roosevelt seemed to be ever present, listening and prodding as his team drafted a legislative agenda.

FRANKLIN D. ROOSEVELT AND THE FIRST NEW DEAL, 1933-1934

Clearly one of the great political leaders of the twentieth century, Franklin Delano Roosevelt casts a long shadow across American history. In part, the times made Roosevelt a great president, forcing him to lead the nation through its greatest domestic trauma and its worst international crisis of the twentieth century. But Roosevelt brought unique gifts to his difficult task. His personal fortitude unbroken by polio, he infused the nation with the pluck to endure the Depression. Although he was not a deep thinker with a clear philosophical vision, Roosevelt had enormous political skills: in public an unswerving ability to tap the emotions of the common people, and in private a legendary charm. Especially in the dark days of 1933, Roosevelt brought to the nation hope and courage.

FDR faced unprecedented challenges from the day he took office. During his first two years as president

he recommended, and Congress passed, a broad array of legislation designed to relieve suffering and stimulate the economy. Although the early New Deal lacked a coherent philosophy, Roosevelt and his advisers generally accepted the inevitability of economic concentration and favored some form of government regulation and planning. For models, they reached back to the federal boards of the World War I era. Roosevelt hoped to gain broad support from both business and labor in the struggle for recovery. But by 1935, a number of the most important initiatives of the First New Deal (as the years 1933-34 have been named) had either failed or run afoul of the conservative Supreme Court, forcing him to launch the so-called Second New Deal. It was especially during this Second New Deal, from 1935 on, that Roosevelt presided over the creation of institutions that define the nation's modern welfare state.

❧ *The Roosevelt Persona*

The only child of "old money," moderately wealthy parents, reared in an idyllic rural environment in Hyde Park, New York, Franklin Delano Roosevelt's childhood bequeathed to him a love of farming and nature, an amorphous but unwavering faith in God, and an irrepressibly confident spirit. Educated at Groton (an exclusive private school) and at Harvard College, where he was editor of the *Crimson,* Roosevelt embodied the *noblesse oblige* of his social class. While a student at Columbia Law School he courted his distant cousin, Eleanor Roosevelt, Theodore Roosevelt's niece, and the two were married in New York City in March 1905. By 1918 the Roosevelts had drifted apart, and FDR had at least one romantic entanglement, which remained the secret of his family and a few close friends. Eleanor, who had been a painfully shy girl growing up, was a woman of strong religious conviction who matured into a powerful advocate for the oppressed — particularly African Americans. The couple maintained the dignity and decorum expected of the presidency despite their personal estrangement. Of course, in these years the private life of the president was considered off-limits to reporters.

Roosevelt's political career began in 1910 when, at age twenty-eight, he was elected a Democratic state senator in New York. He subsequently served eight years as Wilson's assistant secretary of the Navy, and in the 1920 presidential election became James M. Cox's running mate. Roosevelt was a moderately progressive Democrat and an ardent supporter of Woodrow Wilson. But he was sufficiently non-ideological to adore his distant cousin, TR.

Handsome, debonair, and well spoken, Roosevelt had intended to run for the Senate in 1922, but in August 1921 his up-and-coming political career was tragically interrupted. At age thirty-nine he was struck down by polio. Roosevelt fought bravely to regain the use of his legs, making frequent visits to Warm Springs, Georgia, for therapy. However, he was never again able to walk more than short distances, painfully dragging his legs in heavy braces and having to be carried up stairs. But Roosevelt's robust appearance and his nonchalance made it difficult to think of him as

disabled. When he returned to campaigning in 1928, winning the governorship of New York, his handicap transformed him from a dashing aristocrat into a courageous underdog.

After the onset of the Depression, Roosevelt inaugurated a precursor of the New Deal in New York by increasing public works, pressing for bank reform, and establishing an Emergency Relief Administration headed by social worker Harry Hopkins. A proven politician with a demonstrated willingness to experiment, by 1932, Roosevelt was poised to challenge Hoover. Like others in 1932, he did not have a clear understanding of the Depression and its causes, nor did he grasp the enormous magnitude of the task facing him. But Roosevelt brought to the nation in 1933 the things it most needed — hope and self-confidence.

Few presidents have been as persuasive as Roosevelt. His speeches had an intimate quality that endeared him to the public. The first president to master radio speak-

FDR One of the most famous photographs of Franklin D. Roosevelt is this, taken as he met with reporters at his home in Hyde Park, New York. (By using special equipment, Roosevelt was able to drive an automobile despite the paralysis of his legs.) The jaunty jut of his jaw and tilt of his cigarette holder communicated to millions of Americans his message that the Great Depression could be overcome and the American Dream realized.

ing, Roosevelt became famous for "fireside chats" in which he discussed public affairs like a father talking things over with his family. Roosevelt used his personal charm to develop an extraordinary rapport with the White House press corps. Year in and year out, twice weekly, the White House was opened for reporters to ask impromptu questions and engage in friendly exchange with the president. Roosevelt knew the reporters by name, joshed with them, impressed them with his command of detail, and displayed his renowned skills as a raconteur.

Though Roosevelt was no intellectual, and lost interest or became annoyed when discussions got too theoretical, he was not anti-intellectual. He and his advisers embraced a wide variety of ideas that derived from most of the earlier American reform traditions. From populism came a distrust of finance and Wall Street; urban social reform contributed a concern for the aged and indigent; many early New Deal advisers had progressive backgrounds and some had worked in settlement houses. Among the original brains-trusters, only Adolph Berle displayed the strong background of evangelical Protestantism that had been the hallmark of turn-of-the-century progressivism, but most New Dealers shared John Dewey's conviction that society could be shaped by organized social intelligence.

Probably the boldest theoretician in Roosevelt's brains trust was Rexford Tugwell, but he came to represent a path to recovery that the New Deal ultimately renounced. Tugwell rejected progressive support for competition, small economic units, and free-market decisions. He was a planner and believed that the government should make management decisions for the whole economy. Tugwell did not wish to socialize ownership, only management, but his views had a limited impact on the New Deal. Tugwell's fellow brainstruster Raymond G. Moley represented another potential direction for the New Deal, far more pro-business, and ultimately he would break with the president and become one of the New Deal's harshest critics. But as Roosevelt assembled his team amid a deepening national economic crisis, these future differences hardly mattered.

Eleanor Roosevelt and Friends   Eleanor Roosevelt was the first presidential wife who projected her own message to the public. By nature a shy, upper-class woman, conscious of her looks and enduring an unhappy marriage, she learned to absorb energy and inspiration from ordinary citizens. They responded with an outpouring of warmth. She was also one of the first American public figures to make a point of treating blacks with dignity and without condescension, as when she met this group of children in Baltimore.

Roosevelt's cabinet exemplified the diversity of the administration. Cordell Hull of Tennessee, a firm supporter of lower tariffs, was named secretary of state. Roosevelt picked two Republicans for critical domestic posts: scrupulously honest Harold Ickes became secretary of the interior, and Henry Wallace, an Iowa farm-newspaper editor and plant geneticist whose father had been in Harding's cabinet, was named secretary of agriculture. Secretary of Labor Frances Perkins, a former social worker, became the first woman appointed to the cabinet. As postmaster general (an office important primarily for overseeing political patronage), Roosevelt's campaign manager James A. Farley gave the cabinet a Roman Catholic presence.

Roosevelt has been labeled a poor administrator because the New Deal quickly became a maze of overlapping agencies and because he refused to remove inefficient aides. Some historians believe that Roosevelt tolerated these inefficiencies by design, viewing them as necessary experiments. If Roosevelt was displeased with subordinates, even cabinet-level appointees, he bypassed them and gave authority to personal confidants, the most powerful being social worker Harry

Franklin D. Roosevelt's First Inaugural Address, 1933
In his first inaugural address, Franklin D. Roosevelt tried to calm the rising fears of the American people that the Great Depression was unconquerable.

I am certain that my fellow Americans expect that on my induction into the Presidency I will address them with a candor and a decision which the present situation of our Nation impels. This is preeminently the time to speak the truth, the whole truth, frankly and boldly. Nor need we shrink from honestly facing conditions in our country today. This great Nation will endure as it has endured, will revive and will prosper. So, first of all, let me assert my firm belief that the only thing we have to fear is fear itself — nameless, unreasoning, unjustified terror which paralyzes needed efforts to convert retreat into advance. In every dark hour of our national life a leadership of frankness and vigor has met with that understanding and support of the people themselves which is essential to victory. I am convinced that you will again give that support to leadership in these critical days.

Hopkins. Eleanor Roosevelt was the informal conscience of the administration; she traveled widely to advertise the cause of the most oppressed, particularly African Americans.

In 1939, in a far-reaching executive order, Roosevelt established the Executive Office of the President. First composed of six administrative assistants, the Bureau of the Budget was soon added to the Executive Office. This reorganization introduced the modern executive branch with its powerful aides hidden from public scrutiny, which in recent decades has grown prodigiously.

❧ *The Hundred Days*

Franklin D. Roosevelt's first inaugural address on March 4, 1933, was one of those rare speeches that in itself shaped history. The new president solemnly conceded that want gripped the nation, even though "plenty is at our doorstep." He laid the blame on the stubbornness and incompetence of the "rulers of the exchanges of mankind's goods." In a biblical allusion that also revealed his patrician disdain for grubby profiteering, Roosevelt announced that "the money changers have fled from their high seats in the temple of our civilization. We may now restore the temple to the ancient truths." But by far the most famous phrase of his celebrated speech was Roosevelt's confident declaration that "the only thing we have to fear is fear itself." In truth, in the spring of 1933 there was much to fear, and Roosevelt's speech offered no concrete basis for hope. Nonetheless, millions took faith, believing that they had elected a leader who intended to set things right.

The "Hundred Days" following Roosevelt's inauguration witnessed a legislative upheaval that amazed even the president's supporters. On Sunday afternoon, March 5, Roosevelt issued two presidential edicts — one

calling Congress into special session on the following Thursday, March 9, and a second declaring a four-day bank holiday. Acting on questionable legal authority, Roosevelt closed all of the nation's banks, ordered a swarm of inspectors to audit the books of every financial institution, and assured the public that any bank that reopened was sound. Within three days, about 75 percent of the banks that were members of the Federal Reserve System had reopened. This bold move restored confidence in the financial system and sparked a climb in the stock market. On March 12, when Roosevelt addressed the nation by radio in the first of his "fireside chats" to explain the steps he had taken to stabilize the nation's financial system, an estimated 60 million people were listening.

Roosevelt's actions during his first week in office steadied the nation's financial system. So desperate was the situation that he probably could have taken far more drastic steps, including nationalizing the banks, without significant opposition. Exaggerating only slightly, Moley said that "capitalism was saved in eight days." During the next two years the RFC loaned around $1 billion to rescue marginal banks, and nearly 1,800 others were refused licenses by the Treasury Department. The banking crisis was ended, but an estimated $3.26 billion in deposits had been lost in just three years.

True to his campaign promises of "bold experimentation," FDR was willing to try a variety of possible solutions to the economic crisis. When Congress convened, the White House sent fifteen presidential messages and a stream of bills to Capitol Hill. Some of the legislation passed during the special session originated in Congress, but most had been drafted by Roosevelt's advisers. The president had extraordinary powers; some bills left the White House, passed both houses of Congress, and returned for Roosevelt's signature on the same day. When Congress adjourned on June 16, exactly one hundred days after it had convened, it had appropriated huge sums for relief and public works, had extended federal regulation of the nation's financial network, and had initiated a new approach to solving agricultural problems. Some of these measures were radical, some deeply conservative; some were meant to create inflation, while others were designed to restrict demand. No one could grasp the meaning of all that had been done, but most people applauded the president's actions. "If he had burned down the house," quipped Will Rogers, "people would say, 'Well, at least he got a fire started.'"

During its regular session, which began in late 1933, the Seventy-third Congress passed another barrage of legislation, most of it originating in the White House. By the end of 1934 the basic programs of the First New Deal were in place and a broad theoretical outline had appeared.

Rather than follow Tugwell's path to central planning, the First New Deal nurtured "interest group democracy," a political settlement more in keeping with progressive notions of private decision-making aided by government guidance. Roosevelt saw the government as the arbiter of clashes between classes, regions, and various minority groups. A "broker state" emerged. Critics argued that a broker state would be easily captured by powerful interest groups and subject to manipulation by shrill activists. Roosevelt's intent, however, was to greatly expand the variety of groups that had the ear of the government, and one reason for creating a profusion of agencies and programs in the 1930s was to attempt a balance between the divergent and sometimes contradictory interests of hundreds of special-interest groups. But, many economists and historians maintain, Roosevelt's rejection of planning and of massive government spending probably made recovery impossible during the First New Deal.

Beginning with the Hundred Days, Washington was thronged by young New Dealers from all over the country. They drafted legislation, staffed the "alphabet soup" of new agencies, or found jobs as staff assistants to Democratic members of Congress. Usually idealistic but often affecting a pose of "unsentimental" realism, these lawyers, accountants, ex-social workers, and ex-academics found FDR's Washington both exhausting and exhilarating. Few of them would ever leave voluntarily. They made the nation's capital into what it remains: the magnet for men and women who dream of a lifelong career at the center of power.

❧ *Roosevelt and the Moneychangers*

On March 9, the first day of the special session, Congress passed the Emergency Banking Relief Act, giving legal standing to Roosevelt's closing of the banks and granting him broad discretionary powers over the currency and the trading of gold and silver. In thirty-eight minutes the House of Representatives passed the bill without ever seeing it in print. The measure was far from the radical reform of the banking system that some had hoped for; one congressman complained that "the president drove the money-changers out of the Capitol on March 4th — and they were all back on the 9th." More onerous to stock market speculators was the Federal Securities Act that passed in May. An effort to curtail the irresponsible trading that had contributed to the crash, the law required the registration of all new securities with the Federal Trade Commission (later with the Securities and Exchange Commission).

Other financial measures initiated during the Hundred Days were highly contradictory. In an effort to balance the budget (in which he believed as strongly as Hoover), Roosevelt cut federal workers' salaries 15 percent, slashed veterans' benefits, and reorganized government agencies to effect savings. The president retained his commitment to a balanced budget throughout the Depression; when budget deficits grew to unprecedented size, Roosevelt made a distinction in his mind between emergency and temporary spending and endeavored to balance the general budget.

On June 16 Congress enacted the Glass-Steagall Act, the most important banking legislation of the Hundred Days. The act broadened the powers of the Federal Reserve System to curb irresponsible speculation by banks and established the Federal Deposit Insurance Corporation (FDIC) to guarantee individual bank deposits up to $5,000. (Since then, the limit has been raised much higher.) In combination with the New Deal's other financial legislation, the Glass-Steagall Act succeeded brilliantly in restoring stability to the banking industry. For the remainder of the decade fewer banks failed each year than in any year during the twenties.

In the most ill-advised actions taken during his early months in office, Roosevelt resorted to monetary manipulation to try to raise prices and increase foreign trade. First, on April 19, he took the nation off the gold standard, invoking the historic populist panacea. By 1933, almost all the capitalist world except France and the United States had abandoned the gold standard, and today most economic historians regard this ac-

Remedies Roosevelt did not really know how to "cure" the Depression; his genius lay in his willingness to experiment with different policies (some of them having diametrically opposite effects) while inspiring a majority of citizens with hope that the crisis could be overcome. Conservative Washington *Star* political cartoonist Clifford Berryman was generally critical of the New Deal, but in this 1935 caricature he captured the essence of FDR's strategy.

tion as both inevitable and necessary for eventual economic stability. But both Roosevelt's motives and his methods were questionable, and conservatives were horrified. (Aghast, his own director of the Bureau of the Budget declared that going off the gold standard marked "the end of western civilization.") Although the result was a sharp decline in the international value of the dollar, the move did little to stop the disastrous

slide of prices in the United States. Roosevelt also tried several schemes to manipulate the price of gold and silver, hoping to devalue the dollar and raise prices. But once it was obvious that these maneuvers had failed, the administration stabilized the dollar in January 1934 at 59 percent of its former value. The famed British economist John Maynard Keynes observed that Roosevelt's currency manipulation "looked to me more like a gold standard on the booze than the ideal managed currency of my dreams."

Roosevelt's desire to weaken American currency to attain international advantage effectively undermined the London Economic Conference that met in June and July 1933. Some economists of the 1930s, including Keynes, believed that going off the gold standard was a positive step, and that the London Economic Conference was destined to fail anyway. Nonetheless, Roosevelt was justly accused of torpedoing the conference because he knew that stabilizing international exchange rates would clash with his plans to raise U.S. prices unilaterally. FDR misled others about his intentions, reneged on earlier promises, and showed that he had little grasp of the intricacies of international finance. Roosevelt meant to "go it alone" in combating the Depression.

However, if Roosevelt sabotaged international efforts (originally planned by Hoover) to restore monetary stability, at least he had a far better understanding than his predecessor of the crucial role of international trade in promoting recovery and ensuring long-range economic growth. Honoring the traditional Democratic preference for freer trade, Roosevelt directed Hull to begin negotiating reciprocal treaties lowering tariff barriers with specific American trading partners. These treaties would prove to be the first steps toward the liberalization of global trade that would sustain the nation's remarkable economic surge after World War II.

❧ Relief and Public Works

With millions out of work, out of resources, and often out of hope, dealing with the immense human misery spawned by the Depression was an urgent priority for the new administration. In May, at Roosevelt's behest, Congress funded the Federal Emergency Relief Administration (FERA) to dispense $500 million to the states for direct relief to the unemployed. Roosevelt appointed his close confidant Harry Hopkins to head the agency. FERA grants required states to supply matching funds, sparking relief efforts in many states that were labeled "little New Deals." In a show of energy, Hopkins allocated over $5 million in his first two hours in office in May 1933. This infusion of money helped relieve the worst privation in the summer of 1933.

Roosevelt, like Hoover, never liked outright relief, and he did not want to create a permanent welfare class, but the establishment of the FERA and other relief programs in 1933 did launch an American welfare system that would be one of the most controversial legacies of the New Deal. To provide a broad program of work for the unemployed, in June Congress established the Public Works Administration (PWA). Roosevelt named Secretary of the Interior Ickes to head the agency, and Congress appropriated more than $3

PWA Housing   A family sits on the steps outside their home in a Public Works Administration housing project for African Americans in Omaha, Nebraska.

billion to fund it. The PWA became a New Deal fixture; between 1933 and 1939 the agency helped construct 70 percent of the nation's new school buildings, built hundreds of courthouses, sewage plants, public housing units, and hospitals, and launched the aircraft carriers *Yorktown* and *Enterprise*. In the short term, however, the PWA provided little relief in 1933. The tightfisted Ickes planned carefully, determined not to waste tax dollars on useless make-work. Roosevelt became increasingly frustrated that the slow-moving PWA did little to provide the jobs needed to stimulate the economy.

In one of the most innovative experiments of the New Deal, the PWA utilized a National Planning Board to coordinate its diverse activities. In 1934 that agency, under the leadership of Roosevelt's uncle, Frederick A. Delano, became the National Resources Committee. The most serious New Deal effort to develop a plan for the use of the nation's resources, the committee would become a steady target of congressional New Deal opponents, who saw it as a precursor of a collectivist state, and the agency was abolished during World War II. But the committee left behind a legacy in scores of state and municipal planning agencies.

Exasperated, Hopkins ridiculed the PWA's emphasis on long-rang planning: "People don't eat in the long run." He pressed Roosevelt to provide additional emergency aid for the millions who remained unemployed in 1933, and in November the president established a new agency, the Civil Works Administration (CWA), funding it with appropriations made to the PWA and FERA and with contributions from local governments. Roosevelt placed Hopkins in charge of a new public works agency, which during the next year pumped nearly $1 billion into the economy. The CWA launched thousands of hastily conceived projects; employing at its peak 4,230,000 persons. Popular with workers and the local officials who directed its projects, the CWA was regarded by Roosevelt as a stopgap measure. He dismantled the agency in the spring of 1934, returning the basic responsibility for emergency relief to the FERA. The president was alarmed by the enormous cost of the CWA and by the whiff of corruption in its operations. Furthermore, CWA projects were often transparently wasteful. New Deal critics derisively labeled the public works programs "boondoggling."

By the end of 1935 New Deal agencies had aided millions of unemployed Americans with direct relief, and millions more had been given a government job, though often a make-work one. But none of the First New Deal relief programs had been entirely satisfactory. The gigantic relief appropriations had not solved the problem of unemployment, and the wastefulness of some public works projects provided critics with easy targets. Neither FDR nor Hopkins nor most of the other leading New Dealers wanted to see the emergence of a permanent welfare state, in which dependence on government handouts came to be viewed as a way of life rather than a helping hand in an emergency — but that was beginning to happen anyway. Complained a Chicago social worker as early as 1934: "There is a noticeable tendency to regard obtaining relief as another way of earning a living. The former stigma attached to a family dependent on relief is gone and each family in a given neighborhood knows what, why, and how much every other family in a given neighborhood is obtaining from an agency." People who went on relief, rightly or wrongly, quickly came to regard the dole's paltry assistance as theirs by right.

The Dust Bowl This scene, photographed during a dust storm in Cimarron County in the Oklahoma Panhandle in April 1936, captures the total devastation that the prolonged Great Plains drought brought to the region's farm families.

Moreover, surviving older charities — often faith-based — resented the "intrusion" that they saw in federal relief agencies' efforts to reach their former clients. Roman Catholic agencies, for example, sometimes complained that the coming of federal assistance was undermining people's loyalty to the church, which expected its clergy to vouch for the "worthiness" of those who received emergency help. Italian, Polish, and other ethnically oriented charities also claimed that receiving New Deal aid blurred old immigrant loyalties. Such complaints had a point, for the New Deal was part of still larger cultural, social, economic, and political changes that in the 1930s were giving urban working people a new sense of identity.

❧ Conservation and Regional Planning

Some New Deal experiments provided a measure of relief while being more broadly conceived as conservation projects. The Depression era revealed that farming had pushed much too far onto the semiarid plains of the trans-Missouri West and that inappropriate farming methods had damaged, or even ruined, the soil. A series of dry years in the early thirties began blowing the topsoil away. In 1934 the National Resources Board estimated that 35 million acres of previously arable land had been destroyed and that more that 200 million more had been seriously damaged or were endangered. Nearly 800 counties in nineteen different states had become a Dust Bowl, focusing national attention on the need for conservation.

Roosevelt, like TR, believed strongly in conservation and planned land use. A dozen New Deal agencies reflected the president's interest; Roosevelt added more lands to the national forests than all preceding administrations and extended the national and state park systems.

In March 1933, Congress established the Civilian Conservation Corps (CCC), authorizing the employment of 250,000 young men between the ages of eighteen and twenty-five. Working under the supervision of army officers and living in quarters resembling military

CCC Boys The Civilian Conservation Corps was one of the most popular and effective of all the New Deal agencies. It enlisted unemployed young men for outdoor work, paid most of their small earnings to their out-of-work parents, and was administered at very low cost. It completed many useful projects, including reforestation and much of the work of building the Appalachian Trail. A few young women also served in the CCC, strictly segregated from the boys' camps.

camps, the young men worked mostly on conservation projects such as reforestation, prevention of soil erosion, and building improvements in national forests and parks. CCC workers received $30 per month and were required to send a portion of their wages home, thus becoming a source of relief for poor families. The CCC proved to be one of the most popular New Deal programs, providing an outlet for young men who were otherwise unemployable and at the same time addressing environmental problems. At its peak in 1935, the agency employed around 500,000; by the time World War II brought the program to an end, more than 2 million young men were CCC veterans.

One of the New Deal's showpieces, the Tennessee Valley Authority (TVA) was both a major source of unemployment relief and, more importantly, a broad experiment in regional planning and the Roosevelt administration's most far-reaching effort to promote economic growth. In the 1920s progressive Republican Senator George W. Norris had led an unsuccessful crusade to use a government hydroelectric plant — originally built during World War I in Muscle Shoals, Alabama — as the nucleus for the sweeping development of the Tennessee Valley region. Norris framed and Congress passed such legislation in 1928 and in 1931, but Hoover vetoed it. Roosevelt visited Muscle Shoals soon after becoming president, became an ardent supporter of Norris's plan, and signed it into law in May 1933.

Essentially, the Tennessee Valley project called for a series of dams to control the floods that regularly devastated the area and eroded its soil. At the same time, the dams would be the source of cheap, plentiful electricity that would encourage economic diversification and industrial development in the area.

The TVA was created as a government-owned corporation under a relatively independent board of managers. Private power producers complained that the government operation was unfair competition, but in general TVA was an enormously popular and successful experiment, attracting much interest from foreign observers. Between 1933 and 1944, TVA built nine large dams and many small ones and became a major producer of electricity, fertilizer, and explosives. Envisioned as a "yardstick" to measure the pricing policies of private utilities, TVA drove down the price of electricity in the region by two-thirds. Although the TVA worked no miracles, it did stimulate the economic development of seven southern states that ever since Reconstruction had been among the nation's poorest.

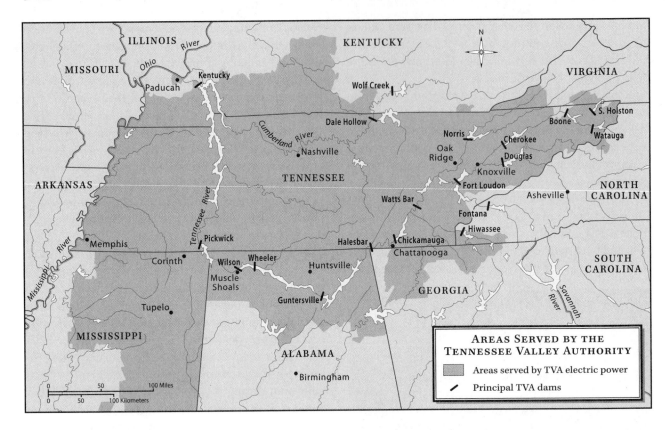

❧ *The Beginning of Agricultural Subsidies*

About a quarter of American farmers whose land was mortgaged lost their farms during the Depression. On March 27, 1933, Roosevelt combined the various federal agencies providing farm credit to form the Farm Credit Association (FCA), and authorized the agency to refinance farm mortgages on long terms at low interest rates. Within eighteen months 20 percent of the nation's farm mortgages had been refinanced. In June 1933 Congress passed a Bankruptcy Act that made it easier to recover lost property. Unfortunately, these measures came too late for many farmers.

The low income of farmers contributed to the decline in purchasing power that fueled the Depression. Even though farmers were among the first to organize politically, all through the twentieth century they subsidized the national standard of living by producing the nation's food supply at a very low cost. The basic New Deal farm program, the Agricultural Adjustment Administration (AAA), attempted to redress this historic imbalance by raising farm prices. As a result, it tended to work against national economic recovery by making food more expensive for hard-pressed, often unemployed urban consumers.

The Agricultural Adjustment Act established a do-mestic allotment plan that granted subsidies to farmers in return for agreements to cut acreage in certain basic commodities, including corn, wheat, rice, cotton, and tobacco. In return for acreage reductions, the prices paid for commodities would be guaranteed at "parity," the average paid for that commodity during the years 1909-1914, when price relationships had been favorable for farmers. The subsidies were funded by a processing tax on the commodities. This policy was supposed to reduce agricultural production and raise prices, thereby increasing farm income and purchasing power. The burden fell on taxpayers, who footed the bill for subsidies, and on consumers in the form of higher food prices than they would otherwise have paid.

Secretary of Agriculture Henry Wallace was anxious to get a farm program in place before the 1933 planting season. He hoped to forestall another year of agricultural surpluses and to stem a rising tide of farm strikes. After the bill passed in May, Wallace immediately dispatched a corps of agents into the South to persuade farmers to plow under 10 million acres of cotton in return for price guarantees. In the Corn Belt, the AAA subsidized the slaughter of 6 million pigs and 200,000 sows; some of the meat was distributed for relief, but most of it was unusable. In 1933, approximately one-fourth of the nation's annual farm production was de-

Okies Three drought refugees from Oklahoma in Blythe, California, in 1936. Such refugees became known as "Okies" because so many were from Oklahoma.

stroyed. These early efforts to cut farm surpluses provoked much prejudice against the AAA; many poor people viewed the destruction as inexcusable waste in the midst of want. Southern farmers found it virtually impossible to force their mules to plow up rows of cotton after years of training them to do exactly the opposite, giving rise to the quip that "a mule has more sense than a New Dealer."

In 1933 the AAA crop reduction program was voluntary, negotiated with individual farmers, but in 1934 the agency placed mandatory acreage controls on cotton and tobacco. Farmers participated in framing the AAA regulations, with a massive referendum held to endorse crop limitations. Millions of farmers voted on AAA policies, including thousands of southern blacks who had never before cast a ballot of any kind. The AAA was administered by 100,000 farmers participating in local associations that made actual crop allotments. Whatever its defects, the AAA was grass-roots democracy in action. Although the Supreme Court invalidated the processing tax and some production control features of the Agricultural Adjustment Act in 1936, the basic principles of acreage reduction and price supports survived. The basic strategies of New Deal agricultural policy — acreage limitations on key crops, price sup-

ports, and the removal of land from production — set the pattern for American agricultural policy until the mid-1990s.

New Deal farm policy did little to promote national economic recovery, although some farmers benefited more than others. Farm subsidies took money from the public sector and transferred it to farmers, who tended to hoard rather than spend their savings. The ratio of farm prices to those of manufactured goods rose steadily, gross farm income climbed 50 percent during Roosevelt's first term, and rural debt fell. Of course, these improvements took place within a Depression setting and farm income did not reach pre-Depression levels until 1941.

The biggest commercial interests, particularly southern cotton barons, benefited the most from the New Deal's agricultural policies, which laid the foundations for post–World War II "agribusiness." But by limiting acreage and encouraging efficient use of land, these policies forced marginal farmers, particularly southern sharecroppers, off the land and worsened the lot of farm laborers. Large numbers of farmers remained tenants (42 percent in 1935), but they had little job security and little interest in protecting the land they worked. Among the most recognizable Depression victims were poor "Arkie" and "Okie" tenant farmers, driven from the land by mechanization, drought, and acreage re-

On the Road to California With all their worldly goods packed into a wheezing old car, another family flees from the Dust Bowl to seek refuge in California. Such sights were common on Southwestern highways like Route 66 during the 1930s.

ductions. By the end of the decade, around a million of these migrants had wended their way westward along U.S. Highway 66 in jalopies crammed with worn possessions. They were immortalized in John Steinbeck's novel *The Grapes of Wrath*. Less celebrated, but no less traumatic, was the migration of rural black laborers from the farms to the cities (see Chapter 28).

❧ The Blue Eagle Soars and Falters

The centerpiece of the First New Deal, passed on the final day of the special 1933 session, was the National Industrial Recovery Act (NIRA). The PWA was established by Title II of the NIRA, but the law's primary aim was the founding of the National Recovery Administration (NRA) to coordinate the nation's industrial recovery. In some ways the most radical of all New Deal programs, the NRA coordinated the nation's industries through codes drafted by owners, labor, and consumers. Setting aside hard-won anti-trust laws, the NIRA gave the government broad powers to approve and enforce cooperation. It was New Deal's the most serious attempt at economic planning.

Headed by blustery General Hugh S. Johnson, the NRA coordinated activities in more than 550 industrial areas employing about 22 million workers. Drawing upon the World War I experience of the War Industries Board (see Chapter 25), the NRA drafted a "fair competition" code for each industry. These codes established minimum wages and maximum hours, theoretically guaranteed quality to protect consumers, and — crucially — freed businesses to coordinate production quotas and (in effect) prices. Johnson dashed about the country in the summer of 1933, assembling committees of business and labor leaders to draft the codes. Business leaders dragged their feet, although some recognized the advantages that big corporations would gain from the government's disregard of monopolistic tendencies. The cotton textile industry adopted the first code, and by September codes had been drafted for the ten largest industrial areas.

During the summer, while the committees were working, Roosevelt asked the nation to voluntarily support a general code that called for a minimum wage of between 30 and 40 cents an hour and a thirty-five- to forty-hour workweek. The blanket code went into effect in July. It became known as the "Blue Eagle" experiment from the image emblazoned on the decal that cooperating businesses displayed showing their cooperation.

The NRA was greeted with patriotic fervor, and thousands of businesses displayed Blue Eagle logos trumpeting the slogan "We Do Our Part." So great was the hoopla surrounding the enactment of the NIRA, and so extravagant were the promises that it would spark a dramatic recovery from the Depression, that many baby girls born in 1933 were named "Nira."

But by 1934 the NRA was in serious trouble. Apprehensions grew about the code's monopolistic concessions as it became increasingly clear that large companies had skewed the code-making process and that business leaders were less interested in economic recovery than in limiting production and hoarding the profits reaped from rising prices. The agency blossomed into a bureaucratic colossus with a staff of 4,500 overseeing more than 700 codes, many of them overlapping. Cork-makers, for instance, were regulated by thirty-four different codes. Soon, NRA efforts to enforce the codes were hopelessly bogged down in litigation; by the end of 1934 more than 150,000 complaints had been filed but less that one-fourth ever reached the court dockets. Critics became more and more vocal. Senator Carter Glass called the NRA "Hitlerism" because of its similarity to the industrial regulations then being established in Nazi Germany. Other detractors started saying that its acronym meant "Nuts Running America" or "National Run-Around."

In early 1934, Roosevelt appointed a National Recovery Review Board, headed by the famous lawyer Clarence Darrow, to evaluate the NRA codes. The president was angered when the board reported that the codes, biased in favor of large businesses, were decimating small businesses. The outspoken General Johnson retorted that the "little fellow" was often a "stingy, sleazy . . . greasy" operator who did not want to "pay code wages." Roosevelt believed that the report was slanted by Darrow's socialist bias, and he continued to support the dubious theory behind the NRA, but by the end of 1934 even he knew that the experiment had failed.

All the evidence supported the Darrow committee's conclusion. Although it was an especially prominent offender, the NRA was not alone among Roosevelt administration's initiatives in helping big business extend its control over the economy all through the New Deal era. Both the Depression and the New Deal's massive regulations tended to push small competitors out of the market. For example, the NRA helped kill off countless "mom-and-pop" groceries in working-class and ethnic neighborhoods by encouraging national chains like the A&P to bring in their more efficient and supposedly antiseptic stores, stocked with national brands marketed by corporate food packagers.

The worst flaw of the NRA was that it was based on the assumption, shared by many during the early years of the New Deal, that the Depression had been caused by overproduction and that it could by cured by constricting production. Such thinking precluded serious efforts to stimulate economic growth.

Like most other New Deal legislation, the NIRA had been challenged in the courts almost immediately, and in *Schechter v. U.S.* the Supreme Court declared portions of the law unconstitutional in 1935. By then, Roosevelt was moving on to the "Second New Deal" and was ready to abandon the attempt to constrict "overproduction."

Labor Supports the New Deal

In the long run, the most important article in the National Industrial Recovery Act was Section 7(a), a concession to organized labor included at the insistence of New York Senator Robert Wagner. Modeled on strategies used by the War Labor Board during World War I, Section 7(a) guaranteed labor's right to organize and bargain collectively. In fact, Section 7(a) gave labor nothing more than a right to compete for power, but aggressive labor organizers seized the opportunity.

John L. Lewis of the United Mine Workers (UMW) was the first union leader to grasp the significance of Section 7(a), labeling it labor's Emancipation Proclamation. The *United Mine Workers Journal* urged unions to seize the opportunity: "The bill will only help those who help themselves." The UMW sent 100 organizers into the field armed with the message that workers were fully protected if they joined a union — and with the much-exaggerated claim that the president wanted every worker to join a union. In fact, throughout much of the New Deal, Roosevelt was lukewarm in supporting industrial unionism. Nonetheless, the impact of Section 7(a) was staggering. Within two months the UMW had increased its membership fivefold and other industrial unions quickly adopted the UMW's recruiting tactics.

Industrialists countered the rise of industrial unionism with a variety of tactics aimed at keeping unions out, and the summer of 1933 was marked by a flurry of strikes. But it was clear that Section 7(a) had transformed labor unions into a much more potent part of the industrial bargaining process.

Completing the First New Deal

Congress passed scores of other important economic measures during the First New Deal. During the Hundred Days a Home Owners Refinancing Act passed, establishing the Home Owners Loan Corporation (HOLC) to stop the stream of home foreclosures that had reached around a thousand per day. By the time the HOLC ceased operation in June 1936 it held about a million mortgages. In June 1934 Congress established the Federal Housing Administration (FHA) to insure loans for the construction and repair of housing.

A final national issue addressed during the Hundred Days was the legalization of alcohol. All but the most diehard "drys" had lost patience with Prohibition, while soaring federal deficits led many to think that the government was forgoing an important source of revenue in the form of excise taxes on liquor. First, Congress passed an act legalizing the sale of beer and wine with a maximum of 3.2 percent alcoholic content. But in December 1933 the Twenty-first Amendment, repealing Prohibition, was declared ratified, and the country toasted the end of the Noble Experiment.

THE SECOND NEW DEAL AND THE EMERGENCE OF THE WELFARE STATE, 1935-1936

The Democrats won a resounding victory in the congressional elections of 1934, giving powerful support to the president and his policies. Some important and popular reforms had been achieved — especially the early relief programs, the cleaning up of abuses in the stock market, and the encouragement that Section 7(a) gave to unionization — and conservatives still smoldered with outrage at the abandonment of the gold standard. Yet much of what the New Deal had so far accomplished actually benefited business interests. By 1935, however, much of the basically conservative First New Deal had either proven ineffective or was threatened by the Supreme Court, and Roosevelt was drawing criticism from both the right and the left. The president was dissatisfied with some New Deal programs, particularly the NRA, and he was particularly angered by the obstructionist tactics of prominent business leaders.

The Second New Deal, as the years 1935-36 were later called, was a response to these developments and represented a turn to the left. In some ways, there was no sharp change in 1935; many older programs continued to be important parts of Roosevelt's plan of recovery, and much of the legislation passed in 1935 had been discussed earlier. On the other hand, the Second New Deal brought discernable shifts in philosophy and substance. Philosophically, Roosevelt ended his flirtation with planning; from now on, he favored a progressive emphasis on regulation. At the same time, in 1935 the government assumed broader responsibility for the welfare of underprivileged groups, including the unemployed, the elderly, and the exploited. The social welfare system established by the Second New Deal was modest by contemporary European standards, but it opened the era of the modern welfare state. To stimulate recovery, the Second New Deal generally dropped the idea of constricting "overproduction" and began gingerly to embrace deficit spending as a way of encouraging the national economic pie to grow.

The Second New Deal fueled anxieties on both left and right. Conservatives and some progressives believed that the broad expansion of government powers signaled a dangerous abandonment of individual responsibility, paving the way for demagogues who would pander to special interest groups. On the other extreme, socialists believed that the welfare state disguised society's real evils, blurred natural class antagonisms, and stilled the voice of dissent. Responding to overblown conservative charges that the New Deal had carried out the Socialist party's program, in 1936 Socialist leader Norman Thomas declared that Roosevelt had carried it out "on a stretcher."

In fact, the New Deal changed the country less drastically than either right-wing or left-wing critics imagined. Despite its bows to the left, the Second New Deal solidified the capitalist foundation of American society. Private property (the right to own the means of production) and free enterprise (the right to manage those means) survived the Second New Deal unscathed, although the government increased its power to require a degree of fairness in operating business. The resulting political and economic compromise prevailed in the last half of the twentieth century, and it became — and remains — the focus for defining the terms *liberal* and *conservative* in American politics.

∻ A Democratic Sweep in 1934

Many political observers assumed that the Democrats would lose a few seats in the congressional elections in

"Come Along! We're Going to the Trans-Lux to Hiss Roosevelt!" Many wealthy Americans hated FDR as "a traitor to his class," as this ironic cartoon from the *New Yorker* suggests. (The Trans-Lux was a New York City movie theater, and the hissing would have been done during the showing of a newsreel featuring the president.)

November 1934, but instead the president's party gained ten seats in both the House and the Senate. The House had only 103 Republicans among its 435 members, the lowest percentage in the party's history. In the Senate the Democrats held sixty-nine seats, becoming the first political party to control two-thirds of that body.

The election of 1934 was a stunning vote of confidence for the New Deal. Participation in the election was up 9.1 percent from the mid-term election of 1930, the turnout clearly indicating that New Deal policies were enlisting swarms of previously alienated or demoralized new voters into the Democratic ranks. Whole blocs of voters — including African Americans, recently naturalized immigrants, the young, those near the bottom of the economic ladder, the unemployed, and those on relief — began to coalesce in a party realignment that continued throughout the 1930s.

The congressional elections of 1934 placed Roosevelt in the most powerful political position of any modern president. "Boys, this is our hour," exulted

Harry Hopkins. "We've got to get everything we want . . . now or never." Roosevelt worried that a left-leaning Congress might run past him and embrace genuinely radical measures. His fears had some substance; had he wished to do so, Roosevelt could have effected dramatic changes in the nation's economic system in 1935.

Nevertheless, Roosevelt by now was drifting to the left himself. His opening address to Congress in 1935 harshly attacked the wealthy and warned that he would tolerate no further interference from business leaders. He had a few supporters among the wealthy, men like Bernard Baruch, Averell Harriman, and Joseph P. Kennedy (the father of John F. Kennedy and a fabulously successful stock market speculator of the 1920s whom FDR had appointed to head the SEC and charged with cleaning up the very practices that had made men like him rich). But some early New Deal measures, particularly the establishment of government control over securities trading, which Kennedy's agency was supposed to enforce, had infuriated the business community. For conservatives generally, Roosevelt was quickly becoming "that man," a "traitor to his class" so loathsome that some even refused to utter his name.

Some business leaders, once they sensed that the nation would survive the Depression, unleashed a vitriolic attack on Roosevelt and the New Deal. In hindsight, their idea that the New Deal posed a radical threat to collectivize the economy was preposterous. Even in his most radical moods, Roosevelt's basic desire was to stabilize prices, increase the profit potential of businesses, increase spending for business subsidies, and expend a minimal amount on public welfare. Nonetheless, in August 1934, a coalition of conservative businessmen and discontented Democrats (including Al Smith, who had broken with Roosevelt for both personal and political reasons) formed the American Liberty League to champion free enterprise, states' rights, the open shop, and the abolition of New Deal bureaucracy. The league was backed by some of the wealthiest and most powerful people in the country, including three Du Pont brothers, newspaper publisher William Randolph Hearst, Sewell L. Avery of Montgomery Ward, and Colby C. Chester, president of General Foods.

The Liberty League's protest grew even more strident in 1935. Many leaders of the Liberty League voiced reasonable concerns about the dangers of a state-dominated economy. More wildly, others charged that the New Deal was a communist plot. Such extreme right-wing rhetoric did not win wide public support.

✥ Radical Alternatives

Politically more troublesome for Roosevelt were several highly visible left-wing critics of the New Deal who offered visionary panaceas. Dr. Charles Francis Townsend, a benign but unsophisticated California physician, urged the federal government to pay $200 per month to every citizen over sixty on the condition that he or she retire and spend the entire sum within the United States each month. Completely unrealistic, the Townsend Plan nevertheless caught fire, fueled partly by a new force in American politics — the elderly. Townsend led rallies that resembled religious revivals all over the country and accurately characterized his supporters as those "who believe in the Bible,

Huey Long   Hated as a demagogue who wielded almost dictatorial power in Louisiana, beloved by millions of poor Americans desperate for a chance to share in the nation's wealth, and feared by Franklin D. Roosevelt as his most formidable political rival in the upcoming 1936 election, Long was at the height of his influence when this photograph was taken in 1935. He was assassinated soon thereafter.

❄ IN THEIR OWN WORDS

"Share Our Wealth," 1934
Originally a supporter of Franklin D. Roosevelt, Senator Huey P. Long broke with Roosevelt by the middle of 1933 and began to propose his own solutions for the economic troubles of the Great Depression. He proposed the establishment of "Share Our Wealth" societies to agitate for changes in national economic policy.

People of America: In every community get together at once and organize a share-our-wealth society — Motto: Every man a king. . . .

There is nothing wrong with the United States. We have more food than we can eat. We have more clothes and things out of which to make clothes than we can wear. We have more houses and lands than the whole 120 million can use if they all had good homes. So what is the trouble? Nothing except that a handful of men have everything and the balance of the people have nothing if their debts were paid. There should be every man a king in this land flowing with milk and honey instead of the lords of finance at the top and slaves and peasants at the bottom. . . .

Title: Share-our-wealth society is simply to mean that God's creatures on this lovely American continent have a right to share in the wealth they have created in this country. They have the right to a living, with the conveniences and some of the luxuries of this life, so long as there are too many or enough for all. They have a right to raise their children in a healthy, wholesome atmosphere and to educate them, rather than to face the dread of their under-nourishment and sadness by being denied a real life.

---

believe in God, cheer when the flag passes by, the Bible Belt solid Americans." In 1935 Townsend claimed that 25 million people had signed petitions supporting his plan; even his detractors admitted that he probably had more than 10 million.

Father Charles Coughlin, a Roman Catholic priest at the Little Flower of Jesus Church in Royal Oak, Michigan, became a more menacing presence (see Chapter 28). In 1930, Coughlin struck a deal with the Columbia Broadcasting System to broadcast his sermons nationwide, and millions of Americans tuned in on Sundays to the "Radio Priest." Coughlin's program, "The Golden Hour of the Little Flower," claimed an estimated weekly audience of 25 to 40 million listeners — the biggest single following of any radio program during the decade. In 1934 Coughlin received more mail than any other person in the United States, including Roosevelt. At first, Coughlin offered a running commentary on the Depression and its causes, identifying Hoover as the foremost villain and a conspiracy of international bankers as the chief cause. Coughlin feared communism and supported Roosevelt's election.

Coughlin's Christian Front flourished particularly in Irish and German Catholic neighborhoods. Seeing "the Padre" as a bridge to the Catholic ethnic communities that he hoped to draw into the Democratic political coalition, Roosevelt courted Coughlin through two Irish-Catholic intermediaries — financier Joseph P. Kennedy and Detroit mayor Frank Murphy. But by 1935 Coughlin turned against the New Deal, and his sermons increasingly focused on political rather than religious themes. In particular, his criticism of law professor Felix Frank-

furter, who had become Roosevelt's trusted adviser, were tinged with anti-Semitism. The radio priest organized his backers into the National Union for Social Justice and began advocating a powerful state that resembled Fascist Italy.

While Townsend and Coughlin endangered the New Deal by proposing schemes that were either chimerical or unacceptable, the most serious political threat to Roosevelt in the 1930s was Louisiana Senator Huey P. Long (also see Chapter 28). Born in bitter poverty in northern Louisiana's hill country, Long completed a three-year law course at Tulane University in eight months, was admitted to the bar at twenty-one, and displayed his virtuosity before the U.S. Supreme Court by winning a case concerning Louisiana schools and gaining the admiration of Chief Justice William Howard Taft. Elected governor in 1928, Long initiated a series of stunning reforms in the schools and highway building. He was the only southern governor of the era to treat African Americans with respect. When the head of the Ku Klux Klan threatened to come to the state to campaign against him, Long told reporters: "Quote me as saying that that Imperial bastard will never set foot in Louisiana, and that when I call him a son of a bitch, I am not using profanity, but am referring to the circumstances of his birth." By 1930, when Long was elected to the Senate, he had dictatorial control of Louisiana — so complete that he continued to act as governor for two more years, holding both offices simultaneously. Long proudly wore the nickname "The Kingfish," taken from a wily character on the "Amos 'n' Andy" radio program (see Chapter 28).

At first, Long supported the New Deal, but in 1934 he

unleashed a withering barrage of criticism, picturing Roosevelt and his advisers as aristocrats out of touch with plain folks. Long labeled the NRA "Never Roosevelt Again," referred to the president as "Prince Franklin," and impishly nicknamed Secretary of Agriculture Henry Wallace "Lord Corn Wallace." Roosevelt reciprocated by privately calling Long one of the two most dangerous men in the country. (The other, in Roosevelt's opinion, was General Douglas MacArthur.)

Huey Long began touting his own program for the nation's recovery. Sometimes his tongue-in-cheek proposals were meant only to twit New Dealers — such as those to turn plowed lands into golf courses and to require that every unemployed citizen with spare time read the interminable novel *The Count of Monte Cristo*. More serious and dangerous was his proposal to redistribute the nation's wealth. In January 1934 Long launched a national political organization to support his "Share Our Wealth" campaign. Among other things, he proposed confiscating large fortunes, placing limits on annual earnings, and distributing money generously to every poor family. Long offered pensions to the elderly and educational assistance to the young, and he advocated a vast public works program, a shortened workweek, and a minimum wage. Long's program of confiscation and steeply progressive income taxes would suffice, he announced, to give to every American family a "household estate" of $5,000 — enough for a home, a car, and a radio — and each family would be guaranteed an annual income of $2,500 — nearly double the median family income at the time. Experts correctly pointed out that the Share Our Wealth scheme was economic fantasy, but the canny Long told the people: "Let no one tell you that it is difficult to redistribute the wealth of this land. It is simple." Long answered his critics with aplomb. Asked if he got his ideas from Einstein, the Kingfish replied: "It's all in the Scriptures," citing the Old Testament Jubilee.

By early 1935 Long had organized more than 27,000 clubs around the nation and his staff had a mailing list of 7.5 million names. Long's organization was headed by a talented Christian Church minister, Gerald L. K. Smith, a powerful speaker characterized by critics as a "combination Savonarola and Elmer Gantry." The Long political machine gave Roosevelt a fright. While the Louisiana senator posed no threat to Roosevelt's reelection in 1936, party leaders feared that he might siphon off as many as 3 or 4 million Democratic votes. By 1940, when Long would be only forty-six, he could be a serious presidential candidate. But that threat ended in September 1935, when Long was cut down by an assassin's bullet in the Louisiana State House. "I wonder why he shot me," Long gasped before lapsing into unconsciousness. His assassin, an idealistic young physician named Carl Austin Weiss, killed Long because his father-in-law, a district judge, had run afoul of Huey in the rough and tumble of Louisiana politics. Weiss's body was riddled by sixty-one bullets fired by Long's bodyguards.

ℰ *Launching the Second New Deal*

FDR's move to the left in 1935 was primarily inspired by his need to head off the combined challenges of Townsend, Coughlin, and Long. In his 1935 address to Congress, Roosevelt called for a broad program of legislation. He recommended an expansion of public works to meet the continued unemployment crisis, a system of social security that would cover the unemployed and the aged, a program to provide slum clearance and better housing, a reallocation of the nation's resources that would bring economic security to all, and specific guarantees of the rights of labor. Congress enacted another staggering corpus of law during the summer of 1935, including every major piece of legislation proposed by the president.

By the spring of 1935 Roosevelt's closest adviser was Harvard Law School professor Felix Frankfurter. Frankfurter was a frequent visitor to the White House, and two of his protégés, Ben Cohen and Tom Corcoran, became powerful White House aides. Advocates of a competitive economy rather than of planning, Roosevelt's new inner circle often seemed more concerned with the regulation of big business than with recovery.

Congress moved toward regulation in 1935 with the passage of the Public Utility Holding Company Act (Wheeler-Rayburn Act), forbidding pyramid ownership and requiring utility companies to demonstrate a localized, useful, and efficient character. Even though the Second New Deal marked a return to progressive notions of competition and regulation, it did not slow business concentration. By 1939 the 250 largest manufacturing firms in the nation owned 65 percent of the nation's productive capacity and in most major areas of the economy a few giant companies were a dominating presence.

ℰ *Extending Relief and Hoping for Recovery*

In January 1935 Roosevelt called for a gigantic public works program that would move people off welfare roles. Still appalled by the expenditure of millions on direct relief, Roosevelt warned: "The Federal Government must and shall quit this business of relief." In April Congress passed an Emergency Relief Appropriations Act that presented the president with the Depression's largest single appropriation ($4.88 billion), giving him broad discretionary powers in the use of the funds. Roosevelt allocated a portion of the funds to existing relief organizations, but by executive order he established a number of new agencies.

The largest single chunk of the appropriation was given to a huge public works organization, the Works Progress Administration (WPA), headed by Harry L. Hopkins. WPA employees were paid a "security wage" based on a sliding scale that took into account regional variations in wages. At its peak in March 1936 the WPA payroll included 3.4 million people; by the time the agency expired in 1943 it had employed more than 8.5 million people. The WPA was the backbone of the Second New Deal's relief efforts; the agency pumped $11 billion into the economy, about 85 percent of that amount being paid in wages.

Often criticized by New Deal opponents as the epitome of waste ("We Piddle Along"), the WPA clearly stimulated the economy and gave a measure of pride to those it rescued from the relief rolls. But despite both the denunciations leveled at it and Hopkins's soaring praise ("Give a man a dole and you save his body and destroy his spirit. Give him a job and you save both body and spirit"), the WPA still left many unemployed jobless. Those who did work for it found their treatment often unpleasant and their wages always pitifully low. Everywhere WPA wages were lower than the rate paid in the private sector. For some workers in the rural South the monthly WPA wage was only $19.

While a majority of WPA projects, like those of the PWA, involved construction of public facilities such as highways, airports, and educational buildings, the agency sponsored some highly visible programs employing skilled people. The WPA's Federal Theater Project employed around 10,000 performers and support personnel in the production of plays, circuses, and vaudeville shows that toured the nation. Many of its productions were amateurish, and the project became highly controversial because of its real and imagined political radicalism, but among its offerings was an innovative Orson Welles production of *Macbeth* featuring an African American cast. The Federal Writers Project published about a hundred books and hundreds of shorter publications, including a highly praised collection of travel guides to the states and territories, the American Guide Series. The Federal Art Project sponsored artists who taught and painted murals in hundreds of

public buildings. While much WPA art was mediocre, among the artists employed by the Federal Art Project were such later luminaries as Jackson Pollock and Stuart Davis. The Art Project also sponsored the collection of thousands of oral interviews with Civil War veterans, jazz greats, Native Americans, and — most important as a historical resource — former slaves.

Roosevelt created a number of other relief agencies out of the funds appropriated in the Emergency Relief Appropriations Act. The National Youth Administration was established in June of 1935 to help young people between sixteen and twenty-five. Most of those aided were students who worked in clerical jobs in schools and colleges.

Agriculture and the Second New Deal

Two agencies funded by the Emergency Relief Appropriations Act addressed rural problems. The Rural Electrification Administration (REA) was created to lend the entire cost of constructing light and power lines to cooperatives in rural areas where private companies deemed it unprofitable to invest. In 1935, 90 percent of the nation's farms had no electrical power, but with REA aid farmers formed cooperatives, borrowed money, and electrified their own farms. By 1941 about 40 percent of the nation's farms had electricity, and in 1950 about 90 percent did.

The most visionary experiment of the Second New Deal, and one that strongly appealed to Roosevelt's love for rural life, was the Resettlement Administration (RA). Headed by Rexford G. Tugwell, the RA loaned funds to small farmers for equipment, supervised their operations and offered advice, and took a percentage of their crops for payment. The RA served as the New Deal's primary agricultural reform organization until it was absorbed by the Farm Security Administration in 1937. Thereafter, the Farm Security Administration continued to help farmers buy land and also aided migrant workers by building a chain of sanitary, well-run migratory labor camps.

Of all the New Deal's programs, the RA was the most color-blind, fighting local prejudices to secure equal benefits for blacks. As its name implied, the philosophical goal of the program was the resettlement of urban slum dwellers in cooperative rural communities. Under the program three "greenbelt" communities were built near Washington, D.C., Cincinnati, and Milwaukee, and a few dozen farm communities were launched. But the RA never received sufficient allocations to undertake major resettlement. Fewer than five thousand families were actually resettled, a far cry from the 500,000 originally targeted.

The New Deal's agricultural policy appeared to be stymied when the Supreme Court nullified the AAA in early 1936, ruling 6-3 that the processing tax was an illegal attempt to regulate production. Congress responded by passing the Soil Conservation Act and Domestic Allotment Act in 1936, as well as a second Agricultural Adjustment Act in 1938. In effect, these laws removed the processing tax but preserved the basic features of the earlier AAA, offering farmers parity price guarantees in return for acreage allotments on certain staple crops. The measures failed to reduce agricultural production, and as surpluses grew, the United States dumped wheat and cotton on the world market. New Deal agricultural policies stabilized farm prices and provided credit for farmers based on their surplus crops, but only World War II saved American agriculture from the effects of huge surpluses.

The agricultural legislation of the Second New Deal frequently embodied conservation principles. Farmers were offered incentives and direct payments to take land out of production and to plant grasslands. In an effort to avert the most harmful side effects of earlier acreage reductions, Second New Deal legislation tried to assure that sharecroppers and tenants would share in the subsidies.

❧ Social Security and the Wealth-Tax Act

The Social Security Act of 1935 was the cornerstone of the emerging American welfare state edifice and is generally considered the most significant single piece of New Deal legislation. Even so, the law was quite limited, and it was enacted several generations after the appearance of similar social programs in Europe.

The act created an annuity financed by taxes on

Launching Social Security   When the Social Security Act went into effect, in 1935, it produced a windfall for wage earners who were at or over the age of sixty-five. Posters such as this urged everyone to apply for a Social Security number. Those excluded were not, however, as "few" as the fine print on the poster implied. Farmers, agricultural workers, and domestic servants—in all, many millions of working Americans in 1935—were not eligible for Social Security. U.S. government employees, also excluded, already had their own pension programs.

workers' wages and employer contributions to provide retirement benefits at age sixty-five. It also set up a system of joint federal and state unemployment insurance and provided matching funds to states for the relief of indigents and some health benefits for the poor. Conservatives attacked the legislation as another infringement on individual self-reliance, while others charged that the Social Security Act did far too little. The program omitted many workers, including agricultural laborers and domestics. The fact that states established the standards for welfare and unemployment relief led to vast regional differences in those programs. Nonetheless, the Social Security Act significantly expanded the concept that the federal government was responsible for protecting certain individual rights.

In a larger sense, the Second New Deal, and especially Social Security, laid the groundwork for twentieth-century entitlement programs in which particular interest groups staked claims to permanent protection. Social Security withstood a test in the Supreme Court; in later years, both Republican and Democratic administrations would expand its benefits.

Conceptually more radical than Social Security, in June 1935 Roosevelt called for a sweeping tax revision to redistribute wealth. The Wealth Tax Act, labeled by its opponents a "soak-the-rich" plan, called for increased inheritance taxes, a gift tax, a steeply graduated income tax, and a corporation income tax scaled according to the size of income. Many felt that the president's tax proposal was a capitulation to Huey Long, but Congress watered it down before passing a version that included only a token corporation tax and dropped the inheritance tax altogether. The result was a mild defeat for the president that neither balanced the budget, soaked the rich, nor redistributed wealth and produced only about $250 million in revenue. Theoretically, the administration had got a progressive tax that would aid the poor, but such measures rarely survive without being seriously diluted.

If the Wealth Tax Act failed to alter the nation's basic class structure, Roosevelt's use of deficit spending during the Second New Deal marked a new and portentous departure in government efforts to counter the effects of economic depressions. Economics had gained prestige in the 1920s as a specialized field. In spite of the almost universal incorrectness of economic predictions during the twenties, the number of professional economists increased during the thirties, and unprecedented numbers filled government positions.

In 1935 John Maynard Keynes, a British genius whose many accomplishments included expertise in the recondite world of international finance, published the most important economic treatise of the twentieth century, *The General Theory of Employment, Interest, and Money.* Virtually inventing macroeconomics, Keynes in the *General Theory* argued that in the aggregate — that is, at the national level — markets worked in ways that were fundamentally different from the expectations of economic orthodoxy. Keynes used powerful analytical tools to show how the Depression had occurred and how it should be combated. His answer was to use governments' enormous powers to tax, spend, and manipulate the money supply and interest rates, all with the aim of ratcheting up aggregate demand. Only by incurring large deficits, sponsoring huge public works, and otherwise placing large amounts of money in consumers' hands could the United States, Great Britain, and other Depression-wracked capitalist nations put themselves back on the road to prosperity.

Economists in the 1930s, as in other times, were sharply divided. Orthodox theorists, whom Hoover and most other political leaders had followed, seemed discredited. Many people in the decade embraced Marxism of various hues (from Norman Thomas's democratic version to the Stalinism of the Soviet Union), all of which saw the Great Depression as capitalism's death throes. Those who still hoped to see capitalism survive but despaired of orthodoxy could follow Keynes — that is, if they were among the handful of experts who understood his highly technical arguments. Much easier to comprehend, and therefore more attractive to New Deal economic strategists, was the theoretical school known as institutional economics. It emphasized government management of the economy through national planning based on careful scientific study, but to a large extent institutionalists despaired of ever reviving a self-regulating market system.

However, one important New Deal official independently arrived at conclusions quite similar to those of Keynes — Utah economist and banker Marriner Eccles. As head of the Federal Reserve System, Eccles drafted the Banking Act of 1935. The law gave the Federal Reserve complete control over credit, greatly increasing the board's ability to stimulate the economy. Although government manipulation of credit could accomplish little in an economic dislocation as severe as that of the 1930s, the restructured Fed functioned well in preventing future recessions and stock market crashes (such as those of 1987 and 1998) from turning into reruns of the Great Depression.

✆ *The Triumph of Labor*

Labor had gained much from the enactment of Section 7(a) of the NIRA, and labor supporters in Congress, led by New York Senator Robert Wagner, moved swiftly to secure new legislation when it became clear that the NIRA would be killed by the Supreme Court. Reflecting congressional rather than presidential initiative (for Roosevelt at first opposed it), the National Labor Relations Act (or Wagner Act) of July 1935 was the most pivotal triumph in American labor history. The law established a powerful National Labor Relations Board (NLRB), and, in effect, threw the weight of the government behind the right of labor to bargain collectively, to strike, and to conduct boycotts. The NLRB supervised elections at the request of workers, defined unfair labor practices, and received broad powers to issue cease-and-desist orders when employers resorted to such practices as blacklists and yellow-dog contracts (in which employees agreed not to join unions). The Wagner Act was a stunning victory for unions, placing them on a near-equal bargaining level with big business.

The Wagner Act was upheld by the Supreme Court in a crucial decision in March 1937, leading to a flurry of state labor laws known as "little Wagner Acts." In addition, the Second New Deal enacted a variety of specific laws that expanded labor rights, notably the Walsh-Healy Government Contracts Act, which controlled the labor practices of all businesses with contracts with the federal government, required minimum wages and a forty hour workweek, and barred child and convict labor.

The Second New Deal's labor laws passed with stunning ease, even though Roosevelt was a less-than-enthusiastic supporter of some of them. But by 1935 it was clear to New Dealers, as well as to Communists and other radicals, that the organized labor movement did not pose a threat to capitalism or property rights. Thus unions, like the elderly and farmers, became part of the Democratic Party coalition. The Democratic Party welcomed the unions as an interest group with legitimate claims on the broker state.

THE LIMITS OF REFORM

The first four years of the New Deal witnessed the most prolific outburst of legislation and growth in the federal bureaucracy in American history. The public endorsed the changes by giving FDR one of the most spectacular victories in American political history in the election of 1936. In the wake of the election, with an unprecedented party majority in Congress, Roosevelt seemed positioned to work his will in directing the nation's recovery.

While some important legislation was added to the New Deal after 1936, the president met increasing resistance in Congress and suffered a series of political defeats. Roosevelt experienced three major setbacks in 1937 and 1938. First, the economy was beset by a round of labor disputes, and a deep recession wiped out much that had been gained during the previous four years. Second, after a bitter battle Congress refused to pass a proposed reform of the Supreme Court. Third, Roosevelt failed when he tried to purge the Democratic party of conservatives during the congressional elections in 1938. By 1938 the New Deal was pretty much finished, and the aggressions of Germany, Italy, and Japan were turning the president's attention to foreign affairs.

✆ *The Democratic Sweep of 1936*

To oppose FDR, the GOP nominated Kansas governor Alfred M. Landon, the only Republican governor reelected in the Democratic landslide of 1934. Landon was a progressive who attracted some Wilsonian Democrats disenchanted with the New Deal, including Al Smith. The Republicans charged that the New Deal had undermined the American virtues of thrift and self-reliance and had replaced capitalism with a collectivist state. Roosevelt, they insisted, had usurped the authority of the other branches of government.

Long's assassination had removed the threat of a major third-party vote, but North Dakota Representative William Lemke caused some concern for Democrats when he accepted the nomination of the Union Party. Backed by Father Coughlin, who in 1936 had begun to call the president "Franklin Double-Crossing Roosevelt," the Union party platform made a pitch for support from Long's following and Townsend's movement. The Lemke candidacy added a note of uncertainty to the campaign; Gerald L. K. Smith, heir of Long's mailing list, promised to deliver 6 million votes for Lemke. To some, Smith's demagoguery seemed to surpass that of his mentor, Long. Mencken labeled him "the deadliest and damndest orator ever heard on this or any other earth . . . the champion boob-bumper of all epochs."

The campaign of 1936 was bitterly fought; few people anticipated the Democrats' landslide victory. About 80 percent of the nation's press was Republican, and its coverage of the campaign distorted the public mood. Although Landon tried at first to present himself as a progressive who would make the New Deal work better, strident right-wingers overwhelmed the Republican message. Roosevelt promised no dramatic new measures to combat the Depression; the vigorous Democratic campaign centered almost entirely on the personal charisma of the president, picturing him as a strong leader capable of saving the country.

Extremist Republican attacks made FDR seem more radical than he really was. But Roosevelt indulged in a little demagoguery himself, loudly denouncing the "economic royalists." "The forces of selfishness and of lust for power," he cried in one speech, "have never before in our history ... been so united against one candidate as they stand today. They are united in their hate for me — and I welcome their hatred." In this decade of intense class antagonisms, such rhetoric was welcome to the many ordinary Americans who felt bitterly alienated from those for whom they blamed the Depression. More movingly — and prophetically — the president also told the nation that "this generation has a rendezvous with destiny."

Roosevelt won the largest electoral majority since the beginning of the two-party system — 523 to 8, carrying every state except Maine and Vermont. He polled a popular vote of 27.7 million to Landon's 16.6 million; Lemke received an unimpressive 882,000 votes. The Democrats amassed huge majorities in both houses of Congress — 77-19 in the Senate and 328-107 in the House. The Democratic majority in the Senate was so large that a dozen freshmen senators were forced to sit on the Republican side of the aisle. The election crippled the Republican Party for years. Less noticed, the election of 1936 revealed that Roosevelt's reform image had virtually destroyed the left wing of American politics. The Communist Party had never won much of a hold in the American electorate and received only about 80,000 votes in 1936. More telling was the decline in popularity of the Socialist Party, whose candidate, Norman Thomas, received fewer than 200,000 votes.

The election of 1936 was a referendum on Roosevelt and the New Deal; the result showed that several groups of voters, including millions of young people, those aided by relief programs, and workers in the expanded federal bureaucracy had shifted to the Democratic Party. Organized labor also vigorously supported Roosevelt in 1936. The CIO contributed the enormous sum of $770,000 to the Democratic Party, nearly $500,000 coming from John L. Lewis's United Mine Workers. The labor vote shifted en masse to the Democratic Party, and was probably decisive in such key states as Ohio, Illinois, and Indiana.

Many of these new Democrats were also first-generation immigrants. In 1936, at FDR's urging, urban Democrats abolished the two-thirds rule that had been required for the Democratic presidential nomination ever since Jacksonian times, a provision that had granted southern Democrats a veto. Roosevelt carefully cultivated the urban, heavily Roman Catholic vote. Significantly, under the Republican presidents of the 1920s only one of twenty-five judicial appointments went to Roman Catholics; under Roosevelt the figure was one in four.

Another new group in the Democratic coalition was blacks. As early as 1932, some Republicans sensed that blacks felt neglected in the party of Lincoln. Nevertheless, Hoover had still won almost three-fourths of the black vote — this at a time when unemployment among African Americans approached 50 percent. (These were *northern* black votes; in the Democratic Solid South, Jim Crow laws almost entirely barred blacks from the polls.) As late as 1936, many black intellectuals believed that Roosevelt had done no better for them than Hoover. But while FDR's record was far from strong, some New Deal agencies honestly tried to be non-discriminatory, and Eleanor Roosevelt and Secretary of Agriculture Henry Wallace were earnest and visible supporters of black rights. The president's executive order in 1935 banning racial discrimination in the WPA may not have been totally effective, but it was a step in the right direction, and blacks appreciated it. African Americans clearly contributed to the Democratic landslide in 1936 by giving Roosevelt three-fourths of their votes. In mid-1938 a *Fortune* magazine poll revealed that nearly 85 percent of blacks considered themselves pro-Roosevelt. "Let Jesus lead you and Roosevelt feed you," preached one black minister. It was a message born more of hope than of reality.

❧ A Faltering Recovery and Labor Unrest

The economy recovered strongly in 1936; by early 1937 unemployment had fallen to between 6 and 7 million. But in the summer a major decline virtually wiped out the gains; by 1938 unemployment had risen to 11 million and other economic indicators suggested similar reversals. Long saddled with responsibility for the Great Depression, Republicans gleefully blamed Roosevelt, and to some extent they were right. During the 1936 campaign and at the outset of his second term, FDR repeatedly asserted that the New Deal was curing the Depression. With unemployment hovering around 14 percent and growth sluggish, it was much too early to make such a claim — but the president's acceptance of his own rhetoric may have led him into a colossal policy blunder. In the summer of 1937, weakened by a battle over the Supreme Court and perhaps truly convinced that the Depression was ending, the president appeased conservative congressional critics by slashing the WPA's budget. Meanwhile the Federal Reserve raised interest rates, just as the new Social Security payroll taxes were starting to bite for workers and employers alike. These negative factors combined in August 1937 to produce a new stock market crash. Within two months, the Dow fell by 60 percent, and by March 1938 unemployment soared to almost 20 percent. Although the administration sought political damage control by calling the downturn a "recession" (a euphemism first introduced on this occasion), what had occurred was no minor blip, but a return to the bleakest conditions of the Great Depression.

The president's desire to cut spending and balance the budget, matched by the Fed's obsessions about inflation, had produced exactly the wrong policies — but Roosevelt simply did not know what to do next. Business-oriented advisers and orthodox economists told him to retrench; New Dealers like Hopkins and Fed chairman Eccles told him to loosen the purse strings. Although they had not studied (or did not understand) his theories, these advisers' stand coincided roughly with Keynes's prescription of heavy government spending to break the Depression's grip. To FDR, however, Keynes's ideas were simply a "rigmarole of figures," and he clung to the orthodox remedy of retrenchment and a balanced budget. Then another sharp drop in the stock market forced Roosevelt and Congress to do something dramatic, and $3.75 billion (even more than the president sought) was appropriated for the WPA. Although it did not restore prosperity, by 1939 the heavy new spending helped stabilize the economy at the early 1937 level — at which point Roosevelt and Congress again tried to economize.

Neither the White House nor Capitol Hill was prepared to follow a sustained Keynesian policy of deliberately incurring large deficits to stimulate recovery

The UAW Flint Sit-down Strike   Workers in the General Motors Fisher body plant in Flint staged a sit-down strike, taking over the plant on December 30, 1936. Their strike lasted over six weeks and triggered a nationwide strike of General Motors facilities.

in times of economic contraction. No president would do that until John F. Kennedy and Lyndon Johnson in the 1960s. As late as 1941, almost 10 percent of the work force was still unemployed, and only the unprecedented federal spending and huge draft calls of World War II would lift the United States out of the Great Depression (see Chapter 29).

Although Roosevelt rejected Keynesianism, he did respond to the economic crisis of 1937-38 by sharpening his rhetoric and reviving the Progressive-Era anti-monopoly crusades. Blaming the nation's economic woes on "the power and privileges of small minorities," FDR for a while let the Justice Department build legal cases against various large economic concentrations (some of which had been encouraged by earlier New Deal policies). Before much headway could be made, however, the military buildup that preceded America's entry into World War II killed off the late New Deal's zeal for trust-busting and gave big business a new lease on life.

Complicating the struggle for recovery was the militancy of organized labor in the wake of the Roosevelt landslide — a victory for which labor claimed much credit. The newly won legal rights of labor unions had precipitated a revolution within the labor movement and a total rejection of the "welfare capitalism" of the 1920s. Grasping the potential to organize trade unions after the passage of the Wagner Act in 1935, militant union leaders, led by John L. Lewis, formed the Committee of Industrial Organizations. These radical leaders operated as an ostensible committee within the AFL until October 1938, when Lewis was expelled and the group changed its name to the Congress of Industrial Organizations (CIO). The aggressiveness of trade union organizers — almost a third of them Communists — triggered a wave of strikes, numbering 4,700 in 1937. The proportion of the nation's work force out on strike rose from 3.1 percent in 1936 to 7.2 percent in 1937.

"Sit-down" strikes, widely used in 1937, were particularly controversial. A tactic devised by French Communists in which workers locked themselves into their factories, the first sit-down in America began spontaneously in November 1936 in the Goodyear Tire factory in Akron, Ohio. In December the tactic was used in a highly publicized strike at the Fisher body plant operated by General Motors in Flint, Michigan. For six weeks sit-downers shut down General Motors, sparking repeated clashes between union and non-union workers, before the company capitulated to union demands in February 1937.

The victory of the United Automotive Workers was followed a month later by a U.S. Steel contract that granted recognition to the union, a wage boost, and a forty-hour week. By the summer of 1937 other major steel companies accepted unionization, as did every major automobile producer except Ford (which brutally fought the unions). Within a year, the tough tactics of the CIO leaders had virtually completed the unionization of American industry.

Labor activism proved to be a divisive issue within the Democratic Party. Middle-class Democrats who supported Roosevelt's efforts at recovery, as well as most southern Democrats, reacted with hostility to labor's assertive demands. Although Roosevelt generally sympathized with the working class, he distrusted labor unions, disliked the questionably legal sit-down strikes, and resented John L. Lewis's insinuations that huge union contributions to the Democratic Party in 1936 had placed him under obligation. Nonetheless, Roosevelt did not intervene in the strikes, as some of his advisers wished; asked in a June 1937 press conference if he agreed with opinion polls showing public distaste for strikers, Roosevelt responded with a lofty Shakespearean quote: "A plague on both your houses." By 1937, 45 percent of respondents in a Gallup poll deemed that the Roosevelt administration was "too friendly" to labor. Conservative, mainly southern Democrats became less and less dependable political allies.

❧ The "Court-Packing" Fight

In his second inaugural address, Roosevelt proclaimed himself a determined reformer, dedicated to improving the lot of the "one third of a nation ill-housed, ill-clad, ill-nourished." The New Deal seemed headed in an even more radical direction. Many expected Roosevelt to launch his second term with a new flurry of legislative initiatives aimed at economic recovery. Instead, his most important proposal called for a sweeping reform of the Supreme Court. Roosevelt's fight with the Court had been brewing for months, prompted by a steady stream of Court decisions invalidating New Deal programs. In 1935, the Supreme Court had four confirmed conservatives (popularly known as the Four Horsemen) who voted consistently against New Deal legislation (James McReynolds, George Sutherland, Willis Van Devanter, and Pierce Butler); three dependable liberals (Louis Brandeis, Benjamin Cardozo, and Harlan Fiske Stone); and two "roving justices," Chief Justice Charles Evans Hughes and Owen Roberts, who sometimes voted with the conservatives and sometimes with the liberals. The conservatives almost always won the support of one of the roving justices, resulting in a series of 5-4 decisions overturning New Deal legislation.

The Court began chipping away at the New Deal in January 1935, ruling that a portion of the NIRA was unconstitutional. By summer, the stream of unfavorable decisions reached a torrent. The Court struck down the NRA and the AAA and ruled that a New York state minimum wage law was unconstitutional. As the Wagner Act and other Second New Deal legislation neared Supreme Court tests in 1936 Roosevelt was frustrated and angry. He felt that he had won a sweeping popular referendum for the New Deal, and that the will of the people was being undermined by the Court.

In February 1937 Roosevelt submitted to Congress a Judiciary Reform Act that provided for the appointment of forty-four new judges in the lower federal courts and the addition of as many as six new Supreme Court justices. Arguing disingenuously that the Supreme Court was overworked, and that many of the justices were too old, the president proposed to add a new justice for each sitting judge over seventy years of age who had been on the court for ten years and who did not wish to retire. The bill offended even the liberals on the court; Brandeis, the oldest justice, and Chief Justice Charles Evans Hughes vigorously denied that the court's workload demanded such reorganization.

Roosevelt for a moment lost his political finesse

and bungled the Court battle. The bill was hatched in secret and foisted on Congress without warning. The Judiciary Reorganization Act stalled in Congress and was finally withdrawn after 168 days. Although Roosevelt insisted that his motives were nonpolitical, the bill was clearly an effort to coerce the Court. When it encountered serious resistance in Congress, Roosevelt refused to compromise and wasted valuable time and influence fighting for a lost cause.

The president paid a heavy price for his obstinacy; the fight left him scared and the myth of presidential invincibility broken. Many Americans who shared Roosevelt's disenchantment with the Supreme Court's conservatism rallied behind the hallowed concept of separation of powers; some people unfairly compared Roosevelt's assault on the court to Hitler's ruthless seizure of power in Germany. Roosevelt's political enemies and those who opposed the New Deal's economic and social reforms, both Republicans and Democrats, got new leases on life.

Roosevelt was bitter and hurt by the defeat, although he boasted afterward that he lost the battle but won the war. Perhaps alarmed by Roosevelt's attack, in the spring Justices Hughes and Roberts joined the court liberals in a series of 5-4 decisions that upheld a Washington minimum wage law, the Wagner Act, and Social Security — assuring the validity of the Second New Deal. In May, Justice Van Devanter retired and Roosevelt appointed liberal Alabama senator Hugo Black to replace him, the first of five justices he would put on the Court during his second term. The "Roosevelt Court" — anchored by three of the most celebrated liberal jurists of the twentieth century, Black (1937), Frankfurter (1939), and William O. Douglas (1939) — greatly extended the government's right to regulate the economy while at the same time jealously seeking to guard the civil liberties of minorities. During the next half century the Supreme Court would not overturn a single piece of significant state or national socioeconomic legislation.

❧ The Primaries Purge of 1938

Franklin D. Roosevelt was an enormously popular president, and Congress granted him exceptional powers during the Depression. But Congress never abdicated all power to Roosevelt during the New Deal; the initiative for much welfare and labor legislation came from Congress. By 1936, many congressional leaders were uneasy about growing executive power, and the "court packing" fight deepened those concerns.

At the same time, Roosevelt's control over his party began to slip. Ironically, the Democrats' extraordinary success weakened party unity and promoted factionalism. In the summer of 1937, as the "Roosevelt Recession" began and labor unrest continued, conservative Democrats joined Republicans in the Senate to block further New Deal legislation. Vice-President Garner headed a coalition of southern Democrats angered by Roosevelt's

---

✳ **I N T H E I R O W N W O R D S**

Opposition to "Court-Packing," New York Herald-Tribune, 1937

When Franklin D. Roosevelt proposed creating six more seats on the Supreme Court, opponents accused him of attempting to destroy the American system of checks and balances by seizing control of the judicial branch of government.

In this one hundred and sixty-first year of the independence of the United States, President Roosevelt has brought forward a proposal which, if enacted into law, would end the American State as it has existed throughout the long years of its life.

The plan is put forward with all the artistry of the President's political mind. He speaks in the name of "youth," always a popular and appealing note. He dangles before the House and Senate fifty new and important jobs, always ripe and luscious bait for the Congressional mind. He ingeniously conveys the impression that all he seeks is a routine and moderate effort to speed up justice and improve the whole Federal bench.

Yet, beneath this veneer of politeness, the brutal fact is that President Roosevelt would pack the Supreme Court with six new justices of his own choosing.

No President of the United States ever before made the least gesture toward attempting to gain such a vast grant of power. Mr. Roosevelt demands it, calmly, artfully. By one legislative act, availing himself of the one loophole in the Constitution — the failure to specify the number of members in the Supreme Court — he would strike at the roots of that equality of the three branches of government upon which the nation is founded, and centralize in himself the control of judicial, as well as executive functions.

It was a French King, Louis XIV, who said, "L'etat, c'est moi" — "I am the State." The paper shell of American constitutionalism would continue if President Roosevelt secured the passage of the law he now demands. But it would be only a shell.

inaction against the sit-down strikers, his failure to balance the budget, and his early support of an anti-lynching bill (which was defeated in Congress by a filibuster). Southern Democrats were particularly restive at finding themselves in a political coalition with organized labor and blacks, and they were furious over Roosevelt's rescinding of the two-thirds rule that had allowed them a veto over Democratic presidential nominations.

Frustrated by this rebellion within the Democratic Party, a caucus of Roosevelt advisers that included Hopkins, Tom Corcoran, Ickes, and the president's son James urged Roosevelt to purge the party of its conservatives. Roosevelt took up the cause in the summer of 1938; he denounced "copperheads" within the party and worked vainly to defeat several southern senators in the primaries. Some of Roosevelt's candidates won, but he failed to unseat senators Walter George in Georgia, "Cotton" Ed Smith in South Carolina, and Millard Tydings in Maryland. Asked after the election whether Roosevelt was not his own worst enemy, the reelected Smith snorted: "Not as long as I am alive." In general, Roosevelt's effort to "purge" the Democratic party in the primaries added new weight to the charges that he wanted to be a dictator — the word *purge* had come to have a sinister meaning in connection with the brutality of Stalin in Russia and Hitler in Germany. Roosevelt's opponents charged that Harry Hopkins had manipulated WPA roles to increase the number of voters on the federal payroll on election day. As a result, in 1939 Congress passed the Hatch Act, forbidding political activity by federal employees.

❧ *The New Deal Ends*

The Democrats suffered broad losses in the elections of 1938. The Republicans picked up eighty-one seats in the House of Representatives and eight in the Senate, and had a net gain of thirteen governorships. The Democrats still held large majorities in both houses of Congress, and Roosevelt boasted that he was the first two-term president since Monroe not to lose control of Congress during his second term. Nonetheless, Republican gains, the conservative southern rebellion within the Democratic Party, and the assumption that he was now a "lame duck" ended FDR's dominance of domestic politics.

Congress did pass some significant legislation as the New Deal drew to a close. The Administrative Reorganization Act passed in 1939 at the president's request, similar bills having been defeated in 1937 and 1938 when Congress was most sensitive to charges that the president had dictatorial ambitions. Congress also passed an important labor law in 1938, the Fair Labor Standards Act. The law set federal standards for minimum wages and maximum hours and banned child labor. Passage of the law required skillful lobbying by Roosevelt; it pitted a coalition of northern liberals, reformers, and supporters of large corporations against those representing small businesses, farmers, much of the labor movement, and the South. Although the bill did not cover many types of laborers, it gave raises to about 12 million workers and set a precedent for later federal wage regulation. "That's that," said Roosevelt prophetically. The Fair Labor Standards Act was the last New Deal reform to be enacted.

In late 1938 Congress began dismantling parts of the New Deal. Relief expenditures were cut and some controversial programs, including the Federal Theater Project, were eliminated. The Senate blocked a number of Roosevelt's appointments. Nothing better illustrated the changing mood in Congress than the creation of the House Committee on Un-American Activities in 1938. Headed by right-wing Texas Democrat Martin Dies, the committee largely ignored fascists (its ostensible target) while conducting highly charged investigations of communist activities. Supposedly nonpartisan, the hearings actually served the purposes of those who believed that the New Deal was communist-inspired and the labor movement communist-infested. The president was angered by the investigations, but by 1939 his attention had turned to the unfolding global crisis. For the first time since his inauguration, in his address to Congress in 1939 Roosevelt asked for no new domestic legislation, stressing dangers abroad.

CONCLUSION: THE DEPRESSION AND THE POLITICAL TRANSFORMATION OF AMERICA

The Depression of the 1930s was a worldwide catastrophe. It contributed to the collapse of liberal democracies around the world and the rise of totalitarian governments, and, in a variety of ways, to the international instability that brought on World War II. Fortunately, in the United States the political changes wrought by the Depression were less cataclysmic than elsewhere. The nation survived with an undiminished faith in popular democracy and equal opportunity — that is, in the American Dream.

Franklin Delano Roosevelt and the New Deal substantially changed the nation's political structure. The

New Deal increased the size of the federal bureaucracy by 50 percent — from 600,000 in 1932 to 950,000 in 1939 — and the numerous new government programs and agencies brought the federal government into contact with millions of citizens. This expanding federal government caused some resentment, but, on the whole, the traditional American distrust of government diminished. Roosevelt also greatly enlarged the powers of the presidency. Theodore Roosevelt and Woodrow Wilson had submitted legislative proposals to Congress, but FDR made the executive branch the major source of planning. By the end of his presidency, Congress expected to be presented with a presidential program, and that pattern endures.

The Depression decade also witnessed a major shift in the balance between the political parties. The Democratic party was transformed from a fiscally conservative, states'-rights, minority party into the "natural party of government" — a majority party that was liberal, urban, sympathetic to the underdog, and strongly supported by Catholics, Jews, African Americans, and union members. While Roosevelt's party remained culturally conservative and unresponsive to civil rights reform pressures, it laid the groundwork for modern economic liberalism. On the other hand, opponents of the New Deal condemned the growth of government bureaucracy and the Democratic Party's appeals to class and minority interests. They joined pro-business advocates to form the modern conservative coalition.

The New Deal resembled the amorphous and experimental mind-set of Roosevelt. While some early New Deal legislation embraced mild forms of national planning, and the AAA perpetuated a degree of planning, the clearest overall intent of the New Deal was to build a pluralistic society in which competing groups would be represented and would receive a fair share of the national wealth. When Roosevelt took office, the white, Protestant, middle-class owners of the nation's industry and farms unquestionably dominated the country politically and economically. Those people remained powerful at the end of the Depression (and still do), but organized labor, immigrants, and Catholics had gained new clout, adding more balance to the nation's power structure.

For the most part, the New Deal was intended to rectify the suffering and injustices brought on by the Depression. Its failures are obvious. The New Deal did little to redistribute national income. It did not eliminate unemployment or poverty. Most of the nation's laborers remained unrepresented by unions, and corporations continued to wield great economic and political power. Although organized labor gained new political clout under the New Deal, other victims of discrimination, including working women and blacks, gained little. In fact, many of the basic social programs of the New Deal, including the Social Security Act (especially Old Age Assistance, Old Age Insurance, Aid to Dependent Children, and Unemployment Insurance) and the Fair Labor Standards Act, ended up creating a system that privileged and catered to white male wage earners and salaried employees. By treating women as wives, argued feminists in later years, New Deal legislation entrenched their status as unequal.

Although the New Deal gave hints that deficit spending by the government could stimulate economic recovery, the actual amounts spent — unprecedented by historic standards — were still insufficient to jumpstart a real recovery. In 1939 the performance of the economy remained significantly below what it had been ten years earlier.

On the other hand, the New Deal could justly claim some successes. Its aim was to provide security to a broad range of Americans, not only to the unemployed and disadvantaged through relief and Social Security, but also to capitalists, labor, business people, and farmers. Social Security, unemployment insurance, and federal relief — all of which immediately became politically sacrosanct "entitlements" — would henceforth constitute a safety-net ensuring Americans that hard times would never again mean utter ruin. For economists, there was another term for the "safety-net": *stabilizers,* the built-in triggers that would tend to keep future recessions from turning into catastrophic depressions. American economic history for the rest of the twentieth century repeatedly showed how well these stabilizers worked.

The New Deal, in short, launched the American welfare state. Later generations of Americans would accept as a matter of course the federal government's primary role in keeping the economy healthy and citizens reasonably secure.

The New Deal was so lacking in philosophical coherence, and its programs were so large and loosely controlled at regional and local levels, that it provided a laboratory for testing a wide variety of ideas. An extraordinary variety of do-gooders and visionaries were scattered through the layers of government bureaucracy, turning government agencies into humane instruments that touched millions of lives. Perhaps most important, Franklin Roosevelt and the New Deal restored the people's confidence in American political and economic institutions, while exalting no ideology except pragmatic experimentalism.

In the long run, the New Deal hastened the nation along the road toward a liberal capitalistic society in which the federal government would balance the interests of various competing forces, becoming a "broker state." While the government assumed more regulatory powers than most earlier progressives had envisioned, the New Deal did not depart sharply from past reform traditions. Economic decision-making remained in private hands, and the free-market economy survived the Depression unscathed. With the minor exception of the TVA experiment in the production of electric power, the United States alone of the major industrial nations of the world established no state-owned enterprises.

The Depression made it clear that the foundation of modern capitalism is an economic expansion that encourages maximum production, consumption, profits, and jobs. During the thirties the government accepted the responsibility for stimulating and stabilizing the market economy. Thus, politicians seeking to escape recessions became the chief benefactors of corporations that provided the jobs necessary for economic growth.

"Before Roosevelt, the Federal Government hardly touched your life," recalled a Chicago worker. "Outside the postman, there was little local representation. Now people you knew were appointed to government jobs. Joe Blow or some guy from the corner." This anonymous Chicagoan exaggerated the extent to which the nation's Joe Blows were getting federal office jobs — though many of their sons, daughters, and grandchildren would. But he was on the mark in grasping how ordinary Americans' understanding of their self-interest was changing as a result of the New Deal. Working-class and ethnic Americans learned how greatly federal policies mattered in their lives. It would make them and their children lifelong Democrats and give them a strong stake in an expansive government. In the longer run, it would seal their full entry into the modern Republic's structure of power.

SUGGESTED READING

Alan Brinkley, *The End of Reform: New Deal Liberalism in Recession and War* (1995). Explores the difficulties encountered by New Deal liberals after 1937.

Frank Freidel, *Franklin D. Roosevelt: A Rendezvous with Destiny* (1990). The standard one-volume biography.

David M. Kennedy, *Freedom from Fear: The American People in Depression and War, 1929-1945* (1999). The most important and sweeping overview of the period, Kennedy's study is weighted heavily toward political

history. A brilliant contribution to the Oxford History of the United States series.

William E. Leuchtenburg, *Franklin D. Roosevelt and the New Deal* (1963). An excellent brief survey of the New Deal.

William E. Leuchtenburg, *The Supreme Court Reborn: The Constitutional Revolution in the Age of Roosevelt* (1995), and *The FDR Years: On Roosevelt and His Legacy* (1995). Two books of essays on various New Deal and Depression topics written by a leading expert.

Joan Hoff Wilson, *Herbert Hoover: Forgotten Progressive* (1975). Portrays Hoover as a surprisingly forward-looking progressive.

SUGGESTIONS FOR FURTHER READING

W. Andrew Achenbaum, *Social Security: Visions and Revisions* (1986).

Edward Berkowitz, *America's Welfare State* (1991).

Michael A. Bernstein, *The Great Depression: Delayed Recovery and Economic Change in America, 1929-1939* (1987).

Alan Brinkley, *Voices of Protest: Huey Long, Father Coughlin, and the Great Depression* (1982).

Blanche Wiesen Cook, *Eleanor Roosevelt: A Life,* Vol 1, 1884-1933 (1992).

Matthew J. Dickinson, *Bitter Harvest: FDR, Presidential Power and the Growth of the Presidential Branch* (1997).

Steve Fraser, *Labor Will Rule: Sydney Hillman and the Rise of American Labor* (1991).

Linda Gordon, *Pitied But Not Entitled: Single Mothers and the History of Welfare* (1994).

Nelson Lichtenstein, *The Most Dangerous Man in Detroit: Walter Reuther and the Fate of American Labor* (1996).

Suzanne Mettler, *Dividing Citizens: Gender and Federalism in New Deal Public Policy* (1998).

Roger Newman, *Hugo Black: A Biography* (1994).

James T. Patterson, *The New Deal and the States: Federalism in Transition* (1969).

Albert U. Romasco, *The Poverty of Abundance: Hoover, the Nation, the Depression* (1965).

Jordan A. Schwarz, *The New Dealers* (1993).

Bruce Shulman, *From Cotton Belt to Sunbelt* (1991).

Harvard Sitkoff, *A New Deal for Blacks* (1978).

Patricia Sullivan, *Days of Hope: Race and Democracy in the New Deal Era* (1996).

Peter Temin, *Did Monetary Forces Cause the Great Depression?* (1976).

Jerry Bruce Thomas, *"An Appalachian New Deal": West Virginia in the Great Depression* (1998).

Robert H. Zieger, *American Workers, American Unions, 1920-1985* (1986).

28

Depression Decade

AS A WHOLE, the American people displayed remarkable resilience during the Great Depression. Some intellectuals and artists in the thirties flirted with radical ideologies, but most people reaffirmed their belief in America's future and scoured the nation's heritage to find new sources of strength. The search for solutions to the nation's suffering greatly empowered the rising generation of social scientists who became the architects of the New Deal.

Ethnicity, gender, profession, region, and religion continued to give millions of Americans an important sense of their identity, defining their needs and aspirations as members of distinct groups. But depression conditions and the New Deal created new clusters of institutions, many of them class-based and government-sponsored. Some older voluntary associations, such as ethnic societies, suffered from declining budgets and loss of purpose in the thirties, but the Depression magnified the importance of class-based organizations such as labor unions, the CCC, the WPA, local farm boards, and REA cooperatives. In every sphere of organized society — whether churches, unions, or government boards — local and regional associations that directly touched the lives of the people fared best during the Depression.

Gone — though not forever — was the 1920s faith that the business system and what Herbert Hoover had celebrated as "rugged individualism" together would build a "new era" of perpetual prosperity. Now, with the old business leadership discredited and unregulated capitalism accused of bringing the nation to its knees, realizing the American Dream seemed to demand a new sense of collectiveness. Capitalism, if it was to survive, needed to be made fairer. "This nation could be made an ideal place to live," wrote an anonymous Minnesota man to Eleanor Roosevelt, "if every one would work together for the common good of every one instead of for selfish purposes." This theme was echoed by every New Dealer from Franklin D. Roosevelt on down.

Almost everyone's life changed during the 1930s, and the specter of deprivation was everywhere visible. But certain groups of Americans suffered disproportionately. Although the United States admitted a relatively small number of Jews fleeing the horrors unfolding in Nazi Germany, the disease of anti-Semitism flared up in this country as well. Economically vulnerable, women workers and blacks were usually the first to lose their jobs. The long-neglected minority most directly touched by New Deal legislation was American Indians, but even so they remained the nation's poorest people.

The Great Depression and the New Deal modified the pace of social change in America but did not alter its direction. Despite vast differences between the lifestyles of the rich and poor, the continued spread of affordable forms of entertainment and recreation, highlighted in the thirties by the enormous popularity of radio, sustained a national mass culture that tied the nation together.

DEPRESSION MOODS

The Depression touched almost everyone in one way or another. In the fall of 1932, *Fortune* magazine estimated that 34 million people, more than a fourth of the nation, belonged to nuclear families without a full-time breadwinner. Beyond these most visible victims were millions of farmers who labored long hours with little return, laborers who worked only two or three days a week, and those who lived in constant fear that their jobs would vanish. Few extended families counted no representatives among the ranks of forgotten men. Serious unemployment continued throughout the 1930s; after the steep recession in 1937, even New Dealers believed that the eventual return of prosperity would still leave 4 or 5 million workers jobless. These stark realities changed the pattern of life in most American families, sometimes breaking them apart, but often drawing people closer together as they faced real physical need.

❋ IN THEIR OWN WORDS

"I'd Rather Not Be on Relief," 1938
The experience of depending on the government was a new and difficult one for many in the Great Depression. This song, written in a Farm Security Administration camp, reflects the despair and shame — but also the necessity — of financial help, as well as the better prospects that might come with union membership.

We go around all dressed in rags
While the rest of the world goes neat,
And we have to be satisfied
With half enough to eat.
We have to live in lean-tos,
Or else we live in a tent,
For when we buy our bread and beans
There's nothing left for rent.
I'd rather not be on the rolls of relief,
Or work on the W. P. A.,
We'd rather work for the farmer
If the farmer could raise the pay;

Then the farmer could plant more cotton
And he'd get more money for spuds,
Instead of wearing patches,
We'd dress up in new duds.
From the east and west and north and south
Like a swarm of bees we come;
The migratory workers
Are worse off than a bum.
We go to Mr. Farmer
And ask him what he'll pay;
He says, "You gypsy workers
Can live on a buck a day."
I'd rather not be on the rolls of relief,
Or work on the W. P. A.,
We'd rather work for the farmer
If the farmer could raise the pay;
Then the farmer could plant more cotton
And he'd get more money for spuds,
Instead of wearing patches,
We'd dress up in new duds.
We don't ask for luxuries

Or even a feather bed.
But we're bound to raise the dickens
While our families are underfed.
Now the winter is on us
And the cotton picking is done,
What are we going to live on
While we're waiting for spuds to come?
Now if you will excuse me
I'll bring my song to an end.
I've got to go and chuck a crack
Where the howling wind comes in.
The times are going to get better
And I guess you'd like to know
I'll tell you all about it,
I've joined the C. I. O.

The Charles L. Todd and Robert Sonkin Migrant Worker Collection, Library of Congress, American Folklife Center

Letter to Franklin D. Roosevelt, 1935

In an attempt to foster grass-roots support for his Social Security Act, President Roosevelt sent a letter to thousands of clergy across the country, asking them to report to him about conditions in their community. Many wrote back to Roosevelt, including this pastor, who conveyed to Roosevelt the difficulty his parishioners faced.

My Dear Mr. President: —

. . . The members of my church are of the industrial class. Needless to say, the past few years have been very hard upon them. . . . They just will not stand forever for the misery which loss of savings, uncertainty and unemployment have wrought while so many all about them are living in luxury. I see no evidence of violent revolution but I do see evidence that many people are coming to the point where they favor trying what seem to those of us who try to think the problem through visionary and impracticable schemes. . . .

The writer of this letter is naturally conservative in his economic and political thinking, but I have been trying to express some of the thoughts which seem to me to be in the minds of a group of people such as those to whom I minister. They have struggled along against great odds in the last few years and helped one another. Many have had to fall back upon relief. Such experiences have shaken the former standards and beliefs.

If this attempt to picture conditions as they are is of any value whatever, I shall feel more than repaid for the effort which I have made. Be assured of our prayers that God will guide you in the great tasks which confront you.

Most respectfully yours,
Clayton R. Stoddard, Pastor
Lowell Avenue Baptist Church
Syracuse, NY
October 25, 1935

In many parts of the world, people turned to radical ideologies on the left and right during the Great Depression, but Americans remained remarkably committed to their belief in individual freedom and equality of opportunity. Many Americans turned to education and to religion for hope and comfort in this time of travail.

❧ *A People Beset*

The human cost of the Depression was horrific. Millions of able-bodied laborers found themselves adrift, unable to provide food for themselves and their families. Many circumspect laborers, thinking of themselves as middle class, had husbanded small nest eggs to protect against hard times, only to see their savings evaporate in failed banks, insurance companies, or mutual-aid societies. Robust and proud men and women stood in long bread lines; self-reliant farmers were thrust from lands tilled by their fathers and grandfathers; thousands of jobless men milled on hundreds of street corners in scores of cities awaiting a chance employer who might offer them a day's work. Writer Sherwood Anderson reported that he had seen "men who are heads of families creeping through the streets of American cities, eating from garbage cans; men turned out of houses and sleeping week after week on park benches, on the ground in parks, in the mud under bridges. . . . Our streets are filled with beggars, with men new in the art of begging."

Many of the unemployed during the Depression had been comfortable professionals. In 1934, Frank Walker, president of the National Emergency Council, wrote: "I saw old friends of mine — men I had been to school with — digging ditches and laying sewer pipe. They were wearing their regular business suits as they worked because they couldn't afford overalls and rubber boots." Harry Hopkins reported that the typical urban worker on relief, however, was a thirty-eight-year-old unskilled or semi-skilled white man who headed a household.

Beyond these typical workers, unemployment fell heaviest on the most vulnerable — women, the elderly, the very young, the least educated, and rural laborers. Investigations into Depression poverty laid bare layers of deprivation — "old poverty," historian James Patterson has called these subcultures — that had long existed in America. Now these marginal workers who had long lived in squalor and hardship were joined by millions of newly out-of-work victims of the Depression. In 1933 Harry Hopkins dispatched veteran reporter Lorena Hickok to tour the country and send to the White House first-hand reports of the suffering she saw. Her letters stunningly portrayed the "one-third of the nation" that Roosevelt described in his second inaugural address in January 1937 as "ill-housed, ill-clad, ill-nourished." From a West Virginia mining town, Hickok wrote of the "old poor": "Some of them have been starving for eight years. I was told there are children in West Virginia who never tasted milk! . . . Most of the women you see in the camps are going without shoes or stockings. It's fairly common to see children entirely naked." Stunned by the suffering in the mining area of eastern Kentucky, Hickok wrote to Hopkins: "I cannot for the life of me understand why they don't go down and raid the Blue Grass country."

The experience left psychic scars on a generation of Americans. Perhaps projecting their own anxieties, many who were lucky enough to keep their jobs (often at drastically reduced pay) resented and feared the unemployed, stereotyping them as loafers or failures and scorning those who accepted relief. And some who failed were bewildered by their inability to make their way, often sharing the prejudices of the fortunate well-off that the poor were themselves somehow responsible for their own misfortune. "I haven't had a steady job in more than two years," a man told a *New York Daily News* reporter in February 1932. "What's wrong with me, that I can't protect my children?" Guilt and self-deprecation cut as deeply into the human spirit as poverty. Overcome by feelings of inferiority, many jobless men sought anonymity, their blank stares speaking more of confusion than of despair. The popularity among intellectuals of psychoanalyst Alfred Adler's concepts of the inferiority complex and individual adjustment betrayed a deep social craving for acceptance on the part of the entire generation. At the popular level, Dale Carnegie's best-seller *How to Win Friends and Influence People* (1936) revealed the same yearning.

A few of the destitute turned sullen and angry, and a handful flirted with communism or violent protest. Sometimes despair won out, as suggested by the decade's rising suicide rates. But most Americans withstood deprivation and humiliation with resignation and courage, unwilling to cast off their beliefs in self-reliance and individualism. Their faces and their letters affirmed the indomitable human will to survive, to "make do," and to help one's neighbors. Their images endure in countless photographs, with babes in arms, looking the grim reaper square in the face. There was a camaraderie among the down-and-out; millions of Americans were poor but proud. They darned their socks and stuffed cardboard soles into worn-out shoes. Thousands of families were evicted by landlords, but they survived to joke about it: "Who was that lady I seen you with last night at the sidewalk café?" a man was asked. "That was no lady; that was my wife. That was no sidewalk café; that was our furniture." Americans clung tenaciously to respectability, and they developed habits of thrift and

caution that remained with them for life. Many poor Americans responded instinctively to the optimistic rhetoric of Roosevelt and, with him, they believed that they would drive the specter of want from the land and bequeath a better inheritance to their children.

❧ On the Road

During the Depression millions of Americans had no fixed address. Migrant laborers had long been a fixture in American agriculture, following seasonal crops from south to north. Since the early nineteenth century another subculture of transient men, known as "hoboes," had wandered the country as a matter of choice. During the Depression, however, untold numbers of other Americans became uprooted wanderers looking for work or opportunity down the road. In one year alone, the Southern Pacific Railroad reported that 683,000 transients had ridden its freight trains. Maury ("Steam Train") Graham, a 1930s hobo, recalled countless thousands of both men and women who "roamed mindlessly across the country, with no destination to reach and no schedule to keep. It was not at all unusual to see a train headed in one direction, loaded with transients traveling in search of work, pass another train, with just as many job seekers aboard, going in the opposite direction, neither group knowing that there was no work either way."

Many of the transients who lived in boxcars and hitchhiked on the roads were youngsters. They learned the ins and outs of towns — where the best missions were, the most generous housewives, the toughest police — and they protected one another. Sociologist Thomas Minehan of the University of Minnesota compared these transients to war refugees. Eric Sevareid, who would later become a distinguished broadcast journalist, entered this "new social dimension" as an unemployed twenty-year-old. It was, he recalled, a "great underground world, peopled by tens of thousands of American men, women, and children, white, black, brown, and yellow, who inhabited the 'jungle' to eat from blackened tin cans, find warmth at night in the boxcars, . . . wander from place to place, tired of it in a day, fretting to be gone again, happy only when the wheels are clicking under them, the telephone poles slipping by."

❧ Family Strains and Future Hopes

Lifestyles turned more conventional during the Depression, for it seemed less stylish to affect rebelliousness, and people sought more stable relationships. Many of

Hoboes Bands of men (and sometimes of women) drifting about the country on freight trains and camping out along the railroad tracks were a familiar sight in early twentieth-century America. Some were unemployable, either by choice or by bad luck; some were alcoholic or mentally ill; some were fleeing failed marriages; some were simply young and restless — and all were disdained and feared by "respectable" citizens as panhandlers and petty criminals. This photograph was taken in the Midwest during the 1920s. The ranks of hoboes swelled with the massive unemployment of the Great Depression.

the writers of the thirties idealized the family and bemoaned the erosion of family life caused by the Depression. Unemployment often undermined the traditional patriarchal family model. "There was certainly a change in our family," said an unemployed male, "and I can define it in just one word — I relinquished power in the family. . . . I don't even try to be the boss. She controls all the money." In other ways, the Depression drove families together. Studies of middle-class families revealed that they spent more time together in family recreation — ranging from playing checkers to listening to the radio. Marital advice emphasized support and companionship more than sex, and people married later and had fewer children.

Between 1929 and 1933 the marriage rate fell 22 percent and the birth rate dropped by 15 percent. The divorce rate also declined by about 25 percent. In some Depression years the number of female babies born was barely sufficient to maintain the population; the 1930s produced 3 million fewer babies than would have been born at 1929 birth rates. Combined with a length-

ening life expectancy as a result of improving medical care, the declining birth rate raised the proportion of people over 65 from 5.4 percent in 1930 to 6.9 percent in 1940, and the nation's rate of population growth fell to 7 percent during the decade.

For most Americans, these were sober times, far removed from the frenetic mood of the twenties. Americans were keenly conscious that the stock market crash had closed an era and opened another. The individualism and carefree spirit of the twenties gave way to a spirit of cooperation and social seriousness. President Roosevelt dismissed the twenties as a "decade of debauch"; the *New York Post* applauded the disappearance

The Trylon and the Perisphere These "futuristic" structures were the symbols of the 1939 World's Fair in Queens, New York. The fair attracted huge crowds in the last years of the Great Depression; Americans responded eagerly to the promise of new technologies and a plethora of consumer goods that it held out. The first public demonstration of television was offered at the fair. Unfortunately, the appearance of all these wonders was delayed by World War II, already brewing abroad. (Today, the New York Mets' Shea Stadium has been added to the World's Fair grounds at Flushing Meadow.)

vailing spirit: "Science Finds — Industry Applies — Man Conforms." The fair's huge pavilions, built by the nation's leading corporations, highlighted the economic survival of big business and a continued fascination with — and confidence in — machines. Streamlining, the dominant new style of industrial design in the thirties, pointed toward the sleeker, more benign future that business had in store for the American consumer. Television, for example, was one of the futuristic technologies developed during the 1930s and displayed at the New York World's Fair, though it would not be made available to consumers until after World War II.

❧ Extremist Echoes in Depression Thought

During the Depression, many European countries turned to totalitarian systems in an effort to restore order and prosperity, sacrificing human rights and individual liberty to those ends. European-style fascism never attracted mass support in the United States, but many Americans worried about whether a Mussolini- or Hitler-style movement could take root in their country. In a 1935 novel, *It Can't Happen Here,* writer Sinclair Lewis described a fascist takeover in the United States, led by a demagogic politician loosely resembling Huey Long (who was still alive at the time Lewis wrote the book). Roosevelt feared Long, confiding to one associate that Long would be "a candidate of the Hitler type for the presidency in 1936." Roosevelt believed that a Long candidacy in 1936 could result in a Republican victory — and "that would bring the country to such a state by 1940 that Long thinks he would be made dictator." Long's assassination in September 1935 removed any real or imagined dictatorial threat he posed. He lingered for two days before dying; his last words were "God, don't let me die! I have so much to do!" "Huey Long was one of those very few men," judged writer William Manchester, "of whom it can be said that, had he lived, American history would have been dramatically different."

of the classic magazine of the twenties, the *American Spectator:* "Nihilism, dadaism, smartsetism — they are all gone, and this, too, is progress." H. L. Mencken, the great iconoclast of the previous decade but now heard from chiefly as a sour critic of FDR, became the target of reproach himself.

Yet Americans did not abandon their belief in progress, nor their confidence in a more humane capitalism. Faith in science and technology — the embodiments of "reason" and "planning" — actually soared. Buoyed by Roosevelt's rosy spirit, most Americans believed that the country was on the path to a brighter future. With great ballyhoo, the two World's Fairs of the 1930s, the Century of Progress Fair in Chicago in 1933-1934 and the World of Tomorrow Fair in New York City in 1939-40, celebrated industry and the promise of technology. The official slogan of the Chicago Fair captured the pre-

Long was the most serious political threat to Roosevelt during the Depression years, but Father Charles

Coughlin was an open advocate of wresting control of the American political system from the established political authorities and moving it in an extremist direction (see Chapter 27). In 1932 he was ferociously attacking communism (which had made some headway among unemployed auto workers in his home city of Detroit) as well as the Hoover administration, and initially he championed Roosevelt. Coughlin's chief target was the old Populist bugaboo, the "Money Power," exemplified by Wall Street and by a dark and conspiratorial nexus of international bankers orchestrated by Jewish directors. But as it soon became clear that Roosevelt had no intention of crushing the banking system, was not interested in a Coughlin scheme to buy silver, and did not share his virulent anti-Semitic prejudices, Coughlin began to attack the New Deal. In November 1934 Coughlin formed the National Union for Social Justice, which at its peak claimed around 8 million members. The "Sixteen Principles" of the National Union called for monetary reforms, the nationalization of key industries, and protection of the rights of labor. While the National Union remained ineffectual, Coughlin's power was considerable. In 1935, he got credit for the defeat of a presidential attempt to affiliate the United States with the World Court in The Hague. Meanwhile his rhetoric became increasingly radical and his criticisms of the New Deal, which he called the "Jew Deal," grew increasingly shrill. At a rally in the Bronx in 1937 he gave a Nazi salute and shouted, "When we get through with the Jews in America, they'll think the treatment they received in Germany was nothing." Forced by his superior to apologize for a particularly vicious slur of Roosevelt, Coughlin's influenced dwindled after 1936.

Although New Deal critics such as Long and Coughlin were often extremist and hateful in their rhetoric, they had their roots in American populist traditions and raised serious economic issues. In short, they were, as historian Alan Brinkley has argued, a part of the American political tradition. European-style fascism probably never seriously threatened American democracy during the Depression, but a number of right-wing organizations, flaunting names such as the Silver Shirts, tried to imitate fascist successes in Europe. In the early years of the Depression it was not unusual for responsible politicians to flirt with the idea of granting dictatorial powers to the president. Republican Senator David A. Reed publicly proclaimed: "If this country ever needed a Mussolini, it needs one now." But such offhanded statements represented no serious threat.

Even though the Bund, a German-American organization supportive of Hitler, packed Madison Square Garden in 1939 with 22,000 members and sympathizers, few Americans had any sympathy for Nazi Germany. Before World War II, in fact, most Americans underestimated Hitler as little more than a ranting, strutting fool.

❧ The Red Romance

At the other end of the political spectrum, leftist radicals believed that the Depression presented an opportunity for revolutionary change. Floyd B. Olson, the big, broad-shouldered, free-wheeling Farmer-Labor Party governor of Minnesota and the most radical official elected during the Depression, advocated a "cooperative commonwealth" in which the government owned key industries. Lorena Hickok reported to Washington in 1933: "This boy Olson is, in my opinion, about the smartest 'Red' in this country." Olson won the admiration of the intellectual left by asserting that "American capitalism cannot be reformed," but he was neither a revolutionary nor a communist. He himself was increasingly disturbed by the rise of radical visionaries on his left. His career was cut short by cancer in 1935, before he could threaten Roosevelt.

During the thirties the Communist Party of the United States of America (CPUSA) was tied closely to the Communist International and slavishly followed the directives of Stalin. The party probably reached its peak in 1932 when its presidential candidate William Z. Foster and his African American running mate James Ford polled 102,000 votes, its all-time electoral high, but still far less than the 884,000 polled by Socialist Norman Thomas, and an insignificant percentage of the whole vote. By the mid-thirties, the American party — on direct orders from the Kremlin — Americanized its methods and language and began cooperating with other leftist groups. In 1935, Stalin himself, alarmed by the threat of fascism in Europe, ordered Communists everywhere to stop attacking socialists and middle-class liberals and instead to join them in a worldwide "popular front."

The CPUSA's militant aura of leather-jacketed "toughness" exerted a momentary appeal to some despairing Americans in the early 1930s. At its peak, the party numbered about 90,000 card-carrying members and had a considerably larger following of "fellow travelers," but by 1934 its appeal was shrinking rapidly, and it counted fewer than 30,000 active members. When Stalin began to stage show trials of Soviet "Old Bolsheviks" in 1935, condemning most of them to death, the CPUSA suffered large defections.

Communists did play a significant role in the rise of the trade union movement. John L. Lewis valued the toughness and dedication of communist recruiters. In 1937-1938 the CIO's organizing drives gave the CPUSA a momentary boost in prestige among those with leftist sympathies, and by the end of the thirties about one-third of CIO field organizers were communists. Lewis welcomed the "red and rebellious" to the United Mine Workers union, believing he could use their talents but block them from gaining control. Communist organizers did gain control of some CIO unions, but the staunchly anti-communist A.F. of L. mounted a successful counterattack that kept the nation's largest labor organization out of communist hands.

Predictably, many American writers and intellectuals in the thirties flirted with communism as an alternative to Fascism. Among the writers joining the party were Waldo Frank, Sherwood Anderson, Richard Wright, John Dos Passos, and Upton Sinclair, and others wrote of social oppression, showed the influence of Marxist ideology, and participated in leftist "popular front" activities. Among intellectuals, communism won some prestige as a bulwark against international fascism when a bloody civil war erupted in 1936 in Spain (where Hitler and Mussolini openly supported General Francisco Franco's right-wing rebel army against the republican government), and as the British and French governments "appeased" Hitler in the late 1930s (see Chapter 29).

Other American intellectuals toyed with leftist ideas during the Depression. The League for Independent Political Action, founded in 1929 by University of Chicago economist Paul H. Douglas, later a highly respected Democratic senator, and influential philosopher John Dewey, declared: "Capitalism must be destroyed." Dewey warned that capitalism was a "decaying system" that was beyond rescue. Among the youthful idealists who joined the party in the 1930s was Alger Hiss, an urbane Harvard law school graduate who served as assistant general counsel in the Agriculture Department where he was a part of a cadre of "boys with their hair ablaze." Hiss joined the CPUSA and first met with his contact, Whittaker Chambers, in the spring of 1934. At the time, such flirtations with leftist ideology seemed innocent enough. Among the intelligentsia communism was radical chic. If you listened carefully, wrote Frederick Lewis Allen, "you might have heard a literary critic who had been gently nurtured in the politest environments referring to *himself* as a proletarian, so belligerently did he identify himself with the masses." For the most part, the intellectual dalliance with communism ended in disillusionment by the late thirties; many of those who embraced the left during the Depression, including Hiss, would pay a price for their youthful idealism in the fifties (see Chapter 31).

The House Un-American Activities Committee (HUAC) was established in 1934 to monitor the spread of undemocratic ideologies. During its first three years the committee focused on its intended target, Fascism, but communist rhetoric made it obvious that democracy was also threatened from the left. Indeed, the *New Masses,* the communist party's most important magazine, openly advocated repression: "We would deny democratic rights to Fascists, to lynchers, to all those who wish to use them as a means of winning mass support for reaction." Not until 1937 did FBI director J. Edgar Hoover receive instructions from the White House to put Communist organizations under surveillance because of fears of espionage. By that time, conservative Texas congressman Martin Dies had turned HUAC's guns on communists in the labor movement and on several New Deal agencies that had been congenial to leftist intellectuals. Dies's attacks helped to kill the Federal Theater Project in 1939. By 1938 a full-fledged conservative backlash against the New Deal was in full swing and the Theater Project was the first of a series of New Deal programs to be dismantled over the next six years. But not until the early Cold War years would serious sanctions — official and unofficial — fall on individuals who had flirted with communism during the 1930s (see Chapter 31).

American intellectuals' "red romance" was always a shaky affair. Most writers were too self-centered and independent to blindly follow directives from the Soviet Union. The communist flirtation reached its peak during the Spanish Civil War from 1936 to 1939; hundreds of American writers supported the unsuccessful Republican fight against Fascism, and the Abraham Lincoln Brigade enlisted several thousand left-wing American volunteers to fight and die for the Spanish Republic. At the same time, the Stalinist purges that began in Russia in 1935 — in which many loyal "Old Bolsheviks" were forced during show trials to confess to preposterous charges and then were summarily shot — repulsed most American intellectuals. The CPUSA suffered another blow when Stalin and Hitler signed a non-aggression pact in August 1939, leading directly to the partitioning of Poland and the outbreak of World War II, although recent revelations from Soviet archives show that most of the party faithful in the United States remained loyal to the cause.

Despite years of depression the party shrank by the late 1930s to less than 30,000 members, a majority of them foreign-born and concentrated disproportionately in New York City. An increasingly exasperated Stalin could never understand why the CPUSA failed to win substantial support from the ranks of labor, African Americans, or the unemployed. In the end, the popularity of Roosevelt and the New Deal, combined with communism's undeniable identification with a foreign ideology, seriously limited the spread of collectivist thought in Depression America.

❦ The Center Holds

The New Deal was so intellectually eclectic and experimental that it disarmed critics on both the right and the left. Conservatives were shocked and disgusted by the proliferation of government agencies, but eventually they begrudgingly acquiesced to the reality of the welfare state. Many of the idealistic Americans attracted by collectivist ideas were interested mainly in exploring the potential of economic planning. Most American intellectuals during the Depression, like other Americans, continued to support the American democratic belief in individualism and capitalism tempered by government regulation. The Depression and the New Deal greatly enhanced the power of the social science experts who had emerged during the Progressive Era and gave an impetus to social engineering that would continue to the end of the century.

The Depression enhanced the prestige of secular-minded, "objective" social scientists such as Dewey. The Depression did nothing to diminish Dewey's faith in the power of reason to bring social improvement, and he remained the most influential American thinker. In *A Common Faith,* published in 1934, Dewey called for the replacement of what he considered outmoded religious traditions with humanistic values such as a sense of community, justice, security, art, and knowledge. Dewey supported Socialist Norman Thomas in 1932 but he soon embraced the New Deal and advocated extensive government planning. In the early thirties Dewey flirted with Soviet communism, in 1934 he founded a journal, *Social Frontier,* that urged teachers to aid the masses. It frequently published contributions from Marxists.

Like Dewey, most social scientists continued to support the progressive vision of a society guided by rea-

son and science. The "legal realism" advocated by Supreme Court Justices Oliver Wendell Holmes and Louis Brandeis, sometimes called "sociological jurisprudence," reigned virtually unchallenged in the nation's prestigious law schools by the 1930s. The most influential legal theorist of the era, Felix Frankfurter, promoted sociological jurisprudence during a long teaching career at Harvard, as a personal friend and confidant of Roosevelt, and, after 1939, as a Supreme Court justice.

Political scientists also became increasingly visible in the government bureaucracy of the 1930s, bringing new concerns for collecting data and introducing the age of political polling. Business leadership had been discredited by the Depression, and social scientists laid claim to being the "scientific" predictors of the future. Modern scientific polling got a boost after the venerable *Literary Digest* (which had fairly accurately predicted elections since 1920) forecast a Landon victory in 1936. The *Digest* poll was skewed because it was based on listings in old telephone books and automobile registrations, tilting the sampling toward those who were better off. By 1940 Elmo Roper headed a more scientific survey team working for *Fortune* magazine and George Gallup had founded the American Institute of Public Opinion.

Because the Depression was a social as well as an economic crisis, the study of sociology broadened during the thirties, spawning such sub-fields as urban, rural, and regional sociology. Other social scientists contributed to Depression thought and politics in important ways. The anthropological studies of Franz Boas, Ruth Benedict, and Margaret Mead and the behaviorist psychological theories of John Watson and B. F. Skinner stressed that human behavior was determined by the environment rather than genetics — considerably deflating the sweeping and rather disturbing claims that had been made for eugenics by earlier progressives. Anthropologists defined culture as a network of ideas, habits, and institutions that existed in all societies and insisted that all cultures had merits and shortcomings. In this highly relativistic anthropological and psychological environment, the source of evil more and more was portrayed as a product of social maladjustments rather than of individual wrongdoing.

❦ The Great Education Debate

Social scientists, educational philosophers like Dewey, and policy makers all recognized the immense importance of educating the American citizenry in the demo-

Science Fiction The Depression decade saw the rise of science fiction as a popular genre, picturing both science's ability to bring about progress and its potential to go awry. This garish illustration of robot war machines wreaking havoc is taken from the cover of *Amazing Stories*, a classic pulp magazine printed on cheap paper and known for its flashy cover art.

cratic ethos and equipping them with the skills necessary for making economic progress. But that task was Herculean, for public education during the Depression had to struggle with severe underfunding, particularly in the South where the annual per capita income fell to only about $200. Public education was almost entirely a local and state enterprise in the 1930s, and hard-pressed states simply could not fund adequate systems of education. In three southern states, annual support for public education fell to less than $40 per child; many blacks and rural whites were illiterate. In 1940, only 25 percent of Americans had graduated from high school and 10 percent from college.

In spite of the deficiencies in public school systems, school attendance skyrocketed during the thirties be-

cause young people lingered in school, unable to find jobs. High school enrollment more than doubled between 1926 and 1932. The New Deal helped public education indirectly in a number of ways. The PWA constructed 12,700 new school buildings; the CCC offered classes for several million young men; nearly 1.5 million people attended adult education classes sponsored by the WPA; the NYA gave part-time employment to more than 300,000 elementary, secondary, and college students. Such aid brought the federal government into a closer relationship with public schools than ever before. That tendency did not escape notice; in the 1930s the National Education Association vigorously opposed federalizing the school system, insisting that schools were extensions of the American family that should be locally controlled.

Dewey's concept of progressive education provided a philosophical base for encouraging practical and useful education and "social adjustment" for mass democracy. In the eyes of progressive educators, the Great Depression confirmed what they had been arguing throughout the 1920s — that individualism and competition were radically evil and must be replaced by cooperation in every sphere of society, beginning with the elementary school, where young minds were first taking shape. Progressive educators of the 1930s redoubled their assault on traditional subjects such as history, mathematics, and science, and with the high schools now overcrowded with students who were there mainly because they could find no entry-level jobs, the argument seemed plausible that schools should prepare children for social life rather than for careers requiring rigorous training in "abstract knowledge." When Depression-era teachers were not worrying about losing their jobs or not being paid their salaries, they were experimenting more enthusiastically with curricular changes designed to supplant traditional content-oriented education. Dewey and his fellow educational progressives, and even some ordinary teachers, professed great interest in "the Soviet experiment" in the early 1930s precisely because they saw the Russians making a heroic effort to use schools for sweeping social transformation. Their admiration for Communist education continued until the mid-1930s, when most of the Russian educators whom Dewey admired (and who had been influenced by Dewey's theories) disappeared in Stalin's purges and Stalin decreed a sharp turn for Soviet education toward a rigidly authoritarian model of schooling, heavily laden with mathematics and science.

Meanwhile, despite what the progressive education experts told the public, most adult Americans clung to their longstanding faith that traditional education offered the best chance for upward social mobility, even during the bleak economic conditions of the thirties. Working-class and lower middle-class people encouraged their children to complete high school. The college population did rise to nearly 900,000, but the cost of a college education, about $450 a year in public universities and $980 in private institutions, still made it a goal out of most Americans' reach.

The Depression dampened scientific research. University support for research declined severely, as did industrial spending for research. Although some New Deal agencies, most notably TVA and the Department of Agriculture, sponsored basic research projects, most government programs focused on bread-and-butter issues. In spite of the unfavorable economic climate, the scientific achievements of the decade were impressive. Although many people lived without the most basic kinds of health care, the use of blood plasma, typhus vaccine, and sulfa drugs helped raise life expectancy from fifty-six in 1920 to sixty-four in 1940. The nation's most famous polio victim, Franklin D. Roosevelt, was among the founders of the National Foundation for Infantile Paralysis in 1938; through an annual "March of Dimes" the foundation raised millions of dollars to support research and assist victims of polio.

The American scientific community was enriched during the thirties as a result of turmoil and persecution in Europe, gaining hundreds of the world's leading scholars and theoretical scientists, most of them Jews, liberals, or leftists fleeing Hitler. By the end of the decade some of the world's foremost physicists, including Albert Einstein from Germany and Enrico Fermi from Italy, had immigrated to the United States. Dewey aided scores of other scientists to find appointments at American universities, including future Nobel Prize winners Hans Bethe from Germany, who was hired by Cornell University, and Hungarian-born Edward Teller, who taught at George Washington University. While the total number of escaping scholars who came to America during the decade was less than a hundred, they helped make American universities the foremost centers of scientific learning in the world. The effect of this intellectual fertilization would be immense in the postwar world.

The rapid accumulation of knowledge in every scholarly and scientific discipline during the twentieth century spawned an unavoidable tendency toward intellectual specialization and compartmentalization. No mind could hope to keep abreast of all the new discoveries; every scholar was forced to concentrate more narrowly on one field of expertise. There was a price to be paid for specialization: an increasing loss of touch with "the big picture" and a growing isolation from what researchers in other specialties were meanwhile learning. This relentless trend toward specialization, as well as realization of its effects, touched off a far-reaching debate within American higher education in the 1930s.

By the 1930s, the elective system had cluttered university curricula with countless specialized subjects, including many courses designed to train students in such technical fields as engineering and in such less cerebral skills as bookkeeping, cooking, and typing. This "service-station conception" of higher education was challenged in the 1930s by Robert Maynard Hutchins, who at the remarkably young age of thirty became chancellor of the University of Chicago in 1929.

With a social detachment that was anathema to Dewey, and that found no echo in the nation's secondary schools, Hutchins argued that true education consisted of a synthesized study that would lead one to grasp the "eternal intellectual verities." Under Hutchins, the University of Chicago became a liberal arts school, endeavoring to instill in students "the arts of reading, writing, thinking, and speaking." The heart of liberal arts education at Chicago was the assignment of one hundred "great books of the Western tradition" that spanned science, philosophy, literature, and history. The Chicago experiment was heralded by many intellectuals like Walter Lippmann, who believed that American society had lost its moral and intellectual moorings, and that college graduates had little understanding of "the Western culture which produced the modern democratic state." Hutchins opened a highly nuanced debate between advocates of general and specialized higher education that would gather momentum after World War II — and that still continues today.

More and more, the complexity of modern scientific disciplines, each with its highly specialized, impenetrable vocabulary, isolated scientists from the masses. Popular thought, while influenced by scientific discoveries, had a life of its own, laden with prescientific religious ideas and grounded in common sense. As the century wore on, many Americans remained fascinated by the powers of science, but they grew less sure that science was an unmitigated force for good. The science fiction writing and films of the 1930s pictured both the benign potential in good science and the awesome destructive potential of science gone mad. World War II and the advent of the nuclear age in 1945 would greatly intensify these anxieties.

❧ Religion Retreats from Reform

Most influential Protestant and Jewish theologians supported the New Deal's moderate, humane social reforms. But meanwhile the historic Protestant churches were losing both members and influence. While most New Dealers came from traditional Protestant backgrounds — and Roosevelt himself was a loyal though theologically vague Episcopalian — the New Deal's morality was decidedly secular. Many liberal Protestant ministers, while not renouncing faith in God, shared the "humanist" and social science belief that social problems demanded secular answers. A poll of 20,000 Protestant ministers in 1934 showed that nearly a third favored socialism and three-fifths supported reforms of capitalism. Under these circumstances, mainstream Protestant laypeople saw increasing reasons to concentrate their faith and energy on secular, political reform and to abandon their churches.

In some ways, the social gospel reached its practical peak during the Great Depression. In 1931, the Federal Council of Churches published a call for "economic justice" that supported many of the reforms enacted in the New Deal. On the other hand, the heady idealism of early twentieth-century social Christianity and the confident optimism of modernistic theology had become so passé by the thirties that modernism as a theological self-description went out of style except in the most liberal seminaries.

The rise of Neo-Orthodoxy, the most significant Protestant theological movement of the 1930s, delivered a considerable jolt to mainline Christianity. The brothers Reinhold and H. Richard Niebuhr — thoroughly American in birth, education, and experience despite their German names — became Neo-Orthodoxy's most prominent advocates in the United States. Drawing on the thinking of Swiss theologian Karl Barth, which stressed such historic Christian themes as human depravity, salvation through Christ, and the authority of the Scriptures, the Niebuhrs warned that the church had been captured by its culture. In *Moral Man and Immoral Society* (1932), Reinhold Niebuhr, who taught at Union Theological Seminary in New York, insisted that social and political institutions could never become moral, and that the world-embracing optimism of modernism was a religious capitulation to materialist

illusions. Only human beings, not institutions, could be redeemed by grace. Politically, Reinhold Niebuhr was no conservative. He supported social reform, ran for Congress in 1930 as a Socialist, and eventually became a firm supporter of Roosevelt; after World War II, he would exert a powerful influence over American liberalism. But his theology attacked the platitudes and glib assumptions of the previous generation of progressives. The problem with religious liberalism, Niebuhr argued, was that it had appropriated an Americanized version of the gospel of progress, blindly accepting "the Social Gospel–John Dewey amalgam, with its faith in the politics of love and reason." In *The Social Sources of Denominationalism* (1929), his brother H. Richard Niebuhr argued that religion had not historically shaped American culture; religion, rather, had been shaped by culture. Protestant churches had given theological consent to an unholy American lust for conquest and power.

Theological traditionalism combined with social activism was not confined to Neo-Orthodox Protestants. Roman Catholic theology remained extremely conservative in the 1930s, dominated by Neo-Thomism, a sophisticated intellectual system rooted in medieval philosophy that stressed churchly authority, highly logical reasoning, and the spiritual value of the sacraments. But meanwhile the Catholic Church remained armed with a social philosophy that supported economic and social reform. In 1919 the National Catholic Welfare Conference issued a statement calling for minimum wage laws, regulation of monopolies, unemployment insurance, and protection for labor. This reform agenda received support from the Vatican in 1931 in the papal encyclical *Quadragesimo Anno,* a strong plea for a fairer distribution of wealth. Many American Catholics saw the New Deal as a response to the church's social philosophy.

The American Catholic church produced an extraordinary spokesperson for social liberalism during the Depression, Dorothy Day. In 1931, Day joined Peter Maurin to found the Catholic Worker movement. The two published a newspaper, the *Catholic Worker,* that was anticapitalist and pacifist and built a network of Houses of Hospitality to minister to the needy. A controversial figure whose 1938 autobiography described a tempestuous youth that included a love affair and an abortion, Day's liberal views often offended church leaders, but she gave Catholics a powerful voice on the left.

Catholicism's identification with the New Deal helped the church continue its march toward Americanization during the Depression decade. Smarting from the anti-

Catholic agitation that had marred the election of 1928, Roman Catholics were gratified to get politically astute attention from Roosevelt. Two Catholics, James A. Farley and Tommy Corcoran, were among the president's inner circle of advisers. Perhaps the most visible Catholic contributor to the New Deal was Catholic University professor John A. Ryan, the director of the Social Action Department of the National Catholic Welfare Conference. Roosevelt named Ryan to the Advisory Council of the United States Employment Service and to the Advisory Committee of the Subsistence Homestead Division of the NRA. Among the scores of other Catholics who were appointed to important positions on New Deal boards was Joseph P. Kennedy, who served as chair of the Securities and Exchange Commission and of the American Maritime Commission and became the highly visible (and controversial) American ambassador to Great Britain in 1937. In short, Roosevelt gave American Catholics the political recognition they had long sought. Significantly, even after Father Coughlin turned on Roosevelt in 1936, the president still garnered an estimated 80 percent of the Catholic vote.

Like mainstream Protestant churches, the synagogues also declined in influence during the Depression. In 1937, the *American Jewish Year Book* estimated that Reform congregations had 50,000 member families, Conservative congregations 75,000 families, and Orthodox congregations around 200,000 families. The combined membership represented no more than 1.5 million people, only about one-fourth of all the Jews in the country.

By 1920, around 80 percent or more of the Jewish population of the United States was of east European descent. If they were religious, most of these immigrants affiliated with Orthodox synagogues upon their arrival, but their children and grandchildren, repelled by the "foreignness" of the religious practices of their parents, gravitated toward more liberal forms of Judaism or became non-observers altogether. For more and more Jews, social centers such as the Young Men's and Young Women's Hebrew Associations became the focal points of Jewish life rather than synagogues.

Zionism was a divisive issue among American Jews in the early 1930s. The leaders of the Zionist movement tended to be nonreligious Jews, but Orthodox and Conservative Jews were draw to Zionism because of their prophetic hopes for the restoration of a Jewish nation. On the other hand, Reform Jews were generally hostile to the idea, viewing Judaism as a religion only and urging Jews to assimilate into American society. The question became less theoretical, however, once Jews began fleeing Hitler's persecution in 1933, and by the mid-1930s all American Jewish leaders had come to support the establishment of a Jewish homeland in Palestine.

THE REGROUPING OF AMERICA: ETHNICITY, CLASS, AND RELIGION IN THE DEPRESSION DECADE

The Great Depression and the New Deal added new layers to the pluralism of American society. Much of

---

❋ **IN THEIR OWN WORDS**

Humanist Manifesto I, 1933

Among the seemingly radical ideas that gained exposure in the 1930s was humanism. Thirty-four educators, philosophers, social scientists, and others signed this manifesto in 1933, including John Dewey and Charles Francis Potter, author of Humanism: A New Religion.

The time has come for widespread recognition of the radical changes in religious beliefs throughout the modern world. The time is past for mere revision of traditional attitudes. Science and economic change have disrupted the old beliefs. Religions the

world over are under the necessity of coming to terms with new conditions created by a vastly increased knowledge and experience. In every field of human activity, the vital movement is now in the direction of a candid and explicit humanism. . . .

There is great danger of a final, and we believe fatal, identification of the word religion with doctrines and methods which have lost their significance and which are powerless to solve the problem of human living in the Twentieth Century. . . .

Today man's larger understanding of the universe, his scientific achievements, and

deeper appreciation of brotherhood, have created a situation which requires a new statement of the means and purposes of religion. Such a vital, fearless, and frank religion capable of furnishing adequate social goals and personal satisfactions may appear to many people as a complete break with the past. While this age does owe a vast debt to the traditional religions, it is none the less obvious that any religion that can hope to be a synthesizing and dynamic force for today must be shaped for the needs of this age. To establish such a religion is a major necessity of the present. It is a responsibility which rests upon this generation.

the political rhetoric of the 1930s praised American nationalism, and artists and writers also rallied to nationalistic themes. But the Depression was also a time when people needed the support of local groups more than ever before. Some of the economic and political changes of the thirties contrived to weaken older subgroups and create new loyalties. New associations and networks appeared, each with its own publications and political agendas; these new associations were often based on class and either supplemented or replaced older group loyalties.

∾ Accelerating Ethnic Assimilation

A number of factors combined to diminish ethnic rivalries and prejudices during the Depression. Restrictions in the twenties and the Depression in the thirties had slowed the inrush of Old World immigrants to a trickle and diminished cross-border migration from Mexico as well. The economic crisis hastened the acculturation of many of those who had arrived earlier in the twentieth century, while also playing havoc with immigrants' cultural, religious, and economic institutions. New Deal agencies provided for many first- and second-generation immigrants an opportunity to work for the government, thus integrating them into the broader culture. Like other poor people, recent immigrants identified strongly with the New Deal agencies that aided or employed them, wearing proudly the badge of being a CCC veteran or an elected official in the loose AAA or REA local associations. The openness of the trade union movement and the strong class antagonisms of the New Deal era also helped break down racial prejudices and stereotypes, while building a greater sense of working-class solidarity. The camaraderie born in violent strikes and sit-downs chiseled away at ethnic and religious prejudices, and union membership weakened ties to ethnic associations.

Even so, strong ethnic enclaves remained in most cities and in many small towns. At the end of the decade, about 25 percent of the population remained first- and second-generation immigrants; in the nation's twenty largest industrial cities the figure was over 50 percent. New York City, for instance, was partitioned into clear ethnic districts — South Bronx was Italian; Brownsville, Jewish; Yorkville, German; Manhattanville, Irish; and Harlem, African American (most of its inhabitants recent migrants from the South). In 1940, English was not the first language of almost 22 million Americans. The number of foreign language newspapers declined during the decade, but about a thousand remained, with a combined circulation of about 7 million, and nearly 200 foreign language radio stations survived to provide programming in German, Polish, Yiddish, and various other languages.

Ethnic minorities were still targets of a good deal of discrimination and insensitivity from the majority white population and that, to some degree, continued to push them together. Most ethnic Americans also retained an interest, and often a degree of pride, in developments in their homeland. Italian Americans and German Americans generally approved of the revived nationalism in their native countries, though only small minorities actively supported Fascist ideology. Japanese Americans, even though they were more stringently segregated in American society, were less likely to feel a pull of loyalty to the old country, which generally viewed them as deserters. In spite of the forces that still worked to isolate ethnic minorities in America, countervailing influences tended to shrink their cultural estrangement.

∾ Decentralizing Tendencies in Unions and Churches

If ethnic distinctions blurred somewhat during the Depression, class cleavages deepened. In terms of income, a worker making $2,500 per year in 1939 would have been considered upper-middle class, but only 4.2 percent earned that much. An average factory worker earned around $1,200; more than half of the employed men and nearly 80 percent of women workers made less than $1,000; millions toiling away on public relief projects made less. The fact that so many were poor during the Depression created a sense of class solidarity among the down and out, and many people began to identify with class-based organizations.

Union growth was the clearest measure of class-based realignment during the thirties. Many workers found in the unions a new focus of institutional loyalty. The A.F. of L. grew from 2.96 million members in 1930 to 3.51 million in 1936. But the explosive growth of industrial unionism during the New Deal followed the passage of the Wagner Act in 1935. Militant CIO leaders nicknamed A.F. of L. head William Green "the All-American mushmouth" and led a virtual revolution in the labor movement. Following the A.F. of L.'s expulsion of John L. Lewis's United Mine Workers and ten other unions in 1937, a new spurt of recruitment pushed the total membership of the A.F. of L. to 4.34 million in 1940, while the CIO reached 2.15

The Radio A Polish immigrant working as a miner listens to the radio after his shift. Perhaps he is listening to a broadcast in his native language; during the Depression almost 200 radio stations offered programming in languages other than English.

million. Union successes revealed the importance of local and regional attachments during the Great Depression. The initiative for union recruitment and strikes, including the sit-downs, usually came from locals rather than national union headquarters.

The CIO's organizing depended significantly on the assistance of women auxiliaries, although such assistance generally reinforced traditional gender roles. "Once you convince the women, and they convince the men, then everything is fine, you know," recalled one organizer. "We were able to sign a lot of cards that way." Moreover, once the CIO unions had been organized they worked hard to keep workers' wives and children involved, cultivated a "family" image, and encouraged after-hours socializing, for example through picnics and bowling leagues — much of this recalling the efforts of 1920s "welfare capitalism" to win employees' allegiance and break down their ties to older ethnic and religious organizations.

Similarly, the Protestant churches that escaped declining membership during the Depression were those that emphasized local and regional leadership and reinforced traditional values. Conservative Protestant churches were the hardiest survivors of the Depression, and during these times of hardship, millions of Americans remained intensely loyal to their local churches. Many liberal Protestants believed that fundamentalism had been irreparably damaged by public ridicule

during the 1920s, but in fact the 1930s and 1940s saw the beginning of a shift in American Protestantism toward the growth in numbers and influence of conservative evangelical churches.

Even though mainstream churches lost members in the 1930s, the spirit of religion remained strong. Pearl Buck, author of the book *The Good Earth,* who had returned to America after years in China (where her parents were missionaries), wrote in 1933 that "I am amazed at all the religion I see everywhere." Conservative churches were in tune with the popular beliefs of average Americans; in 1942 a poll conducted by *Fortune* revealed that 82 percent of Americans believed in "a God who rewards and punishes after death." Symbolic of fundamentalism's survival was the radio success of evangelist Charles E. Fuller of Pasadena, California. Fuller's "Old-Fashioned Revival Hour" went on the air in 1937; two years later he was broadcasting on CBS to an audience estimated at 10 million.

Fundamentalist religion thrived because it nurtured local and regional organizational networks, bypassing unresponsive denominational bureaucracies. Fundamentalist pastors built large churches and clusters of schools, published newspapers, and created missionary boards. While older seminaries languished during the 1930s, conservative Bible schools trained thousands of men and women for service in fundamentalist churches. Regional networks of churches, schools, and other parachurch institutions became surrogate denominations that claimed the loyalty of increasing numbers of poor people alienated from older and richer Protestant denominations.

Most of the fundamentalist institutional networks that appeared in the 1930s centered in the North and Midwest, but local and regional religious networks also flourished in the South. The Southern Baptist church, the most decentralized of the nation's major Protestant denominations, grew to more than 5 million, gaining more than a million members during the decade. Other loosely organized churches whose members were drawn mostly from the working classes and the poor, including the Churches of Christ and various Pentecostal denominations, flourished during the thirties.

Fundamentalist theology spoke clearly and directly to the defeated people of the Depression generation. Conservative Protestant theology still strongly emphasized a sense of individual sin and a hope for supernatural help, both in this life and in heaven. Some powerful fundamentalist pastors, though by no means all, combined conservative theology with virulent strains of anti-Semitism, anti-Catholicism, and anti-radical-ism in politics and the labor movement. The Social Ser-vice Commission of the Southern Baptist Convention justified racial discrimination and remained virtually mute about the rights of labor. Arthur J. Barton, head of the commission, resented Roosevelt's support for the repeal of Prohibition and after 1938 openly opposed the New Deal.

Conservative churches thrived during the Depres-sion preaching a gospel of self-help and traditional morality. But while conservative evangelicals often opposed social reform, they were not indifferent to the needs of the poor. Indeed, most of them were poor themselves, and they could hardly have succeeded had they callously ignored Depression suffering. Thousands of local churches heroically relieved the needy in hun-dreds of communities; many thousands of widows, or-phans, and unemployed survived the Depression with the aid of their almost equally poor fellow Christians.

≈ Gains and Setbacks for Women

Eleanor Roosevelt and Secretary of Labor Frances Per-kins, the first woman cabinet member, gave a level of public visibility to women during the Depression de-cade. Scores of other women, particularly social work-ers trained in settlement houses, moved into New Deal agencies in administrative positions. Nonetheless, the woman's movement sank to its low-est point in the 1930s. In the midst of Depression suffering, such mat-ters as women's personal self-ful-fillment, career advancement, and political participation seemed less compelling, and women's organiza-tions either lost their followings or had no clear reform agenda.

Nonetheless, the image of women did continue to change. The popular media of the thirties no longer portrayed women as friv-olous sex objects. Partly because of the movie industry's self-imposed censorship, but partly because of the changing climate, Hollywood's preoccupation with sex sirens gave way to a more wholesome set of stars, including Katharine Hep-burn and Jean Arthur. The media woman of the thirties was indepen-dent, feisty, and fully capable of competing with men, a full-blown sharer in the triumphs and tragedies of life.

During the Depression, employers routinely dis-criminated against married women. A majority of the nation's cities passed laws excluding women from most non-clerical jobs, assuming that such jobs should be re-served for men who headed households. In most of the nation's school systems a female teacher was forced to resign if she married. Indeed, a national poll taken dur-ing the thirties revealed that 80 percent of Americans (and 75 percent of women) believed that women should be homemakers. In 1939 the respected liberal journalist Norman Cousins was not alone in suggesting a suppos-edly simple way to solve what was by then considered the nation's chronic unemployment problem: Fire the 10 million married women who had jobs and hire the 10 million unemployed men. But this panacea overlooked important realities. Even when the men were working, many families could not survive without the wages brought in by working wives, mothers, and daughters; nor as a practical matter was such "women's work" as domestic service, cooking, sales-clerking, and secre-tarial service open to men. Overall, the Great Depres-

Women and the Depression   The Depression made it even more difficult for women to work outside the home, but women helped support themselves and their families in other ways. Here an Oklahoma City woman whose husband is an unemployed oil-worker offers to take in washing and ironing to supplement the family income.

sion reinforced traditional gender attitudes more than it undermined them.

Even so, the status of women did change during the decade. The proportion of women working for wages grew slightly: In 1930, women had represented 24.3 percent of all wageworkers; in 1940, 25.1 percent. In the same period the number of married women working increased from 11.7 percent to 15.6 percent. Women worked mostly in non-unionized jobs, and, although some profited from the minimum wage laws passed during the New Deal, many women's jobs were specifically excluded from the laws. Women who stayed at home struggled to keep their families together, often assuming increased family responsibilities when their unemployed husbands lost confidence and spirit. Thousands of women took in "boarders" to support their family or did laundry to supplement the meager incomes of their husbands.

Poor women, both black and white, were an almost invisible class during Depression years. Unemployed, "respectable," single women were among the least visible of Depression sufferers. They rarely appeared in breadlines, and there were no flophouses for women, yet many were jobless and homeless. In 1933, *Los Angeles Examiner* reporter Adela Rogers St. John spent two weeks living without money or support and wrote a first-hand description of the trials of the "sisterhood of the damned." She told of weary hours spent in breadlines, employment offices, and county charity offices. She spent days in the public library and nights in a Salvation Army shelter. St. John found most of the charity dispensers in Los Angeles to be tightfisted and arrogant, but she effusively praised the treatment she received at Aimee Semple McPherson's Foursquare Gospel Church, one of the flourishing conservative churches that took seriously its responsibilities to the poor. "God bless her," St. John wrote of McPherson, "Feeding, encouraging, giving hope . . . to the poor, and faith and strength as they jammed Angelus Temple and slept there if they had no place else to go. I saw her begging for them, insulting those with folding money into parting with it for their destitute brothers. Sick women on the floor of her home, old men in her garage, families sleeping in the pews."

❧ *Patterns of Discrimination*

African Americans continued to be the least protected group in American society. Old stereotypes remained deep-rooted. A leading American history textbook

Katharine Hepburn   Shown here in one of her earliest films, from 1933, Katharine Hepburn became one of the most admired and beloved of screen actresses. On-screen and off-screen, for more than half a century she cultivated the image of a feisty, independent woman.

of the 1930s made slavery sound idyllic: "Although he was in a state of slavery, the Negro of plantation days was usually happy. He was fond of the company of others and liked to sing, dance, crack jokes, and laugh." In spirit, Roosevelt supported black civil rights, but he was hobbled by his need for southern congressional support and by the strong prejudices of the times. The president spoke out against lynching and poll taxes, but he did little to ease ingrained patterns of racial discrimination. Political expediency made him unwilling to push an anti-lynching bill through Congress in 1934. "Southerners," FDR explained to NAACP secretary Walter White, "by reason of the seniority rule in Congress, are chairmen or occupy strategic positions on most of the Senate and House committees. If I come out for the anti-lynching bill now, they will block every bill I ask Congress to pass to keep America from collapsing. I just can't take that risk." Some New Deal agencies fought discrimination, but most programs were so decentralized that local officials ignored blacks if they so wished. Only eleven of the ten thousand WPA supervisors in the South were black.

Nonetheless, Roosevelt encouraged his wife Eleanor, who was much more deeply committed to civil rights than he, to become a public advocate for black rights. Because of her, most blacks felt that they had a friend in the White House. Eleanor appeared frequently at black functions and she made the president accessible to African American leaders, particularly Walter White of the NAACP and Mary McLeod Bethune, president of the National Council of Negro Women. In 1939, when the Daughters of the American Revolution blocked a planned Easter Sunday appearance of famed black classical contralto Marian Anderson at their Constitution Hall in Washington, D.C., Eleanor Roosevelt resigned from that blue-blood organization and Secretary of the Interior Harold Ickes (who had been a leader in the bi-racial NAACP) authorized a concert on the steps of the Lincoln Memorial. An audience of about 75,000 attended, including rows of cabinet members, congressmen, and Supreme Court justices. Such gestures were sufficient to win Roosevelt the political loyalty of black voters and to tug at white consciences, but they did little to ease economic and political discrimination.

New Deal agricultural policy and racial persecution during the 1930s hastened the exodus of black workers off the farms into the cities of the South and the North. The cost of transportation and lack of employment opportunities slowed the number of blacks migrating out of the South to 347,000 during the decade — about half as many as in the twenties. In both northern and southern cities, newly arrived blacks found little opportunity; by 1933, fully 50 percent of black workers were unemployed. Long barred by patterns of discrimination from holding many jobs, during the Depression blacks were often displaced from such historic "Negro jobs" as domestic service and garbage collection. One of the few glimmers of hope for working blacks was the CIO's eagerness to organize them in the new industrial unions — a welcome contrast to the stone wall of exclusion that had faced them in the A.F. of L.'s craft unions.

The Depression exacerbated racial tensions. Lynchings increased dramatically in the early 1930s before easing under the spotlight of national media attention

A Lynching, 1930 This chilling photograph was taken not in the Deep South but in Marion, Indiana. The two young black men were accused of killing a white man and assaulting his girlfriend. Taken by a mob from the county jail, they were hung in the town square. The onlookers' smug and gleeful expressions speak for themselves.

at the end of the decade. The most widely publicized racial incident of the thirties involved the indictment of nine black youths in 1931 for an alleged rape of two white prostitutes (who later recanted) on a freight train near Scottsboro, Alabama. The case struck the central nerve of southern race prejudice — sexual intercourse between black males and white women. The youths were given legal aid by the International Labor Defense, an organization with close ties to the Communist party, but, after a hasty trial, they were sentenced to electrocution. After a series of appeals, only one of the nine, Clarence Norris, remained on death row (his sentence was later commuted by the governor); four served prison terms, and four were released.

The NAACP pressed for anti-lynching legislation during the thirties, resulting in repeated debates in Congress, but southern filibusters successfully killed each effort. On the other hand, several court decisions during the thirties hinted at the future course of civil rights reform. In 1938 the Supreme Court ruled that a black student could not be excluded from Missouri's all-white law school, and the court rulings chipped away at southern laws restricting black voting rights. By the end of the thirties, the consciences of educated whites had become more and more uneasy about the

Jesse Owens Americans of all races were thrilled when Jesse Owens won four gold medals, for sprints and (shown here) the broad jump, at the 1936 Olympics in Berlin. Adolf Hitler, who was in the stands, was less thrilled—he stormed out when Owens defeated a German champion. Owens, as a successful business-man, went on to become a role model for younger blacks during the civil rights era.

continuation of racial discrimination. In 1937 Swedish sociologist Gunnar Myrdal began a massive report on race relations in America, *An American Dilemma.* Funded by the Carnegie Foundation, when it was finally published in 1944 Myrdal's study offered a stunning indictment of prejudice in America. Defending his lack of support for anti-lynching legislation in a 1934 conversation with Norman Thomas, FDR predicted that the South would ultimately change: "I'm a damned sight better politician than you are. I know the South, and there is arising a new generation of leaders and we've got to be patient." Indeed, by the end of the decade a coterie of progressive southern leaders had begun to call for an end to lynch law and the poll tax, including editors Ralph McGill of the *Atlanta Constitution* and Hodding Carter, Jr., of the *Greenville* (Mississippi) *Delta Democrat Times.* But more than a generation of determined struggle for African American civil rights still lay ahead as the New Deal was approaching its end.

Baptist, Methodist, and Pentecostal churches remained at the heart of black culture during the Depression, but segregated Afro-American society was also fertile soil for cult leaders. The most noted such figure was George Baker, a black minister who styled himself Father Major J. Divine, and whose followers, mostly black, thought him to be God. In 1933 Father Divine moved his headquarters to Harlem, where he established a Peace Mission, garnering much attention for aiding unemployed blacks, dispensing charity, living lavishly, and posing as a combination mystic, showman, and messiah. Charlatan or true believer, Father Divine offered hope to people disenchanted with conventional churches, and he preached a benign gospel of racial harmony. Father Divine's following was sufficient to attract the attention of politicians, including Roosevelt, and his Peace Movement flourished until his death in 1965.

More important in the long run was the founding of the Nation of Islam (Black Muslims) in Detroit in 1931 by an obscure peddler named Wallace D. Fard. Fard

Eleanor Roosevelt
Protests Lynchings, 1936

*First Lady Eleanor Roosevelt felt very strongly
that the government should protect African
Americans from the scourge of lynchings, but
she was constrained in her efforts to bring
about change, as her letter to Walter White, the
executive secretary of the NAACP, made clear.*

PERSONAL AND CONFIDENTIAL.
The White House
Washington

March 19, 1936

My dear Mr. White:

Before I received your letter today I had been
in to see the President, talking to him about
your letter. . . . I told him that it seems rather
terrible that one could get nothing done and
that I did not blame you in the least for feeling there was no interest in this very serious
question. I asked him if there were any possibility of getting even one step taken, and he
said the difficulty is that it is unconstitutional
apparently for the Federal Government to
step in in the lynching situation. The Government has only been allowed to do anything
about kidnapping because of its interstate
aspect, and even that has not as yet been
appealed so they are not sure that it will be
declared constitutional.

The President feels that lynching is a
question of education in the states, rallying
good citizens, and creating public opinion
so that the localities themselves will wipe it
out. However, if it were done by a Northerner,
it will have an antagonistic effect. . . . I am
deeply troubled about the whole situation
as it seems to be a terrible thing to stand by
and let it continue and feel that one cannot
speak out as to his feeling. I think your next
step would be to talk to the more prominent
members of the Senate.

Very sincerely yours,

Eleanor Roosevelt

disappeared mysteriously in 1934 and was succeeded
by a Georgia minister, Robert Poole, who had taken the
name Elijah Muhammad. Basing much of their doctrine on a distorted reading of the Qur'an, Black Muslims taught that whites were devils created by an evil
scientist, Yakub, and that only blacks were children of
Allah. By the end of the thirties, the group had created
a ritual, formed a hierarchy, and stabilized at around
ten thousand highly disciplined and rigidly moralistic
members. The Nation of Islam competed with similar
groups for the loyalty of alienated urban blacks.

Sports stars continued to offer the most stunning evidence of black resilience during the Depression. In the
Berlin Olympics in 1936, sprinter Jesse Owens enraged
Hitler (who stalked out of the stadium) by winning four
gold medals, confounding Nazi theories of racial superiority. The same point was hammered home in June
1936 when heavyweight-boxing champion Joe Louis
(the "Brown Bomber") knocked out German champion
Max Schmeling in the first round in Yankee Stadium
before a crowd of 75,000. Still, the major team sports
remained rigidly segregated, depriving most Americans of the opportunity to see such great Negro League
athletes as Satchel Paige, in the opinion of many the
finest pitcher in baseball history, except in special ex-

hibition games (in which he frequently struck out the
white major-league batting champions). The integration of professional baseball, football, and basketball
would not even begin until the late 1940s.

The fate of Hispanic Americans during the Depression was much like that of blacks. More than 2 million
Hispanics, mostly agricultural laborers from Mexico,
had been welcomed for their cheap labor by agricultural
employers in the Southwest during the twenties. Competing with white migrant workers, probably half returned to Mexico during the thirties. Those who stayed
in the United States flocked to the cities of the Southwest. Generally deprived of government assistance because they were not citizens, they became some of the
most invisible and helpless survivors of the Depression.

Anti-Semitism intensified during the thirties. When
the Nazi persecution of Jews reached its peak, the
United States granted entry to only a small number of
those trying to flee the impending Holocaust. Anti-Semitic demagogues built large followings; for example,
the Baptist preacher Gerald B. Winrod of Kansas secured 100,000 subscribers for his virulently anti-Jewish
magazine *The Defender*. Many Americans shared Winrod's — and Father Coughlin's — populist-based view
that a conspiracy of international Jewish bankers had

caused the Depression. While anti-Semitism was usually subtler than discrimination against blacks, Jews routinely were excluded from many jobs, exclusive neighborhoods, and private clubs. Many of the leading American universities, including those in the Ivy League, only reluctantly hired Jewish faculty and established quotas for Jewish student enrollments.

Federal Indian policy was revamped during the 1930s under the leadership of Roosevelt's commissioner of Indian affairs, John Collier, who deeply sympathized with the Indians' historical grievances and present plight. Collier's approach was strongly influenced by anthropological theory, particularly Ruth Benedict's influential *Patterns of Culture* (1934) stressing the cohesive values of traditional cultures. Indeed, many anthropologists viewed Indian societies, with their emphases on communal values, intuition, and religious belief, as superior to modern western culture. The primary intent of the Indian Reorganization Act (Wheeler-Howard Act), passed in 1934 at Collier's recommendation, however, was to preserve tribal lands and customs. The intent of the Dawes Act, passed in 1887, had been to encourage the integration of Native Americans into mainstream American society by breaking up reservations and granting homesteads to individual Indians, who were supposed to become white-style farmers. It resulted in a serious reduction in the amount of acreage held by Indians, from 138 million acres in 1887 to 78 million by 1900.

The New Deal's Indian Reorganization Act granted a degree of self-government to Indian reservations, halted the allotment system that had permitted many whites to acquire Indian lands, and created a revolving credit fund to encourage economic development on the reservations. At the same time, the act broadened the powers of the Bureau of Indian Affairs to enforce policies designed by social science experts to improve Indian life. These reforms did not totally allay discontent on the reservations. Many Indians insisted that the New Deal had created a new colonialism that made them servants of an autocratic Collier and his panel of experts. At the end of the decade, the Bureau of Indian Affairs once again veered toward policies that encouraged the integration of Indians into the broader society and the undermining of Native American cultural values — policies that would continue until the 1960s.

❧ *Expanding Regional Sensibilities*

The United States in the 1930s remained a nation with dissimilar regions as well as distinct minorities. Many

Americans still lived on farms. While the census of 1940 reported that nearly 75 million (56.5 percent) lived in areas with a population of 2,500 or over, less than 40 percent lived in towns over 25,000, and the general trend toward urbanization virtually stopped during the Depression. In short, despite impressive urbanization, during the 1930s the United States was still predominantly a nation of small cities, towns, and farms.

The nation's vast regional and local differences attracted a new level of interest and study during the 1930s, highlighted by the publication in 1932 of historian Frederick Jackson Turner's *The Significance of Sections in American History*. Turner's writings, together with University of Texas historian Walter Prescott Webb's *The Great Plains* (1931), revealed a growing western regional consciousness. Many westerners had long been restive under the cultural and economic domination of the Northeast. Turner and Webb emphasized (and probably exaggerated) the historical uniqueness of the frontier West, but western regional consciousness owed more to the legislation of the Progressive Era and the New Deal that gave the region a unique relationship with the federal government. Westerners, more than any other Americans, were brought into close contact with the new federal bureaucracy — the Bureau of Indian Affairs, the Bureau of Land Management, the National Forest Service, and the Bureau of Reclamation. Huge amounts of western lands had been placed in the public domain and set aside as national parks and national forests. A growing anti-government bias in the West was more related to twentieth-century policies than the frontier experience. In addition, the growth of huge and largely autonomous Indian reservations, combined with the influx of legal and illegal Mexican laborers, defined the West as a region with distinctive ethnic minorities and problems.

The South, the land of lynchings and (in Roosevelt's words) "the nation's number one economic problem," remained the country's most self-conscious region. In the South several universities became centers of regional study, particularly the University of North Carolina, where sociologists Howard W. Odum and Rupert Vance led a broad exploration that emphasized the region's strengths and encouraged regional planning. A group of twelve southerners with ties to Vanderbilt University offered a regional critique of the nation in a widely-noted book published in 1930, *I'll Take My Stand*. Known as the "Agrarians" because they praised southerners' historic attachment to the land, these writers urged rural independence as a cure for the Depression

I'll Take My Stand, 1930
Twelve Southern authors came together in 1930 to write I'll Take My Stand, *a manifesto that urged Southerners and others with strong ties to small-town life and farming to appreciate their own past and not to give in to industrialization as the only vision of the future.*

Nobody now proposes for the South, or for any other community in this country, an independent political destiny. That idea is thought to have been finished in 1865. But how far shall the South surrender its moral, social, and economic autonomy to the victorious principle of Union? That question remains open. The South is a minority section that has hitherto been jealous of its minority right to live its own kind of life. The South scarcely hopes to determine the other sections, but it does propose to determine itself, within the utmost limits of legal action. Of late, however, there is the melancholy fact that the South itself has wavered a little and shown signs of wanting to join up behind the common or American industrial ideal. It is against that tendency that this book is written. The younger Southerners, who are being converted frequently to the industrial gospel, must come back to the support of the Southern tradition. They must be persuaded to look very critically at the advantages of becoming a "new South" which will be only an undistinguished replica of the usual industrial community.

and praised the survival of family ties and religion in the South. A diffuse attack on industrialism and defense of southern values, historian Paul Conkin suggested that the book could have appropriately ended with a paraphrase of the Marxist *Communist Manifesto:* "Farmers and poets of the world unite." A reaction against southern boosters' images of the New South and Yankee prejudices about the Benighted South, the writings of the Agrarians exposed the degree to which white southerners considered themselves outsiders in the 1930s and took pride in their regional distinctiveness.

THE ARTS SERVE THE NATION

Technological advances continued to feed the development of mass culture during the Depression years. While the Depression dampened the commercial development of some forms of entertainment, such as movies, it actually encouraged the expansion of radio, which provided free information and culture. To a remarkable degree, American artists joined in the nationalistic mood of the decade, searching in the nation's past for the needed sources of strength to weather the trauma of the Depression. Much of the decade's popular culture was escapist, but some of its enduring works probed the most basic human instincts for individual and family survival.

✸ *Depression Literature: Suffering, Endurance, Patriotism*

The Depression not only seared Americans' lives; its very misery and suffering also offered creative and sensitive writers rich material for pondering the human condition. American readers, likewise, yearned for something that would respond to their pain and fear — explain it, interpret it, or just help them forget it. All of these ingredients combined to make the thirties one of the great creative periods for both "serious" and popular American writing.

The most obvious response to the Depression was to capture the desperation of its victims. A school of "hard-boiled" writers — usually leftists and sometimes Communists — won considerable critical acclaim writing socially conscious novels that cast workers as heroes and capitalists as villains. Most of this writing is today largely forgotten, but among the best of it, James Farrell's trilogy *Studs Lonigan* (1932-35) was a moving, naturalistic portrayal of the exploitation of an Irish immigrant family in Chicago.

By far the most popular and artistically enduring of the era's "naturalistic" novels was published near the end of the Great Depression: California writer John Steinbeck's *The Grapes of Wrath* (1939), a tale of migrant farm laborers fleeing the Oklahoma Dust Bowl. The story of the Joad family, *The Grapes of Wrath* described the hardships and handicaps of migrant laborers, but the book was more a story of family heroism than a book of political protest. The beleaguered migrants endured their pain and shared suffering with an unshakable hope for a "better tomorrow." Although not stylistically important, Steinbeck's moving depiction of Depression suffering won a Pulitzer Prize in 1940, and in 1962 (largely on the basis of this work) he was awarded the Nobel Prize for Literature. In her newspaper column, Eleanor Roosevelt wrote: "*Grapes of Wrath* by John Steinbeck both repels and attracts you. The

John Steinbeck's *The Grapes of Wrath*   A poignant 1939 novel that was made into a powerful film, Steinbeck's epic account of the Joad family's journey from Oklahoma to California was one of the Depression decade's greatest literary events. This is the cover of the first edition.

horrors of the picture, so well drawn, made you dread sometimes to begin the next chapter, and yet you cannot lay the book down or even skip a page." By the end of 1939 the novel had sold 430,000 copies, and John Ford's movie version of *The Grapes of Wrath*, which appeared the next year, became one of the most popular motion pictures of the era.

Despite the leftist leanings of many writers, most serious fiction in the thirties either ignored the social crisis or appealed to the patriotism of the nation's besieged people. Ernest Hemingway, the twenties writer who moved most gracefully into the Depression decade, turned more and more to probing human beings' primal needs for food, drink, sex, and physical exertion. Hemingway's writing was not totally void of a social concern; in *For Whom the Bell Tolls* (1940), a novel that drew on Hemingway's experiences in the Spanish Civil War, the hero, Robert Jordan, dies fighting for the loyalists, vaguely perceiving that he had defended the same principles of freedom and democracy that his father once fought for in the American Civil War. John Dos Passos best illustrated the intellectual migration of the decade's serious writers. Dos Passos supported communist causes in the 1920s and early 1930s, and his massive and stylistically brilliant trilogy, *U.S.A.* (1930-36), catalogued American capitalism's villainies. But a later book, *The Ground We Stand On* (1941), was an inventory of American virtues, foreshadowing Dos Passos's later move far to the political right. Similarly, in 1936, the literary critic Van Wyck Brooks, who in the twenties had sneered at his country as a cultural wasteland, published a celebration of nineteenth-century American literature entitled *The Flowering of New England.*

The southern literary renaissance of the 1930s was deep-rooted in the South's delayed encounter with modernity. The region caricatured by H. L. Mencken in a 1920s essay as "The Sahara of the Bozart" ("Bozart" = *beaux arts,* or fine arts) in the 1930s became a fertile seedbed for some of America's greatest novelists. The region's most celebrated writer, William Faulkner, wrote brooding tales that superficially seemed oblivious to the Depression. In 1929, Faulkner began exploring his native Mississippi in *The Sound and the Fury.* Writing in a complex and demanding modernist style, Faulkner chronicled the degeneration of the fictional Compson family. Some critics pigeonholed Faulkner as a regionalist, but his themes, played out amidst the dark history of his native Mississippi, were universal. Faulkner riveted on the battle between flesh and spirit in stories about the Sutpen family with resounding biblical titles such as *Absalom, Absalom!* (1936) and *Go Down, Moses.* Although Faulkner's novels probed the depths of human perversity in its characteristically Southern guise, in his acceptance of the 1949 Nobel Prize for Literature he insisted that his writings also spoke of courage, honor, hope, pride, compassion, pity, and sacrifice. Faulkner's tragically short-lived contemporary, Thomas Wolfe of Asheville, North Carolina, in a brilliant and lyrical semi-autobiographical novel, *Look Homeward, Angel* (1929), also focused on the tension between southern regional traits and modernity.

Even more than serious fiction, popular writing in the 1930s highlighted the human will to overcome adversity. Dismissed by many critics as hack writing, the most popular (and profitable) fiction work of the thirties was *Gone with the Wind* (1936), written by Mar-

A Photograph by Walker Evans Art in the Depression years — such as this haunting 1936 image of an Alabama sharecropper and his young son — turned its focus onto the lives of ordinary people.

garet Mitchell, the wife of an Atlanta advertising executive. The story of southern belle Scarlett O'Hara's strong-willed survival during the Civil War and Reconstruction sold 2 million copies within two years (more than 25 million by 1990), was translated into seven languages, and published in thirty-seven countries. The book reminded Depression Americans that the nation had survived worse calamities before, and also offered escape into a more romantic past (which modern historians have thoroughly demolished). The film version opened amid unparalleled publicity at Loew's Grand Theater in Atlanta on December 16, 1939. The movie won a record nine Hollywood Oscars, and for many years it was the longest film (231 minutes) produced in America.

Pulp novels, a fixture in American popular literature since the 1890s, sold millions of copies during the Depression. By the beginning of the thirties, mysteries, westerns, science fiction, and crime stories were well-established pulp genres. While much of the writing in these cheap books was formula rubbish, some talented writers wrote pulp fiction, including Zane Grey, Isaac Asimov, Erle Stanley Gardner (the creator of Perry Mason), and Dashiell Hammett (the author of *The Maltese Falcon* and other detective thrillers).

Publishers introduced new pulp series almost monthly during the thirties, many of them featuring valiant, sometimes superhuman, heroes, including Street & Smith's *Shadow Magazine* (1931), *Doc Savage* (1933), and *Nick Carter* (1933). Paper shortages cut into the publication of pulps as World War II approached, and the industry encountered new competition after the war, particularly from television, but during their heyday the pulps published more good and bad prose fiction, to be read by more people, than at any other time in American history.

The most influential new periodical of the Depression decade was *Time,* a jauntily written magazine of news and commentary. Founded by young Yale graduates Henry Luce and Briton Hadden in 1926, *Time's* circulation reached more than a million in 1940. Luce built Time, Inc., into a formidable publishing empire in the 1930s, launching *Fortune* magazine in 1930 and *Life* in 1936, both quality magazines of their respective genres. *Life,* featuring the work of some of the nation's best news photographers, was a spectacular success, reaching a circulation of more than 3 million by 1940, and *Fortune* was one of the most intelligent of business-oriented publications. All of the Luce publications were intended to teach as well as inform the public; the stirring photographic history of the Depression published in *Life* did much to sharpen the national vision of the decade's tragedies and triumphs. On the other hand, Luce was never particularly well-disposed toward Roosevelt, and (except for the popular *Life*) the reach of his publications was confined largely to educated professionals.

Newspapers consolidated under the pressures of Depression economics, but they continued to be the public's major source of news. Comic strips became an enormously popular addition to newspapers in the thirties; most of them imparted time-honored moral messages and furnished millions of Americans with new heroes cast in old morality plays.

The resurgent patriotism of the thirties stimulated studies of ordinary people, their lives and sufferings, and their culture. Constance Rourke, a cosmopolitan woman educated at Vassar, returned to her home in Grand Rapids, Michigan, during the Depression, where she wrote a series of books on folk culture, including the widely read *American Humor* (1931). The New Deal contributed to the renewed interest in folk culture. The WPA Federal Writer's Project collected folklore, folk songs, and tombstone inscriptions and pioneered the field of oral history, collecting the recollections of marginal Americans such as tenant farmers, ex-slaves (published in 1947 as *Lay My Burden Down*), and American Indians; these collections are now invaluable to modern historians' research. A new genre of documentary literature that combined the work of reporters and photographers focused on the lives of ordinary people. In 1936 Walker Evans produced a haunting collection of photographs of tenant farming and poverty in Alabama for *Fortune* magazine; his pictures were subsequently published along with James Agee's stream-of-consciousness narrative in *Let Us Now Praise Famous Men* (1941).

❧ Art and Architecture Turn Serious

"Serious" art during the Depression, like "serious" writing, became more conservative and nationalistic. Although avant-garde artists often suffered grievously as patronage withered after the Wall Street crash, the work of the established modernists found places where it could be exhibited regularly with the founding of the Museum of Modern Art in 1929 and the Whitney Museum of American Art in 1930 in New York City. The Museum of Modern Art sponsored important exhibits in 1936 and 1937 featuring cubism, surrealism, and other abstract forms. Although economic conditions and public tastes still presented formidable barriers, the foundations were being laid for the emergence of New York as the center of the international art world after World War II.

For the broad public, however, the most successful art of the 1930s was realistic. The Federal Art Project favored traditional techniques that would create a popular art expressing the nation's aspirations and achievements. Although some American painters were influenced by the leftist Mexican muralists and painted socially pertinent themes, the cultural nationalism of the decade turned American art toward a discovery of things American. By far the most popular artist of the thirties was Norman Rockwell, whose *Saturday Evening Post* covers captured the mythic strengths of American life and religious faith.

Critics called the decade's leading school of paint-

ers regionalists because of their Midwestern roots and their strong preference for rural subjects, but they considered their work an expression of American nationalism. Leading regionalists John Steuart Curry, Grant Wood, and Thomas Hart Benton were conservative in style, disdaining modern art forms as decadent. The regionalists were not political conservatives; Wood was a New Deal Democrat and Benton's paintings of sharecroppers and blacks were influenced by left-wing Mexican muralists. Nonetheless, their work celebrated the strength and vigor of ordinary Americans. Grant Wood's *American Gothic,* the most popular painting at the Chicago Century of Progress Exposition in 1933 and probably of the decade, spoke of the harshness and courage of life in rural America.

Modernism made little headway among architects during the thirties, as most architectural firms — in a time of relatively low commissions — had to play it safe. There was a distinctly anti-urban bias in the modern architecture of the decade. Lewis Mumford, an influential architectural critic and editor of *The New Republic,* urged "a more organic utilization of the entire environment" aimed at decentralizing urban population. The great architect Frank Lloyd Wright was a more strident critic of modern life, denouncing cities as scars on the natural landscape. Wright's "Fallingwater" house at Bear Creek, Pennsylvania, the most famous residential structure in America in the 1930s, idealized life in the country. Wright's disdain for cities and his respect for the environment led many to regard his work as America's primary contribution to the field of architecture.

Urban architecture during the 1930s moved toward functionalism, the use of materials for architectural expression as well as practical ends. The skyscraper was established as a major American contribution to modern architecture by 1930. During the Depression the New York skyline added the Chrysler Building (1930), the Empire State Building (1931), and Rockefeller Center (1932-1940), the first integrated group of skyscrapers. All these buildings used setbacks as a means of bypassing a 1916 zoning law that limited the height of buildings at street level to allow sunlight into the urban canyons; all were notable works of art — although most of them remained short of tenants until after World War II. The continued building of skyscrapers, most of them bearing the name of a corporate owner, also symbolized the survival of big business in the midst of the country's darkest economic hour.

A WPA Mural   The murals painting by WPA artists for public places like post offices and government buildings generally imitated the heroic style of the Mexican and Soviet revolutionary art of the 1930s. This mural, by Anton Refregier, glorifies the building of the California missions of the eighteenth century by Franciscan friars and their Indian workers.

❧ Radio Unites the Nation

The Depression did little to slow the growth of a national mass culture; the paramount carrier of that culture was radio. In the world of culture, the economic collapse had hit hardest at local or ethnic-oriented institutions, facilitating their replacement by nationally oriented mass media — above all the radio and the movies, which in the thirties came to be recognized as art forms, "the lively arts." Radio was a free entertainment bonanza during the Depression, available in virtually all households, and it had a powerful homogenizing impact on the nation. In 1939, a *Fortune* magazine poll indicated that 70 percent of Americans relied on the radio (rather than newspapers) as their primary source of news. Newscasters such as H. V. Kaltenborn, William L. Shirer, and Lowell Thomas, all of them male and each with a distinctive style, became trusted authorities on the stirring and disturbing events of the decade in millions of households. Nearly everybody in the country laughed at the antics of characters in the most popular regular programs, such as "Amos 'n'

Andy." Millions of people also received regular doses of high culture by way of radio. "Good music" was widely broadcast and the combined audience of weekend broadcasts by the NBC Symphony Orchestra, directed by famed anti-Fascist émigré Arturo Toscanini, the Metropolitan Opera, the New York Philharmonic, and the Detroit Symphony surpassed 10 million listeners. Thus radio continued to close the gap between high and mass culture in America.

Many independent local stations were crushed by the Great Depression, and even if they survived the hard times, they had trouble dealing with the competition presented by the emerging national networks. In 1933, the National Broadcasting Company (NBC) dominated the broadcasting industry, operating two successful networks of stations. The company advertised its success by moving into its imposing new "Radio Center" headquarters in Rockefeller Center on Fifth Avenue in New York City. By the mid-thirties, NBC had a serious competitor, the Columbia Broadcasting System (CBS), a network put together by former cigar mogul William S. Paley. These two major networks suffered declining revenues during the Depression, but they consolidated their dominance of the medium because hard times made it almost impossible for independent stations to survive. Government regulation of radio, begun in 1927 with the establishment of the Federal Radio Commission and expanded with the founding of the Federal

Communications Commission in 1934, upgraded the quality of transmission and greatly improved the quality of broadcasting — but also effectively eliminated weaker competitors.

By the mid-thirties nearly 70 percent of American homes owned a radio, and it became a favored medium for advertisers. The latter half of the 1930s was the golden age of radio, available in nearly all American homes, and, by 1941, in 7.5 million American cars. Between 1935 and 1941 the number of houses with radios climbed from 7 million to 28.5 million, and around half the homes in the nation had two radios. During the last half of the decade about 200 new radio stations were constructed. Most stations reached urban audiences, but in 1934 the first 500,000-watt superpower station, WLW, began broadcasting from Cincinnati with a signal that reached much of the rural Midwest and South. The burst of new stations made possible the founding of the Mutual Network in 1934.

Radio stations steadily increased the amount of airtime during the 1930s, creating an insatiable demand for programming. More than half of the programming was music, most of it taken from electrical transcriptions and records. However, live musical performances were common, both on local stations and the networks. Popular bandleaders such as Benny Goodman, Tommy Dorsey, Russ Morgan, and Sammy Kaye were local radio celebrities before becoming network stars. One of the most popular network programs of the decade, "Your Hit Parade," featured the top rated songs of the week performed live by an all-star cast.

Other types of programs found important niches. Religious programming made up about 5 percent of airtime in the 1930s, and some preachers, like Father Charles Coughlin and Charles E. Fuller, had national audiences. Nearly 10 percent of radio programming was news; in 1930 NBC introduced the first regular fifteen-minute network news program. Professional sports, especially baseball, were also brought into virtually every home by a colorful array of radio sportscasters. (It was during these years that future president Ronald Reagan found his first job as a local radio sportscaster before moving on to Hollywood.) By the end of the decade radio surpassed newspapers as the most popular source of news. Only about 20 percent of radio airtime was filled by talk shows and drama, but those programs contributed much to the popularity of the medium in the 1930s. The quintessential success story was the situation comedy "Amos 'n' Andy," an NBC show begun in 1929 that starred the former

blackface vaudeville minstrel performers Freeman F. Gosden and Charles J. Correll. Featuring comical adventures in a setting including the Freshair Taxicab Company and the fraternal lodge, the Mystic Knights of the Sea, the show was such a phenomenal success that its cast of characters, and their quirks, became familiar to virtually every American. "Amos 'n' Andy" caricatured American black society, and the show's popularity underscored the easy acceptance of racial stereotypes during the thirties. In spite of the stereotyping, however, the characters were plucky, indomitable, and resourceful (especially the wily Kingfish), and the program was a favorite of blacks as well as whites. Other situation comedies became immensely popular in the thirties, including "Baby Snooks," in which actress Fanny Brice "terrorized" her father and brother.

By the end of the decade, radio had explored most of the dramatic forms that would later be adapted to television: situation comedies, quiz shows, soap operas, adventure series, and serious drama. All of the networks broadcast hours weekly of soap operas (so-called because most of them were sponsored by the manufacturers of soap powder and other products aimed at housewives). Adventure series flourished during prime time. "Gangbusters" played on the decade's fascination with crime fighting; "The Lone Ranger" played out the same morals after school hours in a western setting; and "The Green Hornet," begun in 1938, took the war on crime to new technological levels.

The networks also produced a steady stream of serious drama in the late 1930s, often presenting versions of recent movies. The most famous single moment in 1930s radio history came on October 30, 1938, when CBS broadcast Orson Welles's production of H. G. Wells's science fiction novel *War of the Worlds* on its "Mercury Theater on the Air." The program was creatively produced, appearing to be a conventional broadcast being repeatedly interrupted by news flashes reporting a Martian invasion of New Jersey. Thousands of listeners tuned into the program after the opening explanation, and many panicked, believing the reports authentic. (The radio public may have been primed to learn of sudden disasters, for this same month Europe went to the brink of war when Hitler threatened to invade Czechoslovakia; see Chapter 29.)

The reaction to the "War of the Worlds" broadcast symbolized the enormous influence of radio. Americans embraced the medium not only as entertainment but as a source of truth. That power served various interests in the thirties. Big business used radio's popu-

The Radio Goes to Camp These boys are at summer camp near Chicago listening to the radio. Sets were donated by manufacturers to keep campers happy and in touch with their favorite programs. Americans depended on radio in the 1930s, as their children and grandchildren would come to depend on television and the Internet, to stay in touch with the world and with popular culture.

larity to build huge communications corporations and through advertising to reach vast audiences to sell a variety of wares. Radio also served government agencies and politicians well — none better than Franklin D. Roosevelt.

❧ Movies Come of Age

Motion picture audiences declined early in the Depression, a victim of hard times and increasing competition from radio, but began to revive by the end of the decade. The movie industry fought back by offering double features — two films for the price of one — and between features local movie theaters often featured

games and contests offering prizes. By the end of the decade, about 85 million Americans of all classes, ages, and educational levels attended a movie each week.

In the early 1930s the most popular theme in Hollywood was gangster movies. Films such as *Little Caesar* (1930) and *Public Enemy* (1931) catapulted into stardom tough guys Edward G. Robinson and James Cagney. While the gangster movies of the 1930s unswervingly ended with right triumphing over wrong, the gangsters were often portrayed sympathetically; their brashness, energy, and audacity in the face of a hostile world all seemed to give hope to people during the Depression.

Comedy films were also popular during the 1930s. Charlie Chaplin climaxed his career in *The Great Dictator* (1940), playing a Jewish barber whose native country, "Bacteria," had been taken over by a dictator whose emblem was a double-cross. An obvious and clever spoof of Hitler that ended with Chaplin's ringing defense of democracy and human rights, the movie lost some of its poignancy because cautious financial backers delayed its release for fear that it was too controversial. The Marx brothers, Groucho, Chico, and Harpo, reached the zenith of their popularity in a series of Depression films that featured outrageous appearances and the acerbic wit of Groucho.

The decade's most notorious screen persona was Mae West; the voluptuous actress became a legend for delivering wisecracks in a sultry voice from the side of her mouth. In *Night after Night* (1932), a hat check girl, eyeing West, gasped, "Goodness, what beautiful diamonds." West, in a line that stole the show, retorted, "Goodness had nothing to do with it, dearie." West's co-star in the film, George Raft, complained that she "stole everything but the cameras"; West, in turn, revealed that she and Raft had sex in a broom closet — "It was love on the run with half the buttons undone." Moviemakers during the thirties came under increasing pressure to tone down the racy offerings of the twenties, particularly from the Catholic-led Legion of Decency. Acting to head off outside censorship, in 1930 the Motion Picture Producers and Distributors of America adopted a Production Code that banned anything causing the "sympathy of the audience [to be] thrown to the side of crime, wrongdoing, evil or sin." "Impure love," if portrayed in film, could not be "presented as attractive and beautiful" or so as to "arouse passion or morbid curiosity on the part of the audience." The film *Extase* (1933), starring sixteen-year-old Hedy Lamarr, was widely banned in the United States as pornographic, though it won awards in Europe. It was a measure of how strait-laced movies had become that actor Clark Gable's closing words in *Gone with the Wind* — "Frankly, my dear, I don't give a damn!" — shocked the nation as "profanity." In spite of the code, moviemakers found ways to titillate audiences with displays of flesh; the women in Cecil B. De Mille's famous series of biblical epics wore gowns that had more to do with sex than piety or history.

Technological advances in two areas improved 1930s movies. Better sound made possible the filming of complex song and dance routines. Many early talkies contained some singing, but during the 1930s full-scale musicals became popular. Many of the musicals of the 1930s were scored by famous theater composers, including George and Ira Gershwin, Cole Porter, Richard Rodgers, and Jerome Kern, and they starred such Broadway musical stars as Maurice Chevalier and Jeanette MacDonald. In 1935, Irving Berlin wrote the score for the decade's most popular musical, *Top Hat*, a film featuring the dancing team of Fred Astaire and Ginger Rogers.

Color filming also began in the 1930s. The Technicolor Corporation perfected its process in 1933. Technicolor was used sparingly in the 1930s: it was costly and most producers felt more comfortable working in black and white. Color adapted more easily to animation, and Walt Disney, who in the late 1920s had taken the lead in the field of cartoon production with his popular character, Mickey Mouse, quickly outdistanced competitors in films. Disney's full-length animated cartoon, *Snow White* (1937), was a technical masterpiece and a smashing box office success.

The most spectacular full-length movie produced in perfected technicolor in the 1930s was Victor Fleming's *Gone with the Wind* (1939). Brilliantly photographed and skillfully acted, the movie challenged no clichés of the day about race and the South. The most celebrated artistic production of the pre–World War II American movie industry was Orson Welles's *Citizen Kane* (1941). Welles starred in a leading role that was loosely but obviously modeled on the life of publisher William Randolph Hearst — who tried but failed to have the film suppressed. The movie was a triumph of both realism and symbolism, and Welles used a variety of innovative techniques in camera angles, lighting, and sound that are still imitated.

Like radio, the movies of the thirties appealed to certain themes that obviously met the psychic needs of the Depression generation. Many films celebrated the human capacity to survive tragedy and hardship. In addition, 1930s movies heralded such virtues as selfless love, honesty, and justice. The Production Code may have contributed to the simple morality of thirties films, but in truth the films highlighted those virtues that most Americans esteemed most highly during the Depression.

❧ Life Goes On

The popularity of music on the radio and in films encouraged creative artists to synthesize new popular forms of music. Irving Berlin continued to mix ragtime and jazz in his successful musicals, doing much to define the popular music of the day. Before George Gershwin's tragic death in 1937 at age thirty-eight, he created a brilliant work of synthesis of African American, Latin-American, and classical music in the opera *Porgy and Bess* (1935), a work that included such popular songs as "Summertime," "I Got Plenty o' Nuttin'," and "It Ain't Necessarily So."

Jazz continued to be the most popular music in the

early thirties. Black artists such as Louis Armstrong remained on the cutting edge of the development of jazz, and the popularity of white bandleaders such as Paul Whiteman and Benny Goodman exposed the work of black artists to wider audiences. In 1934, Goodman formed an orchestra in New York that played a fast, pulsating variation on jazz that was labeled "swing." Others contributed to the development of swing, including Tommy and Jimmy Dorsey, and, beginning in 1938, the Glenn Miller Band. Based on simple melodies played in a highly disciplined orchestration dominated by saxophones, swing was the dance and record rage at the end of the decade. In the twenties jazz symbol-

Hedy Lamarr   An Austrian-born star, Lamarr shocked American movie audiences with her sexuality. Some of her European-made films were banned in the United States as indecent. This picture dates from 1932.

ized modern vitality to some and decadence to others, but the popularity of swing was nearly universal.

Another form of music that gained greater audiences in the thirties because of radio exposure was "hillbilly," or country, music. Especially popular in the South, country music owed much to the tradition of church music, and usually featured simple accompaniment by such instruments as the guitar, harmonica, mandolin, and violin. By the end of the decade country music had its own circle of superstars of film and radio, including Gene Autry and Hank Williams.

To a remarkable degree, the automobile continued to serve rich and poor alike during the Depression, a luxury most would not sacrifice until all else failed. The influence of cars was apparent everywhere. The first industrially designed service stations appeared during the thirties, enamel-paneled Texaco stations, and the

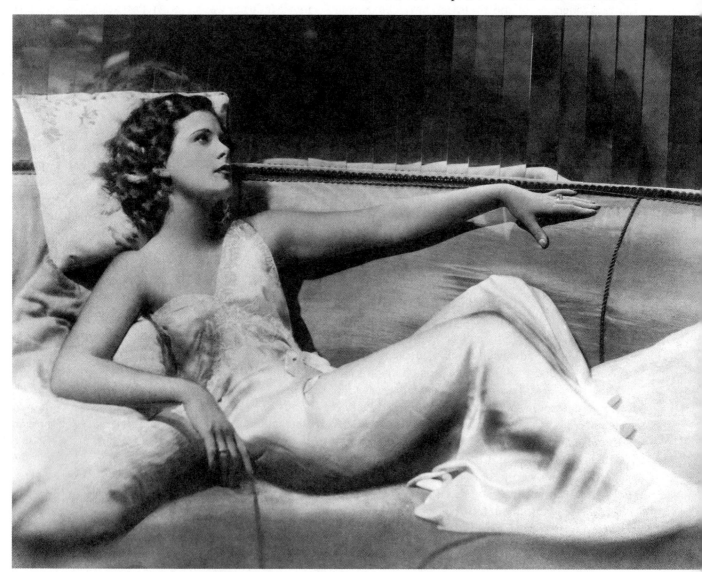

word *motel,* combining *motor* and *hotel,* made its appearance in the language. America's continued fascination with the automobile could be seen in the increased number of racetracks built specifically for auto racing.

Other forms of recreation survived hard times. Pari-mutuel gambling was legalized in 1933; the racetrack provided a last hope for many of the down and out, as well as a recreation for the wisecracking and unmoralistic New Dealer Harry Hopkins. Legalized gambling also encouraged bingo parlors and bank nights at the movies. Dancing remained one of the most popular social diversions during the thirties; by the end of the decade jitterbugging, a frantically acrobatic dance done to swing music, rocked the dance halls of the rich and the poor. Dance marathons were a rage in 1933, somehow capturing the fierce will to survive that characterized life in the Depression.

Benny Goodman   One of the greatest white jazz musicians, Goodman was a product of New York City's Lower East Side. He learned to play the clarinet as a boy in a Progressive Era settlement house. Goodman was also an accomplished classical musician, but as he readily admitted there was far more money to be made in jazz. Here he performs in New York City in 1939.

CONCLUSION: THE DEPRESSION LEGACY

The generation of Americans who survived the Depression was deeply scarred by the nation's encounter with want and fear. Later Americans who had never stood in breadlines or seen their savings vanish in failed banks criticized the political goals of the Depression generation as too materialistic. The dignity of human life was about as lofty an idea as one could market in the 1930s.

Most Americans did not embrace radical ideologies on either the left or the right during the thirties. They continued to believe in such cherished values as individualism and democracy, though those words often had different meanings to different people. Still, most Americans remained confident that the nation would right itself and continue its sacred mission. In many ways, the decade's suffering brought Americans together in an effort to discover a national culture that would sustain them through their common troubles and prepared them for the horrors of war that lay just

ahead. Radio, pulp magazines, and movies continued to build a national culture that transcended the barriers of region, class, and ethnicity.

But the Depression did alter the nature of the nation's cultural diversity. More than ever before, Americans turned to local and regional associations to find identity and aid. Generally, ethnic associations and churches declined in influence, but those that survived the Depression best were groups that related closely to the lives of the people. Many new economic subgroups came to define Americans in the 1930s, ranging from labor unions to various organizations of farmers. Finally, many of the new associations that appeared during the decade related in one way or another to the federal government. The New Deal brought the national government into direct contact with millions of citizens; many joined new communities defined by New Deal agencies and programs. After the Depression, fewer and fewer Americans could be pigeonholed into a simple ethnic, religious, or regional sub-identity.

SUGGESTED READING

Many of the works cited in the previous chapter include information on life during the Depression. Sources that are particularly pertinent for the material in this chapter include the following:

Alan Brinkley, *The End of Reform: New Deal Liberalism in Recession and War* (1995). Examines the evolution of liberal thought after 1937.

Alan Brinkley, *Voices of Protest: Huey Long, Father Coughlin, and the Great Depression* (1982) is an excellent survey of two of Roosevelt's challengers.

Joel A. Carpenter, *Revive Us Again: The Reawakening of American Fundamentalism* (1997). Describes the network building in conservative Protestant churches during the Depression.

Lizabeth Cohen, *Making a New Deal: Industrial Workers in Chicago, 1929-1939* (1990). An analysis of the ways in which mass culture and the Depression forged a new class consciousness among American laborers.

David M. Kennedy, *Freedom from Fear: The American People in Depression and War, 1929-1945* (1999). Includes helpful sections about life during the Depression.

Studs Terkel, *Hard Times: An Oral History of the Great Depression* (1970). Oral history interviews that detail the personal suffering of the Depression era.

Susan Ware, *Beyond Suffrage: Women and the New Deal* (1981). Tells of the network of women who served in the New Deal.

SUGGESTIONS FOR FURTHER READING

Anthony J. Badger, *The New Deal: The Depression Years* (1989).

Robert F. Burk, *The Corporate State and the Broker State: The Du Ponts and American National Politics, 1925-1940* (1990).

Lester V. Chandler, *America's Greatest Depression, 1929-1941* (1970).

Lewis A. Erenberg, *Swingin' the Dream: Big Band Jazz and the Rebirth of American Culture* (1998).

George Flynn, *American Catholics and the Roosevelt Presidency* (1968).

Linda Gordon, *Pitied but Not Entitled: Single Mothers and the History of Welfare* (1994).

James N. Gregory, *American Exodus: The Dust Bowl Migration and Okie Culture in California* (1989).

Jack Temple Kirby, *Rural Worlds Lost: The American South, 1920-1960* (1987).

Harvey Klehr and John Earl Haynes, *The American Communist Movement: Storming Heaven Itself* (1992).

Richard Lowitt and Maurine Beasley, eds., *One Third of a Nation: Lorena Hickok Reports on the Great Depression* (1981).

Mark G. Malvasi, *The Unregenerate South: The Agrarian Thought of John Crowe Ransom, Allen Tate, and Donald Davidson* (1997).

William Manchester, *The Glory and the Dream* (1974).

David J. O'Brien, *American Catholics and Social Reform: The New Deal Years* (1968).

James T. Patterson, *America's Struggle against Poverty, 1900-1980* (1981).

Leo F. Ribuffo, *The Old Christian Right: The Protestant Far Right from the Great Depression to the Cold War* (1983).

Theodore Saloutos, *The American Farmer and the New Deal* (1982).

Ronald Takaki, *A Different Mirror* (1993).

William Vance Trollinger, Jr., *God's Empire: William Bell Riley and Midwestern Fundamentalism* (1990).

T. Harry Williams, *Huey Long* (1969).

Donald Worster, *Dust Bowl: The Southern Plains in the 1930s* (1979).

29

The Dilemmas of Power: America and the World, 1921-1945

ONE OF THE great bestsellers of 1920s America was the novel *All Quiet on the Western Front.* The author, Erich Maria Remarque, was a young German writer who had survived the carnage and become a pacifist. In graphic detail, Remarque told the story of enthusiastic students like himself who had joined the Kaiser's army in the first days of World War I. Remarque's protagonist survives the "sausage grinder" of trench warfare almost until the end, when senselessly he becomes one of the millions of victims. The novel, and the 1930 film based on it, impressed upon millions of sympathetic Americans the dual message that war is horrible and that no single nation bore exclusive blame for the catastrophe of 1914-1918. Many Americans concluded that the dead had died for nothing. A group of American historians asserted that Germany had been innocent of starting the war and that Wilson had been a British dupe. Expounding this thesis, Walter Millis's *America's Road to War, 1914-1917,* became a nonfiction best-seller.

In 1933, North Dakota's progressive Republican Senator Gerald Nye launched a two-year investigation of how American munitions makers such as DuPont had reaped enormous profits from the war and — Nye charged — had been responsible for American intervention in it. At a time when the public was blaming businessmen and financiers for the Great Depression, it became easy to believe that the "merchants of death" had caused the Great War, too — although the Nye Committee offered little proof. Thousands of Americans concluded that American participation in the Great War had been a mistake. Pacifism swept the nation's campuses; at one Ivy League school, 72 percent said they opposed compulsory military service during wartime, and collegians everywhere signed pledges that they would never fight under any circumstances. Beginning in 1934, students and faculty staged one-day antiwar walkouts all across the country. This pacifist protest became an annual campus rite until 1939.

Then came another war. On September 1, 1939, Adolf Hitler — like Remarque, a volunteer front-line soldier in the Great War — unleashed new German armies against Poland. By the following summer, he had overrun most of Western Europe, including France, and threatened Britain with invasion. In June 1941, after bombs had failed to crack British resistance, Germany attacked Soviet Russia and came close to conquering it. Americans watched anxiously from their supposedly impregnable shores until on December 7, 1941, Hitler's Japanese allies destroyed much of the American Pacific fleet at Pearl Harbor. Hundreds of thousands of former antiwar protesters found themselves in uniform, many as volunteers. America, Great Britain, and the Soviet Union formed an alliance that by 1945 crushed Germany and Japan.

World War II irreversibly changed America. The United States recoiled from isolationism and emerged the greatest power on earth. An American-led international scientific team unlocked the secret of atomic power, permitting the United States to end the war by destroying two Japanese cities with the first (and to the present, the last) nuclear weapons ever used in combat.

Apart from Pearl Harbor and America's Pacific territories, the war inflicted no material damage on American soil, and the immense productivity of the American war effort not only ended the Great Depression but also provided the sinews of victory. A powerful government, a vast military-industrial complex, and a huge migration of southern African Americans into northern cities were some of the many permanent changes that the war brought to American society. The devastating blow that the war struck to Western colonialism around the globe, the destruction of the balance of power in Europe, and the Soviet Union's determination to extend its sphere of influence virtually ensured that the United States could never again retreat into isolation. Throughout the remainder of the century the United States bore the burden of global power, with all the moral complexities for dealing with an imperfect world — a burden that millions of Americans had rejected after World War I.

THE AMBIVALENT GIANT

"I don't know anything about this European stuff," President Warren G. Harding airily replied to a reporter's question about international affairs. "They hired the money, didn't they?" was the dry retort of his successor, Calvin Coolidge, to proposals that the United States help stabilize the postwar world by writing off the wartime loans it had made to the Allies. Herbert Hoover had a more sophisticated understanding of world affairs — he made his prewar fortune as an international mining consultant and he won fame by directing relief programs for Europe's millions of starving war victims — but his preoccupation with America's economic crisis after October 1929 paralyzed his ability to put together what might otherwise have been an effective foreign policy.

The Republican administrations of the 1920s and early 1930s were not ostrich-like isolationists. All three presidents supported various initiatives aimed at securing world peace. They also vigorously upheld the United States's imperial position in the Pacific and the Caribbean. In 1920, voters' overwhelming rejection of the Democratic ticket of James Cox and Franklin D. Roosevelt, advocates of joining the League of Nations, attested to popular determination to shun responsibility for enforcing the Great War's outcome. But it did not signal an American withdrawal from the world. In economic policy, the Republican administrations of the 1920s were aggressively internationalist.

❧ Internationalism and Its Limits in the 1920s

Abroad, the Republican faith in laissez-faire government and economics translated into a new version of dollar diplomacy. The Republican administrations believed that the government had an obligation to help American business at home and abroad, and that such aid promoted domestic stability and prevented wars. Thus they continued efforts, begun by the Wilson administration, to promote American corporate interests overseas. In 1918, Congress had exempted American firms operating abroad from antitrust legislation, and the following year it authorized American banks to establish branches in foreign countries. Under Harding and Coolidge, the Commerce Department (headed by Hoover) acted as a kind of international chamber of commerce for American business. A massive informal network of contacts between governmental bureaucracies and corporate headquarters facilitated trade and investment between Europe and America.

The Republican administrations were willing to promote foreign trade by aiding private interests, but not to put the taxpayers' funds or the nation's credit to such use. The United States emerged from the Great War as the world's primary creditor nation. In 1914, foreign investment in the United States exceeded American investment abroad by $3 billion dollars; by 1920, the balance had shifted to favor the United States by $22 billion. America was in a position to assume Great Britain's role as world banker. Instead, Washington acted as if international finance were analogous to personal finance: Fiscal conservatives refused to see that foreign nations could not buy American goods unless credit were available, unless their own economies were healthy, and unless they could sell their products in the United States.

During the period from 1917 to 1919 the United States had lent its principal allies approximately $10.5 billion in government-to-government credits, all of these monies being spent in the United States, thus benefiting American stockholders and wage earners. Harding and his two successors insisted that these loans be repaid with interest, putting immense pressure on Europe's war-ravaged economies as they were trying to recover. Resentment against "Uncle Shylock" naturally ran high in Europe. Throughout the decade, America's creditors tried to convince Washington that there was a connection between war debts, reparations, and U.S. investment in Germany — that in fact U.S. funds, badly needed to restart Europe's economies, were just flowing back to their source. In 1931, Hoover finally agreed to a one-year suspension or "moratorium" on war debt and reparation payments, primarily to protect private American investments in Germany. By the end of the year, however, proceeds from those investments had become frozen and Washington in 1932 insisted that war debt repayments resume.

To make matters worse, the Republicans imposed high tariffs — Fordney-McCumber in 1922 and Hawley-Smoot in 1930 — that made it virtually impossible for America's creditors to sell their products in America, thus earning the dollars with which to pay their debts. Protectionism was one of the reasons that the 1920s economy was basically unhealthy, and it played a major role in turning the stock market crash of 1929 into a decade-long depression.

America's isolationism dictated the parameters of its foreign policy in the 1920s. Secretary of State Charles Evans Hughes — a capable statesman and one of Harding's abler appointees — believed that the United States should play an active role in world affairs. He caved in to Republican isolationists, though, when it came to Europe. Having refused to ratify the Treaty of Versailles, the United States simply signed a treaty with Germany ending the state of war. Initially, the State Department declined to answer mail from the League, though later in the decade the United States sent permanent observers to the League headquarters in the Netherlands. In 1925 the United States also agreed to join the Permanent Court of International Justice, a League organ that posed little threat to any country's sovereignty because accepting its jurisdiction was always optional. Even when this modest agreement was submitted for senatorial ratification, Wilson's old nemesis William Borah and his fellow irreconcilables attached five reservations that forced the United States into prolonged haggling with the other member states. At the end of these talks, in 1935, isolationist sentiment was so strong that the Senate rejected court membership. By then, international disintegration was already well under way, and an ominous new shadow of war was falling over the world.

In 1928 French foreign minister Anatole Briand suggested that his country and the United States sign a pact outlawing war between them. Acutely aware that it had barely managed to defeat a more powerful Germany, and then only in alliance with Great Britain and the United States, France felt intense insecurity during the interwar period. The French made defensive alliances with several east European states created by the postwar settlement, but they desperately wanted a tie with the United States as well. Secretary of State Frank Kellogg understood Briand's motive and proposed that all nations be invited to sign. By the end of the year, fourteen countries (including Germany, Japan, and Italy) accepted the Pact of Paris, renouncing war. The Senate approved it by 85 to 1. A congressional cynic, however, recognized the Kellogg-Briand Pact for what it was: "an international kiss."

❧ Assertiveness in Latin America

Few Latin Americans saw the United States as isolationist. All three Republican administrations of the 1920s furthered American economic interests in the Western Hemisphere by undercutting European, especially British, influence and by working toward better relations with America's sister republics — relations that still suffered from the ill will generated by the interventionist policies of Roosevelt, Taft, and Wilson. The timing seemed propitious. Germany's defeat had

Nicaragua, 1932   American troops occupying Nicaragua display the captured flag of the rebel leader Sandino, whose uprising failed to dislodge the *gringos* and their Nicaraguan allies. Out of the American intervention would come the corrupt and brutal rule of the Somoza family, lasting until 1979, when left-wing rebels claiming to represent the *Sandinista* tradition would again challenge what they condemned as American hegemony over their country.

eased fears of extra-hemispheric threats to the Panama Canal. In addition, the Great War had dramatically weakened Great Britain, giving the edge in the region to the United States.

During the 1920s the United States withdrew its troops from the Dominican Republic and recognized the revolutionary Mexican government, acknowledging Mexico's ownership of subsoil mineral and water rights. The United States thus acquiesced in Mexico's expropriation of American-owned oilfields and plantations, although the Mexican government accepted continued American ownership of oil companies acquired before 1917. Washington felt that it could make such concessions because of the overall growth of U.S. investment in the hemisphere. By the 1920s, more than a thousand American companies, including Standard Oil of New Jersey, International Telephone and Telegraph, and United Fruit, dominated the economies of three-quarters of the Latin American states. American investments there doubled between 1914 and 1929.

Yet there were limits to Yankee benevolence. Since 1912, American military authorities had virtually run Nicaragua. In the mid-1920s Nicaraguan nationalists rallied around Cesar Augusto Sandino and, using Mexico as their base, took up arms to drive out the U.S. Marines and the American-supported right-wing government. After years of bitter fighting, the U.S. forces withdrew in 1933. All was not lost, however. Sandino and two close associates were subsequently assassinated by the American-trained National Guard led by Anastasio Somoza Debayle, who together with his sons would run a ruthless, corrupt, but pro-American dictatorship in Nicaragua until 1979.

Tensions with Japan and Russia

America also pursued an active East Asian policy. Postwar administrations, like all their predecessors since McKinley, defended the Open Door to China and intended to retain American territories in the western Pacific. Those objectives brought America into direct conflict with Japan, bent on its own imperial goals.

During World War I, Japan had joined the Allies. By 1918 it had not only occupied Germany's Marshall, Caroline, and Marianna Islands but also forced China to grant it a sphere of interest on the Shantung Peninsula and in southern Manchuria. Wilson denounced these acquisitions as violating the principle of self-determination, and at the Paris Peace Conference he sought to compel the Japanese to relinquish them. The best he could do, however, was to have the former German islands defined as Japanese-administered League of Nations mandates. Japanese diplomats agreed to relinquish military control of Shantung on condition that Japan retain its predominant economic position there.

Instead of canceling the naval building program they had started during World War I, both Japan and the United States continued to launch warships. This arms race and other tensions badly strained Japanese-American relations in the immediate postwar years. International pressure mounted for a conference to defuse the dangerous situation. In July 1921, Secretary of State Hughes invited eight other countries to meet in Washington to discuss Pacific and Asian problems. America entered the Washington Naval Conference with three objectives: to end its naval race with Japan, to cancel the Anglo-Japanese alliance of 1902, and to gain worldwide acceptance of the Open Door.

The United States achieved all its objectives, thanks largely to British cooperation. In the Five Power Pact, the United States, Great Britain, Japan, France, and Italy agreed to build and maintain "capital ships" (cruisers and larger naval vessels) in a ratio of 5:5:3:1.67:1.67. The United States took the lead in destroying its own ships above this ratio. Japan acquiesced when Britain and the United States agreed to build no new fortifications east and north of Singapore or west of Hawaii — thus conceding Japanese naval supremacy in East Asia. The Five Power Pact divided dominance of the world's oceans among the three major naval powers: Britain from the North Sea to the Indian Ocean, the United States in Western Hemisphere waters, and Japan in the western Pacific. The old Anglo-Japanese alliance was replaced by the Four Power Pact between the United States, Great Britain, France, and Japan, which guaranteed existing borders and promised consultations should a threat to peace arise in the Pacific. Finally, all sides signed the Nine Power Pact, accepting the territorial integrity and independence of China.

The Harding administration had won its major diplomatic achievement, but the lack of enforcement provisions meant that final resolution of Japanese-American tensions was merely postponed. Japan's fortification of its new Pacific islands would cost the United States dearly twenty years later.

Russia took no part in the Washington Conference.

Until 1933, the United States refused to recognize Soviet Russia.[1] Repelled by Bolshevism — revolutionary, dictatorial, socialistic, and antireligious — the United States justified nonrecognition on the grounds that the Soviet government had seized power illegitimately and would not last. Ironically, pressure for normalizing ties with the Soviet regime came mainly from American business. By 1930, Americans were conducting a $100-million-a-year trade with the Soviet Union, and they were convinced that with recognition this commerce would increase dramatically.

American recognition of the Soviet Union came only after Franklin D. Roosevelt's election. In 1933, FDR and Soviet foreign minister Maxim Litvinov worked out a deal calling for American recognition in return for the Kremlin's promise to forswear subversive activities in the United States and to make payments on czarist Russia's war debts to Americans. Ideological differences, including most Americans' repugnance at Stalin's bloody purges during the 1930s, ensured that mistrust still permeated Soviet-American relations,[2] and hopes for more trade never materialized.

THE LONG SHADOWS OF WAR

The peace structure established by the Paris Peace Conference lasted only twenty-one years. The factors responsible for the coming of Word War II are complex and arguable — but the essential fact is that the Treaty of Versailles had humiliated Germany while leaving it capable of rebuilding its power. When the Great Depression swept the world, economic and social insecurity distracted the victors of World War I — the nations that had assumed responsibility for enforcing the peace. The global economic crisis stimulated the growth of fascism throughout the world, turning Germany, Italy, and Japan into aggressive predators.

Although the U.S. was still the world's most formidable economy, Depression-era Americans denied that their responsibilities were global. FDR concentrated

---

1. Called the Union of Soviet Socialist Republics (U.S.S.R.), or Soviet Union, after 1922.
2. Some Americans, including prominent journalists and FDR's ambassador in Moscow, Joseph Davies, insisted that the Moscow purge trials, in which high-ranking Communists confessed to all manner of devious plots, were genuine. We now know that such "confessions" were extracted by torture and threats to the defendants' families. Throughout World War II and into the early Cold War years, Davies was a leading advocate of Soviet-American cooperation. A wealthy businessman, Davies was incurably naive about the nature of the Stalinist system.

on domestic recovery and, despite his internationalist instincts, barely challenged congressional and public isolationism.

Latin America was a different matter. Acting on the assumption that the United States could preserve its security as a purely western hemispheric power, the Roosevelt administration sought to win friends in Central and South America by renouncing intervention. In return, Washington hoped, the American republics would agree to participate in a U.S.-led hemispheric security system. One thing the United States did not renounce, however, was its support for local dictatorships who seemed to serve American national interest. Not only the Somozas in Nicaragua but also such military tyrants as Fulgencio Batista in Cuba and Rafael Trujillo in the Dominican Republic thrived with American blessing, spawning resentment that the United States would reap in years to come.

Not until 1937 did Roosevelt publicly warn that unchecked aggression in Europe and Asia posed a threat to American security. Even then American opinion recoiled from his suggestion that aggressors be "quarantined." Not until Europe actually went to war, in 1939, did the United States begin to prepare to confront the dangers of European and Asian aggression, and not until American forces were actually attacked by the Japanese at Pearl Harbor did the United States formally enter the war.

ॐ The Rise of the Axis Powers

Three major expansionist states emerged during the interwar period to threaten the status quo: Fascist Italy, Nazi Germany, and imperial Japan. Germany craved reversing the outcome of World War I, while Italy and Japan felt that they had not received the spoils of victory they deserved. Following a flirtation with democracy in the 1920s, Japan fell under the sway of army extremists who argued that the nation's survival as a great power depended upon its ability to build an empire. Although they were deeply divided ideologically, all three powers shared the common objective of upsetting the balance of power. They were what journalists called the world's "Have-Not" countries — and they intended to become "Haves."

The flamboyant demagogue Benito Mussolini and his nationalistic Fascist party had seized power in Italy in 1922. Mussolini established a dictatorship that boastfully called itself "totalitarian." Though in fact Mussolini often did not know what was going on in It-

aly, the state claimed the power to control all facets of the economy and daily life. Abroad, Mussolini wanted nothing less than the restoration of the Roman Empire. The Mediterranean, he said, was *Mare Nostrum* ("Our Sea"), and he promised to rule all the lands washed by its waters. As a first step, Mussolini in 1935 invaded the militarily insignificant East African kingdom of Ethiopia. With the League of Nations helplessly standing by, the mechanized Italian army defeated Ethiopia's horse-mounted spearmen. Next, Mussolini cast his imperial gaze on Yugoslavia and southern France, and moved toward an alliance with his German admirer and fellow-dictator, Adolf Hitler.

Ravaged by the Great Depression, the democratic postwar German republic in 1933 succumbed to Hitler, an Austrian-born ne'er-do-well who was the most ruthless of Germany's many political extremists. Racism, aggressive expansionism, and totalitarianism were the three fundamental aspects of Hitler's National Socialist (Nazi) party. Most Americans considered Hitler a strutting, hysterical, but slightly comical figure, brilliantly caricatured (along with Mussolini) in Charlie Chaplin's 1940 film "The Great Dictator." Those few who had read *Mein Kampf*, Hitler's rambling, hate-filled autobiography and political manifesto, understood that he blamed the Jews for Germany's problems and envisioned a world dominated by the "pure" Aryan race whose homeland was Germany. Unfortunately, most Germans and virtually no foreigners bothered to explore the past and the credo of the new *Führer* ("Leader"). Once Hitler was legally appointed chancellor, his storm troopers hounded opposition parties into extinction, and he became absolute dictator. In 1935, Hitler renounced the disarmament provisions of the Versailles Treaty, and the following year he ordered German troops into the Rhineland region that had been demilitarized under the peace settlement. Although he had ordered his generals to retreat at the first sign of resistance by the Western powers, Britain and France refused to enforce the treaty, and Hitler plotted his next moves.

Japan became the third great threat to world peace in the 1930s. A densely populated island nation lacking in the natural resources necessary to support its modern industrial economy, it had to look beyond its shores for petroleum, iron ore, zinc, lead, and rubber, as well as for markets to absorb its surplus production. Liberals in Japan argued that the nation's goals could be achieved through peaceful economic expansion, but they gradually lost out to extreme nationalists, mainly military men.

Virtually everyone in Japan agreed that Manchuria, China's northeasternmost province, was vital to Japan achieving its ambitions. This huge, underdeveloped region was rich in raw materials and offered a tempting market for Japanese products. Liberals in Japan, mostly civilian politicians but including some naval officers as well, opposed annexing the region for fear of precipitating an open break with the United States. The Japanese military disagreed, insisting that their nation's future could be secure only by taking direct control of Manchuria.

By 1931 the Japanese already dominated much of Manchuria. They owned and operated the South Manchurian Railway, controlled the major ports, were the principal investors in the province, and directly governed several towns. During the summer a number of violent clashes occurred between Chinese nationalists and Japanese. On the night of September 18, Japanese military authorities in Manchuria announced that the main railway line was under attack. Thousands of troops poured in, taking physical control of the province. All this was called "the Manchurian incident." China appealed to the League and to the signatories of the Nine Power Pact and the Kellogg-Briand treaty. Secretary of State Henry Stimson, a Republican internationalist in the Roosevelt-Lodge vein, favored a strong response to what he perceived as Japanese aggression. Japan could be pressured, he believed, because it was dependent on the United States for scrap iron (which it used to manufacture steel) and refined petroleum products. Hoover rejected Stimson's advice: He would do nothing to provoke a foreign crisis, which might hinder efforts to end the Great Depression.

Seizing Manchuria and turning it into a puppet-state called Manchukuo did not satisfy Japanese expansionists. In 1937 the Japanese army precipitated full-scale war with China's Nationalist regime, headed by Chiang Kai-shek, which was already fighting a civil war with communist forces led by Mao Zedong. Advancing deeply into China and shocking the world with wanton brutality, Japanese expansionists spoke ominously of creating the so-called Greater East Asian Co-Prosperity Sphere — a Japanese-dominated empire from which

Hitler and Mussolini, 1937 The two dictators review Nazi German troops. At this point, most Americans thought the ranting Führer and the strutting Duce were comical figures rather than serious threats.

European and American interests would be barred. In 1937, Japan took the first steps toward a formal alliance with Nazi Germany and Fascist Italy, called the Axis.

❧ Appeasement and Isolationism

Opposing the "Have-Not" powers stood the victors of World War I — Great Britain, France, and the smaller European countries recognized by the Paris peace settlement, including Czechoslovakia and Poland. In the Far East, the European colonial powers and the United States blocked Japan's ambitions. In reacting to the threats of the aggressor nations, the Western democracies had two ways open to them. They could nip aggression in the bud by confronting the Have-Nots with military force, or they could act on the assumption that the extremist leaders of Germany, Italy, and Japan were reasonable men with legitimate grievances, which should be met with conciliation — or, to use a word that became infamous in postwar years, to resort to appeasement.

Britain and France chose the second course. Partly this reflected public disillusionment with the Great War — a sense that the war had been nobody's fault, had been a ghastly mistake, and had ended with the winners taking unfair advantage of the losers. Partly it resulted from Western policymakers' inordinate fear of

The Only Way We Can Save Her

"The Only Way We Can Save Her"   This cartoon, drawn in 1939 by Carey Orr, conveyed the isolationists' message that only by keeping out of the interminable conflicts of "War Mad Europe" could Americans preserve their democracy. Notice the implied moral equivalence of Nazi Germany and its enemies. Until Pearl Harbor, most Americans clung to hopes that neutrality—and wide oceans—would safeguard the United States.

endless cycle of conflict that had no bearing on American interests. Nor did he accept the prevailing public view that Europe was simply rich, corrupt, and quarrelsome. A member of the eastern elite, FDR had traveled widely in Europe, admired the British and his nationalist cousin Theodore Roosevelt, and as Wilson's assistant secretary of the navy had shown a streak of imperialism. Nonetheless, Roosevelt was elected to pull the country out of the Great Depression. He had no intention of turning congressional isolationists against the New Deal by pursuing interventionist policies in Europe and East Asia. After a brief, unsuccessful effort to get congressional agreement to a measure empowering the president to cut off weapons sales to aggressors while allowing them to their victims, Roosevelt abandoned the field to the isolationists.

Isolationist sentiment crystallized in a series of neutrality acts passed by Congress from 1935 through 1937. In 1935 Senator Nye, partly in response to the threatened Italian invasion of Ethiopia, introduced legislation banning arms sales and loans to all nations at war. Supporters argued that if Congress outlawed activities that had led to involvement in the Great War, America could stay out of future conflicts. The State Department protested that such legislation would hamstring American foreign policy, but Roosevelt refused to oppose these measures. In 1935 Congress banned wartime munitions sales and prohibited travel aboard belligerent vessels. In 1936 it outlawed war loans, and in 1937 it made all three measures permanent.

Isolationists carried the day when a civil war erupted in Spain in 1936. General Francisco Franco, whose Falangist party resembled Mussolini's fascism, waged a bloody war to overthrow the republican government of Spain. Germany and Italy supported the Falangists with supplies and weapons, and the Loyalists (as the supporters of the republic were called) received less substantial support from the Soviet Union. The United States joined the British and French in refusing to offer

the Soviet Union, whose communist doctrines seemed more sinister than the racism and hypernationalism of the Axis powers. And in no small part the West's leaders chose appeasement because it was the path of least resistance. Subsequently, they added still another rationalization: that if only the United States had embraced collective security, confrontation rather than appeasement would have been the policy of choice. Unfortunately, this hindsight claim cannot be tested.

The United States was deeply isolationist during the 1930s and tacitly supported appeasement. Roosevelt did not share the perspective of progressive Senators like Borah and Robert LaFollette, Jr., or of historian Charles Beard, all of whom believed that the imperialist powers, including Japan, were enmeshed in an

assistance to either side. Not only did isolationist sentiment make any other course impossible, Americans were hopelessly divided about the war. Many American Roman Catholics, including Father Coughlin, strongly supported Franco, while American leftists supported the Loyalists. Over three thousand young Americans enlisted in the Abraham Lincoln Brigade where they fought for the Loyalists with volunteers from other countries.

FDR's views during this period continue to be a source of debate. A number of his advisers argued that passage of the neutrality legislation would send the dangerous signal that would-be aggressors could do as they wished with American acquiescence. The measures denied Washington even the option of bluff. Privately, Roosevelt expressed similar concerns. Following the outbreak of the Spanish Civil War and the Sino-Japanese War in 1937, he publicly demanded a "quarantine" of the aggressors — a vague phrase that might mean economic sanctions and perhaps even collective-security measures. But when the public failed to agree, he signed the new neutrality legislation without protest.

❧ The Outbreak of War in Europe, 1938-1939

It was not coincidental that Hitler launched his expansionist program in the spring of 1938. The Führer's stated goal was incorporation of all German-speaking peoples into his Third Reich, and in March, probably with the support of a majority of the Austrians, Germany annexed that country. After absorbing Austria, the Nazis turned their attention to Czechoslovakia's Sudetenland, a border strip given to the country in the Versailles Treaty to provide it with a defensible frontier. The majority of the Sudetenland's population were 3.5 million Germans who raucously demanded reunion with the Fatherland.

As Hitler and his propaganda machine accused the Czechoslovak government (unjustly) of persecuting its German inhabitants, he massed troops along his neighbor's border. The besieged Czechs appealed for support from their allies, Britain and France. They had a strong army and powerful defenses, and it seems likely that they could have held off a Nazi attack had the Western allies backed them. But the Western public and governments saw little reason for involving themselves in what British prime minister Neville Chamberlain dismissed as the quarrels of "faraway people of whom we know nothing." After intensive rounds of what we would now call "shuttle diplomacy," Chamberlain arranged a European summit conference at Munich in late September 1938. No Czech representative attended. There the British and French turned over the Sudetenland to Hitler in return for a promise not to seek an additional square foot of European territory. Chamberlain returned home to be hailed by the British people for bringing "peace in our time." Roosevelt cabled, tersely and enigmatically:

❊   IN THEIR OWN WORDS

The Nye Report, 1936

The rising tide of pacifism in America in the 1930s, along with the Great Depression and the critique of big business it brought, made a ready audience for a Senate committee investigation into whether the munitions industry helped draw the United States into World War I. While the committee's report offered little evidence that big businesses were responsible for America's entry into the war, it was sharply critical of their role nonetheless.

The committee finds, under the head of the effect of armament, on peace, that some of the munitions companies have occasionally had opportunities to intensify the fears of people for their neighbors and have used them to their own profit.

The committee finds, further, that the very quality which in civilian life tends to lead toward progressive civilization, namely the improvements of machinery, has been used by the munitions makers to scare nations into a continued frantic expenditure for the latest improvements in devices of warfare. The constant message of the traveling salesman of the munitions companies to the rest of the world has been that they now had available for sale something new, more dangerous and more deadly than ever before and that the potential enemy was or would be buying it.

While the evidence before this committee does not show that wars have been started solely because of the activities of munitions makers and their agents, it is also true that wars rarely have one single cause, and the committee finds it to be against the peace of the world for selfishly interested organizations to be left free to goad and frighten nations into military activity.

The committee finds, further, that munitions companies engaged in bribery find themselves involved in the civil and military politics of other nations, and that this is an unwarranted form of intrusion into the affairs of other nations and undesirable representation of the character and methods of the people of the United States.

"Good man!" In the aftermath of World War II the word "Munich" would come to be synonymous with "appeasement."

Within six months, the British and French were disabused of any illusions they had harbored about Hitler. In the spring of 1939 Hitler broke his Munich pledge: German troops overran the rest of Czechoslovakia, partitioned it with Hungary, and set up a puppet Slovak fascist state. Then, in the summer of 1939, Hitler signaled his next target by denouncing Poland for persecuting the German minority living within its borders. Belatedly, British diplomats realized that Hitler was bent on the domination of all of Europe. They signed an alliance with Poland and tentatively approached the Soviet Union about jointly opposing Nazi Germany. Convinced that communists and Nazis — who philosophically were archenemies — could never make common cause, British diplomats proceeded at a leisurely pace. Unbeknownst to the West, however, German and Soviet diplomats were already holding secret talks.

On August 23, a shocked world learned that a German-Soviet Nonaggression Pact had been concluded. Its public provisions stated simply that the two nations promised never to make war on each other; but its cynical secret protocols stipulated that if Germany found itself at war with Poland, the Red Army would come to its aid, and that not only Poland but also the three Baltic republics (Lithuania, Latvia, and Estonia) would be divided between Hitler and Stalin.

To no one's surprise, Germany invaded Poland on September 1. Three days later, Britain and France declared war. On September 17 the Soviet Union invaded eastern Poland, and by the end of the month the country had been partitioned between the two totalitarian dictatorships.

ℛ American Response to European War: 1939-1941

As required by the neutrality acts, upon the outbreak of war FDR officially proclaimed American neutrality. While the fateful events of the summer of 1939 had been unfolding, the president, like the British and French leaders, had recognized the threat posed by Germany. He sounded out Congress about modifying the arms embargo to allow the United States to help bolster those who stood up to Hitler. But the Senate leadership adamantly refused. In November 1939, however, with Europe now at war, the president called Congress into special session and persuaded it to substitute provisions allowing "cash-and-carry" arms sales instead of an absolute ban. This would permit belligerent states to purchase arms in the United States if they paid cash and carried away the goods in their own ships. Seemingly evenhanded, in fact the proposal favored the Allies, for the Royal Navy controlled the surface of the Atlantic. (Beneath the ocean, German U-boats roamed.) Public opinion strongly supported the president, and Congress passed the legislation by wide margins.

It would be two years before the United States actually entered the war. During that period, America moved from neutrality first to "nonbelligerency" (as a nonfighting ally of the anti-Axis powers) and then, late in 1941, to undeclared war with Germany. Roosevelt acted carefully. He understood that Hitler posed a mortal threat to America, but he was determined not to lead a divided nation into what would surely be a cataclysmic war.

From 1939 through 1941, debate raged among the American people about how the nation should respond to the dangerous events abroad. A tiny minority favored the Axis — mainly a fringe group of German Americans[3] and a few Italian Americans who admired Mussolini. Most Americans argued that the war did not involve American national interests. But some influential Americans and a minority of the general public believed that America's survival depended upon supporting the Allies, if necessary by intervention.

In the fall of 1940, isolationists formed the America First Committee. "America-Firsters" spanned the political spectrum. They included German and Irish Americans who, while not pro-Nazi, were anti-British and feared a return of the excesses of the World War I era. They were joined by conservative nationalists such as Charles Lindbergh (who had pro-German sentiments), Republican Senator Robert A. Taft of Ohio, and Herbert Hoover. But although isolationism appealed strongly to New Deal haters, it also included midwestern progressives and leftists. Political insurgents such as Borah and Nye joined intellectuals such as Socialist Party leader Norman Thomas and neo-Marxist historian Charles Beard in opposing support for the Allies. Until Hitler invaded the Soviet Union in 1941, the American Communist Party also attacked the war as an imperialist plot engineered from London,

---

3. A very small number of them belonged to the pro-Nazi "German American Bund," which held noisy rallies and otherwise aped Hitler and his stormtroopers. The Bund was investigated by Congress for "un-American activities" in the late 1930s.

and supported the isolationist line. America-Firsters argued that the United States was secure within the Western Hemisphere. They likened the Atlantic and Pacific unto two great moats and argued that foreigners' wars were indigenous, perpetual, and incurable. Many echoed the warnings of George Washington and Thomas Jefferson against soiling American virtue with European corruption.

Interventionists had their organization, too: the Committee to Defend America by Aiding the Allies. Many interventionists were Jews, appalled by Nazi anti-Semitism; others were people of British ancestry or who traced their descent from a nationality that Nazi Germany had conquered, such as Polish Americans. Some belonged to the eastern elite, with strong cultural and economic ties to Europe, a sophisticated knowledge of world affairs, and often an allegiance to the Republican Party. Interventionists also included most liberal New Dealers, some of them frustrated by FDR's reluctance to take a more public pro-Allied stand.

Realizing the depth of public disillusionment with Wilsonianism, interventionists tended to downplay idealistic arguments or appeals to collective security. Instead, they emphasized that once he had overwhelmed Europe and the British Isles, Hitler would turn to the Western Hemisphere. They argued (correctly) that modern air and naval warfare had made the Atlantic and Pacific highways, not moats. Better that the United States act while it still had allies, argued William Allen White, the famous Kansas newspaper publisher and an outspoken interventionist, than wait — and face the aggressors alone.

Although the interventionists' case was compelling, events on the battlefield had a much greater impact on American opinion. After joining Hitler in wiping Poland off the map, Stalin attacked Finland in the winter of 1939-1940, inspiring many Americans to cheer the Finns' stubborn resistance. In the west, however, this period was labeled the "phony war" as the enemy armies sat behind their respective fortifications. In April 1940, fighting suddenly erupted when Germany seized Denmark and Norway, and in May Hitler unleashed his *Blitzkrieg* ("lightning war") against the French army and the British expeditionary force in France. With tanks, mobile infantry, and dive bombers, the German army pushed deep into northern France and drove a wedge between French and British armies. Between May 26 and June 6 a flotilla of civilian and naval crafts evacuated around 335,000 Allied troops and civilians where they were pinned down at Dunkirk on the English Channel and the French stood alone against Hitler's army. On June 14 the German army entered Paris and on June 22 France capitulated, signing a humiliating surrender agreement in the very railway car in which Germany had submitted after World War I. A pro-German regime (called Vichy France from its capital) was set up in the part of that once-proud nation that the German army did not occupy. A resistance movement arose inside France, and a few "Free French" troops escaped to Britain. Their leader, General Charles de Gaulle, was a high-minded but haughty soldier whom the British and Americans would find a difficult ally.

Beginning in July Hitler's air force, the *Luftwaffe,* launched devastating raids first on British airfields and radar installations, and then, beginning in September, German bombers in a campaign known as the blitz battered London and other British cities night after night. The British Royal Air Force (RAF) faced more than 2,600 German bombers and fighters with only about 700 airplanes, but by the end of the year the RAF fighter pilots had turned back the German effort to control British air space and inflicted serious losses on the *Luftwaffe* in what came to be called the "Battle of Britain." In May 1941 the blitz ended and Churchill expressed the nation's gratitude to RAF fighter pilots with the famous words: "Never in the field of human conflict was so much owed by so many to so few."

The speed and success of Hitler's onslaught, vividly captured by newsreels and live radio broadcasts, shocked the American public. As the Germans massed troops after the fall of France in preparation for a cross-channel attack on England, most Americans feared that the impending German invasion would succeed. A frightened Congress dramatically increased the defense budget, and the president asked for — and in September obtained — congressional approval for the nation's first peacetime draft. In a more controversial move, by executive order in September Roosevelt transferred fifty surplus destroyers to Great Britain in return for permission to build bases on eight British possessions in the Western Hemisphere. Defending himself from conservative attacks, Roosevelt insisted that the destroyers-for-bases deal was just part of the effort to perfect the defenses of Fortress America, a term that had found popularity among isolationists.

In the midst of the international crisis, Roosevelt decided to run for an unprecedented third term in 1940. He anticipated that he would be running against an isolationist Republican opponent, but the Republicans nominated Wendell Willkie, a former Democrat businessman who had backed much of the New Deal and was supportive of Roosevelt's foreign policy. Trailing badly in the campaign, however, Willkie attacked Roosevelt as a warmonger, challenging particularly the destroyers-for-bases deal. The defensive president replied with a famous pledge: "Your boys are not going to be sent into any foreign wars." The president's victory was smaller than that in 1936, but he won easily, 27.3 million votes to 22.3 million votes and 449 electoral votes to 82.

⚬ *Toward Belligerency*

Reelected, the president became more and more responsive to British appeals for help in the Battle of the Atlantic where German submarines were sinking a large percentage of Allied freighters carrying goods purchased in the United States. During these critical months, an extraordinarily close personal relationship

Roosevelt and Churchill off Newfoundland, August 1941
On board HMS *Prince of Wales*, with Admiral E. J. King (commander of the U.S. Atlantic Fleet) and Admiral Harold Stark (chief of naval operations) looking on, Roosevelt and Churchill signed the Atlantic Charter. The United States was still officially neutral in World War II, but the two leaders promised to work for a peaceful global order. The emotional high point was the singing, by the entire Anglo-American contingent, of the Navy Hymn, Roosevelt's favorite: "Eternal Father, strong to save.../ Hear us as we cry to Thee/For those in peril on the sea."

blossomed between Roosevelt and British prime minister Winston Churchill. Between 1939, when Churchill was Lord of the Admiralty, and Roosevelt's death in 1945, the two exchanged almost two thousand messages (often hand written) and telegrams that cemented an unprecedented personal bond between two national leaders. Churchill signed his notes "Naval Person" up to his elevation to the post of prime minister after the fall of France in June 1940 and thereafter he signed "Former Naval Person." The two shared many common interests — a love for the navy (FDR having been undersecretary of the navy in Woodrow Wilson's administration), a fascination with the English language, and a deep belief in the superiority of British and American institutions. Above all they shared a dread of the threat posed by Nazi Germany, and to a lesser degree by Japan, to Western civilization.

By the spring of 1941, the president could no longer avoid a confrontation with isolationists in Congress. Churchill thanked the president for the opportunity to purchase the munitions that were enabling Britain to hold off Hitler; unfortunately, he reported, by late summer his country would no longer be able to pay for these supplies. The president responded by asking Congress to pass the Lend-Lease Bill. Under this deceptively titled measure, the United States would "lend" or lease arms, raw materials, machinery, and other items to nations fighting aggression. Managing one of the few jokes of his public career, Senator Taft remarked that lending bullets or food to someone was like lending chewing gum; you really did not want it back. Despite isolationist opposition, Congress handily passed Lend-Lease.

With Lend-Lease, the United States crossed a watershed: it became a nonfighting member of the anti-Axis coalition. From then until the war's end, the United States provided the British Empire with over $25 billion in Lend-Lease aid. Billions more went to other nations fighting against Germany.

In August 1941 Roosevelt and Churchill met on board a British warship in the North Atlantic off the coast of Newfoundland. While Roosevelt could not and did not

The Atlantic Charter, 1941

Franklin D. Roosevelt and Winston Churchill shared not only an extraordinary friendship, but also deep concerns about the threats posed by the Axis powers. The charter they signed was intended to demonstrate their solidarity against these foes and what they stood for; much of its language recalled Wilsonian hopes for the world after the First World War and would echo in postwar efforts to establish independent nations as well as such international organizations as the United Nations.

The President of the United States of America and the Prime Minister, Mr. Churchill, representing His Majesty's Government in the United Kingdom, being met together, deem it right to make known certain common principles in the national policies of their respective countries on which they base their hopes for a better future for the world.

FIRST, their countries seek no aggrandizement, territorial or other;

SECOND, they desire to see no territorial changes that do not accord with the freely expressed wishes of the peoples concerned;

THIRD, they respect the right of all peoples to choose the form of government under which they will live; and they wish to see sovereign rights and self-government restored to those who have been forcibly deprived of them;

FOURTH, they will endeavor, with due respect for their existing obligations, to further the enjoyment by all States, great or small, victor or vanquished, of access, on equal terms, to the trade and to the raw materials of the world which are needed for their economic prosperity;

FIFTH, they desire to bring about the fullest collaboration between all nations in the economic field with the object of securing, for all, improved labor standards, economic adjustment and social security;

SIXTH, after the final destruction of the Nazi tyranny, they hope to see established a peace which will afford to all nations the means of dwelling in safety within their own boundaries, and which will afford assurance that all the men in all the lands may live out their lives in freedom from fear and want;

SEVENTH, such a peace should enable all men to traverse the high seas and oceans without hindrance;

EIGHTH, they believe that all of the nations of the world, for realistic as well as spiritual reasons, must come to the abandonment of the use of force. . . .

Franklin D. Roosevelt
Winston S. Churchill

---

make any military commitments to the British, the two leaders drafted a declaration, the Atlantic Charter, which called for "the final destruction of Nazi tyranny" and was a virtual statement of war aims. The Charter listed "certain common principles" shared by the two countries and set out the objectives for establishing a peaceful world at the end of the war.

By the time of the North Atlantic meeting the nature of the war had been dramatically changed by a massive German invasion of the Soviet Union launched on June 22, 1941. After the signing of the Nazi-Soviet Pact, Americans had been as hostile to the Soviet Union as to Germany, but attitudes changed quickly after the German invasion. For the beleaguered British, Hitler's diversion to the east was an enormous blessing; the conservative Churchill embraced the Russians as allies, announcing that he would make a deal with the devil if Hitler invaded hell. Roosevelt quickly persuaded Congress to extend Lend-Lease to the Soviet Union.

As the Nazis drove toward Moscow and Russia's survival seemed increasingly doubtful, interventionists urged the president to authorize U.S. naval vessels to escort Allied transports and permit American merchant vessels to carry war materiel to Europe. Iso-

lationists replied with a steady drumbeat of "America First" appeals. Echoing the sentiments of many Americans, Missouri Senator Harry Truman suggested that Hitler and Stalin should be allowed to finish each other off — though, he added, Hitler must not be allowed to win.

Still fearful of outstripping public opinion, Roosevelt only agreed to authorize "neutrality patrols" in the western Atlantic. Although Hitler had ordered sub commanders not to attack American vessels, incidents were bound to occur. In September, a German U-boat fired on an American destroyer carrying supplies to GIs in Iceland, which had been occupied by the British in a strategic move in 1940 (they were replaced by Americans in 1942). Roosevelt denounced this "unprovoked" attack and issued a "shoot-on-sight" order. (Only after the war did the public learn that the U.S. destroyer had been following the German submarine, broadcasting its position to nearby British warships.) On October 17, 1941, a German submarine damaged the U.S. destroyer *Kearny*; ten days later, another U-boat sank the *Reuben James*, killing more than one hundred American seamen. When in November Congress acceded to the administration's request to remove the "carry" from cash-and-carry (meaning that American ships could carry war supplies to Britain) and American destroyers began convoying U.S. and British ships, the navy found itself virtually at war with German U-boats.

Step by careful step, Roosevelt had moved the United States from neutrality to undeclared war. Interventionists accused him of being too timid, isolationists of leading the nation into an unnecessary war by trickery. Although a declaration of war on Germany seemed unavoidable by the beginning of December 1941, a poll taken in September 1941 showed that 80 percent of the American people wanted to stay out of the war, and Roosevelt did not want to enter the war without public support.

❧ The Open Door Shuts

When war broke out in Europe the Japanese army was bogged down in China. The Japanese had conquered most of the coastal regions but were unable to finish off Chiang's nationalists and Mao's communists, who continued to resist from deep in the interior of China. On the other hand, Great Britain, France, and the Netherlands had suddenly been removed from the Pacific balance of power. The militarists in Tokyo turned their attention to the Europeans' colonies in Southeast Asia. These colonies — French Indochina, British Malaya and Singapore, and the Dutch East Indies — were rich in rubber, tin, and petroleum and they had been rendered defenseless by the European war.

In the summer of 1940, the United States tried to step into the breach, exerting its considerable economic leverage to stop Japanese expansion. The State Department imposed quotas on most exports of strategic materials to Japan and banned the export of high-octane aviation fuel altogether. Unintimidated, or perhaps provoked, the Japanese successfully pressured the German-dominated Vichy French government to permit them to occupy northern Indochina. Britain and the United States feared that this was the first step toward making Indochina a Japanese colony.

In the spring of 1941, still seeking to end American economic sanctions and to obtain Washington's agreement to a Japanese sphere of interest in the Pacific, Tokyo ordered its ambassador to the United States, Admiral Kichisaburo Nomura, to begin negotiations with Secretary of State Cordell Hull. Their positions proved irreconcilable: Nomura insisted that the United States give Japan a free hand in East Asia, while Hull ended each session with a lecture on the evils of aggression.

In June, talks were broken off. Japanese-American relations took a dangerous turn for the worse, just as Nazi Germany was invading the Soviet Union.

Hitler's attack on the U.S.S.R. benefited Japan, whose expansionist plans had been constrained by worry about an uncommitted Soviet Union to its north. Although Hitler wanted Japan to join in the attack on the seat of world communism, the Japanese decided to move south. In July, Japanese troops occupied the rest of Indochina.

The Roosevelt administration learned of Japan's plans even before the move into Indochina had begun. Using a decoding device known as MAGIC, earlier that spring American intelligence had broken the Japanese diplomatic-military code. Washington responded to the occupation of southern Indochina by imposing a total embargo on trade with Japan and seizing Japanese assets in the United States. Japan had approximately a twelve-month supply of petroleum, and if it did not secure new sources by then, its economy and war machine would grind to a halt.

❧ Pearl Harbor

In October, an army militant, General Hideki Tojo, became premier of Japan, and he set in motion plans to seize the East Indies and go to war with the United States. To mask its preparations, Japan sent yet another negotiator to Washington. As the two sides traded proposals that essentially restated positions taken in the spring, MAGIC enabled American diplomats to evaluate Japan's proposals and declare them unacceptable even before the Japanese diplomats in Washington presented them. Roosevelt's military advisers pleaded with him to avoid steps that would lead to war, because they needed time to shore up inadequate defenses in the Philippines. Hull refused to compromise, however, and on November 26 he sent Japan a stiff reply. Among other things, it called for an immediate Japanese withdrawal from China.

Despite MAGIC, American intelligence did not know that a huge Japanese task force had left its base in the Kuril Islands on November 25, bound for Pearl Harbor while maintaining radio silence. Meanwhile, on December 6, Japanese diplomats issued a reply to Hull's ultimatum (which naval intelligence actually decoded faster than the clerks in the Japanese embassy). "This means war!" Roosevelt exclaimed when he read the Japanese message. Early on December 7, messages warning of imminent war were sent to American outposts in the Pacific — but it was too late, and in any case the Americans expected the blow to fall in the Philippines. The administration and America's Pacific Ocean commanders were taken unaware when, later that morning, Japanese dive-bombers and mini-subs caught most of the U.S. Pacific fleet bottled up in Pearl Harbor. The surprise attack sank or crippled eight battleships — fortunately for the Americans, the fleet's aircraft carriers escaped because they were out at sea. Still, in one brilliant tactical stroke, the Japanese had crippled American naval power in the Pacific. Had Japan known how vulnerable the Americans were and sent a second attacking wave, the disaster would have been even worse.

The Japanese attack on Pearl Harbor, which cost the lives of 2,400 American military and naval personnel, unified the nation as nothing else could have done. The next day Roosevelt told Congress that December 7 was "a date which will live in infamy" and asked for a declaration of war on Japan. Except for Montana's pacifist Representative Jeannette Rankin, both houses unanimously agreed. On December 11, Hitler and Mussolini declared war on the United States — a huge blunder, because it is unlikely that FDR could have persuaded Congress to enter the European war as well. The debate between isolationists and interventionists was over.

THE UNITED STATES AT WAR

When the United States entered the war, the Allied cause was in desperate straits. Hitler and Mussolini controlled virtually all of Europe. German warplanes continued their nightly assault on British cities, while on the eastern front Hitler's army, the *Wehrmacht*, reached the Caucasus Mountains of southern Russia in the spring of 1942. In North Africa, General Erwin Rommel's *Afrika Korps* pushed the British back into Egypt and threatened the Suez Canal.

The situation was equally grim in the Pacific. Simultaneously with their raid on Pearl Harbor, the Japanese

Pearl Harbor   President Roosevelt called December 7, 1941, "a date which will live in infamy."

attacked British Hong Kong and Malaya, the East Indies, and the Philippines. Filipino and American troops under General Douglas MacArthur were overwhelmed by the Japanese advance, and after they surrendered many perished in the brutal and infamous Bataan "Death March." After occupying the Dutch East Indies, Malaya, and the supposedly impregnable British fortress of Singapore, Japanese forces invaded New Guinea and Burma. India and Australia seemed in danger. The crippling of the U.S. Pacific fleet allowed Japan to take Guam and to complete its Pacific island defenses.

❧ Forging Allied Strategy

Determined to avenge Pearl Harbor, most Americans favored a Japan-first strategy for waging war. So did the U.S. Navy. But to Britain's great relief, Roosevelt and the American chief of staff, General George C. Marshall, held to the Europe-first approach that had prevailed since the passage of Lend-Lease. Partly this reflected the European orientation of Roosevelt and his advisers, but mostly it rested on the correct assumption that Hitler posed the greater danger and must be defeated first.

Attack on Pearl Harbor, 1941

The attack of Japanese forces on the American naval base at Pearl Harbor caught the base's inhabitants completely off guard, and was the setting for many acts of heroism, as related here by Corporal B.C. Nightingale of the U.S. Marine Corps.

At approximately eight o'clock on the morning of December 7, 1941, I was leaving the breakfast table when the ship's siren for air defense sounded.... Suddenly I heard an explosion. I ran to the port door leading to the quarter deck and saw a bomb strike a barge of some sort alongside the *Nevada*, or in that vicinity.... I was about three quarters of the way to the first platform on the mast when it seemed as though a bomb struck our quarterdeck. I could hear shrapnel or fragments whistling past me....

The bodies of the dead were thick, and badly burned men were heading for the quarterdeck, only to fall apparently dead or badly wounded.... Charred bodies were everywhere....

I made my way to the quay and started to remove my shoes when I suddenly found myself in the water. I think the concussion of a bomb threw me in. I started swimming for the pipe line which was about one hundred and fifty feet away. I was about half way when my strength gave out entirely. My clothes and shocked condition sapped my strength, and I was about to go under when Major Shapley started to swim by, and seeing my distress, grasped my shirt and told me to hang to his shoulders while we swam in. We were perhaps twenty-five feet from the pipe line when the Major's strength gave out and I saw he was floundering, so I loosened my grip on him and told him to make it alone. He stopped and grabbed me by the shirt and refused to let go. I would have drowned but for the Major.

In 1942, America was totally unprepared to mount a land campaign against Hitler. The highest priority was to bolster Soviet resistance to 3.3 million invading Axis troops — and to forestall the risk that Stalin might make a compromise peace with the Germans. In early 1942 Soviet foreign minister V. M. Molotov came to Washington to demand a second front in Europe at once, a refrain that Soviet diplomats would repeat for two years. To the dismay of his military chiefs, who knew what American capabilities were, Roosevelt promised to engage the Axis in the west by the year's end.

Making good on FDR's promise — but not satisfying the Soviets — in November 1942 American soldiers commanded by Dwight D. Eisenhower landed in Morocco and Algeria. The Vichy forces in these French North African colonies quickly laid down their arms (leading an enraged Hitler to occupy Vichy France). Soon thereafter, British field marshal Sir Bernard Montgomery halted Rommel's drive on the Suez Canal. Defeated in a massive battle at El Alamein in Egypt, the "Desert Fox" turned west and inflicted a stinging defeat on green American troops at Kasserine Pass in Tunisia. Slowly, however, the Anglo-American forces closed the ring on the German army, which was trapped in North Africa. The last Germans there surrendered in May 1943. The fighting in North Africa had cost the Germans dearly — around 350,000 in dead and captured troops — and the Mediterranean was opened to Allied traffic.

The North African campaign did little to placate Stalin, however, whose Russian army was bearing the full force of the German war machine. In perhaps the most critical battle of World War II, the Red Army made an epic defense of the city of Stalingrad (present-day Volgograd). From August through November 1942, the German Sixth Army besieged the city, which had great strategic and (because of its name) symbolic significance. Despite tens of thousands of civilian deaths, the Soviets refused to give way. Neither would Hitler. As the Russian winter began, the Red Army took the offensive. On February 2, 1943, the Germans, having lost 140,000 men, surrendered. The tide of battle had turned in the east, and the Soviets renewed their demand for a second front in the west.

The western allies were still not prepared to assault the Continent. An Anglo-Canadian raid on the French coast in 1942 had underscored both Allied unreadiness and the high risks of failure. Whether such an invasion should even be attempted sharply divided the British and the Americans. Remembering the horrendous slaughter of British troops in World War I, Churchill and his military advisers argued for subjecting Hitler's Europe to relentless bombing, economic strangulation, and attacks along what the prime minister called the enemy's "soft underbelly" — the Mediterranean coast and the Balkans. American strategists countered that Hitler could be beaten only by hurling a huge Allied army into France and then invading the heart of Germany. Roosevelt agreed, but he compromised by accepting Churchill's pleas to attack Italy first before an invasion of France.

In July 1943, American and British troops landed in Sicily. The invasion succeeded, emboldening anti-Axis Italians to overthrow Mussolini. On September 8 Italy surrendered unconditionally. German troops occupied the peninsula, however, freeing Mussolini and installing him as the head of a puppet regime. When, soon thereafter, Allied troops attempted to outflank the Germans in an amphibious landing at Salerno, they faced stubborn German resistance and had to battle to retain a beach head (creating more fears about a cross-channel invasion of France). The Allied advance up the Italian "boot" was slow and costly. Rome did not fall to an American army until June 1944. By that time, the main focus of the war in Europe had moved to France.

❧ Turning the Pacific Tide

In early 1942, American naval and Marine forces tasted bitter defeat throughout the western Pacific. Then, through MAGIC, U.S. intelligence learned that Admiral Isoroku Yamamoto, Japan's naval commander and ar-

chitect of the victory at Pearl Harbor, had dispatched a naval task force toward Port Moresby on the southern tip of New Guinea. If Port Moresby fell, Australia's defenses would be breached and the continent would be open to invasion. The U.S. aircraft carriers *Lexington* and *Yorktown* intercepted the attacking Japanese flotilla. In the ensuing Battle of Coral Sea (May 4-8, 1942), the Americans lost the *Lexington* and the *Yorktown* was damaged, but the Japanese also lost a carrier. More important, they called off their raid on Port Moresby. In that sense, the battle was an important Allied victory. It also showed that the struggle for control of the Pacific would be decided by aircraft carriers, from which combatants could project firepower hundreds of miles. Coral Sea was the first naval battle in history that consisted almost entirely of air attacks.

At Coral Sea the Japanese southward advance had been stopped, but the decisive engagement in the Pacific was the Battle of Midway in June 1942. Making a feint toward Alaska and simultaneously sending the flotilla to capture Port Moresby, Yamamoto ordered a larger fleet to take Midway Island, the stepping-stone to Hawaii. Again forewarned by MAGIC intercepts, American carriers lay in wait northeast of Midway. After hours of furious struggle (in which the damaged *Yorktown* was sunk), a squadron of thirty-seven American dive-bombers caught four Japanese carriers with their planes on deck being refueled and rearmed. Without air cover and with their decks littered with fuel and bombs, the Japanese vessels were perfect targets. The Japanese lost an entire car-

MacArthur Returns   On October 20, 1944, Douglas MacArthur (fourth from right) strode ashore on Leyte Island in the Philippines, fulfilling his vow "I shall return," which he had broadcast after being driven out by the Japanese invaders in early 1942. MacArthur repeated the wade through the surf several times, until the photographers had captured the scene to his satisfaction.

rier fleet and had their air superiority in the Pacific severely compromised. Between 1942 and 1944 Japan could build and launch only four new carriers; American shipyards produced fourteen.

The long process of rooting the Japanese army out of the stifling, mosquito-infested jungles in the islands of the Pacific began with a marine attack at Guadalcanal Island in August 1942. By the time that long, bloody battle finally ended in February 1943, army and marine units under the command of General Douglas MacArthur had secured a foothold on the islands of the Southwest Pacific and the coast of New Guinea.

American military leaders now had to decide on a grand strategy for the Pacific. MacArthur proposed to advance from New Guinea and retake the Philippines, from which he had ignominiously fled a year earlier. Admiral Chester Nimitz, however, wanted to use naval and air power to advance directly across the Pacific, taking key islands and finally besieging Japan itself. The military chiefs decided to combine the approaches. After an American task force destroyed eight Japanese troop ships and ten of the war vessels guarding them, the Japanese decided that it was too risky to try to reinforce their island outposts. This made it possible for Nimitz to "leapfrog," dispatching American forces to overwhelm selected island strongholds while cutting off and bypassing others.

The strategy worked. Nimitz's island-hopping began in the fall of 1943 at Tarawa in the Gilbert Islands. In one of the fiercest battles of the Pacific War, nearly a thousand marines died in taking on four thousand Japanese defenders, almost all of whom fought to the death. From bases on the Gilberts, planes from the Seventh Air Force attacked Japanese positions in the Marshall Islands to the north. In June 1944, Americans wrested control of the Marianas. Using airstrips in these islands — the last great island chain guarding the approaches to Japan — B-29s began a devastating bombardment of Japan itself.

Meanwhile MacArthur closed in on the Philippines from the south. First, in the Battle of the Philippine Sea on June 19-20, 1944, U.S. ships and planes destroyed three more Japanese carriers and nearly three hundred enemy aircraft. Then, on October 20, MacArthur strode ashore on the Philippine island of Leyte,[4] announcing dramatically to assembled journalists: "People of the Philippines: I have returned." The Japanese high com-

mand, desperate to avoid being cut off from vital supplies in Southeast Asia, ordered three battle fleets to converge on Leyte. Beginning on October 25, the largest naval battle in history raged. The United States won decisively, destroying most of what remained of Japanese sea power. From that point on, Japan was forced to rely for its defense on the suicidal attacks of "kamikaze" pilots. Crashing their bomb-laden planes into American warships, kamikazes inflicted serious damage but could not stop the Allied juggernaut. By the end of the year, MacArthur's troops had reconquered the Philippines.

℣ Mobilizing "the Arsenal of Democracy"

Yamamoto — who had studied at Harvard and knew America well — had predicted that victory at Pearl Harbor could give Japan only a temporary advantage. He hoped that a stunned American public and government would sue for peace. Should this not happen, he warned correctly, the outcome of the war would be decided on the home fronts.

Although news from the battlefield remained bleak, it was clear by the end of 1942 that American industry could produce planes, tanks, and guns much faster than the Axis could destroy them. In 1943, American industrial output exceeded that of all the Axis powers. When the war ended, American industry had turned out more than twice as many goods than the German and Japanese economies combined.

World War II ended the Great Depression and gave a powerful stimulus to the nation's economy and technology, laying the foundation for postwar affluence. Plants that had lain idle for years suddenly were running at full capacity. To meet wartime demands, Henry Ford built the huge Willow Run plant in Michigan, which at its height employed 42,000 workers and turned out a B-24 bomber every hour. Henry Kaiser's California shipyard lowered the time required for the construction of a merchant vessel from 105 to 14 days.

Although the rich grew richer during World War II, working-class Americans prospered too. In 1941, 53 percent of all families had incomes below $2,000 a year, while 24 percent lived on $1,000 or less. During the war, average weekly income increased by 70 percent, more than enough to offset a 47 percent inflation rate. For the first and only time in the twentieth century, the United States experienced a downward redistribution of income. The share of the nation's wealth taken by the top 5 percent of the population declined from 22 to 17

---

4. Actually he landed several times, as photographers shot and reshot the scene before he was satisfied.

percent, with most of the difference going to the bottom 40 percent. Excess-profit taxes and a 94 percent marginal income tax rate for the top bracket limited income growth for the rich to 20 percent.

By the time of Pearl Harbor, the draft had been in effect for almost a year. At that point Congress extended the term of military service to cover the duration of the war. Although 15 million American men and women would serve in the armed forces, some 60 million adults remained to operate the nation's factories and farms.

World War II accomplished what the New Deal had never done: It spent federal money on a scale sufficient to end the Great Depression, produce full employment, and benefit such previously marginalized workers as women, blacks, and Hispanics. Government expenditures during the war amounted to two times *all* federal appropriations prior to 1941. These massive infusions rolled through the economy, doubling the gross national product between 1940 and 1945. Prosperity spread at all levels, and the private sector both expanded and consolidated. In 1942 alone, 300,000 businesses closed, many of them absorbed by larger concerns. The biggest businesses proved most efficient — and were most apt to be favored in the awarding of government contracts.

Predictably, trade unions flourished during the war. Encouraged by the pro-labor stance of the Roosevelt administration and led by the CIO, American workers in the 1930s had successfully organized the automobile, steel, and textile industries. From 1941 through 1945, union membership increased from 10.5 million to 14.8 million.

Along with expenditures, massive federal intervention into the domestic economy was another consequence of the war. The state of emergency proclaimed in 1941 permitted the president to allocate manpower and resources. Putting American industry on a war footing, in 1942 Roosevelt created the War Production Board (WPB) headed by affable Sears executive Donald Nelson — who, however, was quickly bypassed by the military, which preferred to deal directly with de-

"The Arsenal of Democracy" Winston Churchill used this memorable phrase to praise the immense output of the machinery of warfare by the revved-up American industrial economy during World War II. Here, on February 12, 1943, B-24 Liberator bombers are on the production line of the Ford Motor Company's Willow Run plant near Detroit. Willow Run was the largest factory in the world.

fense contractors. Public ire boiled as the WPB began approving lucrative "cost-plus" contracts and awarded huge tax breaks to war manufacturers, and as military demands created shortages in the domestic economy, from sugar and coffee to rubber and gasoline. New automobiles were simply not manufactured: The nation's carmakers retooled to build tanks, trucks, and jeeps. The government's answer was rationing and price controls, overseen by the Office of Price Administration. The OPA was perhaps the most universally detested government agency in the nation.

Despite some confusion and profiteering, there were many remarkable success stories in America's wartime production. The government created fifty-one plants to manufacture synthetic rubber. The Office of Scientific Research and Development employed thousands of scientists to develop such crucial weapons as the proximity fuse, the bazooka, the high-altitude bombsight, radar, and sonar. In deepest secrecy, the

Manhattan Project (see below) unlocked the secrets of nuclear energy.

✆ *Loyalty on the Home Front*

To an extraordinary degree, Americans at home felt themselves to be in common cause with their besieged allies in Stalingrad and London. Because it lay remote from any battlefield, that sense of public commitment was fanned by a variety of advertising techniques; after all, as one British visitor noted, among the great powers, only the United States was "fighting this war on imagination alone." The first of the great propaganda efforts during the war was a campaign to sell War Bonds introduced by Secretary of the Treasury Henry Morgenthau, Jr., in 1942. The gigantic bond drives, often headed by celebrities, raised significant amounts of money for the war effort, but they also attracted millions of small wage earners with their messages of patriotism and support for the troops, thus serving to promote national solidarity behind the war effort. In 1942, Roosevelt established the Office of War Information (OWI), headed by respected newspaperman and radio newscaster Elmer Davis, to promote support for the war effort both at home and abroad. The OWI secured the services of leading advertising writers and Hollywood filmmakers to sell the war at home. The army hired director Frank Capra to produce a series of films portraying the unity and valor of the Allies. The controversial agency distributed much information, but its domestic activities were seriously constrained as an increasingly conservative Congress viewed it as an agency designed to further Roosevelt's political career and the New Deal. In the end, American patriotic zeal was whetted more by inflammatory reporting in the popular press than by government information. The movies were particularly important in building national morale.

As in all wars, the depictions of the enemy were framed to promote support for the war effort. Even before American entry into the war, most Americans had come to view the Allies favorably (including the Chinese) and both the Germans and Japanese as treacherous and warlike. While Hitler and the Nazis became targets of American ha-

tred, it was the "Japs" who drew the most stereotypical characterizations as "murderous little ape-men." Often, racist assumptions showed through in public depictions of the Japanese. In the movies, comic strips, and in popular literature during the war, the enemy was depicted in the starkest contrasts of good and evil, stripped of humanity, and promoting the conclusion that only unconditional surrender could rectify the wrongs committed.

✆ *The Return of Prosperity and the Wartime Consumer*

Some 9 million Americans moved to cities, not only in the North but also on the West Coast and Gulf Coast to work in the defense industry. The "Sunbelt," which would become the most important new demographic region in postwar years, had its origin in the wartime boom of California, Texas, Alabama, and Florida, where countless shipyards, aircraft factories, and munitions plants sprang up with government encouragement. California alone gained 2 million residents. This mass migration fattened paychecks but also caused considerable discomfort. Since virtually no new housing had gone up during the Depression, wartime dislocations caused an acute housing shortage. Entire families were

War Workers   These African American women do their part in a World War II defense plant. By providing skilled, dignified, well-paying, and generally non-discriminatory employment, the war effort helped propel blacks into the post-1945 civil rights movement. Off the job, however, African Americans often faced blatant racism.

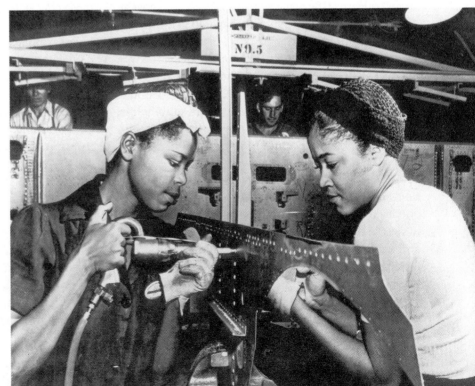

Women at Work on the Homefront

"Rosie the Riveter" was a popular image that came to represent the work of many women in factories and shipyards during the Second World War. One such "Rosie," Katie Grant, recounts her experience here.

I worked the graveyard shift 12:00-8:00 a.m, in the shipyard. I took classes on how to weld. I had leather gloves, leather pants, big hood, goggles and a leather jacket. They said you weld like you crochet.

Well, I did not know how to do that, but I could sew and make a neat stitch. We held the welding rod with one hand and the torch fire in the right hand. Placed the rod in a seam and melted it down in a small bead seam and brushed it off with a steel brush.

They put me forty feet down in the bottom of the ship to be a tacker. I filled the long seams of the cracks in the ship corners full of hot lead and then brushed them good and you could see how pretty it was. The welders would come along and weld it so it would

take the strong waves and deep water and heavy weight. I liked it pretty good.

I don't remember how much I got paid for working. Lots of people came to Richmond to work in the shipyards. Lots of women went to work to help with the war. I told [my husband] Melvin later that I helped to make a ship for him to come home in.

---

forced into single rooms. Prefabricated homes and trailers became the uncomfortable abodes of tens of thousands of defense workers and their families.

Nonetheless, the new prosperity of the wartime economy set off a consumer boom. The race for scarce consumer goods led to hoarding as well as rationing. One early study of fourteen cities found Americans stocking up on a range of products, foods such as sugar, coffee, and spices; rubber goods from tires to golf balls; and clothing, particularly men's suits and shoes. As supplies of such textiles as cotton, wool, and nylon dropped, the government ordered a 10 percent reduction in the amount of cloth in a woman's bathing suit. As a result, the *Wall Street Journal* observed that the "two-piece bathing suit now is tied in with the war as closely as the zipperless dress." When clothes and cars became unavailable, Americans spent their money on entertainment and theater revenues soared as war workers flocked to the films. The war particularly empowered women consumers who for the first time had earnings of their own to spend, as well as the military pay or wages of their husbands, giving them an opportunity to buy, or to save and buy, the conveniences and luxuries identified with the middle class.

❧ Women at War

World War II forced Americans to change their attitudes toward gender roles in the workplace. In the first place, women constituted a significant portion of the armed forces. Approximately 200,000 women enlisted into the Women's Army Corps (WAC) and its naval equivalent, the WAVES; and the Marines and Coast Guard accepted women in lesser numbers. In the second place, female Americans took up the slack in the civilian workforce created by the enlistment and drafting of millions of men and the expansion of industry. The federal government encouraged women to become sheet metal workers, millers, welders, lumberjacks, machinists, and stevedores. The number of women employed in the workforce increased from 14 million in 1940 to 19 million in 1945. By 1944, one-third of all adult American females worked outside the home. Although women continued to be paid less than men for the same work, the average paycheck for female workers increased during World War II by 50 percent. The chance to "get out of the kitchen" and earn money gave American women independence that many would be loath to surrender after the war, although traditional attitudes remained strong and some women intended to leave their jobs when the war was over. Many did not leave, however, and some of those who did later returned to the workforce.

❧ Wartime Roots of the Civil Rights Movement

Even before hostilities began, African American leaders were demanding that their people receive a prominent role in the war effort and that there be no discrimination in either the military or the defense industries. Said one black activist: "Negroes in America want some concrete assurance by direct proof that they will fight not only for others, but that they are fighting for gains of their own." Eventually, more than a million African Americans served in the armed forces, nearly all as enlisted men under white officers. Secretary of the Navy Frank

Knox typified official attitudes when he barred blacks from the rank of petty officer: there was, he said, no way that "men of the colored race" could maintain discipline among "men of the white race." Stereotyped as unreliable under fire, African American soldiers were much less likely to see combat than whites. Perhaps the cruelest irony was that German prisoners of war interned in the South were taken to movie theaters and lunch counters from which local Jim Crow laws excluded African Americans.

In February 1941, A. Philip Randolph, the militant head of the Brotherhood of Sleeping Car Porters, threatened a massive march on Washington unless Roosevelt by executive order banned discrimination in the defense industry and armed forces. Dreading racial turmoil as the shadow of war hung over the nation, FDR got Randolph to call off his march by signing an executive order requiring nondiscrimination clauses in all defense contracts and creating a Fair Employment Practices Committee to police the private sector. These measures had a major long-range impact. The number of African Americans working for the federal government jumped from 60,000 to 200,000 by the war's end, and some 2 million African Americans were employed in war-related jobs.

The lure of industrial jobs drew immense numbers of African Americans out of the South: between 1940 and 1950, 300,000 to the West and 500,000 each to the Midwest and Northeast. This dramatic population shift helped make civil rights a national rather than a regional issue, but it also brought severe racial tensions to the North. As white and black war workers competed for scarce housing and goods, resentments mounted. On a hot Sunday evening in the summer of 1943, black and white swimmers traded insults at Detroit's Belle Island recreation park. The next day a race riot erupted. When after twenty-four hours the National Guard intervened, twenty-three blacks and nine whites lay dead. Later that year, only the intervention of Mayor Fiorello La-Guardia prevented a similar outburst in Harlem.

Whites sensed correctly that African Americans intended to use the war to knock down racial barriers in the workplace, the voting booth, and public facilities. Participation in the military and expanded economic opportunity generated a new sense of confidence and militancy in African Americans. NAACP membership leaped from 50,000 to 450,000. In 1944 the Supreme Court in *Smith v. Allwright* ruled Texas's all-white primary unconstitutional. Thus did the United States take the first step toward enfranchising its people of color. As

black historian Walter White observed: "World War II has immeasurably magnified the Negro's awareness of the disparity between the American profession and practice of democracy."

The war years saw the birth of strategies that, in the 1950s and 1960s, would finally destroy Jim Crow. Employing the nonviolent civil resistance techniques pioneered by Mohandas Gandhi in India, black activists attacked racial barriers both north and south. Founded in 1942, the biracial Congress on Racial Equality, or CORE,[5] staged the first "freedom ride" to fight segregation in interstate transport. Travelling south by bus from Washington, black and white CORE volunteers were arrested in Durham, North Carolina. CORE also staged lunch-counter sit-ins in Washington, D.C., New York, New Jersey, and other northern states. The protesters were frequently beaten and arrested, but a growing number of northern restaurants ended discrimination.

❧ Other Outsiders

Around 25,000 Native Americans served in the armed forces during World War II. Most famous of those who served were the Navajo "code talkers" who were widely used in the Pacific theater to relay secret messages, befuddling Japanese efforts to decipher the code. Many thousands of other Native Americans left reservations during the war to work in factories. Those who left the reservations shared in the sharp economic improvement experienced by other Americans and some remained outside the reservation after the war and assimilated into the mainstream culture. On the other hand, Native Americans living off reservations continued to meet with informal and formal discrimination and returned to the reservations after the war ended. At the same time, pressure mounted during the war to reduce tax commitments to reservations, and to combat that notion Native Americans in 1944 organized the National Congress of American Indians.

Hispanic Americans also profited from some of the same upward social and economic mobility during the war. Tens of thousands left rural New Mexico, Texas, and California for city jobs in the aircraft and petroleum industries. Wages were lower than those paid to whites, and unions sometimes tried to exclude them, but Hispanic Americans benefited nonetheless. In addition, in

---

5. The original name was the Committee on Racial Equality; it became the Congress on Racial Equality in 1944.

1942, the United States and Mexico agreed to the *bracero* program that permitted Mexican laborers to enter the U.S. to work on short-term contracts. Although they generally suffered from discrimination in the workplace, an estimated 200,000 Mexicans seized the economic opportunity offered by the *bracero* program. Around half of these workers settled in California where most lived in segregated communities called *colonias*. While most Mexican laborers continued to perform agriculture labor with little real protection, thousands did escape the farms and found jobs in the manufacturing sector.

An estimated 350,000 Mexican Americans served in the armed forces during World War II, volunteering in numbers that far exceeded their proportion of the population. They also received a disproportionate percentage of citations, including seventeen Medals of Honor. Many served in the Eighty-eighth Division, the highly decorated "Blue Devils" who won acclaim in the Italian campaign.

Alongside this, however, were the violent Los Angeles "Zoot Suit" riots of 1943. During four days of rioting white servicemen invaded Mexican American neighborhoods attacking members of street gangs, presumed to be draft dodgers, who wore ducktail haircuts, wide padded shoulders, pegged pants, wide-brimmed hats, and dangling watch chains. The Los Angeles police largely ignored the rioting and responded only by arresting zoot suiters. In short, while the war offered economic opportunities for Mexican Americans, old patterns of prejudice and discrimination remained once the war ended.

❧ The Japanese Internment

Several American ethnic groups, including Italian Americans, faced suspicion during World War II. But most European immigrants had assimilated somewhat into American society by 1942 — and they were white. On both counts — a resistance to assimilation and because of their racial identity — Japanese Ameri-

An Internment Camp for Japanese-Americans Uprooted from their homes, farms, and businesses after Pearl Harbor, most Japanese American families spent the bulk of the World War II years crowded into rough barracks like this.

cans were the most vulnerable to wartime hysteria. The war with Japan enflamed the West Coast's smoldering anti-Asian sentiments. Throughout the country, most whites believed that both *Issei* (naturalized Americans born in Japan) and *Nisei* (persons of Japanese ancestry born in the United States) were disloyal. Shortly before Pearl Harbor, one journalist predicted that Nisei "will sow mines across the entrance of our ports.... Sierra passes and tunnels will be blocked.... Japanese farmers ... will send their peas and potatoes and squash full of arsenic to the markets." Once the war began, General John L. DeWitt, head of the West Coast Defense Command, warned: "A Jap's a Jap.... It makes no difference whether he is an American citizen or not.... There is no way to determine their loyalty." Bowing to such fears (and to the demands of California's attorney general — later governor and Supreme Court chief justice — Earl Warren), Roosevelt ordered the deportation of 120,000 Japanese Americans to ten hastily built camps in seven western states. Forced to leave their homes and sell their businesses at cut-rate prices, "evacuees" lived in shacks surrounded by barbed wire and armed guards.

Internees sued in federal court, claiming that the government was violating their civil liberties. In 1944 a divided Supreme Court ruled that incarceration of Japanese Americans was justified on grounds of national security. According to the majority, "residents having ethnic affiliations with an invading enemy may be a greater source of danger than those of different ancestry." After 1943, individuals could escape the camps by swearing allegiance to the United States and taking a job away from the West Coast. During the two years that followed, 35,000 internees left the camps, but at war's end some 5,000 Japanese Americans returned to Japan. The detention centers remained in operation until March 1946, and only in 1983 did the government officially admit its mistake and pay compensation to survivors and their heirs.

❧ God at War

Pearl Harbor presented Christians and Jews with a dilemma. The "day of infamy" and the racism and oppression inherent in fascism presented most believers with what seemed an undeniable "just war," in which the taking of life in behalf of freedom and self-preservation was sanctioned by religious tradition. At the same time, memories of World War I's slaughter lingered in the consciences of religious people. Nonetheless, churches and clergy who had been prominent in the pacifist movement of the 1930s quickly embraced the crusade against Japanese and Nazi aggression; idealistic pacifism largely vanished in the wake of the attack on Pearl Harbor.

Within the historic peace churches (such as Quakers and Mennonites) a few thousand young men chose to become conscientious objectors. The ranks of conscientious objectors reached about 12,500, including Jehovah's Witnesses, whose refusal to pledge allegiance to any human government failed to impress draft boards. A small number of young Catholics, evangelical Protestants, and Jews who had religious scruples against war often faced draft boards composed of fellow believers unsympathetic to what they perceived as a lack of patriotism. Government policy required conscientious objectors either to go to prison or to work in an approved alternative public service position financed by their religious bodies. Because many of the larger churches refused or failed to fund such activities, the historic "peace churches" funded

the placement of most conscientious objectors of all persuasions.

Most Christians and Jews wholeheartedly supported the war effort. More than 8,000 clergy served as chaplains in the military during World War II and churches sponsored many campaigns to provide relief supplies. In a typical response to mobilization, the National Catholic Welfare Conference placed its "institutions and their consecrated personnel" at the service of the country.

World War II had a powerful impact on American religion. Many young men thrust into combat found themselves dependent on God and many in the heat of battle dedicated themselves to Christian service. Those commitments, combined with the opportunities to export American values in the postwar world, would fuel a boom of missionary work in the 1950s. In 1942, conservative Protestants, under the leadership of Boston minister and educator Harold John Ockenga, formed the National Association of Evangelicals, preparing to assert themselves in the postwar era. The ecumenical movement also gained strength during the war, setting the stage for the founding of the World Council of Churches in 1948. The cooperation of almost all religious groups in supporting the armed forces and the war effort at home — including Roman Catholics and Jews — did much to foster ecumenical ideals and break down religious barriers, as did the personal associations of soldiers on the battlefield.

The American religious community also had a profound impact on postwar planning. The center of this activity was the Federal Council of Churches Commission on a Just and Durable Peace, chaired by prominent Wall Street lawyer John Foster Dulles. The son of a minister, Dulles was a leading Presbyterian layman who hoped to infuse world order — an abiding interest ever since his participation in the Paris Peace Conference — with a spiritual core. The report of the commission, which also included such prominent theologians as Henry P. Van Dusen and Reinhold Niebuhr, blended world-order utopianism and Christian realism. It was to serve as a basis for the plan that would become the United Nations.

❧ "Dr. Win-the-War" and the 1944 Election

World War II pushed American politics decidedly to the right. Widespread prosperity undercut the economic discontent and class hostility that gave the New Deal much of its momentum, and voters grew increasingly aggrieved over government intrusion into their lives. Price controls, rationing, and a hundred other irritations combined to create a "throw the rascals out" mentality. Republicans also benefited from low voter turnout due to absent servicemen and the inability of newly displaced workers to vote. As a result, in 1942 the GOP made substantial gains in both houses of Congress and captured the governorships of California and New York. Republican legislators joined with conservative southern Democrats to turn the country to the right. In 1943, Congress abolished the WPA, the CCC, and the National Youth Administration. With the draft and the disappearance of unemployment, these agencies had lost much of their reason for being, but conservatives had larger aims in mind. "Many of them [newly elected Republicans] think they have a mandate to repeal all New Deal reforms," *Fortune* magazine observed.

The conservative turn in American politics spelled troubled for organized labor. Unions made significant gains during the war, but strikes in 1943 and 1944 by the United Mine Workers led by the irascible and militant John L. Lewis prompted Congress to authorize presidential seizure of plants essential to the war effort, to require unionwide votes before strikes, and to bar unions from making political contributions. In 1944, Florida and Arkansas passed anti-union "right-to-work" laws that would be emulated elsewhere in postwar years.

As early as 1942, FDR (ever sensitive to public opinion) announced that "Dr. New Deal" had given way to "Dr. Win-the-War." There was never much question that Roosevelt would run for a fourth term in 1944, but partly because of the country's conservative drift, he dumped his liberal vice president, Henry Wallace, in favor of a middle-of-the-road Senator known chiefly for his investigations of wartime profiteering, Harry S Truman. In spite of these pragmatic compromises, Roosevelt retained a firm commitment to the liberal ideals of the New Deal. In his 1944 State of the Union address he presented an Economic Bill of Rights that asserted that every citizen had rights to decent jobs, sufficient food, shelter, and clothing, and security during old age and illness.

To challenge Roosevelt, the Republicans picked New York governor Thomas E. Dewey, who had attracted attention as a crime-fighting prosecutor. Dewey represented the more liberal, internationalist eastern wing of his party, and he made it clear that if he were elected there would be no reversion to isolationism, nor any widespread attack on the New Deal. The increasing velocity of Allied victories undermined Republican efforts to imply that the war had been mismanaged. Roosevelt swamped Dewey in the electoral college, 432 to 99. The popular vote was closer; the president's margin of 3.6 million was the smallest of his four elections, indeed, the narrowest since 1916. Roosevelt appeared weary and frail in 1944 and was suffering from hypertension and heart disease; still, he embraced the victory and embarked on an unprecedented fourth term as president.

VICTORY

In 1944 and 1945, the world changed in stunning ways. Hitler's Third Reich collapsed under relentless military assaults by the Allies on eastern and western fronts, leaving the United States and the Soviet Union as the dominant forces in the postwar world. The shape of the postwar world had been generally agreed upon by Allied leaders before a conference in Yalta in February 1945 formalized the postwar settlement. After Germany surrendered, the Allies turned their attention to the defeat of Japan. Troop ships loaded with Allied soldiers headed from Europe to the Pacific to make ready for a final assault on Japan. That bloody action never took place because in August 1945 the world was shocked by two atomic blasts which led to a Japanese surrender. Much remained to be done, but V-E Day (May 7) and V-J Day (September 2) were welcomed with delirious celebration throughout the United States.

Wartime Diplomacy

As the war progressed, it became evident that the Big Three — the United States, Great Britain, and the Soviet Union — had very different expectations for the world that would emerge after the Axis defeat. Churchill and his advisers were practitioners of the art of balance-of-power politics. They insisted that the fate of Europe would continue to determine the fate of the world. Churchill looked forward to the quick rehabilitation of France, Germany, and Italy to prevent the Soviet Union from dominating the continent. And he bluntly announced that he did not intend "to preside over the dissolution of the British Empire."

Stalin believed that because his country had borne the brunt of the war in Europe, it ought to be free to carve out a sphere of interest in Eastern Europe and the Near East. From the moment Hitler attacked the U.S.S.R., Stalin and his emissaries insisted that the primary Soviet goal was physical security — preventing another Napoleon or Hitler from ravaging their homeland. In 1942, Stalin stated his minimum territorial objectives: the full fruits of the Nazi-Soviet Nonaggression Pact, that is, annexation of Latvia, Estonia, Lithuania, and portions of Poland, Romania, and Finland. Beyond that, the Kremlin insisted on having "friendly" — that is, procommunist — governments in the buffer lands between the Soviet Union and Germany. In short, even as Hitler drove relentlessly toward Moscow and Stalingrad, Stalin stood ready to seize any opportunity and utilize every tactic short of global war to extend Soviet power as far into Europe as possible.

Roosevelt's vision of the postwar world is extremely difficult to define precisely. Just as he had done in facing the Great Depression, so in setting his wartime strategy, FDR preferred to leave options open and shunned binding himself to any one course of action. He seems to have envisioned using the offer of massive American aid for reconstruction to ensure Stalin's good behavior in the postwar world. To secure postwar international security, he spoke of "the Four Policemen" — the United States, Great Britain, the Soviet Union, and Chiang Kai-shek's China — dominating their respective spheres of influence, promoting democracy, and forestalling aggression. Sensing that colonialism was doomed, he tried (with no success) to persuade Churchill and French leader Charles De Gaulle to begin decolonialization.

In 1944, responding to a surge of popular enthusiasm for internationalism, the administration announced with great fanfare that it favored establishing a new collective security organization to keep the peace and promote social justice around the globe. In reality, though, Roosevelt never abandoned his Four Policemen idea. The United Nations, which American policy largely shaped (see below), combined the concept of collective security with that of spheres of interest. Above all, Roosevelt was determined to prevent a third world war by holding the Big Three together and promoting national self-determination — goals that would prove incompatible.

Roosevelt resisted discussing boundaries, reparations, and spheres of influence as long as possible. He feared that wrangling over such issues would tear the Grand Alliance asunder and, at worst, might induce Stalin to sign a separate peace with Hitler. But by the end of 1944, Nazi Germany's defeat seemed only a matter of time, and FDR could no longer avoid specific postwar commitments.

❦ *Liberating Western Europe*

The Soviet Union became increasingly restive in 1943 because of the failure of the Allies to launch a second front in France and Roosevelt sought reconciliation through personal diplomacy. In December, Roosevelt, Churchill, and Stalin met in Tehran to discuss an invasion and other postwar matters. Stalin dismissed Churchill's excuses for delaying the invasion and American military chiefs brushed aside the prime minister's plea for an Allied thrust through the Balkans where they could block postwar Soviet expansion. Because the United States was supplying the major portion of the men and matériel for the Allied war effort in the Western European and Pacific theaters by 1943, it called the strategic shots, and the U.S. and Britain promised a cross-channel invasion in early 1944. The leaders also discussed other postwar questions at Teheran, including the establishment of an international organization at the end of the war and the promise of Soviet aid in the Pacific once Germany had surrendered.

As Stalin impatiently waited, for two years the Allies massed and trained 3 million troops — Americans, British, Canadians, De Gaulle's Free French, and refugee Poles — in Great Britain, stockpiled millions of tons of equipment, and assembled a fleet of landing craft. General Dwight D. Eisenhower, the supreme commander, needed all his talents as a strategist, organizer, and diplomat to hold the massive effort together. By the spring of 1944, *Operation Overlord* was ready to invade the Germans' "Fortress Europe."

On June 6, 1944, the Allies struck during a lull in stormy weather that had threatened to delay the entire operation. Deceiving the Germans into thinking that the real thrust would come farther north, they landed on the Normandy coast, chosen because it possessed few natural harbors and was therefore relatively lightly defended. The invading armada was the largest the world had ever seen. *Overlord*'s 6,483 ships disembarked 176,000 men and 1,500 tanks on the first day of the operation. The ferocity of fighting varied, with the American First Division suffering especially heavy losses on Omaha Beach. The 12,000 Allied planes assigned to *Overlord* quickly destroyed the 169 German fighters available to defend Normandy. A week later, more than 300,000 troops were pushing the Germans back. Not until July, however, were the Allies able to break out of Normandy and open a tank-led drive across the plains of northern France. On August 25, Paris surrendered, and by September Allied troops reached the

Normandy Allied forces swarmed ashore on these beaches on D-Day: June 6, 1944. This photograph, taken after the initial beachheads had been secured, testifies to the immensity of the attack that was unleashed.

upper Rhine. There, Eisenhower ordered a halt so that his troops could resupply. A British-led attempt to cross the Rhine with paratroops in the Netherlands failed.

Hitler made a desperate bid to stop the Allied advance in December 1944, throwing most of his remaining tank divisions into a daring counterattack that the American press called the Battle of the Bulge. Taking advantage of bad weather that denied the Allies air cover, German armor and infantry blasted through a weak point in Eisenhower's lines in the Ardennes forest of Belgium and Luxembourg. Hitler hoped to cut off and isolate up to a third of the Allied army. Although the German offensive pushed the Allies far back in places, the 101st Airborne Division held out at the crucial crossroads Belgian town of Bastogne. Clearing skies finally gave Eisenhower the air cover necessary to take the offensive. In the end, the battle's chief result was to deplete the Wehrmacht's petroleum reserves, destroy much of its remaining armor, and greatly damage its ability to defend German soil. As the Germans fell back toward the Rhine, the Red Army

in January 1945 launched a massive offensive in the east. In a month, it swept westward from the rubble of Warsaw to within fifty miles of Berlin.

Allied forces tightened the noose on Nazi Germany in early 1945. Allied bombers pounded German cities relentlessly, causing immense losses of civilian lives. The worst — and most senseless — instance of such attacks was the Anglo-American firebombing on February 13-14, 1945, of undefended Dresden, a city without military significance packed with refugees and world-famous for its art galleries; as many as 135,000 perished in this and subsequent raids. Then, on March 7, Americans commanded by General Omar Bradley found and crossed the only intact Rhine bridge. Eisenhower, taking his cue from Washington's policy, overruled British appeals that Western troops seize Berlin before the Red

General Eisenhower's
Order of the Day, June 5, 1944
General Eisenhower began drafting his order for
the launch of the Allied forces on the beaches of
Normandy nearly four months before D-Day. It
was distributed to the 175,000 member expedi-
tionary force on the eve of the invasion.

SUPREME HEADQUARTERS
ALLIED EXPEDITIONARY FORCE

Soldiers, Sailors, and Airmen of the Allied
Expeditionary Force!
     You are about to embark upon the Great
Crusade, toward which we have striven these
many months. The eyes of the world are upon
you. The hope and prayers of liberty-loving
people everywhere march with you. In
company with our brave Allies and brothers-
in-arms on other Fronts, you will bring about
the destruction of the German war machine,
the elimination of Nazi tyranny over the
oppressed peoples of Europe, and security for
ourselves in a free world.
     Your task will not be an easy one. Your
enemy is will trained, well equipped and
battle-hardened. He will fight savagely.
     But this is the year 1944! Much has hap-
pened since the Nazi triumphs of 1940-41. The
United Nations have inflicted upon the Germans great defeats, in open battle, man-to-
man. Our air offensive has seriously reduced
their strength in the air and their capacity to
wage war on the ground. Our Home Fronts
have given us an overwhelming superiority in
weapons and munitions of war, and placed at
our disposal great reserves of trained fighting
men. The tide has turned! The free men of the
world are marching together to Victory!
     I have full confidence in your courage,
devotion to duty and skill in battle. We will
accept nothing less than full Victory!
     Good luck! And let us beseech the bless-
ing of Almighty God upon this great and
noble undertaking.

Army got there. Instead, the Allies advanced across a broad front, capturing the Ruhr Valley, the industrial heart of Germany, and meeting the Russians at the Elbe. Meanwhile the Red Army fought its way into Berlin. With the Russians a hundred yards from his bunker, Hitler committed suicide on April 30. A week later, Eisenhower accepted the unconditional surrender of all German forces.

Roosevelt did not live to see Hitler's end. On April 12, 1945, while trying to regain strength at his retreat in Warm Springs, Georgia, he died suddenly of a massive brain hemorrhage, leaving some of the most fateful of all wartime decisions to his untested vice president, Harry Truman.

✈ Ending of the War in the Pacific

As the war in Europe drew to a close, fierce fighting continued in the Pacific. The United States approached the final stages of the Pacific War with apprehensive determination. In February 1945, U.S. Marines fought furiously for twenty days to capture the small island of Iwo Jima — located 700 miles south of Tokyo — from 21,000 Japanese troops living in caves, pillboxes, and trenches. Nearly 7,000 Americans were killed in the bitter fighting and all but 200 of the Japanese defenders lost their lives. The next month American forces stormed the southernmost island of the Japanese archipelago, Okinawa, and in two months of fighting more than 7,000 Americans were killed on land and another 5,000 were

reported killed or missing as a result of kamikaze attacks on American ships.

Nonetheless, Japanese leaders refused to accept defeat. At least they hoped to escape unconditional surrender and to protect the emperor. So, in the spring of 1945 American planes continued devastating bombing of Japanese cities, including a staggering attack on Tokyo on May 23, 1945, which set off a firestorm that razed the city and killed an estimated 83,000 people.

In July, Harry Truman found himself negotiating with Stalin at Potsdam and pondering his options for ending the Pacific War. The first option was to launch a conventional invasion, with an American force led by MacArthur striking from the south and an Anglo-American army, transferred from Europe, descending upon Japan from the Aleutians. D-Day was set for November 1945. Military leaders estimated that the campaign would last a year and cost a minimum of 100,000 Allied lives (and at least a million Japanese, who it was expected would fight to the death). A second option, urged upon Truman by certain diplomatic advisers, was to offer Japan a negotiated settlement. Suffering terribly from Allied bombing, the Japanese would surely surrender, it was argued, if assured that they could retain the emperor, whom they regarded as a sacred figure. At the Potsdam Conference, Truman and Clement Atlee, who had replaced Churchill as prime minister, urged Japan to surrender but promised no concessions. The Japanese ignored the demand. A stunning scientific achievement quickly overtook all of these speculations on August 6, 1945.

❧ The Manhattan Project and the Beginning of the Nuclear Age

Einstein's theory of relativity and other developments in atomic physics in the early twentieth century theorized that mass could be converted into huge amounts of energy. Inevitably, the potential of such ideas in the development of new weapons attracted the attention of militarists in Germany and elsewhere. In 1939, Einstein, who was teaching at Princeton, warned Roosevelt that German scientists were exploring the building of an atomic bomb and urged the U.S. to do the same. The building of a bomb had become feasible because of the discovery of the radioactive characteristics of uranium in the 1930s by Italian physicist Enrico Fermi. Fermi immigrated to the U.S. in 1938 and achieved the first controlled fission chain reaction at the University of Chicago in 1942.

In 1941 Roosevelt initiated a huge and highly secret project to build an atomic bomb. In 1942, the massive undertaking — known as the Manhattan Project — was reorganized under the supervision of the army general Leslie Groves. During the next three years the government invested more than $2 billion in a crash effort to split the atom and produce a nuclear explosive device before Hitler's scientists could. Scientists in Oak Ridge, Tennessee, proved that plutonium was capable of providing the fuel for an atomic bomb, and a team of scientists under the direction of J. Robert Oppenheimer was assigned the task of building the actual bomb at Los Alamos, New Mexico.

U.S. atomic scientists set off an atomic blast in the New Mexico desert near Alamogordo on July 16, 1945. That first device, named Trinity by its builders, produced a blinding fireball and a mushroom cloud that rose 40,000 feet in the sky. "From ten miles away," recalled engineer Philip Morrison, "we saw the unbelievably brilliant flash . . . We wore welder's glasses. The thing that got me was not the flash but the blinding heat of a bright day on your face in the cold desert morning. It was like a hot oven with the sun coming out like a sunrise."

When news was secretly flashed to Harry Truman in Potsdam of the successful New Mexico test, the president, who had not even known of the Manhattan Project when he took office, had another alternative means of winning the war at his disposal. He could shock the Japanese into surrender by dropping an atomic bomb on a Japanese city. After the war some critics would question the morality of Truman's decision to use atomic weapons, and a few advisers at the time suggested giving the Japanese a warning demonstration, but that idea was rejected. He issued an ultimatum (signed by the British as well) demanding that the Japanese surrender by August 3 or face utter destruction. When the Japanese failed to respond to the ultimatum, with little hesitation Truman ordered the Army Air Corps to use the bomb quickly to end the war.

On August 6, a B-29, the *Enola Gay*, dropped a single atomic bomb on Hiroshima, an industrial city and military base with 350,000 civilian inhabitants. By American estimates, more than 80,000 inhabitants of the city died and many others suffered crippling effects from radiation. Still, Japan did not give up. Its leaders were stunned by the attack but were unable to agree on a response. On August 8 the Soviet Union invaded Manchuria. The United States dropped a second nuclear bomb on Nagasaki on August 9, inflicting around 100,000 deaths and devastating the city. On August 14, Japanese leaders announced that they were ready to surrender, and on September 2, 1945, on board the battleship *Missouri*, which was anchored in Tokyo Bay, Japanese officials signed the articles of surrender. World War II was over.

To the end of his life in 1972, Truman insisted that his sole reason for ordering the atomic bombing was to save American lives. Japan, he said, would not surrender, and had the invasion taken place with the American people subsequently learning that the president could have prevented it, he would rightly have been held accountable for the loss of American lives. Furthermore, the two atomic bombs probably killed far fewer Japanese than the number who would have perished with the continuation of conventional bombing and an invasion of the Japanese homeland. Years later, Truman observed that the atom bomb was no "great decision. . . . merely another powerful weapon in the arsenal of righteousness." Whatever the cogency of his reasoning on political grounds,[6] and its seeming inevitability amidst the hatreds that existed in 1945, to many, America's use of atomic bombs seemed both callous and an ominous threat to the future. A New York clergyman expressed those fears: "Everything else seemed suddenly to become insignificant. For I knew that the final crisis in human history had come. What that atomic bomb had done to Japan, it could do to us."

6. These are further discussed in Chapter 30.

Hiroshima　A nuclear weapon was used in warfare for the first time over Hiroshima on August 6, 1945. Somewhere between 70,000 and 80,000 people were killed instantly, and untold thousands more died later from the effects of radiation exposure.

❧ *The GI's War*

Millions of young Americans fought bravely and sometimes idealistically during World War II. When the war began around 1.6 million Americans were in the army; by 1945 that number had swollen to more than 7 million; another 3.9 million served in the navy, 2.3 million in the army air corps, and 600,000 in the marines. Millions of young teenage men either volunteered or were swept into service through the draft. In the training camps and at the front they experienced a cultural diversity that broke down many provincial barriers; southerners fought side by side with Yankees; Catholics with Protestants and Jews; and recent immigrants with old-stock Americans. A disproportionate percentage of the training camps were in the South, and their presence did much to further weaken the historic isolation of that region.

Minorities enlisted in large numbers during the war. Chinese Americans served in the highest percentage of any group of Americans and Mexican Americans had a higher enlistment rate than the general population. Filipinos and other Asian Americans were fiercely loyal during the war, embracing the opportunity to fight alongside other Americans as an equal, and, by and large, in places like California some barriers began to disappear. Only American blacks remained seriously alienated. Black soldiers were strictly segregated and generally assigned to noncombat units commanded by white officers, although the army desegregated officer candidate schools in 1940. The navy accepted blacks only as cooks and stewards, and at the beginning of the war the air force and marines would not accept them at all. Nonetheless, more than a million blacks served during the war and before it ended many were in black combat units. At Tuskegee Institute in Alabama a separate flight school turned out nearly six hundred black flyers; they established an enviable combat record and won eighty Distinguished Flying Crosses.

Many young men volunteered for service with high idealistic notions and visions of glory. Particularly in the early months of the war, when raw and unprepared American troops faced seasoned German veterans in North Africa and Italy, they were often battered and embarrassed. After months of combat, the image of the American soldier, captured so vividly in Bill Mauldin's cartoons, was that of a war-weary veteran trying to survive the horrors and inanities of war. Like all soldiers, they were preserved in war by their loyalty to one another, and to survival, more than to lofty causes or war aims. And they were sustained by memories of home and loved ones who awaited their return.

While American losses were minuscule compared to those of Russia and Germany, nearly 400,000 Americans lost their lives and 600,000 more were wounded. As in most wars, the infantry sustained around 90 percent of the casualties. World War II was fought in spurts in which long preparation preceded such massive campaigns as the D-Day invasion and the repeated amphibious invasions in the Pacific War. Large numbers of men in the armed services spent the war providing the logistical support for the massive military campaigns. Even combat soldiers spent much of their time waiting. At the front they waited in their foxholes, often more threatened by diseases (in the Pacific malaria, typhus, and dysentery were constant enemies) and homesickness than by the enemy.

❧ Learning of the Holocaust

As Allied troops moved across Germany, their worst fears about the fate of Europe's Jews were confirmed. "We passed large stacks of what appeared to be wastepaper and garbage piled in rows six feet high and 400 feet long," reported Captain Belton Cooper. "To my absolute horror, it dawned on me that these stacks contained the bodies of naked human beings." In early 1942 Hitler and his associates, spurred on by rabid anti-Semitism, launched the "final solution" to "the Jewish problem." During the next three years German secret police and SS units, as well as civilians (many of them non-German collaborators), sent millions of Jews to death camps like Auschwitz. The best estimate is that 6 million Jews perished, not only in death camps but also in thousands of smaller-scale massacres and countless individual murders. Four million other "undesirables," including gypsies, Slavs, homosexuals, and the mentally ill, also perished. "We are told that the American soldier does not know what he is fighting for," declared Eisenhower. "Now at least he will know what he is fighting against."

As early as 1942 government officials in Washington were conscious of the massive executions by the Nazis. But, aside from defeating the German army, there was probably little that could have been done at that

"Fresh, Spirited American Troops, Flushed with Victory, Are Bringing in Thousands of Ragged, Hungry, Battle-Weary Prisoners"   Or so reported the stateside newspapers in the spring of 1945. Bill Mauldin, at the time a young U.S. Army sergeant, created the two memorable characters "Willie and Joe" for an armed forces newspaper during the land war in the European theater. They spoke for the experiences of untold thousands of GI "grunts." Mauldin won a Pulitzer Prize in 1945 for this cartoon, and he went on to become one of the greatest American postwar political cartoonists.

point. Appeals to bomb the notorious death camp at Auschwitz in Poland were rejected as unacceptable diversions from the effort to defeat the enemy. Nonetheless, the American government was justly criticized in the aftermath of the Holocaust for refusing to admit into the country significant numbers of European Jewish refugees fleeing the massacre that began in 1939 (as the British did as well). The U.S. could hardly escape the charge of moral insensitivity when the full force of the genocide was made known in 1945.

❧ Creating a New International Order

As it became clear in early 1945 that Nazi Germany's defeat was only months away, Roosevelt finally agreed to a major diplomatic conference to discuss the shape of the postwar world. In late February, the Big Three gathered at the Crimean resort of Yalta. A number of the agreements made at the Yalta Conference were sim-

The Legacy of Hitlerism   Every Nazi concentration camp liberated by the Allied armies at the end of World War II disclosed scenes like this, of the emaciated corpses of victims who had starved to death or had been hastily killed by fleeing guards. This photograph was taken in April 1945.

ply confirmations of agreements made at the Tehran meeting of the Big Three in November 1943. With much of Eastern Europe in his grip, Stalin could bargain hard to protect the interests of the Soviet Union in East Europe. The result was an agreement that set general guidelines for the postwar world, but was often vague and evasive in dealing with the real points of disagreement among the major powers.

Particularly sticky was the issue of Polish independence. The Nazi invasion of Poland had been the trigger for the entry of Britain into World War II and during the war the British had supported a Polish government-in-exile in London. At the same time, the Russians had sponsored a procommunist government in exile in Lublin. Once the Russian army entered Poland, the Russians installed the procommunist Lublin gov-

ernment and gave no more than vague promises at Yalta to allow the integration of pro-Western Polish politicians into the government. In the Declaration on Liberated Europe — formulated primarily with Poland in mind — the Big Three promised "free and unfettered elections" in the lands they occupied as soon as possible, but there was no means of enforcement. In fact, both Soviet and Western leaders knew quite well that pro-Western democratic forces would win any such elections. The Soviet Union also insisted on retaining the Polish territory annexed as a result of the Nazi-Soviet Pact, as well as border rectifications with Finland and Romania, which were given reluctant consent by the Western leaders. Other European nations were to be reconstructed on the basis of elections that enfranchised "all democratic elements."

The three leaders also disagreed in general about the fate of Germany. Roosevelt seems to have envisioned a reunified Germany in the postwar world that could be rebuilt to be a responsible part of the postwar world. Stalin, on the other hand, wanted heavy reparation imposed on Germany and the nation to be permanently divided in the future. The final agreement at Yalta was once again vague and subject to later dispute. Germany was split into zones of occupation, with the Russians controlling the east, the British the northwest, the Americans the southeast, and France a small area in the southwest. Because of its symbolic importance Berlin was divided into zones of occupation as well, even though it was located within the Soviet zone of occupation. The agreement stipulated that at some unspecified future date Germany would be reunified. But no mechanism was provided to bring that about.

In accord with the agreement reached at Tehran, Stalin promised to enter the war against Japan sixty days after Germany surrendered. In return, Roosevelt assured the Soviet leader that the U.S.S.R. would receive the Kuril islands and southern Sakhalin,[7] as well as dominance in Mongolia and Manchuria. FDR made these concessions because his military advisers insisted that Soviet participation was crucial in order to defeat Japan. Two million Japanese soldiers guarded the home islands — but another 1.5 million garrisoned Manchuria, and these troops had to be prevented from returning home to join an expected last stand in Japan, where American troops faced a long, bloody invasion.

Many of the problems of the postwar world were clearly foreshadowed in the Yalta Agreement. Nonetheless, both Roosevelt and Churchill felt that they had done the best they could under the circumstances. In the weeks that followed, Roosevelt watched with alarm the Soviet Union's systematic installation of procommunist governments in East Europe and Poland, but he continued to believe that Stalin was a reasonable man and that, given the proper assurances, he would be amenable to a reasonable postwar settlement.

❧ Constructing the United Nations and an International Framework

The United Nations organization was conceived by American, British, and Russian representatives meeting at the Dumbarton Oaks Conference in the autumn of 1944 and the charter was drafted when delegates from fifty nations met in San Francisco from April through June 1945. There they hammered out the charter of the new collective security organization that Americans overwhelmingly hoped would succeed where the League

of Nations had failed — to prevent aggression and ensure that there were no more wars and no more Holocausts. Inducing the Soviet Union to participate in the San Francisco conference had been a major objective of both Roosevelt and Truman, for which they made significant concessions in their negotiations with Stalin.

The delegates at San Francisco created a three-branch United Nations: a General Assembly in which all member states were represented, a Secretariat to carry out the UN's orders, and a Security Council with rotating and permanent members (the latter being the United States, the U.S.S.R., China, Great Britain, and France). The council could impose economic sanctions on aggressors and, if need be, ask member states to supply troops for an international police force.

The charter contained major concessions to national sovereignty, however, which often prevented the UN from being more than a debating forum. One provision reserved to member nations "matters which are essentially within the domestic jurisdiction of any state," and another sanctioned regional security arrangements. Most important, each permanent member of the Security Council had an absolute veto. As the postwar East-West split emerged (see Chapter 30), that meant that the UN was going to find it difficult to define "aggression," much less stop it. Nonetheless, the United Nations would be a much more significant international force in the last half of the twentieth century than had been the League of Nations, and it increasingly expanded its role as a peacekeeping force.

Two other far-reaching international organizations were established at an American-led conference with delegates from forty-four countries that met in Bretton Woods, New Hampshire in July 1944. The Soviet Union refused to participate because the capitalistic aims of the conference were to promote multilateral international trade and to promote private investment. Convinced that much of the tragedy of World War II had resulted from the worldwide economic disarray of the 1930s, the conference proposed the establishment of the International Monetary Fund (IMF) and the International Bank for Reconstruction and Development, later known as the World Bank. The IMF was designed to stabilize currencies around the world and to break down trade barriers and the World Bank became an important force in postwar reconstruction projects and in stimulating the economies of developing nations around the world. Both organizations received contributions from many nations, but the United States was the major early contributor.

---

7. Territories that Russia had lost after the Russo-Japanese War of 1904-1905.

CONCLUSION: A NATION TRANSFORMED BY WAR

The nuclear holocausts at Hiroshima and Nagasaki were not the deadliest air raids of World War II: the most devastating of all were the attacks on Dresden and the American firebombing of Tokyo in May 1945, in which 100,000 people died — events gleefully reported in the press. Such horrors indelibly mark World War II as a struggle — unleashed, it is true, by irrational dictators contemptuous of human life — in which civilized values were eroded by hatred and revenge.

The road to World War II had begun in the aftermath of World War I. America bore some guilt for what happened because of its abdication of global leadership in 1919-1920, its narrow-minded protectionism during the twenties, and its retreat into outright isolationism just as Hitler and the Japanese militarists began their aggression. But all of the Western democracies shared in the blame. Scarred by the Great War, the democracies only slowly awoke to the Axis menace — too late to prevent war from erupting in Europe in September 1939. Even then, Americans desperately wanted to stay out, though Roosevelt slowly led the nation toward engagement and alliance with England. But American reluctance vanished after Pearl Harbor. Stiffened with American matériel and manpower, the Grand Alliance held the line in 1942 and took the offensive in 1943. Before victory came, Europe and East Asia were devastated and some 40 to 50 million people died.

The war transformed America. Massive military spending pulled the nation out of the Great Depression. Wartime industries drew millions of southern African Americans into cities and millions of women into paid jobs. The aspirations of millions of disadvantaged Americans were kindled by hopes for equality and economic opportunity. And all Americans shared a longing for peace, prosperity, and an effective United Nations. Still, in 1945, overshadowing these dreams loomed the ominous mushroom cloud of the atomic bomb and the portents of a confrontation with the Soviet Union.

SUGGESTED READING

Michael C. C. Adams, *The Best War Ever* (1994). Succinct look at the war and its aims. Provides good insight into the personal strains felt by soldiers.

P. M. H. Bell, *The Origins of the Second World War in Europe*, 2nd ed. (1989). Looks at the causes of World War II.

Akira Iriye, *The Origins of the Second World War in Asia and the Pacific* (1987). A good survey of American-Japanese relations before and after World War II and an account of Japanese motivations and strategies during the war.

David M. Kennedy, *Freedom from Fear: The American People in Depression and War, 1929-1945* (1999). An unsurpassed survey of the war years.

Geoffrey Perrett, *There's a War to Be Won* (1991). Examines the combat experience.

Gerald Weinbert, *World at Arms: A Global History of World War II* (1994). A comprehensive military history of World War II.

SUGGESTIONS FOR FURTHER READING

Sean Dennis Cashman, *America, Roosevelt, and World War II* (1989).

Wayne Cole, *Roosevelt and the Isolationists, 1932-1945* (1983).

Robert Dallek, *Franklin D. Roosevelt and American Foreign Policy, 1932-1945* (1979).

John W. Dower, *War Without Mercy: Race and Power in the Pacific War* (1986).

Robin Edmonds, *The Big Three: Churchill, Roosevelt, and Stalin in Peace and War* (1991).

John Ellis, *Brute Force: Allied Strategy and Tactics in the Second World War* (1990).

Lloyd Gardner, *Spheres of Influence: The Great Powers Partition Europe, from Munich to Yalta* (1993).

Manfred Jones, *Isolationism in America, 1935-1941* (1966).

Warren F. Kimball, *Forged in War: Roosevelt, Churchill, and the Second World War* (1996).

Warren F. Kimball, *The Juggler: Franklin Roosevelt as Wartime Statesman* (1992).

Gerald D. Nash, *The Crucial Era: The Great Depression and World War II*, 2nd ed. (1992).

William O'Neill, *A Democracy at War: America's Fight at Home and Abroad in World War II* (1993).

Geoffrey Perrett, *Days of Sadness, Years of Triumph, 1939-1945* (1973).

Michael Schaller, *The U.S. Crusade in China, 1938-1945* (1979).

Mark A. Stoler, *Allies and Adversaries: The Joint Chiefs of Staff, the Grand Alliance, and U.S. Strategy in World War II* (2000).

Studs Terkel, ed., *"The Good War": An Oral History of World War Two* (1984).

Russell F. Weigley, *The American Way of War: A History of United States Military Strategy and Policy* (1973).

John E. Wiltz, *In Search of Peace: The Senate Munitions Inquiry* (1963).

Allan M. Winkler, *Home Front U.S.A.* (1986).

Bryce Wood, *Making of the Good Neighbor Policy* (1961).

Randall B. Woods, *A Changing of the Guard: Anglo-American Relations, 1941-1946* (1990).

Gordon Wright, *The Ordeal of Total War, 1939-1945* (reprinted 1997).

30

In the Shadow of the Bomb: The Cold War in the Truman Years

WHILE VICTORY IN World War II brought relief and exhilaration to the nation, the beginning of the Atomic Age hung ominously like a cloud over the future. "Anglo-Saxon science has developed a new explosive 2,000 times as destructive as any known before," announced the stentorian voice of NBC's star newscaster H. V. Kaltenborn on the evening of August 6, 1945. "For all we know, we have created a Frankenstein!" Unable to sleep, country music singer Fred Kirby on August 7 wrote a somber hit song, "Atomic Power." "They're sending up to Heaven to get the brimstone fire," the song began; it ended: "We will not know the minute, and we will not know the hour." On August 8, the *Milwaukee Journal* published a map with concentric circles to show what the Hiroshima bomb would have done to Milwaukee. "If we, a professedly Christian nation, feel morally free to use atomic energy in that way," declared the leaders of the Federal Council of Churches on August 9 in a statement signed jointly by Methodist bishop G. Bromley Oxnam and John Foster Dulles, the chairman of the FCC's Committee on a Just and Durable Peace and a future secretary of state, ". . . men elsewhere will accept that verdict. Atomic weapons will be looked upon as part of the arsenal of war and the stage will be set for the sudden and final destruction of mankind." "Instead of congratulating ourselves," editorialized the *Christian Century* on August 15, "we should now be standing in penitence before the Creator of the power which the atom has hitherto kept inviolate." Still, some 80 percent of Americans polled approved of the decision to drop the bomb to end the war. Among the American troops poised to invade Japan, the reaction was nearly universal: "Thank God for the atom bomb!"

The world had entered the Atomic Age, a phrase at once heard everywhere. Mixed with stunned realizations that something almost apocalyptic had happened were promises that atomic power would mean lightning-fast transportation, miracle cures, and power so abundant that the need for human labor would practically vanish. There were also the usual crass jokes and commercial hype inseparable from American life: bars offered "atomic cocktails," department stores touted "atomic sales," and a Los Angeles burlesque house invited customers to ogle its "Atom Bomb Dancers."

Though spared the devastation experienced by many of the warring nations, Americans were emotionally exhausted at the end of the struggle, and they yearned to spend their wartime savings on things that had been denied them during the war. They aspired to get out of cramped housing, to find good jobs, buy a car, and have a good family home. Yet memories nagged of all-too-recent privations: what guarantee was there that troop demobilization would not bring back the Depression?

PATHS BACK TO NORMAL LIFE

World War II changed the face of American society in many ways. Women, for example, had entered the workforce in large numbers. At war's end, some wanted to resume being housewives and mothers, but some relished life outside the home, valued the security that a steady job could bring, and wanted the freedom to choose what they would do. Sometimes their aspirations clashed with the eagerness of thousands of returning servicemen to get back their old jobs or find new ones.

The war had also stirred African American aspirations. Blacks who had defended their country or migrated to wartime jobs in northern cities believed that the time had come to recognize blacks as full citizens. Millions of whites, however, were as determined as ever to cling to old patterns of segregation and discrimination.

A swollen federal government was one of World War II's enduring legacies. During the war, the government set prices, allocated workers, rationed food and consumer goods, and, to some extent, combated workplace racial discrimination. Every wage earner faced the burden of taxation (before the war only the rich had paid income taxes), and the national debt seemed astronomical.

These strains produced a conservative reaction. Wartime prosperity for millions of working-class Americans had dissipated much of the energy driving New Deal social reforms. The president of the National Association of Manufacturers, long an opponent of the New Deal, expressed a widely held view when he argued for "jobs, freedom and opportunity" and demanded that "enterprise must be free of restraint and government regulation." Congress reflected this desire to move away from economic and social reform. Since 1942, Congress had been dominated by a conservative coalition of Republicans and southern Democrats who believed that the federal government should end economic controls and not tamper with race relations.

◈ Harry S Truman

Americans had a new president when the war ended, one who was not very well known. "Who the hell is Harry Truman?" demanded Admiral William D. Leahy upon hearing that FDR had suddenly died on April 12, 1945. Millions asked the same question.

Harry Truman was born in rural Missouri in 1884 and was the last president to lack a college education. After serving with distinction in the Great War, he opened a Kansas City haberdashery in 1919. Within a year, he went bankrupt. Desperate, he turned to politics. In 1926, with the support of the Pendergast machine, which dominated Kansas City–area politics, he was elected county judge. In 1934 he became the machine's nominee for Senator, and he won in the Democratic landslide. Washington insiders, however, disdained him as a hack. In 1940, FDR had supported a rival in Truman's senatorial primary, and the machine dropped him. But Truman stumped the state and won by building a coalition of farmers and workers, whites and blacks.

During World War II, Truman's unwavering support for the New Deal brought him the highly visible chairmanship of a Senate committee supervising the awarding of government contracts and exposing corruption. When FDR decided to drop his staunchly liberal vice president, Henry Wallace, in 1944, Truman's acceptability to all party factions made him Roosevelt's compromise choice as a running mate.

As he readily admitted, Truman came to the presidency ill equipped. Roosevelt had shut him out of crucial policy discussions; he knew nothing of the Manhattan Project or the Yalta negotiations until after he became president. Lacking experience in foreign

"The Buck Stops Here!"   President Harry S Truman at his desk in the Oval Office.

affairs, at the outset he tended to view the world in terms of local politics. He cultivated the image of a no-nonsense man of action; on his desk a sign read "The Buck Stops Here." But his bravado masked deep insecurity. Truman feared that he was unprepared to be president — but he also felt that if a man of the people could not do the job, something was wrong with the system. Some of the new president's personal qualities got him into trouble. Personal loyalties made him prone to cronyism. He quickly replaced much of FDR's cabinet with friends, infuriating veteran New Dealers. And his hot temper was often on display. When a music critic denigrated his daughter's attempt at concert singing, he publicly threatened to punch "the son-of-a-bitch" in the nose.

But Truman was a man of immense integrity. He readily accepted responsibility for all aspects of his administration and was resolutely committed to the interests of his country as he perceived them. He felt that the government should care for those unable to care for themselves. He shared some of the racial prejudice of his day, but he also hated discrimination. Above all, he was persistent and resilient in defending the policies he had inherited from his predecessor.

As FDR's successor, Truman tried to maintain the New Deal. In September 1945 he asked Congress to bring millions of new workers under Social Security, raise the minimum wage, establish national health insurance, launch new regional development projects similar to the TVA, guarantee full employment, and reorganize the executive branch. He was, however, a committed believer in the virtues of the free enterprise system.

Congress did pass an Employment Act in 1946 — but it gutted provisions requiring the government to launch public works projects when unemployment reached a specific level. The act simply set up a Council of Economic Advisers to recommend policies to prevent depressions. Congress also approved a modified version of the president's plan for governmental reorganization. But the conservative-leaning Democratic Congress would do no more to continue the New Deal.

❧ Reconversion and the Baby Boom

After V-J Day, American servicemen and the American public wanted a return to a peacetime society — and they wanted it quickly. "Bring the boys home," the public clamored — and they were heard. The armed forces shrank from 12 million in 1945 to 1.6 million in 1947.

Rapid demobilization and "reconversion" — the transition to a peacetime economy — brought dislocations but not the dreaded return of the Great Depression. The New Deal's safety net — unemployment benefits and Social Security — cushioned the impact of lost wartime jobs. More important, under the Servicemen's Readjustment Act of 1944, or "GI Bill of Rights," the federal government spent $13 billion for veterans' benefits, including unemployment compensation, housing subsidies, education, and small-business loans. By 1947 over a million ex-servicemen were among the 2.5 million Americans attending college. Furthermore, pent-up consumer demand in the form of unspent billions in forced wartime savings stimulated the private sector and created tens of thousands of jobs.

Reversing a steady drop in fertility rates since the early nineteenth century, postwar America experienced a demographic surge known as the baby boom. The birth rate, at a historic low of 19.4 per thousand in

Upward Mobility   This Penn State student, a veteran photographed in February 1946, was one of the early beneficiaries of the GI Bill. He lived with his wife and daughter in a trailer, paying $28 monthly rental. His desk was built out of orange crates, and he earned three or four dollars a night by selling sandwiches in fraternity houses to purchase such "extras" as clothing and entertainment. Many of the parents of the postwar "baby boom" generation got their college education under the GI Bill — and lived under such conditions.

1940, hit 24 per thousand in 1946 and did not fall again until the 1960s. In the 1950s, three- and four-child families were the norm.

Having grown up amid depression and war, young Americans of the late 1940s and early 1950s seemed serious and focused. Those attending college under the GI Bill rushed through the curriculum so they could begin earning money and raising families. They were more security-conscious than their parents had been — or their children would be. Shunning risk, they preferred working for corporations, not opening their own businesses. "Security has become the big goal," reported *Fortune* magazine. "[They] want to work for somebody else . . . preferably somebody big."

❧ Prices, Wages, and Strikes

Reconversion caused Truman innumerable headaches. Businesses and farmers pleaded for wartime controls to be scrapped so they could buy desperately needed equipment. Workers demanded raises, and consumers wanted to spend their savings. The administration, however, feared runaway inflation if controls were lifted too rapidly. Soon after V-J Day it was announced that the Office of Price Administration (OPA) would continue to control prices. Business groups raged; one overheated Republican orator denounced OPA administrators as "the single most important collection of American fascists we've got."

Labor unions, increasingly militant, faced the president with difficult economic decisions immediately after the war. As union leaders scrapped wartime no-strike pledges, strikes crippled key industries. Truman asked Congress for authority to declare an emergency and assume direct control over any industry he deemed vital to the national interest. He wanted the power to order workers back on the job, to fine or jail resisting labor leaders, to set wages and prices, and to draft anyone refusing to work. Labor pressured Congress into rebuffing the White House. Still, the administration mediated settlements in which unions won approximately two-thirds of their wage demands and made hefty gains in fringe benefits. Management passed along the costs to consumers.

In the spring of 1946, bushy-browed John L. Lewis led his 400,000 United Mine Workers out on strike. "I have pleaded your case not in the quavering tones of a mendicant asking alms, but in the thundering voice of the captain of a mighty host, demanding the rights to which free men are entitled," he roared. For the average American, Lewis was at best self-serving and at worst a traitor, and the new strike threatened to shut down every steam-driven apparatus in America. When mine owners refused to negotiate, Truman seized the mines. After fifty-nine days the president brokered an agreement in which the miners got modest gains. Meanwhile the railroad brotherhoods called a nationwide walkout. Even though his legal authority to do so was in doubt, Truman went before Congress to announce that the government was taking over the railroads. As he began speaking, an aide rushed up the aisle with the message that all but one of the brotherhoods had agreed to a compromise. Eventually it too gave in.

Through his decisive actions, Truman had restrained organized labor and held inflation to 7 percent in the first ten months after V-J Day, but his refusal to scrap controls offset whatever public good will he might have won. As the July 1, 1946, expiration date for the OPA approached, Truman appealed to Congress to extend the hated agency's authority — which it did, but only after stripping the OPA of most of its powers. Truman vetoed the bill, allowing the OPA to expire on schedule — and in two weeks inflation skyrocketed to

25 percent. "Prices Soar, Buyers Sore, Steers Jump Over the Moon," headlined the *New York Daily News.* On July 15, a humbled Congress restored controls for a year.

Americans had endured the war with high hopes for postwar life. Instead, returning veterans found shortages, rationing, controls, black markets, inflation, and gridlock. The 1946 film *The Best Years of Our Lives,* portraying veterans returning to an indifferent, squabbling nation, caught the bittersweet mood. Democrats and the president received the blame. "To err is Truman," said wags. "Had enough?" asked the Republicans in the 1946 election. Voters had. A landslide gave the GOP control of Congress for the first time since 1928.

The Eightieth Congress

The leader of the new Republican Congress was Senator Robert A. Taft of Ohio. The son of William Howard Taft, "Mr. Republican" was a foe of the New Deal, a champion of business, a prewar isolationist, and a stern anticommunist. Yet Taft favored some social reform, including federally sponsored public housing and aid to education, and he saw himself as defending workers against union bosses and a president who threatened to draft strikers. He and Truman confronted each other with open contempt.

When the Eightieth Congress convened in early 1947, much of the public, angered by the postwar strikes, strongly supported the centerpiece of the conservative program: the Taft-Hartley bill. Its object was to correct the widely perceived tilt in favor of unions that came with the enactment of the New Deal's Wagner Act of 1935. In June 1947, Congress passed the Taft-Hartley Act by large margins. Although the bill did not go as far as some conservatives wanted, it outlawed the closed shop (in which union membership was a condition of employment) and banned a list of "unfair labor practices." It permitted employers to sue unions for breach of contract and to petition the National Labor Relations Board for elections to determine bargaining agents. When the president found that a strike imperiled national health or safety, he could impose "cooling off" periods and seek court injunctions suspending the job action. Unions were forced to submit annual financial statements to the government and were forbidden to contribute to political parties, and union officials had to swear that they did not belong to the Communist Party.

Unions and liberals viewed Taft-Hartley as an attempt to destroy organized labor. So did Truman, who despite his fulmination against greedy union leaders and strikers knew that he needed organized labor's support in the 1948 election. Truman vetoed the bill, but Congress promptly overrode his veto.

The Eightieth Congress took a postmortem slap at Franklin Roosevelt by sending to the states (which quickly ratified it) the Twenty-second Amendment, limiting future presidents to two terms. Ironically, Democrats would benefit most from the amendment, which in the future would deny third terms to popular GOP presidents Eisenhower and Reagan, though it may have thwarted a third-term run by Bill Clinton as well.

Toward the Good Life

Truman and the Republicans fought their political battles in the midst of rising prosperity spawned by a burgeoning technological revolution. Between 1945 and 1950, consumers encountered the automatic transmission, the long-playing record, the electric clothes dryer, the automatic garbage disposal — and, above all, television, experimentally introduced in 1939 but delayed by the war. When, over liberal objections, price controls ended in mid-1947, families started buying all the TVs, appliances, and gadgets that their paychecks and savings could bear.

In 1945, massive housing shortages created a nightmare. Not since 1929 had there been a good year for new housing starts. Now, almost 19 percent of American families were doubled up, another 19 percent were hunting for housing, and 13 percent had given up looking. Over the next decade Americans would require 16 million new homes, *Life* magazine predicted. Even the ugliest subsidized units were often too expensive. *Fortune* estimated that veterans would have to earn $58 a week to afford the average new house. The mean weekly wage was $46 a week.

The housing problem was solved by a private-public partnership. Traditionally, banks and other lenders had followed a very tight mortgage policy, demanding as much as 50 percent of the total cost as a down payment and allowing no more than ten years to pay off the loan. When the Federal Housing Administration and the Veterans Administration began guaranteeing private construction loans, banks offered 30-year mortgages at 4.5 percent. New home construction jumped from 117,000 in 1944 to 1.7 million in 1950, by which time the housing industry had become the engine of a booming economy.

In 1946, William Levitt began to change American life when he bought 1,200 acres on Long Island and named the tract Levittown. Within months, using war-

Levittown, Long Island By 1955, when this photograph was taken, the "little houses made of ticky-tacky" had become a substantial community. The two Levittowns (on Long Island and outside Philadelphia), quickly built in the late 1940s, became the archetype for the postwar suburban housing boom. Architectural critics sneered, but the first Levittowners were glad to have an affordable place to live after the privations of the Depression and the war.

time mass-production methods, he built 10,000 homes, selling for $7,000 to $10,000; veterans could buy for a home for payments of $56 a month. Even bigger Levittowns soon followed elsewhere.

Some intellectuals sneered at the "little boxes made of ticky-tacky"; the *New York Times*'s architecture critic derided the tract developments as an "urban planning disaster." But the need was desperate, and even the critics realized that the "Levittown houses turned the detached, single-family house from a distant dream to a real possibility for thousands of middle-class American families."

❧ *"To Secure These Rights"*

Wartime labor shortages, coupled with pressure from civil rights activists and a few unions, had modestly increased blacks' share of jobs in defense industries. In addition, a million African American soldiers served in Europe and the Pacific. "I spent four years in the Army to free a bunch of Frenchmen and Dutchmen, and I'm hanged if I'm going to let the Alabama version of the Germans kick me around when I'm back home," vowed

a black veteran. The NAACP and CORE targeted job discrimination, disfranchisement, and racially motivated beatings and lynchings. They won some successes immediately after the war. Many southern African American veterans headed straight for voter registration offices. In spite of intimidation, there was progress. The number of registered black voters in the South increased from 2 percent in 1940 to 12 percent in 1947.

In 1946, Truman appointed the President's Committee on Civil Rights composed of distinguished Americans of every race and region to make recommendations to improve race relations. Their 1947 report, *To Secure These Rights,* described pervasive segregation and discrimination that reduced blacks to second-class citizenship. It called for the "elimination of segregation based on race, color, creed, or national origin, from American life." In February 1948 the president urged an unenthusiastic Congress to turn the recommendations into law. In the first special civil rights message by a president, Truman demanded a federal law against "the crime of lynching, against which I cannot speak too strongly" — something FDR had never attacked for fear of losing southern white support. As Truman expected, Congress failed to respond. On July 26, 1948, the president by executive order banned racial discrimination in federal hiring, and four days later he ordered an end to segregation in the armed forces — in spite of opposition from such military heroes as Generals Marshall and Eisenhower, who feared racial tensions in the ranks would destroy morale. Those worries proved unfounded. In coming years the military would give millions of black men and women dignified, merit-based career opportunities.

Another significant improvement in race relations in the United States during the immediate postwar years was the integration of major league baseball. To break the racial barrier, in 1945 Brooklyn Dodgers owner Branch Rickey handpicked Jackie Robinson, a sharecropper's son who had starred at UCLA and served as an officer during the war. In April 1947, Robinson debuted as a Dodger, often enduring verbal and physical abuse. Robinson prevailed with remarkable self-discipline as well as magnificent talent. By the time he retired in 1956, numerous other black athletes were becoming stars.

THE COLD WAR BEGINS

Americans emerged from World War II hopeful that with the defeat of the Axis the world would enter an era of unbroken peace. Perhaps it did. Some recent students of postwar international relations see the Cold-War era as the "long peace," pointing out that for nearly sixty years since V-J Day the great powers have avoided direct military conflict. Nevertheless, out of the Soviet-American confrontation came a great arms race, a threat of nuclear holocaust, and "proxy wars" that would kill millions around the globe.

At one level the Cold War represented the clash of competing ideologies. Marxism-Leninism assured Soviet leaders that the Soviet Union and its Communist Party stood at the vanguard of the "progressive" working class, confronting imperialistic capitalism bent on subjugating the globe. There might be truces, as when the Soviet Union and the capitalist states joined forces against Nazi Germany, but there would never be true peace until the working class triumphed. On the other hand, virtually all Americans, from Truman and his advisers to ordinary voters, believed that "life, liberty, and the pursuit of happiness" were inalienable human rights, and that dictatorships were intrinsically evil — particularly if they were anti-religious and anti-American. During the 1930s Americans had heard about the *totalitarian* nature of Nazism — its demand for total state control, its aggressive expansionism, and its contempt for traditional values. Americans had learned from the Holocaust that pure evil could motivate an enemy. As the East-West clash unfolded, most Americans came to see Communism as the equally menacing totalitarian successor to Nazism.

Jackie Robinson Steals Home Joining the Brooklyn Dodgers in 1947, Jackie Robinson had become one of baseball's greatest stars by 1952 — and a trailblazer for African Americans' drive for civil rights and personal dignity.

But the East-West struggle grew also out of the conflicting geopolitical goals of the Soviet Union and the Anglo-American powers. The objectives of the Big Three were indeed irreconcilable. The Soviet Union's determination to dominate Eastern Europe as a security zone and to cripple Germany clashed with the principle of self-determination dear to American policymakers and with the balance-of-power and geopolitical precepts that guided British diplomats.

The confrontation began even before World War II was over. Days after Nazi Germany's defeat, Washington abruptly canceled Lend-Lease aid — an action that grated harshly on the Soviet leaders, even though it resulted from bureaucratic clumsiness and targeted Great Britain as well as the U.S.S.R. In July 1945, after Germany's defeat but before Japan's surrender, Truman, Churchill,[1] and Stalin met in the Berlin suburb of Potsdam. "I told Stalin that I am no diplomat," the president recorded in his diary, "but usually said yes and no

1. Midway through the conference, Churchill was replaced by Clement Atlee, the leader of the Labour Party, after it won Britain's first postwar general election.

to questions after hearing all the argument." The Soviet dictator's reaction remains a mystery, but Truman felt that the first encounter went well. "I can deal with Stalin," he wrote. "He is honest — but smart as hell." Britain and the United States reluctantly accepted Polish occupation of Germany's eastern territories and the Soviet annexation of prewar eastern Poland. In conversations with his British and American counterparts, Stalin was candid: "Any freely elected [Polish] government would be anti-Soviet," he said, "and that we cannot permit." Truman and his advisers were unhappy about the emerging Soviet sphere in Eastern Europe, but there was nothing they could do short of going to war — which Western public opinion would not allow.

❧ The Iron Curtain Descends

During his first eighteen months in office, Truman alternated between bombast and conciliation in his dealings with Soviet diplomats, acutely aware of his inexperience in foreign affairs and hoping that Stalin would live up to the promises about holding free elections in Eastern Europe.

American hesitancy to confront the Soviet Union in deed as well as word was due to a number of factors. First, the rapid demobilization of America's armed forces made the threat of confrontation incredible. Second, Truman was indecisive about dropping Roosevelt's generally conciliatory policy toward the Soviet Union. Third, although polls showed that in the five months following V-J Day Americans' belief in the chances of cooperation with the Soviet Union dropped from 54 to 35 percent, the public remained reluctant to abandon the good feelings about Russia that the wartime alliance had generated.

Eventually the Kremlin did hold elections in Eastern Europe, but only after eliminating or intimidating all opposition. In Hungary, Bulgaria, Romania, and Poland, similar scenarios were played out between 1945 and 1947, culminating in one-party elections and the proclamation of "people's democracies." In Yugoslavia and Albania, Communist guerrillas who had led the anti-fascist resistance seized power on their own but made clear their intent to ally with Moscow.

The atomic bomb also loomed as a serious obstacle to good relations with the Soviet Union. While some American strategists, including Secretary of State James F. Byrnes, believed that the U.S. should use the bomb to pressure the Soviet Union, others, including Secretary of War Henry L. Stimson, believed that flaunting the bomb would only serve to deepen Soviet insecurities. Although American military strategists knew that the Soviet Union was working desperately to build its own bomb (which was successfully tested in September 1949), no realistic plan surfaced to control the arms race that was about to begin. President Truman backed the so-called Baruch Plan, proposed by financier Bernard Baruch at the first meeting of the United Nations Atomic Energy Commission in June 1946. In it, the U.S. offered to turn over its stockpile of nuclear weapons to an international control agency under United Nations supervision if all other nations would pledge not to produce their own and agree to an adequate system of inspection. The plan was rejected by the Soviet Union because it precluded any effort on their part to catch up with the U.S. in the nuclear race and because they believed that the United Nations would not be evenhanded in such a role.

Truman's attitude toward Moscow gradually hardened. One signal came in March 1946, when he accompanied former prime minister Churchill to Fulton, Missouri, to make what was billed as a major foreign policy address at Westminster College. With Truman applauding on the platform, Churchill warned that an "iron curtain" had fallen across Europe, and he asserted that there was nothing the Russians had "less respect for than weakness, especially military weakness." Continuing, he warned: "What they desire is the fruits of war and the indefinite expansion of their powers and doctrines." The only thing that stood between Western Europe, devastated by World War II, and the five hundred Soviet divisions in Eastern Europe was the United States. He called for a renewal of the "fraternal association" between English-speaking peoples. While some Americans denounced Churchill as a warmonger, others recalled that he almost alone had sounded the alarm bell against Hitler in the 1930s. Perhaps he was right again.

Churchill's warning came while the Western and Soviet foreign ministers wrangled over peace treaties to be signed with Germany's former allies. The treaties gave Britain and America control of occupied Italy, but the West acquiesced in the Soviet domination then emerging in Hungary, Romania, and Bulgaria, as well as in Poland.

❧ Planning for National Security

Truman's views on the Soviet Union, and those of other American policymakers, were strongly influenced by a group of American foreign service officers who knew the Soviet Union well and distrusted it deeply. None was more important than George F. Kennan, an expert on Russian history and culture and the American chargé d'affaires in Moscow before and immediately after the war. Having spent years closely observing the Soviet Union, Kennan hated Communism. Lenin, Stalin, and their henchmen were "a swarm of rats" who were seeking to destroy Western civilization, he once observed. During and immediately after the war, he had repeatedly questioned FDR's tendency to rely on goodwill and personal relationships in dealing with Stalin and in 1946 sent a highly pessimistic and influential "long telegram" insisting that the fanaticism of Soviet leaders made any short-term compromise with them impossible.

Truman's secretary of state, James F. Byrnes, was a South Carolina politician known more for his ability to manipulate Congress than for his diplomatic expertise. By the time Truman accompanied Churchill to Fulton, Missouri, he and Byrnes had decided that British and American interests in Europe and the Near East were identical and that Soviet expansion must be stopped. But the persistence of neo-isolationism, coupled with ongoing liberal sympathy with the Soviet Union, had kept Truman from publicly confronting Moscow and pursuing a consistently hard-line policy. In the fall of 1946, however, former vice president Henry Wallace — now Truman's secretary of commerce — forced the president's hand. A staunch liberal, Wallace had grown alarmed as East-West relations deteriorated. "Communists everywhere want eventually a Communist world," he conceded, but "for the moment I believe they are essentially interested . . . in strengthening the Soviet Union as an example of the kind of socialism they have in mind." He became convinced that the president had fallen under the influence of doctrinaire anti-Communists. On September 17, Wallace delivered a nationally broadcast address at Madison Square Garden, supposedly stating administration policy. Unwisely, Truman had approved the speech without carefully reading it. Wallace attacked "getting tough" with the Soviet Union and called for Soviet-American friendship to be the cornerstone of American foreign policy. From Germany, where he was promising the people of the western zones that America would not abandon them to the Soviets, Byrnes demanded that the president choose between him and Wallace. Unhesitatingly, Truman demanded Wallace's resignation. "I don't understand a dreamer like that," he subsequently wrote in his diary. "The Reds, phonies and the 'parlor pinks' seem to be banded together and are becoming a national dan-

ger. I am afraid they are a sabotage front for Uncle Joe Stalin." It was a major policy decision.

In January 1947, Byrnes was replaced as secretary of state by General George C. Marshall. Unlike Byrnes — who tended to conduct foreign policy without consulting the White House — Marshall was unswervingly loyal to the president, an austere, inspiring leader, and a strong advocate of standing up to the Soviets. A superb administrator, Marshall's practice was to select able subordinates and delegate authority.

Marshall revitalized the notoriously hidebound State Department, which neither FDR nor Truman respected. The three most important men on whom Marshall relied did much to shape America's Cold War strategy. As his chief deputy, Marshall retained Dean Acheson, a political realist and disciple of theologian Reinhold Niebuhr. Acheson, who was to become Truman's closest foreign policy adviser, readily accepted that the U.S. should have "limited objectives" in the postwar world, but by 1946 he saw it as his moral duty to stand up to the threat posed by Marxism-Leninism and Soviet imperialism. An Atlantic-oriented elitist, Acheson viewed Western Europe as crucial to American interests and believed that foreign policy should be left to experts who would periodically inform Congress and the public of their goals, but otherwise operate independently — generally in secret. For assistant secretary for economic affairs, Marshall chose Houston cotton broker Will Clayton, an international businessman committed to molding the non-Communist world into an interdependent economic unit by lowering trade barriers and establishing stable exchange rates. And Marshall named Kennan to head the department's new policy planning staff, ensuring that at last the not-so-subtle Kremlinologist would be heard.

❧ *The Truman Doctrine and the Marshall Plan*

In February 1947, an economically ailing Great Britain quietly informed Washington that it could no longer dominate the eastern Mediterranean, through which ran its strategic lifeline to Middle Eastern oil and India. Two Mediterranean countries were then being threatened by Communism. Greece had been torn since 1944 by civil war between Communist-led partisans and the pro-British but repressive monarchy. And Soviet troops were massing on Turkey's borders as Moscow ratcheted up demands for a naval base and free access to the Mediterranean. Both countries had been Great Britain's strategic responsibility, but the British could no longer carry the primary burden.

At Acheson and Marshall's urging, Truman stepped into the breach. Acutely aware that the Republicans had won the 1946 elections, the State Department informally sought bipartisan support from congressional leaders. Acheson painted a dark picture. A Communist victory in Greece and the establishment of a Russian military presence on the Turkish Straits "might open three continents to Soviet penetration." The Soviets were "engaging in one of the greatest gambles in history," and only the United States could call their bluff. "Not since Rome and Carthage" had the West faced such a grim challenge. The Republican chairman of the Senate Foreign Relations Committee, Michigan's Arthur Vandenberg, shed his isolationist past (in part thinking of his large constituencies of Polish-Americans) and now supported aiding nations threatened by "international communism." But, he warned, to gain support for such a break with isolationism, the president must "scare hell" out of the American people.

Truman did just that. On March 12, 1947, he made a dramatic appearance before Congress to ask for $400 million in aid to Greece and Turkey. More important, he requested approval of a sweeping declaration of opposition to Soviet imperialism. "It must be the policy of the United States," he said, "to support free peoples who are resisting subjugation by armed minorities or by outside pressure." After brief debate, Congress approved both the aid and the policy statement.

Truman's promise to stand by societies threatened by Communism became known as the Truman Doctrine. It was endorsed by many New Deal liberals, by internationalist businessmen, by converted isolationists led by Vandenberg, by émigrés and ethnic groups from Eastern Europe, and by anti-Communist ideologues of various hues.

By early 1947 war-ravaged Western Europe was in dire straits. Journalists reported its "plague and pestilence, suffering and disaster, famine and hardship, the complete political and economic dislocation." Bombing had destroyed most of the continent's industrial base. Drought had killed much of the 1946 wheat crop, and food reserves were dangerously low. Millions of displaced persons wandered the countryside and glutted cities. German coal production was moribund, and in England the coal shortage was so great that power had to be shut off for hours every day. Prices rose in Italy to 35 times their prewar level, and in Hungary inflation reached 11,000,000,000,000,000 pengos to the dollar. American officials knew that extremism tended to flourish in conditions of economic and social insecurity. The French and Italian Communist parties were those countries' most powerful organizations, and it appeared that they would dominate future governments if nothing was done to provide food, clothing, and shelter.

Responding to this crisis in a June 1947 Harvard commencement speech, Secretary of State Marshall outlined a massive aid program. A notable feature of Marshall's proposal was his call to European nations to frame an *integrated* plan for recovery. If it agreed upon a joint approach to rehabilitation, Europe could count on the United States to supply "friendly aid." Marshall made

---

✾ IN THEIR OWN WORDS

The Truman Doctrine, 1947

When it appeared that the Soviet Union was poised to extend its influence beyond Eastern Europe and into the Mediterranean, President Truman went before Congress to ask for aid for Greece and Turkey, as well as to ask for congressional approval of a declaration of opposition to Soviet imperialism. In the process he articulated what became known as the Truman Doctrine.

One of the primary objectives of the foreign policy of the United States is the creation of conditions in which we and other nations will be able to work out a way of life free from coercion. This was a fundamental issue in the war with Germany and Japan. Our victory was won over countries which sought to impose their will, and their way of life, upon other nations....

At the present moment in world history nearly every nation must choose between alternative ways of life. The choice is too often not a free one.

One way of life is based upon the will of the majority, and is distinguished by free institutions, representative government, free elections, guarantees of individual liberty, freedom of speech and religion, and freedom from political oppression.

The second way of life is based upon the will of a minority forcibly imposed upon the majority. It relies upon terror and oppression, a controlled press and radio; fixed elections, and the suppression of personal freedoms.

I believe that it must be the policy of the United States to support free peoples who are resisting attempted subjugation by armed minorities or by outside pressures.

I believe that we must assist free peoples to work out their own destinies in their own way.

Germany Emerges from the Rubble   This pair of news photographs carried the following caption in 1950: "Drive to Victory and Six Years After [in] Germany.... Six years ago American forces fought their way ashore on the beaches of Normandy and began the drive that was to end in victory and the liberation of Europe from the Nazi heel. Many places familiar in the headlines of war news six years ago present a different aspect today, although nearly all still bear the scars of war.... [Above:] Fifth Division troops advancing through the rubble of Frankfurt. Bottom: the exact spot as it looks six years after with streets and battered buildings repaired."

three things clear: the United States would not fund a collection of national shopping lists; the scheme would have to provide for the economic reconstruction of Germany and its integration into the European economy; and the Soviet Union and its satellites were welcome to join. Kennan, Acheson, and Clayton believed that for a variety of reasons they could not exclude the Communist powers. Aside from wanting the United States to appear magnanimous, American officials feared that if the East European nations were not invited, French and Italian Communists would prevent participation

by their governments. Washington hoped that the prospect of integrating their economies with those of the West would ensure either that the USSR and its client states opened up their economies (and hence their political systems) to Western influence — or else that they never joined.

American planners correctly anticipated the Kremlin's reaction. Stalin ordered the Polish and Czechoslovak governments to reject American aid (which, despite their pro-Soviet orientation, they had hoped to get). In the fall of 1947, Moscow began tying Eastern Europe's economies to the Soviet Union in highly disadvantageous ways for the smaller countries. Europe's division into hostile blocs was gelling. But in Western Europe the Marshall Plan's success was not yet certain.

In the United States, leftists denounced the "Martial Plan," while Taft and the Republicans fumed about "pouring money down foreign ratholes." Administration representatives insisted that the Marshall Plan was a weapon in the struggle against world Communism. In the spring and summer of 1947 the French and Italian coalition governments, at Washington's urging, expelled their Communist members. But if Europe's economic woes did not ease, State Department officials told Congress, Communists would win the upcoming elections.

❧ Strategies for the Cold War

To improve coordination among the armed forces and increase the nation's intelligence capacity, Congress passed in July 1947 the National Security Act. It created a unified military establishment by setting up a cabinet-level Department of Defense, with the Army, Navy, and Air Force becoming subcabinet departments answerable to the secretary of defense. A new body, the National Security Council (NSC), composed of the president, vice president, the secretaries of defense, state, and treasury, and the chief of intelligence, would meet regularly for strategic planning. The act made permanent the Joint Chiefs of Staff, a creation of World War II, and established the Central Intelligence Agency (CIA) to coordinate intelligence gathering abroad. The CIA replaced the wartime Office of Strategic Services (OSS) and it was authorized to use both open and secret methods in the collection of information to protect national security. In later years the CIA also planned and carried out covert military and political operations in behalf of American interests abroad.

In 1948, Congress established what has been called a "cultural Marshall Plan," the Fulbright Exchange

Program. Named for Senator J. William Fulbright of Arkansas, himself a Rhodes Scholar and former university president, the program sponsored exchanges of students and intellectual elites between the U.S. and a growing number of nations. Many of the critical leaders of foreign nations in the postwar years were participants in the Fulbright Program and hundreds of American professors taught abroad as Fulbright professors.

The U.S. also made military linkages around the world in the early days of the Cold War. In 1946 the U.S. granted independence to the Philippines but retained military bases in the islands and remained a strong presence there. In 1948 the U.S. led the way in founding the Organization of American States (OAS) in an effort to promote hemispheric solidarity, and American military advisers visited a number of Latin American nations to offer advice on strengthening their armed forces. In a move with profound implications for the future, in 1948 President Truman, over the objections of the State Department (where Middle East specialists feared the reaction in oil-rich Arab nations), recognized the new state of Israel. Truman's decision was partly to court the Jewish vote as the election of 1948 approached, but he also surmised that Israel would be a strategically critical ally in the Middle East.

❧ "Containment" Takes Shape

In the summer of 1947 an anonymous article entitled "The Sources of Soviet Conduct" appeared in the prestigious journal *Foreign Affairs*. It soon became known that the author, "Mr. X," was George Kennan, and opinion-makers viewed the article correctly as official policy. Russian wartime and postwar expansion, Kennan argued, was another example of the age-old westward push of aggressors from the Eurasian heartland, and the United States — the heir and guardian of Western civilization and the most powerful of the Atlantic democracies — must lead in confronting the Communist menace. Kennan called his policy *containment*. The policy did not suggest aggressively seeking war, but rather keeping Communism out of the industrialized centers of paramount American strategic interest: Western Europe and Japan. If the Communist advance could be parried there, Soviet expansionism would stall and the Soviet system would eventually crumble. The Communist challenge was a blessing in disguise, Kennan concluded, because it would force the American people to accept "the responsibilities of moral and political leadership that history plainly intended them to bear."

As the rationale of containing Communism took hold in the United States, "cold warriors" of three different kinds appeared among politicians, policymakers, and opinion-molders, as well as among citizens who paid attention to foreign affairs. First were the many prewar isolationists who had become aggressive nationalists after the Pearl Harbor attack showed that the oceans were not great barriers protecting "Fortress America," but rather highways across which hostile ships and airplanes could rain down destruction on the Western Hemisphere. Led by *Time-Life* publisher Henry Luce, many America-Firsters decided that if the United States could not hide from the rest of the world, it must flex its economic and military muscles to control it.

The second group of cold warriors were internationalists in the Wilsonian tradition. Unlike the America-Firsters, they tended to see American interests as tightly bound to those of the democracies of Western Europe. Before Pearl Harbor, they had typically advocated giving maximum aid to Britain, even at the cost of becoming embroiled in the war. The United Nations — a more effective and American-led version of the League of Nations — had been their brainchild. But Soviet brutality in Eastern Europe and intransigence in the Security Council (which crippled the UN's ability to act), as well as growing fears of Communist intentions in Western Europe, by 1946-1947 led most internationalists to oppose what they perceived as Soviet expansionism. In doing so, they largely adopted the containment ideas of the third group of cold warriors — the small but now influential circle of men like Kennan and Averill Harriman, who knew Stalinist Russia from firsthand experience and had no illusions about it.

In February 1948, Communists staged a coup in Prague and seized control of Czechoslovakia, a move that jolted Congress into action. President Truman immediately requested authorization to reinstate conscription and universal military training, which had been allowed to expire after the war in keeping with American preferences for a small, volunteer military during peacetime. More important, the stalled Marshall Plan legislation passed both houses by lopsided margins. To maintain conservative support, the White House named automobile executive Paul Hoffman to head the administering agency. Under the Marshall Plan, between 1948 and 1952 the United States delivered about $12.4 billion in aid to Western Europe (today's equivalent would be about $86 billion). The Marshall Plan proved to be one of the most farsighted policies ever initiated by the United States, for it launched the economic recovery that may well have saved Western Europe from Communism and certainly rebuilt the region into a partner for American trade and investment.

❧ *Reviving Western Germany and the Berlin Blockade*

In many ways the postwar fate of Germany became the most critical focus of the Cold War. At first, the Soviets stripped their eastern Germany zone of occupation of most of its remaining industrial assets as reparations, but were thwarted in their efforts to extract similar reparations in the West. It became increasingly clear that the Soviets intended to treat East Germany as a Communist satellite. On the other hand, in 1946 American secretary of state Byrnes assured German leaders that the U.S. would promote the economic rehabilitation of Germany and support the prompt establishment of a provisional government. The Truman administration built on these commitments to Germany; in January 1947 the American and British zones merged as a single economic unit, and the French (who for obvious historical reasons initially opposed the economic and political rebuilding of Germany) joined reluctantly in June. In July the U.S. extended Marshall Plan aid to the three western zones of occupied Germany.

The first great test of the containment policy in Europe came on June 24, 1948. In response to the American policy of establishing a unified economic and political unit in West Germany, Moscow decided to apply pressure on the western sector of Berlin, located 110 miles inside the Soviet zone and connected to West Germany only by a highway and a railroad. Soviet authorities suddenly suspended overland (but not air) access to Berlin that the American, British, and French forces in the former Reich's capital enjoyed under the Potsdam agreement. Stalin seems to have been motivated by the West's refusal to set up a four-power government for all of Germany, as promised by the Potsdam accords. He feared that Britain and the United States intended not only to rehabilitate but to rearm West Germany and unleash it against the Soviet Union. If his former allies could cut off German reparation shipments from their zones, reasoned Stalin, then the Soviets could prevent access to the 2.4 million Berliners inside the Soviet zone of occupied Germany. Stalin calculated that by blockading West Berlin he could either force the West out of the city and allow Moscow complete control over eastern Germany, or else get Western agreement to four-power governance over all of Germany, permit-

ting Moscow to block creation of a pro-Western government and to lure a neutralized Germany into the Eastern orbit.

When the Berlin crisis erupted, Truman seemed on the ropes. His party was splintering, his popularity was at an all-time low, and the Republicans had just nominated a formidable candidate, New York governor Thomas E. Dewey, to run against him in the election of 1948. Some of his advisers argued for abandoning Berlin as strategically untenable. Others, including the U.S. commander in Germany, General Lucius Clay, favored breaking the blockade by force. Truman did neither. He believed that if America surrendered West Berlin, all of non-Communist Europe would lose heart and be vulnerable to Communist takeovers. On the advice of General Omar Bradley, chairman of the Joint Chiefs of Staff, Truman rejected Clay's advice that American troops fight their way into Berlin. Instead, he mounted a massive airlift, joined by the Royal Air Force, to provide Berliners with needed supplies. If there were to be hostilities, the Soviets would have to initiate them by shooting down Allied aircraft. Truman also announced that sixty "atomic capable" American B-29s were being based in Britain, presumably ready to bomb the Soviet Union.

The B-29 ploy was a bluff. The planes had not yet been adapted to carry a nuclear payload; indeed, the United States had fewer than fifty nuclear bombs in 1948, and many of them were not usable. Stalin probably knew this through his intelligence sources, but he chose not to challenge the airlift.

West Berlin required 2,500 tons of food, coal, and medicine a day. Within a week American and British cargo planes were supplying Berliners with that minimum, and later the daily volume reached 4,000 tons. With the frustrated Soviets standing by, the morale of West Germans soared, and the U.S. reaped a propaganda bonanza. Truman decided to keep the airlift going indefinitely, and at its peak the remarkable operation delivered 13,000 tons a day to the besieged city. After 324 days of blockade, on May 12, 1949, the Kremlin backed down and reopened ground routes. Containment had withstood its first test.

The Berlin blockade further polarized Europe and ensured that Germany would remain divided for forty years. When in the course of 1949 the United States and its allies (including the reluctant French) created a West German state — the Federal Republic of Germany — the Soviets immediately set up the Communist German Democratic Republic in the east.

The Berlin Blockade On May 5, 1949, Berliners cheer an American cargo plane as it approaches to land at the city's Tempelhof Airport. At the time this photograph was taken, it had just been officially announced that the eleven-month Berlin Blockade would be lifted in a few days. Notice the apartment houses being reconstructed in the background.

TRUMAN'S SECOND ADMINISTRATION: THE FAIR DEAL AND A GLOBAL COLD WAR

Harry Truman won the presidency in his own right in the election of 1948. While such polls vary dramatically over time, one survey of fifty-eight historians conducted in 2000 ranked Truman fifth in its list of "greatest presidents." Ranked behind Lincoln, the two Roosevelts, and Washington, Truman finished ahead of such notable presidents as Wilson and Jefferson. Granting such an elevated stature to Harry Truman is partly explained by his transparent honesty and willingness to make tough decisions, but it also recognizes his importance in laying the groundwork for the post–World War II Western alliance that confronted and contained the Soviet Union for more than four decades.

Truman was not very successful in shepherding his domestic program through Congress. However, much of his domestic agenda, the "Fair Deal," would reappear on the agenda of liberal reformers throughout the remainder of the century. In foreign affairs Truman made a long series of critically important decisions aimed at rebuilding Western Europe and Japan, building a military alliance capable of halting Soviet expansion, and, finally, committing American troops to a war in Korea to keep the south from being overrun by the Communist north.

❧ *Truman's Stunning Victory*

Despite Truman's popular stand in Berlin, Republicans had high hopes as the 1948 election approached. The president's low poll numbers and a splintering of the Democratic coalition made it seem that the White House was theirs for the taking. Conservatives favored Taft, but northeastern Republicans, mildly liberal and internationalist, wanted an alternative and feared that the dour Taft would repel voters. They approached the immensely popular Eisenhower, but he was not yet ready to run. So moderate Republicans turned to New York governor Dewey, the loser in 1944. His liberal record as governor (including support for black civil rights) and his advocacy of military alliances and foreign aid put him in the mainstream, while his suave manner made him seem the antithesis of the abrasive Truman. The GOP chose progressive California governor Earl Warren for the vice presidency and endorsed most New Deal reforms and Truman's foreign policy.

The Democrats were coming unraveled. On the left, former vice president Wallace campaigned as the champion of social and racial justice and the advocate of friendship with the U.S.S.R. After breaking with Truman, Wallace, who refused to disavow Communist support, tried to rally old New Dealers to his Progressive Party. Democratic liberals admired Wallace, but in the end most labor leaders and New Dealers decided that embracing his new Progressive Party would tar them with the pro-Communist brush. Anti-Soviet liberals like Eleanor Roosevelt, theologian Reinhold Niebuhr, historian Arthur Schlesinger, Jr., and CIO chief Walter Reuther formed the Americans for Democratic Action (ADA), which supported Wallace's call for extending the New Deal at home but resolutely opposed Communism abroad. After Eisenhower turned them down (as he had also rebuffed the GOP), the ADA and CIO reluctantly decided to stick with the man from Missouri.

On the right, many southern Democrats were angered by Truman's steps toward desegregation. At the Democratic convention Truman's backers sought to appease southern delegates with a policy statement criticizing discrimination only in vaguest terms. Liberals, however, demanded a plank attacking lynching and promising broad support for civil rights. Young Minneapolis mayor Hubert Humphrey electrified liberals by calling on the party to "get out of the shadow of states' rights and walk forthrightly into the bright sunshine of human rights." As some southerners walked out, the dispirited convention renominated Truman and named an old party warhorse, Kentucky Senator Alben W. Barkley, as his running mate.

As the 1948 election approached, Truman's approval rating had improved only slightly from the dismal low of 32 percent recorded in 1946. Nonetheless, the president gamely defended New Deal liberalism, and he and his chief political aide, Clark Clifford, developed a sound campaign strategy. Accepting the nomination, he announced that he would call Congress into a special session and dared the Republicans to enact the moderately liberal GOP platform — and when they failed to do so, he relentlessly lambasted the "do-nothing Eightieth Congress." To capture the midwestern and western farm belts, Truman demanded agricultural price supports and stressed his rural Missouri origins. In metropolitan areas he sought union and African American votes by reminding them of his veto of Taft-Hartley and his civil rights recommendations. The president's decision to recognize Israel weaned many Jewish liberals away from Wallace.

The White House hoped to hold most of the Solid South. But that seemed unlikely, as alienated "Dixiecrats" formed the States' Rights Democratic Party and nominated Governor Strom Thurmond of South Carolina for the presidency. Their plan was to win enough electoral votes to throw the election into the House, where they could bargain for their conservative agenda.

The confident Dewey conducted a dignified, bland campaign. According to the *Louisville Courier-Journal,* his four major speeches could be condensed into four sentences: "Agriculture is important. Our rivers are full of fish. You cannot have freedom without liberty. The future lies ahead."

Harry Truman was one of the few people in the United States who believed that he could win. He went on a 31,000-mile whistle-stop tour, making short, fiery speeches. Sometimes available money seemed insufficient to keep Truman's train rolling. But the voters re-

AT THE HOW-DID-IT-HAPPEN CLUB
NOVEMBER 7, 1948

The Experts Stumped   After Harry Truman's surprise victory, the *St. Louis Post-Dispatch*'s cartoonist D. R. Fitzpatrick on November 7, 1948, shows puzzlement everywhere "At the How-Did-It-Happen Club." Actually, the answer is easy: Polling ceased long before votes were cast, so that the last-minute surge of "undecideds" to Truman went unnoticed. Such a gross error in opinion sampling would not be made today.

sponded with shouts of "Give 'em hell, Harry!" He was the first presidential candidate to campaign in Harlem. The growing success of the Berlin airlift helped him, but still, pollsters predicted a GOP landslide.

On election night, as the first returns dribbled in, the *Chicago Tribune* ran a headline trumpeting "DEWEY DEFEATS TRUMAN!" But in a stunning upset that made him forever the underdog's hero, Truman garnered 24 million popular votes to Dewey's 22 million. Wallace and Thurmond trailed far behind with slightly more than 1 million each, and Dixiecrat hopes of throwing the election into the House fizzled as Truman took a majority of electoral votes — 303, to Dewey's 189 and Thurmond's 39. Truman's coattails even gave the Democrats razor-thin majorities in both houses of Congress.

The pollsters had missed a massive last-minute shift to Truman. The Dixiecrat rebellion reassured black voters who had questioned Truman's commitment to civil rights, while Wallace's challenge made it difficult to accuse Truman of being "soft on Communism." Dewey came across as cold, arrogant, and boring. "You have to really know Dewey well in order to dislike him," one Republican insider said. Bitter Republicans swore never again to wage a "me-too" campaign.

❧ *The Fair Deal*

In his State of the Union message in 1949, Truman unveiled a domestic program that he called the Fair Deal. He proposed raising the minimum wage from forty to seventy-five cents an hour, extending Social Security, repealing Taft-Hartley, providing low-cost federal housing, guaranteeing farmers' income, providing federal health insurance, and passing civil rights legislation. Truman's Fair Deal defined the liberal Democratic agenda for the second half of the twentieth century.

Bits of the Fair Deal were enacted. Congress raised the minimum wage and Social Security benefits and brought more than 10 million additional people (including some of the country's most disadvantaged workers) under Social Security. With Taft's backing, funds were provided for slum clearance and the construction of 810,000 units of low-cost housing. And Congress gave the states federal matching grants to build non-profit clinics and hospitals.

But most of Truman's legislative initiatives failed. Taft-Hartley was not repealed, largely because Truman (feeling beholden to the unions) rejected compromise. Federal aid to education (on which Truman and Taft agreed) foundered because Roman Catholics demanded direct support for parochial schools — something anathema to Protestants, Jews, and liberals. Southern Democrats filibustered to death the president's plan for a Fair Employment Practices Commission empowered to penalize job discrimination in the private as well as public sectors. A complicated and costly proposal for farm income support failed when the two most powerful farm lobbies clashed over the issue: Agribusiness interests, nurtured by New Deal policies and thriving thanks to agricultural exports under the Marshall Plan, denounced the plan for threatening to "socialize" American farming, while small farmers, in the midst of an ongoing exodus from the land, supported it. Finally, the administration's proposals for national health insurance — a major gap in the Social Security program — were rejected by Congress under heavy pressure from the American Medical Association, which attacked the idea as "socialized medicine."

Truman failed to enact most of his Fair Deal for several significant reasons. Unlike the Depression decade in which New Deal legislation had been passed, the late 1940s were a period of overall economic expansion and rising personal expectations. White Americans were not yet ready to support meaningful attacks on racial discrimination or stubborn pockets of poverty — which few in the middle class had firsthand knowledge of. The class conflict of New Deal days was giving way to a public consensus that viewed class resentments as un-American and considered Truman's appeals to various interest groups divisive. Although he had reassembled the New Deal coalition for his dramatic electoral victory, the president could not draw industrial workers, farmers, Catholics, "ethnics," Jews, liberals, blacks, and southerners into coalitions to pass legislation. Increasingly, the issues that seized public attention were Communist expansionism abroad, fears of subversion at home, and the prospect of a nuclear war. America during the Truman years was simply not in the mood for reform.

Finally, Truman's administration was buffeted by charges of corruption and cronyism. Although Truman was never personally implicated in "the mess in Washington," many of his closest associates were — and Truman answered Republican attacks on his friends with equally partisan counterblasts. By the time his presidency ended in 1953, most voters were glad to see him go.

❧ *Ever-Colder War*

During Truman's second term the United States poured $13 billion into Europe and worked with various national governments to establish institutions and processes that would rehabilitate Western Europe's economies. By 1952 industrial production in Europe had increased 30 percent over prewar levels and agricultural output rose by 11 percent. Trade within Europe, virtually destroyed by World War II, was resuscitated by the establishment in 1952 of the European Payments Union, which along with the European Coal and Steel Community, a remarkably successful step toward removing restrictions on the movement of those commodities in six European countries, laid the foundation for the subsequent European economic integration and ultimately the Common Market. The economic recovery of Europe, combined with strong support from the U.S., also aided in decisive election defeats for Communists in Italy and France in 1948. The Marshall Plan also served U.S. economic interests. Most of the money poured into European countries was spent in the U.S., and with the revival of its economy, Western Europe became America's largest trading partner.

By 1948, events made it clear that the Cold War was becoming more and more complicated. The first crack in the Iron Curtain in East Europe appeared in 1948 when Yugoslav leader Josip Broz Tito successfully broke with Stalin and established an independent Communist regime. Truman's decision to recognize Israel, over the objections of Secretary of State George Marshall, placed the U.S. squarely on a collision course with Arab nationalism. In the Far East, the rapid crumbling of Nationalist Chinese government gave a new global significance to the Cold War and forced on the United States difficult decisions about selecting allies around the globe.

In 1949, Dean Acheson, who had left the State Department in 1947, replaced Marshall as Truman's secretary of state. Truman relied heavily on Acheson until his departure from office in 1953. The urbane Acheson had great respect for Truman's willingness to make tough decisions, and Truman regarded the secretary of state as "my good right hand." Regarded by conservatives as soft on Communism, but on the other hand too confrontational to suit Kennan and some liberals, Acheson was probably the single most influential architect of America's postwar policy of containing the Soviet Union.

❧ NATO and the Building of the Western Alliance

In the spring of 1949 the Truman administration took another momentous decision: to have the United States sponsor and join the North Atlantic Treaty Organization (NATO). By entering into its first formal alliance since 1778, the nation committed its troops to Western Europe's defense. Under the treaty the United States announced its willingness to go to war in the common defense — that "an armed attack against one or more . . . shall be considered an attack against them all." NATO initially linked the United States, Canada, Great Britain, France, Belgium, the Netherlands, Luxembourg, Denmark, Norway, Iceland, and Portugal.[2] Five days after the formation of NATO the Soviet Union assembled representatives of its seven East European satellites in Warsaw, where they signed a mutual de-

Dean Acheson   Truman's last secretary of state was reviled by conservative Americans as a haughty elitist and "appeaser" of Communism. It is true that he did not suffer fools gladly, sported a natty mustache, and spoke with a clipped, upper-class accent, but he was also a fervent anti-Communist and a very effective diplomat. Here he is shown arriving at London's Heathrow Airport in 1950.

fense treaty that established the Warsaw Pact Organization, comparable to NATO. In fact, however, in the 1950s the Warsaw Pact operated entirely as an instrument of Soviet military domination in the east; joint military exercises were not conducted until 1961.

Fear of Soviet expansionism was not all that motivated the establishment of NATO; it was also intended to reassure the French in particular that Germany would never again threaten West Europeans. It assured that an eventually rearmed West Germany could be re-

---

2. Greece and Turkey joined in 1952, West Germany in 1955, and Spain in 1979. After the Cold War, most of the formerly Communist states of Eastern Europe eventually also joined.

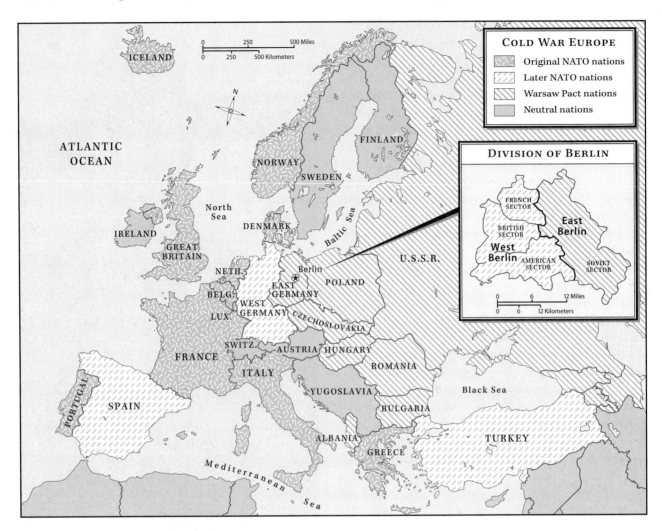

garded as a safe partner, well integrated into the Western military and economic alliance. NATO's purpose, in the words of Lord Ismay, its first secretary-general, was "to keep the Russians out, the Americans in, and the Germans down."

In 1948 Stalin had launched a "peace offensive" whose goal was to enlist European leftists and neutralists in a movement to disarm Germany. This alarmed American planners, because they feared above all a neutralized Germany that might become a Soviet ally. Thus the U.S. embarked on a program to build West Germany's military and economic ties with the Atlantic powers. In turn, this meant beefing up Western forces in Germany so that if an invasion came, Soviet troops could be stopped before they reached the Rhine — thus assuring West Germans that the West would neither abandon them nor drop nuclear bombs on Soviet forces occupying them. In 1950 Truman named Dwight D. Eisenhower to be supreme NATO commander, and he sent four American divisions to Eu-

rope to form the core of a NATO army. These troops were to serve as a tripwire if Soviet troops attacked. In effect, Western Europe had been placed behind an American atomic shield. There was no evidence of a Russian plan to invade the West, but the Soviets continued to maintain hundreds of divisions in Eastern Europe and East Germany. American officials felt that they could not gamble that the hundreds of thousands of Red Army soldiers were in Eastern Europe for purely defensive purposes or that at some future date the Soviet Union might not either miscalculate or formulate more aggressive strategies.

❧ The Soviet Atom Bomb and the Remobilization of the American Military

The condition of American military forces in 1948 was deplorable. Truman and Secretary of Defense Louis Johnson believed that American interests around the globe could be defended on a budget of $14 billion a year and an ill-equipped, undermanned American army of ten divisions. The atomic bomb, they thought, was protection enough. But then, on July 14, 1949, the Soviet Union shocked the West by exploding an atomic device, several years earlier than American experts had predicted.

The Soviet bomb forced a swift reevaluation of the West's military strategy in Europe, and President Truman ordered the National Security Council to undertake a comprehensive reevaluation of American policy. In April 1950, State and Defense Department officials led by Paul Nitze, Kennan's successor as chief Cold War strategist,[3] produced a secret document known as NSC-68. Abandoning Kennan's plea that American strategic interests be confined to Western Europe, the Middle East, and Japan, NSC-68 saw *any* extension of the area under Communist control as a direct threat to the United States. This was not a new idea: American planners had for several years recognized that access to markets and key raw materials (petroleum, rubber, and various strategic metals) was essential for the security and prosperity of Western Europe, Japan, and indeed the United States. But NSC-68 turned this operating assumption into the strategic decision that no significant territory around the globe should be yielded to Communism.

Underlying NSC-68 was an assumption that the American economy was vastly expandable. The paper attacked the parsimony that caused Truman to try to defend American security on the cheap. "One of the most significant lessons of our World War II experience," NSC-68 pointed out, "was that the American economy, when it operates at a level approaching full efficiency, can provide enormous resources for purposes other than civilian consumption while simultaneously providing a higher standard of living." NSC-68 urged in strong language that the United States "strike out on a bold and massive program of rebuilding the West's defensive establishment to the point that it would surpass that of the Soviet world" and meet "each fresh challenge promptly and unequivocally."

Pursuing these objectives meant sharply increasing the size and firepower of American armed forces, and the deployment of large numbers of American ground forces in Europe. NSC-68 also recommended the immediate development of the thermonuclear (hydrogen)

bomb. The first American "Super" bomb was successfully tested at the end of 1952, followed nine months later by the explosion of a Soviet thermonuclear device in August 1953. Many of Truman's advisers balked at the military expansion envisioned because of the costs involved, but Secretary of State Dean Acheson persevered, and the president supported the expanded definition of containment.

Cold War in Asia

The Soviet atomic bomb was not the only shock to American planners in late 1949. On October 1, 1949, Mao Zedong announced the establishment of the People's Republic of China. "China has stood up," he proclaimed, as his nation became a Communist state of 800 million people. America's wartime ally, Chiang Kai-shek, fled to Taiwan with discredited remnants of his corrupt regime.

The relatively few American policymakers who understood China knew that Mao was no Soviet puppet and believed that the United States might be able to exploit Sino-Soviet tensions. Stalin distrusted Mao as a potential rival and was surprised by his victory, won with a peasant-based army that consistently ignored Soviet experts. But for the moment the People's Republic of China became Moscow's ally. One-third of the human race was now ruled by Communist regimes.

The rapidity of China's "loss" horrified the many Americans who had long thought of that country as the beneficiary of Christian evangelism and the Open Door Policy. American business traditionally had viewed China as a huge potential market for exports. "With God's help, we will raise Shanghai up and up, ever up, until it is just as good as Kansas City," a Senator had boasted in the 1930s. The fact that China had succumbed to Communism seemed to millions of Americans the result of someone's stupidity — or betrayal.

In fact, the United States could have done nothing to forestall Communist victory in China. All across Asia, nationalist revolts were brewing against Western imperialism, and the devastation of World War II made China ripe for revolution. Mao's Communist army in China's far northeast had mounted the only vigorous resistance to the Japanese; rather than fighting Japan, Chiang had stockpiled American military gear with an eye to a postwar showdown with Mao, which broke out shortly after V-J Day.

Prewar isolationists — who during World War II had tended to advocate an "Asia-first" strategy — blamed

---

3. Kennan left the State Department in late 1949, convinced that American policy was taking on more commitments than it could handle and was coming to rely excessively on a military response to the Soviet threat.

Chiang's fall on the Truman administration.[4] Supported by *Time* publisher Henry Luce, congressional Republicans blasted the Democrats for what they termed one of the greatest foreign policy failures of the twentieth century. Taft accused Truman and Acheson of pursuing an erroneous Europe-first policy and of appeasing the Soviets, and demagogues like Joseph McCarthy (discussed below) claimed that treason lay at the bottom of the collapse of China.

The Truman administration, however, saw industrialized but devastated Japan, not chronically impoverished China, as the focal point of the Cold War in Asia. Excluding the Soviet Union from any significant role, the United States occupied Japan after 1945 and forever changed the face of that nation. Authoritarian and paternalistic, General Douglas MacArthur headed the occupation regime and quickly won the respect of Japanese from the emperor to ordinary people.

American policy was to remake Japan as a democratic and peace-loving society. MacArthur drew up a constitution for Japan in 1947 patterned after that of the United States. Under it, Japan "forever renounced war as a sovereign right of the nation." American occupation officials reformed Japanese education, safeguarded civil liberties, including those of women, barred high military and civilian officials from office, and conducted war-crimes trials.

As tensions with the Soviet Union grew, MacArthur and the Truman administration began to envisage Japan as a balance to Soviet influence in the western Pacific — and a country that, like western Germany, must not be allowed to fall to Communism after the withdrawal of American occupation forces. Abandoning early attempts to break up large Japanese industries and redistribute land, occupation authorities now promoted industrial production and managerial efficiency, began to furnish economic aid, and encouraged former Japanese leaders to run for office. To the Soviet Union and China, all this seemed like the ominous rebuilding of a former enemy.

Concern with ensuring Japan's economic recovery and with placating France combined to lead the Truman administration to take the first small steps toward involvement in Vietnam. Before World War II, France

The Conqueror   At their first meeting, General MacArthur towers over formally clad Emperor Hirohito, who had come to call on the American proconsul. MacArthur strikes a deliberately nonchalant pose beside the emperor, who before and during the war had been revered as a divine figure by his subjects. The Japanese public came to admire MacArthur greatly for his work in overseeing the rebuilding of their country.

had ruled Indochina, but Japan occupied the colony in 1941. During World War II, the United States encouraged Indochina's Communist-led but also nationalistic Vietminh movement under Ho Chi Minh, which (like Mao's Communists in China) constituted the only effective anti-Japanese movement. FDR had opposed returning the colony to postwar French rule. But with Roosevelt's death, the onset of the Cold War, and the perceived need to placate France and rebuild Japan's export economy, the United States tacitly supported French efforts to regain control of Indochina. From 1946 through 1954, France and the Vietminh fought a bitter war.

4. A major step along this road, they charged, had been the failure of George Marshall's effort, at Truman's behest, to mediate between Chiang and the Communists in 1945-1946. Acknowledging the hopeless incompetence of Chiang's regime, Marshall recommended — and Truman agreed to — the abandonment of active American aid to the Nationalists after full-scale civil war resumed in 1947.

Cold War ideologies soon engulfed the Indochinese struggle. France in 1950 created an anti-Communist South Vietnamese puppet state. In the north, Ho set up the Communist-dominated Democratic Republic of Vietnam, which Moscow and Beijing recognized — making it, to the Truman administration, an agent of international Communism. During the next three years, the United States gave France $775 million to fight the Vietminh, and also sent a few military advisers to help South Vietnam fend off Communist guerillas.

❧ The Korean War

The Cold War first turned hot in Korea. After World War II, the former Japanese colony had come under Soviet occupation north of the 38th parallel and under American occupation south of that line. Efforts by the United Nations to unify the country in 1947 failed, largely because of Soviet intransigence. In 1948 the Kremlin set up a Communist regime in the north, headed by Kim Il Sung; that same year, the equally dictatorial but fiercely anti-Communist Syngman Rhee took power in South Korea after elections sponsored by the United States. The two regimes hated each other, and each vowed to reunite the peninsula under its own rule.

WOULD AMERICA FIGHT?

Although the United States signed an agreement with Rhee's regime in 1948, granting substantial military and economic assistance, there was some question about American willingness to defend South Korea militarily. Partly this was a consequence of the lack of readiness of U.S. conventional forces. Moreover, by early 1949 neo-isolationists within the GOP launched a campaign claiming that the greatest danger to America came not from abroad but from internal Communist subversion. Even mainstream conservatives such as Taft insisted that, because America's resources were limited, the United States ought to give first priority to ensuring its own prosperity by balancing the budget. Neo-isolationists not only opposed stationing of American troops in Europe but also warned against involvement in an Asian land war. In addition, many of Truman's own advisers recoiled at the expense of a global containment policy. Perhaps responding to these critics (scholars still debate why), Acheson announced in January 1949 that South Korea lay outside the American defensive perimeter and should rely on UN protection. Other statements by Acheson and MacArthur indicated that neither South Korea nor Taiwan could automatically expect U.S. intervention in case of attack.

The Communists could have easily concluded that America was writing off South Korea. Recently disclosed Soviet documents reveal that in early 1950 both Moscow and Beijing gave tacit approval to Kim Il Sung's determination to reunify Korea. American actions may also have provoked the North Koreans. In May 1950, the administration announced plans to negotiate a peace treaty with Japan as quickly as possible, with neither the Soviets nor the Chinese allowed to participate and with the United States gaining the right to construct military installations in Japan. For Moscow and Beijing alike, unifying Korea under Communist control would counter a rehabilitated and pro-American Japan.

On June 25, 1950, the well-trained and well-equipped North Korean army swept down the peninsula, scattering South Korea's small and undisciplined army. From the beginning, Truman and Acheson assumed that the invasion was part of a wider Communist thrust to conquer all of Asia — or perhaps a diversionary feint before a Soviet attack in Europe. They swiftly brought Korea and Taiwan back within the American line of defense. On June 26 the president directed the Seventh Fleet to protect Taiwan and authorized a military response in Korea. He regarded the North Korean attack as a test of the "free world's" determination to defend democracy.

The Soviet Union was boycotting the sessions of the U.N. Security Council at the time of North Korea's attack because of America's veto of membership in the organization for Communist China. This blunder allowed the United States to obtain U.N. resolutions condemning the North Koreans as aggressors and calling upon member nations to contribute to an American-led force to defend South Korea. Truman at once named General MacArthur to command the army of liberation. The military effort in Korea was thoroughly American-dominated. The United States supplied 50 percent of the ground forces (most of the remainder came from South Korea), 86 percent of the naval power, and 93 percent of the air power.

GRIM REALITY OF WAR

After six weeks of fighting, remnants of the South Korean army and a small U.N. (chiefly American) force held only an enclave around Pusan. Then, on September 15, MacArthur made a daring landing at Inchon on Korea's western coast. Against light resistance, American marines and South Korean troops advanced inland while their comrades in the south drove northward from Pusan. Seoul was recaptured on September 26.

At this juncture, the Truman administration faced a major decision. MacArthur urged invading North Korea and reunifying the peninsula. He insisted that neither the Soviet Union nor Communist China would intervene. Acheson agreed. Truman was not so sure, but he was persuaded by the argument that if UN forces merely restored the boundary at the 38th parallel, North Korea would attack again in the future. On September 27 the president instructed MacArthur to advance north unless he encountered Soviet or Chinese troops. Ten days later the UN approved reunifying Korea. By November 21 American troops could see Chinese sentries posted across the Yalu River, separating China and North Korea, and MacArthur announced that most American soldiers would be home for Christmas.

Instead, thirty-three Chinese divisions crossed the Yalu and shattered MacArthur's unwisely divided columns. Fighting the bitter cold, the mountainous terrain, and Chinese human-wave charges, American and South Korean soldiers retreated. At Chosin Reservoir, 23,000 were captured or killed. Three weeks later, the front line of battle reached well south of Seoul, and it was the Communists' turn to talk about reunifying Korea. By the end of January 1951, American forces halted the Chinese advance, allowing UN forces to retake the initiative. By March, Seoul was back in UN hands, and soon the 38th parallel was regained.

MACARTHUR VS. TRUMAN

Truman had learned his lesson, but MacArthur had not. MacArthur demanded a naval blockade of China, air attacks on Chinese military and industrial targets, and the introduction of Chiang Kai-shek's troops in Korea. He wanted not only to conquer North Korea but also to "sever Korea from Manchuria by laying a field of radioactive wastes across all the major lines of enemy supply." The administration knew that such acts would risk a global conflict, and — to MacArthur's rage — the State Department on March 20 began considering a negotiated settlement with the North Koreans and Chinese. Three days later the general issued a statement threatening to attack China's "coastal areas and interior bases." He also wrote a public letter to the Republican minority leader in the House, calling for an all-out war in Asia to defeat the Communists and criticizing "the diplomats" for being willing to fight with words only. Such insubordination flouted the American tradition of civilian control of the military. Tru-

man was outraged. "The son of a bitch isn't going to resign on me," the president told General Omar Bradley. "I want him fired." With the concurrence of the Joint Chiefs, Truman on April 11 relieved MacArthur of his command.

Fully aware of MacArthur's popularity, the Republicans blasted the Democrats once more as soft on Communism. The conqueror of Manila and Inchon had not been in the United States for fourteen years, and the nation welcomed him as a hero. After a series of ticker-tape parades, MacArthur made his "farewell" speech to a joint session of Congress. "Old soldiers never die, they just fade away," he intoned — hardly expecting such a fate for himself. For a while there was talk of the GOP running MacArthur for president. Testifying before two senatorial committees in May and June 1951, MacArthur pinned responsibility for the lack of a clear-cut victory on pusillanimous politicians and political generals. He called for an all-out military effort to defeat Communism in Asia, even if it meant a fight to the finish with China, because the course of events in that region would determine the course of world affairs for the "next ten thousand years."

In what was perhaps its finest hour, the Truman administration fought back, making clear that not only American security interests were at stake in the dismissal of MacArthur but also the hallowed principle of civilian control of the military. "Taking on Red China," Bradley told the Senators, would have led only "to a larger deadlock at greater expense." Because the United States regarded the Soviet Union as its main adversary and Europe as the principal Cold War prize, MacArthur's course "would involve us in the wrong war at the wrong place at the wrong time and with the wrong enemy."

ARMISTICE AND CONTAINMENT

Gradually the logic of the administration's argument took hold, and furor over MacArthur's firing faded. When in June 1951 the Soviets suggested an armistice along the 38th parallel, Washington welcomed the move. Tense negotiations began between the Communist and U.N. sides, dragging on through 1952 while thousands of American troops — and far more Koreans and Chinese — continued to die. (One issue was whether Communist POWs should be returned against their will. Many feared to go home.) The stalemated talks became an issue in the 1952 election when the Republican candidate, Dwight D. Eisenhower, promised to go to Korea to end the war. He made good on his promise, secretly threatening the Communists with nuclear attack if they did not agree to a compromise.

The Korean War was a "limited war," a frustrating byproduct of the Soviet-American nuclear stalemate, as well as a Korean civil war. Though the United States possessed atomic devices that could have been used to devastate North Korea and China, it dared not use them for fear of Soviet nuclear retaliation. Thus began nearly forty years of covert and limited, conventional East-West conflicts; a sweeping military triumph was unthinkable in view of the threat of atomic annihilation.

In a sense, however, Korea marked a clear-cut victory for containment. The United States and its allies "held the line" against Communist aggression. Just as the Berlin blockade reassured non-Communist West Europeans that the Americans would stand by them, so the Korean War demonstrated that the United States would defend what was left of non-Communist East Asia — even at the price of uncritical alignment with autocrats like Rhee. It globalized containment, and was a natural outgrowth of NSC-68's call to confront Communist expansionism everywhere. In the long run, the development of a democratic, industrialized, and capitalist Republic of Korea in the South made the war seem a triumph for American aims in Asia.

ESPIONAGE, ANTICOMMUNISM, AND McCARTHYISM

From the beginning of the Cold War until the end of the fighting in Korea, a mounting anti-Communist hysteria swept through every aspect of American life. Partly, the reaction was the result of real and imaginary fears of Soviet espionage. Particularly troubling was Russia's success in stealing nuclear secrets. Only after the collapse of the Soviet Union did the extent of American Communist support for Soviet espionage become fully clear. While these revelations hardly exonerate the excesses of the anti-Communist crusaders, they make more understandable the fears and concerns that gripped many American policymakers and politicians.

The anti-Communist movement also revealed a growing social and cultural divide in the country that had important political consequences. To some extent, the furor was part of a larger nativist backlash, manifest in white supremacists movements and new outbreaks of anti-Semitism. But it also demonstrated a traditional American distrust of social and political

elites, who during the postwar years were portrayed as being soft on Communism. Republican opportunists exploited these fears in the hopes of discrediting New Deal programs and liberalism in general. Some modern political observers date the party realignment of the last half of the twentieth century to the success of the Republican Party in rallying a vast body of Christian, working Americans through its opposition to "godless Communism."

Just as the Truman administration turned to stronger measures to draw the line in Western Europe and stop Communist advances in East Asia, hysterical anti-Communist witch-hunting erupted at home. Careers were ruined, lives disrupted, liberties trampled, trust destroyed, fools taken seriously, scoundrels empowered, and a few citizens hounded to suicide. The nation passed through one of the darker moments in its history — years indelibly associated with the name of the sinister junior Senator from Wisconsin, Joseph McCarthy.

❧ *Espionage and Security*

Between the 1919 "Red Scare" and the early post–World War II years, Communism did not inspire hysterical fear among most Americans. But, inevitably, Cold War tensions changed the mood. In 1945 the House Un-American Activities Committee (HUAC), the descendant of the prewar Dies Committee set up to investigate pro-fascist groups, gained permanent status and began targeting domestic Communism. HUAC's activities were spearheaded by Mississippi Democrat John Rankin, a virulent segregationist and anti-Communist conservative. The Republican victory in the 1946 election brought to the chairmanship of HUAC J. Parnell Thomas of New Jersey, who immediately targeted Hollywood as a center of a dangerous Communist conspiracy.

There *were* Communists in Hollywood. During the Depression, in the 1930s, many movie writers had been a part of the flirtation with the far left. On October 20, 1947, HUAC began hearing anti-Communist testimony from "friendly witnesses" encouraged by the studio bosses to cooperate with the committee, including the popular actor Gary Cooper. Then came a parade of writers and directors who were or had been members of the American Communist Party. Most sought refuge in the First Amendment's guarantee of freedom of speech rather than in the Fifth Amendment's protection against self-incrimination. Several were defiant and abusive. The "Hollywood Ten" were convicted of

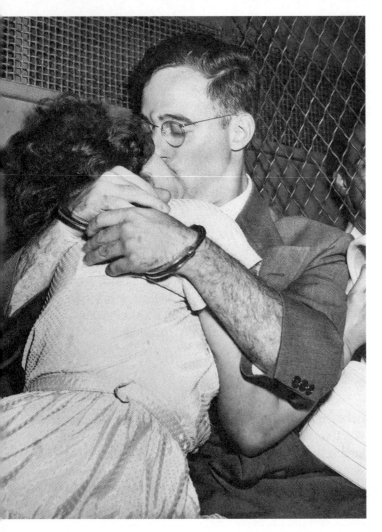

The Rosenbergs This poignant photograph was taken in August 1950, immediately after Julius and Ethel Rosenberg were arraigned and jailed—in separate cells—on espionage charges.

contempt of Congress and, after the Supreme Court upheld their convictions, were sentenced to a year in prison.[5]

HUAC's investigation intimidated the motion picture industry. All major studios pledged not to hire Communists or Communist sympathizers. Dozens of writers, directors, and actors in the United States found themselves blacklisted. Soon the witch-hunt spread to the new television industry.

Even before HUAC declared war on Communism in Hollywood, reacting to fears of Soviet espionage and hoping to forestall GOP charges that Democrats were

5. J. Parnell Thomas also wound up in prison after being convicted of corruption. He and one of the Hollywood Ten met on a work detail, shoveling manure. When Thomas sneered something about "still carrying the old hammer and sickle?" the Communist retorted: "Still throwing around the old chickenshit, Thomas?"

soft on Communism, the Truman administration took drastic steps against Communist subversion. On March 21, 1947, just as he was proclaiming the Truman Doctrine, the president issued Executive Order No. 9835, mandating a loyalty investigation of each applicant for a federal job. Agency heads became "personally responsible" for their underlings' loyalty. The review was to be carried out by the Civil Service and FBI but supervised by a central Loyalty Review Board.

During the next five years the Civil Service conducted more than 3,000 investigations and the FBI made some 14,000 inquiries. Of 380 employees dismissed, only 221 were subsequently indicted, and most of these were never convicted. More significantly, 2,500 individuals resigned under suspicion. In most cases, the charge was not sabotage, espionage, or treason, but rather "sympathetic association" with alleged subversives or with members of organizations identified by the attorney general as subversive. But at the time such charges could ruin an individual. Nor was there any check on the attorney general's authority to designate groups as "subversive." Truman's order led to a massive expansion of the FBI and to the accumulation of hundreds of thousands of "loyalty files." Contradicting accepted notions of justice in American society, loyalty tests in 1951 placed the burden of proof on the person being investigated.

In 1949 and 1950 several sensational incidents of Soviet espionage in the United States came to light, worsening the hysteria. One recent study based on post–Cold War Soviet secret documents concluded that Soviet espionage in the U.S. during World War II was far more extensive than imagined, and that 349 American citizens who were members of the American Communist Party participated in Soviet espionage, many of them still unidentified. "Not every American Communist was a spy," historian Harvey Klehr concluded, "but almost every spy was a Communist." In February 1950, on the heels of the first Soviet nuclear test and the fall of China, physicist Klaus Fuchs — one of the Manhattan Project scientists — was arrested in Britain. Fuchs confessed to betraying atomic secrets to Moscow during World War II. Within months, several Americans, including Julius and Ethel Rosenberg, were arrested in the United States as members of the same spy ring. Tried before a militantly anti-Communist federal judge in 1951, the Rosenbergs were executed in 1953, causing a furor of protest from those who believed them innocent. Recently revealed Soviet evidence seems to show that Julius was both a veteran Communist and a "handler" of other agents and couriers, but that Ethel's involvement was peripheral. Her execution seems to have resulted from prosecutors' futile efforts to pressure Julius to confess.[6]

The most celebrated spy case of the century was that of Alger Hiss, a career bureaucrat in the Treasury and State departments who had accompanied FDR to Yalta. As early as 1939 Whittaker Chambers, a former Soviet agent, had confidentially named Hiss as a spy but showed no proof. In 1948 Chambers repeated his charges before HUAC, this time producing microfilm of documents that he said Hiss had passed to him in 1938. Hiss denied the charges, but was indicted for perjury. (The statute of limitations for espionage had expired.) Truman denounced the accusations as a "red herring," and State Department officials, including Hiss's friend Dean Acheson, defended Hiss. Nonetheless, in January 1950 Hiss was convicted and sentenced to five years in prison.

Recently declassified American and Soviet documents reveal that Hiss had belonged to a clandestine Communist "cell" since 1935, that for years he passed documents to the Soviet military intelligence, and that Moscow secretly decorated him in 1945, soon after he had accompanied Roosevelt to Yalta. When public accusations were leveled at Hiss, the U.S. government evidently chose not to reveal all that it knew about him in order to avoid compromising its intelligence sources. So for half a century the Hiss case polarized the nation. Liberals saw Hiss as the victim of a witch-hunt, condemned for his New Deal sympathies and upper-class manner. Conservatives — whose only proof of Hiss's guilt was the circumstantially confirmed word of the turncoat Chambers — saw Hiss as the incarnation of the elitist traitor. "It was the Hiss case that completely changed the public's perception of domestic Communism," Richard Nixon, a member of HUAC who would use anti-Communist rhetoric to further his national aspirations, later wrote. "People were now alerted to a serious threat to our liberties."

Meanwhile the federal courts had begun moving against the American Communist Party. In July 1948 a federal grand jury indicted twelve party leaders on charges of violating the Smith Act — a 1940 law (originally directed mainly against pro-Nazis) that made it a federal crime to conspire to overthrow the government or to belong to a group advocating its overthrow. In 1951 the Supreme Court upheld the Smith Act and the

conviction of those Communist leaders who had been tried under it.

Determined to leave no room for doubt, Congress in 1950 passed the McCarran (or Internal Security) Act. That measure branded the international Communist conspiracy an immediate threat to the United States. Members of Communist-affiliated organizations were required to register with the federal government, on pain of being fined up to $10,000 and imprisoned for up to five years. The act also authorized the government to deport naturalized citizens and alleged subversives during periods of national emergency.

❧ The Politics and Religion of Anti-Communism

In reality, during the Cold War the Soviet Union sponsored massive espionage efforts that threatened American interests. The anti-Communist campaign spawned by the threat, however, was often marred by political demagoguery, opportunism, chicanery, and downright deceit. Much that was done obscured distinctions between politics and spying — often combining such terms as Communist, sympathizer, fellow traveler, and liberal. In such a political mix, anti-Communist demagogues tainted real efforts to thwart espionage. In the end, the red-baiting furor hobbled real efforts to find Communist infiltrators. By the late 1950s, noted one conservative, the sins of the witch-hunters had made it impossible to accuse anyone of being disloyal for fear of being "hauled up for committing McCarthyism."

Nonetheless, it would have been impossible to keep the issue out of politics. GOP strategists remembered that in the spring of 1948 a Gallup poll had found that 65 percent of the public thought that foreign policy problems were the most important issue in the campaign, and that 73 percent saw Truman as too easy on the Russians. Party leaders also recalled that Dewey had barely mentioned foreign affairs in his campaign. The lesson was clear. If the Republicans were to regain the White House, they would have to blast the Democrats as soft on Communism. "I look at that fellow [Dean Acheson]," said a disgusted Senator Hugh Butler of Nebraska, "I watch his smart aleck manner and his British clothes and that New Dealism, everlasting New Dealism in everything he says and does, and I want to shout, Get Out! Get Out! You stand for everything that has been wrong in the United States for years." Anti-elitist class prejudices were always near the surface in the anti-Communist crusade. "No feature of the Hiss case is more obvi-

---

6. Even the hardened J. Edgar Hoover was privately shocked by this tactic and its outcome.

"The American Idolatry," 1950

In the tense atmosphere of the Cold War, many churches and church leaders felt compelled to make vigorous denunciations of Communism and defenses of the American way of life. Reinhold Niebuhr, one of the most respected theologians of the day, cautioned against a too-fervent championing of national interests.

If the ministers of our great urban churches become again the simple priests and chaplains of this American idolatry, subtly compounded with a few stray Christian emphases, they will merely add one more dismal proof in the pages of history that a religiously sanctified self-idolatry is more grievous than its secular variety. This is how the gospel becomes a salt that has lost its savor.

The gospel cannot be preached with truth and power if it does not challenge the pretensions and pride, not only of individuals, but of nations, cultures, civilizations, economic and political systems. The good fortune of America and its power place it under the most grievous temptations to self-adulation. If there is no power and grace in the Christian church "to bring down every high thing which exalteth itself against the knowledge of God," the church becomes not merely useless but dangerous.

We Protestants speak critical words about the idolatrous pretensions of the Roman Church. But some of these pretensions are actually more plausible than this miserable identification of the "laws of God" with a particular form of democracy. . . .

---

ous or troubling as history," Chambers wrote, "than the jagged fissure, which it did not so much open as reveal, between the plain men and women of the nation, and those who affected to act, think and speak for them. It was, not invariably, but in general, the 'best people' who were for Alger Hiss." The anti-Communist crusade was, in the words of one supporter, "Americanism with its sleeves rolled up."

Some historians have argued that the anti-Communist movement contributed in critical ways to modern conservatism in America by creating a bond between working-class Americans and the Republican Party. The growing fissure between a liberal-leaning intelligentsia which was increasingly loyal to the Democratic Party and a militant anti-Communist conservatism that leaned toward the Republican Party was nowhere more apparent than in the fault lines that appeared in American religion in postwar years.

Church membership increased dramatically during and after the war, triggering a great religious boom in the 1950s. In 1948 the World Council of Churches was founded, and in 1950 the Federal Council of Churches assumed a new name, the National Council of Churches of Christ in the U.S.A. Both of these bodies included mainstream Protestant denominations and Eastern Orthodox churches. Many conservative Protestant churches and the Roman Catholic Church spurned the ecumenical movement.

In an expansive and triumphant mood, mainstream Protestants aspired to speak with one voice for American values. "The Council has nothing to fear from the times, though it has much to desire of them," declared the NCC's founding message. "The Council stands as a guardian of democratic freedom. . . . The revolutionary truth that men are created free follows from the revelation of God in Jesus Christ." But, in truth, the NCC's liberal social agenda represented only one segment of American religion.

As fears grew of Communist subversion and nuclear holocaust, differences between various religious groups and thinkers were thrown into sharp relief. Like the conservative Pope Pius XII, American Catholic leaders took a militantly anti-Communist stand. Joseph McCarthy was a Catholic, and many of his followers were working-class Catholics whose virulent anti-Communism stemmed from their fear of atheism and from their anger at Communist control of their ancestral homelands. McCarthyism's targets were often agnostics, Jews, or liberal Protestants. In particular, many Jews worked in academia or the media, the primary areas under investigation; and many of them, drawn to social justice, civil liberties, and antifascist causes, had joined groups advocating radical change. Increasingly, these Catholic conservatives would find common cause with a rising fundamentalist/evangelical revival in American Protestantism, led by a charismatic and staunchly anti-Catholic young evangelist, Billy Graham (see Chapter 31).

Ultimately the anti-Communist campaign focused on the liberal agenda of the major Protestant denominations. On March 26, 1947, J. Edgar Hoover (a prominent Presbyterian layman) testified before HUAC: "I confess to a real apprehension so long as Communists are able to secure ministers of the Gospel to promote their evil work and espouse a cause that is alien to the religion of Christ and Judaism." Methodist bishop G. Bromley Oxnam, whom various HUAC reports repeatedly labeled a Communist dupe, replied for the Protestants. He denounced both Communism for its atheism and HUAC for its violation of civil liberties. McCarthyism, he declared, represented "the rule of men and not of law." The ongoing confrontation between liberal religion and the anti-Communist stance of Roman Catholics and Protestant evangelicals polarized American churches in the 1950s at the time when religion seemed most settled and pervasive in the culture. In many ways, the religious fault line that developed paralleled the one that was becoming increasingly clear in American politics.

❧ McCarthyism

The Hiss trial and the arrest and confession of Fuchs set the stage for the greatest of the anti-Communist demagogues, Senator Joseph McCarthy. A menacing-looking man[7] of mediocre talents, corrupt habits, and no scruples, he had been elected to the Senate in 1946 on a grossly inflated war record. His lackluster first-term performance made him seem a loser. But early in 1950, after dining with two advisers (one a staunchly anti-Communist Catholic priest), McCarthy was persuaded to revive his waning fortunes by raising the issue of Communist infiltration into American government.

In February 1950 (a month after Hiss's conviction), McCarthy brandished before the Republican Women's Club in Wheeling, West Virginia, what he said was a list of 205 card-carrying Communists in the State Department. Or was it 57? No one could tell because of his mumbling, and in a subsequent speech he claimed 81 card-carriers. Asked for proof, he produced new charges — that Owen Lattimore, a professor at Johns Hopkins University and an expert on China who advised the State Department, was a top espionage agent who had been responsible for America's numerous foreign policy "disasters" in East Asia. When the FBI cleared Lattimore, McCarthy turned on Philip Jessup,

7. Revealing his own class prejudice, liberal journalist Richard Rovere memorably called McCarthy "a truckdriver in a blue serge suit."

McCarthy at Work　　In the 1952 election campaign, Senator Joseph R. McCarthy brandishes a document purporting to prove that Democratic presidential candidate Adlai Stevenson has a record of associations with alleged subversive groups and endorses "the suicidal Kremlin-shaped policies of this nation."

the American representative in the United Nations.

To look into McCarthy's charges, the Senate established a subcommittee under conservative Maryland Democrat Millard Tydings, which found the accusations to be "a fraud and a hoax." But McCarthy dismissed the committee as packed with reds, and in November 1950 he brought about Tydings's electoral defeat. (Maryland McCarthyites circulated a faked photograph showing Tydings and American Communist leader Earl Browder together.) The Democratic Party was, according to McCarthy, "the property of men and women who have bent to the whispered pleas from the lips of traitors who wear the political label stitched with the idiocy of a Truman, [and] rotted by the deceit of a Dean Acheson."

After the Republicans won control of Congress in 1952, McCarthy's "investigative" role widened. He attacked the United States Information Agency, a government agency charged with airing the Voice of America radio broadcast across the Iron Curtain and with maintaining libraries abroad. McCarthy charged

Joseph McCarthy on the Attack, 1950

When Senator Joseph McCarthy originally gave this speech to the Republican Women's Club in Wheeling, West Virginia, he declared that he had a list of 205 members of the Communist Party who were employed in the U.S. Department of State. When he later entered the speech in the Congressional Record, as printed here, he reduced the number to 57. He did not actually have such a list, but in the charged atmosphere of the early years of the Cold War, such claims were enough to grab news headlines and spark fear.

As one of our outstanding historical figures once said, "When a great democracy is destroyed, it will not be because of enemies from without, but rather because of enemies from within."

The reason why we find ourselves in a position of impotency is not because our only powerful potential enemy has sent men to invade our shores, but rather because of the traitorous actions of those who have been treated so well by this Nation. It has not been the less fortunate or members of minority groups who have been selling this Nation out, but rather those who have had all the benefits that the wealthiest nation on earth has to offer — the finest homes, the finest college education, and the finest jobs in Government.

This is glaringly true in the State Department. There the bright young men who are born with silver spoons in their mouths are the ones who have been the worst. . . . In my opinion, the State Department, which is one of the most important government departments, is thoroughly infested with Communists.

I have in my hand 57 cases of individuals who would appear to be either card carrying members or certainly loyal to the Communist Party, but who nevertheless are still helping to shape our foreign policy. . . .

---

that the USIA stocked its libraries with "leftist" books, and sent two abrasive young staffers to Europe to root them out and intimidate State Department officials into cooperating.

McCarthy continued HUAC's assault on the media and then took on academia. State legislatures, swept up by the fervor of his purge, imposed loyalty oaths on state university faculties. About 500 state and local government employees lost their jobs after they were accused of disloyalty. Some 600 schoolteachers and 150 professors were also fired, mostly for invoking the Fifth Amendment. Blacklists, usually the products of gossip and innuendo, ruined the careers of dozens of journalists, particularly in the broadcast field.

The Truman-era red scare was a product, first, of early Cold-War fears. Even the authors of NSC-68 noted that as a free society the United States was at a disadvantage in waging the Cold War and that the federal government might have to curtail freedoms. Equally dreading the Communist "tide" and nuclear annihilation, Americans searched for scapegoats — and many thought that they found traitors burrowing within.

Second, red-baiting also grew out of Republican efforts to discredit the Democratic administration. Normally intelligent and decent Republicans like Taft, frustrated by defeat in 1948, egged McCarthy on. The threat of Communist subversion was the perfect political issue, reconciling (as British philosopher Bertrand Russell noted) the two principal fears of Americans — taxes and Communism. If American reverses abroad

were due to betrayal at home, there was no need for huge new expenditures on defense and foreign aid; all that was required was a domestic house cleaning.

Third, McCarthyism appealed to former isolationists, particularly German- and Irish-Americans, and to many Catholics worried about "Godless Communism." Themselves victims of nativist and Protestant suspicion, and often members of the working or lower middle class who resented liberal "WASPs" and Jews, "hyphenated" Americans could "prove" their patriotism by joining McCarthy's chorus. Many did. Responding to anti-foreign sentiment, in June 1952 Congress passed (over Truman's veto) the McCarran-Walter Act, which kept the national-origins quotas established in 1924 to limit immigration — and also barred "subversives."

Polls showed that McCarthyism, even at its height, appealed only to a minority of Americans. The majority, however, gave the inquisitors the benefit of the doubt — and seldom criticized red-baiting too vigorously, lest they themselves become suspect. Fear bred hysteria, which bred more fear.

McCarthy's downfall began when he attacked the U.S. Army. Investigating an alleged spy ring in the military in 1954, he heard about Dr. Irving Peress, a dentist drafted during the Korean War who had "taken the Fifth" when questioned about alleged Communist activities. McCarthy denounced as Communist sympathizers Peress's commanding officer, the secretary of the army, and even George Marshall.

But the secretary of the army counterattacked, filing twenty-nine charges against McCarthy and his staff. McCarthy responded with forty-six charges of his own. During hearings held from April 22 through June 17, 1954, McCarthy dominated the proceedings. For thirteen days he browbeat the secretary of the army before a national TV audience. It became apparent — as one of McCarthy's Senate colleagues put it — that "Joe couldn't tell the difference between Karl Marx and [comedian] Groucho Marx." Constantly interrupting witnesses with insinuating comments or shouts of "Point of order!" McCarthy gave the nation a firsthand display of his tactics. Finally the army's counsel, Joseph Welch, articulated the disgust felt by much of the committee and most viewers: "Have you no sense of decency, sir, at long last?"

Technically, neither the army nor McCarthy emerged victorious from the hearings, but the grand inquisitor had clearly lost. A Gallup poll revealed that by the close of the hearings McCarthy's approval rating dropped to 35 percent. He had at last become a liability to the GOP.

On July 30, 1954, Senator Ralph Flanders, an elderly Vermont Republican, introduced a resolution calling for McCarthy's removal from the Committee on Government Operations. Journalist Edward R. Murrow ran a series of film clips on TV, showing McCarthy at his worst. After months of debate and parliamentary maneuvering, the Senate voted on March 2, 1955, to censure him. He remained in the Senate, a spent force, and died of alcoholism in 1957.

CONCLUSION: AN ANXIOUS AGE

The first postwar years were ones of recovery, consolidation, prosperity, limited social reform — and deep anxiety. Victory had drawn the nation together, bolstered people's confidence, and whetted their desire to enjoy life. At the same time, the dawn of the Atomic Age meant that human beings had unlocked the power to destroy life on earth, and deteriorating relations with the Soviet Union kindled fears that World War III might be brewing.

Return to normality, for which everyone hungered, meant different things to different people. Prosperity bred by the war continued throughout the late 1940s and early 1950s, lifting millions of working-class Americans into the middle class and ensuring that a majority of Americans became conservative, committed to the status quo. For others — unorganized workers, some

women, and most minorities — the good life was far more elusive.

Despite all the passions it had aroused, the New Deal was neither expanded nor rolled back during postwar years, but it was consolidated. Republicans as well as Democrats accepted its basic structure, and the federal government continued to play a large role in the national economy. Though bitterly reviled, Harry Truman won the White House in his own right because he represented qualities prized by middle-class Americans: integrity, self-reliance, sympathy for the underdog, candor, and courage.

Victory did not bring the national security for which everyone had hoped and prayed during World War II. Although it did not crystallize until 1947-1948, the Cold War came to pit what most Americans saw as democracy and free enterprise against a new totalitarian foe. Then, in late 1949, the Communist world broke the American monopoly on nuclear weaponry and extended its reach to China. The nation became preoccupied with the search for Communist subversives, and domestic anti-Communism became a pervasive force that distorted domestic politics, threatened civil liberties, and sometimes warped foreign policy.

The Cold War created a powerful anti-Communist consensus in American public life, spanning most of the political spectrum. Farthest to the right were the often naive, sometimes cynical, and always shrill subversive-hunters. Mainstream conservative anti-Communists, preoccupied with economic markets and military bases and allied to an emerging military-industrial complex,[8] argued that America could be safe in a hostile world only if it dominated the globe through alliances and an overwhelming nuclear arsenal. Liberal internationalists and even some on the far left, many of them intellectuals, saw America's welfare as inseparable from that of the rest of the world. Besides building alliances and dispensing military aid, the liberal internationalists urged the eradication of injustice around the globe, which they perceived as the breeding ground for Marxist revolution.

Liberal anti-Communists insisted that the United States could not morally qualify as the Free World's leader against Communist tyranny if it did not commit itself to social justice at home; conservative anti-Communists seldom saw the urgency of such a coupling. But not until after 1965, when the United States under a lib-

---

8. For this concept, first publicly mentioned in 1961 by the outgoing President Eisenhower, see Chapter 31.

eral administration combined a military stand against Communist revolutionaries abroad with a massive effort to enact Truman's agenda of domestic reform at home, did the Cold War consensus collapse.

SUGGESTED READING

Larry Ceplair and Steven Englund, *The Inquisition in Hollywood: Politics in the Film Community, 1930-1960* (1980). A study of the impact of McCarthyism on Hollywood and the motion picture industry.

Bruce Cumings, *The Origins of the Korean War*, 2 vols. (1990). The Korean conflict as seen as part of the United States's effort to "roll back" the Iron Curtain.

Alonzo Hamby, *Man of the People: A Life of Harry S. Truman* (1995). The best biography of the man from Missouri.

George Lipsitz, *Class and Culture in Cold War America: "A Rainbow at Midnight"* (1981). A history of American popular culture and civic aspirations in the immediate postwar period.

Elaine Tyler May, *Homeward Bound: American Families in the Cold War Era* (1988). An account of family life during the early Cold War with an emphasis on the roots of conformity and "the feminine mystique."

David M. Oshinsky, *A Conspiracy So Immense: The World of Joe McCarthy* (1983). A mini-biography of Joseph McCarthy and a political history of McCarthyism.

Randall B. Woods and Howard Jones, *Dawning of the Cold War: The United States' Quest for Order, 1947-1950* (1991). A description of the evolving confrontation between the United States and the Soviet Union that depicts U.S. policy as a reasonable if error-prone reaction to Stalinist aggression.

Daniel Yergin, *Shattered Peace: The Origins of the Cold War and the National Security State* (1977). An analysis of the early Cold War with an emphasis on the conflicting ideologies of Marxism-Leninism and liberal capitalism.

SUGGESTIONS FOR FURTHER READING

Paul S. Boyer, *By the Bomb's Early Light: American Thought and Culture at the Dawn of the Atomic Age* (1985).

John P. Craven, *The Silent War: The Cold War Battle Beneath the Sea* (2001).

Mary L. Dudziak, *Cold War Civil Rights* (2000).

Richard M. Fried, *The Russians Are Coming! The Russians Are Coming! Pageantry and Patriotism in Cold-War America* (1998).

Hal M. Friedman, *Creating an American Lake: United States Imperialism and Strategic Security in the Pacific Basin, 1945-1947* (2001).

John Lewis Gaddis, *Strategies of Containment: A Critical Appraisal of Postwar American National Security Policy* (1982).

John Lewis Gaddis, *We Now Know: Rethinking Cold War History* (1997).

John Lewis Gaddis, *Cold War Statesmen Confront the Bomb: Nuclear Diplomacy Since 1945* (1999).

Zachary Karabell, *Architects of Intervention: The United States, the Third World, and the Cold War, 1946-1962* (1999).

Melvyn P. Leffler, *A Preponderance of Power: National Security, the Truman Administration, and the Cold War* (1992).

Melvyn P. Leffler and Eric Foner, *The Specter of Communism: The United States and the Origins of the Cold War, 1917-1953* (1994).

David McCullough, *Truman* (1992).

Gregory Mitrovich, *Undermining the Kremlin: America's Strategy to Subvert the Soviet Bloc, 1947-1956* (2000).

Thomas D. Parrish, *Berlin in the Balance, 1945-1949: The Blockade, the Airlift, the first Major Battle of the Cold War* (1998).

James T. Patterson, *Grand Expectations: The United States, 1945-1974* (1995).

Richard H. Pells, *The Liberal Mind in a Conservative Age* (1985).

Arch Puddington, *Broadcasting Freedom: The Cold War Triumph of Radio Free Europe and Radio Liberty* (2000).

Ron T. Robin, *The Making of the Cold War Enemy: Culture and Politics in the Military-Intellectual Complex* (2001).

Lisle A. Rose, *The Cold War Comes to Main Street: America in 1950* (1999).

W. R. Smyser, *From Yalta to Berlin: The Cold War Struggle Over Germany* (1999).

Stephen J. Whitfield, *The Culture of the Cold War* (1996).

Randall B. Woods, *Fulbright: A Biography* (1995).

31 Containment, Contentment, Discontent: Eisenhower Republicanism and the Fifties

AMERICA AT MID-CENTURY was the world's greatest power, unrivaled militarily, economically, scientifically, and educationally. The Soviet Union challenged but trailed badly.

Despite the Cold War, the mood of the nation was optimistic. Dozens of giant corporations rode the boom to dizzying heights of size and power. The United States became the most prodigious consumer society in history, and unprecedented numbers of people defined themselves as middle-class. A majority of Americans believed that the future would be bright so long as political leaders provided a stable, secure public order that would protect the nation's prosperity.

The Republican Party thrived in such an environment. Internationally, during his two terms as president, Dwight Eisenhower confronted and contained Communism without involving the United States in war. At home, he accommodated the civil rights movement without encouraging it and criticized New Deal institutions without dismantling them. Republicans successfully resisted action on the liberal agenda proposed by Harry Truman without diminishing the federal government very much in size or power. Business interests gained the most from government activism.

The expansion of the middle class during the fifties bred both contentment and conformity. The majority voiced enthusiastic support for traditional beliefs in family, church, prosperity, and country. Television, which became ubiquitous, brought new significance to the term "mass culture," producing unprecedented cultural uniformity as millions watched the same news programs and entertainment every night.

Yet anxieties lurked under the surface. Internationally, the threat of Communism grew steadily more ominous. As the Soviet Union developed thermonuclear weapons and made spectacular progress in missile technology, the possibility of a nuclear holocaust became a frightening specter. Domestically, the African American struggle for civil rights turned into the consummate American moral reform of the twentieth century.

Breaking ranks from conformity, some Americans voiced discontent. Blacks were by far the most visible group to challenge the mood of self-satisfaction, but other dissenting intellectuals offered unsettling critiques of the culture. And teenagers — some of whom would be sixties rebels — embraced rock 'n' roll and idolized Hollywood symbols of rebellion.

DWIGHT D. EISENHOWER AND THE NEW REPUBLICANISM

The end of the Truman administration saw the United States deeply divided. Frustrated by the Korean stalemate, angry over price and wage controls, frightened of nuclear war, and anxious over McCarthy's charges of Communist infiltration, Americans longed for security and stability.

That is precisely what Dwight D. Eisenhower — universally known as "Ike" and famous for his friendly grin — and the Republican Party proposed to give the American people. The watchword of "new Republicanism" was moderation. Eisenhower was an orthodox conservative, favoring a balanced budget, a reduced federal role in American life, and states' rights. But he opposed trying to roll back the New Deal; the federal government, he agreed, should provide a safety net while guaranteeing equality of opportunity and promoting free enterprise. Although he did not embrace the civil rights movement, neither did he oppose it. He warned against the dangerous influence of the military-industrial complex, and he restrained military spending.

❧ The Election of 1952

Discontent was in the air as the 1952 presidential election approached. Beset by Republicans and the media, the Truman administration seemed to many corrupt, irresolute, and incompetent, and the president's standing in the polls hit rock bottom. Nonetheless, Republican leaders took nothing for granted. If another 1948

upset were to be averted, they would have to nominate an electable candidate.

Foreign policy issues divided Republicans. Senator Robert Taft was the choice of conservatives. Not, strictly speaking, an isolationist, Taft did favor a modified Fortress America strategy, in which the nation's security would be anchored by an alliance with Great Britain and island bases in the Pacific. But the eastern, more liberal Republicans — including Henry Cabot Lodge Jr., John Foster Dulles, and Thomas Dewey — remained powerful and internationalist in outlook. Their candidate was Ike, the architect of Allied victory in Europe.

Although he had never voted[1] and disdained the "pandering" aspects of democratic politics, Eisenhower considered Taft dangerously isolationist and slowly warmed to running for president — which he had declined to do in 1948. Belatedly, on June 12, 1952, he announced that he would resign as NATO commander to seek the Republican nomination.

A few weeks later, when the Republican convention opened in Chicago, Taft remained the favorite. But some delegates' credentials were contested. The general's supporters, including Lodge and California Senator Richard M. Nixon, saw to it that Eisenhower delegates got most of the contested seats. Then, with Taft backers seething, the convention nominated Eisenhower on the first ballot. Nixon, best known for his pursuit of domestic Communists, was rewarded with the vice-presidential slot.

The Democratic nomination was also up for grabs as the convention opened. At Truman's urging, Governor Adlai E. Stevenson of Illinois entered the race late, and he won the nomination on the third ballot. The vice-presidential nomination went to Senator John J. Sparkman of Alabama. The Democratic platform called for repeal of Taft-Hartley, enactment of the Truman civil rights program including a Fair Employment Practices Commission, and high price supports for agriculture.

Initially, Eisenhower tried to pose as a national leader above politics. Increasingly, however, he became convinced that his goals could not be realized without Republican victories at all levels. In a highly publicized meeting with Taft, Ike and his rival signed "articles of cooperation" to heal the ideological split in the party. The two men agreed on the need for fiscal responsibility, including a balanced budget, and promised to defend individual liberty and free enterprise against "creeping

---

1. Before World War II, career officers generally abstained from voting out of respect for civilian supremacy over the military.

socialism." In spite of McCarthy's attacks on Eisenhower's hero and mentor, General George Marshall, Ike endorsed the demagogue's bid for reelection and blasted the Truman administration for its supposedly lackluster performance in rooting Communist sympathizers out of the federal government. Furthermore, he charged, Truman's blunders had helped cause the Korean War. If elected, he promised, he would "go to Korea" to bring the war to an "early and honorable" end.

A Princeton-educated lawyer, Adlai Stevenson was witty, urbane, and self-effacing. His articulate attacks on Republicans and McCarthyites appealed to liberals and intellectuals, but he never established rapport with working-class Americans. The GOP attempted to portray Stevenson as an extreme liberal, though he was actually more conservative than Truman. He supported civil rights but believed that in most cases the enforcement of racial justice should be left to the states. Stevenson refused to back Truman on the repeal of Taft-Hartley, farm policy, or federal aid to education. During the campaign he attempted to portray Eisenhower as a political novice and criticized him for not standing up to McCarthy, but beyond that he refused to indulge in political posturing.

"Ike and Dick" appeared headed for an easy victory when in mid-October the New York *Post* charged that Nixon had used for personal expenses $18,000 from a "slush fund" raised by wealthy Californians for his political campaign. Eisenhower distanced himself from his running mate, declaring that everyone associated with his campaign had to be "clean as a hound's tooth." An audit cleared Nixon of doing anything illegal, but Eisenhower insisted that his running mate go on television and justify himself to the American people. In a famous broadcast from Hollywood, Nixon, his wife Pat beside him, denied any wrongdoing and pleaded that he was just an average man, struggling financially like other Americans. Pat owned "only a plain Republican cloth coat," not a mink. (Mink coats were then a symbol of Democratic corruption.) Only one gift from his supporters would he never give up, he said: a cute little black dog named Checkers, whom his young daughters loved. Though maudlin and self-serving, Nixon's "Checkers

Ike and Dick   General Eisenhower proved to be a tremendously effective campaigner in 1952. In these anxious times, Ike's friendly grin and welcoming wave reassured voters as much as his record as a winning World War II general.

Speech" was a masterful use of the new medium of television for establishing a political persona. Polls instantly showed that most Americans felt sympathy for Nixon. Eisenhower promptly and publicly embraced him.

Eisenhower and Nixon won a landslide victory, 33 million to 27 million in the popular vote and 442 to 89 in the electoral college. Presaging the later drift of the region toward the Republicans, Eisenhower broke the Democratic hold on the Solid South by carrying Texas, Tennessee, Florida, and Virginia. Ike's political coattails were long enough to give the Republicans majorities in both houses of Congress for only the second time since 1932.

❧ An American Hero

Dwight David Eisenhower was born in Dennison, Texas, on August 14, 1890, and grew up in Abilene, Kansas. In this agricultural community, not long removed from frontier times, young Eisenhower absorbed the values of small-town America. He was a good student and a superb athlete. Eisenhower was reared in a solid, religious, working-class family — his mother was a member of the River Brethren, a small pacifist German church. Lured by the promise of a free education, Eisenhower won an appointment to West Point through a competitive examination. He graduated in 1915 in the top half of his class but without academic distinction. After serving an uneventful tour during World War I as a tank instructor, Eisenhower graduated first in his class at the prestigious Command and General Staff College. After Pearl Harbor, General Marshall made Eisenhower chief of operations in recognition of the young officer's talent for planning and coordination. Subsequently Roosevelt put him in command of the European theater.

Eisenhower entered the White House with no direct exposure to political life. His military career had accustomed him to hierarchy and command, and he initially found the give and take of conventional politics frustrating. Yet Eisenhower's success in the army owed much to innate political skills. As supreme commander of Allied forces in Europe, Eisenhower had had to reconcile divergent interests, conciliate powerful and difficult personalities, and direct vast operations. When he became president, opponents portrayed him as intellectually superficial — interested mostly in golf and bridge, in Westerns and hunting. In fact, Eisenhower worked quite effectively behind the scenes to achieve his objectives, by persuading, threatening, and conciliating.[2] He was particularly at home in the international realm. That his activism was frequently directed toward the static goals of peace and prosperity made him no less effective.

At home, the new president proved to be a traditional conservative. He wanted to cut taxes, balance the budget, shrink the federal government, and promote business interests. So laden with businessmen was Eisenhower's cabinet that it was dubbed "eight millionaires and a plumber." (The latter was Secretary of Labor Martin Durkin, head of the Plumbers and Steamfitters Union. He soon left.) His secretary of defense, Charles Wilson (the former head of General Motors Corporation), told the Senators at his confirmation hearing that "what was good for the country was good for G.M. and vice versa."

Adlai Stevenson Democratic candidate Adlai Stevenson inherited FDR's large following among non-southern black voters (African Americans in the South generally could not vote). But he had no special rapport with them—nor, indeed, with most ordinary Americans. Witty and erudite-sounding, he was widely regarded as an "egg-head," or intellectual, and not just because of his bald pate. Here, African American journalist Ethel L. Payne interviews him in 1952.

Unlike his most conservative cabinet members, Eisenhower had no desire to dismantle all New Deal agencies. He described himself as a "conservative when it comes to money and liberal when it comes to human beings." Despite his background, Eisenhower was determined to contain military spending. He feared the insatiable appetite for defense spending, and in his farewell speech to the nation at the end of his presidency he would echo radical political warnings against a "military-industrial complex," which had a vested interest in the Cold War.

Republicans delivered on at least a portion of their economic promises. Taxes were cut for individuals and corporations, and Eisenhower submitted a budget that reduced spending for fiscal 1954 by $6.5 billion (then a significant amount of money). Savings were achieved by scaling down foreign aid, defense spending, and the federal bureaucracy; 200,000 civilian employees were removed from federal payrolls during Eisenhower's first term. At the same time, the Federal Reserve raised interest rates and reserve requirements.

These deflationary policies sent the economy into a

2. Even his much-derided tendency to give rambling, unclear answers to awkward press-conference questions had a purpose: to avoid precision when that seemed undesirable. Privately, he could write and speak with great clarity.

mild recession in late 1953. Fiscal conservatives learned that reduced federal expenditures coupled with deflationary monetary policies slowed rather than accelerated economic growth. Moreover, the downturn reduced tax collections, which along with tax cuts made balancing the budget difficult.

These economic troubles did not dent Ike's popularity. Following his overwhelming reelection in 1956 (see below), Eisenhower adopted a more flexible economic policy. Abandoning his goal of a balanced budget, the president supported government spending to restore prosperity. As a result the federal budget grew steadily, from $29.5 billion in 1950 to $76.5 billion in 1960. But Eisenhower could balance the budget in only three of his eight years in office. Increased government spending did not prevent another economic tailspin in 1957-58. The Eisenhower recession differed from previous slumps in that prices remained high while investment and employment figures continued to drop. In 1958 the Federal Reserve eased credit and leading economic indices improved, but the revival was short-lived. By 1960 the economy was again in trouble, with unemployment hovering around 7 percent and steel mills, then the engine of the economy, operating at only 50 percent capacity. Democrat John F. Kennedy's promise to "get the country moving again" economically was one of the reasons for his narrow victory in the 1960 election.

Curtailing Federal Influence

Even during the good economic times of the fifties, the farm sector remained weak. The system of price supports initiated during the New Deal had become a vicious cycle; the more the federal government spent to prop up prices, the more farmers produced. Increased production sent prices still lower, forcing the government to shoulder an even larger burden. Following a heated battle in Congress between farm state Democrats and Republican budget cutters, the administration won passage of the Agricultural Act of 1954. It established flexible price supports, effectively lowering guaranteed prices on agricultural commodities to 75 to 90 percent of parity.[3]

As surpluses bulged out of storage elevators and government costs surged, the administration tried New Deal–style programs to reduce production. In 1956 a

"soil bank" program was established, which paid farmers to take a percentage of their acreage out of production. Designed primarily to cut production, the program also had the ecologically laudable intent of allowing some farmland to lie fallow and replenish itself. Once again, however, modern technology and farmers' ingenuity combined to thwart the scheme. Farmers used scientific farming and chemical fertilizers to produce more on fewer acres. By 1958, Washington was spending more than ever on price supports.

The Eisenhower administration tried hard to keep the federal government out of areas it had not yet entered. California and the Gulf states had long pressed the federal government to recognize their ownership and right to exploit the rich oil deposits off their coasts. During World War II and the Truman years, Washington refused to do so. Eisenhower came into office pledged to support the oil states, and in 1953 Congress passed the Submerged Lands Act, which granted to states title to coastal lands within their "historic" boundaries.

Not surprisingly, the president was an outspoken critic of public power, including the Tennessee Valley Authority. Dismantling the TVA was a political impossibility, much as Eisenhower would have liked to do so, but he was determined to prevent further expansion of public power. The administration soon became embroiled in an effort to force the TVA, rather than expand its capacity, to buy additional power from a private syndicate, Dixon-Yates. A political battle loomed, especially when administration critics charged that special interests would benefit from the deal. Threatened by a potential scandal, the embarrassed administration was relieved when the city of Memphis decided to build an energy facility that would relieve the shortage and add generating capacity.

The Interstate Highway System

By 1953 the deterioration of the nation's transportation infrastructure demanded serious action. Since the close of World War II the railroads, chronically in debt, had cut passenger service and abandoned thousands of miles of track. The nation's road system, a state and local responsibility, was totally inadequate to handle the burgeoning automobile and truck traffic.

The decision facing the federal government was not whether to act but what mode of transportation to support. Throughout 1955, railroads, auto manufacturers, and road construction companies slugged it out for billions of federal dollars earmarked for the nation's

---

3. "Parity" was the objective born of Henry Wallace's New Deal–era farm policies. It was the ratio of farm prices to farm income that had prevailed during the relatively prosperous years 1909-1914, supposedly the golden age of American farming.

infrastructure. Highway safety and civil defense experts weighed in on the side of the road lobby, arguing that an interstate highway system would reduce traffic deaths and facilitate evacuation of populated areas in a nuclear attack. The American military agreed, having gained a profound respect for Hitler's fabled Autobahn system in Germany.

In 1956 Congress passed, and Eisenhower signed, the Interstate Highway Act — the largest public works program in American history. The act won the support of Republicans interested in government-business co-operation and of Democrats concerned about stimulating employment; for the administration, it promised a powerful boost to the economy. Massive federal subsidies were provided for an interstate system initially consisting of 42,000 miles of controlled access, four- to eight-lane highways linking major population centers, to be completed by 1970 at a cost of $27.5 billion. Washington provided 90 percent of the money.

Building the interstate system turned the American love affair with the automobile into a tumultuous marriage. Once completed, the system allowed Americans an even higher degree of mobility, but it also spelled doom for U.S. passenger rail traffic, increased Americans' dependence on automobiles and imported petroleum, and hastened inner-city decay.

❧ The Election of 1956

Although liberal Republicans (like liberal Democrats) grumbled about the president's "blandness," and some conservatives dismissed him as a weak-kneed moderate, the only question about Eisenhower's renomination concerned his health after he suffered a heart attack in 1955. He recovered and announced that he would run for reelection. The Democrats once again selected Stevenson and named a crusading investigator of organized crime, Senator Estes Kefauver, as their vice-presidential candidate. (Kefauver beat out the handsome young Senator from Massachusetts, John F. Kennedy, in an open convention fight for the number-two slot, giving Kennedy valuable exposure on national television.)

The 1956 election lacked the tension and excitement of the 1952 campaign. The country was prosperous, at peace, and (after the downfall of McCarthy) relatively united. The Republican campaign, observed one political pundit, was as smooth and dent-proof as an "I Like Ike" button. Stevenson labored gamely to outline an alternative to "the politics of complacency," but in vain.

Building the Interstate   In Utah in 1960, workers descend a cut through the mountains to set explosives. Launched by the Eisenhower administration, the Interstate Highway System was the greatest public-works project ever undertaken in the United States, dwarfing anything attempted by the New Deal.

Eisenhower won in a landslide, capturing 457 electoral votes to Stevenson's 73. His margin in popular votes was a whopping 9 million out of 62 million cast.

Ike's popularity and his appropriation of the political center had allowed him to make serious inroads into the New Deal coalition. He appealed to the expanding pool of white-collar, suburban voters, both Republicans and independents. Furthermore, the president demonstrated the potential for the Republican Party to tap the innate conservatism of southern white voters, long a loyal minority within the Democratic coalition. Most of all, Americans simply liked Ike and judged him a strong and honorable leader. Amid foreign crises during the 1956 election (see below), most Americans deemed Eisenhower to be the cool-headed and experienced leader that the nation needed.

Eisenhower could not transfer his popularity to his party. Blue-collar voters in the North might "like Ike," but they were still loyal to their Democratic congressional representatives. And in the South, although Ike won many white votes in a region where few blacks could vote, at the state and local levels only Democratic organizations existed, again assuring the Democrats scores of seats in Congress. Thus, in 1956 the Democrats retained control of both houses of Congress, making Eisenhower the first president since Zachary Taylor in 1849 to begin his term with both the Senate and House in opposition hands.

Eisenhower remained popular during his second term, although his prestige suffered from a series of reverses. Most of the setbacks had to do with foreign affairs, but a scandal in 1958, in which the powerful White House chief of staff was accused of influence peddling, forced the president to reshuffle his top advisers. The Democrats increased their majorities in both houses of Congress in 1958. In the ensuing deadlock, no substantial legislation was produced during Ike's second term.

THE SECOND RECONSTRUCTION

The African American struggle for civil rights overshadowed all other domestic concerns during Eisenhower's second term. In 1954, the long legal battle for equality, led by an uncompromising group of young NAACP attorneys, won its greatest victory when the Supreme Court struck down the nation's segregated system of public education. Then, in the second half of the decade, a new generation of southern black leaders turned the civil rights movement into a powerful yet peaceful popular protest. A majority of southern whites resisted — some for ugly, racist reasons and others because they were convinced that such momentous social change could only come slowly. But by the end of the decade the civil rights movement clearly transcended the courts and ordinary politics. The courage and resolve of the movement's leaders and their young supporters, and the obvious righteousness of their cause, caught the world's attention. Civil rights, the consum-

mate American moral crusade of the twentieth century — and the one reform movement that genuinely moved most mainstream Americans — was well underway by the end of Eisenhower's presidency.

So important was the mid-century civil rights movement in the long perspective of the nation's history that it is often known as the "Second Reconstruction." A century after the Civil War destroyed slavery and promised African Americans citizenship and the vote, tasks left undone and gains reversed after the first Reconstruction Era were now addressed by blacks and their white supporters.

❧ *Patterns of Inequality*

In some ways, African Americans lost ground in the early fifties. Reversing a pattern begun during the Depression, African American income began to decline relative to white. Between 1937 and 1952, black earnings climbed to 57 percent of that of whites, but during the next five years it dropped to 53 percent. Throughout the South, segregation remained firmly institutionalized — in schools, public transportation, hotels and restaurants, social clubs, hospitals, the work place, and frequently labor unions. Neither Roosevelt nor Truman had followed up the Supreme Court's 1944 invalidation of the white primary, which in the largely one-party South had disfranchised blacks. The discriminatory application of existing laws, violence, threats of economic reprisals, and other forms of intimidation kept the voting booth lily-white in most of the South. In eleven southern states in 1957, only 25 percent of African Americans were registered — and far fewer voted. By the fifties, lynching was uncommon, though as late as 1955 a black youth visiting from Chicago was killed in Mississippi for "admiring" a white woman.

There were fewer legal and institutional barriers in the North, but informal racism existed there too. Most African Americans were trapped in low-paying jobs. Northern black workers earned about $800 per year more than their southern counterparts, not an inconsiderable sum in view of the fact that in 1954 the average yearly income of non-white families was $2,410. Still, black families lagged far behind their white counterparts, whose average annual income was $4,339. Banks and insurance companies openly discriminated against blacks, and many white social institutions shunned them. Discrimination in the North sometimes took legal form, such as restrictive housing covenants that kept African Americans (and often Jews) from moving outside segregated areas. President Eisenhower was ambiguous toward the issue of civil rights, and his advisers were divided. During the 1952 campaign Ike expressed hopes for a United States that would provide "a true equality of opportunity," but he was convinced that the federal government must do nothing smacking of "statism" or "paternalism." He cautioned that the executive could do little to bring about reforms that require support from society as a whole. Thus he opposed reestablishing Truman's Fair Employment Practices Commission, insisting that compulsory federal intervention not replace state, local, and private responsibility for preventing job discrimination.

❧ Judicial Action and Southern Resistance

Blocked in Congress and faced with a passive executive, African Americans turned increasingly to the courts. From its founding in 1909, the National Association for the Advancement of Colored People had recognized the potential of a legal strategy of confronting white America with the Constitution's embedded civil rights guarantees. NAACP lawyers now targeted public-education segregation.

In 1950 Thurgood Marshall, one of the NAACP's brightest young lawyers, argued the case of George McLaurin, a black student admitted to the University of Oklahoma on "a segregated basis." McLaurin was allowed to attend class with whites but was required to sit in a segregated area in the classroom, as well as in the library and cafeteria. Marshall argued that this physical separation denied McLaurin access to the company of his professors and the intellectual stimulation of his fellow students. It was, moreover, a humiliating badge of inferiority. In *McLaurin v. Board of Regents* the justices ruled in McLaurin's favor, declaring that equality required far more than states providing comparable physical facilities and funds for the education of both races. In 1950, in *Sweatt v. Painter,* the Court went further, finding that separate legal education was inherently unequal. The decision forced the University of Texas to admit a black student who chose not to attend a state-supported law school for African Americans.

In the early 1950s NAACP lawyers concentrated on making local and state authorities live up to the letter of the 1896 *Plessy v. Ferguson* decision, which had called for "separate but equal" facilities. Increasingly, however, social scientists argued that "separate" could never be equal. To challenge segregation directly constituted a dramatic change, but, after much debate, Marshall and

his colleagues decided to do so. By the spring of 1954 the NAACP was pressing five separate cases that challenged the principle of educational segregation.

The first to reach the Supreme Court was the suit of Linda Brown, a Topeka, Kansas, schoolgirl who walked past a neighborhood white school to attend an all-black facility farther away. Rallying impressive sociological and psychological evidence, Marshall argued that separation implied inferiority. Moreover, denying access to any educational institutions purely on the basis of race violated the Fourteenth Amendment's equal-protection guarantee. On May 17, 1954, the Supreme Court, in *Brown v. Board of Education of Topeka,* unanimously agreed. "Does segregation of children in public schools solely on the basis of race . . . deprive the children of the minority group of equal educational opportunities?" asked Chief Justice Earl Warren, writing for the Court. He answered: "We believe that it does. . . . Separate educational facilities are inherently unequal. . . . Any language in *Plessy v. Ferguson* contrary to these findings is rejected."

The *Brown* decision boldly struck down segregation in American public schools, a historic symbol of racial inequality that had been legally mandated in seventeen states and was optional in four others (not all of them southern). The critical issue now became enforcement. Millions of white southerners were determined to defend segregation, and millions of other Americans who accepted the logic and morality of *Brown* believed that the change could only come gradually. Eisenhower was one of them. "The decisions," he confided to an aide, "set back progress in the South at least fifteen years." He also privately regretted having nominated Earl Warren to be chief justice.

The Court itself was loath to follow up on *Brown*. In 1955 the justices simply placed responsibility for implementation on local authorities; under the supervision of the federal courts, they were ordered to proceed with desegregation plans with "all deliberate speed."

White supremacists in the South quickly began organizing to fight *Brown*. By the end of 1955, more than five hundred segregationist organizations, including a revived Ku Klux Klan, were rallying the opposition. White Citizens Councils were formed in many communities across the South, often with the tacit approval of local leaders. During the 1950s these organizations used ostracism, boycotts, and sometimes violence to block public school integration.

More ominous was the resistance of the responsible southern political leaders. In 1956, nineteen southern Senators and eighty-one members of the House, most of them powerful Democrats with years of seniority, signed a "Southern Manifesto" that pledged to use "all lawful means" to stop the integration of southern schools. The manifesto accused the Court of a "clear abuse of judicial power" in its attempt to "legislate, in derogation of the authority of Congress." They argued that the decision had created an "explosive and dangerous condition" in the South that was being "inflamed by outside meddlers." Virginia's Senator Harry Flood Byrd called for "massive resistance." Invoking the memory of John C. Calhoun, the Georgia, Mississippi, and Virginia legislatures passed resolutions of "interposition" that asserted the supremacy of state authority over federal authority and invalidated all mandates requiring integration.

Integration proceeded slowly in 1956 with few real success stories. Louisville, Kentucky, successfully integrated 85,000 white and 13,600 black students under a well-prepared program that Eisenhower praised, but efforts to enroll a few black children in several other places in Tennessee and Kentucky resulted in mob protests that were quieted only when the governors called in the National Guard.

The first major test of *Brown* and the federal government's will to enforce it came in Arkansas in the fall of 1957. On the day following the announcement of the school integration decision, the Little Rock school board instructed Superintendent Virgil T. Blossom to draw up a plan for compliance. Neither Blossom nor the board was enthusiastic about integration, but neither did they wish to defy the Supreme Court. Then, with nine black children scheduled to enter Central High on September 3, 1957, Governor Orval Faubus appeared on television the evening before. To "avoid violence," he declared, the state's National Guard would be stationed around Central to prevent the black children from entering. On September 4 the "Little Rock Nine" braved the mob that had gathered at Central, only to find the National Guard barring the way.

On September 21 the local federal judge ordered Faubus to cease his obstructionist tactics. The gover-

The End of Segregation   Often it took a long, hard struggle to end segregation in the South, but not always. Here, on September 8, 1954, on the first day of classes and just weeks after the Supreme Court's *Brown* decision, an elementary school is integrated in Fort Myer, Virginia. This school served the children of military personnel, and immediate desegregation was ordered by the Defense Department. The children seem to take it all in stride. All too frequently during the decade or more that followed, white parents and communities did not.

nor promptly removed the National Guard, departed for a southern governors' conference, and predicted violence if black students again attempted to enter Central. On Monday morning, September 23, desegregation began under local police protection. The nine black youths, carefully trained by local civil-rights leaders, walked through a gauntlet of abuse. By lunchtime the mob outside the school had become so large and belligerent that the students were removed, and that afternoon the mayor asked the Eisenhower administration for federal troops to restore order. The president immediately federalized the National Guard. By evening, units of the 101st Airborne had arrived in Little Rock. The following morning federal troops escorted African American students into Central and cleared the mobs from the school area.

Little Rock had become the focus of southern white resistance. "I must vigorously protest the highhanded

***Brown v. Board of Education,* 1954**

In its 1954 decision in Brown v. Board of Education of Topeka, *the Supreme Court broke with the doctrine, established fifty-eight years earlier in* Plessy v. Ferguson, *that schools for blacks and whites could be "separate but equal."*

We come then to the question presented: Does segregation of children in public schools solely on the basis of race, even though the physical facilities and other "tangible" factors may be equal, deprive the children of the minority group of equal educational opportunities? We believe that it does. . . .

Segregation of white and colored children in public schools has a detrimental effect upon the colored children. The impact is greater when it has the sanction of the law, for the policy of separating the races is usually interpreted as denoting the inferiority of the negro group. A sense of inferiority affects the motivation of a child to learn. Segregation with the sanction of law, therefore, has a tendency to [retard] the educational and mental development of negro children and to deprive them of some of the benefits they would receive in a racial[ly] integrated school system.

Whatever may have been the extent of psychological knowledge at the time of Plessy v. Ferguson, this finding is amply supported by modern authority. Any language in Plessy v. Ferguson contrary to this finding is rejected.

We conclude that, in the field of public education, the doctrine of "separate but equal" has no place. Separate educational facilities are inherently unequal. Therefore, we hold that the plaintiffs and others similarly situated for whom the actions have been brought are, by reason of the segregation complained of, deprived of the equal protection of the laws guaranteed by the Fourteenth Amendment.

and illegal methods being employed by the armed forces of the United States . . . who are carrying out your orders to mix the races in the public schools of Little Rock, Arkansas," Georgia's powerful Senator Richard Russell cabled Eisenhower. Segregationist agitators poured into the city from across the South, and Central looked like an armed camp. The events in Little Rock were reported in depth on national television, shocking viewers with images of the white resisters' rage and touching them with the daily ordeal of the African American children. The incident began to sensitize white, middle-class Americans to the dignity and morality of the black quest for civil rights. In addition, the federal government, however reluctantly, had at last used force to support integration and quell racial violence.

᪉ *New Strategies and New Leaders*

Perhaps the most difficult task facing twentieth-century civil rights leaders was convincing African Americans that they controlled their own fate. By the mid-1950s, however, a new sense of black solidarity and hope began to emerge, and civil rights became a true mass movement.

Some of the landmarks in the civil rights movement were planned events, but others were spontaneous moments that changed American history. On December 1, 1955, in Montgomery, Alabama, black seamstress Rosa Parks refused to give up her seat on a bus and move to the segregated rear. Parks, who was later dubbed "the

mother of the Civil Rights movement," had long been a civil rights activist in Montgomery and had worked for the NAACP, but her act of defiance on this evening was an expression of personal dignity by a weary woman who insisted that she would endure no more degradation. She was arrested. The next night, African American community leaders gathered at the Dexter Avenue Baptist Church to discuss possible responses. That evening, with the church's young pastor, Martin Luther King, Jr., in the forefront, the black leaders of Montgomery formed the Montgomery Improvement Association and called for a bus boycott. It lasted for months and cost the city dearly.

The boycott originally aimed to force the bus authority to make seating available on a first-come, first-served basis. But after Mrs. Parks decided to appeal her conviction, the organizers set their sights on getting Alabama's segregated-seating law invalidated. An effective carpooling system enabled the protesters to bring the municipal transport system to the brink of bankruptcy. The boycott ended only after the Supreme Court invalidated Alabama's segregation laws in November 1956, scoring another major victory for NAACP attorneys. The boycott drew massive coverage by the national and international media, making King famous and affording the boycotters a degree of protection.

The Rosa Parks incident sparked the first mass movement of what became known as the Second Reconstruction, opening a decade of public protest led by southern blacks. More than any other person, Martin Luther King,

Jr., provided the philosophy and personal inspiration for the movement. As the child of a prominent black minister in Atlanta, King had been spared the grosser aspects of southern racism and thus seemed an unlikely candidate to galvanize the impoverished, poorly educated African American population, but King stepped into a role with an extensive tradition: ministers had long been spokespersons for the black community. A graduate of Morehouse College, a respected all-black institution in Atlanta, King secured a seminary education at Crozer Seminary in Pennsylvania and earned a Ph.D. in theology from Boston University. King's studies familiarized him with neo-orthodoxy (his Ph.D. thesis was on the theologians Paul Tillich and Henry Wieman), as well as the social gospel writers of the late nineteenth and early twentieth centuries. As a student, he was intrigued by Henry David Thoreau's writings on non-violent civil disobedience and by Mohandas Gandhi's application of these concepts in the Indian liberation struggle.

This privileged background prepared King for his role of leadership, but his basic persona was that of black preacher. By the end of his first year of service at the Dexter Street Baptist Church in Montgomery, King had become a charismatic preacher, and his eloquence raised the Montgomery protest to an exalted moral level. "No white person will be taken from his home by a hooded Negro mob and brutally murdered," he told the group assembled in his church the evening after the arrest of Rosa Parks. "We will be guided by the highest principles of law and order." When King was indicted for violating Alabama's anti-boycott law, he responded: "If we are arrested every day, if we are exploited every day, if we are trampled over every day, don't ever let anyone pull you so low as to hate them. We must use the weapon of love. We must have compassion and understanding for those who hate us." The Montgomery confrontation had unveiled a prophet who in the years ahead would prick the consciences of millions of his fellow Americans in both North and South; his persuasive genius was recognized in 1964 when he became the youngest Nobel Peace Prize winner.

CONFRONTING INTERNATIONAL COMMUNISM: THE EISENHOWER STRATEGY OF CONTAINMENT

Despite his election-year lambasting of the Truman administration in 1952 for "losing" China and failing to "roll back" the Iron Curtain, Eisenhower was not fundamentally at odds with American postwar foreign policy. As NATO supreme commander under Truman, he had filled a key position in America's containment scheme. He believed that monolithic "international Communism," directed from Moscow, threatened global peace and American security, and that as leader of the Free World the United States must resist Soviet goals through military alliances and foreign aid. Though the Eisenhower administration never "rolled back" the Iron Curtain, neither the Soviet Union nor "Red China" could expand their empires significantly on Ike's watch. And he contained these global rivals' challenge without fighting the "brushfire" wars that plagued his predecessor and would bedevil his successors.

✣ *John Foster Dulles: Moralist and Pragmatist*

Eisenhower's foreign policy philosophy paralleled that of his powerful secretary of state, John Foster Dulles. A partner in a prestigious New York law firm, Dulles was the grandson of one secretary of state and the nephew of another. As a prominent Presbyterian layman, he had helped plan the postwar international order and had been deeply troubled by the unleashing of the threat of nuclear war in 1945. An intelligent, intense man, Dulles had written extensively on international relations and doubtless would have been Thomas Dewey's secretary of state had he been elected in 1948. As Eisenhower's chief diplomat, Dulles earned a reputation as a hard-line anti-Communist. Sometimes he talked of going "to the brink of war" to defend Free World interests — leading critics to define his foreign policy as "brinkmanship." For him, Communist China and the Soviet Union were not only dangerous, but also evil. Such words as "immoral," "banditry," and "enslavement" laced Dulles's speeches about the Soviets.

But with a few glaring exceptions, Dulles proved to be a capable crisis manager and a flexible negotiator. Much of his rhetoric was designed to placate conservative Republicans.

In practice, Eisenhower and Dulles quickly demonstrated that they had no intention of risking World War III to liberate the "captive peoples" of Eastern Europe. In June 1953 workers in East Germany rioted to protest factory speedups and food shortages. When Soviet tanks put down the uprising, Washington ventured only to "deplore" the action and praise the heroism of the rioters.

In 1956 the Eisenhower administration confronted once again a test of its willingness to free "captive peoples." Stalin had died in 1953, and for two years his would-be successors had struggled for ascendancy. In 1955 Nikita Khrushchev emerged from the pack to become first secretary of the Communist Party of the Soviet Union. The next year, at the CPSU's Twentieth Congress, he exposed many of Stalin's crimes and hinted at a relaxation of repression.

Encouraged, that fall Hungarian dissidents tried to institute democratic reforms. Quickly, their protests escalated into a full-scale anti-Soviet rebellion. The United States had no intention of intervening, but Radio Free Europe broadcasts urged Hungarians to fight — and irresponsibly implied that Western help would be forthcoming. On November 4, 1956, Soviet tanks rolled into Budapest, resisted by rebels with Molotov cocktails and small arms. Thirty thousand Hungarians and 7,000 Soviet soldiers died. Thousands of Hungarian refugees fled, and many eventually resettled in the United States. Over empty protests from Washington, Communism was forcibly restored in Hungary, albeit at the cost of considerable embarrassment to the Soviet Union.

❧ Leashing Chiang

A corollary to the Eisenhower administration's loose talk of liberating Eastern Europe was its promise to "unleash" Chiang Kai-shek (Jiang Jieshi) to reconquer the Chinese mainland. Chiang and his Nationalists had fled to Taiwan (also called Formosa) in 1949, but they still claimed to be the only lawful government of all China — a claim that the United States vigorously backed. In reality, Taiwan was under threat of "liberation" by the Communist People's Republic of China, which the United States refused to recognize and had blocked from entering the UN. In late 1954, PRC artillery batteries began intensive bombardment of Quemoy and Matsu, two tiny Nationalist-held islands just off the mainland. Fearful that the shelling was a prelude to a general attack on Taiwan, Dulles signed a Mutual Defense Treaty with Chiang.

In January 1955, after the Communists seized another tiny Nationalist offshore island, Eisenhower asked Congress for authorization to use American troops to defend Taiwan. He refused to say whether "related islands in friendly hands" would also be covered, but both houses readily passed the Formosa Resolution. The Chinese Communists stopped shelling Quemoy and Matsu for a time, but resumed in August 1958. By then, Chiang had stationed fully one-third of his army on the two islands. Eisenhower announced

that the United States would fight to defend the two islands, but Dulles, less belligerently, declared that Chiang had been "rather foolish" in so distributing his troops. The secretary of state indirectly signaled to Beijing that if China would agree to a de facto cease-fire, he would persuade Chiang to reduce his garrisons on the disputed islands. The United States, he added, had "no commitment of any kind" to aid the Nationalists in regaining the mainland. In response, the Chinese Communists eased their rhetoric, but they reserved the right to shell Quemoy and Matsu on alternate days of the week.

❧ Nationalism and Marxism in the Third World

A Cold War battleground that would be much more serious in the long run was shaping up in Southeast Asia. Despite massive economic aid from the Truman administration, the French effort to maintain a colonial foothold in the region was near collapse by 1954. Gambling, the French commander in Vietnam concentrated 13,000 troops near the northern town of Dienbienphu. He hoped to stop supplies from China reaching the Communist Vietminh insurgents and to draw Vietminh general Vo Nguyen Giap into a pitched battle in which superior French firepower would prevail. Instead, in March a Vietminh army of nearly 50,000 surrounded the isolated garrison. In the midst of a horrific, 56-day-long siege, the French chief of staff arrived in Washington and informed the Eisenhower administration that only direct U.S. military intervention could save the day. Dulles and Nixon supported air strikes to relieve the beleaguered French. But Eisenhower, after getting negative signals from congressional leaders and the British, sent the French emissary home empty-handed. On May 7, 1954, the Vietminh's red flag went up over Dienbienphu, marking a stunning victory of Asian rebels over a modern Western army. The next morning at Geneva delegates from nine countries assembled to decide the fate of Indochina.

By the time the Geneva Conference opened, the Vietminh controlled most of northern Vietnam, the Communist-led Pathet Lao was fighting French colonial rule in Laos, and the war-weary French were ready to abandon Southeast Asia. The United States refused to participate in the conference lest it be tainted with the inevitable compromise and be bound by its outcome, but Dulles worked behind the scenes to ensure that at least part of Vietnam remained non-Communist. Under the terms of the Geneva Accords, signed in June, Cambodia and Laos obtained independence and Vietnam was divided at the seventeenth parallel, the north ruled by Vietminh leader Ho Chi Minh and the south by a pro-French regime. All foreign troops were to leave Vietnam within a year, and an international commission was to supervise nationwide elections scheduled for July 1956.

As in Korea, a "temporary" dividing line hardened into an impermeable boundary. In the South a staunch Catholic, Ngo Dinh Diem, became prime minister and then a dictatorial president. With American support, Diem rejected unification elections in 1956, knowing that the Vietminh would win. Bitter but determined, the Communists lay low and built up military strength.

Concerned about keeping Communism out of the Western Hemisphere, in 1948 the United States created a hemisphere-wide collective security organization, the Organization of American States. Latin American nations were far more concerned about the deplorable state of their economies than about the international Communist menace. Regional leaders appealed to the United States for a "Marshall Plan for the Americas," an aid package that would convert their coffee, banana, beef, wheat, and mineral-producing economies into modern, balanced economies that could raise living standards. But U.S. policymakers' top postwar priority was rebuilding Western Europe and Japan. Meanwhile U.S. corporations that had invested heavily in Latin America before World War II were intent on protecting those interests. Often those same corporations also regarded Western Europe and Japan as better places to invest fresh capital. Clearly, both government and business decision-makers in the U.S. tended to regard Latin America as a Cold War sideshow. This attitude was readily communicated to — and understood by — Latin Americans, feeding anti-*yanqui* anger everywhere "south of the border."

The Eisenhower administration was more willing to intervene militarily in Latin America than elsewhere in the world, and it soon confronted what it interpreted as a Soviet effort to establish a beachhead in the Western Hemisphere. In 1951 Colonel Jacobo Arbenz Guzman became president of Guatemala. In the name of social justice and economic modernization, he began confiscating large landholdings and taxing the rich more heavily. Washington paid little attention until August 1953, when the Guatemalan government seized lands belonging to the United Fruit Company.

Shortly thereafter, the State Department charged Guatemala with "openly playing the communist game."

On May 17, 1954, the State Department announced that 1,900 tons of arms from Communist Czechoslovakia had arrived in Guatemala, dangerously tipping the military balance in Central America. Hurriedly, Washington concluded security pacts with neighboring Nicaragua and Honduras. A Guatemalan exile force began training in Honduras with the CIA's help, and on June 18 these few hundred men invaded their homeland. Deserted by the army, the Arbenz regime collapsed. Washington immediately recognized a new conservative government and extended it substantial economic aid. The White House and State Department were convinced that the United States had helped an indigenous anti-Communist movement thwart a "Red" takeover in the strategically important Caribbean basin. To many Latin Americans, however, it appeared that the United States had once again participated in a thinly veiled intervention in an effort to protect powerful vested interests.

❧ *The New Look for Defense*

As the Guatemalan episode demonstrated, Eisenhower, Dulles, and Secretary of Defense Wilson deemed covert operations in which U.S. interests were defended by local political factions and paramilitaries as far preferable to direct American intervention. Allen Dulles — John Foster's brother, who headed the CIA — strongly agreed. The Korean conflict had convinced these and other Republican leaders that it was a mistake to get bogged down in a conventional war. Even had Eisenhower wanted to fight a Korean-type operation, he would have found it difficult because of the weakened state of America's conventional military forces. The neglect was intentional, a byproduct of the administration's defense strategy. Treasury secretary George Humphrey and other administration leaders believed that big, expensive government, with bloated defense budgets, would undermine the currency, drain private capital, and do what the Soviet Union could never do — destroy America from within. Humphrey and Secretary of Defense Wilson ensured that total military expenditures fell from about $50 billion in 1954 to $35 billion in 1957.

Yet the Communist challenge was real and global. Early in Eisenhower's first term, he and his closest advisers settled on a strategy that would reconcile a reduced budget with a militantly anti-Communist foreign policy.

"Massive retaliation" was the sobering name John Foster Dulles gave to the administration's strategic defense policy. In any direct confrontation with international Communism, America would brandish its nuclear arsenal. To get "more bang for the buck," the Pentagon concentrated funding on the air force, specifically the Strategic Air Command (SAC) — which in a nuclear war would drop the atomic bombs. (Massive retaliation, of course, was a credible threat only if the United States maintained superiority in weaponry and delivery systems.)

Besides massive retaliation, the other foundation of Dulles's containment strategy was a series of interlocking alliances. He sought to build a comprehensive military fence around the Sino-Soviet Bloc. In 1955, at Manila, Dulles presided over creation of the Southeast Asia Treaty Organization (SEATO) — a mutual security alliance of the United States, Great Britain, France, Australia, New Zealand, the Philippines, Thailand, and Pakistan. That same year he sponsored another mutual defense treaty, the Central Treaty Organization (CENTO) that brought together Great Britain, Turkey, Iraq, Iran, and Pakistan.

❧ America and the Third World

These alliances were of dubious value. Many of the new nations emerging from colonial rule in the 1950s and 1960s chose to remain neutral in the Cold War — so much so that these countries began to be referred to as the "Third World," aligned neither with the capitalist West (the "First World") nor with the Communist Bloc

(the "Second World"). These "nonaligned" nations, led by India, the "world's largest democracy," were deemed by Dulles to be "immoral" because of their embrace of neutrality. The Soviet Union wooed Third World nations, seeking to project its power not through military aggression but rather by forging ideological links with anti-colonial revolutionary movements and by offering nonaligned governments economic and military aid. In the decades ahead, Third World nations would "tilt" toward one of the superpowers or the other in accordance with their own self-interest.

America's quest for Third World allies was fraught with difficulties. Dulles's Asian allies were not as yet politically and economically stable enough to be reliable partners, and few of their leaders were interested in promoting either democracy or economic revitalization. The success of NATO and America's containment strategy in Europe rested on shared values that in the 1950s simply did not exist in Asia.

The Middle East became one of the most volatile of Third World arenas of Cold War confrontation. For centuries the Ottoman Turks had ruled Middle Eastern lands from Egypt to Iraq. World War I broke up the Ottoman Empire, but Britain and France took its place when the League of Nations named them protectors of Egypt and of the newly created, semi-independent, and essentially artificial states of Palestine, Iraq, Transjordan, Syria, and Lebanon. Meanwhile a tribal ruler, Ibn Saud, forcibly unified much of the Arabian Peninsula into a new kingdom, Saudi Arabia, dominated by the austere Wahhabi sect of Islam.

By the close of World War II the Middle East seethed

❁ IN THEIR OWN WORDS

**John Foster Dulles
on Massive Retaliation**

The rhetoric of John Foster Dulles, President Eisenhower's secretary of state, resonated with the anxious Cold War mood of the American public during the 1950s. He proposed offsetting the superior numbers of the Soviet armed forces by use of "massive retaliation" with superior American weapons technology.

The Soviet Communists are planning for what they call "an entire historical era," and we should do the same. They seek, through many

types of maneuvers, gradually to divide and weaken the free nations by overextending them in efforts which, as Lenin put it, are "beyond their strength, so that they come to practical bankruptcy." Then, said Lenin, "our victory is assured." Then, said Stalin, will be "the moment for the decisive blow."

In the face of this strategy, measures cannot be judged adequate merely because they ward off an immediate danger. It is essential to do this, but it is also essential to do so without exhausting ourselves....

We need allies and collective security.

Our purpose is to make these relations more effective, less costly. This can be done by placing more reliance on deterrent power and less dependence on local defensive power....

What the Eisenhower administration seeks is a similar international security system. We want, for ourselves and the other free nations, a maximum deterrent at a bearable cost....

The way to deter aggression is for the free community to be willing and able to respond vigorously at places and with means of its own choosing.

with anti-Western resentment, expressed both by Arab and Iranian nationalism and by the early stages of an Islamist revival. Anti-Western feelings were exacerbated by Arab and Muslim perceptions of the United States and its European allies as champions of Zionism, the international movement to establish a Jewish homeland in Palestine.

In 1953 the Eisenhower administration, secretly working through the CIA, engineered the ouster of a nationalist regime in Iran that was threatening to expropriate Western — largely British — oil interests. In Iran, the beneficiary of America's exercise of covert power was the country's ruthless young monarch, Shah Reza Pahlevi. He became a staunch American Cold War ally. The Shah was an advocate of forcible modernization modeled on Mustafa Kemal Ataturk's reform of Turkey after World War I, and he often used brutal methods to suppress religious radicals. With American aid, the Shah built a formidable army and did much to modernize the nation, but he was hated by many Iranians, and was overthrown in a vehemently anti-American Islamic revolution in 1979.

In the wake of World War II, Holocaust survivors from Europe poured into Palestine, seeking a secure future. In May 1948 Great Britain withdrew from Palestine, which it had been administering, and Zionists there proclaimed the independence of a Jewish state, Israel. The Truman administration immediately extended diplomatic recognition, but Arab Palestinians (Muslims and Christians alike) declared war on Israel. All the surrounding Arab states supported the Palestinians, expecting an easy victory. But the new Israeli army routed their foes, driving a million Palestinians from their homes. For the next forty years the humiliated Arab states refused to recognize Israel, tried to strangle the new state economically, and continually threatened to annihilate Israel in a new war.

Maldistribution of the region's oil reserves also fanned unrest. Saudi Arabia, once a poor desert land and the home of Islam's two holiest cities, Mecca and Medina, found itself — or, rather, its huge royal family — enriched by fabulous petroleum discoveries. King Saud protected these assets during World War II by making himself a strategic and business partner of the United States. By the 1950s Arab rulers with petroleum deposits had worked out arrangements with Dutch, British, and American companies under which they received 50 percent of all profits from extraction and refining. Unfortunately, those nations with the largest and poorest populations — Egypt, Syria, and Jordan — had no oil and watched restively as the royal families of Saudi Arabia, Kuwait, and Qatar grew ostentatiously rich.

Nowhere was Arab nationalism stronger than in Egypt. There, in 1952, the corrupt and hedonistic King Farouk was ousted in a coup led by Colonel Gamal Abdel Nasser. Nasser hoped to raise the living standard of his impoverished people, but he also wanted to make Egypt the center of a Pan-Arab movement that would destroy Israel and end Western influence in the Middle East. In 1955 he obtained a pledge from the Eisenhower administration of $56 million in aid to help build a massive dam on the Nile River at Aswan, increasing Egypt's arable land by one-third. When Nasser mortgaged his country's 1956 cotton crop in a huge arms deal with Communist Czechoslovakia and formally recognized the People's Republic of China, however, the U.S. withdrew its offer. Retaliating, Nasser nationalized the Suez Canal, which was owned and operated jointly by the British and French.

Feeling their vital interests at risk, London and Paris decided to intervene, along with Israel — which Nasser had repeatedly threatened to attack. On October 29, 1956, the Israeli army invaded the Sinai Peninsula in order, Tel Aviv said, to destroy Palestinian guerrilla bases on Egyptian territory. Britain and France warned that they would not permit the fighting to interfere with the operation of the Suez Canal. When Nasser refused to offer guarantees, the two Western powers, without informing the United States, dropped paratroops into Egypt and seized the canal.

The Eisenhower administration could hardly condone this blatant aggression without further alienating the Arab world and other Third World countries, but Britain and France were America's two principal allies. On October 30 the United States placed a resolution before the Security Council calling on Israel and Egypt to stop fighting and demanding that Israel withdraw its troops. Britain and France vetoed the American resolution and a similar one offered by the Soviet Union.

Making the most of the situation, the Kremlin threatened to send "volunteers" to Egypt and to rain missiles down on London and Paris. (At this very moment, Soviet tanks were preparing to crush the Hungarian revolt.) Eisenhower responded by announcing that the United States would use force to prevent Soviet intervention. The UN subsequently negotiated a cease-fire, British and French troops withdrew, and the Egyptians began administering the canal fairly and efficiently.

Washington's efforts to restrain Britain and France

won some plaudits in Third World capitals, but overall American interests suffered as a result of the Suez crisis. NATO was split, and Arab nationalism became even more strongly anti-Western. In the wake of the debacle, Anthony Eden resigned as British prime minister, and many British and French leaders concluded that they should frame a more independent foreign policy. Nasser was driven into uneasy alliance with the Soviet Union. It was largely irrelevant that on January 5, 1957, Eisenhower announced that the United States would defend the nations of the Middle East against Soviet attack. With some difficulty, the administration persuaded Congress to pass a joint resolution approving that warning, called the Eisenhower Doctrine.

Later in 1957, Eisenhower found himself doing what he had always feared: intervening militarily in the Middle East. Amid passions enflamed by the Suez Crisis, a radical revolt toppled the pro-Western king of Iraq and brought to power the first of a series of military dictators, preaching secularist Arab nationalism, who would rule that oil-rich country for the rest of the century. Similar forces threatened to engulf pro-Western Jordan and Lebanon. Eisenhower sent Marines into Lebanon, which helped stabilize the situation and bolster King Hussein of Jordan. His action was only the first step in what would be an increasingly deep involvement of the United States in trying to maintain the shaky Middle Eastern balance of power.

❧ The "Missile Gap"

In the 1950s Americans, like their allies and enemies, lived continually under the threat of nuclear annihilation. Bomb shelters were prominently marked in American public buildings, and American school children regularly practiced taking cover under their desks.

In 1949, responding to the brilliant theoretical arguments of the Hungarian-born physicist Edward Teller and to Cold War tensions, nuclear scientists and the U.S. military reluctantly endorsed a research project to develop a hydrogen bomb, "Super." On November 1, 1952, on Eniwetok Atoll in the western Pacific, the first American thermonuclear device was exploded. Whereas the energy released in Hiroshima-type atomic bombs was measured in kilotons — thousands of tons of TNT — the yield of hydrogen weapons was expressed in megatons — millions of tons of TNT. The public was inundated with reports of the Armageddon-type destruction that would accompany a nuclear confrontation. The Joint Congressional Committee on Atomic

Nuclear Jitters   In May 1955 this "Kidde Kokoon" is lowered into a backyard hole eleven feet deep to shelter a family of seven in the New York suburb of Garden City, on Long Island. Thousands of anxious Americans invested in such refuges during the 1950s and early 1960s—and debated the morality of using firearms to defend them against unprotected neighbors in the event of an imminent attack. This model was designed by the reassuringly named Walter Kidde Nuclear Laboratories, Inc., and was made of 3/16-inch steel plate. It boasted a gasoline generator, a chemical toilet, and a filter to remove radioactive particles from the air. When buried under three feet of earth, it was supposed to protect a family for three to five days after a hydrogen bomb blast, three to twelve miles away. No money-back guarantee was mentioned, however.

Energy reported in August 1959 that an attack on the United States might kill 50 million people and seriously injure an additional 20 million, destroying or making uninhabitable half of all the nation's dwellings. That estimate surely understated the consequences of all-out war with *many* nuclear weapons being detonated.

The American public grew increasingly uneasy as news leaked of Soviet increases in the production of nuclear warheads and advances in rocketry. Under these circumstances, basing defense policy on "massive retaliation" and foreign policy on "brinkmanship" seemed to many to be reckless. On October 4, 1957, the Soviet Union shocked the West — hitherto complacent about its technological superiority — by sending into orbit the world's first earth satellite, Sputnik (Russian for "traveling companion"). That accomplishment, achieved before the United States had perfected its own missiles or launched its first satellite, seemed to upset both the scientific and the military balance between the two countries. Even Dulles admitted that Russia had overcome the "preponderance of power" that the United States had enjoyed since 1945.

Public anxiety over the "missile gap," a term coined by Democratic politicians, was ill founded. During Eisenhower's presidency the Atlas, the first U.S inter-continental ballistic missile (ICBM), became operational, and plans for Titan, a liquid fuel rocket, got underway in 1955. The navy began development of the Polaris submarine-launched missile and the air force the Minuteman, a solid-fuel ICBM that could blast off from concrete silos in sixty seconds. These programs were in place by the early 1960s, giving the United States a powerful triad of deterrence: the B-52 bomber, the seaborne Polaris, and the land-based Minuteman. But once established, the "missile gap" became a myth that the Eisenhower administration could not deflate without revealing the sources of secret intelligence about the true — and more modest — state of Soviet military capabilities.

❧ The Cold War Warms and Thaws

To ease Cold War tensions and slow the arms race, Eisenhower attended what the press dubbed a "summit conference" at Geneva in July 1955, meeting the leaders of Great Britain, France, and the U.S.S.R. Nothing came of discussions about disarmament, German reunification, and East-West cultural and commercial contacts. But the atmosphere was surprisingly cordial, leading to talk of "the Spirit of Geneva." Khrushchev and Soviet premier Nikolai Bulganin repeatedly called for "peaceful coexistence" and "the relaxation of world tensions." Eisenhower — ignoring Dulles's advice to appear in public stern and unsmiling — was at his most amiable. When he declared that "the United States will never take part in an aggressive war," Bulganin replied, "We believe that statement."

The "Spirit of Geneva" soon evaporated. The Soviet invasion of Hungary and the Kremlin's fishing in troubled Middle Eastern waters convinced many Americans that the Cold War was still on. Soviet-American

relations took a new nosedive when on November 27, 1958, Khrushchev suddenly demanded that the United States, Britain, and France withdraw their 10,000 soldiers from West Berlin, declare the city a demilitarized zone, and negotiate directly with the Communist German Democratic Republic for terms of access. He set a six-month deadline and threatened to sign a separate peace treaty with East Germany and withdraw Soviet occupation forces if his terms were not met. The West did not recognize the GDR, and the threat of a Soviet pullout implied a new Berlin blockade. Negotiations dragged on throughout 1959, with Khrushchev several times extending his deadline. (At Eisenhower's invitation, he also made a highly publicized visit to the United States in 1959, the highpoint of which was Khrushchev's press-conference tantrum after being barred from Disneyland because of security concerns.) Finally, the Soviet leader agreed to meet Eisenhower and other Western leaders at a summit in Paris in May 1960.

Two weeks before that meeting, on May 1, Moscow announced the downing of an American U-2 reconnais-

At the Summit: Geneva, July 1955   Forgetting his advice to Eisenhower that he keep his grin under wraps, the normally grim-visaged Secretary of State John Foster Dulles breaks into a smile as he meets Soviet premier Nikolai Bulganin (center) and Communist Party first secretary Nikita Khrushchev (right) for lunch. Khrushchev was famous for wearing baggy Soviet-made suits and was widely derided as a mercurial bumpkin; the goateed Bulganin's tastes ran to Western tailoring. Despite all the talk of goodwill, not much was accomplished at Geneva.

sance plane inside Soviet airspace. Washington feigned ignorance, admitting only that an American weather plane might have drifted off course. Then the Kremlin sprang its trap. In fact, the U-2 was not a weather plane, but a CIA spy plane. It had been shot down 1,300 miles inside the U.S.S.R. by a missile, its cameras filled with photos of top-secret Soviet military installations. The Soviets had captured its civilian pilot, Francis Gary Powers, who confessed in a televised press conference in Moscow.

Once the extent of evidence in Soviet hands was clear, Eisenhower grudgingly assumed public responsibility for the flights. Only hours into the summit meeting, Khrushchev demanded that Eisenhower apologize for the violation of Soviet airspace and punish those responsible. That was an impossible demand, for the United States relied on U-2 flights to keep informed about Soviet missile and nuclear programs in the absence of arms-control inspections. When the grim-faced president refused to back down, Khrushchev walked out. He subsequently canceled Eisenhower's planned visit to the U.S.S.R. and made it clear that there could be no serious negotiations on Berlin or any other issue until a new president took office.

SOCIETY AND CULTURE AT MID-CENTURY

While the Cold War made the 1950s an anxious time, Americans reaped the material fruits of being the dominant power to emerge from World War II. Fueled by Cold War military expenditures, by vast consumer spending, and by unchallenged global economic power, the American economy settled into unprecedented affluence. For the majority, the American dream seemed within reach. *Consensus* was the word most often used to describe the fifties mood for many; prosperity swelled the middle class just as slowing immigration made the population less diverse.

Of course, not all Americans were prosperous or content. Discontent rumbled under the surface. By the end of the decade, the civil rights movement had thoroughly shaken simplistic notions about equal access to a fulfilled American dream. Influential writers criticized the rampant consumer culture. Some women began to question the traditional roles assigned them by the dominant culture. The discontents that erupted in the sixties had deep roots in the critical thought of the fifties.

❧ Affluent America

In 1955 the United States, with 6 percent of the world's population, consumed more than one-third of the world's goods and services. Real GNP (which factors in inflation) rose by 51 percent during the decade, raising the already high American standard of living to astonishing levels compared to the rest of the world.

All this convinced most Americans that a life of success and comfort was within reach. In 1950, *Life* magazine featured one Junius P. Shaw, supposedly the first American born in the twentieth century. *Life* concluded that Shaw had turned out to be the "average man," at fifty a "chubby, cheerful and successful businessman." Like many, Shaw had been penniless and jobless during the Depression, but in the 1940s he became a successful salesman for Gates Rubber Company and subsequently established his own auto parts business. By 1950 he owned a "comfortable house" with "every modern luxury, including television" in the "fashionable St. Louis suburb of Ladue." Shaw, it was said, had lived the dream life of the American middle class.

A variety of factors contributed to American economic expansion in the 1950s. Pent-up postwar demand for consumer goods and Korean War spending fueled growth in the early years. Foreign aid stimulated American exports throughout the decade. Growth slowed in the second half of the fifties, but consumer purchases, driven by an ever-growing use of credit, took up much of the slack. By the mid-fifties, purchases of housing and automobiles were growing rapidly, swelled by population growth. The government stimulated purchasing power in a variety of ways, including expanded welfare expenditures, hikes in the minimum wage, and rises in farm subsidies. In addition, the government itself was by 1953 the largest single consumer, purchasing about 17 percent of GNP.

Thus encouraged, American business stepped up investments at home and abroad. From 1946 to 1958, American concerns invested more than $10 billion a year in new plants and machinery, more than three times the rate of investment during the boom of the 1920s. U.S. corporations spent unprecedented sums on research and development during these heady years of expansion. Between 1953 and 1960 industrial expenditures on research and development nearly tripled; in 1960 the federal government provided 63.7 percent of those research funds, but corporations more than doubled their own share. In addition, universities rapidly increased spending on scientific and industrial research, mostly

Southern Poverty Not all Americans shared in the relative prosperity of the 1950s. Living in a shack in Montgomery, Alabama, without water, sewage, or garbage disposal, and with a fireplace as the only heat source, this African American woman and her five grandchildren had to come up with about $25 per month in rent to a white absentee landlord, a prominent Montgomery judge.

The increase in American industrial production, combined with the huge sums of money required for research and development, encouraged the rise of ever-larger corporations. In 1958, 574 of the nation's 573,000 corporations received half of all income earned by American industry. General Motors, the country's largest corporation, employed nearly 700,000 people.

Organized labor, which had made strong gains during the New Deal and World War II, viewed with apprehension both the size of the industrial giants of the 1950s and the trend toward automation. Their fears were justified, because many unskilled jobs would be eliminated by machines, though the process created new jobs for more skilled laborers. The real earnings of American workers rose around 50 percent during the decade, as union membership held steady. The labor movement lost some of its radical image as unions increasingly concentrated on improving benefits and pensions for their workers.

The most striking result of the postwar boom was the broad expansion of the middle class. The proportion of families and individuals with an annual income of $10,000 or more (in 1968 dollars) rose from 9 percent in 1947 to 33 percent in 1968. During the same period, the percentage of families and individuals making less than $3,000 fell from 34 percent to 9 percent. The income of the richest fifth of the population stood at 43 percent of the nation's income at the beginning of the decade, but that percentage declined steadily while the percentage received by the other four-fifths rose. The earnings of the top 5 percent, around one-third of the national total in 1929, declined to 18.1 percent by 1950 and 16.7 percent in 1960.

from state and federal grants. This research provided a flood of new products. For instance, chemical giants DuPont, Monsanto, and Dow provided the consumer culture with aerosol sprays, Dacron, and improvements in and new uses for nylon, Orlon, and Teflon.

More portentous was the advance of information technology, although the computer's impact was largely hidden from the average person. Bell Laboratories' development of the transistor chip opened the door for a stream of new products. The production of computers — huge machines at the time — grew from 20 in 1954 to 1,250 in 1957 and 35,000 in 1967. By the end of the fifties, computers had made more efficient many complex operations, from airline reservations systems to TV evangelist Oral Roberts's responses to millions of prayer requests. IBM turned out a steady stream of new products and improvements as a result of its heavy research and development investments and led to the emergence of "Big Blue" as the giant of the computer industry.

But many Americans remained desperately poor, cut off from the education needed for advancement and deprived of basic standards of housing and health care. Sociologists estimated that as much as 20 percent of all Americans lived below the poverty line, defined in 1960 as an annual income of $3,000 for a family of four and $4,000 for a family of six. Poverty was concentrated among four groups: African Americans, increasingly isolated in ghettos; mill and factory workers in the deteriorating industrial areas of New England and the Carolinas; Appalachian hill inhabitants in the coal region from western Pennsylvania to northern Georgia; and rural southerners, both black and white. Despite these realities, most Americans during the fifties remained unaware of or callous toward poverty. Desperately poor Americans did not find a champion until 1962, when Michael Harrington's book *The Other America* swept away simplistic notions about a uniformly affluent America and challenged the nation to help its poor. Harrington called himself a socialist. He was a disciple of Dorothy Day, the radical activist who was the moving spirit of the Catholic Worker movement, which did selfless work among America's poor.

❧ Dwindling Diversity

The United States became a more homogeneous society in the decade after World War II. A booming birth rate and slowing immigration diluted population diversity at the same time the Depression and World War II were integrating some ethnic minorities, such as Italians and East Europeans, into American society.

The population grew from 130 million in 1940 to 151 million in 1950 and 180 million in 1960. Two main causes were a hefty surge of the birth rate, which remained around 24 per 1,000 women of childbearing age throughout the decade, and a continual rise in life expectancy. But immigration remained low, hovering around 250,000 per year. The foreign-born population in the United States had reached a high of 14.2 million in 1930, or more than 11.6 percent of the population; by 1960 it dropped to 9.7 million, or about 5.4 percent. Furthermore, most fifties immigrants were easily assimilated, coming mainly from Canada and from European countries such as Germany, Great Britain, and Italy.

Internal population trends followed familiar patterns. Farm population continued to fall, dropping from 23 million in 1950 to 15.6 million in 1960 — a decline from 11.6 to 8.7 percent of the population. The number of farms also dropped during the decade even though farm acreage remained unchanged, highlighting the continued growth of agribusiness. So did the extraordinary growth of farm productivity. In 1940, 10.7 people were supplied per farm worker; the number was 15.5 in 1950 and 25.8 in 1960.

The African American population grew rapidly, reaching 19 million by 1960. While the number of blacks increased by more than 1 million in the South, postwar migration sharply cut the percentage of African American population there. The number of blacks in the North grew by nearly 50 percent, to more than 2 million.

❧ The Flowering of American Education

The G.I. Bill had a powerful impact on American higher education. With its funding, 2.2 million veterans completed bachelor's degrees and almost the same number received industrial, technical, or farm training. In 1950, American colleges more than doubled the number of degrees granted in any year before 1945.

The education boom was only partly explained by the G.I. Bill. Education seemed more than ever the key to entering the middle class, leading some critics to charge that schools and colleges were filled with students who were indifferent to culture and public affairs, intent only on materialist goals. There was some truth to that, although a desire to train for a profession had always been the primary goal of those seeking higher education.

Below the college level, enrollments and attendance also vastly exceeded Depression-era figures, similarly reflecting economic recovery and growing public respect for education. The enrollment of school-age children rose to nearly 85 percent — and to 81.5 percent among traditionally deprived African American children. School retention rates reached nearly 75 percent by 1960. Fewer parents were so poor as to withdraw their children from school early to help support the family, and the civil rights movement forced states to improve educational opportunities for African American children, pushing up the percentages of African American students at every level.

The blossoming of American education also reflected an almost euphoric popular faith in the potential of science. "There is little that can be imagined which is too fantastic to become reality before the year 2000," gushed *Life* magazine. The dramatic ending of World War II with atomic weapons put scientists in the limelight — usually as admired geniuses, but occasionally (in the popular media) as crazed monsters. Foreign-born scholars and scientists, joining the brilliant refugees from fascism in the 1930s, made the generously funded American universities leaders in virtually every area of postwar research.

Two internal battles plagued the educational establishment during the decade. Progressive education, with its "child-centered curriculum" and other fruits of John Dewey's theories, dominated the professional educational establishment. But critics, including Eisenhower, charged that the results were an "education wasteland." The Soviets' launch of Sputnik in 1957 frightened the public with the apparent loss of scientific leadership, and many blamed the schools. Calls resounded for reassessment of the American educational system and a return to "basics."

McCarthyism also roiled American education. More than 90 percent of Americans believed that Communists should be barred from teaching, and many school systems purged suspected "reds." In New York City, where Communist organizations had been relatively strong before World War II, 321 public-school teachers and 58 professors lost their jobs because of alleged associations or refusal to cooperate in investigations of subversive activities. Many states imposed loyalty oaths, requiring teachers to swear they had never belonged to subversive organizations, and several hundred teachers who refused were fired. The experiences of the fifties convinced many educators that strong tenure guarantees were necessary to protect faculty in secondary schools and colleges from political purges.

∾ Fifties Families

The divorce rate more than tripled during and immediately after the war, driven up by the stress of separations (and of many hasty unions), but in the 1950s the rate fell to a level only slightly higher than during the early years of the century. At mid-century, nothing symbolized the American belief in the good life more than a stable family. On average, people married younger than at any previous time in the twentieth century (in 1950, at 22 for males and 20.3 for women) and the birth rate approached India's. The baby boom generation was being born. A few signs of problems surfaced in the 1950s, but throughout the decade the family seemed among the most stable of American institutions.

The postwar American family sometimes seemed obsessed with the rituals of child rearing, and the norms of parent-child relationships clearly changed during the decade. Deeply influenced by Dr. Benjamin M. Spock's *Common Sense Book of Baby and Child Care,* the decade's best selling book, and Dr. Arnold Gesell's *The Child from Five to Ten,* many parents saw offspring not as miniature adults needing rigid boundaries and stern discipline but as sensitive human beings deserving freedom and nurture. In the new view, a child's wants and needs were said to be the same. Baby boom children, who would reach maturity during the

TV   During the 1950s, almost all American families acquired a black-and-white television set, which usually replaced the radio as the focal point of family life. Along with the TV came the frozen TV dinner, a bland concoction that just had to be popped into the oven so that everyone could eat without missing favorite programs. Microwaves, cable, and color TVs were wonders still to come.

turbulent sixties, were in general reared in more liberal and permissive household environments than any previous American generation.

The emphasis on family and the surging birthrate reinforced older American notions about domesticity. Women had entered the work force in large numbers during World War II, but most went home after the war to become wives and mothers. Although much (not all) of this return to the hearth was voluntary, both legally and by social assumption men got preference in employment and education.

Magazines, movies, popular literature, and advertisements all reinforced popular notions of the "ideal woman" of the fifties. She was pretty and popular, married by twenty, well dressed, well groomed, an emotional and sexual helpmate to her husband, and an efficient homemaker who befriended her fellow housewives. Career women did not fit the stereotype. Of course, none of this was new in the 1950s. Only rarely were traditional gender roles questioned, and they were supported by some of the leading intellectual fashions of the day, including Freudianism (which emphasized gender differences) and the widely accepted sociological theory of functionalism (which assigned to women a biologically determined social role). Adlai Stevenson and Dr. Spock publicly averred that motherhood, not career, was the normal role for a woman.

Some women challenged these assumptions. If millions of women left the work force after World War II, far more stayed on the job than ever before in American history. By 1960 twice as many women were employed as in 1940; women workers grew at a rate four times that of men, and in 1960 nearly 40 percent of all women over 16 held a job. In 1940, 16.7 percent of wives worked; in 1960, 31.7 percent did.

Changing patterns of women's employment in the fifties were mostly responses to economic pressure. Many couples needed a second income. Often these needs put new strains on families — and particularly on women trying to balance home responsibilities, work, and stereotypes. By the end of the decade a few critics were asking questions about the picture of the placidly happy wife and mother. Skyrocketing consumption of tranquilizers and reports of alcoholism among women pointed to a culture of suburban housewives plagued by boredom and a lack of fulfillment. These simmering discontents did not receive a name until the 1963 publication of Betty Friedan's *The Feminine Mystique,* the opening salvo of modern feminism.

Belying the fifties' staid reputation, hints of a sexual revolution were in the air. *Playboy* magazine, which began publication in 1955, was an unprecedented marketing success, combining provocative pictures of female "playmates" with articles by leading literary figures. Publisher Hugh Hefner battled in the courts against local censors and built a substantial economic empire by debunking American prudishness and promoting a more freewheeling lifestyle.

The postwar years also produced one of modern history's greatest sexual iconoclasts, Alfred C. Kinsey. An Indiana University zoologist, Kinsey turned in the late 1930s to the study of human sexuality. He first compiled the sexual histories of students. Later, disregarding scientific standards of sampling, he began collecting information from the inmates of boardinghouses, prisons, and mental wards. In two large tomes published in 1948 and 1955, popularly known as the Kinsey Reports, he set about demolishing many myths surrounding American sexual habits. Kinsey's conclusion that women could and did enjoy sex as much as men was hardly revolutionary, but it did challenge more traditional notions about sexual behavior. Some were upset by Kinsey's revelations about the normality of masturbation. Even more disturbing was his conclusion that heterosexuality and homosexuality were not exclusive alternatives but poles on a normal behavioral continuum. Kinsey's estimate of the numbers

of people with what many considered "deviant" sexual habits were clearly shaped by his skewed sample — for instance, he reported that 90 percent of men had sex with prostitutes by age 35. But his studies were not challenged by social scientists for nearly forty years. For a generation, meanwhile, his studies powerfully influenced American thinking about sex.

❧ Cars and Subdivisions Alter the Landscape

Nothing changed the American scene more than the proliferation of automobiles. In the fifteen years after World War II, the percentage of American families owning automobiles rose from 54 percent to 77 percent. By 1960 the automobile population was growing faster than the human. Automobiles were the fifties' quintessential status symbol, each year getting bigger, more powerful, and flashier. Road builders struggled to keep up. In 1947 Congress authorized the construction of 37,000 miles of new highways; by 1960 work on the interstate highway system was well underway. By then, many cities were devoting as much as two-thirds of the downtown area to streets and parking areas.

Americans began traveling in unprecedented numbers, and the tourism industry began courting the masses. Thousands of service stations opened; motel and hotel receipts increased 2,300 percent in 1945-1960. Disneyland, opened in 1955, proved a stunning commercial success. Meanwhile well-to-do Americans routinely vacationed abroad — more than 8 million in the fifties.

Migration to suburbia accelerated. Usually financed by the G.I. Bill or the Federal Housing Administration (FHA),[4] the rate of homeownership increased by 50 percent from 1945 to 1960. Most new homeowners lived in suburbs. In 1947 William Levitt, a New York developer, built 10,600 houses on 1,200 acres of cheap Long Island farmland. The low-cost three-bedroom homes sold almost immediately, and within a year Levittown boasted a population of 40,000. Other Levittowns followed in Pennsylvania and New Jersey, and developers all over the country began laying out subdivisions. They were often dreadfully monotonous, but they filled a need.

The housing boom — 13 million new homes were constructed in America between 1950 and 1960, 11 million of them in suburbia — promoted one of the largest internal migrations in American history. By 1960, 18

---

4. By insuring loans for up to 95 percent of the value of a house, the FHA enabled contractors to borrow money for construction and young couples to buy homes.

million Americans were rearing their families on the suburban "crabgrass frontier."

The flight of middle-class families (mostly white) to the suburbs hastened inner-city deterioration. In 1950, 58 percent of Americans who lived in metropolitan areas resided in the "central city." By 1960 that percentage had decreased to 52; the percentage of whites living in the central city declined from 56 percent to 48 percent. At the same time, the percentage of African Americans living in the urban core actually rose slightly to 79 percent in 1960. While all American cities still boasted white majorities in 1960, the pattern of white flight to the suburbs and the concentration of blacks in inner cities had already been well established.

❧ Consumer Goods and Entertainment

Novelties in 1945, shopping centers numbered more than four thousand by 1960. In the middle-class culture spawned by cars and suburbs, shopping centers became community focal points, and shopping itself became a recreation for adults and teens alike. The baby boom

generation enjoyed more disposable income than any of its predecessors, and they created a vast, specialized market for transistor radios, teen fashions, and 45 RPM records — one pop song on each side.

America was awash in a sea of beguiling consumer goods. Spending on advertising increased 400 percent, to almost triple the national expenditure on education. Ads created needs and desires, and the credit card, first introduced in 1950 by Diner's Club, provided instant gratification. At first limited to a few wealthy New Yorkers, the use of "plastic money" soon became commonplace throughout the middle class.

Nothing did more to fuel the consumer boom of the 1950s than the spectacular entry of television into American homes. TV ownership became a badge of consumerism fulfilled. In 1946 thirty commercial stations received licenses and eight thousand Americans owned primitive sets. By 1960, 45.8 million American households (about 90 percent) owned TVs, and more

I Love Lucy   America loved Lucy during the fifties. Lucille Ball is on the right, and her husband Desi Arnaz on the left, in this 1952 still from one of the decade's most popular and zany TV hits.

than six hundred commercial and public stations were broadcasting. *TV Guide* was the fifties' fastest-growing periodical.

Family-life comedies were popular in the early days of television. They reinforced the fifties conviction that trauma and trouble could not disrupt true love and family solidarity. One of the most popular programs was *The Honeymooners,* which ran from 1952 to 1957. Jackie Gleason played an irascible bus driver; Audrey Meadows was his strong-willed, sharp-tongued, but compassionate wife. The blue-collar bickering and undercurrent of love in the series proved to be a magical mixture. The decade's foremost success was *I Love Lucy,* a situation comedy featuring zany comedienne Lucille Ball and her loving and forgiving (and real-life) Cuban husband, Desi Arnaz.[5] The episode "Lucy Goes to the Hospital," coinciding with the actual birth of the couple's first child, was viewed by 44 million people, about twice as many as watched Eisenhower's inauguration the next day.

Comedy extravaganzas and variety productions also attracted huge audiences. As television audiences increased, such hour-long serious theatrical productions as *Playhouse 90* multiplied. But by the end of the decade high-quality drama was giving way to Westerns, "cop-and-robber" thrillers (often showing heroic FBI agents), and quiz shows like *The $64,000 Question.*

The "electronic hearth" changed the way Americans thought, dressed, and acted. More and more people were exposed to a common culture. Late in the decade, intellectuals worried about the medium's impact on American life, fearing that its banality and escapism were impoverishing the national spirit. Such critiques were but a prelude to the onslaught led in the 1960s by Newton Minnow, chairman of the Federal Communications Commission, who labeled the medium "a vast wasteland." And even before the fifties were over, the TV industry was rocked by a major scandal when Columbia University instructor Charles Van Doren (the son of a famous family of scholars) confessed that he had been given answers while a contestant on *The $64,000 Question.* An investigation revealed systematic rigging in most of the quiz shows.

The rise of television shook the movie industry. Before 1939, Hollywood had received 67.4 cents of every American entertainment dollar. Just after World War II, weekly movie attendance hovered around 90 million; it fell to 60 million by 1950 and to 44 million by 1960. At first disdainful of the new medium, in the fifties the movie industry learned that Americans would exchange a huge screen and expensive productions for the convenience of home viewing. Desperate filmmakers concentrated on striving for effects — and on treating subjects — that TV could not match. In 1957 the French film *And God Created Woman* featured a nude Brigitte Bardot, opening the floodgates for sexual frankness in the movies.

The number of movies produced fell dramatically during the 1950s. But some of Hollywood's efforts were of very high quality and — like *From Here to Eternity, On the Waterfront,* and *The Bridge on the River Kwai* — became classics. John Wayne and Gary Cooper thrilled American audiences in their roles as traditional heroes, and several brooding young actors were introduced whose restlessness and defiance tapped into youthful discontent — most notably the scornful, mumbling, engaging rebel Marlon Brando in *The Wild One* and James Dean, an instant star in *Rebel Without a Cause* who died in a 1955 crash of his speeding Porsche.

In 1947 Hollywood came under scrutiny by the Communist-hunting House Un-American Activities Committee (HUAC). The widely publicized hearings exposed the leftist leanings of some actors during the 1930s. Hollywood celebrities divided into three factions — HUAC's friends, headed by young Ronald Reagan and Gary Cooper, intent on purging leftists; a dozen performers and writers who openly supported Soviet Communism and refused to answer questions on Fifth Amendment grounds; and a larger group of liberals who called the investigation a witch hunt. These included such icons as Humphrey Bogart, Lauren Bacall, Katharine Hepburn, and director John Huston. The investigations deeply divided the country and the industry. Conservative producers compiled a blacklist that ended the careers of some, including Charlie Chaplin and African American singer Paul Robeson.

❧ *Art and Literature, Popular and Critical*

Most Americans in the 1950s continued to enjoy realistic art, and the decade produced some notable practitioners, including Andrew Wyeth and Georgia O'Keeffe. But by the mid-1950s art critics were most interested in the new school of abstract expressionism, sometimes called the New York School. Its virtuoso was Jackson Pollock, trained in the realism of Thomas Hart Benton. In the 1950s, Pollock astonished the art world by creating

---

5. Their real-life marriage was more turbulent than their on-screen one, and they later divorced.

huge canvases covered with seemingly random (but actually carefully plotted) drippings of acrylic paint. New York City replaced Paris as the capital of the art world.

The advent of abstract expressionism intensified a debate over modernism that still continues. Cultural modernism's emphasis on discontinuity, fragmentation, and introversion, and its insistence that thought and expression defy rational analysis, found quintessential expression in abstract expressionism. A few art critics denounced "nonrepresentational" art as a sham. Most defended it; some maintained that the essence of great art was mystery, not clarity.

Few American writers took modernism that far, but many of the best clearly stood alienated from the era's affluence and complacency. Playwright Eugene O'Neill ended his brilliant career with *The Iceman Cometh* (1946) and *Long Day's Journey Into Night* (1956), probing an America of failed dreams and empty lives. Tennessee (Thomas Lanier) Williams, who won Pulitzer Prizes for *A Streetcar Named Desire* in 1948 and *Cat on a Hot Tin Roof* in 1955, was equally skeptical of the seemingly simplistic optimism of the decade. Arthur Miller's 1949 Pulitzer Prize–winning play *Death of a Salesman* was in many ways the most poignant critique of postwar America. Miller's antihero, Willy Loman, is an aging traveling salesman who has relentlessly pursued his American dream — success — with bravado and hustle, teaching his two sons to do the same. But Willy is at the end of his career. His small-town salesman skills become obsolete and he loses his job. All his assumptions prove illusory. Never having built close relationships with anyone, alone in a world that denies the validity of his existence, Willy commits suicide.

Overall, postwar fiction writers failed to match the brilliance of the post–World War I literary renaissance. The two most honored novelists of the fifties were distinguished writers from before the war: William Faulkner (who won the Nobel Prize in 1949) and Ernest Hemingway (the Nobel Laureate of 1954). Both were nearing the end of their productive careers. Hemingway shot himself in 1961, and Faulkner struggled with alcoholism before his death in 1962.

Beats   In 1956, outside Lawrence Ferlinghetti's famous City Lights Bookstore in San Francisco, notables of the beat generation pose together. Ferlinghetti is on the right. Allen Ginsberg, wearing glasses but not yet sporting the heavy beard and long hair that later made him the archetypal "beatnik," is in the center of the group. On his right is Neal Cassady, the lover of a number of male beats including Ginsberg.

Most of the serious young novelists of the 1950s portrayed characters scurrying for survival rather than scaling the ladder of success. The central characters in John Updike's *Rabbit, Run,* in Philip Roth's *Goodbye, Columbus,* and in Saul Bellow's *The Adventures of Augie March* were all displaced persons. Roth and Bellow were among the best of a talented generation of postwar writers who probed the dilemmas of tradition versus assimilation that contemporary life was thrusting upon American Jews.

A more radical literary rebellion arose among some 1950s New York intellectuals who distanced literature from liberal reform and other political causes. Inspired by Columbia University literary critic Lionel Trilling, a few alienated young writers attempted an existential as well as an artistic rebellion against the conforming culture. One of Trilling's most promising pupils, Allen Ginsberg, who was expelled from Columbia for writing obscenities on a dormitory wall, went to San Francisco in the early fifties to become the guru of a growing band of dropouts rejecting the conventional life called for by the dominant culture.

These alienated intellectuals gathered in tearooms to imbibe marijuana and poetry. There in 1955, in a moment often called the birth of the "beat" movement, Ginsberg read his poem "Howl." In the audience was Jack Kerouac, another Columbia alumnus, whose stream-of-consciousness novel *On the Road* became a smashing publishing success in 1957.

In 1956 the City Lights Bookstore, a soon-to-be famous establishment owned by poet Lawrence Ferlinghetti, published Ginsberg's rambling 118-line poem. "Howl" was a dizzying kaleidoscope of travel, insanity, art, atheism, sex, drugs, and alcohol. It was also a lament for what Ginsberg saw as the demoralization and degradation of his generation.

The San Francisco police seized "Howl" as obscene. In the trial that followed, a host of literary authorities testified to its artistic and literary merit; the court agreed and lifted the ban. The trial was not only a landmark in the free speech movement, but also brought the rebellious "beat generation" to national attention. The rebels came to be called "beatniks."[6] "Beat" was both a literary and a social movement, seeking fulfillment in poetry, jazz, sex, drugs, and meditation. Beat writers denounced mainstream Western literature and criticism, turning to the East for inspiration. Some have pictured the beat generation as the ideological progenitor of sixties counterculture and the New Left. But the connections are far from direct, and Ginsberg was the only obvious bridge.

❧ Music: Serious, Popular, and "Rock 'n' Roll"

Music became widely accessible to everyone as long-playing records and hi-fi and stereo sets replaced old Victrolas. Jukeboxes became standard in many places. FM radio and (occasionally) television broadcast "serious" music. Every Sunday, the charismatic young conductor Leonard Bernstein introduced classical music to millions of viewers on *The Joy of Music*. Jazz, now becoming accepted as "serious" art, lost its appeal to ordinary people. The "cool" jazz of such masters as Dave Brubeck or the sophisticated bebop style of Thelonious Monk, for example, was almost as far from popular tastes as classical music. Most adults favored music from Broadway shows, dance-band leader Lawrence Welk's bland "champagne music," or crooners like Perry Como and velvet-voiced Nat "King" Cole.

For young people, however, a new sound was born.

6. A term of disputed derivation but obviously affected by the fame of *Sputnik*.

In 1952, a Cleveland disc jockey featured rhythm and blues (hitherto dismissed as black "race music") on a radio program called "Moondog's Rock 'n' Roll Party," coining the term "rock 'n' roll." Embraced by white middle-class youth, rock obliterated boundaries between black and white music, fusing rhythm and blues, country, gospel, and popular jazz styles.

Record producers and studios needed a white performer who could present this new fusion music to white teens. Several talented young musicians competed for that role, including Buddy Holly, whose brief but brilliant career was cut short by a plane crash in 1959. The answer to promoters' dreams was Elvis Presley, a poor young man from Tupelo, Mississippi, who had taught himself to play the guitar. Elvis was performing on regional radio shows around the South by 1954, and in 1956 his career skyrocketed when four of his records sold more than 15 million copies each. "Elvis the Pelvis" flabbergasted parents with his raw sexuality and screaming audiences of young people. Controversially, TV host Ed Sullivan booked Presley for his Sunday night show but kept camera shots of Elvis above the waist. Presley tapped into the latent rebelliousness embodied by film stars James Dean and Marlon Brando. He gave teenagers an identity that they obviously longed for in the midst of one of the nation's most conformist decades.

❧ The Religious Boom

Given the general conservatism of the times, it is not surprising that there was a religious boom in the fifties. Church membership soared from 64.5 million (49 percent of the population) in 1940 to 125 million (64 percent) in 1965. Sunday schools were flooded with baby boom children as upwardly mobile middle-class parents found in the churches moral support for their affluence and patriotism. Critics charged that the bulging churches were vacuous, convictionless bastions of middle-class conformity; the term *civil religion* — signifying a piety laden with patriotic baggage and a state sanctified by religious symbols — seemed particularly appropriate in the 1950s. Dwight Eisenhower, who attended Presbyterian services, gave frequent utterance to such bland, nonsectarian piety — often in the same breath condemning "godless Communism." In 1954 Congress added the words *under God* to the Pledge of Allegiance, and the following year "In God We Trust" was emblazoned on the nation's currency.

All religions and denominations gained during the 1950s, but the growth of the so-called "mainline" churches was the most obvious. Mirroring the homogenization of American society, ecumenical efforts flourished. In 1950, the National Council of Churches of Christ in the U.S.A. became a center for coordinating the work of twenty-nine Protestant denominations, including the Episcopalians, Methodists, Presbyterians, Congregationalists, and Northern Baptists, as well as the formerly non-cooperating Eastern Orthodox churches.

The growing tolerance of the mainstream Protestant churches was accompanied by a decline in the more rancorous forms of anti-Catholicism. This reflected an accelerated movement of the American Catholic

Young Elvis, 1957   Elvis Presley is shown here in a still from his 1957 film "Loving You," at the height of his youthful flamboyance. The next year he was drafted into the U.S. Army.

church toward the American mainstream — though not yet ecumenical outreach. The popularity of a number of highly visible Catholics during the decade, including television personality Bishop Fulton Sheen (see below), reflected new levels of Catholic-Protestant goodwill. The election of a Roman Catholic to the presidency in 1960 took place in a religious environment seriously changed by Protestant ecumenism and a mellowing Catholic church. Reservations that the famous Protestant clergyman Norman Vincent Peale (see below) voiced about entrusting the presidency to a Roman Catholic, presumably subject to papal dictation, were widely condemned by other mainstream Protestants.

In spite of critics' charges that the churches were smug and complacent, mainstream American religion did voice concerns about social problems. In 1952 the National Council of Churches condemned segregation. Responding to pressure from social liberals, the Northern Presbyterians began ordaining women in 1955, and the following year the General Conference of the Methodist Church banned racial segregation among its congregations. The leaders of the National Council of Churches, headed by Methodist bishop G. Bromley Oxnam, were sufficiently liberal to rouse McCarthyite suspicion. In his controversial 1951 book *God and Man at Yale,* young Catholic intellectual William F. Buckley, destined to become an articulate spokesman for political conservatism for more than half a century, charged that liberal Christianity had united with secular humanism to capture Yale University and the intellectual life of the nation, creating an intolerant liberal hegemony.

Seared by memories of Depression-era sufferings and by the rampant horrors revealed by World War II (including the Holocaust and Hiroshima), liberal theology gave way to neo-orthodoxy in many postwar Protestant seminaries. Originally formulated by Swiss theologian Karl Barth, neo-orthodoxy took seriously the traditional

Protestant stress on inherent human weakness and the need for redemption. American Protestant theology took on a decidedly Germanic cast, personified by the German-born theologian and philosopher Paul Tillich, who after the war taught in the United States. The writings of the German Lutheran theologians Dietrich Bonhoeffer and Martin Niemöller — the former executed by the Nazis and the latter imprisoned for years in Nazi concentration camps — profoundly influenced American Protestantism. On the one hand Bonhoeffer and Niemöller called on the church to take seriously its Reformation heritage; on the other they urged it to engage actively with the world's most pressing problems, including war and social justice. In a similar vein the American-born Niebuhr brothers, Reinhold at Union Theological Seminary and H. Richard at Yale, continued to emphasize human sinfulness, the church's tendency to be captured by culture, and the need to rise above the sin of self-love and accept responsibility for improving a morally imperfect world. Yet the somber tone of neo-orthodoxy fit the ebullient fifties little better than the simplistic liberalism of the twenties. By the end of the decade, serious theologians were increasingly focusing on the challenges of secularism.

Judaism felt the same pull of traditional values. After the war, struggling to comprehend the evil that had led to the Holocaust, Jews (and many Christians) found comfort in the German-born Israeli philosopher Martin Buber, who brought Hasidic piety to scholarly and popular attention. His *I and Thou*, a slender but dense book first translated into English in 1937, invited readers to open themselves to a personal encounter with God, beyond all dogmas that reduced God to an object — an "It."

❧ Religious Superstars and Media Religion

Four religious figures gained national reputations and large followings that transcended denomination or faith. Each represented a distinct religious subculture, and each used the mass media to reach broad audiences throughout the nation.

The most surprising of the decade's religious superstars was Fulton J. Sheen, whose hit TV program brought him national fame and appointment as auxiliary bishop of New York in 1951. A respected Roman Catholic academic theologian, Sheen's television program *Life is Worth Living* was broadcast between 1951 and 1957; it attracted 30 million viewers each week and won Sheen an Emmy and a cover story in *Time*. Sheen

Oral Roberts   One of the most famous evangelists of the mid-twentieth century appears here, in 1956, just as he was beginning to reach mass audiences through television. Sophisticated Americans, if they noticed him at all, sneered, but by the end of the century millions of Pentecostal and Charismatic Christians honored him for spreading his message of hope and healing around the world.

appealed to Catholics and non-Catholics alike with his combination of common sense, patriotism, anti-Communism, and traditional Christian morality. His popularity illustrated the extent to which Roman Catholics were entering — and being accepted by — the mainstream of American life.

Sheen's Protestant counterpart in capturing the mood of middle-class America was Norman Vincent Peale, pastor of the oldest existing Protestant church in the United States, the Dutch Reformed Marble Collegiate Church in New York City. Peale combined psychology with therapeutic prescriptions from the Scriptures, offering simple principles for successful living. *The Power of Positive Thinking,* his 1952 book, remained atop the *New York Times* bestseller list for three years. Peale's ideas were widely spread through his lectures, a radio program, a steady flow of books, and a popular periodical, *Guideposts.* Peale was an unabashed conservative Republican and champion of capitalism; his critics charged that his ideas were a simplistic perversion of both psychology and Christianity with purely materialistic goals. But Peale's message of self-help and inspiration mirrored the hopes and beliefs of millions of Americans.

Billy Graham's success outshone that of any other Protestant preacher in the twentieth century. Graham was the spokesman for a resurgent evangelical Protestantism, which in the fifties occupied a middle ground between the mainstream leaders of the National Council of Churches of Christ and the radical fundamentalists, largely isolated culturally since the 1930s.

A jaunty and ambitious young preacher who emerged after World War II, Graham gained a reputation among conservative Protestants while preaching in revivals sponsored by Youth for Christ, a postwar "parachurch" organization ministering to the young. He was thrust into national prominence during a Los Angeles tent crusade in 1949. Impressed by the young evangelist's political and moral conservatism, veteran publisher William Randolph Hearst issued a famous directive ordering his publications to "puff Graham"; the evangelist became the subject of sympathetic news-

paper stories and was featured in *Time* and *Newsweek.* In 1950 Graham began a stunning, professionally organized preaching career that would take him back and forth across America; beginning in 1954 in London, he took his "crusade" all over the world. He launched an enormously successful radio program in 1950, and with his 1957 crusade in New York's Madison Square Garden, he began televising selected crusade services. Graham became one of the most admired people in America and the confidant and adviser of every president after Truman. While many critics viewed him as naïve at best and a conservative dupe at worst, Graham considered himself, and was considered by many political leaders in the nation, to be the moral voice of the American masses.

A man of unquestioned integrity and apparent humility, Graham combined biblical literalism with a fervent emphasis on saving the lost; millions answered his invitation to come to Christ. In his early years Graham also preached an impassioned anti-Communism, though by the end of the decade his social message became more nuanced. Supported strongly by fundamentalists and other conservative Protestants in the early fifties, Graham became the focus of a division in that community later in the decade. During a crusade in Madison Square Garden, he worked cooperatively with some liberal churches and ministers, a move condemned by hard-line fundamentalists. Graham's moderate stance was called neo-evangelicalism. In 1956 the evangelist backed a new magazine, *Christianity Today,* that became the voice of middle-of-the-road Prot-

---

❋ **IN THEIR OWN WORDS**

American Popular Religion in the 1950s
Bishop Fulton Sheen, Norman Vincent Peale, Billy Graham, and Oral Roberts were very different personalities, but all of them became immensely popular thanks to messages that were in many ways similar.

"If you believe the incredible, you will end up doing the impossible!"
— Fulton Sheen

"All we need do is to voice these two petitions: Dear Lord, illumine my intellect to see the Truth, and give me the strength to follow it."
— Fulton Sheen

"Believe in yourself! Have faith in your abilities! Without a humble but reasonable confidence in your own powers you cannot be successful or happy."
— Norman Vincent Peale

"Change your thoughts and you change your world."
— Norman Vincent Peale

"There is nothing wrong with men possessing riches. The wrong comes when riches possess men."
— Billy Graham

"Something good is going to happen to you!"
— Oral Roberts

"He that is in me is greater than he that is in the world."
— Oral Roberts

estantism and the most widely read serious religious journal in the United States.

A fourth religious leader who gained a national reputation was Oral Roberts. Roberts was the foremost evangelist in a remarkable revival that erupted in the Pentecostal subculture after World War II, emphasizing divine healing. Hundreds of thousands of Pentecostals (and others afflicted by illness or disability) flocked to charismatic healers during the early 1950s in search of a miracle. Ignored or ridiculed by most Americans, the extraordinary revival sparked a surge of missionary zeal among Pentecostals that led them to take their message around the world.

More than any other religious figure in the 1950s, Roberts grasped the potential of television. In 1954, having built a solid financial organization in Tulsa, Oklahoma, he began televising his services. Many people were shocked by the spectacle of the healing line, but millions of non-Pentecostals were also intrigued by the raw faith under the tent, blazing the trail for Pentecostalism's remarkable expansion in the 1960s. Always seeking to expand his ministry, Roberts announced in 1960 that he would found in Tulsa what is now Oral Roberts University.

✳ Consensus, Conformity, and Criticism

Despite dissenting voices, the unity of American culture was more visible in the 1950s than its diversity. American intellectuals of the fifties focused increasingly on understanding the apparent serenity and conformity. Historians saw the decade as an example of consensus that illustrated the cohesion in American culture, highlighting the "exceptionalism" of the American experience. Some of the "consensus" historians had been political radicals in earlier decades; now they sought to explain the failure of class conflict in American politics. For the most part they lamented the one-dimensional character of American civilization. In *The American Political Tradition* (1948), Richard Hofstadter pictured a conservative undercurrent running throughout American political history. Movements such as populism and progressivism, which seemed so radical to conservatives of the times, were to Hofstadter actually conservative movements aimed at preserving traditional social and political values from powerful groups who wanted to exploit American society for their own purposes. Intellectual, social, and economic support for this consensus view was offered in Louis Hartz's critical *The Liberal Tradition*

in America (1955). More positive assessments of the unique American character were suggested by Daniel Boorstin in *The Genius of American Politics* (1953) and by David Potter in *People of Plenty* (1954).

Some social scientists applauded American exceptionalism. In *The End of Ideology* (1960), Harvard's Daniel Bell explored the social cohesion of democracy and argued that apocalyptic ideologies, including Marxism, offered little to promote social reform. They would eventually disappear, Bell predicted, and he denied that contemporary social trends either demanded mindless conformity or stunted intellectual creativity. Bell's writings typified the shift of disciplines such as sociology away from broad theorizing — and toward the collection of data and the microanalysis of specific social conditions. The most influential sociological theory of the 1950s, associated with Talcott Parsons (also of Harvard), was called "structural functionalism." It emphasized the organic nature of human society and the sanctity of individual roles that had been worked out over time and institutionalized. For many of these writers, social systems replaced religion as the moral arbiter in modern society.

Three influential and widely read books summarized American conformity and tried to explain its origins. Each found the drive for conformity a troubling symptom of the collapse of older American values. William H. Whyte, a former editor of *Fortune* magazine, wrote a devastating critique of American business, *The Organization Man* (1956). Whyte believed that such virtues as hard work, risk-taking, and self-reliance had been replaced among the nation's business leaders by an emphasis on "togetherness" and being well liked. Whyte concluded that those bastions of American individualism, the giant corporations, had themselves become stifling islands of conformity.

Will Herberg, in *Protestant, Catholic, Jew* (1960), drew a similar picture of fifties religion. While it was true that expressions of religiosity and church membership flourished in the 1950s, Herberg believed that it was largely superficial, typified by Eisenhower's statement that the government must be "founded on deeply felt religious belief — and I don't care what it is." Americans rushed to define themselves as members of one of the three socially acceptable religious communities in the 1950s not out of conviction, but to locate themselves in the community — in short, to conform.

In what was to become a sociological classic, *The Lonely Crowd* (1950), David Riesman summarized fifties conformity. Riesman argued that Americans had

The "Military-Industrial Complex"

Despite his reputation as an effective Cold Warrior, by the end of his presidency Dwight Eisenhower could see ominous byproducts of the Cold War. In his farewell address, he expressed concerns about the influence of what he called the "military-industrial complex."

A vital element in keeping the peace is our military establishment. Our arms must be mighty, ready for instant action, so that no potential aggressor may be tempted to risk his own destruction. . . .

This conjunction of an immense military establishment and a large arms industry is new in the American experience. The total influence — economic, political, even spiritual — is felt in every city, every state house, every office of the Federal government. We recognize the imperative need for this development. Yet we must not fail to comprehend its grave implications. Our toil, resources and livelihood are all involved; so is the very structure of our society.

In the councils of government, we must guard against the acquisition of unwarranted influence, whether sought or unsought, by the military-industrial complex. The potential for the disastrous rise of misplaced power exists and will persist. . . .

The prospect of domination of the nation's scholars by Federal employment, project allocations, and the power of money is ever present and is gravely to be regarded.

---

moved from being an individualistic and ideologically motivated people in the nineteenth century, from a mind set he called "inner-directed," to a conformist mass whose attitudes and values were determined by peer groups and society's demands. Thus, modern Americans were "other-directed" people.

CONCLUSION: CONSERVATISM, CONSENSUS, AND CONSCIENCE

Whyte, Herberg, and Riesman all rued the apparent shallowness of American society in the 1950s. America had become a dreary conformist landscape where the cardinal sin was being different. But most Americans believed that they were living in the best of times. Their optimism was in some ways warranted; victory in World War II had, for America, ushered in unparalleled prosperity, expanded educational opportunities, and triggered an explosion of consumer goods. Many concluded that God truly had blessed America, and people flocked into the nation's churches giving thanks. Yet social and religious conservatism was also fed by anxieties bred of international tensions and a booming but shallow consumer culture.

Given the trauma of World War II, the apprehension associated with the Cold War, and the prevailing prosperity, it is not surprising that the politics of the decade was solidly conservative, though not reactionary, and that the electorate made Dwight D. Eisenhower one of the most popular presidents in history. Moderate Republicans and centrist Democrats did not dismantle the Depression-born welfare state, but they did slow the growth of the federal government.

In foreign affairs the Eisenhower administration managed to contain Sino-Soviet imperialism while keeping America out of a major war. Fortunately, the Cold War never erupted into all-out conflict while the great powers jockeyed to limit one another's global influence. Both the United States and the Soviet Union suffered embarrassments and scored victories, but fears of a global war ebbed until Sputnik soared into space in 1957. By the decade's end, tensions were ratcheting up again. Americans were frustrated by the Cold War, a nuclear confrontation looming ominously, but most people believed that the nation's hero general-president would protect the national interest and advance the cause of freedom.

Critics bewailed the rampant consumerism and complacency in American society. Seeds of the sixties upheavals were sown by some American intellectuals in the fifties and in the decade's glimmers of youthful cultural rebellion. But it was the civil rights movement that ultimately convinced most Americans that all was not well in their country. By the end of the decade, a moral and legal revolution was fully underway; it had begun to change the pattern of racial relations that had denied basic rights to African Americans. More than that, the civil rights movement convinced a generation of Americans that they had been accomplices in a great evil and that it was time to take a look at their country's soul.

SUGGESTED READING

C. C. Alexander, *Holding the Line: The Eisenhower Era* (1975). An excellent brief interpretation of the Eisenhower years.

Stephen E. Ambrose, *Eisenhower: Soldier and President* (1990). A good standard biography of Eisenhower.

William Chafe, *The Unfinished Journey* (1986). A standard text on the postwar years.

John Lewis Gaddis, *We Now Know: Rethinking Cold War History* (1997). A recent summary of Cold War policymaking that uses new archival materials.

David Halberstam, *The Fifties* (1993). An encyclopedic overview of the decade.

Martin E. Marty, *Modern American Religion: Under God, Indivisible, 1941-1960*, vol. 3 (1996). An excellent overview of religion in the fifties.

J. Ronald Oakley, *God's Country: America in the Fifties* (1986). This work highlights the problems and challenges of the fifties.

Herbert Parmet, *Eisenhower and the American Crusades* (1972). A solid treatment of the period and Dwight Eisenhower's role in it.

SUGGESTIONS FOR FURTHER READING

Numan V. Bartley, *The Rise of Massive Resistance: Race and Politics in the South During the 1950s* (1969).

George Carney, ed., *Fast Food, Stock Cars, & Rock'n'Roll* (1995).

John Patrick Diggins, *The Proud Decades, 1941-1960* (1989).

Saki Dockrill, *Eisenhower's New-Look National Security Policy, 1953-61* (1996).

John Fousek, *To Lead the Free World: American Nationalism and the Cultural Roots of the Cold War* (2000).

Robert A. Gorman, *Michael Harrington: Speaking American* (1995).

Peter Guralnick, *Last Train to Memphis: The Rise of Elvis Presley* (1994).

David Edwin Harrell, Jr., *Oral Roberts: An American Life* (1985).

Jeffrey Hart, *When the Going Was Good: American Life in the Fifties* (1982).

Walter L. Hixson, *Parting the Curtain: Propaganda, Culture, and the Cold War, 1945-1961* (1997).

Eugenia Kaledin, *Mothers and More: American Women in the 1950s* (1984).

Christopher Owen Lynch, *Selling Catholicism: Bishop Sheen and the Power of Television* (1998).

Elaine May, *Homeward Bound: American Families in the Cold War Era* (1988).

William O'Neill, *American High: The Years of Confidence, 1945-1960* (1986).

David Potter, *People of Plenty* (1954).

Peter J. Roman, *Eisenhower and the Missile Gap* (1995).

Michael S. Sherry, *In the Shadow of War* (1995).

Harvard Sitkoff, *The Struggle for Black Equality, 1954-1980* (1981).

Herbert Stein, *The Fiscal Revolution in America* (1969).

32 The Climax of Liberalism in the Sixties and Seventies

I N 1960, IT would have been difficult to predict the intensity and contentiousness of the national strife that began in the second half of the 1960s and persisted through the 1970s. In many ways, the optimism and national confidence of the 1950s continued unabated into the 1960s; the nation's greatest heroes, the astronauts, were vintage 1950s characters — clean-cut, scientific, and adventurous. After the election of the charismatic young John F. Kennedy to the presidency in 1960 the nation seemed ready to pull together. Liberal intellectuals and politicians were confident that the nation had entered an era of "affirmative government" in which the use of federal power in good causes would bring to fruition the hopes and dreams of earlier progressive reformers.

Instead, during the 1960s and 1970s a wide-ranging, sometimes raucous, debate about the meaning of the American dream erupted, fueled by rising impatience over persistent patterns of inequality and by self-doubts stirred by international tensions and a disastrous war in Southeast Asia. During these two decades a long series of divisive events and movements undermined American confidence and laid bare deep social cleavages. At every step, the nation's internal traumas were reported graphically on television. The assassinations of John Kennedy in 1963 and of Robert Kennedy and Martin Luther King, Jr., in 1968 highlighted the violent and factious mood that seemed to grip American society. Student radicals and black militants unleashed a stream of revolutionary rhetoric and occasionally violent behavior, and the long war in Vietnam, perceived by many Americans as the first military defeat ever suffered by the nation, brought the ugly violence of war into the living room of every American home. The long Watergate drama, which ended with the resignation of the president, deeply eroded Americans' confidence in their political leaders. It seemed fitting that the decade of the seventies ended with the American embassy in Tehran occupied by Iranian militants and sixty-three American citizens held captive. By the end of the 1970s American national spirit had reached low tide.

The growing sense of unrest in the mid-1960s had many sources. The American civil rights movement stirred the hopes of people around the world that felt that they had been oppressed. In the United States, African American activists turned more confrontational after 1965, and a new wave of feminists and advocates of other minorities and interest groups joined them in demanding that American society become more inclusive. Their causes were aided by an activist Supreme Court that greatly expanded the legal protection of defendants and minorities but was unable to compel equal opportunity.

A second source of dissent in the sixties and seventies, only partly related to the civil rights revolution and other social movements of the era, was a stunning rebellion by young people against the nation's leading institutions and conventional codes of conduct. The youth "counterculture" that emerged in the late 1960s was a diffuse phenomenon. Mostly from within the nation's universities, intellectuals loosely called the New Left launched wide-ranging attacks on American institutions, conventional economics, and Western foreign policy. These academic and public intellectuals, in turn, inspired a generation of student radicals who, though they never constituted more than a small minority among the student population, became highly visible (and vocal) political activists. Their rebellion climaxed in their powerful protest against the Vietnam War. Far greater numbers of young people participated in a milder form of rebellion against their elders by embracing new tastes in music, dress, and grooming and new attitudes toward sex, drugs, and the environment.

Amid the clamors of the sixties and seventies, it was easy to lose sight of mainstream American culture. Most Americans were neither hippies nor social radicals, a fact grasped by such wily politicians as Richard Nixon and by his instinctively conservative heir, Ronald Reagan. Some reacted angrily to the confrontational methods and the demands of the new movements, believing that their own problems were exacerbated by the aggressive tactics of others, and they struck back. But a majority of Americans simply continued to live their daily lives through days of dramatic headlines and cultural upheaval.

THE IDEOLOGICAL AND CULTURAL SOURCES OF SIXTIES LIBERALISM

Liberal ideas in the 1960s and 1970s inspired the rhetoric and agendas of many of the political leaders of the era, in turn raising the aspirations of millions of people. More than anything else, it was the moral fervor of the civil rights movement led by Martin Luther King, Jr., that forced Americans to rethink their commitment to equality of opportunity. The civil rights revolution and other liberal triumphs of the 1960s came amid a rising torrent of demands from radical reformers, who quickly outflanked moderate liberals. By the mid-sixties, militant black leaders were becoming increasingly confrontational, as both racial antagonism and social despair spawned inner-city violence. By the end of the sixties, the civil rights movement had become a model for other interest groups whose members saw themselves as victims of discrimination.

⤋ *The Flowering of Postwar Liberalism*

The conservative temper of the immediate postwar era partly reflected the returning prosperity and consequent contentment of Americans in those years, but it also owed something to a crisis in American liberalism. Throughout the 1950s, liberals — those who believed that the government had a major responsibility for ensuring social justice at home and abroad — had struggled to reconcile their optimistic ideas about human nature with the grim realities of World War II and its aftermath: the Holocaust, Hiroshima and the dawn of the nuclear age, Communist totalitarianism, McCarthyism, and a slowly awakening consciousness of American racial inequality.

Gradually, liberal intellectuals crafted a new vision for achieving economic and social justice. The liberalism of the early 1960s contained no hint of radicalism, little disposition to revive New Deal–era crusades against concentrated economic power, and no intention to fan class passions or redistribute wealth or restructure existing institutions. Internationally, it was strongly anti-Communist. It aimed to defend the free world, to encourage economic growth at home, and to ensure that the resulting plenty was fairly distributed. This was the message of leading liberal intellectuals such as Harvard historian Arthur Schlesinger, Jr., and economist John Kenneth Galbraith, as well as of respected journals of opinion such as *The New Republic*. Their agenda — much influenced by Keynesian economic theory — envisioned massive public expenditure that would speed economic growth, thus providing the public resources to fund larger welfare, housing, health, and educational programs. Galbraith's influential book, *The Affluent Society* (1958), which scolded his fellow-citizens for permitting "public squalor" to persist in America because of irresponsible private consumption, became an economic bible for postwar liberals. Liberals rejoiced in the nation's economic and technological boom during the 1950s and 1960s, sure that an ever growing economic "pie" would make it possible to distribute the nation's wealth more equitably — and painlessly. They believed it would be possible to mobilize the nation behind a reform agenda without dividing it. America, liberals believed, could have quality, quantity, and unity.

❧ *The Accelerating Civil Rights Revolution*

The greatest liberal cause of the 1960s was the civil rights movement. But it was black activists, not white liberals, who ignited the civil rights revolution. White liberals in the 1940s and 1950s had viewed segregation as a distasteful and ugly blemish on the American soul that would have to be wiped away through gradual reform imposed from above; even the *Brown* decision had called for change with "all deliberate speed." They were little prepared for the civil rights revolution that would be launched and led by a new generation of black leaders.

SIT-INS, BOYCOTTS, AND FREEDOM RIDES
In 1957, Martin Luther King, Jr., decided to institutionalize the nonviolent civil disobedience techniques he had first tested in the Montgomery bus boycott. With his friend and ally Ralph Abernathy, he brought together more than a hundred black ministers to found the Southern Christian Leadership Conference (SCLC). The SCLC added a new nonviolent, direct-action civil rights component to the NAACP's traditional legal-action approach. The vibrancy of the civil rights movement of the 1960s owed much to the black churches. The church had long been the most visible independent institutional network within the black communities

of the South, and, since the 1930s, church leaders had been more assertive in defending black rights. Membership in the SCLC grew rapidly, but even so, in the late 1950s the civil rights movement lacked a new focus and seemed to be losing momentum.

The movement was dramatically revived in 1960 by a group of black college students at North Carolina Agricultural and Technical College in Greensboro, who rebelled against segregation laws that allowed them to spend money in white-owned establishments but not to eat, drink, or share restrooms with white patrons. On February 1, 1960, four A & T freshmen sat down at the segregated Woolworth's lunch counter in Greensboro, North Carolina. When, as expected, the white staff refused to serve them, the students remained seated until closing. The next day two dozen supporters joined them, and on the third day, black students occupied all sixty-six places at the lunch counter. The subsequent arrest of forty-five students galvanized the local black community, whose boycott of Greensboro merchants brought an end to decades of legalized segregation. On July 25 an

Dr. Martin Luther King, Jr. The great civil rights leader speaks at Selma, Alabama, on January 22, 1965, encouraging participants in one of the crucial struggles of the Second Reconstruction.

Sit-In This photograph, taken in February 1960, documents the sit-in movement in Greensboro, North Carolina, which ignited the sixties drive for full African American equality. Here, college students occupy seats at a drugstore lunch counter in their effort to dramatize and break patterns of legalized segregation.

African American ate lunch at the Woolworth's counter. "I probably felt better on that day," reported one participant, "than I've felt in my life.... I felt as though I had gained my manhood, so to speak, and not only gained it, but had developed a lot of respect for it." Greensboro was the first of a wave of sit-ins that swept through the South during 1960 and 1961. Altogether some 70,000 people, most black but some white, sat in at a variety of segregated public facilities. "It was like going to church, I guess," John Lewis remembered. "You would put on your ... Sunday clothes, and we took books and papers and did our homework at the lunch counter, just quiet and trying to be as dignified as possible."

While most African Americans supported the sit-in and boycott movements, not all did. Many in the traditional black elite — teachers, politicians, owners of service businesses, and lawyers — had made money and gained influence by cooperating with the white power structure. Some felt threatened by student protests and boycotts, and this generational and philosophical gap spawned a new organization, the Student Nonviolent Coordinating Committee (SNCC, pronounced "snick"), founded in April 1960. SNCC organizers insisted that student protesters should retain control of their move-

ment, and they stressed democracy, grassroots leadership, and Gandhian civil disobedience. In the fall of 1960, SNCC field workers spread out across the South in an effort to stimulate community-based activism.

In the spring of 1961, another group that dated back to World War II, the Congress on Racial Equality (CORE), headed by civil rights veteran James Farmer, planned a series of "freedom rides" to test southern compliance with recent court orders banning segregation on interstate transportation. With financial aid from SCLC and NAACP, Farmer actively sought confrontation. "Our intention," he later declared, "was to provoke the southern authorities into arresting us and thereby prod the Justice department into enforcing the law of the land." The first week in May 1961, thirteen black and white freedom riders took buses from Washington, D.C., to Alabama and Mississippi in two groups. At first they encountered only sporadic harassment, but at Anniston, Alabama, a white mob smashed bus windows and slashed tires. Soon thereafter, en route to Birmingham, the bus was firebombed. On May 20, a fresh group of twenty-one riders boarded a bus in Birmingham destined for Montgomery; when the passengers disembarked they were attacked by a mob, leaving one rider paralyzed. Montgomery police stood by, offering the freedom riders no assistance. Television and news coverage of the violence in Montgomery shocked the nation and forced the somewhat reluctant Kennedy administration to support the freedom riders.

KING AND KENNEDY

In response to these events, President Kennedy, who did not want to divert attention from his efforts to confront Communism abroad and get the American economy moving again, announced a plan to desegregate higher education in the South. Most civil rights leaders deemed this initiative too little, too late, and they launched new campaigns to hasten the pace of civil rights. In the spring of 1963, Martin Luther King, Jr., targeted Birmingham, Alabama ("the most segregated city" in the country, he called it), for a series of protest marches and sit-ins. The nonviolent black protests were met with savage opposition from the Birmingham police force, led by Commissioner Eugene "Bull" Conner. Thousands of blacks were arrested, and demonstrations were broken up with high-powered water hoses, electric cattle prods, and snarling attack dogs. Night after night, network television news broadcast the attacks throughout the world, crystallizing moderate white support for the civil rights movement in both North and South. A behind-the-scenes compromise negotiated by civil rights activists and moderate white political and business leaders resulted in a desegregation of Birmingham stores and the opening of new jobs for black workers. These painful and traumatic events stirred the consciences of many whites in both North and South and, ironically, set Birmingham on a path to becoming one of the nation's more racially progressive cities by the end of the twentieth century.

King's demand for "Freedom Now" in Birmingham forced the reluctant Kennedy administration to move toward a more activist role in the civil rights battle. Still, dissatisfied with the federal government's timidity, on August 28, 1963, Martin Luther King, Jr., led a March on Washington, organized by the major civil rights groups, the AFL-CIO, and both black and white religious leaders. Nearly 250,000 people converged on the Mall to hear King's inspiring speech from the steps of the Lincoln Memorial, describing his dream for America; a dream that would come to pass when "all of God's children, black men and white men . . . will be able to join hands and sing in the words of the old Negro spiritual, 'Free at last! Free at last! Thank God Almighty, we are free at last!'"

BLOODSHED CONTINUES

By the spring of 1964 a "Second Reconstruction" was clearly underway, spurred on by a sense of national sorrow in the wake of John F. Kennedy's assassination and by Lyndon B. Johnson's genuine commitment to black

---

✳ IN THEIR OWN WORDS

"Letter from Birmingham Jail," 1963
While being held in the Birmingham Jail, Martin Luther King, Jr., wrote a response to eight fellow clergy who had publicly criticized his acts of civil disobedience.

MY DEAR FELLOW CLERGYMEN:

While confined here in the Birmingham city jail, I came across your recent statement calling my present activities "unwise and untimely." Seldom do I pause to answer criticism of my work and ideas. . . . But since I feel that you are men of genuine good will and that your criticisms are sincerely set forth, I want to try to answer your statements in what I hope will be patient and reasonable terms. . . .

I must confess that over the past few years I have been gravely disappointed with the white moderate. I have almost reached the regrettable conclusion that the Negro's great stumbling block in his stride toward freedom is not the White Citizen's Counciler or the Ku Klux Klanner, but the white moderate, who is more devoted to "order" than to justice; who prefers a negative peace which is the absence of tension to a positive peace which is the presence of justice; who constantly says: "I agree with you in the goal you seek, but I cannot agree with your methods of direct action"; who paternalistically believes he can set the timetable for another man's freedom; who lives by a mythical concept of time and who constantly advises the Negro to wait for a "more convenient season." Shallow understanding from people of good will is more frustrating than absolute misunderstanding from people of ill will. Lukewarm acceptance is much more bewildering than outright rejection. . . .

I hope this letter finds you strong in the faith. I also hope that circumstances will soon make it possible for me to meet each of you, not as an integrationist or a civil rights leader but as a fellow clergyman and a Christian brother. Let us all hope that the dark clouds of racial prejudice will soon pass away and the deep fog of misunderstanding will be lifted from our fear-drenched communities, and in some not too distant tomorrow the radiant stars of love and brotherhood will shine over our great nation with all their scintillating beauty.

Yours for the cause of Peace and Brotherhood,

MARTIN LUTHER KING, JR.

April 16, 1963

rights. The federal government, with the support of moderate American whites, at last openly committed itself to fulfill the promises made to black Americans during the first reconstruction after the Civil War. Meanwhile, in the wake of the March on Washington, the civil rights movement began to focus on voting rights. Early in 1964 Bob Moses of SNCC and David Dennis of CORE launched Freedom Summer, organizing and training black and white college students in the techniques of nonviolent resistance and political activism, with the aim of registering black voters in Mississippi. Although African Americans comprised 42 percent of Mississippi's population, only 5 percent were registered to vote. During the summer the young workers fanned out across Mississippi trying to persuade blacks to register. "There is a relationship between your not being able to feed your children and your not registering to vote," SNCC workers told the black tenant farmers and laborers of the South. The organizers of Freedom Summer anticipated violence, and they were right. On June 21 three young project workers — Andrew Goodman, Michael Schwerner, and James Chaney — were reported missing in Neshoba County. Goodman and Schwerner were white, Chaney black. Six weeks later the three men's bodies were discovered, and an FBI investigation subsequently uncovered a conspiracy to murder them, implicating local law enforcement officers and members of the Ku Klux Klan. Although the Freedom Summer workers succeeded in registering only around 1,200 voters, they enrolled nearly 60,000 blacks in the Mississippi Freedom Democratic Party, an organization that challenged the state's all-white Democratic Party, and raised politicians' consciousness about the need to protect black voting rights in the South. It also proved to be a training ground for a group of radical black civil rights leaders who would reorganize the movement in the last half of the decade and a number of young white radicals who would later surface as leaders of the radical student movement and anti–Vietnam War protest.

After the election of 1964, in many areas of the South white resistance to black enfranchisement remained strong. In 1965 Martin Luther King, Jr., once again planned a dramatic protest to provoke action, organizing a series of demonstrations in Alabama. Outside Selma, Alabama, in January 1965, civil rights workers marching from that city to Montgomery to petition arch-segregationist Governor George Wallace were attacked by two hundred state and local police with tear gas, clubs, and cattle prods. Television cameras once again relayed scenes throughout the nation that were as shocking and violent as those from Birmingham in 1963, and an outraged nation gave its support to demands for protection for the voting rights of African Americans (see Chapter 33).

❧ The Black Pride Movement and the Rise of Black Militancy

The civil rights movement had created a rising level of expectations among African Americans and released anger and resentment that had been pent up for decades. When traditional forms of protest and nonviolent civil disobedience failed to end discrimination and create equal opportunity, young African Americans rejected the gradualist approach espoused by the NAACP and the SCLC.

Less than a week after President Lyndon Johnson signed the 1965 Civil Rights Act (see Chapter 33), marking the high water mark of legislative civil rights reform in America, young African Americans, many of them unemployed, began looting and razing businesses in the Watts district of Los Angeles. Their objective, they announced to the media, was "to drive white exploiters out of the ghetto." Firemen were attacked with rocks and bottles, and the police and the National Guard moved in to restore order. When at long last the rioters had exhausted themselves, the ghetto lay in smoldering ruin; thirty-four people had died and the property damage was estimated at $200 million.

In one urban ghetto after another during the "long hot summers" of the late 1960s, the Watts debacle was repeated. While a majority of blacks continued to embrace nonviolence and political reform, King, the SCLC, the NAACP, and the black churches increasingly found themselves pushed out of the limelight. New voices now were shouting the slogan "black power." The label "black militant" was applied by the media to a variety of leaders with different agendas, but most of them drew on the broad spirit of rebellion that also blossomed on American university campuses in the late sixties, as well as on the seething discontent in urban ghettos. In the minds of many black militants, liberals, both black and white, were dangerously misguided. In 1966 student activist Stokely Carmichael first used the expression "black power" to argue that blacks must control their own institutions, such as schools and businesses. Increasingly radical black organizations of the 1960s, including SNCC, of which Carmichael assumed leadership, and CORE, now led by Floyd McKissick, purged whites from their memberships and repudiated the long-time civil rights goal of an integrated American society.

An even more militant black group was the paramilitary Black Panthers, led by Huey P. Newton and Eldridge Cleaver. The Panthers emerged as a protest against alleged police brutality in Oakland, California. They embraced Marxism and staged highly publicized confrontations with the police that ended in a number of deaths and the imprisonment of both Newton and Cleaver. Although they were never more than two thousand strong nationwide, the Black Panthers raised the specter of armed rebellion.

In the long run more significant than the Black Panthers was the Nation of Islam, or Black Muslims, under the militant leadership of Elijah Muhammad. Combining the teachings of Islam and the black separatist writings of the prophet W. D. Fard, who had begun the movement in the 1930s, Black Muslims were extremely successful in recruiting and often transforming criminals, drug addicts, and other social outcasts. By the early sixties the most visible Black Muslim was a streetwise minister, Malcolm Little, who changed his name to Malcolm X. Malcolm and other Black Muslims preached black pride and self-reliance, arguing that the only way blacks could liberate themselves — spiritually, politically, and economically — was through violent struggle. "If someone puts a hand on you," he told his followers, "send him to the cemetery." After a pilgrimage to Mecca in 1964, Malcolm abandoned the racist rhetoric of the Black Muslims and sought to identify himself with orthodox, racially inclusive Islamic beliefs. He was murdered on February 21, 1965, by Black Muslims who believed he had betrayed their leader and their faith. Upon the death of Elijah Muhammad in 1975, the leadership of the Black Muslims fell to his son, Wallace D. Muhammad, who was more moderate than his father, but the group continued to represent a separatist alternative for the most alienated African Americans.

The urban riots and the rise of black separatist movements were symptoms of larger problems. Civil rights movements had raised black expectations. As manufacturing establishments left central cities for the suburbs or smaller towns in search of lower taxes and more skilled workers, African Americans remained stranded, lacking transportation to reach jobs or the means to relocate, and often without the skills to compete in the changing job market. Big-city political machines wooed black voters but provided little funding to rebuild the

Malcolm X   Intense, acerbic, and unyieldingly militant, Malcolm X galvanized young African Americans both inside and outside the Black Muslim movement, of which he was originally a charismatic spokesman.

decaying inner cities. Many blacks seeking to escape the ghettos found it impossible because unwritten covenants excluded them from white neighborhoods, and they were forced to pay high rents for crumbling apartments in crime-infested inner cities.

Despite the efforts of liberal politicians to break historic patterns of discrimination and segregation, every city retained black enclaves of poverty. During the unsettled economic conditions in the 1970s, inner-city blacks experienced a 21 percent increase in poverty. Divorce rates ran nearly twice as high for blacks as for whites, and the number of African Americans reporting marital separations was roughly five times as high. Black children were born into poverty at approximately four times the rate of whites. The incidence of fatherless black households grew steadily, and more and more black families were headed by unmarried teenage mothers who relied on welfare to support themselves and their children.

While the plight of poor inner-city blacks remained dire through the sixties and seventies, a rapidly growing black middle class also became more visible. The number of black college students increased from 282,000 in 1966 to more than 1 million in 1976. By the end of the 1970s at least 30 percent of African Americans were defined as middle class, and many had moved to the suburbs. By that time, one-third of all black high school graduates entered college, about the same proportion as whites. By the end of the 1970s, two black Americas were quite visible — one poor, underemployed, and angry; the other a middle class that looked much like other Americans. Successful African Americans often found themselves trapped between continuing patterns of discrimination from whites and the disdain of more militant blacks.

By 1967, after a Detroit race riot left thirty-three black and ten white Americans dead, it seemed to a majority of white Americans that the black power philosophy had come to a dead end. Rioting eroded white sympathy for civil rights, slowing the pace of political reform. While the nonviolent civil rights movement had pricked the consciences of many white Americans, by the end of the seventies racial tensions had once again hardened, and many issues remained contentious and unsettled.

❧ The New Women's Movement

Aside from African Americans, no group derived greater benefit from the new cultural awareness of the 1960s and 1970s than a revived feminist movement, even though it was more amorphous and more difficult to organize than the struggle for African American rights. Since the 1920s the women's movement had lain somewhat dormant, defused first by success in winning the suffrage and then by the privations of the Depression and World War II, and no new broad feminist agenda had appeared for several decades. Nonetheless, during these years women's status in American society continued to change. By 1970 more than 43 percent of all

women were employed outside the home, and in 1978 that figure passed 50 percent for the first time in American history. By the end of the seventies, women constituted nearly 42 percent of the American labor force, they were more likely to be high school graduates than men, and they were entering the work force at an unprecedented rate. Still, the workplace remained starkly discriminatory.

A sense of uneasiness among American women manifested itself in a variety of ways by the mid-1960s. Surveying the lives of young wives in 1960, *Newsweek* noted that middle-class American women were healthier, better educated, and more financially secure than any previous generation, and yet they seemed to have a "disenchantment syndrome." Betty Friedan's *Feminine Mystique*, published in 1963, articulated many of the unspoken discontents of middle-class American women. Countless women agreed with Friedan's contention that they were imprisoned by a society that told them only what they should be rather than empowering and encouraging them to be what they could be.

Women activists took part in all the protest movements of the 1950s and 1960s, and many women were radicalized by the student movement that began in the early sixties, the civil rights revolution, and the antiwar movement. Nonetheless, the radical left, not to mention conventional political liberals, tended to be as sexist as more traditional Americans were. In the student protest movement women activists were generally relegated to such menial tasks as cooking and washing. Many black militant leaders were blatant male chauvinists. Asked to comment on a position paper on "Women in the Movement" during a staff retreat in 1964, SNCC's Stokely Carmichael delivered a notorious quip that captured the gender insensitivity of many sixties radicals: "The only position for women in SNCC is prone." "The New Left has been a hell hole for women," complained one Berkeley veteran. "It's the most destructive environment sexually I've ever encountered."

In this turbulent milieu, a new women's movement began to take shape. In 1967 Betty Friedan led in the formation of the National Organization for Women (NOW). Bringing together both female and male advocates of women's rights, as well as experienced feminists and young veterans of the civil rights movement, NOW became the foremost organization in the women's rights branch of the diffuse feminist movement. NOW grew from a thousand members in 1967 to 40,000 in 1974. Through litigation, political pressure, and public information campaigns, women's rights advocates pushed to guarantee equality under the law and equal opportunity.

The civil rights movement served as a model for women committed to both protest and political action. A Commission on the Status of Women appointed by President Kennedy in 1963 proposed an Equal Pay Act and urged adding gender to the language of the 1964 Civil Rights Act. As a result, the Civil Rights Act of 1964 did include a ban on discrimination in employment on the basis of sex as well as race, and experienced women activists used the new legislation to organize and launch a national women's rights campaign. In the late 1960s and early 1970s women's rights activists won battle after battle that brought about tangible results in the 1970s. In a major equal rights decision, the Supreme Court ruled that women in the armed forces were entitled to the same benefits for their spouses as those accorded male servicemen. In 1967 women were included in affirmative action guidelines, along with blacks and other minority groups. Congress passed an Equal Rights Amendment and submitted it to the states for ratification in 1972. Twenty-eight states quickly ratified the amendment, and it seemed at the time that its addition to the Constitution was inevitable.

All of this resulted in some clear changes in the lives of women in the 1970s. The number of women enrolled in college rose by nearly half in the early 1970s. Nevertheless, certain harsh realities slowed the economic advances of women in the 1970s, including a glutted job market. The women's movement's greatest achievement, many of its advocates believed, came when in 1972 the Supreme Court legalized abortion in the *Roe v. Wade* decision. Feminists regarded the abortion issue as a critical test of their rights, and supporters also pointed out that the number of abortion-related deaths dropped from 320 in 1961, when all abortions were illegal, to only 47 in 1973. The number of legal abortions rose from around 580,000 in 1972 to more than 1.5 million in 1980. In the years ahead, issues surrounding abortion would be among the most divisive and factious in American politics.

While one group of feminists concentrated on economic and political issues, others identified a range of psychic and cultural injustices that they regarded as social impositions designed to relegate women to subservience. These activists, sometimes called the women's liberation movement, were both angrier and more aggressive than the generally conventional women grouped around NOW. Kate Millett's *Sexual Politics* (1970) was one of many militant books that not only

challenged the legal, economic, and political inequality of the sexes but also attacked sexual double standards and sex-role stereotypes. The women's liberation movement argued that girls were trained in childhood to be feminine, solicitous of men and willing to take subservient jobs. The term that united women's liberation activists was "sexism," an obvious coinage from "racism." While virtually all "women's libbers" decried the cultural sexism they saw in *Playboy* magazine and the Miss America pageant (which a group of women picketed in 1968), the movement splintered into factions when some lesbian and extremist leaders denounced all heterosexual love and sex as strategies of male oppression. Outside the formal political sphere, the women's liberation movement used "consciousness-raising" sessions, which were held with increasing frequency on campuses and in communities all across the country.

While the women's movement wrought important changes in American society, older patterns of American family life persisted. Millions of American women continued to be homemakers, and working women discovered that their domestic duties and family role changed little even though they were employed outside the home. Some feminists complained that liberation had simply added to the burdens of women. Nor was it clear that the new sexual morality, however liberating for some women, was an unmixed blessing. Divorce rates shot up during the 1960s and 1970s. In 1960 about 2.5 percent of American men between the ages of 25 and 54 who had ever been married had been divorced, as had 3.8 percent of women. By 1980, those figures reached 8.2 percent for men and 11 percent for women.

No single group ever spoke for all American women. Movement activists were mostly white, middle-class, educated women. Black women generally shunned the women's movement, identifying rather with black causes, and many homemakers resented the feminists' tendency to sneer at domesticity and family values in the quest for autonomy and career. By the end of the decade of the seventies, many women seemed to be losing interest in the feminist agenda. In 1981, in a book entitled *The Second Stage*, Betty Friedan urged feminists to broaden their agenda to include the interests of those women who felt excluded.

Nonetheless, the women's movement refocused and redefined the liberal political agenda, creating a powerful new interest group within the Democratic Party that focused on gender equality. Increasingly, support for or opposition to the *Roe v. Wade* decision on abortion became a divisive litmus test for American politicians.

Gay Rights Rally, 1974 These supportive parents were part of a parade that climaxed one of New York City's earliest gay pride weeks. They had particular reason to celebrate this year; in 1974 the American Psychological Association removed homosexuality from its list of mental disorders.

In 1974 the gay community achieved an important symbolic victory when the American Psychiatric Association removed homosexuality from its list of mental disorders. The movement for homosexual rights in the 1960s and 1970s was bolstered by the flawed findings of the Kinsey Reports, which had concluded that 10 percent of American men had long periods of more or less exclusive homosexuality and that 4 percent were homosexual all of their life. Society's general tolerance for protest meant that the gay rights movement's demands for equal treatment under the law and for cultural legitimacy were for the first time taken seriously; many gay and lesbian Americans first found their voices as part of the general minority consciousness of the sixties and seventies.

❧ Gay and Lesbian Rights

Gay and lesbian communities have existed throughout American history, but not until the 1960s and 1970s did homosexuals begin to "come out of the closet" in significant numbers and to mobilize to defend themselves against discrimination. The feminist movement contributed to gay awareness through its consciousness-raising groups, which often discussed the issue. Lesbians, forced out of NOW in 1969 and 1970, were readmitted in 1971 in a move that symbolized the growing effectiveness of their crusade.

In 1960 homosexuality was generally judged to be either a disease or a crime, and most states imposed some legal penalties for sodomy. Professional psychologists for the most part concurred in diagnosing homosexuality as abnormal; armed with the writings of Sigmund Freud, psychoanalysts spent countless hours trying to "cure" homosexuals of their "perversion." Not until 1969 did the National Institute of Mental Health recommend the legalization of private homosexual acts between consenting adults. These changes were clearly linked to the new political climate of the late 1960s; by the 1970s many communities throughout the country were increasingly hesitant to enforce sodomy laws. By that time many organizations offering support, community, and advocacy to gays and lesbians had formed, and the movement had given birth to thousands of entrepreneurial endeavors catering to the gay community, including publications, bookstores, bars, and coffeehouses.

❧ The Rising Hispanic Consciousness

Several other American minority groups gained new momentum in their struggles for civil rights during the sixties. One of the most important changes in American life during the 1960s and 1970s was the growing visibility of Hispanics, who by the end of the 1970s would replace blacks as the nation's largest ethnic minority. Before 1960 the three major Spanish-speaking groups in America — Mexicans, Puerto Ricans, and Cubans — had largely been confined to the Southwest, southeastern Florida, and New York City. Large migrations from Mexico and Puerto Rico began after World War II, and most Cuban immigrants arrived in the wake of Fidel Castro's Communist revolution in 1959. Inspired by the civil rights movement, activists attempted to forge a common Hispanic identity during the 1960s and 1970s, but cultural, historical, ethnic, and geographical divisions made it difficult to establish a unified identity or agenda among Spanish-speaking Americans.

Because of a weak economy in the island, around 1 million Puerto Ricans immigrated to the mainland

United States after World War II, mostly to New York City. As citizens of the United States, island residents could move freely between Puerto Rico and the mainland, and many returned home after a few years. While the most successful blended into the American society, mainland Puerto Ricans typically congregated in urban neighborhoods where they encountered poverty, crime, and discrimination. In the 1970s some Puerto Rican activists reached out to other Hispanics in an attempt to form alliances, but with limited success. Tensions between different Spanish-speaking communities remained high. For instance, the 350,000 Cubans who arrived in 1959 showed little interest in identifying with other Hispanics. Mostly professionals, business people, and former government workers, they tended to be of European descent and politically conservative.

Mexican Americans had been living in the West and Southwest long before 1848, when the United States annexed the region and significant Anglo settlement began. Like Native Americans, Mexican Americans were often victims of exploitation and discrimination. In 1928 Mexican American activists founded the League of United Latin American Citizens (LULAC), and it, along with the GI Forum established in 1948 in Texas, tried to improve the lives of Mexican Americans by promoting English literacy and encouraging political activism. By the 1960s they had won some victories. In 1947, in *Mendez v. Westminster,* the Supreme Court upheld a lower court ruling that prohibited

the segregation of Mexican Americans in public facilities. Subsequent court rulings attacked other forms of discrimination.

The number of Mexican nationals coming to the United States increased dramatically during World War II, when the American and Mexican governments had cooperated in the Bracero Program. Some 300,000 Mexicans entered the United States as temporary laborers, working primarily on farms and railroads. Because the labor shortage in the Southwest continued in the postwar period, the Bracero Program was extended by the Eisenhower administration. Farmers in the West and Southwest became dependent upon this cheap source of farm labor, and, despite harsh working conditions, low pay, and a lack of social services, thousands of poor Mexican laborers were attracted by the lure of earning American dollars. Some of these workers became American citizens, while others took their earnings and returned to Mexico.

During the 1960s and 1970s the Mexican American community grew at a faster rate than any other segment of the population, both because of immigration and because of high birth rates. In addition to the officially documented Mexicans in the United States, by the end of the 1970s an estimated 8 to 12 million undocumented workers, or illegal aliens, were in the United States. Illegal Mexican laborers flooded across the largely un-

¡Viva la Huelga! Non-Spanish-speaking Americans of the 1960s became well acquainted with la Huelga—"the Strike"—through which César Chávez and his United Farm Workers union refused to pick for produce growers who refused to bargain with migrant workers and sympathetic middle-class consumers refused to buy non-union grapes and lettuce in their supermarkets.

guarded border during the 1970s, and in 1979 Congress initiated a study of the situation, raising the possibility of granting amnesty for illegals. By that time, one of four Texans and one of five Californians was a Mexican American.

Like African Americans in the South, many Mexican Americans were forced to move to cities to seek employment because of agricultural mechanization. In the 1970s, about 85 percent lived in urban ghettos, called *barrios,* in scores of cities such as Los Angeles, San Antonio, and El Paso. Mexican American immigration, like earlier migrations of Italians and Poles, brought millions of devout members into the American Catholic church, swelling its numbers and influence and once again adding to its cultural diversity. Millions of Hispanics were also drawn into the burgeoning Pentecostal and charismatic movement, attracted by a message of hope and prosperity and by the opportunity to construct their own independent religious communities. Slowly a body of skilled workers, middle-class professionals, and entrepreneurs emerged among Mexican Americans; nonetheless, the average income of Hispanic families lagged far behind that of other Americans.

Perhaps the most visible Hispanic activist of the 1960s was César Chávez, a Mexican American farm worker who formed the National Farm Workers' Association in 1963. Between 1965 and 1969 Chávez led a series of dramatic and highly publicized strikes and boycotts that forced grape growers to recognize the union and sign a contract with it in 1970. Chávez was something of a cult hero in the 1960s; in 1968 Robert Kennedy called him "one of the heroic figures of our time." An enigmatic figure who modeled his labor protests on the tactics of Gandhi, he failed to build a strong, lasting labor organization, and by the time of his death in 1993 Chávez had become estranged from most of his early supporters.

In the sixties and seventies, aware of their increasing numbers and encouraged by the success of the black civil rights movement, Hispanic Americans established more militant political and cultural organizations. In 1960 the Mexican-American Political Association was formed to encourage political participation; in 1964, four Mexican Americans were elected to Congress. By the 1970s the Mexican American political party La Raza Unida had become a force in the Southwest and in East Los Angeles. The cultural programs and political organizations that sprang up in the 1960s were collectively known as the Chicano movement.

❧ Native Americans Assert Their Rights

In the years after World War II Congress reversed some of the policies by which the Roosevelt administration had recognized the cultural independence of Native Americans and had sought to deal with the tribes as sovereign entities. Partly in response to pressure from timber and mining companies, Congress in 1953 passed Concurrent Resolution 108, which provided for the "termination" of Indian treaties and sovereignty rights. During the next eight years Congress passed twelve specific termination bills covering sixty tribes, nearly all in the West. Native American lawyers filed a series of suits in federal court designed to protect the tribes, their historic rights, and their reservations. They won a landmark case in 1978, *U.S. v. Wheeler,* which reasserted the principle of "unique and limited" sovereignty for American tribes. Essentially, Native Americans retained their historical right either to integrate themselves into American society as citizens or to remain on reservations that retained a degree of autonomy.

Despite some legal successes in the 1970s, Native Americans remained extremely alienated and economically depressed — Ford Foundation President McGeorge Bundy called them in 1970 "the country's most disadvantaged minority." By then some 300,000 Native Americans had left their reservations to make their way in American society. Most of these "urban Indians" settled into low-paying menial jobs; many suffered from discrimination and a sense of cultural deprivation because of their separation from their native culture. For the nearly half-million Native Americans who remained on reservations, life was often harsh. Schools on most reservations were inferior, unemployment ranged from 20 to 80 percent, and rates of alcoholism and suicide far exceeded those of the general population. The life expectancy of Native Americans in 1970 stood at 44 years, compared to the national average of 71.

During the late 1960s and early 1970s Native American militancy bourgeoned. In November 1969 a group of militants occupied Alcatraz Island in San Francisco Bay, claiming the deserted prison site under a treaty provision that made unused federal lands available to Native Americans. They remained until the summer of 1971. Two years later members of the American Indian Movement (AIM), led by Russell Means, seized eleven hostages on the Pine Ridge Reservation at Wounded Knee, South Dakota. Their seventy-one-day confrontation with federal marshals ended with a government agreement to reassess the treaty rights of the Oglala Sioux. Means and other activists sounded a recurrent charge that the government and the Bureau of Indian Affairs had been at the same time negligent and paternalistic in its treatment of Native Americans. A spate of documentaries and historical novels, including Vine Deloria's *Custer Died for Your Sins* (1969) and Dee Brown's *Bury My Heart at Wounded Knee* created a new awareness of the historical wrongs suffered by the American Indian.

THE NEW LEFT AND THE COUNTERCULTURE

Beginning in the middle of the 1960s an extraordinary counterculture emerged among American young people. The youth revolt of the 1960s drew on the civil rights movement and other reform impulses of the period, in which many participants were activists, but the counterculture had a life and history of its own. This far-reaching and diverse revolt among young people crystallized in the second half of the sixties and flourished into the early 1970s, when many in the movement united in opposition to the war in Vietnam. The counterculture unfolded on a variety of stages — in political protest, and especially the anti-war movement, a heightened environmental consciousness, and experimentation with drugs, sex, and new styles of dress. Battle lines were drawn not on the basis of class or ethnicity but on age; for many, the rallying cry was "Don't trust anybody over 30." Drawing on the thinking of leftist intellectuals from earlier generations, the student radicals in the sixties, known as the New Left, insisted that American society was innately repressive and unjust, and that "law and order" were code words for repression.

Well into the 1970s, many sympathetic observers believed that the countercultural revolt of the young represented an unprecedented reform movement that would initiate profound changes in the structure of American society. Historian William McLoughlin likened the counterculture to a new religious awakening, thrusting the nation into a post-Christian age. The movement fell far short of such predictions, though it was an extraordinary moment of both national idealism and narcissism. Nonetheless, by the end of the seventies, the counterculture seemed more like an aberra-

Wounded Knee, March 1973 At the site of the 1890 massacre, a member of the American Indian Movement named Oscar Running Bear enforces the standoff with federal officials on the Pine Ridge Indian Reservation in South Dakota.

tion, a romantic interlude of youthful rebellion against authority and modernization.

❧ The Rise of the New Left

By the early 1960s much of the conventional liberal thought that had spawned the New Frontier and the Great Society was being loudly challenged by more radical New Left thinkers who became increasingly influential on university campuses. This relatively small group of radicals lumped liberals and conservatives together as the "establishment," a repressive and arrogant hegemony incapable of solving the injustices of society. By the late 1960s many student activists had embraced the vision of radical Columbia sociologist C. Wright Mills, who in *The Power Elite* (1956) argued that "pragmatic liberals" were a part of an "establishment" that was incapable of bringing real reforms.

While radical remedies varied widely, most agreed that liberalism in both its political and intellectual forms was bankrupt. The general mood among New Left intellectuals was pessimistic and foreboding; all agreed that "establishment" liberal timetables for reform were too slow and needed to be replaced by a direct transfer of power to the people. Of course, like most elites, they also insisted that they, as ideologically enlightened, understood better than ordinary Americans what had to be done.

At its most cerebral level, the radical intellectual crisis of the sixties and seventies meant a questioning of the very foundations of Western culture. Theologians and philosophers turned away from general theories and speculative thinking to focus on specific social reforms; scientists acknowledged their inability to solve social problems; and in the social sciences and humanities militant critics challenged older interpretations of history. In literary scholarship, the school known as postmodernism flourished, deeply influenced by the writings of French theorists Jacques Derrida and Michel Foucault, whose "deconstructionist" approach emphasized the ways in which ruling elites used ideas to control others. In the social sciences, an influential group of New Left historians, led by foreign policy specialist William Appleton Williams, wrote a revisionist history that pictured Western civilization in general, and the United States in particular, as an imperialistic monolith united by capitalistic greed. German-born philosopher Herbert Marcuse, who called for a radical overthrow of the establishment, became the foremost guru of disenchanted student radicals.

At a more popular level, a whole new genre of publications, known as the "alternative" or "underground" press, joined older Marxist publications such as *The Guardian* and *Monthly Review* to carry the message of the sixties rebellion on to many college campuses and into counterculture enclaves like Berkeley, Cambridge, and Greenwich Village. Perhaps the most widely read of the new underground publications, the *Berkeley Barb,* bristled with the most extreme and irreverent rhetoric of the New Left; others, such as the *Village Voice* and *Ramparts,* simply moved the demands of traditional liberal thought sharply to the left. While some older liberal journals, most notably *The New Republic,* survived the decade with only slightly lessened influence, much of the liberal press seemed so tepid that it lost much of its readership.

❧ Revolt on Campus

Many factors combined to make university campuses the center of radical thought and protest by the mid-1960s. Exposed to the ideas of New Left intellectuals, many young people responded with idealism to the challenge to rethink American institutions. In addition, American universities had become the focus of much of the social change of the 1950s and 1960s, whether in the breaking of racial barriers or in support for the war in Vietnam. Perhaps most important, in the word coined by University of California-Berkeley chancellor Clark Kerr, universities had become "multiversities," serving a variety of constituencies and operating much like big businesses. To disenchanted students, the university seemed a microcosm of "the establishment" — impersonal, arbitrary, supportive of the status quo, and "corporate." The new student radicals saw universities as the most effective instruments used by elites to manipulate people.

As an explicitly political protest movement, the origins of the radical student movement may be traced to 1960, when Al Haber and Tom Hayden, two University of Michigan graduate students who had been influenced by beat generation writers like Jack Kerouac and by C. Wright Mills's radical sociology, founded the Students for a Democratic Society (SDS). Hayden had grown up in a lower middle-class Detroit suburb and had been an altar boy in the Roman Catholic parish of Father Charles Coughlin (long since silenced politically; see Chapters 27 and 28). Haber, of working-class background, was writing a doctoral dissertation on Mills.

Student political activism increased in the 1960s, and many of the older, far less radical, student organizations, including the strongly anti-Communist National Student Association, also gained members. But student political activism swung dramatically to the left in 1962 when a group of forty SDS students met at a run-down union lakeshore retreat center at Port Huron, Michigan. For that meeting, Hayden, who had been beaten and radicalized while participating in the Mississippi civil rights protest, penned the Port Huron Statement, a call for university students to overthrow the immoral establishment. Only about 60,000 copies of the document were ever printed, and few readers got very far into it, but by reputation it became the most important statement of the political counterculture. Among other things, Hayden condemned racism, poverty in a land of plenty, corporations, the Cold War, and nuclear weapons. The declaration gave some coherence to the student movement, and all embraced the slogan "power to the people," but student radicals subscribed to various, often conflicting, and generally half-understood ideologies — Marxism, black nationalism, anarchism, and pacifism. Some believed in gradual change, but others celebrated the revolutionary tactics of Mao in China and of Fidel Castro and Che Guevara in Latin America.

Influenced to an extent by the Port Huron Statement, students at Berkeley reacted to a campus confrontation in October 1964 by launching the first major student revolt of the decade. It began when Chancellor Kerr banned sidewalk solicitations by student political groups in some campus locations, resulting in the ex-

pulsion of a student recruiting for CORE. In a spontaneous reaction, the Free Speech Movement took shape under the leadership of Mario Savio, a veteran of the Mississippi Freedom Summer and a philosophy graduate student. Several hundred students staged a sit-in in the administration building, and within days demonstrations by thousands of students brought the university to a virtual standstill. Kerr threatened to expel the students, but in the end he relented, granting that the only restrictions on free speech on the campus would be those that applied to society at large.

The Free Speech Movement at Berkeley became a model for student protests around the country. Student strikes became common by 1967 and 1968. Sometimes student radicals attacked the social taboos targeted by earlier rebellious generations — language, dress, drugs, and sex. Much of the behavior of the rebels was calculated to shock. But the student movement also addressed larger political issues, turning its ire on "corporate liberalism" and the war in Vietnam.

The number of student revolts continued to mount, a few becoming violent in the early 1970s, but the student movement increasingly lost momentum. Frustrated by their inability to win significant backing in either political party, the movement's leaders either became more radical or abandoned political activism altogether. The last SDS national convention, in 1969, disintegrated into bitter factional fighting, some members embracing anarchism and others calling for armed revolution.

❋ IN THEIR OWN WORDS

From the Port Huron Statement, 1962
When Students for a Democratic Society convened in Port Huron, Michigan, in 1962, they were presented with a manifesto written by Tom Hayden, who tried to sum up the concerns and aspirations of the burgeoning but diverse student movement.

We are people of this generation, bred in at least modest comfort, housed now in universities, looking uncomfortably to the world we inherit.

When we were kids the United States was the wealthiest and strongest country in the world: the only one with the atom bomb, the least scarred by modern war, an initiator of

the United Nations that we thought would distribute Western influence throughout the world. Freedom and equality for each individual, government of, by, and for the people — these American values we found good, principles by which we could live as men. Many of us began maturing in complacency.

As we grew, however, our comfort was penetrated by events too troubling to dismiss. First, the permeating and victimizing fact of human degradation, symbolized by the Southern struggle against racial bigotry, compelled most of us from silence to activism. Second, the enclosing fact of the Cold War, symbolized by the presence of the Bomb, brought awareness that we

ourselves, and our friends, and millions of abstract "others" we knew more directly because of our common peril, might die at any time. We might deliberately ignore, or avoid, or fail to feel all other human problems, but not these two, for these were too immediate and crushing in their impact, too challenging in the demand that we as individuals take the responsibility for encounter and resolution. . . .

Our work is guided by the sense that we may be the last generation in the experiment with living. But we are a minority — the vast majority of our people regard the temporary equilibriums of our society and world as eternally-functional parts.

✎ *Hippies and the Counterculture*

Many of the young people who embraced the counterculture of the sixties showed little or no interest in political activism. Their revolt was more personal. The rise of the broad countercultural youth rebellion and its narrower component, the student movement, owed something to the decades of boom in the 1950s and 1960s. Distinctive for their uncombed appearance, their anti-authoritarianism, and their embrace of drugs and sex, nearly all the "hippies" were disaffected children of middle- and upper-class families whose parents' affluence, against which they rebelled, ironically made a counterculture lifestyle possible. A mixture of self-indulgent dropouts and thoughtful idealists, the counterculture youth were always a minority of their age group, but they were vocal and visible.

During the mid-1960s student political protest and the adoption of alternative lifestyles — long hair and non-traditional clothing, experimentation with drugs, a flouting of traditional sexual taboos and attempts at communal living — had tended to go hand-in-hand, reinforcing each other. As antiwar protests became more confrontational and the authorities more repressive, many young people dropped out of the political student movement and out of society. Thousands sought fulfillment through LSD and other drugs, through sexual freedom, and through living in environmental or religious communes.

The counterculture of the 1960s had something in common with earlier periods of social experimentation in the United States, such as the 1830s. The hippies of the sixties were attracted both to the individualism of Henry David Thoreau and the mysticism and discipline of Asian philosophy and religions, including Zen Buddhism and various forms of Hinduism. Many bright young people questioned the materialistic lifestyles of their parents, and they searched broadly for alternatives to the canonical principles of Western thought, questioning conventional science as well as conventional morality.

The destination of choice for many who embraced alternate lifestyles was the West Coast, especially San Francisco, which had been the spiritual nursery of the counterculture since the late 1950s. There, in January 1967, a group assembled for a spontaneous "Human Be-In," featuring such countercultural icons as Allen Ginsberg, the Grateful Dead, and the Jefferson Airplane. Later that year, thousands of apolitical "flower children" moved into San Francisco's Haight-Ashbury neighborhood for a famous "summer of love." The run-down area blossomed with shops selling drug paraphernalia and with an outpouring of Eastern (and pseudo-Eastern) literature, psychedelic painting, communal living, and free love.

The quintessential countercultural happening was Woodstock, which unfolded spontaneously on a thirty-five-acre farm in upstate New York in 1969. A crowd estimated at 400,000 gathered for three days of music, which turned into what a participant called a "total experience, a phenomenon, a happening." Hard rock artist Jimi Hendrix opened the festivities with his famous dissonant rendition of "The Star Spangled Banner"; performances followed by virtually every major rock group then performing in the United States. With no violence, no rules, no power structure, and no discipline, Wood-

Woodstock Audience members sit out of view of the stage at the free Woodstock Music and Art Fair. The festival took place on Max Yasgur's dairy farm, which he rented to event organizers for $75,000. About 450,000 people attended the three-day concert, which turned into chaos due to the crowds, heavy rains, and traffic jams. It is nonetheless romantically remembered as a symbol of the liberal spirit of the hippie generation.

stock seemed to the celebrants to represent the dawn of the New Age.

In fact, by 1969 the counterculture was on the wane. The ruinous consequences of drug use became increasingly clear. The voluntary, "ennobling" poverty embraced by the students of the sixties came to be regarded as a vacuous absurdity by those who were genuinely poor. Sexual freedom proved to have its own exploitative dangers, even in those more innocent pre-AIDS days. Furthermore, commercialism quickly undermined the innocence of the counterculture. Its rebellious style spawned a generation of immensely wealthy rock bands who embarked on elaborately staged and highly lucrative tours. Foods with new appeal such as herbal tea, granola, and natural foods launched entrepreneurial empires. By the middle of the 1970s, the counterculture had been seduced by the society it had purported to reject.

On the other hand, the "hippies" left a lasting imprint on American society. They symbolized and energized the anti-Vietnam War movement. Less visible were the hundreds of communes that survived the sixties in the West and in cities throughout the nation. The counterculture left behind a rash of new religious movements, a new awareness of Eastern thought, and the New Age movement. Finally, the counterculture deeply and permanently influenced American music and dress and the public's attitudes toward drugs, sexual mores, and the environment.

ॐ *From Folk to Rock*

While most young people in the 1950s were attracted to what was then called rock 'n' roll, there was also a growing interest in folk music, highlighted by the commercial success of a rather bland but popular group, the Kingston Trio. Joan Baez and Bob Dylan raised serious folk music to new levels of popularity. They performed at the 1963 March on Washington, offering stirring renditions of "We Shall Overcome" and Dylan's "Blowin' in the Wind." Dylan was a particularly gifted

Bob Dylan and Joan Baez   Two of the best-known singers of the folk-music revival relax together in England in 1965. Dylan was famed for his gravelly-voiced songs of protest for which he wrote both words and music; Baez, for her clear and haunting renditions of both classic ballads and contemporary songs— some of them by Dylan himself. They were in many ways the "conscience" of the Sixties activists.

lyricist who captured the moral fervor and rebelliousness of his generation.

In the early 1960s popular music lost much of the initial rebelliousness associated with the rock 'n' roll of the 1950s, becoming sentimental and overwhelmingly commercial. In 1964 a new sound and a new era in popular music arrived when Beatlemania broke out in the United States. Four young working-class Englishmen from Liverpool — John Lennon, Paul McCartney, George Harrison, and Ringo Starr — caused an immediate sensation with their sentimental, rhythmic ballads. The Beatles' earliest songs, such as "I Want to Hold Your Hand," were little more than an updated form of crooning, and their early American concerts were distinguished mostly by the frenzy of their screaming audiences. But the Beatles were talented and entertaining, and in the decade that followed their American debut their music created a gigantic following and sold hundreds of millions of records. Their modish clothes, youthful faces, and long hair made them icons of the emerging youth culture of the early 1960s. Along with other groups such as the Rolling Stones, the Beatles reconnected young American audiences with rhythm-and-blues and rock 'n' roll traditions and elevated popular music to new creative levels.

Eventually both Bob Dylan and the Beatles brought together rock music and the counterculture. Until 1965 Dylan played strictly folk music (mostly of his own writing), but to the dismay of adoring folk fans in the late sixties he donned a leather jacket and began using an electric guitar. As he entered a new musical phase, Dylan's lyrics became more rebellious. The Beatles drifted closer to the center of the counterculture after a journey to India, where they studied transcendental meditation.

At the same time, some black musicians reached a broad commercial audience by taking a less overtly politicized approach. The civil rights movement made black artists such as Aretha Franklin and Ray Charles particularly popular with white performers and led to the rise of a self-conscious soul music. While soul music was distinctly the voice of African Americans, it was not protest music but dwelt on traditional personal themes. Barry Gordy, Jr., a Detroit entrepreneur, established a record company, Motown, that became associated with a distinct sound and style. The Motown sound combined gospel, blues, and jazz into a form popular with white and black audiences, one that led to the rise of such talented artists as Diana Ross, Stevie Wonder, and eventually Michael Jackson.

❧ Drug Use and New Sexual Mores

The "beats" of the fifties were the precursors of the drug scene of the sixties. The guru of drug experimentation in the 1960s was Timothy Leary, a Harvard psychologist fired in 1966 because of his experimental use of LSD. Leary moved on to lecture around the country on the joys of hallucinogenic drug use — which, he explained, led to new levels of consciousness — and he became something of a cult hero in the counterculture. In *Sgt. Pepper's Lonely Hearts Club Band* the Beatles sang of trips taken with "Lucy in the Sky with Diamonds" — widely assumed to be a reference to LSD — and drugs were as much a part of Woodstock as music.

The lightheartedness of the drug scene in the 1960s gave way to second thoughts in the 1970s as the harm-ful effects and addictive nature of drug use became more apparent and as organized crime came to dominate distribution. While marijuana remained a popular symbol of rebellion in the 1970s, hard drugs became a national nightmare. By 1970, a heroin epidemic had erupted among urban young people; estimates of the number of addicts in New York City ranged as high as 100,000.

Repudiation of the establishment meant rejection of traditional sexual mores, and the young rebels of the sixties vowed to "Make Love Not War." They embraced much more permissive attitudes toward sex and family relationships. The new sexual openness, like other countercultural ideas, proved to be a bonanza for creative entrepreneurs. No one cashed in on the sexual revolution more successfully than Hugh Hefner, whose *Playboy* magazine achieved a circulation of around four million by the end of the sixties, along with an empire that included glitzy resorts and nightclubs encouraging freer sexual expression. A clinical study that seemed to document the new sexual era — and turned sex therapy into a veritable industry — was *Human Sexual Response,* authored by William H. Masters and Virginia E. Johnson. The study's findings caused nearly as much stir as had Alfred Kinsey's reports a decade earlier.

❧ Environmentalism

The antimodernism of the counterculture and its romanticization of nature placed the preservation of the environment at the center of the agenda of many of the young rebels. But their embrace of environmental concerns was only part of a much broader reform movement that was well under way by the 1960s.

In 1948 a temperature inversion immersed the industrial town of Donor, Pennsylvania, in a smothering fog, sickening nearly half of its 14,000 inhabitants and killing twenty. In December 1952 a black fog over London reduced visibility to a yard; British doctors estimated the total deaths related to that winter's polluted smog at more than 10,000. The scene was repeated in London in 1956 and 1962, and in 1953 New York City experienced a severe smog that contributed to the deaths of more than 400 people.

By the 1960s the dangers of environmental pollution were everywhere apparent. Rachel Carson's *Silent Spring,* a bestseller in 1962, broadened the environmentalist agenda by convincingly arguing that the pesticide DDT was a serious hazard to the health of all living things. Although chemical companies panned her book, forty state legislatures passed laws restricting the use of the chemical. Industrial pollution of the environment also drew increased attention in the wake of a series of highly publicized accidents, including an oil leak by Union Oil Company that blackened five miles of Santa Barbara's beaches in 1969, destroying much of the area's rich wildlife. In 1965 the Senate passed the Water Quality Improvement Act, aimed at cleaning American rivers and lakes; after the Santa Barbara disaster, fines were levied on oil companies responsible for spills.

Throughout the 1960s, concern about clean air, clean water, and biodegradable products captured headlines not only in the "alternate press" but also in *Time* and *Newsweek*. In April 1970 the first Earth Day was celebrated; Congress adjourned for the day, and ten million schoolchildren picked up litter and planted trees around the country. By then, a healthy environment had become a popular political cause, and in 1972 the United Nations sponsored a World Conference on the Human Environment.

The deterioration of the nation's environment was easy to identify anecdotally, but by the 1970s the environmental movement was carefully and scientifically monitoring environmental problems and documenting the slow improvement in some areas. In 1979, sophisticated air quality measurements confirmed that in Los Angeles the air quality was "unhealthful" during 158 days, "very unhealthful" during 112 days, and "hazardous" during 10 days. Auto emissions were the major source of air pollution in Los Angeles, including 80 percent of carbon monoxide emissions, but industrial pollution was primarily to blame for bad air quality in many other American cities. While changes were gradual, virtually every measure of air pollution in the United States showed improvement in the 1970s; carbon monoxide levels, for example, dropped by around 20 percent. Federal funding for pollution abatement and control increased from a little more than $1 billion in 1970 to more than $8 billion in 1980.

Ralph Nader, a young graduate of Harvard Law School, thrust himself into the forefront of the envi-

Smog This smog-clouded view of Grand Avenue in Los Angeles, in which cars and buildings just a few short blocks away disappear into a thick haze, depicts perfectly one of the environmental movement's greatest concerns.

ronmental movement with the publication in 1965 of a book entitled *Unsafe at Any Speed: The Designed-in Dangers of the American Automobile*. The study highlighted the design flaws of the Corvair, a sporty General Motors product. It was a bestseller and set in motion a groundswell of support for regulation of automobile manufacturers. Reinvigorating the idea of consumer rights, in 1969 Nader established a Center for Study of Responsive Law in Washington, D.C. A corps of idealistic young lawyers supported by the center, known as "Nader's Raiders," pressed environmental causes on a broad front in the 1970s.

CONSERVATISM AND MAINSTREAM AMERICAN CULTURE IN THE SIXTIES AND SEVENTIES

Liberal political ideas rightly claimed the responsibility for much of the social and political reform of the 1960s, and liberals bore the brunt of radical attacks on the "establishment." At the same time, a substantial, though less noticed, conservative movement gained ground in the 1960s. The strength of the new conservatism was symbolized by the presidential nomination of Republican Barry Goldwater in 1964 and the rise to political prominence of Ronald Reagan in the last half of the 1970s. The resurgent conservatism was rooted partly in the writing and teaching of such academics as political scientists Leo Strauss and Russell Kirk, and partly in popular discontent with the pace and coerciveness of liberal reforms. In the 1970s conservatives began building a political coalition that included disenchanted blue-collar whites who flocked to the populist campaigns of George Wallace, conservative Protestants and Roman Catholics, and economic conservatives.

❧ The Postwar Conservative Intelligentsia

Perhaps the most influential of the conservative intellectuals during these decades was Leo Strauss, a German immigrant who was a professor of political science at the University of Chicago. Strauss wrote fifteen books, many of them rather obscure studies of pre-modern political philosophers, but he also was an extraordinarily influential teacher whose students reshaped political science departments throughout the nation. He argued that modern liberal theories that predicted social-political progress based on enlightened, secular philosophy had proven to have many undesirable side effects. Premodern philosophy and political theory provided a more humane and practical base for supporting human societies. More widely influential were the writings of Russell Kirk. According to the *New York Times*, Kirk's book, *The Conservative Mind*, published in 1953, "gave American conservatives an identity and a genealogy and catalyzed the postwar movement." In his thirty-two books, Kirk commented on a wide variety of topics, including politics, culture, educational theory, literary criticism, and ethical theory, and for forty years he wrote a page on education for the leading conservative magazine in the nation, *The National Review*.

The National Review was founded in 1955 by 30-year-old William F. Buckley, Jr. Five years earlier, Buckley had won acclaim among conservatives for a frontal assault on the pervasive liberal and secular bias in higher education in a book about his alma mater, *God and Man at*

✸ IN THEIR OWN WORDS

From the Sharon Statement of the Young Americans for Freedom, 1960

Young Americans for Freedom, an organization founded at the Connecticut home of William F. Buckley in 1960, eventually gained membership that surpassed the size of more prominent radical groups of the decade. Its manifesto could hardly have been more different from the values espoused by the counterculture and more radical student groups.

IN THIS TIME of moral and political crises, it is the responsibility of the youth of America to affirm certain eternal truths.

WE, as young conservatives believe:

THAT foremost among the transcendent values is the individual's use of his God-given free will, whence derives his right to be free from the restrictions of arbitrary force;

THAT liberty is indivisible, and that political freedom cannot long exist without economic freedom;

THAT the purpose of government is to protect those freedoms through the preservation of internal order, the provision of national defense, and the administration of justice;

THAT when government ventures beyond these rightful functions, it accumulates power, which tends to diminish order and liberty;

THAT the Constitution of the United States is the best arrangement yet devised for empowering government to fulfill its proper role, while restraining it from the concentration and abuse of power. . . .

THAT we will be free only so long as the national sovereignty of the United States is secure; that history shows periods of freedom are rare, and can exist only when free citizens concertedly defend their rights against all enemies. . . .

THAT the forces of international Communism are, at present, the greatest single threat to these liberties;

THAT the United States should stress victory over, rather than coexistence with this menace; and

THAT American foreign policy must be judged by this criterion: does it serve the just interests of the United States?

Yale. Throughout the 1960s and 1970s, Buckley's sophisticated and acerbic *National Review* offered intellectual support for conservative causes ranging from anti-Communism to attacks on the welfare state, ensuring that a conservative intelligentsia survived in the liberal postwar years.

In September 1960 Buckley invited ninety young people to his Sharon, Connecticut, estate, where they issued a conservative manifesto and founded the Young Americans for Freedom (YAF). The YAF manifesto called on the government to protect the political and economic freedom of the people, to refrain from expanding its powers "beyond these rightful functions," to protect a free market economy, and to fight for victory over the forces of "International Communism." The membership of YAF exceeded that of more visible radical groups in the 1960s, and the organization played a critical role in the nomination of Barry Goldwater in 1964. Ronald Reagan joined the YAF National Advisory Board in 1962; his presidency brought to fruition the planning of a generation of young conservatives.

❧ Popular Conservatism

Most Americans, including most young people, did not drop out and "turn on" in the sixties. They continued to live middle-class lives. In 1966, at the moment the counterculture was beginning to become highly visible, *Time* magazine named Americans under 25 years of age as its "Man of the Year." Acknowledging the younger generation had a mind of its own, the magazine pointed out that less than 5 percent had been involved in campus protests and that most remained intent on pursuing careers, getting credit cards, and joining the consumer culture. In 1970, *Time* chose as its man and woman of the year "Middle Americans," a silent majority that patronized macho John Wayne movies such as "The Green Berets," elected Richard Nixon president, and enthusiastically sang the national anthem at sports events. Young people in the seventies, the magazine reported, were generally focused on such older themes as "security, stability, and material comfort."

Some saw the conservatism of the seventies as a retreat from a higher idealism of the counterculture into a "Me Decade." The country had lost a war, been humbled by the limits of its economic power, faced increasing threats from international terrorism, and endured politically what some termed a "low, dishonest decade." But the national spirit was resilient, and at the end of the 1970s there were faint signs that the national confidence seemed to be rebuilding. The editor of *Time* wrote: "There is an impression now of national unity, a feeling that the U.S. is emerging from the divisions of the Me Decade."

❧ Backlash against Social Change and Disruption

Conservative backlash against the rapid social change and the disruptions caused by protesters during the 1960s was widely visible by the end of the decade. Some public establishments posted dress codes that banned long hair and beards, and most Americans favored serious penalties for marijuana smoking. There was widespread public support for police suppression of campus violence and the crushing of such violently radical groups as the Black Panthers. Polls taken after nine students were killed by National Guardsmen during a demonstration on the campus of Kent State University in Ohio in 1970 showed that four of five Americans supported the actions of the guardsmen.

Sometimes the backlash targeted particular groups. Many whites resented the gains made by racial minorities which they believed came at their own expense, and most resented the confrontational rhetoric and tactics of black militants. As more blacks entered the middle class in the 1970s, working-class whites often felt that they were being victimized by "reverse discrimination," and there were outbreaks of violent protest in Louisville and Boston. While most working-class whites never embraced radical racist organizations, membership in the KKK doubled to 10,000 between 1978 and 1980. Government support of affirmative action for minorities became a major source of litigation in the 1970s. Some businesses and schools established quotas for minorities and women that seemed to some to establish lower standards for members of those groups.

The most serious legal challenge to affirmative action was the *Bakke* case. In 1973 Allan Bakke, a Marine veteran who had twice been denied admission to the University of California Medical School at Davis, filed a federal suit claiming discrimination on the grounds that sixteen minority students with college grades and MCAT scores lower than his had been admitted. In 1979 the Supreme Court decided that he had been unfairly excluded because of quotas. But the Court also held that affirmative action programs themselves were constitutional.

The backlash included radical feminism as well as black power and affirmative action. A conservative

Kent State, May 4, 1970 A young woman lies dead as National Guardsmen open fire on student demonstrators protesting President Nixon's invasion of Cambodia. Public opinion of the time overwhelmingly supported the actions of the Guardsmen.

women's movement challenged feminists on a range of issues, including the Equal Rights Amendment, efforts to redefine the family, and abortion. Anita Bryant and Phyllis Schlafly were the most visible female leaders of those who saw feminism as a threat to traditional American family values. Insisting that the ERA would destroy all gender distinctions and legalize homosexual marriages, Schlafly led a successful campaign to block the amendment's ratification. Submitted by Congress in 1972, the amendment failed to garner the necessary support from the states, even though Congress extended the period of ratification by three years to 1982.

❧ Mainstream Issues: Crime and Education

Few things galvanized many Americans in their conviction that the liberal reforms of the sixties had failed more than rising crime rates and a seeming deterioration in the nation's educational system. Between 1960 and 1980, crime rates rose from 5 to 10 percent annually. Most disturbing was the rapid escalation of youthful crime, and how much of it was drug-related. While the crime rate among people over 25 actually declined during the two decades, the rate among people under

that age skyrocketed. The homicide rate in the country more than doubled from 1960 to 1979; the rate of black men murdered reached an alarming 6.46 percent. By 1981 the population of federal and state prisons in the United Sates surpassed 350,000, and approximately 35 percent of the inmates were African Americans. In 1980, the U.S. homicide rate was around ten times that of most other developed nations.

Americans continued to believe that education was the key to alleviating cultural and economic problems, but public education failed to meet public expectations. Although schools received large increases in funding, they had to deal with complex social issues that included busing to create racial balance and an increased role for special education. Funding for education increased dramatically, from $24.7 billion in 1960 to $169.6 billion in 1980. Most of the new money for K-12 education came from the federal government; state and local taxes had once carried virtually the whole burden. In 1960, only 1.7 percent of the nation's total educational expenditures came from federal funds, but by 1980 the percentage had risen to 18.4. Increasingly, institutions of higher education also came to depend on federal largess, in the form of grants or student loans.

The proportion of Americans who completed four years of high school or more rose sharply, from around 41 percent in 1960 to 68.6 percent in 1980. Although the percentages for blacks remained far below those of whites, by 1980 more than half of African Americans had graduated from high school, and the percentage of those who graduated from college doubled during the two decades. In spite of these increases, the numbers of school dropouts remained quite high — more than 3 million persons between the ages of 16 and 21 in 1980. High school dropouts were more likely to be black than white, and nearly twice as likely to be male as female. Devoid of the skills needed in modern society, dropouts constituted more than 30 percent of the unemployed labor in the country by 1980.

Perhaps the most factious education issue in the country was school busing. Distressed by the lack of progress in desegregating public schools, the Supreme

Court rendered a number of decisions that compelled schools to transport children out of their home districts in order to create racial balance in the schools. By 1971 many school systems were operating under court orders to balance their racial ratios by busing students. Many whites and some blacks resented having their children bused to distant schools, although most African Americans saw busing as a means of providing a better education for their children. In the South, court-ordered busing proceeded slowly, and sometimes prompted the opening of private schools beyond the reach of desegregation orders, but it proceeded peacefully nonetheless. Resistance from northern urban whites was often more forceful. Between 1975 and 1978 violence erupted in the schools and on the streets of South Boston as frustrated working-class whites protested the busing of black students into their neighborhood schools. Forced busing inadvertently undermined the public school system in certain areas and contributed to "white flight" from the nation's inner cities. Offended by forced busing, many white middle-class parents switched their children to private and parochial schools, moved to the suburbs, or both. White flight left the cores of the nation's urban areas primarily African American and Hispanic — and overwhelmingly poor.

❧ Trouble in the Religious Mainstream

Like American society in general, many Protestant churches were troubled by internal bickering and infighting during the sixties and the seventies. The nation's so-called mainline Protestant churches, including Methodists, Presbyterians, Congregationalists, Episcopalians, and Disciples of Christ, had seemed robust in the 1950s, when their growth rate exceeded that of the population. But by 1965 these historic churches began losing members. By the end of the century many mainline denominations had lost as much as one-third of their memberships. Their decline weakened the prestigious National Council of Churches of Christ, to which they provided most of the leadership and support.

There is no simple reason for the decline in the historic Protestant denominations, and contemporary scholars suggest that these groups' loss of vitality began well before the 1960s. It is, however, certain that the increasingly liberal stance of denominational hierarchies and the clergy in general alienated more conservative church members and deepened a growing clergy-laity divide. As denominational agencies concentrated more and more on social "peace and justice" issues,

traditional doctrine was de-emphasized. Denominational meetings often turned into heated debates on such matters as the roles of women, minorities, and gays and lesbians in the church, and on new interpretations of the Bible that called for reevaluation of much traditional Christian dogma.

Like political liberals, Protestant liberals were also assaulted from the left. A group of radical theologians, including Thomas Altizer and William Hamilton, argued that "God is dead" and that the only hope for the future lay with human beings themselves. In an influential book published in 1965, *The Secular City,* Harvard theologian Harvey Cox maintained that Christ must be sought through humanistic actions in a secular world.

❧ The Changing Face of American Catholicism

For the huge Roman Catholic Church, both in America and around the world, the 1960s and 1970s were a period of reform followed by a conservative reaction. In 1962, Pope John XXIII convened the first general church council since 1870, Vatican II, in the hope of bringing the church "up to date." The former patriarch of Venice, born Angelo Roncalli, John XXIII was a stark contrast to his predecessor, the conservative, intellectual, and strongly anti-Communist Pius XII. Although John XXIII died in the midst of the council's deliberations, in three years of meetings the assembled clergy modernized the liturgy, authorizing the substitution of modern languages for Latin, and initiated an ecumenical openness that greatly lessened tensions between Catholicism and Protestant denominations, and with other religions as well. Together, these changes and redefinitions of traditional practice suggested that the Roman Catholic Church was no longer a monolith but was willing to listen to the voices of the laity and reformers.

In 1965, in considerable measure through American initiative, the Vatican issued a "Declaration on Religious Freedom" that brought to an end the church's historic claim that secular states should grant the Roman Catholic Church official preeminence. This acceptance of the American belief that the separation of church and state was not only tolerable, but preferable, represented a historic triumph for the ideals advocated by American liberal Catholics from the "Americanizers" of the late nineteenth century (condemned at the time by the Vatican) to John F. Kennedy.

The new openness following Vatican II encouraged many priests and sisters to reflect on their vocations, and some chose to marry and pursue secular careers.

Enrollment in American seminaries plummeted, and an acute shortage of priests arose. While many American Catholics approved of the reforms initiated in the sixties, others were dismayed by the pace of change. Small numbers of Catholics supported a traditionalist movement that maintained the Latin liturgy, but few conservative Catholics defected from the church.

John XXIII's successor, Paul VI, was more conservative. He disappointed liberals who anticipated even more radical changes in the church in the wake of the Vatican II reforms. In 1968 he issued an encyclical entitled *Humanae Vitae* ("On Human Life"), which, contrary to expectations, did not moderate the church's historic prohibition of contraceptives, but instead strongly reaffirmed the church's opposition to any artificial form of birth control. American Catholic bishops had drifted toward liberalizing the church's teachings in such areas, and polls indicated that large numbers of Catholic women ignored the prohibitions. The new conservatism in the Vatican thus ensured clashes within the church in the years ahead.

A series of issues soon emerged that deepened the divide between liberals and conservatives in the Roman Catholic Church. The role of women in the church became increasingly contentious during these decades. Catholic women had long been passive, or at least nonconfrontational, about their subordinate posture in the church, but they became increasingly assertive in the 1960s and 1970s. Reformers pressed for greater roles for women in public worship, and some advocated the ordination of women to the priesthood.

On most of the contentious political issues of the sixties and seventies, Roman Catholics divided in much the same ways as the rest of the nation. Many Catholic priests and women religious were conspicuous participants in the civil rights marches of the 1960s, but some southern Catholics resisted the integration of parochial schools, and ethnic Catholics in the North proved to be as resistant to school busing as their Protestant neighbors. In 1967, Jesuit priest Daniel Berrigan and his brother Philip became celebrities in the antiwar movement when they were arrested and jailed for destroying draft records. At the same time, other prominent Catholic leaders were outspoken supporters of the war. Not until the 1980s did the official policies of the American church tilt toward the left on foreign policy issues. In 1983 the National Conference of Catholic Bishops, with Chicago's irenic Joseph Cardinal Bernardin as its spokesman, issued a denunciation of nuclear proliferation, riling conservative Catholics in the Reagan administration.

The national debate on abortion rights was particularly troubling for the American Catholic church. Many prominent Catholic politicians, including 1984 Democratic vice-presidential candidate Geraldine Ferraro, insisted that such moral questions should be matters of individual choice and found themselves at odds with conservative American church leaders. While some Catholics publicly challenged the church's blanket condemnation of abortion, such dissent elicited a strong response from the Vatican and found little support in the church's hierarchy.

Another new development in the church in the closing decades of the century was the emergence of the Catholic Charismatic Renewal movement. The liturgical reforms that followed Vatican II opened the way for experimentation in worship, and in 1966 students at Duquesne University in Pittsburgh reported that they had received the Pentecostal baptism of the Holy Spirit and spoken in tongues. The new emphasis on the Holy Spirit was greeted at first with skepticism and unease by church leaders, but the Charismatic Renewal spread rapidly in America and around the world; by the end of the century millions of Roman Catholics, including bishops and cardinals, were seeking gifts of the Holy Spirit. By the end of the 1970s the Vatican had become supportive of the Charismatic Renewal movement, seeing it as a tool for deepening the religiosity of church members and for curtailing the inroads of Pentecostals among Hispanics and other Catholic ethnic groups.

❧ New Religious Movements

The countercultural revolt of the sixties and a self-fulfillment craze of the seventies had creative religious side effects. A broad array of new religious movements appeared in the United States, some with deep roots in serious Eastern religious literature and others of more dubious origin. In some areas of the country, the practice of meditation flourished; for the first time, large numbers of Americans showed interest in the ancient teachings of Zen Buddhism. Transcendental Meditation received a boost when the Beatles became disciples of Maharishi Mahesh Yogi in the 1970s. In the early 1970s the movement claimed 350,000 adherents and supported 200 training centers. A number of authoritarian and tightly structured new cults attracted young dropouts from the counterculture, including the Unification Church, headed by the Reverend Sun Myung Moon. Moon's teachings were a syncretistic mix of Eastern religious ideas, evangelical Christianity, and anti-Communism.

Central was the belief that Moon was a father to his disciples, and many "Moonies" believed that he was the reincarnation of the Messiah. Moon's young followers lived highly regimented lives, spending most of their time fundraising and studying the church's teachings in a tightly controlled environment. Another new group was the International Society for Krishna Consciousness, or Hare Krishnas, founded in the United States in 1965. A familiar sight in many American cities by the end of the sixties, young Hare Krishna devotees with shaved heads and saffron-colored robes chanted mantras to Hindu deities and solicited funds with a fervor many Americans found disquieting. Several of the new religious groups were accused of brainwashing, and some parents hired anti-cult specialists in efforts to "deprogram" their children.

A Mass Wedding   Eight thousand friends and relatives gather in a gym in Seoul, South Korea, on October 21, 1970, to witness the arranged weddings of 790 couples—all members of the Reverend Sun Myung Moon's Unification Church, one of the rigidly authoritarian new religious movements that sprung up in response to the sixties counterculture. The majority of these couples are Korean, but several are American.

A tragic episode of religious liberty gone awry occurred in 1978, focusing attention on the capacity of cultic movements to lead their followers to the point of self-destruction. During the 1970s, charismatic preacher Jim Jones built a large and controversial People's Temple church in San Francisco, but when rumors of illegal financial transactions arose, threatening an investigation of his church in 1977, Jones moved his followers to Guyana and established a colony named Jonestown. During a visit by California congressman Leo Ryan in 1978, Jones became convinced that the United States government was plotting to destroy his colony, and on November 18, 1978, he orchestrated a mass suicide and murder of his followers that left more than 900 people dead. The Jonestown tragedy once again strained the American commitment to religious diversity and freedom of belief.

❧ The Evangelical Revival and the Rise of the Religious Right

Anxieties about the changes occurring in the 1960s and 1970s encouraged a vigorous religious revival among conservative churches. Nothing signaled more clearly the lasting influence of conservative evangelicalism in the nation than the extraordinary popularity of evangelist Billy Graham, whose crusades continued to attract millions of people each year. His Billy Graham Evange-

listic Association funded several World Evangelization Congresses in the sixties and seventies that inspired Christian evangelism around the world, and he was a personal friend and confidant of Presidents Lyndon Johnson and Richard Nixon. By the 1960s, *Christianity Today,* a magazine founded with the backing of Graham, was one of the most popular Protestant publications in the United States.

Soon, however, Graham's relatively benign form of conservative Protestantism, called neo-evangelicalism, was being challenged on the right by more militant preachers who proudly resurrected the name "fundamentalist." The most influential of the new breed of fundamentalists was Jerry Falwell, pastor of an Independent Baptist church in Lynchburg, Virginia, which by the mid-1970s boasted more than 15,000 members. Falwell's church televised its services as "The Old Time Gospel Hour," offering a mix of old-fashioned preaching, patriotism, and scathing attacks on social liberalism. In 1971, Falwell established Liberty University, which quickly became the leading fundamentalist educational institution in the nation.

Political resentment contributed to the evangelical resurgence in the 1960s and 1970s. Religious conservatives bridled at the sweeping social changes of the times, which they saw as assaults on the moral underpinning of the nation, led by a "secular humanist" elite that controlled the government. While urban rioting, antiwar protests, and the countercultural flaunting of drug use and sexual permissiveness angered religious conservatives, symbolically more important were a 1962 Supreme Court decision that outlawed prayer in public schools and a decision the following year forbidding Bible reading and recitation of the Lord's Prayer. By the middle of the 1970s religious conservatives had also become belligerent opponents of abortion rights, upheld in the Supreme Court's 1973 *Roe v. Wade* decision.

Conservative evangelicals and fundamentalists were as encouraged by the 1976 election of a born-again Christian, Jimmy Carter, as liberal and secular Democrats were dubious and uneasy about Carter's forthright religious persona. But evangelicals were quickly disappointed by Carter's stands on such issues as abortion and gay rights. In the two-year period from 1978 to 1980 an extraordinary organizing frenzy engulfed conservative evangelicals, resulting in a bevy of political action groups collectively labeled "the Religious Right" by the media. Jerry Falwell's Moral Majority, formed in 1979, was for a time the most influential of these groups. Ronald Reagan embraced the ideals of the Religious Right, and the conservative religious groups contributed both funds and votes to his election.

❧ The Pentecostal Revival and the Rise of Televangelism

A second extremely influential, though less visible, religious revival unfolded in the 1960s and 1970s under the leadership of American Pentecostals. By 1980 the Pentecostal emphasis on miracles and gifts of the Holy Spirit had changed the landscape of American religion, and, indeed, had altered the religious demography of the world. Across the country and around the world little Assemblies of God congregations blossomed into huge megachurches, hundreds of independent "Spirit-filled" churches appeared, and the charismatic movement took Pentecostal beliefs and worship style into mainstream Protestant churches and had a major impact on the Catholic church as well.

In many ways the chief catalysts in the transformation of American Pentecostalism were a group of evangelists who established independent ministries in the 1950s and became creative pioneers in religious television in the 1960s and 1970s. The prototype leader of that group was Oral Roberts, a Tulsa evangelist who built a large base of financial supporters by taking his healing crusades onto television in the late 1950s. After establishing a university in 1967, Roberts revolutionized religious television programming at the end of the 1960s by producing a number of entertainment specials that were aired in prime time.

Some non-Pentecostal ministers, such as Billy Graham and Jerry Falwell, used television to good effect in the 1970s, but it was Pentecostal and charismatic leaders, building on Roberts's innovations, who fashioned the modern electronic church during the decade. Pat Robertson, Paul Crouch, and Jim Bakker began cable television networks, and the talented musician and preacher Jimmy Swaggart used his telegenic skills to create a huge ministry. Together, these charismatic leaders borrowed for religious purposes virtually every form of entertainment television, ranging from talk shows to variety shows. They themselves became media celebrities. While Pat Robertson espoused conservative political causes, most of the other charismatic television superstars of the 1970s were largely apolitical, remaining intent on selling their upbeat brand of positive religion.

❧ Television, Movies, and Popular Music

Television, stereo, and other musical equipment continued to devour more than 20 percent of the American entertainment dollar, increasing by more than 100 percent in each decade. Two new technologies drove the television industry in the 1960s and 1970s: the expansion of color sets and the development of cable television technology. Beginning in the mid-1960s color television sets began to replace black and white sets. While standard monochrome television sales slowly declined, the number of color set sales rose from 2.6 million in 1965 to 11.8 million in 1980. The expansion of cable television systems allowed the reception of multiple channels, thus opening television to highly specialized networks, such as sports and religious channels. In 1960, 640 cable systems offered services to fewer than 700,000 homes, but 4,225 cable systems reached 16 million homes in 1980.

The dramatic expansion of television was made possible by the industry's ever-escalating advertising revenue. Television advertising revenues had reached nearly 12 billion by 1960, and that figure rose to nearly 55 billion in 1980. In 1960 advertisers still invested as much in newspapers and magazines as in television, but by 1980 the amount spent on television was more than twice that expended in any other medium.

The American intelligentsia continued to decry the vacuousness of popular television programming. The most popular programs of the 1960s were light comedies such as the *Beverly Hillbillies* and the *Andy Griffith Show* and westerns such as *Bonanza*. On the other hand, television did not lack programming that intended to influence public opinion. A number of popular programs in the 1970s, including *Rowan & Martin's Laugh-In* and *All in the Family,* a situation comedy produced by Norman Lear that led television ratings for five years from 1971 to 1976, featured traditional comedy mixed with a degree of social commentary on controversial issues. The 1977 television production of Alex Haley's book *Roots,* based on his tracing of his family tree back to a Gambian ancestor named Kunta Kinte who was sold into slavery, brought new attention to black history. The immense television audience that watched the eight-part series (estimated at 130 million) was undoubtedly resensitized to the horrors of slavery. Whether the critics liked it or not, Americans were hooked on television, and it was clearly possible to air programs that were both serious and popular.

The number of cinemas actually declined in the sixties before beginning a slight upward trend in the 1970s. In the early 1960s musicals such as *The Sound of Music* (1964) and *My Fair Lady* (1965) were box office hits. But many of the most acclaimed movies of the 1960s reflected the changing values of the entertainment industry. Two 1967 films, *In the Heat of the Night* and *Guess Who's Coming to Dinner,* featured Sidney Poitier and candidly explored racial stereotypes. *The Graduate* (1967) cast Dustin Hoffman in his first film role as a bewildered, affluent college graduate drawn into an affair with an older friend of the family. *Easy Rider* (1969), starring Peter Fonda, Dennis Hopper, and Jack Nicholson, explored sympathetically the countercultural world of drugs, hippies, and sex.

Folk and rock music dominated the sixties, particularly among young people, but by the late 1970s disco was the music of young professionals. Millions of Americans flocked to clubs to dance to the light beat of disco music; by 1980 more than 10,000 discotheques were eclipsing traditional nightclubs, and millions of Americans danced away their evenings in the glitter of flashing lights.

The music of many working-class Americans in the 1960s and 1970s was a brand of country music with deep roots in the South. In 1961, only eighty "all-country" radio stations existed in the United States, but by the mid-1970s the number had risen to more than a thousand. Partly, the growing popularity of country music reflected a growing national acceptance of the South, after decades during which the region had been stigmatized as a land of racial bigotry, economic backwardness, and cultural narrowness. The export of southern country music paralleled the growing popularity of southern literature and of southern religious styles. Country music tapped into the patriotic sentiments that had in part propelled George Wallace into national politics and made it clear that the South was perhaps the most traditionally patriotic of all the sections of the nation. Merle Haggard's "Okie from Muskogee" in 1969 voiced the anti-counterculture beliefs of many working-class Americans. While some of the bevy of nationally famous country singers of the 1970s, among them Johnny Cash and Willie Nelson, identified with the down-and-out, particularly after Cash's 1967 album recorded at California's Folsom Prison, for the most part country music heralded traditional values

Sixties TV Stars   Andy Griffith, Don Knotts, and Ron Howard starred in the popular sixties sitcom "The Andy Griffith Show." Plots concerned the simple, funny, and well meaning but often tangled daily lives of the residents of a fictitious little town called Mayberry, North Carolina — an old fashioned, all-American sleepy town where people went to the fishing hole on a nice afternoon and got pie at the diner. The show was the antithesis of the era's counterculture.

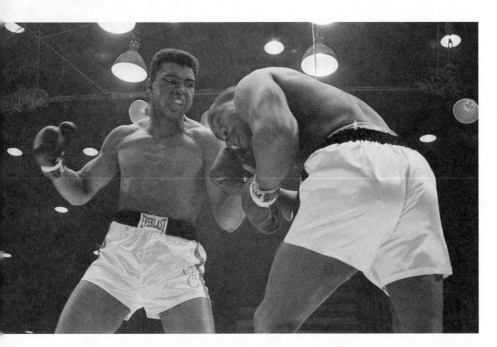

"The Greatest" Cassius Clay converted to the Nation of Islam and changed his name to Muhammad Ali after defeating Sonny Liston in this 1964 heavyweight title bout. He is considered one of the greatest boxers in history — "the greatest," by his own frequent proclamation. He became a controversial figure when he refused to serve in the Vietnam War, but his dynamic personality and prolific skill won admirers all over the world.

or focused on tales of personal depravity and hardship that were devoid of social commentary.

♏ *The Burgeoning Sports Craze*

America continued to be a nation of sports fanatics through the 1960s and 1970s. If anything, the popular appetite for sports increased. The amount expended in the nation for recreation rose from $17.8 billion in 1960 to nearly $107 billion in 1980.

The sixties and seventies produced a new generation of sports heroes and heroines. Jack Nicklaus became the most famous golfer of all time and was named the athlete of the decade in the 1970s. Running back O. J. Simpson of the Buffalo Bills became the first football player to run for more than two thousand yards in one season, and when his career ended he became a popular television movie personality. But the preeminent sports hero of the era was Muhammad Ali, who began his boxing fame by winning an Olympic gold medal in 1960 as Cassius Clay before becoming a member of the Nation of Islam in 1964 and changing his name. Ali, who dubbed himself "the greatest," won the heavyweight championship of the world in a stunning upset of Sonny Liston in 1964. He was stripped of his championship and

jailed in 1967 when he refused to serve in the armed forces because of his religious convictions, but Ali remained enormously popular all over the world. He subsequently won the championship again in 1974. When he retired from boxing in 1978, almost everyone agreed that Muhammad Ali had indeed been "the greatest."

Participation sports continued to consume the largest portion of the nation's recreation expenditures. In 1980, Americans spent nearly $30 billion on sporting equipment and supplies. James Fixx's *Complete Book of Running* (1977) heralded the age of Nike, Adidas, and New Balance, and health spas and racquetball courts appeared throughout the country. Huge numbers engaged in hunting and fishing — 58.8 million people reported that they had hunted or fished during 1980. The number of golfers tripled during the two decades and the number of golf courses in the country doubled. Tennis also became popular, like golf transcending its earlier identification with upper-class leisure pursuits.

♏ *The Arts and Literature*

The affluence of the 1960s stimulated a revival in American performing and creative art. Both the Kennedy and Johnson administrations actively promoted the arts and high culture. The National Arts and Humanities Act passed by Congress in 1965 provided millions of dollars in grants for innovators in the creative and performing arts. Federal appropriations for the National Endowment for the Arts increased from $6.3 million in 1970 to $97 million in 1980, and funding for the National Endowment for the Humanities rose during the same period from $6.1 million to $100.3 million. This public funding supported a wide variety of educational and artistic programs and institutions, some of them quite controversial. Perhaps the most visible recognition of the arts by the federal government was the opening of the Kennedy Center on the banks of the Potomac River in Washington, D.C., in 1971. The funding for a National Cultural Center had been provided by bipartisan legislation and signed into law by President Eisenhower in 1958. Two months after the assassination of Presi-

Jackson Pollock at Work   Pollock prepares to drip paint on a canvas in this 1950 photograph. Pollock's art may appear random and chaotic, but it was actually carefully planned—as modern computer studies of his works are now revealing.

dent Kennedy, Congress voted to make the Center a "living memorial" to John F. Kennedy, who had been a strong supporter of the arts. Constructed with $70 million in public and private funds, the Center opened with a spectacular Requiem mass in honor of President Kennedy written by Leonard Bernstein. In subsequent years the Center helped make Washington a cultural as well as political capital.

American writers during the 1960s and 1970s looked at themes old and new. The tradition of portraying the foibles of middle-class America was carried forward by John Updike. His trilogy *Rabbit, Run* (1960), *Rabbit Redux* (1971), and *Rabbit Is Rich* (1981) depicted the life of former high school athlete and car dealer Harry "Rabbit" Angstrom; the last won him a Pulitzer Prize in 1982. The central character's nickname was an obvious play on Sinclair Lewis's character George F. Babbitt. Books by African Americans about the black experience were a conspicuous new addition to postwar American literature. The classic offerings of the fifties, such as Ralph Ellison's *The Invisible Man* (1952) and James Baldwin's *Go Tell It on the Mountain* (1953), were followed by a series of angrier and more confrontational books, including Baldwin's *The Fire Next Time* (1963).

Above all, the novels of the sixties and seventies were dominated by the anti-hero. One of the most famous of the era's tarnished central characters was Yossarian in Joseph Heller's *Catch-22,* an antiwar novel full of farce and black humor that became a favorite among college students. The protagonist in Ken Kersey's *One Flew Over the Cuckoo's Nest* was an antisocial inmate in an insane asylum who led a wrenching and unsuccessful rebellion against institutional paternalism and conformity. Truman Capote's heroes in *In Cold Blood* (1966) were two mass murderers caught in a system of criminal justice that refused to grant that they were victims in the same sense, if not to the same degree, as the people they killed. Like Norman Mailer's *The Executioner's Song* (1979), it was a protest against capital punishment.

Literary criticism in the 1960s and 1970s was powerfully influenced by postmodernism. Linked particularly to the writings of continental academics Michel Foucault and Jacques Derrida, postmodernism attempted to deconstruct literary texts to rid them of the meanings imposed on them by self-interested elites. Postmodernists attacked the notions of a literary canon that excluded as inferior the literature of oppressed groups, and, in academic circles at least, broadened the body of writing to be taken seriously.

CONCLUSION: COMING APART AND HOLDING TOGETHER

The 1960s and 1970s witnessed a high tide for American liberal ideology. Liberal assumptions came to be a kind of orthodoxy in many areas of intellectual leadership in the country, including academic institutions, the media, large foundations, and mainline Protestant churches. This intelligentsia combined with powerful new interest groups such as government employees and teachers to forge a new liberal political alliance.

But the liberal triumph was never complete; one can clearly see in these decades the seeds of discord that would later bloom into culture wars. Some time in the middle of the 1960s, exuberance began to give way to anger. While much was accomplished by the social activists and political reformers of the early sixties, many of those whom liberals intended to help felt that the effort was too little too late, and radicals turned on "establishment" liberalism as the enemy. To the right of mainstream liberalism, meanwhile, a few influential intellectuals and thousands of young conservative students began constructing a neoconservative ideology that would gain momentum in the 1980s. And in the midst of this intellectual ferment, a majority of Americans continued to live more or less traditional lives. Sometimes this "silent majority" was moved by pleas for change; at other times it was repelled by the tactics of radical protesters. At different times in the 1960s and 1970s each of these groups of Americans dramatically influenced the course of the nation's political life. In many ways, politics of these two decades did not cause the divisions in American society; rather, it was shaped by them.

During the early sixties, popular culture, foreign affairs, and economics seemed to come together as the United States prepared to defend the Third World from the scourge of international Communism and lift its own population out of the morass of poverty, discrimination, and sexism. Keynesian economics would pay for it all. Then, however, Americans were reminded of theologian Reinhold Niebuhr's maxim that all human institutions are corrupt, all intentions flawed, and that what humanity would perfect, it would destroy. Beset by race riots in the cities, escalating drug abuse and crime, and distrust in the nation's political system, many Americans came to feel frustrated and pessimistic about the future.

And yet there were positive signs at the end of the 1970s. The political reforms of the early 1960s had substantially improved the lives of millions of Americans, and, while much remained to be done, the status of many historically disadvantaged groups in American society did begin to change during these two decades. Furthermore, Americans ended these years keenly aware of their manyness — their cultural and ethnic pluralism — and to some degree informed about the plight of those who had been marginalized by bigotry and insensitivity.

SUGGESTED READING

Taylor Branch, *Parting the Waters* (1988) and *Pillar of Fire* (1988). Classic studies of the civil rights struggle.

William Chafe, *The Unfinished Journey* (1986). Provides a sweeping overview of the postwar years.

David Garrow, *Bearing the Cross: Martin Luther King, Jr., and the Southern Christian Leadership Conference* (1986). Another important study of the civil rights movement.

William Martin, *A Prophet with Honor: The Billy Graham Story* (1991). Describes the evangelical religious revival.

W. M. O'Neill, *Coming Apart: An Informal History of the 1960s* (1971) and Godfrey Hodgson, *American in Our Time* (1976). Deal broadly with the period.

Rosalind Rosenberg, *Divided Lives: American Women in the Twentieth Century* (1992). Provides an introduction to the women's movement.

Irving Unger, *The Movement: A History of the American New Left, 1959-1972* (1974). A scholarly account of the rise of the New Left.

SUGGESTIONS FOR FURTHER READING

Terry Anderson, *The Movement and the Sixties: Protest in America from Greensboro to Wounded Knee* (1995).

James L. Baughman, *The Republic of Mass Culture: Journalism, Filmmaking, and Broadcasting in America Since 1941* (1991).

Howard Brick, *Age of Contradiction: American Thought and Culture in the 1960s* (1998).

Michael F. Brown, *The Channeling Zone: American Spirituality in an Anxious Age* (1997).

Morris Dickstein, *Gates of Eden: American Culture in the Sixties* (1977).

Adam Fairclough, *To Redeem the Soul of America: The Southern Christian Leadership Conference and Martin Luther King, Jr.* (1987).

David Farber, *Chicago '68* (1988).

Todd Gitlin, *The Sixties: Years of Hope, Days of Rage* (1987).

David Goldfield, *Black, White, and Southern: Race Relations and Southern Culture, 1940 to the Present* (1990).

Wouter J. Hanegraaff, *New Age Religion and Western Culture: Esotericism in the Mirror of Secular Thought* (1997).

David E. Harrell, Jr., *All Things Are Possible: The Healing and Charismatic Revivals in Modern America* (1975).

Susan M. Hartman, *From Margin to Mainstream: Women and American Politics since 1960* (1989).

Gerald Horne, *Fire This Time: The Watts Uprising and the 1960s* (1995).

Nicholas Lemann, *The Promised Land: The Great Black Migration and How It Changed America* (1991).

David Lewis, *King: A Biography*, 2nd ed. (1978).

Joan London and Henry Anderson, *So Shall Ye Reap: The Story of Cesar Chavez and the Farm Workers Movement* (1970).

Andrew M. Manis, *A Fire You Can't Put Out: The Civil Rights Life of Birmingham's Reverend Fred Shuttlesworth* (2000).

J. S. Olson and Raymond Wilson, *Native Americans in the Twentieth Century* (1984).

James T. Patterson, *Grand Expectations: Postwar America, 1945-1974* (1996).

W. J. Rorabaugh, *Berkeley at War* (1989).

Barbara Rose, *American Art Since 1900* (1967).

Gregory L. Scheider, *Cadres for Conservatism: Young Americans for Freedom and the Rise of the Contemporary Right* (1999).

Harvard Sitkoff, *The Struggle for Black Equality, 1954-1980* (1981).

Marek Tushnet, *Making Civil Rights Law* (1994).

33

The Liberal Hour: Politics in the Sixties

THE PATRIARCHAL IMAGE Dwight Eisenhower projected made him the ideal president for a nation exhausted by the Depression, the reformist zeal of the New Deal era, World War II, and the early Cold War. But in the early 1960s, political liberals reemerged with a renewed sense of hope, buoyed first by the election of a bright and captivating new president and heartened by the sweeping domestic reforms put in place by Great Society legislation in the middle of the decade. During the presidencies of John F. Kennedy and Lyndon B. Johnson, liberalism had its most promising opportunity in the second half of the twentieth century.

Much legislation was passed by the Democratic administrations of the sixties, and the sweeping expansion of federal programs during the mid-sixties led to the establishment of a welfare state. Although they were debated and revised over the next three decades, the basic reforms of the Great Society remained in place at the end of the century. But the liberal experiment had serious flaws. Those groups who were the intended benefactors of the reforms of the period — African Americans and other minorities, the poor, and women — and who, indeed, did profit most from the reforms, became restive with the pace of change. Some of them turned into critics of liberalism as it had been defined in the sixties. And Richard Nixon's election to the presidency in 1968 revealed the deep internal tensions that were the legacy of the liberal politics of the age.

The deathblow to the liberal political experiment of the 1960s came not from within but from without. John F. Kennedy and Lyndon B. Johnson, like the Republican presents who preceded and followed them, were Cold Warriors, veterans of World War II who believed they must stop aggression around the world — although Johnson, more than the others, was preeminently interested in domestic affairs. Under their leadership, the United States sank ever deeper into a war in Southeast Asia that lacked clear moral justification, appeared militarily unwinnable, and aroused a level of criticism at home that undermined public support. Furthermore, the war, combined with the vast budget expansions demanded by liberal domestic programs, undermined the prosperity that the United States had enjoyed since World War II.

JOHN F. KENNEDY AND THE NEW FRONTIER

In 1960 the American people elected as their president the young Bostonian John Fitzgerald Kennedy. Kennedy projected an image of energy, wit, and good looks. In fact, the young president's health was frail, and he had to spend long hours in bed. Nonetheless, his glamorous public persona, and his articulation of a vision of expanding opportunities at home and competition with the Soviet Union abroad, presented the nation with a sharp contrast to the fatherly Dwight D. Eisenhower, revered by most Americans as the guardian of the values and achievements of the past.

Kennedy was not a doctrinaire liberal. Above all he wanted to win the Cold War, and one of his foremost heroes was Winston Churchill. Domestically, he was a hardheaded, pragmatic politician who favored a moderate expansion of the New Deal – Fair Deal, without unbalancing the budget or interfering with the private sector. His initiatives on behalf of the underprivileged were ambitious, but they were only modestly successful because of his political inexperience. Kennedy might have been a bolder reformer in a second term had he been elected with a stronger mandate and had not his presidency been tragically cut short by his assassination.

❧ *The Election of 1960*

Sensing Republican vulnerability because of the late-1950s recession and the Soviet Union's apparent global gains, several United States Senators sought the Democratic presidential nomination in 1960. John F. Kennedy swiftly came to the fore. None could match the lavishly funded Kennedy organization or the personal charisma of Kennedy himself. JFK also had liabilities — his youth, his early support of Senator Joseph McCarthy, and, most problematic, his Roman Catholic religion. After winning the Democratic primary in Wisconsin, Kennedy faced a major challenge in overwhelmingly Protestant West Virginia, where many felt that his Catholicism would present insurmountable problems. Kennedy boldly addressed the religious issue: "Nobody asked me if I was a Catholic when I joined the United States Navy. Nobody asked my brother if he was a Catholic or Protestant before he climbed into an American bomber to fly his last mission." He won an impressive victory in West Virginia, and when the Democrats gathered at their convention in July, Kennedy swept to victory on the first ballot.

In a move that shocked liberals in the Democratic Party, but that undoubtedly strengthened the ticket, Kennedy asked his leading rival for the nomination, Texas Senator Lyndon B. Johnson, to be his running mate. It was an agonizing political decision, and it was opposed by Kennedy's younger brother and campaign manager, Robert, who three times went to Johnson's hotel suite urging him to decline the offer. But Johnson accepted, and never forgave the younger Kennedy. A feud between the two simmered beneath the surface for eight years.

The race for the Republican nomination was a comparatively closed affair. Vice President Richard Nixon had been highly visible and won the nomination easily. The GOP was still the minority party, divided into conservative and liberal wings. Its leaders knew that the main reason they had controlled the White House for eight years was Dwight D. Eisenhower's popularity. Republican liberals, led by New York governor Nelson Rockefeller, pushed through a platform that promised to preserve the New Deal–Fair Deal reforms and to support civil rights for African Americans. Nixon moved away from his earlier image as a right-wing anti-Communist to join his party's move to the center. Conservative Republicans felt shunned, as did doctrinaire liberals in the Democratic Party after Kennedy's nomination, as both candidates attempted to occupy the political center in the quest for victory.

Nixon, clutching Eisenhower's mantle about him, emphasized that he rather than the youthful-looking Kennedy had the experience to stand up to the Soviet Union. Like his Republican predecessors, he implicitly agreed not to dismantle Social Security and other federal programs. The vice president was much more widely known than the young Massachusetts Senator, and he led in early polls. Embracing the role of under-

Hoping to cut into the Republican lead, Kennedy challenged Nixon to four televised debates, and Nixon unwisely agreed. In the first debate, Kennedy put to rest doubts about his inexperience and immaturity by displaying an impressive command of facts and appearing self-assured. Nixon went into the debate fatigued and looked drawn and tentative, while his perspiring face caused his makeup to run, leaving him looking unshaven and grim. Most Americans judged that the last three debates were a draw, but analysts felt that the first debate swayed a significant number of voters to Kennedy.

The Nixon campaign made other tactical errors. While Kennedy concentrated on the heavily populated industrial areas of the country, Nixon wore himself out visiting all fifty states. Nevertheless, Kennedy's margin of victory was razor thin.

Nixon and Kennedy Debating, 1960   The televised Nixon-Kennedy debates were the first such encounters in the history of presidential elections. Kennedy understood the medium better than Nixon. The favorable impression that Kennedy made — rather than the two men's sparring over the issues (they agreed more than they disagreed) — helped him overcome Nixon's supposed edge as the more "experienced" candidate.

dog, Kennedy promised to "get the country moving again" and played on American fears of losing the Cold War. He charged that the Eisenhower administration had stood by apathetically while Communism made inroads in the Third World and claimed that it had allowed a "missile gap" to open. No such gap existed, but the Eisenhower administration and Nixon could not refute Kennedy's claim without breaching national security. Kennedy promised increased funding for the nation's nuclear arsenal, but also promised to contest the Soviet-backed "wars of liberation" by rebuilding the nation's conventional armed forces. In domestic affairs, Kennedy promised to divert resources to rebuild the nation's neglected infrastructure and to expand opportunities for the disadvantaged. Convinced that Johnson would help him garner crucial votes in the South, and genuinely moved by the heroism of civil rights activists, Kennedy gingerly endorsed the growing civil rights movement led by Martin Luther King, Jr.

Out of a total of 68.8 million votes cast, he garnered just 119,450 more votes than Nixon — and opponents charged that some of these had been fraudulently manufactured by political machines in Illinois and Texas. Kennedy's margin in the electoral college was 303 to 219 — with 15 for ultra-conservative Senator Harry F. Byrd of Virginia, for whose "independent electors" many diehard southern whites had voted — and Kennedy actually carried fewer states than Nixon. Democratic gains among minorities and in urban areas had provided the slim margin of victory. Many felt that a telephone call made by Kennedy to Martin Luther King, Jr.'s wife, expressing concern when King was jailed for his civil rights activities, secured the critical African American support that tipped the balance in his favor.

❧ The Kennedy Mystique

John F. Kennedy's inaugural address, delivered beneath a brilliant winter sun, was a Cold War call to arms. "Let the word go forth to friend and foe alike," he announced, "that the torch has been passed to a new generation of Americans, born in this century, tempered by war, disciplined by a hard and bitter peace, proud of our ancient heritage." Under his leadership

Jack and Jackie John F. Kennedy and his bride, Jacqueline Bouvier Kennedy, cut their wedding cake at their fashionable wedding in Newport, Rhode Island.

movies, and imported liquor as soon as Prohibition ended. The elder Kennedy's courtly, attractive wife was the daughter of John F. ("Honey Fitz") Fitzgerald, mayor of Boston. Kennedy's parents earmarked Joseph, Jr., their eldest son, for a political career and Jack, who had been sickly as a child, for academia. Jack attended Choate Academy and Harvard. His senior thesis, a study of British democracy's fumbling attempts to deal with the rise of European fascism, was published as a book, *While England Slept,* after his father hired a journalist to rewrite it.

Soon after World War II erupted, Jack enlisted in the Navy, becoming a PT boat commander in the South Pacific. In an incident that his father took care to publicize, Kennedy's boat was sliced in two by a Japanese destroyer on August 2, 1943. Demonstrating courage and coolness under fire, Kennedy guided his surviving crew to a nearby island and then swam to a neighboring atoll to radio for help. The death of his brother, Joseph, in a bombing mission over France in 1944 made Jack the heir to the Kennedy clan's political ambitions.

In 1946, Jack Kennedy ran for and won a seat in the House of Representatives. After three terms in the House, in 1952 Kennedy upset Henry Cabot Lodge, Jr., to become a Senator representing Massachusetts. Within a year of his senatorial victory, America's "most eligible bachelor" married Jacqueline Bouvier in Newport, Rhode Island. The bride was a beautiful and bright debutante, and the wedding was high society's event of the year. Even though Kennedy had numerous extra-marital affairs, because he still lived in an age when a president's private indiscretions were never publicized, the nation viewed Jack and Jackie as the ideal happily married young couple. In the Senate, Kennedy concentrated on building political relationships rather than sponsoring substantive legislation. In a move that infuriated liberals in the Democratic Party, he carefully avoided voting to censure Joseph McCarthy, who was popular among Massachusetts Catholics and supported by his father.

the nation would "pay any price, bear any burden" to preserve liberty and advance the cause of freedom. He urged peoples in the developing nations to resist totalitarianism, and he promised American aid in their struggle to eliminate poverty and achieve social justice. At his gala inauguration, the youthful president, accompanied by his elegant young wife, charmed both the press and the public. Throughout his years in the White House, Kennedy enjoyed excellent relations with the media. At his televised press conferences, Kennedy's easy mastery of detail, self-effacing humor, and celebrity good looks made him very effective.

Born on May 29, 1917, John Fitzgerald Kennedy was the second of Joseph P. and Rose Fitzgerald Kennedy's nine children. Joe Kennedy was an intensely ambitious self-made Boston Irishman who had attended Harvard College at a time when few Irish Catholics did so, and then made a fortune in the stock market, produced

The Best and the Brightest

After his election to the presidency in 1960, Kennedy surrounded himself with a coterie of gifted intellectuals from the academic and business world. The best and brightest of them all was probably McGeorge Bundy — a summa cum laude graduate of the elite Groton School, the first Yale student to earn three perfect scores on his college entrance exams, and dean of Harvard College at age thirty-four. Bundy became national security adviser. Systems analyst *par excellence* Robert McNamara, the former CEO of Ford Motor Company, became secretary of defense. To head the State Department, Kennedy chose Dean Rusk, a former Rhodes scholar and head of the Ford Foundation. Arthur Schlesinger, Jr., a Pulitzer Prize–winning historian who was "court historian" in the Kennedy administration, remarked, "One's life seemed almost to pass in review as one encountered Harvard classmates, wartime associates, faces seen after the war in [Americans for Democratic Action] conventions, workers in Stevenson campaigns, academic colleagues, all united in a surge of hope and possibility." Another key member of the president's team was his brother Robert, who was appointed to the cabinet as attorney general.

The New Frontier at Home

Kennedy began his presidency by focusing on five "must" bills: an increase in the minimum wage, health insurance for senior citizens, federal aid to education, housing legislation, and aid to depressed areas. From the beginning, however, Kennedy's proposals faced stern opposition from a coalition of conservative Republicans and southern Democrats. In February the administration introduced an education bill providing the states $2.3 billion to build public schools and supplement teachers' salaries, but the bill foundered when, for different reasons, Catholics and southern segregationists opposed it. Other Kennedy proposals also failed to garner support in Congress, including a proposed increase in Social Security taxes to pay hospital and nursing bills for the elderly. On the other hand, Kennedy achieved several successes during his first two years as president. In 1961, a bill raising and extending the minimum wage passed; and Congress appropriated $4.88 billion to fund slum clearance, to build housing for the poor, elderly, and college students, and to provide low-interest home loans for middle-income families.

In 1962, at Kennedy's behest, Congress passed the Trade Expansion Act, the first significant trade revision measure enacted since Franklin Roosevelt's time, which gave the president authority to cut tariff duties

First American in Space   Colonel John Glenn poses beside the space capsule *Friendship 7* in which he became the first American to go into orbit around the earth—two years after Soviet cosmonaut Yuri Gagarin. Glenn's space flight helped restore American self-confidence in competing with the U.S.S.R. in the "space race."

by 50 percent, to eliminate tariffs altogether on certain goods, and to retaliate against certain "unfair" trade practices. The bill led to increased trade with European nations, helped correct the imbalance of payments, and served as a major foundation for the prosperity of the rest of the decade.

Congress eagerly embraced the New Frontier's space program, largely because the nation felt threatened and humiliated by Sputnik and the putative missile gap. Kennedy urged Congress to commit the United States "to achieving the goal, before this decade is out, of landing a man on the moon and returning him safely to the earth." The cost — estimated at $30 to $40 billion over ten years — daunted even Kennedy, but he was convinced that the project was justifiable on scientific and national security grounds. Congress doubled NASA's budget in 1962 and again in 1963. Talk of a missile gap began to subside after the incoming Kennedy administration discovered (or acknowledged) that it did not exist, and especially when on February 20, 1962, Lieutenant Colonel John H. Glenn orbited the earth three times in the *Friendship 7* space capsule. More significant in the long run, on June 10, Telstar, an experimental communications satellite developed by AT&T's Bell Laboratories, was placed into orbit. It soon began relaying the first live transatlantic television pictures.

Kennedy had entered the White House with the United States still mired in its fourth postwar recession. More people were out of work in 1960 than in any year since 1945, and the unemployment rate hovered near 7 percent. During the previous three-and-a-half years the annual growth rate had averaged 2.5 percent, well below what economists calculated it should be at full employment. (Full employment as defined by modern economists means an unemployment rate low enough so that only persons who are between jobs, entering the workforce for the first time, or virtually unemployable are out of work. Most economists of the 1960s considered that even under full employment somewhere around 5 percent of those seeking work would be jobless.) Kennedy had criticized Eisenhower for neglecting the economy, but he entered the presidency as a fiscal conservative himself — opposing, for example, unbalanced federal budgets. However, by 1962 President Kennedy had been converted by his chief economic adviser, Walter Heller, to the view that temporary budget deficits were acceptable if they stimulated economic growth. Kennedy, however, did not embrace creating jobs and stimulating demand through public works and welfare expenditures.

Instead, in the fall of 1963 the Kennedy administration introduced a measure providing for a tax reduction of $13.6 billion — $11 billion for individuals and $2.6 billion for corporations — spread over three years. At the time of Kennedy's death, the bill was hopelessly stuck in Congress, but it later was passed as the Revenue Act of 1964. Together with trade expansion, the tax cut had a significant impact on the economy. By the end of 1965 the unemployment rate had plummeted to 4.5 percent and the annual growth rate had increased to 6.3 percent. The most unquestioned accomplishment of the Kennedy years as president was the beginning of a robust economic boom.

Kennedy and Civil Rights

By the time John F. Kennedy became president, the civil rights movement had gained new momentum, particularly as a result of the student sit-in movement. Although Attorney General Robert Kennedy favored a vigorous enforcement of civil rights laws, the president's attitude was more equivocal. During the 1960 presidential campaign Kennedy had praised the sit-ins, seeing them as a symbol of the general reform spirit he was trying to arouse. Ever conscious of his foreign-policy objectives, Kennedy was disturbed by the damage done by racial strife to American prestige abroad, especially in the post-colonial nations emerging in Africa. At the same time, the president and his advisers wanted to retain the political support of southern whites and hesitated to alienate moderates in the region.

During the violent attacks on the CORE freedom riders in 1961 (see Chapter 32) the Kennedy administration felt increased pressure to protect the activists and to enforce integration of interstate transportation. After a white crowd surrounded Montgomery's First Baptist Church to break up a rally in support of the freedom riders, Robert Kennedy sent four hundred federal marshals to the city. The Justice Department then petitioned the Interstate Commerce Commission to issue clear rules prohibiting segregation on interstate carriers. In spite of these initiatives, James Farmer, the head of CORE, and other civil rights leaders continued to be dismayed by the Kennedy administration's tepid support for African American constitutional rights.

The Kennedy administration focused on plans to banish segregation in southern institutions of higher education. Events at the University of Mississippi in the fall of 1962 did little to allay the misgivings of civil rights activists. At the insistence of Mississippi's diehard seg-

Integrating Ole Miss, October 8, 1962   It took federal troops and John F. Kennedy's determination to enforce a court order that Air Force veteran James Meredith be allowed to register as a student at the University of Mississippi. Howling mobs of students and segregationist agitators, egged on by Mississippi governor Ross Barnett, had threatened to turn the campus into a battleground.

regationist governor, Ross Barnett, "Ole Miss" rejected the admission of James H. Meredith, a black Air Force veteran. Meredith had obtained a federal court order requiring the university to register him, and for trying to block this Governor Barnett was found guilty of civil contempt. Two days later, on September 30, Meredith was escorted onto the campus by federal marshals. Meanwhile, in a statewide radio address, Barnett incited resistance to the "oppressive power of the United States," and an angry mob of several thousand whites, many of them armed, laid siege to the campus. In several days of violence, two people were killed and hundreds injured, but the marshals, several of whom were seriously wounded, held off the rioters with the help of three hundred federalized National Guardsmen.

After the desegregation of the University of Mississippi, racial barriers quickly collapsed in other southern universities. In June 1963 the Kennedy administration forced Alabama governor George Wallace to capitulate to a court-ordered desegregation of the University of Alabama, which he had vowed to thwart by standing in the schoolhouse door.

At least partly in response to Martin Luther King, Jr.'s highly visible civil rights protests in Birmingham and the March on Washington, in 1963 Kennedy proposed a broad-based civil rights law. Some Kennedy administration officials participated in the March on Washington, though the Kennedys did not. In the end, southern Senators wielding the filibuster managed to block passage of any significant legislation. The only real legislative achievement in the civil rights area during the Kennedy years was passage in 1962 of the Twenty-fourth Amendment to the Constitution, barring the poll tax as a requirement for voting in federal elections. Hardcore opposition to integration continued in the South, symbolized by the tragic bombing of a black Baptist church in Birmingham in September 1963 that killed four young girls who were attending Sunday school. Not until 2001 would the sole surviving perpetrator, a Ku Klux Klansman, finally be found guilty.

THE PERILS OF CONTAINMENT: THE KENNEDY FOREIGN POLICY

John F. Kennedy's overriding interest was foreign affairs. Most of his inaugural address was laced with Cold War rhetoric, and he frequently justified initiatives designed to "get the nation moving" by invoking the need to contain the forces of international Communism.

Kennedy and his advisers did not object to Eisenhower's intervention in the affairs of other nations; rather, they criticized his reputed "ineptness" and his failed attempts to prop up the status quo. In a special address to Congress in May 1961, the president declared that "the great battleground for the defense and expansion of freedom today is . . . Asia, Latin America, Africa, and the Middle East, the lands of the rising peoples." He and his advisers hoped to cooperate with less authoritarian governments, even leftist ones, in order to facilitate "democratic development." Specifically, the administration projected an ambitious foreign aid program that would be used to promote social justice, economic progress, and anti-Communist policies in developing nations. At the same time, the administration viewed any significant change in the world balance of power as a threat to American security. Kennedy and his advisers interpreted Soviet leader Nikita Khrushchev's January 1961 speech offering support for "wars of national liberation" as evidence of a new Communist campaign to seize control of the brewing anti-colonial revolutionary movements throughout the Third World.

During his two-and-a-half years in office, President Kennedy launched a major arms buildup, which included massive expansion of the nuclear arsenal and the beefing up of conventional military forces, especially counter-insurgency units. Moreover, from his first days in office, Kennedy clashed repeatedly with Khrushchev over Cuba, Berlin, and Southwest Asia, going to the very brink of nuclear war.

☙ Cold War Legacy

Determined to deal with the Kremlin from a position of strength, Kennedy and Secretary of Defense McNamara announced that America's nuclear arsenal would increase until it contained one thousand intercontinental ballistic missiles. "We dare not tempt

[the Soviets] with weakness," the president declared. The nuclear buildup frightened Khrushchev; he well knew the Soviet Union already lagged far behind the United States in delivery vehicles. Instead of stability, the Kennedy-McNamara buildup touched off an arms race that came close to precipitating nuclear war in 1962, and by 1963 it saddled the United States with a massive $50 billion annual military budget. During his first year in office, Kennedy also increased spending for conventional forces by 15 percent. Impressed by counterinsurgency theories espoused by retired General Maxwell Taylor and various academic experts, Kennedy instructed the Special Warfare Center at Ft. Bragg, North Carolina, to train a new type of soldier capable of meeting Communist guerrillas on their own terms. The Special Forces unit at Ft. Bragg — the Green Berets — increased from fewer than 1,000 to 12,000 during Kennedy's presidency.

The Kennedy administration saw the Peace Corps as a civilian counterpart to the Special Forces. It was to be America's effort to identify with anti-colonialist and nationalist currents in the Third World. Under its first director, Sargent Shriver (a Kennedy brother-in-law), the organization sent idealistic volunteers to forty-four countries to teach English, train native peoples in modern farming and home economics, build hospitals, and combat disease. Together, the administration hoped that Green Berets and Peace Corps volunteers would offer developing nations help in defending themselves and in building prosperous and democratic institutions modeled on the West, thus avoiding more revolutions like the one in Cuba.

☙ The Bay of Pigs

From 1934 until 1959 Cuba was governed by a military dictator named Fulgencio Batista, whose rule favored Cuba's wealthy upper classes and U.S. business interests, including organized crime. Predictably, revolutionary nationalism took root among the island's impoverished masses, and in 1959 Batista was overthrown by a seemingly idealistic, appealing young revolutionary named Fidel Castro. The Eisenhower administration recognized the new government six days after its formation, and American businessmen rushed to pay their taxes, which they had often neglected under Batista's corrupt rule. Uncertain about Castro's intentions, most experts in Washington believed that the American-trained Cuban military would not tolerate anti-American leanings in the new government. They were wrong. It soon became clear that Castro would change the Cold War equation.

Castro announced that 1959 was the Year of the Revolution, and the following year he declared himself a Marxist-Leninist. A roundup of former Batista supporters turned into a state-sponsored effort to crush all dissent. The following year Castro launched the Year of Agrarian Reform, seizing land throughout the island, including approximately $1 billion of American-owned property. The Cuban leader was confrontational, calling Eisenhower a "gangster" and a "senile White House golfer." In the fall of 1960, Castro traveled to New York for the opening of the United Nations, delivered a four-and-a-half-hour harangue to the General Assembly, and publicly embraced Khrushchev in the Harlem hotel where the Cuban delegation was staying. Alarmed by the penetration of the Western Hemisphere by a pro-Soviet Communist regime, the Eisenhower administration secretly authorized the training and arming of a Cuban exile army of liberation under the direction of the CIA.

Almost as soon as he took the oath of office, Kennedy was briefed on the covert operation to train anti-Communist Cubans to retake the island. After the Joint Chiefs of Staff endorsed the plan, Kennedy authorized landing a detachment of 1,450 Cubans trained in Guatemala, but he forbade overt participation by U.S. armed forces, fearing that it might escalate into a war with the Soviet Union. Early in the morning of Monday, April 17, 1961, the Cuban Exile Brigade landed at the Bay of Pigs on the southern coast of Cuba. Although they achieved tactical surprise and fought well, events quickly turned against them. On the second day of the operation, with their ammunition running out and casualties mounting, the exiles surrendered.

American sponsorship of the invasion violated the charters of the United Nations and the Organization of American States, and Kennedy accepted full responsibility for the fiasco. The Bay of Pigs was an American propaganda disaster; it revived fears of Yankee imperialism in Latin America and undercut the nation's position throughout the developing world. The *New York Times* lamented, "We looked like fools to our friends, rascals to our enemies, and incompetents to the rest."

The Kennedy administration responded in two different ways to the humiliation of the Bay of Pigs. Fearing that Castro would spread his revolution elsewhere in the hemisphere, the president announced that the U.S. would seek to alleviate poverty and promote social justice throughout Latin America. In August 1961 economic and finance ministers from all American republics except Cuba signed the charter of the Alliance for Progress. It promised Latin America $20 billion for economic development, spread over the rest of the decade, half to come from the United States. At the same time President Kennedy approved a CIA-supervised effort to overthrow Castro by covert operations. By 1962 four hundred Americans and two thousand Cubans were spending $50 million a year in this "secret war."

Kennedy and Khrushchev

The Cuban confrontation was only one manifestation of the larger Soviet-American rivalry. East-West relations deteriorated sharply during the summer of 1961 as the two superpowers became embroiled once again over the divided city of Berlin. The crisis was precipitated by a "brain drain" of East Germany's intellectual and technical elite, who could easily escape to freedom by taking the subway from the Communist eastern sector of Berlin to West Berlin, which American, British, and French troops still occupied. By 1961, the number of refugees had reached around four thousand a week, and the East German regime felt that it had to stop the flow or risk collapse. The Soviets and East Germans thus demanded that the Western powers agree to turn West Berlin into a "free city" whose borders could be closed.

At a summit meeting in Vienna in June 1961, Khrushchev attempted to intimidate the younger president over Berlin. If the West did not agree to terms of a formal peace treaty with Germany by the end of the year, Khrushchev warned, the Soviet Union would sign a separate treaty with the Communist German Democratic Republic. That would put West Berlin at the mercy of East Germany's hard-line government. Influenced by advice from Harry Truman's secretary of state, Dean Acheson, who still smarted from Republican charges that he had been "soft on Communism," Kennedy took a tough line on Berlin. In a July 25 address to the nation, the president declared that the United States would stand by the people of West Berlin: "We cannot and will not permit the Communists to drive us out of Berlin, either gradually or by force." Americans, he said, "do not want to fight, but we have fought before." He requested and obtained from Congress $3.5 billion more for the armed forces, doubled and then tripled the monthly draft call, and, most ominously, announced a civil defense program that included subsidies for establishment of nuclear fallout shelters in existing structures.

On Sunday, August 13, came the Soviet answer: they began building the Berlin Wall, a concrete and barbed-wire structure that physically divided the city and sealed off East Germany from West. Though the non-Communist world expressed shock and outrage, Kennedy privately welcomed the development. He did not want to go to war over Berlin, and he recognized that the wall was a face-saving device for Khrushchev. On October 17 Khrushchev terminated the deadline for the German peace treaty. Soviet-American tensions eased — but the interlude was just a calm before the storm.

❧ The Cuban Missile Crisis

Responding to Castro's charges that the United States was plotting to overthrow his government, the Soviet Union began sending weapons and troops to Cuba. The buildup included bombers and medium-range ballistic missiles capable of raining down nuclear warheads on American cities. Republican Senator Kenneth Keating got wind of this, probably through Cuban exile circles, and, partly to score points against the Democrats on the eve of the 1962 midterm elections, Keating announced that he had evidence that there were 1,200 Russian troops in Cuba and they were building "concave metal structures" that could very well be the

The Cuban Missile Crisis   Aerial photographs such as these, taken by U-2 spy planes, convinced the Kennedy administration that the Soviet Union was installing offensive missiles in Cuba. Until the missiles were withdrawn and the launch sites dismantled, Kennedy threatened to blockade, bomb, and perhaps invade the island.

beginnings of a "rocket installation." The administration brushed off the charges as "politics," and in the first week of September Soviet ambassador Anatoly Dobrynin promised Kennedy that his country would do nothing to upset the international status quo before the elections and stated specifically that no offensive weapons would be placed in Cuba.

Dobrynin was either lying or deceived by his own government. Photographs taken by a U-2 reconnaissance flight on October 15 revealed that Soviet technicians were building sites from which both 1,000-mile medium-range ballistic missiles and 2,200-mile intermediate-range missiles could be launched against the United States. Subsequently, the U.S. discovered that nuclear warheads for these missiles, as well as nuclear bombs for Soviet bombers, were also on the island. The president was dismayed and angry. It seemed to him that Khrushchev was deliberately and deceitfully upsetting the global balance of power.

To monitor the situation and suggest options, the president created the Executive Committee of the National Security Council (ExComm), consisting of senior political, military, and foreign-policy advisers. During the following week, ExComm focused on two possible responses: an air strike to destroy the missile sites or a naval blockade to prevent the landing of nuclear warheads. Initially, most members of ExComm favored an air strike, but the consensus shifted in favor of a blockade. An air strike would kill Soviet personnel, and, conceivably, Khrushchev could respond by blasting American missile sites in Turkey. On Monday, October 22, Kennedy somberly addressed the nation on television, revealing the presence of the missiles and announcing a naval "quarantine" — the term he used rather than "blockade," which under international law would have been an act of war — to prevent additional equipment and warheads from landing. He called upon the Kremlin to "halt and eliminate this clandestine, reckless and provocative threat to world peace and to stabilize relations between our two nations." Khrushchev denounced the move as "piracy" and ordered the Soviet ships headed for Cuba to proceed. Two days later, however, as the world held its breath, the Soviet flotilla stopped just short of the naval line. Nevertheless, aerial photographs showed that Soviet technicians were continuing work on the missile sites.

As sentiment mounted within Kennedy administration councils for an air strike, Khrushchev sent the president two contradictory letters. The first, an absolutely confidential communication, offered to dismantle the

❋ I N   T H E I R   O W N   W O R D S

**Dobrynin's Cable to the
Soviet Foreign Ministry, 1962**

*The Cuban missile crisis was one of the most
anxious moments of American history, and
the anxiety reached all the way to the White
House, as this cable from the Soviet ambassador to the United States shows.*

Late tonight R. Kennedy invited me to come
see him. We talked alone.

    "The Cuban crisis," R. Kennedy began,

"continues to quickly worsen… the situation
might get out of control, with irreversible
consequences."…

    I should say that during our meeting R.
Kennedy was very upset; in any case, I've
never seen him like this before. True, about
twice he tried to return to the topic of "deception," (that he talked about so persistently
during our previous meeting), but he did so in
passing and without any edge to it. He didn't
even try to get into fights on various subjects,

as he usually does, and only persistently
returned to one topic: time is of the essence
and we shouldn't miss the chance.

    After meeting with me he immediately
went to see the president, with whom, as
R. Kennedy said, he spends almost all his time
now.

27/x-62 A. DOBRYNIN

Soviet missile sites in return for an American promise
not to invade Cuba. "If you have not lost your self-control," he wrote the president, "we and you ought now to
pull on the ends of the rope in which you have tied the
knot of war." In a subsequent letter, apparently written
under pressure from Kremlin hard-liners, Khrushchev
offered to remove the missiles in return for the withdrawal of American missiles in Turkey — in addition to
the previously demanded promise not to invade Cuba.

After much discussion, several members of ExComm
suggested that the president ignore the second letter
and respond to the first. In a telegram the White House
proposed that in return for the removal of the offensive
missiles from Cuba under UN supervision, the United
States would lift its quarantine and give assurances
against an invasion. Allowing Khrushchev maneuvering room, Kennedy verbally indicated his willingness
to discuss American weapons installations, such as those
in Turkey, and within a few months American Jupiter
missiles (which had become obsolete) were removed
from Turkey. On Sunday morning, October 28, Radio
Moscow broadcast Khrushchev's reply. He agreed fully
with the president's proposal, ignoring his second letter, as had President Kennedy.

The Cuban missile crisis almost caused a nuclear
war — and for no good reason, most scholars and even
participants subsequently agreed. Post–Cold War discussions revealed that the Soviet commander in Cuba
had tactical nuclear weapons and the authority to
use them if there was an American invasion of Cuba.
ExComm was unaware of this and did not take such
a possibility into its deliberations. Frightened by the
cumbersome and antiquated channels of communication open to the two nations' leaders during the tense

crisis, in 1963, Kennedy and Khrushchev installed a hot-
line for immediate and direct communication between
the White House and the Kremlin. In the final analysis,
both leaders had shown restraint and the world was
spared a nuclear holocaust.

Chastened, Kennedy and Khrushchev welcomed a
thaw in Soviet-American relations. On June 10, 1963,
Kennedy announced that Soviet, British, and American representatives would meet in Moscow to negotiate a nuclear test ban treaty. Within days, the delegations signed a pact outlawing all nuclear tests in the
atmosphere, in outer space, on land, and under water.
During the following months, nearly a hundred nations
signed the test ban treaty, although neither Communist China nor France ratified it. Under heavy administration pressure the United States Senate approved the
treaty by a vote of 80 to 19.

❧ Growing Crisis in Vietnam

In Cuba, Kennedy confronted a dilemma that faced
all Cold War presidents: What could the United States
do when anti-colonial, nationalist revolutionaries embraced Marxism-Leninism? Despite his oft-repeated
endorsements of anti-colonial movements and support
for economic justice in the developing world, Kennedy's first priority was anti-Communism. Kennedy was
determined to contain the Cuban revolution, and he
made a similar choice in Vietnam.

By 1960, Ho Chi Minh had established in North Vietnam a totalitarian Marxist-Leninist regime. It did not
help matters that the counterpart government in South
Vietnam was neither enlightened nor democratic. In
1955, a year after the Geneva conference, Ngo Dinh

Diem ousted Emperor Bao Dai and made himself president. Diem, a principled, patriotic, but also rigidly autocratic man, briefly attempted land and constitutional reform, but he proved unsuited to the task of building a social democracy. A Roman Catholic and traditional mandarin, both temperamentally and philosophically, he distrusted the masses and disliked democratic politics. Increasingly Diem relied on his family and loyal Catholics in the military and civil service to rule a 90 percent Buddhist country. As corruption increased and the meager efforts to establish a democracy disappeared, organized resistance began to appear in the south. In 1960, North Vietnam began giving formal aid to the newly formed revolutionary movement in the South, the National Liberation Front.

Kennedy was determined to hold the line in South Vietnam. He viewed the conflict in Southeast Asia as another of Khrushchev's wars of national liberation, just as much a test of his administration's resolve as Berlin or Cuba. Kennedy and his advisers fully accepted Eisenhower's "domino theory," assuming that the fall to Communism of one government in a region would destabilize other non-Communist governments in the area and quickly lead to Communist takeovers there as well. As the guerrilla war between the NLF and the Diem regime intensified, the Kennedy administration pumped more aid and additional military advisers into South Vietnam. The number of American uniformed personnel in South Vietnam grew from around 800 in early 1961 to 16,000 by 1963.

Despite American aid, the Diem regime grew increasingly autocratic and isolated from its people. By 1963, South Vietnam teetered on the brink of chaos. The Viet Cong (the military branch of the NLF) controlled much of the countryside and had wide support among the peasantry. Urban South Vietnamese students and intellectuals staged anti-government protests in the leading cities, while high-ranking military officers hatched various coup plots. In front of American television cameras, several Buddhist monks burned themselves to death in protest against the Diem regime. ("Buddhist barbeques," sneered Diem's sister-in-law, Madame Nhu, sometimes referred to as the "Dragon Lady," and widely suspected of being the power behind the throne in the Diem regime.) Shortly before his own assassination, Kennedy approved a military coup in Saigon, which led to the deaths of both Diem and his brother on November 1, 1963. The president sensed that the United States was on the verge of plunging into a morass from which it could not extricate itself

— and yet, for both political and strategic reasons, he was unwilling to allow Vietnam to fall to Communism. Not only would America lose credibility with its allies, Kennedy feared, but also a Republican-led anti-Communist backlash could set off a new wave of McCarthyism. Furthermore, in the early sixties, Kennedy and most liberal Democrats believed that it was the responsibility of the United States to promote profound social and political changes in the developing nations of the world.

❧ Assassination and Legacy

During the fall of 1963 President Kennedy and his advisers turned their attention to politics and the election of 1964. Speechwriter Theodore Sorenson and Robert Kennedy were particularly worried about shoring up the president's political base in the South. Following a visit to Florida in mid-November, the president flew to Texas for speaking engagements in several cities, an inspection of the space facilities in Houston, and talks with party leaders. The entourage that included Vice President Johnson and Texas governor John Connally was greeted by enthusiastic crowds in Houston, San Antonio, and Ft. Worth. In Dallas, the last stop on the tour, the president's motorcade passed large and supportive crowds. But as it drove past a large brick

Lyndon B. Johnson Takes the Oath, November 22, 1963
Aboard Air Force One, LBJ is sworn in as president. He is flanked by his wife Lady Bird and by Jacqueline Kennedy, still stunned and blood-spattered after her husband's assassination.

building, the Texas School Book Depository, shots rang out. Two bullets struck Kennedy in the head and neck. Governor Connally was also wounded, but not fatally. Rushed to a hospital, the president was pronounced dead at one o'clock in the afternoon. Secret service agents escorted Vice President Lyndon B. Johnson to Air Force One, where he was sworn in as president.

Only an hour after the assassination, the Dallas police arrested Lee Harvey Oswald for the murder. A deeply disturbed former Marine and self-professed Marxist, Oswald had lived in the Soviet Union for a time, married a Russian woman, and once had been a member of the pro-Castro Fair Play for Cuba Committee. Two days later, in a bizarre twist that has never been fully explained, Oswald was himself shot and killed in front of the TV cameras while being moved to another jail. His assassin was Dallas nightclub owner Jack Ruby, a police informer with underworld ties.

Kennedy's death was followed by a somber and ceremonious state funeral and burial in Arlington cemetery. There was an outpouring of sympathy for the newly widowed Jackie Kennedy and her young children, and most Americans felt a deep sense of personal loss. Kennedy was transformed almost overnight into a heroic figure, his every action encased in an aura of romance, his thousand-day presidency reinterpreted as a modern-day Camelot.

From the perspective of history, Kennedy's legacy is mixed. His admirers still point to the potential for greatness that was cut short by the assassin's bullet, and to his style and eloquence that elevated the image of America around the world. Furthermore, he helped to begin a vigorous economic recovery, moved the civil rights reform forward steadily if not rapidly, and lowered tensions in the Cold War in the wake of the missile crisis. On the other hand, for all of his rhetorical flourishes, Kennedy was a Cold Warrior who backed huge increases in defense spending, escalated the nation's ill-fated support of South Vietnam, and brought the world to the brink of nuclear holocaust. Domestically, the Kennedy administration passed only about one-third of its legislative agenda, and it expended far more on arms and space exploration than on such liberal reforms as Social Security, public housing, and healthcare.

While the accomplishments of the Kennedy years hardly fulfilled the promise of New Frontier rhetoric, perhaps the president's most important legacy was the rhetoric itself. In the years ahead, it was the imagined Camelot, headed by the young and dynamic leader surrounded by the best and the brightest, that provided inspiration for many of the decade's reformers and idealists.

LYNDON JOHNSON AND THE RESHAPING OF AMERICA

John F. Kennedy hoped to make modest advances in the New Deal–Fair Deal reform tradition, but Lyndon Johnson declared a full-scale War on Poverty. Kennedy's successor was an admirer of Franklin Roosevelt who believed that the government could guarantee opportunity for all and provide security for those who could not compete. Aided by the outburst of public sympathy following the assassination of Kennedy and by a landslide Democratic victory in 1964, President Johnson pushed through Congress a staggering array of new programs that greatly increased the scope and power of the federal government and marked the high-water mark of welfare-state reforms in the twentieth century. Before the expanding war in Vietnam curtailed Johnson's plans for what he called the Great Society, legislation was passed that provided health care for the elderly, job training for the underemployed, development funds for depressed areas, federal aid to education, and community development programs to aid inner-city residents. Though a white southerner, the president championed two far-reaching civil rights bills. The administration embraced environmentalism and provided federal funding for the arts and humanities. Many of the Johnson administration's programs were hurriedly conceived and fell short of achieving their lofty goals, but by the time the president left office, the quality of life for many of the country's most disadvantaged had improved dramatically. Not coincidentally, it did so for the white middle class as well.

❧ A Rage for Reform: The Political Character of Lyndon Johnson

Lyndon Johnson took the oath of office aboard Air Force One as it prepared to take John F. Kennedy's body back to Washington. One of Johnson's first acts, after Kennedy's funeral, was to address a subdued Congress. Noting that Kennedy had begun his inaugural address with the phrase, "Let us begin," the new president declared, "Let us continue." He urged Congress to pass the legislation that the Kennedy administration had proposed, but he also announced that he had a vision of his own, a sweeping agenda that included ending racial discrimination, finding employment for all who wanted to work, broadening Social Security benefits for the elderly, and peacefully coexisting with the Soviet Union. Johnson aimed to complete Roosevelt's New Deal, to realize the unfulfilled agendas of Truman's Fair Deal and Kennedy's New Frontier, and surpass all his predecessors by creating a "Great Society" that would focus on quality as well as quantity. He was not a man of small ambition.

Lyndon Johnson was born on August 27, 1908, in a farmhouse near the central Texas town of Stonewall. When he was five the family moved to Johnson City, a town founded by a distant relative. Johnson attended Southwest Texas State Teacher's College in nearby San Marcos, and upon graduation began teaching secondary school in Houston. After one year he took a job as secretary to newly elected Congressman Richard Kleberg, owner of the famous King Ranch. Within months he had mastered the legislative process and committee system, and ingratiated himself with veteran Capitol Hill operatives. In 1934 he married Claudia Alta (Lady Bird) Taylor, whose dignified loyalty and family wealth served Johnson well during the remainder of his life.

In 1937 Johnson ran for Congress himself, and won. He quickly became a White House favorite, supporting a variety of New Deal programs that benefited both the nation and his home district. Following a non-combat stint in the navy during World War II, Johnson ran successfully for the Senate in 1948 against former governor Coke Stevenson, a dyed-in-the-wool Texas conservative. Johnson's margin of victory over Stevenson in the crucial Democratic primary election was minuscule (87 votes). Throughout his political career his enemies claimed that fraud had made the difference; they derisively nicknamed him "Landslide Lyndon." In 1952, Johnson became Senate minority whip, at forty-four the youngest person to occupy a leadership position in the upper house. When the Democrats gained control of the Senate in 1955, he was elected majority leader. For the next five years he cooperated with Eisenhower to shape both foreign and domestic policy. His refusal to sign the Southern Manifesto opposing integration in 1955, and his role in crafting the Civil Rights Acts of 1957 and 1960, were sufficiently strong statements of his opposition to southern white racism to make him an acceptable nominee for the vice-presidency in 1960.

Lyndon Johnson was an imposing figure, both in stature and demeanor. He cajoled and coerced legislators, interest groups, and the press into supporting his programs. A man of immense accomplishments and ego, but also beset by intense insecurity, Johnson was determined to prove to the eastern establishment that he could outdo his Ivy League predecessor. Personally, he was a paradox. Constantly working to turn his soaring ideals into political reality, he exuded confidence and iron determination on the one hand, while giving in to fits of doubt and self-pity on the other. He could be kind and cruel, thoughtful and insensitive, crude and sophisticated, cunning and naive.

A white southerner who had grown up in a depressed region, Johnson showed many of the traits of traditional southern populism; his concerns for the poor and deprived seemed entirely sincere. He also accepted the populist and progressive prescription of positive governmental action to ensure opportunity. The Great Society, said Johnson, was to be "a place where the city of man serves not only the needs of the body and the demands of commerce but the desire for beauty and the hunger for community."

The new president moved quickly to satisfy the national curiosity and rampant speculation concerning Kennedy's assassination. Johnson appointed Chief Justice Earl Warren to head a commission to investigate the killing. The report of the Warren Commission appeared on September 27, 1964. The 296,000-word, exhaustive report concluded that the murder had been the isolated act of a single individual. The commission knew that the report would not end speculation: "the facts of the assassination itself are simple, so simple that many people believe it must be more complicated and conspiratorial to be true." Although the spinning of theories about wider conspiracies has never ceased, the Warren Commission Report remains the official — and the most widely accepted — explanation of the assassination.

❧ Johnson Takes Charge

Johnson retained the Kennedy cabinet and initially depended heavily on Secretary of Defense Robert McNamara and Secretary of State Dean Rusk. For both philosophical and political reasons, the new president pressed Congress to pass Kennedy's tax reduction proposal. Determined to placate business and financial leaders who had considered Kennedy hostile and fiscally irresponsible, Johnson ordered spending cuts in federal agencies and submitted a lean budget request that was well below what had been anticipated. This show of frugality mollified Senate conservatives, and the tax cut measure passed. Coming as it did during

Head Start These youngsters in Emeryville, California, are getting preschool instruction under the new Head Start program in January 1969. Head Start has proved one of the most enduring and popular of Lyndon Johnson's Great Society programs.

a period of almost no inflation, the tax cut seemed to work as planned. In the year following its passage, the gross national product increased by $52 billion and unemployment fell to 4.5 percent.

Lyndon Johnson felt both a moral and a political responsibility to end discrimination against African Americans. He threw the full weight of the presidency behind the Civil Rights Act of 1964. Johnson and his staff skillfully aligned a congressional coalition of liberal Democrats and moderate Republicans to vote to invoke cloture when the bill encountered the inevitable filibuster by die-hard southern opponents of civil rights, and in June the Senate passed the landmark law, 73 to 27. The Civil Rights Act of 1964, sometimes known as the Public Accommodations Act, prohibited discrimination in hotels, theaters, and buses, cut off funds to federal programs that discriminated, outlawed discrimination in employment on the basis of "race, color, religion, sex or national origin," authorized the Justice Department to institute suits to facilitate school desegregation, created the Equal Employment Opportunity Commission, and provided technical and financial aid to communities to facilitate the desegregation of school systems. The Civil Rights Act was loosely drawn, allowing great latitude to the courts and the federal bureaucracy to devise remedies in the years ahead, such as affirmative action.

Johnson's reform vision went far beyond civil rights, however. The day following Kennedy's assassination, Johnson told an aide: "I am a Roosevelt New Dealer. . . . Kennedy was a little too conservative to suit my taste." With an eye on the 1964 election, Johnson declared "unconditional war on poverty," and in August Congress passed the sweeping Economic Opportunity Act in response to the president's proposal. While the new law retained the New Deal–era Aid to Families with Dependent Children (AFDC) as the centerpiece of the welfare system, it proposed a new plan, the Community Action Program (CAP), to break the cycle of poverty by encouraging welfare recipients, local governments, and businesses to rebuild communities. In addition, the law created the Office of Economic Opportunity, an independent executive agency that was authorized to coordinate the War on Poverty and to direct programs not already supervised by existing cabinet departments. Overall, the Economic Opportunity Act created ten separate programs, including the Head Start program to help preschoolers from disadvantaged backgrounds; Upward Bound, a program designed to ready impoverished teenagers for post-secondary education; Volunteers in Service to America (VISTA), a domestic peace corps; and the Job Corps, which provided vocational training for the unemployed.

❧ The Election of 1964

In a commencement address at the University of Michigan, Johnson launched his 1964 presidential campaign with a shimmering vision of the future. He and Congress would create a "Great Society," banishing poverty, ignorance, and discrimination from the land. Remembering Roosevelt's New Deal coalition, Johnson envisioned his Great Society programs as the means to open the American dream to all citizens, while also serving as a rallying point for a political coalition to ensure his own and his party's triumph. Johnson's nomination was a foregone conclusion. The segregationist governor of Alabama, George Wallace, made a brief run for the nomination in several early primaries on a states' rights, segregationist platform, but his successes were little more than a shot fired across the bow warning of rising white backlash against urban riots and black militants.

To Lyndon Johnson's good fortune, the Republican Party in 1964 vacated the political center the president was plotting to capture. Deeply divided into a conservative wing that still hated the New Deal and lived in fear of an overweening central government and a liberal wing that closely resembled the Demo-

cratic mainstream, the GOP was also frustrated by the Democratic resurgence in Congress in the late 1950s and capture of the White House in 1960. Rejecting Governor Nelson Rockefeller of New York as too liberal, the Republican rank-and-file veered sharply to the right in 1964, nominating a bona fide conservative for the first time since World War II.

In some ways, Arizona Senator Barry Goldwater's nomination was a belated triumph for the traditional conservatives in the Republican Party who felt that Senator Robert Taft had been unfairly denied the party's nomination in 1952. But the international and domestic uncertainties of the late fifties and early sixties had nurtured a rejuvenated conservative political movement that *Time* labeled "the ultras." In part, the new conservatism reflected a rising discontent among intellectuals and college students that was underestimated by liberals (see Chapter 32). But the new conservative movement drew on many sources of discontent, and they were particularly strong in the South and Southwest. Among the diverse elements attracted to the new right were militant patriots who saw no difference between liberalism, socialism, and Communism; religious conservatives who were convinced that the federal government was undermining traditional values; and southern segregationists angered by federal enforcement of civil rights. More and more, the issue that most united the New Right was a disdain for the ever-expanding federal government, symbolized by the activist Supreme Court and Johnson's proposed War on Poverty.

At the time of his nomination, Goldwater had become the unquestioned political leader of the New Right. The son of a department store tycoon who had converted from Judaism to Episcopalianism, and a reserve air force general, Goldwater forthrightly titled his 1964 campaign tract *Conscience of a Conservative*. In it, he called for reduced government expenditures, elimination of government bureaucracies, an end to "forced" integration, reassertion of states' rights, abolition of

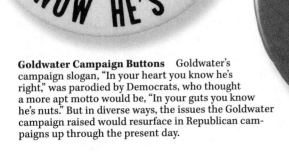

Goldwater Campaign Buttons Goldwater's campaign slogan, "In your heart you know he's right," was parodied by Democrats, who thought a more apt motto would be, "In your guts you know he's nuts." But in diverse ways, the issues the Goldwater campaign raised would resurface in Republican campaigns up through the present day.

Barry Goldwater's Acceptance Speech, 1964

The following is an excerpt from Barry Goldwater's speech at the 28th Republican National Convention, accepting the nomination for president, where he set forth a conservative vision in clear, bracing rhetoric.

The good Lord raised this mighty Republic to be a home for the brave and to flourish as the land of the free — not to stagnate in the swampland of collectivism, not to cringe before the bully of Communism.

Now, my fellow Americans, the tide has been running against freedom. Our people have followed false prophets. We must, and we shall, return to proven ways — not because they are old, but because they are true. We must, and we shall, set the tide running again in the cause of freedom. And this party, with its every action, every word, every breath, and every heartbeat, has but a single

resolve, and that is freedom — freedom made orderly for this nation by our constitutional government; freedom under a government limited by laws of nature and of nature's God; freedom — balanced so that liberty lacking order will not become the slavery of the prison cell; balanced so that liberty lacking order will not become the license of the mob and of the jungle. . . .

I would remind you that extremism in the defense of liberty is no vice. And let me remind you also that moderation in the pursuit of justice is no virtue.

farm subsidies and welfare payments, and additional curbs on labor unions. Abroad, he demanded "total victory" over Communism.

The November elections brought a Democratic landslide of staggering proportions. Johnson buried Goldwater in a popular vote of 43.1 million votes to 27.1 million, carried forty-four states and the District of Columbia for 486 electoral votes, and left Goldwater with only 52 electoral votes from the Deep South and his native Arizona. Johnson's 61.1 percent of the popular vote remains the highest percentage ever recorded in a contested election. The landslide resulted in huge Democratic gains in Congress; when the Eighty-ninth Congress convened in 1965, political liberals held clear majorities in both houses for the first time since the New Deal.

In a sense, the election of 1964 was a dividing line for both political parties: the high-water mark for postwar liberalism, and the moment at which a new Republican conservatism, eventually led by Ronald Reagan, began to coalesce. The most effective weapon in Goldwater's generally ineffective campaign had been a widely broadcast television pitch by Reagan. Just two years later, the movie star and neophyte politician would be elected governor of California, and from that platform he began propounding much of Goldwater's message in less confrontational language.

❦ *Constructing the Great Society*

Lyndon Johnson's commitment to liberal reform and his consummate political skills, combined with the

backing of the "class of 1964," the sixty-five Democrats newly elected to Congress, unleashed a torrent of legislation. He won a stunning victory for the Great Society with the enactment of the Medical Care Act of 1965. Ever since the Truman administration had attempted to pass a national health care program, groups such as the American Medical Association and private health insurers had stalled federal action by labeling it "socialized medicine." The $6.5 billion measure established a basic plan — Medicare — that was compulsory and financed by a payroll tax. Administered by the Social Security Administration, this system covered most hospital and some nursing home stays, diagnostic costs, and home-healthcare visits for those over sixty-five. A second provision of the act, called Medicaid, provided federal funds to the states to help cover the medical expenses of the indigent. Lyndon Johnson's creation of the Medicare system was comparable to Roosevelt's launching of Social Security. It triggered an enormous shift of national resources to the elderly, while at the same time providing relief to many middle-class people who had been burdened with the caring for relatives whose lifespans were steadily lengthening. Politically, Medicare — like Social Security — became an "entitlement," a sacred cow beyond attack. But in future years, a combination of relentlessly rising healthcare costs, heavy payroll taxes, and shrinking numbers of workers relative to retirees would threaten the financial soundness of the system.

Like the New Deal, the Great Society tried to give something to everyone. Johnson wanted to be known as "the education president." In the one-room school house near Stonewall, Texas, where he had begun his own education, he signed into law the Elementary and Secondary Education Act in 1965. The first federal aid to education measure in U.S. history, it provided $2 billion to help local school districts equalize educational opportunity for poor children. The law also made funds available for textbooks, library facilities, adult education, and special education for the handicapped. The Johnson administration followed up its victory by persuading Congress to enact the Higher Education Act of 1965, which expanded basic aid to the nation's colleges and universities and established a program of low-interest student loans. Federal funding for education inevitably ceded to the federal government powers of supervision of the public school system that had long been controlled by state and local interests.

Great Society activism reached broadly across American society. Despite Johnson's image as an uncouth Texan fond of telling crude jokes, the president was also an effective patron of the arts and humanities. At his urging, Congress established the National Endowment for the Humanities and the National Endowment for the Arts, both of which made grants to scholars, artists, and performers. He also addressed environmental concerns. The Wilderness Preservation Act of 1964 incorporated unspoiled federal lands into a National Wilderness System, and with White House support, Congress passed legislation establishing the Water Pollution Control Authority and imposed the first federal standards on automobile emissions.

Along with a strong commitment to civil rights, the War on Poverty was Lyndon Johnson's top domestic priority. The Economic Opportunity Act passed in 1964 was, for the president, only a beginning. In 1965 Congress more than doubled the first year appropriations for VISTA, the Job Corps, and other youth and community action programs. The next year, Congress approved the Model Cities Act, which funneled development funds directly to city governments. The administration also pushed through the Appalachian Regional Development Act, which provided $1.1 billion for highway construction, regional health centers, and resource development intended to stimulate that depressed region's economy.

By late 1966, Lyndon Johnson's Great Society vision began to dim. Partly the program was the victim of structural and philosophical flaws; partly it slowed because the Democrats lost forty-seven House seats in the elections in 1966, and, perhaps most important, the deepening war in Vietnam had begun to drain the nation's finances and splintered the Democratic Party. As rioters, black militants, and antiwar protesters seized center stage in the late 1960s, the Johnson administration began to lose support among moderate whites that had embraced the vision of a Great Society.

Attacked by both friends and foes by the end of his administration, Lyndon Johnson's domestic programs left a legacy that both extended and rivaled that of the New Deal. Many charged that the War on Poverty was irresponsibly expensive, but Great Society domestic programs cost only a little more than $6 billion between 1964 and 1967 — about one-twentieth the cost of waging war in Vietnam. Many of the programs put in place during the sixties remain pillars in the American welfare state. If Johnson's programs fell short of eliminating poverty in the nation, they nevertheless changed many lives for the better.

✳ IN THEIR OWN WORDS

From Justice Hugo Black's majority decision in *Engel v. Vitale*, 1962
This Supreme Court ruling against prayer in public schools became a lightning rod of controversy among religious conservatives in subsequent years.

There can, of course, be no doubt that New York's program of daily classroom invocation of God's blessings as prescribed in the Regents' prayer is a religious activity. It is a solemn avowal of divine faith and supplication for the blessings of the Almighty. The nature of such a prayer has always been religious. . . .

The First Amendment was added to the Constitution to stand as a guarantee that neither the power nor the prestige of the Federal Government would be used to control, support or influence the kinds of prayer the American people can say. . . .

Under that Amendment's prohibition against governmental establishment of religion, as reinforced by the provisions of the Fourteenth Amendment, government in this country, be it state or federal, is without power to prescribe by law any particular form of prayer which is to be used as an official prayer in carrying on any program of governmentally sponsored religious activity.

❧ *The Warren Court under Siege*

Ever since his appointment as chief justice by President Eisenhower in 1953, Earl Warren had made the Supreme Court a bastion for judicial activism and social reform. Conservatives increasingly complained that the Court was assuming the prerogative to "make law," imposing the will of liberal elites under the guise of upholding the Constitution. The activism of the Court increased dramatically as its composition moved to the left during the sixties. Kennedy appointed two liberal justices, Byron R. White and Arthur J. Goldberg, and Johnson led the Court even further to the left with the appointment of Abe Fortas and the first African American justice, Thurgood Marshall.

In the early 1960s the Supreme Court rendered a series of decisions that angered a variety of conservative constituencies. Religious conservatives were distraught by the 1962 decision in *Engel v. Vitale,* which ruled that the state could not sanction prayer in public schools, and the 1963 decision in *Abingdon v. Schempp,* which held that in public school classrooms, Bible-reading for religious purposes and recitation of the Lord's Prayer were unconstitutional. The impact of these rulings trickled down into school systems around the nation. A growing murmur of discontent in many deeply religious communities would grow into a substantial religious political movement in the 1970s. Other religious people, not always the same as those who objected to the school decisions, were outraged by Court rulings abolishing the right of states to control the use of contraceptives and limiting the power of local communities to censor books and films.

Equally objectionable to conservatives, and more important in the long run, were several political decisions rendered by the Court. In the case of *Baker v. Carr* (1962), the Supreme Court established the principle of "one person, one vote" in state as well as federal elections, and claimed for the courts the authority to redraw legislative districts in cases where political solutions were not forthcoming. Even more controversial in the short run were a series of decisions that protected the rights of the accused in the criminal-justice system at the very time that both crime rates and public concerns about them were mounting. In addition to requiring the state to provide an attorney for indigents charged with crimes, the *Miranda v. Arizona* decision in 1966 required police to advise all suspects of their rights upon arrest.

The rulings of the Warren Court in the 1960s signaled a major shift in American constitutional history. Apart from the specific reforms mandated by the Court, the logic behind the Court's rulings greatly expanded the oversight of the federal government, in a sense nationalizing the Bill of Rights. That is, many matters that had formerly remained in the domain of state jurisprudence became literally "federal cases." In addition, the Court gave great weight to new rights (such as a right to privacy) that had had limited or no legal standing previously. The ideological shift of the court and its theoretical broadening of the Constitution's reach were far more important than any single decision it rendered.

By the middle of the 1960s conservatives were deeply angered by the Court's activism. "Impeach Earl Warren" billboards sprouted along the highway in rightwing enclaves around the country following the Court's landmark desegregation decisions in the mid-1950s; they multiplied following the unpopular decisions of the 1960s. In the election of 1968 both Richard Nixon and George Wallace played to smoldering resentment against what many conservatives viewed as a seizure of power by the judiciary.

❧ *Johnson Presses Civil Rights*

When he became president, Lyndon Johnson wanted to move rapidly in the area of civil rights. "Every day while I am in office," he told an aide, "I'm going to lose votes. I'm going to alienate somebody.... We've got to get this legislation fast. We've got to get it during my honeymoon." Johnson's commitment to equality for African Americans was sincere, and it earned him the support of black leaders. Having pushed through the Civil Rights Act of 1964 in the wake of the Kennedy assassination, Johnson wanted to move into the areas of voting rights and school desegregation, but he hoped to be able to control the pace and direction of the civil rights movement. Ironically, Johnson was himself a victim of a civil rights rebellion in the Democratic convention of 1964. As a result of the efforts of the Freedom Summer workers in Mississippi, blacks formed the Mississippi Freedom Democratic Party (see Chapter 32) and attempted to have their delegates seated at the Democratic national convention in 1964 in place of the white delegation sent by the segregationist regular Democratic party of the state. Unwilling to alienate the southern white Democrats at the convention, Johnson engineered a compromise that offered the MFDP two at-large seats. The compromise satisfied neither side. Even after the all-white Mississippi delegation walked

"We Shall Overcome"   Some 100 civil rights demonstrators kept an all-night vigil before the Democratic Convention Hall in an attempt to seat members of the Mississippi Freedom Democratic Party. President Johnson, a strong supporter of civil rights for African Americans, was ironically caught in the middle of this conflict.

out of the convention, Johnson's people refused to seat the MFDP delegates, thus driving another wedge between civil rights activists and other members of the Democratic Party.

After the election of 1964, Johnson was deeply concerned about hardcore southern resistance to black voting, symbolized by the violent mistreatment of protesters marching from Selma to Montgomery, Alabama. At the president's initiative, in July Congress passed the Voting Rights Act of 1965. The law authorized the attorney general to appoint federal election supervisors for states or districts that had literacy tests or other restrictive devices and in which fewer than 50 percent of eligible voters had cast ballots in 1964. The Civil Rights Act of 1965, combined with Supreme Court decisions that eliminated poll taxes, dramatically increased black voter registration in the South; between 1964 and 1971 the number of eligible blacks registered to vote in Mississippi rose from 6 percent to 60 percent. By the 1970s, African American voters were a force to be reckoned with in state elections. In several southern states, black voters became the mainstay of an increasingly liberal Democratic Party. At the same time, increasing numbers of southern whites abandoned the Democratic Party and began building the Republican Party into a genuinely competitive alternative in the South for the first time since Reconstruction.

Both because of its victories and because of white resentment against urban rioting and black militancy, by the late 1960s the civil rights movement had lost much of its political momentum. Lyndon Johnson's last real achievement for civil rights came with the appointment of Thurgood Marshall, a distinguished civil rights lawyer, as the first black Supreme Court justice.

❧ The Johnson Domestic Legacy

Both Lyndon Johnson's critics and his admirers agree that his was a watershed administration in domestic American politics. Johnson's determination to be all things to all people and his sense of urgency produced programs that were sometimes ill conceived and contradictory; many of his initiatives were starts without finishes. Yet his accomplishments were large and lasting, changing American life in areas as diverse as civil rights and immigration. Nevertheless, by the 1980s, he was often pictured at best as a tragic figure and at worst a Machiavellian demagogue who manipulated and distorted American society for his own psychic gratification. Why?

First, the Great Society did represent a considerable swing to the left, particularly in its efforts to empower the poor, and it thus exposed the president to attacks from conservatives on the right. At the same time, Johnson did not move fast enough to satisfy some liberals. Second, Johnson offended and alienated the press, which had been captivated by the Kennedys. Overly sensitive to criticism and jealous of his reputation, Johnson tried to manipulate the press (as Kennedy had done quite skillfully), but he estranged the very journalists he was trying to woo. Johnson also had fatal personality flaws. He was domineering, often contemptuous of those surrounding him, even those who were potential allies. And, finally, as the Camelot myth grew in the years after JFK's assassination, many observed that Johnson's chief liability was simply that his last name was not Kennedy.

Despite these defects, all of them flaws to some degree present in other presidents, the fatal blow to Johnson's domestic program, and to his legacy, came from wounds he suffered in Southeast Asia.

Lyndon Johnson, the Cold War, and the Dilemma of Vietnam

Lyndon Johnson was in basic agreement with the foreign policies of the Kennedy administration; indeed, as vice president he had helped to shape them. Military preparedness and realistic diplomacy, he believed, should be used to contain Communism within its existing sphere. Johnson was keenly aware of the growing split between the Soviet Union and Communist China and of the possibilities inherent in this split for dividing the Communist world. He also took a flexible, even hopeful, view of the Soviet Union and Nikita Khrushchev, thinking that Russia would eventually become a defender of the status quo, and therefore a force for global stability. Johnson embraced Kennedy's policy of "flexible response," including military aid, economic assistance, and technical and political advice in response to the threat of Communism in the developing world, while at the same time negotiating with the Soviets in an effort to reduce tensions.

Above all, Lyndon Johnson wanted to hold the line in foreign affairs to avoid plunging the United States into a major confrontation with the Communist superpowers in a "brushfire war" that might lead to an escalating commitment. But the situation he inherited in Vietnam made that impossible. When Johnson assumed office the anti-Communist regime in South Vietnam was under siege from the armed forces of the National Liberation Front (NLF) and North Vietnam. Despite convincing evidence that North Vietnam's Communist leader Ho Chi Minh was seen by a majority of Vietnamese as an authentic nationalist and that the regime in the South lacked broad political support, in 1964-65 the Johnson administration decided to initiate a bombing campaign against the North and to introduce ground combat troops into the fighting. Although Johnson eventually agreed to negotiations, he had no intention of abandoning the American goal of ensuring a non-Communist South Vietnam. As a result, when he left office, the United States remained deeply mired in a war in Southeast Asia that it seemed unable to win, and bitterly divided at home over the wisdom of staying the course.

❧ The Vietnam Quagmire

Like his predecessor, Lyndon Johnson was unwilling to withdraw from South Vietnam unilaterally or to seek a negotiated settlement that would lead to "neutralization" of the area below the seventeenth parallel, the line dividing North and South Vietnam. Quite likely such a settlement would have resulted in the subsequent fall of the Saigon regime to Ho Chi Minh's revolutionaries, and indirectly to their Chinese Communist sponsors. Like so many other Americans of the World War II generation, Johnson believed that the lesson of the negotiations with Hitler in Munich was that aggression could not be rewarded with appeasement anywhere in the world, including Southeast Asia. And as vice president he seemed genuinely to be smitten with South Vietnamese president Diem, and with what he assumed was the determination of the "brave people of Vietnam" to resist a Communist takeover.

At home, Johnson feared that right-wing adversaries would question his anti-Communist resolve if he abandoned South Vietnam, undermining his hopes for building a Great Society in the United States. Having lived through the McCarthy era and its "Who lost China?" polemics, he knew how disruptive such an issue could become if the Right attacked the Democrats for "losing" Vietnam.

Finally, Johnson was trapped by bureaucratic momentum. Aware of his inexperience in foreign affairs, Johnson retained and relied heavily on Kennedy's top advisers. Secretary of State Dean Rusk, Secretary of Defense Robert McNamara, and National Security Adviser McGeorge Bundy had all played prominent roles in shaping Kennedy's Vietnam policy, and they had a deep personal stake in the success of the war. On November 24, 1963, two days after he had assumed the presidency, Johnson instructed Ambassador Henry Cabot Lodge, Jr., to assure the South Vietnamese generals whose American-backed coup had overthrown Ngo Dinh Diem that they had the full support of the United States government.

The new government of General Nguyen Khanh, which took power in South Vietnam in January 1964, faced insurmountable problems. The countryside became increasingly insecure as peasants either joined or passively supported the rebels in the South, the Viet Cong (the originally derogatory name given to the National Liberation Front by the South Vietnam government). In the cities, students and Buddhist clergy demonstrated against the war and against the corrupt, abusive military junta. Saigon became an armed enclave, and General Khanh isolated himself from the populace and his own government alike.

In the spring of 1964, in an effort to bring closure to the war, Johnson appointed General William Westmoreland as commander of U.S. forces in Vietnam. A decorated veteran of both World War II and Korea, Westmoreland was intelligent, loyal, and confident — an executive in uniform. During the next nine months the United States increased the number of American advisers in Vietnam from 16,300 to 23,300 and poured in $50 million in aid. By the summer of 1964 American uniformed personnel were working with South Vietnamese officers at virtually every level, while civilian technicians fanned out to build hospitals, train civil servants, and teach Vietnamese peasants scientific farming. But South Vietnam grew less, not more, secure. By American estimates, in the late spring of 1964 half of the land area and 40 percent of the population was under Communist control. Furthermore, in the spring of 1964 North Vietnam began extending direct military support to the Viet Cong. In that year alone, 10,000 regular troops from the North made their way down the Ho Chi Minh Trail, a web of improved jungle pathways through Laos and Cambodia that entered South Vietnam at various points.

❧ Gulf of Tonkin and the Expansion of the War

To halt further deterioration in the situation in South Vietnam, some of Johnson's advisers devised a plan that called for the president, after obtaining congressional permission, to authorize an escalating bombing campaign against North Vietnam. The needed provocation for such a campaign came on August 1, 1964, when an American destroyer, the U.S.S. *Maddox,* was attacked while patrolling North Vietnam's coast in the Tonkin Gulf. The ship's mission, undisclosed at the time, was to support South Vietnamese seaborne commandos who were raiding north of the seventeenth parallel. Briefed on the incident, Johnson ordered the destroyer to continue its patrol and ordered a second destroyer, the U.S.S.C. *Turner Joy,* to join it. The night of August 4, in heavy seas, the *Maddox* reported contact with the enemy, and the American ships fired at what they supposed were Communist gunboats; however, American naval personnel involved in the incident were not certain that the second North Vietnamese attack had occurred. When doubts surrounding the authenticity of the second attack later became public, many Senators and Representatives concluded that the White House had deliberately deceived them.

Johnson ordered retaliatory attacks on North Vietnamese torpedo-boat bases and asked the permission of Congress to take "all necessary measures to repel any

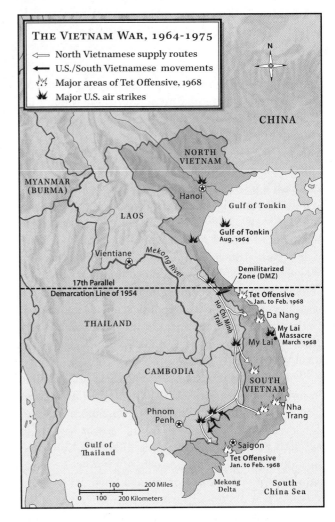

armed attacks against the forces of the United States and to prevent further aggression." Following a brief debate, the Senate approved the Tonkin Gulf Resolution by 88 to 2; discussion in the House lasted only 40 minutes, and the vote was unanimous. The overwhelming support for the resolution convinced President Johnson that he could take whatever military actions he deemed necessary to crush North Vietnam. Johnson ran in the fall presidential election as something of a peace candidate, and the Democrats made much of the risk inherent in allowing Goldwater's presumably itchy finger to be on the "nuclear button." While millions of Americans assumed that Johnson's approach to the conflict would be restrained, planners in the Pentagon prepared for the introduction of American ground troops and a heavy bombing campaign in the North.

On February 6, 1965, Viet Cong units attacked a United States Army barracks in Pleiku and a nearby helicopter base, and a month later guerrillas destroyed an enlisted men's barracks at Quinhon. Using these attacks as a pretext, the president ordered a bombing campaign against the North, called "Rolling Thunder," in an effort to stop the infiltration of troops into the South. Anticipating retaliatory attacks against the giant American air base at Danang, General Westmoreland asked for combat troops to protect the facility. On March 8, 1965, two Marine battalions splashed ashore, the first regular combat units sent to Vietnam. In April, a decision was made to continue the bombing missions, send more troops to the South, and pursue an enclave strategy in which American troops would protect a fifty-mile area around major bases. Controlling the countryside was to remain the responsibility of the South Vietnamese army. The president continued to assure the American people that bombing the North and sending combat troops to the South were responses to specific Communist provocations, not long-range strategic moves aimed at shoring up a tottering dependency.

The bombing of North Vietnam stimulated the infant antiwar movement. Faculty at increasing numbers of American universities conducted "teach-ins" opposing the war, and in April, twelve thousand activists assembled in Washington to protest the military es-

B-52s Bombing Vietnam   Flying under radar control, air force pilots bomb a military target under low clouds over the southern panhandle of North Vietnam on June 14, 1966.

calation. That same month, in a speech at Johns Hopkins University, the president made a thinly concealed effort to shortcut the antiwar movement by offering "unconditional negotiations" with North Vietnam and outlining plans for a billion-dollar Tennessee-Valley-Authority-like system of dams and power plants for the Mekong Valley if the Communists called off their attacks. But as long as the United States was committed to maintaining an independent, non-Communist state south of the seventeenth parallel, there could be no negotiation. Ho Chi Minh was determined to reunify the country, expel foreign troops, and establish his version of a Marxist-Leninist state.

❧ New Tactics — Search and Destroy

Meanwhile, General Westmoreland and American military leaders pushed Johnson to abandon the enclave system and authorize a "search and destroy" strategy by which American troops would seek out and attack the enemy anywhere in the South. Johnson kept close tabs on developments in Vietnam, and he was very reluctant to support escalation. Despite his misgivings, the president agreed to a broadening of the war. The United States intensified its bombing of a limited area of the North, and Johnson authorized saturation bombing by B-52s in areas of South Vietnam where the Communists were particularly active. Most significant, the president granted Westmoreland's request for an additional 100,000 troops and approved the search-and-destroy plan.

Even as the Johnson administration dramatically escalated the war in Vietnam, it failed to come to grips with the question of whether, politically and economically, South Vietnam would be able to survive. Nor did it precisely define America's strategic goals in the region or correctly calculate the cost of achieving those objectives. American policymakers repeatedly underestimated North Vietnam's will, assuming that the U.S. could simply apply more firepower, introduce more troops, and promote more "modernization," until the Communists gave up. They were wrong.

❧ The United States at War

American bombing of North Vietnam intensified and broadened from 1965 through 1967. U.S. pilots attacked not only troop concentrations and transportation networks, but also supply dumps and eventually steel mills and petroleum storage facilities. The tonnage of American bombs dropped on the North increased from 63,000 in 1965 to 226,000 in 1967, inflicting an estimated $600 million in damage. Nevertheless, northern troops continued to pour into the South. Teams of engineers supervising peasant conscripts repaired damage almost as soon as the sound of attacking bombers had faded. Entire munitions plants were rebuilt underground. The Soviet Union and China vied with each other in replacing destroyed tanks, trucks, and munitions. By 1967 major population centers in the North were surrounded by anti-aircraft systems, and by the end of that year some five hundred U.S. aircraft had been shot down. Captured American airmen gave Hanoi great leverage when peace negotiations finally got underway, and in the meantime they were subjected to brutal treatment, including torture, in an effort to get them to confess to war crimes.

By the end of 1966, 431,000 American military personnel were in Vietnam, equipped with sophisticated computers that were supposed to predict enemy movements. The U.S. command declared areas in which the Viet Cong and North Vietnamese army were particularly active "free fire zones," and from 1965 through 1967 American B-52s dropped more than a million tons of bombs on South Vietnam. To deny the enemy cover, more than a hundred million tons of defoliants, including the highly toxic Agent Orange, were sprayed on South Vietnamese forests. Nonetheless, the Saigon government could not control the countryside. Recognizing the weakness of the government in the South, and aware of the growing American antiwar movement, the Viet Cong generally avoided large engagements and resorted instead to guerrilla raids that were difficult to counter. Because the Viet Cong often did not wear uniforms, Americans found it impossible to tell friend from foe. With no fixed battle lines, a daily body count became the measure of failure or success. By late 1967, even allowing for inflated numbers, U.S. and allied South Vietnamese forces had killed around a quarter of a million of the enemy.

❧ Growing Dissent at Home

By 1967 the war had spawned a bitter, divisive debate within the United States. At one end of the spectrum, "hawks" insisted that the administration was not doing enough. Comprised primarily of conservative Republicans and southern Democrats, the hawks were staunch Cold Warriors who saw Communism as an unmitigated evil and the regime in Hanoi as an extension of Chinese and Soviet imperialism. At the other end of the spec-

Agent Orange Over a hundred million tons of the highly toxic herbicide Agent Orange was sprayed on the tropical forests of Vietnam as a defoliant. It was intended to deny cover to enemy soldiers, but its long-term effects were devastating, causing, among other things, cancer in American soldiers who were exposed to it, and birth defects in children—like this boy, born several years after the war ended—whose parents were exposed.

trum was a growing and diverse collection of "doves" who opposed the war as immoral, illogical, counterproductive, or all three. The antiwar coalition included some Washington insiders, including Arkansas Senator J. William Fulbright, who in 1966 held televised Senate hearings on Vietnam that stirred unease throughout the country. While many religious leaders supported the war in Vietnam, others joined in antiwar protests during the mid-sixties. Early opposition to the war came from traditional peace churches such as the Quakers, but other outspoken religious critics included William Sloane Coffin, minister of New York's Riverside Church, and two fiery Roman Catholic priests, Philip and Daniel Berrigan. Other prominent doves included such celebrities as Martin Luther King, Jr., actor Jane Fonda, pediatrician and popular writer Dr. Benjamin Spock, and heavyweight champion Muhammad Ali. Increasingly, however, the most visible antiwar protest came from left-wing students and intellectuals, who saw the war as the fruit of American imperialism and arrogance.

Most Americans supported the country's soldiers in Vietnam, and disapproved of the radical student movement, but as American television displayed the horrors of Vietnam on a daily basis and the escalating American military involvement brought about a dramatic expansion of the draft, the student-dominated antiwar movement gained momentum. The intensity of the protest was horrifyingly demonstrated in November 1965, when a young Quaker pacifist, Norman Morrison, burned himself to death outside the Pentagon. That month, some 30,000 people convened in Washington to stage the largest demonstration against the war up to that time. Young antiwar protesters burned their draft cards, and others fled to Canada to escape the draft. A few mutilated themselves to protest the war and to avoid the draft, and far more got sympathetic physicians or psychiatrists to certify them as "medically unfit." By war's end around 570,000 young Americans had violated the draft law and 563,000 less-than-honorable discharges had been issued by the military. But it was mass demonstrations, televised nationally, that had the greatest impact on the public and the White House. In the spring of 1967, 500,000 marchers of all ages converged on New York's Central Park chanting, "Hey, hey, LBJ, how many kids did you kill today?" Student activist Dave McReynolds summed up the situation: "Everything now revolves around Vietnam. It's no longer a distant, bloodied, tedious spot half way across the planet. Vietnam is here."

Though there were still many Americans who supported the war, countless acts of defiance created a sense of disunity that sapped the national will. Public support for the war, at least for President Johnson's handling of it, dropped off sharply during 1967. In early August the president was forced to ask Congress for a 10 percent surtax on incomes to help cover mounting deficits. Suddenly business leaders began to voice doubts about the war, and such formerly hawkish publications as *Time* called for a reassessment of American policies. As the number of young men drafted each month reached 30,000 and the American death toll passed 13,000, many former supporters of the war effort reluctantly came to conclude that it was a mistake. Beset from all sides, Johnson saw his approval rating in the polls plummet precipitously.

❧ *The Wages of Globalism — Latin America, the Middle East, and Détente*

While the Johnson administration was consumed by the troubles in Southeast Asia, it faced a series of other international problems, including fears of Cuban-inspired revolutions in Latin America. When political instability erupted in the Dominican Republic in 1965, Johnson and his stridently anti-Communist assistant secretary of state for Latin American affairs, Thomas Mann, assumed that "another Cuba" was in the making. Claiming a need to protect American lives, the ad-

ministration landed 20,000 Marines and army troops to prevent the return of a mildly left-wing former president, Juan Bosch, whom they improbably saw as a potential Castro. "We don't intend to sit here in our rocking chair with our hands folded and let the Communists set up any governments in the Western Hemisphere," the president declared. Senator Fulbright led a chorus of critics inside and outside the United States, arguing that there were no more than a handful of Communists in the Dominican Republic and that unilateral intervention violated both the charter and the spirit of the Organization of American States, but to no avail.

The Middle East offered even more serious challenges to America's efforts to maintain a stable world order. After the 1956 Suez crisis, relations had remained tense between Israel and the Arab world, whose most charismatic leader was Egypt's Gamal Abdel Nasser. In May 1967, Nasser persuaded the United Nations to withdraw the peacekeeping force that had separated Egyptian and Israeli forces for a decade, leaving the two adversaries facing each other directly across a huge demilitarized zone covering most of the Sinai Peninsula. Nasser moved quickly to fill the void, ordering his forces to occupy the Sinai. At the same time, Palestinian guerrillas increased attacks against Jewish settlements from bases in the Sinai, Jordan, and Syria. Convinced that an Arab attack was imminent, on June 6, 1967, the Israelis struck first, destroying Nasser's air force, as well as those of Jordan and Syria, before the planes got off the ground. In a rapid six-day advance the Israeli army occupied the Sinai, the old city of Jerusalem, the West Bank of the Jordan River, and the Golan Heights just inside Syria, completely rearranging the strategic balance in the Middle East.

Neither the United States nor the United Nations could control the events in the Middle East. Still, in November 1967, the UN General Assembly approved Resolution 242, calling for a negotiated settlement in the Middle East. In exchange for a multilateral guarantee of Israel's borders, Israel was called upon to return the territory seized in the Six Day War. Israel was promised free access to "regional waterways," while Palestinians were guaranteed "a just settlement of the refugee problem" — a vague provision that they interpreted to mean Palestine's transformation into a state for Jews and Arabs.

The United States supported Resolution 242, while at the same time remaining sympathetic to Israel's security fears. Israel insisted that the Arab nations would have to extend formal recognition and guarantees against aggression before the land seized in the Six

Day War would be abandoned. When the United States continued to replace Israeli military equipment and to subsidize the Israeli economy, an angry Nasser severed diplomatic ties with Washington, and Moscow broke off relations with Tel Aviv. While Israel ruled the territories under its control with an iron hand, Palestinian border raids and terrorist attacks increased, and the region remained ripe for another explosion.

While strongly opposing Communist expansion in Southeast Asia and Central America, and supporting Israel in the Middle East, Johnson was also working quietly trying to lessen tensions with the Soviet Union. This softer strategy toward the Soviet Union, begun during the last days of the Kennedy administration, was called "détente" (a French word meaning a lessening of tensions). Even though enemies in the Kremlin suddenly deposed Khrushchev in October 1964, his successors, Leonid Brezhnev and Alexei N. Kosygin, seemed willing to better relations with the West. Three years of difficult negotiations followed, in which the Soviet Union, the United States, Great Britain, and fifty-eight other nations finally agreed to a nuclear nonproliferation treaty that forbade the nuclear powers from transferring atomic weapons technology to third parties and committed non-nuclear powers not to manufacture or acquire nuclear weapons.

⚬ *Tet and the Devolution of the Johnson Administration*

The Six Day War and the threat it posed to American economic and strategic interests increased pressure on President Johnson to end the war in Vietnam. There was no dearth of peace initiatives; officials counted some two thousand official and unofficial attempts between 1964 and 1968 to bring about a negotiated settlement. In June 1967 Johnson met with Soviet premier Kosygin at Glassboro, New Jersey, hoping to find a way to jointly relieve tensions in the Middle East and Vietnam, but nothing concrete emerged. Opinion polls taken that fall indicated that a majority of Americans considered U.S. intervention in Vietnam a mistake.

Sensing mounting war-weariness in the United States, the North Vietnamese leadership and the NLF launched a major offensive, hoping to spark an uprising in South Vietnam's cities and to demonstrate that no part of South Vietnam was secure. Regular units of the North Vietnamese army were used to lure American forces into diversionary battles while Viet Cong cadres infiltrated the cities of South Vietnam, poised to make surprise attacks on military, police, and government facilities.

In some respects, the Communist strategy worked. In January 1968, during the Vietnamese New Year holiday called Tet, Viet Cong detachments struck Saigon, Hue, and scores of other cities, including thirty-six of sixty-four provincial capitals. Americans at home were stunned to see televised pictures of a Viet Cong team occupying the courtyard of the American embassy in Saigon. American and South Vietnamese forces quickly rallied, however. Within days, the capital was cleared, and over the next few weeks the Communists were driven from most of the territory they had occupied and pushed deep into the countryside, suffering heavy casualties. The infrastructure of the Viet Cong lay shattered, never fully to recover. The Communists themselves considered the outcome a defeat.

Yet the Viet Cong's tactical setback turned into a major strategic victory. Military reports in 1967 had led most Americans to believe that a final victory was near, but during the fierce Tet attack U.S. and South Vietnamese forces suffered heavy casualties. "The rockets came in so loud they would scramble your brains," remembered one helicopter pilot. Recalled another veteran, "Though I didn't do any front line stuff, I did receive a lot of on-the-job training, mostly in how to put guys in body bags." "What the hell is going on?" demanded respected CBS television anchor Walter Cronkite. "I thought we were winning the war." The Tet offensive caused Americans to verbalize their nagging doubts. Was there really a viable nation south of the seventeenth parallel? If so, why were the Vietnamese not willing to fight and die to defend their own country? How could the U.S. military command have been caught so off guard? Did Tet indicate that American strategic thinking was either fatally flawed or totally unrealistic?

In the wake of Tet, Johnson rejected a request from General Westmoreland and the Joint Chiefs of Staff for 205,000 additional troops and refused to strike at Communist sanctuaries in Laos and Cambodia. Late in 1967, a shaken Robert McNamara resigned as secretary of defense, and newly appointed secretary Clark Clifford advised Johnson to resist further buildup while the war was reassessed. Approval of Johnson's handling of the war plummeted to 26 percent during Tet; 78 percent of the public thought that the United States was making no progress in the war. In Washington, a group of veteran diplomats and policy analysts, labeled "the Wise Men" by the press, which included former secretary of state Dean Acheson, called for the "gradual disengagement" of the United States from the war.

WINDING DOWN THE LIBERAL EXPERIMENT

Even before Tet, antiwar Democrats had decided to work against Johnson's renomination in 1968. Their favorite was Robert Kennedy, but he held back, intimidated by the difficulty of defeating a sitting president. Those committed to ousting Johnson turned to Eugene J. McCarthy, a quiet, thoughtful, quixotic, and strongly antiwar Democratic Senator from Minnesota. McCarthy entered the New Hampshire primary and won 42.4 percent of the vote, compared to Johnson's 49.5 percent. Antiwar groups contributed heavily to McCarthy's vote, but so did "hawks" in the Democratic Party who cast a protest vote against what they thought was Johnson's insufficient vigor in waging the war.

A few days after the New Hampshire primary, and after his decision to oppose further expansion of the war, a somber, haggard Johnson went on television to announce that henceforward bombing of North Vietnam would be limited to the area just north of the demilitarized zone. The United States, he declared, was ready to engage in comprehensive peace talks anywhere, anytime. Then he dropped a bombshell: "I shall not seek, and I will not accept, the nomination of my party for another term as president." Johnson had personal as well as public reasons for his stunning decision; he had suffered a massive heart attack while serving in the Senate, and his wife feared that he would not survive another term as president. But McCarthy's showing in the New Hampshire primary had been a bitter blow, and Johnson believed that even if he were reelected, it would only deepen the divisions in the country, making further domestic reform impossible. Finally, Johnson did not wish to bear the stigma of being the president who would have to concede defeat in Vietnam.

❧ More Assassinations

Robert Kennedy entered the race for the Democratic nomination two weeks before Johnson withdrew, reason-

The Tet Offensive These U.S. Marines are battling to retake the old imperial capital of Vietnam, Hue, which was seized by North Vietnamese and Viet Cong fighters in January 1968. On February 4, after bloody fighting, they prevailed. Communist forces suffered devastating losses but won a major battle by convincing the TV-watching American public that victory in the war was still a long way off.

ing that he would make a stronger opposition candidate than McCarthy. Kennedy attracted huge crowds, appealing not only to antiwar liberals, African Americans, and the poor, but also to some working-class Catholics who were political moderates.

Among the potential backers of Robert F. Kennedy was Martin Luther King, Jr. In 1968, King launched his own campaign — the Poor People's Campaign. King's new agenda was to highlight the plight of the nation's poor, regardless of color. He appealed to middle-class consciences, but he hoped to mold all poor people — blacks, Hispanics, and whites — into a formidable political coalition. On April 4, King traveled to Memphis to lead a demonstration in behalf of striking garbage workers. That evening, he was shot and killed by a white racist and ex-convict, James Earl Ray. Although Ray apparently acted alone in the assassination, swirling rumors of a conspiracy involving White Citizens Councils and the FBI touched off riots in a dozen cities, the worst in Washington, D.C., and Chicago.

The King assassination set the tone for the bitter political campaign of 1968. Johnson's heir apparent, Vice President Hubert Humphrey, was a veteran Senator from Minnesota with an impeccable liberal record, but as the campaign unfolded he became marked as the insider candidate of Democratic Party leaders. Ironically, he was scorned by most liberal Democrats because of his loyalty to President Johnson and his support of the war in Vietnam. So while McCarthy and Kennedy waged high-profile primary campaigns, Humphrey concentrated on quietly lining up convention delegates in non-primary states.

King had planned to "get behind Bobby," and after his death the SCLC and other black organizations rallied to Kennedy. By May his well-financed campaign was in full gear. On June 4, Kennedy crushed Humphrey in the California primary and seemed on his way to the nomination. But as he was leaving a victory celebration, a Jordanian immigrant, Sirhan Sirhan, gunned him down. Although his exact motives remained unclear, Sirhan was an Arab zealot who apparently killed Kennedy because of the support he and JFK had given to Israel.

❧ The Raucous Democratic Convention in Chicago

Following the assassinations of two of America's most charismatic political reformers, riots erupted in cities across the nation; America seemed to be coming apart at the seams. When the Democratic convention convened in Chicago in August, the delegates quickly polarized into antiwar and prowar factions. The "hawks," led by Chicago mayor Richard Daley, voted down a "peace" plank calling for "an unconditional end to all bombing in North Vietnam." Although McCarthy won over most of the 300 delegates pledged to Robert Kennedy, Humphrey had the support of party regulars and easily captured the nomination on the first ballot. The Democratic platform, reflecting the political ideas of Humphrey, was generally liberal. The convention refused to seat the segregated white Mississippi delegation, and it democratized the process for selecting future convention delegates, a procedural change that would transform the Democratic Party and American politics in the years to come.

While Democratic delegates clashed within Chicago's cavernous Amphitheater, an army of antiwar activists and student radicals descended on the city. From the earnest and well-scrubbed supporters of Eugene McCarthy to a boisterous and nihilistic group of "Yippies," the crowds spanned the antiwar spectrum. Most were bent on peaceful demonstration, but the Yippies, led by activist Abbie Hoffman (who told reporters that his "conception of revolution is that it's fun"), set out to provoke violence. Mayor Daley assembled an army of 12,000 policemen to control the demonstrators. Confronted with crowds screaming obscenities and hurling plastic bags filled with urine, the Chicago police made war on the mobs. For three days the Democratic convention shared television coverage with scenes of the Chicago police attacking and beating demonstrators, and sometimes innocent bystanders as well.

❧ The Political Reincarnation of Richard Nixon

Most Americans were repulsed by the spectacle in Chicago, and the Republicans met in Miami gleefully relishing the opportunity to oppose a party in such disarray.

❋ **IN THEIR OWN WORDS**

The "Statement From Yip," 1968
Months before the Democratic convention, the Yippies released an initial call to come to Chicago, called "A STATEMENT FROM YIP."

Join us in Chicago in August for an international festival of youth, music, and theater. Rise up and abandon the creeping meatball! Come all you rebels, youth spirits, rock minstrels, truth-seekers, peacock-freaks, poets, barricade-jumpers, dancers, lovers and artists!

It is summer. It is the last week in August, and the NATIONAL DEATH PARTY meets to bless Lyndon Johnson. We are there! There are 50,000 of us dancing in the streets, throbbing with amplifiers and harmony. We are making love in the parks. We are reading, singing, laughing, printing newspapers, groping, and making a mock convention, and celebrating the birth of FREE AMERICA in our own time.

Everything will be free. Bring blankets, tents, draft-cards, body-paint, Mr. Leary's Cow, food to share, music, eager skin, and happiness. The threats of LBJ, Mayor Daley, and J. Edgar Freako will not stop us. We are coming! We are coming from all over the world!

The life of the American spirit is being torn asunder by the forces of violence, decay, and the napalm-cancer fiend. We demand the Politics of Ecstasy! We are the delicate spores of the new fierceness that will change America. We will create our own reality, we are Free America! And we will not accept the false theater of the Death Convention.

We will be in Chicago. Begin preparations now! Chicago is yours! Do it!

Following his defeat in 1960, Richard Nixon had run for governor of California and lost. His second defeat in two years embittered him — particularly toward the press, who he believed had always treated him unfairly. "You won't have Nixon to kick around any more," he sulkily told reporters at his farewell press conference after his gubernatorial defeat. But no other twentieth-century politician proved as resilient as Richard Nixon. After his defeat, he joined a prestigious New York law firm and settled into the role of elder statesman in the Republican Party. He dutifully campaigned for Goldwater in 1964 and, after the party's disastrous losses that year, began lining up delegates for 1968. Liberal Republicans posed little threat to Nixon's nomination in 1968, but he was challenged by a rising conservative wing headed by the newly elected governor of California, Ronald Reagan. Nixon protected his right flank, however, assuring southern conservatives like Senator J. Strom Thurmond — the 1948 "Dixiecrat" presidential nominee and a recent defector from the Democratic Party — that he shared their opposition to the busing of students to achieve racial balance and supported "law and order." Essentially, "law and order" was Nixon's euphemism for a promise to crack down hard on student demonstrators, campus radicals, and ghetto rioters. At the GOP convention in Miami Beach, Nixon was nominated on the first ballot. As his running mate, he selected Spiro T. Agnew, the little-known Maryland governor chosen because of his grandiloquent denunciations of urban rioting. The platform called for a national war against crime, reform of the welfare system to encourage the poor to work, and a stronger national defense.

❧ *The Election of 1968*

The campaign of 1968 was complicated by the entry of Alabama governor George Wallace as a third-party candidate. Wallace made a brief run at the Democratic nomination, making surprisingly strong showings in several northern state primaries, before forming the American Independent Party. Wallace appealed to many of the older prejudices that still lingered throughout the country, and he offered simplistic explanations for the nation's ills. He blamed urban rioting on black power advocates and their "socialist" white allies, and he hinted that integration ought to remain a personal choice. He railed against the federal government, and especially the Supreme Court, for encouraging racial unrest, "coddling" criminals, and tolerating "welfare cheats." Wallace launched a national campaign, predict-

ing that "the people of Cleveland and Chicago and Gary and St. Louis will be so . . . sick and tired of Federal interference in their local schools, they'll be ready to vote for Wallace." Wallace was a shrewd populist politician who sensed the deep discontent felt by many working-class Americans at the dissent and disrespect dividing the country. Selecting Air Force general Curtis E. LeMay for his running mate, Wallace promised victory in Vietnam, presumably by (as LeMay put it) bombing North Vietnam "back into the Stone Age."

Nixon managed to seize the political middle while at the same time seeking to address the anxieties that Wallace exploited. The "new Nixon" appeared relaxed and self-confident — a consensus builder who would be an antidote to the angry and divided Democrats and the overt racism of Wallace. But Humphrey was a skilled, experienced campaigner, and as the election neared some of Wallace's labor supporters began to return to the Democratic fold, as did many party liberals. On November 1, President Johnson announced a total halt to the bombing in North Vietnam, and Humphrey drew virtually even with Nixon in the polls. The final results were extremely close. Nixon polled 31.7 million votes (43.7 percent of the total), Humphrey 31.2 million (42.4 percent), and Wallace 9.9 million (13.5 percent).

CONCLUSION: THE LEGACY OF SIXTIES LIBERALISM

The American people had entered what magazines like *Time* billed as "the Soaring Sixties" with high expectations. The razor-thin election of John F. Kennedy to the presidency in 1960 hardly marked a repudiation of the policies of the Eisenhower administration — containment of Communism abroad and maintenance of the New Deal–Fair Deal reform structure at home — but it did signal a new openness in American society and an acceptance of the need to press on to new frontiers. Kennedy and his advisers believed that their mission was to demonstrate to the world the superiority of liberal capitalism over Marxism-Leninism. The charismatic young president became immensely popular, especially in death, but he lacked political leverage and legislative skills, and his domestic achievements were modest.

In 1963 Lyndon Johnson succeeded to the presidency promising to continue the policies of his predecessor. As good as his word, Johnson went far beyond what Kennedy could have done. Johnson's Great Society programs boldly attacked the problem of poverty, raising millions of Americans above a subsistence level. It also created a federally supported health care system for the elderly, community action programs to regenerate the inner city, and area redevelopment initiatives to eradicate rural poverty. Johnson signed the two most important pieces of civil rights legislation in the twentieth century, the first federal aid to education bill, and a landmark revision of American immigration policy. There was something in the Great Society for everyone, including new national arts and humanities foundations and a beefed-up space program. Johnson dreamed of a new America, prosperous, self-fulfilled, and unified. But it was not to be. Like Woodrow Wilson's progressive vision and Franklin Delano Roosevelt's New Deal, the reform impulse of the 1960s was stifled by a foreign war.

The war in Vietnam drained the resources needed to carry on the liberal reforms of the sixties, and disenchantment with the war drove a deep wedge into the ranks of American liberalism. Kennedy had hoped to align the United States with the forces of anti-colonialism and nationalism in the developing world and simultaneously to contain Communism on every front. Those two objectives were difficult to combine. In the end, Kennedy's commitment to Cold War containment led him perilously close to a nuclear war with the Soviet Union over Cuba and pulled America inexorably into a war in Vietnam. Just as determined as Kennedy to hold the line in Vietnam, Johnson expanded the war in hopes of finding a way to win. As the war dragged on year after bloody year, the nation resounded with angry voices on the right and the left, and Lyndon Johnson's hopes of building the Great Society dissolved. By the time Richard Nixon was elected to the presidency in the factious election of 1968, the country was poised for a tactical retreat from the liberal activism that dominated politics in the sixties.

SUGGESTED READING

Irving Bernstein, *Promises Kept: John F. Kennedy's New Frontier* (1991). Surveys the Kennedy domestic agenda.

Robert Dallek, *Lone Star Rising: Lyndon Johnson and His Times, 1908-1960* (1991) and *Flawed Giant: Lyndon B. Johnson, 1960-1973* (1998). These two books provide the most balanced treatment of Lyndon Johnson and his presidency.

John Lewis Gaddis, *We Now Know: Rethinking Cold War History* (1997). An overview of American foreign policy since World War II, making use of new archival materials in the post–Cold War era.

David Garrow, *Bearing the Cross: Martin Luther King, Jr., and the Southern Christian Leadership Conference* (1986). A compelling study of King and the civil rights movement.

George Herring, *America's Longest War* (1986), and Stanley Karnow, *Vietnam: A History*, rev. ed. (1991). These two works provide balanced overviews of the war in Vietnam.

Herbert Parmet, *Jack: The Struggle of John Fitzgerald Kennedy* (1980), and *JFK: The Presidency of John Fitzgerald Kennedy* (1983). Balanced treatments of Kennedy and his presidency.

Thomas G. Paterson, ed., *Kennedy's Quest for Victory: American Foreign Policy, 1961-1963* (1989). An exploration of Kennedy's foreign policy objectives.

SUGGESTIONS FOR FURTHER READING

David M. Barrett, *Uncertain Warriors: Lyndon Johnson and His Vietnam Advisors* (1994).

David W. Belin, *Final Disclosure: The Full Truth about the Assassination of President Kennedy* (1988).

Larry Berman, *Lyndon Johnson's War: The Road to Stalemate in Vietnam* (1989).

Richard Bett, *The Irony of Vietnam: The System Worked* (1979).

H. W. Brands, *The Devil We Knew: Americans and the Cold War* (1993).

Carl Brauer, *John F. Kennedy and the Second Reconstruction* (1977).

Robert Caro, *The Years of Lyndon B. Johnson: The Path to Power* (1982) and *Means of Ascent* (1990).

Paul Conkin, *Big Daddy from the Pedernales* (1986).

Robert Dallek, *An Unfinished Life* (2003).

Charles DeBenedetti, *An American Ordeal: The Anti-war Movement of the Vietnam Era* (1990).

Adam Fairclough, *To Redeem the Soul of America: The Southern Christian Leadership Conference and Martin Luther King, Jr.* (1987).

John Lewis Gaddis, *Strategies of Containment: A Critical Appraisal of Postwar American National Security Policy* (1982) and *The United States and the End of the Cold War* (1992).

Robert Goldberg, *Barry Goldwater* (1995).

Guenter Lewy, *America in Vietnam: Illusion, Myth and Reality* (1978).

Robert McNamara, *In Retrospect: The Tragedy and Lessons of Vietnam* (1995).

Norman Podhoretz, *Why We Were in Vietnam* (1982).

Gerald Posner, *Case Closed: Lee Harvey Oswald and the Assassination of JFK* (1994).

Thomas C. Reeves, *A Question of Character: The Life of John F. Kennedy*, rev. ed. (1998).

Robert D. Schulzinger, *A Time of War: The United States and Vietnam, 1945-1975* (1997).

Orrin Schwab, *Defending the Free World: John F. Kennedy, Lyndon Johnson, and the Vietnam War, 1961-1965* (1998).

John Schwarz, *America's Hidden Successes: A Reassessment of Twenty Years of Public Policy* (1983).

Mark White, *Missiles in Cuba: Kennedy, Khrushchev, Castro and the 1962 Crisis* (1997).

34

A Nation Beset:
Politics from Nixon to Reagan

THE GHETTO RIOTS, antiwar protests, and political assassinations of 1968 set the tone for the contentious and often dispirited 1970s. Richard Nixon, given new political life by the glaring divisions within the Democratic Party, narrowly won the White House by appealing to Americans' nostalgia for the calmer mood of the fifties. Nixon sometimes used right-wing rhetoric and had a reputation for orthodox conservatism in domestic affairs and for hard-line anti-Communism abroad. But as president he proved to be a pragmatist. His election blocked further experimentation with social welfare programs and new civil rights legislation, but it did not significantly reduce the New Deal–Great Society structure that had been put in place, nor did it roll back the civil rights revolution. In fact, the Nixon administration significantly advanced the liberal agenda in such areas as affirmative action and environmental regulation.

In foreign policy — the president's area of primary personal interest — Nixon and his advisers tried to place America on a non-ideological footing, defining that policy as the containment of Soviet expansionism and the protection of American economic and strategic interests. The Nixon administration had some stunning diplomatic successes; it ended direct American participation in the war in Vietnam, albeit grudgingly and belatedly, and it set in motion dramatic breakthroughs in American relations with the Soviet Union and China. These were initiatives that, had a liberal Democratic president attempted them, would undoubtedly have brought howls of Republican outrage. But the long-term consequences of the Nixon administration's quite brilliant foreign policy did much to establish a stable balance of power in an increasingly prosperous Asia in the decades ahead.

But President Nixon also became the first American president to resign, driven from office on the eve of almost certain impeachment and conviction, leaving the presidency in the hands of his vice president, Gerald Ford. Two years later, with Nixon's political crisis still fresh in their minds, voters in 1976 chose for the presidency a Washington outsider, Jimmy Carter. A former governor of Georgia, Carter exuded innocence and idealism, qualities that served him well in his election campaign but not so well in his presidency. Carter was sympathetic to many traditional liberal causes that called for new programs for the poor and disadvantaged, and he significantly expanded the federal bureaucracy, but he was also committed to balancing the budget. Faced with a bewildering array of economic and diplomatic problems abroad, the Carter administration placed human rights at the fore of its foreign policy. That stance both baffled and irritated the nation's traditional adversaries and inevitably generated charges of Yankee imperialism and led to greater conflict with the Soviet Union.

Between 1973 and 1980, a series of crises — Watergate, America's humiliating withdrawal from Vietnam, the nation's growing dependence on Middle East oil, soaring inflation, and the challenge to U.S. economic supremacy posed by Japan and Europe — profoundly shook the country's self-confidence. The Carter presidency, which appeared to wrestle ineffectually with many accumulated problems, seemed to millions of Americans both symptom and symbol of the nation's decline.

THE NIXON YEARS ON THE HOME FRONT

Despite his reputation as a hard-line conservative in domestic affairs, earned during his years of partisan attacks on the New Deal, the Fair Deal, and the Great Society, Richard Nixon proved to be pragmatic and opportunistic in his social and economic policies. Indeed, the Nixon administration's commitment to equality of opportunity, a social safety net for the chronically disadvantaged, a balanced budget, and minimal support for civil rights initiatives made it seem an expansion of Dwight Eisenhower's "modern Republicanism." When classical economic remedies did not rescue the country

from its economic woes, the president shocked his conservative supporters by turning to deficit spending and by imposing wage and price controls.

Understanding full well that he had received only 43 percent of the popular vote in 1968, and forced to work with hostile Democratic majorities in both houses of Congress, Nixon developed a centrist political agenda. Perhaps the attitude that most separated Nixon from Eisenhower's moderate Republicanism, and that increasingly divided Democrats and Republicans, was the president's desire to rein in the federal bureaucracy. The White House was unremitting in its efforts to scale back governmental agencies, especially the huge bureaucracy created by the Great Society.

∾ *The Political Persona of Richard Nixon*

Richard Nixon was born of Quaker parents in Southern California, the second of five sons. He grew up in Whittier, California, graduated from Whittier College, and after a successful stint at Duke University Law School returned to Whittier to practice law and marry a local schoolteacher, Thelma "Pat" Ryan. During World War II, Nixon served as a naval supply officer in the South Pacific. He entered politics in 1946, winning a seat in the House of Representatives from California. Taking full advantage of anti-Communist anxieties in the postwar years, Nixon used his membership on the House Un-American Activities Committee to build his political reputation. He later surmised that it was the "[Alger] Hiss case [that] brought me national fame." Ambitious and driven, Nixon proved his political mettle in 1950 in winning a close Senate race in California, in which he resorted to Joseph McCarthy-like attacks on his opponent. In the Senate, Nixon railed against the Truman administration over the loss of China to Communism, and in 1952 he was chosen as Eisenhower's running mate to give a conservative balance to the ticket.

Nixon was simultaneously crude and shrewd, complex and simple. He saw himself as the protector of basic American virtues of fidelity to family, God, and country and as the preserver of personal liberty, free enterprise, and law and order. He believed that he represented the great "silent majority" whose rights and interests were trampled on by arrogant elites and attacked by unruly demonstrators. On the other hand, he trusted no one, and was consumed with weeding out traitors and "enemies." He particularly distrusted the press, which he saw as a liberal phalanx determined to undermine his policies and question his personal integrity.

❧ *The Southern Strategy and the Building of Modern Republicanism*

Whatever else he may have been, Richard Nixon was a skilled politician. Buoyed by his victory in 1968 and encouraged by such conservative intellectuals as William F. Buckley and Kevin Phillips, Nixon believed that he had an opportunity to bring about a major realignment in American politics. In *The Emerging Republican Majority* (1969), Phillips identified a new conservative political alliance composed of suburbanites, blue-collar workers, business people, Roman Catholics, and philosophical conservatives that would supplant the Democratic New Deal coalition. Nixon was also aware of the growing discontent of evangelical Christians. He genuinely admired Billy Graham and frequently invited him to the White House (as had Lyndon Johnson). More than any other American president, Nixon consulted Graham about political strategy, especially about winning the support of evangelical Christians in the South. Republican leaders believed that they could attract these groups and form a centrist party to the right of Democratic liberalism without capitulating to the racist ideology of George Wallace on the far right. According to this strategy, Republicans would recast themselves as the party of responsible government and the defenders of law and order in the United States and throughout the world, in opposition to a Democratic party that had been captured by special interests, bureaucrats, and liberal ideologues.

Richard Nixon recognized, as had John F. Kennedy when he chose Lyndon Johnson as his running mate, that a successful presidential candidate needed a political base in the South. He also realized that the South was pervasively conservative and potentially a Republican stronghold. The key to controlling the South, he thought, was the formulation of a civil rights strategy that would be acceptable both in that region and to a majority of Americans elsewhere. The plan backed by Nixon called for rhetorical support for integration and a quiet acceptance of affirmative action, while opposing court-imposed school busing and also insisting that increased power for enforcing integration be

Billy Graham and Richard Nixon   Shown here at Graham's "Crusade for Christ" rally in Knoxville, Tennessee, in 1970, Nixon courted the popular evangelist and sometimes sought his political advice. Graham was a friend of other presidents as well, but his friendship with Nixon was particularly close.

given to states. Civil rights activists, however, saw the president's southern strategy as an effort to rescind the hard-won gains of the sixties.

The pace of desegregation slowed as Nixon's Justice Department and other federal agencies dealt more gently with recalcitrant districts, although both the courts and the federal bureaucracy still contained many liberals intent on pressing for affirmative action to achieve racial balance. In the summer of 1969 the administration announced that desegregation deadlines would be enforced in all southern school districts except those with "bona fide educational and administrative problems." Yet the administration demonstrated little sympathy for the busing of children to achieve racial balance. In March 1970, Nixon asked Congress to approve $1.5 billion in aid for school districts under court order to desegregate, but he drew an important distinction between *de facto* and *de jure* segregation; in the former, school segregation existed because of residential patterns resulting from choice; in the latter — which for Nixon, were the only legitimate targets for busing — segregation had resulted from discriminatory laws or practices. To the dismay of the proponents of busing, but with strong support from millions of middle- and working-class parents, the president promised that "transportation beyond normal geographical school zones for the purpose of achieving a racial balance will not be required."

In civil rights, however, the Supreme Court counterbalanced the executive, consolidating and even extending its earlier rulings. In 1969 Nixon instructed the Department of Health, Education, and Welfare to petition the Fifth District Court asking for a delay in the desegregation of twenty-three Mississippi school districts. For the first time in the modern civil rights era, the federal government intervened to slow the pace of integration. The NAACP filed suit, and the Supreme Court ruled in *Alexander v. Holmes County* that desegregation must proceed "at once." In 1971 the Court handed down a long-awaited busing decision in *Swann v. Charlotte-Mecklenburg Board of Education,* upholding the mandatory busing of some 13,300 children in the Charlotte, North Carolina, area to achieve integration. The ruling insisted that bus transportation was an "integral part of the school system" and as such a legitimate tool to achieve racial balance. Recalcitrant parents found little consolation in the Court's ruling that prohibited busing over distances sufficient to threaten the integrity of the education process or the health of the children, although this provision did open the way for the Justice Department to delay the expansion of busing.

✃ *The Supreme Court Moves to the Right*

Like most conservatives in the late 1960s, Nixon saw the Supreme Court as a major culprit in the nation's move to the left, and he fully intended to shift its balance back to the right. Consequently, when Chief Justice Earl Warren retired in 1969, Nixon appointed as his successor the conservative judge Warren Burger. Burger's tenure as chief justice, which lasted until 1986, was not marked by the same sort of activism as the Warren Court. But neither did he move the Court as sharply to the right as Nixon had hoped.

When Johnson protégé Abe Fortas resigned from the Supreme Court in 1969 amid charges of financial improprieties, Nixon instructed Attorney General John Mitchell to come up with a southern "strict constructionist" — a judge who would avoid Warren-style broad, expansive interpretations of the Constitution. On Mitchell's recommendation, Nixon first nominated Judge Clement F. Haynsworth of South Carolina, a less-than-distinguished jurist with a segregationist background. After Haynsworth's nomination was rejected by the Senate, Nixon's second choice, G. Harold Carswell, another un-

distinguished southerner, was also voted down by the Democratic majority in the Senate. Not until 1970 was Nixon's third nominee, Harry Blackmun, approved by the Senate to fill the vacancy. Blackmun proved to be an independent-minded jurist who moved to the left and retired in 1994 as a liberal icon.

In 1971 Nixon did succeed in placing two conservative voices on the Supreme Court following the death of Justice Hugo L. Black and the resignation of Justice John Marshall Harlan. The new appointees were Lewis F. Powell, a respected Virginia lawyer, and Assistant Attorney General William H. Rehnquist of Arizona, who would in 1986 be appointed chief justice by President Ronald Reagan. Powell ended his tenure as something of a centrist, but in the 1970s, he and Rehnquist formed the nucleus of a center-right majority that began to chip away at the Warren Court's rulings, especially in the area of criminal law.

✃ *The War on Crime and Radicalism*

In proposing strict constructionists for the Supreme Court, Nixon was attempting not only to implement his southern strategy but also to fulfill his campaign promise to restore "law and order" to a nation that felt threatened by the prominent protests of radicals and by the undeniable rise in crime. Like many Americans, Nixon believed that the Warren Court had contributed to the rise of crime by protecting criminals. Particularly galling to conservatives were the Court's rulings in *Gideon v. Wainwright* (1963), which held that all defendants in criminal cases, regardless of their ability to pay, were entitled to legal counsel, and in *Miranda v. Arizona* (1966), in which the justices, by a 5-4 margin, ruled that before questioning suspects police must inform them of their right to remain silent and to legal counsel, and that anything they said might be used against them.

Conservatives at the end of the sixties were as angered by the disruptions of political radicals as they were by the growing crime rate. President Nixon was determined to use the power of the federal government to quell those intent on disrupting American society. FBI undercover agents infiltrated Students for a Democratic Society and black radical groups and cooperated with local police in their confrontations with the Black Panthers. Soon after Nixon's election, his administration authorized a widespread use of wiretapping and other electronic surveillance devices in the war against organized crime, and it persuaded Congress to provide increased support for the Law Enforcement

Assistance Administration. The Organized Crime Act of 1970 limited immunities granted under the Fifth Amendment and permitted judges to lengthen the sentences of particularly dangerous criminals.

The president also used a variety of tactics to try to undermine the antiwar movement, including compiling a notorious "enemies list" of his political foes. Nixon was infuriated when Daniel Ellsberg, an analyst for the Department of Defense, turned over to the *New York Times* the Pentagon Papers, a secret documentary study on American involvement in Vietnam commissioned by Robert McNamara when he was secretary of defense. The papers, stolen and leaked by Ellsberg, gave the appearance to some that the Kennedy and Johnson administration officials had involved the United States in the war without clear objectives or a long-range strategy, and while doing so had repeatedly misled the American people. Although the papers included nothing about the Nixon years, they laid bare a pattern of foreign intrigue and government deception under Kennedy and Johnson, and Nixon feared that these revelations would undermine his efforts to bring the war to an honorable close. When government efforts to bar the publication of the papers were blocked by the Supreme Court, the White House launched a covert operation, known as "the plumbers," which embarked on an illegal search for information that would discredit Ellsberg.

"God Bless Ellsberg"   Daniel Ellsberg was the Defense Department official who leaked the Pentagon Papers to the press, and this graffito, spray-painted on a wall in November 1972, spoke for the antiwar activists critical of U.S. involvement in Vietnam. President Nixon feared the Papers would undermine his efforts to end the war.

❧ Opening the Debate on Welfare and the Family Assistance Program

Conservatives who had supported Richard Nixon in 1968 worried not only about forced integration, crime, and radicalism, but also about the mushrooming welfare state. The cornerstone of the federally supported welfare system was the Aid to Families with Dependent Children (AFDC) program, which dated back to the New Deal's original Social Security system, though it had grown enormously since the Depression. Conservatives zeroed in on what seemed to be the AFDC's subsidy, even incentive, to women who bore children out of wedlock. (Poor married couples with children did not qualify for aid.) At a more fundamental level, conser-

vatives believed that AFDC and other War on Poverty programs were undermining the American work ethic. And they argued that the expenditures demanded by the Great Society entitlement programs were unbalancing the national budget and harming the economy.

Nixon was a moderate conservative, hoping to do away with Great Society programs that did not work and to reform the welfare system without abandoning the poor. He was not a reactionary ideologue who wanted to jettison the safety net that protected the poor — he knew very well that such a policy would be political suicide. To head his planned reform of the welfare system, Nixon chose Daniel Patrick Moynihan, a brilliant Harvard professor who had been an assistant secretary of labor in both the Kennedy and Johnson administrations. A trained social scientist as well as an ambitious politician, Moynihan belonged to the tradition of progressive Catholic social thinkers who combined compassion for the poor with a determination to maintain the nuclear family. Moynihan proposed a striking and innovative solution — a guaranteed annual income. Under the Family Assistance Plan introduced into Congress in late 1969, the federal government would make direct cash payments to ensure each poor family an income of $1600 a year. Such a family unit would be eligible, in addition, for up to $820 a year in food stamps. Each head of a household would have to work in order for the family to receive such a subsidy. FAP would replace all federal welfare grants to the states, and the armies of welfare caseworkers would be swept away.

To the dismay of the Nixon administration, FAP satisfied neither liberals nor conservatives. On the right, the Chamber of Commerce denounced the plan as a first step toward socialism. On the left, the National Welfare Rights Organization condemned FAP as "anti-poor and anti-black" and demanded a guaranteed annual income of $5,500 a year, a proposal that would have affected half the families in America and cost $71 billion in 1970. A liberal-conservative coalition defeated the Family Assistance Plan in the Senate in 1970 and again in 1971. Welfare reform was stymied for another twenty-five years.

❧ The New Federalism

In his 1971 State of the Union address, Nixon asked Congress to join him in launching a "new American Revolution" that would reverse the inexorable growth of the federal government. The president proposed a system of "revenue sharing" whereby the federal government would gradually eliminate specific programs, refunding tax monies to states and local governments to use for community development as they saw fit. His "new federalism," Nixon promised, would eliminate intrusive federal bureaucracies. The program was enacted in 1972, providing for the distribution of $30.2 billion over a five-year period.

Within months, however, mayors and governors complained that the federal government was taking away with one hand what it was giving with the other. Soon it also became clear that during economic downturns towns and municipalities used block grant monies to pay for operating expenses rather than to fund social services. In response, Congress in 1973 passed the Comprehensive Employment and Training Act (CETA), setting aside block grant funds for the vocational training of the poor. Over the next ten years, 600,000 people made their way through the program.

❧ Seeking a Balance on the Environment

Nixon was ambivalent toward environmental issues. Initially, it appeared that his administration would continue the initiatives begun by his Democratic predecessors, but, pressured by business interests, Nixon began to retreat. The politics of environmentalism were not simple. Blue-collar workers often saw the movement as a threat to their jobs, and they scorned the environmentalist movement as a hippie aberration. Business leaders complained that the movement had spawned a bureaucratic nightmare, placing huge and unnecessary burdens on American manufacturers that made them uncompetitive in the world market. By the early 1970s "Nader's Raiders" and other consumer advocates (see Chapter 32) had gained increased support and credibility, but the president still resisted. In November 1970, Nixon fired Secretary of the Interior Walter J. Hickel, who had persuaded the Justice Department to prosecute Chevron Oil Company for polluting the Gulf of Mexico, and in 1971 Nixon overrode his own Department of Transportation and blocked regulations requiring the installation of seat belts in automobiles.

The Alaska Pipeline These caribou do not seem bothered as they graze on the tundra beneath the pipeline at Prudhoe Bay on Alaska's North Slope. But environmentalists bitterly opposed the pipeline, arguing that it would cause irreparable harm to the Arctic terrain and wildlife.

In the 1970s, environmentalists supported a wide variety of causes, including a failed attempt to block an 800-mile pipeline across Alaska's wilderness planned by a consortium of oil companies. They also fought other specific issues such as government support for the development of a commercial SST aircraft and building an airport near the Everglades, all projects supported by the administration. But environmentalism and consumer protection were issues whose time had come, and in 1970 the Democratic-controlled Congress passed the Occupational Safety and Health Act, which set new health standards in the workplace, and the National Air Quality Control Act, which called for a 90-percent reduction in pollution from automobile exhausts by 1975. President Nixon backed a number of pieces of important environmental legislation, including the National Environmental Policy Act of 1969, which required environmental impact statements for most public projects. Nixon also supported the total banning of DDT and established the Environmental Protection Agency to help enforce the growing body of environmental laws.

✣ Stagflation and the Decline of the American Economy

The nation continued a pattern of economic growth throughout the 1960s and 1970s, marred, however, by a serious recession in 1974 and 1975. Between 1962 and 1968, the country experienced a real growth rate of 5 percent, a pace not reached since the rapid industrialization of the Gilded Age. The growth rate for the 1960s had been 4.4 percent, surpassing that of the 1950s. The seventies were a bit more troubled, particularly because of the recession that occurred in the middle of the decade, but overall economic growth during the decade remained a strong 3.2 percent.

As the 1960s came to an end, the country suffered both mounting inflation and increasing unemployment — a combination that journalists called "stagflation." The inflation rate in 1967 had been a tolerable 3 percent, but by 1973 it reached 9 percent, and the next year 12 percent. The inflation rate remained in double digits for the rest of the decade. At the same time, unemployment, at a low of 3.3 percent when Nixon took office, climbed to 6 percent by 1973 and remained high throughout the decade. The stunning inflation of the 1970s had a variety of causes, including a catastrophic rise in oil prices that dislocated the economies of all industrial nations, and by the vast expenditures demanded by Medicare and

the war in Vietnam. Stagflation was also accompanied by other troubling developments, including a deepening pattern of deficit spending by the federal government and a growing trade imbalance.

Stagflation mystified many economists and economic journalists, largely because they were doctrinaire Keynesians. Stagnant growth and rampant inflation were not supposed to occur at the same time, according to Keynesian theory. Many experts overlooked or dismissed such underlying causes as the enormous amounts of federal money being pumped into an economy that was not generating sufficient gains in productivity and the skyrocketing costs of raw materials (particularly oil) and newly enacted federal regulations.

Nixon focused on domestic issues only intermittently during a first term that was often consumed with foreign problems. Increasingly, however, he was forced by economic realities to try to devise a plan for dealing with a set of economic problems that were unprecedented in kind. Not surprisingly, the president initially took a conservative approach to solving economic problems. He pledged never to impose wage and price controls, and, acting in concert with the Federal Reserve Board, tried to curb the inflationary spiral with sharp hikes in interest rates. In an effort to slow the growth of the deficit the administration reduced social spending, but outlays for the war in Vietnam and the space program more than offset the meager savings. Economic problems grew ever more severe. In 1971, with the economy slipping into the doldrums and gold flowing out of the country at an alarming rate, the president changed course. For the first time in peacetime American history, the president imposed a ninety-day freeze on wages and prices. Equally dramatically, Nixon broke with the Bretton Woods system of international monetary policy that had been a cornerstone of the capitalist world's economic structure since 1945. To lower its trade deficit, the United States severed the link between the dollar and gold, allowing American currency to float freely against other currencies in international markets. (Since the Bretton Woods agreements of 1945, the value of the dollar and other major trading currencies had been fixed in terms of gold, that is, its value had been determined by international agreement rather than the open market.) Finally, the administration slapped an immediate 10-percent surtax on imports. These steps were largely symbolic. Like most modern Republicans, Nixon believed fervently in the benefits of international trade. In December 1971, at an international economic meeting in Washington, the United States agreed to reduce the exchange rate on the dollar by about 12 percent and to abolish the surtax in return for a commitment by the other major trading nations to increase the value of their currencies. The trade deficit still increased, but at a slower pace.

Hoping to break the grip of stagflation, in 1971 Nixon announced himself a convert to Keynesianism, which Republicans had hitherto attacked as a liberal scheme to justify heavy social spending and unbalanced budgets. Over the protest of economic conservatives, the White House submitted to Congress a "full employment" budget for 1972, one that envisioned an $11.6 billion deficit. With federal funds stimulating the private sector, the Dow Jones index topped 1,000 for the first time, and many hoped that the economic crisis had been resolved. But the upswing was temporary. Inflationary pressures remained and interest rates began to rise again in 1974, hitting 11 percent, and unemployment reached 8.5 percent the following year. Americans began to sense, correctly, that the nation's economic woes were due to long-term, systemic problems beyond the ability of any one presidential administration, government agency, or economic theory to remedy. Ironically, just as Nixon was proclaiming that "we are all Keynesians now," a growing body of conservative economists were beginning to question the ability of Keynesian theory to "fine-tune" the economy.

Equal Rights?

Not surprisingly, the Nixon administration distanced itself from the feminist movement that emerged in the late 1960s and early 1970s. The president opposed ratification of the Equal Rights Amendment and backed the growing "right to life" movement that opposed abortion. He would do everything in his power, he said, to protect "the sanctity of human life — including the life of the yet unborn." Perhaps most significant, Nixon vetoed a bill passed by the Democratic majority in Congress that would have established a national system of day-care centers. In his veto message Nixon declared that he opposed legislation that would pledge "the vast moral authority of the national government to communal approaches to child rearing, over against the family centered approach."

NIXON, KISSINGER, AND REALPOLITIK

Richard Nixon entered the White House determined to create a new international order that would simul-taneously contain Communism and restore America's freedom of action. Specifically, Nixon and his national security adviser, Henry Kissinger, wanted to secure "peace with honor in Vietnam" by weakening the Viet Cong and North Vietnamese and strengthening South Vietnam. Freed from the Vietnam quagmire, with its prestige restored and its military undistracted, the United States would be able to reassume the role of arbiter of world affairs. The new Republican administration accepted the necessity of opposing Communism on every front, but it sought global containment through diplomacy rather than force of arms. While maintaining an intimidating nuclear and conventional force, the United States would coerce or cajole regional rivals into signing peace agreements rather than fighting prolonged and bloody wars. Nixon's foreign policy was often insensitive to the social and economic injustices that fed nationalist or leftist movements in many developing nations, and American neglect of those concerns continued to fuel the kinds of revolutions that Washington hoped to contain.

Nixon and Kissinger realized that the war in Vietnam was draining American resources and willpower, thus reducing its ability to contain Communism and defend its vital interests elsewhere. They recognized the threat posed to Western democracies and their client states by the Soviet Union and Communist China, but they believed that if ideological rhetoric could be muted and western military superiority maintained, a working relationship with the two Communist great powers could be established. To this end, Nixon engineered diplomatic openings to both Moscow and Beijing. This improvement of relations, or détente, did not end the Cold War, but it did reduce the chance of nuclear confrontation and buy time for a world desperately hoping to avoid Armageddon.

Nixon and Kissinger

As his national security adviser, Nixon chose a brilliant Harvard professor, Henry Kissinger. A German-born Jew, Kissinger and his family had escaped Nazi persecution by immigrating to America in 1938. After serving in army counterintelligence during the war, he earned a Ph.D. at Harvard, and from 1958 to 1971 he was director of the Harvard Defense Studies Program through which many of the world's future political leaders passed. The author of a number of books on European diplomacy, Kissinger was fascinated by the Realpolitik policies of such wily nineteenth-century diplomats as

Metternich and Bismarck. Though in many ways Nixon and Kissinger were different, there were also similarities between the two men. Both were egotistical loners, intensely ambitious, distrustful of bureaucracies, and fond of intrigue. Each found the other useful. Kissinger perceived that through Nixon he would be able to create and influence a new world order led by the United States. For Nixon, his national security adviser provided both support and a philosophical rationale for his planned openings to Russia and China. Furthermore, Nixon hoped that Kissinger could find a way to end the war in Vietnam.

❧ *"Peace with Honor" in Vietnam*

Prior to taking office, Nixon had stoutly defended America's commitment to South Vietnam. Kissinger thought that earlier policymakers had exaggerated Vietnam's importance to American interests, but once committed, the United States could not back down. By the time he was inaugurated, Nixon realized that the war in Vietnam had to be ended, but he also believed that the United States had to conclude a "peace with honor."

Nixon and Kissinger's strategy was to couple great power diplomacy with force in an effort to win an "honorable" peace at the negotiating table in Paris, that is, one that left a non-Communist regime in place in South Vietnam. Encouraged by the military, the president hoped that renewed threats of retribution would break the North Vietnamese will. In March the president sent a personal message to Ho Chi Minh expressing his firm desire for peace and proposing as a first step the mutual withdrawal of American and North Vietnamese troops from South Vietnam and restoration of the demilitarized zone as a temporary political boundary. At the same time he authorized the bombing of enemy supply routes and staging areas in neutral Cambodia, something Lyndon Johnson had avoided. In the ensuing operation, code-named Menu, 3,360 B-52 raids were flown over Cambodia, on which American planes dropped more than 100,000 tons of bombs, killing an untold number of civilians and accelerating the destabilization of Cambodia.

In May Nixon once again offered to withdraw American forces from Vietnam according to a specified timetable if Hanoi would withdraw its troops from South Vietnam, Cambodia, and Laos. When the North Vietnamese delegation dismissed the proposal, Nixon leaked a report that he was contemplating massive bombing attacks on North Vietnam's major cities, a blockade of the country's principal ports, and the use of tactical nuclear weapons if China intervened directly. Ho refused to be bluffed, but the North Vietnamese did agree to begin secret peace talks outside the

Nixon and Kissinger Just before returning to peace talks with North Vietnam's representatives in December 1972, Henry Kissinger strolls and strategizes with Nixon at the president's Key Biscayne, Florida, vacation home.

deadlocked Paris framework, and on August 4, in the first of a long series of contacts, Kissinger met privately with North Vietnamese diplomat Xuan Thuy.

Congress was meanwhile taking its own steps to prevent future Vietnams by trimming presidential power to involve the United States in foreign wars. In June 1969, with strong support from both liberals and conservatives, the Senate approved a resolution requiring the president to secure congressional approval before entering into any national commitment demanding the "use of the armed forces on foreign territory or a promise to assist a foreign country, government or people by the use of the armed forces or financial resources of the United States, either immediately or upon the happening of certain events." Though Vietnam was specifically excluded from the provisions of the resolution, the *Washington Post* declared that "throughout the debate, it was apparent it [the resolution] was the Senate's answer to the U.S. involvement in Vietnam."

❧ Arms Control Stalemate

In 1966 United States intelligence discovered that the Soviet Union was developing a rudimentary anti-ballistic missile (ABM) system designed to ring Moscow and other cities with ground-to-air defenses that could destroy incoming enemy missiles and bombers. If one but not both superpowers possessed such a system, a nuclear "first strike" without danger of retaliation became a distinct possibility. An ABM race appeared to loom on the horizon, dangerously escalating the arms race and raising the specter of huge boosts in military budgets. In 1968, Lyndon Johnson persuaded a reluctant Congress to appropriate $1.195 billion for the construction of an American ABM system, and the Nixon administration wanted the system expanded.

Nixon and Kissinger had little confidence in arms control, believing that the United States should deal with the Soviet Union "from a position of superiority." They were unenthusiastic about the Nuclear Non-Proliferation Treaty and refused to push France and West Germany to ratify it. At a time when Soviet and American diplomats negotiated furiously in Geneva on an arms limitation treaty, the Nixon administration went to Congress in February 1970 and asked for $1.5 billion to fund the second phase of an ABM system. Despite the opposition from Senator J. William Fulbright and others committed to arms control, Congress approved the Nixon request.

❧ Mounting Opposition to the War in Vietnam

Frustration over the stalled peace negotiations in Paris inevitably revived the antiwar movement, which had been disorganized and largely dormant since the disastrous Democratic convention in Chicago. In 1969, demonstrations once again erupted. In June, the Vietnam Moratorium Committee called for a nationwide work stoppage to demonstrate opposition to the war, and in November 45,000 individuals, each carrying a lighted candle and a placard inscribed with the name of a dead American serviceman, marched solemnly to Arlington National Cemetery. Following that demonstration, around a half-million people gathered on Saturday morning, crowding onto the Mall between the Capitol and the Washington Monument, in one of the largest mass protests in American history. For five hours they listened to an array of speakers that included Coretta Scott King and Senators George McGovern and Eugene McCarthy, disproving the Nixon administration's prediction that the Moratorium march would be dominated by radicals and hippies and would turn violent. By 1969, the leadership of the antiwar movement had passed into the hands of activists working within the system rather than protesters.

Privately, Nixon railed against the antiwar students, but he was more even more critical of the "new isolationists" — people like Senators Fulbright, McGovern, and McCarthy — who, he thought, would have the United States "turn its back on the world." He let it be known that during the Moratorium he had barricaded himself in the White House and watched football on TV. But while Nixon rhetorically chastised opponents of the war, he bent his policy to appease them. In June he announced the withdrawal of 25,000 troops from Vietnam, the first step in his "Vietnamization" plan designed to gradually turn the fighting over to the army of South Vietnam. In a televised address to the nation in November, the president reported that the South Vietnamese army was growing stronger every day and that the beleaguered country would soon be able to defend itself. He appealed to the "great silent majority" in the country to stay the course and help him achieve peace with honor.

Nixon's strategy of defusing the antiwar movement by promoting Vietnamization and gaining support from conservatives by promising victory for South Vietnam seemed to work. Polls continued to show solid support for the administration, and the antiwar movement grew quiet again. In a series of hard-hitting speeches before Republican audiences, Vice President Agnew charged that radicals and antiwar activists had unleashed "a spirit of national masochism." Appealing to the traditional mainstream of Americans who were concerned about the decline in national pride and the contentious spirit unleashed by dissenters, Agnew blamed the nation's woes on liberal academics, "an effete corps of impudent snobs," and news executives, "a small and unelected elite." His charges reinforced the deep-seated beliefs of many conservative working-class Americans.

❧ *Cambodia and Kent State*

By the spring of 1970, however, it was clear that Vietnamization was not a magic formula for "peace with honor." In April 1970, the president announced that he would withdraw another 150,000 troops during the next year. Still, North Vietnam showed no willingness to negotiate a settlement that would leave the Saigon government intact. The North Vietnamese government perceived that it had only to refuse concessions, and eventually the Americans would leave. Then the pitifully weak South Vietnamese regime could be summarily dispatched.

The conviction grew within the administration that further military action was needed to ensure the survival of South Vietnam. For years, the American military had urged ground incursions into Cambodia to destroy North Vietnamese and Viet Cong sanctuaries there that had not been destroyed by bombing. In March 1970, the neutralist government of Prince Norodom Sihanouk was overthrown by Cambodia's intensely anti-Communist military commanders, opening the way for U.S. military action. On April 29, South Vietnamese units with American air support attacked an enemy sanctuary on the Parrot's Beak, a strip of Cambodian territory thirty-three miles from Saigon, and a few days later American forces assaulted a North Vietnamese base area in Cambodia. In a televised speech, the president justified the invasion as a response to North Vietnamese "aggression" and limited the invasion to sixty days. The Cambodian campaign did relieve pressure on the South Vietnamese army and government, thereby buying some time for Vietnamization. But it also shattered

Bombing Cambodia   American airborne attacks on villages such as this in hitherto-neutral Cambodia, where Viet Cong and North Vietnamese forces maintained bases, helped cause the massive destabilization of that fragile country and set in motion the rise of the savage Khmer Rouge revolutionary movement.

Cambodian neutrality, paving the way for a bloody civil war in that country and its eventual takeover by a savage Communist revolutionary movement.

At home, the Cambodian invasion triggered a new wave of antiwar protests. In Cambridge, Massachusetts, students occupied Harvard buildings to protest the university's refusal to oppose the war. California governor Ronald Reagan mobilized a battalion of police to confront more than five thousand students and community residents in Berkeley who had seized a vacant lot and turned it into a "people's park." During the first week of May, Kent State students protested the Cambodian invasion by staging demonstrations and perpetrating some acts of vandalism, including an attempted firebombing of the ROTC building. Ohio governor James Rhodes dispatched three thousand National Guardsmen to the campus, setting the stage for a tragic confrontation on May 4. Around two hundred protesters heckled and threw rocks at the soldiers, but the crowd swelled to around 1,500 as other students stood by watching the spectacle. The National Guardsmen first advanced on the students to disperse them and then one detachment opened fire, leaving four students dead and nine wounded. Within days a million-and-a-half students were participating in a boycott of classes, shutting down about a fifth of the nation's campuses for periods ranging from one day to the rest of the school year. While subsequent investigations by the FBI and a presidential commission found the Kent State shootings to be unjustified, polls indicated that a majority of the public blamed the students for the Kent State shootings.

The situation was equally tense on the campus of all-black Jackson State University in Jackson, Mississippi, where relations between students and the local white police had been troubled for some time and sporadic clashes had occurred near the campus. Festering racial resentment among Jackson State students was heightened by Nixon's Cambodian incursion and by the Kent State shooting. On the evening of May 14 police responding to reports of a burning dump truck near the campus were confronted by an angry gathering of students in front of a women's dormitory. Responding to what they believed was sniper fire from inside the dormitory, the police opened fire, killing two students and wounding ten others.

In the wake of the Cambodian demonstrations, Nixon hardened his resolve to make war on those "enemies" whom he judged to be intent on undermining the will of the people. In the spring of 1970 the president authorized an inexperienced young White House aide named Tom Huston to assemble a team of "counter subversives" to ferret out and neutralize his opponents. Under the Huston Plan, intelligence agencies were directed to install wiretaps, open mail, and even break-and-enter to gather information that could be used to thwart opponents of the administration. A siege mentality settled over the White House.

❋ **IN THEIR OWN WORDS**

Investigating My Lai, 1969

One year after the My Lai massacre, details of the incident finally came to light, thanks in large part to a serviceman named Ron Ridenhour, who wrote a letter to various U.S. government leaders describing what had happened.

One village area was particularly troublesome and seemed to be infested with booby traps and enemy soldiers. It was located about six miles northeast of Quang Nhai city at approximate coordinates B.S. 728795. It was a notorious area and the men of Task Force Barker had a special name for it: they called it "Pinkville." One morning in the latter part of March, Task Force Barker moved out from its firebase headed for "Pinkville." Its mission: destroy the trouble spot and all of its inhabitants.

When "Butch" told me this I didn't quite believe that what he was telling me was true, but he assured me that it was and went on to describe what had happened. The other two companies that made up the task force cordoned off the village so that "Charlie" Company could move through to destroy the structures and kill the inhabitants. Any villagers who ran from Charlie Company were stopped by the encircling companies. I asked "Butch" several times if all the people were killed. He said that he thought they were men, women and children.... It was so bad, Gruver said, that one of the men in his squad shot himself in the foot in order to be medivaced out of the area so that he would not have to participate in the slaughter. Although he had not seen it, Gruver had been told by people he considered trustworthy that one of the company's officers, 2nd Lieutenant Kally (this spelling may be incorrect) had rounded up several groups of villagers (each group consisting of a minimum of 20 persons of both sexes and all ages). According to the story, Kally then machine-gunned each group. Gruver estimated that the population of the village had been 300 to 400 people and that very few, if any, escaped.

Congressional Revolt and the Deterioration of Public Support

In the spring of 1971 a new series of incidents undermined public support for the war. On March 29, after a sensational and highly publicized court martial, Lt. William Calley was convicted by a military tribunal of killing "at least twenty-two" civilians in the Vietnamese village of My Lai. In fact, in March 1968, Calley and other members of his company had killed an estimated 200 villagers whom they suspected of having harbored a Viet Cong cadre. By mid-1971, public disenchantment with the war reached an all-time high, with more than 70 percent of Americans telling pollsters that it had been a mistake to become militarily involved in Southeast Asia. Among the more convincing of the antiwar critics was a recently discharged and highly decorated navy veteran, John Kerry. In televised testimony before the Senate Foreign Relations Committee in April 1971, the charismatic and politically ambitious young Kerry blasted the war as immoral. White House counsel Charles Colson, in a secret memo, revealed that he had targeted Kerry, hoping to "destroy the young demagogue before he becomes another Ralph Nader." But Kerry remained visible as a veteran against the war.

Five days after Nixon announced the Cambodian incursion, several members of Congress accused him of usurping the legislature's war-making power and denounced the "constitutionally unauthorized, Presidential war in Indochina." In the first week in July, after six weeks of tumultuous debate, the United States Senate voted to cut off funds for U.S. military operations in Cambodia — the first time the upper house had passed a clear-cut anti–Vietnam War resolution. By late June, polls indicated that nearly 50 percent of Americans advocated getting out of Vietnam immediately. In response, Nixon accelerated American troop withdrawals. By the end of 1971, only 175,000 U.S. military personnel remained in Vietnam, of whom 75,000 were combat troops. At the same time, Nixon authorized a major ground operation against Communist sanctuaries in Laos. The administration insisted that it was trying to buy time for Vietnamization by disrupting enemy supply lines.

To the Brink of Peace

Richard Nixon never let his eye stray very far from the next election. With the implementation of the Twenty-sixth Amendment to the Constitution in 1971 lowering the voting age to eighteen, the president believed that he needed peace in Vietnam to ensure reelection. The withdrawal of troops enabled him to end the draft, dramatically quieting campus protests. He directed Kissinger to make a new secret proposal to the North Vietnamese: the United States would withdraw from the South within seven months after the signing of an agreement if, in return, Hanoi would return all American POWs and refrain from major military operations in the South. The new plan foundered, however, when the South Vietnamese objected, and Nixon decided that it would be politically more damaging to abandon his ally than to sign a peace accord without Saigon's approval.

Openings to Beijing and Moscow

Nixon hoped that foreign policy achievements in other areas might compensate for the failure to reach a peace accord with North Vietnam. In July 1971, he stunned the world by announcing that he intended to accept an invitation to visit China. It was a bold and resourceful move that began the reentry of the most isolated of the world's great powers into international politics. Only an American politician with the untarnished anti-Communist credentials of Richard Nixon could have risked such a daring move.

In February 1972, Nixon, his wife, Henry Kissinger, and a huge entourage of officials and reporters toured China amid lavish press coverage. The president met both Mao Zedong and Premier Chou En-lai. In the short run, the visit produced only a series of innocuous communiqués, but in the long run it proved to be the first step in a dramatic reversal of America's China policy. Nixon declared that the "ultimate relationship between Taiwan and the Mainland is not a matter for the United States to decide," and in August the State Department announced that it supported admission of the People's Republic of China to the United Nations.

The opening to China was part of Nixon and Kissinger's larger effort to manipulate the international balance of power. Beijing cooperated because China needed trade with the West and craved the respectability that admission to the United Nations would bring. For its part, the Nixon administration hoped that normalizing relations with China would isolate North Vietnam and hasten a peace agreement that would end the war. But that scheme necessitated a change in the Cold War relationship with the Soviet Union as well as with China.

Kissinger believed that both the Soviet Union and China could be enmeshed in a network of economic ties that would make war with the United States out of the question. Shortly after Nixon announced his trip to Beijing, the Kremlin invited him to attend a summit in Moscow, and the meeting took place in May 1972, barely three months after his Beijing triumph. Out of Nixon's far-ranging talks with Soviet leaders emerged the Strategic Arms Limitation Treaty ("SALT I"), which included two basic agreements. The first, an official treaty, limited each side to 200 anti-ballistic missiles; the second, a five-year executive agreement, limited land-based and submarine-launched missiles.

NIXON'S DISASTROUS SECOND TERM

Although Richard Nixon had not been able to bring the Vietnam War to a conclusion by the end of his first term, he had neutralized the war's harshest critics and scored stunning diplomatic successes in China and the Soviet Union. At the same time, Nixon had been modestly successful in forging a new moderate Republican domestic policy. In all of this, Nixon had quite consciously striven to build a centrist political coalition composed of the "silent majority" disgusted by years of liberal policies, protest, and radicalism.

Measured by public support, Nixon had clearly succeeded in most of his objectives during his first term. In 1972, he would win a stunning electoral victory when the Democrats nominated a candidate from the left wing of their party. Yet Richard Nixon seemed bent on becoming a tragic figure. Deeply embittered against the accumulated enemies of a lifetime, he responded to success with arrogance and contempt for the law and ultimately plunged his presidency into a vortex of crimes and cover-ups from which there was no escape.

❧ The Election of 1972

With the Vietnam peace negotiations on hold, Nixon turned his attention to the 1972 election. The early leading contender for the Democratic nomination was Senator Edward M. Kennedy of Massachusetts. "Ted" Kennedy was fourth in the line of succession among the Kennedy males, and many political commentators judged him to be a man of less substance than his older brothers. But the violent deaths of his siblings and his relentless championing of organized labor and the poor had made him a force to be reckoned with in the Dem-

McGovern For President, 1972   George McGovern, a much-decorated World War II bomber pilot, openly embraced the peace movement when he ran for president against Nixon. He went down to a crushing defeat.

ocratic Party. Kennedy's political career changed permanently, however, when late on the evening of July 19, 1969 — the same night on which the world's attention was transfixed by live telecasts of the Apollo spacecraft's landing on the moon — his car ran off a bridge while returning from a cookout on Chappaquiddick Island, off Martha's Vineyard. A young woman campaign worker who was the only passenger in the car drowned despite what Kennedy later said were his repeated efforts to save her. The Senator left the scene of the accident, hid in the woods, filed no police report for many hours, and according to some accounts considered concocting an alibi for himself in the interim. Kennedy subsequently made an emotional television speech in which he explained his confused actions after the tragedy, but the incident effectively ended his chance to be president.

With Kennedy out of the picture, the front-runner for the Democratic nomination became Senator Edmund

Muskie of Maine — an opponent of the war in Vietnam, a dedicated environmentalist, and a man respected for his centrist views and temperate speech. But during the New Hampshire primary, Muskie broke down with tears of rage and frustration when faced with personal charges unjustly leveled against him by a conservative paper in the state. The incident damaged his image and scuttled his candidacy. With Muskie gone, the Democratic primaries pitted a strongly antiwar and leftist George McGovern against a charging George Wallace on the right. While campaigning in Maryland, Wallace was shot by a deranged young man, leaving him paralyzed from the waist down, and his withdrawal left McGovern alone in the race. He easily won the nomination at the Democratic convention and selected Senator Thomas F. Eagleton, a liberal Senator from Missouri, as his running mate.

In nominating McGovern in 1972 the Democratic Party moved as far toward its left as the Republicans had gone to their right with Goldwater's nomination in 1964. An idealist who downplayed his own heroism as a World War II bomber pilot, McGovern believed that he could realize his full policy agenda without compromising. And that agenda was sweeping: he favored legalizing abortion and marijuana, endorsed a tax that would redistribute wealth by granting every American $1,000 annually, and (to the horror of the military and defense workers) proposed a $30 billion cut in the Pentagon budget. Finally, McGovern called not only for an immediate withdrawal from Vietnam but also for a sweeping amnesty for draft resisters and deserters. To make matters worse, Eagleton withdrew as the vice presidential nominee after it became known that he had once been hospitalized and given shock treatment for "nervous exhaustion and fatigue." To replace him, McGovern (after failing to recruit a more prominent Democrat to run with him) selected Sargent Shriver, the former Peace Corps director, whose chief claim to fame was that he was the Kennedys' brother-in-law.

Nixon, backed by a well-heeled Committee for the Reelection of the President (inauspiciously called CREEP), was delighted with McGovern's nomination, seeing him as the most beatable of potential opponents. Actually, the elimination of Wallace as a third-party candidate had removed the only real challenge to Nixon's reelection. The Democrats sensed an opening when the news broke that on June 17, 1972, five men had been caught burglarizing the headquarters of the Democratic National Committee in the Watergate complex in Washington. Among the intruders were two former White House aides and a member of CREEP. The White House dismissed this "third-rate burglary attempt" and the American people attached little significance to it during the campaign.

Nixon won reelection by a stunning margin. He received 47.1 million popular votes (60.7 percent) and 520 electoral votes, only three votes short of the record number cast for Franklin D. Roosevelt in 1936. With 29.1 million votes (37.5 percent), the inept Democratic candidate won a majority only in Massachusetts and the District of Columbia. Nixon entered his second term with a striking mandate that fed a sense of invincibility in the White House. Such hubris proved to be the proverbial pride before the fall.

❧ Exiting the Quagmire

With the secret talks in Paris still deadlocked, Kissinger advised breaking off negotiations and launching a massive bombing campaign against the North. The purpose would not be a military victory, but rather to convince Nguyen Van Thieu, South Vietnam's president, that the United States had "gone the extra mile" in his behalf. The "Christmas bombing" of the North caused extensive damages and significant losses of American aircraft. Shortly after the raids ended, negotiators in Paris concluded an agreement calling for an American withdrawal but leaving North Vietnamese troops in the South and recognizing the Provisional Revolutionary Government, the political apparatus established by the National Liberation Front. In return, North Vietnam guaranteed the return of all American prisoners of war. President Thieu of South Vietnam protested, but to no avail. After Nixon threatened to cut off all aid, the South Vietnamese government acquiesced, and on January 27, 1973, a peace pact was signed in Paris. By the end of March all American combat troops had left Vietnam.

Nixon had delivered on his promise to end American involvement in the war, but his promised "peace with honor" had come at a high price. During the final four years of the war, American troops had suffered an additional 20,553 battle deaths, bringing the total to more than 58,000. The fighting from 1969 through 1973 cost the lives of more than 100,000 South Vietnamese troops and of 500,000 Communist fighters. The conflict had fueled an alarming inflationary trend in the United States and shaken the nation's confidence to its core. America had taken up the burden of world leadership in the wake of World War II believing that it was fighting to save freedom, democracy, and indigenous cul-

"It's All Over" American soldiers relax with their baggage at Camp Alpha in Vietnam on March 28, 1973, as they await departure back to the U.S. The last American serviceman left South Vietnam the next day, ending an involvement that lasted twelve years.

tures from the scourge of totalitarian Communism, but many Americans came to feel that none of those causes was at stake in Vietnam.

Hoping to prevent future Vietnams, in the fall of 1973 a rebellious Congress cut into the war-making powers of the president by passing, over a presidential veto, the War Powers Act. This law provided that the president must inform Congress within forty-eight hours of the deployment of American military forces abroad and withdraw them within sixty days unless explicitly authorized by Congress to continue the operation. Many legal authorities believe the War Powers Act is unconstitutional, but it has never been tested in the federal courts. Shortly thereafter, Congress attached an amendment to the Military Procurement Authorization Act banning the funding of any U.S. military action in any part of Southeast Asia.

✑ *The Yom Kippur War*

In the midst of the Vietnam War, the Nixon administration was forced to deal with critical foreign policy issues in the Middle East. Following the death of Egypt's charismatic president Nasser in 1970, his little known successor, Anwar Sadat, became increasingly frustrated by his inability to lessen tension in the region. With Egypt's lead-

ership of the Arab world threatened by the militant Syrian government of Hafez al-Assad, and with both the United States and United Nations unable to wring concessions from Israel, in 1973 Sadat decided on war. On October 6, while Israelis were observing the holiest day of the Jewish calendar, Yom Kippur, Egyptian troops attacked across the Sinai Peninsula, driving the surprised Israeli army before them. At the same time, Syrian forces advanced up the Golan Heights.

For the moment, Israel's situation seemed desperate. Israeli prime minister Golda Meir requested a massive emergency American airlift of planes, tanks, and ammunition. Then, assured of this American support, the Israelis launched a devastating offensive. Israeli troops drove into Syria, and a tank force encircled an entire Egyptian army and crossed and seized the Suez Canal. By October 17 Israel appeared poised for another sweeping triumph.

On that same day, the Persian Gulf members of the oil producers' cartel — the Organization of Oil Exporting Countries (OPEC) formed in 1960 — voted to raise the price for their petroleum by 400 percent. Arab delegates voted to suspend all oil shipments to the West until the United Nations carried out UN Resolution 242, which demanded the withdrawal of Israel from all Arab occupied lands. In response to the American arms airlift and to Nixon's request that Congress appropriate $2.2 billion to pay for more jets for Israel, Saudi Arabia embargoed oil exports to the United States. In the final weeks of 1973, gasoline prices skyrocketed all over the Western world and in Japan.

The United States by this time depended on the Middle East for 12 percent of its petroleum. Thus the Arab oil boycott, which lasted from October 1973 through March 1974, created grave diplomatic, political, and economic problems for the country. The situation was even more difficult for Western Europe and Japan, which imported around 80 percent of its oil from the Arab states. In the United States, the price of gasoline soared, and Americans waited in long lines at filling stations to get gasoline. America's allies clamored for a settlement of the Middle East crisis. Only after months of "shuttle diplomacy" by Kissinger, who had become secretary of state in 1974, did Israel allow the reopening of the Suez Canal and begin withdrawing from the territories its troops had occupied. In return for these concessions, OPEC ended its embargo, and the energy crisis temporarily eased.

❧ *Watergate*

Amid these high-level foreign policy negotiations and the domestic crisis caused by the oil embargo, the Nixon White House also found itself increasingly preoccupied with the unfolding of the saga of Watergate. During the 1972 campaign McGovern had complained repeatedly about Republican "dirty tricks" — using fake letters to identify Democratic candidates with unpopular or unsavory causes, planting hostile questioners or hecklers at Democratic rallies, and, especially, the attempted Watergate break-in. His complaints found few sympathetic ears at the time.

Nixon later claimed that he had no prior knowledge of the Watergate break-in. He may not have had prior knowledge, but through his approval of the Huston Plan and the "plumbers" unit, he certainly authorized it. The scandal was also the product of the overzealousness of the Committee for the Reelection of the President (CREEP). Enriched with a lucrative campaign chest, CREEP was determined to win a huge victory in 1972 at any cost. The membership of CREEP reached into the top echelons of Nixon's advisers, including his chief of staff, H. R. Haldeman, and Attorney-General John Mitchell. Haldeman's former assistant, Jeb Stuart Magruder, the deputy director of CREEP, along with White House counsel John Dean, recruited G. Gordon Liddy and former CIA agent E. Howard Hunt to head the "plumbers" unit to carry out covert, illegal operations. In March 1972, Mitchell approved a plan for wiretapping the Democratic National Committee and gave Liddy $10,000 to do it.

The third week in June, Nixon learned the details of the break-in from Haldeman and realized how deeply Mitchell and other White House staffers were implicated. The president decided to hunker down and contain the damage using the full force of his official powers. A massive cover-up began. That week Nixon instructed Haldeman to order Richard Helms, the head of the CIA, and General Vernon Walters, the president's military aide, to tell the FBI to back off its probe of the Watergate burglary because pursuing it would compromise national security. The president thus embarked on a conspiracy to obstruct justice.

❧ *The Unraveling of the Presidency*

As the crisis deepened in 1972, White House and CREEP spokesmen downplayed the Watergate incident as a petty offense and denied any connection between themselves and the burglars. In his *Memoirs,* Nixon acknowledged that his reaction to Watergate was based on a political "cynicism born of experience," confessing that he "could not muster much moral outrage over a political bugging." Neither did the public pay much attention to the charges.

But gradually the story unraveled like a mystery novel, exposed by the sensational investigative stories of *Washington Post* reporters Carl Bernstein and Bob Woodward, who traced the flow of CREEP's campaign funds through banks in Miami and Mexico to members of the "plumbers" unit. They claimed that top officials in the administration were involved in organizing the break-in. On January 8, 1973, the trial of the Watergate burglars opened before federal judge John J. "Maximum John" Sirica, known for his toughness and long sentences; that same week the Senate named a special committee to investigate Watergate. The committee chairman, North Carolina Democrat Sam Ervin, a folksy and independent defender of states' rights, proved a relentless and engaging investigator. During the televised Senate Watergate Committee hearings the cover-up began to unravel. On April 20, White House counsel John Dean announced that he would not be a "scapegoat in

---

❋ IN THEIR OWN WORDS

A Senator Reflects on Watergate, 1974
Senator Sam Ervin (D-N.C.) was chairman of the committee appointed to investigate the Watergate scandal. He became a national figure and a hero to many Americans.

. . . I think that the Watergate tragedy is the greatest tragedy this country has ever suffered. I used to think that the Civil War was our country's greatest tragedy, but I do remember that there were some redeeming

features in the Civil War in that there was some spirit of sacrifice and heroism displayed on both sides. I see no redeeming features in Watergate.

Web of Lies Satirist Robert Pryor depicts the now-resigned Richard Nixon as entangled in a web of lies and audiotapes in this 1975 image.

the Watergate case." In his testimony before the committee Dean implicated the president's closest advisers, H. R. Haldeman and John Erlichman, in the Watergate burglary and the president himself in the cover-up.

Congress pressed the investigation. Before confirming the appointment of Elliot Richardson as Nixon's new attorney general, the Senate Judiciary Committee secured a promise that he would appoint an independent special prosecutor to investigate the Watergate affair. Richardson, a Massachusetts patrician and a political moderate, selected for this job his old law school professor Archibald Cox (a Democrat), and promised that he would neither remove nor interfere with him. In the meantime, hearings continued in the Senate, highlighted by Dean's testimony and an off-handed revelation from a White House staffer about a secret taping system in the White House. Dean confirmed that Nixon had tape recordings of meetings where these issues were discussed.

A yearlong battle ensued as Congress endeavored to secure copies of conversations between the president and his aides. In October the White House offered to submit summaries of the conversations but not the tapes themselves, an offer that special prosecutor Cox refused to accept. Nixon ordered Attorney General Richardson to fire Cox. He refused and resigned, as did his deputy William Ruckelshaus. Solicitor General Robert Bork agreed to step in as acting attorney general and fire Cox. But this "Saturday Night Massacre" in the Justice Department touched off a huge national protest. Nixon responded by submitting some of the tapes and by reopening the special prosecutor's office under Houston attorney Leon Jaworski.

The momentum toward impeachment moved inexorably forward, and in May 1974 the House Judiciary Committee opened impeachment hearings. In a futile last effort to survive Nixon released 1300 pages of transcripts of conversations about Watergate. Even though the transcriptions were carefully edited ("expletive deleted" recurred endlessly in the text), the crudity and cynicism of the conversations shocked the public. In the meantime Leon Jaworski had continued to press for the release of all White House tapes, and, on July 24, 1974, the Supreme Court ruled unanimously that the president must surrender them. Under extreme pressure, Nixon finally supplied transcripts of all of the tapes, although some of them contained important and lengthy gaps, allegedly erased accidentally by the president's secretary. A March 21, 1973, conversation between Nixon and presidential counsel Dean included a devastating exchange:

John Dean: We have a cancer within, close to the presidency, that is growing. Basically it is because we are being blackmailed.

Richard Nixon: How much money do you need?

John Dean: I would say these people are going to cost a million dollars over the next two years.

Richard Nixon: You could get a million dollars. You could get it in cash. I know where it could be gotten.

By late July, the president's involvement in the cover-up was quite clear.

In the last week of July the House Judiciary Committee recommended three articles of impeachment against the president, charging him with criminal conspiracy and obstruction of justice, a series of abuses of power, and the unconstitutional defiance of committee subpoenas. Nixon invited three old friends and supporters, Senate Republican leader Hugh Scott, House Republican leader John Rhodes, and the silver-haired patriarch of the Republican Party, Senator Barry Goldwater, to the White House to give him their assessment of his chances for survival. Goldwater's appraisal was frank: "Mr. President, this isn't pleasant, but you want to know the situation, and it isn't good." The three leaders estimated that Nixon could count on between 15 and 18 votes for acquittal in the Senate. Fully aware that the House was on the verge of passing articles of impeachment and that he would not survive trial by the Senate, he resigned as president of the United States on August 9, 1974.

Thus ended one of the most extraordinary political careers of the twentieth century, filled with amazing highs and lows. Richard Nixon was an intelligent, at times insightful man with critical character flaws that ultimately undid his presidency and undermined the good that he meant to do the nation. In his resignation speech, Nixon seemed genuinely convinced that his wrongdoings had always been motivated by national, not personal, interest: "I would say only that if some of my judgments were wrong — and some were wrong — they were made in what I believed at the time to be in the best interest of the nation." Yet Nixon had clearly been guilty of obstructing justice, and was fortunate to be pardoned by his successor, sparing him trial and conviction.

Nixon turned the presidency over to Vice President Gerald R. Ford. Almost as a footnote to the events leading up to Nixon's resignation, Vice President Agnew had also been forced to resign in 1973, receiving immunity from prosecution after pleading "no contest" to charges of bribe-taking and tax evasion. Ford, the Republican minority leader in the House, had been approved by Congress as the replacement vice president. His appointment in October 1973 was the first usage of the Twenty-Fifth Amendment, adopted in 1967 to provide for filling vice presidential and presidential vacancies.

Watergate was one of the American republic's darkest hours. Twenty-five members of the Nixon administration, including four cabinet officers, were convicted

Nixon's Departure, August 9, 1974   Bidding farewell to his staff, Richard Nixon waves for the last time from the presidential helicopter before lifting off from the White House. He has just signed his resignation, effective shortly after he will be airborne.

of crimes, and most spent time in prison. Watergate also demonstrated the vitality of American democracy: the nation's institutions emerged from the crisis largely unscathed. But the price of this demonstration had been high.

AMERICA ON HOLD

Distrust of government has long been a part of the national character, but Americans' cynicism about their country's political institutions sank to new depths on account of Vietnam and Watergate. To make matters worse, the economic situation continued to deteriorate. The cost of living increased 7 percent in 1973 and skyrocketed 11 percent the following year. Ford, and his successor Jimmy Carter, faced gargantuan problems in trying to rebuild the nation's international image, stop the economic decline, and heal the nation's self-inflicted wounds. Both Ford and Carter were men of integrity and ability, but neither could stem the descent into the doldrums at the end of the seventies.

Gerald Ford and Vietnamese Refugees   As refugees from Vietnam began to stream into the United States in the spring of 1975, President Ford posed with this Vietnamese baby on a bus at an airbase in California. Ford's presidency was a period of humiliating reverses for the United States, and he paid the price when he was defeated in the 1976 election.

❧ Interregnum: *The Presidency of Gerald R. Ford*

Born in Omaha, Nebraska, on July 14, 1913, Ford grew up in Grand Rapids, Michigan. He attended the University of Michigan, where he was a star football player, before studying law at Yale University. After working his way through Yale Law School, Ford served in the navy in the Pacific during World War II and was discharged as a lieutenant commander. First elected to Congress in 1948, he served twenty-five years in the House of Representatives, eight of them as Republican Party leader. An orthodox conservative, Ford was an affable, open, unpretentious man, without a hint of corruption in his political career — a breath of fresh air following the Nixon years. Most people welcomed the new president, though many were disappointed when, one month after taking office, he pardoned Nixon for "all offenses against the United States" he may have committed while president. The pardon proved to be a political liability for Ford, but he insisted that the nation should be spared the pain of seeing a former president brought to criminal trial.

Ford proved himself to be a traditional Republican, advocating free enterprise, a balanced budget, and a reduced role for the federal government. He launched a campaign of voluntarism aimed at combating the wrenching inflationary cycle that he inherited. Wearing a "Whip Inflation Now" (WIN) button, the president called upon management and labor to exercise self-discipline, holding wages and prices at existing levels. Predictably, Ford was soon at loggerheads with the Democratic Congress. Democrats demanded governmental action, including lower interest rates, a tax cut, and increased spending for welfare and job programs. During his two years in office Ford vetoed more than forty bills, including Democratic proposals to expand federal health care and federal aid to education. On over fifty occasions Congress rejected legislation proposed by the White House.

It fell to the new president to preside over the tragic finale in Vietnam. Never having observed the peace terms worked out by Nixon and Kissinger in 1973, the North Vietnamese saw their chance to finish off the weakened Saigon regime early in 1975 by launching a massive offensive. When several divisions of North Vietnamese regulars overran government positions in the Central Highlands, South Vietnamese troops fled in panic, and a rout began. With the American public and Congress sick of the war and unwilling to recommit American resources to the South, by mid-April it was clear that the end was near. All that the Americans could do was evacuate their own personnel and a handful of "essential" South Vietnamese. On April 29, with television cameras recording the events, the final American helicopter lifted off the roof of the American embassy as panicked South Vietnamese fought to clamber aboard. The next day remnants of the South Vietnamese government surrendered to the North Vietnamese commander, who gave Saigon a new name — Ho Chi Minh City. In May, Congress appropriated funds to fly 140,000 South Vietnamese refugees to the United States.

Communist victories in Vietnam, Cambodia, and Laos brought neither peace nor social justice to Indochina. The regime set up by the victorious guerrilla leader Pol Pot in Cambodia promptly launched one of the twentieth century's most horrific genocides by forcing millions of city dwellers to "resettle" in rural areas.

This combination of forced labor, terrorism, and mass murder cost an estimated 3 million lives. Hundreds of thousands of ethnic Chinese and other minorities fled Indochina as "boat people," desperately trying to stay alive on the South China Sea until they could make it to Hong Kong or the Philippines. Vietnamese intervention in Cambodia ended in a full-scale invasion in 1979 that swelled the refugee population and contributed to widespread starvation in the devastated region.

Such were some of the most visible signs of the American defeat in Indochina — though what a generation of American policymakers had most feared, the domino-like fall of other Southeast Asian nations to Communism, never happened. Indeed, the 1980s would see the emergence of dynamic "Asian tiger" economies in several of the region's non-Communist nations, including Malaysia, Singapore, Thailand, and the British colony of Hong Kong.

Ford and Kissinger, who had stayed on as secretary of state, tried to continue improving relations with the Soviet Union, but they were constrained by conservatives who insisted that any framework that they negotiated should maintain U.S. military superiority and by liberals who demanded concessions from the Soviets on human rights issues. In the fall of 1974, Ford met Soviet leader Leonid Brezhnev in the Siberian city of Vladivostok. They concluded a preliminary and modest arms limitation agreement focusing on missiles. Then in July 1975 in Helsinki, Finland, Ford joined other leaders from East and West in signing a major agreement recognizing all European boundaries as they had been established at the end of World War II. In return, the Soviet Union acceded to a declaration of human rights that endorsed freedom of migration, expression, and religion. At the time, it seemed that the West had made a major concession in return for empty promises. But over the long run, the West gained most from the Helsinki Accords, which encouraged the rise of dissent in the Soviet Bloc and helped promote economic reform. Fifteen years later, those changes contributed to the collapse of Communism in the Soviet Union and its satellites.

❧ The Election of 1976

In the fall of 1975 two mentally unstable women made attempts on President Ford's life. The president was also assaulted politically from all sides by 1976. Ford had antagonized the right wing of his own party by signing the preliminary SALT II accords and by firing his hawkish secretary of defense, James Schlesinger, in the fall of 1975. When Ford's wife Betty hailed the Supreme Court's decision legalizing abortion as "a great, great decision," irate social conservatives within the GOP openly rebelled. California Governor Ronald Reagan declared his candidacy for the nomination and defeated Ford in a series of western and southern primaries, but the president relied on party machines in the Midwest and Northeast to win the nomination by a narrow margin.

In the aftermath of Watergate and a sweeping victory in the 1974 midterm congressional elections, the Democrats looked forward to the 1976 election with great anticipation. The Washington scandal left the race open to a candidate who had not been a part of the long, divisive fight, and Georgia governor Jimmy Carter emerged as the front-running candidate. A self-effacing man with a warm smile, Carter was a devout Southern Baptist who spoke openly about his "born-again" faith. Many northern Democrats and urban liberals were dismayed — or amused — by Carter's overtly religious character, and free-spending congressional Democrats were even more disturbed by Carter's outspoken support of a balanced budget and his opposition to busing. Yet many Americans welcomed Carter as an antidote to the sordidness of Watergate and an exemplar of traditional values who could restore the nation's trust. Winning the nomination, Carter chose as his running mate a liberal Senator from Minnesota, Walter Mondale, and promised the American people, "I will never lie to you."

Carter began the race with a substantial lead, but it melted away in a campaign filled with gaffes by both candidates. Carter granted an ill-advised interview to *Playboy* magazine in which he confessed that he had "committed adultery in [his] heart many times," a failure that was well understood by his fellow evangelical Christians but seemed bizarre to the urban liberals whom the interview was intended to impress. On the other hand, Carter's use of such slang terms as "screw" shocked his evangelical backers. In a televised debate, Ford asserted that "there is no Soviet domination of Eastern Europe, and there never will be under a Ford administration," despite the obvious existence of a Soviet Bloc in Eastern Europe under the Warsaw Pact. The Ford campaign explained that the candidate had meant to say (correctly, as later events proved) that the Polish people would never give in to Soviet domination, but the damage was done. *Time* labeled his remark "The Blooper Heard Round the World."

President Jimmy Carter   Hoping to strike a more "human" note after Nixon's "imperial presidency," Jimmy Carter often carried his own bags on presidential trips or—as in this photograph—lugged an armful of briefing books. The effort backfired. Many thought the gestures insincere, diminishing to the presidency, and a symbol of the United States's "comedown" in the world.

The election revealed little about the future direction of American politics. The Democrats won, but not by the kind of landslide vote that many had expected in the wake of Watergate. Carter took 50.1 percent of the vote to Ford's 48 percent. The tally in the electoral college was narrow, 297 to 241. Carter won in the South, demonstrating the advantages to the Democratic Party of having a southerner head the ticket. Carter had no doubt been aided in the South by evangelical Christians who felt he was one of them. They would be not only disappointed in his presidency, but embittered by it. Another important trend in the election was the increasing

importance of black voters in the South. African Americans voted in large numbers and gave around 80 percent of their votes to the Democratic Party.

❧ Discovering Jimmy Carter

Jimmy Carter was born on October 1, 1924, the oldest of four children. His father operated a successful peanut brokerage firm in tiny Plains, Georgia. Carter studied at Georgia Tech before graduating from the Naval Academy in 1946 in the top 10 percent of his class. Immediately thereafter, he married Rosalynn Smith, another Plains native. To Carter's delight, he was admitted to the navy's newly established atomic submarine program. After leaving the navy, he returned to Plains to take over the family peanut business and devote his free time to public service. In 1966 Carter ran for governor of Georgia, but lost to a strongly segregationist candidate. Rationalizing that it was morally permissible to use equivocal means to achieve righteous ends, he appealed to white supremacists during his successful second run for the governorship in 1970. Once in office, however, Carter proved to be anything but a racist, and during the single term to which the Georgia constitution limited governors he compiled an impressive record as a moderate progressive. In his gubernatorial inaugural address he announced that "the time of racial discrimination is over," and during his term he increased the number of African American appointees on major state boards and agencies from three to fifty-three.

Though the national media called him a populist, Carter was generally a progressive in style and a liberal in substance. Carter was the first president with an engineer's training (and outlook) since Herbert Hoover. A stickler for detail (who even saw fit to involve himself with scheduling his staffers' turns on the White House tennis courts), he championed efficiency and honesty in government and continually invoked the public interest against special interests. Carter saw himself as a trustee of the public welfare and a man above politics — a view of the presidency that had not been much in evidence since the days of John Quincy Adams. He was a true moralist who attributed sordid motives to those who opposed his ideas and programs, a tendency that should have evoked uneasy memories of Woodrow Wilson.

Carter's progressive ideals made him support many traditional liberal programs. He was committed to equality for all regardless of color and gender, and he proved to be an outspoken champion of nondiscrimination. He understood the corrosive effect of entrenched poverty on American society, but he was also distrustful of an unbalanced budget and unwilling to back large increases in federal spending. To the dismay of liberals in Congress, the new administration showed more determination to reduce inflation than unemployment. When the Carter White House tackled the problem of reforming the welfare system and establishing an effective energy policy, it found solid resistance in Congress.

In the end, Jimmy Carter's inexperience in national politics doomed his presidency. He campaigned as a Washington outsider and promised open government. The first alienated him from the federal bureaucracy and Congress, while the second created the image of a divided, out-of-control administration. Carter committed a number of political blunders in the early days of his presidency that squandered much of his political capital. Urging reconciliation, on his first day in office the president offered a "full, complete and unconditional pardon" to Vietnam-era draft resisters. The head of the Veterans of Foreign Wars called the day of the announcement one of the saddest in American history, while peace activists denounced the president for not including deserters and those receiving less than honorable discharges. Shortly afterward, Carter abruptly canceled nineteen water projects located principally in the South and West. Although the action was justified on economic grounds, it alienated important Democratic senators and congressmen and boded ill for the president's subsequent legislative initiatives.

✆ The Economic Crisis and Carter's Domestic Agenda

Of necessity the Carter administration turned its attention first to the stagflation-beset economy. The White House proposed a modest recovery package that included an across-the-board $50 per person tax rebate,

a $900 million increase in corporate taxes, and small increases in public works and job-creating programs. But Carter was unable to control Congress. On May 5, 1977, the House and Senate passed a much more ambitious economic recovery plan that provided $20.1 billion to increase employment through various job programs, reduced corporate taxes by $34 billion over a three-year period with incentives for employers who hired new workers, and increased the minimum wage. The jobless rated dropped below 6 percent in 1978, but the president received little credit.

Perhaps Jimmy Carter's chief liability as president was his penchant for backing liberal causes on some occasions and at other times siding with conservatives. His approach to welfare reform reinforced his image as a conservative. The administration's plan would furnish jobs for welfare recipients who could work and a "decent income" for those who could not, such as the disabled and single parents with small children. Assailed in Congress by liberals and conservatives alike, the administration's welfare reform program as it finally emerged from the House and Senate merely provided $2.8 billion in additional spending to help the states manage their welfare systems. Warned that the Social Security fund faced bankruptcy by the end of the century if current tax rates and payment schedules remained in place, Carter and Health, Education, and Welfare secretary Joseph Califano tried to address the issue by placing the system on a sound financial footing. They estimated that inflation coupled with a rapidly aging population would require an additional $83 billion in taxes over the next five years alone. Though they sensed the political consequences of supporting large new levies, Carter and Congress agreed on a plan that tripled payroll taxes over a period of ten years. Califano's suggestions for long-range reform of the program, including raising the beginning age for benefits, were too politically divisive to have any hope of passage.

In the fall of 1977, Carter's poll ratings began a slide that continued throughout his presidency. By the spring of 1978, only 29 percent of the American people told pollsters that the president "inspired confidence." The decline was in part due to specific events. In September 1977, one of Carter's closest advisers, Office of Management and Budget head Bert Lance, resigned under fire, accused of unethically manipulating bank stock, and the president defended his long-time friend. To make matters worse, the administration divided publicly over the Bakke case, the first reverse discrimi nation case to reach the Supreme Court. The case pitted important Democratic constituencies against each other. American Jewish leaders generally favored affirmative action but opposed quotas, which African American organizations strongly defended. Organized labor, jealous of its seniority system, opposed affirmative action, at least with respect to blue-collar workers. Black advocacy groups urged the Justice Department to file an *amicus curiae* brief in the case defending the right of the University of California–Davis to operate an admissions system with dual standards. Attorney General Griffin Bell opposed affirmative action quotas, while HEW secretary Califano and Vice President Mondale strongly supported the affirmative action policies that had led to the Bakke case. Thus the administration wound up offending both sides.

Jimmy Carter was aware of his growing unpopularity, and he tried to reverse his political decline by promoting himself as the "citizen president," dispensing with bands playing "Hail to the Chief" on ceremonial occasions, enrolling his daughter Amy in a Washington public school (rather than a private school, as virtually all other prominent politicians and bureaucrats did), carrying his own suit bag when he traveled, and periodically holding "town meetings" throughout the country. But such gestures seemed to diminish his stature in voters' eyes, reinforcing the perception that the power and prestige of the United States was waning.

✎ Losing the Battle for Energy Independence

Like presidents before and after him, Carter's most pressing domestic concern was the economic destabilization caused by inflation. The cause most responsible for the economic chaos of the seventies was the energy crisis that had begun with the OPEC embargo in 1973. Carter unveiled his energy program before a national television audience, declaring the struggle to hold down inflation and decrease foreign dependency the "moral equivalent of war." Unkind critics derided the slogan — a quotation from philosopher William James — as "MEOW." The administration subsequently introduced an unwieldy bill that taxed all domestic oil production, created a standby gasoline tax to go into effect when consumption exceeded certain levels, imposed a "gas guzzler" tax on autos that used excessive fuel, required a certain number of new utilities and power plants to burn coal or other fuels instead of oil and natural gas, penalized wasteful industrial users, and established tax credits and other incentives for conserva-

tion. Such a program, if fully enacted, would have been an enforcement nightmare, unparalleled since the days of World War II price controls and rationing. Showing a lack of political foresight, the president failed to consult the groups most affected by the bill. As a consequence, Congress gutted his proposal, removing all energy taxes except those on inefficient automobiles. The energy bill that Congress finally passed attempted to conserve energy through deregulation and tax credits rather than through taxation, and it was an important first step toward establishing a national energy policy. But at the time, it was judged a failure, and Carter took the blame.

✎ The Carter Foreign Policy — Human Rights and Open Diplomacy

The principal themes of the Carter administration's foreign policy were the not-always-easily-reconciled goals of human rights, open diplomacy, and containment of international Communism. Running for president, Carter had lashed out at Kissinger for his secret diplomacy and balance-of-power approach to foreign affairs. "Our Secretary of State simply does not trust the judgment of the American people," Carter had told the Chicago Council on Foreign Relations. He called for open covenants openly arrived at, echoing Woodrow Wilson's Fourteen Points, and his promise to have American foreign policy conform to its lofty principles also seemed to echo Wilsonian rhetoric. As secretary of state, Carter selected Cyrus Vance, a wealthy New York attorney who had served as deputy secretary of defense from 1964 through 1967 and participated in the Paris peace talks from 1968 through 1969. His national security adviser was Zbigniew Brzezinski, an astute Polish-born Columbia University Kremlinologist and — in striking contrast to the liberal Vance — a tough hardliner with no illusions about Soviet benevolence.

The president declared that he would make the human rights declaration in the Helsinki Accords — which committed the signatories to the principles of freedom of expression, freedom of migration, and freedom from economic exploitation — the criteria for U.S. dealings with other countries. Carter and his advisers were mindful of the "lessons" of Vietnam: Vance, for example, insisted that in most of the developing world nationalism, decolonization, and social and economic justice were the driving forces of change rather than Cold War ideologies. Therefore, declared the president, the United States would not aid countries whose rulers oppressed and exploited their populations, and it would feel free to condemn violations of human rights even among those who supported the U.S. against the Soviet Union. Applying these lofty moral standards in foreign affairs consistently proved to be difficult, and sometimes impossible.

❧ *A Freeze on Détente*

Despite Brzezinski's rabid anti-Communism, Carter believed that the United States and Soviet Union could work out a way of getting along that would avoid nuclear war and introduce a period of global peace and stability. He ardently supported the 1972 SALT I agreement, which placed limitations on several types of intercontinental ballistic missiles (ICBMs). With the treaty due to expire shortly, in 1977 disarmament discussions reopened in Geneva. The Soviets had a huge lead in land-based launchers and resisted American proposals for sweeping cuts in this category. Eventually the Americans agreed to accept a limit of 2,400 strategic launchers as a starting point, and in return the veteran Soviet foreign minister Andrei Gromyko indicated that his country would seriously consider an agreement that would reduce both nations' strategic arsenals by 10 percent. The two sides also consented to a protocol that suspended plans for the development and deployment of American cruise missiles (pilotless aircraft that could maneuver close enough to the ground to evade Soviet radar) and the Soviet backfire bomber, which Washington believed could be modified to attack the United States. The resulting SALT II treaty did not compel the drastic reductions many had hoped for, but it kept the disarmament dialogue going.

The 1977 arms negotiations were complicated by the Carter administration's public denunciations of the Soviet Union for violations of human rights and calls for the Kremlin to stop persecuting dissidents and to allow Russian Jews to emigrate to Israel. Such statements infuriated the Soviet leaders, who regarded Carter's human rights campaign as an ideological offensive and an inexcusable meddling in internal Soviet affairs. But in the years ahead Carter's commitment to human rights grew more rather than less strident.

In spite of annoyance caused by Carter's human rights pronouncements, in June 1979 the two nations agreed upon a SALT II treaty in Vienna. Although the agreement did not benefit one party at the expense of the other and did not significantly reduce the arms race, the Senate balked, and Carter reluctantly withdrew the SALT II treaty. This denouement coincided

with the Soviet invasion of Afghanistan. In 1978, the Kremlin engineered a coup that installed a Marxist regime in that remote, mountainous, but strategically important Muslim country. Under siege from Islamic fundamentalist guerrillas angered at the antireligious bent of the new regime, the pro-Soviet puppet government grew weaker. During the Christmas holidays of 1979, Moscow dispatched 85,000 troops to prop up a new, more vigorous pro-Communist ruler. Russia's Vietnam had begun.

The invasion of Afghanistan alarmed, angered, and disillusioned President Carter. It marked the first time that Soviet troops had directly intervened in a nation outside Eastern Europe. The president vehemently denounced the Afghan adventure, broadened and deepened ties (including opening diplomatic relations) with China, and approved covert CIA aid to the Afghan rebels (many of whom would in the 1990s prove to be as anti-American as they were anti-Soviet). Recalling Thomas Jefferson's ill-fated attempt to use commerce as an instrument of national policy, Carter embargoed grain sales to the Soviet Union, thereby enraging American farmers who profited from the trade. He also alienated many sports fans by insisting that American athletes boycott the Olympic Games scheduled for Moscow that summer. The unpopular and largely ineffective posturing cost Carter crucial public support and undercut the force and long-range significance of his State of the Union address in January 1980, in which he enunciated what journalists promptly labeled the "Carter Doctrine:" "An attempt by any outside force to gain control of the Persian Gulf region will be regarded as an assault on the vital interests of the United States of America, and . . . an assault will be repelled by use of any means necessary, including military force."

❧ *The United States and the Developing Nations*

Vance and America's UN ambassador, Andrew Young (an African American from Atlanta with roots in the civil rights movement), had little trouble convincing Carter that large areas of the developing world were unaffected by and unconcerned with the Cold War. During the first part of his administration, Carter resisted the tendency of every administration since World War II to view every regional conflict in the world through the prism of U.S.-Soviet tensions. Despite the claims by white minority governments in Africa that their continuance in power was crucial to the success of the struggle against international Communism, Carter repeatedly declared his support for black majority rule. The president backed up his rhetoric by persuading Congress in 1977 to impose economic sanctions against the white minority government of Rhodesia (today the black-ruled Republic of Zimbabwe).

In Latin America, Washington attempted to use economic aid to pressure several military governments to improve their human rights records, and it took steps to reassure the republics in the region that the U.S. respected their sovereignty. Latin Americans widely believed that a military coup in Chile in 1973 that had unseated the government of leftist president Salvador Allende and replaced him with a military regime led by General Augusto Pinochet had been orchestrated by the United States. Henry Kissinger admitted that in September 1970, Nixon had ordered him to organize a coup against Allende, but he insisted that he dropped the idea a month later. Recent lawsuits by Chilean citizens against Kissinger and the United States government have resurrected charges that the American government was responsible for deaths and other rights abuses perpetrated under the Pinochet regime.

Carter's commitment to this new attitude of respect was most clearly manifest in his treatment of Panama. Both the Johnson and Nixon administrations had promised in principle to negotiate a new Panama Canal Treaty. The original pact, signed in 1903 during the presidency of Theodore Roosevelt, gave control over a ten-mile-wide strip across Panama to the United States "in perpetuity" and had long been interpreted by Panamanians as an infringement on their sovereignty. (The provision had been the price that Panama paid for American support in gaining independence from Colombia.) In the fall of 1977, an American delegation signed two agreements with Panamanian representatives. The first stipulated that the United States would continue to operate the canal until 2000, when Panamanians would take control. The second guaranteed that the canal would remain open to the shipping of all nations and gave the United States the right to defend the canal until 2000.

For six months a bitter debate raged in the United States over the wisdom of ratifying the Panama Canal treaties. Many conservatives condemned the treaty as another sacrifice of America's strategic interests and a symbol of its waning influence. ("We stole it fair and square," huffed one Senator.) The Carter administration fought back, pointing out that less than 10 percent of the nation's trade passed through the canal, and that it had become strategically irrelevant. With bipartisan sup-

port from Democratic leader Robert Byrd and Republican leader Howard Baker, the Panama Canal treaties were approved by the Senate by a margin of one vote.

Although the Carter administration's policy toward Nicaragua and El Salvador began on an idealistic plane, the relationship between the United States and these two countries quickly degenerated into a Cold War free-for-all. Since 1934 the United States had supported the anti-Communist dictatorship in Nicaragua of General Anastasio Somoza Garcia. By the late 1970s, however, Nicaraguans had become restive under Somoza's ruthless and corrupt rule. In 1978, the Sandinista National Liberation Front (named for Cesar Augusto Sandino, who had led a guerrilla movement against American occupation forces in the 1920s) drove Somoza into exile.

Shortly after the Somoza regime fell, Carter persuaded Congress to appropriate $75 million in aid for the new Sandinista regime, hoping it would institute democratic and economic reforms in Nicaragua. Many conservative foreign policy experts warned that Sandinista leader Daniel Ortega and his closest lieutenants were Marxists, but to no avail. Ortega remained a heroic figure to many on the American left throughout the 1970s, in spite of his authoritarian rule at home and

increasing evidence that he was aiding leftist rebels in neighboring El Salvador.

Like almost all Latin American republics, El Salvador had historically been ruled by a tiny land-holding plutocracy in close alliance with the military and the Catholic Church. The peasants were uneducated, exploited, and politically disenfranchised. In October 1979, a group of reform-minded but anti-Communist officers seized control of the government. They installed a regime headed by Jose Napoleon Duarte, who subsequently enraged the plutocracy by attempting land reform and progressive taxation. Members of the former ruling clique, in league with right-wing military officers, organized "death squads" that assassinated an estimated 13,000 Salvadorans during Duarte's first year in office. Carter initially embraced Duarte's reform government and persuaded Congress to vote an aid package. When, subsequently, the government proved too weak to take action against the death squads, including a group of soldiers who assassinated the archbishop of El Salvador and raped and killed four female American missionaries, Washington withdrew its support. Thereupon civil war broke out between the government and the left-wing Democratic Revolutionary Front. Under pressure from anti-Communists in and out of Congress, the Carter administration resumed the shipment of both armaments and non-military aid to the Salvadoran government.

❧ *The Middle East: Breakthrough and Hostages*

Although Central America, and Panama in particular, dominated American media coverage during the first eighteen months of Carter's term, the president devoted much of his attention to the powder keg in the Middle East. In an effort to convince the Arab world that the United States was not blindly pro-Israel and could be trusted as an "honest broker" in

Burning the Flag Demonstrators perched atop the U.S. embassy in Tehran, Iran, burn an American flag, the fourth to be burned there since Iranian students seized the embassy and took more than sixty hostages. They also burned an effigy of President Carter.

any negotiations, Carter announced in March 1977 that he favored a settlement based on the establishment of fair boundaries in the region, including a "homeland" for the Palestinians. Partly in response, that summer the Israeli public voted into office the ultra-nationalist, right-wing, and intransigent Likud Party. The new prime minister, Menachem Begin, was an ex-terrorist (having fought against both the British and the Arabs) who had long resisted making any concession to the Arabs. Dismayed by the ongoing stalemate in the Middle East, Carter in September 1978 invited Begin and Egyptian president Anwar Sadat, who favored a land-for-peace deal, to Camp David, the presidential retreat in Maryland, for discussions that lasted for nearly two weeks. Scrutinized minute-by-minute by the national and international media, and with Carter serving as a virtually full-time go-between, the Egyptian and Israeli leaders eventually succumbed to presidential blandishments (including promises of lavish American financial aid) and signed two vague pacts. One called for "transitional arrangements for the West Bank and Gaza" and promised "full autonomy to the inhabitants," while the second recognized the "legitimate security concerns" of Israel. Both to acknowledge this achievement and to express hope for further progress, in 1978 the Nobel Peace Prize was awarded to Begin and Sadat. Then, after another period of intense negotiation, Carter flew to the Middle East in early March 1979, where he persuaded Sadat and Begin to come to Washington later that month and sign a bilateral peace treaty. That agreement provided for gradual Israeli withdrawal from the Sinai, the establishment of formal diplomatic ties between the two countries, and negotiations on Palestinian rights in the West Bank and Gaza.

But Carter's accomplishments in opening the way for peace between Israel and Egypt were soon overshadowed by America's humiliation in Iran. When Carter became president, Iran was one of America's strongest allies in the Middle East, under the firm control of Mohammed Reza Shah Pahlavi, an autocratic and staunchly anti-Communist monarch whom the CIA helped into power in 1953. The cornerstones of the Shah's rule were a political autocracy maintained by a huge military establishment, westernization and modernization, and good relations with Western petroleum companies. But almost everything the Shah stood for deeply offended the fundamentalist leaders of Iran's Shi'ites, the religious community that included 90 percent of Iran's population. American policymakers, to say nothing of the American public, were profoundly ignorant of the

Reagan for President, 1980   Ronald Reagan ran for the presidency promising to restore American pride, self-respect, and optimism.

explosive anti-Western animosity brewing in the Islamic world in general and Iran in particular. By the late summer of 1978, the Iranian government was under attack by an Islamic Revolutionary Guard loyal to charismatic religious leader Ayatollah Ruhollah Khomeini, then in exile in Paris. With his army rapidly losing control of the country, the Shah, now gravely ill with cancer, fled Iran in January 1979. Khomeini flew home the next month and proclaimed an Islamic Republic, with him as its spiritual head. Under pervasive clerical supervision, the new republic would be ruled by the strictest standards of Islamic law, banishing Western dress, music, and other influences. Fanatical religious leaders whipped up nationalist sentiment against the "Great Satan, the United States," while Khomeini announced that he was cutting off oil shipments to America but permitting them to continue to Western Europe and Japan.

The Carter administration was deeply disturbed by the overthrow of one of America's staunchest allies and the establishment in Iran of a rabidly anti-Western government. Against the advice of the U.S. embassy in Teh-

ran, Carter in October 1979 granted asylum to the dying Shah, who sought medical treatment in America. In retaliation, young Islamic Revolutionary Guards seized the American embassy on November 4, taking its four hundred officials and functionaries hostage, including fifty-two Americans. As the price for their release, the Iranian government demanded that the international community seize and repatriate the Shah's immense personal wealth and that he be returned to Iran to stand trial.

The Carter administration responded with a mixture of confusion and anxiety. Night after night American television audiences were forced to endure an orgy of humiliation as blindfolded American hostages were publicly abused and threatened by their captors. The United States froze $8 billion in Iranian assets in the United States and suspended the sale of arms to Tehran, but America's principal allies — Britain, Germany, and Japan — refused to level sanctions lest they lose their supplies of Iranian crude oil. In desperation, President Carter authorized on April 24, 1980, a commando operation in which a contingent of helicopter-borne Marines was to swoop down on the embassy, kill the captors, and rescue the hostages. When a sandstorm in the Iranian desert caused one of the helicopters to crash into a C-130 transport plane, the president called off the mission. The hostages were then separated and relocated, making another rescue attempt impossible. Secretary of State Vance, who had not been forewarned of the mission and had opposed provoking Iran, resigned in protest.

❧ The Election of 1980

As the election of 1980 approached, it seemed that events were conspiring against Carter. The American flag was being desecrated nightly in Iran, and the U.S. economy stubbornly resisted administration efforts to control inflation and stimulate growth. Conditions actually worsened after OPEC's fourth and largest price hike sent gas prices soaring again in July, touching off the nation's first energy riot. In Levittown, Pennsylvania, truckers barricaded Interstate 95, and two nights of violence left one hundred injured. Confronted with public opinion polls showing a growing lack of confidence in his leadership, Carter secluded himself for eleven days at Camp David to consult with prominent individuals from business, labor, government, academia, and the religious community. The object of the conferences, according to the White House, was to deal with the "crisis of spirit" that seemed to be dragging the country down.

Hoping the country had forgotten about Chappaquiddick, Senator Edward Kennedy challenged Carter for the Democratic nomination. Kennedy ran as a staunch liberal and fared well in several early primaries in the Northeast, but Carter swept the contests in the South and Midwest. When the convention met, Carter almost had enough votes for renomination. Still, Kennedy drove a tough bargain, dropping his challenge only after the president agreed to support a $12-billion jobs program and promised not to seek a balanced budget if it would result in high interest rates and unemployment. Kennedy's strong challenge to the sitting president, and Carter's humiliating need to negotiate within his party to assure his renomination, underscored his political vulnerability and the disaffection of American liberals, who had never quite accepted Carter as one of their own.

Meanwhile, on July 16 Governor Ronald Reagan of California received the Republican nomination and selected as his running mate George Bush, a moderate East Coast Republican who had represented his adopted state of Texas in Congress and had been a respected head of the CIA. Reagan, a modestly successful actor, had been an effective, popular governor. He was a pragmatic politician who spoke the language of a true conservative. Furthermore, in a bold move that other Republican contenders were unwilling to make, Reagan embraced the so-called "New Religious Right" — evangelical Christians enraged by what they regarded as the anti-family and anti-moral policies of the Carter administration.

Carter tried to convince Americans that Reagan was a dangerous reactionary, incapable of leading a great nation in a complex world. Reagan's background as a movie actor unsettled many, although his record as governor of California had proved that he had become a skilled chief executive. Democratic hopes soared when the forthright Reagan repeatedly spoke his honest sentiments, referring to the war in Vietnam as a "noble cause," expressing personal doubts about the theory of evolution, and proposing to make Social Security voluntary. For the moment, it seemed as if the Reagan candidacy might go the way of Goldwater's in 1964. Polls taken at the end of September suggested that the president had reduced Reagan's lead to 4 percentage points. Then, in late October, a reluctant Carter agreed to a nationally televised debate with Reagan. The president conducted himself well, mastering complex questions with apparent ease, but Reagan gave a glimpse of the telegenic persona that earned him the nickname "the great communicator." "There you go again," said the veteran film star softly, with a wry shake of his head, when Carter tried to pin the "extremist" label on him. Reagan carefully avoided the gaffes that had plagued him earlier in the campaign and toward the end of the debate urged every American to ask two crucial questions: "Are you better off than you were four years ago?" and "Do you feel that our security is safe, that we're as strong as we were four years ago?" Given the perilous state of the economy and the Iran hostage crisis, the questions resonated with the electorate.

In an election in which one out of every four voters settled on a candidate during the last week of the con-

---

✤   **I N   T H E I R   O W N   W O R D S**

Ronald Reagan's Acceptance Speech, 1980

Ronald Reagan instinctively understood and used rhetoric that combined a sense of American exceptionalism with straightforward piety, as this excerpt from his acceptance speech at the Republican National Convention illustrates. It was particularly appealing language for evangelical Christians, who emerged as a political force for change in the 1980 election.

The time is now, my fellow Americans, to recapture our destiny, to take it into our own hands. But, to do this will take many of us, working together. I ask you tonight to volunteer your help in this cause so we can carry our message throughout the land. . . .

I have thought of something that is not part of my speech and I'm worried over whether I should do it.

Can we doubt that only a Divine Providence placed this land, this island of freedom, here as a refuge for all those people in the world who yearn to breathe freely: Jews and

Christians enduring persecution behind the Iron Curtain, the boat people of Southeast Asia, of Cuba and Haiti, the victims of drought and famine in Africa, the freedom fighters of Afghanistan and our own countrymen held in savage captivity.

I'll confess that I've been a little afraid to suggest what I'm going to suggest — I'm more afraid not to — that we begin our crusade joined together in a moment of silent prayer.

God bless America.

test, Reagan scored a solid victory. He won 51 percent of the popular vote to Carter's 41 percent. Republican congressman John Anderson of Illinois, running as an independent candidate, ran a distant third with 7 percent. The electoral vote was even more decisive — 489 to 49. The Carter-Mondale ticket carried only the president's home state, Georgia, Mondale's Minnesota, and the Democratic bastions of Maryland, Rhode Island, West Virginia, and the District of Columbia. Riding Reagan's coattails, Republican candidates won control of the Senate for the first time in twenty-eight years. George McGovern and seven other prominent liberal Democrats went down to defeat.

Carter was partly responsible for his own demise, but, at the same time, he lost to a candidate with uncanny political instincts. Liberal pundits ridiculed Reagan, but it was often they, rather than Reagan, who misread the sentiments of the American people. Reagan did not so much pander to the common mind as share it. At the end of a decade and a half of economic chaos, social confrontation, vast expansions in the federal government, and defeat and disgrace abroad, Americans wanted to be able to stand tall and be proud, and Reagan promised to help them do that.

CONCLUSION: A NATION BESET

American politics in the 1970s, like American society, was characterized to an unusual degree by acrimony. To some extent, Richard Nixon's election in 1968, and his overwhelming reelection in 1972, expressed the majority will to slow the pace of change and restore the nation's honor and influence in the world. It was not to be. For all of his political skills and foreign policy accomplishments, Nixon's relentless sense of insecurity and his quest for personal power led him into the disaster of Watergate and deepened the bitterness of the seventies.

Nixon was followed in the presidency by two decent and honorable men, Gerald Ford and Jimmy Carter. In the end, neither proved to be an effective leader, and neither was reelected. In fact, both Ford and Carter faced devastating economic conditions that were not of their making and were probably beyond their power to remedy. President Carter, while he contributed to a hopeful beginning of peace talks between Israel and Egypt, was also confronted with a series of foreign policy crises that ended in heightened tensions with the Soviet Union and the catastrophic seizure of the American embassy in Tehran. In 1980, the American electorate veered to the right, turning the reins of government over to Ronald Reagan in hopes that he could restore the nation's order and its pride.

SUGGESTED READING

Stephen Ambrose, *Nixon: The Triumph of a Politician, 1962-1972* (1987) and *Nixon: Ruin and Recovery* (1991). Classic presidential biographies.

Peter Carroll, *It Seemed Like Nothing Happened: America in the 1970s* (1982). A critical overview of the seventies.

Burton I. Kaufman, *The Presidency of James Earl Carter, Jr.* (1993). A good overview of the Carter administration.

Gary M. Fink and Hugh Davis Graham, eds., *The Carter Presidency: Policy Choices in the Post–New Deal Era* (1998). A splendid set of essays suggesting that Carter's fiscal conservatism undermined his reform ideals.

Betty Glad, *Jimmy Carter in Search of the Great White House* (1980). This treatment is less sympathetic to Carter.

Allen J. Matusow, *Nixon's Economy: Booms, Busts, Dollars, and Votes* (1998). A penetrating look at the economic policies of Nixon and how they were tied to his political motives.

H. S. Parmet, *Richard Nixon and His America* (1990). This is also an excellent study of Nixon.

Gaddis Smith, *Morality, Reason, and Power* (1986). A survey of Carter's foreign policy.

Tad Szule, *The Illusion of Peace: Foreign Policy in the Nixon Years* (1978). A general treatment of Republican foreign policy.

SUGGESTIONS FOR FURTHER READING

Pierre Asselin, *A Bitter Peace: Washington, Hanoi, and the Making of the Paris Agreement* (2002).

James A. Bill, *The Eagle and the Lion* (1988).

Zbigniew Brzezinski, *Power and Principle* (1983).

James M. Cannon, *Time and Chance: Gerald Ford's Appointment with History* (1994).

John R. Greene, *The Limits of Power: The Nixon and Ford Administrations* (1992).

Joan Hoff, *Nixon Reconsidered* (1994).

Walter Isaacson, *Kissinger* (1992).

Stanley I. Kutler, *The Wars of Watergate* (1990) and *Abuse of Power* (1997).

Michael Ledeen and William Lewis, *Debacle* (1981).

R. S. Litwak, *Detente and the Nixon Doctrine* (1984).

Richard Reeves, *A Ford, Not a Lincoln* (1975).

35

A Turn to the Right: The Reagan and First Bush Presidencies

AFTER TWO DECADES marred by divisive partisanship, strident demands for reform, serious economic dislocation, and a series of international setbacks, a majority of Americans in 1980 longed for stability. The last years of the 1970s saw a resurgent patriotism gaining ground over the self-criticism that dominated the media in the late sixties. These changes in the popular mood played a major role in the election of Ronald Reagan to the presidency in November 1980.

Whatever his flaws — and they have been hotly debated — Reagan restored an increasingly conservative America's confidence in itself. Equally important, he set the political agenda for America for the rest of the century. Reagan's friends viewed him as a man of principle, a conservative idealist who refused to back away from deeply held convictions. His foes saw the former Democrat as a superficial opportunist. As president he proved to be a pragmatist who bargained with Democrats in Congress when unable to implement all of his ideas. Reagan advocated a conservative program of lower taxes, smaller government, a stronger military, and traditional values, all funded by a not-so-conservative budget deficit. By the end of his presidency, he and his ideas were such a potent political force in America that many Democratic politicians had abandoned the "liberal" label and moved toward the political center — which had itself moved perceptibly to the right. Of course, many liberal impulses remained strong. Moreover, Reagan's popularity by no means abolished the nation's sense of cultural division. What became known as the "culture wars" — essentially a conflict between liberal and conservative viewpoints — would rage throughout the 1980s and beyond.

Reagan delivered on much of the political agenda that he promised to Americans disenchanted with the intrusiveness, growth, and cost of government, but his policies, involving large increases in military spending and lower taxes for the wealthy, created huge federal deficits. Reagan and his advisers insisted that their economic ideas were working and that, given time, the American economy would rebound as it always had in the past. Indeed, during the 1980s an economic revolution did begin in the American business community, a downsizing that was painful but that by the 1990s had made American companies more competitive globally and better able to capitalize on the late twentieth century's great technological innovations, though the role of the federal government's policies in the boom remains debatable.

Resolutely determined to stop the spread of Communism all over the world, Reagan was the last, and perhaps the most ideologically committed, of the Cold War presidents. In part, the huge American military budgets of his presidency were designed to be the last straw in breaking the back of the decrepit and technologically outmoded Soviet economy. Perhaps more important, under a new, younger leadership, the Kremlin allowed long-dormant forces of change to emerge and drive the U.S.S.R. toward democracy and a market economy. By 1989, with Soviet coercive force removed from Eastern Europe, the Communist regimes in the Soviet Bloc began falling like dominoes. As the Soviet Union itself collapsed between 1989 and 1991, Reagan's successor, George Bush, encouraged other democratic revolutions and tried to grope toward a post–Cold War "new world order."

To uphold this new world order and to defend the industrialized countries' access to oil, the United States under Bush's leadership fought a war to evict Iraqi dictator Saddam Hussein from Kuwait. Victory in this Gulf War, coupled with the end of the Cold War, did much to restore the nation's sense of confidence as a global superpower. But the Gulf War allies' failure to overthrow Saddam himself underscored how dangerous the post–Cold War era would still be, and left the United States with a situation that deteriorated badly in subsequent years.

Its mood soured by a serious recession in 1991-92, the nation rejected Bush in 1992 and turned to Bill Clinton. Since he was a centrist "New Democrat," Clinton's policies in many ways reflected the traditional conservative agenda. In the wake of the end of the Cold War, he cut federal expenditures and balanced the federal budget, attempted to substitute "work-fare" for welfare, and pursued a restrained foreign policy. He appealed charismatically to ordinary Americans and to minorities, and played to the nation's growing cultural diversity. Since the 1950s the struggle to protect minority rights had been at the center of America's social agenda, but by the 1980s a broad debate about the nature and significance of the nation's pluralism was raging in the media, in the universities, and in political campaigns. By the time Clinton entered the White House, many observers on both sides of the debate believed that, more than ever before, acrimonious "culture wars" were dividing the country into separate political and social camps.

AMERICAN POLITICS TURNS TO THE RIGHT

Ronald Reagan dominated the politics of America and the world in the 1980s. A skillful politician with an uncanny ability to communicate with the average American, and a relentless advocate of neoconservative values, Reagan was sometimes extreme in rhetoric and usually moderate in action. While conservatives in the 1980s continued to praise free enterprise and denounce the expansion of government, they were unable and generally unwilling to dismantle the welfare state constructed by the New Deal and Great Society. Reagan sympathized with social conservatives who wanted to rein in affirmative action, constitutionally protect prayer in school, and outlaw abortion, but he was never willing to take significant political risks to reach such goals. He understood that these were battles he was unlikely to win.

Reagan's policies were a good fit for the 1980s. Alienated from public life by Vietnam, Watergate, and the Iran hostage situation, many Americans turned to the pursuit of wealth and individual happiness. At the end of the 1980s, *Time* magazine proclaimed that the decade's dominant characteristics had been "growth, avarice, and an anything-goes attitude." The young urban professionals — or yuppies, as they were nicknamed — who inspired this description were characterized (and often caricatured) as crass materialists who thrived in cutthroat corporate environments and who prized expensive material goods. No stereotype can sum up an entire decade, however: even in this age characterized by novelist Tom Wolfe as the "Me Decade," individual charitable giving increased at an unprecedented pace, reaching an annual rate of $100 billion by 1990.

ॐ *Ronald Reagan and the Politics of Conservatism*

Ronald Reagan was elected in the midst of a decided turn to the right in the American mood — a time his supporters saw as a return to patriotism and economic freedom and his critics pictured as a time of self-centeredness and introversion. He was born in Tampico, Illinois, and grew up in a series of small Illinois towns along the Mississippi River. His father was an alcoholic, but his mother was a devout woman who encouraged him in an amateur acting career in high school. He attended Eureka College, a small Disciples of Christ school near Peoria, Illinois, where he studied economics and continued to act. Graduating in the midst of the Depression, he had the good fortune to land a job at a radio station in Des Moines, Iowa. In 1937, while covering a Chicago Cubs baseball game on the West Coast, he arranged a screen test with Warner Brothers. Impressed, the studio signed him to a contract, and the former sports announcer moved to Hollywood, where he began a career as a movie star. In his best-known performance in *The Knute Rockne Story,* he played Notre Dame football immortal George Gipp — "the Gipper," a nickname by which he too would eventually be known.

During World War II Reagan remained in Hollywood and made training films for the armed forces. Always interested in politics, he was a staunch New Deal Democrat and in 1947 was elected president of the Screen Actors Guild. He held that position until 1952, becoming convinced during the era's controversial investigations into Communist influences in the film industry that subversive influences in Hollywood had been substantial. Politically, he moved to the right, a transformation perhaps hastened by his 1952 divorce from film star Jane Wyman and his remarriage to another actress, Nancy Davis, who held strong conservative convictions.

In 1954 he took a position with General Electric, and for the next eight years he hosted a television program for the giant corporation and toured the country speaking to workers, executives, and local chambers of commerce. His talks were odes to individualism, free enterprise, and middle-class values. Reagan first came to the attention of national Republican leaders in 1964 when, sponsored by the Republican National Committee, he gave a rousing television speech supporting Barry Goldwater's candidacy for the presidency. The speech was broadcast repeatedly on national television and brought floods of money into Republican coffers. Two years later, with the support of a group of wealthy California conservatives, Reagan defeated the popular incumbent governor, Edmund G. "Pat" Brown. Tuned in to resentment against protest and the youth rebellion, Reagan successfully portrayed Brown as a friend of "welfare cheats," "permissive" judges, and urban rioters, and convinced voters that he would discipline both the state's budget and its youth. In his years as governor he battled campus radicalism, labored to cut taxes, and befriended businesses large and small. But, foreshadowing his actions as president, he also proved a flexible negotiator with a predominantly liberal legislature.

ॐ *Constructing a Republican Coalition*

Unlike Richard Nixon's landslide victory in 1972, Ronald Reagan's trouncing of Carter in the election of 1980 seemed to signal a sea change in American politics. A mere six years after suffering its worst defeat since the Great Depression, the Republican Party had won its greatest victory, causing some pundits to predict that a conservative majority was emerging. Indeed, Reagan's victory coincided with and was in part made possible by the continuing growth and political activism of the New Right.

Reagan conservatism blended old and new. It encompassed traditional positions such as anti-Communism and opposition to government intervention and bureaucracy, as well as the old liberal advocacy of free trade. At the same time the New Right appealed to Americans, many of them working-class Democrats, who were outraged at social problems that they believed attacked and undermined morality, the nuclear family, and religious faith. Still, Reagan's strongest support was in the well-to-do suburbs of America's cities.

The most visible new group of activists in the Republican coalition was the so-called "Christian Right" movement energized by such issues as school prayer and abortion. Socially conservative evangelicals were not a monolithic political group, and for years many had been traditional Democrats or apolitical. But conservative politicians — Reagan among them — recognized the potential of the political action groups formed by religious conservatives in the late 1970s. Evangelicals were angered in the 1960s by the Supreme Court's rulings on prayer and Bible reading in the public schools, as well as by *Roe v. Wade*, but it was Jimmy Carter's tilt

Jerry Falwell and Ronald Reagan The founder of the Moral Majority — in the early 1980s the leading voice of the emerging "Religious Right" — greets the Republican presidential nominee as Reagan arrives in Lynchburg, Virginia, to address a convention of the National Religious Broadcasters. Reagan's embrace of conservative Christians was deemed risky by many of his friends, but it proved to be a resounding political success.

to the left on social issues that energized the new Religious Right, resulting in an organizing flurry in the late 1970s. Jerry Falwell's Moral Majority coalition, which consisted primarily of evangelical Protestants but also counted Roman Catholics, Mormons, and Orthodox Jews among its contributors, claimed much credit for Reagan's triumph. Falwell's movement lost steam in the 1980s, and the Moral Majority was disbanded in 1989, but other Christian political action groups took up the cause of pressing a conservative social agenda.

For a time it seemed that a series of financial and sexual scandals was going to disrupt the growth of the new Religious Right. First came the collapse of the TV ministry of Jim Bakker, who had built a huge media and entertainment empire called PTL. (The initials meant "Praise the Lord" or "People that Love" to insiders, but cynics said they really meant "Pass the Loot.") Bakker was sentenced to prison for fraud, along with a num-

ber of his aides. This overlapped a highly publicized sexual scandal that tainted the reputation of evangelist Jimmy Swaggart, one of the most widely known Protestant preachers in the world in the mid-1980s. These scandals did not demolish the conservative-religious coalition, however; rather, they shifted its leadership into different hands. By the end of the decade the most powerful figure on the Christian Right was Pat Robertson, the wealthy founder of the Christian Broadcasting Network who made a run for the Republican presidential nomination in 1988 before withdrawing and becoming a behind-the-scenes force in the Republican Party. Robertson masterminded a variety of conservative strategies and founded the Christian Coalition, which under the leadership of Ralph Reed claimed a membership of 250,000 workers in 325 local chapters in forty-two states by the end of the decade. The Christian Coalition trained thousands of conservative Christians in techniques of political activism, including how to become delegates in Republican conventions and how to run for local and state office. In many communities and in some states the Religious Right came to dominate the Republican Party. By the 1990s, Republican candidates usually received around three-fourths of the evangelical Christian vote. Conservative politicians in the eighties and nineties, beginning with Ronald Reagan, recognized the political potential of a motivated evangelical community, and strategists searched for issues that would politically invigorate the resentment among religious Americans who felt they were under assault from secular elites.

❧ The Reagan Administration

The new president surprised some of his supporters by naming James A. Baker III as White House chief of staff. A friend of Vice President George Bush, Baker was a pragmatic conservative who advised Reagan to focus on two priorities — a major tax cut to get the nation out of the economic doldrums and massive increases in defense expenditures. Social conservatives wanted immediate action on such burning issues as abortion and school prayer, but Reagan and his advisers understood how deeply those questions divided the country, and even the Republican Party, and so he delayed confronting them.

On the other hand, Reagan sent signals from the start that the tone in Washington had changed. Most symbolic was his handling of a strike by the Professional Air Traffic Controllers Association (PATCO), a group of federal employees. After months of negotiation with the Federal Aviation Administration, almost 13,000 controllers went on strike, threatening to seriously disrupt commercial air traffic throughout the country. While the union insisted that its key concerns were reducing job stress and enhancing safety, its demands for $10,000 across-the-board raises and a 32-hour workweek created little public sympathy. The new president was outraged by the strike and he gave the controllers 48 hours to return to work, threatening to fire those who did not comply. About 30 percent did return to work, and military controllers were assigned to airports around the country to ensure that commercial traffic continued with little disruption. As promised, Reagan fired the 11,350 union workers who refused to capitulate and declared a lifetime ban on rehiring the strikers.

Supply Side Economics

At the beginning of the 1980s the American economy was in trouble, and dire predictions about the future abounded. America, many experts warned, was doomed to decline while state-directed and "cooperatively managed" new economies like Japan's surged. The federal budget deficit was escalating rapidly; private debt and bank failures were rising as well. The unemployment rate in the United States was more than 7 percent in 1980, one of the highest among industrialized nations, and many economists predicted that the "natural rate of unemployment" in future years would be in the 5 to 6 percent range. The new administration saw the nation's economic woes as the chief problem confronting it.

Reagan and his conservative budget director, David Stockman, were influenced by the writings of an economist named Arthur Laffer. Laffer and other writers associated with the *Wall Street Journal* made much of the fact that taxes set too high or too low would either strangle the economy or bankrupt the federal government, and that the task of the latter was to find the ideal tax rate. In the late 1970s two fiscally conservative

Republicans, Representative Jack Kemp of New York and Senator William Roth of Delaware, insisted that a 30-percent cut in personal and business taxes would achieve that ideal balance. They dubbed their theory "supply side economics" in opposition to the "demand side economics" of John Maynard Keynes, which called for government spending to stimulate consumer demand and thus create jobs in the private sector. Supply side economic theory predicted that business and industry would plow the capital that previously went to taxes back into their enterprises. Expanding industry and commerce would create new jobs and increase the tax base. Thus, as tax rates went down, government revenues would go up. The Kemp-Roth plan had languished in Congress during the Carter years, but Reagan embraced it with enthusiasm.

In his first State of the Union address in January 1981, Reagan unveiled his economic program. He called for a 30-percent reduction in personal and corporate taxes (reduced in Congress to 25 percent) over a three-year period. The maximum tax bracket would be reduced from 70 percent to 50 percent, and capital gains, estate, and inheritance taxes would be cut. The resulting budget shortfall would be made up by cuts in funding for government departments and regulatory agencies, and by reductions in social services and welfare programs. Reagan's economic plan was denounced, even by some within his party, as "voodoo economics" and a "riverboat gamble," but it was resoundingly embraced by the public. Overwhelmingly approved by Congress, a tax cut bill provided for nearly $280 million in tax reductions.

But public opinion also resolutely opposed the deep cuts in programs benefiting the middle class that such curtailment required. So, while Reagan delivered on his promise to reduce taxes, he failed to rein in federal spending. Indeed, Reagan and his successor, George Bush, outdistanced all their predecessors in spending tax dollars. As annual deficits rose sharply each year, the national debt skyrocketed. The percentage of federal income required to service the national debt rose from 12.7 percent in 1980 to 22 percent in 1995. Many economists in the 1980s warned that the nation was irresponsibly mortgaging its future and that a "day of reckoning" lay ahead.

Economic Resurgence

Pessimism abounded when Reagan took the oath of office, but the new president insisted that if the nation would only be patient, prosperity would return by 1984. He was right; beginning in 1983 the nation entered a period of economic growth and expansion that lasted until the end of the century, broken only by a recession in 1990-1991 (which contributed to the electoral defeat of George Bush). Like all politicians, Reagan was only too happy to take the credit.

Yet the reasons for the economic resurgence were complex. The tight-money policies of Federal Reserve Board chairman Paul Volker, a Carter appointee, began to pay off, lowering the inflation rate from 14 percent in 1980 to 3.5 percent in 1984 as interest rates fell by nearly 50 percent. Meanwhile, changes in international politics and the discovery of new petroleum sources brought the price of oil down dramatically, stimulating business activity. In 1983-84 the gross national product increased at a remarkable 4.3-percent clip, the economy expanded 6.8 percent — its best showing since 1951 — and real income increased by 2.8 percent. Supply-siders claimed that they had brought back prosperity, and the massive tax cut undoubtedly did stimulate the economy. But government expenditures in the defense-aerospace industries, which triggered rapid economic growth in the Southwest and New England and on the West Coast, served as a Keynesian-style stimulus and likewise contributed mightily to the recovery.

ঙ৹ Expanding the Military

Ronald Reagan was all in favor of fiscal discipline — except when it came to the military. Reagan and his hawkish secretary of defense, Casper Weinberger, insisted that the U.S.S.R. had gained an advantage in nuclear and conventional forces during the Carter years, and they resisted the efforts of budgetary conservatives to curb defense spending, telling Budget Director Stockman and his aides, "Defense is not a budget item." During the first five years of the Reagan presidency the Department of Defense budget rose at a rate of almost 10 percent annually, reaching nearly $1.5 trillion, the largest peacetime military spending in American history. Defenders of the Reagan administration would later claim that its huge defense budgets were part of a carefully calculated strategy designed to drive the Soviet Union into bankruptcy. But it is not certain that Reagan and his advisers had such a strategy in mind; they were more likely concerned with simply reversing what they viewed as the Carter administration's neglect of military readiness.

Whatever its motives, the Reagan administration greatly expanded the nation's arsenal of both conventional arms and new high-tech weapons. In the spring of 1983 Reagan unveiled an ambitious new defense plan that threatened the balance of power between the superpowers and virtually ensured an escalation of the arms race. In order to deal with the Soviet Union's alleged "margin of superiority," Reagan proposed the Strategic Defense Initiative (SDI) to provide a defensive umbrella against attack. The plan was the brainchild of Edward Teller, the father of the American hydrogen bomb, who convinced Reagan of its feasibility. Ridiculed by its critics as "Star Wars," after the popular movie, the proposed defense system would consist of lasers and particle beams projected from ground stations and orbiting satellites. These "death rays" would be designed to destroy incoming enemy missiles before they reentered the earth's atmosphere. Domestic critics of the plan claimed that SDI was both technologically impractical and outrageously expensive. Yuri Andropov, who had become leader of the Soviet Union following Leonid Brezhnev's death in November 1982, denounced SDI as a deliberate attempt by the United States to undermine the concept of mutually assured destruction ("MAD"), the uncomfortable but effective basis for global peace since the late 1950s.

ঙ৹ Cutting Government

In his inaugural address Ronald Reagan bluntly declared that "government is not the solution to our problem — government *is* the problem." The budgets for the Occupational Safety and Health Administration (OSHA), the Securities and Exchange Commission (SEC), and the Environmental Protection Agency (EPA) were slashed. While the cuts were usually presented as budgetary savings, they were also intended to reduce what conservatives regarded as the intrusive expansion of federal regulation. Many of Reagan's appointees set out to curb or redirect the federal agencies they headed. Perhaps the most controversial of the administration's new team was Interior Secretary James G. Watt, who infuriated environmentalists by blocking the creation of preserves, opening federal lands for development by coal and timber companies, and leasing a million acres of offshore land to oil companies.

Furthermore, the administration's cuts often targeted such progressive programs for minorities as affirmative action. The staff of the Equal Employment Opportunity Commission was sharply reduced. Feminists, minority organizations, and advocates for the disadvantaged protested vociferously. Reagan's appointment in 1981 of the first woman justice of the Supreme Court, Sandra Day O'Connor, a judicial conservative, did little to placate angry feminists, and Reagan's support from women lagged far behind his popularity with men. Reagan's forthright rejection of the demands of black and feminist activists further strengthened African American solidarity behind the Democratic Party and signaled a growing "gender gap" in the voting patterns of men and women.

REHEATING THE COLD WAR

Ronald Reagan's view of Soviet Communism harked back to the attitudes of the early 1950s. At his first press conference, the president declared that the Soviets were "prepared to commit any crime, to lie, to cheat" in order to facilitate the spread of Marxism. While Reagan's grasp of facts was sometimes so nebulous that it exasperated even his closest advisers, he was crystal clear about the moral challenge presented by the Soviet Union. It was, he believed, an "evil empire," representative of the negative forces abroad in the world: atheism, state socialism, and totalitarianism. Such talk, while it would have been perfectly acceptable from a liberal in the 1950s and early 1960s, further horrified Reagan's liberal opponents in the 1980s.

Ronald Reagan's rhetoric applied increased pressure on the U.S.S.R. at a time when discernible cracks had appeared in the Soviet empire. In October 1978, Karol Wojtyla, Bishop of Kraków, was named Pope John Paul II; a visit by the staunchly anti-Communist leader to his homeland in 1979 set off an unexpected chain of events. In 1980, strikes in the Lenin Shipyards in Gdansk gained international fame for Lech Walesa and the Solidarity Union he led, and encouraged the formation of some forty other independent unions in Poland. Other less successful dissident movements arose in Czechoslovakia and East Germany. Meanwhile, with considerable American support, Islamic forces in Afghanistan were keeping the Soviet army bogged down in a Vietnam-like quagmire. It became increasingly clear that the Soviet empire and even Marxism-Leninism were vulnerable.

Like his predecessors, the president was particularly concerned about the spread of Communism in the Western Hemisphere. Convinced that Castroism was making inroads in Central America, the Reagan administration labored to overthrow the Sandinista regime in Nicaragua and to crush a leftist-led insurrection in El Salvador. Not content to grapple with Communist insurgencies, Reagan and his advisers sought to undermine and demoralize the Soviet regime by tipping the strategic military balance that had prevailed since the fifties.

❧ Terrorism

In the closing decades of the twentieth century, terrorism — acts of violence committed by groups wanting to intimidate populations or governments into granting their demands — was becoming one of the more troubling aspects of modern life. While terrorists were active in many places in the world, the United States found itself increasingly the target of various Islamic groups who objected to American support for Israel. In a highly publicized act in 1985, a TWA jetliner was hijacked in Athens by two Shiite Muslim terrorists, who took the plane to Beirut and forced the Israeli government to release some 750 Islamic radicals in return for freeing 19 hostages. Increasingly, the ire of the American people and the Reagan administration fell upon Libya and its flamboyant ruler, Colonel Muammar Qaddafi, who championed the cause of the Palestinians and sheltered a number of radical organizations and Islamic revolutionaries.

In April of 1987 a bomb went off in a West Berlin discothèque, killing an American serviceman and a Turkish woman and injuring 230. After receiving intelligence reports that identified Qaddafi as sponsoring terrorist acts against Americans, Reagan denounced the Libyan leader as the "mad dog of the Middle East." Later that month thirteen F-111s, operating out of bases in Great Britain, staged a surprise attack on Tripoli. During the twelve-minute assault the U.S. fighters destroyed the Libyan strongman's living quarters and his command and communications center. They also killed a number of civilians, including one of Qaddafi's children. Whether intimidated by the attack or chastened by subsequent economic and diplomatic pressure exerted by the nations of Western Europe, the Libyan firebrand gradually became more restrained.

America placed itself even more squarely in the line of terrorist fire when Reagan sent American forces into Lebanon. By 1982, this formerly stable and prosperous country, which had a population balanced between Muslims and Christians, teetered on the brink of chaos. The country had been flooded by thousands of Palestinians who established bases in the south, and in the early eighties sectarian militia fought pitched battles for control of Beirut. The Syrian army occupied the northern part of the country, and PLO fighters contested with various Christian factions for control of the south. Seeking to restore order and stop raids into Israel, the United States arranged for a cease-fire and subsequently contributed 800 troops to a peacekeeping force. Caught in a crossfire between Christian and Muslim militias, the Americans were in an impossible position. On October 23, 1983, a suicide bomber drove an explosives-laden vehicle through a checkpoint and into a Marine barrack, killing 283 sleeping troops. By early the next year Reagan had withdrawn the last remaining soldier from Lebanon. It became increasingly clear that American efforts to impose order in the Middle East were likely to make Americans targets of extremists abroad — and, as it turned out, at home as well.

❧ An Easy Victory: Grenada

The bad news in Lebanon was somewhat allayed by a swift, popular military operation on the tiny Caribbean island of Grenada in 1983. Control of the island had fallen into the hands of a militant leftist military council, which had signed a pact with Communist countries and imported Cuban laborers to build an airfield. Responding to appeals from neighboring islands and to a call to protect American students attending a medical school in Grenada, Reagan dispatched Marines and Rangers to the island. In a quick and effective strike, the American forces deposed the government and evacuated the American students. While the United Nations condemned the action, many Grenadians and their neighbors in the Caribbean applauded it, and it was popular with the American public.

❧ A Protracted Mess: Iran, Nicaragua, and Iran-Contra

In 1980, a bloody life-and-death struggle between Iran and Iraq erupted. Iraq, ruled by the secular military strongman Saddam Hussein, and Iran, in the grip of an Islamic revolution led by the Ayatollah Khomeini and fundamentalist mullahs, were age-old rivals. This new chapter in their ongoing struggle was the product of an intense competition for regional leadership and control of petroleum resources, refining facilities, and strategic ports. The U.S. State Department feared both regimes and believed that it would be in the best interest of regional stability if neither side won a decisive victory. From 1981 through 1986 the Reagan administration secretly funneled aid to Iran, but in 1987 it tilted toward Iraq. The Iraq-Iran war, coupled with a bloody conflict in Central America, produced one of the more bizarre incidents in contemporary diplomatic history: the Iran-Contra affair.

By 1985 the Contras, an army of Nicaraguan exiles trained by the CIA who hoped to overthrow the Marxist Sandinista regime in their country, numbered somewhere between ten and twenty thousand. This counterrevolutionary force depended almost entirely upon American aid. Concerned over charges of U.S. intervention into Nicaraguan internal affairs and stories of atrocities committed by the Contras, in 1982 Congress limited U.S. aid to anti-Communist guerrillas and stipulated that no funds be used to overthrow the Sandinistas. Two years later the House and Senate tightened the restrictions, barring the CIA or "any other agency or entity involved in intelligence activities" from aiding the Contras. Congressional opposition only strengthened the White House's determination to aid what Reagan called the "freedom fighters" in Nicaragua. With presidential approval, a team that included CIA chief William Casey, National Security Council (NSC) adviser Robert McFarlane, and NSC aide Colonel Oliver North began raising money from anti-Communist governments abroad and from wealthy conservatives at home to help the Contras.

Meanwhile, Shiite Muslim terrorists bankrolled by the Iranian government had taken seven Americans hostage in Beirut. Reagan was deeply moved by the plight of the captives, and following repeated appeals by the families of the victims directed his subordinates to come up with a plan to secure their release. In the fall of 1985, despite American attacks on Libya and the White House's repeated denunciations of international terrorism, the United States began selling large numbers of antitank missiles to Iran for use in its war with Iraq in hopes of winning the hostages' freedom. Oliver North devised a scheme to transfer the proceeds from these weapons sales to aid the Contras in Nicaragua, believing that he could thereby circumvent congressional restrictions.

In 1986, Congress opened highly publicized hearings on the transfer. After a long and complicated investigation, in March 1988 Special Prosecutor Lawrence Walsh indicted North and several others for their participation in the Iran-Contra scheme. Eventually, all of those charged were convicted, although the Supreme

Court subsequently reversed several of the convictions. Even so, the Iran-Contra investigations failed to implicate Reagan in any wrongdoing, and in many ways the telegenic North dominated the proceedings. Taking the offensive, he declared that his and President Reagan's duty was to protect the national security, a responsibility that transcended congressional mandates. Nonetheless, the affair seemed to confirm the image of Reagan as a chief executive who was often ill-informed and naive.

❧ Reagan, Gorbachev, and Perestroika

Whatever the embarrassments suffered by the administration as a result of the Iran-Contra affair, Reagan's stature was enhanced by the changes that were occurring in the Soviet Union. Soviet-American relations took an abrupt turn for the better in the second half of the decade when new Kremlin leadership opened a door that ultimately led to the abandonment of Communism itself. In March 1985 Mikhail Gorbachev became general secretary of the Communist Party of the Soviet Union. Gorbachev represented a new generation of educated and less ideological Soviet leaders who had shed the paranoia of Stalin's generation. An urbane man who had studied philosophy, law, and agricultural economics, Gorbachev understood that his country had fallen behind the capitalist world and even some developing countries in technological innovation and economic output. The only way to reverse his country's

dramatic decline and to revitalize its Marxist-Leninist ideology, Gorbachev reasoned, was through policies of *perestroika* (social and economic "restructuring") and *glasnost* ("openness" to the international community). Seeking an opening to the West, Gorbachev unilaterally stopped his country's nuclear testing program, halted the deployment of intermediate range missiles in Eastern Europe, and agreed to on-site inspections to enforce future arms control agreements.

Throughout his first five years in office Reagan steadfastly refused to meet face to face with a Soviet chief of state, but sensing that Gorbachev would bring a new attitude to Soviet-American relations, the president agreed to a summit with him in Geneva in November 1985. The meeting appeared to be unproductive. But a year later, with very little prior publicity, Reagan and Gorbachev met again in Reykjavik, Iceland. Gorbachev took the initiative, proposing 50-percent cuts in ICBMs as a prelude to their eventual elimination. Not to be outdone, Reagan astonished his advisers by suggesting scrapping all American, and possibly all British and French, nuclear weapons within ten years in return for Soviet acquiescence in the construction and deployment of the SDI. Gorbachev, suspecting that the Americans were trying to establish clear nuclear superiority, rejected Reagan's proposal, and the Reykjavik meeting broke up. Nevertheless, the two leaders departed on a friendly note. The ideas proposed by both had been breathtaking departures, and it appeared that real progress in disarmament lay ahead.

Ollie North for President   Not all Americans were appalled to learn about White House operative Lieutenant Colonel Oliver North's shady machinations in the Iran-Contra scandal. In the summer of 1987 a "North For President" boomlet began. Unidentified persons paid for this billboard near a San Diego naval installation.

The two leaders met again in Washington in 1987 and this time signed the first arms reduction pact since SALT II. Gorbachev had decided that SDI was probably both scientifically and politically infeasible, and he dropped his demand that Washington abandon the project. That cleared the way for the two leaders to sign the Intermediate-Range Nuclear Forces (INF) Treaty, which called for eliminating all intermediate range missiles in Europe and provided for on-site inspection. The U.S.S.R. and the United States still possessed 30,000 nuclear warheads aimed at each other, but the INF Treaty was an important step toward arms control.

Changes in Soviet attitudes now became increasingly dramatic. The Chernobyl nuclear plant meltdown in the Ukraine in 1987 shook the Soviet public's confidence in the regime's credibility and accelerated the dictatorship's internal disintegration. In 1988 Soviet troops were pulled out of Afghanistan, and Moscow ceased to support civil wars in Africa and Southeast Asia. Gorbachev, who during his trip to America had hosted a party for celebrities such as Paul Newman and Henry Kissinger, actively courted American public opinion, and in fact polls showed him to be one of America's favorite world leaders. In June, as he neared leaving office, Ronald Reagan traveled to the heart of the "evil empire." In Moscow, standing in front of Lenin's Tomb in Red Square, the old Cold Warrior embraced his friend Mikhail. "They've changed," the president announced to reporters. Indeed, by the time Ronald Reagan left the White House the world had changed dramatically, and Americans hoped that the future might bring further advances in the relations between the two superpowers.

FOUR MORE YEARS

Despite rising deficits and a bevy of strident critics, Reagan was a formidable candidate for reelection in 1984. Poised, confident, and an extraordinarily effective communicator on television, Reagan was also an astute politician. His self-effacing humor endeared him to even the most cynical of his congressional opponents, and he manifested a willingness to compromise that enabled him to work with the Democratic-dominated Congress. The president's genuine humanity and personal valor were highlighted in the spring of 1981 when a deranged young gunman made an attempt on his life. Gravely wounded, Reagan remained conscious throughout the ordeal, joked in the emergency room ("Honey, I forgot to duck," he told his wife), and won the respect of many Americans for his pluck. His personal popularity and his ability to inspire earned him the title of "The Great Communicator" from the press.

Once the economy revived, Ronald Reagan was probably unbeatable in 1984, but no shortage of Democratic candidates emerged to challenge him. Senator Gary Hart of Colorado entered the race claiming to be the representative of a "new generation" and the advocate of "new thinking," and indeed he represented the more centrist stance that would later be identified with Bill Clinton. The man who came closest to duplicating Reagan's all-American image was Senator John Glenn of Ohio, the former astronaut known for his fiscal conservatism and anti-Communism, but he proved to be politically clumsy. The choice of African Americans and of many liberal Democrats was the Rev. Jesse Jackson, a protégé of Martin Luther King, Jr., who tried to con-

---

❈ IN THEIR OWN WORDS

From Reagan's "Remarks at the Brandenburg Gate," West Berlin, Germany
This speech was delivered to the people of West Berlin, yet it was also audible on the east side of the Berlin Wall.

And now the Soviets themselves may, in a limited way, be coming to understand the importance of freedom. We hear much from Moscow about a new policy of reform and openness. Some political prisoners have been released. Certain foreign news broadcasts are no longer being jammed. Some economic enterprises have been permitted to operate with greater freedom from state control.

Are these the beginnings of profound changes in the Soviet state? Or are they token gestures, intended to raise false hopes in the West, or to strengthen the Soviet system without changing it? We welcome change and openness; for we believe that freedom and security go together, that the advance of human liberty can only strengthen the cause of world peace. There is one sign the Soviets can make that would be unmistakable, that would advance dramatically the cause of freedom and peace.

General Secretary Gorbachev, if you seek peace, if you seek prosperity for the Soviet Union and Eastern Europe, if you seek liberalization: Come here to this gate! Mr. Gorbachev, open this gate! Mr. Gorbachev, tear down this wall!

June 12, 1987

Reagan and Gorbachev President Reagan and Soviet General Secretary Gorbachev at the first summit in Geneva, Switzerland. These two most powerful men in the world ultimately became warm friends and key actors in the ending of the Cold War.

struct a multiracial political bloc called the Rainbow Coalition. The front-runner, however, was former vice president Walter Mondale, a New Deal–Great Society Democrat who appealed to traditional party supporters. The staunchly liberal Mondale was nominated on the first ballot and chose as his running mate New York Congresswoman Geraldine A. Ferraro. Although Ferraro was not widely known, she was bright, articulate, and an ardent feminist, and Democrats hoped that her presence as the first woman candidate on a major party ticket would exploit the "gender gap."

Democrats tried to highlight the obvious problems of the Reagan administration — the soaring budget deficit, a growing gap between the rich and poor in American society, and tension between the United States and the Soviet Union — but to no avail. Reagan's speeches appealed to the rising tide of American pride and patriotism: "I think there's a new feeling of patriotism in our land, a recognition that by any standard America is a decent and generous place, a force for good in the world." The verdict in 1984 was overwhelming. Dealing a crushing defeat to the Democrats, Reagan captured forty-nine states and 525 electoral votes. The popular vote showed 54.5 million (59 percent) for Reagan and 37.6 million (41 percent) for Mondale.

❧ *The Deficit Spiral*

Basking in his massive election victory, Reagan could no longer ignore the ever-deepening federal budget deficit. Tax cuts coupled with a 41 percent real increase in defense spending sent the deficit soaring from $90 billion in 1982 to $283 billion in 1986, far surpassing any

previous peacetime deficits. To finance the deficit, the federal government borrowed huge sums at home and abroad. These economic trends made it increasingly difficult for American firms to compete in foreign markets, and the American trade deficit increased from $36 billion in 1980 to $170 billion in 1987. To many Americans it seemed that the party of fiscal conservatism had mortgaged the nation's future.

❧ *Deregulation and the Downsizing of American Business*

The positive aspects of the restructuring of American business were not always clear in the 1980s; furthermore, American entrepreneurs continued to give their critics plenty to criticize. Among the villains were financial speculators who manipulated scores of takeovers, mergers, and "buyouts." While some of these deals were responsible efforts to restructure and stimulate companies, others were irresponsible get-rich quick schemes that ended in disastrous losses for investors. Financier Ivan Boesky, the co-inventor of "junk bonds" who had made millions on Wall Street buying and selling large corporations, told the graduating class at Berkeley in 1986 that "greed is healthy." A rash of mergers drove stock prices ever upward and brought about an evitable market crash in 1987. In one week in October, the Dow Jones lost 13 percent of its value. At the end of the 1980s more than 60 percent of people polled claimed to have little or no trust that Wall Street bankers and brokers would act in the best interest of the economy. Critics of the pro-business economic assumptions of the Republican era labeled the free-wheeling tactics of Wall Street "the culture of greed."

Further contributing to the nation's economic woes was the virtual collapse of the savings and loan industry. Near the end of the Carter administration, Congress increased the federal insurance level on savings and loan deposits to $100,000. Then, in 1982, President Reagan signed the Garn–St. Germain Act, which virtually deregulated the thrifts. Free to speculate with depositors' monies without risk to themselves, thrift operators poured billions into undeveloped land, commercial property, shopping centers, and other high-risk ventures. In the mid-1980s, as the economy slowed, a series of savings and loan banks declared bankruptcy and the federal government ultimately was forced to bail out the industry at a cost of around $200 billion to repay depositors for their losses and another $200 to

$300 billion to finance the government bonds required to fund the bailout.

Many judged that a more fundamental flaw in the American economy in the 1980s was the declining health of American industry and its seeming inability to compete with foreign manufacturers. The big three American automakers — Ford, Chrysler, and General Motors — continued to lose market share to European, Japanese, and Korean imports well into the 1990s. In 1985, 76 percent of Americans still bought cars produced in America, but by 1997 that percentage had fallen below 50 percent for the first time. At the same time, American manufacturers found it increasingly attractive to build factories in countries where wage scales were lower, promoting "capital flight" that added to the trade deficit.

Despite these negative observations, in hindsight, many economists argue that the 1980s was not so much a decade of "deindustrialization" as of "reindustrialization" and renewed industrial competitiveness. As American companies reorganized to become more competitive, corporate profits moved sharply downward in the 1980s and early 1990s. Expressed as a percentage of national income, profits fell from nearly 15 percent in 1955 to around 7 percent in 1989. But at the beginning of the 1990s, corporate profits began rising again, reflecting the success of cost-cutting measures, rising productivity, and the globalization of the U.S. economy.

American businesses in the 1980s and early 1990s embarked on a rigorous downsizing that resulted in the firing of many skilled and loyal workers. This painful era created a jargon all its own: those fired were said to have been "de-hired," "disemployed," "downsized," "surplussed," or "vocationally relocated." Downsizing cut across the board. In 1996, the *New York Times* cataloged the job attrition that had taken place in some of the biggest businesses: AT&T eliminated 123,000 jobs (30 percent of its workforce); IBM 122,000 jobs (35 percent); General Motors, 99,400 (29 percent); Boeing, 61,000 (37 percent); Sears, Roebuck, 50,000 (15 percent). Between 1985 and 1995, Chase Manhattan Bank reduced its workforce by 28 percent (more than 10,000 jobs) while increasing its assets by 38 percent. These draconian measures created much anxiety; some critics charged that the American workforce would be so demoralized that it would never feel loyalty to its employers. On the other hand, business leaders insisted that belt-tightening was necessary if American companies were to regain their edge in the world market.

❧ Employment Patterns and Labor Organization

The downsizing of the 1980s and early 1990s did not result in wholesale unemployment, as past business recessions had, but it did cause significant shifts in the types of jobs that were available. In the first half of the 1980s layoffs were most severe among factory, mine, and construction workers, creating serious problems in the "Rust Belt" region of the Midwest and the "Oil Patch" states of the Southwest. Workers who lost their industrial jobs in the early 1980s accepted new jobs at considerably lower wages. But in the layoffs of the early 1990s, a majority of the job losses were among older, better-educated employees, most of whom were white-collar workers. During the fiercely competitive downsizing of American businesses, many workers made concessions to hold their jobs: longer hours, reduced benefits and wages, and greater compliance with employer demands. While about 20 percent of American workers reported that they had actually lost a job between 1980 and 1995, nearly three-fourths of all Americans had been affected by a layoff in some way.

The changing nature of the American labor force in the 1980s and 1990s accelerated the erosion of labor unions' significance and power. Union membership fell from 35 percent of the workforce in 1955 to 15.5 percent in 1995. For the first time since the 1930s, the raw numbers of union members began to drop in the 1980s. While the nation's workforce grew by around 15 percent during that decade, union membership actually fell by more than 1 million. The incidence of strikes declined rapidly in the 1980s, reaching a fifty-year low of 385 in 1995, only 32 of which involved more than a thousand workers.

The waning influence of labor unions seems odd when businesses were laying off employees and real wages were shrinking. But many factors worked to undermine union strength — an increase in the number of educated, high-tech employees who resisted unionization, the ability of many high-tech companies to continue to operate during a strike, a surge in labor-management teamwork, and workers' knowledge that they could easily be replaced. By the 1990s, unionized labor dominated only the older industrial sector of the economy. Still, union workers were older and better paid than the national average, in 1995 earning on an average nearly one-third more than non-union workers.

THE NEW WORLD ORDER, ECONOMIC DRIFT, AND GRIDLOCK: THE BUSH YEARS

The stunning collapse of the Soviet Union in the early 1990s presented the United States with extraordinary opportunities to expand its influence. The United States stood back as the Soviet Union and Warsaw Pact disintegrated, seeking to encourage democracy and free market economies in the former Communist countries of Eastern Europe without threatening their security or sense of national sovereignty. Toward China, both President Reagan and his successor, George H. W. Bush, followed a policy of watchful waiting. Generally speaking, the United States avoided direct involvement in regional conflicts in geographically remote areas or where American interests seemed little threatened, seeking rather to work through international organizations and nations more proximate. Closer to home, however — for example, in Panama and Haiti — as well as in conflicts in which American interests were directly threatened, as in the Persian Gulf, the United States acted decisively.

In domestic affairs, George Bush and his advisers wanted to continue the policies of the Reagan era, though the new president was clearly more moderate than his predecessor. The new administration wished to maintain a social safety net while preventing the Democratic Congress from enacting new entitlement programs or expanding existing ones. Unlike Reagan, the new president worried about the deficit and, in a move that deeply offended conservatives in his party, supported a substantial tax increase. Nonetheless, declining revenues caused by recession, combined with increased spending for the military and the savings and loan bailout, caused an increase rather than decrease of federal red ink. On a variety of social issues George Bush sent out mixed signals, and his administration wound up offending many on both sides of the most divisive issues of the day.

❧ The Election of 1988

With Ronald Reagan ineligible for a third term, Democrats looked to 1988 with cautious hope. When the Republicans nominated Vice President Bush, a man long suspect among GOP hardcore conservatives, hope became anticipation. The early front-runner for the Democratic nomination was Senator Gary Hart of Colorado, an attractive, self-effacing favorite of the media,

but he had to withdraw when pictures were published showing Hart with a bikini-clad model on his lap, confirming oft-denied stories of womanizing. The Hart affair signaled the increasing intrusiveness of the media into the private lives of political leaders. Several weeks later Delaware Senator Joseph Biden withdrew from the Democratic primaries when reporters revealed that he had plagiarized part of a speech from a British politician.

That left as the leading Democratic contender Michael Dukakis, the governor of Massachusetts, who promised to bring to the national scene the expertise that he claimed had turned his home state's economy around. Jesse Jackson once again campaigned for the nomination, promising a war on poverty and racial discrimination, but Dukakis soundly defeated Jackson in the primaries and easily won the nomination. In his acceptance speech, Dukakis emphasized his immigrant roots and his ability to govern a country that was becoming more self-consciously diverse. Dukakis shunned Jesse Jackson for the vice-presidential nomination, selecting instead conservative Senator Lloyd Bentsen of Texas.

George Bush, who fended off a challenge from Senator Robert Dole of Kansas to capture the GOP nomination, selected the relatively unknown Senator Dan Quayle of Indiana to be his running mate. Lightly regarded by many, Quayle made frequent gaffes during the campaign and was a favorite target for ridicule.

Dukakis and the Democrats focused on economic issues, blaming "discredited Bush-Reagan policies" for the deficit. The Republican campaign seized on the general sense of social unease in the nation and attacked "liberals" as the source of much of the evil. The label "liberal" became a major liability in the campaign, but Dukakis, a member of the American Civil Liberties Union, refused to renounce his liberal past. Picturing Dukakis as soft on the punishment of criminals because as governor he had signed a weekend furlough bill for convicted criminals, Republicans ran a television commercial featuring Willy Horton, a Massachusetts inmate convicted of rape and assault who, while free on the furlough program, committed another act of rape.

Hardly a dynamic personality, George Bush made a surprisingly forceful acceptance speech at the Republican convention and seemed almost charismatic compared to the wooden Dukakis during the campaign. Building on the Reagan legacy, George Bush won 53 percent of the popular vote and carried forty states.

❧ *George Herbert Walker Bush*

The son of an investment banker and U.S. senator, George Bush grew up in affluence in Connecticut, attending a top prep school and enrolling at Yale. During World War II, he left Yale, joined the navy, and became the youngest fighter pilot in the Pacific theater. He served with valor and was shot down by enemy fire. After World War II, Bush moved to Texas, where he made a fortune in the oil business. Before becoming vice president, Bush had served two terms in Congress as a representative of the Houston district. He also ran unsuccessfully for the Senate and, in 1980, for the Republican nomination for president. Outside of elective office, Bush held a number of responsible positions — chairman of the Republican National Committee, ambassador to China, and head of the CIA — before become vice president in 1980.

George Bush was popular during his first year and a half in office. Much of that had to do with the widespread sense of relief at the winding down of the Cold War, but in addition, compared to Ronald Reagan, Bush seemed less rigid and more compassionate, willing to negotiate with the Democratic Congress on basic social issues. In his inaugural address he appealed for national unity and bipartisan cooperation, promising "to make kinder the face of the nation and gentler the face of the world." Reagan had replaced the picture of Harry Truman hanging behind his desk in the White House with a portrait of Calvin Coolidge. Bush in turn substituted the likeness of Theodore Roosevelt. While President Bush had no sweeping domestic agenda comparable to Roosevelt's progressivism, he did pursue an aggressive foreign policy that was reminiscent of TR's.

❧ *Holding the Line on the Home Front*

When the first Bush presidency began, American public confidence in politicians was extremely low. Much of the skepticism was aimed at Congress, where scandals surrounding savings and loan failures had implicated a number of Senators. In 1989 the powerful Democratic Speaker of the House, James Wright of Texas, resigned amidst charges that he had sought special favors for a Texas savings and loan that had made improper loans in the 1980s and that he had exerted influence on behalf of a wealthy businessman from whom he had accepted gifts.

In his inaugural address Bush noted the corrosive effect the deficit was having on the economy and promised to cut the budget. Unfortunately, the savings and loan crisis undermined any plans he had for budget reductions. By 1989 hundreds of S&Ls had failed, and thousands of depositors were clamoring for their money. Congress expanded the role of the FDIC, which previously had covered only banks, so that it could reorganize and strengthen surviving savings and loans. Experts guessed that over a period of thirty years, the cost of the bailout of the failing financial institutions would be between $300 billion and $500 billion.

George Bush's most concrete pledge during his campaign for the presidency had been his "read my lips" promise not to raise taxes. But economic reality made the promise seem more and more untenable. By the end of the Reagan presidency the national debt had risen to $2.6 trillion, and the projected budget deficit for 1991 was $260 billion. Reluctantly, on June 26, 1990, Bush announced that "both the size of the deficit . . . and the need for a package that can be enacted" required "tax revenue increases." In October Congress passed and President Bush signed a bill that raised rates on the top 2 percent of earners by eliminating certain deductions, increased taxes on alcohol, gasoline, and expensive consumer goods, and upped Medicare payroll taxes for workers. The budget office predicted savings of $40 billion for fiscal 1991 and $490 billion over a period of five years. Unfortunately for Bush, a sharp downturn in the economy sent tax collections tumbling, and the deficit for 1991 was $300 billion, the largest in history.

In another important and politically risky economic move, President Bush pushed to expand international markets and encourage "free trade." His negotiations to ease the international flow of goods, services, and investments among the United States, Mexico, and Canada by eliminating tariffs and other barriers was finally approved in 1993 when his successor, Bill Clinton, successfully guided the North American Free Trade Agreement (NAFTA) through Congress. But the landmark treaty was largely the work of the Bush administration, and it was George Bush who would bear the brunt of criticism from protectionists during the presidential campaign of 1992.

He tried equally bipartisan approaches on other issues. Bush, who had promised to be the "environment president," was confronted with one environmental disaster after another. The most visible and controversial involved the *Exxon Valdez*, a huge oil tanker that ran aground in Alaska's picturesque Prince William Sound, spilling millions of gallons of crude and spoiling a hundred miles of coastline that included fisheries and animal habitats. The Coast Guard investigated and found that the captain of the tanker had been operating under the influence of alcohol. Exxon was subsequently forced to pay $2 billion to clean up after the spill. The Bush administration called for responsible corporations to clean up toxic waste dumps scattered across the country, but after voters in California and New York defeated tax initiatives to pay for these costly operations, the administration proceeded warily.

By the end of the 1980s the American people were deeply concerned about the nation's ever-growing drug abuse problem. Shortly after his election, Bush named William Bennett, Reagan's conservative education secretary, to be the nation's "drug czar," a cabinet-level position. The Bush-Bennett strategy emphasized law enforcement and interdiction rather than prevention and rehabilitation, illustrating the philosophical gap between conservatives and liberals on this vexing social problem. Indeed, 70 percent of the $7.9 billion earmarked for the war on drugs during the Bush administration went toward the construction of new prisons, additional Drug Enforcement Agency personnel, and new prosecutors.

George H. W. Bush and Dan Quayle   Many eyebrows were raised, and many asked "Who?" when Bush named the little-known Indiana Senator (left) as his running mate in 1988. Although many of the jeers were unfair, Quayle never managed to overcome popular perceptions that he was a political and intellectual lightweight, chosen mainly for his loyalty to Bush and his ties to the Religious Right.

❧ Politics and the Conservative Social Agenda

Ronald Reagan's eight years in the presidency had resulted in the appointment of many conservative justices to the federal judiciary, and conservatives correctly anticipated that the courts would begin to reverse some of the decisions made by the liberal Warren Court in the sixties. In 1989 in *Webster v. Reproductive Services of Missouri* the justices ruled that states could deny access to public facilities to women seeking abortions. Writing for the majority, Chief Justice Rehnquist declared that "nothing in the Constitution requires states to enter or remain in the business of performing abortions." Though conservatives hoped for a wave of laws prohibiting public hospitals and public employees from participating in abortions, that happened only in Utah, Pennsylvania, and Louisiana.

Abortion continued to be a troublesome issue for most politicians, who did not wish to alienate either side, but during these years was especially so for Republicans because of the support the party received from the Religious Right. Moderate Republicans insisted that there was room for both opponents and advocates of abortion rights under the Republican "tent." Bush had come down firmly against abortion during the campaign, but he showed little interest in pressing the issue either as a matter of policy or in his appointments to the Supreme Court.

Social liberals and conservatives watched carefully the impending changes in the makeup of the Supreme Court. Bush's first appointment to the Supreme Court in 1990 was David Souter, a distinguished but little-known New Hampshire judge. Many Democrats had begun using a woman's right to an abortion as a litmus test for confirming justices, but Souter, who had no written record on the issue, skillfully refused to discuss his views because the matter was a subject of pending litigation before the Court. He had no trouble gaining confirmation, but Bush's second nomination to the Supreme Court in mid-1991 proved to be one of the most controversial and divisive in American history.

Oil Spill   Workers clean the oil off a cormorant caught in the *Exxon Valdez* oil spill in Prince William Sound, Alaska.

The Clarence Thomas Confirmation Fight

In mid-1991 the distinguished civil rights lawyer and Supreme Court justice Thurgood Marshall announced his retirement. To replace him Bush selected Clarence Thomas, a Yale Law School graduate who had served in a number of capacities in the federal government before being appointed a judge in the U.S. Court of Appeals for the District of Columbia in 1990. In speeches, articles, and in his judicial decisions, Thomas had consistently expressed conservative views on a variety of topics, including opposition to abortion and affirmative action. The Thomas nomination placed Senators in the awkward position of either swallowing Thomas's clear conservative agenda or publicly opposing an African American nominee to the Supreme Court.

Supreme Court nominations had already become more highly politicized beginning with the failed attempt of Ronald Reagan to nominate conservative Robert Bork to the high court in 1987, but Thomas's confirmation hearings escalated to the sensational when Anita Hill, a University of Oklahoma law professor, testified that Thomas had sexually harassed her when both worked for the Equal Employment Opportunity Commission (EEOC). The televised Judiciary Committee hearings attracted a national audience as Hill quietly but graphically detailed her allegations. Thomas denied all of Hill's charges, picturing her as the pawn of embittered civil rights leaders who despised his break from the victimization agenda of black activists. He charged the white Democratic Senators who questioned him with conducting a symbolic "lynching" of an "uppity" black man. Following a stormy floor debate, the Senate voted to confirm Thomas, 52 to 48.

The Thomas hearings and vote raised the level of political confrontation in the United States. Seething Republican resentment over the treatment of Thomas, as well as the long and extended Democratic investigation of Iran-Contra, would feed the fury of a Republican Congress against President Bill Clinton a few years later. On the other side, Thomas's nomination galvanized the temporarily moribund feminist movement. Anita Hill's ordeal before the Senate Judiciary Committee angered millions of women and rekindled old feminist passions.

A revived feminist movement rallied around the issue of sexual harassment. Republicans and Democrats supported new laws and regulations, particularly on college campuses, that banned unwanted sexual approaches, abusive language, and even "suggestive" sounds and motions. Feminists, gay activists, and civil rights leaders thus placed themselves in uneasy alliance with social conservatives who had long pressed for restriction of the First Amendment's guarantee of freedom of speech. But they argued that sexual harassment, like racial epithets, made life so uncomfortable

Anita Hill   Clarence Thomas's accuser generated bitter partisan arguments across the land when she testified before the Senate Judiciary Committee about her allegations that the conservative African American Supreme Court nominee had sexually harassed her.

for the harassed that the majority must accept some infringement of free speech. More significant in the long run, women's frustrations led to an unprecedented number of female candidates for local, state, and national office in 1992.

✼ *The End of the Cold War*

It was George Bush's good fortune to be president when the Cold War finally came to an end. George Kennan, J. William Fulbright, Walter Lippmann, and other sophisticated Cold Warriors had envisioned a scenario whereby the United States, through alliances and aid, would contain Communism within the Soviet Union's post-1948 sphere of influence until it collapsed under the weight of its own contradictions. They anticipated that collectivization, state control, and a closed society and economy would eventually render the Soviet Union incapable of competing and that a new generation of leaders would transform Lenin's creation into a social democracy. With the rise of Mikhail Gorbachev, glasnost, and perestroika, that vision began to materialize.

Bush and his foreign policy team were well qualified to deal with these momentous events. Like his hero, Theodore Roosevelt, Bush was a pragmatic nationalist, determined to safeguard American interests, economically and strategically defined, short of armed conflict if possible, but through force of arms if necessary. The president and his advisers were keenly aware of the limitations on American power, and they resisted calls for the United States to participate actively in the demise of the Warsaw Pact and the fall of Communism in the Soviet Union.

Shortly after Bush took the oath of office, the first democratic elections since 1917 were held in the Soviet Union. At the same time, encouraged by glasnost and perestroika, anti-Communist, nationalist elements in the Soviet Baltic republics of Estonia, Latvia, and Lithuania began challenging their Communist puppet regimes and demanding the departure of Soviet occupation troops. In Poland, Solidarity, under the leadership of Lech Walesa, pressured the Communist regime into holding free elections that swept away the ruling dictatorship. In July Gorbachev told a meeting of Warsaw Pact leaders that his country would respect the national sovereignty of all nations; in effect, he proclaimed that the Kremlin no longer cared how its neighbors conducted their internal affairs. The way was open for non-Communists to take control of the governments of Hungary and Czechoslovakia peacefully. In Bulgaria the Communist regime held on only by changing its name and promising to institute reforms, and in Romania the Communist dictator was overthrown and shot during a military-backed uprising.

The most dramatic events of 1989 occurred in divided Germany, the premier symbol of the Cold War and a polarized Europe. As thousands of East German citizens fled via Hungary and Austria, those who stayed behind demonstrated against the repressive govern-

End of the Iron Curtain   A German youth waves victoriously from the top of the Berlin Wall after the fall of Communism in Germany.

ment of long-time dictator and Kremlin puppet Erich Honnecker. Aware that Soviet troops would not be forthcoming to repress dissent, Honnecker resisted the urge to use police and troops to crush the demonstrators. On November 9 the government opened the border between East and West Germany, and on November 15, as the world watched on television, wrecking crews moved in and began destroying the Berlin Wall. Less than a year later, on October 2, 1990, the newly democratized East German Democratic Republic merged with the German Federal Republic into a single capitalist, multi-party state.

Throughout this process the Bush administration stood on the sidelines and gave quiet encouragement to democratic leaders. Once it became clear that Gorbachev was truly committed to demilitarization, limited privatization of the Soviet economy, and the principle of self-determination for Eastern Europe, Washington tried not to antagonize any of the elements competing for control in Russia and Eastern Europe. Aware that Gorbachev was opposed to including a reunified Germany in NATO, Washington carefully mediated between its European partners and the Soviets. Gorbachev finally accepted NATO membership for a united Germany in return, ironically, for the continued presence of American troops in Europe, which he believed would act as a guard against a revived German militarism.

In the summer of 1991 Bush traveled to Moscow to sign a Strategic Arms Reduction Treaty with Gorbachev. The agreement committed both parties to a one-third reduction in the numbers of their bombers and missiles, and to cuts in conventional forces as well. Shortly thereafter, on August 18, a group of hard-liners representing the Red Army, the KGB, and the Communist party hierarchy attempted a coup. The rebellious troops surrounded the Russian parliament building in Moscow, but Boris Yeltsin, president of the Russian Republic, and a majority of the legislators refused to capitulate, declaring their support for Gorbachev, whom the plotters had seized. When the coup leaders decided not to use force, the conspiracy collapsed. Gorbachev returned from captivity, but Yeltsin had become the hero of the moment and occupied center stage in Russian politics. As of December 1991 the Soviet Union itself was dissolved and its former republics, including the Russian Federation, became independent. Yeltsin led the way in the creation of the Commonwealth of Independent States (CIS), which allied the Russian Federation with Ukraine and Belarus. Within a month, eleven former Soviet republics had joined the CIS. All the while, the Bush administration maintained an official position of neutrality, although Washington quietly supported first Gorbachev and then Yeltsin. The United States promised economic aid to the Commonwealth so long as its leaders continued down the road toward democracy and a free market economy.

❧ The China Puzzle

The Bush administration was similarly circumspect in its dealings with Communist China. As the Chinese tasted the prosperity that economic reforms and trade with the West brought, and as the older generation of revolutionary leaders passed from the scene, China appeared to be embarking on the path of openness taken by the former Soviet Union. Unfortunately for both Washington and Beijing, militant students in China were not willing to wait. In May 1989 thousands of protesters began gathering in Tiananmen Square. The young people erected a huge papier-maché "Goddess of Liberty" figure that bore a striking resemblance to the Statue of Liberty. As the month came to a close, Deng Xiaoping, Mao's successor, declared martial law, banned television crews from the square, and ordered the army to disperse the protesters. A number of reporters and photographers managed to remain on the scene, however, and on June 3 and 4 they recorded the Tiananmen massacre, as government troops attacked the students and tanks rolled over defenseless protesters. Estimates of the number of deaths ranged from 500 to 7,000 and of the approximately 10,000 dissenters who were arrested, 31 were tried and executed. Deng purged from his regime those who had sympathized with the pro-democracy movement.

Many Americans had reservations about the tactics of the stu-

dent radicals, and the wave of outrage that swept the United States during the Tiananmen Square massacre proved relatively weak. The Bush administration condemned Beijing for its repression and temporarily suspended sales of both military and non-military items. The following month, however, the president assured Deng and his associates that relations would return to normal as soon as the controversy died down.

❧ Policing the Caribbean

The Bush administration's non-ideological approach to foreign policy also was apparent in Central America. In 1987, Costa Rican President Oscar Arias Sanchez persuaded four other regional presidents to approve a peace plan that would end the fighting between insurgents and government forces in both Nicaragua and El Salvador. It also called for an end to all outside military aid to rebel forces and for a commitment by all countries involved to hold elections and move toward "political pluralism." Soon after the Bush administration took office, Secretary of State James Baker halted U.S. aid to the Contras, and in return demanded that the Sandinistas hold free elections. At the same time, Washington pressed the right-wing government of President Alfredo Cristiani in El Salvador to negotiate with dissidents in his country. In Nicaraguan elections held in February 1990, the Sandinistas were resoundingly defeated by Violeta Chamorro, the widow of a newspaper publisher who had opposed both the So-

Marching for Freedom   A young woman waves a banner in a march to Tiananmen Square in Beijing during student demonstrations for democracy and human rights in May 1989.

moza regime and the leftist Sandinistas. In El Salvador the Cristiani government and representatives of the rebels arranged a fragile cease-fire in February 1992 and began negotiating.

Bush's reputation as a peacemaker in Latin America was to some extent overshadowed by his decision to send troops into Panama in late 1989. That small country had been ruled since the 1960s by a brutal and corrupt military dictator, General Manuel Noriega. During the 1980s Noriega had angered the Reagan administration by simultaneously funneling aid to the Contras and working undercover for Fidel Castro. In 1988 two Florida grand juries indicted Noriega on charges that he participated directly in the smuggling of drugs into the United States, that he accepted bribes for allowing Panamanian banks to launder drug money, and that he actually permitted Colombians to manufacture drugs in Panama. All the while, the Panamanian dictator had remained in the pay of the CIA.

Not long after Bush took the oath of office as president, Noriega canceled the results of a Panamanian presidential election that he had failed to win and proclaimed himself "maximum leader." In mid-December Bush approved "Operation Just Cause." On December 29, 27,000 Marines landed in Panama with the objective of protecting the canal, safeguarding American citizens, and interdicting the drug traffic flowing north from South America. Troops loyal to Noriega held off the Marines for several days but then capitulated. The U.S. command installed Guillermo Endara as president and shipped Noriega back to Florida to stand trial. He was convicted and imprisoned. Operation Just Cause cost the lives of 24 U.S. soldiers, 139 Panamanian troops, and at least 300 Panamanian civilians.

Bush's Panamanian expedition, together with Reagan's foray into Grenada, perhaps helped erase memories of the Vietnam humiliation. So confident of popular support had the president been that he did not consult Congress, and, in view of the overwhelming support of the American people, no one in the House or Senate raised any opposition to the operation.

❧ The Gulf War

It is hardly surprising, then, that the Bush administration showed little hesitancy in going to war with Iraq in early 1991. On August 2, 1990, Iraqi strongman Saddam Hussein sent nearly 100,000 troops into neighboring, oil-rich Kuwait. Saddam declared that Iraq was merely reclaiming what was its own, but his real motivations were money and power. Iraq needed money to pay debts from its disastrous war with Iran; control of tiny Kuwait's oil fields would satisfy that need and give Iraq a much larger say in determining world oil prices.

The Bush administration responded to the invasion

Burning the Oil Fields of Kuwait   On March 12, 1991, facing defeat at the hands of coalition armies at the end of the Gulf War, Saddam Hussein ordered his retreating troops to torch the Kuwaiti oil wells. The result was an ecological and economic disaster. The long-term damage to many Gulf War troops' health caused by inhaling the fumes of these fires has still not been adequately determined.

of Kuwait promptly and vigorously. Bush began assembling a multinational coalition capable of driving Iraqi troops out of Kuwait. Several factors underlay the determination of the United States and its allies to resist Iraq's aggression. Many, including most of the Arab states in the region, feared that Saddam would not stop with Kuwait, and in fact the Iraqi dictator followed up his seizure of that country by massing troops along the border with Saudi Arabia. In addition, a fully armed and oil-rich Iraq posed a potential threat to America's chief ally in the region, Israel. Rumors were already rampant that the Iraqi leader, an outspoken champion of the Palestinian cause, was building nuclear weapons, and it was well known that he had used poison gas against Kurdish rebels in his own country, as well as against Iran. But the foremost motive behind the war with Iraq was oil. If Saddam were allowed to keep Kuwait, he would control a quarter of the world's proven oil reserves; if he succeeded in conquering Saudi Arabia, he would own nearly half. At that point he would be able to control the price of oil, with the potential for destroying the economies of America, Western Europe, and Japan.

❧ Desert Storm

Secretary of State Baker carefully constructed an alliance that cleared the way for military intervention against Iraq with little opposition from the international community. Most members of the UN and all members of the Security Council favored military action. Britain, Saudi Arabia, and twenty-six other nations agreed to furnish troops, while the Soviet Union and China quietly acquiesced in the decision to use force. In the Middle East, only Iran and the Palestinians firmly supported the Iraqi cause. With this wide-ranging support, the Bush administration within weeks moved more than 700,000 military personnel into northern Saudi Arabia and the waters off Kuwait.

In November 1990, Bush announced that the coalition would soon liberate Kuwait, and the UN Security Council set a date of January 15, 1991, for Saddam to evacuate his troops or face expulsion. Meanwhile, remembering Vietnam, Bush went to Congress and asked for authority to go to war in accordance with the Security Council's resolutions. On January 12 the House and Senate rejected a Democratic-sponsored resolution asking the administration to refrain from the use of force and

give economic sanctions more time to work, and instead authorized military operations. The deadline for an Iraqi pullout from Kuwait came and went, and the coalition began a month-long aerial bombardment of Kuwait and Iraq. On February 24 some 550,000 allied troops, 250,000 of them from the United States, crossed into Kuwait. Saddam promised that his forces would resist in the "Mother of All Battles," but the Iraqis were no match for allied technology and firepower. In less than 100 hours, the battle was over. At the cost of 136 American lives, the coalition had smashed Saddam's war machine and killed an estimated 100,000 Iraqi soldiers. As a parting shot, the retreating Iraqi army set fire to 650 Kuwaiti oil wells, leaving an inferno that took nine months to extinguish.

The nation seemed to have learned the lessons of Vietnam. The military insisted that the political objectives behind Desert Storm be clearly defined and, once the war began, the U.S.-led coalition applied maximum pressure and did not waver from the stated objectives — the liberation of Kuwait and the destruction of the Iraqi military forces threatening Saudi Arabia. (Here, of course, unlike Vietnam, there were no enemy superpowers waiting in the wings to step in if things went too badly for their client.) The United States had thus been able to project its power quickly and decisively into an area vital to its strategic and economic interests. The Bush administration formally consulted Congress, and once hostilities began, kept a tight leash on the press. Israel, a tacit ally of the conservative Arabian Gulf states, welcomed the humbling of Saddam Hussein, and shortly after the end of the war, agreed to peace talks with its immediate Arab neighbors. Israel not only consented to Palestinian participation in the parleys — albeit as part of the Jordanian delegation — but also agreed to allow the Soviets to become involved in the Middle East peace negotiations.

In later years, the fact that Saddam's regime retained power in Iraq and remained a serious menace in the region made the Gulf War seem less than a total victory. Bush's reasons for stopping the allied troops short of Baghdad when the Iraqi army was in disarray were complex. America's Arab allies feared that a total destruction of the Iraqi government would dangerously destabilize the region, and Bush was afraid that the United States might become mired in a Vietnam-like quagmire in the Middle East. In addition, intelligence estimates that Saddam was so weakened that he would be ousted from power proved to be incorrect — and in any event, Baker's advisers told him and the president that in all likelihood Saddam would simply be succeeded by someone just as bad, or worse. After the war, Saddam brutally repressed Kurds in the north and Shiites in the south who had risen up against him expecting — but not receiving — American support.

THE CULTURE WARS AND THE ELECTION OF 1992

American political debate by the beginning of the 1990s was incomprehensible without an understanding of the powerful economic, social, and religious alignments that divided Americans into antagonistic subcultures. On one side, growing economic conservatism tapped a rising backlash against the reforms of the 1960s and 1970s and allied itself (not always comfortably) with a rejuvenated and assertive Religious Right in a broad array of causes, all of which laid claim to restoring the nation's traditional values. At the other end of the spectrum were those who insisted that the United States was more diverse than it had ever been and that only by recognizing — indeed, by celebrating — the nation's ethnic and cultural pluralism could all Americans be protected from the moralistic and self-serving super-patriotism of conservatives. The most outspoken advocates for minority rights continued to be civil rights activists and feminists, but a broader debate over multiculturalism and the role of government in the everyday lives of Americans raised social discord in the nation to new levels of intensity.

Some dubbed the sharp clashes on social issues the "culture wars." In many ways the conflicts of the 1980s and 1990s were a replay of earlier confrontations over American sameness and manyness, the proper role of government, and the separation of church and state. Loose alliances confronted one another on a wide variety of issues — immigration, affirmative action, feminism, reform of public schools, gun control and crime, environmental issues, gay rights, pornography and regulation of the media, and, perhaps most contentious of all, abortion. The United States was not necessarily more diverse than it had been at other times in its past, but Americans had rarely been more keenly or factiously conscious of their diversity. Like social controversies in earlier times, the culture wars at the end of the century were often dominated by rhetorical extremists; their clashes sometimes turned ugly and mean-spirited, and occasionally violent and deadly. Most Americans did not agree with extremists at ei-

ther end of the cultural debates, and they often ignored them, but agitators sometimes forced politicians to address charged social issues in the public square.

❧ The Challenge of Pluralism, Diversity, and Multiculturalism: The American Salad Bowl

If many Americans in the 1980s and 1990s seemed satisfied with material contentment, religion, and patriotism, others insisted that such thinking obscured the nation's problems and misjudged its true character. To counter the cultural and political myth of a monolithic American culture, advocates of multiculturalism called for a renewed affirmation of the nation's diversity and a new sensitivity to minority rights. Although much of the language of the multicultural debate was new, the clash between ethnic and economic minorities and older hegemonies was a part of the nation's historic dilemma of reconciling sameness and manyness.

Voting patterns confirmed the self-conscious alienation of a variety of interest groups. Throughout the last two decades of the twentieth century, between 80 and 90 percent of black voters supported Democratic presidential candidates. Hispanics were only slightly less politically united than African Americans, with about two-thirds voting Democratic. Recently arrived immigrants also showed a tendency to unite behind one party or the other, as Irish and Italian immigrants had earlier in the century. A majority of Asian Americans, for example, consistently voted Republican. In some ways more significant politically, and more illustrative of the growing multicultural sensibility of America, was the "gender gap" that had begun to appear in the election of 1980. Party voting had shown little gender definition through the election of 1976, but beginning in 1980 women tilted toward Democratic candidates, while men leaned just as markedly toward Republicans. The "gender gap" reflected particularly the Democrats' ability to pull large majorities of single women and African American women into their alliance (married women showed a slight preference for the Republicans). In short, American pluralism at the end of the twentieth century defined itself in a wide variety of ways — ethnicity and race, gender, class, religion, and region.

The appeals for a new "multicultural" understanding of America came largely from academia and the Left, but the growing ethnic diversity of the nation gave credence to demands for a renewed emphasis on the diversity of American society. The 1990 census reported that 32 million people over five years of age spoke a language other than English in their homes; around 20 percent of that number spoke little English. The native tongue of more than half of the non-English speakers was Spanish, but twenty-six languages were spoken by more than 100,000 Americans in their homes, and nine by more than 500,000. Still, while advocates of bilingual education cited such statistics as evidence of the cultural diversity of the nation (and the need to celebrate and preserve the country's manyness), the immigrant parents of school-age children overwhelmingly wished them to become fluent in English.

The discussion over the nation's diversity was laden with political objectives as well as social consciousness. Immigrant groups in America had historically found it in their self-interest to remain hyphenated "ethnic American," becoming, in the words of Senator Daniel Patrick Moynihan, "interest groups." In this way, new immigrants found a place in the political process, competing or cooperating with established interest groups such as farmers, union members, evangelicals, feminists, and businesspeople.

The complexity of cultural identification in America was illustrated by a group of mixed-race Americans, uncomfortable about having to list themselves in any of the traditional categories, petitioning the Census Bureau to provide a "multiracial" designation in the 2000 census. The leaders of traditional ethnic groups, such as African Americans, opposed the move because it would likely diminish the size of their bloc, and the new category was rejected. Census data continued to classify Americans in four racial groups: whites, blacks, American Indians and Alaskan Natives, and Asians and Pacific Islanders. In addition, Hispanics were lumped together on the basis of their language, regardless of their race.

While many continued to see the United States as a melting pot that molded great varieties of people into a single American personality, some multiculturalists argued that a better image was a salad bowl, in which a great variety of ingredients contributed to the rich and complex American whole. Both images had explanatory value in looking at American culture. Ironically, immigrants were among the strongest believers in melting-pot concepts. A 1996 Gallup poll revealed that nearly 60 percent of all Americans, including foreign-born, believed that immigrants should be encouraged to blend into American culture, while less than 30 percent stressed the preservation of ethnic cultures. In a similar poll in 1997, 79 percent of the respondents, in melting-pot language, believed that American culture

was unique because it "blended many different cultures into one culture."

It was as true as ever that new Americans were among the most patriotic Americans. A majority of Asian and Caribbean immigrants in a 1995 poll reported that they had felt the sting of racial discrimination in their new home, but at the same time 90 percent reported that they felt welcome in the United States and 70 percent said that more than half of their friends were American citizens. Most newly arrived immigrants still believed that America was a land of opportunity; 93 percent declared that "people who work hard to better themselves can get ahead in this country," a percentage considerably higher than among all Americans.

Multicultural definitions of America began with the reality of diversity, but they were shaped by intellectual debates among academics and by fierce political battles over a variety of social issues. Much of the political rhetoric of the eighties and nineties came from disenchanted scholars who had lost confidence in liberalism. Historian Christopher Lasch disdained 1960s liberalism as elitist and naive, assuming as it had that history was moving toward a higher and more rational plateau, and called for a "post-progressive" mentality. Literary postmodernists — who dominated most English departments — led the intellectual attack on the notion of an American culture rooted in Western, Judeo-Christian values, ideas, and texts (called "the canon"). Some postmodernists saw rational discourse as a Western tradition that had been used to legitimate white males' intellectual and economic tyranny. This white, male, Western hegemony allegedly devalued all other cultures, often consciously obliterating them from history. The goal of deconstructionist multiculturalism was the eradication of racism, sexism, homophobia, and other prejudices that tried to impose arbitrary and self-serving measures of right and wrong — often with the transparent aim of giving power to dominant groups.

While some multicultural ideas turned campuses into battlefields, tolerance and open-mindedness found wide support. Multicultural reforms were varied, ranging from the expansion of affirmative action and minority recruitment programs for students to revisions of the curriculum that downgraded classical studies (viewing much of the literature and history of Western civilization as a canon imposed by the dominant culture) in favor of area studies that stressed the contributions of the peoples of the Third World. Proponents of multiculturalism often pursued their goals with puritanical zeal; opponents dubbed the crusade "political correctness" and accused university administrations of acting as "thought police" who, in the guise of safeguarding minority rights, threatened basic freedoms. In 1994, a committee of the American Historical Association, headed by UCLA's Gary Nash, formulated a set of standards for teaching American history that illustrated the complexity of the clash. The standards proposed by the committee placed so much emphasis on minority contributions to American history (asserting that American history was formed equally by three cultures in convergence — European, African, and Native American) and were so critical of the history of the majority that they caught the attention and provoked the condemnation of the United States Senate.

❧ The Election of 1992

It was in this setting of growing cultural confrontation that the election of 1992 took place. In the wake of the Gulf War, George Bush's approval ratings reached near record levels, but his popularity proved fleeting. A recession began in July 1990, and although the economy was improving by 1992, nineteen states were still seriously depressed. President Bush seemed genuinely confused by the downturn, acknowledging at one point that "people are hurting." But he sincerely believed that the recession would quickly correct itself. He easily fended off a challenge for the Republican nomination from former Nixon aide and right-wing ideologue Patrick Buchanan, and was renominated. But there were signs of danger within the Republican Party. Many conservative Republicans were miffed by Bush's abandonment of his "Read my lips: no new taxes" pledge. Buchanan's challenge raised issues that would be picked up by the spoiler in the 1992 election, Ross Perot.

The Democratic race was thrown wide open when New York governor Mario Cuomo, the best known of the party's potential candidates, announced that he would not run. That left the door open for forty-five-year-old William Jefferson Clinton, the governor of Arkansas, who turned out to be one of the best political campaigners in modern American history. A former Rhodes scholar and Yale Law School graduate, Clinton hoped that his educational credentials, intelligence, and charisma would offset the disadvantages of being from a rural, underdeveloped state. While at Yale, Clinton persuaded one of his brightest classmates, Hillary Rodham, to marry him and return with him to Arkansas. In 1979, at 32 years of age, Clinton became the youngest governor in the country, and he served almost continuously in that capacity until his nomination for the presidency in 1992.

As his prospects for election or appointment to a national post increased, Clinton positioned himself as a centrist. Beyond recommending a massive aid package for the former Soviet Union and anticipating cuts in the defense budget, he forsook foreign policy issues in his campaign in favor of domestic matters. He rejected Reagan's contention that "government is the problem" and argued that the bureaucracy simply had to be made more responsive to the needs of the people. During the general election campaign, Clinton called for reform of the welfare system to make benefits terminable and tied to work, and he promised a new, universal health care system. In addition, he pledged himself to tax relief for the middle class and a restructuring of the student loan program.

Clinton identified himself with other "New Democrats" who distanced themselves from the liberalism of the Mondale and Dukakis campaigns. He was willing to make peace with the business world and hoped to win increased support from the middle class, but at the same time he remained wedded to the politics of multiculturalism. Convinced that Clinton would be a strong candidate, and that he could win back lost constituencies such as southerners and working-class Americans, Democrats gave him the nomination.

Clinton was an indefatigable campaigner and, carefully reading public opinion, he homed in on pocketbook issues. "It's the economy, stupid," insisted one of his principal campaign officials. Hillary Rodham Clinton, his independent and intelligent wife, was very appealing to liberals and to women in general. But Bill Clinton also brought strong negatives to the campaign. Tales of womanizing that had dogged him as governor followed him on the presidential campaign trail. Clinton's forthright opposition to the Vietnam War, and evidence that he had dodged the draft during the conflict, damaged him with veterans' groups and conservatives in general.

With Clinton's negatives and Bush's apparent unwillingness or inability to address the economic downturn, the way was open for the independent candidacy of H. Ross Perot. A billionaire data processing entrepreneur and friend of Richard Nixon who had made his fortune on government contracts, Perot criticized both political parties for not addressing "real" issues such as deficit reduction. A bitter opponent of free trade, Perot was particularly critical of Bush's efforts to negotiate a trade agreement with Canada and Mexico. His scrappy, self-made image, his credentials as a political outsider, and his attacks on Congress and the president struck a responsive chord with a public tired of a government mired in perpetual gridlock. By July Perot had pulled even with the two major party candidates in the polls. But under attack from Republicans for his opposition to the Gulf War and his pro-choice views on abortion, Perot suddenly withdrew from the race. Two months later, responding to appeals from his disillusioned supporters, he reentered the race, but his credibility was irreparably damaged.

In the resulting three-way race, American voters elected Bill Clinton president. He captured only 43 percent of the popular vote (less than the defeated Dukakis in 1988) to Bush's 38 percent, winning in the electoral college by a vote of 370 to 168. Perot failed to carry any states but tallied 19 percent of the popular vote, the best showing by a third-party candidate since Theodore Roosevelt's Bull Moose campaign in 1912. Perot's unusual candidacy made it difficult to read the voters' mandate in 1992, but the result clearly reflected Bush's inability to project qualities of leadership and to convince the nation that an economic turnaround had begun.

Despite getting less than half the popular vote (in the first of three consecutive presidential elections in which the winner failed to capture a majority of votes cast), Bill Clinton entered the White House under otherwise favorable circumstances. With large Democratic majorities in both the Senate and the House of Representatives, the stage seemed to be set for Democrats to address the social and economic issues that they believed had been neglected since the election of Richard Nixon in 1968.

CONCLUSION: AMERICAN CONFIDENCE AND THE NEW WORLD ORDER

Ronald Reagan was the symbol of the neoconservative resurgence that took place between 1980 and 1992. Under his leadership big business joined with the Religious Right and working-class Americans to fashion a formidable political coalition. Reagan and Bush did

Al Gore and Bill Clinton Running in 1992 as "populists" more in tune with average citizens than the patrician George H. W. Bush, the two challengers hit the campaign trail by bus after being nominated. Clinton's appetite for junk food was legendary, and he spent his presidency trying hard to exercise away its effects on his waistline. But his struggles with diet, weight, and food may have helped him "connect" with ordinary people waging similar battles in their daily lives.

not dramatically change the direction of the country, but they changed its mood. While denouncing the philosophy that underlay it, they accepted the basic programs of the welfare state that had been put in place in the New Deal.

While the nation struggled with an onerous deficit during these years, there was a growing sense of well-being about the future of the American economy. Independent of the political rhetoric, the dramatic restructuring of American business that had been taking place, coupled with relentless technological advance, would help put the United States in a dominant economic position by the middle of the 1990s.

In the area of foreign policy, the Reagan and Bush era witnessed the most significant change in world politics in the last half of the twentieth century — the ending of the Cold War. The international changes that led to the end of the Cold War were complicated and could hardly be credited to the policies of any one American administration, but, generally speaking, Reagan and Bush tried to take advantage of the new conditions to encourage the emergence of a world order that was more democratic and more open to worldwide economic growth.

SUGGESTED READING

Lou Cannon, *President Reagan: The Role of a Lifetime* (1991). A biography of the president by a reporter who covered his administration.

Michael Duffy and Dan Goodgame, *The Status Quo Presidency of George Bush* (1992). A critical assessment of the Bush administration.

Haynes Johnson, *Sleepwalking Through History: America in the Reagan Years* (1991). Another reporter's unsympathetic assessment of Reagan.

M. P. Leffler, *A Preponderance of Power* (1992). This volume offers a sweeping history and interpretation of the Cold War.

Herbert Parmet, *George Bush: The Life of a Lone Star Yankee* (1997). An early overview of the Bush presidency.

William E. Pemberton, *Exit with Honor: The Life and Presidency of Ronald Reagan* (1997). A solid study of Reagan and his presidency.

Michael Schaller, *Reckoning with Reagan: America and Its President in the 1980s* (1992). A brief overview of the Reagan presidency.

Daniel Wirls, *Buildup: The Politics of Defense in the Reagan Era* (1992). Describes Reagan's commitment to a strong defense.

SUGGESTIONS FOR FURTHER READING

Martin Anderson, *Revolution* (1988).

William C. Berman, *America's Right Turn: From Nixon to Bush* (1994).

Barry Bluestone and Bennett Harrison, *The Deindustrializing of America* (1982).

Ethan Bronner, *Battle for Justice: How the Bork Nomination Shook America* (1989).

W. S. Cohen and G. J. Mitchell, *Men of Zeal* (1988).

John Lewis Gaddis, *The Long Peace* (1987).

John Lewis Gaddis, *The United States and the End of the Cold War* (1992).

James Davidson Hunter, *Culture Wars: The Struggle to Define America* (1991).

D. T. Regan, *For the Record* (1988).

Jon R. Stone, *On the Boundaries of American Evangelicalism: The Postwar Evangelical Coalition* (1997).

Ronald Takaki, *A Different Mirror: A History of Multicultural History* (1993).

Strobe Talbott, *The Russians and Reagan* (1984).

Martin Walker, *The Cold War: A History* (1993).

36

The Politics of Equilibrium:
The Clinton and Bush Presidencies

P OLITICALLY, THE UNITED STATES in the 1990s was almost evenly divided between Republicans and Democrats. Each of the two major parties boasted hard-core constituencies (often united by "culture war" issues; see Chapter 37), and they competed vigorously to attract voters with weak party loyalties and the growing numbers who called themselves independents. In 2004 a Gallup poll revealed that 45.5 percent of Americans "leaned" toward the Republican Party and 45.2 percent toward the Democrats. The remaining 9 percent were independents. The three presidential elections between 1992 and 2000 were decided by the votes cast for a third-party candidate. When George W. Bush amassed over 51 percent of the popular vote in 2004, it was the first time one candidate had received a majority since his father's election in 1988.

Bill Clinton, a remarkably skillful politician who tried to hew to a slightly left-of-center line, was the first Democrat to be elected president since Jimmy Carter in 1976 and the first of his party since Franklin Roosevelt to win a second term. Still, Clinton was a minority president, receiving only 43 percent of the popular vote in 1992 and slightly less than 50 percent in 1996. Furthermore, in 1994 the Republican Party won both houses of Congress, so that during the final six years of his presidency Clinton faced a hostile legislature. After some early and unpopular gestures toward the left, Clinton pulled the Democratic Party toward the political center, embracing several key conservative issues. Americans overwhelmingly approved of Clinton's performance, even when he was impeached and tried in 1998. Nonetheless, during the Clinton years neither party dominated the nation's political agenda.

The equilibrium in American politics was graphically displayed in 2000, one of the closest and most controversial presidential elections in history. The disputed outcome was not settled for fifty-four days, when George W. Bush secured victory over Vice President Al Gore. Bolstered by a wave of patriotism that followed the September 11, 2001, terrorist attack and military actions in Afghanistan and Iraq, Bush's ratings soared, and the Republicans made significant gains in the elections of 2002. But by early 2004, as the Iraqi war was followed by a bloody and frustrating effort to construct a stable democracy there, and as job growth was slow to accompany an economic recovery, Bush's poll standings dropped and the election of 2004 turned into a hotly contested fight between the president and Democratic Senator John Kerry. Solid Republican victories in the congressional and presidential elections for the first time in many years seemed to tip the scales toward one of the two parties. Even though his victory was far from a landslide, President Bush announced that he intended to vigorously pursue a conservative agenda during his second term.

Foreign policy was important in defining both the Clinton and Bush presidencies. The end of the Cold War left a multipolar world, in which America economically both competed and partnered with Japan, a more united Europe, a rapidly developing China, and the oil-rich countries in the Middle East. Political instability, however, followed the collapse of the Soviet Union, as newly empowered nationalisms challenged earlier balances of power. The United States, the world's sole remaining superpower, struggled first to identify and then to defend its interests around the world.

Increasingly, America had to confront Islamic fundamentalist terrorism, bred in the cauldron of Middle Eastern unrest. Sporadic violence against Americans during the Clinton administration elicited limited responses. Then the dramatic terrorist attack of September 11, 2001, changed the course of modern history. George W. Bush launched a "war on terror" that led the United States ever more deeply into Middle Eastern politics and into military actions in Afghanistan and Iraq. These crises, and George W. Bush's vigorous use of American military force in response to them, strained American relations with some old European allies, tested the post–Cold War friendship with Russia, and revealed how much Americans' faith in the United Nations had frayed.

Domestic politics during the Clinton and Bush ad-

ministrations continued to wobble between left and right on such culture-war issues as abortion, affirmative action, and the environment. However, on critical economic issues, despite much partisan rhetoric, both presidents supported policies that expanded trade, limited government, and vigorously stimulated the economy.

THE CLINTON PRESIDENCY: TOWARD A CENTRIST POLICY

Bill Clinton proved to be a consummate politician, as well as an effective trustee for the New Deal – Great Society commitment to social justice, whose job approval remained strong despite Republican control of Congress and a damaging investigation of his private life. Throughout his presidency, from 1993 to the beginning of 2001, he was the dominant personality in American public life.

In character, Clinton appeared as an almost exact opposite of Ronald Reagan. Reagan had often seemed uninformed and unable to grasp the complexities of problems, but he exuded conviction and an unswerving loyalty to principles. Clinton was a complex, widely read, and talented man who often seemed unmoored to firm principles. Clinton demonstrated his political genius in his ability to position the Democratic Party near the political center. The most substantial achievements of his administration — and they were sizeable — were the result of his reshaping of proposals that had long been a part of the Republican agenda.

Like his recent Republican predecessors, Clinton embraced free-market economics and a balanced budget. Unlike Republicans, however, Clinton was liberal on social issues, championing feminist and African American causes, and refusing to sacrifice programs benefiting the disadvantaged. Heir of a new post–Cold War environment, Clinton at first sought to balance the budget by cutting military spending. But in 1999, his decision to participate in a NATO action following the breakup of Yugoslavia forced him to request increases for the military.

Clinton benefited enormously from the booming American economy of the late nineties, which poured tax revenues into the federal budget and produced the first surpluses in decades. The new economic stability made it possible for the president and Congress to pass major legislation that had long been discussed by both parties.

After gaining control of Congress in 1994, Republicans pressed a broad conservative agenda and enacted part of it. The Republican majority in Congress launched a series of investigations of the executive branch, just as Democratic Congresses had grilled the Republican Reagan and Bush administrations. Stung by what Republicans viewed as extremely partisan proceedings in the hearings on the Supreme Court nomination of Clarence Thomas, and armed with the Special Prosecutor law passed by Democrats during the Iran-Contra affair, the Republicans launched an investigation of the business dealings of Clinton and his wife in Arkansas, led by Special Prosecutor Kenneth Starr. It would entangle the White House in months of litigation and embarrassing revelations about the personal life of the president, without ever turning up solid evidence of financial wrongdoings by the Clintons.

❧ *The Residual Influence of the Religious Left*

After the rise of Ronald Reagan and the emergence of the Religious Right, Bill Clinton tapped into another American religious and political tradition: the Religious Left. Since the promulgation of the Social Gospel at the turn of the century and even before, many Christians and Jews had embraced the notion that their faith required them to act democratically through duly elected governments to end poverty, ensure racial justice, and guarantee equality of opportunity. Franklin Roosevelt, Harry Truman, Lyndon Johnson, and Jimmy Carter were all Christians whose policy agendas reflected their commitment to social justice. Clinton, like Carter, was a Southern Baptist with a deep sense of obligation to the less fortunate of the nation and the world. Clinton in particular was popular with black evangelicals, whose political agenda diverged in many ways from that of white evangelicals. Citing passages from both the Old and New Testaments, religious liberals called upon the nation to share its bounty for the common good and to show compassion for widows, orphans, and the homeless in America and in other lands as well. The "culture wars" Clinton and others found themselves in the middle of did not simply pit believers against "secular humanists," but sometimes believers against believers as well.

❧ *The Clinton Presidency Begins*

In his inaugural address, Clinton promised to end the "deadlock and drift" in government. More than any previous president, "the man from Hope" (he had been born in Hope, Arkansas) focused on the nation's diversity and culture-war issues in his address. He called on all American citizens to overcome the "ancient hatreds and new plagues" that divided people at home and throughout the world. He promised to address social and economic grievances at home and to protect the nation's interests abroad, but at the same time he announced that he would move cautiously. Clinton proved to be more cautious than many of his supporters had hoped; within two years Garry Trudeau portrayed him in the comic strip *Doonesbury* as a waffle.

Clinton's initial cabinet appointments received quick approval in the Senate. But then, concerned to build an administration "that looks like America," he made some poorly researched and thus controversial appointments. His first two nominees for attorney general were exposed for failing to pay Social Security taxes for nannies. Only when the president nominated Miami prosecutor Janet Reno — who had no children and thus no nanny — did the furor subside. But these and other blunders raised questions about the president's administrative skills.

Throughout his two terms, Clinton kept his commitment to diversity and to his most loyal supporters. He seemed most at home with African Americans, and recognized that much remained to be done in changing American attitudes on race. In 1997 he established a commission on race reconciliation, headed by the distinguished black historian John Hope Franklin.

❧ *A Step to the Left*

During the campaign Clinton and his wife, Hillary Rodham Clinton, never denied their liberalism on major social issues. Because of this commitment, and perhaps because of inexperience in national politics, the president immediately thrust himself into an avoidable controversy over gays in the military. Instead of waiting until the end of his term to take up such a thorny issue, Clinton led off with it. On January 21 he instructed Secretary of Defense Les Aspin to draw up an executive order lifting the ban on homosexuals in the armed forces.

In addition to the millions of Americans who held rigidly anti-gay prejudices, including most military personnel, some people who normally would support gay rights on civil-liberty grounds were troubled by what they perceived as an unfair requirement in an environment of involuntary intimacy. The Joint Chiefs of Staff, supported by such organizations as the Veterans of Foreign Wars and the American Legion, protested vigorously. At length, the administration announced what it termed "an honorable compromise." Under a "don't ask, don't tell" policy, recruiters were prohibited from inquiring about an individual's sexual orientation, but those who openly practiced homosexuality could be discharged. Honorable though the compromise might have been, it was a political disaster, offending gay rights activists, military leaders, and millions of Americans.

❧ Healthcare Reform

One of Clinton's first actions was to appoint his wife to head a task force charged with planning reform of the healthcare system. Following a period of intense but secret study by a huge assemblage of experts, the administration unveiled its plan in September 1993. The president announced that universal healthcare was "the most urgent priority" facing the country. At the center of his proposals was the formation of regional health alliances that would purchase high-quality health care at low cost. A National Health Board would regulate all areas of public and private care; each citizen would have a health security card guaranteeing access to medical care; and the government would subsidize the self-employed and the poor to enable them to purchase health plans.

In the months that followed, an administration team headed by Hillary Rodham Clinton lobbied the public and Congress in behalf of a system that essentially promised federally guaranteed universal healthcare. Critics complained that the scheme would place one-seventh of the nation's economy under the direction of the federal government. The American Medical Association and insurance companies, fearing declining income and reduced profits, countered with a plan calling for a privately funded system to which everyone would be required to contribute. As Congress stalled, public support faded. In the end the administration got nothing from its highly publicized initiative, and the president's retreat made him appear vacillating even to his strongest supporters.

The failure of the Clinton health reform initiative left the nation's huge healthcare problem unresolved. Americans were living longer than ever, and both the government and private charities annually spent hundreds of millions of dollars on medical research. The cost of care continued to rise at a dizzying pace. National health expenditures in 1980 ($247.2 billion) were nearly ten times the amount expended in 1960. That figure jumped to $697.5 billion in 1990 and $949.4 bil-

Battling Over Abortion   Police are called in to keep separate pro-life and pro-choice demonstrators outside a Little Rock, Arkansas, abortion clinic in July 1994. No issue stirred both the left and the right extremes in America's "culture wars" more than the abortion debate.

lion in 1994, in some years rising by nearly 10 percent. Some of the escalation came from such programs as Medicare and Medicaid, and some from super-cures and rescue procedures that were disproportionately, and some said indefensibly, expensive. Nevertheless, by the mid-1990s more than 15 percent of the population, many of them children, lacked health insurance. The appearance of private health maintenance organizations (HMOs) slowed the rise in costs in the early 1990s, but only temporarily. Though many voiced concerns about quality of healthcare under HMOs, by 1997 85 percent of America's workers were members of a managed care system.

No health issue received more publicity in the 1990s than smoking. A coalition of forty-six state governments negotiated a settlement of a lawsuit against tobacco companies for health costs incurred for smokers, extracting $206 billion to be paid over twenty-five years. More and more restrictions were placed on smoking, with California leading the way in anti-smoking legislation. Nonetheless, in the mid-1990s around 25 percent of Americans still smoked.

∂ A Continuing National Trauma Over Abortion

President Clinton was more successful in his support of the causes of women's-rights activists, particularly access to abortion. Two days after his inauguration, he signed a series of executive orders reversing his predecessor's policies that had barred doctors working in federally funded clinics from performing abortions and banned abortions in military hospitals. In addition, he restored American contributions to United Nations programs that funded or promoted contraception and abortion, which the Reagan and first Bush administrations had refused to pay.

Politicians in both parties generally preferred to avoid the issue; a majority of Americans continued to be pro-choice, but religious conservatives remained a power in the GOP and the Democrats had large blue-collar Roman Catholic constituencies in states like Pennsylvania. In the 1990s both sides won minor skirmishes. The election of a pro-choice president galvanized the extremist fringe of the pro-life movement, and sporadic (sometimes deadly) violence against the providers of abortion services continued. In the eighties and early nineties a number of anti-abortion groups, notably Operation Rescue, tried to blockade abortion clinics; in 1994 Congress passed legislation aimed at ending such tactics. Generally, pro-life activists failed to find a unified legal position that provided a rallying point for their political supporters. The courts did chip away at *Roe v. Wade,* giving states some leeway in discouraging abortions, but the decision itself stood.

No issue so turbulently mingled concerns about women's rights, family values, and deeply held religious beliefs than the abortion debate. The number of abortions reported in the country rose from 586,760 in 1972 to a high of 1,429,577 in 1990, before beginning a slight decline to 1,186,039 in 1997. By 1997 the ratio of abortions to live births had fallen to the lowest point in more than two decades.

The public remained deeply divided and ambivalent about abortion; looking back on the twenty-fifth anniversary of *Roe v. Wade* in 1998, pollsters found that the nation was as perplexed by the issue as ever. More than half of Americans in 1998 stated that they believed that abortion was "the same thing as murdering a child," yet 58 percent believed that it was "sometimes the best course in a bad situation." Polls in the 1990s consistently revealed that Americans overwhelmingly favored legal abortion, particularly when a mother's health was endangered; on the other hand, more than 70 percent favored some restrictions on it. By 1999 the number of Americans who considered themselves "pro-choice" had declined from a high of 56 percent to 48 percent, and the number who identified themselves as "pro-life" had risen from 36 percent to 42 percent. In both cases, the numbers of men and women were almost equal.

By the 1990s, abortion opponents, with growing popular support, targeted so-called "partial birth" abor-

Spotted Owl   The battle for the habitat of the spotted owl between conservationists and loggers was one of the most heated environmental struggles of the decade. Conservationists feared the loss of the habitat would lead to the extinction of the spotted owl, while loggers saw their livelihoods endangered by the Clinton administration's enforcement of the Endangered Species Act in their area.

tion, a procedure involving crushing the unborn child's skull in the last trimester of pregnancy, even though less than 1 percent of all abortions took place in this manner. In 1996, a bill banning such abortions passed in both the House and Senate. Clinton vetoed the bill, but supporters of the ban, including substantial numbers of Democrats, rallied enough votes in the House to override the veto before falling three votes short of the two-thirds majority needed in the Senate.

❧ Environmentalism

The environmental movement gained momentum around the world during the last two decades of the century, highlighted by international conferences in Montreal in 1987 and in Rio de Janeiro in 1992. Concerns about global warming led many environmentalists to advocate restrictions on economic development, despite the growth objectives of Western democratic governments. Scientists disagreed about the causes of global warming, but most concurred that international cooperation was needed to limit the burning of carbon-based fuels, deforestation, and the production of aerosols. In a series of reports, the Intergovernmental Panel on Climate Control (a UN-sponsored board of scientists) highlighted "human influence" as a cause of global warming and urged international action. Although all politicians paid lip service to cleaning up the environment, neither Ronald Reagan nor George H. W. Bush had any sympathy for slowing economic growth, and they often saw environmentalism as another intrusive grasp for power by regulators.

In 1997, representatives from more than 150 nations met in Kyoto, Japan, to draft a treaty, the Kyoto Protocol, pledging to reduce the emissions of greenhouse gases worldwide by 5.2 percent by 2012. Clinton signed the Kyoto Treaty, much to the delight of European politicians closely identified with environmental causes, even though many American experts feared that the requirement of a 7 percent American reduction in emissions (the United States produces approximately 25 percent of global emissions) would cripple the national economy. The Senate rejected the treaty 95-0.

At home, the Clinton administration promoted environmental objectives. Even before Clinton's election, the Democratic Congress had passed the Energy Policy Act of 1992, which included incentives to increase the use of renewable energy, established efficiency standards for appliances, and experimented with the use of non-petroleum fuel in some government vehicles. Clin-

Branch Davidians The Davidians' Mount Carmel compound near Waco, Texas, is shown engulfed in flames in this April 19, 1993 photo. An advisory jury in a $675 million wrongful death lawsuit by Branch Davidians against the U.S. government found that federal agents were not to blame for the deaths of about 80 sect members in a 1993 siege and fire, but such findings did nothing to quell the rage of anti-government activists who believed the government had overstepped its bounds in the Davidian standoff.

ton's vice president, Albert Gore, had written an environmentalist manifesto, *Earth in the Balance*, and was named to head the administration's "green team." Gore promised to reverse federal environmental neglect by working to boost energy efficiency, preserve wetlands, and combat global warming. In a move that divided the environmentalist community, Clinton's Department of Energy began selling licenses giving manufacturers the right to emit specified amounts of sulfur dioxide, a cause of acid rain, and to sell their allotments to "dirty" factories if they kept their own emissions below the limit. In theory, the cleanest companies would profit by selling pollution "credits," while dirtier utilities would pay for their excesses, but environmental purists found the concept immoral.

The Endangered Species Act pitted environmental activists against logging companies and local communities by giving the federal government power to protect imperiled habitats. Under Clinton, the United States Forest Service vigorously defended the 191 million acres of national forest (about 8 percent of U.S. land area) and endangered species like the spotted owl against lumbering and mining interests, though angry loggers deeply resented the interference of environmentalists in their livelihood.

❧ *Militant Militias and Radical Discontent*

Discontent about government regulation grew more violent, even as the Clinton administration insisted that it would make government decisions more "open" to public scrutiny. In a step purported to symbolize such openness, in December 1993 Energy Secretary Hazel O'Leary released documents revealing that the federal government had not only conducted more than two hundred previously undisclosed underground nuclear tests between 1963 and 1990, but also that during the 1940s and 1950s American citizens had been used as guinea pigs in government-sponsored nuclear experiments. Whatever the intent of the releases, they hardly cleared the air of growing discontent on both the left and the right over federal intrusiveness.

Anti-government hatred reached paranoid, dangerous levels in a small and radical minority of self-described militias. The worst confrontation with such groups was the siege of the Branch Davidian compound outside Waco, Texas. In January 1993 federal agents tried to arrest David Koresh, the leader of the small radical Adventist religious community called the Branch Davidians, on gun-dealing charges. The standoff with Koresh's community ended in April when federal agents forcibly entered the sect's compound. In the final conflict and the fire it touched off, seventy-five members died. The siege had been televised daily after an abortive effort by agents to storm the compound in February left four agents dead; the final confrontation was watched by millions. The government's tactics outraged many people who could hardly be classified as radicals, and the incident sparked the formation of more armed militias.

On the second anniversary of the Waco tragedy, April 19, 1995, Timothy McVeigh set off a powerful truck bomb next to the Alfred P. Murrah Federal Building in Oklahoma City. In the blast 168 people perished. McVeigh was quickly apprehended, tried and convicted in federal court, and executed on June 11, 2001, the first federal execution since 1963. McVeigh was not a militia member, and many questions about his possible links with radical groups remain unanswered, but he seems to have been influenced by the pronouncements of various militia leaders.

❧ *The Economic Boom of the Clinton Years*

Bill Clinton had focused heavily on economic issues in his first presidential campaign, and his administration made the maintenance of prosperity its primary objective. Most economists opposed the ambitious "stimulus package," which included significant new government spending, that Clinton initially proposed. Republicans and conservative Democrats blocked Clinton's initiative, largely on ideological grounds (the "peace dividend" from the end of the Cold War and Clinton's elimination of federal jobs probably would have paid for the program by themselves), and the recovery continued despite — conservatives said because of — rejection of that policy. The Federal Reserve's careful management of the money supply and interest rates, the increasing American presence in the global marketplace, and technological innovation exerted strongly positive effects on the economic recovery. Clinton balanced the budget by trimming the federal bureaucracy, by elimi-

Oklahoma City Bombing   Rescue workers and industrial cranes sift through the rubble of the destroyed Federal Building in the aftermath of the Oklahoma City bombing. On April 19th, 1995, a fuel-and-fertilizer truck bomb exploded in front of the Alfred P. Murrah Federal Building, killing 168 people. Timothy McVeigh, convicted on first-degree murder charges for the worst terror attack on U.S. soil at that time, was executed for the crime.

nating some wasteful government programs, and by reducing military spending through scrapping the Strategic Defense Initiative and closing 92 overseas bases and 129 domestic installations. Finally, by raising taxes on the affluent and corporations, Congress and the administration actually reduced the huge budget deficit and thus helped hold down interest rates.

The budget deficit had been for many in the 1980s a sign of long-range American economic trouble. But tax cuts and spending programs benefiting the upper and middle classes were popular during the Reagan-Bush years, helping swell the deficit to $290 billion in 1992. In 1997, the total federal debt stood at $5.4 trillion, or about $20,000 per American. Although Republicans, ironically, argued that the burden was modest — measured against the gross domestic product, it was much lower than corresponding levels of debt in other developed countries — political pressure mounted to cut spending and require a balanced federal budget.

Later in the decade, however, the surge in national income (and therefore tax revenues) made it possible, for the first time in three decades, to aim plausibly for a balanced budget. A compromise between Clinton and Congress in 1997 included a promise to end budget deficits by 2002, and booming tax collections and reduced expenditures resulted in a 1997 federal deficit of only $22.6 billion. By 1999, there was a surplus, and projections predicted trillions in the excess of federal revenue over outlays.

At the beginning of his administration, Clinton was as committed to free trade and American participation in a global economy as his Republican predecessors. (Not since 1933-39 had an American administration been protectionist.) He boldly ensured ratification of the North American Free Trade Agreement (NAFTA) in 1994, with critical help from congressional Republicans, in the face of stiff resistance from Ross Perot and his followers, environmentalists, organized labor, and Democrats from the Rust Belt. The agreement provided for the gradual elimination of most tariffs and other trade barriers between the United States, Canada, and Mexico. The president also exerted his influence to try to promote trade with nations in Asia.

❧ The Republican Insurgency and the Contract With America

While much of Clinton's agenda had been a part of his political campaign, particularly his emphasis on economic growth and free trade, a resounding Republican victory in the congressional elections of 1994 created renewed interest in such issues as crime and welfare reform. For the first time since the Eisenhower administration, Republicans controlled both houses of Congress, which they kept for the remainder of Clinton's presidency. Not a single Republican incumbent in 1994 lost, and among the Democrats forced into retirement was Speaker of the House Thomas Foley, the first holder of that office to lose since 1862. Eleven Democratic governors went down to defeat, including Mario Cuomo of New York, the nation's most eloquent and high-profile Democratic governor.

The leader of the Republican revolt was Congressman Newt Gingrich from suburban Atlanta. Abrasive and articulate, Gingrich had made his way into the GOP leadership by relentlessly attacking Democrats. He authored the party's 1994 campaign platform and named it the "Contract With America." It called for procedural changes in the House, a constitutional amendment requiring a balanced budget (which narrowly lost when the Senate failed to override a Clinton veto), a line-item veto (which passed but was ruled unconstitutional by the Supreme Court), anti-crime measures, welfare reform, tax cuts for the middle class, increases in defense spending and prohibition of the use of American troops under UN command, reductions in the federal budget and unspecified cuts in the bureaucracy, and the imposition of term limits on members of Congress (which did not pass). Neither Congress nor the president could misjudge the level of voter discontent after the election of 1994, and both Clinton and the Republican Congress tried to appropriate the issues that underlay the voter revolt.

❧ Clinton Occupies the Center

With the Republicans riding high after their success in the 1994 elections and Gingrich installed as Speaker of the House of Representatives, Clinton sought the political middle ground. No president had ever been more attuned to public opinion polls, and Clinton attempted to co-opt or dilute the most popular planks in the Republican platform. Stung by Republican charges that Democrats were soft on crime, Clinton pushed through Congress a crime bill that appropriated federal funds for hiring 100,000 additional police and shortened the appeals period for death-row inmates. The White House also worked with Gingrich and Senate Majority Leader Bob Dole to hammer out a welfare reform bill. Announcing in his 1995 State of the Union address that

After Columbine   Following the deadly rampage of two students at Columbine High School in Littleton, Colorado, in 1999, schools around the nation were forced to take steps to guard against similar attacks. This Dallas high school, and many others around the country, installed metal detectors in an attempt to keep students safe.

the "era of big government" was over, Clinton promised to streamline the federal bureaucracy.

"Big government" by no means bit the dust. Although the president joined Republicans in pledging to balance the budget by 2002, he locked horns with them over the 1996 budget. A Republican attempt to reduce entitlement programs deadlocked Congress and twice caused a temporary shutdown of the government, allowing Democrats to paint the Republican Congress as obstructionist and insensitive to the poor and elderly. Fearing that Gingrich and the Republicans meant what they said about shrinking outlays for popular programs, the public sided decisively with Clinton and the Democrats.

❧ *Crime, Drugs, Guns, and Violence*

Crime and the cluster of issues connected with it, including drugs and the nation's love affair with guns, were hot issues in the 1990s. While all politicians bemoaned the pervasiveness of violence, the parties mostly divided on solutions. Republicans generally opted for more law enforcement and stricter sentencing, while urban Democrats supported social reform programs and gun control.

For fifty years up to 1980, the number of people incarcerated in correctional institutions in the United States had hovered around 315,000. By 1990 it shot up to 1,148,702, and in 2001 it hit 1,406,031. At the end of the century the United States had more people in prison (both absolutely and per capita) than any other industrialized nation. The huge increase in prison population was attributable to tougher sentencing for drug users as well as drug dealers, to larger police forces, and to heightened efforts to stop drug trafficking. The incarceration of so many prisoners cost an estimated $31.4 billion in 2000, caused serious overcrowding, and raised questions about the wisdom of imprisoning non-violent criminals and prosecuting victimless crimes. On the other hand, removing violent offenders from the streets helped cut crime rates. The incidence of "serious crime" reported by law enforcement agencies headed steadily downward each year in the 1990s.

Conservatives pressed for stricter enforcement of sentences, including the death penalty. In the years between the reinstatement of the death penalty by the Supreme Court in 1976 and the mid-1990s, slightly more than 250 people had been executed, but the number awaiting execution soared above 3,000; the average time spent on death row stretched to 8.8 years. In some states the number of executions began to rise in the 1990s; in 2000 Texas executed forty men. On the other hand, in the twenty-five years between 1976 and 2001 California executed only eight people, and in 2000 it had 586 prisoners on death row. Meanwhile, revelations concerning the mishandling of DNA evidence and conspiracy between police and prosecutors in Illinois raised concerns about misuse of the death penalty.

Drug abuse continued to be a major component of crime. In 2000, 38.9 percent of Americans over twelve years of age had used an illicit drug at least once during their lifetime, and 11 percent had done so in the previous year. Marijuana was by far the most widely used drug, but an estimated 1.2 million Americans were cocaine users, and more than 130,000 were addicted to heroin. As many as 17 million people used marijuana in a given year. In 1994 the government recorded more than 500,000 drug-related admissions to hospital emergency rooms and estimated a national toll of 8,400 drug-related deaths.

Guns and Second-Amendment rights continued to generate emotional debate, although the percentage of Americans who reported having guns in their homes declined between 1959 and 1999, from 49 to 34 percent. The gun-control movement received an unwelcome boost from a series of violent incidents in 1993, and in November Congress passed the Brady Bill, named after James Brady, the former White House press secretary crippled in the 1981 assassination attempt on President Reagan. The legislation imposed a five-day waiting period to allow for background checks on some would-be gun purchasers. Battling die-hard resistance from the powerful National Rifle Association, advocates of controls gained another small victory in 1996 when persons convicted of domestic violence were barred from owning a handgun. Nevertheless, guns and violent crime continued to plague American society. Renewed demands for regulation followed a series of deadly attacks in public schools, including a chilling incident in 1999 in Littleton, Colorado, in which two high-school students murdered a teacher and twelve classmates before shooting themselves as well.

❧ Welfare Reform

As Clinton positioned himself in the political center, pressure to end the "era of big government" produced a sweeping welfare reform in 1996. States were authorized to establish their own welfare programs, funded by federal block grants. The new law severely revised the New Deal–era Aid to Families with Dependent Children program, ending welfare as an entitlement. Henceforth, most adult welfare recipients were required to find jobs within two years, and a lifetime limit of five years was established for receiving welfare assistance. Benefits were sharply cut for non-citizens. Despite liberals' objections, welfare reform was generally hailed as a startling success — aided by a booming

Under Attack   Vice President Gore is shown here offering a public show of support for President Clinton during the scandal surrounding his presidency in 1998. Though impeached, Clinton was not convicted in the resulting Senate trial. Many of his closest allies, including his wife, Hillary Rodham Clinton, remained loyal throughout the scandal, but some were disillusioned by his behavior. Others protested the immense cost and energy expended on an investigation of the president's personal life.

economy that provided plentiful opportunities for employment. In 1998, federal welfare rolls dropped below 10 million for the first time in twenty-five years.

❧ The Election of 1996

In spite of the thrashing the Democrats had suffered in 1994, Clinton was nominated for a second term without opposition. He basked in the glow of the growing economy and seemed the embodiment of moderation and good sense during his budget standoff with Congress. Television commentator Pat Buchanan led an ultra-conservative charge to gain the Republican nomination, but mainstream Republicans secured the nomination for Senate majority leader Robert Dole. A man with a dry wit (and sometimes a hot temper) who was respected by his Senate colleagues, Dole, a decorated and severely wounded veteran of World War II, seemed to represent the American heartland.

Dole often failed to project a positive image during the campaign. His voice sounded more angry than conciliatory, and he did little to distance himself from extremists in his party. Aside from calling for large tax cuts (for which voters showed little enthusiasm), Dole failed to find a solid issue. Republican attempts to make the election a referendum on Clinton's character failed, despite many rumors about the president's indiscretions (and revelations that Newt Gingrich had divorced his wife while she was bedridden with cancer did not help the GOP's character campaign). Republicans charged that the Democratic National Committee had raised millions of dollars in illegal contributions from various Asian countries, including China, and that the White House offered a night in the Lincoln Room to anyone contributing $100,000 to the campaign. Clinton's skills as a fundraiser contributed significantly to his reelection.

Clinton easily won, with nearly 50 percent of the popular vote and 379 electoral votes to Dole's 41 percent and 159 electoral votes. Ross Perot this time captured only 9 percent of the popular vote and no electoral votes. Perot's vote in 1996 was not so critical to the outcome as in 1992, though he likely siphoned off more votes from Dole than from Clinton. Clinton's move to the center had undoubtedly helped his reelection, but his greatest asset was the booming economy. In spite of Clinton's solid victory, both houses of Congress remained in Republican hands.

✒ Farmers Get a New Deal

After a century of decline, the percentage of Americans engaged in farm occupations stabilized in the 1980s and 1990s, at around 2.5 percent of the labor force. The average size of an American farm continued to grow, from 374 acres in 1970 to 428 in 1980, and 469 in 1995. Nonetheless, individuals and families, not corporations, still dominated American farming.

Agricultural goods continued to be one of the nation's primary exports. Farm products constituted about 10 percent of all exports in 1995, and the raw value of American agricultural exports grew dramatically, from around $41 billion in 1980 to an estimated $56.2 billion in 2003. In 2003, the nation's agricultural exports exceeded its agricultural imports by more than $10 billion.

Like American corporations, in the 1980s American farmers had experienced severe economic problems, and thousands of them lost their land through foreclosures. The farm crisis of the mid-1980s was caused primarily by the tripling of farm debt (to more than $100 billion) in the heady expansion of the 1970s. Farmers retrenched during the economic slowdown of the early 1980s; farm debt also began shrinking, settling at about $75 billion in the 1990s.

Renewed prosperity in the 1990s permitted the first major revision of farm policy since the New Deal. In the Freedom to Farm Act of 1997, the government phased out subsidy payments on most major crops over a seven-year period and ended government crop acreage controls. Just as these reductions were due to become fully effective in 2002, Congress passed, and President George W. Bush signed, legislation that once again increased agricultural subsidies.

✒ The Clinton Scandals

Bill Clinton seemed almost designed to infuriate conservatives. As a young man during the sixties, he had tried marijuana, opposed the Vietnam War, dodged the draft, taken part in antiwar demonstrations in England, and otherwise flouted traditional American sensibilities. (Clinton later explained that he had not actually "inhaled" while smoking marijuana.) His political career in Arkansas had been marred by repeated charges of womanizing and shady business dealings. In his 1992 presidential campaign, Clinton denied charges (later proved true) made by a woman named Gennifer Flowers regarding a lengthy sexual relationship. He survived as a candidate partly because of staunch support from his wife Hillary. Given the incivility of American politics by the 1990s and the media's insatiable appetite for scandal, it was apparent that Clinton would be forced to defend himself.

No sooner did the Clinton administration take office than the president and his wife became embroiled in a murky scandal called "Whitewater," involving Arkansas real estate speculations and banking irregularities. Under pressure, in 1994 the president asked Attorney General Janet Reno to appoint an independent counsel to investigate. Kenneth W. Starr, who eventually led the investigation, was a former federal judge and the solicitor general during the Bush administration who had been reared as a member of the staunchly conservative Churches of Christ. Ironically, Starr had drafted the Reagan administration's argument against reauthorizing the independent counsel law, believing that it violated the separation of powers and had been used unfairly by Democrats to try to tar Republican presidents. Eventually the inquest expanded to include the firing of seven long-time employees in the White House travel department and the administration's collecting of FBI files.

Starr's investigation was energized in 1996 when an Arkansas jury convicted three Whitewater defendants — a former governor of Arkansas and two former Clinton business partners. A final report on the Whitewater investigation was submitted in 2000. The independent counsel's office could not find enough evidence to charge the Clintons, but twelve people were convicted of crimes as a result of the investigations, including Justice Department official Webster Hubbell, Mrs. Clinton's law partner.

More damaging to the president than Whitewater was a slow and painful public exposé of his sexual exploits. Administration supporters had hoped that Gennifer Flowers's accusations during the 1992 campaign marked the last of such incidents. But in May 1994 Paula Jones, a former Arkansas state employee, sued the president for making unwanted sexual advances while he was governor. The president denied the encounter and sought to postpone litigation. In May 1997, the Supreme Court ruled that Clinton was not immune from being sued for sexual harassment and could be forced to testify. The administration gained a reprieve when in April 1998 a federal judge threw out the Jones case for lack of evidence either of coercion or job discrimination. But by then another presidential sex scandal had arisen involving a young White House intern, Monica Lewinsky. Paula Jones's attorneys, digging deep into Clinton's sexual past in search of a pattern of harassment, uncovered evidence of a relationship between the intern and the president. Under oath, Lewinsky denied the charge. In January 1998, Starr's office received secretly taped conversations between Lewinsky and another former White House employee, Linda Tripp, in which Lewinsky talked of having oral sex with the president in the White House. Starr's office was granted authority to include the Lewinsky matter in its investigation.

All through 1998 the press kept the scandal before the public, as Clinton issued categorical denials. The president's defenders insisted that he was the victim of a political hatchet job. Hillary Clinton told a television interviewer that the attack was part of "a vast right wing conspiracy" to overthrow an elected president. However, the story began to unravel slowly before Starr's grand jury in Washington, D.C. In August 1998, Lewinsky testified before it under immunity. Confronted with a growing body of evidence, including a stained dress worn by Lewinsky during one of her trysts with the president, Clinton agreed to testify. For four hours on August 6 he answered questions from Starr's staff on videotape. In a televised speech to the nation

on that same day, Clinton offered the first of what was to be a long sequence of apologies, stating: "I did have a relationship with Ms. Lewinsky that was not appropriate. . . . It constituted a critical lapse in judgment and a personal failure on my part for which I am solely and completely responsible."

On September 9 Starr reported to Congress that he had found "substantial and credible information . . . that may constitute grounds for impeachment." The most serious was the charge that the president lied in his deposition in the Jones civil suit when he testified that he had not had sexual relations with Lewinsky. The report, which the House Judiciary Committee subsequently made public, contained Lewinsky's lurid account of her encounters with Clinton. Perhaps most stunning was the revelation that several of their trysts had taken place during the 1996 election campaign and while the Starr investigation was in full swing.

After several weeks of partisan bickering, on October 8 the House authorized the House Judiciary Committee to conduct an impeachment inquiry after the elections. When the Democrats picked up five seats in the House and polls showed that two-thirds of Americans did not want the president impeached, many thought some compromise resolution of censure might be possible.

All compromise proposals demanded (in the words of one offered by former presidents Ford and Carter) that "President Clinton would have to accept rebuke while acknowledging his wrongdoing and the very real harm he has caused." The president was willing to strike a deal, and on November 13 he agreed to pay Paula Jones $850,000 to drop her lawsuit without admitting guilt. But most House Republicans continued to believe that Clinton's actions warranted impeachment. On December 12, the House Judiciary Committee concluded its televised impeachment hearings and recommended four articles to the House. On December 19, in highly partisan votes, President Clinton was impeached on two articles, one charging perjury and a second obstruction of justice.

Clinton's impeachment trial ran for five weeks, from January 7 to February 12, 1999, when the Senate voted on the two articles. On the charge that the president "willfully provided perjurious, false and misleading testimony" to the grand jury, the vote was 45 Senators yes and 55 (including 10 Republicans) no. On the obstruction-of-justice charge, the vote was 50 yes and 50 no (including 5 Republicans). Since it would have taken a two-thirds vote to convict, Clinton was acquitted.

Throughout, Clinton steadfastly refused to consider resignation, and he was bolstered by unwavering support in opinion polls. Around two-thirds of the public consistently rejected the notion that the president should be removed from office. Even though a majority of Americans believed that Clinton had lied and obstructed justice, his job approval ratings remained high. Immediately after the Senate trial, 64 percent of Americans said that they approved of the decision to acquit, though only 39 percent thought that the decision vindicated Clinton. As a person, however, 57 percent rated Clinton negatively and 35 percent positively.

The president's worst enemies were disgusted and dismayed by his acquittal. "Let's move on," said Senator Bob Smith of New Hampshire. "He won. He always wins." But it was not so clear-cut. Greatly relieved, the president once again spoke contritely to the American people. "Acquittal wasn't cheap," observed *U.S. News and World Report.* Indeed, the scandals had deeply stained both the president and his partisan critics in Congress.

While Clinton could not escape responsibility for the nation's fixation on his sexual misdeeds, probably the most unpopular figure in the whole drama was Kenneth Starr. Although Starr did to some extent rescue his reputation as a partisan, puritanical, right-wing zealot (a reputation played up by the White House and many in the popular media) in an appearance before the House Judiciary Committee, his expensive, seemingly endless investigation convinced most Washington politicians that the Independent Counsel Act should not be renewed, or, at least, that it should be seriously altered. Critics were appalled that the Starr investigation cost tens of millions of dollars, and they also charged that Starr intimidated witnesses. Susan McDougal, for example, spent more than a year in prison for refusing to answer Starr's questions. Democrats and Republicans have long differed over the wisdom of the independent counsel law, depending upon which party has been in control of the White House. The excesses of the Starr team, however, caused unease throughout Congress and among the general populace.

❧ *The Election of 1998*

Many Republicans had believed that the Clinton scandals would produce substantial gains for them in the elections of 1998, but the Democrats retained forty-five seats in the Senate and gained five in the House, shrinking the Republican majority to twelve votes. Republicans retained the governorships in eight of the ten largest states in the country, but the Democrats won the coveted governorship of California. Republicans took heart from the fact that two sons of former president George Bush won governorships in politically important Texas and Florida, but elsewhere, momentum seemed to be turning to the Democrats.

These returns caused Republicans in Congress to rethink their bitter anti-Clinton agenda. Gingrich, already embattled a year earlier by his own scandal involving the use of tax-exempt money for political purposes and giving inaccurate information to the House Ethics Committee about it, resigned as Speaker and from Congress. It was clear that the public was disgusted by the political fighting, and particularly by the extended investigation of the president. The mud that had been slung seemed to stick to everyone in Washington. In 1998, turnout dropped to 36.1 percent of registered voters, the lowest since 1942.

❧ *Soaring Economy, Budget Surpluses, and Post-Scandal Politics*

To some extent, the robust economy eased minds anguished by the political wars in Washington. In 1999, the Congressional Budget Office reached the startling conclusion that the budget surplus could amount to a staggering $2.6 trillion over the next decade. While much of that surplus came from overpayment of Social Security taxes beyond the amount needed for immediate disbursement, even regular tax collections would provide a surplus of $787 billion over the decade. The president's proposed budget for 2000 included billions of dollars in new spending, as well as "targeted" tax cuts, but he also promised not to tap into the surplus and to propose a plan that would pay off the national debt by 2013. To accomplish this, the administration offered a package of new taxes and the closing of corporate tax loopholes. Of course, all of this depended on the economy continuing to grow rapidly and the world remaining peaceful. Insisting that the surplus must be preserved to protect Social Security and Medicare, Democrats hoped to stall a Republican initiative to cut taxes. Because of American involvement in a war with Serbia, Clinton had to request a major increase in military funding in 1999, and the Republicans appropriated far more than the president requested.

Many Washington insiders believed that the Republican Party was still paralyzed by loyalty to its right-wing base and the legacy of Gingrich. So preoccupied had the party been with Clinton's destruction that it failed to articulate an agenda. Many Republicans feared that their party had aided Clinton's adroit political moves to marginalize them by embracing many of their basic demands. A 1999 Gallup poll showed that a majority of Americans still felt that "moral problems" rather than "economic problems" were the most important issue facing the nation, but Republicans felt they must offer more than "moral cleansing" (as the *New York Times* charged) as a party platform. After a summit meeting in 1999, Republican congressional leaders agreed on an agenda that included tax cuts, increased defense spending, local control of schools, and privatization of Social Security, pointedly omitting such divisive issues as partial birth abortion and abolition of the National Endowment for the Arts.

❧ *Searching for a Foreign Policy*

Aside from his vigorous promotion of free trade, Clinton's early foreign policy seemed tentative. He had promised, in broad generalities, to address the problems of the post–Cold War era. Indeed, there was an idealistic Wilsonian quality to Clinton's foreign policy statements. Advancing democracy should be the object of "a long-term Western strategy," he said, but he openly acknowledged that the future focus of American foreign policy would be expanding the global economy. Clinton seemed to echo former president Jimmy Carter in calling for a global American-led campaign to ensure respect for human rights. During the 1992 campaign he had blasted the Bush administration for not doing more to stop conflict in former Yugoslavia. Given his youthful opposition to the war in Vietnam and his uneasy relationship with the military, it was ironic that Clinton used American armed force at least as generously as had his Republican predecessors. But Thomas Jefferson and Woodrow Wilson had found themselves in similar predicaments. For Clinton and his successors, foreign conflicts would be intra- as well as international, pitting tribes against tribes, religion against religion, ethnic groups against ethnic groups, rather than nations against nations.

New realities faced the world in the 1990s. Everywhere, globalizing economic, political, and cultural trends faced countervailing outbreaks of nationalism. Festering centuries-long conflicts, such as a Kurdish resistance to Turkish rule and the Kosovar Albanians' struggle against Serb domination, broke into the open. These conflicts were not new, but the Cold War had kept them under wraps. During the last two decades of the century, millions died in civil wars or insurgen-

cies in Afghanistan, Turkey, the Basque region of Spain, Sri Lanka, Indonesia, Colombia, Guatemala, Israel and the West Bank, Iraq, Chechnya, and in such African countries as Angola, Mozambique, Ethiopia, Liberia, Rwanda, Sierra Leone, Sudan, and Somalia. The bloodshed in these little-noticed wars was appalling: in early 2002, for example, it was reported that at least three million had perished in civil and tribal strife in Congo over the preceding three years. In 1999, around 14,000 United Nations military and civilian personnel, including 658 Americans, were deployed in peacekeeping missions in seventeen countries.

❧ *Peacekeeping and "Nation Building"*

Bill Clinton inherited an intractable mess in civil war–torn Somalia, where late in 1992 the outgoing Bush administration had authorized a U.S.-led, UN-sanctioned military intervention in hopes of saving the population from starvation. During the Cold War, first Moscow and then Washington had poured weapons into this poor but strategic place, bidding for the support of its dictator, Mohamed Siad Barre. When the Cold War ended he was overthrown, and fighting erupted between clan leaders. Thousands fled, and many who remained faced mass starvation. Although a similar situation existed in Sudan, the American media chose to focus on the swollen bellies and fly-covered corpses in Somalia. In response to public outrage, the Bush administration in December secured UN Security Council approval and landed 28,000 American troops at Somalia's capital, Mogadishu. Fittingly, given the prominent role played by the media in prompting the intervention, the troops wading ashore had to fight their way through scores of reporters and photographers. The expeditionary force set up a relief network but did not disarm the clans, which bided their time.

Clinton pledged to stay the course, but when Somali militiamen shot down a U.S. helicopter and massacred its crew, and then another eighteen Americans died in a firefight in October 1993, the American public lost heart. During the spring of 1995 the last of the U.S. and UN troops withdrew. Although the specter of mass starvation declined, Somalia reverted to anarchy.

Like most of its predecessors, the Clinton administration demonstrated the greatest concern about instability in the Caribbean. After the democratically elected president of Haiti, Jean-Bertrand Aristide, was overthrown in a coup, Clinton sent American troops to the country in 1994, responding to gross violations of human rights, to the prospect of a flood of refugees, and to pressure from African American members of Congress. Just before U.S. troops landed without resistance, former president Carter persuaded Haiti's military dictator to step down. Aristide was returned to power, but despite billions of dollars in American aid, Haiti remained mired in poverty and corruption. Many charged that Aristide's rule was no less tyrannical and corrupt than that of his predecessors. After U.S. aid had been cut off, Aristide was overthrown by another insurrection in 2004, and once again American, French, and other international peacekeepers were called upon to restore order. When international troops left in May, the island seemed once again destined to sink into poverty and military rule.

The collapse of Communism in Yugoslavia in 1991 and the subsequent savage civil wars there severely tested Clinton's commitment to preserving peace and building democratic nations. Yugoslavia splintered into ethnic and religious divisions that the postwar Communist dictatorship had always suppressed. Slovenia and Croatia declared independence, but to achieve it they had to fight the Serbs, who dominated what was left of Yugoslavia and were led by a demagogic Communist-turned-nationalist named Slobodan Milošević. When in 1992 predominantly Muslim Bosnia-Herzegovina also attempted to break away, war erupted between that small country's Serb and Croat minorities on the one hand and the largely Muslim Bosnian government on the other. Over the next three years tens of thousands of people died in civil strife or were uprooted from their homes in brutal "ethnic cleansing" campaigns. The United Nations inserted some 24,000 peacekeeping troops into the combat zones and negotiated one cease-fire after another, only to see all of them fail. When Clinton came into office there was considerable pressure to use American forces to relieve the Serb siege of Bosnia's capital, Sarajevo, and to stop the bloodshed. He insisted, however, that the Bosnian nightmare was a matter for NATO and the United Nations to handle and that the countries closest to the tragedy, particularly France and Germany, should take the lead.

In 1995 American negotiators persuaded Croatia, Bosnia, and the Serb-dominated rump Yugoslav federation to agree to a comprehensive peace plan calling for a Bosnia divided into Muslim-Croat and Serb sectors. The agreement promised protection of human rights and free elections. A cease-fire went into effect in October 1995, and 20,000 American troops were dispatched to Bosnia as a part of a 60,000-strong NATO peacekeeping operation.

In 1998 Milošević began an ethnic cleansing campaign in the Serb province of Kosovo, where a majority of the population was Albanian Muslims, and where a separatist guerrilla war had erupted. Clinton announced in March 1998 that it was a "moral imperative" to end the Serb atrocities in the area. After months of negotiations and threats demanding that Serb forces be removed from Kosovo, on March 24, 1999, NATO launched an American-led air campaign against the Serbs. Air strikes continued for 78 days before Milochseviaac agreed to the withdrawal of Serb troops from Kosovo (which remained nominally part of Serbia) and agreed that the region would be occupied by NATO troops. During the war NATO forces flew 35,000 missions and reportedly destroyed more than half of Yugoslavia's defense industry and 35 percent of its power. The bombs had fallen with amazing accuracy despite several unfortunate mistakes, including destruction of the Chinese embassy (mislabeled on a map), which killed several Chinese diplomats and set off a storm of protest in China. The end to the conflict was hastened by mediation by pro-Serb Russia, but interference by Russian troops in the occupation of Kosovo caused new tension.

The Kosovo campaign was a notable achievement for NATO, which turned fifty years old in 1998. In March 1999 NATO expanded to include three new member states and former Soviet satellites — the Czech Republic, Hungary, and Poland. While NATO hailed the Kosovo settlement as a victory, the future of Kosovo and the entire Balkan region remained clouded.

The Kosovo war won tepid support in Congress. Some in both parties condemned the NATO efforts as either too timid without ground troops, or else as arbitrary intrusion into the internal affairs of another nation. Some Republicans reflexively denounced the war as Clinton's attempt to divert attention from his personal scandals. But the president carefully cleared his actions with Congress, which approved a huge $289 billion military spending bill in June 1999.

The Clinton administration's effort to assist democratic, free-market regimes in replacing the defunct communist systems of Eastern Europe were complicated by relations with Russia, no longer communist, but as nationalistic as ever. He continued Bush's support for the bumbling Russian president Boris Yeltsin, and the United States and international financial institutions poured billions of dollars of investment into rebuilding Russia's economy. When Yeltsin stepped down in 2000, he left a legacy of gigantic financial mismanagement and corruption, a society still teetering on the verge of political and economic collapse, and a successor — Vladimir Putin — with questionable democratic credentials and a shadowy KGB background.

❧ War and Peace in the Middle East

The beginning of Clinton's second term came as tensions continued to rise in the Middle East. In 1997 Clinton faced pressure from human rights groups to halt new Israeli settlements in occupied territory as clashes between Israeli forces and Palestinians escalated. At the same time, American supporters of Israel demanded that Clinton support Prime Minister Benjamin Netanyahu in his determination to protect Israeli interests. After months of negotiations, the Clinton administration persuaded Netanyahu and Palestine Liberation Organization Chairman Yasser Arafat to convene at the Wye River Plantation in Maryland. In October 1997 the two sides signed the Wye River Memorandum, which promised some pullback of Israeli forces from the West Bank in return for renewed Palestinian efforts to control terrorism and to abandon a provision in their charter calling for the destruction of the state of Israel.

As Israeli-Palestinian tensions simmered, Iraq continued to cause problems for the United Nations. In January 1998, Saddam Hussein blocked UN inspectors from a number of suspected weapons sites. Under threat of force from the United States, Hussein finally agreed to admit inspectors to so-called "presidential sites" suspected of housing weapons of mass destruction. Clinton warned that if Iraq reneged on its pledge to let UN inspectors do their job, "then the United States . . . would have the unilateral right to respond at a time, place, or manner of our own choosing." Later that year Saddam again refused to cooperate with inspectors in an attempt to get the UN to end its economic sanctions on Iraq. When negotiations failed, U.S. and British air forces bombed several presidential sites. In the UN, meanwhile, France, Russia, and China, who wished to open trade relations with Iraq, pushed for a lifting of the UN sanctions.

❧ The Clinton Legacy

Scandals aside, Bill Clinton contributed significantly to the reshaping of American domestic policy. Like Jimmy Carter, Clinton was a Baptist southerner who tried to position himself in the political center while holding the allegiance of the left wing of his party. But Clinton was more successful than Carter in striking that balance. It

was a virtuoso act, worthy of another southern Democratic president, Lyndon Johnson. In the Middle East, the Balkans, and Northern Ireland, Clinton sought with some success to persuade ancient enemies that peace and reconciliation were not only possible but inevitable.

The Clinton presidency could never escape the stigma of scandal and impeachment. Days before the end of his term the president struck a deal effectively ending the Whitewater investigation, admitting that he had given false testimony under oath in the Lewinsky case and agreeing to a five-year suspension of his law license. Many of those closest to Clinton, like his friend and political adviser for five years, George Stephanopoulos, wondered "what might have been — if only this good president had been a better man."

PEAKS AND VALLEYS IN THE PRESIDENCY OF GEORGE W. BUSH

George W. Bush assumed the presidency in a nation deeply divided by the disputed election of 2000. A clear loser in popular votes, Bush was declared the winner only after weeks of legal wrangling that ended when the Supreme Court ruled that he had won Florida's electoral votes by a minuscule margin.

When he entered the White House Bush talked of bringing to Washington the consensus-building skills that had served him well as governor of Texas, but his early days did not bring major accomplishments. Then the September 11 terrorist attack vaulted him into the role of national spokesman in a time of national trauma. He acted with resolve and won the resounding support of the American people. Bush's crafting of a vigorous, and to some extent new, foreign policy that asserted America's right to unilaterally use preemptive military strikes when it was in the nation's interest was by far the most important legacy of his presidency, and also his most controversial. By the time his campaign for reelection had begun, Bush had become an extremely polarizing figure, hated by some of his critics with a passion that rivaled the Clintonphobia of rightwingers. The president's victory in 2004 positioned him to push aggressively for his conservative agenda.

❧ The Election of 2000

Both parties entered the 2000 presidential campaign with front-running candidates. Clinton's vice president, Al Gore, faced a challenge from former New Jersey Senator Bill Bradley in the primaries, but he had the backing of the party establishment and easily won the nomination. The leading Republican contender was the governor of Texas, George W. Bush, the son of President George Herbert Walker Bush. Bush, who had raised large sums of money before the campaign began, was challenged in the primaries by Senator John McCain of Arizona. A Vietnam War hero, McCain ardently supported campaign finance reform and attracted many independents. McCain won a surprise victory in the New Hampshire primary, but after Bush's strong showing in the March "Super Tuesday" primaries, McCain was forced out of the race. As his vice-presidential nominee, Gore chose Senator Joseph Lieberman of Connecticut, an observant orthodox Jew who had criticized the moral transgressions of Hollywood and President Clinton. Bush selected former Wyoming congressman Richard B. Cheney as his running mate. Cheney had served as secretary of defense during Bush's father's administration and had since been an executive in the oil industry.

The booming economy and budget surpluses favored the Democrats, and Gore presented himself as an experienced, competent national leader. Bush portrayed himself as a "compassionate conservative," intent on appearing more sympathetic to the suffering of the poor than his father had been portrayed. Bush strategists hoped to make the election a referendum on "character," forcing Gore and the Democrats to answer for the stains left on the presidency by Clinton. Critically important to the final outcome was the candidacy of Ralph Nader on the Green Party ticket. Nader, a long-time icon of the environmental movement, refused pleas from the Democrats to drop his candidacy, and his presence clearly cut into Gore's support.

In spite of George W. Bush's success as governor of Texas, many Democrats believed that he was incompetent. But in their televised debates Bush, though sometimes less knowledgeable than Gore, seemed more articulate than expected, and transparently sincere. On the other hand, Gore appeared stiff and wooden; one cartoonist began to picture the vice president as "Gorbot." Gore failed to present himself effectively as the heir to Clinton's successes. Each party raised unprecedented amounts to finance its campaign and worked diligently to get out its core supporters, and opinion polls indicated that the outcome would be very close.

After the Supreme Court awarded him disputed Florida, Bush won the presidency by 271 to 266 electoral votes. In popular votes, Gore came out on top, with 50,992,335 votes (48.38 percent) to Bush's 50,455,156 (47.87 percent) — a plurality of over half a million votes.

Early in the evening on November 7, 2000, all of the major television networks projected that Gore had won a close race for Florida's electoral votes. But as the night wore on, the networks retracted their Florida projections even as it became apparent that the national election hinged on the outcome in that state. At 2:15 a.m. the next morning the networks concluded that Bush had won Florida and proclaimed him the victor. Gore called Bush to concede defeat. But less than an hour later his aides persuaded him that Florida was still too close to call, and he telephoned Bush to retract his concession. The razor-thin Florida vote automatically triggered a recount, and reacting to claims of irregularities, both sides sent swarms of lawyers into the state. Gore's team requested a hand recount in four Florida counties that were Democratic strongholds. The Democratic challenge in Florida was based on a confusing "butterfly" ballot used in Palm Beach County, which some Gore voters marked incorrectly, and on voting machine problems in three other counties where punch-card ballots had failed to register because of "hanging chads." Florida Secretary of State Katherine Harris, the Republican official responsible for certifying the state's electoral results, insisted that a machine recount of the votes should be used to determine the official result, and on November 26th Harris certified that Bush had won Florida's electoral votes by 537 popular votes. The Florida Supreme Court, composed mostly of Democrats, ordered hand recounts. To the surprise of many observers, the U.S. Supreme Court agreed to hear an appeal of the Florida decision from Bush's lawyers. On December 12, in a 5-4 ruling, the Supreme Court for the first time intervened in a presidential election, halting the Florida recounts. The next day Gore conceded the election. It was the first time since 1888 (when Benjamin Harrison ousted Grover Cleveland) that the electoral-college winner had fewer popular votes, and the first presidential election since 1876 in which the outcome had to be decided by arbitration.

Many Democrats were outraged that the election had been settled by a conservative-majority Supreme Court. A consortium of news agencies undertook a "comprehensive review" of the Florida results, and in November 2001 the groups published findings that defused some discontent: they concluded that had the recount proceeded in the four counties requested by Gore's lawyers, Bush would still have won. On the other hand, the consortium observed that Gore might have won a statewide recount. Inevitably, loyal Democrats charged Bush with having "stolen" the election, and for many he was never the legitimate president. So close was the outcome, however, that the same charges would have been made by Republicans against a victorious Gore. The issue festered until the 2004 election.

The election of 2000 highlighted the nearly even social and political divide in the U.S. at the beginning of the twenty-first century. The Democrats gained four Senate seats, leaving a 50-50 balance; Republicans controlled the upper house only with the vote of the vice president, its presiding officer under the Constitution. Among notable Democratic victories was Hillary Rodham Clinton's capture of the New York seat vacated by Daniel Moynihan. The Democrats gained one House seat, producing a division of 221 Republicans, 212 Democrats, and two independents. In the election of 2000, Democrats carried the populous coastal areas and urban patches across the country, while Republicans won in the heartland. Gore won the popular vote; Bush carried about three-fourths of the nation's counties. Democrats were most at home with labor unions, feminists, gays and lesbians, African Americans and other minorities, liberal Christians and Jews, and city dwellers; Republicans were the favorites of business, white men, the Religious Right, and those from more homogenous areas of the country. In the end, George W. Bush's triumph (like his father's defeat) owed much to a third-party candidate. Ralph Nader received only 2,882,897 votes nationwide (2.74 percent), but in Florida, his 97,488 votes clearly could have swung the state — and the election — to Al Gore.

❧ George W. Bush Takes the Helm

George Walker Bush joined John Quincy Adams as the only presidential son to be elected to the office. Born in 1946 in New Haven, Connecticut, Bush moved with his family to Texas when he was two years old. Later he attended the prestigious Phillips Andover Academy in Massachusetts (as had his father) and graduated from Yale — where he did not have a stellar academic career. Graduating in 1968, Bush served two years in the Texas Air National Guard, where he learned to fly fighter jets, but did not have to serve in Vietnam. Bush acknowledged that he went through a "nomadic" period during the early seventies that included heavy drinking and possible drug abuse. (He subsequently joked that he could pass background checks only as far back as

1974.) He enrolled at Harvard Business School in 1972 and earned an M.B.A; he was the first president to hold a business degree. Bush returned to Midland, Texas, where he formed an independent oil and gas exploration business and in 1977 married Laura Welch, a teacher and librarian.

Bush made his first political foray in 1978, unsuccessfully running for the House of Representatives. Returning to the oil business, he amassed a considerable personal fortune. Disturbed by Bush's heavy drinking, in 1985 his parents arranged a meeting in which evangelist Billy Graham encouraged him to give up alcohol and become a more committed Christian. He began to turn his life around, becoming more serious and religious. George W. Bush was not an official member of the Bush campaign team in 1988, but he was his father's closest confidant and an important point of contact with Christian conservatives in the Republican Party. In 1989 he organized a group of wealthy investors in Dallas to purchase the Texas Rangers baseball team, giving him increased public visibility. He sold his share of the team in 1998 for a handsome profit.

In 1994, Bush ran for governor of Texas and, to the surprise of many political observers, decisively defeated the popular Democratic governor. Despite his lack of political experience, Bush proved to be an effective campaigner; he spoke matter-of-factly and without pretense, promising increased local control of schools and welfare reform. As governor, Bush was affable and personable in one-on-one meetings, and he turned out to be a successful consensus builder, winning unprecedented support from Democrats in the Texas legislature. In 1998, he won reelection by an impressive 65 percent to 35 percent majority. Bush immediately became the front-running candidate for the Republican presidential nomination, and he began amassing a huge campaign chest long before announcing his intention to run.

Bush had pledged a bipartisan approach while running for the presidency, and many applauded his appointment of popular general Colin Powell as the first African American secretary of state. Condoleezza Rice, also an African American, became the president's national security adviser. Other Bush appointments were less conciliatory. Like his running mate Dick Cheney, most of his closest advisors were career Republicans, many of whom had served in previous GOP administrations. In view of subsequent events, his most important cabinet nominees were Secretary of Defense Donald Rumsfeld and Attorney General John Ashcroft. Rumsfeld, a crusty veteran of government service and in the business world, had served as secretary of defense during the Ford presidency. Ashcroft, who narrowly lost his Senate seat in Missouri during the 2000 elections, was known in Washington for his devout Pentecostal background and his strongly conservative views on such issues as abortion and the death penalty. His nomination was vigorously, but unsuccessfully, opposed in the Senate.

9/11

The world changed on September 11, 2001. At 8:02 that morning, American Airlines Flight 11 left Boston's Logan Airport for Los Angeles, but shortly after takeoff it was seized by hijackers. Mohamed Atta, one of five Muslim extremists on board the flight, had attended flight school to learn to fly jets, as had several of his accomplices. Atta's suitcase, abandoned at Logan Airport, contained a video on flying airplanes, a fuel consumption calculator, and a copy of the Koran. Atta flew the plane to New York City. At 8:48 a.m., Flight 11 struck the North Tower of the World Trade Center, between the 95th and 103rd floors. All 92 people onboard the Boeing 767 died, including nine flight attendants and two pilots. Exactly fifteen minutes later, United Airlines Flight 175, a Boeing 757 scheduled to fly from Boston to Los Angeles, crashed into the South Tower at about the 80th floor, killing all 65 people on board. A third plane, American Airlines 77, departed Washington Dulles Airport at 8:10 with 64 passengers and crew on a scheduled flight to Los Angeles; hijacked and flown into the Pentagon, it caused a five-story section of the building to collapse. A fourth flight, United 93, departed Newark, New Jersey, at 8:01 with 44 persons on board, bound for San Francisco. Hijackers commandeered it and steered it toward Washington, D.C., probably intending to crash into either the White House or the Capitol. Hearing of the other crashes by cell phones, several of the passengers decided to overpower the hijackers. Passenger Todd Beamer's "Let's roll" was the last utterance heard by the outside world before United 93 crashed near Shanksville, Pennsylvania. Four commercial airplanes, departing three cities within twelve minutes of each other, had carried out the worst attack on American soil since the bombing of Pearl Harbor.

The horror of 9/11 was graphically recorded on television. Cameras focused on the burning North Tower were able to record the crash of the second jet into the South Tower. At 10:05 a.m. the South Tower collapsed, crushing to death people trying to escape as well as rescue workers from the New York police and fire departments. Twenty-four minutes later the North Tower went down, killing many more. Both buildings had been built to sustain the impact of a jet crash, but the heat generated by the jets' 18,000 gallons of fuel melted the buildings' superstructures and caused them to pancake. It was a scene of unimaginable horror and heroism, filled with images of trapped victims plunging to their death and soot-covered workers rushing to their own death while attempting to save those fleeing the buildings. The final tally of the number of people killed by the terror attacks was estimated at nearly 3,000.

The 9/11 attacks sent shock waves around the world and elicited an outpouring of sympathy for the victims. International leaders, including many Muslim heads of state, condemned the act and pledged to support a new worldwide effort to suppress terrorism. Condemnation of the events of 9/11 was not universal, however; Americans were shocked and angered by scenes of cheering and dancing Palestinians and Jordanians.

In the weeks following the 9/11 attacks, patriotism soared. The public rallied around Bush, whose job approval rating soared to 90 percent, and New York City firefighters, policemen, and Mayor Rudolph Giuliani became national heroes. Congress reacted immediately to assure compensation for those who had been killed in the attacks. To save the major airlines from bankruptcy, Congress overwhelmingly passed a $15 billion bailout package.

The War on Terrorism

Nineteen hijackers died in the suicide attacks. All were from the Middle East; twelve were from the underdeveloped, highly tribal southwestern provinces of Saudi Arabia. It soon became apparent that all were linked to the notorious al Qaeda terror network headed by Osama bin Laden, which had been implicated in earlier attacks of Americans, including a 1993 truck bombing of the World Trade Center in which six people died and more than a thousand were injured. In 1998, al Qaeda terrorists bombed American embassy compounds in Kenya and Tanzania, killing more than two hundred. Just eleven months before the 9/11 attack on the World Trade Center an American destroyer, the U.S.S. *Cole*, was bombed near Aden, Yemen, leaving 17 sailors dead and 39 injured. Five conspirators were convicted and sentenced to long prison terms after the 1993 bombing of the World Trade Center. Four terrorists were captured after the embassy bombings through the efforts of the Kenyan police and the most massive overseas deployment of FBI agents in the history of the agency. In the late 1990s bin Laden transferred his operation to Afghanistan where he operated freely under the protection of the Taliban, ultra-fundamentalist Muslims who seized control of that country some years after the expulsion of the Soviets in 1989.

President Clinton promised to bring to justice those responsible for the bombings in Africa and of the *Cole,* and the United States launched retaliatory missile strikes against terrorist camps in Afghanistan and the Sudan. But the 9/11 attacks raised the issue of terrorism to a new level. Bush declared war on terrorism, vowing that the United States would hunt down the terrorists and those who harbored them. The president's vow received bipartisan support in Congress and promises of cooperation from nations around the world.

The war on terrorism set off feverish activity both at home and abroad. Bush appointed Pennsylvania governor Tom Ridge to a new cabinet-level position, the Director of Homeland Security; later, twenty-two existing government agencies were combined into the Department of Homeland Security, including the Immigration and Naturalization Service, the Customs Service, and the Coast Guard. It was the most sweeping transformation of the government since the formation of the Department of Defense in 1947. Among other things, the new department was charged with revamping the nation's airport security and immediately began training 50,000 airport screeners. The huge new department was also charged with protecting against terrorism through the analysis of intelligence, guarding the nation's borders and airports, and coordinating responses to threatened attacks. Many doubted that the agency would greatly increase security, and conservatives were deeply suspicious of such a huge expansion of the federal bureaucracy. But the agency became a highly visible presence, especially with its color-coded alerts of potential attacks.

Particularly targeted for reform was the system of airport security that had so clearly failed on September 11. Both the FBI and CIA came under heavy criticism. Hearings in Congress revealed lapses in communication that led to a reorganization of the FBI and a large expansion of the counterterrorism section of the CIA.

Attacks continued around the world, including the kidnapping and murder of *Wall Street Journal* reporter Daniel Pearl in Karachi, Pakistan, and a horrific bombing in Bali, Indonesia, in October 2002 that killed more than 200 tourists. By the end of 2002, the Pentagon had

September 11, 2001 As the North Tower of the World Trade Center burns from the first terrorist attack, hijacked United Flight 175 crashes into the South Tower. Within an hour, both towers would collapse. These, and the simultaneous attack on the Pentagon and the apparently attempted destruction of either the Capitol or the White House, were the first serious enemy strikes on the U.S. mainland since the War of 1812.

dispatched American Special Forces to the Philippines, Yemen, and the former Soviet republic of Georgia to train anti-terrorist troops. Some two hundred nations pledged support for the war on terrorism, and by late 2003 more than three thousand suspects had been detained around the world. Perhaps the most successful battle in the War on Terror was the worldwide effort to disrupt the financial resources of al Qaeda, Hamas,

Islamic Jihad, and other terrorist organizations. The most controversial reaction to the terrorist attacks was the passage of the Patriot Act on October 26, 2001, with only one dissenting vote in the Senate and by 357 to 66 in the House. The act gave law enforcement agencies increased surveillance and investigative powers, especially regarding gathering information from the Internet and cell phones. The act was staunchly defended by Bush's attorney general, John Ashcroft, and just as vigorously attacked by civil libertarians. In the two years after the 9/11 attacks, more than five thousand citizens of foreign countries were detained under anti-terrorism provisions in the new law. Without assurances of due process and speedy trials — the constitutional right of American citizens — these detainees could be held without charges and without access to counsel. More than five hundred of those arrested were deported for immigration violations, and others spent lengthy periods in jail before being brought to trial. Islamic organizations and Muslim citizens complained that they were unfair targets in the war on terror, and civil rights cases began to be reviewed by the courts by 2003. But government leaders tried to calm public anger against Middle Easterners in the wake of the attacks, and there were only sporadic episodes of vigilante action.

For months after the attacks anxiety remained high concerning new terrorist threats. In late September and early October four letters were mailed to American political and media figures, including Senators Tom Daschle and Patrick Leahy and NBC anchorman Tom Brokaw, containing deadly anthrax spores. Twenty-three people who came into contact with other such letters contracted the disease, and five died. An expensive cleanup followed, but years later no one had been charged in the incident.

❧ *The War on Terror Goes Abroad: Afghanistan*

George Bush promised to bring Osama bin Laden and al Qaeda to justice. When the Taliban government of Afghanistan refused to cooperate, in early October American and British warplanes launched a high-tech assault on Taliban forces and al Qaeda training camps hidden in the rugged country's cave-riddled mountains. American Marines and Special Forces coordinated attacks with a hodgepodge of anti-Taliban resistance fighters, and before the end of the year the Taliban regime collapsed. However, bin Laden remained at large, and many al Qaeda operatives escaped into Pakistan.

The military action in Afghanistan, and the country's subsequent rebuilding, were supported by most of America's European allies. Several thousand American troops remained in Kabul to help maintain order, but the new government's control of the rest of the country remained tenuous.

One of the legacies of the war in Afghanistan was the detainment of around 650 Taliban and al Qaeda prisoners in a specially constructed prison at the Guantanamo naval base in Cuba. The United States maintained that the prisoners were "enemy combat-

---

❀ IN THEIR OWN WORDS

President Bush Addresses the Nation, September 11, 2001

After the chaos of the day's events, President Bush gathered himself and addressed the nation on the evening of September 11. His themes of national strength and the value of freedom and his use of biblical imagery remain hallmarks of his presidential rhetoric.

Good evening. Today, our fellow citizens, our way of life, our very freedom came under attack in a series of deliberate and deadly terrorist acts. The victims were in airplanes, or in their offices; secretaries, businessmen and women, military and federal workers; moms and dads, friends and neighbors. Thousands of lives were suddenly ended by evil, despicable acts of terror.

The pictures of airplanes flying into buildings, fires burning, huge structures collapsing, have filled us with disbelief, terrible sadness, and a quiet, unyielding anger. These acts of mass murder were intended to frighten our nation into chaos and retreat. But they have failed; our country is strong....

America and our friends and allies join with all those who want peace and security in the world, and we stand together to win the war against terrorism. Tonight, I ask for your prayers for all those who grieve, for the children whose worlds have been shattered, for all whose sense of safety and security has been threatened. And I pray they will be comforted by a power greater than any of us, spoken through the ages in Psalm 23: "Even though I walk through the valley of the shadow of death, I fear no evil, for You are with me."

This is a day when all Americans from every walk of life unite in our resolve for justice and peace. America has stood down enemies before, and we will do so this time. None of us will ever forget this day. Yet, we go forward to defend freedom and all that is good and just in our world.

Security Alert   In the wake of September 11, Americans and travelers around the world became increasingly familiar with having to endure waits and inspections, especially at airports. Here airline travelers wait to pass through security at the Fort Lauderdale airport.

ants" who could be lawfully detained until the cessation of hostilities and resisted efforts by international organizations to gain access to the detainees, though over time opposition to the prison camp grew within the U.S. and abroad.

✤ Operation Iraqi Freedom

In his State of the Union speech in January 2002, President Bush broadened the war on terrorism, naming Iran, North Korea, and Iraq an "axis of evil" — a highly controversial phrase — threatening world peace. In June 2002, the president warned that stateless terrorists were seeking weapons of mass destruction from rogue nations. In this new environment, he said, the United States would not hesitate to strike preemptively if necessary.

The message to Iraqi president Saddam Hussein was clear. In the summer and fall of 2002, Bush began to build a case for removing Saddam from power, publicly asserting on October 7 that Iraq possessed chemical and biological weapons and that Saddam was actively building a nuclear arsenal. For several months, Bush tried to build an international coalition that would use military force, if necessary, to remove the brutal Iraqi

dictator. The Bush administration's embrace of the concept of preemptive war presented a watershed in the history of American foreign relations. But the president's vigorous assertion of America's right to take such action against Iraq failed to gain the support of several key nations, including China, Russia, France, and Germany, as well as many Islamic countries.

On September 12, 2002, Bush addressed the United Nations General Assembly, urging the Security Council to quickly enforce its mandate to verify the disarming of Iraq (which had illegally expelled weapons inspectors in 1998). Otherwise, he warned, the United Nations would become irrelevant. Led by France and Germany, the Security Council pressured Iraq to allow the return of inspectors to search for weapons of mass destruction (WMDs), and Iraq agreed to allow UN weapons inspectors to resume working in the country. But Bush's patience wore thin with the slow pace of inspection and its failure to uncover evidence of Iraqi violations. Citing evidence from both American and British intelligence sources about the imminent danger of Iraqi WMDs, Bush insisted that the United States had no option but to build a coalition to protect the world and, if need be, to act unilaterally. Bolstered by fears of WMDs, Congress passed resolutions authorizing the president to use the U.S. military against Iraq. The resolution received remarkable bipartisan votes of 296-133 in the Republican-controlled House of Representatives and 77 to 23 in the Democrat-controlled Senate.

Blocked from gaining UN approval, the United States and the United Kingdom announced their intention to lead a coalition that would remove Saddam Hussein from power and enforce Iraq's disarmament. France, Germany, Russia, and China continued to oppose using military force, as did Pope John Paul II, but Spain, Italy, Poland, and other former Soviet satellites gave their support. In early March the UN ordered its workers to withdraw from Iraq.

On March 19, 2003, Operation Iraqi Freedom began with air attacks. Coalition troops moved into the country the next day; Saddam Hussein boasted that the invading forces would suffer horrendous casualties. But U.S. and British troops moved rapidly through weak Iraqi resistance, entered Baghdad in mid-April, and fanned out around the country attacking pockets of resistance. On May 1, Bush announced that "major combat operations in Iraq have ended." The Pentagon reported 230 American deaths in the short war. The war enjoyed widespread public support in the United States, and Bush's poll ratings soared to all-time highs.

Bush critics had predicted a long and bloody war, and the swift military success did quiet some criticism. But postwar events proved more problematic. Serious questions were raised about how well the administration had planned for occupying and rebuilding Iraq. Looting and disorder persisted, and it proved difficult to restore order and basic services. More troublesome was the escalating violence against allied troops. Week after week coalition troops were killed by roadside bombs and attacks by small groups of fighters, particularly in the Sunni Muslim strongholds to the west and north of Baghdad. By the end of 2004, American loss of life in Iraq had risen to more than 1,000. Equally damaging to the administration was the failure to find evidence of weapons of mass destruction. Some critics of President Bush and British Prime Minister Tony Blair charged that the two leaders had deliberately misled their countries about the danger posed by Iraq. Even supporters of the war were embarrassed by the misleading intelligence reports regarding weapons of mass destruction and demanded reform of the FBI and CIA.

In 2004, efforts to reconstruct Iraq progressed slowly under the direction of an Iraqi Governing Council and an American-led Provisional Authority headed by Paul Bremer. Congress, after considerable debate, passed legislation appropriating almost $86 billion for the support of American troops and the reconstruction of Iraq. President Bush resolutely insisted that internal control of Iraq would be turned over to an interim government on June 30, and the U.S. cooperated with a United Nations Special Envoy, Lakhdar Brahimi, in selecting the members of the interim regime. This government was to have "full sovereignty" until national elections were held in January 2005. After his installation, Interim Prime Minister Ayad Allawi resolutely insisted that elections should take place as scheduled in spite of diehard resistance by insurgents. When the elections did in fact take place as scheduled, with high levels of voter turnout, support for efforts to rebuild the government increased around the world.

Still, American efforts to establish a stable government in Iraq were hindered by a series of setbacks in the summer of 2004 and beyond. Serious violence in the Sunni city of Fallujah and other cities led to ever-increasing bloodshed and instability. That problem was somewhat alleviated when American and Iraqi forces cleared Fallujah in house-to-house fighting in a fall campaign, but incidents of violence remained numerous in the Sunni Triangle. Adding to American embarrassment and worldwide disgust were revelations of abuse of Iraqi prisoners in Baghdad's notorious Abu Ghraib prison. In May, stunning photos of American soldiers abusing prisoners surfaced causing a media furor and providing new ammunition for opponents of the war. In the midst of such adverse publicity, public support for the war weakened. For the first time in years, the various branches of the armed services were unable to fill their enlistment quotas.

Even after the transfer of political authority to the Iraqi interim government, and some limited success in training Iraqi security forces, it seemed likely that most of the occupation force needed to stabilize a new democratic regime in Iraq would be American. Even after the January election, it was clear that a substantial number of American troops would continue to be needed to provide security.

❧ Assessing the Bush Foreign Policy

In its unilateralism, George Bush's post-9/11 foreign policy was not a radical departure from the past. Without Security Council approval, Bill Clinton used American armed forces in Bosnia in 1995 and in Kosovo in 1999. No serious American policymaker in the 1990s would advocate subordinating American national security to the United Nations. Still, Bush's actions in Afghanistan and Iraq raised new questions about the use of American force in the post–Cold War world. Its justification of preemptive war was a dramatic departure. The president's assertion that the protection of America from terrorist enemies and WMD threats justified preemptive military strikes and the targeting of rogue regimes raised serious questions about the future relationship of the United States to the United Nations, and also threatened the stability of NATO and the Western alliance, not to mention the credibility of the administration for many at home and abroad. Bush's aggressive policies did have some positive effects; for instance, Pakistani President Pervez Musharraf became an important ally in the war against terrorism (and showed a willingness to make peace with India) and Libya's Muammar Qaddafi abandoned his quest for WMD and

Mission Accomplished?   On May 1, 2003, George W. Bush donned a flight suit to make a dramatic landing on the USS *Abraham Lincoln* off San Diego, welcoming home sailors from the war in Iraq. A huge banner boasting "Mission Accomplished" stretched across the carrier's flight deck as Bush made his televised address to the crew and the nation. But in the months that followed, support for the action faltered under the burden of continued violence, prisoner abuses, and a failure to find weapons of mass destruction, though support increased again after successful Iraqi popular elections in 2005.

the United States had embarked on a new period of imperialism, claiming the right to take over and run countries for its own benefit. One critic labeled America a "rogue nation" that had embarked on a "unilateralist" foreign policy. Democratic centrists, including Senator John Kerry, offered a more balanced alternative to Bush's policies, calling for a rebuilding of America's alliance with such traditional allies as France and Germany to face the threats of terrorism and the proliferation of weapons of mass destruction. They believed that Bush's abandonment of the Western alliance and his unilaterialist approach were a dangerous departure from the diplomatic and military system that had provided world security for half a century. On the other side, conservatives (particularly a group often labeled "neoconservatives") believed that the United States, as the sole world superpower, was obliged to maintain world order. They were convinced that some of the nations of "Old Europe" were too willing to appease aggressors and that the United Nations was fatally flawed as an effective means of establishing international order.

Bush continued to try to downplay the severity of the rift between the United States and its traditional allies in Europe and Asia, but only time would tell how much the Iraqi war had done to alter the international landscape. At home, the military successes in Afghanistan and Iraq were at first popular. But questions remained whether the United States could stop international terrorism and construct democracies in the Middle East, and whether the American public would foot the bill and incur the necessary casualties. The Bush administration tried to emphasize its accomplishments, but by 2004 even Defense Secretary Donald Rumsfeld — who had been one of the most aggressive of Bush's advisers in pressing for war — conceded that finishing the job in Afghanistan and Iraq was likely to be a "long, hard slog."

opened his country to renewed economic and political ties with Western countries. On the other hand, North Korea and Iran showed little inclination to abandon plans for nuclear weapons.

Critics of Bush's aggressive foreign policy charged that

❧ *The Economy*

George W. Bush remembered well how economic issues had contributed to the defeat of his father in 1992. He had a Reagan-like confidence in supply-side economic theory, believing strongly both in reducing the size of government and increasing private sector purchasing power. He also, as it turned out, shared Reagan's affinity for deficit spending. Amid rosy projections of huge budget surpluses, Bush spent the first months of his new administration pushing for massive tax reductions. Although the Bush tax cut passed in 2001 was labeled a "compromise" after congressional Democrats negotiated some reductions, it resulted in a $1.35 trillion reduction in taxes spread over the next decade.

Still, in 2002 the economy faltered. Growth slowed, unemployment rose, and consumer confidence fell. Bush reacted dramatically. Heartened by a resounding Republican victory in the mid-year elections in 2002, Bush presented Congress with another proposal for large reductions in income tax rates. A combination of the huge expenses involved in the aftermath of September 11 and the war on terror, the war in Iraq, the slowing of the economy, and the Bush tax cuts pushed budget deficits to all-time highs. In the 2003 fiscal year the federal deficit reached $374.2 billion, more than double that of the year before, and predictions for the next year were even gloomier. But by the middle of 2004 the economy had improved markedly. Hundreds of thousands of new jobs were added during the first two quarters of the year, raising tax revenues but doing little to reduce the huge budget deficit.

❧ *Simmering Domestic Agendas*

Other traditional political battles raged in Washington in predictable ways. Bush infuriated environmentalists by easing regulations on businesses, encouraging the development of natural resources on federal lands, and rejecting out of hand the Kyoto Treaty for cutting greenhouse gases on grounds that it would harm the American economy. The president appointed Vice President Cheney to develop a new energy policy in cooperation with the oil companies, eliciting charges of collusion. An administration push to open oil drilling in the Arctic National Wildlife Refuge in Alaska drew strong resistance from environmentalists and failed to gain congressional approval.

Bush had advocated education reform while governor of Texas and he engaged Congress in a sweeping debate on that subject that resulted in passage of the No Child Left Behind Act in January 2002. The act increased testing requirements and accountability in public schools, and included provisions allowing children in low-performing schools to transfer to better ones, key planks in the Republican education agenda. On the other hand, Democratic public-education advocates were promised large increases in federal funding — which, however, the administration did not fully spend. Perhaps more significant for the future of public education in America, in 2002 the Supreme Court upheld the use of tax money to provide vouchers to students wishing to attend religious schools. President Bush established a White House office to promote "Faith Based and Community Initiatives." While unable to gain passage of a sweeping faith-based initiative bill, Bush continued to press to expand religious groups' access to federal social funding.

On another highly volatile culture-war issue the administration won a hard-fought victory. In October 2003 Congress passed by comfortable margins a bill banning "partial birth" abortions, the first restriction since 1973. Around 70 percent of the public favored the ban.

The Supreme Court remained delicately balanced during these years of political equilibrium, often rendering 5-4 decisions. On such hot issues as abortion rights, affirmative action, and church-state separation, Sandra Day O'Connor was usually the swing vote. Democrats feared that President Bush would push the Court further to the right, although Bush made no Supreme Court appointments in his first term. The Democrats delayed scores of Bush nominations to lower court judgeships; around 100 such appointments were awaiting action at the end of 2003. Senate Democrats on several occasions used the filibuster, a tactic with a long history in American politics, to stop the appointment of judges whose opinions they considered too radical. In May 2005 moderates in the Senate worked out a deal to end filibusters on some controversial judges, but the future promised more conflict over appointments to the federal bench.

❧ *Republicans Gain Momentum: The Elections of 2002 and 2004*

In June 2001, Vermont senator James M. Jeffords left the Republican Party and became an independent, enabling the Democrats to organize and lead the Senate. Suddenly, Bush was forced to work with an opposition-controlled Senate, and with a very small majority in the House. Under these circumstances, the mid-term elections of 2002 loomed large for both parties.

The political balance in Washington was dramatically changed by a Republican victory in the mid-term elections of 2002. The Republicans gained two seats in the Senate, giving them a tiny majority, and unexpectedly gained four seats in the House. Democratic candidates held their own in gubernatorial elections, including the reelection of Governor Gray Davis in the key state of California. (That victory was blunted when Davis was recalled by a popular vote in 2003 and replaced by Republican Arnold Schwarzenegger.) The big winner in the elections of 2002 was President Bush, who put his political capital on the line by aggressively campaigning in fifteen close states and raising $140 million for his party.

Both parties immediately pointed to the presidential election of 2004, and the campaign proved to be the longest and most expensive in American history. After early challenges from eight other hopefuls, including the maverick former governor of Vermont who was an outspoken critic of the war in Iraq, Howard Dean, and North Carolina Senator John Edwards, Senator John Kerry of Massachusetts clinched the Democratic nomination. He selected Senator Edwards as his running mate. Both Bush and Kerry accumulated huge financial caches, and during the summer, before the nominating conventions began, the two parties flooded television with ads, particularly in several "battleground states" where both parties believed they had a chance to win.

John Kerry had one of the most liberal voting records in the Senate, and his nomination marked the recapture of the party by the left wing from Clinton centrists. Early in the campaign Kerry struggled to put forward an identity that placed him in the political mainstream; in the process, his statements often seemed contradictory, as did his life story. A decorated hero during his service in Vietnam, he became a leader of anti-war veterans upon his return home. Kerry was first elected to the Senate in 1984 and was reelected for a fourth term in 2002. Married to the wealthy, accomplished, and independent Teresa Heinz Kerry, the Massachusetts Senator was a spokesperson for traditional Democratic constituencies, including African Americans, labor unions, and feminists. But it was not clear that he could establish the same visceral relationship with these groups that had served Bill Clinton so well. Early in the campaign, besieged by negative ads run by Republicans, Kerry was forced to spend much time and money defending his record and struggling consistently to define himself.

At the same time, George Bush faced formidable hurdles in his bid for reelection. The economic recovery (albeit with slow job growth) blunted Democratic attacks on that important issue, but the escalation of violence in Iraq, the ever-growing list of casualties, and the Abu Ghraib prison scandal caused Bush's job approval ratings to nosedive in the summer. The president's campaign seemed in serious trouble after public opinion polls showed him a clear loser to Kerry in a series of three televised debates. But each candidate had strengths and weaknesses — Kerry was favored by those most concerned about the economy and those opposed to the war in Iraq, and Bush was favored by those most concerned with the threat of terrorism and by declining "moral values."

Anticipating a replay of the contested 2000 election, both parties dispatched thousands of lawyers into the battleground states to assure that no voters were excluded. But George W. Bush won a relatively easy victory, garnering 51 percent of the popular vote (the first majority victory since his father's election in 1988), beating Kerry by more than 3.3 million votes. In the electoral college the margin was 286 to 252. Republican gains in Congress were equally impressive; the party gained four seats in the Senate and five in the House of Representatives, adding substantially to their majorities.

In some ways the election was very close; only three states changed party allegiance from 2000 to 2004 (Iowa and New Mexico from Democratic to Republican and New Hampshire the reverse). On the other hand, the growing Republican monopoly in the South, where the party elected five new Senators and where the president won by comfortable popular votes, and the solid grasp of the party on the heartland between the coasts clearly posed serious challenges for the Democratic Party.

George W. Bush successfully cut into a number of Democratic constituencies in the election of 2004, substantially increasing his vote among women and Hispanics (though still garnering only 47 and 42 percent of those groups). African Americans continued to be the most unshakable Democratic block, voting 89 percent for Kerry. Religion was also a significant vote predictor; more than 60 percent of those who said they attended church weekly voted for Bush.

Exit polls highlighted the fact that 22 percent of voters listed "moral values" as the most important issue in determining their vote, ahead of the economy, terrorism, and Iraq. Among those voters, 80 percent voted for George Bush. This upsurge in the moral vote was probably heightened by the fact that eleven states included on their ballot initiatives banning the recognition of gay marriages. In all eleven states, the measures passed. In an election termed the "most important of our lifetime" by both Democrats and the Republicans, concern for the sanctity of the traditional family clearly played an important role.

❧ *The Bush Record and Persona*

George Bush, like Bill Clinton, seemed destined to infuriate his opponents. Some doubted his intelligence and pictured him as a puppet manipulated by his father's old cronies, Dick Cheney and Donald Rumsfeld. A Chicago newspaper greeted the result of the 2004 election with the headline "RE-DUBYA." Bush did often seem inarticulate. His early defenses of the Iraqi War were laconic and vague, particularly when compared with the detailed and analytical defenses offered by British Prime Minister Tony Blair. September 11, tragic though it was, transformed Bush as a public figure and probably saved his administration. To a majority of the American public he became a heroic symbol of the nation's determination in crisis. And few doubted that Bush the president, like Bush the governor, was effective in face-to-face meetings with world and Congressional leaders.

George W. Bush seemed to a majority of Americans a sincere and honorable man. Princeton political scientist Fred Greenstein judged that his public demeanor revealed "a president who was serious, thoughtful, and neither defensive nor boastful." At his best, he appeared to be a man very much at peace with himself. After the first debate with John Kerry, when he had seemed testy and irritated, his wife Laura, who according to insiders was the person most likely to level with the president, told him, "I don't know what happened. You've got to be yourself, and you weren't."

More than any other American president, George W. Bush displayed his religion publicly, and his personal religiosity combined with his reliance on the Religious Right for support pushed religion to the forefront of American political life. When Bob Woodward asked if he consulted his father, Bush replied, "You know, he is the wrong father to appeal to in terms of strength. There is a higher father that I appeal to." While the president's faith was undoubtedly sincere, he sometimes used religion to justify himself personally to the Religious Right rather than relying on his policy agenda, which has been less uniformly appealing to some of his religiously conservative constituency. From the Religious Left (and the Vatican), critics questioned whether the U.S.

John F. Kerry   Senator John Kerry (D-Massachusetts) speaks with people attending a lunchtime forum at the Concord City Auditorium in New Hampshire. Kerry garnered the Democratic nomination for the presidency, but lost in the hotly contested presidential election of 2004.

action in Iraq met the necessary requirements of classical "just war" doctrine, while others denounced the Iraq war from enduring religious traditions of pacifism. Many believers on the left and the right ultimately had as much trouble finding common ground in the events surrounding the Bush presidency as anyone else.

❧ *A Second Term: Spending His Capital*

Bush announced that his hard-won victory had left him with a largess of political capital that he intended to spend in the upcoming four years. "Let me put it to you this way," said Bush in a post-election press conference, "I earned capital in the campaign, political capital, and now I intend to spend it. It is my style." He immediately began reshaping his team of advisers, replacing several important cabinet members, including Secretary of State Colin Powell, Attorney General John Ashcroft, and Tom Ridge, the head of the Department of Homeland Security. The president nominated Condoleezza Rice to succeed Colin Powell as secretary of state, and Alberto Gonzales, the son of migrant workers from Mexico, to be attorney general.

In spite of the Republican gains in Congress, during his second term Bush faced many thorny problems that would require compromise and statesmanship. The president promised to make major changes in the tax code and in the Social Security system, both formidable tasks. He faced future battles over reining in government spending, controlling soaring medical costs, dealing with a bundle of immigration issues, and an almost certain reshaping of the Supreme Court. The outcome of those battles, along with the success or failure of Bush's foreign policy, would determine his lasting historical reputation.

CONCLUSION: A DELICATE BALANCE

American politics remained delicately balanced between the two parties at the beginning of the twenty-first century. Partly that was because the centers of the two parties were not actually far apart. Domestically, both parties had embraced a limited welfare state, and both parties had more or less accepted the notion that private sector economic growth should be promoted at home and abroad. Plenty of differences remained. The two parties had clearly defined constituencies in the culture-war debates, and there were real differences on economic priorities, but both parties tried to occupy the center of the political spectrum.

Bill Clinton was a master politician with incredible survivability, but he was not able to lead his party to political dominance. George W. Bush also proved to be an effective politician and, in 2002 and 2004, he helped his party make gains that made the Republicans as dominant as either party had been in Washington since the beginning of the 1990s.

In some ways, Bill Clinton and George Bush reacted similarly to world events, although they were vastly different in style. But George W. Bush's vigorous actions against terrorists, and particularly the American intervention in Iraq, represented a new stage in America's relations with the rest of the world. Although much of Bush's threat to use American military might against anyone who harbored America's enemies in the war on

terrorism at first received bipartisan support in Washington, especially in light of the attack on the World Trade Center, criticism of the Iraq war abounded and grew as the effort to reconstruct that nation met stubborn resistance. The relative success of elections in Iraq and the rumblings of spreading democracy in the Middle East raised some hopes about the long-term success of the American mission in Iraq, but dramatic events at every turn demonstrated time and time again the challenges of predicting such matters. As with all of the past, only time will tell who acted wisely, and when.

SUGGESTED READING

James Baughman, *The Republic of Mass Culture* (1992). Explores the media's impact on modern American culture.

David Maranniss, *First in His Class: A Biography of Bill Clinton* (1995). A popular account of Clinton's political rise.

The Starr Report (1998). The official report that triggered the Clinton impeachment.

James B. Stewart, *Blood Sport: The President and His Adversaries* (1996). Considers the various scandals that dogged Bill Clinton's first term.

Bob Woodward, *Plan of Attack* (2004). An analysis of the Bush policies in Iraq based on extensive White House interviews.

SUGGESTIONS FOR FURTHER READING

Douglas Brinkley, *Tour of Duty: John Kerry and the Vietnam War* (2004).

Howard Gilman, *The Votes That Counted: How the Court Decided the Presidential Election* (2001).

Gary L. Gregg II and Mark J. Rozell, eds., *Considering the Bush Presidency* (2004).

Michael Isikoff, *Uncovering Clinton* (1999).

Stephen Mansfield, *The Faith of George W. Bush* (2004).

Roger Morris, *Partners in Power: The Clintons and Their America* (1996).

Gary B. Ostrower, *The United Nations and the United States* (1998).

James B. Stewart, *Den of Thieves* (1991).

Martin Walker, *The President We Deserve: Bill Clinton, His Rise, Falls, and Comebacks* (1996).

Judith Warner, *Hillary Clinton: The Inside Story* (1993).

37

American Society in the New Millennium: A "Culture War," a Stable Center

AMERICAN SOCIETY DURING the presidential terms of Bill Clinton and George W. Bush seemed hopelessly divided over social and cultural issues. A broad array of well-funded advocacy groups skilled in lobbying and litigation kept their causes in the forefront. The leaders of some of these interest groups were veteran champions of political combat; others, such as advocates for the elderly, became increasingly powerful voices. Significant shifts in the makeup of American society fueled cultural tensions. However, the amorphous interest groups that did most to set the agenda for cultural and political debate in the 1990s were, on one side, religious conservatives drawing leadership largely from a politicized evangelical Protestantism that emphasized what they called "family values," and on the other side liberal academic and media supporters of what was broadly labeled "multiculturalism." Sometimes ignored in this clash were religious liberals, who tended to side with the forces of diversity, although for reasons very different from those of "secular humanists."

This polarization continued a familiar historical pattern. Throughout most of the twentieth century, liberals celebrated the nation's diversity (its "manyness"), advocating the rights of newcomers and the disadvantaged, while conservatives spoke of traditional American values (its "sameness"). Both sides insisted that they were defending principles that had made the nation great.

In spite of fierce culture-war battles, most Americans formed a relatively contented majority. Among the things that unified Americans was the rejuvenation of the economy. During the 1990s American capitalism became the envy of the world, and at the turn of the millennium federal budget surpluses kindled hopes of retiring the national debt. An economic slowdown in the early months of the Bush administration, the costs of the war on terrorism and two foreign wars, and tax cuts quickly plunged the nation back into deficit spending. Economists disagreed about the robustness of the recovery; it was marred by a lag in the creation of new jobs, prompting critics to complain about the "outsourcing" of jobs to developing countries.

As the nation entered the new millennium, American values and habits remained remarkably unchanged. Nowhere was this more visible than in the vitality of religious belief and American churches. Public opinion fluctuated, but at the opening of the twenty-first century a majority of Americans remained optimistic about the future.

THE NATION'S CHANGING MAKEUP

The nation's population continued to grow briskly in the eighties and nineties. Birth rates remained low, but the country saw the largest influx of immigrants since early in the twentieth century. While these new Americans contributed to the expanding economy, some Americans saw immigration as an economic and social threat.

Demographic changes brought new challenges. As the ranks of elderly Americans grew, policy questions arose about the future of Social Security and Medicare. Perhaps even more controversial were changes in the family structure and sexual mores that led some to demand new definitions of what constituted a family. Some of the late-twentieth-century population changes placed huge burdens on the nation's systems of health care and education and embroiled them ever more deeply in cultural debates.

✸ *Patterns of Growth and Mobility*

After passing 200 million in the 1970 census, the population of the United States rose to 281 million in 2000. The center of population continued to move to the West and South, crossing the Mississippi River in 1980 to a spot southwest of St. Louis, Missouri. The two chief reasons for continued growth were immigration and high birth rates among certain minority groups. America's historic openness to immigration and its republican conception of national identity stand in sharp contrast

New Americans   This cosmopolitan group of new citizens pledge allegiance to the United States in a mass ceremony in Los Angeles on July 3, 2004.

to the "blood and soil" national self-understandings in many Asian and European societies. As a result, those countries have been much more resistant to immigration than the United States, and, consequently, are more vulnerable to demographic graying. Immigration continued to provide the United States with a base of working people that would otherwise shrink dangerously in the twenty-first century relative to the number of retired persons.

In 2004 the Census Bureau issued a projection of the ethnic composition of the American population by the middle of the 21st century. The bureau acknowledged that its projection assumed no changes in such variables as the admission of immigrants, patterns of fertility, and life expectancy, but, given those limita-

Columbia and many southern states with high African American percentages. In many American metropolitan areas, minority ethnic groups became majorities. Anglos were only about 5 percent of the population of Laredo, Texas, and all along the border region from Brownsville, Texas, to Fresno, California, Hispanics constituted well over 50 percent of the population.

For the first time, the census of 2000 allowed Americans to select from more than one of fourteen boxes representing "races and subcategories" and another labeled "some other race." Thus, a person selecting both "black or African American" and "white" in the 2000 census would be counted as neither, but would be enumerated in the category "two or more races." In addition, the census counted "Hispanics or Latinos (of any race)" as a category distinct from "race." Advocates of these changes — many of them from minority groups — believed that they were necessary to show how diverse and multicultural American society had become. But others feared that the new count would seriously reduce the numbers of people classified in specific minorities, with implications for government funding and political clout.

As it had been since the early nineteenth century, the United States continued to be a nation on the move toward the South and the West. Around 80 percent of New Yorkers in 1990 were born in that state, whereas more than 70 percent of the people living in Florida had moved there. During the 1980s, Florida's population gained 29 percent; the 3.2 million people who settled there during that decade amounted to more than the entire population of the state in 1950. Nearly twice that many new residents moved to California, increasing that state's population by 12.4 percent, boosting its lead as the nation's most populous state, and giving California a record fifty-two congressional seats.

In the 1990s, patterns of internal population migration showed signs of moderating. The baby-boom generation reached their fifties during the 1990s and, having survived the job uncertainties of the 1980s, they appeared less likely to move than in earlier decades. The Sun Belt still grew, though less dramatically, and the Midwest retained more of its natives as new industries to some extent replaced jobs lost by industrial reorganization. In the early 1990s, California's growth slowed because of severe economic recession (driven partly by the federal government's rapid cutback in defense-related spending), although by 1995 the state was once again beginning to grow faster than the nation, this time largely because of foreign immigration.

tions, the predictions were eye-catching. In 2000, 69.4 percent of the population was non-Hispanic white, 12.7 percent black, 12.6 percent Hispanic, and 3.8 percent Asian. The Census Bureau predicted a balance in 2050 of 50.1 percent white, 24.4 percent Hispanic, 14.6 percent black, and 8 percent Asian. In fact, however, the American birth rate, like that in other developed countries, began to decline in the 1990s, dropping to an all-time low of 13.9 births per 1,000 in 2002; by comparison, at the height of the baby boom in 1957 the rate was 25.3 per 1,000. While the birth rate remained at a level that would sustain the population, only immigration assured the nation's future growth.

Racial and ethnic diversity varied widely by region. Considerable ethnic variety was evident in California and New York, with their large immigrant populations; in Florida, Texas, New Mexico, and Arizona, with their sizable Hispanic communities; and in the District of

Las Vegas The landscape of the burgeoning metropolitan area of Las Vegas illustrates the continuing movement of the U.S. population to the West and South. Las Vegas was the fastest-growing metropolitan area in the country at the beginning of the twenty-first century.

African Americans continued to return to the South in large numbers. Both opportunity and familiarity fed the migration. Many of those returning moved back into the rural South, citing a "love for the land and the lure of a simpler life," while southern urban areas such as Atlanta attracted others. While some were fleeing urban ghettos in the North, others were lured back to the South by the region's booming economy and employment opportunities.

In some ways, by the mid-1990s the most auspicious pattern of growth in the United States, and, indeed, all over the world, was the dramatic increase in the number of elderly people. By the 1990s, *Modern Maturity*, the magazine of the American Association of Retired People, would claim a circulation of over 21 million. Citizens over 65, in 1900 only about 4 percent of the population, by 2000 made up 12.4 percent — nearly 35 million people. The Census Bureau estimated that the number would increase dramatically in the first decade of the twenty-first century. The United States was a part of a worldwide "gray wave"; experts predicted that by 2050, some 22 percent of the world's population would be over 60 years of age, more than the number of people 14 or under. Also contributing to the aging of America was a continued increase in average life expectancy. In 2000, the life expectancy of an American male was an all-time high of 74.1 years and that of a female was 79.5. Life expectancy remained substantially higher for whites than blacks; the life expectancy of white women was 80 years and white men 74.8, while that of black women was 75 and black men 65.5 years.

The 2000 census revealed that more than 80 percent of Americans (226 million) lived in metropolitan areas. Around half of all Americans lived in suburbs, far more than in either central cities or rural areas. Most census experts expected the pattern to continue with suburban sprawl spilling into "exurban" areas beyond the suburbs. After reaching a low in the early 1970s, the number of people living in rural areas began to rise slowly as commuters moved to greener pastures beyond cities. Still, growth in non-metropolitan areas lagged, and only a small percentage of those living in the countryside were engaged in agriculture.

Immigration Patterns and Concerns

As has always happened in the United States in times of economic expansion, immigration rates turned sharply upward in the 1980s and 1990s. The Immigration Act of 1990 raised the annual quota of immigrants to 700,000, not counting refugees. Although still not approaching the great European Diaspora that began in the late nineteenth century (when the rate of yearly immigration went as high as 11.5 newcomers per 1,000 residents), in the 1990s the annual immigration rate reached 3.2 per 1,000, up from less than 0.5 in the 1930s. The percentage of Americans who were foreign-born jumped dramatically: after reaching a low of 4.8 percent in 1970, it rose to 6.2 in 1980, 7.9 in 1990, and 11.4 in 2000.

The ethnic composition of newly arriving immigrants also shifted. Hispanics remained the largest group; their number jumped dramatically as a result of an amnesty act passed by Congress in 1986, which accorded legal status to around 1.4 million one-time illegals. In 1995, nearly 7 million American citizens had been born in Mexico. The second-largest category of immigrants was Asians (31 percent of the total), and third was Europeans (14 percent). In addition to the quota allotted for legal immigration, the United States continued to admit around 100,000 political refugees annually. In the 1980s refugees included more than 300,000 Vietnamese, 130,000 Laotians, 109,000 Cambodians, and 105,000 Cubans. New immigrants attracted others: of the 880,014 immigrants admitted to the United States in 1993, 62 percent were relatives of citizens or legal permanent residents. The impact of immigration varied widely in different sections of the country. In addition to the long Hispanic belt along the border with Mexico, most major cities featured a substantial Hispanic population. Hispanics constituted a language grouping rather than a racial category, for they included persons of different races. In 1993, Mexicans accounted for 61.2 percent of American Hispanics; Puerto Ricans, 12.1 percent; Central Americans, 8 percent; and Cubans, 4.8 percent. The West Coast attracted many Asian immigrants. In the West, Asian Americans made up 7.7 percent of the total western population (and in California 9.6 percent), outnumbering African Americans. Most West Coast cities had large, often middle-class, Chinese, Korean, Japanese, Vietnamese, and Filipino neighborhoods.

By the 1990s many East Coast cities once again hosted bustling immigrant neighborhoods. In the first half of the 1990s more than 500,000 legal immigrants poured into New York City, raising the foreign-born population to 2.5 million legal immigrants (as well as an estimated 400,000 illegals).

The end of the twentieth century witnessed massive movements of population across borders all around the world, and these migrations sparked new debates in many places about the effects of immigration. A 1997 poll revealed that nearly two-thirds of the citizens of European Union nations called themselves "racists" and resented immigrants. The reawakening of nativist concerns in the United States was part of a worldwide pattern. By the mid-1990s, twenty-three states passed laws requiring the use of English in government agencies. Conservatives tried to make English the country's official language, and a Gallup poll in 1992 found that 82 percent of Americans felt that such a law should be passed.

The economic belt tightening of the 1980s escalated concerns about immigration. In 1996, three-fourths of those who had been affected by layoffs stated that they believed that immigration should be reduced and 64 percent of all Americans favored more stringent limitations. Large numbers of Americans feared that immigrants would overburden the nation's welfare system, cause further losses of jobs, and add to racial conflict. Particularly objectionable to advocates of reform was the number of unskilled workers admitted on the grounds of family relationship because of the strain these unskilled people placed on the social services of the nation. Yet even conservatives pressed immigration reform reluctantly, acknowledging that the country's greatness stemmed in no small part from its traditional role as cultural melting pot.

Persisting Patterns of Poverty

Hard-core poverty proved to be intractable amid the prosperity of the 1990s. In the early 1960s, more than 20 percent of the nation had been classified as poor. That rate fell in the decades that followed, in part due to the reforms of the Great Society and in part due to economic upturns, staying below 15 percent except during recessions. However, neither political action nor prosperity pushed the figure below 11 percent. The number of people living below the poverty level hovered around 35 million throughout the eighties and nineties.

After 1980, income disparities grew. By 1995, the richest 5 percent of Americans were receiving 20 percent of the national income, but the poorest 40 percent only around 15 percent. The number of people living below the "poverty line" (a family of four with income less than $18,100 in 2001) rose from 13 percent to 13.5 percent from

Homeless in America   By 2002, New York City's homeless population exceeded what it had been in the 1980s. Most of the increase was the result of some 13,000 children trying to live on the streets, such as this Latino boy waiting for a bus to take him to a shelter for the night.

evening. While New York City led all American cities with nearly 25,000 homeless people, few urban Americans had not come face to face with homelessness.

There were other measures of the vast disparities in the lives of the rich and the poor. Rich and upper-middle-class people often lived in "gated" and guarded communities, while the poor clustered in blighted inner cities. Flight from the cities took increasing numbers of Americans into rural areas to live, spatially separating them from the slums and the poor. While racial segregation eased by the end of the century, economic segregation was more visible than ever.

The persistence of poverty and the deepening economic gulf in the country provided steady data for those who supported traditional welfare programs. Liberals charged that the federal government had abandoned the poor because of its unwillingness to expand social programs, even though programs paying money to individuals, excluding Social Security, expanded sharply during the Republican presidencies of Reagan and Bush. Conservatives replied that federal programs had institutionalized poverty and needed reform.

❧ Hope and Alienation for African Americans

African Americans continued to be at the center of much of the debate on multiculturalism. Few Americans questioned the reality of racial progress since the mid-1960s, but blacks and whites differed sharply about its degree. In a 1988 poll, 87 percent of white Americans agreed that "in the past 25 years, the country has moved closer to equal opportunity among the races," but less than half of blacks did.

There was little doubt that American thinking about race had changed by the nineties. In a 1997 Gallup poll, 77 percent of blacks (compared to 60 percent in 1972) and 61 percent of whites (compared to 25 percent in 1972) said they approved of black-white marriage. Asked whether they would be willing to vote for a black candidate for president, 91 percent of blacks answered yes (up from 78 percent in 1958), as did 93 percent of whites (up from 36 percent in 1958). Still, many felt that much remained to be done to change American racial attitudes.

Although at the end of the twentieth century blacks still trailed whites by almost every measure, most of those gaps were closing. More black students than ever were attending colleges — up from 9.3 percent of the college population in 1990 to 11.1 percent in 2000. Though disparities remained, average black income rose sharply in the eighties and nineties. By 1992, about

1980 to 1990, and then declined to 11.3 percent in 2000. Nonetheless, the rich-poor gulf widened. Income disparity was more marked among African Americans and Hispanics than among whites. Around 30 percent of both blacks and Hispanics remained below the poverty line.

Nothing highlighted patterns of chronic poverty more than homelessness. In 1990, the Census Bureau came up with incomplete, but still sobering, figures: 168,309 people in emergency shelters, 10,329 in shelters for runaways, 11,768 in shelters for abused women, and another 49,734 "visible in street locations." Many of those living on the streets suffered from chronic mental illness. The 2000 census counted 280,527 homeless persons, but did not release detailed statistics because it believed its count was inaccurate. A 1996 survey by the Department of Housing and Urban Development estimated that around 470,000 Americans (more than the population of Wyoming) were homeless on any given

4 percent of all American firms were black-owned. Most polls in the 1990s showed that a majority of blacks believed that they would be better off in the next generation; as a group blacks were more optimistic about the future than whites.

Mirroring the nation as a whole, however, African Americans experienced a growing separation between upper and lower income groups. Indeed, the gap grew faster among blacks than in any other group. In 1967, 8 percent of blacks earned less than $5,000 a year and 7 percent more than $50,000. By 1990, 12 percent earned less than $5,000 and 15 percent earned more than $50,000. Two African American communities had emerged by the end of the century — one middle- and upper-class and educated, the other mired in poverty. In 1995, around 10 million African Americans — nearly 30 percent of the black population — lived in families below the poverty line. In female-headed households, the percentage below the line was 45.1 percent.

Racial tensions remained in the spotlight in the 1990s. After an all-white jury acquitted four policemen in the beating of black motorist Rodney King in April 1992, rioting, looting, and arson swept South Central Los Angeles, leaving more than fifty people dead. In 1994, the country divided ominously along racial lines during the murder trial of football star O. J. Simpson, who was accused of killing his white former wife and her friend. In the glare of unprecedented media coverage, Simpson was first found not guilty of murder by a majority-black jury and subsequently convicted in a civil case of wrongful death by an all-white jury.

African Americans continued to be at the center of one of the nation's most contentious political issues: affirmative action. While in retrospect most Americans approved of the civil rights movement, a majority never fully embraced affirmative action if it meant government intervention to ensure equitable outcomes. The strongest objections came from working-class American men who, caught in a shrinking job market, felt that blacks were unfairly pushing ahead of them through preferential treatment. Some conservatives played to these resentments, including North Carolina Senator Jesse Helms, who was reelected in 1990 thanks in part to a controversial television ad in which a voiceover intoned, "You needed that job. You were the best qualified. But they had to give it to a minority, because of a racial quota. Is that really fair?" Many Americans believed that any system of preferences ran counter to the traditional American vision of equal opportunity.

In 1996, California voters approved Proposition 209, banning the use of race as a criterion for admission to state colleges and universities, and the measure was upheld in the courts. In California and elsewhere, affirmative action programs began undergoing revision. Universities intent on promoting diversity, following the example of the University of California at Berkeley, modified admissions standards (including relying less on SAT scores) to overcome the "achievement gap" between Hispanic/black and white/Asian applicants. During the 1990s, federal courts dismantled desegregation agreements that had used racial quotas, generally holding that "racial diversity" was a legitimate goal in school admissions but that race could not be a "predominant consideration."

✳ IN THEIR OWN WORDS

California's Proposition 209, 1996
In 1996 California voters passed a controversial ballot initiative that banned affirmative action in state agencies, including colleges and universities.

Section 31 is added to Article I of the California Constitution as follows:

SEC. 31. (a) The state shall not discriminate against, or grant preferential treatment to, any individual or group on the basis of race, sex, color, ethnicity, or national origin in the operation of public employment, public education, or public contracting. . . .

(f) For the purposes of this section, "state" shall include, but not necessarily be limited to, the state itself, any city, county, city and county, public university system, including the University of California, community college district, school district, special district, or any other political subdivision or governmental instrumentality of or within the state.

(g) The remedies available for violations of this section shall be the same, regardless of the injured party's race, sex, color, ethnicity, or national origin, as are otherwise available for violations of then-existing California antidiscrimination law.

The Supreme Court decided an important case on admissions policies in June 2003. By 5 to 4, the Court upheld the University of Michigan law school's consideration of race in the admission of students, but by 6 to 3 it struck down a point system based on race used to admit undergraduate students. The Court affirmed the legality of affirmative action (while asserting that it would no longer be necessary at some future date), but rigid systems that looked like quotas were rejected, and universities were urged to adopt race-neutral admissions policies "as soon as practicable." The decisions left much unsettled and seemed to ensure further litigation, and public opposition to affirmative action remained strong. According to a Gallup poll following the Michigan decision, 69 percent believed university students should be "admitted solely on merit" without consideration of "racial and ethnic backgrounds," and only 27 percent favored race-based admissions to promote diversity. Among whites, 75 percent favored admission "solely on merit," and 59 percent of Hispanics agreed. African Americans continued to favor giving consideration to racial and ethnic backgrounds by a margin of 49 to 44 percent.

❧ Gender Gains and the Gender Gap

No group gained more from growing national sensitivities about discrimination than women. In 1997, 74 percent of American women and 79 percent of men said that they believed that the status of women had improved over the past twenty-five years. Women closed the earnings gap somewhat during the 1980s and 1990s; as a percentage of men's earnings, women's earnings rose from less than 65 percent in 1980 to 76.4 percent in 1994. Among childless adults between the ages of 27 and 32, women earned nearly 98 percent of men's wages. By 2000, disparities between the earnings of women and men reflected the statistically greater likelihood that males would remain in the workforce throughout their lives, whereas women were more likely to take time out for childrearing, along with lingering discrimination. In the 1980s a majority of women continued to say that they would prefer to stay home rather than work, but by the mid-1990s more than half of American women said they preferred working outside the home. Still, in 2002 the Census Bureau reported that the percentage of children being raised by full-time, stay-at-home moms increased by 13 percent in the last decade of the twentieth century, perhaps because of the prosperity of the late 1990s. By the middle of the nineties there were 7.7 million female-owned businesses in the United States, about one-third of the total number in the country.

In higher education women created a reverse gender gap. For the first time in 1979, more women than men graduated from institutions of higher education; in 1999 women earned more than 57 percent of the bachelor's degrees granted. Boys were more likely to enter the job market after they finished high school, while more girls continued their education. Women began to enter many fields previously dominated by men; in the early 1990s, 20 percent of women college graduates earned degrees in business, more than in any other field. One of the most conspicuous symptoms of a "gender gap" in the job market was the "glass ceiling" that excluded women from the highest levels of corporate leadership. However, as increasing numbers of women accumulated seniority in major corporations, and as residual "old-boy" attitudes faded, more women became CEOs.

The feminist movement, which could justly claim credit for many of these changes, had become less focused by the 1990s. The success of the movement probably contributed to the declining visibility of women's issues, though the movement also had suffered some serious defeats, notably the failure of the Equal Rights Amendment in 1982 after a ten-year struggle for ratification. Asked in the mid-1990s if they had a favorable view of the women's movement, more than two-thirds of Americans responded positively, but less than half of American women believed that the movement had had a positive impact on their lives. The number of women who called themselves feminists steadily declined in the 1990s to less than one-fourth. Nonetheless, a gender gap in American voting grew throughout the eighties and nineties and played a significant role in most elections. Women activists remained particularly important in advocating certain women's causes, including protection from sexual harassment and abortion rights, and women clearly responded differently from men to a variety of political issues.

❧ Grading Public Education

Since the Jacksonian era, the dominant American view has been that education is the bulwark of democracy, but public education became another extremely contentious battleground in the cultural wars of the mid-nineties. In many ways the United States made remarkable progress in education in the years after World War II. Whereas 24.5 percent of Americans had graduated from high school in 1940, by 2000, 84.1 percent had done so, and while the percentage of whites who were high school graduates was still higher than blacks, that gap narrowed significantly in the 1990s. African Americans' progress was impressive, rising from only 7.3 percent graduating from high school in 1940, to 78.5 percent in 2000. In 2000, more than 25 percent of the population had completed four or more years of college (4.6 percent in 1940), including 16.5 percent of blacks (1.3 percent in 1940).

Yet in terms of quality, American education was the subject of withering criticism. Wrote education critic Richard Goodwin: "It is no secret to most parents and concerned citizens that our public schools system is a disaster." There was ample evidence to support such negative assessments. Standardized test scores sank steadily; in a 1995-1996 international test of math and science skills of advanced high school seniors in sixteen countries, American students ranked last in physics and next to last in math. Equally distressing, discipline and order seemed to be breaking down. Drugs, violence, and guns plagued many inner-city schools, turning them into besieged fortresses — and "good" suburban schools were by no means safe, either. This was made clear in the spring of 1999, when two students brought weapons to school and opened fire at Columbine High School in Colorado, killing twelve students and one teacher and wounding more than twenty.

In light of the controversy that increasingly surrounded public education, political discussion turned to possible improvements and alternatives. Many Democrats insisted that existing public schools must be supported by spending more money on hiring teachers, lowering teacher-student ratios, and making computers accessible to all students. President Clinton supported the establishment of charter schools free from bureaucratic regulation and controlled by teachers, community leaders, and parents, to provide an alternative for parents living in inferior school districts. Conservatives increasingly advocated voucher systems that would allow parents to remove their children from failing public schools and finance their education in private, even church-supported, schools. The education debate spawned unusual alliances, illustrated by evidence from opinion polls of strong support for school choice among African Americans, who were otherwise a bastion of Democratic support. For many Americans, however, vouchers threatened the hallowed principle of church-state separation and opened the door to publicly supported religious education.

❧ *Focus on Family Values*

The term *family values* covered a nexus of thorny, often divisive, social issues. It was clear in the 1990s that most Americans living in a nuclear family believed strongly in the importance of the nuclear family. The comfort level of the American public with the single-mother family became a highlight in the 1992 presidential campaign when Vice President Dan Quayle publicly rebuked the popular television show "Murphy Brown" for having a lead character (depicted as a highly paid professional) give birth to a child out of wedlock. Quayle was widely mocked in the media because of his remarks, but he and other conservatives bridled at the notion that the two-parent family should be recognized simply as one more "lifestyle choice," along with the single-parent family. On the other hand, many feminists and gay rights activists argued that the "traditional family" concept had always been more myth than fact. They insisted that *family* was a term based on mutual commitments and that it quite properly included single-parent households and same-sex couples.

Although conservatives were the most aggressive assailants of the alternate family concept, by the mid-1990s politicians of virtually every stripe pledged allegiance to the traditional family. In the 1990s the more traditional approach gained new life, though mothers now worked outside the home. A study by the National Institute of Mental Health in 1997 assured modern mothers that the children of two-parent, two-earner families showed no ill effects and noted that working women generally had higher self-esteem and often seemed happier than stay-at-home mothers.

Beyond the philosophical and religious debate over defining families, most Americans viewed the deterioration of family life among the poor, particularly African Americans, as a tragedy. By the 1990s the social and political consequences of the family breakdown were quite clear. Forty percent of never-married mothers were long-term welfare recipients, compared to only 14 percent of divorced mothers. The growing demand for welfare reform in the nineties reflected concerns about reestablishing families as much as about costs.

❧ *Sexual Patterns and Sexual Politics*

A broad scientific survey of American sexual habits conducted at the University of Minnesota and published in 1994 seriously challenged many long-held assumptions that grew out of Alfred Kinsey's studies. The new

Gay Marriage　The first same-sex couple to wed after Mayor Gavin Newsom of San Francisco ordered municipal officials to legalize such unions, Phyllis Lyon and Del Martin embrace in City Hall. Images of gay and lesbian couples marrying evoked strong responses from both supporters and opponents of same-sex marriage, turning it into a political issue in many states.

inquiry called into question the image of a free-wheeling sexual society portrayed by the media, finding that Americans were largely monogamous (83 percent had either one or no sex partner during a year); most sex was conventional intercourse (96 percent); 75 percent of American men and 85 percent of women said they had never committed adultery and 94 percent of married people said they had been faithful to their partners in the past year. Other surveys seemed to challenge this "Victorian" overview. Student approval of casual sex reached a record 52 percent in 1987, before beginning to decline, reaching 41 percent by 1996.

The University of Minnesota survey also challenged previous estimates of the number of gays and lesbians in the nation, finding that only 2.7 percent of American men and 1.3 percent of women had had homosexual sex in the preceding year. Only 6.2 percent of men and 4.4 percent of women said they were sexually attracted to people of the same gender, significantly lower than the percentages reported during the 1940s and 1950s by

Kinsey. While the numbers varied, such surveys generally concluded that less than 3 percent of Americans considered themselves gay or bisexual and that as few as 1 percent were exclusively gay. Gays were, however, highly visible in certain communities, especially San Francisco and New York, and in such professional venues as the arts and media. Gay-rights advocates continued to campaign for a number of causes, such as the extension of legal rights to gay couples and increased spending on AIDS research. In general, Americans became more accepting of gay rights, and most were appalled by such acts of gratuitous violence as the savage beating to death of a gay student, Matthew Shepard, in Wyoming in 1998.

Perhaps the most controversial gay-rights cause was the demand to make "domestic partners" in both heterosexual and homosexual relationships legally equal. San Francisco allowed registration of "domestic partners" in 1989, thus making homosexual couples eligible for employee and health benefits provided to traditional spouses, and some courts upheld the right of gay couples to adopt children. By the 1990s, hundreds of companies had extended spousal benefits to homosexual partners. Recognizing gay unions as "marriage" raised the debate to a new level. In 1996 Congress passed, and President Clinton signed, a Defense of Marriage Act that freed states and localities from the obligation to recognize same-sex marriages authorized in other jurisdictions. A growing majority of Americans believed that homosexual sex should be legal, and nearly three-fourths told pollsters that gays should have equal job opportunities, but a large majority disapproved of legalizing gay marriage. In 2004 the Massachusetts Supreme Court ruled that gays could legally marry in that state. Thousands of gay couples flooded into the state to wed, promising a new round of court cases to determine the validity of Massachusetts marriages in other states where same-sex unions were banned by law. The Massachusetts action thrust the issue squarely into the 2004 election debate and fed conservative demands for a constitutional amendment defining marriage as a union between a man and a woman.

✨ The AIDS Epidemic

In the decade following the discovery of Acquired Immunodeficiency Syndrome (AIDS) in 1981, the Centers for Disease Control and Prevention estimated that more than 122,000 persons had died from the infection. The number of diagnosed AIDS cases combined with those infected with Human Immunodeficiency Virus (HIV), a non-lethal immune system infection that typically developed into AIDS, increased sharply each year, reaching a peak of nearly 80,000 in both 1992 and 1993. By 2000, an estimated 458,551 Americans had died of the disease; AIDS was the leading cause of death among those between the ages of 25 and 44. The number infected by the disease stabilized in the mid-1990s and then sharply declined. The number of new cases of AIDS/HIV diagnosed in 2001 was under 25,000 for the first time since 1986. Just over half of the 816,147 Americans with AIDS/HIV in 2001 were gay men, and another 25 percent were drug users. By the end of the nineties an estimated 15 percent of those who had the disease had acquired it through heterosexual contact.

Ronald Reagan's surgeon general, Dr. C. Everett Koop, advocated the use of condoms and other measures to stop the spread of HIV; the Clinton administration was much more vigorous in supporting treatment and education aimed at eradicating the disease. The declining number of AIDS-related deaths in the late 1990s was attributed to increased spending by the government on treatment and on the development of powerful new drugs that slowed the progression from HIV infection to AIDS.

ECONOMIC SURGE AND RETREAT

Beginning slowly in the 1980s before gathering momentum as the end of the century approached, the United States underwent a dramatic economic recovery. The recovery was manifested in rising stock prices, and it rested on technological and scientific breakthroughs, on major gains in worker productivity, and on growth-favoring changes in government tax and trade policy. Although many economic problems remained unresolved, including a very serious trade imbalance, and although the run-up in technology stock prices reflected mainly "hype" and hope, by 2000 the American economy was the envy of the world. Then the massive spending de-

The AIDS Memorial Quilt   Created to commemorate by name the Americans who fell victim to AIDS, the Memorial Quilt was displayed on various occasions in the 1990s. This viewing is on the Mall in Washington, D.C., in 1997. Eventually, as the death toll from the disease continued to mount, the quilt became too large to be shown in public.

manded by the war on terrorism and military actions in Afghanistan and Iraq halted the nation's economic recovery. By 2004, the economy was once again in turmoil, marked by the reappearance of huge budget deficits and sharp declines in the value of the dollar.

More than ever before, at the beginning of the twenty-first century all world economies were tied together. American and foreign political leaders faced new trade, labor, and environmental issues raised by globalization and the spread of multinational corporations.

❧ *The Economic Surge of the 1990s*

Even during the worst of the early eighties doldrums, some economists insisted that the nation was going through a natural adjustment and that the United States would remain the most powerful economy in the world. By some measures the GNP of the American economy always out-produced that of any other nation, and the American share of world production never fell. The United States grew more slowly than many other nations in the 1980s, but that seemed inevitable as the recovery of European and Asian nations devastated by World War II accelerated, narrowing differentials in world standards of living. Furthermore, the United States had continued to carry a large share of financial responsibility for world peace, and in 1990 the United States expended $18.6 billion in foreign aid.

During the first five years of the 1990s the American economy grew only slowly, but the rate of growth accelerated in the last half of the decade. Inflation hovered around 3 percent through most of the 1990s, and unemployment reached a low of 4.1 percent, a figure approaching full employment. Family incomes lost ground in the early 1990s but began a sustained recovery in 1994.

By the second half of the nineties, the American economy was booming. Most experts credited the recovery to a surge of worker productivity, aided by the computer revolution and the Internet, and budget surpluses resulting from the end of the Cold War. (This also produced an unhealthy surge in the price of "dot-com" stocks, most of which produced little or no actual earnings.) In a stunning reversal, the economic doldrums gripped several once-booming European and Asian nations. In the United States, steady growth, low inflation, and dramatic improvements in productivity, as well as successful efforts to rein in spending and balance the federal budget, all combined to make the American economy the international model at the end of the twentieth century.

American gross domestic product (GDP) in the 1990s was more than double that of either China or Japan, and five times as large as that of Germany. The American economic recovery could be charted by many measures. The dollar rose against foreign currencies and the stock market moved steadily higher. The rash of bank failures that had marked the 1980s seemed a distant memory.

Getting rich never seemed easier than in the 1990s, and many highly skilled business managers opted for more independence as entrepreneurs and venture capitalists. The heroes of the new generation of entrepreneurs who turned technological innovations into success stories were media mogul Ted Turner and Microsoft's Bill Gates, who amassed two of the largest fortunes of the twentieth century. Equally stunning was the saga of Arkansas native Sam Walton, who died in 1995. By 2000 his Wal-Mart network was the largest U.S. corporation. Belying its hometown advertising imagery, Wal-Mart owed its success to a superb computerized inventory system and to an ability to buy goods in bulk while holding down labor costs.

The new generation of entrepreneurs also had its share of villains. In 2002 a slew of corporations folded, accompanied by accusations of fraud at the highest levels; among other things, ruthless executives had sold off millions of dollars of their own stock, taking advantage of inside information on forthcoming profit-loss reports or had arranged so-called golden parachutes, multimillion-dollar severance packages, before the companies they had mismanaged actually had to declare bankruptcy. Corruption and greed at the highest levels of corporations such as Enron, WorldCom Inc., and Qwest infuriated rank-and-file employees, who often found themselves without a job, a dime of severance pay, or a retirement fund. A number of companies such as Enron had required their employees to take their retirement in company stock. When whistle-blowers uncovered an accounting scandal that hid the company's huge debt and over-inflated profits, Enron collapsed in the largest bankruptcy ever, and its stock became virtually worthless.

Trade deficits remained a highly visible flaw in the American economic success story. Partly, the deficit was caused by the robustness of the American economic upswing as foreign investors poured money into the stable and growing American economy. The deficit was also fueled by a strong dollar and the massive purchasing power that accompanied American full employment, and it continued to hover above $100 million a year until the late 1990s, when it began an alarming annual rise to nearly $490 billion in 2003. In 1995 the trade imbalance with Japan alone was nearly $60 billion, but the United States had a negative trade balance with nearly all of its other trading partners. American businesses complained about the unfairness of foreign competition and demanded that the government exert pressure on foreign countries to open their markets; at the same time, labor leaders and many Americans resented the flooding of the American market with goods produced by cheap (sometimes child) labor. Nonetheless, Bill Clinton and George W. Bush generally remained champions of free trade, believing that deficits would decline if American products got freer access to foreign markets.

❧ The International Impact of Multinational Corporations

The globalization of the world economy accelerated in the 1980s and 1990s, leaving complicated patterns of interdependence. Developing countries feared economic colonization by the United States and other developed countries, but they badly needed investments by multinational corporations to improve their economies. Many developed nations resented the globalization of the world economy because it seemed to mean the transplanting of American culture, a "Coca-Colonization" of the World. When the Walt Disney company opened the EuroDisney theme park near Paris in 1992, French critics sniffed about a "cultural Chernobyl."

Most world leaders believed that an expanding international economy was both inevitable and essential to promote economic growth throughout the world, and that economic globalization foreshadowed a broader movement toward internationalization. The size and complexity of the world economy made it unlikely that any twentieth-century economic entity or interest could establish hegemonic powers, and a multitude of emerging international regulatory agencies offered some protection against multinational corporations.

The impact of globalization in America varied. Some industries, such as automobile manufacturing and steel making, declined dramatically. At the same time, jobs in other fields grew very rapidly. The trade imbalance was largely the result of the fierce competition among developing countries to penetrate the American market. Globalization brought many benefits to American consumers, making a wide variety of products available at lower prices.

❧ The Economic Slowdown and Recovery

In 2001 the Congressional Budget Office predicted a ten-year budget surplus of $5.6 trillion based on the booming economy. The surplus quickly withered away in the months that followed. The turnaround was the product of two large Republican tax cuts passed in 2001 and 2003 and of huge government expenditures in the wake of the September 11 terrorist attack and the war with Iraq.

More disturbing than the return to deficit spending was a general cooling of the economy that threatened to turn into a recession in early 2001. A huge drop in the stock market shocked the economy in January 2001, initiated by the crash of inflated technology stocks. Many erstwhile millionaires saw fortunes evaporate in this "dot-com" crash. More important, scores of companies were thrust into bankruptcy, leaving thousands of highly skilled workers unemployed. Weakened by the crash in technology stocks, the stock market plummeted again in the last half of 2002. This decline reflected the general weakness of the economy and was fueled by revelations of corporate misconduct. The Enron Corporation, an energy trading giant headed by Kenneth Lay, was charged with falsifying earnings reports in order to inflate stock values, aided by the Arthur Andersen accounting firm. By the summer of 2004 several Enron executives had either been convicted and sentenced to prison terms or were under indictment. The bankruptcy of Enron was followed by the largest bankruptcy in American history ($107 billion) at WorldCom, some of whose executives admitted fraudulently inflating profits. While the weakness of the stock market was disturbing, other measures of the nation's economic weakness in the first half of 2002 were more ominous. Consumer confidence fell, the dollar declined sharply, unemployment rose and job creation declined, household incomes fell, and more and more people were reported living below poverty levels. The government responded quickly, and seemingly effectively, to the weakness of the economy. Led by Alan Greenspan, the Federal Reserve imposed a series of interest rate cuts to encourage investment, pushing rates to the lowest level in decades. Republican-sponsored tax cuts in 2001 and 2003 and government spending for military operations and postwar reconstruction in Iraq also stimulated economic growth. By the third quarter of 2003 almost all economic indicators were once again positive. While the recovery remained somewhat sluggish in 2004, particularly in the area of job creation, it was sufficiently strong to defuse Democratic attacks on George W. Bush during the presidential campaign.

THE SEARCH FOR VALUES

In many ways Americans in the 1990s were better off than ever before. Measured by such standards as the quality of housing, declining segregation, improving air and water quality, declining crime rates and infant mortality, and rising opportunity, the United States had clearly made progress. Americans received better healthcare than ever before (though it cost more than ever, too) and faced better prospects for their retirement years.

Technology continued to change the lives of most people at an astonishing rate. Advances in computers gave millions of people access to the Internet and, in turn, consumer demand pushed new developments forward at a dizzying pace. Television remained a dominating presence, and in the 1990s it brought into American homes a bewildering array of high and low culture. Television's insatiable appetite for new programming deepened Americans' love affair with organized sports, creating a new generation of immensely wealthy athletic heroes.

Many Americans feared that the prosperity and materialism of the nineties was once again undercutting the nation's moral character. Anchoring the demands for a return to conventional moral values at the end of the century was a phalanx of moderate and conservative religious groups. If the twentieth century did not turn out to be the triumphant Christian century predicted by evangelical leaders in 1900, neither did it witness the death of God anticipated by secularists. The depth of religious commitment in America has always been difficult to measure; some have suggested that spirituality in the U.S. is "a mile wide and an inch deep." Nevertheless, the pervasiveness of religion is undeniable. At the end of the century, polls found that 73 percent of Americans said that religion was either very or somewhat important in their lives, and only 8 percent said they had no interest in religion. Even secularists at the beginning of the twenty-first century seemed both impressed and perplexed by the continued robust religious vision of Americans entering a new millennium.

The backbone of this national religious identity continued to be provided by the vast network of churches, synagogues, mosques, and temples that seemed to be perpetually under construction in America. Denominational loyalties ebbed and flowed; as in the past, new

The High-Tech Revolution   In August 2001, Microsoft chairman Bill Gates (right) and Intel chairman Andy Grove pose in a San Jose museum with the first IBM PC model, introduced in August 1981. The speed with which computer technology developed during the last decades of the twentieth century was truly mind-boggling for those who lived through it.

and old groups vied to attract the loyalties of believers, and the competition seemed to keep the American religious enterprise robust.

❧ Science, Computers, the Internet, and the Future

One of the continued marks of American leadership in the world was the dominance of the United States in scientific achievement. Americans won an impressive number of Nobel prizes in chemistry, physics, and medicine. It was the pace of technological change that assured the power and prestige of the nation at the end of the century.

Technology made American lives at the end of the century dramatically different from those lived in 1900. At the beginning of the twentieth century, about 5 percent of Americans had telephones in their homes; in 1997, 94 percent did. Two twentieth-century innovations, television and air conditioning, were by 1999 fix-

tures in 98 percent and 73 percent of American homes, respectively. More than half of Americans had telephones in their homes by 1938, had television sets by 1953, had flown on an airplane by 1961, and had personal computers in their homes by 1998.

By the 1980s, "third-generation" computers using incredibly fast and small microchips to process information had triggered a laptop computer revolution. Huge new industries emerged to take advantage of the advances that made computer technology available to the masses. The talented few who understood the potential of the computer revolution made fortunes, including Bill Gates, who dropped out of Harvard in 1977 to develop a software programming company called Microsoft. By 1986, at age 31, Gates was a billionaire. A massive antitrust suit against Microsoft in the 1990s cost the company billions of dollars and forced it to include its rivals' software on computers as well as its own Windows system, but a 2002 settlement between the company and the Department of Justice left the computer giant relatively unscathed. At the end of the century Bill Gates was one of the richest people in the world.

Technology not only changed the lives of Americans in the 1980s and 1990s; it also changed the world. The information revolution spread all over the globe, but the United States led in the number of personal computers in use — more than 150 million by 2000. A new generation of computer-literate young people was able to access and create information, art, and entertainment at a previously unimaginable rate.

Computers were only one of the stunning scientific achievements of the closing decades of the century. Biotechnology industries produced new drugs that enriched and lengthened lives. Some futurists coolly predicted that human beings would eventually live more than 150 years.

✤ Literature, the Arts, and Popular Culture

In the area of serious literature, the Nobel Prize in the 1990s went mostly to authors from developing countries; black novelist Toni Morrison was the only American so honored during the decade. On the other hand, the proliferation of VCRs and cable television provided Americans with an astonishing array of popular culture. Technological advances did much to fragment mass culture in America, offering so many choices that both programmers and advertisers increasingly targeted narrow audiences.

Television had long since become the dominant medium of American popular culture. At the century's end more than 98 percent of American homes had radios and color televisions and nearly 90 percent had VCRs. In 1980 only about 22 percent of American television owners received cable channels, but in 1995 that number had grown to 65 percent. Millions of Americans spent as much as six hours a day in front of the television.

American television offered, and the public watched, both serious news and commentary and light, sometimes mindless entertainment. Nothing seemed to capture the mood of the nineties culture wars more than a spate of talk shows that vied in exploiting the sensational and the bizarre. However, the serious news show *60 Minutes* finished first in the annual ratings four times in the 1980s and 1990s. A lighthearted family comedy, *The Bill Cosby Show,* dominated ratings in the late 1980s. The Super Bowl remained the premiere television extravaganza each year.

The entertainment industry found itself at the center of the era's culture wars. In 1995, 65 percent of Americans claimed to feel that the entertainment industry was "seriously out of touch with the values of the American people," and 83 percent said that the industry should reduce the depiction of sex and violence in movies, popular music, and television. In 1996, Republican presidential candidate Bob Dole characterized Hollywood studios as "nightmares of depravity," and politicians in both parties proffered plans to stem the sex and violence. Still, viewers made such entertainment profitable, and it flourished.

On the other hand, a profoundly religious movie, *The Passion of the Christ,* produced by Mel Gibson in 2004, shocked critics by grossing the seventh largest box office revenue in American history. A graphically violent portrayal of the death of Jesus (garnering it an "R" rating), the film was branded as anti-Semitic and historically inaccurate by some critics, but it reflected Gibson's ultra-conservative Roman Catholic faith. Evangelical Protestants and conservative Catholics swarmed to view *The Passion,* showing the consumer power of religious conservatives.

Bidding Farewell to *Friends* Standing in New York's Times Square, a teary-eyed crowd watches the telecast of the last episode of the popular TV show in May 2004. During its ten-year run, the sitcom about the tangled lives of a group of customers of a New York City coffee shop had won the hearts of millions of young American adults.

❧ Fitness, Sports, and New Heroes

Americans continued on a physical fitness craze into the 1990s. Far more people than ever before reported that they engaged in some physical exercise to increase their fitness — 60 percent in 1998 compared to 24 percent in 1961. On the other hand, the number of people who believed they needed to lose weight had risen from 31 percent to 52 percent. The Centers for Disease Control warned that obesity had increased sharply in the 1990s; in 2002 in thirty states, more than 20 percent of the population was considered obese.

The United States continued to be a nation of outdoors enthusiasts. In 1997 about 35 million people bought fishing licenses, far more than participated in any other sport. But organized sports made the most spectacular gains, financed by huge television contracts fostered by competition among the networks and cable channels. Professional football, baseball, basketball, hockey, and golf all shared in the popularity and profitability. So did NASCAR motor racing, which attracted the largest crowds of any sporting events, as well as flamboyant but phony professional wrestling. The financial impact of television money made the earnings of star players climb into millions of dollars,

and American cities vied with one another, offering incentives, to attract franchises.

Women also made gains in organized sports, particularly at the college level, because of federal legislation that required NCAA colleges to treat men's and women's organized sports equally. Women's sports became a growing presence on television and college campuses.

❧ Values, Habits, and the American Way of Life

The daily cycle of life for Americans changed dramatically in some ways in the twentieth century, and in others it remained remarkably the same. For instance, around 64 percent of Americans reported that they drank alcoholic beverages (the same as in 1969 and slightly more than in 1939), but the proportion of smokers declined from 44 percent of the adult population in 1949 to 23 percent in 1999. The number of people who were fans of major league baseball, around 40 percent, remained almost unchanged throughout the century, but football surpassed baseball as the nation's favorite sport.

New notions of gender equality have changed the routine of life in many homes. In 1938 — with Depression-era unemployment still very high — only 22 percent of Americans approved of a woman holding a job in business or industry if her husband was able to support her. By 1997, 80 percent supported the idea of women working, mostly in order to improve a family's standard of living. Although some protested that the burden of housework still fell disproportionately on working women, 85 percent of women and men polled in 1998 reported that husbands helped with household chores.

The morals and mores of American society have changed in many obvious ways. For instance, in 1939 nearly one-third of Americans believed it was indecent for a *man* to wear a topless bathing suit, and in 1955 a Gallup poll reported that 64 percent disapproved of women wearing Bermuda shorts in public. At the same time, some basic values in the nineties looked like basic values in the fifties; well over half of the population attended church and reported that religious beliefs decided how they should live their lives.

The Passion of the Christ   In February 2004, a customer at a Christian bookstore in Buford, Georgia, examines books and other merchandise marketed to coincide with the release of Mel Gibson's controversial but stunningly successful film about the crucifixion of Jesus.

Mainstream Protestantism Moves Left

Churches remained the most visible and pervasive voluntary associations in American society in the 1990s. Organized religion remained an immense national presence, receiving billions of dollars contributed each year as tax-exempt deductions. While organized religion in general flourished at the end of the century, there were clear numerical winners and losers among the denominations.

The older Protestant churches, long known as "mainstream," continued to lose members. Typical was the fate of the United Methodist Church, which lost members at a rate of more than 50,000 per year in the early 1990s and declined from a peak membership of more than 11 million to 8.5 million in 1995. Other older denominations, including the Presbyterians, United Church of Christ, Disciples of Christ, and Episcopalians, suffered similar attrition. The problem in the mainstream churches was at least partly theological. More liberal clergy found themselves at odds with the more traditional religious beliefs preached by more conservative evangelical churches and embraced by many of their own members. Still, mainstream Protestants were a powerful presence in American life and

politics; Episcopalians, Presbyterians, and Methodists were present in the United States Congress in far larger percentages than they were in the nation's religious population.

The mainstream churches also became battlegrounds in the culture wars, with clergy often clashing with more conservative laity on social issues. Ecclesiastical conferences often ended in factious debates over feminist and gay-rights issues. With considerable success, women pressed for ordination in mainstream Protestant churches and for inclusive language in liturgy and scriptural translations. Methodists and Presbyterians admitted women to the clergy in 1956; in 1976 the Episcopal Church ordained its first women priests; in 1980 Marjorie Matthews became the first female Methodist bishop, and in 1989 Barbara Harris was installed as the first woman Episcopal bishop.

More controversial were revisions of hymnbooks, confessions, and Bible translations using gender-inclusive language. Feminist theologians pressed for recognition of the male/female character of God. Symbolizing the somewhat unresolved status of those issues, in 1991 a new edition of the New Revised Standard Version of the Bible used inclusive language while retaining male designations for God.

Homosexuality was an even more divisive issue, causing much debate in mainstream churches. In the mid-1990s several mainline denominations, including the United Church of Christ and the Episcopal Church, allowed the ordination of non-celibate homosexuals. In 2003 the Episcopal Church found itself on the brink of a division after its General Convention confirmed the election of an openly gay priest, Gene Robinson, as the Bishop of New Hampshire. Indeed, by 2004, the 77 million member worldwide Anglican communion was threatened by schism because of objections from conservatives around the world, particularly in Africa, to the American church's action. In the summer of 2004 the United Methodist Church faced a similarly divisive confrontation over the denomination's failure to expel a practicing lesbian minister.

Roman Catholicism Moves Right

Roman Catholics were thoroughly integrated into American society at the end of the century; in 2000, the 107th Congress counted 150 Catholics among its 535 members. At the end of the century, the Roman Catholic Church claimed more than 61.5 million members in the United States, nearly 23 percent of the population,

Pope John Paul II One of the longest-serving pontiffs in history, John Paul II traveled frequently, and he attracted large crowds around the world, including the United States. In 1995 he celebrated mass in East Rutherford, New Jersey, for a crowd of over 82,000 people who endured a rainstorm to be part of the event.

giving the United States the third largest Catholic population in the world, behind Mexico and Brazil.

The leadership of the Roman Catholic Church moved to the right in the 1980s and 1990s, responding to the theologically conservative leadership of Pope John Paul II, whose pontificate, which began in 1978, was the longest and perhaps the most important of the twentieth century. During his papacy, John Paul II was noted for his extraordinary worldwide visibility, as well as for his staunch resistance to theological change. By the end of the century, the church's hierarchy in America had swung solidly behind the views of the Vatican on such controversial issues as abortion and the refusal to ordain women priests. Although many Catholics still hoped to change the church's views on such questions, in 1999 Francis Cardinal George of Chicago told lay leaders that "liberal Catholicism is an exhausted project." In 1999 the National Conference of Catholic

Bishops voted overwhelmingly to require theology professors at Catholic colleges and universities to obtain a certification from their bishop declaring that they teach "authentic Catholic doctrine."

At the same time, the American Catholic church remained a divided flock, with the laity often picking and choosing whether or not to follow church teachings on such issues as birth control, divorce, and even abortion. Indeed, if mainstream Protestant clergy were more liberal than laity, the Catholic hierarchy was often more conservative than its flock. At the beginning of the twenty-first century, Catholic leaders struggled to contain a scandal involving child sexual abuse by priests and the failure of American bishops to discipline offenders. By 2003 various dioceses had settled more than 500 suits alleging sexual abuses by priests and administrative malfeasance by superiors, and an estimated 1,000 more lawsuits were pending. An official report released in early 2004 asserted that 4 percent of all priests serving since 1950 had been credibly accused of sexually abusing young people. The scandal shook confidence in church leadership among both laity and lower clergy.

❧ The Continuing Acculturation of Old Outsiders

At the end of the twentieth century, around 5 million Americans, mostly from Eastern Europe, traced their religious roots to Eastern Orthodox Christianity, although less than half that number were active members of one of the fifteen autocephalous (self-governing) and four autonomous (self-ruling) Orthodox denominations, which were defined largely by ethnicity. The loosely bound Standing Conference of Orthodox Bishops in America was the most authoritative voice of American Orthodox Christians. Three seminaries trained Orthodox clergy. With unmarried bishops and a rich heritage of ritual and iconography, Orthodox churches seemed a mystery to many Americans, but they remained important spiritual oases for millions of Americans of Greek, Russian, and other East European origin. In the wake of the Cold War, Orthodox leaders in America often lobbied on behalf of causes in their native lands.

Orthodox churches have been bastions of theological and social conservatism in American society. The Orthodox do not share communion with other religious bodies, ordain only males to the priesthood, reject calls for the use of "inclusive language" in the Bible regarding God or the Trinity, and refuse to sanction homosexual behavior. At the same time, Orthodox churches have a long history of ecumenical activity, and in 1950 the Standing Conference of Orthodox Bishops began an uneasy relationship with the National Council of Churches of Christ in America. That association was interrupted in the 1990s as the social agenda of the NCC became more and more liberal, but resumed before the end of the century.

Perhaps the most dramatic twentieth-century success story among the older, non-mainstream, American religious groups was that of the Church of Jesus Christ of Latter Day Saints (Mormons). The church grew rapidly in the late twentieth century and in 2000 claimed more than 11 million members worldwide, including around 6 million in the United States. The church was also extremely wealthy, with annual revenue estimated at $6 billion, and Mormons constructed more than a hundred impressive temples throughout the world. The celebrated 325-voice Mormon Tabernacle Choir based in Salt Lake City was famous for its broadcasts, telecasts, and concert tours. Stressing a wholesome message of family values and exhibiting a spirit of super patriotism, the once-alienated Mormons moved ever closer to the center of American culture.

❧ New Religious Outsiders

Immigration brought a stunning new religious diversity to the United States at the close of the century. By 1995, the number of Muslims in the country was variously estimated at from 1.5 to 5 million. If the higher figures were correct, the number of Muslims in the United States rivaled the number of practicing Jews. Even more striking to many Americans was the appearance of Hindu temples in such places as Atlanta, Nashville, and Indianapolis; by the mid-1990s the number of Hindus in America approached 1 million.

Other new religions bore witness to the continued intellectual and entrepreneurial creativity of America's open religious society. The 1980s saw a rising interest in the New Age Movement, an umbrella term referring to

Muslims in Ohio   The striking visual image of the Islamic Center of Greater Toledo rising in the middle of a midwestern field is a reminder of the growing ethnic and religious diversity of the U.S. population even in the nation's heartland.

a spiritual movement involving a wide variety of individuals, organizations, ideas, and practices. Generally speaking, the movement anticipated the beginning of a New Age of peace, light, and love and sought to unshackle the powers of self. The most recent historical roots of the New Age Movement may be traced to the counterculture of the 1960s, but it draws on many American and Eastern intellectual traditions. New Age ideas influenced not only American religious thought (particularly on the West Coast) but also areas as diverse as music, medicine, psychology, and business. Although some New Age religions had shallow roots in the counterculture of the 1960s, many supporters of these new groups were serious students of Buddhism, Taoism, and Hinduism, and some were particularly attracted by the Dalai Lama's efforts to save Tibetan culture and explain Buddhist beliefs.

The United States continued to exhibit extraordinary religious creativity as new and old groups vied for a place on the religious map. The nation's attention was once again drawn to the eccentric margins of new religious groups in the tragic confrontation in Waco, Texas, between self-styled prophet David Koresh, leader of a maverick Adventist group, and heavily armed agents of the U.S. Bureau of Alcohol, Tobacco, and Firearms in April 1993 (see Chapter 36). Another extraordinary and controversial religious figure in the eighties and nineties was Louis Farrakhan, leader of the Nation of Islam, whose flare for the dramatic captured the nation's attention when he sponsored a "Million Man March" on Washington in 1995 calling for personal responsibility and family commitment from black men.

❧ Resurgent Evangelicalism

In the 1990s, the estimates of the number of people who considered themselves evangelicals ranged from 50 to 80 million, and evangelical leaders powerfully asserted their right to speak for God. Of course, evangelicals were a diverse group, but theologically they shared many traditional Protestant beliefs, including a personal salvation experience, belief in the Bible as the ultimate source of truth, and a mandate to share their faith with others. Many members of the old mainstream denominations considered themselves evangelicals, as did many African American Christians.

The two largest blocks in the evangelical community were millions of Pentecostals and independent Charismatics and the nation's largest Protestant denomination, the Southern Baptist Convention. Pente-

costal denominations swelled in numbers; by 1995 the Assemblies of God reached 2.3 million members, and one black Pentecostal church, the Church of God in Christ, reported nearly 5.5 million members, making it the largest predominantly black denomination. Even more visible was the appearance in American cities and suburbs of scores of "megachurches," with memberships reaching into the thousands. While some of these large churches were affiliated with evangelical denominations, many described themselves as "nondenominational." Among the booming independent charismatic churches at the end of the century (many sponsors of nationally televised programs) was the Lakewood Church in Houston, founded in 1959 by John

Charismatic Explosion   By 2005 Pentecostal and Charismatic churches formed the largest family of Protestant churches. Many large independent megachurches, and their wide-ranging outreaches, were led by African Americans and women. This photo is from Bishop T. D. Jakes's 1999 "Woman, Thou Art Loosed" conference in Atlanta, which attracted over 80,000 participants.

Osteen, a celebrated speaker in charismatic circles. After the founder's death in 1999, his son, Joel Osteen, pastored the 20,000-member church. Black evangelist Creflo Dollar's World Changers Church International, founded in 1986 in College Park, Georgia, claimed 20,000 members in 2003. The Potter's House in Dallas, Texas, begun in 1996 by African American Bishop T. D. Jakes, was probably the fastest growing church in the nation by 2003, boasting 28,000 members after only seven years in existence. In 2001 *Time* magazine featured Jakes on its cover along with the question, "Is This Man the Next Billy Graham?"

By 2000 some independent churches had begun forming incipient denominations. John Wimber, a writer and teacher whose emphasis on miracles fostered a movement called the "third wave," or "Signs and Wonders Movement," was particularly influential among independent charismatic churches whose members had been drawn from the older mainstream denominations. Wimber pastored a 4,000-member congregation in Anaheim, California, and in 1982 he launched the Association of Vineyard Churches. At the time of Wimber's death in 1997, the association was a loose affiliation of more than 700 congregations with around 200,000 members. During the eighties and nineties, celebrated charismatic teacher Kenneth Hagin and his son, Kenneth Hagin, Jr., built a worldwide network of Rhema schools and churches that increasingly functioned like a denomination. Anchored by the 8,000-member Rhema Bible Church and the Rhema Bible Training Center in Tulsa, Oklahoma (which boasted 23,000 graduates by 2002), the Rhema network included hundreds of churches and Bible schools in thirteen nations.

The Southern Baptist Convention slowed in growth at the end of the century, but in 2000 it still claimed more than 15.7 million members. The denomination remained a powerful presence in many communities; a listing of local congregations with more than 2,000 members at the turn of the century included more than 100 Southern Baptist churches. As if to symbolize the ascendancy of evangelical Christianity in general, and the SBC in particular, in 1998 among the politicians who were, or had been, members of the Southern Baptist church were President Bill Clinton, Vice President Al Gore, Senate Majority Leader Trent Lott, and Speaker of the House Newt Gingrich.

While conservative Christians remained a powerful political force at the end of the century, there were signs that the movement had lost some of its political cohesion. In part, the movement had been diminished by its success; politicians of every stripe offered lip service to morality, traditional values, and the protection of families. As a political movement, the Religious Right also made powerful enemies. In 1999, the Christian Coalition chose to reorganize rather than contest IRS charges that its political activities violated the limits allowed for tax-exempt organizations. In some ways the decline of the Christian Coalition signaled only the diffusion of leadership in the Christian Right, often into groups that were more targeted toward specific issues, such as James Dobson's Focus on the Family and Promise Keepers, a religious organization that sponsored rallies to encourage responsible fatherhood.

CONCLUSION: UNTO A GOOD LAND — THE ENDURING AMERICAN VISION

The "culture wars" of the 1990s were real and noisy, fueled by old struggles for rights by established minorities and by new multicultural realities that accompanied the arrival of millions of new immigrants. But the shrillness of the battles over divisive issues such as affirmative action and the rights of illegal immigrants obscured a more stable and serene center in American society. In the 1990s, most people were reasonably satisfied with their lot and optimistic about the future. It would be easy to overlook the fact, in the words of sociologist Alan Wolfe, that "middle-class Americans, black and white, male and female, by and large constitute a 'reasonable majority.'" To a large degree, the culture war was waged between extremists on opposite ends of the political spectrum. The issues they raised were often important, but the rhetoric of zealots rarely captured the mood of Americans in general.

Maintaining a healthy economy was important in keeping the "reasonable majority" satisfied. Politicians of all stripes in America (and indeed throughout the world) seemed to have accepted the notion that economic growth and full employment were the keys to social and political stability. Economists and politicians differed about how best to stimulate economic growth, and how to fairly divide the benefits of prosperity, but no one doubted the importance of a fully employed populace.

As nations go, the United States is still very young, but it is the world's oldest democracy. During its short history, the nation's embrace of democracy, individual liberty, and equality of opportunity came in fits and starts and was often deeply flawed. Still, in its best moments the United States did become a "city on a hill," a symbol of freedom. Generation after generation, the American vision provoked millions of the best and brightest from around the world to leave their homes to become Americans. Lofty ideas, as well as the hope for a better life, continued to attract millions of immigrants at the beginning of the twenty-first century. The good land the American people inhabited was bountiful beyond imagination, and Americans became richer than any people before them.

In Europe, many of the political ideas of the eighteenth and nineteenth century became inextricably linked with secular, anti-religious sentiments. American democracy, based on an unprecedented commitment to separation of church and state, viewed religion as compatible with the aims of liberal politics and economics. Indeed, religion became a partner in American democracy, and it provided much of the vocabulary for expressing American ideals. At the beginning of the twenty-first century, America's moral envisioning of itself still set the country apart from many more secular Western nations. To the consternation of much of the rest of the world, Americans continued to believe that they lived in a God-blessed land whose mission was to oppose evil and uphold righteousness.

From one end of the political spectrum to another, from John Winthrop to Thomas Jefferson, from Abraham Lincoln to William Jennings Bryan, from Martin Luther King, Jr., to George W. Bush, American leaders have bathed American aspirations and actions in religious rhetoric. All nations and people profess a commitment to acting correctly, but few share the enduring American legacy of appeal to religious language and belief. Those who came to America four centuries ago, and those who have most recently arrived, all set out to find a good land. They hoped to build a good country that would provide a model for others throughout the world. Noble or naïve — and it has been both — such thinking has kept alive a powerful myth about America's meaning and destiny.

SUGGESTED READING

James Baughman, *The Republic of Mass Culture* (1992). Explores the media's impact on modern American culture.

Godfrey Hodgson, *The World Turned Rightside Up: A History of the Conservative Ascendancy in America* (1996). A good account of the rise of conservative values.

David A. Hollinger, *Postethnic America: Beyond Multiculturalism* (1995). Presents a good summary of the debates over multiculturalism.

Arthur Schlesinger, Jr., *The Disuniting of America: Reflections on a Multicultural Society* (1991). A liberal historian and Kennedy adviser offers a unique take on multiculturalism.

Garry Wills, *Under God: Religion and American Politics* (1990). Wills offers an insightful account of the rise of the conservative religious/political coalition in modern America.

Daniel Yergen and Joseph Stanislaw, *The Commanding Heights: The Battle Between Government and Marketplace That Is Remaking the Modern World* (1998). A sweeping overview of the economic changes in the last half of the twentieth century.

SUGGESTIONS FOR FURTHER READING

Mary Jo Bane and David Ellwood, *Welfare Realities: From Rhetoric to Reform* (1994).

Alan Brinkley, *Liberalism and Its Discontents* (1998).

Stephen L. Carter, *God's Name in Vain: The Wrongs and Rights of Religion in Politics* (2000).

Andrew Hacker, *Two Nations: Black and White, Separate, Hostile, Unequal* (1992).

Geoffrey T. Holtz, *Welcome to the Jungle: The Why Behind Generation X* (1995).

Michael B. Katz, *The Price of Citizenship: Redefining the American Welfare State* (2001).

Gary Nash, Charlotte Crabtree, and Ross E. Dunn, *History on Trial: Culture Wars and the Lessons of the Past* (1998).

Henry R. Nau, *The Myth of America's Decline: Leading the World Economy in the 1990s* (1990).

Sam Roberts, *Who We Are: A Portrait of America Based on the Latest U.S. Census* (1995).

Randy Shilts, *And the Band Played On: Politics, People, and the AIDS Epidemic* (1987).

David K. Shipler, *A Country of Strangers: Blacks and Whites in America* (1997).

Stephen Thernstrom and Abigail Thernstrom, *America in Black and White: One Nation, Indivisible* (1997).

Robert Wuthnow, *The Restructuring of American Religion: Society and Faith since World War II* (1988).

Appendix

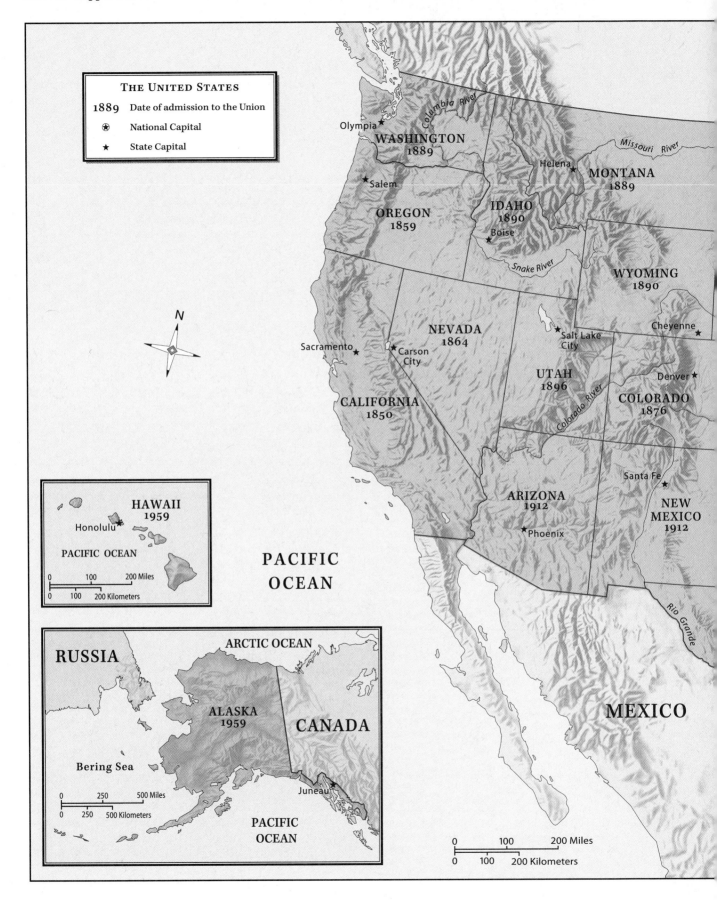

THE UNITED STATES

1889   Date of admission to the Union

✦   National Capital

★   State Capital

Columbia River

Olympia ★

WASHINGTON
1889

Missouri River

Helena ★

MONTANA
1889

★ Salem

OREGON
1859

IDAHO
1890

Boise ★

Snake River

WYOMING
1890

Cheyenne ★

N

NEVADA
1864

Salt Lake ★
City

UTAH
1896

Denver ★

Sacramento ★

★ Carson
City

Colorado River

COLORADO
1876

CALIFORNIA
1850

Santa Fe ★

ARIZONA
1912

NEW
MEXICO
1912

★ Phoenix

PACIFIC
OCEAN

HAWAII
1959

Honolulu ★

PACIFIC OCEAN

0   100   200 Miles

0   100   200 Kilometers

Rio Grande

RUSSIA

ARCTIC OCEAN

ALASKA
1959

CANADA

Bering Sea

0   250   500 Miles

0   250   500 Kilometers

Juneau ★

PACIFIC
OCEAN

MEXICO

0   100   200 Miles

0   100   200 Kilometers

The Declaration of Independence: A Transcription

www.archives.gov

May 23, 2005

The Declaration of Independence: A Transcription

IN CONGRESS, July 4, 1776.

The unanimous Declaration of the thirteen united States of America,

When in the Course of human events, it becomes necessary for one people to dissolve the political bands which have connected them with another, and to assume among the powers of the earth, the separate and equal station to which the Laws of Nature and of Nature's God entitle them, a decent respect to the opinions of mankind requires that they should declare the causes which impel them to the separation.

We hold these truths to be self-evident, that all men are created equal, that they are endowed by their Creator with certain unalienable Rights, that among these are Life, Liberty and the pursuit of Happiness.—That to secure these rights, Governments are instituted among Men, deriving their just powers from the consent of the governed, —That whenever any Form of Government becomes destructive of these ends, it is the Right of the People to alter or to abolish it, and to institute new Government, laying its foundation on such principles and organizing its powers in such form, as to them shall seem most likely to effect their Safety and Happiness. Prudence, indeed, will dictate that Governments long established should not be changed for light and transient causes; and accordingly all experience hath shewn, that mankind are more disposed to suffer, while evils are sufferable, than to right themselves by abolishing the forms to which they are accustomed. But when a long train of abuses and usurpations, pursuing invariably the same Object evinces a design to reduce them under absolute Despotism, it is their right, it is their duty, to throw off such Government, and to provide new Guards for their future security.—Such has been the patient sufferance of these Colonies; and such is now the necessity which constrains them to alter their former Systems of Government. The history of the present King of Great Britain is a history of repeated injuries and usurpations, all having in direct object the establishment of an absolute Tyranny over these States. To prove this, let Facts be submitted to a candid world.

He has refused his Assent to Laws, the most wholesome and necessary for the public good.

He has forbidden his Governors to pass Laws of immediate and pressing importance, unless suspended in their operation till his Assent should be obtained; and when so suspended, he has utterly neglected to attend to them.

He has refused to pass other Laws for the accommodation of large districts of people, unless those people would relinquish the right of Representation in the Legislature, a right inestimable to them and formidable to tyrants only.

He has called together legislative bodies at places unusual, uncomfortable, and distant from the depository of their public Records, for the sole purpose of fatiguing them into compliance with his measures.

He has dissolved Representative Houses repeatedly, for opposing with manly firmness his invasions on the rights of the people.

He has refused for a long time, after such dissolutions, to cause others to be elected; whereby the Legislative powers, incapable of Annihilation, have returned to the People at large for their exercise; the State remaining in the mean time exposed to all the dangers of invasion from without, and convulsions within.

He has endeavoured to prevent the population of these States; for that purpose obstructing the Laws for

Naturalization of Foreigners; refusing to pass others to encourage their migrations hither, and raising the conditions of new Appropriations of Lands.

He has obstructed the Administration of Justice, by refusing his Assent to Laws for establishing Judiciary powers.

He has made Judges dependent on his Will alone, for the tenure of their offices, and the amount and payment of their salaries.

He has erected a multitude of New Offices, and sent hither swarms of Officers to harrass our people, and eat out their substance.

He has kept among us, in times of peace, Standing Armies without the Consent of our legislatures.

He has affected to render the Military independent of and superior to the Civil power.

He has combined with others to subject us to a jurisdiction foreign to our constitution, and unacknowledged by our laws; giving his Assent to their Acts of pretended Legislation:

For Quartering large bodies of armed troops among us:

For protecting them, by a mock Trial, from punishment for any Murders which they should commit on the Inhabitants of these States:

For cutting off our Trade with all parts of the world:

For imposing Taxes on us without our Consent:

For depriving us in many cases, of the benefits of Trial by Jury:

For transporting us beyond Seas to be tried for pretended offences:

For abolishing the free System of English Laws in a neighbouring Province, establishing therein an Arbitrary government, and enlarging its Boundaries so as to render it at once an example and fit instrument for introducing the same absolute rule into these Colonies:

For taking away our Charters, abolishing our most valuable Laws, and altering fundamentally the Forms of our Governments:

For suspending our own Legislatures, and declaring themselves invested with power to legislate for us in all cases whatsoever.

He has abdicated Government here, by declaring us out of his Protection and waging War against us.

He has plundered our seas, ravaged our Coasts, burnt our towns, and destroyed the lives of our people.

He is at this time transporting large Armies of foreign Mercenaries to compleat the works of death, desolation and tyranny, already begun with circumstances of Cruelty & perfidy scarcely paralleled in the most barbarous ages, and totally unworthy the Head of a civilized nation.

He has constrained our fellow Citizens taken Captive on the high Seas to bear Arms against their Country, to become the executioners of their friends and Brethren, or to fall themselves by their Hands.

He has excited domestic insurrections amongst us, and has endeavoured to bring on the inhabitants of our frontiers, the merciless Indian Savages, whose known rule of warfare, is an undistinguished destruction of all ages, sexes and conditions.

In every stage of these Oppressions We have Petitioned for Redress in the most humble terms: Our repeated Petitions have been answered only by repeated injury. A Prince whose character is thus marked by every act which may define a Tyrant, is unfit to be the ruler of a free people.

Nor have We been wanting in attentions to our Brittish brethren. We have warned them from time to time of attempts by their legislature to extend an unwarrantable jurisdiction over us. We have reminded them of the circumstances of our emigration and settlement here. We have appealed to their native justice and magnanimity, and we have conjured them by the ties of our common kindred to disavow these usurpations, which, would inevitably interrupt our connections and correspondence. They too have been deaf to the voice of justice and of consanguinity. We must, therefore, acquiesce in the necessity, which denounces our Separation, and hold them, as we hold the rest of mankind, Enemies in War, in Peace Friends.

We, therefore, the Representatives of the united States of America, in General Congress, Assembled, appealing to the Supreme Judge of the world for the rectitude of our intentions, do, in the Name, and by Authority of the good People of these Colonies, solemnly publish and declare, That these United Colonies are, and of Right ought to be Free and Independent States; that they are Absolved from all Allegiance to the British Crown, and that all political connection between them and the State of Great Britain, is and ought to be totally dissolved; and that as Free and Independent States, they have full Power to levy War, conclude Peace, contract Alliances, establish Commerce, and to do all other Acts and Things which Independent States may of right do. And for the support of this Declaration, with a firm reliance on the protection of divine Providence, we mutually pledge to each other our Lives, our Fortunes and our sacred Honor.

The 56 signatures on the Declaration appear in the positions indicated:

Column 1
Georgia:
 Button Gwinnett
 Lyman Hall
 George Walton

Column 2
North Carolina:
 William Hooper
 Joseph Hewes
 John Penn
South Carolina:
 Edward Rutledge
 Thomas Heyward, Jr.
 Thomas Lynch, Jr.
 Arthur Middleton

Column 3
Massachusetts:
 John Hancock
Maryland:
 Samuel Chase
 William Paca
 Thomas Stone
 Charles Carroll of Carrollton
Virginia:
 George Wythe
 Richard Henry Lee
 Thomas Jefferson
 Benjamin Harrison
 Thomas Nelson, Jr.
 Francis Lightfoot Lee
 Carter Braxton

Column 4
Pennsylvania:
 Robert Morris
 Benjamin Rush
 Benjamin Franklin
 John Morton
 George Clymer
 James Smith
 George Taylor
 James Wilson
 George Ross
Delaware:
 Caesar Rodney
 George Read
 Thomas McKean

Column 5
New York:
 William Floyd
 Philip Livingston
 Francis Lewis
 Lewis Morris
New Jersey:
 Richard Stockton
 John Witherspoon
 Francis Hopkinson
 John Hart
 Abraham Clark

Column 6
New Hampshire:
 Josiah Bartlett
 William Whipple
Massachusetts:
 Samuel Adams
 John Adams
 Robert Treat Paine
 Elbridge Gerry
Rhode Island:
 Stephen Hopkins
 William Ellery
Connecticut:
 Roger Sherman
 Samuel Huntington
 William Williams
 Oliver Wolcott
New Hampshire:
 Matthew Thornton

Page URL:
http://www.archives.gov/national_archives_experience
/charters/declaration_transcript.html

U.S. National Archives & Records Administration
8601 Adelphi Road, College Park, MD, 20740-6001,
• 1-86-NARA-NARA •
1-866-272-6272

Articles of Confederation

To all to whom these Presents shall come, we the undersigned Delegates of the States affixed to our Names send greeting. Articles of Confederation and perpetual Union between the states of New Hampshire, Massachusetts-bay Rhode Island and Providence Plantations, Connecticut, New York, New Jersey, Pennsylvania, Delaware, Maryland, Virginia, North Carolina, South Carolina and Georgia.

I.
The Stile of this Confederacy shall be "The United States of America".

II.
Each state retains its sovereignty, freedom, and independence, and every power, jurisdiction, and right, which is not by this Confederation expressly delegated to the United States, in Congress assembled.

III.
The said States hereby severally enter into a firm league of friendship with each other, for their common defense, the security of their liberties, and their mutual and general welfare, binding themselves to assist each other, against all force offered to, or attacks made upon them, or any of them, on account of religion, sovereignty, trade, or any other pretense whatever.

IV.
The better to secure and perpetuate mutual friendship and intercourse among the people of the different States in this Union, the free inhabitants of each of these States, paupers, vagabonds, and fugitives from justice excepted, shall be entitled to all privileges and immunities of free citizens in the several States; and the people of each State shall free ingress and regress to and from any other State, and shall enjoy therein all the privileges of trade and commerce, subject to the same duties, impositions, and restrictions as the inhabitants thereof respectively, provided that such restrictions shall not extend so far as to prevent the removal of property imported into any State, to any other State, of which the owner is an inhabitant; provided also that no imposition, duties or restriction shall be laid by any State, on the property of the United States, or either of them.

If any person guilty of, or charged with, treason, felony, or other high misdemeanor in any State, shall flee from justice, and be found in any of the United States, he shall, upon demand of the Governor or executive power of the State from which he fled, be delivered up and removed to the State having jurisdiction of his offense.

Full faith and credit shall be given in each of these States to the records, acts, and judicial proceedings of the courts and magistrates of every other State.

V.
For the most convenient management of the general interests of the United States, delegates shall be annually appointed in such manner as the legislatures of each State shall direct, to meet in Congress on the first Monday in November, in every year, with a power reserved to each State to recall its delegates, or any of them, at any time within the year, and to send others in their stead for the remainder of the year.

No State shall be represented in Congress by less than two, nor more than seven members; and no person shall be capable of being a delegate for more than three years in any term of six years; nor shall any person, being a delegate, be capable of holding any office under the United States, for which he, or another for his benefit, receives any salary, fees or emolument of any kind.

Each State shall maintain its own delegates in a meeting of the States, and while they act as members of the committee of the States. In determining questions in the United States in Congress assembled, each State shall have one vote. Freedom of speech and debate in Congress shall not be impeached or questioned in any court or place out of Congress, and the members of Congress shall be protected in their persons from arrests or imprisonments, during the time of their going to and from, and attendance on Congress, except for treason, felony, or breach of the peace.

VI.

No State, without the consent of the United States in Congress assembled, shall send any embassy to, or receive any embassy from, or enter into any conference, agreement, alliance or treaty with any King, Prince or State; nor shall any person holding any office of profit or trust under the United States, or any of them, accept any present, emolument, office or title of any kind whatever from any King, Prince or foreign State; nor shall the United States in Congress assembled, or any of them, grant any title of nobility.

No two or more States shall enter into any treaty, confederation or alliance whatever between them, without the consent of the United States in Congress assembled, specifying accurately the purposes for which the same is to be entered into, and how long it shall continue.

No State shall lay any imposts or duties, which may interfere with any stipulations in treaties, entered into by the United States in Congress assembled, with any King, Prince or State, in pursuance of any treaties already proposed by Congress, to the courts of France and Spain.

No vessel of war shall be kept up in time of peace by any State, except such number only, as shall be deemed necessary by the United States in Congress assembled, for the defense of such State, or its trade; nor shall any body of forces be kept up by any State in time of peace, except such number only, as in the judgement of the United States in Congress assembled, shall be deemed requisite to garrison the forts necessary for the defense of such State; but every State shall always keep up a well-regulated and disciplined militia, sufficiently armed and accoutered, and shall provide and constantly have ready for use, in public stores, a due number of filed pieces and tents, and a proper quantity of arms, ammunition and camp equipage.

No State shall engage in any war without the consent of the United States in Congress assembled, unless such State be actually invaded by enemies, or shall have received certain advice of a resolution being formed by some nation of Indians to invade such State, and the danger is so imminent as not to admit of a delay till the United States in Congress assembled can be consulted; nor shall any State grant commissions to any ships or vessels of war, nor letters of marque or reprisal, except it be after a declaration of war by the United States in Congress assembled, and then only against the Kingdom or State and the subjects thereof, against which war has been so declared, and under such regulations as shall be established by the United States in Congress assembled, unless such State be infested by pirates, in which case vessels of war may be fitted out for that occasion, and kept so long as the danger shall continue, or until the United States in Congress assembled shall determine otherwise.

VII.

When land forces are raised by any State for the common defense, all officers of or under the rank of colonel, shall be appointed by the legislature of each State respectively, by whom such forces shall be raised, or in such manner as such State shall direct, and all vacancies shall be filled up by the State which first made the appointment.

VIII.

All charges of war, and all other expenses that shall be incurred for the common defense or general welfare, and allowed by the United States in Congress assembled, shall be defrayed out of a common treasury, which shall be supplied by the several States in proportion to the value of all land within each State, granted or surveyed for any person, as such land and the buildings and improvements thereon shall be estimated according to such mode as the United States in Congress assembled, shall from time to time direct and appoint.

The taxes for paying that proportion shall be laid and levied by the authority and direction of the legislatures of the several States within the time agreed upon by the United States in Congress assembled.

IX.

The United States in Congress assembled, shall have the sole and exclusive right and power of determining on peace and war, except in the cases mentioned in the sixth article — of sending and receiving ambassadors — entering into treaties and alliances, provided that no treaty of commerce shall be made whereby the legislative power of the respective States shall be restrained from imposing such imposts and duties on foreigners, as their own people are subjected to, or from prohibiting the exportation or importation of any species of goods or commodities whatsoever — of establishing rules for deciding in all cases, what captures on land or water shall be legal, and in what manner prizes taken by land or naval forces in the service of the United States shall be divided or appropriated — of granting letters of marque and reprisal in times of peace — appointing courts for the trial of piracies and felonies committed on the high seas and establishing courts for receiving and determining finally appeals in all cases of captures, provided that no member of Congress shall be appointed a judge of any of the said courts.

The United States in Congress assembled shall also be the last resort on appeal in all disputes and differences now subsisting or that hereafter may arise between two or more States concerning boundary, jurisdiction or any other causes whatever; which authority shall always be exercised in the manner following. Whenever the legislative or executive authority or lawful agent of any State in controversy with another shall present a petition to Congress stating the matter in question and praying for a hearing, notice thereof shall be given by order of Congress to the legislative or executive authority of the other State in controversy, and a day assigned for the appearance of the parties by their lawful agents, who shall then be directed to appoint by joint consent, commissioners or judges to constitute a court for hearing and determining the matter in question: but if they cannot agree, Congress shall name three persons out of each of the United States, and from the list of such persons each party shall alternately strike out one, the petitioners beginning, until the number shall be reduced to thirteen; and from that number not less than seven, nor more than nine names as Congress shall direct, shall in the presence of Congress be drawn out by lot, and the persons whose names shall be so drawn or any five of them, shall be commissioners or judges, to hear and finally determine the controversy, so always as a major part of the judges who shall hear the cause shall agree in the determination: and if either party shall neglect to attend at the day appointed, without showing reasons, which Congress shall judge sufficient, or being present shall refuse to strike, the Congress shall proceed to nominate three persons out of each State, and the secretary of Congress shall strike in behalf of such party absent or refusing; and the judgement and sentence of the court to be appointed, in the manner before prescribed, shall be final and conclusive; and if any

of the parties shall refuse to submit to the authority of such court, or to appear or defend their claim or cause, the court shall nevertheless proceed to pronounce sentence, or judgement, which shall in like manner be final and decisive, the judgement or sentence and other proceedings being in either case transmitted to Congress, and lodged among the acts of Congress for the security of the parties concerned: provided that every commissioner, before he sits in judgement, shall take an oath to be administered by one of the judges of the supreme or superior court of the State, where the cause shall be tried, 'well and truly to hear and determine the matter in question, according to the best of his judgement, without favor, affection or hope of reward': provided also, that no State shall be deprived of territory for the benefit of the United States.

All controversies concerning the private right of soil claimed under different grants of two or more States, whose jurisdictions as they may respect such lands, and the States which passed such grants are adjusted, the said grants or either of them being at the same time claimed to have originated antecedent to such settlement of jurisdiction, shall on the petition of either party to the Congress of the United States, be finally determined as near as may be in the same manner as is before prescribed for deciding disputes respecting territorial jurisdiction between different States.

The United States in Congress assembled shall also have the sole and exclusive right and power of regulating the alloy and value of coin struck by their own authority, or by that of the respective States — fixing the standards of weights and measures throughout the United States — regulating the trade and managing all affairs with the Indians, not members of any of the States, provided that the legislative right of any State within its own limits be not infringed or violated — establishing or regulating post offices from one State to another, throughout all the United States, and exacting such postage on the papers passing through the same as may be requisite to defray the expenses of the said office — appointing all officers of the land forces, in the service of the United States, excepting regimental officers — appointing all the officers of the naval forces, and commissioning all officers whatever in the service of the United States — making rules for the government and regulation of the said land and naval forces, and directing their operations.

The United States in Congress assembled shall have authority to appoint a committee, to sit in the recess of Congress, to be denominated 'A Committee of the

States', and to consist of one delegate from each State; and to appoint such other committees and civil officers as may be necessary for managing the general affairs of the United States under their direction — to appoint one of their members to preside, provided that no person be allowed to serve in the office of president more than one year in any term of three years; to ascertain the necessary sums of money to be raised for the service of the United States, and to appropriate and apply the same for defraying the public expenses — to borrow money, or emit bills on the credit of the United States, transmitting every half-year to the respective States an account of the sums of money so borrowed or emitted — to build and equip a navy — to agree upon the number of land forces, and to make requisitions from each State for its quota, in proportion to the number of white inhabitants in such State; which requisition shall be binding, and thereupon the legislature of each State shall appoint the regimental officers, raise the men and cloath, arm and equip them in a solid-like manner, at the expense of the United States; and the officers and men so cloathed, armed and equipped shall march to the place appointed, and within the time agreed on by the United States in Congress assembled. But if the United States in Congress assembled shall, on consideration of circumstances judge proper that any State should not raise men, or should raise a smaller number of men than the quota thereof, such extra number shall be raised, officered, cloathed, armed and equipped in the same manner as the quota of each State, unless the legislature of such State shall judge that such extra number cannot be safely spread out in the same, in which case they shall raise, officer, cloath, arm and equip as many of such extra number as they judge can be safely spared. And the officers and men so cloathed, armed, and equipped, shall march to the place appointed, and within the time agreed on by the United States in Congress assembled.

The United States in Congress assembled shall never engage in a war, nor grant letters of marque or reprisal in time of peace, nor enter into any treaties or alliances, nor coin money, nor regulate the value thereof, nor ascertain the sums and expenses necessary for the defense and welfare of the United States, or any of them, nor emit bills, nor borrow money on the credit of the United States, nor appropriate money, nor agree upon the number of vessels of war, to be built or purchased, or the number of land or sea forces to be raised, nor appoint a commander in chief of the army or navy, unless nine States assent to the same: nor shall a question on any other point, except for adjourning from day to day be determined, unless by the votes of the majority of the United States in Congress assembled.

The Congress of the United States shall have power to adjourn to any time within the year, and to any place within the United States, so that no period of adjournment be for a longer duration than the space of six months, and shall publish the journal of their proceedings monthly, except such parts thereof relating to treaties, alliances or military operations, as in their judgement require secrecy; and the yeas and nays of the delegates of each State on any question shall be entered on the journal, when it is desired by any delegates of a State, or any of them, at his or their request shall be furnished with a transcript of the said journal, except such parts as are above excepted, to lay before the legislatures of the several States.

X.

The Committee of the States, or any nine of them, shall be authorized to execute, in the recess of Congress, such of the powers of Congress as the United States in Congress assembled, by the consent of the nine States, shall from time to time think expedient to vest them with; provided that no power be delegated to the said Committee, for the exercise of which, by the Articles of Confederation, the voice of nine States in the Congress of the United States assembled be requisite.

XI.

Canada acceding to this confederation, and adjoining in the measures of the United States, shall be admitted into, and entitled to all the advantages of this Union; but no other colony shall be admitted into the same, unless such admission be agreed to by nine States.

XII.

All bills of credit emitted, monies borrowed, and debts contracted by, or under the authority of Congress, before the assembling of the United States, in pursuance of the present confederation, shall be deemed and considered as a charge against the United States, for payment and satisfaction whereof the said United States, and the public faith are hereby solemnly pledged.

XIII.

Every State shall abide by the determination of the United States in Congress assembled, on all questions which by this confederation are submitted to them. And the Articles of this Confederation shall be inviolably observed by every State, and the Union shall be perpetual; nor shall any alteration at any time hereafter be made in any of them; unless such alteration be agreed to in a Congress of the United States, and be afterwards confirmed by the legislatures of every State.

And Whereas it hath pleased the Great Governor of the World to incline the hearts of the legislatures we respectively represent in Congress, to approve of, and to authorize us to ratify the said Articles of Confederation and perpetual Union. Know Ye that we the undersigned delegates, by virtue of the power and authority to us given for that purpose, do by these presents, in the name and in behalf of our respective constituents, fully and entirely ratify and confirm each and every of the said Articles of Confederation and perpetual Union, and all and singular the matters and things therein contained: And we do further solemnly plight and engage the faith of our respective constituents, that they shall abide by the determinations of the United States in Congress assembled, on all questions, which by the said Confederation are submitted to them. And that the Articles thereof shall be inviolably observed by the States we respectively represent, and that the Union shall be perpetual.

In Witness whereof we have hereunto set our hands in Congress. Done at Philadelphia in the State of Pennsylvania the ninth day of July in the Year of our Lord One Thousand Seven Hundred and Seventy-Eight, and in the Third Year of the independence of America.

Agreed to by Congress 15 November 1777 In force after ratification by Maryland, 1 March 1781

Source: Documents Illustrative of the Formation of the Union of the American States. Government Printing Office, 1927. House Document No. 398. Selected, Arranged and Indexed by Charles C. Tansill. http://www.yale.edu/lawweb/avalon/artconf.htm

Historical Election Results

Year	Presidential Candidates	Vice Presidential Candidates	Parties	Popular Vote	Electoral Vote
1789	**George Washington**	**John Adams**	Federalist	No record	69
	John Adams		Federalist		34
	Others				35
1792	**George Washington**	**John Adams**	Federalist	No record	132
	John Adams		Federalist		77
	George Clinton				50
	Others				5
1796	**John Adams**	**Thomas Jefferson**	Democratic-Republican	No record	71
	Thomas Jefferson		Democratic-Republican		68
	Thomas Pinckney				59
	Aaron Burr				30
	Others				48
1800	**Thomas Jefferson**	**Aaron Burr**	Democratic-Republican	No record	73
	Aaron Burr		Democratic-Republican		73
	John Adams				64
	Others				65
1804	**Thomas Jefferson**	**George Clinton**	Democratic-Republican	No record	162
	Charles C. Pinckney	Rufus King	Federalist		14
1808	**James Madison**	**George Clinton**	Democratic-Republican	No record	122
	Charles C. Pinckney	Rufus King	Federalist		47
	George Clinton	Others			6
1812	**James Madison**	**Elbridge Gerry**	Democratic-Republican	No record	128
	De Witt Clinton	Jared Ingersoll	Federalist		89
1816	**James Monroe**	**Daniel D. Tompkins**	Democratic-Republican	No record	183
	Rufus King	Others	Federalist		34
1820	**James Monroe**	**Daniel D. Tompkins**	Democratic-Republican	No record	231
	John Quincy Adams	Others	National Republican		1
1824	**John Quincy Adams**	**John C. Calhoun**	Coalition	113,122	84
	Andrew Jackson		Democratic-Republican	151,271	99
	William Crawford	Others			41
	Henry Clay				37

Year	Presidential Candidates	Vice Presidential Candidates	Parties	Popular Vote	Electoral Vote
1828	**Andrew Jackson**	**John C. Calhoun**	Democratic	642,553	178
	John Quincy Adams	Richard Rush	National Republican	500,897	83
		William Smith			
1832	**Andrew Jackson**	**Martin Van Buren**	Democratic	701,780	219
	Henry Clay		National Republican	484,205	49
	John Floyd	Others			11
	William Wirt				7
1836	**Martin Van Buren**	**Richard M. Johnson**	Democratic	764,176	170
	William Henry Harrison		Whig	550,816	73
	Hugh L. White	Others			26
	Daniel Webster				14
	William P. Mangum				11
1840	**William Henry Harrison**	**John Tyler**	Whig	1,275,390	234
	Martin Van Buren	Others	Democratic	1,128,854	60
1844	**James K. Polk**	**George M. Dallas**	Whig	1,339,494	170
	Henry Clay	Theodore Frelinghuysen	Democratic	1,300,004	105
1848	**Zachary Taylor**	**Millard Filmore**	Whig	1,361,393	163
	Lewis Cass	W. O. Butler	Democratic	1,223,460	127
1852	**Franklin Pierce**	**William R. King**	Democratic	1,607,510	254
	Winfield Scott	William A. Graham	Whig	1, 386,942	42
1856	**James Buchanan**	**John C. Breckinridge**	Democratic	1,836,072	174
	John C. Frémont	William L. Dayton	Republican	1,342,345	114
	Millard Filmore	Andrew Donelson			8
1860	**Abraham Lincoln**	**Hannibal Hamlin**	Republican	1,865,908	180
	John C. Breckinridge	Joseph Lane	Democratic	848,019	72
	John Bell	Edward Everett			39
	Stephen A. Douglas	Herschel V. Johnson			12
1864	**Abraham Lincoln**	**Andrew Johnson**	Republican	2,218,388	212
	George B. McClellan	George H. Pendleton	Democratic	1,812,807	21
1868	**Ulysses S. Grant**	**Schuyler Colfax**	Republican	3,013,650	214
	Horatio Seymour	Francis P. Blair Jr.	Democratic	2,708,744	80
1872	**Ulysses S. Grant**	**Henry Wilson**	Republican	3,589,235	286
	Horace Greeley		Democratic	2,834,761	—
	Thomas A. Hendricks	Others			42
	Others				21
1876	**Rutherford B. Hayes**	**William A. Wheeler**	Republican	4,034,311	185
	Samuel J. Tilden	Thomas A. Hendricks	Democratic	4,288,546	184
1880	**James Garfield**	**Chester A. Arthur**	Republican	4,446,158	214
	Winfield S. Hancock	William H. English	Democratic	4,444,260	155
1884	**Grover Cleveland**	**Thomas A. Hendricks**	Democratic	4,874,621	219
	James G. Blaine	John A. Logan	Republican	4,848,936	182

Year	Presidential Candidates	Vice Presidential Candidates	Parties	Popular Vote	Electoral Vote
1888	**Benjamin Harrison**	**Levi P. Morton**	Republican	5,443,892	233
	Grover Cleveland	Allen G. Thurman	Democratic	5,534,488	168
1892	**Grover Cleveland**	**Adlai E. Stevenson**	Democratic	5,551,883	277
	Benjamin Harrison	Whitelaw Reid	Republican	5,179,244	145
	James B. Weaver	James G. Field	People's	1,027,329	22
1896	**William McKinley**	**Garret A. Hobart**	Republican	7,108,480	271
	William J. Bryan	Others	Democratic People's	6,511,495	176
1900	**William McKinley**	**Theodore Roosevelt**	Republican	7,218,039	292
	William J. Bryan	Adlai E. Stevenson	Democratic People's	6,358,345	155
1904	**Theodore Roosevelt**	**Charles W. Fairbanks**	Republican	7,626,593	336
	Alton B. Parker	Henry G. Davis	Democratic	5,082,898	140
1908	**William H. Taft**	**James S. Sherman**	Republican	7,676,258	321
	William J. Bryan	John W. Kern	Democratic	6,406,801	162
1912	**Woodrow Wilson**	**Thomas R. Marshall**	Democratic	6,293,152	435
	Theodore Roosevelt	Hiram W. Johnson	Progressive	4,119,207	88
	William H. Taft	Nicholas M. Butler	Republican	3,483,922	8
1916	**Woodrow Wilson**	**Thomas R. Marshall**	Democratic	9,126,300	277
	Charles E. Hughes	Charles W. Fairbanks	Republican	8,546,789	254
1920	**Warren G. Harding**	**Calvin Coolidge**	Republican	16,153,115	404
	James M. Cox	Franklin D. Roosevelt	Democratic	9,133,092	127
1924	**Calvin Coolidge**	**Charles G. Dawes**	Republican	15,719,921	382
	John W. Davis	Charles W. Bryan	Democratic	8,386,704	136
	Robert M. LaFollette	Burton K. Wheeler	Progressive	4,822,856	13
1928	**Herbert C. Hoover**	**Charles Curtis**	Republican	21,437,277	444
	Alfred E. Smith	Joseph T. Robinson	Democratic	15,007,698	87
1932	**Franklin D. Roosevelt**	**John N. Garner**	Democratic	22,829,501	472
	Herbert C. Hoover	Charles Curtis	Republican	15,760,684	59
	Norman Thomas		Socialist	884,781	—
1936	**Franklin D. Roosevelt**	**John N. Garner**	Democratic	27,757,333	523
	Alfred M. Landon	Frank Knox	Republican	16,684,231	8
1940	**Franklin D. Roosevelt**	**Henry A. Wallace**	Democratic	27,313,041	449
	Wendell L. Willkie	Charles L. McNary	Republican	22,348,480	82
1944	**Franklin D. Roosevelt**	**Harry S. Truman**	Democratic	25,612,610	432
	Thomas E. Dewey	John W. Bricker	Republican	22,117,617	99
1948	**Harry S. Truman**	**Alben W. Barkley**	Democratic	24,179,345	303
	Thomas E. Dewey	Earl Warren	Republican	21,991,291	189
	J. Strom Thurmond	Fielding L. Wright	State's Rights	1,169,021	39
	Henry A. Wallace		Progressive	1,157,172	—

Year	Presidential Candidates	Vice Presidential Candidates	Parties	Popular Vote	Electoral Vote
1952	**Dwight D. Eisenhower**	**Richard M. Nixon**	Republican	33,936,234	442
	Adlai Stevenson	John Sparkman	Democratic	27,314,992	89
1956	**Dwight D. Eisenhower**	**Richard M. Nixon**	Republican	35,590,472	457
	Adlai Stevenson	Estes Kefauver	Democratic	26,022,752	73
	Walter B. Jones	Herman Talmadge			1
1960	**John F. Kennedy**	**Lyndon B. Johnson**	Democratic	34,226,731	303
	Richard M. Nixon	Henry Cabot Lodge	Republican	34,108,157	219
	Harry F. Byrd	J. Strom Thurmond			15
1964	**Lyndon B. Johnson**	**Hubert H. Humphrey**	Democratic	43,129,566	486
	Barry M. Goldwater	William E. Miller	Republican	27,178,188	52
1968	**Richard M. Nixon**	**Spiro T. Agnew**	Republican	31,785,480	301
	Hubert H. Humphrey	Edmund Muskie	Democratic	31,275,166	191
	George C. Wallace	Curtis E. LeMay	American Independent	9,906,473	46
1972	**Richard M. Nixon**	**Spiro T. Agnew**	Republican	47,169,911	520
	George S. McGovern	R. Sargent Shriver	Democratic	29,170,383	17
	John Hospers	Theodora Nathan			1
1976	**Jimmy Carter**	**Walter F. Mondale**	Democratic	40,830,763	297
	Gerald R. Ford	Robert Dole	Republican	30,147,793	240
	Ronald Reagan				1
1980	**Ronald Reagan**	**George Bush**	Republican	43,904,153	489
	Jimmy Carter	Walter F. Mondale	Democratic	35,483,883	49
1984	**Ronald Reagan**	**George Bush**	Republican	54,455,075	525
	Walter F. Mondale	Geraldine A. Ferraro	Democratic	37,577,185	13
1988	**George Bush**	**James Danforth Quayle**	Republican	48,886,097	426
	Michael S. Dukakis	Lloyd Bentson	Democratic	41,809,074	111
	Other				1
1992	**William J. Clinton**	**Albert Gore Jr.**	Democratic	44,908,254	370
	George Bush	James Danforth Quayle	Republican	39,102,343	168
1996	**William J. Clinton**	**Albert Gore Jr.**	Democratic	45,590,703	379
	Robert Dole	Jack Kemp	Republican	37,816,307	159
	H. Ross Perot		Reform	7,866,284	—
2000	**George W. Bush**	**Richard B. Cheney**	Republican	50,460,110	271
	Albert Gore Jr.	Joseph Lieberman	Democratic	51,003,926	266
	Ralph Nader	Winona LaDuke	Green	2,883,105	—
2004	**George W. Bush**	**Richard B. Cheney**	Republican	62,040,606	286
	John F. Kerry	John Edwards	Democratic	59,028,109	251

Sources: U.S. National Archives and Records Administration, http://www.archives.gov/federal_register/electoral_college/scores.html; Dave Leip's Atlas of U.S. Presidential Elections, http://uselectionatlas.org/USPRESIDENT/index.html.

United States Population Growth

Year	Number of States	Population	Percent Increase	Population per Square Mile
1790	13	3,929,214		4.5
1800	16	5,308,483	35.1	6.1
1810	17	7,239,881	36.4	4.3
1820	23	9,638,453	33.1	5.5
1830	24	12,866,020	33.5	7.4
1840	26	17,069,453	32.7	9.8
1850	31	23,191,876	35.9	7.9
1860	33	31,443,321	35.6	10.6
1870	37	38,558,371	22.6	10.9
1880	38	50,189,209	30.2	14.2
1890	44	62,979,766	25.5	17.8
1900	45	76,212,168	21.0	21.5
1910	46	92,228,496	21.0	26.0
1920	48	106,021,537	15.0	29.9
1930	48	123,202,624	16.2	34.7
1940	48	132,164,569	7.3	37.2
1950	48	151,325,798	14.5	42.6
1960	50	179,323,175	18.5	50.6
1970	50	203,302,031	13.4	57.5
1980	50	226,542,199	11.4	64.0
1990	50	248,709,873	9.8	70.3
2000	50	281,421,906	13.2	79.6

Source: U.S. Bureau of the Census.

Credits

Index